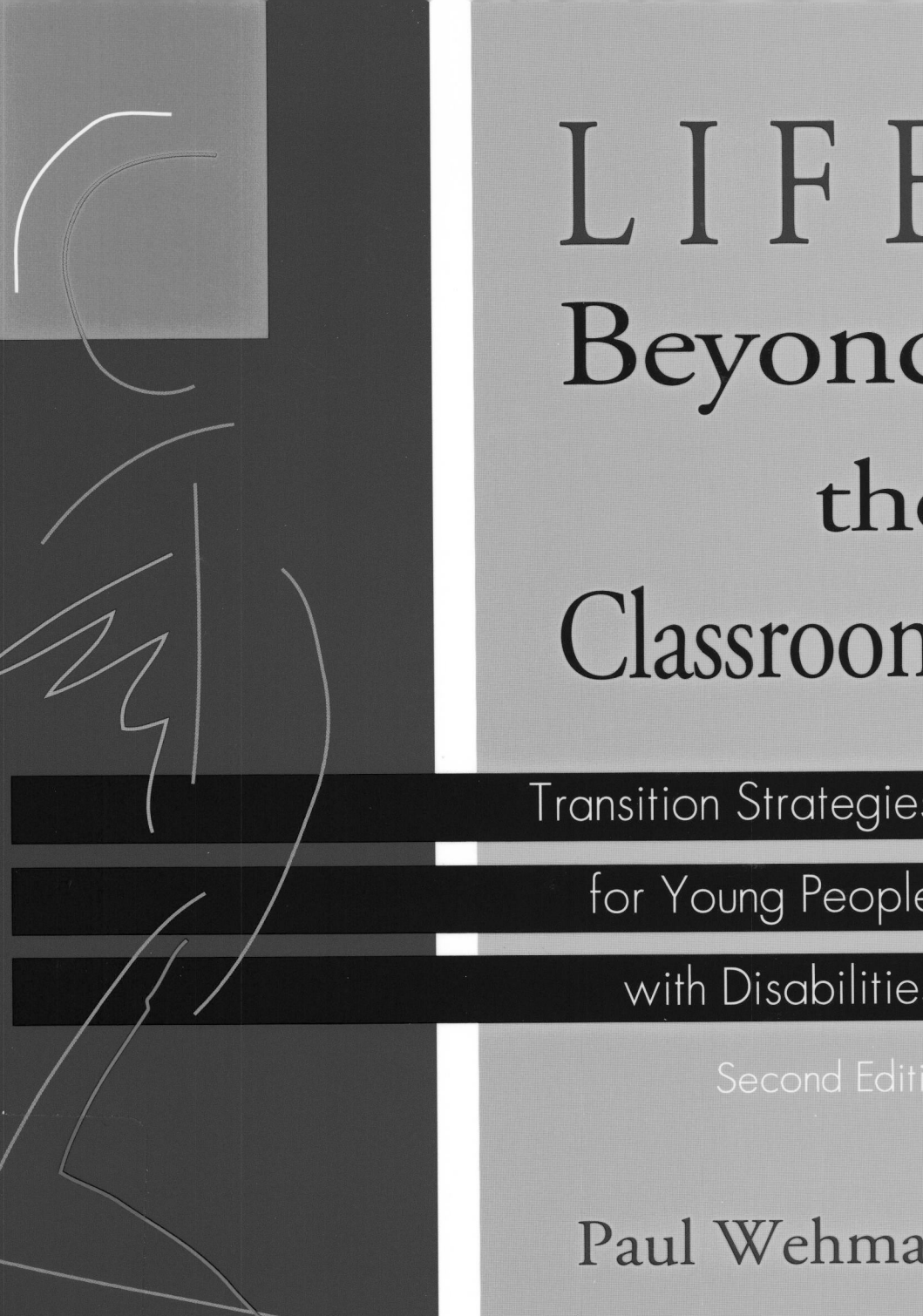

LIFE
Beyond
the
Classroom

Transition Strategies
for Young People
with Disabilities

Second Edition

Paul Wehman

Life Beyond the Classroom

Life Beyond the Classroom

Transition Strategies for Young People with Disabilities

Second Edition

by

Paul Wehman, Ph.D.
Virginia Commonwealth University
Richmond

with invited contributors

·P·A·U·L·H·
BROOKES
PUBLISHING C?

Baltimore • London • Toronto • Sydney

Paul H. Brookes Publishing Co.
Post Office Box 10624
Baltimore, Maryland 21285-0624

Typeset by Zeko Graphics, Kansas City, Missouri.
Manufactured in the United States of America by
The Maple Press Co., York, Pennsylvania.

Library of Congress Cataloging-in-Publication Data

Wehman, Paul.
 Life beyond the classroom : transition strategies for young people with disabilities / by Paul
Wehman ; with invited contributors. —2nd ed.
 p. cm.
 Includes bibliographical references and index.
 ISBN 1-55766-248-7
 1. Vocational guidance for the handicapped—United States. 2. Handicapped youth—
Employment—United States. 3. Handicapped youth—United States—Psychology.
4. School-to-work transition—United States. I. Title.
HV1568.W43 1996
331.3'4'087—dc20
 96-5882
 CIP

British Library Cataloguing-in-Publication data are available from the British Library.

Contents

About the Authors

Paul Wehman, Ph.D., Professor of Physical Medicine and Rehabilitation, Rehabilitation Research and Training Center on Supported Employment, Virginia Commonwealth University, 1314 West Main Street, Richmond, Virginia 23284-0211

Paul Wehman is a professor in both the Department of Physical Medicine and Rehabilitation, Medical College of Virginia, Virginia Commonwealth University, and the School of Education, Virginia Commonwealth University. Dr. Wehman has taught many courses in special education, published various special education articles, and been involved in teacher training. Internationally recognized for his service and scholarly contributions in the fields of special education, psychology, and vocational rehabilitation, Dr. Wehman has received numerous awards in both special education and rehabilitation, including the 1990 Joseph P. Kennedy, Jr., Foundation Award in Mental Retardation; a 1992 Leadership Award from the Association for Persons in Supported Employment; and the Distinguished Service Award from the President's Committee on Employment for Persons with Disabilities in October 1992. He is the author or editor of more than 100 books, research monographs, journal articles, and chapters in the areas of traumatic brain injury, mental retardation, supported employment, and special education. He is also the editor of the *Journal of Vocational Rehabilitation,* an international journal published by Elsevier. His specific research interests include transition from school to work, supported employment, developmental disabilities, and brain injury.

Patricia Brown-Glover, M.Ed., Transition Planner, Richmond Public Schools, Exceptional Education, 301 North Ninth Street, Richmond, Virginia 23219

Patricia Brown-Glover is the transition planner for Richmond Public Schools. She is responsible for developing and coordinating transition-related guidelines and activities for all students in Exceptional Education programs. Prior to her appointment as transition planner, she served as a training associate with the Rehabilitation Research and Training Center on Supported Employment at Virginia Commonwealth University and taught students with mild disabilities in both rural and urban settings.

Mike Cosel, 13 Pleasant Drive, Setauket, New York 11733

Mike Cosel is in construction and property management. He serves on the Board of Directors of Island Harvest, a food service program; the Assistance Dog United Campaign; and Suffolk County Special Olympics.

Ronne Cosel, 13 Pleasant Drive, Setauket, New York 11733

Ronne Cosel has recently embarked on a second career as a full-time professional artist following a career as a public librarian. She is also on the Board of Directors of Freya's Sensory Center.

Elizabeth Evans Getzel, M.A., Rehabilitation Research and Training Center on Supported Employment, Virginia Commonwealth University, 1314 West Main Street, Richmond, Virginia 23284-0211

Elizabeth Evans Getzel is Research Associate with the Rehabilitation Research and Training Center on Supported Employment at Virginia Commonwealth University. She has worked for a number of years conducting analyses of federal and state policies to assess their impact on services and programs for individuals with disabilities, developing and implementing evaluation studies to identify effective strategies and programs within service delivery systems, and providing technical assistance to accommodate students with disabilities in secondary and postsecondary settings.

Karen Gibson, M.S., Rehabilitation Research and Training Center on Supported Employment, Virginia Commonwealth University, 1314 West Main Street, Richmond, Virginia 23284-0211

Karen Gibson holds a bachelor's degree in Administration of Justice and a master's degree in Rehabilitation Counseling from Virginia Commonwealth University. Ms. Gibson has been employed in the human services field since 1988, holding such positions as a supported living residential counselor and an employment specialist. Before joining the Rehabilitation Research and Training Center on Supported Employment, Ms. Gibson worked for 3 years as a senior employment specialist for a local community services board. In her present position as a vocational employment counselor, she is responsible for providing supported employment services for individuals referred to the Natural Supports Transition Project using the Community and Workplace Support Model. In addition, Ms. Gibson has had extensive experience identifying and developing supports within the community and workplace to address both work-related and non–work-related issues as they pertain to individuals referred to the Natural Supports Transition Project.

Cary Griffin, M.A., Director of Training, Rural Institute on Disabilities Research and Training Center, 52 Corbin Hall, University of Montana, Missoula, Montana 59812

Cary Griffin is Director of Training for the Rural Institute on Disabilities Research and Training Center and the University Affiliated Program. Mr. Griffin has extensive experience as a direct services worker, a job developer, and an adminstrator of adult vocational programs for individuals with severe disabilities. He consults internationally in the areas of career

development, natural supports, management/leadership, organizational change, and resource development. He is especially interested in creating community partnerships, facilitating leadership in business and human services, self-advocacy, and systems change.

Susan Lehmann Griffin, Ph.D., Senior Research Associate, Developmental Disabilities Training Institute, CB 3370, Carr Mill Annex, University of North Carolina at Chapel Hill, Chapel Hill, North Carolina 27599-3370

Susan Lehmann Griffin is Senior Research Associate at the Developmental Disabilities Training Institute (DDTI) at the University of North Carolina at Chapel Hill. She is also involved in research and training involving customer service within human services delivery systems and person-centered planning/innovative service delivery. Prior to her position at Chapel Hill, Ms. Griffin worked with individuals who have visual impairment or blindness at the Rehabilitation Research and Training Center on Supported Employment at Virginia Commonwealth University, focusing on supported employment.

John J. Gugerty, M.S., Center on Education and Work, University of Wisconsin–Madison, 964 Educational Sciences Building, 1025 West Johnson Street, Madison, Wisconsin 53706

John J. Gugerty has been an academic staff member of the Center on Education and Work since 1975. He has staffed and directed a number of state and federally funded projects that addressed one or more facets of career/vocational preparation of youth and adults with disabilities and, specifically, staff development activities. In addition, he has volunteered with state and county parent groups (Learning Disabilities Association, The Arc) and local/state Consumer Advisory Groups sponsored by the Wisconsin Division of Vocational Rehabilitation. He is also a member of Wisconsin's State-Level Oversight Committee for the Implementation of the Americans with Disabilities Act, known as the ADA Wisconsin Partnership, which serves as the steering committee for Wisconsin's Disability and Business Technical Assistance Center. Mr. Gugerty also serves on the statewide Special Population Transition Action Team, whose goal is inclusion of those who learn differently or with difficulty in Technical Preparation and School-to-Work Programs.

Christine Hess, M.Ed., Senior Associate, Stetson and Associates, Inc., 13910 Champion Forest Drive, Suite 208, Houston, Texas 77069

Christine Hess has more than 20 years' administrative and teaching experience in special and general education, from early childhood through postsecondary, with emphasis in severe disabilities, community-based instruction, transition, and inclusive education. Before joining Stetson and Associates in 1992 as Senior Associate, she worked as a regional education consultant, an assistant principal for instruction, a supervisor, and a classroom teacher. Ms. Hess has assisted hundreds of school districts and state agencies in the implementation and evaluation of recommended practices for all students.

Kelly Kane, Rehabilitation Research and Training Center on Supported Employment, Virginia Commonwealth University, 1314 West Main Street, Richmond, Virginia 23284-0211

Kelly Kane holds a bachelor's degree in psychology and is taking graduate courses in special education at Virginia Commonwealth University. Since 1992, Ms. Kane has been employed in the supported employment field for people with severe disabilities, working for 2 years as an employment specialist and for 1 year managing a team of employment specialists in Syracuse, New York. Since 1994, she has worked at the Rehabilitation Research and Training Center on Supported Employment at Virginia Commonwealth University as a vocational employment counselor, providing supported employment services for individuals referred to the Natural Supports Transition Project. Ms. Kane has had extensive experience identifying and developing supports within the community and workplace to address both work-related and non–work-related issues as they pertain to these individuals.

John Kregel, Ed.D., Professor of Special Education, Associate Director and Research Director, Rehabilitation Research and Training Center on Supported Employment, Virginia Commonwealth University, 1314 West Main Street, Richmond, Virginia 23284-0211

John Kregel is Professor of Special Education and Associate Director and Research Director of the Rehabilitation Research and Training Center on Supported Employment, both at Virginia Commonwealth University. Dr. Kregel has experience as a special education teacher and administrator. He is the author or co-author of numerous books, journal articles, book chapters, research monographs, and other publications on school-to-work transition and supported employment.

Melinda Mast, 137 Long Tree Road, Springfield, Illinois 62704

Melinda Mast is Project Director for United Cerebral Palsy Associations (UCP) employment initiatives. She also assists UCP affiliates nationwide and other agencies to convert to a system of community-based services. She is a strong promoter of an individualized approach to services for people with the most severe disabilities. Her background includes teaching and directing vocational services for people with disabilities.

Pam Sherron, M.Ed., Program Manager, Employment Services Division, Rehabilitation Research and Training Center on Supported Employment, Virginia Commonwealth University, 1314 West Main Street, Richmond, Virginia 23284-0211

Pam Sherron is Program Manager for the Employment Services Division of the Rehabilitation Research and Training Center on Supported Employment at Virginia Commonwealth University. She has been involved in the implementation of supported employment since 1986. Before then, she taught adult basic education classes and personnel management.

Darlene Unger, M.Ed., Rehabilitation Research and Training Center on Supported Employment, Virginia Commonwealth University, 1314 West Main Street, Richmond, Virginia 23284-0211

Darlene Unger is Project Coordinator for the Natural Supports Transition Project at the Rehabilitation Research and Training Center on Supported Employment at Virginia Commonwealth University. She has been responsible for developing and implementing a natural supports approach to providing supported employment services. She is particularly interested in working with employers and community organizations in developing and providing support for people with disabilities. Ms. Unger is a doctoral student in the Urban Services Program at Virginia Commonwealth University.

Michael D. West, Ph.D., Rehabilitation Research and Training Center on Supported Employment, Virginia Commonwealth University, 1314 West Main Street, Richmond, Virginia 23284-0211

Michael D. West holds a master of education degree in Special Education and Habilitative Services from the University of New Orleans in Louisiana, and a doctorate of philosophy in education from Virginia Commonwealth University. His direct service experiences have included projects in special education, residential programs, vocational services, and general community functioning. He is Research Associate with the Rehabilitation Research and Training Center on Supported Employment at Virginia Commonwealth University. He has also authored or co-authored numerous journal articles and book chapters on supported employment, special education, and other disability-related issues.

Preface

The education and employment of young adults with disabilities in the United States must remain a leading priority. The education of individuals with disabilities is critical to the foundation of adult adjustment and success in work and the community. Without an education that focuses on the development of personal competence, life skills, and employment opportunities, young adults with disabilities are greatly handicapped in the complex modern society in which we live. Their education should focus on functional activities taught in real-life situations (e.g., community environments in close proximity to students without disabilities).

The other major building block for successful inclusion in the community is employment. Competitive employment is the most desirable alternative for young adults with disabilities and may take place in many different types of businesses, industries, and settings. Some individuals will choose to become self-employed; others will choose to work part time and continue school; others will go on to technical schools; and still others will enter the work force full time with the help of job coaches and other technological aids, such as voice recognition devices and computers. All students, however, need a chance to work *before* they leave school.

Translating educational experiences into meaningful employment is what transition from school to adulthood is all about. One cannot intelligently examine transition without simultaneously considering education and employment. Yet, transition involves more than employment. Community living, meaningful leisure pursuits, and confidence in personal relationships are also important aspects of transition. In both editions of *Life Beyond the Classroom,* we emphasize the importance of independent living skills and other nonvocational activities; yet, one of the most important vehicles to a successful adjustment in the community and personal happiness remains satisfaction with one's job. Although the specific job or working conditions may not be ideal, the fact remains that any employment is an important milestone for everyone in American society. Therefore, the careful planning of individualized transition from school to community life is absolutely essential.

In this second edition of *Life Beyond the Classroom,* a number of important themes emerge. For example, the value of supporting people with disabilities in work and community environments and providing them with experiences with classmates without disabilities in neighborhood schools is highlighted. We think that it is very important for these two groups of young people to be regularly exposed to one another and to learn how to manage the frustration and difficulties that are associated with a heterogeneous community environment. The continued protection and segregation of people with disabilities will not benefit them in their quest for greater self-esteem and inclusion in the community and workplace.

For too long, the well-meaning professionals who work with individuals with disabilities (e.g., counselors, special educators) have underestimated the very significant

potential of most people with disabilities. This book evidences our efforts to emphasize this potential. Having high aspirations for success can influence the actual outcomes of people with disabilities. We live in a rapidly changing society, both politically and techno-logically, and it can become easy to feel inept or overwhelmed. Yet, positive self-esteem and confidence can directly alter one's level of success. There are substantial doubts on the part of many in society about the quality and credibility of education for people with dis-abilities. Unfortunately, as long as thousands of students leave school every year without employment or a meaningful career pathway, the skeptics are given more ammunition for their position. This type of thinking is enhanced when there is a shortage of funds for expanding good programs or when misguided social priorities predominate.

Whatever the political climate (and these philosophies do move in cycles), there will always be young adults in need of education and work opportunities. Transition from school to adulthood has remained a major priority of state legislatures, as well as the U.S. government, primarily because intelligent and informed people know that the country's future rests upon the education and employment of its young people, thousands of whom have specialized needs or disabilities. As society becomes more complex and as technol-ogy and jobs become more specially designed, upgraded equipment and facilities, as well as a more sophisticated approach to training, will be required. Greater work experiences in the community, more intensive apprenticeships, greater use of business mentors, and employment during school all constitute a more successful approach to transition plan-ning, according to observations since 1980.

Why would anyone, regardless of his or her political persuasion, argue against real work with benefits for people with disabilities? This should be the consummate bipartisan issue and should receive endorsement from all parties. All players involved benefit by employ-ing people with disabilities. The individual with a disability has—often for the first time—a real job, benefits, and dignity. The employer gets a good worker and often will receive specialized support to train and maintain the individual's lifestyle. The family will be able to see their family member in a competent role in the workplace. Taxpayers will save money as the individual will no longer require services in a segregated day program year in and year out. The question then remains: Why do the vast majority of individuals with significant disabilities remain unemployed?

The answer to this question lies in the inability of advocates and people with disabil-ities to sufficiently market their capabilities and work potential. The existing adult services system in the United States, as well as around the world, has been deeply entrenched for several decades. To change this way of providing services, particularly in times of reduced funding due to a serious fiscal crunch, is extremely difficult. Hence, there is an over-whelming necessity to market the positive attributes of supported employment for people with disabilities on a local and national level.

Important gains and progress have been made in the education and employment of young people with disabilities since 1990, yet only in certain parts of the country. There is an unfortunate disparity among communities in successfully helping their young adults. In this second edition, we endeavor to provide many more individualized examples of transition planning in order to give the reader more specific and concrete examples of how to collaboratively plan individualized transitions with meaningful adult goals for people with disabilities. There is also a stronger focus on person-centered planning and career

development with a clear message that, unless businesses and industry are involved in a more direct fashion, those training activities generated exclusively in the school environment are doomed to fail, being largely ungeneralizable.

It is hoped that this book will successfully touch the lives of thousands of university students and professionals who wish to accumulate more information and knowledge in the important areas of education and employment for young people with disabilities. The challenge is greater than ever. There is a critical need for professionals to take a more significant leadership role in the community on behalf of people with disabilities. Advocacy and involvement are essential to making transition work in a community. This book is based upon the notion that any community can have a successful transition program, but individuals with disabilities and their families and advocates must be actively involved and committed to envisioning successful employment and community outcomes for students after school.

For the Reader

Each chapter in this volume opens with a list of learning objectives that serve to introduce the chapter and preview its major points. Each chapter also closes with study questions that we hope the reader and, in some cases, the university professor will find helpful in understanding the major points. The study questions are offered as a way to help the reader to synthesize the information in the chapter in the most effective way.

The case studies that appear in this book are based on synthesized composites of the authors' experiences in the transition field. They are presented to help the reader to understand the basic underlying concepts of each chapter.

Each chapter features profiles of U.S. leaders in the fields of education and employment of young adults with disabilities. Choosing only 16 individuals to showcase in this volume was quite difficult because of the number of outstanding leaders working in the field. Nonetheless, it is hoped that the profiles presented here will provide role models for others.

In May 1992, the American Association on Mental Retardation (AAMR) approved a new definition of mental retardation. Rather than using the specific IQ of 70 as a criterion for mental retardation, this new definition includes individuals with IQs ranging from 70 to 75. The new definition also focuses more specifically on assessment of adaptive skills and needed supports, basing the categorization of mental retardation on support required instead of labeling individuals as having mild, moderate, severe, or profound mental retardation. Levels of support (e.g., intermittent, extensive) are a very important aspect of this book. We believe that supports are crucial in determining how successful individuals with disabilities will be; yet, there remains a necessity to communicate broad differences between individual abilities. For that reason, we have continued to refer to some individuals as having mild levels of retardation (i.e., needing a more minor level of support than those with severe mental retardation). Also, because some of the studies discussed in this book were conducted before the new AAMR definition of mental retardation was approved, it is necessary to refer to the formerly used categories in order to accurately reflect the data.

Acknowledgments

I am so grateful to many people who contributed to the development of this second edition of *Life Beyond the Classroom*. There are many colleagues with whom I have worked and from whom I have learned and benefited while developing this book. It is difficult to know where to start, insofar as there are so many who have very much influenced my work. This is actually the third transition-related book with which I have been involved: *Transition from School to Work* was published in 1988, and the first edition of *Life Beyond the Classroom* followed in 1992. I mention this because there are a number of people who have been involved in these projects who have helped to shape my thinking.

I am blessed to work with some wonderful people at the Rehabilitation Research and Training Center on Supported Employment at Virginia Commonwealth University. Some of these people have strongly influenced the direction of my writing; they include Dr. Katherine Inge, Dr. Michael D. West, Dr. John Kregel, Dr. Wendy Parent, Pam Sherron, Vicki Brooke, Mike Barcus, Grant Revell, and Karen Flippo. They have helped to give me insight into the future direction of transition for young people with disabilities. In addition, I am grateful to Elizabeth Evans Getzel, Patricia Brown-Glover, Christine Hess, Susan Lehmann Griffin, Stacy Dymond, and Cary Griffin for their contributions to this book. They have greatly enriched this effort.

In addition to this important group of people, I would be remiss if I did not acknowledge leaders in the transition and disability fields at large who have helped to provide the foundation for many of the chapters in this book: Rebecca McDonald, David Mank, Lou Brown, Rud and Ann Turnbull, Ernie Pancsofar, Marty Agran, Susan Hasazi, Michael Wehmeyer, Jim Patton, Wendy Wood, Sherril Moon, Jane Everson, Frank and Janis Rusch, Edna Syzmanski, Sharon DeFur, Teresa Grossi, Margo Izzo, and Katina Karoulis, for example, immediately come to mind in considering the significant effects of their work on this book. There are many others who have also published excellent work and who work in the field in an outstanding fashion. Although it is impossible to recognize everyone by name, they have helped shape my thinking as well.

The next group of people I feel compelled to acknowledge are the parents, individuals with disabilities, and advocates who have continually shown us the way in terms of their wishes, demands, requests, and so forth. They have asked us as professionals to be responsive to their needs. I only wish that more of us could be more responsive and hear them more clearly.

Finally, I acknowledge Jeanne Dalton for typing and guiding the technical development of the manuscript for this book. She has spent hundreds of hours helping me improve this book by tracking down references and permission releases and communicating with contributors on my behalf. I could not have completed either the first or second edition of this book without her willing and positive help, especially in providing me with chapter after chapter of clean manuscript.

To Brody, Cara, Blake, Le Le,
Colin, Neal, Kent, and Therese

Life Beyond the Classroom

I

Defining and
Planning Transition

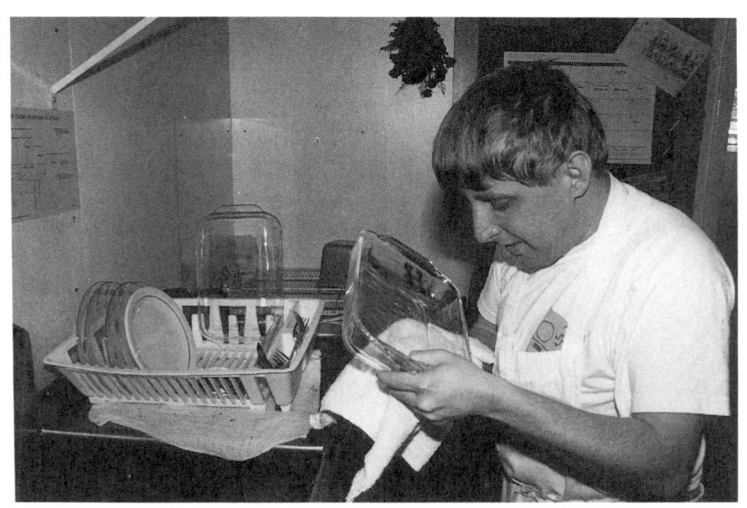

1

Identifying the Scope
and Vision of Transition

Upon completion of this chapter, the reader will be able to do the following:

- Define *transition* as it has been used to describe secondary and postsecondary services
- Understand seven types of transitions faced by youth with disabilities
- Recognize the nine guiding principles critical to understanding the transition from school to adulthood
- Discuss various legislation pertaining to children with disabilities, including the Individuals with Disabilities Education Act (IDEA) of 1990
- Discuss the role and importance of student choice in transition planning

Susan Susan is a cheerful 17-year-old girl who is deaf in both ears (sensorineural bilateral loss), has only partial use of her vision (some light perception), and has mental retardation requiring intermittent support. Susan exhibits some stereotypic behaviors such as eye pressing and body rocking when she is nervous or agitated and occasionally has seizures, which she keeps under control with medication. She was institutionalized between the ages of 5 and 8 but now lives at home with her parents and an older brother. Susan is currently enrolled in a class for students with multiple disabilities in her neighborhood high school, where she is learning skills, such as self-help, work, and community mobility skills, that will enable her to be more independent. Part of Susan's school week is spent with a mobility instructor, who works with her on using a cane and utilizing trailing tech-

niques. At home and school Susan signs using the American one-hand manual alphabet. When she is with others who are unfamiliar with signing, she uses a communication board. Although Susan can communicate effectively, she usually does not initiate interactions.

At school, Susan is involved in community-based instruction, meaning she and other classmates learn necessary skills in the community rather than the classroom. Currently, Susan participates in biweekly shopping trips, eating out at restaurants, and a half-time placement at a jobsite. Because of Susan's age, she and her parents are looking into possible work and residential settings for the future. They will face a terrible shock if they have not planned accordingly for the transition into adulthood (Gallivan-Finlon, 1994; Hanley-Maxwell, Whitney-Thomas, & Pogoloff, 1995).

Consider the tremendous challenges Susan will face as she enters adulthood. The dual loss of hearing and sight is thought to be one of the most isolating disabilities, as it limits both the amount and manner in which information in the environment is received and assimilated. Despite these challenges, Susan, with the aid of training and technology advancements, can have a good quality of life but not without appropriate planning and self-advocacy on her part.

This book presents ways to help Susan and millions of other young adults like her adjust to the challenges of adulthood—and in particular, the workplace—in today's complex society. There are over 4 million children with disabilities in special education in the United States; a significant number of them are in middle and secondary schools. Table 1.1 shows the distribution of these children in 1992. Across the country, these young people with disabilities are leaving the public schools and looking for postsecondary opportunities in community colleges and the work force, searching for their rightful places in the community. However, as Table 1.2 indicates, in 1992, 229,000 students exited school and faced these transitions alone. The unemployment rate for people with disabilities continues to hover between 50% and 75%, an unacceptable and discouraging figure reaffirmed by a 1994 Louis Harris and Associates Poll. Equally disturbing is the 25%–30% dropout rate of young people with disabilities (Holsch, Karen, & Franzini, 1992; MacMillan, Balow, Widaman, Bosthwick-Duffy, & Hendrick, 1990; MacMillan et al., 1992). It has become increasingly clear to professionals in the disabilities field and concerned family members that the only way to alter these rates is by emphasizing greater work opportunities and experiences in the schools. Consequently, public schools must critically self-examine their curriculum offerings.

This book also focuses on how to build connections throughout the community for young adults with disabilities. Businesses, community colleges, recreation centers, and places to live are all key connections to facilitate transition. This book addresses not only people with mental or physical disabilities but also those with cognitive, hearing, visual, and emotional disabilities. Transition is for all young adults. In fact, literature, demographic trends, and movements that affect young adults without disabilities are also addressed in this book, as studying this age group in its entirety is the only way to plan and implement effective transition programs. For example, why do some students, regardless of level and/or type of disability, do well at work? Why do others perform poorly? The days of exclusively identifying vocational programs for people with disabilities as isolated from business, industry, and the work force, in general, are gone. And people are finally realizing that transition issues apply to all students.

Table 1.1. Disability of students ages 6–21 served under Part B and Chapter 1: Number and percentage, school year 1992–1993

Disability	Part B	
	Number	Percentage[a]
Specific learning disability	2,333,571	52.4
Speech-language impairments	990,718	22.2
Mental retardation	484,871	10.9
Serious emotional disturbance	368,545	8.3
Multiple disabilities	86,179	1.9
Hearing impairments	43,707	1.0
Orthopedic impairments	46,498	1.0
Other health impairments	63,982	1.4
Visual impairments	18,129	0.4
Autism	12,238	0.3
Deaf-blindness[b]	773	0.1
Acquired brain injury	2,906	0.1
All disabilities	4,452,117	100.0

Source: U.S. Department of Education, Office of Special Education Programs, Data Analysis System (DANS).

[a]Percentage sum within columns.

[b]Coordinators of the State and Multi-State Services for Children with Deaf-Blindness have identified 8,404 people between the ages of birth and 21 in the United States. They are required under law [20 USC 1422 (c)(1) and (2)] to conduct an annual census of all people under age 22 who meet the federal definition for deaf-blindness (*Federal Register*, 1991, p. 51585). For a full report, contact the Severe Disabilities branch of the Office of Special Education Programs.

In a 1994 address, one of the most prominent politicians of the era, Senator Robert Dole, spoke of his concerns and hopes for people with disabilities:

The National Organization on Disability recently released an update of the groundbreaking 1986 Louis Harris survey of disabled Americans. The 1986 survey asked people with disabilities for the first time how they saw their lives and what was important to them. Taken together, the 1986 and 1994 Harris surveys allow us to determine America's progress in closing the gap in participation by those with disabilities—and the work that remains.

There is both good and bad news. First, the good news: Education levels have risen—the percentage of people with disabilities who have completed high school has grown from 60 to 75 percent. And fully 60 percent say things have changed for the better—including access to businesses, attitudes, public transportation, and portrayal of people with disabilities.

But there is bad news as well. In 1986, 33 percent of disabled Americans were working. In 1994, 31 percent. That is right—over the past 8 years employment among people with disabilities has not improved.

In my view, the new medicine we need is a national strategy on employment of people with disabilities. A year ago, I suggested we translate our good intentions into a national goal. Consider again that goal—by the year 2000, employment among the disabled will increase to that of the nondisabled. That would involve putting perhaps 3 million people to work. Alan Reich, president of the National Organization on Disability, has called for a goal of 2 million. Less ambitious, but maybe more realistic. But the point is the same. Let us set a goal, then figure out how to reach it. If a program makes a difference, fine, let us keep it. If not, let us spend our money another way and try something else. (Dole, October 7, 1994, pp. 1–3)

For too long, young people with disabilities have been treated as a separate group, segregated from "normal" people and excluded from the curricula, service delivery, and post-

Table 1.2. Basis of exit for students with different disabilities, number and percentage: School year 1991–1992

Disability	Diploma		Certificate		Maximum age		Dropout		Status unknown		Total	
	Number	Percent	Number	Percent	Number	Percent	Number	Percent	Number	Percent	Number	Percent
Specific learning disability	65,851	49.7	14,318	10.8	662	0.5	28,257	21.3	23,409	17.7	132,497	100
Speech-language impairments	3,562	43.9	596	7.3	87	1.1	1,633	20.1	2,230	27.5	8,108	100
Mental retardation	14,088	36.1	10,797	27.7	2,359	6.0	7,650	19.6	4,099	10.5	38,993	100
Serious emotional disturbance	9,557	28.1	2,217	6.5	338	1.0	11,894	35.0	9,995	29.4	34,001	100
Multiple disabilities	1,560	38.7	977	24.3	529	13.1	546	13.6	416	10.3	4,028	100
Hearing impairments	1,900	55.8	587	17.3	69	2.0	444	13.0	403	11.8	3,403	100
Orthopedic impairments	1,379	50.2	439	16.0	123	4.5	252	9.2	556	20.2	2,749	100
Other health impairments	1,771	48.6	614	16.9	67	1.8	606	16.6	584	16.0	3,642	100
Visual impairments	879	60.7	172	11.9	55	3.8	166	11.5	177	12.2	1,449	100
Autism	82	28.2	75	25.8	29	10.0	27	9.3	78	26.8	291	100
Deaf-blindness	72	50.3	42	29.4	15	10.5	6	4.2	8	5.6	143	100
Acquired brain injury	41	64.1	5	7.8	4	6.3	8	12.5	6	9.4	64	100
All disabilities	100,742	43.9	30,839	13.5	4,337	1.9	51,489	22.4	41,961	18.3	229,368	100

Source: U.S. Department of Education, Office of Special Education Programs, Data Analysis System (DANS).

Note: Percentage may not total 100% because of rounding.

secondary opportunities for youth without disabilities. However, if optimal ways to a smooth transition into adulthood are to be discerned, the work opportunity and likelihood for successful integration into the community for all students must be examined.

The idea of educating youth with and without disabilities together is not simply a philosophical notion, but one that is born out of pragmatic sense and, in 1993, judicial support. In the Third U.S. Circuit Court, Judge Edward Becker ruled that public schools must teach students with disabilities in general education classrooms as much as possible. ("Neighborhood school," 1993). This case, along with prevailing philosophies in the field, are leading to increasing numbers of students with disabilities receiving education in general education classrooms and neighborhood schools.

Defining Transition

Much has been written about transition since the 1980s (Syzmanski & Parker, 1995). More literature is needed, however, to specifically address the nature of these transitions and the challenges they present for 16- to 25-year-olds. Transition from school to adulthood may be defined as the life changes, adjustments, and cumulative experiences that occur in the lives of young adults as they move from school environments to more independent living and work environments. Examples of transitions include changes in self-awareness, body, sexuality, work and financial needs, and the need for independence in travel and mobility. Successful transitions also increase success, confidence, and competence in one's work skills.

Transition was defined in 1994 by the Council for Exceptional Children, Division on Career Development and Transition, as the following:

> Transition refers to a change in status from behaving primarily as a student to assuming emergent adult roles in the community. These roles include employment, participating in postsecondary education, maintaining a home, becoming appropriately involved in the community, and experiencing satisfactory personal and social relationships. The process of enhancing transition involves the participation and coordination of school programs, adult agency services, and natural supports within the community. The foundations for transition should be laid during the elementary and middle school years, guided by the broad concept of career development. Transition planning should begin no later than age 14, and students should be encouraged, to the full extent of their capabilities, to assume a maximum amount of responsibility for such planning. (Halpern, 1994, p. 116)

The best way to address the various dimensions of transition encompassed in this definition is to focus attention on how transition planning should occur. This process includes four major components:

1. An emerging sense of student empowerment that eventually enhances student self-determination within the transition planning process
2. Student self-evaluation, as a foundation for transition planning
3. Student identification of postschool transition goals that are consistent with the outcomes of their self-evaluations
4. Student selection of appropriate educational experiences to pursue during high school, both in school and within the broader community, that are consistent with their self-evaluations and their postschool goals

Transition to Adulthood for Youth with Disabilities

Young people with disabilities face many different types of transitions that must be successfully approached in order for students to be able to move beyond them into a stable adulthood. The following seven are the most common transitions that youth with disabilities face:

1. Employment
2. Living arrangements
3. Getting around the community
4. Financial independence
5. Making friends
6. Sexuality and self-esteem
7. Having fun

Employment

Most young people, regardless of disability, have concerns about what they will do after they finish high school. But not knowing how to find a job and lacking specific vocational skills that lead to employment are added sources of anxiety for people with disabilities. Without some form of employment, departing students are immediately dependent upon their parents or society, in the form of Social Security allowances. In addition, studies show that U.S. business and industry greatly value attitude, communication skills, and work experience when deciding to hire young people leaving school—assets to which many students with disabilities are never exposed (see Table 1.3). Perhaps these shortcomings explain the discouraging results[1] presented by Louis Harris and Associates (1994) regarding the employment of people with disabilities:

1. Two thirds of Americans with disabilities between the ages of 16 and 64 are not working.
 - Two in 10 (20%) are working full-time, and 11% are working part-time.
 - As in 1986, it is true that "not working is perhaps the truest definition of what it means to be disabled" (Louis Harris and Associates, p. 81).
2. The overwhelming majority of unemployed people with disabilities in the working-age population want to work.
 - Fully 79% of unemployed people with disabilities age 16–64, including 84% of people age 16–44, say they would like to have a job.
 - The proportion of these unemployed working-age people who want to work has increased by 13 percentage points, rising from 66% in 1986.
3. Adults with disabilities who are working are employed in a range of occupations:
 - Sixteen% hold professional or managerial positions or are proprietors.
 - Fourteen% are service workers.
 - Thirteen% are clerical or sales workers.

[1]These results were first published by the National Organization on Disability. (They are shown here from Louis Harris and Associates [1994]. *The ICD Survey II: Employing Disabled Americans* (pp. 6–8). Washington, DC: National Organization on Disability; reprinted by permission.)

Table 1.3. Qualities that count with employers

Factor	Rank
Attitude	4.6
Communication skills	4.2
Work experience	4.0
Recommendations from current employees	3.4
Recommendations from previous employer	3.4
Industry-based credentials, certifying skills	3.2
Years of schooling completed	2.9
Academic performance (grades)	2.5
Experience or reputation of applicant's schools	2.4
Teacher recommendations	2.1

Source: New York Times News Service (1995, April 6).

Note: Question posed to employers: When you consider hiring a new nonsupervisory production worker, how important are the following in your decision to hire?

Key: 1 = Not important, 5 = Very important.

- Twelve% are unskilled laborers or farmers.
- Seven% are skilled craftspeople.

These proportions are not very different from the employment patterns of employed people without disabilities.

4. Most adults with disabilities who are working or are willing and able to work (69%) do not need special equipment or technology in order to perform effectively at work; one quarter (26%) of these adults do need special equipment or technology.
5. A substantial minority of people with disabilities who are employed or are willing and able to work confront discrimination, unfavorable attitudes, and physical barriers in the workplace.
 - Three in 10 have encountered job discrimination.
 - Two in 10 have encountered physical barriers in the workplace.
 - Almost half of working-age people with disabilities who are not working believe that employers are insensitive to people with disabilities.
6. In this same poll, however, Americans also indicated that their attitudes toward integrating people with disabilities into all aspects of life, including employment, are more open and positive than ever before—an encouraging trend in a period marked by serious economic recession.

The ability to be employed upon leaving school, therefore, is important for at least three reasons: 1) working in competitive employment provides an opportunity to receive wages and benefits that lead to greater independence and mobility in the community at large, 2) being productive on a daily basis in a meaningful vocation is critically important for one's self-esteem and dignity, and 3) establishing new friendships and networks of social support in the community is facilitated by having a job.

Hence, the first aspect of transition that teachers, service providers, rehabilitation personnel, family members, and others should focus on is reducing students' anxiety over unemployment and economic insufficiency by effective occupational training. This should

occur through real jobs (i.e., paid employment in local business and industry) while the students are still in school.

Living Arrangements

The second aspect of transition most individuals concern themselves with involves their postschool living arrangements. They ask questions such as, "Must I always live with Mom and Dad?" and "Will I have to live in a room by myself?" These are very important questions that significantly influence the way people look at themselves and the types of friends they have.

Burchard, Hasazi, Gordon, and Roe (1991) looked at lifestyle normalization, community integration adjustment, and personal satisfaction for 133 adults with mental retardation requiring intermittent to limited support living in small group homes. The study indicated that people who lived in supervised apartments achieved the most typical lifestyles. They had greater personal independence and community integration and reported levels of lifestyle satisfaction and personal well-being similar to that of people living with their own families. Other studies, such as the work of Rotegard, Bruinicks, Holman, and Lakin (1985), repeatedly reinforce the critical nature of this transition. In fact, Halpern (1985) made community living one of the major components of his model. Clearly, one cannot consider movement from school to adulthood without closely examining the types of living arrangements available (Lakin, Proutry, Smith, & Braddock, 1995).

Getting Around the Community

A third aspect of transition is mobility. The ability to move around both within the community and in and out of the community is often taken for granted. Most people drive automobiles or have access to public transportation or friends who can help them to get around. Independent movement in the community is critical for going to movie theaters, convenience stores, grocery stores, parks, church, and work, as well as for feeling independent. One of the great difficulties that people with disabilities face is a lack of independent mobility.

Lack of mobility can be caused by ambulation problems or inaccessibility of public places. More often than not, however, lack of mobility is caused by the person's inability to drive an automobile or to obtain a driver's license or having a limited number of friends who are able to drive. Lack of mobility may also reflect living in an area without public transportation.

Financial Independence

Economic self-sufficiency is a major goal that most citizens desire—individuals with disabilities are no different. Unfortunately, education does not help students learn financial planning, investment strategies, or the basic knowledge necessary to evaluate the quality of retail sales and merchandising. Not surprising is that individuals with disabilities are among those most vulnerable to scams and unfair marketing practices.

Financial/income security transition goals should rank in importance just behind employment and postsecondary education transition goals, especially when considering that the majority of money spent on disability in the United States is on Social Security pay-

ments and medical assistance. Individuals with disabilities need to be educated in their rights and entitlements as related to these payments. Although the details of Social Security regulations are almost too complex to understand, an individual should know how to get help and resolution to specific questions. In 1995, the Social Security Administration made available an excellent resource, *Graduating to Independence,* for students who need information on Social Security.

Financial planning and income security involve a range of issues from the simplistic, such as money management, saving money, and making purchases, to more complex topics, such as estate planning, using credit, or long-term financial planning. For example, consider Laura, 21 years old, whose parents have saved $250,000 for her. They may decide, upon discussion with the education team, that an annual structured annuity payout over the next 40 years will be most advantageous to Laura. The transition plan should reflect this type of specificity. Remember, the plan needs to be a blueprint that sufficiently integrates all major aspects of the student's life.

Making Friends

Peer relationships and making friends are a fifth aspect of transition. Beginning in the the late 1980s, the transition literature has increasingly stressed the importance of and need for friendships in the lives of people with disabilities. In addition, there must be sensitivity to the changing nature of peer relationships as students move from middle school to high school, and then out of high school into adult environments. Once in adult environments, young people are expected to be increasingly independent in identifying friends, socially networking with people, and initiating social activities. Obviously, some people are better and more successful than others in developing such relationships. However, this is clearly a cause of stress and anxiety for many people with disabilities who have not been sufficiently empowered to have a network for meeting people.

Joblessness, poor living quarters, and/or restricted mobility are factors that can inhibit peer relationships. Developing new friendships, maintaining old friendships, and meeting the challenge of changing peer relationships are critical aspects of transition for all people with disabilities.

Sexuality and Self-Esteem

The development of sexuality and self-esteem is a sixth aspect of transition. As most teenagers grow into adulthood, they begin to establish their own values. Their confidence levels and how they choose to interact with members of the opposite sex are very important in establishing good self-esteem. People express sexuality, both in dating formats and in groups, through their clothes, hairstyles, and recreational activities. Too little attention has been paid to this important transition; but with increased focus in this area, some of the other transitions will fall into place more smoothly.

Having Fun

Finally, simply having fun and appreciating life constitute the seventh aspect of transition. There have been many wonderful materials and curricula developed that reflect age-appropriate leisure activities (Kelley & Frieden, 1989; Moon, 1994; Schleien, Meyer, Heyne,

& Brandt, 1995; Schleien & Ray, 1988). The key to selecting appropriate individualized transition plan (ITP) recreation goals hinges on the following criteria:

- What recreational interests does the student demonstrate and are these interests consistent with his or her intellectual and physical capabilities?
- What opportunities are available in the home and local community to actually enjoy this leisure activity?

Participating on the swimming team, walking or jogging, working out in an aerobics class, taking an arts and crafts class, or learning a game that other friends play (e.g., Super Nintendo) are some examples of leisure goals. Usually these goals are facilitated through local parks and recreation specialists, instead of in the classroom. With insight and creativity, an educational team can find scores of activities in which students can participate; however, planning will be necessary to make leisure options a reality. The use of adaptations for the leisure program and/or materials can also play a major role in identifying viable recreation goals.

Frequently, materials and equipment used in a recreational activity act as barriers to participation as they are usually designed for individuals without disabilities and do not take into account the severe physical or sensory impairments of those with disabilities. Therefore, it is often necessary to adapt or modify the equipment or materials to eliminate these barriers to recreation.

Related Disability Legislation

Congress has put a number of related laws into place that influence the transition from school to adulthood for young people with disabilities. Together, they form an important foundation for understanding the transition process. As of 1996, however, several of these laws are under review as the composition of Congress changes.

The Individuals with Disabilities Education Act (IDEA) of 1990

In 1975, PL 94-142, the Education for All Handicapped Children Act, mandated a free appropriate public education in the least restrictive environment for all children with disabilities. Since then, there have been a number of amendments to this act. In 1990, new amendments were reauthorized that expanded PL 94-142 under a new public law number, PL 101-476, which renamed the original act and its earlier amendments in a composite law, the Individuals with Disabilities Education Act—commonly referred to as IDEA. IDEA changed the term "handicapped" in the law's language to "with disabilities" and allowed private citizens to sue states or state departments of education for violations.

IDEA's new definition of "transition services" requires that students themselves be included in their individualized education programs (IEPs) and authorized changes in transition plans:

> Transition services means a coordinated set of activities for a student, designed within an outcome oriented process, which promotes movement from school to postschool activities, including postsecondary education, vocational training, integrated employment, including supported employment, continuing adult education, adult services, independent living or community participation. The coordinated set of activities shall be based upon the individual student's needs

taking into account the student's preferences and interests and shall include instruction, community experiences, employment development, and other postschool adult living objectives, and when appropriate acquisition of daily living skills and functional vocational evaluation. (PL 101-476, 20 U.S.C., 1401 [a][19])

Under PL 101-476, IEPs must include annual statements of the needed transition services for students, with the first document being written no later than a student's 16th birthday. If the school system determines that it is appropriate for a student, a statement of needed transition services is required at age 14 or younger. These statements should include descriptions of the interagency responsibilities and/or linkages needed before the student leaves the school setting. IDEA also encourages federally funded transition programs to develop and disseminate exemplary programs and practices that meet the unique needs of students who utilize assistive technology and services.

Although IDEA does not mandate ITPs, it does provide a requirement and challenge to the more than 16,000 local education agencies to include transition planning and implementation in IEPs for all children with disabilities. This was a major improvement over previous legislation, which addressed transition only in passing and did not provide a definition of transition, an explanation of the comprehensive nature of transition services, or a discussion of the role of interagency responsibilities related to transition. IDEA defines transition services as the following:

A coordinated set of activities for a student, designed within an outcome-oriented process which promotes movement from school to postschool activities, including postsecondary education, vocational training, integrated employment (including supported employment), continuing and adult education, adult services, independent living, or community participation. (Section 602[a])

The Individualized Education Program and Individualized Transition Plan The IEP has been required since the passage of PL 94-142 in 1975. It is a legally binding document that describes the student's annual goals and short-term objectives, along with a detailed level-of-performance assessment and necessary diagnostic data. The IEP can be enforced through due process and can advance to the federal court level. Because of its legal ramifications, most school systems have learned that they must responsibly fulfill an IEP's requirements. Table 1.4 outlines specific aspects of IEPs.

However, the concept of transition planning as part of IDEA and the IEP is relatively new. In the process of transition planning, the family, student, and education team can develop an ITP as part of the IEP, but an ITP is not legally required and does not hold the same specificity of structure as an IEP—schools have no statutory responsibility to provide ITPs. Furthermore, the concept of an ITP was introduced only with the 1990 passage of IDEA. Previously, the concept of transition was discussed in a more general or theoretical way.

Often, as many teachers and other education personnel will attest, the ITP is only a stepchild to the IEP. It is not uncommon for an IEP meeting to last 1–1½ hours, while the following ITP meeting lasts only 15–30 minutes. In school systems where this is the practice, it is most unfortunate because the idea underlying the ITP is to create a design or blueprint with a futures orientation in collaboration with the student and family—a task that can hardly be achieved in 15–30 minutes. Smith, Edelen-Smith, and Stodden (1995) list seven transition planning pitfalls (see also Chapters 3–6):

Table 1.4. Individualized education program: A closer look

An individualized education program is a written statement that does the following:
- Describes the special education program for an exceptional student
- Describes in general terms what an exceptional student can do (i.e., his or her present level of functioning)
- Describes the specific direct and indirect services the student will receive while in the special education program
- Describes how much time a student will spend in special and general education classes
- Lists the dates on which special education will begin, end, and be reviewed
- Describes what an exceptional student is expected to learn and how progress will be evaluated
- Lists the people who developed the plan and indicates their agreement with its content

An individualized education program is not any of the following:
- A daily lesson plan that describes each little thing that will happen to a student while in a special program
- A report written by a psychologist or educational diagnostician to describe a student's strengths and weaknesses
- An agreement that promises all services that are needed will be provided or that guarantees that services that are provided will work
- A ticket to unlimited mainstreaming or to full-time placement in a special education program
- Inflexible
- A substitute for a report card or other daily, weekly, or monthly progress reports
- A formal contract that places legal obligations on the people who develop it or the parents and professionals who agree to it

From Ysseldyke, J., & Algozzine, R. (1995). *Practical approach for teachers* (3rd ed., p. 131). Boston: Houghton Mifflin; reprinted by permission.

1. Failing to plan at the appropriate level
2. Confusing means with ends
3. Failing to involve all relevant educational partners
4. Selecting programs before identifying program destinations.
5. Failing to consider evolving future realities in the community
6. Being unaware of the process elements of strategic planning
7. Assuming that all systematic planning approaches are basically the same

Furthermore, planning for transition is difficult, at best, given the fact that multiple local agencies must be involved. An effective transition plan cannot be managed solely by a local rehabilitation agency, a local chapter of The Arc (formerly the Association for Retarded Citizens of the United States), or a local school system; all must work together.

The Rehabilitation Act Amendments of 1992

The Rehabilitation Act Amendments of 1992, PL 102-569, is quite significant, being the primary federal law that encourages access to disability support services and vocational rehabilitation for individuals with disabilities after school. This Rehabilitation Act has been improved over several decades with frequent amendments, but the law passed in 1992 (the Rehabilitation Act Amendments of 1992) is perhaps the most significant in terms of choice and consumer control over vocational outcomes. This law is far reaching and implemented in all 50 states in the United States through a combination of federal and state matched

dollars. Every state has local vocational rehabilitation (VR) offices, giving people with disabilities the opportunity to obtain vocational and independent living help as needed.

However, there have been a number of criticisms over the years about the Vocational Rehabilitation program. Specifically, some believe that only those clients with mild disabilities have been served with the limited funds that are available. Furthermore, many critics believe the Rehabilitation Act does not provide enough direct services and is too laden with administrative bureaucracy (Government Accounting Office, 1991; Salkever, 1994). Although these limitations do exist, this remains the sole program for many people with disabilities and has proven itself to be responsive to changes at a local or state level, depending on the nature of leadership.

The following is a list of the major features included in the Rehabilitation Act Amendments of 1992:

- *Employment outcome:* "Must be consistent with the abilities, capabilities, and interests" of the individual
- *Helping students make transitions:* State plan must contain policies designed to facilitate the transfer of responsibilities for helping students to make the transition students from school to work
- *Competitive employment:* "Compensation at or above minimum wage is required"
- *Extended employment:* Replaces the term *sheltered employment,* "work in a nonintegrated setting with compensation at or above the minimum wage, unless a lower wage based on individual productivity is permitted in accordance with . . . the Fair Labor Standards Act"
- *Making informed choices:* Each individual must be provided a list identifying all of his or her options for services and the providers of services of interest, also requires other information on "quality, accessibility, and consumer satisfaction be made available . . ."
- *Integrated setting:* A setting where the majority of individuals with whom individuals with disabilities interact meaningfully, excluding service providers, are not other individuals with disabilities. If there is a "distinct work group of only individuals with disabilities, the work group consists of no more than eight . . ."
- *Use of profit-making organizations for on-the-job training:* Increases state flexibility to use profit-making organizations to provide employment services
- *Supported employment plan:* Requires each state to have an acceptable plan for providing supported employment (SE) services
- *Eligibility:* Requires a presumption that the person can benefit from vocational rehabilitation, unless "there is clear and convincing evidence" otherwise. The eligibility determination must be made "within 60 days of the date on which an application is submitted"
- *Movement to more integrated employment:* States must make a "maximum effort" to provide services to promote movement from extended employment to integrated employment

The Americans with Disabilities Act (ADA) of 1990

On July 26, 1990, President George Bush signed into law PL 101-336, the Americans with Disabilities Act (ADA) of 1990, which many have hailed as a civil rights law for all people

with disabilities (J. West, 1992). This act was followed exactly 1 year later by a comprehensive set of regulations (*Federal Register,* July 26, 1991). These regulations provide for accessibility, nondiscrimination, and greater entrance into workplaces, community facilities, public transportation, and telecommunications. If this law achieves a reasonable degree of successful implementation, young adults should enter a world that is less discriminatory against people with disabilities. More rigorous legislation that reflects advances in medical rehabilitation, vocational rehabilitation, and behavioral intervention is expected to continue to develop as the 21st century approaches.

Already, the law has been increasingly phased in, as the following timeline demonstrates:

- 1990—Congress passed the Americans with Disabilities Act, a comprehensive law that prohibits discrimination on the basis of a disability.
- January 1992—Employers were required to make public areas accessible to people with disabilities.
- July 1992—A portion of the law went into effect prohibiting employers with 25 or more workers from discriminating on the basis of disabilities in hiring, firing, promoting, or compensating employees.
- July 1994—The law was expanded to apply to employers with 15 or more workers.

The United States has developed specific, protective policies and regulations designed to promote the employment of individuals with disabilities that are very different from those used in most other parts of the industrialized world, which are usually not so defining. In the United States, civil rights laws, specifically the ADA and Section 504 of the Rehabilitation Act of 1973, PL 93-112, protect individuals by prohibiting discrimination in employment on the basis of disability.

Under the ADA, employers are prohibited from discriminating against otherwise qualified individuals with disabilities during recruitment, hiring, evaluation, promotion, or any other facet of employment. Employers are further required to provide "reasonable accommodations" to enable individuals with disabilities to successfully perform their jobs, when accommodation can be provided without an employer sustaining an "undue hardship." Reasonable accommodations may include such things as restructuring jobs or work schedules, modifying equipment or providing assistive devices, providing an interpreter or reading aids, or improving the overall accessibility of the worksite. Employers found to be in violation of the law face the same legal penalties as those found guilty of discrimination based on gender or race. Table 1.5 lists aspects of the ADA that employers must be sure to implement to ensure fair treatment for workers with disabilities.

The ADA affirms that people with disabilities are willing and able to make valuable contributions to the economic life of their local communities. Under this approach, federal or state governments should not provide unwarranted financial incentives to employers. On the contrary, employers must only be required to provide individuals with disabilities open and fair opportunities to succeed—the biggest obstacle facing individuals with disabilities is the discrimination they face as they live in and move about their communities. The ADA is founded on the belief that people with disabilities are not burdens to business and industry who necessitate large government subsidies to offset anticipated increased costs. The barriers to employment they face are most often around them, not within them (Blanck, 1994).

Table 1.5. Questions for employers regarding the implementation of the ADA

- Do you provide information to job applicants and current employees about their rights under the ADA?
- Have you informed managers and supervisors about their responsibilities under the ADA?
- Do you recruit from nontraditional sources, including organizations that serve people with disabilities?
- Have you reviewed your employment practices and procedures to ensure that they do not discriminate against applicants or employees with disabilities?
- Are your interview sites and workplace facilities accessible to people with disabilities?
- Do you provide reasonable accommodations for applicants during the selection process and for employees as needed?
- Can you identify the essential functions of your jobs, and do your interview questions focus on the applicant's ability to perform them?
- Do you administer medical examinations only *after* an offer of employment is made?
- If you have medical records, do you keep them in separate, confidential files?
- If you have collective-bargaining agreements, do they support ADA implementation?
- Do you involve employees with disabilities in social and recreational activities?
- Is your employee benefits program accessible to all employees?

Source: President's Committee on Employment of People with Disabilities (1986).

The implementation of the employment provisions of the ADA presents a significant challenge to private business, as well as local, state, and federal governments. In 1993, the National Council on Disability (NCD) submitted a report to the President and Congress reviewing the progress made during the ADA's first 2 years of implementation and concluding that employers who were aware of the ADA requirements were making serious efforts to comply with the law (National Council on Disability, 1993). Most large companies appear to have designated an individual to be responsible for ensuring compliance with the ADA and efforts to modify recruitment and hiring processes are well underway in most major corporations. As of 1993, however, some companies (particularly smaller employers) were not aware of all the requirements of the ADA. In many instances, employers have struggled to gain accurate information. The NCD report also indicated that the entrepreneurial activities stimulated by the ADA have led to a proliferation of inaccurate training and technical assistance materials that have adversely affected implementation.

Goals 2000: Educate America Act of 1994

PL 103-227, Goals 2000: Educate America Act of 1994, commonly referred to as Goals 2000, contains two major components: 1) a system for helping states and localities establish high, voluntary academic standards; and 2) a system to support business, labor, educators, and the public in developing occupational skill standards. The two components are inextricably linked. A new generation of workers—those prepared for high-skill, high-wage jobs—will emerge from a restructured American education system that produces workers firmly grounded in core academic subjects and equipped with skills that are in demand in today's labor market.

To further these goals, the legislation establishes a National Skill Standards Board to encourage and assist partnerships in developing and adopting standards that are relevant to industry. The partnerships, including broad-based representation from business, labor, and education, actually develop the standards. The board's function is to provide financial and technical assistance in developing the standards and to endorse standards that meet

objective criteria. Standards endorsed by the board would be linked to the highest international standards and would promote the transition to high-performance work organizations.

Through the development of broadly defined skill standards, the United States will be able to set goals for skill achievement, competencies, and performance that will help create a lifelong learning system for all Americans and will drive the nation's economic growth into the next century and beyond. The law aims to accomplish the following goals by the year 2000:

- School readiness—All children in America will start school ready to learn.
- School completion—The high school graduation rate will increase to at least 90%.
- Student achievement and citizenship—All students will leave grades 4, 8, and 12 having demonstrated competency in challenging subject matter, including English, mathematics, science, foreign languages, civics and government, economics, arts, history, and geography. Every school in America will ensure that all students learn to use their minds well so they may be prepared for responsible citizenship, further learning, and productive employment in our nation's modern economy.
- Mathematics and science—U.S. children will be the best in the world in mathematics and science achievement.
- Adult literacy and lifelong learning—Every American adult will be literate and will possess the knowledge and skills necessary to compete in a global economy and exercise the rights and responsibilities of citizenship.
- Safe, disciplined, and alcohol- and drug-free schools—Every school in the United States will be free of drugs, violence, and the unauthorized presence of firearms and alcohol and will offer a disciplined environment conducive to learning.
- Teacher education and professional development—The nation's teaching force will have access to programs for the continued improvement of professional skills and the opportunity to acquire the knowledge and skills needed to instruct and prepare all American students for the next century.
- Parental participation—Every school will promote partnerships that will increase parental involvement and participation in promoting the social, emotional, and academic growth of children.

The Technology-Related Assistance Act for Individuals with Disabilities Amendments of 1994

The Technology-Related Assistance Act for Individuals with Disabilities Amendments (Tech Act) of 1994, PL 103-218, was signed into law on March 9, 1994, and provides access to assistive technology services and devices for individuals with disabilities of all ages. There are three specific purposes of the Tech Act:

1. To provide discretionary grants to states to assist them in developing and implementing a "consumer-responsive, comprehensive, statewide program of technology-related assistance for individuals with disabilities of all ages"
2. To fund programs of national significance related to assistive technology
3. To establish and expand alternative financing mechanisms to allow individuals with disabilities to purchase assistive technology devices and services

With the passage and reauthorization of the Tech Act, Congress acknowledged the powerful role that assistive technology can play in maximizing the independence of individuals with disabilities. This law emphasizes being responsive to the needs of consumers and has the potential to open many new opportunities for individuals with disabilities and their families to receive appropriate assistive technology services.

The act's state-grants program is intended to be a catalyst for statewide systems change to increase access to appropriate assistive technology devices and services. These funds are to be used to support systems change and advocacy activities, which will increase the availability of, funding for, and access to assistive devices and services (see Chapters 11 and 12).

The School-to-Work Opportunities Act of 1994

The School-to-Work Opportunities Act of 1994, PL 103-239, was signed into law by President Bill Clinton on May 4, 1994, and authorized $300 million for fiscal year 1995 to develop and establish school-to-work transitions for all young people, including those with disabilities. The Council for Exceptional Children promoted recommendations to include children with special needs in school-to-work transition programs that were incorporated into the final legislation. Among the law's specifications, career awareness and exploration/counseling must begin no later than seventh grade, and paid work experience is not required. This law, when taken in conjunction with others, holds tremendous promise. Table 1.6 compares the School-to-Work Opportunities Act with IDEA. As this book went to press in 1996, this law was being repealed with other work-related legislation and Congress was discussing the best way to consolidate these laws.

Although these laws do not guarantee change, they do provide an important national framework for people with disabilities. Understanding their basic intent will help in the development of relevant transition planning, especially in finding necessary resources to implement programs.

Nine Guiding Principles for Transition Implementation

Despite the fact that there are myriad political interests and differences in ideology in Congress for helping youth with disabilities, a number of guiding principles for effective transition implementation remain.

This book discusses many concepts related to individualized transition planning, teaching for transition, and involvement in work and community living, while the transition literature since the 1980s has coined many terms and concepts related to the transition from school to adulthood. It is important to sort out the most significant elements of transition and establish a foundation of principles. The following sections describe and relate nine principles related to the transition process (see Table 1.7).

Self-Determination and Student Choice

The transition models advanced in the early- to mid-1980s (Halpern, 1985; Wehman, Kregel, & Barcus, 1985; Will, 1984) did not adequately focus on student choice, family choice, and self-determination. Choice of school, type of job, type of work arrangement, and nature of

Table 1.6. Interrelationship of transition service requirements of IDEA and the School-to-Work Opportunities Act of 1994

School-to-Work Opportunities Act of 1994	Individuals with Disabilities Education Act (IDEA) of 1990
School-based learning component • Career awareness, exploration, and counseling to identify career interests and goals • Selection of a career major by the 11th grade • Program of study designed to meet the standards set by Goals 2000: Educate America Act of 1994 • Integration of academic and vocational learning • Regularly scheduled student evaluations • Entry into additional postsecondary education	• Include instruction, community experiences, development of employment and other postschool adult living objectives, and, if appropriate, acquisition of daily living skills and functional vocational evaluation • Annual planning and review meetings, functional vocational assessment, assessment of students' needs and interests • The IEP for each student, beginning no later than age 16 (or younger, if determined appropriate)
Work-based learning component • Work experiences • Job training experiences relevant to student career • Workplace mentoring • Instruction in general workplace competencies • Instruction in all aspects of the industry	• "Transition services," meaning a coordinated set of activities for a student, designed within an outcomes-oriented process that promotes movement from school to postschool activities, including postsecondary education, vocational training, integrated employment (including supported employment), continuing and adult education, adult services, independent living, or community participation
Connecting activities component • Match students and employers • School-site mentor to serve as liaison among employers, educators, case managers, and others • Provide technical assistance and services to employers, educators, case managers, and others • Provide technical assistance to schools and employers to integrate school-based and work-based learning • Encourage active participation of employers • Collect and analyze information regarding postprogram outcomes of students • Postprogram planning and assistance • Link youth development activities with employer strategies for upgrading worker skills	• Development of employment and other postschool adult living objectives based on students' interests • Provision of related services to achieve transition goals • The IEP must include a statement of transition services including, if appropriate, a statement of each public agency's and each participating agency's responsibilities or linkages, or both, before the student leaves the school setting • Student participation is required in the development of transition plans • Graduation assistance is provided • Postprogram reconvening of the IEP team

Source: Norman & Bourexis (1995).

instruction were assumed to be controlled unilaterally by the special education teacher and school system. Fortunately, more progressive thinking has entered the field, suggesting a much greater focus on choice, self-determination, self-advancement, and, generally speaking, freedom. A number of professionals, parents, and advocates have begun to write

Table 1.7. Nine guiding principles for transition implementation

1. Self-determination and student choice
2. Level and intensity of support
3. Family and student attitudes
4. Person-centered planning
5. Secondary curriculum reform
6. Inclusion
7. Career development
8. Longitudinal curriculum
9. Business connections and alliances

in this regard (Turnbull, Turnbull, Bronicki, Summers, & Roeder-Gordon, 1989). This philosophy is a very important aspect of planning for transition because the focus of control shifts from the service providers to the service recipients, who should be making decisions (Wehmeyer, 1992). This is more than an initiative, priority, or theme. It should be the only way to provide services. If service providers do not honor this need for a student- or client-focused way of planning services, they will eventually be out of business.

In the eyes of many, particularly those Americans with disabilities who have experienced discrimination, self-determination means empowerment: the right to assume control in one's life and the right to define quality of life for oneself. Two key issues must be addressed to support individuals with disabilities in becoming self-determining adults. First, opportunities to learn and practice skills of choice and decision-making must be made available early in life and exist across multiple environments. Second, legislation that increases accessibility and opportunities in multiple environments must be implemented and leveraged so that home, school, and community environments create and nurture choice and self-determination for people with disabilities (Kearney, Durand, & Mindell, 1995).

The implications for a student- and family-oriented approach to transition planning are significant. They include students participating in educational experiences in meaningful ways, going to workplaces and identifying the jobs they want, vetoing unfair vocational evaluation practices, and choosing the type of skills that they think will be useful.

Level and Intensity of Support

Supports are ways to help people with disabilities become more independent and capable of controlling the direction of their own lives. In designing education and human services programs, there is a strong movement to emphasize the role of supports in enhancing the success of people with disabilities. This has been considered by some as a "paradigm shift" from "curing" people of their disabilities to supporting them to the fullest extent possible (Bradley, Ashbaugh, & Blaney, 1994; Middendorf, 1995). Every individual needs some level of help or assistance to succeed. There are some people, for example, with very severe disabilities who need a great deal of support to succeed in school, work, home, and the community, while others may need only minimal assistance.

Supports can be identified from community organizations or agencies. Those found to be the most productive include personal connections through friends, acquaintances, or

personal experiences, the telephone book, the newspaper, and other colleagues. Five general types of support option categories have been identified: 1) employer supports, 2) transportation supports, 3) community supports, 4) personal and independent living supports, and 5) recreation and social integration supports (see Chapters 10 and 11; Newton, Olson, & Horner, 1995).

However, people with severe disabilities rarely take full advantage of all the support resources available to assist people in achieving their education, community living, or employment goals. Simply because a support is available at the workplace or in the community does not necessarily mean that an individual will automatically use it or benefit from its use. It is quite common for individuals to not know what potential supports are available to them, how to choose among the alternatives, or how to go about gaining access to desired support. A critical factor in the use of a variety of supports is often a teacher who helps the individual with identifying, choosing, and using needed supports at whatever level of assistance he or she prefers (Parent, Unger, Gibson, & Clements, 1995). This process is important since it comes from the individual perspective.

Family and Student Attitudes

Prior to 1975, young adults with severe disabilities could not even attend school. These students were fortunate if they could get into The Arc for a partial day program. The Education for All Handicapped Children Act of 1975 changed that. In the 1980s, students and their families were happy to be bused to schools, to have services from 9 A.M. to 3 P.M., and to exercise their due process—when appropriate—to receive occupational, physical, speech-language, or other related therapies. As the decade drew to a close, however, it became increasingly clear to those individuals and families that more functional, real-life community work experiences, and even job placements, before exiting school are necessary and essential means for transition. Finally, in 1996, the focus is turning to what the students and their families want instead of what teachers or school systems want.

Parents and other family members play an extremely important, even critical, role in the transition process. However, many parents do not attend to the necessary planning activities and indicate they do not know how to use the system or where to go for help (Campbell & Lehr-Essex, 1994; Llewellyn, 1995).

It is appropriate at this point to introduce two people, Ann and Rud Turnbull, who are nationally recognized as transition leaders and parents of a young man with a disability (see Transition Leader Box on p. 23).

Person-Centered Planning

All person-centered planning approaches begin with a focus on the wants and needs of an individual and recognize the importance of both formal and informal supports in assisting the person to achieve his or her dreams (Mount, 1994). O'Brien (1987) summarizes three characteristics of all person-centered planning approaches:

1. Everyday activities should be the focus of planning efforts.
2. Services are less important than family and community connections.
3. No single person can or should do everything.

Ann P. Turnbull Dr. Turnbull is the co-director of the Beach Center on Families and Disability and a professor in the Department of Special Education at the University of Kansas–Lawrence. Her research focuses on family systems and family-centered services. She has been the principal investigator on more than 20 federally funded research grants and has authored 12 books (many in second and third editions) and more than 100 articles, chapters, and monographs.

In addition to her professional credentials, she is the mother of three children, one of whom is an adult son with mental retardation and autism. She frequently participates in meetings as a family representative and is an active participant in national and international consumer organizations.

H. Rutherford Turnbull, III Mr. Turnbull is the co-director of the Beach Center on Families and Disability and a professor of special education and a courtesy professor of law at the University of Kansas–Lawrence. His training is in political science (B.A., Johns Hopkins University) and law (L.B., University of Maryland; L.M., Harvard Law School).

Mr. Turnbull concentrates his research and training in four areas: special education law and policy, mental disability law and policy, public policy analysis, and ethics as related to disability policy and service provision.

Since developing his specialization in the mid-1970s while a professor of public law and government at the Institute of Government, the University of North Carolina at Chapel Hill (1969–1980), Mr. Turnbull has authored more than 125 articles, books, chapters, monographs, technical reports, reviews, and commentaries related to disability issues. Mr. Turnbull has been "of counsel" on amicus briefs in two disability cases heard by the U.S. Supreme Court; has been the author and draftsman of North Carolina's special education law and limited guardianship law; has been the draftsman of PL 100-407, the Technology-Related Assistance for Individuals with Disabilities Act of 1988 (in his role as special staff to the Senate Subcommittee on Disability policy); and has testified numerous times on behalf of people with disabilities.

The Turnbulls are widely acknowledged as the preeminent leaders in the disability field on issues of families and parenting. They are "hands-on" people who have shown themselves to be incredible advocates for parents and their children with disabilities. Their expertise is wide ranging, from early childhood to transition, inclusion, and law. They are truly leaders in the field.

Personal futures planning does not in any way usurp the transition services component of the IEP but rather is used to dramatically expand or alter the traditional system-centered planning services. This is done by guiding teams in using, gathering, and managing assessment data; developing instructional interventions; and creating packages of supports that are more person centered and visionary (see Chapters 3 and 4). For exam-

ple, a teacher might seek to understand a student's vision for employment and vocational education by asking questions such as those listed below:

1. What job would you like to be doing 2 years from now? Five years from now? Ten years from now?
2. What kind of work experiences have you had? What kinds of things do you think you are good at? What are you not good at?
3. What skills will you need to do the kind of job you want to do? What kind of training or education do you need for this kind of job?
4. What things are important to you in a job (e.g., salary, benefits, transportation, schedule, location, personality of your boss)?
5. What hobbies and interests do you have that might be related to a future job?
6. How can service providers help you get a job? How can family members and friends help you get a job?

Secondary Curriculum Reform

Transition into adulthood for all youth with disabilities should be viewed as a right, and the goal of education should be to prepare students with disabilities to live and to work in their communities. This change in focus will expand the role of education from preparing individuals for transition to include making initial placements in appropriate community settings with sufficient time for adjustment before they actually exit school. As Edgar (1987) has noted, a very critical look at the quality of the secondary special education curriculum is in order. Although all blame cannot be attributed to the public school system and, specifically, the secondary special education teacher, there is little question that there must be a much closer relationship between instruction in the schools and the requirements of business and the workplace.

As these new attitudes permeate the school systems and more parents begin to expect these services, there will be a compelling pressure on all school systems and boards to alter their curricula to include functional skills training that reflects those skills required for success in business and industry. School systems must train students to be able to work in hotels, retail stores, fast-food restaurants, factories, warehouses, offices, libraries, and hospitals. Students must be able to take orders, work in teams, take initiative, and be cross-trained into other jobs fairly quickly. If schools are not prepared to teach students these skills, then the American labor force is going to be unable to meet the demands of the 21st century.

Edgar (1987), Edgar and Polloway (1994), and Wehman (1992) have eloquently called for the field of special education to be much more functional in secondary curriculum approaches and design; Clark and colleagues (1994) and Sternberg (1993) have echoed this plea. Although most parents want their children, regardless of disability, to be able to read, write, and compute, they also expect their children to be able to function in the community with an increasing degree of competence as the children grow older.

Functional curriculum involves making the skills that are presented interesting and useful. It is not difficult to teach from a workbook or run off ditto sheets; it is more challenging to individualize every student's program according to what each needs for his or

her age and skill level and base instruction in community, home, or work settings. Brown and Lehr (1993) have written about the importance of making activities meaningful for students with severe multiple disabilities, but this is true for all students. They suggest that for an outcome to be meaningful it must result in participation in daily routines according to the student's strengths. In additional, instruction should result in the student's having more meaningful control over personal routines and events in the environment.

However, until this transformation is made in the more than 16,000 local education agencies (LEAs), youth who are economically disadvantaged and young adults with disabilities are less likely to succeed as the curriculum that they currently receive is often grossly inappropriate for their needs. (Examples of nonfunctional materials and activities are listed in Table 1.8.) Yet, no amount of federal legislation can change this error in the way special education services are delivered; only teacher trainers, principals, school board representatives, central office administration, and, above all, special education teachers will be able to begin to make these changes (Blackosby & Wagner, 1996).

Inclusion

Since the early 1990s, educators have made great progress in developing models for educating children with disabilities in the least restrictive environment (Cipani, 1995; Janney, Snell, Beers, & Raynes, 1995). The focus of many of these efforts has been to educate children with disabilities within general education programs and, whenever possible, in the general classroom. A number of school systems have developed methods of educating students with severe disabilities in general education classes (Eichinger & Woltman, 1993) through techniques such as team teaching (Jones & Carlier, 1995). In fact, experienced teachers can be the critical factor in the success of inclusion in the high school classroom environment (Worlery, Werts, Caldwell, Snyder, & Lisowski, 1995). Fostering greater inclusion of individuals with disabilities during the school years rests on two premises: 1) If society is for everybody, then schools should be for everybody. Therefore, the first measure of a school should be the extent to which it can serve all its students. 2) Schools are responsible, not only for the education that students receive but also for what students are prepared to do once they graduate; that is, the schools are responsible for providing services in ways that ensure their graduates' success. For the typical student, success is measured in outcomes such as meaningful work, a place to live, and personal fulfillment that includes a social network of friends and family; these goals are equally valid for students with disabilities. Education in an integrated environment is the best way to prepare students to live in integrated communities as adults.

The Association for Persons with Severe Handicaps (TASH) has been one of the leading proponents of inclusion. The TASH resolution (1993) lists five key aspects of inclusion:

1. The provision of specialized staff, resources, and services to meet individual needs in the general education classroom, neighborhood school, home and family, and community program and setting

2. The substantive training and retraining of personnel, both special and general service professionals, to prepare them to provide instruction to a variety of heterogeneous groups of learners

Table 1.8. Examples of nonfunctional materials and activities

Domain	Functional task	Nonfunctional because of material	Nonfunctional because of activity
Domestic/ self-help	Student puts arms through coat held by teacher prior to community-based instruction.	Student puts arms through holes in sleeveless practice vest.	Student identifies pictures of children putting on coats.
Leisure	Student uses switch-activated tape player.	Adolescent plays with switch-activated dancing bear.	Student is guided in putting pegs in a pegboard.
Community	Student takes items from store shelves and puts them in shopping cart.	Student bags toy "food" in classroom vocational area.	Student watches videotape of appropriate bus-riding behavior.
Vocational	Student tears plastic off bagged items in stockroom of department store.	Student sorts plastic toy nuts and bolts into slots on a form-board.	Student listens to a story about community helpers.

From Reid, D., Parsons, M., McCarn, J., Green, C., Philips. J., & Schepis, M. (1985). Providing a more appropriate education for severely handicapped persons: Increasing and validating functional classroom tasks. *Journal of Applied Behavior, 18,* 292; adapted by permission.

3. The systematic shifting of service delivery design and services away from a categorical, homogeneously grouped, and separate model to one that requires integration and thrives on a variety of grouping arrangements
4. The philosophical and administrative merger of special and general education and specialized and generic services into one service delivery system, evidenced by the integration of both professional staff and students
5. An unambiguous model of the least restrictive environment (Osborne & Dimattia, 1995; Yell, 1995), which is marked without exception by integration into normalized community environments and proximity to family, peers, and other citizens who do not have disabilities

Lipsky and Gartner (1994), who have written forcefully on inclusion in the past, indicate that parents need to be encouraged to take a stronger role in moving beyond separate to equal. Laski (1994), who has been a major pioneer in the movement toward inclusion, writes the following:

On June 14, 1994, the U.S. Supreme Court issued the final order in the *Rachael Holland* litigation. In formal terms the Court's denial of the Sacramento, California School District's petition for *certiorari* simply means that the U.S. Supreme Court decided not to hear the case bringing in the Holland litigation. In real terms the U.S. Supreme Court order means much more. It means an end to routine placement to children in handicapped only classes. It means an end to thoughtless rejection of parents' request for full inclusion. It means that the Supreme Court has decided not to disturb the strong set of legal principles and rules available to parents to protect the presumption of regular education classes. Because the Sacramento School Board entreaties and arguments to the U.S. Supreme Court were in vain, future threats by the school districts to string out parents in due process and resist inclusive education were stopped. Now when parents and

teachers join to plan and provide education in regular classes, they can do so with confidence knowing the standards and rules are clear and certain. (p. 3)

Stainback and Stainback (1984) discuss the merits of including all children in general education classrooms and having one unified system as opposed to two distinctively different systems (see also Table 1.9). The following 10 points[2] are suggested as key reasons for full inclusion:

1. *Reduction of stigma*—Serving students with disabilities in general education classrooms reduces the chances of stigma associated with students who have to leave the classroom for special services.

2. *Better understanding across disciplines*—Inclusion encourages special education teachers and general classroom teachers to work together. This reduces the mystique of special education and facilitates collaboration among professionals.

3. *On-the-job training for general educators in special education skills*—Individualization and other special interventions, such as task analysis, behavior management, and curricular adaptation, can be learned by classroom teachers with special education teachers serving as role models.

4. *Reduction of mislabeling*—Serving all students in general education classrooms, including those with special needs, reduces the requirement for labeling and, therefore, the possibility of mislabeling.

5. *Spillover benefits to all students*—Students without disabilities are able to benefit from interactions with their peers who experience various learning and behavior problems.

6. *Suitability of the model to the needs of secondary school students*—Serving students with special needs in general education classes enhances the likelihood of adaptations to instruction and content in various content courses.

7. *Prospect for master teacher staffing in special education*—Inclusion, which can be implemented using the consultation/collaboration model, encourages the chances for developing a master teacher professional who can meet the needs of a divergent student population. This benefits not only students with identified learning needs, but also those at risk for developing learning and behavior problems.

8. *Streamlines system*—The dual system of education has numerous problems, making it difficult to provide appropriate education to many students, including those with disabilities and others who have special needs.

9. *Reduction of duplication is cost-effective*—The dual education system is cost-ineffective in that it maintains duplications.

10. *Guarantees equal education opportunity*—Merely having access to general education programs is not sufficient to guarantee equal education opportunity for students with disabilities and those at risk for developing disabilities; the dual system of education is discriminatory and programmatically ineffective.

Segregation often leads to the isolation of children with special needs. It can limit their opportunities for social interaction and make it difficult for them to develop appropriate

[2]These 10 points are adapted by permission from Stainback, W., & Stainback, S. (1984). A rationale for the merger of special and regular education. *Exceptional Children, 51,* 107; Copyright 1984 by The Council for Exceptional Children.

Table 1.9. Comparison of dual and unified systems

Concern	Dual system	Unified system
Student characteristics	Dichotomizes students into special and regular	Recognizes continuum among all students of intellectual, physical, and psychological characteristics
Individualization	Stresses individualization for students labeled special	Stresses individualization for all students
Instructional strategies	Seeks to use special strategies for special students	Selects from a range of available strategies according to each student's learning needs
Type of educational services	Eligibility generally based on category affiliation	Eligibility based on each student's individual learning needs
Diagnostics	Large expenditures on identification of categorical affiliation	Promotes cooperation through sharing resources, expertise, and advocacy responsibilities
Professional relationships	Establishes artificial barriers among educators that promote competition and alienation	Emphasis on identifying the specific instructional needs of all students
Curriculum	Options available to each student are limited by categorical affiliation	All options available to every student as needed
Focus	Student must fit regular education program or be referred to special education	General education program is adjusted to meet all students' needs

From Stainback, W., & Stainback, S. (1984). A rationale for the merger of special and regular education. *Exceptional Children, 51,* 107; Copyright 1984 by The Council for Exceptional Children; reprinted by permission.

interpersonal skills, which creates obstacles to proper adjustment. Without the experience of living and working in community settings, it is more challenging for students with disabilities to live and work in the "real world" after they leave school. In addition, separate placements can stigmatize children with special needs. A sense of being different may cause a child to develop a negative self-image, which can prove to be a greater obstacle to living a fulfilling life than any disability or learning problem.

Consider the case[3] of Nathan, a 10-year-old boy with mental retardation who lives in Iowa. He has had positive experiences since being placed in a neighborhood school.

Nathan Hi! My name is Nathan, S.P. I'm 10 years old. You may be wondering about the letters after my name. I did, too. My mom said I needed them before I could start school. They stand for severe/profound. I started at River Hills, a special school for kids with disabilities in Cedar Falls, Iowa, at age 2. (Talk about pushy mothers!) But I love school! I liked River Hills, especially the popcorn machine in the office, and there were nice people there.

When I was 6, my mom heard that River Hills might be closing. We didn't know where I would go to school if River Hills closed so we checked around. We found Hansen Elementary School in

[3]This case study is from *Topics in Inclusive Education* (1994). Minneapolis: University of Minnesota; reprinted by permission.

Cedar Falls. I enrolled in kindergarten at Hansen. I was included in the kindergarten class with all the other kids. It was great! I loved Hansen! I went there for first grade, too.

In 1992, I transferred to West Cedar Elementary School in Waverly. (My mom has a hard time making up her mind.) No really—West Cedar is my neighborhood school. I like going to school in Waverly. I like riding the bus, but the ride to Cedar Falls was really long.

It took some planning for me to come to West Cedar. I'm in the regular class here, too. West Cedar didn't have kids like me in the regular classroom until me. My mom and my integration facilitator and associate from Hansen met with Dr. Book, the Superintendent of Waverly-Shell Rock School District, in July of 1991, to discuss an inclusion program for me in Waverly for the fall of 1992. After Dr. Book had time to review some information we provided him and he met with Roger Wilcox, my principal, they said they didn't know why it wouldn't work!

Everyone has been great! My teachers and my associates are wonderful! My mom says Waverly-Shell Rock and AEA 7 have collaborated to make this program a success. (I'm not sure what that means but I know everyone has been working together.) I've made a lot of friends here. My guidance counselor, Ms. J., helped by teaching my classmates about disabilities and about the circle of friends.

Career Development

The majority of research related to transition focuses on school-to-work transition. The subject of transition from postsecondary preparation and training to the world of work is critical, not only to meet the career needs of students with disabilities, but also to ensure the development of a cadre of professionals with disabilities to provide role models for children and adolescents with disabilities. Researchers are exploring the use of various vocational and career counseling methods, identifying barriers to career achievement, and developing intervention strategies. Many researchers are also beginning to address the problems that students with disabilities face in higher education.

A common theme that runs throughout much career development literature is that, although the process of career development is similar for all students, many issues are unique to the individual and the group of people with disabilities. Given this, most authors believe that career development should be individualized to meet the unique needs of people with disabilities. This may include such interventions in higher education as social skills training, developing career awareness, self-advocacy training, experience-based education, mentor programs, and career education courses. According to Symanski, Turner, and Hershenson (1992), two important factors to keep in mind when working with students with disabilities are type of disability and the age of onset—both of which can have a major impact on the career choice, development, and achievement of students with disabilities.

A second theme repeated by many authors is that environmental attributes conspire to limit the early social and vocational experiences of people with disabilities, excluding them from participation in extracurricular activities or volunteer experiences. Experiential learning opportunities are needed to encourage the typical development of career exploration, preparation, and maturity. Postsecondary education must provide these experiences for students with disabilities, although students without disabilities are generally exposed to them at an earlier age.

The Division on Career Development and Transition of CEC has expressed five key aspects of career development and transition education at the elementary level (Clark, Carlson, Fisher, Cook, & D'Alonzo, 1991) that help form the foundation for this book:

1. Career development and transition education is for individuals with disabilities at all ages.
2. Career development is a process that begins at birth and should continue throughout life.
3. Early career development is essential for making satisfactory choices later.
4. Significant gaps or periods of neglect in any area of basic human development affect career development and the transition from one stage of life to another.
5. Career development is responsive to intervention and programming when the programming involves direct instruction for individual needs.

Longitudinal Curriculum

All elementary and middle school programs for students with disabilities need to have an active vocational component, making career and vocational education a fairly prominent role in the child's daily educational program. It is not too early for the 11-year-old with a behavior disorder, learning disability, or cerebral palsy to begin considering the range of available career options. This is not to say that students who are 11–12 years old should go out and work on a jobsite. Instead, teachers must focus on real-life work experiences, opportunities, visits, and career-oriented field trips throughout a student's educational career. Most families are not accustomed to vocational experiences and intervention during the ages of 9–13, but research suggests that this level of intervention is extremely important (Wehman, 1992). Table 1.10 shows how vocationally related activities can occur longitudinally across the school year. Ultimately, the responsibility falls upon the schools to communicate and plan for the long term.

Business Connections and Alliances

There will be an increasing demand for a diversified work force in the 21st century (Kregel & Tomiyasu, 1994). Work opportunities will abound in selected areas, such as entry-level service occupations in the hotel and restaurant industries, the child care sector, the technologies, inventory management, and clerical support. These are areas in which people with disabilities, if sufficiently trained and exposed to the work environment, can make contributions to society, business, and industry while bettering their own lives.

The connections with business and industry have been underlined in importance as a result of post-21 follow-up study research data. Findings from many studies show that students are most likely to be employed after leaving school if they held paid jobs while they were in school (Chadsey-Rusch, Rusch, & O'Reilly, 1991; Edgar, 1987; Frank, Sitlington, Cooper, & Cool, 1990; Hasazi, 1985; Hasazi, Gordon, & Roe, 1985; Levine & Edgar, 1995).

Halpern, Doren, and Benz (1993) argue eloquently for the need to bring the secondary curriculum much closer to the needs and demands in the local business environment:

> So long as school and adult agency personnel are basically uninvolved in helping students to find their jobs during the school year, or are perceived to be uninvolved, and as long as school-sponsored work experience is infrequently a part of the student's program, it is at least questionable whether or not the jobs that are found by or for any given student will fit into an overall educational plan for that student. (p. 37)

Table 1.10. Vocational environments and activities across grade levels

Grade level	Environments	Examples of potential activities
Elementary	*Integrated school* General education classroom	• Take attendance to the office • Lunch count • Milk count and delivery • Keep time • Feed classroom pets • Water plants in classroom • Line leader • Pass out snack
	School office	• Clean pencil sharpener/erasers • Prepare school newsletter: collate, staple, deliver, print on the computer
	Lunch room	• Sort out and roll coins from milk and lunch money
	Art room	• Organize/sort materials
	Gymnasium	• Set up/put away gym equipment
	Library	• Reshelve books
	Neighborhood	• Fundraising in neighborhood for school functions
Junior high	*Integrated school* Lunch room	• Lunch room duties: portioning food, wiping tables, room monitor
	Gymnasium	• Take tickets at games and dances • Sell refreshments at school functions • Cashier at school bake sales
	School store	• Stock supplies, cashier
	Library	• Deliver audiovisual equipment
	School office	• Photocopy materials for classroom • Laminate materials for classroom
	Theater (school)	• Usher at plays, concerts
	Neighborhood	• Fundraising for school functions • Paper route
	Community businesses Music stores	• Price items, stock shelves
	Video rental stores	• Rewind films/reshelve returned films, log new films into computer
	Clothing stores	• Price, tag, hang up, and steam clothing
	Movie theaters	• Take tickets
	YMCA/Health clubs	• Wash/fold towels
	Fast-food restaurants	• Prepare salads, prepare take-out packages
	Hospitals	• Package surgical supplies
	Banks	• Microfiche checks, operate coin machine
	Hotels	• Housekeeping/laundry
	Offices (e.g., insurance)	• Prepare mailings, collating, stapling
	Computer stores	• Copy computer disks, mail orders, inventory supplies
	Grocery store	• Stock items, package produce, bag groceries
	Florist	• Prepare standard bouquets, water plants
High school and transition	*Integrated school* Student-run business or sales	• Cashier, participate in producing products, stock items
	Community businesses Same options as junior high	• Same options as junior high

In order for such a connection to emerge between the basic school curriculum and paid work, much more is needed than simply advocating for "better jobs" (see Chapter 3).

> Employers will need to be educated about the purposes of work for students, and incentives will have to be developed or improved in order to make such 'employment' profitable to the employers. Curricula within the schools will have to be improved or developed in order to build clear and relevant bridges between school and the world of paid employment. (p. 37)

However, the key role of business cannot be overemphasized (Benz & Halpern, 1993).

Conclusion

A new generation of teachers who fully comprehend the importance of transition in the special education curriculum and the adult services system is needed to empower young people with disabilities. This book proposes several basic tenets for professionals.

1. The student or family (i.e., the customer) is usually right. Listen to the student. Listen to the family. What are they saying? What hints are they giving in terms of what they need? These ideas are the critical features of a student-oriented transition program.
2. It is essential to look closely at what business and industry require of their work force. The new generation of teachers will examine their daily curricula and critically evaluate whether the skills, objectives, and activities they are currently emphasizing have direct relationships to what local employers need to maintain a dependable work force. These teachers will also determine whether their curricula are being influenced by what business says is required and needed or by objectives generated by bureaucrats who have no real-life experience.
3. All young people with disabilities should have the opportunity to be included in the workplace and schools. Special schools, segregated work activity centers, and programs that are designed only for people with disabilities must become institutions of the past. People with disabilities consistently perform better in typical work environments and natural community environments—perpetual segregation hinders transition. Integration must be an outcome, not a process, that educators, parents, and professionals work toward together.

This chapter has discussed a legislative and philosophical framework for promoting school to adulthood transition. Strategies for enhancing transition services for young people with disabilities are developed in subsequent chapters.

1
Study Questions

1. What seven areas should be addressed in transition planning?

2. What are four major components of transition planning?

3. What requirements are placed on educational systems by the Individuals with Disabilities Education Act (IDEA) in regard to transition?

4. What are some major features of the Rehabilitation Act Amendments of 1992 and the Americans with Disabilities Act (ADA) of 1990?

5. What are three characteristics of person-centered planning?

6. How can educational systems improve the choice and self-determination of students with disabilities and their families?

7. What are the primary attributes of transition as defined by the Council for Exceptional Children, Division on Career Development and Transition?

8. What are five of the arguments for inclusive education as presented by Stainback and Stainback (1984)?

2

Expanding Participation and Choice of Students and Families

Upon the completion of this chapter, the reader will be able to do the following:

- Describe the role of the family in transition planning
- Discuss family expectations for children with disabilities in terms of transition outcomes
- Be aware of ways that youth with disabilities can communicate their transition needs
- Understand what family support programs are and why they are important
- List at least six recommendations for developing family support plans

Students with disabilities and their families must be the focal point for transition planning and implementation (Hanley-Maxwell, Whitney-Thomas, & Pogoloff, 1995). Student and family input in planning instructional objectives, career goals, and community living are critical, yet remain the missing link in most transition programs across the United States. In too many instances, meetings to review student progress include only professionals who can determine merely what they *think* students and families need or want. Although most professionals are well intentioned, the fact remains that specific student and family views are not well represented, which causes school programs and long-term transition plans to become functions of what professionals believe is required, instead of what students and families actually require (Stineman, Morningstar, Bishop, & Turnbull, 1993; Thorin & Irvin, 1992).

In addition, too often, school systems have a monopoly on services, forcing students with disabilities and their families to accept whatever curricula, service delivery models,

and transition plans are offered, whether they like them or not. In reality, however, these students and families have a legal right and entitlement to challenge schools and school boards for appropriate public education that reflects the students' needs. More families need to exercise these rights in order to change the archaic behavior of many rigid school systems. Consider, for example, how businesses operate: Years ago, most successful companies in the United States learned that in order to earn a profit and meet the needs of customers, they must first understand what their customers want. Potential customers were surveyed repeatedly to determine their needs, attitudes, opinions, and wishes. Companies that did not engage in this behavior (i.e., marketing and outreach to customers) quickly lost business. Customers went to other shops to purchase similar products. Similarly, families need to "shop around" for the most appealing and appropriate services.

There is, therefore, an incumbent responsibility on families to exercise their rights. Many professionals become quite frustrated when they are unable to involve families in the process, as such apathy clearly hampers the development of truly responsive transition plans. Students and their families must be willing to determine their career choices and preparatory life experiences by indicating what they want and taking responsibility for their own transition planning. This chapter shows how students with disabilities and their families can become major participants in transition planning and demonstrates how they, as customers, can direct their individualized transition planning for the best results. It also includes descriptions of some of the strategies that students with disabilities and their families can utilize to become more involved and more assertive in the transition planning process. The philosophy of this chapter, and indeed this book, is that students and families know their needs better than anyone.

Students and Parents: Getting Involved in the Transition Process

The first aspect of involvement is to be aware of the individualized education program (IEP) and knowledgeable about how an individualized transition plan (ITP) should be developed. If a school does not offer individualized transition planning, transition goals must be incorporated into the IEP or, better yet, parents and students can appeal to administrators and teachers for ITPs. As ITPs are broader based than IEPs and require professionals from outside of the school system, services that involve many agencies, and a long-term approach (i.e., more than 1 year), students and families must speak for themselves in establishing annual transition plans. Consider Addie Comegys, one of the most outstanding parents in the United States, and the role she has played on behalf of her adult daughter who has severe multiple disabilities. Ms. Comegys has been a major transition leader and advocate for change, never afraid to "get involved" (see Transition Leader Box on p. 37).

The second aspect of involvement requires regular follow-up with the school system to ensure that the transition plan is being implemented. Even the most well-meaning schools sometimes abandon the detailed implementation of ITPs in the face of the bureaucratic challenges inherent in daily administration. Students and families who are most outspoken and follow up regularly with the schools for the services identified in their ITPs are most likely to receive them.

In following up, usually a telephone call, followed by a letter, and eventually a visit are effective means of communicating interest. If these attempts make no progress, visits to

Addie Comegys Twenty years ago when Kate Comegys was born with severe mental retardation, cerebral palsy, deafness, and an inability to speak, doctors told her parents to institutionalize her and adopt a child. Instead, Addie and Brock Comegys listened to their "immediate instincts" and kept their daughter with them. Today, Kate is a senior at Hamilton-Wendham Regional High School and wants to get a job in town after graduation. She works part time in competitive employment at a cable television company.

Through the years, her mother, Addie, has been Kate's greatest advocate and supporter—challenging the notions and the systems that produced inadequate and inappropriate services to support her family in meeting Kate's needs. Addie began advocating for Kate with two basic beliefs: 1) that Kate's potential far exceeded professional expectations, and 2) that Kate should and could be an active and included community member—revolutionary ideas 18 years ago. Six years ago, Addie successfully fought for supported employment training for Kate in an integrated setting. She has also prevailed in obtaining an age-appropriate, public school placement for Kate in her local high school. Her efforts have not stopped with Kate.

As an executive board member, chair of the family committee, and a member of the media committee at The Association for Persons with Severe Handicaps (TASH), Addie has been instrumental in conveying the needs and interests of families and finding ways to meet those needs. Her leadership has been felt in Massachusetts and across the country, where she is frequently called upon to share her experience and expertise.

key administrators within the central office of the local education authority are helpful. As a general rule, however, the best way to get an ITP implemented is to develop an ongoing level of rapport and positive communication with those professionals responsible for its actual daily implementation. Students and families must learn to use professionals for help in furthering their goals.

The third element of involvement is accountability, the area where most parents and students fall short. Accountability means determining if the ITP is working and resulting in positive differences. Consider, for example, Marvin—a student whose transition plan includes 25 hours of competitive employment in a stocking job at the local grocery store. Marvin, who has never worked before, continues to cut, paste, and color with the idea that this is a meaningful prevocational activity. The school system continues to say that it cannot find a job for him and that the local rehabilitation counselors are too busy. In this situation, Marvin and his parents should stand up for themselves and request that his vision of a part-time competitive job at the grocery store be implemented by the school. However, Marvin and his family will eventually give up, worn down by the school system's bureaucracy. It is this lack of accountability on the part of the customer (i.e., the student and family) that leads to high postschool unemployment rates and many unsuccessful transitions. Families and students must hold school systems accountable for their promises. Again, families who are the most outspoken and assertive—even those considered nuisances—

will receive more services than families who are passive and apathetic (Ryndak, Downing, Lilly, & Morrison, 1995).

Ultimately, transition practices will change only when school systems become more progressive and more responsive to families, which will lead, in turn, to better transition planning and implementation. In 1996, however, only a limited number of students were receiving the types of quality services necessary for work and independent living.

This makes it essential for customers to know what services they want. Better informed customers will be much more successful in incorporating quality services into ITPs and implementing those ITPs than people unable to express what their child needs. Therefore, families who educate themselves about available community services and how these service delivery systems work will obtain services much more easily than uninformed families.

How Should Students with Disabilities Voice Transition Needs?

Most professionals would probably agree that very few teenagers and young adults with disabilities actively participate in their transition planning, a practice that goes directly against the way that most teenagers without disabilities plan their futures (i.e., by working with their guidance counselors or trying different jobs in the community) (Fullerton, 1995). Clearly, youth with disabilities need special assistance to assert themselves. There are several ways that these students can become involved in the transition process and taught to voice their concerns.

First, it is very important that parents help build confidence in their children and continuously remind them to indicate their desires to their teachers and other professionals in the school system. Obviously, the family plays a critical role in teaching the student self-advocacy and assertiveness. Family members should regularly talk to their child about transition and future planning, thus reinforcing the importance of the issue in the student's mind. Parents and family members can also follow up with the school to see that the students' concerns are being addressed. After the student has been given assistance in goal identification and ways to voice concerns, he or she becomes increasingly empowered and independent in dealing with teachers and other power figures within the school.

Second, teachers can involve students by including this kind of training in their curricula. Very few IEP objectives reflect self-advocacy and assertiveness training or ways to plan for the future. These are, however, very viable instructional objectives for students who lack these skills. The special education professional should also actively teach students how to plan for their transitions. This involves a variety of career education experiences, which makes students knowledgeable about what to select and, more important, shows them how to assert themselves in the overall process so that if a student does not like the way the transition goal-setting process is proceeding, he or she will know how to modify or even stop it. In order for these to be useful, students must be educated about their rights.

Wehmeyer (1995) has developed The Arc's Self-Determination Scale—an excellent way to help teachers, families, and students to individually assess the level of self-determination experienced by the student. This scale is comprehensive across all life-skill areas.

A third way to develop greater student involvement is through student peer groups, in which friends, who are also students with disabilities, meet with or without professional guidance to discuss their transition goals (e.g., where they want to live, where they want

to work, how they are going to get to work). These support groups can become vehicles for creating a more assertive climate and disseminating information to students. It is increasingly accepted and widely known that many people with disabilities and their families respond better to peers than to professionals. The idea of student involvement in transition and appropriate transition training are also well-suited for the support group arrangement.

For years, however, the goal of self-advocacy/future planning was not included as part of the transition plan. Only with the passage of the Americans with Disabilities Act (ADA) in 1990, PL 101-336, and literature published since the early 1990s has the consumer movement in disability been documented. Self-advocacy is grounded in the roots of freedom, choice, and self-determination—fundamental values for all U.S. citizens. Unfortunately, too many of the approximately 49 million people labeled as "disabled" by the U.S. Bureau of the Census (1992) do not know how to advocate for themselves in an appropriate fashion. Many individuals with disabilities, particularly severe disabilities, have been taken care of and made highly dependent on others.

Increasing numbers of programs purport to teach self-advocacy skills to people with disabilities by calling for these individuals to acquire greater amounts of knowledge about their rights and, more important, the choices that might be available to them in the community. Unfortunately, the empowerment gained from this knowledge is still insufficient for many people who lack the assertive personality so often required to make one's interests and needs known. This is especially true in the disability field, where individuals must fight for scarce resources against other human services agencies in the community, such as drug prevention, teenage pregnancy, and early intervention programs. The concept of self-advocacy as an instructional goal should be infused throughout the school experience and learning self-management is a good first step.

For example, students can be taught how to ask for assistance or file a complaint with the manager while visiting a shopping mall. They can be shown how to contact the Bureau of Consumer Affairs if they believe that they have been treated unfairly. Educators must go beyond simply inculcating basic threads of knowledge to help shape individuals to be more active in helping themselves. The goal of self-advocacy is very important for people with disabilities as they 1) fight for the best services to which they are entitled, 2) gain information and knowledge about the financial entitlements that they may be eligible to receive from the state and federal governments, and 3) gain awareness of community happenings that could affect them (Turner, 1995).

Although there are probably dozens of other ways to enhance student involvement in transition planning, what is important here is that teachers understand that writing a transition plan without student involvement is insufficient and unacceptable and that a student who passively sits at the end of the table does not constitute student involvement. Although it may not always be possible for students and family members to actively participate, it is important that all education personnel give them the resources and opportunities to be able to do so.

Family Expectations for Their Children

Ann Turnbull and H. Rutherford Turnbull, III, national leaders profiled in Chapter 1, have written extensively about parent attitudes and expectations for young people with disabilities. The Turnbulls, who are parents of a child with a disability as well as children

without disabilities, have unique perspectives as both family members and professionals on which to base their writings. In a 1988 article, they note that summer jobs, chores, friendships, and personal decision making are critical elements of job success and transition planning. They note, for example, the following: The dream for the 21st century must be that families, people with mental retardation, and professionals will understand how powerful technology can be in assisting a person with mental retardation to work. Families need support in learning to acquire and appropriately use that technology (Turnbull & Turnbull, 1988, p. 341).

Perhaps the most in-depth study of parent attitudes toward the working conditions of their adult children with mental retardation comes from Hill, Seyfarth, Banks, Wehman, and Orelove (1987). In this study, a mail survey was sent to 660 parents and guardians whose adult children were receiving mental retardation services in Virginia asking questions about the parents' perceptions of their child's current and preferred working conditions. A return rate of 47.5% was obtained and a series of one-way analyses of variances showed that parent attitudes toward vocational services for their children were not influenced by the age or sex of the adult child or the educational or occupational status of the parent. Measured intelligence levels showed highly significant effects on parental attitudes, however, even when differences in level of satisfaction with current placement were controlled. Parents of individuals with moderate, severe, and profound mental retardation[1] generally showed less interest in improving their children's earnings, integration, responsibility, and so forth than parents of individuals with borderline or mild mental retardation. Parents and guardians in this sample expressed low interest in specific improvements in work conditions. They indicated satisfaction with the current program placements for their adult children and a positive attitude toward work in general for the adult children. Only 12% indicated a preference for competitive employment for their adult children who were then enrolled in day program services.

In the mid-1990s, however, there has been a positive shift in these perceptions and parents now hold somewhat greater hopes and aspirations, as Collins (1995) has noted:

> Parents of children with severe or profound disabilities who had been served in segregated school settings in Kentucky were interviewed prior to and following the placement of their children in integrated school settings. Using the questionnaire developed by McDonnell (1987) as a basis for the interviews, the parents were asked to predict and later to report mistreatment by nondisabled peers, isolation within the school, and loss of services. In addition, they were asked to rate their satisfaction with the segregated versus the integrated program. The results indicate that parents' perceptions of integration change when their children are placed in integrated school settings. While the change was positive for the most part in the present study, results indicate that the type of change is dependent on the quality of the program and that integration alone does not ensure program quality. (p. 64)

It is important to remember that the Hill et al. (1987) study was conducted as state and federal transition initiatives as well as supported employment were just beginning on a

[1]Although this terminology was used in the 1987 study, the authors acknowledge that these labels are no longer acceptable, preferring instead to label the level of support needed. (From Luckasson, R., Coulter, D.L., Polloway, E.A., Reiss, S., Schalock, R.L., Snell, M.E., Spitalnik, D.M., & Stark, J.A. [1992]. *Mental retardation: Definition, classification, and systems of support* [9th ed]. Washington, DC: American Association on Mental Retardation.

national level. Although these results were clearly discouraging to those who wished to see individuals with disabilities working competitively, they probably accurately reflect parents' thought processes at that time. This parent/guardian attitude survey, included in Figure 2.1, can be modified for service providers interested in obtaining the views of the parents and guardians with whom they work.

Brotherson et al. (1988) conducted telephone interviews with 48 parents of young adults with mental retardation and physical disabilities. This study examined aspects of parent planning for adult needs and the relationship of that planning to family functioning. The greatest needs identified by parents were 1) residential, 2) socialization skills, and 3) employment; and the study found a positive relationship between planning for adult needs and family functioning. This study reaffirmed that, even in 1988, parents were more interested in having their children's basic needs met in the areas of physical care, residence, socialization, and leisure—work was not as critically important an outcome for parents of students with disabilities.

McNair and Rusch (1991) reported on a study that sent surveys to 200 families, asking parents what they thought their child would be doing after completing school. Of these 200 surveys, 108 were returned. In 63% of the cases, parents had plans, and 67% of the parents indicated that they would like to see their child holding a job in the community. It is interesting to note that 48% believed that their son or daughter would hold a job in the community, while only 28% thought their child would be working in a sheltered workshop. This may be the first study that discovered positive improvements in parent attitudes and expectations toward the work potential of their adult children, possibly reflecting the effects of 78 years of transition initiatives, research literature, and, perhaps most important, the implementation of PL 94-142, the Education for All Handicapped Children Act of 1975 (i.e., special education entitlement).

The quickest route to raising parent and family expectations involves two steps:

1. It is absolutely critical to show that young people with disabilities can work competitively and for a substantial duration of time.
2. There must be a support system in place so that if their jobs are lost, people with disabilities can reenter the work force with minimal difficulty.

Once people come to expect those with disabilities to work competitively, education, training, public awareness, and parent communication become paramount. The major problem that McNair and Rusch (1991) found is that a significant number of parents were unaware of any transition programs for their children, although virtually all desired involvement of some kind. It also appears that structured transition programs as well as demonstrated competitive employment programs are very limited. Until both of these alternatives become available, significant parent involvement in advocacy or elevated parental expectations are unlikely (Ferguson, Ferguson, & Jones, 1988).

There are some exceptions: "I expect my 12-year-old daughter who is in a behavioral disabilities self-contained class to have viable job skills when she gets out of school. In fact, by the time she is 21, I expect her to have a job that pays a decent wage so that she can live independently or perhaps in an apartment with support. I will make sure that vocational education and postsecondary education are included in her ITP/IEP and that the schools are providing real work experiences." This statement was made by Trisha, a well-informed

Parent/Guardian Attitude Survey

As a person with responsibility for a person with mental retardation, your knowledge and experience are needed to help educators to develop better programs for people with mental retardation of all ages. By taking 10 minutes to answer these questions about your son or daughter, you will be performing a service for all people with mental retardation. Because this questionnaire goes to parents and guardians of both children and adults, some of the questions will be more appropriate than others to your situation. Choose the best response for each item and write its corresponding numbers in the box provided. If you care for more than one person with mental retardation, answer these questions about the oldest one. If you and other caregivers share responsibility for the person, the person with the most knowledge of the individual's daily life should complete the questionnaire. The information you provide will be strictly confidential.

1. What is the sex of your son or daughter?
 1. Female
 2. Male
2. What is his or her age?
 1. 17 years or less
 2. 18–22 years
 3. 23–30 years
 4. 31–40 years
 5. 41 or over
3. What is his or her approximate developmental (IQ) level?
 1. Profound retardation (IQ 19 or below)
 2. Severe retardation (IQ 20–35)
 3. Moderate retardation (IQ 36–51)
 4. Mild retardation (IQ 52–67)
 5. Borderline (IQ 68–83)
4. Where does he or she live?
 1. In a state residential facility
 2. In an intermediate care facility
 3. With his or her own parent(s) or guardian(s)
 4. In a group home
 5. In an apartment with other people with disabilities
 6. Other (Please describe)

5. What is his or her primary way of communicating with others?
 1. Does not communicate meaningfully
 2. Communicates with sounds or gestures
 3. Speaks in one- or two-word phrases
 4. Uses limited manual sign or picture/symbol communication (vocabulary under 10 words)
 5. Speaks in sentences but speech is not clear to others
 6. Speaks clearly in sentences
 7. Uses manual sign or picture/symbol communication in a fluent manner

6. How much help does your son or daughter require in personal care (e.g., feeding, toileting, dressing, bathing)?
 1. Nearly total assistance required
 2. Major assistance required
 3. Some assistance required
 4. Minor assistance required
 5. No assistance required
7. Please check one or more of the items below that describe(s) the physical abilities of your son or daughter.
 ____ 1. Has no physical, visual, or hearing impairment(s)
 ____ 2. Has visual or hearing impairment(s) not correctable by glasses or hearing aid
 ____ 3. Has impaired use of one or both hands
 ____ 4. Uses wheelchair regularly but is usually pushed by others
 ____ 5. Uses wheelchair regularly but usually propels chair independently
 ____ 6. Usually walks but needs some help or is very slow

Questions 8–27 ask about the daily activities of your son or daughter in a day program or on the job.

8. At present, how much money does your son or daughter make, on the average, for his or her daily work activities?
 1. No pay
 2. Less than $1 hour
 3. $1.01–$2.50 per hour
 4. $2.51–$3.35 per hour
 5. Above $3.35 per hour
 6. Don't know or not applicable
9. In your opinion, under ideal working conditions, how much do you believe your son or daughter *should* earn?
 1. No pay
 2. Somewhat less than now

Figure 2.1. Parent/guardian attitude survey. (Developed by Hill et al., 1987.)

(continued)

Figure 2.1. *(continued)*

3. Same as now
4. Somewhat more than now
5. Much more than now

10. At present, how often does your son or daughter have contact with people without disabilities other than supervisors or teachers in daily work activities?
 1. Never
 2. Rarely
 3. Sometimes
 4. Frequently
 5. Don't know or not applicable

11. In your opinion, how much contact with people without disabilities would be *best* for your son or daughter during his or her work activities?
 1. Much less than now
 2. Somewhat less than now
 3. Same as now
 4. Somewhat more than now
 5. Much more than now

12. At present, how often does your son or daughter have the opportunity to advance to a job that pays more or has more responsibility?
 1. Never
 2. Rarely
 3. Sometimes
 4. Frequently
 5. Don't know or not applicable

13. In your opinion, how often should your son or daughter have the opportunity to advance to a job that pays more or has more responsibility?
 1. Much less than now
 2. Somewhat less than now
 3. Same as now
 4. Somewhat more than now
 5. Much more than now

14. At present, how often does your son or daughter perform tasks on his or her own, without a supervisor nearby to help?
 1. Never
 2. Rarely
 3. Sometimes
 4. Frequently
 5. Don't know or not applicable

15. How much of the time would you *prefer* that your son or daughter perform tasks on his or her own without a supervisor nearby to help?
 1. Much less than now
 2. Somewhat less than now

3. Same as now
4. Somewhat more than now
5. Much more than now

16. At present, how often is your son or daughter expected to look and act as a "normal" adult in his or her work activities?
 1. Never
 2. Rarely
 3. Sometimes
 4. Frequently
 5. Don't know or not applicable

17. In your opinion, how often *should* your son or daughter be expected to look and act as a "normal" adult in his or her work activities?
 1. Much less than now
 2. Somewhat less than now
 3. Same as now
 4. Somewhat more than now
 5. Much more than now

18. At present, how often does your son or daughter complete the same work tasks as people without disabilities?
 1. Never
 2. Rarely
 3. Sometimes
 4. Frequently
 5. Don't know or not applicable

19. In your opinion, how *often* should your son or daughter complete the same work tasks as people without disabilities?
 1. Never
 2. Rarely
 3. Sometimes
 4. Frequently
 5. Don't know or not applicable

20. At present, how often is your son or daughter teased or taken advantage of by others during work activities?
 1. Never
 2. Rarely
 3. Sometimes
 4. Frequently
 5. Don't know or not applicable

21. In your opinion, how capable is your son or daughter of protecting him- or herself from being teased or taken advantage of during work activities?
 1. Not at all capable
 2. Slightly capable
 3. Somewhat capable
 4. Very capable
 5. Don't know or not applicable

(continued)

Figure 2.1. *(continued)*

22. How do you feel about the following statement, "Work should be a normal part of life for my son or daughter"?
 1. Strongly agree
 2. Mildly agree
 3. Not sure
 4. Mildly disagree
 5. Strongly disagree
23. Are the work activities that your son or daughter performs most of the time too easy, too hard, or about right, considering his or her ability?
 1. Too hard
 2. About right
 3. Too easy
24. Overall, how satisfied are you with your son's or daughter's present work activities?
 1. Not very satisfied
 2. Somewhat satisfied
 3. Satisfied
 4. Very satisfied
25. At present, where does your son or daughter spend most of his/her working hours?
 1. Activities center with other individuals with mental retardation (e.g., training may include cooking, recreation, and work skills development but clients are generally not paid)
 2. Sheltered workshop (e.g., he or she works with other persons with disabilities performing assembly or production contract work for piece-rate wages, usually below minimum wage)
 3. Enclave (e.g., he or she is still enrolled in a workshop program but works in a group or crew with other persons with disabilities in a regular community business or industry)
 4. Competitive employment (e.g., he or she works for a regular community business or industry with nondisabled persons performing regular jobs for at least minimum wage)
 5. Other (Please describe)

26. If you have your choice, where would you prefer your son or daughter to spend most of his or her working hours? (Refer to question 25 for descriptions)
 1. Activities center with other individuals with mental retardation
 2. Sheltered workshop
 3. Enclave

4. Competitive employment
5. Other (Please describe)

27. For how many years has your son or daughter been in his or her current job or program?
 1. Less than 1 year
 2. 1–2 years
 3. 3–4 years
 4. 5 years or more

Questions 28–32 ask for information about you and your family.

28. How far did you go in school?
 1. Grades 1–8
 2. Grades 9–12
 3. After high school technical school
 4. College
29. What type of job is held by the main wage earner in your household?
 1. Farmer or rancher
 2. Protective or service worker (firefighter, police officer, domestic worker, repair person, attendant, sales person, etc.)
 3. Manual worker (laborer, carpenter, etc.)
 4. Clerical worker (office worker, secretary, typist, etc.)
 5. Business person (outside sales, insurance, real estate, banker, etc.)
 6. Proprietor or manager
 7. Professional
 8. Not working
30. What is your sex?
 1. Female
 2. Male
31. What is your relationship to the person with mental retardation asked about in these questions?
 1. Mother or father
 2. Other relative (Please describe)

 3. Legal guardian
 4. Foster parent
 5. Counselor
 6. Friend
 7. Other (Please describe)

32. Are you or anyone in your household a member of The Arc?
 1. No
 2. Yes

Please return this questionnaire in the enclosed business reply envelope.

mother who knows her child's potential for employment. She is well aware of what schools and adult agencies are supposed to be doing and is actively involved in guiding their activities. Furthermore, she has definite expectations of what an effective secondary education program should look like, as well as knowledge about what does not work. Trisha is a new breed of parent, one that has grown up with PL 94-142 and PL 101-476, the Individuals with Disabilities Education Act (IDEA) of 1990. She knows her child's rights and will not be intimidated by professionals.

To help ensure this kind of effective parent/guardian involvement in the transition process, school systems and families can follow the measures listed below:

The school program should do the following:
- Encourage parents to plan optimistically for the employment of their son or daughter, beginning at the elementary-school level.
- Educate parents about employment alternatives available for their son or daughter in the local community and describe those that should be available.
- Provide parents with information about model employment programs throughout the country.
- Orient families to community agencies, explaining the responsibilities of each.
- Show parents what they can do at home to help promote the employability of their son or daughter.
- Involve parents in the design and implementation of a written, formal transition plan for employment 3–5 years before their child graduates.

Parents or guardians should do the following:
- Make sure that vocational education is part of their child's IEP as early as 10–11 years of age.
- Actively support teachers' efforts to provide training in a variety of jobs in community-based sites.
- Know what training programs and employment options are available for their child.

Parent Roles and Involvement

Of the many roles that parents and other family members can assume in planning for transitions, four levels of involvement emerge:

1. Someone who provides support and care for a young adult but may not consistently attend or provide input during IEP team meetings
2. Someone who consistently attends IEP meetings, provides input to other team members, and advocates for quality services
3. Someone who acts as a member of a personal futures planning team
4. Someone with a membership or leadership role in a local- or state-level interagency team whose mission is to address transition and/or other education services

Research has generally found that family participation in ITP meetings is a good indicator of successful completion of the plan and that educational personnel want parents to be involved in transition planning (McNair & Rusch, 1991; Sale, Metzler, Everson, & Moon, 1991). This research has also found, however, that school personnel do not necessarily value the suggestions or concerns of family members or believe that they can con-

tribute substantially to the process (Gallivan-Finlon, 1994; Stineman et al., 1993). In fact, the more vocal family members are often perceived to be troublesome, obtrusive, or perhaps even delusional about their child's potential. A common example is planning for postschool employment: Parents push for competitive employment, and educators suggest sheltered employment at best.

Federal law requires that the student and parents or other family members be allowed to participate as members of ITP teams if appropriate. If the goals and concerns of the family and student are to be fully addressed, however, then participation is not enough. They must also assume a leadership role in planning, including determining appropriate postschool goals, environments, and support services. This may produce some skepticism or resistance from the school ITP members and will likely be difficult for parents who are accustomed to relinquishing control to education professionals. McNulty (1995) lists five questions, presented in Table 2.1, for parents to consider while transition planning for their child's future. These questions are focused upon the outcomes they want the school to help provide.

Vocational Planning

Vocational planning for students who have disabilities should begin in elementary school and continue into the adult years. During each educational phase, appropriate vocational IEP objectives should be incorporated; these objectives should increasingly emphasize vocational training as students grow older. It is also important that students receive opportunities for real work experiences in a number of community-based job settings during their school years. Parents should request that their children receive job training outside the classroom that is based on viable employment options in the immediate area.

Job Placement

Ideally, if a student has received appropriate preemployment training, he or she should be ready for actual job placement toward the end of the educational career. Parents—along with teachers, rehabilitation counselors, and community adult mental retardation agency service coordinators—must be actively involved in this process. It is during this phase of a supported work approach to job placement and training that parents must commit themselves to allowing their children to enter the adult work world.

Before someone is placed in a job, his or her job counselor (e.g., teacher, rehabilitation professional) must meet with the parents on several occasions to gather information about the worker's abilities and preferences and discuss parental concerns. Topics such as the loss of Social Security benefits, transportation, and job rules must be discussed with the family before a person begins work. Parents should always ask questions and receive factual information prior to making a commitment.

Professionals are obligated to respect and understand families' skepticism and to help them learn the benefits of employment for their son or daughter with a disability. Some of the things job counselors should do include setting up appointments with local Social Security officials, introducing the parents to the employer and co-workers, teaching transportation skills and/or helping the family make arrangements for transportation, intro-

Table 2.1. Questions for parents concerning transition services

1. As a parent of a child who is deaf-blind, what is most important to you about your child's transition from school to adult services?

2. What supports are most critical to you, your child, and other family members during this transition period?

3. What role or roles do you think parents should play in their child's transition from school?

4. What transition services outcome would you like to see for your son or daughter? For example, where will he or she live, work, enjoy leisure activities, and socialize?

5. Speaking from your own experiences, what should service providers, family members, and friends know about young people who are deaf-blind that would help to improve their lives?

From McNulty, K. (1995). Parents speak out: Perspectives on transition services. In J.M. Everson (Ed.), *Supporting young adults who are deaf-blind in their communities: A transition planning guide for service providers, families, and friends* (p. 88). Baltimore: Paul H. Brookes Publishing Co.; reprinted by permission.

ducing the family to other parents with a family member with a disability who is already working, and assuring the parents that someone will be on the jobsite with their son or daughter until he or she has adjusted.

Jobsite Training

Once a job placement is made, parents must be prepared for their child's first few critical months on the job during which he or she will receive intensive training from an employment counselor. During this period, parents play an important role by providing emotional support for their son or daughter. Beginning any new job is a stressful experience, and for workers with disabilities, the stress is even greater. Parents must also provide logistical support at this time, such as ensuring that lunches are prepared, uniforms are clean, and the worker is punctual.

During jobsite training, the employment counselor should keep parents informed. By regularly sharing information about the student's progress, the professional can do much to help parents maintain their peace of mind.

Follow-Along

Once jobsite training is completed and the employment counselor has largely faded his presence, the student enters the follow-along phase. Here, students utilize the assistance of co-workers, supervisors, and other people more natural to the work environment. The employment counselor does stay in touch to perform ongoing assessment, which involves periodic site visits to speak with the work supervisor and co-workers. Follow-along also provides for on-the-job behavioral observation and written feedback from the employer. This kind of continual assessment allows the professional to provide additional intervention as needed, such as jobsite training, arranging needed medical treatment, or teaching the client to use a bank.

Parental support remains important in this phase of the employment process, as workers with significant disabilities may continue to need a higher level of assistance with job-related concerns than their peers without disabilities. Parents should be careful, however, to avoid overinvolvement at their daughter's or son's workplace. Some contact with

the employer is appropriate, but an employer typically does not have the time or patience to humor a family that makes constant demands on his or her time; such demands can negatively affect a supervisor's perception of the worker. Therefore, if family members believe that some problem needs to be dealt with on behalf of their son or daughter, the employment counselor should be consulted. Parents should avoid unannounced visits to the workplace.

Parental Concerns

Many parents are skeptical of the relatively new concept of competitive employment, which has successfully placed people with significant disabilities only since 1985. In an effective vocational program, the employment counselor will address concerns with parents until they believe they have enough information upon which to base a decision. Of the many concerns that might arise, a few of the more common are addressed below. Figure 2.2 addresses ways that parents can prepare for these concerns.

How Can I Be Sure that My Son or Daughter Is Ready for a Job?

There are never any guarantees that someone is ready for a job, but experience has shown that most people with disabilities can succeed in jobs with the help of a supported work approach. Important success factors include parental support, availability of transportation, good social skills, and a desire to work on the part of the student; parents can usually judge for themselves whether these are present.

How Will My Child's Working Affect
Supplemental Security Income (SSI) and Medicaid?

Because government regulations are so complex, especially with the massive Social Security/Medicare/Medicaid overhaul of the Clinton administration, families with a student with disabilities should visit their local Social Security Office to obtain case-specific information.

Generally, though, as long as a person receives any SSI payment, however small, she retain eligibility for Medicaid. If a person becomes ineligible for SSI—by, for example, working full time for 9 months—he or she automatically becomes ineligible for Medicaid benefits as well. Unless the worker has medical insurance as part of a fringe benefit package, this can create problems. Therefore, parents and professionals must make this a priority when planning for employment for a student with disabilities. A job with good benefits, such as full medical insurance comparable to Medicaid, may be better than a job that pays a higher wage but offers few benefits.

Typically, if a person consistently earns more than $400 a month, he or she will lose SSI eligibility after 9 months of employment. If less than $300 a month is earned, SSI payments will be partially reduced based on earnings—the exact amount varies among states. In most cases, however, the person will come out ahead financially by working. If he or she does not hold the job for at least 9 months, SSI eligibility will be retained, which allows a grace period in which a person with a disability can determine if he or she is able to hold a job.

If you have questions or concerns about what your son or daughter with disabilities is going to be doing after leaving high school, joining a Community Transition Interagency Committee (CTIC) may help you find the answers. Every school district, special education cooperative, or education district that provides special education for students ages 14–22 must belong to a CTIC, and CTIC membership must include parents of and youth with disabilities.

Are you a member of your CTIC? If you are a CTIC member, are you active and do you speak out by asking questions or raising your concerns?

Listed below are five things parents can do to help their sons or daughters receive appropriate services when they leave high school settings:

1. Join your CTIC. Get in touch with other parents who have young adults similar in age to your child and take them with you when you join.

2. Identify current services, programs, and funding sources in your community for young adults with disabilities. Do those services and programs meet the needs of young adults in your community? If not, speak out at your CTIC meetings.

3. Help identify creative ways for different adult services providers to work together to meet the transition needs of young adults in your community. Parents are great at cutting through the red tape to get things done.

4. Write your local policy makers (members of your county board, city or town council) to let them know of the transition needs of young adults with disabilities. Encourage them to provide services that help young adults with disabilities to live and work as independently as possible within your community.

5. Serve as a transition resource person to other families in your community who have youth in transition. Encourage them to become involved, and together you can improve transition services in your community.

Figure 2.2. A brochure to help parents prepare for the day their children leave high school. (From Minnesota Pacer Center. [1994, June]. *How to prepare for the day your child leaves high school.* Minneapolis: Author; reprinted by permission.)

How Will My Son or Daughter Get to Work without Driving?

Experience has shown that people with significant disabilities who can hold a competitive job can also learn to use public transportation. This may require careful training by a teacher, family member, or employment counselor over a period of weeks or even months. Local resources can also provide such training and should be available from the supported work program that trains the worker at his or her jobsite. In locations with no public transportation system, alternative means must be found, often by a parent. This may include

riding with a family member or neighbor with similar work hours or joining a car pool. This is the type of problem that should be dealt with before a placement is made.

Conclusion

Students with disabilities and their families are directly affected, for better or worse, by the transition services offered by school systems. Therefore, they should direct—not merely influence—transition planning and service delivery. Families have ongoing service needs during and after transition, and only they truly know the nature of these needs. Family-directed support services should empower families with the knowledge and freedom to choose the types of services that meet their unique needs and goals.

Study Questions

1. How can students with disabilities and their families help ensure the accountability of the school system in transition?

2. What are some ways that school systems can ensure parent/guardian involvement in transition?

3. What are four levels of involvement that parents/guardians can assume in transition planning?

4. What are the rights of parents/guardians in the transition process?

5. Why is self-advocacy an important educational outcome for students with disabilities?

Appendix A

Questions and Answers
About Competitive Employment

QUESTION: Can people with disabilities work in competitive settings? What about people with mental retardation? What about those with chronic mental illness?

ANSWER: Yes, many people with mental retardation can fill jobs in the community given the proper training and support. The same holds true for people with chronic mental illness and people with developmental disabilities, even though the type of support they require is different from that of people with mental retardation.

QUESTION: What types of competitive jobs can people with severe disabilities hold?

ANSWER: Types of employment are not restricted to any field; however, because the service sector is growing, most employment opportunities for people with disabilities have been in that area. Some examples of supported employment opportunities in the service sector include maid, janitor, orderly, assembler, auto mechanic helper, food services worker, porter, hand packer, kitchen helper, and laundry room helper.

QUESTION: What are the benefits of competitive jobs over work activity centers and sheltered workshops?

ANSWER: The most obvious difference is that wages are significantly higher for competitive jobs. Workers in competitive jobs are around people who serve as positive role models and exemplify more socially appropriate behavior. In these jobs, people with severe disabilities are challenged to produce in ways comparable to other members of the community. Furthermore, as workers with disabilities become wage earners and taxpayers, they contribute to the community instead of merely being supported by it. This is the hidden benefit of increased social integration.

QUESTION: If people with severe disabilities have the ability to work in competitive settings given proper support, why do we have so many sheltered workshops and work activity centers?

ANSWER: There are several reasons for this. One major reason is that, until 1996, there have been no vocational options for people with mental retardation or other disabilities. Long waiting lists are common for those programs, which attests to the need for long-term vocational services for these people. Also, until 1987, the Rehabilitation Act Amendments of 1986 (PL 99-506) did not contain a provision that required supported employment services to be available to those who would not have access to vocational rehabilitation services. Prior to 1987, many parents and professionals were skeptical of the employment potential of people with disabilities. This attitude is changing as the

The author is most appreciative for the assistance of the Virginia Commonwealth University Rehabilitation Research and Training Center training division staff in the development of this appendix.

benefits of supported employment are becoming evident. Vocational programming for those with chronic mental illness is a relatively new priority. More funds and effort must be put into providing staff for supported work services at jobsites. Supported employment services providers should work in an ongoing fashion with employers to provide assistance after clients are employed (see Chapter 7).

QUESTION: How long should I expect a person with disabilities to be able to work if he or she is able to get a job?

ANSWER: With a supported employment model of assistance, someone with disabilities should be able to hold a job as long as many other workers, including those without disabilities. There are, of course, numerous reasons people leave jobs; however, if professional staff are on hand for periodic assistance, there is no reason why, with proper placement, a person receiving supported employment services should lose his or her job.

QUESTION: Is a person with disabilities safe on the job?

ANSWER: Places of business are structured environments. Everyone has a job to do, and there is limited time available for any employee to harass another. Usually there are a number of people in a work area to observe any misbehavior, and there are strong codes in society against taking advantage of people with disabilities. Even break areas and lunch rooms are consistently safe places in most businesses. The supported employment services provider should make sure that the jobsite is free of obvious safety hazards before the worker is selected for the job.

QUESTION: What are the best ways to determine if a person with a severe disability has good potential for competitive employment?

ANSWER: The three most critical aspects of an individual's capacity for employment are 1) family support, 2) social skills or the ability to get along with others, and 3) a desire to work. IQ scores, test scores, and academic abilities are not necessarily important features of the successfully employed worker with severe disabilities.

QUESTION: Why aren't supported employment services more widely available?

ANSWER: The most obvious reason is that the concept of supported employment is a relatively new one. In many states, few providers exist. A goal of the Oklahoma Supported Employment Project, for example, is to create a statewide network of supported employment services providers. As with all new concepts, there are many problems to work out to ensure ongoing funding. Furthermore, not all professionals understand this approach to serving people with severe disabilities. Innovative approaches to providing services are not always quickly accepted without demonstrated success.

Appendix B

Questions and Answers About the Job Coach

QUESTION: The job coach seems to be an important part of competitive employment. What exactly does this role entail?

ANSWER: The role of the job coach is dual in nature. On one hand, he or she represents the employee with disabilities. On the other hand, he or she acts as a business consultant to employers. The skills required of personnel representing and training people with severe disabilities include the following:

1. Job coaches must be able to respond to a variety of community-based work settings. This means that the job coach must dress, behave, and speak the same language as the business community in order to help people with disabilities better fit in to the various companies in the community.
2. Job coaches are responsible for developing the worksites at which training and development will occur.
3. Job coaches must be able to capture all of the requirements and needs of a particular job; this activity is called *job analysis.* In addition, the analysis must include all of the related and subtle skills that affect the employee's success in that job.
4. Job coaches might be required to restructure a job to facilitate success. This task requires negotiation with the employer for approval of any restructuring of work routines.
5. Job coaches must apply systematic training skills to assist people with disabilities to perform their jobs effectively. This includes dealing with inappropriate behaviors that may jeopardize the success of the individual on the job. These skills must include effective strategies for decreasing assistance to the least degree possible while maintaining acceptable worker output. This concept is called *fading.*
6. The job coach must be willing to participate actively at the worksite whenever necessary to ensure that the employer's production expectations are met, to provide relief in emergencies, and to encourage the employee to assume gradually increasing job responsibilities.
7. Job coaches must be able to foster relationships among the co-workers, supervisors, and people with disabilities. This is most important for ensuring lasting success.
8. Job coaches must provide services on a long-term basis for as long as necessary for each worker. To do so, they must develop many individualized agreements with employers about the form of ongoing support necessary to keep the worker on the job.
9. Job coaches must be prepared to offer assistance and training for needs and skills outside the worksite. This may include transportation, financial assistance, resolution of family and personal problems, and similar non-workplace concerns.
10. Job coaches must communicate regularly with the employee and the family about

how things are going at work. Effective job coaches recognize that a person's work life and home life are closely connected.

11. Job coaches "troubleshoot" problems that occur in worksites, such as production problems, the method of performing tasks, relationships with co-workers, boredom, frustration, and attendance.

QUESTION: I understand that the job coach is responsible for developing a job and training the person with disabilities on the job, but what happens if the person does not like the job? What care is taken to ensure that the job matches his or her needs?

ANSWER: Before anyone is considered for a job, it is important to find out whether he or she wants to work. If an individual wants to work, then every effort must be made to ensure that the worker and the work are matched. The family can play an important role in promoting compatibility between the worker and the workplace by helping the job coach develop a worker profile of their child. Family knowledge about the person with disabilities can save having to take standardized tests that often predict failure. Job developers, parents, and guardians are asked to consider the needs, skills, and preferences of the individual and the potential jobsite during the job development planning stage. Ideally, the job and the worker should "fit like a glove" once the jobsite has been actually secured. The parents or guardian should be careful that the person with disabilities has a say in the selection of the job. Too often this right can be overlooked in the push to find a job. It is more important that a match makes sense in relation to a person's life than to try to predict success.

3

Transition Planning
with the Community

Upon completion of this chapter, the reader will be able to do the following:

- List at least six important components that should be in any effective model of transition
- Discuss the role of business and industry in transition
- Describe the principles of shared responsibility
- Compare and contrast at least three career education and transition models
- Discuss the importance of student choice and involvement in transition planning

Of the many concepts related to the transition from school to adulthood, that of community is perhaps most important. Planning must be done with the entire community system in order for a given community to have effective transition programs. Transition is not exclusively a school-driven experience, nor is it simply an array of postschool vocational choices. For too long, there has been the misperception that the school systems bear the exclusive responsibility for transition from school to adulthood. Although the school plays a key role, by initiating the planning process and prescribing an individual curriculum for each student based on his or her needs, wishes, and desires, others need to be heavily involved as well. Public schools, community colleges, universities, adult services programs, Social Security, vocational rehabilitation, and, perhaps most significant, the business community must be invited to participate and feel a sense of responsibility for what happens to students with disabilities.

Without continual involvement, planning, and collaboration from key local agencies, the visions that students create for themselves will not occur. For example, assume a student wants to work competitively, but receives Supplemental Security Income (SSI). These benefits may be adversely affected if the student works more hours per week than the law allows. Although all students should be encouraged to work on a full-time basis, it is important that the student and family be aware of the consequences of competitive employment on SSI incomes. Involvement and participation by a Social Security Administration representative would be critical for this student's transition planning.

If a student with a learning disability wishes to attend the local community college but requires assistance, the college may be asked to provide an accommodation for note taking. In this case, the community college must be involved in the transition planning. Without its participation, the transition may fail (Rojewski, 1996).

Clearly, the school system alone cannot solve all transition problems. Vocational rehabilitation needs to take responsibility for helping to provide counseling, placement, and funding when necessary for students as they leave school. The community colleges, universities, and adult services programs at the post-21 level need to take responsibility for students as they prepare to exit their school programs. Fortunately, in some communities, representatives from different agencies have learned to communicate with each other and identify the necessary services to deliver based on their customer's desired outcomes. Those communities that try to deliver services rotely and neglect to provide opportunities for competitive employment and good community living options invariably end up with disgruntled students and families who feel that they have been grossly shortchanged.

This chapter identifies components to consider when planning transition across the entire community of schools, businesses, and families. Furthermore, it reviews the different types of transition models in practice. Although transition planning can be considered on an individualized level, this chapter focuses on planning in the broader community.

Sharing Responsibility for Transition

Before identifying components of transition being utilized in schools and communities for career education and transition planning, it is helpful to review the work of Steere, Pancsofar, Wood, and Hecimovic (1990). The writings of this group represent a departure from ideas on the transition initiative of the early 1980s, which continue to be applicable in the 1990s. With the virtue of being able to reflect on some earlier trains of thought that were, perhaps, somewhat superficial, Steere, Pancsofar, et al. were able to provide more depth. What they have termed *the principles of shared responsibility* have been developed to emphasize the necessity for "all parties in the transition planning process to adhere to a consistent set of guiding principles" (Steere, Pancsofar, et al., 1990, p. 144). The notion of sharing responsibility across different agencies, students, families, and businesses is an important concept and helps to form the basis for the analysis of models in this chapter.

Sharing responsibility has also been a major theme in the work of Rebecca McDonald, one of the best known leaders in community transition planning in the country. Ms. McDonald has been a catalyst for mobilizing communities in person-centered transition planning for more than 20 years.

Rebecca McDonald Rebecca McDonald, M.S., has more than 20 years of experience in the field of special education and rehabilitation for people with disabilities. She has held clinical, administrative, teaching, and training positions in university settings, school systems, governmental agencies, and nonprofit organizations. As Director of Technical Assistance Services for the University Affiliated Program of New Jersey, she coordinates training and technical activities throughout the state in conjunction with governmental agencies, school systems, consumers and families, advocacy organizations, and service providers.

Ms. McDonald is recognized nationally for her work in integrated employment, transition from school to adult life, systems change, interagency planning and service coordination, training technology, and person-centered service planning and design. She is also a founding board member of the International Association for Persons in Supported Employment and its current president. In the field of transition, she is known as a fierce advocate and someone who is able to get things done. Her greatest skill is her ability to mobilize communities to become more effective at providing transition and employment services.

Key Components in Transition Models

A meaningful transition includes postsecondary educational opportunities such as admission to a community college program or employment in real work. It also includes moving toward postsecondary residential independence and individual competence in community living. To achieve these goals, there are actual components on which local planning groups should focus. Some of the more prominent transition components are presented in Table 3.1. These components provide for check-off questions that the transition team can review.

Students and Their Families Should Take an Active Role in the Community

Parents must take a proactive role in the planning for their child during his or her secondary school and post-21 years. Students and families must be the focal point of services. If this principle is ignored, service providers will begin to plan curricula and services around what they think is necessary rather than what students and families consider important.

Students Should Learn Functional Community-Referenced Skills During Their Educational Years

Students need to acquire community-referenced skills while they are in high school. This has been a frequently described tenet for a number of years (Falvey, 1989) and, in fact, most researchers have concluded that these attributes are critical for students, especially those with severe disabilities, to have effective transitions.

Table 3.1.　Transition components in local communities

The establishment of a system for ensuring that individuals with disabilities are involved in transition planning at the individual and community levels.	How many individuals with disabilities work at the school and other participating agencies?
The establishment of a system for ensuring that families of individuals with disabilities are involved in transition planning at the individual and community levels.	What is the process for students and families to make their needs, wants, and wishes known in a nonintimidating way?
The development of a process to determine what services students with disabilities need after leaving high school and to communicate this information among adult services providers.	Has the school system established an annual survey to see how previous students are doing?
The development of a process to address the transition needs of students and families of diverse cultures.	Is the educational team composed of people from different backgrounds and heritages?
The development of a smooth transition process using interagency linkages among the key agencies of education, county social services, and vocational rehabilitation services.	What is the plan for agencies to share resources and planning time to help the "customer" (e.g., student and family)?
The development of a process for the ongoing collection and use of postschool follow-up information.	Are the other community agencies as well as the school locating and using information related to students after they leave school?

Services Should Be Aimed at Preparing Supports, Not People

The pivotal point is not so much to "manage" a person's life, but rather to work with him or her to determine the elements that can help one achieve independence. Later in this chapter, there is more discussion on this point in the context of person-centered planning.

All Necessary Connections with Adult Services and Funding Agencies Should Be Established and Maintained

It is the responsibility of the transition planning team to establish and maintain relations with adult services and funding agencies, a job that is easier said than done. There is little doubt that all students and their families would like to know that a planning team is available at school or within the community that will take care of all matters that affect transportation, accessibility, community recreation, and nondiscriminatory employment—important goals that all transition models should embrace. (See Chapter 4 for some of the ways to create these interagency agreements that allow planning teams to be more effective and less restrained by bureaucracy.)

Each Student Should Graduate into Paid Community Employment

The availability of paid community employment after graduation is a major outcome that must be established in all school systems. As Senator Robert Dole has noted (see Chapter 1), full employment for all people with disabilities who want to work must be a national goal. This goal will not be attained unless the schools actively promote employment,

ideally while the student is still in school. Local planning teams must be involved in planning for job placement as few rehabilitation counselors will have the resources or the time to place every student.

Transition Planning Should Result in Employment Experiences that Allow Each Student to Attain an Improved Quality of Life

Placement into sheltered employment into positions with very few paid hours per week or into such poor working conditions that the person is unhappy or dissatisfied does not meet the goals of effective transition outcomes. These negative outcomes can be avoided by building a plan around what the student wants. Vocational placements present significant challenges to school personnel and transition planners because a job is not enough. It must be of a quality that matches the individual's satisfaction level.

These points make the importance of each student's choices and the family's role apparent. These principles will not permit job developers and job placement specialists to mandate the jobs people with disabilities can have or paternalistically pass over people for certain jobs without even letting them know what options are available. The student and job developer or specialist must learn to work together as a team, look for jobs together, and communicate in a respectful, professional way.

The Role of Business in Transition Planning Should Be Emphasized

The role of business and industry in a local community needs to be emphasized. People who work in business and industry have a vested interest in their local school system, which produces their labor force. They can also be a tremendous resource for information about the most promising careers and future job availability. It is extremely naive for school programs and other human services agencies to design programs without regularly consulting with local businesses. The existing vocational technical centers that are in place in many cities and towns, which typically offer a standardized vocational curriculum, such as auto mechanics or nursing, have limitations. These centers do not usually respond directly to the unique labor market needs of a given community. A more appropriate approach would be to design vocational and employment curriculum around a survey taken by the local chamber of commerce, retail merchants association, or other trade groups that indicate where the community's labor market needs are.

One model that has successfully shown the significant role that businesses can play in transition leadership is the Bridges From School-to-Work Program—a national program spearheaded by the Marriott Foundation for People with Disabilities—already in place in several large U.S. cities (see Figure 3.1) (Tilson, Luecking, & Donovan, 1994). In this program, all students with disabilities work closely with employer representatives who help to place and support them in business-sponsored internships (see Table 3.2). Tilson et al. (1994) note the following:

> An unexpected outcome of the Bridges program in all five cities is the high percentage of students offered continued employment with their host companies. This is unexpected because it is understood by all parties that the internship is time-limited and there is no obligation on the part of the employer or the student to continue the employment relationship. While more study of this phenomenon is warranted, this outcome suggests that employer exposure to disability as

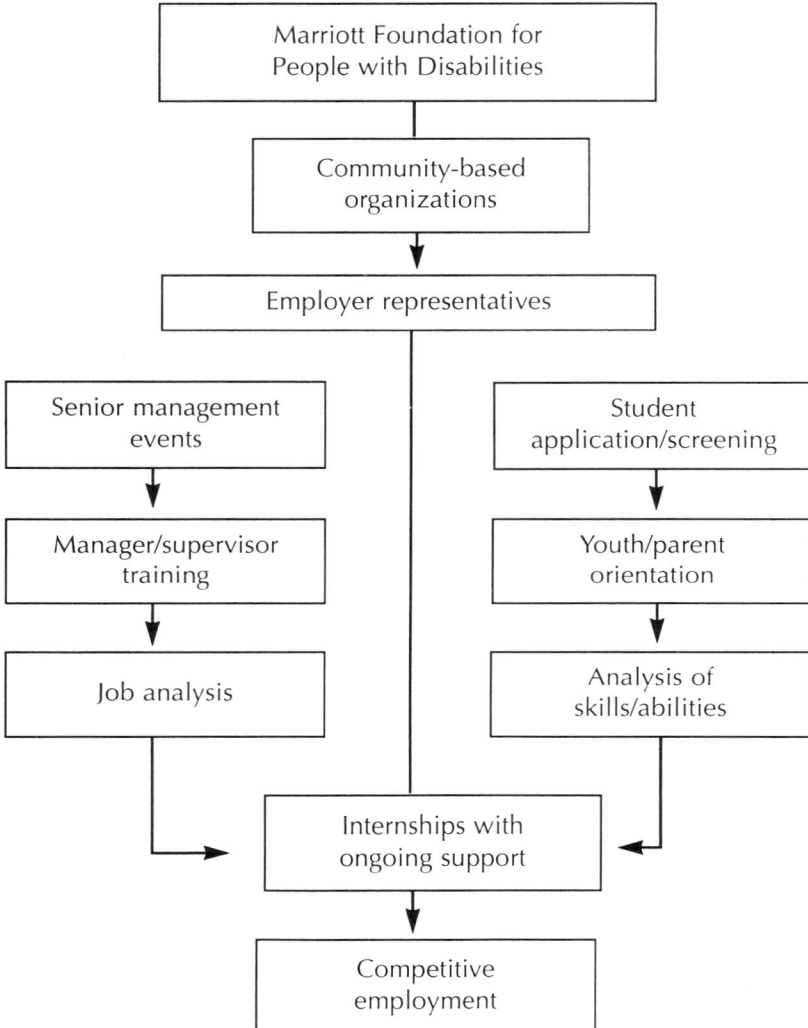

Figure 3.1. Components of the Bridges From School-to-Work Program, spearheaded by the Marriott Foundation for People with Disabilities. (From Tilson, G.P., Luecking, R.G., & Donovan, M.R. [1994]. Involving employers in transition: The Bridges model. *CDEI, 17*[1], 84; reprinted by permission.)

well as the support and training they receive remove many of the barriers which otherwise inhibit positive hiring behavior.

While the Bridges placement rate suggests an effective placement process, there remains the need to examine the reasons for the non-placement of 103 young adults (14% of those referred to and accepted into the program). In addition, the 82% internship completion rate indicates that the support students receive on the job is appropriate in the large majority of cases; however, reasons for termination should be studied to determine the influence of such factors

Table 3.2. Businesses hiring Bridges interns

Primary industry	Number	Percentage
Retail trade	198	30
Food service/restaurant	79	12
Health services	45	7
Research	40	6
Finance, insurance	38	6
Public utilities	32	5
Lodging	35	5
Manufacturing	23	4
Amusement/recreation	23	4
Business	17	3
Educational services	19	3
Communications	12	2
Personal (laundry, etc.)	12	2
Public administration	14	2
Automobile services	9	1
Construction	6	1
Transportation	4	1
Real estate	3	a
Other	35	5

aLess than 1%.

as job matching, support needs of both the employer and the student, pre-internship educational preparation, parental support, and other non-work life needs. (p. 82)

The use of internships as a vehicle for promoting transition and, more important, including business into the community planning process can be very effective. Business should be used not only for hiring but for their resources and expertise as well. Following are 15 types of activities that can help build connections between students and employers:

1. Include employers on advisory committees. A simple way to continually improve the quality of the school–business partnership is to involve businesses in leadership. This may involve the following:
 - Establishing a collaborative team including students, educators, and business employees
 - Creating a focus group of business representatives that meets each May to answer the question, "How can we improve our partnership next year?"
2. Develop an employer speaker bureau where company employees can present issues such as employee trends, quality-improvement techniques, global competition, sales, and marketing. A school can suggest development of a bureau.
3. Create linkages between general and special education business-related activities.
4. Have local businesses review school curricula and strategies. Once the best practices have been identified and curricula have been revised, new teaching strategies should be shared with businesses.
5. Have social services professionals intern at workplace and schools.
6. Pursue vocational–technical curriculum in community colleges to train for skilled

jobs. Community colleges are playing a greater role in the education of students for high-skilled jobs.

7. Use shadow programs, especially for middle school students. In these programs, students simply shadow employees of community businesses for all or part of their work day.

8. Have business representatives visit schools. The initial stages of occupational awareness result in knowledge of businesses in the community.

9. Use mentor programs to connect individual students with a peer or older person who acts as example, confidante, and adviser.

10. Do job tours. Students indicating interest in a particular field (e.g., medicine) may benefit from job tours.

11. Have students keep notebooks of job interests, which are useful for identifying early vocational interests.

12. Have career fairs for students in elementary and middle school. Teachers organize career fairs to take place at school and include various career areas (e.g., medicine, education, agriculture, retail sales, forestry, wood products).

13. Have each student learn a job and share with other students. This helps prepare students to become employee/trainers.

14. Promote awareness of students with disabilities in businesses. Most employees in today's work force grew up during a time when students with and without disabilities were separated. This separation created fear and misunderstanding that remain in the work force regarding the productive capacity of employees with disabilities.

15. Hold school classes at worksites. Once relationships are developed with business, primary and middle school teachers will find many opportunities to hold class at worksites.

Participation in Postsecondary Institutions of Higher Education Should Be Expanded

Involvement in colleges and universities has been limited for young people with disabilities (Greenbaum, Graham, & Seeles, 1995), even though these connections can be as important as those in business and industry. Movement into postsecondary institutions of higher education is critical as strategies such as Goals 2000 are implemented. In an effort to study the issues surrounding community college involvement, the Board for Rights of Virginians with Disabilities conducted an extensive survey of young adults with disabilities in Virginia (West & Kregel, 1991). This survey examined the types of specialized and generic services and program accommodations both utilized and needed by students with disabilities in Virginia's institutions of higher education. Student satisfaction with the services provided, barriers encountered by students with disabilities, improvements in disability-related services, and the students' roles in the development of policies and procedures were also investigated.

Survey forms were developed with input and direction primarily from students with disabilities and service coordinators at a number of Virginia postsecondary schools. Coordination of services across the state was used as the point of access to students with dis-

abilities for survey distribution. A total of 761 surveys were returned following 2 semesters of distribution.

Results indicated that students utilize a variety of services during their educational experiences. Although students generally expressed satisfaction with the services they received, they also identified numerous barriers to their postsecondary education, including the following:

- Misunderstanding, distrust, and unwillingness to make accommodations from instructors, professors, and other school staff
- Discrimination on the part of faculty, staff, and students as a result of modifications in course requirements or procedures requested by students with disabilities
- Poor access within and between buildings
- Limited parking areas designated as handicapped only; noncompliance with handicapped parking regulations by other students, faculty, staff, or state personnel; and lack of enforcement of handicapped parking
- Unavailability of tutors, readers, and other assistants, as well as limited special equipment and aids such as tape recorders and texts in alternative media

Respondents expressed great concern about the limited financial and personnel resources devoted to services for students with disabilities. They also expressed fear that budget cuts in Virginia's institutions of higher education will reverse the gains in services and accessibility that have been made.

A number of recommendations for further study and action have been made to address these problems. Key recommendations include the following:

- Greater efforts should be made to educate faculty, staff, and other students regarding disabilities, accommodations, services, and the legal rights of students with disabilities.
- Appropriate action should be taken against instructors or professors who repeatedly refuse to make course or examination modifcations and other accommodations for students with identified disabilities.
- Postsecondary schools should initiate more creative measures to advertise disability-related services to prospective students in need.
- Support groups and clubs, if not organized in particular schools, should be encouraged and supported by postsecondary schools.
- Students with disabilities should be included in formulating disability-related policies and services.
- Consistency should be developed both within and among postsecondary schools regarding the types of services and accommodations that are available to students with disabilities. At present, too much ambiguity exists in availability and delivery of services, which limits the access of students with disabilities to services and accommodations.
- Models of exemplary services for postsecondary students with disabilities should be identified and examined for adaptation in Virginia's postsecondary institutions.

Tables 3.3 and 3.4 reflect the types of services and accommodations that are viewed as important by students with different disabilities.

Table 3.3. Services and accommodations most frequently used

School type	Services and accomodations	Percentage providing service or accommodation
Four-year public colleges and universities	Priority registration/advising	57.4
	Flexible testing arrangements	53.8
	Information about services	44.5
	Personal counseling	40.0
	Preadmission information	32.7
	Tutors	31.9
	Career counseling/placement	28.8
	Diagnostic testing/assessment	28.6
	Financial aid	25.3
	Accessible classrooms	21.7
Two-year community colleges	Personal counseling	55.1
	Priority registration/advising	53.3
	Preadmission information	52.9
	Career counseling/placement	49.3
	Information about services	47.6
	Flexible testing arrangements	43.2
	Tutors	41.4
	Financial aid	41.4
	Diagnostic testing/assessment	38.8
	Library assistants	38.8
Private colleges and universities	Tutors	64.7
	Flexible testing arrangements	52.9
	Diagnostic testing/assessment	49.0
	Information about services	49.0
	Library assistants	45.1
	Personal counseling	45.1
	Study skills training	45.1
	Career counseling/placement	39.2
	Accessible on-campus housing	37.3
	Preadmission information	37.3
	Personal skills training	37.3

From West, M., & Kregel, J. (1991). *Results from the Board for Rights of Virginians with Disabilities Survey of the concerns, needs, and satisfaction with services of Virginia's postsecondary students with disabilities* (p. 42). Richmond: Virginia Institute for Developmental Disabilities; reprinted by permission.

Career Education and Transition Models

A number of career education and transition models have been available since the 1980s and 1990s, including the Life-Center Career Education Model by Brolin and Kokaska (1979); the Life-Planning Program Model by Schumaker, Hazel, and Deshler (1985); Brown's (1984) Four-Stage Transition Process; Will's (1983) Three-Step Transition Model; Wehman, Kregel, and Barcus's (1985) Secondary Vocational Program; the Independent Living and Community Adjustment Model by Halpern (1985); A School-Based Career

Table 3.4. Services and accommodations most frequently used

Disability type	Services and accommodations	Percentage receiving service or accommodations
Physical impairment	Priority registration/advising	60.7
	Personal counseling	49.7
	Handicap access parking	49.5
	Information about services	47.6
	Flexible testing arrangements	47.1
	Accessible elevators	46.5
	Preadmission information	46.3
	Accessible rest rooms	45.7
	Financial aid	43.6
	Accessible classrooms	41.2
Sensory impairment	Priority registration/advising	45.9
	Flexible testing arrangements	44.4
	Personal counseling	42.9
	Career counseling/placement	40.5
	Preadmission information	38.1
	Information about services	37.1
	Financial aid	36.6
	Tutors	35.6
	Diagnostic testing/assessment	30.2
	Accessible seating	28.8
Learning disability	Flexible testing arrangements	58.4
	Priority registration/advising	53.3
	Information about services	49.5
	Personal counseling	48.1
	Tutors	46.7
	Diagnostic testing/assessment	41.9
	Preadmission information	35.3
	Career counseling/placement	31.3
	Study skills training	29.4
	Special equipment for students	28.3
Other impairments	Financial aid	55.3
	Personal counseling	55.3
	Information about services	50.0
	Diagnostic testing/assessment	34.2
	Preadmission information	34.2
	Career counseling/placement	34.2
	Tutors	31.6
	Flexible testing arrangements	26.3
	Study skills training	23.7

From West, M., & Kregel, J. (1991). *Results from the Board for Rights of Virginians with Disabilities Survey of the concerns, needs, and satisfaction with services of Virginia's postsecondary students with disabilities* (p. 43). Richmond: Virginia Institute for Developmental Disabilities; reprinted by permission.

Development and Transition Education Model for Adolescents with Disabilities by Clark and Kolstoe (1995); and Person-Centered Planning, forwarded primarily by Vandercook, York, and Forest (1989).

The Life-Centered Career Education Model

Because so many models have been developed since the 1970s, it is useful to start with one of the earliest and most popular, the Life-Centered Career Education Model (Brolin & Kokaska, 1979; Kokaska & Brolin, 1985). This model has identified many features of special education work-study programs and has been expanded repeatedly to encompass the concept of career education for individuals of all ages. Specifically, this model identifies 22 major competencies in the areas of daily living skills, personal social skills, and occupational guides and preparation. This model reflects a broad approach to infusing competencies into the general curriculum and considers the variety of daily life and work skills that are necessary for success in the real world (Brolin, 1989). It tends to focus on the high-incidence student, or youth with mild disabilities, as opposed to those with the most severe and profound disabilities. Brolin and Kokaska are pioneers in the transition field and their work, field tested over a number of years, is a beacon for others to follow.

The Life-Planning Program Model

In a model for secondary students with learning disabilities, Schumaker et al.'s (1985) Life-Planning Program Model involves instruction in cognitive compensatory strategies, problem solving, and goal setting in instructional implementation, usually by a professional at the high school level. Because a limited number of transition models are specifically targeted at youth with learning disabilities, this program meets an important need.

Brown's Four-Stage Transition Process

A model for individuals with mild disabilities has been advanced by Brown (1984). Brown suggests that students with disabilities experience difficulties during the transition process, and, in response, presents strategies to overcome this dysfunction. The four-stage transition process in this model includes assessment, planning, implementation, and evaluation. Suggested in each stage are combined activities applicable to a secondary education setting to facilitate and train for transition.

Will's Three-Step Transition Model

One of the most widely disseminated transition models was advanced by Will (1983), former assistant secretary for special education and rehabilitation at the U. S. Department of Education. Her transition model features three major components. The first involves finding typical jobs for young adults with mild disabilities and establishing them without any special services. Students follow the same routes in the community as people without disabilities.

The second aspect of this employment-driven transition model makes time-limited services available to a large number of people with disabilities who require modifications to perform typical community jobs. Time-limited services draw on human services in the community, particularly vocational rehabilitation, but stop service at a specific time (i.e., once the person becomes sufficiently independent at the job).

The last component of Will's model requires ongoing services for young adults with disabilities who need continuous support in order to maintain employment. This calls for the creation of supported employment options, such as work crews, competitive employ-

ment with support, and specialized enclaves in business and industry—options intended to replace traditional nonvocational adult activity programs.

Wehman, Kregel, and Barcus's Secondary Vocational Program

Wehman, Kregel, and Barcus (1985) have also advanced a model of transition oriented toward vocational services. This model's three stages focus on a secondary vocational special education program. First, functional curricula, integrated school environments, and community-based services are seen as critical to effective secondary special education programs. Second, this model utilizes the individualized program planning process, which includes interagency cooperation and consumer input from the parent and student. The third aspect of this model is the vocational outcome, such as competitive employment, work crews, or other specialized work arrangements. This model has been useful for all levels of disability, but is limited by its focus on vocational services as well as its lack of emphasis on consumer control and leadership in decision making. However, it does provide a simplified description of the sequence of events from school to adulthood.

The Independent Living and Community Adjustment Model

One of the few transition models that focuses more heavily on postsecondary independent living and community adjustment, rather than only on employment, was advanced by Halpern (1985). By making community adjustment a critical outcome of transition, he dramatically advanced the employment-oriented models of the early 1980s. This comprehensive model of community adjustment encompasses residential outcomes, employment, and social interpersonal skills. Halpern has also been a major leader in the transition field and done outstanding work in post-21 follow-up studies.

A School-Based Career Development and Transition Education Model for Adolescents with Disabilities

One of the best models on which to pattern services was introduced by Clark and Kolstoe (1995). This model, titled "A School-Based Career Development and Transition Education Model for Adolescents with Disabilities," is presented in Figure 3.2 and includes all of the critical components of the previously mentioned models. For example, adult and continuing education, graduate schools, universities, community colleges, and community rehabilitation facilities are all identified. Furthermore, cooperative education, work evaluation, and technical education are included. The model's foundation of special education services reflects values, attitudes, human relationships, occupational information, and specific acquisition of job and daily living skills. This model offers something for everyone in terms of the long-range planning that is necessary for students with disabilities from middle and high school through the early stages of adulthood.

Person-Centered Planning

One concept is missing from each of these models—consumer orientation. Clearly, as thinking continues to become more responsive to students and families, a much greater emphasis must be placed upon providing consumer-oriented services, as with the Personal Futures Planning work of Mount and Zwernik (1988) and Vandercook et al. (1989).

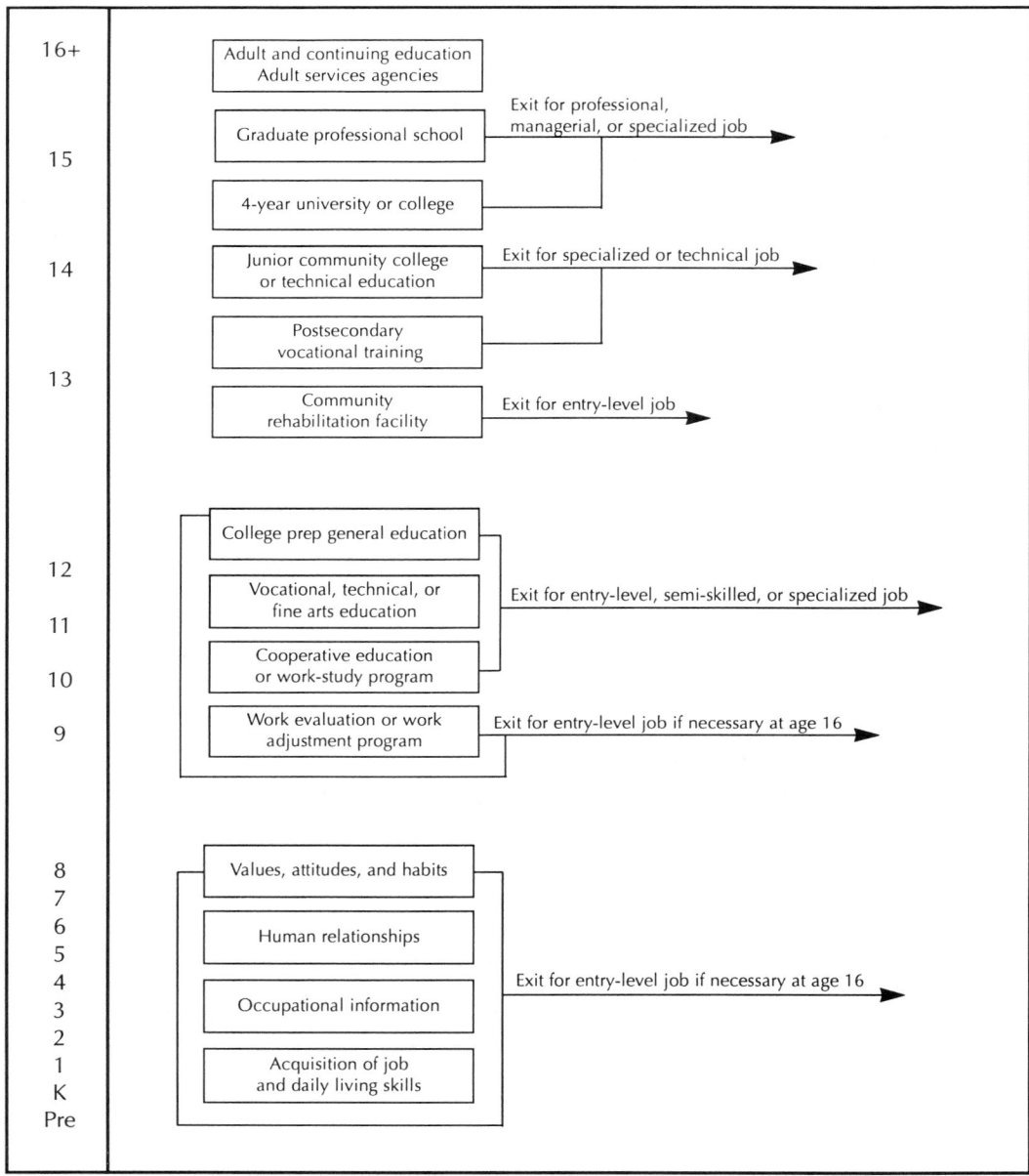

Figure 3.2. A school-based career development and transition education model for adolescents with disabilities. (From Clark, G.M., & Kolstoe, O.P. [1995]. *Career development and transition education for adolescents with disabilities* [p. 45]. Needham, MA: Allyn & Bacon. Copyright © 1990 by Allyn & Bacon; reprinted by permission.)

The person-centered planning approach has been a wonderful addition to the transition planning models. With a person-centered approach the entire focus is on individual students and the key people in their lives who can affect their futures. This approach establishes a blueprint for the future and helps to remove the ceiling of expectations that many professionals unwittingly place on students. In the traditional educational team model, professionals usually confer with each other, sit around the table, and make final decisions about what the student's educational plan will look like, often without any concrete input from the student or family. When a school system moves from this traditional approach to a more person-centered orientation, it puts the locus of control in the hands of the student and family, asking them to determine their future direction themselves. Obviously, this pathway greatly influences the types of curricula and learning environments that the student will experience. Furthermore, educational assessment data rather than the student's vision are a major source of information for planning the future. Table 3.5 compares the characteristics of a more traditional educational team approach with the person-centered planning approach.

Personal futures planning consists of three main components: a personal profile, a planning meeting, and the futures plan document. The first involves creating a personal profile of the *focus person*—the person with disabilities for whom the plan is being developed. The profile is completed prior to the initial planning meeting through a group interview that includes the focus person and a few others who care about and know the individual well. The profile contains a record of the person's life, including important relationships and places, past events, preferences, dreams for the future, barriers, and opportunities. Most important, however, it asks what this person wants for the future. Information gathered in the profile session can be graphically organized in a series of "maps" using colors, pictures, and symbols.

At the planning meeting, the group collectively works to develop a vision of a desirable future. A facilitator trained in personal futures planning leads the meeting, but the focus person and key people—usually a circle selected by family members—in his or her life are included. If the focus person is unable to speak on his or her behalf, an advocate or spokesperson is included. Often, a family member will choose to play this role.

Clearly, this approach is an excellent embodiment of self-determination and student choice. It is, however, at odds with the highly traditional approach of the educational team formulating a plan for or on behalf of the student. Chapter 4 discusses how to reconcile these two approaches by showing how a person-centered planning approach can be merged into most existing school structures.

Waiting Lists for Adult Services

For each of these programs, however, waiting lists have become a national problem because resources are so limited. As Table 3.6 indicates, there are more than 186,000 people with disabilities awaiting some form of community services. The majority of students with severe disabilities leaving school are, unfortunately, joining an ever-expanding waiting list with little hope of timely placements in valuable community-based programs. Families,

Table 3.5. A comparison of personal futures planning and traditional transition planning concepts

Traditional transition planning	Personal futures planning
A team of service providers meets annually, or more frequently if needed, with the parents and student to develop a plan for educational related services.	A circle of support made up of the focus person with a disability, parents, and other family members meets with service providers and general community members monthly or as frequently as needed to develop a future vision for the focus individual and to implement an action plan to achieve the future vision.
A transdisciplinary team conducts and interprets assessment data using standardized and nonstandardized assessment mechanisms.	A circle of support gathers, organizes, and manages assessment information into a personal profile and future vision using highly visual graphics known as MAPs.
The student with a disability is invited to participate in the team meeting as appropriate.	The circle defines a role for every focus person and assists the person in assuming the roles in a respected and competent manner.
Parents are invited to participate in the development of the individualized service plan.	Parents, other family members, friends, and general community members define the personal profile and future vision and look to service providers for support.
An IEP with a statement of needed transition services is mandated to guide services.	A future vision and action plan guide the circle's activities and should be used to drive the IEP/transition plan content.
Implementation of the plan is ensured through provision of entitlement services, due process, and professional services.	Implementation of the plan depends upon the commitment and energy of the circle of support and their connections with the focus person and family.

From Carr, T. (Ed.). (1993). Transition services and personal futures planning. *HKNC-TAC News, 6*(3); reprinted with permission from the Helen Keller National Center, Technical Assistance Center.

educators, adult services providers, and advocates must develop strategies that work to improve this situation, created by tight budgets and misplaced fiscal priorities. It is senseless to maintain a student for 10–15 years in public schools and then place him or her on a waiting list for services for 30 years.

Perhaps the solution is to emphasize in-service training. Many teachers have been in their field for as long as 5 years and have never had any of the transition training that personnel preparation programs are finally beginning to provide. It is crucial that discretionary programs meet these needs by funding competent in-service providers to reach teachers through innovative techniques, such as video courses, computer networking, technical assistance, and other revitalizing strategies. For the most part, teachers need immediate help in their schools or agencies from professionals who have been directly involved in transition planning and implementation in the past.

Table 3.6. Type of services people are waiting for by state

State (reference number)	Date data were collected	Residential	Day habilitation/ vocational services	Residential vocational	Support	Other	Total
				Type of services/supports			
AL(6)	6/9/90	1,086	1,325	–	776	–	3,187
AK(20)	5/1/90	–	–	–	517	601	1,118
AZ(21)	12/11/90	145	416	–	–	701	1,262
AR(37)	1990	271	272	–	7	338	888
CA(28)	3/9/92	–	–	–	–	–	–
CO(41)	11/30/90	1,616	1,202	–	–	–	2,833
CT(24)	1/1/92	937	453	–	–	15	1,390
DE(27)	4/1/91	179	24	–	–	–	203
DC(48)	10/2/91	210	52	–	–	–	262
FL(32)	1/14/91	–	–	–	–	–	4,673
GA(51)	11/29/89	1,179	–	–	–	–	1,179
HI(51)	9/30/90	201	277	–	–	–	478
ID(N/A)	–	–	–	–	–	–	–
IL (9) (29)	1986	10,000	1,989	–	–	–	11,989
IN(42)	4/30/91	2,048	1,096	–	–	–	3,144
IA(9)	1986	2,000	1,700	–	–	–	3,700
KS(39)	1/15/91	932	672	–	156	48	1,808
KY(31)	11/15/91	4,503	3,087	–	–	807	8,327
LA(45)	4/18/90	0	550	–	1,400	1,750	3,700
ME(2)	1/91	732	872	–	–	1	1,605
MD(46)	7/1/91	2,392	2,968	–	3,917	–	9,277
MA(25)	2/18/92	1,749	513	265	2.000	–	4,527
MI(N/A)	–	–	–	–	–	–	–
MN(15)	1991	560	1,272	–	340	–	2,172
16	1991	–	–	–	–	963	963
MS(36)	5/31/91	240	–	–	–	–	240
MO(3)	1/1/92	1,617	–	–	–	1,925	3,542
MT(7)	1/27/92	719	852	–	561	–	2,132
NE(33)	4/20/90	–	–	–	–	–	539
NV(4,13,18,22)	11/13/91	116	–	–	–	171	287

(continued)

73

Table 3.6. *(continued)*

State (reference number)	Date data were collected	Residential	Day habilitation/ vocational services	Residential vocational	Support	Other	Total
NH(34)	12/91	494	381	–	104	–	979
NJ(14)	2/92	3,023	360	–	–41,089	4,472	–
NM(8)	12/18/91	127	274	–	172	442	1,015
NY(19)	2/15/92	9,674	5,251	–	16,007	–	30,932
NC(38)	1989–1990	–	1,727	–	–	300	2,027
ND(30)	1/15/91	–	–	–	–	–	–
OH(49)	10/91	2,719	1,242	–	535	227	4,723
OK(17)	5/20/91	391	–	–	486	306	1,183
OR(23)	1987	–	–	2,000	4,600	–	6,600
PA(44)	1990–1991	3,995	–	–	–	–	3,995
RI(12)	–						
SC(1)	7/17/90	847	441	–	–	–	1,288
SD(5)	7/91						
TN(35)	12/31/91	544	869	–	–	–	1,413
TX(43)	1989	–	–	–	–	–	25,313
UT(52)	12/2/91	370	205	207	43	1,262	2,087
VT(50)	12/91	140	160	–	72	194	566
VA(11)	1991	2,100	–	–	–	–	4,479
(19)	1989	–	1,130	–	–	1,249	2,087
WA(47)	7/90	1,640	2,208	3,848	–	–	7,696
WV(n/a)	–						
WI(40)	9/1/90	1,380	1,255	–	1,209	1,884	5,728
WY(26)	1989	–	–	–	–	–	4,301
Total reported		60,876	35,095	6,320	32,902	14,273	186,272

From Hayden, M.F., & Depaepe, P. (1994). Waiting for community services: The impact on persons with mental retardation and other developmental disabilities. In M.F. Hayden & B.H. Avery (Eds.), *Challenges for a service system in transition: Ensuring quality community experiences for persons with developmental disabilities* (pp. 178–180). Baltimore: Paul H. Brookes Publishing Co.; reprinted by permission.

74

Conclusion

In this chapter, key elements of transition models, such as community factors, individual student choice, business connections with the schools, resources, and rehabilitation counselors, are identified. There is little question that many of the models developed in the 1980s have tremendous potential for vocational and independent living planning in the schools as well as in communities at large. However, a stronger emphasis on students, families, and their choice in transition outcomes as they enter adulthood is necessary.

3

Study Questions

1. Why is it important to involve communities in transition planning and program development?

2. How can transition programs "prepare supports, not people"?

3. How can businesses be involved in transition program development and individualized transition planning?

4. What is the Life-Centered Career Education Model, and for whom is this an effective approach?

5. What is person-centered planning, and how does this approach differ from traditional planning meetings?

6. What are typical services and accommodations needed by students with disabilities entering postsecondary education?

4

Individualized Transition Planning

> Upon completion of this chapter, the reader will be able to do the following:
>
> - Discuss the differences between individualized education programs (IEPs) and individualized transition plans (ITPs)
> - Know the seven major steps involved in designing and implementing ITPs
> - Write sample ITPs for students with three types of disabilities

This chapter expands upon the transition planning process and the importance of cooperation between agencies that serve youth and adults with disabilities by discussing guidelines for individualizing transition planning for students.

Challenges in Individualized Transition Planning

A major problem in transition planning involves the fact that teachers, parents, and others involved in developing ITPs are often limited to the services students are already receiving and have no access to the services they actually need. Furthermore, most plans are influenced by what is available in the community, rather than what students need to succeed in the community. For example, many students with mental retardation may need supported employment. Because there are no supported employment programs available in the community, however, the designers of the ITPs may not list supported employment as a desirable outcome. Similarly, educators and students may feel that a community-based work program would be very useful for a student but not include it in the ITP if such an opportunity is not available in the typical curriculum.

Implementing Individualized Transition Planning Procedures

Initiating transition planning for students with disabilities is the responsibility of the local education agency (LEA) because the school is the primary provider of services to youth during the transition planning years. Furthermore, with the Individuals with Disabilities Education Act (IDEA) of 1990, PL 101-476, transition planning is mandated by law. The local interagency agreement (see Chapter 5) is one mechanism that enables school systems to initiate, implement, and monitor interagency ITP processes. LEAs, however, cannot be solely responsible for individualized transition planning without the cooperation of local adult services providers.

The steps below describe, in sequence, the activities necessary for developing ITPs for students with disabilities who are leaving the public school system. Suggestions are also offered regarding schedules and service personnel responsible for the completion of each step. There are many transition planning manuals available that have been developed for specific states and localities (e.g., Goodson, 1995; Horton, Maddox, & Edgar, 1983; Izzo & Shumate, 1991; Lambrou et al., 1986; McDonnell & Hardman, 1985; Stodden et al., 1986). These manuals, as well as this chapter, provide specific and tested guidelines for individualized transition planning that can be adapted to the unique needs of particular students in certain communities.

Step One: Organize ITP Teams for All Transition-Age Students

Identify All Students Formal transition planning should begin when students are 16 years of age. For students at high risk of dropping out of school, 14 years old might be the targeted age. A teacher, social worker, guidance counselor, or other designated personnel may assume the role of transition planning coordinator or school transition liaison. This person operates within the procedures that have been determined by the core team and documented in a local interagency agreement. The designated person is responsible for compiling the list of transition-age students and overseeing the remaining steps in the transition process.

Identify Appropriate School Service Personnel School personnel (e.g., teachers, therapists, counselors) who have been involved with individual students targeted for transition planning should be identified to participate in the individualized transition planning process. When enlisting school staff for involvement, the organizer should be careful to select staff from all relevant disciplines who have had recent and meaningful contact with the student. However, the number of participants should be kept to a minimum so that teams are not too large to work productively as a group.

The members of the individual transition team will vary from situation to situation depending on the vision that the parents and student have for a long-term transition plan. Typically, however, a special educator will be involved, along with a vocational educator and a vocational rehabilitation counselor or representative. In addition, frequently there will be a service coordinator from an adult services agency. The following lists outline the primary responsibilities that several of the major participants have in the transition planning process:

Parents
- Attend ITP planning meetings
- Focus the team's planning and provide input on the individual student's and family's needs
- Provide informal home and community skills training, if possible
- Provide information to the team on various issues that the family will need to address, such as sexual, medical, social, financial, or guardianship issues

Special educators
- Target names of students for transition planning and coordinate data management
- Organize and attend ITP planning meetings
- Identify key referral needs and ensure that referrals are made to appropriate adult services agencies
- Coordinate the development and implementation of transition plans
- Ensure that student and parent choice and participation are maximized

Vocational educators
- Attend ITP planning meetings for all students who require vocational training or placement
- Consult with the ITP team on local employment trends and specific skills required for jobs
- Help identify and analyze community-based vocational training sites
- Provide instruction at community-based vocational training sites as necessary
- Provide leadership roles and job placements for students during their final years of school

Vocational rehabilitation counselors
- Serve as consultants to the ITP planning team throughout student's secondary years
- Coordinate the vocational training, job placement, and supported employment of post-secondary students
- Provide oversight and direct assistance into the eligibility process for vocational rehabilitation, including initial evaluations and job placements

Service coordinators from adult services agencies
- Share responsibility for assessment of students' needs as necessary
- Conduct home visits as needed
- Attend ITP planning meetings for students in their final years of school or for students at high risk of dropping out
- Provide follow-along services once students have been placed in supported living or supported employment work arrangements

Identify Adult Services Agencies In order to involve adult services agency representatives when their services can be utilized best and avoid overloading them with involvement at a time when they cannot be active participants, arrangements should be made for representatives to participate in the ITP process for students in their last 2 years of school.

In some cases, it may be necessary to involve this representative before the last 2 years of school. However, school officials should be aware of the very large caseloads of adult services workers and should refrain from requesting their early involvement except as required for certain students. But, typically during the early secondary years, adult services providers may assist ITP team members best in an informal consultative role.

During the crucial transition years, adult services representatives can provide valuable input on the available and most appropriate services for a particular student as he or she leaves the school program. Community agencies from which representatives may be drawn include mental health, mental retardation, vocational rehabilitation, social services, local organizations of The Arc (formerly Association for Retarded Citizens of the United States), and or the United Cerebral Palsy Associations (UCP). The likelihood that the student will benefit from an agency's participation or will be using its services in the future determines that agency's involvement. The more knowledgeable the school liaison or transition planning coordinator is regarding the functions and service capabilities of adult services providers and agencies, the better able he or she is to identify appropriate agency representatives for participation in ITP meetings.

Step Two: Organize a Circle of Support

Much of the anxiety about putting together any kind of service plan can be minimized by making the person with disabilities the focus of the plan development. Together, the focus person and family, staff, and friends can begin implementing new values and choices while letting go of old assumptions. "Deficit-finding" planning must be eliminated, and viewing people with disabilities with respect as people who are capable and gifted and being prepared to build goals on their strengths, unique talents, and interests must be adopted.

Person-centered planning offers the most information about a person and has the most opportunity for reward. This is a process that focuses on people's gifts, talents, and skills, instead of their impairments, which allows people to become involved in planning for their own future, including where to work, where to live, and what to do in the community. Person-centered planning searches for opportunities and capacities through the development of a personal profile. The facilitator meets with the focus person and a small group—usually called a circle of support—of friends, family members, co-workers, neighbors, church members, and staff to describe the focus person's life story and find out about the following:

- People in the focus person's life, both paid and unpaid
- Where the focus person spends his or her time
- Things that people see as contributing to a positive reputation
- Things that people see as contributing to a negative reputation
- Choices
- Preferences—things that motivate the person and create interest
- Things that do not work and that create frustration and upset the person
- Images of desirable future (i.e., goals)
- Most important things to work on now (2–4 months) and in the future (1–5 years)
- Opportunities—things or people who can help the focus person achieve his or her personal goals (desirable future)

- Obstacles/barriers—things that are getting in the way of achieving desirable future
- Strategies to achieve a desirable future

Successful implementation of a person-centered plan is made possible by the presence of this group of people who are committed to getting together regularly to solve problems, develop strategies, and make commitments to act on behalf of the focus person. As they develop the personal profile, the circle of support should also discuss strategies for implementing the ITP. Figure 4.1 is a positive student profile for Sam. Note the emphasis on the good things in Sam's life, not the negative things.

Step Three: Identify Key Activities

Throughout the meetings, key items emerge as important to the individual, such as the need for greater travel skills and mobility or help with communication and language skills. Some students will be highly motivated to have a paid job before leaving school while others may be more concerned with improving academic skills to sufficiently enter community college. These activities are influenced by the needs, wishes, and capabilities of the student as well as the supports that family members and friends can provide. Once these target activities are determined, the student and family are ready to move into the more formal, school-based IEP/transition meetings.

Step Four: Hold Initial ITP Meetings as Part of Annual IEP Meetings

Schedule the ITP Meeting Individualized transition planning meetings must be scheduled for each eligible student so that the student, parent(s) or guardian(s), relevant school personnel, and adult services representatives can attend. The student should always be included in the transition meeting so that he or she can have an active role in planning his or her future.

As decided by the core team and included in the local interagency agreement, the transition meeting may be conducted as part of the IEP meeting. This way, IEP goals and objectives can be written to reflect those of the ITP. Coordination of IEP skills and ITP services link the two agendas together.

Before the ITP meeting, the school liaison should make arrangements for cross-agency sharing of information about transition-age youth. These arrangements are essential because the LEA is prohibited from releasing confidential information on students in special education programs without the signature of a parent, a guardian, or the student.

Conduct the ITP Meeting Transition meetings should progress through definite stages to ensure that the goals and objectives are specific enough to achieve the desired outcomes. An ITP should identify adult residential and employment goals and the support services required to achieve and maintain these goals. In contrast, an IEP identifies skill impairments and remediation strategies. An effective ITP matches the specific strategies and behavioral objectives of the IEP with employment, residential, and community goals that a student must achieve in order to become an independent adult. The meeting format outlined and discussed below is based on a transition planning strategy used in several Virginia LEAs. These procedures should help professionals, parents, and students to develop ITPs that include 1) clearly defined outcomes, 2) selection of appropriate services to achieve those outcomes, and 3) objectives that must be met to arrive at the outcomes.

Who is Sam?
- Sam was born April 1, 1980. He is the middle child in his family.
- Sam has an older sister who is a physician and a younger brother who is a junior in high school.
- Sam is a sophomore in an inclusive high school and loves to read.
- Sam is shy around large groups of people.
- If Sam is comfortable, he is very talkative and interested in every thing going on in and around his life.
- Sam has a very supportive family.
- Sam likes basketball, computer games, swimming, Nintendo, and Sega.
- Sam likes to keep up with current and world events and has weekly discussions on such with his family.
- Sam likes animals—he has two dogs and a Bare-Eyed Cockatoo.
- Sam loves to help and exhibits a great need for independence.

What are Sam's strengths?
- His memory and retention of facts
- His reading abilities
- Expressing himself, when allowed time to do it
- Being able to care for himself
- Academics
- Is usually nonjudgmental
- Does well traveling with family and friends and in inclusive settings

What are Sam's greatest challenges and needs?
- Travel training
- Gainful employment and a career
- Community independence in leisure, recreation, and living
- Empowerment and/or self-determination curriculum
- Money
- Speech
- Computer skills

What supports are needed for Sam?
- Computer literate teacher or peer
- Calculator
- Writing software to strengthen writing skills
- Inclusive schooling, adapted collaboratively by Sam's special education teacher, general education teacher, and parents
- Peer tutors for schoolwork and peer partners for after-school activities
- Continued speech therapy to reinforce fluency and to develop inferential language and social problem solving

What are our dreams for Sam?
- For Sam to live as independently as possible
- For Sam to continue to have a substantial circle of support
- For Sam to have a meaningful career and friendships
- For Sam to always have a pet
- For Sam to continue to travel
- For Sam to attend sports events and belong to a golf club
- For Sam to attend town meetings, especially political ones
- For Sam to have private time

Figure 4.1. An example of a positive student profile.

Open the Transition Meeting The person conducting the meeting should welcome and introduce all meeting participants. An informal atmosphere is recommended so that the student and his or her parents will feel as comfortable as possible. It is the professionals' responsibility to encourage honest and open participation from everyone in attendance.

Generate a Discussion of Desired Outcomes and Available Support Services Students' post-school living and employment preferences and their specific competencies or talents should be strongly emphasized in the establishment of transition goals. Sarkees-Wircenski and Wircenski (1994) suggest using an ongoing career portfolio, similar to a job résumé, to catalog the transition/vocational competencies of the student. In addition, parents should verbalize what they want for their child's postschool life. It is important to encourage parents to express themselves openly so that any fears or uncertainties may be addressed in the discussion. A school representative should discuss the postschool outcomes he or she believes the student can achieve given the appropriate support services. For example, the vocational teacher may believe that the student can be successful in a full- or part-time job with supported competitive employment services or rehabilitation engineering. Such an assessment would, of course, be supported by evidence that the vocational training that has taken place throughout the school years has been appropriate and successful. The adult services representatives should discuss the postschool support services that are or will be available to the student. It is helpful to provide ITP meeting participants with a written list of available service options.

Certain programs or models considered may not be available in some communities. However, possessing information about these services can still be useful, for example, in providing community leaders with valuable ongoing needs assessment information. One of the agency liaisons should be responsible for compiling the information into a report at the conclusion of each year's ITP and submitting it to the administrators of the appropriate agencies.

Identify Transition Goals Having determined long-term employment and residential objectives and the appropriate service delivery model, short-term transition goals should then be developed and documented by the group. A goal should include the desired outcome (e.g., full-time employment) and the appropriate service delivery model to achieve the goal (e.g., a supported competitive employment approach). Some examples follow:

- Employment, such as part-time employment in an enclave program
- Residence, such as group home living
- Recreation, such as participation in an integrated recreation program (e.g., beginners swimming at the YMCA) or a peer-advocate program
- Community access, such as use of public bus systems to get to the jobsite and recreation program

Include with each goal the following:

- Projected date for achievement of goal, specifying completion before or after graduation
- Names of the agencies that will work toward this particular goal
- The person who is primarily responsible for seeing that the goal is achieved by the date set for completion

Determine Objectives and Steps to Accomplish Goals The objectives and/or sequence of steps needed to accomplish transition goals must be determined. This can be done in much the same way as writing a task analysis.

On page 85 is a plan developed for a student with a learning disability, labeled LD. Zina is 16 years old. She has been integrated into four of six classes a day. Currently, Zina is very concerned about social and recreational issues. She wants to do the right things, but she feels that she has a limited community with her father and older male siblings. She wants to develop a social relationship with a mature female. Zina's mother's death seems to bother her more these days. She has questions about sex, acquired immunodeficiency syndrome (AIDS), relationships, careers, and expectations.

On page 89 is an ITP written for a 19-year-old student with moderate to severe mental retardation. Larry has some verbal skills but is still very difficult to understand. He can point to pictures to make his needs understood but does not read, although he can identify some letters and numbers. He is very distractible and easily frustrated and will punch his fist in the air when he gets angry. Larry does not respond well to constructive criticism and will often gesture in an aggressive manner to peers and female staff. He lives with his parents and elder sister in a low- to middle-income home in a rural area. There is not a good work ethic in the family, and it is presumed that Larry will go to an adult activity center after school.

On page 93 is an ITP for a 21-year-old student with mental retardation. Garland is verbal and ambulatory. He can read approximately 30 sight words and complete simple written math problems with a calculator. He knows coin values but cannot count change. Garland can print his name and copy other words. He is strong and frequently engages in unorganized sports with classmates and family. Garland lives with his parents and younger brother and sister in a low- to middle-income suburb.

In these transition plans,[1] notice that each student has a "vision" developed by the student, family, friends, and others on the educational team. This vision helps the team as they try to provide concrete steps to implementation. This plan should be part of every IEP.

Devise a Services Referral Checklist Actions beyond those listed in the ITP objectives or in the "steps to accomplish goals" may be necessary to effect a smooth transition. Based on the goals and services needed as identified by the ITP meeting participants, agency representatives should be designated as "persons responsible" to begin the formal referral and application processes that will initiate the appropriate adult services. Application and referral forms must be completed by each of the adult services representatives identified as having a role in the student's postschool life. These include representatives from the Department of Rehabilitation Services, Social Services, Community Mental Health and Mental Retardation Services, the Social Security Administration, and the local sheltered workshop.

End the Meeting At the end of the meeting, all participants should sign the ITP document. The school liaison should send copies of the ITP to all participants as soon as possible. Information describing adult community services should be given to the parents or student at this time. This may be a community services booklet prepared by the transition planning core team (see Chapter 5) or brochures and pamphlets from the above agencies.

[1]Each of these ITPs is reprinted by permission from Wehman, P. (1995). *Individual transition plans: The teachers curriculum guide for helping youth with special needs.* Austin, TX: PRO-ED.

Description of Student's Future Vision

Zina would like to have a career as a beautician. She also values her mobility within the community and knows that she needs to purchase an automobile. Zina would also like to develop better peer relationships and acquire more friends.

Individualized Transition Plan

Student's Name ___Zina___

Birthdate _____

Student's Identification Number _____

Participants:

Name	Position
Zina	_Student_
Warren	_Father_
Maurice	_Guidance counselor_
Tom	_Accountant_
Sid	_Vocational evaluator_

School ___Eastland High School___

ITP Conference Date _____

Career and Economic Self-Sufficiency

Employment Goal *Zina will seek a career in cosmetology.*

Level of present performance: *Zina enjoys styling her hair and nails. Like many teenagers, she spends her allowance on various skin, hair, and nail products.*

Steps needed to accomplish goal: *1. Teacher will assist student in securing catalogs from beauty academies. 2. Zina will use a grid to compare course offerings, price, job placement, and credentials of schools. 3. She will apply for top two choices. 4. Zina will enroll in a beauty academy that offers job placement.*

Date of completion: *January 1996*

Person(s) responsible for implementation: *Teacher and Zina*

Vocational Education/Training Goal *Zina will participate in paid work experience in a beauty salon.*

Level of present performance: *Teacher and vocational evaluator are working together to complete a functional assessment while developing a job in a salon as an attendant, shampoo person, or receptionist.*

Steps needed to accomplish goal: *1. Teacher and vocational evaluator will complete an assessment that provides information on what level of instruction student needs, transportation issues, preferred work days and hours, orientation skills, and sequence skills. 2. They will use classified ads and networks to gain employer interviews, jobsite analysis, and job analysis.*

Date of completion: *December 1994*

Person(s) responsible for implementation: *Teacher, vocational evaluator, and Zina*

Postsecondary Education Goal *N/A*

Level of present performance:

Steps needed to accomplish goal:

Financial/Income Needs Goal *Zina and her father will meet with a financial planner to discuss how to manage her money from her trust fund.*

Level of present performance: *Zina will be 18 years old in 2 years. She would like to attend a beauty academy and purchase a car. Father has asked teacher to identify a financial planner to assist Zina in making good investments.*

Steps needed to accomplish goal: *1. Teacher will set up a meeting with an accountant, Zina, and her father. 2. The three will develop a financial plan.*

Date of completion: *September 1995*

Person(s) responsible for implementation: *Teacher, Zina, and father*

Career and Economic Self-Sufficiency

Independent Living Goal *N/A*

Level of present performance:

Steps needed to accomplish goal:

Date of completion:

Person(s) responsible for implementation:

Transportation/Mobility Goal *Zina will purchase a car.*

Level of present performance: *Zina has earned a driver's license.*

Steps needed to accomplish goal: *1. Zina will meet with an accountant. She will develop a financial plan. 2. Zina and father will shop for a car. She will develop a grid to compare cars. Zina and her father will select vehicle. 3. She will purchase car insurance, county tags, and licenses after purchasing vehicle.*

Date of completion: *June 1996*

Person(s) responsible for implementation: *Zina and father*

Social Relationships Goal *Zina is interested in developing a social relationship with an adult female as she misses the relationship she had with her mother.*
Level of present performance: *Zina is lonely and has become quite isolated. Her social skills need to improve.*

Steps needed to accomplish goal: *1. Zina will use telephone book to locate numbers to several community organizations. 2. Zina will call to get information on how to join the organizations. 3. She will complete applications and necessary paperwork. 4. Zina will follow up with applications if necessary.*

Date of completion: *August 1994*

Person(s) responsible for implementation: *Zina*

Recreation/Leisure Goal *Zina will practice and try out for the majorette squad.*
Level of present performance: *Zina is interested in becoming a majorette next school year. She has spoken with the teacher/sponsor and members of the current squad.*

Steps needed to accomplish goal: *1. Zina will attend meeting for prospective squad members. 2. Zina will attend practice sessions. 3. Zina will ask for additional help if needed to master baton twirling. 4. Zina will prepare routine for tryouts.*

Date of completion: *September 1994*

Person(s) responsible for implementation: *Zina and teacher/sponsor*

Personal Competence

Health/Safety Goal *Zina will gain knowledge of AIDS and pregnancy prevention.*
Level of present performance: *1. Zina has asked guidance counselor for information on AIDS and pregnancy prevention. 2. Zina admits that she is sexually active.*

Steps needed to accomplish goal: *1. Counselor will seek permission from Zina to include father in future meetings. 2. Counselor will refer Zina to school nurse. 3. Counselor will help her to make an appointment with a counselor from the health department. 4. Counselor will help Zina make an appointment with a doctor for a checkup.*

Date of completion: *June 1994*

Person(s) responsible for implementation: *Guidance counselor, Zina, and father*

Self-Advocacy/Future Planning *ITP will be updated in June 1995.*

Level of present performance: *Zina appears to have very specific goals. However, Zina will lead discussion around independent living, social development, and recreational leisure areas to develop new goals.*

Steps needed to accomplish goal: *1. Zina will be prepared to discuss future plans, identify existing supports, and predict other supports that will be needed to accomplish her goals.*

Date of completion: *June 1995*

Person(s) responsible for implementation: *Zina*

Student Career Preference

Career in cosmetology

Student's Major Transition Needs

1. Employment
2. Social relationships

Additional Notes

Description of Student's Future Vision

Larry wants to develop his physical fitness skills and would also like to develop a better network of friends than those in his immediate neighborhood. He also wants to have a real job in competitive employment and avoid being placed in a sheltered workshop after he leaves school.

Individualized Transition Plan

Student's Name _Larry_

Birthdate _____

Student's Identification Number _____

Participants:

Name _Larry and family_
 Julia
 Li-Shing
 Washington

School _Litton_

ITP Conference Date _____

Position _Student and parents_
 Teacher
 Service coordinator
 Vocational evaluator

Career and Economic Self-Sufficiency

Employment Goal _Larry will work full time as an assembler of bicycle brakes in a local factory with job coach and co-worker help._

Level of present performance: _Larry has worked on serveral different unpaid manufacturing sites with a school-supported work crew. He likes to earn money._

Steps needed to accomplish goal: _1. Obtain supported employment services through vocational rehabilitation. 2. Arrange observation of Larry at work with work crew by rehabilitation counselor. 3. Arrange for transportation by STAR._

Date of completion: _March 1995_

Person(s) responsible for implementation: _Teacher, parents, and factory supervisor (if available)_

Vocational Education/Training Goal _Larry will receive individualized vocational assessment at three or more manufacturing sites._

Level of present performance: _Larry has worked for up to 1½ hours with a crew. He requires frequent reinforcement and prompting to stay on task, with specific prompting on difficult descriptions._

Steps needed to accomplish goal: _1. Locate jobsites with tasks that are repetitive. 2. Provide individual training at three or more sites. 3. Explore appropriate, natural reinforcers for Larry with positive co-workers. 4. Evaluate job performance at sites. 5. Share information with vocational rehabilitation counselors._

Date of completion: _December 1994_

Person(s) responsible for implementation: _Vocational evaluator and teacher_

Postsecondary Education Goal *N/A*
Level of present performance:

Steps needed to accomplish goal:

Financial/Income Needs Goal *Larry will provide for his own clothing and recreation.*
Larry's parents are of low income and have not yet obtained SSI for Larry.

Level of present performance: *1. Apply for SSI. 2. Budget for clothing and weekly recreation. 3. Open account for Larry and assist him with gaining access to funds.*

Steps needed to accomplish goal:

Date of completion: *December 1995*

Person(s) responsible for implementation: *Service coordinator and parents*

Career and Economic Self-Sufficiency

Independent Living Goal *Larry will live in a group home with two to three housemates.*
Level of present performance: *Larry needs assistance with daily living activities such as shopping and cooking. He can independently shower and dress.*

Steps needed to accomplish goal: *1. Apply for residential services. 2. Continue instruction in shopping, cooking, and household activities at training sites. 3. Provide training during Larry's transition from his parents' home to the group home.*

Date of completion: *June 1995*

Person(s) responsible for implementation: *Service coordinator, teacher, and designee from the Center for Independent Living*

Transportation/Mobility Goal *Larry will learn how to ride the public bus from his house to a jobsite.*
Level of present performance: *Larry requires supervision in the community. He does not look before advancing across streets and has not shown independence in bus travel.*
Steps needed to accomplish goal: *1. Work with bus driver on Larry's route. 2. Provide bus training through teacher-assisted instruction on the bus.*

Date of completion: *June 1995*

Person(s) responsible for implementation: *Teacher*

Social Relationships Goal *Larry will engage in two activities per week with peers without disabilities.*

Level of present performance: *Larry has difficulty communicating and acting appropriately with peers. He does not spend time with peers outside of school.*

Steps needed to accomplish goal: *1. Obtain a volunteer "lunch buddy" for Larry from the high school. 2. Rotate volunteers quarterly. 3. Provide Larry with a discreet picture communication book and regularly update it.*

Date of completion: *January 1995*

Person(s) responsible for implementation: *Teacher*

Recreation/Leisure Goal *Larry will use a fitness facility regularly.*

Level of present performance: *Larry is healthy but uncoordinated and has difficulty playing sports. He watches wrestling and collects body-building magazines; peers in the neighborhood make fun of him.*

Steps needed to accomplish goal: *1. Teach Larry to use the fitness equipment at school (Nautilus, stationary bike, etc.). 2. Budget for membership to fitness center (YMCA or other) near home. 3. Arrange for transportation to center. 4. Seek volunteer to attend center with Larry.*

Date of completion: *January 1995*

Person(s) responsible for implementation: *Physical education teacher and parents*

Personal Competence

Health/Safety Goal *Larry will avoid strangers in the community.*

Level of present performance: *At school, worksites, and other community settings, Larry will try to engage stranger in "conversation" or activities.*

Steps needed to accomplish goal: *1. Continue instruction in appropriate social interactions in various settings. 2. Teach Larry to identify community "helpers" versus strangers. 3. Teach Larry to use an identification card.*

Date of completion: *March 1995*

Person(s) responsible for implementation: *Teacher*

Self-Advocacy/Future Planning *Larry will learn how to gain access to rehabilitation services.*

Level of present performance: *Larry's family members are slow to obtain services for him. They rarely attend school meetings, often refuse home visits, and have shown no interest in vocational rehabilitation (VR) services.*

Steps needed to accomplish goal: *1. Maintain frequent contact with vocational rehabilitation. 2. Provide information about services to Larry. 3. Teach Larry how to call and ask for VR help.*

Date of completion: *January 1995*

Person(s) responsible for implementation: *Teacher*

Student Career Preference

Working as an assembler in a manufacturing site

Student's Major Transition Needs

1. Employment
2. Vocational training
3. Advocacy
4. Residential services
5. Social skills

Additional Notes

Description of Student's Future Vision

Garland wants to live independently of his parents and be able to manage his own money with very little help. He also hopes to extend his school work experiences into a permanent job at the local supermarket. Garland would like to make arrangements with his co-workers for long-term transportation help and support.

Individualized Transition Plan

Student's Name ___Garland___

Birthdate _____

Student's Identification Number _____

School ___Turner High___

ITP Conference Date _____

Participants:

Name	Position
Garland	_Student_
Sam and Susan	_Parents_
Mary	_Teacher_
Miller	_Service coordinator_
Lawrence	_Vocational rehabilitation (VR) counselor_

Career and Economic Self-Sufficiency

Employment Goal Garland will work full time in the deli department of a local grocery store with supported employment.

Level of present performance: Garland has been employed by school enclaves at two sites and has taken a vocational food preparation course at school.

Steps needed to accomplish goal: 1. Assist Garland with applying for jobs at local grocery stores. 2. Arrange for transportation by carpool. 3. Provide job training assistance and support as needed.

Date of completion: _June 1995_

Person(s) responsible for implementation: _VR counselor_

Vocational Education/Training Goal Garland will work part time with supported employment prior to graduation.

Level of present performance: Garland has received vocational situational assessment at two grocery stores and has been assigned a Department of Rehabilitative Services (DRS) counselor.

Steps needed to accomplish goal: 1. Meet with DRS counselor and assist in job application as needed. 2. Arrange Garland's school schedule to accommodate work schedule. 3. Provide staff for jobsite training. 4. Provide transportation. 5. Share information and responsibilities with DRS counselor.

Date of completion: _December 1994_

Person(s) responsible for implementation: _Teacher_

Postsecondary Education Goal *Garland will attend classes of interest offered by Parks and Recreation.*

Level of present performance: *Garland can follow modeled instructions and is interested in working on cards, with wood, and other manual activities.*

Steps needed to accomplish goal: *1. Seasonally obtain brochures of classes. 2. Budget for classes. 3. Complete applications. 4. Arrange for transportation.*

Date of completion: *March 1995*

Person(s) responsible for implementation: *Service coordinator*

Financial/Income Needs Goal *Garland will be independent of his parents for basic financial needs.*

Level of present performance: *Garland receives a paycheck and SSI. He has a savings account. His parents provide basic needs and make deposits for him.*

Steps needed to accomplish goal: *1. Assist Garland in planning a budget for basic needs. 2. Initiate payment of rent to parents until alternative residence is secured. 3. Assist Garland in budgeting for and purchasing food and clothing.*

Date of completion: *May 1995*

Person(s) responsible for implementation: *Parents*

Career and Economic Self-Sufficiency

Independent Living Goal *Garland will live in a supervised apartment with one to two roommates, close to his parents.*

Level of present performance: *Garland is close to his family but wants to be independent. Garland is independent in personal hygiene and basic household chores.*

Steps needed to accomplish goal: *1. Apply for residential services. 2. Provide instruction in responding to emergencies.*

Date of completion: *March 1995*

Person(s) responsible for implementation: *VR counselor and teacher*

Transportation/Mobility Goal *Garland will use a taxi to travel to destinations nearby but not within walking distance.*

Level of present performance: *Buses are not available in Garland's area. He can ride a bike, use a telephone (given a written number), and cross streets safely.*

Steps needed to accomplish goal: *1. Teach Garland to arrange taxi service by telephone. 2. Teach Garland to identify list of unusual destinations by name and street. 3. Teach Garland to use "Dollar-more" strategy to pay for taxi.*

Date of completion: *March 1995*

Person(s) responsible for implementation: *VR counselor and teacher*

Social Relationships Goal *Garland will enjoy safe social/sexual relationships with female peers.*
Level of present performance: *Garland likes the company of girls and has several "girlfriends" among his peers without disabilities.*

Steps needed to accomplish goal: *1. Provide family life instruction. 2. Participate in appropriate co-ed recreational group activities.*

Date of completion: *December 1994*

Person(s) responsible for implementation: *Teacher and parents*

Recreation/Leisure Goal *Garland will join a Saturday bowling league.*
Level of present performance: *Garland's parents have been on bowling teams. Garland is a good bowler but cannot keep score.*

Steps needed to accomplish goal: *1. Assist Garland in joining a team. 2. Obtain a teammate mentor for Garland. 3. Assist Garland in budgeting for leagues and obtaining transportation.*

Date of completion: *March 1995*

Person(s) responsible for implementation: *Parents*

Personal Competence

Health/Safety Goal *Garland will maintain control over seizures.*
Level of present performance: *Garland had infrequent tonic-clonic seizures as a young child. He has remained seizure-free since age 15 but still takes low doses of Dilantin.*

Steps needed to accomplish goal: *1. Assist Garland in taking daily medications as recommended. 2. Continue regular checkups with family physician.*

Date of completion: *December 1994*

Person(s) responsible for implementation: *Family*

Self-Advocacy/Future Planning *Garland will benefit from family estate planning. He will assume his own guardianship, and his siblings will act as future trustees.*

Level of present performance: *Garland's parents are his guardians. His siblings are 2 and 4 years younger than Garland. Garland stands to share the inheritance of property.*

Steps needed to accomplish goal: *Obtain legal counsel to advise and prepare plan.*

Date of completion: *June 1995*

Person(s) responsible for implementation: *Parents*

Student Career Preference

Working at a grocery store

Student's Major Transition Needs

1. Employment
2. Residential services
3. Transportation
4. Financial management
5. Social relationships

Additional Notes

Step Five: Implement the ITP

Operating under the terms of an interagency agreement, those designated as responsible for goals or specific steps in the ITP should implement the plans as prescribed. Most of the ITP goals will require cross-agency involvement. Some services may be needed immediately, however, whereas other services may be utilized over a period of several school years and may even extend beyond graduation.

Step Six: Update the ITP Annually and Implement Follow-Up Procedures

As the student nears graduation and the ITP is implemented, adult services agencies should increase their involvement with the student. At this point, the schools should concentrate on transferring their information and services to these agencies. It is important that one of the agency liaisons be designated to follow up on the progress of the ITP throughout its implementation. This may mean calling the ITP coordinator to check on the status of individual goals or items. Follow-up should occur at least quarterly to ensure completion of all steps and, thus, increase the likelihood of achieving desired goals. Follow-up also may involve organizing and scheduling another meeting of ITP participants if it is found that goals are not being achieved as planned. Annual or more frequent revisions of the original ITP may be required.

Step Seven: Hold an Exit Meeting

Toward the end of a student's last year in school, the school liaison and adult services representatives should plan an exit meeting with graduating students and/or their parents to finalize plans for the transition from school to work. At this time, any final needs relevant to the transition process can be addressed. The group should examine goals that have and have not been achieved by their scheduled completion dates and verify goals that are scheduled for completion shortly after graduation. Those goals that have not been achieved as scheduled and those scheduled for postgraduation should be reviewed by the group for acquisition and relevancy. Achieved outcomes should also be discussed to determine how the student and his or her family are faring with the new activities.

In one of the best summaries of how the school-based transition process occurs, Izzo and Schumate (1991) have delineated six steps that show how the IEP is used as the administrative vehicle overriding the transition plan:

1. Prepare for the student's transition from school to work. Obtain or update information on the student's vocational skills, including the use of the following:
 - Vocational interest inventory
 - Formalized vocational assessment
 - Informal assessment, including behavioral observation
 Establish a transition file for each student.
 - Obtain or update information concerning the student's disabling condition, including medical and psychological evaluations.
 - Gather or update information about agencies (public and private) or individuals, including family members, that may be involved in the student's eventual transition, placement, or support.

- Collect information from the bureau of employment services and local chamber of commerce regarding local labor market needs.
2. Establish the transition team.
 - IEP chairperson reviews updated student information to determine individuals and agencies necessary to implement a successful school-to-work transition.
 - IEP chairperson ensures that agencies will have entered into a working interagency agreement with the school system.
 - IEP chairperson convenes the first full transition meeting.
 - IEP chairperson assigns transition coordinator as student advocate who will monitor the transition process.
 - Transition coordinator completes referral forms to adult services agencies and monitors services provided by adult agencies to ensure a well-coordinated transition process.
3. Set broad transition goals via the IEP/ITP.
 - The team determines the type and nature of the school and/or community placement that will be the context for the student's transition.
 - The team determines appropriate community living goals, including living arrangements, medical needs, estate planning, social options, and so on.
 - The team determines appropriate short- and long-term employment goals, including job training and employment options.
 - The team writes the goals on the IEP/ITP.
4. Establish the transition objectives.
 - Attach objectives with specific initiation and completion timelines to each of the goals specified on the ITP.
 - On the ITP, write the name of the individual assigned to be responsible for monitoring each objective.
 - Affirm the ITP team coordinator's role in monitoring the objectives with each team member throughout the year.
5. Update the transition plan based on the student's progress.
 - Reconvene the ITP team at least once to evaluate progress on the plans, goals, and objectives.
 - Modify or update the ITP based on reports by team members responsible for transition objectives.
6. Establish follow-up and follow-along services.
 - Determine scope and nature of follow-up.
 - Establish agency or individual responsibility for follow-up and follow-along.
 - Forward information gathered in course of ITP process to the follow-up coordinator.
 - Update school and agency files to reflect changes in the student's plans.

Strategies for Transition Planning

Team members must listen very carefully to what the student and family are indicating to the team in terms of what it is they want, where it is they want to go, and what their priority of goals are. Few ITPs can be completely comprehensive; because of limitations on resources or time, some goals are inevitably not implemented. Therefore, the ITP team must decide, with the student and family, which areas to focus on most extensively in the early

stages of the transition period. Students and families need information and guidance; they do not need to be told what to do or be patronized. Table 4.1 gives tips for professionals helping students and families implement their vision for a challenging future in adulthood.

Consider Angela,[2] who unfortunately represents thousands of young people with mild intellectual disabilities in the United States in the 1990s. The purpose of effective transition planning is to avoid the dilemma that Angela's story portrays.

Angela *Angela is a vivacious 22-year-old woman who graduated from high school in 1994. In one way, she is very typical of many young adults with mental retardation who require intermittent supports and who exit special education programs upon graduation: She is waiting for community services.*

Angela's educational program attempted to prepare her for integration into the community by providing vocational training prior to her graduation. According to her mother, Angela had enjoyed school and had many friends there; she never wanted to miss a day. But, in discussing her school experience, Angela said, "They always put me on work instead of helping me with reading or math, which are really hard for me. I was not happy because I had to go to work." The school staff had believed that job skills were a higher priority than academic skills for Angela. She does know the alphabet, however, and once spelled out street signs to her mother on the telephone when lost.

Angela received supported employment services from the community following graduation as stipulated by her educational transition plan. Upon graduation, Angela worked at a fast-food restaurant but later requested a different job. She then secured employment in the housekeeping department of a local hotel—a job she enjoyed. Angela said, "I made a lot of friends on the job. It was great! The first time I walked in, they joked with me. I miss them." In an attempt to live more independently, Angela also moved into an uncle's home at this time.

After 8 months, however, she began to call in ill frequently and lost her job at the hotel. She said that she was having problems with her seizures and was unable to work mornings, when the seizures primarily occurred: "I told them I have to have a night job instead of working mornings because it is really hard for me with seizures going on, so they fired me." Angela also admitted that there may have been other problems during this time. She missed her family a great deal, and also said, "I did not have my cat there either, so I probably wanted to move back home because I was missing my cat, too."

A month after losing her job, Angela moved with her family from the city to a suburban home. Since then—a period of 18 months—she has been out of work. When asked about her life and daily routine, Angela says, "It's boring. I really don't do all that much. I watch television. I do the laundry, and sometimes I dust or vacuum while Mom is at work. I sleep a lot." She says she often feels depressed, explaining, "I get cranky and take it out on my mom and dad and sister. I get cranky often, but today is not too bad. I'm expecting company later, so I am getting excited about that."

Other than her boyfriend, whom she met 7 months ago while rollerskating with her family, Angela has made no new friends since moving. Her family's home is relatively isolated, with few neighbors nearby. She rarely sees her old friends from school and work because "I took the city bus from

[2]This case study is adapted with permission from El-Afandi, B. (1994). Barriers to support: Waiting lists. *IMPACT: Feature Issue on Self-Advocacy, 1*(1), 1–4. Minneapolis: University of Minnesota, Institute on Community Integration, Research and Training Center on Community Living.

Table 4.1. Do's and don'ts for transition planning

Do:

- Provide formal transition planning for students when they are 16 years of age, or younger for those at risk of dropping out.
- Utilize all appropriate school staff.
- Involve the student actively in the transition meeting, as well as parents or other family members.
- Make sure the IEP parallels the ITP, but with more specific strategies and behavioral objectives.
- Make sure that ITP goals are stated in such a way that they provide a meaningful desired outcome.
- Establish a checklist that provides a careful sequence of services that the student will need to be matched with in the community.
- Ensure that there is a lead person identified for implementing each of the goals on the ITP.
- Arrange for increased involvement by select adult services agencies as the student nears graduation.

Don't:

- Involve numerous adult services programs that are not going to be able to help the student.
- Involve adult services programs too early in the transition planning.
- Hold the transition meeting so that parents, families, or students feel they are being patronized or controlled.
- Give up easily on gaining input from the student and parents.
- Craft interagency agreements that have no specific outcomes or resources allocated to goals.
- Discontinue communication with parents simply because the ITP is signed and the meeting completed.
- Fail to follow up after the student leaves school.

where I used to live, but I do not know how to get there now." Her social life currently consists of going to the movies or tractor pulls or just "sitting around watching television" with her boyfriend, Tim, and her family.

In the future, Angela would like to get a small apartment in a secured building. She would take her cat with her and remember to call her mother whenever she felt lonely. Ideally, it would be on a bus line, somewhere near her job and Tim. She says that she would still need someone "to help me pay my bills and get to the grocery store. I cannot do that by myself." She says she feels older and more mature now, better able to handle life on her own.

Her most important goal right now, however, is finding a job. When she moved with her parents to the suburb, she and her mother went to the local social services agency to change her Medical Assistance and request assistance in finding a job. Later, a social worker came to their home and told them that Angela's name would be put on a waiting list for supported employment and transition services, as nothing was currently available. Nearly 18 months later, Angela is getting impatient. She and her family are also still waiting for her records to be transferred to their new county. She says, "I really want to go back to work. It is boring here. There is really nothing to do. The only thing that I am concerned about is that they are not helping me with a job. It is really bugging me!"

Angela has always been encouraged by her family to be involved in decisions regarding choices that will affect her life. They encouraged her to take an active role in her school planning process, which failed. Angela says, "I was there. I told them what I wanted. I tried, but they never listened to me. They said just go for jobs." Angela also tried to advocate for herself later when dealing with the agency providing her supported employment services, again to no avail. She says, "I tried to tell

them, but my mom was not there at that point. I told them I cannot work mornings because it's real hard for me. I tried to tell them, but they never listened." She feels that only her decisions to leave, and subsequently return to, her family's home were controlled entirely by her.

She has recently requested that information regarding the People First organization be sent to her. Both she and her mother feel that a self-advocacy group could enhance Angela's skills and help her form meaningful friendships. Angela and her mother recently began working on a reading skills program at home; learning to read is still difficult but for Angela it is an important goal. For now, however, finding a job is her top priority.

One person who has helped people with mild disabilities like Angela on a national level is Professor Andrew Halpern of the University of Oregon. He has been a leading career educator for years and a major proponent of all aspects of adult life planning, not just employment (see Transition Leader Box on p. 102).

Communication with Parents

Parental support is crucial to successful implementation of the ITP and in helping young people like Angela avoid frustration and disappointment. Therefore, communication with parents must begin in the first transition planning meeting and continue throughout all phases of implementation. Parents will be concerned about their child's move from the sheltered environment of the classroom to unprotected environments, such as employment or community living settings. They may voice concerns about transportation to and from work, co-workers' attitudes toward their child, the pressures of the job, Supplemental Security Income (SSI) and health care benefits, and supervision and safety in a group home. In particular, parents must understand how employment will affect their child's SSI and health care benefits. It should be stressed that care will be taken to maintain health care benefits through the employment situation or, if possible, by maintaining SSI eligibility.

It is critical that the goals and objectives of the ITP reflect the desired priorities and lifestyle of the student and his or her parents or guardians. As a youth makes the transition from the mandatory and intensive involvement of the school service system to a nonmandatory adult services system, the responsibility for carrying out the goals and objectives as decided by the ITP team will shift to them. If the goals are a reflection of what the professionals think is best and most appropriate for the student rather than what is desired by the youth and the family, then it is likely that achievement of targeted outcomes will not occur.

Conclusion

Three factors are critical to the successful implementation of an individualized transition plan:

1. The involvement of ITP members who are knowledgeable about the availability of local services

Andrew Halpern Dr. Andrew Halpern has been actively involved in the field of special education since 1966, focusing much of his effort on the areas of assessment, independent living, and secondary special education and transition. From 1971 to 1988, he was the director of a rehabilitation research and training center in mental retardation at the University of Oregon. Since 1988, he has directed a collection of projects dealing with secondary special education and transition. During this time, he has also published several papers dealing with the foundations of the transition movement.

During the mid-1960s and early-1970s, his efforts were focused largely on evaluation and improvement of cooperative work-study programs involving collaborations among special education, vocational education, and vocational rehabilitation. For the next 10 years, he pursued projects in test and curriculum development, which eventually resulted in the production and publication of several standardized tests along with structured curriculum materials in the social and vocational domains of secondary special education.

In the 1990s, he has worked extensively on the development and implementation of a systems change model for improving secondary special education and transition services at both state and local levels. The system, known as the *Community Transition Team Model*, has been implemented in several states, including Alabama, Arizona, Idaho, Kansas, Nevada, Oregon, Utah, and Washington, and in New South Wales (Australia). He is presently developing a curriculum that will teach high school students how to do their own transition planning. His research has helped hundreds of school systems and communities establish transition planning strategies for young people with disabilities.

2. A process that ensures the identification of all desired outcomes within the least restrictive service options
3. The ability of community agencies to provide or procure the needed services.

Communities with well-written interagency agreements, a wide array of community service options, and a collaborative plan to address service needs will have the best chances of achieving desired outcomes for each student.

4

Study Questions

1. What are the seven basic steps in formulating and implementing individualized transition planning?

2. What are some of the challenges faced by educators in implementing transition planning for the student with disabilities?

3. Who are the individuals most likely be involved in transition planning and what others might be involved and why?

4. What are five factors that influence key activities important for the student's transition?

5. What are the eight steps for conducting an initial ITP meeting?

6. What roles do adult services agencies play in the development and implementation of the ITP?

7. What are the six steps identified by Izzo and Shumate (1991) for a school-based transition process?

8. How might Angela's outcome have been affected by a person-centered transition plan?

II

Facilitating and Supporting Transition

5

Interagency Cooperation

Upon completion of this chapter, the reader will be able to do the
following:

- Explain what an interagency agreement is and why it is im-
 portant
- Understand the role and importance of local planning, espe-
 cially by a community care team
- Discuss the activities of a local community care team
- Review and describe key items that should be included in
 writing interagency agreements
- List and describe briefly the agencies that should participate
 in transition planning

Effective transition planning and service provision depend on functional linkages between
school and adult services agencies (Everson, 1995; Fenton & Keller, 1981; Hasazi, 1985;
Rachal, 1995). Although the agencies that are primarily responsible for serving individuals
with disabilities are seeking the same or similar outcomes for their clients, they have, in
many instances, been operating in isolation or even in opposition to each other.

Statistics indicating the lack of successful employment outcomes for students leaving
public school special education programs are revealing. A 1994 Louis Harris and Associ-
ates Poll indicated that 66% of people with disabilities remain unemployed. The data point
out transition-related problems, such as the inability of different agencies to coordinate
services and resources to accomplish meaningful postschool outcomes in the areas of em-
ployment and community living. Many follow-up studies of public special education
graduates show similar data indicating low rates of employment (Benz & Halpern, 1993;
Hasazi, Gordon, & Roe, 1985; Holsch, Karen, & Franzini, 1992; Mithaug, Horiuchi, & Fan-
ning, 1985; Scuccimarra & Speece, 1990; Sitlington, Frank, & Carson, 1990; Wehman, Kregel,
& Seyfarth, 1985).

In order for interagency cooperation to occur and tangible goals for individuals with disabilities to be achieved, state and local community leader must follow federal examples of leadership. Terms for cooperation must be designed and written for local-level agencies, and staff and participating agency resources must be committed to accomplishing transition-related outcomes. Plans must be developed and implemented to provide for regular and frequent face-to-face interaction of interagency teams at the service delivery level (Everson, Rachal, & Michael, 1992).

This chapter discusses ways to develop cooperative interagency agreements so that transition planning activities are implemented and targeted outcomes are achieved. A list is provided that will facilitate the implementation of written interagency agreements. Interagency agreements at the state level are discussed along with several options for interaction at the local level. Finally, in the chapter Appendix is an example of a three-way, community-level agreement as a model for implementing individualized transition planning and supported employment services.

Interagency Cooperation at the State Level

For state level interagency collaboration to bring about changes in local-level activities, the leaders must have a strong and visible commitment to common missions (Rachal, 1995). This sense of mission is necessary to focus the activities of an organization (Beer, 1980; Tichy, 1983). For most agencies serving individuals with disabilities, the mission is service provision.

The purpose of providing educational programming to children and youth with disabilities is to maximize their independence as adults. Education should prepare children and youth for adulthood. In contrast, adult services providers do not begin their service provision to individuals with disabilities until these individuals are adults. The goal of service provision is the same for schools and adult services providers; it is their deadlines for accomplishing the goal that differ. In order to use time more efficiently, adult services providers look for more immediate and varied means to accomplish their goal.

Because their missions are the same but different approaches are being utilized by agencies, the methods of each agency should be examined and efforts should be coordinated. Gaining a better understanding of how and why the different agencies operate as they do will improve efficiency and reduce instances of duplicated services.

One example of duplication is the repetition of expensive diagnostic evaluations because one state agency does not accept the records of another state agency or because an agency is required to conduct its own evaluations as a part of eligibility determination. Yet, some agencies continue to complete diagnostic evaluations in advance, assuming they will meet the receiving agency's eligibility requirements. This duplication, however, is senseless. Individuals who have received services while in public school special education programs must have been determined eligible for those services because of a disability; procedures for eligibility determination are carefully prescribed in the regulations specified by the Individuals with Disabilities Education Act (IDEA) of 1990, PL 101-476. The existence of an individualized education program (IEP), as required by law for each student with disabilities, should therefore be sufficient documentation that there is a disability and that the individual is eligible for adult services for individuals with disabilities.

Programs with similar service provision goals for people with disabilities include the vocational education program—Joint Training Partnership Act (JTPA)—and developmental disabilities programs. Unlike educational services, however, these are eligibility programs, not entitlement programs, which means there is no guarantee of service.

In order to demonstrate how these service providers are similar in mission, it is necessary to restate or reexamine each agency's mission and then to recognize common goals—also a useful tool for initiating interagency cooperation. Once a common mission is identified across agencies, the purpose of formalizing interagency collaboration—efficient provision of services—becomes clear and logical.

After recognizing that interagency cooperation is advantageous, the leader at the state level must begin to work with agencies to commit staff and resources to initiating the transition process. For example, designating middle-level management personnel to develop interagency activities is a logical starting point. Management designees from the different agencies must come together as a core team to examine the need for interagency cooperation by conducting state- and local-level needs assessments to define necessary changes. The core team also develops strategies and deadlines for planning and implementing transition services (McCarthy, Everson, Inge, & Barcus, 1985).

It is important for the agency designees to have equivalent levels of authority so that they will have similar power for planning and implementing interagency programs. Unequal appointment of leadership-level staff indicates an unequal commitment to the implementation of interagency transition planning activities. A balance of leadership across the participating agencies is important so that there is relatively equal power and ability to allocate and mobilize personnel to disseminate information regarding transition and interagency activities and to utilize agency resources.

For most state-level agencies, plans for interagency cooperation should be built into the agencies' working documents (Ashby & Bensberg, 1981). Most state agencies are required to write state agendas that illustrate their plans of operation for a 5-year period. A state plan that includes procedures for transition planning is likely to show evidence of interagency service coordination. Without explicit procedures for interagency interaction in an agency's working document, interagency agreements may be safely filed away, resulting in little or no change in actual service provision. Management staff should develop and implement schedules of interaction between agency representatives, devise a list of activities and deadlines for their completion, and identify expected outcomes.

Implementation of any new activity also requires a commitment of funds. The information gathered by the state-level core team is useful for budget allocations, which ultimately affect local-level programs and service delivery to consumers.

Agency representatives involved in interagency cooperation for transition planning activities must keep consumer needs as their primary goal. Representatives should also remember that the service system also benefits from combining and coordinating resources to accomplish outcomes for consumers. At this point it is appropriate to recognize one of the most talented transition leaders providing interagency technical assistance, Dr. David Johnson of the University of Minnesota. Dr. Johnson has visited local and state agencies throughout the United States, helping them work out transition issues.

David Johnson Dr. David Johnson is Director of The National Transition Network and Research Associate in the Institute on Community Integration (ICI) at the University of Minnesota and several other federal and state projects in the areas of transition programs, interagency collaboration, special education, supported employment, vocational rehabilitation services, and other education issues. He is also responsible for orchestrating the design and procedures for the identification and validation of proven models and exemplary practices that are a part of the overall activities of the North Central Regional Information Exchange, Research and Rehabilitation Training Center on Community Living, and Research and Rehabilitation Training Center on Children and Youth with Chronic Illness and Disability at the University of Minnesota.

Dr. Johnson has a master's degree in rehabilitation counseling and a doctorate in special education policy and administration, with a specialization in the design of transition and employment training systems for people with disabilities. He has also served as a consultant to a number of national and state organizations on public policy and evaluation issues. He has published numerous journal articles, book chapters, monographs, and technical reports, on such topics as school-to-work transition, interagency cooperation, cost–benefit analyses of special education and supported employment programs, and postschool outcome studies, among others.

Dr. Johnson is one of the foremost technical assistance experts in the United States on transition. More than a scholar, he is highly skilled in working closely with parents and professionals in crafting interagency agreements and meaningful collaborations. He is known as a person who can "get the job done"—an innovator yet someone who can adapt to changing conditions. David Johnson is a true leader.

Interagency Cooperation at the Local Level

The steps outlined and discussed for state-level cooperation should be repeated by agency leaders at the local level. A local core team must be organized to write a local-level interagency agreement that establishes the operating and interaction procedures among agencies for planning and implementing transition services. This plan for interaction should include an interorganizational structure with responsibilities outlined for each participating agency. A local community needs assessment should be conducted soon after the core team is established.

The needs assessment information is valuable for the development and writing of the local interagency agreement and for the implementation of the agreement from year to year. Therefore, the needs assessment activity is important because it gathers initial planning information. For this information to be useful in the implementation of the interagency agreement, it must be updated at least annually.

Organization of a Local Community Core Team

The core team in a local community must include members from all of the key agencies providing services to individuals with disabilities. Agency representatives might include

the special education director from the local school system, the director of vocational education services, the regional director or program supervisor from the local rehabilitation services office, the director of community services from the local mental health and mental retardation agency, a representative from a local client advocacy group, and parents of children with disabilities. Other agencies serving individuals with disabilities in a given community should also participate in core team interagency planning activities. (See Chapter 3 for a discussion of initiating development of community-level transition planning core teams.)

The initial activities of the local community core team are 1) to establish a reason for its existence (i.e., to improve and coordinate the provision of services for youth making the transition from school to adult community living); 2) to delineate the goals of the transition planning core team, which include completing a local-level needs assessment and writing an interagency agreement; 3) to list and rank by priority the activities that will enable the team to accomplish its goals; 4) to divide the list of activities and assign people or work groups to be responsible for completion of activities; and 5) to establish deadlines for completion of all activities.

Johnson and his associates (1993) stress the importance of "ownership" by all participants in the transition planning process. They suggest that all who are involved, also known as "stakeholders" in the process, be asked the following questions:

- What are the desired or positive outcomes students should achieve 1 year after they graduate from high school?
- What attributes or characteristics of current school programs and transition planning processes currently support or limit students in achieving these outcomes?
- What fundamental changes in special education and transition services need to be made to improve postschool outcomes?
- What types of information should be assembled and included in the information system to aid staff decision making in improving student service planning and program improvement efforts?

Table 5.1 provides a checklist to help stakeholders to ensure they achieve meaningful goals and outcomes for youth with disabilities.

Local Community Needs Assessment

A community-level needs assessment should be conducted by the core team to gather information needed for optimum service delivery. This information is also useful in determining how to reallocate resources for the development of new programs as they are

Table 5.1. Checklist for stakeholders

- Do students, family members, and community services representatives consistently participate in student IEP and ITP meetings?
- Are transition goals and objectives incorporated within current IEPs?
- Are students participating in appropriate transition-oriented school programs and services related to their IEP goals and objectives?
- Has a transition plan been developed that identifies specific postschool outcomes and desired adult services?

needed. The community-level needs assessment should be conducted to identify 1) how many individuals will graduate from public school services in the next 5 years, 2) how many adults are being served in each existing program, 3) how many adults are waiting for services, 4) what services are available in the community, 5) what the current programs' service capacities are, and 6) what program or service options are still needed in the community.

Figure 5.1 can be used to gather relevant information for a local community needs assessment. Once completed, the chart contains a summary of programs available in the community; provides quantitative data to indicate where, when, and the extent to which each service option is needed; and shows which types of services have demands either over or under their existing service capacity. Instructions for compiling information for a local community needs assessment are as follows:

Column One: Projected Number of Individuals to Initiate Demands on the Adult Services System The following instructions help agency staff to calculate the number of individuals who will require adult services in the next year.

1. List the number of special education graduates who began using adult services programs during the specified 12-month period (A).
2. List the number of students who will use adult services programs during the specified 12-month period prior to graduation (B).
3. Estimate the number of adults who may be initiating demand for adult services programs during the specified 12-month period (C). Include those individuals entering the target area from other localities, those reentering from institutional care, or those identified as appropriate for services after a period of not being served.
4. Add the numbers from rows A, B, and C to arrive at a total number of individuals estimated to initiate demands for adult services during the specified 12-month period (D) (e.g., between July 1996 and June 1997).

$$A + B + C = D$$

Column Two: Program Type and Service Capacity The transition planning core team should identify the program types (e.g., job placement, transitional employment, supported competitive, enclave, mobile crew, sheltered workshop, adult activity) that are available and the number of individuals who can be served in each program type. If a program type is not available in the community, indicate this fact on the form.

Column Three: Number of Individuals from Column One Targeting Specific Program Types From the individualized transition plans (ITPs), individualized program plans (IPPs), and individualized written rehabilitation plans (IWRPs), compile the number of people targeted for each program type. Requests or demands for program type(s) not currently available in the community should be noted and included in the needs assessment information.

Column Four: Number of Individuals Currently on Waiting Lists For each program type, identify and list the number of individuals on the providers' waiting lists for services.

Column Five: Projected Number of Program Openings Per Year Based on the previous year's information, list the number of program slots projected to open in each program type. Adjust this projection with the current funding and staffing levels as well. Include

1	2	3	4	5	6	7	8
Projected number of graduating students to initiate demands on adult services system	Program type and service capacity (SC)	Number of candidates from Column 1 targeted for specific program types	Number of candidates currently on waiting list	Projected number of program slots to open per year	Projected percentage of program slots to open	Total number to be over program's service capacity	Percentage of change in funding resource allocations indicated
A. Number of special education graduates to begin utilizing adult services between 7/96 and 6/97 <u>115</u>	Job placement SC = <u>50</u>	44	8	35	70	17	+34
	Transitional employment SC = <u>40</u>	28	15	21	52	22	+55
B. Number of special education students to utilize adult services prior to graduation between 7/96 and 6/97 <u>8</u>	Supported competitive employment SC = <u>60</u>	31	18	35	58	14	+23
	Enclave SC = <u>11</u>	12	3	1	9	14	+127
C. Number of students expected to begin utilizing adult services programs between 7/96 and 6/97 <u>20</u>	Mobile crew SC = <u>NP</u>	6	3			9	+100
	Sheltered workshop SC = <u>65</u>	16	15	9	13.8	22	+34
D. Total number of new individuals to potentially demand adult services between 7/96 and 6/97 <u>143</u>	Adult activity SC = <u>22</u>	6	8	1.5	6.8	12.5	+57
	No services requested	36					

Figure 5.1. Local community needs assessment. (Instructions for completion of this form are in text.) (Adapted from Wehman, Moon, Everson, Wood, & Barcus, 1988.)

the approximate number of individuals moving out of the target area, completing the program, discontinuing the program, or requiring a level of service that allows the program to accommodate new referrals.

Column Six: Projected Percentage of Program Turnover Compute the percentage of program turnover by dividing the projected number of program openings per year (i.e., the number in Column 5) by the service capacity (i.e., the number in Column 2), then multiply by 100. The resultant number is a projected percentage.

(Column 5/Column 2) x 100 = Projected turnover percentage

The projected turnover percentage indicates the number of people expected to move from each program type (e.g., 66% of the consumers may move out of the program or may require a level of service that allows the program to accommodate new referrals).

Column Seven: Total Number to Be Beyond Program's Service Capacity Add the number of graduating students targeted for specific program types (i.e., the number in Column 3) and the number of candidates on waiting lists (i.e., the number in Column 4). From this sum, subtract the projected number of program openings per year (i.e., the number in Column 5).

(Column 3 + Column 4) – Column 5 = Number over service capacity

This number indicates the projected waiting list numbers for each program type in the upcoming 12-month period. This figure is based on current funding and staffing levels.

Column Eight: Indicated Percentage of Change (+ or –) in Funding or Resource Allocation(s) To calculate the indicated percentage of change in funding or resource allocations, divide the number of individuals projected to be over the program's service capacity (i.e., the number in Column 7) by the service capacity and multiply the quotient by 100.

(Column 7/Column 2) x 100 = Indicated percentage of change

This figure gives planners an estimate of the amount of increase or decrease in budget allocation that may be necessary to meet service demands for each program type in the upcoming year.

After compiling these data, the local core team will have information that should be useful in indicating where agency resources must be concentrated and in what proportion. Using this method of community analysis, the service programs can be planned based on actual needs. Agency resources can be shifted to programs that are most effective and to those areas with the greatest demand for services.

Community Services Program Effectiveness Survey

Further needs assessment information can be gathered by using the form in Figure 5.2. This form is difficult for some program and service providers to complete because of the detailed information it requires. Specifically, the form requests a careful delineation of the targeting goals of each program plus an estimation of the expected duration of the program services required to achieve the targeted outcomes. Although it may be difficult, or even uncomfortable, for some service providers to complete, the information it yields is extremely valuable to program planners as well as the purchasers and consumers of the actual program services. Similar to commodities in private industry, human services can be viewed as a buyer–seller arrangement. With a delineation of targeted goals in hand, the "buyer" can make better decisions regarding the "purchase" of a goal rather than investing in an undefined service process. Use of the form may encourage users to clarify the outcomes that consumers want and candidates need. Instructions for completion of the community services program effectiveness survey follow.

1	2	3	4	5	6
Name of services provider and program type	Targeted outcome(s) of service (months)	Prescribed duration of service (and/or preservice referral period) to achieve targeted outcomes	Number of consumers achieving targeted outcome within prescribed service duration in last 12-month period	Total number of consumers served by program in last 12-month period	Percentage of program effectiveness
Vocational rehabilitation–job placement services	Candidates will be placed in competitive employment situations earning minimum wage or above and will retain employment for at least 60 days.	3	25	45	55
Carl County public schools vocational education job placement services	Candidates will be placed in competitive employment situations earning minimum wage or above and will retain employment for at least 60 days.	3	15	30	50
Supported employment of Carl County Competitive Employment	Candidates will be competitively employed earning minimum wage or above, require less than 10% job coach intervention time by the end of a 5-month period, and will retain employment for a period of 6 months. Candidates will be accepted for ongoing follow-along services by the appropriate agency.	8	18	24	75
Carl County Arc supported competitive employment	Candidates will be competitively employed earning minimum wage or above, require less than 10% job coach intervention by the end of a 5-month period, and will retain employment for a period of 6 months. Candidates will be accepted for ongoing follow-along services by the appropriate agency.	8	9	20	45
Supported employment of Carl County enclave program	Candidates will be employed in an enclave employment program earning 50% of minimum wage by the end of a 4-month delivery period.	8	8	12	66
Name of service provider and program type	Targeted outcome(s) of service.				
Carl County sheltered workshop program—Level I	Candidates will achieve earnings to equal 25% of minimum wage by the end of a 6-month delivery period.	6	7	10	70
Carl County sheltered workshop program—Level II	Candidates will achieve earnings to equal 50% of minimum wage by the end of a 6-month delivery period.	6	14	20	70
Carl County sheltered workshop program—Level III	Candidates will achieve earnings to equal 75% of minimum wage by the end of a 6-month delivery period.	6	8	15	53
Carl County sheltered workshop program—Level IV (competitive placement)	Candidates will be placed into competitive employment situations by the end of a 6-month service delivery period.	8	6	8	75

Figure 5.2. Community services program effectiveness (i.e., percentage of candidates reaching targeted outcomes). (Instructions for completion of this form are in text.) (Adapted from Wehman, Moon, et al., 1988.)

Column One: Name of Service Provider and Program Type List each service provider (e.g., Carl County Arc) and the specific program (e.g., supported competitive employment) it operates. If a service provider operates more than one type of program (e.g., supported competitive employment, mobile work area), each should be listed separately.

Column Two: Targeted Outcome(s) of Service Define in measurable terms the providers' targeted outcome and the desired consumer result from the provision of the named service.

Column Three: Prescribed Duration of Service (and/or Preservice Referral Period) to Achieve the Measurable Targeted Outcome Based on intervention records, list the average duration of service provision necessary to achieve the targeted outcome (i.e., Column 2).

Column Four: Number of Clients Achieving Targeted Outcome(s) List the number of clients who achieved the targeted outcomes as defined in Column 2 in the last 12 months.

Column Five: Number of Clients Served by the Program List the number of clients served by the program over the past 12 months.

Column Six: Percentage of Program Effectiveness Calculate the percentage of program effectiveness by dividing the number of clients achieving targeted outcome(s) (i.e., the number in Column 4) by the number of clients served by the program (i.e., the number in Column 5). Multiply the quotient by 100.

(Column 4/Column 5) x 100 = Percentage of program effectiveness

This form is helpful because it requires the provision of information that reflects program effectiveness. Service providers are asked to provide data regarding the number of individuals who achieve targeted outcomes in a prescribed time period or over an expected duration. The precision required to answer the questions on the form is justified from a service purchaser's point of view. It would be inefficient for service purchasers, such as vocational rehabilitation agencies, to spend funds on programs that are not effective.

Some examples of targeted outcomes for program services follow:

1. **State department of rehabilitative job placement services**—Competitive employment situations, located by the state department of rehabilitative job placement services, in which candidates earn minimum wage or above and will remain employed for a period of 60 days.

2. **Placement in a local sheltered workshop**
 Level I—Candidates achieve earnings that equal 25% of minimum wage by the end of a 6-month service delivery period.
 Level II—Candidates achieve earnings that equal 50% of minimum wage by the end of a 6-month service delivery period.
 Level III—Candidates achieve earnings that equal 75% of minimum wage by the end of a 6-month service delivery period.
 Level IV—Candidates are placed in competitive employment situations by the end of a 6-month service delivery period.

3. **Supported employment by a local nonfacility company**
 Competitive employment services—Candidates are competitively employed earning minimum wage or above, requiring less than 20% job coach intervention by the end of a 5-month service delivery period. They remain employed for a period of 6 months. Ongoing follow-along services are arranged.

Enclave employment services—Candidates are employed in an enclave employment program earning 50% of minimum wage by the end of a 4-month service delivery period.
4. **The Arc adult activities center**
 Independent living skills (Level I)—Candidates are approved to enter the county's supervised apartment program by the end of a 6-month service delivery period.
 Independent living skills (Level II)—Candidates are approved to enter a group home through the county's residential services department by the end of a 6-month service delivery period.

The delineation, in measurable terms, of targeted outcomes offers both consumers and purchasers of services important information that will affect their decisions regarding the services they want. In the past, candidates and service purchasers paid for a service, such as work adjustment training, without a statement of expected results. However, the achievement of a candidate's individual goals should not be confused with the targeted or desired outcome of the service.

The key activity in the cooperative effort of transition planning is the dissemination of information to individuals who are best able to use it in meaningful ways. As competition among service providers for limited funds increases, service purchasers—such as vocational rehabilitation agencies—are likely to place greater demands on programs to demonstrate their effectiveness.

Developing and Writing Local-Level Interagency Agreements

Too many state- and local-level interagency agreements do not achieve their goals and, thus, never have any direct impact on service provision. Table 5.2 lists items that facilitate the implementation of written interagency agreements. A well-written document that only proclaims the rationale of interagency cooperation and the desired goals of the agreement and only lists each agency's available services will not result in improvements in service provision or service outcomes. A written interagency agreement must specify behavior changes for the staff of the participating agencies in order for implementation of services and achievement of outcomes to be effected. For example, a written interagency agreement should designate a staff member, such as a secondary special education teacher, to coordinate ITP meetings every year. Activities necessary for this coordination include contacting all appropriate participants, scheduling meetings, and obtaining information release forms signed prior to meetings.

Models of Interagency Interaction

Interagency cooperation can be characterized by three basic interaction models. These three models are used to illustrate degrees or levels of interaction between agencies with regard to 1) communication and information exchange, 2) service planning and implementation, and 3) cost sharing. Figure 5.3 illustrates these levels of interaction.

In Model A of Figure 5.3, there is little or no planned procedure for communication between agencies. Information is transferred from one agency to another in the form of stacks of paper that usually consist of the educational, psychological, vocational, social, and medical histories of the individuals who have been served by one agency and are

Table 5.2. Interagency agreement checklist

The agreement should include or address the following:
1. Mission statement or purpose of agreement
2. Number and names of agencies involved in the agreement
3. Measurable goals to be accomplished by core team as preliminary activities to the writing of the interagency agreement
4. Definitions of terms
5. Descriptions of roles and responsibilities of each agency in agreement implementation
6. Description of eligibility determination processes for each agency
7. Delineation of referral procedures for each agency's services
8. Description of staffing allocations from each agency for transition and interagency operations
9. Implementation procedures
10. Plan for dissemination of agreement
11. Plan for interagency in-service
12. Time overlapping/service coordination
13. List of service options available (direct or purchase)
14. Procedure for development of new services
15. Provisions for individuals with severe disabilities
16. Time-limited and ongoing service provision
17. Cost sharing
18. Data sharing (formative and evaluative)
19. Procedures for information release and confidentiality policy
20. Attendance of IEP/ITP meetings
21. Schedule for implementation
22. Schedule for renegotiation or modification of agreement terms
23. Policy on service delivery (e.g., duplication, repeating, initiation dates)
24. Identification of agency liaisons to participating agencies
25. Schedule of interaction between liaisons
26. Desired outcomes of agreement
27. Dissemination of services available to parents and candidates
28. Procedure and schedule for ongoing needs assessment

being referred for the services of another. In many instances, services are repeated by a receiving agency that may doubt the success of any services dispensed by another agency. Similarly, staff at the receiving agency may repeat evaluations to gather the same data because the information they received is out of date or the sending agency is not considered a reliable information source. In this model, services are unnecessarily duplicated and funds are utilized inefficiently because of poor communication and a lack of coordinated planning.

In Model B, efforts to arrange services are carefully coordinated among agencies so that as soon as one agency's involvement with an individual ends, another agency's involvement begins. The services are preplanned in the interagency ITP meetings so that service delivery is smooth and uninterrupted. Ongoing communication and comprehensive planning among agencies provides for procedural consistency, which facilitates the continuation of a logical and comprehensive service plan and prevents inefficient backtracking and repetition of service activities.

In Model B, the interagency ITP team determines the sequence of service activities necessary to achieve the greatest success in effecting the transition of students from school to work. Each agency is responsible for providing or procuring the mutually agreed-upon

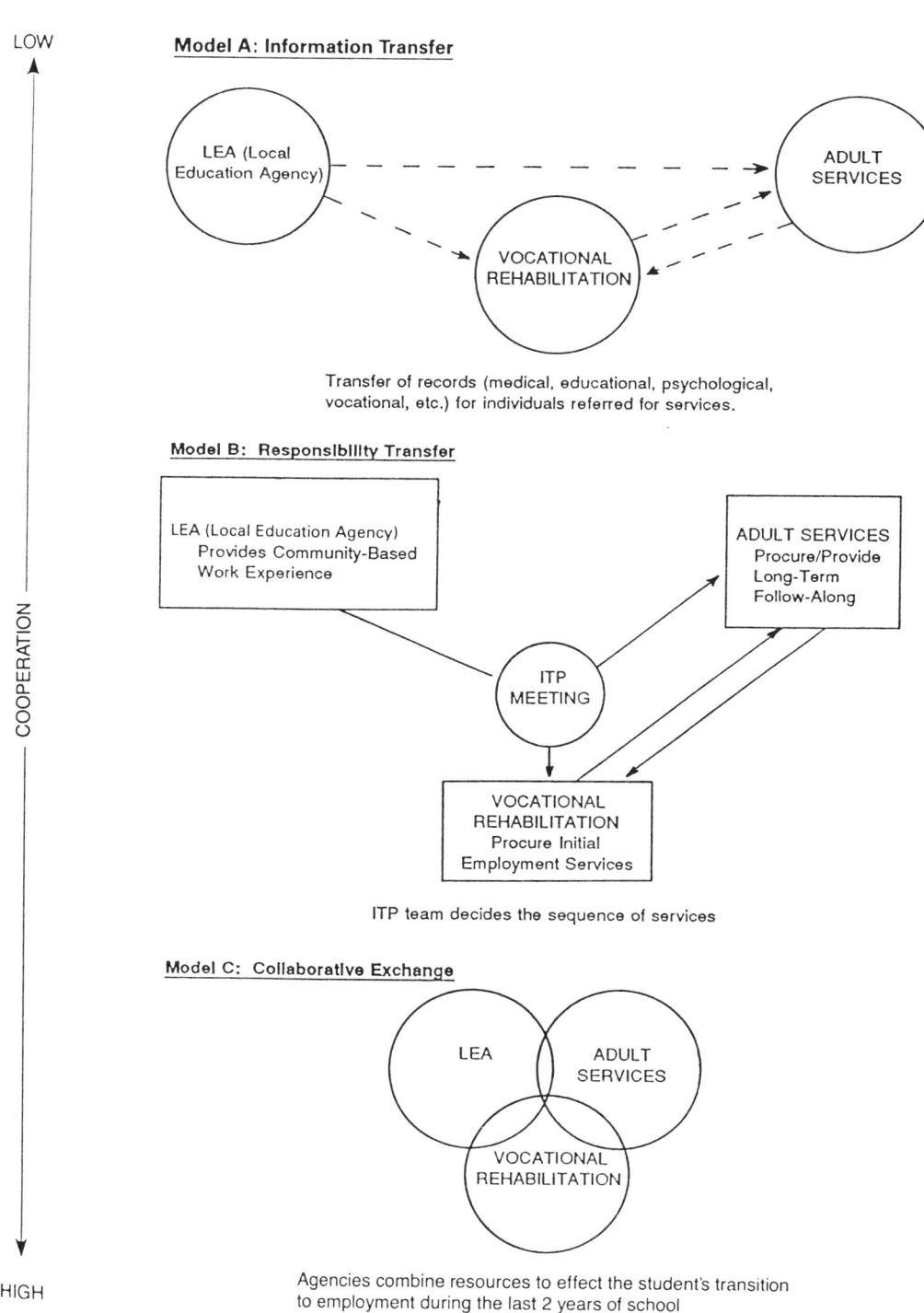

LOW

HIGH

COOPERATION

Model A: Information Transfer

LEA (Local Education Agency)

VOCATIONAL REHABILITATION

ADULT SERVICES

Transfer of records (medical, educational, psychological, vocational, etc.) for individuals referred for services.

Model B: Responsibility Transfer

LEA (Local Education Agency) Provides Community-Based Work Experience

ITP MEETING

ADULT SERVICES Procure/Provide Long-Term Follow-Along

VOCATIONAL REHABILITATION Procure Initial Employment Services

ITP team decides the sequence of services

Model C: Collaborative Exchange

LEA

ADULT SERVICES

VOCATIONAL REHABILITATION

Agencies combine resources to effect the student's transition to employment during the last 2 years of school

Figure 5.3. Models of agency interaction. (Adapted from Wehman, Moon, et al., 1988.)

119

services at the times set at the ITP meeting. For example, for Steven to succeed in community employment, the team has decided that supported competitive employment is the most appropriate service delivery option. The activities outlined for each agency might be as follows:

Schools—The school will provide work experience for Steven during his last 2 years of school in at least two different community-based work experience training sites. This will occur at least 4 days each week, 4 hours each day, prior to graduation from school. If a competitive employment position is identified prior to graduation and conditions permit, the school will confer with the agency liaisons. If it is deemed appropriate, the placement will be made. Training in the use of public transportation in the local community will be included as part of work experience training.

Rehabilitation—The rehabilitation counselor will procure supported employment services for Steven immediately following graduation. Or, if he has already been placed by the school system and still requires 2 or more hours of job coach or employment specialist intervention 3 times per week, the counselor will arrange these services. The rehabilitation counselor must arrange for these services far enough in advance that the school and the service provider can cooperate for a smooth transfer of services.

Mental retardation adult services—The mental retardation agency representative will initiate long-term follow-along services for Steven after he has adjusted to the employment situation and the rehabilitation counselor has terminated service involvement with the candidate. The mental retardation services representative will allow time for transfer of information in the event of a change in service delivery personnel. In such a situation, the employment specialist who is providing jobsite training intervention, the student, the parent or guardian, and the employer should be informed of the change and properly introduced to the new employment specialist.

In this service delivery arrangement, each agency has a definite point for relinquishing responsibility to the next agency. Adult services agencies, rehabilitation, and mental retardation community services do not provide services while students are still in school, but a comprehensive sequence and plan for service responsibility can ensure continued employment support.

Model C depicts interagency interaction that provides for coordinated overlap of service implementation without spending overlap. This overlap of service implementation occurs because agencies combine resources to serve a targeted population of students during their last 2 years of school. Using this model, all agencies are involved with the planning and implementation of services, but there is no duplication of spending for individual students.

This model is an example of the interagency agreement developed for Smithfield County, Virginia, a rapidly growing suburban county. The three key agencies in Smithfield County work together to develop ITPs and to implement supported competitive employment services. In this agreement, there is a planned procedure for communication and information sharing, service implementation arrangements prevent duplication, and cost sharing is equitable—an important feature as financial resources for public agencies serving individuals with disabilities are limited. Therefore, efficient and effective use of funds is important. Duplication of services or misappropriation of funds due to lack of communication or coordinated planning is undesirable for agencies and candidates.

A Three-Way Interagency Agreement for
Transition Planning and Supported Employment Services

The following is a three-way interagency agreement[1] for the implementation of transition planning and supported employment services. The agencies participating in this agreement are the Smithfield County Public Schools, the Smithfield County Mental Health and Mental Retardation Community Services Board, and the Virginia Department of Rehabilitative Services serving the Smithfield area.

Mission Statement

The purpose of this agreement is to provide for meaningful postschool employment outcomes for youth with severe disabilities who are leaving the public school system. It is understood that the students targeted for services in this cooperative agreement will be in their last 2 years of school. All of these students, at the point of graduation, will become the responsibility of the adult services systems. Formal transition planning for individual students will begin at age 16 or before for the purpose of implementing meaningful functional and community-based instructional programs in integrated environments.

The transition process begins with each agency participating in the provision of employment, independent living, recreation and leisure options, and community integration outcomes for graduating students. By coordinating the efforts of the three key agencies during the 2 years prior to graduation, several advantages can be identified:

1. The school's knowledge of individual students can be channeled directly into decisions regarding the employment of the students making the transition from school to work.
2. The number of personnel assigned to employment outcomes is increased, at no cost to the adult services system, by involving the schools in the supported employment service provision. Instead, a portion of the up-front costs are borne by the school system.
3. This interagency agreement provides for jobsite instruction as well as at other community settings, rather than in the prevocational classroom.
4. Direct involvement by school personnel in actual employment situations provides important program evaluation and feedback to the schools. This information can be used to facilitate school curriculum improvements regarding work in the "real world."
5. With the involvement of the schools, costs are shared in a three-way split between rehabilitation and mental retardation/developmental disabilities services (see Figure 5.4).

Cooperating Agency Liaisons

Each cooperating agency agrees to designate at least one individual to act as a transition liaison. These liaisons are primarily responsible for maintaining frequent and regular contact among the three agencies and for coordinating services for all students moving from school to adult services. An agency liaison might be the mental retardation services' employment specialist or the rehabilitation counselor assigned to serve the school popula-

[1]This section is taken from Wehman, P., Moon, M.S., Everson, J.M., Wood, W., & Barcus, J.M. (1988). *Transition from school to work: New challenges for youth with severe disabilities* (pp. 116–129). Baltimore: Paul H. Brookes Publishing Co.; adapted with permission.

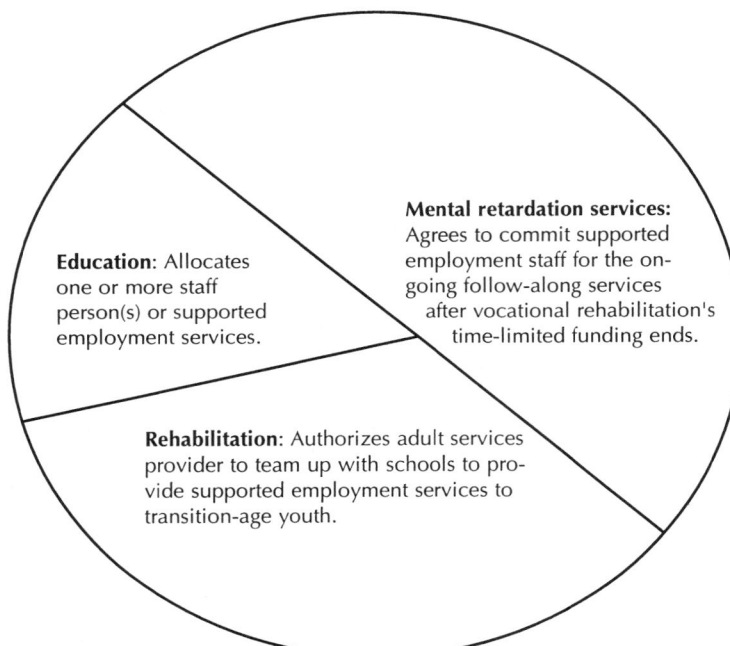

Figure 5.4. Three-way cost sharing for the implementation of supported employment services with transition-age youth. (Adapted from Wehman, Moon, et al., 1988.)

tion. Each agency liaison must be responsible for his or her agency at all ITP meetings. The agency liaisons may attend all or part of the meetings themselves or they may assign a designee to attend. Each agency liaison is responsible for providing ITP meeting designees with information regarding his or her agency's capacity to provide agency services and/or resources. Agency liaisons are responsible for training their agency's designees in areas of receiving referrals, services eligibility, and schedules for authorizing or committing agency services or resources.

Schedule of Interaction of Cooperating Agency Liaisons

Participating agency liaisons will meet on the third Thursday of every month during the first year of this interagency agreement's implementation. Relevant service delivery personnel or other involved participants should be invited to these meetings as necessary. The group's meeting agenda will include discussion of ITP meeting schedules, services currently available in the community, examination of transition planning outcomes, and cooperative service delivery efforts.

Individualized Transition Planning Meetings

The Smithfield County Public Schools agree to initiate the planning and scheduling for individualized transition planning meetings for a mutually agreed-upon target group of stu-

dents age 16 or older. The development of ITPs should be completed as part of the IEP meeting, with transition planning issues being discussed first, so that school outcomes follow. The ITP goals and service provision plans will be developed as an addendum to the IEP document. The rehabilitation counselor and the Mental Handicaps/Mental Retardation (MH/MR) services representative should incorporate ITP goals into the individualized written rehabilitation plan (IWRP) and the individualized program plan (IPP).

The school liaison is responsible for ensuring that the information release authorization forms are signed by the appropriate person(s) prior to scheduling ITP meetings. Information release forms must be signed for all students who are in their last 2 years of school. Copies should be forwarded to the adult agency liaisons prior to scheduling ITP meetings.

The school liaison will notify the cooperating agency liaisons of ITP meetings at least 5 days prior to each meeting. When circumstances prohibit giving advance notice, the schools will do whatever possible to communicate scheduling arrangements or other information to the other agency liaisons. ITP meeting participants should include the following:

- Student
- Parent, guardian, or primary caregiver
- Rehabilitation counselor
- Mental retardation service coordinator
- School employment specialist
- Mental retardation employment specialist
- Special education administrator
- Agency liaisons (if different from any of the above)
- Special education administrator
- Current or previous employer; medical doctor; or occupational, physical, or speech-language therapist, as applicable

The ITP meeting is the appropriate forum for the agency representatives to develop long-term service provision plans for graduating students. Each agency representative should assume responsibility for referral to and delivery of the various services required for an effective transition from school to work. Agency representatives should bring referral/service application forms, program or agency brochures, and information on program eligibility to ITP meetings for parents and candidates.

School Services The Smithfield County School system agrees to provide community-based work experience for students in actual work settings in the community. The settings can be paid or unpaid. Unpaid training programs must meet the criteria for nonpaid training situations as described by the U.S. Department of Labor (see Chapter 11). Students should have work experience in at least two community-based work settings prior to graduation, with the last experience requiring 4 days per week, with at least 3 hours per day, for a period of at least 6 months. Other community-based training positions in integrated environments will also be provided for students prior to graduation from the public schools. These will include public transportation training, grocery shopping, and integrated programs for recreation in the community. Other services to be offered by the schools include vocational evaluation, vocational education/training, guidance and coun-

seling, job placement, time-limited job coach services, community access training, leisure and recreation training, and domestic skills training.

Mental Handicaps/Mental Retardation Adult Services The Smithfield County MH/MR Services agrees to provide case management services to transition-age students. These services will entitle candidates to assistance in areas such as exploring residential options, providing for advocacy needs, adult day support, respite care, follow-along supported employment services, or other services necessary for maintaining integrated community living.

Rehabilitative Services The State Department of Rehabilitative Services agrees to provide or procure services for transition-age youth either before or immediately following graduation from the public school system. As outlined in the ITP or IWRP, services may include the following: vocational evaluation, job-seeking skills training, counseling, work adjustment training, time-limited job coach or employment specialist services, independent living training, on-the-job training (OJT), time-limited sheltered employment, and rehabilitation engineering.

Supported Employment Services

Intensive Training Role: Schools The Smithfield County Public Schools agree to provide one full-time certified teacher to act as an employment specialist to place and train specific students in competitive employment settings utilizing a supported competitive employment approach. The full-time teacher must be completely free from the day-to-day operation of the school building (e.g., bus or lunch duty, weekly staff meetings). The employment specialist's schedule must be flexible enough to allow planning around the work hours of any given student in any given employment situation.

Students identified for supported employment services must first be considered eligible for receipt of services by the Smithfield County MH/MR Community Services Board agency representative. These criteria must be met before the agency will commit its resources for ongoing follow-along services for supported employment candidates.

Mental Handicaps/Mental Retardation Services The Smithfield County MH/MR Community Services Board agrees to designate at least one full-time employment specialist to team up with one full-time school employment specialist. These individuals will place and train designated school-age youth in competitive employment situations utilizing a supported competitive employment approach.

The organization agrees to assume responsibility for the ongoing follow-along services for all employment candidates who are placed in jobs by the supported competitive employment team prior to graduation. A firm commitment to this model is critical prior to placement of any individual in a job that utilizes the supported competitive employment approach. The employer, the client, and the client's parent or guardian will depend on the continuation of these services.

Rehabilitative Services The rehabilitation counselor representing the Virginia Department of Rehabilitative Services (DRS) agrees to authorize funds for supported competitive employment intervention hours to be provided by one in-kind match employment specialist employed by the Smithfield MH/MR Community Services Board. The Smithfield MH/MR Community Services will provide supported competitive employment services as prescribed in the agreement with the Virginia DRS. The MH/MR Services employment specialist will work with the school employment specialist to place people between ages 20

and 22 into jobs 2 years prior to their graduation. Supported competitive employment services will be billed based on a prearranged fee, at a rate of $29.75 per hour. Records of intervention time will be maintained utilizing a consumer-specific intervention time recording sheet with billing to the Virginia DRS on a monthly basis.

Students served by the school employment specialist will be placed on the Virginia DRS caseload, but the training and other intervention hours provided by the school employment specialist will not be billed to the rehabilitation counselor. These clients will be rehabilitation clients, whose full records are provided to the assigned rehabilitation counselor.

The rehabilitation counselor should make sure that all students targeted for supported competitive employment services have been accepted for services by the MH/MR Community Services Board so that ongoing follow-along services will be provided. Those students who do not need follow-along services may benefit from transitional employment services (e.g., job coach services) that are provided for limited periods only.

Data Collection The Smithfield County Public Schools, Rehabilitation, and MH/MR Community Services representatives agree to use the Virginia Commonwealth University, Rehabilitation Research and Training Center (VCU/RRTC) data management system by completing the prescribed forms according to the established schedules. The VCU/RRTC agrees to provide data analysis services and program evaluation feedback for the three co-operating agencies beginning March 1, 1996.

Interagency In-Service Cooperating agency liaisons should coordinate at least one interagency in-service training program during each school year that addresses issues surrounding transition, employment, residential options, secondary or postsecondary education, adult services, and so on. The agency liaisons are responsible for issuing invitations to cooperating agency staff to attend transition-related in-service sessions provided by any agency. The interagency transition liaisons must work together as a team to plan or conduct at least one transition-related in-service training session.

Exchange of Information

List of Upcoming Graduates The Smithfield County Public Schools agree to provide the Smithfield County MH/MR Community Services Board (the agency liaison) and the Smithfield County DRS liaison with a list of names of upcoming graduates who are in their last 2 years of school. Information release forms must be signed by students before names can be released. The school is responsible for obtaining signatures.

Projected Graduates Over a 5-Year Period The schools agree to provide the number of students scheduled to graduate for the next 5 years. This information will assist the two adult services agencies in projecting future service needs.

Adult Services Programs in the Smithfield County Area The Smithfield County MH/MR Community Service Board and the Virginia DRS serving the Smithfield area agree to provide a list of currently available adult services and programs accessible to youth who are making the transition from school to the adult services system. The list will also include the service capacity (i.e., number of individuals who can be served) of each program and the projected number of slots to open by July 1 each year.

Adult Services Selected for Graduating Youth from ITP Meetings The school liaison has access to all completed ITP meeting forms and, therefore, is responsible for compiling and disseminating information from those forms to the MH/MR Community Services

Board and to the Virginia DRS liaisons. The report should indicate the number of students selected for each type of program or service, including those currently available and those that have been requested but are not currently available to Smithfield County citizens with disabilities.

Postgraduation Follow-Up Data MH/MR Community Services and DRS agree to provide the schools with follow-up data (employment or residential services) concerning graduates from the program for at least 2 years following their graduation. This will ensure the ongoing commitment of the schools to the interagency agreement and will provide educators with continuous information about the graduates' employment and independent lives.

Expected Outcomes

Past data from supported employment programs indicate that, in a 12-month period, one skilled employment specialist can place and train 410 individuals in competitive employment situations, depending on each individual's skill level compatibility with the requirements of the job (i.e., the more complex the job, the higher the probability that the candidate will require extended training time). Ensuring compatibility involves striving to match candidates to jobs that are complex enough to avoid boredom and apathy. Positions should require skills that are challenging yet obtainable with intensive training and ongoing support, thus providing for improved employment retention.

Given a school and mental retardation services supported employment team of two employment specialists (with the school specialist operating on a 10- or 11-month contract), the supported employment team should provide services to 10–18 student candidates (depending on skill level of candidates) between the ages of 20 and 22 years. Employment retention for these individuals should be 65% at the time of graduation from school.

Administrative Considerations

Staff Competency All staff from the three participating agencies will attend training internships on supported employment and transition planning. The employment specialists will also spend a 20-day period in intensive field work training. This training is to be done by experts in supported employment.

Liability Employment specialists and other staff providing training in community-based settings will have liability insurance coverage provided by their employing agency. In case of an accident while training on employment sites or other community settings, the agency's insurance will provide coverage unless gross negligence is apparent on a community training site.

Office Space The Smithfield County MH/MR Services will provide office space, telephone service, and office supplies for the supported employment service delivery staff, which includes the school employment specialist. This arrangement will provide opportunities for staff to interact frequently.

Transportation Each agency will provide its staff with mileage reimbursement for travel expenses incurred as a result of jobsite training, community-based training, or other travel needs or services related to the job. With two or three employment specialists, travel costs usually amount to $200 per month.

Dissemination of Agreement Written copies of this agreement will be disseminated to all core team members, designated agency liaisons, service delivery administrators, and other relevant agency personnel. All participants in the process must be aware of arrangements.

Review and Modification of Agreement The transition planning core team members will plan to meet quarterly in January, March, July, and October to reevaluate this interagency agreement. Written reports, program outcome reports, and yearly needs assessment information will be included in this evaluation.

Procedures for Development of New Services At the quarterly meetings, the local core transition team will examine community services and needs assessment information to determine if there is need for expansion or development of new programs. Some modifications should be anticipated within 6 months to a year of enacting a program.

Conclusion

This chapter has provided an in-depth look at how three different parties (i.e., schools, vocational rehabilitation, and local community services) can plan an outcomes-oriented agreement for resources sharing. Formal interagency agreements at both the state and local levels are necessary in order for comprehensive planning and service implementation to occur. Leadership at the state and federal levels should provide impetus and guidance to leaders at the community level to work together. Community-level leadership is charged with the responsibility of developing terms for interagency cooperation. These terms should provide for actual changes in service implementation and achievement of outcomes. Issues of territorialism and notions that one agency is superior to other agencies serve only to inhibit efficient and effective utilization of available resources.

All of the agencies need to be knowledgeable about the capabilities, strengths, and weaknesses of the other participating agencies. Staff at the level of actual service provision must be experts at coordinating and making available whatever resources are necessary to achieve the desired outcomes of transition planning.

Community leadership must be aware of needs and demands for new services that may allow individuals to achieve desired outcomes. It is not the responsibility of the candidate to "fit" into available services. Rather, it is the responsibility of the service agencies and providers to offer services that "fit" the candidates' needs.

To accomplish effective transition planning, participating agency leadership and service delivery personnel must remember that the mission of the agencies is to provide successful outcomes to candidates. Service provision alone is not the goal; it is the means to an end. The goal, the desired result of the services, is to provide people with disabilities with employment and the opportunity for independent living as adults in integrated communities.

5

Study Questions

1. Name three types of adult services agencies with which transitional programs should collaborate.

2. Who should be members of the local community transition core team?

3. What are the types of information that should be collected in an initial community needs assessment?

4. What are the steps to completing a community services program effectiveness survey?

5. What are the major differences between the three models of interagency cooperation?

6. List the types of participants in an ITP meeting.

Appendix

Sample Interagency Programs

Collaborative Planning for Supported Employment

Mankato District 77 and Maple River District 72
Division of Rehabilitation and Mankato Rehabilitation Center, Inc.
Contact: Terri Trexler, Education Specialist
 1000 North Broad Street, Mankato, Minnesota 56001; (507) 387-1818

Overview

Mankato District 77 and Maple River District 72, along with Division of Rehabilitation (DRS) staff and managers from the Mankato Rehabilitation Center, Inc. (MCRI), have developed a plan in which students with special needs are provided supported employment opportunities within the Mankato area. This plan was the result of numerous meetings and visits to other sites by all parties over a period of 18 months.

The Need

This collaborative effort began as a result of student needs for increased supported employment opportunities and the loss of professional staff due to budget cuts. With the cuts in staff in the school Work Experience Program in Mankato and the lack of employment opportunities in the rural town of Mapleton, the needs of the students with disabilities became increasingly difficult to meet. Within the Mankato Area Community Transition Interagency Committee (CTIC), we realized we had four separate organizations within the Mankato area looking for and coordinating worksites for individuals with special needs. Rather than have each district try to address vocational needs on its own, we used our CTIC as the focus in developing a plan that maximizes resources.

Meeting the Need

Based on information gathered from members of the IEP team on student interest and family involvement, a referral to DRS would be initiated. Confirmation of DRS eligibility was the next step in the process. Once the student became eligible for DRS services, his or her DRS counselor referred the student to Mankato Rehabilitation Center for community-based supported employment.

This appendix is reprinted by permission from Johnson, D.R., Rydell, C., & Hunt, P. (1994). *Transition strategies that work* (Vol. II, pp. 14–19). Minneapolis: University of Minnesota, Institute on Community Integration.

At this point, the team—which included staff from all the agencies involved as well as the student and family—would develop an individual plan based on how best to support the student in an employment setting. The type of work in which the student would be interested would be evaluated. The availability of worksites in the area of interest would also be discussed. Once these concerns were met, the logistics of meeting these needs and funding considerations would be determined.

The funding for this program is a cost shared between DRS and the local school district. MRCI bills the local school district for the cost of providing supported employment services. The local school district then bills DRS for 48% of that cost. Since the district receives 52% state reimbursement for this program, the cost to the local district is for transportation.

When a student already has a one-to-one Management Aide through the local school district, the aide serves as a job coach.

Students in this program receive pay for their work and MRCI is responsible for handling all payroll, worker's compensation, and subminimum wage documentation. The local school district still provides classroom training in a job seminar class. Six-week progress reports are scheduled and the training plan is then used by MRCI, DRS, and local school districts through the Work Experience Training Plan.

Results

The logistics of transportation seem to be the major scheduling problem. It is the feeling of all concerned, however, that transportation would be a barrier regardless of who coordinated the program. The biggest gain that can be seen at this time is that the collaborative efforts among schools, DRS, adult service providers, and the community result in positive gains for the student as well as being fiscally sound, with the elimination of duplication of services among all parties.

Comments

As local school systems work to maintain programs for students with special needs despite funding reduction, collaborative efforts to achieve meaningful programs are imperative. This program allows agencies to work together to achieve the goal set forth by each individual agency in the most cost-effective manner. The opportunities for students increase and make for a much smoother transition for the student and family into the world beyond high school.

Groups Collaborating

- Mankato Public Schools
- Mankato Rehabilitation Center, Inc.
- Maple River Public Schools
- Minnesota Division of Rehabilitation Services
- Minnesota Valley Action Council

Participant Disabilities

- All disabilities are welcome—the only requirement is a current IEP.
- Students ages 14–21 are invited to participate, but the program gives a special focus to those students in their junior and senior years of high school.

Areas of Collaboration

- Information sharing
- Staff sharing
- Co-funding
- Joint training plans
- Program sharing
- Assessment sharing

Leadership for Empowerment (LEP)

Ridgedale YMCA
12301 Ridgedale Drive, Minnetonka, Minnesota 55305
Contact: Polly Harrison (612) 544-7708

Overview

Leadership for Empowerment is based on a partnership between a middle school and YMCA or other local community agency. In an effort to promote inclusion, the youth involved in LEP include individuals with and without disabilities. After a program site is established, the school determines the most appropriate program format, whether it be after school or during the school day. In addition, the school recruits a balanced ratio of youth to enhance possible friendship building among individuals with and without disabilities. The community agency proceeds with programming, which includes youth providing service to the community in a variety of options (i.e., benefiting the community environmentally, creatively, educationally, etc.). Youth are then referred to other existing programs as they graduate into high school. The program is flexible and capable of being adjusted to meet the needs of the collaborating agencies. The Ridgedale YMCA acts as the liaison between partnerships, intervening when any specific problems arise.

The Need

Recognizing that socialization and self-determination skills are key factors in the successful development of any youth, the need to offer youth with developmental disabilities the same opportunities to achieve such skills as youth without disabilities is significant. Research shows that individuals are more sensitive to diversity the younger they are exposed to it. While a large percentage of inclusive programming is currently being offered on the high school level, little is available for students in junior high or younger. The LEP program is an effort to plant the seeds of awareness and sensitivity toward youth of all abilities in junior high school for successful inclusion in high school. This program targets middle school-age youth to experience diversity in a nonthreatening environment. In addition, by strengthening programming by using two separate community agencies, youth are inadvertently exposed to a variety of community opportunities and the larger impact of team effort. Thus, all youth, regardless of differences in ability, are empowered to become fully contributing members in the social, economic, political, and spiritual life of their community.

Meeting the Need

Through funding from the Governor's Planning Council on Developmental Disabilities, the Ridgedale YMCA began implementation of LEP in an effort to achieve the following goals:

- **Inclusion**—LEP supports inclusion by recruiting youth both with and without disabilities to participate in a semester-long program.
- **Integrated friendships**—By balancing the ratio, youth have more of an opportunity to develop friendships with youth they might not have met.
- **Empowerment**—By keeping the program flexible, youth are given a variety of opportunities to make decisions together.
- **Community service**—The culmination of the program includes providing a service for the community. Services have included performing a play for a nursing home or hospital, participating in community clean-ups, and volunteering for various community events.
- **Transition steps**—LEP lays the foundation for self-determination and leadership skills. Youth in the program are recruited to participate in a variety of existing leadership conferences that include high school–age youth such as Youth in Government, an annual mock government experience for grades 8–12. In addition, adult conferences to develop leadership skills have been adapted and geared toward middle school–age youth. Also, youth who have graduated to high school often maintain a connection with LEP by continuing to assist in program implementation. Finally, LEP refers youth to become a part of other programs available for youth in high school.

Results

The connections between youth with and without disabilities are a measure of LEP's success rate. Examples, such as that of a usually violated youth who became more assertive and outgoing during a conference, acknowledge LEP's success. In addition, with the program doubling its size in its second year, professionals can easily see the immediate impact of the program and its positive effects on agencies and youth alike.

Comments

The crucial element in replicating this program is a willingness for two community-based agencies to develop a partnership. Proper funding would ideally provide a single overseeing agency to act as the liaison between the collaborating organizations. Together, the partnership sites would be responsible for sharing the necessary resources to fuel the program.

Groups Collaborating

- Albert Lea Family YMCA/Albert Lea Middle School
- Itasca County Family YMCA/Grand Rapids Junior High School
- Minneapolis Ridgedale Branch YMCA/Minnetonka Junior High School
- Anwatin Middle School
- Moorhead Community Education at Moorhead Junior High School
- Minneapolis Southdale Branch YMCA/Central Middle School

Areas of Collaboration

- Shared programs
- Shared staffing
- Information sharing
- Recruitment efforts
- Model development

Occupational Skills Program

Brainerd Staple Technical College, Brainerd Campus
300 Quince Street, Brainerd, Minnesota 56401
Contact: John Wallin (218) 828-5355, or Karl Samp (800) 247-2574

Overview

The Occupational Skills Program is a 1-year, individualized occupational educational program that supports adults with disabilities in receiving a technical college diploma. The program provides occupational skills training in the least restrictive environment and enables graduates to achieve one or more of the following goals:

- To obtain competitive employment
- To live independently
- To seek additional education

The Need

Many young people with mild disabilities do not qualify for ongoing social support services through the counties and other agencies, yet are unable to compete in the work force and live independently without additional training after they leave school. This is especially true for young adults coming from small, rural school districts with limited options for work experience and independent living skills training.

Other young adults who do qualify for ongoing public support services may not need that level of support for an extended period of time. After a year of occupational and independent skill training, they have the skills to work competitively and live independently.

Based upon the number of inquiries and enrollees the program has had in the past 2 years, there is a large number of young adults who can benefit from a year of postsecondary education and training.

Meeting the Need

By providing equal access for adults with disabilities to the technical colleges, the Occupational Skills Program (OSP) does the following:

- Helps students make appropriate career choices
- Provides supplemental services as needed
- Assists in the transition of students with disabilities from secondary education to postsecondary technical education

- Reduces the dependency of individuals with disabilities
- Prepares individuals with disabilities for optimum adult participation in society

The OSP helps students gain occupational experience and training by developing partnerships with community organizations and businesses with which students can receive hands-on training, or by having the students enroll in technical college courses in an area of interest. They are provided with support services and accommodations to increase their opportunities for learning and success.

Independent living skills are taught in a series of settings, including apartments. Community participation is addressed through Service Learning, a method of teaching/learning that connects community service with academic learning. Students receive credit in Service Learning experiences. Job placement is done in close collaboration with Department of Rehabilitation Services (DRS) staff. OSP is staffed with three full-time licensed faculty who do classroom instruction, service coordination, and training activities coordination, and are academic supervisors. There are two part-time paraprofessional staff who provide job training, technical and academic tutoring, and transportation to job training sites. Student/peer tutors are also used to supplement the technical tutoring.

Each student has an ITP that is written twice per year—once, in the fall by the service coordinator for the transition into OSP, then again in the spring for the transition out of OSP and into employment and independent living. Students also have individual technical education plans (ITEPs) that are developed in the fall from the ITP to establish the training and education plan for the students' year in OSP—identifying outcomes, support services, and accommodations.

Least restrictive environment (LRE) documentation must be completed by the student's team before enrolling in the program, indicating that the student did not complete a traditional technical college program.

Results

There are approximately 30 OSP students enrolled each year. Most have received a high school diploma; however, several attended under a high school contract for services after participation in graduation ceremonies with their classmates and remain on an IEP for 1 or more years. Students complete at least 48 credits, including a 6-credit, 1,600-hour internship in which they demonstrate the skills necessary to maintain employment. They often remain in these intern jobs after graduation.

Job placement records show a 90% placement rate for graduates in the second year after program completion. Most are also living independently in the community or with some support through semi-independent living services (SILS). OSP provides some services to high schools through contracts for services in conjunction with DRS.

Comments

The OSP in Brainerd was recognized as a 1993 Minnesota Exemplary Youth Service Program for the Service Learning component of the program.

Groups Collaborating

- Brainerd Staples Technical College
- Division of Rehabilitation Services
- Social Services
- Center for Independent Living
- Various School Districts
- Businesses/Community Organizations
- Community Education

Areas of Collaboration

- Transition planning
- Career awareness planning
- Vocational training
- Independent living skills
- Community participation

6

Teaching for Transition

Upon completion of this chapter, the reader will be able to do the following:

- Understand the rationale for a selection of instructional transition objectives
- Discuss at least three curriculum resources for transition
- Define community-based training and discuss the values of this approach
- List four problems and their solutions in implementing community-based training
- Know the sequence of response prompts, task analysis, and reinforcement in implementing transition instruction

To this point, this book has been devoted to planning for transition, working with other agencies, and designing individualized transition plans (ITPs). Very little attention has been focused on individualized instruction for transition or what the teacher should do in the classroom. A number of books are available that provide more in-depth assessment, instruction, behavior management techniques, and other types of systematic training (e.g., Snell, 1993). The purpose of this chapter, however, is to discuss what the educator must do to enhance the likelihood of transition from an instructional perspective. Clearly, the responsibility falls on the shoulders of the teacher in terms of implementing the instructional aspects of any student's program and increasing the likelihood that the student will have the confidence to make the transition into independent living in the community.

Therefore, this chapter addresses the following questions: What should educators teach transition-age students? What resources should teachers draw upon for curriculum development? Where should instruction take place? Is the community superior to the classroom for such instruction, and, if so, how does one implement such a program logis-

tically? How should teachers arrange the instructional environment so that teaching techniques are used most effectively?

Curriculum Design for Transition: What Should Teachers Teach?

Many facets of curriculum development should be examined as a secondary teacher designs and implements an ITP. However, this chapter focuses on three specific facets: 1) the rationale for selecting instruction objectives, 2) descriptions of different curriculum resources that may be used by teachers, and 3) a sample of different types of curriculum sequences that can be taught with the use of selected instructional programs.

Rationale for Selecting Transition Instructional Objectives

The most important activities that the student will need to perform independently in the vocational, residential, and community environments must guide selection of transition objectives. One of the most important instructional tasks for teachers is selecting the most necessary skills in which each student needs instruction. This process cannot be conducted exclusively by the teacher; it requires ongoing collaboration with the student and family. In order to truly use a self-determined approach, the student must be the starting point in the plan. This rationale for skill selection continues to be one of the most overlooked aspects of instructional planning and implementation in special education.

After an initial ITP is designed, the teacher should obtain direct input from the student and family, members of the community, and others who are interested and concerned about this student's future. The teacher's primary responsibility is to teach those skills the student will need for a successful future. This does not mean that the teacher purchases a variety of curricula and then teaches all the skills on those curricula hoping to teach something that the student may be able to use. On the contrary, this "shotgun" approach should be abandoned for a targeted approach that identifies the most essential skills for independence in adulthood. This process is more time-consuming and requires greater thought than simple identification of objectives from a set curriculum or checklist. The teacher must have the intelligence, creativity, and, above all, diligence to work closely with the family in narrowing down those skills that are most necessary and realistic for completion.

The strategy for developing this kind of functional curriculum involves identifying and prioritizing key activities. Table 6.1 describes these points and should be followed by teachers who are designing transition programs.

Selected Transition Objectives

There are many transition objectives that can be developed as the student and family draw up a plan for the student's desired future direction. These objectives can and should intersect with real-life daily environments. For example, in Table 6.2, Cronin and Patton (1993) provide examples of how 48 target life skills can be infused into daily curricula. These activities illustrate how a curriculum can be practical while still emphasizing selected academic skills such as reading and writing.

Table 6.1. Establishment of priority activities for instruction

1. With the student and his or her family, evaluate the student's performance in each of the domain categories and identify desired future environments in which the student will function.
2. Identify activities and skills relevant to the student's current environment and skills necessary to function in projected future environments.
3. Review all relevant current and future activities and indicate those activities that occur in two or more domains and that are age appropriate.
4. List these activities from most to least frequent in occurrence.
5. From this list, identify activities that are crucial for the student's safety. Next identify activities critical for functioning independently in the desired future environments.
6. Select for immediate instruction:
 • Activities essential to the student's safety within current environments
 • Activities that the student must perform frequently in order to function independently within his or her current and identified future environments
7. Select remaining objectives from the list of activities (see #4).

The development and utilization of social skills is also a critical area of competence for transition-age students. Brown and his colleagues (1989) have developed a series of social relationship objectives to be used in neighborhood high schools (see Table 6.3).

Selected Work Skills for Transition Planning

Sowers and Powers (1991) have presented a set of vocational tasks (see Table 6.4) targeted for students with physical disabilities; however, these tasks have merit for all young people with disabilities. The tasks in Table 6.4 are suggested only to give the teacher ideas for curriculum objectives and areas in which possible task objectives may be identified. Many of these work skills can be found in a variety of local settings.

Where Should Teachers Provide Instruction?

Increasing numbers of educators are accepting that community-based instruction is best for implementing transition programs for young adults with disabilities. Often, classroom instruction does not generalize into the community well, which frequently makes instruction nonfunctional. In community-based instruction, however, educational objectives are taught, in natural community environments, such as worksites, shopping malls, and restaurants. Regardless of the student's disability or its severity, community-based training experiences appear to be the most functional. It is recommended that teachers identify sites for community-based instruction for at least 50% of their curricula. These sites can involve vocational training, home living skills instruction, recreational instruction, and community skills development.

Creative teachers who understand that leaving the school grounds to go to community sites may not always be possible will identify sites and tasks within the school or on the grounds that can approximate natural community environments, ideally beginning at 10–13 years of age, instead of the typical 16 or 17 years of age. Possible sites for work experience in school include the following:

Table 6.2. Integrating life skills into the curriculum

Subject	Employment/ education	Home and family	Leisure pursuits	Community involvement	Emotional/ physical health	Personal responsibility/ relationships
Reading	Reading classified ads for jobs	Interpreting bills	Locating and understanding movie information in a newspaper	Following directions on tax forms	Comprehending directions on medication	Reading letters from friends
Writing	Writing a letter of application for a job	Writing checks	Writing for information on a city to visit	Filling in a voter registration form	Filling in medical history on forms	Sending thank-you notes
Listening	Understanding oral directions for a procedure change	Comprehending oral directions about making dinner	Listening for forecast to plan outdoor activity	Understanding campaign ads	Attending lectures on stress	Taking turns in a conversation
Speaking	Asking boss for a raise	Discussing morning routines with family	Inquiring about tickets for a concert	Stating opinion at the school board meeting	Describing symptoms to a doctor	Giving feedback to a friend about the purchase of a compact disc
Math applications	Understanding difference between net and gross pay	Computing the cost of doing laundry in a laundromat versus at home	Calculating the cost of a dinner out versus eating at home	Obtaining information for a building permit	Using a thermometer	Planning the costs of a date
Problem solving	Settling a dispute with a co-worker	Deciding how much to budget for rent	Role-playing appropriate behaviors for various places	Knowing what to do if victim of fraud	Selecting a doctor	Deciding how to ask someone for a date
Survival skills	Using a prepared career planning packet	Listing emergency phone numbers	Using a shopping center directory	Marking a calendar for important dates (e.g., recycling, garbage collection)	Using a system to remember to take vitamins	Developing a system to remember birthdays
Personal/ social	Applying appropriate interview skills	Helping a child with homework	Knowing the rules of a neighborhood pool	Locating self-improvement classes	Getting a yearly physical exam	Discussing how to negotiate a price at a flea market

From Cronin, M., & Patton, J.R. (1993). *Life skills across the curriculum for youths with special needs* (p. 33). Austin, TX: PRO-ED; reprinted by permission.

Table 6.3. Social relationships that can develop between students with and without disabilities

Social relationship	Example
Peer tutor	Leigh role-plays social introductions with Margo, providing feedback and praise for Margo's performance.
Eating companion	Jennifer and Rick eat lunch with Linda in the cafeteria and talk about their favorite music groups.
Art, home economics, industrial arts, music, or physical education companion	In art class, students were instructed to paint a sunset. Tom sat next to Dan and offered suggestions and guidance about the best colors to use and how to complete the task.
General class companion	A fifth-grade class is doing a "Know Our Town" lesson in social studies. Ben helps Karen plan a trip through their neighborhood.
During-school companion	After lunch and before the bell for class rang, Molly and Phyllis went to the student lounge for a soda.
Friend	David, a member of a varsity basketball team, invites Ralph, a student with severe disabilities, to his house to watch a game on TV.
Extracurricular companion	Sarah and Winona prepare their articles for the school newspaper together and then work on the layout in the journalism lab.
After-school project companion	The sophomore class decided to build a float for a homecoming parade. Joan worked on it with Maria, a nondisabled companion, after school and on weekends in Joan's garage.
After-school companion	On Saturday afternoon, Mike, who is not disabled, and Bill go to the shopping mall.
Travel companion	David walks with Ralph when he wheels from last-period class to the gym, where Ralph helps the basketball team as a student manager.
Neighbor	Parents of nondisabled students in the neighborhood regularly exchange greetings with Mary when they are at school, around the neighborhood, at local stores, at the mall, and at the grocery store.

From Brown et al. (1989). The home school: Why students with severe disabilities must attend the schools of their brothers, sisters, friends, and neighbors. *Journal of The Association for Persons with Severe Handicaps, 14,* 4; reprinted by permission.

- Main office
- Attendance office
- Library
- Audiovisual room
- Athletic office
- Teachers' work room
- Nurse's office
- Counselor's office
- Cafeteria
- Physical plant and grounds

Dozens of tasks can be identified for experience and specific instruction within the school. For example, students' attendance information or semester grades can be entered on a computer in the attendance office. In the main office, students can take telephone messages, deliver faxes, and photocopy documents. In the library, checkout cards can be filed, protective covers can be put on new books, and old book covers can be repaired.

Table 6.4. Vocational tasks for students with physical disabilities

Vocational tasks	Examples/descriptions
Typing	Type membership cards at banks, associations, clubs, and libraries. Type file folder labels. Type addresses on mailing labels or envelopes.
Computer data entry	Input customer, patient, or client information and complete billing and inventory information for businesses and medical offices. Input mailing list information for associations and commercial businesses.
Word processing	Word process memos and letters in almost any office. It requires the ability to read cursive writing.
Filing	Place papers in individual file folders, placing folders in file drawers, and retrieving files. Complexity varies depending on file system.
Telephone answering	In small, informal offices, one person may answer telephone and then tell coworkers they have calls. Larger and more formal offices put callers on hold and transfer calls. This job typically requires taking messages (usually written, but potentially recording messages).
Photocopying	Few businesses are without a photocopy machine. The type of copying done varies among companies. Some only need copies of single-page documents; others need copies of large documents and books or manuals. In most cases, the person who photocopies is also responsible for collating (if it is not done by the machine) and stapling.
Collating/stapling	Companies that perform a large amount of photocopying or have materials printed elsewhere may hire persons to collate and staple. Examples include print shops, direct mail businesses, and associations.
Mail preparation	Fold letters, stuff envelopes, place labels and stamps on envelopes, and run postage meter machines.
Packaging	Package products in manufacturing or distribution businesses. Type of product and packaging process will vary greatly.
Unpackaging/pricing	Most stores require merchandise received from distributors to be unpackaged, and in some cases repackaged for sale, and a price tag or label placed on it. Pricing may be done by hand or with a price gun. May also include placing the items on shelves.
Delivery	Deliver food for restaurants, items from central supply or pharmacies to floors in hospital, fax messages and documents from one office to other offices (e.g., legal documents from law office to courthouse).
Light assembly	Electronics assembly is a common type of light manufacturing task. There are hundreds of other products assembled in large and small businesses in most communities.
Light cleaning	Most offices desire some light clean-up and straightening in addition to the more heavy cleaning done by a janitorial service (e.g., banks need to have someone straighten up the lobby a couple of times a day).
Microfilming	Microfilming is becoming less prevalent due to the advent of computers. However, some businesses still employ microfilming for recordkeeping. Some banks microfilm checks. Hospitals and government offices also typically maintain microfilm records.

From Sowers, J.A., & Powers, L. (1991). *Vocational preparation and employment of students with physical and multiple disabilities* (pp. 30–31). Baltimore: Paul H. Brookes Publishing Co.; reprinted by permission.

Health status information can be entered on the computer for the school nurse. In the audiovisual room, records of equipment can be maintained, and audiovisual equipment can

be delivered to appropriate classrooms. Cleaning and landscaping can be done on the grounds.

In Table 6.5 is a description of the variety of potential vocational activities that can be taught throughout a student's educational career. It is, however, important that these tasks are introduced to students at a young age.

In order to successfully implement any community-based training program, however, a philosophical commitment to the training must be made. Commitment goes beyond community experiences to involve identifying specific program objectives and the target age and populations of students who should participate. From this identification process, different types of jobs, community activities, and resources can be selected for specific students. Potential training sites where initial contacts can be made with business owners or employers will then become apparent. These sites can be visited to determine whether a sufficient array of skills and activities could be acquired by the student. Once it appears that the site is appropriate, the teacher should be ready to negotiate to use the site for training. This usually entails writing a training agreement and asking the employer to sign it.

Implementing Community-Based Training

After the school has verified that all program operation procedures adhere to U.S. Department of Labor Standards,[1] the necessary skills for instruction can be analyzed in detail (Moon, Kiernan, & Halloran, 1990; Simon & Halloran, 1994). Typically, one to three students are assigned to a community site, then detailed schedule and transportation arrangements are made. From this point, systematic instruction procedures (Falvey, 1989) can be developed and implemented, and a means of monitoring student performance can be designed. It is, of course, necessary to maintain contact with employers, owners, co-workers, and any supportive people at the training site. The appropriateness of the training site should be reviewed at least monthly. At the beginning of such a program, only a limited number of sites should be used until their success is shown.

Characteristics of Successful Vocational Training Sites

Several characteristics of successful vocational training sites have emerged over the years. First, employers should understand that students are there primarily to receive training and experience, not necessarily to produce large amounts of work. If an employer feels that the main reason the students are there is to complete work, the program will likely fail. There must be a clear understanding that the work will get done but may require the efforts of several students and the teacher working together.

Second, worksites should offer opportunities to perform a variety of tasks. The ideal worksite yields four to six different tasks and allows for interaction with a variety of co-workers—both necessary to teach for generalization and to enhance the likelihood of "cross-training" of skills.

Third, the purpose of work experience is to provide maximal opportunities for individuals to work and interact with employees without disabilities. Hence, when analyzing

[1]For an in-depth discussion of U.S. Department of Labor standards, see Chapter 12.

Table 6.5. Teaching for transition

Student	Domestic	Community	Leisure	Vocational
Tim (elementary age)	—Picking up toys —Washing dishes —Making bed —Dressing —Grooming —Practicing eating skills —Practicing toileting skills —Sorting clothes —Vacuuming	—Eating meals in a restaurant —Using restroom in a local restaurant —Putting trash into container —Choosing correct change to ride city bus —Giving the clerk money for an item he wants to purchase —Recognizing and reading pedestrian safety signs —Participating in local scout troop —Going to a neighbor's house for lunch	—Climbing on swing set —Playing board games —Playing tag with neighbors —Tumbling activities —Running —Playing kickball —Playing croquet —Riding bicycles —Playing with age-appropriate toys	—Picking up plate, silverware, and glass after a meal —Returning toys to appropriate storage spaces —Cleaning the room at the end of the day —Working on a task for a designated period (15–30 minutes) —Wiping tables after meals —Following two- to four-step instructions —Answering the telephone —Emptying trash —Taking messages to people
Mary (junior high age)	—Washing clothes —Preparing simple meals (e.g., soup, salad, sandwich) —Keeping bedroom clean —Making snacks —Mowing lawn —Raking leaves —Making grocery lists —Purchasing items from a list —Vacuuming and dusting living room	—Crossing streets safely —Purchasing an item from a department store —Purchasing a meal at a restaurant —Using local transportation system to get to and from recreational facilities —Participating in local scout troop —Going to a neighbor's house for lunch on Saturday	—Playing volleyball —Taking aerobics classes —Playing checkers with a friend —Playing miniature golf —Cycling —Attending high school or local basketball games —Playing softball —Swimming —Attending craft class at city recreation center	—Waxing floors —Cleaning windows —Filling lawn mower with gas —Hanging and bagging clothes —Busing tables —Working for 1–2 hours —Operating machinery (e.g., dishwasher, buffer) —Cleaning sinks, bath tubs, and fixtures —Following a job sequence

(continued)

Table 6.5. *(continued)*

Student	Domestic	Community	Leisure	Vocational
Sandy (high school age)	—Cleaning all rooms in place of residence —Developing a weekly budget —Cooking meals —Operating thermostat to regulate heat and air conditioning —Doing yard maintenance —Maintaining personal needs —Caring for and maintaining clothing	—Utilizing bus system to move about the community —Depositing checks into bank account —Using community department stores —Using community restaurants —Using community grocery stores —Using community health facilities (e.g., physician, pharmacist)	—Jogging —Archery —Boating —Watching college basketball games —Playing video games —Playing card games (e.g., UNO) —Attending athletic club swimming class —Gardening —Going on a vacation trip	—Performing required janitorial duties at J.C. Penney —Performing housekeeping duties at Days Inn —Performing grounds keeping duties at college campus —Performing food service at K Street cafeteria —Performing laundry duties at Moon's Laundromat —Performing photocopying at Virginia National Bank headquarters —Performing food stocking duties at Farm Fresh —Performing clerical duties at electrical company —Performing job duties at company standards

a site, staff should note how much the employees interact with each other and assess the extent to which the assigned task will require them to work with the other employees. The Vocational Integration Index developed by Parent, Kregel, and Wehman (1992) provides a means of determining the opportunity for physical and social integration. (The 32 indicators that can be used are listed in Chapter 8.)

Community-Based Training Problems and Solutions

A number of papers and books have been written about the challenges associated with moving from classroom instruction to community-based training sites (e.g., Falvey, 1989). Essentially, however, the major problems revolve around staffing and scheduling, transportation, liability and safety, and costs.

Staffing and Scheduling The first issue for educators designing community-based training programs is locating the staff to manage students who are dispersed throughout the community. Usually, these educators fail to be resourceful enough to identify team teaching and the use of volunteers, paraprofessionals, and peer tutors as potential instructors; they typically also fail to utilize the services of university student teachers, practicum students, and graduate students. A given site should have at least a 1:4 teacher–student ratio. Student training schedules can be staggered, but students should be grouped heterogeneously so that the students with the most severe disabilities are not congregated at one site. An important aspect of coordinating services is using occupational therapists, recreational therapists, and other support personnel in an integrated therapy model. Computers can also be very helpful in terms of responding to scheduling issues.

Transportation There are many ways to facilitate movement of students from classrooms to different community sites. Often the regular bus schedule can be coordinated with the training schedule, and school district vehicles—such as vans, teachers' cars, or other vehicles—can be used throughout the day. School district vehicles are used for many student functions and can also be made available for community-based instruction. In many school systems, teachers have conveniently transported the students to their worksites and been reimbursed for mileage. Also, in some urban areas, training sites can be identified that are within walking distance of the schools.

Liability and Safety The local school board must have a district-wide policy agreement regarding liability and safety. Furthermore, specific school and/or student agreements with participating companies or sites are essential. District liability insurance policies usually cover teachers and students while they are in the community. Students can be insured through school accident funds or employers' policies. If students are being paid, their worker's compensation insurance will be drawn from their wages. Volunteers can register with a school system volunteer training program for insurance coverage. Although liability and safety issues take time and thought to resolve, they require little attention once they are in place.

Costs The issue of how to pay for community-based instruction is paramount; but with planning and thought, this problem can usually be solved. For example, most classrooms have supply budgets that can be used for community-based costs as well as classroom supplies. Community-based instruction costs should also be included in proposed budgets. Most school districts have career and vocational education funds that could rightfully be used. Furthermore, a number of local businesses and community groups, such as Kiwanis Clubs and Lions Clubs, make donations for specific uses such as bus passes or training. Finally, educators should try to structure training around regular purchases, using the family supply list for funds. Clearly, teacher creativity and resourcefulness as well as school and community resources are key to resolving cost issues.

Community-Based Instruction in Action[2]

Frances *Frances is an 18-year-old African American woman with severe mental retardation. Frances communicates using simple sign language (e.g., EAT, DRINK, BATHROOM) to express her needs. She also uses one-word utterances in conjunction with sign language. She responds best to one-step directions but will frequently wait for specific verbal or gestural prompting even when familiar with a routine. When too many demands are placed on Frances or she is uncertain of what to do next, she withdraws from the task and asks to go to the restroom.*

Frances lives with her grandparents and has attended a segregated public school for students with disabilities for 10 years. Frances's educational domain includes functional communication, adaptive skills, domestic skills, leisure skills, community integration, and vocational/workshop skills. Frances first received community-based vocational training for 2 hours a week at a local church. The teacher worked with three students, providing intermittent one-to-one training performing tasks, such as dusting, washing windows, and sweeping. Frances then received vocational training 2 hours a day, 4 days a week at two community-based sites, each for a period of 6 weeks.

The first training site was at a local shopping mall where Frances was required to work in a large area. Frances was instructed in emptying and lining trash cans around the outside of the mall, cleaning trash can lids, and wiping off column ledges using a cloth. Other job-related duties included getting supplies (e.g., rag, trash bags), and pushing and navigating a cart. At the end of the training session, her skill acquisition score for emptying trash cans was 55%; putting in new liners, 0%; and cleaning trash can lids, 0%.

Frances's second training site was at a local grocery store where she worked in the deli. She worked at a stable work station and was instructed on packaging potato salad, macaroni salad, and cole slaw in large and small containers and putting lids on the containers. The system of least intrusive prompts (Snell, 1990) was used to teach the majority of the task. Because Frances had difficulty determining how much salad to scoop onto her spoon to fill the containers, the instructional strategy was changed to graduated guidance. By the end of the training session, Frances was completing 78% of the task of filling small containers and 64% of the task of filling large containers.

Once Frances had completed 12 weeks of community-based training, she was targeted for competitive employment. Based on her performance from the two training sites, it was evident that Frances would perform best in a stable work setting with frequent contact with co-workers who could provide intermittent supervision. She would also perform best in a position that is highly structured and repetitive and involves minimal fine discrimination skills.

A position as a silverware roller was secured in an area restaurant, for 20 hours a week with a starting wage of $4.25 per hour. This position was chosen because it involved a repetitive task in a stable work setting with frequent contact with co-workers and because the employers were willing to adapt the position to Frances's abilities. Co-workers helped to arrange Frances's work station each morning, clocked her in and out, and told her when to take lunch breaks and return to work.

[2]These case studies were developed by Katherine J. Inge, Training Manager at Virginia Commonwealth University Rehabilitation Research and Training Center; Chris Johnston, Employment Specialist at Virginia Commonwealth University; and Stacy Dymond, Coordinator of The Technical Assistance Center for Students with Severe and Profound Handicaps.

Frances learned to negotiate several locations in the restaurant, including the employee entrance, the restroom, the time card rack/time clock, and her work station. In each area the instructor used the system of least intrusive prompts with a hierarchy of natural cue, verbal cue, then gestural cue. Within the first month of employment, Frances was able to negotiate these areas independently.

The training strategy of backward chaining and graduated guidance with physical assistance (Snell, 1990) was used to teach the task of rolling silverware. This strategy was chosen for several reasons. During the community-based training sessions, Frances showed difficulty learning the sequence of a task. Using backward chaining, she learned each step before being introduced to the next step. Graduated guidance with physical assistance was chosen because the task involves discrimination and fine-motor dexterity. The instructor was able to physically guide Frances through the steps and gradually decrease the assistance as these skills improved. This has also been an effective strategy because it gradually introduces the task as it is being learned, thus decreasing Frances's frustration. It is also effective in increasing work stamina.

Bobbie *Bobbie is a 16-year-old Hispanic female with an IQ of 36 as measured by the Stanford-Binet Intelligence Scale (Binet & Simon, 1916). She is obese (in excess of 250 pounds) and has partial paralysis on her left side, although her ambulation and mobility are not impaired enough to interfere with typical functioning. Her sight, hearing, and fine motor skills are unimpaired. Bobbie communicates primarily through sound and gestures but also has demonstrated limited use of manual signs (e.g., BATHROOM, WORK, EAT).*

Behaviorally, Bobbie's teachers described her as "single-minded" and say, "If she wants to do something, she will do it." Her teachers also report that Bobbie engages in self-stimulatory behaviors and is permitted to do so behind a screen in the classroom. Other behavior problems include stomping her feet and sitting down on the floor when she does not want to follow instructions, biting, pulling hair, grabbing items, and rocking. The teacher deals with many of her behaviors by physically reinforcing Bobbie with hugs and allowing her to manipulate stuffed toys in the classroom. Bobbie had not received any community-based instruction or paid employment experiences at the time of the referral. She had not been targeted for supported employment or transition services within the school due to her severe mental retardation and behavior problems.

The teacher identified three community-based training sites for Bobbie. An employment specialist was assigned to implement instruction for 6 weeks at each site. Each training session lasted for 2 hours per day, 4 days per week.

Bobbie's first training site was a discount clothing store. Her job duties included putting clothes (e.g., shirts, pants, coats) on hangers, emptying boxes, changing hangers, and removing plastic bags from clothing. Approximately six people performed these job duties at any given time during store hours. Production rates were slow to average, depending on the time of day and season of the year. Communication was minimal and not required for job completion. The back stockroom where Bobbie worked was of moderate size, uncrowded, and noisy from a loud radio playing through an overhead speaker.

Bobbie learned some parts of her tasks rather quickly. She had difficulty with tasks that required putting new items on hangers, because each item was placed on the hanger in a slightly different manner. After this was noted, the employment specialist modified the steps in the task analysis so that the task remained consistent no matter what style of garment she was hanging.

During training, Bobbie was curious about the items in the work setting. Most of the objects that attracted her were small and shiny with moveable parts. Initially, she would stop and pick up items from the shelves on the way to her work station, examine them, and put them back on verbal request. Difficulty occurred, however, when she discovered that the store sold stuffed toys. She would attempt to grab the toys and could not be physically moved from the store area to her work station. This behavior developed during the last week of her training at this site, and a behavior management program was not successful in reducing the behavior. On one occasion, Bobbie grabbed a toy away from a child in the store; however, she did release it when physically prompted.

It was apparent from this training site experience that several issues should be considered for Bobbie's future job placements. First, all tasks must be consistent with minimal changes in routine. Second, her environment should be free of distracting items, such as toys, because she has been allowed to play with these as reinforcers in her school program. In addition, a behavior management program should be implemented that does not incorporate the use of age-inappropriate items. Bobbie is unable to recognize what is hers and what belongs to someone else. Continued use of stuffed toys could greatly decrease her integration in the community.

Bobbie's second training site was a large shopping mall with outside stores. The job required her to push a cart around the outside of the mall and service the trash cans. She had to remove the trash, put it in the cart, line the trash cans with new bags, and clean the lids. The area where she worked was an outdoor sidewalk circling the mall where trash cans were spaced at regular intervals along the way. While Bobbie was servicing the trash cans, customers walked along the area where she worked.

Bobbie was ready to go to work on most days and was always dressed appropriately. She worked well in the 9:45 A.M.–11:45 A.M. time slot, smiled on most days, and seemed to enjoy her job. Bobbie always did well for the first hour of training. She had difficulty when there were distractions, such as soft drinks and stuffed animals. She would stop work and investigate them or would sit on the ground and not get up. Efforts to decrease these behaviors included redirecting her to work and reinforcing her for appropriate work behaviors. In the last 5 days of training, Bobbie's inappropriate behaviors decreased significantly and were no longer a problem. In general, Bobbie improved a great deal in staying on-task, and she learned to ignore some of the things that distracted her.

Bobbie's third training site was a motel laundry room. Her job duties included folding a variety of laundry and storing it on a shelf. One to two people performed this job daily, and they were also responsible for washing and drying the linens. Production rates ranged from slow to fast, depending on the number of guests in the hotel and the number of workers on duty. Co-workers socialized with Bobbie on a regular basis when she took her breaks. The room was small, uncrowded, and noisy from a loud radio playing in the room.

Bobbie seemed to enjoy this job from the first day of training. She demonstrated that she could perform each laundry folding task independently for 3 consecutive days by the end of the third week. The tasks were extended to include placing laundry on the appropriate shelves. Bobbie began to pay attention to detail in her job, a behavior that had not been noted previously. In the laundry room, Bobbie neatly matched the corners of the towels and smoothed them appropriately.

Overall, this was an excellent job for Bobbie, and she demonstrated many mature work behaviors on the job. She obviously found the work itself reinforcing, often refusing to take a break in order to continue folding the laundry. The employer remarked that she was very helpful and would be an excellent candidate for a job there.

Community-based instruction is a very effective means of implementing a transition program. In fact, teaching for transition is not effective unless at least some instruction occurs in real community environments. Training away from the school takes more planning and time and can be more logistically difficult to implement. However, student interest is heightened, and skill selection is usually more functional.

Teaching for Transition

This section describes strategies and techniques teachers must understand and consider when implementing systematic instruction programs in classrooms and community-based settings. Systematic instruction strategies are used to instruct students with challenging learning behaviors to perform skills such as folding laundry, putting away silverware, washing windows, crossing streets, ordering fast food, and making purchases. Factors that affect the effectiveness of instruction include complexity of the skill, the instruction site, and the teacher's instructional skill capabilities. It has been widely documented that students with more challenging learning disabilities and behavior problems, such as those with autism, require more precise and intense systematic instruction techniques. An overview of some of these techniques is provided here, but the reader should understand that strategies such as these can be modified for students who have less severe disabilities.

Task Analysis

Most teachers arrange curricula using task analysis and skill sequencing. Task analysis involves dividing a set of activities or skills into smaller components for the students to learn. Generally, the extent to which a skill should be broken down is determined by the severity of the individual's disability.

Careful sequencing of skills greatly enhances the speed with which students with severe disabilities learn. Many teachers have begun to arrange the sequence of activities in a functional manner (i.e., one that makes sense in the context of a given environment), moving away from dividing skills into incrementally small steps without maintaining the context of the activity.

As Wilcox and Bellamy (1982) have pointed out, there is greater merit in teaching community skills, such as ordering a hamburger in a fast-food restaurant, when a number of such skills are chained together. This type of "chaining" involves going into the restaurant independently, going to the cashier, knowing which items to select, using appropriate communication devices to select the items, and paying for the items. The student then must know how to take the food to a table and eat independently.

In the 1970s, many teachers focused exclusively on teaching one or two small components of a skill without putting all of the links in the instructional chain together. In the 1990s, thinking has led to repeated instruction of the entire sequence of tasks. Also, community visits should occur at a less stressful time of the day, and more people should be introduced gradually as the students exhibit competence. Obviously, it does not make sense to take three students with histories of self-injurious behavior into McDonald's during the noon rush hour. Dr. M. Sherril Moon is an outstanding national transition leader in the area of instructional and curriculum.

M. Sherril Moon M. Sherril Moon is a professor of special education in the secondary, transition, and severe disabilities areas at the University of Maryland. She has worked as a special educator, adult services provider, teacher trainer, and researcher in transition and supported employment. She has provided in-service training to educational and adult services agencies and employers across the United States. She currently works with several school systems, revamping their community-based curricula for students with severe disabilities and developing their transition procedures. She has written textbooks, articles, monographs, and curriculum guides in the areas of transition and community living for people with severe disabilities.

Dr. Moon has provided special leadership and expertise in the area of adaptive physical education and recreation for students with severe disabilities. She gets great joy out of directly working with young people with the most severe disabilities, especially in sports and leisure activities where she has been an outstanding role model for others.

Response Prompts

Prompts should be used during instruction to help students demonstrate correct answers. These include verbal instructions, gestures, modeling, and physical help. Any of these techniques can be used during transition skill training. The most important factor to consider when choosing prompts, however, is selecting those that more naturally occur within a specific community domain. For example, if a student is working in an industrial laundry facility, model prompts may be the most natural since the student can watch others use the machines or put away clean items. Before any prompts are used, however, the skill sequences should be task analyzed. As a general rule, instructors should use as little prompting as possible.

Verbal Instructions Verbally instructing students is usually the most natural form of help because most people learn this way. Instructions for individuals with autism, severe communication disorders, or severe mental retardation should be short, direct, and related to each part of the task sequence.

Gestures Pairing verbal instructions with gestures, such as pointing, tapping, or touching, is another form of assistance. Gesturing is a form of communication that allows employees with hearing impairments, for example, to participate in work and social interactions with supervisors and co-workers.

Models A teacher can also model a step of a skill sequence. This involves demonstrating that step and then waiting for the student to copy it (Mank & Horner, 1988). Modeling should always be performed beside the student rather than across from or in front of him or her. This allows the student to view the skill as it is to be performed, and it does not require him or her to reverse the direction of the model step. Modeling is especially effective with students who have receptive communication problems or do not pay attention well or with skills that are hard to learn without direct observation.

Physical Assists Hands-on assistance, also known as physical prompting, may be required for some students to complete portions of a skill sequence. For example, when instructing a student to sweep the floor for the first time, the teacher may stand behind the student, place his or her hands with the student's hands on the broom, and move it in the sweeping pattern. Clearly, fast-paced work environments are not the best place for this type of assistance.

Most students who enter transition-age programs at 15, 16, and 17 years of age should already possess a number of community and vocational skills. At this age, teachers should not have to devote large amounts of initial training time to simple skills acquisition. By their mid- to late teens, students should be performing these skills and learning how to do them more effectively in the community. Many of these skills must be learned, regardless of the disability or the severity level, by students 8–15 years of age. By the time they arrive in the secondary school environment, students should have an array of transition skills in their repertoire. The mission of the secondary-level teacher should be to help students utilize those skills in the community in preparation for adulthood.

Least Intrusive Assistance

One way to systematically fade the types of prompts described previously is to use a system that Snell (1990) has called least intrusive prompts. This system allows teachers to progress from verbal prompts to model or gestural prompts to physical prompts for various components of a skill sequence. Most important, the student is not given the opportunity to make an error. The teacher should always be ready to interrupt with the next degree of assistance as the student begins to make a mistake or if the student does not respond. Table 6.6 includes guidelines for using a response hierarchy of less intrusive assistance with a student worker who is expected to wash windows in a mall.

The teacher must gradually fade his or her presence as the student becomes more confident at a job or community site. Ultimately, the teacher should leave the immediate instructional area so that the student can show increased competence. Paychecks can be used as reinforcement in this process (see Table 6.7).

Reinforcement Procedures for Transition Training

Providing positive reinforcement for students when they demonstrate correct instructional behaviors is essential in any good teaching situation. Effective teachers know that positive attention and tangible reinforcers, such as points and tokens, are not only highly effective, but absolutely essential to increase the speed at which students learn behaviors.

Timing The timing of reinforcement delivery is critical. All positive reinforcements should be given immediately following the occurrence of desired behavior. For example, when a student picks up a glass with both hands, the teacher immediately says, "Good using both hands!" By immediately praising this specific skill, the teacher increased the likelihood of its repetition.

Sometimes, however, it is not feasible to deliver a reward immediately. This is especially true at community-based sites where there may be several students working at one time or if tangible rewards, such as a cup of coffee or a magazine, have been selected. In

Table 6.6. Development and implementation of Michael's new program

Consumer: Michael
Jobsite: Mall
Position: Janitor
Schedule: Monday–Friday, 7:00 A.M.–11:30 A.M.

Program: Teaching independent performance on cleaning upper window panes of the main entrances at the mall. Each window set must be cleaned one time per week. Michael currently cleans the lower panes at each entrance using a horizontal wiping pattern. Cleaning the upper panes will require the following task modifications:

1. Use of an extended step ladder to obtain the height needed to clean each upper pane
2. Correct positioning of the step ladder in front of each window pane to be cleaned
3. Fitting an extension pole on the handles of the squeegee and sponge to increase the area that can be covered with this equipment
4. Use of a vertical wiping motion, moving from the top to the bottom of each window pane

Skill training will be implemented in order to assist Michael in learning the new job task.

Consumer characteristics: Michael demonstrates the ability to acquire new skills with verbal, gestural, and physical prompts. He responds to both verbal and tangible reinforcements by increasing the quality of his work.

Data collection: Five separate, but identical, task analyses will be used to monitor Michael's progress at each of the five window sets. The use of five separate recording forms will allow the trainer to assess Michael's performance across different locations and time periods. Due to Michael's work schedule, probe and prompt data will be recorded once per week at each of the five window sets. Multiple opportunity probe data will be taken on the first single window pane cleaned each day. Correct performance will be defined as initiation of work within 3 seconds. A (+) will be used to designate correct performance of the step in the task analyses. Incorrect performance is designated by a (–). Prompt data will be recorded during cleaning of the second single window pane cleaned each day.

Baseline performance: Michael independently completed 12 of 41 steps (29%) in the task analysis.

Behavior change procedures:

1. A system of least intrusive prompts will be implemented to fade response prompts needed during initial training. A three-prompt hierarchy, including verbal, gestural, and physical prompts, will be used in conjunction with this system. Training will occur simultaneously on all steps of the task analysis (total task presentation). The criterion for skill acquisition is 100% performance on three consecutive probe trials.
2. Training will begin with the trainer within 3 feet of the base of the ladder. The trainer should be ready to mount the ladder at any time during the training period when physical assistance is needed for correct performance of a step in the task analysis. Movement from this distance is determined by the procedure outlined below. The trainer will initiate the training session with the cue, "Michael, clean the window." If no response is given within 3 seconds or Michael begins to make an error, the trainer will introduce the first level of prompting (verbal) in the three-prompt hierarchy. If correct performance is not demonstrated at this level of prompting, the trainer will introduce the next more intrusive prompt of the hierarchy. At no time will the trainer allow Michael to make an error.
3. Verbal reinforcement will be delivered on each completed step of the task analysis during the first 3 days of training at a particular window set. For example, if Michael correctly wipes the window ledge with a physical prompt, the trainer will say, "Good wiping the window ledge, Michael," at the completion of this task. Beginning on the fourth day of training at a particular window set, verbal reinforcement will be delivered on only those steps of the task analysis that have not been performed correctly for three consecutive probe trials. This process will continue until reinforcement is required only at the conclusion of the entire task. When all steps of the task analysis are completed independently for three consecutive trials, the trainer will step back to a distance of 6 feet. When Michael independently performs at this distance, the trainer will move back to a distance of 30 feet. When independent performance is demonstrated at this distance, the trainer will fade from the worksite. Probe data will continue to be recorded on a weekly basis at each particular window set.

Table 6.7. Establishing John's paycheck as a reinforcer

Phase 1:

The workday was divided into 5-minute intervals.

John could earn a check on a card for working during an entire 5-minute interval.

After he earned two checks for working, John immediately received a nickel.

The workday was divided into four segments/breaks during which John could spend the nickels he had earned.

After 2 consecutive days of John not refusing to work, the program moved to phase 2.

Phase 2:

The workday was divided into 10-minute intervals.

The other elements of the program remained the same.

After 2 consecutive days of John not refusing to work, the program moved to phase 3.

Phase 3:

The workday continued to be divided into 10-minute intervals. Checks were earned on a card for working during an entire interval.

As soon as two checks were earned, John received a nickel.

However, John could use his nickels only to buy preferred items during two scheduled breaks. One occurred during the midpoint of the day and the other at the end of the day.

After 2 consecutive days of John not refusing to work, the program moved to phase 4.

Phase 4:

The workday was divided into 15-minute intervals.

John no longer earned a nickel after every two checks were earned. Instead checks were added during the midpoint break and at the end of the day for spending.

After 2 consecutive days of John not refusing to work, the program moved to phase 5.

Phase 5:

The workday was divided into 20-minute intervals.

At this point, checks were added up at the end of the day, and John was able to spend his money on a preferred item.

After 2 consecutive days of John not refusing to work, the program moved to phase 6, and so forth.

Note: John's program was written to gradually increase the length of the intervals before John received a check on his card. The amount of the payment also gradually increased until payment at the end of the day was one dollar. Payment every day faded to payment every other day, and so forth, until payment occurred naturally on payday.

these cases, the teacher could use reinforcers, such as tokens, points on a card, or checks on a calendar, that can be exchanged later for an item or activity.

Schedule of Delivery Teachers must determine how often reinforcement will be delivered. There are two types of reinforcement schedules. Continuous reinforcement schedules should be used during new skills training, meaning that students receive reinforcers for every correct step in a skill sequence. As students become more independent, an intermittent reinforcement schedule can be instituted. In these schedules, delivery of the reinforcer occurs only after a predetermined number of responses or a predetermined time period.

Common sense suggests that the teacher should be located beside the student initially to provide direct instruction. As the student becomes increasingly independent, however, a planned sequence of withdrawal should be implemented. For example, the teacher should move further away from the student as he or she successfully completes more components of the task. Eventually, the teacher will not be visible to the student. In Table 6.8, Paul's teacher fades as Paul becomes more competent at the jobsite.

Table 6.8. Fading Paul's instructor from the jobsite

Program: Fading during task acquisition
Worker: Paul
Jobsite: The Center
Instructor: Martha

Objective: Paul will complete all tasks with 100% accuracy with the employment specialist out of sight for 3 consecutive days.

Worker characteristics: Paul is a hard worker who learns the unchanging portions of his tasks very quickly. He has some difficulty with changes in routine. He responds well to verbal praise and smiles but does not like being corrected. Any error correction should be phrased very tactfully. Paul can become sullen and abrasive if corrected, and the best response seems to be silence until a positive action can be reinforced. Then an economy of positive words should be used—for example, "That's it," or "You've got it." Paul enjoys working independently. He has excellent problem-solving skills and finds the most efficient way to accomplish a task. The order of the TA steps need not be strictly followed in order for him to complete the task correctly.

Data collection: Task analyses of each task should be used to record progress in task independence as well as employment specialist distance. Data should be taken daily. No prompts should be given unless errors occur.

Reinforcement: Verbal reinforcement will be used during training. Praise for independent work will be given unless an error occurs.

Fading procedure: During acquisition (performance of less than 100%), employment specialist should remain 3–10 feet from Paul (closer than this seems to annoy Paul). Move to 3 feet for problem areas of the task as indicated by previous data, and back to 10 feet for steps Paul has completed correctly for several days. Give reinforcement for correctly completed steps that had been trouble spots and responses done correctly after prompting. Reinforce at task completion.

Phase 1:
When Paul completes the task independently with 100% accuracy for 3 consecutive days, fade to 10–20 feet. Reduce verbal praise so that it is given at task completion only. Smile instead of praising verbally during task, and look at his hands instead of making eye contact to reinforce attending to task rather than looking up. If an error is made, step in and tactfully correct, maintaining positive attitude. Praise correct response (e.g., "That's it," "You've got it"), and move back to 10–20 feet.

Phase 2:
When Paul completes the task with 100% accuracy for 3 consecutive days independently with the instructor at 10–20 feet, fade to over 20 feet. Continue to smile during correct work and add periods of looking away or doing something with hands when Paul is performing steps with which he has had no trouble. If an error is made, follow procedure in phase 1 and step back to over 20 feet. Verbally praise task completion and reinforce independent work.

Phase 3:
When Paul completes the task with 100% accuracy for 3 consecutive days independently with the trainer at over 20 feet, fade to out of sight (preferably to area of next task if it is performed out of sight of the current work area). When Paul moves on to next task, approach and reinforce independent task completion and moving on to next task. Inspect work completed when possible (during another task at phase 3 or during Paul's break). If no error is apparent, continue phase 2 the next day and inspect. If no error is apparent, continue phase 3 the next day. If no errors are found for 3 consecutive days, inspection may be done on an intermittent basis.

It does little or no good for students to learn to perform skills only under the watchful eye of one teacher. It is essential that other teachers be faded in and out, with the ultimate goal that the students be able to demonstrate transition skill competence independently.

Analyzing an Instruction Plan

The teacher must be continuously mindful of what he or she is doing with the student during instruction. Too many teachers continue an instruction plan for weeks or even months at a time without reviewing the progress that is being made. The teacher must analyze the effectiveness of the training strategy and whether the skill sequence has been individualized sufficiently to match the individual's abilities. Furthermore, all of the reinforcement strategy issues should be reviewed. Table 6.9 provides a list of points to be considered as a teacher analyzes an instructional plan. Because, at times, it is very difficult to engage in a meaningful analysis of one's own plan, it is helpful for a teacher to consult with another professional. This person may be better able to determine where the plan is breaking down, if, in fact, it is.

Teaching Strategies: The Logistics of Scheduling[3]

Although the process of assessing students and developing appropriate education goals is difficult, creating a schedule that accommodates each student's goals and objectives during the school day is equally challenging. Factors such as staffing patterns, natural routines within the school day, the availability of desired integrated classes, transportation schedules, and students' community jobsite hours must all be coordinated. Although there is no one established way of developing a schedule, there are several components that all good, functional, structured classroom schedules share.

Why Is it Important to Have a Schedule?

Schedules are an integral part of any program because they identify how each IEP goal will be accomplished within a functional activity. With a schedule, staff understand their instructional responsibilities, "downtime" is minimized, and transitions between activities proceed in a smooth, organized fashion. A structured schedule also encourages a positive environment where challenging behaviors are less likely to occur.

Who Should Be Involved with Creating a Schedule?

It is important to involve all team members in the process of developing a class schedule. Typically the classroom teacher is viewed as the primary person responsible for scheduling; however, almost all decisions regarding the schedule will depend on the availability of staff. Many people find it helpful to schedule a team meeting prior to school so that teachers, therapists, and paraprofessionals can review students' individualized education program (IEP) goals and plan effective staffing patterns that will help each student to achieve his or her goals. Throughout the year, these teams may need to reconvene specifically to review the schedule and make appropriate changes.

What Information Is Needed to Develop a Schedule?

The first step involved with designing a structured classroom schedule is to review each student's priorities for instruction. These priorities should be the goals and objectives

[3]The author is indebted to Stacy Dymond for her contribution of this section of the chapter.

Table 6.9. Analyzing an instruction plan

Analyze the effectiveness of the training strategy.
 Does the training strategy match the learning style of the individual?
 Is the person responding to the type of prompt(s) selected?
 Is he or she attending to the task?
 Are too many skills being taught at the same time?
Has the task analysis been individualized to match the individual's abilities?
 Has the task been broken down into steps that are small enough?
 Have the physical limitations of the consumer been taken into consideration, or was the task analysis
 written for someone without physical limitation?
 Can the task oe taught in sections rather than in the entire chain?
 Does the task analysis eliminate the need to make quality judgments (e.g., four times around the sink
 results in a clean sink by employer standards)?
 Would external cues or adaptive equipment help the person learn the task if they were added to the
 task analysis?
Have all of the components of delivering reinforcement been considered?
 Is the reinforcement given immediately after the desired response?
 Has the amount of reinforcement been reduced too quickly?
 Does the reinforcement match the individual's current abilities (i.e., does the person need a material
 or food item paired with social praise?)?
 Does the individual have a behavior that is interfering with learning the task? Should a behavior pro-
 gram be developed in addition to the skills acquisition program?

listed in the IEP. Although all IEP objectives will need to be addressed, some may be em-
phasized more than others depending on the priorities of the parents and other IEP team
members. These priorities will influence the settings selected to teach the skill and the
amount of time spent in each setting. For example, if the priorities for a student surround
social skills with age-appropriate peers, the schedule may reflect a majority of instruc-
tional time spent teaching social skills in activities with peers without disabilities. Like-
wise, if the instructional priorities for a student focus on learning work skills, the schedule
for that student would emphasize vocational training in a variety of school and community
work environments.

What Are the Components of a Good Schedule?

Functional Age-Appropriate Activities IEP objectives need to be addressed within
the context of meaningful activities that are appropriate for each student's chronological
age. If the IEP objective is stated in terms of an isolated skill (i.e., grasp and release an ob-
ject) rather than an activity-based skill (i.e., grasp a washed plate from a peer and release
it in the dish rack), then the first step is to translate the objective into functional activities
that are age appropriate for the student. Using the same isolated skill of grasp and release
as an example, one might target grasping blocks and releasing them in a toy box for a pri-
mary school student during leisure time; however, an age-appropriate activity for a mid-
dle school student might be grasping the dice and releasing them during a Yahtzee game.

Natural Routines Schedule activities so that, whenever possible, they are taught at
the natural time(s) and in the actual location(s) where the skill is required. Begin by looking
broadly at the types of activities that occur within a typical school day. Each student will

have routines surrounding arrival, toileting, getting out work materials and putting them away, eating lunch, and departing school. For lunch, the natural location is the cafeteria and the natural time for lunch is when other students of the same age are having lunch. During arrival and departure at the high school level, dressing and social skills may be targeted to occur at a hall locker whereas in elementary school, the natural location to work on these goals may be at the cubby/closet inside the classroom. It should be noted that some routines such as toileting, tube feeding, or receiving medication may need to accommodate the student's required schedule rather than the school or classroom's natural schedule.

Number of Opportunities to Use the Targeted Skills It is better to schedule priority skills for a short period every day than for a long period once or twice a week. In general, the more significant an individual's disability, the more opportunities he or she needs to practice targeted skills. The reason for this is that many students with severe disabilities have difficulty learning tasks that they perform on an infrequent basis. Limited training opportunities can increase students' frustration with the task, diminish their motivation, and ultimately prevent them from acquiring the targeted skill. For example, rather than targeting an entire morning once a week to teach students purchasing skills in the community, schedule the activity for an hour, three times a week. If a priority goal for a couple of students is meal preparation, the schedule might reflect time each day for the students to prepare a bag lunch (and take it to the cafeteria to eat) rather than preparing a large classroom meal once every other Friday.

Generalization and Maintenance Almost all IEP objectives can be taught in a variety of different environments. Even an activity such as toileting can occur in a number of environments. There are toilets in classrooms, on different school halls, in the gym locker rooms, at home, and in the community. Chances are that none of these bathroom environments is exactly the same. Many students with severe disabilities are unable to adapt to subtle changes in their environment. If they learn to perform a skill in one setting, they may not be able to perform the same skill in a similar setting. By scheduling IEP objectives in a variety of functional activities, students learn to generalize and maintain the skill in different settings and with different people. An IEP goal for "wiping" might be taught by having a student wipe tables in the cafeteria after lunch, wipe the art table as part of the clean up procedure in art class, brush sawdust off the machines in a wood shop class, dust shelves in the library, or wash a car during a school car wash fundraiser.

Embedding Skills If the schedule is to reflect functional, meaningful activities for each student, then it is important that IEP objectives become embedded within the activities and not practiced in isolation. Social, communication, and mobility goals can become part of each activity within the daily routine. For example during center time in an elementary school, a student with severe orthopedic impairments might work on communication skills by using eye gaze to choose a picture of the center in which he or she wishes to participate. Gross motor goals would be addressed by helping the student move to the desired center and transfer from his or her wheelchair into a prone stander. At the audiotape listening center, the student's objectives would be to greet a friend by raising a hand, select a story using eye gaze, and activate a switch to listen to the story. Once center time was finished, the student could use eye gaze again to indicate "finished," raise a hand to say goodbye to his or her friend, and return from the prone stander into the wheelchair.

Available Resources The schedule time, setting, and frequency of any activity will ultimately depend on the classroom's resources. These resources may include staff time, program funds, and transportation availability. Although few schools ever have the degree of resources they desire, there are several ways that creative scheduling can be used to maximize school resources. During the initial team meeting, staff should map out their roles and responsibilities including specific schedules of when they will be working in the classroom. Naturally, there will be some gaps in the schedule when there do not appear to be enough staff to support the scheduled activity. This is where the team can play an important role. If activities are not running smoothly, the team may need to brainstorm ideas regarding how students can be grouped differently, how the activity can be restructured, or how staff time can be reallocated. Strategies such as team teaching, integrated therapy, block scheduling, cooperative learning groups, and the use of peer tutors, peer buddies, and volunteers in the classroom may help to maximize staff resources.

Integrated Therapy Therapy services should be scheduled in the classroom environment within the context of a functional activity. This strategy helps to maximize staff resources and allows students to maintain their identity as part of the group; it also allows all staff to learn new skills for working with the student that can be carried over into other activities when the therapist is not present. Block scheduling—one integrated therapy strategy—involves condensing the therapist's usual time with one student into a larger block of time. Instead of working with a child three times a week for 20 minutes, the therapists might provide a 1-hour block where some of the time was spent in direct therapy and some of the time was devoted to a team meeting or consultation. Although block scheduling decreases the frequency of the therapist's contact with the student, it does allow the therapist more flexibility in working with the student's needs in his or her learning environment.

Community Training Scheduling activities off school grounds requires coordination with school transportation services and local businesses. Whenever possible, instruction should be provided in the community where the student lives and in the businesses frequented by the student and his or her family. This will ensure that the student has opportunities to socialize in the community and learn skills that will be applicable in the family's community environment. In schools with limited transportation availability, community-based instruction may need to be the first activity on the classroom schedule. This is particularly true for high school students who are participating in time-limited, nonpaid vocational training placements. Because the labor regulations require students to change placements after a specific amount of job training, new vocational training placements must be located and worked into the schedule on a regular basis.

Schedule Design Once the schedule has been developed to incorporate each student's IEP objectives, the final step is to post it in the classroom. For each time period in the day, the schedule should indicate the activity that will occur, the location of the activity, which staff member will be working with each child, and the IEP objective(s) that will be targeted during the activity. The schedule should be written in such a way that it can be followed and understood by each staff member. Once the classroom schedule is developed, it can easily be broken down so that each student has his or her own schedule that outlines the activities in which he or she will be participating on that day. .

Conclusion

This chapter has provided an overview of what to teach, where to teach, and how to teach students in transition. Transition planning and implementation consist of far more than instruction plan development and transition instruction as competence in transition skills is necessary for entry into the workplace, independent home living, and the community. A number of books and resources delve into this in greater detail (Falvey, 1989; Moon, Inge, Wehman, Brooke, & Barcus, 1990; Snell, 1990).

The teacher is the "point" person for leading the instruction. All other instructional personnel and transition team members look to the teacher for leadership in the area of critical transition skills. If the teacher is unable to identify the appropriate skills for entry into adulthood, the student will never acquire the appropriate skills for adult competence. Still worse, a number of students with mild disabilities will become so disillusioned, disappointed, and bored with school that they will drop out. Once these students drop out, they will embark on a path of underemployment or no employment. They become potential offenders in the criminal justice system and often end up out of the mainstream of society and community networks.

If the teacher chooses to provide instruction exclusively in the school and the classroom, there is far greater likelihood that nonfunctional skills or activities will be presented. Then, the likelihood of high dropout rates and ineffective instruction increases.

Teachers who do not understand the most effective instructional practices are unable to equip their students with necessary skills. Therefore, teachers must be aware of the variety of teaching techniques that are reported in the professional literature. Transition instruction must be powerful and precise for students with the most challenging learning and behavior problems; however, all teachers who are working with any students with disabilities must be cognizant of different ways to individualize instruction and be as effective as they can be.

6

Study Questions

1. What should be the key criterion for selecting transition objectives for students with disabilities?

2. What are the steps for prioritizing instructional activities for students with disabilities?

3. What are some ways that social skills and relationships can be fostered at school?

4. What is community-based instruction, and why is it valuable for students with disabilities?

5. What are some key considerations in establishing and utilizing community-based work experience sites?

6. What are common problems encountered with community-based work programs, and how can those problems be addressed proactively?

7. What are task analysis and chaining?

8. What are four types of response prompts, and what is meant by "least intrusive assistance"?

7

Finding Jobs for
Young People with Disabilities

Cary Griffin and Pam Sherron

Upon completion of this chapter, the reader will be able to do the
following:

- Describe three methods for identifying business contacts
- Discuss how to make an effective presentation to a potential
 employer
- State ways to overcome specific employer objections
- Describe how job carving can create work opportunities

Job development is a phase of supported employment in which the employment specialist,
in pursuit of identifying work opportunities, contacts the business community to learn
about employer needs and establish relationships. Through job development efforts, cur-
rent or future work opportunities are identified. Prior to developing jobs, the employment
specialist should have an understanding of the type of work the job seeker desires (Goodall,
Groah, Sherron, Kreutzer, & Wehman, 1991; Moon, Goodall, Barcus, & Brooke, 1986; Sher-
ron & Groah, 1990).

At times, the job seeker may be able to learn to do a job without modification of the
existing job description. Often, however, an applicant with a severe disability may not pos-
sess the range of skills specified in an employer's job descriptions and may be viewed as

All lists and dialogue that appear in this chapter are reprinted by permission from Wehman, P.,
& Sherron, P. (1995). *Off to work: A vocational curriculum for individuals with neurologic impairment*
(pp. 143–151). Verona, WI: Attainment.

unqualified, with or without reasonable accommodations. If a job seeker possesses very specific functional abilities, creating a position through "job carving" may be an effective way to invent a work option.

Job carving requires the employment specialist to demonstrate to the employer how the individual with a disability could increase business efficiency with the use of his or her unique skills and talents. One approach to job carving involves analyzing different positions within an organization and having the workers prioritize the importance of their tasks. Tasks rated as low priority are targeted as potential duties for a new job. Consider the following example: In one company, multiple job analyses revealed that many staff members spent up to 10% of their time photocopying documents. When presented with this information, the company manager was quick to agree that it made good business sense to relieve highly paid professionals from this task, and a part-time office aide position was created.

Job Development

Developing jobs for people with disabilities necessitates that the employment specialist establish relations with businesses that can benefit from the services the job seeker offers, as well as locate or create work that suits the job seeker's preferences and expectations. There are basically two approaches the employment specialist can take: 1) assess the client's skills and then find or create a job that maximizes their use, or 2) assess the needs of a business and match it to the job seeker's skills. Employment specialists will most likely use a combination of the approaches. No matter which approach is used, prior to initiating the search for work, the employment specialist should know what is being offered, be able to intelligibly respond to employer queries, and have a clear understanding of the job seeker's expectations and vocational strengths.

Value of Services

An understanding of the program's values, methods, and procedures that guide interactions with business is essential. Supported employment program staff should be able to answer the following questions:

- What is the program's philosophy relating to securing and creating employment opportunities?
- How will job seeker participation be encouraged in the job placement process?
- How will job seekers be represented during an employer contact?
- What materials will be used to represent the program and job seeker to the business world?

This vital information should be readily accessible to staff as part of the program's policy and procedures manual.

Services Offered

Potential employers will want to know exactly what is being offered by a supported employment program. In order to be effective, the employment specialist should know the nature of the services represented and be well versed in how to respond to questions or

concerns without hesitation. Many employers will be more open to listening and considering the low-risk nature of a proposal if the employment specialist appears to be a skilled professional. The employment specialist should be able to respond to the following typical inquiries:

- How will these services benefit this organization?
- What abilities does the job seeker possess that will meet my needs?
- What other businesses have used this service?
- How much is this going to cost in terms of time and resources?
- How long have you or the company been in business, and how successful have you been?

Job Seeker Expectations

Developing an understanding of what the job seeker expects from work and has to offer to the community is an important aspect of consumer assessment. With this information, the employment specialist should be able to identify or create positions that suit individual preferences and needs. The employment specialist should be able to answer the following questions about the job seeker:

- What are the person's vocational strengths?
- What functional skills can be performed with accommodation?
- What approach or combination of approaches will be used to detect work?
- Will an existing position be sought and possibly restructured by elimination of marginal duties?
- Will businesses be approached about creating a job from combining low-priority tasks of other workers?
- When creating work, will the job seeker's special skills be presented to employers who might have a need for such service, or will employer needs be assessed and then matched to applicants?
- How will the job seeker be represented and what is his or her stand on disclosure?
- Will the job seeker participate in job development activities and if so, how?

In the long run, efforts that encourage participation in the job search process are likely to improve job retention. The person with a disability may choose to participate in job development in a variety of ways, such as telephoning employment specialists with job leads, cold-calling potential employers, and networking with friends and family. This collaborative effort provides an excellent opportunity for the employment specialist to gain additional insight into the person's skills and abilities; it also empowers the job seeker.

Identifying Business Contacts

Once the employment specialist is familiar with the services offered and the job seeker's expectations, he or she should identify businesses to approach. Any business with positions that do what the job seeker is able or wants to do should be considered a potential employer. There are a variety of ways to target these businesses including surveying and developing personal networks, responding to recruitment advertisements, or contacting businesses that are not advertising.

Surveying and Developing Personal Networks

Personal connections are a rich source of business leads and a personal referral network can be easily developed during a home visit. Those in attendance are asked to brainstorm regarding people who may be appropriate for the following lists: family and friends, neighbors, church members, social club members, volunteer supervisors or co-workers, professionals (e.g., teacher, hair stylist), and employees in local, frequented businesses (e.g., convenience store, dry cleaners). Next, a plan of action for communicating with these people is established; for this, creativity is essential. For example, one job seeker posted a notice in the church bulletin requesting assistance from the congregation; another person delivered flyers to neighbors in his apartment complex. In both cases, the job seeker received remarkable support. During communication with leads, one should aim to schedule a meeting. Also, keep in mind that the referral chain can be continuously expanded by asking every contact for a referral to others.

A system for obtaining leads from the state rehabilitation agency should be established. Many state offices have a marketing coordinator, who assists by ensuring job leads are shared with service providers in a timely manner. Some agencies hold monthly networking meetings where employers present information on their organization's employment needs and often arrange site tours for interested parties.

Social networking through active membership in a club or organization is also an effective way to make business contacts. Attendance at community events can provide insight into issues that affect employment needs as well as introduce the employment specialist to new people.

Plan of Action An excellent way to increase the odds of discovering work is to make new contacts and follow up with existing contacts on an ongoing basis. A tickler file to re-contact employers quarterly should be maintained and used to keep the program in the forefront of the employers' mind. Some find that writing a job placement plan of action that states specific goals to be achieved helps them to focus during job search activities; once a goal is set, the employment specialist must strive until it is reached. Setting realistic and achievable goals on a weekly basis can also increase the confidence of an employment specialist. Often, employment specialists report feeling down due to employers' rejections.

Responding to Recruitment Advertising

Recruitment advertisements offer a way to identify immediate job openings and employers to contact. Advertisements may be found in the daily newspapers, government listings, job hotlines, and so on. When reviewing classifieds, if the employment specialist's interest is in researching a specific type of position, he or she should be sure to scan the entire employment section, as positions sought may be listed under a variety of job titles. When attempting to secure an advertised position, competition will be inevitable. However, some positions have a high turnover rate, and many employers should recognize and be interested in the benefits of using supported employment.

Businesses Not Advertising

Arrangements to meet with employers who are not recruiting is typically an excellent way to identify current jobs or future work, especially if the goal is to create a position for the job

seeker. The Yellow Pages of the telephone book can be used to identify types of organizations that may have a particular position being sought or may need the service offered by the job seeker. Review of specialized reference books and periodicals, such as *National Business Employment Weekly* or *Directories in Print*, and published sources of employer information, such as the Chamber of Commerce Directory or newspaper articles, can be useful as well. A drive around the job seeker's community is another way to identify businesses to reach.

Making Contact

A study by Hagner and Daning (1993) revealed that job developers who focused on establishing personal, trusting relations with employers, rather than filling a job opening, were most successful. In fact, successful job developers rarely asked about job openings. Instead, they found ways to work with employers to create jobs to fill the employer's need or accommodate the job seeker.

The idea of building relations is more fully explored in Bissonnette's (1994) book, *Beyond Traditional Job Development*, which states that the relationship between an employer and employment specialist should be dynamic and ongoing and evolve and change as either party's needs or interests change. The employment specialist should function as a consultant, focusing on establishing a mutually beneficial relationship.

Using this paradigm, the emphasis shifts from making cold calls to calls of introduction. As Bissonnette (1994) states, an introductory call does not seek a "yes or no" answer from an employer but establishes the rapport needed to develop a creative response to employer needs or concerns and offer services, rather than persuade. Additionally, the one-sided sales pitch becomes a two-way conversation in which the employer can determine the relevance and value of what is being offered. When making introductory calls, there is no failure, only feedback.

Approaching businesspeople requires excellent communication skills, patience, confidence, perseverance, and, above all, a positive attitude. Initial employer communications may occur via a telephone call, personal visit, or written correspondence. No matter which approach is used, the employment specialist should be well prepared and know why the business is being called and the desired outcome of the contact (i.e., secure an interview for a job seeker, receive information on the company and future hiring needs, analyze positions in the organization to identify job creation or carving opportunities, or gain referrals to similar businesses). The desired outcome can vary depending upon whether the employment specialist is looking for a specific type of work based on the job seeker's skills or has several job seekers in mind. Over time, some employment specialists may find themselves better at one approach. Their favored approach, however, may not be effective with all employers all of the time. Whenever an employer appears unresponsive, an alternative approach should be used. Using a variety of strategies can also reduce monotony throughout the workday.

Business Contacts by Telephone

Business contacts by telephone can be very effective if the employment specialist can get beyond the receptionist, who is there to decide if the call is valuable enough to forward.

Prior to making calls, it might be useful for the employment specialist to script an approach. Foreknowledge of to whom to speak and confidently requesting to be connected to that person is often effective. For example, "Good afternoon. This is Eileen Cassidy of Acme. Would you please connect me with John Freeman?" In case this direct and assertive approach does not work, the employment specialist should be prepared to respond to receptionist replies. Table 7.1 gives alternative strategies.

If the person requested is not available after another call, the employment specialist should leave a message that includes full personal identification, the name of the service represented, and the telephone number. The employment specialist should also be prepared to leave messages on voice mail. To eliminate long pauses and "ums" in message content, the employment specialist may want to write out what to say in advance. If the desired contact is repeatedly unavailable or not returning messages, the employment specialist should attempt to identify the best time of day to reach that person or an alternative contact.

Once contact is made, the employment specialist should be ready to ask the employer for a personal meeting. This contact should be brief and to the point. The following outline should be used to script the approach:

- Greet the person.
- Identify who you are.

Table 7.1. Strategies for contacting a business person through cold calling

Receptionist response
Perhaps I can help you instead?

Strategy 1
Talk slowly and deliberately and begin a long and detailed explanation about who you are and what you are attempting to do. If a receptionist is answering a number of lines and feels you are long-winded, he may forward your call.

Strategy 2
Use service lingo, which may make the receptionist feel unqualified and forward the call to someone more experienced.

Strategy 3
Ask a question that can only be answered by the person you want to reach.

Strategy 4
Recontact the person throughout the day; perhaps you will eventually get a less-experienced relief receptionist who will put your call through.

Receptionist response
We are not hiring right now.

Strategy 1
Reaffirm that this is understood and then explain you are interested in meeting with a company representative at his or her convenience so you can explain the valuable free services you have to offer.

Receptionist response
That person is not available. May I take a message?

Strategy 1
Reply that you would rather not and call back later. Ask for the receptionist's name and thank her personally for her willingness to help.

- Identify whom you represent.
- Briefly state the nature of the service offered.
- Briefly state how the service offered may benefit the employer.
- Request an informational interview to learn more about the business or a specific job.

Even with advanced preparation, this can be an unnerving event. The following tips for business contact by telephone might be useful:

- Calls should be made in a quiet office away from distractions. (Music, talking, or laughing in the background during a telephone call sounds unprofessional.)
- Smiling while talking can give the voice lift and a cheerful enthusiastic tone.
- Always be clear and honest about the specific purpose for calling.
- Set aside a block of time each day for making calls.
- Convey to the receiver through the use of active listening skills that you understand.
- Performance should be evaluated on an ongoing basis by peer review and being attuned to the receivers' reactions.
- Good communication skills are critical; take inventory of existing skills and if improvement is warranted, take action to upgrade ability.

If a position has been identified through the classified advertisements, unless otherwise specified, the first contact will be by telephone. If the company representative is too busy to meet and requests an application be dropped off instead, the employment specialist should inform the person that a meeting would take only 20 minutes or that he or she would like an opportunity to see the job prior to submitting applications to ensure only viable candidates are referred. If the employer still refuses, the employment specialist should determine the value of the opportunity and act accordingly.

Drop-In Visits

A drop-in visit has the obvious advantage of getting a "foot in the door"; however, sensitivity must be given to the time constraints placed on an employer who has not set aside time for the visit. This method may be most suitable for the service industry and larger companies that regularly post job leads. Often, an appointment to meet with the employer at a later date will need to be scheduled. However, if the employer is interested and has time, a presentation should be made on the spot.

The employment specialist should always be on the lookout for opportunities. For example, if an opportunity is spotted while shopping, it should be noted and followed up on during office hours. Opportunities present in a variety of ways, such as help wanted signs or noticing a lack of quality service due to an understaffed workforce.

Letters of Introduction

If the above efforts fail, written correspondence should be considered. The letter should explain the difficulty, acknowledge the value of the person's time, state the benefits of a meeting, and set a time for future telephone contact.

Posting, faxing, or e-mailing letters of introduction to a targeted or mass audience might also be used to introduce a service to businesses. All correspondence should lead to a request for a personal meeting. Mailing letters might be more effective with small businesses as large companies are often inundated with mail. The employment specialist

should always keep in mind that the quality of the message may determine whether a response is received.

Employer Presentation

There is virtually no way to predict in advance which employers will be receptive to supported employment programs. Decisions will be based on a number of factors, such as current needs and underlying values. Regardless, the employment specialist should try to enhance the odds of being well received by using a professional approach, including a well-groomed appearance. Role playing and observing professionals in action can be useful training activities for a novice employment specialist.

Appearance

Reportedly, an interviewer will decide whether or not to consider an applicant for a job within the first 5 minutes of an interview—a decision partially based upon the interviewee's personal appearance. Likewise, an employment specialist's image also has the potential to affect the outcome of a meeting. In *Martin's Magic Formula for Getting the Right Job*, Martin (1987) offers advice to assist college graduates in their career searches—recommendations that are also useful to employment specialists. When approaching a professional place of business, clothing should be conservative, such as a skirt or tailored suit for women and a jacket and trousers for men. In a factory setting, a more casual look may be acceptable. Shoes should always be polished and comfortable. If jewelry is to be worn, it should be conservative; male employment specialists may want to avoid more than a school or wedding ring.

It is always useful to become familiar with what the employees are wearing at the jobsite and then dress a little nicer for the interview. Dressing in sync with the company's image can give the employment specialist an edge. For instance, a dark suit might be best for a meeting with a law firm, whereas more stylish and colorful clothing is appropriate for a meeting in the fashion industry. Because it is likely that the employment specialist will be meeting with various industries, such a specialized approach to dressing might not be possible. Whenever meeting with an array of employers or when in doubt, the employment specialist's look should be neat, clean, and conservative.

Employment specialists should remember that their body language and nonverbal messages also affect an employer's outlook. Posture should be alert, expressions should convey a pleasant attitude, and eye contact should be comfortable. One way to gain insight into personal appearance is to videotape the employment specialist in a role play of an employer meeting.

Positive Attitude

Attitude and knowledge on how to build relations will directly affect an employment specialist's success at job development. If a knowledgeable employment specialist is not seeing results, then his or her strategies for implementation may need improvement. The attitude of an employment specialist should be positive. Employment specialists who believe they have no control will, in fact, have none. One person who has reflected a positive atti-

tude throughout his career as a national transition leader is Larry Naeve, who has directly helped hundreds of people with disabilities find and hold jobs.

> ***Larry Naeve*** Larry Naeve is the main director of C.I.T.Y. community services, one of the most widely known, and most emulated, transition and supported employment programs in California. He has been a leader in Los Angeles and across the country in setting policy for competitive employment opportunities for young adults with disabilities. His program is recognized as one of the best and is certified by the Commission of Accreditation for Rehabilitation Facilities. He has made many presentations and is highly recognized nationally for his innovative and creative thinking in terms of the best way to deliver transition/employment services for people with disabilities. As a transition leader, he is active on the front lines every day.

In *Job Strategies for People with Disabilities: Peterson's Guides,* Witt (1992) introduces positive reframing as a method for moving away from negative beliefs toward positive beliefs. Shifting from a powerless to empowered perspective might allow some to approach job development in a positive frame of mind. To illustrate the power of reframing, consider the examples in Table 7.2, adapted from Witt's advice to people with disabilities who are involved in an independent job search.

If the employment specialist focuses on developing relationships instead of getting a job lead, he or she cannot be rejected. Each employment specialist must view him- or her-

Table 7.2. Negative beliefs reframed into positive beliefs

Negative beliefs	Reframed positive beliefs
The job market is in recession. There are no jobs.	What recession? Obsessing over negative statistics only drags me down.
It's not what you know; it's who you know. I don't know anyone.	Everyone knows someone. I must figure out who I know and how I can expand that connection into 10.
The job seeker does not have the right skills.	I have an array of services and accommodations to offer employers. My challenge is to effectively present to employers how these services can benefit them. If things do not work out, I will assist the person in finding different work.
The competition is overwhelming.	I will look for opportunities to create jobs.
Employers do not want to hire someone with a disability.	Employers want to hire someone to get the job done. The people I represent would be dedicated and hard-working employees any employer should be happy to have on the payroll.
The job seeker cannot compete with applicants who do not have disabilities.	The ADA helps, but I must convince the employer he has nothing to lose.
Employers will not be willing to make the job accommodations as needed.	Many employers will voluntarily make job accommodations for qualified applicants. Most employers are required by law to make reasonable accommodations.

self as an educator and builder of employer relations rather than a salesperson who expects an immediate payoff. If the employment specialist feels continually rejected perhaps he or she needs to reconsider this career choice.

Business Meeting Guidelines

Some employers will want a brief, well-organized presentation, while others may invite a detailed description of services. Some might be interested in personal accounts of success stories, while others will want to know facts and program statistics. The content of the employer presentation may also vary depending upon whether the employment specialist is pursuing an available position or is interested in gaining more information about future work opportunities. The following outline lays a foundation for the employer presentation.

Set the Stage At the start of the meeting, the employment specialist should explain what he or she would like to achieve. For example, "Thank you for agreeing to meet with me today. As I mentioned over the telephone, my organization offers free services to employers. These services might be able to improve your organization's efficiency as well as increase the diversity of the workforce. The people I am working for—workers with disabilities—have a range of skills and abilities. Some people are qualified for existing employment opportunities, while others have very specialized abilities. These people are looking for a way to benefit business through the use of the abilities they have. All of the services I have to offer will be provided at no cost to you. Services may include a free work environment analysis, referral of prescreened job applicants, and on-the-job skills training to the new employee, to mention a few."

Cover the Basics Next, the employment specialist should inform the employer of issues to be addressed and proceed to cover these issues in a straightforward and logical way. The employment specialist should be sure to focus on the benefits offered rather than model implementation. Employer benefits might include saving time and money on recruitment costs, reducing lag time in filling vacant positions, improving employee morale and community reputation, and attracting positive press. An example of an employment specialist's presentation is as follows:

> Today I would like to have the opportunity to learn more about your business so I can provide you with the information you need to determine if this service can be beneficial to you. In addition, I would like to establish a protocol for future relations in case you do not need services now but may desire them at a later date. The goal of this program is to identify ways to help employers meet their business demands while giving an individual who experiences disability a chance to gain or regain a position in society as a tax-paying citizen.
>
> If you are interested in exploring how we might be able to increase efficiency, a job analysis will be conducted and compared to the job seeker's strengths. Then, the data will be used to determine if any of the people I am working for can fill existing positions or offer their services in other ways. This service involves observing employees at work and then making suggestions on how the person I represent can assist you in making the best use of your resources. As an employment specialist, it will be my duty to accompany the new employee to the jobsite and arrange for any needed accommodations. These services are highly individualized and may include specialized job skills training, again at no cost to you. I will also contribute to completing the job until the new employee develops the speed and endurance needed to perform the duties independently.

Once the worker is able to perform the job to the standards you have set, I will gradually reduce my presence from the jobsite. I will, however, continue to monitor the worker's performance and will be available for additional support as necessary, such as retraining a task or teaching a new duty.

After describing the service, the employment specialist should inform the employer about available financial incentives, such as the targeted jobs tax credits (TJTC) and tax deductions for making accommodations.

Discuss Business Needs Next, the employment specialist should request permission to ask questions and discuss the employer's business needs. It may be useful to prepare a list of questions in advance—asking relevant and intelligent questions should help establish credibility with the employer. If an employer feels the employment specialist is genuinely interested in his or her needs and concerns, it may inspire confidence about establishing a relationship with the program.

The following are examples of questions that may help the employment specialist learn more about current business needs:

- Can you tell me about your business?
- How is business going?
- Do you foresee any trends that will affect your industry?
- Can you describe some of the entry-level positions?
- Do you experience a high turnover rate in any positions?
- Have you worked with a supported employment program in the past?
- Do you feel this service can augment what you are already doing?

Address Concerns and Questions Prior to concluding the meeting, invite the employer to ask questions but only after anticipating answers to some typical employer questions or objections, which unfortunately include misperceptions about working with people with disabilities. Consider the examples of employer concerns in Table 7.3.

Employment specialists may find it useful to know some statistics about workers with disabilities. The following facts from the 1994 poll by Louis Harris and Associates may come in handy when addressing employer questions or concerns.

- More than three fourths of managers surveyed say the costs of employing both workers with and without disabilities are about the same.
- Employers surveyed say the costs of accommodations virtually never drive the cost of employment above the average range of costs for all employees.
- Almost all employers surveyed reject the argument that workers with disabilities do not fit in with most workers without disabilities.
- Nearly half of employers surveyed agreed that workers with disabilities have fewer accidents on the job than workers without disabilities. (The survey did not report how many employers say workers with disabilities have an equal number of accidents on the job.)
- Three fourths of department heads and line managers surveyed rate workers with disabilities as equally or more productive than workers without disabilities.
- More than three fourths of department heads and line managers surveyed who have supervised workers with disabilities say they are no more difficult to supervise than workers without disabilities.

Table 7.3. Employer concerns

An employer had a "bad experience" with an employee with disabilities in the past, so he or she is reluctant to consider your program.
- Be empathetic.
- Explain how supported employment can address his or her concerns.
- Stress the individuality of applicants and the motivation of the people for whom you work.

A personnel manager expresses interest in your program; however, he or she suspects that the hiring supervisor may have reservations.
- Acknowledge that this is not uncommon.
- Solicit specific information.
- Explain how services can address concerns.
- Request to provide a group in-service program or to meet with the supervisor individually.

A store manager informs you that he or she has a maintenance position available but that one of the job duties involves climbing a ladder. Currently, none of the people in your referral pool are able to climb ladders.
- Explore the possibilities of trading a job duty with a person who can climb ladders.

A supervisor has positions available but continues to express the opinion that all of the positions are too demanding for someone with a disability.
- Acknowledge concern and explain that there are many accommodations that can assist with production issues.
- Explain the diversity among individuals in the referral pool.
- Explain a 100% job completion guarantee (if appropriate).

An employer expresses a concern that his or her insurance rates will rise.
- Provide information that negates this myth and offer to investigate the concern with the employer's insurance company.
- Refer the employer to others who have used the service.

A personnel director raises concerns about the possibility of the employment specialist being injured while on the premises.
- Provide a letter from your agency stating that you are covered under their policy.
- Provide a copy of the employee handbook or policy that states how worker compensation claims are handled.

- More than three fourths of department heads and line managers surveyed rate workers with disabilities as being equally or more punctual and having equal or better attendance records than workers without disabilities.
- More than three fourths of department heads and line managers surveyed rate workers with disabilities as equally or more reliable than workers without disabilities.
- More than three fourths of department heads and line managers surveyed rate workers with disabilities as equally or more willing to work hard compared with workers without disabilities.

Wrap Up At the close of the meeting, employment specialists should ask for what they want. If this is a job placement, they should emphasize the practicality of the idea and explain why it is a no-lose proposition. In addition, they should stress that the work is going to be done with little risk. If the employer is agreeable, the employment specialist should arrange to analyze the position and set up times for job interviews. If the employer is not able to grant the employment specialist's request, he or she should remain open and receptive to different opportunities.

Unusual Occurrences

During the course of an employer meeting, the employment specialist might encounter some unusual developments. Consider the following examples and possible techniques for dealing with them:

- *Issue*—Being kept waiting
 Technique—Be patient; however, if you are kept waiting for longer than 20 minutes, ask the receptionist to offer the person an opportunity to reschedule. Do not appear annoyed and be sure to reschedule while on the employer's premises.
- *Issue*—Rude reception or response
 Technique—Inform the person that he or she appears very busy and ask if you should reschedule for an alternative time or with another person. Thank him or her and leave early if needed.
- *Issue*—Periods of silence
 Technique—Plan in advance and have a list of employer assessment questions ready.
- *Issue*—Interruptions
 Technique—If the meeting is unexpectedly interrupted by a telephone call, provide a perception of privacy by focusing on a wall object or looking out the window. If an apology is offered, respond that it is no problem and proceed with the presentation.

Skill Enhancement

Job development takes an array of skills and savvy that are developed only with experience. With confidence and determination, success will occur. Every contact made offers the employment specialist an opportunity to reflect upon existing skills and determine ways to make improvements. Also consider the following methods.

- Pair up with colleagues from time to time for performance feedback.
- Videotape a simulated employer meeting with your supervisor playing the role of employer.
- Observe experienced personnel in the field to gain insight on how to strengthen your approach.
- Survey employers visited by mail or telephone. Be sure the survey is brief, concise, and easy to do and provide a self-addressed stamped envelope for its return.
- Compile data on characteristics of companies that do become involved with the program, including information about the person who was hired and those who developed the relationship.

Job Analysis

At the close of the employer meeting, the employment specialist should ask for a time to return to the business to perform a job analysis (Moon et al., 1986; Sherron & Groah, 1991). No two people have the same ability or disability, thus each job seeker presents a need for a unique worker–job situation. Job analysis involves gaining insight into what a position requires and comparing this to the job seeker's skills. The outcome of an analysis is to determine if an existing position suits the job seeker or what positions might be created to

improve overall business efficiency. During job analysis, the employment specialist should also explore the types of accommodations that would allow the job seeker to succeed in the job. Consider the following types of accommodations that can be provided to ameliorate the functional limitations of a job seeker.

Job Restructuring

Job restructuring involves the redistribution of job functions that cannot be performed by the job seeker. An employer may assign a nonessential job function to another worker, often in exchange for a task the person who experiences a disability can do (Moon et al., 1990).

Modifying Equipment, Acquiring Adaptive Device, or Reorganizing the Work Station

Assistive technology ranges from high-tech and costly, such as voice synthesizing software for a computer operator candidate who is blind, to low-tech and cost-free, such as raising a desk for an office aide due to mobility problems (Moon et al., 1990). The job analysis can reveal ways to adapt the environment to promote independent performance on the job.

There are a number of resources available to assist in identification of accommodations. One of the most comprehensive services is the Job Accommodation Network (JAN). The employment specialist can telephone a JAN consultant toll-free who will search (free of charge) the computer base for a listing of accommodations.

Hiring a Personal Assistant

Sometimes a job seeker may want to hire an assistant for help in performing a job. In this case it is important to be sure that the assistant is not doing the job for the employee but providing a support service.

Building Employer Awareness of the Need for Jobs

Understanding the suitability of work from the viewpoint of the person with the disability is always foremost. However, employers have begun taking a more active role in the job search, analysis, placement, and supervision activities necessary in supported employment. In the northern Colorado towns of Fort Collins and Greeley, for instance, the Center for Technical Assistance and Training (CTAT), an organization that promotes employment for citizens with disabilities, and the Colorado Division of Vocational Rehabilitation (VR) developed a Corporate Partnership Initiative that is largely directed at a grass roots level by people with disabilities and local business.

As the first step in building employer awareness of the need for jobs, professional staff from CTAT and VR began joining local business and service groups, such as the Chamber of Commerce, Rotary, and Kiwanis, as active members, willing to participate and contribute to products and events (publicity newsletters, fundraisers, etc.). Simultaneously, individuals with disabilities needing jobs and/or family members were involved in meeting members of the local business community. In only a few weeks, enough connections were made to form Business Advisory Councils (BACs) in each community dominated by local employers representing both small business and large corporations (e.g., Hewlett-Packard;

Sykes Enterprises, Inc.; Bank One; NORWEST Banks; Electronic Fab Tech Corporation; Professional Finance Company; Teledyne; Express Personnel; State Farm Insurance; United Airlines) and people with disabilities, with a few human services and school personnel to explain and manipulate disability systems.

These councils meet monthly and each member is required to bring the Corporate Initiative manager and the local VR counselors at least one employment lead or "contact." Consumers enrolled in Vocational Rehabilitation are asked if they have an interest in exploring employment in the "contact's" business. This contact is then called and given the name of the BAC member who suggested calling, and an appointment to discuss employment opportunities is made. Often, these contacts are suppliers of the BAC member's business and a natural business relationship already exists that can be leveraged into job development. Often, too, the BAC members find that they have jobs available in their companies and help minimize the red tape and other roadblocks inherent in employment. Because the BACs include the active participation of business and consumers and the expectation that employment outcomes are the absolute priority for all BAC activity, mutually beneficial and respectful relationships form that create a force for job development in the community (Griffin & Hammis, 1994).

Critical lessons that seem to have universal applicability to all communities are being learned through Corporate Initiatives across the United States:

1. In order to create employment and act as a representative for people with disabilities, the job developer should be well known in the business community and should have people with disabilities take the lead in creating business and personal relationships.

2. Businesses are particularly concerned about the future of students leaving public schools and most service organizations such as Chambers of Commerce, the Elks, the Rebekahs, local churches, and city/county governments all seem to have committees studying school improvement that welcome contributing committee members and can assist with job development efforts.

3. The use of Social Security Work Incentives, such as Plans for Achieving Self Support (PASS), are especially intriguing to people with disabilities and their families. PASS allows individuals receiving Social Security payments to shelter that income and set it aside to purchase employment enhancing assets such as transportation, cosmetic surgery, computers, and training. Typically, citizens with disabilities live in poverty, unable to earn a living for fear of losing medical benefits and unable to own employment-related assets that most people leverage to make themselves employable. A case in point is a mechanic applying for a job. Without a comprehensive set of tools, the mechanic is of little use; but with tools, the employer can exploit this resource in exchange for salary (Hammis, 1994). PASS has allowed a number of individuals working with CTAT to gain employment by protecting benefits while the individuals purchased cars, electric wheelchairs, training, computerized sewing machines, and so on.

4. Employers are intrigued by the use of Social Security Work Incentives and understand that taxpayer savings are an economic resource and that the supports available for purchase through such incentives as PASS help make employment possible for people once considered "too disabled" to work.

5. Employers understand their workforce and production needs much better than people who do not work daily in those businesses. Therefore, forging alliances with employers who can assist in job restructuring and on-site training is more efficient and natural than imposing outside human services personnel who typically must first learn jobs, then teach the new worker. In numerous cases, co-workers effectively instruct new workers with disabilities in task performance with employment specialists offering instructional support to the pair or to the experienced worker regarding effective teaching and supervision strategies.

6. Peer marketing—using an employer to influence other employers to hire an individual with a disability—is much more powerful and effective than having a human services representative act as the sole job developer. Employment development can benefit from creative rehabilitation professional expertise, but businesspeople should also work face to face with people with disabilities in need of employment and their peers. Hiring people with disabilities is, unfortunately, still viewed as a business risk. Hearing of successful employment from both a business and workers with disabilities provides powerful support to employers who have not hired a worker with disabilities. Human services roles seem most appropriate in the context of getting these constituents together and providing technical and strategic support until a quality relationship is solid.

Job Carving

The process of breaking jobs down into their key components and reassigning those pieces in more efficient or understandable ways is called *job carving*. This strategy is a creative extension of job development that results in job restructuring or job creation (i.e., typical work duties are reassigned to one or more workers with disabilities or a new job is created to address efficiency needs). Although full-time employment is certainly a reasonable outcome, job carving is typically utilized with individuals in transition from school to work or supported employment who, for a variety of reasons, including physical disability, psychiatric illness, diminished intellectual capacity, medical fragility, unavailable supports, and choice, may not be in the market for full-time employment (Griffin & Winter, 1988). Care must be taken not to create jobs that devalue people with disabilities by physically separating them from other workers or by having them perform tasks that are considered bothersome, dangerous, or unpleasant.

Many variables are associated with the job carving process. For instance, the marketing approach in job carving should be deliberate and businesslike. Job developers should approach potential employers as diagnosticians, ready to determine needs and offer solutions to productivity challenges. Another variable is student or adult services consumer employment objectives. No job development effort can take place without a thorough understanding of the type of work that is suitable and acceptable. The attitude of co-workers is also an issue. In creating employment opportunities, the "corporate culture" (i.e., the unwritten rules of a particular workplace) must be taken into consideration.

A job was once carved for an individual to pick up and deliver parts for an automobile dealership. Employing a designated parts delivery driver as a financially efficient method for this dealership resulted

in problems. The dealership's traditional method involved taking a parts order from a local garage and then pulling a parts department, services department, or repair employee from his or her current task to deliver the part. This was very inefficient, but the employees enjoyed it because they got to leave the building for a while and take a break from their regular duties. The job created for a person who wished to work under 30 hours a week did not last because the other employees saw this new worker as taking one of the few benefits associated with their jobs. Careful observation of the worksite culture might have indicated the need for a different employment approach and avoided this job loss.

Observation, in addition to frequent employer contact, is the key to job carving. Without spending time in the actual business setting or one very closely associated with it, the job creation process will not succeed. Every workplace is different in culture, quality standards, personalities, and procedures (Deal & Kennedy, 1982). To ensure a good employer–employee fit, the job match process must include jobsite research based upon consumer desire and employer need.

Steps Involved in Job Carving

Table 7.4 illustrates the steps associated with the creation of new employment opportunities. The first step, determining the student's needs and desires, is critical to employment success. Efficacious job development must be based upon student choice. Many transition-age students, for instance, have had little exposure to the variety of vocational options found in the employment marketplace. Creating a series of specific work experiences by carving tasks amenable to and manageable by a student can provide valuable information regarding work tolerance, likes and dislikes, learning styles, support needs, and necessary social skills. The teacher or job coach relies upon this information when a real first job is considered.

The second and third steps are to research and visit targeted businesses. These steps concern the prospecting phase of job development. Here, there are few shortcuts. In order to develop a niche for a prospective worker, some diagnosis of employer need must occur. Most employers do not know that they could benefit from hiring people with disabilities,

Table 7.4. Creation of employment opportunities

Step	Action
1	Determine student needs and desires.
2	Research target businesses, including personnel, training, retention, competition, and technical issues.
3	Visit sample target businesses.
4	Inventory activities of typical workers performing target tasks.
5	Observe corporate culture, including rules and rituals.
6	Task analyze duties and determine consumer capabilities, training, and assistance needs.
7	Negotiate with employer.
8	Teach and refine tasks.
9	Build on typical supports and relationships.
10	Fade.
11	Maintain consultative role.

so a deliberate, carefully paced, employer-education phase must be initiated to provide specific information on the benefits of working with the school or agency. Typically, those benefits include prescreening of applicants, on-the-job training, and increased efficiency through task analysis and environmental modifications. Positive outcomes from this education phase generally develop slowly and methodically. Specialized services have kept people with disabilities out of the public eye and created many prejudices, which take time and effort to overcome.

The employment specialist usually spends a few hours in the target business to complete the fourth step: recording the actions and interactions of workers performing their jobs. Step five, observing the corporate culture, is also addressed during this phase. In both steps, patterns of work accomplishment and social activity are inventoried and later considered when determining employment possibilities.

The sixth step is a task analysis of duties and a determination of the candidate's capabilities. In this step, a job concept or a grouping of job tasks materializes, and the job matching and training plan process should proceed. In the next step, this information is taken to the employer, who has been kept up-to-date throughout the process; and negotiations of placement, pay, hours, benefits, supports, and supervision are undertaken. The assumption is that the student or adult consumer is an active participant in this process and agrees to the job specifics being explored.

The eighth and ninth steps involve teaching at the jobsite and enlisting the co-workers to build supports and relationships for the student. Involving the assigned company supervisor in the early phases of training, asking a co-worker to help explain and demonstrate production shortcuts, and making sure that the new employee interacts with other personnel at clock-in and clock-out times and during breaks and lunch are critical to acceptance and job retention.

Fading, step ten, is critical to worksite integration. Professional human services presence in the worksite carries a stigma that impedes the sense of belonging necessary for the new worker to become a vital participant in the workforce (Nisbet & Hagner, 1988). Fading of the trainer or job coach should be planned and systematic. The employer and others in the business should be informed, as appropriate, of the fading process (Moon, Inge, et al., 1990).

Finally, the adult services agency that supports the new worker should remain in low-profile contact with the employer. If a business-service approach was used in creating the employment opportunity, a consultative role with the employer should be maintained. The goal here is not necessarily to develop more jobs for people with disabilities, but rather to assist with advancing the career of the person placed or to refill the position if the person chooses to leave the business. There is a risk of creating worker and employer dependence on the service agency. Hence, care should be exercised to serve unobtrusively in a consultative problem-solving role.

Illustrations of Successful Job Carving

A few examples of job carving follow to illustrate the strategies or approaches employed in developing work experiences and employment options for individuals with severe disabilities.

Business Efficiency and Productivity Strategy The business efficiency and productivity strategy can be utilized with a variety of service and manufacturing operations.

Jim *Jim's Texaco is located in a Southwest town of approximately 10,000 people that is slowly becoming a year-round resort due to its proximity to mountains, fishing, hiking, camping, and skiing. Jim has operated the gas station for more than 10 years and usually works alone. He has had part-time help but finds local college students unreliable and hard to supervise.*

An employment specialist observed Jim over an 8-hour day. His tasks were recorded, and he was later questioned concerning income, demand for his mechanical repair services, and so on. The inventory revealed that Jim spent approximately 4 hours a day performing mechanical repairs, for which there was always ample demand. The rest of Jim's day was consumed with the activities listed in Table 7.5. A quick check of these activities and a little behind-the-scenes research, which included calls to the local gasoline wholesaler, the National Automobile Dealers Association, and General Motors, revealed that Jim earns $34 per hour when performing mechanical repairs and tune-ups, but only $.05 per gallon when pumping gasoline. However, Jim must sell gasoline to keep the Texaco franchise. The other activities, which account for half the work day, have little direct revenue-generating impact on Jim's business.

Further discussion revealed that Jim takes home approximately $26,000 per year. If Jim were to spend 8 hours per day performing mechanical repairs, which he enjoys and for which there is a waiting market, his annual salary would double to $52,000. By carving out the activities that are vital to the operation of Jim's Texaco and creating a job for an individual with a severe disability, the owner can concentrate on the more profitable activities. The new position might have an annual salary of $12,000 (a very reasonable salary for this type of job), thereby reducing Jim's take-home pay to $40,000 per year. This new salary represents a marked increase over the original $26,000 figure and will appeal to Jim if a cautious, relationship-building sales approach is utilized (Griffin, 1991). The actual job created, of course, depends upon consumer choice, competence, and available supports, as well as local market conditions and the general climate of the work environment.

Table 7.5. An inventory of Jim's duties at his gas station

Jim's inventory (nonsequential)	Efficient and productive for Jim	Valued or useful labor for an assistant
Answer telephones	Sometimes	Yes
Pump gas	No	Yes
Check oil	No	Yes
Trouble shoot	Yes	N/A
Wash windshields	No	Yes
Clean tools	No	Yes
Wash/detail cars	Sometimes	Yes
Make mechanical repairs	Yes	No
Go to post office	No	Yes
Restock shelves/islands	No	Yes
Check-in deliveries	No	Yes
Talk with customers	Sometimes	Maybe
Perform tune-ups	Yes	No/maybe
Fix flat tires	No	Yes
Clean facility	No	Yes

The business efficiency and productivity strategy, which might seem beneficial to all employers, is not always workable. In a variety of bureaucracies, such as government offices, university departments, and some social services entities, increased efficiency does not have a cash payoff and, therefore, is difficult to engineer.

Shelly A student, Shelly, was identified who had good interactive and communication skills, could orient well to landmarks, could match and sort items by color, and enjoyed walking. The job developer observed that university department secretaries left their desks at various times in the morning and again in the afternoon to pick up incoming mail and to deliver outgoing mail at the campus post office. The job developer recorded this activity and estimated that approximately 15 civil service secretaries spent more than half an hour per day walking to and from the post office. The developer then checked with university personnel to determine the average salary of a department secretary, broke that down into an hourly wage, and multiplied that by half an hour.

The activity of the 15 secretaries was costing the university approximately $20,000 per anum. The job developer reasoned that a 4- or 5-hour-a-day job could be created for the individual with disabilities at $5 per hour, plus benefits and vacation, for under $7,000 per year. This would save the university $13,000 in lost productivity and quell complaints by the secretaries who did not enjoy having to leave their other assigned duties twice each day.

This information was well received by the university vice president. The efficiency increase would benefit staff morale and improve service to faculty and college students; however, the personnel system was such that all available positions were filled, and funding for new positions was restricted by the state legislature. No new positions could be added without significant maneuvering, which would be inconvenient, time-consuming, and potentially politically hazardous for the vice president.

In short, the rigid employment systems of some bureaucracies may dictate that other approaches or long-term efforts are required to break into these markets.

Consultative/Employment Service Strategy The consultative/employment service strategy can be utilized with a variety of businesses, especially those that have high personnel turnover or seasonal market fluctuations. Jobs typically having high turnover may not be choice jobs for anyone, however. These positions should not be utilized as dumping grounds for people with severe disabilities and may indeed result in heightened anxiety about work demands, job loss, and employment expectations. These jobs should be approached with common sense and the understanding that such positions can be great first jobs or seasonal jobs—and a step on the career ladder. Again, it is important to note the corporate culture and work environment of businesses that appear to have high personnel turnover.

There was a motel that had a high turnover rate, but after a few days of on-site observation, a core group of stable employees became apparent. This group of housekeepers had long-term employment records and shared a highly ritualized culture that was hard to infiltrate. Admission was gained through showing work stamina and a strong sense of insider humor, and by contributing to the purchase of donuts, soda, and snacks for team members to share. Failure to understand the culture and

take slow, decisive action to fit in led quickly to exclusion. New employees who failed to perceive these rites were left to fend for themselves. In this situation, many workers simply moved on to the next job.

A good job developer recognizes these worksite traits and develops strategies to make consumers members of the workforce, thus protecting the job and the individual.

In the consultative/employer service strategy, research is performed to find business trends conducive to job development (Griffin, 1989). In keeping with the motel example, research was performed in a Western city to assist in the creation of a service niche for a local supported employment agency. The research included the identification of motels near the homes of individuals seeking first and second jobs in housekeeping departments. Calls were made to the owners of a dozen small- to moderate-size motels.

Almost all of the owners were willing to discuss their turnover, recruitment, and training issues. From these discussions, it was determined that the average moderate-size motel in this area employed five housekeepers, one of whom was the head housekeeper with additional duties, responsibilities, and pay. The average work week for the housekeepers was 40 hours in 6 days, and the average pay was $4.50 per hour with varying benefits. Head housekeepers made $6–$8 per hour. Average annual turnover was approximately 200% with a range of 80%–300%. Turnover varies by city and motel, necessitating case-specific research.

When the housekeeping department terminates the employment of a staff member, the manager or the head housekeeper performs the work or sees that the duties are covered. Head housekeepers get the first option to work extra hours for overtime pay in many cases. Usually, overtime is split between the head housekeeper and the other housekeepers. In any case, the managers or owners view this as a possible time for reduced work quality, poorer customer service, and additional cost. The search for another housekeeper is vital and is initiated through classified advertisements, calling a pool of former employees, or through word of mouth to friends of the other housekeepers.

Once a new employee is identified, a week is often required for training on company standards. This pulls the head housekeeper away from typical duties and requires more overtime expenditures. When recruitment and training are completed, the expense to the employer can range from $500 to $2,000, largely in hidden costs. If the motel employs five maids and has an average turnover rate of 200%, the employer stands to lose as much as $20,000 per year in hiring and training costs. The job developer must create a problem-solving relationship with the motel manager or owner and approach the discussion of these costs over time. A rush to accomplish this can cause the owner to feel incompetent or angry, inhibiting employment opportunities.

A job developer can approach the manager with a possible employment service strategy. This service might include hiring, screening, training, and follow-up. Charging for this service, based on an analysis of what the employer stands to save by hiring one or two people through the service agency, is also a reasonable business activity. When people get something for nothing, their dedication to it is minimal, and if the provider agency does not value the employment services it offers, ongoing service accountability to the employer is diminished. Good employment services are worth paying for, and the addition of a market-based price may raise the expectations and accomplishments of all involved parties.

Another strategy is to perform an analysis of housekeeper routines, and, in a fashion similar to Jim's Texaco, carve out unproductive or duplicative efforts to make all workers more productive. This also reduces the inconvenience associated with a team member quitting. Such carved duties at a motel might include stripping beds, emptying trash cans, stocking supply carts, and replenishing towels in towel carts. All of these activities save time and make the workers more productive.

Making people more productive can have the short-range effect of lowering weekly paychecks, however. This event can lead to trouble for the new employee if he or she is viewed by the others as the cause for their misfortune. If this situation occurs, a strategy should be developed with the employer. Perhaps increased productivity dictates that the next vacancy not be filled, thus guaranteeing full employment for those remaining while securing the need for the newly created assisting position.

Many businesses and offices of all types face similar circumstances and can benefit from consolidating activities into a new core job or jobs. Grease Monkey, a quick oil-change franchise company, has carved a number of duties to speed production and smooth operations. Customers at Grease Monkey are greeted by an attendant who takes vital information on the service desired. Quickly, an employee begins to vacuum the carpets, while another cleans windows. The vehicle is pulled inside a work bay, and one employee, stationed in the grease pit, drains the oil and lubricates the chassis. While topside, employees check tire pressure, fill fluid reservoirs, and add new oil. The whole process takes less than 15 minutes and costs a little less than typically slower service at a local garage. The labor costs for Grease Monkey can be higher than other companies in the oil change business because Grease Monkey has as many as four employees working on one car; however, customer satisfaction, resulting from convenient service hours, short wait periods, and quality service, brings an increase in highly profitable, repeat business.

Employment specialists looking for summer employment for students can also find the consultative/employment service strategy useful. One possible avenue to creating employment is to simply walk around the community and note all of the odd jobs that the city or county government has overlooked. This might include painting sign posts or buildings, cleaning and mowing vacant lots, watering flower beds in the city park, or performing maintenance on city vehicles and equipment—tasks predictably overlooked by city officials during the summer due to the activity of road repair, the impact of tourism in some locales, and the shortage of staff due to vacation schedules. By approaching the city manager, the mayor (who probably chairs the ubiquitous mayor's committee on disability), or the public works director and explaining that there is a waiting workforce, temporary summer employment can be created. These jobs represent valuable evaluation and experiential opportunities for transition-age students, teachers, and new job coaches. Towns and cities often utilize summer youth employment programs operated by entities such as the local JTPA vendor. Supervision, training, and wage assistance is available and should be utilized by schools, families, employers, and adult services providers.

The Interactive Duties Strategy The interactive duties strategy shares aspects with the others but is presented to show how job restructuring can lead to the creation of natural or typical supports.

A welding shop operation was observed and inventoried to determine a possible job match for an individual with severe mental retardation. The shop employed four welders who performed all duties associated with business, except accounting, which was handled by an outside agency.

In order to create a naturally supportive environment and minimize job coach presence, the inventory of daily activities facilitated the identification of tasks that could be carved for this individual to perform. This also included duties that normally would be accomplished by two welders working together. The sales approach here emphasizes that now, instead of having two welders, who each earn $12 per hour, to perform a task, one welder and the newly hired assistant, earning less, can perform the same job at reduced cost and greater efficiency.

This example can be modified to fit many industries. Table 7.6 illustrates the tasks that are performed routinely, possible carved tasks, and the duties that can be performed by the assistant with other workers or performed in the presence of co-workers. The interactive duties strategy decreases job coach presence and stigma, emphasizes natural supervision and co-worker involvement, and reduces consumer reliance on service systems (Rogan, 1990).

White-collar employment also offers diverse opportunities to create employment. In one case, an inventory was performed of an office administrative assistant's duties and interactions. Core duties included answering telephones, word processing, preparing bulk mailings, filing, desktop publishing, bookkeeping, ordering supplies, photocopying documents, running errands, and coordinating company travel logistics. As the business grew, juggling all of these duties became increasingly difficult.

The job developer identified a student interested in office work, contacted several employers, performed job duty inventories by observing and interviewing clerical staff, and approached one of the employers with an efficiency plan. The business manager, consumer, administrative assistant, and job developer created a clerical assistant position that is supervised by the administrative assis-

Table 7.6. Job carving at a welder's shop

Welder's inventory (nonsequential)	Carved tasks	Interactive and shared tasks
Clock-in	Yes	Yes
Drink coffee and talk	Yes	Yes
Get work orders	Yes	Yes
Design and trouble shoot	No	No
Weld	No	Maybe
Change welding tanks	Yes	Yes
Sort scraps	Yes	Maybe
Carry scraps to recycling or trash bin	Yes	Sometimes
Clean work area	Yes	Yes
Clean facility	Yes	Maybe
Label stock and supplies	Yes	Yes
Check-in and stock deliveries	Yes	Yes
Talk with customers	No	Maybe
Lunch/breaks: Talk and joke	Yes	Yes
Check-out; ride home	Yes	Yes

tant. The individual in this position performs filing, bulk mail preparation, and photocopying. The job is part time, working with a variety of professionals who are well connected in their community, and all of the work is performed with or near co-workers without disabilities. No job coach is necessary on site due to management's commitment to use co-workers in the mentoring process. The employer saw immediate improvement in work quality, customer service, and office efficiency. The administrative assistant got a helping hand and lessened his work stress.

Conclusion

In carving and analyzing jobs for individuals with disabilities, the employment specialist must be open to learn and willing to grow. Approaches must be flexible, creative, and adaptable to the employer's needs. If at first the employment specialist does not get a placement, he or she must continue to believe in the power to effect change in nonresponsive attitudes. The key is education; no contact can be viewed as a failure if the employment specialist remembers his or her role as an educator. The decision to accept circumstances as they exist or accept the responsibility to make changes is definitely within the employment specialist's control.

The information presented in the job development and job carving examples is related to specific research or to individuals with unique employment goals. Specific market situations and worksite cultures vary drastically by region and town; however, the general concepts presented here should generalize to a variety of employment settings and situations. The implementation of a job carving approach is at first quite time-consuming and, therefore, not readily utilized in its more sophisticated forms. If the process outlined here is considered, and significant attention is given to addressing both student/adult consumer and employer concerns, lessened reliance on service system supports and increased job tenure should result. Employers understand job carving and regularly re-engineer workplace processes to accommodate new equipment, changing personnel, and variable production schedules. Employers and prospective employees who have disabilities must play an active role in the design of individualized jobs and job carving. Corporate partnerships and supported employment all function together in an integrated quality employment development approach.

7
Study Questions

1. What is "job carving," and what are the benefits to individuals with disabilities and businesses?

2. What are three sources of job contacts, and how can each be utilized effectively?

3. What are five steps in a business contact "script"?

4. How can employment specialists address the concerns and questions of managers and supervisors?

5. What are some ways that employment specialists can improve their job development skills?

6. What are three ways of accommodating workers with disabilities? Give an example of each.

7. What is the "consultative/employment service" strategy, and how can this model be utilized by teachers?

8

Vocational Placements and Careers

Upon completion of this chapter, the reader will be able to do the following:

- Name four values that should be associated with quality work programs
- Understand vocational integration and its importance
- Discuss the process of obtaining vocational rehabilitation services
- Present six models of vocational placement and give examples of each
- Know what supported employment is and how it differs from sheltered work
- Discuss the role of natural supports in the workplace
- Contrast the features of integrated employment with those of segregated employment
- Describe major aspects of PL 101-336, the Americans with Disabilities Act (ADA) of 1990

David *David*[1] *is 19 years old and has acquired brain injury. He resides at home with his parents and a 13-year-old sister. David presents himself as being meticulously groomed and extremely talkative and sociable. Just prior to David's 10th birthday, he was hit by an automobile while walking.*

[1]This case study is taken from West, M.D., Gibson, K., & Unger, D. (1996). The role of the family in school-to-work transition. In G.H.S. Singer, A. Glang, & J.M. Williams (Eds.), *Children with acquired brain injury: Educating and supporting families* (pp. 208–209). Baltimore: Paul H. Brookes Publishing Co.; reprinted by permission.

He was in a coma for 3–4 days, with further coma induced to reduce his pain and discomfort. He sustained damage to the right frontal part of the brain with generalized swelling. David reportedly did not have a history of serious injury, illness, or seizures prior to his injury and reached developmental milestones well within typical or advanced limits prior to his injury. As a result of his injury, David has no peripheral vision and a hearing loss in his right ear that is not correctable with a hearing aid. Often, his voice tone and volume are loud, possibly due to his hearing loss. Although he speaks clearly and in sentences, he appears to have some difficulty with expressive language, especially in formulating his thought process and word retrieval. David also has significant difficulties in both short- and long-term memory and a limited attention span.

Prior to his current educational placement, David had been integrated with the assistance of a full-time aide. David was able to maintain progress for many years following his injury because there were minimal demands for higher level, independent reasoning. However, as educational demands increased, David encountered extreme difficulty in advanced reasoning skills. He currently attends a self-contained class for students labeled as having mild to moderate mental retardation. The class focuses on teaching students functional academics and appropriate work behaviors and also provides students with nonpaying, community-based work experiences. David has participated in a community-based work experience at McDonald's and worked in a cafeteria performing stocking.

A representative from the school system met with David and his parents to discuss referring David to a local supported employment program for job placement and training while David was still in school. After hearing about the program, David and his parents decided that they were interested in his receiving these services. David's VR counselor made the referral to the supported employment provider, and a home visit was scheduled so that a representative from the supported employment program and the state Department of Rehabilitative Services could meet with David and his parents.

During the home visit, the job coach described the services that the program offered and asked David and his parents questions regarding David's prior work experiences, his general likes and dislikes, what types of things might be important to David in working in the job of his choice (e.g., location, type and size of business, work hours, transportation), his vocational goals and experience, and who might be available to assist David in any areas where support might be needed. For example, David said that he was interested in working full time and would like to work during school at a business close to where he went to school. His parents had suggested that it might be good for David to begin working part time and build up his stamina and then he could ask for more hours if the job permitted.

After the home visit, the job coach initiated a community-based situational assessment with David. At one assessment site, a buffet-style restaurant, David worked side by side with another employee who prompted David on what to do. He was responsible for filling pans and bowls with food items and then placing them in the appropriate spot on the buffet table. David needed frequent prompting in order to remember where to return the leftover food items after he was through filling the pan or bowl. He had no difficulty reading the chart that showed where the item was to be placed on the buffet table and was able to count the number of spaces to place the pan or bowl accordingly. The co-worker did not seem to mind that after David returned from the buffet table, he needed to be prompted to the next task. The job coach noted that a checklist would be extremely useful for David in making him more independent on the job.

Because David was very social and wanted contact with the public, his school teacher, parents, and job coach agreed that David would need a job where there would be a lot of interaction with people and support from co-workers to stay on task. From the information that the job coach obtained from the assessments and David's records, it was evident that David would also require a job that was repetitive in nature and would be performed in a predictable environment. David would also benefit from the use of memory strategy training techniques, such as notebooks or calendars and schedules.

After the job coach visited the restaurant, the teacher called and said that David had asked the employer for a job at the restaurant. The teacher felt that the employer was very receptive to working with a supported employment program and might be willing to hire David. The job coach is currently in the process of following up on the lead that was provided by both the consumer and the teacher and hopes that a potential job for David can be identified at the restaurant.

David is a good example of the many students with special needs who must decide on what type of postschool placement and career path they will follow. As most children leave middle school and enter high school, their thoughts turn to college, jobs, careers, and, essentially, what they are going to do with their lives. For tens of thousands of young people with disabilities, the questions are as follows: Can I get off a waiting list and into a vocational training program? Will Vocational Rehabilitation (VR) find me eligible for services? Can I get a job that pays more than $4.50 an hour? Will I be stuck in the same job for the rest of my life? Will I always be in an adult activity center or a sheltered workshop? For decades, the answers to these questions were not very encouraging. In fact, most people with disabilities were happy if they received any level of service. The opportunity to choose a different job, particularly one that came with decent wages and 40 working hours a week, was a rare occurrence.

With the advent of supported employment for people with disabilities, the passage of PL 101-336, the American with Disabilities Act (ADA) of 1990, and the concomitant thinking, there is greater vocational opportunity than ever for young people with disabilities. In rehabilitation and other postsecondary agencies, there is an increasingly strong feeling that vocational services should make transition-age students a priority—a feeling that has been intensified by the large investment in resources for special investment entitlement programs. This chapter is about vocational placement options and models for providing vocational services as well as different types of jobs, careers, and opportunities that can and should be made available to young people with disabilities (Siegel, Avoke, Paul, Robert, & Gaylord-Ross, 1991).

Sheltered workshops or part-time, entry-level service jobs are no longer appropriate end points for young people with disabilities leaving schools; most of them and their families have much higher aspirations. Although for some, segregated day programs may be the only placement option, most students with disabilities need to aspire to competitive employment in a career as their first option and work to achieve that before settling for less. If people with disabilities do not view themselves positively and have high vocational aspirations, then the expectations of advocates, family members, friends, and others working on their behalf will reflect that position.

Important Values in Vocational Programs

Before reviewing the vocational options that are available to transition-age youth, it is necessary to understand the values that should be present in any vocational option model or arrangement. Educators and employment specialists must know what to look for in a given job situation in order to help students to make decisions. Therefore, descriptions of some aspects of attractive jobs are provided below.

Student Satisfaction with the Job

Motivation is one of the most important elements of good work performance. In order for students to want to work and do a good job, they must be sufficiently motivated. Motivation can be developed in a number of ways, but it helps if the person wants to do the job, likes the work environment, and feels that he or she is useful and productive. Student satisfaction with a job can be shaped by reinforcement given by school personnel, such as counselors, teachers, work-study coordinators, and principals. Reinforcement is best delivered by jobsite visits and telephone calls. In addition, family members, particularly parents, can encourage a strong work ethic to enhance the likelihood of job satisfaction. Finally, employers or co-workers can provide reinforcement by giving the new workers frequent feedback about how they are doing and how valuable they are.

Test, Hinson, Solow, and Keul (1993) have stressed the importance of job satisfaction for supported employees, linking job satisfaction to the social validity of supported employment:

> The direct consumer of supported employment is the worker with severe disabilities. Thus determining job satisfaction of workers in supported employment would be one potential measure of the social validity of supported employment. Job satisfaction data provide a means by which persons in supported employment can begin to socially validate empirically demonstrated outcomes. (p. 222)

All school personnel involved in finding jobs for young people with disabilities should strive for student satisfaction (West & Parent, 1992). If the student does not feel that he or she had a choice in selecting a job, then the probability of a meaningful work experience is low. Wehmeyer's 1994 study seems to further affirm this belief, showing that, of more than 200 people with disabilities, those in competitive employment felt substantially greater control over their lives than their counterparts in sheltered workshops—a finding echoed by Parent (1994), who conducted more than 250 interviews with people working in competitive employment. Clearly, successful work experiences are a key element to one's satisfaction and quality of life.

Wages and Fringe Benefits

Most people are not intrinsically motivated to work; they need decent pay and reasonable fringe benefits. Students and other young adults with disabilities are no different. The opportunity to earn competitive wages, to receive time off for illness and vacations, and to be enrolled in insurance programs is viewed very positively. However, competitive pay and compensation arrangements are often hard to find for young people with disabilities who are starting their vocational careers. Therefore, it is not unreasonable to assume a less than optimal arrangement initially (West, Kregel, & Banks, 1990). However, these factors are important in determining the value with which the job will be viewed.

Amount of Work Available and Scheduling

Another value to consider when developing jobs for people with disabilities is the number of hours that are available for the person to work each week. In too many cases, employers try to assign people with disabilities and other economic disadvantages only 15–20 hours of work per week to avoid paying fringe benefit costs. Furthermore, their schedules may be erratic and undependable. As most young people with disabilities are not able to advocate exclusively for themselves with employers and in the workplace, rehabilitation counselors and school vocational personnel should show them how to negotiate for better work arrangements.

Career Focus

Vocational training and job placement programs should extend into careers. Isolated jobs and episodic attempts at different training experiences are very discouraging to people with disabilities; this is also a very inefficient way to go about long-term vocational planning. Jumping from job to job will not yield much in the way of occupational satisfaction (Syzmanski, Hershenson, Ettinger, & Enright, 1995). Career development should begin at an early age (i.e., middle school) with the student having ample opportunities to learn about the relative merits of different types of careers (Blalock & Patton, 1996). One of the most outstanding transition leaders in the area of career development and disability is Edna Mora Syzmanski from the University of Wisconsin–Madison.

Edna Mora Syzmanski Edna Mora Syzmanski is a professor in the Department of Rehabilitation Psychology and Special Education and Director of the Rehabilitation Research and Training Center on Career Development and Advancement at the University of Wisconsin–Madison (UWM). She joined the UWM faculty in 1989. Professor Syzmanski also worked for 5 years as a vocational rehabilitation counselor and 7 years as a unit supervisor for the New York State VR agency. She has also authored numerous publications and served on several research committees.

Ms. Syzmanski is an incredible role model for rehabilitation counselors to emulate. She is highly oriented toward helping those with the greatest need and is outstanding at promoting advocacy for people with disabilities. As a university educator, she is an especially strong force on behalf of women who aspire to leadership roles in the disability field.

Vocational Inclusion

As more and more children with disabilities are attending general education schools and being educated next to children without disability labels, these students and their families are becoming more interested in being included in competitive employment arrangements. They do not wish to be segregated in vocational settings—often considered stigmatizing—that highlight their disabilities. The value of inclusion in the workplace is a major element of supported employment and influences the type of jobs, businesses, in-

dustries, and even geographical locations where people may be placed. Those who truly value integration may take somewhat less pay and stay on waiting lists longer in order to get more attractive vocational arrangements.

The Vocational Integration Index (Parent, Kregel, & Wehman, 1992) lists indicators of job quality, such as advancement into better paying jobs within the company, minimal transportation requirements, and perceived status of a given job. It is incumbent upon school counselors, vocational personnel, and particularly teachers to help students identify desirable job features when the students are 10–13 years old. Only after these values have been ascertained will there be a likelihood of student satisfaction and motivation. Unless school personnel and family members work in tandem to identify these features, reasonable vocational aspirations and positive work ethics will never be developed. As Schloss, Alper, and Jayne (1993) have observed, the issues of choice, risk, and dignity affect people with disabilities more than ever as they attempt to enter the labor force. Everybody should have the opportunity to choose what type of work they wish to do and be allowed to experience the risk of failure.

Vocational Placement Options: What Are the Choices?

Historically, there have been very limited vocational choices for people with disabilities. Those who were labeled as such were referred to rehabilitation counselors, and if the counselors could place them, they were considered lucky. In the 1960s and 1970s, the number of sheltered workshops and assorted types of day program arrangements increased dramatically, which increased the options for rehabilitation counselors but left people with disabilities looking for competitive jobs with the same poor quality of choice (Weaver, 1994). Furthermore, as Weaver has observed, many rehabilitation services are not competitively offered. As progressive thinking has prevailed, however, inclusionary work opportunities in competitive employment arrangements have become the highest goal and vocational option of choice. There is an increasing recognition that individuals with disabilities need to be heavily involved in planning their own futures (Wehmeyer & Lawrence, 1995). The following sections review different vocational options that are available in some communities in the United States. More progressive communities have better vocational options and models from which people with disabilities can choose. In addition, some of these communities have limited or stopped the development and expansion of the less desirable choices, such as large adult day activity centers.

The federal–state vocational rehabilitation program, also known as the Rehabilitation Act Amendments of 1992, PL 102-569, is the primary program through which people with disabilities apply for vocational rehabilitation assistance. However, this program is not an entitlement, meaning that some people with disabilities are not accepted into the program. Eligibility requirements vary from state to state. The sequence of activities required for entry into vocational rehabilitation is outlined in Table 8.1.

Adult Day Programs

In the United States, there are approximately 5,000 adult activity centers or day programs that serve people with mental, physical, and emotional disabilities (McGaughey, Kiernan, McNally, & Gilmore, 1993). These programs are sponsored by The Arc, United Cerebral

Table 8.1. The basic vocational rehabilitation process

Application	People who apply or are referred to the state department of vocational rehabilitation must complete applications for service. Every state has such a department.
Eligibility determination	Each person is then evaluated to determine eligibility and potential for employment. Eligible people: • Have a physical, mental, or emotional disability • Have a disability that is a substantial barrier to employment • Are reasonably expected to be employable after receiving rehabilitation services
Rehabilitation plan	Eligible individuals have been determined to work with counselors to prepare individualized written rehabilitation plans (IWRPs) that include • A vocational goal with estimated start and completion dates • Counseling and guidance activities • Specific services and their providers • The individual's rehabilitation responsibilities • Intermediate objectives • Financial services (when necessary) • Job placement activities
Services provided to eligible individuals	Rehabilitation counselors may provide any or all of the following 15 services: • Guidance and counseling • Vocational evaluation • Physical health, mental health, and medical services • Vocational training • Financial maintenance • Transportation • Family services • Interpreter services • Telecommunication aids and devices • Recruitment services in public service employment • Job placement, including supported employment placement • Postemployment services • Occupational licenses needed to enter specific occupations or employment • Rehabilitation engineering services • Any other services that can reasonably be expected to benefit an individual with a disability in obtaining employment
Job placement	At the conclusion of rehabilitation, the counselors work with the clients to find and secure suitable employment. Cases are considered closed when clients have been employed at least 60 days in suitable jobs.

Palsy Associations, local churches, and other community organizations. The bulk of community funds for mental health and mental retardation are still allocated to these types of local arrangements for people with developmental disabilities. Usually these programs offer activities of daily living, training, prevocational training, "make-work" vocational activities, field trips, recreation, and other types of special education–related curricula that people with severe intellectual disabilities are assumed to require.

Generally, these programs operate on a 9 A.M.–3 P.M. day. Often transportation is provided, and as many as 50–75 people congregate in a center. Studies have repeatedly shown that people who are placed into these centers do not leave them and never "graduate" to workshops or into competitive employment (Buckley & Bellamy, 1985). They are, in effect,

day care programs with very limited instruction for progression into real-life activities. Staffing ratios tend to be unfavorable, and staff generally work year round for low salaries. Although staff in these programs tend to be very committed to delivering the best services they can, the general notion of the adult day program operates from a flawed perspective.

Traditionally, the philosophy of the adult day program is that adults with severe disabilities should learn skills in center-based programs and, ultimately, generalize those skills into competitive employment and independent residential life. This notion is essentially based upon a medical model of training, which aims to "fix" someone's disability to make him or her well enough to successfully enter the "real world." Although a nice idea, this does not work and proves grossly inefficient when compared to providing support to people with disabilities in natural work environments and real home living environments.

In fact, there are very few positive endorsements for the large-scale maintenance of adult day programs. Most agree that they should be shut down or phased out by the year 2000, with funds transferred to providing support to people in more productive and dignified community pursuits. People with disabilities can perform quite nicely in the real world with help and support.

As community services providers become more skilled at the technical aspects of vocational program development, job development, assistive technology, and working with business and industry, there will be little or no interest or demand for adult day care services.

Rehabilitation Facilities

In the United States, sheltered workshops, which are increasingly becoming known as rehabilitation facilities, have been the predominant vehicle for providing vocational services to people with developmental disabilities. Sheltered workshops are licensed by the U.S. Department of Labor to pay less than minimum wage on a piece-rate basis for contractual work, and contracts are obtained from local businesses and industries. Traditionally, sheltered workshops have delivered services to 50–100 people with disabilities at a given time. Sheltered, nonprofit workshops exist in most parts of the United States and some have grown quite large (e.g., Goodwill Industries, Jewish Vocational Service Program).

Since the early 1970s, many sheltered workshops have been run by managers with considerable skill at operating businesses. These managers have moved toward diversifying the type of vocational services that are provided and relying less on sheltered work, which is directly tied to only one or two community contracts. For example, some facilities offer job placement services for youth with mild disabilities and a supported employment program for people with severe mental illness or traumatic brain injury. Vocational evaluation and work adjustment services may also be provided to the local rehabilitation counselor for a fee.

Typically, sheltered workshops have not been well funded by vocational rehabilitation, mental health, mental retardation, or other state agency sources. Therefore, it has been necessary for workshops to identify more funding sources and to expand in order to establish economies of scale and efficiency. A number of rehabilitation facilities were built with a lot of equipment and built-in overhead, however. Unfortunately, these costs have made rehabilitation facilities quite expensive to operate, drawing on funds that could be used for other activities, such as direct job placement services. In most states, associations for rehabilitation facilities were established as trade groups.

For most of their history, parents and families have supported sheltered workshops, pleased with their services in the absence of other viable alternatives. Sheltered workshops seemed the only vehicle for postschool service delivery for many children; because of the recommendations of professionals, many families had diminished vocational expectations for their children. Over the years, sheltered workshops have served thousands of Americans with mental disabilities. However, the U.S. Department of Labor and Buckley and Bellamy's (1985) study have documented that people with disabilities who enter sheltered workshops generally remain in them. These placements tend to be final, with extremely limited movement into competitive employment or careers in the outside world.

Bill Bill has been labeled with autism, severe retardation, mental retardation, and multiple disabilities. His parents are anxious for him to enter the local sheltered workshop even though his teachers, among others, feel that he might benefit from a competitive employment or supported employment program. But Bill's parents have already spoken with the director of the local sheltered workshop, and arrangements have been made for Bill to go to the sheltered workshop each morning during his last year of school.

At the sheltered workshop, Bill puts paper clips in boxes. He is responsible for doing 100 boxes an hour and is supposed to put 20 clips in a box. He is paid 2 pennies for every box he completes. Bill is surrounded by people with mental retardation or physical disabilities. Most of them are nonverbal or only marginally verbal. Bill's placement has no fringe benefits, no room for advancement, and only limited likelihood that Bill will be placed in competitive employment. If he is placed in competitive employment and support is not available, Bill cannot be expected to generalize any skills that he has learned into a new, faster-paced competitive environment because he has not been trained. This course, although chosen by him and his parents, will lead to a path of segregated employment and, subsequently, a dependent vocational lifestyle. Service providers, advocates, special education teachers, and families must ask themselves whether they have made the right choice when people like Bill are placed in sheltered workshops.

In the 1980s, a great deal was learned about the abilities of people with severe disabilities to work in competitive employment; with job coaches in supported employment; or with adaptive aids, compensatory strategies (Kreutzer, Wehman, Morton, & Stonnington, 1988), and rehabilitation engineering at jobsites. As thinking progressed, consumers and families demanded more jobs in competitive employment and fewer sheltered work placements. This pressure began to manifest itself in the form of conferences, journal publications, books, and—eventually—changes in state and federal policies. Less emphasis was given to center-based work activities, and industry-based and competitive employment activities received more attention. Obviously, these changes placed financial, philosophical, and programmatic pressure upon rehabilitation facilities. Clearly, maintaining the status quo was not sufficient for their long-term survival or acceptance in communities. Hence, with the support of the National Association of Rehabilitation Facilities (1989), sheltered workshops have dramatically reduced the number of staff and clients they serve and have begun to allocate more resources to supporting people in jobs in the community.

A 1991 survey conducted in 50 states found that approximately 20% of all day programs were planning to convert or redirect many of their resources into integrated employment activities (Wehman, Kregel, & Revell, 1991). This means that more money will be spent on placing people with disabilities into real jobs and less for adult activity center supervision. Furthermore, the same survey indicated that programs providing supported employment services increased from 300 to more than 2,600—a change that reflects a move away from exclusively center-based activities.

The role of community rehabilitation programs in transition planning for young people with disabilities should be community based and consumer oriented. It should not be a predominantly segregated approach. The best community-based organizations are those that can respond to the varied vocational needs of the many young people with disabilities exiting schools.

Job Placement

For years, the preferred vocational option for people with disabilities has been job placement in the competitive employment market. Employment is typically gained in one of two ways. The first is through the use of rehabilitation counselors who are located in most cities and towns through state and federal vocational rehabilitation programs and funded primarily by the federal government through the Rehabilitation Act Amendments of 1992.

Rehabilitation counselors usually have bachelor's and master's degrees in counseling, work adjustment, evaluation, and placement services. They are expected to understand all disabilities and carry extraordinarily large caseloads (i.e., 100–200 cases at a time). Subsequently, it is very difficult for counselors to provide the individualized service coordination and specialized placement services that increasing numbers of people with severe disabilities require. Furthermore, most counselors are unable to provide the extended follow-up and on-site services—such as regular visitation, telephone contact, and training—that are required to help some people with disabilities maintain employment.

Rehabilitation counselors have come under fire because of these heavy caseloads and their subsequent inability to handle the most challenging cases. In fact, several studies (Hasazi, Gordon, & Roe, 1985; Hess, Kregel, & Wehman, 1991; Wehman, Kregel, & Barcus, 1985) indicate that a family–friend network—the second method of job placement—is often a more valuable way of quickly getting jobs for people with disabilities. The family–friend network reflects an increasing reliance on people in the community—that is, employers, friends, and other individuals not involved in the vocational rehabilitation system who are willing to try to find jobs for people with disabilities. These contacts have resulted in many job placements for people with disabilities in local businesses and industry.

Mitchell Mitchell, who is 20, is diagnosed as having attention-deficit/hyperactivity disorder (ADHD), learning disabilities, and neurological impairments. He has multiple auditory and visual learning disabilities, represented by his inability to read and compute as well as his disorganized memory and planning skills. Mitchell was referred to a rehabilitation counselor by both his vocational and special education teachers. His rehabilitation counselor recently completed a special course on adults with learning disabilities and spent several hours counseling Mitchell about vocational options. Specifically, the counselor wanted to know what Mitchell liked most about work and what his "ideal job" would be.

Mitchell's father is a vice president in a bank, and Mitchell wanted to work in a similar environment. Therefore, a concerted effort was made to find a placement in a community financial institution. One of the major banks in town had a job opening for a service specialist in the car loan department. This job entailed entering all loan payments in the general ledger system and checking them against the correct account numbers. Because much of this job had been automated, the supervisor had to work specifically with Mitchell for a number of weeks. Because of Mitchell's motivation and prior interest in his father's work, however, Mitchell was able to perform this job successfully without specialized on-site help. Within 3 months, Mitchell was very pleased and satisfied with his employment.

Initially, the bank gave Mitchell only 20 hours of work per week, questioning his ability to do the job quickly enough. He has since been elevated to 40 hours per week and has even been working overtime. The major reasons for the success of this placement were 1) Mitchell's interests were given careful consideration, 2) his father's background in the field had a positive family influence, and 3) the counselor communicated frequently with the employer to verify Mitchell's progress.

Job placement for young people can and should be a reality before they exit the public school systems. Once students leave school, it becomes more difficult for them to enter the work force. Whether they acquire jobs through the rehabilitation system or through their families and friends, these students need to be directed into the mainstream work force and taught marketable skills before they become so discouraged that they choose not to work.

Transitional Employment

One of the most popular forms of vocational placement and rehabilitation that has traditionally been used for people with mental illness is called transitional employment (Beard, Probst, & Malamud, 1982; Gervey & Shafer, 1995), which is being expanded to serve more individuals. With the transitional model, rehabilitation counselors or other vocational staff are assigned to work with people who need specialized help on jobsites. Generally, there is an understanding among the client, employer, and staff person that the amount of help the individual receives will last from 2 weeks to 3 months. Furthermore, there will be limited follow-up—the employer will maintain the supervision and training of the employee just as he or she as would with an employee without disabilities.

Robert Robert, who is deaf and has mild cerebral palsy, is 26 years old. He has been in an institution for 5 years where he received office training. Robert has been referred to vocational rehabilitation, which has placed him in two different jobs. He has lasted less than 2 weeks at each because of communication problems at the jobsite. Robert was then referred to a third job. At this time, a transitional counselor, Marika, was assigned to work with Robert for approximately 60 days. Marika is a certified interpreter and spent time working with the co-workers, the supervisor, and Robert to facilitate the adjustment process. She also made several physical accommodations at the jobsite so that Robert could maneuver around the area better. Over several weeks, Robert became increasingly independent and no longer needed Marika—he had adjusted to his position. His co-workers learned how to communicate with him better and began to get to know him as a person.

Although this approach to vocational rehabilitation takes a little more time than others and is a bit more individualized, it lends itself to steady and frequent communication with employers and jobs of much higher quality for people who have been consistently failed by the current system. It can be adapted to people with physical disabilities, hearing impairments, visual impairments, and mild mental disabilities.

Supported Employment: An Overview

Since the 1980s, perhaps one of the most popular programs in rehabilitation—sparking discussion and controversy—has been supported employment. The Rehabilitation Act Amendments of 1992 define *supported employment* as paid employment in integrated, real-work situations in which one must work at least 20 hours a week. According to this act, services must be given to those with the most severe disabilities.

Intense interest in the program has consistently amazed many experienced rehabilitation professionals. For example, in the 1991 hearings held around the country by the U.S. Department of Education, Rehabilitation Services Administration, more than 600 comments were generated for or about supported employment. Only nine comments were heard about the general vocational rehabilitation program and all other aspects of that program. Many still fail to realize, however, that supported employment provides an outlet and a source of vocational hope for thousands of disenfranchised and excluded people with severe disabilities. This program has very broad-based appeal in that it cuts across numerous disciplines and most disability populations (Kregel, Shafer, Wehman, & West, 1989; Kregel, Wehman, & Banks, 1989). As Figure 8.1 shows, there has been a dramatic growth rate in the number of participants with severe disabilities in supported employment from 1986 to 1993 (Revell et al., 1994).

Accounting for its popularity is the fact that, in the hands of good service providers, it is a program that satisfies all parties. Holding a real job is an elevating experience for a person with a severe disability who has never before had the opportunity to work. Many of these people, considered unable to hold a job, formerly attended day programs or worked in sheltered workshops making only $.84 per hour. With the $4.25 per hour they can earn in the work force, more and more people with disabilities are paying for their own support, as many as 52%—as opposed to 8% before supported employment (Kregel, 1995). Following are the major challenges faced by those interested in providing or receiving supported employment services (Wehman & Kregel, 1994, 1996):

- Increasing the effectiveness of programs so that a better variety of higher paying jobs can be offered
- Improving the program so that even people with severe disabilities can participate
- Increasing the number of hours that people are able to work (i.e., providing them with 35–40 hours per week instead of 20–25)
- Solving some of the challenging service delivery and system issues (e.g., long-term funding, reducing long waiting lists, expanding business and industry involvement and responsibility)
- Increasing natural supports to decrease the time and expense of job coaching needed for the long-term maintenance of people with disabilities
- Continuing to move away from center-based programs into industry-based programs, and maintaining this momentum by changing attitudes

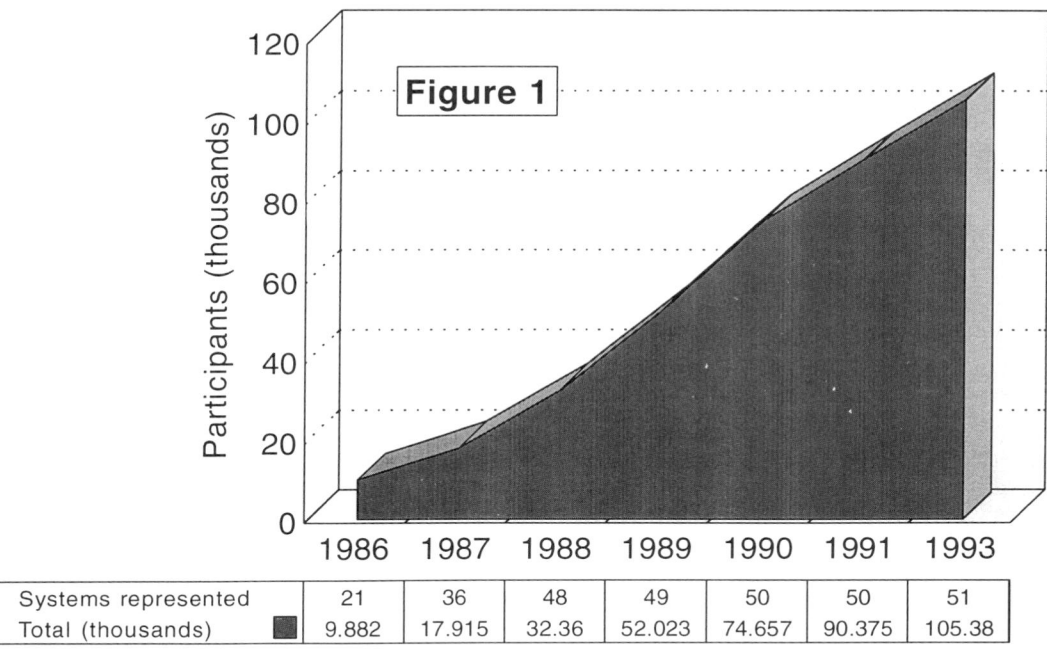

	1986	1987	1988	1989	1990	1991	1993
Systems represented	21	36	48	49	50	50	51
Total (thousands)	9.882	17.915	32.36	52.023	74.657	90.375	105.38

Figure 8.1. Total number of participants in supported employment (FY 1986–FY 1993). (From Revell, W.G., Wehman, P., Kregel, J., West, M., & Rayfield, R. [1994]. Supported employment for persons with severe disabilities: Positive trends in wages, models, and funding. *Education and Training in Mental Retardation and Developmental Disabilities, 29*[4], 256–264; adapted by permission.)

Individual Placement Model Two basic types of supported employment models have been implemented since the 1980s. The first—known as the *individual placement* or *job coach model*—provides an employment specialist, or job coach, to help a person with a disability to find and train for a job. The job coach stays with people on the job until they have attained a sufficient level of independence and their employers are comfortable. Unlike transitional employment, most people who participate in supported employment require ongoing support intervention for the duration of their employment. As the employment specialist should only go to the jobsite for those people whom a co-worker or supervisor cannot help, supported employment should be reserved for people with the most challenging disabilities. The employment specialist is also responsible for on-site training and any necessary periodic counseling, travel training, assistance to parents or families, and other areas that could impair job retention. A community employment specialist is the key aspect of successful supported employment. Brooke, Wehman, Inge, and Parent (1995) have described the employment specialist's roles in detail in Table 8.2.

Margaret Margaret is 20 years old and has Down syndrome with a measured intelligence of 36. She also is deaf. For the last 5 years, Margaret's mother and father have been trying to get the public schools to increase her time at community worksites. Last year, Margaret was assigned to a com-

Table 8.2. Community employment specialist: Roles and functions

Roles	Definition of roles	Functions of position				
		Customer profile	Career development	Employment match	Jobsite supports	Extended services
Planner role	Responsible for analyzing the services that the customer is seeking and assisting the customer in the development of a plan to achieve the identified outcomes.	X	X	X	X	X
Consultant role	Responsible for entering into a consultant relationship with customers of supported employment services and providing recommendations based upon knowledge and expertise.		X		X	X
Head-hunter role	Responsible for staying current with the community labor market and maintaining strong personal relationships with the employment community. This role includes a host of different types of marketing activities ranging from the development and dissemination of promotional information about supported employment services to identifying strategies for an individual to market himself/herself to a prospective employer.		X			
Technician role	Responsible for staying well versed in the latest high and low rehabilitation technologies to be able to identify appropriate strategies for teaching a needed skill, provide training when necessary, and to fade assistance systematically to ensure acquisition and maintenance of a skill/behavior.			X	X	X
Community resource role	Responsible for having a thorough knowledge of community resources and services to include transportation options, recreational opportunities, social establishments, housing services, independent living programs, and other community organizations and agencies. Conducting community analysis activities specific informations should include contact person, address, application process, and availability of services.			X	X	X

From Brooke, V., Wehman, P., Inge, K., & Parent, W. (1995). Toward a customer-driven approach of supported employment. *Education and Training in Mental Retardation and Developmental Disabilities, 30(4)*, 308–319; reprinted by permission.

munity rehabilitation counselor with a strong faith in supported employment. In the last 6 months of the school year, Margaret was hired as an electronics assembler for 32 hours a week at the local Hewlett-Packard factory. The job paid $6.16 an hour and provided complete fringe benefits for those who worked 35 hours a week. After Margaret passed the 6-month trial period, she was able to increase her hours enough to receive the benefits. The rehabilitation counselor provided an interpreter to help co-workers learn to communicate with Margaret and a job coach to help the supervisor train Margaret in the necessary skills of electronics assembly.

In the first weeks of placement, Margaret was very nervous and withdrawn and refused to communicate. After 3 weeks, she became friends with one of her co-workers who happened to have a partially deaf sister. This co-worker began to drive Margaret to and from work and has introduced her to other co-workers.

One year and approximately 230 hours of job coaching intervention later, Margaret is working 40 hours per week at Hewlett-Packard and only requires approximately 20 hours per month of job coach visitation. Above all, she is very satisfied with work and feels that she has a future with Hewlett-Packard.

Typically, vocational rehabilitation agencies pay for the necessary initial job coach services. As a person becomes more proficient at his or her job and is maintained over time, long-term funding is drawn from mental health or mental retardation sources. Generally, long-term support for all disabilities costs much less than initial job development and training.

According to a 1993 survey, the individual placement model has been used in over 70% of the more than 105,000 supported employment placements that have been reported in the United States (Wehman, Revell, & Kregel, 1996). This figure reflects the positive attitudes of most service providers and consumers regarding the integration and pay benefits typically assumed with the individual placement model.

Group Placement Models There is also a steady interest in several other types of models, commonly known as *group placements.*

Mobile Work Crew Model First, there is the *mobile work crew model* where a supervisor without disabilities leads several people usually with disabilities in doing service work around the community. The crew may do cleaning, landscaping, or any other type of activity that necessitates moving from one area to another. The mobile work crew concept has enjoyed some popularity, particularly in areas where there are very few jobs available.

This model does, however, require somewhat specialized equipment and transportation—a significant drawback. For example, a van, cleaning equipment, and machinery may need to be purchased and supplies replenished. Hence, a contract for services rendered must include compensation for the workers, the supervisor, and the equipment if the operation is to be totally unsubsidized.

Kendall *Kendall has mental retardation requiring extensive support and a measured intelligence of 22. She has a severe behavior problem and, on occasion, has exhibited self-injurious behavior (SIB) such as head banging. For the last 6 years, she has been in and out of state institutions. Although paid work had seemed like a remote possibility for Kendall, in her last few years of school she received excellent vocational instruction on a number of cleaning skills. In her last year, she has*

had the opportunity to participate in a mobile work crew responsible for cleaning several Days Inn hotels.

Kendall and her mother, who is a single parent, were very excited about the possibility of her working on this crew every day instead of sitting in a classroom. Therefore, she began employment at the beginning of the second semester of school earning $4.25 an hour and working 30 hours per week. Her responsibilities included helping to clean the bathrooms and the rooms and making up the beds in approximately 50 rooms in the three hotels that the crew serviced. Kendall worked with four other women, three of whom had severe disabilities. A supervisor without any disabilities provided transportation and overall supervision. The crew worked Monday through Thursday and all day Saturday. Although this schedule was very tiring, it helped Kendall reduce her behavior problems to a minimum and avoid reinstitutionalization.

———

The Industrial Enclave Another group placement model that has enjoyed even greater popularity is the *industrial enclave.* Within this model, a small number of people with disabilities are placed at a business, usually a manufacturer, and a staff person is assigned to work with them providing the necessary training and support. Enclaves generally occur in electronic manufacturing companies, shoe factories, sewing machine shops, and warehouses, as well as countless other types of manufacturing operations. Ideally, workers should not be congregated but instead should work throughout the company worksite, especially once increased confidence is attained.

The major advantages of the enclave model are 1) the cost-efficiency of placing more than one person to every staff member, 2) the sedentary nature of the jobs that allows less ambulatory people to be employed, and 3) the possibility for job-sharing especially among those who are very slow. However, this model often does not lend itself to integration and, generally, there is no fading.

In fact, the enclave approach has come under increased pressure as more and more service providers have begun to competently place people with challenging disabilities into individual placements; subsequently, there is increased skepticism about the need for an enclave arrangement. Nevertheless it would appear that small enclaves, with the prospect of dispersal, good pay, and highly supportive co-workers, have promise in selected industries and communities. This is particularly true for young people with very severe disabilities who are just entering the working world.

The Small Business Model A third group placement model that was utilized quite frequently for a time but has faded in popularity is called the *bench work* or *small business model* (O'Brien, 1987). This model was originally designed (Bellamy, Horner, & Inman, 1979) for those individuals with the most severe disabilities. The small business model recommends placing a small number of people with severe disabilities (10–12) into a manufacturing operation for contract work. The primary difference from the traditional sheltered workshop is the small business model's very small size and frequent employment of a few workers without disabilities. Also, all of its workers require extended, intensive training in a long-term, ongoing fashion in order to complete work assignments and have historically been institutionalized for long periods of time.

The small business model has never really caught on with supported employment primarily because it is very expensive and the staff required to make it effective are very dif-

ficult to recruit, train, and retain. Finally, the actual quality of such a model is not particularly enticing as people who work in these arrangements are significantly segregated and out of the mainstream. Increasingly, the thinking has been on integrating these people in some fashion into competitive work environments.

Peer Counseling

One of the most popular forms of vocational placement is peer counseling, which developed through the national network of Centers for Independent Living (CIL) that predominantly assists people with severe physical disabilities who have been shut out of the competitive labor market because of their physical and/or communication disabilities. The majority of these people can and want to work (Louis Harris & Associates, 1986) but have been discriminated against due to the limited perceptions and poor attitudes of many business and industry employers. Circumstances such as poor accessibility and lack of telecommunication capability or physical accommodations all impede their vocational placement.

At CILs, all vocational counseling is from other individuals with physical disabilities. This type of peer counseling has great credibility and provides a crucial form of emotional, moral, and informational support for people who feel that there is no hope for them vocationally.

An illustration of the problems experienced by talented individuals with severe physical disabilities follows. This autobiographical sketch is by Thomas L. Hock, who works at the Virginia Commonwealth University Rehabilitation Research and Training Center (VCU–RRTC) on Supported Employment.[2]

> The community of people with disabilities has come a long way in the past 10–15 years. At one time you would never see a person with a disability having a good job, being married, or going out among the general public. Instead, people with disabilities were locked up in nursing homes and warehoused.
>
> I have been asked to talk about the needs of people with disabilities who are participating in supported employment and how state systems can do a better job in helping to meet those needs. I will also comment on some of the obstacles I have experienced as a supported employment consumer, how services should be made more accessible to individuals with various disabilities through consumer involvement and self-advocacy, and what I feel the next steps should be for supported employment. Perhaps it would be best to begin by describing some of my life experiences so everyone will understand how the service delivery system is perceived by the consumer.
>
> As a child, I attended a special school for children with cerebral palsy. At the age of 18, I had to stop going to that school even though I had not completed enough credits to earn my high school diploma. The local school board allowed me to attend regular school and take three classes a year toward the completion of my diploma. The teachers there had limited knowledge of persons with disabilities, and my parents had to help me take my tests at home. It took me an additional 2 years to graduate. In 1978, I enrolled at Virginia Commonwealth University (VCU).
>
> At that time, VCU did not have many services available for students with disabilities. A man had just been hired to help make the campus more accessible, and he was of some help because he talked to my instructors about my disability. I needed to get the names of the textbooks before each semester started because I had a hard time reading. Because I understood when

[2]This speech was delivered by Thomas L. Hock at the National Meeting of Supported Employment Directors on September 7, 1991, in Washington, D.C.; reprinted by permission.

somebody read to me, I got the books taped from Recordings for the Blind. (I do not know if they would have given me the service if they had known I was not blind, but I did not volunteer this information because I needed the tapes.) When the university decided to help me get my textbooks taped, another lady sent the list of textbooks, and I received a taped list of the books, instead of the books! At this time, a family member began to read my textbooks on tape for me.

Vocational rehabilitation had long since closed my case because they thought I was unable to become employed. After seeing my progress in college, they elected to reopen my case. After a series of evaluations, I still received no vocational guidance to assist me in selecting an area of study in which to concentrate. I decided to major in information systems, contrary to the evaluators' recommendations. Vocational rehabilitation refused to assist me in purchasing the necessary equipment until my last year in college when they offered to buy me a computer and to pay my tuition. My parents still paid for my helper to write my tests for me.

I got some work experience the summer before I graduated from college. VCU's rehabilitation department had a grant to place persons with physical disabilities in employment, and I was one of the first to participate. The inclusion of persons with physical disabilities in supported employment was furthered due to the appropriation of funds for follow-along services by the state legislature a few years later. In August 1986, after 8 years of going to classes and taking 2–3 courses a semester, I received my bachelor of arts degree in information systems. I had a GPA of 3.2 (3.4 in my major). I thought it might take a couple of months or even 6 months to find a programming job because I had an excellent college record and I already had some work experience in my field. I was dead wrong.

First, I had to fight with the vocational rehabilitation department to get help. I had a good counselor during my last year of college, but as soon as I graduated, they transferred my case to another counselor. I had a hard time getting him to do anything and made an appointment that September to see him and try to push him to get on the ball. After 5 minutes, he told me that he could not work with me because he had trouble understanding my speech. I could not believe a counselor would tell clients that. So, I asked him to pay the Cerebral Palsy Center to arrange my supported employment. In December 1986, he finally approved 100 hours of assistance from them.

One year after graduating from college and staying at home, I began an internship at the Department of Parks and Recreation where I worked for 10 months for no pay. I then worked for a friend in a part-time job with no benefits as a programmer for about a year and a half. My friend's small business got into financial trouble and he had to let several employees go. I was back to where I had started from with no job. I went back to vocational rehabilitation, and it took them 6 months to reopen my case. During that time, I sent out résumés, wrote letters, and interviewed for jobs on my own and with the help of friends. I felt that if vocational rehabilitation had helped me after I had been laid off, I would have had a good chance of finding another job. On the recommendation of the Cerebral Palsy Center, I also bought a $3,000 talking machine with my own money to help me with job interviews.

Finally, vocational rehabilitation gave my case to the supported employment counselor. I never met a vocational rehabilitation employment counselor who wanted to help more and who put more effort into her job. She called me almost every week and asked if I wanted to apply for jobs she had seen advertised. We went to several interviews. Although my last job coach was highly motivated, when I wanted to give her many copies of my résumé that I had printed on good paper, she instead took one copy and made copies on a photocopier machine, and you know how cheap that looks. I was taught better in business school. If we have people with disabilities who have college educations, we have to have job coaches who know how to help them.

In August 1990, I interviewed at the Rehabilitation Research and Training Center at VCU and began working there on a part-time basis in October. I am still working there, and, as of June, am a full-time programmer with benefits. Although I am pleased to be employed at a job that I like and in an environment in which I feel comfortable, I feel that it is a shame that it has taken me so long to get a good job when I could have started working 5 years ago when I graduated from college.

The main problem persons with severe disabilities experience when seeking a job is employer apprehension. If I were an employer with no experience in dealing with persons with dis-

abilities, I don't know if I would hire a person who could not talk or needed a walker. The general public does not know much about persons with disabilities. It is getting better, but it will be a long time before much progress is made. It seems that companies are more willing to hire persons in wheelchairs who can talk than persons with severe speech problems.

Employer apprehension is even a problem after getting a job, as I experienced during my summer internship. The department director was very wary of my abilities at first and wanted to have little to do with me, but after I was there for a while and had proven myself, he became just the opposite and even assisted me in later years when I was job hunting. I don't know how to overcome this apprehension. Perhaps training or information sharing by fellow business people could be an effective way to educate employers to overcome their fears of hiring people with disabilities.

Another problem that workers with disabilities face is that they are likely to lose financial support such as Supplemental Security Income (SSI) or Social Security Disability Insurance (SSDI) from the government. These financial disincentives prevent many who are capable of working from choosing to work. When I was only working part-time, I could not have afforded to live independently and lose my SSDI. If I had to live on that without my family's assistance, I would have been out of luck. Now that I am employed full time, increased independence is a reality, but it took me many years to reach this point.

The following are some recommendations that I would like to make regarding the direction I feel supported employment should take and some of the systems changes that should be examined:

- First, develop some good courses on self-advocacy for those in their later teens. If I had known earlier what Section 504 of the Rehabilitation Act of 1973 (PL 93-112) contained, I could have demanded that my college help me much more than it did. Now, with the Americans with Disabilities Act (PL 101-336), it is even more important that persons with disabilities know the laws.
- Because I could not speak and walk well, prospective employers discriminated against me in hiring. We must work to help employers obey the laws and, more important, to not be afraid to hire persons with severe disabilities.
- Vocational rehabilitation agencies should investigate alternative systems for vocational rehabilitation personnel to use to enhance the quality of the services they provide to persons with severe disabilities and to combat counselor apathy. For example, extra rewards to counselors who successfully close cases of persons with severe disabilities may be beneficial.
- Because most people with severe physical disabilities have difficulty taking standardized evaluations, state systems must investigate better ways to measure the potential of persons with disabilities and to educate counselors to have more understanding of people who have severe disabilities. These counselors must be shown that they have to work with their clients and may arrange for situation assessments without relying on evaluations.
- Employment specialists should be trained how to work effectively with persons with physical disabilities who are of normal intelligence. Too many times, people perceive individuals with disabilities as having mental retardation. The services a person with physical disabilities requires to obtain and maintain employment are very different from those required by a person with mental retardation.
- Finally, I would like to see more people with physical disabilities receiving supported employment. In 1990, less than 2% of those people receiving supported employment nationally have cerebral palsy. Supported employment is a good tool to place those with disabilities in employment, and we have to make sure it continues and grows across disability labels.

As this poignant speech indicates, people with disabilities sincerely need employment and community access. The ADA provides the civil rights framework to make the 1990s a period of great opportunity for people with disabilities and should influence the future for

young people leaving schools. (See Appendix A for more information about Title I of this law.) Figure 8.2 is a checklist for determining building accessibility and usability to help teachers and rehabilitation counselors who work with young people with disabilities.

Moving Toward a Customer-Driven Model of Supported Employment[3]

Although the individual and group placement models provide a useful overview of supported employment, they do not reflect the strong move toward a customer orientation. As Brooke and her associates (1995) note, services must place a much greater emphasis on treating people with disabilities as "customers" of rehabilitation services.

Many individuals with disabilities have characterized their typical relationships with human services and/or rehabilitation professionals as paternalistic or as having a "professionals-know-best" attitude (Chumbley et al., 1992; Kregel, 1992; Turner, Dofny, & Dutka, 1994). This general air of condescension has many negative and far-reaching implications that can ultimately affect the full integration of people with disabilities into their communities. When professionals view these people as "helpless," employers, family members, and the general public adopt this same attitude, which perpetuates the negative attitudes about and stereotypic images of people with disabilities. This "paternalistic" attitude also exists in the field of supported employment. Rehabilitation counselors, service coordinators, job coaches, and program managers for years have been directly or indirectly transmitting messages to people with disabilities that say "We, the professionals, are in charge."

With the passage of the ADA, among other laws, people with disabilities are beginning to perceive themselves differently and act in a more assertive manner (Field, 1996; Field & Hoffman, 1994, in press). People with disabilities are seeking community-integrated, competitive employment and increasingly referring to themselves as customers (Chumbley et al., 1992; Turner et al., 1994). They maintain that they want and need the assistance of a professional as they work to obtain and uphold competitive employment (Kregel, 1995; Kregel & Tomiyasu, 1994; Kregel & Unger, 1993). However, they are demanding that supported employment services be developed, marketed, and delivered based upon what would best fit their needs instead of what is convenient for the existing service system.

Because communities often have multiple supported employment service providers, customers must research each program to determine which is best for them. A good example of this exists in communities that have instituted a voucher system to pay for services. Here, rehabilitation customers with vouchers exercise their rights to purchase supported employment services from friends, human services organizations, or community employment agencies. Once a customer selects an organization, he or she should interview the direct services staff to determine which individual would be best suited to meet his or her service delivery needs. One of the key factors related to job retention is the rapport established between the direct services provider and the new employee.

[3]Portions of this section were drawn from Brooke, V., Wehman, P., Inge, K., & Parent, W. (1995). Toward a customer-driven approach of supported employment. *Education and Training in Mental Retardation and Developmental Disabilities, 30*(4), 308–319; reprinted by permission.

Yes	No	

Passenger arriving–leaving space

____ ____ Is there a safe place designated for passengers to get into and out of cars (maybe on the street or off the street)?

____ ____ Is that space zoned to prohibit parking?

____ ____ If space is at curbside, is the curb ramped up to the sidewalk?

Walks

____ ____ Are public walks at least 48 inches wide (60 inches needed to facilitate passing where wheelchair traffic is heavy)?

____ ____ If a walk is sloped, is the grade not greater than 5% (1 foot of rise for 20 feet of length)?

____ ____ If there are steps in the walks, are there also ramps to bypass the steps?

____ ____ If doors open into walks, is there a level platform at least 5 feet by 5 feet?

Parking

____ ____ Is parking available for persons with disabilities either at end of rows or in diagonal or head-in (perpendicular) stalls 12 feet wide?

____ ____ Are pedestrian (wheelchair) inclines or sloped walks provided in place of, or in addition to, curbs and steps from parking area?

Entrances

____ ____ Is there at least one ground-level or ramped primary entrance usable by persons in wheelchairs?

Doorways

____ ____ Do doorways have clear, unobstructed openings of at least 32 inches? (Revolving doors are unacceptable unless accompanied by a side leaf door with 32-inch minimum opening.)

____ ____ If there are two leaf doors side by side, does one leaf provide at least 32 inches of clear opening?

____ ____ Do doors in series (i.e., vestibule doors) have at least 84 inches between sets?

____ ____ Are thresholds flush with the floor? If not, are they less than ½ inch?

Ramps

____ ____ Do ramps rise no more than 1 foot every 12 feet of length?

____ ____ Does the ramp have handrails 32 inches from the surface on both sides?

____ ____ Do handrails extend 1 foot beyond the top and bottom of the ramp?

____ ____ For rest and safety, do long ramps and sloped walks have level platforms at least every 30 feet?

Elevators

____ ____ Are elevators accessible on the same level as entrance?

____ ____ If this facility is more than one level (including basement, balcony, etc.) are all levels served by an elevator?

____ ____ Does the elevator doorway provide at least 32 inches of clear, unobstructed opening?

____ ____ Is the elevator cab at least 4 feet wide by 6 feet deep?

____ ____ Is the space between the building floor and the elevator floor ½ inch or less?

____ ____ Are the controls, including emergency switches and light, no more than 48 inches from the floor?

Stairs

____ ____ Do steps have rounded nosings with sloping risers?

____ ____ Are there handrails on both sides of all stairways?

(continued)

Figure 8.2. A checklist to evaluate buildings and facilities for their use by people with physical disabilities. (From Clark, G.M., & Kolstoe, O.P. [1990]. *Career development and transition education for adolescents with disabilities* [p. 401]. Needham, MA: Allyn & Bacon; reprinted by permission.)

Figure 8.2. *(continued)*

_____ _____ Are stairway handrails mounted 32 inches above front edge of stair tread?
_____ _____ Do handrails extend 1 foot beyond top and bottom step?
_____ _____ Are step risers no greater than 7 inches in height?

Toilet rooms

_____ _____ Do doors in toilet room (men and women) have at least 32 inches of clear opening?
_____ _____ Is there at least one toilet stall that is a minimum of 3 feet wide by 5 feet deep?
_____ _____ Does the toilet stall have a doorway with 32 inches of clear opening?
_____ _____ Does the toilet stall door swing out?
_____ _____ Is that toilet stall also equipped with handrails on both sides, 33 inches from the floor?
_____ _____ Is the toilet seat 20 inches from the floor?
_____ _____ Will the area from the toilet room entrance to the stall allow a wheelchair to pass (32 inches of unobstructed space)?
_____ _____ Is the bottom edge of at least one mirror no higher than 40 inches above the floor?
_____ _____ Are lavatories (sinks) mounted so that persons in wheelchairs can use them (29 inches from floor to top of wheelchair armrest)?
_____ _____ Are soap, towel, and other dispensers mounted no higher than 40 inches above the floor?

Tubs

_____ _____ Is a handrail (e.g., grab bar) securely mounted at either the foot or head end of the tub that can easily and safely be reached for getting in and out of the tub?
_____ _____ Is a handrail mounted parallel to the length of the tub to safely facilitate sitting or rising?
_____ _____ Does the bottom of the tub have an abrasive, antislip surface?

Showers

_____ _____ Does shower stall doorway have at least 32 inches of clear opening?
_____ _____ Is shower stall floor level with room floor without an obstructing riser or curb between?
_____ _____ Does shower stall have an antislip surface?
_____ _____ Is there a handrail on at least one side of the shower stall when facing the shower and also near the stall entrance to facilitate going in and out?
_____ _____ Is there a seat in the shower stall? (A hose-type, detachable shower head is preferable.)

Drinking fountains

_____ _____ Are water fountains both hand and foot operated?
_____ _____ On wall-mounted fountains, is the spout no higher than 36 inches from the floor?
_____ _____ On floor-mounted models, is there a side fountain 30 inches from the floor?

Telephones

_____ _____ Do telephone booth doorways have 32 inches of clear opening?
_____ _____ Are coin drops not higher than 48 inches from the floor?
_____ _____ Are some telephones equipped with receiver volume control for the hard of hearing?
_____ _____ Are phones for the hard of hearing readily identifiable?

Controls

_____ _____ Are switches and controls within reach from wheelchair position (not higher than 48 inches from the floor)?

Warnings for deaf and blind

_____ _____ Are there raised letters or numbers for identifying rooms?
_____ _____ Are the numbers at the side of the door 5 feet above the floor?
_____ _____ Are potentially dangerous areas identified by knurled door handles or knobs?
_____ _____ Are warning signals both audible and visible?
_____ _____ Are signs, lights, and hazardous hanging objects at least 7 feet above the floor?

Within a customer-driven model of supported employment, the community employment specialist's job functions are linked to the major components of the support service and include 1) the customer profile, 2) career development, 3) employment match, 4) job-site training and supports, and 5) long-term supports or extended services. The specific activities that the community employment specialist actually performs, however, will vary depending upon the needs of the individual requesting service (Wehman, Parent, Unger, Gibson, & Clements, 1994). A good community employment specialist does not focus solely on the "consultant role" or the "planner role" to the exclusion of the other areas. It is also important to remember that the specialist must work closely with the customer, employer, co-workers, family, and others, providing as little or as much assistance as the individual needs to accomplish his or her identified outcomes.

Toward Competitive Employment for All People with Disabilities

It is clear that day programs must be abandoned for community employment, and individuals with disabilities must lead the way. Not only are the state and federal investments associated with maintaining large adult centers enormous, but redirecting these funds into community support and career development activities will greatly benefit people with disabilities. Individuals with disabilities must demand the opportunity to choose from a variety of career alternatives that will provide satisfying wages and fringe benefits, suitable working conditions, and opportunities for career advancement, rather than just choosing whether to stay in an activity center, sheltered workshop, or at home.

Who Is Receiving Competitive versus Segregated Employment?

West, Revell, and Wehman (1992) identified 74,657 supported employment participants for fiscal year 1990. In 1994, Revell and his colleagues found that 105,000 people were receiving supported employment nationally. With an estimated 1.3 million individuals served by rehabilitation services, clearly the majority of individuals with disabilities continue to be served in segregated day programs. In fact, Schalock, Kiernan, McGaughey, Lynch, and McNally (1993) found that 86% of individuals with mental retardation or developmental disabilities were served in segregated facilities.

In particular, West et al. (1992) found that the primary recipients of supported employment were individuals with mild mental retardation (48.8%); 36.0% had moderate mental retardation, and 12.2% severe and profound mental retardation. Similarly, Schalock et al. (1993) found that three fourths of supported employment recipients had mild or moderate levels of disabilities. West et al. (1992) also found that while the number of individuals with long-term mental illness served by supported employment has dramatically increased, the relative percentages of people with other disabilities has decreased. McAllister (1991) found that individuals with severe disabilities are the least likely to receive supported employment.

McGaughey et al. (1993) reported that 18% of services provided to people with mental retardation and other developmental disabilities by state Mental Retardation/Developmental Disabilities (MR/DD) agencies in 1990 were in integrated environments. This was a modest improvement over 1988 figures, which showed that only 13% of services were provided in integrated environments. Yet, states have reported that about one third

of new participants enter into integrated employment. Students leaving school are given top priority for integrated services, followed by adults not currently receiving services, individuals in sheltered employment, and, finally, day program participants.

State-by-State Data

There are many variations among states in how the state agencies allocate their funds to serve people in employment and day services. Table 8.3 ranks states on the inclusiveness of the services they provide (McGaughey et al., 1993). Among the states serving more than 50% of people in integrated settings are New Hampshire (52.36%), Washington (50.33%), New Mexico (50.05%), and Alaska (50%).

Natural Supports in the Workplace

The movement to emphasize the use of community and workplace supports has become a topic of interest to individuals with disabilities and local programs providing supported employment services (Hagner, Butterworth, & Keith, 1995). The notion underlying the "natural supports" approach reflects an increased recognition of the ability of employers to accept and accommodate a diverse array of employees; the potential role of family members in locating jobs; and the willingness and ability of co-workers to provide training, assistance, and support (West & Parent, 1995). Although credible evidence documenting the effectiveness of the natural supports approach is lacking, few can argue with the overall intent of these efforts. Of the numerous types of natural supports, two have emerged as being among the most popular: 1) the employer or supervisor as a training mentor, and 2) co-worker assistance.

Employer or Supervisor as Training Mentor

For a number of individuals with severe disabilities, the immediate employer or supervisor will be the best trainer for a number of reasons. In some cases, the job is simply too complex or specialized for a job coach to grasp without an extended learning period. Sometimes, companies simply prefer to use their own personnel for training. Other companies are committed to affirmative action hiring, but do not wish to have noncompany personnel on the premises.

A particular benefit of this approach is that the employer/supervisor feels additionally empowered to handle difficulties that may arise on the job. A job coach or rehabilitation counselor still may be involved in the initial framing of the training, assisting with a behavioral management plan, or be available for troubleshooting, but the primary responsibility is assumed by the supervisor or employer. On-the-job training funds can be used as a means of compensating the employer or supervisor for the training time. It may be helpful for both parties to understand that the company is being financially compensated for this effort, which can further establish commitment to the training endeavor. These on-the-job training agreements are frequently developed for periods of 3–6 months using state rehabilitation agency funds or Job Training and Partnership Act (JTPA) monies, among other means.

Table 8.3. Integrated employment services provided by state/district MR/DD agencies

Rank	States/districts	Total serviced	Integrated service	Percent integrated
1	New Hampshire	1,413	740	52.37
2	Washington	3,952	1,989	50.33
3	New Mexico	927	464	50.05
4	Alaska	422	211	50.00
5	Connecticut	5,666	2,423	42.76
6	Arizona	2,443	1,035	42.37
7	Colorado	4,349	1,793	41.23
8	Oregon	3,480	1,416	40.69
9	Virginia	5,370	1,842	34.30
10	Utah	1,362	407	29.88
11	Vermont	776	224	28.87
12	Minnesota	7,167	2,057	28.70
13	Pennsylvania	13,389	3,520	24.46
14	North Carolina	5,579	1,340	24.02
15	Maryland	6,060	1,449	23.91
16	South Carolina	5,934	1,359	22.90
17	Mississippi	1,701	383	22.52
18	Wisconsin	13,095	2,948	22.51
19	Kentucky	2,654	572	21.55
20	South Dakota	1,400	291	20.79
21	Florida	9,138	1,891	20.69
22	Maine	1,991	374	18.78
23	Delaware	607	114	18.78
24	Nevada	679	124	18.26
25	Kansas	3,585	635	17.71
26	Massachusetts	7,625	1,324	17.36
27	Illinois	20,854	3,368	16.15
28	West Virginia	2,486	400	16.09
29	Hawaii	895	140	15.64
30	California	28,290	4,440	15.55
31	Iowa	6,579	998	15.17
32	New Jersey	5,407	799	14.78
33	Nebraska	2,194	302	13.76
34	Montana	1,348	176	13.06
35	Tennessee	3,591	451	12.56
36	Wyoming	370	46	12.43
37	Oklahoma	2,691	329	12.23
38	Louisiana	2,037	246	12.08
39	Georgia	6,607	783	11.85
40	Ohio	17,186	1,815	10.56
41	New York	42,010	4,127	9.82
42	Indiana	12.551	1,209	9.63
43	Rhode Island	3,500	330	9.43
44	Idaho	1,664	147	8.83
45	Texas	13,600	1,000	7.35
46	Michigan	13,009	911	7.00
47	Alabama	3,615	236	6.53
48	District of Columbia	1,026	46	4.48
49	Missouri	2,673	83	3.11
50	Arkansas	2,494	13	0.52
51	North Dakota	932	0	0.0
	Total	309,373	53,280	17.22

Source: McGaughey, Kiernan, McNally, & Gilmore (1993).

Co-worker Assistance

Although a relatively new job placement model in vocational rehabilitation, the co-worker assistance approach appears to have considerable potential. The co-worker's roles include trainer, observer, and advocate for the client within the workplace, including the education of other staff about a client's specific cognitive assets and impairments. This typically leads to co-workers who are more cooperative and supportive of the client.

Shafer, Tait, Keen, and Jesiolowski (1989) reviewed the limited, but growing, literature regarding the involvement of co-workers in the supported employment process, underscoring the following benefits: 1) the data on performanced-based feedback collected from co-workers is more likely to be reliable and to provide a realistic perspective on employment performance, and 2) a performance-based feedback structure provides co-workers with a framework and reminder for giving feedback.

Unfortunately the natural supports model has been presented as the sole alternative to the traditional job coach model, which is viewed by some as ineffective or even detrimental to individuals with disabilities. The job coach model is not the "problem" with supported employment, however. Minimizing the major impact of employment specialists who work closely at the jobsite with individuals with disabilities is unjustified and unproductive. Instead, we should ask whether employment specialists are using all available resources and strategies to meet the needs of workers and companies.

In order to find out the value of an employment specialist, ask the people participating in supported employment what they want from their job coaches. This is exactly what Parent (1994) did through a series of intense, face-to-face interviews with supported employment participants at the VCU–RRTC on Supported Employment. She found that people did not want their job coach to stay away from the workplace, but, they wanted their job coaches to be there only when they needed them. Consumers desire and demand the support of a skilled employment specialist.

The vast majority of employers view the job coach as a positive presence within the workplace, as opposed to an intrusive or disruptive influence. They want the job coach to be immediately accessible and responsive to their needs (Kregel & Tomiyasu, 1994; Kregel & Unger, 1993; Petty, 1994). Denying employers the opportunity to hire individuals because they need more assistance and support than employers can provide does a disservice to the individuals and the employers. The key to successfully using natural support is knowing how to identify the best types of community and workplace supports. Parent, Unger, Gibson, and Clements (1995) have developed an excellent form (in Figure 8.3) to address these issues.

It makes little sense to continually discuss the pros and cons of job coaches versus support facilitators, as the job coach model has enabled more than 100,000 individuals to gain and retain competitive employment. Efforts are only now underway to fully determine the effectiveness of natural support approaches. Yet, neither approach has been particularly effective in allowing individuals with significant cognitive disabilities to participate in competitive employment, and neither has fully encouraged consumers to choose their own jobs and plan their own careers. Framing the argument in an "either/or" manner trivializes the real problems and hides the fact that supported employment needs to move beyond all current models. New strategies that empower consumers must be identified that

enable all individuals with significant disabilities to benefit from employment. To do this, the best components of the job coach model and natural support strategies must be combined, as well as assistive technology, person-centered planning, compensatory strategies, personal assistant services, and many other strategies and approaches. Mank (1994) eloquently notes the following:

> Millions of individuals continue to be denied access to high quality employment programs that would enable them to take charge over their careers. The ADA continues to be assailed as an "unfunded federal mandate" which places burdensome constraints on well-meaning businesses. Finding solutions to these challenges will require a renewal of the spirit of innovation and risk-taking which has been a defining characteristic of supported employment since its inception.

As a means of summarizing the points made previously, Table 8.4 is provided. Obviously, the ways to interfere with vocational placement are listed in a somewhat "tongue-in-cheek" manner to illustrate what educators and services providers should not do; however,

Community and Workplace Support Form

Date: _____ Provider ID: _____
Consumer Name: _____ Employment Specialist: _____
SS#: _____ ID Code: _____
Currently Employed? yes _____ no _____
 Company Name: _____
 Street _____
 City, State, ZIP: _____
 Date of Placement: ____ /____ /____ (month/day/year)

Please answer the following questions for each support need. Complete a separate form for each area of need that is identified regardless of whether it is new or one that has been previously addressed.

1. What type of support is needed or desired? (check only one)
 _____ 1. Determining job choices
 _____ 2. Developing a résumé
 _____ 3. Finding a job
 _____ 4. Learning how to do the job
 _____ 5. Remembering how to do the job
 _____ 6. Orienting around the workplace
 _____ 7. Completing all regular job duties
 _____ 8. Being able to perform infrequent duties associated with the position
 _____ 9. Arranging work schedule/hours
 _____ 10. Signing in/out at work
 _____ 11. Calling in sick or late
 _____ 12. Attending company meetings
 _____ 13. Taking lunch and/or breaks

(continued)

Figure 8.3 Community and workplace support form. (From Parent, W., Gibson, K., Unger, D., & Clements, C. [1994]. The role of the job coach: Orchestrating community and workplace supports. In P. Wehman & J. Kregel [Eds.], *New directions in supported employment* [pp. 12–18]. Richmond: Virginia Commonwealth University, Rehabilitation Research and Training Center on Supported Employment, Natural Supports Transition Project; reprinted by permission.)

Figure 8.3. *(continued)*

_____ 14. Receiving a raise or increased benefits
_____ 15. Getting along with co-workers
_____ 16. Developing friendships
_____ 17. Participating in social activities during work hours
_____ 18. Finding transportation to and from work
_____ 19. Finding transportation not associated with work
_____ 20. Getting a learner's permit or driver's license
_____ 21. Using public transportation
_____ 22. Learning how to use public transportation (e.g., taxi, bus, subway)
_____ 23. Using specialized transportation
_____ 24. Making ride arrangements (e.g., co-worker, volunteer, friend, family member)
_____ 25. Meeting people outside of work
_____ 26. Pursuing recreational interests
_____ 27. Purchasing/selecting/maintaining uniforms or clothing for work
_____ 28. Arranging volunteer opportunities
_____ 29. Attending social outings after work hours
_____ 30. Participating in programs/activities offered by community or civic organizations
_____ 31. Locating a place to live
_____ 32. Learning independent living skills
_____ 33. Getting up and/or ready for work
_____ 34. Picking up/cashing a paycheck
_____ 35. Managing money/paying bills
_____ 36. Using money/making purchases
_____ 37. Applying for SSI, SSDI, or other government subsidy
_____ 38. Handling SSI or SSDI issues
_____ 39. Using Social Security work incentives (e.g., PASS, IRWE)
_____ 40. Taking care of personal hygiene and grooming
_____ 41. Dealing with substance abuse issues
_____ 42. Changing something about the job
_____ 43. Attending school/college
_____ 44. Addressing sexual issues
_____ 45. Pursuing career advancement opportunities
_____ 46. Learning how to do something new at work
_____ 47. Finding a different or a second job
_____ 48. Addressing communication issues
_____ 49. Dealing with aggressive, disruptive, or problem behaviors
_____ 50. Handling family issues
_____ 51. Handling legal matters
_____ 52. Addressing/monitoring medical or medication issues
_____ 53. Requesting time off from work
_____ 54. Addressing fatigue or stamina issues
_____ 55. Arranging follow-along job coach services
_____ 56. Recording and monitoring work schedule/hours
_____ 99. Other

2. a. Has this support need been addressed previously while being served by this program?
 _____ 1. Yes
 _____ 2. No
 b. If yes, what type of assistance was received? (please describe briefly)

 c. What is the reason for developing another support option? (check only one)
 _____ 1. Consumer handled on own and now would prefer outside assistance
 _____ 2. New/additional supports were identified/needed
 _____ 3. Consumer no longer needed assistance/issue reoccurred

(continued)

Figure 8.3. *(continued)*

_____ 4. Consumer chose to stop using the support/has changed mind
_____ 5. Consumer preferred to find a different means of support
_____ 6. Person providing support was no longer willing/able to continue
_____ 7. Support was not successful/did not meet individual's needs
_____ 8. Support was too costly/funding no longer available
_____ 9. Support or assistance no longer available/situation changed
_____ 10. Support was not available/could not be located
_____ 99. Other

3. What is the status of this support need? (check only one)
_____ 1. Critically needed immediately
_____ 2. Critically needed in the future
_____ 3. Possibly needed/desired sometime
_____ 4. Not needed but desired immediately
_____ 5. Not needed but desired in the future

4. a. What support resources have been identified to address this need? (check all options)
Finding a Job
_____ 1. Family/friends assisting with identifying job leads or getting applications
_____ 2. Consumer pursuing job leads and/or picking up applications
_____ 3. Assistance from community employment agencies with résumé writing, job leads, getting/completing applications (e.g., State Employment Commission)
_____ 4. Employment specialist assisting with job development activities
_____ 5. Job placement assistance by members of the community, volunteers, civic organizations (e.g., JayCees)
_____ 6. Job placement assistance by school personnel, human services agencies (e.g., vocational rehabilitation, mental health/mental retardation [MH/MR] services)
_____ 98. Consumer accompanied to different businesses to find out about the type of job and/or company
_____ 99. Exploring interests and experiences/talking with the consumer and others (e.g., family, rehabilitation counselor, teacher, job coach)

Learning How to Do the Job
_____ 7. Co-worker mentoring
_____ 8. New employee training provided by the company (e.g., orientation, videos)
_____ 9. Supervisor training and/or prompting
_____ 10. Employment specialist training
_____ 11. Observing workplace personnel perform the job (e.g., co-workers, supervisor)
_____ 12. Retired person/company employee providing training
_____ 13. Standard company training procedures expanded/modified/extended
_____ 14. Restructuring job duties, making accommodations, developing compensatory strategies
_____ 15. Co-worker training and/or prompting
_____ 16. _____

Assistance with Completing the Job
_____ 17. Co-worker assisting, training, and/or prompting
_____ 18. Modifying job duties/arranging a work routine
_____ 19. Purchasing something to make job easier/better (e.g., toys, lock, raincoat)
_____ 20. Employment specialist training
_____ 21. Modifying/changing work hours
_____ 22. Utilizing a self-monitoring strategy (e.g., checklist, flip cards, diagram)

(continued)

Figure 8.3. *(continued)*

_____ 23. Consumer handling it on his/her own (e.g., asking, using natural cues)
_____ 24. Utilizing external cues (e.g., pictures, color code)
_____ 25. Supervisor assisting, training, and/or prompting
_____ 26. Making job accommodations, utilizing compensatory strategies/assistive technology

Addressing Work-Related and Non–Work-Related Issues

_____ 27. Consumer doing it on his/her own (e.g., making arrangements, self-monitoring)
_____ 28. Employment specialist assisting, training, arranging, and/or supporting
_____ 29. Family members assisting, arranging, monitoring, and/or supporting
_____ 30. Supervisor/employer arranging, prompting, training, monitoring, and/or supporting
_____ 31. Company providing and/or managing (e.g., direct deposit, programming timeclock)
_____ 32. Community or civic organization providing assistance and/or information
_____ 33. Human services agency providing assistance, information, and/or services (e.g., vocational rehabilitation, independent living center, MH/MR services)
_____ 34. Friend or advocate assisting
_____ 35. Self-managing behavior, walk away, re-direct anger
_____ 36. Member of the community or volunteer assisting
_____ 37. Training or classes through a school or human services agency (e.g., residential services, MH/MR, independent living center, technical center)
_____ 38. Establishing/modifying work hours, job duties, and/or break routine
_____ 39. Residential staff prompting and/or assisting
_____ 40. Arranging a flexible work schedule/hours and/or time off
_____ 41. Co-worker prompting, assisting, training, and/or monitoring
_____ 42. Utilizing an external cue (e.g., alarm watch, color code)
_____ 43. Utilizing a compensatory strategy (e.g., list of names and numbers, letter with blanks, posting schedule, contract, calendar book)
_____ 44. College or university students assisting/tutoring
_____ 45. Training and/or advocacy with co-workers, employers, the community, etc.
_____ 46. Training and/or role-playing with the consumer
_____ 47. Help from a paid personal assistant
_____ 48. Counseling (e.g., individual/family, private/public)
_____ 49. Consultant or specialist assisting (e.g., private company, independent business, Social Security specialist)
_____ 50. Receiving medical treatment/services (e.g., physician, neuropsychologist)
_____ 51. Receiving legal assistance/services (e.g., lawyer, public defendant)
_____ 52. Participating in peer and/or community support groups
_____ 53. Training or classes through a community or civic organization
_____ 54. Participating in community activities/events
_____ 55. Exploring interests, opportunities available, and support resources
_____ 56. Enrolling in college or university courses/program
_____ 57. Teaching personal hygiene and/or grooming
_____ 58. Purchasing something (e.g., extra keys, alarm clock, radio, razor)
_____ 59. Contacting people, friends, others with similar interests
_____ 60. _____

Arranging Transportation

_____ 61. Family member or relative drive
_____ 62. Walk
_____ 63. Take a taxi
_____ 64. Friend, neighbor, community member, volunteer/hired person drive

(continued)

Figure 8.3. *(continued)*

_____ 65. Use specialized transportation
_____ 66. Carpool or ride with a co-worker
_____ 67. Ride a bus
_____ 68. Drive self
_____ 69. Ride a bicycle
_____ 70. Attend driving school
_____ 71. Family member train and/or assist
_____ 72. Employment specialist train, assist, and/or drive
_____ 73. Receive assistance with purchasing or repairing a car
_____ 74. Utilize a compensatory strategy (e.g., list of phone numbers, availability)
_____ 75. Assistance and/or services from a community or civic organization
_____ 76. Assistance and/or services from a human services agency

Other

_____ 77. _____
_____ 78. _____

b. Which support resources has the consumer chosen to use? (place corresponding number of the support resource identified in above question in the blank beside primary choice of the consumer and any other options being used concurrently or as an alternative or back-up support option)

_____ 1. Primary
_____ 2. Concurrent or alternate/back-up
_____ 3. Concurrent or alternate/back-up
_____ 4. Concurrent or alternate/back-up
_____ 5. Concurrent or alternate/back-up
_____ 6. Concurrent or alternate/back-up

5. What type of support option has been selected? (check only one)

_____ 1. *Employer or workplace support* (e.g., assistance provided by the consumer, employment specialist, or workplace personnel to address work or work-related issues at the job)
_____ 2. *Community support* (e.g., assistance provided by the consumer, employment specialist, or community to address work-related or non–work-related issues outside the workplace)
_____ 3. *Transportation support* (e.g., assistance provided by the consumer, employment specialist, workplace, or community to address transportation issues to and from work or not related to work)
_____ 4. *Recreation and social integration support* (e.g., assistance provided by the consumer, employment specialist, workplace, or community to address social and recreational issues with co-workers or persons outside the workplace after work hours)
_____ 5. *Personal and independent living support* (e.g., assistance provided by the consumer, employment specialist, workplace, or community to address personal, independent living, and residential issues outside the workplace)

6. Who has primary responsibility for arranging or obtaining the support? (check only one)

_____ 1. Consumer
_____ 2. Parent/family member
_____ 3. Friend/acquaintance/neighbor
_____ 4. Employment specialist
_____ 5. Rehabilitation counselor
_____ 6. Case manager
_____ 7. Teacher
_____ 8. Workplace personnel
_____ 9. Residential staff
_____ 99. Other: _____

(continued)

Figure 8.3. *(continued)*

7. a. Does the support require someone to function in the role of provider?
 _____ 1. Yes
 _____ 2. No

 b. If so, who is the primary person? (check only one)
 _____ 1. Consumer
 _____ 2. Supervisor
 _____ 3. Co-worker
 _____ 4. Other workplace personnel
 _____ 5. Parent/family member/spouse
 _____ 6. Friend/acquaintance/neighbor
 _____ 7. Member of the community
 _____ 8. Student
 _____ 9. Volunteer
 _____ 10. Tutor
 _____ 11. Retired person
 _____ 12. Consultant/specialist
 _____ 13. Rehabilitation counselor
 _____ 14. Teacher
 _____ 15. Case manager
 _____ 16. Employment specialist
 _____ 17. Community/civic agency representative (name: _____)
 _____ 18. School
 _____ 19. Business
 _____ 20. Residential staff
 _____ 21. Human services agency representative (name: _____)
 _____ 99. Other: _____

8. What has been the role of the employment specialist in addressing this support need?
 (check all that apply)
 _____ 1. Identifying support options
 _____ 2. Contacting support resources
 _____ 3. Assisting consumer with choosing type of support
 _____ 4. Helping/training consumer to obtain/use the support
 _____ 5. Advocating
 _____ 6. Training person providing support
 _____ 7. Working together with the consumer and support provider
 _____ 8. Overseeing the support arrangement
 _____ 9. Ongoing monitoring of support
 _____ 10. Providing additional support as needed
 _____ 11. Providing the support (continued)
 _____ 12. Employment specialist not involved
 _____ 13. Making support arrangements
 _____ 14. Making alternative arrangements if support breaks down
 _____ 99. Other: _____

9. a. Are any costs associated with providing the support?
 _____ 1. Yes
 _____ 2. No

 b. If so, what is the approximate amount? (Round off to the nearest dollar)
 $ _____

 c. Who is the primary funding source for the support? (check only one)
 _____ 1. Supported employment program
 _____ 2. Employer
 _____ 3. Consumer or his/her family
 _____ 4. Vocational rehabilitation

(continued)

Figure 8.3. *(continued)*

```
            _____  5.   School
            _____  6.   Private business (other than the employer)
            _____  7.   Community or civic organization/agency (name: _____ )
            _____  8.   Social Security work incentives (e.g., PASS/IRWE)
            _____  9.   Human services agency (name: _____ )
            _____ 99.   Other: _____
```
10. Who is primarily responsible for overseeing the ongoing monitoring of the support? (check only one)
```
            _____  1.   Consumer
            _____  2.   Parent/family member/spouse
            _____  3.   Friend/acquaintance/neighbor
            _____  4.   Employment specialist
            _____  5.   Rehabilitation counselor
            _____  6.   Case manager
            _____  7.   Teacher
            _____  8.   Workplace personnel
            _____  9.   Support no longer needed/short-term
            _____ 10.   Residential staff
            _____ 99.   Other: _____
```

these ideas often reflect the state of current vocational education in the United States, and teachers should carefully examine their policies and practices.

Table 8.4. Guidelines for vocational placement

Promoting vocational placement
1. Talk about the importance and value of work with the student regularly in school and at as early an age as possible. Point out the merits of having a job and emphasize the opportunities available to people who work.
2. Take students to jobsites where they can see other students or recent graduates working. Let them see firsthand what it is like to be employed in a real job. Talk about this visit repeatedly and emphasize the importance of work by showing models.
3. Enlist the help of parents and family members in helping students to select jobs that are appropriate and in providing encouragement for students who are reluctant to work.
4. Invite employers into the school and classroom to talk about the importance of work ethic, good work habits, and employment opportunities.
5. Let students try different jobs for several days at a time.
6. Do everything you can to help students become employed even on a part-time basis well before they exit school. It is essential that they have the experience of succeeding and also failing in real work environments.
7. Teach work skills and social skills, such as going to the Social Security office, filling out job applications, and arranging interviews. Teach these skills in a context of real jobs, not workbooks.
8. Encourage rehabilitation counselors, the local employment commission, and other adult agencies to visit and talk to students about the importance of getting work experience early.
9. Make the daily curriculum as vocationally and career oriented as possible. Emphasize how this can affect vocational placement.

Interfering with vocational placement
1. Make sure that all of the work activity in the classroom is make work and simulates real work; don't have students work in real jobs, but instead make sure that they practice a simulation of it extensively in the classroom until boredom sets in.
2. Be sure that the students consistently demonstrate that they can do sheltered workshop tasks successfully before considering "promotion" to a competitive tract.

(continued)

Table 8.4. (continued)

3. Emphasize that work is only part of the overall adult life and do not push them too hard into career development.
4. Never raise the expectations of the student or generate high vocational aspirations; after all, he or she may fail and this could crush his or her self-esteem for life.
5. Remind the student that there are numerous Social Security programs that can be taken advantage of if he or she doesn't want to work. Point out that Social Security is there for him or her as an option to not work if he or she doesn't want to.
6. When working with parents who have concerns about their children working in competitive employment, don't bother to educate them about new approaches and new research. Never disagree with parents or suggest that they try competitive employment even on a trial basis.
7. Make sure the student goes through extensive amounts of vocational evaluation. Be sure to spend at least a year on different types of standardized evaluation tools that will yield process information.
8. Never emphasize the relationship between work and money and fringe benefits that accrue to people who work.

Conclusion

This chapter described available vocational placements and models and the values associated with responsive and quality employment programs. Case studies of young people with disabilities working in the different vocational arrangements illustrate the strengths and weaknesses of each model. As national data indicate, the range of vocational models in place for people with disabilities is increasing (Shafer, Wehman, Kregel, & West, 1990); however, there must be a greater focus on career development and upward mobility into more challenging jobs for people with disabilities.

8

Study Questions

1. What are five aspects that make jobs attractive and motivating to students with disabilities?

2. What are four vocational options for students with disabilities? List advantages and disadvantages for each.

3. What are the five steps in the vocational rehabilitation process?

4. What are the differences between the individual and group models of supported employment?

5. What percentage of people receiving vocational services are in segregated and integrated programs?

6. In what ways can employers and co-workers be sued if they do not provide support to student workers with disabilities?

Appendix A

The Americans with Disabilities Act, Title I Employment

QUESTION: Which employers are covered by the ADA, and when is the coverage effective?

ANSWER: The employment provisions, which apply to private employers with 25 or more employees, were effective as of July 26, 1992. Employers with 15 or more employees were covered beginning July 26, 1994.

QUESTION: What practices and activities are covered by the employment nondiscrimination requirements?

ANSWER: The ADA prohibits discrimination in all employment practices, including job application procedures; hiring; firing; advancement; compensation; training; and other terms, conditions, and privileges of employment. It applies to recruitment, advertising, tenure, layoff, leave, fringe benefits, and all other employment-related activities.

QUESTION: Who is protected against employment discrimination?

ANSWER: Employment discrimination is prohibited against "qualified individuals with disabilities." People discriminated against because they have a known association or relationship with an individual with a disability are also protected. The ADA defines an "individual with a disability" as a person who has physical or mental impairments that substantially limit one or more major life activities, a record of such an impairment, or a person who is regarded as having such an impairment.

The first part of the definition makes clear that the ADA applies to people who have substantial, as distinct from minor, impairments and that these must be impairments that limit major life activities, such as seeing, hearing, speaking, walking, breathing, performing manual tasks, learning, caring for oneself, and working. An individual with epilepsy, paralysis, a substantial hearing or visual impairment, mental retardation, or a learning disability would be covered, but an individual with a minor, non-chronic condition of short duration—such as a sprain, infection, or broken limb—generally would not be covered.

The second part of the definition includes, for example, a person with a history of cancer that is currently in remission or a person with a history of mental illness.

The third part of the definition protects individuals who are regarded and treated as though they have substantially limiting disabilities, even though they may not have such impairments. For example, this provision would protect a qualified individual who has a severe disfigurement from being denied employment because an employer feared negative reactions of others.

QUESTION: Who is a "qualified individual with a disability"?

ANSWER: A qualified individual with a disability is a person who meets legitimate

skills, experience, education, or other requirements of an employment position that he or she holds or seeks, and who can perform the "essential functions" of the position with or without reasonable accommodation. Requiring the ability to perform "essential" functions ensures that an individual will not be considered unqualified simply because of inability to perform marginal or incidental job functions. If the individual is qualified to perform essential job functions except for limitations caused by a disability, the employer must consider whether the individual could perform these functions with a reasonable accommodation. If a written job description has been prepared before advertising or interviewing applicants for a job, this will be considered as evidence, although not necessarily conclusive evidence, of the essential functions of the job.

QUESTION: Does an employer have to give preference to a qualified applicant with a disability over other applicants?

ANSWER: No. An employer is free to select the most qualified applicant available and to make decisions based on reasons unrelated to the existence or consequence of a disability. For example, if two people apply for a job opening as a typist, and one is a person with a disability who accurately types 50 words per minute and the other is a person without a disability who accurately types 75 words per minute, the employer may hire the applicant with the higher typing speed if typing speed is needed for successful performance of the job.

QUESTION: What are "reasonable accommodations"?

ANSWER: Reasonable accommodation is any modification or adjustment to a job or the work environment that will enable a qualified applicant or employee with a disability to perform essential job functions. Reasonable accommodation also includes adjustments to ensure that a qualified individual with a disability has the same rights and privileges in employment as employees without disabilities.

QUESTION: What are the limitations on the obligation of employers to make a reasonable accommodation?

ANSWER: The individual with disabilities requiring the accommodation must be otherwise qualified, and the disability must be known to the employer. In addition, an employer is not required to make an accommodation if it would impose an "undue hardship" on the operation of the employer's business. "Undue hardship" is defined as "an action requiring significant difficulty or expense" when considered in light of a number of factors. These factors include the nature and the cost of the accommodation in relation to the size, resources, nature, and structure of the employee's operation. Where the facility making the accommodation is part of a larger entity, the structure and overall resources of the larger organization would be considered, as well as the financial and administrative relationship of the facility to the larger organization. In general, a larger organization would be expected to make accommodations requiring greater effort or expense than would be required of a smaller organization.

QUESTION: Must an employer modify existing facilities to make them accessible?

ANSWER: An employer may be required to modify facilities to enable an individual to perform essential job functions and to have equal opportunity to participate in other employment-related activities. For example, if an employee lounge is located in a place inaccessible to a person using a wheelchair, the lounge might be modified or re-

located, or comparable facilities might be provided in a location that would enable the individual to take a break with co-workers.

QUESTION: May an employer inquire as to whether a prospective employee has a disability?

ANSWER: An employer may not make a pre-employment inquiry on an application form or in an interview as to whether, or to what extent, an individual has a disability. The employer may ask a job applicant whether he or she can perform particular job functions. If the applicant has a disability known to the employer, the employer may ask how he or she can perform job functions that the employer considered difficult or impossible to perform because of the disability and whether an accommodation would be needed. A job offer may include conditions based on the results of a medical examination, provided that the examination is required for all entering employees in the same job category regardless of disability and that information obtained is handled according to confidentiality requirements specified in the act. After an employee enters on duty, all medical examinations and inquiries must be job related and necessary for the conduct of the employer's business. These provisions of the law are intended to prevent the employer from basing hiring and employment decisions on unfounded assumptions about the effects of a disability.

QUESTION: Does the ADA take safety issues into account?

ANSWER: Yes, the ADA expressly permits employers to establish qualification standards that will exclude individuals who pose a direct threat (i.e., a significant risk) to the health and safety of others if the risk cannot be lowered to an acceptable level by reasonable accommodation. However, an employer may not simply assume that a threat exists; the employer must establish through objective, medically supportable methods that there is genuine risk that substantial harm could occur in the workplace. By requiring employers to make individualized judgments based on reliable medical evidence rather than on generalizations, ignorance, fear, patronizing attitudes, or stereotypes, the ADA recognizes the need to balance the interests of people with disabilities with the legitimate interests of employers to maintain a safe workplace.

QUESTION: Can an employer refuse to hire an applicant or fire a current employee who is illegally using drugs?

ANSWER: Yes, individuals who currently engage in the illegal use of drugs are specifically excluded from the definition of a "qualified individual with a disability" protected by the ADA when an action is taken on the basis of their drug use.

QUESTION: Are people with acquired immunodeficiency syndrome (AIDS) covered by the ADA?

ANSWER: Yes. Legislative history indicates that Congress intended the ADA to protect people with AIDS and human immunodeficiency virus (HIV) from discrimination.

QUESTION: How does the ADA recognize public health concerns?

ANSWER: No provision in the ADA is intended to supplant the role of public health authorities in protecting the community from legitimate health threats. The ADA recognizes the need to strike a balance between the right of people with disabilities to be free from discrimination based on unfounded fear and the right of the public to be protected.

QUESTION: What is discrimination based on "relationship or association"?

ANSWER: The ADA prohibits discrimination based on relationship or association in order to protect individuals from actions based on unfounded assumptions that their relationship to a person with a disability would affect their job performance and from actions caused by bias or misinformation concerning certain disabilities. For example, this provision would protect a person with a spouse with disabilities from being denied employment because of an employer's unfounded assumption that the applicant would use excessive leave to care for the spouse. It also would protect an individual who does volunteer work for people with AIDS from a discriminatory employment action motivated by that relationship or association.

QUESTION: How are the employment provisions enforced?

ANSWER: The employment provisions of the ADA are enforced under the same procedures now applicable to race, sex, national origin, and religious discrimination under Title VII of the Civil Rights Act of 1964. Complaints regarding actions that have occurred since July 26, 1992, may be filed with the equal employment opportunity commission or designated state human rights agencies. Available remedies include hiring, reinstatement, back pay, and court orders to stop discrimination.

Appendix B

The ADA: Separating Myth from Reality

There is a backlash in the United States that threatens to wipe out much that is good in the federal government. Nowhere is it more apparent than in swipes at disability protections—most especially the ADA. We have all read the misstatements about the ADA—how it is wiping out small businesses, creating incredible financial burdens on public accommodations and local governments, how it is intruding on the rights of employers, and so forth. Most people waging these attacks have little understanding of the statutory language, regulations, and current implementation of the act. The following myths and realities of ADA were compiled by members of the disability rights community in Washington as a means of countering the misstatements that are found daily in the public arena. We encourage you to use this piece in response to any myths and/or misstatements that you may encounter.

MYTH: *The Americans with Disabilities Act is "an example of feel-good law" with no apparent economic rationale undergirding the decisions Congress and the administration made when they passed and signed this statute.*

REALITY: People who promote this myth completely overlook the overriding purpose of this act. As cited by the Bush administration and the bipartisan majority of both houses of the 102nd Congess, the ADA is intended to eliminate the disastrous impact of disability discrimination on the American economy. More than two thirds of adult working-age individuals with disabilities are unemployed and receiving some form of public benefits. During the development of the act, former President George Bush frequently noted that the federal, state, and private sectors were spending over $200 billion per year (in 1984 dollars) to keep individuals with disabilities in programs that facilitate dependency rather than independence.

MYTH: *The ADA is an absolute right whose "magnitude of [negative] economic consequences is only beginning to become apparent."*

REALITY: Nothing could be further from the truth. ADA specifically states that no public entity or business can be forced to take any action that would result in undue financial burden. The entire structure of this act is based on balancing the need for access of people with disabilities with the legitimate concerns, including costs, of business and government entities. The law requires only that a reasonable accommodation to disability, such as auxiliary aids and services, like interpreters, must be provided for individuals with disabilities unless an "undue burden" or "significant difficulty or expense" would result. The purpose of making a reasonable accommodation to a disability is to permit an "equal opportunity" to participate or benefit from the business or service (e.g., to get through the door or to reach the shelf and purchase or utilize what everyone else can obtain). While physical barriers must be removed if "readily achievable," that is, "able to be carried out without much

difficulty or expense" (e.g., installation of ramps over steps), alternative methods are permitted if readily achievable, such as curbside service. In determining what is an undue burden or what is readily achievable, the nature and the cost of the accommodation can be taken into account regarding the resources of the company. This allows small businesses in particular to address accommodations to disabilities in creative and inexpensive ways.

MYTH: *The Americans with Disabilities Act is a gold mine for bureaucrats and lawyers with regulators specifying detailed minutiae required for compliance.*

REALITY: In contrast, the ADA regulations give business and government room to exercise judgment and common sense. According to Justin Dart, former Chair of the President's Committee for the Employment of Persons with Disabilities, in testimony before the Senate Governmental Affairs Committee in January 1995, "The ADA provides the proper balance between the civil rights of people with disabilities and the legitimate concerns of state and local governments, employers and private businesses." Similarly, in 1989 Attorney General Dick Thornburgh described the ADA to Congress as "fair, balanced legislation [that] builds on an extensive body of statutes, case law, and regulations to avoid unnecessary confusion [that] allows maximum flexibility for compliance [and] does not place undue burdens on Americans who must comply." One example of the balanced approach is the U.S. Department of Justice architectural barrier removal requirement for existing government facilities that, instead of specifically mandating accessibility for every facility, requires access to programs, allowing an entity to utilize nonstructural methods for compliance (e.g., moving a town meeting from an inaccessible town hall to an accessible public school).

MYTH: *Lift-equipped buses are required in lieu of door-to-door paratransit services because people with disabilities want to be mainstreamed.*

REALITY: Congress recognized that accessible transportation is the linchpin to ensuring that people with disabilities are integrated into society's social and economic mainstream, which is why they required all new buses to be equipped with lifts. However, the law's emphasis on lift-equipped transportation rather than door-to-door service is purely economic. Door-to-door paratransit is very expensive—averaging from $20 to $50 per trip—which is why Congress did not choose paratransit as the exclusive option in the ADA. The law limits its use to people who cannot use (board, ride, or disembark) mainline lift-equipped systems. Congress found this dual approach to be far most cost-effective than reliance on paratransit.

9

Independent Living

Michael D. West, Karen Gibson, Darlene Unger, and Kelly Kane

Upon completion of this chapter, the reader will be able to do the following:

- Describe key differences between continuum-based residential models and models based on individualized supports
- List at least three nonfacility options for supporting individuals where and with whom they wish to live
- List the steps for identifying and utilizing community and workplace supports
- Provide an overview of person-centered services and how this process can assist with assisting individuals with disabilities to live in the community
- List at least three options for providing transportation support to individuals living in the community
- Describe behavioral supports and give an example of how an individual with challenging behaviors can be supported in the community

The development of this chapter was supported by Grant No. H235J20014 from the U.S. Department of Education, Rehabilitation Services Administration. The opinions expressed are solely those of the authors and no official endorsement by the Rehabilitation Services Administration should be inferred.

Beth and Robert Beth and Robert live in the same city. Both have mental retardation, and both are employed. They are very similar in their behaviors, their learning capacities and limitations, and the adaptive skills they have developed, such as bathing, grooming, dressing, cooking, housekeeping, and attending to other personal needs. Robert lives in a group home with five other individuals with mental retardation—they have three 8-hour shifts of supervision. He wants to live in his own apartment, but the staff of the agency that runs his group home do not believe he is ready for such independence. Beth lives in an apartment with a roommate without mental retardation who helps Beth in many ways, although she is not a paid staffperson. How is it that Beth is ready to live in her own apartment but Robert is not, despite their comparable levels of functioning and skill development?

Changing Paradigms of Independent Living

These cases illustrate two different organizational views of independent living for people with disabilities. Robert's agency maintains that different types of residential settings require different skill levels or competencies. They organize their residential programs along a continuum that might include large congregate facilities, small group homes, clustered apartments, and semi-independent or independent apartment living. Their service recipients are expected to progress through this continuum as they acquire more skills and, in the process, gain greater independence, achieve community integration and participation, and enjoy a more normalized lifestyle. This paradigm is often referred to as a *readiness model* because individuals must prove themselves "ready" to function in increasingly integrated environments.

In a critique appropriately entitled "Caught in the Continuum," Taylor (1988) described a number of logical and ethical dilemmas posed by this model:

- It confuses the types and extent of *services* that individuals need with the *locations* in which they are provided, as if services were necessarily linked to particular types of residences.
- It makes it virtually impossible for individuals with more severe disabilities to move out of the most segregated and least normalized settings.
- It supports the primacy of professional opinions over people's choices of where they would like to live, work, or socialize.
- It forces people to move as they develop and change, thereby disrupting relationships with family, friends, and neighbors.

The readiness model is perhaps best exemplified by Siperstein, Reed, Wolraich, and O'Keefe's (1990) study of 477 residential program staff members to identify those skills they consider essential for adults with mental retardation to function in different residential situations. Figure 9.1 presents the capabilities that at least 80% of the respondents agreed were essential for functioning in supervised and unsupervised apartments. Although there were no skills considered essential for functioning in a group home setting, 8 were identified as essential for supervised apartments, and 21 as essential for unsupervised apartments.

	Supervised	Unsupervised
Drink from a cup unassisted	✓	✓
Dress and toilet independently	✓	✓
Eat with utensils	✓	✓
Follow a one-stage command	✓	✓
Act appropriately toward strangers	✓	✓
Anticipate hazards	✓	✓
Recognize traffic signs	✓	✓
Use a lock and key	✓	✓
Address two people by name		✓
Join in a simple conversation		✓
Indicate symptoms verbally		✓
Choose appropriate clothes to wear		✓
Tell time		✓
Make change for a dollar		✓
Use public transportation		✓
Find way in unfamiliar surroundings		✓
Use pay phone		✓
Schedule daily activities		✓
Budget for monthly expenses		✓
Cook a meal		✓
Do own laundry		✓

Figure 9.1. Essential skills identified by residential specialists for living in supervised and unsupervised apartments. (From Siperstein, G.N., Reed, D., Wolraich, M., & O'Keefe, P. [1990]. Capabilities essential for adults who are mentally retarded to function in different residential settings. *Education and Training in Mental Retardation, 25,* 45–51; adapted with permission.)

These lists of "essential skills" give rise to some speculation. If an individual needs help to complete dressing and toileting, does that mean that apartment living is an unachievable goal? Must an individual avoid an unsupervised apartment in an area where there are no bus lines if other means of transportation can be arranged? Are individuals who are nonverbal due to deafness or motor delay—and, therefore, unable to perform three of the essential skills—inappropriate candidates for independent living?

Even proponents of the readiness model would have to agree that the answers to these questions are an unequivocal "no." Many individuals with severe disabilities are already living contented and fairly independent lives with personal assistants who help them with dressing and toileting or other personal needs. Many individuals with disabilities walk; carpool with co-workers, family members, or friends; or use specialized transportation

services to jobs or recreational activities. Even those who are nonverbal can communicate with other members of their communities through gestures, word or picture cards, or communication devices. In fact, there are numerous ways to reconcile the absence of "essential skills" (e.g., through training, adaptation, or support) while the individual resides in the more integrated and independent setting.

Consider the example of Beth. The staff working with Beth understand that community living is not an all-or-nothing proposition where, if one fails to meet certain preselected criteria for "independent" living, then congregate living is the only alternative. They understand that no one, with or without disabilities, truly lives independently, but that all members of a community are interdependent, conducting their individual affairs through mutual reliances upon one another (Klein, 1992; O'Brien & O'Brien, 1992). They believe that a person with even very severe disabilities can be a valued and contributing member of an interdependent community. They understand that the lines between "independent," "semi-independent," "supported," and "supervised" living are rapidly becoming blurred and irrelevant, and perhaps even detrimental to service consumers. Instead of putting their efforts into operating different types of facilities or programs, an increasing number of service providers are adopting a new orientation that focuses on the preferences, strengths, and support needs of every individual (O'Brien, 1994). Ferguson, Hibbard, Leinen, and Schaff (1990) wrote the following:

> A one sentence summary of this new orientation states the goal simply: People, regardless of their disabilities, should live in the community where they want, with whom they want, for as long as they want, with whatever supports they need to make that happen." (p. 18)

This orientation can open up an array of residential options for individuals with disabilities, options that are common and readily available to people without disabilities. For example, once residential service staff have identified the community or area in which an individual desires to live, they can creatively explore such options as roommates, housing cooperatives, boarding with families, living with friends or family members, and even home ownership (Racino & Taylor, 1993).

This chapter describes methods to assist individuals with disabilities in living "where they want and with whom they want." It presents a model for identifying and utilizing community support needs through a planning process that emphasizes the needs and desires of the individual with a disability. A number of key areas in which planning should occur are also presented. Throughout the chapter, case studies detail the lives of individuals with severe disabilities who are being supported in the neighborhoods and homes of their choice.

Identifying and Filling Community Support Needs

Support can be very broadly defined as "an array, not a continuum, of services, individuals, and settings that match the person's needs" (Luckasson & Spitalnik, 1994, p. 88). Using a broad array of support technologies, such as training, adaptations and modifications, assistive technology, personal assistance, and family and friends, offers consumers more options from which to choose how their community living needs will be met.

Since 1992, the Rehabilitation Research and Training Center on Supported Employment at Virginia Commonwealth University (VCU–RRTC) has operated a research and

demonstration project for developing community and workplace supports for individuals with severe disabilities. The VCU–RRTC approach relies on the use of paid service staff, family, friends, neighbors, and community supports to enable individuals with severe disabilities to obtain and maintain jobs and homes of their choosing. Within the VCU–RRTC model, the role of the agency shifts from that of a provider of services to a provider and facilitator of services and supports that enhance each participant's integration, interdependence, and value at work and in the community (Parent, Unger, Gibson, & Clements, 1994).

A systematic process for identifying support needs and utilizing community and workplace supports has proven useful for meeting both work-related and non–work-related support needs (see Parent et al., 1994, for a detailed description of the process). First, the effectiveness of a method of support is determined by 1) whether the support actually fulfills the need, and 2) whether the consumer is comfortable and satisfied with the support method. Second, ongoing monitoring of support mechanisms is crucial to maintain levels of independence because relationships and circumstances change over time. For example, a friend who gladly provides transportation to an individual with a disability may eventually find it burdensome. Also, as an individual becomes part of a social network within the community, new sources of support begin to emerge that may be more convenient or comfortable. Several elements are critical to the successful implementation of this model, including relationship building, person-centered services, circles of support, and total community involvement.

Relationship Building

Taking time to become acquainted with the individual and develop a trusting relationship is the basic foundation of and essential first step in the service delivery process. It is likely that most individuals with disabilities have had some unpleasant or disappointing experiences with professionals and may be hesitant to open up to yet another service provider. This hesitation is sometimes interpreted as noncompliance or lack of motivation. Spending time with the individual and learning more about him or her, such as past experiences, present lifestyle, hobbies or interests, interpersonal relationships, community connections, and desired goals, will clear up misconceptions and provide valuable insight for planning community supports. Meeting in an informal, comfortable location of the individual's choosing (e.g., the individual's home, school, job, day program, or clubhouse; a restaurant) provides an excellent opportunity for establishing rapport and gathering essential information.

Person-Centered Services

The type of supports that are utilized, the manner with which they are provided, and the frequency of their use should be determined by each individual's support needs and preferences. The VCU–RRTC project uses a planning process similar to Personal Futures Planning (Mount, 1991, 1994), which emphasizes positive images of individuals with disabilities, maximizes their gifts and talents, and provides for informed choices that truly reflect their preferences.

During the planning meetings, it is important for all participants to offer ideas about any possible resources, to keep an open mind about the potential options, and to collec-

tively brainstorm for creative ways to provide support. Rather than assuming that a desired goal cannot be accomplished due to a perceived lack of support, it is much more productive to develop supports that can assist in achieving the desired outcome.

Gina Gina, an individual served by the VCU–RRTC project, found a job with assistance from a job coach but had no way of getting to and from work. Short-term provisions were put into place for the duration of the training, with the job coach driving her to work and a family member picking her up. Meanwhile, alternative arrangements were explored that resulted in the following outcome: Gina chose to walk if weather permitted, to use a taxi when running late or during inclement weather, and to ride with a specific co-worker after completing late-night shifts. The job coach assisted by making the arrangements, writing down pertinent information about each option, posting the contact information beside the telephone for quick reference as needed, and implementing ongoing monitoring provisions by the supervisor and family to ensure that the plan was working as intended.

Circles of Support

During the course of establishing a relationship with the consumer and facilitating community involvement, a variety of support resources are likely to be identified and put into place even if they are not needed at that time. Being prepared to respond to a particular need often reduces its intensity and minimizes its consequences. Just knowing that assistance is in place and available if needed can be a tremendous support in and of itself.

Luckasson et al. (1992) presented supports as a "constellation," or concentric circles of support, with the individual at the center. The closest circle would consist of the individual's family and friends. Unpaid support providers, including co-workers, neighbors, church, or community groups, make up the next circle. The next support circle involves generic services—supports and formal services that are available to all members of the community—such as public transportation, housing assistance, and company-sponsored employee assistance programs. The outermost circle includes specialized support services, which are formal services developed primarily for use by individuals with disabilities, such as vocational rehabilitation, mental health services, and counseling. Typically, the circles of support closest to the individual are the least stigmatizing and obtrusive and should be given preference; however, consumer choice should be the ultimate factor in choosing a support source. One person who has been a major leader in forming circles of support with both parents and professionals is Sharman Jamison (see the Transition Leader Box on p. 237).

Total Community Involvement

Central to the "circles of support" model is the need for a coordinator or facilitator (Luckasson & Spitalnik, 1994). In many disability service systems, that may be a case manager or service coordinator. In the VCU–RRTC project, the individual's job coach fulfills this function primarily because the focus of the project is employment. As employment is the catalyst that enables and enhances life in the community, project staff also assist individu-

Sharman Jamison Long regarded as one of the preeminent leaders on helping parents and families in the transition planning process, Sharman Jamison is the parent of a 23-year-old daughter who is deaf and has autism and an 18-year-old son.

Ms. Jamison holds a Bachelor of Science in Speech and Hearing Sciences. She has been an advocate for people with disabilities, serving for 4 years as Project Coordinator of the Supported Employment Parent Training–Technical Assistance (SEPT/TA) Project (a national, federally funded project at PACER Center). There, Ms. Jamison assisted in the development and implementation of a parent training course about supported employment in 50 states and Puerto Rico. In addition, she has organized national conferences and small group meetings and has presented at numerous national conferences about supported employment and transition from school to work.

Ms. Jamison is responsible for assisting parent training courses and information centers in developing and implementing strategies 1) to enhance their leadership capabilities to affect transition and supported employment systems, and 2) to foster and expand each center's capacity to train and inform more families about transition and supported employment. She also coordinates the Technical Assistance about Training on the Rehabilitation Act (TATRA), a national technical assistance project that assists projects to train families and consumers about the Rehabilitation Act.

Through all of these efforts, Ms. Jamison has helped people with disabilities and their families achieve independence and self-determination in their lives.

als in locating supports to improve their housing situation, independent living skills, transportation, friendships, leisure pursuits, and any other needs that might potentially impinge upon employment success.

There are multitudes of people and organizations within communities that can be utilized as sources of support for individuals with severe disabilities. Table 9.1 provides a list of some of the support options that have been developed by the VCU–RRTC project to facilitate independent living for participants.

Types of Support Needs

Although there are specific areas in which support planning should occur, no specific list of supports exists. All individuals have unique skills, characteristics, and needs that influence the types of support needs that must be addressed, among them housing options, transportation, social and recreational activities, shopping and financial management, health and safety, and behavioral support.

Housing Options

A home is more than a place to eat, sleep, and relax. It is a place where people can exercise personal control, express individuality, and experience a sense of ownership (O'Connor & Racino, 1993). *Personal control* means that the individual decides not only where and with whom he or she lives, but also who enters the home and for what reasons, what activities

Table 9.1. Examples of support resources

Transportation supports
Taxi
Carpool with co-worker
Walking
Bicycle
Parents
Public transportation

Community supports
Cooperative Extension Service
Independent living center
College students
State assistive technology systems
Planned Parenthood
Neighbors
Red Cross safety courses
YWCA safety courses
Auto club driving school
Employment commission
Community-sponsored child care courses

Personal and independent living supports
Roommates/housemates
In-home support staff
Budgeting assistance
Personal security systems
Private counseling
Housing assistance

Recreational and social integration supports
Volunteering
Jaycees
YMCA
Neighborhood community association
Employer-sponsored social activities
Parks and recreation programs

will take place there, and daily routines and "house rules," among other aspects of occupancy. *Individuality* means that the person decides how the home is decorated, including the placement of personal effects such as pictures and mementos. *Sense of ownership* refers to feelings of security and confidence that one will not be forced to move at some arbitrary point.

Many service agencies focus on providing "home-like facilities" or "housing" rather than helping people find and maintain homes (Racino & Taylor, 1993). Nothing is inherently wrong about operating group homes or apartments solely for people with disabilities unless people are forced to accept only that option, and no attempts are made to give people choices or to customize their services for individual preferences.

Upholding the principle that people should live "where they want and with whom they want . . ." involves much more than just having residential programs. It also means creating individualized housing supports, such as the following:

- Providing support services to people living in their own apartments
- Matching individuals with disabilities to roommates without disabilities or with families that may be compensated for providing needed assistance
- Supplying in-home supports to people with disabilities and their families who choose to remain intact
- Assisting people with disabilities to become homeowners via housing cooperatives, federally backed home loans, low-interest loans, or low-cost homes through the U.S Department of Housing and Urban Development (HUD), family trusts, and other options

Carrie *Carrie is an 18-year-old student who attends a rural high school where she has just completed her sophomore year. Carrie has resided with a foster family since she was 3 and has no contact with her natural family. A Department of Social Services service coordinator serves as her guardian and Social Security payee. Carrie has an active case with the local Community Services Board (CSB) and is eligible for all services, which include service coordination and vocational and residential placement. Carrie recently was employed in her first job with the assistance of supported employment. In planning her most recent individualized education program (IEP), participants discussed goals for her future, whether Carrie was benefiting from classroom instruction, and if she should continue in school until age 22. Her foster placement ends upon graduation; therefore, additional concerns were raised as to where Carrie would live.*

Carrie currently has no independent living skills and wishes to continue living with her foster family. The foster family, although willing to have her stay, is not sure if this is allowed and wishes to have her live as independently as possible. They do not want to hold her back. Her CSB service coordinator is willing to put her on a residential waiting list for the local group home, but Carrie's Social Services service coordinator is in a different locality and Carrie may need to change jurisdictions, thereby ending her involvement with her current CSB.

Carrie decided to stay in school and continue her employment. She will stay with her foster family but be placed on the group home waiting list. In the interim, she will work on independent living skills at school. More information will be gathered regarding the logistics of her potential move for future planning and referral to other necessary agencies. In addition, other community living arrangements will be explored such as continuing to live with her foster family, renting her own apartment, utilizing a paid companion, applying for an auxiliary grant for a low-income apartment or adult home, and utilizing a Social Security Plan for Achieving Self Support (PASS) to purchase employment-related residential assistance such as readying for work, which might include personal hygiene, laundering uniforms, or preparing her breakfast and lunch.

Transportation

Transportation is a critical consideration in all areas of independent living, including work, continuing education or training, recreation, social activities, friendships, shopping, and use of community resources. Safe, affordable, and reliable transportation opens up options in all areas of people's lives, thereby enabling them to lead the lifestyle of their choice (West, Barcus, Brooke, & Rayfield, 1995). Without reliable and affordable means of getting about, many individuals with disabilities are forced into segregated

schools and workplaces, social and physical isolation, and economic dependence (Piep-meier, 1992).

Unfortunately, far too many individuals with disabilities lack transportation, which limits their community participation and often bars employment. Many disabilities pre-clude driving as an option or require such extensive supports to drive (e.g., lift van, cus-tomized automobile) that the possibility is financially infeasible. Despite the mandates for accessibility under the ADA, public transportation remains largely inaccessible because of route limitations (particularly in rural or suburban areas) or the absence of any public transportation.

One solution is to encourage people to relocate in urban areas. This is not always the best approach, however, and sometimes creative solutions are needed to transport people with disabilities. Within the work arena, co-workers can be solicited for rides to work and back. In fact, some companies encourage and sponsor carpooling among employees, and these companies can be targeted during job development. Apartment bulletin boards, pub-lic service announcements, or volunteer exchanges can also be used to advertise for pur-chasing or locating rides to work. Many human services agencies (e.g., The Arc, Red Cross, elderly services) run van or bus routes for their consumers and may be willing to let some-one with a disability who lives and works on or near the route purchase a seat. In addition, training in the use of public transportation (or even driver's education) can be explored. These strategies can be utilized for social or recreational outlets as well.

Mary *Mary is a 23-year-old woman with mild mental retardation and autism who currently resides in a group home. When she was referred to a supported employment program to obtain a clerical job a year after graduation from high school, transportation to and from work was a critical need. After considerable brainstorming the many different transportation possibilities with Mary, her co-workers, and support staff developed a transportation support plan. Her group home staff now take Mary to work, and two co-workers share the responsibility of giving her a ride home.*

Social and Recreational Activities

As noted by Dattilo and Schleien (1994), social and recreational services for people with disabilities tend to focus on a narrow range of stereotypic activities, such as bowling, swimming, arts, and crafts. In addition, most formal programs to increase social partici-pation tend to focus on segregated, disability-only activities instead of assisting individ-uals to develop the skills and have the opportunities to participate in activities of their own choosing (Dattilo, 1991). Programs that force people to engage in activities in which they have little or no interest disregard the primary purpose of leisure activities: to do things we like to do, with people with whom we enjoy doing them. The following are some practical guidelines for helping individuals with disabilities develop and experience leisure activi-ties of their own choosing:

- Because of lack of experience in integrated leisure activities, some people with disabil-ities may need to experiment with different types of recreational pursuits and social events in order to develop their preferences.

- Targeted leisure activities should include an array of both solitary and group activities.
- When looking for leisure supports for people with disabilities, it is important to remember that they do not necessarily have to be good at something to enjoy it or to participate with individuals without disabilities. Likewise, individuals do not necessarily have to engage in activities in the ways that people without disabilities do but can use adapted equipment or rules without meeting any objections from their teammates.
- Individuals may choose to participate in segregated activities; however, they should also be able to engage in similar activities with people without disabilities. A support person, often called a "leisure coach," can facilitate those opportunities.

Frank *Frank has cerebral palsy that affects his limb movement and speech, but he can ambulate short distances with a walker. He is a sports fan and spends much of his free time watching sports on television. Frank's service coordinator assigned a leisure coach to him to help develop more social and recreational outlets, and sports seemed a logical place to start.*

Frank's city has a minor league baseball team. At the start of the season, the leisure coach purchased season tickets for Frank and himself. Because season ticket holders keep the same seats for the season, they encountered the same individuals repeatedly, individuals who were also avid fans. The leisure coach began to facilitate contacts between Frank and the other fans based upon their common interests. The leisure coach also served as an intermediary when the others could not understand Frank's speech. One group of fans in particular took an interest in Frank and invited him to their homes to watch the team play away games as well as other types of sports.

Frank's leisure coach does not go with him to his new friends' homes. He was careful to allow Frank's friendships to develop naturally and then withdrew when he was not needed anymore. Also, because Frank wants to be actively involved in sports, the leisure coach will be getting him involved in a bowling league, perhaps using a portable ramp or other adaptation to send the ball down the lane.

Shopping and Financial Management

Many individuals with disabilities, particularly cognitive impairments, need assistance with household budgeting, shopping, locating income supports (e.g., Social Security, housing assistance, cash subsidy programs), obtaining credit, and paying bills. This type of assistance is critical for ensuring that individuals with disabilities are able to maintain their homes and improve their quality of life. In many cases, these supports can be provided by family and friends or paid staff members. There are also organizations that provide this type of assistance to anyone in need, such as a credit counseling agency, Cooperative Extension Agency, church, or business organization. Requiring assistance with shopping or financial management should not preclude community living.

Erica *Erica lives in an apartment with two other women who, like Erica, have cognitive disabilities. Support staff take the women shopping for clothing and food and assist them with paying rent and utilities. Yet, Erica wanted and needed to learn to make small purchases on her own, such as at the neighborhood convenience store and fast-food restaurants. Her support staff attempted to teach*

her to count dollars and coins, but she could not count out the correct amount of money in response to a verbal prompt.

Erica can, however, count to 10. Since it would be unlikely that Erica's purchases would ever total more than $10, her support staff have her carry ten $1 bills when she goes out, and have taught her to make purchases using the "next-dollar" method. Beginning in the apartment and then moving to nearby stores, they instructed Erica to attend to only the number of dollars told to her by the clerk or counter person. She then counts out that many dollars plus one more. For example, if the clerk says, "That will be $5.15," Erica counts out five dollars and one more, then waits for her change. Staff have also taught her to discriminate the rare occasions when a purchase totals an even number of dollars and to eliminate the step of giving the clerk the next dollar. Erica can now make small purchases independently and naturally, and she always has plenty of change for the snack machines at her job.

Health and Safety

Perske (1972) first wrote of the *dignity of risk* for people with mental retardation and other developmental disabilities. Living in the community brings risks of rejection, disappointment, and potential harm. Recognizing risk and emphasizing personal control, however, does not mean that unhealthy or unsafe practices are ignored or tolerated; rather, potential risks are balanced against the benefits of participation in integrated environments, and areas that seem "too risky" for a particular individual receive some form of intervention. Table 9.2 presents areas of safety and health that may need to be addressed in planning independent living supports and services.

Art Art, age 21, has a significant psychiatric and learning disability. When he was 18, his doctor recommended that he not reside at home with his mother because of dependency issues. At that time, he and his mother sought alternative housing. Art was offered a vacancy at a nursing home facility that had a young adults section. Given his difficulty managing his medication and his lack of independent living skills, he was willing to reside there. Art was also referred to a Center for Independent Living (CIL) for skills training and other assistance, but he withdrew from the center because he did not like being around other people with disabilities.

However, Art began receiving supported employment and soon found a job. He had several life needs that required assistance and training: time management, personal hygiene and grooming,

Table 9.2. Health and safety issues for independent living

Avoiding unsafe areas	Handling stress
Avoiding unsafe relationships	Home cleanliness and clutter
Avoiding victimization	Home security
Electrical hazards	Nutrition
Emergency preparation	Personal hygiene
Exercise	Proper lighting
Family planning	Sexual precautions
Fire safety	Substance abuse
First aid	Traffic safety
Food storage	Use of medication

money management, care of his uniform and laundry, transportation, medication management, and meals. Art and significant people in his life addressed each need by exploring all options available and utilized the resources of Art's choice. He devised a routine that fit comfortably with his lifestyle pattern. His preference was to sleep late and stay up late; therefore, his work hours were evenings. Because he was unable to judge when to bathe and how much time to allow for eating and travel, his time was structured. The schedule was monitored by facility staff who would prompt him when he needed assistance. To assist with money management, he and his mother worked out an agreement where she would assist him with safely picking up his check and depositing it at a bank; prior to working, she was accustomed to bringing him a weekly allowance so this replaced that activity.

Art left the nursing facility and moved into an apartment with a friend. He took his medication independently with the help of a pill box that held a week's supply by days and times of dosage. He also referred to a written medication schedule. His friend replaced the staff prompting for preparing for work and assisted with meal selection and preparation. His mother continued the money management assistance. Art chose to leave his job and applied for food stamps. He sought other assistance through volunteers with the Cooperative Extension Service, university students, and a paid personal assistant.

Art is moving to his own efficiency apartment as he no longer wants a roommate and has gained the skills to live independently. He will continue to utilize his current supports and will explore additional supports as they are needed.

Behavioral Support

Individuals with disabilities sometimes exhibit inappropriate or stigmatizing behaviors that can limit their participation in integrated living, work, or social activities. The methods of altering or eliminating these behaviors have primarily evolved from the science of behaviorism (Skinner, 1953), which argues that changes in behavioral response rates routinely occur in the presence or absence of either reinforcements or punishments. Behavior management procedures attempt to manipulate individuals either to increase desired behaviors or decrease undesired ones. Typical procedures for reducing rates of undesired behaviors include shaping, fading, extinction, and differential reinforcement strategies for increasing the rates of alternative, incompatible, and appropriate behaviors (Gast & Worley, 1986; Kazdin, 1980).

An emerging application of support technology involves positive behavioral support in community settings (Horner et al., 1990; West, Rayfield, Clements, Unger, & Thornton, 1994). Horner et al. (1990) list aspects of a behavioral support program:

- The success of a behavioral support program depends upon positive lifestyle change in addition to behavior change. Behavior change is of no value in and of itself but should increase the individual's access to preferred settings, people, and activities.
- Emphasis is placed on determining the function that a behavior fulfills for the individual (i.e., functional analysis) and using that determination to drive intervention.
- While behaviorism seeks to direct a specific intervention at a specific behavior, behavioral support utilizes multicomponent interventions as part of an overall plan that may address a number of similar behaviors.
- Where behaviorism emphasizes the manipulation of immediate antecedents and con-

sequences of behavior, a program of positive behavioral support will emphasize instruction in adaptive behaviors and the manipulation of environments and precipitating conditions as means of eliminating the individual's need for the undesirable behaviors and the opportunities for exhibiting them.

- Positive behavioral support minimizes the use of punishments and instead emphasizes the use of interventions that promote the dignity of the individual.

Roger *Roger is a young man with profound deafness and mild mental retardation. He lives in an apartment complex operated by a community services agency. Roger is employed but has some behaviors that are causing problems at work and in the community. After using a public restroom, he restores his clothing while he is exiting, which sometimes results in his "flashing" his co-workers or complete strangers. He also sometimes offers to shake hands with others (particularly women), but after taking the other person's hand he will sometimes grab it and move it to his chest or groin. His support staff feel that these behaviors may cost him his job and his chances at making friends in his neighborhood.*

Because Roger's bathroom behavior at home is identical to that in public, his staff hypothesize that it may be a result of poor learning. Roger came to his community services agency from a state institution, where in all likelihood his bathroom behavior was not a high priority. Rather than use a behaviorist model of rewards and punishments for the behavior, staff instituted a functional training program to model appropriate fixing of one's clothes after using the restroom and using the mirror to make a final check before exiting.

Although Roger's bathroom behavior might initially have been a result of poor learning, the shocked responses he was receiving were undoubtedly reinforcing it. Staff also hypothesized that his behavior of putting others' hands in inappropriate places on his own body were his efforts to gain attention as well. Given the fact that Roger could not communicate with those around him, staff speculated that he was a very lonely man and preferred the negative attention he was receiving to no attention at all. His support staff began to explore ways in which Roger could interact appropriately with those around him and gain the social contact and attention he wanted and needed. They began to teach some of Roger's repertoire of simple signs to co-workers, neighbors, and others with whom he comes in contact regularly. They also began to explore ways of integrating him into recreational outlets where he could associate with people without disabilities. Thus far, Roger's problem behaviors are decreasing as his circle of friends grows.

Conclusion

A growing movement in disability-related services and legislation is *self-determination*, a belief that the power to choose and have choices is the predominant factor in the progress of one's life (Wehmeyer, 1992). Everyone, with or without disabilities, should have the same opportunity to select where and with whom he or she lives. In contrast to the traditional continuum of residential facilities and services, the emerging service paradigm focuses on supporting individuals with disabilities where they choose to live instead of where facilities or programs are located.

9

Study Questions

1. What are some criticisms of the "readiness" model presented by Taylor?

2. What does "interdependence" mean and how does it relate to community living for people with disabilities?

3. What are the steps for identifying and utilizing community and workplace supports for people with disabilities?

4. What are the four circles of support and how can they be utilized in community living for people with disabilities?

5. What are three ways of locating transportation support?

6. What are four guidelines for assisting someone with disabilities to engage in recreation and social activities?

III

Designing and Implementing Individualized Transition Plans

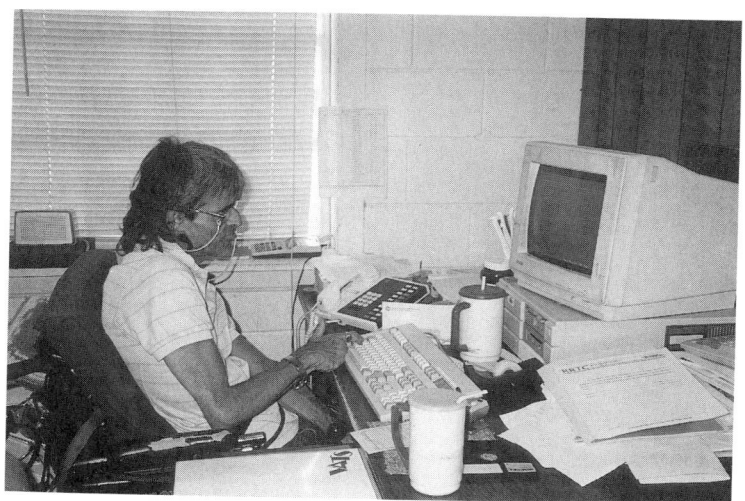

10

Applications for Youth with Mild Mental Retardation

Patricia Brown-Glover and Paul Wehman

Upon completion of this chapter, the reader will be able to do the following:

- Identify some of the characteristics of students with mild mental retardation
- Understand challenges that parents, students, and schools face when trying to provide educational services for students with mild mental retardation
- Describe and develop learning objectives using the ecological inventory method of curriculum development
- Be aware of the positive outcomes of transition planning
- Understand the team approach to transition planning and identify the players in the process
- Discuss the importance of good follow-up information as it relates to program development

The ability of individuals with mild mental retardation to succeed in the community is directly related to the amount of training and support that they receive while they are in school. These individuals have enormous potential to be extremely successful in independent community living and a career of their choosing (O'Brien, 1994). Their only limitations are those that are placed upon them by themselves, their teachers, and paid professional staff—individuals fortunate enough to receive instruction from a teacher with high aspirations typically do very well. Much of the success or failure of people with mild mental

retardation is directly related to their own personal outlook as well as the motivation and support that they receive from the circle of key people in their lives (Colond & Wieseler, 1995).

All young people in transition require some support, especially those with intellectual challenges who do not learn as quickly as the average student (D'Zamko & Hedges, 1985; Kolstoe, 1976). Many of the more complex aspects of community living and social adjustment can be successfully overcome with a little bit of well-placed help and support. In fact, without this assistance, many people with mild mental retardation develop social-emotional and psychological problems that cause them significant difficulty in holding employment and being successful in their home and community living arrangements (Newton, Olson, & Horner, 1995).

This chapter focuses on practical solutions for helping these individuals manage the challenges inherent in any community. In some areas, including physical appearance, these students are no different from their peers without disabilities (D'Zamko & Hedges, 1985; Wang, Reynolds, & Walberh, 1990). For example, in a learning environment, they are able to effectively deal with concrete concepts and master motor and vocational skills. They can acquire and maintain meaningful employment as well as manage their daily lives with great independence (Kolstoe, 1976; Payne, Kauffman, Patton, Brown, & DeMott, 1979). The mainstreamed environment is manageable for these students when individualized and small-group instruction is provided. And with thoughtful vocational and social curriculum planning, students can increase their chances of leaving the school system for positive and productive adult lives (Karge, Patton, & de la Garza, 1992; Payne et al., 1979).

Changes in the Population of Youth with Mild Mental Retardation

In the 1980s and early 1990s, the characteristics of students who attended classes once provided exclusively for individuals with mild mental retardation changed substantially—decreasing in number but possessing more severe and varied additional disabilities (Epstein, Polloway, Patton, & Foley, 1989; Heflinger, Cook, & Thackrey, 1987; MacMillan, 1988). These students now constitute a very heterogeneous group. But, generally, they are usually male, from racial or ethnic minority groups, and often from single-parent homes (Epstein et al., 1989). They exhibit problems in adaptive behavior and academic achievement (Kolstoe, 1976; Lilly, 1979; MacMillan, 1977). In addition, the majority of these students are in need of language and behavior remediation (Epstein et al., 1989).

Several factors have contributed to the changes in the makeup of this group of students. First, the ceiling score on IQ tests was lowered from 85 to 70 and an adaptive behavior proponent was added to the requirements for admission into special education programs—both of which contributed to classes of students with more severe disabilities; those individuals with higher functioning no longer meet the eligibility requirements on national, state, and local assessments (Polloway & Smith, 1983). Despite marked impairments in intellect and academic achievement, they continue to be found ineligible for special services and are usually placed in general classrooms (Heflinger et al., 1987), which are fine if students are afforded the necessary academic, vocational, and social supports. Academic placement alone will not prepare students with mild disabilities for adulthood but must be accompanied by strong vocational and community-referenced skills training, especially if the students do not view higher education as a transition planning goal.

Second, litigation has allowed parents and professionals to challenge the placements of a disproportionate number of ethnic and minority students in special education programs (Polloway & Smith, 1983). Although these numbers remain high, school officials are being more cautious about the identification procedures used in student placements (Wang et al., 1990).

Third, attempts to streamline the identification process have led to the use of various adaptive behavior assessments. Professionals are now considering factors such as academic achievement and adaptive behavior skills when attempting to place students in special education programs (Lilly, 1979). More specifically, the use of the System of the Multicultural Pluralistic Assessment (SOMPA) by some professionals, which focuses on adaptive behavior outside of the school rather than exclusively addressing school difficulties, has contributed to a decline in the number of students identified as having mild mental retardation (Heflinger et al., 1987).

Fourth, professionals believe that early intervention programs, such as Head Start, affect the placement of students in special education programs by attempting to alter the intellectual abilities of students at high risk, therefore reducing the prevalence of students with mild mental retardation in special education (Polloway & Smith, 1983).

This changing population has raised an important question: What curriculum is best for students challenged with intellectual disabilities (Edgar & Polloway, 1994)? The curriculum is of unequivocal importance as it determines what students will or will not have the opportunity to learn (Beirne-Smith, Patton, & Henbach, 1994). A curriculum should be molded by the learning characteristics of students, which—for children with mental retardation—have rapidly shifted (Edgar & Polloway, 1994; Polloway et al., in press). In 1996, our understanding of how these children learn is based on outdated research data (MacMillan, 1988), necessitating a serious reconsideration of current curricula. Guidelines for developing a comprehensive curriculum are provided by Polloway, Patton, Epstein, and Smith (1989):

1. Be responsive to the specific needs of an individual at the specific time.
2. Provide a balance for peer interactions with students without disabilities.
3. Directly relate it to the specific placement of a student.
4. Consider transitional needs across the life span.
5. Be outcome based.
6. Consider diploma goals.

If these goals are carefully followed, curriculum will be responsive to students' specific needs and be delivered in a manner that will accommodate their learning potentials.

Challenges of Working with Youth with Mild Mental Retardation

Parents and students are frustrated with the curricula for youth with mild mental retardation as it too often resembles that of the general classroom (D'Zamko & Hedges, 1985; Wang et al., 1990). Curricula that combine general and special education requirements are beneficial if the students are on an academic tract, but can be detrimental if more systematic skills training is needed.

Many students, parents, and professionals are confused about what specifically should be included in the curriculum. These students are labeled only during formative school placement (Lilly, 1979), yet have functional problems that originate in school and carry over into adult life (Wang et al., 1990). Clearly, these students require special services, such as community-based training, vocational education, and career planning—services that are addressed in functional and ecological curricula, which are derived from the identification of skills necessary for community functioning. These students also need the opportunity to earn an occupationally oriented diploma through a program that teaches functional academic skills, as well as paid work skills—occupational and career orientations in middle and secondary school are absolutely imperative for this group of students.

Many students reject specialized, outcomes-oriented curricula because they are often implemented in stigmatizing ways. This is particularly difficult for students with mild mental retardation who are not labeled in their communities but are in school (Cartwright, Cartwright, & Ward, 1989; Lilly, 1979). In other cases, these students follow schedules and curricula that closely resemble those used in general classrooms without being afforded the necessary individualization and support services, which causes them to fall further and further behind both academically and vocationally (Wang et al., 1990). Therefore, professionals are challenged to deliver needed services in ways that preserve the respect and dignity of the students and their families.

Choice and Empowerment

Many people with mental retardation have not been allowed to participate in the direction of the services they receive, how they are administered, or what their outcomes should be (Brotherson, Cook, Cunconon-Lehr, & Wehmeyer, 1995). All too often, both providers and recipients seem to believe that people with mental retardation should feel grateful simply to get into a program; however, the notion that consumers should gain power over human services, and, in the process, gain or regain power over their own lives is becoming increasingly popular (Rosen, 1994). This type of *self-determination* or *empowerment* can be broadly defined as the transfer of power and control over the values, decisions, choices, and directions of human services from external entities (i.e., government agencies, service providers, social forces) to the consumers of services. This is likely to give consumers increased independence, greater motivation to participate and succeed, and a greater degree of dignity (Syzmanski, 1994).

Choice is defined as "the act of an individual's selection of a preferred alternate from among several familiar options" (Sigafoos, Roberts, Couzens, & Kerr, 1993, p. 222). This implies that choice making involves two parts: 1) identifying one's preferences, and 2) expressing those choices. Individuals with severe disabilities may have difficulty with one or both of these skills as a result of a lack of training on how to make choices, inexperience with choice making, little knowledge about possible alternatives, and limitations with communication. (See Sigafoos et al., 1993, for an excellent training package on incorporating choice making and turn taking into leisure activities for individuals with multiple disabilities.)

Wolfensberger (1995) speaks eloquently to the fact that choice needs to be real and that caregivers should not set their values on the person with a disability:

> It seems that the "choices" of societally devalued people in general are vastly more likely to be honored if they are for segregation or things that are bad for them than if they are for good things

available to other people. But aside from that, the current "choice" craze seems to be part of the broader contemporary craze of "give them what they say they want," a logical endpoint of which is to help people kill themselves, or do it for them if they ask for such help. (p. 10)

Ferleger (1994) also writes of the importance of informed choice. For people with mild mental retardation who can be more easily taken advantage of in society, this is a critical issue.

Individuals with disabilities frequently respond positively to a question or answer in a manner they feel the questioner would prefer because often they do not understand what is being asked, are not aware of the given alternatives, or do not want to jeopardize the chance to receive help. Unfortunately, these "choices" often translate into service delivery that does not reflect what the individual actually wants. Typically, individuals with mental retardation require additional assistance, support, or time in order to express their preferred choices.

The concepts of choice and empowerment are a dramatic departure for thousands of people with mental retardation who have experienced decades of limited choices (Altman & Cunningham, 1993), have been sent to live in institutions, have been told to work in a sheltered workshop, and have been shunned from public education.

The Nature of Supports and the AAMR Definition

Supports are a key aspect of helping people with disabilities achieve their goals and succeed (Brooke, Wehman, Inge, & Parent, 1995) and a guiding principle of this book. In 1992, the American Association on Mental Retardation (AAMR) changed its definition of mental retardation to incorporate the concept of supports and how they are provided. This definition reflects the 1990s philosophy that the success of people with mental retardation is directly based upon the availability and quality of supports in their homes, communities, and workplaces (Bradley, Ashbough, & Blaney, 1994; Newton, Horner, Ard, LeBaron, & Sappington, 1994)—a serious departure from the way services have been traditionally provided and a new vista of hope. The new definition of mental retardation is as follows:

Mental retardation refers to substantial limitations in present functioning. It is characterized by significantly subaverage intellectual functioning, existing concurrently with related limitations in two or more of the following applicable adaptive skill areas: communication, self-care, home living, social skills, community use, self-direction, health and safety, functional academics, leisure and work. Mental retardation manifests before age 18. (Luckasson et al., 1992, p. 5)

This definition accounts for the likelihood that the individual can and will change over time (Smith, 1994). It is formulated to broaden the conceptualization of mental retardation, prevent the assigning of a disability label based on IQ, and determine the appropriate support based on an individual's needs. Furthermore, it strongly supports the expectation of individual potential and growth (Schalock et al., 1994). It also recognizes that not all people with mental retardation will have the same limitations, which is important for young adults mild mental retardation, giving them a tremendous opportunity to successfully blend into society without odious labels.

In the AAMR definition the following assumptions are considered essential:

1. Valid assessment considers cultural and linguistic diversity as well as differences in communication and behavioral factors.

2. The existence of limitations in adaptive skills occurs within the context of community environments typical of the individual's age peers and is indexed to the person's individualized need for supports.
3. Specific adaptive limitations often co-exist with strengths in other adaptive skills or other personal capabilities.
4. With appropriate supports over a sustained period, the life functioning of a person with mental retardation will generally improve. (Luckasson et al., 1992, p. 5)

These are critically important assumptions that reflect the research of the 1980s and 1990s. They establish the fact that some people with mental retardation may eventually acquire sufficient competence through supports as to no longer be considered as having mental retardation.

Two transition leaders who have devoted their professional lives and provided meritorious leadership to show how people with mental retardation can develop with supports are Drs. Janis Chadsey-Rusch and Frank R. Rusch, who have produced much of the critical research on the subject.

Janis Chadsey-Rusch Janis Chadsey-Rusch is an associate professor in the Department of Special Education at the University of Illinois and is affiliated with its Transition Research Institute. She also worked for 10 years as a speech-language pathologist. She is recognized for her research, which focuses upon social integration issues in employment contexts and has been instrumental in confirming valued social behaviors that exist in employment contexts and developing different strategies that can be used to promote social relationships. In particular, she has taken an ecological perspective toward studying social interactions, recognizing the mutual influences that environments and people have on one another. Dr. Chadsey-Rusch is also known for her work on transition; she has contributed numerous chapters, articles, and presentations. She is one of the coordinators of the Moderate and Severe Disabilities Program that prepares teachers to work with students who have severe disabilities.

Frank R. Rusch Frank R. Rusch is a professor of special education and Director of the Institute for Research on Human Development at the University of Illinois, Urbana–Champaign. For the last 10 years, he has been Director of the Transition Research Institute—a federally funded institute formed by the Office of Special Education and Rehabilitative Services to address the problems faced by youth in making the transitions from school to adulthood. He has also served as Education President of the American Association on Mental Retardation. Professor Rusch focuses upon integration and employment. He has published numerous books, chapters, and articles related to learning (self-instructional strategies), relationships and supports in the workplace (co-worker involvement), and program evaluation (cost–benefit analysis) that have been cited by colleagues throughout the world.

The 1992 AAMR definition provides four levels of supports as guideposts in determining how much help a person with mental retardation may need:

1. *Intermittent*—special help that an individual might need only periodically, perhaps upon losing a job
2. *Limited*—supports that occur somewhat frequently but are less intense, such as time-limited job training
3. *Extensive*—help that occurs regularly in a person's life, such as living in a group home with a 24-hour counselor
4. *Pervasive*—support that is all-encompassing in a person's life and very expensive (e.g., extended medical care or behavioral support)

These supports are taken in conjunction with 1) the diagnosis of mental retardation, and 2) the description of the person's adaptive skills and intellectual functioning to form the initial basis of the classification system.

Natural Supports for Youth with Mild Mental Retardation

The job coach is a critical factor in the use of a variety of supports. A job coach helps the consumer to identify, choose, and utilize needed supports at whatever level of assistance he or she prefers (Parent et al., 1995). A systematic process for utilizing community and workplace supports in supported employment is provided in Figure 10.1.

The first step in utilizing an array of support options is determining what type of assistance is potentially available in the community and in different employment settings by becoming familiar with the local community and its resources available to and used by individuals both with and without disabilities. Similar to the community job market analysis typically conducted by most supported employment programs, identifying community and workplace support options requires that personal contact be made with various agencies, organizations, associations, and businesses. Those contacts found to be the most productive include personal connections through friends or acquaintances, the telephone book, the consumer and his or her friends, the newspaper, and other colleagues. Five general types of support option categories have been identified, including 1) employer supports, 2) transportation supports, 3) community supports, 4) personal and independent living supports, and 5) recreation and social integration supports. Several examples of different kinds of support options identified within each of these categories are listed in Table 10.1.

Assessment of Youth with Mild Mental Retardation

Special education students are identified and placed in school programs based on their general intellectual functioning. Intelligence tests are presumably used to set the parameters for which and to what extent students are served in special classes and programs; however, it has been proven that special placements were already occurring before the development and widespread use of these tests (Reschly, 1988). Although student achievement and ability must be measured for distribution of appropriate services and maintenance of fiscal policies, efforts should be made to use other means of assessment to gain information for curriculum development and leverage in educational decision making (Shapiro & Derr, 1987). Commercially prepared, standardized norm-referenced tests have been used for evaluating and classifying students academically and vocationally. Achievement tests have been used to determine students' levels of mastery in basic academic skills, such as

Figure 10.1. A systematic process for utilizing community and workplace supports in supported employment.

reading and math (Shapiro & Derr, 1987). Vocational evaluation has played a crucial role in determining eligibility for rehabilitation services and in predicting vocational success (Menchetti & Rusch, 1988). In academic and vocational assessments, only a small percentage of skills emphasized in the curricula have counterparts on standardized tests (Shapiro & Derr, 1987).

The major purpose of vocational testing has been to measure a student's ability to master skills associated with real work settings. This testing is designed to determine who is eligible for services and which services are appropriate for specific individuals with disabilities in the rehabilitation field. Some critics, however, suggest that the purpose of vocational assessment may be unrelated to the identification of specific training needs. Determinations of low IQ scores or poor aptitude do not provide practitioners with clear instructions about what should be included in the curriculum for vocational training. When testing procedures do not provide training-related information, they serve little purpose in the educational setting.

The testing approach that predicts the general vocational ability of students is known as the mental testing approach. Rehabilitation professionals have relied upon this approach for years (Menchetti & Rusch, 1988). Many professionals, however, are beginning to rely upon the counseling orientation approach. This approach is more functional than the mental testing approach because it measures variables that can be used to identify students' specific training needs and, subsequently, for curriculum development and instructional planning associated with vocational training (Cobb, 1972; B.M. Menchetti, personal communication, October 15, 1991).

Table 10.1. Support option resources

Employer supports	**Transportation supports**
Co-worker mentor	Taxi
Company videotape training	Riding with a co-worker
Co-worker training or monitoring	Walking
Company-sponsored computer accommodation program	Riding a bicycle
Employee assistance program	Driven by parents
Restructuring job duties	Bus/public transportation
Scheduling flexibility	**Personal and independent living supports**
Supervisor prompting or monitoring	Counseling
Job duty checklist provided by employer	Purchased digital watch or alarm clock
Supervisor and co-worker advocacy	Advocate for assisting with housing
Employee counseling	Housemates
Community supports	Community residential workers
Cooperative extension service (financial management)	Purchased security items (e.g., keys, flashlight, reflective vest)
Independent living center	**Recreation and social integration supports**
College students as peer mentors or tutors	Jaycees
State assistive technology systems	YMCA
Planned Parenthood courses	Neighborhood community association
Red Cross safety courses	After-work social activities with co-workers
YWCA safety prevention courses	Parks and recreation programs
Social Security Incentives specialist/consultant	Volunteer at local rescue squad
Auto driving school	Company-sponsored activities (e.g., bowling)
Employment Commission	Linking up with a friend (e.g., skating, lunch)
Community-sponsored child care course	
Neighbors	

From Parent, W., Gibson, W., Unger, D., & Clements, C. (1994). The role of the job coach: Orchestrating community and workplace supports. In P. Wehman & J. Kregel (Eds.), *New directions in supported employment* (pp. 40–52). Richmond: Virginia Commonwealth University, Rehabilitation Research and Training Center; reprinted by permission.

The consensus among many professionals is that vocational assessment should aid in the identification of training needs more than measurement of prior learning. Individual strengths and weaknesses should be assessed and considered as goals are outlined in individualized education programs (IEPs) and individualized transition plans (ITPs). Including test results in IEPs and ITPs allows individual and group instruction and constant monitoring of student progress (Menchetti & Rusch, 1988).

Curriculum Strategies for Youth with Mild Mental Retardation

Individuals with mild mental retardation are experiencing problems with employment, independent living, and community access, which began when they were students. Historically, these students have been educated through workbooks, ditto sheets, and blackboard work, instead of training for practical community-referenced skills, such as driver's education, substance abuse education, sexually transmitted diseases (STDs) and acquired immunodeficiency syndrome (AIDS) education, job-seeking skills, and socialization skills (Smith & Puccini, 1995). These skills must be introduced to students early in their educational careers. Krom and Prater (1993) indicate that very little career and vocational edu-

cation efforts are begun in middle school. Furthermore, they noted that teachers write IEP goals based on their own curriculum, not student needs:

> Although the teachers in this study stated they used students' present levels of functioning to determine IEP goals, all of them also reported that they wrote annual goals to fit the content of the curriculum they taught. At the intermediate level, teachers may be confronted with the dilemma of whether to meet students' needs or to meet water-downed general education course requirements. The trend to require higher academic standards for receipt of a high school diploma may force special educators to emphasize academic curricula and spend less time on career and vocational experiences.
>
> Research suggests that training in vocational areas usually begins in high school (Edgar, 1987; Polloway et al., 1989). Postsecondary outcomes of students with MMR indicate that waiting until high school to provide students with life skills may be too little, too late. Preparing all students in systematic and deliberate ways for their adult future must commence early in their schooling. (p. 36)

Most curriculum guides present activities in general terms, but good teachers can design creative ways to involve members of the community in the learning process, especially for instruction in vocational, community, and recreational domains.

It is also essential that each student has an IEP, not a program that has been mass produced for all of the students in a class. Although this is more costly in terms of aides, time, and planning, it would cost society more in the long run not to individualize these programs. Community-referenced skills training that interests students must take the place of dry, boring, and nonfunctional curricula.

Many of the criticisms by Edgar (1988), in which he questions the justifiability of special education, rest on the assumption that the curriculum used with most young people with mental retardation is static and does not encompass community and society needs. Only a proactive teaching approach will change this situation.

The research on exiting special education youth strongly supports the importance of gaining community-referenced skills through paid work as part of the school experience. In Table 10.2, Nixon and the Williamston, North Carolina, Martin County Schools (1995) provide one way to earn an occupational diploma in a program that emphasizes work over academics. This schedule can be revised to focus more intensely on work as the student's needs and interests dictate.

The ultimate goal of education is to prepare students to function in their future environments. Therefore, schools should analyze the demands of these environments and organize curricula that prepare students to function with as much independence as possible. The curricula must provide principles and generic skills that are applicable for solving problems and meeting challenges in adult life (Chadsey-Rusch, DeStefano, O'Reilly, Gonzalez, & Collet-Klingenberg, 1992).

Toward an Occupational Diploma

In general high school programs, students with mild retardation have repeatedly engaged in activities that are not very relevant to their needs. Until the late 1980s, these students were not given full consideration for admittance into vocational programs and services that support positive transition into employment, independent living, and community programs (Cobb & Hasazi, 1987). Programs are needed that enhance self-direction and

Table 10.2. Occupational preparation for students with special needs: Curriculum courses for grades 9–12

Grade 9
Employment English I
Employment Math I
Life Skills Science
Career Preparation I (1 class period)—school factory
Electives (2 or 3)

Grade 10
Employment English II
Employment Math II
Career Preparation II (2 class periods)—in-school jobs, community career exploration

Grade 11
Employment English III
Employment Math III
Career Preparation (2 class periods)—nonpaid community-based training, job shadowing

Grade 12
Employment English IV
Applied Work Science (3 credits for work)—paid part-time employment
Career Preparation IV (1 class period)
Electives (optional based upon needed courses and work situation)

Developed by Dr. Cindi Nixon, Martin County Schools, Williamston, North Carolina (1995).

Note: This schedule of courses is currently being offered at two high schools, with three staff people sharing the teaching responsibilities at each school. An aide, who is also a certified driver, is available between the two programs. The transition coordinator serves both of the schools through weekly staffings, offers assessment services, operates a Job Club program for middle school students, and chairs the community-level transition team.

teach both generic and specific problem-solving skills in the classroom, in the community, and at vocational worksites.

As of 1996, schools have begun to move away from providing educational services within classroom settings and are moving toward offering experiences and training in actual community settings. Students' current skill levels are compared to those necessary for future success in adult settings. As a result, the ecological curriculum provides a true set of individualized goals.

Student Involvement in Curriculum

Students with mild mental retardation must be heavily consulted in the learning process and curriculum (see Table 10.3) as they need the concrete involvement of participating in meaningful learning activities and performing necessary skills (Brotherson et al., 1995). This means that teachers must directly relate a curriculum area, such as health education, to the challenges of living in the 1990s, including concerns about unexpected pregnancies, sexually transmitted diseases, and social problems within the criminal justice system (e.g., committing crimes against others, becoming victims of crimes).

These students must also be educated about how to be good citizens. In the 1990s, more young people have been incarcerated and executed in states where capital punishment is allowed than ever before. Special education personnel and rehabilitation counselors must actively help these students learn the rules and guidelines for appropriate behavior and guide them in obtaining legal counsel if needed.

Table 10.3. Curriculum recommendation for children with disabilities

"Do"s

1. Ask each student the types of activities and skills that he or she would like to work to develop during part of every day.
2. Actively involve students in career education and job-seeking activities.
3. Invite outside speakers from different careers to come into the classroom and share information about their jobs. Encourage students to visit different jobs to gain an understanding of what is involved in holding a job.
4. Teach students how to complete job applications.
5. Teach skilled students how to develop résumés.
6. Make sure every student has a Social Security card.
7. Teach students how to look for jobs in the classified advertisements.
8. Teach students how to find different recreational activities and events in the newspaper. Take them to some of these activities and events and teach them to involve themselves in community activities.
9. Teach students how to get around town using public transportation or learning how to identify a network of people who will give car rides.

"Don't"s

1. Do not rely heavily on workbooks, which are essentially simulations of what the real work activity is.
2. Do not rely on large volumes of ditto sheets and desk work.
3. Do not try to simulate regular education academic-based curricula.
4. Do not spend extensive time doing blackboard work.
5. Do not let students repeatedly fail tasks or activities. Instead try to modify the tasks or make them easier or more interesting.
6. Do not segregate the more capable from the least capable students in class. Slower students can learn from more capable students. Also it is not necessarily true that because students are slow in one area that they will be slow in another area or that they will stay slow in a given area.
7. Do not plan curricula on the basis of a curriculum guide or book that comes from a state agency or book publisher. Plan curricula around the students' needs and interests.
8. Do not arrange teaching environments so the teacher does all of the teaching and the students do all of the listening. Design environments where students are heavily involved in the learning process.
9. Do not mass duplicate IEPs.

A Community-Oriented Approach

The community-based, or ecological, curriculum model equips students to function in their primary living environments with as much independence as possible (Cronis, Smith, & Forgnone, 1986). In order for the ecological curriculum to be implemented, however, traditional teacher roles must be abandoned. Flexibility is needed to go out of the classroom and to identify the specific needs of each student and the cultural and ethical nuances of their individual communities. With the help of individual students, parents, and other family members, future environments (e.g., living, community, vocational worksites) must be assessed and cataloged. Because of cultural, political, and family dynamics, each student's inventory of skills is different.

During the assessment and inventory of curriculum domains, the home and school partnership should identify skills that are currently needed and predict skills that will be needed for the students to function independently in the future. Domains may include the following:

1. The *vocational domain* involves skills related to employment and work experience.
2. The *community domain* relates to skill attainment for independence; for example, stu-

dents should have skills related to shopping, banking, and participating in community activities. Furthermore, appropriate health education curricula must include sex education, substance abuse education, and information about AIDS and other sexually transmitted diseases.

3. The *leisure domain* includes skills for recreation in the community.
4. The *domestic domain* identifies skills needed for residential independence.

After the domains have been identified, they must be broken down into natural environments. For example, if the domain is community, then the bank would be a natural environment of the community. Subenvironments of the bank are assessed next, for example, the bank lobby where activities and skills such as knowing how to make deposits or how to cash checks can be taught. These types of skills should be identified and targeted as a part of the instructional plan outlined in Figure 10.2. In the vocational domain, one illustration of a skill that many students need to acquire is appropriate job interviewing. Making a good impression and presentation is very important, especially with employers who have limited knowledge about workers with disabilities. Mozingo, Ackley, and Bailey (1994) present a validated job interview training program.

Setting Transition Goals

After all of the necessary domains and subenvironments have been cataloged, the teacher serves as the coordinator of the data. The teacher, vocational specialist, and family members collaborate to prioritize goals and skill attainment (Snell & Grigg, 1987). The goals are included in the IEP for daily use in the classroom as students move toward ITP objectives. Obviously, students cannot work toward all goals at the same time. Teachers, parents, and students must prioritize goals and tasks and work toward the goals that will be needed first. After individual goals have been developed, a workable daily schedule must be implemented. Today's class schedule should not look like schedules of the past. They should be more flexible, they should reflect general and special education class goals as well as related services provisions. In addition, no two IEPs should look the same. Some objectives may cross over several different IEPs; but mass duplication of IEPs is not acceptable. The practice of photocopying IEP pages and inserting them into individualized programs does not ensure individualization of curricula development for students. Figure 10.3 illustrates a flexible schedule of a student who attends school and is employed at a local grocery store. This student is concentrating on community, vocational, and domestic skills attainment as he moves toward completion of secondary school.

Teacher Role

In order for flexible scheduling to work, the traditional teacher role must be abandoned. The teacher may be called on to provide transportation to and from training sites; to conduct job placement, training, and follow-along; or to provide instruction in the community. Resources that are usually allocated for the purchase of books and classroom materials should be channeled into financing travel, extra personnel, and community training. Speech-language and physical therapies are no longer conducted in isolation but incorporated into schedules. For example, the speech-language therapist might accompany a student during instruction in the community where the remediation is actually needed.

Ecological inventory of skills

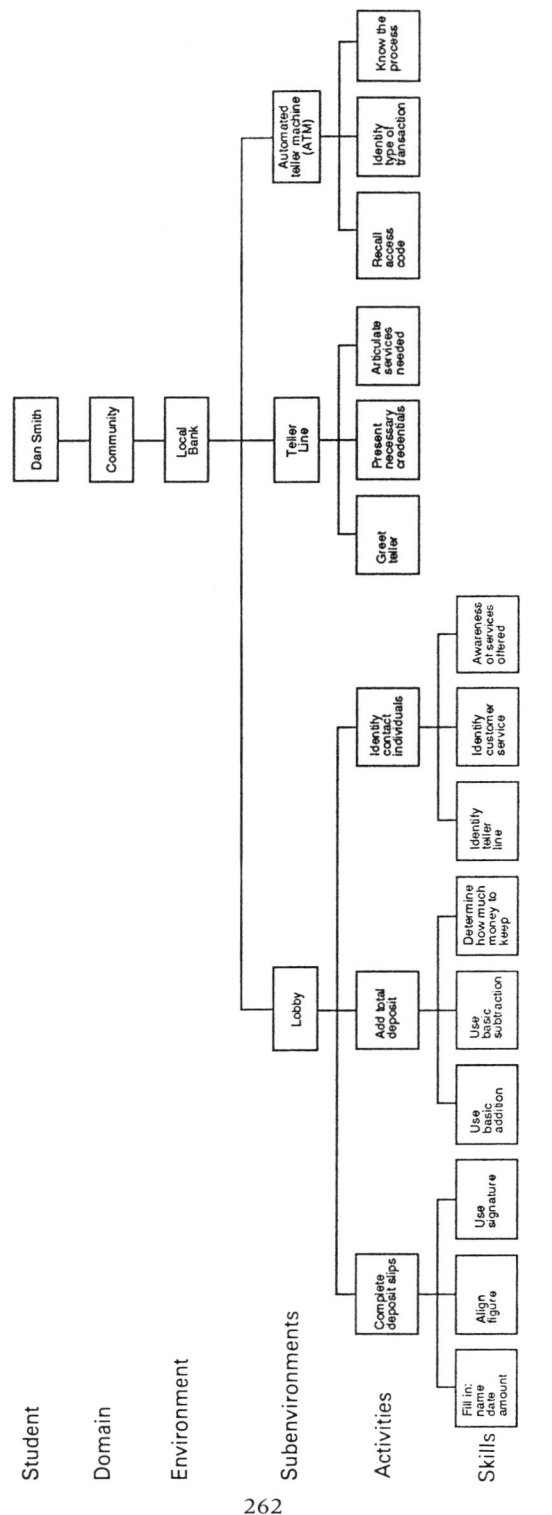

Student

Domain

Environment

Subenvironments

Activities

Skills

Figure 10.2. An example of an instructional plan. (Adapted from Snell & Grigg, 1987.)

Monday	Tuesday	Wednesday	Thursday	Friday
8:30 A.M.– 1:30 P.M. **Work-Ukrops**	8:30 A.M– 4:30 P.M. **Work-Ukrops**	8:30 A.M.– 8:40 A.M. **Regular homeroom**	8:30 A.M.– 4:30 P.M. **Work Ukrops**	8:30 A.M.– 4:30 P.M **Work Ukrops**

8:30 A.M.–
1:30 P.M.
Work-Ukrops

1:45 P.M.–
2:15 P.M.
Lunch

2:15 p.m.–
3:00 P.M.
**Functional
 academics**
Complete simple
 applications
Complete budget
Recite personal data
Functional site words
Prepare shopping lists
Use calculator to man-
 age checking account
Complete deposit and
 withdrawal slips
Read simple picture
 recipes

3:00 P.M.–
 3:20 P.M.
Library
Appropriate behavior
Locate and check out
 books and magazines
Use photocopier

8:40 A.M.–
11:15 A.M.
**Recreation/
leisure**
Select appropriate
 activities
Bowling—select
 shoe size and
 ball, lane courtesy,
 knowledge of rules
Fitness center—aerobic
 routine, weight equip-
 ment, ride stationary
 bike
Swimming—enter pool,
 walk through water,
 submerge head, follow
 directions

11:30 A.M.–
 2:15 P.M.
Group home
Prepare lunch
Laundry—wash, dry, and
 fold clothes
Household tasks—sweep,
 vacuum, dust, and clean
Community access
Make purchases
Manage money
Order food and eat

3:00 P.M.–
 3:20 P.M.
Library
Appropriate behavior
Locate and check out
 books and magazines
Use photocopier

Figure 10.3. An example of a flexible student schedule.

Within this flexible schedule, students participate in general class placements, especially in electives such as auto shop or home economics.

In Dan's case study, each of these concepts is illustrated. Readers should pay careful attention to the differences in student outcomes as the old and new modes of teaching are demonstrated.

Dan *Dan is a 16-year-old student in an eighth-grade special education program. He attends a classroom for students with mild mental retardation. Dan has been in similar classrooms since he was tested and found eligible for special education placement 6 years ago.*

Before that time, Dan attended a general day care in his community and general kindergarten and first-grade classes. Dan's first-grade teacher referred him for testing because he was not mastering his basic skills at the same rate as other students. He also displayed some signs of aggression toward other students and figures of authority. Dan experienced more and more frustration as time passed. By the end of first grade, Dan had been labeled a behavior problem and a poor learner.

Dan's mother, Ms. Smith, was contacted sporadically about her son's progress and problems. She was asked to come to school only to give her permission for testing and other administrative procedures. The teachers did not make any effort to include Ms. Smith as a part of Dan's planning team. It was assumed that his behavior was typical for a student from a low economic status and a broken home (Dan's older brother had also utilized special education) and that his parent did not want to be involved in the process.

Dan had an IEP that looked like every other student's IEP in the class. It included objectives pertaining to the mastery of academics, such as sentence dissection, American history, civics, and algebra. Dan was not interested in school or his studies. He fell further and further behind academically. He started to miss a lot of school and was always in the principal's office for one thing or another.

Under pressure from the central office to produce "good" statistics, Dan was promoted to the next higher grade 1 year but then retained the following year for no apparent educational rationale. The teacher completed and mailed his IEP home, and Dan's mother was required to sign it and mail it back to school. Dan and his mom were not involved in any functional curricula or individualized planning for classroom activities or community transition training.

By 16 years of age, Dan was very streetwise, had no regard for figures of authority, intimidated other students, and did not attend any classes or engage in any constructive learning when he went to school. At this point, Dan's mother refused to go to the school for a conference because she felt that the school system had failed her child. Initially, she felt that a special placement was in his best interest and would allow him to catch up in school and afford him some good survival skills. She felt helpless and suspicious about why her involvement was solicited at this late stage. Dan's teacher was contacted 1 week later. Dan had been arrested for murder. Before the school year ended, Dan was sentenced to 99 years in jail.

Dan with Educational Intervention *Dan is a 16-year-old student in a secondary special education program. He is placed in a classroom for students with mild mental retardation but spends most of his time in the community where he is employed as a bus boy in a local restaurant. At school, he attends general elective classes, such as physical education and woodworking. He is also involved in functional academics and community training activities. Both Dan and his mother, Ms. Smith, have been very active in Dan's curricula planning. They are very satisfied with his class placement and work training.*

Even though Ms. Smith is a single parent and once attended a similar class, she feels that she can manage her son's education and assist in making sound educational and vocational decisions for him. As a matter of fact, Ms. Smith has signed an agreement with the school to be responsible for making sure that Dan is picked up from work because he gets off work after school hours. In turn, the school's aide, Mrs. Jefferson, drops Dan off at his job in the morning on her way to the community training sites.

Dan and his mother have decided that he will stay in school until he turns 18. He will then receive a special diploma and leave the school system with a transition plan in place for entry into the workforce.

These two scenarios are very real for many inner-city students as they navigate through the web of special services. It cannot be emphasized enough that flexible, empowering, outcome-oriented curricula planning is needed. In Dan's case, the second scenario proved successful because of two important factors. First and most important, the family and student had an equal and active role in the decision-making process. Second, the student could take ownership and pride in his schedule because it was independently tailored to meet his needs. Community site trainings were not field trips; rather they were strategies used for goal attainment. Dan's IEP was not a photocopy of a master form; it was a legal and binding document that was produced through collaboration.

School administrators must advocate for all students and allocate resources equally. Aides, community business resources, and volunteers must be encouraged to participate in the process. In order for teachers to provide necessary leadership, the support of central office and local school-level administrators is needed. All school personnel must be concerned about promoting the most productive and least restrictive environments as the major tools of learning for all students. Classroom teachers must examine their ethics and priorities. Services must be delivered that are consistent with the belief that all students are entitled to an appropriate and free education.

Implementing Individualized Transition Plans for Youth with Mild Mental Retardation

The gap between school and adult life for students with disabilities continues to receive national attention (Goodall & Bruder, 1986). During the 1980s and early 1990s, much attention was focused on the postschool adjustment of special education students—a movement that stems from the discouraging patterns of postsecondary employment of youth with disabilities (Wehman, 1990). Specifically, the postschool unemployment rate of students with mild disabilities ranges from 30% to 75% (Bates, Suter, & Poelvoorde, 1986). Generally, these students are underserved because of the lack of structured activities that lead to positive adult outcomes. A follow-up study done by Hasazi, Johnson, Hasazi, and Gordon (1989) continues to document a high unemployment rate among individuals with disabilities who leave school. When these people do find employment, they usually receive lower wages, fewer fringe benefits, fewer available hours, and less skilled jobs than people without disabilities. Halpern (1990) suggests that these students experience difficulty in community adjustment. He cites inappropriate living conditions, inadequate financial re-

sources, restricted opportunity for postsecondary educational opportunities, and feelings of noninvolvement in the community as some of the personal and social problems former special education students experience.

As a result of these concerns, federal initiatives are being implemented to ensure structured, formalized planning for postsecondary outcomes of students with disabilities. The Individuals with Disabilities Education Act (IDEA) of 1990, PL 101-476, and its amendments include transition planning as one of the services that should be accessible to all special education students. Transition services are defined as coordinated sets of activities for students, designed with an outcomes-oriented process that promotes smooth movement from school to postschool activities. Wehman, Moon, Everson, Wood, and Barcus (1988) define transition as an interagency planning and implementation process. This includes activities that lead to admission into postsecondary education programs, employment, residential independence, and positive community living.

Although transition planning can be viewed as a generic process, some aspects of the process should be modified or emphasized for students with mild mental retardation. First, it is particularly important that these students be included in all of the planning stages. In many cases, these students have distinct opinions about what they want to do vocationally, socially, academically, and residentially. However, students sometimes have unrealistic views about the types of jobs they can perform. The teacher's role is to help these students to identify realistic goals by including career exploration in the curriculum and to explain the requirements and expectations of various jobs. While helping the student to develop realistic job expectations, teachers should also take into consideration the types of jobs about which the student exhibits interest or distaste. For example, many students find work in fast-food restaurants to be stigmatizing and demeaning but are very comfortable working in hotels. Students have said that their friends do not know what they do in hotels, but that they are too visible in fast-food restaurants. Implementing career exploration goals into ITPs can help to target appropriate vocational and community training objectives and alleviate unrealistic expectations about job choices.

Second, social skills training should be a part of the transition planning process for students with mild mental retardation, many of whom have problems with managing their behavior appropriately (Epstein et al., 1989). Transition planning goals should reflect the teacher's effort to work with students to develop coping strategies and to identify community services that may further alleviate problems. Table 10.4 shows problems some students encounter in interviewing for a job. Behavior training and coping strategies should be implemented during community training time, general classroom placements, jobsite training time, or any other time that lends itself to resolving problems and issues.

Postsecondary education is a realistic outcome of transition training for some students with mild disabilities (Polloway et al., in press). In cases in which the student and his or her family have chosen higher education as a transition planning outcome, vocational and community-referenced skills should continue to be taught; however, academic readiness is very important. Teachers must be sure that students are prepared to take minimum competency and other tests that are offered in general classrooms. Teachers must work with students to be certain that the necessary academic credits have been obtained. Informal decisions must be made while the student is in middle school so that teachers, students, and parents can modify transition plans to reflect the requirements needed for academic or vocational tracts.

Table 10.4. Rating criteria used with six people with developmental disabilities in job interviews

Question and ratings	Examples
1. How old are you?	
• Poor—shows the interviewer that student does not know how old he or she is	*I don't know.*
	My momma knows.
• Weak—states an age but shows that student is unsure about answer	*33, I think.*
	Uh, uh, 20, 22.
• Good—states an age	*28.*
• Best—states an age in a complete sentence	*I am 31 years old.*
	I just turned 25.
2. How do you dress and groom for work?	
• Poor—insinuates that student does not understand the question, or does not always dress and groom well	*What groom?*
• Weak—tells the interviewer that the student tries to dress and groom well	*Good.*
• Good—tells the interviewer that the student always dresses and grooms well or tells what he or she does to accomplish good grooming	*I try to look nice.*
• Best—tells the interviewer that the student dresses and grooms well, how he or she accomplishes this, and implies that he or she could dress and groom appropriately for the job at hand	*Good, I shave and bathe every day and wear clean clothes.*
3. What days and hours can you work?	
• Poor—shows that student does not understand the question	*I don't know.*
• Weak—student does not directly answer the question but hints that he or she will work when needed	*When do you want me to work?*
• Good—student tells the interviewer the exact number of days he or she is available with confidence	*I can work any time but night shift.*
• Best—student tells the interviewer the days and hours he or she can work but says he or she can also be available when needed	*I can work Monday through Friday anytime and weekends if you need me.*

From Mozingo, D., Ackley, G.B.E., & Bailey, J.S. (1994). Training quality job interviews with adults with developmental disabilities. *Research in Developmental Disabilities, 15*(5), 396; reprinted by permission from Elsevier Science Ltd., Oxford, England.

Note: The questions, ratings criteria, and examples upon which this table is based are derived from an empirical analysis of the local hiring community and provide objectives of interview response quality.

Although many students with mild mental retardation can learn to acquire meaningful employment and manage their daily lives, some individuals have problems when they leave school (Wang et al., 1990). Residential options are important as families and professionals approach transition planning including knowing which community resources are available and how to use them (O'Brien, 1994). Skills needed to function in specific residential environments must be highlighted and included in transition plans (Benz, Lindstrom, & Halpern, 1995; Clark, Field, Patton, Brolin, & Sitlington, 1991; Wehmeyer & Kelchner, 1995).

The most important thing to remember while working with students with mild mental retardation is that they can and should make their wants and desires known. Professionals must know how to draw out the best in each student as they make decisions, acquire new skills, plan, and resolve conflicts.

Dorothy *Dorothy is a 16-year-old student with mental retardation. She is ambulatory with an unusual gait and verbal but has a slight speech impediment. Dorothy can recognize her name and the names of familiar students but cannot read other sight words or recognize numbers. She can recite numbers 1–15 and the days of the week. Dorothy is very friendly and speaks to almost everyone she sees. She easily remembers names and routines related to the school day. Dorothy is easily distracted and has difficulty staying on task unless it involves helping another student or staff member. She lives with a cousin, nephew, and older half-brother in the home of her grandmother.*

Once a student's wishes and desires have been obtained, an interagency transition team should be formed to plan the ITP. (Pages 269–272 contain an ITP for Dorothy.) The team should include representatives from various agencies and backgrounds. These representatives should be from the local school division (e.g., administration, special and vocational education); vocational rehabilitation; mental health and mental retardation agencies; private rehabilitation facilities; postsecondary education institutions; and parents, students, and employers. Individuals with mental retardation will usually require these resources or at least some of them during the transition planning process.

Each ITP team member has a role (see Table 10.5). The roles interact, resulting in a collaboration of ideas and resources with each role being equally important. The special education teacher is responsible for the provision of functional school and community-based training, retrieval and analysis of data, and serving as the educational consultant to the team. The rehabilitation counselor's role is to provide funding for adaptive equipment and transportation needs related to employment and to participate in the assessment process. The school administrator's role includes facilitating community-based instruction and transportation and promoting parent, personnel, and public awareness training programs. The role of the service coordinator involves providing follow-along services after graduation; advising all parties about policies associated with Social Security benefits, medical benefits, and employment incentives; and working closely with families throughout the transition process. The role of the vocational education teacher includes providing specific training skills, locating job training sites, and assisting in the collection and analysis of data from vocational evaluations. The employer provides input of business community needs and access to job training sites. All of these representatives of various agencies work together to plan and project the most efficient and productive outcomes for students and their families (Sarhees-Wircenski & Wircenski, 1994).

The student and his or her family are the most important partners in the individualized transition planning process (Bates, 1990). With foresight and planning of transition services, students with disabilities can look forward to brighter futures. Every effort should be made to accommodate family members so that they and the student can attend all meetings. Both parents and students should be encouraged to express their personal

Description of Student's Future Vision

Dorothy wants very much to engage in sports and recreation activities, especially with peers without disabilities in regular community activities like bowling or softball. She knows she needs to improve her social skills as well as independent track abilities and these are both important aspects of her personal futures planning.

Individualized Transition Plan

Student's Name _Dorothy_

Birthdate _____

Student's Identification Number _____

Participants:

Name _Dorothy_

Cindy

Tom

Mary

School _Hanover High_

ITP Conference Date _____

Position _Student_

Teacher

Service coordinator

Work coordinator

Career and Economic Self-Sufficiency

Employment Goal _Dorothy will work part time as an activities assistant in a nursing home with supported employment._

Level of present performance: _Dorothy has had limited work experience. She has difficulty focusing on sedentary, repetitive tasks but enjoys helping._

Steps needed to accomplish goal: _1. Obtain supported employment services. 2. Seek placement at site on bus line. 3. Provide travel training._

Date of completion: _June 1995_

Person(s) responsible for implementation: _Service coordinator and work coordinator_

Vocational Education/Training Goal _Dorothy will volunteer in the activities department of an area nursing home 2 days per week._

Level of present performance: _Dorothy has worked at three different unpaid worksites with a small work crew. She does not do well with repetitive tasks._

Steps needed to accomplish goal: _1. Obtain appropriate sites. 2. Arrange for school staff to train and supervise Dorothy at sites. 3. Arrange for transportation to and from sites._

Date of completion: _December 1994_

Person(s) responsible for implementation: _Teacher_

From Wehman, P. (1995). *Individual transition plans: The teachers curriculum guide for helping youth with special needs.* Austin, TX: PRO-ED; reprinted by permission.

Postsecondary Education Goal *N/A*
Level of present performance:

Steps needed to accomplish goal:

Financial/Income Needs Goal *Dorothy will obtain her own bank account for part of SSI funds and full paychecks.*

Level of present performance: *Dorothy needs assistance in all financial matters. Her grandmother also has difficulty with finances and does not let Dorothy handle money.*

Steps needed to accomplish goal: *1. Meet with Dorothy's grandmother to discuss setting up an account. 2. Assist Dorothy in opening an account. 3. Appoint a trustee for long-term financial assistance to Dorothy.*

Date of completion: *December 1994*

Person(s) responsible for implementation: *Service coordinator*

Career and Economic Self-Sufficiency

Independent Living Goal *Dorothy will live with a foster family.*

Level of present performance: *Dorothy's grandmother has difficulty caring for those in her household. Dorothy's physical, financial, and emotional needs are often neglected.*

Steps needed to accomplish goal: *1. Discuss options with Dorothy's grandmother. 2. Place Dorothy on waiting list for foster placement. 3. Visit several homes so Dorothy can observe different homes.*

Date of completion: *June 1995*

Person(s) responsible for implementation: *Service coordinator and Dorothy.*

Transportation/Mobility Goal *Dorothy will learn to cross streets safely.*

Level of present performance: *Dorothy orients herself quickly to locations. She is easily distracted and does not look both ways before starting across streets.*

Steps needed to accomplish goal: *1. Identify a variety of locations for training in Dorothy's neighborhood. 2. Provide community-based instruction on street.*

Date of completion: *March 1995*

Person(s) responsible for implementation: *Teacher*

Social Relationships Goal *Dorothy will exhibit appropriate behavior in the presence of male staff or peers.*
Level of present performance: *Dorothy is aggressive to most people. She has begun to seek attention from males by kicking them or calling them names.*

Steps needed to accomplish goal: *1. Develop a behavioral intervention plan to encourage appropriate behavior at school. 2. Provide opportunities for appropriate peer modeling at school social activities. 3. Continue family instruction.*

Date of completion: *January 1995*

Person(s) responsible for implementation: *Teacher*

Recreation/Leisure Goal *Dorothy will become a member of a unified sports program pairing a volunteer without disabilities with a partner with disabilities in recreational league sports.*
Level of present performance: *Dorothy enjoys physical activities. She has no regular activities outside of school and little opportunity for integration.*

Steps needed to accomplish goal: *1. Enroll Dorothy into program. 2. Budget for transportation as needed. 3. Continue instruction in sports at school.*

Date of completion: *January 1995*

Person(s) responsible for implementation: *Teacher*

Personal Competence

Health/Safety Goal *Dorothy will exercise caution with strangers.*
Level of present performance: *Dorothy speaks to everyone everywhere and will stop strangers to ask them questions.*

Steps needed to accomplish goal: *1. Provide instructions on safety in the community. 2. Teach Dorothy to identify community workers versus strangers. 3. Provide many opportunities for Dorothy to receive attention appropriately.*

Date of completion: *January 1995*

Person(s) responsible for implementation: *Teacher*

Self-Advocacy/Future Planning *Dorothy will benefit from alternative guardianship.*

Level of present performance: *Dorothy has a large extended family. Her grandmother is currently caring for her out of necessity and would be relieved if an appropriate guardian could be named in her place.*

Steps needed to accomplish goal: *1. Meet with other family members. 2. Provide information on rights and responsibilities of guardians and those with disabilities. 3. Appoint alternative guardian.*

Date of completion: *January 1995*

Person(s) responsible for implementation: *Grandmother and service coordinator*

Student Career Preference

Helping elderly people

Student's Major Transition Needs

1. Foster care
2. Employment
3. Vocational training
4. Social skills
5. Advocacy

Additional Notes

Table 10.5. The roles of ITP team members

Special education teacher
- Provides community and school-based training in all four curricular domains
- Gathers and analyzes assessment data
- Serves as instructional consultant to team members

Rehabilitation counselor
- Provides funding for adaptive equipment and transportation needs related to employment
- Participates in assessment process
- Serves as consultant to team on local job trends and job descriptions

School administrator
- Facilitates community-based instruction and transportation
- Promotes parent, personnel, and public awareness training programs

Service coordinator
- Provides follow-along services after graduation
- Advises on SSI/SSDI and medical coverage and employment incentives
- Works closely with family throughout entire transition process

Vocational education teacher
- Provides specific skill training
- Locates job training sites
- Assists in the collection and analysis of vocational evaluation data

Employer
- Provides input on business community needs
- Provides access to job training sites

Parent(s) and student
- Conduct home training
- Advocate for full community integration of offspring
- Participate in selection of ITP goals
- Participate in selection and implementation of ITP goals

Adapted from Wehman, Moon, Everson, Wood, and Barcus (1988).

Abbreviations: SSI/SSDI = Supplemental Security Income/Social Security Disability Insurance; ITP = individualized transition plan.

goals and views of needed services (Bates, 1990). Students should provide information about the jobs they want, how they want to spend free time, and how they wish to spend their money (Wehman, 1990). Parent and student responsibility to the planning team include conducting home training, advocating for full community integration, and participating in the selection of IEP and ITP goals (Everson, 1995).

As the evaluation is completed, professionals, parents, and students should feel that something special has been accomplished in the ITP process. Plans and visions for the future should have been set in motion to secure the dignity of students as they make transitions from school to adulthood. Furthermore, these visions need to take into account the different ways to include youth with mild mental retardation into the mainstream of school activities, as well as classrooms. Inclusion must be planned—it will not happen by chance. Table 10.6 is a list of several types of inclusion activities that can help this to occur.

Table 10.6. Questions about inclusion

1. Do we genuinely start from the premise that each child belongs in the classroom he or she would otherwise attend if he or she did not have a disability? (Or do we cluster children with disabilities into special groups, classrooms, or schools?)

2. Do we individualize the instructional program for all children whether or not they have disabilities and provide the resources that each child needs to explore individual interests in the school environment? (Or do we tend to provide the same sorts of services for most children who share the same diagnostic label?)

3. Are we fully committed to maintenance of a caring community that fosters mutual respect and support among staff, parents, and students in which we honestly believe that children without disabilities can benefit from friendships with children with disabilities and vice versa? (Or do our practices tacitly tolerate children teasing or isolating some as outcasts?)

4. Have our general educators and special educators integrated their efforts and their resources so that they work together as integral parts of a unified team? (Or are they isolated in separate rooms or departments with separate supervisors and budgets?)

5. Does our administration create a work climate in which staff are supported as they provide assistance to each other? (Or are teachers afraid of being presumed to be incompetent if they seek peer collaboration in working with students?)

6. Do we actively encourage the full participation of children with disabilities in the life of our school including co-curricular and extracurricular activities? (Or do they participate only in the academic portion of the school day?)

7. Are we prepared to alter support systems for students as their needs change through the school year so that they can achieve, experience successes, and feel that they genuinely belong in the school and classes? (Or do we sometimes provide such limited services to them that the children are set up to fail?)

8. Do we make parents of children with disabilities fully a part of our school community so that they can experience a sense of belonging? (Or do we give them a separate PTA and different newsletters?)

9. Do we give children with disabilities just as much of the full school curriculum as they can master and modify it as necessary so that they can share elements of these experiences with their classmates? (Or do we have a separate curriculum for children with disabilities?)

10. Have we included children with disabilities supportively in as many as possible of the same testing and evaluation experiences as their classmates without disabilities?

Source: Rogers (1993).

Evaluation of Transition Outcomes for Youth with Mild Mental Retardation

Follow-up studies continue to document the bleak futures of students with disabilities. Therefore, each locality must take responsibility for its own students. Active involvement must be sought from families and the community to make the system work for all students. More specifically, outcome issues such as higher education, competitive employment, access to the community, integrated living, and recreation must be examined in terms of goals for future living. Foresight and vision must be a part of this decision-making process because each student's curriculum must reflect goals that will enable him or her to function with as much independence and autonomy as possible in the adult world.

All localities must be committed to tracking their own students. In doing so, problems and issues can be identified and addressed in a proactive manner. Program development and curriculum adjustments can lead to the most appropriate delivery of services. The student and his or her family must be active participants in the curriculum planning process to ensure that they are receiving the services they want and that the services are not being delivered in demeaning or stigmatizing ways.

Follow-up studies allow school systems to look within themselves and to assess available resources by asking questions such as the following: Are our former students employed? What types of jobs do they have? What wages do they earn? Where do they live? To what extent do they use community services? What services do they need? Without a formal method of answering these questions, school personnel cannot respond to students' curriculum and transition needs.

Money, time, or personnel alone cannot determine whether schools need follow-up information. If a system is truly committed to providing the best educational opportunities to all of its students, then this information is needed so that services and resources can be allocated and implemented in the most cost-effective way to ensure quality programming and brighter futures for all students.

Conclusion

The education of secondary students with mild mental retardation is a major challenge. These students present a range of problems and issues that require creative, practical, and flexible solutions. With increasing budget cutbacks and greater demands on community services, young adults with mental retardation are more at risk than ever for not receiving the necessary supports for community adjustment. Without these supports and assistance, they will be more likely to be unemployed and live in poverty-like conditions. This chapter has presented ways that schools and communities can help to overcome the barriers and improve the outcomes of these students.

10
Study Questions

1. What are the five guidelines for curriculum development for students with mild mental retardation?

2. What are some considerations in offering choices to students with mild mental retardation?

3. What are the steps to identifying and obtaining community and workplace supports for students with disabilities?

4. What are five categories of community and workplace supports and an example of each?

5. What are some postschool employment and individual living outcomes for students with mild mental retardation?

6. How do those outcomes compare with students without disabilities who exit school?

7. What are some practical implications of a community-oriented approach to skill instruction?

11

Applications for Youth with Severe Disabilities

Paul Wehman, Christine Hess, and John Kregel

Upon completion of this chapter, the reader will be able to do the following:

- Understand the important characteristics of transition education for students with severe disabilities
- Be aware of the problems of using a school-only approach to vocational training
- List the steps involved in developing community-based vocational sites
- Have knowledge of U.S. Department of Labor regulations associated with community training
- Define and give examples of personal futures planning
- Discuss the supported employment potential and outcomes for individuals with severe disabilities

There was a time in the not-so-distant past when people who were labeled as having severe disabilities were considered to be hopeless and placed in state institutions for most of their lives. These people, even by the 1970s, were not legally entitled to free and appropriate educations in the public school systems nor were they considered to be employable, able to live in the community, or capable of performing simple personal hygiene activities such as tooth brushing, dressing, or toileting. Since then, however, an enormous amount of research has suggested that the potential of individuals with severe mental retardation is much greater than once thought (Lakin, Braddock, Smith, & West, 1994, 1995).

It is entirely possible, and even likely in some communities, that these people could be competitively employed in the local bakery, library, print shop, or grocery store. For an individual with mental retardation who is earning money, operating the local ATM machine, and sharing an apartment with another individual in the community (with periodic visits from a social worker), navigating the community is no problem. Aside from the typical obstacles of community living, individuals with disabilities can usually fare well as independent adults.

Contrast this scenario with that of an individual with disabilities in the same community in 1972. That person probably did not live in the community. He saw his parents only periodically on visits home from the state institution, which was probably in a very rural area away from people and any real work prospects. In fact, this person was considered incapable of employment and made to do free work around the institution grounds. There was no individual participation because he was also considered incapable of choosing appropriate leisure activities. Community recreation typically involved transporting institution residents by bus to the State Fair for a day to walk around with 50–75 other people with mental retardation (Erb, 1995; Smith & Polloway, 1995).

One of the primary reasons for this historic discrimination is the lack of research on people with severe disabilities and the resultant negative and misguided perceptions about their capabilities. One of the great transition leaders whose involvement, influence, and research has served to reverse this discrimination is Dr. Lou Brown.

Lou Brown Lou Brown received both a bachelor's and a master's of arts in Social Studies and Clinical Psychology from East Carolina University, and a doctorate in Special Education from Florida State University. Since 1969, he has been a professor in the Department of Rehabilitation Psychology and Special Education at the University of Wisconsin.

In the field of education, he has focused his efforts on the development of service delivery models, curricula, and values that prepare individuals with significant disabilities to live, work, and play in integrated society. His dream is for all such people to live in decent family-style settings containing no more than two people with disabilities, to perform real work in the real world, to enjoy rich and varied recreation and leisure lives with their friends and neighbors without disabilities, and to have access to all community environments someday soon.

In the past, many considered his views radical and extreme because he believed so strongly that citizens with significant disabilities could become productive members of integrated society and because he called for the termination of institutions, special schools and classes, sheltered workshops, activity centers, enclaves, group homes, and other manifestations of segregation. Such views are now commonplace. Dr. Brown also believes that many educational and vocational training programs do not prepare people to function in integrated society and calls for massive changes in the ways we serve and prepare others to serve.

This chapter examines ways students with some of the most challenging disabilities can participate in transition planning. The characteristics of appropriate school programs for individuals with mental retardation, including essential components of vocational training and administrative guidelines for developing vocational training sites, are explored. Procedures for developing individualized transition plans (ITPs) are outlined, and methods for evaluating transition outcomes are provided.

Who Are Individuals with Severe Disabilities?

For the purpose of this chapter, individuals with severe disabilities are those students with the lowest intellectual functioning, comprising 1%–3% of the school-age population. They include a diverse group of individuals who may also have severe mental retardation, multiple disabilities, autism, deafness, blindness, or physical disabilities (Falvey, 1989; Snell, 1993). Rather than focusing on definitions, it is more important to understand the unique learning characteristics of individuals with severe disabilities, which include difficulties in generalization and transfer of training, decreased number and complexity of skills that can be learned, problems in retention and recoupment of skills, the inability to synthesize information and apply it in new settings, and an increased number of instructional trials required to reach competence in learning skills. Brown et al. (1983) have noted the following:

> Envision someone who can learn, but who cannot learn as much as 99% of his or her age peers; who needs more time and trials to learn and to relearn than almost all other persons; who has difficulty transferring that learned in one environment to another; and who rarely synthesizes skills acquired from several different experiences so as to function effectively in a novel situation. (p. 74)

This description of individuals with severe disabilities is meant not to limit their options but to expand their opportunities. By understanding how individuals with severe disabilities learn, appropriate education programs can be designed to best meet their unique needs.

Characteristics of Appropriate Education Programs

Before 1980, most programs for students with severe disabilities were based on a developmental approach to curriculum development. This approach used assessments based on typical development. An individual with severe disabilities was assessed and assigned a developmental age or score in various skill areas, including fine motor, gross motor, communication, self-help, and cognition. A curriculum was then planned using typical developmental sequences as the guide for instructional planning and priorities. The traditional developmental model operated from a "bottom-up" approach in which a student moved through firmly established prerequisite skills before age-appropriate skills were attempted. For example, a student was required to stack blocks and put pegs in pegboards before he or she could progress to purchasing a drink from a soda machine. Although students with severe disabilities made progress, instructional opportunities and environments were restricted, and teacher and parent expectations were low. More important, students exited school programs unprepared to function in the real world.

Teachers in the 1990s throughout the United States are implementing a different

approach to curriculum development for students with severe disabilities. Instead of a bottom-up approach, teachers are using a top-down approach in which skills necessary for independence as adults are the focal point for curriculum development (Moon & Inge, 1993; Wehman & Kregel, 1996). This top-down approach, or *community-based instruction*, focuses on the development of functional, chronological age–appropriate skills taught in a variety of integrated environments. It prepares individuals to function in four basic life-spaces or domains: 1) domestic, 2) community, 3) recreation and leisure, and 4) vocational environments.

Community-based instruction uses an ecological inventory approach to determine curricular content (Figure 11.1). In using this approach, the environments in which a student functions at the present time and will in the future are identified and analyzed to determine critical activities and skills for instruction in each domain. This curriculum development strategy facilitates the attainment of age-appropriate, functional skills; prepares the student for a more independent lifestyle; allows greater flexibility for the student and teacher; and verifies the appropriateness of the goals selected for instruction.

Parents are interviewed in order to ensure the development of relevant goals and objectives. Conducting a parent/guardian inventory allows everyone to become more aware of the future needs and preferences of the student with severe disabilities. Figure 11.2 provides an example of questions that may be asked as part of a parent/guardian inventory.

Information also is gathered from students' cumulative records. All of the information is summarized and evaluated in order to establish current and subsequent priorities for instruction. Priorities for selecting instructional environments and activities should be based on several factors including, but not limited to, the following:

- Student preference
- Parent preference
- Functionality
- Age-appropriateness
- Safety
- Social significance
- Opportunity for interactions with peers without disabilities
- Longitudinal nature
- Development of daily routines

Individualized objectives and appropriate adaptations are determined through a discrepancy analysis process. The student's performance is compared with that of an individual without disabilities and the differences in performance are analyzed. Individualized adaptations are designed to promote the participation of the student in at least some component of the activity. The instructional program is designed and implemented in the context of integrated natural environments.

Determining whether the natural environment is an integrated general classroom or instruction in the community depends upon the chronological age of the student. As the student with severe disabilities gets older, the amount of time spent in nonschool instruction should increase. In order to facilitate a smooth transition to adult life, very little time should be spent on the school campus during the last 2 years of school (Brown, Schwarz, et al., 1991; Sailor et al., 1989).

Figure 11.1. The seven phases of an ecological inventory approach are used to develop curricula. (Adapted from Learning in Functional Environments [LIFE]. [1986]. Adapted with permission).

Inclusion Experiences

Youth with severe mental retardation need the opportunity to be educated alongside students without disabilities (Janney, Snell, Beers, & Raynes, 1995). This may be at a vocational technical center in an after-school photography club, during physical education class, or in any of a number of meaningful school experiences. Selection of appropriate inclusion experiences should be based upon the student's educational needs, and specific strategies for inclusion in community settings must be planned for as early as elementary or middle school (Beck, Baers, Hogue, Shipstead, & Knowlton, 1994; Clark, Carlson, Fisher,

Job preferences

1. Are there any jobs in which your child seems particularly interested?

2. Are there any jobs that your child does not seem to like?

3. Do you have any preferences for your child's occupational placement?

4. Are there any occupations that you would find objectionable for your child?

5. What do you see as your child's greatest strength that is applicable to the workplace?

6. What do you see as your child's most significant weakness that may affect him or her in the workplace?

7. Are there any time or day restrictions for your child in relation to a schedule?

Transportation

1. Because the area does not have public transportation, getting to and from work can be a problem. Since transportation for students in competitive employment is the responsibility of the student and parent, how do you anticipate your son or daughter getting to work?

2. Is there any way that the district can help with transportation and ease concerns?

Long-range planning

The years can pass very quickly as we get older, and when we reflect, we often wish we had begun certain activities or preparation earlier that would have made our lives happier or less stressful. One of the best ways to prepare for the future and be ready to take advantage of opportunities as they come our way is to have a goal or plan of action for what we would like to see for our children and ourselves. Please think very carefully about these questions and answer them as best you can so that the districts can make every effort to enhance reaching those goals. We want to make sure that we do not hinder your progress or waste valuable time.

1. Job placement: Where do you see your child working 5 years from now? 10 years from now?

2. How do you plan to support your child's job 5 years from now? 10 years from now?

Figure 11.2. An example of a parent/guardian inventory. (*Source:* Spring Independent School District, Houston, TX. [1992].)

Cook, & D'Alonzo, 1991; Field, Leroy, & Rivera, 1994; Hilton & Liberty, 1992). Table 11.1 gives tips for inclusion.

School-Based Vocational Instruction

Vocational training programs for students with severe disabilities have traditionally utilized a school-based model of instruction and emphasized prevocational activities. In this approach, simulated workstations, or "make-work," are arranged in the classroom, and students rotate through various jobs during the school day. In some settings, teachers arrange for work to be brought into the classroom and the students complete contract jobs. Sometimes the classroom is expanded to include on-campus worksites around the school building. Using the school-only approach to vocational training poses problems for teachers and their students with severe disabilities, including the following:

- Difficulty with skill transfer and generalization to community-based employment settings (Soto, Toro-Zambrana, & Belfiore, 1994)
- Lack of opportunity to interact with individuals without disabilities (Hilton & Liberty, 1992)
- Difficulty teaching job-related skills (e.g., getting to and from work, locating the breakroom, interacting with co-workers at breaktime)
- Inability to simulate real-work environments in school settings
- Difficulty in persuading parents to envision their son or daughter with severe disabilities participating successfully in an employment setting

Essential Components of Community-Based Vocational Instruction

Individuals with severe disabilities do have the opportunity to perform meaningful work in the community. Through the development of supported employment technologies, individuals who previously attended work activity centers and sheltered workshops are now able to consider a variety of employment options. School programs play an important role in preparing students for real work, but several program characteristics must be in place to increase the likelihood of supported employment for students with severe disabilities, as well as participation and competence in meaningful community activities such as travel skills (Sowers & Powers, 1995; Soto et al., 1994).

Students need community-based instruction with frequent opportunities to demonstrate skills in the actual settings where they will be used (i.e., vocational training in real work settings). The training should last long enough for students to sample a variety of occupational skills and learn to interact with their peers in a variety of settings. Individuals with severe disabilities must learn to meet the social standards associated with a variety of environments and work settings—an important life skill that students with severe disabilities usually learn at a much slower pace (Clark, Field, Patton, Brolin, & Stillington, 1994).

Vocational training must start early for students with severe disabilities (Meers, 1992) and include learning to pay attention to natural cues and corrections, to monitor themselves, and to delay reinforcement. These things are necessary to be successful at vocational sites later. As a student ages, he or she should spend more time in high-quality vo-

Table 11.1. Tips for Inclusion

1. Identify one or more students without disabilities who can help the student with severe disabilities at lunch, during art class, or on the playground.
2. Design general classroom activities in such a way that the student with severe disabilities can participate through use of volunteers, student teachers, or other classroom helpers.
3. Individualize curricula for students with severe disabilities by providing learning objectives consistent with life skill/functional needs.
4. Provide for necessary adaptations, assists, and supports in teaching techniques to minimize the severity of the student's disability.

cational training (Bellamy, Horner, & Inman, 1979; Belfiore, Lim, & Browder, 1993, 1994). Through a variety of instruction sites, students participate in job-sampling and résumé-building activities for ongoing assessment and instruction in generalized work behaviors. By the time a student is 14–15 years old, information should have been gathered regarding student preferences, capabilities, and skills in each type of job (Polloway, Patton, Epstein, Smith, & Rodriguez, 1991). This information is used to select paid employment during the student's latter years in school. Paid employment should occur prior to graduation so supports are firmly in place before the student leaves the public school system (Revell & Wehman, 1996). The vocational program also must be coordinated with the other areas of the student's life, especially for students with very severe disabilities for whom life skills are usually far more important. These community access activities, such as eating lunch at work or shopping for clothes, and leisure pursuits should also be chained.

The teaching of academics, if necessary, can be incorporated into the vocational program (see Cronin & Patton, 1993) by assessing the site for math, reading, and writing skills opportunities. For example, the student may need to look at the clock to know when to take a break, count a certain number of items for packing, or read simple labels. Skills like these can be taught using pictures or other cues (Robertson, Gravel, Valconte, & Mavern, 1992). Equal attention should also be paid to the individual's communication system. Developing augmentative systems and sharing information with co-workers is an extremely important variable for long-term success on a job. Table 11.2 provides some tips for curriculum development for young adults with severe disabilities.

Community-Based Vocational Training and the Fair Labor Standards Act

Post-21 alternatives for individuals with severe disabilities have historically been limited and segregated. Community-based vocational training programs now provide students with opportunities to gain the skills needed to successfully perform on the job. With the increased emphasis and the federal mandate on transition planning in the Individuals with Disabilities Education Act (IDEA) of 1990, PL 101-476, schools—in cooperation with vocational rehabilitation agencies—facilitate actual job placement prior to graduation. Because of these changes, knowledge concerning community-based vocational instruction and federal labor laws is vitally important to school district personnel (Hess & Horton, 1990). (See Table 11.3 for answers to various questions regarding U.S. Department of Labor work regulations.)

Table 11.2. Curriculum development

Suggestions
1. Spend increasing amounts of time in vocational training placement.
2. Teach skills that are likely to be used regularly by students.
3. Focus on developing community functioning skills that allow for greater competence in shopping malls, recreation events, and so on.
4. Select vocational skills that have marketability in the local community.

Cautions
1. *Don't* use preschool materials and activities. Use real materials.
2. *Don't* confuse once-a-month field trips with the intensity of effective community-based training.
3. *Don't* teach from behavior checklists, developmental tests, or commercial curricula that have little relationship to community needs.
4. *Don't* provide instruction primarily in the school.

Community-based vocational instruction is a nonpaid, secondary model that rotates students through clusters of vocational training sites. During this rotation, vocational assessment, instruction, and job sampling are conducted and empirical information is gathered regarding students' strengths, weaknesses, likes, dislikes, and necessary adaptations in a range of vocational options. Unlike work–study programs, this is not an employment program. Traditional work–study programs focus on proficiency in a single job, and students are paid and considered employees of that company.

When a school district develops a vocational training program, the U.S. Department of Labor regulations must be consulted to guarantee that students are behaving as trainees, rather than employees, among other issues (see Table 11.3). Only at the end of community-based vocational training, when a student is placed in paid employment, does a change in status from trainee to employee occur.

The goal of community-based vocational training is assessment and instruction, not development of proficiency in a single job. One of the issues of concern is whether this benefits the business training site. In fact, many assert that community-based vocational training—with its legal requirements mandated by the Fair Labor Standards Act (see Table 11.4)—may actually impede the functioning of the business for the following reasons:

• Students usually train with employees, which may impede the employees from completing their job responsibilities.
• Students do not perform up to usual employee expectations and there is a reduced production rate or instances of materials being ruined, which causes waste for the business training site.
• New students are continuously starting with various job titles in a business and training program—a turnover that impedes business.
• Students do only portions of employees' full job descriptions.
• This model of programming operates on a zero-reject basis, so students of all ability levels are on the sites.
• Collection of data concerning independent performance is critical to documenting maintenance of trainee status. The U.S. Department of Labor's position is that if a student can perform a job description independently, from that point on, the student is providing a benefit to the business. Documentation of student progress toward

Table 11.3. Key information related to community-based instruction and U.S. Department of Labor (DOL) regulations

1. *Which students may participate in community-based vocational education under these guidelines for nonemployment relationships?*

 Students who meet state guidelines for special education may participate in community-based vocational education if it is determined appropriate for them.

2. *How is it determined which students might need community-based vocational education?*

 The determination should be based on the individual student's needs taking into account the student's preferences and interests. Community-based vocational education would be considered a major change in placement for most students and would require a change in the IEP. The education agency must invite the student to any meetings considering transition services or participation in community-based vocational training.

3. *The criteria in the guidelines also indicate that community-based vocational education is intended for students who will need "intensive ongoing support" to perform in a work setting. Does this mean that it is intended for students with more severe disabilities?*

 Community-based vocational education is intended for those students with more severe disabilities; however, the level of severity must be based on skills and behaviors necessary to function in a work setting. Examples of ongoing support services include job redesign, environmental adaptations, personal assistance services, transportation, and social skills training (Rehabilitation Act Amendments of 1992, Senate Report 102-357).

4. *What type of documentation is needed?*

 It is important in community-based vocational education programs to document that all participants—the student, the parent or guardian, the employer, and instructional staff—understand that:
 1. If at any point the community-based vocational activity is no longer a learning experience, it cannot be considered a nonemployment relationship.
 2. The community-based vocational program must meet all the requirements outlined in the guidelines for nonemployment relationships.
 3. Students are not entitled to employment at the worksite where they are receiving instruction and training.

 Three types of documentation must be employed to meet the requirements of these guidelines: 1) an IEP reflecting vocational instruction and training goals and objectives relevant to the community-based vocational experience; 2) a letter of agreement outlining the DOL/ED requirements listed above and signed by all participants; and 3) ongoing case notes (e.g., attendance records, progress reports).

5. *Is special or extra liability coverage for students required?*

 Community-based vocational education is considered part of the student's individualized education program. In nonemployment relationships, the worksite is perceived as an extension of the school. In other words, the student is pursuing instructional objectives in a work setting. Since these students are not employees, they are not eligible for the usual worker's compensation or insurance coverage provided to employees. If the student is a paid employee of the business, then the employer is responsible for offering him or her the same liability coverage offered to other employees. If the student's participation in the workplace activity can be considered instructional and part of a nonemployment relationship, then the school may be responsible for liability coverage. Generally, the same insurance and liability policies that apply to other off-site school experiences (e.g., athletic events, field trips) should apply. Each school district must work out its own policies regarding liability.

(continued)

Table 11.3. *(continued)*

6. *Is it necessary that the vocational goals and objectives in the IEP specify exact site placements?*

 No. It is possible for the IEP to identify only general goals and objectives to be pursued (e.g., job clusters to explore or in which to conduct assessments; assessments of general work behavior skills; training in a specific occupation). The IEP should, however, expressly limit the amount of time students will spend at any one site or in any one distinguishable job classification. Additional written agreements with parents, students, and employers should reflect the exact location and document the specific nature of the education and training involved.

7. *Given these guidelines, could an employer move students around to different work stations or occupational areas not specified in their written agreement?*

 No. As stated earlier, goals and objectives for the student have been outlined in the IEP and written agreements between the student, parent, employer, and school personnel detail specific activities for the community vocational experience. Thus, the community-based vocational experience can be considered a valid educational experience under the supervision of school personnel. Employers must feel free to remove students from any work activity if they determine that removal is necessary for safety or other reasons; however, under no circumstances should the student be placed in a work station or occupational area not specifically outlined in the written agreement.

8. *What is the educator's role in ensuring that regular employees will not be displaced by the student trainee in the workplace?*

 The community experience must be primarily for the benefit of the student. Also, regular employees must not be displaced or relieved of assigned duties and vacant positions should not go unfilled. Two strategies are available to educators for ensuring that this criterion is met. First, the educator can confirm that all parties—the employer, the student, and the parents—understand that students in the program must not displace regular employees. An agreement documenting this understanding should be signed by all involved. Second, those who provide direct supervision to the student at the worksite may observe when employment displacement and other violations are occurring and takes steps to correct the situation.

9. *Can students accept an offer of paid employment at a worksite where they were placed for community-based education?*

 Yes. Students may accept an offer of paid employment at a worksite where they received instruction and training. The student would then become an employee of the business and an employment relationship would ensue. This means that the employer is responsible for full compliance with the Fair Labor Standards Act, including minimum wage and overtime pay provisions.

10. *Could the student be paid less than the minimum wage?*

 Yes. Employment below the minimum wage rate is permitted in instances when a worker's disabilities impair his or her ability to perform the job. This special minimum wage rate is based on the productivity of the worker with disabilities as compared to the productivity of a worker without disabilities. Employees must apply to the U.S. Department of Labor for authority to employ workers with disabilities at these special minimum wage rates.

independence is provided through regularly collected data in the areas of level of supervision, work adjustment behaviors, specific task acquisition skills, and production rates. School personnel should keep anecdotal data or descriptive notes at the end of each instructional session concerning work quality, type of support needed, and incidents of maladaptive behavior.

- There should be a clear understanding on the part of the employer that there is no guarantee of work to be performed or completed by the students. This should be noted in the agreements between the businesses and the school districts.

Table 11.4. Vocational trainee legal requirements

The Fair Labor Standards Act (1938) defines situations in which students with disabilities may be considered "trainees," rather than "employees," while participating in community-based vocational training. The act states that each of the following six criteria must be met in order for the student to be considered a trainee:

1. The training, even if it includes the actual operation of the employer's facility, is similar to that given in vocational schools.
2. The training is for the benefit of the trainees.
3. The trainees do not displace regular employees, but work under their close supervision.
4. The employer providing the training derives no immediate advantage from the activities of the trainees, and on occasion his or her operation may actually be impeded.
5. The trainees are not necessarily entitled to a job at the conclusion of the training period.
6. The employer and the trainees understand that the trainees or students are not entitled to wages for the time spent in training.

- Differentiated training sites and potential employment sites must be maintained. If employers are seen as using the community-based vocational training program as a training ground from which to hire employees, then the employer is benefiting from the process. The U.S. Department of Labor usually asks each employer how many students he or she has hired in order to determine if the employer is using the program as a market to find new employees, thereby overriding the training purposes of the program. If a business is located in a rural area where there are limited employment options, however, a student may be hired for a paid position in a training site, which is acceptable as long as this does not become a regular practice.
- If a student holds a part-time job outside of school hours, no job training may occur within the same job title for which he or she is employed.
- Student trainees are not to supplant usual employees or to cause employees to have reductions in work hours. While on the site, students may complete a variety of tasks; however, these should not equal the job description of a usual worker. Students often perform parts of jobs, rather than complete jobs. At times students may be paired so that two individuals "job share" in order to perform tasks. No employee's job description changes as a result of the training program. The training program, therefore, does not alter the crew structure of the business.

Clearly, the U.S. Department of Labor regulations are complex. All personnel involved in community-based vocational training, including administrators, teachers, and paraprofessionals, should have a clear understanding of the issues before they implement community-based vocational instruction.

Individualized Transition Planning for Youth with Severe Disabilities

Setting Transition Goals

Transition planning ensures that the most appropriate adult options for a student are put into place before he or she exits school. Because of this, transition planning has been defined as an "outcomes-oriented process" (Bates, 1989, p. 11). It is essential that the out-

comes and the planning are individualized and meaningful. It should not be assumed that all individuals with severe disabilities automatically exit into a particular program or service delivery model.

Courtney *Courtney is a 16-year-old student with severe mental retardation. She attends her local high school, where she is eligible to receive education until she is 21. With only 5 more years in school, school district personnel must begin asking Courtney and her family the following questions: Where do you want to work as an adult? In what type of job? Where do you wish to live and what types of activities would you like to do after work? Answers to these questions should form the basis of Courtney's ITP.*

In the early 1980s, efforts in transition planning emphasized the transition from school to work and considered integrated employment as the only goal. Minimal attention was paid to activities outside of the employment arena. Since then, however, the emphasis has shifted to quality-of-life issues that reflect full participation in all aspects of community life (Steere, Wood, Pancsofar, & Butterworth, 1990).

Personal futures planning, or *lifestyle planning,* is a process that assists transition teams in creating visions of the future for individuals with disabilities and gives families the opportunity to explore issues that will assist them in making decisions about the future. It is important that representatives from the postschool services provider system participate in futures planning with the family so that they understand the goals, dreams, and desires of each individual and his or her family and are involved in the total planning process. Transition teams should consider conducting personal futures planning sessions prior to the development of an ITP or listing of transition goals.

A personal futures planning meeting should last approximately 2 hours and include the individual with the disability and his or her family members or other important individuals. The facilitator arranges the logistics carefully, seating people in a semi-circle, providing name tags for all participants, and having flipcharts and pens available for use during the session. Before the meeting starts, the facilitator outlines the general process and reminds participants that the purpose is to create a vision of the future for the individual. Participants are reminded to be positive. Professional jargon should be limited, and everyone should be viewed as an equal member of the team. O'Brien (1987) describes a step-by-step guide that teams can follow, in which they examine the following:

- The present quality of life for the individual
- Changes that will influence the quality of life
- The desired adult lifestyle
- The most critical barriers
- Changes in service practices that will assist the individual

Steere, Wood, et al. (1990) used a version of futures planning in developing an outcomes-based process for transition planning. Their process views employment as the means for attaining quality-of-life outcomes. Through brainstorming, teams focus on assisting individuals in identifying the priority outcomes they wish to attain from employ-

ment (e.g., the development of friendships through work). Through this process, decisions are made *with* an individual and his or her family, not *for* the individual with disabilities (see Chapter 6; Halvorsen, Doering, Farron-Davis, Usilton, & Sailor, 1989). Lifestyle planning also allows for prioritization of goal areas and identifies individuals or agency representatives who may need to be invited to a formal meeting. Although initially time consuming, implementing this approach is critical to the development of meaningful transition planning. Figure 11.3 is an example of a form that can be used to summarize this planning process. Karen's story and ITP illustrate the process in action.

Karen *Karen is a 19-year-old student with severe disabilities. She is nonverbal and uses approximately 20 manual signs to express her needs. She is ambulatory but obese. Karen lives with her mother and younger brother. Her interaction with peers is limited to school-day activities guided by staff. In the first 8 years of her life, Karen lived in a state institution where she was physically restrained due to behavior problems. Karen needs to acquire an array of community living skills before her transition into adulthood. An ITP specifically drafted for Karen begins on page 291.*

If it is not possible to conduct futures planning sessions with all students, input from students and families should be obtained prior to formal transition goal development. Home visits, questionnaires, school conferences, and telephone conferences are just a few of the ways to obtain information concerning future goals.

Evaluating Transition Outcomes of Youth with Severe Disabilities

The most common method of evaluating transition outcomes is to conduct a follow-up study of graduates, school dropouts, and/or people who are "aged out" of high school. For individuals with severe disabilities, follow-up studies indicate high levels of unemployment and underemployment, low enrollment in postsecondary training, and continued dependent family living (Bove, Nevin, Paolucci-Whitcomb, & McNeil, 1991; Wehman, Kregel, & Seyfarth, 1985). Frank, Sittington, Cooper, and Cool (1990) conducted a survey of recent graduates with mental retardation in Iowa and found that slightly more than 8% of the total group interviewed met their criteria for being successful as adults. Individuals are leaving educational programs and exiting to waiting lists and an adult services system unprepared for the quality or quantity of needed services (Ward & Halloran, 1989).

A 1992 evaluation of ITPs for students with mental retardation in the Houston area indicated that 28% of individuals with mental retardation exited into competitive employment and more than 60% needed supported employment services. Sheltered employment was predicted for only 3.2% of the individuals (Bates, Bronkema, Ames, & Hess, 1992).

The majority of postschool outcome assessments analyze the employment, postsecondary school enrollment, and residential status of individuals with disabilities (DeStefano & Wagner, 1992). Most employment surveys ask questions regarding employment status, current wages, hours worked, benefits received, and employment history. Independent living outcomes are measured by where and with whom the individual lives. Postsecondary education questions center on enrollment in courses and completion of

Description of Student's Future Vision

Karen's vision is having a good job with many friendly co-workers and other people. She and her family want her to become markedly more competent in travel, personal hygiene, and safety skills. At this point in Karen's life, she is most concerned about weight control and better health.

Individualized Transition Plan

Student's Name _Karen_
Birthdate _____
Student's Identification Number _____
Participants:

School _____
ITP Conference Date _____

Name		Position	
Karen		_Student_	
June		_Mother_	
Ellen		_Teacher_	
Janelle		_Nurse_	
Annie		_Vocational evaluator_	
Shane		_Employment specialist_	
Leon		_Vocational rehabilitation (VR) counselor_	

Career and Economic Self-Sufficiency

Employment Goal _Part-time supported employment performing repetitive tasks in retail outlet such as Wal-Mart._

Level of present performance: _Karen has shown interest and abilities in performing tasks such as folding laundry, assembling boxes, and hanging clothes. She wanders on sites requiring movement to various areas. She shows signs of discomfort when carrying packages over 25 pounds._

Steps needed to accomplish goal: _1. Referral to vocational rehabilitation and Dare County Enterprises for supported employment services. 2. Help arrange funding for supported employment. 3. Provide assistance in identifying an appropriate job coach._

Date of completion: _January 1995_

Person(s) responsible for implementation: _Parent, service coordinator, VR counselor, and teacher-invite employer to watch_

Vocational Education/Training Goal

1. Complete situational assessment on three or more job-sites. 2. Increase endurance at work. 3. Expand range of jobs.

Level of present performance: _Karen works for an average of 60 minutes on one task. Learns two- to three-step tasks quickly. Works steadily at moderate pace on repetitive basis._

Steps needed to accomplish goal: _1. Refer to Vocational Assessment Center for situational assessments. 2. Increase time at jobsites. 3. Utilize a variety of training sites in different retail outlets._

Date of completion: _January 1995_

Person(s) responsible for implementation: _Teacher and situational assessment coordinator_

From Wehman, P. (1995). *Individual transition plans: The teachers curriculum guide for helping youth with special needs.* Austin, TX: PRO-ED; reprinted by permission.

Postsecondary Education Goal *N/A*
Level of present performance:

Steps needed to accomplish goal:

Financial/Income Needs Goal *Karen will open a savings account and learn to sign/write name for checks/documents.*

Level of present performance: *Karen is supported by her mother and has no income. She is dependent for all uses of money and cannot write her name.*

Steps needed to accomplish goal: *1. Initiate SSI application. 2. Assist Karen in opening savings account. 3. Karen to receive instruction on modified signing of her name.*

Date of completion: *June 1995*

Person(s) responsible for implementation: *Parent, service coordinator, and teacher*

Community Integration and Participation

Independent Living Goal *Karen will increase independence in hair care, menstrual care, and food preparation.*

Level of present performance: *Karen lives with single mom and brother and is dependent in meal preparation but helps at home with domestic chores. She does not initiate menstrual care.*

Steps needed to accomplish goal: *1. Apply for residential services. 2. Receive food preparation instruction. 3. Refine self-help skills to include hair care and thorough menstrual care.*

Date of completion: *June 1995*

Person(s) responsible for implementation: *Parent, service coordinator, and teacher*

Transportation/Mobility Goal *Karen will learn how to get to and from job and exhibit safety awareness in parking lots and at bus stops.*

Level of present performance: *Depends on others for all transportation and requires assistance to travel/walk in the community.*

Steps needed to accomplish goal: *1. Apply for STAR transportation. 2. Receive instruction on safety/street crossing in the community.*

Date of completion: *March 1995*

Person(s) responsible for implementation: *Teacher and parent*

Social Relationships Goal *Make social friendships and new connections outside of family and school.*
Level of present performance: *Karen is close to her family and friendly to school staff. She does not engage in activities away from home or school.*

Steps needed to accomplish goal: *1. Attend church activities with a peer. 2. Contact Big Brothers/Big Sisters. 3. Utilize summer and weekend camp services (e.g., Camp Jaycees). 4. Join local photography club.*

Date of completion: *June 1995*

Person(s) responsible for implementation: *Parent, service coordinator, and local community recreation specialist*

Recreation/Leisure Goal *Karen will develop interest and abilities in age-appropriate personal and community activities, which are use of a camera, aerobics class, swimming, and drawing.*
Level of present performance: *Karen currently spends most of her free time alone. She has been exposed primarily to toys and preschool materials.*

Steps needed to accomplish goal: *Teach Karen to engage in two to three community recreation activities and increase by two to three her repertoire of personal age-appropriate activities.*

Date of completion: *June 1995*

Person(s) responsible for implementation: *Teacher, parent, and local community recreation specialist*

Personal Competence

Health/Safety Goal *Karen will learn to control diet, decrease weight.*
Level of present performance: *Karen eats healthy foods but constantly seeks more; her physical activity is limited. She does not sufficiently communicate need for help or feelings of pain.*

Steps needed to accomplish goal: *1. Extinguish requests for too much food at mealtime and pair with physical activity after meals. 2. Provide modified instruction on human sexuality. 3. Teach functional use of help/hurt feelings.*

Date of completion: *January 1995*

Person(s) responsible for implementation: *Teacher, parent, and school nurse*

Self-Advocacy/Future Planning *Karen will learn to use 30-40 functional signs and pictures to make community choices and personal needs known.*

Level of present performance: *Karen uses signs in limited way. Her mother and guardian is a single parent.*

Steps needed to accomplish goal: *1. Teach functional use of more signs. 2. Increase opportunities for choice-making throughout day. 3. Make connections with alternative guardian. 4. Seek legal advice regarding guardianship/will.*

Date of completion: *August 1995*

Person(s) responsible for implementation: *Parent, teacher, and service coordinator*

Student Career Preference

Employment in a small department of a retail setting.

Student's Major Transition Needs

1. Employment
2. Social relationships
3. Effective communication
4. Independent self-care and health management
5. Safety awareness

Additional Notes

Individualized transition planning guide

Name _____ Date _____

Skills, abilities, competencies:

Likes, dislikes, preferences:

Projected outcomes:

Support needs:

Suggested ITP team members:

Figure 11.3. An example of an individualized transition planning form that can be used during lifestyle planning by the transition team. (Adapted from Steere, Wood, et al., 1990.)

degree and certificate requirements. For individuals with severe disabilities, these measures should be expanded to include an analysis of the quality of life and the community integration of the individual. Only then can the success of transition be truly assessed.

In the area of employment, social integration is critical (Parent, Kregel, Wehman, & Metzler, 1991), and the following questions must be answered during outcome evaluation: Are individuals with severe disabilities merely working alongside co-workers without disabilities or are they truly socially integrated into the culture of the workplace? Do individuals with severe disabilities have the opportunity to develop friendships and establish social networks (Stainback & Stainback, 1985)? Is the employment environment conducive to the development of such relationships? What effect does integration have on individuals, their co-workers, and the business? Do individuals with disabilities have friendships and supports outside of the workplace (Strully & Strully, 1985)? Answers to these questions are still unknown. Research in this area would be useful in developing future programs and priorities.

For individuals with severe disabilities, integration in community living should not be measured by independent living (Condeluci, 1996), as most individuals with severe dis-

abilities require lifelong support in this area (Nisbet, Clark, & Covert, 1991). Instead, questions should be asked about participation in decision making and choices (Newton, Horner, Ard, LeBaron, & Sappington, 1994; Newton, Olson, Horner, & Ard, 1996). These questions include the following: Who decides how income is spent? Who does the grocery shopping? To which environments outside the home does the individual with severe disabilities have access? How frequently do individuals participate in outside activities? With whom do they spend the majority of time? Do they have friends? Do they spend time with friends without disabilities? Are recreation activities planned by others? Are the recreation activities ones in which the general community participates, or are they planned specifically for individuals with disabilities?

Typically, postsecondary school environments have not been available to individuals with severe disabilities. There has been a move among community colleges to change that outcome. In the Houston area, several community colleges have begun classes for individuals with severe disabilities. As part of their transition plan, some students are enrolling in typical continuing education classes. Support is provided through a combination of community college and school district efforts. Evaluation of success in this area should focus on the integration of the individual in the classes and surrounding environments, not the completion of a degree or licensure in a vocational area.

Helping Individuals with Mental Retardation Enter Supported Employment

As a more in-depth analysis of transition outcomes, it is useful to explore the competitive and/or supported work potential of people with severe mental retardation, which has only recently become a viable possibility via supported employment programs. Leading writers in this area have noted the following:

> Since auspicious beginnings, a decade of investment and implementation have passed. More than 110,000 people have had access to supported employment. Nearly $100 million has been (or will soon have been) invested in state systems change grants (U.S. Department of Education, 1993). More than $10 million has been invested by the Rehabilitation Services Administration in community demonstration projects for supported employment (U.S. Department of Education, 1993). Several hundred millions of dollars each year provide for long-term support for people in supported employment through state developmental disabilities or mental health agencies. More than 2,500 community programs provide some supported employment. A plethora of newsletters, professional publications, videotapes, conferences, long- and short-term training programs, seminars, and forums has emerged. A new international association, the Association for Persons in Supported Employment, specific to the issues of supported employment, has come into being with more than 1,300 paying members representing all 50 states and 6 other countries. (Mank, 1994, p. 3)

Since the 1970s, there has been a growing realization that people with mental retardation are capable of competitive employment in many different industries, in part due to a number of isolated case studies in the late 1970s and early 1980s.

For example, Wehman, Hill, and Koehler (1979) showed how a young man with Down syndrome could work successfully in a competitive job at a college campus food service station. Through the use of a job coach, this individual became increasingly competent at a variety of kitchen utility tasks and among co-workers and customers without disabilities (see also Rusch & Mithaug, 1980; Wehman, 1981). In 1987, Wehman, Hill, Wood, and Parent reported the successful competitive employment outcomes of 21 individuals with se-

vere mental retardation, which was quickly followed by more sophisticated and in-depth analyses (Kregel & Wehman, 1989b; Kregel, Wehman, & Banks, 1989). One of these studies (Kregel, Wehman, & Banks, 1989) looked at how individual client characteristics related to key employment outcomes such as increased earnings after supported employment participation. This study was very important because it showed a marked lack of participation by people with severe mental retardation, even though they experienced earning increases of over 500% after participation in supported employment.

Following this research, Wehman and Kregel (1989b) reported and analyzed the successful work outcome in competitive employment of 109 individuals with severe mental retardation. The mean age of the group was 28 years and mean intelligence quotient (Stanford-Binet) was 30. The data were drawn from over 90 local community programs in the United States. Results indicated that all people were in supervised residential situations and 93% were competitively employed with a mean wage of $3.63 per hour and 22 mean hours of weekly employment. After 12 months of placement, 81.5% of the clients were still employed.

These studies, and several others (Albin, Rhodes, & Mank, 1994; Rhodes, Sandow, Mank, Buckley, & Albin, 1991; Thompson, Powers, & Houchard, 1992; Wacker et al., 1994) have helped to establish a body of literature that provides a framework for understanding the work potential of people with severe mental retardation. Moon, Inge, Wehman, Brooke, and Barcus (1990) have utilized some of this research to develop a job training text for people with mental retardation. Ford (1995); Smith, Belcher, and Juhrs (1994); and Sowers and Powers (1991) have done likewise for people with severe mental illness, severe autism, and multiple physical disabilities, respectively.

In 1994, Kregel completed a follow-up study analyzing several key features of how best to help people with severe mental retardation gain competitive employment. He contrasted the work histories of 161 individuals with severe mental retardation in 34 programs across four states with those of 153 supported employment workers with mild mental retardation. Table 11.5 summarizes some of the key characteristics associated with workers who have been labeled as having severe mental retardation. In reviewing Table 11.5, it is interesting to see how behavior technology has emerged to help these workers become competent employees. This does not mean, unfortunately, that every transition program has the personnel with the skills to provide the necessary training for these students. Charlie's case study below demonstrates how supported employment can help maintain an individual in competitive employment.

Charlie Charlie[1] *is a 31-year-old man with Down syndrome. He has measured IQ of 27 and requires extensive support. He lives with his family and holds a job. Prior to his competitive placement, Charlie spent 4 years in a segregated vocational education program and 1 year in a work activity center.*

[1]From West, M., Rayfield, R., Clements, C., Unger, D., & Thornton, T. (1994). An illustration of positive behavioral support in the workplace for individuals with severe mental retardation. In P. Wehman & J. Kregel (Eds.), *New directions in supported employment* (Vol. 1, pp. 88–102). Richmond: Virginia Commonwealth University Rehabilitation Research and Training Center; reprinted by permission.

Table 11.5. Characteristics associated with the likelihood of individuals with severe mental retardation finding employment

1. *What are the demographic and functional characteristics of people with severe mental retardation participating in local supported employment programs?*

 It is clear that for the vast majority of consumers with severe mental retardation, their participation in a supported employment program is their first opportunity to hold a job with the local labor market. Results of the Kregel (1994) study indicated that only 8% of all supported employment participants with severe mental retardation had ever worked previously.

2. *Do people with severe mental retardation differ from other supported employment participants in terms of functional characteristics and employment outcomes?*

 The comparison of employment outcomes between individuals with severe mental retardation and individuals with mild or moderate mental retardation produced several important findings. First, supported employment participants with severe mental retardation are able to achieve equivalent levels of integration at the jobsite and were equally as likely to retain their jobs for a period of 12 months. Furthermore, the hourly wages earned by the individuals with severe mental retardation were only 5% lower than those earned by those with mild retardation. These outcomes are particularly noteworthy in light of clear differences in previous employment experience, functional capacities such as communication and functional academic abilities, and numerous work-related behaviors.

 Second, only one third of the consumers with severe mental retardation reported that they were able to work full time. The reasons underlying this lack of availability and the applicability of this finding to all supported employment participation with severe mental retardation should be investigated in detail. Factors such as medical conditions, transportation difficulties, potential effects on SSA beneficiary status, personal or parental concerns, or other considerations may be limiting the number of hours per week people with severe mental retardation are able to work. This in large part may account for differences in earnings between individuals with severe mental retardation and other supported employment participants.

 Third, people with severe mental retardation worked fewer hours per week and were less likely to receive fringe benefits than members of the comparison group. Assuming that there is a direct relationship between full-time employment status and fringe benefits (i.e., part-time employees are less likely to receive health insurance or paid vacations), this finding reinforces the need to investigate the tendency among supported employment participants with severe mental retardation not to be engaged in full-time employment.

3. *What is the relationship between functional characteristics and work-related behaviors and the selected employment outcomes of job retention and number of hours of service received from employment specialists?*

 The analysis of work-related behaviors in relation to the employment outcomes of job retention rate and amount of job coach intervention hours has significant implications for consumers, clinicians, and policy makers. First, the analysis identified a set of behaviors that statistically correlated with an individual's ability to remain employed 12 months after initial placement. Second, a subsequent analysis identified a second set of behaviors that correlated with the number of job coach intervention hours that individuals received during employment. The results are striking in that the two sets of variables bear little relationship to one another. In other words, the factors that enable an individual to quickly learn a job and perform it independently (i.e., fewer job coach hours are required) have little to do with the likelihood that the individual will be able to retain the job for an extended period of time.

At Charlie's current job, his primary work area is a dining room for students, faculty, and staff with a seating capacity of approximately 110 patrons. Charlie works 30 hours a week and performs a variety of tasks independently, including wiping tables, stocking shelves, sweeping, mopping, and trash disposal.

Charlie is nonverbal but communicates with co-workers, students, and friends through vocalizations and gestures. Charlie's jovial personality is widely known and has been generally accepted by all of the university community who patronize the food services. Throughout Charlie's nearly 10-year competitive work history, behavior management has been a focus of intervention. Recurring problems include 1) blowing his nose into his hand and wiping the mucus onto his apron or shirt sleeve; 2) inhaling mucus (snorting) loudly in the dining area without covering his mouth; 3) coughing, clearing his throat, or vocalizing loudly while wiping tables so as to disrupt diners; and 4) disturbing diners by sweeping underneath tables as they attempt to eat. These problem behaviors are most frequent following spring, summer, and holiday breaks. A number of management strategies, including aversive procedures, have been employed over the years without significantly altering this pattern.

A regular component of Charlie's long-term job retention plan was for supported employment staff to monitor his behavior and intervene in the days immediately following those extended absences from work. During the early months of 1996, several complaints were made by patrons concerning escalation of two unappetizing behaviors: inappropriate nose wiping and making loud snorting noises. They threatened notification of the city's health department. Charlie's manager indicated that the frequencies of these behaviors were intolerable and needed to be addressed immediately.

Training *A training program was designed that included the following components: 1) direct intervention through differential reinforcement of low rates of behavior (DRL) to decrease the two target behaviors (Kazdin, 1980); 2) the use of a permanent prompting system (Berg & Wacker, 1983); and 3) the enhancement of co-worker supports to deal with his behaviors.*

DRL and verbal reminders had previously been used with Charlie for these two behaviors with some success. The procedure entailed giving Charlie verbal praise for working without performing the behaviors for increasing periods of time. To enhance social support, Charlie's co-workers were included in this procedure, providing Charlie with reminders to use his handkerchief frequently and go to a nonpublic area to wipe and blow his nose.

The permanent prompt employed was a personal cassette tape player with headphones that Charlie was allowed to wear while wiping tables. Country music (Charlie's favorite) was dubbed onto the cassette tapes, with a delay of approximately 10–15 seconds between songs. Into these intervals were dubbed verbal instructions from Charlie's preferred job coach—gentle reminders not to perform the two target behaviors and to use his handkerchief when necessary. The cassette player was selected as a permanent prompting system because it was unobtrusive and acceptable in Charlie's work environment and because Charlie had previously been able to decrease his behaviors with regular verbal reminders. Several of Charlie's co-workers voluntarily checked to see that Charlie was wearing the headphones, to ensure the tape player was working properly, and to turn over the tape when needed.

During the baseline phase, nose wiping averaged about 30% of intervals and snorting about 15%, but neither behavior showed a stable baseline or direction. Intervention was initiated anyway because of the acute situation. Nose wiping was then decreased in level to between 0% and 20%. During follow-up (with continued use of the headphones and co-worker support), the behaviors were observed in 0%–10% of the intervals. Charlie's snorting behavior also stabilized during the intervention phase. Near the end of intervention, an increase was observed, but this was believed to be caused by illness that included increased nasal discharge. Low rates of this behavior were also observed during the follow-up phase.

The results of this study indicate how the use of positive behavioral supports in the workplace can help individuals with mental retardation (Parent et al., 1994). Although Charlie's most job-threatening behavior was diminished, he continues to display other behaviors that are stereotypical, stigmatizing, and problematic. These include interrupting students who are studying, waving to people real and imagined, and persistent vocalizations. However, a level of tolerance was achieved that allowed Charlie's supervisor, co-workers, and customers to ignore those minor behaviors as immutable elements of Charlie's personality.

Although only a minor change was effected in Charlie's most serious behaviors, it is notable that his supervisor and co-workers were extremely positive in their assessment of the intervention's impact. Their perceptions that his behaviors had improved significantly are not shown by the data. It is likely that the attention given to the situation, and their involvement in the behavioral support intervention, positively influenced their perceptions of Charlie and his behaviors; that is, occurrences of the problem behaviors came to be viewed as exceptions rather than the norm. In short, it was the continuance of Charlie's employment and the relationships he had developed that made the intervention successful, not the measured impact on his behavior.

Conclusion

Transition planning benefits everyone. It benefits the individual with severe disabilities because it ensures that appropriate adult options and support mechanisms are in place before the individual graduates so that an integrated lifestyle can be maintained. The school district benefits because graduates attain productive and satisfying lives—one of the goals of public education. Transition planning benefits the service delivery system by examining the effectiveness of current programs and by becoming the driving force for the development of new opportunities for individuals with disabilities. Without transition planning, there is a higher probability that the individual will exit into waiting lists, sheltered workshops, and segregated living options without the appropriate services or supports.

Implementing individualized transition planning for individuals with severe disabilities is both challenging and complex. Conducting futures planning activities prior to the development of transition planning is one of the ways local school districts can begin to address the process. However, the development of a transition plan alone does not ensure that students with severe disabilities will exit into integrated community lives as adults. School districts still must provide appropriate curriculum, vocational training in community settings, integrated age-appropriate school environments, and interagency linkages in order for transition planning to be successful. Most important, parents and individuals must be empowered with the skills and knowledge to make the best decisions (Fullerton, 1995; Nozoki & Mochizuki, 1995; West, 1995b). Only then will the vision of full participation in the community for the individual with severe disabilities become a reality.

11

Study Questions

1. Students with severe disabilities constitute what percentage of the school-age population?

2. What is the difference between a "bottom-up" and "top-down" approach to curriculum development?

3. What are some advantages and disadvantages to community-based, vocational instruction as opposed to school-based vocational instruction for students with severe disabilities?

4. What is a "personal futures planning" approach, and what are some of the issues explored during the planning meeting?

5. What are five critical issues to be addressed in follow-up surveys of students with severe disabilities?

6. How do individuals with severe intellectual disabilities in supported employment compare to individuals with mild disabilities in terms of service needs and outcomes?

12

Applications for Youth
with Sensory Impairments

Susan Lehmann Griffin and Paul Wehman

Upon completion of this chapter, the reader will be able to do the following:

- Have increased knowledge of demographic information concerning youth with sensory impairments
- Be aware of some of the unique learning and behavior characteristics of youth with sensory impairments
- Understand assessment strategies and processes for youth with sensory impairments
- Be aware of effective teaching and instruction strategies for youth with sensory impairments
- Have increased knowledge about developing effective individualized transition plans (ITPs) for youth with sensory impairments
- Be aware of critical questions to ask in assessing the quality of transition services implementation
- Understand the major technologies available to help youth with sensory impairments and be able to give five examples of useful technology
- Describe community travel strategies for youth with visual impairments

Individuals with sensory impairments (i.e., auditory and/or visual) compose a heterogeneous group of people with challenging transition needs. The severity and age of onset of an individual's sensory loss along with the frequent existence of one or more physical, cognitive, perceptual, and/or medical disabilities present a variety of transition needs. Approximately 50,000 individuals across the United States have dual sensory impairments (i.e., are deaf-blind). The number of individuals with single sensory impairments and associated disabilities is far greater but difficult to quantify, and reports from supported employment studies indicate that, nationally, individuals with sensory and multiple impairments are underserved by rehabilitation programs for numerous and complex reasons.

First, confusion surrounds the definitions and labeling. As a result of program eligibility requirements and definitions, assessment and testing procedures, and personnel limitations, many individuals with sensory impairments are hidden within labels of mental retardation, multiple disabilities or, simply, vision or hearing impairments. Depending upon the age of onset of the disability and/or the occurrence of related disabilities, these individuals may or may not be eligible for developmental disabilities services.

Second, there is a shortage of skilled personnel to address vision or hearing loss support needs, especially in community-integrated employment settings. Low vision specialists, orientation and mobility (O & M) specialists, audiologists, communication specialists, and rehabilitation technologists can all play important roles in providing employment support services for consumers with hearing and vision impairments. But combining the skills and experiences of these personnel with those of vocational rehabilitation personnel will enhance the success of competitive employment placements for individuals with dual sensory impairments and other multiple disabilities.

People with visual, hearing, or dual sensory impairments compose approximately 75% of people with severe disabilities (Center for Independent Living, 1991). An increasing number of articles have addressed the needs of youth with dual sensory impairments, but little attention in the transition literature or in model programs has been directed toward the needs of students with singular sensory disabilities (Allen, Rawlings, & Schildroth, 1989; Bullis, Bull, Johnson, & Peters, 1995; Hanley-Maxwell, Griffin, Szymanski, & Godley, 1990; Irwin & Macdonell, 1988). These are the students who tend to drop out of school and slip through the cracks of transition planning (Allen et al., 1989). Through their 1989 study of deaf students in transition from school to work, Allen et al. determined that only approximately 52% of deaf youth graduated with high school diplomas and 29% dropped out of school without transition planning having occurred. Similar results can be anticipated for students who are blind or have visual impairments, and even higher dropout rates are expected for students with dual sensory impairments.

As of 1989, the transition literature indicated that neither the education nor the adult services system was well prepared to assist youth with sensory impairments in transition (Allen et al., 1989; Bullis et al., 1995; Covert, 1988; Danek & McCrone, 1989; Everson, 1995; Hayden & Abery, 1994; Irwin & Macdonell, 1988). Adult services resources are severely limited, and communication with the student is a significant barrier. As with any disability group, this low-incidence population needs and deserves quality transition planning from school to adulthood. This chapter focuses on the transition process exclusively for people with sensory impairments. In particular, it examines the needs of students who

have singular sensory impairments, such as any degree of deafness or blindness without secondary cognitive or physical disabilities, for whom traditional transition planning efforts have been too extensive (i.e., involving too many services) or ineffective (Bullis & Egelston-Dodd, 1990).

Defining Students with Sensory Impairments

Visual Impairment

The question of defining a visual impairment is very complex as the possible differences far outweigh the similarities. In fact, there are widely varying types and effects of visual impairments, and only approximately 10% of people with visual impairments are completely blind.

Terminology that refers to a person's amount and range of vision also may vary. The generic term *blind*, as used by the general public, implies that a person receives no information through vision and learns mainly through touch or listening. The term *legal blindness* is very different. It is used by some agencies and educational systems to decide whether an individual qualifies for services. People with *legal blindness* have an acuity of less than 20/200 with best correction or a field loss of 20 degrees or more. Although a person whose acuity is 20/200 has difficulty resolving fine visual detail, that person recognizes and identifies objects and learns a great deal through vision. Many people with *legal blindness* are very visual learners; those who are *blind* have little usable vision.

Several terms are used to describe vision that is significantly different from that of a typical person. The term *low vision* describes a person who is "still severely visually impaired after correction, but who may increase visual functioning through the use of optical aids, nonoptical aids, environmental modifications and/or techniques" (Corn, 1980, p. 3). In some regions of the country, the term *partially seeing* refers to people who have a relatively mild vision difference that falls within the corrected range of 20/70–20/200 and does not qualify the person for services as *legally blind.*

Regular unbiased assessments and evaluations are needed to make decisions about appropriate interventions to increase performance and determine the effectiveness of previous strategies. Through this approach, a systematic method of teaching visual images, social skills, and career and vocational skills enables the educational system to maximize development and learning. Again, the importance of visual efficiency and function must be emphasized when defining students with visual impairments in terms of age-appropriate curricular demands.

Hearing Impairment

A hearing loss is classified by hearing sensitivity at various frequencies within the audible range. These frequencies are termed decibels (dB). An individual is considered to have typical hearing if the hearing threshold is at least 25 dB. Hearing sensitivity within the 25–40 dB range is considered a mild loss; within the 40–55 dB range, a moderate loss; within the 55–70 dB range, a moderately severe loss; within the 70–90 dB range, a severe loss; and exceeding 90 dB, a profound loss or deafness. There are three terms—*deaf, hard of hearing,* and *hearing impaired*—that are frequently used to describe people with hearing impairments.

1. **Deaf**—a loss of hearing from severe to total where speech is not understood with or without the use of hearing aids (There is controversy over the use of this term because some children with profound hearing losses have succeeded in hearing with hearing aids and speech communication. Also, the term *deaf* is used by others culturally to include the larger population of individuals with hearing impairments who share common experiences.)
2. **Hard of hearing**—a loss of hearing where speech is commonly used
3. **Hearing impaired**—any loss of hearing

Characteristics of Youth with Sensory Impairments

Adult members of the deaf and blind communities are widely known for their strong group advocacy efforts. In fact, the strategic planning, attraction of media attention, and tenaciousness of people with visual impairments have increased the group's Social Security benefits. Similar advocacy efforts can be noted on the part of the Deaf culture. Acts of self-assurance and advocacy, however, are not intuitive or automatic in youth with sensory impairments but must be taught by school personnel, friends, and family members.

Youth with sensory impairments can also incur many undesirable behavioral characteristics that are directly related to the loss of one or more senses. A diminished sense hinders input, which seriously skews perceptions of the world (Scholl, 1986). Unfortunately, it is difficult for seeing and hearing people to imagine the profound loss that accompanies the partial or total diminishment of a sense. Imagine the perceptions and related emotions experienced when one witnesses two people looking directly at him or her while whispering. These feelings of personal and social mistrust and diminished self-esteem hinder confidence and thwart the self-advocacy efforts of people who are deaf or hard of hearing, with daily or hourly occurrences that become devastating over time.

Lowered Social Competence

Youth who are deaf or blind are usually born into hearing and seeing families. Thus, social isolation begins early in life. Long-term social isolation typically results in slower social development and, therefore, social problems (Danek & McCrone, 1989), which is problematic because social skills are necessary for success in adult life. Interventions that promote social skills should occur before and during the transition process (Sacks & Wolffe, 1992). Sacks and Wolffe also suggest that competent social role modeling prior to and during employment training is an effective strategy for increasing the social capabilities of youth with sensory impairments.

Lowered Vocational Competence

Because of social characteristics, communication barriers, and inadequate vocational training, youth with sensory impairments are typically underemployed or unemployed (Allen et al., 1989). Danek and McCrone report that most deaf individuals who are employed are craftspeople or work in the manufacturing industry; few hold professional positions. In their large-scale study of American Deafness and Rehabilitation Association (ADARA) members, Allen et al. arrived at similar findings, which they attributed largely to oral and

written communication barriers. These findings are also similar to those for people with visual impairments and exacerbated for people with dual sensory impairments (Covert, 1988).

Lowered Academic Competence

Youth with sensory impairments generally do not perform as well in academic and vocational courses as their hearing and seeing peers. Communication barriers can again be cited as a major cause of lowered performance, which are compounded by lack of adequate teacher training and/or resource personnel. However, Allen et al. (1989) and Bullis and Egelston-Dodd (1990) reported that students with sensory impairments attending integrated schools fared about the same as students with sensory impairments attending private, specialized schools.

Other Common Characteristics

People with sensory impairments have in common several other characteristics related to their levels of disability. Decreased social participation is typical, primarily as a result of communication hurdles. Interacting with hearing and seeing peers requires work on behalf of both parties, and it is often easier to interact with peers who have similar disabilities or to remain alone. These students also tend to have lower aspirations, often achieving less in the social, educational, and vocational realms based upon what others have told and, subsequently, reinforced them to believe.

Many youth with dual or congenital sensory impairments experience significant cognitive and behavior delays. It is not unusual to encounter self-stimulation, passiveness, unresponsiveness, aggressiveness, or anger with these students (Downing & Eichinger, 1990).

All of these characteristics affect students' transitions from school to adulthood. Roberts (1990) suggests that no matter what the activity, people with sensory impairments always have difficulty with mobility and understanding and completing projects.

Unique Learning Challenges Presented to Professionals by Youth with Sensory Impairments

Perhaps one of the most unique challenges presented by youth with sensory impairments is to professionals who must hurdle the communication barrier effectively. Communication issues, which vary according to the degree of disability, are quite complicated. People with singular sensory impairments are likely to skew information that they receive from the other major senses; for example, a person who is blind may misinterpret conversations when the speakers rely heavily on body language. People with profound dual sensory impairments receive little information from the outside world and preventing isolation is more of a factor when communicating with them. Teachers and adult services representatives must therefore be prepared for and skilled in communicating with all kinds of youth.

Professionals must also remember to incorporate the disability's etiology (i.e., whether it is congenital, had an early onset, or occurred later in childhood) and progression, both

of which can influence the student's learning style and, thus, the professional's teaching style. Professionals and paraprofessionals must always remember that no two individuals are alike. Two students may share similar degrees of blindness, but one may have congenital blindness while the other's is the result of an accident. One student may prefer to tape instructional information, while the other student relies on braille material or a reader plus tactile instruction. These individual preferences must be assessed and discussed.

Another unique challenge for professionals working with students with sensory impairments is ensuring that instruction and interventions foster the highest possible degree of generalizability and adaptability (Roberts, 1990). People with sensory impairments receive only partial or fragmented pieces of information, making generalization from task to task difficult. Although instruction or interventions that are designed specifically for one task or event may be easier to implement, they are not very beneficial to students in the long run. The goal of transition is to help youth become as independent as possible. Therefore, programs should be designed to allow the students the greatest control and highest applicability across situations.

Professional competence is essential to deal with the challenges presented by people with sensory impairments and to ensure the success of each individual's transition. Communication issues and adaptability and independence issues arise frequently during assessment and instruction and the design and implementation of ITPs. Preservice preparation programs for teachers and services providers of youth with sensory impairments are beginning to surface (Irwin & Macdonnell, 1988). It is hoped that teachers and service providers who exit these programs will be better able to perform their jobs without the addition of resource teachers, interpreters, or other outside specialists. One of the most effective transition leaders in the area of dual sensory impairment and transition has been Dr. Jane M. Everson, who has developed some of the leading materials in transition for people with sensory impairments.

Jane M. Everson Jane M. Everson, Ph.D., is the director of the Helen Keller National Center–Technical Assistance Center on Transitional Services (HKNC–TAC) located at the Helen Keller National Center (HKNC) in Sands Point, New York, but works from a regional office in New Orleans, Louisiana. She is also an associate professor with the Louisiana State University Medical Center, School of Allied Health Professions. Dr. Everson is an experienced educator, job coach, and residential services provider for students and young adults with low-incidence disabilities. Her areas of interest include the development and refinement of interagency services and the application of person-centered planning concepts to education and adult services.

From a young age, Dr. Everson has been a fierce advocate on behalf of young adults with disabilities. She is readily available to work with individuals with the most severe sensory and intellectual disabilities. She is incredibly positive and in continual demand from professionals for specialized help with transitions, especially in the highly complex and challenging area of deaf-blindness.

Assessment of Youth with Sensory Impairments

The transition coordinator or team leader must bring essential assessment information into initial ITP meetings. The information gathered assists transition teams in making the most appropriate decisions based upon the data and each student's wants and needs. A complete assessment does not necessarily need to include a multitude of standardized tests and batteries, of which there are more than 52 that can be used with people who are deaf and more than 50 for people who are blind. These tests actually provide the team with little usable information (Allen et al., 1989). Rather, a complete functional assessment should incorporate the following components: 1) a full medical evaluation, 2) a functional assessment of residual hearing or vision, 3) observational and interview data concerning the student's functional abilities, 4) pertinent scholastic records, and 5) student interview information.

Team leaders who work with youth with visual impairments have a slight advantage over leaders who work with youth in other disability groups in that an O & M specialist or a rehabilitation teacher can assist in performing the assessment for these students (Zimmerman, 1992). The O & M specialist determines how the student can move most efficiently and effectively around the environment. This specialist can also be responsible for performing the functional vision examination and beginning a training program (Griffin & Kendall, 1989). The rehabilitation teacher can assist in assessing how the student utilizes natural and artificial cues in learning tasks. The rehabilitation teacher is instrumental in designing instructional programs for any of the following domains: work, social and leisure, residential, and community participation.

Team leaders who work with deaf students benefit from the opinions of a speech-language therapist and an auditory specialist. Because most individuals who are deaf or severely hard-of-hearing must use some key words, a speech-language therapist can assess the student's current level of oral communication ability and functional ability. An auditory specialist can assist the team leader in assessing and recommending various devices and strategies to assist the student in learning.

Full Medical Evaluation

Several causes of vision or hearing loss can also affect other large organs of the body. For example, a student who has a congenital loss of vision may also have heart or kidney dysfunction; diabetes and vision loss may be found together; and students affected by Usher syndrome (i.e., congenital deafness and progressive visual impairment) often have accompanying medical problems. Many of these medical conditions have a significant impact on the lifestyles the students will lead as adults (i.e., job, residence, physical/recreational activity). Thus, transition teams need recent medical reports from which to plan.

Functional Assessment of Residual Hearing or Vision

Transition teams are too often presented with detailed medical reports instead of functional assessments. To most team members, statements such as "distinguishes human voices at 90 dB" and "has ocular occlusion and 20/400 vision in right eye" have little functional meaning. A functional evaluation of residual vision and hearing might contain statements such as "can distinguish human voice over minimal background sound" and

"has an 80% occlusion in middle of right visual field; surrounding vision is limited to shadows." This type of information about remaining vision and hearing abilities better demonstrates how students can apply their remaining vision and hearing. The functional vision assessment should also contain information about visual or hearing aids and devices the students currently use or have been tested to use, indicating how well the students functioned with each device. In Table 12.1, Ferguson (1995) provides an excellent functional assessment for determining work and employment capabilities that focuses on the strengths of the person with sensory impairment.

Observational and Interview Data
Concerning the Student's Functional Abilities

Several summary forms and methods are available to gather functional information regarding student abilities (Falvey, 1989; Inge, Dymond, & Wehman, 1996; Wehman, Moon, Everson, Wood, & Barcus, 1988). Regardless of how assessment data are summarized, the transition team leader should make certain that information regarding a student's functional abilities is obtained in the home setting, school setting, and, if applicable, the community-based instruction site (Bradfield, 1992). Information concerning the student's work habits, tardiness or timeliness, physical capabilities, instruction needs, reinforcement needs, assistive technology needs, coping abilities, social skills, resource development skills, and adaptability should be noted in detail (Corn, 1985). If information is collected across settings, it is more reliable. Care should be taken to stress the person's abilities and to note the areas where intervention might be necessary.

Table 12.1. Functional assessment for work potential

Vision	• Analyze lighting source for high or low illumination with light source on side of the "better eye."
	• Check height and angles of work surfaces and reduce reflective areas as necessary.
	• Determine if enlarged print, colors, symbols, or pictures can be used for direction/work supplies.
	• Assess usefulness of tactual clues added to materials, equipment, or environment to focus consumer's residual vision on key aspects.
Hearing	• Note noise level within work environment and determine if work station needs to be repositioned.
	• Determine if sound discrimination is a critical factor of the job.
	• Analyze work area to assess employee's need to localize the origin of sound (e.g., fire alarm).
Orientation and mobility	• Determine systematic methods of traveling across or between landmarks to reduce complicated orientation patterns.
	• Analyze methods of maintaining direction regardless of environmental obstacles.
	• Critically review all environmental safety factors affecting this area (e.g., fire drills, crowds).
Modifying task requirements	• Check the availability of support to include both natural and artificial systems.
	• Determine how other senses might be used.
	• Identify job components that lend themselves to technology solutions that will meet consumer needs.

Source: Ferguson (1995).

If a summary form—preferable for ease of discussion—is used, it can often be "matched" with a job analysis form, which should be completed when the student is seeking employment (Bradfield, 1992; Wehman, Moon, et al., 1988). Although this process of matching skills to job requirements gives the counselor or employment specialist some idea of how the student might perform in a given job and where interventions might be needed, it should not replace the skilled intuition of the professional or the preferences of the student.

Pertinent Scholastic Records

Scholastic records can assist team members as they make transition plans by presenting academic or vocational areas in which the student excelled as well as those the student found troublesome or did not like. Scholastic records may also show which learning strategies worked best for the student in the classroom (e.g., taping sessions, using a reader, having an interpreter).

Student Interview Information

None of these assessment tools, however, should stand alone as a complete assessment. An assessment is not complete until information is obtained directly from the student and his or her family regarding their aspirations for the student's adult life. Questions to address before the first ITP meeting include the following: Where does the student want to live? Does he or she want to go to college? What kind of job does he or she want? Would he or she be comfortable with the assistance of an employment specialist?

Teaching Strategies for Youth with Sensory Impairments

A number of strategies can be used to instruct youth with sensory impairments. Instruction for transition should begin during the early childhood years when perceptions about adulthood are being formed, and each strategy should be applied throughout the student's educational career.

Integrated Instruction

Because research has indicated that students with sensory impairments do not show better achievement in segregated settings, it makes little sense to separate these students from their peers without disabilities; as adults, these two groups of students will be expected to live and work together. Research has also shown no evidence that students with singular sensory impairments who are mainstreamed fall through the transition cracks any more often than their segregated peers (Allen et al., 1989). Although integrated instruction makes sense, teachers must upgrade their communication skills and strategies to depend less on resource teachers in the classroom.

Focus on Adaptation and Coping Skills

Allen et al. (1989), Corn (1985), and Roberts (1990) agree that people with sensory impairments must learn coping and adapting skills rather than a series of separate, more traditional skills, such as typing, home repair, sewing, cooking, and so forth; however, this is

not to suggest that these skills are not important. Research also shows that academics, such as English, math, courses emphasizing spatial relationships, and vocational education, are critical for youth with mild or singular sensory impairments. But the teaching approach must not be centered on a particular traditional skill or activity; it should instead be centered on assisting the student in learning adaptive strategies that can be transferred across tasks. Corn (1985) suggests using a matrix that breaks down each individual skill acquisitions in terms of resource development, problem-solving ability, self-advocacy, and social skills development. Corn contends that if all skills are examined and instructed based upon these four basic skills, the student will be able to make better independent choices later in life. An example of this teaching method and how it could apply to the transition process is shown in Table 12.2.

Community-Based Instruction

Community-based instruction integrates the skills that the student learns at school with those necessary for his or her home, employment, and community environments (see Chapters 8 and 12; Hanley-Maxwell & Syzmanski, 1995). Community-based, or off-site, instruction should begin several years prior to graduation for 1–2 half-days per week, gradually increasing as the student ages. Community-based instruction is more effective when sites are rotated because the student with sensory impairments learns to generalize orientation and mobility, social, and vocational skills across a variety of settings. Instruction within typical environments enhances the student's coping and generalizing skills. Allen et al. (1989) found that employment while still in school enhanced the ability of deaf people to find work after graduation. Many of the jobs these people found, however, were "dead ends"—not the type of jobs that students would want after graduation. The majority of students with singular sensory impairments utilized classroom teachers, rehabilitation teachers, and school counselors for assistance in finding and learning jobs; few utilized employment specialists.

Instructional Procedures

Instruction should occur in natural surroundings, if possible, and should utilize naturally occurring cues and reinforcers. Such strategies foster independence and social interaction for the students. Students, whether they learn from systematic instruction, tactile teaching, or counseling, should learn to expect natural consequences from their behaviors, should develop problem-solving and self-correction behaviors, and should learn to receive and respond to feedback from peers and supervisors. These are strategies used constantly in adult life and can ease the transition process considerably.

As important as effective instruction and reliable assessment procedures are, new advances in technology can have a dramatic impact on all individuals with disabilities and especially those with sensory impairments. Teachers, counselors, and others involved in helping must be aware of technology and how it can be prescribed for a given student's needs.

Table 12.2. An example using the four basic skills necessary for an independent adult life

Subject	Resource development	Problem-solving ability	Self-advocacy	Social skills development
Travel	Cane to get to the lunch room Sighted guide Walk independently	Which method is most efficient? Which method does the student like? Can the student get help from a friend? What should a friend do if chosen method does not work? How much time does the student have?	Can student talk to person with him or her? If the co-worker and student do not want to sit together, how do they part ways? Will it benefit the student to talk with co-workers?	Can student locate assistance if he or she walks alone? How should student explain the sighted guide approach to co-workers?

Technology and Transition for Youth with Sensory Impairments[1]

The Internet

Miller (1993) described the Internet as "the fastest-growing telecommunications system ever built, surpassing even the telephone network in its prime" (p. R4). As of July 1993, the Internet hosts 1,766,000 computers, with traffic increasing as much as 15% per month. In 1993, the Internet was used to facilitate communication at several levels, including listing messages to the public by President Bill Clinton and releasing Supreme Court decisions to the public in less than 1 day. On an average day in 1993, approximately 35,000 messages were posted on Usenet (a subnetwork of the Internet) by 80,000 users, which filled 44 megabytes of disk space (Hunt et al., 1993).

People in a university setting can access the Internet simply by obtaining an account on a mainframe computer that is connected to the National Science Foundation (NSF) backbone. Others can connect their personal computers into a local area network (LAN), which is connected to a regional network hooked to the NSF backbone. Another means of access to the Internet is to subscribe to one of the commercial on-line services (e.g., CompuServe, Delphi, America Online, Prodigy) that allow electronic mail (E-mail) to flow to and from the Internet for an additional fee. One of the newest trends is to operate a bulletin board system (BBS) that allows access to the Internet. For a small fee, approximately $25 per year, a person can send E-mail to and from others using the Internet. Other BBSs offer more extensive services on the Internet. Several of the services available on the Internet are listed below:

- International E-mail—sending and receiving messages
- Usenet—international discussion groups on thousands of topics
- File Transfer Protocol (FTP)—retrieving files from an Internet host

[1]Much of this section is reprinted by permission from Fullmer, S.L., & Walls, R. (1994). Exploring the Internet: The rehabilitation community's access to the growing communication network. *Technology and Disability, 3*(3), 235–242.

- Telnet—logging on to other Internet hosts to access anything on them
- Gopher—a menu-driven program that gives the user access to on-line databases and services (Full texts of many documents, song lyrics, graphic images, and books can be copied directly to a user's computer using Gopher [Gaffin & Electronic Frontier Foundation, 1994].)
- Internet Relay Chat (IRC)—allows real-time group discussions in text

The Internet can be viewed as a vast computer universe, containing many other computer networks with over a million computers and several million users. On-line, computerized communication has suddenly gained such popularity because the Internet and its subnetworks provide timely access to a vast amount of information, some of which is of interest and/or use to almost anyone. The services that are available to the user are continually expanding. Of relevance here is how access to this universe can help those with sensory impairments.

The Internet and the Rehabilitation Community

In order for rehabilitation providers and individuals with disabilities to plan rehabilitation intervention effectively, they must become adept at gathering and synthesizing information that will facilitate eligibility determination, formulate transition and rehabilitation plans, and determine the services that are necessary to complete the plan. To make informed choices, a person should have access to information concerning his or her disability, coping strategies, adaptive devices, and appropriate types of training, education, and employment opportunities. There is a wealth of disability-oriented information available on the Internet. The Internet gives providers and consumers access to information that will help them find a map through the maze of coping strategies, adaptive equipment, and employment opportunities. Opportunities previously missed can be seized. The ability to communicate with others having similar disabilities, to share strategies and horror stories, and to find resources for employment and entertainment makes access to the Internet a prime vehicle for promoting informed choices in a rehabilitation program and beyond.

E-mail If a person is severely limited by a disability, other knowledgeable people may have valuable input as to the feasibility of the individual's future independence and employability or know of accommodations that would allow the person to obtain services and employment. Using E-mail to discuss available services and training in other geographical areas is also a potential benefit. Information, especially that from someone with a similar disability, can be exchanged, such as information concerning similar side effects, limitations, strategies, and peer counseling, which can help a person with a disability to maximize his or her potential. E-mail can expand the number of experts a person can reach if one knows only the individual's E-mail address in advance.

Discussion Groups Rehabilitation practitioners also use Internet discussion groups as information-gathering tools, which can remedy the E-mail address requirement. Discussion groups are clusters of E-mail users who share a common interest. Users can post (i.e., send) messages addressed to the group, which are automatically redirected to all members who can then respond. A thread, or continuing discussion, on any subject is common, with many posts and replies. There are two types of groups: News groups are ac-

cessed through an Internet new-reader program, and mailing lists send and receive messages via regular E-mail.

Among these discussion groups are several rehabilitation-related conferences (discussions). Participants in these discussion groups include consumers, researchers, rehabilitation practitioners, vendors, and software developers, among others. These users typically ask questions (many times concerning specific disabilities), reply to others' questions or previous responses, and post messages noting new software or devices. From a rehabilitation standpoint, both consumers and practitioners can benefit from the information about functional limitations, possible strategies used to cope with these limitations, new devices and software that could be used to accommodate the disability, and a wealth of information concerning employment, legislation, or transportation, which come from a large and knowledgeable audience. Following are some examples of discussion groups available on the Internet (Gibbs & Smith, 1994):

- Attention deficit disorder—(add-parents) includes information on support, research, and autism/developmental disabilities
- Blindness—(blind-1) a discussion group dedicated to computer use by and for people with visual disabilities
- Carpal tunnel syndrome—(sorehand) an information exchange about repetitive motion and related problems
- Stuttering—(stut-1) discusses research and clinical practice on stuttering
- Technology—(1-hcap) exchanges information about the technological needs of people with disabilities

Telnet A third tool available on the Internet is remote log-in to access many of the Internet host computers around the world. The individual's terminal responds as if it is directly connected to the remote host. This procedure of logging on and using a host computer is called Telnet. An Internet user can use Telnet to access programs and databases containing meteorological data, statistical data, or the full text of many documents. On-line libraries around the world can be accessed and their catalogs searched. For example, the Assistive Technology Database Interface (ATDI) at the University of Texas allows access to descriptions of assistive devices. In addition, the ATDI has a list of vendors who provide services in particular geographical areas.

File Transfer Protocol File Transfer Protocol (FTP) is a service that allows an Internet user to log on to another Internet host and transfer computer files to and from that host. Any type of information that can be stored on a computer file can be transferred. There are several sites that allow access to graphics files depicting subjects from weather maps to the Dead Sea Scrolls.

Three sources of disability-related files can be accessed by the rehabilitation community using FTP. The first is called the Handicap News Archives (Internet address: handicap.shel.isc-br.com). There are 60 directories containing text files, shareware, and demo programs, including 12 directories dedicated to files and programs for people with visual impairments. Titles of these directories range alphabetically from the *Americans with Disabilities Act* to *Work and the Handicapped*. Following are some examples:

- ADA—the Americans with Disabilities Act, contains files such as the ADA text and the NARIC ADA Resource Guide

- Hearing—contains files such as a PC/TDD communications program and a list of TDD relays in all states
- MS—(Multiple Sclerosis Information) contains files about MS moods and other related topics
- Pain—contains *Back Pain* magazine and a list of back pain books
- Speech—has files and programs for speech synthesizers such as demos of the Accent speech synthesizer and the FLIPPER speech program

The FTP also allows access to electronic texts available on the Internet, which can be transferred to a personal computer and read using a word processor and a speech synthesizer. Examples of subject matter are classics such as *Great Expectations* by Charles Dickens (Oxford Archives), the Supreme Court Decisions in the 1993–1994 session (Case Western University), and the Fiscal Year 1995 Federal Budget (The White House) (Samizdat, 1994).

Gopher Telnet and FTP have been the traditional methods of remote log-in and the means to obtain files from Internet sites for quite a long time. To use these processes, the user has to know the Internet addresses, various log-on procedures, operating commands on the different operating systems, and subdirectories where the files were stored—a barrier to many potential users because this is hard to use and hard to remember. A software program developed at the University of Minnesota named Gopher has streamlined the Telnet and FTP services into a menu-driven, easily accessible process. Gopher sites all use standard mechanisms for storing and retrieving files, but do not advertise what they contain. A user must still know exactly where to go to get information on a particular topic.

From a rehabilitation standpoint, there is significantly more information available via Gopher than via FTP and Telnet. Gopher can be used to explore the job market through a submenu titled Employment Opportunities and Resume Postings, which contains additional submenus that provide employment information about job openings at many universities, in the government, and in private industry all over the world. For people finishing a college education or technical training, these information sources provide many opportunities that may well have been previously overlooked.

Assistive Devices and Accommodations
for Individuals with Sensory Impairments

Braille labels, modifications to telephone equipment, and handrails are examples of inexpensive modifications that can improve a worker's productivity. For example, vibrating pagers can be rented through a telephone-paging service for approximately $15 per month. There are many of these types of assistive devices and accommodations that can be used with young adults with hearing impairments. Table 12.3 provides guidelines for determining accommodations.

Below are listed 14 types of assistive technology devices that can help youth with sensory impairments.

1. Sign language—a visual, gestural language used predominantly by those closely connected with the deaf community, includes American Sign Language (ASL) and signed English
2. Fingerspelling (manual alphabet)—signs are made while individuals face each other and hold hands to feel the movement

Table 12.3. Accommodations for people with hearing impairments in postsecondary environments

1. Can students use their interpreter well? Do they have the facilities for effective use of the interpreter in the classroom (e.g., understand signs well and/or read lips well)? Is the student able to understand the instructor without the aid of an interpreter?
2. If students are able to understand the instructor with or without the aid of the interpreter, are they able to take their own notes in the classroom? If so, how good are their notes? Are they helpful to them in their study sessions?
3. If students are not able to take a complete set of notes, is it possible for them to just jot down their own thoughts, concepts, or key terminology that can help them to study and compare them with other sets of notes provided by a trained notetaker or someone else?
4. What kind of notetaking assistance would be most appropriate for students? Would a trained note-taker be required, or would a volunteer notetaker be sufficient? Would the student be satisfied with the notes provided by the instructor, if any?
5. Do students use their notes or notes from someone else as one of the primary study sources? Do the students compare the notes from a trained notetaker or someone else with their own jotted notes, if any, and rework the notes?
6. If students are not able to use an interpreter and none of them are able to understand the instructor, would notes provided by a trained notetaker help? Would they need a tutor? Is it the best way to pro-vide a service to the students? If not, what are some alternatives?
7. What additional services are needed for the students? For instance, do the students have reading problems? Are the students academically prepared for the course? Do the students have any other problems (e.g., emotional, social) that may be hindering their academic progress in the classroom in spite of the services being provided? Can a tutor effectively help the students to develop study skills and classroom participatory skills?

Source: *Technology and Disability* (1993).

3. Tactual sign—words are spelled using a series of finger positions, each representing a single letter
4. Print-on palm—tracing capital block letters in consumer's palm using index finger
5. Speech reading (lipreading)—people with good residual vision may use this method; however, only 30%–40% of spoken English can be understood using this method alone
6. Tadoma—a rarely used method of speech reading using touch in which the consumer places thumb on lips of the speaker, with fingers on throat
7. Gestural systems—includes natural gestures; behavior showing likes, dislikes, and choices; and touch cues or tactile prompts
8. Pictures/photos—use of pictures and symbols to communicate with others
9. Written notes—use black pen and glare-free paper to communicate expressively and receptively
10. Pre-written cards—use for predictable everyday occurrences and basic wants and needs
11. Raised alphabet card—speaker places consumer's index finger on braille letters, thereby spelling words (alphabet is printed above same letters in braille)
12. Tellatouch—portable typewriter-like machine enabling a person to type a message the consumer receives in braille
13. Tactile speech indicator (TSI)—enables a consumer with good speech to communicate on the telephone
14. Electronic devices—includes a device to magnify print, computers with programs to enlarge print and give large print or braille output, and telecommunication devices (e.g., TDDs)

TT/TDD Equipment A Text Telephone (TT) or Telecommunication Device for the Deaf (TDD) has a standard keyboard, screen display, and either an acoustic coupler or direct phone connection that enables individuals who cannot speak or hear well enough for voice phone communication to communicate. TT/TDD technology requires no special installation, but necessitates that both parties have the essential equipment. TT/TDD equipment generally costs between $160 and $600. Any worker who is deaf or hard of hearing and required to use phone communication can benefit from this technology.

The ADA mandates that each state implement a TT/TDD relay service. Relay service operators speak everything typed to them via TT/TDD to the hearing party and type the responses to the party on the TT/TDD. Some relays offer voice carry-over where the caller who is deaf or hard of hearing, but verbal, speaks directly to the person he or she called, and the relay service operator types the responses through the TT/TDD.

Although the intended use of TT/TDD technology was to parallel voice telephone service, other uses have been explored. For example, a bank teller who is deaf uses two TTs/TDDs and a training device to facilitate face-to-face communication with customers with accuracy and speed.

Telephone Amplification Telephone communication can be enhanced through amplification. Amplified headsets, replacement handsets, and in-line and portable amplifiers all increase the volume of the call. One telephone increases the volume, allows the user to adjust the frequency range, and has noise cancellation to increase the clarity of the call. Some headsets and replacement handsets also have noise cancellation features. Many hearing aids have a "T switch" that acts as an additional receptor for the signal. A foam pad can also be used to acoustically couple the hearing aid to the phone handset. This system eliminates feedback that may result from covering the hearing aid.

Tape Transcription Another accommodation not specifically developed for use by people who are hard of hearing, but appropriate, is a Pressure Zone Microphone (PZM)—available from an electronics supply store for approximately $50. Feedback from all workers—both with and without disabilities—has indicated that the investment has resulted in increased productivity for any worker who uses taped conversation in his or her work.

For example, a city employee with a profound bilateral hearing loss who can read lips, wears hearing aids, and uses FM systems needed to take minutes at commission meetings in the course of her job. Previously, she would take the notes and send the tape for transcription, which involved a high turnaround time and cost. Her Job Accommodation Network (JAN) consultant suggested attaching a PZM to the recorder to enhance the quality of the tape.

Amplified Stethoscope An example of a more specialized technology is a piece of equipment for medical professionals who are hard of hearing—the amplified stethoscope. Stethoscope amplifiers were developed for use in noisy environments, but can serve the needs of those who are hard of hearing. The small amplifying unit is attached to the tubing of the user's stethoscope. One limitation at this time is using any stethoscope with hearing aids. The person who is hard of hearing must remove his or her hearing aids to use the stethoscope effectively.

Paging Systems People in the workplace often need to communicate over distance. Paging systems are useful to reduce barriers in distance communication. Some pagers operate over the telephone lines. Others are stand-alone units with a more limited range.

Pagers can be used to alert people to a task to be done, to an emergency situation, or to report to a co-worker. Pager communication is one way. A message is sent, but the response must be made by telephone or in person. The message can be a simple vibrating signal or flashing light that alerts the receiver to make a prearranged response. For example, a signal may alert the grocery store employee that he or she is needed at the registers. Pagers with light-emitting diode (LED) displays of alphanumeric information can be used to send a more complicated message. For example, the housekeeper in a hotel can be advised of problems or needs in a particular room. Pagers can be used to alert people in emergency situations. For individuals who work alone or in remote areas, pagers can be akin to the buddy system by providing access to a co-worker even though that person is in another location.

Computer-Assisted Note Taking Technologies to assist communication in meetings, seminars, training sessions, and conferences are available using existing computer and stenographic equipment. These technologies provide alternatives to the use of certified interpreters. Finding a qualified interpreter may be difficult and is not economically feasible over the long term. An alternative approach is to use a personal computer (PC) and a PC projector. Typically, a projector is connected to a port in the computer and projects the text image onto a screen. PC projectors that have their own light source are available, but a less expensive option is to use a liquid crystal display panel with an overhead projector. Another option is to have several computer monitors available for individual viewing. The typist then records the conversation using standard word-processing software. The typist uses abbreviations and summarizes the content being presented. Some organizations recommend using software that allows variable-size print. It is usually recommended that the typist have a vocabulary list, list of attendee names, and notes of the content to be discussed before the meeting takes place. There are interpreter services that provide this service, but a less expensive method is to use someone in-house. The main drawback is that the conversation is not being recorded verbatim. If it is important that every word be transcribed, then the stenographic model is a better approach.

The stenographic model uses a stenographic keyboard attached to a computer and special software to translate the phonetic symbols entered by the stenographer into English. The same methods of projection or individual viewing can be used with this system. The drawback is both the equipment and software are expensive. Stenographic notetakers are an option for meetings and training situations, but will cost more than $2,000 for their equipment and compensation. In addition, the compensation for a court reporter will be costly. The advantages are that verbatim transcriptions are recorded and every attendee can have a record of the proceedings with diskettes or hard copy printouts of the text.

Visual and Tactile Cues Other modifications address unique workplace problems. For example, computers that send auditory cues to alert to errors or other problems with the equipment or software can be modified to substitute screen or cursor flashes for the auditory signal. Depending on the type of computer used, software may be commercially available to switch the auditory signals to visual. Macintosh computers have this as a built-in option. Turning the volume all the way down signals the use of visual cues. For example, an essential function of a postal employee's job was to monitor the performance of a sorting apparatus. The machine made a clicking sound when it was operating correctly. The machine was modified so that a light flashed to alert the worker if the machine failed

to click as a piece of mail went by. The manufacturer of the metering machine used its design engineering group to adapt the equipment.

Another mechanism to alert a worker to sounds in the environment is a vibrating signal that responds to noise. A meter-reader used this device in a suburban area to alert him to potential danger from dogs, approaching cars, or other hazards as he read meters in the field. These devices are more effective in relatively quiet environments where the worker needs to be alerted to abnormal sounds. They were designed for use in speech-training situations, but the technology has proven useful in this work setting as well.

Designing and Implementing Individualized Transition Plans for Youth with Sensory Impairments

Although there are many wonderful types of technology to help people with sensory impairments and other disabilities, these devices are of little value if the student does not have accessibility to them. Transition planning can play a large role in enhancing this accessibility.

Professional literature is filled with articles concerning the necessity of transition planning for youth with disabilities (Bullis et al., 1995; Everson, 1995; Sacks & Wolffe, 1992; Sisson & Babeo, 1992). These articles range from citing career and social development theories to citing vocational programming as the backbone of transition planning. Several professional works, including Wehman, Moon, et al. (1988), cite the elements of the planning process as the crux of any successful transition from school to adulthood. The process of designing and implementing a transition plan is much like combining the ingredients of a recipe. If all ingredients are combined in the correct order and in the right measures, the transition is most likely to be successful. If elements are combined out of order or in incorrect amounts, however, the transition is destined to deviate from the plan. This section describes the elements and conditions of transition planning that ensure positive and expected outcomes for people with sensory impairments, according to the seven basic steps below:

1. Organize education teams for all transition-age students.
2. Organize the circle of people, including students, who can craft visions of transition.
3. Identify the key activities identified in this vision.
4. Hold an initial transition planning meeting as part of annual individualized education program (IEP) meeting.
5. Implement the ITP through secondary school and adult services providers.
6. Update the ITP annually.
7. Hold an exit meeting.

As mandated in the Individuals with Disabilities Education Act (IDEA) of 1990, transition planning for students with disabilities should begin no later than 16 years of age. The dropout rate for students with sensory impairments, particularly those with singular sensory impairments, is high. For those students at risk for dropping out, transition planning should begin at 14 years of age. According to IDEA, all students who participate in annual IEP meetings are required to participate in transition planning. Teachers, parents, and administrators should be conscious of the tendency to concentrate on students with more

severe or multiple disabilities and should adjust screening and implementation processes to compensate.

Once the teams are organized, a variety of individuals will be invited to participate as the circle of people who help the student identify the vision for the future. Once this vision is crafted and activities generated, it is then time to advance to the more formal school-based transition plan. The activities reflect a period of brainstorming in which many difficult ideas are put forth by the circle of friends. Core members of this group tend to be the student, the parents, the school transition coordinator (if one is designated), the school-based rehabilitation counselor (if one is available), the school administrator and/or teacher (if the student attends a resource class or segregated classroom), and the state rehabilitation counselor (if one has not been placed within the school setting). Additional members are usually called as needed or as the student approaches his or her graduation date. Typical "consulting members" for students with visual impairments include the O & M specialist and rehabilitation teacher (Zimmerman, 1992). A "consulting member" for students with hearing impairments might be a speech-language therapist. Students with dual sensory impairments typically utilize all of these consultants to varying degrees.

Additional consulting members for people with sensory impairments may include physicians, auditory specialists, low vision specialists, psychologists (as adaptation to additional loss of vision or hearing is traumatic and people with sensory impairments typically have difficulty adjusting to life changes), and independent living staff members.

Particularly in rural communities, people other than agency personnel may be formally used to assist the student in transition (Bickford & Sheldon, 1988). These paraprofessionals often serve as links between the school system, adult services agencies, and community. Paraprofessionals may be parents, concerned business leaders, church representatives, or civic group representatives who become to some degree responsible for activities such as career development, community orientation, community-based instruction, transportation, or organized recreation.

After the transition team has been determined for each student with sensory impairments, planning for the initial meeting can occur. Typically, the initial meeting occurs as a part of the student's IEP meeting (Wehman, Moon, et al., 1988). The meeting should be scheduled at a time when all of the core members of the planning team can be present, but it is most important that the student and his or her parents attend. It is preferable that the meeting occur on a weekday when consulting members can be reached by telephone during the meeting. An initial part of the IEP/ITP plan will be where the student should receive school services. Services in neighborhood high schools are preferable for students learning how to function in the community. Table 12.4 provides several tips for inclusion into general education classrooms.

The transition coordinator or school-based rehabilitation counselor is responsible for organizing the transition meeting and for gathering all available pertinent information about the student prior to the meeting. The team leader should be able to quickly summarize key information regarding the student's educational history, medical, educational, and vocational assessments, and past activities and interests. Up-front organizational efforts by the team leader ensure more actual planning time for the transition team.

Typically, the transition coordinator or school-based rehabilitation counselor serves as the team leader during the transition planning in an IEP meeting. The leader makes cer-

Table 12.4. Tips for inclusion of youth with visual impairments

Find out about who is available to help you. (Also, learn what their titles mean and what they do.) One very important person who typically works with students with visual impairments is the itinerant teacher. Itinerant teachers move from school to school working with individual students, and usually translate students' classwork into braille. Students may also receive training from an orientation and mobility instructor, who will teach them to move independently.

Learn how to adapt and modify materials and instruction. (The changes you make might also help other students.) Teachers face a wide variety of students with diverse abilities, styles of learning, and cultural and linguistic systems, as well as disparate economic situations, family structures, and value systems. The good news about the variety in the classroom is that teachers' efforts at individualizing instruction and materials for students with the greatest difference may result in adaptations that will benefit all students.

Learn as much as you can, and encourage the professionals you work with to do the same. One of the key ingredients for successful inclusion of students with disabilities is adequate education and support of the professionals who work with students who have disabilities.

Find out about training that may be available and ask to go. Often in-service training will be provided by your local school district, a regional service center or co-op, a nearby university, or a regional or national conference. Get your name on the mailing list of organizations whose focus is on visual impairments.

Suggest that others become informed, especially students, who may have access to programs like the "Kids on the Block" puppet shows that teach about disabilities. Use your local library and bookstores to find print material that you can read and share.

Call parents and ask questions when you don't understand terminology, equipment, or the reasons for prescribed practices. Then, keep an open mind.

Teach other students to assist in social as well as academic settings. Most young children are able and willing to help students with disabilities as they adjust to their new situation in a general classroom. Students can offer assistance at lunch, on the playground, and in fine arts classes, where there is less structure and routine.

From Viadero, D. (1989, November). Side by side. *Teacher Magazine Reader,* p. 4. Needham, MA: Allyn & Bacon; copyright © 1989 by Allyn & Bacon; reprinted by permission.

tain that all members know each other and encourages open and honest communication within the group. The team leader is also responsible for discussing the "ground rules" for participation and decision making in the planning process. One of the most important ground rules is that the student and family always provide input and make the final decision about participation in an activity.

The transition team leader is also responsible for initiating discussion about transition outcomes and possible support services available to the student. The student with a sensory impairment should decide which outcomes are most important in the following domains: employment and higher education, social and leisure activities, community participation, and residential options. The rest of the group members should generate adult support services to assist the student in attaining the chosen outcomes. Figure 12.1 lists adult support services available to people with varying degrees of sensory impairment. Transition teams benefit from generating a checklist of support services to be used during the planning process. The major benefit of such a checklist is to prevent the team from excluding or forgetting potential sources of support for the student. The team leader should encourage all members of the group to voice opinions or concerns about potential outcomes or support services during the ITP meeting rather than allowing a decision to occur without the full support of the group.

Employment/higher education

Vocational rehabilitation (VR) (Many states have specialized agencies for vision and hearing.)
 Interpreter services
 Reader services
 Brailling
 Transportation (usually time-limited during job training)
 Counseling
 Evaluation for employment, O & M, and assistive technology
 Job placement (transitional)
 Job development and supported employment
 Sheltered employment
 Higher education or trade school
 Note: VR for people with blindness is "birth through death"; therefore, some services are
not time-limited

Residential

Vocational rehabilitation through independent living services
 Location of Section 8 housing
 Assistance with housing or roommate search
 Evaluation for and provision of assistive technology devices
 Rehabilitation testing of domestic skills
 Counseling and assistance with home management
 Assistance with Social Security benefits
Mental retardation/developmental disabilities agencies for students with sensory impairments
 Group home or ICF/MR placement
 Supervised apartment placement
 Location of Section 8 housing
 Service coordination
 Attendant care (if needed)

Recreation

Vocational rehabilitation (blind services)
 Counseling on finding recreational options
 Assistance in networking
 Updates on recreation options available
 O & M instruction
Mental retardation/developmental disabilities agencies for students with sensory impairments
 Sponsored recreation programs
 Individualized instruction and support for participation
 Service coordination

Community participation

Vocational rehabilitation through independent living services
 Interpreter services
 Brailling (Library for the Blind)
 Orientation and mobility
 Adaptations and assistive technology
 Rehabilitation teaching
Mental retardation/developmental disabilities agencies for students with sensory impairments
 Service coordination
 Instruction
 Structured programs for participation

Figure 12.1. A sample checklist of adult services available to people with sensory impairments.

The student's ITP should at least consider all 10 of the following goals:

1. Employment
2. Vocational education/training
3. Postsecondary education
4. Financial/income needs
5. Independent living
6. Transportation/mobility
7. Social relationships
8. Recreation/leisure
9. Health/safety
10. Self-advocacy/future planning

According to Wehman (1995) each goal should include 1) a projected date for accomplishment, 2) a designation of whether the goal will be completed before or after graduation, 3) names of support programs and personnel who will work with the student, and 4) the name of the individual responsible for monitoring this aspect of the ITP.

Tashell *Tashell is an 18-year-old African American woman with a severe visual impairment and occasional self-abusive/self-stimulatory behavior. Tashell can see shadows and bright light and can read enlarged print magnified on a portable screen.*

Enrolled in a public high school college preparatory studies program, Tashell is completing her junior year. She plans to be a child care assistant for preschoolers with disabilities. Tashell is sometimes loud and, on occasion, verbally abusive to staff and peers when corrected. She ambulates independently, using a white cane.

The reader should keep in mind, however, that the ITP on pages 325–328 is written only for Tashell. Other individual's plans may be similar but no two should ever be identical.

The responsibilities of the core and consulting members of each ITP team are numerous. Most teams and team leaders find comfort in utilizing a services referral checklist (Wehman, Moon, et al., 1988) to initiate and monitor referrals to the various adult services agencies. The checklist does not need to be elaborate. It only needs to convey services to which the student has been referred, the referral date, the name of the contact individual, and the dates by which the services are expected to begin and end.

Each ITP member should leave the initial ITP meeting with a sense of satisfaction that the student's interests have been fully examined and actions have been taken. Members should also know what their responsibilities are in the actual implementation of the plan. If any issues have not been resolved (e.g., an assessment is needed on remaining vision or on an assistive device), team members should set another meeting time at the initial meeting to discuss the results of further investigation and to finalize the ITP. A key to good planning is never to leave loose ends without a plan to resolve them.

Description of Student's Future Vision

It is Tashell's dream to complete high school and work in the child care field. She loves children and wants to develop these skills as well as make friends with others who have similar vocational interests. Tashell wishes to expand her church activities as well.

Individualized Transition Plan

Student's Name _Tashell_

Birthdate _____

Student's Identification Number _____

Participants:

School _Godwin_

ITP Conference Date _____

Name	Position
Tashell	_Student_
Cleone & Samantha	_Parents_
Tim	_Transition coordinator_
Steve	_DRS coordinator_
Mary	_Child care coordinator_
Paula	_Guidance counselor_
Bonita	_Teacher of students with visual impairments_

Career and Economic Self-Sufficiency

Employment Goal _Tashell will gain employment as a child care worker._

Level of present performance: _Tashell has completed her second semester in child care prep. She has no paid work experience to date._

Steps needed to accomplish goal: _1. Enroll in work-study for Fall 1994. 2. Enroll in work experience for Summer 1994 to work with preschoolers at the Richmond Cerebral Palsy Center. 3. Develop a resume of work experiences/references._

Date of completion: _June 1994_

Person(s) responsible for implementation: _Tashell and transition coordinator_

Vocational Education/Training Goal _Completion of a 2-year child care preparatory program._

Level of present performance: _Tashell has a "B+" average in her child care class (6 credits). She is extremely patient with 3- and 4-year-old children, particularly with self-care skills._

Steps needed to accomplish goal: _1. Complete 1st semester, senior-year academic/child care courses. 2. Visit off-site child care centers with VR counselor._

Date of completion: _December 1994_

Person(s) responsible for implementation: _Tashell, VR counselor, and transition coordinator_

From Wehman, P. (1995). *Individual transition plans: The teachers curriculum guide for helping youth with special needs.* Austin, TX: PRO-ED; reprinted by permission.

Postsecondary Education Goal *Completion of a 2-year (associate-level) junior college early childhood education worker program (Project PAVE).*

Level of present performance: *Tashell currently has a "C" average in academic areas. She has experienced some difficulty adjusting to a new laptop and frequently refuses to turn in homework.*

Steps needed to accomplish goal: *1. Take a refresher course in word processing, Summer 1994, to maintain skills. 2. Apply to PAVE (J. Sargeant) by 10/94. 3. Visit PAVE by 12/94. 4. Graduate with "B" average in 6/95.*

Date of completion: *June 1995*

Person(s) responsible for implementation: *Tashell, parents, and guidance counselor*

Financial/Income Needs Goal *Tashell currently receives SSI and SSDI. She will earn an income and develop a PASS for her first year of employment.*

Level of present performance: *Tashell has no earned income.*

Steps needed to accomplish goal: *1. Tashell will develop a work history with earned income. 2. Parents will work with accountants and DRS to develop PASS.*

Date of completion: *December 1994*

Person(s) responsible for implementation: *Tashell, parents, and work coordinator*

Career and Economic Self-Sufficiency

Independent Living Goal *Tashell will live independently with minimum support.*

Level of present performance: *Tashell can cook frozen meals using a microwave oven.*

Steps needed to accomplish goal: *1. Attend Center for Independent Living (CIL) classes Summer 1994, with a teacher for students with visual impairment. 2. Attend CIL classes Fall 1994 independently (Tuesday evenings). 3. Work with family to foster domestic independence. 4. Apply for independent Residential Options Service, 6/94.*

Date of completion: *June 1995*

Person(s) responsible for implementation: *Tashell, parents, and transition coordinator*

Transportation/Mobility Goal *Tashell will utilize public/private transportation independently.*

Level of present performance: *Tashell can call a cab. She has never utilized the public bus system. Her parents frequently drive her places.*

Steps needed to accomplish goal: *1. Enroll in Center for Independent Living mobility classes 9/94. 2. Work with mobility instructor, Summer 1994. 3. Apply for STAR Transporation, 6/94.*

Date of completion: *May 1995*

Person(s) responsible for implementation: *Tashell and Division of Visual Impairment*

Social Relationships Goal *Tashell will attend school dances with her friends.*

Level of present performance: *Tashell currently attends school functions only with her younger sister or cousin. She does not trust others for support, although she is fairly well liked by some peers. Her head scratching (self-stimulating) has diminished somewhat lately.*

Steps needed to accomplish goal: *1. Tashell will attend the "Junior Pre-Summer Blast" 6/6/94 with Sherron (classmate). 2. Tashell will attend one dance per quarter, 1994-1995.*

Date of completion: *December 1994*

Person(s) responsible for implementation: *Tashell and parents*

Recreation/Leisure Goal *Tashell will join her church and school choirs.*

Level of present performance: *Tashell has a beautiful voice. She sings at home/church but has just recently expressed an interest in joining choir.*

Steps needed to accomplish goal: *1. Join church choir by 6/15/94. 2. Attend all Wednesday and Sunday evening practices June, July, and August. 3. Audition for school choir 9/94. 4. Attend all practices/ recitals with next door neighbor (choir member).*

Date of completion: *September 1994*

Person(s) responsible for implementation: *Tashell, mother, and neighbor (has agreed) specialist*

Personal Competence

Health/Safety Goal *Tashell will accept assistance from peers and others when necessary.*

Level of present performance: *Tashell currently places herself in danger by refusing assistance and becomes verbally abusive to others.*

Steps needed to accomplish goal: *1. Meet with minister (to whom she is close) to discuss power struggles, and 2. Incrementally accept assistance with appropriate attitude by 6/95.*

Date of completion: *June 1995*

Person(s) responsible for implementation: *Tashell, Reverend Graves, and parents will monitor*

Self-Advocacy/Future Planning *Tashell will develop a stronger self-concept and understand/ accept both physical limitations and strengths.*

Level of present performance: *Tashell has made tremendous gains in the past 12 months but occasionally loses confidence in her ability.*

Steps needed to accomplish goal: *1. Join a support group for older teens with visual impairments by 10/94. 2. Maintain a typed journal of fears and hopes (autobiography). 3. Submit autobiography to a confidante to measure growth (Tashell's plan).*

Date of completion: *March 1995*

Person(s) responsible for implementation: *Tashell and parents (to assist with schedules)*

Student Career Preference

Child care position

Student's Major Transition Needs

1. Complete child care certification (high school)
2. Complete high school
3. Develop work experience
4. Maintain mobility/academic independence
5. Develop social circle of friends

Additional Notes

Community Integration for Youth with Visual Impairments

Enhancing Travel Skills

The transition team and student may consider many different forms of travel when planning for the transportation needs of students with visual impairments. Depending on the person's mobility and expressed needs, the O & M specialist—in cooperation with relevant team members—might consider teaching the individual a safe walking route to and from the local recreation center. For some individuals, solo foot travel to and from work is common. If the person chooses this means of transportation, the O & M specialist should monitor the individual's applicable safety techniques and use of the various senses. If the O & M specialist determines that the individual's safety is in jeopardy, various long cane techniques may be taught to assist the individual in locating curbs and objects in the foot path. In addition to acting as a bumper, the long cane alerts drivers that the individual has a visual impairment. This is usually helpful at street crossings where there is moderate to heavy traffic.

Other types of mobility devices such as electronic travel aids, assistive technology, and low vision devices, such as telescopes, may also be useful in assisting the individual with a visual impairment to travel to and from the work setting. These devices can be expensive however, and may require extensive training for successful use. The teacher must evaluate whether the individual would benefit from such instruction. Figure 12.2 gives an example of how a girl who is deaf-blind ambulates around her community.

An alternative to these technical devices is to teach the individual with a visual impairment the safe method for walking with a sighted individual. In the sighted-guide technique, the individual who is blind grasps the sighted guide's arm directly above the elbow, forming a 90° angle with his or her arm. The individual walks one half-step behind and to the side of the sighted person. In this position, the individual can feel the guide's movements and react to turns, proceed up and down stairs, and pass through doors and narrow areas safely. Sighted-guide skills are often used in combination with other mobility devices.

When evaluating a potential worksite, it is important to consider whether the individual's work schedule includes evening duties and responsibilities. If so, the O & M specialist will need to plan accordingly for potential O & M instruction in this area, for example, a long cane in conjunction with a wide-angle mobility nightlight.

Public Transportation

Some destinations will be too far for the individual with a visual impairment to travel to by foot, and alternative methods of transportation will need to be explored. Public transportation may be chosen as the best method for traveling to and from the work setting.

When preparing to use public transportation, certain questions need to be considered by the O & M specialist: What public transportation systems are available in the community and useful to the individual? Is the transportation schedule consistent enough to match the individual's work or social schedule? Are there adequate sensory landmarks at the pickup and destination points to assist the individual in locating and distinguishing those places? Is the individual capable of using that system?

Using Public Transportation To gain access to the public transportation system, the individual with a visual impairment must get to the bus stop or subway station platform,

Carol Kaplin, a high school student, uses many different types of assistive technology in a typical day's activities to make her life run smoothly.

Carol, please tell me about yourself.

My name is Carol Kaplin. I am 19 years old, and I am deaf-blind. I have macular degeneration and a 20/70 acuity loss in both eyes. I don't see objects or people clearly, especially in my central field. My hearing loss is mild to moderate in both ears. I hear some speech and most environmental sounds—cars, trains, planes—if there's no background noise.

Mornings I go to Roosevelt High School. In the afternoon, I'm learning work skills for a job after graduation. My mom works the night shift and my dad works days, so I'm pretty independent at home.

How do you travel?

I learned how to use a cane to travel indoors. I also use a visual and tactual map, large print compass, telescope, and various cane techniques. Recently, I attended a dog guide school and received a dog guide, Sasha. She and I travel indoor and outdoor routes that are familiar to both of us.

How do you communicate when you travel?

Some people who don't know me well have a hard time understanding my voice. Most of them don't understand American Sign Language (ASL) either. If an interpreter isn't with me, I use communication cards or a print-on-palm system. People print letters of the alphabet on my palm to talk to me. I print on paper or sometimes on their palm to talk to them. It works, especially for emergencies.

What types of "tech aids" do you use?

I use a folding cane with a marshmallow tip, communication cards, map, note pad, and my dog guide for indoor travel. When I leave my house, I use a large print compass, telescope, cane, communication cards, note pad, and my dog guide. I don't use all of them each time I travel. I choose "tech aids" based on where I'm going and the activity. I tend to use different aids for familiar and unfamiliar settings.

Tell me about the ones you used today.

This morning, at home, I trailed to find the different rooms. But when I needed to go downstairs to the laundry room for my wash (it's full of things I could trip over), I used my cane. The marshmallow tip helps it glide over uneven surfaces.

Before school, I took my dog Sasha for a walk. This way we both get some exercise. I took my pre-printed communication cards in case of an emergency or if I get confused. I wore my telescope around my neck on a string and used it to cross a quiet road. It enlarges and expands my viewing area to make up for my central field loss. And, Sasha helps me cross streets. She's trained not to move when I give her a command if a car is in my path. Once she knows the route, I won't need the telescope for our morning walk.

This afternoon, I went to a job interview across town. My mobility teacher reviewed the route with me last week. I use a large print compass and a telescope to cross low-traffic streets. My cane skills are good. Based on my skills and comfort level, my instructor and I agreed to meet at the building. I didn't take Sasha because she didn't know the route. I located the right bus with my telescope and showed my pre-printed communication card to the driver before sitting down. It must have been my lucky day! He remembered to tap my hand so I knew when to get off. I found the direction with my compass, walked to the building using my cane, and identified the address with my telescope.

I had a visual and tactual map of the building, with landmarks on it so I knew where I was in the building. My mobility instructor was there but I didn't need her. The hallway was too dark to see the office numbers, so I stopped someone and asked for help. I wrote "Office #237?" on my note pad. He wrote, "two more doors" and pointed down the hallway. I found it. Luckily, I left my house early. Being on time for a job interview is important!

Figure 12.2. Examples of how assistive technology enhances Carol's life. (From Carr, T. [Ed.]. [1994]. *Assistive technology: Enhancements for daily life. HKNC–TAC News, 7*[2], 3; reprinted with permission from the Helen Keller National Center, Technical Assistance Center.)

identify the correct bus or car, board and pay the fare (possibly ask for a transfer), locate a seat, and exit at the proper destination. The O & M specialist should teach the individual how to obtain information over the telephone regarding schedules, the amount and type of fare, location of pickup and destination points, and whether transfers are needed. This teaches the individual solicitation skills that are generalizable to other settings in the community.

Of all of the transportation options listed above, travel on buses and trains requires the greatest amount of O & M skill and ability. Using minibuses and taxis requires the least amount of travel ability, and many people with visual impairments choose these options over travel by foot or on public transportation. In the case of the scheduled minibuses and taxis, the individual has to telephone the transportation office and schedule a pickup time and destination point. Usually, reservations must be made in advance. Unlike the scheduled minibus, taxi pickup is usually more flexible in scheduling, but fares are generally more expensive.

Dog Guides

The use of dog guides is yet another possible method of travel that dates back to the 19th century. Systematic mobility training of dog guides began in Germany toward the end of World War I. In 1929, The Seeing Eye, Inc., became the first dog guide training facility in the United States. Initially airlines, restaurants, hotels, bus lines, and schools were reluctant to allow the dog and the individual with a visual impairment entrance. Because of the ADA and more tolerant public attitudes, people with dog guides now have access to all facilities open to the general public, including public transportation. To enhance an individual's placement prospects, the teacher may recommend that the student use a dog guide for travel purposes. Training usually takes up to 6 weeks, so adequate time must be included in the placement schedule.

The ultimate decision regarding modes of travel is the responsibility of the student and the teacher or specialist. Weighing the possibilities of available transportation systems and matching those options with the individual's travel abilities require a complete and thorough analysis of the risks and hazards involved in traveling to and from the work setting.

Evaluation of Transition Outcomes for Youth with Sensory Impairments

An ITP is worthless without monitoring, evaluation, and follow-up. In the past, many transitional IEPs and standard IEPs have been written to comply with federal and state regulations and suggestions; however, they were never acted upon to a sufficient degree (S.W. Smith, 1990), as mandated by IDEA.

The best evaluation of transition outcomes includes a variety of measures. These measures are both qualitative and quantitative and occur at several different levels. At the planning level, the evaluator should ask the following questions:

- Are interventions and services designed to be maximally under the control of the individual with the disability?

- Do the interventions, programs, and services encourage independence, problem-solving abilities, self-assurance, and needed social skills (Corn, 1985; Sacks & Wolffe, 1992)?
- Are naturally occurring cues and consequences used first so that human services intrusiveness is kept to a minimum?
- Are interventions designed for generalizability and the promotion of problem solving?
- Are monitoring points built into the plan where feedback can be obtained from the service providers and the student with sensory impairment?

At the implementation level, the evaluator should continue to monitor the issues outlined above and add these questions:

- Are the parents and the student periodically met to discuss progress and areas that need further attention?
- As a result of planning and progress toward independence made in each domain, is the student able to achieve other personal goals above and beyond those listed?
- Is the student able to wean from assistance and rely more heavily on self-help?
- Is the student building lasting, nonpaid friendships?
- Can the student, at any point during the process, call a meeting and change the transition plan to better suit his or her needs?

At the exit level, the evaluator should examine the following issues:

- Have all transition goals been met or changed for a better outcome?
- Does the student know who his or her service provider contacts are after graduation?
- Does the student have a stable, integrated place to live?
- Is the student employed or enrolled in a postsecondary educational program?
- Does the student have friends, and is he or she involved in recreational activities within his or her community?
- Does the student frequently exhibit the ability to solve problems and adapt to new situations with minimal or no assistance from paid caregivers?
- Are the student and his or her family happy with the transition outcomes?

These measures should not be answered with simple "yes" or "no" responses. They are intended to be the basis for further exploration in each domain and for the overall ITP.

Sandra *Sandra[2] is a 29-year-old woman who has no functional vision and a severe bilateral hearing loss as a result of rubella. Based on the results of an Inventory of Client and Agency Planning (ICAP) completed in 1988, Sandra needs close supervision and ongoing assistance in performing personal care activities. Sandra uses some sign and tactile cards (textures and parts of objects) to communicate with those who do not sign. She has no physical impairment and uses both hands efficiently to perform work tasks. Sandra uses a sighted guide for safe travel. She lives at home with her parents.*

[2]From Downing, J., Shafer, M., Brahm-Levy, A., & Frantz, M. (1992). Supported employment for individuals with dual sensory impairments and mental retardation: Current practice and future challenges. *Journal of Vocational Rehabiliation, 2*(1), 28–38; reprinted by permission.

Work History *Sandra graduated from a state school for the deaf and blind in 1982 and attended a sheltered workshop program for 16 months before going to the Helen Keller National Center for Deaf-Blindness for a 12-month evaluation. Sandra returned to the sheltered workshop for 4 years. Like many sheltered workers, Sandra was socially isolated from others and experienced frequent amounts of downtime with little training or support. Her typical work pattern included performing one piece of the task, signing to herself GOOD, and hitting a counter to tabulate her piece rate. At that time, Sandra was reported to be very slow, requiring frequent prompting, and failing to ask for additional work materials when needed. Sandra's files also indicated that she engaged in vocalizations that were highly distracting, acted out frequently, and regularly stole soda from others. Sandra did not communicate with other employees (all of whom had disabilities) and did not initiate communication with her trainers. During lunch or breaks, Sandra typically sat by herself.*

At her parent's request, Sandra stopped work and stayed home for 6 months. At that point, COPD initiated an assessment of Sandra's strengths and areas of concern, which led to her placement in the enclave. Sandra's work tasks entail breaking plastic parts of sheets, sorting parts, bagging, heat sealing, and assembling. Sandra sits physically close to other people with severe disabilities while she performs these tasks and also works with workers without disabilities in other jobs, such as cleaning the restrooms for employee use. Once Sandra learns a job, she is completely independent, does not need to sign GOOD to herself to continue, requests more work materials, and initiates conversation with others.

Sandra continues to engage in vocalizations, but the work environment is relatively noisy and allows for individual displays of such behavior without distracting other employees—a factor taken into consideration during her assessment.

Support Needs *While at the sheltered workshop, Sandra had little opportunity to interact with others, especially those who signed, and was virtually isolated. As part of the work enclave and the larger typical work environment, Sandra's opportunities for communication and social interaction have increased. Because of her severe dual sensory impairment and reliance on some signing for receptive and expressive communication, however, support for increased interactions was necessary. COPD staff devised a system of 15 tactile and textured cards (with written messages) that allow her to interact with individuals who do not understand signing. Vocabulary was developed based on her social needs at the work setting. Sandra uses this system both expressively and receptively. In addition, an augmentative communication wallet was developed to help Sandra gain access to the bank and other community facilities near her worksite. This wallet holds the money necessary for the purchase and a written message to the cashier regarding the desired order and how to handle the transaction. This device also signals to Sandra that she is about to use such a community facility.*

In addition to these augmentative communication devices, Sandra's primary support consisted of job adaptations and initial intensive instructions to learn individual tasks and the various routes needed to move safely in this environment. Tasks were analyzed into separate components and each component was identified by a tactile cue. To assist in the organization of her work and aid in efficiency, bins were set up to keep her work materials separated. Once Sandra had attained mastery of each task (after approximately 20 hours of training), support was faded. Sandra consistently requires support to aid in task changes and worksite mobility.

Employment Outcomes *Sandra has now been employed in the Concor enclave for approximately 2 years. During this time, she has displayed a marked decrease in her vocalizations and she now frequently interacts with others and purchases her own sodas rather than stealing them from others. During the past year, she averaged 27 hours of work per week and earned an average*

hourly wage of $0.76 (range of $0.22–$1.33). Obviously, her hourly wage is far from ideal, and strategies for placement into a better paying position or production enhancement procedures are being explored. Unfortunately, current funding levels limit the expansion or refinement of supported employment opportunities for Sandra.

Conclusion

Students with sensory impairments can and do benefit greatly from individualized transition planning. This group of students, like students with learning disabilities, tends to fall through the cracks of the educational and adult services provision systems. Value-based transition planning that promotes and monitors self-esteem, self-advocacy, problem solving, and emphasis on quality of life will help to ensure that people with visual and hearing impairments live and work within their own communities.

12

Study Questions

1. What are the differences among the diagnoses of *blindness, legal blindness, low vision,* and *partially seeing?*

2. What are the differences among the terms *deafness, hard of hearing,* and *hearing impaired?*

3. What are some common social, academic, and vocational characteristics of youth and adults with visual and hearing impairments?

4. What are the components of a "functional assessment" of youth with visual and hearing impairments?

5. What are some Internet resources that can be utilized by individuals with hearing and visual impairments?

6. What are three types of assistive technology specifically for individuals with hearing impairments?

7. What are some methods for improving travel and mobility skills for individuals with visual impairment?

13

Applications for Youth with Learning Disabilities

Elizabeth Evans Getzel and John J. Gugerty

Upon completion of this chapter, the reader will be able to do the following:

- Describe the impact of having a learning disability and its pervasiveness upon a student's life
- Understand the critical factors in gathering information through an assessment process
- Be aware of some of the unique challenges presented by students with learning disabilities and strategies to work effectively with them and their families
- Present alternative transition strategies for students entering postsecondary education or employment settings
- Know steps to take when conducting a postschool follow-up
- Describe the role of the transition team and the importance of student and family involvement on the team

Learning disabilities (LD) can be viewed from at least three perspectives: definitional, data, and individual experience. A working knowledge of definitions and a familiarity with aggregate data are key tools in the effective professional's repertoire; however, professionals who wish to develop a more accurate understanding of LD and their manifestations in personal, social, and work situations must develop and internalize an understanding of their impact on the lives of real people. In doing so, it becomes apparent that those with LD, even in milder forms, face severe problems in developing and maintaining employment, independence, and interpersonal relationships.

Defining Learning Disabilities

Addressing the needs of students with learning disabilities is an important component of American education, but as a service category it is characterized by inconsistency and disagreement (Keogh, 1986). Differences in identification of LD have also been shown to be related to disciplinary or professional perspectives and techniques, to the specific formula used for determining a discrepancy between ability and achievement, to the techniques and measures used in diagnosis, and to a variety of institutional or organizational constraints (Keogh, 1986).

Algozzine and Ysseldyke (1986) reviewed the history and status of diagnostic and classification practices, and concluded that because LD screening and diagnostic activity are so flawed and limited, it is time to redirect resources toward corrective and preventive educational interventions. They saw no reason to believe that observed trends in screening and diagnosis would improve programs for individuals with learning disabilities and thus recommended that resources used for screening, diagnosis, and classification be diverted to making all education more special.

Nonetheless, the diagnosis, classification, and program design controversies continued unabated (Bryan, 1989; Coles, 1987; Coplin & Morgan, 1988; Graham & Harris, 1989; Leong, 1989; McLeskey, 1989; Miller, 1990; Rispens, van Yperen, & van Duijn, 1991; Siegel, 1989a, 1989b; Stanovich, 1989; Swanson, 1987; Torgeson, 1989). Hammill (1990) reviewed efforts made since 1962 to define learning disabilities. He quoted 11 widely known and historically influential definitions, compared and contrasted their content, and concluded that the field could and should form a consensus around the National Joint Committee on Learning Disabilities (NJCLD) (1988) definition:

> Learning disabilities is a general term that refers to a heterogeneous group of disorders manifested by significant difficulties in the acquisition and use of listening, speaking, reading, writing, reasoning, or mathematical abilities. These disorders are intrinsic to the individual, presumed to be due to central nervous system dysfunction, and may occur across the life span. Problems in self-regulatory behaviors, social perception, and social interaction may exist with learning disabilities but do not by themselves constitute a learning disability. Although learning disabilities may occur concomitantly with other handicapping conditions (for example, sensory impairment, mental retardation, serious emotional disturbance) or with extrinsic influences (such as cultural differences, insufficient or inappropriate instruction), they are not the result of those conditions or influences. (p. 1)

Work by Levine (1989, 1990) and Viadero (1991) support the role of neurobiological factors in learning disabilities.

At the postsecondary level, Brinckerhoff, Shaw, and McGuire (1993) support the NJCLD definition for the following reasons:

- It has a broad base of support, including that of the Association on Higher Education and Disability (AHEAD).
- It is consistent with the concept of intraindividual differences in a range of areas, including reasoning.
- It clearly specifies that learning disabilities exist throughout the life span.
- It does not require identification of central nervous system (CNS) etiology.
- It recognizes that problems with related psychosocial skills may exist but does not include them as part of the definition.

- Although it acknowledges possible concomitant disabling conditions, it deals with LD as the primary condition.
- It does not rule out the possibility that LD can occur in people with superior intellectual functioning.

Bateman (1994) recommends a three-stage identification process for kindergarten to grade 12 students suspected of having LD.

> This process examines discrepancy, causality, and the need for special education in a way that is consistent with all legal requirements. It also improves upon the too common practice of relying on a mathematical formula which reduces the child to two test scores and falsely equates learning disabilities with discrepancy. (p. 95)

Hagin, Kugler, and Ellsworth (1994) discuss general principles in assessing adults suspected of having LD, as well as describing "markers" on the Wechsler Adult Intelligence Scale–Revised (WAIS–R) subtests (Wechsler, 1981) and other assessment strategies that they associate with the presence of LD. Individuals working for or with the state–federal rehabilitation staff will find the Rehabilitation Services Administration (1995) operational definition of *specific learning disabilities* useful for vocational rehabilitation (VR) purposes.

Experiences of Individuals with Learning Disabilities

Primary School Experiences

What is it like to be a kindergartner with dyslexia? Richie, now an adult, remembers:

> Maybe someone like me was a new thing for the teacher I had in kindergarten. At the time she was also new to me. As life went on, I met up with more and more people like her; it's no longer new to me.
>
> I vividly recall her segregating the class into ability levels. The A students sat in one row, followed by the B and C students. The three worst students in the class sat in front of the room facing the rest of the students and were made constant examples of what would happen should you not do well on the next project. I spent the entire year facing that class, but I never looked back at them; I kept my head low.
>
> By the time I was in first grade, teachers knew something was very wrong. I was reading from right to left and all my letters and numbers were completely written in reverse. If it had been up to those teachers, nothing would have been done. But, luckily, I had parents who really cared. My parents say these were terrible years for them. They were even worse for me. I came home screaming, "I'm dumb, I'm dumb, I wish I were dead!" At the time, I didn't realize what kinds of battles my parents had to fight to get me help.
>
> While all the politics were taking place I had already flunked from first grade back into kindergarten. Sometimes the teachers would try to encourage me; they would say, "Come on Richie, you know what that word is." Only, I didn't and it was embarrassing. I just felt dumb. And dumb is how the kids treated me. They'd make fun of me every chance they got, asking me to spell "cat" or something like that. Even if I knew how to spell it, I wouldn't; they'd only give me another word. It was awful. More than anything I wanted friends. I was 7 years old in the first grade. The oldest in the class. As I inhaled deeply to blow out the seven candles on my cake, my parents made a wish. They wished to find out what my problem was; they wished they could make me happy. I still remember that I didn't wish that I could read or write. I wished that the kids would like me. (Menzia, 1990, pp. 6, 8)

Social isolation and the need for friendship are major problems faced not only by many first graders with learning problems, but also by individuals throughout their school years and adulthood.

Secondary School Experiences

Some older students with learning problems describe their experiences in vivid and colorful language (Levine, 1990):

My head is just like a television set except it has no channel selector. So I get all the programs on my screen at the same time.

When I sit in class, I keep having these "mind drifts." I never know when my mind is gonna drift away so I lose what's happening.

I like to move around a lot. When I sit still, I get tired. I get bored. I need action.

I think I'm a "busticator." A busticator is someone who busts things up all the time. He doesn't mean to. He's real fast and keeps getting into trouble for not thinking. You know it's not really his fault that he does things fast, but I guess he has to take the blame when he causes trouble or bothers someone. Anyway that's me. I'm a real busticator.

I was looking at the bulletin board. I noticed that there were seven thumbtacks in the bulletin board but only six of them were being used. I wondered about the seventh thumbtack. Why was there nothing underneath it? Maybe someone had pulled something off, or maybe it had fallen off. I thought about pulling the thumbtack out of the bulletin board. I thought it might even be cool to put it on the seat of the kid in front of me. I noticed that this thumbtack was red and all the others were either blue or green. I wondered why the red thumbtack was the one with nothing under it. Maybe there was a reason for it. I tried to think of some reasons. Then, all of a sudden, the teacher called on me, and I realized I had no idea what had been going on in the classroom. The teacher was telling us important stuff while I was busy with that dumb thumbtack. That keeps on happening to me. I'm so distractible. All kinds of things pull me off track. (pp. 35–36)

Many individuals with learning disabilities develop ways to mask or cope with their painful school experiences. Karen Campbell (1988) describes her situation:

Memories of my early childhood are filled with frustration, pain and occasions of constant failure. I always knew I was different from the other kids and I was reminded of it every day. I couldn't remember which hand to raise to salute the flag even though instructions had just been given me. In every attempt at writing something, my letters came out backward and I can remember that heat of tears as I struggled to do the simplest task and failed all too often.

I was really quite verbal so I learned how to get by in classroom discussions, but when it came time to read, my mind would dance away and I couldn't remember what I had just read. I couldn't spell the simplest words. I learned how to write poorly, and to clown around or get defensive about my writing and my trouble carrying out instruction. I never knew it at the time, of course, but I later discovered that the reason for all the trouble I had in school was due to a learning disability, a condition that had nothing to do with intelligence, attitude, or personality, but was simply a matter of birth. . . . I had come into the world with a disability that would make learning a struggle, and a tremendous challenge. Not everyone recognized it as such. In school, it had always been the same story, "Karen's such a bright, attractive girl. Her mind just seems to wander. She doesn't pay attention, nor does she seem to want to try."

My mother knew from an early age that I would avoid confrontation and that I would clown around about my problems. What she didn't know was that I was trying my best, because I wanted so badly to please my parents, but I just couldn't keep up. I used to hide during recess because the other kids used to tease me.

Despite my problem, I was able to get through elementary, junior high and high school with minimal difficulty because I know how to drop classes, copy papers, get into study groups with better students, and cheat. I never felt good about any of that, but I knew I had to go to college to please my parents, and it was the only way I knew to get through. (pp. 42–43)

College Experiences

Amazingly, some individuals with disabilities do not discover or understand their learning disabilities until they are in college or even later. Carolee Reiling is one such individual. As a freshman at Stanford University, she heard another student with learning disabilities describe his experiences (Reiling, 1990):

All of a sudden, my mind clicked. It was as if someone had turned on the light in the dead of night. . . . As I tried to resist, each illustration that Andy gave of his learning disability pierced further into my mind. The extreme feeling of sickness before every exam or other measure of ability; the lack of reading comprehension; the inability to communicate thoughts and ideas; the sense of isolation. These difficulties came back to haunt me once more. But weren't these problems common to most people? I had always assumed so because I knew no differently. I realized that I studied more than my friends and that I was a slower reader, but I idealistically had considered them to be the exceptions. I did not consider myself to have weaknesses, but rather my friends to have strengths. It soon dawned on me that it was me who was the exception. . . .

I do not think that I have ever felt so alone in my whole life. Even though essentially nothing in my life had physically changed, it was ironically as if everything in the whole world had changed. My self confidence seemed to vanish into thin air. I instantly found myself, who was once so secure in my friendships, unable to relate to anyone, including my parents. I was very apprehensive about how others would react to my diagnosis. And for good reason too. I could just look to myself and my unfavorable response for the needed proof. If I could not even understand and accept this situation that was my own, how could I expect others to do so?

As a result, I set out on a sole expedition to find and conquer these problems which caused me to be identified as learning disabled. I questioned. I thought. And then I questioned and thought some more. I became so preoccupied with myself and my condition that I unknowingly evolved into a changed person. My joking and energetic attitude became serious and depressed. . . . Since I had always carried around the idea that I might be learning disabled in the back of my mind, I thought that it would be a great relief for me to be diagnosed. It explained many hardships in my life and allowed me to direct many past criticisms on my inability in certain areas from myself to the disability. However, this was a very painful process since it brought out many unhappy memories from the past. . . .

As I continued to reflect on my past, I also connected my disability with my poor performance in and great dislike for English. At least now there was something to explain why I could read and comprehend an English assignment one night and then the next morning could fail a simple quiz to see if you had read. The material was somewhere in my brain, but the question was where. It was like the information was misfiled and so when I went to draw on it, I could not locate it. I always knew that the answers were somewhere in my brain not far from my reach. However, the harder that I tried to recollect them, the farther away they went. I was so close, and yet so far. And yet even though there was now an explanation for many of my difficulties, I was not ready to accept it. I was not ready to accept the fact that I was different, that I had problems. Furthermore, it meant accepting this condition as one of my inherent characteristics with which I was to spend the rest of my life. And the scary part was that there was not a single thing that I could do to cure myself of it. I could compensate for it, as I had already innately been doing, but it would always be lurking and hiding, ready to surprise me at any given moment. "I am not disabled," I would think to myself. "I may need a little help once in awhile. I may be a little slow. I may be a little stupid. But I will tell you right now that I am not dyslexic."

These thoughts were quickly contradicted once I went through the evaluation process and the reality of my learning disability was established. And yet to what extent? I quickly redirected my energy from continuous denial of my situation into preparation for war. I was ready to fight. I was not going to let this thing beat me. I had done quite well throughout my life and nothing was going to change now. I had mustered up all of my effort throughout high school and had put everything in the whole world that I had towards getting into Stanford. And I was not going to be conquered after I had succeeded. As a result I wanted to know what I was up against, who

my opponent was. I wanted to know which problems, errors, and frustrations I could attribute to the disability and which to my own carelessness and stupidity.

My excitement mounted when I received a thick letter from the Morrissey/Compton Educational Center, Inc. I thought that finally the long awaited end to my anxiety had arrived. I was expecting to find out precisely how disabled I was or wasn't and how exactly I compared to everyone else. But all that I found was that I have "significant disabilities of the dyslexic type." Rather than answering my questions and concerns, this statement served to arouse new ones. How does one characterize the "dyslexic type"? Where does "significant" place me in relation to everyone else? Exactly how significant is "significant"?

As a result, I have endeavored to evaluate the degree to which I am afflicted by my learning disability. For ten days, from Wednesday, February 28, 1990, to Friday, March 9, 1990, I have monitored and kept track of my errors, difficulties, and frustrations which are generally attributed to the presence of a learning disability. This was a very difficult process because it brought me face to face with the effects of my disability. However, I feel that I have learned a lot more about myself and my thought process. For example, I did not just discover that I misspelled, miswrote, misread, and misspoke things infinitely more times than I would previously ever have admitted to doing, but I also began to realize why. While it was a very awakening and almost disheartening self-evaluation, it was also very interesting.

Throughout the ten day time period, I monitored my problems and errors as they corresponded to a learning disability characteristics summary and I also had a log in which I recorded my academic frustrations. The statistical summary, while very informative, is far from as accurate as I would like it to be because often my mistakes and difficulties would be so numerous that I did not include many of them. I rather attributed them to anxiety, lack of careful attention, or just general incapabilities like in reading or writing. The general areas in which my difficulties exist are writing, reading, spelling, testing, concentration, speech, orientation, memory, foreign language, and everyday manifestations such as feelings of stress, isolation, and inadequacy. I definitely had problems in all of these areas. (pp. 1–4)

Reiling used an outline of learning disability manifestations to structure her self-monitoring exercise. Due to space limitations, only selected descriptions of her experiences are presented.

Writing Tendency to work out specific parts of the paper laboriously instead of focusing on the paper as a whole:

> Once again since it is hard for me to conceptualize the overall idea of papers and so contributes greatly to their lack of organization. I tried to record the number of my problems with this. I averaged 12.2 times a day, with a high of 22 and a low of 3, depending on how much time I spend on my paper that day. (p. 4)

Freezing up when trying to write:

> This is a difficulty which seems to constantly affect me academically. I have difficulty taking class notes, writing letters, and of course writing papers. Writing is something that for some reason has always seemed to be very forced for me. It is not natural for me to express myself through writing. (p. 5)

Sentences seem to vanish before being written down:

> This is a problem that contributes greatly to my problems with writing because often when I finally think of a good way to express something, it is a race for me to get it written down before it disappears, never to come back. This also happens many times every day in trying to take class notes. It is really frustrating because I will get the first part and then just put a bunch of question marks for the second part. Here I am at a loss because when I take notes in class, I never understand the lecture at the same time and so I can never improvise and put things in my own words. My lecture notes are essentially quotes of the professor. The statistics for this average about 18 times a day with a high of 32 and a low of 5. (p. 5)

Words and letters out of sequence in sentences:

This is something that I do quite frequently and had previously just ignored or overlooked. This week I spent a lot of time thinking about as to why I do it. What I think happens is that when I am either writing or just taking notes I will get a sentence or phrase in my head that I need to write down before I forget it. So while I am writing I am also trying to remember and so I end up switching things or completely omitting them. However, I do not realize that I am doing this at the time and so I end up with a lot of incomprehensible statements. I did this on the average about 37.8 times a day with a high of 63 and a low of 13, depending on how much I wrote and also if I had my CIV (Culture, Ideas, and Values) lecture on that day. (p. 5)

Writing the exact opposite of what one meant to do—thinking one thing and writing another:

This is a very frustrating mistake especially when it occurs on tests and you don't catch it. I don't know why it occurs. I guess that maybe I am thinking in my head that I should not write something and so I get confused and end up writing it. I did this approximately 10.4 times a day with a high of 21 and a low of 4. (p. 6)

Writing things that make absolutely no coherent sense:

This results from things in my mind not coming out on paper in the right order. By switching and omitting words and phrases, I found many sentences in my writing and especially in my lecture notes that even I would not understand. Usually I can understand most of what I write for notes, even though others cannot. This explains why when people would borrow my notes in high school, they would quickly return them saying they could not understand. I found that I did this about 7.9 times a day, with a high of 14 and a low of 5. (p. 6)

Reading Slow reader (estimates range up to four times as long to read a page as others):

Reading has always been very difficult for me. It takes me an extremely long time, primarily because I have to reread things 3–4 times in order to try and understand them. If I cannot get them within four times, I get so frustrated that I just give up. I read out loud which greatly detracts from my speed. It is also very hard for me to conceptualize overall ideas or themes, which makes CIV terrible since that is all that we are supposed to discuss. A sad result of my reading problems is that I do not read anything, even including magazines and the newspaper, outside of that which is required of me. (p. 6)

Mistaking one word for another (e.g., *for* instead of *from*, *to* instead of *of*):

I have always done this, but I just thought that I was trying to read the material too fast without paying enough attention. I found that I do this too frequently and unconsciously to keep track of. (p. 7)

Spelling Reversals common (e.g., *b* instead of *d, freind* instead of *friend, probadly* instead of *probably, 0137* instead of *0317*):

This is a difficulty that I always have seemed to possess, but previously I just thought it was because I was not paying enough attention to what I was doing. I did this approximately 34.8 times a day, with a high of 48 and a low of 10. This varied a lot depending on my classes and how much written work I had. (p. 7)

Frequently dropping, adding, or reversing letters and word parts (e.g., *now* instead of *know, dab god* instead of *bad dog*):

This is a very broad category and embodies a lot of the mistakes that I make. I averaged about 31.2 times doing this a day, with a low of 20 and a high of 62. (p. 7)

Testing Seldom able to complete exams in class:

This generally would be the case with me, but now I take all of my exams for extra time. The time that I use is usually up to me. For example, on my last Chemistry midterm, there were so many numbers involved that I spent two hours on what was a fifty minute test. In Japanese I spend about two hours also on each test. I feel bad about this, but it is the only thing that allows me to have a fair chance at doing well in my classes. (p. 8)

Difficulty with multiple-choice questions; difficulty filling in the bubbles on forms:

This is something that I could never seem to do, but I thought that it was that way for everybody. By the time I even located the correct bubbles, I had forgotten which one I was supposed to fill in. Then I was always worried that I filled in the wrong one, and for good reason too. (p. 8)

Misinterprets directions or questions on exams:

This is something that I seem to do on every test without fail. It ends up costing me a lot of time and usually a lot of points. On my Physics 61 midterm last quarter, I wasted about 45 minutes of a two hour exam by misreading just a couple of words, which completely changes a problem. I did not realize this and could not get my answer to make sense. I figured out my mistake after the teacher mentioned a hint that was not even remotely connected with the way that I did my problem. I then really questioned my work and finally found my error. But by that time I was so flustered and frustrated that the test just went downhill for me from there. I was very lucky to get a 36% on it. Misreading things on tests is so terrible, and yet so easy to do. You are in a high pressure situation and your mind is set on making sure that you do not forget that formula that won't stick in your head. This makes it really easy to screw up. I have now gotten into the habit of also rereading the questions when I am checking my work because often I instead give answers for things that were not asked or I will forget to do a second or third part of a question. During my period of self-evaluation, I had to take my third chemistry midterm. I only messed up severely twice. The first was misreading something and so I spend 1.5 pages trying to prove something that I did not have enough information to do. I realized this but just thought that I screwed up. I finally discovered my problem. The second thing was forgetting to do part B of two problems, but fortunately I found them when I checked my test. (p. 8)

Extreme test anxiety:

I know that everybody gets nervous before tests, but I always knew that there was something wrong with me. I cannot count the number of tests that I have literally almost thrown up before. I usually start shaking and get very short of breath. I can't talk to anybody because my mind is so focused on the ordeal ahead of me. My hands get sweaty and my adrenalin rises to such a height that it is like I am getting a workout while just sitting in one place. I don't know why I feel such a pressure to perform, but I wish it weren't there because I would probably do better. (p. 9)

Concentration Focusing requires extraordinary effort:

It has always been extremely hard for me to concentrate completely, especially when reading, studying, or listening. I have the attention span to read about 3–4 pages. I constantly have to set goals with myself, like saying after I read 5 more pages I can take a short break. This is a pain because I feel like I waste a lot of time. But if I push myself to keep on going then I don't get anything out of it, so either way I lose. I try and move around from my desk to my bed to the floor to the lounge and try and rotate what I am doing. I intersperse reading with math, which helps break up the monotony and dread of reading. I can never stay focused in my classes, but if I get the notes I can understand the rest later. (p. 9)

Easily distracted by noise and movement:

This is a problem that I always associated with my inability to focus for periods of time. In high school, I would always yell at my brother or parents for making too much noise when I was try-

ing to study. They thought that I was insane and told me just to wait until I got to college where nothing would ever be quiet. However, they did comply because I was so emphatic about it. Noises that really bother me a lot are ticking of clocks or people making noises like flicking their pens because of nervous habits. I guess that these things make me more nervous and pressured than I already am. I quickly get to the point where I am about to go crazy and then I ask them to cut it out, please. Movement also does not allow me to concentrate. For some reason, when people next to me in class are nervously doing something with their hands or legs it never fails to catch my attention. When someone is doing that I have to move or else I cannot concentrate on lecture or even take notes. I figure that this happens to me about 10.6 times a day with the high being 17 and the low being 2. (p. 9)

Speech Difficulty in communicating ideas clearly:

I often say something exactly the opposite of how I should have said it. (e.g., "Does the dog have the ball?" = "Does the ball have the dog?"). I have gotten into the habit of going over in my head what I have just said hoping to catch stuff like that, and sometimes I do. But often I don't and people just say, "What?" and look at me weird. I also have problems conveying my ideas to others even if I say them how I meant to. This is why I am terrified of public speaking or even talking to a group of peers. For example, in CIV section one day I made a point and referred to a passage that I thought supported it. The teacher did not understand what I was trying to get across and I could not explain it right. Finally he pretended like he understood (I am used to that) and we went on. About 10 minutes later he raised my point to the class. I almost jumped out of my seat when I told him that his point was exactly what I had been trying to say. Needless to say, it was very embarrassing and frustrating. I did this about 18.1 times a day, with a high of 32 and a low of 9. (p. 10)

Orientation Difficulty in distinguishing left and right:

I always have had problems with left and right, but I considered them to be over. However, when I was talking to someone one night this week and he asked me to get a folder out of the right-hand drawer, I said no problem. I put out my hand like I usually do to remember which side I am looking for, but this time I put out my left hand. I did not realize it until I saw that there were no drawers on the left. (p. 11)

Directions, map reading, and navigating difficulty:

Nothing will make you feel more stupid than getting lost in Meyer Library trying to follow their stupid map. When I was trying to get books for my CIV research paper, it took me forever to find where my book should have been. However, it was not there, nor was its section. I was so lost. I finally decided to start over and try again and it was then I realized that I was on the wrong floor. (p. 11)

Feeling lost in a familiar setting; becoming disoriented easily:

I always seem to get lost. I had severe problems trying to find Sweet Hall from Meyer Library last week since I thought it was in the opposite direction to that in which it really is. Until just recently, I had thought that to get to crew practice, which I have been doing all year, we went the exact opposite direction on El Camino than we do. Also one day our crew bus stopped about 25 feet from where it usually stops and I got off and had no idea where I was until I saw my bike right in front of me. I cannot count the number of times that I have gotten lost running. One afternoon first quarter I was out for 1 hour and 45 minutes because I got lost and could not figure out how to get back. I finally had to ask someone and they showed me the road I was looking for was about 300 feet in front of me. Too bad I had been looking the other way for it. (p. 11)

Memory Difficulty recalling familiar things like one's telephone number, address, age, names of friends, and so forth:

I am the worst person on this whole world with names. There are so many names and different kinds of people that I cannot associate them and so I usually forget. The worst thing that always happens to me is that people will remember my name and so I just pretend that I know theirs. Ages are also very difficult for me. By the time I learn mine it seems that it is the next year and it changes. I do not know my brother's, mom's, or dad's. As far as my phone number is concerned, I did not learn it until about half way through winter quarter. I have it posted big on my desk and so it is reinforced in my memory about a hundred times a day. However, when people asked me what it was, I could not remember. Whenever I am on the phone and I need to leave it, I can't remember. Fortunately I have it posted where I can always easily find it. (pp. 11–12)

Frequently misplacing, losing, or forgetting things:

Ever since I was young, I have been called "senile" so many times that it is like part of my name. My parents always said that if my head wasn't attached to my shoulders I would forget where I put it, too. One of my biggest problems at Stanford has been remembering where I put my bike. I cannot begin to estimate how much time I have wasted walking around in circles looking for it. As for things that I have to remember, I write everything down. I make an extremely detailed daily schedule each night of my next day's activities. I also line up all of the books and homework that I will need for each class since chances are very good that I would otherwise omit them like I used to do in high school. An example is first quarter when I had my Physics 61 midterm. It was open-notes and open-book and so I had spent a long time making a 40 page review sheet of all the things that I knew I would forget or confuse. I had it laid out to take with me to the exam, but I completely forgot it. When I got there I realized this and also realized how lost I was without it. I do not think I have ever biked so fast in my whole life and fortunately I made it back before the test started. I tend to do this many times a day, only some of which I can probably attribute to my disability. On the average I did this about 8.3 times a day with a low of 3 and a high of 11. However, this is not as accurate as it would normally be because I compensate very much for this forgetfulness. (p. 12)

Everyday Manifestations Feeling constantly behind:

Even if I am caught up on all my work, I never find myself at a loss for something to do. Just because I read the chapter once doesn't mean that I remember any of it. However, many times I find myself having the attitude of thinking that the teacher only said that I had to read it and he did not say anything about comprehending or remembering it. And yet it is only me who is getting hurt by this. (p. 14)

Isolation resulting from fear of being misunderstood:

I often feel like I live my life in a different world. I have a very difficult time communicating my thoughts, especially when I am speaking to more than just one person and all of the attention is on me. This results in a very high level of frustration. My level of frustration further mounts when the people to whom I am speaking do not understand my thoughts. After several attempts I usually give up in despair. Needless to say, I feel very isolated when ideas that are all so clear in my mind cannot be made understandable to others. I often get a similar feeling when things that others say go so far above my head that they are beyond my reach. (p. 15)

Feeling inadequate because of difficulty doing tasks others find easy:

I feel that this statement summarizes for me the primary difficulty of being learning disabled. Even though my slow reading rate has become a joke with all my friends and myself, it still really hurts my self-image. I cannot help being jealous of the ease with which they read, understand, write, speak, remember, and concentrate. It is so easy to feel inadequate and get a low esteem of oneself. Even though I know that I am not stupid because of my learning disability, sometimes I feel that there is no other word with which to describe my incapabilities. (pp. 15–16)

This discussion by Reiling (1990) illustrates what it is like to go through life when one cannot rely on the accuracy of what one reads or expresses either in speech or in writing. It documents the anxiety and stress an individual with LD experiences and the energy he or she must expend to cope with tasks that most people perform automatically, accurately, and with minimal effort. Her story also points out that "dyslexia" does not do justice to the complexity of the experience, the effort required to compensate and cope, or the many other aspects of life that are affected by LD.

It is also important to note that the evaluation report Reiling received explained nothing, especially omitting the implications of her situation for daily life, academic life, and future employment. Few individuals with LD are able to analyze themselves as thoroughly as Reiling did in order to develop a better understanding of her situation. In the absence of assistance from knowledgeable professionals, many individuals with learning disabilities—even those who were identified in primary or secondary school—have a very incomplete understanding of their disabilities, few use self-monitoring or compensatory strategies, and most have little awareness of how their disabilities influence their abilities to obtain employment and perform successfully on the job. Yet, Reiling makes many references to the long-standing nature of several of her problems—reversals, omissions, misperceptions, direction problems, memory problems, and the fact that she completed high school without any of the staff noticing manifestations of what was later diagnosed as a severe learning disability.

Reiling's situation reflects what Shaywitz and colleagues (1990) found when they studied more than 400 Connecticut children from 12 towns in kindergarten through third grade. Using some of the same kinds of testing instruments that the school used, the researchers tested each child for reading disabilities and contrasted those findings with the number of students the schools identified as having reading disabilities. After testing each second grader, the researchers found 17 of 198 boys and 15 of 216 girls to have reading disabilities; in contrast, the schools had identified 27 boys but only 7 girls with reading disabilities. By the third grade, the researchers found 18 boys and 13 girls with reading disabilities; the schools identified 20 of 199 boys, but only 9 of 215 girls. In contrast, Shaywitz et al. theorized that such imbalances occur because girls typically exhibit more acceptable classroom behavior and are usually not as active or inattentive as boys. Therefore, boys are often inaccurately identified, and girls with difficulties may be overlooked. "Our data indicate that school-identified samples are almost unavoidably subject to a referral bias" (1990, p. 3).

Employment Issues

As Lemke (1991) stated, 60%–80% of people with LD are employed, but most face a high job turnover rate. They may be unable to keep jobs, unable to find jobs that maintain their interest, or do things that cause them to lose their jobs. Many are also underemployed and commonly complain that they do not get the same promotions their peers do.

Although there are successful people with LD, many adults with learning disabilities continue to struggle with the same problems that affected their performance while in school. On the job, they tend to make frequent errors, to have more accidents than the

average worker, to have difficulties in learning sequences of tasks, to be inefficient because they are disorganized, and to be unable to make change or read instructions. In addition, impulsivity and unrealistic expectations of the world may impair their abilities to maintain jobs. For example, one individual with learning disabilities walked off his job angry because his supervisor asked him to sweep the warehouse floor. He felt it was not in his job description (Goodman, 1988).

The main reason most people with LD lose jobs is not the skill level required by the job but the individual's lack of organizational, self-monitoring, and self-correcting skills, all of which resulted from faulty executive functioning. "It is easy to measure reading and math levels but difficult to measure executive functioning because it is very subtle and sophisticated" (p. 8).

Theis (as cited in Bosch, 1991) defines the comparable executive processing as, "those cognitive functions that are responsible for organizing, coordinating, and directing mental activity and behavior" (p. 5). Executive processing includes attention, formulation of goals and plans to achieve those goals, monitoring and evaluating behavior, and correcting behavior as needed to continue toward the goals. This involves appreciating the situation, managing time, and controlling actions. The flexibility required to evaluate and change behavior, a necessity for attaining goals, is one of the most difficult areas for adults with LD. They cling to routine because of the amount of energy required to learn new tasks.

Gerber et al. (1990) studied the persistence of LD in 133 adults categorized as highly or moderately successful in employment. Findings showed that both groups deteriorated markedly in the areas of functioning typically included in diagnostic and remediation efforts. On every item (i.e., listening, speaking, reading, writing, spelling, math, visual perception, auditory perception, coordination, impulsivity, distractibility, hyperactivity, and attention span), roughly a quarter or more of all of the respondents with learning disabilities reported increasing difficulties in adulthood.

> It is very possible that developmental deficits are exacerbated by increasing demands in adulthood. . . . The reported persistence of problems by the subjects may also stem from increasing demands of their work and daily routines. The added complexity of tasks in adult life may highlight a multiplicity of self-perceived problems or inadequacies in their lives. . . . It must be kept in mind that, while the population studied may be typical in some respects, the subjects are skewed in the direction of successful to highly successful vocational functioning. . . . The data presented in this study directly support the notion that learning disabilities is a lifelong problem. (Gerber et al., 1990, p. 572)

Unfortunately, many individuals with LD cannot be characterized as even moderately successful in their career development efforts. Okolo and Sitlington (1988) found that adults with LD who were employed were often part-time workers and minimum wage earners. High school dropouts fare poorly in the labor force in terms of employment and earning power. In Table 13.1, the national dropout rates for individuals with learning disabilities are shown, along with the dropout rates of other groups for comparison.

Unique Challenges Presented by Youth with Learning Disabilities

Learning disabilities have often been called the "hidden" disabilities. Because these disabilities are not readily visible, students with specific learning disabilities often report that

Table 13.1. National dropout rates of special education students

Year	Number of students with disabilities	Percentage who received a diploma	Percentage receiving a certificate	Percentage who aged out	Percentage who dropped out	Percentage who left for other reasons	Percentage of students with learning disabilities	Percentage of students with emotional disabilities	Percentage of dropouts with cognitive disabilities	Total percentage of dropouts
1984–1985	212,000	39.0	15.0	4.0	21.0	18.0	36.0	57.0	38.0	39.0
1985–1986	213,623	43.0	17.0	2.0	26.0	11.0	37.5	56.0	31.7	39.0
1986–1987	209,114	46.0	13.0	3.5	25.0	13.3	34.0	54.7	31.3	38.3
1987–1988	238,579	42.0	11.0	2.5	27.4	16.8	43.0	62.5	37.9	44.2
1988–1989	248,590	43.9	9.7	2.5	26.6	17.3	41.7	61.5	36.0	43.9
1989–1990	221,418	44.8	12.4	2.5	27.0	13.3	37.6	61.0	31.4	40.3
1990–1991	223,229	45.7	13.3	2.0	23.3	15.8	36.9	60.1	31.5	39.1
1991–1992	229,368	43.9	13.4	1.8	22.4	18.3	39.0	64.3	30.1	40.7

Source: U.S. Department of Education, Office of Special Education and Rehabilitative Services (1987–1994).

Note: The 1987, 1988, and 1990 annual reports state that the vast majority of students classified as "left for other reasons" were, in fact, dropouts who did not inform anyone; they just stopped attending school. The 1991 annual report qualifies this by noting that in four large states, a number of students with speech-language problems were put in the "left for other reasons" category when, in fact, they were reclassified as general education students. The 1992 annual report stated that OSEP-sponsored research showed that some states are including in this category students who transferred to other school districts but were not known to be continuing their education, students who did not formally withdraw from school but simply stopped attending, students who returned to general education, and students who died.

it is difficult to make others understand and accept the problems they experience. One student commented, "I have constantly run up against misunderstanding and the unwillingness to accept learning disability as a disability. The typical response I get is that everyone has trouble with learning, which is totally an inadequate response and narrow one" (Board for Rights of Virginians with Disabilities Technical Assistance Project [BRVD-TAP], 1991, p. 20). Further challenges include difficulties with problem solving, decision making, and social skills, especially in the area of communication.

Understanding One's Disability

Students with LD often deny that they have learning problems. Zetlin and Hosseini (1989) report that, in a follow-up study of six young adults with mild LD in high school, one young man never admitted to having a learning disability and dismissed any conversation implying such an idea. It was not until he was out of high school and had not been able to keep a job or complete any postsecondary training program that he began to admit that he might not have a "normal" future (p. 407). Because these students are anxious to leave school and remove themselves from special education labels, they often do not seek postschool services in the community (Schwarz & Taymans, 1991; Zetlin & Hosseini, 1989). However, these students are realistic in their concerns that only their weaknesses will be noticed (Garnett & LaPorta, 1984).

In addition, parents must learn to accept and understand their child's LD. Some parents of children with LD believe that once their child has participated in special education classes for several years, disabilities will disappear (Alexander & Clements, 1975; Kinnison, 1987; Marion, 1981). This belief may result in parents' unwillingness to consider options for their children other than going to college, not consenting to vocational testing that explores interest areas, requiring their children to register for academic coursework rather than vocationally oriented classes, or denying permission for further testing of the student's specific learning disability. Transition team members must be aware of and sensitive to parents' expectations about their child's future goals. Often their reluctance to accept other potential career goals stems from their misunderstandings of difficulties their child experiences and fears about the child's future after school.

It is becoming increasingly apparent that teaching self-determination skills to students with LD is a critical component of their gaining a greater understanding of themselves and learning how to communicate their strengths and accommodation needs both in school and the community. Adults with LD have identified making the decision to take charge of one's life and making the necessary modifications to achieve one's goals as important keys to success (Reiff, Ginsberg, & Gerber, 1995). Students with LD who are able to understand their skills, effective learning strategies, and how to acquire information or services are able to obtain a sense of control over their lives (Wille-Gregory, Graham, & Hughes, 1995). Incorporating self-determination skills as part of a student's learning experience is critical. In secondary schools, accommodations may be part of the students' experience, but in most postsecondary or employment settings the student or worker with disabilities is part of the mainstream and must self-advocate to obtain them (Gugerty, Tindall, Gavin, & Gribbon-Fago, 1993).

There are several skills, behaviors, and attitudes that are used to define self-determination and should be taught to individuals with disabilities at an early age (Phillips, 1990;

Scheiber & Talpers, 1987; Ward, 1988). Examples of some of the skills include 1) knowing about oneself, including interests, strengths, and needs; 2) understanding what resources are available for assistance and how to use them; 3) being able to set goals and pursue them; and 4) taking responsibility for one's accomplishments and setbacks (Hoffman & Field, 1995; Scheiber & Talpers, 1987; Serna & Lau-Smith, 1995; Ward, 1988). These skills enable the development of a positive self-concept that helps to encourage strong self-determination skills. Parents, teachers, friends, and other significant individuals should foster the personal growth and independence of individuals with LD throughout the individual's life (Goldberg, 1991; Ward, 1991).

An important method for assisting students with disabilities to take ownership to achieve their goals is through the development of an individualized transition plan (ITP) as part of their individualized education program (IEP). All too often, students are not active members in their IEP meetings, even though they attend them (Lovitt, Cushing, & Stump, 1994). In their study, Lovitt et al. (1994) asked students to describe their experiences at IEP meetings. Most of these students indicated that they just sat there and did not understand what was going on. Typically, parents and professionals have taken on the role of advocates for students, which limits their opportunities to become active participants in the process. The IEP/ITP process can enable students with LD to assess their interests, limitations, and needs and practice decision-making and problem-solving skills to reach their goals (Hughes, 1992a).

Wille-Gregory and colleagues (1995) have identified examples of programs that educators can incorporate into their curriculum to assist students with LD to develop the skills to help them become more active participants in their IEP and transition planning meetings. Two of these curricula are described below.

- *The Education Planning Strategy: I PLAN [revised version is called Self-Advocacy]*—I PLAN is a megacognitive strategy focused on developing effective planning and communication skills in preparation for participation in the IEP meeting. The strategy can be taught to students in upper elementary and higher grades in about 6 hours over a 1- to 2-week period. With minimal modification, the I-PLAN strategy can be used to prepare students to participate in a variety of planning or problem-solving meetings with teachers, employers, or co-workers.
- *The ChoiceMaker Self-Determination Transition Curriculum: Self-Directed IEP*—This curriculum teaches students how to manage their own IEP meetings in 11 steps. The methods and materials can be used with a broad range of students, including those with mild to moderate learning and behavior problems. (Wille-Gregory et al., 1995, p. 2)

Problem-Solving and Decision-Making Skills

Individuals with LD may have difficulties in problem solving and decision making, which are critical skills for students entering employment or seeking postsecondary training. Students with LD often exhibit difficulties in setting priorities, managing their time, and recalling information (Szymanski, Gugerty, Tindall, & Schmidt, 1989)—skills important for identifying and solving problems.

Students with LD need skills that enable them to identify problems or tasks that must be completed, to list the choices or options involved with problems or tasks, to determine possible outcomes or consequences, and to select the best course of action. The amount of practice and hands-on experience these students receive in accepting environments increases the likelihood that they will use these skills in all areas of their lives (Izzo, Pritz, & Ott, 1990).

Students with LD may have difficulties managing their time. They may miss appointments or other scheduled events. Even if they have clocks or calendars, they may forget to look at them or may misread what they have written. On the job, they may schedule a number of activities in a row, not allowing enough time to complete each one (Gavin, Tindall, & Gugerty, 1990; Szymanski et al., 1989). They may also have difficulties with jobs that require tasks to be completed in certain amounts of time and in required sequences. Setting priorities is another challenge for students with learning problems. Although these students may appear organized if they keep lists or other techniques to organize their activities (Gavin et al., 1990; Szymanski et al., 1989), they are often unable to determine what to do first. They spend a great deal of time on relatively insignificant tasks and do not focus on the essentials. Many students with LD have difficulty with final decisions and obtaining closure for issues.

Another issue confronting many students with LD is the ability to remember something that has been taught previously, even on a daily basis. Often these students have been labeled "passive learners," meaning they are not actively involved in the learning process (Izzo et al., 1990; Torgeson, 1982), which is necessary for acquiring problem-solving skills. Short-term memory problems can also contribute to difficulties in remembering information over a period of time. Izzo and her colleagues (1990) identified two basic criteria for instruction that are particularly helpful for people with LD: 1) connecting the instruction to the learners' prior knowledge, which helps students to link new information with what they already know; and 2) using real-life and employment situations to encourage learner motivation and ability to apply new skills.

Social and Communication Skills

Social skills can present particular challenges to people with LD. As a result of perceptual difficulties, these individuals may have problems understanding others. They may not be able to differentiate between a stare and a thoughtful glance. They may appear to be rude by breaking into conversations or making inappropriate remarks. Individuals with auditory problems may have problems telling the difference between angry and excited voices (Brown, 1982). They may also find that they must concentrate so intently on what is said that they miss the nonverbal messages that accompany the spoken words (Brown, 1982). Because of this, they may respond incorrectly. In addition, individuals with LD may appear inattentive because they are easily distracted or maintain poor eye contact with the person who is speaking.

Difficulties in depth perception can lead to sitting or standing too close to other people. This invasion of "personal space" can create social interaction problems for students with LD without them knowing why. They may also stand or sit close to other people to block out competing noises, enabling them to concentrate on what is being said (Career Services for the Handicapped, n.d.).

Zetlin and Hosseini (1989) illustrate how problems with social skills, especially communication, can affect an individual's life. They describe a woman who had very poor expressive skills and relied upon others to supply words or phrases to complete her thoughts. She had difficulty getting along with her peers. However, her disability was discussed only in the context of educational goals so she lacked an understanding of how it could affect her socialization. Another individual was eager to learn everything about his workplace.

He persistently asked his co-workers questions and made suggestions about how they could do their jobs better. His co-workers felt that his actions were inappropriate, creating difficulties for him. He needed someone to explain the rules of turf and territory in the workplace (President's Committee on Employment of People with Disabilities, 1986).

Because of the inability to socialize with their peers, these students tend to isolate themselves, which delays social development and can result in immature social skills development. Students need feedback about behaviors that create problems for them if they are to learn creative ways to overcome communication obstacles. Students can be taught to identify possible mentors (Robinson, 1984)—people they trust and with whom they feel comfortable. Mentors can offer advice on how to interact with others in employment or school settings. If students both understand the impact they have on others and know how to improve their skills, they will be able to increase their self-esteem—an essential asset for pursuing goals.

Vaughn and La Greca (1993) suggest that social skills training focus on the areas of communication, social perception (how behavior is interpreted to understand the thoughts and feelings of others), and social problem solving. They recommend that social interventions be developed for those students with LD who have been identified as having specific sociobehavioral problems.

Assessment for Transition

Assessments of all kinds are part of the transition experience for youth with identified LD. School personnel who are responsible for arranging or conducting assessments can enhance their value by keeping the following points in mind:

1. Do not assume that an individual has a thorough, accurate understanding of his or her disability or its ramifications. Support staff at many postsecondary schools have discovered that 65%–80% of new students with previously identified LD cannot articulate what having a learning disability means or describe its implications to others (Dalke & Schmitt, 1987). Vocational rehabilitation counselors, who often deal with individuals with more severe disabilities, state that up to 90% of applicants with LD demonstrate little understanding of what their learning disabilities mean or the employment implications of those disabilities (M.A. Greco, personal communication, June 2, 1992).
2. Explain in terms that the individual can understand why more tests are necessary, what will happen, and what can be learned from these tests. Remember that individuals with communication difficulties may need several explanations, presented in different ways. (Assurances of understanding must be verified.)
3. After all testing has been completed, review the results with the individual. Again, remember to accommodate any perceptual and communication difficulties. Do not accept assurances of understanding without verifying that the individual does in fact comprehend.
4. If you purchase assessments from other agencies or independent professionals, discreetly check that the person performing the assessments understands testing accommodations that must be made for the individual. Advanced degrees alone do not

guarantee that understanding. In addition, some private testing organizations and professionals actually have psychometricians or paraprofessional staff members administer the assessments while the highly credentialed and highly paid professional reviews the results and writes the reports. Sometimes the importance of appropriate testing accommodations and environment is not fully appreciated by those actually carrying out the assessment.

It is also important to check the testing environment, in person if necessary, to see that it is free of distractions. A surprising number of testing environments are noisy or contain visual distractors (e.g., ceiling fans, intricate wallpaper, large windows overlooking busy streets). Validity, and thus relevance, of assessments require that all involved pay close attention to the details of test administration, the details of an individual's known strengths and weaknesses, and the details of the environment in which the assessments occur.

5. Many individuals with LD perform well in the quiet, orderly, systematic environments of classrooms but fail in the noisy, hectic environments of jobs. These latter environments may be replete with interruptions, incomplete or overwhelmingly extensive information, and fluid (i.e., fluctuating, changing) responsibilities. Understanding the conditions under which tasks must be performed is a critical component for success of many individuals with disabilities in the work world.

6. Since it is very possible that other members of the individual's family may also experience LD, take great care to ensure that the purpose, procedures, results, and implications of assessment are conveyed completely and accurately to the individual's parents. Do not rely on the individual to do this unless no other option is possible. When an individual with perceptual or communication problems communicates with others (e.g., parents), who may also have perceptual or communication problems, serious misunderstandings may occur. Preventive actions may result in good working relationships with families and few hostile confrontations.

7. Be sure to address social and interpersonal skills in assessments for transition planning purposes.

 People with positive self concepts tend to persevere toward their goals, and those with negative concepts tend to avoid tasks they consider difficult. In like manner, social relationships are affected by feelings and beliefs about ourselves. Students with learning disabilities are found to have more negative self-concepts than their classmates when they are asked to rate their academic performance, though not when scales are used that assess feelings of self-worth. Moreover, these negative academic self-concepts do not seem to respond to teachers' attempts to improve perceptions through failure-free instruction and nongraded classrooms, and they extend beyond the school years into young adulthood. Because students' self-concepts are the products of their own experiences, observations, and messages from others, effective interventions involve not just the student but significant others in students' lives. Research findings have indicated that individuals with learning disabilities also have problems gaining social acceptance . . . Such was the case even at the kindergarten level before the LD child was identified. In a recent study of learning disabled youngsters, it was found that over half were socially rejected or neglected, and that the rejected tended to become aggressive and disruptive while the neglected became shy and withdrawn. . . . Finally, some studies have found that females with learning disabilities are at greater risk than males. (Bryan, 1990, p. 6)

8. Review the eligibility criteria for adult services agencies and comply whenever possible in order to minimize repetitive and unnecessary testing. Rehabilitation agencies, for ex-

ample, require recent diagnostic information from professionals with specific credentials. If these requirements are met as part of a multidisciplinary team process, the individual is saved from another, frequently onerous, testing situation; the service delivery process is more efficient; and cooperating agencies' resources are used more efficiently.

Assessment Reports

Assessments are only as good as the information they generate, and reports are useful only to the extent that they contain information that guides the design of transition programs and implementation of services. Assessment reports should include a description of the individual's functional strengths and limitations in executive processing skills, a description of how the individual learns or acquires information, coping and compensation strategies used by the individual, demonstrated basic and vocational skills (including the conditions under which performance was measured), social and interpersonal skills, self-advocacy skills, and the vocational implications of all of these items.

Because assessments should be individualized to meet the person's needs and tailored to be useful to those providing services, a standard assessment package is inappropriate. The following examples, however, are worthy of consideration as parts of transition assessment packages.

The first of these, the SLD (Specific Learning Disabilities) Behavior Checklist (Figure 13.1), was developed by staff at the Vocational Rehabilitation Center of Allegheny County, Pittsburgh, Pennsylvania. Educators can use this checklist to determine how accurately a student with LD understands his or her strengths and difficulties and whether the individual requires additional counseling about his or her LD and/or practice in explaining strengths and difficulties effectively.

Individuals with LD can use the checklist to develop a complete functional statement of their strengths and difficulties. This functional description could be used when describing one's LD to people without a technical background in the field, such as supervisors or co-workers.

The second instrument, the Functional Skills Inventory (Figure 13.2), was developed by staff from the Wisconsin Division of Vocational Rehabilitation (VR), Learning Disabilities Association of Wisconsin, and Vocational Studies Center, University of Wisconsin–Madison, as part of a project funded by the U.S. Department of Education, Office of Special Education and Rehabilitative Services (OSERS). This inventory is designed to provide rehabilitation counselors with detailed functional information about each individual with LD who seeks VR services. The questions on the inventory address many functional skills that have a profound impact, by their presence or absence, on an individual's chances for success in the work world. Thus, parents, educators, and other professionals can use this inventory as a means to develop training content for a student's IEP or ITP.

The third instrument, the Work Personality Profile (Figure 13.3), was developed by Bolton and Roessler at the Arkansas Research and Training Center in Vocational Rehabilitation at the University of Arkansas. Educators and other professionals could use this to assess students' performance in work-study or other community-based employment training programs. The resulting profile of work-related skills and difficulties can form the basis of a training plan designed to improve students' on-the-job performances, and thus enhance the likelihood of their employment success as adults.

SLD Behavior Checklist

Name: _____ Date: _____

Instructions: Ask the client the following questions and have him or her state one of the following responses: NO, NOT AT ALL; YES, JUST A LITTLE; YES, PRETTY MUCH; or YES, VERY MUCH. Hand the client a reminder in order to help him or her remember the four possible answers.

Questions	Not at all	Just a little	Pretty much	Very much
Auditory compensation				
1. Do you have problems following spoken directions?	____	____	____	____
2. Do you have problems remembering what you heard?	____	____	____	____
Spoken language				
3. Do you have problems telling stories so that people understand?	____	____	____	____
4. Do you have problems recalling the exact word you want to use?	____	____	____	____
5. Do you have problems remembering the names of people or things?	____	____	____	____
Orientation				
6. Do you lose track of time?	____	____	____	____
7. Do you have problems keeping to a schedule?	____	____	____	____
8. Do you get lost?	____	____	____	____
9. Do you have problems judging distances?	____	____	____	____
10. Do you have problems judging weights?	____	____	____	____
11. Do you have problems concentrating on your work?	____	____	____	____
Motor coordination				
12. Do you have trouble walking?	____	____	____	____
13. Do you have trouble running?	____	____	____	____
14. Do you have trouble climbing?	____	____	____	____
15. Do you have trouble playing sports?	____	____	____	____
16. Do you have trouble keeping your balance?	____	____	____	____
17. Do you have trouble using hand tools?	____	____	____	____
18. Do you have trouble writing so that people can read what you wrote?	____	____	____	____
19. Do you have trouble seeing clearly?	____	____	____	____
20. Do you have trouble drawing pictures?	____	____	____	____
Personal and social behaviors				
21. Do you dislike your present job?	____	____	____	____
22. Do you have problems keeping friends?	____	____	____	____
23. Do you avoid social functions (parties, dances, etc.)?	____	____	____	____
24. Do other people have problems understanding you?	____	____	____	____
25. Do you have problems understanding other people?	____	____	____	____
26. Do others have problems getting along with you?	____	____	____	____
27. Do you have problems getting all of your work done?	____	____	____	____
28. Do you make many mistakes?	____	____	____	____
29. Do you need help from others?	____	____	____	____

(continued)

Figure 13.1. SLD (Specific Learning Disabilities) Behavior Checklist. (From Goyette, C.H., & Washburn, C. [1984]. *Vocational rehabilitation of learning disabled adults, participants manual* [pp. 13–14]. Pittsburgh, PA: Vocational Rehabilitation Center of Allegheny County; reprinted by permission.)

Figure 13.1. *(continued)*

30. Do you get upset easily? ___ ___ ___ ___

Visual comprehension

31. Do you have problems remembering what you saw? ___ ___ ___ ___
32. Do you have problems reading maps? ___ ___ ___ ___
33. Do you have problems reading newspapers? ___ ___ ___ ___
34. Do you have problems doing math? ___ ___ ___ ___
35. Do you have problems when someone shows you how to do something? ___ ___ ___ ___
36. Do you have problems using directions to put something together? ___ ___ ___ ___

Comments

Please describe the client's observed work performance using the five options listed below to complete the 58 behavioral items.

(4) a definite strength, an employability asset
(3) adequate performance, not a particular strength
(2) performance inconsistent, potentially an employability problem
(1) a problem area, will definitely limit the person's chances for employment
(x) no opportunity to observe the behavior

1) _____ Sufficiently alert and aware.
2) _____ Learns new assignments quickly.
3) _____ Works steadily during entire work period.
4) _____ Accepts changes in work assignments.
5) _____ Needs virtually no direct supervision.
6) _____ Requests help in an appropriate fashion.
7) _____ Approaches supervisory personnel with confidence.
8) _____ Is appropriately friendly with supervisor.
9) _____ Shows pride in group effort.
10) _____ Shows interest in what others are doing.
11) _____ Expresses likes and dislikes appropriately.
12) _____ Initiates work-related activities on time.
13) _____ Accepts work assignments and instructions from supervisor without arguing.
14) _____ Improves performance when shown how.
15) _____ Works at routine jobs without resistance.
16) _____ Expresses willingness to try new assignments.
17) _____ Carries out assigned tasks without prompting.
18) _____ Asks for further instructions if task is not clear.
19) _____ Accepts correction without becoming upset.
20) _____ Discusses personal problems with supervisor only if work-related.
21) _____ Accepts assignment to group tasks.
22) _____ Seeks out co-workers to be friends.
23) _____ Responds when others initiate conversation.
24) _____ Conforms to rules and regulations.
25) _____ Maintains satisfactory personal hygiene habits.
26) _____ Changes work methods when instructed to do so.
27) _____ Pays attention to details while working.

(continued)

Figure 13.1. *(continued)*

28) _____ Maintains productivity despite change in routine.
29) _____ Recognizes own mistakes.
30) _____ Asks for help when having difficulty with tasks.
31) _____ Comfortable with supervisor.
32) _____ Gets along with staff.
33) _____ Works comfortably in group tasks.
34) _____ Appears comfortable in social interactions.
35) _____ Initiates conversations with others.
36) _____ Displays good judgment in use of obscenities and vulgarities.
37) _____ Arrives appropriately dressed for work.
38) _____ Maintains improved work procedures after correction.
39) _____ Maintains work pace even if distractions occur.
40) _____ Performs satisfactorily in tasks that require variety and change.
41) _____ Initiates action to correct own mistakes.
42) _____ Performance remains stable in supervisor's presence.
43) _____ Supportive of others in group tasks.
44) _____ Joins social groups when they are available.
45) _____ Listens while other person speaks; avoids interrupting.
46) _____ Listens to instructions or corrections attentively.
47) _____ Expresses pleasure in accomplishment.
48) _____ Moves from job to job easily.
49) _____ Needs less than average amount of supervision.
50) _____ Offers assistance to co-workers when appropriate.
51) _____ Is sought out frequently by co-workers.
52) _____ Expresses positive feelings (e.g., praise, liking for others).
53) _____ Displays good judgment in playing practical jokes or "horsing around."
54) _____ Transfers previously learned skills to new task.
55) _____ Handles problems with only occasional help.
56) _____ Assumes assigned role in group tasks.
57) _____ Expresses negative feelings appropriately (e.g., anger, fear, sadness).
58) _____ Controls temper.

WORKSHEET

Scale		Total	Average
S1	1 __ 12 __ 13 __ 24 __ 25 __ 36 __ 37 __ 46 __ 53 __ 58 __		
S2	2 __ 14 __ 26 __ 38 __ 47 __ 54 __		
S3	3 __ 15 __ 27 __ 39 __		
S4	4 __ 16 __ 28 __ 40 __ 48 __		
S5	5 __ 17 __ 29 __ 41 __ 49 __ 55 __		
S6	6 __ 18 __ 30 __		
S7	7 __ 19 __ 31 __ 42 __		
S8	8 __ 20 __ 32 __		
S9	9 __ 21 __ 33 __ 43 __ 50 __ 56 __		
S10	10 __ 22 __ 34 __ 44 __ 51 __		
S11	11 __ 23 __ 35 __ 45 __ 52 __ 57 __		
F1	2 __ 3 __ 5 __ 14 __ 17 __ 18 __ 26 __ 27 __ 28 __ 29 __ 30 __ 38 __ 39 __ 40 __ 41 __ 42 __ 47 __ 48 __ 49 __ 54 __ 55 __		
F2	9 __ 10 __ 22 __ 23 __ 34 __ 35 __ 43 __ 44 __ 46 __ 50 __ 51 __ 52 __		
F3	4 __ 12 __ 13 __ 15 __ 16 __ 21 __ 33 __ 56 __		
F4	11 __ 19 __ 20 __ 24 __ 36 __ 45 __ 53 __ 57 __ 58		
F5	1 __ 6 __ 7 __ 8 __ 25 __ 31 __ 32 __ 37		

Functional Skills Inventory

Name of person being rated _____

Rater _____

Date _____ Phone _____

Independence

1. Will need parental support to arrange and complete interviews with DVR counselor — yes _____ no _____
2. Follows a schedule if someone else prepares it. — yes _____ no _____
3. Prepares and follows own schedule. — yes _____ no _____
4. Can tell time to the minute. — yes _____ no _____
5. Meets new people easily. If "no," please explain:

6. Accurately *states* his or her:
 - Social Security number — yes _____ no _____
 - Phone number — yes _____ no _____
 - Complete mailing address — yes _____ no _____

Reading

7. Can read, understand, and interpret a single-sentence statement or question. — yes _____ no _____
8. Can read, understand, and interpret a paragraph-length statement or question. — yes _____ no _____
9. Can read, understand, and carry out instructions that are:
 - Typed — yes _____ no _____
 - Handwritten — yes _____ no _____
 - In paragraph form — yes _____ no _____
10. Can read and understand a job application. — yes _____ no _____
11. Can read and understand newspaper articles. — yes _____ no _____
12. Summarize this individual's reading skills. Be specific in relation to the individual's career goals and expected achievement in postsecondary education and/or job performance.

Math

13. Counts to 100 accurately. — yes _____ no _____
14. Performs the following accurately 99%–100% of the time:
 - Adding whole numbers — yes _____ no _____
 - Adding fractions — yes _____ no _____
 - Subtracting whole numbers — yes _____ no _____
 - Subtracting fractions — yes _____ no _____
 - Uses a pocket calculator correctly — yes _____ no _____
15. Can make correct change for purchases under $20. — yes _____ no _____

(continued)

Figure 13.2. Functional Skills Inventory. (From Wisconsin Division of Vocational Rehabilitation Counselors, Wisconsin Association of Children and Adults With Learning Disabilities, and Vocational Studies Center. [1988]. *Best practices: Successful vocational rehabilitation of persons with learning disabilities* [pp. 133–138]. Madison: University of Wisconsin–Madison; reprinted by permission.)

Figure 13.2. *(continued)*

16. Summarize this individual's math skills. Be specific in relation to the individual's career goals and expected achievement in postsecondary education and/or job performance.

Writing
17. *Accurately* writes his or her:
 - Social Security number yes _____ no _____
 - Phone number yes _____ no _____
 - Complete mailing address yes _____ no _____
18. Can correctly fill in an application for a job, a school, or a training program. yes _____ no _____
19. Has prepared a complete résumé yes _____ no _____
20. Summarize this individual's writing skills. Be specific in relation to the individual's career goals and expected achievement in postsecondary education and/or job performance.

Physical coordination and orientation
21. Has this person been observed to have any physical coordination problems? yes _____ no _____
 Describe how this might limit the individual's employment possibilities.

22. Has this person been observed to have any directionality problems?
 not observed _____ no _____ yes _____
 The problems are:

Health and hygiene
23. Practices good grooming and hygiene. yes _____ no _____
24. Implements good health practices:
 - Balanced diet yes _____ no _____
 - Exercise yes _____ no _____
 - Medical checkups yes _____ no _____
 - Dental checkups yes _____ no _____
25. Missed more than 4 days of school per year. yes _____ no _____
26. If yes, why?

(continued)

Figure 13.2. *(continued)*

Travel

27. Uses public transportation. If yes, describe type(s) used.
 yes _____ no _____

28. Possesses valid driver's license.
 yes _____ no _____
29. Knows route to:
- Place of work yes _____ no _____
- DVR office yes _____ no _____
- Grocery store yes _____ no _____
- Bank yes _____ no _____
- Laundromat yes _____ no _____
30. Can determine routes to new locations without assistance. yes _____ no _____
31. Can follow verbal directions to a new location. yes _____ no _____
32. Can follow written directions to a new location. yes _____ no _____
33. Must be "walked through" route to a new location in order to learn it.
 yes _____ no _____

Employment

34. Can use telephone directory to obtain addresses and phone numbers of potential employers and social services agencies.
 yes _____ no _____
35. Will need assistance and encouragement to arrange and complete successful job interviews.
 yes _____ no _____
36. Determines appropriate time to arrive at work or other scheduled events (not too early nor too late).
 yes _____ no _____
37. Once at work, finds own work station. yes _____ no _____
38. Asks questions of supervisor if he or she does not understand work assignment.
 yes _____ no _____
39. Reacts well to changes in work assignment yes _____ no _____
40. Learns and follows safety procedures. yes _____ no _____
41. Can read and understand technical manuals. yes _____ no _____
42. Understands that work can result in earning money. yes _____ no _____
43. What does this individual do if assigned work is finished?

44. If work is completed ahead of schedule, uses unassigned work time appropriately.
 yes _____ no _____
45. Works cooperatively in a group of three or more. yes _____ no _____
46. Works appropriately alone. yes _____ no _____
47. Behaves appropriately during work breaks. yes _____ no _____
48. Behaves appropriately during lunch breaks. yes _____ no _____
49. Handles criticism from fellow workers appropriately. yes _____ no _____
50. List the work history of this individual and state how he/she obtained these jobs.

Jobs performed in the school setting: _____

Jobs performed in the community: _____

(continued)

Figure 13.2. *(continued)*

51. Can accurately describe *verbally* what he or she did on these jobs. yes _____ no _____
52. Can accurately describe in *writing* what he or she did on these jobs (e.g., when asked to fill out a job application). yes _____ no _____

Other skills

53. Understands and follows three-step verbal directions. yes _____ no _____
54. Can explain how he or she learns best. yes _____ no _____
55. List other skills that this individual has (e.g., musical, athletic).

Learning style and strategies

56. Needs extra time to answer questions
 • Verbally yes _____ no _____
 • In writing yes _____ no _____
57. Gets distracted by sounds (e.g., people talking). yes _____ no _____
58. Gets distracted by visual stimuli not related to the task at hand (e.g., people, birds). yes _____ no _____
59. What approaches work best if this person needs to learn or practice a new skill that involves eye/hand/body coordination?

Learning style/strategies

60. What approaches work best when teaching this person information that he or she does not know?

61. Describe this individual's attitudes and abilities in regard to his or her career choice. Include work habits, initiative, teacher comments, and so forth.

Personal statement

62. Attach a paragraph written by this individual that explains: 1) why he or she is seeking DVR assistance, 2) his or her career objectives, and 3) why he or she feels that he or she will be successful in that career.

Setting Transition Goals

Many youth with LD leave secondary education with insufficient vocational, functional, or academic skills to be successful in either career entry jobs or postsecondary education (deFur, Getzel, & Kregel, 1994). Improved transition planning while the students are in high school is critical to ensure that they exit school with the necessary skills and knowledge to acquire the needed supports and services in the community. Establishing transition goals help to provide a framework for the curriculum that students with LD will pursue while in high school and to identify independent living skills that students will need in the community.

REPORT

Name		Sex		Age	Race

Education		Disability	

Employability ASSET		Employability PROBLEM	Percentile Equivalent		
4	3	2	1	%	

```
0 9 8 7 6 5 4 3 2 1 0 9 8 7 6 5 4 3 2 1 0 9 8 7 6 5 4 3 2 1 0
I I I I I I I I I I I I I I I I I I I I I I I I I I I I I I I        _____ S1   Acceptance of work role
I I I I I I I I I I I I I I I I I I I I I I I I I I I I I I I        _____ S2   Ability to profit from
                                                                                 instruction or correction
I I I I I I I I I I I I I I I I I I I I I I I I I I I I I I I        _____ S3   Work persistence
I I I I I I I I I I I I I I I I I I I I I I I I I I I I I I I        _____ S4   Work tolerance
I I I I I I I I I I I I I I I I I I I I I I I I I I I I I I I        _____ S5   Amount of supervision required
I I I I I I I I I I I I I I I I I I I I I I I I I I I I I I I        _____ S6   Extent trainee seeks assistance
                                                                                 from supervisor
I I I I I I I I I I I I I I I I I I I I I I I I I I I I I I I        _____ S7   Degree of comfort or anxiety with
                                                                                 supervisor
I I I I I I I I I I I I I I I I I I I I I I I I I I I I I I I        _____ S8   Appropriateness of personal
                                                                                 relations with supervisor
I I I I I I I I I I I I I I I I I I I I I I I I I I I I I I I        _____ S9   Teamwork
I I I I I I I I I I I I I I I I I I I I I I I I I I I I I I I        _____ S10  Ability to socialize with co-workers
I I I I I I I I I I I I I I I I I I I I I I I I I I I I I I I        _____ S1   Social communication skills

I I I I I I I I I I I I I I I I I I I I I I I I I I I I I I I        _____ F1   Task orientation
I I I I I I I I I I I I I I I I I I I I I I I I I I I I I I I        _____ F2   Social skills
I I I I I I I I I I I I I I I I I I I I I I I I I I I I I I I        _____ F    Work motivation
I I I I I I I I I I I I I I I I I I I I I I I I I I I I I I I        _____ F    Work conformance
I I I I I I I I I I I I I I I I I I I I I I I I I I I I I I I        _____ F5   Personal presentation
```

Critical employability deficits (i.e., behaviors rated "1" or "2")

"1" Problem areas "2" Problem areas

Figure 13.3. Work personality profile. Instructions for the worksheet follow: Ratings on the 58 behavioral items are reduced to 11 scale scores by summing the keyed items and dividing by the number of items completed. Disregard items rated X. Instructions for the report follow: Record the scores obtained from the worksheet on the 4-point scale appearing on page 358. For example, if a score is 1.5, place a mark on the number 5 on the scale below the large number 1. Follow this procedure for all the scores obtained and once this is completed, a line may be drawn through the numbers marked, creating a graph. Record at the bottom of the report number 1 and 2 problem areas. This will help to prioritize behaviors that must be addressed. When communicating the results of the profile, it is important to also include the strengths that the individual exhibited. This profile is to be used as a planning tool to improve the individual's employability. It is not designed to diagnose the presence or absence of a learning disability. (From Bolton, B., & Roessler, R. [1986, December]. *Work personality profile* [p. 212]. Fayetteville: Arkansas Research and Training Center in Vocational Rehabilitation; reprinted by permission.)

Teaching Strategies

Several factors should be considered when determining appropriate teaching strategies for students with LD. These factors can be divided into three categories. The first area focuses on the student. The development of specific teaching strategies is based on the unique learning characteristics of the student as identified through formal or informal assessments. The cultural backgrounds of the students and their effects on learning should also be considered.

The second category concerns the transition and postschool goals of the students. For some students with LD, further education in a postsecondary setting is a goal. Others may seek employment upon leaving school. Teaching strategies and the emphasis on what these students must know will differ based on their transition goals. No matter what their goals are, however, many students need assistance with daily living skills so that they can live independently in the community.

The classroom environment is the final category to consider when selecting teaching strategies. Helping students to feel motivated to learn is especially important for students with LD. Many of these students have not had positive experiences in school and, by the time they reach high school or postsecondary settings, are likely to have negative self-images, poor self-concepts, and lack of motivation (Sarkees & Scott, 1995). Creating an atmosphere that reinforces the strengths of the students and helps them to feel comfortable with learning is not an easy task. By enabling these students to feel that they can achieve in certain academic or vocational areas, they gain invaluable tools to cope with the many decisions they will make as they move from school to the community.

Instructing Students

To understand how the student can effectively learn, it is important to determine the student's strongest learning mode(s). The three primary learning modes are visual, auditory, and tactile (i.e., hands-on) learning. Information about how the student learns can be gained by asking the student directly, interviewing the student's family or guardian, and analyzing formal or informal assessment results, psychological reports, and school records. The first step in determining appropriate teaching strategies is focusing on the learning styles of each student and adapting the curriculum accordingly. The second step is for teachers to conduct self-assessments of their teaching styles to determine whether changes are needed to teach students with a variety of learning modes. The curriculum does not always require alterations, however. By offering students a variety of ways to learn material, all students may learn more effectively (Heron & Jorgensen, 1995; Scheiber & Talpers, 1987).

Visual Learners The techniques discussed here are but a few of the many methods that can be used to instruct students with LD. Instructing a student whose strongest learning mode is visual essentially means assisting the student to turn spoken words into pictures. The student must learn how to "visualize" the information that is presented in lecture formats. Whenever possible, lectures should include visual cues to help the student to understand the information that is being presented. Giving students lecture outlines before class may help them to prepare for class and review the material after it is presented. When presenting class material, a variety of visual aids should be used to reinforce infor-

mation. Examples of techniques include 1) writing or drawing on the blackboard; 2) using an overhead project with materials that are highly visual, such as maps, graphs, or colored overlays; and 3) incorporating movies or videotapes into lessons (Gavin et al., 1990; Gregory, 1994; Sarkees-Wircenski & Scott, 1995). Students should also be encouraged to complete assignments with graphs or drawings to illustrate their comprehension of the material.

When students are reading class materials, they should be encouraged to underline key points. They should also be taught how to take notes that clearly separate different concepts. Students who are visual learners should get into the habit of making notes to themselves and writing down assignments and other information that must be learned. Teachers may suggest that the student always carry a notepad or notebook (Gavin et al., 1990; Gregory, 1994; Sarkees-Wircenski & Scott, 1995).

Auditory Learners Gavin and colleagues (1990) have suggested several techniques for instructing students who are auditory learners. Teachers should emphasize sound when presenting material and speak slowly and clearly. Students should be taught to listen for cues when information is given. For example, phrases such as, "The most important point is . . ." or "To summarize, we have discussed . . ." are cues that extra attention should be given. Students should be permitted to tape-record information presented in class to review what was presented. Visual cues, such as maps, charts, or overheads, can also be used as long as the information is accompanied by a clear explanation.

Auditory learners may benefit from oral tests or role play (Gavin et al., 1990; Gregory, 1994; Sarkees-Wircenski & Wircenski, 1995). In role play, students present information to other class members and answer questions they may have. This technique is helpful because the student verbalizes obtained information.

Tactile Learners Students who learn best through hands-on experiences are tactile learners. For them, instructors should structure learning situations to include activities (Gregory, 1994). If these students are involved in training programs, they should begin to use tools or equipment as soon as possible (Gavin et al., 1990).

General Techniques and Strategies In addition to specific techniques utilized for each type of learner, several general techniques should be considered when teaching students with LD. These common strategies may assist teachers as they develop and organize classroom materials (Gavin et al., 1990; Sarkees-Wircenski & Scott, 1995).

- Use concrete examples when presenting material. Abstract concepts can confuse and frustrate students with LD.
- Try to make all printed materials clear and readable. Materials that are not clearly reproduced will add to the students' difficulty with comprehension.
- List assignments in steps. Too much information or direction given at once can confuse students with LD. It is easier for them to follow one step at a time.
- Allow more time, if necessary, for students to complete activities.
- Use a multisensory approach including visual, auditory, and tactile strategies. These techniques can be helpful to all students in the class, not only students with LD.

Assistive technology can be an invaluable support to students with LD, although its uses and benefits have been given little attention in the literature for people with LD (Raskind, 1994). Assistive technology can provide a method for coping in a variety of settings (Raskind, 1994). Laptop computers, pocket-size spellcheckers, tape recorders, and

personal data managers can be easily taken from one setting to another. For example, computers in school settings can help students complete assignments by offering a multisensory approach to learning and can give them immediate feedback on how well they are doing and where errors are occurring. Software can supplement demonstrations, problem solving, and other learning skills. Tape recorders can be used to assist students in listening to books or lectures. Personal data managers with a calendar can help individuals keep track of class schedules, deadlines for assignments, and exam dates. It is important that students with LD have access to available assistive technology.

Tables 13.2, 13.3, and 13.4 have been included to provide additional and more specific ideas about how to assist students with LD in the classroom. These techniques include assistance with speaking, math, and writing and are only a few examples of the methods that have been developed to help facilitate the learning process.

Creating Positive Learning Environments

By the time students with learning disabilities reach the secondary school setting, they are often discouraged about school, have negative self-concepts, and lack motivation for learning (Vogel, Hruby, & Adelnan, 1993). These feelings typically result from a series of negative experiences associated with school. It is important for teachers to create classroom environments that are nonthreatening and build on the strengths and capabilities of the students. West (1987) described several functions of instructors who develop positive learning environments (Gugerty & Gavin, 1991), including 1) serving as good role models, 2) being prepared and organized, 3) developing equitable grading policies, 4) possessing varying teaching styles, and 5) encouraging teamwork among students to develop skills (e.g., employability skills). Students should experience success and feel that they are participants in the class (Brolin, McKay, & West, 1978).

A variety of methods and strategies exist for motivating students to learn (Sarkees-Wircenski & Scott, 1995; Van Reusen, 1993). Cohen and Beattie (1984) offer the following suggestions:

- Provide students with choices. Give them alternative ways to finish assignments or to take exams.
- Provide students with opportunities to take responsibility for their education (e.g., solicit ideas for field trips or other activities, have students evaluate their own progress in class).

Table 13.2.　Techniques for helping students with speaking

- Be sure students are enrolled in supplementary speech classes, reading labs, or remedial reading courses.
- Make glossaries of key words related to specific vocational skills. Provide pictures of the processes or items to help students with learning disabilities to pronounce and learn words.
- Encourage students to demonstrate skills and explain to their classmates how to perform tasks.
- Encourage students to think about what they will say before they speak.
- Provide students who are hyperactive talkers with a separate place to study. Arrange for them to listen to tapes. Remove them from situations in which they disrupt other students and themselves.
- Provide or recognize opportunities to build self-confidence and give praise.

From Gavin, M., Tindall, L.W., & Gugerty, J.J. (1990). *Still puzzled about educating students with disabilities: Vocational preparation of students with disabilities* (p. 159). Madison: University of Wisconsin–Madison, School of Education, The Vocational Studies Center; reprinted by permission.

Table 13.3. Techniques for helping students with mathematics

- Encourage students to learn the basic units of standard and metric measures. Rules and other measuring instruments should be available to give students hands-on practice.
- Allow students to use calculators to help them solve problems and eliminate errors.
- Use visual and tactile materials in addition to demonstrations to solve vocational math problems.
- Work with special education and math teachers to help students with learning disabilities build and use math skills. Inform the math teacher of the skills the student needs and ask the learning disabilities specialist to help to teach these skills.

From Gavin, M., Tindall, L.W., & Gugerty, J.J. (1990). *Still puzzled about educating students with disabilities: Vocational preparation of students with disabilities* (p. 160). Madison: University of Wisconsin–Madison, School of Education, The Vocational Studies Center; reprinted by permission.

- Assign pertinent topics. Select topics of interest and relate their content to the students.
- Information related to potential careers or vocational opportunities can assist students in learning about opportunities in the community.
- Give students feedback that focuses on their actions, not on the teachers' opinions. Provide information about incorrect answers. Let them know about their progress in class.

Creating an environment that enables students with LD to feel motivated about learning and builds their self-esteem is important. To increase their chances of success in the community, students with LD need many opportunities to learn and practice appropriate behaviors before and during the transition process. If students are given these opportunities in settings that allow them to feel comfortable in making mistakes, asking questions, and acquiring new skills, they will be interested in and excited about preparing for their transitions into the community. The attitudes and beliefs of teachers regarding their students is fundamental for developing positive learning setting (Fuchs, Fuchs, Hamlett, Phillips, & Karns, 1995); as one teacher commented when analyzing positive learning environments:

> In the final analysis, my experience has convinced me that the main ingredient in developing a positive learning environment in the classroom is the teachers' unconditional love for their stu-

Table 13.4. Techniques for helping students with writing

- Encourage students to write out ideas to the best of their abilities, preferably in sequenced outline form. Downplay spelling and mechanics.
- Encourage students to draw simple pictures or diagrams where appropriate.
- Keep samples of successful work outlines for each student.
- Review earlier work to demonstrate progress.
- If a student is reluctant to do outlines or diagrams, ask him or her to express ideas orally. Outline ideas as the student talks to show how they would appear in writing.
- Allow students with learning disabilities to use classmates' notes to learn important points from class.
- Record lectures and demonstrations and allow students to borrow the tapes for home or out-of-class review.
- Give oral exams if necessary.
- Teach students notetaking skills, such as recording key words or concepts and organizing notes.

From Gavin, M., Tindall, L.W., & Gugerty, J.J. (1990). *Still puzzled about educating students with disabilities: Vocational preparation of students with disabilities* (p. 160). Madison: University of Wisconsin–Madison, School of Education, The Vocational Studies Center; reprinted by permission.

dents. I'm further convinced that none of my motivational gimmicks or techniques would have worked if my students didn't feel or sense the positive regard I had for each of them. (Colby, 1987, p. 33)

Instructing Multicultural Students

When discussing teaching strategies, it is important to consider working with culturally diverse students with LD (Harry et al., 1993). Careful and comprehensive evaluations should be performed to ensure that these students are not incorrectly identified as having LD as a result of language differences or other cultural influences (Graham, Harris, & Reid, 1990). When assessing the needs of students who are members of ethnic groups, information should be gathered concerning all of the developmental domains, cultural and linguistic influences, and family and community data (Walker, 1988). Suggestions for assisting students with limited English proficiency in the classroom include the following (Inestroza, 1990):

- Allow students to provide information nonverbally (e.g., solving math problems on the blackboard, pointing to answers on graphs or charts).
- Use synonyms and antonyms, or paraphrase to convey classroom material. Redundancy is allowable when instructing these students.
- Use demonstrations and visual cues when instructing. Concrete examples are better than pictures.
- Respond to students' intended meaning when answering questions. The instructor can rephrase what the students have said to enable them to hear how to state an answer correctly. The instructor should build on the information already provided by the students.
- Do not correct a student's pronunciation more than three times consecutively. Excessive correction may make the student afraid to speak. Correction of grammar is best done through writing.
- Do not change students' names to make them sound more American. Doing so deprives students of their cultural identities.

In order to increase their involvement and understanding of the educational process and to assist their children in planning futures beyond the transition process, the students' families should be included in the development of educational and transition plans (Posey & Hollenback, 1990; Walker, 1988). Transition planning for students with culturally diverse backgrounds can be enhanced with understanding of cultural and family expectations.

Preparing for Transition

Postsecondary Settings

Students with LD comprise 25% of all students with disabilities in postsecondary settings (Henderson, 1992). Postsecondary training and education can occur in a number of settings. Examples of programs include junior or community colleges, 4-year colleges or universities, technical schools, private schools and agencies, special stations in business and industry, and instructional opportunities in community agencies (Schloss, 1984). Although

the number of youth with disabilities enrolling in postsecondary education has tripled since 1978 (Wille-Gregory et al., 1995), their enrollment rates still fall well below those of their peers without disabilities. In particular, individuals with LD participate at a significantly lower rate than those without disabilities (Fairweather & Shaver, 1991). To assist these students in making a successful transition from high school to postsecondary settings requires collaboration among secondary school staff and postsecondary service providers (Durlak, Rose, & Bursuck, 1994).

All too often students with LD are unable to manage their education on the postsecondary level and eventually drop out. Low retention and completion rates remain a problem for these students (Aune, 1991). Barriers that students must overcome when attending postsecondary schools include lack of appropriate coursework to prepare them for advanced education or training, lack of awareness of support services or how to use them, limited knowledge about their rights, and inadequate services to meet their unique needs (Aune, 1991; Brinckerhoff, 1994).

Tindall and Gugerty (1990) asked postsecondary instructors in 2-year technical training institutions to name issues they face when teaching students with disabilities. Their responses included the following:

- Information about specific students with disabilities should be shared as they make transitions from secondary settings.
- Methods are needed to identify students with disabilities who have been out of school for some time.
- Instructors must know more about support services (i.e., who to refer, how to refer, and where to refer).
- Instructors must know how to vary curricula to meet the needs of students with disabilities.
- Students with disabilities often do not express that they need assistance.
- Instructors need more information about what is considered reasonable accommodation in the classroom.
- Instructors need further training to overcome preconceived ideas about students with disabilities in postsecondary settings.
- Instructors are unsure whether developing classroom accommodations gives an unrealistic view of the ability of students with disabilities to become competitively employed.
- Instructors expressed some doubt about the availability of jobs for students with disabilities after the students have received training.

Many of the questions and concerns expressed by these instructors exist in other settings. Students with LD in Virginia's 2- and 4-year colleges and universities who responded to a survey on their satisfaction and need for services on the postsecondary level (Board for Rights of Virginians with Disabilities Technical Assistance Project [BRVD-TAP], 1991) expressed frustration over many of these same questions and concerns. One student stated, "My instructors think if I can't manage without extra help, I can't manage in the real world" (p. 20). Another student expressed, "My main problem has been the teachers. They don't know what I'm talking about when I explain my learning disability. One said I just had a lack of confidence" (p. 21).

Students with LD experience other changes when entering postsecondary settings. These changes are in many respects results of the differences between secondary and postsecondary settings. Dalke and Schmitt (1987) cited four primary changes that students experience:

1. In postsecondary settings, students have less contact with teachers. Classes tend to be larger with teachers instructing the class 2 or 3 days a week.
2. Instructors on the postsecondary level tend to anticipate higher levels of academic competence because the students have entered advanced training and education beyond the secondary level.
3. Changes occur in the available personal support systems. Students who enter postsecondary schools often do not have the same level of support from family and friends. This is especially true if they enter schools in other cities or states. In addition, students do not have the support of special education staff and other support staff that was available to them in high school.
4. In postsecondary settings, there are greater expectations for students to achieve independently. Postsecondary settings do not offer the structure and guidance that secondary schools do. Students with learning disabilities are expected to meet the demands of structuring their time and meeting class or training requirements of the classes or training on their own.

Smith (1983) found that students with LD are more likely to have poor organizational skills (e.g., time management and study skills), poor self-concepts, and a lack of appropriate self-advocacy skills. These difficulties, along with the changes that occur from secondary to postsecondary schools, compound already difficult transitions for many students.

There are several activities that can occur on the high school level before students with LD enter postsecondary programs. Suggested activities include the following (Wille-Gregory et al., 1995; Wren, Adelman, Pike, & Wilson, 1987):

- Make sure students understand their disabilities and can describe their strengths and needs.
- Teach students to describe the accommodations that they need.
- Locate students already enrolled in postsecondary programs to describe their experiences and to answer questions.
- Teach students the necessary self-advocacy and decision-making skills.
- Involve appropriate agencies and postsecondary personnel at the beginning of the transition planning process.
- Teach study skills, time management skills, and learning strategies.
- Provide parents and students with information about colleges, vocational schools, and available support services.
- Ensure that ACT and/or SAT tests are taken with accommodations and that all testing results are current (preferably only 1 year old).

It is also important to find out as much as possible about the postsecondary programs that are being considered by students and their families. Visiting the schools under consideration provides information about the schools and the support services available. Whether a specific student is able to visit a school or inquiries are done by telephone, some

specific questions are helpful in obtaining information about the range of services the school or program offers. Table 13.5 lists some of the questions that should be asked.

Suggested activities for postsecondary personnel have been identified to facilitate the transition of students into postsecondary programs (Boyer-Stephens, 1990; Tindall & Gugerty, 1990):

- Develop support groups for students. Approximately 20% of the students who participated in the BRVD-TAP (1991) study expressed a need for a support group or club.
- Tailor in-service training for faculty and instructors to meet their specific needs.
- Encourage high school personnel, students, and parents to tour schools to learn more about the academic or training offerings and available support services.
- Encourage faculty and staff to make all students aware of special services available for students with disabilities.
- Develop informational packets on the support services available. Disseminate the packets to community groups involved with individuals with disabilities, high school personnel, and the school's recruitment office.

Participating in a summer orientation program to prepare students for their transition to the community college or college they are planning to attend can be an excellent way to help facilitate their transition. An example of an orientation program designed to meet the needs of incoming students with LD is the Summer Prep Program at the New River Community College in Dublin, Virginia (Gugerty et al., 1993). The community college's Southwest Virginia Regional Center for the Learning Disabled offers a 5-week program providing students with tutoring, counseling, and instruction in study methods. To enhance their chance for success in a college curriculum, Summer Prep participants receive instruction in basic English and mathematics skills and an orientation to study and survival skills for college. Students also receive an orientation to the college's facilities and available resources, learn about the college's existing programs of study, and establish a rapport with students, faculty, and the Regional Center staff. In Wisconsin, a similar program exists that features orientation days held prior to the students' enrollment to help them to become familiar with the school and to meet with the support staff and instructors (Tindall, 1980). Assistance is available in completing applications for school or obtaining funds for financial help. The support staff also provides help with daily living needs (e.g., locating housing when necessary, assisting students in finding doctors or opening checking accounts). This program provides extensive support to students and staff, which is not always available at postsecondary institutions.

When considering postsecondary programs, information and resources should be identified to assist in the decision-making process. Often, transitions can be facilitated by learning about recommended practices in the area of transition for students with learning disabilities (Greenbaum, Graham, & Seeles, 1995). Ideas about assistance during the transition process can be obtained by contacting universities and asking questions about their practices and projects. Other ideas for collecting information or developing ties with the community include 1) forming working relationships with the area private industry council (PIC), which is the organization that determines how Job Training Partnership Act (JTPA) funds are spent for job instruction; 2) learning about national projects that have been funded to develop resources for recommended practices in vocational preparation

Table 13.5. Questions about accommodations in postsecondary education

Admission
What are the admission requirements for students with learning disabilities?

Diagnosis
Is diagnosis of learning disabilities available on campus? If so, is there a charge for it? If not, where can
 students go to be tested?
Is testing expensive?
Does student health insurance pay for diagnosis?
Will the parents' health insurance cover the student?
If the student was diagnosed as a child, is new testing necessary?
How will a diagnosis be of use to the student?

Tutoring
For which subjects is tutoring available?
How do students find tutors?
Is there a charge for tutoring?

Seminars
Are there special seminars for students with learning disabilities? If so, what do the seminars address?
How will the seminars help students with learning disabilities?
How do students register for these seminars?

Classes for credit
Are there classes designed for students with learning disabilities that can be taken for credit? If so, which
 courses?
Are these courses available every term?

Advocacy and accommodations
Is there someone who will help students to obtain accommodations if they need help?
Is there someone who can explain the student's rights and responsibilities?
Is there a person or committee that considers petitions such as requesting to be excused from taking a
 second language or taking a lighter class load?

Personal and career counseling
Is counseling available from someone experienced with learning disabilities?
What areas does personal counseling include?

Support groups
How do students with learning disabilities get to know each other?
What kinds of topics are addressed in support groups?
When and where do support groups meet?

Specific programming for learning disabilities
Are there any programs just for students with learning disabilities?

Taping texts
Is there a program for taping textbooks?
How do students enroll in such programs?
If there is no program, what do students with print disabilities do?
How do students contact Recording for the Blind?

Extra tuition charge
Is there an extra tuition charge for the services provided for students with learning disabilities? If so, what
 is the charge?

Source: Szymanski, Gugerty, Tindall, & Schmidt (1989).

Quoted from: Association on Handicapped Student Service Programs in Postsecondary Education. (1987). *Unlocking the doors: Making the transition from secondary to postsecondary education* (pp. 8–9). Columbus, OH: Author; reprinted by permission.

and transition from school to the community; and 3) identifying resources to assist in locating postsecondary institutions with established programs for students with disabilities. One resource is the HEATH Resource Center, National Clearinghouse on Postsecondary Education for Individuals with Disabilities (Getzel, 1990).

Employment

For students who wish to obtain employment after exiting school, it is important to provide them with numerous opportunities to explore career options throughout their secondary school experience. This will help them to set realistic goals about occupations to pursue. Students working cooperatively with their transition team members and other school staff should consider the following points (Wille-Gregory et al., 1995):

- Develop an awareness of the range of career opportunities and the requirements for those careers.
- Create opportunities for career exploration and work experience during high school, even for students who are planning to attend a postsecondary school.
- Obtain part-time employment or volunteer experiences to help develop work habits, enhance social skills, and explore vocational interests.

Typically, teachers who are responsible for providing instruction to students with LD have backgrounds in special education and have limited experience with vocational training (Hasazi & Cobb, 1988). However, strategies can be incorporated in the curriculum in addition to occupationally specific training, including academic and vocational instructors working together to incorporate academic competencies into vocational courses or to make academic curricula more vocationally relevant by using vocationally oriented examples when teaching academic subjects. Cooperation among school personnel is essential to ensure that students' academic and vocational skills are integrated.

Neubert and Foster (1988) found that students with LD who participated in postsecondary transition programs had limited awareness of their strengths and weaknesses, were unrealistic about attaining higher education degrees, lacked knowledge about education and training options other than college, and had limited awareness of local employment opportunities. Neubert and Foster developed a transition program to enable students to learn more about their strengths and weaknesses and gather information to make career choices. In addition, the program offered these students exposure to their local community through community-based exploration activities.

Each student participating had his or her own employability profile before exiting school. The profiles consist of information about the students' reading levels, math levels, tested vocational interests, dexterity skills, work habits, learning styles, work environment preferences, recommendations from vocational evaluation reports, and overall strengths and weaknesses. Neubert and Foster suggest that the profile can easily be a part of students' ITPs; can serve as a starting point for vocational exploration; and can be used to identify appropriate employment, school, or training requirements.

Students should be made aware of certain techniques that they can use as "survival skills" on the job. Robinson (1984) listed several on-the-job tips for individuals with LD, including taking notes or using tape recorders and noting when discussions occurred and with whom. To help compensate for perceptual problems, Robinson suggested that indi-

viduals organize their work so everything they need is in a specific place. For individuals with eye–hand coordination problems, the author recommends that the employees practice the required job skills when they are not under pressure to perform. Individuals with LD should also learn how to talk about their disabilities with co-workers.

Other resources are available to assist students with LD as they prepare for employment. Table 13.6 offers information that should be used by employees with LD. Table 13.7 summarizes ideas that can assist supervisors of employees with LD. It is important for students to understand the perspectives of potential supervisors, and this information can be used by school staff to emphasize employment survival skills in the curriculum and training experiences.

Designing and Implementing ITPs for Youth with LD

Identifying Team Members

Developing transition plans requires cooperation among a number of service providers, students, and their family members. Building teamwork is an evolving process. The 1989

Table 13.6. Suggestions for employees with learning disabilities

1. Be prepared to spend extra time learning the job even if you are not paid extra. Bring price lists home to memorize. Practice completing forms. If you are working at a chain of restaurants, go to a different restaurant within the chain and watch the workers. If you are slower, be willing to take extra time to finish your share of work.
2. Ask for help as you need it. Even though other employees and the supervisor may act impatient, it's better than making errors.
3. Never ask for help if you don't need it.
4. In most jobs, accuracy is more important than speed. Take the time to do it correctly, even if people pressure you to go faster.
5. Take advantage of your first few days on the job. During this "honeymoon period," you can ask many questions. Try to find someone who will watch you do the job correctly. Repeat information. Say, "Please listen to me tell you, so I can be sure I understand." Don't let them interrupt you and tell you what to do. Be sure they are listening to you. Some people like helping others. Try to find them.
6. Offer to perform tasks that you can handle but others consider unpopular. Then, you can ask others to assist you with jobs that you can't do.
7. Develop ways to remember important facts. Everyone has a particular technique. Write things down, say them aloud when you are alone, or ask your friends or parents to drill you.
8. When you make mistakes, apologize and correct them immediately.
9. Report on time. If you have trouble being on time, arrive early.
10. Try hard and appear to make an effort. Sometimes, when people make mistake after mistake, it is tempting to act indifferent or as if you are doing it on purpose. That isn't helpful. Make your effort obvious:
 • Appear to pay attention. Look everyone in the eye. Nod your head occasionally as they speak. Respond to what they have said.
 • Look at your work as you do it. Don't let your eyes or mind wander when you are on the job. Walk purposefully from place to place.
 • Always work, except during breaks or lunch.
 • As you improve, tell your supervisors and co-workers. Say, "Thank-you for your help. As you can see, I did it correctly this time."

Adapted from Alabama Department of Education, Division of Rehabilitation and Crippled Children Services (1989).

Table 13.7. Ways that supervisors can help employees with learning disabilities

1. Be direct and specific. Say exactly what you mean. Make important points without sarcasm or "hints."
2. Help the employee with a learning disability to understand the hidden rules in your organization. Don't expect this person to "pick them up." Explain inappropriate behavior and help him or her to overcome it. Tell the employee what behavior is making others uncomfortable and what changes you expect.
3. Be understanding of his or her problem, but be firm about any limits you set.
4. Be especially thorough in your orientation of this employee. Go over every work rule. Make sure that the person understands all of the components of a successful work day.
5. Treat the disability matter-of-factly and use common sense. Realize that a person with learning disabilities can be a productive team member.

Source: Syzmanski, Gugerty, Tindall, & Schmidt (1989).

Quoted from: Brown, D.S. of The President's Committee on Employment of People with Disabilities. (1986). *Supervising adults with learning disabilities.* Washington, DC: U.S. Government Printing Office; reprinted by permission.

yearly summary of Minnesota's Community Transition Interagency Committees concluded that the following minimal requirements were necessary for effective interagency planning: 1) a common understanding of the mission and philosophy of the planning effort, 2) knowledge about what each of the representatives from agencies on the committee do, 3) understanding each individual's role on the committee, and 4) a universal feeling that each member's participation is important (Graham, 1992).

Transition team members must ensure that all necessary community agencies are represented on the committee; representation differs according to the transition needs of the student. One method to identify potential team members is to use a checklist, such as the example in Figure 13.4, which identifies some of the adult role dimensions of an individual.

Identifying Roles and Responsibilities

Two of the most important elements in developing effective cooperation are an understanding of the range of supports and services provided by other agencies represented on the team and an understanding among the members of their roles. The process of developing one's role as a member of a team is ongoing, but can be aided by developing a basic definition of the agency's responsibilities on the team as agreed upon by all members. This type of description can establish a common understanding among the members and can facilitate the further development of each role as the team begins to work together over a period of time. It is important that the responsibilities of the student and his or her family members are also included, which can help to develop a shared responsibility for the student's transition by all involved parties.

Bob *Thomas Dale High School, located in Chesterfield County, Virginia, has a student enrollment of 1,300. The school serves both rural and suburban communities, and the staff face a mixture of problems in educating its students. Although the school is close to a large metropolitan area where students can participate in a variety of employment and postsecondary training opportunities,*

Adult role dimensions	Agencies				
	Department of vocational rehabilitation	Postsecondary institutions	JTPA	Services for independent living	Other
Career planning options					
Employment options					
Postsecondary training					
Financial assistance/income support					
Community participation					
Advocacy/legal services					
Leisure/recreation					
Transportation					
Self-advocacy					
Socialization/friends					
Personal management					
Living arrangements					
Medical needs					
Insurance					
Other					

Figure 13.4. Potential transition team members checklist. (Adapted from Graham, 1992.)

problems related to rural communities are relevant. Transportation is a critical issue because the school is located in an area not served by public transit. Employment and training opportunities in the more rural sections of the county are also not accessible by public transportation.

The school's transition teams include a special education teacher, a vocational education teacher, a guidance counselor, a community-based organization representative(s), the student, and family members. The team assists in identification of academic and/or vocational goals with appropriate modifications, general services, counseling and guidance services, postsecondary training and education options, and agencies to provide support for needed services.

Bob is a student with learning disabilities in his junior year of high school. He is the youngest of three children and has always been sheltered by his family. Both of his parents work outside of the home in professional careers. Bob's two older brothers completed high school and are attending 4-year universities. Bob's parents have not allowed him to obtain a driver's license or to explore potential part-time employment during the school year or summer because they feel that he is not mature enough to handle a great deal of responsibility.

Bob shows limited interest in his academic classes. His grades are fair. He maintains "C"s and "D"s. Bob reads at grade level, but his math skills are two grades below what they are expected to be. Bob's handwriting is poor, and he has difficulty listening to classroom instructions and taking notes. Information gathered by his teachers indicates that Bob understands written instructions better than verbal ones and is easily distracted by noises around him. Bob is able to organize his work to complete his homework on time and shows increased effort to do well when he is interested in a subject.

One of Bob's biggest problems is his social skills. He has difficulty relating to his peers and frequently misunderstands what is being said to him because he cannot distinguish an individual's tone of voice or facial expressions. When he enters a group of students and attempts to initiate a conversation, he usually interrupts whoever is talking. Typically, his comments are inappropriate and he ends up in fights. Bob becomes frustrated easily and has difficulty handling anger. He has been unsuccessful in dating and spends most of his time alone.

Bob's resource teacher and guidance counselor met to discuss his situation. One of their primary concerns was Bob's lack of direction for adulthood. It was apparent that his career goals were very different from his parents' expectations for him. His family has indicated that they want Bob to enroll only in academic courses because everyone in the family has attended college. His parents believe that Bob could attend college if he would work a little harder and try to concentrate more on his studies, but they are also considering his entering the armed services—an option in which Bob is very interested. They believe that if Bob does not enter the service or attend a college he will be unable to make a living and have a lifestyle similar to other members of his family. Bob has expressed that he feels pressure to please his parents. He has stated that he does not want to go to college but cannot persuade his parents to consider other alternatives.

The transition team notified Bob and his parents that they planned to work with them during the IEP meeting to develop career objectives and review Bob's coursework. At their meeting, the team discussed the possibility of a vocational assessment to determine Bob's interests, strengths, and weaknesses. Bob said that he wished to explore career options that did not involve college, and his parents finally agreed to a vocational assessment. When school personnel approached Bob's parents about obtaining a vocational assessment during the 10th grade, his parents refused to sign the permission slip.

The transition team suggested that Bob take a drama class to improve interpersonal skills and build self-esteem. It was also decided that Bob would meet regularly with the guidance counselor to discuss difficulties he may be experiencing.

Soon after the meeting, Bob went to the technical center for a variety of assessment activities. During this time, he attended some vocational classes to see what the training program offers. Bob was particularly interested in the plumbing class and returned later to talk with the instructor about the class.

The vocational assessment results were consistent with the results from earlier school testing and indicated that Bob enjoys activities that require hands-on experience. The transition team determined that Bob would be able to handle a vocational program like plumbing if some modifications were made in training (e.g., extra assistance with necessary math). The vocational teacher on the transition team gathered information about apprenticeship's potential earnings to present to Bob and his parents.

At the next meeting, the team carefully reviewed the information obtained from the assessment. Bob was very excited about the possibility of entering the plumbing program. The vocational teacher discussed her findings, and Bob's parents were surprised by the income potential and that Bob could earn money while receiving advanced training. They agreed to permit Bob to enroll in the technical center's vocational program in his junior year. Included in Bob's plan was for the resource teacher to coordinate with the vocational teacher to help Bob with math and with material presented during lectures. The plan also heavily emphasized entering the Navy or some other branch of the armed services where a trade such as plumbing could be formally developed.

Other goals established at the meeting included getting a driver's license, pursuing summer

employment through the local JTPA program, and opening a checking account. The staff also discussed some long-term goals around other independent living skills. The team members suggested that they continue to work with Bob to prepare him for more independent living after graduation. The team planned to increase Bob's awareness of programs and services located in the community. The team also suggested that Bob receive further evaluation concerning his LD, but his parents refused, saying that they wanted to wait and that perhaps enough information had already been gathered. Bob's ITP is on pages 379–382.

Evaluation of Transition Outcomes for Youth with LD

Evaluating what happens to students after they exit school is an important part of the transition process. Collecting information on the training programs, educational experiences, employment opportunities, and the recreational and leisure activities in which they are involved assists transition planning teams to better assess the strengths and needs of their processes. Studies have found that many students with learning disabilities are not able to move into the community successfully. D'Alonzo, Faas, and Crawford (1988) cite several follow-up studies that indicate that a large number of people with LD have difficulty obtaining employment, and if they secure positions, are unable to keep them. This unemployment is not necessarily related to the geographic labor market, but to the students' lack of employment-related knowledge and experience (Schwarz & Taymans, 1991). Respondents in the Schwarz and Taymans study reported that people with LD were not receiving services through adult services agencies in their communities and were unable to name the services that might be available.

Evaluation activities conducted as part of the transition process provide a mechanism to obtain feedback about the programs and activities developed for students with LD.

> Successful participation in vocational education and completion of a high school program is not a guarantee that individuals with LD will exit the school system to become fully employed. It is imperative that vocational educators and special educators work together to better prepare these youths for gainful employment. (Schwarz & Taymans, 1991, p. 19)

Their conclusion is appropriate for all members participating in the transition planning process. It also supports the need for feedback on students who have already exited school to determine the effectiveness of the preparation and planning activities they experienced.

There are several steps in the development and implementation of an evaluation process. The basic components include identifying information the transition team should collect and the type of evaluation instrument to use to gather information and determining how often the evaluation should occur, who should be responsible for implementing it, and how the results should be used. It is recommended that both graduates and dropouts be included in follow-up studies (Szoke & Vest, 1975).

Collecting Appropriate Information

The transition team members should consider the type of information that will assist them in determining the effectiveness of their process and the scope of the evaluation process.

Description of Student's Future Vision

Bob would like to become increasingly self-sufficient, graduate from high school, and enter the U.S. Navy to obtain training as a boilermaker.

Individualized Transition Plan

Student's Name ___Bob___

Birthdate _____

Student's Identification Number _____

Participants:

School ___Thomas Dale___

ITP Conference Date _____

Name	Position
Bob	_Student_
Sonya	_Mother_
Terrence	_Teacher_
Mickey	_Navy recruiter_

Career and Economic Self-Sufficiency

Employment Goal *Bob will be employed as a boilermaker.*

Level of present performance: *Bob has expressed an interest in building and repairing metal structures. Mother says student has a natural talent for building and fixing things.*

Steps needed to accomplish goal: *1. Bob will earn Carnegie units to finish high school. 2. Bob and mother will visit the Armed Services Recruitment Office. 3. Bob will complete application and pass physical test for admission into the U.S. Navy. 4. Teacher will follow up and be ready to assist.*

Date of completion: *January 1995*

Person(s) responsible for implementation: *Bob, mother, and teacher*

Vocational Education/Training Goal *Bob will enter the U.S. Navy upon graduation from high school to get training as a boilermaker and to serve his country.*

Level of present performance: *Bob is enrolled in an LD resource class. All classes are in mainstreamed environments except the study skills/test-taking class.*

Steps needed to accomplish goal: *1. Bob will continue to work toward a high school diploma. 2. He will use the LD class to gain specific skills in studying, improving test-taking momentum, critical thinking, advocacy, and completing necessary paperwork for admission into the U.S. Navy. 3. He will designate boilermaker occupation as area of training.*

Date of completion: *July 1994*

Person(s) responsible for implementation: *Teacher (lead), Bob, Navy recruiter, and guidance counselor*

From Wehman, P. (1995). *Individual transition plans: The teachers curriculum guide for helping youth with special needs.* Austin, TX: PRO-ED; reprinted by permission.

Postsecondary Education Goal *N/A*

Level of present performance:

Steps needed to accomplish goal:

Date of completion:

Person(s) responsible for implementation:

Financial/Income Needs Goal *While in the Navy, Bob will invest in U.S. Savings Bonds and set up an account for his mother.*

Level of present performance: *Bob is currently working to help his mother with household expenses. He wants to establish a plan to save with little risk and continue to be able to help out at home.*

Steps needed to accomplish goal: *1. Bob and his mother need to discuss financial benefit information with Navy recruiter. 2. Teacher will help family interpret information in order to make best decisions. 3. Student will sign the appropriate forms for payroll deductions.*

Date of completion: *January 1995*

Person(s) responsible for implementation: *Bob, mother, teacher, and Navy recruiter*

Career and Economic Self-Sufficiency

Independent Living Goal *N/A*

Level of present performance:

Steps needed to accomplish goal:

Date of completion:

Person(s) responsible for implementation:

Transportation/Mobility Goal *Bob will purchase a car.*

Level of present performance: *Bob enjoys activities that allow him to build things. He has always had an interest in model cars and trucks.*

Steps needed to accomplish goal: *1. Bob needs to identify his level of expertise with the activity. 2. He needs to purchase the vehicle of choice. 3. He needs to purchase all tools and supplies needed.*

Date of completion: *June 1995*

Person(s) responsible for implementation: *Bob*

Social Relationships Goal *N/A*

Level of present performance:

Steps needed to accomplish goal:

Date of completion:

Person(s) responsible for implementation:

Recreation/Leisure Goal *Bob will pursue his hobby of putting together model cars.*

Level of present performance: *Bob enjoys activities that allow him to build things. He has always had an interest in model cars and trucks.*

Steps needed to accomplish goal: *1. Bob needs to identify his level of expertise with the activity. 2. He needs to purchase the vehicle of choice. 3. He needs to purchase all tools and supplies needed.*

Date of completion: *June 1995*

Person(s) responsible for implementation: *Bob*

Personal Competence

Health/Safety Goal *Bob will maintain a healthy body and mind through weight training and exercises offered by his school or job.*

Level of present performance: *Bob is on the school's wrestling team. He is very athletic and wants to maintain a healthy body and mind.*

Steps needed to accomplish goal: *Bob will visit the weight room several times a week at school and then in the Navy.*

Date of completion: *Ongoing*

Person(s) responsible for implementation: *Bob*

Self-Advocacy/Future Planning *Bob will continue to advocate and make decisions that are consistent with his values.*

Level of present performance: *Initially, Bob was discouraged from enrolling in the armed services. However, he was not persuaded. He wants to pursue a career in the armed services because his older brother is a Gulf War veteran.*

Steps needed to accomplish goal: *1. Bob will continue to be a self-advocate. 2. Bob will gather pertinent information and analyze the information to make the best decision.*

Date of completion: *June 1995*

Person(s) responsible for implementation: *Bob, teacher, and mother*

Student Career Preference

Enter the Navy

Student's Major Transition Needs

1. To enter the U.S. Navy
2. To invest and save money and resources
3. To purchase a car

Additional Notes

This involves deciding which outcomes they wish to measure and how the information collected will determine their impact. Essentially, the team defines the evaluation parameters and chooses the most important components. Rusch and DeStefano (1989) suggest that quantitative and qualitative outcomes should be used to monitor the progress of former students. They divided outcome information into two areas. The first centered on the employment of the students (e.g., types of jobs held; wages earned; benefits received; hours worked; job tenure; employer performance ratings; degree to which employers, parents, and students were satisfied with the outcomes of the transition process). The second area concerned the integration of the students into the community (e.g., leisure or recreational activities, living arrangements, community-related activities occurring outside of the realm of employment or training activities).

The team must consider whether to use a minimal or maximal approach (Chatham, Johnson, & Peterson, 1981), especially when considering the outcomes related to employment. The minimal view would measure a successful employment outcome as earning at least minimum wage and demonstrating personal characteristics necessary to obtain and keep a job (e.g., punctuality, attendance, grooming). The maximal view is more longitudinal and defines success as achieving a satisfactory pattern of employment over an extended period of time, not simply obtaining a paid job (e.g., having a positive self-concept, being self-directed, possessing good thinking and planning skills). Because of the need for better information on the transition needs and employment histories of students with disabilities (Neubert, Tilson, & Ianacone, 1989) and the need for more intense and appropriate secondary-level programming, transition teams should take a more maximal view when planning and implementing a system to monitor former students.

Developing an Evaluation Instrument

The method the transition team chooses to gather information affects the type of questions that are asked and the length of the form used. Former students may be contacted by telephone, in person, with a survey mailed to their residence, or with a reunion letter or newsletter (Szoke & Vest, 1975). The availability of resources affects the method selected. In addition, the respondents should be considered. A mailed survey may not be as time consuming as telephone or personal contacts, but it may present problems for individuals with LD. The team may obtain better results through telephone interviews.

When developing an evaluation form, transition team members must ensure that the length of the survey does not prevent former students from completing it. The survey should include questions with responses provided for the individual to check or circle. Some open-ended questions may allow the students to answer in depth. The instrument should present a mix of question types. Team members should be sensitive to the wording of questions to avoid confusing respondents. Survey instructions must be clear and accompanied by a letter describing why the survey was sent to the individual, its purpose, who will see the answers, and how the information will be used. Figures 13.5 and 13.6 (see pp. 387–389) are examples of evaluation forms developed for follow-up studies.

The transition team can develop surveys to assess the impact of the transition process from a number of perspectives. Team members can survey parents and employers to obtain their views on the success of the students' transitions into the community. The team must consider who will be the primary sources to receive follow-up forms. It is essential

Student Follow-Up Survey

1. Name _____

2. Program
 _____ Cooperative School Work Program (VAC)
 _____ Vocational education
 _____ Modified vocational education
 _____ Individual Vocational Training (IVT)/Community classroom
 _____ None
 _____ Graduate

3. Classification
 _____ Behavioral disordered (BD)
 _____ Learning disabled (LD)
 _____ Educable Mentally Handicapped (EMH)
 _____ Educational Resource Teacher-Learning Disabled (ERT-LD)
 _____ Other

4. Did you discuss your choice of classes with anyone at school?
 _____ yes _____ no

5. Whom did you discuss this with?
 _____ Special education teacher
 _____ Classroom teacher
 _____ Vocational evaluator
 _____ Vocational resource educator
 _____ Counselor
 _____ Principal
 _____ Vocational teacher
 _____ Other, please specify _____

6. Which of these things did you do?
 _____ Vocational evaluation (evaluation lab)
 _____ Career exploration (What class did you do it in?)
 _____ Toured or discussed vocational classes

7. Did you attend your IEP meeting?
 _____ yes _____ no

8. Did you choose the classes you would take?
 _____ yes _____ no

9. Are you employed?
 _____ yes _____ no

10. How long have you been at your present job?
 date employed _____

11. What type of employment?
 _____ Part time _____ Full time

12. Are you in a field related to your training?
 _____ yes _____ no

(continued)

Figure 13.5. A student follow-up survey used to evaluate the transition process. (From Tindall, L.W., Gugerty, J.J., Dougherty, B.B., & Heffron, T.J. [1987]. *Replicating jobs in business and industry for persons with disabilities: Vol. II* [p. 53]. Madison: University of Wisconsin, School of Education, The Vocational Studies Center; reprinted by permission.)

Figure 13.5. *(continued)*

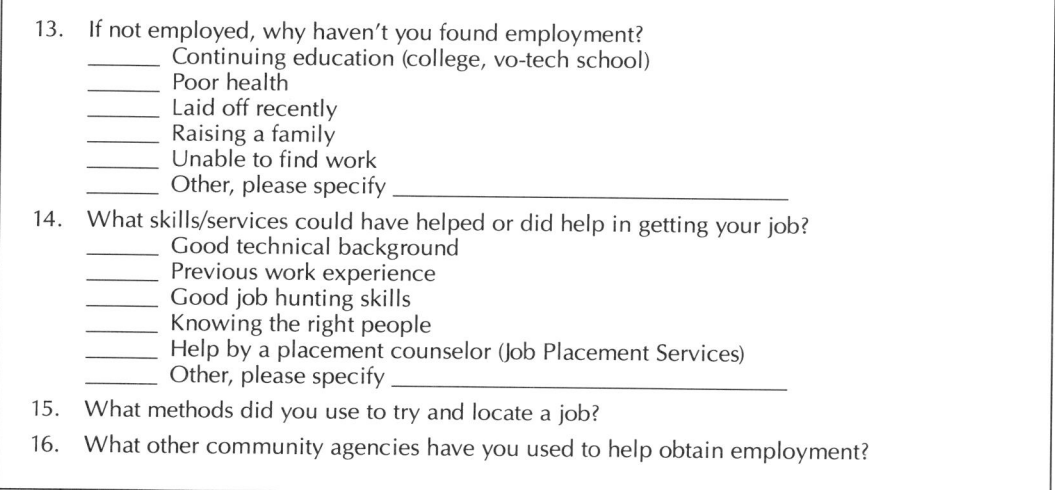

13. If not employed, why haven't you found employment?
 _____ Continuing education (college, vo-tech school)
 _____ Poor health
 _____ Laid off recently
 _____ Raising a family
 _____ Unable to find work
 _____ Other, please specify _____

14. What skills/services could have helped or did help in getting your job?
 _____ Good technical background
 _____ Previous work experience
 _____ Good job hunting skills
 _____ Knowing the right people
 _____ Help by a placement counselor (Job Placement Services)
 _____ Other, please specify _____

15. What methods did you use to try and locate a job?

16. What other community agencies have you used to help obtain employment?

that the team at least contact former students because they are the primary consumers of transition planning and implementation.

After the form is developed, a small sample of former students with LD should complete the form and provide feedback about any problems they might have had in completing it. The team should ask whether the wording is clear, approximately how long it took to complete the form, and if the students have ideas for other questions that should be asked. Results of a trial indicate whether the survey will elicit the range of information needed.

Implementing the Evaluation Process

The transition team must consider how often to contact former students with learning disabilities. It is believed that periodic contact is essential to obtain the necessary amount of information (Bruininks, Wolman, & Thurlow, 1989). Szoke and Vest (1975) have suggested that former students be contacted on a 1-, 3-, and 5-year basis to truly evaluate the effectiveness of preparing students for the community. They also stated that one real measure of an effective preparation process for students is how well they are doing 5 years after leaving school, not just whether they have employment 6 months after graduation. This idea of compiling data over a span of years supports the earlier discussion of a maximal view of evaluating outcomes. Decisions about how frequently to conduct follow-up study are dependent on the resources of the team. Szoke and Vest also believe that the students and their parents should be informed while the students are in school that a follow-up study will be performed after they exit. This will help the parents and students to understand the reasons for the evaluation before they become participants.

The team must also designate an individual to ensure that the surveys are distributed and the results are compiled after they are returned. Resources should be identified and the school administration should confirm that adequate resources will be available to per-

form evaluation activities. One of the major transition leaders in the United States who has been a pioneer with such follow-up surveys is Dr. Susan Brody Hasazi.

Susan Brody Hasazi Susan Brody Hasazi, Ed.D., is a professor in the Department of Education and Director of the Center for Transition and Supported Employment at the University of Vermont. She has directed personnel preparation projects for training special educators, vocational educators, and adult services professionals in the skills necessary to meet the transitional and postsecondary needs of youth with disabilities. In addition, she has been involved in a variety of research and evaluation efforts related to conducting follow-up/follow-along studies for program improvement and evaluating the effectiveness of vocational and secondary-level curriculum and interagency collaboration between schools and adult services.

Dr. Hasazi received a 1983 Mary Switzer Research Fellowship from the National Institute on Disability and Rehabilitation Research (NIDRR) for her work related to the vocational and transitional experiences of youth with disabilities. She was a 1982 Joseph Kennedy Fellow in Public Policy and Mental Retardation and spent 6 months working for Senator Robert Stafford on the Senate Subcommittee on the Handicapped, where she assisted in the reauthorization of the Vocational Rehabilitation Act Amendments of 1965, PL 89-333; the Carl D. Perkins Act Vocational and Applied Technology Education Act of 1990, PL 101-392; and the Education of the Handicapped Act Amendments of 1986, PL 99-457. Dr. Hasazi serves on a variety of state and national advisory boards and is active in advocacy efforts related to increasing consumer-directed services and supports.

In 1995, Dr. Hasazi received the highly prestigious Education Award in the Joseph Kennedy Foundation competition for outstanding professionals in the field of mental retardation. Dr. Hasazi has been one of the leading women in the world on behalf of young adults with disabilities, especially in the area of analyzing the post-21 outcomes for students leaving special education and entering adulthood.

Using the Results of the Evaluation Process

After the results of the evaluation process are gathered, the transition team should summarize the results for their use and share them with individuals who can use the information to improve programs for students (Fourqurean, 1994). Ideally, a report would include recommendations by the transition team and a discussion of resources needed to conduct the next cycle of the evaluation.

The evaluation results should be reviewed within the context of the outcomes identified by the team during the initial phase of the evaluation system. The team should determine whether the transition process has achieved desired outcomes. The evaluation results may identify problems that former students encounter in the community, which were not addressed in the transition process. If specific issues are identified, the team should take steps to modify the transition process. Follow-up information also identifies ways in which the transition process is working for students with LD.

Student Follow-up Survey

Name: _____ Birthdate: _____
Current Address: _____

City: _____ State: _____
ZIP Code: _____ Phone Number: (_____) _____
Year you finished vocational/technical school _____

Work

Please check the answer that fits you now:

_____ Employed full time (35 hours a week or more)
_____ Employed part time (34 hours a week or less)
_____ Military service
branch of service _____
your military job _____
_____ Unemployed and looking for work
_____ Unemployed and **not** looking for paid work

If you are working at a job for pay, please answer the following:

Employer's name: _____
Employer's address: _____

Job title: _____
Main tasks you must perform on this job: _____
How long have you been working at **this** job? _____
May we contact your employer to see how well you are doing?
_____ yes _____ no
If it's OK to talk to your employer, please **print** your supervisor's name below:

and **sign** your name here _____
How much do you earn per hour? $_____ /hour
How many hours do you work each week? _____
Please check all fringe benefits you get on this job:

_____ None _____ Worker's compensation _____ Paid vacation
_____ FICA _____ Pension _____ Paid holidays
_____ Life ins. _____ Unemployment comp. _____ Medical ins.
_____ Dental ins. _____ Paid sick days _____ Other

Who helped you get the job you have now? Please check the appropriate choice:
_____ Vocational teacher
_____ Special needs counselor
_____ Other teacher from school
_____ Vocational rehabilitation counselor
_____ Job Service counselor
_____ Your parents, or other family member
_____ A friend or neighbor
Have you changed jobs since leaving school? _____ yes _____ no
If yes, how many jobs have you had since leaving school? _____

(continued)

Figure 13.6. A student follow-up survey used to evaluate the transition process. (From Gugerty, J.J., & Gavin, M.K. [Eds]. [1991]. *Designated vocational instruction: A cooperative process for change* [pp. 55–58]. Unpublished manuscript, Wisconsin, Department of Public Instruction, Madison; reprinted by permission.)

Figure 13.6. *(continued)*

How long did it take you to find your first job after leaving school? _____

School

Are you going to school now? _____ yes _____ no

If yes, check one:

_____ A technical college 1-year diploma program

_____ A technical college 2-year diploma program

_____ A 4-year college program

_____ An apprentice program

_____ An on-the-job training program

_____ Other, please describe _____

If yes, which school? _____

If yes, what field do you study?_____

Income

What are your sources of income? Check all that apply.

_____ Your job _____ Social Security

_____ Your family _____ Welfare

_____ Your roommate _____ Workfare

_____ Your spouse _____ Vocational rehabilitation

_____ Other _____

Living Situation

With whom are you living? Please check one.

_____ Self _____ Parents _____ Other relatives _____ Spouse

_____ Roommate _____ Other _____

If you live in your own home or apartment, did anyone help you get this place to live?

_____ yes _____ no

Does anyone help you budget your money? _____ yes _____ no

Does anyone help you buy your food? _____ yes _____ no

Does anyone help you get your meals ready? _____ yes _____ no

Travel

How do you get to work and back home again? _____

How do you get to the grocery store, or other stores? _____

Do you have a driver's license? _____ yes _____ no

Recreation

What do you do when you are not at work? Check all that apply.

_____ Play sports _____ Read _____ Take naps

_____ Watch TV _____ Do crafts _____ Do hobbies

_____ Go to movies _____ Drive around _____ Walk around

Personal Needs

Do any of the following people work with you? Check all that apply.

_____ Service coordinator _____ Social worker _____ Job coach

Medical Needs

Do you have a "green card"? _____ yes _____ no

Other Information

Was there anything you now wish you had learned in vocational/technical school but did not?

_____ yes _____ no

(continued)

Figure 13.6. *(continued)*

If yes, what did you wish you had learned? Check all that apply.
_____ How to manage your money
_____ How to manage your time
_____ How to stand up for yourself
_____ How to handle emergencies
_____ How to get medical help if needed
_____ How to keep yourself neat and clean
_____ How to buy and cook food
_____ How to keep your house/apartment neat and fixed up
_____ Other _____
What services do you need now but are not getting? Check all that apply.
_____ Job or career counseling
_____ Personal counseling
_____ Transportation
_____ Job club or other support group
_____ Other _____

Figure 13.7 summarizes the ideas discussed here and describes some of the common problems encountered by staff and solutions for overcoming these problems.

Conclusion

This chapter has presented a number of experiences from the perspective of the individual with LD. Readers should understand the complexity of the problems and issues faced by these individuals and how their disabilities can affect all aspects of their lives. A number of transition alternatives have been discussed for use when working with these students and their families as they move from school to the community. Individuals with LD are too often viewed in terms of what they are unable to do and not provided the opportunities to develop their skills and talents. Through appropriate services and supports and a shared commitment, these students may be able to pursue their dreams and aspirations as they enter their adult lives.

Transition Evaluation Outline

Task list

Define study objectives and choose survey method.
Design survey to meet objectives considering survey methods.
Perform a survey "trial run."
Revise as needed.
Select survey population
List population graduates.
Design a student profile to organize preliminary information.
Collect preliminary information (e.g., address, phone number, special education programming, exit/graduation date).
Make final revision; print copies.
For mailed survey, write a cover letter explaining objectives, instructions, etc.
Mail survey, or begin survey interviews.

Periodically do the following:

Revise survey methods.
Revise survey content to fit needs.
Revise student profile.
Determine best calling times/locations from graduate's family or friends.

Common problems	Some solutions
Graduate records are hard to compile.	Organize a comprehensive record-keeping system from the start.
Survey vocabulary can confuse students, causing their responses to be clouded.	Write surveys at student reading levels, including many examples and definitions.
	Mail written copies of the survey that students can follow during phone interviews.
	Explain terminology and system practices to keep confusion to a minimum.
Former students may be difficult to contact because of relocation, job schedules, or lifestyles.	Use both direct interview and mail survey methods.
	Contact family members and friends when possible for pertinent information.

Figure 13.7. Transition evaluation outline. (From Gugerty, J.J., & Gavin, M.K. [Eds.]. [1991]. *Designated vocational instruction: A cooperative process for change* [p. 62]. Unpublished manuscript, Wisconsin Department of Public Instruction, Madison; reprinted by permission.)

13
Study Questions

1. What are at least 10 effects a learning disability can have on an individual's academic and daily living experiences, according to Reiling? How do problem-solving, decision-making, social, and communication skills difficulties commonly experienced by students with LD often affect academic performance and peer relationships?

2. What are four of the skills, behaviors, or attitudes used to define *self-determination* and how can a student's development of self-determination skills affect the individualized education programming process?

3. How can school personnel who arrange or conduct assessments enhance the value of a student's assessment to the education and transition planning process?

4. What are some factors to consider in determining appropriate teaching strategies for students with LD? What accommodations (including assistive technology) might be provided for a student who learns best through visually presented material? How might strategies for this student be different from those that would be most helpful for an auditory learner? A tactile learner?

5. How can the instructor facilitate a positive learning environment and enhance motivation for students?

6. How can the secondary school education planning process facilitate transition to a postsecondary or work setting?

7. What are the benefits of and the steps involved in the evaluation of the transition planning process for students with LD?

14

Applications for Youth
with Behavior Disorders

Upon completion of this chapter, the reader will be able to do the
following:

- Understand the mental health needs of students with behavior
 disorders
- Describe six behavioral characteristics of students with be-
 havior disorders
- Understand how work experience and employment can pos-
 itively ameliorate behavior impairments and excesses
- Discuss the role of student choice in transition planning and
 vocational placement
- Be aware of several types of self-control and techniques for
 teaching self-control
- Understand the concept of the job club for youth with behav-
 ior disorders
- Discuss supported employment outcomes for individuals
 with behavior disorders

Children and youth who are classified as having behavior disorders represent the third
largest category of students with disabilities in the United States (Pullis, 1991), following
only those with speech impairments and learning disabilities. Because of the size of this
population, it is particularly disturbing to find the paucity of literature and resource ma-
terials regarding career and vocational education, transition planning, and employment
programming for those with behavior disorders. Although there are many issues, prob-
lems, and challenges in the field of special education, few can compare in complexity to

serving these youth. This group requires appropriate curricula and service delivery models and, perhaps most important, ongoing mental health care.

Most teachers and education personnel of students with behavior disorders possess backgrounds and training only in special education. However, teachers of these students should also have especially close liaisons with trained psychiatric and counseling personnel. Many of these students are filled with rage or are depressed or continuously anxious or paranoid, unable to learn or perform effectively at jobsites and often suspended or expelled from school. It is critical to realize that most of their mental health issues can be significantly ameliorated with community integration and real work activities (*Vocational Training News*, 1991).

This group of students also has a range of emotional disorders. For example, within this group, there are people with mild behavior disorders, severe behavior disorders, and long-term histories of institutionalization; there are those who have been abused and neglected by parents or diagnosed with autism. These are students with particularly difficult problems that will not disappear as these students age. In fact, these problems will become increasingly prevalent and more complex to resolve unless frequent and intense community-based activities are incorporated into their lives from an early age.

Defining Behavior Disorders

The Individuals with Disabilities Education Act (IDEA) of 1990, PL 101-476, defines students as being "seriously emotionally disturbed" when any one of the following characteristics occurs over a long period of time, to a marked degree, and adversely affects educational performance:

- An inability to learn that cannot be explained by intellectual, sensory, or other health factors
- An inability to build or maintain satisfactory interpersonal relationships with peers and teachers
- Inappropriate types of behavior or feelings under normal circumstances
- A general pervasive mood of unhappiness or depression
- A tendency to develop physical symptoms or fears associated with personal or school problems (p. 44802)

In addition, the definition includes children who are schizophrenic but excludes those who are socially maladjusted unless they are also seriously emotionally disturbed (*Federal Register*, 1992).

Characteristics of Youth with Behavior Disorders

Young people with behavior disorders can be overwhelmed by the demands in the community and the workplace, making the transition from school to adulthood particularly difficult (Ford, 1995; Unger, 1995). These are not typical children who have periodic behavior problems at different points in their lives. Their problems (e.g., disruptive, withdrawn

behavior) tend to present themselves over the long term with significantly higher frequencies of occurrences than those seen in children without behavior disorders.

The most important aspect of the majority of these youth is their inability to control behavior, specifically impulses to do unusual or bizarre things. Reactions to anxious or stressful situations usually lead to behavior that is inappropriate and viewed negatively by peers or adults. Kortering and Elrod (1991) discuss the crucial role of social competence and citizenship that these students must learn.

> Educational programs must prepare students for social roles, for being good citizens and responsible adults who respect and understand others, their culture, ethics, and values. A first step toward such a goal is to provide the kinds of experiences that will help the student develop the level of competency necessary to secure a place in the social structure of school. To help students attain the required competency for participating in the school, programs would need to offer learning experiences that serve to facilitate engagement in school activities. It is indeed perplexing that during the adolescent years, when peer influence, dating, uncertainties about the future, and increasing independence are dominant themes in adolescent development (and opportunities to develop), social competency is often ignored or given a secondary role. For most students, the school is the most important institution in their lives, yet our programs make little, if any, effort to take advantage of this opportunity. While it is true that most schools do offer representations of social groups (e.g., athletic teams, social clubs, band), participation in these events is generally limited to those who already possess adequate social skills. (p. 151)

Many behaviors and actions are associated with behavior disorders. It is important to remember that these characteristics are not considered symptoms of a behavior disorder unless they occur frequently and for an extended period of time (i.e., are observable). Specifically, these behaviors include 1) frequent mood changes, severe depression, and/or strange mannerisms; 2) being highly distractible and lacking concentration abilities; 3) continuous withdrawal from others; 4) displaying annoying habits, such as talking to oneself or tapping feet repeatedly; 5) poor control of impulses, such as not thinking before acting; 6) blaming others for problems and refusing to consider changing habits; and 7) making inappropriate and irrelevant comments and jokes in class.

Young people with these behavior patterns become easily frustrated with the demands of school and the community. They exhibit resistance to authority and a desire to ignore discipline attempts. Teachers must develop confidence in these students and teach them how to succeed by developing vocational competence, community living skills, and independence. One way to improve these social skills is to develop leisure skills that are appropriate (see Chapter 9). Schloss et al. (1995) developed an excellent instructional program to teach students with mental retardation and behavior disorders functional sight words for use in community recreation settings. These words (e.g., SWIMMING) provide constructive alternatives to disruptive behavior—achievements that provide important foundations for better adjusted adult lives and more successful vocational outcomes (Bond, 1978; Bond & McDonnel, 1991). Vocational outcomes in integrated settings are extremely important aspects of these students' transition plans. As Fabian (1989, 1992) noted, work and quality of life are often inextricably entwined. One of the most widely known transition leaders in the United States, career educator and counselor Donn E. Brolin, is a leading advocate for vocational training.

Donn E. Brolin Dr. Donn E. Brolin is internationally recognized for his work in education including the creation of Life-Centered Career Education (LCCE). He was recipient of the Council for Exceptional Children's 1990 J.E. Wallace Wallin Award for outstanding contributions to the education of children with disabilities. He is a professor emeritus at the University of Missouri–Columbia in the Department of Educational and Counseling Psychology, where he has taught since 1975. He is an active lecturer, consultant, and director of in-service workshops on career development.

Since 1969, Dr. Brolin has led efforts to establish training programs in special education, rehabilitation services, and vocational assessment, and has initiated several federal and state grant projects on career and vocational education.

Dr. Brolin's 22 life-skill competencies, which serve as the focus for the LCCE curriculum, have become a foundation point of reference for professionals dealing with career education or transition education for people with disabilities. This curriculum includes many practical or functional activities, such as domestic skill training, travel, and other important community living skills. This curriculum is viewed as a classic by many teachers working with youth who have mild disabilities.

Integrated vocational training and placement are important for students with behavior disorders, who are often denied the opportunity to work because they are viewed as being too aberrant. Work can be very therapeutic in remediating many of the behavior problems that these students exhibit, but their negative behaviors limit their chances of participating in programs that could reverse the adverse cycles in which they function.

Unique Challenges of Youth with Behavior Disorders

Millions of children and youth experience significant psychological and behavior problems (Pullis, 1991). The National Institute of Mental Health (NIMH) reports that approximately 12% of children in the United States require mental health services. The Council for Exceptional Children's Council for Children with Behavior Disorders estimates that about half of these students need special education (Pullis, 1991): 5%–6% of the school population. Since 1976, however, the actual number of reported children with behavior disorders in the schools has never exceeded 1%. The most revealing evidence about the difficulties that these youth experience comes from the evaluations of drop-out data.

Approximately 50% of students with behavior disorders drop out of school (Pullis, 1991). Only 17% of students with behavior disorders attend postsecondary school programs as compared to almost 50% of students without disabilities (Knitzer, Steinberg, & Fleisch, 1990); only 40%–50% of students with behavior disorders are employed—a stark contrast to the 85% employment rate for the general population of adults and students.

One study conducted in the greater Houston, Texas, area indicated similar findings for people with behavior disorders (Hess, Kregel, & Wehman, 1991). Of 230 young people with disabilities, only 36.6% were employed full or part time, and 27% had never held a job. Only 4.9% of students with behavior disorders had received vocational training or em-

ployment services from the Texas Rehabilitation Commission. In those cases where students with behavior disorders were employed, 43% had gotten help from a parent, 29% found jobs on their own, 15% received help from a friend, and school personnel found jobs for 7%. No young people with behavior disorders had received direct help from a rehabilitation counselor.

This study also found that young people with behavior disorders were unlikely to work even in the summer. Only 14% worked full time in the summer and over 46% were not employed at all. During the school year, less than 5% of youth with behavior disorders were engaged in full-time employment. It also presented additional data that show that students with behavior disorders are spending too much time in the classroom, little time out of school in community-based training, and virtually no time in paid work experiences. If the supposition that work can be therapeutic for remediating behavior impairments and excesses is true, then the existing practices in many schools help to explain why post-21 outcomes for young people with behavior disorders are so poor.

Focus on Jobs

The first major challenge that educators and counselors must face in working with these students is helping them to obtain both paid and nonpaid work experiences while still in school. It is critical that they are not kept from work because of behavior problems but instead are supported at the jobsite with appropriate behavioral interventions.

Smith (1990), one of the leaders in providing supported employment for adults with autism and other severe behavior problems, has placed more than 55 people with behavior disorders in jobs. Her Rockville, Maryland, program demonstrates how people who engage in head banging, self-stimulatory behavior, screaming, and property destruction can work in competitive work environments if they are given job coach and/or teacher support and high-quality psychological/behavior management training.

Nonaversive Intervention

The second challenge educators and counselors face is providing humanistic, nonaversive behavior and psychological interventions in natural environments for young people with behavior disorders. Training in the community, instruction in the workplace, and teaching mobility within the community are essential elements for promoting transition. Often, however, designing and implementing behavior interventions in natural environments is preempted for training in controlled environments, such as classrooms or institutions.

Individualizing Curricula

A third challenge is individualizing curricula to meet the unique and specific psychological and education needs of students with behavior disorders. Teachers must be able to interface the psychological needs of each student with his or her educational and vocational needs, ideally with concrete instruction in real-life environments. Instead of trying to solve and eradicate the student's underlying problems, time is better spent developing an array of competent vocational and community skills, especially for those with autism, as the limited data on this population show. Regardless of disability, it is critical that teachers understand and follow this approach in transition planning.

Drop-Out Issues and Expulsion

Information is limited about students with behavior disorders and almost nonexistent for students who drop out (Frank, Sitlington, & Carson, 1991). Studies have found that, nationally, about 50% of students classified as having behavior disorders drop out of school before completing their programs. In a follow-up study interviewing 70 students who dropped out of school, most indicated personal problems as their reason for leaving. Another frequent response was a desire to quit school, and approximately 14% indicated that the school had recommended that they leave (Frank et al., 1991). When students' behaviors are so severe that they interfere with the operation of the school or school regulations are defied, schools will usually move to expel students (Katsiyannis & Prillaman, 1989). However, the courts have ordered that schools ensure that the rights of students are always respected (Yell, 1989, 1990, 1995).

Assessment for Transition

The philosophy of assessing the vocational and transition needs of youth with behavior disorders is similar to that of all students with disabilities. The focus must be on a community-referenced approach to assessment that specifically asks students about their career and vocational goals. Because of difficulties with the reliability of their responses, it is important to ask about career goals several times and, more important, to observe what their preferences seem to be. Figure 14.1 lists questions teachers and vocational counselors can ask students—their answers should be shared with parents or guardians. Positive vocational experiences can lead to positive adjustments in the transition process as job moti-

What jobs can you do now?

What jobs do you think you might like to do in 2 years?

What jobs do you think you might like to do in 10 years?

To do the jobs you want 2 years from now, what skills will you need to improve?

To do the jobs you want 10 years from now, what abilities will you need to improve?

What are your biggest problems with the jobs you can do now?

What problems do you have getting a job now?

What can you do about these problems?

Figure 14.1. A sample career planning questionnaire. (From Hammill, D., & Bartel, N. [1986]. *Teaching students with learning and behavior problems* [4th ed.]. Needham, MA: Allyn & Bacon; copyright © 1986 by Allyn & Bacon; reprinted by permission.)

vation and interest are key factors in job satisfaction, which can improve many negative behaviors.

After determining what each student's career and vocational interests are, teachers must also ascertain each students' community living, mobility, recreation, and personal goals. Assessing curriculum targets within these areas is the key to designing good secondary special education programs and effecting positive transitions. Without such an assessment, disgruntlement, boredom, and exacerbation of the students' problems are likely to occur, which often leads to suspension, expulsion, or dropping out.

After making a reliable determination of students' choices and needs, efforts should be channeled into vocational situational assessments. Situational assessments (i.e., the objective quantitative evaluation of student performance in different work experiences) are valuable for determining work responses under varied conditions. By varying the stress conditions of the work assessments and modifying the nature of commands and tasks, work performance data can be compiled and potential can be determined. Assessments include observations of students both in school and in the community at various worksites; on-the-job tryouts; classroom performance examples; tests to measure interests, aptitudes, or learning styles; and work samples (i.e., simulated tasks of particular jobs) (National Information Center for Children and Youth with Disabilities [NICHCY], 1990). Utilization of standardized vocational evaluation testing for this population, however, has not been promising except in unique circumstances such as determining aptitudes for computer, health care, and automotive repair occupations. Instead, real-life situational assessments yield more practical information.

Vocational assessments should help to obtain information about a student's aptitudes, interests, work habits, socialization skills, work attitudes, and work tolerance (Sarkees & Scott, 1985; West, Revell, & Wehman, 1992), and can also be used to help structure students' planning and preparation for further postsecondary training. Vocational assessments provide information in response to the following questions:

- Where is the student in the vocational awareness, exploration, or preparation process?
- In what occupational area does the student show the greatest interest?
- In what occupational area(s) does the student show aptitude and ability?
- Are there specific learning requirements that will need to be incorporated into a student's educational program to help him or her prepare for a particular occupation?

Behavior assessment can occur on worksites by using a very common procedure of defining the behavior, evaluating what happens before the behavior, and recording what happens after the behavior. Good behavior analysis can lead to strategies that will help the teacher in changing aberrant behavior (Smith, 1990).

Teaching for Transition

Too many teachers who work with youth with behavior disorders focus their curriculum and instructional efforts exclusively on academic skills, neglecting career and vocational education curriculum. The following list of units of instruction provides teachers with ideas for developing opportunities to participate in community activities:

- Financial and legal aspects of employment
- Attitudes and skills that may lead to promotion

- Job applications and interviews
- Requirements of different occupations
- Occupational interests
- Private and other employment agencies
- Managing time and activities
- Getting along with co-workers
- Dealing with frustration and failure at a job
- Identifying different sources of employment
- Understanding employer and supervisor expectations

Creative teachers turn these units into real-life experiences for students, using guest speakers, such as students who are working effectively in the community and panels of professionals. The optimal way to teach these skills, however, is through placement in paying jobs. Concrete actions and practices are particularly important for students with behavior disorders. These students are usually bright enough to determine whether an activity is real or "make believe." For example, a 3-day internship at a dry cleaning shop, where a teacher can help the student to manage his or her frustrations and develop work motivation, is far more useful to students than viewing filmstrips or overhead projections in the classroom. Students learn best when they receive repeated practice and reinforcement, especially in learning how to manage their own behavior. It is essential that teachers, job coach counselors, aides, volunteers and/or university students provide frequent on-site communication with employers and students.

 Economic self-sufficiency and greater independence in controlling personal finances should be tackled after the student is performing reasonably well in his or her job. Examples for lessons in this area include 1) managing money through budgeting, 2) learning how to use catalogs, 3) understanding costs of goods and services, 4) considering price versus quality factors when shopping, 5) understanding sales, 6) reading advertisements, 7) making simple home furnishing purchases, 8) caring for personal possessions, 9) understanding banking services, 10) understanding credit and bank loans, 11) understanding and selecting insurance, and 12) saving money—skills necessary for competent and well-adjusted transitions. Because many students with behavior disorders are not intellectually slow or delayed, they can acquire many of these skills. They must, however, be taught in a stimulating and creative fashion, with an emphasis on competence, not process. Worksheets, ditto sheets, blackboard work, and extensive bookwork will not elicit optimal learning from students with behavior disorders. Verbal instruction, modeling, ample feedback, and other reinforcements also enhance curriculum and instruction efforts.

Teaching Self-Control and Self-Management Strategies

The primary obstacle in the community transition process for youth with behavior disorders is developing self-control. According to Kazdin, "self-control refers to those behaviors and individual activities taken to achieve self-selected outcomes" (1975, p. 192). Self-control may include strategies such as self-observation and self-reinforcement and, if well-established, can effectively help youth with behavior disorders to resolve many of the problems and frustrations they face in the community or workplace, such as developing self-directed behaviors with minimal external supervision. Teaching self-control to youth

with behavior disorders is invaluable as it is the most typical and realistic goal for these students and it enables them to feel in control of their lives and choices.

Self-control training can take place in the community where the process of independent living presents many decision-making situations. Self-control may be required in the following activities: 1) maintaining a balanced diet, 2) staying on a regular work schedule, 3) washing and caring for clothes, 4) managing money, and 5) using discretion in choosing friends and deciding whom to trust. Situations that arise in public places where frustration tolerance may be low are perfect opportunities to practice self-control, such as riding crowded buses, waiting in lines, following directions, dealing with cab drivers, and interacting with hostile service clerks.

Self-management strategies can also be utilized in the workplace (Furlong, Jonikes, Cook, Hathaway, & Goode, 1994). For vocational adjustment, self-control should be used in task performance and social skills. Social behavior, such as the proper use of breaktime, being prompt, and giving appropriate social greetings, can be incorporated into curriculum objectives. It may also be appropriate to allow students to determine their own work criteria in conjunction with their employer and then self-administer some form of reinforcement. Frequent self-reinforcement for gradually doing more work shapes improved performance.

Modeling is one means of teaching self-control behaviors. Another strategy for teaching self-control is role-playing, which can be used in group counseling sessions or one-to-one sessions. A third approach is social reinforcement, which is appropriate for the student who already engages in independent decision making and self-direction. As in shaping any new behavior, reinforcement should be given quite often initially and then gradually limited as the student becomes more confident in development of self-control.

Reid and Harris (1993) conducted a study that looked at the self-monitoring of attention versus the self-monitoring of performance with students who have learning and behavior disabilities. Learning self-regulation is very important for students who lack impulse control. The specific steps for teaching self-regulation vary somewhat but generally include the following (Alberto & Troutman, 1982; Cooper & Mank, 1987; Worlery et al., 1988):

1. Identify the target behavior
2. Define the behavior
3. Develop the data collection system
4. Teach the student how to use the self-management system
5. Implement the system
6. Evaluate the effectiveness of the system

Instruction should include a rationale for students to engage in the behavior change program, teacher modeling of the procedure, and structured practice and feedback as students use the procedure. Carr and Punzo (1993) have shown that self-monitoring can have a positive impact on academic accuracy and productivity in students with behavior disorders.

Self-control strategies are not always as easy to develop and implement as strategies in which the teacher assumes total control over the student. They have major positive consequences for teaching long-term independence and interdependence with other people in the community; however, students with behavior disorders must learn self-management strategies at early ages so that they will be prepared to move into more complex and challenging community environments.

Various Components of Self-Management In the early 1970s, researchers first began to differentiate the various components of self-management. Among the components identified as frequently used in employment settings are self-recording, self-monitoring, functional assessment, self-instruction, and self-reinforcement.

Self-recording simply refers to the use of conventional observation and data collection strategies to measure one's behavior. For example, an individual attempting to meet a production standard of eight units per hour might simply record each unit as it is completed. Sowers and Powers (1995) used self-recording in conjunction with picture cues to teach 13 vocational tasks to a group of adolescents with developmental disabilities. After pictures of individual tasks were presented in a photo album sheet to prompt independent performance, self-recording was used to check off each task picture as completed. Students quickly learned to use the picture sequencing and recording procedures to independently sequence and complete tasks. Performance was maintained after the physical presence of the investigator was removed from the jobsite.

Self-monitoring is similar to self-recording, except that the individual generally compares his or her performance to some predetermined standard. Ackerman and Shapiro (1984) used self-monitoring to maintain productivity increases in the vocational performance of individuals with mental retardation. Productivity was initially increased through goal setting and verbal praise. Subjects were then taught to record their daily work rates and compare the rate to a standard. The self-monitoring procedure was successful in maintaining higher work rates, even when verbal praise was no longer provided. Some professionals suggest using videotapes in classrooms to help students develop and monitor their own behavior control program. The advantage of an "instant replay" is particularly valuable with these students.

Functional assessment involves an examination of the events, antecedents, and consequences of the target behavior to determine the controlling stimuli and the function of the behavior itself. For example, Eric, an individual who worked as a stock clerk in a large department store, indicated that he was having a problem getting along with his co-workers. After agreeing to participate in a self-management plan, he was first taught to keep simple Antecedent–Behavior–Consequence records of his interactions with co-workers. While examining his data with his employment specialist, he discovered that he most frequently had arguments with co-workers when he felt he was under pressure to meet a deadline established by his supervisor. Furthermore, Eric discovered that after arguments occurred, his co-workers tended to ignore him and not help him with his tasks, making it less likely that he would meet his supervisor's deadlines. Eric and his employment specialist were able to use this information to design a self-management plan that involved self-recording and self-reinforcement and focused not only on his interactions with co-workers, but also on his ability to meet performance deadlines and request the assistance of his co-workers.

Self-instruction refers to a number of self-management program strategies in which the individual delivers a visual or auditory prompt that sets the occasion for the targeted behavior to occur (Hughes, 1992). For example, Rusch and his colleagues (1994) used self-instruction to promote on-task performance of two food service workers. Prior to intervention, both individuals were reported at risk of job termination as a result of an inability to perform three tasks to employer standards. Both workers were taught to provide a self-

instructional set in which they asked questions about the task to be performed, answered the questions (cognitive rehearsal), and then guided their own performance by verbalizing specific self-instructional prompts. In the Rusch et al. study, the individuals were able to learn the procedures quickly and maintain them after training. The package had the further effect of markedly improving the individuals' on-task behavior.

Other investigators have attempted to simplify the traditional self-instructional paradigm for use with individuals with significant cognitive disabilities. Referred to as *self-labeling*, the procedure emphasizes only the verbalization of the specific self-instructional prompts and eliminates the more complex cognitive rehearsal components. Agran, Moore, Fodor-Davis, and Deer (1989) combined picture cues with self-generated verbal prompts to teach instruction-following skills to a group of adolescents with severe disabilities participating in a vocational skills training program. Shafer (1986) used verbal labeling to address the poor work skills displayed by two supported employment participants. The first individual, employed to clean doorways and escalators in a shopping mall, utilized a self-labeling procedure in which he verbalized the most critical components of the task. The procedure dramatically improved and helped him maintain the quality of his work. For a second worker employed as a porter in a large interstate truck stop, the verbal labeling procedure did not significantly improve his performance on the work task of cleaning shower stalls. A supervisor-mediated feedback procedure was then introduced to produce moderate improvements in his performance.

Self-reinforcement techniques consist of individuals delivering reinforcers to themselves contingent on the performance (or absence) of particular target behaviors. While applying self-reinforcement, the individual must be taught to evaluate him- or herself and determine whether the criterion for self-reinforcement has been met. In vocational settings, self-reinforcement is frequently used to address both production and behavior problems. For example, a motel maid assigned to clean 16 rooms might reward herself on a fixed ratio schedule with a 10-minute break after completing sets of four rooms. Other individuals may reward themselves with compact discs, meals in restaurants, or other activities after arriving at work on time for a prescribed number of days.

Designing Self-Management Programs Smith (1993) provides some useful guidelines for use in designing self-management programs. First, the individual should be involved in setting the goal of the program. The goal must be practical and attainable. If an individual is not committed to the goal of the program or does not feel a need to change his or her behavior, the likelihood of successfully designing and implementing a self-management plan is minimal. Second, when designing self-management programs, it is important to remember that all the principles of behavior management apply to self-management programs as well. Principles such as reinforcement schedules, fading, maintenance, and generalization must all be considered and addressed in the design and implementation of the program. Third, it is not necessary to design a plan entirely by oneself in order to be considered a behavior management program. In vocational settings, employment specialists, rehabilitation counselors, employers, and family members may all assist the individual with a disability to develop a plan appropriate to a particular situation. To be effective, however, the designers should be competent in the development of behavior management programs and involve the individual who will be implementing the program.

Teaching Social Skills

Most students with behavior disorders lack social skills. Teachers working with these youth must teach these skills in addition to academic and vocational skills. Social skills should be taught in a variety of community settings as well as in inclusive high schools in interactions with peers without disabilities. Table 14.1 gives tips for inclusion that can be infused into the curriculum resources below.

There are a number of curriculum packets for social skills instruction. An extremely popular program—called the ACCEPTS Program (Walker et al., 1983)—uses scripted lessons and a videotape that emphasizes proper social interactions, making new friends, and getting along with others, particularly in mainstream general education settings.

Another program—called Think Aloud—is a social problem-solving program created for elementary school students, but it has merit at the middle and secondary school levels as well. This program is especially beneficial for students who lack self-control in social situations and have shown themselves to be aggressive.

A third program—called Skill Streaming—uses a structured learning approach for teachers engaged in modeling, role playing, and direct feedback (Goldstein, Sprafkin, Gershew, & Cline, 1980). Content areas include dealing with feelings while managing aggression, alleviating stress, and planning.

A number of other social skills curricula are also appropriate for students with behavior disorders; unfortunately, virtually none of these provide for social skills assessment and instruction in the workplace.

Individualized Transition Planning

The Job Club for Youth with Behavior Disorders

Although it is agreed that most students with behavior disorders require structure, assistance, and specific help in finding employment, there is little consensus on how to provide this support. Traditional methods of vocational education, prevocational training, sheltered work, and other modes of vocational education are not always successful for students with behavior disorders. In addition to being at risk for unemployment, these young people are vulnerable to breaking laws in the community. No amount of appropriate curricula or self-control strategies will lead to employment unless other more proactive vocational efforts are taken on behalf of these young people.

The job club approach has merit for youth and adults with behavior disorders. Pioneered in 1979 by Azrin and Besalel, the job club model employs a very structured behavioral focus for vocational counseling and continues to be a popular way of helping people with behavior problems gain employment (Ford, Oswald, & Dineen, 1995). The teacher or counselor responsible for leading the club identifies concrete behavioral components that are critical links to job placement. The goal of the job club counseling method is to obtain jobs of the highest feasible quality in the shortest possible time for all participating students. This approach is distinctive because each procedure in the behavioral sequence is used consistently with every job seeker. Some of the procedures of the job club strategy follow:

Table 14.1. Tips for inclusion of youth with behavior disorders

Instructional strategy	Description	Advantages	Disadvantages
Modeling	Exposing target student to display prosocial behavior	Easy to implement	Not sufficient if used alone
Strategic placement	Placing target student in situations with other students who display prosocial behaviors	Employs peers as change agents, facilitates generalization, is cost effective	Research data inconclusive when used alone
Instruction	Telling students how and why they should behave a certain way and/or giving rules for behavior	Overemphasizes norms/expectations	Not sufficient if used alone
Correspondence training	Positively reinforcing students for accurate reports regarding their behavior	Facilitates maintenance and generalization of training, is cost effective	Very little documentation of effectiveness
Rehearsal and practice	Structured practice of specific prosocial behavior	Enhances skill acquisition	Not sufficient to change behavior if used alone
Positive reinforcement or shaping	Prosocial behaviors or approximations followed by a reward or favorable event	Strong research support for effectiveness	Maintenance after treatment termination is not predictable
Prompting and coaching	Providing students with additional stimuli/prompts that elicit the prosocial behavior	Particularly effective after acquisition to enhance transfer to natural settings	Maintenance after treatment termination is not predictable
Positive practice	A consequence strategy in which student repeatedly practices correct behavior	May produce immediate increases in prosocial behavior	Long-term effectiveness not documented; less restrictive approaches should be used first
Multimethod training packages	Multicomponent instructional package that incorporates several behavioral techniques	Greater treatment strength and durability, applicable to a range of children and settings	

From Carter, J., & Sugai, G. (1989). Social skills curriculum analysis. *Teaching Exceptional Children, 22,* 38. Copyright 1989 by the Council for Exceptional Children; reprinted by permission.

- Friends, relatives, and acquaintances may be sources for job leads.
- Standard scripts and forms should be used by all job seekers.
- Group support is provided by other job seekers in the club.
- A buddy system encourages the participants.
- Unpublicized jobs should be sought through family and friends.
- One job lead often uncovers another.
- Personal and social skills are emphasized.

- Résumés are developed for each job seeker.
- Each job seeker undergoes interview training.
- An interview checklist is established for key interview skills.

These 10 items are only part of the overall process, which has more than 20 components that are taught by the leader and reinforced by other club members. A major strength of this approach is the singular focus on job identification and placement. Too many vocational education activities focus on getting people ready for placements but do not provide the necessary follow-through for placements to occur. The job club approach provides a daily or weekly schedule of activities for structured job seeking and job placement. Issues, such as the number of students in a job club, the focus of job searches, and optimal ways for teaching the strategy components, are flexible and limited only by the leader's creativity.

Participation in a job club should begin no later than a student's 16th birthday—the age at which most students drop out of school. As Azrin and Besalel (1979) indicate, once students are successful in attaining some level of employment within the club, others become motivated. Many of the self-management and self-control strategies described in this chapter are appropriate for the job club approach. Furthermore, this approach does not foreclose the use of job coaches, mentors, or volunteers who could help with initial transition employment support. In designing and implementing individualized transition plans (ITPs) for students with behavior disorders, a highly practical, community-based approach is ideal for attaining transition goals established in the plans. The job club approach and similar forms of group counseling have all of the necessary characteristics for helping students with behavior disorders to make successful transitions into the workplace. However, the job club approach could be enhanced by involving youth of without disabilities. In particular, the buddy system could be strengthened and the additional pool of families and acquaintances could add to the job lead repertoire.

Job Possibilities for Youth with Behavior Disorders

Students with behavior disorders are capable of working in a variety of jobs with help, training, and support (Smith et al., 1995). It is very important to focus on training constructive and productive work activity with these students as unstructured or empty time usually leads to inappropriate behavior. There are several industries in which these workers have done especially well (see Table 14.2), providing tasks that teachers should look for in forming functional curriculum.

Manufacturing Jobs

Workers with behavior disorders can work in a variety of jobs in the manufacturing field. They can assemble computer cables, air conditioning parts, electronic parts, venetian blinds, fuses, and dental supplies. They can also perform other manufacturing duties, such as lamination, rolling and labeling posters, and enlarging and copying microfiche. Manufacturing jobs typically have the advantages of providing spacious—sometimes isolated—work spaces, requiring little or no language, requiring little or no social skills, providing well-established routines, and involving repetitive jobs.

Table 14.2. Jobs for people with behavior disorders

Computer cable assembler

Job description This job involves assembly line production of computer cables according to consumer specification.

Worksite description This is a medium-size company that manufactures and installs computer cables and connections; the company employs about 15 workers to assemble cables.

Job tasks • Measure and cut cable according to specifications.
 • Strip the ends of each cable with a razor blade.
 • Operate a crimping machine.
 • Place pins in the connection by matching a numbered slot to a colored wire.
 • Assemble hood over connection.
 • Label cable for length and assembler initials.
 • Test cable using a volt meter.

Equipment, machinery, and hand tools needed to complete job tasks
 • Hand-operated cable measurement device
 • Hydraulic crimping machine
 • Volt meter
 • Razor blade

Receiving clerk/stock clerk

Job description This job involves working in the stockroom, preparing price tags, and pricing merchandise.

Worksite description This job is with a large catalog discount store, which is part of a chain; the store employs approximately 30 workers, including one employee with autism.

Job tasks • Make price tags.
 • Open boxes of merchandise.
 • Apply price tags to merchandise and repack boxes.
 • Price merchandise using a hand gun.
 • Pull up computer printouts of orders.
 • Fill orders by locating merchandise in stockroom.
 • Stock shelves with merchandise.

Equipment, machinery, and tools needed to complete job tasks
 • Order forms
 • Map used to locate items in warehouse
 • Pricing gun

Warehouse worker

Job description This job involves managing inventory for a lighting fixture warehouse.

Worksite description The job is with a division of a large corporation that distributes lighting fixtures to retail stores; there are approximately 100 workers in the warehouse, 4 of whom work in the same area as the 2 with autism.

Job tasks • Pull ordered items from shelves.
 • Pack items for shipping.
 • Price items.
 • Restock shelves.
 • Sweep and clean.
 • Assemble wheelbarrows and other items.

Equipment, machinery, and hand tools needed to complete job tasks
 • Boxes
 • Tape gun
 • Box labels
 • Pricing gun
 • Screwdrivers
 • Hammers

(continued)

Table 14.2. *(continued)*

Bindery worker

Job description	This job involves completing various steps in the assembly of books, booklets, pamphlets, and other printed matter.
Worksite description	This job is with a medium-size, family-owned printing company; there are 16 rooms in the company, 4 of which are used by employees. There are approximately 40 workers in the company—2 with autism who work with 4–8 other employees in the bindery performing similar jobs.

Job tasks
- Separate and pack books from the printer.
- Collate inserts into brochures.
- Punch holes in book covers.
- Bind booklets.
- Wrap books in plastic using a shrink-wrap machine.
- Keep inventory of completed work.
- Retrieve materials from storage.
- Assemble cardboard boxes.
- Sweep work area.

Equipment, machinery, and hand tools needed to complete job tasks
- Binding punch
- Tape gun
- Tape dispenser
- Jacks
- Binding machine
- Carts and skids for moving materials
- Razor blades and scissors
- Shrink-wrap machine

From Smith, M.D., Belcher, R.G., & Juhrs, P.D. (1995). *A guide to successful employment for individuals with autism* (pp. 110, 141, 179, 228). Baltimore: Paul H. Brookes Publishing Co.; reprinted by permission.

Retail Jobs

Workers with behavior disorders can be employed in various retail settings including clothing stores, toy stores, hardware stores, housewares stores, department stores, and drug stores. Job duties have involved stocking and restocking shelves, straightening displays, tagging merchandise, filling orders, retrieving merchandise from the stock room, sorting merchandise, collecting damaged items, peeling stickers from incorrectly priced items, and organizing merchandise. Retail jobs can be found that require minimal or no interaction with public, so that emphasis on language or social skills competencies is not needed.

Delivery Jobs

Delivery jobs have the advantages of being out-of-doors and requiring a great deal of walking. Some individuals with autism enjoy pacing and walking, and these jobs may be good

sources of employment. They typically require no spoken language, few social skills, and no fine motor skills. If behavior problems do occur or if productivity slows for some reason, there is no disruption to co-workers, because these are relatively solitary jobs. People with behavior disorders have been successfully hired by companies to prepare items for delivery and to deliver the items to residents in the community such as advertisements for pizza delivery services and newspapers.

Jobs in Warehousing and Distribution

Workers with behavior disorders can work in numerous warehouses and distribution centers. Warehouse jobs include a variety of tasks, such as cleaning rental glassware, folding rental party linens, packaging items for display in vending machines, filling orders for music tapes and compact discs, filling orders for electronic parts, and doing inventory. These jobs allow students to focus on specific work tasks and not become emotionally involved in a negative fashion.

Jobs in Printing

Typically, jobs in printing companies are held by workers with spoken language, although there have been some exceptions. Work in printing companies often involves limited interaction with the public, and tasks are often done alone, in an assembly-line fashion in spacious work areas with a high background noise level. Printing is a business that is becoming computer based, which people with behavior disorders can learn to operate. Although there might be a variety of job tasks for the worker to learn, each task is usually done in the same way each time, according to rigid routines. Work is usually precise and requires good visual motor and fine motor skills.

Charles *Charles is a 16-year-old sophomore who was classified as having a behavior disorder in the first grade. Since then, he has been placed in a variety of different classrooms. Charles also has a mild case of cerebral palsy (CP) that affects his right arm; subsequently, he is left-handed and his writing is very difficult to read. Charles's CP is due to a birth trauma for which his parents sued the doctor and were awarded a structured settlement that will provide for Charles into adulthood. Charles is socially isolated by choice. His hygiene and manners are very haphazard, and he tends to behave in a very unsocialized manner. When Charles is acclimated to being around people, he can be articulate and sensitive.*

Charles has been evaluated by the local rehabilitation center and has a strong need for a good vocational training program. His parents are investigating fiduciary management for their son, but know his social, hygiene, educational, and vocational needs are paramount for his success as an adult.

On pages 410–413 is a detailed outline of the ITP that Charles, his family, friends, and the school team developed. Note the interest in working within the computer industry.

Description of Student's Future Vision

Charles needs and wants to make new friends. His hope is to improve his living situation so that he can eventually have a good roommate(s) for a friend. Charles aspires to a career in the computer industry.

Individualized Transition Plan

Student's Name _Charles_

Birthdate _____

Student's Identification Number _____

Participants:

Name	Position
Charles	_Student_
Family	_Mother_
David	_Teacher_
Kendall	_Vocational rehabilitation (VR) counselor_
Juan	_MR service coordinator_

School _Miranda High School_

ITP Conference Date _____

Career and Economic Self-Sufficiency

Employment Goal *Charles will work competitively in the computer industry.*

Level of present performance: *Vocational evaluation suggests that Charles shows an aptitude for skill in this area.*

Steps needed to accomplish goal: *1. Charles will take the education for employment course. 2. He will develop computer literacy by performing different computer strands of work. 3. He will be evaluated at local vocational center (VoTech) in the computer track.*

Date of completion: *June 1995*

Person(s) responsible for implementation: *Teacher, family, Charles, VoTech staff, and service coordinator*

Vocational Education/Training Goal *Charles will receive vocational training in a computer job at the local government building.*

Level of present performance: *Charles is minimally computer literate but is extremely interested in developing this area; he will continue high school toward a regular diploma.*

Steps needed to accomplish goal: *1. Charles will be placed in a worksite at the government building. 2. He will receive training from a co-worker mentor.*

Date of completion: *June 1995*

Person(s) responsible for implementation: *Charles, guidance counselor, and mentor*

From Wehman, P. (1995). *Individual transition plans: The teachers curriculum guide for helping youth with special needs.* Austin, TX: PRO-ED; reprinted by permission.

Postsecondary Education Goal *N/A at this time*

Level of present performance:

Steps needed to accomplish goal:

Date of completion:

Person(s) responsible for implementation:

Financial/Income Needs Goal *Charles will receive funds through a structured settlement; needs fiduciary advisement to be arranged for him.*

Level of present performance: *Charles is covered under his parents' health plan but will need his own after he turns 18 or after school ends.*

Steps needed to accomplish goal: *1. Parents will begin reviewing Charles's needs with legal advisers. 2. They will contract with one to start a financial conservatorship for Charles. 3. They will train Charles in long-term planning.*

Date of completion: *June 1995*

Person(s) responsible for implementation: *Parents, Charles, and legal advisers*

Career and Economic Self-Sufficiency

Independent Living Goal *Charles will live independently or with roommate, life partner, or spouse.*

Level of present performance: *Charles does very little for himself at home and will need training to achieve this goal.*

Steps needed to accomplish goal: *1. Charles will take creative living to begin to learn basic self-help skills. 2. Mother will work at home to teach Charles skills. 3. Charles will enroll in Center for Independent Living Program on weekends.*

Date of completion: *June 1995*

Person(s) responsible for implementation: *Charles, mother, service coordinator, and guidance counselor*

Transportation/Mobility Goal *Charles's parents are deferring Charles's involvement at this time and will continue to provide transportation.*

Level of present performance: *Charles's parents wish to wait until he is more trustworthy for a driver's license.*

Steps needed to accomplish goal:

Date of completion:

Person(s) responsible for implementation:

Social Relationships Goal *Charles will engage in more social activities and make two new friends.*

Level of present performance: *Charles has few friends and doesn't try to involve himself in activities; he can be difficult to get along with.*

Steps needed to accomplish goal: *Charles will join a club during the 1994-1995 school year.*

Date of completion: *June 1995*

Person(s) responsible for implementation: *Charles, parents, and physical therapist*

Recreation/Leisure Goal *Charles will get involved with a recreational activity of his choosing.*

Level of present performance: *Charles does not get out much and his physical therapist is working with him to develop an interest.*

Steps needed to accomplish goal: *Charles will work with his physical therapist and do a physical activity, hobby, or sport to increase his physical activity.*

Date of completion: *June 1995*

Person(s) responsible for implementation: *Charles, parents, and physical therapist*

Personal Competence

Health/Safety Goal *Charles will improve his personal hygiene.*

Level of present performance: *Charles's personal hygiene is inadequate.*

Steps needed to accomplish goal: *1. Charles will work with his service coordinator and guidance counselor to increase his awareness of his personal hygiene. 2. His parents will reinforce this awareness at home.*

Date of completion: *June 1995*

Person(s) responsible for implementation: *Charles, parents, service coordinator, and guidance counselor*

Self-Advocacy/Future Planning *Charles will require service coordination and possibly conservatorship in his adult life.*

Level of present performance: *Charles is generally cared for by his parents. He is an only child and at this point very reliant on his parents.*

Steps needed to accomplish goal: *1. Charles and his parents will explore self-advocacy and create experiences to allow Charles to begin to initiate some self-determined activities geared toward adult living. 2. They will also initiate a referral for developing disability services.*

Date of completion: *June 1995*

Person(s) responsible for implementation: *Charles, parents, service coordinator, and developmental disability counselor*

Student Career Preference

Employment in computer industry

Student's Major Transition Needs

1. Employment
2. Residential services
3. Transportation
4. Financial management
5. Social relationships

Additional Notes

Evaluation of Transition Outcomes for
Students with Behavior Disorders

Before examining specific variables that should be considered by educators and counselors for transition outcome evaluation, it may be helpful to mention one of the largest studies conducted with adults with psychiatric impairment. In 1991, MacDonald-Wilson, Revell, Nguyen, and Peterson reported supported employment outcomes for 212 people with a primary psychiatric disability and 1,588 people with a nonpsychiatric primary disability. Results from this study were organized into areas such as 1) service patterns through analysis of types of job coach intervention; and 2) outcomes from supported employment services, such as wages earned and hours worked. The results indicated that people with psychiatric disabilities consistently earn higher wages across a variety of service models than individuals in the other group. Differences between the two populations were also found in types of jobs, job retention, and reasons for separation from employment. Over 88% of people with psychiatric impairments indicated having moderate-to-frequent integration with workers without disabilities. The total mean average job coach time for this group over 52 weeks was 95.5 hours, while the nonpsychiatric impairment group averaged 177.6 mean hours. Both groups primarily performed food service and janitorial work; 20% were in stock clerk warehouse work and 13% performed clerical and office work.

Job retention of people with psychiatric impairments was considerably worse than those with other disabilities and nonpsychiatric impairments. After 12 months, even with use of a job coach, only 36% retained their first jobs, while over 50% of the nonpsychiatric population was still at work. Most notable is that the majority of reported job coach time for the psychiatric population is administered at the jobsite, which is contrary to popular assumptions. However, more emphasis is placed on advocating for the supported worker with supervisors, co-workers, and customers, and less time is spent with the individual worker in training as compared to the nonpsychiatric population.

This study provides an important baseline to determine the type of outcomes that should be targeted for young people with behavior disorders. Very few individuals in this study came from inclusive schools and had previous work experience in integrated employment. For most of these people, this was their first job, which supports the post-21 follow-up data, most of which supports the notion that paid work and work experience are important precursors of stable competitive employment (Peraino, 1992).

Supported Employment Outcomes for
Individuals with Behavior Disorders

A number of descriptive articles have focused on modifications to the supported employment model for individuals with behavior disorders (Anthony & Blanch, 1987; Bond, 1987; MacDonald-Wilson, Mancuso, Danley, & Anthony, 1989; Trotter, Minkoff, Harrison, & Hoops, 1988). Those modifications include 1) a greater emphasis on personal job values in identifying jobs, 2) a longer preemployment phase to choose a job, 3) a greater variety of job types, 4) an emphasis on careers and advancement, 5) a greater emphasis on educating employers and co-workers, and 6) an emphasis on support services away from the job.

More extensive data have revealed additional ways to significantly influence employ-

ment services for individuals with severe psychiatric impairments. After studying numerous types of work programs, Bond, Dietzen, Vogler, et al. (1995) reported that supported employment was most cost-effective for individuals with long-term mental illness. Gervey, Parrish, and Bond (1995) surveyed 12 exemplary supported employment programs for people with psychiatric disabilities and found excellent performance rates once service coordination modifications were made to the job coaching process—results that parallel those of Becker and Drake (1994); Bond, Dietzen, McGrew, and Miller (1995); Cook and Rosenberg (1994); Drake et al. (1994); and Drake, Becker, Xie, and Anthony (1995). The research by these leading investigators suggests the following[1]:

> The field of vocational rehabilitation for people with psychiatric disabilities is characterized by tremendous potential. Yet the growth of new approaches has heretofore been hindered by a lack of valid reliable knowledge about effective rehabilitation practices and how to encourage them. The most recent research offers many promising and suggestive avenues to program development. (Cook & Pickett, 1994, p. 10)

As educators, guidance counselors, and rehabilitation counselors work together to determine how to evaluate outcomes appropriately, several variables should be considered. First, does the student have a job? Having a job in which one works a minimum of 15 hours per week, receives at least minimum wage, and learns how to get along with co-workers should be a priority of any transition evaluation checklist. Second, what is the student's self-esteem, confidence, and happiness level? Does he or she seem excited and motivated about the prospect of coming to school, participating in community-based training, and having a job? If not, then activities, such as teaching self-management and exposing students to the positive consequences of work, can be very beneficial. Third, what level of behavior is the student exhibiting daily? Are there periodic outbursts of frustration or frequent unpredictable and explosive outbursts? Clearly, the likelihood of a satisfactory level of confidence and self-esteem should be influential in reducing these types of negative behaviors. A fourth form of transition evaluation is examining how many important community living skills the student gains competence in over a 1-year span.

Teachers cannot identify behaviors to evaluate without a clear sense of what must be targeted for intervention and change. Therefore, at the beginning of the school year, these items must be compiled as goals for intervention and adjusted throughout the year as necessary. Given the volatility and unpredictability of a number of students with behavior disorders, however, it may take much longer to determine the effectiveness of a given program (e.g., the job club) and make the necessary modifications.

Conclusion

Work experience, paid work, and high levels of activity at community-based instruction sites are very important vehicles for improving the quality of behavior in students with be-

[1]This rapidly growing body of outstanding research has given validity to a superb text by Ford (1995) on designing employment programs for people with long-term mental illness. In this text, Ford provides a blueprint for performing effective supported employment outcomes, emphasizing the important integration of psychotherapeutic supports with practical behavioral supports in the workplace.

havior disorders. New skills and activities are being generated that are providing important ways to reduce aberrant behavior therapeutically in this population, regardless of the level of behavior disorder, emotional disturbance, or autism. The use of self-management, self-control, self-reinforcement, and self-observation strategies are underutilized by educators. Students with behavior disorders must feel that they have control over their environments and help to choose what they want to do. They need choices as well as explicit structure. An activity, such as a job club, can be a useful means of structuring a student with a functional and meaningful purpose. There are a number of important behaviors associated with job seeking and employment—travel, training, use of money, banking, and social and personal skills at the jobsite—that are important curriculum material for teachers who are responsive to individual transition needs.

14

Study Questions

1. What are five possible indicators (i.e., behavioral manifestations) that a student may have an emotional or behavior disorder?

2. What are three possible causes of emotional or behavior disorders?

3. What three conditions must be met for a student with unusual or difficult behaviors to receive an *educational diagnosis* of emotional or behavior disorder?

4. Approximately what percentage of school children have emotional or behavior disorders?

5. What is the approximate drop-out rate for students with emotional and behavior disorders, and what are some reasons these students leave school early?

6. How do students with emotional and behavior disorders fare after leaving school in terms of employment, postsecondary education, and social engagement?

7. What is self-regulation, and what are the six steps for teaching self-regulation to students with emotional and behavior disorders?

8. Describe five strategies for teaching behavioral self-management to students with emotional and behavior disorders.

15

Applications for Youth with Orthopedic and Other Health Impairments

Michael D. West, Melinda Mast, Ronne Cosel, and Mike Cosel

Upon completion of this chapter, the reader will be able to do the following:

- List five orthopedic and five health impairments
- Understand potential implications of orthopedic and other health impairments on transition planning in functional areas
- Describe three potential postschool employment or educational environments and the implications of each for transition planning
- Describe at least four strategies for adapting or supporting work tasks or work-related activities of students with orthopedic or other health impairments
- Know how to develop an evaluation plan for transition services for youth with orthopedic and other health impairments

Since the 1970s, adult services providers and education organizations serving people with disabilities have attempted to design programs around certain values, among them integration in a variety of community settings and activities, normalized lifestyles, enhanced quality of life, productive employment with meaningful wages, and, most recently, choice and empowerment. Among education personnel, there has been increased awareness of the need to prepare youth with disabilities for the same goals as youth without disabilities:

to live, work, and participate in recreation as independently as possible in their home communities after leaving school. Individualized transition plans (ITPs) have been the primary vehicle for this preparation (Wilcox & Bellamy, 1982).

Despite a proliferation of theoretical models and research efforts in transition services, the vocational preparation and employment outlook for youth with disabilities exiting school programs have improved little over the years, and youth with orthopedic and other health impairments are not exceptions. As evidence, data from the National Longitudinal Transition Study (NLTS) of Special Education Students are presented in Table 15.1. The NTLS was contracted by the U.S. Department of Education, Office of Special Education Programs (OSEP), and conducted by SRI International in 1987 with follow-up data collected in 1990. The NLTS collected information on education programs and postschool outcomes for a nationally representative sample of more than 8,000 students with disabilities. Table 15.1 shows the generally poor involvement of students in various vocational activities within 2 years from school exit and 3–5 years from exit. In contrast, 59.1% and 69.4% of a cohort of youth without disabilities were employed competitively at the 2-year and 3- to 5-year milestones, respectively.

Moreover, despite a body of research indicating that involvement in vocational training and work experience in secondary programs enhances students' employment outlook as adults (Hasazi, Gordon, & Roe, 1985; Hasazi, Johnson, Hasazi, & Gordon, 1989; Mithaug, Horiuchi, & Fanning, 1985; Schalock et al., 1986), few students with orthopedic or other health impairments were found to be involved in school- or community-based work experience programs, occupationally based vocational education, vocational counseling, career development, job training, job placement assistance, or other vocational activities during or after secondary education. Furthermore, contact between the school and adult services agencies was minimal for the majority of these students (Valdes, Williamson, & Wagner, 1990). For the majority of secondary students with orthopedic and other health impairments, and for students with disabilities as a group, transition planning and implementation continue to lag far behind generally accepted "recommended practices."

This chapter discusses issues and guidelines related to school-to-work transitions and postsecondary education for youth with orthopedic and other health impairments presenting examples of the transition process in action.

Behavior and Learning Characteristics
of Youth with Orthopedic and Other Health Impairments

By statutory definition, orthopedic impairments are severe physical or motor disabilities caused by disease, trauma (excluding brain trauma, which is a distinct educational classification [see Chapter 16]), or congenital anomalies, which adversely affect a student's educational performance. Other health impairments are acute or chronic health problems that limit a student's strength, vitality, or alertness. Some common orthopedic and health impairments are listed in Table 15.2, although not all students with any of these types of problems are automatically considered to have educational disabilities. The determination of disability depends upon the degree to which the impairment affects learning or performance.

In the education literature, students with orthopedic and other health impairments

Table 15.1. Competitive employment rates following school exit for youth with orthopedic and other health impairments

	Orthopedic impairments (%)	Other health impairments (%)
Within 2 years of school exit		
Employed part time	15.2	18.3
Employed full time	5.0	14.8
Not competitively employed	79.8	66.9
Three to five years following school exit		
Employed part time	10.8	13.3
Employed full time	10.9	26.5
Not competitively employed	78.3	60.2

Source: Wagner, Blackorby, Cameto, Hebbeler, & Newman (1993).

are frequently considered together because the physical manifestations and educational implications of their disabilities tend to be similar. These manifestations frequently include impaired movement and mobility, fatigue, tendencies for injury and illness, and secondary visual or auditory impairments (Umbreit, 1983). Because many types of orthopedic and health impairments can be caused by or result in damage to the brain (e.g., anoxia, fever, infection, trauma), these students may also experience difficulties in learning, visual-motor perception, auditory perception, and receptive and expressive communication (Umbreit, 1983). In addition, these students are at risk for problems with self-esteem, social maturity, and emotional or behavioral adjustment (Bywater, 1984; Gortmaker, Walker, Weitzman, & Sobol, 1990; Magill & Hurlbut, 1986; Whitt, 1983).

Unique Challenges Presented by Youth with Orthopedic and Other Health Impairments

Students with orthopedic and other health impairments present many unique challenges for transition planning teams and the transition process. Two major challenges for these students are 1) the need for personal assistance services in postschool environments, and 2) the need for assistive technology and rehabilitation engineering in postschool environments. In addition, student self-advocacy is necessary for an effective transition.

Personal Assistance Services and Transition

Personal assistance services are broadly defined by Nosek (1991) as "assistance from another person with activities of daily living to compensate for a functional limitation" (p. 2) and include assistance with personal hygiene, meal preparation, housekeeping and other household chores, and community mobility. In the words of Litvak, Zukas, and Heumann (1987), these services are "tasks . . . that individuals would normally do for themselves if they did not have a disability" (p. 1). Personal assistants allow people with severe physical or health impairments to participate more fully in community settings and activities, including employment.

Table 15.2. Common orthopedic impairments and other health impairments

Orthopedic impairments	Other health impairments
Cerebral palsy	Tuberculosis
Spasticity	Rheumatic fever
Athetosis	Nephritis
Rigidity	Asthma
Dystonia	Sickle cell anemia
Hypotonia	Hemophilia
Mixed	Epilepsy
Spina bifida	Lead poisoning
Spinal cord injury	Leukemia and other childhood cancers
Traumatic brain injury	Cardiac defects
Curvatures of the spine	Ventricular septal defects
Scoliosis	Atrial septal defects
Kyphosis	Pulmonary valve stenosis
Lordosis	Aortic valve stenosis
Congenital limb absence	Metabolic disorders
Hip conditions	Hurler syndrome
Legg-Perthes disease	Phenylketonuria (PKU)
Congenital dislocation	Cystic fibrosis
Poliomyelitis	Diabetes mellitus
Rheumatoid arthritis	Acquired immunodeficiency syndrome (AIDS)
Muscular dystrophy	
Bone tuberculosis	
Amputation	
Contractures	
Club foot	

Source: Umbreit (1983).

Because personal assistance services are frequently dependent on public funding, most states impose age and income limits on eligibility, causing most people to rely predominantly on informal supports (i.e., family, friends, neighbors) (Nosek, 1991).

During childhood and adolescence, the personal assistance needs of students with orthopedic and health impairments are typically filled by parents and other family members; in school, teachers, aides, or other students provide assistance. During the transition process, personal assistance needs—as they relate to the workplace and other community-based environments—are of prime interest to the student and his or her family (Nehring, 1990). The ITP team should identify the anticipated personal assistance needs of the student as well as the available resources, formal and informal, for meeting those needs. For many daily functions, family, friends, or volunteers can provide work-related assistance without stigmatizing the student. For example, transportation to and from work can be provided by a family member or co-worker. In many, if not most, workplaces, supportive co-workers can be found who will assist the student with getting from one area to another or with feeding; however, it is unusual to find co-workers willing to assist with toileting at work, to clean up after toileting accidents, to administer injections, or to take care of other personal and medical needs. For those students who would feel stigmatized by having a family member come to the workplace for these purposes, a paid assistant is a viable option. Although the use of a personal assistant in the workplace may initially seem unusual

to co-workers, the arrangement should eventually become accepted, particularly if the student hires, trains, and pays the assistant.

Assistive Technology, Rehabilitation Engineering, and Transition

Students with severe orthopedic and health impairments are frequently referred to as *technology supported* or *technology assisted* (Condry, 1989; Odom & Chandler, 1990) when they utilize specialized equipment and procedures to gain more control, independence, and efficiency in day-to-day activities and to participate more fully in community-based vocational and social activities. When technology is applied to people with disabilities, it is termed *assistive technology* (Franklin, 1991). When assistive technology is applied in education, employment, or independent living settings, it is frequently termed *rehabilitation engineering* and, in most states, is a service offered by vocational rehabilitation (VR) agencies (Langston, Coker, & Smith, 1989; Stack, 1988).

Examples of technological support for students with health impairments are ventilators to aid respiration, intravenous nutrition, drug therapy, mobility aids, and artificial or transplanted organs. For students with orthopedic impairments, technology can include an array of assistive devices, from very simple pointing devices to motorized wheelchairs, robotic limbs, and voice and eye gaze–activated computer programs that help users to achieve greater independence in communication and environmental control.

In the 1990s, assistive technology has received considerable attention from the rehabilitation field, consumers, manufacturers, and legislators, with a corresponding surge in funding for technology and in the sophistication and precision of assistive devices (Fee, 1991; Franklin, 1991). Assistive technology can enable students and adults with even the most severe physical and health impairments to have more options, choice, and self-determination in their lives (Powers, 1994). Obviously, for the purposes of transition from school to work, it is important to develop and utilize technological adaptations that have utility in integrated workplaces, such as adaptations that assist the student in completing a specific work task, maintain health or physical functioning, or contribute to general independence or social integration (Carlson & Vervena, 1995; Flippo, Inge, & Barcus, 1995; Nehring, 1990). The following guidelines for using assistive technology have been adapted from works by Sharpton and West (1991) and Williams (1991):

1. Is the technology effective? Does the use of the technology result in correct task completion or improved social integration or functioning?
2. Does the technology maintain the dignity of the individual? Devices should be developed or purchased that are appropriate to the age of the individual and do not draw negative attention to him or her.
3. Is the technology durable? Can it be used as it was intended without quickly becoming unusable from wear and tear?
4. Is the technology portable? An assistive device should be designed so that it can be easily taken by the student to the place where it is needed. Assistive devices are particularly useful if they can be used in a variety of settings.
5. Can the assistive technology be understood and used by the employer and co-workers after the teacher or VR staff have left?
6. Has the student had the opportunity to evaluate the technology and suggest alterna-

tive means to accomplish the same purpose? The student has spent a lifetime developing personal adaptive techniques and may prefer an "antiquated" but comfortable method or device.

7. Does the technology accomplish its purpose in the least intrusive and most simple way possible? Complex technologies can often lead to complex glitches that are counterproductive to the reasons for utilizing technology.

Self-Advocacy and Transition

As individuals and groups, citizens with disabilities are increasingly seeking forums and opportunities to speak for themselves and to educate one another about the rights and responsibilities of citizenship (Gould, 1985). Within human services, the self-advocacy movement translates into *consumer empowerment*, which may be broadly defined as the transfer of power and control over the values, decisions, choices, and directions of human services from external entities (i.e., government agencies, services providers, social forces) to the service consumers (Gradel, 1991; Turner, 1995; West & Parent, 1992). The desired outcomes of empowerment are increased independence, greater motivation to participate and succeed in adult roles, and more dignity for the consumer (Sowers & Powers, 1995; Wehmeyer, 1994; West & Parent, 1992).

According to Gould (1985), self-advocacy has three benefits within transitional school-to-work programs. First, self-advocacy can help to ensure that the wishes, desires, needs, and goals of parents and students are considered in the planning process. Second, self-advocacy allows students and their families to build and maintain community social support systems and to develop decision-making skills. Finally, self-advocacy allows students and their families to seek more individualized and cost-effective services and opportunities.

Training models for students in transition have been developed to increase knowledge of rights and to improve self-advocacy skills. One model available to school systems is Students in Transition Using Planning (Odom & Chandler, 1990). For students with physical impairments, this format consists of three class sessions with activities, scripts, handouts, and overheads. The first session focuses on future planning and goal setting for 1-, 3-, and 5-year intervals. Planning areas typically include training and employment, residential options, and financial resources. The second session provides information on human and civil rights, including specific laws and regulations, and the third session focuses on self-advocacy and communication skills, using role-playing and scripted exercises for securing services, employment, and housing. The Students in Transition Using Planning materials are available from the PACER Center or through the ERIC Document Reproduction Service.

Parents should also practice self-advocacy skills during the transition process. It is the family and the student who will have to live with the decisions that the team makes. Therefore, parents can and should make their concerns and desires known prior to the initial ITP meeting and throughout the transition process (West, Gibson, & Unger, 1986).

Andrew *Andrew's diagnosis of cerebral palsy (CP) and developmental delay provided him access to infant stimulation programs and physical and speech-language therapy at the age of 9 months. Since that time, he has been involved in structured therapeutic and educational settings. Although the majority of the programs were segregated for children with disabilities, Andrew was main-*

streamed in life as much as possible. As Andrew grew, opportunities for inclusion in the community began to seem more and more limited. He had few friends that he could visit after school because the children who attended his programs came from all over the county. Each time his parents approached the school district to request appropriate integrated placement, they were informed that there were no suitable classes.

When Andrew was an infant, his doctors repeatedly said that he had "minimal CP." As time passed, it became apparent to his parents that his multiple disabilities would affect his life more than the word "minimal" implied (e.g., a limp or some slight difficulty with fine motor skills). Although Andrew began to ambulate using braces and crutches for short stretches and a wheelchair for long distances, his speech remained impaired and his fine motor skills limited his ability to write and dress himself. His educational progress was extremely slow.

When Andrew was 16 years old, his parents realized that they should begin to consider Andrew's future as it required a great deal of planning. It was very difficult for them to talk at length about possibilities and alternatives. Although they did not begin any formal planning immediately, they shifted the focus of their reading and research to concentrate on adult concerns and increased their efforts to integrate Andrew into the local community. At that time, Andrew was in a special school program for children with orthopedic impairments. His parents made inquiries about the school's vocational program and Andrew went for an evaluation. The program was not prepared to deal with the realities of workers with fine and gross motor impairments or those facing significant intellectual challenges. Andrew's interest in car repair was met with an unqualified response that it was too unsafe to be considered as a setting for him. The teachers were not prepared for, or educated in, adapting curricula and tools for students with disabilities. Andrew's parents were upset and discouraged.

Andrew's parents began to think about other alternatives and broached the subject with the school district's committee on special education (CSE). The principal of the special school Andrew was attending supported their efforts to take Andrew out of the rarified atmosphere of the "orthopedically handicapped program." They were able to mainstream Andrew into the larger school population for some classes for students classified as having neurological impairments. This meant that he interacted with a group of 200–300 students rather than a group of 87.

About this time, Andrew's parents learned of the United Cerebral Palsy Associations (UCP) National Demonstration Project on Supported Employment. As a result of their research, his parents revised Andrew's individualized education program (IEP) and brought the concept of supported employment to the attention of the school district. More important, they began to talk to the CSE about community-based work experiences for Andrew while he was still in high school in order to prepare him for supported employment. They contacted several local businesses to make preliminary inquiries about supported employment opportunities and were encouraged by the results.

Simultaneously, Andrew's parents requested that the school district make preparations to include Andrew in the local high school. A compromise plan was worked out for Spring, 1996. Andrew continued to attend the special school, but was bused to the general high school on a trial basis two afternoons each week. Andrew's bus was met at the high school by an aide and a student volunteer. The student was extremely active in student government and extracurricular sports and acted as Andrew's buddy, making Andrew more approachable for the rest of the students.

In response to his parents' repeated inquiries about Andrew's future options, they were directed to a parents' tour of sheltered workshops and day treatment programs. On the tour they questioned the guides about productivity standards, advancement from one level of programming to another,

competitive employment possibilities, and other issues. It was a terrible day for them. They came away as dejected as they had been when they first realized the challenges Andrew would face. The workshops and programs offered little room for individuality, modification, adaptation, or advancement. In addition, no one was able to speak knowledgeably about the concept of supported employment. They decided that whatever Andrew's future would be, it would not include a sheltered workshop or a day treatment program.

Andrew's integration into the high school on a twice-weekly basis was a success, leading his parents to request that Andrew return to the district full-time beginning the next fall. The meeting with the CSE did not go smoothly. Both the parent member and psychologist on the committee questioned the appropriateness of exposing Andrew to the high school. They said he might want to date or befriend individuals who would reject him, or he might have extremely frustrating experiences and become angry. They asked how his parents could justify subjecting Andrew to such uncontrolled, potentially dangerous situations as the cafeteria and hallways filled with 1,300 students. Andrew's parents responded that he had as much right to failures and disappointments as to successes and achievements. With the support of the assistant principal and the director of special education, Andrew was allowed to return to the high school on a trial basis, subject to review after 3 months.

That fall, Andrew began a full-time program at the high school. A supportive team of teachers, paraprofessionals, health professionals, and building-level administrators was instrumental in integrating Andrew into daily student life. Concerns with finding a job coach, jobsites, insurance, and transportation temporarily stymied his parents' insistence on a community-based work experience. They offered to assist and, in fact, developed a job at a local department store. They were unable to start the program, however, and the community-based work experience was not realized during the 1995–1996 school year. Andrew did have an in-school job assignment during this time. He delivered attendance sheets from the office to various classrooms.

In the fall of 1996, Andrew returned to his high school and began his last year in the school system. Before his return to school, his parents met with the CSE and requested that everything be in place to begin community-based work experience immediately. Over the summer, the district had recruited a creative and innovative teacher to spearhead the high school vocational program. Using the groundwork Andrew's parents had laid with several local businesses, this teacher arranged numerous potential worksites for the students in vocational special education. Andrew began to work in a local family-owned department store, delivering and picking up receipts from all departments. The main problem with this placement was that it was too little, too late—2 hours twice a week was not enough to develop job proficiency.

Andrew's next job will be at the University Hospital affiliated with the State University of New York at Stony Brook. At his parents' request, his work schedule will be increased to 3 half-days. This large and complex environment promises to provide many opportunities to develop jobs appropriate for Andrew. At least in the beginning, they anticipate a mail delivery route. After talking with several people involved in supported work programs, Andrew's parents will try to ensure that his work is structured to balance the time he spends moving from place to place and in a single department. This is important so Andrew will spend time in a stable environment and have an opportunity to form friendships with his co-workers. Andrew's parents made it known in their initial interactions with the University Hospital that they hope a paying job will evolve from this student work program.

Andrew has several months left in the local high school. He will continue the academic program with an increasing emphasis on work aspects. His parents will meet with his VR counselor and make

more definite requests and plan for Andrew to receive VR services. In the spring, his parents will convene a circle of support to assist in future planning. In preparation for this, they are sharing descriptive materials on this process and recruiting friends, teachers, and family members. They recognize the importance of creating a supported living situation for Andrew and envision him in his own home with one to three roommates. Their primary emphasis is on finding and securing an appropriate job for Andrew. Second, they talk to everyone they meet, investigating any possibility and keeping their eyes open for houses that might be made accessible. They plan to contact the established agencies sponsoring group homes and discuss the possibility of their supplying supports to Andrew and his roommates.

During the next year, his parents must become thoroughly familiar with a completely different service delivery system. Through personal and business connections, they must continue the hard work of finding Andrew a place of employment, recreational opportunities that provide peer interaction and stimulation, and a living situation that provides a measure of independence and support. As hard as the research and planning has been to this point, Andrew's parents believe that the hardest part is still in front of them: building an adult life that allows Andrew to be integrated into his surrounding community.

Assessment of Youth with Orthopedic and Other Health Impairments

Regardless of a student's academic skills and educational goals, assessment for transition needs should take a very functional approach. School- and community-based work experience programs are ideal for assessing functional abilities and limitations in work environments. This section briefly describes assessment questions that should be addressed by ITP teams. These assessment areas are discussed in detail by Sowers (1991) and Sowers and Powers (1991).

Bathroom use: Many students with orthopedic and other health impairments have problems with incontinence, accidents, catheterization, transferring to toilets, and using handheld urinals, and require assistance with toileting and other personal needs. Those who use wheelchairs also require accessible bathrooms. Transition planning, therefore, involves assessing future bathroom needs and planning for their provision.

Work endurance: Students with orthopedic and other health impairments often have problems with fatigue. During school-based work experience programs, a student's endurance can be assessed on a multitude of tasks, which drive job placement decisions and adaptation needs.

Eating and drinking: The amount of assistance required for eating and drinking must be assessed. This includes time requirements, messiness, special diets, and any implications of these factors in transition to work or postsecondary education.

Communication: Meeting communication needs requires an assessment of the means of communication the student uses and the student's proficiency in receptive and expressive communication. Secondary communication modes may need to be developed if those within the student's repertoire are not functional in work settings.

Grooming: Grooming includes the student's personal hygiene and the type and appear-

ance of clothing. Grooming can be problematic for some students because of limited use of hands and arms, visual or perceptual problems, or simply lack of experience with taking care of one's appearance. Because drooling or toileting accidents can occur, assessment should be conducted at the beginning of and throughout the work period.

Hand use: Hand use assessment includes the ability to grasp and manipulate objects, hand and arm strength, and amount of control over hands and arms.

Medical needs: For many students with health impairments, and to some extent those with orthopedic impairments, health limitations and the ongoing need for medical monitoring may be issues in future employment. For example, a student with a seizure disorder who experiences tonic-clonic seizures may need to have a place at the job where he or she can go to rest following a seizure or work-time adjustments for unpredictable "breaks" due to seizures. School personnel should include plans to "bridge the gap" between pediatric and adult health services and financing as a part of the ITP process (Bauer, 1994; Rinehart, 1994).

Mobility: Mobility assessment areas include the means that the student uses, distances that can be safely or independently traversed, and needs for accessible entrances, elevators, and so forth. Mobility assessment should also include the need for assistance from others and the need for adaptations to work areas due to limited range of motion or other motor impairments.

Transportation: Getting to work and back is a critical issue for students with orthopedic and, to a lesser degree, health impairments, particularly if the student uses a wheelchair or walker or lives in an area with limited or no public transportation (McGaughey, Kiernan, McNally, & Gilmore, 1993). The ITP team may need to develop creative solutions to transportation problems.

Social interaction: Assessment of social interaction includes appropriate and inappropriate social behaviors and responses to stress, criticism, pressure to perform, and so forth. Social assessment should occur in a variety of community-based environments, not just in educational settings.

Academic skills: An assessment of reading, writing, and mathematics skills leads the ITP team in targeting jobs and adaptation strategies. Academic assessments should also help the ITP team to identify appropriate postsecondary education or training needs and goals.

Teaching Strategies for Youth with Orthopedic and Other Health Impairments

As with assessment, teaching strategies for students with orthopedic and other health impairments in transition should take a very functional approach. This approach is summarized by Sharpton and West (1991): "If a work skill or task can be taught, teach it; if it can't be taught, adapt it; if it can't be taught or adapted, support it" (p. 16).

For students with orthopedic and health impairments, jobsite interventions focus less on training in specific job tasks and more on adaptations of the work environment or job duties and support for the student/worker, the supervisor, and co-workers (Cooper & Mank, 1989; West, Callahan, Lewis, Mast, & Sleight, 1991). The use of adaptation and support strategies in work settings for students with physical limitations has been termed

jobsite enabling (Sowers & Powers, 1991; Wood, 1988), which captures the importance of adaptation and support for future employment success.

For problems or performance impairments in each of the functional areas described in the preceding section, the ITP team members should explore the feasibility of the following adaptation and support strategies suggested by Sowers and Powers (1991):

1. Redesign the sequence of the task or activity to eliminate difficult steps.
2. Determine alternative means of performing the task or activity that are within the student's physical capacity.
3. Rearrange the environment to permit easier access to work areas and materials.
4. Position the equipment or materials to make the job easier for the individual to reach or manipulate.
5. Enhance existing cues (e.g., signs, buttons, instructions) or develop alternative types of cues the student can discriminate.
6. Make or purchase assistive devices that alleviate difficulties with mobility, movement, discrimination, work speed, visual acuity, and so on.
7. Have a co-worker or other support person complete tasks that the student cannot.

Designing and Implementing ITPs for Youth with Orthopedic and Other Health Impairments

Although the transition planning process is generally perceived as focusing on "school to work," it is important to recognize that transition planning involves not only the student's future job and work environment, but his or her living situation, recreational and social activities, community mobility, and use of community services.

Tom *Tom is a 19-year-old student with severe cerebral palsy and mild mental retardation. He is nonambulatory and has very limited use of his hands. His speech is very difficult to understand, but he can recognize 30–40 sight words and can add and subtract using a calculator. He uses augmentative communication and can operate his motorized wheelchair.*

Tom lives in a small house with his parents. His father is retired, and his mother has never worked outside the house. Tom's parents have difficulty in caring for his personal needs because of Tom's size and their ages. They depend on Tom's older, married brother to take Tom to appointments and on occasional recreational outings. An ITP developed specifically for Tom appears on pages 430–433.

Transition from School to Competitive Employment

In many cases, individuals with even severe orthopedic or health impairments are able to locate, obtain, and maintain employment without specialized services or through time-limited vocational education or VR services that teach job-seeking and interviewing skills and provide career exploration, work experience, or work adjustment training. Individuals with orthopedic and health impairments may also need occasional assistance from co-workers, friends, and general employee assistance programs to complete tasks and solve work-related problems.

Description of Student's Future Vision

Tom would like to be employed full time in a career in computers, data entry or programming, and live independently with personal assistance.

Individualized Transition Plan

Student's Name _Tom_

Birthdate _____

Student's Identification Number _____

Participants:

Name _Tom_

 Claire

 Lauren

 Sue

School _Smithville_

ITP Conference Date _____

Position _Student_

 Parent

 Teacher

 Service coordinator

Career and Economic Self-Sufficiency

Employment Goal Tom will work full time in a computer data entry position in the Department of Motor Vehicles.

Level of present performance: Tom has a strong desire to be employed. He utilizes a computer in class using a head pointer.

Steps needed to accomplish goal: 1. Tom will take computer classes. 2. Tom will be referred to VR. 3. Arrangements will be made for Tom to take STAR. 4. Tom will apply for Personal Assistance Service. 5. Tom will be evaluated for equipment modification needs.

Date of completion: June 1, 1995

Person(s) responsible for implementation: Teacher and service coordinator

Vocational Education/Training Goal Tom will complete computer training courses.

Level of present performance: Tom has used a computer for academics and recreation but has not taken any occupation-related courses.

Steps needed to accomplish goal: 1. Review course/program options at community high school. 2. Enroll in classes. 3. Arrange for transportation and classroom assistance as needed.

Date of completion: December 1994

Person(s) responsible for implementation: Teacher and service coordinator

From Wehman, P. (1995). *Individual transition plans: The teachers curriculum guide for helping youth with special needs.* Austin, TX: PRO-ED; reprinted by permission.

Postsecondary Education Goal *Tom will take computer courses related to his job at the community college.*

Level of present performance: *Tom's position will be at the entry level. He will need to keep up with computer technology advances.*

Steps needed to accomplish goal: *1. Identify course options (i.e., in-service training, community college course). 2. Meet with admissions officer at community college. 3. Budget for course and transportation. 4. Budget for personal assistance as needed.*

Date of completion: *December 1994*

Person(s) responsible for implementation: *Service coordinator, guidance counselor, and community college admissions*

Financial/Income Needs Goal *Tom will be financially independent of his parents.*

Level of present performance: *Tom is dependent upon his parents for basic needs. He rarely obtains cash from his Social Security income to make purchases.*

Steps needed to accomplish goal: *1. Assist Tom in opening bank accounts. 2. Place SSI and wages in his personal accounts. 3. Teach Tom budgeting skills. 4. Identify computer software to help him manage funds.*

Date of completion: *March 1995*

Person(s) responsible for implementation: *Service coordinator, teacher, and Tom*

Career and Economic Self-Sufficiency

Independent Living Goal *Tom will live with a roommate without disabilities in an accessible apartment.*

Level of present performance: *Tom wants to live independently. He requires assistance for all daily living activities.*

Steps needed to accomplish goal: *1. Arrange for residential services. 2. Arrange for personal assistance services for designated times daily. 3. Modify appliances for safety and increased independence. 4. Train Tom to use adaptations for self-care and safety.*

Date of completion: *August 1994*

Person(s) responsible for implementation: *Service coordinator and Center for Independent Living*

Transportation/Mobility Goal *Tom will travel safely in his wheelchair in the community.*

Level of present performance: *Tom has had limited experience traveling on sidewalks or crossing streets. He can travel to familiar destinations on the school campus.*

Steps needed to accomplish goal: *1. Provide community-based instruction on safe travel in traffic areas. 2. Teach Tom, roommate, and personal assistant basic wheelchair maintenance.*

Date of completion: *March 1995*

Person(s) responsible for implementation: *Teacher and service coordinator*

Social Relationships Goal *Tom will functionally use an appropriate augmentative communiation device.*

Level of present performance: *Tom has used a variety of devices to communicate, some of which were cumbersome and inflexible for various environments.*

Steps needed to accomplish goal: *1. Determine Tom's communication needs in different environments. 2. Schedule assistive technology evaluation at Cerebral Palsy Center. 3. Acquire funding for needed equipment. 4. Train Tom to use communication equipment.*

Date of completion: *January 1995*

Person(s) responsible for implementation: *Teacher and speech therapist*

Recreation/Leisure Goal *Tom will use the public library weekly.*

Level of present performance: *Tom enjoys videos, music, and books on tape. He does not have a VCR or tape player at home. Tom does not live close to a library.*

Steps needed to accomplish goal: *1. Assist Tom in obtaining library card from area library. 2. Budget funds for tape player and/or VCR. 3. Teach Tom how to use library. 4. Arrange transportation to library. 5. Teach Tom how to use tape player/VCR with adaptations.*

Date of completion: *April 1995*

Person(s) responsible for implementation: *Teacher and service coordinator*

Personal Competence

Health/Safety Goal *Tom will receive regular dental care.*

Level of present performance: *Tom has difficulty maintaining proper dental hygiene and rarely sees a dentist.*

Steps needed to accomplish goal: *1. Teach Tom methods for daily dental care. 2. Locate appropriate dentist. 3. Determine source of funding for dental care fees. 4. Maintain regular dental appointments.*

Date of completion: *November 1994*

Person(s) responsible for implementation: *Service coordinator and teacher*

Self-Advocacy/Future Planning *Guardianship by Tom's parents will be transferred to limited guardianship by Tom's brother.*

Level of present performance: *Tom's brother has maintained close contact with him. Tom's parents are elderly and depend on Tom's brother for assistance in legal and financial affairs.*

Steps needed to accomplish goal: *1. Obtain legal services. 2. Document Tom's choices/desires for employment and independent living. 3. Transfer guardianship.*

Date of completion: *August 1995*

Person(s) responsible for implementation: *Family and service coordinator*

Student Career Preference

Working with computers

Student's Major Transition Needs

1. Employment
2. Residential services
3. Transportation
4. Assistance with self-care
5. Self-advocacy

Additional Notes

Outcomes-Based Planning Although models range from the practical to the esoteric, transition planning typically focuses on finding and obtaining employment, not necessarily achieving quality-of-life outcomes (e.g., reduced financial dependence, friendships, increased self-esteem and self-direction). Steere, Wood, Pancsofar, and Butterworth (1990) present an outcome-based planning model of transition for students with disabilities— based on a career planning model—that can be useful in identifying and achieving quality-of-life outcomes for all students with disabilities.

The outcomes-based model has three appealing features for students with orthopedic and health impairments. First, this model does not assume that employment is an end in itself, but is instead a means of achieving a happy and productive adulthood for the student. Second, with the outcomes-based planning model, ITP goals and processes are consumer driven, based upon the desired outcomes of the student and his or her family. Third, this planning process encourages the ITP team to explore transition creatively to achieve an array of potential postsecondary outcomes. The six-step approach to outcomes-based planning is described below:

1. During an orientation session, the team members are introduced, along with the student and family members, and a team leader is named to coordinate the efforts of the group. The steps of outcomes-based planning and a rationale for integrated employment are given during this orientation.
2. A brief biographical sketch of the student is presented, which details his or her noteworthy characteristics and achievements. This may also include likes and dislikes, special interests, and support needs. The intent is not necessarily to identify skill limitations, but to focus on ways of building competencies.
3. A brainstorming session is initiated for generating possible quality-of-life outcomes with input from the student. This may involve some interpretations of the student's communication abilities and behaviors and possibly some preconference discussions with the student. From this brainstorming, a priority list of outcomes and definition statements, or descriptors, is generated through team consensus.
4. A measurement system is then identified for determining whether desired outcomes are being or have been attained. In Andrew's case, the outcome goal of developing friendships through work has as one descriptor "participation in after-work social events." A measurement standard would be to go out after work with co-workers a specific number of times per month.
5. The list of outcomes, descriptors, and standards is then used for initial compatibility screening with potential employment situations as they become available. As each is considered, team members also consider possible barriers and challenges that impede movement to the position. Possible solutions and action plans may be developed to serve as a framework for achieving optimum employment experiences.
6. The members of the team continue to meet to follow up on progress in the completion of action plans and meeting desired outcomes. The process can be repeated as deemed necessary to accommodate the student's growth and changing needs.

This method of planning can be used in conjunction with both the ITP and the IEP (Steere, Wood, et al., 1990). It can also serve as a guide for selecting postschool employment.

Judith *Judith has congenital spastic diplegia cerebral palsy but is mobile with Canadian crutches or a scooter. She has a learning disability and a visual problem that causes her to walk looking down at all times, resulting in a severe problem with balance and frequent falls. Judith attended school at a special education center until she reached high school age, when she was mainstreamed into general education classes with resource help provided as needed.*

Judith had some difficulty adjusting to life in high school. The size of the school itself, with more than 1,200 students, overwhelmed her. She had difficulty maneuvering around the building and was frequently late for classes, which tended to upset her more than her teachers. Judith was initially reluctant to ask for help from the resource staff but did when she found it necessary to keep up with other students in her classes. She was able to maintain average grades.

Judith's high school has two types of transition program options. One option is special education in a self-contained classroom in which students work on required subjects for graduation as well as job readiness and life skills. Frequently, students from this program make transitions to day programs or workshop facilities or sometimes to supported employment programs.

The second option is JOBS—a program that includes general high school classes in addition to a job readiness class. Students begin JOBS in their junior year and frequently work a portion of each day by their senior year. Transition options are supported by the VR system, and students are served by a VR counselor.

During her junior year, at age 17, Judith was referred to the transition program and the VR agency. She worked with the VR counselor to establish a program that would result in employment upon graduation. She was enrolled in the JOBS program that met at 7:30 A.M. (Judith eventually came to hate the early morning and initially wanted a job that began at noon.) During Judith's junior year, the JOBS class included exploring types of jobs and careers and preparing mentally and physically for work. A transition team, which met quarterly during the year, was established that included Judith, her parents, the VR counselor, her JOBS teacher, and her high school guidance counselor.

Each spring the VR agency sponsored a transition fair for students and their parents to learn about available programs. Included in this fair are representatives from workshops, skills training programs, residential programs, day training, and supported employment programs. After attending the fair, Judith and her parents were enthusiastic about a clerical skills training program that teaches people with disabilities entry-level clerical skills and places them in clerical jobs. They discussed this option with the transition team, and another meeting was arranged with a representative from the training program. The program includes 6 months of individualized training, meeting every day for 6 hours. The next session began in July, but Judith still had 1 year of school left before graduation. After several meetings with the program staff, it was arranged that Judith would begin full-time training with the class in July until school began in September. Then, she would attend the training for a half-day during the entire school year. She would attend training during the morning and be back at the high school for afternoon classes. She would continue to attend the 7:30 A.M. JOBS class at the school. A school bus would be provided to get her to the training by 9:00 A.M.

Judith spent the summer with her VR counselor learning to ride the bus. She also attended a cooking class at the local UCP affiliate and learned to prepare her own meals so her mother no longer had to come home to make lunch for her.

In July, Judith began the training program with 12 other people. She was very enthusiastic and

enjoyed the contact with others in the class. Her courses included filing, basic bookkeeping, typing, word processing, and receptionist techniques.

In September, Judith started her senior year in high school. She attended JOBS class from 7:30 A.M. to 8:30 A.M. at the school, then took a school bus to the clerical training program at 9:00 A.M., which picked her up again at noon to return to school. She had lunch and at 12:45 P.M. began her afternoon classes. Because of the structure of the training, it was decided that the process should be reversed during the second semester.

Monthly meetings were held with the ITP team, which now included the training instructor from the clerical program. As graduation and completion of the clerical program approached, the focus shifted to finding jobs. The job developer from the training program worked with the VR counselor, the JOBS teacher, and Judith in selecting types of employment situations appropriate for her skills. Judith did very well at filing and receptionist tasks. Her typing was slow as a result of the spasticity in her hands, but it was very accurate. They made a list of employers who could possibly use Judith's skills and made appointments with several of the employers on the list. The job developer from the training program made the initial contacts with the employers. After 2 months of searching, a job was found for Judith as a receptionist with a large agency. She would be the first person encountered by visitors, signing them in and out, and monitoring people entering and leaving the building. In addition, she would answer incoming calls to the general information number, switch callers to extension numbers, and take messages on a computer.

The starting date was set for September 1. This provided some time to work on another of the family's requests—helping Judith to move out of her parents' home. Judith had been associated with an agency that provided residential services, and she qualified for a community independent living program. She and a roommate moved into their own apartment in August. Together they were able to take care of most of their needs, requiring an aide only 3–4 hours a day.

When Judith began work, several adaptations were needed: very simple additions to the computer, a telephone headset, and an enlarged office directory. The job developer from the training program made weekly visits to help Judith to make a smooth transition to work. After several months, visits were reduced to one per month. This visiting schedule continues.

Transition from School to Supported Employment

Supported employment became a service option in state VR programs through the Rehabilitation Act Amendments of 1986 (PL 99-506), which defines *supported employment* as paid work for people with severe disabilities in integrated settings with ongoing support services (*Federal Register*, 1987). Supported employment is designed for people who could not achieve successful employment without extended services, such as periodic job skills reinforcement and continuing monitoring and assessment (Moon, Goodall, Barcus, & Brooke, 1986). This ongoing assistance and support to employers and employees is the defining characteristic of supported employment.

The Individuals with Disabilities Act (IDEA) of 1990, PL101-476, has legitimized supported employment as a potential transition goal for school systems and adult services providers (Wermuth, 1991), and demonstration projects have explored "recommended practices" in the delivery of supported employment services to meet the unique needs of people with severe physical and health impairments (Callahan et al., 1990; Cooper &

Mank, 1989; Sowers & Powers, 1991; West et al., 1991; Wood, 1988). Because ongoing support services can be expensive, intrusive, and stigmatizing for workers with disabilities, it is imperative that those who receive supported employment truly need and want this level of support to maintain their employment. For students with orthopedic or other health impairments, appropriateness for supported employment services might be indicated by a very severe physical impairment that requires extensive adaptations in the workplace, multiple disabilities, or the presence of additional behavior or personality characteristics that may affect the student's employability. Although predetermining need for supported employment is not always exact, work experience programs can provide invaluable information for school and adult services ITP team members.

The planning process for transition to supported employment is similar to planning for the transition to unsupported competitive employment. Because the level of support needed for the student to obtain and keep employment is high, however, planning for these needs is critical. Sowers (1991) recommends a three-step process for developing an employment support plan:

1. A student's work skills, experiences, and anticipated support needs in the areas of toileting assistance or bathroom accessibility, work endurance, eating and drinking, communication, grooming, hand use, vision and hearing, medical needs, mobility, transportation to and from work, social interactions and behaviors, and academic skills are summarized.
2. At an ITP meeting attended by the student, his or her family, educational staff, and adult services agency representatives, the student's available resources are identified, including both formal and informal support mechanisms.
3. The ITP team develops a plan for identifying appropriate employment options, the types and minimum amounts of supports to be provided, and the providing and funding entities.

Susan Susan was a student in the self-contained classroom of a high school transition program. She was born with cerebral palsy and was classified by the school district as having mild mental retardation. Susan walks with Canadian crutches and has a severe drag of her left leg and foot. She attended a special education center until she was 14, when she was enrolled in the public high school in special education classes.

After 2 years in high school, at age 16, Susan entered the transition program. From the beginning she was a reluctant participant. Her family situation contributed to her poor attitude toward school, transition, and work. She had learned as a young child how to work her divorced parents against each other effectively. Susan's mother was employed and engaged to be married. Her father had remarried but had been unemployed since before he and Susan's mother divorced. He did odd jobs, such as yard work and carpentry, but wanted to start his own business and provide lifelong employment for Susan. Susan wanted to be a nurse in a nursery for children at high risk; and her father encouraged this goal, telling her he would find a way to pay for college training. Susan lived with her mother but wanted to live with her father.

A transition team was formed that included Susan, her parents, her teacher, the high school special education coordinator, and the VR counselor. At the initial meeting, school members tried to help Susan and her parents to understand and accept that Susan was not eligible for college or nurses'

training. They convinced Susan's parents that she could work successfully in the right job with necessary supports. They discussed jobs in hospital settings where children would be present. After several meetings, Susan and her parents agreed to try supported employment and she was referred to a program.

At their first meeting, the supported employment program staff found themselves in the middle of a very heated argument among Susan, her father, and her mother. Susan became verbally abusive, started shouting and crying, and quickly left the room, slamming the door and swearing at everyone as she left. Her father shouted abusive language after her, but Susan kept going. This set the pattern for monthly meetings during the following 6 months.

In addition to these group meetings, a job coach met with Susan every other week to get to know her. Susan was excused from her first class to attend these meetings. The meetings were held at the school because of Susan's behavior and her father's wishes. Individually, Susan was more cooperative and enthusiastic. She worked well with the job coach as they completed a historical assessment and was willing to improve her appearance for these sessions. Her usual appearance was described as "shaggy." The job coach insisted she bathe before each meeting, and Susan usually complied with this request.

The job coach and Susan made good progress together. Susan continued to state that she really wanted to work with children or in a hospital. The job coach arranged for Susan to observe various jobs in the hospital and to speak with different people. Susan also observed in the nursery for infants at high risk and spoke with one of the nurses who was very frank about the job and the skills necessary to do the job. Susan realized she would be unable to hold an infant safely.

Team meetings were another story. When her parents attended, Susan would become very obstinate. She would remind everyone that it didn't matter what the supported employment staff did because her father was going to start his own business and give her a job. These meetings frequently ended in her becoming upset, crying, swearing, and leaving the meeting.

During the summer between her junior and senior year, Susan's mother remarried and her father sued for custody of Susan. Susan's mother relented, and Susan went to live with her father. When school began in the fall, Susan's father wanted her to be employed immediately, and he tried to exclude Susan's mother from the team meetings. He thought Susan's weekly meetings with the job coach were a waste of time and focused only on immediate employment.

Susan's father's uncooperative attitude prevailed for much of the fall semester. During that time, a job was found for Susan in the special education office, supervised by the special education coordinator. Susan was to do collating and answer the office telephone. This job lasted 6 weeks, ending because Susan was frequently late and unable to complete her assigned tasks without constant supervision, which could not be provided. During the time that Susan had been employed, she and her father decided that they were no longer interested in supported employment and refused to continue to work with the job coach. Even after this first job ended, they would not consider supported employment. After several months, school staff members and the VR counselor found another job for Susan in a child care center, but she was fired after 3 days.

In January, after a serious argument, Susan moved out of her father's house and into an apartment with a girlfriend, which created new problems. Susan frequently missed school and was uncooperative with the transition staff when she did attend. Her VR counselor also had little success with her. Susan wanted nothing to do with her father and did not want him involved in any way.

Susan eventually moved into her cousin's home. Both of Susan's parents told her that they would not support her after she graduated. Susan decided she needed a job and agreed to work with

the supported employment program. By this time, her former job coach was working with another person so a new coach was assigned to Susan. During the middle of summer following graduation, Susan began missing the meetings with her new job coach. When told that she would be dropped from the program, she became more cooperative. She knew that she needed to support herself and was anxious to have a job. For 5 months, Susan worked with the job coach and the VR counselor in locating employment. A job was developed in an agency that worked with children where Susan would be responsible for answering the telephone, sorting the mail, photocopying materials, and filing. Simple adaptations were made that included a telephone headset, an electric letter opener, and color-coded file headings.

The job coach was required to be on the job with Susan full time for about 9 months. She had difficulty following instructions and anything that seemed like a direct order. In these cases, she would get angry and say, "I don't need this job!" She knew, however, that she did need the job, and, in fact, liked it and several of the people in the unit.

Susan's biggest problem continues to be her temper. The job coach sees Susan and talks with her supervisor daily. Several co-workers are beginning to help her to control her temper. Susan continues to have minimal contact with her parents.

Transition from School to Postsecondary Education and Training

Students with disabilities are enrolling in postsecondary schools in increasing numbers, although the exact proportion is not known because disability disclosure is voluntary. Students with disabilities continue to lag far behind those without disabilities in terms of participation in postsecondary education and training, however. Table 15.3 summarizes data about the participation of students with orthopedic and other health impairments in different types of postsecondary settings.

One person with a physical disability who is an excellent example of being successful in postsecondary education is Dr. Michael Ward—one of the leading experts in the United States on transition and self-determination.

Michael Ward Michael Ward is currently the chief of the Secondary Education and Transitional Services Branch within the U.S. Department of Education, Office of Special Education Programs (OSEP). His responsibilities include administering the Postsecondary Education Programs for Individuals with Disabilities. He previously worked as a vocational rehabilitation counselor and as an education specialist in policy research.

Throughout his life, Dr. Ward—who has a physical disability, cerebral palsy—has been a tireless advocate on behalf of self-determination for people with disabilities. He has been instrumental in developing and directing OSEP grant-funded priorities for demonstrating new curricula and methods for increasing choices and choice-making skills of children and youth with disabilities. Through his writings and presentations directed to educational programs and families, he has promoted self-determination as a meaningful and desirable outcome.

Table 15.3. Postsecondary education and training for youth with orthopedic and other health impairments

Educational institution	Orthopedic impairments (%)	Other health impairments (%)
Postsecondary vocational program	12.6	33.9
Two-year college	32.3	28.4
Four-year college	12.9	21.9

Source: Fairweather & Shaver (1991).

Section 504 of the Rehabilitation Act of 1973, PL 93-112, prohibits discrimination on the basis of disabilities by programs and activities receiving or benefiting from federal financial assistance—a protection that was extended to all citizens with disabilities through the Americans with Disabilities Act (ADA) of 1990, PL 101-336. Subpart E of the rules and regulations for Section 504 (*Federal Register*, 1977) addresses postsecondary educational services and specifically prohibits discrimination in recruitment and admissions, academic and athletic programs and activities, student examinations and evaluations, housing, financial aid, counseling, and career planning and placement. In addition, schools are required to make modifications to academic requirements and other rules that discriminate against students with disabilities; to provide auxiliary aids, such as taped texts and readers, to students with disabilities; and to ensure that social organizations supported by the school do not discriminate on the basis of disability.

In a 1993 survey of higher education students in Virginia (West et al., 1993), the majority indicated that they had encountered significant barriers in their educational endeavors. For students with physical and health impairments, these barriers included poor access within and between buildings, limited handicapped parking spaces and poor enforcement of parking regulations, limited numbers of paid or volunteer staff to assist with school-related functions, and poor compliance with Section 504 regulations by university faculty and staff despite intervention from the school's coordinator of services for students with disabilities—findings that have implications for the transition planning process:

1. The ITP team cannot assume that services and accommodations at the postsecondary level will be available when they are needed. A number of factors, including funding and staff shortages, inflexible instructors, historical architecture, and overburdened disability services, can intervene, resulting in students with disabilities being denied their legal rights to services and accommodations.
2. Students with disabilities and their parents need to be informed of their right to accommodations in pursuing postsecondary education and training and trained in self-advocacy to ensure that their rights are protected.
3. The transition planning process includes decisions about to which educational institutions the student will apply for admission—decisions based on physical accessibility, available accommodations, and the student's educational goals and abilities. The student and his or her family should be encouraged to arrange visits to schools to meet with service coordinators, tour the campus and buildings in which the student will have classes, and talk with instructors and other students with disabilities. If student housing will be needed, the accessibility of rooms and the availability of domestic as-

sistance can be assessed. These site visits provide more valid information than any college catalog.

4. After acceptance at a postsecondary school, the coordinator of services for students with disabilities at that school should be invited to become a member of the ITP team so that proactive planning can occur, even if services will not be sought immediately upon admission. If the student's health or physical condition worsens and problems with attendance or classwork arise, prior knowledge of the student and his or her disability will help the service coordinator to make arrangements with the student's instructors before the student's grades are affected.

———

Cary *Cary is a 19-year-old man with sickle cell anemia, resulting in jaundice, fatigue, infections, and occasional vaso-occlusive episodes requiring medical care and even hospitalization. Despite periodic absences during relapses and treatments, he maintained good grades in high school and wanted to attend college to pursue a business degree. Cary's parents were supportive of his goals and willing to finance his education to the extent they were able.*

During Cary's junior year, his high school guidance counselor convened an ITP team to help him and his family select a university. During the first meeting, the team members established three criteria: 1) the university they select should offer a business program up to the graduate level in case Cary decides to pursue an MBA, 2) it should be designed so that Cary could get around without excessive fatigue, and 3) the faculty should be willing to make allowances for Cary's periodic absences from class. Cary also stated during the meeting that he wanted to attend an out-of-town university. When questioned, he stated that he felt overprotected by his parents and wanted to gain more independence. Although surprised by his request, his parents agreed to consider not only the two universities in their city but any other state-supported schools as well.

Over the course of his junior year, Cary and his parents visited four universities, meeting with business faculty and service coordinators. The fourth university they visited, located approximately 2 hours from his hometown, seemed ideal and they decided to concentrate their efforts on getting Cary enrolled there. Several factors led them to choose this university. Although the campus was large, it had an extensive bus system that connected the residence halls, library, and most of the buildings in which Cary would have classes. The university had comprehensive student health services with on-campus clinics. Faculty members of the school of business met with Cary and his parents and assured them that they would accommodate Cary's absences and would help him to keep up with his courses. The disability services coordinator impressed them with her knowledge of sickle cell anemia and its implications on Cary's educational career. She also assured them that she could arrange for notetakers or other assistance on short notice when Cary would have to miss class or could not get out to do library research or other class requirements. She had also made arrangements prior to their visit for them to talk with a student with a coronary disorder who had received similar services.

During Cary's senior year, the other members of the ITP team helped him and his family with the application process by planning for unforeseen contingencies. The disability services coordinator joined the ITP team and was instrumental in identifying problems they might encounter. For instance, Cary had applied for on-campus housing, but the service coordinator informed them that there are never enough dormitory rooms to meet the demand. In case on-campus housing was unavailable, their contingency plan was that Cary and his family would find an apartment on a bus

route and advertise for a roommate to share expenses. Fortunately, Cary was accepted for a residence hall, and the contingency plan was not needed.

Another problem area was finances. Cary's parents could afford his tuition, housing, and meal plan, but not much else. The service coordinator brought financial aid applications to the ITP meeting for Cary to complete and Cary applied for scholarships and work-study. Between ITP meetings, the service coordinator met with the university's work-study coordinator and identified available jobs that would not fatigue Cary and were flexible enough to allow for periodic absences.

Cary's transition went very smoothly, thanks to the thorough troubleshooting and contingency planning of the ITP team. Cary is now in his sophomore year and is still in the business program. He works 15–20 hours per week in a computer lab, helping other students learn to use word processing, graphics, and spreadsheet programs. His health has been relatively stable, and he has not missed many classes for health reasons; his 7:30 A.M. classes, however, are another story.

Evaluation of Transition Outcomes for Youth with Orthopedic and Other Health Impairments

Evaluating transition programs includes process and outcome evaluation. Process evaluation involves determining whether individual students in transition are meeting ITP objectives, and outcome evaluation involves conducting follow-up or follow-along studies of students who have been through the program. There are four purposes of conducting outcome evaluations:

1. To assess the postsecondary employment or educational status of students who have received transitional services
2. To assess adaptive behavior competence of students who have made transitions
3. To evaluate the degree of coordination of different agencies in the community and their effects on the adjustment of special education graduates
4. To evaluate the satisfaction of students and their families with the transition services they have received and to solicit their suggestions for improving transition

Educational agencies must translate these objectives into a series of survey questions and a viable methodology for obtaining answers to those questions. Halpern (1990) provides a list of desirable features of an outcome survey and 67 questions that mirror the four purposes listed above. Among the desirable features are the following:

1. A follow-along strategy (i.e., longitudinal assessment of status at periodic intervals from school exit) is superior to a follow-up strategy (i.e., a "snapshot" from a single point in time).
2. If the purpose of the survey is descriptive and a sample is drawn from the total transition pool, the sample should be representative of the transition population for generalization purposes. If the purpose of the survey is explanatory, the sample should be large enough to permit statistical analysis of predictor and outcome variables.
3. Telephone or face-to-face interviews are desirable; mail surveys should be avoided.
4. Multiple dimensions of community adjustment and involvement should be used,

rather than the narrow focus of employment. Other dimensions for surveying could be use of community support services, social and recreational activities, and use of public accommodations (e.g., transportation) and commercial businesses (e.g., shopping and restaurants).

Some special education researchers (Affleck, Edgar, Levine, & Kottering, 1990; Hasazi et al., 1989) have recognized that students with disabilities are making transitions into a general economic and social climate that is equally favorable or inhospitable to students with and without disabilities. Surveying representative samples of students without disabilities is suggested as another desirable feature for outcome studies. For students with orthopedic and health impairments, primary questions for follow-along surveys include student mobility within the workplace and the community, use of and need for assistive technology and rehabilitation engineering services, use of and need for personal assistants or volunteer assistants on the job, involvement in postsecondary education and training, and satisfaction with transition services and the quality of adult life. Answers to these questions allow transition programs to individualize services for their communities and students.

Conclusion

This chapter has reviewed issues and strategies for successful transitions for students with orthopedic and other health impairments to postschool work, educational, and training environments. Key issues include the need for assistance technology and/or personal assistants, self-advocacy, and the identification of appropriate postschool environments. Additionally, students with orthopedic and health impairments and their families should be trained in the rights and assurances provided to them under IDEA and other disability-related legislation, such as the Rehabilitation Act and the ADA, and effective means of advocating for those rights. Functional assessment, primarily of mobility, endurance, medical needs, transportation, and physical assessment needs, helps to ensure smoother transitions.

Study Questions

1. What are three common physical manifestations of orthopedic and other health impairments?

2. Do most people who require personal assistance rely on formal (i.e., paid) assistants or informal (i.e., unpaid) assistants?

3. Why is self-advocacy important in transition planning?

4. What are some postschool employment outcomes for students with orthopedic and other health impairments?

5. What are the 11 areas of functional assessment for students with orthopedic and other health impairments?

6. What are the six steps to outcomes-based transition planning?

7. What are some special considerations for students with orthopedic and other health impairments who are making the transition to postsecondary education?

16

Applications for Youth with Traumatic Brain Injury

Paul Wehman, Michael D. West, and Pam Sherron

Upon completion of this chapter, the reader will be able to do the following:

- Describe traumatic brain injury, including information about its incidence and prevalence
- Understand at least five unique challenges and difficulties faced by young people with traumatic brain injury
- Discuss the transition from the hospital back into the school
- Discuss the strategies necessary for conducting employment assessments
- Be aware of ways in which compensatory strategies can help youth with traumatic brain injury to enter the workplace

Since the 1980s, emphasis has been placed on the rehabilitation, education, intervention, and, ultimately, transition of people who have experienced traumatic brain injury (TBI). More people than ever before are surviving moderate and severe traumatic injuries sustained in motor vehicle and other accidents because of advances in neurosurgery and emergency evacuation procedures, rehabilitation techniques, and psychopharmacology. Unfortunately, most of these people are young (i.e., less than 30 years of age) and require specialized vocational services if they are to return to the work force.

Walter *Walter was recently discharged from the U.S. Navy. At 22 years old, he was ready to enter graduate school to study engineering until he sustained massive injuries to his brain and chest when hit by a drunk driver at a crosswalk. Walter was taken to the nearest hospital trauma center, where he became medically stable a few days after the accident. He remained unconscious for several months, however. During the months after his return to consciousness, Walter began to recover, but cognitively and emotionally he still has problems. He has memory difficulties, his planning and organizing skills are limited, and he becomes angry and frustrated for no apparent reason.*

Students with TBI face two difficult transitions: 1) the transition from typicality to disability, and 2) the transition from adolescence to adulthood. Although this population is now recognized by the Individuals with Disabilities Education Act (IDEA) of 1990, PL 101-476, the emotional and physical trauma associated with their injuries is often devastating.

Characteristics of Youth with Traumatic Brain Injury

Biomechanics of Traumatic Brain Injury

Traumatic brain injury, also termed craniocerebral trauma, is defined by Vogenthaler (1987a) as "damage to living brain tissue that is caused by an external, mechanical force" (p. 113). TBI is typically followed by a period of altered consciousness, either coma or posttraumatic amnesia (PTA), and seizures, headaches, vomiting, or a discharge of cerebrospinal fluid from the nose or ears (Vogenthaler, 1987b).

When the brain undergoes impact, the forces of acceleration, deceleration, compression, and shear (i.e., twisting) act upon the brain matter, causing tears and bruises in the nerve fibers (i.e., contusions). Because of the brain's jelly-like consistency and its surrounding cushion of cerebrospinal fluid, there may also be a "rebounding" effect, in which additional injuries are sustained on the side of the brain opposite the point of impact (Vogenthaler, 1987a). These are the primary effects of the impact. Secondary damage may come from raised intracranial pressure due to swelling, hematomas, ischemic lesions, posttraumatic epilepsy, and hydrocephalus (Jennett & Teasdale, 1981).

Distinctions are often made between open and closed brain injuries. Open brain injuries are penetrating and often caused by a bullet or other projectile and tend to result in localized damage and relatively predictable disabilities based on the location and extent of the damage (Jennett & Teasdale, 1981; Lishman, 1973). Closed brain injuries, however, are most often a blow to the brain and tend to produce more diffuse brain damage resulting in highly variable and unpredictable consequences (Vogenthaler, 1987b).

Severity of Injury and Course of Recovery

A number of measures have been developed to determine the severity and outcome of TBI. One of the first reported and perhaps most valid measures of severity is the duration of PTA. Russell (1932) first correlated PTA with outcome and produced an assessment scale based on his findings; the scale was subsequently expanded by Jennett and Teasdale (1981) (see Table 16.1). This duration has proved to be a valid indicator of the person's future out-

Table 16.1. Duration of posttraumatic amnesia and injury severity

PTA duration	Severity
Less than 5 minutes	Very mild
5–60 minutes	Mild
1–24 hours	Moderate
1–7 days	Severe
1–4 weeks	Very severe
More than 4 weeks	Extremely severe

Source: Jennett & Teasdale (1981).

comes in terms of independent living, productivity, and rehabilitative potential (Jennett & Teasdale, 1981).

Jennett and Teasdale (1977) also devised their own assessment scale based on the level of responsiveness in eye opening, motor response, and verbal performance, called the Glasgow Coma Scale (see Table 16.2). Individuals are rated in each area, and the combined score is used to determine a level of severity. This scale has produced consistent and reliable ratings of levels of responsiveness and consciousness across settings and raters (Teasdale, Knill-Jones, & Van der Sande, 1978)—a formidable feat considering that coma is often a loosely defined term that can refer to various levels of consciousness.

Other formal and informal means of assessing injury severity include focal neurological signs, cognitive functioning, neurological complications from the injury (i.e., epilepsy, hematoma), and physical and behavioral sequelae (Jennett, 1976; Jennett & Teasdale, 1981; Ylvisaker, Hartwick, Ross, & Nussbaum, 1994). However, duration of PTA and the Glasgow Coma Scale remain the most commonly cited and are frequently described as the most reliable indicators of severity of injury and potential for recovery (Jennett & Teasdale, 1981).

Recovery from TBI is dependent upon a number of factors, including the severity and location of the injury, the preinjury personality and coping strength of the individual, and the types of resultant medical and psychological problems. Individuals who sustain minor injuries may experience mild complications, such as nausea, dizziness, or headaches, and may not seek or receive treatment. A long-held assumption was that there is no permanent damage or long-term effects to people with mild injury (Vogenthaler, 1987a); however, evidence has shown that some of these people continue to have sensory, motor, cognitive, or psychological difficulties that inhibit return to their preinjury lifestyle (Griffith, 1983; Karzmark, Hall, & Englander, 1995).

For individuals who sustain moderate or severe injuries, treatment typically follows a three-stage process described by Bond (1978) and Vogenthaler (1987a). The first stage—acute care—is characterized by the maintenance of essential supports to the patient, including oxygenated blood, nutrition, and a clear airway. Acute care also involves medical maintenance to lessen the complications from the injury, such as bleeding and fever. The acute care phase ends when the patient responds to speech (Bond, 1987) or PTA ends (Long, Gouvier, & Cole, 1984).

Acute rehabilitation then begins. This second stage is characterized by continued medical treatment and maximum recovery of physical and mental functions through spontaneous recovery or therapeutic interventions (e.g., physical therapy, occupational therapy,

Table 16.2. Glasgow Coma Scale

Area of responsiveness	Examiner's test	Injured person's response	Assigned score
Eye opening	Spontaneous	Opens eyes on own	4
	Speech	Opens eyes when asked in a loud voice	3
	Pain	Opens eyes when pinched	2
	Pain	Does not open eyes	1
Best motor response	Commands	Follows simple commands	6
	Pain	Pulls examiner's hand away when pinched	5
	Pain	Pulls a part of body away when pinched	4
	Pain	Flexes body inappropriately to pain (decorticate posturing)	3
	Pain	Body becomes rigid in an extended position when examiner flinches (decerebrate posturing)	2
	Pain	Has no motor response to pinch	1
Verbal response	Speech	Carries on a conversation correctly and tells examiner where he or she is, who he or she is, and the month and year	5
	Speech	Seems confused or disoriented	4
	Speech	Talks so examiner can understand but makes no sense	3
	Speech	Makes sounds that examiner cannot understand	2
	Speech	Makes no noise	1

Summed scores
Vegetative state = 3
Severe disability = 4–8
Moderate disability = 9–11
Good recovery = 12 or greater

Adapted from Jennett & Teasdale (1977).

cognitive therapy, neuropsychology). These interventions are typically provided in a rehabilitation hospital or rehabilitation unit of a hospital. Family services may also be provided. Many individuals recover sufficiently with these services to resume typical or near typical activities. For those who do not, postacute rehabilitation is indicated.

Vogenthaler (1987b) describes the third stage of postacute rehabilitation as a "plateau" period in which gradual improvement occurs for 6 months to 1 year following the injury. After that point, the rate of improvement decreases or ceases. Although slow, gradual improvements may be observed over many years (Thomsen, 1984), intensive rehabilitation is required to make effective changes in the quality of life for individuals in the plateau stage (Griffith, 1983). These rehabilitation efforts may include teaching independent living skills, psychological services, behavior management, and vocational training and placement.

A number of scales have been developed to assess the course of recovery of people with TBI and provide general impressions of both the speed and extent of recovery during acute and postacute rehabilitation stages. Eson, Yen, and Bourke (1978) devised a recovery scale based upon typical developmental sequences and patterns (i.e., birth to 4 years, 4–8 years, 8–12 years, and 12–16 years). Selected standardized instruments assess the return of functional abilities during each developmental period. Smith, Fields, Lenox, Morris, and Nolan (1979) based their scale upon the Glasgow Coma Scale. With both of these scales,

individuals are assessed regularly from the time of the injury until they show a failure to improve.

Incidence, Prevalence, and Population Characteristics

A number of studies have established that TBI is a common occurrence in the United States. Caveness (1979) reviewed data from the National Health Interview Survey (NHIS) and estimated that approximately 7.8 million cases of TBI were reported from 1970 to 1975. This number represented approximately 4% of the nation's entire population during that period. Caveness also estimated that approximately 25% of these injuries were major injuries, resulting in either death or permanent and substantial brain damage. Results from the 1974 National Head and Spinal Cord Injury Survey (Kalsbeek, McLaurin, Harris, & Miller, 1980) indicated that the incidence rate for TBI was approximately 2 per 1,000 people with 422,000 new cases in 1974. Additionally, 926,000 people were experiencing the effects of TBI to the extent that they required hospitalization. Results also showed no significant differences in incidence rates across geographic regions.

More recently, Frankowski (1986) and Jennett (1983) estimated the number of new cases of TBI to be approximately 500,000 people annually—a figure some (i.e., Stonnington, 1986) believe to be misleading on the presumption that there are a large number of unreported injuries. McMordie, Barker, and Paolo (1990) concluded that the incidence rate for traumatic brain injury is higher than that for epilepsy, Parkinson disease, multiple sclerosis, Huntington disease, and amyotrophic lateral sclerosis combined. Its occurrence is 34 times that of mental retardation.

Most TBI survivors experience some physical or cognitive problems as a result of their injuries regardless of severity, but it has been estimated that annually 44,000–90,000 people sustain injuries that result in severe and chronic disability (Jennett, Snoek, Bond, & Brooks, 1981; National Head Injury Foundation [NHIF], 1986; Traphajan, 1988). The Brain Injury Foundation (formerly NHIF) (1986) concluded that more people have severe and permanent disabilities from brain injuries than from cerebral palsy, muscular dystrophy, or multiple sclerosis.

Frankowski (1986) reviewed descriptive epidemiological studies of TBI in the United States and concluded that they have a number of methodological limitations. These studies have typically lacked uniform definitions, clinical criteria, and mutually exclusive diagnostic categories, and have been geographically restricted, making comparisons across studies difficult. Results do, however, reveal some consistent findings: 1) peak incidence years are from the late teens (age 15) to young adulthood (mid-20s to early 30s); 2) males are at least twice as likely as females to sustain brain injuries; 3) motor vehicle accidents account for about half of all traumatic brain injuries, with falls, sports accidents, and assaults comprising most of the remaining cases; and 4) there do not appear to be any significant differences in incidence rates for Caucasians and non-Caucasians. Additionally, Rimel and Jane (1984), reviewing demographic research on people with TBI and information from a brain injury data bank in central Virginia, concluded that 1) people who are unemployed are three times more likely than employed individuals to sustain TBI; 2) lower socioeconomic classes are overrepresented in the TBI population; and 3) individuals who are alcohol and drug abusers are at greater risk for TBI, as are individuals with psychiatric illnesses.

Cognitive, Psychosocial, and Physical Characteristics

Traumatic brain injury often results in myriad cognitive behavior and physical disabilities. Cognitive disabilities can include degrees of short-term memory loss; difficulty in concentrating; problems in processing abstract information; poor retrieval of stored information; and impaired processing in planning, initiating, and carrying out actions (see Table 16.3).

Physical and sensory disabilities can include impairments in speech, vision, hearing, fine and gross motor skills, and balance. Behavioral and emotional difficulties can result from a combination of specific neurological damage and feelings of frustration or being overwhelmed by the inability to cope with the effects of TBI (Morton & Wehman, 1995).

Costs of Traumatic Brain Injury

Costs to Survivors and Their Families It is surprising, but little literature addresses the financial costs of TBI on individuals and their families (McMordie & Barker, 1988; Wehman, Kregel, West, & Cifu, 1994). Watson (1987) studied 19 people with TBI and found that acute care averaged 49 days and $60,009; acute rehabilitation averaged 140.6 days and $33,650. Watson did not report the proportion of these costs that were borne by the individuals and their families, but it is logical to assume that they were faced with some of the direct costs and lost earnings for a substantial time period.

McMordie and Barker (1988) also examined the ongoing costs of care and treatment for people with TBI. Of the respondents, 55% reported yearly medical costs averaging $18,480; 14% reported ongoing therapy costs averaging $5,749; 15% reported costs for institutional care averaging $24,337; and 11% reported yearly costs for specialized therapeutic programs averaging $25,779.

McMordie and Barker's (1988) information on the financial hardships associated with TBI reported that over 47% of the respondents had to borrow money to pay for the care and treatment of the person with TBI, and 26.3% lost personal possessions as a result of the injury. A small percentage (5.7%) reported that they declared bankruptcy, with spouses of survivors more likely to do so than parents. Less than half of the respondents (42.7%) reported that they received benefits or entitlements (i.e., Supplemental Security Income, worker's compensation) following the injury, and approximately 17% reported that they received a legal financial settlement following injury.

McMordie and Barker's (1988) study also examined personal and family incomes prior to and following injuries. Almost 89% of parent respondents reported a decrease in income, with the remaining 11% reporting an increase in income. The average annual decrease was approximately $6,000. Over 90% of spouse respondents reported a decrease in the annual income of the individual with TBI, with the average decrease equaling almost $18,000. Perhaps even more telling, family incomes also decreased substantially, an average of $2,100 for parent respondents and nearly $14,000 for spouses. The difference in family income pre- and postinjury is probably the result of parents or spouses giving up their jobs, working fewer hours, or missing substantial amounts of work in order to be with or provide care for their loved one. Thus, McMordie and Barker (1988) conclude that families may experience a substantial decrease in income even in cases in which the member with TBI does not contribute to family income. Moreover, they write that specialized programs that assist these individuals to return to employment are frequently unavailable or beyond

Table 16.3. Sequelae of closed brain injury

Physical impairments[a]

Epilepsy	Hemiparesis
Ataxia	Hemiplegia
Loss of balance	Dysarthria
Loss of endurance	Apraxia
Spasticity	Rigidity
Tremors	Motor weakness
Loss or limitations of sensory function (visual, auditory, taste or smell)	
Speech impairments (stuttering, articulation, etc.)	

Cognitive impairments[b]

Disorientation	Memory deficits
Illogic	Reasoning deficits
Poor initiative	Poor judgment
Distractibility	Visual/auditory
Reduced eye–hand coordination	perception deficits
Impaired executive function	
Loss of intellectual functioning	
Problems with attention or concentration	
Problems with processing or sequencing information	
Difficulty with generalization	
Inability to perceive own deficits	
Inability to use words	
Loss of language skills	

Psychosocial, behavior, and emotional impairments[c]

Psychosocial problems

Dependency	Social isolation
Affective disorders	Neurosis
Personality disorders	Psychosis
Poor interpersonal relations	Alcohol or drug abuse

Behavior problems

Passivity	Restlessness
Impulsivity	Aggressiveness
Childishness	Slovenliness
Sexual dysfunction	Loss of inhibitions
Lack of goal-oriented behavior	
Inability to self-monitor	
Inappropriate social behaviors	

Emotional problems

Emotional instability or lability	Disturbed self-image
Low self-esteem	Apathy
Anxiety	Irritability
Depression	Denial of disability
Unrealistic expectations	Egocentricity
Low frustration tolerance	

[a]*Sources:* Jennett (1983); Smith (1983); & Vogenthaler (1987a).

[b]*Sources:* Ben-Yishay & Diller (1983); Corthell & Tooman (1985); & Vogenthaler (1987a,b).

[c]*Sources:* Lishman (1973); Long & Webb (1983); Olson & Henig (1983); Rosenthal (1983); & Vogenthaler (1987a, 1987b).

the financial means of the individual or the family. Based on their findings, they conclude that TBI frequently transforms taxpayers into lifelong tax burdens.

Costs to Society Irving (1969) provided one of the earliest estimates of the social costs of TBI—$2 billion for the year 1967, with medical costs, lost wages, and insurance administrative expenses totaling $330 million and compensation to people with TBI $160 million.

More recent estimates (Kalsbeek et al., 1980; Stonnington, 1986) have suggested that the social costs are much higher, not only because of increasing medical costs and economic inflation, but also because more individuals survive severe injury and require long-term vocational and economic support. In 1986, Stonnington estimated that direct costs for hospital, physician, and nursing care exceed $6 billion annually, with indirect costs, such as lost wages, productivity, and long-term care, exceeding $22 billion.

Using the Interdisciplinary Team Approach

Practitioners have found that using an interdisciplinary team approach is the most effective way to accomplish goals for people with TBI. Members of the team—including the individual and his or her family—work together, communicate frequently, and set mutual goals for recovery. An advantage of the team approach is that each member has a unique set of skills to contribute to the treatment and intervention plan.

One of the great transition leaders in the United States who is a leading advocate of the significance of the family of individuals with TBI in the rehabilitation process is Dr. Al Condeluci. Dr. Condeluci is one of the most inspirational leaders of our time.

Al Condeluci Dr. Al Condeluci has been an advocate and catalyst for innovative community services in western Pennsylvania since 1970. Holding a master of social work and a doctoral degree from the University of Pittsburgh, Dr. Condeluci is internationally known for programs and systems advocacy work, conducted through the United Cerebral Palsy Associations (UCPA) of Pittsburgh.

UCPA is working toward a community that includes members of the Center for Personal Development, Residential Supports of Allegheny County, and Community Associated Projects. Each of these divisions offer entrepreneurial, inclusionary activities that focus on building community.

Dr. Condeluci has spoken and consulted throughout North America. His writings are well respected; his first book, *Interdependence: The Route to Community* (1991), received an honorable mention by the Non-Profit Management Association's Terry McAdams Book Award. His second book, *Beyond Difference,* was released in early 1996.

Team composition varies depending on the individual's needs and phase of recovery. Following are brief descriptions of each member of an education and treatment team involved in assisting an individual with TBI regain the ability to function as independently as possible.

Teacher

The teacher is the leader of the educational team and helps the student and family make choices about transition goals, curriculum, and types of community placement.

Employment Specialist

An employment specialist, also known as a job coach, is knowledgeable about the employment challenges of individuals with TBI and provides specialized assistance in locating, learning, and keeping jobs. The employment specialist also communicates with rehabilitation counselors, employers, workers, and family members regarding job-related concerns.

Employment specialists take on a variety of roles, responding to the skills and support needs of each individual during each component of the supported employment process. He or she provides jobsite support and training and assumes the role of a service coordinator, continually monitoring and assessing an individual's employment situation and corresponding needs. Knowing how to respond effectively in specific situations is critical to successful employment outcomes for people with TBI.

In addition, throughout the employment process, the employment specialist directs the consumer to a variety of resources, such as housing, transportation, reassessment of Social Security benefits, substance abuse treatment, marital and/or individual counseling, support groups, and social/recreational programs.

Rehabilitation Counselor

The vocational rehabilitation counselor is a specially trained professional who coordinates an array of multidisciplinary services involving medical, therapeutic, and vocational services that lead to employment (Goodall, Lawyer, & Wehman, 1994). A rehabilitation plan, formulated and monitored by the counselor, specifies physical, cognitive, and/or emotional supports necessary to enhance employability. These services are provided by the counselor or contracted out to service providers. The counselor is involved in counseling the individual and the family regarding work-related and independent living needs.

Neuropsychologist

A neuropsychologist understands how problems with the brain and nervous system affect emotions and intelligence and performs evaluations to diagnose emotional problems as well as intellectual problems involving memory, learning ability, and arithmetic reasoning. Special therapy is provided by the neuropsychologist to help the individual to compensate for intellectual problems, and counseling is often made available to the individual and the family.

Nurse

A nurse is responsible for carrying out the physician's orders and managing day-to-day medical care. A nurse educates families regarding medical care, condition, and prognosis. In the early stages of injury, he or she is primarily involved in maintaining and improving the individual's medical condition. In later stages, a nurse is more likely to assist the individual in carrying out daily living activities and various therapies.

Occupational Therapist

An occupational therapist is a specially trained professional who helps individuals to regain their ability to carry out activities of daily living. Therapeutic exercises provided by the occupational therapist improve strength and the coordination skills required for eating, dressing, toileting, and bathing.

Physiatrist

A physiatrist is a physician who specializes in the field of rehabilitation. He or she typically has primary responsibility for managing the individual's day-to-day care after discharge from neurosurgical care. The physiatrist often prescribes rehabilitation treatments, including physical, occupational, and speech-language therapies.

Physical Therapist

A physical therapist is a professional who is specially trained in understanding how muscles work. Exercise and instruction by a physical therapist improves control over muscles with the goal of increased ability to walk, stand, and sit properly. Wheelchair use and transfer skills are taught if necessary. Physical therapists also work with comatose individuals to reduce muscle stiffness.

Social Worker

Social workers are trained to recognize financial and daily living needs. A social worker is likely to be involved in arranging for insurance coverage and placement for an individual after discharge. He or she may also be involved in educating, counseling, and communicating with family members.

Speech-Language Pathologist

Speech-language pathologists have special knowledge regarding communication and language and help with basic problems in oral comprehension and expression. A speech-language pathologist may teach exercises for mouth and tongue muscles so the individual can develop better control in speech and eating. A speech-language pathologist teaches the use of adaptive devices if the individual is unable to communicate orally.

Unique Challenges Presented by Youth
with Traumatic Brain Injury

Young people with TBI have myriad complex problems, some of which are acute and others that are ongoing (i.e., chronic). The major problems these youth experience in job placement and retention have been related to unrealistic vocational aspirations, substance abuse problems, and psychiatric or interpersonal difficulties (Eames, 1988). An effective transition-operated work reentry program considers these problems throughout the job development and job placement process. Figure 16.1 lists 18 critical employment compatibility issues that should be analyzed prior to or concurrent with placement. These issues are divided into seven categories, each of which is discussed below. The specific compatibility issues are presented as guidelines for program planning, not as rules.

		Yes	No
I.	Preinjury vocational competence and motivation		
	1. The client showed a stable work history for at least 12 months prior to injury.	___	___
	2. The client showed an interest in work advancement.	___	___
	3. The client has specific vocational skills.	___	___
II.	Postinjury vocational competence and motivation		
	4. The client has shown a stable work history for at least 12 months since the injury.	___	___
	5. The client consistently indicates a desire and willingness to work.	___	___
	6. The client has specific job or vocational preferences.	___	___
III.	Physical and medical status		
	7. The client has no physical problems other than the brain injury.	___	___
	8. The client has been medically evaluated within the past 6–12 months.	___	___
	9. The client takes medication as prescribed by a physician.	___	___
IV.	Psychiatric or maladaptive behavior		
	10. The client has no history of persistent psychiatric problems or maladaptive behavior.	___	___
	11. The client has no history of persistent socially inappropriate behavior in a variety of setting	___	___
	12. The client has no history of consistent physically or verbally abusive behavior.	___	___
V.	Substance use or abuse		
	13. The client has no history of substance use or abuse that caused social problems.	___	___
	14. The client currently abstains from alcohol.	___	___
	15. The client currently abstains from the use of illicit drugs.	___	___
VI.	Family or marital stability		
	16. The client's family is supportive of his or her employment.	___	___
	17. The client and/or the family has received counseling or support services for adjustment to consequences of the injury.	___	___
VII.	Vocational goals and expectations		
	18. The client consistently indicates the type of job and pay he or she likes and dislikes.	___	___

Figure 16.1. Traumatic brain injury employment compatibility analysis. (From Wehman, P., & Goodall, P. [1990]. Return to work: Critical issues in employment [p. 4]. In P. Wehman & J. Kreutzer [Eds.], *Vocational rehabilitation for persons with traumatic brain injury*. Rockville, MD: Aspen; adapted by permission.)

Preinjury Vocational Competence and Motivation

A person's preinjury vocational competence, specific work history, and interest in advancement are important for vocational staff. This information provides the clinical data necessary to direct appropriate job development. Three questions must be asked in every complete evaluation.

1. Did the student show a stable school or work history for at least 12 months prior to the injury?
2. Did the student show an interest in work advancement?
3. Did the student have specific vocational skills?

Accurate answers to these questions give the vocational staff information on the type of worker an individual was in the past, the quality of work habits, and the industry in which to initially focus job development efforts.

A number of people with TBI who require services may not have had a good preinjury work record, which can further complicate the job development and job placement process.

Postinjury Vocational Competence and Motivation

Wehman, Kreutzer, West, et al.'s (1989) study noted that 42 people with TBI worked only 13% of the months that they could have following hospital release, instead of almost 75% of the months as they did before they sustained TBI.

The 12-month period after hospital release is a time when people with TBI experience discouragement, frustration, anger, and indecision about work. It is during this critical time, however, that the tone and direction of the work reentry program are set.

Prigatano (1988) has suggested that people who experience long-term (i.e., more than 12 months) postacute rehabilitation might be more ready for placement after working out frustrations and unrealistic expectations. Others have suggested that immediate vocational intervention after hospital release is most beneficial (Stonnington, 1986). No clear data exist to guide clinicians in this regard.

Some observations indicate that postinjury vocational competence may be more affected by the amount of motivation and competence a person has or can develop rather than by length of time since injury. In many cases, people with TBI require two, three, or even four job placements before stability is established (D.A. Ellerd, personal communication, January 18, 1989). Wehman, Kreutzer, West, et al. (1989) also support the need for additional placements.

Physical and Medical Status

Whether caused by motor vehicle accidents, firearms, assaults, falls, or pedestrian accidents, people with moderate and severe TBI often require extensive hospitalization as a result of coma or other conditions. They may also require weeks and months of intense physical and cognitive rehabilitation. Even then, many individuals continue to experience physical, social, and cognitive problems that interfere with gaining and maintaining employment (Brooks, McKinley, Symington, Beattie, & Campsie, 1987). In the supported work approach to job placement, clients are not excluded on the basis of cognitive or physical disabilities (Wehman, Kreutzer, Wood, et al., 1989).

To ensure the safety of an individual and to assist in the job matching process, it is necessary to obtain detailed information about a client's physical and medical status. Each individual referred for supported employment should undergo a physical and medical evaluation within the 12 months before placement. The evaluation by a physician should approve and release the individual for employment and indicate physical strengths and problems (e.g., seizures, diabetes). The physician should list medication prescribed for the client, including dose and frequency, which should be used to increase the likelihood of success on the job.

Psychiatric or Maladaptive Behavior

Major barriers to achieving stable employment and job retention for individuals with traumatic brain injury are emotional or interpersonal difficulties (Hendryx, 1989; Wehman, Kreutzer, Stonnington, et al., 1988). During job development, information from client records, family members, and other professionals should be examined to discern if the individual has a history of psychiatric or emotional difficulties, severe and persistent maladaptive behaviors, or physically or verbally abusive behavior.

If severe depression or aggressive outbursts can be controlled and stabilized with therapy and/or medication, the individual probably will remain a candidate for supported employment. At the worksite during supported employment, a professional employment specialist helps the client to adjust socially and manage inappropriate behavior using behavior management techniques (Wehman & Kregel, 1985).

Severe and persistent behavior that is dangerous or grossly inappropriate will adversely affect job placement and job retention, causing further frustration and loss of self-esteem for the client. At this point, the employment specialist should refer the client to a neuropsychologist or psychiatrist.

Substance Use or Abuse

Research studies show a relationship between alcohol use and traumatic brain injury (Goodall, 1989). Although most of these studies focus on alcohol or other drug use at the time of injury or preinjury, a recent Medical College of Virginia survey found that approximately 23% of surveyed individuals with TBI were problem drinkers 18 months after their injuries (Kreutzer, 1988).

Postinjury substance abuse may be as serious a problem as the brain injury itself (National Head Injury Foundation, 1986). Beyond the physical dangers, such abuse may be an added reason for loss of employment (Eames, 1988; Wehman, Kreutzer, Wood, Morton, & Sherron, 1988).

Some professionals believe abstinence from alcohol and other drugs should be a requirement for people referred for supported employment services who exhibit substance abuse problems (Kreutzer & Goodall, 1989). One supported employment program lists "absence of evidence indicative of substance abuse" as one of its criteria for accepting a candidate for placement (Wehman, Kreutzer, Wood, et al., 1989, p. 110).

Supported employment programs can screen for evidence of substance use via a questionnaire and/or structured interview (Wehman, Kreutzer, Stonnington, et al., 1988). A history of alcohol or other drug use, particularly at the time of the injury, should be carefully noted. If the client and the family indicate that the client does not use alcohol or other drugs, then it can be assumed that no problem currently exists; however, assessment for substance abuse should occur throughout an individual's employment, especially if there were signs of use or abuse before or at the time of injury.

Any evidence of current substance abuse must be addressed by a trained substance abuse or addiction specialist before job placement. A substance abuse problem is not alleviated by employment; in fact, employment may provide additional income with which to purchase alcohol or illicit drugs.

Family or Marital Stability

Family systems theory posits that when something happens to anyone within a system, all members within that system are affected (Minuchin, 1974). If a family member experiences TBI, the entire family is affected and altered by the consequences of the injury, which include physical, emotional, and behavioral changes in the individual (Livingston & Brooks, 1988). Lezak (1987) found that the role changes that inevitably occur when an adult becomes dependent can be emotionally distressing for all concerned, particularly for spouses.

It is generally accepted that the family of an individual with a disability is important in the successful implementation of supported employment services (Moon, Goodall, Barcus, & Brooke, 1986; Wehman & Kregel, 1985). Rosenthal and Young (1988) stated that "a failure to understand family dynamics following head injury . . . is likely to limit the potential success of any rehabilitation program" (p. 42). Some families may be overprotective or unsupported; others may be dysfunctional and in need of family counseling or therapy. It is common for relationships to dissolve following an injury (Peters, Stambrook, Moore, & Esses, 1990).

In light of the changes that occur within the family and the family's importance in rehabilitation efforts, family members must be included as a vital part of the supported employment team. The employment specialist's role includes providing the family with information about supported employment services and assessing the family's feelings about employment for the family member with TBI.

Vocational Goals and Expectations

Most quality vocational programs for people with TBI concentrate on an individual's interests and preferences (Fraser, 1988) because people work most effectively in jobs they like—a particularly relevant assumption for people with TBI who often feel a need to gain control over at least some aspects of their lives. In determining vocational goals and expectations for an individual referred for supported employment services, the following should be considered:

- What type of work is the client interested in doing?
- What type of work has the client done preinjury? Postinjury?
- What are the family's work expectations for the client?
- What are the client's existing skills?
- What is the client's ability to learn new skills?

If these issues are not considered before job development, clients may repeatedly refuse potential job interviews, sabotage job placements, or be placed in jobs in which they are unhappy.

Unfortunately, many individuals hold unrealistic vocational expectations because their brain injuries themselves cause diminished self-sight and lowered ability to solve problems and perceive situations correctly. Families may contribute to denial by predicting a complete recovery in which the individual will return to preinjury employment (Corthell & Tooman, 1985; Kreutzer, Wehman, Morton, & Stonnington, 1988). Intervention through education or counseling may be necessary if the desires and work expectations of the client and family conflict with the professional options of the supported employment staff.

Job Match Matching specific characteristics of a client and a given job is critical to a successful job match. In the supported employment approach, an employment specialist engages in client-specific job development. A job match is the culmination of the employment specialist's thorough analysis of job requirements and client abilities. Based on existing skills and the potential to learn certain tasks, the client is matched to a suitable job (Kreutzer et al., 1988; Wehman & Kregel, 1985; Wehman, Kreutzer, West, et al., 1989).

Moon et al. (1986) describe the job-matching process as locating and analyzing a potential job. If the employment specialist believes the client can perform or learn the job duties involved and will be comfortable in that job environment, a job interview is arranged. The employment specialist also considers issues of transportation, family support, physical and medical status, and social and behavioral skills.

Assessment for Transition

The purpose of student assessment in transitional employment programs is to develop a realistic, appropriate, and acceptable vocational direction for the student with TBI. In conducting assessment activities, supported employment program staff seek insight into a consumer's interests, personality characteristics, vocational strengths, and support needs in addition to establishing rapport with consumers and family members.

Several approaches can be used to gather information and define a vocational goal, including a home visit, an informal psychosocial assessment, a situational assessment, a career search exercise, and writing a functional résumé.

Home Visit

During a home visit, program staff have an invaluable opportunity to learn about the individual's residential environment, observe family interactions, discuss any family members' concerns about pursuing a vocational direction, and collect information on hobbies or chores that the individual performs at home. For students with TBI, home interviews and observations should focus on 1) vocational expectations of the student and family; 2) the types of vocational support that family members can provide (e.g., transportation, financial support); 3) the independence that the student experiences in the home and community; 4) evidence of family stress and dysfunction caused by the injury, its aftermath, or other related reasons; and 5) any assistance the family can provide in identifying preferred jobs or in developing leads for work experience sites or future employment. Although program staff may find it useful to conduct structured interviews during home visits, a wealth of information can be gathered simply by spending a couple of hours chatting informally in people's homes.

Informal Psychosocial Assessment

In order to gain insight into behavioral functioning, build rapport, and expose students to different work environments, program staff may want to accompany students with TBI to a variety of community-based settings, such as malls, libraries, restaurants, museums, and college campuses. In addition to giving students an opportunity for recreation away from the home, observing the interactions of the student in these settings can help teachers to

anticipate behaviors that may be problematic on a jobsite. One student who was taken to a restaurant by an employment specialist finished his own lunch, crammed numerous "free" sugar packets into his pockets, and requested that he be permitted to eat the employment specialist's leftover lunch. The employment specialist was naturally concerned about social interaction skills at the time of placement.

Situational Assessment

Actual work settings are used in situational assessments to enable students to test their interests in job duties and work environments, to observe consumers' responses to training strategies, and to identify needs for support. Because a real worksite offers characteristics that are common to most work environments (e.g., interruptions in routine, distractions), this approach to assessment has a greater likelihood of yielding information relevant to a job placement than assessments performed in an office or facility-based setting. Although a situational assessment should not be mandatory for all consumers, it can be a useful tool for students with TBI when more information is desired to determine the feasibility of a vocational direction, to allow the student to explore career options, and to see firsthand how the student interacts with co-workers, reacts to work pressures, and responds to work-related suggestions and supervision, among other areas of concern (Kreutzer & Morton, 1988). Table 16.4 outlines the basic steps for developing situational assessment sites.

 Setting Transition Goals Once assessments are completed, the transition goals need to be established (Mira, Tucker, & Tyler, 1992; Savage & Wolcott, 1994). The student, family, and friends must confer to identify their needs and wishes. The transition team can then take this information and begin to formalize a plan.

Career Search Exercise

Numerous tools, such as standardized career interest inventories and computerized vocational assessment programs, are available to programs that have the resources or inclination to use them. Consider, though, that many of these tools were not specifically developed for people with physical and/or cognitive disabilities associated with TBI. Nonetheless, working through a career search exercise with a student can yield valuable assessment information in addition to helping the student to identify potential jobs.

Writing a Functional Résumé

The process of writing a résumé can be useful to students with TBI and program staff in clarifying and defining vocational goals. Depending on the type and level of position to be pursued, an employer may require a résumé instead of, or in addition to, a job application. Although a traditional chronological résumé can be utilized, sometimes a functional résumé is more useful. A *functional résumé* portrays an individual's broad skill areas developed as a result of employment, volunteer, recreational, and educational experiences and is ideal for individuals who have limited pre- and/or postinjury work experience or for those who have not retained many of their preinjury cognitive, academic, or physical skills. In these cases, a functional résumé is an effective way of focusing on the unique abilities, interests, and characteristics that each person can bring to a job situation.

Table 16.4. Developing a situational assessment site

1. Identify jobs in the local community that are available, generally appropriate for people in the refer-
 ral pool, and offer some variety. Although it would be ideal to assess each consumer in his or her
 specific area of interest, this is probably not feasible. Targeting jobs that are representative of a num-
 ber of different vocational areas, however, can make the experience more relevant for the consumer,
 who has options from which to choose.

2. Identify businesses in the local community that have the targeted jobs. Since hospitals and universi-
 ties typically possess a variety of positions, they are usually excellent assessment sites.

3. Contact the personnel director by letter and a follow-up phone call, and schedule an appointment
 to visit the company. During the visit, describe the supported employment program, the purpose of
 situational assessment, and the responsibilities of the employer, job trainer, and consumer during an
 assessment. If the personnel director approves the company's participation in a situational assess-
 ment, schedule an appointment to meet with department supervisors.

4. Meet with department supervisors and identify positions suitable for situational assessment. Arrange
 to observe workers performing the targeted jobs and develop task analyses.

5. Identify consumer(s) to participate in the assessment and schedule times. Depending on the type of
 position being worked, the amount of information desired, and the needs of the consumer and em-
 ployer, the length of time required for an assessment might range from hours to several days, and
 possibly longer in some cases.

6. Complete the assessment and record observations. It is recommended that observations focus on the
 items listed on the consumer screening form so that information derived from various sources can
 be compared.

7. Finally, provide feedback on the experience to the consumer, family members, program staff, and re-
 ferral source. If the program is receiving funds for conducting situational assessments, a formalized
 written report is likely to be necessary.

Adapted from Moon, Inge, Wehman, Brooke, & Barcus (1990).

Although a functional résumé should honestly reflect the student's skills and interests, there is ample opportunity during job placement activities to discuss the job candidate's support needs with an employer. A functional résumé consists of the six following areas:

1. *Job objective:* Traditionally, a job objective briefly defines a job seeker's career direction. Such information as the type of position desired, the type of organization for which the job seeker would like to work, and examples of skills the job seeker would like to use are included in the job objective. For example, a job objective for someone with an interest in a clerical field might read:

 To obtain a clerical position in a financial institution using my skills in bookkeeping, typing, and oral communications

 Obviously, using a résumé with a job objective that is as well defined as the example limits the student to applying for positions that match his or her stated objective. For those whose career direction is less focused or those who would like to consider a variety of positions, a résumé can be developed to fit each objective, the objective can be written more generally, or it can be omitted entirely.

2. *Education:* Identified in this section are the name, location, year of graduation or years attended, type of degree, and program of study (if applicable) of the educational institution last attended. Information pertaining to vocational training, seminars, or relevant coursework can also be included in this section.

General diploma, Richmond High School, Richmond, Virginia, June 1986. Courses include typing, word processing, bookkeeping, business math, and composition.

3. *Skills:* Identifying the broad skills areas that an individual possesses is perhaps the trickiest aspect of developing a functional résumé. In general, any abilities, gifts, instincts, or strengths exhibited should be listed. For example, one woman with TBI demonstrated her abilities in oral communication by speaking to the state legislature on behalf of people with disabilities. Another utilized his entrepreneurial talents by collecting aluminum products from friends and neighbors, taking them to a recycling plant, and depositing the profits in a savings account. For the student with TBI, behavioral and personality sequelae of the injury can sometimes be used to advantage as well. For example, a student with a low tolerance for error or disorganization, which frequently is an annoyance at home or school, can be attractive to an employer if this trait also means "attention to detail." When portraying skills areas on a functional résumé, the skills selected should be relevant to vocational goals and specific evidence reflecting each skill should be provided. Items listed under experience and interests may demonstrate these skills.

4. *Experience:* All paid and volunteer experiences, both pre- and postinjury, should be listed in reverse chronological order.

Oral and written communication skills
- Presented to members of state legislature on the need to improve accessibility of public facilities for people with disabilities
- Read books to elementary school children at local library
- Receptionist/office assistant, Bank of Virginia, Richmond, Virginia, 1988–1990

5. *Interests:* If space permits, a functional résumé may be enhanced by listing any interests, hobbies, or unusual life experiences.

Gardening, fishing, running, reading, swimming, and needlework

6. *References:* Because most employers generally request the names and telephone numbers of at least two references, it is helpful to type this information on a separate piece of paper prior to the job interview so that it is readily available.

Figure 16.2 is an example of a functional résumé composed using a worksheet format. When program staff have finished gathering information during the intake and assessment phase, all information pertaining to a case should be reviewed and compared so that general trends and inconsistencies can be identified.

Enhancing Academic Reentry and Inclusion

Savage (1991), a leading writer in the area of educational identification and classification of children with TBI (see also Savage & Wolcott, 1994), noted that there are two major issues related to classification. The first issue concerns the usefulness and validity of medical classifications such as mild, moderate, and severe traumatic brain injury. The second issue concerns classification of educational services versus rehabilitation therapy (e.g., occupational, physical, speech-language) that schools are required to provide under IDEA. Physicians usually make clinical evaluations in the emergency room that may have very little or

Functional resume worksheet

Name ———————————————————— Phone ————————————

Address ————————————————————————————————————

Job objective (optional)

To ——

Education

——

Degree Major/program School

——

Location of school

Skills **Accomplishments**

———————————————— ————————————————————

 ————————————————————

———————————————— ————————————————————

 ————————————————————

 ————————————————————

Experience (most recent)

——

Job title Employer City State Years employed

——

Job title Employer City State Years employed

Interests

References—available upon request

Figure 16.2. A functional résumé worksheet. (From Goodall, P., Groah, C., Sherron, P., Kreutzer, J., & Wehman, P. [1991]. *Supported employment services for individuals with traumatic brain injury* [p. 75]. Richmond: Virginia Commonwealth University, Rehabilitation Research and Training Center on Supported Employment; reprinted by permission.)

no utility in classifying and placing a student into educational arrangements. The definition of TBI presented earlier in this chapter provides a necessary starting point for an interdisciplinary team to make an initial determination of the nature of the disability; however, this information is descriptive at best and, along with the problematic issues surrounding classification, makes an impending placement very difficult.

The development of the individualized education program (IEP), amid the recommendations of the interdisciplinary team, should lead to an appropriate placement in a general education class, resource class, or self-contained class. As a result of the multiplic-

ity of problems that are usually presented by these children, it is very difficult to determine which type of placement will be best. To a large extent, the appropriateness of the placement depends on the flexibility with which the teachers and therapists are willing to provide services. Students with TBI should be given every opportunity to be included in as many general education activities as possible, academic as well as extramural. But continuing failure can lead to frustration, aggression, and greatly lowered self-esteem.

In helping the IEP team make an appropriate placement, it may be helpful to determine whether the child can 1) follow simple directions, 2) function within a group of two or more students, 3) engage in some type of meaningful communication, 4) tolerate 20–30 minutes of general classroom stimulation, and 5) attend to a task for at least 10–15 minutes. In reviewing the numerous issues related to placement into different educational arrangements that may be offered by the school system, Savage (1991) articulates that the following points that should be considered.

1. Does the school know the definition of traumatic brain injury?
2. Does the school know what the child can do now?
3. Does the school know what the child needs to do next?
4. What environmental program changes does the child need in school?
5. Who will be responsible for the child's educational program?
6. How will the family know that the educational program is working for the child?

Savage further notes that students with traumatic brain injury often make such rapid changes in the first few months following a brain injury that their initial IEP should be written for a shorter period of time, such as 6–8 weeks. Eventually, the IEP goals can be extended over a longer period of time. Goals and solutions should be highly functional and practical. Issues such as safety can become paramount (see Table 16.5).

The challenges of identifying, classifying, and placing students with disabilities are only further compounded when a child sustains a moderate or severe traumatic brain injury. As special education personnel know very little about traumatic brain injury, it is not surprising that these children are somewhat lost in the public education system. Because TBI is the primary cause of pediatric mortality, however, it is essential for special educators to improve their knowledge base.

Managing the Transition from Hospital to School Some (Ylvisaker, 1985; Ylvisaker, Feeney, & Mullins, 1995; Ylvisaker, Hartwick, & Stevens, 1991) have indicated that there are a number of points that need to be understood during the all-important school reentry process:

1. Initial reentry planning
2. Reentry activities through the rehabilitation admission
3. Reentry activities shortly before discharge
4. Transitional classrooms
5. Support to general classrooms

The initial reentry planning should involve determining whatever academic or social support the child may need, who the significant people in the child's environment are (e.g., teachers, peers), and what will be necessary to effectively modify and monitor the child's

Table 16.5. Problems and solutions for a student with TBI

Problem	Solution
Mary is unable to utilize emergency assistance via telephone.	A Duo/Speaker Phone is preprogrammed with emergency numbers (e.g., police, fire, ambulance) so that Mary can call them with the push of a button. Each word is paired with a symbol (i.e., "fire" and a flame). Her mother's work number is also programmed so that Mary can contact her at any time.
Mary's speech is difficult to understand over the telephone.	The Real Voice System, a full-featured Duophone-based speech synthesizer with natural sounding rhthym and intonation, allows Mary to better communicate over the telephone.
Mary opens the door indiscriminately because she cannot see who is there.	A surveillance camera allows Mary to turn on the television set to identify visitors visually. If Mary does not recognize the visitor, she is not to open the door, unless the individual provides appropriate identification.
Mary is unable to safely use appliances in her home.	Electronic buzzers installed on the stove and microwave alert Mary when an appliance has not been turned off.
Mary has difficulty remembering time and date.	A digital calendar watch helps Mary keep track of the date, month, and time.
Mary is unable to keep appointments, pay bills on time, or meet other deadlines.	Mary consults an electronic calendar daily to obtain information about appointments and deadlines. The calendar is programmed monthly, and instructions are listed sequentially. For example, the day before a medical appointment, the electronic calendar instructs Mary to call the taxi company to arrange transportation; the next day, the calendar informs her of the arrival time of the taxi as well as the time of the appointment.

program. Initial contact with the school is an important feature of a successful reentry. This means that the hospital service coordinator, social worker, or other outreach coordinator must make immediate communication with school personnel.

Reentry activities throughout the rehabilitation administration will include activities such as family education (including siblings), peer education, and increased communication with the school and former classmates. This may mean developing material on traumatic brain injury for targeted school personnel who will be working or interacting with the child. The tips for inclusion found in Table 16.6 are useful strategies to help youth with TBI reenter the general education school environment.

Designing Transition Programs for Youth with TBI

When planning a transition program for youth with TBI, especially those 18–21 years of age, it is paramount to focus extensively on work and vocational placements. Specifically, these youth should experience placements in real employment situations (Clark, 1996).

Table 16.6. Tips for inclusion of youth with TBI

Receptive language
Limit the amount of information presented at one time.
Provide simple instructions for only one activity at a time.
Have the student repeat instructions.
Use concrete language.

Expressive language
Teach the student to rehearse silently before verbally replying.
Teach the student to look for cues from listeners to ascertain that he or she is being understood.
Teach the student to directly ask if he or she is being understood.

Maintaining attention
Provide a study carrel or preferential seating.
After giving instructions, check for proper attention and understanding by having the student repeat them.
Teach the student to use self-regulating techniques to maintain attention (e.g., asking "Am I paying attention? What is the required task?").

Impulsiveness
Teach the student to mentally rehearse steps before beginning an activity.
Reduce potential distractions.
Frequently restate and reinforce rules.

Memory
Teach the student to use external aids such as notes, memos, daily schedule sheets, and assignment sheets.
Use visual imagery, when possible, to supplement oral content.
Teach visual imaging techniques for information presented.
Provide repetition and frequent review of instruction materials.
Provide immediate and frequent feedback to enable the student to interpret success or failure.

Following directions
Provide the student with both visual and auditory directions.
Model tasks, whenever possible.
Break multistep directions into small parts and list them so that the student can refer back when needed.

Motor skills
Allow the student to complete a project rather than turn in a written assignment.
Have the student use a typewriter or a word processor to complete assignments.
Allow extra time for completing tasks requiring fine motor skills.
Assign someone to take notes for the student during lectures.

Adapted from Mira, Tucker, & Tyler (1992).

Therefore, the transition program presented in the following section includes information on how to support people in competitive work environments.

Susan *Susan is a 19-year-old who experienced TBI at age 15. She lives with her mother, a single parent. She has an older brother who does not live with them. As a result of her injuries, she has had difficulty controlling her inappropriate behavior at times and is subject to frequent depression. Susan has full use of her right side but no functional use of her left hand and minimal use of her left foot. She uses a wheelchair for mobility but can stand with minimal support. Susan can read and write but becomes easily frustrated and apathetic. She wishes to work as a cashier in a retail store.* *An ITP for Susan follows on pages 467–470.*

Description of Student's Future Vision

Susan would like to improve her physical and mental health, increase her mobility and independence, and find employment as a cashier.

Individualized Transition Plan

Student's Name *Susan*

Birthdate _____

Student's Identification Number _____

Participants:

School *Virginia Randolph*

ITP Conference Date _____

Name		Position	
Susan		*Student*	
Aurelia		*Mother*	
Melissa		*Teacher*	
James		*Service coordinator*	
Sandra		*Principal*	

Career and Economic Self-Sufficiency

Employment Goal *Susan will work as a (stationary) cashier.*

Level of present performance: *Susan reads at third-grade level, can add and subtract up to 3-digit numbers, and has money skills (count, make change).*

Steps needed to accomplish goal: *1. Obtain VR services. 2. Arrange for transportation through STAR. 3. Provide assistance with personal care before work via personal assistance services.*

Date of completion: *January 1995*

Person(s) responsible for implementation: *Service coordinator, mother, and VR counselor*

Vocational Education/Training Goal *Susan will complete situational assessments at two or more sites using stationary cashiers (e.g., Piccadilly Cafeteria, Morrison's).*

Level of present performance: *Susan has worked at various unpaid sites, including the mailroom of Henrico Personnel, the Office of Henrico Public Utilities, and Dumbarton Library.*

Steps needed to accomplish goal: *1. Locate sites. 2. Schedule training times. 3. Train at two or more sites. 4. Share information with family, case manager, and Department of Rehabilitative Services.*

Date of completion: *December 1, 1995*

Person(s) responsible for implementation: *Teacher and vocational assessment center*

From Wehman, P. (1995). *Individual transition plans: The teachers curriculum guide for helping youth with special needs.* Austin, TX: PRO-ED; reprinted by permission.

Postsecondary Education Goal *Susan will attend two selected classes per year offered by Henrico Parks and Recreation.*

Level of present performance: *Susan is unable to do work samples from the GED but often states that she will be attending college. She spends most of her unstructured time watching television.*

Steps needed to accomplish goal: *1. Identify course options (i.e., in-service training, community college course). 2. Meet with admissions officer at community college. 3. Budget for course and transportation. 4. Budget for personal assistance as needed.*

Date of completion: *March 1995*

Person(s) responsible for implementation: *Service coordinator*

Financial/Income Needs Goal *Susan will open a checking account and learn how to make three department store purchases.*

Level of present performance: *Susan receives SSI but no other income. Her mother provides for her basic needs. Susan currently spends money frivolously and has not developed shopping skills.*

Steps needed to accomplish goal: *1. Assist Susan with opening a checking account. 2. Teach Susan how to budget her monthly income. 3. Guide Susan through practice in appropriate shopping skills.*

Date of completion: *March 1995*

Person(s) responsible for implementation: *Teacher and mother*

Career and Economic Self-Sufficiency

Independent Living Goal *Susan will be independent of her mother's assistance for personal care.*

Level of present performance: *Susan and her mother wish to continue living together but her mother is unable to assist Susan with all her personal care needs.*

Steps needed to accomplish goal: *1. Apply for personal assistance service through VR for preparation at work. 2. Occupational therapist should evaluate modifications as needed in the home. 3. Susan should receive instruction at home for self-care.*

Date of completion: *June 1995*

Person(s) responsible for implementation: *Occupational therapist and VR counselor*

Transportation/Mobility Goal *Susan will initiate her own transportation needs through STAR (to and from work and recreational activities).*

Level of present performance: *Susan can travel independently in her wheelchair at school and at home. She uses the telephone independently.*

Steps needed to accomplish goal: *1. Arrange for STAR services. 2. Instruct Susan on budgeting for transportation. 3. Instruct Susan on scheduling transportation.*

Date of completion: *December 1994*

Person(s) responsible for implementation: *Service coordinator*

Social Relationships Goal *Susan will develop platonic peer relationships and engage in activities with friend(s) weekly.*

Level of present performance: *Susan often speaks of wanting a baby and has made inappropriate advances toward male teachers and other students. She spends little time with peers.*

Steps needed to accomplish goal: *1. Susan will continue to attend Family Life classes. 2. She will attend a TBI support group. 3. She will join a school club (e.g., newspaper).*

Date of completion: *December 1994*

Person(s) responsible for implementation: *Teacher and parent*

Recreation/Leisure Goal *Susan will engage in daily aerobic exercise with friends.*

Level of present performance: *Susan spends much of her unstructured time watching TV and eating snacks, leading to decreased mobility and stamina.*

Steps needed to accomplish goal: *1. Prepare an "individualized" exercise video. with exercises appropriate for Susan's needs. 2. Instruct Susan in performance of the exercises.*

Date of completion: *April 1995*

Person(s) responsible for implementation: *Physical therapist*

Personal Competence

Health/Safety Goal *Susan will continue counseling sessions through the local mental health department.*

Level of present performance: *Susan has frequent bouts of depression. She has threatened to commit suicide several times since her accident.*

Steps needed to accomplish goal: *1. Maintain monthly contact with Susan and her mother. 2. Provide transportation as needed.*

Date of completion: *October 1994*

Person(s) responsible for implementation: *Service coordinator*

Self-Advocacy/Future Planning *Susan will become knowledgeable about available services and legislation related to people with disabilities.*

Level of present performance: *Susan and her mother depend on service coordinators and school personnel to gain access to services.*

Steps needed to accomplish goal: *1. Provide Susan and her mother with information on legislation. 2. Provide list of phone numbers for service agencies.*

Date of completion: *March 1995*

Person(s) responsible for implementation: *Teacher*

Student Career Preference

Susan wants to work with money in a cashier situation.

Student's Major Transition Needs

1. Part-time or full-time employment
2. Social activities with peers
3. Self-care training
4. Transportation
5. Continued counseling

Additional Notes

Compensatory Strategies on the Jobsite

Compensatory strategies are effective for helping students with TBI regain functional skills for living and working efficiently. Compensatory strategies consist of external and internal aids used to accomplish specific tasks. External aids are objects—such as watches, grocery lists, alarm clocks, or appointment books—that assist people with remembering and organizing their environments. Internal aids include techniques such as mental rehearsal, visual images, or mnemonics to assist memory or the comprehension of abstract concepts. Techniques such as personalized checklists and schedules ensure routine and minimize the effects of memory and attention impairments.

To increase their effectiveness, compensatory strategies must be functional and unobtrusive in work settings, and they should be developed in conjunction with family members and the individual who will be using them. Because they know about compensatory strategies that have been used successfully in the home, family members are especially resourceful. As people with TBI return to employment, their independence and productivity can be enhanced through the development of effective compensatory strategies and physical adaptations. The following are compensatory strategies that can be used by teachers in employment settings to foster independence:

- Use lists to compensate for memory problems. Information can be written in a pocket notebook or an appointment book or listings posted where a particular task or behavior is to occur. Checklists can be used to remind the student that certain activities have been completed.
- Use individualized auditory or visual cues. Tape-recorded messages or instructions are excellent auditory cues. Different colored containers can serve as visual cues for specific items.
- Structure the environment to enhance functioning. Accommodate endurance levels and stress tolerance by sequencing tasks (e.g., schedule more difficult tasks first to alleviate fatigue). Change the environment, if possible, to decrease stress resulting from excessive noise or temperatures.
- Use physical adaptations. Use trays or jigs to help students to keep materials in place and improve work speed. Materials such as electric staplers, rubber band holders, rubber fingertips, and laminated work materials increase work efficiency.
- Rearrange the immediate work area. To save time, reduce confusion, and compensate for specific limitations, arrange the workspace, the sequence of job tasks, and the overall workday so that the majority of time on the job is productive. For example, place work materials on the left if the student has problems with the right visual field or situate an individual apart from other workers if distractibility is a concern.

Helping Individuals with TBI Go to Work

A number of researchers attempting to determine the variables that influence return to work have consistently found that the severity of injury—measured by a Glasgow Coma Scale score, length of hospitalization, or duration of PTA—is negatively related to the likelihood of returning to work (Ezrachi, Ben-Yishay, Kay, Diller, & Rattok, 1991; McMordie, Barker, & Paolo, 1990; Prigatano et al., 1994.) It is important to note, however, that some in-

dividuals sustaining very severe injuries are able to return to employment relatively un-hindered (McMordie et al., 1990; Rao et al., 1990), and not all investigators have found a re-lationship between injury severity and return to work (Brooks, Campsie, Symington, Beat-tie, & McKinlay, 1987). The specific types of cognitive, physical, and psychosocial impairments associated with an individual's TBI may be more predictive of his or her re-turn to work than the measure of injury severity. For example, the presence of significant physical disability, psychosocial impairment, and memory/reasoning deficits have all been linked to poor work outcomes.

The types and duration of postinjury rehabilitation efforts have also been shown to af-fect return to work. For example, Vogenthaler, Smith, and Goldfader (1989) found that the amount of postinjury rehabilitation services received (primarily physical and occupational therapy) was a significant predictor of work or other productive activity. Participation in vocational adjustment services also appears to improve work outcomes.

Supported Employment

The value of supportive work environments and financial rewards in long-term job reten-tion has been empirically established for members of the general work force and, to a lim-ited extent, other disability groups; yet, this work factor for people with TBI has only begun to receive attention. A prospective study by West (1994) found that individuals with TBI who experience positive supported employment outcomes had been placed in posi-tions that offered more opportunities for socialization with co-workers, more company-sponsored supports such as employee assistance programs, and other types of "natural" supports. In addition, work outcomes were enhanced by placement in jobs that offered fringe benefits, particularly medical insurance and regular reviews for raises and ad-vancement. No other factors, including preinjury variables, injury-related variables, or postinjury services or work histories, appeared to influence supported employment out-comes.

Since the 1990s, new information has been generated relative to the complexities of helping people with TBI—who are difficult to employ—return to work (Fraser & Weh-man, 1995; Morton & Wehman, 1995; Wehman, West, Sherron, Kregel, & Kreutzer, 1995). These are usually people who have been through many different attempts and approaches to improve their community adjustment. An examination of their service history data is re-vealing as it shows the lack of a consistent and succinct set of effective interventions. What is most interesting about these services, many of which were very costly, is how, for the most part, they did not lead to useful outcomes. Based on the available published litera-ture, however, a number of vocational program guidelines do emerge. This information is targeted to practitioners as well as patients, families, and professionals.

The evidence is overwhelming that brain injury severity has a clear and powerful effect on going back to work. Research literature supports this finding and is useful for practitioners planning on the amount of time and effort that will need to be expended in return to work (RTW) interventions. Similarly, severe neuropsychological impairments in-fluence work outcome. Those with the most severe cognitive impairments are more likely to reenter the work force successfully than those with mild dysfunctions.

This is not to suggest, however, that return to work is unlikely and intervention is in-effectual. Emerging technologies, including supported employment, assistive technology,

job carving, and workplace accommodations, can mitigate the effects of cognitive, physical, and psychosocial impairments resulting from TBI. Public policy initiatives such as the Americans with Disabilities Act (ADA) of 1990, PL 101-336, and the Rehabilitation Act Amendments of 1992, PL 102-569, demand that these technologies and accommodations be available to individuals with even the most severe disabilities. Successful RTW can be fostered by training in work skills and behaviors as well as by recognizing discrimination, fostering choice and self-determination, encouraging self-advocacy, and ensuring the right to receive appropriate services, accommodations, and supports.

People with severe TBI in supported employment tend to move from job to job before settling; such instability may be the result of medical or health problems, economic layoffs, slow or poor quality work, a poor job match, and inappropriate behavior, among other reasons (Kregel, Parent, & West, 1994). Yet, like many members of the general population who are beginning their careers, many individuals with severe TBI achieve success in second, third, or later positions. A defining characteristic of supported employment is the availability of follow-along services throughout the client's work history, including periods of unemployment, which requires a reconceptualization of the concept of return to work. The ability to achieve employment should not be measured by results from one or two jobs because repeated placements may be necessary for individuals to develop or regain work goals, skills, and behaviors. Return to work with supported employment should be conceptualized as labor force participation, using measures such as the employment ratio, rather than single job retention.

Community-based work experiences—either paid or unpaid, part time or full time— are extremely valuable activities that should be provided as early as during the postacute phase. Engaging regularly in productive community work experiences helps individuals discover their work preferences, ambitions, and needs.

Evidence suggests that significant determinants of success in supported employment are the pay and benefits received and the types and extent of social support found on the job (West, 1994). The likelihood of successful work following TBI can be enhanced by assisting individuals to find jobs that are financially and socially rewarding to them. Specifically, employment outcomes can be improved by paying close attention to the structure and culture of the workplace before a placement is made and targeting positions that offer fringe benefits, opportunities for raises and advancement, formal and informal supports, and opportunities for socialization and friendships with other employees.

Return to Work and the Family

Going back to work is a complex interplay of differing interests and motivations, and those of the family cannot be overlooked. Family support and adjustment have been shown to promote employability for individuals with TBI and other types of disabilities. Motivated family members can assist with job leads, transportation, psychosocial and substance abuse treatments, and other supports and interventions. Work outcomes can be enhanced by fully exploring employment goals with both the individual with TBI and the family. For example, if health or medical issues are a concern, then positions offering extensive medical insurance benefits are optimal. If the individual and family are more interested in developing friendships or occupying time, then these factors should drive the job development process.

Ultimately, people with severe TBI should no longer be led to believe that returning to work is impossible. Legislative initiatives give individuals with severe disabilities protection from discrimination and mandates for workplace accommodations and appropriate rehabilitative services, including supported employment for those with the most severe disabilities. With an appropriate work program in place (i.e., one that focuses heavily upon community-based work experiences with support from a job coach), employment is possible for most individuals with severe TBI who want to work. The motivation of the individual and his or her family, acceptance of limitations, and supportive assistance from the rehabilitation agency and the work environment are the key elements of success.

Allen *Allen is a 24-year-old who sustained a traumatic brain injury in a serious car accident. He was in a coma for over 2 months and was hospitalized for more than 4 months. Since the injury, Allen walks with a leg brace and cane and has static nerve palsy in the right leg. He has right-hand ataxia and visual impairment in the left eye. Prior to his injury, Allen worked part time as a maintenance assistant, spray painter, and animal care attendant for varying lengths of time. During a 3-year period in the Marine Corps, he performed clerical work. After leaving the hospital, Allen indicated a desire for a full-time office job based on his previous clerical experience. A neuropsychological report recommended a desk job that involved calculator skills.*

A 40-hour per week job as a microfilm processor at a large electronics retailer was located. The job consisted of two major tasks: processing expense and merchandise checks and microfilming documents. Allen learned all of the steps in the processing portion of his job within 30 days. Initially, there were 30–40 quality control checks per hour by the employment specialist, until a level of 98%–100% accuracy was established. In the microfilming area, accuracy levels exceeded 85% after 1 month; after 3 months, Allen was completing 250–300 units per day with 99% accuracy.

Despite Allen's rapid skills acquisition, problems with work quality and skill maintenance occurred during the first 4 months of employment. These problems included forgetting the steps involved in the job, slow production rate, difficulty in operating the equipment, and sequencing and addition errors. The following job modifications and adaptations helped to improve the speed and quality of Allen's job performance:

1. *The worktable was elevated using two wooden two-by-fours.*
2. *Written notes were posted as visual cues.*
3. *Pen caps were placed on the switches of the microfilm machine to prevent incorrect hitting.*
4. *Large paper clips were substituted for small ones.*
5. *An electric stapler replaced the manual one.*
6. *Plexiglas file dividers, rather than cardboard, were used.*

Allen had off-site problems as well, notably periodic drinking binges and chronic poor nutrition. Budgeting was also a persistent concern. Many hours of intervention time, away from the jobsite, were devoted to addressing these problems.

A total of 712 staff hours have been spent with Allen. However, the initial, heavy involvement of the employment specialist was reduced as Allen became increasingly independent and competent on the job. One month after Allen was hired, the company upgraded his status from trial to permanent worker; his hourly wage also increased from $4.50 to $5 per hour with full fringe benefits.

Allen continues to work a 40-hour week with opportunities for overtime. He has been employed

for almost 2 years. As result of his job, Allen is able to live independently. He purchased a stereo and a car, and he goes out socially more frequently than he did before he got his job. Allen's work quality remains stable; the employment specialist is on site only during planned periodic visits as part of follow-along services.

Cal Cal is a 32-year-old who experienced traumatic brain injury after falling asleep while driving and crashing his car. He was not discovered for nearly 12 hours. Cal was in a coma for 21 days. Following the injury, Cal had decreased short-term memory, difficulty following instructions, poor concentration, occasional confusion, and reduced physical mobility on the left side.

Prior to the accident, Cal, who graduated from college with a degree in journalism, was employed as a sportswriter for a local newspaper. He returned to his former job 9 months after his injury but was terminated within 6 months because of his inability to meet story deadlines.

Cal then attended a state residential rehabilitation center and received certification as an office helper. He was employed in a mail processing position but left the job 1 month later because he could not meet the productivity standards. Cal was unable to locate employment on his own and worked for 2 years as a volunteer physical therapy aide at an outpatient rehabilitation center.

A position as an activities aide at a convalescent center became available. The job was for 20 hours per week at $3.55 per hour. Job duties involved one-to-one visitations with residents who were unable to leave their rooms independently. The job also required documentation of these visits on a patient interaction report for Medicare purposes.

Cal's interest in working with people, his good communication skills, and his preference for non-repetitive work made him a good candidate for the position. In addition, the job duties would place minimal demands on his visual/motor skills, and the working environment was fairly quiet, which would increase Cal's ability to concentrate on job tasks.

The employment specialist played a major role in structuring and organizing the visitation schedule and the documentation procedures, which enabled Cal to perform his job duties independently. The employment specialist also modeled appropriate ways to interact with residents during room visits and provided Cal with feedback on his performance.

Total teacher/job coach intervention time has been 234 hours to date. The employment specialist contacts Cal and/or the employer twice a month to ensure that the job is being completed to the employer's satisfaction. Cal, the employment specialist, and the activities director meet quarterly to update the visitation schedule. Cal has been employed for 20 months and expresses a strong desire to continue working in this field; he hopes to obtain a full-time position in the future.

Implementation of Compensatory Strategies, Adaptations, Modifications, and Restructuring

The implementation of compensatory strategies, adaptations, and modifications, in addition to restructuring the work environment, can enhance an individual's learning and promote the ability to perform independently at a jobsite. Adjustments can be cognitively oriented, providing the individual with effective ways to remember what to do and how to do it (e.g., a worksheet outlining the steps needed to balance a cash drawer, a map that outlines a route to follow when cleaning apartment grounds, detailed written instructions to

follow when cleaning plants). Other implementations may be used to compensate for physical limitations (e.g., providing a lap board for individuals involved in data entry to reduce ataxia, use of a stand to reduce unsteadiness in upright positions while an individual sorts mail). Development and implementation of strategies usually occurs when an individual encounters difficulty in learning a new task, shows great variability in task performance, or is unable to meet the required production standard. A review of probe data can reveal where difficulties arise.

It is crucial that the individual perceive the usefulness of compensatory strategies and participate in the planning process, which increases compliance with strategies. The guidelines listed in Table 16.7 may be useful when discussing the development of a compensatory strategy, adaptation, modification, or job restructuring with an individual.

E.Z.　*E.Z. is employed as an order entry operator at a national pizza company chain. His duties include taking incoming calls from customers, ordering pizza, and routing orders to the appropriate distribution centers via computer terminal. E.Z. had minimal problems learning the necessary skills for his job. He reached 100% accuracy by the second week of employment. Because of physical and cognitive limitations (i.e., left hand ataxia; right side hemiplegia; slowed, disorganized thinking), however, E.Z. is unable to consistently work fast enough to meet the required production rate.*

Factors contributing to his slow speed are an inability to press the shift key and other keys simultaneously, periods of increased extraneous movement caused by ataxia, and poor fine motor skills. E.Z. also has difficulty turning the pages of a city map used to locate customer delivery areas.

At times, E.Z. cannot recall procedures for exceptions to the basic routine (e.g., remembering to calculate a 10% discount if a customer orders 10 or more pizzas). Finally, E.Z. makes frequent requests for special considerations. Some modifications, adaptations, and interventions that might be effective in alleviating these problems follow:

The problem　*Inability to press shift key and other keys simultaneously (E.Z. types with left hand due to right hand paralysis)*

Possible solutions　*Computer accessory: shift key device*
　　　　　　　　Program computer to allow sequential pressing of certain keys

The problem　*Slow rate of data entry due to periods of increased extraneous movement caused by left hand ataxia*

Possible solutions　*Lap board to give arm stability*
　　　　　　　　Raised surface on keyboard created by doublesided tape to give hand stability

The problem　*Difficulty turning pages of city map book due to left hand ataxia, right side hemiplegia*

Possible solutions　*Automatic page turner*
　　　　　　　　Laminate pages of map in a binder and use tabs
　　　　　　　　Laminate map and place on wall

The problem　*Inability to remember exceptions to basic routine (i.e., poor memory)*

Possible solutions　*Program computer to "flag" special exception orders*

The problem　*Frequent requests for special considerations (e.g., request for longer lunch break because of his disability)*

Possible solutions　*Provide counseling on appropriate versus inappropriate requests*
　　　　　　　　Encourage employee to discuss appropriate requests with employer

Table 16.7. Guidelines for developing compensatory strategies

1. Review consumer assessment information to determine the individual's strengths and learning style.
2. Commend job performance to date in areas in which the individual is competent.
3. State employer concerns about enhancing performance in the desired area.
4. Review data, indicate the individual's current performance, and explain the objective of the strategy.
5. Request input on potential strategies to use in order to enhance current performance. Explain that strategies may be removed at some point in time.
6. Reinforce ideas. If ideas are unrealistic, guide the individual through a decision-making process that will lead to the agreed-upon objective.
7. Whenever possible, give the individual control (e.g., what size the checklist should be, what color notebook it should be).
8. Commend the individual for selecting a strategy.
9. Discuss the positive aspects of using the strategy (i.e., continued employment and independence).

Source: Goodall, Groah, Sherron, Kreutzer, & Wehman (1991).

Behavior Counseling

The employment specialist should be aware of how individuals interact with others in the work environment. Behavioral counseling techniques are useful in assisting workers to adjust to work environments. Table 16.8 illustrates possible behaviors that may impede employment and corresponding strategies.

One method used to gather and analyze behavioral data is the antecedent-behavior-consequence (ABC) analysis approach (see Chapter 15). The employment specialist first defines the behavior as specifically as possible using concrete, observable descriptions. Next, the employment specialist identifies antecedents that occur prior to occurrence of the targeted behavior and the consequences of that behavior. Documenting behaviors in

Table 16.8. Behaviors that can impede employment

Behavior	Strategies
Paranoia	• Investigate causes of insecurity. • Explain that thoughts are misguided.
Self-centeredness or egocentrism; impulsiveness or lack of inhibition	• Instruct co-workers and supervisors to provide direct feedback. • Convince the individual that he or she can control him- or herself by reinforcing controlled behavior. • Establish a key phrase, such as "chill out," to be repeated when the individual feels that he or she is losing control of a situation. • Investigate the use of alcohol and other drugs that lower inhibition. • Investigate prescribed medication effectiveness and compliance. • Have jobsite personnel express their feelings. • Provide immediate feedback on how behavior affects self and others (e.g., role play). • Provide a short command, such as "stop!" that signals the individual to recognize the behavior.
Agitation, irritability, or verbal outbursts	• Model calm behavior; keep nonverbal cues relaxed. • Acknowledge the individual's feelings and frustrations and provide a time for further discussion after work hours, then redirect the task.

(continued)

Table 16.8. *(continued)*

Behavior	Strategies
Agitation, irritability, or verbal outbursts *(continued)*	• Reinforce the consumer for regaining self-control after an outburst. • Remove the individual from the situation if possible and provide feedback about how the outburst may affect others. • Comment on the behavior, not the person. • Provide structure in the environment to minimize frustration; eliminate environmental distractions. • If co-workers become agitated, stay calm and redirect the individual to avoid manipulation. • Teach the individual relaxation techniques. • Learn to detect signs of increasing agitation. • Investigate outside stressors (e.g., interpersonal relationships, financial insecurities). • Investigate medication compliance and effectiveness. • Investigate the possibility of substance abuse or use. • Investigate work stressors (e.g., fear of not meeting expectations).

Source: Goodall et al. (1991).

this format identifies issues that need resolution and provides information to be included in the development of an overall behavior management plan.

Conclusion

This chapter has described the characteristics of youth with traumatic brain injury and how to develop transition programming for them. The unique challenges of these young people are formidable and include distorted vocational aspirations, serious cognitive and psychological problems, and ongoing physical disabilities. Work is an important medium for therapeutically overcoming many of the obstacles they face. A combination of work and school (i.e., a part-time job and participation in the community college) is often an effective bridge from school into the world of work. The education and intervention team members play an important role in this process. Personnel who would not be involved in the planning for young people with other disabilities should be involved in planning transitions for youth with TBI.

16

Study Questions

1. What is traumatic brain injury (TBI)? What are some of its causes and its economic impact on the individual, the family, and the community?

2. How is severity of TBI assessed and what are some factors that influence recovery?

3. Who typically comprises the individualized education program (IEP) planning team for a person with TBI and what are their roles?

4. What information in each of the following areas should be obtained to facilitate vocational outcomes: preinjury vocational competence and motivation, substance abuse, family or marital stability, physical and mental status, vocational goals and expectations?

5. What are five approaches that can be used to gather information and define a vocational goal for transition planning? Describe each.

6. What are some examples of compensatory strategies and physical adaptations that can be used to accommodate injury-related disability?

7. What factors typically enhance the likelihood of a successful vocational outcome for individuals who have sustained TBI?

References

Ackerman, A.M., & Shapiro, E.S. (1984). Self-monitoring and work productivity with mentally retarded adults. *Journal of Applied Behavior Analysis, 17*, 403–407.

Affleck, J.Q., Edgar, E., Levine, P., & Kottering, L. (1990). Postschool status of students classified as mildly mentally retarded, learning disabled, or nonhandicapped: Does it get better with time? *Education and Training in Mental Retardation, 25*, 315–324.

Agran, M. (Ed.). (1996). *Student directed learning: A handbook on self-management*. Pacific Grove, CA: Brooks/Cole.

Agran, M., Madison, D., & Bown, C. (1995). Teaching supported employees to prevent work injuries. *Journal of Vocational Rehabilitation, 5*(1), 31–42.

Agran, M., Moore, S., Fodor-Davis, J., & Deer, M. (1989). The application of a self-management program of instruction-following skills. *Journal of The Association for Persons with Severe Handicaps, 14*, 147–154.

Akabas, S.H. (1994). Workplace responsibilities: Key employer characteristics in support of job maintenance for people with mental illness. *Psychosocial Rehabilitation Journal, 17*(3), 91–101.

Alberto, P., & Troutman, A. (1982). *Behavior management*. Englewood Cliffs, NJ: Prentice Hall.

Albin, J.M., Rhodes, L., & Mank, D. (1994). Realigning organizational culture, resources, and community roles: Changeover to community employment. *Journal of The Association for Persons with Severe Handicaps, 19*, 105–115.

Alexander, R.N., & Clements, E.J. (1975). Parent training: Bringing it all back home. *Focus on Exceptional Children, 10*, 1–11.

Algozzine, B., & Ysseldyke, J.E. (1986). The future of the LD field: Screening and diagnosis. *Journal of Learning Disabilities, 19*(7), 394–398.

Allen, T.E., Rawlings, B.W., & Schildroth, A. (1989). *Deaf students and the school-to-work transition*. Baltimore: Paul H. Brookes Publishing Co.

Altman, B., & Cunningham, P. (1993). Dynamic process of movement in residential settings. *American Journal on Mental Retardation, 98*(2), 304–316.

American Association for Mental Retardation. (1992). *News and Notes, 5*(1), 1–8.

Americans with Disabilities Act (ADA) of 1990, PL 101-336, 42 U.S.C. § 12101 *et seq.*

Anthony, W.A., & Blanch, A. (1987). Supported employment for persons who are psychiatrically disabled: An historical and conceptual perspective. *Psychosocial Rehabilitation Journal, 11*(2), 5–23.

Ashby, S., & Bensberg, G.J. (1981). *Cooperative occupational preparation: Exemplary models*. Lubbock: Texas Technological University, Research and Training Center.

Aune, B., & Ness, J. (1994, Fall). *ParaLink*. Minneapolis: University of Minnesota, University Affiliated Program of Minnesota.

Aune, E. (1991). A transition model for postsecondary-bound students with learning disabilities. *Learning Disabilities Research & Practice, 6*, 177–187.

Avernson, L., Joseph, C., Ripke, V., & Schweitzer, K. (1994–1995, Winter). Strategies to increase job tenure for people with psychiatric disabilities: An overview of the back to work program. *American Rehabilitation, 20*, 13–17.

Azrin, N., & Besalel, V. (1979). *The job club counseling manual*. Champaign, IL: Research Press.

Barker, L.T. (1994). Community based models of employment services for people with psychiatric disabilities. *Psychosocial Rehabilitation Journal, 17*(3), 212–218.

Bateman, B. (1994). Toward better identification of learning disabilities. *Learning Disabilities, 5*(2), 95–99.

Bates, P. (1989). *Illinois transition planning program and program guide*. Southern Illinois University, Illinois Transition Project, Carbondale.

Bates, P. (1990). *Best practices in transition planning: Quality indicators*. Southern Illinois University, Illinois Transition Project, Carbondale.

Bates, P., Bronkema, J., Ames, T., & Hess, C. (1992). State-level interagency planning models. In F.R. Rusch, L. DeStefano, J. Chadsey-Rusch, L.A. Phelps, & E. Szymanski (Eds.), *Transition from school to adult life: Models, linkages, and policy* (pp. 115–129). Sycamore, IL: Sycamore Publishing.

Bates, P., Suter, C., & Poelvoorde, R. (1986). *Illinois Transition Project: Transition plan development for special education students in Illinois public schools*. Southern Illinois University, Illinois Transition Project, Gover-

nor's Planning Council on Developmental Disabilities, Carbondale.

Bauer, D.K. (1994). School health services: Supporting students with special health needs. *Impact*, 7(2), 8–9.

Beard, J.H., Probst, R.N., & Malamud, T.J. (1982). The Fountain House model of rehabilitation. *Psychosocial Rehabilitation Journal*, 5, 47–53.

Beck, J., Baers, J., Hogue, E., Shipstead, J., & Knowlton, H.E. (1994). Strategies for functional community based instruction and inclusion for elementary aged children with mental retardation. *Teaching Exceptional Children*, 26(2), 44–48.

Becker, D.R., & Drake, R.E. (1994). Individual placement and support: A community mental health center approach to vocational rehabilitation. *Community Mental Health Journal*, 30, 193–206.

Beer, M. (1980). *Organization change and development: A systems view*. Pacific Palisades, CA: Goodyear Press.

Beirne-Smith, M., Patton, J., & Henbach, R. (1994). *Mental retardation* (4th ed.). Columbus, OH: Charles E. Merrill.

Belfiore, P.J., Lim, L., & Browder, D.M. (1993). Increasing the efficiency of instruction for a person with severe disabilities: The applicability of (FITTS) Law in predicting response time. *Journal of Behavioral Education*, 3, 247–258.

Belfiore, P.J., Lim, L., & Browder, D.M. (1994). The effects of task design remediation and response efficiency on work productivity in adults with moderate and severe mental retardation. *Education and Training in Mental Retardation and Developmental Disabilities*, 29(3), 202–212.

Bell, K., & Tallman, C. (1995). Community reentry of long-term institutionalized brain injury persons. *Brain Injury*, 9(3), 315–322.

Bellamy, G.T., Horner, R., & Inman, D. (1979). *Vocational training of severely retarded adults*. Austin, TX: PRO-ED.

Ben-Yishay, Y., & Diller, L. (1983). Cognitive deficits. In M. Rosenthal, E.R. Griffith, M.R. Bond, & J.D. Miller (Eds.), *Rehabilitation of the head injured adult* (pp. 167–182). Philadelphia: F.A. Davis.

Benz, M.R., & Halpern, A.S. (1993). Vocational and transition services needed and received by students with disabilities during their last year of high school. *Career Development for Exceptional Individuals*, 16(2), 197–211.

Benz, M., Linderstrom, L., & Halpern, A. (1995). Mobilizing local communities to improve transition services. *Career Development for Exceptional Individuals*, 18(1), 21–32.

Berg, W., & Wacker, D. (1983). *Effects of permanent prompts on the vocational performance of severely handicapped individuals*. Paper presented at the Association for Behavior Analysis, Milwaukee, WI.

Bickford, J., & Sheldon, M. (1988). Breaking the transitional model: A preservice preparation program to serve rural areas. In *Alternative futures for rural special education: Proceedings of a national conference*. Eugene: University of Oregon.

Binet, A., & Simon, T. (1916). The development of intelligence in children. *Training School Bulletin*, 11, 18–28.

Bissonnette, D. (1994). *Beyond traditional job development*. Washington, DC: Milt Wright & Associates.

Blackosby, J., & Wagner, M. (1996). Longitudinal outcomes of youth with disabilities: Findings from the National Longitudinal Transition Study. *Exceptional Children*, 62(5), 399–413.

Blalock, H.R., & Patton, J.R. (1996). Transition and students with learning disabilities: Creating sound futures. *Journal of Learning Disabilities*, 29(1), 7–16.

Blanck, P.D. (1994). *Communicating the Americans with Disabilities Act: Transcending compliance: A case report on Sears, Roebuck & Co*. Iowa City: University of Iowa Law School.

Board for Rights of Virginians with Disabilities Technical Assistance Project (BRVD-TAP). (1991). *Results from the Board for Rights of Virginians with Disabilities' survey of the needs, concerns, and satisfaction with services of Virginia's postsecondary students with disabilities*. Richmond: Virginia Commonwealth University, Virginia Institute for Developmental Disabilities.

Bolton, B., & Roessler, R. (1986, December). *Work personality profile* (pp. 212–218). Fayetteville: Arkansas Research and Training Center in Vocational Rehabilitation.

Bond, G.R. (1987). Supported work as a modification of the transitional employment model for clients with psychiatric disabilities. *Psychosocial Rehabilitation Journal*, 11(2), 55–75.

Bond, G.R., Dietzen, L., & McGrew, J. (1995). Accelerating entry into supported employment for persons with severe psychiatric disabilities. *Rehabilitation Psychology*, 40(2), 18–32.

Bond, G.R., Dietzen, L.L., McGrew, J.H., & Miller, L.D. (1995). Accelerating entry into supported employment for persons with severe psychiatric disabilities. *Rehabilitation Psychology*, 40(1), 17–37.

Bond, G.R., Dietzen, L.L., Vogler, C.H., Katuin, J.H., McGrew, J.D., & Miller, L.D. (1995). Toward a framework for evaluating cost and benefits of psychiatric rehabilitation: Three case examples. *Journal of Vocational Rehabilitation*, 5(2), 75–88.

Bond, G.R., & McDonnel, G. (1991). Vocational rehabilitation outcomes for persons with psychiatric disabilities: An update. *Journal of Vocational Rehabilitation*, 1(3), 9–20.

Bond, M.R. (1978). The stages of recovery from severe head injury with special reference to late outcome. *International Rehabilitation Medicine*, 1, 155–159.

Borus, M. (1984). A description of employed and unemployed youth in 1981. In M. Borus (Ed.), *Youth and the labor market* (pp. 13–55). Kalamazoo, MI: Upjohn Institute.

Bosch, H. (1991). Postsecondary issues for adults with learning disabilities. *Postsecondary LD Network News*, 13(5), 37–39.

Bove, M.E., Nevin, A., Paolucci-Whitcomb, P., & McNeil, M.E. (1991). What have we accomplished in the

education of persons with severe challenges? *Teacher Education and Special Education, 14*, 110–115.

Bowe, F. (1987). Section 504: 10 years later. *American Rehabilitation, 13*(2), 2–3, 23.

Boyer-Stephens, A. (1990). Transition to postsecondary education. *Missouri Lincletter, 13*(2), 1–3.

Bradfield, A.L. (1992). Environmental assessment and job site modifications for people who are visually impaired. *Journal of Vocational Rehabilitation, 2*(1), 39–45.

Bradley, V.J., Ashbaugh, J.W., & Blaney, B.C. (Eds.). (1994). *Creating individual supports for people with developmental disabilities: A mandate for change at many levels.* Baltimore: Paul H. Brookes Publishing Co.

Brickey, M., Browning, L., & Campbell, K. (1982). Vocational histories of sheltered workshop employees placed in projects with industry and competitive jobs. *Mental Retardation, 20*(2), 52–57.

Brickey, M., Campbell, K., & Browning, L. (1985). A five-year follow-up of sheltered workshop employees placed in competitive jobs. *Mental Retardation, 23*(2), 67–73.

Brinckerhoff, L.C. (1994). Developing effective self-advocacy skills in college-bound students with learning disabilities. *Intervention in School and Clinic, 29*, 229–237.

Brinckerhoff, L.C., Shaw, S.F., & McGuire, J.M. (1993). *Promoting post secondary education for students with learning disabilities: A handbook for practitioners.* Austin, TX: PRO-ED.

Brolin, D.E., Durand, R., Kromer, K., & Muller, P. (1989). Post-school adjustment of educable retarded students. *Education and Training for the Mentally Retarded, 24*, 144–148.

Brolin, D.E., & Kokaska, C.J. (1979). *Career education for handicapped children and youth.* Columbus, OH: Charles E. Merrill.

Brolin, D.E., McKay, D.J., & West, L.L. (1978). *Trainer's guide to life centered education.* Reston, VA: Council for Exceptional Children.

Brooke, V., & Green, H. (in press). The path to real jobs. *Exceptional Parent.*

Brooke, V., Wehman, P., Inge, K., & Parent, W. (1995). Toward a customer-driven approach of supported employment. *Education and Training in Mental Retardation and Developmental Disabilities, 30*(4), 308–319.

Brooks, D.N., Campsie, L., Symington, C., Beattie, A., & McKinlay, W. (1987). The effects of severe head injury on patient and relatives within seven years of injury. *Journal of Head Trauma Rehabilitation, 2*(3), 1–13.

Brooks, D.N., McKinley, W., Symington, C., Beattie, A., & Campsie, L. (1987). Return to work within the first seven years of severe head injury. *Brain Injury, 1*, 5–19.

Broome, S., & White, R. (1995). The many uses of videotapes in classrooms: Serving youth with behavioral disorders. *Teaching Exceptional Children, 27*(3), 10–13.

Brotherson, M.J., Cook, C.C., Cunconon-Lehr, R., & Wehmeyer, M. (1995). Policy supporting self-determination in the environments of children with

disabilities. *Education and Training in Mental Retardation and Developmental Disabilities, 30*(1), 3–12.

Brotherson, M.J., Turnbull, A.P., Bronicki, G.J., Houghton, J., Gordon, C.R., Summers, J.A., & Turnbull, H.R. (1988). Transition into adulthood: Parental planning for sons and daughters with disabilities. *Education and Training in Mental Retardation, 23*(3), 165–174.

Brown, D. (1982). Rehabilitating the learning disabled adult. *American Rehabilitation, 7*(3), 17–22.

Brown, F., & Lehr, D.H. (1993). Making activities meaningful for students with severe multiple disabilities. *Teaching Exceptional Children, 25*, 12–16.

Brown, J.M. (1984). A model for enhancing the transition of mildly handicapped youth into postsecondary vocational education. In J. Chadsey-Rusch (Ed.), *Enhancing the transition from school to the workplace for handicapped youth* (pp. 40–55). Champaign: University of Illinois, College of Education, Office of Career Development for Special Populations.

Brown, J.M., Bohns, C., & Gardner, H. (1991). Integrating academic skills into postsecondary vocational education programs through accommodation teams. *TASPP Bulletin, 3*(1), 1–3.

Brown, L., & Lehr, D.H. (1989). Why students with severe disabilities must attend the schools of their brothers, sisters, friends, and neighbors. *The Journal of The Association for Persons with Severe Handicaps, 14*, 4.

Brown, L., Long, E., Udvari-Solner, A., Davis, L., VanDeventer, P., Ahlgren, C., Johnson, F., Gruenewald, L., & Jorgesen, J. (1989). The home school: Why students with severe intellectual disabilities must attend the schools of their brothers, sisters, friends, and neighbors. *Journal of The Association for Persons with Severe Handicaps, 14*(1), 1–7.

Brown, L., Nisbet, J., Ford, A., Sweet, M., Shiraga, B., York, J., & Loomis, R. (1983). The critical need for nonschool instruction in educational programs for severely handicapped students. *Journal of The Association for Persons with Severe Handicaps, 8*, 71–77.

Brown, L., Schwarz, P., Udvari-Solner, A., Kampschroer, E.F., Johnson, F., Jorgensen, J., & Gruenewald, L. (1991). How much time should students with severe intellectual disabilities spend in regular education classrooms and elsewhere? *Journal of The Association for Persons with Severe Handicaps, 16*, 39–47.

Bruininks, R.H., Wolman, C., & Thurlow, M.L. (1989). *Issues and guidelines in designing follow-up systems for special education service programs.* Minneapolis: University of Minnesota, University Affiliated Program.

Bryan, T. (1989). IQ and learning disabilities: A perspective from research on social factors. *Journal of Learning Disabilities, 22*(8), 480–481.

Bryan, T. (1990, Spring). Social vulnerability of students with learning disabilities. *The Lantern, 6.*

Buckley, J., & Bellamy, G.T. (1985). *National survey of day and vocational programs for adults with severe disabilities: A 1984 profile.* Unpublished manuscript, Johns Hopkins University, Baltimore.

Bullis, M., Bull, B., Johnson, B., & Peters, D. (1994). Young adults who are respondents in a transition

study: Did they and their parents apply similar data? *Exceptional Children, 60*(4), 323–333.

Bullis, M., Bull, B., Johnson, B., & Peters, D. (1995). The school to community transition experiences of hearing young adults and young adults who are deaf. *Exceptional Children, 28*(4), 405–423.

Bullis, M., & Egelston-Dodd, J. (1990). Priorities in the school-to-community transition of adolescents who are deaf. *Career Development for Exceptional Individuals, 13*(1), 71–82.

Bullis M., & Reiman, J. (1992). Development in preliminary psychometric properties of the transition confidence battery for deaf adolescents and young adults. *Exceptional Children, 59*(1), 12–26.

Burchard, S.N., Hasazi, J.S., Gordon, L.R., & Roe, J. (1991). An examination of lifestyle and adjustment in three community residential alternatives. *Research in Developmental Disabilities, 12*(2), 127–142.

Butler-Nalin, P., & Padilla, C. (1989, March). *Dropouts: The relationship of student characteristics, behaviors, and performance for special education students.* Paper presented at the meeting of the American Education Research Association, San Francisco.

Bywater, E.M. (1984). Adolescents with cystic fibrosis: Psychological adjustment. *Archives of Diseases in Childhood, 56,* 538–543.

Callahan, M., Everson, J., Hollahan, J., Gradel, C., Cohen, R., Button, C., Franklin, K., & Brady, P. (1990). *Getting the job done* (Rev. ed.). Washington, DC: United Cerebral Palsy Associations.

Campbell, J., & Lehr-Essex, E. (1994). Factors affecting parents in their future planning for a son or daughter with developmental disabilities. *Education and Training in Mental Retardation and Developmental Disabilities, 29*(3), 222–228.

Campbell, K. (1988). Learning: A struggle and a challenge. In *Their world* (pp. 42–43). New York: The Foundation for Children with Learning Disabilities.

Career Services for the Handicapped. (n.d.). *Helpful hints for employers of persons with learning disabilities.* Albuquerque, NM: Author.

Carlson, J.M., & Vervena, L. (1995). Bringing assistive technology to transition-age youth in rural Minnesota. *Impact, 8*(1), 12–13.

Carr, S., & Punzo, R. (1993). The effects of self-monitoring of academic accuracy and productivity on the performance of students with behavioral disorders. *Behavioral Disorders, 15*(3), 141–148.

Carr, T. (Ed.). (1993). Transition services and personal futures planning. *HKNC-TAC News, 6*(3).

Carr, T. (Ed.). (1994). Assistive technology: Enhancements for daily life. *HKNC-TAC News, 7*(2), 3.

Carter, J., & Sugai, G. (1989). Social skills curriculum analysis. *Teaching Exceptional Children, 22,* 38.

Cartwright, G.P., Cartwright, C.A., & Ward, M.E. (1989). *Educating special learners* (3rd ed.). Belmont, CA: Wadsworth.

Caveness, W. (1979). Incidence of craniocerebral trauma in the United States in 1976 with a trend from 1970 to 1975. In R. Thompson & F. Green (Eds.), *Advances in neurology* (pp. 1–3). New York: Raven Press.

Center for Independent Living. (1991). *Disability: A profile of facts, figures and history.* Berkeley, CA: Author.

Chadsey-Rusch, J., DeStefano, L., O'Reilly, M., Gonzalez, P., & Collet-Klingenberg, L. (1992). Assessing the loneliness of workers with mental retardation. *Mental Retardation, 30*(2), 85–92.

Chaffin, J., Spellman, C., Regan, C., & Davison, R. (1971). Two follow-up studies of former educable mentally retarded students from the Kansas work-study project. *Exceptional Children, 37,* 733–738.

Chatham, K.M., Johnson, J.N., & Peterson, R.M. (1981). *The concept of employability: A review of the issues.* Washington, DC: National Institute of Education.

Chumbley, C., Collins, M., Elliot, J., Geake, L., Grant, M., Hague, J., Hock, T., Moore, J., & Toth, T. (1992). Supported employment service issues: Consumer advocacy and supported employment: A vision for the future. Richmond: *Virginia Commonwealth University, Rehabilitation Research and Training Center Monographs,* 14–32.

Cipani, E. (1995). Inclusive education: What do we know and what do we still have to learn? *Exceptional Children, 61*(5), 498–501.

Civil Rights Act of 1964, PL 88-352 U.S.C. § 241.

Clark, G. (1996). Transition planning for secondary level students with learning disabilities. *Journal of Learning Disabilities, 29*(1), 79–92.

Clark, G., Carlson, B., Fisher, S., Cook, I., & D'Alonzo, V. (1991). Career development for students with disabilities in elementary schools: A position statement of the Division on Career Development and Transition. *Career Development for Exceptional Individuals, 14,* 109–120.

Clark, G., Field, S., Patton, J., Brolin, D., & Stillington, P. (1994). Life skills instruction: A necessary component for all students with disabilities: A position statement of the Division on Career Development and Transition. *Career Development for Exceptional Individuals, 17*(2), 125–134.

Clark, G.M., & Kolstoe, O.P. (1990). *Career development and transition education for adolescents with disabilities.* Needham, MA: Allyn & Bacon.

Clark, G.M., & Kolstoe, O.P. (1995). *Career development and transition education for adolescents with disabilities* (2nd ed.). Needham, MA: Allyn & Bacon.

Cobb, B., & Hasazi, S. (1987). School-aged transition services: Options for adolescents with mild handicaps. *Career Development for Exceptional Individuals, 10,* 15–23.

Cobb, H.V. (1972). *The forecast of fulfillment.* New York: Teachers College Press.

Cohen, M.W., & Beattie, J.R. (1984). What works with LD adolescents. *Academic Therapy, 19*(4), 397–402.

Colby, C.R. (1987). Developing a positive learning environment. *Journal for Vocational Needs Special Education, 12,* 33.

Coles, G.S. (1987). *The learning mystique: A critical look at "learning disabilities."* New York: Pantheon Books.

Collins, B.C. (1995). The integration of students with severe and profound disabilities from segregated schools into regular public schools: An analysis of

changes in parent perceptions. *Journal of Developmental and Physical Disabilities, 7*(1), 51–64.

Colond, J.S., & Wieseler, N.A. (1995). Preventing restrictive placements through community supports sources. *American Journal of Mental Retardation, 100*(2), 201–206.

Condeluci, A. (1991). *Interdependence: The route to community.* Delray Beach, FL: St. Lucie Press.

Condeluci, A. (1996). *Beyond difference.* Delray Beach, FL: St. Lucie Press.

Condry, S. (1989). *A literature review of topics concerning children who are technology-supported and their families.* Lawrence: University of Kansas, Beach Center on Families and Disability.

Cook, J.A., & Pickett, S. (1994–1995). Recent trends in vocational rehabilitation for people with psychiatric disability. *American Rehabilitation, 20,* 1–13.

Cook, J.A., Razzano, L., Straiton, D.M., & Ross, Y. (1994). Cultivation and maintenance of relationships with employers of people with psychiatric disabilities. *Psychosocial Rehabilitation Journal, 17,* 103–116.

Cook, J.A., & Rosenberg, H. (1994). Predicting community employment among persons with psychiatric disability: A logistic regression analysis. *Journal of Rehabilitation Administration, 18,* 6–22.

Cooper, A., & Mank, D. (1989). Integrated employment for people with severe physical disabilities. *American Rehabilitation, 15*(3), 16–23.

Coplin, J.W., & Morgan, S.B. (1988). Learning disabilities: A multidimensional perspective. *Journal of Learning Disabilities, 21*(10), 614–622.

Corn, A. (1980). *Development and assessment of an inservice training program for teachers of the visually handicapped: Optical aids in the classroom.* Unpublished doctoral dissertation, Columbia University, Teachers College, New York.

Corrigan, J., Lamb-Hart, G., & Russ, E. (1995). A program of intervention for substance abuse following traumatic brain injury. *Brain Injury, 9*(3), 221–236.

Corthell, D.W., & Tooman, M. (1985). *Rehabilitation of traumatic brain injury.* Menomoniee: University of Wisconsin-Stout, Research and Training Center.

Covert, A.M. (1988). Introduction. In A.M. Covert & T.S. Carr (Eds.), *Value-based services for young adults with deaf-blindness* (pp. 1–4). Long Island, NY: Helen Keller National Center for Deaf-Blind Youth and Adults Technical Assistance Center and The Associate for Persons with Severe Handicaps Technical Assistance Project.

Cronin, M., & Patton, J.R. (1993). *Life skills across the curriculum for youths with special needs.* Austin, TX: PRO-ED.

Cronis, T.G., Smith, G.J., & Forgnone, C. (1986). Mild mental retardation: Implications for an ecological curriculum. *Journal of Research and Development in Education, 19*(3), 72–76.

Cypress-Fairbanks Independent School District. (1989). *Perspectives on the transition to young adulthood: A follow-up study of handicapped students.* Unpublished paper, Houston, TX.

Dalke, C., & Schmitt, S. (1987). Meeting the transition

needs of college-bound students with learning disabilities. *Journal of Learning Disabilities, 20*(3), 176–180.

D'Alonzo, B.J., Faas, L.A., & Crawford, D. (1988). School to work transition: Project M.E.A.L.: Model for employment and adult living. *Career Development for Exceptional Children, 11*(2), 126–140.

Danek, M.M., & McCrone, W.P. (1989). The mandate for transition services: Myth or reality? In T.E. Allen, B.W. Rawlings, & A.N. Schildroth (Eds.), *Deaf students and the school-to-work transition* (pp. 1–29). Baltimore: Paul H. Brookes Publishing Co.

Dattilo, J. (1991). Recreation and leisure: A review of the literature and recommendations for future directions. In L.H. Meyer, C.A. Peck, & L. Brown (Eds.), *Critical issues in the lives of people with severe disabilities* (pp. 126–137). Baltimore: Paul H. Brookes Publishing Co.

Dattilo, J., & Schleien, S.J. (1994). Understanding leisure services for individuals with mental retardation. *Mental Retardation, 32,* 43–52.

Deal, T.E., & Kennedy, A.A. (1982). *Corporate culture: The rites and rituals of corporate life.* Reading, MA: Addison-Wesley.

DeFur, S., Getzel, E.E., & Kregel, J. (1994). Individual transition plans: A work in progress. *Journal of Vocational Rehabilitation, 4*(2), 139–145.

DeStefano, L., & Wagner, M. (1992). Outcome assessment in special education: What lessons have we learned? In F.R. Rusch, L. DeStefano, J. Chadsey-Rusch, L.A. Phelps, & E. Szymanski (Eds.), *Transition from school to adult life: Models, linkages, and policy* (pp. 173–207). Sycamore, IL: Sycamore Publishing.

Dikmen, S., Timkin, M., Machamer, J., Holuvkov, A., Fraser, R., & Winn, R. (1994). Employment following traumatic head injuries. *Archives of Neurology, 51,* 177–186.

DiLeo, D. (1994). *Supported employment: How to help your family member with a disability develop a meaningful career.* St. Augustine, FL: Training Resource Network.

Dole, R. (1994, October 7). Employment for persons with disabilities. *Congressional Record.*

Downing, J., & Eichinger, D. (1990). Instructional strategies for learners with dual sensory impairments in integrated settings. *Journal of The Association for Persons with Severe Handicaps, 15*(2), 98–106.

Drake, R.E., Becker, D.R., Biesanz, J.C., Torrey, W.C., McHugo, G.J., & Wyzik, P.F. (1994). Rehabilitative day treatment vs. supported employment: (I) Vocational outcomes. *Community Mental Health Journal, 30*(5), 519–532.

Drake, R.E., Becker, D.R., Xie, H., & Anthony, W.A. (1995). Barriers in the brokered model of supported employment for persons with psychiatric disabilities. *Journal of Vocational Rehabilitation, 5*(2), 141–149.

Durlak, C.M., Rose, E., & Bursuck, W.D. (1994). Preparing high school students with learning disabilities for the transition to postsecondary education: Teaching the skills of self-determination. *Journal of Learning Disabilities, 27*(1), 51–59.

D'Zamko, M.E., & Hedges, W.D. (1985). *Helping exceptional students succeed in the regular classroom.* New York: Parker.

Eames, P. (1988). Behavior disorders after severe head injury: Their natural causes and strategies for management. *Journal of Head Trauma Rehabilitation, 3*(3), 1–6.

Edgar, E. (1987). Secondary programs in special education: Are many of them justifiable? *Exceptional Children, 53*(6), 555–561.

Edgar, E. (1988). Transition from school to community. *Teaching Exceptional Children, 20*(2), 73–75.

Edgar, E., & Levine, P. (1987). *Special education students in transition: Washington state data 1976–1986.* Unpublished manuscript, University of Washington, Seattle.

Edgar, E., Levine, P., Levine, R., & Dubey, M. (1988). *Washington state follow-along studies 1983–1987: Students in transition.* Unpublished paper, University of Washington, Seattle.

Edgar, E., & Polloway, E. (1994). Education for adolescents with disabilities: Curriculum placement issues. *Journal of Special Education, 27*(4), 438–452.

Education for All Handicapped Children Act of 1975, PL 94-142, 20 U.S.C. § 1400 *et seq.*

Eichinger, J., & Woltman, S. (1993, Fall). Integration strategies for learners with severe multiple disabilities. *Teaching Exceptional Children,* 18–21.

El-Afandi, B. (1994). Barriers to support: Waiting lists. *IMPACT: Feature Issue on Self-Advocacy, 7*(1), 1–4.

Elliott, N., Houser, N., & Alberto, P. (1991). *Administrative and implementation guidelines for school community-based vocational instruction based on the Fair Labor Standards Act.* Unpublished manuscript, Project SETS, Georgia State University, Atlanta.

Epstein, M.H., Polloway, E.A., Patton, J.R., & Foley, R. (1989). Mild retardation: Student characteristics and services. *Education and Training of the Mentally Retarded, 24*(6), 7–16.

Eson, M.E., Yen, J.K., & Bourke, R.S. (1979). Assessment of recovery from serious head injury. *Journal of Neurology, Neurosurgery, and Psychiatry, 41,* 1036–1042.

Evans, E.D., & Richardson, R.C. (1995). Corporal punishment: What teachers should know. *Teaching Exceptional Children, 27*(2), 33–36.

Everson, J.M. (Ed.). (1995). *Supporting young adults who are deaf-blind in their communities: A transition planning guide for service providers, families, and friends.* Baltimore: Paul H. Brookes Publishing Co.

Everson, J.M., Rachal, P., & Michael, M.C. (1992). *Interagency collaboration for young adults with deaf-blindness: Toward a common transition goal.* Sands Point, NY: Helen Keller National Center–Technical Assistance Center.

Ezrachi, O., Ben-Yishay, Y., Kay, T., Diller, L., & Rattok, J. (1991). Predicting employment in traumatic brain injury following neuropsychological rehabilitation. *Journal of Head Trauma Rehabilitation, 6*(3), 71–84.

Fabian, E.S. (1989). Work and the quality of life. *Psychosocial Rehabilitation Journal, 12,* 39–49.

Fabian, E.S. (1992). Supported employment and quality of life: Does a job make a difference? *Rehabilitation Counseling Journal, 36,* 84–87.

Fabian, E.S., Edelman, A., & Leedy, M. (1993). Linking workers with severe disabilities to social supports in the workplace: Strategies for addressing barriers. *Journal of Rehabilitation, 59*(3), 29–34.

Fabian, E.S., & Luecking, R.G. (1991). Doing it the company way: Using internal company supports in the workplace. *Journal of Applied Rehabilitation Counseling, 22*(2), 32–35.

Fabian, E.S., Luecking, R.G., & Tilson, G.P. (1994). *A working relationship: The job development specialist's guide to successful partnerships with business.* Baltimore: Paul H. Brookes Publishing Co.

Fair Labor Standards Act, PL 99-150, (1985), 29 U.S.C. § 201 *et seq.*

Fairweather, J.S., & Shaver, D.M. (1991). Making the transition to postsecondary education and training. *Exceptional Children, 57,* 264–270.

Falvey, M.A. (1989). *Community-based curriculum: Instructional strategies for students with severe handicaps* (2nd ed.). Baltimore: Paul H. Brookes Publishing Co.

Fardig, D., Algozzine, R., Schwartz, S., Hensel, J., & Westling, D. (1985). Postsecondary vocational adjustment of rural, mildly handicapped students. *Exceptional Children, 52*(2), 115–121.

Fareta, G. (1981). A profile of aggression from adolescence to adulthood: An 18-year follow-up of psychiatrically disturbed and violent adolescents. *American Journal of Orthopsychiatry, 51*(3), 439–453.

Federal Register. (1977, May 4). Nondiscrimination on basis of handicap: Programs and activities receiving or benefiting from federal financial assistance. Washington, DC: U.S. Government Printing Office.

Federal Register. (1987, August 14). Final regulations. Washington, DC: U.S. Government Printing Office.

Federal Register. (1991, July 26). Americans with Disabilities Act (ADA): Accessibility guidelines for buildings and facilities. Washington, DC: U.S. Government Printing Office.

Federal Register. (1992, June 24). 34 CFR 363, *57* (122), 28432–28442. Washington, DC: U.S. Department of Education.

Fee, J.W. (1991). Rehabilitation robotics for individuals with disabilities. *Journal of Vocational Rehabilitation, 1*(2), 65–69.

Fenton, J., & Keller, R.A. (1981). Special education–vocational rehabilitation: Let's get the act together. *American Rehabilitation, 3,* 26–30.

Ferguson, P.M., Ferguson, D., & Jones, D. (1988). Generalization of hope: Parental perspectives on the transitions of their children with severe retardation from school to adult life. *Journal of The Association for Persons with Severe Handicaps, 13,* 177–187.

Ferguson, P., Hibbard, M., Leinen, J., & Schaff, S. (1990). Supporting community life: Disability policy and the renewal of mediating structures. *Journal of Disability Policy Studies, 1*(1), 10–35.

Ferleger, D. (1994). *Choice and decision making in the lives*

of persons with disabilities. Albany: New York Department of Mental Health.

Field, S. (1996). Self-determination: Instructional strategies for youth with learning disabilities. *Journal of Learning Disabilities, 29*(1), 40–52.

Field, S., & Hoffman, A. (1994). Development of a model for self-determination. *Career Development for Handicapped Individuals, 17*(2), 159–169.

Field, S., & Hoffman, A. (in press). *Steps to self-determination.* Austin, TX: PRO-ED.

Field, S., Leroy, B., & Rivera, S. (1994). Meeting functional curriculum needs in middle school general education classrooms. *Teaching Exceptional Children, 26*(2), 40–43.

Flippo, K.F., Inge, K.J., & Barcus, J.M. (Eds.). (1995). *Assistive technology: A resource for school, work, and community.* Baltimore: Paul H. Brookes, Publishing Co.

Ford, L.H. (1995). *Providing employment support for people with long-term mental illness: Choices, resources, and practical strategies.* Baltimore: Paul H. Brookes Publishing Co.

Ford, L.H., Oswald, S., & Dineen, J. (1995). *Job clubs revisited.* Newsletter of the Center for Continuing Education in Rehabilitation, Western Washington University, Bellevue.

Fourqurean, J.M. (1994). The use of follow-up studies for improving transition planning for young adults with learning disabilities. *Journal of Vocational Rehabilitation, 4*(2), 96–104.

Frank, A.R., Sitlington, P.L., & Carson, R. (1991). Transition of adolescents with behavioral disorders—Is it successful? *Behavioral Disorders, 16*(3), 180–191.

Frank, A.R., Sitlington, P., Cooper, L., & Cool, V. (1990). Adult adjustment of recent graduates of Iowa mental disabilities programs. *Education and Training in Mental Retardation, 25,* 62–75.

Franklin, K.S. (1991). Assistive technology: Where are we? Where are we going? *Journal of Vocational Rehabilitation, 1*(2), 6–7.

Frankowski, R. (1986). Descriptive epidemiologic studies of head injury in the United States: 1974–1984. In L. Karger & T. Basel (Eds.), *Advanced psychosomatic medicine: Vol. 16. Trauma treatment in practice: The head injured patient* (pp. 152–172). New York: Elsevier.

Fraser, R.T. (1988). Refinement of a decision tree in traumatic brain injury job placement. *Rehabilitation Education, 2,* 179–184.

Fraser, R.T., & Wehman, P. (1995). Traumatic brain injury rehabilitation: Issues in vocational outcomes. *Neurorehabilitation, 5,* 39–48.

Fuchs, D., & Fuchs, L.S. (1994). Inclusive schools and the radicalization of special education reform. *Exceptional Children, 60*(4), 294–309.

Fuchs, L.S., Fuchs, D., Hamlett, C.L., Phillips, N.B., & Karns, K. (1995). General educators' specialized adaptation for students with learning disabilities. *Journal of The Association for Persons with Severe Handicaps, 20*(2).

Fullerton, A. (1995). Promoting self-determination for adolescents and young adults with autism. *Journal of Vocational Rehabilitation, 5*(4), 337–346.

Fullmer, S.L., & Walls, R. (1994). Exploring the Internet: The rehabilitation community's access to the growing communication network. *Technology and Disability, 3*(3), 235–242.

Furlong, M., Jonikes, J., Cook, J.A., Hathaway, L., & Goode, S.C. (1994). *Providing vocational services: Job coaching and ongoing support for persons with severe mental illness.* Chicago: Threshholds National Research and Training Center on Rehabilitation and Mental Illness.

Gaffin, A., & Electronic Frontier Foundation. (1994). *Big dummy's guide to the Internet.* (Available by anonymous ftp from ftp, eff.org, directory pub/Net——info/Big—— Dummy, file name bigdummy.txt.)

Gallivan-Finlon, A. (1994). "Their senior year": Family and service provider perspectives: On the transition from school to adult life for young adults with disabilities. *Journal of The Association for Persons with Severe Handicaps, 19*(1), 11–23.

Garnett, K., & LaPorta, S. (1984). *Dispelling the myths: College students with learning disabilities.* New York: Hunter College of the University of New York.

Gast, D.L., & Worley, M. (1986). Severe maladaptive behaviors. In M.E. Snell (Ed.), *Systematic instruction of persons with severe handicaps* (3rd ed., pp. 300–332). Columbus, OH: Charles E. Merrill.

Gavin, M., Tindall, L.W., & Gugerty, J.J. (1990). *Still puzzled about educating students with disabilities? Vocational preparation of students with disabilities.* Madison: University of Wisconsin–Madison, School of Education, The Vocational Studies Center.

Gaylord-Ross, R.J., & Haring, T. (1987). Social interaction research for adolescents with severe handicaps. *Behavior Disorders, 12,* 264–275.

General Accounting Office. (1991). *Vocational rehabilitation: Clear guidance could help improve services on those with severe disabilities* (Report No. HRD-92–12). Washington, DC: Author.

Gerber, P.J., Schnieders, C.A., Paradise, L.V., Reiff, H.B., Ginsberg, R.J., & Popp, P.A. (1990). Persisting problems of adults with learning disabilities: Self-reported comparisons from their school-age and adult years. *Journal of Learning Disabilities, 23*(9), 570–573.

Gersuny, C., & Lefton, M. (1970). Service and servitude in the sheltered workshop. *Social Work, 15*(3), 74–81.

Gervey, R., Parrish, A., & Bond, G. (1995). Survey of exemplary supported employment programs for persons with psychiatric disabilities. *Journal of Vocational Rehabilitation, 5*(2), 115–125.

Gervey, R., & Shafer, M. (1995). Introduction to psychiatric impairment issue. *Journal of Vocational Rehabilitation, 5,* (73–74).

Getzel, L.E. (1990). Entering postsecondary programs: Early individualized planning. *Teaching Exceptional Children, 23*(1), 51–53.

Gibbs, M., & Smith, R. (1994). Rehabilitation-related

discussion, list, and e-mail resources on Internet. In *Navigating the Internet.* (Available in Gopher: Internet Resources, Virtual Reference Desk, Disability Information, Rehabilitation-Related Discussion, List, and E-Mail Resources on Internet menu items.)

Goals 2000: Educate America Act of 1994, PL 103-227, U.S.C. § 5801 *et seq.*

Goldberg, M. (1991, September). Choices—A parent's view. *The PACESETTER*, 10.

Goldstein, A.P., Sprafkin, R.P., Gershew, R., & Cline, T. (1980). *Social skills curriculum.* New York: Yeshiva University.

Goodall, P. (Ed.). (1989). *Return to work following traumatic brain injury* (special issue newsletter), 5(1). (Available from Virginia Commonwealth University, Rehabilitation Research and Training Centers on Supported Employment and Traumatic Brain Injury, Richmond.)

Goodall, P., & Bruder M.B. (1986). Parents and the transition process. *The Exceptional Parent*, 16(2), 22–28.

Goodall, P., Groah, C., Sherron, P., Kreutzer, J., & Wehman, P. (1991). *Supported employment services for individuals with traumatic brain injury: A guide for service providers.* Richmond: Virginia Commonwealth University, Rehabilitation Research and Training Center.

Goodall, P., Lawyer, H., & Wehman, P. (1994). Vocational rehabilitation of TBI: A legislative public policy perspective. *Journal of Head Trauma Rehabilitation*, 9(2), 62–81.

Goodman, C.R. (1988). Learning how to work. *Their World*, 67, 82–94.

Goodson, L.A. (1995). Roles for success in community living: A report on the development of self-determination. *Journal of Vocational Rehabilitation*, 5(4), 347–356.

Gortmaker, S.L., Walker, D.K., Weitzman, M., & Sobol, A.M. (1990). Chronic conditions, socioeconomic risks, and behavior problems in children and adolescents. *Pediatrics*, 85, 267–276.

Gothelf, C.R., Crimmins, D.B., Mercer, C.A., & Finocchiaro, P.A. (1994). Teaching choice-making skills to students who are deaf-blind. *Teaching Exceptional Children*, 26(4), 13–16.

Gould, M. (1985). Self-advocacy for youth in transition from school to work and adult life. In M. Gould & G.T. Bellamy (Eds.), *Transition from school to work and adult life* (pp. 78–89). Eugene: University of Oregon, Specialized Training Program.

Gozali, J. (1972). Perception of the EMR special class by former students. *Mental Retardation*, 10, 34–35.

Gradel, K. (1991). Customer service: What is its place in assistive technology and employment services? *Journal of Vocational Rehabilitation*, 1(2), 41–54.

Graham, J.W. (1992). Transition through interagency coordination. *Missouri Lincletter*, 14(3), 1–3.

Graham, S., & Harris, K.R. (1989). The relevance of IQ in the determination of learning disabilities: Abandoning scores as decision makers. *Journal of Learning Disabilities*, 22(8), 500–503.

Graham, S., Harris, K., & Reid, R. (1990). Learning disabilities. In E.L. Meyen (Ed.), *Exceptional children in today's schools* (2nd ed., pp. 207–217). Denver, CO: Love Publishing.

Green, F., Schleien, S., Mactovish, J., & Benepe, S. (1995). Nondisabled adults perceptions of relationships in the early stages of arranged partnerships with peers with mental retardation. *Education and Training in Mental Retardation and Developmental Disabilities*, 30(2), 91–108.

Greenbaum, B., Graham, S., & Seeles, W. (1995). Adults with learning disabilities: Education, social experiences during college. *Exceptional Children*, 61(5), 460–471.

Gregory, M.W. (1994). *How to provide accommodations for students with learning disabilities.* Columbia: University of Missouri–Columbia, Department of Special Education.

Griffin, C.C. (1989). *Get a job: Selling, marketing, and winning community employment* [Videotape]. Syracuse, NY: Program Development Associates.

Griffin, C.C. (1991, April). *Relationship marketing: Job development as if people really mattered.* Presentation at the meeting of the Minnesota DACA/MARF Developmental Disabilities Conference, St. Paul.

Griffin, C.C. (1992). Typical, generic, in vivo, in situ, normal, informal, typical (a.k.a. natural) supports. *The Advance*, 3(2), 1–3.

Griffin, C.C., & Hammis, D. (1994). *The Northern Colorado Corporate Partnership Initiative.* Project proposal submitted to Colorado Vocational Rehabilitation, Greeley.

Griffin, C.C., & Winter, L. (1988, September). *Employment partnership: Job development strategies in integrated employment.* Presentation at the training session of the Winter Group Marketing, Rocky Mountain Resource and Training Institute, and Colorado Developmental Disabilities Planning Council, Denver.

Griffin, S.S., & Kendall, E.D. (1989). Supported employment for persons with visual impairment or blindness. *Journal of Applied Rehabilitation Counseling*, 20(3), 44–49.

Griffith, E.R. (1983). Types of disability. In M. Rosenthal, E. Griffith, M. Bond, & J. Miller (Eds.), *Rehabilitation of the head injured adult* (pp. 23–33). Philadelphia: F.A. Davis.

Gugerty, J.J., & Gavin, M.K. (1991). *Designated vocational instruction: A cooperative process for change.* Unpublished manuscript, Wisconsin Department of Public Instruction, Madison.

Gugerty, J.J., Tindall, L.W., Gavin, M.K., & Gribbon-Fago, B. (1993). *Serving students with learning or cognitive disabilities effectively in two-year colleges: Seven exemplary approaches.* Madison: University of Wisconsin–Madison, Center on Education and Work.

Hagin, R.A., Kugler, J., & Ellsworth, N.J. (1994). Assessment of adults with severe learning disabilities. *Learning Disablties*, 5(1), 35–50.

Hagner, D., Butterworth, J., & Keith, G. (1995). Strategies and barriers in facilitating natural supports for employment of adults with severe disabilities. *Journal of The Association for Persons with Severe Handicaps*, 20(2), 110–120.

Hagner, D., & Daning, R. (1993). *Opening lines: How job*

developers talk to employers. Syracuse, NY: Syracuse University, Department of Special Education and Rehabilitation.

Hagner, D., & Dileo, D. (1993). *Working together: Workplace culture, supported employment and persons with disabilities*. Brookline, MA: Brookline Books.

Hagner, D., Rogan, P., & Murphy, S. (1992). Facilitating natural supports in the workplace: Strategies for support consultants. *Journal of Rehabilitation, 58*(1), 29–34.

Halpern, A.S. (1985). Transition: A look at the foundations. *Exceptional Children, 57*(6), 479–486.

Halpern, A.S. (1990). A methodological review of follow-up and follow-along studies tracking school leavers from special education. *Career Development for Exceptional Individuals, 13*(1), 13–27.

Halpern, A.S. (1994). The transition of youths with disabilities to adult life: A position statement of the Division on Career Development and Transition, Council for Exceptional Children. *Career Development of Exceptional Individuals, 17*(2), 115–124.

Halpern, A.S., Doren, B., & Benz, M. (1993). Job experiences of students with disabilities in their last two years in school. *Career Development for Exceptional Individuals, 16*(1), 63–74.

Halvorsen, A.T., Doering, K., Farron-Davis, F., Usilton, R., & Sailor, W. (1989). The role of parents and family members in planning severely disabled students' transition from school. In G.H.S. Singer & L.K. Irvin (Eds.), *Support for caregiving families: Enabling positive adaptation to disability* (pp. 253–267). Baltimore: Paul H. Brookes Publishing Co.

Hammill, D.D. (1990). On defining learning disabilities: An emerging consensus. *Journal of Learning Disabilities, 23*(2), 74–84.

Hammill, D.D., & Bartel, N. (1986). *Teaching students with learning and behavior problems* (4th ed.). Needham, MA: Allyn & Bacon.

Hammis, D. (1994). Ask another question. *The Field Report, 4*(3). (Available from Center for Technical Assistance & Training, University of Minnesota, Minneapolis.).

Hanley-Maxwell, C., Griffin, S.L., Szymanski, E.M., & Godley, S.H. (1990). Supported and time-limited transitional employment services. *Journal of Visual Impairment and Blindness, 84*(4), 160–165.

Hanley-Maxwell, C., & Szymanski, E.M. (1995). School to work transition and supported employment. In R.M. Parker & E.M. Szymanski (Eds.), *Rehabilitation counseling: Basics and beyond* (2nd ed., pp. 327–355). Austin, TX: PRO-ED.

Hanley-Maxwell, C., Whitney-Thomas, J., & Pogoloff, S. (1995). The second shock: A qualitative study of parents perspectives and needs during their child's transition from school to adult life. *Journal of The Association for Persons with Severe Handicaps, 20*(1), 3–15.

Harchik, A., Sherman, J., & Sheldon, J. (1992). The use of self-management procedures by people with developmental disabilities: A brief review. *Research and Developmental Disabilities, 13*(3), 211–228.

Haring, K., & Lovett, D. (1990). A follow-up study of special education graduates. *Journal of Special Education, 23*(4), 465–477.

Harry, B., Grenot-Scheyerm, M., Smith-Lewis, M., Park, H., Xin, F., & Schwartz, I. (1995). Developing culturally inclusive services for individuals with severe disabilities. *Journal of The Association for Persons with Severe Handicaps, 20*(2), 99–109.

Hasazi, S.B. (1985). Facilitating transition from high school: Policies and practices. *American Rehabilitation, 11*(3), 9–16.

Hasazi, S.B., & Cobb, R.B. (1988). Vocational education of persons with mild handicaps. In R. Gaylord-Ross (Ed.), *Vocational education for persons with handicaps* (pp. 331–354). Mountain View, CA: Mayfield Publishing.

Hasazi, S.B., Gordon, S., & Roe, R. (1985). Factors associated with the employment status of handicapped youth exiting high school from 1979–1983. *Exceptional Children, 51*(6), 455–469.

Hasazi, S.B., Johnson, R.E., Hasazi, J.E., & Gordon, L.E. (1989). Employment of youth with and without handicaps following high school: Outcomes and correlates. *The Journal of Special Education, 23*(3), 243–255.

Hasazi, S.B., Johnston, A.P., Liggett, A., & Schattman, R. (1994). A qualitative policy study of the least restrictive environment provision of the Individuals with Disabilities Education Act. *Exceptional Children, 60*(6), 491–508.

Hayden, M.F., & Abery, B.H. (1994). *Challenges for a service system in transition: Ensuring quality community experiences for persons with developmental disabilities*. Baltimore: Paul H. Brookes Publishing Co.

Hayden, M.F., & Depaepe, P. (1994). Waiting for community services: The impact on persons with mental retardation and other developmental disabilities. In M.F. Hayden & B.H. Avery (Eds.), *Challenges for a service system in transition: Ensuring quality community experiences for persons with developmental disabilities* (pp. 173–206). Baltimore: Paul H. Brookes Publishing Co.

Heal, L., & Rusch, F. (1995). Predicting employment for students who leave special education high school programs. *Exceptional Children, 61*(5), 472–488.

Heflinger, C.A., Cook, V.J., & Thackrey, M. (1987). Identification of mental retardation by the system of multicultural pluralistic assessment: Nondiscriminatory or nonexistent? *Journal of School Psychology, 25*(2), 177–184.

Heiden, J. (1989). A ten-year follow-up study of former students at the Wisconsin School for the Handicapped: 1978–1987. *RE:view, 21*(2), 81–87.

Helms, B.L., Moore, S.C., & McSewyn, C.A. (1991). Supported employment in Connecticut: An examination of integration and wage outcomes. *Career Development for Exceptional Individuals, 14*(2), 159–166.

Helmstetter, E., Peck, C.A., & Giangreco, M.F. (1994). Outcomes of interactions with peers with moderate or severe disabilities: A statewide survey of high school students. *Journal of The Association for Persons with Severe Handicaps, 19*(4), 263–276.

Hemming, H. (1986). Follow-up of adults with mental retardation transferred from large institutions to new small units. *Mental Retardation, 24,* 229–235.

Henderson, C. (1992). *College freshmen with disabilities: A statistical profile.* Washington, DC: HEATH Resource Center.

Hendryx, P.M. (1989). Psychosocial changes perceived by closed-head-injured adults and their families. *Archives of Physical Medicine and Rehabilitation, 70,* 526–530.

Heron, E., & Jorgensen, C.M. (1995). Addressing learning differences right from the start. *Educational Leadership, 52*(4), 56–58.

Hess, C., & Horton, J. (1990). *Planning for transition.* Houston, TX: Region IV Education Service Center, L.I.F.E. Steps Training Project.

Hess, C., Kregel, J., & Wehman, P. (1991). *Houston area post-21 follow-up study.* Houston, TX: Region IV Education Service Center.

Hill, J., Seyfarth, J., Banks, P.D., Wehman, P., & Orelove, F. (1987). Parent attitudes about working conditions of their adult mentally retarded sons and daughters. *Exceptional Children, 54*(1), 9–23.

Hilton, A., & Liberty, K. (1992). The challenge of ensuring educational gains for students with severe disabilities who are placed in more integrated settings. *Education and Training in Mental Retardation and Developmental Disabilities, 27,* 167–175.

Hoffman, A., & Field, S. (1995). Self-determination through effective curriculum development. *Intervention in School and Clinic, 30,* 134–141.

Holsch, S.A., Karen, R.L., & Franzini, L.R. (1992). Two-year follow-up of the competitive employment status of graduates with developmental disabilities. *Career Development for Exceptional Individuals, 15*(2), 149–155.

Horner, R.H., Dunlap, G., Koegel, R.L., Carr, E.G., Sailor, W., Anderson, J., Albin, R.W., & O'Neill, R.E. (1990). Toward a technology of "nonaversive" behavioral support. *Journal of The Association for Persons with Severe Handicaps, 15,* 125–132.

Horton, B., Maddox, M., & Edgar, E. (1983). *The adult transition model: Planning for post school services.* Seattle: University of Washington.

Hughes, C. (1992a). It's my life! Facilitating self-advocacy through the transition planning process. *Lincletter, 15*(1), 22–24.

Hughes, C. (1992b). Teaching self-instruction utilizing multiple exemplars to produce generalized problem solving among individuals with severe mental retardation. *American Journal on Mental Retardation, 97*(3), 302–314.

Hughes, C., Rusch, F.R., & Curl, R.M. (1990). Extending individual competence, developing natural support, and promoting social acceptance. In F.R. Rusch (Ed.), *Supported employment: Models, methods, and issues* (pp. 181–197). Sycamore, IL: Sycamore Publishing Co.

Hunt, P., Haring, K., Farron, S., Staub, D., Rogers, J., Porter, S., Karasoff, P., Goetz, L., & Sailor, W. (1993). Factors associated with the integrated educational placement of students with severe disabilities. *Journal of The Association for Persons with Severe Handicaps, 18*(1), 6–15.

Hurwitz, S., & Kersting, H. (1993). Advances in technology for persons with disabilities. *Technology and Disability, 2*(2), 12–18.

Hutchins, M., Renzaglia, A., Stahlman, J., & Cullen, M. (1986). *Developing a vocational curriculum for students with moderate and severe handicaps.* Charlottesville: University of Virginia.

Individuals with Disabilities Education Act (IDEA) of 1990, PL 101-476, Title 20 U.S.C. § 1400 *et seq.*

Inestroza, R.A. (1990). Integrating basic skills for IEPs in vocational education. *Journal for Vocational Special Needs Education, 13*(1), 41.

Inge, K., Dymond, S., & Wehman, P. (1996). Community based vocational training. In P. McLaughlin & P. Wehman (Eds.), *Mental retardation and developmental disabilities* (pp. 297–316). Austin, TX: PRO-ED.

Iowa Department of Education. (1989). *Iowa statewide follow-up study: Adult adjustment of individuals with mental disabilities one year after leaving school.* Unpublished manuscript, Des Moines.

Irving, J.G. (1969). Impact of insurance coverage on convalescence and rehabilitation of head-injured patients. In A.E. Walker, W.F. Caveness, & M. Critchley (Eds.), *The late effects of head injury* (pp. 483–490). Springfield, IL: Charles C Thomas.

Irwin, J., & Macdonell, P. (1988). Access to transition services: Integral part of curriculum. *Journal of Visual Impairment and Blindness, 82*(2), 69–70.

Izzo, M.V., Pritz, S.G., & Ott, P. (1990). Teaching problem-solving skills: A ticket to a brighter future. *Journal for Vocational Special Needs Education, 13*(1), 23–26.

Izzo, M.V, & Schumate, R. (1991). *Transition planning guide.* Columbus: Ohio Department of Education.

Janes, C., Hesselbrock, V., Myers, D., & Penniman, J. (1979). Problem boys in young adulthood: Teachers' ratings and 12-year follow-up. *Journal of Youth and Adolescence, 8*(4), 453–472.

Janney, R.E., Snell, M.A., Beers, M.K., & Raynes, M. (1995). Integrating students with moderate and severe disabilities into general education classes. *Exceptional Children, 61*(5), 425–439.

Jennett, B. (1976). Assessment of severity of head injury. *Journal of Neurology, Neurosurgery, and Psychiatry, 39,* 647–655.

Jennett, B. (1983). Post-traumatic epilepsy. In M. Rosenthal, E.R. Griffith, M.R. Bond, & J.D. Miller (Eds.), *Rehabilitation of the head injured adult* (pp. 119–124). Philadelphia: F.A. Davis.

Jennett, B., Snoek, J., Bond, M., & Brooks, N. (1981). Disability after severe head injury: Observations on the use of the Glasgow Coma Scale. *Journal of Neurology, Neurosurgery, and Psychiatry, 44,* 285–293.

Jennett, B., & Teasdale, G. (1977). Aspects of coma after severe head injury. *Lancet, 1,* 878–881.

Jennett, B., & Teasdale, G. (1981). *Management of severe head injuries.* Philadelphia: F.A. Davis.

Johnson, D.R., Rydell, C., & Hunt, P. (1994). *Transition strategies that work: Volume II.* Minneapolis: University of Minnesota, Institute on Community Integration.

Johnson, D.R., Thompson, S.J., Sinclair, M.F., Krantz, G.C., Evelo, S., Stolte, K., & Thompson, J.R. (1993). Considerations in the design of follow-up and follow-along systems for improving transition programs and services. *Career Development for Exceptional Individuals, 16*(2), 225–238.

Jones, M.M., & Carlier, L.L. (1995, Spring). Creating inclusionary opportunities for learning with multiple disabilities: A team-teaching approach. *Teaching Exceptional Children, 23*–27.

Kalsbeek, W.D., McLaurin, R.L., Harris, B.S.H., & Miller, J.D. (1980). The national head and spinal cord injury survey: Major findings. *Journal of Neurosurgery, 53*(Suppl.), S19–S43.

Karge, B.D., Patton, P., & de la Garza, B. (1992). Transition services for youth with mild disabilities: Do they exist, are they needed? *Career Development for Exceptional Individuals, 15*(1), 47–68.

Karzmark, P., Hall, K., & Englander, J. (1995) Late-onset post-concussion symptoms after mild brain injury: The role of premorbid, injury-related, environmental, and personality factors. *Brain Injury, 9,* 21–26.

Katsiyannis, A., & Prillaman, D. (1989). Suspension and expulsion of handicapped students: National trends and the case of Virginia. *Behavioral Disorders, 15*(1), 35–40.

Kazdin, A.E. (1975). *Behavior modification in applied settings.* Homewood, IL: Dorsey Press.

Kazdin, A.E. (1980). *Behavior modification in applied settings* (2nd ed.). Homewood, IL: Dorsey Press.

Kearney, C.A., Durand, V.M., & Mindell, J.A. (1995). It's not where but how you live: Choice and adaptive/maladaptive behavior in persons with severe handicaps. *Journal of Developmental and Physical Disabilities, 7*(1), 11–24.

Kelley, J., & Frieden, L. (1989). *Go for it: A book on sports and recreation for persons with disabilities.* San Diego, CA: Harcourt Brace Jovanich.

Kennedy, C., Horner, R., & Newton, J. (1990). The social network and activity patterns of adults with severe disabilities: A correlational analysis. *Journal of The Association for Persons with Severe Handicaps, 15*(2), 86–90.

Kennedy, C., & Itkonen, T. (1994). Some effects of regular class participation on the social contacts and social networks of high school students with severe disabilities. *Journal of The Association for Persons with Severe Handicaps, 19*(1), 1–10.

Keogh, B.K. (1986). Future of the LD field: Research and practice. *Journal of Learning Disabilities, 19*(8), 455–460.

Kiernan, W.E., McGaughey, M.J., & Schalock, R.C. (1988). Employment environments and outcomes for adults with developmental disabilities. *Mental Retardation, 26,* 279–288.

Kinnison, L.R. (1987). Do parents know best? Parents'

participation: The weak link in career decision making. *The Journal for Vocational Special Needs Education, 10*(1), 13–16.

Klein, J. (1992). Get me the hell out of here: Supporting people with disabilities to live in their own homes. In J. Nisbet (Ed.), *Natural supports in school, at work, and in the community for people with severe disabilities* (pp. 277–339). Baltimore: Paul H. Brookes Publishing Co.

Knitzer, J., Steinberg, Z., & Fleisch, B. (1990). *At the schoolhouse door.* New York: Bank Street College.

Kokaska, C.J., & Brolin, D.E. (1985). *Career education for handicapped individuals* (2nd ed.). Columbus, OH: Charles E. Merrill.

Kolstoe, O.P. (1976). *Teaching educable mentally retarded children* (2nd ed.). New York: Holt, Rinehart & Winston.

Kortering, L., & Blackorby, J. (1992). High school dropout and students identified with behavioral disorders. *Behavior Disorders, 18*(1), 24–32.

Kortering, L.J., & Elrod, G.F. (1991). Programs for mildly handicapped adolescents: Evaluating where we are and contemplating change. *Career Development for Exceptional Individuals, 14*(2), 145–157.

Kregel, J. (1992). The subtle and salient points of program evaluation: An illustration from supported employment. *Journal of Vocational Rehabilitation, 2*(2), 53–61.

Kregel, J. (1995a). *Facts and figures about supported employment costs.* Richmond: Virginia Commonwealth University, Rehabilitation Research and Training Center.

Kregel, J. (1995b). Personal and functional characteristics of supported employment participants with severe mental retardation. *Journal of Vocational Rehabilitation, 5,* 221–231.

Kregel, J., Parent, W., & West, M. (1994). The impact of behavioral deficits on employment retention: An illustration from supported employment. *NeuroRehabilitation, 4*(1), 114.

Kregel, J., Shafer, M., Wehman, P., & West, M. (1989). Policy development and public expenditures in supported employment: Current strategies to promote statewide systems change. *Journal of The Association for Persons with Severe Handicaps, 14*(4), 283–292.

Kregel, J., & Tomiyasu, Y. (1994). Employer attitudes toward workers with disabilities: The effect of the ADA. *Journal of Vocational Rehabilitation, 4*(3), 165–173.

Kregel, J., & Unger, D. (1993). Employer perceptions of the work potential of individuals with disabilities: An illustration from supported employment. *Journal of Vocational Rehabilitation, 3*(4), 17–25.

Kregel, J., & Wehman, P. (1989a). An analysis of employment outcomes of young adults with mental retardation. In P. Wehman & J. Kregel (Eds.), *Supported employment for persons with disabilities* (pp. 232–248). New York: Human Sciences Press.

Kregel, J., & Wehman, P. (1989b). Supported employment for persons with severe handicaps: Promises deferred. *Journal of The Association for Persons with Severe Handicaps, 14*(4), 293–303.

Kregel, J., Wehman, P., & Banks, D. (1989). Effects of consumer characteristics and types of employment models of individual outcomes in supported employment. *Journal of Applied Behavior Analysis, 22*, 407–415.

Kregel, J., Wehman, P., Seyfarth, J., & Marshall, K. (1986). Community integration of young adults with mental retardation: Transition from school to adulthood. *Education and Training of the Mentally Retarded, 21*, 35–42.

Kreutzer, J.S. (1988, September). *Alcohol, drugs, and crime: Before and after injury.* Paper presented at the second annual meeting of Cognitive Rehabilitation, Community Reintegration Through Scientifically Based Practice, Richmond, VA.

Kreutzer, J.S., & Goodall, P. (1989, June). *Incidence, assessment and treatment of substance abuse.* Workshop conducted at the Postgraduate Course in Rehabilitation of the Brain-Injured Adult and Child, Williamsburg, VA.

Kreutzer, J.S., & Morton, M.V. (1988). Traumatic brain injury: Supported employment and compensatory strategies for enhancing vocational outcomes. In P. Wehman & M.S. Moon (Eds.), *Vocational rehabilitation and supported employment* (pp. 291–311). Baltimore: Paul H. Brookes Publishing Co.

Kreutzer, J.S., Wehman, P., Morton, M.V., & Stonnington, H. (1988). Supported employment and cognitive compensatory strategies for enhancing vocational outcome following traumatic brain injury. *Brain Injury, 2*(3), 205–223.

Krom, D.M., & Prater, M.A. (1993). IEP goals for intermediate-aged students with mild mental retardation. *Career Development for Exceptional Individuals, 16*(1), 87–95.

Lakin, K.C., Braddock, D., & Smith, G. (1994). State institution closings. *Mental Retardation, 32*, 77.

Lakin, K.C., Braddock, D., Smith, G., & West, R. (1994). Trends and milestones. *Mental Retardation, 32*(1), 77.

Lakin, K.C., Proutry, R., Smith, G., & Braddock, D. (1995). Trends and milestones: Places of residence of medicaid HCBS recipients. *Mental Retardation, 33*(6), 406–408.

Lambrou, J., Lowder, M., Leslie, J., Jensen, L., Heidelberger, J., Zeller, D., Moure, C., & Steirer, J. (1986). *Transition! School to community.* Boise: Idaho State Department of Education.

Langston, A., Coker, C.C., & Smith, C.A. (1989). A descriptive study of rehabilitation technology utilization in state vocational rehabilitation agencies. *Journal of Rehabilitation Administration, 13*(5), 45–50.

Laski, F. (1994). On the 40th anniversary of Brown versus Board of Education. *TASH Newsletter, 20*(6), 3–4.

Learning in Functional Environments (LIFE). (1986). Region 4, Education Service Center, Houston, TX.

Lemke, A. (1991). Keeping them on the job: Ways to assist employees with LD in upgrading their skills. *Puzzle People News, 4*(4), 10–13.

Leone, P., Fitzmartin, R., Stetson, F., & Foster, J. (1986). A retrospective follow-up of behaviorally disordered adolescents: Identifying predictors of treatment outcome. *Behavioral Disorders, 11*, 87–97.

Leong, C.K. (1989). The focus of so-called IQ test results in reading disabilities. *Journal of Learning Disabilities, 22*(8), 507–512.

Levine, M.D. (1989). Learning disabilities at 25: The early adulthood of a maturing concept. *Learning Disabilities, 1*(1), 1–11.

Levine, M.D. (1990). *Keeping ahead in school.* Cambridge, MA: Educator's Publishing Service.

Levine, P., & Edgar, E. (1994). Respondents and agreement in follow-up studies of graduates in special and general education programs. *60*(4), 334–343.

Levine, P., & Edgar, G. (1995). An analysis by gender of long-term postschool outcomes for youth with and without disabilities. *Exceptional Children, 61*(3), 282–300.

Lezak, M. (1987). Relationships between personality disorders, social disorders, social disturbances, and relative's psychiatric and social functioning. *Journal of Head Trauma Rehabilitation, 2*(1), 57–69.

Lilly, M.S. (Ed.). (1979). *Children with exceptional needs.* New York: Holt, Rinehart & Winston.

Linden, B., & Forness, S. (1986). Post-school adjustment of mentally retarded persons with psychiatric disorders: A ten-year follow-up. *Education and Training of the Mentally Retarded, 21*, 157–164.

Lipsky, D., & Gartner, A. (1994). Beyond separate to equal: Changes in rights and rules. *TASH Newsletter, 20*(7), 5.

Lishman, W.A. (1973). The psychiatric sequelae of head injury: A review. *Psychological Medicine, 3*, 304–318.

Litvak, S., Zukas, H., & Heumann, J.E. (1987). *Attending to America: Personal assistance for independent living: A survey of attendant service programs in the United States for people of all ages with disabilities.* Berkeley, CA: World Institute on Disability.

Livingston, M.G., & Brooks, D.N. (1988). The burden on families of the brain injured: A review. *Journal of Head Trauma Rehabilitation, 3*(4), 6–15.

Llewellyn, G. (1995). Relationships with social support: View of parents with mental retardation and intellectual disability. *Mental Retardation, 33*(6), 349–363.

Long, C.J., Gouvier, W.D., & Cole, J.C. (1984). A model of recovery for the total rehabilitation of individuals with head trauma. *Journal of Rehabilitation, 50*, 39–45.

Long, C.J., & Webb, W.L. (1983). Psychological sequelae of head trauma. *Psychiatric Medicine, 1*, 35–77.

Louis Harris and Associates. (1994). *The ICD Survey II: Employing Disabled Americans* (pp. 6–8). Washington, DC: National Organization on Disability.

Lovitt, T.C., Cushing, S.S., & Stump, C.S. (1994). High school students rate their IEPs: Low opinions and lack of ownership. *Intervention in School and Clinic, 30*(1), 34–37.

Luckasson, R., Coulter, D.L., Polloway, E.A., Reiss, S., Schalock, R.L., Snell, M.E., Spitalnik, D.M., & Stark, J.A. (1992). *Mental retardation: Definition, classification, and systems of supports* (9th ed.). Washington, DC: American Association on Mental Retardation.

Luckasson, R., & Spitalnik, D. (1994). Political and programmatic shifts of the 1992 AAMR definition of mental retardation. In V.J. Bradley, J.W. Ashbaugh, & B.C. Blaney (Eds.), *Creating individual supports for people with developmental disabilities: A mandate for change at many levels* (pp. 81–95). Baltimore: Paul H. Brookes Publishing Co.

MacDonald, J. (1987). The integration of students with severe handicaps into regular public schools: An analysis of parents' perceptions of potential outcomes. *Education and Training in Mental Retardation, 22*(98), 111.

MacDonald-Wilson, K.L., Mancuso, L.L., Danley, K.S., & Anthony, W.A. (1989). Supported employment for people with psychiatric disability. *Journal of Applied Rehabilitation Counseling, 20*(3), 50–57.

MacDonald-Wilson, K., Revell, W.G., Nguyen, N., & Peterson, M. (1991). Supported employment outcomes for people with psychiatric disability. *Journal of Vocational Rehabilitation, 1*(3), 30–44.

MacMillan, D.L. (1977). *Mental retardation in school and society.* Boston: Little, Brown.

MacMillan, D.L. (1988). Issues in mild mental retardation. *Education and Training in Mental Retardation, 23*(4), 273–284.

MacMillan, D.L., Balow, I., Widaman, K., Bosthwick-Duffy, S., & Hendrick, I. (1990). Methodological problems in estimating dropout rates and the implications for studying dropouts from special education. *Exceptionality, 1,* 29–39.

MacMillan, D.L., Widaman, K., Balow, I., Bosthwick-Duffy, S., Hendrick, I., & Hemsley, R. (1992). Special education students exiting the educational system. *Journal of Special Education, 26*(1), 20–36.

Madison, D., & Agran, M. (1995). Safety skills training in supported employment: A survey of current practices. *Journal of Vocational Rehabilitation, 5*(1), 15–24.

Magill, J., & Hurlbut, N. (1986). The self-esteem of adolescents with cerebral palsy. *American Journal of Occupational Therapy, 40,* 402–407.

Mallik, K. (1990). Rehabilitation engineering and environmental modifications. In P. Wehman & J. Kreutzer (Eds.), *Vocational rehabilitation for persons with traumatic brain injury* (pp. 89–102). Rockville, MD: Aspen.

Mank, D. (1994). The underachievement of supported employment: A call for reinvestment. *Journal of Disability Policy Studies, 5*(2), 1–24.

Mank, D.M., & Horner, R.H. (1988). Instructional programming in vocational education. In R. Gaylord-Ross (Ed.), *Vocational education for persons with handicaps* (pp. 142–173). Mountain View, CA: Mayfield Publishing Co.

Marion, R.R. (1981). *Educators, parents, and exceptional children.* Rockville, MD: Aspen.

Martin, P. (1987). *Martin's magic formula for getting the right job* (2nd ed.). New York: St. Martin's Press.

Martino, L.R. (1993). A goal setting model for young adolescent at risk students. *Middle School Journal, 24,* 19–27.

McAllister, M., & Mank, D. (1992). *Rehabilitation facility implementation of supported employment: A survey of five states in the Pacific Northwest.* Eugene: University of Oregon, Specialized Training Program.

McCarthy, P., Everson, J.M., Inge, K., & Barcus, J.M. (1985). Transition from school to work: Developing the process for individuals with severe disabilities. *Techniques: A Journal for Remedial Education and Counseling, 1*(6), 463–472.

McCord, W., & Sanchez, J. (1983). The treatment of deviant children: A twenty-five year follow-up study. *Crime and Delinquency, 29*(2), 238–253.

McCrea, L.D. (1993, June). Frequency of job skills appearing on individualized plans of students with moderate retardation. *Education and Training in Mental Retardation,* 179–185.

McDonnell, J. (1987). Supported employment: Delights and dilemmas. *The Rehabilitation Advocate, 6*(1), 1–12.

McDonnell, J., & Hardman, M. (1985). Planning the transition of severely handicapped youth from school to adult services. A framework for high school programs. *Education and Training of the Mentally Retarded, 20*(4), 275–286.

McGaughey, M.J., Kiernan, W.E., McNally, L.C., & Cooperman, P.J. (1991). *Supported employment for persons with severe physical disabilities: Survey of service providers.* Boston: Children's Hospital, Training and Research Institute for People with Disabilities.

McGaughey, M.J., Kiernan, W.E., McNally, L.C., & Gilmore, D.S. (1993). *National perspectives on integrated employment: State MR/DD agency trends.* Boston: Children's Hospital, Training and Research Institute on Developmental Disabilities.

McGaughey, M.J., Kiernan, W.E., McNally, L.C., Gilmore, D.S., & Keith, G.R. (1994). *Beyond the workshop: National perspectives on integrated employment.* Boston: Institute for Community Inclusion.

McLeskey, J. (1989). The influence of level of discrepancy on the identification of students with learning disabilities. *Journal of Learning Disabilities, 22*(7), 435–438, 443.

McMordie, W.R., & Barker, S.L. (1988). The financial trauma of head injury. *Brain Injury, 2,* 357–364.

McMordie, W.R., Barker, S.L., & Paolo, T.M. (1990). Return to work (RTW) after head injury. *Brain Injury, 4,* 57–69.

McNair, J., & Rusch, F.R. (1991). Parent involvement in transition programs. *Mental Retardation, 29*(2), 93–101.

McNulty, K. (1995). Parents speak out: Perspectives on transition services. In J.M. Everson (Ed.), *Supporting young adults who are deaf-blind in their communities: A transition planning guide for service providers, families, and friends* (pp. 87–98). Baltimore: Paul H. Brookes Publishing Co.

Meers, G.D. (1992). Getting ready for the next century. *Teaching Exceptional Children, 24*(2), 36–39.

Menchetti, B.M., & Rusch, F.R. (1988). Vocational evaluation and eligibility for rehabilitation services. In P. Wehman & M.S. Moon (Eds.), *Vocational rehabilitation*

and supported employment (pp. 79–90). Baltimore: Paul H. Brookes Publishing Co.

Menzia, R. (1990). Why can't you spell? *The MATC Times, 31*(8), 6.

Middendorf, K. (1995). Presidential address of 1995: The shifting paradigm from rhetoric to reality. *Mental Retardation, 33*(6), 394–398.

Miller, J.L. (1990). Apocalypse or renaissance or something in between? Toward a realistic appraisal of *The Learning Mystique. Journal of Learning Disabilities, 23*(2), 86–91.

Miller, M. (1993, November 15). Contact high: Computer networks have transformed campus life and the changes hint at what may be ahead for us all. *Wall Street Journal,* R4.

Minnesota Pacer Center. (1994, June). *How to prepare for the day your child leaves high school.* Minneapolis: Author.

Minuchin, S. (1974). *Families and family therapy.* New York: Basic Books.

Mira, M., Tucker, B.F., & Tyler, S. (1992). *Traumatic brain injury in children and adolescents.* Austin, TX: PRO-ED.

Mitchell, S., & Rosa, P. (1981). Boyhood behavior problems as precursors of criminality: A fifteen-year follow-up study. *Journal of Child Psychology and Psychiatry, 22,* 19–33.

Mithaug, D.E., Horiuchi, C., & Fanning, P. (1985). A report on the Colorado statewide follow-up survey of special education students. *Exceptional Children, 51*(5), 397–404.

Moon, M.S. (Ed.). (1994). *Making school and community recreation fun for everyone: Places and ways to integrate.* Baltimore: Paul H. Brookes Publishing Co.

Moon, M.S., Goodall, P., Barcus, M., & Brooke, V. (1986). *The supported work model of competitive employment for citizens with severe handicaps: A guide for job trainers* (Rev. ed.). Richmond: Virginia Commonwealth University, Rehabilitation Research and Training Center.

Moon, M.S., & Inge, K. (1993). Vocational preparation and transition. In M. Snell (Ed.), *Instruction of students with severe disabilities* (4th ed., pp. 556–587). New York: Macmillan.

Moon, M.S., Inge, K.J., Wehman, P., Brooke, V., & Barcus, J.M. (1990). *Helping persons with severe mental retardation get and keep employment: Supported employment issues and strategies.* Baltimore: Paul H. Brookes Publishing Co.

Moon, M.S., Kiernan, W., & Halloran, W. (1990). School-based vocational programs and labor laws: A 1990 update. *Journal of The Association for Persons with Severe Handicaps, 15*(3), 177–185.

Morton, M.V., & Wehman, P. (1995). Psychosocial and emotional sequelae of individuals with traumatic brain injury: A literature review and recommendations. *Brain Injury, 9*(1), 81–92.

Mount, B. (1991). *Person-centered planning: A source book of values, ideals, and methods to encourage person-centered development.* New York: Graphic Features.

Mount, B. (1994). Benefits and limitations of Persons

Futures Planning. In V.J. Bradley, J.W. Ashbaugh, & B.C. Blaney (Eds.), *Creating individual supports for people with developmental disabilities: A mandate for change at many levels* (pp. 97–108). Baltimore: Paul H. Brookes Publishing Co.

Mount, B., & Zwernik, K. (1988). *It's never too early, it's never too late: A booklet about personal futures planning.* St. Paul, MN: Metropolitan Council.

Mozingo, D., Ackley, G.B.E., & Bailey, J.S. (1994). Training quality job interviews with adults with developmental disabilities. *Research in Developmental Disabilities, 15*(5), 389–410.

Murphy, S.T., & Rogan, P.M. (1995). *Closing the shop: Conversion from sheltered to integrated work.* Baltimore: Paul H. Brookes Publishing Co.

National Association of Rehabilitation Facilities. (1989). *Supported employment in context: NARF's national scope supported employment survey of policy implications.* Washington, DC: Author.

National Head Injury Foundation. (1986). *Trauma: The silent epidemic.* Framingham, MA: Author.

National Information Center for Children and Youth with Disabilities (NICHCY). (1990, December). Vocational Assessment: A guide for parents and professionals. *NICHCY Transition Summary,* 6.

National Institute of Mental Health (NIMH). (1986). *National statistics on the mental disorders.* Washington, DC: U.S. Government Printing Office.

National Joint Committee on Learning Disabilities (NJCLD). (1988). *Letter to NJCLD member organizations,* p. 1. Austin, TX: PRO-ED.

National Longitudinal Transition Study (NLTS). (1989, March). *The transition experiences of youth with disabilities: A report from the NLTS.* Presented at the annual meeting of Division of Research, Council for Exceptional Children, San Francisco.

Neel, R., Meadows, N., Levine, P., & Edgar, E. (1988). What happens after special education: A statewide follow-up study of secondary students who have behavioral disorders. *Behavioral Disorders, 13*(3), 209–216.

Nehring, W.M. (1990, April). *Transition needs for children with chronic illness into adulthood: Alleviating the concerns of families with information and knowledge.* Paper presented at the 11th Annual International Conference on Developmental Disabilities, Young Adult Institute, New York.

Neighborhood school decision held for severely handicapped. (1993, May 30). *Philadelphia Inquirer, 2,* 16–18.

Neubert, D.A., & Foster, J. (1988). Learning disabled students make the transition. *Teaching Exceptional Children, 20,* 17–21.

Neubert, D.A., Tilson, G.P., & Ianacone, R.N. (1989). Postsecondary transition needs and employment patterns of individuals with mild disabilities. *Exceptional Children, 55*(6), 494–500.

Newton, J.S., Horner, R.H., Ard, W., LeBaron, N., & Sappington, G. (1994). A conceptual model for improving a social life of individuals with mental retardation. *Mental Retardation, 32*(6), 393–402.

Newton, J.S., Olson, D., & Horner, R.H. (1995). Factors contributing to the stability of social relationships between individuals with mental retardation and other community members. *Mental Retardation, 33*(6), 383–393.

Newton, J.S., Olson, D., Horner, R., & Ard, W. (1996). Social skills of the stability of social relationships between individuals with intellectual disabilities and other community members. *Research in Developmental Disabilities, 17*(1), 15–26.

Nietupski, J., Verstegen, D., Hamre-Nietupski, S., & Tanty, S. (1993). Leveraging community support in approaching employers. *Journal of Vocational Rehabilitation, 3*(4), 38–45.

Nihira, K., Foster, R., Shellhaas, M., Leland, H., Lambert, N., & Windmiller, M. (1990). *AAMD Adaptive Behavior Scale.* Odessa, FL: Psychological Assessment Resources.

Nip, R., Doman, J., & Schenthek, C. (1995). Traumatic brain injury: Factors predicting return to work or school. *Brain Injury, 9*(5), 517–532.

Nisbet, J. (Ed.). (1992). *Natural supports in school, at work, and in the community for people with severe disabilities.* Baltimore: Paul H. Brookes Publishing Co.

Nisbet, J., Clark, M., & Covert, S. (1991). Living it up! An analysis of research on community living. In L.H. Meyer, C.A. Peck, & L. Brown (Eds.), *Critical issues in the lives of people with severe disabilities* (pp. 115–144). Baltimore: Paul H. Brookes Publishing Co.

Nisbet, J., & Hagner, D. (1988). Natural supports in the workplace: A reexamination of supported employment. *Journal of The Association for Persons with Severe Handicaps, 13,* 260–267.

Nisbet, J., Rogan, P., & Hagner, D. (1989). Squeezing long-term supports out of a short-term program: Independence issues and supported employment. *Journal of Applied Rehabilitation Counseling, 20*(3), 21–25.

Nixon, C., & Williamston, North Carolina, School System. (1995). *Occupational preparation: Occupational diploma for special needs student curriculum courses.* Kinston, NC: Authors.

Norman, M.E., & Bourexis, P.S. (1995). *Including students with disabilities in school-to-work opportunities.* Washington, DC: Council of Chief State School Officers.

Nosek, M.A. (1991). Personal assistance services: A review of the literature and analysis of policy implications. *Journal of Disability Policy Studies, 2*(2), 1–17.

Nozoki, K., & Mochizuki, A. (1995). Assessing choice making of a person with profound disabilities. *Journal of The Association for Persons with Severe Handicaps, 20*(3), 173–175.

O'Brien, J. (1987). A guide to life-style planning: Using *The Activities Catalog* to integrate services and natural support systems. In B. Wilcox & G.T. Bellamy (Eds.), *A comprehensive guide to The Activities Catalog: An alternative curriculum for youth and adults with severe disabilities* (pp. 175–189). Baltimore: Paul H. Brookes Publishing Co.

O'Brien, J. (1994). Down stairs that are never your own: Supporting people with developmental disabilities in their own homes. *Mental Retardation, 32,* 1–6.

O'Brien, J., & O'Brien, C.L. (1992). Members of each other: Perspectives on social support for people with severe disabilities. In J. Nisbet (Ed.), *Natural supports in school, at work, and in the community for people with severe disabilities* (pp. 17–63). Baltimore: Paul H. Brookes Publishing Co.

O'Brien, P., & Schiller, W. (1979). Evaluation of a transitional training program for mentally retarded, multiply handicapped high school students. *Rehabilitation Literature, 40*(8), 232–235.

O'Bryan, A. (1985). The specialized training program (STP) benchwork model. In P. McCarthy, J. Everson, S. Moon, & M. Barcus (Eds.), *School to work transition for youth with severe disabilities* (pp. 183–194). Richmond: Virginia Commonwealth University, Rehabilitation Research and Training Center.

O'Callaghan, R., & Toomey, J. (1983). Adult status of mildly retarded past-pupils from special education: Part one: Employment. *International Journal of Rehabilitation Research, 6*(1), 19–28.

O'Connor, S., & Racino, J.A. (1993). "A home of my own": Community housing options and strategies. In J.A. Racino, P. Walker, S. O'Connor, & S.J. Taylor (Eds.), *Housing, support, and community: Choices and strategies for adults with disabilities* (pp. 137–160). Baltimore: Paul H. Brookes Publishing Co.

Odom, S.L., & Chandler, L. (1990). Transition to parenthood for parents of technology-assisted infants. *Topics in Early Childhood Special Education, 9*(4), 43–54.

Okolo, C., & Sitlington, P. (1988). The role of special education in LD adolescents' transition from school to work. *Learning Disability Quarterly, 11,* 292–306.

Olson, D., & Henig, E. (1983). *A manual of behavior management strategies for traumatic brain injured adults.* Chicago: Rehabilitation Institute of Chicago.

Osborne, A.G., & Dimattia, P. (1995). Counterpoint: IDEA's LRE mandate: Another look. *Exceptional Children, 61*(6), 582–584.

Parent, W.S. (1994). *Consumer satisfaction at the workplace: A survey of individuals with severe disabilities who receive supported employment services.* Unpublished doctoral dissertation, Virginia Commonwealth University, Richmond.

Parent, W., Gibson, W., Unger, D., & Clements, C. (1994). The role of the job coach: Orchestrating community and workplace supports. In P. Wehman & J. Kregel (Eds.), *New directions in supported employment* (pp. 40–52). Richmond: Virginia Commonwealth University, Rehabilitation Research and Training Center on Supported Employment.

Parent, W., Kregel, J., & Wehman, P. (1992). *Vocational integration index: A guide for rehabilitation and special education professionals.* Austin, TX: PRO-ED.

Parent, W., Kregel, J., Wehman, P., & Metzler, H. (1991). Measuring the social integration of supported employment workers. *Journal of Vocational Rehabilitation, 1*(1), 35–58.

Parent, W., Unger, D., Gibson, K., & Clements, C.

(1994). The role of job coach: Orchestrating community and workplace supports. *American Rehabilitation, 20*(3), 2–11.

Payne, J.S., Kauffman, J.M., Patton, J.R., Brown, G.B., & DeMott, R.M. (1979). *Exceptional children in focus* (2nd ed.). Columbus, OH: Charles E. Merrill.

Peraino, J.M. (1992). Post-21 follow-up studies: How do special education graduates fare? In P. Wehman (Ed.), *Life beyond the classroom: Transition strategies for young people with disabilities* (pp. 21–70). Baltimore: Paul H. Brookes Publishing Co.

Perotti, F. (1985). A comparison of the vocational adjustment of educable mentally retarded adults after completion of work-study, vocational-technical and resource room high school programs. *Dissertation Abstracts International, 45*(8), 2487-A.

Perske, R. (1972). The dignity of risk and the mentally retarded. *Mental Retardation, 10,* 24–27.

Peters, L.C., Stambrook, M., Moore, A.D., & Esses, L. (1990). Psychosocial sequelae of closed head injury: Effects on the marital relationship. *Brain Injury, 4,* 39–47.

Peterson, L., & Smith, L. (1960). The post-school adjustment of educable mentally retarded adults with that of adults of normal intelligence. *Exceptional Children, 26,* 404–408.

Petty, D., & Fussell, E. (1995). *Supported employment trend analysis.* Knoxville: Tennessee Initiative on Employment, Tennessee University Affiliated Program.

Phillips, P. (1990, October). A self-advocacy plan for high school students with learning disabilities: A comparative case study analysis of students', teachers', and parents' perceptions of program effects. *Journal of Learning Disabilities, 23*(8), 466–71.

Piepmeier, J.M. (1992). *The outcome following traumatic spinal cord injury.* Mount Kisco, NY: Futura.

Polloway, E.A., Patton, J.R., Epstein, M., & Smith, T.E.C. (1989). Comprehensive curriculum for students with mild handicaps. *Focus on Exceptional Children, 21*(8), 1–12.

Polloway, E.A., Patton, J.R., & Smith, J.D. (1991). Issues in program design for elementary students with mild retardation: Emphasis on curriculum development. *Education and Training in Mental Retardation, 26,* 142–148.

Polloway, E.A., & Smith, J.D. (1983). Changes in mild mental retardation: Population, programs, and perspectives. *Exceptional Children, 50*(2), 149–159.

Polloway, E.A., Smith, T.E.C., Patton, J.R., Edgar, E., Clark, G., & Lee, S. (in press). Individuals with mild mental retardation: Postsecondary outcomes and implications for educational policy. *Education and Training in Mental Retardation and Developmental Disabilities.*

Posey, V.K., & Hollenback, K. (1990). Serving language minority and multicultural special populations in rural areas. *Journal for Vocational Special Needs Education, 12,* 23–27.

Powers, L. (1994). Self-determination and assistive technology. *Reporting on Assistive Technology, 2*(4), 3–12.

President's Committee on Employment of People with Disabilities. (1986). *Employment Status Report.* Washington, DC: U.S. Government Printing Office.

Prigatano, G. (1988). Rehabilitation interventions after traumatic brain injury. *Brain Injury, 4*(2), 30–37.

Prigatano, G.P., Klonoff, P.S., O'Brien, K.P., Altman, I., Amin, K., Chiapell, B., Shephard, J., Cunningham, M., & Moore, M. (1994). Productivity after neuropsychologically oriented milieu rehabilitation. *Journal of Head Trauma Rehabilitation, 9*(1), 91–102.

Project proposal submitted to Colorado Vocational Rehabilitation, Institute on Community Integration (UAP), University of Minnesota

Pullis, M. (1991, October–November). No bridges over troubled waters: Transition services for students with behavioral disorders. *Missouri Lincletter, 14*(2), 1–3.

Rachal, P. (1995). Interagency approaches to transition services for young adults who are deaf-blind. In J.M. Everson (Ed.), *Supporting young adults who are deaf-blind in their communities: A transition planning guide for service providers, families, and friends* (pp. 301–324). Baltimore: Paul H. Brookes Publishing Co.

Racino, J.A., & Taylor, S.J. (1993). "People first": Approaches to housing and support. In J.A. Racino, P. Walker, S. O'Connor, & S.J. Taylor (Eds.), *Housing, support, and community: Choices and strategies for adults with disabilities* (pp. 33–56). Baltimore: Paul H. Brookes Publishing Co.

Rao, N., Rosenthal, M., Cronin-Stubbs, D., Lambert, R., Barnes, P., & Swanson, B. (1990). Return to work after rehabilitation following traumatic brain injury. *Brain Injury, 4,* 49–56.

Raskind, M.H. (1994). Assistive technology for adults with learning disabilities: A rationale for use. In P.J. Gerber & H.B. Reiff (Eds.), *Learning disabilities in adulthood: Persisting problems and evolving issues* (pp. 152–162). Boston: Andover Medical Publishers.

Reagan, M., Murphy, R., Hill, Y., & Thomas, D. (1980). Community placement stability of behavior problem educable mentally retarded students. *Mental Retardation, 18,* 139–142.

Rees, L.M., Spreen, O., & Harnadek, M. (1991). Do attitudes towards persons with handicaps really shift over time? Comparison between 1975 and 1988. *Mental Retardation, 29,* 81–86.

Rehabilitation Act of 1973, PL 93-112. 29 U.S.C. § 701 *et seq.*

Rehabilitation Act Amendments of 1986, PL 99-506, 29 U.S.C. § 701 *et seq.*

Rehabilitation Act Amendments of 1992, PL 102-569, 29 U.S.C. § 701 *et seq.*

Rehabilitation Services Administration. (1995, March 5). *Definition of learning disability: Program policy directive* (RSA PPD-85-7). Washington, DC: U.S. Department of Education, Rehabilitation Services.

Reid, D., Parsons, M., McCarn, J., Green, C., Philips, J., & Schepis, M. (1985). Providing a more appropriate education for severely handicapped persons: Increasing and validating functional classroom tasks. *Journal of Applied Behavior, 18,* 292.

Reid, R., & Harris, K. (1993). Self-monitoring of attention vs. self-monitoring of performance: Effects on attention and academic performance. *Exceptional Children, 60*(1), 29–40.

Reiff, H.G., Ginsberg, R., & Gerber, P.J. (1995). New perspectives on teaching from successful adults with learning disabilities. *Remedial and Special Education, 16*(1), 29–37.

Reiling, C. (1990). *How significant is "significant"? A personal glimpse of life with a learning disability.* Columbus, OH: Association on Handicapped Student Service Programs in Postsecondary Education.

Reschly, D.J. (1988). Assessment issues, placement litigation and the future of mild mental retardation classification and programming. *Education and Training in Mental Retardation, 23*(4), 285–299.

Revell, W.G., & Wehman, P. (1996). Best practices in transition. *Journal of Vocational Rehabilitation, 7*(1), 48–56.

Revell, W.G., Wehman, P., Kregel, J., West, M., & Rayfield, R. (1994). Supported employment for persons with severe disabilities: Positive trends in wages, models, and funding. *Education and Training in Mental Retardation and Developmental Disabilities, 29*(4), 256–264.

Rhodes, L., Sandow, D., Mank, D., Buckley, J., & Albin, J. (1991). Expanding the role of employers in supported employment. *Journal of The Association for Persons with Severe Handicaps, 16*, 213–217.

Rhodes, L.E., & Valenta, L. (1989). Industry-based supported employment: An enclave approach. In P. Wehman & J. Kregel (Eds.), *Supported employment for persons with severe disabilities: Focus on excellence* (pp. 53–86). New York: Human Sciences Press.

Rimel, R.W., & Jane, J.A. (1984). Patient characteristics. In M. Rosenthal, E.R. Griffith, M.R. Bond, & J.D. Miller (Eds.), *Rehabilitation of the head injured adult* (pp. 9–20). Philadelphia: F.A. Davis.

Rinehart, P.M. (1994). Moving on: Transition from pediatric to adult health care. *Connections: The Newsletter of the National Center for Youth with Disabilities, 5*(1), 1–5.

Rispens, J., van Yperen, T.A., & van Duijn, G.A. (1991). The irrelevance of IQ to the definition of learning disabilities: Some empirical evidence. *Journal of Learning Disabilities, 24*(7), 434–438.

Roberts, A.H. (1990). Generic adaptions to blindness: An alternate method of rehabilitation. *Journal of Visual Impairment and Blindness, 4*, 151–154.

Robinson, E. (1984). Techniques for job hunting. *Journal of Rehabilitation, 50*(2), 93–95.

Rogan, P. (1990). *Strategies for facilitating natural supports in the work place.* Presentation at the meeting of the Virginia Commonwealth University, National Symposium on Supported Employment, Virginia Beach.

Rogan, P., Hagner, D., & Murphy, S. (1993). Natural supports: Reconceptualizing job coach roles. *Journal of The Association for Persons with Severe Handicaps, 18*(4), 275–281.

Rogers, J. (1993). *Research Bulletin.* Bloomington, IN: Phi Delta Kappa, Center for Evaluation, Development, and Research.

Rojewski, J.W. (1996). Educational and occupational aspirations of high school students with learning disabilities. *Exceptional Children, 62*(5), 463–476.

Rose, T. (1989). Corporal punishment with mildly handicapped students: Five years later. *Remedial and Special Education, 10*(1), 43–52.

Rosen, J., & Burchard, S. (1990). Community activities and social support networks: A social comparison of adults with and adults without mental retardation. *Education and Training in Mental Retardation, 25*, 193–204.

Rosen, M. (1994). Empowerment: A two edge sword. *Mental Retardation, 32*(1), 870–873.

Rosenthal, M., & Young, T. (1988). Effective family intervention after traumatic brain injury: Theory and practice. *Journal of Head Trauma Rehabilitation, 3*(4), 42–50.

Rotegard, L.L., Bruinicks, R.H., Holman, J.G., & Lakin, K.C. (1985). Environmental aspects of deinstitutionalization. In R.H. Bruiniks & K.C. Lakin (Eds.), *Living and learning in the least restrictive environment* (pp. 55–184). Baltimore: Paul H. Brookes Publishing Co.

Rusch, F.R., & DeStefano, L. (1989). Transition from school to work: Strategies for young adults with disabilities. *Interchange, 9*(3), 1–2.

Rusch, F., & Mithaug, D. (1980). *Vocational training for retarded adults.* Champaign, IL: Research Press.

Rusch, F.R., Wilson, P., Hughes, C., & Heal, L. (1994). Matched-pairs analysis of coworker interactions in relation to opportunity type of job and placement approach. *American Journal on Mental Retardation, 32*(2), 113–122.

Russell, W.R. (1932). Cerebral involvement in head trauma: A study based on the examination of 200 cases. *Brain Injury, 55*, 549–603.

Ryndak, D., Downing, J., Lilly, J.R., & Morrison, A. (1995). Parents' perceptions after inclusion of their children with moderate or severe disabilities. *Journal of The Association for Persons with Severe Handicaps, 20*(2), 147–157.

Sacks, S.Z., & Wolffe, K. (1992). The importance of social skills in the transition process for students with visual impairments. *Journal of Vocational Rehabilitation, 2*(1), 46–55.

Safer, D., Heaton, R., & Parker, F. (1981). A behavioral program for disruptive junior high school students: Results and follow-up. *Journal of Abnormal Child Psychology, 9*(4), 483–494.

Sailor, W., Gee, K., Goetz, L., & Graham, N. (1988). Progress in educating students with the most severe disabilities: Is there any? *Journal of The Association for Persons with Severe Handicaps, 13*(2), 87–99.

Sailor, W., Gee, K., & Karasoff, P. (1989). Full inclusion and school restructuring. In M. Snell (Ed.), *Systematic instruction for students with moderate and severe disabilities* (pp. 1–30). New York: Macmillan.

Sailor, W., & Guest, D. (1989). *Severely handicapped students: Instructional design.* Boston: Houghton Mifflin.

Sale, P., Metzler, H., Everson, J., & Moon, J.S. (1991). Quality indicators of successful vocational transition programs. *Journal of Vocational Rehabilitation, 1*(4), 47–63.

Sale, P., Revell, W., West, M., & Kregel, J. (1992). Achievements and challenges (II): Analysis of 1990 supported employment expenditures. *Journal of The Association for Persons with Severe Handicaps, 17*(4), 236–246.

Salkever, D. (1994). Access to vocational rehabilitation services for persons with severe disabilities. *Journal of Disability Policy Studies, 5*(2), 45–64.

Sandow, D., Olson, D., & Yan, X. (1993). The evolution of support in the workplace. *Journal of Vocational Rehabilitation, 3*(4), 30–37.

Sarkees, M.D., & Scott, J.L. (1985). *Vocational special needs* (2nd ed.). Homewood, IL: American Technical Publishers.

Sarkees-Wircenski, M., & Wircenski, J. (1994). Transition planning: Developing a career portfolio for students with disabilities. *Career Development for Exceptional Individuals, 17*(2), 203–214.

Savage, R.C. (1991). Identification, classification, and placement issues for students with traumatic brain injuries. *Journal of Head Trauma Rehabilitation, 6*(1), 1–9.

Savage, R.C., & Wolcott, G.F. (Eds.). (1994). *Educational dimensions of acquired brain injury.* Austin, TX: PRO-ED.

Schalock, R.L., & Genung, T. (1993). Placement from the community based mental retardation program: A fifteen year follow up. *American Journal on Mental Retardation, 98,* 400–407.

Schalock, R.L., Kiernan, W.E., McGaughey, M.J., Lynch, S.A., & McNally, L.C. (1993). State MR/DD agency information systems and available data related to day and employment programs. *American Journal on Mental Retardation, 31*(1), 29–34.

Schalock, R., Stark, J., Snell, M., Coulter, D., Polloway, E., Luckasson, R., Reiss, S., & Spitalnik, D. (1994). The changing conception of mental retardation: Implications for the field. *Mental Retardation, 32*(3), 181–193.

Schalock, R., Wolzen, B., Ross, I., Elliott, B., Werbel, G., & Peterson, K. (1986). Post-secondary community placement of handicapped students: A five-year follow-up. *Learning Disability Quarterly, 9,* 295–303.

Scheiber, B., & Talpers, J. (1987). *Unlocking potential: College and other choices for learning disabled people—A step-by-step guide.* Bethesda, MD: Alder & Alder.

Schleien, S.J., Meyer, L.H., Heyne, L.A., & Brandt, B.B. (1995). *Lifelong leisure skills and lifestyles for persons with developmental disabilities.* Baltimore: Paul H. Brookes Publishing Co.

Schleien, S.J., & Ray, M.T. (1988). *Community recreation of persons with disabilities: Strategies for integration.* Baltimore: Paul H. Brookes Publishing Co.

Schleien, S.J., Ray, M.T., & Green, F.G. (1996). *Community recreation and people with disabilities: Strategies for inclusion* (2nd ed.). Baltimore: Paul H. Brookes Publishing Co.

Schloss, P.J. (1984). Postsecondary opportunities: The role of secondary educators in advocating handicapped young adults. *The Journal of Vocational Special Needs Education, 7*(2), 15–19.

Schloss, P.J., Alper, S., & Jayne, D. (1993). Self-determination for persons with disabilities: Choice, risk, and dignity. *Exceptional Children, 60*(3), 215–225.

Schloss, P.J., Alper, S., Young, H., Arnold-Reid, G., Aylward, M., & Dudenhoeffer, S. (1995). Acquisition of functional sight words in community-based recreation settings. *Journal of Special Education, 29*(1), 84–96.

Scholl, G.T. (1986). *Foundations of education for blind and visually handicapped children and youth.* New York: American Foundation for the Blind.

School-to-Work Opportunities Act of 1994, PL 103-239, 20 U.S.C. § 6101.

Schumaker, J.B., Hazel, J.S., & Deshler, D.D. (1985). A model for facilitating postsecondary transitions. *Techniques, 1,* 437–445.

Schwarz, S.L., & Taymans, J.M. (1991). Urban vocational/technical program completers with learning disabilities: A follow-up study. *Journal for Vocational Special Needs Education, 13,* 15–20.

Scuccimarra, D., & Speece, D. (1990). Employment outcomes and social integration of students with mild handicaps: The quality of life two years after high school. *Journal of Learning Disabilities, 23*(4), 213–219.

Serna, L.A. (1995). Teaching self-determination skills to adolescents. *Intervention in School and Clinic, 30,* 132–133.

Serna, L.A., & Lau-Smith, J.A. (1995). Learning with purpose: Self-determination skills for students who are at risk for school and community failure. *Intervention in School and Clinic, 30,* 142–146.

Shafer, M.S. (1986). Competitive employment for workers with mental retardation. In M. Hersen, R.M. Eisler, & P.M. Miller (Eds.), *Progress in behavior modification* (pp. 213–231). New York: Academic Press.

Shafer, M.S., Tait, K., Keen, R., & Jesiolowski, C. (1989). Supported competitive employment: Using coworkers to assist follow-along efforts. *Journal of Rehabilitation, 55*(2), 68–75.

Shafer, M.S., Wehman, P., Kregel, J., & West, M. (1990). National supported employment initiative: A preliminary analysis. *American Journal of Mental Retardation, 95*(3), 316–327.

Shapiro, E.S., & Derr, T.F. (1987). An examination of overlap between reading curricula and standardized achievement tests. *Journal of Special Education, 21*(2), 59–67.

Sharpton, W.R., & West, M. (1991). Severe and profound mental retardation. In P. McLaughlin & P. Wehman (Eds.), *Handbook of developmental disabilities: A guide to best practices* (pp. 16–29). Austin, TX: PRO-ED.

Shaywitz, S.E., & Shaywitz, T. (1990). Boys unfairly singled out as reading disabled. *Education of the Handicapped, 16*(18), 1–3.

Sherron, P., & Groah, C. (1990). Supported employment phase I: Job placement. In P. Wehman & J. Kreutzer (Eds.), *Vocational rehabilitation for persons with traumatic brain injury*. Rockville, MD: Aspen.

Siegel, L.S. (1989a). I.Q. is irrelevant to the definition of learning disabilities. *Journal of Learning Disabilities, 22*(8), 469–486.

Siegel, L.S. (1989b). Why we do not need intelligence test scores in the definition and analyses of learning disabilities. *Journal of Learning Disabilities, 22*(8), 514–518.

Siegel, S., Avoke, S., Paul, P., Robert, M., & Gaylord-Ross, R. (1991). A second look at the lives of participants in the career ladder program. *Journal of Vocational Rehabilitation, 1*(4), 9–24.

Sigafoos, J., Roberts, D., Couzens, D., & Kerr, M. (1993). Providing opportunity for choice making and turn taking: Two adults with multiple disabilities. *Journal of Developmental and Physical Disabilities, 5*(4), 297–233.

Simon, M., & Halloran, W. (1994). Community-based vocational education: Guidelines for complying with the Fair Labor Standards Act. *Journal of The Association for Persons with Severe Handicaps, 19*(1), 52–60.

Sinnott-Oswald, M., Gliner, J.A., & Spencer, K.C. (1991). Supported and sheltered employment: Quality of life among workers with disabilities. *Education and Training in Mental Retardation, 26,* 388–397.

Siperstein, G.N., Reed, D., Wolraich, M., & O'Keefe, P. (1990). Capabilities essential for adults who are mentally retarded to function in different residential settings. *Education and Training in Mental Retardation, 25,* 45–51.

Sisson, L.A., & Babeo, T.J. (1992). School-to-work transition of students with blindness or visual impairment. *Journal of Vocational Rehabilitation, 2*(1), 56–65.

Sitlington, P.L., Frank, A., & Carson, R. (1990). *Iowa state follow-up study: Adult adjustment of individuals with behavior disorders one year after leaving school*. Des Moines: Iowa Department of Education.

Sitlington, P.L., Frank, A.R., & Carson, R. (1992). Adult adjustment among high school graduates with mild disabilities. *Exceptional Children, 39*(3), 221–233.

Skinner, B.F. (1953). *Science and human behavior*. New York: Macmillan.

Slobodzian, J. (May 30, 1993). Court sets rules on technology disabled. *The Philadelphia Inquirer, 2,* 16–18.

Smith, C.R. (1983). *Learning disabilities: The interaction of learner, task, and setting*. Boston: Little, Brown.

Smith, D., & Polloway, G. (1995). Patterns of deinstitutionalization and community placement: A dream deferred or lost? *Education and Training in Mental Retardation and Developmental Disabilities, 30*(4), 321–328.

Smith, G., Edelen-Smith, P., & Stodden, R. (1995). How to avoid the seven pitfalls of systematic planning: A school and community plan for transition. *Teaching Exceptional Children, 27*(4), 42–48.

Smith, J.D. (1994) The revised AAMR definition on mental retardation: The MRDD position. *Education and Training in Mental Retardation and Developmental Disabilities, 29*(3), 179–183.

Smith, M.D. (1993). Introduction to autism issue. *Journal of Vocational Rehabilitation*. New York: Elsevier.

Smith, M.D., Belcher, R.G., & Juhrs, P.D. (1995). *A guide to successful employment for individuals with autism*. Baltimore: Paul H. Brookes Publishing Co.

Smith, R.M., Fields, F.R., Lenox, J.L., Morris, H.O., & Nolan, J.J. (1979). A functional scale of recovery from severe head trauma. *Clinical Neuropsychology, 48*–50.

Smith, S.W. (1990). Individualized education programs (IEPs) in special education: From intent to acquiescence. *Exceptional Children, 57*(1), 6–14.

Smith, T.E.C., Polloway, E., Patton, J.R., & Dowdy, C. (1995). *Teaching children with special needs in an inclusive setting*. Needham, MA: Allyn & Bacon.

Smith, T.E.C., & Puccini, I.K. (1995). Position statement: Secondary curricula and policy issues for students with mental retardation. *Education and Training in Mental Retardation and Developmental Disabilities, 30*(4), 275–281.

Snell, M.E. (1990). *Systematic instruction for persons with moderate and severe handicaps* (2nd ed.). Columbus, OH: Charles E. Merrill.

Snell, M.E. (1993). *Systematic instruction for individuals with moderate and severe disabilities* (4th ed.). Columbus, OH: Charles E. Merrill.

Snell, M.E., & Grigg, N.C. (1987). Instructional Assessment and curriculum development. In M.E. Snell (Ed.), *Systematic instruction of persons with severe handicaps* (pp. 64–109). Columbus, OH: Charles E. Merrill.

Social Security Administration. (1995). *Graduating to independence*. Baltimore: Author.

Soto, G., Toro-Zambrana, W., & Belfiore, P. (1994). Comparison of two instructional strategies for social skills acquisition and generalization among individuals with moderate and severe mental retardation working in an isolated setting. *Education and Training in Mental Retardation and Developmental Disabilities, 29*(4), 307–320.

Sowers, J. (1991). Transitioning students with physical and multiple disabilities to supported employment. *Journal of Vocational Rehabilitation, 1*(4), 25–37.

Sowers, J.A., & Powers, L. (1991). *Vocational preparation and employment of students with physical and multiple disabilities*. Baltimore: Paul H. Brookes Publishing Co.

Sowers, J., & Powers, L. (1995). Enhancing the participation and independence of students with severe physical and multiple disabilities in performing community activities. *Mental Retardation, 33*(4), 209–220.

Spring Independent School District. (1992). *An example of a parent/guardian inventory*. Houston, TX: Author.

Stack, R.P. (1988). The rehabilitation engineer and technological services. In P. Wehman, W. Wood, J.M. Everson, R. Goodsyn, & S. Conley (Eds.), *Vocational education for multihandicapped youth with cerebral palsy* (pp. 173–196). Baltimore: Paul H. Brookes Publishing Co.

Stainback, W., & Stainback, S. (1984). A rationale for the merger of special and regular education. *Exceptional Children, 51*, 107.

Stainback, W., & Stainback, S. (1985). Facilitating friendships. *Education and Training in Mental Retardation and Developmental Disabilities, 22*, 18–25.

Stanovich, K.E. (1989). Has the learning disabilities field lost its intelligence? *Journal of Learning Disabilities, 22*(8), 487–492.

Steere, D., Pancsofar, E., Wood, R., & Hecimovic, A. (1990). *The principles of shared responsibility.* Hartford, CT: Institute of Human Resources.

Steere, D.E., Wood, R., Pancsofar, E.L., & Butterworth, J. (1990). Outcome-based school-to-work transition planning for students with severe disabilities. *Career Development for Exceptional Individuals, 13*, 57–69.

Sternberg, L. (1993). Individuals with profound disabilities: Definition and characteristics. In L. Sternberg & X. Taylor (Eds.), *Individuals with profound disabilities* (pp. 1–21). Austin, TX: PRO-ED.

Stineman, R.M., Morningstar, M.E., Bishop, B., & Turnbull, H.R. (1993). Role of families in transition planning for young adults with disabilities. *Journal of Vocational Rehabilitation, 3*(2), 52–61.

Stodden, R., Browder, P., Boone, R., Patton, J., Hill, M., Fickens, J., Lau, R., Nishimoto, J., & Shirachi, S. (1986). *Overview of transition and the Hawaii Transition Project.* Honolulu: University of Hawaii at Manoa, Hawaii Transition Project.

Stonnington, H. (1986). Traumatic brain injury rehabilitation. *American Rehabilitation, 22*(4,5), 19–20.

Strully, J., & Strully, C. (1985). Friendship and our children. *Journal of The Association for Persons with Severe Handicaps, 10*, 224–227.

Swanson, H.L. (1987). Information processing theory and learning disabilities: An overview. *Journal of Learning Disabilities, 20*(1), 3–7.

Sweeney, H.M., & LeBlanc, J.M. (1994). Effects of task size on work related and aberrant behaviors of youth with autism and mental retardation. *Research and Developmental Disabilities, 16*(2), 97–116.

Szoke, C.O., & Vest, S. (1975). Procedures for program evaluation to serve those who are handicapped (Rev. ed.).

Szymanski, D., Gugerty, J.J., Tindall, L.W., & Schmidt, G. (1989). *Successful vocational rehabilitation of persons with learning disabilities: Best practices.* Madison: Wisconsin Association for Children and Adults with Learning Disabilities and Vocational Studies Center, University of Wisconsin.

Szymanski, E.M. (1994). Transition: Life span and life span considerations for empowerment. *Exceptional Children, 60*(5), 402–410.

Szymanski, E.M., Hershenson, D.B., Ettinger, J., & Enright, M. (1995). Career development theories, constructs, interventions, and research: Implications for people with disabilities. In E.M. Szymanski & R.M. Parker (Eds.), *Work and disability: Issues and strategies in career development and job placement* (pp. 442–462). Austin, TX: PRO-ED.

Szymanski, E.M., & Parker, R. (Eds.). (1995). *Work and disability: Issues and strategies in career development and job placement.* Austin TX: PRO-ED.

Szymanski, E.M., Turner, K.D., & Hershenson, D. (1992). Career development of people with disabilities: Theoretical prospective. In F.R. Rusch, L. DeStephano, J. Chadsey-Rusch, A. Phelps, & E.M. Szymanski (Eds.), *Transition from school to adult life: Models, linkages, and policy* (pp. 391–406). Sycamore, IL: Sycamore.

Taylor, S.J. (1988). Caught in the continuum: A critical analysis of the principle of least restrictive environment. *Journal of The Association for Persons with Severe Handicaps, 13*, 41–53.

Taylor, S.J., Bogdan, R., & Lutfiyya, Z.M. (Eds.). (1995). *The variety of community experience: Qualitative studies of family and community life.* Baltimore: Paul H. Brookes Publishing Co.

Teasdale, G., Knill-Jones, R., & Van der Sande, J. (1978). Observer variability in assessing impaired consciousness and coma. *Journal of Neurology, Neurosurgery, and Psychiatry, 41*, 603–610.

Technology-Related Assistance for Individuals with Disabilities Act of 1988, PL 100-407, 29 U.S.C. § 2201 *et seq.*

Technology-Related Assistance for Individuals with Disabilities Amendments of 1994, PL 103-218, 29 U.S.C. § 2201 *et seq.*

Test, D.W., Hinson, K.B., Solow, J., & Keul, P. (1993, March). Job satisfaction of persons in supported employment. *Education and Training in Mental Retardation, 38*–46.

The Association for Persons with Severe Handicaps. (1993, February). *Inclusion resolution.* Seattle, WA: Author.

The seven phases of ecological inventory approach are used to develop curricula. Learning in Functional Environments (LIFE). (1986). Region IV Science Center, Houston, TX.

Thompson, L., Powers, G., & Houchard, B. (1992). The wage effects of supported employment. *Journal of The Association for Persons with Severe Handicaps, 17*(2), 87–94.

Thomsen, I.V. (1984). Late outcome of very severe blunt head trauma: A 10–15 year second follow-up. *Journal of Neurology, Neurosurgery, and Psychology, 47*, 260–268.

Thorin, G.R., & Irvin, L. (1992). Family stress associated with the transition to adulthood of young people with severe disabilities. *Journal of The Association for Persons with Severe Handicaps. 17*(1), 31–39.

Tichy, N.M. (1983). *Managing strategic change: Technical, political, and cultural dynamics.* New York: John Wiley & Sons.

Tilson, G.P., Luecking, R.G., & Donovan, M.R. (1994). Involving employers in transition: The Bridges Model. *Career Development for Exceptional Individuals, 17*(1), 77–89.

Tindall, L.W. (1980). *Puzzled about educating special needs students? A handbook on modifying vocational curricula for handicapped students.* Madison: University of Wisconsin–Madison, Vocational Studies Center, School of Education.

Tindall, L.W., & Gugerty, J.J. (1990, December). *Issues in educating special needs students in postsecondary programs.* Paper presented at the American Vocational Association Convention, Orlando, FL.

Tindall, L.W., Gugerty, J.J., Dougherty, B.B., & Heffron, T.J. (1987). *Replicating jobs in business and industry for persons with disabilities: Volume II.* Madison: University of Wisconsin, School of Education, Vocational Studies Center.

Topics in inclusive education. (1994). Minneapolis: University of Minnesota.

Torgeson, J.K. (1982). The learning disabled child as an inactive learner: Educational implications. *Topics in Learning and Learning Disabilities, 2,* 45–51.

Torgeson, J.K. (1989). Why IQ is relevant to the definition of learning disabilities. *Journal of Learning Disabilities, 22*(8), 484–486.

Traphajan, J. (1988). *Community re-entry.* Southborough, MA: National Head Injury Foundation.

Trotter, S., Minkoff, E., Harrison, K., & Hoops, J. (1988). Supported work: An innovative approach to the vocational rehabilitation of persons who are psychiatrically disabled. *Rehabilitation Psychology, 33*(1), 27–36.

Turnbull, A.P., & Turnbull, H.R., III. (1988). Toward great expectations for vocational opportunities: Family–professional partnerships. *Mental Retardation, 26,* 337–342.

Turnbull, H.R., III, Turnbull, A.P., Bronicki, G.J., Summers, J.A., & Roeder-Gordon, C. (1989). *Disability and the family: A guide to decisions for adulthood.* Baltimore: Paul H. Brookes Publishing Co.

Turner, E. (1995). Self-advocacy: A key to self-determination. *Journal of Vocational Rehabilitation, 5*(4), 329–336.

Turner, L., Dofny, E., & Dutka, S. (1994). Effective strategy and attribution training on strategy maintenance and transfer. *American Journal on Mental Retardation, 98*(4), 445–454.

Umbreit, J. (Ed.). (1983). *Physical disabilities and health impairments: An introduction.* Columbus, OH: Charles E. Merrill.

Unger, K.V. (1995). Unfinished business: Providing vocational services to transition-aged youth with serious emotional disturbance. *Journal of Vocational Rehabilitation, 5*(2), 159–165.

University of Minnesota. (1994, Fall). *Inclusive education: Nathan's story: Topics in inclusive education.* Minneapolis: Author.

U.S. Bureau of Census. (1992). *Selected social characteristics, 1990.* Washington, DC: Author.

U.S. Department of Education (1987–1990). *To assure the free appropriate public education of all handicapped children: The ninth, tenth, eleventh, and twelfth annual reports to Congress on the Education of the Handicapped Act.* Washington, DC: Office of Special Education and Rehabilitative Services.

U.S. Department of Education. Office of Special Education Programs, Data Analysis System (DANS)

Valdes, K.A., Williamson, C.L., & Wagner, M.M. (1990). *The National Longitudinal Transition Study of Special Education Students: Statistical almanac: Vol. 8. Youth categorized as orthopedically impaired.* Menlo Park, CA: SRI International.

Vandercook, T., York, J., & Forest, M. (1989). The Gill Action Planning System (NISSA): Strategies for building inclusion division. *Journal of The Association for Persons with Severe Handicaps, 14,* 205–215.

Van Reusen, A.K. (1993). Learning disabled adolescents and motivation. *Their World,* 28–31.

Van Reusen, A.K., & Dos, C. (1994). Facilitating student participation in individualized education programs through motivation strategy instruction. *Exceptional Children, 60*(5), 466–475.

Vaughn, S., & La Greca, A. (1993). Social skills training: Why, who, what, and how. In W.N. Bender (Ed.), *Learning disabilities: Best practices for professionals* (pp. 251–271). Austin, TX: PRO-ED.

Viadero, D. (1989, November). Side by side. *Teacher Magazine Reader,* 1–5.

Viadero, D. (1991). New study ties dyslexia to vision abnormalities. *Education Week, 11*(4), 10.

Vocational Training News. (1991, December 12). Students with behavior disorders in work experience. Washington, DC: Author.

Vogel, S.A., & Adelman, P.B. (1992). The success of college students with learning disabilities: Factors related to educational attainment. *Journal of Learning Disabilities, 25*(7), 430–441.

Vogenthaler, D.R. (1987a). An overview of head injury: Its consequences and rehabilitation. *Brain Injury, 1,* 113–127.

Vogenthaler, D.R. (1987b). Rehabilitation after closed head injury: A primer. *Journal of Rehabilitation, 53*(4), 15–21.

Vogenthaler, D.R., Smith K.R., & Goldfader P. (1989). Head injury, a multivariate study: Predicting long-term productivity and independent living outcome. *Brain Injury, 3,* 369–385.

Wagner, M. (1989). *The transition experiences of youth with disabilities: A report from the National Longitudinal Transition Study.* Menlo Park, CA: SRI International.

Wagner, M., Blackorby, J., Cameto, R., Hebbeler, K., & Newman, L. (1993). *The transition experiences of young people with disabilities: A summary of findings from the National Longitudinal Transition Study of Special Education Students.* Menlo Park, CA: SRI International.

Walker, H., McConnell, S., Holmes, D., Todis, B., Walker, J., & Golden, N. (1983). *Walker social skills curriculum.* Austin, TX: PRO-ED.

Walker, J.L. (1988). Young American Indian children. *Teaching Exceptional Children, 20*(4), 45–51.

Wang, M.C., Reynolds, M.C., & Walberg, H.J. (Eds.). (1990). *Special education research and practice: Synthesis of findings*. Elmsford, NY: Pergamon.

Ward, M.J. (1988). *The many facets of self-determination: Transition summary*. Washington, DC: National Information Center for Children and Youth with Handicaps.

Ward, M.J. (1991, September). Self-determination revisited: Going beyond expectations. *NICHCY Transition Summary*. Washington, DC: National Information Center for Children and Youth with Disabilities and HEATH Resource Center.

Ward, M.J., & Halloran, W.J. (1989). Transition to uncertainty: Status of many school leavers with severe disabilities. *Career Development for Exceptional Individuals, 12*, 71–81.

Weaver, C.L. (1994). Privatizing vocational rehabilitation: Options for increasing individual choice and enhancing competition. *Journal of Disability Policy Studies, 5*(1), 53–76.

Wechsler, D. (1981). *Wechsler Adult Intelligence Scale—Revised*. New York: The Psychological Corporation.

Wehman, P. (1981). *Competitive employment: New horizons for severely disabled individuals*. Baltimore: Paul H. Brookes Publishing Co.

Wehman, P. (1990). School to work: Elements of a successful program. *Teaching Exceptional Children, 23*(1), 40–43.

Wehman, P. (1992). *Life beyond the classroom: Transition strategies for young people with disabilities*. Baltimore: Paul H. Brookes Publishing Co.

Wehman, P. (1995). *Individual transition plans: The teachers curriculum guide for helping youth with special needs*. Austin, TX: PRO-ED.

Wehman, P., Hill, J., & Koehler, F. (1979). Placement of developmentally disabled individuals into competitive employment: Three case studies. *Education and Training of the Mental Retarded, 14*(2), 37–52.

Wehman, P., Hill, J.W., Wood, W., & Parent, W. (1987). A report on competitive employment histories of persons labeled severely mentally retarded. *Journal of The Association for Persons with Severe Handicaps, 12*(1), 11–17.

Wehman, P., & Kregel, J. (1985). A supported work approach to competitive employment of individuals with moderate and severe handicaps. *Journal of The Association for Persons with Severe Handicaps, 10*, 3–11.

Wehman, P., & Kregel, J. (1994). Toward a national agenda for supported employment. *Journal of Vocational Rehabilitation, 4*(4), 3–12.

Wehman, P., & Kregel, J. (1995). Supported employment: At the crossroads. *Journal of The Association for Persons with Severe Handicaps, 20*(4), 286–299.

Wehman, P., & Kregel, J. (1996). *Teaching independent living skills to individuals with special needs: A longitudinal curriculum appeal*. Austin, TX: PRO-ED.

Wehman, P., Kregel, J., & Barcus, M. (1985). From school to work: A vocational transition model for handicapped students. *Exceptional Children, 52*(1), 25–37.

Wehman, P., Kregel, J., & Revell, G. (1991). *National analysis of supported employment implementation: FY 1986–FY 1990*. Richmond: Virginia Commonwealth University, Rehabilitation Research and Training Center.

Wehman, P., Kregel, J., & Seyfarth, J. (1985). Transition from school to work for youth with severe handicaps: A follow-up study. *Journal of The Association for Persons with Severe Handicaps, 10*(3), 132–136.

Wehman, P., Kregel, J., West, M., & Cifu, D. (1994). Return to work for persons with traumatic brain injury: An analysis of cost. *American Journal of Physical Medicine and Rehabilitation, 73*(6), 280–283.

Wehman, P., Kreutzer, J.S., Stonnington, H.H., Wood, W., Sherron, P., Diambra, J., Fry, R., & Groah, C. (1988). Supported employment for persons with traumatic brain injury: A preliminary report. *Journal of Head Trauma Rehabilitation, 3*(4), 82–90.

Wehman, P., Kreutzer, J., West, M., Sherron, P., Diambra, J., Fry, R., Groah, C., Sale, P., & Killam, S. (1989). Employment outcomes of persons following traumatic brain injury: Pre-injury, post-injury, and supported employment. *Brain Injury, 3*(12), 397–412.

Wehman, P., Kreutzer, J., Wood, W., Morton, M.V., & Sherron, P. (1988). Supported work model for persons with traumatic brain injury: Toward job placement and retention. *Rehabilitation Counseling Bulletin, 31*(4), 298–312.

Wehman, P., Kreutzer, J., Wood, W., Stonnington, H.H., Diambra, J., Sherron, P., & Fry, R. (1989). Helping persons with traumatic brain injury return to work: Three case studies. *Archives of Physical Medicine and Rehabilitation, 70*, 109–113.

Wehman, P., & Moon, M.S. (Eds.). (1988). *Vocational rehabilitation and supported employment*. Baltimore: Paul H. Brookes Publishing Co.

Wehman, P., Moon, M.S., Everson, J.M., Wood, W., & Barcus, J.M. (1988). *Transition from school to work: New challenges for youth with severe disabilities*. Baltimore: Paul H. Brookes Publishing Co.

Wehman, P., Parent, W., Unger, D., & Gibson, K. (in press). Supported employment providing community-based employment for persons with Down syndrome. In S. Pueschel (Ed.), *Adolescents with Down syndrome* (2nd ed.). Baltimore: Paul H. Brookes Publishing Co.

Wehman, P., Parent, W., Wood, W., Kregel, J., & Inge, J. (1989). From school to competitive employment for young adults with mental retardation: Transition in practice. *Career Development for Exceptional Children, 12*(2), 97–105.

Wehman, P., Revell, G., & Kregel, J. (1996). *Supported employment: A national program that works*. Manuscript submitted for publication.

Wehman, P., & Sherron, P. (1995). *Off to work: A vocational curriculum for individuals with neurological impairment*. Verona, WI: Attainment.

Wehman, P., West, M., Kregel, J., Sherron, P., & Kreutzer, J. (1995). Return to work for persons with severe

traumatic brain injury: A data-based approach to program development. *Journal of Head Trauma Rehabilitation, 10*(1), 27–39.

Wehmeyer, M.L. (1992). Self-determination and the education of students with mental retardation. *Education and Training in Mental Retardation, 27,* 302–314.

Wehmeyer, M.L. (1994). Employment status and perceptions of control of adults with cognitive and developmental disabilities. *Research in Developmental Disabilities, 15*(2), 119–131.

Wehmeyer, M.L. (1995). *The Arc's Self Determination Scale.* Arlington, TX: The Arc.

Wehmeyer, M., & Kelchner, K. (1995). Measuring the autonomy of adolescents and adults with mental retardation. *Career Development for Exceptional Individuals, 18*(1), 3–20.

Wehmeyer, M.L., & Lawrence, M. (1995). Whose future is it anyway? Promoting student involvement in transition planning. *Career Development for Exceptional Individuals, 18*(2), 68–84.

Wehmeyer, M.L., & Metzler, C. (1995). How self-determined are people with mental retardation? The National Consumer Survey. *Mental Retardation, 33*(2), 111–119.

Wermuth, T. (1991). Impact of educational legislation on transition and supported employment programs. *The Advance, 3*(1), 3–4.

West, J. (1992). *The Americans with Disabilities Act: From policy to practice.* New York: Milbank Memorial Fund.

West, L.L. (1987). Designing vocational programs for special needs individuals. In G.D. Meers (Ed.), *Handbook of vocational special needs education* (2nd ed., pp. 222–242). Rockville, MD: Aspen.

West, M. (1992). Job retention: Toward vocational confidence, self-management and natural supports. In P. Wehman, P. Sale, & W. Parent (Eds.), *Supported employment strategies for integration and workers with disabilities* (pp. 176–203). Austin, TX: PRO-ED.

West, M. (1994). Aspects of brain injury in the workplace. *Brain Injury, 8*(4), 232–234.

West, M. (1995a). Aspects of the workplace and return to work for individuals with brain injury in supported employment. *Brain Injury, 9,* 301–313.

West, M. (1995b). Choice, self-determination, and VR services: Systematic barriers for consumers with severe disabilities. *Journal of Vocational Rehabilitation, 5*(4), 281–290.

West, M. (1995c). Common sense is alive and well: Comments on Arb (1995). *Mental Retardation, 33,* 400–402.

West, M., Barcus, M., Brooke, V., & Rayfield, R.G. (1995). An exploratory analysis of self-determination of persons with disabilities. *Journal of Vocational Rehabilitation, 5*(4), 357–369.

West, M., Callahan, M., Lewis, M.B., Mast, M., & Sleight, L. (1991). Supported employment and assistive technology for individuals with physical impairments. *Journal of Vocational Rehabilitation, 1*(2), 29–39.

West, M.D., Gibson, K., & Unger, D. (1996). The role of the family in school-to-work transition. In G.H.S. Singer, A. Glang, & J.M. Williams (Eds.), *Children with acquired brain injury: Educating and supporting families* (pp. 197–220). Baltimore: Paul H. Brookes Publishing Co.

West, M., & Kregel, J. (1991). *Results from the Board for Rights of Virginians with Disabilities survey of the concerns, needs, and satisfaction with services of Virginia's postsecondary students with disabilities.* Richmond: Virginia Institute for Developmental Disabilities.

West, M., Kregel, J., & Banks, P. (1990). Fringe benefits available to supported employees. *Rehabilitation Counseling Bulletin, 3*(2), 126–134.

West, M., Kregel, J., Getzel, E.E., Zhu, M., Ipsen, S., & Martin, E.D. (1993). Beyond Section 504: Satisfaction and empowerment of students with disabilities in higher education. *Exceptional Children, 59,* 456–467.

West, M., & Parent, W. (1995). Community and workplace supports for individuals with severe mental illness in supported employment. *Psychological Rehabilitation Journal, 4,* 12–18.

West, M., Rayfield, R.G., Clements, C., Unger, D., & Thornton, T. (1994). An illustration of positive behavioral support in the workplace for individuals with severe mental retardation. *Journal of Vocational Rehabilitation, 4*(4), 265–271.

West, M., Revell, W., & Wehman, P. (1992). Achievements and challenges (I): A five-year report on consumer and system outcomes from the supported employment initiative. *Journal of The Association for Persons with Severe Handicaps, 17*(24), 227–235.

West, M.D., & Parent, W. (1992a). Consumer choice and empowerment in supported employment. In P. Wehman, P. Sale, & W. Parent (Eds.), *Supported employment: From research to practice* (pp. 29–48). Stoneham, MA: Andover Medical Publishers.

West, M.D., & Parent, W.S. (1992b). Consumer choice and empowerment in supported employment services: Issues and strategies. *Journal of The Association for Persons with Severe Handicaps, 17,* 47–52.

Whitt, J.K. (1983). Children's adaptation to chronic illness and handicapping conditions. In M.G. Eisenberg, L.C. Suthior, & M.A. Jansen (Eds.), *Chronic illness and disability through the lifespan* (pp. 69–102). New York: Springer-Verlag.

Wilcox, B., & Bellamy, G.T. (1982). *Design of high school programs for severely handicapped students.* Baltimore: Paul H. Brookes Publishing Co.

Will, M. (1983). *OSERS programming for the transition of youth with disabilities: Bridges from school to working life.* Washington, DC: Office of Special Education and Rehabilitative Services.

Will, M. (1984). *Supported employment services: An OSERS position paper.* Washington, DC: U.S. Department of Education.

Wille-Gregory, M., Graham, J.W., & Hughes, C. (1995). Preparing students with learning disabilities for success in postsecondary education. *Transition Line, 8,* 1–6.

William T. Grant Foundation Commission on Work, Family, and Citizenship. (1988) *The forgotten half: Noncollege youth in America.* Washington, DC: Author.

Williams, R.R. (1991). Assistive technology in the eye of the beholder. *Journal of Vocational Rehabilitation, 1*(2), 9–11.

Wisconsin Division of Vocational Rehabilitation Counselors, Wisconsin Association of Children and Adults with Learning Disabilities, and Vocational Studies Center. (1988) *Best practices: Successful vocational rehabilitation of persons with learning disabilities.* Madison: University of Wisconsin–Madison

Witt, M. (1992). *Job strategies for people with disabilities; Peterson's guides.* New York: Longman.

Wolfensberger, W. (1994). A personal interpretation of the mental retardation scene in light of the "signs of the times." *Mental Retardation, 32*(1), 19–33.

Wolfensberger, W. (1995). "A normalization" lifestyles, the special olympics, deinstitutionalization, mainstream, integration, and caveages and kinks. *Mental Retardation, 33*(2), 128–131.

Wolffe, M., & Wild, J. (1984). The occupational success of visually handicapped adolescents in the first year after leaving school for the partially seeing. *International Journal of Rehabilitation Research, 7*(4), 399–407.

Wood, W. (1988). Supported employment for persons with physical disabilities. In P. Wehman & M.S. Moon (Eds.), *Vocational rehabilitation and supported employment* (pp. 341–363). Baltimore: Paul H. Brookes Publishing Co.

Worlery, M., Werts, M.G., Caldwell, N.K., Snyder, E.D., & Lisowski, L. (1995, March). Experienced teachers' perceptions of resources and supports for inclusion. *Education and Training in Mental Retardation and Developmental Disabilities,* 15–26.

Wren, C., Adelman, P., Pike, M.B., & Wilson, J.L. (1987). *College and the high school student with learning disabilities: The student's perspective.* Chicago: DePaul University.

Yell, M. (1989). Honig vs. Doe: The suspension and expulsion of handicapped students. *Exceptional Children, 56*(1), 60–70.

Yell, M. (1990). The use of corporal punishment, suspension, expulsion, and timeout with behavior disordered students in public schools legal considerations. *Behavior Disorders, 15,* 100–110.

Yell, M. (1995). The least restrictive environment mandate and the courts' judicial activism on judicial restraint. *Exceptional Children, 61*(3), 578–581.

Ylvisaker, M. (1985). *Head injury rehabilitation: Children and adolescents.* Austin, TX: PRO-ED.

Ylvisaker, M., Feeney, T.T., & Mullins, K. (1995). School reentry following mild traumatic brain injury: A proposed hospital-to-school protocol. *Journal of Head Trauma Rehabilitation, 10*(6), 42–49.

Ylvisaker, M., Hartwick, P., Ross, B., & Nussbaum, N. (1994). Cognitive assessment. In R. Savage & D. Wolcott (Eds.), *Educational dimensions of acquired brain injury* (pp. 311–347). Austin, TX: PRO-ED.

Ylvisaker, M., Hartwick, P., & Stevens, M.B. (1991). School reentry following head injury: Managing the transition from home to school. *Journal of Head Trauma Rehabilitation, 6*(1), 10–22.

Ysseldyke, J., & Algozzine, R. (1995). *Special education: Practical approach for teachers* (3rd ed.). Boston: Houghton Mifflin.

Zasler, N. (1989). Editorial: Employment outcomes of persons following traumatic brain injury. *Brain Injury, 3,* 331–333.

Zetlin, A.G., & Hosseini, A. (1989). Six postschool case studies of mildly learning handicapped young adults. *Exceptional Children, 55*(5), 405–411.

Zimmerman, G.L. (1992). Orientation and mobility training: Enhancing the employment prospects for people with blindness or visual impairment. *Journal of Vocational Rehabilitation, 2*(1), 66–72.

Zirpoli, T.J. (1990). Physical abuse: Are children with disabilities at greater risk? *Intervention, 25*(1), 6–11.

Appendix

Review of Post-21 Studies for Youth with Disabilities

This appendix provides an in-depth review of post-21 studies for populations of youth with disabilities. Some populations, such as students with learning disabilities and mental retardation, provide a large number of studies from which to draw conclusions, while others, such as students with sensory or hearing impairments and physical disabilities, have yielded very few studies.

Learning Disabilities

Fifteen studies of the adult outcomes of students with learning disabilities are discussed; however, two include students with varying disabilities as well, making specific interpretation difficult. Eight of these studies included graduates only, three dropouts only, and the remaining two included both graduates and dropouts. The studies include published articles as well as state and national studies. Of the studies reporting gender distribution, male distribution averaged 71%.

Educational experiences are frustrating for youth who have learning disabilities, and their dropout rates are high (38% as opposed to a 25% dropout rate for youth without disabilities). In addition, most do not have the study skills, reading and math levels, or academic coping skills to successfully persevere through a 4-year college career. These characteristics place them at risk for a stressful social, emotional, and health life adjustment.

The employment rate of recent high school graduates with learning disabilities is similar to the national rate for youth without disabilities. Of the non–college-bound students, 49% of male high school graduates and 42% of female high school graduates were working full time 1–2 years after graduation (William T. Grant Foundation, 1988). Although many of the reviewed studies did not break down employment into full-time and part-time positions, it can be estimated that two thirds of these students are working full time (National Longitudinal Transition Study, 1989), which is comparable with the national employment rate of 70%.

For a detailed discussion of post-21 studies, please refer to Peraino, J.M. (1992). Post-21 follow-up studies: How do special education graduates fare? In P. Wehman, *Life beyond the classroom: Transition strategies for young people with disabilities* (pp. 21–70). Baltimore: Paul H. Brookes Publishing Co.

Yet, these youth with learning disabilities are often underemployed in entry-level positions that offer low pay and little esteem—leaving workers distinctly disadvantaged in a competitive society. Salary comparisons with young adults without disabilities are not available, although some have suggested that this discrepancy is a result of the low rate of attendance in postsecondary educational institutions by students with disabilities (28% versus 56%) (Jones et al., 1986). Also, age seems to correlate with employment status, at least within a few years of high school exit, and rates 5–10 years after graduation may be revealing. Long-term follow-up, preferably of a longitudinal nature, will help to clarify these results.

Predictive factors for occupational and educational attainment are few: Being male, graduating from high school, and having parents with above-average intelligence and socioeconomic status, however, indicate positive outcomes. Other positive factors include, for adult employment, paid work experience in high school and specialized vocational education. Factors affecting educational attainment include social integration, a lack of behavior problems, and success in school. There are likely a number of predictive factors that have not yet been identified.

The implications of these results suggest that a considerable amount of effort should be directed toward 1) studying programs that prevent females from achieving higher rates of employment and postsecondary education, 2) developing programs aimed at reducing the dropout rate for students with learning disabilities, and 3) making school a successful experience despite low intelligence and/or academic achievement skills. This is particularly true for low-income and minority youth. Program development should include directing youth to work for pay during high school, developing study and academic coping skills, and teaching social skills.

Mental Retardation

Twenty-one outcome studies pertaining to students with various degrees of mental retardation were uncovered in the literature. The studies include reports from 10 state studies as well as the NLTS. Of the subjects, 62% were male; and a distinction was often made between studies that sampled high school graduates, dropouts, or both.

The employment rate of young adults with mild mental retardation (51%) is below the national rate for young adults without disabilities (62%) and those with learning disabilities (70%). This rate further declines when students have severe retardation (20%) or drop out (16%). Students with mental retardation participate in postsecondary education only one fourth as often as youth without disabilities; yet, graduation rates are similar. Independent living rates are approximately half of those of adults with learning disabilities, while rates for living with parents are similar.

Many of the predictors of outcome identifiers for those with mental retardation do not change (i.e., intelligence, gender, age, minority membership). The only variable predictors are vocational education/training, graduation status, and social/interpersonal skills. It remains unclear whether independent living skills training is effective.

Behavior Disorders

A 1986 survey by the National Institute of Mental Health reported that 20% of all Americans have a diagnosable mental disorder, with children and adolescents showing the largest rate increases. Yet, 20% of our children are not in special education and, thus, are not receiving the curricula they require to extinguish antisocial and negative behavior patterns and increase socialization skills.

Drug use and abuse is probably high among this group, and drug abuse prevention programs should be considered. There is also the indication that this group experiences low self-esteem, poor anger control, poor peer relations, and identity confusion. These students are at high risk for continued behavior and legal problems. Often, family problems exist and many of these youth leave home early and drop out of school. Schools are often hard pressed to deal with these kinds of issues; one solution is to let the school serve as a community center for these and other youth in need.

Although the employment rate for young adults with emotional or behavior disorders is favorable (59%) compared to youth without disabilities (62%), it is lower than that for students with learning disabilities (70%) and only slightly higher than the rate for those with mental retardation. Their participation in postsecondary education is low (23%) and their dropout rate is high (47%)—about 30% are not engaged in any productive activity whatsoever. Nineteen percent of people with emotional or behavior disorders live independently, a comparable number, and fewer live with their parents. Given the nature of their disorder, however, many do not have the support network to facilitate a healthy transition into adulthood.

Hearing Impairments

Three transitional outcome studies of former students with hearing impairments were reviewed. Two of these are from Washington State (on graduates with hearing and visual impairments), and one is from the National Longitudinal Transition Study (on graduates and those who dropped out with hearing impairment only). The Washington study reported a 51% female population. Overall, 402 deaf individuals and 470 individuals with hearing impairments were studied.

Individuals with hearing impairments have transition outcomes that rival those of individuals without disabilities, lagging behind only in employment status. High school graduation and postsecondary participation rates are similar, as are the average salaries. Students with hearing impairments also tend to utilize agencies and services (e.g., rehabilitation agencies) at higher rates, which suggests higher levels of social integration.

Visual Impairments

Four outcome studies, including those who are blind as well as those with partial sight, were identified that specifically reported adult transition outcome data. One of the stud-

ies employed a follow-along strategy of graduates from the Wisconsin School for the Visually Handicapped (WSVH) from 1978 to 1987. The three remaining studies utilized a longitudinal design, conducting its first assessments 1–2 years after high school exit. The average female distribution was 43%. Most of the studies focused only on graduates; however, one included dropouts as well. The conclusions drawn are tentative.

Most of the graduates with visual impairment worked or went to school, but did not do both. Combined scores of employment, postsecondary education participation, and unengagement rates totaled 96%. These students attend postsecondary institutions (46%) as often as individuals without disabilities; yet, employment rates are relatively low.

Factors associated with successful outcomes include the following: 1) for occupational success, being male and having a high school diploma—better visual acuity and positive attitudes toward disability may also be helpful; 2) for educational success, graduating from high school, being socially integrated, and having an above-average IQ and family socioeconomic level; and 3) for social adaptation, receiving adaptive living skills training.

Physical Disabilities

Three studies reported data on the postsecondary outcomes of people with physical disabilities—two from Washington State and one from NLTS. The two longitudinal studies separated those with orthopedic impairments from those with other health impairments. Gender distribution varies from 63% male to 49% male, while sample sizes ranged from 388 to 51.

The following conclusions are tentative—definitive conclusions cannot be drawn because of the limited data. First, people with health impairments appear to be employed, engaged, and living independently more often than those with orthopedic impairments. A difference that, perhaps, exists because use of a physical aide is associated with employment status and people with orthopedic disabilities tend to use this kind of assistance more often than others. Second, people with orthopedic impairments show a slightly higher rate of educational attainment, with higher postsecondary participation and lower dropout rates.

Recommendations

Based on this extensive review of the research literature, a number of suggestions are offered:

1. Systematic cooperative ventures between special education and vocational departments and between special education departments and public agencies are necessary to facilitate transition.

2. Specific mandates detailing who is responsible for developing the individualized education program (IEP) with individualized transition components are also necessary to minimize confusion and increase the likelihood of transition into adulthood. If such an agency is determined to provide an IEP, then a specific designee within the agency must be chosen to lead coordination.

3. Increased parent involvement, which appears to be effective with those with more severe disabilities, for all categories of disabilities would serve as a model for students in special education and also increase their chances of a smooth transition.

4. Given the research and its general conclusions, compliance monitoring can be instituted through its recommendations of programmatic elements. If a work-study program, for example, was deemed to be an important programmatic element for people with mental retardation, then compliance monitoring can be instituted through a requirement of such a program. As the field of research ventures into the transition of special education, an increasing number of programmatic elements can be incorporated through the use of a monitoring system.

5. There is no single essential element for a special education curriculum across all disability categories. The needs of someone with autism, for example, are quite different from those with mild hearing impairments or those who have learning disabilities. The development of essential elements, however, can occur through the use of programmatic elements.

Index

Page numbers followed by "f" indicate figures; those followed by a "t" indicate tables.

HV 1568 .W43 1996

Wehman, Paul.

Life beyond the classroom

A

himself, scratching at his stubbled, gray beard, and turned away from the huge mass of people thronging the courtyard. He passed under an orange tree whose branches were filled with chattering, laughing children—all peering wide-eyed at the steps leading up into the hall of Shishinden, hoping for a glimpse of the new Emperor—and then forced his way against the press of citizens flowing into the royal complex from the streets. Once beyond the Imperial precincts, the traffic eased and he sighed with relief. He shrugged his shoulders, loosening his muscles, tucked both arms inside his kimono, and found his feet on the great Nara road, heading west. The night sky was clear, showing the moon in quarter-crescent, and the stars were twinkling like jewels strewn on black velvet.

Breathing deeply, feeling free for the first time in a decade, the old man started home.

strike carrier for only a day, the Nisei officer had already grasped the leap in power and confidence of the Knights. Seeing the ship's crew at work in the command spaces, in the medbay, even in the shuttle which had brought him over to the *Naniwa*, an old, old story from the naval history of old Earth had come to mind. A Danish admiral had once said, when judging his people's many enemies: "Nothing shows the temper and ability of a nation more clearly and concisely than the crew of a ship of war—be it an aircraft carrier or an attack submarine—everything else can be disguised, hidden, faked . . . but not the natural camaraderie and interplay of an experienced crew."

"Susan, I am still an Imperial officer. My name remains on the List, my commission stands. I can tell you this much of the Knights: the *Pilgrim* is a match in gunnery, speed, crew, and systems for any carrier in the Fleet. Her crew is dedicated, resourceful, and enthusiastic. And yes, I have seen with my own eyes—I have in fact *used* to excellent effect—an emissions dampening system which rendered a Temple-owned freighter *invisible* to Khaid sensors at point-blank range."

Koshō did not answer immediately, setting down her own cup and adjusting the tray carefully. When she did look up, Hadeishi felt a tiny cold shock. Her expression was pinched and wan. "Do you think—" She paused, reordering her thoughts. "Has the Order decided to break with the Empire? Is the *Pilgrim* on a combat footing?"

"Combat?" Mitsuharu shook his head. "No, they've stood down. There are fighter wings on patrol . . . but I've seen *nothing* which indicates they are hostile to us."

Then she did seem to relax, a brittle tension flowing away from her, and she raised the cup again. "Greetings, *Chu-sa*. I did not think I'd see you again, when we parted at Toroson."

"I either!" Hadeishi laughed softly, feeling his heart lighten. "Who could have guessed we'd come together again in such a remote fastness, or by such a circuitous path?"

"Who indeed?" Koshō offered a faint smile, though her eyes were shadowed again. "It must have been fate."

The temple bells were ringing the length and breadth of Kyoto, filling the warm night air with a glad clamoring sound. Uncounted voices were raised, singing a song of welcome and unbridled joy. Musashi nodded to

Koshō looked around at the gleaming wood-paneled walls—the tatami-patterned g-decking—and laughed softly. "Pretty—but all this doesn't give me another meter of armor, another sixteen hard-points. . . ."

"Don't think it useless!" Mitsuharu admonished. "You must find rest *somewhere* or your alertness will be dulled."

"How does it compare to a Templar ship?" Susan slid a panel aside on one of the walls, revealing a compartment holding a black iron kettle and a rack of cups. "Tea?"

"*Dōmo, Sho-sa*." He knelt gingerly on a nearby mat, settling with a hiss of pain. Koshō began measuring *matcha* into the cups. "What I have seen of the *Pilgrim* matches the best the Fleet has put underway. Their captains—well, I've experience with two—are able."

"Hm." Susan whisked steaming hot water into the green powder. "Are you oath sworn now, to the Temple?"

"No." Hadeishi tilted his head inquisitively. He could see Koshō's attention was fixed on the molten jade swirling in the two cups, but something in her voice sharpened his interest. "I've command of the *Kader* under the terms of a commercial contract as a serving crewman on a Temple-owned ship—as salvage officer. But I am not yet a Knight of the Temple, or even a poor brother. . . ."

She turned, holding a small enameled tray in her hands, and knelt as well, pale blue cups and rice cakes between them. "You wish to be?"

"They have use of my poor talents, it seems. As a salvage driver, if nothing else." He shrugged, and then lifted his cup. "*Dōmo arigatō, Sho-sa*. It is good to sit with you again, even in such a strange place, so far from home."

She inclined her head. "You're welcome, *Chu-sa*. Magister De Charney would be a fool to refuse your talents. Not as a tug captain, either! I've recently reviewed all of the Mirror briefs on the *Fratres Milites Templi*—and while they have an excellent reputation in counterpiracy activities, and even in some border skirmishes—there is *no* evidence they have put main line-of-battle vessels like the *Pilgrim* into service before. Nor deployed ships displaying a countermeasures system which can handily defeat our sensors!"

With this, she paused, watching him carefully. For the first time in their long association, Mitsuharu suddenly felt a distance between them. *She's suspicious? Of me?* Hadeishi set down his cup. *And why not? I've arrived in the colors of a foreign power.* Having been aboard the

"Yes?" she said, not bothering to look up.

"Somehow," he said, amused, "you've brought your office through in fine shape, *Sho-sa*. Mine always seemed to take the worst of it, riding such a rough passage. Everything would always be ruined. . . ."

Koshō's head lifted, eyes widening at the sight of the thin, weary-looking Nisei officer. She stood, tucking a stylus into the twisted bun of hair behind her head, and stepped around the end of the desk.

"You're here?" She paused a polite distance away, the carefully impassive mask of her face subtly transforming. Without meaning to, Susan began to smile. "You were very foolish to come through the Pinhole after us—there was no safety to be found in our company."

"So we discovered!" Mitsuharu bowed, dark eyes twinkling. "But things would have been worse if we ran the other way. . . . I had no choice, really, knowing you were here."

She nodded, looking him up and down. Then she shook her head, seeing quickheal gel shining on his neck, his wrists. The trim brown and white uniform seemed to fit him well enough, though it was strange to see him out of Fleet colors. "You've been in the infirmary again, *Chu-sa*. And I've seen your poor ship—kindling and splinters are all that remains."

"Yes," he said ruefully, shrugging thin shoulders. "She had a brave heart, though, even to the end."

"Your crew is aboard," Koshō offered, "under the best care we can provide." She stepped closer, pursing her lips disapprovingly, and took the hem of his jacket sleeve between thumb and forefinger. "Lost all your clothes, I see. Is this a loaner?"

Hadeishi shook his head, straightening the half-jacket. "I've a new commission, *Sho-sa*. Brevet-captain of the *Kader*—that same poor wreck lying in tow off the *Pilgrim*—mine now that I'd found her, brought her to worse state than when she fell into my hands. But—"

"A ship, still. A starship." Koshō stepped back, her expression turning wan and drained. "I can offer you nothing better, *Chu-sa*. Not even as an unfounded promise."

"I know." Hadeishi smoothed back his hair from forehead to nape in a terribly familiar gesture. "It is strange—not to be in dress whites, not to hear the piping when coming aboard." He looked around her cabin, at first sad, but then whistling softly in appreciation. In comparison to his old quarters on the *Cornuelle*, the *Naniwa*'s accommodations were refined, even luxurious. "This suits you, *Sho-sa*."

I felt, holding any of my babies in my arms. This was his great failing, I think, having no children of his own."

With this, Anderssen finally lay back on the bed, her eyes turned to the ceiling and some distant vision. Koshō watched her for a minute, and then for five. But the Swedish woman said nothing more. At last, the *Chu-sa* turned away, motioning for Helsdon to follow.

When the door had cycled shut, Susan tapped open a comm channel to Oc Chac, who was acting duty officer on the bridge. "*Sho-sa*, can you connect me to Captain De Charney aboard the *Pilgrim*? Extend my regards and let him know we're ready for the rest of the wounded to come aboard."

Then she turned to the engineer, who was waiting silently, head slightly bowed as he tried to digest all they had heard in the medbay. "*Kikan-shi*, find Hennig and let him know we'll be underway and out of this cursed place as fast as his crews can get the hypercoil in operation."

Koshō's face was calm and composed but her eyes were dark with troubled thoughts as Helsdon departed in haste. She could think of only one thing to do, given the intricacy of the situation. *It's at least seven days to get in range of one of the big t-repeaters on the Rim. If we push it, six. If I can manage a secure channel to Obasan Suchiru, then perhaps an accommodation can be made between the Mountains. Emperor Ahuizotl cannot be pleased to learn I've lost his son—not even an honorable corpse to bring home—as well as any possible prize from this tar-pit.*

The thought of facing her grandmother with a disaster of this scale made Susan's stomach clench, but despite this she walked steadily to the nearest lift, nodding to the doctors and corpsmen hurrying here and there in the medbay. When the doors cycled closed, she was perfectly composed, her white uniform shining in the gleam of the overheads.

"Main Command," she requested.

Hadeishi pressed two fingers against a battle-steel door and heard, muted and distant through the metal, a chiming sound. A moment passed as he stood at ease, hands clasped behind his back, and then the door receded into the bulkhead with a soft *hsst!* Within, kneeling behind a low desk of teak and rosewood, her fine-boned face pale in the light of a single task-light, Susan Koshō was considering an array of v-displays, all filled with reports, forms, and colorful graphs displaying the state of her ship.

rules the Hjo, from what I gather. But the Guide is not a Vay'en any-more, just some old fart of a Hjogadim pissing around a palace. So do the great powers pass!"

During this Helsdon had said nothing, but now the engineer stirred, moistening his lips before venturing: "You are saying the elder Vay'en had discovered how to live forever by impressing their memories and personality patterns upon the newborns of their *own kind* as they emerged from the birth-caul. They murdered their own children, so they might live on themselves?"

"Not just kin-murderers, either. They had no care for others of any race." Gretchen's voice was flat with anger. "You saw how Sahâne viewed *us*. A pale echo of the attitude of his Gods. I think when the Vay'en de-parted their puppets en masse and descended to renew themselves, the Hjo rose up, seizing their *one* moment to escape. We have stumbled across the traces of a successful slave revolt."

"But they didn't all rebel, did they?" Koshō lifted her chin at the nav plot, where the vast shoals of broken leviathans still drifted in the abyss. "Even within the shield-reed, there must have been those who re-mained true to their masters."

"Yes, many remained loyal. Quite a vicious little struggle they had. It was brother against brother . . . so much for the legacy of the glorious Vay'en. A squalid play of infanticide, kin war, and murder played out on a galactic scale, just to forestall death *one more day*."

"And now? What will happen to the children you've released from slow-time?"

Anderssen shrugged, managing the faintest smile. "I don't know. It's not much of a gifting day present, but they are freed from a cruel past." *And free of Lord Serpent, I hope.* A nagging feeling of unease began to steal over her. *Did that one escape the rebellion? How would you kill something like that? How long do they live?*

"Was that what Hummingbird wanted?" Susan's old anger began to return, thinking of the old Nahuatl. "Was that the choice of a *nauallis*? You said the end result was much as he desired—"

"His desire?" Gretchen snorted incredulously. "No, this was a tired mother's choice, one who has seen both happy children and sad in full measure. No child was ever so blessed as to grow without the hand of expectation on her neck! Those which are let be, flourish, while those who are pressed hard wither. The Crow had no comprehension of what

"Their children."

Helsdon and Susan stared at her, uncomprehending.

"That clever little bronze tablet Hummingbird gave me? He must have thought it a personal comp, or a ship-comm of some kind. But it was a teaching device for immature Vay'en. It tried to reprogram *my* mind and failed because my poor old ape brain just wasn't capable of following the lessons. But it was a piece of the puzzle—and a twisty, nasty one at that. You see, the tablet was very old, even to the Vay'en. It was something they'd put aside—a failed, melancholy experiment—in favor of another, more promising way to cheat death."

Koshō said nothing, hands clenched tightly behind her back. The Swedish woman's voice had a queer, atonal quality and her face seemed marked by some last remnant of a hot golden glow. Helsdon drew back, shaking hand reaching for his sidearm.

"The Vay'en were—are—energy creatures," Gretchen continued. "We would consider them sentient wave structures. And I would guess they could manipulate electromagnetic fields in close proximity to themselves with great dexterity. But in turn, their *own* physicality could be manipulated by quantum resonance. With the tablet, they were trying to bring their offspring 'up to speed' by exposing them to the already established mentation pattern of an accomplished elder. The mind in the tablet had been a poet, I think. Some kind of great artist. They wanted to keep his essence alive, even when chaos claimed him at last.

"In the beginning, the Vay'en evolved in the interface around a black hole. They could live far beyond its confines, but from all we saw, it seems they returned there to breed." Gretchen halted, watching her two companions digest what she'd said.

Susan spoke first, musingly. "It was a nursery."

Anderssen nodded, digging around for a threesquare in her blankets.

"They were betrayed, then," the Nisei officer continued. "Their most loyal servants turned upon them at a most crucial juncture—their great fleet shattered by their own weapons. The Vay'en had to descend into the singularity to birth a new generation? But the Hjogadim trapped them too close to the event horizon, in slow-time. Then the treacherous Hjo abandoned the artifact and fled—to assume custody of the Vay'en dominions—to become Gods themselves."

"Plagiarists," Anderssen mumbled around the chewy bar. "Doesn't sound like the traitors told anyone, though. A 'Guide of Thought' still

hands. "The Vay'en *assembled this*. They dragged these suns into position, spun up a black hole of their own, wrapped in the wall of knives—everything within ten light-years is here by the will of Lord Serpent, who perished nearly a million years ago!" She caught Koshō's eye with a piercing, exasperated glare—then jabbed a finger at Helsdon. "We can barely perceive their works with our instrumentality—and you expect the Mirror, or the Fleet, to grasp their technology?"

"In time." Susan lifted her hands, conceding the point. "But what else can we do? Even if we are beneath the notice of these great powers, that must surely change. When that black day comes, we'd be remiss in all duty if we had not prepared as best we could. Even to the point of waking—as you say—a power like the Vay'en and seeking their alliance."

"Foolish. Very foolish." Gretchen buried her head in both hands. "At least this temptation is banished—none of the sleepers will return from the pit." She made a casting-away motion. "The balance in the system has been destroyed. Structures you cannot perceive have descended deep into slow-time, quite close to the event horizon of the singularity. The tidal stress on the Thread broke apart the *Chimalacatl*—the Pylon, the great chrysalis chambers, the warehouses for the hosts—all gone."

"We saw." Helsdon sounded sick, but his face was alight with interest for the first time. "How—how did they do it? Hold something in balance deep in the gravity well? A platform—for the Vay'en themselves?"

"There were two lattices," Anderssen replied, growing weary. What little strength had returned to her while recuperating in medbay was beginning to flag. "One fell while the other raised—not much, in the scale of their works, but enough. Enough for them to feel time quicken again."

"Who?" Helsdon frowned, glancing to Koshō for support. "You said the Vay'en fell to oblivion—but something else rose up out of slow-time? What else was dwelling in this place? Something that will issue forth, as these Vay'en would have done?"

"Not yet, maybe never." Gretchen made a vague motion towards the floor. "Eventually they might escape the gravity well, as their ancestors did. Or not. They have"—a small, fierce smile flitted across her face—"free will at least. They'll have to choose, just like the rest of us."

"Who? If the Vay'en perished in the singularity, what was on the *other structure*?"

espousing the same goals, I'm sure, but embracing markedly different means to reach the end." She tapped the *croix fiché*. "Three crosses, each composed of three arms, surmounting a spear. I—I saw something like that when I was aboard the *Moulins*. The sense of it was a warrior brotherhood, standing watch on the edge of infinity, much like the Judges. . . ."

"Three of three?" Helsdon blinked. "Like the patterns on the surface of the *Chimalacatl*?"

"Aping the Vay'en and their symbology." Gretchen scowled. "The Hjogadim were the same way, thinking the oversize robes and scepter of their overlords would grant them the power of Lord Serpent! Fools. The strength of the Vay'en was—is—beyond our ability to grasp." She laughed harshly, thinking of the hundreds of thousands of Hjo corpses desiccating in the garbage disposal chutes throughout the massive artifact. "The same fate awaits us—our puny little principality—if the great houses, the Emperor and the Order all fall out amongst one another over the prize. It is better the Sunflower is gone—safer by far for everyone. Much better."

Hearing a change in the Swedish woman's voice, Koshō's jaw tightened and she glanced sideways at Helsdon. The engineer was watching Gretchen as well, and the same dawning suspicion was showing in his face. "You destroyed the artifact, Doctor? You—what *did* you do?"

"And why? Just to protect humanity from some hypothetical civil war?" Susan seemed genuinely curious. "Are you certain such a fate would befall us?"

"Look around you, Captain!" Gretchen rang her knuckles on the damaged wall beside her. "An Imperial Judge betrayed the Prince's expedition to the barbarians! Just to keep the Emperor's hand from the hilt of this infernal blade! The unity of the Temple is already divided, one faction intriguing against the other—and it will not end here, no— it will not end until Anáhuac is a burning ruin and all our colonies and settlements are laid waste." Her voice had gained a harsh, hectoring edge. "Because even should we seize this power for ourselves and learn its use—*others* will come which we cannot withstand, even with this weapon! Remember the lesson from the Hill of Grasshoppers!"

The Swedish woman winced, feeling her bruised torso twinge. Angrily, she stabbed at the field comp with her stylus, invoking a projected image of the rosette—the three brown dwarves, the distant demarcation of the Barrier, the singularity—then she cupped the holo in her

here—the Mirror, the Judges, and presumably the Emperor himself—
who else could have dispatched Sayu with a newly minted super-
dreadnaught? It is very likely the Knights are *also* divided amongst
themselves—if not, why send some of their agents in secret, and others
arrive with such overwhelming force as to seize the prize openly? Also
weigh that they have *not* attacked us, though at least a day has passed
since the missing Templar from the Sunflower should have reached the
Pilgrim."

This gave Gretchen pause, and she settled back, searching her mem-
ories. "That is . . . possible. Hummingbird had not intended to reach
this place aboard the *Moulins*—we were supposed to meet another
ship—one carrying an ally, he said—but the Khaid had intercepted
them. I think—I got the impression we were going to meet Captain
Hadeishi on that other ship. And he's here, now, right?"

"Yes." Susan nodded, her eyes dark. "I've been told he is aboard the
Pilgrim. They took him aboard, along with many survivors from the
Imperial ships destroyed outside the Pinhole. I've spoken with one of
his officers—a Mirror technician, actually—who was brought over
from their medbay. He was on a ship called the *Wilful*, commanded by
a woman *Sencho* named De Molay."

"Really? How curious . . ." Anderssen opened her field comp again.
"Yes—I thought that sounded familiar. A famous Templar surname,
actually. So two Templar spy-ships—and a fleet to back them up—but
maybe only *one* of the freighters was intended to be here. The other—
the crewmen on the *Wilful*—they had an insignia, a tattoo actually, of
a—ah, here it is: the *Croix recroisetée au pied fiché*, in crimson on a
white field."

She turned the comp so Koshō and Helsdon could see a cross com-
posed of three smaller squared crosses—for the crossbar and crown—
then the long end of the cross was more like a spike, or spear, pointing
downward.

"Striking," Susan commented, "but not the insignia of the Knights of
the Order. They bear a cross with equal arms and rounded ends, fit to a
circle, not a rectangle."

"This one," Gretchen said, tapping up a second image, which matched
the Nisei officer's description.

"So there are your two factions, *Chu-sa*." Anderssen shrugged again.
"Probably representing a political split within the Temple hierarchy; each

unknown threat is the alternative." Susan flexed her hands angrily. "One of the first lectures Chapultepec beats into the heads of the lower form is that the realm of the México, for all its power, pomp, and majesty, is a tiny principality in a galaxy filled with mammoth empires. It is easy to forget that we are weak and ill-regarded." She laughed bitterly. "They do not tell you, however, anything about these great powers . . . that is ring-zero information. Only the Emperors will know how low on the mountain we truly are."

"Hummingbird implied the same to me, when first we met." Anderssen closed her field comp. "When you work for the Honorable Company, it's very clear your purpose is to poke and pry and dig in the dead cities and ruined worlds, not for scientific benefit, but for tools—weapons—knowledge from the ancients that will benefit the Empire. Make it stronger, make it more powerful. Climb another step on that mountain. . . ." She sighed, shaking her head. "The Mirror was trying the same thing here. They found *something* and wondered if it could make them great—but they were only a cat's paw. The Templars came prepared. Hummingbird came prepared. Even Xochitl was sent by someone who *knew what was here already*."

"What about the Khaid?" Helsdon ventured. "Why bring them into the equation?"

"The Judges—or Hummingbird—must have decided that the Mirror fleet had to be destroyed. And *they* didn't know the Order was also in play with a powerful fleet." Gretchen smiled ruefully at Koshō. "He had great faith in you, Captain, expecting you and your ship to survive when everyone else was slated to die. The arrival of the *Tlemitl* threw all of those plans into question—he was almost frantic when the Prince arrived."

"And the Knights of the Temple," Susan said, her lip curling in distaste. "Stood by waiting to clean up the survivors—on either side!—and take the prize."

"And now they have it." Helsdon's pale face was drawn with worry. "*Chu-sa*, we're not ready to fight or even run. Perhaps—perhaps we should give her over, if that will obtain our safe passage?"

Gretchen nodded in agreement, but Koshō's expression turned obstinate. "She's all we have for a bargaining chip—I'm not going to *offer* her to anyone." She raised a slim hand to forestall Anderssen's rejoinder. "Consider this as well—at least three *Imperial* factions were involved

Prince's ship had entirely new security systems—none like those used by the Judges, or the Mirror. I doubt that would have been allowed if there were proper political officers aboard!

"And after all of this business was done—if you survived—then you'd be sent off on patrol, and then *I* would be the one dropping in unexpectedly when *I* needed a ship for some dirty work."

Koshō grimaced. "You're one of the *Tlamantinime* now, are you? I thought there were no female Judges."

"There aren't." Anderssen bit at the edge of her thumb. "But once I heard the Crow and two others talking—a female counterpart to the *nauallis* exists—and they were pressing to take on a similar role along the frontier. I think that now—driven by fear—the old strictures are breaking down. I think Hummingbird hoped I would become his apprentice—take on his responsibilities—and the two of us would replace him and Hadeishi, if they died or grew too old to act."

"How interesting." Susan's displeasure radiated from her as a sharp, prickly heat. "I have no appetite for his schemes—and now that he's dead, then all of this can die with him."

"Can it? If he spoke truly—if the Templars were correct in their belief—then *someone* must walk the fences, watch in the shadows, do all the things Hummingbird and his brother Judges have been doing."

Koshō shook her head. "He arranged the deaths of thousands of Fleet crewmen. He, and whoever decided to poke this nest of ants with a stick, and whoever dispatched Sayu to his death. Do you want that kind of hideous *karma* upon *your* soul?"

"No." Gretchen's voice faltered. "It's already cost me my boy. A wise woman once said—almost immediately after meeting the Crow—that he stank of 'broken shells and ash.' She was right—he would not hesitate to sacrifice a fleet, a planet, even a whole species to achieve the ends he thought necessary. But I begin to perceive there are other players in the game, perhaps those on the very summit of the Heavenly Mountain, who will sacrifice even more to *win*, or just survive."

She tapped the navigational plot. "Alliance with the Vay'en would have cost us our humanity. Even if our bodies endured—they would have been no more than husks filled with a living flame—and every human being alive would have been their slave. Yet someone, somewhere, believes it was absolutely necessary to do so."

"This implies the annihilation of our species at the hands of this

had something to do with the Templars being here—the rest? It seems doubtful."

"He arranged—he arranged the Khaid." Helsdon looked more uncomfortable than ever. "We've found traces in the comm system of t-relay activity between the *Naniwa* and the Khaid fleet during the fighting outside the Pinhole."

"Ah." Gretchen nodded, remembering. "I helped him assemble a t-relay when we first came aboard."

"And he arranged for *Chu-sa* Hadeishi to be here." Susan's expression was positively glacial. "Both to further his own ends—and as leverage with me, if needed."

"Yes." Anderssen was watching the Nisei officer again and smiling faintly. "I didn't like the Crow—hate might be too weak a word—but he had something in mind for you, Captain Koshō, and for me as well. You'd served with Hadeishi for a long time, hadn't you?"

"Five years," Koshō said grudgingly, regarding the archaeologist with suspicion. "What do you mean—*in mind*?"

"So you'd seen Hummingbird come and go over those five years, always dropping in unexpectedly, getting your ship and your captain into some kind of dodgy situation? Always on off-the-books business for the *Tlamantinime*?" Gretchen didn't wait for a response from Susan. "He had the same pattern in mind for you, and for me. Once you had your own ship—this ship!—you'd be put on frontier duty, patrolling alone at the edge of cultivation—one step out into the darkness—with no support, no backup, and no oversight."

She paused, running one hand through her tangled, greasy hair. Koshō looked like she'd swallowed a sour pickle. "Where is your political officer, Captain? Where are the Mice? I haven't seen any—isn't that *very strange?*"

"We—" Susan halted, considering. "I had assumed Oc Chac, my new *Sho-sa*, was the Mirror representative aboard—but you're right, there should be a whole complement on a ship this size." She glanced at Helsdon, who had retreated again and was swallowing nervously. "All of the other ships in the squadron were drawn from units tasked to support the Mirror science teams. They would have been crawling with political officers. But not us?"

"You see? The *Tlemitl* was free of them as well. Hummingbird mentioned at one point—I don't think he realized I was listening—that the

Helsdon cursed under his breath, rubbing his palms on his thighs. "The Barrier. The *Naniwa* and the *Moulins* could reach the Sunflower because all three of you were aboard!" He laughed, a little hysterically. "All my work to identify the Barrier threads—for nothing! Good thing we didn't get too close while the security system was still operational!"

"Wait—" Koshō's eyes narrowed in suspicion. "The builders of this place were obviously fond of threes and multiples of three. I can understand the ambassador, if his people had once been the servants of the Vay'en. But how did *you* and *Sayu* qualify as keys to the structure? You're not Hjo!"

"I was." Anderssen knuckled her brow-line with one fist, feeling an enormous migraine coming on. "Hummingbird had exposed me to that corroded-looking bronze tablet—let me use it as a comp—and the Vay'en 'instructor' within began to rewrite my neurology. The tablet led us through the Barrier—you saw the effects as it revised the ship's interfaces and systems—the same was happening to me, though I didn't realize it until too late. While I was under its influence, the *Chimalacatl* treated me as a Hjo as well."

"And the Prince?"

Gretchen pursed her lips, examining Susan's face with great care. "Did you care for him?"

"Me? For Sayu?" Koshō looked horrified. "He pursued me, momentarily, at Chapultepec when we were in the lower form. But I was not what he expected, so—nothing came to pass. After that, there was open rivalry between us, and—I must confess—he often came up short." She paused, remembering. "Later he did better—after third year he seemed to collect himself. Then he was the popular one, the pretty one. Captain of the *Ullamaliztli* team—everything expected of a scion of the Imperial house."

Anderssen nodded to herself. "Like me, he had an overlay which allowed him entrance, made him seem enough of a Hjogadim to qualify for the machine. I don't think he realized, even at the end, why he was here. Whoever sent him must have known what would happen . . . but you know, Hummingbird was surprised to encounter Xochitl out here. Surprised when the big battleship arrived." She ran her fingertips along the outside of her field comp. "You said the Crow *arranged all of this*— but I don't agree. I think he was trying to manage a situation that kept escalating out of his control. Some of it—yes, he brought me here, he

approaching. One which we—humanity—cannot withstand without the assistance of the kind of powers which once dwelt here."

Helsdon stiffened in his chair, fear stark in his features. "My God, woman, this place was built by a race with the power of the Gods! We won't have this level of technology for thousands of years!"

Susan nodded in agreement, her complexion growing waxy. "Do you know what they fear? Do the Templars?"

"They believe they know." Gretchen smiled sadly. "I do not. But I can tell you the Order Knights are being used, as you and I were used by Hummingbird, by *another* agent—another puppet master hiding in the wings, out of our sight. This seems to me a skirmish—an opening move—where greater powers than the Empire are jockeying for position on the field of combat."

"These Vay'en," Koshō said, after considering the Swedish woman's words. "The Templars believed they were still alive, after millions of years? That they could be woken, or summoned? And bargained with?"

Anderssen nodded. "Yes. It is even possible they were right—but none of the Vay'en remained, only their machines and devices. Of course, given the disparity of power between us, I don't think *bargained with* would be the appropriate term. Subjecting humanity to slavery and servitude—yes, that would have been the likely outcome."

Helsdon glanced at Susan, who nodded, wondering what the engineer intended.

"Doctor Anderssen—what happened to disrupt the equilibrium of the system? Did—did *you* do something?"

Gretchen looked at him, seemingly puzzled, before saying, "Ambassador Sahâne attempted to harness the machine. But his exocortex was insufficient to the task. There was an interruption during the process—and what he intended did not come to pass."

Susan's forehead creased sharply. "Why was the ambassador here? Did he know something about the artifact? Did his race—these Hjo—know something?"

"*He* knew nothing." Anderssen sighed. "But his race—yes, they had once served the Vay'en—long ago, they were servants, soldiers, bureaucrats . . . the linchpin of the Vay'en demesne. Like the Prince, like me, his presence had been *arranged* by those who set all this in motion. Three of us were needed to unlock the mechanism, so three were delivered by Hummingbird."

Susan made a soft, strangled sound. "He wanted the Sunflower destroyed?"

"More than that," Gretchen replied. "He needed—or the Judges needed—to ensure that not only was the artifact obliterated—but everyone who had come seeking its power was slain, denied, or convinced it did not exist. The Prince is dead, the Khaid massacred, the Order Knights left with empty hands . . . we are witnesses to the immolation of the evidence. The navplot shows that the entire Barrier will be swallowed up in time, pulled into the black sack and made to vanish."

She laughed nervously. "Only three people remain who saw the heart of the structure, who know what happened there—me and an Order Knight who escaped, the one who departed in the *Moulins*. He will certainly carry the news to his masters—and I wonder how they will react?"

"They came well equipped," Koshō admitted grudgingly. "The *Pilgrim* is the core of a full-scale squadron and seems more than capable of mopping up the leftovers of our ill-fated expedition. If we're on the books to be marked off—we won't last long."

"If you give me to them, they will let you go." Gretchen's statement carried an odd weight of certainty. "I think they are very keen to know the fate of the Vay'en, and the *Chimalacatl*, and what transpired within."

"That seems, to me, Doctor Anderssen, an excellent reason *not* to put you into their hands." Susan offered a tight, bitter smile. "I am still an officer of the Fleet and the Emperor's servant. If we escape, then duty requires that I report what transpired in this benighted place. It seems unwise to leave *all* of the witnesses in the hands of the Temple. But what becomes of you after we return—I cannot say."

"It does not matter." Gretchen's expression was bleak. "I've done all I can. Like Hummingbird, my death or disappearance evens the books, leaving almost no trace of our passing."

"Untrue." Koshō lifted her chin, indicating the icons of the Templar ships on the plot. "They are still here—they have possession—but what do they gain from all this, Doctor? Are they now an enemy of the Empire?"

"No." Anderssen scratched the back of her head, where a sore had developed from wearing her helmet so long. "They came seeking to ally themselves with something—with someone—they thought remained in this funereal place. Hummingbird alluded to needing *time*. He believed—and the Templars believe—some enormous calamity is fast

Gretchen shook her head, all expression draining from her tired face. "No. I had been waiting for him, or someone like him, to come nosing around. After everything that happened on Jagan, when I came home empty-handed, without a bonus check from the Company, I found that my boy Duncan had been killed while working on a trawler in the Northern Cape Sea. That—"

She stopped, her attention suddenly far away from the medbay and the two officers. Susan waited, watching the subtle play of emotions on the blond woman's face, until Helsdon stirred, looking at his commander beseechingly.

"Anderssen-*tzin*, we don't have much time. Please tell us what the Hummingbird was doing here."

"Oh." Gretchen shook herself, grinding the heel of one palm into her left eye. "I have a recording, I think. My suit comm was on when he told me. You can hear it from his own lips."

She tapped up a sequence on her field comp, and then slid the volume to three-quarters. The sound of static and harsh breathing filled the little room, and then the old Nahuatl was saying: . . . *the annihilation of the Prince, the Khaid, even the poor Ambassador and my own life in the bargain. A clean set of books—nothing falling into the Emperor's hands to upset the balance at home—and time. Time we desperately need.*

The recording stopped and Anderssen made a face. "We came here in little tramp freighters and mail-boats before the *Moulins*, which seemed like more of the same. Hummingbird didn't have anything on his side but some fancy comps in a case, me—for whatever I was worth—and his own invincible self assurance. Do you hear him? He was hurt when he said that, and afraid—not of dying, no, but of failing at the task he'd taken upon himself."

She stopped, running her finger across the navigational display. The *Chimalacatl* was already gone, torn to shreds as it fell. Comp projections showed the delicate balance holding all three of the brown dwarves was beginning to fail. In a hundred years, or a thousand, the entire rosette would succumb to the black hole and obliterate all traces of the Vay'en and their works.

"I thought," Gretchen continued, "when I sent them down into oblivion, that I defeated him. But listening to his voice now, I think I did exactly what he wanted . . . even better than he could have managed himself."

officer indicated the ship, the rosette, the universe with an encompass-
ing wave of her hand. "I know these things: that my ship is alone,
wounded and in desperate need of resupply. A presumably friendly
fleet—including a strike carrier easily the size of the *Tlemitl*—has come
to our aid, is providing medical assistance, and has sent across dozens
of wounded rescued from other Fleet ships lost in the recent series of
battles. But at the same time, you tell me that Knights of the Temple
have murdered an *Imperial Prince,* the ambassador of a friendly realm,
and also an Imperial Judge, and . . . I wonder if we are next, if the
Knights decide to clean up this little mess before they go on their way."

"Oh." Gretchen leaned her head on one hand, eyes half closed. "That
is a problem, I guess."

"It could be . . . serious." Koshō stood beside the bed, her attention
fully upon the Swedish woman. "You came here with Hummingbird. I
know he was at the center of all this. I have a horrible suspicion that he
arranged all of this. But I do not know why—and I hope that you will
tell me, for the sake of my crew, if not out of courtesy to me."

Anderssen regarded Susan sidelong, her expression still and distant
for nearly a minute. Then she lifted her head, attention returning to the
present, and she looked at Koshō with great curiosity. "Captain, do you
remember that this is the third time our paths have crossed? Each time,
great events have been in play—at Ephesus III, on Jagan, and now
here. . . . I wonder, is *Chu-sa* Hadeishi here as well? I know you've your
own ship now, but—"

"He is." Koshō's stoic expression was suddenly and subtly trans-
formed, cycling from glad relief to concern to suspicion and then grim
certainty. "He *is* here. Hummingbird brought him here. Hummingbird
brought *me* here, and the Prince, and—what in the Nine Hells was he
doing? What were *you* doing with him?"

"Do you really want to know?" Gretchen spread her hands. "You will
find no ease to your worries!"

"Tell me." Susan's voice sounded stretched and brittle.

"The Crow found me on New Aberdeen," Anderssen said, "and he
needed help with something beyond his 'capacity to evaluate.' *I* thought
he needed my technical skills as a xenoarchaeologist—but that was a
gravely incorrect assumption. *He* never said—he never does, you
know?—what he expected me to do."

"And you just came when he beckoned?" Koshō sounded disgusted.

in determining what happened to Prince Xochitl and Ambassador Sahâne. Can you tell me?"

"Oh," Anderssen blinked, and then rubbed her face, trying to remember. "I had forgotten all about the two boys . . . they are dead, Captain. One of the Templars shot Xochitl in the face with an assault rifle, and Sahâne—well, he was burned alive by a plasma burst and then cut in half. Old Crow, he—" She nodded to herself, feeling light-headed. "He was shot, then stabbed, and then fell down a very, very deep pit. But—but I could not say for certain he perished, not being able to see the bottom of that pit. It was quite deep."

Susan's expression congealed into a cold, immobile mask. "My marines found you drifting on a jury-rigged grav-sled outside the artifact, Doctor Anderssen, in the company of a half-dead, blinded Jaguar Knight who had been *Cuauhhuehueh* of the Prince's guard detachment. The ship Xochitl commandeered—the *Moulins*—has disappeared. Do you know what happened to the freighter?"

Gretchen shrugged. "One of the Templars survived the melee with the Prince and his men. He must have taken it out of the landing cradle— she was gone when Koris and I reached the garbage disposal port."

"I see." Koshō's jaw tightened in frustration. "Do you know how the freighter avoided our notice—assuming the ship left the vicinity of the *Chimalacatl* and boosted outbound, to join the rest of the Templar battle-group? Helsdon here and my techs have gone over the sensor logs at least three times—finding nothing."

"It was a military ship," Anderssen offered. "Disguised as a freighter. But the crewmen were all Order Knights and they were using—at the end—powered armor and modern weapons. Better than the Prince's men had, from what I saw."

Susan looked to Helsdon, clicking her teeth. "Then the *Moulins* could have been equipped with the same stealthing technology the *Pilgrim*'s fighters were showing off against the Khaid."

"No reason," the engineer coughed, covering his mouth, "to believe otherwise, *kyo*."

"Why are you asking me, Captain?" Anderssen was watching them both with an odd, distant expression. "I'm just an archaeologist caught up in something far, far bigger than she expected."

"I need any information you can give me, Doctor, because I'm beginning to wonder if *we* will be allowed to leave this place." The Nisei

ABOARD THE *NANIWA*

In company of the *Pilgrim* and her support flotilla

Chu-sa Koshō nodded in greeting to the two Imperial marines standing watch outside medbay pod twenty-seven, and then stepped inside without a pause, followed by *Kikan-shi* Helsdon. The pressurized door whispered shut behind them and Susan paused a moment, letting the portal seal, before turning around, hands clasped behind her back. The *Naniwa*'s commander looked civilized again—she'd had a shower, been out of her z-armor for nearly a day, and gotten a few hours of sleep. Helsdon, now sitting nervously in a corner chair, looked little different than usual. The engineering teams had been working around the clock to repair secondary hull damage and return normal living conditions to the hab rings and command compartments.

"Anderssen-*tzin*, good afternoon."

Gretchen looked up from her field comp, face mottled with bruises, her tangled blond hair tied back in a ponytail. Her bare arms and neck were shining with quickheal, and her ruined civilian z-armor had been replaced by a matte black Fleet skinsuit while she remained in med-bay. She was sitting on a bed of crates, spare insulation, and blankets—the regular pod bed had been moved somewhere else. A portable lamp hung from the ceiling, shedding a bluish-white glow. On her field comp's screen, a relayed feed from the main navigational array was unspooling, showing the singularity and its attendant stars. The icon of the Sunflower was nowhere to be seen.

"It's gone." The Swedish woman set the comp down, shoulders slumping in weariness. "Dragged down by irresistible gravity. The last sanctuary of the Vay'en is no more."

Koshō glanced to Helsdon, who shook his head in ignorance. The Nisei woman pursed her lips, frowned once, and then tilted her head questioningly at the xenoarchaeologist.

"I do not know who these *Vahyyyen* might be, but I am very interested

De Molay produced a data crystal, bound with gold and white bands. "If you recall, *Chu-sa* Hadeishi, you signed aboard the merchanter *Wilful* as an engineer's mate. After *Wilful's* unhappy experience with marauding Khaid, you assumed emergency captaincy until such time as you engineered the capture of the Khaiden light cruiser *Kader*. You served as *de facto* captain aboard her until the vessel was evacuated. From our point of view, you are still captain of the *Kader*, but her fate is yet to be decided. And you are still our employee, bound by contract. One possibility is to scuttle the cruiser and add her remains to the debris along the Barrier. Another is to affect sufficient repairs to allow transit to the nearest Temple shipyard where she may either be reborn, or recycled. In any case, she is your charge. These orders—" She tapped a fingernail against the crystal. "Affirm your employment and responsibilities."

De Molay reached for his hand and closed his thin, newly scrubbed fingers over the crystal. It seemed tremendously heavy, possessing a weight in his mind far in excess of the tiny dimensions.

Hadeishi's glance shifted to Ketcham. "What time is it and when does the next watch begin?"

De Molay turned a snort of laughter into a sneeze.

Ketcham shook his head, putting on a forbidding expression. "You, *Chu-sa*, are on medbay time. Down here, I'm XO of the *Pilgrim* in name only. When the Infirmarian lets you go, you can take your duty station. Until then—well, you'll have time to sleep at last."

"Interesting." Musashi yawned, hands behind his head. "But the militia does not ride war horses."

Hadeishi awoke to find a sandy-haired man with knight-commander's tabs standing beside his gurney. The familiar sounds and smells of medbay surrounded them, and De Molay was loitering behind the Templar. Her gray eyes wrinkled up in amusement at the look on Hadeishi's face when he recognized Ketcham.

"You were in a bad way the last time I saw you, *Chu-sa* Hadeishi," the European observed.

Mitsuharu smiled wryly, "Aside from far too much radiation exposure, I believe my wounds are only of the heart, Præceptor Ketcham. You found another ship, I see, and one better suited to you than wildcatting with an illegal ore refinery."

"I did." Ketcham scratched the back of his head, failing to suppress a huge grin. "You seem to have gotten back into the hot-chair, too, by hook and by crook."

"By stealing my ship," De Molay grumbled. Her good humor made the elderly woman seem a dozen years younger. "Twice!"

"I returned it," Hadeishi said quietly. He looked around the room, hoping for a comm panel.

"Much the worse for wear!" De Molay objected, jutting out her chin pugnaciously.

"He has that way." Ketcham laughed. "You will want to know, *Chu-sa*, that Commander Koshō is well, though busy aboard her ship, which is somewhat . . . battered. We intend to ship your men across to the *Naniwa* as soon as she has atmosphere restored on all decks, and proper facilities prepared."

Mitsuharu felt his heart ease at the news of the battle-cruiser's survival and lay easier on the gurney. "Then I can sleep at last."

He closed his eyes, feeling the tug of tremendous weariness, and wondered idly if it were possible for him to sleep for a full week. Then he sat up again, frowning at the two Templars. They had not moved, and were waiting for him expectantly.

"My men, you say, to the *Naniwa*. Where am I bound, if not with them?"

Norsktek *Galahad*-class hull with—by what I saw from the shuttle viewport—an entirely upgraded drive array. Out of the yards on New Malta?"

"It is indeed," De Molay said, pleased. "And it is appropriate that you have attended to all her details."

Mitsuharu's thin black eyebrows lifted in query.

"In good time, *Chu-sa*," De Molay said with no emotion whatever. "If you will step over here, please." She guided him away from the others. Templar medical staff were everywhere in the bay, triaging the rescued Imperials. A line of grav-sleds was waiting to take the survivors away. "Come with me, there is someone who has waited a long time to see you again."

In the tube-car, Mitsuharu closed his eyes—for just a moment—and fell sound asleep against the upholstered chair.

Tap-tap-tap went the blind man's bamboo cane on the side of the road, ticking against the mossy rocks laid at the border. Musashi was dozing, nearly asleep in the shelter of the little shrine. Rain was drumming on the slanted, tiled roof, but his head was dry on a bundle of cloth holding the rice-paper book he'd been so laboriously writing in. He opened one eye halfway as the shuffling mendicant ducked under the eaves. "Ah, pardon," wheezed a tired voice. "Just getting out of the rain."

"Welcome, brother," Musashi replied, moving his legs out of the way. Both shins were bound in bandages. "I'd offer you tea—if I had any—or a rice ball—if I had one. But I've neither, so you're welcome to the dry roof at least."

The blind man laughed, his stout face creasing into a merry smile. "The tamghachi *have left this whole province hungry—or so they tell me in the inns, when there is nothing to eat." He settled down on a little bench, head bowed over his cane.*

Outside, the drumming sound of the rain was supplemented—then replaced—by the rattle of hooves on the metaled road. At first one horse, then a dozen. "Hm." The blind man dug vigorously at one ear with a blunt finger. "Someone is coming in a great hurry. I wonder—could it be the militia? I've heard there is a murderer loose—he slew a tax collector some days ago."

OUTSIDE

The shuttle's cargo door swung up with a whine and spacers in white-and-brown z-suits helped Hadeishi and the remains of his crew out into a huge, brightly lit boat-bay. Mitsuharu looked over the faces of his men with a measuring eye. They were all bloody, bruised, and pale with exhaustion. *Some of these men have crewed three ships in this one venture.* In spite of the heavy losses, he felt great relief and pride at the spirit of his surviving crew. Not one of them seemed impressed by the shining new ship surrounding them, or the ranks of armored men arrayed across the floor of the bay. Enormous banners hung from the walls, showing a crimson cross on a white field. *And now another ship, another berth. Lost travelers on the road to the holy city, redeemed from bandits and rogues by the cross-men.* Then he caught sight of a familiar face and smiled broadly through the grease and carbon he knew crusted his face and helmet. "*Konnichi-wa, Sencho-sana.*"

Captain De Molay was waiting impatiently, arms crossed, one foot tapping on the deck. She was kitted out in the same white-and-brown space-armor as the ship's crew. Her rank insignia was quite polished; a squared cross crimson flamed on her breast. She saluted stiffly. *Wounds from the Khaiden ambush not yet mended.*

"*Chu-sa* Hadeishi, welcome aboard the *Pilgrim.*"

Mitsuharu nodded, and then returned the salute with a hand trembling with fatigue. "Our fortune improves. And my men?"

"We've taken almost sixty aboard already, and there are more on shuttles inbound." The elderly woman offered him a sombre expression. "*Our* medical facilities are first-rate."

"*Infirmus fui et visitastis me.*" Mitsuharu returned soberly.

De Molay stared at him in surprise, the corner of her mouth quirking into a smile. " 'I was sick and you visited me.' That is—"

"The twentieth rule," he said, nodding to the cross on her breastplate. "This is a strike-carrier of the Order of the Temple; I would say a refitted

across the mirror-bright floor. His good hand scrabbled wildly on the surface—then he tipped over the edge, just like Sahâne and the pilot.

The comm circuit cut off, leaving only Anderssen's harsh, bellowslike rasp echoing in her ears.

It's done. It's all done.

gasped. "I was used in turn, Doctor, by a *Senescalcus* of Templars. He—it—is stronger than I understood. It *pushed* my mind, sent me down this course—sent them along, the Knights, to ensure the message we heard from Piet's lips was delivered!"

Gretchen froze, a flash of memory resurfacing. *One survived. One still survives.*

Then she moved again, vastly relieved. The last shred of conscience which had lain upon her, holding back her fury, evaporated. Something in her expression must have transformed as well, for Hummingbird hissed in anger and darted away from her, trying to cut across the gap between the consoles and the pit. Anderssen leapt after him, feeling a joyful strength filling her body. She caught him two paces from the edge of the shaft, dodged past his outflung arm, and smashed the tool across his faceplate and shoulder. Sparks leapt back, the old man crashed to the floor, and atmosphere hissed, obscuring his faceplate.

"Ahhh!" His cry of pain echoed on her comm. Anderssen pounced, pinning him to the floor with one knee. The point of the tool ground against his armpit, tearing at the gel.

"Anderssen, please! Remember your family, remember they need you to come home—to provide for them! Isabelle, Tristan—they can still benefit—the *calmecac* schools *can* be moved to accept them. Ahhh!"

The spike punched through into his side, blood boiling away into vapor as it welled around the metal.

"There's nothing you can offer me, Crow, which will buy your life." Gretchen's voice was cold, her heart filling with a tremendous pressure as his face contorted behind the faceplate. "You can promise only ash and broken shells. Your gifts are only death and suffering—"

"Duncan," he gasped, trying to catch her eyes, his old face tight with terrible pain. "There are universities on Anáhuac who will still take him; he can be all you desired, you can—"

"My son is dead," she said, wrenching the field tool free and standing up. "My son *is dead.*"

Atmosphere hissed from the gaping wound. Hummingbird's faceplate frosted over and she could hear a tight, harsh gasp of pain over her comm. The *nauallis'* body jerked spasmodically, limbs stiffening. He tried to roll over, to get his feet beneath him. Gretchen took a step back, and then jammed her boot into the old man's side, sending him sliding

up, broken arm clutched against his thin chest. For the first time, she saw a glint of real fear in his limpid green eyes. The scarred, impassive face was suddenly showing signs of humanity. He scuttled back, finding himself caught in the wedge-shaped corner of two of the consoles.

"Doctor Anderssen, you know the kinds of things I must do. You know my purpose. I have never misled you about my aims. This place—"

"Is exactly the kind of trap you've always gone on about!" Gretchen snarled, circling to put herself between him and the stairs. "A fortune no one can spend, a tool no one dare wield. Do you grasp the enormity of what lies below us, incubating in the forge of creation? Do you know how long you would last under their influence?"

Hummingbird—sidling along the console—stopped, a questioning expression stealing over his scarred old features. "Do *you* know? Have you seen them, comprehended them?"

What? Oh Lady of the Seven Stars, he has no idea what is going on here! Anderssen hefted the field tool, finding a surety of purpose in the heavy, oiled metal. "Goddamned Crow, you didn't even know what you might unlock when you set the Prince against this place? What were you hoping to gain? The weapons technology behind the barrier of knives? Some fragments of the wisdom of the Vay'en themselves?"

"At the most," he said, voice settling into something like its old calm, "the annihilation of the Prince, the Khaid, even the poor Ambassador and my own life in the bargain. A clean set of books—nothing falling into the Emperor's hands to upset the balance at home—and *time*. Time we desperately need."

"Against what black day?" Gretchen eased closer, the tool raised, her eyes fixed on his midsection. "Opening this tomb door would vomit up the annihilation of our entire species—isn't that your eternal fear?— well, here you were right!"

She lunged again, snapping the tool around in a fast, sharp arc. Hummingbird bolted, twisting his shattered arm into the path of the spike. The point gouged into his z-suit, bouncing from a metal plate and snagging in the gel at the elbow. Gretchen wretched the tool away, but the *nauallis* slammed his working forearm into her faceplate, cracking a metal wristband against the glassite with a ringing blow. Stunned, Anderssen skipped back, desperate to retain her weapon.

"I never meant to wake the powers sleeping here!" Hummingbird

Templar turning towards her, assault rifle swinging up. It was Captain Locke. Gretchen swallowed against a dry, dry throat; a prayer to the Virgin of the Roses on her lips.

"Traitor—" Locke jerked as a very small hole appeared in his faceplate. Water vapor, blood, and atmosphere jetted out, condensing into dirty-red frost. The Templar pitched to one side, quite dead. Gretchen saw Hummingbird, one arm shattered, crouched at the edge of the platform, a tiny black gun in his hand.

"You do carry a pistol," Anderssen said, crawling towards him. She was feeling so very, very cold. Her med-band shone solid red. "I always knew you did."

"Not mine," Hummingbird wheezed, his pupils huge from the meds coursing through his system. Shaking, he tossed the pistol aside. The weapon clattered away, fetching up at the foot of one of the consoles. "There is a grav-sled below, Anderssen, we can—"

He stopped, suddenly apprehending the bleak expression on her face, the cold, lifeless light in her eyes as she staggered up on both feet. Her field tool was in one hand as she limped towards him, the trenching spike extended.

"You just saved my life, Crow, but we are *not even.*"

Alarmed, the *nauallis* edged away from her advance, barely able to crawl.

"You drew that damned bronze block across my path as a lure, letting the teacher inside infest my mind—you brought the Prince and Sahâne here against their will, just so you could cut out their hearts on this hell-bound altar—yes, a nice symmetry, bringing three keys to the doors of the tripartite temple." Her voice rose, ringing harshly on the suit-comm. "And you've your back up—these soldier-priests with their superb armor and unflinching resolve—but—by my eyes—they are *all dead* now, Crow, and only you and I are left."

"Anderssen!" Hummingbird's voice was ragged, but he managed something of his old strength. "Stop this foolishness! You need me to get out of here; we need each other to survive the next ten hours, we—"

"There is no *we!*" Gretchen lunged, slamming the field tool down at his face with a convulsive, rage-fueled stroke. The *nauallis* rolled away with a gasp at the last second, his face blanching white, and the pick screeched on the Vay'en metal of the floor. Hummingbird scrambled

a meter from Piet and Sahâne in a stunning blast of flame and armor-piercing shrapnel.

The Hjo bio-armor crumpled. Sahâne's helmet flew backward and the plasma-flare boiled the priest's flesh from his skull. The blast flung Piet and the corpse into the Thread. Like the bronze tablet, both Templar and Hjo were diced neatly in half before disappearing from sight.

The blast also slapped aside the other armored Templars. One hurled forward down the steps to crash into the Jaguar Knight in a tangle of arms and legs. The other slammed against the edge of a console, but bounced back, shaken but unharmed. The Templar vaulted the nearest control panel and skidded down the side of the pylon, showing fabulous dexterity in remaining upright. Two more marines opened fire on the Order Knight as he alighted, but neither was clad in battle armor.

Gretchen looked away as she heard the two Imperials die over the open circuit on her suit-comm. She clung by her fingernails to the base of the console, her feet dangling over a hundred-foot drop. Anderssen could see that the fight on the stairs was over, the remaining Templar having shattered Koris' faceplate and flung him aside. Anderssen pulled back from the edge of the platform, wheezing, her damaged z-suit once more hissing air. Lacking the time to fumble out another cylinder of quickseal, Gretchen dragged herself up to the viewing screen. The surface was undamaged, and a quick glance showed pulsating warning symbols surrounding a new control constellation. *An override,* she guessed, her hand poised over the half-understood symbology.

Is it right for me to make this choice, Gretchen's conscience ventured. *For an entire race? One I've observed only in fragmentary dreams and through teaching-illusions? Guided by an untested hypothesis which could be so, so wrong? . . .*

Lord Serpent stared back at her out of memory. A brilliant, golden glare of unfettered, unparalleled power. Brighter even than the plasma-blast incinerating its host. *Eat then, of the fruit of knowledge, and you shall know the truth.*

Anderssen's fingers moved on the console and the override blinked out.

The entire great machine groaned once more as the Thread whined to life. Far below, one structure rose, the other fell. Out of the corner of her eye, almost obscured by the helmet, she caught a glimpse of the last

"All," Hummingbird interjected very smoothly, before Piet could answer, "seek Guidance."

"Then what can I do?" Sahâne's nervousness was palpable.

Anderssen took his hand, feeling a cool shock as her fingers passed through the aura of glyphs surrounding the young alien. "We will move these constellations like . . . so . . ."

Codes unlocked at the priest's touch and the great machine trembled awake. The Thread emitted an audible wail. Enormous energies, long held in abeyance, were released. Mechanisms spun to life, twisting the pattern of space, dragging at infinity like Herakles against the Promethean chain.

Gretchen heard someone's swift, measured breathing rasp on her suit comm and the soft clink of metal on metal.

We're out of time.

Far far below, at the mouth of the abyss, two structures moved—one up, one down. The consoles flared alight with warnings, flashing glyphs and symbols of all kinds. Sahâne goggled at the displays, dark eyes filled with the hot glow of the lights. Simultaneously, his exo bleated a warning just as Anderssen's fingertips—no more than a millimeter from his body—*adjusted* the drifting pattern of glyphs which controlled the alien's body armor. The z-suit helmet suddenly detached with a *thonk!* as the retaining ring popped loose. The Hjo screamed, clawing at his neckring—atmosphere warmer than the sub-freezing atmosphere in the chamber rushed out, frosting the inside of his helmet solid white.

Her blood surging with adrenaline, Anderssen took the first chance for protection and heaved herself over the console just as Löjtnant Piet, shouting in alarm, lunged forward to catch Sahâne. The other two Templars turned hastily towards the near stairway, their guns coming up. Hummingbird hurled himself to one side, but too late as they both squeezed off a burst. Flechettes pocked the *nauallis'* chest and shoulder, punching him back. His footing lost, Hummingbird toppled down the steps, directly past the Jaguar Knight crouching at the edge of the platform.

Koris sidestepped the Judge nimbly. One powerful arm pitched a bundle of short-fuse grenades onto the platform. Löjtnant Piet turned awkwardly, Sahâne's armored body clutched to his chest. The Hjo's z-suit was rippling into spiked bio-armor while his clawlike hands struggled to replace the helmet. The grenade-bundle exploded less than

THE THREAD

Gretchen turned to Sahâne, her hands light on the console, fingertips floating a millimeter over the softly glowing hieroglyphs. "Holy One, it is blasphemy for me to complete this task. This is the abode of your Gods and you are their priest. Stand by me, give me your blessing, and I will rouse them from the long sleep. Let them guide your people again, if they wish."

The Hjo goggled at her; suspicion, fear, and slowly growing wonder lighted his eyes. "You lie, toy. You will . . . you will . . . what *will* you do?"

"Look around, Holy one. You saw the bodies of the fallen at the last door. The Guard Imperial fell here—to the last man—defending this place. The enemies of your people could not pass that portal, not against their sacrifice. The traitors fled, unable to reach this"—once more she spread her arms, taking in the entire panorama of the accretion disk, the pylon, and the endless rows of cradles—"sanctuary." She leaned towards him, voice fading to barely a whisper.

Almost against his will, Sahâne stepped within an arm's reach. Gretchen continued. "But your Gods *did not die*. They are sleeping far below. Those Hjo who remained faithful to the end did that much. They sent the Wise One to safety."

Sahâne's fur rippled erect. His voice was hushed, barely audible even over the comm. "He . . . he is here?"

Anderssen met his eyes and nodded assent. "Why else should the Banner Crimson and Black fly *here*, save he was present?" *And perhaps he was,* she thought, remembering the Lord Serpent. *Perhaps he was.* "Will you help me lift him up, into the land of the living?" She tilted her head towards Löjtnant Piet. "Their message is for *him*, you know. They seek *his* help, to be guided, as The People are guided."

Sahâne looked at Piet in puzzlement, and then he nodded as understanding slowly took hold. "I . . . I see. I did not know—that you believed as we believe."

In the threatwell, the *Chimalacatl* loomed, growing steadily larger with every passing second.

"Up speed a quarter-point," she spoke sharply at Olin, startling the México officer. "*Sho-sa*, prepare a combat team—if any of our marines are left alive—for a boarding action."

No one is going to miss a spare Judge amid all this slaughter. No one.

"Time to safety limit?" Koshō felt a great lightness steal over her as the *Naniwa* slipped past the last of the gargantuan wrecks. They were once more in open space, with nothing between her battle-cruiser and the distant speck of the artifact but vacuum. Somewhere ahead the ionized clouds of two *Hayalet*-class battleships marked the edge of the thread-weapon guarding the Sunflower. She hoped they would be able to use that—somehow—to their advantage in dealing with the rest of the Khaid. Her attention snapped to Helsdon, who was still crouched over his consoles, stylus tapping intermittently as he tried to tune the sensor array to detect the quantum distortions caused by the alien weapon.

Her other earbug was filled with bursts of chatter from out-system, where Pucatli's sensor booms were trying to capture and decipher the enemy battlecast.

"The Khaid have counterattacked," Oc Chac reported. He, too, was watching the sensor plot closely.

Thai-i Olin laughed nastily. "If what I've heard is true, these Maltese would match Xipe himself in flaying them to the bone."

"The Khaid assault anyone who assaults them," Susan replied softly, her mind filled with disquiet. "They are ambitious. Destroying even one Order ship would win the survivors enough respect among the *Kovan* planets and stations." *Those men on the little ship,* she suddenly realized, *were Order Knights. The* Moulins . . . *Hummingbird arranged all this!*

An instant of pure fury was ruthlessly suppressed. Susan breathed in sharply, steadying herself. *Hummingbird arranged everything. Even the Khaid. Everything. The deaths of all those Mirror scientists and their support ships. He used me. He even used Sayu! Gods of mountain and stream, his ambition is without limit! He's traded an entire Fleet battle-group— all of my dead crew—a super-dreadnaught fresh from the yards for that thing.*

Yielding to chaos. But still, neither set of control symbols would move. *The controls are jammed,* she realized with a sinking feeling. Her focus turned to the second set.

This is birth; borrowed memory told her, *rejuvenation.* Images of a blossoming flower invaded her vision—opening, wilting, dying, budding, opening, wilting—*no, not just any bloom, but a perennial. But why—*

Gretchen grasped the totality of the puzzle in one shining instant. Many details were lacking, but the shattered pot suddenly fell together in her hands. *What cold calculating horror.* She knew what must be done. *Hummingbird is going to be displeased with me.*

Anderssen laughed aloud, drawing a strained look from everyone arrayed around her.

No, old Crow, I won't tell you what I'm going to do. Not now, not ever again.

She suppressed a start of alarm when the still-open secondary comm channel squeaked in her ear. *Oh oh, not much time left!* Rubbing her gloves together, Anderssen placed her hands on the console.

The control surfaces gleamed like water under her touch. The glyphs swam to and fro in her unsteady vision. She closed both eyes, letting her mind grow quiet, feeling the pattern of the ancient machinery radiating against her outstretched hands. *Somewhere here . . .*

"This is truly a construct of the Vay'en?" Hummingbird's voice was reasonable, quiet, and far distant from her hurrying, busy thoughts. "A curious turn, to find the Hjogadim here in such numbers. . . ."

"I do not know of these *Vahyyyen*," Sahâne replied testily. "My people built this fastness long ago, for our signs and symbols are everywhere. Even the passage-signs are in archaic Hjogadim, just as you might read in the Perfect Path. You trespass! This female of yours cannot have the first conception of how to—"

Gretchen moved along the control surface, following fragmentary memories, until a collection of glyphs under her hands suddenly felt *incorrect.*

A constellation of meanings, she perceived, *where specific arrangements of the glyphs equal actions. Not verbs and nouns, but hieroglyphs. Like in the transit core outside.* She adjusted two of the outermost symbols, letting them flow under her fingertips into their long-accustomed, proper orientation.

A rippling groan permeated the air, rising up from the floor below the pylon. Everyone tensed, but nothing happened immediately. Anderssen craned her neck over the edge to see that the endless rows of cradles had tilted upright. Their restraining wings were unfolding. *Ready for the next fifty thousand passengers!*

"I did that," she said idly to the onlookers. Then she returned to letting her awareness expand and hoped against hope to grasp the meaning of these . . . *That is odd.* Two whole sequences of the controls were suddenly and clearly out of joint. *These feel . . . stuck.* She tried to move them back into what was so-obviously their proper configuration. Intermittent thought-images from her gold-tinged dreams surfaced, colliding with the glyphs on the control surface, but yielding faint guidance to her. *Yes, this first is a control constellation which means death. Transfiguration.*

dead, taking them away to be properly disposed of . . . A frown creased her forehead. *But not by the great doors? Wouldn't they . . . ah, but everything there is in a great untidy pile. Collected by the automated janitors, for something else, something larger to take away. But it couldn't? Because the doors were locked tight, sealed. . . .* She suppressed an automatic reaction to look around the platform for the corpse of the last technician, the one that had sealed the doors, trapping himself inside, and then expired in due time. *Not here, not here . . . some chamber where he'd cached a bit of food and water, until he knew the tomb was forgotten and no one would return.*

So, treachery. *Battle and slaughter in the midst of the great undertaking. Millions of stasis racks, all empty. Storage for the bodies drained of guiding flame. Waiting for their masters—their operators?—to return. . . .*

Gretchen's tongue awoke. "I don't think you want him to do *anything* with that console, Löjtnant Piet."

The pilot turned, politely curious.

"His race views ours as *slaves* and *toys*. I do not think the honorable Lord Sahâne will treat us kindly once he's figured out how to work the controls of this fortress." She forced a grin. "I think war-machines will come and we will all die. And then *he* will be in control of this place, and all that it contains."

Piet stared first at her, then at Hummingbird, and finally at Sahâne. Gretchen was woefully aware of his sudden confusion, and fear, and the absolute depth of his ignorance. *If a penny will not do, then a pound must suffice.* She coughed wetly. "We don't have much time, but I think I can deliver your message to his Gods—to the Vay'en who are sleeping far below us, in the singularity." Another cough, this one unforced. "Even without the bronze tablet."

Sahâne's eyes were black as ink, his long face unreadable.

Piet blinked at Gretchen, and then eyed Sahâne suspiciously. Nodding, he raised his weapon. "Away from the console, creature."

The Hjogadim moved back, slender hands raised.

"And him, too, get *him* away from *everything*," Gretchen said, feeling her weakness returning, indicating Hummingbird with a tilt of her helmet. "You mustn't trust him *at all*."

The Templars were quick to action. They forced the *nauallis* away, to the top of the steps. Hummingbird went without complaint, though his eyes were fixed on Anderssen, his entire body tensed.

could anything have survived that plasma blast? She turned in amazement to get a better look. But the apparition was already gone. The ghost-world was fading now, consumed by the chaos of ancient battle. Too many fleeting events to leave a lasting mark on the substance of the consoles or the time-worn floor. Only one last glimpse of the Lord Serpent wicking through the air as a burning ribbon. Then it plunged into the cowering body of a still-living blue-black technician.

In a last burst of memory, the slim, now-radiant alien escaped over the edge of the pylon.

A vampire. Gretchen realized, falling back into the waking world, her limbs clammy with shock. *A parasite of some kind, that . . . something like that was in the tablet! It was controlling me, guiding my mind! Xochitl was right—and there are hundreds of thousands more of them, down there, in the abyss . . . the deities of the Hjogadim.*

"I will say these words, to the Gods," Sahâne announced, breaking her train of thought. The priest made an elegant, human-style bow. "If you give me leave to do so."

The three Templars shared a glance and nodded, almost as one. Piet gestured with his assault rifle, pointing Sahâne towards the nearest console. "Waste no time, then."

Gretchen watched curiously as the Hjo paced deliberately to the largest, most centrally located console and then pressed fingertips to forebrain, a swift, mumbled litany on his lips. *What is he? . . .* Anderssen felt suddenly the fool. Her ghost-sight quickened, and she saw the air around Sahâne come alive with flickering glyphs and signs. *His masks are on overdrive and—spouting nonsense? They must be trying to decipher the control systems . . . but are too new to understand these older mechanisms.*

Despite the confusion of symbols, the subaudible hum in the floor changed pitch. At once the consoles flickered awake, glowing with dappled green and gold. The air in the enormous chamber stirred. Long lines of lamps began to shine among the abandoned cradles. Anderssen crawled to the nearest panel and felt it becoming aware under her hands, waiting for guidance. She realized that despite the echoes of destruction reverberating in the ghost-world, the gargantuan machine around her was intact and functioning.

Automated maintenance, she guessed. *Little bots or nanites always working to clean and fix and repair . . . gathering up the bodies of the*

THE PYLON

Gretchen flinched away from a sudden, titanic plasma blast. The air erupted with blinding flame and a whirlwind of shrapnel. She lost her balance, teetering at the edge of the platform. Both Piet and Hummingbird lunged forward, gloved hands seizing her arms. Only then did she realize the burning cloud was passing through the two of them without harm. Eons in the past, the technicians at the consoles were strewn about like matchsticks. The mighty Hjogadim Lord burned like a torch while the golden serpent suddenly, violently, escaped from its physicality. The great hall, to its farthest corners, boiled with unforeseen catastrophe.

Anderssen blinked tears from her eyes, trying to focus on the present. Meanwhile, Piet had torn away her utility rig and was digging through the pockets.

"I saw her stash it . . . back in the ship," his voice rasped over the comm. "It must be here somewhere!"

"It is gone," Sahâne barked in amusement. The Hjogadim gestured towards the shaft. "Cast into the abyss."

Piet glared at the alien. "Then you will serve in her place."

Sahâne nodded and rose to his feet, helped by one of the other Templars. To Gretchen it was plain that something in the Hjo had found surety at last, banishing his chronic fear. "What will you have me say?"

Confused, Gretchen eyed the Europeans, Hummingbird, and the alien. *A message? To the dead? No . . . to those sleeping below? But they cannot hear us—not without a Voice—uh oh . . .*

Piet paused, squaring his shoulders, and then recited: "That we await their coming and are prepared to aid, as did their servants of old. That we pledge true service, where so many failed them before. That we have need, for a great peril will soon return."

Sahâne's snout twitched in amusement, but he nodded.

Out of the corner of her eye, Gretchen caught a glimpse of a thin blue-black furred shape shrouding the pilot like a ghostly cloak. *How*

Hadeishi felt his skin burning painfully from residual heat the z-suit could not disperse and gasped, blinded by even the microsecond of exposure to the antimatter reactor annihilating itself. When his vision cleared, the compartment was filled with drifting corpses, the walls discolored by the blast of radiation.

"Report," he croaked, "any survivors, report!"

For a minute, or more, there was silence—stunned, wordless silence—but he could hear someone breathing harshly. Then a handful of voices babbled back, reporting status of their teams and their compartments.

"*Chu-sa*, what happened?" Cajeme's voice was suddenly clear and sharp; and the thought of the little Yaqui's survival released a tiny fraction of the bone-crushing despair Mitsuharu had been struggling to wade through.

"A *Neshter*-class destroyer," Hadeishi managed to croak out, "blew to atoms within visual of us. I do not know why, or how, but nothing else has hit us in the last sixty seconds, so I claim victory."

"No, *Chu-sa*," worried voices replied. "It's been quiet on either side of us for maybe five minutes."

Just as Hadeishi thumbed the all-channel push control on his z-suit comm, the partially open bay doors flared into a white-hot bar. The debris cloud outside was ionizing as a particle beam ripped across the surface of the *Kader*. The impact reverberated through the frame of the ship seconds later, transmitting itself to Mitsuharu as a keening shriek rising from his boot-soles. Screams on the comm channels were snuffed out abruptly as the beam punched through the central ring of the cruiser.

The boat-bay doors crumpled as the primary hull twisted, suddenly torqued by a series of explosive blasts. Hadeishi dropped to the floor, crouching over Lovelace's body, and felt the walls and floor ripple. Glassite shattered as the boat-bay windows tore from their frames. A second colossal impact followed as a shipkiller rammed into the gap torn by the particle beam. The missile vented plasma into the shipcore, immolating the dozens of Imperials still trapped within the secondary hull.

The concussive wave transmitted to the primary hull as well, tearing the bay doors away entirely. The old cruiser split open, though Mitsuharu knew only that he and Lovelace were thrown against the far wall of the compartment along with everyone else in the makeshift med-bay. Cries of agony filled his ears, but the *Chu-sa*'s attention was fixed on the violently glowing dust-clouds now visible through the gaping hole where the boat bay had been. What tiny bit of atmosphere had remained in the management compartment now vented out into hard vacuum, crystallizing as frost on their suits.

Hadeishi's suit visor flickered, trying to focus on the abyss outside, then suddenly picked out—and enhanced—the outline of a Khaid destroyer sliding past at ten thousand kilometers, a long black shape with a blue-white flare where the drive nacelles were burning at one-quarter power. The first thing springing to mind was the image of a missile hatch cycling open as he watched . . .

"We've got to get out"—he forced himself away from the wall, one arm snaking behind Lovelace's shoulders to pull her with him—"of here."

Before he could drag her away a stabbing white glare flooded the compartment, momentarily polarizing Hadeishi's visor to black.

"What is—" someone shouted on the channel, before being drowned out by a tidal wave of static.

garbage as could be found through the doors to discourage the Khaid from trying to land in them.

Lovelace was tacked to the floor, her body wrapped in a survival blanket, leaving only the status readouts of her z-suit visible. Her rounded face was pale behind the faceplate, eyes closed. On her wrist, the med-band was a softly glowing bracelet of amber and green.

"Not dead yet," Mitsuharu said softly, squinting at the tiny readout. "But you're not going to last without proper facilities."

"Sorry, *kyo*." The Mirror Comms officer's voice was a broken rasp. "They sealed the hull splinter in with me, but I can feel the knife twisting when I breathe."

"Don't talk then." Hadeishi sat, his back against the wall, her wrist held lightly between thumb and forefinger. "We've all run out of time in any case. And the Khaid are sadly lacking in regen pods. They don't eat their own dead, but do employ a species of shipbug blessed by their priests for the very purpose."

"I taste terrible," the girl said; her voice very, very faint.

Mitsuharu nodded, watching her respiration flutter. The pale blue light of the glowbeans painted her cheekbones a deathly hue. "I'm sure you do, *Sho-i*. It was an honor to serve with you. I am sorry I did not listen—you tried to keep me from this fool's errand."

"We—" A bubbling wheeze stopped her for a moment, but then she managed to say: "We were dead if we tried to run out past those two destroyers. You bought us another sixteen hours, at least."

I did that, he thought. *To no good end, save to bring down a few more Khaid before the black sea takes us all.*

One of the lights on her med-band began to pulse red. Feeling a terrible sense of *déjà vu*, he gently dialed the band to send the Comms officer unconscious. *Plum petals are falling, sickle moon sharp as—*

The poem faltered in his memory, the pace and tenor of the chatter and background noise on his comm suddenly changing. Hadeishi looked away from Lovelace, eyes closed, letting the voices of his men, his subcommanders, the sound and feel of the ship penetrating his back, his hands, the soles of his feet wash over him. On one of the channels, Tocoztic's familiar voice—his breathing labored—said: "Is this getting easier, or is it my imagination?"

Mitsuharu stiffened, rising from the floor. "All units report. Are you currently in contact with the enemy?"

six of them ripping loose with suppressive fire to shred the ceiling tiles and shatter the remaining lights. The vanguard loped forward, looking to clear the "ambush" zone, while the rear-guard fell back to the closest intersection, ensuring their line of retreat was secured.

Hadeishi popped up as the lead Khaid sprang past a fallen beam, and the *Yilan* tucked into his shoulder stuttered, flash-suppressor spitting flame in a brief, brilliant cross. At point-blank range, the armor-piercing munitions tore up the chest, faceplate, and shoulder of the hunter's armor, knocking him back into the Khaid following behind. The other Imperials also let loose, all fire concentrated on the same lead figure. By the time the hunter had collided with his companions, the armor had been punctured twice by the hundreds of rounds and he drifted limply away.

"Go!" Mitsuharu barked, ducking back. One of his men tossed a grenade—their last—into the midst of the enemy vanguard and then kicked off, sailing down their escape route. The other Imperials were already gone as the grenade cooked off in a sharp, hot blast. The Khaid hunters were thrown back by the pressure wave, but it was an even chance any of them suffered any lasting damage. Their armor was too tough for the lightweight weapons Hadeishi's crew had managed to scavenge. The blast did collapse the roof, however, which had already been weakened by an engineering crew.

The spitting howl of a squad support weapon replied—Mitsuharu didn't remember the code-name assigned by Fleet intelligence—but the flechettes tore a horizontal gap across the fallen debris and hot sparks chased him down the hallway.

Twenty minutes later, the *Chu-sa* ducked under a haphazardly strung line of glowbeans and went to one knee, his face seamed with worry. The main med-bay had been abandoned an hour ago, when the Khaid attack into the shipcore had focused on the secondary command ring, which also held the medical section. The surviving Imperials needing a corpsman—and there were many now—had been hauled out by grav-sled or z-line to the armored compartment managing the boat and cargo bays in the primary hull, which had escaped the initial assault. On a properly equipped Fleet ship, Hadeishi might have had one or two spare shuttles tucked away in the boat bays. But the *Kader* had nothing spare, so they'd cut power to the bays and vented as much debris and

THE KADER

Humanoid shapes moved abruptly in the shadows, armor glinting in the intermittent strobe of emergency lights. Some sections of the old *Spear*-class cruiser had their own generators to run critical subsystems, which meant there were pockets of atmosphere and occasional overheads still working. Hadeishi was crouched down behind a shattered section of interior wall, watching the advance of the enemy through a remote v-eye tucked into a dead lighting socket. A good dozen Khaid marines were leapfrogging up the main corridor into the habitat ring, five of the aliens in powered armor in the lead. Mitsuharu guessed they were a combat team detached from the main body of the attackers, who had managed to fight their way into the shipcore.

The Nisei officer turned, signing *Stand by* to the four Imperials behind him with their motley assortment of weapons. When he checked the v-eye again, the Khaid were shifting smoothly from door to bulkhead frame to door, their heavy shipguns shining oily in the flickering light.

Now. Hadeishi flashed a quick sign, and then tripped the switch on a portable fuel-cell generator they'd lugged down from the Command ring. Electrons flooded the local circuits and every light and door activated. The room hatches being forced by the Khaid suddenly cycled open, sending at least one of the invaders sprawling into the compartment beyond. The overheads flared to life, shedding a bright warm glow over the wreckage strewn along the corridor. The Khaiden marines swiveled, guns quartering the nearest openings—and found nothing. Their advance paused for an instant as each hunter assessed every possible threat within his field of view.

Heated to flashpoint by the lights in the overheads, twenty or thirty pounds of fuse paper—all they had left from the landing site clearing supplies the Khaid had been dragging around—ignited with a rippling *bang-bang-bang* and the overhead panels popped free, swinging wildly in the oozing clouds of smoke. The Khaiden marines reacted violently,

line of metrics displayed on the console. "I've seen that kind of signature once before, *Sho-sa*, but not in such numbers. This is something like a Maltese assault carrier launching its complement. But I've never heard the Knights had something which could simultaneously deploy over three hundred fighters!"

"Don't know, *kyo*." Pucatli grimaced, indicating the flood of contacts now racing across the plot. "But they're at high-v and rolling right down the drive plume laid by the Khaid battlegroup!"

"Huh!" Koshō's attention switched to the Khaid light cruiser, which had suddenly exposed a pinpoint hot-spot on its shipskin. "We're in line with a comm laser?"

Oc Chac nodded, keying up a directional indicator. "Snap transmit to the main fleet, *Chu-sa*, but see—it's already too late."

A brace of drive signatures suddenly flickered into view on the telemetry; ships a fraction the size of the Khaid light cruiser racing past the long black hull, and then the stuttering flare of shipkiller detonations rippled from one end of the warship to the other. In the remote's camera view, a flurry of white-hot pinpoints appeared in the darkness and then the bright, sudden blossom of the cruiser's containment failing enveloped the ship.

The tiny ships had already vanished, just before the remote's telemetry stopped cold.

"They found our remote, too." Susan clasped her hands behind her back, teeth clicking thoughtfully. "*Sho-sa*, did you notice how well shielded their drives are? Like ghosts . . ."

The Mayan barked a hoarse, exhausted laugh. "Like they weren't even *there*, *Chu-sa*. Until they were on that cruiser and firing."

"*Kyo?*"

Susan opened her eyes, alarmed that she'd fallen asleep in her shockchair. Oc Chac and Pucatli were at the Comms console, and the *Sho-sa* seemed quite agitated.

"What has happened?" Koshō sat up, feeling every bone and sinew complain.

"Our remote at the Pinhole is gone." Pucatli shook his head in disgust. "We've some telemetry from the aperture right before we lost contact, but it makes no sense."

"Show me." Susan rolled her neck and flexed her fingers, trying to force some warmth back into them. Secondary Command seemed to have lost pressure and temperature control while she'd been sleeping. Oc Chac rotated a large v-pane towards her, and then tapped up a series of glyphs to replay the feed.

"We'd picked up what seems to be a Khaid light cruiser about sixty minutes ago." The Mayan's stylus indicated a faint outline against the riot of color glowing from the Barrier clouds. "Lying dark, under full emissions control. Watching the back trail of the main squadron, of course. Doing a good job, too—the *Thai-i* only caught him out by replaying the gravity plot from our passage through the region."

Oc Chac patted Pucatli on the shoulder. "Then we get a gravity-spike from the Pinhole—see, here? Massing like a dreadnaught, *kyo*. As though the *Tlemitl* picked herself up and came after us. But then—wait, I'll rewind again." Susan had started, watching the emissions signature on the plot suddenly break apart.

"Not one ship, but hundreds of smaller ones." The *Sho-sa* shook his head in puzzlement. "Look at all the drive flares! Like they came in packed together, then deployed in a cloudburst. We're still crunching the signatures in comp, trying to match a known profile but—"

Susan's eyes narrowed in speculation, a fingertip drifting across a

Gretchen managed a sickly grin, and on the other side of the shaft, Sahâne made a barking sound like a dog choking on a too-large bone. *Was that laughter?*

"Tablet?" she said innocently. "I don't have any tablet."

Piet went quite still. Hummingbird's eyes did not leave her face, but they grew large with surprise.

platform, tattered brown cloak drifting behind him. "Particularly now that the Prince is dead. You will need this Hjogadim to explain why Xochitl had to be killed. The Grand Master will want to know the *Tlatocapilli* was sent to seize this place for the Empire in defiance of the Pact."

Three black-snouted rifles swung 'round, fixing on the old man. The *nauallis* nodded genially to the Templars. "Though my lord Sahâne is entirely competent for the task at hand, Miss Anderssen has your master's tablet in her safekeeping. Help her to a console, if you will."

That's Mrs. *Anderssen to you, Crow,* Gretchen thought blackly, refusing to budge from the nice comfortable floor even when the tangleweb strands were cut away. Hummingbird and the wavering ghost-image of the serpent-headed Hjogadim Lord interpenetrated in her Sight. At that moment she perceived they were cut much of the same cloth, though they stood millennia apart. *Equally calculating and barren of compassion, using entire civilizations as their . . . what did Sahâne call us? As their toys?*

Piet reached down and dragged her up, grimacing at the ruin of her chestplate, now bubbled shut with quickseal foam. "She's been shot," he said in an annoyed snarl.

Hummingbird was at Gretchen's side in an instant. He gently prodded at her z-suit, checking the med readout. She met his gaze with a cold, angry stare. He drew back minutely. She felt his thumb, hidden under her arm, adjusting the channel on her suit comm.

"I'm sorry, Anderssen," he said, face turned away from the three Europeans. "But these men have not the least respect for my authority."

"I'll bet," Gretchen growled, feeling faint. The ghostly Hjogadim lord was stalking amongst his servants, and the entire great chamber was lit from below by a wavering bronze-colored fire. Even without looking over the edge, she knew every Hjo body in every cradle was yielding up its guest, a serpentine ribbon of living flame, all of them flowing into the thread leading down into the singularity. "That was a dirty trick with the tablet. . . ."

"I warned you the first time we met," Hummingbird said, voice tinged with melancholy. "There are many things best left undisturbed."

"Will she live?" Piet broke in, leaning over the old man's shoulder.

"She will," Hummingbird said. Gretchen realized he had switched the comm channel back. "But she is badly wounded. . . ."

"Give me the Old One's tablet, then," the pilot said eagerly. "I can serve as his messenger, if she cannot."

one could react, exploded. A web of glittering silver filaments sprayed out, tangling Gretchen, Sahâne, and the Prince. Xochitl cursed in two languages as he struggled to draw a monofilament knife.

The gray-eyed navigator from the *Moulins* appeared in Gretchen's field of view. Absurdly, she was relieved to see no trace of a golden glow emanating from his helmet. *A regular old human, thank Christ the Sacrifice!*

Piet gave her an evaluating look, swinging a short-barreled assault rifle in her direction, but when his eyes fell upon the México—still struggling to cut away the webbing—his face contorted into open hatred and the Frisian squeezed off a burst into the Prince's faceplate. At such short range Xochitl's glassite faceplate shattered as the armor-piercing rounds struck, spraying blood across Sahâne's helmet. The Prince's corpse contorted violently, but the México's last movements barely moved the tangleweb. The Hjo squealed, as though he were the one who had been murdered. Gretchen felt a paralyzing shock run through her body.

That was as cold and calculated an execution as I ever pray to see.

Two more crewmen from the *Moulins* appeared. They quartered the platform, checking the bodies of the fallen marines in a business like way. Their battle-armor was scarred and pitted, but seemed to have held up far better than that of the dead Imperials. Their insignia—a red cross formed of three smaller crosses surmounting a descending spike— gleamed hot in the pale light of the accretion jet. Now, seeing them in motion with arms, armor, and heraldry revealed, Anderssen grasped who they were: *Knights of the Order of the Temple of Jerusalem—the Templars of New Malta! But—they're allies of the Empire, servants of the Emperor—aren't they?*

Though her abdomen was beginning to warm, her z-suit working overtime to replace the heat lost through the punctured chestplate, she felt a chill memory surface. *The Jehanan warred upon one another, each clan seeking to seize the false secrets of the* Kalpataru *for themselves, and so their unity was destroyed and—in time—their civilization fell into ruin, burned away by thermonuclear fire.*

"Which one do we need?" Piet inquired of his companions. His rifle muzzle indicated Gretchen and Sahâne in turn. "Her . . . or him?"

"I suggest you keep both of them alive," the voice of Green Hummingbird urged over the comm. The old Nahuatl stepped up onto the

the intersections between the triangular sectors. The hiss of her suit atmosphere escaping failed to register upon Anderssen's conscious mind. Despite the cold pricking her chest as her clothing turned brittle in the near-zero atmosphere, Gretchen crawled unhindered to the edge of the shaft at the center of the pylon.

Far below, the singularity swelled in her sight: a pulsating void streaked with fire as a constant, thin stream of matter plunged down to annihilation. The Thread descended beyond the limit of her sight, a cable of nine atoms stretched enormously thin, forming an unbreakable path into the abyss. The wavering mercury-sheen of some kind of force field blocked the full glare of annihilation from blinding her. *Is this their heaven? They are below, somewhere between here and the event horizon. Millions of them, basking in the crucible of creation—are they healing? Giving birth to a whole new generation? Sleeping until it is time to wake again? Is this a natural cycle? A serpent's egg warmed by the cascade of dying mass from three carefully-balanced suns?*

The stuttering roar of an assault rifle firing wildly only meters away broke her concentration. Gretchen scrambled back into the shelter of a console, gasping as bones ground raw in her chest and side. A Fleet marine staggered across her field of view, blood hissing to vapor from rents in his armor. Across the gaping maw of the shaft, she saw Prince Xochitl and Sahâne crouched behind another console. The Prince's attention was on his attackers, his visage grim, teeth bared in a snarl of defiance. As she watched, he ejected an ammunition spool from his rifle and slammed in a fresh one. The Hjogadim, its long snout wrinkled up in fear, stared wide-eyed across at Gretchen. *Is he capable of pleading for mercy?*

A priest, she remembered. *Like those toiling on the field of abandoned husks below. But that isn't right . . . a technician. A medical technician?*

Xochitl nosed his rifle around the corner of the console and squeezed off a burst of flechettes in the direction of the stair.

But the cubbyholes in the halls were all empty, Anderssen thought, her mind drawn inexorably back to the puzzle at hand. Wheezing, she lay back and fumbled quickseal from a thigh pocket. Even in her elevated state, she could now feel bitter cold biting at her heart. *Where did all the Hjo bodies . . . oh, the garbage disposal port. Outside, then, and into the maw of the black hole. Discarded servants.*

A little black cylinder bounced up onto the platform and before any-

THE PYLON OF THOUGHT

Burning shapes impressed themselves upon Gretchen's perception, even with her eyes squeezed tightly closed, even without the power of the bronzed tablet flowing through her nervous system. A shining rainbow streak coiled around the Thread tethered at the center of the shaft. The low consoles and the floor itself were filled with quiescent corkscrewlike patterns of brass and silver. Far above, the roof of the enormous room was flowing with filmy curlicues drawn in white, rose, and violet. Dimly, she felt these were the sleeping patterns of control systems, comp nodes, and other undecipherable systems.

In her ghost-sight, the phantasmal bodies of uniformed Hjogadim congealed from the air, busy at the control consoles on either side of the platform. There were other beings with them—slighter of form, indigo-blue-pelted, with thin, ancient-seeming faces and depthless eyes. These creatures stood apart from the Hjo operators though they were intensely focused on the work underway.

Are those the Vay'en themselves? she wondered for an instant, before *something else* climbed onto the platform. The powerfully built physicality of the Hjogadim was barely visible as a vaporous skeleton. The organic frame was obscured by the scintillating golden glare of *something* coiled at the top of the inhuman spine.

A serpent of fire, was the first image springing to mind. *Naga-kanya, the bringer of wisdom. Where are the five heads?*

The crack of assault rifles and the darting transparencies of the Prince's marines were ephemeral to her. The shapes of the ancient past were far, far clearer. She rolled to her knees, taking in the valley-sized chamber below in one sweeping glance. Hundreds of thousands of ancient ghosts thronged the rows of platforms. Countless golden-haloed Hjogadim lay within the crystalline cradles, while swarms of slightly built blue-black creatures tended to the machines. Platoons of armored Hjo—massive in powered red-and-black battle armor—stood ready at

He's ejected pods, she thought, feeling an enormous distance open in her heart. *Reactors are offline. She's just scrap metal now, falling into infinity. Not even worth—*

The two Khaid destroyers cut their drives as well, and on the plot, the paths of the three vessels began to converge.

"Why are—" Pucatli fell silent, seeing that Oc Chac was nodding to himself.

The Mayan scratched at a tiny fringe of beard he'd started to accumulate. "The coil on that ship might still be intact, *Thai-i,* and her reactors are still working—even if they've had to shut them down. Some quick work by the engineers on those two *Mishrak*-class boats might salvage the whole ship. No reason to waste a shipkiller *and* a working starship."

Oc Chac looked to Koshō, a speculative expression on his face. "And the captains of those two destroyers haven't read *Chu-sa* Hadeishi's service jacket, have they?"

"No." Susan sat up, feeling an enormous, crushing weight begin to dissipate. "They have no idea the evacuation pods are empty. No idea at all."

Then she scowled forbiddingly at the *Sho-sa* and the rest of the crew. "Back to work! We need our drives back on line, missile racks refreshed, guns working!" She clapped her hands sharply, making a fierce explosive sound that made everyone in Secondary jump in alarm. "*Banzai!*"

The pilot shrugged. "No guarantees, *kyo*. Comp has tagged this one"—he highlighted one of the icons—"As the *Kartal*—an *Aslan*-class heavy cruiser—and presumably the Flag for the remains of their squadron. She's building vector away from the *Chimalacatl* and away from us. The others might be converging on her, but there's no guarantee yet."

Koshō nodded, considering the dimensional model herself. After a minute, she said: "They may have found the chase too hot to follow—or they may be resolving internal differences of *surtu* hierarchy. Set course for the Sunflower—but keep us well back from the destruction point of those two Khaid ships."

Then she smiled tightly at Helsdon, who had looked up from his console for a moment.

Blanching, he set himself to work again.

"*Kyo*?" Pucatli looked up from the Comms console, where he was sharing space with the duty officer. "We've synched a channel to the remote at the Pinhole. You should see this . . ."

Susan tapped up the feed on her own console and pursed her lips, whistling in surprise. The relay telemetry showed three ships erupting from the aperture, engaged in a long-distance missile duel. All three of them popped up on the display with the familiar collection of Khaid glyphs. The pursued—a light cruiser tagged "*Kader*" by shipnet from the 'cast traffic they'd captured during the initial fighting—was taking a beating, shedding a coiling cloud of debris and weaving drunkenly. In comparison, the two pursuers seemed sleek and fast, shrugging aside any counter-fire with contemptuous ease.

"A clan dispute, *kyo*? Did one of the ship commanders try a coup?" Oc Chac peered at her display.

"No." Susan's hand clenched on the armrest beside the shockchair. *He tried to reach me.*

"No," she continued. "This must be the Khaid ship captured by *Chu-sa* Hadeishi. He found himself in the same predicament as we did—and passed through the Pinhole as well."

"To no avail, *Chu-sa*." The Mayan shook his head sadly. "See, they've lost that last drive—they're ballistic now. If they don't lose containment, the Khaid will finish them off with a single shipkiller."

Koshō nodded, feeling sick. The *Kader*'s maneuvering drives had sputtered out, leaving the cruiser a hulk coasting into the void. A cloud of tiny pinpoints popped, spilling away from the dying ship.

to the Home Islander sitting at the Pilot's station. "We need to move closer to the *Chimalacatl* at every opportunity. The Khaid will fear it now, and we'll take every advantage the Goddess sends us."

Oc Chac looked up from the other end of Secondary. "*Chu-sa*, won't we fall prey to the same fate, if we move too close to the device?" His gloved fingers tapped restlessly on the back of his helmet. "That Khaid ship was destroyed well out from the artifact—when we dropped off that freighter we were much closer—" The *Sho-sa* suddenly stopped, having reached an unpalatable conclusion. "How will we tell what our safe distance is *now*?"

Susan looked pointedly at Helsdon. The engineer grimaced, wishing he could clear the taste of ashes from his throat, and immediately fell to work at one of the consoles. "For now," the *Chu-sa* said, "we will assume it's safer near the Sunflower than in the crosshairs of a Khaid missile battery."

Oc Chac nodded in agreement, and then pointed wordlessly at the compartment status v-panes showing a wild mixture of red, orange, and yellow on his display. Koshō leaned in, feeling a slow trickle of despair at the state of her fine new ship.

"Release emergency air to decks thirteen and fifteen. Close down atmosphere to the rest of the compromised compartments."

Turning back to the threatwell—what a relief to have some view of the battle, even if the display had substantial arcs of darkness where there was simply no data to be had—Susan tilted her head, puzzled for a moment by the latest positions of the enemy.

"*Chu-sa*, they're regrouping—the destroyers hunting us are shifting vector out of the shoal." Pucatli sounded wary, and Koshō shared his concern.

"Assume they *are* taking stock of the situation, *Chu-i*. They will need to set some priorities—so keep a close eye on any movements in our direction. See if that remote at the Pinhole can pick up their 'cast traffic."

Then she sat, at last, and drank some more water and managed to force down a threesquare. Everyone else remained furiously busy with damage control and trying to get updated inventory and arranging for the wounded and the dead. Susan sat quietly in the commander's shockchair, watching the 'well update.

"Can you project their rendezvous point?" Susan asked Fujiwara as the minutes crawled by.

"What about the remote we dropped at the Pinhole?" Susan folded her arms, glaring at Oc Chac and Helsdon working on the door. Being denied the threatwell or any kind of proper information feed was making her almost violently nervous. The *Sho-sa* was now cutting into the doorframe with a plasma torch, which was generating a huge cloud of sparks and smoke droplets. "Do we still have a t-relay connection?"

"*Hai, kyo.*" Pucatli was working the comp as fast as he could, but no good answers were coming back. "But it's six light-years from the *Chimalacatl*—so we've nothing on sensor or visual. Gravity plot now . . . here we go."

The *Chu-i* turned the comp, showing Susan a navigational plot. Multiple tracks arrowed inbound from the Pinhole, showing a line-pattern indicating they'd gone superluminal to leap across the six light-year interval to the immediate region of the Sunflower. One of the traces ended abruptly—and the timestamp on the vector indicated they'd ceased to exist less than fifteen minutes ago.

"See that, *Chu-sa*?" Pucatli could not help but grin, teeth white behind his grimy faceplate.

"That last *Hayalet* stepped too close to the sun," Susan stated flatly.

"Boom-boom, *kyo*," the Comms officer observed, rubbing fine particles of ash from his screen.

Now we know what happened to this fleet, Koshō thought, feeling the weight of the dead pressing against the hull of her ship. *Did they try and attack the artifact? No—they weren't warships. Whoever—whatever— controlled the weapon system turned upon them.*

She turned up the filters on her z-suit against the electrical smoke now obscuring their vision. *Anderssen and Hummingbird must have had some way to slip us past before, when we were so close to the artifact. Damn the old man . . . somehow he knows how to control the weapon.*

Thirty minutes later, in Secondary Command, Susan stretched gingerly and sucked down some water. She'd taken a bad crack on the shoulder while the command team had scrambled downdeck. Most of her ship was seriously damaged, though they'd been lucky enough not to lose the shipcore entirely.

"The main squadron will be coming back this way, Fujiwara," she said

IN THE DEAD FLEET

Oc Chac, Helsdon, and Konev cursed in unison, levering at the hatchway into Main Command with a magnetic ram. The compartment frame had warped in the last exchange of shipkillers, though their continued survival spoke volumes to the resistance afforded by the hexacomb armor between the primary and secondary hulls. Koshō hung back, one arm tucked around a stanchion, paying only partial attention to the efforts of the bridge crew to force an exit from the ruined compartment. Her earbug was still live, and she could monitor the chatter from Secondary Command, which was in operation. She could have used one of the escape hatches that led to an evac pod, but there was still work to be done, and her ship to fight.

Chu-i Pucatli was nearly helmet-to-helmet with her, a field comp tucked into his elbow while the Comms officer tried to keep track of everything happening elsewhere on the ship.

We've broken contact, Chu-sa, reported the second watch pilot from Secondary. *That last exchange blinded the destroyer and we've gone to ground between two of the leviathans.*

"How much clearance do we have?" Susan did not like the thought of getting too close to something that might wake up at any time, though she admitted to herself that *beggars cannot be choosers.*

Enough, kyo. But once they start hunting, we'll have to run for it and drives are at sixty percent.

Koshō shook her head in displeasure, eyeing Pucatli. "Are you picking up anything from their 'cast traffic?"

The Comms officer's lips twisted into a puzzled grimace. "Fragments, *kyo*—I think something's happened in-system from us." The younger officer clipped his z-suit to the stanchion and crossed his legs, pinning the field comp in place as he floated. "Most of our sensors are blocked by the wrecks, but—"

he'd reached the steps leading down into the courtyard below, the first of the Mongol spearmen were swarming over the lower curtain wall. The sight of them sent a shock of vigor through his limbs. Here was an enemy within the length of his blade!

to travel. All hands to arms, all hands to battle stations. Form up on your section leaders, check your sidearm loads, and regroup to the Command deck."

Mitsuharu paused, checking the v-panes arrayed on his console. Some of the ship's automatic systems were still in operation. He'd lost touch with Cajeme and the engineering crew on comm, but the 'net v-eyes in cargo one and two showed ranks of evacuation pods lined up and ready. Mentally saluting the little Yaqui, the Nisei officer punched in a launch code, then watched with half-lidded eyes as both cargo bays vented to space. The pods scattered, some of them retaining enough maneuvering fuel to kick off preprogrammed escape vectors.

Dandelion seeds on the last breeze of autumn.

Tocoztic had been watching, his display updating with scattered icons. "Capsules away, *kyo*. They'll be on the Khaid sensor plot already."

I don't think they're going to take the bait, Hadeishi thought, feeling his stomach clench. A horrible pain was starting to pierce his heart, stealing the strength from his limbs. *Another ship lost . . . another crew killed.*

On passive sensors, the two Khaid destroyers were unmistakably clear as they closed in on the coasting-cruiser, each properly spaced to overlap point-defense while retaining a clear field of fire for their missile racks and hardpoints. Mitsuharu hoisted the *Yilan* shipgun from the scabbard at the side of his shockchair and checked the magazine charge. *Six hundred rounds, armor-piercing.*

Then he thumbed an override glyph on the console, sending the main reactor into shutdown and cutting all internal power. The dimmed lights flickered and went out. In the sudden darkness, Mitsuharu toggled his suit-comm alive and said: "Stand by to repel boarders."

Musashi crouched beneath the battlement of Shimabara Castle, his armor in tatters. A huge ringing sound filled his head, as though an enormous gong had been cloven by a giant. Blood was everywhere, streaking the rough-hewn stones. At the edge of his stunned vision, a gaping section of the wall had been torn away by the impact of a Mongol bombard stone. All of the samurai on the parapet had been cast to the ground as jackstraws. He groped fruitlessly for his bōkuto, but the weapon was nowhere to be found. Despite the stunned weakness of his limbs, Musashi rose up, finding a katana still scabbarded in the belt of a dead man. By the time

AT THE PINHOLE EXIT

The *Kader* limped out of the Barrier passage, coughing clouds of debris and leaking radiation. In Command, Hadeishi watched the plot stonily as the Khaid destroyer *Han'zhr* nimbly avoided the last of their makeshift mines and closed to gun-range with a flare of her engines.

Tocoztic coughed hoarsely, his z-suit patched up with quickseal, and stabbed a series of glyphs on his console. "Another contact emerging from the Barrier, *Chu-sa*." He squinted at the v-display, which was fluctuating as shipnet nodes crashed and rebooted themselves in quick succession. "Looks like another *Mishrak*. No ident confirm . . . I don't think the 'net is going to hold up through another hit."

Mitsuharu nodded, jaw clenched, and surveyed the wrecked bridge. A penetrator had chewed through part of the Command compartment, killing more than half of the men standing watch. Lovelace had been carried away by the corpsmen, but Inudo and the weapons officer were left. "Pilot, can we still maneuver?"

"Barely anything left, *kyo*. Adjustment thrusters are wrecked, we only have one drive nacelle in operation and there's nowhere to go." The Nisei pilot indicated the navigational scanners with a shaky hand. "The nearest object here is about three light-years away and our hypercoil is shot to hell."

The race is over, Mitsuharu thought bleakly. *The Naniwa is nowhere to be found and our sensor suite is reduced to almost nothing . . . two destroyers are more than a match for this cripple, and there's nothing stopping that* Hayalet *from coming through the Barrier after us.*

"Pilot, cut thrust to zero."

Then he switched his comm to ship-wide channel, hoping the crews of men struggling to keep them spaceworthy were all within range of a repeater or a shipnet node in operating condition. "All hands, this is *Chu-sa* Hadeishi. We can see Fuji-san, but there is still one last kilometer

was so clear in the golden light—Anderssen's hand twitched in horror and the bronze block skittered away across the floor of the platform. Sliding on the smooth metal, the tablet encountered little or no resistance.

Meters away, the others jerked around as the tablet sailed across the shaft opening and was sliced cleanly in half by an invisible thread running vertically through the open space. Both halves vanished into the depths without a sound.

"The singularity is down there," Gretchen gasped out. She rolled over and punched her med-band override. She felt a sharp pinching in her chest and the cool flood of meds rushing into her bloodstream as the little device reacted in confusion, thinking the collapse of the neural overlay represented her own imminent demise. A raging headache from fighting the gold-tinged invader in her consciousness faded with the onslaught of painkillers. "Down at the root of all this . . . a string tied to a stone cast into a deep dark pool . . . *aaaaah!*"

Anderssen felt her own native sight awaking, pricked by the stabbing pain in her chest. *Focus,* she commanded and went limp on the platform. Her sightless eyes stared up into the darkness. *Focus,* she commanded, and her mind fell quiet.

Distantly she heard one of the marines say. "Someone's coming up the steps,"

Another—this one very close by—said, "her band has redlined."

"I think," Sahâne said, making a sign of command at the Prince. "That you should kill it right now."

Xochitl jerked around with a gasp, combat automatic flying out of his holster, and there was a sharp *snap-snap!* A cloud of flechettes slammed into Anderssen's chest, knocking her across the platform to crash into a console near the outer edge of the pylon. She gasped, spat blood from a split lip, and clawed weakly at the smoking wound.

Seeing that the Prince had taken action, the marines lunged forward to throw themselves between Xochitl and Sahâne. The Hjo coughed out a bitter laugh. "Tell your servants to step away, *toy*. Tell them to—"

"No," Xochitl grated out, crashing his exo again. With relief he found his vision abruptly clear of the strange artifacts. The muttering drone in his mind fell quiet. "Those patolli beans only get one throw, and you've used up all your luck, you worthless coward."

Sahâne blinked in surprise and hastily made another sign of command. The Prince shoved past the marines. "No Hjo-designed exo," Xochitl said tightly, his automatic sighted on the creature's faceplate. "No *magical* control of me. No more wastrel Sahâne, he was lost in some *accident* in the back of beyond." The México lord essayed a grim smile. "No one will ever miss you, assistant-under-attaché to the ambassador. Let's see how long your bio-armor lasts against this—"

The whine of a grav-sled echoing on his comm brought the Prince up short.

Out of sight and out of mind, Gretchen crawled away, leaking atmosphere in a deadly hiss from her punctured suit, nerveless fingers scrabbling into the ruin of her field jacket to drag out the corroded bronze tablet. The device was now pierced with dozens of pinpoint, smoking holes. The golden glare in her mind had dissolved into confusion with hundreds of voices chattering away. Random images flared across her retinas. Then the memory of a raspy, irritating old voice speaking impeccable Nahuatl forced its way through into her stunned, shocky consciousness: *The second enemy of perception is seeing too much. You must learn true focus for the first time in your life.*

Then, those were not *my thoughts! All the events I could see! Everything*

Gretchen hardly noticed the Prince. Her consciousness was suffused with data pouring into her perception from all sides. Here, everything was thick with meaning. Even node $3^3 3$ seemed barely able to keep up with the flood of information. Something in the flow—so many glyphs and icons and ghost-images were popping up around her she could barely process the visual stimuli—caught at her. *This isn't right—there's something broken somewhere—no, not broken, a translation matrix is throwing errors.*

"How . . . how does this all work?" Xochitl's voice came as if from a great distance.

Gretchen struggled to focus on the man standing in front of her. When she could separate out the visual channel, the Prince was sweating behind his faceplate. Gretchen knew beyond doubt that his "mask" was gabbling unknown languages into his mind and troubling his vision with intermittent flashes of undecipherable symbols. She felt pummeled by the same forces. Xochitl reached out, seized Gretchen's suit-collar, and dragged her close. "Where is . . . where is the command interface?"

Anderssen felt immortal, weightless, and unassailable. Xochitl's problems did not concern her—or were so remote to her experience he was negligible in any calculation involving her attention. "Didn't they tell you what it looked like?" Part of her regarded him coolly. "When they sent you out here? No diagrams, no pictures of your goal?"

"No! Yes—a theory—just to find a control interface." Xochitl blinked, looking away. He batted jerkily at the air between them. "Is this hot light in my mind—or is it—"

"It is she," Sahâne accused in a wheezy growl as he finally reached the top of the long stair. The marines, growing more and more nervous for the Prince's safety, twitched toward the Hjogadim. The alien looked worse, as the inside of his helmet was smeared with bruised-plum-colored vomit. "It's been this female all along. She and the queer old ape with the bright eyes. They are the ones that brought us to this terrible place."

Gretchen nodded calmly. She hoped no one would see her hands clench into claws. The golden overlay was seeping so quickly through her synapses that the ability to command her body was running thousands of cycles behind her consciousness. *These biological interfaces are so slow!* "This is so."

THE ALTAR OF THE UNDYING FLAME

BURNING AT THE SUNFLOWER'S HEART

Prince Xochitl reached the top step of a pyramidlike stair ascending from the enormous floor. He glanced down at the others still toiling upward on the wide, gleaming steps, and then strode onto a platform marking the summit of the pylon. By the pale light of the distant accretion jet, he began to comprehend the scope of the massive chamber. *Scaled for giants! Or the gods themselves!* The floor stretched away for kilometers in both directions. *In a place like this, clouds will form. Rain will fall. Lightning might strike. Surely a First Sun artifact!* He turned slowly, taking everything in. He became aware of a strange, singing hum permeating his suit and vibrating through every surface on his body.

Piercing the center of the pylon was a six-meter-wide shaft, a nine-pointed star in cross-section which plunged down into darkness. Poised directly above this unfathomable hole was a second pyramidal shape, apex pointing down from the unseen ceiling. At the junction between these mirror-like pyramids, the platform measured at least thirty meters on each side. The surface was composed of a metallic alloy bearing the endlessly repeating design of two nested, equilateral triangles, while each side was circumscribed by three raised, angular consoles. Their upper surfaces were glassy-smooth, though Xochitl's exo was beginning to annotate the featureless expanse with faint glyphs indicating minute imperfections of the surface.

At much the same time, his z-suit environmental sensors began to register that the tremendously cold air in the chamber had warmed a degree, and the atmospheric mixture, which had been almost entirely nitrogen was now beginning to percolate with oxygen.

Perhaps there . . . The Prince's thought broke off as the others clambered up to the last of the steps and stopped to goggle in wonderment as he had done.

hammered her, shredding armor and turning hard-points into plasma-consumed hells. The battleship swerved away, rotating to bring fresh guns to bear on the remaining missiles boosting towards her.

"Pilot," Mitsuharu croaked, seeing that Inudo was still alive and clinging to his console. "Hold course and get us out of here!"

ing orders. A cloud of debris, atmosphere, and chaff spewed out behind the damaged cruiser.

Hadeishi watched the streaking missile tracks on the plot with cold eyes. Inudo was pushing the maneuver drives for all they were worth—and making gradient inside the Barrier itself was obviously impossible. The transit metrics were off the scale.

"Forty seconds to the second wave," Tocoztic announced, sweat gleaming on the sides of his face. "Point-defense is down to thirty percent, shipkillers are exhausted. One salvo of penetrators and two spoofer pods left—"

"Weapons, drop pods," Mitsuharu snapped, switching his attention to the navigation plot. The track of the Khaid fleet was marvelously clear—their battleship drives coughed high-order radiation with reckless abandon—and he was praying the Barrier had not already shifted enough to swing a lattice of knives into their path. The two spoofer pods spun out from their launchers and Lovelace was waiting to key them up as duplicates of the *Kader* as soon as they had separated from her signature. "Pilot, cut drives and rotate fresh armor!"

Another ship icon popped up on the plot—a hundred thousand k behind the *Kukumav*—pulling high g acceleration. For an instant, Hadeishi thought it might be the *Moulins*, but then shipnet crunched the emissions signature and a whirl of hostile glyphs surrounded the contact.

"*Mishrak*-class destroyer *Han'zhr* on the board," Tocoztic barked.

"Rotating aspect," Inudo followed as the main drives cut out.

Mitsuharu snarled, lips drawing back. The *Kukumav*'s second missile volley slammed into the *Kader* at a bad angle. Perhaps a quarter of the shipkillers had swerved away, following the two spoofer pods, but the remainder rained in on her aft-ventral quarter. Inudo had swung them round hard, bringing an undamaged section of shipskin into line with the attack, but the guttering flare of penetrators and bomb-pods ripped aside their point-defense and tore at the primary hull in a wave of explosions.

Command lost power entirely for a microsecond, and Hadeishi felt the carapace lining the shockchair splinter as the g-decking failed. He slammed hard into the frame, and then bounced back. Secondary mains cut in, and their consoles flickered back to life in time for him to see the *Kukumav*'s icon flicker. The weapons cloud from the *Tlemitl* had

Hello, old friend. The voice on the comm channel was so unexpected, yet so familiar, that Mitsuharu could not place it for a seeming eternity. *I knew you would come, if anyone could win through, and you would need every tool at your command.* The sigil vanished, Hummingbird's voice faded, and Lovelace drew back at her station in alarm, watching as the *Tlemitl's* fragmentary shipnet unfolded before her on the Comms console.

"We're in," Hadeishi barked, watching the intercept solution for the Khaid missile storm wind down towards their destruction. "Lovelace— shift control to Tocoztic—Weapons, you have full control over anything still working in the hulk of the *Firearrow*—dump it all! Everything! Now!"

The *Kader's* hull shuddered again as the point-defense guns lit up, filling the rapidly shrinking interval between the Khaid shipkillers and the fleeing cruiser with a wall of hyper-accelerated depleted uranium pellets. Bomb-pods began to stutter in sun-bright flares, stabbing at the shipskin with invisible beams of high-energy X-rays. The first wave of shipkillers rode in hot behind the suppressive fire, tearing through the *Kader's* counter-measure.

Hadeishi felt the cruiser heave, hull hammered by a dozen impacts. His status displays flashed wildly, shading red. Dozens of compartment alerts howled as pressure vented from the secondary hull. The primary hull shredded, gouged open by massive explosions.

Tocoztic, his face bone white, stabbed a command glyph on the v-display relayed from the ruin of the *Tlemitl*. "Dumping ordnance, now!"

All along the flank of the *Tlemitl's* carcass, hard-points woke up, draining local emergency power, and went into remote mode. The launch rails and missile racks surviving the dreadnaught's dissection cycled open. They could not hurl their weapon loads into battle at high v, but approximately eighty shipkillers separated from the hull and immediately locked onto the *Kukumav*, which was building velocity past them at a relatively low speed. At the same time, the kinetic weapons began firing, spitting a cloud of ballistic munitions towards the Khaid ship.

For her part, the *Kader* punched deeper into the Pinhole at maximum burn on her engines, her flight punctuated by the flare of shipkillers and penetrators detonating across her hull. The *Kukumav's* gunners cycled their launch rails, subcommanders howling new target-

Frowning thunderously, Lovelace stared over at the pilot, whose expression had gelled into a stoic mask. "*Chu-sa* . . ." The Mirror officer caught Hadeishi's eye, her face filled with raw appeal. "The drive trail from the battle-cruiser is fragmentary now—and the Barrier *moves!* We couldn't possibly—"

"We don't need the *Naniwa*'s trace, *Sho-i*." Mitsuharu nodded to the plot as the console under his fingertips began to shiver with the engines igniting. "The Khaid fleet has already blazed the trail for us—their emissions will be impossible to miss."

"Underway, *kyo*." Inudo's report was mechanical. "Building v—we'll be out of the shadow of the *Tlemitl* in five—four—three—two—"

"Contact, *kyo!* We have contact!" Tocoztic's blurt of alarm overrode the Pilot. "Bearing eleven high, she's massing like a battleship! Cast analysis says she's the *Kukumav!*"

The noise level in Command jolted upward, but now Hadeishi felt everything extraneous—even the joyful howl from the Khaid channel— drop away. "Weapons—launch everything you have, dead on. Pilot—get us out of here!"

The cruiser's hull shuddered, groaning as the drives kicked up to all nodes combusting full-bore and the launch rails and hardpoints belched a cloud of shipkillers and a hammering stream of kinetic warheads. Tocoztic's countermeasures display was already alight with the incoming Khaid missile storm, which outmassed theirs by five or six to one.

"Cast relay active, *Chu-sa!*" Lovelace's fingers were flying across her panel, the *tik-tik-tik* of her styli a seamless stream, like the clicking of spinning gears. "We're synching to the *Tlemitl*—wait one, wait one— she needs authorization!"

A fresh v-pane popped up on Hadeishi's console, showing the Fleet authentication interface. Cursing to himself—there was no chance the *Tlemitl* would have the authorization glyph cluster for a cashiered reserve officer—Mitsuharu framed his face in the pickup window, got a green rectangle and then keyed his sequence. The v-pane flickered, showing an IDENTITY REJECTED message for a fraction of a second, and then suddenly blanked. In its place, an oblong glyph of intertwining roses appeared, holding a black-on-white flame. Hadeishi felt a shock of recognition, though he'd only seen the icon once before, while another was manipulating a ring-zero system.

We're locked out hard—the *Sho-i* tried breaking in, but found not a single loose bean."

Lovelace nodded, looking equally grim. "We found some survivors, *kyo*. One of the compartments is still intact and—"

"Do they have shipnet access?" Hadeishi cut her off coldly, his mind rotating the problem through every angle he could conceive. "Do they have power? Sensors? Anything?"

The young woman's face went blank, stung by his tone. "*Chu-sa*, they're on emergency power, but yes—they have 'net access and access to the node in their fragment. . . ."

"Put me through." Hadeishi turned to the plot, lips a tight, compressed line. "Pilot, are we ready to maneuver?"

Inudo nodded, his face wan with exhaustion. "Drives are hot, *Chu-sa*, standing by."

"Survivors on channel sixty-three, *kyo*," Lovelace said, her voice far more formal than she'd offered before. Hadeishi wasn't even aware of the change, his whole attention focused on the wavering, jittery v-pane which popped up on his display. Two z-suited figures were framed in the pickup, a room filled with floating debris behind them.

"This is Mitsuharu Hadeishi, *Chu-sa* of the *Kader*. I am your new commanding officer. I need you to open a 'cast feed to my Comms officer—*Shoi-i* Lovelace—and do *everything* you can to allow her to relay through your subsystems. Do you understand?"

The sharp, harsh edge to his voice galvanized both men, though he knew they must be running low on air, were probably out of water, and had little chance of surviving even to see another watch pass. A ragged "*Hai, kyo!*" echoed back to him across the circuit. The Nisei officer nodded sharply to his Comms officer. "Get me a sensor feed from the far side of the hulk—there's another Khaid out there, we need to find it immediately."

Then he paused, considering the plot for a long, endless three seconds and then—resolving an internal struggle—his stylus sketched out a new maneuvering vector on the plot. "Pilot, get us underway. I want maximum acceleration while holding to this path. Weapons, stand by to engage the enemy. Expect a missile exchange at a blade's distance."

Inudo stared at the new vector, then nodded jerkily to himself. "Plotting course, *Chu-sa*."

THE *KADER*

Command was awash in confused voices as the last of the evacuation pods was winched into the cargo hold. Hadeishi tapped his med-band, injecting another dose of anti-inflammatory to suppress a spiraling migraine. Five or six conflicting channels of information were vying for his attention, and the low-level confusion amongst his scratch crew kept jarring his attention away from the Khaid battlecast. The enemy had started to frequency-hop, but Lovelace was keeping up, though the translator always seemed to be five or six words behind what he could make out himself.

One of the new officers—his name had escaped Mitsuharu in the latest round of introductions—signaled cargo one was sealed, and the armored partitions were rotating closed over the bay doors. The *Chu-sa* switched to Cajeme's team, catching the exhausted-looking Yaqui as they were hauling two corpses from the pod, along with one midshipman who looked like she might live.

"*Nitto-hei*—how many pods do we have aboard?"

Cajeme stared back blankly for a moment, then shook himself, saying: "Eleven, *kyo*, we have eleven."

"Get them prepped to eject," Hadeishi said sharply, a hard edge in his voice. "A Weapons team is on their way to you now—there were fifteen thermonukes in munitions storage—I want those pods refitted as fast as you can."

"*Hai*"—Cajeme wheezed, his face black with carbon from the backwash of the cutter he'd been slinging for the past eighteen hours—"*kyo*."

Mitsuharu turned his attention back to Command, feeling his shoulder blades itching in anticipation. *They're coming . . . more than one of them.* "*Thai-i* Tocoztic—any progress on connecting to the *Tlemitl's* sensor array?"

The Islander shook his head, expression mournful. "Nothing, *kyo*.

Susan saw the wreckage occlude the pursuing destroyers as Holloway put them into a jinking curve, fleeing past another of the dead behemoths. "Weapons, tight pattern—rear launchers only—delayed fuse while we're in scan-shadow."

"*Hai, kyo!*" Konev cycled his launchers, stylus darting across his console. Preconfigured munitions packages punched outbound, venting from the eight rearward rails at nearly a hundred g's.

At the same moment, Olin's voice cut across the Russian's. "New contact! New contact! *Aslan*-class cruiser to ventral—range sixty thousand kilometers—enemy is launching now, thirty missile tracks incoming! Impact in eighty seconds!"

"Now, *Sho-sa*," Susan said, her voice preternaturally calm, "Now we're in the brawl."

Behind them, the *Hayalet* held course at an angle away from the *Naniwa* and her running firefight. Susan watched the vector firm up, heading in-system at a good clip.

How could they fail to notice the singularity? The sensor suite on one of those battlewagons must be the equal of ours—some daring hunt-lord sees the realization of an entire race's dreams of empire riding on that thread.

This reminded her of Prince Xochitl and the missing Hummingbird, and her heart lifted at the thought of the Khaid howling in behind those two "gentlemen," well stoked with blood lust.

They're all suited to one another, she thought bitterly. Then Susan felt a pang of conscience, just for an instant. *An Imperial officer should be mindful of her duty.*

A proximity alarm sounded—the battle-cruiser sped past an outlier of the vast shoal of wreckage—even as the first wave of Khaid shipkillers began to flare around her. The *Naniwa* groaned, shipskin hammered by the stabbing flare of fusion detonations. Now the plot was filled with the tracery of outgoing kinetics, the flash of bomb-pods erupting and Command was loud with the swift, urgent voices of her crew reacting. Konev's counter-missile wave banged away, shaking the secondary hull with the violence of launch rails cycling.

Adrenaline flushed her limbs with a quivering, bright energy. The only thing missing was Hadeishi's voice in her earbug, calm and controlled, his presence radiating a contained focus as he put the ship through her paces. *I am alone.* Susan felt a tight, stabbing pain in her diaphragm. On the plot, the density of the wrecks was soaring, and Holloway's brow was dappled with sweat as he maneuvered. *Here we go.*

Koshō detached a series of v-panes showing the movement of the Khaid battleship towards the Sunflower to her Executive console.

A good six hours for them to reach the artifact, she saw. *Long time to stay in this dance.*

A shipkiller blew only three compartments away, shredding the *Naniwa*'s shipskin and venting a huge gout of atmosphere and flotsam. In Command, the overheads flickered, half the consoles cut out and someone cursed violently as their v-display shorted, spilling smoke globules and hot sparks into the air.

Oc Chac was at the man's side in an instant, a portable extinguisher spitting foam into the splintered console. "Damage control, this is Main Command, we've lost a 'net node and five consoles."

scan is showing a lot of small fragments between the hulks—no good avenues for us to maneuver down—no holes yet, to hide in."

"Find us something, *Thai-i*. Quickly now." Koshō's voice was pointed. "We have two minutes . . ."

"Launch signatures!" Konev's voice was relaxed, almost a drawl, but the tenseness in his arms was as clear to Susan as an ash-cloud over Mount Talol. "Sixty missile tracks are on the board."

"Initiating countermeasures." Pucatli—at Comms—dumped the first of her spoofer pods.

"Counter-fire, *kyo*?" Konev looked to Koshō with a fierce gleam shining in his eyes. "If we concentrate, we might knock one or two out before they close to gun range."

"Save your launchers, *Thai-i*. We need to conserve every shipkiller we have left." Susan had already considered the fire rate from the onrushing destroyers and their range of engagement. "Engage the missile cloud with kinetics and ECM starting at six minutes."

"Isn't this a brawl, *Chu-sa*?" Oc Chac looked at her questioningly, his face pale with fatigue. "Even one or two of the enemy down at this range will even the odds appreciably."

Koshō lifted her chin, indicating the 'well. "Not yet, *Sho-sa*. This is 3-v *Ullamaliztli* with only one player left on our side. You played at Academy, I'm sure—"

A warning Klaxon honked, cutting her off. A fresh icon popped into view on the 'well.

"A *Hayalet*-class battleship, *kyo*." Konev's voice was tight as he reeled off the specifications of the new indicator. "Punched straight through from the Pinhole, right on our track."

Susan swiveled, lifting an eyebrow at Olin and Holloway. "Time to enter the maze?"

"Five minutes, *Chu-sa*." The pilot's eyes were wide with fear. "I've picked up some options but—"

"They'll have to do. Pilot, take us in."

On the plot, the destroyers continued to close, their launchers cycling a new spread of missiles every one hundred and twenty seconds. The first wave was still three minutes out, but the *Naniwa*'s point-defense was already hammering away at the incoming targets. Pucatli's spoofer pod was squealing, flooding the spectrum with distorting noise and false signals. Khaid penetrators began to flare, and then wink off of the plot.

AMONG THE FALLEN

In quick succession, a handful of widely spaced icons popped up enemy-red in the *Naniwa*'s threatwell. The gravity spike of the Khaid ships dropping from transluminal reached the Imperial ship only instants after they emerged into realspace. Koshō was watching, elbow on the armrest of her shockchair, eyes hooded. Command was fully staffed, everyone having gotten a least a round of the showers and an hour off duty.

"Confirming five transits," Konev announced, the icons beginning to annotate with glyphs indicating expected speed, throw-weight, and countermeasures. "All cruisers or smaller—*Mishrak* and *Aslan*-class— acceleration and emissions are within expected ranges."

"Undamaged." Oc Chac grimaced, tapping through a series of v-panes showing the wreckage being cleared from the battle-cruiser's downship compartments. "Are they fresh, *Chu-sa*?"

"Doubtful, *Sho-sa*. Their captains are pushing hard—the Khaid have little need of patience. They will be wounded, like us, but keen to bring us to ground. Time to cover?"

Holloway eyed the plot. Fully half of the threatwell was a blizzard of icons representing the dead fleet. "Fifteen minutes to the nearest wrecks, *Chu-sa*. About twelve minutes until we're inside the Khaid launch envelope."

"Deflector status, Chac-*tzin*?" Susan looked back to the Mayan. "Are we still running hot?"

Oc Chac shook his head. "No, *kyo*. We can pull another three, four gravities."

"Give us a boost, Holloway-*tzin*. But don't open the throttle wide— we need to be able to turn once we're in the debris field."

The console under Susan's fingers began to thrum with the vibration of the antimatter reactors chewing mass. "Nav—what are our options?"

Thai-i Olin looked up from his console, shaking his head. "Active

Mitsuharu blinked and everything seemed to slow. *The* Naniwa? *The missing battle-cruiser is—*

"How did they get through?" Tocoztic demanded of Inudo. "How can they track her—*we* can barely see her signature in this mess!"

"Do we have comm to the *Naniwa*?" Hadeishi's expression made Lovelace stiffen in her seat.

"No, *Chu-sa!* We're just picking up fragments of battlecast from a re-lay the Khaid dropped behind them. I'm getting five or six different emitter tags—one per ship probably." The *Sho-i* swallowed nervously. "She won't last long if she's alone."

"The *Naniwa* will fight to the last missile, the last gun . . ." Mitsuharu viciously suppressed an urge to order Inudo to take them to maximum acceleration and to the Eight Hot Narakas with the rest of the evacuation capsules. Despite this, his voice was a harsh growl which made every man and woman in Command straighten up in alarm. "*Chu-i*, I want to see a ticker on the plot telling me how long the engineers have to get those capsules inboard. Tocoztic-*tzin*, get your crews to their guns, get me status on anything we have left to throw. Pilot—lock down that drive plume signature and stand by for battle acceleration."

The howling and yammering of the *surtu* pounded in his ear, though Hadeishi felt their bloodlust only as a ticking sense of time falling away into darkness. He eyed the plot—still no sign of the enemy moving against them—but now he was certain at least one of the *surtu* was loitering in the *Tlemitl*'s sensor shadow, waiting for them to break cover.

"Comms. Broadcast on the last frequency we had for the *Wilful*. Say only, "We are visiting Osaka." Do not repeat the message."

Lovelace stared back at him, pale brow furrowed as she resolved the reference, her stylus poised over the v-pane. "Do you think Captain De Molay will hear?"

"Perhaps."

"A little boat like hers—what could she—?"

"Much depends upon the purity of one's intent, *Sho-i*. Send the mes-sage."

the pods they'd recovered initially. Cajeme and his engineers downdeck were busily shuffling off the newly recovered ratings and officers, which looked to swell the *Kader*'s complement by another eighty or ninety bodies. Most of those recovered, however, had been injured to greater or lesser degree.

Now for the second act, he thought, gaze settling on *Sho-i* Lovelace at the Comm's station, despite being—perhaps—the junior-most tech aboard. The ensign had tucked two spare console styli into her hair, which was bound up in a blond bun behind her head. The young woman's expression was distant, all attention focused on sorting out the confusion of signals picked up by their sensor booms.

Hadeishi caught her eye. "*Sho-i?* Are we still synched with the Khaid battlecast?"

"No, *kyo.* I'm getting intermittent bursts of traffic, but we're out of the loop now." She offered a crooked smile. "I'm sure they've figured out we're no longer running with the *surtu.*"

"Very well. Route what you have to my earbug on sixty-three and—"

Lovelace started to nod in acknowledgment, then became quite still. "Wait one. Wait one."

She stared at her console, gently adjusting the signal filtering, before scowling. "We're picking up a rebroadcast, *kyo.* It's the Khaid 'cast channel, but not from our immediate area. Routing to sixty-three."

A babble of excited Khadesh flooded Mitsuharu's hearing. The translator kicked in, but the hunt-lords were yowling so quickly, and overlapping one another, that the software produced only a garbled mess on the secondary channel.

"Fix a vector, *Sho-i!*" he ordered, barely able to hear himself think. "Are they behind, or ahead?"

I want that ship! popped out of the howling. *She escaped once, not again!*

Hadeishi twisted the earbug around, frustrated. *That sounds like the one named Sylahdeposu—he's quick off the mark, but who does he have in his sights? Has another Imperial combatant dropped into the area, or . . .*

"*Chu-sa* Hadeishi!" Inudo had turned in his seat. The pilot had a finger to his earbug, his voice loud over the chatter on the *Kader*'s crowded bridge. "I think he means the *Naniwa.* Comp says she is the one that survived the ambush and ducked into the Pinhole—a squadron of the Khaid must have slipped past us, following their drive track."

THE *KADER*

Hadeishi frowned, his jaw clenched tight as Cajeme's voice burred in his earbug. *Capsule lock is completely jammed—we're having trouble cutting through without frying the nitto-hei inside—and there are four more capsules outside we can't bring onboard until we've got these men out.*

The Nisei officer's eyes darted to the nav plot, which still showed the *Tlemitl* between them and the Khaid fleet—or what of the enemy they could see with their sensors greatly obscured by the Barrier, the radiation clouds from discharged weapons, and the sensor shadow of the broken dreadnaught. From his vantage, several Khaid destroyers were hanging off at a distance, but the rest of the enemy had disappeared.

"*Thai-i*, do we have a remote we can run out to the edge of the wreck?"

Tocoztic shook his head in disgust. The Arawak's beard was starting to grow in, which made him look particularly disreputable. "Nothing, *kyo*. We've got nothing *useful* aboard. I'd use an evac pod, but their maneuvering jets are exhausted once we get them into cargo one . . ." He gestured angrily at the plot. "Something is going on out there—I can pick up gravity-wave changes and some partial drive emission signatures—but we can't see anything directly."

Mitsuharu's expression darkened further, considering the movements of the enemy. *Out of sight is not out of my mind . . . that battle-cruiser's drive emissions could easily be visible to these new-model battleships of theirs. This* Spear *does not carry the most advanced electronics quills can buy. Not like the . . . wait a moment.*

"What about the *Tlemitl*? Are there any sensor booms or subsystems we can connect to and use?"

"The—" Tocoztic stopped himself, initial disbelief replaced by curiosity. "I don't know, *Chu-sa*, but she hasn't lost *all* power to systems—just her mains. One moment . . ."

Hadeishi swiveled his shockchair, feeling the carapace creak under him. All of the Command stations were now filled with crewmen from

bird slipped out into the dim, chaotic vastness of the landing bay. Packing foam lay scattered at the base of the landing cradle. He grimaced, seeing that the Order crewmen had brought, and assembled, a grav sled. *Prepared, were they?*

He ducked back inside the ship and returned moments later with a single-rider grav-ski. The device unfolded in swift, programmed motions. A bit of a smile shone in the old man's face, remembering long summers wasted skidding around the alleys and avenues of Coyoacán with his classmates, a tight noisy pack of boys. Then the sense of fleeting time gripped him. He hopped on and grasped the controls.

"Go now." He sped away with the wide flare of the running lights searching the enormous corridor ahead.

fully awake and feeling quite limber. The compartment door was locked, but liquefying the suit had also deposited a number of tools from the gel matrix on the floor. He found them by feel, sorted them with deft fingers and then cut open the locking mechanism with a tiny plasma torch no longer than his little finger. Then he duck-walked out into one of the crew cabins and—thankfully—stood up.

As Hummingbird did so, the dissonance of his thought patterns concerning the crew of the *Moulins* finally caught his attention. An initial sensation of puzzlement was swiftly replaced by shock. *I've been "pushed,"* he realized. *That "Old One" is stronger than I suspected.* Disgusted, he spat on the floor of the empty room. *I've made a deadly mistake in helping an Order ship come here. They are after the same prize as the Prince. Christ the Guardian curse them down through all nine hells!*

Fifteen minutes later having recovered his clothing and z-suit, he padded onto the mess area and found the marines had been taken away. Worried, the old *nauallis* moved carefully through the rest of the little ship. Finally, he found the Imperials laid out on the floor of a cargo area above Engineering, trapped in their dead armor. Hummingbird squatted next to the squad leader with a pleasant smile. *Something to salvage. We are all "friends" here . . . the Order hasn't broken fully with the Empire yet.* The marine glared back at him, sullen-eyed and gagged.

"*Go-cho* Pequah," the old crow greeted him amiably, running practiced fingers down the desealer strip at the marine's shoulder. The wrecked armor sighed; tension released from the gelcore, and it fell away in a limp pool of black oil and plexisteel laminate. The Iroquois flexed his fingers, toes, and then rolled up—clad only in his service skinsuit, his body stiff as lightning with restrained fury. The other four marines made angry, muttering sounds behind their gags.

"We've all been played dirty," Hummingbird commented, peeling a flattened sleepytime capsule from Pequah's neck. "And I appreciate your natural desire to eviscerate someone, but your first concern must be the Prince's safety."

Released, all five marines nodded slowly, grudgingly, as they flexed oxygen-deprived limbs. For a long moment the *nauallis* met their eyes in turn, then nodded, satisfied. "Leave the Europeans to me. The Prince has a tracker in his suit. Follow the repeaters until you find him and make sure he gets back here in one piece."

Leaving the marines to scavenge for weapons and tools, Humming-

ON THE *MOULINS*

A groan escaped Hummingbird's lips as consciousness returned in fits and starts. He opened his eyes, finding nothing but darkness. He tested the movement of his arms and legs, and found they were tightly bound. Shifting his head from side to side, the old Nahuatl determined that something—a rubbery plastic—had been stretched over his eyes. He was not gagged, which indicated to the *nauallis* that there was no one within shouting distance. In any case, he did not like to make noise when he could not see who might be listening.

On my own, am I? Hummingbird shifted his shoulders, feeling walls on either side. *A closet perhaps? But they were in a hurry—I am still wearing my skinsuit.*

The old Nahuatl twisted his head from side to side, testing the limits of his ability to move. Discovering that both knees could reach his chin, he managed to roll forward gently and get both feet beneath him. Then, Hummingbird stood up slowly and found the roof of the confined space less than a meter above his resting position. *A bit cramped, but then I am not the largest of men.*

He twisted one shoulder around to bring the sealing strip of the skinsuit within range of his lips and then spent a good fifteen minutes trying to catch the recessed plastic tab in his teeth. Finally, after relaxing all of the muscles in his neck, back and arms individually, he was able to do so. When the tab popped free, the skinsuit puddled to the ground in a pool of gelatinlike oil, leaving only the neckring. With a two-millimeter clearance between his bonds and skin, the *nauallis* was able to shimmy free in another twenty minutes of hot, sweaty work in the closet.

As he worked, he felt a slow, steady sense of outrage building in his mind. *A pity they couldn't accept me as a fellow brother of the Order! Srá Osá will be most displeased by their shortsightedness. Protecting humanity from itself requires broader thinking.*

Pulling the skinsuit back on was also a bit of work, but now he was

one taken from the enemy at that." Despite herself, she started to grin in delight.

Oc Chac shook his head in astonishment. "A tremendous feat, if true. But, *Chu-sa*, this could easily be a trick—a stratagem of the Khaid to lure us into a trap!"

"It could." Koshō straightened her shoulders, trying to quell a fierce and unexpected joy blooming in her heart. "But *this* officer was recently forced to the beach and the Fates would truly be against us if the Khaid intelligence services were so far-thinking as to capture *his* voice patterns for use against *me*. No, fantastic as it sounds I believe that *Chu-sa* Mitsuharu Hadeishi is—somehow!—beyond the Barrier, that he has captured a Khaid ship, and is using that same vessel to recover our lost evac capsules."

The Mayan's expression became dour. "Sounds brave as the deeds of Hunahpu and Xbalanque in the heroic stories of my people, but doomed, surely. There is a full Khaid *fleet* at the other end of the Pinhole, *Kyo*. And against them, one ship will not last long at all. . . ."

Susan laughed out loud. "Your twin heroes were fashioned from mortals who excelled at contests to the death, *Sho-sa*. In this living world, there is no ship commander more likely to achieve the impossible than the man whose voice we've just heard."

Then her expression darkened, lips drawing tight. "But more likely, the Khaid fleet is no longer waiting outside the Barrier. No—they have likely found a way through as well, and will soon be upon us. Then *we* will be the lone lion amongst the wolf pack."

Koshō turned to the pilot. "*Sho-i* Holloway, bring us about and prep the coil to punch gradient. We need room to maneuver. Weapons, prep your launchers!"

THE NANIWA

Koshō felt her stomach quail and the lighting in Command pulsed twice as the battle-cruiser dropped gradient into realspace. Brisk, well-practiced chatter flowed across the bridge stations as the officers of the watch confirmed they had made transit properly, that ship's systems were on-line and they had a solid navigational fix. The threatwell began to refresh as the remote watching the Pinhole unspooled the last eight hours of captured data. Oc Chac was working his checklist in a low fast voice, ensuring they still had maneuvering drives, nothing had lost pressure or vented during the transition, and all compartments were secure for combat.

Only Pucatli was frowning, and the tense line of his head drew Susan's eye like a magnet from her consideration of the survey plot. "Comms?"

Puzzlement clouded the *Chu-i*'s face. "*Chu-sa*, there's a recorded transmission on one-hundred-ten you need to hear."

Koshō tapped her earbug, cycling channel. Immediately, she heard: *All Imperial evac capsules, converge on this signal. . . .*

"An Imperial broadcast! Someone's alive? How could . . ."

We have captured a Khaid vessel and come to take you home. Converge upon this signal with all haste. The familiar voice spoke quickly, concisely. It hummed with adrenaline; its familiar tone was inextricably connected in her mind, in her body, to imminent violence and battle. Susan's gaze tracked back to the threatwell—but there was nothing to be seen. The gravity-plot around the Pinhole remained quiescent.

"Mitsuharu?" she said aloud, without meaning to. Oc Chac—who had switched his own earbug to listen in—caught her eye, his head canted in a questioning pose.

Koshō replied to the unspoken question. "The Khaiden are not alone outside the Pinhole. That is the voice of a Fleet officer well known to me—it seems he is gathering up the fallen. But . . ." She paused, rewinding the message. "He can only have one ship under his command, and

Peregine, Pervicax transmito. Cohortes imperatoris deletae sunt. Khai sepulchrum intraverunt. Quinque custodes Khaianes consisti sunt, whispered out into the aether.

De Molay felt a mingled sense of relief and wary anticipation. There had been a dozen times in the last week that she'd expected to be incinerated, or captured, or simply vanish in the blossoming flare of an antimatter detonation. But—somehow—she had won through, and now her entire purpose had been discharged with a single message. *One which will likely go—*

The console chimed softly, indicating an incoming message spooling through the relay. She stiffened, startled to receive such a quick reply.

The message read*: Venimus. Signa transitu pone pro insertio directio teleportano. Evigila.*

Ready we shall be, then. By the Lord, they must be close by.

Her attention shifted to the plot. All four Khaid destroyers on sentry duty remained in their watchful pattern. No missile launches were detected by the forest of sensors extruded from the hull of the *Wilful*, no movement towards her on their part. De Molay settled back, wincing a little at the enduring pain in her face, her side, and her leg. *I am far too old for this,* she grumbled mentally.

Which, said a voice much like her own—damnable conscience!—*is why you'd retired. Why exactly did you volunteer for this excursion?*

Patzanil clattered onto the bridge, a large bowl tucked under one arm. The smell washed over her like the tidal return from Port Valletta on a long, hot summer day.

"Is it meatlog?" she asked politely.

The *Thai-i* gave her a devil-may-care smile. "I don't know, but if the Khaid can eat it, I can, too."

De Molay suppressed a laugh. "Back to sleep for me, then. Nothing new on the plot."

"*Chu-sa* Hadeishi has something in mind, I'm sure." The old woman scratched at the edges of the gel sealing her face wound. On the plot, the Khaid battlewagons had formed into an evenly spaced line and were picking up velocity. The other, smaller ships were also in motion—save one.

"What are they leaving behind, *Thai-i?*"

Patzanil was already correlating the emissions data. "Something in a destroyer's mass-range, *kyo*. Might be a *Mishrak*-class—we'd identified a couple of them in the attacking force before the *Gladius* went down."

"We'll stay well away," De Molay said, settling back into her cocoon. "Any others left behind?"

"*Hai, kyo*. Three others—same general class—at the corners of the box."

"Sentries, then." On the plot, the last of the Khaid heavies had disappeared behind the seemingly invisible veil of the Barrier. She nodded to herself, making some mental calculation. "Very good."

The boy looked at her expectantly for a moment, but De Molay closed her eyes again.

"Ah, *Sencho-sana?*" His voice was tight, hinting at an internal conflict between well-ingrained Fleet duty and the plain fact that the old woman was *not* a Fleet officer.

"Yes, *Thai-i*," De Molay responded. "You can get something to eat."

"Thank you, *kyo!*" He was up and out of his seat and through the hatchway before she could open both eyes. When she had sat up fully, he was long gone. De Molay laughed softly to herself, then keyed into her console and—after negotiating several authorization screens—brought up the t-relay interface. Then she sat for a moment, considering the plot and tapping her fingers slowly on the edge of the console.

Not that much time to dither, the old woman thought. *The boy will be back soon, and I've no surety the Khaid will not return swiftly, or that reinforcements have not been summoned. The iron is hot, so we must strike.* She wondered if Hadeishi and his reclaimed cruiser were still busy recovering the crew of the super-dreadnaught, but her window of opportunity was terribly short. *The Order masters would say to act in the moment of balance*, De Molay remembered from an old book she'd been forced to read in the *collegium*.

She shook her head and keyed open a comm channel. The message had been composed in her mind for at least a day, but she had needed the bridge to herself before risking a transmission.

THE *KUUB*

Loitering in the dark, shipskin aligned to full absorptive mode, the *Wilful* lay at the edge of the debris cloud generated by the destruction of the Khaiden battleship *Khorku*. The region of radioactive metal ash left behind by fusion containment failure served the little freighter as an extra screen, hiding her from the intermittent lidar scans emitting from the enemy ships still in the vicinity of the Pinhole. On her bridge, De Molay had moved back to the captain's station, her puffy black jacket, blankets, and the shepherd's cap supplemented by thick woolen gloves. The environmental systems were still trying to recover from their ill-use during the rescue efforts.

The old woman had her eyes closed, and a faint snore escaped her lips.

Thai-i Patzanil—who seemed very young to De Molay, far too young to be aboard a ship-of-war, much less acting as her navigator—was watching the plotting projection and the status boards. Weary himself, he stood and paced around the periphery of the tiny Command, peering at the old-fashioned dials on the equipment and idly fingering the cracked leather seat-backs. When he'd returned from the head, something had changed on the plot and he sat down hurriedly, red-rimmed eyes scanning the boards.

"*Sencho? Sencho* De Molay?"

The old woman opened one eye halfway, squinting at the boy.

"The Khaid main fleet is in motion, *kyo*. They're making for the Pinhole."

De Molay sat up, rolled her neck, and gestured for him to update the plotting projection. When the holo had refreshed, she pursed her lips, brows drawing tight. "Tired of testing the waters, hey? Has there been any sign of the *Kader?*"

Patzanil shook his head. "They've been down behind the radar shadow of the *Tlemitl* for at least two hours. Recovery operations must be complete by now, so I don't know—"

waste-tube and wept purple tears into his matted, unkempt facial pelt. He trembled uncontrollably, leaning against the door frame, overcome by stunned fear. *Oh Guide of Thought,* he blubbered to himself, *why have you sent your worthless servant into such a terrible place? I am no priest, no demagogue—I know nothing of the rituals of greeting or awaking! What cruel, cruel fate has placed me here, among barbarians and slaves and discarded toys, at such a time? To place me before the Gods themselves?* He could not bring himself to step across the threshold.

But the toys are already inside the Holy of Holies. The voice in his mind was faint and hard to understand; by far the most ancient of all his teachers. The others, who had begun babbling in counterpoint, fell silent.

You must go in, young smoot. Your only way home lies forward.

mechanisms, allowing a pale roseate light to shine through the opening. Armored corpses spilled into the nonagonal room, tumbling away from the hulks of shattered war-meka. Even Xochitl jumped back in surprise as a cascade of broken battle-steel bounced away across the floor.

There was a buzz of static on their comm channel, but then the ear-bugs cycled frequency and the irritating sound died away. The Prince was the first to regain his composure. He whistled in astonishment at the size of the chamber revealed behind the long-dead combatants.

"Now, Swede, now you've found us something." Xochitl felt a great lightness rise in his chest. "We are the first beings to look upon this vista in ten thousand years," he said. "Marines—patrol pattern! There may be automatic defenses left active, even after so long . . ."

Sahâne's long snout peeled back from his fore fangs in horror to see the faded signs and symbols emblazoned upon the shattered fragments of armor. Hundreds of corpses slithered down out of the doorway, many of them bearing recognizably similar diagrams.

"The place of the Celestials," the Hjo whispered, unable to believe his eyes. "And The Fallen Thousand . . . the Banner Crimson and Black. My revered ancestors. This is . . . *impossible. This is a children's fable!*"

"All too real, Esteemed One," Gretchen said in a thick, hollow voice. Her facial muscles jumped randomly as her old self struggled to regain neural control from the gold-tinged invader. "My Lord Prince, your *control structure.*" She pushed his assault rifle aside and stepped down from the sled, hands spread wide to frame the vast chamber lit through a clear wall by the glare of the accretion disc's light-year-long plasma jet shining far, far away to her left. Beyond the wreckage at the doorway, where some ferocious battle had denied an equally forgotten, unknown enemy entrance, long rows of triangular crystalline cradles rested upon the floor in such numbers as to vanish, uncountable, into the distance. Far, far away, a tall pylon rose from the flame-lit darkness. It shone with subdued green and gold lights, crowned in shadow.

Xochitl pushed past a seemingly frozen Sahâne, following Anderssen cautiously, gun at the ready. The xenoarchaeologist moved slowly, try-ing to keep control of her limbs, the visible world a riot of conflicting data. The México prince signed for one of his marines to shadow her, while the other four set themselves to the points of the compass. Koris followed slowly in the sled.

Left alone in the transit core, the Hjogadim heaved violently into his

revealing the shadow of a greater pattern. Anderssen found she could not—did not want to—look away, but at the same time she felt her own memories begin to fray. . . . *Hummingbird,* she howled mentally. *You evil old man! Nothing ever happens around you by accident.*

"Your eyes are . . . quite golden," Sahâne said in puzzlement. The Hjo didn't remember if this toy had expressed such a peculiar appearance before. Then he flinched back as the Prince's *Macana* assault rifle jammed past his snout and against Gretchen's head, muzzle wedging in between her neckring and helmet.

"Where are we going, Swede?" Xochitl's voice was flat, menacing, much like the flash-suppressor digging into her ear. "Is this a transit car?"

"You know it is, *Tlatocapilli,*" she squeaked, forcing her unwilling tongue to form human words. The peculiar jolt in her perception made her aware of two distinct identities occupying the same physicality—her old self and now something new. This evolving Gretchen rode at the edges of her nerves, altering her perceptions of the universe . . . supplying meaning, context, and direction. Constellations of glyphs began to appear in silhouette around the Prince, the marines, the Jaguar Knight— even Sahâne had his own annotations. A Hjogadim epithet suddenly sprang to mind: *A sure and certain Guide to my thought!*

"I assure you, Lord Prince, we are going where you wished to go."

"I do not think so," he said, eyes narrowed. His exo—and by the Risen Christ, it was a vast relief to have his exocortex operating again— was reporting a flurry of unexpected changes in Doctor Anderssen's breathing, in her kirlian field, in the tension visible in her skin and bone. "I think you have become *infected* with something."

Gretchen raised her arms, turning fully towards him. The flash-suppressor clinked across her helmet, coming to rest square on her faceplate. "I am very sure, now, that Hummingbird did not expect you to be here, Lord Prince, nor indeed, the Holy One." She opened her hand towards Sahâne. "He expected to need just *one key*—myself."

"Key?" Sahâne said, curiosity winning out over naked fear. "Key to what?"

The transit core suddenly came to a halt and everyone froze as they felt the ancient device grow still. In motion, none of them had been aware of anything, but now that the room had completed its travels, each of them felt their equilibrium settle. The door that showed the worst battle damage ground up, shedding dust from long-unused

Eight of the walls shuddered, spilling faint clouds of dust into the air. Behind them, the triangular door slid down with unexpected violence, grinding along hidden tracks with a squeal. The party turned in alarm, their lights sending a cluster of gleaming circles dancing across the battered walls. The door failed partway down, momentarily revealing the hallway beyond dropping away with dizzying speed. This brief visual cue was the only indication they were in motion. Then the door closed as firmly as its eight counterparts, vanishing into the larger expanse of the wall without leaving a visible join.

Xochitl cursed—a long, bitter oath—and his face suddenly cleared, dark eyes glinting through his faceplate. Anderssen felt his "mask" stir. In her Sight, hidden signs and symbols flared to life around the México lord as though he were wreathed in ghostly flame. Fascinated, she watched them solidify first into a wholly alien symbology and then flicker into the more recognizable glyphic alphabet of the México.

Customized, she had time to think, before a dissociative jolt jarred her mind. There had been no noticeable physical sensation of movement, but Anderssen was suddenly sure they had passed over a threshold. *What a peculiar sensation—as though we'd stepped through a doorway within a doorway, leading into a room within the room where we were already present.*

Slowly, she withdrew her gloved hand from Sahâne's arm and turned to stare at the alien. "Revered Sahâne," she breathed, as though addressing him for the first time.

"Get away from him," the Prince ordered. The marines and Koris turned as well, catching a peculiar tone in her voice.

Ignoring the threat in Xochitl's command, Gretchen marveled as the Hjogadim's periphery gleamed brightly with a dizzying array of symbols. Far more in number, and far more varied, than the ghostly effusion accompanying his outburst in Secondary Command on the *Naniwa.* Now his z-suit and fur were literally crawling with signs and symbols of all varieties. Yet as she watched, they began to settle down, consolidating into a rotating, half-seen mesh of glyphs which almost entirely obscured the alien.

Apparently unaware that *he* had changed, Sahâne returned her gaze with one of great curiosity.

Her awareness of the symbology congealed as the glyphic aura around the creature settled down. Vectors of meaning began to emerge,

DEEP WITHIN THE SUNFLOWER

The very long hallway ended in a sloping wall of dark metal pierced by a triangular door. This particular portal seemed to have become jammed, for at the top of the triangle they could see a portion of the valve itself. The edges of the massive frame were also mottled and streaked with carbon scoring and sections of the metal had melted before cooling into odd shapes. Beyond the door, illuminated by the hard white radiance of their helmet and hand lights, stood a nonagonal chamber of moderate size—only thirty or forty meters across.

"Nine walls." The Prince's voice was filled with irritation. "Three was sacred to them, then? And a dead end, Doctor."

"I think, Lord Prince, that they are doors," Gretchen amended. "All alike save this one, which has been damaged."

"Massive." Xochitl did not spit on the floor, but his impatience was very clear.

"They fought hard here." *Cuauhhuehueh* Koris traced his light across the signs of ancient battle—huge discolorations from plasma discharges covered the walls, there were melted panels here and there, and the inlaid floor was scored with deep gouges. The Jaguar Knight dug at the wall with his monofilament combat knife, but left no mark. "Huh!"

Sahâne offered no comment, standing amid them with his shoulders tucked in, radiating unease.

The glyphs and signs ghosting across Anderssen's vision pointed her to the right, collecting like ephemeral birds over a collection of interlocking triangles scribed into the floor.

"Which way?" the Prince snarled, nervously swinging his assault rifle from side to side. "Is this a transit nexus? Swede, all we need is—what are you doing?"

Gretchen had nudged Sahâne down onto the floor, just where he could step onto the triangles illuminated by her hand light. At the touch of the Hjogadim's boot, there was an almost imperceptible tremor.

of the mess area. When the captain removed a breakerbox from his jacket, Hummingbird decided that he was impressed by Locke's resources and expertise. *These men can only be Knights out of New Malta, and see—he is being so very careful not to violate the compact between the Grand Master and the Emperor.*

To that end, Locke shorted out the combat armor on all three marines before tucking the tool away.

"Deft," Hummingbird said quietly, watching the Maltese with intense interest. "Am I still a captive?"

Locke nodded as he removed the comm crystals from the marines' headsets and pocketed them. When he did look up, his greenish eyes were cold. "The Old One said you would be carrying the tablet, but you're not. Regardless, the Saints smile upon us. Better by far for *her* to be his messenger than one of your kind."

Hummingbird's eyebrows rose and he shifted slightly, testing the zipcuffs. *Patience!* he reminded himself. The Templar raised the slim little weapon. One *pfft* and Hummingbird felt a chill wash over him. Then . . . darkness.

The great unknown in the *nauallis'* mind was—were they Maltese, or some other as-yet-unknown faction who had decided to step into the great game? The Knights he believed he understood and could manage, if they kept their tempers, but if it were some other organization? *There is no path to take, yet, while they—ah, now, how interesting!*

From his vantage in the mess, Hummingbird could pick out the respiration of the navigator and Captain Locke on the bridge, as well as two crewmen climbing up from downdeck. And in this very moment, each of the four men was breathing quietly and deeply in unison.

Now, a path is opening. Hummingbird tensed without open movement, preparing for violence.

"Captain, want a *kaffe*?"

Through the hatch opening onto the bridge, the *nauallis* saw the gray-eyed Pilot stand up, his motions easy and assured. Captain Locke looked over from his console, shaking his head. "No, not right now. But—"

Without the slightest hesitation, Piet slapped a gel-tab against the neck of the marine watching the main boards. The man stiffened, paralyzed before he could shout a warning. The Imperial toppled backward into Captain Locke's waiting arms. Hummingbird, watching with interest, noted that both civilians moved with an admirable and soundless efficiency.

The other two marines on the bridge were out of sight, but Piet and Locke both produced slender, matte-black pistols from their jackets—sighted—and there was an almost unnoticed *pfft*. A series of clunking sounds followed, which drew the attention of the marine *Heicho* sitting across the mess from Hummingbird. The corporal rose, shipgun in his hand, eyes swinging to check the *nauallis*, then darting back to the two crewmen coming up the gangway—they were chattering about a zenball scandal on Langkasuka colony—and in that moment of inattention, Piet was behind him. Another gel-tab downed the Imperial, and the two crewmen were across the mess deck at a run to secure the fallen marine.

Locke emerged from the bridge, exchanged a series of complex hand motions with the other three—patterns which, to Hummingbird's great interest, were neither Fleet nor Army battlesign—and then remained behind while Piet and one of the other men disappeared down the gangway.

Ignoring the old Nahuatl, Locke and the remaining crewman dragged the three marines from the bridge and lined up all four men in the middle

ABOARD THE *MOULINS*

Green Hummingbird found himself in the tiny mess area of the freighter, two seats down from the *kaffe* dispenser, his hands secured with a pair of zipcuffs. The Fleet marines remaining aboard had sorted themselves out—three were on the bridge, one was keeping an eye on the *nauallis* and the shipcore, while the remaining man was downdeck in engineering. All of them had armored up while the first team deployed into the landing chamber, but the men inside the ship had slung their helmets over their shoulders on a lanyard.

No one, the old Nahuatl observed, *likes breathing their own recycled waste.*

For his part, Hummingbird was sitting quietly, being as unobtrusive as possible, while the marines and the crew went about their business. Captain Locke and his men, particularly Piet the navigator, had acquired a still, waiting quality over the last hour. The marines were all listening to the chatter of the Prince and his party banging around amongst the dead corridors of the artifact. The expedition had been dropping repeaters at every junction as they moved. The Europeans—Hummingbird had made careful note that all of the freighter crew were of a distinct genotype—were listening as well, but for something else.

The old Náhuatl could do nothing at the moment—guarded and bound as he was—but Hummingbird could let himself become aware of the tenor of men's voices, the speed and direction of their movements, even their smell if they passed by close enough. What he absorbed from all of this was troubling. The very character of the *Moulin's* crew had gradually transformed from the ne'er-do-well collection of roustabouts he and Anderssen had first encountered, to a far more focused team with a well-defined air of something he could only describe as *fierce intent*.

They, too, have a mission here. One unknown to the Prince, or he would have warned his men.

slew sixteen adversaries with only a wooden bokutō *when they ambushed him at prayer. Not one of them believed he was truly in danger.*

The *Kader* cut her main drives, lighting off a hard deceleration burn as soon as the ship had rotated aspect. Inudo laid the light cruiser into the shadow of the *Tlemitl* as they slowed. Hadeishi watched him handle the old *Spear*-class cruiser with great appreciation. The helmsman was exceeding himself today, despite wrestling with an archaic control system. The Nisei officer was gladdened by his men's undaunted spirit.

"All boat-bay doors open, recovery teams stand by." Mitsuharu ordered. Then he tapped open a broadcast channel to the cloud of Imperial evac capsules hiding in the shelter of the stricken flagship. "All Imperial survivors, stand by for identity confirmation."

The shuttle floated delicately into the open boat bay of the *Sokamak* and set down in a rush of maneuvering jets. As soon as the landing pads had touched the deck, the entire boat blew neatly apart into six sections. Four Khaiden penetrator pods deployed out of the debris cloud. Their on-board comps recognized the environment, sorted out targeting in a nanosecond, and burst away from the broken shuttle.

The Khaiden sub-officer in the boat-bay shrieked "Penetrators aboard! Incoming! Incoming!" into his comm an instant before being obliterated by an energy flare. The penetrators raced away down loading corridors and access ways, their plasma cutters shearing through locks and bulkheads.

Mitsuharu considered the likely effects within the *Sokamak* with satisfaction. *It is a poor Khaiden commander who has not prepared for the day when he must put the knife to his superior.*

As the severed wing spun away behind the *Kader*, the on-board weapons systems woke up and spewed a cloud of free-seeking missiles, bomb pods, and chaff. The other two *Hayalet*-class battleships reacted to the sudden appearance of live munitions on their plot by lighting off their own engines and swerving away from both the invisible Barrier and the "weapons accident." The attendant destroyers and support ships followed, while their commanders were tremendously amused to see a brace of sprint missiles from the "accident" flare across the prow of the proud *Sokamak.*

Their 'cast chatter was quick and violent, but now Hadeishi was beginning to pick out sentences and phrases:

"See, Begh-Adag covers himself with glory again!"

"Fireworks to celebrate his demotion."

"What other captain could guide his ship to such renown, eh Hunt-lord Zah'ar?"

"Are you volunteering for something, Geh'zir?"

"No!"

"God of a Thousand Eyes forefend! The Sokamak!*"*

The battleship was still quite clear on Mitsuharu's v-display. The massive hull convulsed, ripped by four fusion blasts deep within its core. Then it shattered as jets of plasma erupted from gaps in the outer hull, tearing apart in a rapidly expanding cloud of superheated radioactive debris.

Hadeishi smiled, nodding to himself. *At Kurētāko Shrine, Musashi*

THE KADER

"Pilot, acceleration up a point," Hadeishi announced, preternaturally calm. The light cruiser moved forward, picking up speed as the real-space drives burned mass. In his earbug he could hear a sudden rise in chatter from the Khaiden battleship. *Someone is paying attention—but the shuttle is far more interesting than we are.* Before him on his plot, a faint, faint trail gleamed.

"Pilot, course one-quarter point to starboard. And not one meter more."

Warning! the navigation officer on the *Sokamak* barked in alarm. *You're too close to the . . .*

"All hands, brace for impact!" Hadeishi snapped into his shipside comm.

The *Kader*'s starboard wing, a long pylon holding missile racks, bomb pods, and an array of other weapons, sheared directly into a Thread and neatly separated with a squeal of metal Mitsuharu could hear in Command, and then spun away from the light cruiser. Secondary explosions cauterized the shattered pylon almost immediately. Damage control parties rushed down suddenly vented corridors to patch the ruptures. Mitsuharu felt the whole ship tremble. He punched new course settings into the plot. "Full speed, *Thai-i.*"

A stabbing azure flare burst from the engines and the *Kader* leaped forward like a scalded cat, racing away from both Thread and the *Sokamak* at maximum acceleration. An instant later, the México officer at the *Kader*'s comm station punched up a prerecorded distress call—translated to Khadesh—on all frequencies, interspersed with pleas for "a clear path, give us a clear path!"

Hadeishi's attention stayed on the plot as the battleship receded in the viewing screen. The shuttle carrying the "Imperial scientist" was only seconds from entering the assigned docking bay. Mitsuharu nodded to Lovelace, who was poised with a preprogrammed transmission burst ready to send. "Comm, go."

Anderssen at the cargo rail. She scrutinized what she could see of his face within the helmet. *He's interested. Not as tired. Not as fearful.*

The Jaguar Knight turned the sled, sending them down another long vaulted hallway. More rows of compartments appeared, yet like the others they were spotless and empty.

of gold. Glyphs inscribed beside the entrance swam and cavorted in her sight, a vision now drenched in brassy light. On the floor, on the walls, as high as their hand lights could reach, meanings leaped out, indicating direction and time and purpose in an ever-dancing overlay to the solid world. Murals began to emerge from the plain-seeming walls, showing the edifice of a great civilization—towers piercing cloud-streaked skies; endless multitudes moving below, in enormous cities. Thousands of races were represented and not one of them seemed to be placed above the others, though the massive Hjogadim were well represented.

Oh boy, Anderssen thought. *Is this how the structure functions? Or did the ancient Hjo see the world this way all the time?*

"Keep moving," Xochitl gritted. They stepped out into a leviathan hallway, stretching off far beyond the reach of their lights in either direction. Only a few meters from the doorway, a row of diamond-shaped compartments was visible at floor level. The Prince, curious, advanced to the closest one—his marines pacing him ahead and behind. As their lights moved, Gretchen bit her lip, seeing another row of compartments above the first, and then another, and then another. . . .

Xochitl rapped on the closest door, then shone his light inside. "It's like glassite. Sealed, but empty." He stepped away from the dark, silent chamber and swung with the beam of his lamp off into the distance, following the wall.

"They go way up, too," the marine behind Gretchen added. "Way up."

Sahâne stared morbidly into the sealed spaces as he passed by. The gleam of the helmet lights was swallowed up by the enormous spaces surrounding them. After walking fifteen minutes without seeing any end in sight, Xochitl ordered a halt.

"Koris—take two men back and get us a grav-sled from the freighter."

Once aboard the sled, they made excellent time, zipping along the massive passageway. After nearly an hour of travel, they reached an intersection.

"I think, this way," Gretchen urged, seeing the glyphs flowing and dancing in the air congregate around the right-hand avenue. "Yes, definitely."

Sahâne peered into the darkness, staring at the patterned sigils cut into the walls of the intersection, and then shuffled over to stand beside

He's removed his mask again. Only a frightened man remains in Huitzilopochtli's place.

"Sahâne-*tzin*, what do you say to this?" Xochitl asked.

The living Hjo's face greatly resembled that of the long-dead priest walking in Gretchen's golden vision, a ghastly mask of suppressed horror. His limpid gray-black eyes fixed on Gretchen for the first time. "*You* know what this place is . . . how can this be? How can a *toy* know what I—one of the Guided Race—do not!"

"There are legends," she replied carefully, "and fragments out of the past that still endure. Not all fantastical tales are false . . . but all that *I* know is that this whole enormous structure"—she extended her arms, taking in the entirety of the *Chimalacatl* and the singularity—"is the work of *your* people. Are you not pleased to look upon their greatness?"

"I despair," Sahâne croaked, voice thick with emotion, "to find myself amid this ruin and find the greatness of my people is ash!"

Xochitl seemed confounded. His face went blank. Gretchen caught a fragment of his helplessness, but made no move to enlighten him.

Sahâne favored them both with a contemptuous stare. "Apes! Such skills as tore suns from their orbits and compressed matter into ultimate annihilation, such skills as made this . . . this mausoleum . . . are *lost to us*. This place, it might as well have been made by the gods themselves! By the Living Flame which Guides! We are so petty now . . ." His voice trailed away into a disgusted, lamenting mumble.

A flicker of emotion lighted Xochitl's face. He scrutinized Gretchen warily. "Team one, to me." The Prince ordered half of his men forward. "Team two, secure the ship. Doctor Anderssen, you help the Esteemed Sahâne here *find a command structure!*"

With the heavy black assault rifles of the marines at her back, Gretchen reached up to place a gentle hand on the young Hjogadim's armored wrist. "Lord Sahâne, let us go further on. Is this not a cathedral of your caste? Has not the place of it been lost to your line? Have a care here. So many lie untended."

She led the Hjo onward, picking their way out of the disposal chamber through a triangular doorway. As they passed through, Gretchen caught sight of a faint radiance shining in the metal. *After all this time there are still glimmers within the material. What marvelous alloy could this be? Or are there bioluminescent organisms trapped within?*

"Ah!" The pale gleaming strengthened rapidly, becoming a floodlight

in cross-section. Perhaps only a difference in nutrition, but if I could look at the whole thing, it might turn out to be a genetic difference. Maybe the old Hjogadim were a different sub-species. Wouldn't that be interesting!

Curious, Gretchen moved off across the midden, her fingers brushing lightly across the most exposed of the corpses. Most of them seemed morphologically similar, though there were other, more alien-seeming races among the dead. *Has the history of these others been wholly lost? Is this where they became extinct? How long ago did all this occur?*

She stopped, going to one knee, and pulled out her field comp.

"This is your *suitable entrance?*" Xochitl crunched over to her, his voice a harsh rasp. "How far are we from a control structure? From whatever mechanism manages the entrance to the Barrier?"

Anderssen flashed a wintry smile up at the Prince. Her field comp had flickered awake and she was scanning one of the better-preserved skulls with her sensor wand turned to short-focus x-ray. "I am not sure *we* can enter the control spaces of this device. But I believe that *he* can." She indicated Sahâne with a tilt of her helmet. "If he chooses to lead us there."

Looking back at the alien, the now-familiar sense of disassociation stole over her, filling her chest with pleasant warmth, drawing her mind far from her body, which seemed to recede below her. Standing in this ancient place, her eyes filled with glorious Sight. The snap and glare of plasma guns, the screams of the wounded and dying dinned against her ears. A swirl of faint ghosts washed over her, as the ancient Hjogadim struggled and died, slaughtering each other in the corridors and control spaces. Then machines came, bearing the dead, laying them in ordered rows in the disposal bay, even as the tide of battle washed on to other shores. In her vision, a solitary Hjo—in comparison to the others, seeming almost solid—moved among the dead, giving some kind of last blessing. His skin and armor were anointed with the same glyphs and markings as Sahâne bore.

Watching the—priest?—passing among the dead, Gretchen became peripherally aware of a golden tinge tainting her sight. Tentatively, her fingers moved, drifting to touch the bronze block. They stopped short, encountering an aura of heat, almost hot enough to scald.

"We had best move on—if we are to stay," she said, forcing herself to focus on the Prince. "If you intend to carry through with your purpose. . . ."

"I do," Xochitl said, his face pinched and pale.

WITHIN THE SUNFLOWER

Forty minutes after the *Moulins* was secured in the landing cradle and Captain Locke's crew had completed their set-down checklist, the marine fire team disembarked from the freighter in full combat armor, assault rifles at the ready. They confirmed what the exterior cameras had already shown Gretchen and the others on the bridge.

The rest of the chamber was filled with an enormous drift of bones, plasma-scored metal, and the desiccated corpses of thousands of inhuman creatures. Fifteen minutes after the marines had signaled the all-clear for the immediate vicinity, the Prince, Gretchen and a very nervous Sahâne stepped out of the cargo elevator and crunched their way across a slope of crumbling bones to a platform facing an exit door.

There Xochitl stopped, panning his helmet light across the ossuary in grudging wonder. "Battle," he commented, eyes drawn to the shattered limbs and broken armor thigh-deep in the bay. "But not here . . . these bodies were dumped." His gaze traveled upward, the light picking out the angled shape of a monstrous crane hanging over the chamber, and beside it another, and another. They were folded up against the ceiling like a resting spider's knobby legs. The Prince turned to Gretchen. "What kind of entryway did you choose for us?"

"Garbage disposal," Sahâne said, his alien voice thick with bitterness. He knelt and lifted one of the cadaverous skulls. It was long-snouted, with a tapering jaw, and a mouth filled with rows of crushing molars aft and shredding incisors forward. Some remnant of a pelt remained, preserved by vacuum, apparently a mottled black or dark gray. "For discarded husks which could not be properly cremated."

Looking over his shoulder, Anderssen nodded, unsurprised. *I will send Professor Griffiths in the Comparative Languages Department a thousand roses, should I ever see Imperial space again!*

She wanted to handle the bones, but wondered if the ambassador would take offense. *A skull much like that of a Hjogadim, though larger*

creature were not part of the old witch's plan. Another ugly thought came to her. *He has his own ship—if he knows a way out of here, then we've been left behind to decoy and delay the Khaid. But even so—I would not trade places with Sayu now.*

"Tens of thousands of cargo containers—suspension pods, I would guess—are held in each of those three lobes. But that's only what we see nearby in this image. In the whole of the debris swirl, there are over four thousand ships, the comp says . . ."

Koshō's eyes widened, taking in the lift capacity of the dead fleet. "Troop transports for a million-man army?"

"Colony ships?" Helsdon shook his head. "I don't know what to make of it. Maybe refugees? A million isn't much to lift from some dying world—but it's sure better than what *we* could pull together."

"Was all this a fortress?" Susan wondered softly, her eyes turning to the system plot and the delicate balance of the brown dwarves, the singularity, and the *Chimalacatl*. "It must have been, hidden behind the wall of knives. But not a refuge, not in the end . . ." Her voice strengthened. "Engineer, can you find out if these ships were empty or full when they were destroyed?"

Helsdon nodded. Koshō turned to Oc Chac. "Meanwhile, we need another way out of this pocket, one that is not barred by the enemy. You've the search-pattern set?"

"*Hai, Chu-sa* . . . starting from the Pinhole and spiraling out."

"Excellent." Susan nodded approval.

"But *Chu-sa*, if what Engineer Helsdon mentioned is true—if the whipping knives destroyed this great fleet of souls—why haven't we been attacked?"

"I do not know, *Sho-sa*, but I hope our luck holds." Koshō returned to her station, intending to comm up Engineering and see how Hennig was getting along, then stopped, looking quizzically around Command. *Something's not right* . . . Frowning, she tapped open a v-pane showing the guest quarters, then scanned through a series of empty cabins with rising alarm. *Damn his scrawny bones!* She commed Ship Security, "*Thai-i*, can you determine if either of our diplomatic guests are available to meet me in the command bridge conference room? This is urgent."

Beside her, Oc Chac glanced up nervously, saw her stormy expression, and ducked back to the search pattern. Five minutes went by with no word from the brig. "Very well," Susan said. "Full speed ahead, *Sho-sa*. We've no time to waste." *Hummingbird would not have taken that "ambassador" with him—contravening the Prince's express order—if the*

THE *NANIWA*

The battle-cruiser had clawed its way back up out of the interlocking g-fields wrapped around the singularity in realspace, finally reaching a point where the hypercoil could punch them through to transluminal. In Command, Koshō sat in her shockchair, one slim leg crossed over the other, watching the threatwell rotate slowly. The cloud of broken ships was fast approaching as they climbed gradient, and the sight of such colossal devastation weighed heavily on her thoughts. Helsdon, having completed his mandatory sleep cycle, was sitting at the Nav station with *Thai-i* Olin. Together they had reconfigured nearly half of the shipskin to watch for the kind of quantum disturbances the engineer suspected heralded the movement or presence of the Barrier threads.

Better than nothing, Susan thought tiredly, *but I am already missing Doctor Anderssen's presence.*

She paced over to their console. "Any luck, *Kikan-shi?*"

"There must be a defensive Thread array associated with the Sunflower," Helsdon muttered, one pale hand trembling over a plot of the broken armada. "Most of these ships were cut apart, just as ours were. . . ."

"An attack?" Koshō leaned over his shoulder, puzzled. "They're bunched together so tightly . . ."

"No . . ." Helsdon replied, scratching nervously at a week's beard. "They've fallen into a balance point in the gravitation of this system. This is an eddy of flotsam . . . the ships might have all been destroyed out by the Barrier itself . . . or even closer to the artifact."

"Why not a battle?"

Helsdon seemed to shrink, shoulders hunching in, and an expression of pain flitting across his face. "These weren't warships, *Chu-sa.*" His stylus tapped unevenly across the control panes and a series of comp-projected reconstructions sprang to life. The alien craft were revealed as sixty-kilometer-long trihedrons with bulky drive fairings at the rear.

The light cruiser matched velocity with the *Sokamak*, and the shuttle jetted away on an intercept course for the battleship. A v-pane on his console showed Mitsuharu the boat-bay-three doors cycling closed.

"Shuttle away, *kyo*," Cupan confirmed.

Hadeishi shifted uncomfortably in the shockchair, one eye on a replay of the missing battle-cruiser's escape, the other on a series of panels showing thermal readings from the profusion of broken ships, fusion detonations, and other hot-spots in the immediate area. The dust clouds, which seemed to have thickened around the invisible Barrier, were slowly shifting color as the component particles soaked up the hard radiation.

"Pilot, turn two points to starboard, one point dorsal."

Inudo nodded, his neck shining with sweat. "*Hai, kyo*. Two points starboard, one dorsal."

The *Kader*'s maneuvering thrusters flared briefly as she turned away from running parallel with the *Sokamak*, her nose angling towards the entrance to the Pinhole itself. There, the walls of dust were burning with a deep orange and azure, making a sea of fire to blind the unwary eye.

Against this background, Hadeishi thought, *the thrust-signature of our so-able friend would be nearly undetectable if one did not know exactly what to look for.*

But Lovelace and Tocoztic had painstakingly reassembled the course taken by the battle-cruiser, and now Mitsuharu was watching for traces of her drive plume wending its way amongst the hidden shoals and reefs of the depthless ocean.

Musashi stands poised on the bridge at Windlodge, goose-feathers brushing the enamel of his cheek-guard, the Iroquois swarming up the levee in a numberless, copper-skinned mass. One of their ohnkanetoten *surges through the ranks of charging pike men astride a roan stallion . . . sun-dogs gleaming from his garishly ornamented plate-mail, his long sword shining silver in the summer light.*

him with a bellicose stare, saying, "If you were my fosterling, I would rap your knuckles sharply, *Chu-sa*. You play recklessly, risking yourself at every turn—but I cannot fault your consideration for the other children. They are always in your thoughts, and you are always the first to offer them a hand up from the ground. I hope—and I doubt we will meet again—that you will consider that *your* life may be just as precious, to others."

The *Wilful* had slipped away hours before, vanishing into the vastness of the *kuub*, leaving no trace of its passing which the *Kader*'s sensors could detect.

"All stations secure?" Mitsuharu asked on the command channel. A frenzy of confused activity followed amongst the Imperials on the unfamiliar bridge. "Weapons—confirm that guns are cold? Missile racks and penetrator pods are locked down? All hands, brace for combat acceleration."

A ragged chorus of *Hai, Chu-sa* arose, both in Command and on the channel from downdeck.

Hadeishi nodded to Inudo. "Pilot, point-and-a-quarter to ventral. Begin deceleration burn."

The *Thai-i* rotated a glyph on his display just a fraction and then slid a gauge lower. "*Hai, kyo*. Point-and-a-quarter, ventral. Beginning deceleration burn."

On the plot, the *Kader*'s icon closed swiftly with that of the *Sokamak*, the largest of the Khaid battleships. Lovelace's translation of the 'cast chatter had gleaned only fragmentary information for Hadeishi, but he knew some of the ship designators now, and a little bit about his enemy. He knew that one of the more vocal Khaid commanders was named Za-h'ar, and he had at least two rivals. The late, unlamented captain of the *Kader* had been Begh-Adag—and that fellow seemed to have been the least respected of the clan-lords involved in this escapade.

"*Chu-sa*, point-and-a-half turned. Deceleration burn complete." Inudo shook out his shoulders and hurriedly called up a new slate of course and speed settings on a side pane.

"*Joto-Heiso* Cupan, ready shuttle in bay three for launch," Hadeishi said into the throatmike. "Damage control parties, starboard wing, stand by for decompression."

The chief petty officer from the *Asama* tapped in amongst the chorus of *Hai, kyo* from the damage control teams. "Shuttle in bay three, ready for launch, *Chu-sa*."

THE KADER

Hadeishi listened intently to the z-suit radio, his throatmike replaced by a vocoder Cajeme had assembled from the components of an entertainment 3-v scavenged from the main mess deck. As he listened, the eager voice of a Khaiden *Kabil Rezei* aboard the battleship *Sokamak* buzzed away into silence.

"Yes, my lord." Mitsuharu keyed into a v-pane on his display. A second later, the 'coder produced a yipping bark ending in a sibilant growl. To Hadeishi's poorly trained ear, it sounded like proper Khadesh. . . . "One of the Imperial capsules had a scientist aboard—he sought to barter service—and questioning has revealed a way to detect the Wall-of-Knives. I am bringing him to you now with his instrumentation."

Out of the corner of his eye, Hadeishi observed the other officers standing watch in Command were keeping their mouths shut, as ordered. They were, however, grinning and signing "victory" to one another. *Morale is good,* he thought, waiting for a response. *As befits those snatched from Mictlantecuhtli's dreadful embrace.*

The *Kader* plowed through the dust at a swift pace, transit deflectors up full, shrouding the ship in a cascade of brilliant interference. The Pinhole was now only moments away. The *Hayalet*-class battleships deployed around the broken hulk of the Imperial research station showed clearly on her sensors.

Five minutes to deceleration burn, Thai-i Inudo keyed to each of the other stations.

Hadeishi bid proper farewell to the hunt-lord, then closed the circuit. *I miss Captain De Molay. But she has her ship back, only a little worse for wear.* The old woman had not been happy about the mess they'd left behind on the *Wilful,* but accepted it as the cost of survival. A handful of the walking wounded had been left with her as well, to crew the little freighter.

In their last conversation, on comm between the two ships, she fixed

the alien warily, but they kept their distance. The Hjo licked his lips, long head darting from side to side.

Hummingbird affected no notice of the activity: "My duty to your father compels me to try and save your life."

Xochitl drew his sidearm, thumbing off the safety. "Unwise choice, old man. You are utterly—"

"Lining up a new approach vector," Gretchen's voice cut in. She had ignored the Prince and the Judge and their spat, even the appearance of Sahâne, instead watching the progress of the diamond-hard light which had traversed the hull. Now the radiance flickered out as swiftly as it had appeared, and the Navigator's panel in front of her woke to life again. Now, however, all of the v-panes and controls were displaying the tight curlicues of the alien hieroglyphics which had come and gone from her vision over the past days.

Landing beacon locked, one of them suggested to her and, nodding in acknowledgment, Anderssen tapped the glyph. The nav system on the freighter kicked in, adjusting their approach. Piet started in alarm— then looked to the captain for guidance—his face tight with distress. Locke shook his head *no*, the movement barely visible even to Gretchen, who was seated only two meters away. Both men watched her intently and Gretchen suddenly tasted a little of their desire, which matched tone and color with hers.

Let us see what lies beyond, a memory echoed, bringing with it the smell of oiled wood and a perfume she'd last worn as an undergraduate. *Beyond the door of the unopened tomb, beyond the rise of the next hill, within unplumbed space, beyond our conception. This is the fever which drives us to create, to innovate, to overcome.*

Outside, the mottled black wall had divided into three parts, and each triangle receded from sight. Beyond, in a chamber whose comprehensible size—only a few hundred meters in each dimension—seemed puny and cramped, was the age-etched shape of a landing cradle.

"Entering an active g-field," Piet reported, taking over the controls. "Docking jets adjusting . . ."

Then a point of hard jewel-like radiance appeared at the center of the innermost diamond. A distinct collimating beam stabbed out and washed over the *Moulins*, causing the forward cameras to polarize, reducing their view to nothing but a scintillating white point. In Anderssen's equipment rig, the bronze block stopped vibrating and went cold. Gretchen gasped in pain as her perceptual gestalt abruptly collapsed, leaving her blinking owlishly at her console, which had terminated all of the v-panes simultaneously.

Behind her, the Prince stiffened in alarm.

The vision overlay generated by Xochitl's exo was awash with unknown and indecipherable datagrams and hieroglyphs. Voices were speaking in his mind in a lilting, singsong tongue like calling birds; but though the cadence of the sounds seemed terribly familiar he knew none of the words. Alarmed, he surged upward out of his shockchair. "What the—"

"A Gate opens before you," said an unexpected voice. A seamed old hand, hard as bog oak, settled on the Prince's shoulder and forced him back down. The México looked up, astounded to see that Green Hummingbird—now clad in a Fleet z-suit—had slipped quietly into the back of the bridge. The dyspeptic face of the Hjogadim Sahâne peered down over his shoulder, red-rimmed eyes staring accusingly at the Prince. The *nauallis* met Xochitl's gaze with a serious expression. "I advise you not to enter this structure."

"You would exhaust God's patience, sorcerer." The Prince threw aside the old Náhuatl's arm and pushed up from his seat. "You *do not* command me! You serve the Empire and in this place I am—"

"It is my purpose, *Tlatocapilli*," Hummingbird interrupted, "to keep humanity from harm—and this *place* is beyond our skill to use, our power to hold, and our intellect to understand. We must leave before we come to grief. Or worse, bring disaster home with us."

"You threaten me?" Xochitl bit out the words, struggling to keep his temper.

The Prince's exo had already summoned *Cuauhhuehueh* Koris and the marines, who now appeared in the hatchway. The Jaguar Knight ducked inside, shipgun leveled on Hummingbird's back.

Sahâne found himself surrounded by the marines, who were watching

"They are closed to us," Gretchen said, attempting to smile reassuringly at him over her shoulder. The resulting expression was almost feral, for a wild, heedless light had come into her face. "We need just the right kind of way in . . . nothing fancy, *Tlatocapilli*. That would be dangerous."

"And you can tell that which is dangerous and that which is not?" His attempt at sarcasm sounded shrill, for his voice was tight with fear.

"We are still alive, aren't we?" Gretchen turned back to her console. *Oh, what is this?*

Illuminated by the *Moulin's* running lights, a constellation of new structures emerged from the darkness. Tall pylons ascended from pooled shadow below to disappear into equal indigo above. Between them, another of the structures which seemed to be a portal door had appeared: a triangular shape several hundred meters high, comprised of four smaller triangles. Each of the inner triangles contained a further inverted, and recessed, triangle. This arrangement, unlike many others they had passed, held a darker hue—almost night-black itself, but irregularly mottled.

Anderssen's console flickered, all of the v-panes abruptly closing and then reopening again. She stiffened, feeling a flood of heat warm her chest, even through the z-suit and the equipment rig. The edges of the analysis displays on the console began to distort, the lettering transforming into the unintelligible glyphs which had overcome the *Naniwa's* navigational system during their transit of the Pinhole.

Uh-oh. Node 333 is connecting—but it's not plugged in! Gretchen felt the pattern of her analysis matrices shifting. The pulsing back-and-forth of her comps and storage nodes shaded as well, starting to move faster— much faster than she could follow. Dreading what she might feel, Anderssen slipped her right hand under her jacket, fingertips brushing against the surface of the bronze block. It was very warm and vibrating faintly. She looked down and was stunned to see that a hot, golden glow was shining between her fingers. *What the—*

"Anderssen, what *is* that?" Xochitl had finally noticed the grouping of pylons.

"We are very close," she managed to say. Löjtnant Piet, without even a look to Captain Locke, had turned the freighter towards the four-sided diamond. Their speed slowed, now the *Moulins* was inching along. The exterior floods angled forward, trying to illuminate the blackened surface. The beams played across the portal, but did not even generate a reflection, as though the material were drinking in the light.

WITHIN THE SUNFLOWER

The *Moulins* crept forward through the dark, exterior floods stabbing into a colossal empty space. Hints of enormous structures wreathed in shadow ghosted by on either side. On the bridge, Gretchen had her eyes half closed, fingers drifting lightly across her console. The *oliohuiqui* she'd taken was burning at the back of her throat, and the flood of data populating her v-displays had coalesced in her perception, becoming a fluid thing, shifting and deforming with each passing moment, as more and more information flowed into the array of comps. Dozens of passageways branched off in all directions as they moved, but only one thread through the maze seemed proper to her. If pressed, she would have said the volume of the channel they were following felt the *most used*, though nothing obvious about the ranks of triliths they passed would have indicated this.

"Six hundred k from the entrance now," the pilot said quietly. "How deep are we g—

"As deep as necessary," Xochitl snapped. His mood, if possible, had worsened while sitting in the darkness at the back of the bridge. *He doesn't like it that Europeans are handling the ship.* Gretchen clearly felt the nervous tension throbbing in the Prince, as though a wire were being twisted tighter and tighter around some fulcrum. His discomfort was now beginning to cause *her* physical pain.

Xochitl stirred, glaring accusingly at Anderssen. "We have passed several hundred thousand openings into the structure, Swede. Why haven't we stopped?"

Though her attention was focused far from the Prince, after a lengthy pause Gretchen remembered to reply: "None of them are suitable."

"How so?" The Prince brought up the internal map of the structure being constructed by the sensors on the Navigator's console. "We've passed numerous secondary openings—are these doors?—large enough for a dreadnaught to enter—how are they not suitable for *our* entry?"

shadow of the dreadnaught's hulk. We are going to go in and get them out." A smile lit his face for a moment. "And if some Khaiden ships fall afoul of our passage, well then—all the better."

"Impossible," breathed an ensign, now the sole officer remaining from the *Gladius*. "We haven't a third the weight of a single *Hayalet!* We'll be shot to bits within moments of our initial missile salvo!"

"Therefore," Hadeishi said, turning and surveying them all, "we will not attack until it is too late for them to respond. And preferably, we will not attack *at all* while achieving our goal."

The Imperial officers stared at him in confusion. Then there was a babble of questions.

"Show us," De Molay said loudly. That quieted the group. Her seamed old face showed skepticism, but Hadeishi saw that her eyes were merry with anticipation. "Show us what you plan to do, *Chu-sa.*"

"Attention the bridge," Hadeishi announced, standing up. The low murmur in the circular room died away. The regular watch had swollen to include the leaders of the various ships' crews rescued from the abyss. Mitsuharu looked about slowly, considering each man and woman as though seeing them for the first time. He stepped to the center of the bridge, where Lovelace had rigged up a holocast projection in place of the old-fashioned plotting display which had formerly served the *Kader*. *It's no threatwell*, Hadeishi thought, *but will do for now*. He marked off the area of interest with his stylus. A series of vector tracks appeared in the 'cast.

"The *surtu*, as the Khaiden name their hunting pack, has dispersed over the last forty-eight hours." Mitsuharu's tone was crisp. "Four of their *Hayalet*-class battleships remain at the entrance to the Pinhole. They are supported by six destroyers, several tenders, and what seems from message traffic to be a troop ship. It is difficult to keep track of their movements under the current conditions, but I would hazard they are making a serious attempt to chart the outlines of the aperture. The other surviving ships have scattered to police the battleground, and to search along the periphery of the Barrier for another way through." The corners of his eyes tightened minutely. "One of their prey—an Imperial battle-cruiser of the *Provincial*-class—has escaped the battle by navigating through the Barrier itself."

"How?" An officer from the *Mace* blurted without thinking. "Our sensors can't even . . ."

"We do not know how," Hadeishi said quietly. "But the telemetry we've deciphered from *this* ship indicates they did so. It is also possible that the battle-cruiser took aboard at least one evac capsule from the super-dreadnaught which was destroyed in the Pinhole itself—"

"Surely your Prince Xochitl left the field of battle in haste, then!" De Molay said loudly, drawing a round of glares from the Imperials seated or standing around her.

Hadeishi continued, unperturbed. "Speculating about who may have lived or died is useless.

"And we are not concerned with the Prince." The stylus in his hand circumscribed a constellation of glowing dots on the plotting board. "There are sixteen evac capsules from the *Tlemitl* hiding in the sensor-

into the formation . . . we'd trip ourselves up the first time someone commed to discuss the weather!"

De Molay spread her hands. "Then we give up and go home. No loss."

Her nonchalant expression sparked a flare of anger in the Nisei officer. He glowered at the freighter captain, which drew an amused snort from the old woman, and then he sat back in the uncomfortable chair again, thinking furiously.

The youngest of the Seven Sisters pressed her forehead to the straw matting covering the floor of Musashi's hut. "Please, sensei," she begged earnestly, "none of us can defeat Möngke; he is a monster, gifted with inhuman powers, surrounded by an army of tens of thousands of men. Osaka castle itself is a maze of fortifications, towers, moats . . . We've tried sneaking in, but he's suborned the ninja clans as well, and they watch by night while his archers watch by day."

"He only has one weakness," Eldest said, kneeling beside her irrepressible sibling. "He believes himself the finest swordsman in all of Asia—not just Nippon—and if you challenge him, then he will come forth to meet you in single combat, for his pride will admit no other rival."

"I no longer travel the sword-saint's road," Musashi croaked, his voice raspy from disuse. He indicated a small stone statue of the Buddha with a seated bow. "I no longer seek conflict in the world of men. Ieyasu and I strove to overthrow the Yuan seven years ago, and failed utterly. Now he is dead and I have found sanctuary here on Mount Iwato. Only the Dokkōdō remains." He gestured to a series of scrolls sitting on a small side table.

Eldest glanced sidelong at Squeaker's twin, who was standing in the doorway, keeping watch.

"What if the Emperor summoned you, called you forth to do battle with the invaders? Would you deny him, foreswear your duty to all Nippon?"

Musashi shook his head sadly. "The last Emperor fell at Nara generations ago."

"Not so." The third Sister turned in the doorway. "The Imperial line is sustained even today. Would the plea of the Son of Heaven move you to action?"

The hermit fell silent, eyes downcast, for a long time. When he looked up, at last, the sunset was gilding the rough-hewn timbers of his hut. "It would."

The third Sister extended his hand. "Then stir yourself, Musashi Miyamoto, Nippon calls you."

"We have comm intercept available, *Chu-sa*," De Molay announced in an offhand way.

Hadeishi's command chair rotated to face her with an audible whine. Apparently the Khaid refit had failed to properly seal the gimbals, and fire suppression foam was eating away at the mechanism. The Nisei officer shifted restlessly. "We're synched into their battlecast? Is the translator running?"

"Such as it is." De Molay shrugged, her thin shoulders swallowed by the expedition jacket. "Channel eleven."

Mitsuharu pressed a finger to his earbug, jumping channels until the hissing growl of the enemy flooded in, making him wince. Dialing down the volume, he found the jury-rigged translator circuit could use a great deal of improvement—about every fourth word of Khadesh echoed back in Nihongo on channel two. He grimaced, feeling a truly staggering migraine coming on, before settling back with his eyes closed, trying to parse some kind of meaning from the staticky roaring.

After thirty minutes, he wrenched the earbug free and stared cross-eyed at Lovelace and De Molay. Hadeishi said nothing for a moment, keying his med-band to dispense as much painkiller as it would allow.

"This won't work. Your efforts are tremendous, but the shipnet comps just can't keep up with all of the cross-conversations. Have you been recording all of this traffic?"

The *Sho-i* nodded vigorously. "We have sixteen hours in the can, *Chu-sa*."

"Can we translate that, if the comp has time to grind away?"

"*Hai, Chu-sa.*"

Mitsuharu shook his head slowly, beginning to despair. "Without following the 'cast in real time, there's no way we can insert ourselves

sequence. "Go on, enter," she directed. "We'll be shielded from the radiation storm inside."

The freighter passed in, maneuvering drives flaring, and was swiftly enveloped by abyssal darkness. Behind them, the constellation of triliths reformed with admirable speed, abruptly cutting off sight of the hot, glowing sky outside.

"It seems the artifact is not entirely dead," Gretchen said cheerfully. "No matter. I believe we can open the passage again, when the need arises."

In the suddenly dim bridge, Xochitl scratched his nose and—taking a deep breath—began to compose a series of numbers in his thoughts. *Zero, one, one, two, three, five, eight, thirteen, twenty-one . . .*

and pressed the acidic tablet beneath her tongue. Her skin was singing with the tension congealing in the Command compartment, but the promise of so many wonders to come pushed all of her concerns away.

"Radiation levels are rising," Piet reported, tapping a winking glyph on his display to expand the warning message. "Captain?"

"Reconfigure the shipskin for maximum protection," Locke replied without bothering to consult with the Prince. "Let's try not to fry!"

Anderssen paid them little attention, though part of her mind wondered what had happened to the shipskin, for the flow of data into her analysis array did not diminish at all. The exterior configuration of the ship *had* changed however, shifting into an unfamiliar alignment.

But for the moment, Gretchen didn't care about the crew's machinations. *As long as we're capturing clean data . . . wait a moment.* A subtle change had occurred in the visual flow of the artifact. Nothing obvious—the intersecting triangles had a vertiginous effect on the eye—but the consistency of the shadows pooling in their depths had begun to thicken. "There!" Anderssen suddenly spoke, half-rising from her seat. "Quadrant six by sixteen—that's a lock entrance."

"How can you tell?" Xochitl glared over her shoulder in disgust at the flurry of bizarre glyphs and patterns dancing across her v-displays. "What *is* all of this static?"

"Our eyes in the darkness, Lord Prince," she replied distantly. "Löjtnant—slow a bit . . ." Her stylus danced across a v-pane cross-connected to the comm system. A burst of indecipherable noise flooded from the ship's tachyon array. "Now, wait . . . wait . . . there!"

One of the triliths moved—its motion obvious even to the naked eye—receding into sudden darkness. The constellation of other triliths around the missing triangle followed, sliding backward into shadow without evident mechanism. An opening emerged with fluid suddenness—a channel or corridor leading into the interior of the structure. Measurements popped up on Gretchen's console and she whistled softly, breaking into a huge grin. "Six kilometers on a side, Lord Price. I think the *Moulins* will make easy passage."

"This was built for truly giant ships," Xochitl said, his voice tinged with awe. "Like the thousands of wrecks in the debris cloud."

No one replied. Locke and Piet were motionless, their faces settled into expressionless masks. Gretchen felt a current of raw fear circulate among the men in Command, but the taste was distant and of little con-

kind of lord who likes strangers—particularly inquisitive ones—to come knocking around.

"But Harriet especially liked taking a gaggle of impressionable students out to do big ground surveys and to excavate just enough of an old city to intrigue the historical agencies, who would then give her more money and permits to do whatever she wanted so they could learn the next bit of the story she was telling. I think the reason *she* did it was because the challenge of facing sudden death and coming home with the bacon got her out of bed in the morning.

"As long as I knew her, she specialized in visiting the resident gang lord with a gift bottle of *uisge-beatha*. By the time she'd spent an hour chatting with him in an entirely charming manner, the fearsome and despicable toad had been transformed into her special, professional chum. I never knew her to break any laws, and somehow she always brought her crew home with all their fingers and toes."

Green Hummingbird raised an eyebrow. "An enviable record, Doctor Anderssen." He stood up, patting his pockets. "I believe you are going to need all of your equipment in a very short time."

Six hours later, the *Moulins* had reached the edge of the *Chimalacatl*.

Gretchen had appropriated the Comm station from the Jaguar Knight and now watched her v-displays eagerly. Endless ranks of jagged architectural forms glided past as the freighter plowed along at right-angles to the surface of the artifact. The structure was apparently composed entirely of triangular sections, each holding a second inverted triangle recessed within. The bronze block was tucked into a pocket of her equipment rig, now strapped on over her z-suit. Her field comp and secondary equipment were tacked to the console, all components recording at maximum fidelity. Just for good measure, her interface to the *Moulin*'s shipskin, cameras, and the single sensor boom was running bidirectional—which allowed her to offload some processing to the shipnet itself when needed.

For the moment, she had not connected the bronze block to anything. Despite this measure, it seemed heavy against her chest, and warm to the touch, as though some internal process was underway.

Even without node 3^3 in operation, however, enough data was flowing into her conceptual models and analysis matrices to leave her feeling slightly drunk. Fingers trembling, she unwrapped an *oliohuiqui* packet

pair of folding kitchen tables. As she moved aside the last of the ammunition crates with a grunt, his lips fluttered with a soft snore.

"Does the Prince know you've come along, Crow?" Anderssen pinched his brown old ear as hard as she could. The old Náhuatl opened one eye, squinting at her, then sat up carefully and eased out of the tiny space under the tables. Briskly chafing his wrists and ankles, he observed: "*Tlatocapilli* Xochitl is noted for his admirable qualities in battle, not for his legendary acumen. *Chu-sa* Koshō, on the other hand, is beginning to understand how to operate in the wide world, as befits a gifted student with an excellent master."

Gretchen shook her head, retrieving her pack. She began digging through the compartments, confirming that everything she'd stowed was still in place and undamaged. "Why did they send him then? They knew what was out here, right?"

Hummingbird shrugged. "I believe he was judged the most expendable of the Emperor's sons."

"More so than the one that's always on the 3-v? Tezozómoc the Glorious?" Anderssen was appalled.

"Not all stone flakes the right way," the old man replied, pulling on a pair of boots he'd lifted from one of the other duffels. "What use is a pretty piece of flint if it cannot take an edge?"

"And Tezozómoc *can*?"

Hummingbird did not reply, instead he dug around in the bottom of his gear and came up with a plastic container filled with cheesecloth. Holding the jar up, the old Náhuatl turned it this way and that, checking the contents. Then he turned back the lid, smelling the small egg-sized rounds inside.

"Lady of Light!" Gretchen coughed, eyes smarting. "Those are strong! Is that *opium*? What the devil are you doing with a basket of knuckles?"

He smiled serenely at her, tucking the container inside a field jacket he'd stolen from someone, somewhere. "My traveling companion needs a little coaxing to leave his shipping container."

Anderssen shook her head in dismay. "You know, Crow, I had a friend who had a fascination for doing archaeology in the ancient home of the Chichimecas. It was always dangerous, uncomfortable work. The land is harsh, the people were poor, running contraband was the only way to make money. All social hierarchies began and ended with some *pilli* in his fortified house surrounded by an army of goons. Not the

Then while she waited for the alarms to sound, most of her attention was on the supply manifests *Thai-i* Goroemon had forwarded up from Logistics for her review. They were desperately low on every kind of munitions, and only marginally better off for parts, meds, and food. *Six months of supplies left, eh? Only if you don't get a quarter of your stowage vented by a penetrator.*

Some time later, the tramp freighter *Moulins* maneuvered out of the rear cargo hold under its own power. The ship had been hurriedly re-supplied with water, food, and other perishables. Reaction mass for the engines had been topped off and Prince Xochitl, his remaining Jaguar Knight, Doctor Anderssen, and a handful of marines borrowed from the *Naniwa* were on board. In the cramped Command space, Captain Locke and his pilot were watching the external cameras and docking control status with a weather eye. The Prince and his bodyguard had appropriated the Navigator and Comm officer's seats and were glowering at the backs of the Europeans during the delicate maneuver.

Gretchen watched them all from the hatchway while the ship was de-coupling, then left them all to stew and banged downdeck to the cargo area where all of their luggage had been piled by the middies from the *Naniwa*. Her duffle had disappeared, to her disgust, under an enormous quantity of marine gear.

And, she thought, rather morosely, *here I am again on this damned tiny ship with these fanatics.*

Locke had accepted this new commission without protest, having apparently spent his time in the brig playing cards and smoking a suc-cession of foul Novo French cigarettes. Now free of the battle-cruiser and at the helm of his own ship again, his hostility towards the Prince and the Fleet marines cluttering up his decks was banked, but simmer-ing. Löjtnant Piet was doing less well at hiding his antipathy, but Xo-chitl apparently did not care, showing not the slightest awareness of their anger.

They'll find a way to get along, Anderssen thought cheerfully, dragging olive-gray duffels aside. "There's my—oh, what the hell are you doing in there?"

Beneath the pile of luggage, with his head resting on Gretchen's field pack, Green Hummingbird had made himself a bit of a nest using a

welling up within her, suffusing her arms, legs—even her thoughts—with anticipation.

Two hours later, Koshō looked up at a soft tapping at the door to her private office. "Enter."

The door slid open and Green Hummingbird stepped in, his feet bare, attired in a simple Fleet undershirt and off-duty trousers. Without his usual cloak and hood, he seemed surprisingly small—until one met his dusky green eyes and then his true stature asserted itself.

"*Chu-sa* Koshō," he said politely. "A word with you, if I may."

"I believe," she said, rising and stepping to the door. "That you were confined to the brig, by order of the Prince Imperial himself."

No one was in the corridor, though Susan was unpleasantly aware that nearly every centimeter of the *Naniwa* was under surveillance by some kind of recording device.

The old Náhuatl nodded. "I am. Thank you for your concern for my comfort. Your hospitality has been most adequate, but I am on my way to pay respects to the Esteemed One and shall not keep you further."

With that, he made a polite bow and then slipped out the door again. Koshō stared after him, wondering if she should summon the marine ready squad, have the *nauallis* clapped in chains and then, perhaps, locked in a room for which there was no key. *But then,* she thought, starting to feel rising amusement at the thought of seeing the Prince's face when the escape was discovered, *he would wrinkle his way out of that, too. I wonder . . .* Another thought brought her up short. *Does Hummingbird believe he will cheat death, too, in the end?*

Juggling the possibilities in her mind, Koshō came to the unpleasant conclusion that letting the *nauallis* go about his business without interference was less dangerous than following the Prince's orders. Particularly since she was quite certain that Hummingbird knew what he was doing, even if she couldn't stand him personally. *However,* she thought, *I do need to keep an eye on the future.*

Susan then went to her console and tapped open a channel to the brig. The marine officer on duty responded immediately, his young face intent and dutiful.

"*Heicho* Adamsky, has someone thought to provide the prisoner in cell one with something to eat?"

"Then we have a problem," he declared. "The *Naniwa* must leave this area immediately. My noble guest, the *sian-fengh*, has made his desire to flee very clear. I cannot refuse him. Yakka, I need you to keep a close eye on him for me. He's truculent, difficult and, as you saw—unexpectedly dangerous, but I don't think he'll give you much trouble if you put a nargile and some opium back in his hands."

"Where are *you* going?" Koshō clasped both hands behind her back, falling into an easy parade rest.

Xochitl smiled, showing a large number of perfectly formed white teeth. "I've been thinking about what you said before, about my father— I'm going to do *exactly* as he asked. I'm taking that little merchant ship in the rear cargo hold and staying behind, while you return to the Barrier wall. I understand she's well shielded, and won't cost you something off your manifest if we suffer the same fate as that cargo shuttle."

He tapped the side of his head sharply. "Find us a way out, Yakka. We have to get out of here before we starve or are baked inside the shipskin, and there's no sense in you wasting time *here* while we poke and pry."

"Thus your *problem*," Koshō said coolly. "I'll need Anderssen-*tzin* and her comp models to find a way out, but *you* can't get inside the artifact without her. She can't be in both places at once, can she?"

The Prince nodded, clapping his hands lightly together. "That would seem a puzzle, save I have an answer." He smiled tightly at the *Chu-sa*, an expression which made the little hairs on Gretchen's neck rise.

"That pale, nervous Anglishman you've got stowed away in Engineering—yes, I know where he is—give him the telemetry from your passage through the Pinhole and he can reconfigure your sensors to reveal the spiderweb trapping us."

Beyond a slight nostril flare, Koshō showed no reaction. But Gretchen could feel the woman's entire body stiffen from across the room, and the answering surge of pleasure in the Prince. *What a foul dog he is,* she thought, watching the two of them as from a great distance.

"Helsdon is not wholly himself—"

"All the better," Xochitl snapped, "near-mad as he is may prove to your advantage! I am taking Anderssen here into the artifact, *Chu-sa*, while you find us a way out of this hole. Is that perfectly clear?"

"*Hai, Gensui.*"

Anderssen felt an enormous surge of delight, like golden honey

I'm a cripple. The thought was bitter ash in his mouth. *While the Hjo remains in my proximity.*

This, Xochitl realized, was both the core of the problem and the obvious solution. He stood up abruptly and paced over to the xenoarchaeologist at the comm station.

"Follow me," he said before turning away, scanning the doors leading off of Secondary Command for a room which would suffice. *There! Thank Yacatecuhtli, Guide of the Lost, that someone's put up a sign in Nahuatl!*

Xochitl gestured for Anderssen to enter the conference room, and then closed the door lightly behind them. She sat on the edge of a fine-looking red mahogany table which made a hollow circle. The base apparatus for a holocast projector filled the center of the room. Gretchen looked the Prince up and down with open interest, wondering what was on his mind. *Something is, for certain.* Then she narrowed her eyes, trying to gain a sense of him, wondering if her gift—if it was a gift, and not the product of drugs or the unknown influence of the *Adh'atr*—would work on a person as well as a potsherd.

Xochitl said nothing, leaning against a cedar-paneled wall ornamented with recessed watercolor paintings of flowers—they looked like pansies to Anderssen's eye, but she was no expert on the flora of old Earth—and scowling at her with a disturbingly unblinking gaze.

This is very strange, Gretchen thought—but she played along, saying nothing, idly kicking her feet and trying not to fidget. She felt the desire to be back at her console, digging through the reams of 3-v data, or the spatial model, or measurements of the enormous structure, as a physical pain. But still, she waited.

After quite a long time, the door recessed into the wall with a soft *chuff* and *Chu-sa* Koshō stepped in, her white dress uniform as immaculate as ever, her fine-boned face perfectly composed.

Seeing her, the Prince snorted rather rudely in amusement and then lifted his chin at Anderssen.

"This is the one who led you through the Barrier?"

Koshō paused at the edge of the conference table, regarding him levelly, and then nodded slightly.

THE *NANIWA*

Though proper quarters had been provided for him, Prince Xochitl remained in Secondary Command, staring fixedly at the incomprehensibly large shape of the artifact four thousand kilometers from their bow, and doodling on his console. Doctor Anderssen and a rotating set of sensor techs and weapons officers had been working through all of the data captured by Konev's shuttle before its destruction, along with everything else flowing into their limited set of radiation-hardened sensors.

Chu-sa Koshō, who seemed to have taken up permanent residence in Main Command, had directed the technical team to modify one of the remotely controlled bots used for hull repairs and use the resulting "probe" to plumb the convoluted architecture of the structure without loss of life.

Xochitl found it interesting, in a nasty way, that the Nisei officer was concerned for the life of even the least of her crewmen. *Yakka won't last long in the Fleet,* he decided, *without someone to sponsor her. I wonder . . .* He paused a moment, half expecting his exo to kick in and present a list of advantages and disadvantages accrued by his patronage. When nothing happened, Xochitl felt the absence as a kind of unquenchable hunger, twisting his stomach into emptiness. He had not realized, having the exo present his entire adult life, how heavily he relied on the device.

My eyes are flawless, the Prince reminded himself, *but how do I see when the world around me is not annotated, described, outlined?* It was difficult for him to even navigate the hallways of the ship—no map presented itself, directing his steps, and the *kanji*-lettered signs and warnings were unreadable. Xochitl was a little stunned to realize that he did not actually know the meanings of all of the rank badges, flashes, and glyphs which informed the knowing observer of all of the hierarchies and authorities within the Fleet. Exo had always been whispering in his mind, guiding his interactions with the military, with the provincial governors, with—with everyone in his life.

notice by shrinking down into his seat. "With time and experience, that which was once obscure becomes clear," Hadeishi said softly. Then he picked up his stylus, eyes again fixed upon the little display, his whole attention focused on the tactical puzzle before him.

complained when he used so many computing cycles. De Molay and Lovelace had settled back into their seats, some kind of hot, nasty-smelling beverage in their hands. He rotated the shattered hulk of the *Tlemitl*, examining the debris field the super-dreadnaught had generated.

Sure enough, a cloud of evac capsules is huddling behind the wreck. He scratched behind one ear with his stylus.

The warship had lost two major sections to the Barrier weapon, but had remained largely intact. Whoever remained aboard had managed to cut the engines, contain the reactors, and get the surviving crew away into the evacuation pods. They had not kept the two severed sections from continuing forward, to be diced into ever smaller debris by whatever lay beyond . . . but the main mass of the hull had halted its rush to destruction. *Affording a paltry shelter to the survivors.*

"Here, *Sencho*, here are the ones who need us most. Their oxygen, water, and food is ebbing away like the outgoing tide. Even the *Firearrow*'s corpse will not shield them from the Khaid much longer."

He turned to find De Molay regarding him pensively. "You don't intend to leave a single man behind, do you?" she asked. "Even if this means risking nearly two hundred lives you've already saved and this fine ship you've taken?"

"It is not my ship," Hadeishi replied absently. "I cannot be held to account for its loss. But there are skilled officers and men out there waiting to die in the dark, either by fire or from cold, and their spirits will weigh heavy upon me if I do not try."

"Even if they would leave *you* behind without a second thought?"

Hadeishi gave her a sidelong look. The rest of the men and women on the bridge had paused in their work and were listening intently—though, out of deference to the two senior officers, not openly. Save Lovelace, of course, who was just staring at the two of them in dismay.

Mitsuharu tapped the helmet ring of his captured Khaiden armor, which he had not had time to take off since boarding the *Kader*. "I am already dead," he said quietly. "While they still live and breathe. I would keep grave-dust from their mouths as long as I can. In this way, even a spirit can serve."

De Molay made a disbelieving face. "I do not understand this fatalism, *Chu-sa*. It is not my way."

Hadeishi spared a moment to regard Tocoztic, who had taken the weapons officer's station. The young man looked pale, trying to escape

eye, structure was slowly emerging from the seeming chaos of racing ships and sun-bright detonations. One ship, in particular, stood out amongst the confusion. An Imperial battle cruiser. A brand new one, he guessed, from the drive-flare and the outline the Khaid cameras had captured during the fighting.

Ah, she is beautiful. And her commander will win himself more than one medal if he sees home again. See how deftly he handles her . . . so sure in every maneuver, parsimonious in his launch patterns . . . and if my eye does not deceive, still alive, having fled down this opening in the Barrier wall.

"*Chu-sa?*" Leaning over from her console, De Molay broke his concentration. "I think our toil is showing fruit. Listen, isn't this the Khaiden battlecast?"

"Wait." Hadeishi signaled Command for quiet. "Please confirm that we are not broadcasting, *Sho-i* Lovelace. The Khaid have acute hearing." The old women handed over her earbug—though internal comm was operating again, the Khaid-specific systems were still cut from the main loop. He wiggled the uncomfortable object into his ear, listening closely to the resulting ebb and flow of alien chatter.

After a few minutes he nodded to himself and signaled for Lovelace to kill the circuit.

"I think you're right. Now we need a working real-time translator." He smiled wanly at the two women. "In about twelve hours?"

De Molay made a face, looking sideways at Lovelace. The *Sho-i* shook her head in dismay. "I don't think that's *possible*, *Chu-sa*. I know they exist—but *we* don't have one!"

Mitsuharu frowned, sitting back in the beetle-chair. Now he was thankful for the rigid armor which kept him from being stabbed in the side every time he moved. "Do we have a lexicon at least? My Khadesh is very poor—is anyone on-board fluent?"

"You mean besides the four Khaid we've captured?" The old woman shook her head. "Can we get a couple hours of shuteye, then try and work a new miracle for you?"

"Of course, *Sencho*. There are mats in those rooms down the main corridor. Lovelace-*sana* can show you where they are."

A full watch later, Hadeishi had coaxed the display into allowing him to zoom in on sections of the battle, even though the *Kader*'s shipnet core

Hadeishi sighed, and then picked up his stylus again: *Our mission continues to be successful. We have found and destroyed nine Imperial escape pods. Additionally thirty useable z-suits, numerous small arms and edged weapons were recovered. Return to the hunting pack is expected within twenty-three hours.*

A firm tap on the running-man glyph spooled the message off into the t-relay system. *Done,* he thought, *with that exercise—for another six hours.*

"Isn't that strange," De Molay said from her seat at Navigation. Somehow the old woman had acquired a puffy black expedition jacket and mittens. Hadeishi didn't think it was so cold in Command, but he allowed that the Khaid had not set environmental to warm either. "The ship's previous course indicates they took no prisoners, captured no equipment . . . just a missile or beam into each pod and on their way."

Mitsuharu tried to swivel the beetle-chair at the captain's console, found that the chitin was sticking again, and stood up. He had been sitting too long in any case. "That is an odd course for a military so very in need of technical expertise, as well as slave labor. Haste overthrew their normal procedure, I think. They always took the time to dig every last beet from the fields before."

The old woman shook her head. "Wasteful."

Then she frowned, indicating the navigational plot on his console. "Do these raiders believe they can pick up the mystery weapon and use it like a shipgun? Every vessel we've seen is a warship—have they no scientists along, to analyze these phenomena?"

"That is an excellent point." Hadeishi nodded thoughtfully. "Do we have a breakdown of the battle around the science station yet?"

"Five minutes, *Chu-sa*." De Molay yawned and turned back to where Lovelace had continued unraveling the encoded Khaid 'cast logs. "Five minutes."

An hour later, Mitsuharu was sitting on the edge of the uncomfortable chair, wholly engrossed in stepping through the debacle around the science station one more time. The *Spear*-class light cruiser had gone out of service fifteen years before his old *Cornuelle* had even been laid down, so it lacked a wide variety of modern innovations. No threatwell, no reconfigurable consoles. But the dedicated v-display built into the side of the captain's station was enough to show him what he needed to see. To his

wrinkled up her nose. The thick musk of Khaid blood was mixed with the astringence of fire suppression foam to make a particularly foul smell. Beyond that, the chair at the weapons officer's console she'd been offered by a slightly built, worried-looking *Sho-i* gave her serious pause. "A beetle shell?"

"Yes, ma'am." Lovelace offered an apologetic smile. "Haven't found anything better."

De Molay shrugged and fitted an instafoam pillow into the peculiar dished chair back, then sat down gingerly. "We're underway again? I felt the drives light up while that big fellow hauled me up ten decks on his back...."

"*Hai, Sencho*." The *Sho-i* called up a navigational plot, showing the past track of the *Kader*, as well as the projected patrol pattern. "I recovered this from one of the engine control nodes—when we flashed the whole ship, temporary storage went too—but some of the secondary systems had working copies, and this was one of them." The route spidered out from the main Khaid elements near the Pinhole, covered an irregular section of the stellar vicinity, and then angled back to join the pack again. "The *Chu-sa* wants us to be as inconspicuous as possible—so we follow the ordered route, submit status reports at the requested times, and so on. I've already sent one, cobbled together from the last transmit from the t-relay system, but we're due for five more before getting back to tau zero."

"This course was intended to cover the area of battle?"

"*Hai, Sencho*. The Khaid commander peeled off these three ships to mop up."

De Molay smiled, tapping through the navigational interface. "Well, let's press on then, shall we? I believe these three signals are Fleet evac capsules." Her stylus sketched in a slight change in vector to overrun all three icons on the plot.

Mitsuharu frowned, reviewing a comm-system composition pane. *The Monkey of Fate,* he thought with considerable irritation, *is laughing. Now I have to submit status reports to some Khaid overlord!* He looked over at Inudo, lately of the Scout *Corduba*, who was now sitting pilot for the *Kader*. "How many men have we recovered in total, *Thai-i*?"

"Over a hundred now, *Chu-sa*."

"Fortune has smiled," Hadeishi replied, glad himself that she still lived. "Did you take any damage?"

De Molay shook her head. "Your wounded have been coming over in a steady stream—didn't someone tell you?" She looked off-screen. "There are at least a dozen more laid out in what space we can spare. But we're entirely out of meds and ancillary supplies."

Mitsuharu levered up his faceplate, scratching a terrible itch beside his nose. "The sickbay here is all Khaid supplies, but I'll have *Gun-so* Ad-Din peel someone off to search the holds—there may be useful meds somewhere . . ." A shipbug scuttled across the console, wearing a crown of foam. "Are you low on vermin? We have more than I can stomach over here."

She shook her head. "I can live without them. How stands your new ship? Does she have a name?"

"The Khaid called her the *Kader*. I haven't found a hull-plate or record to indicate the Fleet designation." Mitsuharu rubbed one eye. Adrenaline was draining from his system, leaving only the ache of lactic acid buildup. "The Khaid failed to destroy the communications equipment and their sensor records. *Sho-i* Lovelace reports we have all of the telemetry of the attack on the *Tlemitl*, the Research Station, and the IMN escort fleet—if I understand her correctly. But she is speaking far too quickly today for me to follow. Can you come across and take over cleanup here in Command? I need to go back downdeck and make sure the Khaid holdouts are run to ground."

De Molay nodded, pursing her lips. "You want me to break down the Khaid battlecast?"

"With Lovelace's help, yes." Hadeishi suddenly looked thoughtful. "Also, you will want to bring a cushion."

"A cushion?"

He shrugged. "Khaid chairs do not fit us so well. There's no sign any of the Fleet interior fittings survived, which is a great pity."

De Molay laughed in delight. "You *are* having trouble sitting down these days. I will see you in an hour or two."

Three hours later, after one of the burlier Team Four *kashikan-hei* had carried her up from the cargo bay where the *Wilful* was now docked, De Molay stared around at the wreckage of *Kader*'s Command deck and

Hadeishi wiped a coating of yellowing foam from the captain's console of the light cruiser. His armor was blackened and scored by flechette impacts and all of his grenades were gone. Cajeme and the other Team One survivors were dragging the last of the Khaid corpses away, for the enemy had tried to make a stand on the Command deck. The console was flickering in and out of focus—part of the glassite surface had shattered—and the Nisei officer shook his head in dismay. Disgusted, he shut down the entire console, then went to the Navigator's station where he was pleasantly surprised to see the Fleet standard interface was up and awaiting input.

He clicked channel. "Found one working, *Sho-i.*"

Lovelace was still far down the ship, barricaded into the Engineering compartment, with the remains of Team Four as her guardians. Between them, the shipcore was momentarily in Fleet hands, but there were still gangs of Khaiden roaming the side passages, exchanging intermittent gunfire with the Team Three commandos. Locked out of all of the control interfaces, the enemy had little chance of mounting an effective defense, but the Khaid were nothing but persistent. In some places they had cut their own way through the internal doors—but none of them had any heavy equipment, which meant the frame bulkheads and the main hatches were a serious barrier. "Keying in."

Got your login, kyo, she responded a moment later. *Handing off shipnet on deck one to your console.*

"Received." Weary, he sat down in the chair, ignoring the foam which spilled onto the floor. His first thought was to check in with De Molay, so he activated the intership channels and pinged around until one of them locked onto the *Wilful.*

The freighter captain's face appeared on the display a moment later and she brightened to see him. "Well, if it isn't our Engineer's Mate, gone missing the last day."

The remaining Jaguar had brought the old Náhuatl to a primary security cell and stripped him naked before locking him inside. Oc Chac, at Susan's direction, had already scrambled the codes and reviewed the list of those crewmen with access to the compartment.

His kind will not remain contained for long, Sayu.

Alone in the bare room, the old man looked up into the cameras and the faintest hint of a smile crossed his lips as he lowered himself gingerly into a cross-legged position on the floor.

Koshō sneered back, wishing once more that her *sensei* Hadeishi were on hand to deal with his "old friend" and all these intrigues. *I am not cut out for this,* she thought darkly. *We should flee this place, not stay, poking at a dark hole in the cliff with sticks . . . no matter what the Emperor demands.*

a rock-face which had grown so impossibly detailed and distinct in her vision that she could barely process the flood of sensation streaming into her from the totality of the world. But now there was a sensation of discrimination and all of the extraneous data could be discarded, leaving the Flowery Prince isolated in her perception and laid bare before her.

She absorbed all of the Prince's frailty, fear, doubt, ignorance. She glimpsed a fading half-image of a peculiar, inhuman second self which had shrouded him like a ceremonial mask. A façade which had worn *him*, completing his persona, investing him with a thousand subtle cues to authority and rule. Without that, he was only a shadow, less than half himself.

"No, *Tlatocapilli*." She said, supremely confident. "But if you give me leave, I will peel back all of its secrets for you—every last one. But . . . didn't you tell the ambassador we were leaving? What will you do about him?"

Xochitl swallowed, blinking again, his hand trembling in physical memory of incandescent pain twisting in every nerve. "I'll have to kill it—kill him—and atomize the body. Or, or cast it into the sun—or . . ." The Prince seemed paralyzed by the decisions before him. Without his exo providing summaries and risk-vectors, everything seemed suddenly gray and murky.

In Main Command, *Chu-sa* Koshō watched the Prince and Doctor Anderssen discussing the attributes of the *Chimalacatl* on her surveillance cameras. Though her mien was impassive and controlled, she was deeply troubled by what she'd seen. A command sequence was waiting on her console, constructed in great haste during the scuffle and now refined, to vent the entire compartment to the void, and flood the evacuated rooms with hard radiation. *Would that be enough to kill this "ambassador" with the self-generating combat armor?* She was furious with herself for not attaching more security to the alien.

Susan had never encountered a "Hjogadim" before, and shipnet had nothing for her—no detail, no rumors, and no warnings—despite the fact that the creature spoke passable Nahuatl and was obviously well known to both the Prince and the *nauallis*. The thought of Hummingbird loose upon her ship made Koshō's stomach twist. Brow growing thunderous, she tapped up the security cameras for the ship's brig.

Xochitl looked the *nauallis* up and down, realizing he did not know who the old man was or where he'd come from. "Who the devil are—wait, you're one of the *tlamatinime!*" His face contorted in a snarl. "*Cuauhhuehueh* Koris—get this old witch off my bridge! Put him in the brig—someplace locked tight! With nothing on him but his skin."

The remaining Jaguar Knight rose from inspecting the body of his comrade. The master sergeant's visor was opaque, having shifted into combat mode, but his voice boomed hollowly. "As you bid, Lord Prince."

Hummingbird clasped his hands behind his head without a fuss and was escorted away. Gretchen watched him go with interest, wondering what the old Crow was up to now. *He'll be closeted with that alien in sixty seconds,* she wagered with herself. *He doesn't really want us to leave—just nudge the Flowery One in some direction of his choosing. But,* she thought, *two can play that game.*

Seeing the initial results from her analysis of the *Chimalacatl*'s surface—even just on the battle-cruiser's shipnet, much less after node 3^3 had taken the datastream apart and put it back together—had solidified a chaos of options vying for her attention. *I need to set foot on this thing, if that can be managed safely; even for a half-hour would make all of this worthwhile.* Another certainty had formed in her heart, crystallizing out of a thousand points of long-held despair, anger, hatred, and delighted curiosity. *Hummingbird needs to be there, too. Oh yes, he does.*

"Now you, woman, what is your name?" Xochitl blinked owlishly at her, trying to glare in a properly Imperial manner.

"Doctor Gretchen Anderssen, xenoarchaeologist, University of New Aberdeen, Lord Prince."

"Are you now?" The Prince sat up straight in his chair, surprised and pleased at the same time. "How did you get out here?"

Gretchen said the first thing that came to mind. "I was supposed to be with the others, but I missed the survey ship, so I came on this one." She spread her hands, encompassing the whole of the *Naniwa.*

"How fortunate for you. . . ." Xochitl's attention, now that he still lived and breathed, was drawn inexorably back to the enormous shape of the Sunflower. He bit nervously at his thumb. "Do you . . . do you know what this thing is?"

Anderssen felt something like an electrical shock, a tingling jolt from crown to toe. In that instant, something blossomed in her mind and, for an instant, she was back under that overhang on Ephesus III, staring up

in their thousands to come—we must be away from this accursed place swiftly and *this one*"—the *nauallis'* boot toed the Prince's side—"is their Authority. Through him, you control the others and may achieve a swift departure."

«*Four seconds to cortical failure.*»

Xochitl fought to form a coherent thought, and found he *could* still command his conscious mind, despite the annoying overlay of the exo. Desperate, feeling his mentation slipping away, he brought to focus a string of numbers—*three, five, five, seven, eleven, thirteen, seventeen, nineteen, twenty-nine* and . . . the voice of the exo abruptly stopped. There was no audible sound, no flashing overlay informing his vision of the event—but the fail-safe tripped, shutting down his implant.

Wheezing, his chest thudding with pain, the Prince closed his eyes, hoping to avoid further agony. His mind, suddenly, seemed quiet and empty—desolate. His limbs weak, helpless. The Prince began to panic, realizing that his interface to the shipnet would now have to be managed manually—and he didn't even have a hand-comp stowed in his luggage.

"Get us underway, *nongmin.*" The Hjogadim stepped away from Xochitl's body, careful to keep his eyes averted from the vast panorama filling the v-display. Then he loped from Command, making a beeline for the lift a corridor away.

Gretchen looked up questioningly from her pirated console, trying to catch Hummingbird's attention. The *nauallis* had tilted his head, watching with great interest as the Prince struggled to his feet. Xochitl's skin had turned waxy and he blinked incessantly. Without the exo to re-fine his vision, he did not see well at all.

"My Lord?" The old Náhuatl offered the Prince his hand.

"We're not leaving," Xochitl rasped, his throat raw. He slumped weakly into the command shockchair. He pointed at Gretchen. "You—the one with the ugly hair—what happened to our probe?"

Turning slightly in her chair, Anderssen shrugged. "The relic is guarded by the same kind of protective lattice as the whole star system." She caught the Prince's eye and grinned. "But if we stay, I can get you inside."

"We should leave," Hummingbird snapped, glaring across at the Swedish woman.

expression. "We must determine the provenance of this—object—and if it poses a threat to México space! Then we can—"

"*Stand away*, toy!" Sahâne yelped, frightened by the Prince's fierce movement, reflexively making a form of obedience with his hand, as though the human were a servant in the house of his fathers. Xochitl staggered, eyes wide, his face draining of color.

«*Heart failure induced,*» his exo said brightly. «*Cortex shutdown expected within ten seconds.*»

The Prince collapsed to his knees, and then tipped to one side when his arms failed to support his weight. A great rushing sound roared in his ears. He saw the two Jaguar Knights lunging forward, weapons out, striking at the Hjo with all the speed they could muster. Sahâne's exposed fur shifted color and tone, and the first bodyguard to reach him—butt of his shipgun reversed as a club—saw his knockout blow glance away from a sudden effusion of spiked scales which covered the Hjo's z-suited arm in a blur.

The creature, furious and sick at the same time, backhanded the marine with a long, gray arm. There was a *crack* of electricity and the Jaguar Knight was flung back, armor coiling smoke, to strike the floor, limp and lifeless.

«*Cortex shutdown in seven seconds.*»

Everyone in Secondary Command froze. The other Jaguar fetched up, weapon raised, suddenly unsure of how to attack the fully armored apparition. Sahâne stared down at his arm, the dark, rune-scribed z-suit now glittering with a spiked metallic shell, in astonished horror. "I did not do that," he declared in a weak voice. "I could not. This is *impossible.*"

"Esteemed One, stay your merciful hand!" Hummingbird's voice was clear and direct, ringing in the air as the *nauallis* prostrated himself on the deck. "These *shiau har-e* will not serve without their lord being *shun tzing.* If he bends to your will, then all will be harmonious and we may flee this accursed place in speed and safety!"

Xochitl, barely able to see, gasped for life on the deck. The exo's implacable voice continued to count down the seconds left before his brain starved from oxygen deprivation. The Hjo loomed over him, blocking out the light of the overheads. A pair of black eyes stared down and the long mouth twisted in a snarl.

"Let this toy live, when it has raised a paw against me? Why should I?"

"Think, Esteemed One," Hummingbird said, his voice controlled—persuasive—without a hint of disobedience, "Think of your offspring

in him. "I've a remote going aboard that structure within moments, and we'll—"

Out of the corner of her eye, Gretchen caught sight of an entire console filled with v-panes wink out. The comm officer sitting at the station cried out in alarm.

"*Chu-sa!* My Lord Prince!" A man's voice echoed in the air. "We've lost contact with the shuttle."

A section of the Prince's console unfolded into a large v-pane, showing *Chu-sa* Koshō's face, which was now cold and alert, her eyes flickering from side to side. Xochitl stepped back to his shockchair, intent on the Nisei officer.

"Well?" he demanded.

"The cargo shuttle has exploded, *Gensui.*" Susan's lips were a tight line, her brow furrowed. "No warning, no energy emissions . . . we're rewinding the telemetry, but I don't believe there is anything left to recover."

The Prince cursed, unable to keep rein on his temper a moment longer, and slammed a fist into the side of the shockchair. The Hjo recoiled, though Hummingbird's grip was tight enough to keep the creature from falling down. "We must flee," Sahâne wailed, "reverse your course, human. Reverse now!"

Without considering the ramifications, Gretchen slipped free of the Jaguar's grip—the Knight was staring at the console display, his attention distracted for a moment—and slid into a shockchair beside the horrified comm-tech.

"Roll that feed back, my dear," she said, voice calm and commanding. "Frame by frame."

The parchment envelope was opened and one of the octopus arms snaked from her pocket into a socket on the console without anyone noticing. Gretchen snugged her earbug tight against the background noise. The Prince and Koshō were disputing the merits of sending another shuttle towards the Sunflower. "Give me broad-spectrum passive scan at 20X for surface of the structure directly adjacent to the explosion . . ." *Should be some impact scarring now, from the debris. Crude— but I'll take the infopoints.*

"My lord . . ." Xochitl turned away from Susan's impassive visage, feeling thwarted at every turn, and advanced on the Hjogadim with a fierce

life—but then caught sight of the Prince's face and felt a bolt of adrenaline flush through her limbs. *He is furious, though!*

The Jaguars picked up the wave of displeasure radiating from Xochitl as well, and the one holding Anderssen seized her neck with an armored hand. Servos whined in her ear and the metallic grip dug into her flesh. *Oh god, he'll just twist and—*

"Esteemed One." With a visible effort, the Prince halted his angry pace and bowed, face contorted with the effort of mouthing peaceful words. "I am relieved to see you are feeling better, but I urge you to return to Medical. You will be safe there and your diverse stomachs set in order."

The Hjo trembled from head to toe, but managed to squeak out: "Turn us about, mad creature! The radiation levels in this sector must be immense. Have you no care for your offspring to come? We must depart immediately!"

Anderssen experienced a strange sensation, watching the ambassador swaying before the Prince. The jolt of fear which had struck the alien dumb now seemed to supplement the earlier sense of assurance. She could taste a stark, unadulterated desire to live, and wondered if the creature had ever felt that particular spike of self-awareness before. Then Gretchen blinked rapidly, half-blinded by the glare from the v-display, and wondered if she was hallucinating. The air around the creature seemed to be flickering or twisting with tiny fleeting gleams of light. *A reflection? But of what?*

As she turned her head—feeling the armored fingers still digging into her neck—the spectacle on the v-display drew her eye like a magnet. The panorama seemed terribly familiar—something she'd seen, or read in a book, or—*What is it? Those triliths are . . . damn, but it's just beyond reach!*

Behind her, Hummingbird had somehow moved closer to the Hjo, a supportive hand under one arm, and she could hear him whispering: "Departure, yes. An excellent idea, Esteemed One."

Anderssen and the Prince spoke simultaneously: "It is not!"

Xochitl turned towards her with a scowl, jaw tight. "Get her out—"

"This object can only be a First Sun artifact," she blurted, catching his eye. "The Ik-Hu-Huillane tablets speak of an 'abode of the waking mind' which is formed in threes and multiples of three—this structure is the very image the Yithians speak of!"

"Yes . . . At last." The Prince's face cleared, the words striking a chord

and Gretchen slipped inside as well, keeping to the corners and out of the way of the long, furred arms. The creature swung its head from side to side as the lift raced between decks.

By the time the blast-doors to Secondary Command irised open, the ambassador had managed to straighten up to his full height and—somehow—his z-suit and exposed fur had shed the vomit. Anderssen found the creature tremendously interesting; when first she'd set eyes upon it, the Hjo seemed shrunken and withered. *He—yes, this is a male, I'm sure of it—felt incomplete. But now it is filling out, becoming more sure of itself.* She eyed the armored suit curiously. Was a med-band at play here, injecting some kind of confidence-building med into the creature?

"Account for this wretched treat—" Sahâne stopped, long mouth yawning open, his dark eyes reflecting a hot white glow. All of his newly won assurance staggered, quailed, and then fled. A pained whimper emerged from his throat. Gretchen looked away from the creature in surprise and then her own eyes went wide with delight.

Secondary Command had been reconfigured to create one massive v-display which stretched from floor to ceiling and wrapped around three-quarters of the chamber. The Command consoles had been relocated to the sides and back of the room, their smaller v-displays filled with ever-changing data. On the vast canvas, a live camera feed of the Sunflower filled the room with the hot white glare of the ejection jet boiling up out of the singularity. The three bloated orbs of the brown dwarves studded the sky and the dark mass of the accretion disc formed a backdrop for the tri-lobed structure. Those surfaces at an angle to the jet glared with reflected light, throwing the *Chimalacatl* into high relief.

"How big . . ." whispered Anderssen, fumbling in her jacket pockets for a hand-comp. "My god, it's five thousand kilometers on a side!"

A Jaguar Knight in combat armor suddenly blocked her view, a gauntleted hand crushing her fingers and plucking the comp from her grasp. Another *Ocelotl* had moved in on the other side, immobilizing Hummingbird, who was standing quite still, all of his attention focused on the Hjo and a slim, handsome man of middle age rising from a shockchair placed at the center of the room. Seeing him in the flesh, Gretchen felt a pang of disappointment—*he's not nearly so pretty in real*

Gretchen was holding the parchment envelope by her fingertips, careful not to actually press against the bronze-colored block inside. She shook her head angrily. "Why do you think I'll come anywhere with you? You've used me as an experimental test subject to see if this . . . tool . . . would do me harm. Do you really think I would continue helping you, once I found out?"

Hummingbird paused in the doorway, watching her with an inscrutable expression. "If you do not come, Anderssen-*tzin*, then you will not see what they have found." Then he nodded to the envelope. "Bring the device—one text I have seen names it the *Adh'atr*, which is the easiest for us to say—I think you will need its capabilities soon."

Goddamnit. Gretchen tossed the block from hand to hand, then stowed it in her backpack. Dragging everything with her, she hustled out into the corridor, where she found the Esteemed One clinging to Hummingbird's shoulder, its face a ghastly hue. The plastic bucket had disappeared, but the z-suit—or armor or carapace—was liberally streaked with regurgitated fluids. Together, they were shuffling towards the nearest lift.

"I will compel action," the Hjo declared loudly, long gray nose raised in defiance. "Someone will be Instructed for this. There is a Certainty!"

"If I may suggest—" Hummingbird said, his voice low, "there is a small but well-equipped ship aboard that could easily receive your person and take you to a safer location. . . ."

"No!" The creature's reaction was abrupt and violent, though for the moment it lacked the strength to do more than flail one arm. "Order and harmony must be restored without resort to flight! Flight in a tiny, ill-equipped cylinder, crowded with apes and their acrid stench . . ." Sahâne muttered. "*They* will try again to destroy me, the last of a noble and laudatory descent. No . . . Take me to the place of authority!"

"But Esteemed One, the Prince is at the focus of action, in Secondary Command . . ." Gretchen started to speak—seeing Hummingbird gesture towards the glyph for deck thirty-nine on the lift controls—but kept her peace, wondering what the old Nahuatl intended.

"Yes. There shall be a confrontation." The creature was mumbling again. "And explanation!"

Hummingbird bowed obediently and pressed the call button for the lift. When the doors cycled open, the Hjo lurched inside—making a snuffling whine upon seeing the confined space—and then Hummingbird

Gretchen peered out to see a pair of marines escorting a wretched-looking creature—obviously nonhuman, nose deep in a white plastic bucket—into the adjoining medbay. Medical staff converged on the alien from all directions, though most of them were taken aback by its peculiar appearance. To Anderssen it seemed most closely to resemble a grayish black anteater or perhaps a kind of erect sloth or tapir. A cloud of alcohol fumes drifted in their door and she grimaced at the smell of regurgitated rum. Then Hummingbird quietly closed the door, his head tilted in an attitude of listening.

"A heavy guard for such a pitiful-looking specimen," the Crow said after a moment.

"It doesn't look particularly dangerous. What species is it?"

Hummingbird gave her a considering look. "You heard the soldiers—an ambassador."

"From where? Out here?" Gretchen's eyes narrowed in suspicion. "Wait a moment . . . is this whole business an embassy to—whatever is hiding in this place?"

The old Náhuatl tilted his hand this way and that. "The Flowery Prince brought this one along at another's command. But despite his poor appearance, the ambassador is quite dangerous—to us, to humanity. He is Hjogadim and they are quite rare in Imperial space."

To Anderssen's eye the Crow seemed to hop from one foot to the other, wings rustling nervously, before he took hold of the door latch again. "I need to speak to the ambassador—find your clothes, get dressed, and packed up. The *Chu-sa* needs you, remember?"

Then he slipped out quietly, the door barely making a noise as he passed over the threshold.

"Huh!" Gretchen began digging through the storage bins. *Now I do truly need Magdalena and Parker and even Dai Bandao, if he were available. I need backup. I should not have lost my temper with the Crow.* She sighed, suddenly weary. *I am an idiot. I could have done this just as easily back home on New Aberdeen. But no—I have to come haring out here to the back of beyond, just on the off-chance I'll touch the face of the unknown one more time.*

Finding a shirt, spare field pants, and the leather jacket, Anderssen had managed to get herself together by the time Hummingbird reappeared, radiating pleased satisfaction. "Quickly now, Doctor Anderssen—we are accompanying the Esteemed Sahâne to the bridge."

"That," Gretchen said, drawing a breath to steady herself, "is the kind of insanity which gives rise to racial genocide, and forced breeding, and tyranny! Human beings are *all the same* at the genetic level, Crow! That's been shown thousands of times, on multiple worlds! Our differences are minute, one or two pairs of chromosomes fallen out in some random coupling of mitochondrial mitosis!"

The old Náhuatl shook his head in disagreement. Anderssen found herself reduced to glaring at him in outrage.

"This," he said at last, "is not so. There are distinct and identifiable differences between the Firsts, Seconds, and Thirds. There is—" Hummingbird paused, jaw clenched against what he had almost said. "I cannot provide you proof *out here*, Doctor. But it does exist. You are a Third and the only one with your specific gift we have yet found amongst the current human population."

"Current?" Anderssen gave him a mocking look. "What about the past, then? Who falls into your special society that I might, say, know from a history book? Or have seen on the 3-d, or perused in some wet-dream *manga* peddled by evil old meddlers like yourself!"

Her shout echoed from the walls of the medbay and Gretchen was suddenly aware that all of the noise outside, in the main sickbay, had stopped. She felt furious—used and deceived—and it was an effort to keep from picking up her breakfast tray and smashing it across Hummingbird's masklike face.

In the moment before the door opened, the old Náhuatl said: "One of your distant relatives had a similar power—she could see what other men intended, sometimes even before they decided a course of action themselves. You would know her—the brightest star in the firmament of your people's history—for she saved mankind from a truly dark path. But over seven hundred years have passed since—"

One of the medical orderlies opened the door and poked his head in, a professionally cheerful smile on his olive-skinned face. "Up and around, are we? Feeling better? Excellent—*Chu-sa* Koshō has been comming me for your status, Doctor Anderssen, at regular intervals."

"Great." Gretchen looked around for her jacket, fingering the medical tunic they'd put on her. "Where did my clothes go?"

The orderly was about to answer when a sudden noise erupted in the corridor outside. Someone shouted: "Ho there! Corpsman, secure quarters for the ambassador immediately!"

but he cannot lead them beyond the disguise unless their heart opens of itself to become *neltiliztli*—well-rooted, authentic. When the second group express their belief it is not because they are infected by communal memes. When they worship, they do not do so because all around them do, but because of their own undiluted vision, whether it be false or true. If they do not believe in a thing, you cannot make them. For them the Mother of Tepeyac is seen to come down Her hill, roses rising with each footstep, to lift their chin and pour mercy into their eyes, *or* She does not. You *cannot* make them become believers, though they may *tell* you that they are believers—but if they are not, they cannot become so, even under the lash or when put in irons." A second finger raised.

Gretchen snorted. "I know both of those sets of people!"

"Then there is the third group who are born with the potential for full wisdom and revelation," and now the old Nahuatl's voice shaded into an unconscious gravity. "Who need neither a church, nor a sermon, nor a book. They *know* the truth, the flower-and-song of reality, the constant becoming and motion of the world, and only the confusion of men and machines and the roar and tumult of society drives this sight from their minds." The third finger joined the first two. "And these men and women are whence the saints and prophets come, the greatest artists and poets, the worst madmen and monsters without conscience or humanity—for they see that which most cannot, finding either everlasting splendor or unending horror behind the placid mask of the universe."

Anderssen made a face, drawing back from Hummingbird, whose face had contorted into a tight forbidding expression. "You," he continued, "are among a minute fraction of the third population—a genetic pool which is quite small to begin with—but then hidden among them, are those with the propensity to *see*."

"You have got to be—"

"I am *not* joking, Doctor Anderssen." The Crow's voice was hard and flat, cutting her off. "I may be able to focus my mind, attain clarity of vision which eludes other men, perform feats which seem miraculous—but I am only a Second, not a Third. I was *taught* the arts of intuition to perceive the authentic world. And thus . . ." He gestured at the parchment envelope. "Such mechanisms are beyond my capacity to understand."

"A tool." The old Náhuatl stood up, leaning heavily on the bed. "One you can operate, where others cannot—where I cannot."

"Really?" The Swedish woman looked up at him sidelong, tasting deception in the air. "A tool that you needed working when you came— here, to this hidden place."

He nodded, face somber. "My powers are not infinite, Dr. Anderssen. Even beyond your professional skills—which are well regarded, you should know—your other talents have not escaped notice."

"By who?!" Gretchen felt chilled at the thought. *How long have I been under surveillance?* Another part of her mind answered, mockingly, *Always, idiot!*

"Not all of the *nauallis* are . . . are Judges," he said, framing his words carefully. "There are those who collate data, who watch for trends—not the trivial ones of concern to the Emperor or the Mirror—but who sift for changes in *who we are*."

"Humanity, you mean?" Anderssen frowned, gaining an unmistakable impression he was skirting around a deep and slippery pit. "What kind of changes?"

Hummingbird did not answer immediately, pursing his lips and watching her with a steady, unwavering gaze. At last he said: "It is not well known, Doctor, but there are—in broad strokes—three perceptual capacities expressed within the human species. There are those who accept the conceptual framework of cultural memes, who perceive only the *nahualli*, the disguise or mask of the world; they live and work and bear their children happily within this house of paintings. What they perceive is *ahnelli*, unrooted, inauthentic, a montage of lies and expectations, merely the replication and self-deception of contagious beliefs. There are those—to take a specific example—who express a belief in the Heavenly Creator, in the Risen Lord, in God—if they are asked. These are the people who attend religious services because everyone else does— who find a sense of community there, a sense of sharing which comforts them, or an avenue to power over their fellow men." He raised one finger.

"Then there are those who do not partake of these collective memetic frameworks, who must question, seek out for themselves the *nelli*—the rooted, true, authentic cosmos. They must look beyond the world of dreams and illusion towards the *teotl*—the heart of things. They seek, but few succeed. A *tlamatini* instructs and teaches his pupil,

the sound of their feet on the floor, their bright, carefree chatter, and heavy tread of the protectors watching over them. With stately grace, she descended a phalanx of steps. As she moved, the nearest of the Chosen looked up, their faces emerging from the haze like flowers opening before the rays of the first sun. Three of them cried out, seeing her, raising their hands in greeting. Now she was close enough to touch Isabelle's hair, see Tristan's bright blue eyes shining. Duncan was looking away, his attention caught by something speaking in enormous, earth-shaking tones. She put her hand on his shoulder, and he turned. Anderssen saw—

—the roof of the medbay as she blinked away tears. Anderssen gasped, drawing a ragged breath into lungs starved for air. A queer humming died away, replaced by the sound of someone drinking soup and the distant rattle and clink of men and women working in an enclosed space. The smell of the soup—picken, she guessed—struck her hard, turning her stomach into a twisted ball of hunger.

"Oh sweet Jesus." Gretchen rolled sideways, feeling utterly drained. A parchment envelope slipped from her hands, landing amongst the blankets. "There had better be a liter of that for *me*, Crow, or I'll murder you where you stand."

Hummingbird looked back at her, dark green eyes curious over the edge of his bowl. "There has been a full breakfast the last two days, Anderssen, but you have been sleeping—so I've done you the favor of cleaning the plate."

Lacking even the moisture to spit, Gretchen managed to sit up and found that—indeed—there was a full tray set beside her bed. More soup, a bowl of red gelatin, kaffe, two bottles of hydrofast. Fingers shaking a little, she popped the top from the first of the orange bottles and began sipping carefully.

After a few minutes, Hummingbird set down the bowl and Anderssen drained the last of her bottle.

"So, Hummingbird—I confess confusion about the purpose of the Judges. Once you said to me your duty was to protect humanity from those powers or even ideas which could destroy us, particularly alien influences we might encounter in the depths of space."

He nodded minutely, watching her with an impassive face. Gretchen drifted her fingertips over the parchment envelope and the block hidden within. "What is this, then? An experiment with my mind, my physiology? Do you even know what this is?"

shield-reed, doesn't it, *Chu-sa*?" he remarked, looking up as she approached.

Susan nodded. *If the Gods made sunflowers as big as a large moon, and gave them long, spiked metallic petals, and a center formed from triangles within triangles . . .*

Xochitl's face was visible on Chac's console as well, his visage equally bright—though not with the joy of exploration or curiosity, but naked greed. "Each petal is comprised of hundreds of thousands of folds—do you see them? Set one within another . . . such scale! We're still waiting for an estimate of age, but surely this is something from the First Sun!"

Koshō felt her gut clench. She looked to Pucatli. "No erosion rates from the surface?"

"Nothing, *kyo*. The skin should be pitted by micrometeoroids or cosmic ray impacts—but we're seeing nothing at all—just like came from the fab yesterday."

"*Chu-sa*." Oc Chac's voice shaded into awe. He was indicating a fresh set of scan data, from shipborne receptors pointed towards the singularity itself. "Look at this. . . . A tether or beanstalk of some kind?"

Something with barely any cross section at all traced a hard, straight line down from the "flower" towards the boiling fury of the accretion disk and—one supposed—the event horizon of the black hole.

The Mayan rubbed a hand across the back of his head. "Could they be *powering* this structure from the electromagnetic field generated by the infall? Gods, that would give them almost unlimited capacity!"

"It is possible," Susan replied, resisting the urge to fold her arms. Instead, she kept both hands clasped behind her back, forcing her mind to consider the implications of such a place to her ship. Her gut churned, triggering her med-band to dispense antianxiety meds in a sharp, cold burst.

Gretchen was standing in a portal, her tripartite shadow thrown sharp on a glassy floor by a harsh, brassy glare at her back. Before her, a massive chamber stretched off into a hazy distance, the room spined with endless ranks of sharp vaults. Everywhere there was motion—long streams of the white-garbed Chosen flowed up from the vaults below, and then passed out through the triangular exits, shepherded by guardsmen who loomed above them, armor glinting black and crimson. The air reverberated with

to operate during a bomb-pod storm. Despite stepping down the fidelity of their data capture by orders of magnitude, the "structure" was of such colossal size they could not help but make out some detail.

General silence prevailed in Command as they watched the visuals unspool. *Nothing in the natural world contrived this,* Koshō thought, trying to wrap her mind around the sheer scale of what they beheld. *Nothing in the world of men could have built it. It cannot even hail from this eon in time. Why aren't we dead right now?*

She tore her gaze away, looking to the Prince for fresh orders. He was silent, eyes hooded, fingertips steepled beneath his noble nose. *Now which way will Sayu jump?*

Presently, Prince Xochitl frowned hugely at Susan and grumbled, "I agree that caution is required in dealing with . . . with this relic. Dispatch an exploratory team in a combat shuttle as soon as possible. They can perform a short-range scan and begin detailed mapping of the surface."

"*Hai*, Lord Prince."

Koshō gestured for Konev to join her at the command station. When the weapons officer was within range of a quiet conversation, his hands clasped behind his back and veritably vibrating with desire, she looked him up and down, troubled by the eager expression on the Russian's face.

"If you wish to try your luck—out there—find two other volunteers and refit one of the cargo shuttles to fly by wire. We'll run the boat out, and you can fly in on camera." She raised her hand sharply, cutting off the boy before he could protest. "If you're successful with a close-in approach, and can drop some sensor packs onto the surface with the shuttle's cargo arm—then we'll work up a manned landing. But until then—you've your orders."

"*Dōmo arigatō, Chu-sa!* I know just who to ask."

Bowing, he left. Koshō stared after him for a moment, and then flicked the Prince's v-pane away from her display. *Now the Prince owes me a shuttle,* she thought, suppressing a wave of irritation. Unable to sit any longer, she rose and paced over to Oc Chac's station, where the *Shosa*, Pucatli, and Holloway were poring over the detailed model of the structure being assembled by the ship's comp as measurements flowed in from the shipskin.

The Mayan's face was filled with delight as he shifted views, drilling down to successive levels of detail. "Looks like a *Chimalacatl*—the

Prince Xochitl interrupted before Susan could reply. "A waste of time! I need something in operation, *Chu-sa*. This is all"—he made an angry motion towards the wraparound v-display configured in Secondary Command—"a diversion."

That would be "no," thought Koshō, hiding her reaction behind an impassive, cool mask.

"*Hai*, Lord Prince," she replied, then shook her head at the Russian. "Not one energy source has cropped up in the scan data, *Thai-i*. We'd need a proper science team to evaluate all of this."

Xochitl nodded, satisfied, and then turned away to stare at the vista playing out on his screens.

Susan was not pleased. *So we leave Chekov's famous pistol lying beside the road at our backs. What can the man want with an "operating mechanism?" Does he believe that we can divine or control something of this magnitude without any technical resources to draw on?*

More troubling was the intuition that the Prince believed exactly that. Koshō tried to put the issue from her mind, tapping up the latest data from the remote she'd dropped at the Pinhole. Nothing had yet appeared from out of the Barrier, but she didn't believe her luck would hold in that respect either. *Wish we'd had more mines left. . . .*

Six hours later, they had completed their passage of the wrecked fleet and come within viewing range of the structure, which stood at a resonance point formed by the gravity wells of the three brown dwarves— now huge, distorted discs on the display, shedding a ruddy glare which the v-panes automatically blocked out—and the swirling vortex of the accretion disc hiding the singularity. Each sun was distended, extruding a long tail of mass corkscrewing down into the black hole.

"*Kyo?* We've lost hyper gradient—the local g field is tremendously distorted." *Thai-i* Olin licked his lips nervously. "Something emanating from that—object—is maintaining field equilibrium. While we're inside its influence . . . there's no way we can punch through to superluminal."

At this close range, the *Naniwa*'s hull was completely locked down, all booms drawn inboard. Hull temperature was rising as well, for the ambient radiation storm in this area of space was intense. Their external sensors were now limited to a set of battle-hardened scanners built

time, leaving us only traces of their titanic struggle? And Queen of Heaven, four thousand ships? There might not be four thousand starships of this size in the entire Empire!

Oc Chac sat down again, spreading his hands to indicate the spectra telemetry duly generated by ship-comp. "This is all old. Ancient. Who were they, *Gensui?*"

Xochitl did not respond, seemingly lost in his own thoughts. Koshō stirred herself, saying: "We have more pressing concerns, *Sho-sa*. Radiation levels from that accretion disc are climbing by the hour. Reconfigure the shipskin for maximum protection and pull in any sensor booms or nodes which may be adversely affected."

In his v-pane, the Prince stirred, anger shading his expression.

"However," Susan continued, shooting Xochitl a quelling look. "We want as detailed a scan as we can manage, while maintaining hull integrity and our protection, as we pass through the wreckage. Pay close attention for energy sources! *Thai-i* Holloway, please find us a path through with as little debris as possible."

The *Naniwa* edged through the ancient armada, her engines at one-quarter, booms extended, and the shipskin deployed for maximum data absorption in those parts of the battle-cruiser which were not inhabited. Koshō was back on the bridge, a great feeling of unease riding her shoulders, as the massive shapes drifted past on the camera displays. The alien vessels were enormous—far larger than even the *Tlemitl*—and formed of three "wings" joined at a central core. Most were shattered, showing gaping wounds in the unknown metal, but despite this—to her eye— Susan was gaining the uncomfortable impression that all of the ships were of a very similar kind.

"Even the smallest is the size of one of our colony stations," the Prince mused. He had not left Secondary Command in almost thirty-six hours, obsessively reviewing every data-point as it flowed across the sensor network.

"*Chu-sa.*" Konev's voice barely concealed his eagerness. "Should we dispatch an exploration team? We could board one of the smaller wrecks! Maybe there is something useful to be gleaned, like a memory core or a switch capable of controlling the thread-barrier? Even a training manual?"

THE *NANIWA*

The battle-cruiser had accelerated inbound at superluminal, having found the hyper gradient dropping off precipitously as they moved away from the Barrier. Now, having leapt three light-years from the Pinhole to the immediate vicinity of the rosette, her forward big eye filled with the ever-growing glare of the ejection jet. With initial repairs complete and Command fully staffed again, Koshō watched the plot unfold with a weather eye. The near edge of the vast shoal of debris was quickly approaching and she was on edge. There were more spectators on hand than she was used to. Prince Xochitl was still camped out in Secondary Command, and a v-pane showing his handsome but worn face had acquired a permanent—and unwelcome—place on her console.

The camera displays revealed static undulations of deep purple hue, crested with orange from the glare of the plasma stream, which gradually resolved into strings of gigantic beads, and then into enormous individual entities drifting in a black soup of smaller, irregular material. Ship's comp began scanning, trying to pattern-match the jagged shapes.

Susan stood up slowly, both eyes on the screen, one hand on the edge of her console. She had already recognized what lay before them and the sheer scale of it held her speechless for a moment.

At the XO's console, Oc Chac stiffened as the first models began to flow onto his display from the comp analysis. "Ships!" he exclaimed. "They're starships."

"All wrecked." Holloway started to bite at a fingernail, before forcing his hands to the console.

"A fleet of hundreds—no, thousands!" Prince Xochitl's expression was a study in mingled awe and excitement. He looked off-screen, and then said: "Initial analysis detects four thousand, thirty-four objects in this debris field which are likely starships of some provenance."

"The Prince is impressed," Susan said without emotion. *What will he want to do with an armada of leviathans that perished deep in the abyss of*

When it did, he keyed the reset code distributed by the Fleet to all commanding officers in the event of their encountering—or capturing—a starship of Imperial manufacture in inhuman hands. There was a tidy business in reselling retired Fleet spacecraft—some of which found their way into service with hostile powers. Too, the Fleet did—occasionally—lose ships in battle, ships that might be refurbished or rebuilt by those with the technical infrastructure to do so.

Another blast, larger than the last, smashed at the doorway, flinging the *Gunso* back into the room. Smoke billowed from something burning, filling the air with thousands of tiny black globules. A hulking figure, easily a meter taller than any of Hadeishi's team, bounced through the opening.

The *Yilan* bucked twice in quick succession against Mitsuharu's shoulder, his thigh braced against the console, and the Khaid was thrown back, chest armor splintering as the blast hit him square-on. Lovelace squealed, ducking under the console.

"*Sho-i*, back to your station!" Hadeishi shouted, dodging across the room with a kick. He got an angle on the corridor, saw there was hand-to-hand fighting amongst a swirl of figures—nearly all of them in Khaid armor—and double-tapped the tallest attacker he could see. "Seal every hatch, door, ventilator, and compartment partition from frame four up-deck, and flood the Command ring with fire-suppression foam!"

lowed with smoke, shrapnel, and the whine of flechettes. Two sharp *booms* followed, and then the marine *Gunso* ducked back in.

"They're coming again, *Chu-sa*—I can hear 'em howling up past the bathrooms at that junction."

"One minute," Hadeishi replied. "Jacking power to the console—now."

Lovelace rose up enough to see the display, watching as the interface flickered to life. An unfamiliar set of v-panes unfolded, filled with the tight columns of technical Khadesh, but the arrangement was familiar enough, and some of the icons were still Fleet standard issue. "Panel's coming up; switching to maintenance—"

Under the console, Hadeishi rotated the comm node to face him and saw the main power feed was still in place. Gingerly—there was no telling if the Khaid up on Command would decide to flip the mains back on— he levered the connector out. "Node is dead, no power!"

"I'm in maintenance mode on the console, *Chu-sa*. Overwriting the diagnostics suite now."

Lovelace's field comp, plugged socket-to-socket into the sub-comp running the console itself, chuckled and whirred for approximately four seconds, reloading the tools, interface image, and 'net matrix which ran the display itself. All of the v-panes went blank for an instant, and then reappeared, now showing the Fleet-standard interface.

"We're live," Lovelace said, keying a blur of commands with a stylus in either hand.

The *Gunso* at the door caught Hadeishi's eye, signing *They're coming*.

Mitsuharu nodded, flipping himself out from under the console. He had the second powercell in his hand, thumb on the safety switch. "Twenty seconds, *Sho-i*, and you'll be back on the shipnet."

"Ready," she snapped, back in her element, thin-boned face gleaming with the reflected light of the v-panes unfolding like a thousand blooming flowers on the display. Hadeishi flipped the switch, feeling the cell come to life, and his earbug suddenly woke up as an Imperial-standard comm frequency flooded the room. "Hit it."

Lovelace keyed a complicated, thirty-six ideogram sequence. A screaming howl rose on their radios—the sound of a hunting pack in full cry— and the *Gunso* at the door ducked out, his shipgun hammering away at some unseen target. A pane popped up on the display, filled with warning notices in white lettering on a red background. Mitsuharu leaned over the panel, waiting for the authorization glyph to appear.

Engineer. There's a lockout after fifteen tries in the base software—and we don't have time to work around that." He shoved aside a handful of hardwired data threads, and found—by feel—a comm node nestled behind them in the kind of socket that Defense Consortium salesmen liked to say was "easy to service, but hard to dislodge accidentally."

"*Sho-i*, you ready up there?" Mitsuharu plucked a multitool from his belt and wiggled half his shoulder into the panel.

"Ready, *Chu-sa*." Lovelace's voice was tight and trembling on the edge of open panic. "Are you really sure—"

"It worked before," Mitsuharu said, trying sound as cheerful as possible. *At the academy, on a different class of training cruiser—but from the same manufacturing yard and design shop—if memory serves.* "Shorting the shipnet relay for this compartment—now." He jammed the tool's screwdriver into the node's service socket and twisted to the right, grinding his wrist against the bundle of data threads. There was a sharp, bright flash and he felt his glove spark. "Done!"

The lights went out. There were a series of explosions very close by, followed by the high-pitched whine of shipguns on full automatic opening up. *I didn't mean to do that.*

"They're in the corridor," barked the *Gunso* on the team radio. "Power's down in the whole compartment!"

"Hachiman's spear, they've cut the mains!" Hadeishi popped up from under the console, finding the room had cleared save for *Sho-i* Lovelace, who was staring at him with wide eyes. The engineering panel was dead, along with the overheads and everything else in the room save one emergency light which had flickered on to shed a feeble reddish glow.

"No power," she bleated, pointing at the lightless displays.

Mitsuharu glared around the room, and then caught sight of her field comp, which was still humming away. "Powercell—pull the powercells from everything you've got. Move!"

Lovelace's face cleared and she tore open the satchel, dragging out two Fleet-standard cells, just like the ones that ran her comp. "Here—and I've an adapter!"

Hadeishi was back under the panel, one ear listening to the scrum in the hallway, with both cells in his hands and the adapter wrapped around one wrist. The *choonk* of a grenade launcher punched through all the other noise and he hooked an arm out, grabbing the *Sho-i* by the foot. "Down!" She yelped, pitching over backward, just as the doorway bil-

Then he—and the others—were thrown violently to one side as the light cruiser went into some violent evolution and the g-decking on their whole ring fluctuated. Hadeishi hit the wall hard, feeling chitin splinter, and then bounced back as the decking failed entirely. He tucked in tight, getting his feet under before hitting the far wall. The marine had done the same. One of the *kashikan-hei* was floating limp, his faceplate filled with crimson bubbles.

"Move!" Mitsuharu pulled himself along the guiderail set into the wall, heading downdeck as fast as he could. The *Gunso* followed with the other *kashikan-hei*, the two men dragging a spool of comm-wire and a repeater with them. The hammering roar of shipguns swelled in on the radio feed, and from the sound of his team commanders shouting, the *Chu-sa* guessed the Khaid on board were counterattacking along the shipcore.

Fifteen minutes later, Hadeishi swung himself through a jagged hole hacked from a sidewall and into the engineering station at frame four. The room, controlling the cruiser's dorsal power mains and shipskin sensor nodes, was tucked in behind a thermocouple relay and the motors for a pair of the big cargo elevators. Dead Khaid were webbed to one of the walls, and everything was scorched by plasma-cutter backwash.

Lovelace had found the main console, but she was engaged in a furious shouting match with one of the engineers when Mitsuharu reached her.

"*Kyo,*" the *Kikan-shi* pleaded, turning towards him, "she's going to get us all killed—she wants to—"

Hadeishi stopped the engineer with a cold glance. His face was rigid when he turned to the comm officer. "We're four minutes behind schedule and you've already been here at least that long. What's wrong?"

"This idiot," Lovelace spat, wrenching her field comp from the *Kikan-shi's* hands. "Is trying to convince me we can crack the authorization codes for the shipnet interface by *guessing them* with something he's hacked together on his hand-comp."

"We don't have time. Give me that cutter." Hadeishi hooked one boot under the console, took the proffered plasma cutter—a small one, not the big industrial version they'd used on the wall—and sliced open the paneling directly under the display panel. "There are thirty-six billion combinations allowed in the authorization interface of a *Spear*-class cruiser,

crouched at the edge of the hatchway, urging them on. As far as he could tell, the *Wilful* had entirely vanished. He couldn't see maneuvering jet flare, star-occlusion, anything to tell where she was. Despite this, he guessed De Molay was waiting it out, hiding in plain sight, so when the last of his men had dropped inside the hull, Mitsuharu climbed down himself, squirting "twenty-four seconds" on his earbug before the shipskin cut off the transmission.

The maintenance hatch airlock was a wreck, all plasma-burns and torn metal. The inner airlock was no better, and as soon as Hadeishi was inside the hull proper, his radio burst alive with the combat-chatter of men running, fighting, being killed, the roar of gunfire and the distant unmistakable whine of a monofilament saw cutting into hexacarbon. The interior of the ship seemed mostly unchanged, at least on this deck, though the old Imperial signage had been torn down and replaced, or pasted over, with Khadesh equivalents.

The marine *Gunso* commanding Team Three was waiting as Hadeishi kicked through a secondary interior door, just past the corridors servicing the cargo bay. "Shut this hatch," the *Chu-sa* snapped. "We've artillery incoming."

A pair of Team Four *kashikan-hei* slammed the portal closed, rotating the manual locking mechanism. "Report, sergeant."

The marine grinned, his faceplate scored with black streaks. "*Kyo*, this compartment's secure and we've punched through to the shipcore along the immediate axis. Cargo elevators are knocked out, as is the tube car system. There's atmosphere is most compartments, but not all. We blew out a set of blast doors at frame three and I've got the combat team pushing downdeck towards frame four—"

At that moment, the ship groaned and everything shuddered. The overheads flickered, shading from a Khaid-friendly bright white to a more normal yellow tone, then popped back. The alarms, which had been blaring since Mitsuharu had entered the primary hull, shifted tone—now they squealed like a pierced bladderfish.

"We're hit!" The *Gunso* stared at the ceiling. "Sounded like a bombpod going off at short range."

Hadeishi shook his head, starting to grin ferally. "The freighter's lit off her maneuver drives. I doubt she'll punch through the shipskin, but we need to abandon this corridor. Move everyone downdeck towards the engineering ring. That's where we'll settle this."

"Team Three, go!" Mitsuharu rotated in a quick circle, picking out the rest of his men, spread out across the hull. "Cargo doors first, then punch through to the shipcore." He clapped a hand on the *Sho-i's* shoulder. "We need to get Ensign Lovelace as far into the hull as we can!"

Then he toggled the throatmike channel. "Get out of here, *Sencho*; they can't miss seeing you now."

We'll hold on just a little longer. I have an idea, but you've got to get clear of the outer hull.

Hadeishi's heart skipped, catching a wild tone in the freighter captain's voice. "You have to leave *my* ship in one piece, too, *Sencho*."

De Molay laughed and at this short distance, he could see the black outline of the *Wilful* rotate on her maneuvering jets, swinging the main drives 'round to face him. Marines were dropping through the hatch as fast as they could, but Mitsuharu was suddenly certain they wouldn't all get through before De Molay lit off her drives.

"One hundred eighty-six seconds to get them all inside," squeaked a tiny voice at close range. Hadeishi looked down, seeing Lovelace crouched on the hull, her satchel clutched to her chest and one hand gripping a twisted piece of metal. Her eyes were huge and he suddenly realized she was susceptible to vertigo. "Three seconds for a marine, five seconds for a crewman."

"You're next," he barked, seizing her by the lanyard loop on her belt and handing her off to the last of the Team Three marines ducking into the hole. "Get her core-ward, *Gunso!* There's an engineering console at the junction of the fourth spaceframe and compartment ninety-six on this class—she needs to be there, and working, in eleven minutes!"

Get inside, Chu-sa; I've got gun emplacements in motion up here.

"My men are still outside, *Sencho*, keep your rotation and head back down the drive-wake. They'll punch you full of holes other—"

The *Wilful* suddenly rippled from one end to the other as a wave of burning pinpoints and wild color swept across her. Mitsuharu gaped, watching in stunned surprise as the freighter pulled the raiment of heaven over her head and disappeared from visual sight. "Goddess of the dawn," he breathed, "I've been sold a lame horse!"

Team Four was inside the hatch in less than one hundred and sixty seconds, though the time lag dragged into an eternity for the *Chu-sa* as he

marine was cursing, his right arm injured, and the comm officer was just clinging in panic to the hull with both hands and feet.

"Up you get, *Sho-i*," Mitsuharu growled, seizing her by the shoulder. The ensign yelped but got her feet beneath her. "*Joto-hei*, are you mobile? We've thirty seconds to get inside."

The marine nodded, his face parchment-pale behind his helmet visor. "Good to go, *kyo!*"

The hull shivered under Hadeishi's feet and he moved left, a lanyard snapped to the *Sho-i*'s belt, another cast to the marine. Cajeme had already scuttled towards them, sparing only seconds for himself before the demo plastic he'd slapped down around the periphery of a maintenance hatch offset from the set of massive cargo doors blew—a hard white flash stabbing at their eyes, sending everyone's visor polarized—and the shipskin peeled away from the edges of the portal. A pair of remote-controlled antipersonnel guns had also taken the brunt of the explosion, and their short, stubby barrels were now pointed off at the distant stars.

"Team One, go!" Mitsuharu was at the side of the two crewmen with the magnetic rams as they slammed them into place at the edge of the hatchway, where the locking bolts were now exposed. Each ram consisted of a half-circle of molybdenum-steel wrapped around the magnet array and a fusion-pumped capacitor. The crewmen snapped the adhesion arm into place, stamped down on the locking mechanism to fix the rams to the shipskin and then—bracing themselves—triggered the two devices on a count of "And one!"

Hadeishi's radio squealed, flooded with radiation, and the bolts tore free. Chunks of metal spalled away, spiraling off into the void. The crewmen cranked back the rams, peeling away the hatch.

"Team Two, go!" The engineers' mates with the blasting plastic swarmed into the hole, their tethers taut in the hands of the men behind them. Mitsuharu spared a glance for the comm officer, seeing she still had hold of her comp and the data-crystals. The marine was right at her side, shipgun at the ready, his face a blur of sweat. The two engineers popped back out of the hatch, shouting "Clear!"

A jet of plasma erupted from the hatchway, boiling the shattered edges and licking out thirty or forty meters into the jewel-hot sky.

You've got company coming, De Molay suddenly announced in his earbug. *We're getting a storm of chatter on that circuit you pirated.*

pect and we need to match v on her. No step-through, repeat no step-through. We're going to make contact in free flight."

There was a flurry of activity, but the Nisei officer had already turned to watch the bay doors thud back into the hull. A vast expanse of boiling dust and hidden, gleaming stars opened before him, swallowing all sight and vision. The beauty of the *kuub*—the intricate traceries of debris plumes and the shining coronas of distant stars—poured in, filling the cargo bay with a hot jeweled light.

The appearance of the black shape of the Khaid ship was an abrupt jolt as the *Wilful* went into a hard burn herself. It loomed up suddenly, still in the middle of its own maneuver, the drive-plume blazing like a rising sun off to starboard as the massive ship turned inside their own course.

"Velocities match!" Tocoztic and De Molay's voices overlapped. "Gantries away!"

Rail one slammed forward, safety interlocks disengaged, and Mitsuharu and his two crewmen were suddenly blown out of the side of the freighter as the tray slammed into the end of the rail and flipped down and out of the way. The successive trays on the gantry banged away, one every three seconds. Clouds of men hurtled across the void between the two ships, suddenly enveloped in a coruscating radiance.

The Khaid light cruiser continued her burn, the hull swelling before them like a basalt cliff, a jagged landscape of thermocouple fins, airlocks, gun emplacements . . . Hadeishi's eye grasped her outline in a flash and exulted. His intuition had been right, the drive signature confirmed.

"She's an old *Spear*-class cruiser," he barked on both channels, hands light on his suit propellant controls. "Cargo locks are dorsal mount, to our right and high. All hands, maneuver on my mark. Mark!"

Mitsuharu angled to the right, jets hissing, and the black wall came rushing on. Even without a suit-comp to feed him intercept times and distances, his eye was keen enough to gauge the right moment.

"Team one, braking!" He blew the last of his propellant, but even this was not enough to avoid slamming hard into the shipskin of the old *Spear*. The junior comm officer hit next, then the marine. Off to their left, Cajeme and his team had done a better job, touching down at almost zero delta. "Team One is down, repeat Team One is down."

Hadeishi staggered up, letting his boots adhere to the shipskin. The

the trusty bokutō *had shattered on whale-bone armor, leaving him with nothing. He tossed the splintered rattan away, keeping his balance with a shift of his hips. The beach itself was hard and flat, the sand gleaming wet as the tide ran out. Heke and his retinue were waiting, weapons drawn, some of the younger men leveling muskets at the ronin.*

"Nowhere to run, Pākehā," *the chieftain shouted, his tattooed face twisting with anger. "Put down your sticks and take up a man's blade!"*

One of the other Maori overhanded a bolo *at Musashi, which he caught from the air with a twisting motion. The long, flat steel blade felt tremendously heavy in his hands—far heavier than any katana. Then Heke and his men came on at a run, their war-cries booming against the counterpoint of the surf.*

"One minute, thirty seconds, *Chu-sa*." Tocoztic announced, his voice barely a whisper. "Maneuvering burn—now!"

The ship quivered, the motion magnified by the cargo-rails, and Hadeishi felt the engines tick up to barely a g of acceleration. The momentary burst, he hoped, would be obscured by the Khaid ship's own engine flare. The immediate roar of static faded slightly as the little freighter slipped out of the drive plume.

"Cycling bay doors," the *Thai-i* announced. Warning lights along the sides of the fifteen-meter-wide cargo doors flared to life as the motors kicked in. An audible alarm blared in their ears. "Vector match in—wait one, wait one."

Hadeishi stiffened, suddenly wild to see the navigation plot and the holocast. The bay doors rolled aside, revealing the glare of the Khaid ship's drive plume falling away above them.

She's lit off her own maneuvering burn, De Molay snapped, her voice tight. *She's preparing to roll aspect and change direction. But we don't know which way—*

"He's turning a dog-leg, doubling back on his trail." Mitsuharu's blood was singing. "This one alternates in thirds—he's going to swing to port, *Sencho*, to port. Match course and give me thirty percent power for seventeen seconds, then snap the gantries and we'll take it from there."

You are *mad.*

"Do it!" Hadeishi reached down and unsnapped his tether from the cargo tray. "All teams! Release your tethers. The Khaid ship is rolling as-

Mitsuharu clicked his teeth, switching channels. "The cruiser's still off-vector?"

By a point and a half. The freighter captain's voice was very dry. *You'll only have three minutes and you won't be coming in at a right angle.*

"As long as our velocities match, we'll be fine." Hadeishi felt his blood quicken, his vision sharpen, everything begin to grow preternaturally clear. "Just keep a steady hand on the tiller, *Sencho*."

"Five minutes." Tocoztic's voice had settled, becoming hard and flat. "We're in their wake. Powering up the gantries."

A set of rails embedded in the roof and floor of the cargo bay rattled to life, warning lights blinking and their motors whining. Team One was on the ventral rail, crouching in their successive loading trays—each a large, X-shaped rectangle a few centimeters larger than an Imperial-standard cargo pod. Team Two had already secured themselves to the second tray—and directly "below" them the rest of the teams were swarming into the second rail.

We're in the drive-plume full-on, De Molay reported, though Mitsuharu could already hear a roar of background static on the Khaid radio as the exhaust of the Khaiden ship's antimatter drive washed over the *Wilful*'s hull. *Three minutes and we're popping out like an appleseed. Primary hull temperature is soaring and we're getting radiation damage to the secondary.*

"All teams, secure yourselves!" Hadeishi craned his neck, eyeballing everyone. He secured his tether to Cajeme, who was already linked to the others. "Three minutes, thirty seconds to the bay doors, four minutes to contact!"

Time dragged as Mitsuharu breathed slowly and steadily through each nostril in succession, steadying his heartbeat. The radio circuit was filled with tiny noises—men praying under their breath, the rasp of someone with smoke-damaged lungs, the *tic-tic-tic* of someone nervously clicking their teeth together.

Musashi's sandals slid on black sand, the whole slope under his feet breaking free and cascading down towards the beach. Behind him, the jagged crown of Suribachiyama loomed up against a darkening sky, filled with the outriders of the taifun blowing up out of the Western Ocean. This time

him hear the rasping breath and muttering of every man and woman crowded into the bay with him. The alien armor was lacking any number of features—no personal vitals, no med-band-style dispensers—but it would hold pressure, the chitin-scale armor was tough, and the maneuvering jets had propellant. *No complaints.*

"All teams, equipment check," Hadeishi announced, rotating to the crewmen who'd drawn Team One duty with him. There were five—Cajeme and his two assistants, who were heavily laden with demolitions packs and a pair of magnetic rams—then a marine for security, and the junior comm officer from the *Eldredge*, who had survived the destruction of her ship by an utter miracle, and was kitted out with the most powerful field comp they could salvage from the *Wilful* and a satchel filled with tools, spare parts and data crystals. Mitsuharu ran through a careful check of Cajeme's z-suit and his demolition packs. "Can't have you lose air while we're working, *Nitto-hei*. You might drop something that makes a loud bang."

The Yaqui's leathery face remained impassive as he waited, but his nut brown eyes were sparkling. "The *Chu-sa* relates an excellent joke, *kyo*. Knowing how difficult it is to drop things in z-g."

"Eight minutes," The *Thai-i*'s voice was growing tenser by the second.

"All teams, sound off by section," Mitsuharu ordered as Cajeme finished checking the *Chu-sa*'s armor. Team Two was also six men—two engineer's mates and the rest of the blasting plastic, along with a portable monofilament saw from the *Wilful*'s shop and a plasma cutter carried by two more able-bodied men—then another two marines with salvaged Khaid grenade launchers. Team Three was next—eighteen men in the heaviest armor and shipguns, either Fleet or Khaid, they could scrape together—and then Team Four, the cleanup crew, which comprised the remaining twenty-five. These men were armed, in some cases with no more than their personal sidearms.

"Six minutes, *kyo*. Target is holding steady course."

Hadeishi nodded to Cajeme and the junior comm officer. "Load up."

Cajeme and his cutters swung up into the first tray on the cargo gantry. Hadeishi and the comm officer followed, spacing themselves equidistant across the second tray, with the marine to her left.

I'll miss our little talks, De Molay's voice came in his earbug, *when you've had your guts pulverized on the side of that ship.*

lation. "Unless . . . can your absorptive mode swallow our engine flare as well?"

"No, it cannot!" De Molay sat up, wincing at the pain in her side. "It is a passive system, as you can well guess. It is not a weapon, but a defense."

Hadeishi laughed, brightening for a moment. "We will make do, *Sencho*."

Feeling well enough to stand, the old woman limped over to him and examined the Khaid armor from top to bottom, testing the dark black-and-green fittings and running a fingertip along the tight, blocky lettering on the upper arms. Nodding in approval, she said, "You make a fine raider, *Chu-sa* Hadeishi. I think you've been in the wrong business all along!" Then her face grew more serious. "How many are you taking in with you?"

"I leave you our esteemed *Thai-i* here as pilot," he said, "plus two in Engineering and Galliand in medbay. But not Cajeme, he's in the first team with me."

De Molay's expression darkened and she rapped him sharply on the arm, making the chitinous armor ring hollowly. "That would be fifty-five men sent to their deaths, *Chu-sa*, if your calculations are wrong."

"*Wilful* carries no missiles, no guns, *Sencho*. We cannot overcome this Khaid from a safe distance. We must do this the hard way, as *your* ancestors did in the old days." He flashed a brief smile. "And so we need at least eight minutes at zero-delta, but thirteen would be better."

"We could abandon this place, take these men to the nearest Fleet depot." The old woman's voice was beginning to sound tired. Her fingers tightened on his arm. "Saving some would be better than losing all, would it not?"

Hadeishi shook his head. "These men and women are Fleet, *Sencho*. It is not in them to flee the battlefield when their comrades can still be saved, or when they can still strike out at our enemies."

Then he carried her back to the shockchair, and the *Thai-i* helped him tuck her into the blankets.

"Ten minutes to intercept." Tocoztic's voice echoed in Mitsuharu's ear-bug. Within the *Wilful*'s port cargo-bay, ship-comm was still working. The *Chu-sa* had the Khaid radio in his armor working as well, which let

Mitsuharu stood up, straightened his battered leather jacket, and gave her a very proper bow. "Then we've a great deal of work to do. Thank you, *Sencho*."

Several hours later, Hadeishi climbed awkwardly up one of the gangways to the command deck, having trouble adjusting to the restricted field of vision and clumsy weight of his new armor. The bandolier of grenades strapped across his chest and the bulky *Yilan*-class shipgun over his shoulder banged against him with every movement. *Maybe,* he thought—a little late—*this wasn't a good idea.*

Clomping in his heavy boots, the Nisei made his way onto the bridge and fetched up beside Tocoztic's station at Navigation. The *Thai-i* looked up at the sound, about to snarl something rude, and yelped in alarm. Trying to leap backward while snatching out his service sidearm earned the lieutenant a hard collision with the second chair, a bruise, and a seat on the deck.

"Resume your station, *Thai-i*. I am no Khaid." Mitsuharu opened the visor of the salvaged combat armor to expose his features. His face seemed a little small inside a helmet designed for the larger Khaidite cranium and jaw, but the foundation of the suit itself was composed of a gel similar to that used by the Fleet, and had sized itself to his frame as best it could. The chitin plates riding on the gelcore were now awkwardly distributed, but he hoped they'd still serve.

Tocoztic recovered himself smartly, climbing up from the floor with a doughty, "*Hai, Chu-sa!*"

"Status of that light cruiser, *Thai-i?*"

"Still holding course, dead on for the end of our burn, *kyo*."

"Hm." Hadeishi frowned, turning to the holocast to check their vector.

De Molay, working on a thermos of tea, raised an eyebrow at the Nisei officer. "I thought you wanted them to come hunting for you?"

"I *want* them to come—look—find nothing—and return to their initial patrol pattern." He tugged a stylus from the holder at the edge of the Navigator's console and sketched out a trajectory in the air. "Like so. Then, when we overlap course here—roughly—we'll match velocity for nearly thirteen minutes."

Mitsuharu looked over at the old woman, his face filled with specu-

tempting to reconnoiter. *So one of us got away with a working ship—excellent piloting—but now De Molay's "whipping knives" are shown to have a chink in their armor. And what might lie beyond? That is a powerful draw for the* Kabilizar. . . .

Movement in the active holocast caught his eye. Three of the smaller Khaid ships had gotten underway, each building velocity with a steady burn. The corona flare of their engines stood out on his plot—and each seemed to be departing the main group on a different vector. Hadeishi scratched the back of his head, reached for a plastic jug of water someone had left in Command, and then grew very still.

Three drive flares, three ships—but not the same engine signature. His stylus was immediately busy on the console, capturing all three emissions profiles and then routing them into a spectral analysis module the freighter's comp maintained for finding hydrogen strata in gas giants. *There! There she is.*

One of the three ships—perhaps a light cruiser from the mass index—was what he was waiting for.

"The Goddess watches over the patient," Mitsuharu said to himself. His stylus tapped rapidly on the console, setting a new course. He frowned as the nav comp calculated the intercept, as the resulting numbers were not good. *This gives us a very poor angle of approach. We need to trim that up.*

De Molay opened one eye as the timbre of the *Wilful*'s vibration changed, the maneuver drives going into their pre-ignition sequence. "And now?"

"We need to pick up some velocity, *Sencho*. How high can I push these engines?"

Both of the old woman's eyes opened. "Are you mad? If you go to maximum burn, the Khaid will pick us up on long-range scan."

"I know." Hadeishi offered her a lopsided smile. "I want one of their light cruisers to come looking for us—or at least change their course enough to scan our area." He paused, thinking. "The absorptive mode will work again, correct? It wasn't a one-time getaway device?"

"Yes," De Molay said, sounding wary, "it will work again. . . ."

"And unless a Khaid camera is pointed directly at us as we occlude the star field—which is luckily very sparse here—or move across one of the more excited dust clouds, their sensors won't pick us up?"

"That is the idea." An acerbic tone crept into her voice.

OUTSIDE THE BARRIER

Once more, Hadeishi was sitting in the darkened bridge, the *Wilful*'s day having wound down into the third watch, watching sensor traffic spool past in the holocast. De Molay was seemingly asleep in her chair—she rarely moved now, having given up her cabin to the worst of the wounded—and Tocoztic and a Mirror comm officer who just needed a place to lay her head were snoring on mats on the floor behind the Navigator's station. The Khaid fleet at the Pinhole was still busy, various scattered ships returning to the main group, and the battleships standing watch were now gathering up and accelerating battle debris into the opening. At this range, Mitsuharu couldn't follow the details of their mapping process, but he was certain they were making headway.

His hand moved on the controls, rewinding the last thirty-six hours of data, then letting it run forward at sixty-speed over and over again. *Where are you*, he wondered, keying up the commercial registry one more time. *I can feel you're there, given a fresh coat of paint, or at least a new nameplate . . .*

His earbug fluttered with snatches of Khaiden message traffic as well. Their encryption was spotty, and sometimes they broadcast in the clear—though, to their credit, only on line-of-sight laser when in close proximity—but Mitsuharu had time, and the passive scanners stitched into the hull of the *Wilful* were very good, just as the old woman had promised. What he heard was mostly unintelligible, but occasionally he made out the names of ships, or *Kabil*-commanders, or perhaps curses used over and over again.

They are not pleased. That much was very clear. Mitsuharu also gained the impression that an argument was underway between the ship captains—some seemed bent on leaving, the others on wrinkling out the one Imperial ship to escape their trap. A battle-cruiser which, from what he could gather from fragmentary appearances on their long-range scan, had disappeared into the "passage" the Khaid were at-

stone. "All of this was built, you say? The whole of the *kuub* and this hidden realm as well?"

"Almost certainly, *Gensui.*" Susan remembered the raw greed on Gretchen's face very clearly. "I will keep you—"

"Let us consider our situation carefully, *Chu-sa* Koshō."

The cold formality in the Prince's voice stood the small hairs of Susan's neck on end.

"The Khaid will have summoned reinforcements," he continued. "They will not abandon the watch at our badger-hole. Indeed, they will be aggressively seeking a way in after us. A six-light-year-diameter surface will take years to search properly, and I do not believe we have years of supplies aboard this ship. If all of this is a "made-thing," then the structure at its core will be a control apparatus of some kind—"

"Or cheese!" Koshō interrupted in irritation. "Or the hostile fortress all of this was built to protect! Certain destruction in any case, as it will be defended—"

"Make course for the structure, *Chu-sa*," the Prince growled. "Every recording device aboard on continuously. Dispatch message drones with the contents every half-hour."

"Of course, Lord Prince." Koshō closed the comm connection, then stifled a sigh and picked up a stylus to lay in a new plot. "So, down into the black heart of the *kuub*," she muttered. "And then out again as quickly as possible." *Grubbing for something to show his beneficent father, some prize to buy back favor. There's a cold thread of fear in his heart now . . . and we'll all likely pay for it. I should not have suggested he'd been sent out here to die.*

Holloway and Oc Chac were waiting, faces pensive, when she looked up again.

"Yes, *Sho-sa*?"

The Mayan made a disgusted face. "And where, *kyo*, does he expect these message drones to *go*?"

"It was." She looked him up and down, nodding to herself. "I am glad to see you back on duty, however. Look at this." Koshō turned to the executive 'well displayed by her console, stylus light in her hand, and marked a semicircular area deeper into the Pocket, partway between the *Naniwa* and the singularity and its attendants.

A dark mass emerged from the scan as the 'well zoomed in.

"There is an enormous amount of debris," Susan said, "between us and the event horizon. Shoal after vast shoal of matter, all of it dark and cold. The dispersion pattern is very stable—only in a few places have we been able to pick out infall from the cloud towards the black hole. And it seems to be old."

"Ancient!" Oc settled at his own console, keying up a copy of what she was looking at. He grimaced at the figures displayed on the sidebar v-panes. Other displays unfolded, showing him the results of the latest navigational scans. "We're not receiving much data from deeper in the system, either, but look at the initial analysis on this formation: very heavy—metals, radioactives, high-order elements. And the size of the field—I wonder if the planetary systems from those brown dwarves made this up—after something pulverized them into rubble."

Koshō nodded, rubbing her chin. "Or something cut them up into tiny pieces."

Thai-i Holloway, who had been poring over the same data, hoping to find some clue in the pattern of dust clouds to indicate another Pinhole-like exit, looked up and caught Susan's eye. "*Chu-sa*, I think there's something solid down at the horizon." He stepped to the main threatwell and jabbed his stylus deep into the projection. "I can see just a faint ghost—here—on my long-range plot."

The *Chu-sa* nodded. *It must be enormous to show up at this range, but what else could we expect? All of this didn't come into being by accident.*

Kosho straightened her uniform, keyed up her own image in a v-pane looping from the comm system, and then tapped open a channel to Prince Xochitl in Secondary Command.

"Lord Prince?" she said briskly, when his grim visage appeared. "Status update. Still no way out, but we've confirmed the pocket is just more than six light-years across. We have also found indications of an artificial structure very near the event horizon of the singularity."

Xochitl frowned, his expression impassive, as though carved from

Be joyful, there are intoxicating flowers
in our hands.
Put on these necklaces
of flowers, flowers from the season of rain,
fragrant flowers opening their corollas.
Here flies a bird, he chatters and sings,
he comes from the house of the Risen Lord.
With flowers in our hands, we are happy.
With songs upon our lips, sadness disappears.
O great-hearted ones, in this way,
your sorrow is put to flight.
The Giver of Life, the Sacrificed One, he has sent them.
He invents them, the joyous flowers,
These put your sorrow to flight."

When the Mayan's basso voice fell silent, Susan realized the hummingbird dancer had vanished like smoke among the fir trees and the faces of all the engineers and Backbone *kashikan-hei* were open and glad, empty of fear or fatigue. Even she felt refreshed, in a strange way, as though some of the weight upon her shoulders had been lifted.

Several hours later, after taking her station in Command, Koshō saw Oc Chac enter, once more in his usual Fleet uniform. She beckoned him over, her expression curious. "*Sho-sa*, my thanks for this morning's invitation."

The Mayan nodded grudgingly. "You were most welcome, *kyo*."

"Did you need me to be present?" She tilted her head to one side, watching him closely. "Should the commanding officer attend these ceremonies?"

"*Chu-sa* . . . No, it is not necessary. Most captains do not appear."

"Was my presence helpful?" Koshō leaned back a little in the shockchair. "You let me stand—you made me part of the ritual. Were I absent, would you have taken my place?"

Chac shook his head. "No, *kyo*. The officer in charge of the damaged area would usually represent the Risen Lord—but Goroemon was off-watch, having stood in for mine, and I thought . . . I thought you might find it interesting."

his bare feet swallowed by the deep voice of the drum. Watching him, seeing the rapt faces of her crewmen and feeling a tension singing in the air, Susan felt chilled. Back and forth along the section of rail, the *Huitzitzilnahualli* danced as though flying, an irregular, swooping motion. From one end of the watching crowd he passed to the other, sometimes spinning, sometimes leaping in short, tightly controlled hops. The walls of the tubeway began to vibrate in time with the drum—faster now, as the dancer pushed himself, speeding through the intricacy of the pattern—and both of the Mayan's hands were a blur on the *huehuetl*.

Suddenly, as the hummingbird dancer completed a high leap, the drum stopped cold.

The boy landed, instantly still, wings draped over his face, covering his head and shoulders.

Not even a breath disturbed the silence. Susan could feel her heart thudding in her chest.

A new sound entered—the soft wail of a conch-bellied mandolin—and the dancer contorted, flinging back his wings, exposing his iridescent chest to the roof of the tubeway. Koshō stiffened and more than one crewman gasped aloud. A thick crimson streak had appeared over the boy's heart. It seemed as if blood were leaking from beneath the feathers, pooling under the green and gold. The *Huitzitzilnahualli* leapt straight up, flinging himself backward in a stunning reverse, and as he did so, the white mantle and the gleaming wings became speckled with irregular black spots.

He landed square on both feet, but now his stance had changed. No longer did he move with such delicate grace—instead he spun, wings inward, showing his broad back and mantle to the watching men—and with every revolution, swinging into ever tighter circles, the whiteness was pierced again and again by black, corrosive streaks. In a flurry of motion, the dancer was suddenly prostrate before Chac and Koshō at the end of the lines of watching men—and his mantle, his chest, his legs were all but consumed by stippled gray-on-black darkness, as though his limbs had washed away in a tide of corruption.

BOOM. The drum sounded fully one more time, the boy head down on the platform before them, his breath coming in audible gasps. Then Oc Chac struck the sides of the drum sharply with stiffened fingers, drawing everyone's attention away from the *Huitzitzilnahualli* and onto himself.

"A poet once said:

sides of the tube ahead of her was surprising. There were at least thirty *kashikan-hei* with logistics flashes on their z-suits lined up along the walkways on either side of the rail. At the far end of the group, she could see Oc Chac's polished visage watching for her, though the slim figure at his side was unfamiliar.

The Mayan's companion was young, no more than a cadet, and what she could see of his face indicated he was straight from the Center, possibly from Tenochtitlán itself, with shining black hair like smoke tied back behind a smooth copper-colored neck. What piqued her interest, however, was the elaborate and beautiful costume he was wearing. A classical Nahuatl mantle formed of tiny gleaming white feathers was draped across his shoulders and back, leaving the front open to reveal a fitted shirt ablaze with green and gold and iridescent yellow. The shirt was also made of feathers, even smaller and more downlike than the mantle. Most of his face was hidden by a hummingbird mask figured in black and red and green—and the mask itself seemed to be formed of beaten gold inlaid with semiprecious stones and jade. His feet were bare on the platform, though tiny conch shells were braided around his ankles. As she approached, the *kashikan-hei* lining the side walls bowed respectfully, their caps pressed over their hearts, and Oc Chac saluted smartly.

The Mayan officer had set aside his z-suit and uniform and was wearing a hooded cotton cloak and tunic. Like the young man, his feet were bare, though unadorned.

"*Chu-sa* on deck," Juarez announced, his voice echoing in the tubeway. With a rustle, everyone knelt save the *Huitzitzilnahualli* and Susan. She glanced questioningly to Oc Chac, who motioned for her to step to the edge of the tube beside him and remain standing. When she had done so, the Mayan squatted down with a drum between his legs. A flat, calloused palm struck the stretched leather and a deep, basso *boom-boom* sounded. In the rail tunnel, the sound reverberated in each direction, generating a skin-tingling vibration.

In the first silence, the hummingbird dancer raised his arms, lifting one foot. As he did, the white mantle stiffened, conforming to his muscular arms, and the ends extended, becoming proper wings.

Stamp! His bare foot fell, striking the platform. In the same instant, Oc Chac struck the drum again. *BOOM!*

Thus the youth danced, first in an irregular pattern which wended this way and that, each light footstep ringing in the tubeway with the slap of

ABOARD THE *NANIWA*

Koshō woke to the sound of a reminder chime from her comp. Lying in the dimness of her cabin, she felt perfectly fine for approximately three seconds—then she moved her head, looking over at the screen to see what needed doing—and every muscle, joint, and tissue in her body complained. *Oh Queen of the Heavenly Mountain,* she thought blearily, *did I take that many meds in the last two days?*

The bone-deep achiness in her back, legs and shoulders argued that she had, in fact, taken way too many stayawakes for her body to process in only four hours of sleep. Regardless, she swung out of her bunk and padded on bare feet to the comp.

Ventral end of magazine conveyor thirty-two, in fifteen minutes? Susan scratched her head, feeling an irritating graininess in her scalp, and realized she'd collapsed into bed without even washing her face. The sensation of grime clogging every pore on her body made the Nisei woman shudder, so she tapped a quick "acknowledged" into the comp and fled to the shower.

Fourteen minutes later, in a fresh uniform and with a bulb of tea in her hand, Koshō stepped out of the tube—and nodded in greeting to a junior engineer waiting for her in the little offloading station. *Socho* Juarez had attached himself to her as soon as Susan had left her cabin.

"*Kikan-shi* Ige, good morning. *Sho-sa* Chac is waiting for me?"

"They all are, *kyo.* This way please." The Mixtec engineer gestured for her to precede him.

They all *are?* Curious, Koshō drained the rest of the bulb and followed along. *What is Chac up to now?*

Almost immediately they descended a gangway passing through two layers of battle-steel and stepped out onto a hexacarbon walkway running the length of a railway tube. Susan recognized part of the Backbone from all the work they'd done during trials to get the maglev system up and running, but the number of crewmen standing along the

"You're going to stand in the Noyan's way? You are a man of great bravery."

"Not the Noyan." The elderly samurai essayed a grin. "A local gang— no more than bandits, forty or fifty of them—the governor has parted out the collections, being too indolent to do this himself."

Musashi felt a spark of interest flare in his breast, so he settled his shoulders, picked up the bokutō and bowed politely. "Now this I need to see," he said. "How many of us are there?"

"Five others," Kambei said. "Did I mention all the farmers can pay is our meals?"

have capsules on the plot, but nowhere to bunk the survivors for more than a few hours. Where to put them . . ."

"Success will defeat you if we do not find a way." De Molay settled back into her blankets. "Or you will have to be satisfied with the souls you've already saved, and let the rest go."

"No." He shook his head vehemently. "I won't abandon them."

"Then what will you do?" The old woman's exasperation was clear. "There is *no room* at the inn."

Hadeishi nodded slowly, his face clearing. "Your point is taken. Plainly, we need another ship."

"Another ship?" Tocoztic—who had come in while they were talking and sat down quietly at his station—exclaimed. "But—"

"Then get one." De Molay replied tartly, glaring at Mitsuharu. "I am content to watch from here while you do the heavy lifting, but I would appreciate just one tiny favor, *Chu-sa.* I would like *my ship back* in operable condition!"

"Of course."

Musashi swung the axe in a light, looping arc—striking the end of the log square center—gravity and the full power of his shoulders splitting the wood from end to end with a sharp crack! *He reached down, tossed the two sections aside into a large and growing pile, and then reached for another log.*

"Pardon me, sir," came a polite but authoritative voice. Musashi looked over his shoulder, tattered kimono stretching over his muscular arm. An elderly, balding man was standing at the edge of the inn's wood lot—no, not just a man, someone who had once been a samurai officer. That much was instantly apparent to Musashi from his horseman's stance, his calm and level gaze. Such men were rare in Japan under Mongol rule—well, rare that they walked the streets and were not in chains, or laboring in some work gang in shackles.

"I understand that you are ronin—and needful of employment?" The stranger tilted his head slightly, indicating the woodpile.

"I need to eat, like all men," Musashi replied, straightening up. "What's the job?"

"Tax collectors are going to level their village." The samurai gestured politely to two farmers cringing behind him, their faces drawn with hunger, their bodies thin with starvation. "As the harvest has been short this year."

The old woman scratched at the half-healed wound on her cheek. "So—how is our new crew adjusting to their reduced circumstances?"

"Some of the wounded won't last, but their spirits are good." Hadeishi sat, his good mood evaporating. "We'll lose nearly ten, I think, if we can't find better medical facilities for them."

De Molay nodded, watching him closely. "My apologies, but I cannot offer anything better . . ."

"That you—that we—are here has already given them a priceless gift." Hadeishi's eyes narrowed, thinking of the hidden compartments he knew existed downdeck. "Now, *Sencho*, is that really true? This is a ship of many surprises! I've not gone through every centimeter of the holds—have you a whole medbay down there? Along with this"—he indicated the hull with a wave of his hand—"very interesting shipskin and heat exchanger?"

In response, she frowned, jutting her chin forward. "So far the rescue campaign is going well, you would say?"

Hadeishi started to nod, his expression brightening. "Very well! We need to kit up some more bunks, as you've said, and take a close inventory of our supplies, but—"

"*Chu-sa*," De Molay said sharply. "How many men and women have we taken aboard?"

"Sixty," he said after a moment of mentally reviewing the rosters from each capsule.

"We are at one hundred twenty-five percent of environmental capacity, *Chu-sa*. The scrubbers are showing amber across the board, the sewage recycler is backed up, and we're out of hot water. In fact, we're going to be out of water *period* very soon because there is waste and leakage in these *Knorr*-class freighters and we're pushing the system too hard! But that," she concluded, her voice rising angrily, "won't be an issue much longer because we are almost out of *food*."

Hadeishi sat back, scratching at his beard, which had begun to twist into an ungainly white-streaked tangle. Reluctantly, he walked mentally through the ship, comparing the numbers of compartments to the number of men aboard. *These capsules are coming in with some emergency rations aboard, but this freighter didn't come prepared for a search and rescue mission. We're just over carrying capacity.*

"You're right," he said at last, brow furrowed in thought. "We still

THE *WILFUL*

Hadeishi stepped onto the bridge—such as it was—of the little freighter, with a light heart. The search pattern laid down by De Molay had let them recover no less than five evacuation capsules from a variety of Imperial ships. In each case the capsule had been maneuvered into one of the cargo bays with the *Wilful*'s z-g loading cranes and clamped down. Gunner's mate Tadohao and *Nitto-hei* Cajeme had grown quite proficient in the art of undogging the capsule hatches and sorting out the dazed, wounded, and confused men inside. Nearly every *Sho-i* and *Thai-i* they'd rescued had protested the command structure, complained vehemently, threatened mutiny, and finally settled down after a thorough reading of Mitsuharu's papers.

Hadeishi found it quite interesting—more so with each conversation—that none of the Fleet officers seemed to find it strange or unusual to be rescued by a tramp freighter commanded by a reserve *Chu-sa* in the uttermost wilderness. *But then*, he remembered, *this was a Smoking Mirror operation, which means every man and woman of them came expecting the strange, the untoward and the downright peculiar to happen.*

Mitsuharu stepped to the captain's chair, seeing that De Molay was dozing at her station, still wrapped in a variety of blankets and now wearing a hand-knit shepherd's cap. He was about to sit when he noticed the shockchair had been reduced to nothing but the bare frame, without even the cracked leather seat he'd grown used to.

"What have you done to my chair?" He gave the old woman a questioning look.

"Hm? Oh, the cushions?" De Molay yawned elaborately, stretching both skinny old arms. "All of your lost children needed something for their heads; these floors are quite cold if you've not even a blanket."

"Yes . . . that is true." He fingered the hexacarbon framing and eyed the recessed bolts in the seat.

ghost of a smile. In his other Eye, the z-suited alien had removed his helmet and was stuffing a long-snouted face with fried dumplings, a veritable buffet table of freshly delivered food laid out before him. Beside the table, a trolley cart had been provided, filled with gleaming glass bottles of liquor.

Now our feet are on the proper road.

this cursed murk, and they came loaded for capital ships . . . so tell me this, is it safe to take my ship back into Imperial space with you aboard?" Her expression flattened. "Are you running from someone, Lord Prince? We've been out of comm contact for weeks—is your father dead? Is there some new Emperor on the Quetzal throne? One that finds you displeasing?"

"What do—" Xochitl stopped, his expression suddenly frozen. "Yakka, that is a cold, cold thought."

"The Princes of the México are notoriously cruel, my Lord. Particularly when they war upon one another."

"My father sent me *himself*," Xochitl allowed confidently, but felt his jaw twitch as he gave the words life. Susan shook her head minutely in disbelief, her eyes filling with pity. Suddenly, he felt naive. "He . . . no one else knew my destination or intent. No one. We left Anáhuac under complete blackout and emissions control; my own ship, my own picked men. He . . . couldn't send anyone else . . ." The Prince's voice trailed off and his vision grew dark with growing fury.

Now I know how sensei *felt at Jagan,* Susan thought, abruptly gripped by despair. *The fate-cursed retainers of a doomed Prince, conveniently sent into a wilderness from which they will not return . . .*

"No," Xochitl said slowly as he tried to rally his wits. "No, I will not believe that, not yet. Many hands touched the planning of the Mirror expedition—or the Khaid may have been snooping here already—anyone might have . . ." A thought occurred to him and his face lightened with relief. "The embassy! Someone had informed the—" He stopped abruptly, blinking as an overlay appeared in his field of vision.

«*Security Warning! Koshō, Susan, Chu-sa in command of IMN BC-268, does not hold ring-zero clearance!*»

Susan looked at him expectantly. Xochitl felt suddenly, terribly alone. *I can't tell her. She's not cleared to know such things. How—*

"There is another explanation," he said coldly, rising and going to the door. "Which is a privy matter. Expedite your repairs, *Chu-sa*. We will need to be underway as soon as possible. As soon as it is safe to move, begin looking for a way out of this . . . place. And send all current telemetry to the secondary bridge for my review."

Susan watched him leave with a frown. *Now what did he almost say? What "embassy" was involved with this?*

Down in Medical, Hummingbird's impassive face showed the faint

"You make that title sound positively dirty," Xochitl jested weakly, trying to summon even a spark of his usual ebullience. The anger had already faded from him, leaving only a pensive weariness. He groped for a chair, found a low-cut Nakashima fiddleback, and collapsed into the elegant seat. "How many men did you lose, Yakka?"

"Nearly a hundred. I welcome the replacements you brought."

"Huh!" The Prince's laugh—to his own ear—was a tired bark from an exhausted dog.

"You still owe me ninety-three more."

In the darkness of the med-bay, Green Hummingbird frowned, watching the Prince and the captain stare at each other in weary silence. He blinked, switching the feed to another of his *dorei* infesting the shipnet.

This v-cam showed the armored alien who'd come aboard with the Prince. The creature was cowering in the corner of a well-appointed cabin with its long tapering head hidden in his hands. A constant muttering wail issued forth from the helmet, which was loud enough for the room security camera to pick up and relay to the *nauallis*. The sounds were unintelligible, though the México had a more than passing knowledge of the Hjo trade language used in Imperial space.

What a pitiful creature, the old man thought, and subvocalized a series of commands into his throatmike. *A pity the zhongdu didn't send someone more . . . aware. Still, one uses what tools are to hand.*

"How are we going to get out of here?" Xochitl paced back and forth across the bamboo-parquet flooring of the *Chu-sa*'s private office. His boots ground into the sealant layer protecting the light-grained panels, leaving tiny gritty black marks. "How did you navigate through the Barrier? Can you get us back out?"

"Don't you wonder," Koshō said, in a musing tone, "if the Khaid knew our full strength when that pack made transit . . . or do they habitually hunt Imperial scouts with such numbers? It seems very odd their *Kabil Rezei* would go loping around in this wasteland with a *fleet*."

The Prince glared at her. "You are *still* just as annoying as in school."

Koshō shrugged, meeting his eyes with a calm, direct gaze. "They were hunting for you, Sayu. They jumped in hot, right on top of us in

wall. She seemed entirely unimpressed by his battered appearance and lank hair. He, in turn, could not help but see the *Chu-sa* was worn almost to the point of exhaustion. And that, somehow, she had aged during the past ten years, becoming a formidable-looking woman with more than a passing resemblance to her maternal grandmother.

"I'm the ranking officer here," Xochitl growled, trying to summon an authoritative snap in his voice.

"Then you'll be on the secondary bridge," Koshō replied evenly, not even bothering to look up from her personal comp. "As befits the *Gensui* commanding the battle group. My apologies—we are not fitted with a flag bridge. Be aware, *Tlatocapilli*, that *I* will remain in command of *my* ship and all operational matters at all times."

"You will follow *my* orders!" Xochitl responded, outraged.

"Only if they exhibit a shred of sense." Susan turned, looking him up and down with a measuring eye. The Prince stiffened, not used to such judgmental scrutiny, or the sensation that he had been found wanting.

"Right now," Koshō continued, her voice harsh with exhaustion, "there is only *one* thing to do—get out of here as quickly as possible. We're in no shape to deal with the Khaid, much less the powers which might dwell in this benighted sinkhole. My ship has been hammered up one side and down the other, our magazines are low, we've battle damage in every department and almost every section. Do you honestly think we can do *anything* here, other than blunder into another defensive system and make a quick exit to Mictlan?"

Xochitl started to speak, and then paused, his attention drawn away, listening to some voice only he was privy to. Then, with a sharp, deep breath he stepped back and rubbed his brow fiercely. Beads of sweat glistened at his temples.

"No," the Prince said, having collected himself. "You're right. Without our science teams and the support ships, we have no way . . ." He paused, seeming to look inward again. "Thrice-cursed Huss and his league of devils! I am a fool and fool's fool." Xochitl glared at Susan, eyebrows drawn together as his whole face transformed into a furious mask. He ground a fist his palm. "*Someone* brought the Khaid down on us, didn't they? The raiders haven't been reported operating in this area before."

"No." Koshō's lips twitched and she clasped her hands. "Not in the last ten years of working the Rim. Someone was expecting *you*—Lord Prince, or someone like you—to come along."

shroud himself. The monitoring panel on the stretcher beeped questioningly, to which the *nauallis* responded by keying an override into the machine.

With his bed showing nothing but green status lights, Hummingbird padded to Anderssen's shroud, raised the cover, and then drifted his right hand over her face, forehead, shoulders, and then down the length of her body. He was careful not to touch her skin or the fabric of her shirt or trousers. Instead, eyes half-lidded, he seemed to be feeling for something perceptible only a centimeter or less from her body.

"Hsss . . . that was near too much for you, child." He frowned, green eyes dark with worry. His gnarled old hands had paused over her wrists, where there was a sensation of terrific heat. So, too, at her clavicles and the right side of her face. This was apparently unexpected, for Hummingbird drifted his hands away from each location and then back again several times.

Still frowning, his lips tight with concern, the *nauallis* opened the stowage bin under the stretcher and drew out the parchment envelope holding the bronze-colored block from Gretchen's jacket. Curious, he examined the device carefully—but could see no signs of change or transformation in the corroded metal. Shaking his head, he put everything back where he'd found it, closed Anderssen's shroud, and then crawled back into his own bed. This time, before strapping himself down and closing the glassite cover, he made sure both earbugs were inserted and responding, then yawned mightily—activating his dropwire—and pressed a fingertip into the cavities beneath either side of his jaw, turning on his throatmike.

Immediately, his earbugs filled with interesting chatter. As he lay motionless, his heart slowing, diagrams and images began to play out on the inside of his eyelids. One of his search *dorei* active in the v-network stitched through the fabric of the battle-cruiser was waiting with a video feed—complete with sound. Prince Xochitl had been shown into *Chusa* Koshō's private quarters.

The México lord stared around obstinately at the subdued colors and simple, even spartan furniture that Susan maintained in her suite of rooms. Koshō was sitting at her desk, the collar of her uniform undone and her jacket hung on the back of a chair which swiveled out from the

with tremendous pain hidden behind a wall of meds, and now the rest of her had seemingly converted into an enormous ache. *At least the bees are gone,* she thought blearily. Her skin had settled down, which was a mercy. Whatever had happened when her hands had been on the corroded bronze block seemed to have faded, leaving only a faint golden tinge at the edges of her vision.

The stretcher whisked through a double-wide hatchway, and she was suddenly enveloped by the smell of antiseptics, blood, and urine. A face appeared above her—a junior medical officer, his lean visage spotted with crimson, his eyes hollow with sixteen hours on watch. Despite his appearance, however, he flashed a cheerful smile and palpated her arm. His touch made everything whirl around her like a sudden *tchindi* and someone, somewhere, groaned aloud in terrible pain.

"This temporary block is shot," a voice said. "Load her up and knock her out. Back to room eight for her, with the old—"

There wasn't even a needle-prick, just sudden sleepiness and then . . . nothing at all.

The orderly guided the stretcher into the second base station in the assigned room, confirmed the med-interlocks were set and showing green on their little status panel, then covered Anderssen with a blanket and adjusted the pillow under her head. Given the possibility that the g-decking might fail if combat resumed, he strapped her down and lowered a protective glassite shroud from the ceiling. Then, given he was in the room, the medic raised a similar covering over the old Nahuatl man in the next bed and tested his retinal responsiveness with a hand-light.

"Nothing," muttered the orderly, shaking his head in dismay. "Facial pallor, weak and thready breath, heart arrhythmia . . . grandfather is in poor condition." He charted the necessary notes with his stylus, then turned out the lights and closed the door behind him.

Once the room was dark and empty, however, Green Hummingbird let out a long, slow breath, and then wiggled his fingers and toes. After a moment to let his body stabilize, the old man turned his head sideways, looking at Gretchen's supine form in the next bed. His forehead creased with worry, wrinkles drawing up at the corners of his mouth and eyes. Deftly, he worked an arm free of the restraints, and then raised the

A pair of corpsmen had arrived with orderlies and stretchers. They immediately climbed in through the mangled airlock to help out the men still inside the capsule. The first to emerge was the hulking, seven-foot-high shape of the alien, in its unfamiliar armor. The marines and engineers stiffened, hands going to personal weapons. The creature looked around; head tilted back a little, and then saw the Prince. Xochitl looked back to the warrant officer.

"Take me to the *Chu-sa* immediately. Quarters for my men can wait. I will not. This one"—he pointed to Sahâne—"send to whatever cabin is reserved for *me*. I will take something else, anything else."

Von Bayern nodded amiably, apparently unaffected by the fury radiating from the Prince like a furnace draft. "Of course, my lord Prince, our transport is standing by." He gestured to a nearby grav-sled—a regular cargo carrier which had a pair of bench-seats bolted on and draped with fabric in colors approximating the Imperial eagle crest. Xochitl shook his head, now beyond words, and climbed aboard.

As the grav-sled whined away, one of the corpsmen helped Helsdon out of the capsule, supporting his shoulder. The engineer looked ghastly, but was able to keep his head up as they loaded him onto a stretcher. The *Joto-Heiso* from the work crew was waiting with a flask, along with Juarez and four of the marines.

"Welcome aboard, *kyo*. The *Chu-sa* says you're straight to a spare cabin and twenty, thirty hours of sleep." The engineer flashed a broken-toothed smile behind his white mustache, pressing the flask into Malcolm's hands. "Here, this'll set you right. She sent it down. A twenty-year malt *uisge-beatha*—like velvet!"

Helsdon laid his head back on a pillow, puzzlement pushing aside his exhaustion for a moment. "Who—who sent this?"

"*Chu-sa* Susan Koshō, Engineer." Juarez patted him gently on the shoulder, and then motioned for the marines to escort him away. "Welcome aboard the *Naniwa*. The captain apologizes for keeping you in the can so long, but there wasn't time to peel you out properly until now."

All Gretchen could see was corridor roof, gleaming with overheads, and occasionally the superstructure of a hatchway as the grav-stretcher zipped along. A corpsman was jogging along beside her, though she could hear his voice only intermittently. Her left arm was throbbing

capsule at speed, while the *Naniwa* barreled past in the Pinhole—though its landing in boat bay one had been . . . rougher . . . than the navigator intended.

"Clear!" barked the *Joto-Heiso* bossing the team of engineers. He stepped back, swinging the saw up onto his shoulder. Hot hexacarbon fragments littered the deck, filling the air of the cargo bay with thick spirals of smoke. "Get 'er open."

The hatch squealed as pry bars dug in around the periphery, then popped free with a *ting!* Four of the *Joto-hei* on hand seized hold with magnetic grapples and wrestled the enormously heavy block of battle-steel, hexacarbon, and glassite onto a waiting grav-sled. As soon as the portal was removed, there was movement inside the capsule and two battered-looking Jaguar Knights emerged, shipguns at the ready. The *Joto-Heiso* stood his ground, unsuccessfully hiding a sneer behind a thick walruslike mustache. "Muddies," he muttered under his breath to the engineers standing behind him.

"Xochitl-*tecuhtzintli*, welcome." *Heisocho* Von Bayern was waiting for the next man to emerge. Prince Xochitl stamped out, his armor streaked with vomit and stippled with fresh dents. The México lord's face—his helmet was now canted back—was glacial with fury, his dark eyes flashing dangerously. One of his high, chiseled cheekbones had acquired a dark, purpling bruise. The Diplomatic Service warrant officer bowed appropriately, and then saluted sharply. "*Gensui* on deck," he barked.

A dozen meters back, *Socho* Juarez and the full remaining complement of marines aboard the battle-cruiser stamped their right feet in unison, presented arms—they'd scrambled to unpack their Macana assault rifles—and then held rigid while the cruiser's piper wailed through the Imperial March.

Xochitl stared at the welcoming committee, his expression congealing into something very much like icy mud. Nothing about the reception was in the least irregular, though rousting out a piper for the March was generally falling from fashion. Von Bayern offered the Prince a gracious smile, hands clasped behind his back, until the drone of the bagpipes had ceased.

"My lord, I hope you will accept our apologies for detaining you and your crew within your evac capsule during transit. Your physical safety is of tremendous concern to *Chu-sa* Koshō. And . . . here are the medics."

the yards, the *Naniwa* had experienced very few outright component failures. "What I need you to do, *Thai-i,* is—"

She turned to the navigational plot shipnet had pieced together from data recorded during their passage. Oddly, the changes made to the navigational interfaces—and to the threatwell and other Command systems—when Anderssen had taken them over, had all reverted to their Fleet-standard configurations. Even the massive rush of topology information which had allowed Susan to navigate through the Pinhole had purged itself. Only second-by-second Command camera images of the threatwell remained, but from them shipnet had reverse-engineered a model of their exit point and the surrounding area.

"—find us a place to lie up while all immediate repairs are completed. We've moved into a peculiar area of space—one without charts, and which may obey different physical laws than we're used to—so I don't want to rush about until we've laid down a tight nav plot. But here"—Koshō indicated a convoluted set of folds in the nearest dust clouds—"is a region free of the Barrier threads, and excited and dense enough we may be masked from passive sensors if someone comes along, banging on the temple-wall with a stick. Drop a remote to watch the Pinhole for us, and then move the *Naniwa* in there and go to zero-v. The engines need maintenance as well—we've taken enough dings, dents, and outright punctures to warrant a thorough inspection."

"*Hai, kyo.*" Goro covered a yawn with her salute and settled herself gingerly in the command chair.

Susan looked around the bridge one last time, saw that Anderssen had already been taken away, nodded to herself, and strode off to find her own cabin.

A monofilament saw shrieked, cutting away at the airlock on a badly battered evac capsule. Two burly engineers, their combat armor awash in a flood of sparks, were sawing away the last of the hinges holding the hatch closed. The portal itself was badly scarred and had been slightly twisted in the framing socket by some massive impact. The evac capsule had fared no better—carbon-scoring had turned nearly the entire surface black and the view ports were milky with tiny fissures. Another crew of engineers were dragging away a couple hundred meters of high-v cargo netting—the net *Thai-i* Holloway had arranged to snatch up the

THE *NANIWA*

The last of the officers and ratings who'd ridden through the Pinhole had crawled off to their bunks by the time *Thai-i* Goroemon managed to reach Command. Koshō was still in her shockchair, reviewing the telemetry captured by shipnet during their passage, looking for somewhere to hide her battered ship.

"*Chu-sa?* Holloway-*tzin* said you needed me to stand officer of the watch?"

"I do, *Thai-i*. I am very glad you survived. Can you handle another eight hours awake?"

Goro shrugged, broad shoulders stretching the gel of her z-suit. "Hard to sleep with all the racket, *kyo*—but we didn't get hit too hard down in the Backbone. Two magazine conveyors went down due to jams, but nothing punched past into the inner hull where we were."

The lieutenant rarely stood a Command watch, though she was technically fifth on the roster. Her usual duty station was in the munitions roundhouse controlling the network of high-speed magnetic railways threading between the primary and secondary hulls of the battle-cruiser. The *Naniwa*'s main magazines were spaced along the shipcore itself, as far from hostile fire as possible, while a network of secondary—or "ready"—depots served each hard-point, launch-rail, or gun-pit. Managing the Backbone ammunition network was third in complexity among the ship's systems, behind the engines and shipskin.

"How soon will we be reloaded?" Susan asked, frustrated with herself that she hadn't already checked in with logistics.

"Another hour, *kyo*, and we'll have all the conveyors back in operation," Goro replied. "*Kikan-cho* Hennig's men have both of the jammed ones torn apart right now. He said there's some fabrication problem with the pass-along sensors, so they're getting pulled, hand-tested, and replaced as needed."

"Better than I expected." Koshō was pleased. For a ship so fresh from

but Mitsuharu was having a hard time believing the data before him. *Every engineer in the Empire would fall on his sword to bring this secret home. Someone has developed an effective thermodynamic shunt. And it's working and it's on this ship, on my ship.*

"*Thai-i* Tocoztic, eyes on your console, mind on the mission." Hadeishi's voice was sharp, ringing with hidden elation. The tone gained the younger officer's complete attention. "Pilot De Molay, plot a course for the next surviving evac capsule. We still have work to do, even if the Khaid are careless and blind. The next patrol ship may be more attentive."

"*Hai, Chu-sa!*"

Hadeishi felt something tight in his chest release at the long-familiar words: *Ah, now my heart is beating again!*

The thought gave him a chill down the back of his neck.

"Here it comes," the *Thai-i* breathed, "we'll have visual in—"

The Khaid destroyer emerged from a screen of stellar dust, black bulk dwarfing the *Wilful*, flanks etched with the landing lights outlining her boat bay doors. On the camera display, Mitsuharu could make out rows of launcher hard-points, the shallow pits of particle beam emitters and point-defense guns. The hypercoil ring to aft and the maneuver drives were arranged in an unfamiliar pattern, but close up the Nisei could guess at her manufacturer. *A refitted Megair* Vampyre-*class light cruiser. Interesting—the Khaid Zosen must have bought her as a hulk and replaced all of the internal systems—the Khaiden body form doesn't fit very well to the arthropod. Those drives look new, too.*

Regardless of her provenance, the destroyer sailed on past, showing every sign of being unaware of their presence. Tocoztic stared at his console, stylus busily tapping away. He checked and double-checked the paltry stream of data available. "Their active scan is pinging right over us!" he whispered loudly.

Suddenly Hadeishi had to suppress a full-on grin; not a proper hint of a smile or a careful mask of command, but a fierce, predatory snarl.

The Khaid rolled on past, and the *Wilful* shuddered a little as the wash of radiation from her engines pelted the shipskin. Mitsuharu, properly somber again, paid close attention to the status displays from the hull configuration. *What excellent engineering*, he thought. *The emission wave from the enemy radar failed to spike our surface temperature. The drive wake has been absorbed as well. But . . . how could shipskin cool to relative zero so fast?*

The Nisei sat back, nearly overcome with wonder. Then he noticed that the subsonic vibration of the reactor interface had soared up, almost to an audible level. He looked to De Molay in concern, but the old woman just shook her head minutely. Her gray eyes rested steadily on him. For the first time in a long time, Mitsuharu felt nervous, jumpy. *A tramp freighter, eh? I am six kinds of a fool.*

Tocoztic squirmed in his chair, looking around curiously at the walls. "What's that weird vibration?"

"Engine phase-transition, *Thai-i*. Every ship has its own quirks and noises," Hadeishi replied with deliberate calm as he reviewed his console again. *Power output is up 300 percent. But—we're not leaking heat, the internal temperature is actually cooling. . . .* The reason was obvious,

for the *Wilful.* "We're going to have to go to zero-power and lose steering way, hope they pass over us as wreckage. We're too close to—"

Tocoztic gave him a sick look. "They're sure to catch us on active scan—we're not Imperial, we're not Khaid—they will *know* we're a scavenger that didn't get caught up in the battle. That fate"—he stabbed a finger at the location of the obliterated capsule—"will be ours!"

"Going dark," De Molay announced, when Hadeishi failed to respond immediately. Her face drew tight with concentration and Mitsuharu could see that another set of v-panes had appeared on her console. The markings—and he could not see them clearly from his vantage point—did not seem to be formed of human letters.

"Hostile is less than a light-second away," Tocoztic breathed, sounding anguished. "She's accelerating. We're getting side scatter from an active scanning array—"

"There!" The old woman sighed in relief. "Memory still holds true!"

At the same moment, the *Wilful's* engines died and the lights dimmed markedly. The constant vibration of the reactor drew down, and then entirely faded away. Hadeishi watched with intense interest as each on-board system shut down in swift succession. On his console, the myriad v-panes and controls faded away—the threatwell went dark—and the environmental monitors indicated that every compartment had dialed down air circulation and scrubber activity to the absolute minimum. The only activity registered on the shipskin, which was assuming a new aspect—one that Mitsuharu had never seen before. Part of the forward hull was visible in the camera display, which was still active, and there he saw that the hull had deformed into a strange, "fuzzy" configuration, the surface extruding millions of what appeared in close-up to be tiny matte-black cilia.

Truly we have turned into a creature of the abyss!

He gave De Molay a curious glance. "We're in an absorptive mode?" he asked quietly.

"We are," she replied with the hint of a smile. Hadeishi hid his reaction, suddenly mindful of Tocoztic and the other Fleet ratings who might be listening down deck. *There's no heat sump on this ship capable of absorbing the impact radiation on the skin. Nothing big enough to swallow our own emissions, not for more than a few seconds. So—what lies behind those closed-off compartments on the Engineering deck? Something to hide us completely?*

THE WILFUL

The Khaid destroyer—another classified as *Neshter*-class by the com-mercial registry, though Mitsuharu's practiced eye had already picked out a number of differences between this ship and the *Qalak*—loomed in the threatwell, its icon surrounded by a constellation of informative graphics.

"Launch signature," Tocoztic announced suddenly, his voice tight. "Looks like a one-rail sprint missile." In the 'well, a glowing streak ap-peared, following the track of the weapon. "Vectors do not overlap."

Hadeishi had already seen the target and his face stiffened in fury.

"An evac capsule," De Molay said, a moment later. "We picked up their signal about an hour ago."

"As did the Khaid," Mitsuharu bit out with difficulty. "They haven't a chance."

The missile icon intersected the capsule's graphic and both winked out. A quarter-second later, a tiny bright flare appeared on one of the camera displays, and then faded away. Against the slow roll of the dust clouds—all ruddy red, purple, and orange luminescence—the explo-sion went almost unnoticed.

Hadeishi was motionless, his face in shadow on the darkened bridge, staring at the 'well. *And I was unable to do even the slightest thing to save the men aboard.*

"She's turning," the *Thai-i* announced into the silence. "We have—we have vector overlap if they hold course."

The Nisei stirred, forcing his attention back to the 'well and the move-ment of ships, wreckage, anything else which might affect his tiny command. He rewound the 'well through the last three hours of data, the myriad icons a blur of motion. "They're into the return leg of their patrol pattern."

He clicked his teeth, seeing that the intercept solution was very poor

muscle and bone throb violently. "*Thai-i* Holloway, we need to get third watch on duty stations and send everyone else to the showers. Myself included. Chac is busy, and you and Konev are due for a break, so see if *Thai-i* Goroemon survived the last sixteen hours and get her up here to stand in as officer of the watch."

"*Hai, kyo!*"

Stiff beyond measure, Koshō limped through a slow circuit of Command, checking in with each duty station. As she approached Comm, Pucatli popped up with his hand extended. The young México was holding a glass vial filled with a pale rose-colored fluid. "For you, *Chu-sa.*"

Susan frowned. "An antibiotic?"

"No, no, *Chu-sa.*" Pucatli grimaced. "Those are poison! What's bad for microbes can only be bad for people. This is a tincture for the weary, made from the root and flowers of *chunuli* plants in my mother's garden. Mix it with very hot water and partake gently."

Drink it with sayu? Susan converted the near-hysterical laugh that rose in her throat to a polite nod. "Thank you for the kind thought, *Chu-i.*"

passed over some kind of equilibrium point, where the curve of physical space has inverted—we can't make transit out of this . . . this *pocket*. That inversion is forcing gradient well beyond ships' capacity to punch through into hyper."

Susan suppressed a curse. "What about inside the pocket? Can we reach superluminal *here*?"

"Perhaps." The Mayan adjusted the scan controls on the navigational console. "We'll need to move deeper in—see if gradient slopes off abruptly." He turned back to Koshō, jaw clenched. "It may be, *kyo*, that the pinhole we've slipped through has taken us into a captive universe."

"What do you mean?" Susan felt the tide of cold reach her sinuses, which abruptly made her head feel both light, empty, and clear. The engineer's statement hung before her, seemingly profound, but also beyond practical reach. "What does that mean to us, *Sho-sa*?"

"It means, *kyo*," Oc Chac said, considering his words carefully, "that *here* we may be able to punch through to hyperspace—but we won't have anywhere to *go*. The Barrier itself may be wrapping gravity—and the core fabric of realspace—back around to the other side of the pocket. Indeed, if we traveled the six light-year-width of this place from end to end, we may well wind up at our starting point."

Holloway—who seemed as confused as Susan—scratched the back of his head, then said: "But there's a break in the fabric, right, because we just came through from the "outside." So the only way out, would be right back the way we came—and into the waiting claws of that Khaid battle-group."

The Mayan shrugged. "*Thai-i*, such may be our fate." He lifted his chin, giving Koshō a questioning look. "Hennig's crews are ready to tear into the coil and replace those damaged cells—if we're done maneuvering at high-g for a couple hours."

Koshō nodded. "Get to it, *Sho-sa*. Keep the duty officer informed of your progress and estimated time to complete. As soon as we can find somewhere to lie up, we'll go off battle-stations."

Gretchen stirred expectantly, her parchment-wrapped block tucked under one arm. The Swedish woman looked ghastly—her face was a sallow frame for enormous, fatigue-blackened eyes—but she was still game to plunge ahead into the unknown, seeking the thrill of first-light shining upon something lost eons ago.

"I said *no*." Susan eased herself out of the shockchair, feeling every

lap around the suns. The dim stars were shedding long sinuous trails of mass, drawn down into the hidden maw of the singularity.

The sound of the main bridge hatch cycling open was jarringly loud in the silence.

Koshō looked over her shoulder, seeing an exhausted and work-stained Oc Chac limp onto the bridge. His combat armor—a necessity for engineers working in the midst of battle—was scored with dozens of impact dimples on the battle-steel. The Mayan's face was uncharacteristically open, his lips parted, the muted glare of glowing night reflecting in his eyes.

"Mictlan," the *Sho-sa* sighed. "Beneath the cold lands of the north from whence Quetzalcoatl retrieved the bones of the first people, a tomb filled with decay and rivers of ash, where reigns the dreadful god Mictlantecuhtli, his face covered with a bony mask, sitting amongst owls and spiders, ruling the land of the dead: The destination an unfortunate corpse must strive towards for four long years: first through a whirlwind of knives, then against icy winds, daring all the dangers of the underworlds, at last to cross nine waters and dissolve into the void. A dreadful place where the living dare not tread. . . ."

"Approximately three light-years from us—three superjovian brown dwarfs in perfect balance," Susan said quietly, fingernails brushing across the navigational plot. The images tightened, zooming in. Her med-band was pulsing, flooding her with stimulants to keep onrushing fatigue from overwhelming her mind. The tension of battle and headlong flight was beginning to fade, leaving her entire body throbbing with pain. "And a singularity at their center, drinking their mass like blood."

At the navigational console, Gretchen stirred—tearing herself away from the wonder resplendent before them—and looked back to Koshō. The civilian's face was fairly glowing with desire.

"No." Koshō's eyes were half-lidded, but her voice was firm. "We'll be going no closer. Pilot, find us somewhere to lie up and rest the crew. We'll repair what we can, and then we'll move a goodly distance away from the Pinhole and see if we can reach gradient. . . . Yes, *Sho-sa*?"

Oc Chac had moved to Holloway's station at Nav and was shaking his head. "Even when repairs are complete, *Chu-sa*, and the coil is back in operation . . . Gravitometric readings around us are off the scale—we've

THE LAND OF THE DEAD

The *Naniwa*'s acceleration faded off a point, and under Koshō's gentle direction, the battle-cruiser slid around a particularly dense accretion of the veils. Beyond this—to her surprise—there was nothing on the navigational display. No queer, interlocking geometry of billions of infinitesimal razors, only emptiness. The *Chu-sa* blinked, easing off on the engines, dropping her acceleration to almost zero. The ship continued to speed ahead, but she left her velocity undiminished.

"I think we're clear," Anderssen announced to a hushed bridge crew. She took her hands away from the corroded bronze rectangle. As she did the threatwell's sketchy, alien display faded away—showing only a few trailing quantum distortions at the edges—and then, nothing. The normal navigational plot flickered in and out of view, and then stabilized. A moment later, keyed up by *Chu-i* Pucatli, the long-distance camera feeds appeared on the main v-displays behind the threatwell.

There was a hiss of surprise from nearly every member of the bridge crew. Susan smoothed back her hair and then turned to the communications officer. "*Chu-i*, pipe this to all of the news displays shipside. I'll make an announcement momentarily."

Then the *Chu-sa* turned to consider the long-range scan display now building on her console.

The plot confirmed what the eye beheld. Beyond the Barrier, deep at the heart of the *kuub*, the protostellar debris folded back to reveal three diminutive stars in a tight cluster. Between their sallow pinpoints, the hard white slash of an ejection jet speared "up" and "down," bisecting the visible universe. Illuminated by its radiance, towering plumes and great walls of dust glowed with a brilliant, jeweled fire. If the gravity scan was to be believed, the rosette of stars concealed an infinitesimal black hole in their center. On the ship's plot, the gaudy roil of an accretion disc spiraling into a maelstrom of distorted gravity reached out to

afraid of death. I am an officer and sworn to sacrifice my life for the Emperor."

"He said: If you put death foremost in your thoughts, if you resolve yourself to death each time you wake, then you will always strike your enemy with the utmost force."

"To embrace death so readily! I don't—This has nothing to do with—"

Hadeishi's face suddenly became calm and still, as though the grief and weariness and fear etched in his features had been washed away by a sudden, unseen rain. His eyes were upon the holocast, looking far beyond the puzzled face of the *Thai-i*. De Molay's attention snapped around, following his gaze.

"Stand to battle stations!"

Before the command was fully uttered, De Molay had activated the ship's internal alarm. Tocoztic jumped, startled by the blaring sound, and then switched all his attention onto the pilot's console. Thousands of hours of Imperial drill seized him up and put his hands, his thoughts, his entire purpose on the right path.

At the limit of their sensor range, a Khaid destroyer nosed through the dark towards them.

seemingly clear space, by which he assumed the weapon was actually blocking passive scan on some level. *There is a hidden pocket here, tucked away inside this wall of knives.* "Against these Khaid we need at least a heavy cruiser. Anything less will only buy us tea in Yomi. *Thai-i* Tocoztic, switch your panel to run sensor analysis. We must be about our business."

The *Thai-i* pushed Mitsuharu's identity papers away with a scowl. "You lost your ship!" he said in an accusing voice. "You were discharged from service by the court of review! And you still—"

De Molay glared at the pilot, but Hadeishi's rueful laugh cut him short.

"You were aboard the *Falchion*, *Thai-i*?" Mitsuharu gave the young man his full attention.

Tocoztic nodded stubbornly. "What does that—"

Hadeishi drifted his hand across the holocast controls. A section of nearby space expanded, revealing the scattered wreckage of a heavy cruiser. "There she lies," he said sadly, grief plain in his voice. "A fine ship, now gone to destiny, to die in the service of our lord. . . . I fear, *Thai-i*, you are the last of her officers to survive." Mitsuharu fixed him with a steady, unnerving stare. "Have I done you disservice, by saving you and your men from death? Did you wish to join your ship, your *Chu-sa*, your fellows in final repose, in this funereal pyre of cooling plasma? That is a noble end."

"No!" Tocoztic drew back, horrified. "A useless death—"

"And there you have my own desperate strait," Hadeishi said quietly. "My ship died—as yours has done—yet I lived. Do you know the *Hagakure* of Tsunemoto?"

"Of course," The *Thai-i* replied huffily. "It is required reading in the Academy. . . ."

"Have you hit your target?"

Tocoztic frowned, not grasping the reference. "I do not—It is an old text. Written by one long dead. How do those legends apply here?"

Mitsuharu nodded. "An excellent question. Tsunemoto relates the words of a vain young samurai: 'If you die before striking your enemy, then you die the death of a dog.' Many believed this to be a truth, and thereby found cause to avoid battle, to avoid sacrifice, to avoid risk. What did Tsunemoto say to those men?"

Tocoztic's face turned a rather mealy color. "I am México. I am not

Mitsuharu looked expectantly at the old woman. "Do *we* know, Captain?"

De Molay avoided his eyes, taking a long drink of hot tea. "These raiders seem to have come out of nowhere. What do you suppose brought them here in such numbers? And at just the right moment to encounter and destroy so many Imperial ships?"

Hadeishi's lips twitched, closely observing De Molay. "Why—it could only be treachery, Captain. But now—they know there is a prize to be won, as well, and I do not think they will wish to give it up." He lifted his hand, palm up. "The Khaiden *Kabil Rezei* commanding this hunting pack has paid a dear price—he will want payment in kind. And this— weapon—if it is such, would make him more than a chieftain—it would make him king, or emperor."

"I doubt they have the means to mount a long campaign." The old woman made a circular gesture, encompassing the whole of the *kuub*. "It's very expensive to field three squadrons in this wasteland, no matter how rich you are." Then she peered curiously at Tocoztic, who had made a strangled noise in reaction to something he was reading.

"The prize is too great," Mitsuharu replied. "When you are a pirate, the taking of even one treasure ship can secure your clan for a lifetime. If left alone indefinitely, these Khaiden *will* find a way, even if they have to bargain with Mictlantecuhtli himself and take his skull and meatless bones for their own."

"A cheerful assessment." De Molay gulped the rest of her tea and indicated the holocast. "Now only two remain."

Hadeishi leaned forward, tapping through the various sensor logs and displays. Neither ship matched anything in the commercial registry, but then he suspected these were a brand-new class, quite possibly the first the clans built and fielded themselves. *They're surely not stolen from us, not with those drive signatures and hull outlines. And they don't look like anything the Kroomākh would build—they would be the most likely power to sell the Khaid some heavy metal.*

"Battleships—probably the least damaged," he said at last.

De Molay shrugged. "If they remain near the station wreckage, then we will know they are playing watchdog. After all, any ship that exits might reveal the gap in the Barrier."

"And would be attacked." Hadeishi thought of the lone battle-cruiser they'd seen escape on long-range scan. That ship had vanished into

THE *WILFUL*

From a discreet vantage inside a cloud of radioactive debris leaking from one of the broken Khaid destroyers, the little freighter waited to see if the raiders would dare to cross the Barrier in force. Hadeishi watched the situation unfolding on their jimmied-up holocast with interest, forefinger smoothing his ragged mustache. The Khaid squadron had resorted to pitching missiles one at a time into the Pinhole.

"They're stuck," Tocoztic offered, looking up from the Fleet identity packet. "They'll never get anywhere that way."

Mitsuharu raised an eyebrow. "In comparison to the Khaid commanders I've encountered before, *Thai-i*, this one is the very model of a modern naval officer. He is circumspect, wary, and mindful of the resources he has to hand—which are greatly reduced from considerable strength."

"We would do no better, Lieutenant," De Molay remarked, only her eyes visible above a pile of blankets Tadohao had brought up from the living quarters. "They—my sources—say the guardians of this place are like whipping knives, and they move from place to place, unaccountably."

"Interesting." Hadeishi looked across the darkened bridge at the old woman. "Perhaps their pattern mimics the changing currents of some ancient sea. And the dreadful weapons drift like shoals of kelp on an unseen, ethereal wind."

"Or schools of stinging jellyfish, O poet," De Molay retorted. She was tired and cold, despite the blankets. "Dare we continue with your good work while they are fishing?"

"Not yet. They are in motion again." As they watched on the holocast, the Khaid squadron began a maneuvering burn. Soon the majority of ships withdrew from the area around the Pinhole entrance. The lighter vessels that remained began quartering the area of battle, apparently recovering survivors. "They will not go far. They *know* something valuable is here—even if they do not comprehend what that might be."

"—annoying little girl." Gretchen finished with a grimace. Her head was throbbing. She groped for her medband, mashing the override glyph, hoping for a flood of cool relief.

"Or in a gruesome tale my grandmother was fond of telling on stormy nights, a goblin."

whipped through the personnel manifests of the ships reported on station. Helsdon's record popped up a moment later. She skipped through a lengthy entry detailing his assignment to the *Calexico* and his ordeal in the wreck. *One of my old Cornuelles is in trouble. That, I will not have.*

"Recovery crews, stand by," Koshō announced abruptly. "All stations—we're slowing to one-quarter speed. Damage control crews, stand by. Prepare for missile impacts! *Socho* Juarez—get down to the forward boat bay with a medical crew and an honor guard. Now!"

A flurry of acknowledgments came back to her, settling on her shoulders and in her heart like evil crows. Relieved of having to fly the ship for a moment, Susan sank into her combat chair, her heart filled with great foreboding. *If* Naniwa *is lost because of him—if even one of my men dies on his account—there will be no death evil enough for this cursed Prince.*

Just forward of the command chair, Gretchen suddenly roused herself, straightening up as though from a deep sleep, and looked around, blearily aware of an immediate world of physical things she could touch and feel once more. Her whole body was buzzing, as though millions of tiny golden bees were dancing just beneath her skin. "We're stopping?"

"We're slowing, but don't let the navigational updates stop," Koshō replied. There was a surly edge to her voice. "We're taking aboard survivors from the flagship. As soon as they're secured, we'll have to press on." She considered the threatwell, seeing that the latest Khaid barrage had outlined the thread-veil in spectacular manner. But beyond the illusion of safety, the enemy was in motion.

Gretchen frowned, memories of the immediate past finally forcing themselves past the brilliant geometries which had filled her sight, informed her hearing, and ordered her thoughts. "You called him *hot water*?"

The corner of Susan's mouth twitched. Her eyes slid sideways, checking to see if anyone was standing close, then she said: "On the Hill of Grasshoppers, Old Chapultepec, you could not keep your child's name, and you could not yet take an adult name. So the Sisters chose one for you. Randomly, they said, but they always picked ones which fit—or we grew to fit them, I suppose. He was *sayu*—water almost boiling, hot enough to scald—and they called me *yakka*, which is—"

"*Chu-sa*, I didn't tell him what you said!" Holloway was obviously terrified at the prospect of bartering for the life of a member of the Imperial household. Susan's expression hardened. Holloway shook his head. "I cannot, *Chu-sa*."

At least he has enough gumption to say no to me.

"Very well." Furious, Koshō overrode the comm channel from her console. A sharp close-up of the Prince appeared on her holo. He had aged a little since the last time she'd seen him. "Hello Sayu, can I help you?"

"Yakka?" Xochitl grinned in a strained way. "Get me out of here!"

"I'm sorry, did you say something?" Desperate to keep her heading and velocity, Koshō finessed the *Naniwa* around a spiral of filaments, and now the wreck of the *Tlemitl* was dead ahead. She aimed the battlecruiser a quarter-point off, intending to slide directly over the shattered dreadnaught. "Did *you* ask *me* for help?"

"Yes," the Prince hissed. "*Please,* Yakka, slow down and pick us up. I've got a capsule full of men."

"Do you?" Koshō kept her face impassive, throwing in a little shrug for good measure. "Sycophants, bodyguards, a concubine or two . . . just like in school, eh? I'm so sorry, Sayu, but *Regulations* are very clear—evac capsules are recovered *after the battle is over.*"

"Yakka!" A glint of real fear was in his eyes. The Prince licked his lips as he slumped back in his seat. "What do you want? If you're going to tithe me, tell me how much! Give me a chance."

"I'm not asking you for *anything, Sayu.* I'm just doing my duty." She finally let the tiniest fraction of old, old anger leak through into her expression. "Sit tight, and we'll be back for you after the—" Koshō stopped in midsentence. Behind the Prince, she suddenly caught sight of a familiar profile—sandy hair, a habitual hunch; the man's attention was far away, working some problem on a console—in the second chair.

Helsdon.

The Prince's eyes followed her gaze. "My engineer is reprogramming the sensor-suite here. To detect the weapon's knives, but our equipment is not—"

"One moment."

Susan closed the channel with a fierce, sharp motion. "Pilot, assume maneuvering on my mark—three—two—one. Hold current course for the next eighteen seconds." She ignored Konev's curious stare and

tight, wintry grin as her fingers danced lightly on the control console. The threatwell was now fairly choked with gleaming strands of Barrier threads, yet the "passageway" had not completely closed. A fresh plume of the invisible razors now emerged from the chaotic storm on the sensors. The constant detonations of Khaid missiles were fouling the ship's perceptions, and the *Naniwa* had lost enough shipskin to seriously degrade her capabilities in the best of circumstances.

"Incoming!" The ship rolled aspect, jets of propellant erupting along her flanks. A second later the decking vibrated violently as the dorsal point-defense erupted—clouds of counter-missiles erupting from the launch racks; beam nacelles discharging, the smaller gun-pits hammering away with ballistic munitions. The Khaid missile cloud staggered, nearly two-thirds of the incoming birds shattered or knocked aside. Konev's spoofing pods and emitters whined into high-output, sending another sixth of the sprint missiles into electronic catatonia, or off into the void, chasing phantoms.

The dorsal armor took the rest head-on. Koshō felt the ship lurch, hammered by nearly a hundred impacts. Huge swathes of shipskin went dark, ruptured, and the damage control board—just visible off to her left—flared red along a jagged S-curve. The ship crabbed behind the plume of threads she'd picked out.

"*Chu-sa*, we're down to minimal load on the external batteries," Konev reported. "I've no shipkillers left on the rails and resupply is backed up. Magazines three, four, and seven are off-line."

The bridge was filled with a sea of beeping alarms and the tense chatter of damage control teams reporting in. Only Holloway was still turned towards her, finger pressed to his earbug, his face growing longer by the moment. The *Thai-i* shook his head. "*Chu-sa*, he orders you to retrieve the capsule."

"What does the Prince offer in return? What does he have to say to me?" Susan's voice was Kelvin-zero cold. Holloway flinched back, saying nothing.

"Konev," Koshō said levelly to her weapons officer, "let the next wave of missiles break on this plume"—her stylus indicated the formation—"don't engage them with point-defense so far out. Be frugal—we're a long way from a Fleet depot."

"*Hai, kyo!*" The Russian nodded, then tried to focus on the threatwell. Susan turned back to the Pilot. "Well?"

THE *NANIWA*

Once the battle-cruiser had entered the Pinhole proper, Koshō was tempted to put on more speed. Unfortunately, only a thousand kilometers into the aperture the topology of the threads grew more complex, and she was forced to cut speed to three-quarters. This ended the brief respite from Khaiden bombardment. Fusion detonations began to flare around them, scattering the clouds of chaff which Konev and his crews had been liberally ejecting to mask their position. The scavenged remotes had been expended on their approach, so the *Naniwa* was back to her own resources.

The space-frame shook, rattling the consoles in Command, as a series of bomb-pods blew apart off their ventral quarter. The Khaid battleships were refining their firing solutions. Compartment alarms sounded, but Susan had no attention to spare for them.

"*Chu-sa*, we've about three hundred sixty sprint-class contacts incoming," Konev warned.

"Understood," Koshō gritted out through clenched teeth. She cast about in the topology rushing towards her, looking for a pocket she could lay the battle-cruiser into. Nothing sprang into view. . . .

"*Chu-sa!* We have to try and rescue the Prince!" Holloway had muted the comm channel, but his voice was near panic at the thought of abandoning the most superior officer he'd ever come into contact with.

"Sixty-five seconds to missile storm impact," Konev announced, his voice flat. The weapons officer's fingers were flying across his control surface. "All point-defense engaged."

"Weapons, rolling aspect in thirty-five seconds." *That'll bring the dorsal batteries into play.*

"*Hai, kyo!*"

Susan spared a glance for Holloway. "I won't lift a finger for the Prince, not if it places my crew and ship in danger—he won't be the first great lord of the México to die gloriously in battle." Koshō managed a

De Molay nodded, head held high. Her fingers were not as quick on the controls as they once had been, but in a few moments the navigational displays were reconfigured into a pattern closely approximating those used by the Fleet. Hadeishi clapped his hands, unexpectedly pleased to have all of the v-panes, slide controls, and other mechanisms in their familiar places.

"Thank you," the old woman said, sketching a bow from her seat. "Now there's one thing more you're missing, I believe." She tapped through a series of obscure panes, hunting for *something*, and then, after changing this and that, the air forward of the captain's chair and behind the pilot and navigation stations shimmered with the distinctive heat-haze of a holocast projector. After several false starts, De Molay—frustrated by her inability to remember where the proper settings were—conjured up a threatwell. Not a large one, or as detailed as the data collection allowed by a warship, but a threatwell nonetheless.

"Excellent." Hadeishi smiled in thanks. Then he leaned forward a bit, studying the display, while rolling a stylus between the fingers of his left hand.

"How about this one? Not too far away," he said. "This heat signature implies a cooling plasma cloud, if the color coding is accurate."

"This analysis program is at least as good as anything you've ever worked with, *Chu-sa*." The old woman's voice was aggrieved. "But one lifeboat is as good as the next. Engaging drives on your mark."

"Underway then, Pilot."

The *Wilful's* maneuver drive flared briefly, and then the secondary thrusters kicked in, reorienting the freighter. On their new heading, the little ship glided forward into the darkness, hurrying towards its next rescue.

Mitsuharu reached into the document pocket of his z-suit and then paused; realizing he'd discarded every trace of his old life while languishing in Shinedo. He laughed softly. "I am—"

"Hadeishi, Mitsuharu; captain of the Imperial México Navy," croaked De Molay from the hatchway. Both men turned. The old woman was leaning heavily on *Joto-hei* Tadohao, but still had both feet under her. "Late of the IMN CL-341 *Henry R. Cornuelle*, discharged from active duty four months ago. Service ID 9874662. Decorated three times for valor under fire, credited with eleven capital-ship kills against Khaid, Megair, pirate, and Kroomākh opponents."

Wincing, De Molay slumped into the navigator's chair next to the lieutenant. "Here"—she said, rather breathless from the effort, tossing Tocoztic an identicard packet—"are his papers."

The *Thai-i* caught them, flinching as though from a water moccasin, and stared at the Fleet packet as though the snake itself were winding its coils around his hand. "A forgery—" he started to say.

"Read them!" De Molay growled, before leaning back in the chair with a relieved sigh. "I have—they are quite interesting. Particularly his duty jacket."

Tocoztic made a sour face, but began paging through the packet, brows furrowed over dark eyes. While the youth convinced himself, Hadeishi studied the mosaic of v-panes from the cameras. Cajeme had made his way halfway down the shipcore, taking apparent delight in stripping the Khaid bodies, but he was alone. Mitsuharu looked up, catching the old woman's eye.

"Another hand is needed with the cleanup. Can you spare your assistant, Captain?"

"Indeed. Thank you for your help, *Nitto-hei*." She crooked a finger at Hadeishi. "There's no point in wasting time making this gunner play pilot. I was a navigator in the old days; I can lay a plot for you better than he—with my own ship, no less!"

"He needs something to do, Captain, and he needs to be up here." *Where I can keep an eye on him,* went unsaid.

"Second seat then," sniffed De Molay. She made a puckered, terrible face, as though sucking on a salted tamarind. "You'll be useless yourself unless you've my spot—I knew it from the first."

"Well then," Mitsuharu said, settling himself into the captain's chair. "We are certainly overqualified on this watch, aren't we?"

The marine drew himself up. "Repair hand first class, *kyo*."

Hadeishi nodded smartly. "There is much to do, *Nitto-hei*. If one of your fellows is able-bodied, round him up on the way to Engineering. I've shut off environmentals in nearly all the compartments, but we'll start flushing in atmosphere as you work. Khaiden dead go out the airlock—but strip their gear first, even z-suits if they are operable condition. We don't want to give up *anything* which might be useful later—guns, ammunition, identity packets, even shoes. Secure what you find along the main shipcore until someone can do inventory. If we are fortunate, there will soon be other hands to help you."

Mitsuharu tapped a printed map of the ship tacked up on the bridge hatch. "Med-bay is one deck down from the roundabout outside, and to port-side."

Cajeme nodded, checked the equipment belt on his z-suit, accepted a spare hand-lamp, and double-timed out the hatch.

His immediate concerns addressed, Hadeishi turned his attention back to *Thai-i* Tocoztic, who had swung his pilot's chair around and was giving him a sullen, obstinate glare. The Nisei affected to ignore this, pointing with his chin at the navigational display. "Check the plot, *Thai-i*. There were twenty or thirty evac capsules within range of our sensors when last I looked. Route us to the nearest—but take care with our engine signature. We should be underway at the first opportunity, but we want no attention."

"I won't take your orders, civilian," Tocoztic declared, eyeing the ship-gun angrily. "Certainly not under duress. Never at gunpoint!"

"I am not a civilian," Hadeishi said calmly, keying up the internal surveillance cameras on the captain's console with his free hand. A mosaic of v-panes arranged themselves and he could see the wounded man was under care in the med-bay. De Molay—and a helper—were on the move.

He then settled his grip on the shipgun and met the young México officer's eyes directly. "I am a Fleet reserve officer of superior rank," Mitsuharu said patiently. "Commanding this ship in a theater of war. Now that you are aboard, *Thai-i*, you will take my orders or I will consider you mutinous." He frowned at Tocoztic. "And I would be well within Regs to shoot you for a treacherous and disloyal dog if you continue to be obstinate."

The youth's face assumed a mulish expression. "You can't be a reserve officer—"

send him back to you as quick as I can. I am certain you'll have great use for him soon."

"*Hai, kyo!*" Both men nodded in agreement, chewing noisily. De Molay leaned heavily on the Iroquois *Joto-hei* and took a moment to get the worst of her hair tucked back and the Bulldog stowed inside her jacket. "Your *Thai-i* and my new XO need us, Tadohao, before they both need the med-bay!"

Meanwhile, Hadeishi had managed to chivvy Tocoztic and the marine up to the tiny bridge, where they stared around uneasily. The Nisei could tell they were put off by the ancient-seeming equipment, the cramped quarters, and the grime apparent on often-used surfaces. *It takes time to see her noble heart,* Mitsuharu thought to himself. *For she is a willing steed, and does not complain of the load.*

"This is a small ship," he said aloud, drawing their attention back to him, "compared to your *Falchion*, but you will find her able. Do not underestimate the quality of the ship's fittings. Though not much to look upon, she is neither antique nor decayed. All critical components are in first-rate condition. I will wager they are the equal of anything found in the Fleet. *Thai-i.*" Hadeishi pointed to the pilot's chair with the muzzle of his shipgun. "Your duty station."

Expressionless, the México officer sat. Immediately he began wiggling around, trying to find a comfortable spot on the old, cracked leather.

"Marines?" Hadeishi tilted his head towards the little *Nitto-hei*, who—despite the Nisei's paltry height—was still shorter, though nearly as wide as the doorframe. "Cajeme, I believe?"

"*Hai, kyo.*" The marine clasped his hands behind his back for a moment, then—glancing sidelong at the lieutenant, who was grimacing at the Pilot's controls—offered Hadeishi a proper salute.

Mitsuharu returned the gesture, trying to keep from bursting into a wide smile. The little man's accent had confirmed his guess—*Out of the Atoyaatl Mayo, if my ear is still good.*

"What was your duty station, *Nitto-hei* Cajeme? Your badging reminds me of the engineers."

"This and that—*Chu-Sa.*" The Yaqui shrugged.

"You can be specific. I've been below-decks of late, plugging boilers and shoveling coal."

"*Hai, kyo*. I'm Ensign Galliand, *gun-i* from the *Falchion* and this is Gunner's Mate Tadohao."

"Well met, gentlemen," she said, then gestured weakly at the med closet controls. "Do what you can for him. . . ."

Galliand wiped his face, which was caked with soot and sweat, then began unsealing the injured man's z-suit. Tadohao joined in, holding the man steady. After a few moments, medpaks were secured to the damaged leg and their status lights were winking amber. The corpsman paused again, using some antiseptic towelettes from the bay to clean his hands and the rest of his face. Tadohao didn't seem to mind the grime, hunkering down beside De Molay with his head in his hands.

"I am Captain De Molay," the old woman said. "Your z-suits are severely damaged. The *Falchion* was destroyed?"

Galliand nodded. "She's gone, *kyo*. We were in the throughway between the forward magazines and the gun-deck—Tado and I were clearing out some men wounded when one of the launch rails jammed with a sprint missile in the tube. No one noticed it had hung fire, and then the weapon blew—taking out the whole rail and an adjacent compartment. Then we got hit by something big and the throughway was engulfed in flame. The *Thai-i* dragged us out—I must have been unconscious for a bit—but we made it to a cargo shuttle." He shook his head, only just beginning to grasp what had happened. "Risen Christ, that was close!"

De Molay nodded, and then patted Tadohao on the shoulder. "*Joto-hei*, can you help an old woman stand up?"

Both men moved to assist her, and the freighter captain took a moment to look them over carefully.

"You need new z-suits. If you look through the cabins on this deck, you'll find something that fits—but hurry. *Sho-i*, I need you to prep this whole area for multiple injuries and the swiftest triage you can manage. I believe there are more paks for the cabinet in those bins down there. We will be recovering more evac capsules and who knows how many more wounded."

Galliand nodded and began stripping off his z-suit, which started to disintegrate as soon as he released the seal. De Molay dug in the pockets of her jacket, finding a threesquare. She broke the peanut-flavored ration bar in half, giving each of them a section.

"Now, *Sho-i*, I need Tadohao's help to get up to Command, but I will

THE WILFUL

Well away from the Khaid squadron concentrated at the Pinhole, the little freighter went about her salvage work. She loitered amongst the dust clouds, letting the dim violet glow wash over her, while the passive sensors on the hull boom listened hopefully for the sound of Imperial distress beacons, or the drive signatures of shuttles or other Fleet boats.

On deck two, the pair of Fleet ratings arrived at the medical closet, their companion unconscious between them. Captain De Molay was standing at the entrance to the med-bay, one hand clutching the edge of the platform, the other resting on the grip of her Bulldog. Her pallor matched theirs, though she was in better color than the man who'd lost his foot.

"Stop right there, *Sho-i*."

All of the *Falchion* crewmen halted, their eyes fixed on the remarkably steady muzzle of the Webley. The ensign managed a "*Hai, kyo!*" and the start of a salute. The other *Joto-hei* just stared, struggling to support the wounded man.

"At ease, gentlemen," she said, lowering the pistol. "And raise your faceplates. I'm breathing decent air. Let your recyclers take a rest—you may need them again! I'm not going to shoot you. At least, not yet."

The two able-bodied men opened their helmets. Together, they hoisted the wounded sailor into the med-bay, though his limbs were limp and difficult to manage. De Molay examined the severed foot, which was tightly bound in someone's shirt. The fabric was caked with blood. Her lips drew into a tight, pale line. "Has this man had treatment?" Her sharp gray eyes raked over each of them in turn.

"Only the tourniquet," the *Sho-i* said wearily. "I lost my medpak and trauma kit when we blew atmosphere. There were only the most minimal supplies on the shuttle. . . ."

"You're a medic, then?" De Molay took the opportunity to slide to the floor, breathing fast, and get her back to the wall. "Your name, please."

A winking dot appeared in the threatwell, drifting steadily towards an effusion of threads.

"We're maneuvering to intercept you . . ." Xochitl continued, pausing to wipe his forehead. He was sweating profusely.

"No!" Holloway turned, staring hopelessly at his captain. "*Chusa* . . . it's the *Gensui!* He's on that evac—"

"Tell him to *stop* and wait." Koshō's patience had long since reached its limit. In her hands the battle-cruiser jerked and jumped from side to side, swerving around individual threads. Her nerves were stretched tight, tensed for the instant when she missed one of the deadly filaments and the *Naniwa* squealed in agony as armor and shipskin parted before an unbreakable razor. "*Thai-i*, if you can devise a way to bring them aboard at speed—I'm open to suggestions—but I am *not* slowing down. Not for him."

navigational feed of the various ships in motion around the periphery of the Pinhole. His t-relay—despite being bounced around a bit—was still in operation. A quick diagnostic check indicated the unit was receiving and transmitting. *Good.* Hummingbird gauged distances and times, then toggled open a subaudible channel.

Have done, winged out into the night, directly to one of the Khaid command ships.

"It *is* ours," Xochitl snarled as his exo whispered the name of the approaching Imperial ship and her commander, along with pertinent details of crew, tonnage, and weapons systems. "Set an intercept course, Engineer, and speedily, too. She's faster than Lucifer himself and will not wait!"

He turned away from the engineer, his exo supplying a visual overlay for the communications controls in the capsule. Ghostly images emerged in his sight, highlighting the necessary mechanisms. The Prince keyed up a comm channel and sought handshake with the fast-approaching battle-cruiser.

Behind the *Naniwa*, the Khaid fleet—now minus another battleship—had regrouped again. This time they did not speed in pursuit, but watched with interest, waiting for the reckless Imperial commander to obliterate his ship in the same spectacular way that had consumed so many of their fellows. The Khaid destroyers were already beginning to withdraw to a safe distance.

"Incoming comm," *Chu-i* Pucatli blurted in surprise. "Flash traffic from the Flag!"

The corner of Koshō's lip curled up. Her whole attention was devoted to gentling the battle-cruiser through the drifting shoals of threads as fast as Gretchen could pump navigational data into the threatwell. Holloway—the only officer now at loose ends on the bridge—was obliged to take the call and blanched to find himself face-to-face with a ragged-looking Imperial Prince in smoke-stained combat armor. A cluster of other faces peered over the *Tlatocapilli*'s shoulders, and none of them looked at all well.

"Slow and take us aboard," the Prince demanded, "I'm transmitting our coordinates now."

quiescent, dumbed-down state. Now, with the flood of information rolling in from the *Naniwa*'s sensor array, the device had improved itself, or recalled capabilities long left idle.

Now she was giddily happy that the only communications method between her and the machine was a keypad—a stylus—what her visual perception could reveal. A more direct connection, she was sure, would had rendered her insensate. *And mad, very definitely mad.*

"I can't fly this thing," Anderssen gasped. "I'll draw a path. You'll have to follow."

"Piloting control to console one," Koshō commanded, settling her shoulders. Holloway was frozen, agog at the transformation of his control surfaces. In the threatwell, patterns of constantly shifting veils were beginning to emerge from the confusion of symbols and diagrams. Susan tried to focus, finding the hubbub amongst the Command crew distracting and the gelatinlike fluidity of the new control surfaces difficult to grasp.

Despite this, the *Naniwa* plunged through the Pinhole and into the unknown spaces beyond. Koshō's grasp of the new controls—and of the information contorting her threatwell—grew rapidly. Her hands light on the flight interface, she sidestepped past both a stricken Khaiden destroyer and the spray of filaments which had torn the warship to shreds.

To Susan's right, on the second tier of Command, Anderssen was beginning to groan in a peculiar way, as though iron nails were being driven into her eyes.

Down in medical, Hummingbird opened one eye to a bare slit. He'd heard nothing for the past fifteen minutes, which augured well. The second eye opened and he turned his head gently. No one was in sight— not a marine guard, not a medical officer, not even his lovely assistant. Alone at last, the old México sat up, moving slowly, letting his heartbeat return to normal, blood flow resuming.

The poor vitals showing on the med-panel ticked up to normal after a few minutes. The *nauallis* listened again—now hearing and feeling the vibrations of a ship operating at high velocity—ignored the warning lights blinking on the med-panel, and jacked his remaining comp into the nearest access port. Then he lay back down, clasped both hands on his chest, and closed his eyes again.

Streams of data played out on the inside of his eyelids, including a

separating into dozens of laser emitters. A stabbing white glare rippled from one end of the Khaid battlewagon to the other, shredding shipskin and gun nacelles, cracking open the hardpoints at each rail launcher. The ship shuddered, veering off, and then two of the big maneuver drives blew apart, disgorging clouds of debris.

"Secondary remotes going to full burn . . . now."

The other Khaiden ships burst away from the impact point, assuming she was trying to catch them edge-on, where their own fire would be blocked by friendly ships. Missiles and beam-weapons licked out at the speeding Imperial ship. The *Naniwa* swerved, punching into the dispersing formation where the battleship had fallen from line. The battlecruiser's beam-weapons lashed across the nearest Khaiden battleship. Anion impacts rippled over the flank of the bulky ebon vessel, but Koshō had no interest in going toe to toe with such a behemoth. Instead, the *Naniwa* slipped past, spewing a tight cloud of decoys—the last of the scavenged remotes—that raced off at a sharp angle, breaking for open space, away from the Barrier.

The Khaid ships swung round, belching more shipkillers and penetrators, their formation coalescing again. The *Naniwa*, engines dead for the moment, plunged into the Pinhole along the drive-plume of the stricken battleship. Only moments from crossing the Barrier line, Koshō jerked back from her executive threatwell as the entire constellation of icons and designators shifted abruptly. Looking up at the main holocast, she saw the familiar symbols winking out, replaced by a crude new array of glyphs flaring to life in the holo.

"What—"

Holloway pointed at Gretchen, his face ashen. Most of the navigator's v-panes now showed a stream of unintelligible symbols and distorted images. "Shift piloting control to console two," Susan barked, startling the Command watch from stunned panic.

"No," Gretchen choked out, barely able to speak. The information density flowing across her v-displays was so dense, even with the assistance of the *oliohuiqui* to focus her mind she could barely process a tenth of the flood of images, sounds, models, and diagrams rushing past. She was grappling with an overwhelming—and terrifying—sensation that node $3^3 3$ had woken from some ancient sleep. That the interfaces she had discovered—and prodded and poked—had been operating in some

up at him in puzzlement, and as if at an equal. *You shall not think me incapable of the task!* Xochitl took a deep breath. "Can this sensor array be reconfigured? Tweaked to detect the barrier?"

"It will be slow work." Helsdon squinted at the intentionally simple capsule controls. "But we—" He paused, staring at the navigational plot. "Isn't that one of ours?"

Koshō watched with interest as the Khaid flotilla in the area around the Pinhole—at last—reacted to the *Naniwa*'s approach. Intermittent bursts of message traffic came and went on the enemy channel and now they were chattering away again. The enemy battleships began to accelerate, swirling out and away from the entrance to the gap like a flock of huge, ungainly birds. Her eyes narrowed to see they were keeping reasonable cohesion and spacing, even when forced to redeploy from disorder.

But they had reacted a little too slowly, given her approaching speed.

"Salvo one away," Konev reported, and the rumbling echo of launch rails discharging followed hard on his words.

A flight of shipkillers winged away from the *Naniwa* in a black wedge—exhausting the last of her ready magazines. Konev had been refining their attack vector for the past sixteen minutes and a formation of the remote platforms winged in, leading the swarm of *Tessen* missiles. With the response time from the remotes looping back through the main t-relay, the weapons officer had shortened his reaction time to the counter-missile storm erupting from the lead battleships. They had also pushed forward the reach of *Naniwa*'s countermeasures.

"Lead remotes going to rapid-fire," the *Thai-i* announced.

The flare of antimatter detonations began to spark in the darkness, almost lost against the fantastic roil of colors from the dust clouds. The *Naniwa*'s course shifted a point, driving hard against the edge of the Khaid formation, running in hot behind the glare of the sprint missiles discharged from the remote platforms. A secondary cloud of anti-missile munitions had also hared away from the remotes and these slashed into the midst of the Khaiden point-defense, confusing their targeting and ripping up their own counter-missile launch.

The wave of *Tessens* hammered into the most exposed of the Khaid battleships. A cluster of brilliant flares erupted, each shipkiller warhead

neatly into three sections, receding, plumes of burning atmosphere jetting from the black hull. A Khaid cruiser—now no more than a shattered hulk—was within sight as well. The Prince, his helmet faceplate levered up, bit at the corner of his thumb and considered a nav-plot on his tiny control console. There were other capsules in range, and at the edge of sensor capacity, an able-bodied Khaiden destroyer was edging back out of the danger area.

"We cannot detect the threads," rasped a voice from behind him. Xochitl turned, surprised to see the engineer crouching in the door of the miniscule bridge. Looking more haggard than ever, fear radiating from him in waves, Helsdon gestured at the viewport. "Our sensors just aren't designed to recognize such a distortion of quantum law. You will want to halt our movement, before we strike one of them."

Though he was feeling something that—in a lesser mortal—might be termed terror, the Prince essayed a feeble joke: "There are laws at the quantum level?"

"As far as these pitiful computers are concerned, there are." Helsdon squeezed in beside Xochitl, ignoring centuries of protocol and policy which would have relegated the commoner to some distant precinct of the Prince's daily routine. The engineer's fingers trembled as he jacked a hand-comp into the control console. "We were right in the middle of reprogramming everything to ignore known laws, to assume that the Planck-length components of these threads were . . . well then, you shut us down." Helsdon laughed ghoulishly, his own fear cutting through any sense of social hierarchy.

Xochitl stiffened, his jaw clenching. *Whom do you think you address, Anglishman? No one reproves me. Not even the Imperial family. It is not permitted. My father depends on my judgment. He sent me here to secure this situation. He—*

Then the Prince realized his mind was wandering, even his exocortex had fallen silent while his human consciousness whirled in a dozen directions.

«*Cognitive capability is impaired,*» the exo finally announced, «*by chemical reactions to the perception of incipient destruction. Injecting stabilizing compounds.*» Xochitl felt a cool tickling sensation in his wrists and raised his hands in confusion. A moment passed before the thudding of his heart slowed and his mind cleared.

When the Prince focused again on the engineer, Helsdon was looking

which had previously been inactive or inaccessible. The discovery algorithm she'd loaded into her own field comp had mutated, evolved, and returned, rippling across the Imperial systems with blinding speed. Her model was now tremendously detailed, with some kind of interpolative subprocess filling in the gaps in the quantum data feeding back from the battle-cruiser's sensor suite.

The science probes had been lost in the fighting, though in comparison to the *Naniwa's* shipskin, they were tiny black birds, pecking at a leviathan wall of basalt blocks. The warship drank data with every surface, and node 3^33 swallowed it up just as fast. There was only one jarring note in the rising symphony. Gretchen was suddenly aware that something was out of place in the block pressed between her fingers.

You're broken, she realized, feeling that same rushing sense of *rightness* which had first come to her when the last fragment of an Old High Martian Period III bowl had fit into place on Old Mars and the entire object was whole and perfect in her hands, restored after five thousand years of separation. *This piece of you is out of place.* She felt the mechanism—was it like a clock? No, more a series of orbitals constantly in motion like the arms of an astrolabe, each ring a pressure-wave interlocking with the others in their emptiness—slip and side under her attention. But then, when she focused her internal image of what *should be,* the whirling rings suddenly conformed to the pattern she desired.

The block seemed to change, under her fingertips, though she was sure nothing visible about it had altered, and felt—for the first time—as though it was in *proper* form. Unblemished, unbroken, at last intact.

In her elevated state, Anderssen's perceptions shifted, the command deck and the tiny humans there falling away, her vision expanding to taste the dust clouds, the wreckage, the hot flare of the ship's drives like brilliant jeweled stars. Agitated waves spun away from them as they built velocity, shifting the dust, even brushing the threaded veil which lay ahead, stirring its components with a hot wind.

The gap—the Pinhole—loomed, no more than a long jagged gap of darkness within darkness.

Prince Xochitl's evac-capsule sped away from the wreck of the *Tlemitl,* the momentum imparted by the launch rail carrying them forward. Through one of the viewports Xochitl could see the great ship, now cut

Holloway and Konev both distracted her from the thought by abruptly stiffening in alarm. A second later her own console flashed a series of warnings. Something had entered the shipnet and begun altering the code controlling the navigational interfaces—or replacing modules wholesale—at fantastic speed.

"*Chu-sa!*" The navigator had half-risen from his shockchair. "Are you *certain* this is a good idea?"

"It is the best chance we have," Koshō replied softly. She directed her gaze at the Swedish woman. "Anderssen-*tzin*, can your mechanism perceive the Barrier as it ebbs and flows? Can it relay the telemetry we need fast enough to move through at high-v?"

Gretchen turned towards her and Konev hissed in horrified surprise. The woman's pupils had grown huge, dilated by the drugs now coursing through her bloodstream. Her face had acquired a peculiar waxy sheen. "Zaryá protect us from all witches!"

"I do not know," Anderssen said, her voice tight and distant, "if your interfaces are fast enough."

"We will do our best," Susan answered, nodding to Holloway. "Stand by for our entry run. Bring up main drives, angle deflectors tight in on the hull. Konev—*Thai-i* Konev!"

Startled, the Russian turned to face her, once more composed and alert.

"Bring the remote platforms in as well, inside our deflector array. I don't want to lose them, but we're going to be moving erratically. Gun crews stand by for a hot passage. *Chu-i* Pucatli, sound battle stations and acceleration alert." Immediately, Klaxons began to blare.

Koshō turned back to Gretchen. "Anderssen-*tzin*, you have the con."

Deep in the bowels of the ship, reaction mass channels opened fractionally and the main maneuver engines roared as Holloway advanced both of his speed controls. The *Naniwa* surged ahead, building v as fast as she could. The internal frame, already battered by multiple missile impacts, groaned with the stress. In every compartment, crewmen secured their stations and prepared for a rough ride.

At the navigation console, Gretchen settled back, letting the holocast unfold before her. Attached directly to the shipnet's fastest interfaces, node $3^3 3$ seemed to expand, releasing hundreds of the processing nodes

"*Kyo*, what are we doing?" Konev's voice was very soft. Koshō nodded, accepting the bold question.

"Finding two more hours for *Sho-sa* Chac to complete repairs on the coil." The *Zosen* were behind schedule, for the damage to some of the hypercells was worse than initially estimated. Susan lifted her chin, indicating the partial gap amongst the thready pattern. "We have this much of a map, and I hope—" She glanced over at Anderssen, who was carefully removing a bronze-colored comp from a parchment envelope and securing the device to the navigation console. The Nisei officer blinked, suddenly certain that the corroded-looking surface was actually gleaming very brightly, as though burnished and new. "I hope we have the rest near to hand."

Gretchen spread her hands on either side of the block, took a deep breath, and then tapped open a pair of v-panes on either side. *Thai-i* Holloway, who had been watching her closely from his neighboring chair, stiffened and shot a panicky glance at Koshō.

Susan met his eyes, nodding. *We're only alive now,* she thought, *because of what Anderssen deduced. If we try and flee into open space, the Khaid will run us to ground in no more than an hour. Chac needs time, and that means we need safe haven. Even a quarter-light-minute inside that barrier, drawing a veil behind us where the Khaid cannot follow, will be enough to complete our repairs.*

Holloway swallowed, eyes dragged back to a flurry of geometric diagrams opening and closing on the console. Anderssen was now breathing deeply and steadily through her nose, fingers digging in another envelope from her jacket pocket. Two pale yellow tablets emerged, held gingerly between thumb and forefinger.

Oliohuiqui? wondered Susan. A nauallis *drug—ah now, how is our other passenger?*

Mindful of the security risk he represented, Koshō attached one of her v-panes to the datastream from the security cameras in Medical. Green Hummingbird was in bay three, his small brown body curled up in a fetal position. The dull gray mantle, hooded brown cloak, and trousers he affected were stained and torn—though those limbs exposed to her sight were unmarked. The vitals feed from bed telemetry showed his heartbeat was slow, his breathing shallow, and his condition marked UNCONSCIOUS.

Susan frowned at this. *I wonder . . .*

Koshō looked up, sparing an instant's attention from the threatwell, at the sound of someone gasping in pain as a grav-stretcher floated into Command. The Swedish woman, Anderssen, arrived in the company of two *gun-i*. Her left arm was splinted, her face and visible arm badly bruised. An extra med-band had been strapped to her off-wrist, leaving her face drawn and pale. Despite this, she met Susan's gaze with equanimity.

"Put her next to *Thai-i* Holloway at Navigation," Koshō said, inclining her sleek, dark head towards the semicircular console on the second tier. "Secure the shockchair, we can't have her jolting about."

Turning back to the 'well, the *Chu-sa* considered the movements of the Khaid ships at the Pinhole once more. Konev, now moved over to the XO spot, had dialed up a series of secondary schematics, showing the historical track of the enemy contacts over the last hour.

"They're not leaving, *kyo*," the Russian said, rubbing his eyes. He, like the rest of the command crew, was now standing their second straight watch.

"No, they are regrouping. They are curious—did the *Tlemitl* have a true goal in mind, or did it act in equal ignorance, hurling itself to certain doom?"

"They're trying to guess the outline of the passage, *kyo*?" Konev sounded dubious.

Susan smiled, watching a series of darting lights emerge from one of the Khaid ship-icons. "But—wisely—they've stopped throwing ships into the grinder's teeth." Her stylus circled the minute flecks, directing the 'well to zoom in. "Instead they are testing the opening with missiles from this leeward battleship."

On the threatwell, the cluster of missiles sailed effortlessly into the Pinhole. Some interpenetrated with the nearest veil, winking out in seemingly empty space, while others sped on, unmolested.

"And my Fleet rank," the Nisei continued, "exceeds yours. You may dispute me, or demand satisfaction at a later time. But not today, for there is a great deal of work to be done."

"Your rank? You have no rank! You're . . . you're a smuggler, an outcast in a grimy z-suit! Barely human." Tocoztic's face flushed red as he struggled to express his outrage.

the viewport, the shuttle tumbled away, one more fragment of debris swallowed by the greater sea of the *kuub*.

"We should not abandon that shuttle!" The wounded *Thai-i* objected. "We'll need her if this vessel suffers the same fate as the *Falchion*."

"I do not intend to lose *this* ship," Mitsuharu replied evenly. "And a cargo shuttle will only take up valuable stowage we will soon need for the others."

The airlock chuffed, separating from its seal, and then swung aside. Hadeishi nodded at the lieutenant, whose face had acquired a formidable glower. "If you are truly concerned, we have an escape pod aboard. Welcome to the *Wilful*. Medical is that way."

The lieutenant, despite his injuries, did not follow the four ratings. He and the marine *Nitto-hei* remained in the roundabout off the airlock while Hadeishi secured the hatch. "I am *Thai-i* Tocoztic, gun deck officer from the heavy cruiser *Falchion*."

Hadeishi turned and gave a slight bow. He kept his expression meticulously polite. "Mitsuharu Hadeishi at your service, *Thai-i*, Engineer's Mate of the *Wilful* and her acting XO."

Tocoztic looked Hadeishi up and down, jaw thrust forward. The México officer was taller and wider than the norm, with a dark *chocolatl* tone to his complexion. From his slight accent, Mitsuharu guessed the young man hailed from Ciguayo or Arawak—islands in the Eastern Sea which had been part of the Empire since the fourteenth century. The Nisei was pleased to see that despite falling into poor circumstance, the boy had lost none of his fighting spirit or sense of duty. *Whether dead or alive, within two campaigns he will be worthy of his braid.*

"I am an officer of the Imperial Fleet. In the name of Emperor Ahuizotl and by the Regulations covering the use of civilian assets in a time of war, I am assuming battlefield command of this vessel! *Nitto-hei* Cajeme, secure his sidearm."

"I am also the Emperor's servant," Hadeishi said softly, his shipgun already centered on the *Thai-i*'s chest. The marine private had failed to leap into action, despite his officer's command. His demeanor remained watchful, his movements contained. Mitsuharu was impressed, for the young *Thai-i* had quite a snap to his voice. *Could the marine be a Yaqui from the south? He commands excellent stillness.*

fellow stared uncertainly into the lighted, but vacant gangway. "Hello the ship?"

"I'm stepping out," Hadeishi called, "no trouble, *Sho-i.*"

Then he stood up, shook out his shoulders—offered a quick prayer to Ameratsu to preserve him for just a few more minutes—and stepped around the corner, the muzzle of his shipgun pointed at the deck. The ensign had disappeared, though Mitsuharu was certain he—and his friends, if any—were only just out of sight. "We're the *Wilful*, shipping out of Shinedo *uchumon*. My name is Mitsuharu Hadeishi—I'm the Engineer's Mate. We are prepared to lend you aid, if you need it. Have you wounded aboard?"

The *Sho-i* reappeared, looked him over, and then held up two fingers. Behind him a tall México with lieutenant's flashing on his torn and bloody z-suit pushed past on the arm of a smaller man, a wiry little marine. Hadeishi stood aside while they limped into the freighter's airlock. Three more followed, one rating in the middle—with no boots and only one foot—was being carried by his fellows. The ensign remained on the shuttle, face pale under the black coating of volatilized plastics.

"We have no medic," Hadeishi said, watching the injured rating's face grow paler by the second. "But there is an amputee kit in the medical closet." He glanced over the five men in the *Wilful*'s airlock—to his naked eye, they all seemed properly human—before turning to the ensign in the shuttle doorway. "Are there others?"

Without waiting for an answer, the Nisei stepped far enough inside to scan the interior of the shuttle. The boat was bare, even of equipment, and stank of burning.

"No, *Kyo*. We were lucky to get out ourselves. The ship was . . ." The *Sho-i*, who seemed even younger than usual for an ensign, twitched every time Mitsuharu moved. "They came in fast. *Thai-i* Tocoztic says they—they were Khaiden."

"They still are. We cannot keep the shuttle, *Sho-i*. Move over there with the others."

He took one last look around, in case there were useful supplies to bring with them, and then cycled the shuttle hatch closed. The gangway rang hollowly under his boots and then he was back aboard the *Wilful*, fingers quick on the locking mechanism. Another *thunk* boomed around them and the gangway separated. Hadeishi keyed open the inner lock to the freighter, his refugees huddled uncertainly together. Out

The old woman shook her head. "I would not!" She paused, thinking. "Our decrepit appearance will suggest we are some kind of scavenger."

"Just as you planned, *Sencho*," Hadeishi offered a faint smile. "Just as you planned. But as fortune has provided, they are *not* deceived by our appearance. They are correct. *Wilful* is a scavenger—of the lost. Matching airlocks now."

"Very poetic," De Molay muttered. Mitsuharu did not reply, his whole attention on matching the lock interfaces and running out the freighter's gangway. A moment later, a faint *tunk* echoed through the decking and he had a string of green lights on the airlock status board. Then he double-checked the seal on the *Wilful*-side of the lock, making sure everything was secure, set the drive controls to automatic, and hurried downstairs.

His captured shipgun slung under-arm, Hadeishi looked in on De Molay in the medical closet. He'd gathered up a portable medpak and a bag of threesquares and water bottles. The silver-haired captain was trying to sit up in the tiny bunk, which was not as easy as it seemed.

"Lie quiet, *Sencho*. I'm going to cycle the lock in a moment—so I've switched Command to this console." He reached under the medbay overhead and reconfigured the display. "You've got full control of environmentals and even the drives, if need be. But try not to run about, you'll do yourself an injury."

The look she gave him eased his worry for her safety. "And yourself, Engineer. I can manage from here." She smiled tightly, tapping the grip of the Bulldog, whose holster and gunbelt were strapped across her chest. "Watch yourself, this wouldn't be the first time the Khaid have booby-trapped an Imperial evac-capsule, or shuttle."

"Or put a half-dozen marines aboard an unsuspecting rescue ship," Hadeishi added brightly.

The shuttle hatch irised open, battle-steel partitions folding back into the hull. Mitsuharu crouched just out of sight around the corner of his own lock—standing wide open—watching the other end of the gangway via a remote. There was a long still minute, and then a wary, soot-stained Fleet ensign peered out—his own shipgun at the ready. The

"Yes. A reaction mass tank from a battle-cruiser or strike carrier."

Hadeishi sighed deeply. Remembered faces and fragments of conversation distracted him. A tremendous feeling of sorrow was welling up in him. Thoughts of the *Cornuelle* were prominent in his memory. Now he wished he'd carried the samisen up from Engineering. Lacking the instrument, he tapped his fingers on the console, setting a slow, mournful beat.

> *"A phantom greenish gray,*
> *Ghost of some wight,*
> *Poor mortal wight!*
> *Wandering*
> *Lonesomely*
> *Through*
> *The black*
> *Night."*

Then he stopped, the shattered cylinder falling away behind them.

"What more can you offer?" De Molay shook her head, silver hair falling into her eyes. She brushed the strands away. "This is the fate of all sailors on this dark sea, to perish at last in the void, and find repose on the surface of the deep."

Mitsuharu did not respond, his thoughts far away. Then, as he sat quietly, watching the dust clouds slowly change color, one of his scan alerts chirped. The Nisei's head turned, eyes focusing once more on the present. A familiar silhouette coalesced on the main viewer. Using the vector from passive scan, two of the cameras had focused, picking out the outline of a vessel. Ship's registry reported an initial identification—a Fleet *Varanus*-class cargo shuttle.

"See, *Sencho*? A sheaf of wheat is still standing among the broken stalks."

Though the ship's boat seemed intact and free of obvious battle damage, there was no sign of life aboard. The portholes were dark, engines cold, and the shuttle was tumbling end to end. Hadeishi steered alongside, smoothly matching her rotation with a deft play on the drive controls.

De Molay pursed her lips, eyes narrowed. "A derelict, do you think?"

"Sensors can lie, *Sencho*. If there are survivors aboard, would they advertise themselves?"

IN THE *KUUB*

The *Wilful* moved stealthily through the debris of battle. Hadeishi had the little freighter's engines pulsing only intermittently, letting momentum carry them through the wreckage as silently as possible. With only the two of them aboard, he'd isolated all of the compartments save the bridge, medical closet, and the passages connecting them. Everything else was powered down to reduce signature. Though it made no difference to a hunter's active scan, Mitsuharu had also dialed down the lights on the bridge. He sat at the command station in darkness, his face lit only by the glow of the console and the ruddy gleam of light from the external camera displays.

Bodies, broken equipment, ruptured evac capsules, chunks of decking floated past the *Wilful*'s cameras. Where he could, Hadeishi angled the little ship to hide in the emissions shadow of larger sections of blasted hull, or to follow the agitated particle trails of now-dead ships. Where he was forced to cross unbroken "ground," he moved as swiftly as the *Wilful*'s engines would carry them.

"You make a fine mouse hunting in a stubbled field," De Molay observed, her voice low and quiet, though she could have shouted wildly and none of their putative enemies would have noticed.

"An eye out for owls and foxes all the while, *Sencho*," Hadeishi nodded companionably. "You've lived on a farm?"

"My grandmother's. May Our Blessed Lord guard her soul."

"Ours as well." Hadeishi put the helm over a point, nav plot revealing a cluster of wreckage ahead. A light tap on the engine control shifted their heading and a long cylindrical panel drifted past on the dorsal cameras. The structure—seventy or eight meters long—had been ravaged by a plasma detonation. The battle-steel was puckered and wrinkled. In the coppery glare, some fragments of warnings and informational inscriptions remained on the outer surface.

"Imperial?" De Molay asked softly.

Jaguars and his face grew still. "Yes. The capsule's intact. The launch rails are clear and the release subsystems are showing green across the board. We just have to get the hatch open."

Xochitl could see the pod was last in queue on the shared maglev launch tube. *A rough ride out of Firearrow's guts. And then where?*

«Staying mobile and capable of reacting to circumstance improves our chances of survival by several orders of magnitude,» the exo stated, displaying a variety of helpful graphs and comparison metrics on the Prince's field of view.

Without orders, the Jaguars bulled forward and gestured the sailors away from the hatchway. Two of them—a cook and a midshipman from laundry—started to protest, but the engineer waved his companions back. He was watching Xochitl with a wary expression, his mouth a tight line.

The Prince met his gaze with a level stare. "How many of us will fit?"

The man's eyes lost focus for an instant, and then he looked down at his hand-comp. "This one holds ten, Great Lord."

Xochitl's eyelid twitched. Including his Jaguars, there were twelve people floating in the compartment, most staring at him with suddenly wide eyes. His expression hardened as he considered the larger-than-human-size of his guest with a sidelong glance.

"Three of you must remain behind," Xochitl declared, his exo whispering details of skills, time in service, and political reliability in one ear. A pistol-model shipgun was already in his hand and leveled on the two cafeteria attendants. They froze. The Prince's face remained utterly cold as the pistol snapped twice, punching a flechette through each of their suit masks.

Everyone else jerked in surprise, stunned. One of the petty officers cried out, horrified, and jetted away down the corridor. One of the Jaguars raised his shipgun, but Xochitl waved him off. "Let him go—the rest of you, get the hatch open!"

Five minutes later, the Hjo clambered into the capsule, helped by the *Cuauhhuehueh*. The Prince watched the creature, whose mere existence had caused the loss of two Imperial lives, with barely controlled fury, then followed.

Moments later there was a reverberating *bang* and the evac capsule accelerated violently down the launch rail.

"Status of our hypercoil? How long to make gradient?"

The Mayan *Zosen* stared at her blankly, one dark-complected finger pressed to his earbug. "*Kyo?*"

"How long," she said steadily, staring at him with a cold, considering expression, "to make transit to hyperspace?"

Oc Chac swallowed, dark eyes darting to his status panel. "Coil is down, *Kyo*. We've taken fragmentation damage along cells nineteen to thirty-six." He looked up, expression impassive. "I need two hours to make her right, *Chu-sa*."

Susan nodded, looking back to the threatwell. "We have no more than thirty minutes before they come at us again, *Sho-sa*. Take direct command of the repair crews."

"*Hai, kyo!*" The engineer bolted from Command, speaking rapidly into his throatmike as he ran.

Plasma detonations blossomed in the threatwell, bracketing the *Naniwa* as she maneuvered.

"They're getting our range, *kyo*," Konev reported, voice hoarse. "We've lost two of the remotes."

Susan's gaze swept across her console. Though mauled, the battle-cruiser was still game for a fight, but against so many Khaid? Her eyes flicked up, fixing on the long-range sensors. The Pinhole was still abroil with radiation and shattered ships. Their emissions blocked any sign of what lay beyond in the ever thicker dust-clouds. She grimaced, tapping her earbug.

"Medical? Get our Swedish passenger up here—awake—*right now!*— with all of her possessions."

Xochitl, the suited creature, and his *Ocelomeh* arrived at the evac-capsule cluster to find only one pod remaining. The other access-doors showed only empty cradles beyond thick glassite windows. The door to the last capsule was apparently stuck, as a motley collection of officers and ratings was banging away at the hatch with pry bars and other tools cribbed from the nearest damage control closet.

"Is it working?" the Jaguar Knight *Cuauhhuehueh* demanded, his voice booming on the local circuit.

A pale, sandy-haired man with Engineer's insignia turned to face the Prince's party. His light brown eyes registered the unit insignia of the

THE *NANIWA*

Susan watched her bank of displays with a fixed, stony glare. The threatwell showed their situation only too well. On the hull of the once-great *Firearrow*, the last of the battle-shield projectors flickered and died. The Khaid ships which had survived the reckless pursuit were underway at last, pulling back from the unexpected weapon which had consumed their fellows. From what she saw on her 'well they would be successful in escaping the trap if they just reversed along their own drive trails.

They're going to figure this out pretty fast, she mused, her thoughts filled with foreboding. *They've got too much data on hand, and now they have the time to let it all sink in. . . .*

But for the moment, her way forward was clear. Behind, however, the flotilla of destroyers that had been nipping at the *Naniwa's* heels was still there, slowly closing range, their beam weapons snapping past or flaring out as the aft point-defense knocked them down. None of these hounds had the missile throw-weight to punch past her counter-missiles and Konev had gathered up fifteen or sixteen remote weapons platforms initially deployed by the *Tokiwa* and *Asama* in the early stages of the battle.

The platforms were low on munitions, but still had some capacity left. They were keeping pace, extending both her missile intercept envelope and the battle-cruiser's sensor range, and in this kind of knife-fight Koshō would take anything she could get. Susan sat stiffly, back ramrod straight, and her eyes flickered across the arrayed data one more time. "We need to determine if there are any survivors," she said softly, drawing Oc Chac's attention. "We can take on several thousand, if we triple-bunk."

The Mayan shook his head in dismay. "*Chu-sa!* We'll overtax environmentals in a few days with that sort of passenger load! Only we remain," he ventured. "We dare not help them—"

There is no time for reckless gestures, Susan realized, brow furrowing sharply. *We have to get out.*

"Come, Esteemed One," Xochitl commanded, barely polite. "We must get you to safety."

He was answered by a long, violent harangue in a lilting, sing-song tongue, and entirely inhuman growling. The noise was abrasively loud on point-to-point comm. The Prince grimaced, his ears ringing, and then he gestured at the two Jaguar Knights.

"No one can stay here, Esteemed One. We're taking you to a place of safety."

The Knights seized the creature's shoulders and kicked off, carrying the Hjo towards the door. There was another outburst of growling and snarling, interspersed with a long tirade in the unknown tongue. But the Hjo remained tightly curled up, trying to hide its long tapering head, and this made it possible for the two *Ocelotl* to hustle the alien along.

Back outside, once they'd left the security corridor and its intrinsic shielding, Xochitl's exo conjured up a deck plan in his field of view. "Ah, good," the Prince said aloud on the local comm circuit. "There's an escape pod rail not far from here."

The Jaguars looked at him, puzzled. Their sergeant gestured at the comp built into his suit. "Nothing on shipnet, my lord. Everything's down. . . ."

"No matter, *Cuauhhuehueh*, I've a backup copy. This way."

They turned left, jetting down a main corridor—large enough to drive two grav-sleds side-by-side—filled with drifting debris. Constellations of smoke globules parted before them, bumping into their facemasks as they sped along. Though they passed scattered corpses and even some wounded, Xochitl did not stop. Hidden by his facemask, the Prince's expression was set and hard.

lay hands on the engineer. "Anyone see an evac capsule sign? That way? Chop-chop, everyone, let's go."

A grav-sled had been thrown the length of the entryway to the flag admiral's quarters, smashing into the stone pillars framing the monumental door. Broken chunks of stone floated in a slow eddy, making Xochitl's progress difficult. Both sets of mural walls had shattered, adding a glittering drift of glassite which flared and shimmered in the suit lights as he moved. One of his Jaguars led the way, combat suit jets puffing whitely, and another followed. Here in officer's country, the internal damage seemed worse—there had been more ornamentation to rip free from the walls and smash into things—than down on the deck holding secondary command.

His men hadn't asked what had happened, but the Prince had an excellent idea.

«*The Mirror plotting data was flawed,*» his exo supplied, completing his thought.

"I know," he whispered, forgetting to concentrate on the thought-interface between them. "I know."

The Jaguar sergeant in the lead pushed aside the fallen statuary—his powered combat armor made the task possible—and forced open the door beyond. Xochitl swung through the opening, thankful for the moment that they were in z-g. With proper EVA gear, they had made very swift progress through the wreckage. The sitting room beyond was utterly destroyed—tables, screens, personal artifacts all jumbled together in a drifting cloud of flotsam—but in one corner, curled up into a turtle-like shell, was a larger-than-human figure in a dark metallic z-suit. In their suit-lights, the metal surface gleamed with thousands of tiny, incised glyphs and markings. Their meanings were unknown to the Prince.

«*Recording,*» the exocortex reported, tucking away thirty seconds of high definition video for later analysis. «*Seven hundred and twenty-nine distinct ideograms identified. Spawning subtasks to collate comparisons against known Hjogadim character sets.*»

Xochitl drifted close to the figure—careful not to touch the alien z-suit—and oriented himself face-to-face. The suit mask was almost opaque, but he could make out the gleam of helmet lights flickering in a pair of deep-set eyes.

THE *TLEMITL*

Emergency lighting sputtered, flickering on and off in a red-lit haze, along the corridor. Helsdon rotated slowly in midair, disoriented. Then his eyes caught on a doorway swinging past and his mind snapped back into focus. "We've lost the g-decking," he wheezed, suddenly aware that his chest and side were throbbing with pain. "Damage control team, report."

A chorus of groans and cursing answered him. The engineer tucked in, giving himself a little momentum, and his boots adhered to the nearest surface. Stable, he found himself standing on the wall of the passageway. Debris was loose everywhere, filling the air with clouds of paper, broken bits of furniture, loose shoes—anything which hadn't been secured when the *Tlemitl* had suffered an enormous blow.

Swallowing against a very dry throat, Helsdon retrieved his hand-comp—which was attached by a retractable cord to his tool-belt—and thumbed the device awake. Status lights flickered and then a display came up. "Power is down across the whole grid," he said aloud. The others were gathering, hauling themselves along the walls and floor. "No gravity, no environmental control." He blinked rapidly.

"What the hell happened?" One of the midshipmen was staring around wildly.

"We hit the—we hit the phenomena," Helsdon croaked, feeling a horrible constriction in his chest. "Part of the ship—most of the ship?—has been cut away from—from us."

A cook caught his shoulder, holding the engineer steady. "We've gotta get off, chief."

"There's nowhere to go," Helsdon whispered, watching his hand-comp scan uselessly for a live shipnet node. "The reactors are in shutdown, but who knows how long that will last?"

"Help the chief, he's hurt." The cook gestured for the midshipmen to

horror as another infinitely thin razor dissected the super-dreadnaught, shearing through decks, bulkheads, hapless crewmen. . . . Now they were close enough for the cameras to interpolate, picking out the disintegrating flagship through iridescent streamers of dust.

"Gods," Konev blurted, his face shining with sweat. "They're sure to lose containment now!"

We're alone, Koshō thought, forcing herself to look away. A tight knot was forming in her stomach. *The Khaid are as badly shaken as we are—but they still outnumber me by five to one, at least.*

way divided by the Mirror probes. But the newer information the Swedish woman had loaded into the *Naniwa*'s nav system clearly showed one of the veils had begun to occlude the opening. The phalanx of Khaid battleships and lighter elements charged in directly behind the crippled dreadnaught and catastrophe ensued.

Koshō couldn't help but grin ferally as first one and then a dozen of the enemy ships interpenetrated with the invisible Barrier—a rippling string of icons winked out abruptly on her 'well plot. Moments later, the camera views on the side panels studded with the blue-white flare of ships disintegrating. A storm of chatter erupted on a channel Pucatli had picked out of the storm of electromagnetic noise. Susan couldn't understand the Khaid traffic—the message bursts were encrypted and in a tongue foreign to her—but the cadence of the staticky noise said nothing but *panic*.

For another minute the *Tlemitl* dodged and weaved, exercising her maneuver engines to the utmost, following a corkscrew path known only to—and then the dreadnaught brushed against one of the invisible threads. The battle-shields, which were mostly active at that moment, did *nothing* to prevent nearly a third of the behemoth from being cloven away in one dumbfounding instant.

At this distance, on the cameras, there was nothing to see but a jagged smear of light where the hull rupture was decompressing explosively.

On the *Naniwa*'s bridge, however, there was loud confusion. Konev and Holloway, who had access to enhanced telemetry feeds from the battle-cruiser's sensors, shouted aloud in alarm. Pucatli and the others turned, staring at Koshō in raw, open fear. The threatwell updated, showing the enemy ships in disarray.

"What happened, *Chu-sa*?" The comm officer ventured. "The Khaid battleships—"

"Are gone," Susan said steadily. "Holloway-*tzin*, tracking update please."

"Ten containment failures, *kyo*," the navigator reported, shaken. "Three more badly damaged and losing way. The Khaid battle-group is trying to reverse course. The *Tlemitl* . . . she's . . . she's a dead ship, *Chu-sa*. Battlecast status is flickering in and out, but the last report says she's lost nearly a quarter of her compartments. Reactors are intact, but her drives are dead. She's coasting . . ."

Belching atmosphere and debris, the giant ship spun inexorably into another thread. Aboard the *Naniwa*, the Command crew watched in

"The fool! He should swing back to meet us."

In her executive 'well, Susan watched the *Tlemitl* barrel towards the Pinhole, closely followed by a phalanx of Khaid battleships, the entire conglomeration ablaze with the snap of beam-weapons, streaking missiles, and the constant stuttering flare of fusion detonations. The massive radiation signature from the battle was threatening to wash out passive scans and hide the whole affray from view.

"They're not going to make it," she hissed to herself. Dragging her attention away from the doomed flagship, Koshō checked in with the repair crew cutting away the door to cabin nine on deck six. A medical team was lifting the body of the Swedish woman and the old *nauallis* out on stretchers. Susan tapped her earbug, jaw clenched. "Are either of them alive?"

In the v-pane, the *gun-i* holding a medpak to the old México's chest nodded, *Yes.*

Anderssen raised her head feebly, a bronze-colored comp clasped tight to her chest. "Captain, you've . . . got to slow the ship. . . ." She coughed as the medical team loaded the stretcher onto a grav-cart. "The outer surface of the Barrier shifts and moves, billowing like a sail . . . or a permeable membrane . . . it's not stable. All of the Mirror data is outdated, too old to use."

"Get her to medical," Koshō snapped, "stabilized and jacked into shipnet with her comp!"

What next? she wondered, turning back to the threatwell. "Pucatli! Get me *someone* on the flagship—I don't care who, the kitchen staff supervisor will do!"

Three hundred thousand kilometers ahead, the *Tlemitl* swerved into the confines of the Pinhole. Susan could see they were following the path-

"You bear a simple cross of silver at your breast, *Sencho*. Would you leave all these travelers abandoned in the dark, prey to our enemies? Where is your charity then?"

The old woman did not reply, her eyes narrowing to tight slits.

Mitsuharu shook his head. "I cannot abandon them, *kyo*. We go forward."

"You should take us out of here, back into hyperspace—" De Molay was frowning.

"Not while we can rescue some of these men." Mitsuharu felt strange—alive again, with the v-panes of a starship under his fingers. He felt the hum of the engines through the deck, the tickle of a comm implant snug in his ear canal. But he had a sensation of riding in emptiness, alone on a deserted road, astride a strange horse with no known companions. *Where is the chatter of my crew? Where is Susan's slim, fierce shape at the secondary console? There are only ghosts.*

"We're not equipped to fight, Engineer. This is not an IMN ship of war!"

"I know." Hadeishi settled himself in the command chair, feeling the cracked leather dig at his skin. Even the shape of the civilian shockchair was odd and unfamiliar. The console was too far away for his taste, and could not be adjusted. There was no threatwell, or even a holotank to give him a working view of the field of battle!

Dishes rattled in the kitchen of the little noodle shop. Musashi was hungry—starved would be a better word, he thought—and was busy shoveling udon into his mouth, feeling the first hot rush of chicken broth like the wind from Nirvana, with a pair of chopsticks. The yakuza, four of them, entered with unusual swiftness, their faces blank as Nōgaku masks, and before even he could react, their leader had snatched up his bokutō and hurled the wooden blade away, out into the night-shrouded street.

"This is the one," the gangster barked, his own katana rasping from a cheap bamboo sheath. His arms bulged with muscle, gorgeously colored tattoos peeking from beneath both kimono sleeves.

Musashi looked up, expressing dumb astonishment and curled his left hand around the bowl of soup. "The one, what?"

"Haiiiii!" The other three yakuza drew their swords with a great flourish, kicking mats and tables aside.

Musashi turned slowly to face them, rising with the bowl in one hand, the chopsticks between his middle fingers in the other. "Pardon?"

But the scanner display was dusted with the signatures of evac-capsules. Mitsuharu lifted his hand towards the screen: "We're the only chance they have to escape a slow agonizing death, or slavery. We'll save as many as we can, before we have to run."

"I gather Command has spoken," De Molay replied, her expression pinched.

Much better, he thought, seeing a whole series of v-panes unfold, all seeming very modern and closely modeled on the standard Fleet executive interface. *I do believe this ship has illegal software loaded. Excellent.*

For a moment he considered drilling into the ship's manifest and construction logs, looking to see who—exactly—had updated the freighter. But then Hadeishi brushed those panes aside. His suspicions could wait, for there was far more interesting business afoot.

He shut off the transit alarm and then ran through a postgradient checklist. The hyperspace coil was still in operation, though now quiescent, and maneuver drives were primed and idling. Exterior cameras showed the *Wilful* drifting in a region of fantastically colored dust and gas plumes. As the little ship's passive sensors woke one by one, they revealed distant shoals of wreckage, multiple radiation sources, shattered ships, and the far-off wink of distress beacons. His hand lingered over a set of controls which would initiate an active scan, but then he passed on, unfolding up a comm channel to the medical closet.

"We've come to the right place," Hadeishi said, when De Molay's face appeared. "Hachiman has passed this way with scythe and spear. I'm picking up both Khaid and Imperial transmissions, so the outcome is still in doubt."

The *Wilful* crept forward through the murk, emissions signature as low as Mitsuharu could manage with his rough understanding of the freighter's capabilities.

"Where are you taking us?" De Molay asked, watching his face intently through the monitor. Now that she was lying down and had proper meds, her color was improving rapidly. The trauma unit had also dispensed a drinking tube of complex carbohydrate-based rehydration fluid. This substance was a lambent green, but the old woman didn't seem to mind the taste.

"There are Imperial evac-pods within range," Hadeishi answered, eyes flitting from screen to screen. "And this ship needs a crew to be useful."

De Molay did not respond immediately, though Hadeishi could hear her breathing tensely as he double-checked the feed from the scanners. Their immediate area *seemed* to be clear of combat—he couldn't pick up any missile drive plumes, anion beam spikes, or the gravity dimples of mainline starships. *But then, the sensor suite on this barge is . . . limited.* His fingers tapped briskly on the console.

the first IV tabs. De Molay shivered from head to toe, and then her eyes fluttered open. She gave a short breathy laugh when she saw the image of her mashed thigh on the overhead display. "Just a flesh wound," she gasped.

Hadeishi peeled away the press-pak from her leg. Bright red blood oozed in tiny pinpoints from an enormous bruise easily the length of his forearm.

"Severe tissue damage. No broken bones," an androgynous voice announced from the trauma unit. "Apply anti-inflammatory agents as needed. Apply fresh press-pak. Leave on forty-eight hours. Set patient medband to dispense pain control agents as needed. Bed rest is recommended to speed recovery."

De Molay made a face at Mitsuharu. "Give me those press-paks. Where's the Bulldog?"

Hadeishi fished out the Webley and checked the magazine before handing the automatic over. "Full up, *Sencho*. But I think we've finished off the other gunslingers."

De Molay shot him a pained glare. "You're a clever engineer with the toxic air, but I'll keep my old Humbert handy. He is very reliable. Now"—she paused, clenching her teeth and waiting for the medband to kick in—"I'm already a patient. I can be my own corpsman. You— you're all the command crew we have."

Hadeishi nodded, rummaging through the trauma station. He laid out the necessary medpaks, made sure her comm bracelet was responding and the overhead v-display toggled to show shipnet. "You're the only backup I have, *Sencho-sana*."

"So I'm not permitted to die, then? I'll consider the suggestion."

Stepping around the bodies fallen at the entryway to the bridge, Mitsuharu entered gingerly—a Khaid shipgun cradled in his hands, safety off—and checked all the corners before turning his attention to the command station.

The Khaid officer was still slumped against the console. Hadeishi grunted with effort, heaving the body onto the floor with a clatter. Then he cleared the session on the boards—the Khaid had loaded some kind of interpreter to allow them to enter transit coordinates—and authorized himself with De Molay's codes.

The main hatch to Engineering cycled open with a pained groan and Hadeishi slipped through the opening. The machete was sheathed, the serrated knife tucked away in his tool belt. Two bandoliers of shipguns—in a wide variety of models—were slung over his shoulder. De Molay was leaning heavily on the console, her face tight with pain.

"You're tracking blood on my deck, Engineer. But," she gestured at her leg and side, "who am I to complain?"

Mitsuharu laid down the captured weapons and knelt beside her. His lips pursed, gentle fingers tightening the press-pak on her leg wound. The bandage was saturated and the status strip across the blue material had shaded to red as well. The old woman's color had deteriorated in his absence.

"No geisha ever had a whiter brow than you, *Sencho.* I will carry you to the medbay."

Moving the freighter's captain would not improve her condition, but Hadeishi saw no other option. He was not a corpsman and there were no doctors to hand. He rigged a sling, eased her into the fabric, and then set off, his own weariness offset by a jolt of stimulant from his med-band. Dead Khaid sprawled in the nonengineering corridors, their bodies chittering with shipbugs. As they moved slowly through, De Molay glanced at the tight, distorted faces, all gray with the mark of carbon monoxide poisoning. After the first dozen or so, she closed her eyes and leaned her head against his back.

"Don't sleep yet, *Sencho*, you've landing papers to sign, manifests to review . . ." He hoped the medbay, if there was such a thing on the freighter, was equipped with an autobot of some kind. *Aren't all ships as well equipped as a Fleet light cruiser?*

The reality was far more spartan, but the medical bay—more properly a closet with a fold-out bed—did have a diagnostic and treatment module for trauma cases. Hadeishi broke open a shock-pak and applied

Does he even see we're here? Koshō discarded the thought. "*Chu-i*, you find me someone to talk to. If anyone can circumvent the Khaid jamming, the interference from the dust cloud, and the radiation blaze from so many wrecked ships, you can."

"*Hai, Chu-sa, hai!*"

Then she turned to Holloway and Oc Chac, who were heads down over the navigational console.

"*Sho-sa*, can we get a reading on that Barrier? Anything?"

The Mayan shook his head. "Sensors show a clear field, save for the omnipresent dust. Only empty space beckons beyond the shattered dead."

"Not good enough." Susan tapped her fingers rapidly on the edge of her shockchair. "Get me an update from the medical team on six. Now."

alternate course plots at a blinding rate. At main navigation, the *Thai-i* sitting at the station had drawn back, finding his v-panes and control displays no longer responding to his touch. Suddenly the alternates dropped away and the Prince nodded to himself. "New course by my mark, full power. We need breathing room!"

Engines thundering, the decking vibrating with a deep basso roar, *Tlemitl* charged away from the wrecked *Asama*, all surviving launchers and gun nacelles concentrated on two Khaid heavy cruisers which had drawn the unlucky course to stand in the Prince's way. Both broke off, trying to change vector as multiple shipkillers slammed into their deflectors, breaking through to sear armor and shatter their engine rings. Undaunted, the *Firearrow* accelerated towards the Pinhole.

Three-quarters of a million kilometers behind the swirling firefight around the super dreadnaught, Koshō grasped the Prince's intent immediately. The *Naniwa* was already accelerating to join him, having shrugged aside the last of the lighter ships, but now the Khaid battleships had reformed, relocking their point-defense and fire control. Swift as harriers, they came hard on the chase and stood directly between the battle-cruiser and the flagship. Thoughtful, Susan tapped up the channel to deck six.

"Anderssen-*sana*, can you get me better telemetry?"

There was no response, only intermittent static and then a "*cabin inhabitants are unavailable at this time*" message generated by shipboard comm. Face tight with dismay, Koshō switched channels.

"Damage Control, Medical. Get teams to cabin nine on deck six, immediately!"

In the 'well, her course and that of the *Tlemitl* were fast converging on the outer edge of the debris field from the *Can*. Beyond the wrecked station loomed the invisible passage of the Pinhole, though now Susan realized that even if the Scouts had found an opening—there was no surety it led anywhere save into a veil of threads which would gut her ship like a *teppan*-chef.

"Comm, any response from the Flag?"

The comm officer shook her head, eyes huge. "Nothing, *Chu-sa*. She's still moving and fighting, but I've no response from any shipside system, not even on identicast."

The circuit came back up with a few hiccups. "Done here," he shouted. They'd manually switched to a little-used comm channel when the main network went down, but there was still interference. "On to the next."

"Doubt if we have all the holes patched, Engineer," one of the warrant officers remarked with a strained laugh.

"Yeah, only ten or twenty to go," someone else's voice came through the suit-to-suit line. "What now?"

"Wait one." Helsdon grunted with exhaustion, thumbing through a succession of panes on his hand-comp, the team crowded around him, faces expectant for the next task.

The battle-steel hatchway to Secondary Command cycled open and Xochitl and his Jaguars crowded in. The *Sho-sa*, who had found himself commanding the dreadnaught when primary Command and Flag had gone off-line, jerked around, his face ashy.

"*Tlatocapilli*, I'm glad to see you! We've—"

"Out of the chair," the México lord seized the lieutenant commander by the arm and dragged him away from the command console. "You're XO now—get me damage control back on-line and report munitions inventory!"

The main threatwell was still functioning as Xochitl settled into the shockchair, taking stock of the situation. He'd been out of contact for nearly thirty minutes, but his exo jacked in to the main boards and the Prince saw the gun decks were still in operation, hammering away at the swarm of Khaiden battleships pacing the dreadnaught. The new battle-shields wavered in and out of existence, flaring bright with missile impacts.

«*Forty percent coverage remaining,*» exo reported. «*Launchers are at sixty percent, though four port-side are jammed.*»

The *Asama* had fallen away behind, crippled and shuddering from secondary explosions deep in her core, crew bailing out in a cluster of shuttles and evac-capsules.

Xochitl waved his hand and the threatwell reconfigured; the myriad points of Imperial distress beacons vanished, leaving only the combatants.

"Lord Prince," The *Sho-sa* ventured. "We have stowage to take them aboard—"

"Leave them," Xochitl growled, his command console flickering with

free, shaking off bits of burning metal and fabric. Two of his body-
guards were down, along with most of the junior officers and ratings
who had been at their stations.

"Raise damage control," Xochitl ordered his exo. "*Cuauhhuehueh*
Koris, status of the rest of your squad?"

"Only us in comm contact, *Tlatocapilli*." The Jaguar Knight shook
his head slowly. "I'm not getting a response from Command either."

«*Thai-sa Yoemon is dead,*» reported the exo. «*Autonomic systems re-
port that Main Command has lost environmental control due to a pene-
trator hit. No life signs remain in the compartment.*»

"Mains are down," the Prince said aloud, replying to Koris. "Find me
the secondary and let's get moving."

The intership comm channel was fuzzing with static, making even
short-range conversations impossible. "Exo, what is this?"

«*A Khaid disruptor bug has entered the ship via a penetrator. Internal
communications on the regular channels will be impossible until the module
is located and destroyed or damage control reroutes around the infection.*»

"Find me a clear channel, then."

The Jaguars were already moving, hustling the Prince out into the
corridor. The hatchway tried to close behind them and stuck, flat
streamers of black smoke oozing along the roof. A fire suppression sys-
tem kicked in, flooding the hallway with foam. Xochitl wiped his face-
plate clear and jogged on. The assistive mechanisms in his suit would let
him run a long way without tiring.

Four decks away, Engineer Second Helsdon and two of his crew slipped
pry bars behind the cover of a section of shattered comm conduit and
wrenched hard. The cover tore away, revealing six meters of shredded,
blackened crystal. Freezing wind, howling down the passageway from
some hull rupture, pummelled their z-suits, laying down frost on every
surface. Malcolm jammed a cutting tool behind the junction at his end
of the conduit and popped the interface free—off to his right, the other
two men were doing the same.

"Clear!" Two *Jun-i* hustled up, bearing a length of replacement crys-
tal. They shoved the new conduit into place and Helsdon locked down
his end, a hand-comp tucked into his elbow. A moment later, with diag-
nostic leads attached, he had a string of green lights on the status display.

decks nineteen and twenty. Four compartments compromised. I have a radiation fire in compartment eighty-one."

"*Sho-sa*, get your teams in," Susan barked, "Pilot—get me some headway!"

Her engines intact, the *Naniwa* accelerated away on a sharply different vector. Koshō held her breath, watching her ship veer hideously close to the shimmering veils plotted on her 'well.

In their cabin on six, Gretchen and Hummingbird were torn through their restraints and slammed hard against the wall. Gravity fluctuated violently for a microsecond and the comps ripped free as well, smashing into the walls, displays splintering into ruin. Bloody, one arm stabbing with terrible, blinding pain, Gretchen found herself pinned against the ceiling. Alarm Klaxons screamed and the bitter smell of burning insulation flooded the air. Crushed by a giant hand, Anderssen struggled to breathe. "Crow! Crow!"

Hummingbird was pinned as well, though his head lolled limply to one side.

Four hundred thousand kilometers behind the *Naniwa*, the pack of Khaiden ships reacted as well, shedding velocity to make an equally abrupt course change. Three of them managed this quite smartly, matching the battle-cruiser's relative angle. They continued to spit missiles at the Imperial ship, though their rate of fire slacked off sharply. The other five also made the turn, but too slowly. Their icons interpenetrated with the first of the veils plotted on Susan's display and abruptly winked out.

"Score on goal," Koshō breathed, only too aware of how close she'd come to blundering into the same fate. "Pilot, get me a new intercept to the *Tlemitl*!"

Aboard the *Firearrow*, Xochitl grimaced as one of his Jaguars cut away the mangled wreckage of his shockchair. Flag Command was filled with smoke and guttering flames from a shipkiller impact which had torn through the secondary hull. Able to move once more, the Prince crawled

dodged past, their captains and crews alert enough to realize the danger and begin laying down a sweeping pattern of computer-controlled ballistic rounds.

"Pilot, prepare to rotate ship," Koshō announced, glaring at Holloway. "Rotate in one minute, sixteen—"

Stop, you've got to stop!

She jerked, hearing an unfamiliar voice shouting in her earbug.

"Belay that order," Susan snarled, "who is this?"

Gretchen Anderssen, Captain Koshō. Your charts are out of date—I'm updating your display—now!

"Jigoku-e ochiro!" The *Chu-sa's* shouted curse startled everyone on the bridge, and Oc Chac turned to stare at her in surprise. Susan's complexion shaded almost porcelain. The threatwell display mutated wildly, the Mirror coordinates for the invisible Barrier wiped away and replaced by a series of veil-like patterns, overlapping on one another and filled with pockets and eddies.

"Forty seconds to intersection, *kyo*," Holloway yelped, his console throwing a dozen alarms.

"Pilot, hard over!" Koshō snarled, punching the collision alarm glyph on her console. Then her stylus stabbed out, marking a new course in the 'well.

"Thirty-nine seconds!"

Naniwa groaned from stem to stern, engines cutting out as the ship rotated, and then flaring as they slewed around into a new heading. Shedding velocity to make the turn, the battle-cruiser was suddenly seconds "behind" where the constant stream of Khaiden missiles expected her to be. Penetrators rained onto her newly exposed "roof," their onboard comps triggering detonation. Hammerblows boomed across the shipskin, shredding tiles and overloading the thermocouples. Radiating fins splintered all across the *Naniwa's* hull. Secondary plasma charges pierced the shipskin itself, blowing enormous gaps through to the secondary hull. Behind the plasma charge, the penetrator rounds themselves collided with the inner armor at tremendous speed. The triple layer of armor mesh convulsed, trying to shed impact energy across the whole shipframe, but dozens of tiny ruptures punched through, spewing thermonuclear plasma into two compartments just fore of Engineering. Atmosphere vented, blowing out a chaff-cloud of debris.

"Multiple punctures," Oc Chac bawled, "we've lost environment on

Her latest modeling pass had discarded the data preprocessed by the Mirror scientists and culled from the *Korkunov*'s initial telemetry. Something nagged at her, saying it was too old to be accurate. Instead, drawing on the sheer processing power and storage offered by node 3^33, she'd asked the comps to sweep through the most basic data flowing back from the Imperial science probes and break it down, looking for gravitational anomalies at a sub-Planck scale. The descriptions of the damage inflicted on the *Calexico* hinted at a mechanism capable of dissecting battle-steel, which implied the weapon was able to break down the interlocking matrix of the armor without diffusing its impact energy across the enormous, mutually supporting weave of the material.

Her comps now revealed a new "map" of the surrounding space, one far different in detail than the Imperial data they'd received—or stolen. Anderssen cursed, her body jolted with fear. Tearing free of the restraints, she was at Hummingbird's side in the blink of an eye. She seized hold of the old man's ear, drawing a bright crimson pinpoint of blood with the corner of one nail.

"Crow! Come back to me. Captain Koshō is trying to use the Barrier as a weapon, and the Imperial data we have is *no good* for this sector. Break me into the command circuit, right now!"

"Rack eight away," Oc Chac announced, as a fresh cluster of plasma mine icons popped up on the threatwell. "We're done, *kyo*." The Mayan looked back at Susan, his chiseled face questioning.

"Not enough," the Nisei woman said, watching the last of her area denial munitions spin away behind the *Naniwa*. The battle-cruiser was pushing hard at maximum-v for the level of particulates in this area of space, and there were still nine Khaiden cruisers and destroyers racing after her. "Weapons, start dumping delayed-fuse bomb-pods into our wake. I want them on a timer and dark until they tick over on intercept."

Then she swiveled around, considering the threatwell. *Naniwa* was now closing fast on the forbidden area indicated by the Mirror scientists. Stabbing flares started to pop up behind them, catching one of the Khaiden cruisers with a direct hit. The enemy ship staggered, losing way, and then plowed through three more plasma mines. Atmosphere began to vent from dozens of punctures, but the other Khaid ships

stared at her blankly for a heartbeat, then caught himself and nodded abruptly. "*Hai, Chu-sa!* Preparing to roll mines."

Gretchen picked herself up warily and groped from bunk to desk. Gravity wobbled again, the ship groaning around them, but this time she was ready and held on. Hummingbird had wedged himself into a corner of the room, a comp still in his hand—face tight with some tremendous effort of concentration—and she saw his fingers were a blur on the interfaces. All of his equipment, even scattered under the bunks, was still in operation. Gritting her teeth against a series of bad bruises, Anderssen found her own field comp and flipped it open. Her models were still running, and now they had resolved themselves down to only two alternatives.

"Where are we, Crow?" she gasped, fumbling at the control pad. "We've got to get all of this gear secured before we lose g-deck integrity entirely."

All of her equipment shoveled into the backpack without a problem. A roll of stickytape secured the pack to the bunk, which was in turn welded to the wall of the cabin. Her hand-comp stayed with her, though its interface was tiny in comparison to the bigger units. Hummingbird's setup was harder to deal with, particularly when her shoulders were itching at the prospect of the next abrupt maneuver. But in a few moments, all of it was stowed save the t-relay, which was a Yule tree of status lights. Grasping the main unit, she cast around for something to secure the device to.

"Leave be!" Hummingbird spared a dark, furious glance for her. "I've almost broken into the Khaid battlecast and we'll need that to survive the next hour. Pin it to the floor, if you must, but don't move it or disassemble the mechanism."

You'll sing a different tune, carrion bird, if this thing cracks you in the head. . . .

She strapped it down as best she could, feeling the metal radiating hot enough to scorch her fingertips. Then Anderssen crawled back to the other corner, wedged herself into place, and thumbed up the display on her hand-comp. *Plot position,* she ordered the little machine. On the sidebar, Gretchen was heartened to see that node 3^33 was still in synch and processing data at a blistering rate. *Excellent, but—*

"Enough!" Xochitl felt hot inside his armor and now he heard the whine of the air circulation system trying to shed waste heat like the buzz of a thousand mosquitoes. "Enough."

His head was throbbing violently and he groped for the medband override.

The *Naniwa*'s hull shook with repeated explosions as a wave of sprint missiles and penetrators crashed through her point-defense. In Command, Oc Chac was speaking rapidly into his throatmike, his status displays a sea of red and amber indicators. Koshō snarled, seeing three Khaid light cruisers and a pair of destroyers interpose themselves between her and the *Tlemitl*. The enemy ships were formed up tight, and their point-defense interlock had stopped the last salvo of shipkillers Konev and his gunners had spun into them.

"Pilot, time to 'cast interlock with the Flag?"

"Too long, *kyo*." Holloway looked up, wild-eyed, and shook his head. "We'd have to bull right through them to reach interlock range."

"Understood, *Thai-i*." Susan's attention snapped back to the threatwell, where a second pack of Khaid lightweights was barreling in on her flank, trying to get into the shadow of her drive plume. *We need to shed some of these dogs,* she thought, juggling distance, velocity, and time in a heartbeat. Her stylus slashed through the executive 'well at her console.

"Pilot, new heading. Don't spare the horses."

Naniwa responded, still agile despite the burning craters littering her hull and the cloud of vented atmosphere, splintered radiating fins, and other flotsam she was shedding. The battle cruiser shifted course, angling away from the *Tlemitl* and *Asama*, which were at the center of their own hot, constantly strobing cloud of detonations, and headed dead-on to the Barrier coordinates loaded into Susan's threatwell.

"Course correction burn complete, *kyo*," Holloway reported. "Nine hostiles now in pursuit."

"Incoming spread—one-hundred-six contacts," Konev barked. "Point-defense engaging."

Susan hissed, feeling her ship's pain deep down in her gut. "*Sho-sa*, prepare to roll mines."

Oc Chac nodded, attention wrenched away from damage control. He

stormfront of shipkillers, penetrators, and bomb-pods hurtling towards the Imperial ships. Behind their munitions screen, the heavy beam weapons on the Khaiden battlewagons were sparking, searching for a weakness in the battle-shields surrounding the *Firearrow*.

The shield-generator status display was a patchwork of green, amber, and red. Some of the nodes had already failed, having shorted on back-feed from the shields themselves, or failing under the massive stress. Xochitl's teeth bared, gleaming white and sharp, and he cursed the *pochtecas* who had sold his father such junk.

«Projected failure rate of the shield nodes, from field trials, is almost thirty percent. Current failure rate is thirty-four percent.»

"Unacceptable." Xochitl straightened in his chair, attention drawn to the emergence of a second pack of Khaiden heavies which had been screened from the *Tlemitl's* sensors by the oncoming wave of attackers. This formation was accelerating off at an angle and redeploying on the move, smoothly shifting from their initial wedge into an unfolding "flower-box."

«Secondary elements are targeting the Gladius,» exo reported, and the threatwell shifted, focusing in on the heavy cruiser, which was trying to match course with the *Tlemitl* and *Asama*. *«Missile storm intercept in sixteen seconds.»*

The particle beam nacelles covering that quadrant of the envelope began igniting. Yoemon's gunnery team had reached the same conclusion. Khaid shipkillers began to wink out, obliterated by anion impacts. The *Gladius'* point-defense guns were spinning hot, filling the intervening space with ballistic rounds, and her short-range launchers were discharging as fast as the robotic loaders could clear the launch rails. Better than half of the incoming missiles were obliterated, but the remainder detonated in a staggered wave of plasma flares, washing from one end of the ship to the other.

Xochitl jerked back, his face dark, ruddy bronze as the heavy cruiser's glyph vanished from the threatwell plot.

«Three friendly effectives remain,» exo stated, highlighting the glyphs of the dreadnaught and two remaining battle-cruisers. *«Hostile numbers are now sixteen combatants, twelve noncombatants. Point-defense network is suboptimal, ECM cloud is sub-optimal, launcher recycle time is suboptimal, munitions expenditure—all weapon systems—is excessive, and maneuver drive efficiency is—»*

shake the outbound munitions package—but the interceptors frag-
mented on final approach, separating into dozens of smaller missiles,
each radiating as hot as the parent chassis. Point defense lasers and bal-
listic munitions tore through them, causing a sparking cascade of
smaller explosions. Serenely, the *Tessen* sailed through the weak ECM
spewing from the destroyer's emitters and slammed into the smaller
ship's hull at a hundred g. At the instant before impact, the multiphase
warhead ignited, spearing a needle-sized plasma jet into the Khaiden
shipskin.

A seven-meter-wide hole blew through the side of the destroyer be-
fore the *Tessen* blew up inside the hull proper. The destroyer convulsed,
filling with superheated plasma, and then shattered into a cloud of molten
debris.

The other Khaid lightweights scattered, dumping a cloud of missiles
and bomb-pods behind them.

Koshō nodded thoughtfully, then tapped an execute glyph Pucatli
had prepped for her.

Each of the fleeing destroyers had acquired a spoofer pod running pas-
sive when the *Naniwa* had interpenetrated the formation. Now they each
lit off with the battle-cruiser's signature and sped off, keeping pace with
the Khaid ships, each now followed by a swiftly closing pack of missiles.

"Pilot, vector to join the Flag," Koshō snapped, letting her attention
return to the larger battle. "Get us into their envelope and synched up
on point-defense."

She did not have time to give Tloc, his holds full of *chocolatl*, or the
lamentable *Chu-sho* Xocoyotl even the brief parting Muldoon had re-
ceived.

«*Enemy battlecast pattern is adapting,*» exo announced.

Prince Xochitl had sunk back in his chair, expression thunderous as
he realized how heavily the odds had turned against him. The *Tlemitl*
outweighed any single enemy ship by three or six to one, but now his
battle-group was stripped down to only three supporting cruisers. Even
the two Scout frigates had disappeared.

As he watched, the Khaid battleships coalesced—showing admirable
skill, one part of his mind commented—into a tight pack. Now they
veered towards the *Tlemitl*, their point-defense overlapping, with a

"Crow, we'd better get tied down, this is getting rough."

The old México did not bother to look over his shoulder. His displays had reconfigured again and the Swedish woman frowned, not recognizing any of the interfaces he was now navigating. Somehow it seemed freshly minted and new, though still recognizably México in origin. "Hummingbird, are we going to get out of this?"

"I have," he said in a musing voice, "a great faith in *Chu-sa* Koshō's ability to survive."

Then everything lurched violently and Gretchen lost her seat, flying into the nearest wall with a bone-jarring *crunch*. Hummingbird's consoles tore free of the tape, one of them shattering against the wall beside her. Despite this, his attention remained fixed on flipping through the *Tlemitl*'s internal systems as fast as possible.

"Holy Blessed Mary, Bride of Jesus, that hurts!" Anderssen slid to the floor as the g-decking reasserted itself, landing painfully. "*Crow!*"

Six decks away, Koshō watched calmly as the *Naniwa*'s abrupt course change sent the battle-cruiser careening into a pack of six oncoming Khaiden destroyers. The battle-cruiser's deflectors rippled with millions of tiny impacts as irradiated dust and battle debris hammered at the electromagnetic veil. Missiles punched straight through, while particle beam traces speared past as the Khaid gunners lost lock on the elusive Imperial ship. In turn, she was designating priority in her 'well, the stylus stabbing like a dagger into the heart of the enemy.

"Weapons, target number four, give me a tight grouping!"

The *Naniwa* shuddered as the starboard missile launchers went to rapid-fire, spitting a cloud of smaller interceptors around a single big *Tessen* shipkiller. The destroyers had broken ranks, each burning maneuver mass to break away from the oncoming Imperial. The *Naniwa*'s beam nacelles strobed, capacitors discharging with a high shrieking whine that carried through the shipframe like the lament of the damned. Secondary launchers spat out a handful of spoofer pods. Target five flared with a brilliant violet-hued detonation and the ensigns on the lower tier of Command shouted, "*Seikou!*"

Susan nodded to Konev, whose beam gunners had gotten in a choice hit.

To starboard, target four had gone into a corkscrew pattern, trying to

«*IMN BC-261 lost with all hands,*» Xochitl's exo commented, spooling off a log entry.

"Battlecast resynced." Yoemon's voice was harsh and flat. The *Tlemitl* was now turning, still building velocity, with the *Asama* running in tight, well inside the fire control envelope of the dreadnaught's point-defense batteries. With the four Khaid heavies drawn off by killing the battle-cruiser, the two Imperial ships accelerated into the flank of the opposing fleet. Four Khaid cruisers swung towards them, but now the full throw-weight of the *Tlemitl* and *Asama* could focus on the approaching ships.

A storm of sprint missiles and particle beams stabbed out, while the spoofer pods flooded Khaid targeting control with thousands of phantom contacts. The first three cruisers shattered, shipskin ravaged by particle beams, missile racks torn away, and then each hull punched in by a pair of shipkillers—big *Tessen*-class multiphase penetrators.

«*Resource utilization is higher than recommended per target,*» exo commented, but the Prince shook his head. "The weapons officer is showing admirable restraint, given his desire to be sure of the mark. Yoemon has noticed we've no resupply now that the *Hanuman* has fled. Very wise."

'Cast relay beeped cheerfully, showing a fresh Imperial fire-snake glyph boosting towards the protective shell of the *Tlemitl*'s point-defense.

«*IMN CA-1042 Gladius has synched to battlecast,*» exo announced. «*All other cruisers have been lost.*»

Her field of view filled with an intricate schematic of potential Barrier threads, racing ship glyphs, and the still-present necklace of science probes arrayed beyond the radiation cloud which had been the *Can*, Gretchen tried to concentrate on the results from her models. The first pass she'd taken had been discarded and while searching for more computational resources Anderssen had found—to her wary delight—that node 3^33 also boasted well over nineteen thousand processing nodes. Many of them were inactive, or inaccessible to her, but enough remained to offload model calculations for three alternate schemas.

The constant fluctuations in the g-decking field made her work very difficult and Gretchen had resorted to taping down the comps and her other gear.

displayed comparisons of numbers of ships, types, and throw-weight between this battle and more recent encounters with the Khaid raiders.

A proper fleet, the Prince observed, almost impressed. *On our model; with supply ships, a repair tender, lighter elements, some kind of troop transports. . . .*

Swiftly approaching the danger zone marked out on the threatwell in strobing crimson, *Thai-sa* Yoemon's voice cut sharply across the chatter on the command 'cast. "Prepare to change vector, rotating aspect . . . now."

Xochitl's eyes slid to the display showing g-integrity deck by deck on the massive ship. *Time to put everything to the test.*

The constant rumble transmitted through the hull—despite a brand-new dampening system—from the maneuver drives ceased abruptly. The *Tlemitl* rotated aspect on tertiary thrusters. The status displays started to wink amber and yellow—one red spot flared up as a compartment lost its g-decking—and then the *Firearrow* was pointed on a new heading. The exchange of missile clouds and beam weapons had continued unabated throughout the evolution and the Prince was pleased to see his gun crews had kept targeting lock on the lead Khaid battleships. Battlecast was still in sync, though hostile ECM was now starting to interfere, forcing a faster encryption cycle rate.

"Main drives at full," Yoemon snapped and the rumbling vibration kicked in again. Now three compartments flared red and Xochitl cursed, knowing any man in those areas was probably dead or seriously wounded, given the acceleration they were pulling. Still, the dreadnaught had successfully swerved away from the Barrier, the *Asama* keeping pace off her port. The *Tokiwa*, however, had failed to change vector with them. Xocoyotl's battle cruiser had rotated to reverse aspect, but now she was forced to a full-burn to avoid colliding with the invisible weapon.

The fire from all four Khaid battleships retargeted on the *Tokiwa* as she slipped out of the point-defense envelope maintained by the *Tlemitl* and *Asama*. Hundreds of shipkillers rained in, saturating the battle-cruiser's lighter point defense network. Dozens of explosions rippled the length of her hull, stressing shipskin beyond its capacity. A bright pinpoint seared through the plasma clouds as a penetrator pierced containment on the antimatter reactor. Then everything—the *Tokiwa*, the debris clouds spilling from her flanks, the corona of bomb-pod lasers igniting—was washed away by a pure white flare.

Muldoon. May Mor-Ríoghain convey you to the West with all good speed.

The battle-cruiser held fire, munitions racks rolled out with the full weight of her shipkillers and suppression pods ready to launch. Seconds ticked past, and then—

"*Chu-sa*, transit spike!" Holloway's voice was flat and sharp. "Multiple spikes! Incoming transit across the board—estimating thirty contacts inbound."

"Launchers ready for salvo two, *kyo*," Konev barked, running through his readiness checklist one more time.

A wide arc of space shimmered, twisting aside as dozens more Khaiden ships—a swarm of destroyers, light cruisers, Fleet tenders, and assault boats—dropped out of hyperspace. Susan grinned mirthlessly. Months spent far beyond the rim of Imperial space, hunting the Khaid and Megair and being hunted in return, had gained her a hard-won familiarity with their tactics.

The *Naniwa* sprint missiles already launched into the void were now within seconds of a sudden new array of targets. The deadly little weapons sprang awake, autonomic targeting systems fixing on the fresh signatures of Khaiden ships, and blasted forward, exhausting the last of their fuel.

Two Khaiden destroyers staggered as the Imperial missiles streaked past their point-defense and antimatter charges detonated against shipskin. Startlingly violet blossoms of plasma erupted from their engine arrays. An assault boat tore in half. Missiles raced through the Khaiden formation, causing panic. Ships corkscrewed away wildly amid a wave of secondary explosions. A wedge of destroyers rotated towards the *Naniwa*, beam weapons stabbing at her through the incandescent murk.

"Weapons, fire salvo two."

The battle-cruiser shuddered as every launch rail and missile rack triggered simultaneously.

The *Tlemitl* and her two consorts lunged toward the Barrier at maximum acceleration, clawing for room to maneuver. In FlagCom, Xochitl let the threatwell feed wash over him, his attention fixed on the maneuvering of the Khaid main elements. The arrival of their support ships had been expected, though he was surprised to see such numbers. Exo

Someone shouted "Heave!" and the stanchion squealed, trying to slide free of the hatch. At the airlock controls, the Engineer Second wrenched aside the panel covering with a pry bar and shorted the mechanism. The hatch tried to cycle open and the stanchion popped loose. Almost immediately the environmental circuits triggered an alarm—the boat bay had lost its exterior doors and was open to the void—and only the inner airlock hatch, luckily still intact, prevented the entire corridor from venting into space.

Helsdon had his hand-comp clipped in and now he thumbed a counter-override, letting the little unit drop into a blindingly fast response cycle as the hatch requested permission to close, was told *no*, then requested it again. . . . The damage control party dragged the stanchion free with a grinding scrape.

The Engineer Second unclipped the comp—the hatch ground closed, spitting out metal shavings—and he pitched the plastic control cover away.

"Let's go," he broadcast, drawing everyone's attention. "There's a hull puncture two halls leeward and we're venting atmosphere. We've got an emergency repair closet there and one on the way, so get ready to carry what we'll need."

Their faces were blank with incomprehension, or stiff with incipient fear, but Helsdon pushed them along—using the pry bar if necessary. If they stopped, he would stop, and then he knew he'd break down. The specter of another endless time trapped in a broken, disabled ship, waiting for the cold or hunger or radiation to take him was ever-present.

The *Naniwa* sped towards rendezvous with the flagship, steadily building velocity. In Koshō's mind, the invisible, undetectable Barrier seemed only a hands-breadth from her flank. All sections had finally reported in, ready for battle. Damage control crews were standing by, the launchers had recycled, and transit deflectors were at full strength. In her executive 'well, she could see that the *Tlemitl* had brought the new battle-shields on line and Susan was pained by jealousy. *Curse the Prince, he has all the new toys . . . while we fight with flint and wicker!*

Koshō stiffened, agonized to see the *Falchion*—hammered by dozens of bomb-pods—shiver and begin to break apart. A cloud of evac capsules spewed away from the mortally wounded cruiser, but Susan knew her commander would not be aboard one of them.

able job. Initial damage was already being attacked by Engineering damage control parties. Shields were up, the ship was building velocity and the *Tokiwa* and *Asama* were closing vector with all speed.

We need to get point-defense interlock engaged. The Prince scowled, watching the intercept projections update in his 'well. The Khaid were forming up, their main body of battleships—falling somewhere in size and throw-weight between the *Tlemitl* and her battle cruisers—screened from immediate attack by this lead group of four.

The two Imperial battle-cruisers swung in moments later, having reached interlock range on point defense. Both were spewing ECM pods and the new remote point-defense platforms as fast as their launchers could recycle.

"Combat interlock confirmed," *Thai-sa* Yoemon and *Chu-so* Xocoyotl's voices overlapped in each ear. The Prince had already seen his secondary status displays shade green. The *Tlemitl*'s spoofer pods now began to flood nearspace with a hurricane of false data. Subsystems on all three ships had been drinking in the Khaid ECM signatures for almost ten minutes now, and with interlock allowing each ship to differentiate their countermeasures, the attacking ships were suddenly moving in an electronic fog.

«Now?» suggested his exocortex. «*Battlecast synch time is within parameters to implement override.*»

Xochitl shook his head, though no one else could see, or hear, the exo. "No, not yet. The commanders of the other ships haven't been briefed—" Even Yoemon, who had seen the new control overrides in action during trials, wasn't ready to let the *Tlemitl* fight herself. *Well, under my direction,* thought the Prince.

«*Our direction,*» countered his exo. «*We are one.*»

"—they'll panic."

The interior airlock opening onto boat bay nine wheezed, locking motor complaining as it attempted to seal the hatch. A fallen stanchion twisted with a squeal, crushed by the door, but refused to break free. Helsdon, face streaming with sweat, looped a magnetic block ring around the twisted battle-steel, snugged it tight, and stepped back. Behind him, a good dozen cooks, stewards, stray officers, and off-duty ratings leaned into the rope, hauling for all they were worth.

Hanuman had been at the periphery of the attack area and was now only minutes from making gradient to hyperspace.

The battle cruiser *Naniwa*, which had just rotated out on a patrol sweep, was also out of the immediate melee.

Though his first instinct was to comm *Thai-sa* Yoemon for ship's status, Xochitl knew the captain was fully occupied with damage control and fighting for his ship. Instead he confirmed the status of the other ships in the squadron and added himself to the 'cast command channel. Immediately the chatter of six or seven commanders flowed through his earbug, including the harsh bark of *Chu-sho* Xocoyotl on the *Tokiwa*.

"Battle shields coming on-line now," Yoemon reported on a channel specific to the *Tlemitl*.

The overhead lights in Flag Command flickered and the constant shattering vibration of bomb-pod impacts and particle beam detonations ceased. In the threatwell, the *Firearrow*'s glyph changed and Xochitl knew that outside—in the maelstrom of radiation, spinning debris, and streaking missiles—a wavering, rainbow-hued globe had sprung up around his ship. Within the second, one of the v-panes on his threatwell display was strobing, showing impact rates on the various shield cells managed by the massive Tototl-Aerospatiale generators embedded beneath the shipskin.

One corner of the threatwell spiked as an irregular sphere of plasma suddenly occluded the *Can*.

So much for the Mirror's sensor platform, Xochitl thought, shunting the flood of data flowing over him to his exocortex. *Battlecast is up and synchronized . . . Xocoyotl had better get—ah, good, here they come.*

The secondary beam weapons on the *Tlemitl* were now firing in staccato, sweeping the area ahead of the massive ship free of bomb-pods and penetrators. The Khaid were fond of strewing clouds of one-off mines when they engaged the enemy, then working to drive their prey into the shoals which resulted.

Four Khaiden battleships—Xochitl had never encountered the class before and his exocortex could find no references to them in the Fleet briefings and intelligence estimates—were now closing on the dreadnaught, seeking to bring particle weapons to bear behind three speeding waves of shipkillers.

An answering salvo of penetrators was already belching from the *Tlemitl*. Xochitl fought down a fierce desire to override Yoemon and take direct command of the dreadnaught, but the *Thai-sa* was doing an

"*Kyo*, salvo one away," Konev reported, voice tight with adrenaline and fear. "Cycling launchers."

In the center of the spiderweb, caught at a dead stop, battle-shields off-line, the surface of the *Tlemitl* rippled with white-hot explosions. Khaid particle-beam weapons savaged the enormous hull, chewing away at a shipskin four times the thickness of the armor encasing the *Naniwa*. Clouds of shipkillers rained in, flooding the point-defense network with a constant stabbing barrage of detonations. Behind them, bomb-pods stuttered, unspooling long chains of thermonuclear-pumped laser emitters. Despite being caught unawares, the *Tlemitl*'s on-duty gun crews were already in action—city-block-long emitter nacelles swiveled, flaring with the sidescatter radiation from beam weapons igniting. Missile launch rails were cycling as fast as their hardware allowed, disgorging heavy shipkillers in bursts.

In Flag Command on the superdreadnaught, Prince Xochitl—who had been caught by the attack in transit to a meeting with the senior Mirror scientists and their political officers—staggered as a pair of shipkillers detonated against the *Tlemitl*'s hull. The internal g-field was fluctuating and even his coppery skin was noticeably pale as he dropped into a shockchair at the Admiral's console. His Jaguars had been carrying the components for a full EVA suit with them, and now the Prince was locked down and encased in full armor.

The *Tlemitl*'s captain, Ikaru Yoemon, was in Main Command, fifty decks and half the length of the ship away, which left the Prince with whichever duty officers were within reach of FlagCom when the first alarms sounded. Despite being shorthanded, Xochitl tapped into the battlecast directly and immediately upon establishing comm lock, the Flag threatwell sprang to life, showing the whole chaotic scene in vibrant detail.

The *Fiske* and *Eldredge* were already shattered hulks, spewing wreckage and burning with radiation fires on all decks. Two of the heavy cruisers, the *Axe* and the *Mace*, were expanding spheres of ionized metal and plasma—containment lost on their reactors, weapons cooking off in a ripple of secondary explosions. By tremendous luck, the Fleet tender

Chac's attention on her, hot and wavering, an unsteady flame. The other officers were still scrambling to bring deflectors up, or confirm gun crews and missile teams were standing by. Pucatli at comm was speaking rapidly into his throatmike, confirming readiness of the interior compartments and sections.

Koshō caught the Mayan's eyes. "*Sho-sa*, this is a brawl for dreadnaughts. I'll handle maneuver, combat targeting, and tactics; you keep us able to move, fight, and react. Do you understand? We're going to get hit hard, and you're going to have to put us right with all speed."

Oc Chac stared back at her for a second, almost paralyzed with panic, and then nodded sharply. "*Hai, Chu-sa, hai!*"

"Pilot, full ahead," Koshō grated, seeing *Naniwa*'s velocity climb. They had not, luckily, been at full stop when the attack began. The initial confusion around the *Can* had started to stabilize and she could see every Imperial ship was trying to get underway. *They've jumped in "orumchek" formation*, she realized, watching the spiderweb attack pattern of the Khaid ships unfold. *And they've caught almost all of us at zero-v, pants down, finger up the nose.*

"Weapons, all launch racks deploy, give me every sprint missile we can throw, configure for independent terminal tracking." The stylus slashed through her copy of the threatwell, describing a second "shell" of target areas around the periphery of the combat area. "Pilot, full combat power, angle for thirty-two degrees off axis. Take us hard up along the Barrier line. Transit deflectors at maximum power."

The *Naniwa* surged ahead, engines flaring sun-bright, warning lights flashing in every compartment as the crew raced to battle stations. Susan ran through a brief internal checklist, confirming all drives were showing green, no bay doors were open to space, and internal battle compartments were sealing. Already the ship shook with the vibration of the ammunition Backbone shuttling fresh shipkillers to the primary rails, while the missile racks rolled out from the hull.

"*Chu-sa*, targeting solutions are locked." Konev seemed absurdly happy. "Hardpoints are clear to launch."

"Weapons, fire." Koshō felt a sharp bolt of elation as dozens of missile tracks sprang into view on the threatwell, spiraling out from the *Naniwa*, which was now accelerating hard. Holloway was sparing nothing to hit the mark she'd set for him.

pie into his mouth, and then sealed his helmet. He, unlike many of the others present, was still wearing a proper z-suit and carried his full EVA helmet slung over his back on a lanyard. Surviving in the wreck of the *Calexico* had made him intimately familiar with every piece of survival gear Fleet provided.

"Incoming hostiles at all points," bellowed the overhead. "Missile impacts expected in one minute, one minute. Brace for hull rupture, all hands secure compartments and brace for zero-g."

Oh Lord of my Sainted Fathers. Helsdon bolted for the nearest damage control station. *Work to do, I have work to do. I need to do my work*, he chanted as he ran, fearing he'd freeze up if he faltered for even an instant.

Koshō stiffened in her shockchair as the executive threatwell displayed by her console filled with a swarm of angry red icons, each circumscribed by rapidly mutating glyphs. The ship's threat assessment AI triggered, sounding alarms the length of the *Naniwa*.

"Battle stations!" Koshō barked, feeling the shockchair fold around her automatically. A helmet was already lowering over her head and she reflexively tucked her hair in. Combat readiness subsystems were kicking in at every station, discarding the patrol-specific displays and replacing them with battle configurations. The lights shaded to red, and behind her the main hatchway sealed itself. Her eyes flicked across the storm of data flowing into the main threatwell. "We are under attack by a Khaid fleet—repeat, we are under attack by a Khaid fleet."

The Khaiden armada—or nearly so, given the usual size of their raiding squadrons—had dropped gradient directly on top of the Imperial ships loitering around the *Can*. The *Naniwa*'s sensor suite was already flooded with the fury of beam weapons igniting, and the threatwell was filled with swarm after swarm of missiles and bomb-pods spewing into the void.

Koshō spared an instant to thank Hachiman they were in motion and a fair distance from the rest of the squadron.

"Message drone away," Oc Chac barked reflexively. "Transit to hyper in one hundred thirty-six seconds."

Susan's habitual calm turned icy and everything around her narrowed down to the storm unfolding in the threatwell. She could feel Oc

AT THE PINHOLE

Sitting in the junior officer's mess aboard the *Tlemitl*, Engineer Second Helsdon was acquainting himself with a fresh-baked chicken pie and a jug of Ceylon black tea. The Jaguar Knights who had dragged him before the Prince had no interest in escorting him all the way back to the *Can*—so they'd jobbed him off on Logistics to ferry over to the research station when convenient. This left the sandy-haired engineer at loose ends for six or seven hours, so cooling his heels in the well-appointed mess seemed the perfect answer.

But scuttlebutt from the ensigns slouching at the next table indicated the *Can* itself was being abandoned, with the Mirror scientists returning to their transports. Which left Helsdon with nowhere to go, but for the moment he wasn't too concerned about finding a bunk—the chicken pie was excellent and he guessed the engineers aboard the *Tlemitl* would look out for their own in a pinch. He'd hot-bunked himself, more than once, when a fellow mechanic needed a place to sleep and hadn't found an official posting yet.

A steward passed by, and Helsdon flagged her down. "Could I get another cuppa, please?"

She was pouring, the tea shedding curlicues of steam, when an alarm Klaxon sounded. The noise was harsh, shocking to the ear, and unmistakable.

"All hands to battle stations," boomed the overhead, "all hands to battle stations."

The decking itself suddenly shivered; every cup, saucer, and pot rattling on all of the mess tables. Aft of the cafeteria, in the engine ring, the super-dreadnaught's maneuver engines were flash-heating to full combat power. Everyone was already up, on their feet, sealing the regulation shipsuit under their uniforms and scrambling towards the emergency lockers for helmets.

Helsdon seized hold of the edge of the table, stuffed the rest of the

consoles on the far side of the small bridge. These turned, then one of them pointed at an environmental display flashing a warning.

De Molay shook her head. "They see the air warning lights. How quickly will they be overcome?"

Mitsuharu looked thoughtful. "Not long, but it may be enough to cause us mischief. I will stand watch at the lift between decks."

After a swift review of the weapons to hand—his machete and knife were now supplemented by another Khaid shipgun—the Nisei slipped out of Engineering. As the hatch closed behind him, De Molay ventured a crooked little smile, saying: "I'll let you know if anyone resists taking a very long nap."

over, and then stepped in, hacking down. Now the blade fell true and the Khaid's head lolled to the side, half severed. Hadeishi grimaced, feeling his limbs burn with exertion, and then felt enormous exhaustion wash over him.

The books are ruined, his father's voice echoed in memory. *What a pity.*

Hadeishi staggered into the Engineering compartment, the tool belts from both dead engineers looped over his shoulder. He was surprised—but pleased—to see that De Molay had dragged herself down to the still-working console and was trying to secure control of ship's systems.

"You've access to environmental, *kyo*? Good. Pump one percent cee-oh to Command and the cargo bay." Mitsuharu gasped, feeling winded. "Secure air in Engineering and let's get you into a z-suit."

De Molay clung grimly to the console with both hands. "They'll be in the corridors, too."

Struggling with the stylus, the *Wilful's* captain tapped open a new series of v-panes—from cameras Hadeishi had never been able to reach with his own access. The old woman leaned her head over, wheezing: "I can see another figure in the mess as well. Everything else looks clear for the moment."

"Good." Hadeishi took a deep breath and set down the extra tools. "Don't lock the areas where the gas is released. Let them believe free movement is possible." He stood at her shoulder, watching the suddenly superior v-pane displays with envy. "And where was all of this when I was cleaning the bilges?"

"That one knows there's a problem," De Molay observed softly, a blood-caked hand tapping the feed from the bridge. A Khaid under-officer stood uncertainly at the captain's station, rubbing his eyes. "He could signal for help if the comm system has been recoded since they came aboard."

Hadeishi shrugged. "I struck down one reviewing our technical manuals—but how far they've gotten beyond the nav system—"

The crewman sat down in the captain's chair, looked around in apparent puzzlement, and then suddenly pitched forward. The sound of his fall was audible in the camera pickup, and was more than enough to draw the attention of three more Khaid who had been working at

rolling in different directions, and the Nisei lunged, getting an arm under the shoulder joint. The alien was very heavy—massing nearly twice his own weight—and Hadeishi grunted with pain as he eased the corpse to the g-decking. Mindful of leaving a trail, he dragged the body into hypercontrol, wrapped the corpse in a plastic sheet from his other leg pocket, and then wiped off his hands and forearms, which had been spattered with cloying blue-black blood.

Then he continued on, trying to move a little faster. The down-below had never seemed so large before, but now the number of rooms seemed infinite. Finally, having almost completed a circuit of the entire ship, he approached an alcove which served as a crude reference library—there were shelves of data crystals, a comp station, and portable readers hung on the walls. Nearly twenty-five minutes had passed and his chrono was showing time winding down at a swift pace.

But light flickered on the wall of the alcove and there was a singular musk in the air. *Reading up on the new ship, is he? A Khaid seeking to better himself, how excellent.*

Hadeishi crept to a point where he could see the elbow and shoulder of the engineer, who was sitting on the bench in the alcove, thumbing through a series of technical manuals. *Laudatory,* Mitsuharu thought, feeling a pang. *I've had ensigns who refused to do so much. . . .*

At that instant, the ship began to slide gradient and the transit alarm blared. Startled by the unexpected noise, the engineer looked up in time to catch sight of Hadeishi rushing out of the dimness. The Khaid's first impulse was to drag out his comm—a handheld unit instead of the usual Imperial wristband—and sound an alarm. In the heartbeat between impulse and action, Mitsuharu hewed down with the machete, the full strength of his shoulders behind the blow, catching the Khaid's raised hand on the wrist. There was a jarring *crack* and the joint split, along with the z-suit ring.

Howling in pain, the Khaid leapt back, crashing into the shelves. Books and data crystals flew in all directions, rolling wildly on the floor. Hadeishi crabbed in, hacking with the long flat blade, and the edge bit into the engineer's other arm, drawing a deep wound. Blood slicked the floor, making his footing treacherous. The Khaid sounded a deep coughing howl and scrabbled for some weapon—a knife, a gun—nothing came immediately to hand.

Mitsuharu kicked the engineer's knee, making the creature topple

THE WILFUL

De Molay was lying in her hammock over the reaction mass tank, eyes closed, listening to the gurgling and chuckling of the pipes winding over and around her, when Hadeishi emerged from the darkness, his face blackened with grease. "Here," he said, parting her thin fingers and pressing the slim metallic shape of the Webley Bulldog into her hands. "I will return in a little while, but anything may happen between now and then."

She opened one eye, and then the other, seeing the Nisei had acquired a serrated-blade knife about twenty centimeters long to go with his machete. The machete was now enclosed in a crude, handmade scabbard and strapped to his chest at an angle. The knife fit into his belt. She made a face, eyebrows beetling up. "You will need to be quick," she whispered. "Do you hear that whine building in the hypercoil? We're losing gradient fast, we'll drop back to realspace soon. And when we do, even these lax fools will realize something is amiss."

"I know." Hadeishi held up his hand-comp, which was still relaying the nav system telemetry. "About thirty minutes and we'll drop out. I plan to be back before then."

He bowed in parting, and then climbed silently down to the Engineering compartment. By his count there were two Khaiden loose in the down-below decks, and both of them had left their duty stations to do . . . something. So he padded quietly from room to room, working his way around the huge bulk of the maneuver drives. Approaching the access way leading to the hyperspace coil generator he heard the sound of boots on the decking and flattened against the wall.

A Khaid engineer ambled out of the side passage, helmet back, nosily crunching on a heavy, bonelike ration bar. The alien's jagged, double-flanged teeth were making quick work of the claylike brick.

Mitsuharu's arm snapped out, the serrated blade spearing up into the underside of Khaid's jaw. The creature goggled at him, huge eyes

Korkunov route that could explain the blackout. Perhaps we can avoid it the next time around."

Oc Chac frowned at the console for a moment longer, watching the diagnostic run.

"*Chu-i*, if anything flags red on that scan—you let me know immediately."

Things are now afoot to which we are not privy. Shall even the Judges shine dim beside the *Tlaltecutli*, the Lord of the Earth? Surely the human race would be at insupportable risk if we cannot penetrate new secrets as they arise! We must get inside this mystery box that is the *Firearrow*."

"In a minute," Anderssen mumbled.

"Of course," he said, watching her with a sort of cool detachment.

At much the same time, his comp constellation completed the process of dumping a set of infiltrators into the *Naniwa*'s communications network, allowing Hummingbird to open a tachyon relay channel without anyone on the bridge being the wiser. A short, discrete burst of data was dispatched out into the wasteland of the *kuub*. A bit later, the reply filtered back to Hummingbird's console.

Excellent, he thought, setting a timer to run. *Seventeen hours and counting.*

On the command deck, another watch came on duty and *Sho-sa* Oc Chac was once more at his console, monitoring the efforts of the rest of the bridge crew and ancillary departments. Given his background, the Mayan was paying close attention to the efforts of the *Zosen* still rounding out a few tail-end projects. When *Chu-i* Pucatli suddenly tilted his head and stared at the status board in puzzlement, he was up out of his seat and beside the Comms station before the sub-lieutenant could sound an alarm.

"*Sho-sa*, we've lost sync with *Tlemitl*'s battlecast," Pucatli reported, not too surprised to find Oc Chac at his shoulder.

"Have we moved out of range?" Oc Chac asked, reaching over the younger man's shoulder to key up a diagnostic subsystem. "Is there some kind of heavy debris concentration between us and the squadron?"

"*Kyo*, we're on a return leg of the patrol pattern—distance is closing with the *Can* and squadron center-point. But the dust—it's very heavy." Pucatli slid part of the navigational display into view on his console. "I've been seeing irregular gravitational interference with comm, but we've rotated through this sector at least once before and did not lose sync."

"Mark the area. And see if there's anything on our new map of the

those who *used* them left all pretense of humanity behind. How"—he paused, searching for the right words—"how can even a warrior countenance the death of an enemy he has not faced, met eye to eye, and traded blows with in the circle? Anything else is murder. I would say that a murderer has abandoned the common thread which ties us all together."

Anderssen squinted, wondering if the Crow was mocking her, then shook her head. "None of those atrocities were initiated by the *tools*—the rifle, the machine gun, the bomb only had the misfortune to fall into the hands of men who had *already* decided upon atrocity."

Then she set the block down, picked up her stylus, and returned to her work.

Hummingbird became quite still, seeing that the European woman had turned her back on him. He watched her intently for nearly thirty minutes, but Gretchen's attention was wholly devoted to building a new analysis model. Apparently satisfied by what he'd seen, the old crow returned to his own efforts, and the hours passed by in quiet save for the clicking of their styluses on the control surfaces.

At length, Hummingbird pushed away from his comp—breathed out a deep, long sigh—and stared for a moment at the pale blue wall behind his still oblivious companion. "The dreadnaught's shipnet is using an unknown encryption and security system. Not only is it unfamiliar to my tools, but it seems impervious to investigation."

Gretchen made no sign she had heard. Hummingbird scratched the back of his head and surveyed the rest of their cabin. Conversationally, he said: "There are the afterimages of cranes in flight, etched into this ceiling. A former tenant must have needed at least the illusion of the homeworld to ease his mind."

Still Anderssen ignored him. The *nauallis* grimaced and rose, swaying a little. After two cups of thickly sugared *kaffe* he found steadier footing. Then he sat down on the edge of his bunk and unwrapped a threesquare. Even when he'd finished, the Swedish woman was still hard at work.

Experimentally, he said: "The *Tlemitl* is one of the Emperor's personal ships—long rumored but never proven. Never have I encountered an Imperial system which could resist my overrides. Always before, the Judges have contrived to know what transpired in Imperial Space.

proper purpose. But in the comp system? There was a disconnect between the object—or truly the data trying to describe the object—and her ability to grasp its totality.

I can't go EVA and touch the damned thing. She felt daunted. *I have to figure this one out the old way.*

Across the room, Hummingbird stirred, his eyes focusing on her as though from a great distance. "How very interesting," he said. "It would seem the Prince has arrived with no Judge or Mirror oversight. No Seeking Eye commissars, no political officers."

Gretchen gave him a look over the rim of her *kaffe* cup. "A Prince of the realm, riding the finest steed in the land, with not the slightest restraint on his activities? What a marvelous adventure for him!"

"For all of us, I fear," Hummingbird muttered, producing a small paper wrapper from his mantle. He withdrew two small white tablets and placed one of them under his tongue. "Curious—there is only a skeleton crew aboard the *Tlemitl*. Barely enough men to operate her."

"That many fewer to share the loot." Anderssen sat back down, scratching her ear, attention already sliding away into this new puzzle.

"Abominations!" Hummingbird exclaimed in outrage as he peered at one of the v-panes. "I'm bumped out."

"Oh, you'll get back in, eventually," Gretchen assured him. "You are a *nauallis*, after all."

"Anderssen . . ." Hummingbird finally looked at her directly and the shock of meeting his dark eyes drew her full attention. "Have you considered what it means to encounter, to experience a First Sun device?"

Gretchen laughed bitterly. "You mean, will fame and fortune go to my head? Isn't your whole purpose to make sure that *no one* realizes such a thing has even been encountered? There's no fortune there, for me, and certainly no fame."

The old man shook his head slowly. "Such things are only the shell, only the surface of the matter." He pointed with his chin and Anderssen looked down, surprised to find the corroded bronze block in her hands.

"Your ability to use such things imperils your very humanity. You must tread very softly."

"This? This is just a computer—one of the tools at our command. Do you think using tools threatens anyone's humanity?"

He nodded. "The men who devised the first rifle, or machine gun, or thermonuclear bomb let go of something innate in themselves. Then

device did have storage available and there was some kind of pathway to allow access.

Gretchen's first instinct was to yank out the octopus and sever the connection. But then, when her fingers touched the cable, her eyes drifted back to the long string of nines and all of the raw storage they represented. *I could build a nice dataset with all of those probes feeding in . . . I wonder how fast it can process?*

A little guiltily she glanced over at Hummingbird, who seemed entirely oblivious to her activities. His face seemed remote and unapproachable and the *click-click-click* of his stylus was swift and sure, the patter of hail on a tin roof in a high country storm.

One step at a time, she decided, and reconfigured the octopus to allow only one-way communication. *At least,* she thought, *I can store all of the data right now, then disconnect from the probes before someone notices I've hijacked them. That would be prudent.*

Five minutes later the first of the probes was unspooling its history log across the 'net and into the bronze block at a very reasonable speed. Watching the performance metrics built into her comp, Anderssen realized after about ten minutes that the limiting factor on the transfer was the octopus itself, which had not been designed for moving such enormous volumes of data.

I'm going to short the poor thing out. What else do I have available? . . .

Her stylus tapped through a series of panes, looking for alternate methods of transfer, and on the fourth one she paused, eyebrow rising, to see that node 3^3 had registered twenty-seven wireless access ports, all open and unsecured. *I wonder . . . will stellarcast let me multichannel onto this device?* Gretchen poked around some more, cursing at the arcane interface for the shipnet, until she figured out how to assign the data feeds from the sixty-plus probes across all the available access ports. Then she tapped a GO icon and sat back.

All of the probe data was loaded nine minutes later.

Anderssen blinked, smoothed back her straight blond hair, and got up to get a *kaffe*.

Well, well, well, she mused, pouring instacream into the black liquid. *Now how to model all this and find the keyhole I need, or the shape of this . . . or, or . . .* Gretchen hissed in frustration. When she held a physical object in her hands—potsherds, a broken mechanism, a bone— something would usually suggest itself to her, some clue or guide to its

an order of magnitude beyond that of the smaller ships, including the *Naniwa*.

Hummingbird bit at his thumb, eyes narrowed. "Who came with the Prince?" he mused. "What resources does he have to hand? . . ."

The *nauallis* fell silent then, his attention wholly focused on defeating the protections girding the *Tlemitl*. Anderssen lost interest in his struggle. The question of the mysterious weapon and the barrier it had drawn across this whole section of space was far more intriguing. She had never had an opportunity to investigate an artifact of such colossal scale before. *No way I'm passing this up,* Gretchen thought gleefully and rubbed her hands together briskly in anticipation. Her initial forays into the resources available through the 'cast network had already discovered a whole series of robotic probes deployed along the "frontier" of the hidden weapon, probes which had been under the control of the Mirror scientists working on the *Can*, but now they were drifting aimlessly, having been abandoned at the Prince's direction.

Come here my pretties, she thought, grinning. Watching Hummingbird at work had revealed his outgoing stellarcast transmissions were masquerading as authorized 'net access from the *Naniwa*. The probes were happy to recognize her request as official and socket into her network. After handshaking, they began unspooling an enormous volume of data back to her little set of comps. Almost immediately, she received warning errors from the data interfaces. Frowning, she eyed Hummingbird's constellation of devices but decided it would be unwise to steal storage from him. *What about the local shipnet, maybe I can hijack someone's . . . Hold up, what's this?*

A new icon had appeared on her main v-display; one showing a glyph indicating it "belonged" to her set of resources. There was no description and only a generic symbol with the identifier $3^3 3$ attached. Curious, Anderssen queried the storage available and then sat back in surprise when the node responded with a long string of nines. *That is . . . a hell lot of crystal lattice,* she thought, impressed. *Is this the public storage cloud on the* Naniwa? *No, it would have a serial number and description and all sorts of wonky detail . . .*

Now concerned, she flipped from the logical view she'd been operating through to a physical resource diagram and then stared over at the corroded bronze block. "You?" she said aloud, startled. The protocol mapping algorithm had apparently completed, determining that the

"Not at all." The old *nauallis* rubbed the back of his head. "Their beliefs are genuine, but while I have some standing among them, I am not one of them, if you follow my meaning. They agreed to help us come this far, but we will need a better conveyance to move forward. To reach the device."

"Hmm." Gretchen turned the bronze block over in her hands. It was quite dense for its size. The interface strip was reattached and reconfigured. She reached for her portable input panel and v-display. "You don't know where this came from?"

"I know who gave it to me," he answered, in a very dry tone. "But before that? I could not say."

"And what did you trade for it?" Anderssen regretted asking the question immediately, realizing she did not want to know the answer. *He might trade anything, for anything,* she thought, feeling a cool chill trip across her shoulders.

"Services rendered, Anderssen-*tzin*. By another, not by you—or I—if you are concerned."

"Well," Gretchen said, distracted, "then let me see. . . ."

She powered up her input devices, socketed them into the interface strip, and settled back to see what presented itself. Almost immediately a node appeared in her little local network, right alongside the tiny blue birds representing her field comp and hand comp. *Time to negotiate,* Anderssen thought, *initiating conversational algorithm.*

Three hours later, Hummingbird was sitting cross-legged on his bunk, his stylus clicking irregularly on the control surface, when a double-chime sounded from one of the v-panes open before him. A thin line of bloody spots ran along his left arm, where he'd been pricking himself with a maguey spine as he worked. Thoughtfully he nodded, closing a series of other windows and expanding the one demanding attention.

"Squadron 'cast access achieved," he said softly, scarred hand flexing. "Protocols are open with all ships save the *Tlemitl*."

Gretchen had been following along with her own systems, which seemed positively paltry in comparison to what the *nauallis* had brought into play. Still, their activities and agents were now able to move where they willed throughout the battlecast network. Only the flagship remained isolated, but Anderssen had the impression the dreadnaught's shipnet was

dubious, but gestured for her to proceed before turning back to completing his system setup.

Gretchen smiled to herself and began rooting through the bag, looking for the doubled green bands. Almost immediately, she ran across a brick-like object wrapped in—of all unlikely things—a parchment envelope.

"Well now," she said to herself, running a finger across the smooth material. "What is this? A book?"

The envelope was held closed by a silver clasp ornamented with a well-worn device. Peering closer and turning the envelope to throw the sigil into relief, she made out the stylized figures of two men—were they in armor? They seemed to be sporting pointed helmets—riding on a single horse.

I've seen this sigil before, she thought, slipping a fingertip under the clasp and opening the envelope.

A heavy metal block—corroded bronze or brass at first glance—slipped out into her hands. As soon as the device touched bare skin, Gretchen felt there was a fundamental imbalance in the mechanism. Attempting to resolve this, she switched the block around and found one end was fitted with a strip of Imperial-standard interface ports. "A comp," she said aloud, though not meaning to. "It feels so old. . . ."

Puzzled, she ran her fingertips across the corroded surface, but no rust or scale came away. Instead, Anderssen realized that the surface was quite smooth, but had been mottled by tremendous heat at some time in the past. *This isn't right,* she felt, and tugged at the interface strip until it came away. *Better.* She sat down on her bunk and opened her backpack, pulling out her trusty old octopus and jacking the multilead into her own comp. Then, humming softly to herself, she began testing the tiny pits revealed by the removal of the interface strip.

After an hour, Gretchen realized she was thirsty and looked up to see that Hummingbird had quietly completed the assembly of his comp station, including the t-relay, and was running well over a hundred v-panes, all showing a wide range of data and visualizations.

"Who made this, Crow? This little comp I've got here?"

Hummingbird did not turn, but shrugged his wiry old shoulders. "It came to me in trade, Anderssen-*tzin*. I did not think it wise to show while we remained on the *Moulins*."

Gretchen snorted. "You didn't trust Captain Locke and his devout crew?"

the comings and goings of Command, old memories unspooling in her mind's eye.

The *Naniwa* pressed on, following her patrol pattern, wake surging bright with particle decay.

Down on deck six, in an officer's cabin with two bunks, a shower, proper desks, and a real closet, Gretchen threw down her duffle bag and kicked off her boots. "By the Risen Christ, Hummingbird, do you think they have fresh hot water? That would be a relief after bathing in recycled spit for a week. . . ." She sorted out her field comp and notebooks from the backpack, including a little Hesht figurine that Magdalena had given her in parting. *Grrault is the god of travelers, bachelors, and the unlucky, so keep him close and remember to give him bits of meat or bone from time to time,* Magdalena had said in complete seriousness. *See this cavity? Place the sacrifice within and after a moment or two, watch the color of his eyes. Amber means the meat is poisoned, red means it is safe to eat.* Then the Hesht had paused, snout wrinkling up. *Safe for a Hesht to eat, of course. For a cub like you with only one stomach . . . perhaps not. But still, he's sure to bring good luck.*

Parker had laughed, pressing his favorite multitool into her hands and giving her an awkward hug. If you need a ride, he said, sniffling, you just comm, right?

Hummingbird did not reply, and when Anderssen turned around, she whistled in appreciation.

The *nauallis* had unlocked both of his traveling bags. One of them had unfolded cleverly into an entire desktop-style comp station with three large v-displays and two stylus pads. The other bag was packed tight with equipment boxes of all kinds. Hummingbird had already appropriated one of the desks and was plugging in cables as fast as he could.

After watching for a moment, Gretchen dove in beside him and started unpacking comm relays and other devices from the second bag. Hummingbird, obviously in a tearing hurry, flashed her a warning look—to which Anderssen gave a smirk in return, saying: "Don't give me that sour face, Crow, I know which end is which."

"Very well. Find a set of modules marked with double bands of green—they can be assembled into a t-relay station. It would speed things up tremendously if you could get that operational." He seemed

quest has been received from a group of visitors on six—with your chop, *Chu-sa*. Should it be approved?"

Susan nodded, though a nagging feeling of being cheated remained.

Doggedly, Oc Chac pressed on: "*Kyo* . . . this ship we captured, the *Moulins*, her crew is to be kept in the brig, secured? But not the, ah, guests in the cabin on six?"

"Even so, *Sho-sa*."

"*Hai, kyo*! I'll have this data loaded immediately."

"Excellent. Run it as an overlay in the well. I want to see a comparison with the plot provided by the Mirror scientists."

Then she leaned back in her chair, fist pressed to her chin. *We'll have a better picture of this Barrier, but I'm going against the spirit of the operational orders in taking a* nauallis *aboard in the midst of a Mirror obsidian-op.* The Chu-sa *never seemed to mind,* she thought, feeling a pang at the memory of Hadeishi sitting forlorn and directionless in the *fumeiyo-ie* on Toroson. Then her expression hardened. *And so my sensei lost his ship and nearly his entire crew. And now we are forever apart.*

Oc Chac returned from one of the operations consoles, hands clasped behind his back.

"New orders have come from squadron, *Chu-sa*. The *Tlemitl* has taken over battle-cast control."

Koshō lifted one eyebrow. "The whole matrix? Squadron-level targeting and countermeasures? Did this come from *Chu-so* Xocoyotl or from the Prince?"

"Everything, *kyo*, is now routing through the *Firearrow*. The *Tokiwa* is lead for the battle-cruiser squadron, but the Flag has switched ships. Prince Xochitl has also ordered all probes presently monitoring the Pinhole to be withdrawn."

Susan tapped her fingers lightly on the armrest. "And the scientists?"

"Ordered back aboard their transports, *kyo*. All technical personnel have been transferred to the *Tlemitl*. The *Can* is being abandoned."

"The Prince is certainly decisive!" *He is cutting the Mirror out of the picture. That will be his father's direction. So—is this a Fleet operation now? Or are Hummingbird and Xochitl actually acting in concert?*

Oc Chac suppressed a scowl at her sarcasm—one which Koshō was too distracted to notice, or comment upon—and returned to his station. The *Chu-sa* remained in her seat, her expression distant, ignoring

THE *NANIWA*

The lift dinged politely and a battle-steel hatch cycled open, revealing the semicircle of Command. Koshō stepped onto the bridge feeling tense and unsettled. She rolled a heavy, Fleet-style data crystal between her fingers, her expression distant. Hadeishi was close in her thoughts, but not as she often heard his voice—relating advice or giving orders in the midst of battle—rather with new appreciation for the compromises he had made while commanding the *Cornuelle*.

"Transferring ship authority, *Chu-sa*," Oc Chac said, switching the command codes from his console to hers.

"Accepted, *Sho-sa*," she replied absently, settling into her shockchair. Susan held up the crystal again and it gleamed with the reflection of dozens of v-displays circling the deck. She had never felt comfortable with the kinds of company Hadeishi had kept, or the odd side diversions he would turn the light cruiser to. Many of those excursions—too many, really—had been at the behest of shadowy figures like Green Hummingbird, who was now sitting in a cabin on deck six, using her water for a shower and eating food from her dispenser system.

I forced the terms of the trade, so why do I feel I'm the one carrying home a koku *of grass seed?*

"*Sho-sa?*" She beckoned the XO over. "Load this into the navigation system, but do not replicate the data onto the squadron 'net."

"*Hai, kyo!*" Oc Chac took the crystal gingerly, but then he stopped, trying to formulate a properly deferential question.

"It is a copy of the *Korkunov* telemetry, *Sho-sa*. Recovered from a message drone launched by the *Calexico* only moments before she was destroyed." Susan raised a warning hand as the Mayan's face twitched with surprise. "We are lucky to have the data, but do not question how the goat got into the garden."

Oc Chac nodded slowly, and then ventured to say, "*Kyo*, an access re-

"Get up," Xochitl snapped irritably. "Tell us—tell me—what you saw and how you survived."

Helsdon breathed in deeply. *This isn't the real thing, it's only a story about what happened to another person. Just another debriefing. Nothing can reach me here.*

"Light of Heaven, I was going EVA to repair a thermocouple relay," he began.

He related the momentary glimpse of the "blurred thread" which cut *Calexico* in half, leading to so many deaths, and then the long desperate struggle to stay alive in the wreck of the destroyer. Eventually—and by this time his voice was hoarse—another Imperial Scout ship had arrived and recovered him.

When Helsdon finished, he found himself rubbing his hands on his trousers. *Why do they sweat so much?* Then he stood in the awkward silence, trying to focus on the Prince. The room had darkened into night cycle as he'd talked, and now Xochitl was only a vague shape, his light-colored mantle a lesser shadow in the gloom.

"Thank you, Engineer Second." Xochitl stood up slowly.

Wish I could see his face better. Didn't he believe me?

Xochitl spoke to the air: "*Kikan-shi* Helsdon is ready to return to the research station."

Helsdon's mind—which seemed oddly fogged—cleared at the thought of returning to work. *Now there it is again. A sound like a tubercular breathing; such sharp, short gasps. Where is it coming from?*

But then the Jaguars entered and escorted him, gently this time, away.

In the darkness, when the door had closed, Xochitl threw himself down on the sofa and passed his hand over a side-lamp. A dull, orange-tinted glow sprang up and the Prince raised an eyebrow questioningly at the largest of the screens at the back of the room. A pair of lambent, angular eyes gleamed back at him.

"Satisfactory, Esteemed?" Xochitl strove to put the proper deference into his voice, but knew in his heart there was only truculence and barely suppressed anger in the words. "Or shall I interview another?"

At the end of the hall, a massive, blocky stone gate stood closed. Each door post was formed in the shape of a jaguar standing on its hind legs, paws raised, talons unsheathed. The lintel was formed of a line of squared-off skulls, deep-set eye sockets filled with shadow. As the engineer approached, one of the jaguar heads swiveled towards him—and even after serving in the Fleet for nearly ten years, the sight still raised the hackles on the back of his neck—and the feline eyes burned a deep, lambent yellow for a moment. Both Knights paused, and their firm grip on Helsdon's shoulders held him in place while they were scanned. Then the gate swung open, stone valves grinding ominously. The *Ocelotl* officer stepped inside, muttered something, and then gestured for Helsdon to enter.

The engineer presumed such quarters would be filled with every kind of luxury. But instead, he found himself facing a slim, dark-haired, copper-skinned young man with perfectly regular features, in a room stacked with shipping crates and a series of oddly decorated freestanding screens. The young man was sitting on the edge of a table heaped with a fortune in papers and real books. On him, Fleet dress whites seemed more than a uniform, they seemed to glow under the strip lights in the ceiling, and the contrast with his dark skin was very striking. In full court regalia, an Imperial Prince would be almost invisible under the weight of a massive, jeweled feather-cloak and pendants and torques of gold.

But here, in this jumbled room, he exuded an effortless, almost irresistible authority. Only one dissonance caught at Malcolm's attention.

He seems . . . anachronistic, Helsdon thought. *Where are all of his electronics?* The Prince did not wear a medband or comm bracelet, or even an earbug. There was a velour-skinned sofa, but no chairs and no bed. A strange, not-entirely-unpleasant odor of musk and tobacco hung in the air. The engineer was frankly puzzled when he knelt before the Prince. As he did, he noticed the Jaguars had remained outside, leaving him—apparently—alone with the young man. He was no expert on court ritual and etiquette, but it seemed rash to let one slightly deranged Fleet *kika-no* within arm's reach of the Emperor's son. *But he must be well armed of himself. Aren't the Imperial Family supposed to be superhuman?*

"*Tlatocapilli*—great lord, son of the Light of the World—how may I—"

a Fleet Command staff, whole embassies, trade delegations, and a full regiment of marines. But here—as he and his escorts zipped along on a g-sled—most of the offices, or spaces for shops, were empty.

Only a combat crew aboard, he guessed. At one point they passed a pair of technicians rooting around in a series of access panels in an adjacent hallway. *Still doing the fit and finish work. So this heavyweight has been rushed into service.*

The sled passed through two checkpoints—both manned by more Jaguar Knights—and finally they found themselves in a tenanted precinct. Officers, technicians, and staff orderlies filled the passages, each moving with the kind of swift direction which implied a task of tremendous importance.

They dismounted in a double-height corridor lined with enormous mural-sized v-panes.

On the left side, as Helsdon hurried past, two towering volcanoes— the doomed lovers Popocatépetl and Iztaccíhuatl—loomed over a vast, bowl-like city drowned in night. But so great was the glow of lights and fires and refineries in the valley that it seemed filled with rivers of molten gold. Beyond the dim outline of the two peaks, the night sky was split by the blazing white-hot descent of an enormous meteor, which would in just moments smash into the plain of Tlaxcallan a hundred kilometers to the east. The streaking fire-trails of thousands of anti-ballistic missiles—launched by the México in a vain hope to destroy the incoming weapon—were frail in comparison.

That Blow—and even Helsdon, raised on a colony world far from the Center knew the story, which was a foundation stone of Imperial mythology—would shatter the neighboring province, triggering massive earthquakes which would level most of Imperial Tenochtitlán, and inspire a new ice age due to the dust thrown into the upper atmosphere. But all of this would not fatally wound the Empire and, indeed, the México reaction to the attack would carry their armies victoriously to every corner of the globe.

Curiously, Helsdon could not—in his half-addled state—recall the name of the adversary who had struck the Blow. *Must have been one of the European powers—was it Denmark? I cannot remember.*

To the right, the mural panels were dark, showing only intermittent static and a wandering glyph indicating the v-server attached to them had suffered some kind of file corruption problem.

dozens of black spots overlaid on a mosaic of pale blue and yellow lines. Their helmets, the visors currently opaque, rippled with stylized black and white feathers. Though entirely functional, the *Ocelototec* Mark Sixteen articulated combat suit contained a simple stealthing technology which allowed the wearer to adjust the surface patterning at will. At the moment, all three Jaguar Knights had their distinctive regimental colors and emblems dialed down—but Helsdon had seen them on military parade in Tenochtitlán itself, and knew they could, with the addition of brilliantly feathered nanomechanical cloaks, shine like the sun itself.

The officer—there were no obvious markings on his armor to indicate this, but Helsdon had a sense of the Knight from the way he carried himself—surveyed the room. The Jaguar's gaze settled on the engineer, which made Malcolm swallow nervously. *Not good; someone has realized I'm the "survivor."*

"The Prince Imperial will speak with you," the officer declared, his voice underlain by a vocoder-generated growl.

A firm grip helped him to his feet and down the hall. *I guess consent isn't required.* Wisely Helsdon made no protest, simply following along where directed. Any instinct to resist had been suppressed by his tremendous weariness. A tubecar put him and his escort at the main shuttle bay, which had previously been the *Calexico*'s cargo loading hangar. A mint-new shuttle was standing by, hull glittering with protostellar debris. He got a good look at the crest above the hatchway as he was hustled inside. *The Imperial household! They did mean "the Prince." Saint Ebba the Younger, preserve me from the attention of On High.*

The shuttle drifted into a boat-bay on the side of the *Tlemitl* which could have swallowed the *Calexico* whole. The descent of the passenger boat to the landing stage seemed almost ludicrous to Helsdon as he watched acres of freshly constructed pressure wall roll past the porthole. Even the seats on the shuttle were so new they squeaked. Professional curiosity drove him to eyeball the curve of the air intakes, and peer out at the flaps and lifting surfaces on the shuttle wing.

Two versions up, at least, from the last of these Tegus *models I worked on.*

Inside the super dreadnaught, he was struck by the emptiness of the passages. An SDN usually carried an enormous complement; freighting

ABOARD THE *CAN*

Kikan-shi Helsdon, formerly 2nd Engineer on the IMN DD-217 *Calexico*, squinted against the glare of a pair of work lights to see if he could help the shipnet specialist crammed down in the cramped bottom of a holotank housing. "Do we need to run in more power?"

The specialist coughed, his face spotted with flecks of data crystal interface cable. The sound echoed tinnily in the confined space. "Modelers always need more power, Engineer. And memory. And room. And . . . how long before somebody comes down here wanting to see a life-size model of the whole damned *kuub*?"

The other Mirror technicians in the upper chamber laughed. They were busy laying down conduit and hooking up racks of portable computation engines into the shipnet. The whine of cutting saws echoed from the outer corridor, along with the *pang-pang-pang* of a nail gun tacking up temporary wall sections.

Helsdon tried to grin. "Maybe we should have looked around when we appropriated this threatwell tank. Who knows what else Logistics threw in when they loaded up?"

"I could use less chatter in here," one of the other techs muttered, "and more computational help. The volume of this flux data is unbelievable. We're saturating the storage interface!"

"One moment," Helsdon replied, wiping his hands clean. "Got a place for me to work?" He crossed to a computer station jammed in next to the pair of double doors leading into the chamber and took a handheld v-pane unit from the Mirror technician.

The sandy-haired engineer had barely sat down on the floor—no chairs were available—and started to drill down into the configuration of the interfaces when three figures appeared, their imposing bulk blocking the entire doorway. They said nothing, but every technician in the room, including Helsdon, turned instinctively towards them.

The Imperial Jaguar Knights entered silently, their armor etched with

He thumbed a set of commands into the hand comp, one ear listening to the banter of the Khaid technicians below them at the main engineering panel. A red glyph began to flash on the little display and he covered the icon with his thumb, ready to press.

The hyperspace coil buried two decks below keened awake. His thumb mashed down—the glyph deformed—then disappeared. The ship spun up to gradient and then—with a shudder and a queasy slide—the *Wilful* was away as well, racing forward at transluminal speeds.

Vector confirmed, he thought, smiling to himself.

De Molay looked up at him questioningly. "What have you done?" she mouthed.

"A detour," he whispered. "When one door shuts, another opens.' "

On the display, Khaiden icons shook out into new positions.

"That is an odd formation," De Molay wheezed, trying to find a comfortable position. The hammock swayed a little.

"They're preparing for a hot combat jump," Hadeishi replied softly, feeling a trickle of adrenaline start up in his heart. Old familiar feelings—ones he'd thought lost, now welcome in their return—flooded him, watching the alien ships form up. "Heavies pentahedral at the core, lights orbiting at the edge of their combat interlink range. But . . . what is there to attack out here? No planets, no systems . . . not so much as a mining enclave in range."

De Molay snorted softly. She had recovered some color. "The hidden places are always busy, Nisei. There is an Imperial research station. Five or six light-years from here, I would venture. A secret . . . but not well kept, as we see."

He looked over his shoulder, one eyebrow raised. "You were bound there yourself?"

"The *Wilful*? Not directly." She tapped him gently on the shoulder with gnarled fingertips. "*Your* destination, Captain Hadeishi, is a little grander . . . one of our sister ships should have been waiting for us at that moon. I wonder if they suffered our fate, only earlier. Unless they were delayed and have yet to reach rendezvous."

Mitsuharu breathed deeply, calming a sudden burst of outrage. *So— I've been deceived and carted about like a sack of meal! Hmmm . . . but who would want me out in this desolation?*

"Ah, see? The Khaid fleet is underway." De Molay's voice was a bare whisper.

Indeed, the enemy was rippling out of sight into hyperspace.

"Three waves. Then us." *In this soup*, Hadeishi thought, *they'll be on top of the station without the slightest warning.*

He thumbed through a series of other views, tapping each ship's system in turn. The hyperspace coil reported coordinates for transit had been locked in and the freighter was quickly approaching gradient. Mitsuharu's eyes narrowed, but a quick flip back to the navigation feed confirmed what he'd expected—hoped!—when he'd seen the Khaid combat pattern.

We're plotted for a different vector. For some frontier depot with a prize crew aboard. Useless in a fight, but too valuable for these scavengers to leave behind. Excellent.

Hadeishi sat in deep gloom, only the barest slivers of light shining on the pipes overhead. One boot was edged against the fuel valve at the top of an enormous tank of reaction mass, the other tucked under him as a makeshift seat. De Molay, tucked into the hammock again, was only a hand-span away, almost invisible in the darkness. The string net was suspended from a series of overhead pipes. Below them, intermittent sounds echoed up from the engineering spaces as two Khaid engineers banged around, trying to decipher the *Wilful*'s control systems. Hadeishi had put the rest of their supplies—everything he could gather up in the time allowed—in another bag, which also hung from a lanyard.

A burst of harsh chatter rose up to them, and the entire ship shuddered with a sharp, reverberating *clang-clang-clang*. De Molay shifted, and Mitsuharu heard her whisper: "We've separated."

He nodded, judging the sounds the same way. Their suspicions were confirmed a few moments later when the entire ship shivered awake and the pumps attached to the fuel tanks hummed into action. *We're on maneuvering drive,* Mitsuharu thought.

His fingertips reached out, confirmed the location of the machete, and then he leaned close enough to the freighter captain to feel her faint, thready breath on the side of his face. "They are preparing to take us into hyperspace."

Hadeishi twisted around, putting his back to her, and held up a comp he'd appropriated from one of the equipment lockers. The tiny screen displayed a telemetry feed relayed from the navigational system. The whole Khaid fleet was in motion.

"So many ships," whispered De Molay. "That doesn't seem like a raiding party. . . ."

Mitsuharu shook his head. "This is a fleet. The first I've ever seen—or heard—of the Khaid assembling. Something—larger—is underway."

Then she glanced over at Gretchen. "Dr. Anderssen, a pleasure to see you again. Do you know what is happening here? What all of this is about?"

"I do," Hummingbird interrupted at once.

The *Chu-sa* flashed a tiny, cold smile.

Gretchen wanted to smile, too, but thought it wise to mind her own business. She could feel Hummingbird's anger starting to rise. She knew perfectly well the *nauallis* did not like to barter. *He needs something very badly, or he would not be prepared to horse-trade.* She sat down on her duffle—the console was like ice—and reached into her jacket for a Gogozen bar. *Maybe I should record this,* she mused, *for posterity.*

cargo hold was actually part of the exterior hull of the warship, which carried the shipskin, weapons, boat and cargo bays, and so on. The secondary hull—probably twenty meters inward from their current position—would be warm and toasty. Gretchen looked around, sighed, and parked her duffle and backpack against the foot of a control console. Then Anderssen leaned back against the metal, arms crossed, and nodded politely to the Imperial ship captain. *This one looks very familiar, where . . . ah now, it's Captain Hadeishi's second! I haven't seen her since that embassy reception on Jagan.*

Koshō's attention was wholly upon Green Hummingbird, and she radiated an icy distaste which matched the room temperature. The strength of her animosity was refreshing to Gretchen, for the Nisei woman evinced not the slightest fear, respect, or deference for the old Crow. *That is more like it!*

"I see," the *Chu-sa* said, lifting her chin slightly. "Now everything is perfectly clear to me."

"Excellent," Hummingbird replied, setting down his own luggage. "Then I need not explain. We require a private room with bath, shipnet access, and transport to the science station I believe the Mirror Which Reveals is operating not too far from here. And quietly, too," Hummingbird said. "This is a privy matter."

"Is it?" Koshō gave him a steely glare. "I am entirely familiar with *my* operational orders, Hummingbird-*tzin*. Your . . . faction . . . is not welcome here—your presence forbidden." The faintest smile threatened to disturb the cold perfection of her lips. "I could have you both shot, buying myself the favor of the Mirror with the same flechette. A bargain, I think!"

Hummingbird became very still. Gretchen watched, wide-eyed, wondering if the sense of sharp, coiled fury she felt from the Imperial officer was apparent to the *nauallis*. *Damn,* Anderssen thought, *her fingertips are on her sidearm! Is she going to chop him down right here?*

The old México's eyes narrowed and he shifted his stance subtly. Then, apparently rallying himself, he said: "Your *sensei* still lives, *Chu-sa*, as I promised. And he prospers."

"Proof?" Susan tilted her head slightly to one side, almond-shaped eyes bare slits gleaming with reflected light from the boat bay.

"My word upon it."

"Utterly without value." Koshō's free hand made a chopping motion.

Gretchen snorted in disgust, knowing full well there was *no way* the old México had planned this. "You know, Crow, you remind me of my first field instructor. She really didn't know what she was doing. She didn't plan. She was clumsy and forgetful. Disasters followed her everywhere, but something always happened to make her look great. She eventually wandered up a pyramid on Go-Long in the rainy season and was struck by lightning."

Socho Juarez returned, his expression thunderous. "The *Chu-sa* will speak with you." He jerked an armored thumb at two of the marines. "*Heicho* Gozen, Chayle, the captain is waiting for them in the loading bay overlook."

"We'll need our luggage," Hummingbird interjected, radiating an aura of perfect reasonability. "It will only take a moment, and save time later." Juarez just stared in bafflement. The *nauallis* slowly lowered his hands, gathered up his spare mantle, the hand comp, and gestured for Gretchen to precede him out of the control space. Both marine corporals—shipguns at the ready—followed along, a little nonplussed themselves.

Behind them, Juarez shook his head, finger to his earbug. "Are you sure, *Chu-sa*? This whole ship stinks of an infiltrator. . . . *Hai, hai.* They're on their way."

Clattering down the gangway from the *Moulins*, half-blinded by the brilliant glare of the spotlights illuminating the enormous hold, Gretchen shifted her duffle and backpack, feeling the straps dig into her shoulder. "But the native people that lived nearby said they had seen a bright angel escape from her body. So they built a shrine so they could pray to her for good luck."

Hummingbird said nothing, breath frosting in the chill air, his attention fixed on a petite figure in dress-whites looking down upon them from a glassite window halfway up the side of the bay. His two travel bags—made from some heavy synthetic and badly worn, some holes patched over with dozens of transfer stickers—hung heavy in his hands as he walked.

"I like that story," he replied, after a moment. The marines keyed open a passenger door and they stepped aboard the *Naniwa*.

The overlook was entirely lacking any amenities—no chairs, no soft couches, no dispenser filled with cold drinks. No heat to speak of, as the

to hear. Her expression turned quite remarkably sour, as though she'd bitten into a rotten persimmon. Oc Chac waited, his curiosity obvious, while the *Chu-sa* stared distantly at the threatwell. When she turned to him, he straightened, hands clasped behind his back. "*Kyo?*"

"Loading bay one between the engine ring and the main holds—do we have something stowed there?"

"*Iie, Kyo*, Fleet regulations indicate the exterior bays are only for—"

"*Sho-sa*, prep the bay to tether that ship. I want it inside our coil field as quickly as we can." She looked away. "*Socho* Juarez, we're bringing you inboard, but I want a squad on-board at all times, and bring in some *Zosen* to tear it apart—hidden compartments, look for everything. . . ."

"*Hai, kyo!*"

On the bridge of the *Moulins*, Hummingbird watched with equanimity as the gaping maw of the battle-cruiser's rear cargo hold enveloped them. He was keeping an eye on his comp, which chirped pleasantly a moment after they were fully inside the Imperial ship. Anderssen frowned—her hands were clasped on the top of her head, just like Captain Locke and the pilot—and she was staring down the barrel of an Imperial shipgun. The *nauallis'* comp was sitting on a side console, still plugged into the freighter's shipnet, and seemed to be quite busy.

"Who are you talking to with that thing?" she hissed out of the side of her mouth.

"There has been correspondence with the battle-cruiser's navigational system," the *nauallis* said. "Are your bags packed?"

"Of course," she growled, and then fell silent. One of the marines—his black-on-black nameplate seemed to say Juarez—had noticed their conversation and came over, expression grim.

Before the Imperial could say anything, however, Hummingbird nodded pleasantly and said: "*Socho*, please consider my credentials before doing anything rash. I am an Imperial *Tlamantinime*—a Judge—on official business. This woman is my assistant and we appreciate your commander's efforts in picking us up." He twisted his wrist, exposing a comm band, and then submitted quietly as the marine scanned his various forms of identification.

"Huh." Juarez pursed his lips, looked the motley set of them over, and then turned away, speaking into his throatmike.

Then she sat back, feeling a cold shiver of adrenaline course through her limbs as the Klaxon sounded, and her bad mood vanished like the morning frost from the eaves. *Smartly now,* she thought, watching the bridge crew in action. *Mitsuharu would be pleased to see their progress.*

"*Chu-sa?*" Oc Chac looked up from his own console, his chiseled face gleaming as the overheads flashed three times. "Battlecast needs an update on our course correction. Should I—"

She shook her head, *no.* "Let's see what we've beaten from cover, first, *Sho-sa.* Then I'll report to the various admirals."

The *Naniwa* cut in quite nimbly, Susan was pleased to see, using the particle storm kicked up by the *Tlemitl*'s passage as a hunting screen, and Juarez' combat teams had dropped alongside the tiny ship with two shuttles before there was any indication the intruders realized they'd been seen.

Koshō listened intently, a constellation of v-feeds from marine armor cameras unspooling on her main console, as the *Socho* and his men cracked two airlocks simultaneously and secured the ship. There was some chatter from the inhabitants, but by then the engines were locked out.

She raised an eyebrow, looking questioningly at Oc Chac.

"Registry, *Sho-sa?*"

"The *Moulins, kyo.* A 'merchanter for hire' out of Denby 47. No more than an asteroid with a hydrogen cracking station and fueling gantry. If memory serves, Denby lies within the jurisdiction of New Malta."

"A Templar ship?" Koshō was intrigued. "Or even Norsk?"

Oc Chac grimaced. "The Europeans would be mad to meddle in the Prince's affairs, *kyo.* But the knight-priests? They might find it amusing to trick about at his tail, all unseen."

Susan folded her slim arms and stared apprehensively at the multiplane view afforded by the threatwell. *This place is drawing far too many players. All for a hazard to navigation? No—the Mirror must think they can gain control of the weapon, or whatever it is, and turn it to our use. But why did the Prince arrive so late? He was never late to any affaire or affray before . . . curious. Very curious.* She tapped open the Marine command circuit.

"*Socho* Juarez, what do we have for passengers?"

His report, brisk and efficient as it was, was *not* what Koshō wanted

what I think of the Flowery Prince, his personal attributes, or his social history. She tapped her earbug angrily.

"*Chu-i* Pucatli, please send appropriate greetings to Prince Xochitl aboard *Tlemitl* on behalf of myself and the crew of *Naniwa.*"

Then she turned back to her XO. "*Sho-sa* Oc, get us out of the *Firearrow*'s drive plume. Send *Naniwa* wide, then curve back to the patrol pattern. That should avoid any radiation wake behind that behemoth."

"*Hai, Chu-sa!*"

Susan tried to turn her attention back to reviewing the latest supplies and munitions projections from Logistics, but the constant chatter on the battle-group stellarcast—which she had spooling on one of her earbug channels—was afire with speculation. *Tlemitl* had not 'cast the usual greeting or pleasantries, though the massive ship's course was clear—dead on to the *Can.*

The thought of Xocoyotl's reaction to being usurped by the Prince, who outranked the vice admiral in every possible way, did lighten her mood a little. But she did not relish the prospect of managing both of them.

Sixty-two minutes later, as the *Naniwa* completed her course correction, an alarm sounded from the Navigation station.

"*Chu-sa!*" the navigator said sharply, looking up from his console. "Unknown signature on the plot! We have an intruder in our patrol box."

"Where?" *Thai-i* Konev at Weapons looked keen to exercise his systems.

"Report," Susan said, her voice calm and controlled. Her own displays were already adjusting, with threat analysis panes opening up. "Size—heading—something pertinent, *Thai-i* Holloway."

"Pretty small, *kyo*, about sixty meters long. It's piggybacking in the *Tlemitl*'s wake. Signature is intermittent—" Holloway swallowed a curse, as the icon suddenly vanished from the threatwell.

"Project location from the data we've already captured, *Thai-i*. Lock heading as soon as we've caught sight of her again." Koshō looked to Pucatli, who was sitting in at comm for the usual first-watch officer. "Signal battle stations to all hands, *Chu-i*. Immediate intercept. Unauthorized ship of unknown flag. Guns live. This is not a drill. Load missile racks one and two. Direct *Socho* Juarez to ready two teams for board and seizure."

THE *NANIWA*

Koshō happened to be reviewing battle-group dispositions in preparation for ordering a change in heading for the next leg of their patrol pattern, when a bright spark popped into view on the threatwell. Her eyes widened, then flicked to the ident code glyphs popping up around the speeding mote.

"*Kiken-na!*" she snapped, outraged. "Evasive action, *Thai-i*, cut to starboard at maximum burn."

The lieutenants at the navigation and pilot stations were already in motion and acceleration alarm Klaxons blared the length of the ship. *Naniwa's* frame groaned, antimatter-powered drives kicking into maximum thrust, and Koshō watched, face impassive, as they cut away from intercept.

A moment later, as the g-decking stabilized, *Sho-sa* Oc Chac was in Command as well, sliding into his own shockchair. He seemed a little wide-eyed, given the abrupt maneuver.

"*Chu-sa?*"

Susan did not answer for a moment, her face hard-set, brows furrowed. She was watching the conversation between the *Naniwa's* 'cast system and the intruder. Camera images of the oncoming ship began to unfold on her panel, and the ident system chirped, yielding a verified identification.

"IMN SDN-6 *Tlemitl* has joined the battle-group," she said at last, her lips a tight, hard line. "Under the command of the Prince Imperial Xochitl, Admiral of the Fleet." She sat back in her shockchair and forced her hands to stillness. "What is he doing here in the *Firearrow*? There isn't a 3-v camera within light-years! I should . . ."

"*Kyo*," Oc Chac ventured to interrupt, his black eyes curious. "Do you know the *Gensui*?"

"We were in school together," Koshō bit out. *And I will not tell you*

So, she thought, feeling Hummingbird's tension ratcheting up with each second. The pilot had the maneuver engines on restart and Captain Locke had pitched in to bring up the hyperspace coil. But she could tell it was all going far, far too slowly for the Crow's frayed patience.

"Hm," she said, drawing a baleful gaze. "He's the pretty one, isn't he? With the hair?"

Locke nodded, swallowing hard. His hands clenched on the arms of his chair.

Gretchen was glad—she'd had the thought before—she'd already had her quota of children. *Though just one more . . . no, it's too late for that.*

Twelve minutes later the *Moulins* groaned, her hull hammered by successive waves of particles—all hot and glowing with borrowed radiation—as the massive ship rolled past.

"A super-dreadnaught," whispered the pilot in awe, camera interpolation yielding an enormous outline through the curtains of fire. "It must be four kilometers long, or more!"

Hummingbird was working his stylus in a quick, efficient blur on a hand comp. A lead had been jacked from the unit into the control consoles and Gretchen jumped slightly when he suddenly cursed aloud. Locke and the pilot turned in alarm.

"Xochitl!" The sound was harsh, abrupt.

Hummingbird stared at his comp, right eyelid twitching. Then, after a stiff moment with everyone staring at him, he looked up. "Captain Locke, spin up the mains as soon as we're in the thrust shadow of that monster."

"Delicate flower?" Gretchen ventured. "I've heard that name before."

"One of the Princes Imperial has arrived," the old *nauallis* answered, looking at her sidelong. She had been around him long enough to glimpse anger and unease behind his usual stoic mask. *Could our all-seeing sorcerer be worried?* Gretchen struggled to suppress a grin.

"We have to get in there immediately." Hummingbird glared at Locke.

Xochitl—I remember, that's "precious flower"—now where . . . Ah! Of course.

A flurry of 3-v magazine covers, each more lurid than the last, came to mind. Page after page of *Temple of Truth* filled with "candid" snaps of a young, heartbreakingly handsome man. The foremost of the Emperor's "Mighty Sons," Prince Xochitl was not the eldest, but he did shine the brightest in popular culture. A victorious Fleet commander—he'd driven the Kroomākh back from Al-Haram, recapturing two colony worlds and a series of critical mining stations—and a notorious duelist who had left a long trail of broken hearts and honorable deaths behind him.

"Reckless idiot!" Locke shook his head in dismay, and then eyed Hummingbird. "This the one you're waiting for?"

"Target's v is pushing the limit for this particle density." The pilot sounded impressed. "It's big and must be packing a serious set of deflector generators! I wonder if—"

Locke snorted, saying: "I don't think he can see any better in this than—"

"Go dark!" Hummingbird's voice was sharp as a knife and filled with an unmistakable tone of command. Without even thinking, the pilot jerked around in his seat, both hands busy on the controls. The level of ambient noise in the control space suddenly dropped and every light shaded down to a dull red, or turned off entirely. The sound of the air circulators ceased and the constant, low-level vibration in the decking stuttered and then died.

"Captain, we are at zero emissions," the pilot reported in a low voice. "Gravity generators are cold. Engines are cold."

Gretchen was interested in Locke's reaction—Hummingbird had given direct orders on his bridge—but the freighter captain seemed unperturbed. *If he'd noticed at all?* Anderssen found that peculiar, but the captain had been treating the old *nauallis* very deferentially for the last week. *I need to look up what Præceptor means.*

The icon on the navigation board continued to show swift progress and Gretchen, peering over Hummingbird's shoulder, suddenly realized that another icon—one shining green with a blue band around it—must be the *Moulins*. Which meant . . .

On the camera screens, a point of blue-violet light suddenly became visible. As she watched, it grew in size, resolving into a black speck surrounded by a brilliantly colored corona of violently excited particles. The wake of the approaching starship quickly became apparent as a corkscrew-like fan of burning motes.

The pilot cursed, looking first to Locke and then to Hummingbird. "Radiation from that drive plume is going to slam us hard. We need to—"

"Hold position." The Crow's voice was steely and his demeanor inflexible. "They are blinding their own sensors with all that electromagnetic trash. If we remain still, they will race past, unknowing. Otherwise, we'll be a fine target for a sprint missile or a particle beam practice."

puzzle that would elude everyone else, even him. This is not going to be pleasant.

She clipped on her medband and comm bracelet, swung out of the tiny bunk, and found her jacket, comp, and other tools. The *Moulins* had been poking along in the dark, following an uneven, zigzag course for several days. But now, she had a sense the ship had stopped moving. *Have we arrived?* she wondered. "Time to find out."

After a detour by the mess deck to fill her mug with hot, weak *kaffe*—the dispenser seemed programmed to produce the most wretched version of anything requested—Gretchen climbed the gangway to the control spaces. Captain Locke, the pilot, and Hummingbird were sitting, watching the navigational displays with varying degrees of boredom. The screens showing the exterior view of the *Moulins* were filled with gorgeous, glowing dust clouds in every shade of red, violet, and viridian. Streamers of iridescent material arced across the field of view. Embedded in the murk—were they distant pulsars, or stars almost swallowed by this wrack?—were hot points of light.

Anderssen slipped into the creaking, cracked-leather chair beside the old *nauallis* and strapped herself in.

"What's happening?"

Hummingbird turned slightly, his weathered old face impassive. "We've found what seems to be an Imperial battle-group. Most of the ships are stationary, but some are working patrol patterns around this whole area."

"But we're waiting?" She felt itchy, knowing that the artifact—her life's work if she could but touch it—might only be light-minutes away. "What for?"

"The right ship. And the right commander." His voice was very low, only barely audible to her, even sitting in the adjacent seat.

"So, we're thinking weeks parked here in the dark, watching the pretty lights?" Her light tone did not move him.

Instead, he nodded minutely. "If need be."

A chime sounded from one of the console panels and a series of glyphs strobed on the main board. The pilot leaned over, interested. His stylus circled a moving icon on the display and the view focused in. Velocity and heading figures appeared in a sidebar.

NEAR THE PINHOLE

Anderssen woke abruptly, finding herself in near-darkness, and for a moment she was certain the roof above was formed of bronze-colored metal, metal which gleamed and flickered with the light of constantly moving streams of flame. Something like wraiths, or fiery shadows, which moved throughout the tower around her, which tenanted the streets below, and darted through sullen, amber-colored skies above.

Her mouth was filled with a hard, metallic taste and she tried to muster enough spit to clear her palate. *Gods, what did I drink last night?* She could not remember drinking anything harder than tea.

Sitting in the darkness, Gretchen flexed her fingers, tied back her hair, and groped around for her comm band. She found the bracelet by touch and turned the device over. The cool blue glow of the readouts steadied her and the last of the flickering, flame-tenanted shadows faded from the edges of her vision.

"I see," she said aloud, suddenly wishing she'd brought Malakar along to watch over her while she slept. *Or Parker, or Magdalena! Where are my friends, my team? In the old days I would never have hared off like this without them.* The thought brought her up short and Anderssen realized—with a chill shock—that she had placed herself in a very precarious position. *I am out here, in the middle of nowhere, with a crazy old sorcerer and a crew of religious fanatics, looking for . . . something . . . which by all rights aught be left well enough alone. Holy Mary of the Roses, what was I thinking? Magdalena would give me such a cuffing!*

Then she decided that Hummingbird had jobbed her again with his measly five hundred thousand quills. *And why did he pay that out?* she wondered. *He must be desperate for . . . for a washed-up, out-of-work, out-of-her mind xenoarchaeologist. He could rent a graduate student from the Company for almost nothing!*

The obvious reason was disturbing. *He knows about my talent, and how it's grown. He's expecting me to be able to find all of the pieces of some*

howling like a demon, and the chill cut through Musashi's cloak like a
knife. Arrayed across the road, their own furs white and almost invisible
against the blowing snow, stood a line of men with drawn blades. In his
ear, Musashi heard the blind man sniff once, then twice. "Ah, idiot
donkey—why have you angered the shugenja? *Now we shall be late. . . ."*

The engineering panel was not equipped to generate a full-up
threatwell display, but Hadeishi could read the swarm of glyphs and
icons as well as any Fleet officer. De Molay opened one eye, peering at
him from the hammock. "Well, engineer's mate, where are we going?"

"That, I cannot tell. But we have found company . . . two dozen
Khaid warships, I would judge—some of them larger than I've ever
seen under their colors before—and we are all on the same heading."

He stepped away from the console, thinking. "I'm going to have to
find a place to hide you, *Sencho*. The Khaid prize crew will come around
soon enough."

"Main shipnet relay from the bridge to down below, *kyo*."

"And how did you know it was there?" She was frowning, and had the old woman her full strength, her expression would have been formidable.

Hadeishi shrugged. "*Sencho*, I have many bad habits."

Slinging her on his back again, Mitsuharu set off for his old quarters behind the fuel tanks.

Winter rain was pouring down, setting the mountainside streams to rushing, white-frothed torrents. Musashi was climbing the pass under Mount Murou, a plain wooden staff in each hand. A bitterly cold wind howled, nipping at his face, etching white streaks on the wolf-skin he wore as a cape. The old blind man clinging to his back was cursing endlessly, complaining about every jounce and jolt in the road as the swordsman climbed, step by step, his feet bleeding in the straw sandals, towards the summit of the pass. If he missed a step, the old man would strike the side of Musashi's head with a begging bowl and shout—"donkey!"—over the hiss of the wind.

De Molay slumped into Hadeishi's hammock with a relieved groan. Her face was very pale, her skin waxy. Mitsuharu pulled one of the bottles of Mayahuel from his leg pockets and popped the cap. The old woman drank noisily, but seemed a bit revived when he took the empty away.

The main engineering console had been shorted out, which Hadeishi found a crude but effective way to prevent its use, but the secondary panels were still active. He retrieved his stylus from a corner and keyed up the interface. "*Kyo*, what code should I use?" he asked, looking to De Molay.

"Hierusalem," she said, and then spelled out the Latinate word for him. The panel quickened to life, showing a wholly different interface than he'd ever had access to before. Both of Hadeishi's eyebrows rose in surprise, then he quickly navigated through the sensor options to find the transit display.

At the summit of the pass, where Toudai temple had once stood, there was a ring of shattered pillars and broken stones. Here the icy wind was

Moments later, with the bridge hatch propped open once more, Hadeishi was climbing down a service tube running between the decks, with Captain De Molay clinging to his shoulders. The old woman was light enough to carry, but no burden he wanted to freight for hours. A clumsy set of straps tied them together, and he could do no better with the time allowed.

He could feel, from the vibration of the ship, that the *Wilful* was underway, though her engines were still cold. Hadeishi assumed the *Qalak* was accelerating away from the ambush point and spinning up gradient. Hadeishi was hoping to find somewhere for them both to hole up before—

The dim lights in the shaft flickered—his stomach sprang up, reversed, and crawled back down his throat. De Molay groaned, her abdomen clenching in protest. She gagged, but managed to choke down the vomit.

"We're away," Mitsuharu said, when he felt steady enough to resume climbing down. "And who can tell where we're heading?"

"I can," De Molay wheezed, "if we can get access to a control panel in engineering."

"*Hai, kyo.* At our first opportunity." They reached a junction between decks and Hadeishi struggled to step off the ladder and onto the service door landing. De Molay had to help, grasping at a stanchion with her weak hands, while he navigated the corner. Then Mitsuharu keyed through the door and saw they had descended far enough to reach the lower cargo deck.

"Wait here, *kyo*," he muttered, setting her down. "I need to set some insurance."

Back in the maintenance shaft, he tore open a series of access panels until he found an orange-colored conduit the thickness of his wrist. Gingerly—who knew how stable the substance was!—he tacked the blasting putty behind the communications main and then wedged the remote detonator into place. Working his way back to the corridor, he closed and locked the entrance to the shaft and then checked the detonator relay.

Cupped in his hand, the status light shone a pale green.

"What did you mine?" De Molay asked, peering up at him from the floor. She was still too weak to stand.

low idle, reactors were cooking, and every kind of weapon on the ship had been gathered up by the Khaid and hauled away.

Well, he thought, *almost everything*. He patted the machete.

"You're our new engineers-mate then," De Molay wheezed, trying not to cough. "Azulcay said you were showing some promise."

"Kind of him," Mitsuharu replied, glancing over at the main hatchway. The door was locked and barred, though he knew there was a shipbug swarm busily cleaning up the blood sprayed across the floor and walls outside. The thought still turned his stomach. "Are there any explosives on board? Grenades?"

"If the bastards didn't take it," she coughed, pointing at the bridge gun locker—whose door was hanging open, the locks sprung. "There might be some blasting putty in there. I keep some on hand when we have to clear a landing zone."

Hadeishi nodded, distracted by a faint tremor suddenly running through the floor and making his fingertips buzz on the control panes. He checked the exterior camera feeds, and saw the *Qalak*'s shipskin was deforming. The forests of radiating fins were drawing inward, while the destroyer's transit drive foils were unwinding.

"She's prepping to jump and take us with her. Finish that *kaffe*, *kyo*, we're going to have to move."

"Move where?" De Molay managed to lift her mug and drain the rest of the sludge. "Two poor pilgrims are we, with only one tired horse— not even one we can fly out of here!"

"No, not yet." Hadeishi rummaged quickly through the gun locker— twice looted between the *Wilful*'s crew and the Khaid—and came up with a half-used cylinder of grayish putty, no more than a finger in length. "No triggers?"

"Not in there, child." De Molay attempted a smile, which made her cheek twinge. "Stowage bin beside the captain's chair, the one with the broken lock."

"Ah." Hadeishi fished out three putty triggers, one of which was a remote-controlled detonator. "*Dōmo arigatō.*" The triggers went into one pocket, the putty into another.

On the camera pane pointing down the gangway into the *Qalak* there was sudden motion. Mitsuharu leaned over, caught sight of four Khaid in z-suits strolling across the gangway, and motioned to De Molay. "Time to go, *Sencho-sana*."

hear through his helmet. Suppressing an urge to vomit, Mitsuharu kept to the edge of the room and made a quick exit out the far door.

Breathing fast, Hadeishi forced himself to stop—now he was in a short corridor leading back to the roundabout—and he was suddenly afraid he'd walked out in full view of any Khaiden camera pointing down the gangway between the two ships. Luckily, the corridor was not in line with the airlock itself. Breathing a sigh of relief, he ducked across to the other side of the passage and was about to chance angling back to the cross-roads to get to the bridge itself when he realized that the thick trail of blood and offal leading into the charnel room had a companion. Not much more than a scrape of blood here and there, but a clear sign that someone had come out of the slaughterhouse—crawled across the corridor on hands and knees—and through a door at the end of the passage.

Well now, they missed someone on their sweep. He followed the trail down a short maintenance passage filled with racked air filtration membranes and into a space holding the plumbing risers for the bathrooms.

The blood trail led into an opening beneath the gray water return. Taking a risk, Mitsuharu cracked open his z-suit helmet, set down the pry bar, and then knelt on the deck, peering under the pipes.

The dim glow of his helmet lamp glittered back from a pair of pale gray eyes.

An elderly, silver-haired woman was squeezed in among the plumbing, her jumpsuit caked with blood, her face gashed open. Now he could hear her labored breathing and see the muzzle of an automatic—a Webley Bulldog, from what he could see—pointed in his general direction.

"*Sencho*," he said quietly, recognizing the rank tabs on her collar. "I'd better get you out of there."

An hour later, on the bridge, Captain De Molay was lying back on the pilot's shockchair, her face bandaged and a mug of instant *kaffe* clutched in hands shining with antibiotic biogel. She looked only marginally better and her breathing was still hoarse. Hadeishi was sitting at the captain's panel, carefully paging through the onboard cameras, a long machete-like knife close by his hand, and two different earbugs inserted. The *Wilful*'s systems were more of a hodgepodge than he'd believed, but on-board power was up, the transit coil was spun down to a

Why the Khaid—who were not one of the insectoid species known to the México—employed the shipbug, Hadeishi did not know. One intel briefing he had seen suggested the Khaiden themselves had once been a subject race of the Kryg'nth or Megair and had adopted some of their past masters' technologies and practices. Too, he understood they found the insects a delicacy. He found the bugs loathsome and stayed back, out of the room, until the swarm had departed for some other corpse-strewn pasture.

Then he forced himself to search through the remains of the two men, and gathered up their identity cards, pocket multitools, and anything else of use he could find. The refrigerator in the rec area also yielded up more to eat and two bottles of Mayahuel brand beer, which he stowed in the leg pockets of his z-suit.

Do they have a handler? he wondered, thinking of the shipbugs again. *So far they are the only sign of life. . . . Perhaps the Khaid close off the ship, let the bugs scour everything clean, and then come in to gather them up. All fat and juicy and . . .* He spat violently in the sink, then wiped his mouth. *I need to find a real command console with access to all of the security cameras.*

Hadeishi crouched at the junction between the shipcore and an access way to the main passenger airlock, morbidly amused to stand no more than a meter from where he'd been marched out in chains no more than an hour earlier. This time the roundabout was empty— all of the bodies had been dragged away and the Khaid marines were gone. Cautious, Mitsuharu held a small mirror mounted on a telescoping handle around the corner, looking for the expected guards. The airlock itself was open, but no one seemed to be in the gangway leading to the *Qalak. There must be someone just out of sight on the other side. . . .*

Wary of showing himself in the crossroads, Mitsuharu backtracked to the nearest door and slipped inside. The room was one of a set ringing the top of the shipcore and seemed to be sleeping quarters for four. On the far side was a sliding doorway leading into a shared bathroom. Hadeishi wasted no time in passing through, giving the fresher a quick once-over—no weapons or tools—and then easing open the doorway to the second bunkroom.

Here he found the bodies from the roundabout and bridge. They were thrown in a heap—and the *tik-tik-tik* of the shipbugs was loud enough to

could get to his feet, Mitsuharu shuffled down to the cargo master's office—really no more than a closet with controls to manage the gangways and cranes—and rummaged through the storage bins. This yielded up a Gogozen bar—a kind of high-fat candy he usually avoided, but now stuffed into his mouth without delay—and far better, three cans of Kuka-Kolo—a carbonated *chocolatl* beverage sweetened with the sap of the Nopal cactus. When all three were drained dry, Hadeishi began to feel human again. *Ah, sugar. Very delicious. Now I need a weapon, or more than one.*

He missed the grenades, but they seemed to have done well by the Khaid shuttle.

After searching the closet one more time, Hadeishi signed into the shipboard net and paged through the security camera views available to him. Restricted to below-decks, he found nothing in ten fruitless minutes. *No Khaid down below . . . they must be up on the bridge.*

Picking up a long pry bar stowed behind the comp panels, Mitsuharu slipped out of the closet and made his way towards the shipcore with his helmet external audio turned up, listening for anything beyond the usual groaning and hissing of the old ship.

The starboard cargo lift rattled to a halt on the accommodation deck— not an area Hadeishi had ever set foot in before—and he eased out, pry bar in both hands like a bat, and stepped lightly towards the shipcore. Almost immediately he encountered a rec room strewn with burned fabric and paper, fallen *kaffe* cups, and broken plates. His boots crunched on scattered shipgun flechettes, and the walls and cupboards were badly torn up. Two bodies lay sprawled on the floor—both wearing the jumpsuits favored by the *Wilful's* crew—and as he gingerly approached, they convulsed with a rippling wave of motion.

"Shipbugs," Mitsuharu muttered under his breath, skipping backward, face twisting in disgust.

Both corpses collapsed into a tatter of cloth and white bone. The Khaid shipbugs, an insectile omnivore about the length of his thumb, swarmed across the floor, their silvery carapaces making a queer, shimmering mass. Hundreds of antennae turned in his direction, waved about tasting the air, and then the entire swarm turned away with a rustling *tik-tik-tik*, looking for more decomposing organics to consume.

He switched off the plasma cutter and curled himself up into a ball. It was a long fall to the freighter and he hoped—devoutly prayed—that the Khaiden commander on the *Qalak* didn't decide to turn on full active scanning for the immediate volume around his ship. *Then I would fry like a sweet dumpling!*

At two hundred forty-five seconds a wave of metallic debris, intermixed with charred cushions, chunks of piping, internal framing, and bits of z-suit accelerated past him. Buffeted by the flotsam, he looked back and saw that the entire shuttle had vanished in a blast cloud. The Khaid marines—barely visible at this range—were in equal disarray. *Score one for the army! Good thing, too,* he thought. *That combat armor will sport an IR mode for extravehicular combat.* Gritting his teeth, he dialed down his suit temperature regulator. *Can't go to zero, but I can draw down my signature. . . .*

Sixteen minutes later, his limbs numb with cold and his radiation monitor strobing red, Hadeishi collided with cargo hold B on the *Wilful*'s port quarter. Shocked out of a hypothermia-induced daze, he bounced along the pitted, scarred surface of the freighter for five or six seconds until he managed to get his hands flat against the metal hull and his z-suit adhered. The jerky stop sent stabbing pains up each arm, but he managed to hold on. *Ah, now that hurt.*

Now able to dial up his suit temperature, Mitsuharu scrabbled along on all fours, looking for the nearest airlock. If memory served, there was a cargo door between two of the drive fairings. The last six meters seemed a vast distance, but he managed to drag himself to the control panel and punch in his access code. Human-friendly lights flickered on inside the lock chamber and he fell in, feeling utterly drained. Hands shaking, Mitsuharu managed to get the outer lock closed and atmosphere cycling before he collapsed.

Gravity kicked in as he lay on the floor, inner door rotating open. For a long moment Hadeishi couldn't even lift his head, but when he could, the cargo hold access way was empty. No alarms had triggered, no sirens sounded. *Khaid haven't reprogrammed the ship yet.*

Dragging himself over the threshold, Hadeishi managed to prop himself against the nearest wall and close the hatch. His hands and feet were getting warmer, and he felt some strength returning. When he

the edge of the opening, Hadeishi waited for the right moment—then he saw the port-side passenger door slide past—and he sprang outward, hands and feet outstretched.

He hit the side of the shuttle with a heavy thud, let his knees and elbows flex to absorb as much impact as possible, and then flattened himself against the hull. Seconds later, the Khaid shuttle had cleared the *Qalak* and the entire spaceframe shivered as its main engines went into pre-ignition.

Two hundred seconds. A cool sensation tickled his left wrist as his med-band started to inject anti-radiation meds. Ignoring the sensation, Hadeishi scuttled forward to the passenger door and peered inside.

Perfect, he thought, suppressing a laugh. A Khaid sailor in a blue-and-black z-suit was just inside, watching an environmental control panel as the shuttle started to pick up speed. After a moment of preparation, Mitsuharu began banging hard on the porthole with the severed forearm. Then, before waiting to see what happened, he secured the limb with two quick passes of stickytape so that the bloody glove was easily visible in the window, and scrambled up and over the roof of the shuttle.

Crouching, he took his bearings and saw the shuttle was turning away at an angle from both the *Qalak* and the *Wilful.* It was hard to gauge distance with no backdrop, but he guessed the freighter was a good kilometer away. *Two hundred, fifteen seconds.*

Hadeishi pulled out the little plasma cutter, oriented himself towards the *Wilful*—looked back towards the passenger door with a wry twist to his lips—and when he saw the top edge of the door cycle outward, he rotated the strength ring to full and thumbed the control.

The plasma jet flickered out in a long, blue-white line and Hadeishi felt his boots tug—kicking away, he lost adhesion—and then saw the shuttle falling away below him. Long seconds passed . . . he imagined the hatch cycling open, the limb being retrieved, the Khaid sailor stepping back inside to examine the queer artifact. Then the portholes on the sides of the shuttle suddenly flared with a stabbing, orange-red light. The spacecraft shuddered, spilling debris. Out of the corner of his eye, Mitsuharu saw a swarm of combat suits boiling out of the *Qalak*'s boat-bay. EVA carts winged towards the shuttle, which was now leaking spheroids of gray-white smoke as the interior fittings burned.

Two hundred, forty seconds.

Hadeishi worked his way down to the smaller hatchway, trying to keep out of line-of-sight from the window. Just a meter away from the opening, he froze, feeling the hull under his hands and feet begin to tremble.

One hundred and sixty seconds.

The bay doors began to separate, spilling a frosty wisp of atmosphere out into the void, and letting a sharp white light gleam through. Beneath him, the metal doors continued to roll back into the hull, carrying Hadeishi with them. *One hundred, sixty-eight seconds.*

He scrambled to the porthole and risked a look inside before the smaller hatch disappeared. Sure enough there was a boat-bay on the other side, holding a fair-sized shuttle. With the brief glimpse, he picked out a pair of Khaiden pilots visible through the beveled windows of the spacecraft. Then he took in the rest of the bay and froze, heart thudding in his throat, back pressed against the cold metal. The loading deck beside the shuttle was swarming with Khaid marines in combat armor; some of them were climbing onto EVA carts like the ones the *Zosen* used to ferry supplies and work crews around the hulls of larger starships.

Musashi was trudging through mud, in the rain, his head bowed beneath a peasant's bowl-like straw hat, a simple bokutō *over his shoulder, when the gates of the castle swung wide. Perforce, he stopped, moving to the side of the road, and watched in interest as a great column of samurai rode out, their armor gleaming wetly and their spear points bare to the sky. Weary, he squatted as they thundered past, wrapped in silken cloaks, their faces hidden behind armored masks. At the last, the banner man rode out, and though his* uma-jirushi *hung heavy in the pelting rain, Musashi could not avoid seeing the Tokugawa* mon. *Thus knowing the evil lord remained within the castle, his heart was gladdened—for victory or death over the Mongol overlords was close at hand.*

Hadeishi glanced back at the shuttle, saw the bus-sized craft was not mounted on a launch rail like a strike-fighter, and raced to dig into his pouches. An instant later, he'd found the roll of stickytape he needed, then double-checked the grenades and the severed arm. Nerving himself, he moved to the edge of the still-moving bay door. Keeping out of sight of the Khaiden hunting party, he crouched down, tensing his legs.

One chance, he thought, feeling giddy. *Watch for it. . . .*

The bay doors stopped with a *clunk*, and then the shuttle separated from the landing cradle. Ponderously, moving only under low-powered thrusters, the craft wallowed out of the boat-bay. Crouched just beyond

Now the mechanism creaked again, but faster, and then began to rotate smoothly. Letting out a long hiss of relief, Mitsuharu worked the balky key around until a dull *thud* reverberated through his arms and the control panel flashed a magenta icon. At the same time, a pair of handles popped free from the metal.

Now, he thought, *I will truly be on the clock.* Before opening the door, he carefully stowed all of his tools and secured the lanyards and pouches on both belts. Even the severed hand was tacked down. Then he took hold of both handles and pulled. The hatch swung towards him a little ponderously, revealing a dull gray chamber with a perforated grating as the floor. On the opposite wall was a thick glassite panel and beyond that—the wink and gleam of distant stars.

Thirty seconds, Hadeishi counted, watching the airlock cycle. A number of warning lights had come on as soon as he'd secured the inner lock and vented atmosphere. *Thirty-five seconds.*

The exterior hatch opened and the dull, ruddy light of the *kuub* streamed in, throwing harsh shadows on the walls. Mitsuharu checked his wrist, watching the radiation indicator fluctuate and then settle into the orange zone. *Thirty-eight seconds.*

He swung out of the lock, oriented himself, and then dialed up the magnification on his helmet to thirty-x and took a quick three-sixty of the horizon line. To his right a long profusion of radiating fins emerged from the shipskin, blocking most of his view. To the left the hull arced away into nothing but the abyss of stars. Behind him, however, he felt his heart leap to see the drive cowlings of the *Wilful* rising over the horizon.

Forty-four seconds. Watching the radiation detector fluctuate wildly, Hadeishi wished he had a full EVA rig. His z-suit was airtight and temperature regulated, but it was *not* intended for lengthy stays outside of the shielding of a ship. *Beggars cannot be choosers,* he chided himself, and moved off towards the freighter as fast as his boots could adhere to the shipskin.

A hundred meters on he halted, catching sight of a pair of recessed cargo or boat-bay doors ahead. He crouched down and crept to the edge of the opening. The doors were closed, but he could see a porthole-like window not far away, on a smaller access hatch. Carefully he glanced around, checking the horizon. Nothing caught his eye, so

Khaid forearm had been dripping globules of blood behind him as he'd moved and now they gleamed fitfully in the air, drifting past like tiny blue-black planets. He pressed the glove against the touch plate.

Nothing happened.

Then he felt relieved—*Idiot! If they found those bodies, someone will have noticed the missing hand, and shipboard security will be on the lookout for these credentials.* That meant getting through the airlock the old-fashioned way . . . the keypad was a guessing game he didn't have time to play, the card-reader had possibilities—but a quick search through the pouch and the belt he'd stolen didn't find an access card or crystal—and the touch plate was too likely to trigger an alarm. Instead he cast around in the immediate vicinity, looking for an emergency access hatch that would let him cycle the airlock on an override. This led him farther down the corridor without success.

Back at the lock, Hadeishi felt his chances of escape eroding with every chrono tick. At a loss, he examined the control panel and its various components again. This time, something tickled in memory and he found himself staring at the hex-shaped bezel. *A ship built for the Hesht, six fingers on each hand, six packs to a pride* . . . He took out his pry bar and jammed the metal tip under the edge of the bezel, which was not made of the same heavy steel as the rest of the lock. Indeed, the plastic cap popped off, revealing a deep socket—also hex-shaped—running into the hatch.

Emergency access! he gloated, fumbling through both tool belts for something that would fit the keyhole. A moment later he was spraying some unlok into the opening—it was a fair guess no one had manually opened the hatch since construction!—and then he wedged a number six socket wrench into the opening and then ran one handle of the bolt cutters through the socket itself. Then Hadeishi braced himself against the sidewall—thankful for once that he was working in z-g—and put everything he had into cranking his scratch-built key around.

For a long, long minute the socket and cutter combination resisted, going nowhere. His arms started to burn and he felt a twinge in his chest. Then, with a creaky vibration felt through his boots, the wrench rotated a centimeter. Breathing harshly, Hadeishi stopped—sprayed more unlok into the hole—and then put his shoulder into it again.

Regardless, he forced open the access plate and eeled out into a dark, congested room filled with more pipes and machines of unknown provenance. Getting the panel closed behind him was an effort, one that left him exhausted. Hadeishi hooked one leg around a nearby pipe and let himself float.

A search of his pockets found a threesquare bar, which—after checking his environment readings—he ate. That quieted his hunger, but did nothing for his thirst. He licked his lips, trying to remember how many days or hours he could survive without something to drink. *Probably the least of my worries,* he thought. Hopefully, he went through the equipment belt and pouch taken from the Khaid marine, but found nothing edible. He did find a brace of thumb-length cylinders on the belt. Turning them over, he sighed—despairing for his fellow man—for they were México Imperial Army HM-240 grenades long past their expiration date.

Why sir, I found these lying in the street. They must have fallen from an air-lorry.

Fortified, Hadeishi checked his chrono and tried to gauge how much time had passed since the *Wilful* was attacked. *No more than an hour, I hope. I've got to keep moving.* He didn't remember feeling the over-under nausea of punching into transit, which meant the Khaid were probably still cleaning up after their attack on the freighter.

Searching the machine room he found a small door and another access plate. Both seemed temperature neutral, so he eased the door open and found himself looking into a service way lit by only a thin strip of glowlights along the walls. This struck him as a proper maintenance shaft and he looked back, trying to gauge which way was skinside from the heading of the conduit.

That way? he guessed, pulling himself quickly "down" the corridor. Twenty meters on, the shaft turned to the right and a heavy lock-style door emerged from the gloom on his left. *O praise Ameratsu, bringer of daylight!*

Mitsuharu kicked away from one wall and touched down beside the lock. A control panel faced the heavy hatch, but there was no glassite window showing what lay beyond. He wanted to rub his face, but found himself nervously tapping on the faceplate of his helmet instead. The controls had a keypad with twelve buttons around a hex-shaped bezel, some kind of card-reader beside them, and a touch plate.

Time for the old guard to lend a hand, Hadeishi thought. The severed

The panel pulled closed behind him and, duckwalking, he scrabbled along by helmet light. After only a few moments, the shape of the huge heat exchanger conduit loomed up before him. This time the mauve striping had been replaced by bright crimson bands and, to his surprise, lines of a different—familiar—script ran between the warning markings.

This was a Hesht ship? Astounding. I thought they suicided their— well, maybe the Khaid bought it from some bankrupt pack. Or a shipyard switched clients in midstream.

He did remember a bit of low Heshok, as well as most of the more important letterforms, and what he could make out of the warnings indicated that yes, this was an air circulator attached to the heat exchangers. *On one of our ships, that means the outbound air will circulate through shipskin radiators to cool before being returned to the sterilizers.*

Feeling grimly determined—Musashi himself would have been impressed by such a stoic demeanor in the face of such calamity—Hadeishi hurried along beside the conduit until, after squeezing past a number of stanchions, he found an access port to the exchanger itself. *Finally!*

The panel popped loose with a little help from his pry bar, and then—after making sure the things he'd looted from the Khaid guard were secured to his suit by lanyards and his helmet was snugged tight— he crawled inside. Immediately, a hot wind roared around him and his z-suit began to squeak alarms about the mounting temperature. He also felt his stomach quease with the loss of gravity and guessed he'd just moved past the last of the g-decking.

Quickly then, he thought, scrambling along the pipe as quickly as he could. *I wonder how long my temperature regulator will hold out?*

Some time later the character of the conduit changed. The pipe came to an abrupt end in a wall filled with hundreds of dimples, each with a much smaller pipette opening recessed within. Hadeishi stopped, feeling the hot wind beating at his back, and then retreated. This proved difficult—going with the airflow, he hadn't realized how hard it was pushing at him—but three meters back from the diffusion wall he found an access plate. Now he pressed his temperature sensor against the opening, and saw with relief that the plate itself was quite cold.

They'd be fools to have open vacuum adjacent to the air exchanger, right? Don't want to trip a pressure alarm.

gling sort of wail echoing from the dripping walls.—*will be the holding cells we were destined for. Now I do need that shuttle bay.*

Which posed a dilemma: his Khadesh was limited to the barest courtesies—the human palate and tongue couldn't really duplicate the high-pitched yelping and growl undertone that characterized the diplomatic language used by the clans—and he couldn't read most of their written language. The ship itself, even if stolen from another starfaring race, wasn't a model he recognized, so he was going to have a hard time guessing where to find the nearest shuttle bay.

From in here, he realized. *I need to get outside, where I can make better time. . . .*

He cocked his head, listening again, and now—very distantly—he heard something like the roar of gunfire. Some of the overhead lights flickered and Hadeishi felt certain the sailors from the *Wilful* had found an honorable death.

No more distractions for the enemy. He picked a corridor that seemed—if he was not entirely turned around—to lead outward towards shipskin, and ran swiftly along, watching the maze of pipes and conduits overhead as he moved. A dozen meters on, a big pipe emerged from the floor and disappeared through the wall to the left. It was banded with bright mauve stripes and covered with blocky lettering.

Mitsuharu slowed, turning his wristband over to let the temperature sensor pick up the ambient radiation from the conduit. *Five-degree spike,* he saw. *Just what I need.*

Now he felt his shoulders creep with tension and a prickling at the nape of his neck, which usually meant something hostile was close by. He scuttled along the base of the wall, shining a hand-light at the joins in the passage molding. Fifteen meters down he found an unusually thick panel border and stopped.

His helmet was still open, so he squatted down and closed his eyes, listening.

Back the way he'd come, there was an echoing grinding sound. *Hatchway opening.*

The tool-belt produced a cutting torch and he thumbed the plasma emitter to quarter power and bit in along the edge of the panel. The join came apart, revealing a dark access way carpeted with mold. *Ah, brown mushrooms!* he thought, a fragment of an old song unspooling in memory. *In we go.*

Hadeishi hurled himself to the side as the zmetgun roared, barrel smoking red hot, and a spray of flechettes ripped across the ceiling of the passageway.

This is taking too long, flitted across Mitsuharu's mind as he back-handed the Khaid's helmet with the cutters. This time the blunt tool caught the creature in the join between neck-ring and the helmet proper. The z-suit gel—much the same technology as in a Fleet rig and designed to ablate high velocity impacts—gave way and metal jarred on bone. The Khaid staggered, clawing at its neck, and the other two sailors—hands now free—tore its zmetgun away.

One of them, his own faceplate washed red with blood, jammed the rifle barrel into the guard's chest and triggered a burst. The corpse jumped and flechettes spalled across the deck.

"Back to the ship," snarled the other sailor. He'd recovered the other zmetgun and ammunition.

"No!" barked Hadeishi, without thinking. He still had the cutters clenched in both hands and his whole body was shaking with adrena-line. Every instinct screamed to tear down the passage and lose them-selves in the environmental conduits sure to be spidering out from the thermocouple into the rest of the ship. "We need to go down deck and look for a shuttle bay."

"Idiot," growled the other sailor, now armed himself. "Our only way home is the *Wilful*—and we can't let the Khaid capture her. A shuttle will only make a quick coffin. . . ."

"There are—" Hadeishi fell silent. Both men had already run back up the passage towards the main airlock. He shook his head once, and then snatched up the equipment belt from the nearest Khaid, some-thing that looked like a document pouch on the creature's thigh and—using the bolt cutters with a sharp, violent jerk—the guard's right forearm. Then he ran in the opposite direction.

Past the next set of hatchways, Mitsuharu found himself at the top of a gangway leading "down" and paused for a moment to crack open his helmet. The smell of the alien ship was violently awful, but he forced down the urge to vomit and let the heat flowing up from the shaft wash over him.

Definitely a heat exchanger below and that sound—There was a gar-

Hadeishi fell clumsily, knocking into the sailor in front of him. The man turned, snarling. Mitsuharu took the opportunity to lose his footing and fall down. The guard kicked him, catching Hadeishi on the thigh, and then turned to warn off the sailor.

Curled up on the decking, Mitsuharu pulled his cuffed wrists under both tucked-in legs and—once his hands were in front of him—jimmied the bolt-cutters from his tool belt. Groaning with effort, he managed to twist the steel chain into the cutting blade. Seconds later, a heavy gloved hand seized his shoulder and dragged him up.

"Suk korek!" A throaty alien voice snarled in his earbug. At such short range, the conductive comm system in his suit was picking up the 'cast from the Khaid's radio. Hadeishi turned, keeping his head down, and gritted his teeth. The cheap steel in the cuffs was resisting the cutters, and the tight pressure on his wrists was sending sharp, bright pains up his arms. "Napiyorzun?"

That's done it, Mitsuharu gasped. A sharp *ping!* echoed in his helmet and his hands were free.

The Khaid reversed his zmetgun and made to slam the metal stock into Hadeishi's chest, but the Nisei officer bounced up and slashed the alien across the neck of its z-suit with the heavy cutters. The blow sent a shock up both arms, but the creature's trachea—or equivalent—ruptured. Dark blue-black blood suddenly gushed from the Khaiden's mouth, sloshing into the bottom of his neck-ring. Its wide-spaced eyes—set into a skull resembling nothing so much as an Afriqan meerkat mated with a hyena's coloring—glazed with pain.

That was enough—Hadeishi smashed the tool down on the Khaid's gun hand, knocking the zmetgun free. The rifle skittered away on the metal decking. At the same moment, the lead guard—who had whirled at the gurgling cry from his fellow—triggered a burst from his weapon. The first of the sailors was lunging at the Khaid and caught the burst full in the chest and face. Shattered z-suit material, clothing, and blood sprayed back. The second two men rushed the guard, heads down. Hadeishi darted in behind them, desperate to silence the Khaid before he could sound an alarm. The guard knocked one sailor aside, then fired wildly—missing everything—and Mitsuharu speared the cutters into his faceplate.

Glassite splintered, turning the clear material milky white, but did not shatter.

ABOARD THE *QALAK*

Inside the Khaid ship, Hadeishi and the other prisoners were hurried out of the main airlock—a fresh squad of Khaiden marines was crowding into the space, preparing to board the *Wilful*—and immediately down a side passage. As soon as the hatchway groaned shut behind them—Mitsuharu's ear caught the distinctive sound of a pump working overtime to compensate for a fouled hydraulic line—he lifted his head in the dim, fetid darkness and glanced around.

The last time he'd been aboard a Khaiden raider his Fleet sensibilities had been affronted by how poorly maintained the alien ships were. And his reaction had been mild compared to the outrage shown by the Engineering team he'd put aboard . . . that captured heavy cruiser couldn't have been salvaged without a complete interior rebuild. Much of this, he believed, sprang from the paucity of resources afflicting the ill-defined and disorganized Khaid polity. Fleet intelligence bulletins indicated the hostile power was more a fragile alliance of feuding clans and stations than a real nation. In particular, they lacked a unified industrial base—most of their ships were captured, or stolen—and repair facilities were few and far between.

In the same situation, Mitsuharu believed he'd have taken pains to keep his ship—or ships, if he were some lucky Khaiden warlord—in the best possible condition. But then, he suspected the Khaid might do just that, for ships they had built themselves. But for a stolen ship? Some alien vessel jury-rigged to allow Khaiden operation? There was no reason to spend more than the most minimal resources on a captive vessel; particularly when it would likely be destroyed in the next raid.

Now, seeing the interior of the *Qalak*, he guessed they were being herded down to a holding facility—and from the look of the piping overhead, and the steadily growing heat, it would be close on to a thermocouple station. Then the guard behind Hadeishi interrupted his train of thought with a hard jab to the shoulder with a zmetgun.

array, leaving just the tiniest gap . . . but not big enough to avoid destruction when they stepped out-of-bounds."

Sho-sa Chac considered the plot, eyes fixed on the Mirror research ships now snugged up against the station. "They'll be going in, *Chu-sa*, and someone will have to play watchdog . . . pray to the Lady of Tepeyac we avoid such a fate!"

For her part, Koshō felt claustrophobic. The emptiness around her ship seemed suddenly confined, filled with invisible walls. "Keep the coordinates of this . . . barrier . . . in the threatwell at all times," she decided, caution pricked by the object lesson of the three wrecked survey ships. "If we need to maneuver at speed, we don't want to interpenetrate by accident."

"*Hai, Chu-sa!*" Llang was very quick to agree. The others nodded vigorously.

"What else?" Koshō felt the tactical problem beginning to turn over in her mind, options shifting in and out of consideration, alternatives discarded as quickly as they suggested themselves.

Llang tapped through a series of detailed views of the area around the Mirror station itself. "*Kyo*, the only other thing we've found is this . . . probably a good third of the *Calexico* is the core of the *Can* itself. Looks like they dragged half of the scout back out of the danger zone and cut away the damaged sections. The other two ships lost containment on their reactors, but by some miracle the *Calexico*'s power plant survived."

"Frugal." Koshō clicked her teeth together. "Someone must have survived the attack or they'd never have found this opening . . . not without losing another dozen ships blundering around in the dark. Ask around, *Sho-sa* Oc. See if you can get names."

"*Hai, kyo!*" The Mayan nodded, his face impassive. But as he strode away, Susan caught a fragment of a prayer, muttered under the man's breath: "Hear us, O Xbalanque. Lend us your clever mind and subtle hand. Guide us in this foul Darkness which over you has no power."

Now, she thought, feeling the bone-deep ache of being up too long and running on too many cups of tea. *That makes me feel so much better. May it settle his mind, for it does nothing for mine.*

His image of a whirlwind of knives barring the dark road to Xibalba remained with her.

the lift doors rotated away, every duty station was staffed and there were four or five extra bodies present, holding up the walls and checking console diagnostics that had been checked only the day before. Oc Chac nodded as she approached.

"Show me." Koshō nodded to Llang, who slipped into a seat at the comm and sensor station. The *Thai-i*'s stylus skittered across the control surfaces with admirable speed. Immediately a series of navigation diagrams appeared and a holo rotated into view, showing the science platform, the debris clouds in the immediate vicinity and then—three sharp taps zoomed the focus far, far down, showing an indistinct smear a goodly distance from the *Can*, deep into the area marked off by the Mirror as out-of-bounds.

"*Kyo*, it's really hard to see—the remains of the ships are just more radioactive junk in with all of this other radioactive junk, but we believe that this—"

Llang tapped once more, and a camera overlay sprang up, showing a sort of empty wedge in the cloud.

"That this was the *Kiev* after she lost reactor containment. The scout must have been traveling within gun range of the *Korkunov*—that's this other gap off her starboard. When they blew, the force of the explosion actually cleared an area in the nebular cloud. The densities of material around the edges of each of these gaps sort of approximate the mass of the ships themselves. At least we think that's right. And look at this— the *Calexico* has been cut clean in half!" Llang looked up, her face filled with mingled horror and awe. "Have you ever seen anything like that before, *Chu-sa*?"

Susan stared at the enhanced, high-contrast image and marveled at the clean edge of the ship's wound. "How far away is this?"

"Three light-minutes beyond the *Can*, *kyo*, just at the edge of sensor range in the cloud." The *Thai-i* grimaced. "Too much grit to see if there's anything else out beyond them. . . ."

Susan compared the plots and the information from the morning's briefing. Her frown deepened.

"There's an opening," she said, clenching her hands, which had suddenly gone cold. "Survey and the Mirror advance elements have been here at least a week—they'll have seen what we see, guessed what we guess. Their danger zone is well on this side of all three of those ships. The *Kiev* must have blundered into a failed component of the weapon's

"How could—" Susan started to ask, but Tloc interjected:

"My information says a gravitational distortion's been detected around a huge volume, all of it clogged with nova debris. Almost impenetrable to scanning . . . just to twist the screw another thread."

"And I've heard if you run into this phenomena you get cut to bits." Muldoon made a throat-cutting gesture. "Word is a pair of Survey ships tried to break through and ended up literally dissected."

Susan frowned. "Do these lost ships have names? Any detail at all?"

"Not yet, but give me some time," Tloc replied. "I've got about a ton of *chocolatl* and *kaffe* in personal stowage."

Ten minutes later, after arranging a trade to keep the kitchen happy, Koshō signed off. The second watch was in the process of leaving Command, most yawning, some already busy in conversation with their fellows. The comm duty officer and the assistant navigator were a step slow and Susan beckoned them over.

"Rumor says a pair of Survey scouts caught hold of the *Chu-sho's* phenomena by the sharp end. See if you can pick out any wrecked ships in the immediate vicinity. They ought to be the other side of the *Can*. Keep your eyes open for *anything* out of place. Something very odd killed those scouts—and I'd like to avoid the same fate."

The quiet of the off-watch officer's mess was broken by a soft voice: "*Chu-sa* Koshō?"

Susan looked up from her cup of tea. It was Navigator's Assistant Llang, trying to suppress a huge grin. Susan beckoned her over. "We've got 'em, *kyo*." Llang blurted, comp clutched to her chest. "All three. It's—"

"Not to be discussed here." Koshō silenced the girl with a sharp look. The *Chu-sa* picked up her tea and guided the young *Thai-i* back out the door at a brisk walk. "Let's use my station on the bridge instead."

In the lift, as the decklights blurred past, Susan considered the young Tagalog lieutenant. This was the girl's second duty posting—she'd come recommended from the *Mac Allan*, a frigate working shipping lane patrols around Alpha Centauri—and Koshō was sure she had very little political experience. After a moment she said quietly, "There may be those aboard *Naniwa* who will have lost friends or family in those ships. We do not want to break such sad news in a casual way."

Third watch should have found the bridge nearly deserted, but when

shower. For the moment, the bridge was double-staffed as the crew prepared for turnover. Amid all of the commotion, she had taken a moment to comm up the two officers she remembered from the Academy. Both of them—Muldoon on the *Falchion* and Tloc on the *Axe*—had been surprised to hear from her.

"Not often you high-flying battle-cruiser commanders take the time to say hello to the plow horses," said Muldoon after they'd confirmed a private channel and triggered their own encryption. "But it's good to see you again, Koshō-*tzin*."

"Likewise," grumbled Tloc. The Ciguayan captain had acquired a bad set of burn scars on the side of his face since graduation day. "How did you get on Xocoyotl's bad side? I've never heard him rip a junior officer like that before."

"I gave him some advice," Susan said, shaking her head slightly. "I should have known better."

Muldoon laughed. "Admirals know all and see all, remember? Just like the upper form prefects on Grasshopper Hill. The Runner said you'd been the wise woman behind that formation change during transit—but I didn't think he'd take it so hard."

Tloc grimaced. "I'm on my second posting with him—he knows best and likes it that way."

Koshō frowned, feeling worse for having the extent of her misstep made so clear. "My last commander would've expected me to suggest a better course, if I saw one."

"Then you were lucky." Muldoon's normally lively tone flattened. "I heard Hadeishi was beached. That's too bad, everyone said he was a fine ship-handler."

Susan nodded, once. "Too good, sometimes. I have been reminded—repeatedly—that being very good can lead to believing you can do the impossible *one more time* than you can."

Both men nodded, sobered. "That's the truth," Tloc said, touching the side of his face.

"So what about *this* mess?" Koshō felt the memory of Hadeishi weighing on her. "What does Painal the Runner say about this most secret of secrets?"

Muldoon perked up, laying one finger alongside his nose. "My money is on a quantum-level distortion. We could see it from here, except it's invisible to our sensor suite."

by one of the doors. One of the admiral's aides keyed up a projector panel and the lights dimmed. Cuaxicali cleared his throat, looked at the *Chu-sho* questioningly—received a snarl in response—and then began tapping on a slim silver comp with his stylus.

Behind him the projector shifted aspect and a holo of the surrounding region sprang into view. The collection of ships arrayed "south" of the *Can* appeared with Imperial standard glyphs. "North" of them, a broad area of crimson points appeared.

"Avoid this range of spatial coordinates," Cuaxicali said, indicating the beelike swarm of scarlet, "if you wish to keep your ship intact. This is the area of our—ah—*the* phenomenon. And it is exceptionally dangerous."

The assembled captains looked at one another, then a forest of arms went up to ask for details.

"No, no. No questions." Cuaxicali shook his head nervously. "This is a matter of the utmost security. There is no other information available at this time save what I've shown you—a copy of these astronomical charts has already been commed to your navigators."

"Surely you can tell us what sort of peril to expect?" a loud voice boomed across the conference room.

"I could," Cuaxicali agreed, attempting a consoling smile, "But for safety's sake I will not."

A red-haired *Chu-sa* whom Susan remembered vaguely from Chapultepec stood up and asked, "Begging your pardon, Scientist Cuaxicali, but please explain how can it be safe to not know the nature of our opponent? Or even what it looks like?"

An ill-disguised snort of laughter erupted at the back of the conference room.

Cuaxicali's face changed abruptly into a sort of maroon-olive. Susan was not sure she'd seen the exact shade before, on anyone, anywhere.

Chu-sho Xocoyotl stood up and surveyed the assembled officers with one raised eyebrow. The room settled down.

"That is all. Return to your ships. Patrol patterns will be distributed by third watch."

Five hours later, as second watch was winding down, Koshō was back on the Command deck in a fresh uniform, her hair slick from a fast

The staff conference room on the *Tokiwa* was crowded, hot, and noisy as the last of the squadron commanders found their seats. *Chu-sho* Xocoyotl's staff were arrayed along the walls, while everyone else was present at a long oval table which folded up out of the floor. The flag battle-cruiser was an older model than the *Naniwa*, though still in the Provincial class, and this same room did not exist in the current configuration of Koshō's ship. If memory served, a suite of Logistics and Supply offices occupied the same internal coordinates.

"Admiral on deck," barked one of the *Tokiwa*'s marine sergeants and everyone stood.

Xocoyotl was of medium height, carrying a bit too much flesh on his bones, and the color of polished mahogany. His high cheekbones caught a gleam from the overheads as he took his place at the head of the table. "Sit," he growled—his voice was even deeper in person than over stellarcast.

"Our business here comes under purview of the Imperial Secrets Act," he said with a scowl. "The Mirror is leading an investigation of some local phenomena and Fleet is providing security for their operations. Beyond this, I am informed we do not need to know *anything*."

He stopped, glanced around the room at all of the officers, snorted, and continued in the near-perfect silence.

"Survey informs us this area of the *kuub* is tremendously dangerous. It is also uncharted and there are no navigational beacons within range. I expect, therefore, that all watches will be fully staffed and weapons will be maintained in ready status at all times."

Xocoyotl flashed a tight, frosty smile at Koshō. "At least one of our ships—the *Naniwa*—has a fresh crew, a fresh captain and has not yet completed trials. I expect the other combatants to make allowance for this when plotting combat vectors."

To her credit, Susan remained entirely still while the *Chu-sho* went on about the combat patrol pattern he expected of the other ships, and she did not let her outrage show in any obvious way. Out of the corner of her eye, however, she could see some of the cruiser captains glancing sidelong at her in puzzlement. *How could I be more circumspect,* she wondered, *in suggesting that deployment change during transit? Losing one of the support ships would have crippled the entire mission.*

"Scientist Cuaxicali? Your turn." Xocoyotl gestured abruptly at a fat little México civilian in a Survey Service mantle who had been standing

Everything within optical range of the battle-cruiser's cameras was a thick haze of heavy dust and debris. What dim light filtered through the murk from distant, half-hidden stars was diffuse and red-shifted. It made an appalling sight for a Fleet captain. Even a miner's scow would find heavy going in this environment.

"Impact rate?" The *Naniwa* was at very low v as she maneuvered into a parking station a safe distance from the unnamed research station.

"Forty-five percent," responded the weapons officer. "And we're nearly dead slow."

Susan nodded, leaning back in the shockchair. "Holloway, you and Konev work up some velocity metrics for me—how fast can we go, how best to configure the transit deflectors. We need to make headway in this mess. I want something by end of the watch."

"*Hai, Chu-sa!*" both voices chimed together in near unison.

"And get us a name for that station—something simple."

Holloway smiled tightly. He'd already queried the *Temasek*—the lead of the two Survey Service frigates—for the latest news. "They're calling it the *Can, Chu-sa.* Very imaginative."

"That will do." Koshō considered the threatwell for a moment, trying to map out the local terrain in her mind. This was just the situation—some nasty, unknown patch of space filled with hidden opponents, tangled local politics, and unsteady stellar phenomena— that Hadeishi excelled in. *Nothing drains the strength of your opponent,* he would say, *faster than unknown ground. But if you are alert, even the most treacherous swamp can be your ally, a third arm striking at the enemy.*

A message chime on her board interrupted the memory. Susan started to grimace, seeing the *Tokiwa's mon* chopped on the header, but then smiled slightly as the message unspooled.

"*Socho* Juarez, I'll need a shuttle prepped and a guard-party suitable for the squadron staff meeting."

The marine, never far away by earbug, replied immediately: "*Hai, Chu-sa.* We'll be ready in fifteen minutes, boat-bay three."

Good, she thought, relieved to finally get a chance to meet her fellow squadron commanders and exchange proper introductions with *Chu-sho* Xocoyotl. *Now we'll find out what the devil is going on out here.*

THE PINHOLE

"Transit kick in three—two—one . . ."

Susan's stomach flipped, settled, and she swallowed the faint taste of bile. At the pilot's station, *Sho-i* Holloway counted down his post-insertion checklist, announcing all systems green; deflectors intact and the ship in proper spatial position. By then, two minutes had passed.

"Status of the squadron?" Susan had already reviewed her own boards, seeing that all three battle-cruisers had kept station after dropping to normal space, but it never hurt to check. Particularly with a piglike Fleet tender along. The *Fiske* and *Eldredge* had done well in keeping up so far, but she doubted they had any legs at all if things got hot.

"All present and accounted for," Holloway replied. "We have three friendly IFF registers. Fleet says they are—" He reviewed a side-pane on his panel, making sure that the battlecast relays had come up, verified the new ships, that they matched registry entries and the *Naniwa*'s long-range cameras had confirmed their outlines in the heavy murk. "—*Temasek*, *Corduba*, and . . . no name on the third vessel, but she's registered as a 'mobile science platform'—same as ours in the registry, but the silhouette is markedly different."

That will be the Mirror hard at work. Susan nodded. Then the debris density they'd dropped into registered on her consciousness and she felt mildly ill.

In transluminal space, the physical protostellar matter collecting in the wasteland of the *kuub* was represented by both a gravity dimple and a quantum-level spore, or nugget, which interacted with the translated quantum-frame state of a ship much as a physical rock would interact—that is, smash into—the physical hull of a ship in realspace. Here, though, where physicality assumed its usual guise of solidity, the swarms of dust particles, or even micrometeoroids and outright boulders or asteroidal fragments, posed an even greater danger to the *Naniwa* and other ships trying to make realspace headway.

barely enough room for her shoulders, much less her feet, the hurt cur-
dled in her breast. The thought that Grandfather's cause—noble and
doomed as it had been—was still secretly alive in the wilderness out be-
yond the Rim, had lifted a little of the weariness upon her heart. Now
the same cold weight settled again, twice as heavy, and she fell into a fit-
ful sleep, troubled by dreams of men's voices singing beyond a golden
doorway, in a lost tongue she ought to understand.

knuckles were white. *Oh. Well. I guess I don't need Malakar's singing to bring on this . . . this . . . whatever it is.*

The peculiar perceptual gestalt which came and went—incited by stress, or by psychotropic drugs, or the presence of another being in a state of extreme agitation—had been absent from her daily existence while she'd toiled away in the basement office on New Aberdeen. The nightly visions or dream-states which caused her to speak aloud in the tongues of ancient Mokuil had been slowly diminishing as time passed and her body recovered from being exposed to the memory-echo of the *kalpataru*. Malakar's notebooks were filled with drawings, songs, tales long lost to her people—Gretchen's troubled sleep had yielded up an unexpected bounty for the old librarian—but even that had been drawing to an end when the Hummingbird had arrived.

Now, with her mind feeling awake for the first time in months, Anderssen licked her lips in unease. *Is simply being in the presence of the* nauallis *enough to fray the veil blinding my perception? On Ephesus he had to give me a pill—a dose of oliohuiqui to part the shadows—but on Jagan all I needed was the presence of the Tree Which Gives What You Desire. And here? There doesn't seem to be even so much . . .*

The prospect of perceiving the true shape of the world around her, to glimpse the underpinning of men's purposes, was both troubling and exciting. *Now if only I could make it work when I want it to! That would be a bonus. What a tremendous tool. Just seeing the proper pattern of a broken pot would—*

Then, with her mind alert to the present, she heard through the hatchway Hummingbird's low, sharp voice speaking in an unfamiliar language, though the vowel cadence sounded terribly familiar. Locke's astonished reaction was like a bucket of ice water.

"You? *Præceptor*? Impossible!"

Peering through the partially open hatch, Gretchen caught sight of the old México's face. The *nauallis* nodded slowly, his arm lifted as though displaying some symbol to the merchanter.

Ah, a pity. Anderssen's throat felt tight with disappointment. These men were not HKV, not Resistance. *A crimson cross on a white field. A bloody spear and some secret language. No crew-women to be found. Just some marginal religious sect fallen prey to the Crow's blandishments.*

Disappointed, she gathered up her things and crawled back to their tiny cabin behind the food recyclers. Lying in the narrow bunk, with

Both of the crewmen stood up, pitched their cups, and climbed down the ladder to the engineering spaces.

Not their work tools, she realized, watching them go out of the corner of her eye. *They have the same sidearm.* The thought caught in her memory and other fragmentary images suddenly coalesced. *Tattoos— at least two, maybe three of these men have a crimson cross fitche on a white field. Like an insignia. Every one of them has at least one handgun. All about the same size, too, as though they were issued arms. These men must be ex-military.*

She gave the mess deck a considering glance, then cast about in memory for any other details she'd glossed over in the last two days while the ship had bounced from transit point to way station and on- ward into this trackless expanse. The *Moulins* was small; listed as a freighter seeking supercargo passengers, or some kind of high-value, low-mass cargo that couldn't wait for a big liner or cargo-carrier to come by. Or, she realized, for fugitives to smuggle . . . like her, like the Crow. Or information—very low mass; data-crystals or comp discs— and that could turn a tidy profit.

That familiar pressure—the constant, draining, exhausting need for quills which had been omnipresent her whole life—seemed out of place here. *That's not right. This captain, this crew, they don't taste right, feel right; they're not mercenaries.* She couldn't say quite why, but she was suddenly certain that Locke and his men were not out in the back of be- yond looking for money.

A spy-ship? But not an Imperial one. Her heart skipped. None of the crew she'd seen were México or Nisei or Skawtish or any of the other nations bound by the compact of the Four Hundred families. *Could this be an HKV courier? A Resistance ship? Glorious Christ, there is still a Royal Navy at work amongst the stars?* She thought of *her* great-grandfather, a fiery old man with a neat white beard, killed in the Last War. He had served aboard a Swedish cruiser in battle near Saturn. A flood of emo- tion filled her and for an instant—her heart aching—she perceived something of the *shape* of the ship, the crew, even the irritable Captain Locke. She saw a *bloody spear, shining in the darkness, radiating roseate light into the void. Pointed ever outward, fixed upon the heart of an invis- ible, implacable enemy.*

Chilled and sweating, Gretchen slumped back against the bulkhead. The coffee cup squeaked in her hand. When she looked down, her

prickly heat on her face. Before the captain could continue, however, Hummingbird raised a hand and looked over to Anderssen.

"Could you step outside, and see we're not disturbed?"

Meeting his gaze directly, Gretchen felt the adrenaline-heat suddenly flow away, replaced by cool calculation. *He expected this,* she realized. The old *nauallis* didn't seem fazed by the turn of events, though there was a substrate of annoyance in his voice.

"Sure, boss," she said, ducking out through the hatch. The heavy steel drew closed behind her, though she didn't let the panel lock into the socket. Three crewmen were now standing around the dispenser, their attention drawn by her sudden appearance and the clank of the hatch.

"I think," she said brightly, "that you're all going to get a hazard bonus."

The men looked at her quizzically, and then one bustled off downship with three cups balanced in his hands. Gretchen leaned against the hatchway and unwrapped a stick of chicle from her pocket. *I am so very nonchalant,* she thought in amusement as the hot taste of cinnamon filled her mouth. *Very much the idler.*

The remaining two crewmen ignored her and sat down to the table.

Without consciously intending to, Anderssen turned to examine some old bulletins posted on the nearest wall and let her eyes lose focus. Like magic—if sensory prioritization could be called magic—her hearing sharpened and she heard one of the men say: "Spero Lockenem maleficum eum circuagere non permissurum esse."

The other replied, equally softly: "Navarchus non stultus est. Claude os et oculos aperi!"

How odd. They're speaking—

She forced herself to step away from the door and pick up her cup of coffee. The little sound leaking through from the control space indicated a vigorous discussion was under way, and now that these two burly specimens were watching her, it wouldn't be polite to overhear. She swirled the cold liquid around in the cup, frowned, and went to the dispenser. Both of the men at the table turned away as she passed, but something about their clothing—no, their tool belts—caught her eye. *Nothing unusual about them,* she thought, wondering what had set her on edge. *You're getting paranoid . . . that's Hummingbird's business, not yours.*

Hot liquid steamed into the cup and she thumbed the glyph for extra cream, extra sugar-substitute.

"One drive trace," muttered Locke, chewing on the edge of his thumb. "Too big for our contact."

"Maybe two," ventured the pilot. His stylus clicked on the display surface. The navigation holo shifted slightly and Gretchen, now quite alert, could see two vectors illuminated by the computer. "But this big signature is washing out the other."

"Our ship?" Green Hummingbird was watching Locke closely.

The freighter captain rubbed his forehead, and then swung into the navigator's seat. "The commercial shipping registry has some drive signatures on file," he said, uneasy. "Let's see what it kicks up."

Hummingbird waited patiently, while Gretchen—who felt an urge to start tapping her fingers—took the opportunity to examine the little room and the adjacent compartments. In comparison to the mess area, things were cleaner, and some components might have been recently replaced—but even so, there was a sense of age and hard use permeating everything she could see.

No, she suddenly thought, *that's not right—*

Locke cursed, drawing her attention back to the three men. Two ship's schematics had come up on his display—one obviously of considerable size, the other showing an outline almost exactly like their own paltry freighter. The captain sat back, covering his mouth with one hand. He pointed at the larger schematic with his chin.

"This is the flux signature of a Khaid *Neshter*-class destroyer. And the smaller one must be your ride."

The pilot hissed in dismay, looking back to the drive trails on the navigation holo.

"The smaller ship's signature is showing a couple hours newer than the entry-point for that destroyer . . . but their chrono tracks synch up on exit."

"I warrant the freighter went in chains!" Locke stood up, giving Hummingbird a hard look. "There's no ride onward for you, México. We're turning around and getting the hell out of here."

"Our agreement, Captain Locke, says you deliver me and my assistant to our destination." Hummingbird's tone was even, showing neither anger nor concern. "I will provide you with new transit coordinates and we will press on."

Locke bristled and Gretchen could feel his agitation like a sharp,

Her coffee cup suddenly shivered—dark liquid pulsing into a sharp spike and then collapsing. Her stomach did the same thing, at the same time.

The freighter had dropped from transit. The g-decking in the mess area failed momentarily, eliciting curses from a crewman trying to refill his cup from the dispenser. Gretchen's mug had a clear cover, which kept it from disgorging a flight of brown-and-white globules into the air. Without thinking, she put her thumb over the drinking spout—gravity returned—and she wiped her finger on the thigh of her field pants.

Hummingbird ducked into the room, even his short frame needing to bend to get through the hatchway from the passenger cabin they'd booked for this leg of their journey into the unknown. Like the crew, the old México was kitted out in a workaday mantle over his z-suit with a broad leather belt at his waist and deep pockets. As he passed, Gretchen looked up curiously. The old man lifted his chin, indicating the hatchway to the control deck.

"Are you ready to transship?"

Anderssen nodded. *Next bus, now departing* . . . "How soon?"

"We'll see in a few moments."

Though he hadn't invited her, Gretchen slipped out from behind the table—tucked her comp away, drained the coffee cup—and followed along quietly. They had been in motion—hopping from ship to ship—for nearly ten days now and the old sorcerer had yet to speak more than a handful of words to her, none of them concerning their eventual destination.

When she squeezed into the door to the control space—*bridge* seemed too grand a word for the crowded warren of consoles, wire bundles, and creaking shockchairs—the sharp, abrupt impression of fear and adrenaline was a cold splash on her face. *Better than coffee!* she thought, feeling suddenly awake and on edge.

The freighter's master, a short balding little man named Locke, was standing over the pilot's shoulder, peering at the main navigational display. The camera displays were filled with a riot of iridescent color. Thick clouds of dust congealed out of the void on every side, lit with the radiance of distant, unseen stars. In comparison to the usual emptiness of interstellar space, the view seemed dangerously crowded. Hummingbird was also squeezed in, on the other side of the pilot, and his face seemed tight.

ABOARD THE *MOULINS*

IN THE *KUUB*

Gretchen sat squeezed in behind a narrow fold-out table on the mess deck, a mug of coffee clinging to a stickyplate by her right hand and a battered field comp balanced on her left knee. The crew was grumbling in and out of the tiny space, getting their threesquares heated and coffee refreshed, and passing what gossip had managed to evolve in the last shift. The room was cold, crowded, and noisy. Every surface felt worn with age and constant, hard use. Like the rest of the ship—or the parts she'd seen—it was spotlessly clean, but the freighter was of an age that no amount of scrubbing and polishing could make the walkways, walls, or counters seem fresh.

Despite this Anderssen felt almost happy for the first time in nearly six months, her nostrils filled with the stink of cold diesel and burning rubber. Abstracts from a good year's worth of the *Extraplanetary Archeological Review* flipped past on the comp's screen. From time to time she recognized names or remembered the faces of old coworkers or rivals or long-standing dignitaries in her field. Occasionally an obituary cropped up—leaving a small, cold chill behind as she paged to the next document.

How did I get so far behind? All of the time spent toiling at the Technical College seemed to have faded from memory already, as though the whole interlude had been a fever dream, and her last "real" assignment and this one were running together with only a few idle weeks at home in between. *Easy to forget the last half year, I guess.* She hoped that was true.

The articles were the same as ever—plenty of insights promised, but the results were always a few pages of heavily censored data, some half-hearted conclusions, and hopes for further funding. The good stuff, of course, was never in the public journals. The Honorable Company, or the Mirror Which Reveals, saw to that quickly enough. *Our Secret Histories,* she though morosely, *where the truth goes to be stuffed, buried, and forgotten.*

seemed professional and direct once more. "There is work to be done, *Chu-sa.*"

"Dismissed," she replied, and then watched him with interest as he strode off.

Can he really make the men forget—or put aside—this apprehension? That would be a boon indeed.

He waited expectantly. *For what?* she wondered.

"*Kyo*, did they teach you that the México Kingdom of the Dead is but a weak shadow of Xibalba, place of phantoms, place of fear? That deadly trials and cruel, prankish Gods and whirlwinds of knives bar the way to that awful kingdom?"

Susan frowned. The Mayan had her full attention. "You believe we've chosen such a road ourselves?"

"Those who go that way have no choice, *kyo*. It is only for those who are dead."

Before she could reply, Susan's earbug crackled with the peculiar static endemic to the region. Pucatli was speaking, his normally calm voice tight with adrenaline.

"*Hai, Chu-i*, put him through."

"*Chu-sa* Koshō," Xocoyotl's voice rumbled in her ear. "I have decided to reform the squadron. *Tokiwa*, *Asama*, and *Naniwa* will lead with the cruisers forming a secondary wedge. Set your transit shielding at maximum extent and clear a path through the dust for those who follow. New vectors will be on your navcomm within the quarter hour."

"*Hai, Chu-sho!*"

Susan turned, feeling the chair motors kick in quietly. She tapped up the intraship channel and waited for Pucatli to confirm green across his repeater boards. Chac said nothing, his attention turned inward. Koshō's attention lingered on him for a moment, before she shook her head and opened the channel.

"All hands, all section officers. Be advised that *Chu-sho* Xocoyotl has commanded the squadron to reform our flight pattern. We will be shifting vector in fifteen—I say fifteen—minutes. Engineering sections be aware that we are going to full transit shield power. Stand by for maneuver on my mark."

When she closed the circuit, Oc Chac was standing at the edge of the threatwell, seemingly lost in thought.

"Do you truly believe what you just said, *Sho-sa*?" Susan's voice was soft, given they were surrounded by a busy Command deck. "That we've stepped onto some cursed road, leading only to destruction?"

Chac turned, his face somber. "Such thoughts come to me in this place unbidden, *kyo*—and if they assail *my* mind, they will afflict the soldiers, starmen, and scientists aboard the squadron doubly so."

He nodded sharply to her, and now everything about him

"*Hai, Chu-sho!*" Koshō nodded sharply in acknowledgment. Then she paused, wondering if there was enough of an opening to—

The v-cast folded away in the air before her with a soft *ding!*

Shaking her head, Susan returned to the captain's chair, her fingers tapping in thought on the shockframe. Oc Chac was almost immediately at her side.

"What were you going to ask him, *kyo*?" The XO asked in an undertone.

Susan tilted her head, considering the engineer for a moment. Then she said, "What we discussed earlier: live-fire exercises for our command and gun crews. But given the rush, I doubt he'd approve the expenditure of munitions or time that would require." She sat down in her chair and flicked open the v-panes on her control surface. "Not that I am easy about pulling power from the deflectors in this muck—even without the stress of gun exercises—it's eating my ship."

Oc Chac stiffened at the light tone in her words. "This does not seem amusing to me."

He stared at the convoluted patterns in the threatwell for a long moment, then continued in a low voice: "I cannot laugh, *kyo*. All this reminds me of Hunahpu's description of the road to Xibalba:

> *Here there is no light but what we wayfarers bring with us.*
> *We grapple in the dark with degraded, phantom faces.*
> *Only treachery awaits us.*"

Susan frowned. "It's long since I read the *Popol Vuh*; what canto—"

> "*It is as if we are finding our way to the underworld,*
> *To the dark stairs which bisect the sky.*"

The low, chanting tone to his voice began to raise the hackles on Susan's neck. His face—normally striking, given the strength of his features—now seemed cold and still. The long oval shape, the distinctive nose, the wide lips punctured by labrets of jade and turquoise—a living statue dredged up from the wreck of old Palenque or Copán.

"*Chu-sa*, you know the legend of Mictlan?"

"I do, *Sho-sa*. The tutors of Chapultepec are diligent in their application of México history."

The *Chu-i* stiffened and then immediately began speaking into his throatmike. Koshō stood up, stretched, and took a roundabout of the bridge. This caused a wave of activity to move with her, as the staff checked and rechecked their status displays. When Susan came around to the threatwell, she was standing well away from everyone else. Only Oc Chac had remained on-task with the gunnery control officer, testing the launch control relays for the main missile batteries spaced along the "wing" of the battle-cruiser. Six or seven control modules had already been replaced, having failed their workup.

Now the Mayan's attention was fixed on her from across Command, and he lifted one eyebrow in question.

Susan shook her head, then tapped her earbug live as Pucatli reported the channel was open, secure, and the admiral on-line. A holocast of the *Chu-sho*'s face appeared before her, surrounded by a wedge of informational glyphs. Xocoyotl was a little overweight for a México officer, with hard cheekbones and a northern—or Anasazi—cast to his features and a deep, gravelly bass for a voice. So swift had been their departure that Koshō had yet to actually meet her commanding officer in person.

"Report."

"*Chu-sho*, battle-group 'cast is showing increasing shipskin erosion from the cloud. *Naniwa*'s deflectors are fresh from the yards and we're still failing to make a perfectly clean channel—the smaller ships are doing worse, with an increased risk of equipment failure."

"Your point, *Chu-sa*? We are still behind schedule to reach rendezvous. If we slow—"

"Understood, *kyo*. If I may—our projections show that slowing one-half—or reorienting the battle-group for overlapping coverage—will reduce the chances of losing the *Fiske*, *Eldredge*, or *Hanuman* by almost sixteen percent."

The admiral's expression did not change—it was habitually disapproving—but Susan thought there was a brief flicker in the deep-set, black eyes. She missed Hadeishi again—discussing something like this with him would have been brief, efficient, and to the point.

"We've no time to experiment," he said at last. "All ships will stay on course and make do."

Saxony had been long part—he would not have found a posting in the Fleet at all.

Which would be a shame, Susan thought, *because we are short enough of talented officers as it is.*

"Emil," she said aloud, "how does the shielding on the *Fiske* or *Eldredge* compare to ours, in this dust, at our current velocity?"

"Poorly, *Chu-sa.*" He looked off-pane, and Koshō was heartened to see that the engineer already had the 'cast telemetry on his own monitors. "We're pegging up to five or six percent capacity—that last bolus deflected from the port shielding at nineteen percent—but *Fiske* is showing sixty or seventy percent just in the easygoing."

"You'd agree the densities are increasing, the deeper we go?"

He nodded. "*Kyo*, whatever gravitational sources are causing all of this debris to collect are—more or less—dead ahead. The closer we come, the tighter the influx spirals are going to be. Right now, if you plot back to our entry point, you can see we're cutting across deeper 'valleys' in the clouds. The interval between each ridge is growing shorter as well."

"Sensor efficiency?"

"Declining, *Chu-sa.*" Hennig smoothed back short-cropped gray hair. "Have you been watching the cycle-rate on the battlecast itself?"

Susan shook her head, *no.*

"Increasing as well. Tachyon relay times are starting to vary—which indicates we're getting deep into a gravitational eddy as well—and 'cast timing is starting to slow. Not noticeable to you, or I, *kyo*—but our ability to supplement the navigational suites of the smaller ships is starting to degrade."

"And if—when—we're attacked?"

Hennig showed a set of small, pearl-like teeth. "*Chu-sa*, below-decks chatter says the gunnery officer on *Mace* nearly lit off a sprint missile into the *Falchion* two watches ago . . . a distortion interposed between them and he lost ident lock. So it will be interesting."

"Delightful." Susan sat back, her face calm and composed. "Thank you, *kika-no.*"

Thirty minutes later, after reviewing the incident reports from the rest of the battle-group—or at least those she was privy to—Koshō lifted her chin and caught the duty Comms officer's eye.

"Pucatli-*tzin*, I would like to talk to the battle-group commander on the *Tokiwa* directly, captain's line."

THE *NANIWA*

Koshō sat easily in the captain's chair, one leg crossed over the other, comp control surfaces arrayed to the left to allow an unobstructed view of the engineering stations on her right. Midafternoon watch was nearly half over and there were crewmen at every station. The threatwell forming the center of Command was filled with light—the hard diamonds of the battle-group and a contorted maze of filaments representing the dust clouds they had been passing through for the last three days.

On her central board, the transit shielding status displays were flickering crimson and amber much like the fluttering of hummingbird wings—nearly too swift for the eye to follow. One of the graphics surged into red, and then scarlet, and a soft *ding-ding* sounded. Susan looked up from the readiness reports filling her displays and frowned, a sharp crease splitting her forehead.

Gravitational densities were fluctuating in an uncomfortable way, causing the protostellar debris to congeal in ever-moving eddies. The *Naniwa*'s newly installed deflectors were easily shrugging aside the constant stream of impacts, but she was beginning to worry about the other smaller, older, ships in the convoy. At present the combat elements made a widely dispersed globe around the *Fiske*, *Eldredge*, and *Hanuman*. The squadron was currently arrayed to prevent wake overlap and further damage to the smaller ships following the heavy warships.

Koshō brushed the readiness reports closed with a flick of her wrist, then keyed into battlecast with her stylus.

After a few minutes of considering telemetry from the noncombatants, she tapped her earbug awake and paged Engineering.

"Hennig here, *kyo*." The *Kikan-cho* was a dough-faced Saxon of very conservative mind. Koshō found him refreshingly direct and, like many engineers, disinterested in politics of any kind. Had he shown any flickering of concern for the past glories of Imperial Denmark—of which

was a drift of corpses—all of them apparently human—pinned against one wall with a net of sprayfoam. More of the dark-blue-suited Khaiden were busy at the consoles. The doors were pitted with thousands of tiny sparkling blemishes where shipgun flechettes had impacted.

Fierce smugglers in these parts, he thought, seeing a cloud of tiny ruby-colored droplets drifting in the hatchway. Then the momentary vision was gone, and the airlock was cycling around them. Hadeishi tensed, feeling the hot, humid air of a Khaiden ship wash over him.

The Qalak, *then,* he thought. *Into the belly of the carrion bird.*

The guard jammed him in the back with the muzzle of a tribarrel, pushing him forward, and as they passed into the dull, redlit space beyond, his earbug cycled frequency—losing contact with the *Wilful's* shipnet—and for just a moment, before an encrypter kicked in, he caught a burst of Khadesh.

"—blood-drinking Maltese! A pestilence upon their—!"

———————

With two of the enemy in close proximity, there was nothing to be done but clasp both hands behind his back and feel the bite of a heavy pair of steel cuffs through the z-suit gel. Hadeishi kept his eyes lowered as the Khaiden dragged him down the corridor past the bodies of Azulcay and the other starman. The Marocâin's face was invisible behind shattered glassite coated with congealing blood. The Khaiden in front of him kicked the corpses aside, ignoring their tools and comm bands.

They are in a hurry, they haven't taken my tool belt. Mitsuharu hurried along between the two invaders, chin tucked to chest, trying to see anything he could out of the corners of his eyes. The shipcore was swarming with the enemy, most in battle armor—the usual grab-bag of stolen equipment—but some were kitted out in dark blue z-suits with a gold-colored icon of some kind of hunting bird. The tight, blocky script on the sides of their helmets was hard to read, but Hadeishi thought it might be something like *Qalak*, or *Khaerak*. *Those are custom-fitted uniforms,* he realized with a little chill shock. He did not remember ever seeing a Khaiden raider sporting standardized equipment, much less uniforms or heraldry.

Mitsuharu was herded up the shipcore, following a swing-line with three other crewmen from the *Wilful*, and then into a cross-corridor marked with heavy yellow stripes warning of environment change ahead. *The port, forehull airlock,* he guessed. They had passed several more squads of Khaiden, and now he was thinking the dark-blue z-suits were officers. The boarding parties—the equivalent of the Fleet marines—showed little standardization in their arms, armor, or personal gear. *That's business as usual. . . .*

At the entrance to the airlock, he stopped abruptly as the lead guard jammed the other prisoners against the wall without warning. Four Khaiden jetted past, z-suit maneuvering jets spitting exhaust, with two more of their fellows on litters between them. Still keeping his head bowed, Hadeishi smiled tightly. *That little gun did some good.*

Ahead, the airlock cycled open, sending a gust of damp, hot air into the corridor. The medical party disappeared through without a pause. Mitsuharu weighed his chances, but then the guard behind him was pushing him forward. They passed a cross-corridor leading upship and for the first time Hadeishi caught a glimpse of the command deck. There

"What's—" Two crewmen bolted down the passageway towards them, followed immediately by a stabbing flare of gunfire. One of the spacers staggered and spun around, crashing into a wall. The other threw himself down, caught on the nonskid decking, and scrambled past them on hands and knees. Behind the gun-flashes, five or six bulky figures advanced at a quick pace, the muzzle of the leader's gun glowing like a hot star in the gloom.

The sideways, skittering approach of the invaders told the Nisei all he needed to know about the enemy which had overtaken them. *Khaiden*, he thought, a brief flash of memory bringing back visions of a bulky starship breaking apart under the impact of three well-placed ship-killers. The *Cornuelle* had taken severe structural damage in that affray, but shipboard losses had been light. *We were lucky,* part of his mind commented as he moved. *They thought we were too small to—*

Hadeishi squeezed off a burst just low of the enemy gun in his sights, then darted aside into the corridor, his shipgun pointed at the floor. Answering fire raked the wall, shredding the paneling and sending the Marocâin into the nearest room with a yell. One of the Khaiden was down, and the others rushed forward. Mitsuharu stepped in, emptied the rest of his clip into the nearest hostile at point-blank range and then darted past, trying to burst past the following two in the darkness.

The roar of Khaiden guns filled the corridor behind him as the other crewman and the engineer opened up. Flechettes hissed past, spattering from his armor and Mitsuharu felt something clip his shoulder. He stumbled, thrown off balance and into the last of the Khaiden boarders.

The creature towered over the slightly built Nisei by a least a meter and its shipgun lashed out hard, butt-first, to slam into Hadeishi's faceplate. The tempered glassite rang with a clear, bell-like tone and Mitsuharu was thrown to the decking. Teeth clenched, he snatched a fresh clip from the bandolier and snapped open the Bloem-Voss' cartridge bay—then froze, the glowing bore of a Khaiden zmetgun jammed hard into his faceplate. Smoke curled across his vision and the glassite popped with the heat. Hadeishi groped for a suitable *koan. No time left,* he thought sadly. *For a proper parting.*

The Khaiden kicked the human's shipgun away, and then wrenched the bandolier from his shoulder.

Ah, Mitsuharu realized with dismay. *They do prize technicians—a life of servitude awaits. . . .*

sole died again with a massive thud that made the flooring shake. *All the loading bays.*

"We're boarded," cursed the Marocâin.

It wasn't a question. Hadeishi was already sealing up his z-suit as Azulcay fumbled with his. The feeling of the suit gelling around his neck and face brought back a thousand memories. *Wind was rattling the bamboo, making the surface of the stream flowing past at Musashi's feet sparkle with tiny wavelets. A series of mossy boulders made an uneasy path to the far side. Kiyohara was poised on the largest of them, his nodachi slung insolently across his massive shoulders. "Come then," the brigand shouted, "unsheath your famous blade, King of Swordsmen!" Behind him, on the far bank, the sally drew a raucous laugh from the dozens of ronin gathered there.*

"Gun locker code?" Hadeishi was at the armored cabinet, but the battle-steel door was properly secured. The engineer nodded, his face paling. Despite obvious fear, his fingers were steady enough to punch in the authorization code and the gray metal doors swung aside to reveal a brace of shipguns and two bandoliers of ammunition.

"Pretty light," Mitsuharu muttered, pulling a Bloem-Voss TK6 from the padded cradle. The civilian weapon only carried a single kind of round, a ship-safe flechette, and lacked a grenade launcher or a thermal sight. The Nisei had the bandolier over his shoulder and secured, with the gun tucked under his arm and lanyard snugged to his tool belt before the engineer had even managed to get the ammunition and snub-nosed rifle out of the cabinet.

"Let me," ordered the Nisei, quickly righting the civilian's gear. "Follow me and shoot at anything you don't recognize. But, please, not the back of my head." The proper helmet for the z-suit slid down over Hadeishi's brow and he locked the neckring with a practiced twist of his fingers.

A moment later, Mitsuharu eased out into the main corridor connecting the cargo bays to the shipcore. The overhead lights were flickering on and off as something interfered with environmental power, so he tripped the nearest panel and killed them entirely. Azulcay's breathing was harsh and fast in his ear.

"There!" The Marocâin scrambled up from behind the console as the screen flickered to life again, revealing even an ever-thicker murk, now glowing in long striated bands with the light of some distant, unseen star. "Damn, it's worse."

Mitsuharu nodded, though he noted the engineer did not open a comm channel to the bridge, or issue any kind of warning to the captain. *Interesting,* he wondered. *His faith in the command staff is remarkable. In this murk, I would have my damage control crews in z-suits and waiting in the airlocks to go hullside. . . .* The paucity of data irritated him immensely, but there was only a single, shielded comm run connecting the engineering spaces to the bridge. *One camera, one shipnet conduit . . . we're blind down here. Still, I should—*

"What the hell! We're right on a moon." Even as the Marocâin spoke, the rumble of the maneuvering drive hiccupped into a lower pitch. "That's orbit. To stations!"

Mitsuharu immediately took his place at the secondary console. It was the "station" he had appropriated from the beginning, giving him a reasonable view of the engineer's panel and control of some useful secondary systems. *A moon,* he saw, *but without a planet or star in reasonable distance.* Only a dim glow illuminated the indistinct sphere. One could imagine ice-shrouded peaks piercing the roughened surface, but without better sensors it looked dimly red-purple, like the passing boulders.

"Looks like a beat-up billiard ball," Azulcay muttered. He looked curiously at Hadeishi. "Where's the solar system? There's no proper star in sensor range."

"Gravitational eddies could form a moon from stellar debris without forcing an orbit." Mitsuharu shrugged. "Or the star could have lost fuel millions of years ago . . . who could say?"

"See if you can get a read on . . ." The engineer stopped, listening.

Hadeishi heard the sound, too, and reflexively hit the ALERT glyph on his control pane.

"Explosions. Coming our . . ."

The alarm began to blare, but the wailing noise did not drown out a succession of dull, heavy thuds.

"We are attacked." *Who? I wonder. Perhaps Kryg'nth?* A dull *whoomp* came from the direction of the nearest loading bay. Something dark and jagged flickered across the camera pickup before the entire control con-

might have lost deflection . . . and even if the deflectors snapped back in time to push aside something big . . ."

"We'd already be punched full of a thousand little holes." The engineer grunted in agreement and then—with a grudging air—went through his own checklist on the panels. Hadeishi stepped away, keeping a polite distance, and took a moment to make sure his boots were strapped tight and all of the tools in his belt were in place.

When he looked up, Azulcay was peering curiously at the video feeds, one olive-skinned hand scratching at his tight, curly beard. "What *is* this place?" The Marocâin tapped the v-pane with a ragged fingernail. "Can we run for long in this much debris?"

"Depends on how fast the captain tries to go," Mitsuharu said quietly. "May I?"

The man nodded, and Hadeishi folded most of the v-panes away, replacing them with a large single pane containing the camera feed surrounded by a constellation of smaller displays showing hit rates and the status of the various shielding nodes on the outer hull. For some time he scrutinized the ocean of dimly lighted debris streaming alongside as the *Wilful* pressed onward. Thrust rates from the engines seemed to indicate the captain was pressing a hard course. The dust thickened as they watched, showing whorls and patterns in the fitful light.

Mitsuharu weighed the time since last they had passed an Imperial navigation beacon. *Out of range of Search and Rescue, I think.* One of the sensor panels dinged quietly, warning of scattered asteroidal fragments in the murk. The ship shifted course minutely and the engineer let out a soft whistle.

"Someone upstairs is paying attention . . . but we'd better get ready for damage con—"

The comp displays on the main panel wavered, blinked twice, and went dark. The engineer cursed fluently in Norman, then jerked a frayed power cable from its socket in the back of the board. "Gimme those spacers and a meter probe."

Hadeishi had the tools in hand already, and he hid a smile at how quickly the action had become second nature. For all his faults, Azulcay knew far more about the *Wilful*'s systems than anyone else. The *Wilful*'s mix of systems were not up to Fleet standard, and they made a constantly mutating puzzle to unravel.

THE *WILFUL*

Hadeishi woke, feeling the ship drop from transit with a twisting sensation. Almost immediately a subsystem somewhere in the ceiling kicked into operation. With a frown he realized that a capacitor was discharging at sharp, staccato intervals. *Transit shielding is taking a hit;* he thought and swung down easily from the hammock. His boots, a heavy jacket he'd scrounged, and his tool belt peeled off the wall easily enough. Out of habit, he tugged at the bolt cutters, hand-torch, welding arc, and other useful items on the belt. All were secure. Though the ship was under acceleration and there was gravity of a sort, he'd spent too many long-suffering hours as a cadet to trust even Fleet g-decking.

He padded to the engineering boards in the outer room and ran through a quick checklist.

We're running hot, he saw, and tapped open a series of v-panes showing exterior telemetry. There was only one hull camera patched through to Engineering—which was odd of itself—and it revealed only a confused roil of dust clouds shot with intermittent points of reddish light. But the shielding monitors were in constant motion, registering thousands of impacts a second. Hadeishi frowned and his stylus—dug out of a crevice behind the main comp panel—skittered quickly across the control surface. Two more capacitors dropped into the circuit, and the secondary fusion pump shivered awake.

"Captain didn't ask for that," growled a voice at his shoulder. Hadeishi nodded, feeling Azulcay's scrutiny hot on his neck. "What are you thinking?"

"In protostellar debris like this," Mitsuharu said, his voice level and unconcerned, "sensor reaction times degrade—sometimes masking something more massive behind lesser dust. The shielding control relays would have tried to bring more capacity on-line—but by then, we

"Back of beyond . . ." Susan smiled tightly, tapping her own orders packet. "Stepping out into the big dark."

"A bad omen, *kyo*," Chac growled, "a very poor precedent. The festival of *Mictecacihuatl* is underway . . ."

"Prove them wrong, *Sho-sa*. Dispel this apprehension." She paused minutely. "Put on a brave face!"

Two days later, with her comm-panel singed by a vitriolic series of messages from her commander, *Chu-sho*—or Vice Admiral—Xocoyotl, Koshō was on the bridge of the *Naniwa* as she matched velocity with the rest of the battle-group nearly sixty million kilometers off Europa. One pane of her command comp showed their approach to gradient as a sharply narrowing spike.

Below her and to one side, Oc Chac was standing behind the two *Thai-i* on the Navigation boards, gnarled hands clasped behind his back.

"There's the go-ahead, *kyo*," he announced. *Mace* and *Falchion* were in the lead, and both cruisers had cut maneuvering thrust in preparation for transit.

"They're not wasting time." Susan switched to the all-hands channel. "All hands prepare to make gradient. Transit in five minutes. Repeat, transit in five minutes."

Susan sat back, her heart steady, looking for a moment upon the golden orb of Jupiter arrayed behind the blue-black of nightside Europa. *Where now*, she wondered. An ancient *jisei* crossed her mind as the whine of the main coil began to shudder through the decking, lifting the fine hairs on her arms and making her inner ear sing in counterpoint.

> *Rise, let us go—*
> *along the path lies*
> *the clear dew.*

"Then you cannot leave the ship until all is done, can you?"

Chac shook his head sharply. "*Chu-sa*, you cannot have her for—at least!—another three weeks. Then you can catch up with your admiral! I will not authorize release from the yards until then."

"Very well." Susan removed the second packet from her pouch. "*Sho-sa* MacMillan will not be joining us from the *Akashi*. He has been brevetted to command in place of her late captain. And I must replace him with someone the men trust, particularly if they are wary of me and my inexperience."

"Very wise, *kyo*," the Mayan nodded sharply. "You will not interfere with my duties?"

"I will not. But I will guide them, as needed, and expect you to perform admirably." With this she presented the packet and gave an abbreviated, but proper bow. "Welcome to the *Naniwa*, *Sho-sa* Oc Chac. I've had the orderlies move your gear to the XO's cabin—a bit more spacious than your old bunk, I trust, but not palatial!"

Chac stared at the orders packet, then at her in horror. "Impossible, *kyo*. *Zosen* are not Fleet line of battle officers! I've no—"

"Due to his knowledge of the crew, the ship, and all on-board systems," Susan recited from memory, "Oc Chac-*tzin* is the most expedient and effective replacement available for MacMillan."

She squared her shoulders, regarding the older man with a stern expression. He was struggling to frame a response.

"*Sho-sa*, we have sixteen hours to finish loading supplies and get underway. The rest of the squadron is already formed up off Europa—two more battle-cruisers in *Tokiwa* and *Asama*, with the heavy cruisers *Axe*, *Gladius*, *Falchion*, and *Mace* as escorts for the Fleet tender *Hanuman* and the science platforms *Fiske* and *Eldredge*. They're our real purpose, I expect."

Chac let out a long, sober hiss of dismay.

"The Mirror, *kyo*."

Koshō lifted one eyebrow. The battle-group manifest was terse but could not disguise the throw-weight surrounding the two exploration ships. "What suggests this?"

"Sealed orders, *Chu-sa*, we've had no real-time 3-v onto the stellarcast in weeks. No regular mail coming or going. All incoming manifests under crypt, but you're doubled on every kind of ration, repair-part, and munitions they can pack in. Be gone . . ." The Mayan pursed his lips, calculating stowage. "At least nine months."

of course, but the severed limb was too badly damaged by cyanosis by the time the rest of the work crew got him inside."

"And what," Susan asked, now truly curious, "would you have done to prevent this?"

"*Chu-sa*, my purpose is to address *kaach'al*—the things which are broken. To mend them. One of the most curious things to repair is men's apprehension—their fear of ill-luck. Had I been aboard the *Agarwal*, then my *huitzitzilnahaualli* and I would have attended to the compartments where the man was injured. And every crewman aboard would have known of what happened and how any ill-luck was taken away from that place."

"What?" Koshō could not help herself. "How is this *not* wild superstition?"

Oc Chac shook his head in dismay. "How is a dwelling haunted, *Chusa*? There is nothing that can be measured, no true apparitions to behold—but you enter and feel a deadly chill, you walk night-drowned hallways and your heart races with quiet panic. What makes this dreadful place so different from your parent's quiet peaceful garden where your heart finds ease?"

"Nothing! Do not delude yourself, *kyo*, every centimeter of Anáhuac is drenched in blood. No meter of the earth has not seen murder, rape, betrayal, theft . . . if you knew the provenance of every stone in that garden, you would recoil, your mind's eye filling with the blood of the innocent, your ears with the shrieks of those enslaved or betrayed. There is *no difference* between the cursed dwelling and the beautiful garden, save that *you do not know* what has occurred there.

"This is the purpose of the *huitzil*—to go into these dreadful places, to show himself to all, for his feathered cloak to shine alabaster white, to take upon himself the burden of this ill-luck, these curses, this dreadful karma—before an entire crew, a nation, a planet. And by his sacrifice, to ease so many minds and lighten so many hearts that you can, once more, lift the tool, use the chamber, send the ship of war into the face of the enemy with an unburdened heart."

He fell silent, and Koshō did not speak. Instead, she stepped away, circling among the radiating fins, her head bowed in thought. When at last her steps led back to the old Mayan, she regarded him with a new appreciation and a faint smile.

"What is *my* enemy, *Chu-sa* Koshō?"

Susan tilted her head; her face a quiet, still mask. "Tell me."

"Your crew, *kyo*." His left hand stabbed at the hull beneath their feet. "These men and women toiling inside, all effort concentrated to our safety. They are my enemy, and a cunning, devious one they are, too! More than a match for all fail-safes and interlocks, able to overcome every restraint we put upon them."

Koshō attempted to keep her expression still, but Oc Chac snarled at *something* in her countenance. "Still, *Chu-sa*, you do not understand. Listen!"

"The *Agarwal* was a Fleet battleship in the *Vishnu*-class. A planetary commission financed by the colonies around Maghada Prime. Two thousand, five hundred crew. Lost with all hands off Tau Ceti during her second trials. The wreck was recovered and the *Zosen* tore the remains of the ship apart, seeking to understand her death.

"This much they found—" he held his thumb and forefinger apart by the smallest fraction. "One of the waste recirculators failed behind a bulkhead, seeping biochemical sludge into the between-hull. Line-sensors reported the initial leak, but the engineering tech investigating the alert did not enter the between-hull. Instead he checked the flow meters on either end of the line, saw they were within variance of each other, and then suppressed the alert.

"The sludge—containing a robust strain of mycelium—seeped through the between-decks, multiplying vigorously. Now it infiltrated the air circulators for a series of sleeping compartments and poisoned the men occupying those quarters. A contamination alert was triggered, but the men didn't realize they were suffering from mycotoxic infection when they went on shift. A sanitation crew arrived after they had left—and by then it was too late. Two of the *uchu* were gunnery crewmen and began suffering violent hallucinations at their duty station. *Agarwal* was destroyed by a sprint missile ignited in the launch-rack by mistake."

Susan said nothing, waiting for the Mayan to continue. After a long moment, Chac continued: "The technician refused to enter the between-hull because one of his coworkers had suffered a bad injury in the same area during construction. The man had lost his left arm when his z-suit was ruptured by a dislodged stanchion. His z-suit autosealed,

with a long tradition, a great lineage. . . . Your blindness in this matter is of great concern—both to me, and to your men.

"So listen. There is no mechanism yet devised by man which exceeds the complexity of a ship of war. Our *Naniwa* is small, as the great ships go, yet she holds within her every kind of system, every kind of comp-net, sensor, power plant, engine of destruction we can devise. Her armor may be lighter than a dreadnaught, she may lack so many launch-racks as a carrier—but everything is present in her. A capsulation of all we can build . . . and she is fragile. A delicate bubble."

Chac lifted his face to the vast, molten orb hanging over their heads. "Despite all her shielding and armor and bronzed hull, if *Naniwa* were plunged into the heart of Jupiter—tidal pressures would crush her shell, incinerate her inhabitants, and leave nothing but dust."

His hand moved, indicating the radiating fins surrounding them, almost invisible against the ebon backdrop of open space. "If the thermocouples fail, we roast inside, broiled by our own waste heat. If Engineering does not balance containment properly, a fusion rupture obliterates us. In battle, the slings, arrows, and stones of the enemy will seek us—and one penetrator through the point-defense leaves us an expanding cloud of superheated plasma. Everywhere, failure is waiting to consume us.

"All this, beside the unforgiving environment of open space . . . a hideous broil of hard radiation, micrometeoroid swarms, gravitational eddies—you have seen what happens to a ship which loses transit shielding in the run-up to gradient! There is no soft margin upon which to fall, not for us.

"Thus the *Zosen* crawling through every compartment, access way, and control space on this ship. All of them seeking to find and eliminate as many sources of failure in this machine as they can. Your crew, too, is deep in the work. Preparing to take her out—then the real learning begins! And I am here, *Chu-sa*, trying to keep *you* alive with my . . . superstitions."

The Mayan leaned close, the faceplate of his helmet almost touching Susan's.

"What kills more ships, Captain, than pitiless space? More than microscopic black holes, the teeming ships of the Megair or Khaid or Kroomākh? More than solar storms lancing out from the heart of some unseen sun to overwhelm shielding and armor?

sharply. "Do you see why the crew fear you, *Chu-sa*? Why they are on edge? Why my work here is crucial for your success at trials?"

"So all say." Koshō spread her hands, accepting fate. "And are we ready? Could I take *Naniwa* into transit tomorrow? Could I take her into battle in a month?"

"Battle, *kyo*? In a month!" The Mayan laughed out loud. "Oh, *Chu-sa*, you know she is not ready, the crew is not ready! Six or seven months of working up, running the engines through a full maintenance cycle . . . then you can go hunting! A month." He chuckled.

Susan removed a folded orders packet from the document pouch on her suit gunrig. She held it up, letting the light of Jupiter gleam ruddy red and gold from the Fleet seal.

"We have received deployment orders," she said quietly. "To join a battle-group forming up off Europa right now. *Chu-sho* Xocoyotl is already aboard the *Tokiwa*, and the other ships are arriving in short order. *Naniwa* is expected to join them within five days, fully supplied and ready for action."

"Hsst! Impossible!"

"Tell that to the admiral. Will your work be done in time? Will everyone cease giving me such foreboding looks and turn their minds to proper work?"

The Mayan's chiseled old face twisted into a grimace. "*Chu-sa*, you don't believe they have cause to fear? Even with all that has happened to you, even with the engineer's mighty tribute?" For an instant, it seemed as if he would spit in disgust, but then held back. "You called me the *superstitions* officer, as though such a thing had no weight in this world!"

Susan almost took a step back, hearing the fury in the old man's voice. "Instruct me, then, *Zosen*, for I have little time left to waste, not with the admiral—"

"Waste, *kyo*?" Chac cut her off with a harsh bark. "Waste is the root of my business, and the fullness of your ignorance. Listen!" He stopped abruptly, his anger having passed as quickly as it had come. "Listen, *kyo*."

Koshō said nothing, waiting patiently. Grandmother had spent a long time teaching her to grow still, to pause in the instant of action, waiting for balance to emerge from chaos.

"The mind of a warrior must be clear, *kyo*," Chac began, "undiluted by fear, unrestricted by disorderly thoughts. If he hurries the throw, his aim ever goes awry. You know this, you are *samurai*. You family is noble

understand we've finished final inspections on all systems save the ship-skin and the main drive coil?"

Chac nodded, but said nothing. In response, she gave him an abbreviated bow and turned to look upon the face of Jove as well.

"I would like to apologize for my behavior the other morning. It was rude."

The Mayan shifted a little, and Koshō could feel his attention focus upon her.

"I understand," she continued, "that you have been most diligent in your efforts to see construction completed and all systems readied for our trials. Engineering, in fact, sings your praises and promises to spill a thousand cups of *octli* beer in your honor. Which, from my experience with engineers, is heady tribute indeed."

There was a short, abrupt snorting sound. *He laughs. Well, now I have him.*

"These same engineers pressed me, in a most unseemly way, to let you finish your work. I must admit, as I've never served on a *new* ship before, that I do not fully understand your role."

"Truth, *kyo*," the Mayan barked, almost against his will. "Your service jacket bears such a statement out. . . ." Now he was facing her, and Susan could make out his eyes as shadows within shadows. "The *Cornuelle* was far past her time."

He paused. Koshō could hear him click his teeth together. *Thinking, is he?*

"This *Chu-sa* Hadeishi of yours was competent—this I have heard from Painal the Runner, and having read the Book, would believe. But he was reckless! Ah, by the Gods, *Chu-sa*, he was a madman!"

For a moment Susan struggled, trying to frame a proper response. *How can he say this! Mitsuharu was spinning gold from straw for six months! How . . .* Her shoulders sagged for an instant, before she straightened up again. *How could he have risked all our lives? He did. He dared Hachiman over and over again . . . even at Jagan he was still maneuvering for a way to stay out on patrol. Even at the end, when he and the ship and the crew were past exhaustion. . . .*

"He was." The words were harsh, brittle, metallic in her mouth. *But true.* "And so he paid, in the end, in blood—as we all pay."

"Huh!" Chac wrinkled up his prominent nose and clicked his teeth

The officers complement on the *Naniwa*—including junior officers—stood at almost a hundred men and women. After her discussion with the Mayan *hafuri*, their attitude towards her had cooled noticeably. When she'd first come aboard, most of the five-hundred-plus crew were already hard at work, so Susan had found herself out of synch with her subordinates. There had been so much to do, however, they had started to gel into something like the team she expected.

But nothing like we had on the Cornuelle. Koshō knew that had been rare—Fleet crews usually had a high rate of turnover as specialists rotated out and the officers were promoted. A ship's complement which remained substantially intact for three years—particularly under combat conditions—was almost unheard of save in the Clan-supplied squadrons. She missed the comfort long familiarity provided.

Proper respect for the *Chu-sa* was absolutely necessary for the proper functioning of the ship, but there was an uneasy tension Susan could not ignore, particularly when the fitting officer was not in her chain of command. The Fleet was dependent on the *Zosen*—Construction and Supply Service—but did not control the logistics arm of the Imperial military. Like the Army, they were held separate from one another by the Emperor's decree. Each *Kaigun Kyo* reported directly to the Military Council. Her rudeness, therefore, had exacerbated a natural division between *Zosen* and Fleet.

Again, grandmother would have illuminated this error with a bōken *or perhaps a kettle.*

The marine signed an all-clear and Koshō stepped past him, around one of the towering fins, and onto an open area among the heat radiators much like a meadow in a forest of black battle-steel. Oc Chac was waiting, hands clasped behind his engineer's construction suit, helmet turned towards the vast eye of Jupiter burning down upon them. His mirrored faceplate glowed amber and red, as though filled with fire.

"Chac-*tzin*." Susan waved off the marine, who faded back into the "forest," his combat armor dappling to match shadow to shadow. Most Fleet officers seeking a private conversation—particularly of ship-command rank—would have ordered the sergeant-major to stay aboard ship and out of their hair, but Koshō had spent far too long beyond the Frontier to go anywhere without proper security precautions. Indeed, she hadn't even thought of *not* having Juarez accompany her. "I

between Europa and the gas giant were off to her left, though invisible save for the tiny moving flares of shuttles or cargo lighters trolling between the wide-spread components of the Akbal complex.

Koshō stepped carefully, wending her way along the hexacomb pattern of the shipskin tiles. Her combat armor boots were magnetized, as were the narrow walkways installed for the final fit-out of the ship. Primary hull construction had been completed early the previous year—the last sixteen months had been spent by the *Zosen* installing crew compartments, weapon systems, fuel bladders, and so on.

With the loading bays and internal atmosphere operational, the shipskin had been laid down—a quarter-million tiles according to one of the binders now filling up the tiny office in her quarters—and punched down to the shipnet. Each tile was composed of a multi-phase composite which could deform—within limits, of course—upon command. Reflective or refractive surfaces could deploy within milliseconds, absorptive ones as well. They were tough, too. A diamond-bit saw could barely scuff their surface, much less cut the material.

But the *Chu-sa* knew there were gangs of yard specialists running hundreds of tests against the skin, looking for defective linkages, bad command interfaces, or skunky tiles which had—for unknown reasons—lost their ability to deform with acceptable speed. Her boots trampling on the quiescent surface would trigger alarms and lead to unnecessary work.

We have enough to do, she thought pensively. *Naniwa* was still at least thirteen days from being spaceworthy.

The marine walking point in front of her raised a warning hand. They had entered a region of the shipskin where long radiating fins ran out from the hull, making a queer sort of forest—all black limbs and leaf-like extrusions frilled with thousands of tiny heat-exchanging surfaces.

"Priest dead ahead, *kyo*," *Socho* Juarez muttered across the local comm. Susan could tell the sergeant major was unhappy, but who wanted their commander skylarking around outside the ship's armor—even here, deep in Anáhuac space—when they could be safely parked in Command, out of harm's way? "*Chu-sa*, do you want some privacy?"

Susan shook her head.

You're sure? he signed. *There are Mice everywhere.*

Koshō almost laughed aloud. *The Mice are always watching,* she replied with a deft movement of her gloved fingers. "Feel free to listen in. But if you are worried—I will be polite."

operational commander of the Yards—was expecting her on v-cast within the hour. A whole set of Fleet orders packets had arrived during shipnight and they required discussion with the *Zosen* officers responsible for the *Naniwa's* construction, as well as other personnel issues she would have to manage herself.

Grandmother Suchiru would put her cane to the soles of my feet for this. . . . Koshō stiffened at the thought of facing a superior Fleet officer in a less-than-immaculate uniform. *All night and all day. What to do? Improvise. I will improvise.*

Frowning, Susan commed the laundry and asked the petty officer on duty to send someone around to collect everything, then she found a reasonably clean kimono and clipped her hair back.

Laughing a little at herself, Koshō sat at her desk, woke up her main comp, and unfolded three v-panes on the desk surface. *Chapultepec lower form never taught a better lesson than this!*

Her stylus skipped across the control interface in a blur as she called up a skinning module, mapped her proper dress whites onto a splice of the v-cast feed routed back from the pickup nodes to pane two, then set pane three to show her what the admiral would see.

Six minutes before the v-cast started, she was finished tweaking herself and the door cycled open to admit one of the midshipmen.

"*Kyo?*"

"Everything is over there, Jushin-*tzin*." She watched him for a moment, toying with a pair of reassignment packets from the bigger pile, as he bustled around, gathering up uniform tunics. A thought occurred to her while she was waiting. "*Ko-hosei*—do you know if our fitting officer is still aboard?"

"Chac-*tzin?*" Jushin's expression was carefully neutral. "I believe so, *Chu-sa.*"

"Excellent." Koshō considered the packets sitting on her desk, then shook her head. *I will just have to make do with the resources at hand.*

Two hours later, Susan had an excellent view of the construction frame enclosing the six-hundred-meter length of the *Naniwa.* Beyond the spindly web of metal and the hundreds of canisters queuing to be unloaded into the cargo bays, the striated orb of Jupiter blotted out most of the visible sky. The constellation of orbital habitats holding station

Her voice echoed from the unfinished *shoji*. "I will say this—and no more—the *Cornuelle* was well and truly caught in a trap at Jagan. Her captain taken by surprise, myself trapped planet-side when the ship was stricken. The Admiralty made many excuses for us, but none of them are the truth. We had been out on patrol *too long*. We were far past tired, and our ship had worn down to nothing . . . a stupid, deadly mistake her captain rues to this day. *His* soul was in that ship, and now—with *Cornuelle* sent to the breaking yards—he is lost as well."

Koshō inclined her head towards the ensigns sitting near the main door. "Remember this lesson. *Chu-sa* Hadeishi was one of the finest ship-handlers you could ever meet—and even he was caught out— defeated—by an enemy whose first weapon was patience. The odds *always* turn against you."

"So is my belief, *kyo*," Chac said, in a voice too low for the others to hear. "And what did you learn from this excellent teacher?"

Koshō's right hand tightened on the breakfast tray. The Mayan matched her frigid stare without flinching, then raised one eyebrow minutely, bowed, and made his way out of the room. Susan did not watch him go, but stalked to her seat and sat down.

Koshō took two deep breaths, closed her eyes for a moment, and then set to eating the rice pudding. *A fine breakfast with my officers,* she thought, chewing mechanically. *Very fine.*

The next week passed in a blur of construction review, sitting in with *Thai-i* Goroemon while the Logistics officer bartered with Supply Service to fill the ship's holds with perishables and spare parts, and the lengthy business of actually meeting all of her department heads and their staff. In all the confusion of the tribunal at Toroson and the hurry to get to her new command, Susan had neglected to obtain the services of a manservant or—as she might have claimed—a maid. She'd always considered Hadeishi's maintenance of old Yejin some kind of a charitable arrangement . . . until now, when she woke one morning, twenty-one days after reporting aboard the *Naniwa*, and found she had not a single clean uniform left in her closet. The ship, of course, boasted a fine, modern laundry, but *someone* had to gather up the dirty clothes and send them off to be cleaned.

Her comm chimed politely, reminding her that *Thai-sho* Kasir—the

"Should it be replaced?"

He shook his head, *no*.

His silence was both amusing and irritating at the same time, and she was hungry.

Chac frowned, thought for a moment, and then shook his head. "*Chu-sa*, be mindful of this mess hall—always leave one seat empty. Always."

"What suggests this?" She shifted the binders under the tray and started picking at her sliced fruit.

"Saving yours, *kyo*, there are only twenty-five seats." He indicated the tables and Koshō saw this was indeed the case. "The last to sit will be— must be—in the thirteenth chair, regardless of how they enter."

"Ah," she said, suddenly realizing who he must be. "You are our *hafuri* priest."

"No!" He shook his bald head abruptly. "The *jichinsai* rites to consecrate the hull will be performed by others, before you leave the yards. I am your fitting officer, *kyo*."

But our hafuri bonze *should* . . . "You're not our fitting officer," she said, voice suddenly cold. "You're our *superstitions* officer."

Chac's impassive face seemed to congeal, and Susan bit down on further angry words. *That was not polite.*

"Starmen *are* . . . superstitious, *Chu-sa*," the Mayan hissed, trying to keep his voice down. Koshō realized she'd cut him to the quick with the heedless statement. "Do not tempt fate! You bring this ship bad luck enough, *kyo*, without provoking Camaxtli with your rudeness!"

"Bad luck?" Susan's eyes narrowed to bare slits.

"Not that you are a woman!" Chac hissed, standing his ground. Though Koshō would never be accounted tall, she had a good two inches over the tiny Mayan. But he did not flinch away from her. "Your last ship died, her crew disgraced, captain sent down to the List . . . you think no one here *knows* what happened at Jagan? And you survived? Were promoted? How dearly bought was that last golden skull, *Chu-sa*? Did your family pay?—Or did you?"

"I see." Koshō felt still and cold, the Mayan's words a well-placed dart straight to the heart. She turned, sweeping the mess with a sharp, piercing glance. Every officer sat still as a statue—staring at the two of them in varying degrees of interest, horror, and uncertainty. "Rumor is fleet of foot, they say, and your ears will be filled with all manner of calamities."

Her initial postings to the destroyer *Ceatl*, and then the *Cornuelle*, had begun nearly a decade after the light cruiser's commissioning, and though they'd been in dry dock or offlined for repairs many times, Hadeishi had always been in the middle of the actual repair work, leaving her to manage the local authorities and run security while he crawled around in the engines with Isoroku and the grease-monkeys. Under normal conditions, she'd have had the option to task her XO with the engineering review or take it herself—but *Sho-sa* MacMillan had not yet arrived from his previous command—and that left her very shorthanded.

Now *she* was the one in the conduits, banging her head and shuffling around after the construction foremen and *Kikan-cho* Hennig while the engineers talked nonstop about kinetic absorption rates in the between-frame armor and the spalling tendencies of the new model g-decking.

She had never felt better in her entire life, or more exhausted. Every cell in her brain had been stretched in three or four directions, and then snapped back into place. *But she's my ship, and I have—at last—my own command.*

It had not really occurred to her, until now, how long she'd spent on the *Cornuelle*, banging around in the dark, out beyond the fringes of Imperial control. She was years behind the others from her Academy class in achieving a ship command—*but there is a balance,* Koshō reminded herself, *none of the others were given a battle-cruiser.* None of them had her combat experience.

"*Chu-sa* Koshō," the man said, peering up at her with a pair of black eyes. The pupil and irises were almost exactly the same peat-dark brown, leaving only a thin white ring to outline them against his skin. He was wearing the somber black uniform of the Engineering service—not the shipboard branch, which was under the purview of the Fleet, but the station-side arm, which ran the sprawling complex of orbital habitats, forges, construction frames, and fitting stations which comprised the Akbal yards.

A Mayan, she thought with interest. *Of an old, old family. What an astounding profile.*

"Oc Chac, *kyo*," he said, bowing stiffly to her once he'd stood.

"A pleasure," she replied, then paused a split second before saying: "Is there something wrong with this *zabuton*?"

Chac nodded, lips thinning.

THE AKBAL YARDS

Off Europa, the Jovian System

Koshō entered the temporary officer's mess on the *Naniwa* balancing a tray of tea, rice pudding, and sliced fruit on her right hand, while a heavy set of construction binders were tucked under her left arm. The room seemed enormous to her after the cramped quarters on the *Cornuelle*. Due to the rush of work underway to complete fitting out the ship, there were sections of wall panel missing, and several ceiling tiles were pulled up, exposing bundles of comm and power conduit.

Two long tables ran the length of the room and both were crowded with officers of all stripes, busily digging into bowls of rice, fried egg, picken, and chillis. As soon as she'd stepped across the threshold, the nearest ensign shot up out of his place on the tatami and bawled, "*Chusa* on deck!"

Everyone paused, chopsticks in midair, and the veterans cast amused looks at the clean-shaven young man, so fresh from Academy. No one else stood up, though everyone was paying close attention to the new commander's response.

"As you were," Susan announced to the room, which brought a rustling sound as everyone relaxed. Then she nodded politely to the ensign, saying: "We are not so formal at mealtimes, *Sho-i* Deskae. A well-fed crew is a hardworking crew. Please continue with your breakfast."

The boy was back at his bowl of noodles faster than the eye could follow, bronzed skin darkening in embarrassment. Susan hid a smile as she paced along the tables towards her place at the far end. After a dozen paces she slowed, noting an empty *zabuton* between two senior petty officers from Engineering—but there was a little, mahogany-skinned man sitting cross-legged on the floor in just such a way as to block anyone else from sitting on the cushion.

Koshō stopped, looking down at his bald head and was dismayed to glimpse her own reflection. *Ay, I look haggard as a fishwife,* she thought. *Three months of sixteen-hour days wears . . . that it does.*

"This is family business. You must understand that. None else can assume the responsibility." Ahuizotl smiled. "And who, then, should I send? Tezozómoc the Glorious? To command the *Tlemitl*?"

Xochitl laughed nastily. Pleasure at his father's apparent favor flushed his face. "The *Tlemitl*, you say?"

"Yes. She has just cleared the fitting yards. And it is only proper that you should command her. But carefully now," the Emperor went on, a serious tone creeping into his voice. "The Scout Service may have found something *real* out in the back of beyond, and if they have, the single most important thing you must do is make sure this Hjogadim emissary *does not find out* what it is. Too, he must be returned safely to Anáhuac. And of course, we must secure the relic or object for our own use. You understand?"

Xochitl nodded.

Ahuizotl knew his son's blood would be afire with the prospect of reaching high enough to touch the face of *Tonatiuh* itself. As for himself, the Emperor felt exhaustion and sadness settle deeper into his bones. *We cannot afford the loss of a ship like the* Firearrow *. . . not now. I can spare a son, but not her . . . curse the Mirror, the Judges, and all meddlers!*

He tapped the channel closed, an old song coming to mind—something he'd heard long ago, in his innocence, from one of the elders at Chapultepec:

> *Oh youths, here there are skilled men with shield-reeds,*
> *In the flowers of the pendant eagle plume,*
> *The yellow flowers they grasp; they pour forth noble songs,*
> *Noble flowers;*
> *They make payment with their blood,*
> *With their bare breasts*
> *They seek the bloody field of war.*
> *And you, O friends, put on your black paint*
> *For war, for the path of victory;*
> *Let us lay hands on our shields,*
> *Raise aloft our strength and courage.*

"Later." The México tapped up a panel showing the faces of five men. Four were quite alike, handsome and clear-faced, flint-eyed, each radiating a sureness of spirit which would have made another father positively glow with joy. The last was a sallow, dissolute wreck with puffy features and lank hair. Despite his intent, the man's eyes settled there and remained for a long time.

"Tezozómoc, my son," the México breathed at last, running the edge of his little finger along the side of the 3-v pane. "You were such a beautiful child. . . ." Great sadness suffused the *Tlaltecutli*'s face, here in this false privacy. The image before him melted into that of a little black-haired baby held in a woman's arms. His large, bright eyes looked out from the folds of a blanket. "Now look at you . . . my little, little boy. What has become of you?"

After a long moment, the Emperor passed his hand over the pane and it folded away. Only the four mighty brothers remained. Outside the armored windows, the convoy threaded between soaring towers aglow with neon and searchlights. Tenochtitlán the Eternal sprawled out to fill the bowl of the Valley of the México like a lake of living gold. The cold fire of his city lighted Ahuizotl's face while he considered each of his sons in turn. *Four of the finest warriors we can produce,* he mused. *Equipped with the finest training, with dearly bought exocortex overlays, genetically enhanced . . . which should I spend on this useless exercise? Who goes to the eagle's stone?*

Minutes later, he reached out from deep thought to com Xochitl, his second-eldest, popularly know as "precious flower."

"My son," he began without greeting. "I have a task, a mission which I wish you to undertake."

"My father, I . . ."

The Emperor did not permit a response. "Someone exceptionally trustworthy must convey an agent of the *zhongdu* beyond the Rim. It is *possible* that a weapon of the First Sun has been found. Considering your capabilities, I am confident that no one else will serve. Understand that the Mirror is already on station, monitoring the device . . . and a Fleet battle-squadron will be underway within the hour."

Ahuizotl could see the combined suspicion and pleasure in Xochitl's face. *His tutors did train him to be ever wary. But he is my son, and he wishes to earn my good regard.*

"Surely one of the Admiralty would . . ."

He brushed past the others quickly, but still heard the sneering whisper: "Maybe the great Sahâne can bring Right Thought to the humans and their chattels!"

"Yes, a task worthy of our esteemed holy one!"

"I do not need servants to remind me of my family duties," the young Hjo mumbled to himself. "More than a thousand generations of noble duty are more reputation than any one Hjogadim of the Sacred Line should have to bear." Once safely inside his sleeping compartment Sahâne slumped against the hatchway. "Little is more useless," he whispered bitterly to the nearest wall, "than the last priest of a race without need for Gods."

A thousand meters away, the unmarked aircar lifted from the landing stage with a swirl of dust and sped away into the thick, humid sky. A constant layer of cloud lay over the city, trapped beneath the massive dome which enclosed the Capital. The vapors and exhalations of the millions living below rose upward, forming a microclimate beneath the glassite despite the presence of thousands of air circulators in the dome superstructure. The leaden clouds replied with a constant, stinging rain.

Two kilometers from the skytower, four *Tocatl*-class airtanks dropped out of the gloom and settled into formation around the aircar. Now the entire convoy increased speed, racing northwest across the sprawl. In the comfortable passenger compartment, the nobleman coughed harshly and rubbed his temples, trying to banish the remaining chill. The servants had dressed him on the platform, resealing his armored skinsuit, applying a fresh med-band, and pressing a cup of circulatory stimulant into his hands.

The *kaffe* had gone into the disposal as soon as he was alone. He needed the warmth, but his stomach would not stand the acidity of the drink. And now his mind was full again, and ten thousand priorities vied for his attention.

The *zhongdu's* command, however, held sway in his thoughts.

But what could be done? If the Hjogadim wanted to interfere, then he must let them. "There is too much set on this throw to provoke another crisis," he said aloud to the mauve and gunmetal blue compartment.

"Would you care for hot *cacahuatl?*" the CabinComp asked in a soothing feminine voice.

With the toy gone, Ekbanz glared down at the pitiful specimen his servitors now dragged before him. The *zhongdu* felt a painful throbbing in his forebrain, just from considering the doleful aspect of the Hjo at his feet. But, as was proper, he said nothing for a long moment, partaking of the bitter smoke provided by the water pipe.

"A punishment is in order," he declared at last, "for disturbing the right order of *my* heavens. You were sent here with great expectations, Sahâne, but you have only proven how low your noble line has fallen." The *zhongdu* made a gesture indicating large and abiding regret. His nostrils flared wide to inhale the aspect of the young priest suffering deliciously from pure fear. Ekbanz felt almost repaid for having this embarrassment cluttering up the embassy for so many months. "The Hypothesis that brought all of this about was posited by *you*, and you will prove it out."

Sahâne's nose quivered. "Esteemed, I only imagined . . ."

"Pack your bags. You will accompany the local toys to investigate this anomaly."

"Yes, of course. Guide my Thoughts."

"They shall find Guidance."

Sahâne shuffled out into the outer hallway and sank immediately into a dreadful depression. *Isn't it enough that I am exiled to this backwater?* He fished about in his pouch for a box of opium pellets. *I am too large of mind and body to be stuffed into a miniature spaceship! How shall I stand the smell and chatter of these ignorant toys? It will take too long—these foolish exercises are beyond the Rim. The universe is full of worthless stellar clusters. I am no astronomer! This is beneath the station of anyone in my family! Pah!*

"Ah, Most Honored One . . . word has it that you have received a crucial posting, a task from the *zhongdu* himself. Where are you going?"

The young Hjo straightened up, seeing two older members of the embassy approaching. Their fur was lying quite flat and still, indicating hidden amusement and delight.

"As you can well guess," he replied, trying to keep his voice level, "this is a secret mission, and not to be bandied about. I must leave you now. There is little time to prepare."

that the evidence is quite poor. It consists only of three missing ships. We are mounting an effort to examine the area of space and determine if a permanent hazard to navigation exists, and if so, to determine what it might be that all might avoid the region in future."

The *zhongdu* settled back, wrinkling his long leathery snout, and took a protracted drag on a *nargile* sitting beside the chair. The sharp scent reaching the México's nostrils suggested opium, or another derivative of the poppy. *No, not just opium. Something else less subtle. Probably synthetic. Remarkable how much psychoactivity Hjo physiology absorbs without noticeable effect. It is true that in his place I, too, should not be pleased. Nor surprised.*

After a moment, the creature issued a long, coiling stream of smoke from one nostril. Its eyes had settled back in their sockets, leaving only a faint, disgusted gleam.

Ekbanz considered the human with disgust. *Look at the fragile, pink-skinned toy in the heavy jacket and fur-lined cloak! See how it mimics Us, as though taking our seeming would confer our strength! This one seems sick, too. Behold the yellowing of the eyes. But Right Thought has guided it to me, just as my patience with Sahâne wanes. Their ships are fragile—easily lost in the abyss—yes, there is Purpose to be found here.*

"We shall send an expert to review the situation," the *zhongdu* declared. "As we have great experience in such matters."

"Esteemed, such generosity is far beyond our—" the México began.

"*Hsst!* Your fleet's departure requires our emissary aboard the flagship. Do not consider otherwise."

"Of course, Esteemed." The México bowed his head. *I hope your agent is disposable.* "The expedition's departure is imminent. The last shuttle leaves this evening at the second dinner hour."

The *zhongdu* shook its head slowly. "You will wait until the emissary arrives. Go now and prepare. Your presence here is no longer required."

Despite an intense desire to begin running, the man held a measured pace as he removed himself from the chamber. Once outside, in the blue-lit tunnel, he clenched his jaw against a stabbing pain behind both temples. *A migraine and no med-band to alleviate the pressure.*

"Right Thought? *Right Thought?*" The *zhongdu* Ekbanz's brow furrowed sharply and his eyes gleamed with distaste. "Ever we are displeased to hear sacred words from your pitiful lips." A massive hand cut the air sharply. "Though so you must address us, as guided by Law . . ." There was a long, high-pitched hiss as the creature exhaled through a set of multivalved nostrils.

The nobleman neither spoke nor moved. He felt his own naturally smooth brown skin blotching and pitting with the cold in the audience room. He waited an unseemly period for the *zhongdu* to continue, but by continued slow breathing and a focused mind he kept from making an unwise movement, or showing any hint of the grim cold which was stealing into his limbs.

At last, the *zhongdu* stirred from his contemplations and exposed a single claw tip. The appendage gleamed with red and black lacquer as it pointed at the man's chest. "You have neglected Duty. You have broken the third agreement, human. By Law, this entire system should be forfeit to us—an example to be made, of cindered worlds and ashy skies. . . ."

What has come to his attention? And more important, who was the messenger? "Esteemed—"

"You cannot force harmony from this dissonance! My sources are accurate, timely, detailed in their facts."

Just fishing for information? I wonder. "The third agreement?"

The *zhongdu* bared his teeth. Even at this distance, its breath was hot upon the México's face. "With proper concessions, We may be satisfied with a colony world serving as an example. What do you offer to restore proper balance between us?"

"Esteemed, I still await the accusations."

The Hjo grimaced, revealing twin rows of tiny, cutting teeth. "You are a bold servant, human. But this is not a matter for a Speaker of the Law to adjudicate. This is between *us*. Our arrangements require that you provide us with *all* evidence of the Ones-Who-Wait in a prompt and forthright matter. If you have found *anything . . .*"

Ahuizotl felt suddenly, unaccountably sad. *An Imperial security breach. At the highest levels. The Mirror, I would think. Now there must be another purge.* He straightened his shoulders. "Esteemed, I assure you

attempting to conserve some vestige of the summer heat in the folds of his coat. The first time the nobleman had entered this chamber—sixty years ago, more or less—he'd come close to hypothermia and he had no desire to lose fingers or toes to hastiness.

A breathing technique, imparted by a *nauallis* of his acquaintance, settled his mind, slowing his heartbeat and moderating his metabolism. His mind, usually filled to capacity with a thousand and one details, all warring with one another for his attention, fell quiet as well. In other circumstances, the México would have welcomed a moment of quiet meditation.

Here, however, such efforts were part and parcel of his preparations.

No more than an hour later, a creature appeared out of one of the passages opening into the waiting area, and the México was curiously surprised. He guessed—and a review of historical records would later confirm—this was the shortest that either he, or one of his predecessors, had ever waited.

Odd, he allowed himself to think.

The servitor gestured sharply with a wrinkled gray-black hand and then turned away. The México followed without hesitation and moments later had climbed a flight of steep, granite steps into a second room—this one well known to him, and occupied by a being he knew far too well. Like the servitor, the creature, sitting upon a large chair of some bloodred wood, was wrinkled and gray-black with a heavy, close-napped fur. To a human, it seemed as though a two- or three-meter-high tapir had found hind legs and stood up. A pair of shiny, feverish eyes was placed far back in deep sockets on either side of a long, tapering skull which ended in a pair of slit-like nostrils. Though his scientists had not dared to dissect the rare Hjo which fell prey to misfortune in Imperial space, the México knew the alien could withstand tremendously cold temperatures, that it was very fast when startled, and stronger—kilo for kilo—than an equivalent human. In other circumstances, the suffering the Hjo must endure in the Anáhuac summer might have drawn a drop of compassion from the México, but in this case—he often prayed for even worse heat and drought to afflict his city.

"Esteemed Ekbanz." The man bowed precisely as low as required, then stood up straight with benign attention arrayed upon his face. "Guide me to Right Thought."

The pattern word made something *click* in his mind, and the omnipresent exocortex overlay that daily informed his vision faded away.

The Jaguar-Knight stepped away from the man's side, his heavy *Yaomitl* plasma-rifle at half port. The safety interlock was sealed and peace-bonded with a texite strap, but none of the guardsmen could bear to leave their weapons behind, not even here. The circle of iron parted, allowing the México to approach the single door exiting the platform.

The portal was massive—six meters high—and formed of a single anthracite slab. The walls on either side gleamed dully, showing the refractive sheen of battlemetal. When the man's step reached a handspan from the door, there was a soft hissing sound and the entire massive structure folded up and away into a hidden cavity. Beyond, a dark corridor receded, lit only by a line of pale blue lights on the floor. Chill air billowed out around the nobleman, biting at his high cheekbones and stinging his lips. Eddies of fog formed as the near-freezing atmosphere inside the corridor mixed with the thick, warm air of central México.

"Await me," the man said to the Jaguar-Knight before stepping away and pacing down the corridor, fog boiling at his heels. "I will return in due time."

The twenty-meter-long passage was entirely empty—and in truth, in the whole of the man's life this was possibly the only time he was truly alone—and ended in a second titanic slab of stone. As the first had risen, this one receded into the floor at his approach and again the temperature dropped. Hoar-frost now rimed the walls, though the chamber beyond was well appointed with large, heavily constructed chairs, a pair of low waiting tables, and behind them—on walls cloaked in heavy silken tapestries—a vast collection of curious artifacts.

Gorgeous masks and finely wrought amulets, tiny figurines of gold and silver, one or two delicate statues in glossy marble—a collection of treasures, all drawn from the cities, nations, and principalities of Anáhuac—and all well known to the México, who had spent many interminable hours considering them as he waited in this very room.

Thus are our museums plundered, he thought drily. Any anger had long since been schooled from him. *And our history held up to mock us.*

This time he did not pace along the walls, but rather stood quietly,

TENOCHTITLÁN

High on the side of a skytower rising above the neon tumult of the Tlapocan district, a thin, darkly handsome México of indeterminate years stepped from an unmarked aircar and onto a landing platform shining crimson with silken carpet. Six guardsmen had preceded him, each shrouded in combat armor, their faces invisible behind armored masks skinned as jaguars. The nobleman paused, waiting for his bodyguards to check their perimeter and signal an all-clear. While he waited on the open platform, a hot southern wind tousled his long, straight hair, carrying with it the stench of the largest city in the world—burning rubber and plastic, the smoke from countless fires, and the acrid tang of industrial solvents exuded from the endless kilometers of factories, workshops, foundries filling the old city districts climbing the surrounding mountains. Such was the heady air of the Valley of the México people, Anáhuac.

The lead guardsman snapped shut a portable sensor and inclined his head towards the man standing quietly in the center of the platform.

"Clear, my lord," growled the Jaguar-Knight. The nobleman nodded slightly, and then lifted his arms. A manservant stripped away his mantle and undertunic, leaving nothing but bare flesh. A second servant immediately ran his thumb—enhanced with a spurlike ring— along the man's shoulders, arms, sides, and down to his heels. The first servant hurried back from the aircar and now gathered up the almost-invisible skinsuit puddling at the México's feet.

Now the second servant produced a slim metallic wand and carefully ran the device around the periphery of the man's limbs, eyes fixed on a tiny readout. When he was done, the servant nodded sharply to the México, who let out an infinitely small breath of relief. He shrugged his shoulders, loosening the muscles, and then beckoned for the heavy Tatarsky coat just carried from the aircar. A sleek ermine-fur hat followed, and both servants made a careful check of cuffs, belt, and boots before whispering "all is well" in the man's ear.

Much of the ship itself was a mess, showing signs of clumsy repair and refitting, but some things very much in order were not easy to hide. The overly large atmospheric drive fairings on the outer hull were matched by a series of interesting bulkheads ringing the hyperspace coil and the maneuvering drives.

He ran a hand along one of the bulkheads, feeling the metal tremble with the action of hidden engines. *A little overpowered, I think. There's something beyond the usual gear behind these walls.*

Mitsuharu's movements on the ship were limited—there were too many locked doors and hatchways to allow for *all* his curiosity—but he was beginning to feel her out.

She might be fast. He rubbed his hands together and grinned quietly. Not even the foul air seeping into his quarters from the fuel stowage dimmed his cheer. Sitting in the semidarkness, feeling the *Wilful* throbbing at his back, reactor idling in port, Hadeishi counted up the days and was ashamed to find his "abyss of despair" had lasted only twelve weeks. "Barely three months! Addict!"

His soft laugh drew a glare from Azulcay, who had returned from "upstairs."

"You, Nisei. Make yourself useful. The below-decks mess needs a cook. The rest of us need dinner. Move."

The mess proved to need more than a cook, but the simple act of opening the self-heating threesquares and doling out portions gave Mitsuharu a satisfaction out of proportion to the minimal nutrition obtained from the food. Out of long habit, he sat quietly watching the dozen men eating at the single long table while he nursed a cup of tea. *Possibilities,* he mused. *Under the dirt and sloth. Something could be done with them.*

The *Wilful* lumbered into space the next day and a shadow lifted from Mitsuharu's mind. The tug of gravity faded, the ship shivered alive under hand and foot, and even though his spirits sagged momentarily at the tremulous moan the engine emitted, he smiled to be home again.

"Stop smirking," barked the engineer, who was listening to the maneuver drives with a cocked head. "One of the translator circuits is going bad. Get that kit and follow me."

mock slung behind the number two heat exchanger, in a space previously inhabited by a refrigeration unit, and mostly filled with spare boxes of ration bars. A fine layer of grime coated the floor, overlaid by discarded litter, and the walls were mottled with dings and cracks.

The cubbyhole was mostly private and Mitsuharu settled in with his few remaining belongings, including the lamentable *samisen*. Some sticktack and spare wire scavenged from the bins under the engineer's desk made a hanger for the instrument, and then he lay back in the hammock to consider the conclusion of his grand career as a musician. *And well done with,* he thought, relieved. His efforts had only embarrassed the shade of his father, which was doubtless now resting easily once more in the Western Paradise.

A day after Hadeishi had come aboard and been pointed to his hole, the engineer returned—he was a Marocâin, showing faint traces of Swedish blood, named Azulcay. The officer scowled at Mitsuharu, ordered him to "clean things up"—and then disappeared into the upper decks of the tiny ship to consult with the captain. Barely had Mitsuharu started stowing tools and making sure nothing was going to come loose the next time they turned over the engines, than the Bosun returned and detailed him off to help load cargo.

This led to a raised eyebrow on Mitsuharu's part; the cargo holds were some kind of refit—a pair of modernized transfer bays sitting on opposite sides of the ship. Though they had a passable ground-loading configuration with extending ramps and a forklift, to his eye they were custom built for open-space resupply with a matching pair of z-g gantries in each hold.

Realizing this, as he helped two other crewmen guide a heavy cargo pallet up the A-ramp, Hadeishi felt a tiny jolt of adrenaline and a tiny fragment of *chambara* rose out of his memory: *Musashi sitting under a bridge, in the rain, with twenty or thirty other rootless men, listening to them complain about the weather, the lack of food, the cold. And marking they were all missing the same* mon *from their* haori, *and the underlying colors were all of a kind.*

He started to whistle a little tune under his breath as they rolled the pallet into one of the holds.

When the loading was done, the bosun failed to reappear, leaving Hadeishi an opportunity to investigate the farther corners of the *Wilful.*

threatwell, the reassuring chatter of his bridge crew in his earbug. *I'm the crew!* he realized, and perversely the thought heartened him. *Even as Musashi was always alone, yet never lacking companions. And what would the sword-saint think of this ship?*

With a more critical eye, Hadeishi waited for the latest line of lorries to rumble past, then walked quickly across, his boots crunching in the icy slush. The air was thick with fumes and constantly hammered with enormous bursts of noise. Every ten or twelve minutes a ship or shuttle lifted off from somewhere in the sprawling expanse of the *uchumon*, and each time the whole world shuddered. The gate to the pad was half ajar, but he did not enter. Instead, he walked past, craning his head to see the flanks of the little ship, the way she sat on the blast-plates, whether there was rust or grime caking her intakes—what he could see of them, anyway.

The gangway into the lower cargo deck was foul with sooty ash and oil. The painted letters identifying the registration numbers and name were almost unreadable; micrometeoroid scaling had worn them away. He could still see, however, the outline of a string of *katakana* representing the word *Wilful*.

Musashi, he thought sourly, *would be disappointed. This isn't even a smugglers' ship! It's just . . . small, nondescript, and poorly maintained.*

But in the back of his mind, a casual voice said: *She is still a ship, and she can still make transit.*

Hadeishi could not disagree, so he traced his way back to the gate. There he stood for a moment, turning the Rusman Corporation hiring packet over in his wiry hands. This one thing stood out in a peculiar way—the contract chits and packaging were all first rate, the agency far too expensive for the presumed owners of the battered old *Wilful*. There was no lack of "hiring agencies" in the office parks ringing *uchumon*, and none of them would employ an expensive-looking Javan . . . not for a contract as paltry as this.

"Hmm." *An intrigue of some kind.* But whose? Standing in the cold slush, surrounded by the scents and sounds of the port, with an actual ship in front of him, he found he did not care. He pushed aside the half-open gate and went in search of the purser.

The crew did not take to Mitsuharu. The bosun, a stringy Frank in a stained shirt and nondescript work pants, directed Hadeishi to a ham-

struggle between pride and raw greed that seized hold of his tongue and held him helpless.

"A small ship, which has need of a junior engineer. If you are not already contracted here"—Imwa indicated the bar, the sleeping prostitutes, and the spiderwebbed curtains with a wave of her fine-boned hand—"then we may fulfill our obligation by arranging your service."

I've not served in Engineering since I was a cadet. My course seemed so promising then. Hadeishi realized he was gaping at her, while she waited patiently for his response. He resisted the urge to explain what he was doing playing *samisen* in a house of pleasure. *Now it seems I cannot even rate as an officer on some tramp steamer.*

"When—when does she lift?" He croaked out at last.

The Javan smiled prettily and drew a crisp-edged packet from the inner pocket of her jacket. "As soon as there are hands to fire the reactors."

"I will consider it," he said, and with another bow the young woman left.

Hadeishi scanned the papers to see if they were some kind of joke; then he sat down on the edge of the small, dark stage and read through them carefully. Now he regretted parting with his Fleet surplus comp and comm. Both would have made verifying the recruiting company and everything else about Miss Imwa and this . . . this *ship* . . . far easier.

I will have to go see this scow for myself, he thought, amused.

Then he realized just how tightly he was holding the papers, and how fast his heart was beating.

Despite the poor weather—morning rains had turned to sleet and then a nasty, treacly slush in the streets—Mitsuharu found himself loitering across the cargo road from liftpad ninety-two later that afternoon. The bulk of the ship was visible behind a tattered razorwire fence and a series of tar-shingled warehouses held together by broadsheet advertisements.

Small, was his first thought, looking up the sixty-meter-high shape. *Cramped inside . . . but lean. Those atmospheric drive fairings look a little big for this class of barge.*

It felt strange, to be standing groundside, sizing up the tiny starship. He felt crippled, without the constant ebb and flow of data on the

SHINEDO

Winter clung tight to the city. Icy fogs daily filled the darkened streets, driving most inhabitants to hearth and bed. This day the prostitutes were asleep, the bartender dozing. Listless, Hadeishi sat on the stage in the empty tea house, plinking away at a mournful tune. He was regretting the lack of even a few quills to purchase sheet music. *How am I supposed to entertain, when—*

The traditional cloth curtain at the front of the main room parted with the slight shimmer of an environment field, allowing in a gust of chill air and a sleek-haired woman dressed in a conservative pale blue winter suit over a black sweater, pants, and high boots.

"*Konnichi-wa,*" she said, drawing a 3-v card from inside her jacket. The woman held up the tiny pasteboard, which flickered to life when pressed between her thumb and forefinger. After an instant of intense scrutiny—comparing his own face to the picture—she nodded in satisfaction.

"Hadeishi-*tzin*? A pleasure to meet you."

Hadeishi laid aside his instrument and returned the bow.

She tapped a modest pendant hanging at her neck, which generated a full-featured holo in the air before him. A duplicate of the woman's face appeared, surrounded by blocks of text and a variety of commercial *mon*. In more refined circles, his comp would have exchanged greetings and security protocols with hers, verifying her identity. Here he was satisfied her amber-hued eyes matched tone and color from life to holocast.

"I am Bela Imwa, representing the Rusman Corporation. We provide crews for the major shipping concerns and liner companies. I understand you are Listed as an engineer's mate?"

Hadeishi found himself nodding. *Not for long years, woman—*

"There is a ship—"

Hadeishi was nonplussed. His mind raced, trying to frame some response, but the woman continued, blithely unaware of the abrupt

of the 3-v, arguing about the loading capacities of the latest mine crawlers. *I don't need anything anymore.*

Much later, when Gretchen had sent out the last piece of reporting for her "paying work," she stood up from the scarred kitchen table and turned off the dimming solar lamp.

"*Hoooo*, now." The familiar alien voice spoke softly out of the shadows. "This old one does not trust this 'friend' of yours."

Gretchen nodded ruefully. The scrape and rustle of the Jehanan's long furred coat filled the doorway to the main hall. "You shouldn't. He is not a nice man." She moved to pass by, but Malakar placed a long, broad-fingered hand on her shoulder. Though old and hunched, the alien still outweighed Anderssen by twenty or thirty kilos.

"It stinks of disease and death." The triply lidded eyes blinked slowly, revealing deep-set irises tucked into a bony integument. "Broken shells and ash—"

Hummingbird nodded slightly. He felt more at ease now, to Gretchen, as though the two girls had been a particularly hostile audience. *And maybe they are. . . .*

"There was a Survey mission. Telemetry was received."

"And—"

"There seems to be a multiple singularity within the region."

"Black holes inside a dust cloud? Shouldn't the particles have been drawn into the . . ."

"It's artificial. The whole arrangement has to be." Hummingbird's expression—though it had not appreciably changed—seemed pinched to her. His voice dropped even lower. "Something is holding the clouds at bay . . . and there's a weapon that snuffed out three ships in as many breaths."

Gretchen felt a flush of heat on her hands and the back of her neck. "How old?"

"You need ask, given the scale of the artifact?"

"Well, yes, Crow, I do need ask. Are you asking me to look at a First or Second Sun creation that'll fry my brain and that of all of my troublesome friends and relatives in a millisecond? Or something young enough it could actually be *studied*?"

A ghostly smile flitted across Hummingbird's face. "Old enough. Old enough to launch an Imperial task force. Under Mirror command."

Under the table, Gretchen clenched and unclenched her fist. *So. A race. And the Hummingbird is not in the thick of it yet.* "When are you leaving?"

Hummingbird grimaced. "When you come with me. What we find . . . will be beyond my capacity to evaluate properly."

She considered her palms, and the glassy scars and nicks lining her fingers.

"Huh. Well, when five hundred thousand quills are *verified* in my mother's Riksbank account, then I'd be happy to go with you. And that will be in *advance*, if you please."

She felt his inward sigh of relief as a knot uncoiling. In the same moment, she felt a sharp pinch between her shoulder blades. Just the sort of feeling you got in the alpenstand when crossing the trail of a *kilikat*.

Ay, she realized, sweating suddenly, *that was an easy catch for him. Goddamnit! We need that money, though. No, they need it.* Gretchen turned her head, relieved to see the girls and Malakar crouched in front

when Malakar snuffled around him, her snout wrinkled up in suspicion. Anderssen was in no mood to explain anything to the Crow.

Why volunteer, she thought, *that our old friend spends her nights crouched at my bedside with pen and parchment book, listening to me mutter and sing in my sleep, writing down all the fragmentary bits and pieces of Mokuilite poetry so revealed? It is the least I can do to repay her my life, and her friendship.*

After the plates were emptied and cleared away, and the night was fully upon the house, and with all eyes upon him, Hummingbird nodded to them each in turn and then faced Gretchen. "Your particular skills are urgently needed, Dr. Anderssen."

Both girls perked up at this, but Gretchen felt a cool thread of anger boil up in her chest. *That'll get you nowhere, Crow.* She caught her mother scowling from the kitchen door and held up a finger for pause. "Excuse me." Gretchen took a handheld scrambler from the pantry and set it on the table between them. The constellation of lights on the device flickered, formed a series of random geometric patterns, and then settled into a calm blue square.

Hummingbird tilted his head to one side. He scrutinized the sturdy, if outdated, Vosk Model 12 for a moment, and then nodded approval. In a low voice he went on: "Imperial Scout Service has found something enormous, Anderssen, hidden back in the depths. Within an area of heavy interstellar dust clouds navigators name the *kuub*. Are you familiar with this place?"

Gretchen blinked involuntarily in recognition, then eyed Isabelle and Tristan, who were sitting very quietly at the table, trying their best to remain invisible. "Why don't you two show Malakar how to play that new coaling sim?"

Twin pouts met the invitation, but the code for "make yourselves scarce, this is business," was unmistakable. The disappointed girls left, gathering up their gunrigs and taking the shotguns with them. Gretchen frowned at Hummingbird.

He responded to their exit by pulling a flat packet out of his vest pocket. Unfolded, the package proved to be another, far more modern, scrambler.

"A *something*, Crow? You must have more than that? Something won't get you anything here. . . ."

"The Rim." Gretchen's eyebrows twitched. Then she shook her head. "I'm late getting home already. You can't stay here. The night watch would shoot you."

The Anderssen homestead hugged a ridge well above the town. Gretchen's mother had picked the site—there was plenty of open space to discourage surprise attacks, and the house sat with its back to the wind among stands of imported spruce and fir. Night had already fallen under the eaves of the forest as they settled onto bare, rocky ground west of the house that served as a landing pad. Together, they pushed the air-car into a pole barn cut into the hillside. Heavy blocks of stone and turf formed three of the walls. Before crossing the garden—all rows of spindly beans on lattices, with some tomatoes and squash in between— Anderssen took a slow careful look around, hand light on the heavy re-volver slung at her hip. "You carry a weapon, Crow?"

Hummingbird shook his head, though her tension made him wary.

"There are cats here big as jaguars. And half-humans with the same table manners. Out beyond the townfence, you should always go armed. Never know what might come roaming by."

"I don't use them," the old man said quietly, keeping clear of her gun hand.

Inside the house and behind a pair of locked, airlock-style doors, Gretchen started to relax. Curt introductions served to identify the México to Grandmother Anderssen and the two girls. Isabelle and Tris-tan regarded Green Hummingbird with interest, but when the meal ar-rived, they quickly fell to whispered gossip from the day. Gretchen's mother caught the wary look Hummingbird gave their sidearms and monofilament knives as she was setting the table for dinner.

"Not the Center, eh?" Grandmother cracked a betel-nut and grinned at the old man. "Though we do occasionally put on a duel or blood feud for the tourists. Then it's just like Anáhuac, isn't it?"

Hummingbird ignored the aside, his attention fixed on the hulking gray reptilian shape squatting on a broad, leathery tail at the end of the table. Gretchen smiled wickedly at the old *nauallis'* pained expression

fury. "Duncan's applications were lost, so the *calmécac* deans say. So sorry. It is too late, Dr. Anderssen. All the deadlines have passed. Perhaps when your son has obtained a certification from your local collegium, he can apply for graduate school?"

Hummingbird sat quietly, his face still.

Gretchen went on. "The colonial government denied us access to the tuition funds. Your so-subtle influences meant *nothing* to these institutions. You have no power over them. I have no delusion that you are capable of paying me anything for my work. Ever. Go away!"

"How does it happen that you are not, at least, still working for The Honorable Company?"

"I am working *here* because I fit with everything *here*. We are unaligned with any of the great families, the big corporations, or the Imperial government. We cater, in fact, to the sons and daughters of the timbering crews, the land-clearing gangs, the Batrax miners, and the local rural population."

She pointed to the door. "If you leave now, you can still catch the last bus. You'll be back at your transport node by noon tomorrow. Find another fool for your dirty work."

Hummingbird did not stand up. He continued sitting quietly, watching her work. Twice, he attempted to dissipate the suffocating atmosphere of the cell-like room with a movement of his wrinkled hand.

"Stop that!" Gretchen turned and gave him a sharp look. The blue flash of her eyes showed her pent-up anger had not abated. "I like it this way. It keeps managers and other carrion birds out of my hair."

Hummingbird smiled a little at her joke, but did not reply. Instead, he continued to wait.

At last, Gretchen gathered her materials together and stood up. "Why are you still here? I told you 'no.'"

"I cannot leave until you accompany me."

She hissed in annoyance, and then shuffled through papers in one of the drawers. "See—" She handed him a closely printed page. "You must leave no later than tomorrow by eleven in the morning, or you'll be stuck here for three days longer. The bus service only runs four days a week."

"*We* should leave tomorrow, Dr. Anderssen. There are several transport changes between Dumfries and the Rim."

apparently grown up unplanned in one of the quadrangles, he found an unpainted wooden building turned dull silver with age.

Now his hand-comp chimed quietly, indicating the outline of the old laundry matched a six-week-old Identicast from a Colonial Administration surveillance satellite.

Through a scratched metal door at the end of a dirty hallway, in the basement of the building, Hummingbird found Gretchen Anderssen sitting behind stacks of archaic equipment, her desk covered with manila folders, stacks of memory crystals, and a relatively new comp—though he could see the device lacked a *pochteca* maker's mark.

"These computers were old when I was a young man," he said by way of greeting.

Gretchen did not look up. Her fingers, lined here and there by old scars, moved quickly on the old-style interface.

"There's a pitiful ghost in this corner," the *nauallis* said, forcing himself to step through the door despite an uneasy stomach. "There's no proper sign on your door, no windows . . . this whole building feels . . . ill." He patted the chest of his poncho. "My guidebook says this was formerly the Territorial Prison."

"Then leave," Gretchen said, not bothering to look up from her control slate. "I have work to do. *Paying* work to finish today."

He leaned over the table, reading her comp screen. *Disaster Communications Protocols: Classroom Lockdowns.* One of the side panes was filled with thumbnail-sized video feeds from cameras scattered around the campus. The rest of the display surface was filled with text-readers scrolling constant streams of log data. To his eye, even the fonts seemed archaic.

Hummingbird moved a stack of printed manuals aside and sat down. "ISS will make it worthwhile to listen; I've found a contract for you—a lucrative one—if you've need of more quills than this place can afford."

Gretchen's fingers paused in their movement. Now she did look at him, and her expression was cold. "Do you? Paying like the last one? Not a single quill? An oversupply of broken promises? What will it be this time? Do you know my son Duncan is . . . too old for *calmécac,* even if, at long-last, you came up with tuition and an open door!"

Hummingbird stiffened slightly. "What is this? I kept my end of *Chusa* Hadeishi's bargain, Dr. Anderssen."

Gretchen laughed harshly, her oval face suddenly chiseled with tight

DUMFRIES POST STATION

IMPERIAL CHARTERED COLONY OF NEW ABERDEEN

The leaden gray sky poured down rain as a small backwoods settlement lurched into view through streaming windows. Sitting quietly on a cracked dark green vinyl seat, Green Hummingbird watched weather-worn buildings roll past, their windows shuttered tight against a cold, damp summer. The transit bus slid to a halt before a terminal of patched glass and corroded metal. He climbed down behind a crowd of migrant lumbermen and waited patiently for his turn at the baggage claim.

"Here y'go, graunfaither," a red-faced clerk nodded politely, pushing a heavy leather satchel across the counter. "Welcome t' Dumfries."

Hummingbird paused a moment inside the drafty arrival hall, letting the crowd of travelers carrying waterproof luggage tubs swirl past and out the doors. The crowd was mostly dour-faced humans wearing heavy clothing and knee-high boots. They scuffed across a hard-surfaced floor smeared with yellowish mud and out into the rainy afternoon. A collection of heavy-wheeled vans, crawlers, and logging tenders was waiting. There were no taxis or pedicabs in sight.

When the locals had sorted themselves out, the México put away his hand-comp and shrugged into a nondescript Imperial Army surplus poncho. His boots rattled on the slabbed logs making up the sidewalk. Somewhere out of sight, enormous tractors rumbled past heavy with newly cut lumber. Their passage made the puddles filling the street quiver and shake. *On their way to docks at lakeside,* he guessed.

The identifying sign for Dumfries Technical College was far newer than any of the buildings, and each door was marked by irregular patches where older signs had been recently removed. Piles of crumbling, moss-eaten concrete lined the walkways between the classroom halls. Hummingbird passed from building to building, a steadily growing frown etching his face. None of the signage matched what he expected to see. At last, after passing through a grove of dour trueoak which had

the contraband? If I do not hold it in my hand, it will seem I am hiding Truth or have sold something for my own profit.

Cursing, he paced back down the alley and retrieved the crystal, which had gone seemingly untouched. Now it seemed far too heavy in his palm.

The little old Yaqui man sitting on the corner did not look up from stuffing his face with fried *chapultin*, nor show the slightest interest in the creature's self-conscious scrabbling in the garbage bin, but the event had not gone unnoticed.

The Hjo grimaced, wrenching his polluted limb free from the toy's grasp. Beneath his fingers, the warm oozing sensation of a cut was already fading as his scalp-skin crawled back together. "I heal," Sahâne spat. Though his legs felt loose and rubbery, the Hjo fled, staggering up the steps and brushing past a startled-looking youth in vibrant, polychromatic robes carrying a ribbed, dark green effigy pot in his hands.

Behind him, in the dim recess of the restaurant, the young México pretended not to notice the puzzled Xochipilli priest on the stair. He smoothed down his mantle before spraying a biocide on the table and chair where the Hjogadim had rested. Then he glanced around the room to make sure no one was paying any attention and disappeared out through the kitchen.

Down the street, Sahâne stumbled to a halt, leaning against a wall covered with glossy painted tile showing dozens of young boys dressed as bees, birds, and macaws sitting in the branches of a massive tree whose limbs tangled the sun and stars, while the roots twined down amongst the skulls and bones of the dead. Opposite him a stall lined with dozens of flowered cloaks caught the midday sun, casting a hot glow of brilliant hummingbird colors in his watery eyes.

This is a dreadful place, the young alien thought for the thousandth time, pawing in the pouch at his belt for a map token that would lead him to other vendors. *I will just find some alkaloids instead—*

His long fingers brushed against something small, smooth, and cylindrical. The Hjo fell still, hindbrain yielding up a list of everything he'd donned in his cubicle before setting out into the teeming anthill of the human city.

Seconds passed. Sahâne carefully pulled out and regarded the datacrystal with a jaundiced eye. He looked about, saw only the usual throng of humanity, and pitched the irritating little item into the nearest garbage can. Then he stood up, feeling relieved, and loafed off thinking: *Right Thought guides me well, to avoid the complications of lesser creatures at every turn!*

The Hjogadim had gone a good block or more, almost stepping out into the bustling flower market of Tlatelolco to buy his lunch, when another thought intruded: *What if some cunning Eye informs the zhongdu of my meeting, and Demands are made upon me to produce*

did not move him at all. His master the *zhongdu* seemed to take an interest in the chattering and scrabbling of the *humans*, but Sahâne had done his best to stay far, far removed from such things. It was not, after all, his purpose.

"The . . . *hikuli* priest is coming here?" Sahâne whispered tentatively. "How would he know to come—"

"I told him," the human said, unnaturally slim fingers producing a data-crystal, "that you would be a little late, and wished to try authentic Tenochtitlán food. Where else but Tlatelolco would you find such fine grilled dogs? We will need only a moment for our business."

The Hjo's dull black eyes fixed on the message capsule, which was banded with red and seemed to shine with an inner light. "That is one of *ours*," he muttered, feeling his skin heat with distress. "How did you get it?"

The human smiled again. "This is for your master. Will you convey it to the *zhongdu*?"

"I will not," Sahâne hissed. The low ceiling pressed down claustrophobically. "It is not my purpose to exchange messages with your kind! I will be . . ." The Hjo clamped his mouth shut before *severely punished* escaped into the open air. "I am not a Voice," came out instead, as a hiss.

"If you do not accept the gift," the human said, sharp brown eyes watching the nervous alien and wondering what a "Voice" might be, "then your 'priest' will be further delayed and there will be no godhead to accompany you to the consulate."

The Gods are not here! an ancient-sounding voice sneered among Sahâne's thoughts. *Were they, we would be exalted and these toys churned to ash for our gardens. Were the Gods here, we would not need these pasty sulfates and salts to entertain us! We would burn with—*

"I can find another—" Sahâne rose abruptly and there was a dull *clonk* as his head slammed into the iron candelabra suspended over the table. "Aaah!"

Wincing, the Hjo staggered away from the table, long fur-covered fingers clutching his tapered head. His mouth gaped wide, revealing the heavy rows of grinding molars and chisel-shaped cutting teeth lining his fore-jaw.

"I've got you," the Mirror agent said, steadying the alien arm. The smooth human countenance creased with worry. "You're bleeding, Sahâne-*tzin*."

and wondered if the establishment was closed. A handful of other pa-
trons sat at the far end of the long room, but none of them had paid
his entrance the slightest attention. Sahâne's long, tapir-like head
swiveled, looking for the telltale ghosting of a human comm-panel in
the air. *Nothing.* He frowned, the leathery skin around two deep-set
eyes wrinkling up. He could *smell* food, but . . . how did you order a
meal without an interface?

"A *waiter* comes," someone said, in passable Trade. "And you tell him
which ingestibles you desire."

Sahâne's frown deepened into puzzlement. The human settling into
a chair opposite the young Hjo was familiar—Sahâne had been aware
of him dozens of times—but they'd never spoken before. The fine coat-
ing of hollow hairs forming the top layer of his fur shivered, making the
silver-gray gloss ripple. *An Eye should not speak; it is inappropriate! Its
only duty is to spy.*

"Though," the human male continued, tucking a pair of sunglasses
into a pocket of his mantle, "the menu here is limited. You'd be best to
order an *octli* beer and perhaps a plate of *nopalli*, if you are hungry."

"I am not," Sahâne said, after a moment of consternation. "You have
never spoken to me before—is there a . . . a situation? A danger?"

Every member of the Hjogadim delegation on Anáhuac, to the best
of Sahâne's knowledge, had at least three Eyes fixed upon them—not all
at once, of course, but in rotating shifts throughout the swift Terran
day—but always from a distance. This one—tall, as the indigenes went,
with sleek dark fur on its head and regular, waxy-skinned features—
had always been at least a block away for as long as the Eye had ob-
served the Hjo. That it should come closer—or even *speak* to
Sahâne—implied something had gone terribly, terribly wrong.

Ah, the Hjo suddenly realized, *the wretched Eyes don't wish me to
purchase trimethoxyphene from this new vendor. The previous merchant
must have complained—*

"There is no situation," the toy said, quite calmly. It approximated a
Hjo smile, lips tight. "You are perfectly safe. There will be only a slight
delay before the priest comes."

Sahâne blinked, feeling a familiar fog of confusion congealing
around him. He did not like this place—the backwater polity; the
crude, barbarous planet; much less this dreadful bowl of hot smog that
passed for a city—and the intrigues and plots of the local princelings

TENOCHTITLÁN

Sahâne stepped gingerly down a flight of well-worn steps formed from compressed ash, his eyesight adjusting smoothly to the abrupt separation of a hazy, hot day and the cool dimness of a restaurant. The insect-whine of his cooling system fell below audibility and the Hjogadim priest let out a relieved hiss. His long snoutlike nose twitched, assailed by the thick, greasy smell of cooking meat, the acid bite of chilli powder, and the earthy smell of red beans simmering in an iron skillet. With a conscious effort, Sahâne closed his mouth, thick gray tongue rolling back into his jaw.

This species of indigene, young smoot, a gruff, pedantic voice spoke out of memory—one of an interminable number of teachers replaying in response to the situational prompt—*grows uncomfortable, even agitated, when confronted with the sight of our superior dentition.*

"No teeth, no teeth," the Hjogadim muttered to himself, a jaundiced eye roving around the gloomy cavern. Long wooden tables—all too small for his two-meter-plus frame—jammed against the walls, crowded by throngs of chairs. Threatening wrought-iron chandeliers hung from the domed ceiling on chains. "A torture chamber," Sahâne observed, beginning to feel nervous. *To remain demands intoxicants.*

The cool air, however, was a blessing he was loath to abandon so quickly. The superconducting threads running through his heavy fur could only dissipate so much heat when he was walking—no, more like swimming—through the thick hot air of the city. That the natives would build underground, or behind heavy whitewashed adobe walls, or install their own refrigeration systems on a massive scale, did not trouble his mind. Sahâne was keenly aware of his own discomfort, but the theoretical trials of a planet of inconsequential *toys* did not move him at all.

Circling around the wicked ornamentation of the nearest chandelier, the Hjo sat at one of the tables, back against the pleasantly cool wall,

Neon washed his face as he walked, expression vacant, thoughts light-years away. Snow was falling again, dusting his hunched shoulders with white. He'd felt terribly cold then, too, strapped into his shockchair, hands numb with the effort he'd spent to get the ship's nose up, her orbit stable.

If I were not prideful, Mitsuharu thought, feeling his spirit sink even lower. *I could be among the stars again.* But what am I beyond pride, he wondered, *without my uniform, without duty? Am I more than a shell of starched linen and golden ribbon? Is there any reason to be anything else?*

Without a warship to command, he realized, merely shipping out was without purpose.

Lord Musashi, he remembered, *would not compromise his honor at such a pass. He would wait patiently, living on a beggars' charity, until someone deserving of his service called upon him. Even if he waited until death.*

But that was a very cold comfort, on this gray and frigid day.

pile of blankets, eyes fixed on the tiny screen. *Five Rings* was particularly beloved for its setting—Japan itself, during the long struggle of the Restoration, when the Nisei had returned to the home islands and driven out the vile Mongol dynasty which had terrorized their homeland during five centuries of exile.

I will have to buy a knife next week, Hadeishi thought glumly. *When I've a little money again.*

The door of the temple-house slid closed behind him with a soft click. Mitsuharu tucked his chin into the collar of his jacket, frost biting his face. A long walk faced him—back into the upper city, across the lower bridge vaulting the estuary, a hike up over the ridge separating the well-heeled Khahtsalano district from the area around the spaceport, and finally home to his pallet.

Hadeishi was descending the wooden stair into the cemetery proper when a long-drawn-out rumble reached him, carried up from the south in the cold, still air. A laser-boosted shuttle cut through the clouds, a bright red spark racing away to orbit.

They look big from down here, he thought, remembering sitting on the hillside across the river from the main launch-pits at *uchu* with his father. *Gigantic. Leaping into the heavens on wings of flame . . .* But even the largest shuttle was dwarfed by the massive shape of the commercial liners waiting in orbit, much less the vast bulk of a Fleet carrier or dreadnaught. The cold was in his heart now, and an ache was trickling along his spine.

He trudged across the bridge, bitter sea wind piercing his jacket and sweater, cap tugged low. *There was a merchanter's guild office,* Hadeishi remembered, *and I'd qualify for a senior rating's birth. Perhaps even an officer. On a miner, or a cargoman, or a bulk carrier. It would be . . . something. Better than being a samisen player for drunkards.*

The wounded sound of the *Cornuelle's* spaceframe groaning as she twisted into the atmosphere over Jagan was suddenly sharp in his memory. The hoarse rasp of his own breath inside the helmet, the queasy nausea of shattered ribs. Corridors clogged with floating debris, bubbles of smoke, and the drifting bodies of the dead.

I killed my ship. Susan's face appearing out of the darkness, her eyes blazing with worry as her helmet visor levered up. The tightening of dismay around her almond-shaped eyes as she realized what he'd done. *I killed my own children. For pride. Because I was very good at what I did. But not good enough to deny fate.*

But the third spring had brought an unexpected sight—long boats with many rowers toiling up the coast from the south. The handful of Nisei ships which remained seaworthy—many had been cannibalized for nails, lumber, cordage, and other desperately needed fittings—met the Toltec *pochteca* on the low swell at the mouth of Deception Creek. From the front step of this very temple-house, a pillar could be seen on the farther shore where the Emperor's representatives had first held conversation with the emissaries of the great southern kingdoms. By then the Nisei had driven the tribal peoples from their villages along the shore and were beginning to clear the forest for their new city.

Mitsuharu finished his prayers and remained seated, feeling entirely directionless.

I've done what must be done, he realized, *every commission discharged. Honor to Fleet, family, and Emperor satisfied by the most meager effort. My purpose at an end.* His lips twisted in dismay and thin, fine-boned hands patted at his service jacket, feeling for the hilt of a knife or blade of some kind. *Ah, old fool. You traded your service* tantō *for new strings for that useless scrap of wood . . . you have already forgotten yourself, haven't you? A samurai, an officer, without even the least weapon to hand? What would Lord Musashi think of you now?*

Hadeishi grunted, the harsh sound echoing in the silent temple, and answered himself. "Lord Musashi was never bothered by the lack of steel!"

An old, old memory came to mind—the fuzzing screen of an ancient black-and-white two-d set showing the calm, centered face of a samurai framed by the pillars of another temple, one in Japan itself, where a ring of ruffians—not even *samurai*, though their nervous hands held blades aplenty, but bandits and honorless men—circled the lone sword master. A strong wind was blowing, rustling the leaves of ancient trees, bending their creaking limbs. Lord Musashi had nothing in his hands save a length of willow wood.

They were doomed, Hadeishi remembered, the ghost of a child's smile in his eyes. *Though he had nothing but the clothes on his back.* The *Five Rings chambara* had played on the two-d every afternoon throughout Mitsuharu's childhood. Hundreds of episodes, rarely shown in order, depicting the long and remarkably heroic life of the sword-saint Miyamoto Musashi. An excellent reason for a youngster to run home from school and fling himself onto the floor of his parent's house in a

muster. Thirty-six days had passed while the gray vastness of the sea hammered at their boats. Few of the Japanese vessels had been fitted for such a voyage, though in the mad panic to evacuate Edo and Osaka, no mind had been paid to their seaworthiness. More than half of those who fled dying Nippon had perished. But the Emperor himself had survived, carried forth from the wreck of his ancient realm in a massive Chinese *hai-po* taken in a raid off Taiwan. That enormous ship had run aground in Deception Creek, or so the children said, and the last true Emperor to be born in the Immortal Islands had splashed ashore with *katana* in hand and rusted armor upon his breast. Though the shore he faced was crowded with an impossibly thick forest, and his people were sick and weak, there was nowhere else to run.

Mitsuharu made a little space among the grave goods with his fingers and set both sake bottles among the debris left by other mourners. He considered his comm for a long time. The metal surface was chipped and worn, discolored by plasma backwash, and a sixteen-glyph was blinking on the display surface. *Messages of sympathy from fellow officers*, he thought, entirely devoid of curiosity, *I will never view.*

Hadeishi placed the flowers atop the comm and bent his head over clasped hands.

"One leaf lets go," he whispered, eyes squeezed tight, "and another follows on the wind."

I am sorry, mother, father; that I did not come home. News of your illness, your death, reached me by courier off Kodon, when vital repairs were already underway. I am late to bring you these things, to pray for you, to bid you a speedy journey home to the Blessed Isles. I am sorry. I am not a good son. I was not a good captain. Now I am a wretched player in a disreputable tavern. So the wheel turns.

The foundation of the temple-house was laid upon the grave of that first man—a lesser courtier of the Imperial House; a *kugyo* born in Echizen—to die upon *gumshan*. He was not the last. Fell beasts roamed the primordial forest and the natives were quick and sly, slipping unseen through deep shadows with knives of knapped stone. The weather was far fiercer than the nobles of Nara and Kyoto expected, and the refugees accounted barely a handful of men experienced in hunting, fishing, carpentry, blacksmithing . . . by winter's end, another quarter of the survivors were crudely interred around the temple-house. The great cemetery had begun its millennia-long sprawl.

more accurately as a team under fire . . . who needs that here? There is no war in the city.

Very near the shuttle port, in the maze of narrow alleys and bars and tea houses making up the district called Water Lantern, he had managed to secure employment. He played the samisen in a tea house on the evenings, while the off-duty Fleet and merchanter ratings wasted their money on girls and rice beer and gambling at *patolli* or dice or cards. His father—who had been very good with almost any stringed instrument—would have been appalled to see his so-promising son picking away at the kind of cheap lute a tea house *teishu* could afford.

No vinegar left, he thought, passing beneath a wooden arch wound with heavy snow-dusted vines. *All spilled out of me at Jagan with the* Cornuelle *burning up in the atmosphere. With all the dead. . . .*

Beyond the arch was a small clearing laid with fitted stones—swept clean even on such a cold day—surrounding a temple-house of red enamel and dark, polished wood. The smell of incense hung in the frigid air, tapers twining long loops of smoke through the rafters. Hadeishi's Fleet boots made a tapping sound as he walked and his careful eye could make out ideograms cut into each of the paving stones. Ever here, in the Western Chapel, where at winter's end the Emperor came to witness the sun of the vernal equinox settle into the distant sea, surrounded by the great nobles and the deep, throaty roll of massed drums, the dead lay close at hand.

Mitsuharu knelt in the temple, bending his head against the floor in obeisance to the gilded idol. The altar was crowded with candle stubs, pools of melted wax, and drifts of fallen ash. Coins, gewgaws, trinkets, little toys, chicle-prizes, letters, twists of paper folded with prayers covered every flat surface in the shrine.

"The city is expensive," he said aloud, shaking his head in dismay. "I've little to leave you, mother, father." Hadeishi dug in his pockets, found the sake, the flowers, the hard plastic shape of his Fleet comm. "But what I have, I will send to you, beyond the sea."

Beyond the walls of the temple-house, a late afternoon wind guttered among the stones. The first Nisei to be laid to rest in the Western Paradise had been interred within days of the Landing. The fleet had breached upon this shore out of exhaustion. The rough passage between the outer bulwark of Mowichat Island and the rocky, forest-shrouded coastline had taken the last burst of energy the refugees could

Even a dirty industrial neighborhood should be allowed to putter along . . . without improvements, without renovations.

But Shinedo of the Nisei had grown enormously while he'd been gone among the stars. A new high-speed maglev cargo railway now ran day and night to the far eastern coast, moving millions of tons of Asiatic goods from Shinedo's deepwater port to the grimy coastal cities of Oswego and New Canarsie in the Iroquois Protectorate. And from there, onward to Europe and Afriqa. The sprawling spaceport in the wetlands south of the city benefited as well. Though there were larger Fleet installations planet-side, Shinedo *uchumon* handled a constant and lucrative passenger service. The industrial districts Mitsuharu prowled in his youth had moved south to sprawl around *uchu* in a thick belt of newly built factories, smokestacks, and office parks.

But little of that ugliness was visible within the quiet solitude of the preserve. Here—and only here within greater Shinedo metro, still protected by the edict of an Emperor long dead when the first human spacecraft lumbered into orbit from the Nanchao testing range— towering groves of old coastal redwoods remained. The entire park, save for the serpentine meadows containing the cemetery, was filled with the same nearly impenetrable rain forest which had greeted the first Nisei to set foot upon *Gumshan*—the Golden Mountain.

Beneath their broad eaves, heavy with snow, there was a deep sense of quiet.

As befits the honored dead, Hadeishi thought as he turned onto a side path—this one set with wooden steps and a railing—which climbed the westernmost hill in the park. *Let them rest, distant from the garish, uncaring noise of those who still live.*

His Fleet discharge pay had evaporated once he'd stepped off the shuttle. Shinedo was not cheap. Food, lodging, bus tickets . . . everything was expensive. Even the most wretched grade of sake was a full quill the jar. Two ceramic bottles clinked in his jacket pocket, rubbing a handful of wilted flowers to pale yellow dust. There was a dole for the indigent, but Mitsuharu had prided himself on having useful skills. His comp, waiting messages ignored, and other things reminding him of the Fleet, he sold. So his old life had been eaten away by the new.

Solving a four-dimensional puzzle with seventy-six vectors in less than a second has no value in the civilian world. Knowing the little tricks of command, of gaining men's loyalty, of making them work harder, faster,

SHINEDO

A week's tips feeling very light in his pocket, Hadeishi trudged up a long low hill through fresh snow. In summer, the hillside would be covered with neatly cropped grass and the misty forest on either side of the parkland would be a deep cool green, filled with croaking ravens and drifting butterflies. Now everything was crisp and white, the mossy pillars covered with hanging ice. Behind him, where the sea broke against a reddish slate headland, gray waves shone with pearlescent foam. Walking carefully between the ice-slicked walkway and endless rows of grave markers, Mitsuharu picked his way along a turfed horse path. Even in this weather, the springy sod beneath the frost yielded queasily with each step. *Here,* he thought wistfully, *everything is just as I remember. So our dead sleep quietly, shielded from the restless chaos of the city.*

The other places he'd held unchanged in childhood memory were simply gone.

Fifteen years of Fleet service—and at least a decade since he'd spent leave in the bustling commercial capital stretching east and south of this quiet peninsula—had seen his old neighborhood leveled. His parents' single-story house with the green tin roof and white-painted walls was gone. The entire street—ancient cobblestones and crumbling asphalt and peeling advertisements on the garden gates—had vanished. No more little single-door shops, tucked in between the warehouses and old factories, selling tea and cakes and hot noodles. Even the narrow park along Deception Creek—which marked the southern edge of downtown—had been replaced. Ancient rows of cherry and mulberry trees sawn down, replaced by a modern promenade of expensive shops and brisk, gleaming cafés catering to the young and rich.

Civilians. Merchants, he thought, dully angered by the wall of gleaming sea-green-glass apartment towers burying his boyhood memories beneath sixty stories of luxury flats and their attendant hovercar garages.

against the side of the heavy pressure door. Streaks of frost blocked most of the view, but Helsdon had no trouble seeing out.

Grasping what he saw took a heartbeat, then another . . . two breaths to realize he wasn't looking down at an engineering drawing, but rather at the heart of the *Calexico* herself laid bare. Somehow Engineering was falling away from him—along with the great proportion of the destroyer itself—every deck exposed, every hall and conduit pipe gaping wide to open space. A huge cloud of debris—sheets, *kaffe* cups, papers, shoes, the stiff bodies of men already dead from hypoxia—spilled from the dying ship.

Helsdon's helmet jerked to one side, searching for a point of reference—anything that made sense—and fixed on a section of wall jutting out into his field of view to the left. He could see three-quarters of the hallway—flooring with nonslip decking, dead light fixtures, a guide-panel—and then nothing. Only an impossibly sharp division where the ship simply ended.

We've been cut in half.

hyperspace as quickly as possible. A second drone was run out by a sud-
denly frantic deck crew, ready to launch as soon as the results of the
wide-spectrum scan were complete.

A louder alarm was blaring in Engineering, drowning both the warble
of the drive coil and the basso drone of the antimatter reactor and its at-
tendant systems. In the number three airlock, Engineer Second Mal-
colm Helsdon turned in place, his z-suit already sealed, a gear-pack
slung over one shoulder and ten meters of heat-exchange thermocouple
looped around the other. Through the visor of his suit helmet, he peered
back through the closing inner door of the lock, seeing the on-duty crew
moving quickly—*as they should,* he thought—to action stations.

That heat exchanger is going to have to wait. Helsdon's habitually se-
rious expression soured.

The engineer reached out to key the lock override, but the looped
thermocouple bound his arm and he paused, shifting his feet, swinging
the ungainly package around to his other side, to get a free hand on the
control panel. Sweat sprung from his pale forehead, and the usual shag
of unkempt brown hair was in his eyes.

Through the outer door's blast window, the blur of motion was so
swift only the faintest afterimage registered in his retinas.

"What—" *was that?* The overhead lights in the airlock went out.

There was an instant of darkness and Helsdon knew, even before the
local emergency illumination kicked in, that main power had failed cat-
astrophically. Without a second thought, he threw himself back against
the wall opposite the interior lock door and seized hold of a stanchion.
As he moved, local g-control failed and he slammed hard into the
plasticine panel. The *Calexico* was at full burn and only the armored
resiliency of his Fleet z-suit kept Helsdon from breaking both shoul-
der and arm. For an instant, all was whirling lights and vertigo.

A moment later, the engineer steadied himself and ventured to open
his eyes.

Everything was terribly quiet.

Still alive, he thought, blinking in the dim glow of the emergency
lights. The thermocouple had come loose and was drifting in z-g, slowly
uncoiling to fill the airlock with dozens of silvery loops. *Reactor hasn't
fried me yet. . . .* He kicked to the inner lock window, bracing one leg

There were hints of a massive gravity sink down at the heart of the region. A black hole, or maybe more than one. The navigator was starting to see queer distortions in the local hyperspace gradient, though they didn't look anything like the usual fluctuation patterns around a singularity. She tapped her throatmike again.

"*Chu-sa*, we're approaching transit vertex pretty quickly. I think we'd better slow. I'm seeing . . . wait a minute. Hold one. Hold one." Her voice turned puzzled.

Rae, in the midst of offering the *Kiev* an engineering team to tear down a degraded shield nacelle, caught the change in her voice and his reaction was instantaneous. He slapped the FULL STOP glyph on his main console and barked a confirming order to his crew: "All engines, go to zero-v and prepare to rotate ship! All power to transit shielding, all stations report!"

Six seconds later, amid the crisp chatter of his department heads reporting their status, the t-relay from *Kiev* stopped cold.

In the threatwell directly in front of Rae's station, the icon representing the Survey ship winked out. A camera pod immediately swiveled towards the event and two seconds later the *Chu-sa* was watching with gritted teeth as the *Kiev* vanished in a plume of superheated plasma.

"Antimatter containment failure—" Rae's voice was anguished, but then his eyes widened in real horror. The *Korkunov* vanished from the plot three seconds after its sister ship. A second burst of sunfire stabbed through the dust. His fist slammed the crash button on his shockframe.

"Full evasion! Guns hot, give me full active scan! Battle stations!"

A Klaxon blared and every lighting fixture on the ship flashed three times and then shaded into a noticeable red tone. Rae's shockframe folded around him and a z-helmet lowered and locked tight against his z-suit's neckring. A groan vibrated from the very air as the destroyer's main engines flared and the g-decking strained to adjust. The *Calexico*—which had been about to rotate and slow with main drives— surged forward into a tight turn, its radar and wideband laser sensors emitting a sharp full-spectrum burst to paint the immediate neighborhood.

Down on the gun deck, a message drone banged away from the ship, thrown free by a magnetic accelerator and immediately darted back along the expedition's path of entry into the *kuub*. The drone's onboard comp was already calculating transit gradients, looking to punch into

IN THE *KUUB*

The navigator of the IMN DD-217 *Calexico* frowned at her console, tapping her throatmike to life: "*Chu-sa* Rae? We're at barely thirty-percent see-through in this . . . combat reaction range is down to less than a light-minute."

At the other end of the narrow twenty-meter-long bridge, Captain Rae's grimace matched the navigator's wary expression. His destroyer had an upgraded sensor suite to match the two Deep Range scouts for which he was flying gunsight, but in this protostellar murk nothing was working quite to Engineering Board specifications.

"Are *Kiev* and *Korkunov* still in relay? Are we getting a clean telemetry feed?"

"*Hai, kyo,*" the navigator responded, watching the particle collision counts on the forward transit deflectors flicker rapidly in and out of redline on her stat panel. "Feed is clean, but we're edging towards full-stop."

"I see it." Rae had the same readout running on his console. *Calexico* lacked the new battle shielding Fleet was refitting onto the capital ships, and her transit deflectors—though upgraded to match Survey requirements—were finding it hard going in the heavy interstellar dust endemic to this region of space. "Comm, patch me through to the *K* and *K*."

Rae waited patiently while his communications officer rounded up the captains of the two Survey ships. Watching the collision counts surging red did not ease his mind. The *kuub* was notorious for its hazards to navigation. Ancient stellar debris—rumor said the science team was feeling warm about a double-supernova—swirled in a hot murk glowing with radiation from the few suns still embedded in the nebula. There were solid fragments as well, the bits and pieces of planets shattered by the catastrophic detonation, mixed with cometary debris, stray asteroids . . . a nebula of incredible breadth and density.

attention seemed far away, politely ignoring the argument playing out before him, rosary beads clicking one by one through pelted fingers.

"Arrangements could be made," the old México allowed with a grimace.

"Good." Koshō offered the most minimal bow, glanced up to check the transit board, cursed at the time, and then left in haste.

The *nauallis* watched her go, his expression pensive. Hummingbird rubbed the back of his head again, glancing sideways at his wizened companion. "Ah, if only she had a gram of Hadeishi's native circumspection! He will be hard to replace . . . but what is done is done. Once the arrow has flown . . ."

Sra Osá said nothing, ancient face impassive beneath the woolen hood.

Hummingbird nodded to himself, some internal judgment weighed and accepted, checked his bag for the twine-wrapped package, then lifted both cases and moved away.

tounding success of the *xochiyaotinime* in providing Fleet and Army
with such a *vigorous* martial test. And I am very pleased Captain
Hadeishi was not forced to satisfy his honor, or that of the Emperor,
in some . . . final way."

"Are you?" Koshō managed to keep from curling her lip, all in defer-
ence to the old priest watching the two of them with bright, inquisitive
eyes. "Then why have you done nothing to help him, when he has al-
ways rendered you aid—even in defiance of his ordered duty? Is this
how the *nauallis* repay their allies?"

Hummingbird's chiseled face tightened. He was rarely challenged by
anyone, much less a Fleet officer whose career he could destroy with a
comm call. Susan knew this and failed to care. She had never found him
intimidating—dangerous, yes, like a redwood viper loose on your com-
mand deck—but not a source of fear. Though she would be loath to ad-
mit such a thing, the Judge did not exist high enough on the slopes of
the Heavenly Mountain to impress her.

"I have done what I can," he snapped. "He lives, does he not? He will
have a command again, when enough time has passed to dim the mem-
ory of his enemies."

"He only has such enemies," Koshō allowed a faint exhalation of dis-
gust, "because of his association with *you*."

The old *nauallis* became quite still, eyes narrowing, and he seemed to
settle into the lounge chair like a mountain finding its footing in the
earth. "What would you have of me, child, that Hadeishi would not ask
himself? For he has *not* asked me for aid, though I have offered."

*Have you? How many visitors has my captain entertained in his empty
rooms? How many well-meaning friends has he turned away?*

The admission stilled her angry rush, letting unexpected venom
drain from her thoughts.

"He has to be saved," she said, controlled once more. "Before he sim-
ply fades away."

Hummingbird shrugged. "Perhaps you should let him tread his own
path?"

"No." Koshō fixed him with a steady, considering eye. "He will lan-
guish and die if left without purpose. Find him a ship. Put a g-deck un-
der his feet. Give him what he deserves."

Hummingbird rubbed the top of his head, which was brown and
smooth as a betel-nut. He cast a sideways glance at Sra Osá, whose

"Green Hummingbird!" she hissed. Koshō turned on her heel and plunged through a squad of enlisted ratings sprawled on transit couches, the floor around them littered with Mayahuel bottles and *patolli* gaming mats sprinkled with money and dice sticks, to fetch up before two men—no, one human and one alien—sitting in a quiet corner of the huge, bustling room.

"What are *you* doing here?" Susan's voice was cold.

The human was holding a package in his hands, something rectangular wrapped in twine and brown paper. He looked up, catching Koshō's gaze with a pair of green eyes deep as Tuxpan jade, and his polished old mahogany face, etched with tiny scars and sharp wrinkles, expressed nothing more than the most polite interest. "*Chu-sa* Koshō, a pleasure."

"What are you *doing here*?" A horrible suspicion had formed in her mind the instant she'd set eyes on the old México. He was well known to her—an Imperial *nauallis* or Judge, of the sort who traveled the backwaters of the Rim, poking and prying into all sorts of dangerous business, showing up at odd places and times, commandeering the *Cornuelle* or any other Imperial ship on hand as he pleased—he and Hadeishi had some kind of history, for the captain had always been generous, bending rules and regulations with aplomb to accommodate the Judge and his "business." *An Imperial agent, a spy, an assassin, a sorcerer . . . a walking career disaster.*

"I am waiting for my ship, like everyone else," Hummingbird said, showing the ghost of a smile, "and catching up with a recent friend."

His scarred hand—now empty, the package having disappeared into one of the medium-sized travel cases at his feet—indicated the alien in the opposite chair. Susan spared a glance for the creature—a slight shape with a vaguely humanoid face. Thin, ancient-seeming fingers covered with a close-napped blue-black fur held a chain of beads. Much like Hummingbird, the alien was wearing a hooded mantle over tunic and trousers, this one a faded, mottled green with a dull-colored red cross quartering its chest.

"Holy one, this is Captain Susan Koshō. *Chu-sa*, the honored Sra Osá." Koshō bowed politely. "My pleasure, Osá-*tzin*."

Then her whole attention was on Hummingbird again, her face tight with barely repressed anger. "Did you have anything to do with this? With the Tribunal's *compromise*? With what happened to us on Jagan?"

"I had nothing," the old México said carefully, "to do with the as-

ther. The twin suns at the core of the Michóacan system were now re-
duced to sullen pinpoints, no brighter than the other main sequence
stars in the sky.

Susan strode into the base's main departure lounge in a black mood.
Riding alone in the tubecar from the Fumeiyo dome she had turned her
conversation with Hadeishi through all five directions. *He does not wish
your charity, Koshō-sana. He will starve and die rather than ask a friend
for assistance. Idiot. Three kinds of idiot. No, four kinds!*

But it was a familiar idiocy.

*How many of grandfather's retainers went the same way? Wasting
away, living on less and less, refusing to admit their sons and daughters
needed to learn useful skills—would it be so terrible to master a craft?
To . . . to sell goods in the marketplace?*

That Koshō's grandmother had steered her into a military career—
the *one* paying profession which remained honorable for her caste,
though the subject of intense competition—seemed now the most nat-
ural thing in the world. An admirable and direct answer to the nagging
question that plagued all of the old nobility: *How does one pay the rent,
when there are no* koku *of land remaining to till, leasehold, or sell?*
Changes in Nisei tax law under a succession of canny Diet prime minis-
ters, and the constant pressure of the mercantile classes, had eroded the
vast estates of the old families. Susan was sure the Tai-Sho was quite
pleased with the outcome. *No one can raise and arm men from houses
filled with antiques. And the merchants pay their taxes.*

Susan's pace slowed, eyes drawn to the huge transit board filling the
far wall of the lounge. Hundreds of ships were listed, heading in every
direction. One of them was hers—a Fleet personnel liner bound for the
home system, to Anáhuac, and the massive Akbal yards off Jupiter.

*My first command. My own ship . . . the dream of every junior officer
in the Fleet.* For a moment, she felt uneasy, aware of an incipient loneli-
ness, and part of her devoutly wished Hadeishi had accepted her serv-
ice. *I will miss him, but I do not need him to guide my hand.*

Then a half-familiar shape glimpsed from the corner of one eye drew
her head around. The general ill-feeling of anger, resentment, and
thwarted intent endemic to the passages of the base suddenly had a sin-
gular, unmistakably clear focus.

charger . . . you'll need to keep her dancing in the hot of it—no stand-
ing toe to toe—not with the armor she lifts. In and out, missile-work
and raids . . ." The momentary surge of energy failed, and his eyes grew
dull again. "You'll do well . . . a Main Fleet posting, I'd wager . . .
something where you'll be seen, noticed. . . ."

Where my family connections can lift me up, Koshō thought bitterly
as he fell silent. *Where my advantage of birth can show its strength.*
Where the son of a violin-maker and a shop clerk would not even be ac-
corded the time of day by his fellow officers.

"*Chu-sa*—"

"Say nothing, *Sho-sa*. Say nothing."

"No. You are the finest combat commander I've ever met. All of *my*
skill springs from your example. You will be *wasted* on the List, waiting
for some . . . some scow to need a driver. Let me . . ." She struggled to
frame the proper words, failed, and blurted out: "Enter my service, *Sen-*
sei. You've the heart of a *samurai*; let me make you one in truth. Then
you *will* command a ship again! Come with me—"

Hadeishi stiffened, almost recoiled, and a quick play of emotions on
his agile face exposed—just for an instant—astonishment and then a
stunning grief shown by suddenly dead eyes and a waxy tone to his flesh.

"*Sensei*," he whispered, almost too faintly for her to hear. "Your
samurai. This is how you see me?"

"*Hai!*" she said, overcome with embarrassment, and bowed so deeply
in apology her forehead brushed the mat. "Please, you mustn't lose
hope. I can—"

"No, thank you," Hadeishi said faintly, staring at her as though an
apparition had risen through the gleaming floor, a *yakka*-goblin out of
legend to torment him and lay bare every scar carried in his heart. "An
honest gesture, *Sho-sa*, but the weight of my failure will only drag your
star down into shadow."

Susan almost flinched from the icy tone in his voice. She felt short of
breath. Koshō blinked, forcing her face back to accustomed impassivity,
falling back behind her shield of customary remoteness. "*Chu-sa* . . ."

"You should leave now," he said coolly. "Your ship is waiting."

Entirely unsure of what she'd said to put such abrupt distance be-
tween them, Koshō left quietly, gathering up her boots. Outside, the
day-program of the garden had advanced into twilight, yielding mist
from the streams and pools. The panels far overhead dimmed still fur-

mander the illusion of privacy, though they were no more than a meter apart.

"So I am the last, least fish caught in this flowery net."

Susan did not reply, her gaze fixed on the rear wall of the teahouse.

"And I am left with nothing." There was the crisp rustle of parchment. "You are to await the pleasure of the Emperor," he read, "should he have need of your service." Hadeishi sounded utterly spent. "How long, *Sho-sa*, do you think I will wait? A year? Two years?"

Forever, she thought, feeling the tension in her stomach turn tighter and tighter. *You will be forgotten, like so many other disgraced captains before you.*

"There is nothing to say, is there?" Hadeishi lifted a hand and scratched slowly at the stubble on his chin. "There are never enough combat commands for all those who desire them . . . who need them. Not without some great war to force the hand of the Admiralty and inspire a new building program." A tiny spark of anger began to lift the leaden tone from his words. "Not when political favor can be exchanged to see some well-connected clan-scion at the helm of a ship of war—"

He stopped abruptly. For the first time, Mitsuharu focused fully on Koshō's face. A clear sort of penetrating light came into his eyes, wiping aside the despair, but leaving something far more tragic in its place.

"You've your fourth *zugaikotsu*," he whispered, lifting his chin at the gleaming skulls on her collar. "At last."

Hadeishi bowed in place, as one honorable officer might to another. "*Sho-sa*, I regret the words just spoken. I do not impugn the nobility of your birth. Of any man or woman in the Fleet who has borne my acquaintance, you—you are worthy of a ship."

The cable of tension in Susan's stomach bent over on itself, wire grating against wire.

"The *Naniwa*, I hope," Mitsuharu ventured, recalling a dim memory. "She should be out of trials by now . . . did they hold her for you?"

Koshō nodded and felt a sharp pain in her gut, as though the imaginary cable had frayed past breaking and steel wires spun loose to stab into her flesh. "They did. She is waiting at Jupiter for me right now."

There was the ghost of a smile on Hadeishi's lips. "She is a fast ship, Susan, new and bold . . . tough for her size, but still no dreadnaught! I pulled her specs months ago. A sprinter she is, not a plow horse, not a

Koshō—at last—let her properly impassive countenance slip, show-ing a flash of dismay. She dug into her jacket and produced a carefully folded tabloid. The busyink lay quiescent while Hadeishi unfolded the paper, before flashing alive with colorful diagrams, animated graphs, tiny low-res videos . . . all the appurtenances of modern news.

A sallow-faced youth with unmistakable México features popped out, pockmarked walls visible behind his shoulder, smoke coiling away from hundreds of bullet holes, the glossy black of his Fleet shipskin spat-tered with blood, a heavy HK-45B assault rifle slung over one shoulder. The boy—he must have been in his late twenties, but he seemed much younger—was grinning triumphantly.

"The hero of the hour," Koshō drawled, "savior of the legation, captor of the native ringleaders . . . Tezozómoc's public image is shining and bright this week. Someone, somewhere, is very pleased with themselves for this bit of . . . editing."

Hadeishi stared at the picture, impassive, eyes hooded, and then turned the tabloid facedown on the mat beside the parchment envelope. For a moment he pressed both palms against his eyes, head down, breathing through his nose. Koshō waited, wondering if her old captain would react as she had. *I should have brought a sidearm, a ship-pistol, something . . . to stun him with. When he becomes violently angry. When he threatens to—*

"All this . . ." Mitsuharu did not look up. "Our dead—our broken ship—the wreckage on the surface—my career—it was all for *him*? To polish his reputation, to give this dissolute Prince some respectability in the eyes of the *public*?"

"The Four Hundred families cannot allow a Prince Imperial," Susan replied, voice carefully neutral, "to seem the buffoon, to be known as a wastrel, a drunkard, a party-addict . . . the Emperor is no fool. Even the least, most laughable member of the Imperial Clan *must* be seen by the general populace as a potentially terrifying warrior of unsurpassed skill. Particularly when *Temple of Truth* runs a popular weekly fea-turette detailing his latest lewd binge. . . ."

Hadeishi rocked back, eyes still closed, fists clenched white to the knuckle. Susan waited, feeling a tight, singing tension rise in the pit of her stomach. After ten minutes had passed, the man's eyes opened and his shoulders slumped. Hastily, Koshō looked away, giving her old com-

The corners of Koshō's eyes crinkled very slightly. "Great care was taken that no Imperial agency be found at fault. The Fleet Book shows you fought the *Cornuelle* against vicious odds—"

Hadeishi stiffened, astonished. "Fought? Fought! I was taken unawares by a *weather satellite network*—our ship crippled, our crew decimated—our only *struggle* was to stay alive while repairs were underway and the ship kept her nose up!"

Susan nodded, saying. "Representatives of the Mirror-Which-Reveals-The-Truth mentioned this on several occasions—as a mark against you. But the Admiralty has no love for spies and informers, or for the clumsy Flower War priests who sparked the Bharat revolt. They would not let you hang for a botched Mirror project. Not when it meant a smudge on their own mantle!"

"But—"

"They cannot give you a ship, *Chu-sa*. Not with so many powers quarreling over the blame." Susan frowned, then allowed herself a very small sigh. "Colonel Yacatolli fared no better—he's been posted to a sub-arctic garrison command on Helmand—while Admiral Villeneuve was actually *reprimanded*, with a black mark struck on his duty jacket for failing to provide *Cornuelle* with munitions resupply—and Ambassador Petrel has simply left the diplomatic service."

Hadeishi's eyes flickered briefly with anger, before he snorted in cynical amusement.

"Did the tribunal assign *any* blame in this wretched turn of events?"

Susan nodded. "HKV agitators have been blamed for inciting the local population to rebellion against the Empire."

"The—they are blaming the *Europeans* for this?" Astonishment flushed Hadeishi's countenance with a pale rose-colored bloom. "There has not been a *European* resistance movement in extra-Solar space for nearly fifteen years! Not since—"

"I know." Susan's voice was gentle. "Nonetheless, the tribunal has declared a Finn named Timonen ringleader of the whole sorry affair— and he is conveniently dead, his body disintegrated."

Mitsuharu snorted again, dismayed. "Do they even care what *actually happened*?"

Susan shook her head. "They are overjoyed with the Prince's performance."

"The P— No, you make a poor, poor jest, *Sho-sa*. Not—"

The woman removed her boots and padded across the spotless floor to the edge of the mat.

"Oh *Sho-sa*," the man said, shaking his head. "You should not have brought me the honorable blades. A fine gesture, truthfully, but—"

"I bear no swords," Susan Koshō said, kneeling gracefully and drawing a parchment envelope from the inner pocket of her uniform jacket. "The Admiralty tribunal has concluded its deliberations. You will not satisfy the Emperor's Honor for the loss of our ship. As of only an hour ago, you are free to leave this place at any time you please." She set down the envelope, touching the corners to align the rectangle properly between them.

"What is this?" Mitsuharu Hadeishi, recently captain of the ill-starred IMN *Astronomer*-class light cruiser *Henry R. Cornuelle*, eyed the parchment suspiciously. "This is not an orders packet."

Koshō shook her head *no*, gaze politely averted from his, attention unerringly fixed on the hem of his kimono, which was frayed and showing a small tear. She wondered, seeing how shabby his clothing was, what had happened to the old manservant who had tended Hadeishi's personal affairs aboard the *Cornuelle*. The rest of the crew—those who had lived through the disaster over Jagan—had scattered to the five directions. *Even my feet,* she thought, *are on a strange road, every compass awry with the influence of the fates. With every step, a crossroads appears out of the darkness. . . .*

"I have been retired?" Hadeishi's voice was thin with distress.

"No." Susan met his eyes at last. "You have been placed on reserve duty, pending the needs of the Fleet. Your record . . . your service jacket is . . . all references to the incident at Jagan have been removed. A compromise was reached—"

"But I have no ship," he said, blinking, trying to take in the abrupt end of his career as a plain envelope pinched between thumb and forefinger. "No duty, no . . . no . . ."

He stopped, lips pursed, dark eyebrows narrowed over puzzled, wounded eyes. Susan could feel his mind whirling—imagined touching his brow would reveal a terrible, fruitless heat—and her own face became glacially impassive in response to his distress.

After a moment, Hadeishi's eyes focused, found her, remembered her words, and his head tilted a little to one side. "What of the others? Or am I the only one small enough to be caught in the net of accountability?"

THE HOUSE OF FUMEIYO-IE

TOROSON ADVANCED FLEET BASE, IMPERIAL MÉXICA SPACE

A slim Nisei woman, her back straight as a sword blade, glossy black hair coiled at her neck, paused before a *shoji*-panel of laminate cedar and redwood. She took a moment to straighten the crisply starched cuffs of her dress whites, to tuck her cap under one arm, and to adjust the four tiny golden skulls on her collar tabs. Then, prepared, she placed two fingers against the door itself.

There was a quiet chime—the sound of a temple bell filtered through autumnal leaves—and the panel slid soundlessly to one side. The Imperial México Navy *Chu-sa* stepped out onto a covered porch, walked down a flight of broad wooden steps and out into a perfectly manicured Tokuga-period garden. A glassite pressure dome vaulted overhead, half of the armored panels polarized against the glare of the twin primaries of the Michóacan binary. Her boots clicked on a curving stone bridge crossing a swift, silent brook—the recycled water clear as crystal, reeds and tadpoles wavering in the current running over mossy stones—and she passed beneath the rustling branches of a stand of hothouse aspen.

A teahouse stood beneath the golden trees, ancient wood and paper walls meticulously assembled at the heart of the Fleet base, slate roof strewn with leaf litter. The newly minted captain knelt at the door and paused again—taking a measured breath—before drawing aside the old-fashioned panel of rice paper and varnished pine. The large interior room was quite barren. A tatami lay in the middle of the floor, a pale jute-colored island in a sea of gleaming dark fir planking. A man was kneeling on the mat, hands hidden in the folds of a plain civilian kimono. He lifted his head curiously at the sound of the opening door.

His thin face, pale and seamed from long exhaustion, was calm.

Then he recognized her and everything sure and composed about him disappeared in a jolt of surprise—delight—and then slowly dawning grief.

LAND OF THE
DEAD

No maize grew, and the gods of the field
Turned their eyes from the people,
And all the people grew thin, and perished.

The Lord of Heaven cut the heart from his living son,
And so was born the Sixth Sun, which sustains
The universe with infinite light.
Its sign was 4-Flint.
Those who watch the sky say this Sun

Will end in annihilation, when the flint-knife
Severs the birthcord of the Sun, plunging all
Into darkness, where the people will
Be cut to pieces and scattered.

This is the time of the Sixth Sun. . . .

In the beginning was the First Sun,
4-Water was its sign;
It was called the Sun of Water,
For water covered the world,
Leaving nothing but the dragonflies above
And the fishy men below.

The Second Sun was born,
4-Jaguar was its sign;
This was called the Sun of the Jaguars.
In this Sun the heavens collapsed,
So that the Sun could not move in its course.
The world darkened, and when all was dark
Then the people were devoured.

The Giants perished, giving life to the Third Sun.
4-Rain was its sign;
It was called the Sun of Rain,
For this Sun rained fire from bleeding eyes
And the people were consumed.

From the torrent of burning stones,
The Fourth Sun was born.
4-Wind was its sign, and it was called the Sun of Wind.
In this Sun, all which stood on the earth was carried
Away by terrible winds.
The people were turned into monkeys,
and scattered from their cities into the forest.

Now, by sacrifice of the divine liquid, the Fifth Sun was born.
Its sign was 4-Motion.
As the Sun moved, following a course,
The ancients called it the Sun of Motion.
In the time of this Sun, there were
Great earthquakes and famine,

Itto-Hei	Starman 1st Class	Private 1st Class	
Nitto-Hei	Starman 2nd Class	Private 2nd Class	Telpochyahqui *(LEADING YOUTH)*
Santo-Hei	Starman 3rd Class *(RECRUIT)*	Private 3rd Class *(RECRUIT)*	Telpolcatl *(YOUTH)*
Sencho	Captain of a civilian starship		

MILITARY RANKS OF THE IMPERIAL MÉXICA FLEET, ARMY, AND MARINES

NISEI TERM	FLEET RANK	MARINE/ ARMY RANK	MÉXICA TERM
Gensui	Admiral of the Fleet	Commandant	Cuauhnochteuctli *(EAGLE PRICKLY-PEAR LORD)*
Thai-sho	Admiral	General	Ezhuahuacatl *(BLOOD-SHEDDER)*
Chu-sho	Vice Admiral	Lieutenant-General	Tlacoccalcatl *(COMMANDING GENERAL)*
Sho-sho	Rear Admiral	Major-General	Tlacateccatl *(GENERAL)*
Thai-sa	Captain	Colonel	Cuauhtlahtoh *(CHIEF)*
Chu-sa	Commander		Cuahyahcatl *(GREAT CAPTAIN)*
Sho-sa	Lieutenant-Commander	Major	
Thai-i	Lieutenant	Captain	
Chu-i	Sub-Lieutenant	Lieutenant	
Sho-i	Ensign	Sub-Lieutenant	
Sho-i Ko-hosei	Midshipman		
Seito	Cadet	Cadet	Pipiltin
Heisocho Jun-i	Warrant Officer	Warrant Officer	Cuachicqueh *(SHORN ONES)*
Joto-Heiso Socho	Chief Petty Officer	Sergeant Major	Tiahchcacauhtin *(TEACHER OF YOUTHS)*
Itto-Heiso Gunso	1st Petty Officer	Sergeant	Cuauhhuehueh *(EAGLE ELDER)*
Nitto-Heiso Gocho	2nd Petty Officer	Corporal	Tequihuah *(VETERAN WARRIOR)*
SeiHeicho Heicho	Leading Starman	Lance Corporal	Yaotequihuah *(LEADER OF YOUTHS)*
Joto-Hei	Able Starman	Superior Private	

A NOTE CONCERNING MEASUREMENTS

Though her later victories rendered the full terms of the Lisbon Accords moot, the México Empire abides by the common set of weights and measures set forth by the Accord in A.D. 1724. As a result, distances are in kilometers, weights in kilograms, and so on.

A NOTE ABOUT IMPERIAL MÉXICA NAVY SHIP NAMES

Capital ships—dreadnaughts, heavy carriers, and battleships—tend to have México names, usually of gods, monsters, or famous generals from the Conquest.

Midrange ships—strike and escort carriers and heavy cruisers—usually have Nisei, Mixtec, or Skawtish names. Very recently, some *Provincial*-class battle cruisers have come into service bearing city names.

Smaller ships—light cruisers, destroyers, transports, and fleet tenders—come in a wide variety of classes and naming schemes, usually assigned as a sop to some organization or group outside of the Four Hundred families.

THE CONCORDANCE

A wealth of detail about the universe of the Sixth Sun can be found at: http://www.throneworld.com/wiki/index.php?title=Category:Concordance.

For Keith Laumer, K. H. Scheer, and Walter Ernsting: That was some good reading!

Tremendous thanks are owed to my able, witty, and good-looking advisors in matters scientific, mythological, and military: Martin, Annita, Cap'n Paul, Chris W., Chris C., and the "O.W."

This is a work of fiction. All of the characters, organizations, and events portrayed in this novel are either products of the author's imagination or are used fictitiously.

LAND OF THE DEAD

A Tor Book
Published by Tom Doherty Associates, LLC
175 Fifth Avenue
New York, NY 10010

www.tor-forge.com

Tor® is a registered trademark of Tom Doherty Associates, LLC.

Library of Congress Cataloging-in-Publication Data

Harlan, Thomas.
 Land of the dead / Thomas Harlan.—1st ed.
 p. cm.
 "A Tom Doherty Associates book."
 ISBN-13: 978-0-7653-1204-4
 ISBN-10: 0-7653-1204-2
 1. Aztecs—Fiction. 2. Antiquities—Collection and preservation—Fiction.
3. Mexico—Fiction. I. Title.
 PS3558.A624244L36 2009
 813'.54—dc22

 2009013466

First Edition: August 2009

Printed in the United States of America

0 9 8 7 6 5 4 3 2 1

LAND OF THE
DEAD

THOMAS
HARLAN

A TOM DOHERTY ASSOCIATES BOOK

NEW YORK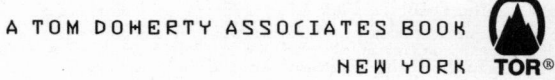

TOR BOOKS BY THOMAS HARLAN

LAND OF THE DEAD

HOME BUYERS GUIDE

The Home Buying Process

Buying a home can be one of the most important decisions a person will make in his or her lifetime. A buyer is required to make several legal and financial commitments. For the first-time buyer, and even some veteran homeowners, this process can be confusing. Therefore, it is vital that the prospective buyer understand the process that must take place between the initial decision to move and the eventual possession of the new home. In this section, a typical home-buying process is followed, and the necessity for each step is explained.

Making the Decision

There are many reasons why people change homes. Frequently, people are forced to move because they change jobs and need to relocate to another town. For these people, buying a new home takes on some amount of urgency. They cannot afford to wait for the perfect house. For others, moving is a way to upgrade or modify their housing. They may desire more space or less space than they currently have. They may seek a more desirable neighborhood. There may be features of a home they do not presently have but want. They may just be renters who are ready to enjoy the benefits of homeownership. These groups can take a more leisurely approach to selecting a home.

A first step in making an intelligent choice is to decide exactly what you want in the new home. It might be helpful to detail the features of the "ideal" home, then decide what you would forego if you have to scale back. (Check the section on housing options, page 5.) Establishing your priorities will help you to evaluate homes and to describe to sales agents what you are looking for.

Setting a Price Range

Before going out and seriously looking at homes, you might call some lenders to get an idea of current mortgage rates. Loan terms will help determine how much you will be able to afford.

When you apply for a mortgage loan, the lender will apply certain criteria to determine how large a loan to make. The amount depends mainly on your income and how much debt you currently have. You can run through a similar analysis to provide an estimate of your loan limit. (See the section on prequalifying, page 9.)

1

Home Shopping

You will need to do some information gathering. First try to get an idea of the prices being asked for homes on the market. Read the classified ads and visit new home subdivisions. You may even pick up variations between certain locations. You should begin to select neighborhoods that appear desirable. A neighborhood can be favored because of the style of homes there, convenience to work or other points, or its reputation for retaining property values. If you know where you would like to live, you can save much time when you begin to look at houses.

Now you are ready to start the search process in earnest. There are several sources for available homes. Some owners try to sell their own homes without the aid of an agent. Check classified ads and *for sale* signs in front yards for these offers. Builders often advertise open house showings and may provide sales offices on the premises. Real estate brokerage firms represent many home sellers and also advertise with newspaper ads and yard signs. However, a visit to the brokerage office allows you to find out about a large number of homes on the market by looking through *exclusive* and *multiple* listings with an agent. (Exclusives are homes that are offered through a single broker; multiple listings are offered in cooperation with all brokers who are members of the service. (See Types of Listings, page 22.) The agent can also help you narrow down the list to the location, features, and price you desire. In addition, the agent can provide an inspection tour of available homes.

Negotiation

When you find the home you wish to buy, you can make an offer by submitting a *sales contract*. (This document may have another name in your state. For example, in Texas it is an *earnest money contract*.) The contract states what you are willing to pay (in most cases, it is not necessary to offer the full asking price), when you would like to take possession, and under what conditions the sale will be completed. These conditions generally include a provision that you are able to obtain financing at certain specified terms. This frees you of the obligation to go through with the purchase if you are turned down for a loan. Another common provision is that the house is free of defects over a specified amount of repairs that the seller agrees to make before closing. Other contingencies can be included, such as a provision that you must first sell your current home. (See the sales contract, page 793.)

Your offer will be accompanied by a check to signify serious intent. This earnest money is typically less than five percent of the price of the home and is forfeited if you back out of the contract. (If the deal falls through because of one of the conditions in the contract, your deposit is returned.) Of course, the contract is not binding until the seller signs it. The seller may accept your offer by signing the contract, reject the offer by sending it back, or propose a counteroffer by modifying the contract and signing it. Since a counteroffer is a substitute offer, it constitutes

2

rejection of the contract. If the counteroffer is acceptable, you may initial the contract to validate it. Alternatively, you may make another counteroffer; or you may reject the counteroffer, refuse to negotiate further, and take back your earnest money. This negotiation can go back and forth until an agreement (or an impasse) is reached. Of course, until a contract is signed by both parties, the seller may entertain offers from other buyers.

The sales contract designates the date at which property ownership will change. This is called a *closing*. In the meantime, you need to arrange financing. Since this typically takes from three to eight weeks, a loan application should be filed soon after signing the sales contract.

Getting Financing

Most home mortgage loans are made by lending institutions, such as savings and loan associations or banks, and mortgage bankers. Information on available terms can be obtained by calling a number of these lenders. There may be several types of loans available. Compare terms since they may vary significantly among lenders. (See the sections on loan sources and loan types, page 11 and page 12.)

When you have decided on a lender and type of loan, you can prepare to make a loan application. Take some time to gather information on your current income, major debts and available cash (or assets that can be converted to cash readily). If you are self-employed or work on commission, you may need income tax returns for the last three years to establish your income. (See page 792 for worksheets that can be used to calculate your qualifying income.)

When you visit the lender, you will need to take along a copy of the sales contract. You will fill out an application form stating your income, debts, and assets. You will also sign forms that allow the lender to verify some of the information you have provided (such as salary and bank account balances). Finally there will be a nonrefundable fee of at least $200 to cover the expense of an appraisal and credit review.

During the next several weeks, the lender analyzes your application to determine if a loan commitment can be issued. The home will be appraised to see if it is worth enough to cover the loan. Your credit history will be reviewed. Your income and debt will be evaluated to see if you can reasonably afford to make the payments on the loan. Finally, the lender will check to see if you have enough cash to make the required down payment on the house. If you require mortgage insurance, you will apply for it during this period.

The final decision to make the loan is generally made by a loan committee that meets periodically. If the decision is favorable, you will be given a commitment for the loan, sometimes with a locked-in interest rate. The commitment is good for a stated period from the time of the application, and the rate is good for a shorter period. For example, the commitment for the loan might be good for six months, with the rate valid for 45 days.

Preparing for Closing

In the time before the closing, there are several things that must be done. Practices vary from place to place. In many areas it is customary for the seller to arrange for a title search and, at closing, purchase a title insurance policy in the name of the lender and/or buyer. This policy assures good title and protects against claims of ownership or partial interests. The buyer must arrange for a hazard and liability insurance policy to be written for the new house. Such a policy is required for the mortgage loan. A new survey will be made of the property to make sure no building is encroaching on surrounding property. A termite inspection is typically required. The buyer may exercise the right under the contract to hire a housing inspector to report any non-functioning equipment or unsafe building condition. Recall that the sales contract may require the seller to repair any broken component up to a certain dollar limit. Such repairs should be completed before closing.

In some cases it may be necessary for the buyer to move into the house before the closing. Possibly a lease has expired or a previous house has closed before the buyer takes possession. If the new house is vacant, the buyer may arrange with the seller to rent the house in the interim. This is usually done at a nominal rental rate or may even be rent-free, particularly if the buyer is merely storing possessions but not actually living in the home.

In any event, the buyer must obtain the seller's agreement to the arrangement, preferably in writing. The buyer should also check with his or her insurance carrier to see if the policy covers the possessions while in the new house.

Closing

On closing day, all parties will meet and execute the necessary paperwork to pass title of the property. (For more details, see section on closing procedures, page 16.) Closing generally takes place at the offices of the title insurance company. The buyer and seller are present or represented, along with legal counsel, if desired. Also present will be the real estate broker, if one has been involved, and a representative of the mortgage lender. Closing day is considered the first day of ownership for the buyer, and all benefits and responsibilities are conferred at this time.

At the closing, the seller delivers a deed to the home, signifying passage of legal title to the buyer. The deed is a document that describes the title conveyed and acknowledges the identity of the new owner. The buyer provides any down payment required and signs the mortgage documents releasing the borrowed funds to the seller. These documents include a note acknowledging the debt and promising to repay the loan in a specific manner and a mortgage pledging the home to back up the borrower's promise. The seller then uses a portion of the money to retire any existing loans on the property (except for those that are

assumed by the buyer), pays the expenses of sale, and receives a check for the balance.

Most of the costs associated with the sale are paid at closing. The agents receive their commissions and the attorneys their fees. There also may be costs involved in inspections, surveys and various legal requirements. The one-time premiums for title insurance are paid. The lender may require payments toward setting up an *escrow* for the payment of future property taxes, insurance premiums and interest to cover the time from closing until the end of the month. From that point on, mortgage interest is paid at the end of the month as part of the regular monthly payment. In most cases, property taxes are due toward the end of the year. To adjust for this, the seller pays the buyer a prorated share of the tax.

After the closing, the buyer can begin to enjoy the full benefits of the new home. The purchase process can be time-consuming and expensive but, if done right, results in security and satisfaction for the new homeowner.

Housing Options

The housing market has developed a number of options that have more to do with the legal rights you possess as a homeowner than with the physical style of the building. Since your ownership interest can be important in determining your satisfaction with the home and the investment rewards of the purchase, try to settle on the type you prefer before you start your housing search.

Single-family Detached

The *single-family detached* unit, which is the most common type of housing structure, is what most people have in mind when they think of buying a home. It is simply a house designed for use by one household that sits on its own plot of land without being connected to a neighboring structure. When you buy a single-family detached home, you own the house and land and are solely responsible for their upkeep. You are free to modify the structure and landscape or build outbuildings as long as you comply with local ordinances and codes and any deed restrictions.

Attached or Cluster Housing

In large cities and areas where space is limited, several housing units may be combined into one structure. Such *attached* or *cluster housing* units are separated by party walls and have individual entrance ways. They may also have small lawns or courtyards in front and/or in back. In some areas, these units are called *row houses* or *brownstones*, but more generally are referred to as *townhouses*. Some townhouse complexes are set up as *condominiums*, which are described in the next sec-

tion. However, many townhouses, particularly older units, are individually owned. In these cases, the homeowner shares ownership of the party wall with each neighbor having an easement legally protecting the integrity of the wall.

In some newer subdivisions, housing units are clustered together to provide additional open space. These may be called *patio homes* or *zero lot line homes*. The arrangement often involves some type of shared wall, driveway or common grounds which are protected by easements as in townhouse units. The practical meaning of any of these types of housing arrangements is that the owner may be restricted in how he or she uses the component covered by the easement. The prospective buyer should become familiar with the specific restrictions that may apply.

Condominiums

The term *condominium*, which describes joint sovereignty, refers to the way individual property rights are exercised among the participating homeowners. Condominiums are made up of a number of dwelling units combined in a single building, complex, or subdivision. In a strict sense, the individual homeowner has ownership of only the interior of the dwelling unit. The structure of the buildings, the grounds, and any facilities on the grounds are common areas controlled by the homeowners' association. Every owner is a member of the association, paying periodic fees and having a vote in deciding its actions. The association generally maintains the common areas and sets rules for their use. In practical terms this means that the homeowner can enjoy common facilities, such as a swimming pool, at a fraction of the cost of providing one for individual use. It also means that the homeowner may be much more restricted in what can be done with his or her home than the owner of a single-family detached home. If you are considering a condominium, you should examine the association by-laws prior to making an offer. Some associations prohibit pets or even children.

Condominiums can be large or small, can be part of complexes with hundreds of units or a few units, and can be in the form of high-rise buildings, garden apartments, townhouses, or detached homes. Some units will be among the lowest priced housing available, while others are among the highest priced. The more inexpensive units are usually designed to take advantage of the lower land costs associated with high density development. The high priced units are usually located in highly desirable areas and include many luxury features. Condominiums appeal to people who don't care to do home maintenance chores.

Cooperatives

Like condominiums, *cooperatives* involve sharing ownership of property with other homeowners. The cooperative buyer purchases shares in a corporation holding title to the building. The shares give the owner the right to occupy an apartment in the building. Each share-

holder pays a portion of all financing, tax, and operating expenses associated with the building. The important differences between a cooperative and a condominium are related to mortgage financing and resales. In a cooperative a single mortgage loan is taken out by the corporation; in a condominium individual loans are obtained by each tenant. The cooperative arrangement may prove advantageous during periods of high interest rates as the new purchaser does not have to obtain new financing. However, failure of some cooperative shareholders to pay their share of expenses places a burden on all other owners to avoid foreclosure of the loan. Regarding resales, cooperative owners are free to offer their shares on the market, but transferring their right to occupy a unit must be approved by the other shareholders. In most cases, this procedure causes no problem, but does present one potential snag to reselling the unit.

Duplexes

Homes designed to accommodate two households are called *duplexes*. There are also *triplexes* and *quadraplexes* for three and four households. The building is divided into separate living areas, each with its own bath and kitchen facilities, as well as outside entrance. A duplex can often be purchased for little more than a single-family home and offers the opportunity to generate rental income. The owner may live in one half and rent the other to help defray housing expenses. If you like the idea of being a homeowner and landlord at the same time, a duplex may be for you.

Manufactured Housing

Once referred to as mobile homes, *manufactured homes* are usually sold without a lot and can be moved to a site that is owned or leased by the buyer. These homes can be as large and luxurious as many site-built homes but cost substantially less. However, the market for used manufactured homes is not as broad as that for site-built homes. This means that a manufactured home will probably have no real appreciation in value. Many communities severely restrict where manufactured homes may be placed, so before you consider this alternative, check on where such homes are permitted.

Lease Options

Sometimes it is possible to try out a home before committing to a purchase. A *lease option* is a lease with an option to buy within some time period. The tenant may be asked to pay a fee for the option. This fee will be applied toward the purchase price if the option is exercised, but forfeited if it is not. In markets where homes are hard to sell, however, option fees are usually not charged. In addition, the seller may be willing to apply some of the rent toward the purchase price. Lease

options are good ways to find out about a home before buying, and may provide a way to save a down payment for a home.

Equity Sharing

One way to buy a home when cash for a down payment is short is to arrange to co-purchase the home with an investor. The investor contributes a large portion of the down payment and you get to live in the home. Generally you must pay some form of rent on the investor's interest in the home. When the home is sold, you and the investor share in the proceeds. Before entering into an equity-sharing arrangement, it is essential to have in writing exactly what your rights and responsibilities are and the conditions under which the home can be sold.

Finding a new home can be a long and trying process. Fortunately, there are experienced professionals who can help in the search. Licensed real estate brokers can show you homes that are on the market, suggest sources of financing and help you in other aspects of the home purchase. Even with this assistance, however, you will find the process less confusing if you know a few basics. You will find it helpful if you know how to estimate the highest price you can afford to pay, how to size up the market, and how to make an offer.

Financing Options and Procedures

By far the biggest hurdle in buying a home is getting a loan. To qualify for a loan, you must have enough cash for the down payment and other closing costs and enough income to handle the loan payments. By comparing these requirements to your income and cash on hand, you may figure out how much you can afford.

Determining your Financial Status

The first step is to put together an accounting of current income and debts. The lender will want to see these items when you apply for the loan. It is a good idea to do this before you look at homes, so you don't waste your time with homes you can't afford.

Salaries Include what you make from your regular job. You may also include a spouse's salary if the job is steady and you can show that the income is dependable. The same goes for second jobs, bonuses and overtime pay. Are they a dependable source of income or just a temporary arrangement? If you are self-employed or work on commission, you should average the income received over the last several years. The object is to total the income you expect to make on a continuing basis.

Investments The money you get from your investments may be included if it is large enough to be meaningful (in most cases, $100 per month). This income includes interest from bank accounts, bonds and mutual funds, and dividends from stocks and bonds. You should not include assets you intend to sell to raise cash to purchase the home.

Once again, the idea is to include sources of income to be used for making the loan payments. If real estate is included, use net income after taking out routine expenses.

Alimony and child support Include these sources of income if they are not subject to termination in the near future. For example, child support is generally terminated when the child reaches a certain age. If you expect to receive this income for only the next few years, it should not be included.

Liabilities Now, make a list of your debts that require periodic payments. Include long term installment debt with a remaining term of more than ten months. Typically, this will include car loans, furniture loans, and other loans for major purchases. If you carry a balance on your credit cards, you should include the average monthly payment. Also include any other real estate mortgages you have, for example, the one on the rental property you listed in the income section. Finally, if you pay alimony or child support, you should include that payment.

Prequalifying: How Much House Can You Afford?

Lenders have different *ratios* they apply to your income alone and to your income minus debt obligations. You can use these ratios to get an idea of the largest loan you can obtain. You should apply both ratios because you must qualify under both criteria.

The most common loan is the conventional mortgage loan. This is one with no government insurance or guarantee to cover the lender's risk that you may fail to keep up the payments. Most lenders require the ratios that are required to sell the loan in the secondary market. Currently, the Federal National Mortgage Association, a major investor in home mortgages, requires that total mortgage payments plus insurance and taxes be no more than 28 percent of gross monthly income. Also, these expenses plus other debt payments can be no more than 36 percent of gross monthly income.

An example will show how these ratios can be used to estimate the maximum affordable loan. Mr. and Mrs. Brown receive $3,500 per month salary plus an average of $500 per month from investments. Their total monthly income is $4,000. Their mortgage payment may be no more than 28 percent of this income, or $1,120. An approximation of monthly escrow payments is one-fifth of the total payment. In the example, that would be $224, leaving $896 for principal and interest. They find that a mortgage loan can be obtained at 10 percent interest for 30 years. They look at a mortgage payment table and find that the largest loan they could afford is for $102,100.

The Browns also pay an average of $400 per month on their credit cards and car loan payments. Using the 36 percent ratio, they have $1,440 to use for all debt payments. Taking out the $400 they spend on current debts leaves them with $1,040 a month for mortgage expenses. After deducting one-fifth for taxes and insurance, the remainder for principal and interest is $832. This payment would support a loan of

$94,800 at 10 percent interest. Since this is less than the amount indicated by the simple income ratio, it represents the effective maximum loan obtainable. With a 20 percent down payment, they could afford a home priced at $118,500. Such a purchase would require a down payment of $23,700 plus closing costs of approximately $3,000, depending on how much the seller is willing to pay toward closing costs.

HOW MUCH CAN YOU AFFORD?
(CONVENTIONAL LOAN EXAMPLE)

1. Using the income to payment ratio

Monthly income

Salary	$3,500	
Investment income	500	
Total	$4,000	
	× .28	
Maximum mortgage payment	$1,120	
Tax and insurance	− 224	(payment divided by 5)
Maximum principal and interest payment	$ 896	

Maximum loan @ 10% (30 years)

Locate page of mortgage payment tables for 10%.

Find column for 30 years.

Find highest payment amount less than 896.

Note amount of loan in far left hand column.

Subtract payment in table from maximum payment.

Repeat previous three steps with the difference.

Maximum Payment	Amount in table	Difference	Loan Amount
$896.00	$877.58	$18.42	$100,000
18.42	17.56	.86	2,000
.86	.88	− .02	100
	Total loan amount		$102,100

2. Using the total debt to income ratio

Monthly income	$4,000
	× .36
Income to pay all debt payments	$1,440
Average credit card payment	− 100
Installment loan payments	− 300
Existing mortgage payments	0
Maximum mortgage payment	$1,040
Tax and insurance	− 208
Maximum principal and interest payment	$832

Tax and insurance: (payment divided by 5)

Maximum principal and interest payment: (Note: if larger than amount in income part, stop)

Maximum loan amount:

Maximum payment	Amount in table	Difference	Loan Amount
$832.00	$789.82	$42.18	$90,000
42.18	35.11	7.07	4,000
7.07	7.03	.04	800
Total loan amount			$94,800

Sources

The first step in getting a loan is to find out what is available in the market. It is a good idea to check on several sources before committing, since the variation in interest rates, discount points and types of loans offered can be great.

Mutual savings banks and *Savings and loan associations.* Thrifts are institutions that specialize in home mortgage loans. Like commercial banks, they take in and pay interest on deposits from individual savers; then they lend these funds out to borrowers. Thrifts should be one of the first places you check for a loan.

Commercial banks do most of their lending on a short-term basis, such as auto loans and business loans. At times, however, they also make long-term mortgage loans.

Mortgage companies are prime sources for mortgage loans. Unlike savings and loans, mortgage companies do not collect deposits from savers. They obtain their funds by selling the loans they originate to investors, other lenders and the major secondary market agencies. Incidentally, it makes little difference to the borrower whether the loan is

11

retained by the lender or sold in the market. In most cases, the originator will continue to collect payments and manage the escrow account. *Credit unions* have been known to make home mortgage loans. This source could be worth checking if you are a member of a credit union. *Home finance companies* rarely make first mortgage loans for purchasing a home, but may be a source for second mortgages to help finance the down payment on a home.

Individuals also make home loans. Most often, these individuals are sellers who are willing to help finance the sale. When interest rates are high, or loans from established lenders hard to find, sellers may offer to take back a note as a way to clinch the sale. Seller financing differs in several important ways from a loan from a third-party lender. The financing is tied to a particular home offered at a particular price (which may be higher than the price you would pay without the financing). The loan is usually short term with a balloon payment. That means you must refinance the loan after a few years. These loans are meant for special situations, but can be worthwhile when those situations occur.

Government agencies sometimes make loans. In general, these loans are highly restricted to certain income groups or other target groups. Some state and local governments have money available from the sale of bonds to make home loans to first-time buyers. The loans are originated by established lenders, so inquire about these when you check out rates.

Federal Housing Administration (FHA) and Veterans Administration (VA) loans are made by private lenders using their own funds. The government backs up these loans if the borrower fails to make payments and the home is foreclosed. For FHA loans, the government provides insurance against default. The borrower pays a premium for this insurance. Similar insurance is provided by private companies for conventional loans. VA loans are guaranteed by the government and are available as a benefit to qualified military veterans. If you qualify, bring your DD214 form to the lender. The main advantage of these types of loans is the lower down payment required. In addition, FHA and VA loans may be assumed without an increase in the interest rate.

Loan Types

In many cases, getting the right loan can determine whether or not you can afford to buy the house you desire. Some loans require large cash down payments, while others call for relatively modest investments. Some have larger monthly payments than others. With some loans, the monthly payments vary over time. You will want to find the least expensive financing that fits your financial situation with adequate security.

Over the last several years, a great number of financial variations have developed for home buyers. At one time, the fixed-rate, fixed-payment loan was used exclusively by home buyers. Now there are loans whose payments vary as interest rates change, and those whose pay-

ments start out low and rise over the years. Loans with relatively short terms (such as 15 years instead of 30) are growing in popularity. This expanded list of options makes the loan selection decision a complicated one.

Fixed rate mortgage The standard loan covers 80 percent of the cost of the home, or the appraised value, whichever is lower. (Some lenders may offer loans in excess of 80 percent, but these higher *loan-to-value ratio* loans usually carry higher interest rates and costs.) The remainder of the cost is the cash down payment that you must provide at closing. Lenders also charge *discount points* as a condition of making the loan. Each point charged requires the buyer to pay an amount equal to one percent of the loan amount in cash at closing. An estimate of all these expenses will be given to you when you apply for the loan.

Each monthly payment on the fixed-rate loan includes interest on the outstanding principal plus repayment of a part of the principal borrowed. In this way the loan will be completely paid off at the end of the mortgage term. If you pay the loan back before the end of the term, the amount of principal you owe will be less than the amount you borrowed. The gradual reduction in principal is called *amortization*. Each payment of principal and interest is equal over the life of the loan. Since you are gradually paying back the principal with each payment, the amount of payment devoted to interest decreases over time. This means the amount of principal paid back increases with each payment. Therefore, the older the loan the faster you are paying the loan off. Each monthly payment may include a payment to an escrow account used for paying hazard insurance premiums and property taxes. While the interest and principal remain unchanged, the total payment may change over time because of increases or decreases in the escrow payment required.

It is possible to get mortgage loans for more than 80 percent of cost if the loan is insured. (This should not be confused with mortgage life insurance, which pays off the loan in the event of death or disability of the borrower.) The FHA insures home loans for up to 97.5 percent of value. Limits on the dollar amount of the loan make FHA insurance appropriate for low to moderate priced houses. Loans not insured by the FHA (or guaranteed by the VA) are called *conventional loans*. These loans can be insured by Private Mortgage Insurance (PMI) companies. PMI loans are not as restrictive in amount as FHA loans. Insurance, either PMI or FHA, requires additional premium payments at closing and may require an annual fee of one-quarter to one-half of one percent of the principal.

Adjustable rate mortgages Since 1980, *adjustable rate mortgages (ARMs)* have become an important part of the mortgage market. One reason is that lenders like the protection that ARMs give them from the effects of rising interest rates. Another reason is that ARMs usually start out with lower interest rates than comparable fixed-rate mortgages. Some home buyers find they can afford to borrow more with an ARM than they could with a higher interest rate fixed-rate mortgage. The main difference between ARMs and fixed-rate loans is that the

13

interest rate on the ARM may vary periodically. At pre-established intervals ranging from three months to five years the lender may change the interest rate. This is done by monitoring an *index of interest rates* and maintaining a set relationship between the interest rate and the index. The index may be the market yield on some government security, the average mortgage interest rate in the nation, or the cost of the money used by lenders to make loans. When the interest rate on the loan is changed, the monthly payment will change accordingly. This means the amount you pay on your loan for principal and interest may vary significantly over time. One way borrowers are protected from large changes in payments is through pre-set limits, or *caps*, placed on the interest rate adjustment. Some loans have caps that apply to the periodic adjustment and a cap on the overall change in the interest rate over the life of the loan. Some loans also have limits on the amount of change in the payment, but not on the interest rate. This type of cap can create *negative amortization*, a situation in which the amount of principal owed may increase over time. (For more information on these loans and helpful tables for analysis, see *Adjustable Rate Mortgages*, in Barron's Financial Guide series.)

Graduated payment mortgages The FHA also insures loans in which the interest rate is fixed, but the payment rises according to a pre-set schedule. These are called *Graduated Payment Mortgages (GPM)* because the payments are increased each year during the early life of the loan. The effect is to reduce the payment level in the first few years and to increase it somewhat in the middle and later years. The GPM is intended for young home buyers whose relatively low income is expected to grow over the years. The predetermined amount of change in the payment is not dependent on the movements of an index, although there are loans which combine the features of the GPM and the ARM. The common type of GPM involves negative amortization for the first several years.

Interest saving loans Some home buyers become dismayed when they learn the amount of money they must spend in interest over the life of a long-term mortgage loan. The total costs may be several times the price of the home. This concern has drawn attention to loans designed to cut down on the interest expense. In all cases, these types of loans require larger or more frequent payments.

One type of interest-saving loan is a fixed-rate loan with a 15-year term. Total interest expense can be reduced significantly, although the monthly payments are somewhat higher. For example, a loan of $50,000 at 10 percent interest requires a principal and interest payment of $438.79 when paid over 30 years. The total interest paid is $107,963. If the same loan is paid over 15 years, the monthly payment increases to $537.30, or about $100 more per month. Total interest paid, however, is only $46,714, a savings of over $60,000.

Other types of loans have been developed to save interest by paying

14

off the loan faster. One type is the Growing Equity Mortgage (GEM) which has a payment that increases periodically. Unlike the ARM or GPM, the increase in the payment is devoted to reducing the loan principal, so that the loan is retired in about half the original term. Another type, the *biweekly*, requires payments at two-week intervals (coinciding with payday for many workers) of half the normal monthly payment. Since there are 26 two-week intervals in the year, the borrower pays the equivalent of 13 months of payments, and the principal is paid down much faster.

Loan assumptions In some cases, it may not be necessary to obtain a new loan. Some sellers have existing mortgage loans that can be assumed by the buyer. When interest rates have risen, existing loans may have interest rates, and payments, much lower than those required with new loans. The buyer may be able to avoid many of the closing costs associated with new loans as well. Assumable conventional loans are becoming rare because in recent years lenders have included "due on sale clauses" in the loans. These provisions entitle the lender to call the loan due or raise the interest rate if the house is sold. Loans insured by the FHA or guaranteed by the VA are generally assumable at the original interest rate.

There are several drawbacks with assumable loans. The seller may want a higher price because of the loan; and the loan may cover a relatively small proportion of the cost of the home. In some cases, the latter problem has been overcome by the seller taking a second mortgage as part of the purchase price.

QUICK GUIDE TO CHOOSING A MORTGAGE LOAN

Borrower Concern	Possible Solution
Need low down payment	Conventional loan with private insurance FHA insured mortgage
Need low monthly payments in early years to help qualify	Adjustable Rate Mortgage with low initial interest rate Graduated Payment Mortgage Assumption with or without seller financing
Desire to reduce interest paid over loan term	Loan with 15-year term Growing Equity Mortgage Biweekly mortgage

The Closing

Closing day marks the time when all accounts are settled and title to the house passes to the buyer. In one simultaneous procedure:

- The seller receives the price of the house and retires the old loan (unless the buyer is assuming the loan).
- The sales agent receives a commission. (The commission may be split between a listing broker and a selling broker.)
- All fees are paid. These include title insurance premiums, survey costs, and fees for filing documents. They may also include attorneys' fees and inspectors' charges if these have not been paid previously.
- The lender supplies the proceeds from the loan and collects origination fees and discount points. This is the first day of the new loan which from then on begins to accrue interest. The lender usually requires interest be paid at the closing to cover the period from closing day to the end of the month. All other interest payments are made at the end of each month.
- The buyer receives documents which signify the passage of ownership of the property from the seller to the buyer.

For all practical purposes, the closing ends all negotiations and contingencies associated with the transaction. For that reason, it is important that all parties clear all these matters before the closing day. If not, the closing may be delayed, which can be very inconvenient for both seller and buyer.

The most common reasons that closings do not proceed as scheduled are connected with failures to make the necessary preparations. Sometimes the seller has a problem clearing a title. There may be existing liens, claims filed by those with partial interests in the property, or an ex-spouse with community property rights that complicate the process. If the property becomes involved in a lawsuit, the title may be impossible to clear for several years. Problems also occur when the buyer has trouble arranging a mortgage loan. The appraisal may be too low to justify the loan amount requested, or the buyer may not qualify. When loan activity is heavy, approval times can be delayed because the lender's staff is inadequate.

The seller can entertain contingent contracts from other buyers after the first contract is signed. These contracts have no effect on the original contract as long as the deadlines on contingencies are not exceeded. However, if the buyer is turned down for a mortgage, the house may be sold to another buyer before the first buyer can reapply.

Here is a good way that you, as the buyer, can prepare for a closing. Assume you have a mortgage commitment already approved. The following steps should be followed:

- Get a good estimate of the cash required at closing. The title company handling the closing can provide a reasonably accurate accounting. Make sure you can provide a certified check for your share of expenses on closing day.
- Have all inspections made and make sure all required repairs are com-

pleted. Unless agreed to in writing, the seller has no responsibility for repairs after closing. If any condition of the property is misrepresented, however, you still have remedies against the seller. Basically, the property is yours *as is* after closing.

- You may want to get an attorney to review all documents and represent you at the closing. Arrange for this beforehand.
- Arrange for a hazard insurance policy to be written on the property. The lender will require the house to be insured for at least the amount of the loan. At closing you will have to pay the first year's premium plus an amount to start the escrow account (usually two or three months prorated premium).
- Make sure the survey is completed as required by the lender.

If it looks as if the closing will be delayed due to some problem in getting everything done, it may be possible to move the closing date. The date stated in the sales contract is understood to be an approximation. Unless the market is unusually active, with many buyers vying for each home, the seller should be willing to comply. If the closing is delayed, you may be caught without a place to move into after vacating your previous residence. You may arrange with the seller to lease the new house on a temporary basis prior to closing if the home will be vacant during that time.

At closing, you will sign several documents. The following are most common:

- *Settlement statement* This shows the closing costs charged to each party in an itemized list. Of special note are the various prorated expenses. Property taxes, insurance premiums and other recurring expenses are generally paid once a year. If already paid by the seller, you are charged a proportional amount based on the remaining number of days in the year. If due after the closing, you will be given a credit for the days in which the seller owned the home.
- *Loan disclosure* This gives you certain information about the mortgage loan. The Annual Percentage Rate (APR) of interest is calculated. This amount takes into account the discount points paid at closing assuming their costs are spread out over the term of the loan. Also shown is the total amount of interest paid over the loan term, the monthly payment of interest and principal, the number of payments over the term and the date at which the first payment is due.
- *Mortgage note* This signifies your responsibility to pay back the amount borrowed on the mortgage.
- *Deed of trust (security deed, bond*, etc.) This pledges the house as security for the mortgage loan.
- *Deed* This transfers the title of the property to your name. In most cases you will receive a *general warranty deed*, meaning that the seller guarantees that the title is clear and will be clear in the future (not clouded by prior claims). In some cases, the seller may give a *special warranty deed*, which guarantees that any claims arising during the seller's ownership have been settled. Any additional liability stemming from a warranty deed are assumed by the title company.
- *Title policy* This provides protection should legitimate claims to the title of the property arise.
- *Additional documents* You may request copies of other documents asso-

17

ciated with the transaction. These include the survey map, the appraisal, and any inspection certificates prepared. These are desirable to have for future reference.

Tax Benefits of Homeownership

Many of the costs of owning a home are deductible from individual federal income taxes. Therefore, tax savings from these deductions may reduce homeownership costs. In addition, there are tax benefits when a home is sold.

Mortgage Interest Payments

The interest portion of mortgage monthly payments is deductible. Each year, the borrower receives a statement from the lender indicating how much interest was paid for the tax year. This amount should be included on schedule A of the 1040 tax form. In addition, for the year of purchase, discount points paid to the lender may qualify as interest payments. When they are a customary charge in the area, paid with a separate check, and not considered an origination fee, points should be deductible. When an origination fee is charged, it normally is only a portion of the discount point payment. Check with the lender to see how much is considered a fee. Remember that each point is one percent of the amount borrowed. For example, if three points were paid on a $100,000 loan, the total charge would be $3,000. Suppose one point was considered a fee and the rest discount points. An amount of $2,000 could be deducted as interest in the year of purchase.

Interest Expense Limits on Home Mortgages

Interest on up to $1,000,000 of mortgage debt to acquire, construct, or substantially improve a home or a second home is fully deductible. Interest on up to $100,000 of home equity debt is generally fully deductible for taxpayers who itemize deductions.

Property Taxes Paid to Local Governments

In most cases, these taxes are paid by the lender from an escrow account kept current by part of your monthly payments. The annual statement from the lender will indicate how much was paid in taxes for the year. If you pay taxes directly, you will have a statement from the

local taxing authority to indicate the amount of taxes paid. When you sell the home, do not forget to include any prorated taxes you may have paid to the buyer.

These benefits also apply to a second home, but not to any additional homes you may own. If you own houses as rental property, a different set of rules apply.

Capital Gains

When you buy your first home, the purchase price becomes the property's basis for calculating capital gains. At resale, taxes may be required on any profits realized. A profit is indicated if the sales price exceeds the basis. However, the cost of selling (commissions, advertising, etc.) may be deducted from the sales price. Major improvements, not just repairs, to the home while you own it may be added to the original basis. All of these things help to reduce the taxable capital gain.

As an example, suppose a home was purchased for $50,000 in 1960. In 1969, a second bath was added at a cost of $5,000. The house is sold in 1993 for $80,000. The seller paid a commission of $4,000 and $1,000 of the buyer's closing costs.

Original cost	$50,000
Improvements	5,000
Basis	$55,000
Sales price	$80,000
Sales expense	5,000
Net sales price	$75,000
Capital gain	$20,000

Capital gains taxes may be deferred if a replacement home is purchased within 24 months of the sale. The 24-month period may extend before or after the sale. The cost of the new home must be at least as much as the net sales price of the home sold. No tax is due in the year of sale but the basis of the new home is reduced by the amount of gain deferred. Suppose the seller of the home above buys a new home for $85,000. The new basis is $85,000 minus the $20,000 of gain deferred, or $65,000. As long as the procedures are followed, deferral of capital gains taxes can go on indefinitely, each time reducing the basis by the taxes deferred. After the age of 55, a homeowner may sell and receive an exemption of $125,000 in deferred gain. This can be elected only once in a lifetime.

HOME SELLERS GUIDE*

The typical American spends less than 12 years in any given house. This is the average. You may be the person transferred by an employer every year, or the one who lives in the same house for your entire life. Sooner or later, however, most of us need to sell a home. It may be because an altered family situation makes a larger or smaller house more desirable. Changing tastes, a job change, or the desire to be closer to schools or shopping facilities are other reasons commonly cited for moving. Hopefully, real estate market conditions will be favorable when you need to sell but this is not always the case. For example, a job or business location change often requires a move from an economically depressed to a booming area; consequently a house must be sold in a sluggish market, and another bought in a vibrant one. Still, the transaction process need not be fraught with hazards. Some considerations are discussed below.

Selling Yourself or Using a Broker

Many homeowners sell their own homes successfully. Those who do so save the sales commission, usually six percent of the home's price, or they may choose to speed up the sale by passing part of the savings on to the buyer. However, most home owners turn the job over to a real estate broker who has the experience, expertise and business connections to locate buyers and offer other services to a seller. After weighing the factors involved, a seller may first proceed without professional assistance, resorting to a broker only if these efforts prove unsuccessful.

If a broker is engaged, a *listing* is the contract of employment between the owner of the property and the broker hired to sell it. Under the terms of the listing contract, the owner agrees to pay the broker a commission when the broker locates a party who is ready, willing, and able to buy the property at its list price. Should an offer be tendered for less than the list price, the broker is entitled to a commission when the transaction is consummated.

Normally, the seller pays the commission at closing. However, it is possible for a buyer to agree to pay a commission in lieu of the seller or in addition to the seller, so long as all parties are aware of the circumstances.

*The authors gratefully acknowledge the contributions of Eileen Snyder and Don Stebbins who wrote, *Preparing Your Home for Sale*, and *Some Important Tax Considerations*, respectively, and the Real Estate Center at Texas A&M for allowing use of some of their materials.

Types of Listings

Listings can be categorized as *Open*, *Exclusive agency*, or *Exclusive right to sell*. In turn, any of these three basic types can be categorized as being, *Net* and/or *Multiple*.

Open listings Using an open listing, the seller or *principal* offers the broker a commission provided that the broker secures a purchaser. The listing is considered "open" because the owner reserves the right to list the property with other brokers or to sell it independently. All open listings are automatically canceled upon a sale of the property, so that the seller pays no more than one commission.

Exclusive agency listings Under an exclusive agency listing, one broker is employed to the exclusion of all others. The owner retains the right to sell the property independently without paying a commission. However, if the property is sold by a broker other than the listing broker, the listing broker is entitled to a full commission.

Exclusive right to sell listings An exclusive right to sell provides the employed broker a commission upon the sale, no matter who sells the property. Such a contract may appear to be to a seller's disadvantage. Even if the seller or another broker finds a buyer, the listing broker earns a commission. But this rigid arrangement, which gives the listing broker complete protection, can work to the seller's advantage. Under an exclusive right to sell, the employed broker has more incentive to spend time and money to promote the sale of the listed property. Brokers employed through other types of listings may not make as much effort precisely because the property can be sold by the owner or another broker. In recognition of this, most real estate boards emphasize the exclusive right to sell listing, particularly for single-family dwellings.

Net listings Any one of the above listings may also be a net listing if the property owner fixes the minimum acceptable net amount from a sale. For example, the seller informs the broker that he or she wants $100,000 from the sale. The broker may keep any amount as a commission so long as the seller "nets" $100,000. Thus, if the sale price is $100,001, the commission is $1; a sale at $104,000 yields a $4,000 commission.

In some states, net listings are illegal. In states where they are permitted, many real estate brokerage organizations suggest that, when offered a net listing, the broker add the customary charge to the net amount and then inform the seller of the resulting list price. For example, a six percent commission rate added to a $100,000 net figure results in a $106,383 offering price. As a check on the math, six percent of $106,383 is $6,383 leaving $100,000 for the seller. The arithmetic is as follows:

$$\frac{\text{Net amount to seller}}{\substack{\text{Fraction of sales price to seller} \\ \text{(100\% less commission)}}} = \text{List price with commission}$$

22

Using the $100,000 net figure and the 6 percent rate of commission, the list price becomes:

$$\frac{\$100,000}{.94} = \$106,383$$

Multiple listings Some brokers in a given geographical area may agree to pool all of their listings. They form a *multiple listing service* (MLS) to coordinate activities. Through this association, brokers agree to share their listings. Then, any cooperating broker may sell property that another has listed. Upon the sale of multiple-listed property, the commission is split between the listing and the selling broker in accordance with the agreement established by the multiple listing association. A small fraction of the commission is paid to the association to cover its expenses of operation. The MLS maximizes exposure of the property to prospective purchasers. Even in areas where there isn't a formal MLS organization, cooperation between brokers is quite common.

Rate of Commission

As a matter of law, commission rates for the sale of real estate are negotiable between the principal and the broker. The rate or amount should be specified in the listing contract to avoid misunderstandings. In most cases the rate is a percentage of the sales price (often four to seven percent), which is paid at closing.

Listing Period

Listing contracts should have a fixed expiration date. Most provide 60 to 120 days for the sale of single-family homes and up to six months for commercial property and apartment complexes. The law does not establish limits, so the actual period is a matter of negotiation.

If a house is unsold at the expiration of the stipulated period, the owner and broker can renew the listing. However, the broker is paid nothing as brokers are typically compensated only upon a sale. An owner may decide to try a different broker if the first one failed to produce satisfactory results or activity.

Occasionally, after having been shown a particular piece of property through a broker, a prospect and the property owner may arrange a sale "behind the broker's back." Together they wait for the listing to expire, then contract for the sale without advising the broker, in an attempt to elude the payment of a commission. Despite the fact that the listing has expired, courts are likely to require payment to a licensed broker, if it can be shown that the broker was the procuring cause of the sale.

Expectations of Broker Services

Upon listing your house, you can expect a broker to help you decide on an offering price, advertise the property, and show the house to prospective buyers. Typically, the broker places a *For Sale* sign on the front

lawn, advertises in newspapers or local magazines, and may hold an open house. The listing will be included in the book or computer of the multiple listing service if your broker belongs to the MLS.

How To Choose a Broker

Try to determine the broker's level of activity in your neighborhood. A broker with numerous for sale signs would be a likely one to select, especially if there is also a liberal sprinkling of "sold" signs. Check for the integrity and professional reputation of the firm by asking people you know to recommend a broker. Ask friends who recently sold a house in your area to describe the transaction. Did they feel they received the best possible personal treatment and financial result? Specifically, ask about pricing, time on the market, selling efforts, courtesy, and procedure for showing the home.

Call brokers and ask them to visit. Usually they will be prepared to discuss how best to market your home, including a suggested selling price or range. Ask the broker for information about transactions in your neighborhood: What has sold? At what price? What hasn't sold and why? Ask what advertising the broker would use: Which media? What frequency? Would he or she hold an "open house." Discuss the type of listing, especially if you have names of prospects who are considering buying from you. A firm that participates in a multiple listing service may increase market exposure, while national franchises or local firms that belong to national referral services are more likely to reach homebuyers who are relocating to your area. Bear in mind, however, that a local firm may give more attention to each listing.

The Real Estate Market

The real estate market is peculiar. Though you need only one buyer for your home, you never know when that buyer will appear. A buyer could come the day your ad first appears or not until a year or so later. When there are plenty of houses for sale and they don't seem to be selling — at least not quickly — there is a *buyer's market*. In this situation, buyers have many houses to choose from and can negotiate a tough bargain.

In a *seller's market*, the opposite is true. There are few houses for sale, and when one does become available, it is snapped up immediately — often at a higher price than was paid earlier for similar houses. Sometimes even a higher price is paid than was originally asked. Obviously, this is the type of market that sellers prefer.

A market is called *balanced* when most houses priced for sale at *market value* sell within a normal period of time. A "normal" or "reasonable" period is 30 to 180 days.

Nearly all home buyers have two concerns. First, they must like the house. Next, the price or payments must be affordable. These two elements must be present before a buyer will make an offer. Buyers can

usually be categorized as either *taste-conscious* or *price-conscious*. *Taste* buyers find the home of their choice and buy it if the price is within reason. *Price* buyers want a bargain. They could easily afford a higher-priced house in which they might actually prefer to live. Instead, they opt for the bargain — something that is not exactly what they want, but they grab it nevertheless because of its low price and resale potential.

Few buyers are guided exclusively by either taste or price considerations; most fall somewhere in between the two extremes and are willing to sacrifice some of the features they want for a good price, or vice versa.

Pricing

It is obvious that sellers want the highest possible price for their home. Buyers want the lowest. Most transactions take place at or near *market value*, which may be briefly defined as the highest price a buyer, willing but not compelled to buy, will pay a seller, willing but not compelled to sell, both acting with reasonable knowledge of the market.

Buyers become acquainted with the market by shopping. After visiting several homes, buyers will get a feel for what homes are worth. They don't know exactly what a house will cost until they try to buy one, but they are told the asking price for each one they visit. They understand they can buy any house for its asking (listed) price, and that most homes will actually sell for less.

As a seller you can sample the market the same way. Read ads in the newspapers. Find out how much neighbors are asking and visit their homes. You'll get a rough idea of what you should ask for your home.

It is also a good idea to phone some real estate brokerage agencies. Good agents will volunteer to visit your home just to meet you and offer their services in the hope that you'll list with them. You won't obligate yourself just by asking how much they would advise listing your home for. Good agents will let you know. They want your business. As a matter of professionalism and thoroughness, agents may offer an analysis of comparable sales ("comps"). Comps that have sold (as opposed to those that are for sale) provide actual prices, which are better indicators than offering prices. Agents will frequently leave a copy of their analyses with you.

Another way of estimating a price is to call a professional independent fee appraiser. Look in the Yellow Pages of your phone book under "Appraisers." Those with professional designations of SRA, ASA, or MAI, have met high professional standards. Ask one or two for an appraisal. Fees typically range from $200 to $400. (Some appraisers will charge more, especially if your hosue is particularly unusual.) In any case, an appraiser's fee may be money well spent, especially since an appraiser may be able to suggest ways to increase the market value of your home.

Consider asking an appraiser these questions:

1. **Which** local mortgage lenders accept his or her valuations. If the appraiser is accepted by most local savings and loan associations, that appraisal can be used for a new loan application without paying another fee. You've saved your buyer some money, perhaps some time, and you can point that out when negotiating on other items.
2. Ask the appraiser what forms will be used. Ideally, the appraiser will use the most recent FHLMC/FNMA standard form. Most lenders want this form so that the loans they produce can be more readily sold.
3. Tell the appraiser you want a market value estimate, and, further, that you would like to know a probable sales price range. *Don't attempt to maneuver an appraisal into a specific amount.* Professional ethics will require the appraiser's resignation from any assignment where a client pushes for a high value. Ask for the price range in which your home is most likely to sell. A good appraiser will understand and oblige. He or she recognizes that the formal estimate is of market value, but that homes sell for more (and less). Generally, an appraiser will provide this range verbally.
4. Ask about market conditions. Is it a seller's market? A buyer's market? A balanced market? How long do houses like yours stay on the market. Is this a good time to sell?
5. Ask the appraiser to give you a list of items that should be repaired or "cured" in your home. The appraiser may be able to point out important things that you have overlooked, such as carpet that should be cleaned, faded paint, or broken fixtures. You should then take care of these things before buyers turn you down.
6. Ask whether you can later ask brief questions about the appraisal. A good appraiser will go over the report with you and later answer questions about how it was prepared.

An appraiser and the appraisal report can really be useful. The $200 to $400 appraisal cost can provide plenty of information. Once you have that appraisal report, study it carefully.

Forget about what you paid for your home. Whether you bought it for $10,000 or $500,000 makes no difference. When you want to sell it, the question is its *current value* — not your cost. The question of value is answered by that appraisal report. An appraisal should not refer to your original cost. That is a historic fact which has nothing to do with its present market value.

After estimating the market value, a seller should consider other matters. First, buyers typically want to negotiate price or other concessions. So the offering price should be raised above market value to leave room for flexibility. (Again, keep in mind whether you are in a buyer's or seller's market.) Next, the seller must consider how quickly a sale is needed. Pricing will be structured differently depending on whether the seller can wait for a good offer or is anxious or even desperate to sell. A lower price normally results in a quicker sale; a higher price could, but doesn't always, materialize only after the home is on the market for some time. Finally, a seller should consider whether the market is rising or falling. In a rising

market time is on the seller's side — there is a tendency to hold out for a high price. However, when prices are falling a seller will want a fast sale.

Some sellers adopt a policy of starting at a high price, then lowering it over time. This approach avoids selling for too low a price. However, a home with several price drops may give the impression that something is wrong with it. Sales agents are more reluctant to encourage the purchase of an overpriced house than one that is priced at the market.

Fixing Up

It is obvious that a house in a good state of repair and maintenance will sell faster and/or for a higher price than one that needs work. Before putting your house on the market, check its appearance and condition of its components.

Exterior Appearance

A prospective buyer will see the exterior first. Since first impressions count heavily, the exterior may well determine whether the prospect will want to look further. A good-looking, well-cared-for exterior is important in setting the value of a home. Consider the following factors:

- Does the house need a fresh coat of paint? Do pulled-away shingles need to be replaced? Do mortar joints need to be repointed?
- Has the roof been checked to ensure there is no cracking or drying out?
- Are the gutters and downspouts free of debris?
- Are there any cracks that need repair?
- Do the window screens need to be repaired?
- Do windows need recaulking and reglazing?
- Is the property well-landscaped, with the lawn trimmed and edged and the yard free of trash?
- Are there any cracks in the patio or driveway?
- Is the fence in good repair?
- Is the swimming pool clean and in good repair?
- Has an exterminator examined the house lately?

Interior Appearance

Particular care must be given to the interior. It is important to keep your home as neat and clean as possible to best display its assets. For example, excessive furniture needs to be removed so rooms do not appear crowded. In addition, the following suggestions should be considered:

- Are the walls faded, wallpaper smudged and woodwork worn? (If the interior needs painting, use neutral colors.)
- Does the carpet or floor need to be cleaned or repaired?
- Loose knobs, sticking doors and windows, warped cabinet drawers, and other minor flaws detract from home value and can be fixed easily.

27

• Kitchen and bathrooms are of particular interest to buyers and need to be kept clean and orderly. Repair caulking in bathtubs and showers.
• Keep stairways clear to avoid a cluttered appearance and possible injuries.
• Spacious closets are important to most buyers, so take the time to clean them.
• Display the full value of your attic, basement and other utility space by removing all unnecessary articles.

Mechanical Systems

After the exterior and interior of the home have been checked, the mechanical systems should be inspected to ensure their proper working order. Plumbing is a prime concern of buyers and can be observed readily. In these days of energy awareness, the heating and cooling plant will also be of great interest to prospective buyers.

Check the pipes and fix any leaky faucets. Old or corroded sections of the pipes should be replaced, loose joints tightened, and broken fixtures replaced.

The heating and cooling units also should be checked. A dirty heating plant tends to break down more frequently and does an inefficient job of heating. Before a home goes on the market, the owner should check the air-conditioner condenser and recharge the freon if necessary. It is unlikely every part of the home checked will require maintenance.

When improvements or repairs are indicated, decide whether the cost will be justified in the selling price.

Showing Your House

When your home is listed with a real estate broker, expect him or her and other brokers to *preview* it. The broker will show the home to prospects while you are away. Unless there is a compelling reason for you to stay, it is best to leave the showing to your broker.

Most active brokers in metropolitan areas are members of an MLS. Weekly or monthly a group of brokers will travel as a *caravan* to see the new listings. Allow them to do so as this enhances market exposure: possibly an agent has been looking for a house exactly like yours on behalf of a client. Your broker may also suggest putting a *lock box* on your door. That is a small metal box, opened by a key, in which your house key is put. All MLS members have a key to the box and, thus, have access to your home. If you have a compelling reason to avoid the lock box — such as fear of burglary — do not allow it. This could cause logistical problems because you, or someone else with a key, must be present to allow entry. However, your peace of mind is worth this inconvenience. (Should you have moved away from the house, a lock box may be the only practical solution.)

Buyers or their brokers should make an appointment to view your home. This will give you time to prepare. Whether you show your own home or leave the showing to a broker, plan your approach, determining

in advance the features to be called to the attention of the potential buyer. Often it is these unique or special features that prove to be persuasive. It could be the oak mantle or the view from the kitchen window that makes the potential buyer want to purchase your home.

It is important to be truthful about both good and negative points of the home. The potential buyer then will be more confident you are being completely honest. Point out the advantages an older home offers over a newly built home: it is in an established neighborhood whose character is apparent; the yard is already landscaped with more mature trees and shrubs; most minor problems with the home already should have been solved.

Before appointment time, pretend that you are the prospect and go on a tour. Start outside. Be sure that there's a place for the visitor to park — either on the street or in the driveway. From the logical parking spots, be certain that there's a clear path to the front door. If there is snow or ice on the ground, clear it or sprinkle sand. Stand just outside the front door. Look up, down and to all sides. Any cobwebs to be removed? Screws to be tightened? Does the doorbell work? Are there any visible cosmetic problems that your prospect will readily observe? Quickly repair them. Do your best to give the front door area an attractive appearance. People want to be proud of their front door area, even if it is seldom used.

Walk through your home with the intent of doing any last minute dusting, vacuuming, replacing electric bulbs, and so on. Your prospective buyers will arrive any minute so there's not time for major repairs. Just do the last minute cleaning and cosmetics.

When showing the home, consider these tips:

• A home that is well lighted is inviting. Open draperies during the day and turn on all lights in the evening.
• Turn off the radio and television so there will be no distractions.
• Keep pets out of the house during inspections.

Helpful Information

Any information that may facilitate the sale should be available to prospective buyers. Try to have the following information readily written and accessible to answer any questions that might arise:

• The date you are planning to move
• Why you are selling
• How old the home is, and who built it
• Records of utility expenses, maintenance costs and annual taxes
• Insulation material
• Draperies, appliances and other items included in the sale
• Recent improvements or additions, such as new appliances or a ceiling fan

Sales Contract

Due to the complexities of a real estate transaction, the most certain way to be sure a sale is properly closed is to use the services of an attorney. Care must be taken to see that both the buyer's and seller's legal rights are fully protected. This involves a knowledge of what these rights are and what must be done to keep them from being violated. State law contains many pitfalls in the sale and purchase of real property. Consequently, counsel by an attorney with experience in residential real estate transactions is advisable.

To consummate any sales agreement, the buyer and seller should sign a sales contract. The contract should contain the following elements:

- Signatures of competent parties
- An offer and an acceptance
- An adequate legal description of the property
- The sales price and the terms of financing
- An escrow deposit to bind the parties to the contract
- A description of the type of *deed* to be used in conveying *title*
- Any other provisions pertinent to the agreement.

A sample contract of sale is shown on page 793. However, a certain form may be preferred or mandated for use in your state.

Parts of a Real Estate Contract of Sale

A contract of sale for real estate will normally contain certain parts. These and their purpose are as follows:

Part	Purpose
Parties	States the names of the seller (*vendor*) and buyer (*vendee*).
Property description	Provides an adequate legal description of the subject property and fixtures included.
Sales price	States the amount to be paid in cash at closing and from the proceeds of financing.
Financing conditions	Purchaser stipulates acceptable conditions of financing, including the type of loan, loan-to-value ratio, interest rate, monthly payments.
Earnest money	The amount of the good faith deposit presented to the seller or agent. Also called *hand money* or *escrow money*.
Type of deed	Describes the type of deed to be given at closing.
Title evidence	Describes the type of evidence to be considered satisfactory assurance that the seller can give title.
Title approval	Describes rights of purchaser and seller in the event that purchaser objects to a flaw in the title.

Property condition	States whatever changes (if any) are required to the property, and required inspections such as for structural integrity, electrical, mechanical, and plumbing systems, and for wood destroying insects.
Prorations	Calls for the proration of prepaid or unpaid taxes, insurance, rents, etc., between buyer and seller.
Loss	Affixes responsibility for casualty losses until closing.
Possession	Establishes a date for possession.
Closing	Establishes a date for closing.
Broker	Acknowledges the existence of a real estate broker, the commission rate, and which principal is to pay the commission.
Default	Describes the obligations of parties in the event one fails to perform.
Miscellaneous provisions	States whatever other provisions buyer and seller agree upon.
Signatures	Principals, brokers, escrow agents.

A worksheet, shown on page 801, can be used to estimate the amount a seller receives upon the sale.

There may be considerable negotiations before prices and terms are agreed to. Usually, a prospective buyer makes an offer on a *sales contract* and tenders *earnest money*. If the seller accepts, the money should be placed in escrow by the broker, or with an attorney or title insurance company. However, if the seller changes any of the terms, it is a rejection of the offer and the substitution of a new offer to sell to the buyer. Negotiations may then proceed until the contract is consummated or may be broken off.

Tax Considerations on The Sale of Your Home

Two major tax provisions pertain to the sale of a taxpayer's principal residence after July 20, 1981.

For Homeowners 55 and Older

The first provision of the act pertains to taxpayers who are 55 or older at the time of the sale (only one spouse needs to be 55). Qualifying taxpayers can elect to exclude from gross taxable income up to $125,000 of any gain realized from the sale of a principal residence ($62,500 for married individuals filing separate returns). However, this election can be exercised only once in a lifetime and is binding on both spouses. Additionally, the taxpayer must have owned and occupied the property

31

as a principal residence for three or more years during the five-year period before the sale.

Since the exclusion may be elected only once, this provision has important implications for married taxpayers who elect it during a marriage which may later be dissolved by divorce or by the death of a spouse. Remarriage will not reinstate the election.

For Homeowners of Any Age

A second provision of the act applies to homeowners of any age. It requires taxpayers to defer taxes on a gain realized from the sale of a principal residence if a replacement residence that costs at least as much as the sale price of the residence sold is purchased or built within 24 months of the sale. Normally, only one tax-deferred sale is allowed during each 24-month period; an exception in the act permits more than one such transaction (usually called a *roll-over*) within 24 months if the taxpayer relocates for employment purposes. The same standards currently in effect concerning deductibility of moving expenses are used to determine if the sale was caused by a change of employment location.

The act permits taxpayers who are 55 or older to use both provisions to minimize taxes on the sale of their home. For example, suppose a 55 or older taxpayer realizes a $200,000 gain on the sale of a principal residence for $400,000. If that taxpayer purchases or builds a replacement for $275,000 within 24 months, taxes on the entire gain are minimized. This homeowner could postpone $75,000 through the roll-over provision and exclude $125,000 by the election available to older taxpayers. This permits those 55 or over to "step down" in the housing market and minimize their tax burden.

IRS Form 2119

The Internal Revenue Service has provided Form 2119, entitled "Sale or Exchange of Principal Residence," to help taxpayers calculate: (1) the gain on the sale of the old residence, (2) the adjusted sales price of the old residence, (3) the amount of taxable gain and (4) the adjusted basis of the replacement residence (if any). Form 2119 is reproduced on page 804.

Moving Expenses: Tax Implications

If you move to a residence 35 miles closer to where you work than you now live, most of your moving expenses may be tax deductible.

For example, if you lived 50 miles from your office and moved to within 15 miles, you moved 35 plus miles closer and qualify. However, if you moved from 50 miles from work to a new residence that is 20 miles from work, the 30 mile difference is not enough to qualify. Generally, one must work in the new area for 39 weeks during the first year after the move.

You cannot deduct the same expense twice. For example, expenses of selling your old home may be used either as moving expenses or subtracted from the old home selling price, but not both.

If you qualify as having moved to a new job location, direct and indirect moving costs are deductible. Direct costs are for moving personal and household goods from the old to the new home, and traveling, including lodging, from old to new. If one's auto is used, the allowance is nine cents per mile, or actual operating expenses but not depreciation. Generally, only 80 percent of the amount spent for meals is deductible. There is no other limit on the amount of deduction for direct expenses.

House hunting expenses are deductible, including meals at 80 percent. The cost of lodging while in temporary quarters at the general area of the new job site is also deductible for up to 30 days. The deduction for house hunting plus temporary living expenses cannot exceed $1,500.

Qualified real estate sale expenses include the real estate broker's commission, escrow fees, advertising expenses, deed preparation, state transfer taxes, points on a buyer's FHA mortgage, and any loss on the sale. On the home purchase, one may deduct legal, title, appraisal, and loan costs (but not interest). The costs of breaking a lease (but not rent) are deductible. Real estate expenses are also indirect expenses, and total indirect expenses may not exceed $3,000. Limits are higher for moves to and from a foreign country.

A sample IRS Form 3903 is provided on page 805.

Closing

Closing, in a real estate transaction, is when money and property change hands. In most states a title company, abstract company, or lawyer is responsible for preparing and recording the necessary documents and accounting for money. A sample form, *Seller's Estimated Receipts*, appears in the Appendix, page 801.

An abbreviated closing statement is shown below.

SAMPLE CLOSING STATEMENT

	Seller		Buyer	
	Debit	Credit	Debit	Credit
Real property		$80,000	$80,000	
Prepaid taxes		670	670	
Sales commission	$2,400			
Survey fee			75	
Cash paid by buyer to close ..				$80,745
Cash received by seller	78,270			
Totals	$80,670	$80,670	$80,745	$80,745

Items that affect only one party will be shown as a debit or a credit only on the statement of the party affected. For example, if the sales commission is paid by the seller, the amount will appear only on the seller's closing statement. If the buyer pays for a survey, it will appear on the buyer's statement only.

Items of value that are sold, exchanged, or transferred between buyer and seller will be shown in *opposite* columns of *both* parties. For example, the transferred property is shown as a credit to the seller *and* as a debit to the buyer. Never should an item transferred, exchanged, or taken over be shown as a credit to both parties or as a debit to both. If an item is transferred, sold, or exchanged, it will be a debit to one party and a credit to the other.

Items usually *debited* (charged) to the buyer include the following:

1. Purchase price of the real property
2. Purchase price of personal property
3. Deed recording fees
4. Title examination
5. Title insurance
6. Hazard insurance
7. Survey
8. Appraisal fee (sometimes charged to seller)
9. Prepaid taxes
10. Loan assumption fees

Items that are likely to be *credited* to the buyer are:

1. Earnest money deposits
2. Proceeds of a loan the buyer borrows
3. Assumption of a loan
4. Mortgage to the seller (purchase money)
5. Current taxes unpaid to closing
6. Tenant rents paid in advance (the seller collected these)
7. Balance due from purchaser to close (paid by buyer to close)

Items likely to be *debited* to a seller are:

1. Sales commission
2. Current but unpaid taxes
3. Existing debt—whether assumed or to be paid off
4. Loan prepayment penalties
5. Discount points for buyer's loan. Discount points on FHA, VA, and *conventional* loans may be charged to buyer or to seller depending on contractual arrangements, custom in the area, local law, etc.
6. Rent received in advance
7. Deed preparation

Items usually *credited* to a seller are:

1. Sales price of real property
2. Sales price of personal property

3. Prepaid taxes
4. Prepaid insurance (only if policy is assumed by buyer)
5. Escrow balance held by lender

When selling your home you may ask the person responsible for closing to allow you to review the figures a day or two prior to closing. If any amount does not appear correct or you have questions concerning charges, get the problem resolved then. It is awkward to resolve matters at the last minute.

Many people are frightened by real estate transactions. There is no need to be apprehensive when one's homework has been properly done.

MEDIAN SALES PRICES OF EXISTING SINGLE-FAMILY HOMES FOR METROPOLITAN AREAS, 1982-1991
(Not Seasonally Adjusted in Thousands of Dollars)

Metropolitan Area	1982	1983	1984	1985	1986	1987	1988	1989	1990	1991
Akron, OH	$51.7	$51.2	$50.4	$52.7	$56.2	$57.1	$59.9	$64.5	$67.7	$71.8
Albany/Schenectady/Troy, NY	47.1	49.4	52.9	60.3	72.7	86.4	92.2	104.9	106.9	110.3
Albuquerque, NM	67.6	70.1	73.4	76.8	81.6	82.6	80.4	83.0	84.5	86.8
Orange County (Anaheim/Santa Ana MSA), CA	131.5	133.4	132.6	134.7	146.6	165.6	203.9	241.7	242.4	239.7
Atlanta, GA	55.4	63.1	66.2	n/a	n/a	n/a	n/a	84.0	86.4	89.3
Baltimore, MD	62.0	n/a	66.1	72.6	74.0	81.1	88.7	96.3	105.9	110.1
Baton Rouge, LA	69.3	n/a	73.5	n/a	71.0	67.8	64.7	63.8	64.9	69.4
Birmingham, AL	60.6	62.8	65.1	64.5	68.3	71.6	75.7	78.5	80.8	86.0
Boston, MA	80.2	82.6	100.0	134.2	159.2	177.2	181.2	181.9	174.2	170.1
Buffalo/Niagara Falls, NY	n/a	n/a	44.8	46.7	52.4	56.7	65.5	72.5	77.2	79.7
Charleston, SC	55.7	57.5	60.9	n/a	n/a	72.7	73.1	74.5	76.2	79.4
Charlotte, NC	n/a	63.8	66.8	64.8	n/a	n/a	n/a	88.1	93.1	101.4
Chattanooga, TN	n/a	49.4	52.3	69.4	55.3	59.0	63.5	65.4	68.0	70.8
Chicago, IL	73.0	76.4	79.5	81.1	86.1	90.8	89.0	107.0	116.8	131.1
Cincinnati, OH	n/a	57.2	58.9	60.2	63.5	66.1	69.7	75.8	79.8	84.9
Cleveland, OH	n/a	n/a	62.7	64.4	66.9	68.1	69.2	75.2	80.6	86.2
Columbia, SC	57.8	59.4	59.9	n/a	67.2	68.4	69.7	73.9	77.1	80.5
Columbus, OH	n/a	n/a	n/a	62.2	65.5	68.7	72.6	77.9	81.6	85.2
Corpus Christi, TX	n/a	n/a	n/a	66.0	65.9	64.9	64.9	63.2	64.3	64.3
Dallas, TX	76.7	80.9	86.8	94.0	93.8	94.2	90.8	93.4	89.5	88.3
Daytona Beach, FL	n/a	n/a	n/a	57.7	57.3	59.4	62.6	63.4	64.1	66.3
Dayton/Springfield, OH	76.2	78.3	82.7	84.3	86.4	88.9	81.8	85.5	86.4	76.3
Denver, CO	n/a	53.0	52.4	52.5	55.9	59.4	63.3	63.4	64.1	89.1
Des Moines, IA	52.6	47.5	48.5	51.7	58.1	55.6	55.8	57.5	60.5	68.2
Detroit, MI	47.5	55.8	57.8	57.6	59.0	65.6	73.1	73.7	76.7	80.6
El Paso, TX	56.8	55.8	48.5	59.0	59.2	59.6	63.1	63.1	63.6	68.2
Ft. Lauderdale/Hollywood/Pompano Beach, FL	74.2	73.9	73.1	74.6	77.7	79.6	81.1	83.9	92.6	89.1
Ft. Myers/Cape Coral, FL	n/a	55.8	57.8	57.6	59.2	59.6	63.1	63.1	66.7	80.6
Ft. Worth, TX	n/a	n/a	n/a	n/a	n/a	62.7	62.7	66.6	69.3	71.3
Grand Rapids, MI	39.1	41.3	42.8	46.7	50.4	53.5	57.9	64.2	68.3	77.6
Greenville/Spartanburg, SC	n/a	n/a	n/a	n/a	64.3	64.2	65.9	68.6	73.9	66.1
Hartford, CT	82.9	81.2	87.4	99.6	129.0	157.4	167.6	165.9	157.3	148.2
Honolulu, HI	n/a	n/a	n/a	172.0	186.0	210.0	270.0	352.0	352.0	341.2

36

MEDIAN SALES PRICES OF EXISTING SINGLE-FAMILY HOMES FOR METROPOLITAN AREAS, 1982-1991
(Not Seasonally Adjusted in Thousands of Dollars)

Metropolitan Area	1982	1983	1984	1985	1986	1987	1988	1989	1990	1991
Houston, TX	$77.2	$79.9	$77.6	$78.6	$69.9	$65.9	$61.8	$66.7	$70.7	$74.0
Indianapolis, IN	50.6	52.8	53.1	55.0	59.0	62.5	66.1	71.2	74.8	79.1
Jackson, MS	n/a	n/a	n/a	n/a	n/a	62.7	n/a	69.0	65.9	68.5
Jacksonville, FL	n/a	51.9	55.7	58.4	62.8	65.1	67.7	69.3	72.4	73.7
Kalamazoo, MI	n/a	n/a	n/a	n/a	n/a	49.9	53.2	57.2	60.4	64.9
Kansas City, MO/KS	58.1	58.8	59.1	61.4	65.4	69.8	70.5	71.6	74.1	76.6
Knoxville, TN	57.1	57.5	59.4	58.2	60.3	65.4	67.0	71.1	75.4	78.8
Lansing/East Lansing, MI	n/a	n/a	48.2	50.3	52.4	54.5	56.6	59.8	63.3	66.7
Las Vegas, NV	n/a	75.1	76.3	75.1	77.5	77.0	78.8	85.7	93.0	101.4
Lexington/Fayette, KY	n/a	n/a	n/a	n/a	67.7	72.5	73.5	77.0	75.0	75.6
Lincoln, NE	n/a	n/a	n/a	n/a	n/a	54.8	55.5	57.0	60.4	62.7
Little Rock/N. Little Rock, AR	n/a	n/a	n/a	n/a	63.2	63.1	63.9	63.7	64.8	67.5
Los Angeles Area, CA	119.6	118.9	121.6	125.2	135.8	147.1	178.9	214.8	212.8	218.9
Louisville, KY	45.0	47.4	48.9	50.6	51.6	51.7	54.5	58.4	60.8	65.4
Madison, WI	n/a	n/a	n/a	n/a	66.4	69.2	72.0	76.5	82.3	87.7
Melbourne/Titusville/Palm Bay, FL	n/a	n/a	n/a	n/a	66.7	66.7	69.9	72.2	72.0	77.7
Memphis, TN	59.3	61.6	64.1	64.6	70.6	75.0	76.3	78.1	78.1	82.5
Miami/Hialeah, FL	n/a	n/a	79.5	80.5	81.1	81.1	82.9	86.9	89.3	93.7
Milwaukee, WI	65.8	68.0	68.2	67.5	69.9	70.5	74.5	79.6	84.4	90.0
Minneapolis/St. Paul, MN	72.4	73.6	74.0	75.2	77.9	80.5	85.2	87.2	88.7	91.1
Mobile, AL	n/a	n/a	n/a	n/a	n/a	55.6	53.0	56.7	59.1	60.8
Montgomery, AL	58.0	61.0	62.9	66.1	61.0	64.5	64.5	68.8	69.3	76.2
Nashville/Davidson, TN	n/a	n/a	n/a	n/a	70.8	75.5	77.6	79.9	81.8	86.9
New Haven/Meridan, CT	n/a	n/a	n/a	n/a	n/a	156.9	169.4	163.4	153.3	153.2
New Orleans, LA	n/a	n/a	n/a	n/a	n/a	n/a	73.1	70.6	67.8	71.8
New York/N. New Jersey/Long Island, NY/NJ/CT	77.1	88.9	105.3	134.0	160.6	183.5	183.8	183.2	174.9	173.5
Bergen/Passaic, NJ	n/a	n/a	n/a	n/a	n/a	n/a	n/a	204.5	187.7	187.1
Middlesex/Somerset/Hunterdon, NJ	n/a	n/a	n/a	n/a	n/a	n/a	174.4	167.0	161.7	158.4
Nassau/Suffolk, NY	n/a	n/a	n/a	n/a	n/a	n/a	172.0	172.0	161.0	159.2
Oklahoma City, OK	58.5	61.6	63.9	64.7	63.0	62.3	56.2	53.5	53.2	57.0
Omaha, NE	52.6	55.3	56.2	58.3	58.8	59.0	59.5	60.6	63.0	66.5
Orlando, FL	63.5	64.4	70.1	70.3	72.5	76.2	79.1	79.8	82.8	86.3
Peoria, IL	n/a	n/a	n/a	n/a	45.7	46.5	45.0	46.8	50.5	55.8

MEDIAN SALES PRICES OF EXISTING SINGLE-FAMILY HOMES FOR METROPOLITAN AREAS, 1982-1991
(Not Seasonally Adjusted in Thousands of Dollars)

Metropolitan Area	1982	1983	1984	1985	1986	1987	1988	1989	1990	1991
Philadelphia, PA	$58.1	$ n/a	$ n/a	$74.0	$82.4	$97.0	$102.4	$103.9	$108.7	$118.4
Phoenix, AZ	n/a	n/a	74.4	74.8	78.4	80.9	80.0	78.8	84.0	85.5
Pittsburgh, PA	n/a	n/a	n/a	n/a	n/a	n/a	n/a	65.8	70.1	74.2
Portland, OR	n/a	n/a	62.9	61.5	62.6	64.2	63.2	65.8	79.5	88.5
Providence, RI	49.7	54.7	59.6	67.5	87.6	121.4	130.2	127.9	n/a	124.3
Raleigh/Durham, NC	n/a	n/a	n/a	n/a	89.5	98.0	97.0	103.6	n/a	100.8
Reno, NV	n/a	n/a	n/a	n/a	93.8	98.0	96.6	102.6	109.7	115.1
Richmond, VA	n/a	n/a	n/a	n/a	n/a	n/a	n/a	87.5	87.5	92.5
Riverside/San Bernardino, CA	78.8	80.4	81.5	85.0	92.1	96.1	106.7	124.1	132.1	135.4
Rochester, NY	49.5	54.8	59.7	64.2	68.3	72.5	75.7	78.5	79.8	81.5
Rockford, IL	n/a	n/a	n/a	n/a	n/a	n/a	n/a	n/a	n/a	n/a
Sacramento, CA	76.4	75.7	76.3	77.9	82.9	87.5	94.6	111.7	136.7	137.7
Saginaw, MI	n/a	n/a	n/a	n/a	n/a	42.7	44.3	46.9	48.1	51.5
Salt Lake City/Ogden, UT	64.6	64.3	65.8	66.7	68.5	69.4	67.7	69.4	69.4	72.8
San Antonio, TX	58.3	62.6	67.5	67.7	69.2	70.2	65.0	64.2	63.6	64.9
San Diego, CA	98.9	99.3	100.6	107.4	118.5	129.2	153.4	181.9	183.2	187.5
San Francisco Bay Area, CA	128.0	133.7	134.1	145.1	166.2	176.7	212.9	260.6	259.3	262.8
Seattle/Tacoma, WA	n/a	n/a	n/a	n/a	n/a	82.6	88.7	115.0	131.5	143.1
Shreveport, LA	n/a	n/a	n/a	n/a	n/a	45.4	49.1	61.6	61.4	64.0
South Bend/Mishawaka, IN	n/a	n/a	n/a	n/a	n/a	51.2	52.2	56.5	55.5	59.1
Spokane, WA	n/a	n/a	n/a	n/a	n/a	n/a	n/a	52.2	56.5	64.5
Springfield, MA	n/a	n/a	n/a	n/a	87.6	105.2	122.0	125.0	120.0	117.1
St. Louis, MO	57.0	58.9	61.8	65.7	70.9	74.4	78.1	76.9	76.7	79.4
Syracuse, NY	45.1	48.7	50.7	58.8	64.3	68.9	74.6	79.3	80.7	77.7
Tampa/St. Petersburg/Clearwater, FL	53.9	55.5	58.4	58.8	61.1	63.8	65.6	71.9	71.4	71.3
Toledo, OH	n/a	51.8	50.7	51.9	56.0	56.3	58.4	60.8	62.8	68.8
Tulsa, OK	63.3	64.1	67.3	66.7	65.5	65.7	65.0	62.6	63.9	65.4
Washington, DC/MD/VA	87.2	89.4	93.0	97.1	101.6	114.2	132.5	144.4	150.2	147.5
W. Palm Beach/Boca Raton/Delray Beach, FL	87.2	86.5	84.8	88.3	92.6	102.6	99.0	102.6	108.0	116.3
Wichita, KS	n/a	n/a	n/a	n/a	n/a	n/a	60.1	62.0	62.4	65.9
Worcester, MA	n/a	n/a	n/a	n/a	n/a	139.1	147.5	141.5	136.8	n/a
Youngstown/Warren, OH	n/a	n/a	n/a	n/a	n/a	46.6	46.9	48.6	51.1	54.5

Source: National Association of Realtors, *Home Sales Yearbook*. Adapted with permission.

ANALYZING REAL ESTATE INVESTMENT OPPORTUNITIES

Real estate investment analysis is the process of determining the suitability of a proposed real estate investment to a specific investor. The process involves weighing the expected benefits of property ownership against the possible risks and matching them with a potential investor. The validity of this analysis rests on the assumptions that are used. When overly optimistic assumptions are input, the investment will appear deceptively attractive. Further, returns from real estate take several forms and are more complex than other investments. For these reasons, real estate investment analysis requires a great deal of knowledge, sound judgment, and careful consideration.

Financial Benefits of Investing in Real Estate

Financial benefits of investing in real estate are classified into four major categories:

1. Cash flow
2. Income tax advantages
3. Capital appreciation (including inflation hedge)
4. Equity build-up via mortgage reduction

These four benefits, plus additional financial and non-financial reasons for investing in real estate, are described below. Because of inherent conflicts in the benefits it is very difficult for an investor to maximize all four from the same property. An investor should seek the one or two that are the most important in satisfying his or her goals.

Cash Flow

Cash flow is the excess of rentals over combined operating expenses and debt service. Cash flow alone may provide a rate of return on equity that is competitive with other investment alternatives.

Income Tax Advantages

Improved real estate can generate income tax losses that may offset income from other sources. Ordinary and necessary operating expenses, depreciation, and interest on indebtedness in a trade or business are allowable tax deductions. If total allowable deductions exceed rental income, a tax loss is generated. Since depreciation is a noncash

39

accounting deduction, rental property can generate a tax loss while providing cash flow and value appreciation. However, the use of such passive losses to offset active or portfolio income was severely restricted by the Tax Reform Act of 1986.

Capital Appreciation

There are good prospects for *capital appreciation* of land and improved properties in addition to inflation gains. Speculators and other landowners in the path of growth can enjoy windfall gains as rural areas become urbanized. Residential owners gain price increases because stricter environmental regulations and building codes, and higher interest rates increase replacement costs. In areas of growth, prices of existing units tend to rise with replacement costs. Higher interest rates require rents to rise before new construction becomes feasible. Furthermore, the number of residential units needed has been increasing due to the trend toward smaller household size.

Hedge against inflation Many investors acquire real estate as a *store of value*. In the long run, land prices tend to rise with inflation, keeping pace with the price level of other commodities. Improvements to and on land are considered to be long-lasting. As the price of bricks, lumber, concrete and other building materials rise along with higher wages, replacement costs for improved real estate increase. Prices paid for existing real estate rise with higher replacement costs.

Equity Build-Up

Equity build-up is a method of forced saving while owning real estate. Most real estate mortgages require at least some *amortization* (principal payments) to reduce the debt over time. The benefit of this payment is returned to the investor upon a sale or perhaps a refinancing of the property.

Additional Financial and Nonfinancial Benefits

Pride of Ownership and Control

The tangible nature of real estate provides advantages. Prestigious location, size, impressive architecture, or even a modest but well maintained property can add much to the psychological satisfaction of the owner. Control and use of property are also important aspects of ownership.

Leverage

Leverage provides the traditional key to building wealth with real

estate. By using borrowed money to purchase real estate, an investor can magnify the benefits of value appreciation. Advisors do point out the risk-return effect of leverage and counsel some middle ground for security. To the investor recognizing the trade-off between risk and reward in investments, there is a prudent amount of leverage.

Estate Building

All investors desire to accumulate wealth, and real estate is recognized as an excellent vehicle for this purpose. Traditional investors recognize the power of appreciation combined with leverage to build wealth. By controlling an appreciating asset using borrowed funds, owner's equity can grow quickly. Experience has shown that appreciation is not universal nor constant over time. Thus, investors spend much effort searching for properties with the best prospects for appreciation and plan to hold each property for five or more years.

Security of Capital

There is a certain security in real estate because it is highly unlikely that the asset will ever become worthless (in contrast to stocks and bonds). If an investor is interested in security, then judicious use of leverage, long-term leasing to high quality tenants, and diversification are advised.

Balancing Investment Portfolios

Spreading the risk among various investments — *diversification* — can serve to preserve principal and income. Diversification relates to the type of investment and to the geographical distribution of holdings. Large pension plans and life insurance companies acquire — in addition to securities — real estate and mortgages in many different locations. Additional diversification can be achieved through investments in different types of real property, e.g., shopping centers, office buildings, or apartments.

Opportunity for Abnormal Returns

Because each parcel of real property includes a unique location in geographic space, its owners enjoy some monopoly power. Investors who can obtain the more desired locations can derive above average returns. Such returns are achieved either by luck or through use of entrepreneurial skill. Consistent winners must be able to find those locations that will be in demand in the near future, create competitive advantages for their development, select the proper time for acquiring and disposing of property through knowledge of business cycles, or know how to overcome government-imposed constraints on the use of land.

Disadvantages of Investing in Real Estate

Among the reasons investors expect to receive relatively high returns from real estate investment are the extensive risks involved. To the careful investor, these risks represent challenges calling for expert knowledge. To the risk-taker, they are minor hurdles that discourage the uninitiated and timid.

Illiquidity

Real property is very costly; it is also time-consuming to buy and sell. Transaction costs are high compared to those associated with other assets. The market is more difficult to evaluate. Selection of a property requires analysis of the local economy and the location, as well as the specific attributes of the property under consideration. Locating a buyer generally requires the services of a professional agent. Furthermore, advantageous purchases and sales depend on proper market timing. Money invested in real estate, therefore, is apt to be tied up for a considerable period of time.

Management Burden

Real property ownership entails the responsibility for maintaining the property and collecting rents. This calls for continuous personal involvement on the part of the investor. Many have found that ownership of property outside their home area is impractical.

Economic Depreciation

Not only do properties require upkeep to offset physical deterioration, but periodic remodeling is needed to keep the property competitive in the market. Keeping a reserve account to handle these tasks is prudent.

Government Controls

The property owner may be restricted in several ways in the use of the property. Zoning and subdivision controls affect changes in the use of the site. Housing codes may require a specified level of maintenance (not necessarily in line with what the market demands). Rent controls can prevent recouping investments spent to upgrade property.

Legal Complexity

The buying and selling of real estate involves a succession of legal commitments with potentially serious consequences. It is not uncommon for both buyer and seller to be represented by legal counsel even in a simple transaction.

Lack of Information

Buyers and sellers of real estate are handicapped by limited information about current market conditions and the properties they are considering. It is important to negotiate the best deal, and up-to-date information is essential to that end. Such information is costly to obtain. (This is not so important for those who intend to use property for personal purposes; the greater part of their evaluation rests on the suitability of the property for their own use.)

Benchmark Example

At this juncture, a benchmark example of a proposed real estate investment will be used to introduce investment analysis. Variations on the basic case will highlight certain points. The benchmark is simplified into basic components from these standpoints:

1. Physical composition
2. Financial composition
3. Rights to use
4. Income and expenses

Physical Composition

Our hypothetical benchmark property is a 50-unit apartment complex which cost $2 million — $200,000 in land value, plus $1,800,000 of depreciable improvements. To simplify the illustration, all of the improvements are depreciated using a 27½ year life. Depreciation was calculated at 3.64 percent of the asset cost annually on a straight-line basis, except for the first year which is $^{23}\!/_{24}$ of that rate because of the midmonth convention introduced by the 1986 tax act. Land is not depreciated; only improvements are depreciable.

The property was expected to increase in value by three percent annually, compounded. Transaction costs to sell the property at the end of the projection period were three percent of the resale price.

Financial Composition

The mortgage-equity components of our benchmark property included a $1,600,000 loan at 11 percent interest, with monthly payments, self-amortizing over a 25-year period. The $400,000 balance of the purchase price was considered to be paid in cash at closing.

Rights to Use

It was assumed that the landlord held all of the rights and privileges of ownership, subject to tenant leases that were arranged on a short-

43

term (typically one-year) basis. Thus, periodic rent increases were likely.

Income and Expenses

Each apartment rents for $550 per month. A 10 percent vacancy and collection allowance was assumed in the example. Miscellaneous income (such as from laundry and vending machines) was $5,000 for the first year. Operating expenses, (such as utilities, maintenance, real estate taxes, and insurance) were $100,000 for the first year.

These figures were incremented annually at three percent for revenues, and five percent for operating expenses. A higher rate of increase was used for operating expenses than revenues because as rental property ages its market appeal diminishes, yet it requires more maintenance.

Computer Simulation

A computer program can be used to project future income expected from the investment, or results can be projected by hand, preferably with a calculator. The computer program used for this illustration allows the user to input separately, the potential gross income, miscellaneous income, vacancy and collection allowance, and operating expenses. A compounded growth rate is allowed for the relevant variables.

A 20-year projection of cash flow and taxable income or loss for the subject property was performed, based on the assumptions stated. Results are shown on the following pages. (Contact the authors at Texas A&M University, College Station, Texas 77843, concerning availability of the computer program which generated this output.)

Column 1 shows the *potential gross income* each year. This is the amount of rental income that would be received if all units were occupied and paid for each month.
Column 2 shows the *vacancy allowance* each year. Some allowance is needed for vacant apartment units, and for the failure to collect some rent.
Column 3 shows *miscellaneous income* each year. Typically, this derives from laundry or vending machine concessions.
Column 4 shows *operating expenses* each year. These expenditures are necessary to operate the property, even if it were bought free of debt. Expenses include insurance, real estate taxes, repairs and maintenance, replacement of worn carpets and appliances, property management, and the like.
Column 5 shows *net operating income (NOI)* each year for 20 years. (Column 1 plus column 3 minus columns 2 and 4.)

Year	1. Potential Gross Income	2. Vacancy Allowance	3. Misc. Income	4. Operating Expenses
1	330,000	33,000	5,000	100,000
2	339,900	33,990	5,150	105,000
3	350,097	35,010	5,305	110,250
4	360,600	36,060	5,464	115,762
5	371,418	37,142	5,628	121,551
6	382,560	38,256	5,796	127,628
7	394,037	39,404	5,970	134,010
8	405,858	40,586	6,149	140,710
9	418,034	41,803	6,334	147,745
10	430,575	43,058	6,524	155,133
11	443,492	44,349	6,720	162,889
12	456,797	45,680	6,921	171,034
13	470,501	47,050	7,129	179,586
14	484,616	48,462	7,343	188,565
15	499,155	49,915	7,563	197,993
16	514,129	51,413	7,790	207,893
17	529,553	52,955	8,024	218,287
18	545,440	54,544	8,264	229,202
19	561,803	56,180	8,512	240,662
20	578,657	57,866	8,768	252,695

Year	5. Net Operating Income	6. Interest Expense	7. Principal Amortization	8. Before-Tax Cash Flow
1	202,000	175,367	12,815	13,818
2	206,060	173,884	14,298	17,878
3	210,142	172,229	15,953	21,960
4	214,241	170,383	17,798	26,060
5	218,353	168,324	19,858	30,172
6	222,473	166,026	22,156	34,291
7	226,594	163,462	24,720	38,413
8	230,712	160,601	27,580	42,530
9	234,819	157,409	30,772	46,637
10	238,909	153,849	34,333	50,727
11	242,973	149,875	38,306	54,792
12	247,005	145,443	42,739	58,823
13	250,994	140,497	47,684	62,813
14	254,932	134,979	53,203	66,751
15	258,809	128,823	59,359	70,627
16	262,613	121,954	66,228	74,432
17	266,334	114,290	73,892	78,152
18	269,958	105,739	82,442	81,777
19	273,473	96,199	91,983	85,291
20	276,864	85,555	102,627	88,682

Year	9. Depreciation Expense	10. Taxable Income	11. Passive Loss Used	12. Passive Loss Carryover	13. Tax Paid (−Savings)	14. After-Tax Cash Flow
1	62,640	− 36,007	0	36,007	0	13,818
2	65,520	− 33,344	0	69,350	0	17,878
3	65,520	− 27,607	0	96,958	0	21,960
4	65,520	− 21,662	0	118,620	0	26,060
5	65,520	− 15,490	0	134,110	0	30,172
6	65,520	− 9,073	0	143,183	0	34,291
7	65,520	− 2,387	0	145,571	0	38,413
8	65,520	4,591	− 4,591	140,980	0	42,530
9	65,520	11,890	− 11,890	129,090	0	46,637
10	65,520	19,540	− 19,540	109,550	0	50,727
11	65,520	27,578	− 27,578	81,972	0	54,792
12	65,520	36,042	− 36,042	45,931	0	58,823
13	65,520	44,977	− 44,977	954	0	62,813
14	65,520	54,433	− 954	0	14,974	51,776
15	65,520	64,466	0	0	18,051	52,577
16	65,520	75,140	0	0	21,039	53,393
17	65,520	86,524	0	0	24,227	53,926
18	65,520	98,699	0	0	27,636	54,141
19	65,520	111,754	0	0	31,291	54,000
20	65,520	125,789	0	0	35,221	53,461

Sale Year	15. Selling Price Before Expenses	16. Selling Expenses	17. Selling Price After Expenses	18. Mortgage Balance	19. Adjusted Tax Basis
1	2,060,000	61,800	1,998,200	1,587,185	1,937,360
2	2,121,800	63,654	2,058,146	1,572,887	1,871,840
3	2,185,454	65,564	2,119,891	1,556,935	1,806,320
4	2,251,018	67,531	2,183,487	1,539,137	1,740,800
5	2,318,548	69,556	2,248,992	1,519,279	1,675,280
6	2,388,105	71,643	2,316,461	1,497,123	1,609,760
7	2,459,748	73,792	2,385,955	1,472,403	1,544,240
8	2,533,540	76,006	2,457,534	1,444,822	1,478,720
9	2,609,546	78,286	2,531,260	1,414,050	1,413,200
10	2,687,833	80,635	2,607,198	1,379,717	1,347,680
11	2,768,468	83,054	2,685,414	1,341,411	1,282,160
12	2,851,522	85,546	2,765,976	1,298,673	1,216,640
13	2,937,067	88,112	2,848,955	1,250,988	1,151,120
14	3,025,179	90,755	2,934,424	1,197,786	1,085,600
15	3,115,934	93,478	3,022,456	1,138,427	1,020,080
16	3,209,413	96,282	3,113,130	1,072,199	954,560
17	3,305,695	99,171	3,206,524	998,307	889,040
18	3,404,866	102,146	3,302,720	915,865	823,520
19	3,507,012	105,210	3,401,802	823,882	758,000
20	3,612,222	108,367	3,503,855	721,256	692,480

Sale Year	20. Passive Loss Released	21. Taxable Gain On Sale	22. Tax On Gain (− Savings)	23. After-Tax Resale Proceeds	24. Internal Rate Of Return On Init Equity
1	36,007	24,833	6,953	404,062	4.47%
2	69,350	116,956	32,748	452,511	10.18%
3	96,958	216,613	60,652	502,304	11.98%
4	118,620	324,067	90,739	553,612	12.77%
5	134,110	439,601	123,088	606,625	13.19%
6	143,183	563,518	157,785	661,554	13.41%
7	145,571	696,144	194,920	718,632	13.54%
8	140,980	837,834	234,539	778,118	13.61%
9	129,090	988,969	276,911	840,298	13.64%
10	109,550	1,149,967	321,991	905,490	13.65%
11	81,972	1,321,281	369,959	974,044	13.65%
12	45,931	1,503,405	420,953	1,046,350	13.64%
13	954	1,696,881	475,127	1,122,840	13.62%
14	0	1,848,824	517,671	1,218,968	13.60%
15	0	2,002,376	560,665	1,323,364	13.57%
16	0	2,158,570	604,400	1,436,532	13.52%
17	0	2,317,484	648,896	1,559,321	13.48%
18	0	2,479,200	694,176	1,692,679	13.42%
19	0	2,643,802	740,264	1,837,655	13.37%
20	0	2,811,375	787,185	1,995,415	13.31%

Sale Year	25. Overall Rate Of Return	26. Debt Service Coverage Ratio	27. Before-Tax Cash Flow To Inital Equity	28. After-Tax Cash Flow To Inital Equity
1	10.100%	107.343%	3.455%	3.455%
2	10.003%	109.501%	4.470%	4.470%
3	9.904%	111.670%	5.490%	5.490%
4	9.803%	113.848%	6.515%	6.515%
5	9.700%	116.033%	7.543%	7.543%
6	9.595%	118.222%	8.573%	8.573%
7	9.488%	120.413%	9.603%	9.603%
8	9.379%	122.601%	10.633%	10.633%
9	9.268%	124.783%	11.659%	11.659%
10	9.155%	126.956%	12.682%	12.682%
11	9.040%	129.116%	13.698%	13.698%
12	8.922%	131.259%	14.706%	14.706%
13	8.802%	133.379%	15.703%	15.703%
14	8.680%	135.471%	16.688%	12.944%
15	8.555%	137.532%	17.657%	13.144%
16	8.428%	139.553%	18.608%	13.348%
17	8.299%	141.530%	19.538%	13.481%
18	8.166%	143.456%	20.444%	13.535%
19	8.032%	145.324%	21.323%	13.500%
20	7.895%	147.126%	22.171%	13.365%

Year	29. Gross Rent Multiplier	30. Break-Even Ratio
1	6.061	87.328%
2	6.061	86.255%
3	6.061	85.243%
4	6.061	84.288%
5	6.061	83.392%
6	6.061	82.522%
7	6.061	81.767%
8	6.061	81.036%
9	6.061	80.359%
10	6.061	79.734%
11	6.061	79.161%
12	6.061	78.638%
13	6.061	78.165%
14	6.061	77.741%
15	6.061	77.366%
16	6.061	77.038%
17	6.061	76.757%
18	6.061	76.522%
19	6.061	76.333%
20	6.061	76.190%

Column 6 shows *interest expense* for each of 20 years based on the $1,600,000, 25-year monthly payment mortgage at 11 percent interest. Note how the interest portion of the constant payment diminishes over time as the principal is retired.

Column 7 shows the *principal payment* on the mortgage: this is the annual equity build-up. Note that principal payments (called *mortgage amortization*) require cash and are not tax-deductible.

Column 8 Before-tax cash flow is the difference between NOI in column 5 and the debt service requirement (principal and interest, the sum of columns 6 and 7).

Column 9 Depreciation was based on 3.64 percent per year, the straight-line rate that approximates a 27½year life. Depreciation provides a tax deduction without a cash outflow. Note: the first year is slightly less than other years because of the midmonth convention under the 1986 tax act.

Column 10 Taxable income (or *loss*) is the result of subtracting interest and depreciation from net operating income, specifically column 5 minus columns 6 and 9. Note that losses occur during the first seven years of ownership; these losses diminish with reduced mortgage payments and increased NOI. In later years taxable income increases sharply; however, projected taxable income is less than before-tax cash flow for the first 15 years. This occurs because depreciation exceeds the mortgage principal payment each year until the sixteenth year.

Column 11 In this projection it was assumed that tax losses generated in early years could not be applied against other income. Instead, the losses are suspended until this property generates positive taxable income; then they are released to offset such income or gain from the sale. *Passive losses* may be used earlier depending on the investor's other income and personal circumstances. An "active" property owner who meets certain requirements may deduct up to $25,000 of passive losses against non-passive income.

Column 12 The *passive loss carry-over* column accumulates the property's passive losses, net of annual application.

Column 13 The owner was assumed to be in the 28 percent marginal and average tax bracket. The *tax paid* column offers the amount of tax attributable to the property. For the first seven years the property offers tax losses but they are suspended because of passive loss limitations. Taxable income generated during the next six years is offset by releasing the suspended losses. Consequently, no income taxes are due for the first 13 years. In the fourteenth year, some taxes are due, continuing through the end of the projection.

Column 14 *After-tax cash flow* is before-tax cash flow (column 8) modified by taxes paid or saved (column 13). The investor keeps these dollars.

Resale Simulation

The eventual resale of our benchmark property will create a taxable gain (or loss) and cash proceeds (or cash deficits). We know that real estate is not a liquid asset, and it may take months or years just to realize market value in a sale. Furthermore, values are subject to fluctuation in an unpredictable manner. In an effort to simplify this analysis, our benchmark property was assumed to grow in value at a three percent rate, compounded annually. Transaction costs, estimated at a one-time charge of three percent, were subtracted. The mortgage balance and adjusted tax basis could be projected mathematically. Other details are shown in the projections.

Please note that columns 15 through 24 may be used for any year of sale and are valid only for that year because the property can be sold only once. All years are shown in the table to offer complete information for decision making purposes. For example, for a presumed sale in year 10, read across the line for year 10 of columns 15 — 24. That is the only relevant line across these columns for a 10 year projection. Results of operations would be applicable for years 1 through 10; but operations in years 11 through 20 should be ignored as they would be extraneous.

Column 15 The *selling price before expenses* is the initial cost increased by three percent compounded annually. The projection offers the price for any year, based on the assumed increase.

Column 16 *Selling expenses*, or *transaction costs*, are three percent of the resale price. This would include a brokerage commission and legal expenses.

Column 17 The *selling price after expenses* is the difference between column 15 and 16.

Column 18 Future *mortgage balances* were based on scheduled amortization. Neither accelerated payments nor delinquencies were considered for this projection. Refinancing was not attempted.

Column 19 The *adjusted tax basis* for each year is the initial cost less annual depreciation.

Column 20 Unused *passive losses* are assumed to be released upon a sale, and reduce the taxable gain.

Column 21 The *selling price* (column 15) minus the sum of selling expenses (column 16), adjusted tax basis (column 19), and passive loss released (column 20) result in a taxable gain or loss on a sale.

Column 22 A 28 percent tax rate was applied to the amount in column 21 to indicate the *tax on the gain*.

Column 23 The *after-tax resale proceeds* are the selling price after expenses (column 17) less the sum of the mortgage balance (column 18) and tax on the gain (column 22). This is the net cash amount the sale will provide.

Column 24 The *internal rate of return* is a complicated mathematical calculation that compares the equity paid with the after-tax cash flows forecast, including the cash proceeds from resale. Suppose the investor had instead put the cash down payment in a bank savings account and withdrew the same annual cash flows as the property is expected to generate. Then, the interest rate that the bank must pay to sustain the withdrawals would be equal to the internal rate of return.

Column 25 The *overall rate of return* is the net operating income (column 5) divided by the selling price before expenses for the previous year (column15 for 1 year earlier). This percentage may provide an indication of whether the estimated resale price is in line with the income at the time of resale.

Column 26 The *debt service coverage ratio* is net operating income (column 5) divided by the combined principal and interest payment (column 6 plus 7). It indicates to a lender whether the property can support the debt service payment.

Column 27 Before-tax cash flow (column 8) divided by initial equity is a percentage rate that compares the equity investor's rate of cash flow to the equity contributed; it is commonly known as the equity dividend rate.

Column 28 After-tax cash flow (column 14) compared to initial equity is an after-tax equity dividend rate.

Column 29 *Gross rent multiplier* is the selling price divided by the potential gross income expected for the next year (column 15 divided by Column 1 for the next year).

Column 30 The *break-even ratio* is the percentage occupancy rate that is needed to pay for operating expenses, interest and principal (sum of columns 4, 6, 7). Divide that sum by column 1 to derive the percentage.

Conflicts Among Financial Benefits

Property may be carved into several pieces to offer different investors the one or two types of financial benefits they desire. However, one investor will not be able to maximize simultaneously all potential financial benefits from the same property because of inherent conflicts. Some of these conflicts are discussed below.

Cash Flow versus Taxable Income

It is difficult to maximize cash flow and tax savings at the same time. Depreciation, a noncash tax deduction, makes possible the simultaneous receipt of cash flow and tax losses. However, further tax losses must be accompanied by a cash flow reduction — such as would result from receiving less rent, incurring higher operating expenses, or a higher interest cost.

Increases in cash flow will be accompanied by increases in taxable income. It is always preferable to receive cash and pay a tax on the income than it is to pay cash and possibly receive tax losses.

Cash Flow versus Mortgage Reduction

An investor can increase the equity build-up benefit by accelerating mortgage principal payments. Most lenders will allow that; however, loans on commercial property often have prepayment penalties of one to five percent and some have closed periods, meaning they cannot be prepaid for the first five to ten years.

Since cash is required to reduce the principal balance, there is an inherent trade-off of cash flow versus equity buildup. Most investors prefer to receive spendable cash flow unless the mortgage interest rate is higher than their earnings rate. Then, it may be preferable to reduce the mortgage debt. Fast mortgage amortization also reduces the future interest payment, so it inherently conflicts with tax savings.

Cash Flow versus Appreciation

An owner can attempt to enhance property value by plowing back cash flow into property maintenance, repairs, and capital expenditures. Conversely, an owner can attempt to maximize cash flow by skimping on maintenance. An owner must make this choice, keeping in mind present needs for cash contrasted with future value enhancement. When choosing, an owner should remember there are many properties that suffer from deferred maintenance or neglect and consequently lose value. The longer this process continues, the more difficult it is to reverse by rehabilitation or modernization.

Tax Shelter versus Appreciation in Value

There is an inherent conflict between tax savings and appreciation. When the effect of general economic inflation is removed, land tends to rise in value with population pressures, while improved real estate tends to wear out. An investor who seeks income tax savings would prefer to purchase depreciable improvements, whereas one who seeks appreciation would prefer land. Consequently, though it is possible to gain some of both benefits, it is very difficult for one investor to maximize both appreciation and tax shelter simultaneously. Furthermore, if appreciation does materialize, the property must be sold to recognize the gain and income taxes paid.

Judging Income Stream Quality

The value of real estate is based on its expected future income. To estimate future income, the following must be considered:

1. The amount of net operating income.
2. When the income will be received.
3. The expected net proceeds from the sale of the property.

Many real estate investors, especially those who are just beginning, may rely on professional appraisers to assist them with these projections. An appraiser should possess knowledge of market rental rates, operating expenses and values for the property being considered.

The Amount of Net Operating Income

Market data on competitive properties will provide benchmarks against which to judge the property being analyzed. This information might include market rental rates, vacancy rates, and typical expense ratios. Appraisal reports on income-producing properties should include these items.

Potential gross income In estimating the potential gross income, there is a difference between *market rent* and *contract rent*. Market rent is the prevailing market rate for similar properties. Contract rent is the sum agreed to between a landlord and a tenant. If the existing leases are for a long term, the contract rent serves as an important ingredient in calculating the investment value of the project. It is possible, for example, that the amount the property owner actually receives for the term of a lease may be considerably less than market rent. In the case of short-term agreements, a potential buyer should determine whether it is reasonable for contract rent to equal the market rent at the time leases are renegotiated. With several leases encumbering a property, it is good to prepare a schedule with the expiration date of each lease. This will assist in estimating the quality and duration of the known portion of the income stream.

Special problems can occur in analyzing projects occupied by a single tenant. One may evaluate the credit worthiness of the tenant and the length of the lease to judge the probability of a vacancy in the future and when this vacancy would be likely to occur.

Vacancy and collection allowance The potential gross income is the amount received if every unit were rented at full rates all of the time. From this must be subtracted the loss from expected vacancies and an allowance for unpaid rents. The vacancy allowance depends on real estate market conditions (overbuilding is often problematical), regulatory requirements, and marketing.

Miscellaneous income Miscellaneous income includes revenues from laundry rooms, concession income, and the rental of parking spaces and storage bins.

Operating expenses Operating expenses are either fixed or variable. *Fixed expenses* do not change as the rate of occupancy changes. *Variable expenses* are directly related to the occupancy rate. As more people occupy and use a building, variable expenses increase.

Fixed expenses include property taxes, license and permit fees, and property insurance. Variable expenses include cost of utilities, management fees, payroll and payroll taxes, security costs, annual landscaping costs, advertising fees, and the cost of supplies and fees for various services provided by local government or private contractors. Operating rental property differs from most other businesses in that, whether a property is fully occupied or mostly vacant, the cost of real estate operations hardly changes.

A prospective purchaser should review utility bills, property tax assessments, insurance policies, receipts and reports from property management companies, title insurance policies, W-2 forms and other wage information for employees, copies of the actual leases in force, and income tax forms pertaining to the operation of the project.

When The Income Will Be Received

Cash flows are negative during *new construction*. The expected duration of construction is estimated by examining schedules and expected times of completion. During this period, interest is to be paid to the construction lender or added to the loan balance. A forecast must be made assessing the expected interest costs during construction, and whether it is to be funded by the construction loan, or paid in cash.

During the *leasing phase*, cash flows will rise as the project is leased to tenants. Upon attainment of break-even occupancy, often 80 to 85 percent, the project generates adequate income to provide cash flow. Hopefully, full occupancy occurs and continues until the project approaches the end of its economic useful life.

The Expected Net Proceeds From The Sale of Property

One of the most difficult tasks is to estimate the net proceeds expected from the resale of the subject property at the end of its holding

period. The following factors should be considered:

Possible appreciation of the land Depending on what happens to the surrounding area, the land could increase or decrease in value. For example, if the local government plans to build a highway interchange at the site, the highest and best use of the land and its value will change accordingly. Conditions of future scarcity of buildable sites with similar location qualities might also be viewed as upward value indications. On the other hand, if future land uses are adverse, the land value may decline.

Depreciation of the improvements In real economic terms, that is, after correcting for price level inflation, the value of improvements is expected to decline over time. The rate of this depreciation can be estimated by the experience of similar properties.

Income taxes Because income tax laws are subject to the political process, over the long run there is no certainty as to how much tax must be paid at the time of disposition. Over the short run, income taxes can be determined with reasonable accuracy.

Inflation Consideration must be given to expected inflationary pressures on real estate values. In times of high inflation, measurements are more difficult especially as investor expectations drive up prices.

Leverage

Leverage is the use of "other peoples' money" in an effort to enhance the equity investor's rate of return. In real estate, leverage can be extensive: while most properties are acquired with some equity, it is possible to borrow the entire property cost in many situations. Leverage is positive when the property provides income at a rate greater than the interest rate; the rate of return to equity is then enhanced.

However, if the property fails to provide income or appreciate faster than the interest rate, leverage is negative. The owner not only loses money, but loses at a rapid rate because the losses apply to the total cost, both debt and equity. The ability to employ leverage successfully can greatly enhance an owner's wealth, while failure results in huge losses.

Techniques to Measure Rate of Return from Real Estate

There are two major techniques to measure rate of return from a real estate investment: *ratio* and *yield*. Ratio involves a simple arithmetic computation that relates some level of periodic income to a corresponding asset value. Yield computation is based on *discounting* future income to account for the *time value of money*. The time (or *present*) value of money is today's value of a future payment, or series of payments, discounted at some appropriate rate. Yield analysis is more

sophisticated than ratio analysis but more difficult to perform. A discussion of both ratio and yield techniques follows for our benchmark example.

Ratio Models

The periodic real estate income can be divided by an asset or investment amount to result in a percentage. Alternatively, the income can be divided into an asset value, which results in a *multiplier*. For example, suppose monthly rent for a house is $800 and its estimated value is $80,000. The ratio, $800/$80,000 tells us that rent is one percent of value. Alternatively, $80,000/$800 provides a rent multiplier of 100, which tells us that value is 100 times monthly rent. The result, whether a percentage or multiplier, provides a unit of comparison to judge proposed investments.

Ratio techniques are numerous and include the *gross rent multiplier, overall rate of return, equity dividend*, and *net spendable income*. Whichever method is used, one must take care to assure that the proper amount of income is compared to the corresponding asset or capital amount. For example, cash flow to equity should be compared to the amount of equity, and not to the total cost of mortgaged property. When preparing computations, avoid a mismatch of cash returns to one investor with money invested by two investors.

Gross rent multiplier The gross rent multiplier (GRM) is the relationship of the purchase price to the gross rental income. As it is defined, either potential gross income (before vacancies and collection allowances have been subtracted) or effective gross income (net of a vacancy and collection allowance) may be used. In the benchmark example, the GRM is 6.061 as shown in column 29, computed as follows:

$$\frac{\text{Purchase Price}}{\text{Annual Rental Income}} \quad \frac{\$2,000,000}{\$330,000} = 6.061$$

This method is one of the most widely used techniques because it is easy to compute and involves readily available figures. However, its widespread use stems from the ease of computation and comparison to other projects—not from its reliability as a measuring device.

The GRM fails to account for operating expense variations among projects, financing, resale prices, and income taxes. It disregards the amounts and timing of after-tax cash flows to the equity investor.

Overall rate of return (OAR) The overall rate of return is computed by dividing the net operating income (NOI) by the purchase price. The result is the rate of return on the entire purchase capital, without regard to the contributor (i.e., equity investor or mortgage lender).

Applied to the benchmark example, the OAR fluctuates as shown in column 25:

$$\frac{\$202,000}{\$2,000,000} = \frac{\text{NOI}}{\text{Price}} = 10.1\%$$

The OAR improves on the GRM in that operating expenses are taken into account. The OAR is a good ranking device for comparable, unmortgaged properties since it evaluates properties free and clear of any financing. However, when property is subject to an existing mortgage, a market-derived OAR fails to acknowledge the particulars of existing debt.

An OAR also fails to reflect an individual's income tax situation. With modifications it can include provisions for specific before-tax equity rates, mortgage loans, loan-to-value ratios, and forecast property appreciation. The OAR is frequently used by appraisers to estimate the market value of property, but it does not necessarily indicate the value to a specific investor.

Equity dividend rate The equity dividend rate is also called the *cash-on-cash return* method, the *cash return on cash invested* method, and the *percentage cash flow technique*. Computation involves dividing the before-tax cash flow (column 8) by the initial equity investment and converting the decimal result to a percentage. Results for each year are shown in column 27.

The equity dividend rate fails to acknowledge income tax implications, resale implications including property value changes, and reductions of mortgage principal. It also fails to describe a yield rate to maturity. Therefore it does not consider the investment life cycle. This technique, however, is commonly used by real estate investors.

As it applies to the benchmark property, the rate is as follows:

Year	Fraction		Equity Dividend Rate
1	$\dfrac{\$13,818}{\$400,000}$	=	3.455%
2	$\dfrac{\$17,878}{\$400,000}$	=	4.470%
3	$\dfrac{\$21,960}{\$400,000}$	=	5.490%

Net spendable income technique. When this technique is used, the rate is computed by dividing the sum of before-tax cash flow and the tax savings or payment (after-tax cash flow) by the initial equity investment. The resulting after-tax cash flow is compared to initial equity, as shown in column 28. The method is deficient for the same reasons as those advanced for the equity dividend rate; further, the rate fails to reflect taxes upon a sale.

As applied to the benchmark property, the net spendable income rate is the same as the equity dividend rate for the first 13 years. Although the equity dividend rate and net spendable income techniques do not account for all income sources from a property, they may be appropriate for certain types of investors. Tax-exempt or low tax bracket investors and those who do not anticipate selling the property (elderly or retired

individuals) might consider these indicators adequate for decision purposes. Also, these techniques may be used to compare a group of properties with similar tax implications and appreciation potential.

Other Ratios

Other ratios are useful in describing characteristics of the property although they are not valuation techniques. These may come from the balance sheet or cash flow statement. Balance sheet ratios include the *improvement*, *loan-to-value*, and *equity* ratios. Cash flow ratios include *vacancy*, *break-even*, *operating expense*, *debt service coverage*, and *operating expense* ratios.

Improvement ratio The ratio of buildings and site improvements to the total price of the property is the improvement ratio. It is 90% for our benchmark example. The improvement ratio generally indicates the fraction of total cost that can be depreciated for income tax purposes. The higher the fraction, the greater the noncash tax deductions.

A low improvement ratio generally indicates that land is a large component of value. While such property offers less to depreciate for tax purposes, it is likely to retain high values as land is not subject to genuine economic depreciation in value.

The improvement ratio generally ranges from 60 to 95 percent. Shopping centers need expensive land for access and driving convenience, as well as lots of land for parking and because buildings are only one or two stories. Consequently, shopping centers tend to have a relatively low improvement ratio. High-rise buildings will have a higher ratio because of the ability to spread the land cost over more improvements.

Loan-to-value ratio The loan-to-value ratio is the ratio of the mortgage debt to the property value — 80 percent in the benchmark example. The ratio indicates the degree of leverage. Higher ratios mean more leverage; lower ratios mean more equity.

From a lender's standpoint, higher ratios imply a greater risk of default and foreclosure. Institutional lenders have certain limits for loan-to-value ratios. (Life insurance companies in many states cannot lend more than 75 percent of the value of property that they finance.)

Equity ratio. This is the reciprocal of the loan-to-value ratio, indicating the percentage of equity included. When additional value is created in real estate it is possible to refinance and extract all of the equity that was paid in. A question then arises as to how much equity is in the project, that is whether equity is based on actual contributions or on current values. For decision-making purposes, use of current market values, although sometimes difficult to obtain, is more useful than historic accounting information.

Vacancy ratio. Collection allowances are usually lumped together with vacancies. Maintaining a low vacancy ratio for real estate is important because most cash outflows are fixed. Real estate taxes, insurance, and debt service show little variation for most properties regardless of occupancy. The variable cost of renting to a tenant is small, so nearly all of

the space should be rented to maximize income. Generally, it is preferable to have a 90 to 100 percent occupied building at slightly below market rates than an 80 percent or lower occupancy rate at above market rental rates.

Vacancy rates range widely with the type of property. Hotels and resorts expect a lower occupancy rate than do stores or apartment buildings. For resorts, this is due to the seasonal nature of their business. Hotel occupancy may vary for this reason or because of weekend traffic and conventions. Managers of apartments and office buildings generally try to maintain 93 to 97 percent occupancy. When leased property is fully occupied, there is an obvious opportunity for a rental rate increase. This may increase total rental income despite an accompanying occupancy rate decline. Conversely, management may offer rental concessions to gain more tenants when occupancy is less than 80 percent.

Break-even ratio Also called *default point*, this is the occupancy ratio needed to cover cash expenses. Shown in column 30, it is the sum of operating expenses and debt service, divided by the potential gross income. For the benchmark, the break-even ratio for the first year is about 87 percent, computed as follows:

$$\frac{\$100,000 \text{ operating expense } + \ \$188,182 \text{ debt service}}{\$330,000 \text{ potential gross income}} = 87.328\%$$

The break-even ratio allows investors to determine the minimum occupancy rate at which there will be some cash throw-off. The term *default point* implies that the owner will default on the mortgage payment when the occupancy rate falls below that point. That suggestion is misleading. Nearly all investors will remain even when the ratio drops below the default point in the hope of income increases and/or capital gain upon resale.

Debt service coverage ratio This is found by dividing the annual debt service into the net operating income. In column 26 of the sample, the debt service coverage ratio is only 1.073 for the first year. Like the break-even ratio, it offers information comparing the net operating income to debt service.

The debt service coverage ratio offers important information that is of concern to both lenders and investors. Many lenders impose minimum coverage ratios which vary according to each property, economic conditions, and the geographic area. For example, a 1.05 ratio may be an acceptable ratio for a free-standing store that is net-leased over a long term (as long as the mortgage term) to an AAA credit-rated tenant. For a shopping center with 50 percent "credit" tenants, a 1.2 — 1.25 ratio would be appropriate. Apartments and some office buildings, will require a 1.25 — 1.50 ratio. The variability of hotel and resort income creates the need for a higher ratio.

Operating expense ratio This is the ratio of operating expenses to potential gross income — 100,000/330,000 = 30% in the benchmark

example. Operating expenses are those necessary to maintain and run the property. Operating expenses include utilities, repairs, replacement reserves, real estate taxes, management, insurance, payroll, payroll taxes, advertising, postage, and other items. Debt service, depreciation, and income taxes are excluded. When property is subject to a net lease, the tenant pays all operating expenses, and the real estate owner incurs none. The ratio then is zero. The ratio may be below 15 percent on semi-net leased property where the owner is responsible for items such as insurance or real estate taxes. For most apartments, the typical ratio is 33 to 45 percent, unless the rental rate includes all utilities; then it may go above 50 percent. Office buildings that include cleaning services and elevators, lobbies, and restrooms, will have a high (45 to 60 percent) operating expense ratio.

Yield Models

Yield models consider an annual compound interest factor that reflect the time value of money. Most models derive the value of equity in this manner, and add that to the mortgage balance. All of the income the equity investor expects to receive during the holding period should be included—specifically, annual after-tax cash flow and the after-tax proceeds from resale.

Small-to-medium sized investors or those who invest in real estate as a part-time activity typically do not use a yield model. More time and effort might be required for appropriate use than benefit received from an occasional application.

There are two major varieties of yield models: those that solve for project value (*net present value*), and those that solve for rate (*internal rate of return*). Both types have strengths and weaknesses. The choice often depends on the income configuration and analyst's approach.

Net present value The net present value (NPV) technique involves discounting and summing investment inflows to a present value at a specified discount rate. The resulting present value is then compared to the investment outflow(s); if the present value of outflow(s) exceeds the present value of inflow(s), the proposed investment is rejected because the investment fails to return the minimum acceptable rate of return. Otherwise, the proposed investment is considered.

In theory, the specified discount rate used for net present value computations is the entity's cost of capital. In practice, however, measurement of the cost of capital is subjective which adds to the difficulty of implementation.

As the NPV relates to the sample property, if a 15 percent or greater rate were used as the minimum acceptable (so called *hurdle*) rate, the subject property would not be acquired because the net present values are negative at 15 percent. Acceptance would be allowed if 10 percent or less were the cutoff point and a projection period in excess of one year was considered.

Internal rate of return The internal rate of return (IRR) is usually defined as the rate at which the present value of investment outflows and investment inflows are equal. The formula, shown below, requires a trial-and-error method for solution.

$$\sum_{t=1}^{n} \frac{\text{periodic } cash\ flow}{(1\ +\ i)^t} = \text{investment amount}$$

where i = internal rate of return
t = each time interval
n = total time intervals
\sum = summation

As it relates to the subject property, the periodic cash flow is the annual after-tax cash flow and any after-tax proceeds from resale, while the investment amount is the cash down payment plus subsequent cash payments.

The IRR, in column 24, shows the annual rate of return on capital generated by an investment. It is a compounded rate of earnings per investment dollar per time period and often is a useful device for ranking alternative investments. One drawback lies in its *reinvestment assumption* — after-tax cash flows from the investment must be reinvested at the internal rate of return for the rate to be a valid indicator of investment profitability.

Conclusion

When an individual considers acquiring real estate, he or she should analyze the potential costs and benefits of that property. Real estate investments can be lucrative by providing cash flow, appreciation, and a hedge against inflation. However, drawbacks include complex transactions, a need for business and management skills, and a potentially high risk of loss especially with financial leverage, and illiquidity. Careful analysis can increase the likelihood of a successful investment.

HOW TO READ
AN APPRAISAL REPORT

An appraisal is an estimate of value of a specific property based on the appraiser's professional judgment. The appraisal report is a detailed description of the process the appraiser used in estimating the stated value. Appraisers collect market data that they analyze by accepted methods. Based on this analysis, they derive the value of the subject property.

Appraisal reports can be presented in different forms, but each includes standard sections and types of information. A typical narrative report contains an introduction, factual descriptions, data analysis, the appraiser's opinions, and an addendum. In reviewing and evaluating the report, the user can work through each section systematically, giving specific attention to the purpose, relationship with other parts of the report, and appropriateness of the data.

Generally, the **introduction** establishes the appraisal's purpose and states limitations. Following that will be a **geographic and market analysis**, a **physical and legal analysis**, a **highest and best use analysis**, a description of **valuation techniques**, and the **reconciliation**—the section that explains the reasoning behind the final value opinion.

The appraisal report is simply a tool or methodology used to aid someone making a real estate decision. The user's instructions to the appraiser about the reason for the appraisal significantly affects the usefulness of the report.

Appraisal reports can be complex, including detailed analyses of market data and structured procedures for estimating value. Unless the user is a trained real estate appraiser, the narrative may be hard to follow and the report's quality may be difficult to evaluate. Worse yet, the meaning of the value opinion may be misunderstood, particularly if the concept of market value is not clear to the user.

Types of Appraisal Reports

The report must be communicated meaningfully and clearly to the client in a way that is not misleading. The appraisal can be presented as an oral report, a letter report, a form, or a narrative report.

An *oral report* is used when the client does not need a written report. This report should include a description of the property and the facts, assumptions, conditions, and reasoning on which the conclusion is based. The appraiser must keep all notes and data with a complete memorandum of the analysis and conclusions.

APPRAISAL REPORT

A *letter report* usually contains only the appraiser's investigations and analyses. To be meaningful, certain items must be included: the certificate, adequate property identification, the valuation date, all limiting conditions, indication of the contributions of others, and a statement of non-bias. Use of the letter report is limited.

The *letter-form appraisal* is used predominately by governmental and financial institutions to expedite the review process and enable standardization for decision makers. The form ensures that no item required in the review process is omitted. Unfortunately, it restricts additional information, which must be introduced as a supplement. The form also allows reviewers to identify and easily locate the information sought. Lenders often use the Federal National Mortgage Association (FNMA) format.

Narrative reports are the most complete appraisal format. This report enables the appraiser and appraisal service user to present and receive thorough documentation of all reasoning and data in the appraisal process (within financially feasible constraints).

The narrative report typically is organized in the following manner:

Part One, or Introduction, includes:
- Title page
- Letter of transmittal
- Table of contents
- Certification of value
- Qualifying and limiting conditions, including general and underlying assumptions
- Summary of important conclusions
- Purpose of the appraisal
- Definition of value and date of value estimate
- Property rights appraised

Part Two, or Factual Descriptions, contains:
- Photographic identification of the property
- Area, city, neighborhood, and location data
- Zoning and taxes data
- Site data
- Description of improvements
- History

Part Three, or Data Analysis, together with the appraiser's opinions, includes:
- Market analysis
- Highest and best use of the land, as though vacant
- Highest and best use of the property, as improved
- Land value
- Sales comparison approach
- Income capitalization approach
- Cost approach
- Reconciliation of the value indications to a final value estimate

The final section, or the Addendum, contains:

• Detailed legal description
• Detailed statistical data
• Leases or lease summaries
• The appraiser's qualifications

Reading the Report

Each part of the report should have a distinct purpose and should add to the user's understanding of the basis for the value determination. The sections should build on one another and point to the same conclusion. Information used to make adjustments and reconciliation in the last portions of the report should be drawn from earlier sections. The following discusses the purpose of each section, how they relate to other parts of the report, as well as several points that the user should consider.

Introductory Material

The introduction establishes the appraisal's purpose and relates any limitations or qualifications to the value opinion. The specific type of value should be identified and, possibly, defined. This should clear up any misunderstanding about why the appraisal was done. Most appraisals estimate market value according to the accepted definition established in the appraisal profession. Most of the limitations stated are routine. However, there may be special considerations that affect the value of a specific property and these should be clearly stated.

Geographic and Market Analysis

The geographic and market analysis describes the market environment and the forces shaping property value. This section details the property's economic setting, ranging from the general market area to the property's specific surroundings.

If the user is unfamiliar with the area around the property, this section can be very helpful. It provides an image of how the local economy is structured and the current condition of its markets. The strength of demand for properties like the subject's should be described, as well as how many similar properties there are in the market. Also, it describes the area surrounding the property and the relative desirability of the location.

Physical and Legal Analysis

The physical and legal analysis describes characteristics of the subject property that will be used later in applying valuation methods. This usually is divided into a description of the site and its improvements.

Even if the user is familiar with the property, it is still worthwhile to see how it is described by a professional trained in critically examining properties. The description should point out features of the property that affect its value, such as the quality of construction and the adequateness of the site for its current use. Legal analysis indicates any restrictions that may exist, either as local ordinances or as components of the property deed, that affect how the property may be used.

Highest and Best Use Analysis

The highest and best use analysis establishes the specific usage that supports market value. Most properties are purchased with the intention of continuing the current way it is used. However, some properties are valued primarily for conversion to, or redevelopment for, an alternative use. Market value, then, is based on the property's highest and best use.

In most cases, this analysis will merely state that the current usage is the most appropriate one for the property. Nevertheless, in some cases, the current use may be for an interim period or where the neighborhood may be changing so that the current use is no longer appropriate. If so, this should be pointed out with a discussion of what types of uses are most appropriate.

Valuation Techniques

The core of the appraisal report is the valuation techniques section, in which all facts and inferences from previous analyses are applied to derive an estimate of property value. In general, the problem is approached from three independent directions: **market comparison**, **cost reproduction** and **income capitalization**. Each approach uses evidence from market data in different ways to reach the same objective. If these techniques faithfully follow market reasoning, the estimates should be similar. However, data limitations may produce significant differences. A final **reconciliation** process is needed to address these and to settle on a defensible estimate.

Market Comparison Approach

The purpose of the market comparison approach is to derive a value based on recent sales prices of similar properties. The method assumes that the typical buyer pays no more for a property than the cost of purchasing an identical property.

Data are collected on recent sales of properties similar to the subject, called *comparables*. How recent and how similar the comparables are depend on the availability of data. Because comparables will not be identical to the subject, some price adjustment is necessary. The idea is to simulate the price that would have been paid if the comparables were actually identical to the subject. Differences that do not affect value are not adjusted. If the comparables are *superior* to the subject, an amount is *subtracted* from the sales price. *Inferior* features require that an amount be *added* to the sales price. From the group of adjusted sales prices, the appraiser selects an indicator of value that is representative of the subject.

How are comparables selected? To minimize the amount of adjustment required, comparables should be closely similar to the subject.

The following are common shortcomings in the selection process:

- The sale is too old (the market may have changed since the sale took place).
- The location is too different (location and surroundings have important effects on value).
- Special financing was used in comparable sales (part of the price may have resulted from favorable financing terms).
- Too few comparables are found (one or two sales may not represent the market).

When the subject is unusual or when market activity is slow, these problems may be unavoidable. However, if this is the case, it should be acknowledged and taken into consideration when the final value opinion is rendered.

Cost Approach

The purpose of the cost approach is to indicate value based on the cost to replace the property, using current materials and methods. The underlying cost is thought to be a basis of long-term value that is not sensitive to market fluctuations. Cost may be the only indication of value for unique properties, or for properties without active markets.

The value of improvements as well as the land are estimated separately. For improvements, *reproduction cost* is estimated. This figure represents what it would cost to produce the building with current methods. It is not necessary to simulate production of an exact replica. The reproduction should be one that a typical purchaser would consider as a perfect substitute. Any *depreciation* on the subject property is estimated and subtracted from the new reproduction cost. Depreciation includes physical wear (incurable physical), needed repair and replacement of components (curable physical), outmoded design and materials (functional obsolescence), and incompatibility with surroundings (locational). Site value generally is estimated by market comparison using site comparables.

Improvements should represent the property's highest and best use. If they do not, then they do not contribute fully to the site's value. Therefore, an estimate of the value of such improvements, even when diminished by accrued depreciation, will overstate the contribution made to property value. Improvements should agree with the previous finding of the property's highest and best use.

Income Approach

The purpose of the income approach is to indicate value based on the capitalized worth of the projected income stream. Accordingly, this approach assumes the property is purchased for its productivity as an investment. For owner-occupied properties, value is based on the value of imputed income in the form of services provided by the property.

Usually, a value indication is derived through *direct capitalization* of net operating income. Net operating income for the subject property is projected based on market level rents and operating expense ratios. If income fluctuations are expected, the net operating income must be stabilized to reflect its long-term level. *Capitalization rates* (net operating incomes divided by selling prices and known as "cap rate") are abstracted from market transactions. The value indication then is calculated as the net operating income divided by the market cap rate.

For properties that do not generate rental income, a related technique is used. Comparables are selected from recent sales of similar properties that do generate rental income. The ratio of sales price to gross rent (*gross rent multiplier*) is calculated for each comparable. A representative gross rent multiplier is selected and multiplied by the market rent for the subject property to indicate value.

In most cases, the cap rate will be selected from market data of actual transactions. The process is similar to the use of comparable sales in the market comparison approach. How well the subject fits its comparables affects the method's reliability. While cap rates should be similar for the same property type in a comparable location, other factors may cause the rate to vary. These factors should be recognized and accounted for in the analysis. They include:

- What is the expected duration of the income stream? In a highly competitive market, income may fall as the building ages, resulting in a higher cap rate.
- What are expected increases or decreases in future value? If neighborhood trends are positive, the cap rate may be lower than for properties in declining areas.
- What are the purchaser's motivations? If comparable sales occurred prior to changes in tax policies or lending rates, the indicated cap rate may be too low or high for current conditions. Rate selection should be supported by the same type of reasoning used to adjust comparable sales prices.

• What if direct capitalization is not used? If a discounted cash flow method is used, all assumptions should be justified. The most important ones are the application of an appreciation rate and a discount rate to derive net present value. One test of an appreciation assumption is to calculate an overall rate (net operating income divided by sales price) at the end of the projection period. If lower than the first year rate, the analyst should explain why the property is expected to be more attractive in the future.

The discount rate should be comparable to currently available yields on investments with similar risks and rewards, such as high-risk growth stocks, new issue stocks, or desired returns of pension funds and real estate investment trusts (REITs).

Reconciliation

This section explains the reasoning behind the final value opinion which generally is expressed as a single figure. However, a range of values may be appropriate in some appraisals.

Reconciliation then is the culmination of the appraisal investigation. It should draw on all of the preceding information and analyses. It is the report's most essential statement.

An appraisal is simply an opinion based on the analysis of economic concerns that can influence the price of the property to be sold. Establishing a price before a sale is necessary for conducting business in a dynamic or even problem economy. The appraisal report is a tool or methodology to aid someone in making a decision; however, it is not an end in itself.

Appraisal Designations

More than 17 appraisal designations are awarded by professional organizations, the best recognized being the Appraisal Institute. Most organizations require specialized course work, professional experience, and preparation of approved demonstration reports. Designations include:

1. Appraisal Institute
 Member, Appraisal Institute (MAI)
 Senior Residential Appraiser (SRA)

2. American Society of Appraisers
 Senior American Society of Appraisers (ASA)
 Accredited Member (AM)
 Fellow American Society of Appraisers (FASA)

67

3. American Right of Way Association
Senior Member Right of Way Appraiser (SR/WA)

4. National Association of Independent Fee Appraisers (NAIFA)
Independent Fee Appraiser (IFA)
Senior Independent Fee Appraiser (IFAS)
Independent Fee Appraiser and Counselor (IFAC)

5. American Society of Farm Managers and Rural Appraisers (ASFMRA)
Accredited Rural Appraiser (ARA)
Accredited Farm Manager (AFM)

6. International Association of Assessing Officers (IAAO)
Certified Assessment Evaluator (CAE)
Accredited Assessment Evaluator (AAE)
Certified Personalty Evaluator (CPE)
Residential Evaluation Specialist (RES)

7. National Society of Real Estate Appraisers (NSREA)
Master Real Estate Appraiser (MREA)
Certified Real Estate Appraiser (CREA)
Residential Appraiser (RA)

REAL ESTATE REGULATIONS

The following offers a brief description of some of the prominent federal regulations that affect real estate. At the end of each entry appears the agency (or agencies) assigned to enforce the described regulation. State and local regulations should also be checked by homebuyers, investors, developers, and mortgage lenders.

Agricultural Foreign Investment Disclosure Act (1978)

Requires foreign persons who acquire, transfer, or hold interests in agricultural land to report transactions and holdings to the Secretary of Agriculture (U.S. Department of Agriculture, ERS, 500 12th St. S.W., Rm. 240, Washington, D.C. 20250) and directs the Secretary to analyze reports for effects these transactions and holdings may have on family farms and rural communities. Department of Agriculture.

Americans With Disabilities Act (1990)

Requires owners and tenants of "places of public accommodation" to modify practices that discriminate against the disabled, provide auxiliary aids to communication, and remove architectural barriers (if removal can be readily achieved). Some examples are: (1) Installing ramps; (2) Making curb cuts in sidewalks and entrances; (3) Repositioning shelves; (4) Installing a raised toilet seat, grab bars in toilet stalls, rearranging partitions to increase maneuvering space. *U.S. Attorney General.*

Black Lung Revenues Act (1981)

Contains language that pertains to rentals to family members and shared-equity mortgages; provides two tax advantages to lessors who rent to family members: (1) larger depreciation deductions because of accelerated cost recovery and (2) more allowable tax losses; provides for participation of parents and other relatives in a shared-equity mortgage with the same tax deductions as an unrelated party. (Circumstances greatly affect the applicability of this tax law; seek tax counseling or legal advice prior to making decisions on provisions.) Internal Revenue Service.

Clean Air Amendments Act (1970) [Amendments (1977)]

Gives the Environmental Protection Agency (EPA) the power to establish standards and gives citizens and public interest groups the right to bring suit against alleged polluters, federal agencies, and the EPA administrator. Amendments establish new standards to protect areas with clean air from deterioration of air quality and extend some deadlines for city and industry compliance with air-quality standards. Federal Energy Regulatory Commission, Environmental Protection Agency.

Clean Water Act (1972 and 1977)

Provides primary authority for water-pollution control, including effluent limitations, wastewater discharge permits, water-quality standards, municipal pollution control, and waste treatment. Environmental Protection Agency.

Coastal Zone Management Act (1972) [Amendment (1976)]

Declares a national policy to preserve, protect, develop, and, where possible, to restore or enhance coastal resources for all generations. Encourages and assists states in effectively exercising coastal zone responsibilities through development and implementation of management programs to achieve wise use of coastal land and water resources, giving full consideration to ecological, cultural, historic, and esthetic values, as well as to the need for economic development. Amendment of 1976 creates an energy-impact fund to assist states in providing public facilities and managing growth in coastal areas. Department of Commerce.

Community Reinvestment Act (1977)

Requires financial institution regulators to (1) encourage banks under their supervision to meet credit needs of their communities, including low- and middle-income neighborhoods and (2) scrutinize a lender's inner-city credit activities when the lenders seek to undertake certain prescribed activities. Federal Reserve System, Federal Deposit Insurance Corporation, Comptroller of Currency, Federal Home Loan Bank Board, Department of Housing and Urban Development.

Condominium and Cooperative Abuse Relief Act (1980)

Seeks to (1) minimize adverse impacts of condominium and cooperative conversions on the housing opportunities of low-income, moderate-income, elderly, and handicapped persons, (2) ensure that fair and equitable principles are followed in the establishment of condominiums and cooperatives, and (3) provide appropriate relief where long-term leases of recreation and other cooperative- and condominium-related

facilities are determined to be unconscionable. Department of Housing and Urban Development.

Consumer Credit Protection Act (1960)

Requires accurate credit reports; allows consumers to correct inaccurate information in their reports; requires that credit reports be kept confidential, allowing access by properly authorized parties only; assures a meaningful disclosure of credit terms, allowing the consumer to compare other available credit terms to avoid uninformed use of credit; and to protect against inaccurate and unfair credit billing and credit card practices. Titles of this act that affect mortgage lending are found in the Truth in Lending Act (I) and the Fair Credit Reporting Act (VI). Federal Deposit Insurance Corporation.

Consumer Home Mortgage Assistance Act (1974)

Authorizes federal savings-and-loan associations to invest an amount not greater than (1) the sum of its surplus and undivided profits and reserves or (2) five percent of its residential real estate loans within 100 miles of its home office or within the state in which such office is located. Federal Home Loan Bank Board.

Depository Institutions Deregulation and Monetary Control Act (1980)

Extends reserve requirements to all financial institutions; provides for orderly phaseout of limitations on the maximum rates of interest and dividends paid on deposits and accounts; allows thrift institutions to offer an expanded range of financial services and increases federal deposit insurance to $100,000 per depositor; preempts state usury ceilings for federally related, conventional, residential first mortgage loans unless a state enacts overriding legislation by April 1, 1983; requires depository institutions to report their liabilities and assets to the Federal Reserve Board at intervals the board determines so that the board can monitor and control finances and credit. Federal Deposit Insurance Corporation, Federal Home Loan Bank Board, Comptroller of Currency.

Economic Recovery Tax Act (1981)

Makes numerous adjustments in the Internal Revenue Code affecting real estate; affects replacement periods on sales of personal residences; contains income-producing property provisions that deal with cost recovery (depreciation) methods, depreciation recapture, rehabilitation expenditures, construction period interest and taxes for low-income housing, investment credit for certain building rehabilitation, investment tax credit for Section 38 property, additional first-year depreciation and imputed interest; addresses tax rate changes regarding

individual income tax rates, corporate taxes, maximum tax, and alternative minimum tax. Internal Revenue Service.

Emergency Home Finance Act (1970) (Title III)

Creates the Federal Home Loan Mortgage Corporation (Freddie Mac) to operate a secondary market in conventional home mortgages. Federal Home Loan Bank Board.

Energy Conservation Standards for New Buildings Act (1976)

Requires Department of Housing and Urban Development to implement building energy standards for new residential and commercial construction. Department of Housing and Urban Development.

Equal Credit Opportunity Act (1974) [Amendment (1976)]

Requires financial institutions and other firms engaged in the extension of credit to make all credit equally available to all credit-worthy customers without regard to sex or marital status. Compliance standards to prohibit discrimination are regulated by credit standards and loan application procedures prescribed by the board of governors of the Federal Reserve System.

The amendment of 1976 prohibits discrimination in lending on the basis of age, color, race, religion, national origin, or receipt by applicant of public assistance. A lender must notify the prospective buyer of action taken on the loan within 30 days of application, and if requested by applicant, a reason for denial of loan must be given. Steady part-time earning must be considered by the lender in evaluating a loan application. Federal Home Loan Bank Board, Comptroller of Currency, Federal Deposit Insurance Corporation, Federal Reserve System.

Fair Housing Laws

Prohibits discrimination on the basis of minority status in the sale or rental of any house, apartment (or other residential structure), and vacant land; requires that each client be treated as an individual and be served according to individual needs and desires.

The major laws that comprise the regulations prohibiting discrimination are:

Civil Rights Act of 1866
Civil Rights Act of 1964 (Title VI, Nondiscrimination in Federally Assisted Programs)
Civil Rights Act of 1968 (Title VIII—Fair Housing)
Department of Housing and Urban Development.

Farm Credit Act (1971)

Provides for the farmer-owned cooperatives system of credit for farmers and ranchers and their cooperatives, rural residences, associations, and other entities on which farming depends, to provide an adequate and flexible flow of money into rural areas and to modernize and consolidate existing farm credit laws to meet current and future rural credit needs. Farm Credit Administration.

Farmers Home Administration (FmHA) Act (1946)

Replaces the Farm Security Administration; continues government loan programs established under the Resettlement Administration; gives FmHA authority to insure loans made by banks, other agencies, and individuals. Farmers Home Administration.

Federal Flood Insurance Program (1968) and National Flood Insurance Act (1968)

Makes flood insurance available at reasonable rates to property owners in flood-prone areas; protects property owners against loss from flood damage not generally covered by commercial insurers at feasible rates. (Bank regulators require flood insurance when a mortgage is made in a flood-hazard area of a community participating in the national flood insurance program.) Department of Housing and Urban Development.

Federal Home Loan Bank Act (1932)

Creates the Federal Home Loan Bank Board and the Federal Home Loan Bank System; establishes a reserve system for home financing to provide a permanent credit source for home mortgage lending institutions. Federal Home Loan Bank Board.

Federal Trade Commission Improvement Act

See Magnuson-Moss Warranty (1975).

Federal Water Pollution Control Act and Amendments (1972)

Establishes regulatory and grant programs to "reach and maintain the chemical, physical, and biological integrity of the nation's waters;" sets up a program of state grants for construction of sewage treatment plants; establishes stiff industrial and municipal pollutant discharge permit programs. Federal Energy Regulatory Commission, Environmental Protection Agency.

Financial Institutions Reform, Recovery, and Enforcement Act (FIRREA) (1990)

Restructured the regulatory and deposit insurance apparatus dealing with savings and loan associations and changed the rules under which federally regulated S&Ls operate. Created the Federal Housing Finance Board, Office of Thrift Supervision, Resolution Trust Corporation.

The FIRREA was intended to address the major problem of failing S&Ls due to mounting nonperforming loans held in portfolio, as well as to make reforms that would prevent the problem from recurring. Often referred to as the "S&L bailout," the law represents a large expenditure of federal funds to pay off depositors at failed associations. Created the Resolution Trust Corporation, which is charged with managing and liquidating the assets of associations seized by the government. The Federal Savings and Loan Insurance Corporation was abolished by law, and its insurance and regulatory responsibilities were brought under the Federal Deposit Insurance Corporation, which also insures commercial banks. *Federal Reserve Board.*

Flood Disaster Protection Act (1973) [Amendments (1975 and 1976)]

Expands the national flood insurance program by substantially increasing limits of coverage and total amount of insurance authorized to be outstanding and by requiring known flood-prone communities to participate in the program; provides for the expeditious identification and dissemination of information concerning flood-prone areas; requires states or local communities — as a condition of future federal financial assistance — to participate in the flood insurance program and to adopt adequate flood plain ordinances and effective enforcement provisions; requires the purchase of flood insurance by property owners acquiring or improving property in flood-hazard areas and assisted by federal programs or institutions. Amendment of 1975 prohibits federally regulated lending institutions from making loans for mobile home purchases or for commercial or personal construction occurring in flood-hazard areas unless flood insurance is available for loan protection. Amendment of 1976 allows certain property exemptions from sanctions in communities not participating in the flood insurance program. Department of Housing and Urban Development.

Foreign Investment in Real Property Tax Act (1980) [Amendment (1984)]

Eliminates techniques by which a nonresident alien (a foreign national temporarily present in the United States) or a foreign corporation could sell U.S. real estate without being subject to U.S. tax laws. Internal Revenue Service.

74

Garn-St. Germain Depository Institutions Act (1982)

Liberalizes procedures for rescuing insured saving and loan associations in distress, gives associations greater freedom to convert to stock form of ownership, expands the type of assets an association may hold, and reduces the differentiation between thrift institutions and banks. Federal Deposit Insurance Corporation, Federal Savings and Loan Insurance Corporation, Federal Home Loan Bank Board.

Home Mortgage Disclosure Act (1975)

Provides information to assist in determining whether depository institutions are serving the housing needs of their communities and neighborhoods; helps public officials determine the distribution of public sector investments in a manner designed to improve the private investment environment, contains a detailed reporting system. Federal Home Loan Bank Board, Comptroller of Currency, Federal Deposit Insurance Corporation, Federal Reserve System.

Interstate Land Sales Full Disclosure Act (1968) [Amendments (1979)]

Requires developers of subdivisions with 25 lots or more to file a property report and a statement of record with the Office of Interstate Land Sales and with the secretary of the Department of Housing and Urban Development prior to promoting or offering subdivision land for sale or lease; applies to land sold or leased in interstate commerce; recent revisions involve property reports and regulations for filing financial reports and advertising. Department of Housing and Urban Development.

Land and Water Conservation Act

Establishes financial assistance and grants to states and their political subdivisions for comprehensive planning, land acquisition, and facility development. Bureau of Resources.

Magnuson-Moss Warranty (Federal Trade Commission Improvement Act) (1975)

Establishes mandatory standards for warranties on consumer products to improve consumer information, prevent deception, and improve competition in the marketing of consumer products; requires written warranty, as required by the rules of the Federal Trade Commission, to fully and conspicuously disclose in simple language the terms and conditions of the warranty; includes new home appliances and other equipment that are an integral part of plumbing, electrical, and heating

systems. (Wiring, piping, and other similar items are not covered; however, home builders are responsible for satisfying warranty claims with respect to any warranties they provide on these items.) Federal Trade Commission.

National Historic Preservation Act (1966)

Authorizes the Secretary of the Interior to (1) expand and maintain a national register of districts, sites, buildings, structures, and objects significant in American history, architecture, archaeology, and culture to be referred to as the National Register and to grant funds to states for preparing comprehensive statewide historic surveys and plans, in accordance with criteria established by the Secretary, for the preservation, acquisition, and development of such properties; (2) establish a program of matching grants-in-aid to states for public benefit, designed to preserve properties that are significant in American history, architecture, archaeology, and culture; (3) establish a program of matching grants-in-aid to the National Trust for Historic Preservation in the United States. Department of the Interior.

National Mobile Home and Construction Safety Standards Act (1974)

Establishes federal standards for the construction, design, performance, and safety of mobile homes. Department of Housing and Urban Development.

Neighborhood Self-Help Development Act (1978)

Authorizes the Secretary of the Department of Housing and Urban Development to make grants and provide other forms of assistance to neighborhood organizations to prepare and implement specific housing, economic and community development projects, other appropriate neighborhood conservation and revitalization projects, and to assist these organizations in implementing such projects in partnership with local government and other public and private entities; designed to involve low- and moderate-income neighborhood residents through their contribution of time and resources. Department of Housing and Urban Development.

Occupational Safety and Health Act (OSHA) (1970)

Establishes OSHA and sets up the Occupational Safety and Health Review Commission and the National Institute for Occupational Safety and Health; gives OSHA the power to promulgate and enforce worker safety and health standards, conduct inspections and investigations, and require employers to keep detailed records on worker injuries and illnesses; gives OSHA power to conduct research. Occupational Safety and Health Administration, Department of Labor.

Real Estate Settlement Procedures Act (RESPA) (1974) [Amendment (1975)]

Encourages homeownership by regulating certain lending practices, and closing and settlement procedures in federally related mortgage transactions to minimize unnecessary costs and difficulties of home purchase; provides the prospective borrower an information booklet on the nature and costs of real estate settlement services when application for a mortgage loan is made. (Booklets may be printed and distributed by lenders if form and content are approved by the HUD Secretary.) A 1975 amendment permits the HUD secretary to exempt certain localities, where settlement statements are not customarily provided, from the required uniform settlement statement and permits the statement to be modified for different parts of the United States. Federal Home Loan Bank Board, Department of Housing and Urban Development, Federal Deposit Insurance Corporation, Comptroller of Currency.

Regulation B (Title VII, Consumer Credit Protection Act) (Amendments)

Requires lenders to notify potential borrowers of action taken on their loan applications and to provide a written report on adverse action or a written statement of the prospective borrower's right to receive this information; addresses the terms under which a creditor can and cannot deny credit. Federal Reserve System.

Regulation BB

Implements the Community Reinvestment Act (CRA) requiring financial institution regulators to encourage state-chartered banks and savings-and-loan associations under their supervision to meet the credit needs of their community; requires financial institution regulators or supervisory agencies to scrutinize lenders' credit activities and compliance with these regulations when considering any application requiring federal approval. (A notice describing the act and written comments on the lender's performance must be posted in the bank or savings-and-loan association and made available to the public.) Federal Reserve System.

Regulation D

Governs certain offers and sales of securities that do not require registration under the Securities Act of 1933; revokes three exemptions under Rules 146, 240, and 242 including the related filing forms; simplifies and clarifies existing exemptions, to expand their availability and achieve uniformity between federal and state exemptions to facilitate capital formation consistent with the protection of investors; allows increased use of private offering investment vehicles to raise equity for

real estate investment. (Regulation D is part of the Securities Act. See Securities Act.) Securities and Exchange Commission.

Regulation Z

Includes regulations pertaining to consumer-credit disclosure issued by the board of governors of the federal reserve system pursuant to Title I (Truth in Lending Act) and Title V (General Provisions) of the Consumer Credit Protection Act. (See Truth-in-Lending.) Federal Trade Commission.

Resource Conservation and Recovery Act (1976)

Sets safety standards for handling and storage of hazardous wastes; requires permits for the operation of hazardous waste treatment, storage, and disposal operations; gives the Environmental Protection Agency authority to make state grants for hazardous waste-treatment programs. Environmental Protection Agency.

Section 8 Program

Assists low- and moderate-income families in obtaining decent, newly constructed, and substantially rehabilitated housing, in accordance with provisions; promotes economically mixed housing; includes a federal rent-subsidy program for low- and moderate-income tenants and permits developers of new or substantially rehabilitated multifamily housing to contract for housing assistance payments on any or all units and be eligible for financing with mortgages insured under the National Housing Act; was created by the Housing and Community Development Act of 1974. Department of Housing and Urban Development.

Securities Act 1933

Requires any firm or individual issuing securities for sale in interstate commerce or through the mail to file financial and other data about the issuer and its securities with the Securities Exchanges Commission before the securities can be placed on the market.

Detailed information on this act, its amendments, and specific sections can be obtained from the Office of Chief Counsel, Securities and Exchange Commission, 500 N. Capitol Street, N.W., Washington, D.C. 20549. A brief description of selected sections follows:

SEC Regulation A Offering Set forth Rules 252 – 263 and affects the registration exemption of qualified small offerings.

SEC Rule 144 Permits holders of restricted securities, and affiliates of an issuer of the securities, to sell their securities publicly without registration.

SEC Rule 147 Removes some of the uncertainties arising under the intrastate offering exemption.

Senior Citizens Housing Act (1962)

Establishes loan programs for low-rent apartments for individuals age 62 and over and authorizes loans to establish recreational facilities. Farmers Home Administration.

Sherman Antitrust Act (1890)

Protects trade and commerce against unlawful restraints and monopolies and establishes a policy in favor of competition; a recent supreme court ruling includes real estate agents under the purview of this pioneer antitrust statute; this ruling establishes that real estate agents who charge identical commissions in the same area may be sued for price fixing. Federal Trade Commission.

Tax Equity and Fiscal Responsibility Act (1982)

Affects real estate investment and development through modification of rules concerning accelerated cost recovery, investment tax credits, corporate construction-period interest and taxes, industrial development bonds, and the completed-contract method of accounting. Internal Revenue Service.

Tax Reform Act (1984)

Increases real estate asset recovery periods under the Accelerated Capital Recovery System to 18 years, places time limits on delayed 1031 exchanges, and establishes Original Issue Discount rules for seller-financed real estate transactions. Internal Revenue Service.

Tax Reform Act (1986)

Greatly reduces the ability to derive tax shelters from real estate investments, lengthens depreciable lives of assets, eliminates favorable treatment of capital gains, restricts use of installment sales, creates Real Estate Mortgage Investment Conduits (REMICs) to assist in issuing of mortgage-backed securities, substantially reduces the number of tax brackets for individual taxpayers, and eliminates or phases out certain itemized deductions. Internal Revenue Service.

Truth-in-Lending Act (1968)

Assures a meaningful disclosure of credit terms so consumers know of the cost of credit and can more readily compare terms and avoid uninformed use of credit; promotes economic stabilization and strengthens competition among financial institutions and other firms that extend consumer credit. Federal Trade Commission, Federal Home Loan Bank Board, Comptroller of Currency, Federal Deposit Insurance Corporation, Federal Reserve System.

Truth-in-Lending Simplification and Reform Act (1980)

Amends the Truth-in-Lending Act of 1968, making significant changes in credit disclosures that creditors must make to borrowers. (Information required by this act must be disclosed conspicuously, and the terms "annual percentage rate" and "finance charge" must be disclosed more conspicuously than any other terms, data, or information provided in connection with a transaction, except information relating to the identity of the creditor.) Federal Trade Commission, Federal Home Loan Bank Board, Comptroller of Currency, Federal Deposit Insurance Corporation, Federal Reserve System.

Uniform Relocation Assistance and Real Property Acquisition Policies Act (1970)

Establishes a uniform policy for the fair and equitable treatment of persons displaced by federal and federally assisted programs so such people will not suffer disproportionate injuries as a result of programs designed for the benefit of the public as a whole. Department of Housing and Urban Development.

Veterans' Housing Benefits Act (1978)

Amends title 38 of the United States Code to improve the housing benefits programs of the Veterans' Administration: provided for increased loan-guarantee and direct-loan amounts, authorized the Veteran's Administration to approve loans for home improvements involving installation of energy-conserving devices such as solar heating and cooling systems, reduced the amount of time of service required for Vietnam veterans to be eligible for loans. Veterans' Administration.

CAREERS IN REAL ESTATE

Opportunities in the real estate business are as varied and versatile as the properties themselves. Whether a person is entrepreneurial and wishes to start a business, or prefers to earn a fixed salary or an income based on productivity, opportunities abound. One of the drawbacks is the cyclical nature of the real estate business, which generally has higher peaks and lower troughs than the economy as a whole.

Real estate businesses and developments are among the few enterprises that one can still enter with little capital. A real estate broker, appraiser, or developer can start "on a shoestring"; a desk and telephone are the essential tools. Overhead can be kept low until enough income and work are generated to justify office space, advertising, and clerical help. Some of the largest real estate businesses in America were started only a few years ago by a single enterprising individual with little or no capital! Energy, a basic knowledge of real estate, and the ability to work with people is all that is needed.

Most jobs in real estate are compensated by commissions. Payment is made according to financial performance, whether it be sales, leasing, or mortgage arrangement. Some property managers are given incentive pay and the same holds for employees of some developers. Working on straight commissions can be extremely lucrative during good times, especially for experienced commercial real estate salesmen. However, those who start in the business must be prepared in every way — emotionally and financially — for the inevitable frustrations and setbacks that will occur during the early years.

Salaried jobs do exist in real estate, but they generally pay less than commissioned jobs. Clerical personnel are needed in every office, and there are some highly compensated opportunities in the production function for those with special skills. These jobs will be competitive in salary with comparable positions in other businesses and may offer more opportunities. Still, salaried workers tend to make less in real estate than those on commission.

As has been stated, the real estate business is rather cyclical. When interest rates are low and local business conditions good, real estate activity booms. However, high interest rates, tight money, or poor business conditions can play havoc with incomes generated from real estate, even for salaried employees. Since these economic factors are beyond the individual's control, people who earn their living from real estate must prepare for slow periods, if they are to remain in the business.

This section offers introductory career information concerning some of the better-defined occupations in real estate. These include appraisers, brokers, salespersons, counselors, developers, subdividers, educa-

tors, mortgage lenders, planners,and property managers. For each occupation, an overview is provided of the nature of the work, responsibilities, opportunities, hours, travel, educational requirements, and professional associations. The list of occupations covered is not intended to be exhaustive. Millions of others are engaged full time in real estate activities. These include lawyers, architects, engineers, accountants, surveyors, building inspectors, and construction workers. Most of these occupations have educational and career paths that are separate from the traditional real estate program.

Real Estate Appraiser

Nature of Work

The *real estate appraiser* answers questions about the value, quality, and use of real property. The appraiser is a problem solver who collects, studies, and interprets relevant facts and information.

A real estate appraiser is likely to evaluate these types of property:

- Single-family dwellings, including condominiums, cooperatives, and townhomes
- Apartment buildings
- Office buildings and complexes
- Shopping centers
- Industrial properties
- Hotels and motels
- Farms and ranches
- Undeveloped land

Appraisers are also sought to comment on the value and use of partial interests in real estate, such as:

- Air rights
- Easements
- Leaseholds
- Life estates
- Mortgage participation
- Partnership shares
- Syndication units

They may be called to testify in zoning hearings or in litigation of various property matters or to give advice on the viability of proposed developments, including subdivisions and income-producing properties. They may also testify in condemnation hearings, which occur frequently and can be quite lucrative.

Responsibilities

Appraisers are responsible for estimating the value of real estate. They are relied upon by individuals, businesses, and financial institutions for various purposes. For example, appraisals are desired by:

- Buyers and sellers, to establish a purchase (or sales) price
- Mortgage lenders who are lending a percentage of appraised value
- Insurance underwriters who want a value estimate of property they will insure
- Governments and public utilities, when condemning land for a public use
- Businesses planning mergers or dissolutions
- Individuals, for such personal reasons as estate planning and divorce settlements
- Publicly held entities including limited partnerships and real estate investment trusts.

The soundness of our nation's financial institutions depends, in part, upon the validity of appraisal reports. Thus, appraisers are responsible for providing decision-making information to individuals, corporations, and governments, and they contribute to the nation's financial soundness.

Advancement Opportunities

Many appraisers aspire to be self-employed independent fee appraisers (those who are paid fees by customers for appraisals) while others strive to be officers and directors of banks, savings and loan associations, or insurance companies. Still others enter the occupation merely to gain experience leading to positions in development, mortgage banking, asset management, and counseling.

Government agencies that employ appraisers include the Federal Deposit Insurance Corporation, Federal Savings & Loan Insurance Corporation, Department of Housing and Urban Development, General Services Administration, Federal Asset Disposal Agency, Justice Department, Federal Home Loan Bank Board, and Federal Reserve Board.

Entry-level positions are typically available as assistants to experienced appraisers. At first, assignments may be limited to field work such as obtaining measurements of homes and land. Getting sales and telephone verification of sales prices and terms are the next step. Once the apprentice gains sufficient experience to learn the appraisal process and sources of market information, he or she would be in a position to draft form reports for residential appraisals.

Depending upon education and experience, a beginner can expect to acquire more responsibility within one to two years. Tasks include field work and report preparation with moderate supervision and assisting in the appraisal of more complex properties. During this time, the professionally motivated appraiser will begin work leading to a professional designation. Most designations require experience, coursework, and examinations. Within five years from entry, the appraiser will be ready to supervise others and to accept more challenging and rewarding experiences.

A professional designation is conferred by appraisal organizations as a sign of a candidate's attainment of professional status. Eight major appraisal organizations and their designations are shown below.

Hours and Travel

Like other professionals, an appraiser can expect to put in far more than 40 hours per week. Providing prompt service to clients, maintaining professional skills, and contributing to one's community and professional associations requires time and commitment. Although some appraisers may regularly shut their office doors behind them at 5 P.M. (particularly those who work for a government or bank), most are constantly concerned with their clients' problems and find that they must work some evenings and weekends.

Local travel to the real estate being appraised and to comparable property that has recently been sold is essential. As an appraiser grows in reputation and status, or develops a unique specialty, he or she will be in demand for out-of-town assignments. Travel may also be needed to support professional associations and to maintain educational skills. It is difficult for the best appraisers to avoid travel, even when there is ample work available in their home town.

Educational Requirements

Education is required for prestigious professional designations; usually a bachelor's degree from a four-year accredited college or equivalent is necessary for the most coveted designations. In addition, the candidate must take certain courses and pass examinations. Some colleges and universities offer a real estate curriculum within the business college that includes appraisal courses, allowing the student to undertake professional association examinations without taking association-sponsored courses.

Professional and Trade Associations

Appraisal Institute
875 N. Michigan Ave.
Chicago, IL 60611
312-329-8538
Professional Designations: SRA, MAI
Publications: *Appraisal Journal*
 The Appraiser

American Society of Appraisers
Dulles International Airport
P.O. Box 17265
Washington, D.C. 20041
703-478-2228
Professional Designation: ASA
Publication: *Newsline*

American Society of Farm Managers and Rural Appraisers
950 S. Cherry St., Suite 106

Denver, Colorado 80222
303-758-3513
Professional Designations: AFM, ARA

International Association of Assessing Officers
1313 East 60th Street
Chicago, IL 60637
312-947-2069
Professional Designations: CAE, CRE
Publications: *Property Tax Journal*
 Assessment Digest

International Right of Way Association
13650 South Gramercy Place
Suite 100
Gardena, CA 90249
310-538-0233
Professional Designations: SR/WA

National Association of Independent Fee Appraisers
7501 Murdoch Ave.
St. Louis, MO
314-781-6688
Professional Designations: IFA, IFAS, IFAC

National Society of Real Estate Appraisers
1265 E. 105th Street
Cleveland, Ohio 44108
216-795-3445
Professional Designations: RA, CRA, MREA
Publications: *National Report*
 Income Property Appraisal and Analysis

Real Estate Broker and Salesperson

Nature of Work

The principal function of a *real estate broker* is to bring together buyers and sellers or owners and tenants. Most brokers secure a *listing* which offers property for sale or lease, from a seller. A fee is earned

when the broker finds a ready, willing, and able purchaser at terms the seller will accept. By law, a licensed real estate broker can also perform other activities such as managing property, appraising, and auctioning.

Most real estate brokers specialize, especially those in metropolitan areas. Residential sales is considered a specialty, although some brokers further limit their activity to a certain price range and/or a certain geographical area. Commercial property brokerage is another specialty, with some brokers working only in the office building market, others in shopping centers, warehouses or industrial properties. Some brokers concentrate on farms and ranches or undeveloped land.

Real estate salespersons in all states must be licensed and associated with a licensed broker. All of their activities must be approved by their broker. (Activities that must be approved include acquiring listings, acquiring sales contracts, and performing appraisal work.) Real estate brokers and salespersons must complete an educational program and pass an exam.

Responsibilities

Real estate brokers are governed by the law of agency. They act in a fiduciary capacity and must place the interests of their clients above their own and be fair to all parties. Brokers must exercise integrity in the discharge of their responsibilities and must be prudent and cautious to avoid misrepresentation by omission or commission. They must be knowledgeable in the real estate business, stay informed on state and local issues that affect the real estate industry, and exercise skill and judgment in performing their work.

Advancement Opportunities

Opportunities in real estate brokerage are very broad and exciting. Many people are content to earn a sales or broker license and maintain it with no further work effort. Some wish to build an empire. Real estate brokerage is one of the few businesses where this is possible because capital requirements for entry are minimal.

With a broker's license a person may operate a business independently, and should feel like an independent entrepreneur. A broker can sell or lease the property of his or her choice, manage others' property or personnel, or open an independent brokerage office. Most states require applicants for broker's licenses to have held a salesperson's license for a certain minimum time, and to meet additional educational requirements.

The promotion ladder, for some brokers, means graduating from one type of property (single-family houses) to more complicated types such as office buildings. Others find property development or syndication a more challenging and/or more lucrative occupation.

Hours and Travel

Some licensees are content to stay home and wait for the phone to ring. However, brokerage is a 24-hour job for those who are truly active. They must sow seeds in the market area they define and develop market expertise and a reputation. Brokers and salespersons must be prepared to meet clients, whether residential or commercial, at a moment's notice. Their family activities are often subordinated to the needs of clients whom the broker may have to meet at an airport or subdivision with no advance notice, any time of day, any day of the week. Commercial real estate brokers may find themselves chasing people and deals all over the city, state, and country. Their lives can be hectic. Salespersons or brokers who find themselves or their families unable to cope with an unpredictable schedule often return to jobs with regularly scheduled hours.

Whether commercial or residential, brokers and salespersons are typically responsible for all of their own business expense. They must pay for the automobile that is used in business, air travel, professional association dues, and educational materials. Most brokerage firms provide a desk and telephone to sales personnel, but some firms charge salespersons for that, too. Commission splits between salesperson and broker firm are negotiable.

Educational Requirements

Typically, to be licensed as a salesperson or broker, one must:

- Be a U.S. Citizen or lawful alien
- Be 18 years or older
- Have been a state resident for 60 days
- Be honest and competent (competency is demonstrated by examination)
- If a corporation, be represented by a designated officer who meets broker qualifications
- Meet educational requirements
- Serve a specified time as salesperson before becoming broker

Professional and Trade Associations

National Association of Real Estate Brokers (NAREB)
1104 14th Street, N.W.
Washington, D.C. 20005
202/966-5100

National Association of Realtors (NAR)
430 N. Michigan Ave.
Chicago, IL 60611
312/329-8200
Publications: *Real Estate Today* and others

Society of Industrial and Office Realtors
777 Fourteenth St., N.W.
Washington, D.C. 20005-3279

Real Estate Counselor*

Nature of Work

A *real estate counselor* provides competent, disinterested, and unbiased advice, professional guidance, and sound judgment on diversified problems in the broad field of real estate. Any and all segments of the business, such as merchandising, leasing, management, planning, and financing, may be involved.

A counselor performs a separate and distinct function from that of the real estate broker. The professional service offered is advice born of experience, blended with wisdom, tempered by judgment, and supported by facts. The relationship between counselor and client is similar to the professional bond existing between lawyer and client.

The counselor translates knowledge of the past into projections for the future. Broad experience equips the counselor to comprehend the most sophisticated situations in the real estate field, which may include conservation of property as well as analysis of its diversified uses and potentials. In studies of the many complicated and challenging problems encountered in the broad spectrum of real estate, the counselor's perspective, professional objectivity, and detachment permit recognition and selection of the alternative courses of action most beneficial to the client. Skills in communicating findings and recommendations to clientele render the counselor's services valuable in the most practical way.

Advancement Opportunities

Few real estate counselors began their careers in that capacity. Most started in a related field such as appraising, property management, or brokerage. After demonstrating an exceptional ability to analyze and solve difficult problems associated with real estate, they find themselves being sought after for advice and counsel. Most counselors are independent professionals who perform their work for a fee, often being employed on a retainer. Some counselors are employees of corporations, developers, or consulting firms.

Hours and Travel

Complex real estate problems that require professional counselors arise infrequently in any one location. Further, owners cannot wait long

*Adapted with permission from "Real Estate Counseling" published by the American Society of Real Estate Counselors.

for solutions. Consequently, counselors must travel to out-of-town engagements and expend intensive efforts until appropriate solutions can be presented. Relatively few counselors have every evening and weekend free for personal pleasure; if they did, it would indicate a lack of demand for their skills.

Educational Requirements

Membership in the American Society of Real Estate Counselors requires, among other things, practical experience in the real estate field for at least ten years. This requirement may be modified on the basis of postgraduate academic achievements and/or degree achievements.

While it is possible to become a counselor with a degree in any field, an education in finance and real estate will be helpful. Real estate courses include investment analysis, appraisal, finance, law, and land use. Also helpful would be building construction, urban planning, and zoning. A broad academic base, such as that offered by a degree in business administration (BBA or MBA), would prove helpful. Courses offered by professional associations should be taken; continuing professional education is an essential part of a counselor's career.

Professional and Trade Association

American Society of Real Estate Counselors
430 North Michigan Ave.
Chicago, IL 60611
312/329-8427
Publications: *Real Estate Issues*

Real Estate Developer and Subdivider

Nature of Work

A *real estate subdivider* acquires a piece of land and makes it usable by rezoning, bringing utilities to the site, creating streets or roads, and/ or providing other amenities such as parks and school sites. The final product is marketed to builders or other consumers.

A *developer* goes one step further. He or she builds a structure on the land. A successful developer or subdivider is like an artist: land is the canvas and the final product is worth more than the cost of raw materials.

Responsibilities

A developer is an entrepreneur — the focal point of a real estate project. He or she must envision a product that has market feasibility. The developer must be concerned with physical, financial, legal, and social

aspects of the property and its infrastructure (streets, utilities, police, and fire protection).

Development is a high-risk business with potentially high rewards. The developer is responsible for acquiring and financing land, then processing it to a buildable state. There are numerous pitfalls for the unwary: financing requirements, legal considerations, the local political situation, environmental concerns, design, and construction. Of course, the project must be sold or leased to yield a profit.

Advancement Opportunities

Most developers are individual entrepreneurs. They see or create their own opportunities, then acquire land using money they borrow from financial institutions. Progress is often measured by the size of their projects. Large developers create high-rise office buildings and regional malls. Small ones develop mini-warehouses, freestanding buildings, and small subdivisions. Few developers remain in a certain niche for very long.

Some individuals gain their first experience by working for another developer. Most developers begin their careers as appraisers, mortgage lenders, or real estate brokers. They envision development activity as offering more lucrative opportunities.

Hours and Travel

A developer's work load may be erratic. One may work around the clock for several weeks, then do virtually nothing for several months. A crash effort may be needed to solve a crisis — and many legal and financial matters have the potential for causing a crisis. When a project is progressing smoothly, there may be time to search for the next project. However, it is sometimes difficult to locate a feasible endeavor, as the local real estate or mortgage markets are not always ripe for continued development.

A developer must be prepared to build in another city when opportunities are greater there than at home. Developers who have exhibited great skill by regularly completing projects on time and within budget are in demand everywhere.

Educational Requirements

There are no special requirements for developers. Those who seem to be most successful have business, architecture, or law degrees. However, many successful developers have little advanced education.

Professional and Trade Associations

American Land Development Association
1220 L Street, 5th Floor
Washington, D.C.
202/371-6700

International Conference of Building Officials
5360 South Workman Mill Road
Whittier, CA 90601
213/699-0541

National Association of Home Builders
15th & M Streets, N.W.
Washington, D.C. 20005
202/822-0200

Urban Land Institute
625 Indiana Ave., N.W. Suite 400
Washington, D.C. 20004-2930
202-624-7000

Real Estate Educator

Nature of Work

Real estate educators teach and provide educational and research materials in real estate matters. Core real estate courses include real estate principles, appraisal, law, finance, marketing, mathematics, brokerage, investments, and property management.

Real estate is taught at different types of educational institutions and instructors at each have different commitments and obligations. The institutions include colleges and universities, junior or community colleges (which provide credit and noncredit courses), and proprietary schools.

Educators at some institutions are only required to appear in class; at others they have a student advisement or counseling role as well. Some educators help students locate jobs and/or work with their local real estate associations to help solve business problems. At colleges and universities, full-time real estate instructors serve on various university committees, perform scholarly research, write books and articles, and are committed to community service (in addition to teaching and counseling requirements).

Responsibilities

Educators are responsible for assuring a minimum level of proficiency for their students. When the primary goal is education for licensing, educators are responsible for efforts that enable their students to pass the sales and broker's exams, as well as for efforts leading to protection of the public (which is the purpose of licensing). Thus, educators impart information and are role models for their students in ethical and legal behavior.

Those teaching real estate courses to the general public are responsible for supplying unbiased information on home buying or selling and

investing in real estate. Those teaching at the college or junior college level are responsible for career preparation of real estate majors.

Advancement Opportunities

Real estate teachers in licensed preparation schools and junior colleges, advance with their teaching skills experience, and reputation. Faculty in senior colleges must hold advanced degrees and publish scholarly works.

Hours and Travel

Schedules will vary with the institution that employs the educators. While most proprietary schools offer courses locally, some cross state boundaries and may require an hour or two of highway travel. Beyond that range, it is generally more efficient to find a local instructor. Most college and junior college courses are offered locally, but professors often travel to present research reports to colleagues or attend meetings of professional associations.

Many real estate courses are offered evenings and weekends. Instructors must be prepared to meet these demands.

Educational Requirements

Proprietary school teachers and those at junior colleges are generally required to be licensed as real estate brokers or salespersons and have three years of business experience. A master's degree is helpful but may not be required.

College and university faculty at fully accredited institutions are generally required to have a master's degree plus professional designation (JD or CPA). Many colleges require a PhD of their permanent full-time faculty, but may offer part-time or full-time non-tenure-track faculty appointments to qualified persons without the PhD.

Professional Associations

American Real Estate Society
c/o J.R. Webb
Dept. of Finance
Cleveland State University
Cleveland, OH 44115
Publications: *Journal of Real Estate Research*

American Real Estate and Urban Economics Association
c/o Mike Miles
Prudential Realty Group
751 Broad Street
Newark, NJ 07102
Publications: *AREUEA Journal*

Real Estate Chairholders and Director's Association
c/o Dr. Peter Colwell
University of Illinois
Urbana, IL 61801

Real Estate Educators Association
One Illinois Center #200
111 E. Wacker Drive
Chicago, IL 60601-4298

Mortgage Loan Officer

Nature of Work

Mortgage loan officers typically work for a mortgage banking firm, savings and loan association, commercial bank, or insurance company. There are four separate functions that a loan officer can fulfill: loan origination, underwriting, servicing, and marketing — all of which may be performed for residential housing or for commercial property. Most individuals specialize in either residential or commercial property; few do both.

Loan originators (loan solicitors) seek out property buyers in an attempt to get their business. Before the loan is approved, however, *underwriters* investigate the likelihood of a default by considering the property and borrower. If the loan is extended, *servicers* make sure the monthly payments are received, property taxes are paid, and the property is adequately insured. *Marketing* refers to selling loans. Mortgage bankers sell nearly all the loans they originate, and savings and loan associations are doing the same in increasing numbers.

In sum, mortgage officers lend and collect mortgage money, which is the lifeblood of real estate activity.

Responsibilities

Mortgage officers are responsible for the safety and security of funds for their institutions and investors. They must exercise skill and judgment in lending money, and consider the property, borrower, and terms of the loan. Although individual home loan amounts may be only in the tens of thousands, a few days' work can run well into millions of dollars — as do most loans on commercial real estate. An interest rate error as small as half of one percent can be very costly. A default is also extremely costly.

Advancement Opportunities

Many successful loan officers started as loan originators or processors, or in supporting functions at a branch office. They progressed to branch manager, then to corporate executive.

Hours and Travel

Loan originators generally enjoy flexible hours. However, most will put in more than the minimum required. When business is good, extra effort pays off handsomely; when business is slow, as it often is when interest rates are high, extra effort is needed to maintain adequate income.

Travel is generally local for residential mortgage bankers. Those in the commercial business may travel all over the country to garner business from lenders or investors.

Educational Requirements

While there are no specific degree requirements for being a mortgage officer, the Mortgage Bankers Association of America suggests that education is a prime factor in recruitment for the income property field. A candidate should have a solid background in finance and banking. Moreover, the candidate should possess a basic knowledge of many aspects of real estate, including appraising, underwriting, negotiating, financial statement, lease analysis, and legal matters, in addition to having established contacts throughout the real estate community. A good mortgage banker will gain the trust and confidence of investors through knowing and even anticipating their investment tastes. A person with good fiduciary judgment, coupled with the ability to develop a bond of mutual respect with an investor, should find a career in income property mortgage banking personally challenging and financially rewarding.

Professional and Trade Associations

The Mortgage Bankers Association of America
1125 Fifteenth St., N.W.
Washington, D.C. 20005
202/861-6500
Publications: *Mortgage Banking*
 Real Estate Finance Today
Professional Designation: Certified Mortgage Banker

U.S. League of Savings Associations
111 East Wacker Drive
Chicago, IL 60601
312/644-3100

Real Estate Planner*

Nature of Work

There are several areas of specialization for *real estate planners*, each entailing diversified challenges. Some planners are employed by cities, others by real estate developers. Specialties include:

Land Use Planning This is probably the oldest area of specialization within planning. It is concerned with the orderly, efficient, and equitable development of land. Important issues include environmental conservation, regulation of the use of land, recreation, ecological balance, and land management.

Housing and Community Development Specialists in this area analyze the housing stock and residential neighborhoods to identify shelter needs and deficiencies. They work to develop strategies to improve environments where housing is substandard or overcrowded, the rental rates are excessive, or the neighborhood is undesirable. These may involve work in developing countries in Africa, Asia, and Latin America.

Planning degrees can lead to opportunities across disciplines and fields such as transportation, economics, program management, environment, government, social policy, international development, research, education, and consulting, in either the public or the private sector.

Responsibilities

Planners formulate plans and policies to meet social, economic, and physical needs, and they develop the strategies to make these plans work. Planning is both science and art. It demands technical competence as well as creativity, hardheaded pragmatism as well as an ability to envision alternatives to the physical and social environments in which we live. It is an excellent career choice for those who desire a role in shaping the future.

The planning process typically involves the performance of a number of roles. Some planners function primarily as technical analysts or researchers, others as designers or program developers, and still others as managers or educators. Some planners will focus on only one of these roles; most, however, will perform several of them at different stages of their lives. In all phases of their careers, planners will find that planning is an interdisciplinary profession, and they will draw upon the resources and expertise of a wide variety of fields. Planners develop comprehensive approaches that attempt to show how best to use a community's land: where residential, commercial, industrial, recreational, and other human activities should take place. More and more, comprehensive plans emphasize the process of change and outline the social, economic, and environmental consequences.

*Adapted from *Had You Planned to Be a Planner?* published by the American Planning Association.

95

Opportunities

Employment prospects for planning graduates during the 1980s will be very good according to the U.S. Bureau of Labor Statistics. Though there have been cutbacks in planning in some areas of government, the slack has been compensated for by the private sector. Communities in rapidly growing areas of the country will be seeking additional professional planning help in dealing with urbanization and population growth. The energy-rich states will offer opportunities for planners to help guide the development of growing towns and to protect the environment. Older cities will continue to need planners to deal with housing, transportation, and redevelopment issues. The many types of private firms mentioned earlier will also be seeking planners. Policy planning and other new fields will provide fresh opportunities for which urban planning is excellent preparation. For a formal forecast of jobs in planning, see the U.S. Department of Labor, Bureau of Labor Statistics, *Exploring Careers: Office Occupations* (Bulletin 2001-3).

Hours and Travel

Most salaried planners keep regular office hours during business days; however, there are times when late hours are required to complete urgently needed plans. Those in private practice do not have such regular hours and may travel frequently to seek and perform out-of-town assignments.

Educational Requirements

Most professionals enter the field by earning a degree from a recognized school of planning. Several schools offer an undergraduate degree in planning, but most planners hold a master's degree with a solid base in a related undergraduate field. The typical graduate program involves two years of study. In many schools the students take part in practical field work during both the summer and in conjunction with courses offered during the academic year.

Students enter graduate planning programs from virtually all undergraduate fields. Most come directly from their undergraduate studies, but more and more have had previous experience in urban and regional planning or allied fields.

Professional Association

American Planning Association
1313 East 60th St.
Chicago, IL 60637
1776 Massachusetts Avenue, N.W.
Washington, D.C. 20036
Publication: *Planning Magazine*
Professional Designation: AICP

Property Manager

Nature of Work

Property managers handle the daily business activities for owners of income-producing real estate, such as apartments, shopping centers, and office buildings. Many developments have an on-site manager responsible for the project in addition to a centralized headquarters that issues instructions for managing all properties.

Property managers handle tenant-related activities of building use, and assure the sound mechanical state of the property and the efficient running of all systems. They may show and lease space to prospective users, determine tenant eligibility, and conduct credit checks. They set up accounting systems for the collection of rent and payment of operating expenses, with appropriate descriptions of accounts to determine income or loss of each profit center.

Property management varies greatly with the type of property — an apartment complex, office building, or shopping center — particularly in the areas of leasing and tenant mix. Since expertise learned in one type of property is not always transferable to another, specialization is important.

Responsibilities

Property managers are responsible for assuring the smooth operation of their property so as to assure the long-run profitability of the project and its value. They must comply with all laws including general commercial business practices, building codes, and affirmative action. Managers must work with tenants and tenant organizations, assure compliance with lease agreements, and report to the owner on the financial situation each month and on legal and marketing aspects when needed.

Advancement Opportunities

Property managers frequently begin as on-site managers of small properties (under 100 apartment units, for example) then move up to larger ones. Experienced personnel have many opportunities to move up in a large property management firm.

In most states a real estate broker's license is needed for most property management situations. Many real estate brokers enter the property management field because it provides a regular source of income regardless of business conditions. Other brokers begin to manage property as a service for owners of property they brokered.

Hours and Travel

On-site property managers may conduct most of their business during normal business hours. However, they may be called upon at any

97

time to show or lease space or respond to a security problem.

Those at higher management levels also conduct their business during normal hours but may be called on at any time for urgent security problems. In addition, they may travel to visit properties they manage out of town and to report to owners who live at a distance from the property.

Educational Requirements

There are no mandatory educational requirements, although courses are offered by several trade associations. Courses deal with on-site management; apartment, office building, and retail space management; and managing investment real estate.

Professional and Trade Associations

Building Owners and Managers Association
1221 Massachusetts Ave., N.W.
Washington, D.C. 20005
202/638-2929
Publication: *Annual Office Building Experience Exchange Report*

Community Association Institute
1630 Duke St.
Alexandria, VA 22314
703/548-8600

Institute for Real Estate Management
430 N. Michigan Ave.
Chicago, IL 60611
312/661-1930
Publication: *Journal of Property Management*
Professional Designation: Certified Property Manager (CPM)

National Apartment Association
1111 14th St., N.W., Suite 804
Washington, D.C.
202/842-4050
Publication: *Units*
Professional Designation: Certified Apartment Manager (CAM)

Alphabetization: All words are alphabetized by letter rather than by word. Thus, for the purpose of arrangement, all multiple word terms are treated as if they were one word. For example, the word "ad valorem" follows "adult," rather than preceding as would be the case if "ad" were treated as a separate word. Abbreviations, in the rare instance that they appear as entries, are treated as if they were a word. The term "MAI," which stands for "Member, Appraisal Institute," appears before "maintenance fee." A separate list of abbreviations is included, so as a general rule, abbreviations and acronyms do not appear as entries. In the case of "MAI," the initials are understood by many who are not familiar with the formal name. Thus, MAI becomes the entry.

Parentheses: Parentheses are used in two instances. The first application is to indicate an abbreviation commonly applied to the term. For example, "ADJUSTABLE RATE MORTGAGE (ARM)" indicates that the abbreviation "ARM" commonly refers to adjustable rate mortgages. The second application is to indicate the context of the term as defined. For example, "TO RETIRE (A DEBT)" indicates the context under which the word "retire" is defined is when it is applied to retiring a debt. The definition is not appropriate to other legitimate uses of the word retire, such as in the expression "retirement benefits."

Cross References: When an entry is used in the definition or example for another entry, the term is printed in **boldface type.** This provides a cross reference in case the term is used in the definition is unclear to the reader. In general, the term is printed in boldface only the first time it appears in the definition. Occasionally, when a term is a closely related concept or provides contrast, it is cross-referenced, even though not used in the definition. In the former case, the term is referenced as follows: "See **cash flow.**" In the latter case, the reference appears as: "Contrast with **net lease.**" When an entry is merely another expression for a term defined elsewhere in the book, a reference rather than a definition is provided; for example, "NOMINAL RATE same as **face rate.**"

Examples and Addresses: At least one example is given for each definition in the book. In the case of organizations listed as entries, a current address is supplied in lieu of an example. The examples are intended to illustrate how the term is used in a sentence or to provide a sample of specific things which fall under the purview of the term. For example, under the entry for "closing costs" a list of specific closing cost items is provided. When an entry has more than one definition, an example is provided for each definition. Where applicable, an illustration is provided as an example. e.g., under "cluster housing," an illustration of a sample cluster housing plan is included.

A

AAA-TENANT same as **triple-A tenant.**

ABANDONMENT the voluntary surrender of property, owned or leased, without naming a successor as owner or tenant. The property will generally revert to one holding a prior interest or, in cases where no owner is apparent, to the state. Abandonment does not relieve obligations associated with lease or ownership unless the abandonment is accepted by the entity to which the obligation is owed.
Example: Abel owns a dilapidated apartment house with 2 years' delinquent property taxes. Rather than pay the back taxes, Abel *abandons* the building by disclaiming ownership.

ABATEMENT a reduction in amount or intensity.
Example: A manufacturing plant may install equipment for pollution *abatement.*
Example: Tenants may ask for an *abatement* in rent over a period when their use of the property has been interrupted or inhibited by actions of the landlord, such as renovation of the structure.

ABSENTEE OWNER an owner who does not personally manage or reside at property owned.
Example: Abel, living in New York, purchases an apartment building in Houston. Abel is an *absentee owner.*

ABSOLUTE AUCTION an auction in which the subject property is sold to the highest bidder regardless of the amount of the winning bid.
Example: Although Amos was disappointed by the amount bid for his house, he had no choice but to sell since the property was sold in an *absolute auction.*

ABSORPTION RATE an estimate of the expected annual sales or new occupancy of a particular type of land use.
Example: The demand for new homes in a market area is estimated to be 500 per year. Developer Abel's new subdivision, when completed, is expected to capture 10% of the market. Therefore Abel's subdivision has an expected *absorption rate* of 50 homes per year (10% of 500 = 50).

101

ABSTRACT OF TITLE a historical summary of all of the recorded instruments and proceedings that affect the title of property.

Example: A title insurance company will have an attorney prepare an *abstract of title* prior to granting a title insurance policy.

Example: An abstract company will compile an *abstract of title* with copies of all recorded instruments affecting title to a specific tract.

ABSTRACT UPDATE making current an existing, but old, **abstract of title** by adding to it copies of all relevant documents recorded since the preparation or most recent update of the existing abstract.

Example: A building that was sold on April 1, 1992, was sold again on July 10, 1992. An abstract of title was provided for the April 1 sale, though an *abstract update* was considered adequate for the second sale.

ABUT adjoining or meeting. See also **adjacent.**

Example: The 2 properties shown in Figure 1 *abut* one another. The property on the right also *abuts* the road.

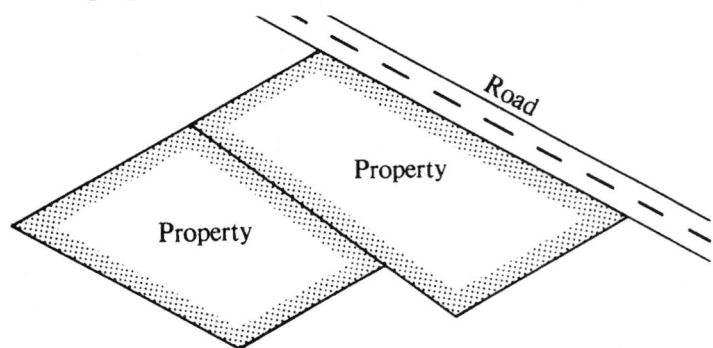

FIG. 1. ABUTTING PROPERTIES

A/C air-conditioning.

ACCELERATED COST RECOVERY SYSTEM (ACRS) a method of depreciation introduced by the Economic Recovery Tax Act of 1981 and modified by the Tax Reform Acts of 1984 and 1986. As *ACRS* applies to real estate, depreciable lives for buildings depend on when they are placed in service. See Table 1 for depreciable lives and rates for real estate acquired after 1986.

Example: If an apartment building were purchased in January 1993 for $1,000,000 exclusive of land, $34,800 (3.48%) could be claimed as depreciation in 1993, and $36,400 each year for the following 26 years.

TABLE 1
TAX DEPRECIATION RATES FOR REAL ESTATE

Post-1986 Recovery Percentages for Residential Rental Depreciable Property

Recovery Year	Month Placed in Service											
	1	2	3	4	5	6	7	8	9	10	11	12
1	3.48	3.18	2.88	2.58	2.27	1.97	1.67	1.36	1.06	.76	.45	.15
2–27	3.64	3.64	3.64	3.64	3.64	3.64	3.64	3.64	3.64	3.64	3.64	3.64
28	1.88	2.18	2.48	2.78	3.09	3.39	3.64	3.64	3.64	3.64	3.64	3.64
29	0	0	0	0	0	0	.05	.36	.66	.96	1.27	1.57

Post-1986 Recovery Percentages for Nonresidential Depreciable Property

Recovery Year	Month Placed in Service											
	1	2	3	4	5	6	7	8	9	10	11	12
1	3.04	2.78	2.51	2.25	1.98	1.72	1.46	1.19	.93	.66	.40	.13
2–31	3.17	3.17	3.17	3.17	3.17	3.17	3.17	3.17	3.17	3.17	3.17	3.17
32	1.86	2.12	2.39	2.65	2.92	3.17	3.17	3.17	3.17	3.17	3.17	3.17
33	0	0	0	0	0	0	.27	.54	.80	1.07	1.33	1.60

ACCELERATED DEPRECIATION depreciation methods, chosen for income tax or accounting purposes, that offer greater deductions in early years. See **accelerated cost recovery system, double declining balance, sum-of-years-digits depreciation.**
Example: One method of *accelerated depreciation* is the double declining balance method (DDB). If straight-line deductions equal 5% of depreciable basis, DDB allows a deduction of 10% (200% of 5%), but applied to the undepreciated basis. Thus the deductions decline each year (Figure 2).

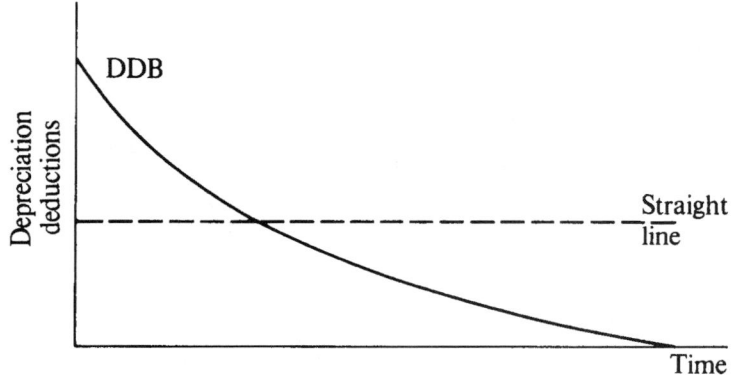

FIG. 2. ACCELERATED DEPRECIATION

ACCELERATION CLAUSE a loan provision giving the lender the right to declare the entire amount immediately due and payable upon the violation of a specific loan provision, such as failure to make payments on time.
Example: Collins sells her house to Baker, who assumes the existing 8% interest rate mortgage. They do not notify the lender of the sale. Clause 17 in the mortgage states that the full principal *accelerates* unless the lender approves of the sale. Collins must now pay the balance of the principal.

ACCEPTANCE the act of agreeing to accept an offer.
Example: Abel offers property for sale, Baker makes an offer to buy the property for a specified price. Upon Abel's *acceptance* a sales contract is complete.

ACCESSION additions to property as a result of annexing fixtures of alluvial deposits.
Example: The lease on a restaurant expires. The proprietor of the restaurant leaves some counters and bar stools. They become a part of the property by *accession*.
Example: Property bordering on a river is legally enlarged by soil deposited by the river (**alluvium**).

ACCESSORY APARTMENT a separate living unit created within a single-family home and occupied by either a family member or a non-family tenant. Generally, such units are outlawed by local **zoning** and **housing codes,** although some cities conduct special programs to encourage such units for specific purposes.
Example: Mrs. Andrews was left with a large home when her husband died. Through a special program conducted by the city, she was able to create an *accessory apartment* in her home and rent it to another widow. This provided low-cost housing for the tenant and additional income and companionship to Mrs. Andrews.

ACCESS RIGHT the right of owners to get to and from their property.
Example: If Baker is granted an *access right* to the property in Figure 3, a curb cut may be made onto the highway.

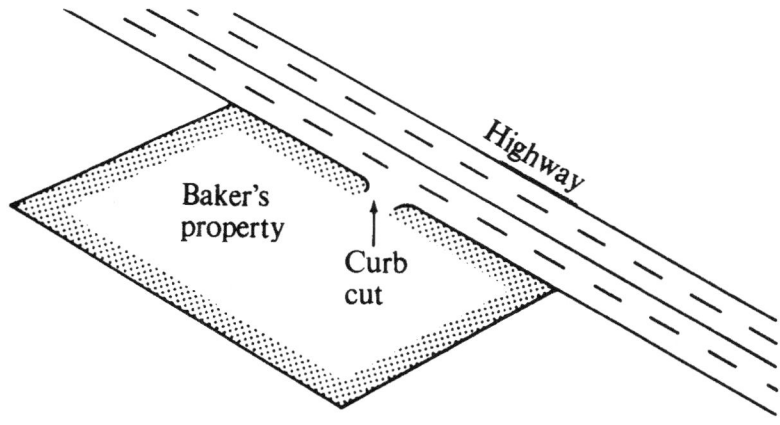

FIG. 3. ACCESS RIGHTS

ACCOMMODATION PARTY one who has signed an agreement without receiving value for it, for the purpose of lending his or her name so that another person can secure a necessary loan or other arrangement.
Example: The young developer asked an experienced friend to act as an *accommodation party*. The experienced developer signed the loan agreement even though there was no monetary benefit to him.

ACCRETION the addition to land through processes of nature, such as deposits of soil carried by streams. See **alluvium.**
Example: Figure 4.

FIG. 4. ACCRETION

ACCRUAL METHOD a method of accounting that requires income or expense to be entered when the amount is earned or the obligation is payable. Distinguished from **cash method** in which amounts are posted when paid or received.
Example: The home buyer bought and paid for a 3-year hazard insurance policy at closing. On the *accural method*, only the current year's expense is indicated.
Example: Interest on a loan is 3 months delinquent. The expense, though unpaid, appears in the current year's financial statement under the *accrual method*. Under the cash method it would appear on the financial statements when paid.

ACCRUED DEPRECIATION same as **accumulated depreciation.**

ACCRUED INTEREST interest that has been earned but not paid.
Example: If 6% interest is earned on a $100 deposit, then $6 of interest has *accrued* to the depositor.

ACKNOWLEDGMENT a declaration by a person who has signed a document that such signature is a voluntary act, made before a duly authorized person.
Example: Figure 5.

I, Albert Abel, hereby deed to Robert Baker, the land that I own in Fair County, further described below.

Albert Abel
Albert Abel

Jack Jones
Witness

Sigs R. Real
Notary Public
Acknowledgment

George Smith
Witness

FIG. 5. ACKNOWLEDGMENT

ACCUMULATED DEPRECIATION in accounting, the amount of **depreciation** expense that has been claimed to date. Same as accrued depreciation. See **adjusted tax basis.**
Example: A building was bought for $100,000. The annual **straight-line depreciation** expense is $2,500. The *accumulated depreciation* in 3 years is $7,500.

ACQUISITION COST the price and all fees required to obtain a property.
Example: Abel purchases property for $90,000 plus $5,000 in **closing costs** (attorney's fees, loan fees, **appraisal** costs, **title insurance,** and loan **discount points**). Abel's *acquisition cost* is $95,000.

ACQUISITION LOAN money borrowed for the purpose of purchasing a property.
Example: The developer negotiated an *acquisition loan* for the purchase of land and a construction loan to improve the land for homesites.

ACRE a 2-dimensional measure of land equaling 160 square rods, 10 square chains, 4,840 square yards, or 43,560 square feet.
Example: A land survey shows that Abel owns 1.3774 *acres* of land (Figure 6).

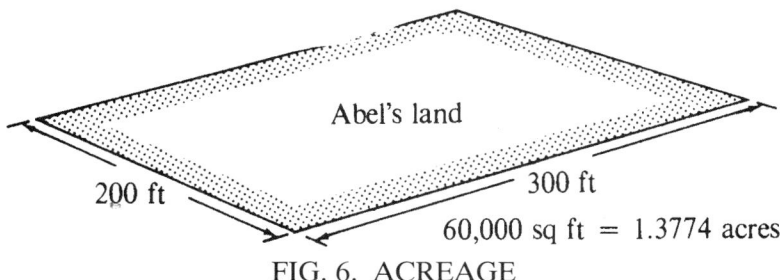

FIG. 6. ACREAGE

ACRS accelerated cost recovery system.

ACTION TO QUIET TITLE see **quiet title (action).**

ACTIVE PARTICIPATION type of investor position which determines how rental income is taxed. Requirements for *active participation* are less stringent than for **material participation.** An investor may have a manager for rental real estate and still be considered an active participant. Indicators of *active participation* in real estate are:
• Approving new tenants
• Deciding on rental terms

• Approving capital or repair expenditures
Active participation excludes:
• Owners of a 10% interest or less
• Limited partners
An active participant with adjusted gross income under $100,000 without regard to passive losses, may deduct up to $25,000 of passive losses against other income. This allowance is phased out on a 50% ratio as adjusted gross income increases from $100,000 to $150,000.
Example: Anna earns $40,000 from her job as an attorney, and is an active investor in an apartment complex. If the apartments generate a tax loss, she may offset up to $25,000 of her salary with the loss.

ACTIVE SOLAR HEATING a system that uses energy from sunlight to heat a structure and/or provide hot water. Contrasted with **passive solar heating** by the use of pumps or fans to move the energy-transporting medium through the system. Installation of active solar heating equipment is eligible for certain income tax credits.
Example: A schematic of a typical *active solar heating* system is shown in Figure 7.

FIG. 7. ACTIVE SOLAR HEATING

108

ACT OF GOD an unpreventable destructive occurrence of the natural world.
Example: A **contract** has a provision that allows the buyer to **default** if the property is damaged by an *act of God*.
Examples of an *act of God* are:
• earthquake
• flood
• hurricane
• lightning
• tornado

ACTUAL AGE in appraisal, the chronological age of an improvement, as contrasted with its **effective age.**
Example: Although the *actual age* of the building was only 5 years, excessively heavy use made it appear much older.

ACTUAL EVICTION see **eviction, actual.**

ACTUAL POSSESSION see **possession.**

ADC LOAN acquisition, **development,** and **construction loan**.
Example: A real estate developer wishes to create a **shopping center** on a **tract** of land that he has an option to buy. His first step is to arrange **leases** with **tenants** for much of the proposed space. The next step is to secure a **commitment** for **takeout financing.** Then, he may **secure** an *ADC loan.* See **construction loan.**

ADDENDUM (plural: ADDENDA) something added, as an attachment to a **contract.**
Example: An *addendum* to the **contract of sale** described the type of **financing** that the buyer must secure to be required to purchase the property.
Example: Commonly added *addenda* in real estate purchase agreements are for financing terms and property **inspection** requirements.

ADDITIONAL FIRST-YEAR DEPRECIATION (TAX) under the 1986 tax act, up to $10,000 of depreciable personal property purchased each year may be expensed, rather than depreciated, provided not more than $200,000 is purchased in a year. The $10,000 is phased out, dollar for dollar, when purchases exceed $200,000 in a year.
Example: Barbara is a real estate broker. She bought a $4,000 computer to assist with her business; she may expense the cost in the year purchased, rather than depreciate the equipment.

109

ADD-ON INTEREST interest that is added to the principal of a loan. The amount of interest for all years is computed on the original amount borrowed.
Example: Abel borrows $1,000 at 8% *add-on interest* for 4 years. Total interest is $320 (8% of $1,000 for 4 years). Abel will repay the $1,320 total in equal monthly installments.

ADJACENT nearby but not necessarily **adjoining.**
Example: Lot B is *adjacent* to lot A (Figure 8).

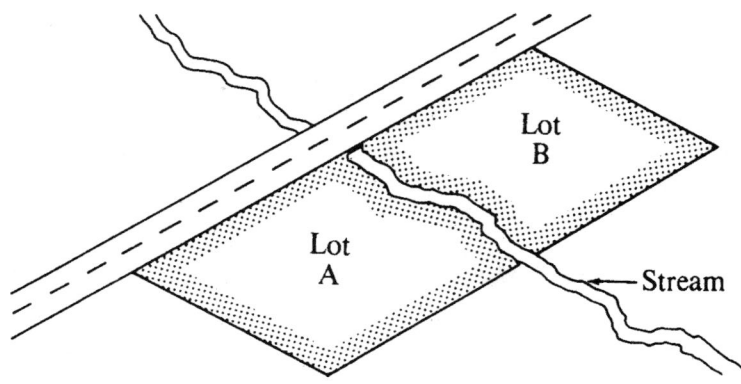

FIG. 8. ADJACENT LOTS

ADJOINING contiguous; attaching; sharing a common border.
Example: A warehouse with *adjoining* office space (Figure 9).

FIG. 9. ADJOINING PROPERTY

ADJUSTABLE-RATE MORTGAGE (ARM) a mortgage loan that allows the interest rate to be changed at specific intervals over the maturity of the loan.
Example: A person obtains an *adjustable-rate mortgage* to finance the purchase of a home. After a 2-year period, the lender may adjust the rate of interest on the loan in accordance with an established index.

ADJUSTED SALES PRICE 1. in appraisal, the indicated price of a comparable property after adjustments have been made to account for differences between comparable and subject properties.
Example: The comparable property is identical to the subject property except that the comparable has an additional half bath. The sales price of $70,000 is adjusted by subtracting $3,000 for the extra bath. The *adjusted sales price* is $67,000.
2. in income taxation, the selling price of a home less expenses of sale, less fixing-up expenses. When the purchase price of a new principal residence equals or exceeds the *adjusted sales price* of a former residence, any gain on the sale of the former residence will be deferred. See **Section 1034.**
Example: A principal residence sold for $90,000. Just prior to the sale the seller had a contractor paint at a cost of $3,000; sales commissions and other seller-paid closing costs were $7,000. If the seller acquires another residence for $80,000 or more, there will be no income tax due on the sale of the former home.

ADJUSTED TAX BASIS the original cost or other basis of property, reduced by **depreciation** deductions and increased by **capital expenditures.**
Example: Collins buys a lot for $10,000. She erects a retail facility for $60,000, then depreciates the improvements for tax purposes at the rate of $4,000 per year. After 3 years her *adjusted tax basis* is $58,000 [$10,000 + $60,000 − (3 × $4,000)].

ADJUSTMENTS (IN APPRAISAL) dollar value or percentage amounts that, when added to or subtracted from the sales price of a **comparable,** provide an indication of the value of a subject property. *Adjustments* are necessary to compensate for variation in the features of the comparable relative to the subject.
Example: An appraisal is to be made of a four-bedroom house. One **comparable** is similar in all salient characteristics, including total size, except that it has 3 bedrooms. This comparable sold for $100,000. The appraiser makes an adjustment of $1,000 to the comparable to account for the difference of bedrooms. The adjusted sales price of the **comparable** is $101,000.

111

ADMINISTRATOR a person appointed by a court to administer the estate of a deceased person who left no will.
Example: The *administrator* of the estate called a meeting of the deceased's relatives for the purpose of dividing the property.

ADMINISTRATOR'S DEED a **deed** conveying the property of one who died without a will (**intestate**).
Example: At the hearing called by the administrator, the heir received an *administrator's deed* to her father's home.

ADR **asset depreciation range.**

ADULT one who has attained the age of **majority.**
Example: Abel enters into a contract to purchase land. Because he is 17 years of age he is a **minor** (not an adult) and may **void** the contract.

AD VALOREM according to value. See **ad valorem tax.**

AD VALOREM TAX a tax based on the value of the thing being taxed.
Example: If the *ad valorem tax* rate is 1%, the tax would be $1 per $100 of assessed value.

ADVERSE POSSESSION a means of acquiring title to real estate where an occupant has been in actual, open, **notorious,** exclusive, and continuous occupancy of property for the period required by state law.
Example: Although the elderly Ms. Davis held no official **deed** to the land, she was awarded title by *adverse possession*, since she had lived on the property all her life and the legal owner was unknown.

AFFIDAVIT a written statement, sworn to or **affirmed** before an officer who is authorized to administer an oath or affirmation.
Example: The *affidavit* affirmed that the landlord was solely entitled to lease out the property.

AFFIRM to confirm; to ratify; to verify.
Example: At a meeting between the buyer, seller, and broker, the voidable sales contract was *affirmed* by the party who could have voided it. All parties are now bound by the stipulations of the contract.

A-FRAME a post-World War II style house with a frame in the shape of one or more "A's."
Example: Figure 10.

"A" shape frame

Steep gable roof

Large windows

Shingles

FIG. 10. A-FRAME HOUSE

AFTER-TAX CASH FLOW **cash flow** from income-producing property, less income taxes, if any, attributable to the property's income. If there is a tax loss which can provide a tax saving from the shelter of income earned outside the property, that savings is added to the **cash flow** that is earned by the property. **Example:** A property generates $1,000 per year of cash flow. In the first year of ownership, depreciation and interest deductions provide a tax loss of $3,000. The loss saves $900 of income taxes that the investor would otherwise pay on salary earned as a teacher. The *after-tax cash flow* is $1,900.

AFTER-TAX EQUITY YIELD the **rate of return** on an equity interest in **real estate,** taking into account financing costs and income tax implications of the investor.
Example: An investor pays $100,000 for an equity interest in a property that is subject to a $900,000 mortgage loan. The investor receives $8,000 of **cash flow** each year, then must pay $2,000 for income taxes. The **after-tax cash flow** is $6,000. Upon resale of the property, the investor receives $120,000 after a 5-year **holding period,** net of taxes on the sale. The $6,000 annual cash flow is combined with the $20,000 gain on resale to provide a 9.3% *after-tax equity yield* rate. See **internal rate of return** for computations.

AFTER-TAX INCOME same as **after-tax cash flow.**

113

AFTER-TAX PROCEEDS FROM RESALE the amount of money left for the investor after all obligations of the transaction and after personal income taxes on the transaction.
Example: Table 2.

TABLE 2
AFTER-TAX PROCEEDS

Resale price	$1,300,000
Less: Transaction costs	– 100,000
Outstanding mortgage	– 900,000
Tax on gain	– 180,000
After-tax proceeds from resale	$ 120,000

AGENCY the legal relationship between a principal and his **agent** arising from a contract in which the principal engages the agent to perform certain acts on the principal's behalf.
Example: Under the law of *agency*, agents must be loyal to their employers. Therefore broker Roberts submits to employer Davis all offers on property.

AGENT one who undertakes to transact some business or to manage some affair for another, with the authority of the latter.
Example: An owner engages a **broker** to act as *agent* in selling real property; the broker in turn engages salespersons to act as *agents* to sell the same property.

AGREEMENT OF SALE a written agreement between seller and purchaser in which the purchaser agrees to buy certain real estate and the seller agrees to sell upon terms of the agreement. Also called **offer and acceptance, contract of sale, earnest money** contract.
Example: Abel's **broker** prepared an *agreement of sale* to sell a home to Baker. Both principals signed it. It states that the price of $50,000 is to be paid in cash at closing, subject to Baker's ability to arrange a $40,000 loan at a 12% interest rate.

AIREA American Institute of Real Estate Appraisers.

AIR RIGHTS the right to use, control, or occupy the space above a designated property. Air rights can be leased, sold, or donated to another party.
Example: The Pan Am Building in New York City is situated in the *air rights* of Grand Central Station (Figure 11).

114

FIG. 11. AIR RIGHTS

ALIENATION to convey or transfer **title** and **possession** of property. May be voluntary (by the owner) or involuntary (without the owner's consent) such as in **condemnation.**
Example: By signing a **deed,** there is an *alienation* of property.

ALLODIAL SYSTEM a legal system that allocates full property ownership rights to individuals. The allodial system is the basis for property rights in the United States.
Example: Under the *allodial system*, an individual may obtain **fee simple** ownership of a parcel or real estate. This allows the individual to enjoy the full set of rights entailed in property ownership, subject to restriction only by governmental powers of taxation, **police power,** and **eminent domain.**

ALLUVIUM (or ALLUVION) soil deposited by **accretion.** Usually considered to belong to the owner of the land to which it is added.
Example: Figure 12.

FIG. 12. ALLUVIUM

115

ALTA American Land Title Association.

ALTERNATIVE MINIMUM TAX (AMT) a type of flat-rate tax that applies to individual taxpayers who have certain types of income. A 21% rate applies to broadly based income. If this tax exceeds the regular income tax, then the *alternative minimum tax* is to be paid instead of the regular income tax. See **tax preference items.**

ALTERNATIVE MORTGAGE INSTRUMENT (AMI) any mortgage other than a fixed interest rate, level payment **amortizing** loan.
Examples:
Various types of *AMI's*:
• **variable rate mortgages**
• **rollover loans**
• **graduated payment mortgages**
• **shared appreciation mortgages**
• **adjustable rate mortgages**
• **growing equity mortgages**

AMENITIES in **appraisal**, the nonmonetary benefits derived from property ownership, such as pride of home ownership.
Example: Graham bought a **condominium** overlooking Lake Michigan with a prestige address, thus enhancing the *amenities* of ownership.

AMERICAN BANKERS ASSOCIATION a trade organization for officers of commercial banks. Publishes the monthly *ABA Banking Journal* and several other specialized banking periodicals.
Address:
American Bankers Association
1120 Connecticut Avenue NW
Washington, DC 20036

AMERICAN INSTITUTE OF ARCHITECTS a professional organization of architects, designers, and developers. Publishes the monthly *AIA Journal* and other periodicals.
Address:
American Institute of Architects
1735 New York Avenue NW
Washington, DC 20006

AMERICAN INSTITUTE OF REAL ESTATE APPRAIS-ERS (AIREA) an organization of real estate appraisers that merged with the Society of Real Estate Appraisers to form the Appraisal Institute in 1991.

AMERICAN LAND TITLE ASSOCIATION (ALTA) a national association of title companies, abstractors, and attorneys established to promote uniformity and quality in **title abstract** and insurance policies.

Example: The title company employed in the purchase of the property is a member of the *American Land Title Association* and, therefore, used standard ALTA forms when underwriting the title policy.

AMERICAN MANSARD OR SECOND EMPIRE STYLE a nineteenth-century-style house whose main and distinguishing characteristic is the roof design. The mansard roof slopes gently back from the wall line and then is topped with an invisible (from the street) section resembling a conventional hip roof. Multiple dormers protrude through the roof.

Example: Figure 13.

Massive cornice and supporting brackets

Mansard roof

Decorative iron work

Many dormers

Colored glass windows

French doors

FIG. 13. AMERICAN MANSARD-STYLE HOUSE

AMERICAN PLANNING ASSOCIATION (APA) a professional organization of regional and urban planners for the purpose of promoting professional standards, research, and education. APA was formed by the merger of the American Institute of Planners (AIP) and the American Society of Planning Officials (ASPO). APA publishes a monthly magazine, *Planning*, and a quarterly journal, *Journal of the APA*.

Address:
American Planning Association
1313 East 60th Street
Chicago, IL 60637

AMERICAN REAL ESTATE AND URBAN ECONOMICS ASSOCIATION (AREUEA) an organization of scholars, researchers, and practitioners concerned with economic analysis of real estate related problems. Publishes the *AREUEA Journal* quarterly.
Address:
AREUEA
College of Business Administration
Indiana University
Bloomington, IN 47401

AMERICAN REAL ESTATE SOCIETY (ARES) an organization of scholars, researchers, and practitioners who are mainly concerned with solving business problems related to real estate. Publishes the *Journal of Real Estate Research* and *Journal of Real Estate Literature.*
Address:
James B. Webb
Dept. of Finance
Cleveland State University
Cleveland, OH 44115

AMERICAN SOCIETY OF APPRAISERS (ASA) a professional organization of appraisers (not restricted to real estate). ASA publishes the biannual journal *Valuation*. It offers the professional designations FASA and ASA.
Address:
American Society of Appraisers
International Headquarters
Dulles International Airport
P.O. Box 17265
Washington, DC 20041

AMERICAN SOCIETY OF REAL ESTATE COUNSELORS (ASREC) a professional organization of real estate investment counselors and consultants. Affiliated with the **National Association of Realtors®**. Awards the designation of Counselor of Real Estate (CRE). Publishes the biannual journal *Real Estate Issues.*
Address:
American Society of Real Estate Counselors
430 North Michigan Avenue
Chicago, IL 60611

AMERICANS WITH DISABILITIES ACT (ADA) federal law that prohibits discrimination against individuals with physical handicaps, including hiring practices and design of buildings intended to serve the public.
Example: There are three deadlines associated with the Act:
• January 26, 1992: Removal of barriers to disabled people. All future renovations must be in compliance.
• July 26, 1992: Companies with 25 or more employees must remove barriers that limit job opportunities of disabled persons.
• January 26, 1993: All new construction must be in compliance.

AMI alternative mortgage instrument.

AML adjustable mortgage loan.

AMORTIZATION a gradual paying off of a debt by periodic installments.
Example: A $100,000 loan is arranged at a 12% interest rate. The borrower pays $13,500 in the first year. Of the payment, $12,000 is for interest, $1,500 for *amortization*. After the payment, the loan balance is amortized to $98,500.

AMORTIZATION SCHEDULE a table that shows the periodic payment, interest and principal requirements, and unpaid loan balance for each period of the life of a loan.
Example: An *amortization schedule* for a $1,000 principal, 5-year self-amortizing loan at 10% interest with annual payments is shown in Table 3.

TABLE 3
AMORTIZATION SCHEDULE

End of year	Payment required	Interest at 10% of unpaid balance	Principal retirement	Unpaid balance at end of year
1	$263.80	$100.00	$163.80	$836.20
2	263.80	83.62	180.18	656.02
3	263.80	65.60	198.20	457.82
4	263.80	45.78	218.02	239.80
5	263.78	23.98	239.80	0
Total retired			$1,000.00	

AMORTIZATION TERM the time it takes to retire a **debt** through periodic payments. Also known as the *full amortization term*.
Example: Many mortgage loans have an *amortization term* of 15, 20, 25, or 30 years. Some have an **amortization schedule** as a 30-year loan, but require a **balloon payment** in 5, 10, or 15 years.

119

AMORTIZED LOAN any loan with at least some payments to **principal.**
Example: A loan of $10,000 at 10% interest requires annual payments of $1,200. Because the payments exceed the interest required, the loan balance will be reduced, so it is an *amortized loan*. Contrast with **interest-only loan.**

AMOUNT OF ONE same as **compound amount of one.**

AMOUNT OF ONE PER PERIOD same as **compound amount of one per period.**

ANCHOR TENANT the main tenant in a shopping center.
Example: Big Buy Foods is the *anchor tenant* in Figure 14. (Note: Large-scale centers may have more than one anchor tenant.)

FIG. 14. ANCHOR TENANT

ANNEXATION the process by which an incorporated city expands its boundaries to include a specified area. The rules of annexation are established by state law and generally require a public ballot within the city and the area to be annexed. Other incorporated areas are generally protected from annexation by an adjacent city.
Example: *Annexation* is generally sought by a city to expand its boundaries by taking in an area to which it may already be providing services. Many unincorporated suburban areas, however, resist efforts to annex them into the city because of possibly higher tax rates and loss of local control over schools and other services.

ANNUAL CAP a limit on the amount of adjustment in the interest rate on an **adjustable rate mortgage** over a twelve-month period. See **cap.**
Example: An adjustable rate mortgage has a current interest rate of 8% and an *annual cap* of 2 percentage points. After one year, the highest the interest rate can be is 10% and the lowest it can be is 6%, due to the cap.

ANNUAL DEBT SERVICE required annual principal and interest payments for a loan.
Example: A loan of $100,000 calls for 300 equal monthly payments to fully **amortize** the principal. Interest is 15% annually. Monthly payments are $1,280.83. *Annual debt service* is the sum of 12 monthly payments, or $15,369.96.

ANNUAL MORTGAGE CONSTANT the amount of **annual debt service** compared to the principal; also expressed as a dollar amount.
The formula is:
$$\text{Annual mortgage constant} = \frac{\text{annual debt service}}{\text{mortgage principal}}$$

Example: A loan, at a 15% interest rate, is amortizing over 30 years with monthly payments. The *annual mortgage constant* is 15.1733%. Total principal and interest payments in a year are $15.18 per $100 borrowed. Note: The annual mortgage constant must exceed the interest rate for **amortization** to occur.

ANNUAL PERCENTAGE RATE the effective rate of interest for a loan per year, disclosure of which is required by the **Truth-In-Lending** Law. See **yield to maturity.**
Example: Abel gets a loan for $50,000 at 10% interest plus 2 **discount points,** payable over 30 years. Because of the discount points $49,000 has been effectively borrowed but $50,000 must be repaid with 10% interest on $50,000. Considering the effective amount borrowed, the *annual percentage rate* is 10.25%.

ANNUITY a series of equal or nearly equal periodic payments or receipts.
Example: The receipt of $100 per year for the next 5 years constitutes a $100 five-year *annuity.*

ANNUITY DUE same as **ordinary annuity.**

ANNUITY IN ADVANCE a series of equal or nearly equal payments, each payable at the beginning of the period.
Example: A landlord leases property for 5 years. The rent, payable at the beginning of each period, constitutes an *annuity in advance* (Figure 15).

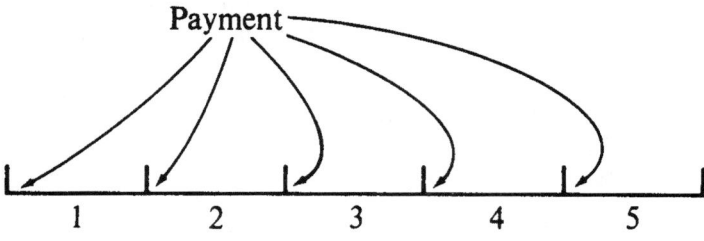

FIG. 15. ANNUITY IN ADVANCE

ANNUITY IN ARREARS same as **ordinary annuity.**

ANNUITY FACTOR a mathematical figure that shows the present value of an income stream that generates one dollar of income each period for a specified number of periods.
Example: Collins is to receive $1,000 each year for 10 years for rental of her land. To value this income, she used an *annuity factor* at a 10% rate that is 6.144. The estimated rent has a present value of $6,144 (6.144 x $1,000).

$$\text{Annuity factor} = \frac{1 - \dfrac{1}{(1+i)^n}}{i}$$

where i is the periodic interest rate in decimal form and n is the number of periods that the income stream will last.

ANTICIPATION, PRINCIPLE OF in **appraisal of real estate,** the principle that the value of property today is the present value of the sum of anticipated future benefits.
Example: A **commercial property** is net-leased to a **triple-A tenant** for $10,000 per year for 30 years. At the end of that time the building will be worthless. The anticipated benefit of $10,000 per year for 30 years at a 10% **discount rate** is $94,269. This value is based on the *principle of anticipation,* because the income is expected to be received in the future.

ANTITRUST LAWS federal and state acts to protect trade and commerce from monopolies and restrictions.
Example: In the early 1960s several real estate boards required all members to charge the same rate of commission. Some boards were found to be in violation of *antitrust laws.* Now there are no boards that require specific commission rates.

APA American Planning Association.

APARTMENT (BUILDING) a dwelling unit within a multi-family structure, generally provided as rental housing. An apartment building is a structure with individual apartment units but a common entrance and hallway. See **multifamily housing.**
Example: *Apartments* may vary in size from small, 1-room efficiencies to large, multibedroom units. *Apartment buildings* may range from a 1-story, 4-unit building to a high-rise building with hundreds of units and retail and office space included.

APP appreciation (in appraisal terminology).

APPEALS BOARD a body empowered with the ability to overturn decisions of the local government permitting agency and code enforcement agency based on appeal by the aggrieved petitioner.
Example: When Ambler was turned down on her rezoning request, she petitioned the zoning *appeals board*, which unfortunately agreed with the zoning board and denied her request.

APPORTIONMENT 1. the **prorating** of property expenses, such as taxes and insurance, between buyer and seller.
Example: A house is sold on July 1. Property taxes, paid in **arrears,** are due on January 1 of the following year. At closing taxes are *apportioned*, so the seller pays the buyer one half of the estimated taxes as his share of the estimated tax payment due in January.
2. the partitioning of property into individual parcels by tenants in common.
Example: A sister and brother inherit a property and hold it as tenants in common. The brother wishes to sell. The property is *apportioned* into 2 separate parcels to allow for the sale.

APPRAISAL an opinion or estimate of the value of the property.
Examples: A property owner may have an appraisal made of a specific property to:
• determine a reasonable offering price in a sale
• determine the value at death for estate tax purposes
• allocate the purchase price to the land and improvements
• determine the amount of hazard insurance to carry

APPRAISAL APPROACH one of 3 methods to estimate the value of property: **cost approach, income approach,** and **market comparison approach.**
Example: An independent fee appraiser generally uses each of the 3 *appraisal approaches* when preparing an appraisal report.

APPRAISAL BY SUMMATION same as **cost approach.**

APPRAISAL DATE in an **appraisal report,** the date to which the value applies.
Example: Some property was condemned by the government for use as a park. The government and the former property owners hired **appraisers** to value the property as of March 13, 1992, because that was the **condemnation** date. The appraisers used that as the *appraisal date* for their reports, and estimated the value based on market conditions as of March 13, 1992, although they were hired several months later.

APPRAISAL FOUNDATION an organization that came into existence in the late 1980s in an effort to encourage uniform requirements for **appraisal** qualifications and reporting standards.
Address:
Appraisal Foundation
1029 Vermont Avenue NW
Washington, DC 20005

APPRAISAL INSTITUTE an organization of professional appraisers that was formed in 1991 by the merger of the **American Institute of Real Estate Appraisers** and the **Society of Real Estate Appraisers.** It offers **MAI** and **SRA** designations. The MAI is qualified to appraise any property, while the SRA is primarily qualified for residences. Both designations require high standards of education and experience for membership. It supports the **SREA, SRPA,** and **RM** designations, though no new ones will be offered.
Address:
Appraisal Institute
875 North Michigan Avenue
Chicago, IL 60611

APPRAISAL REPORT describes the findings of an appraisal engagement. Reports may be presented in the following formats: oral, letter, form, or narrative. See the **Uniform Standards of Professional Appraisal Practices.**
Examples:
• A 150-page narrative appraisal report was prepared for a neighborhood shopping center to fully explain each element that was considered in estimating its value.
• A 4-page form report with blanks filled in was prepared for a single-family home.
• An oral report was requested by a client for a vacant lot, though the appraiser kept full details of the assignment in writing in a file.

APPRAISER one qualified to estimate the value of real property.
Example: One may hire an *appraiser* to render an opinion of a property's market value. In a court of law, an *appraiser* may be called upon for expert testimony.

APPRECIATION an increase in the value of property.
Example: Abel sold for $100,000 land that he purchased 10 years ago for $60,000. During that time the amount of *appreciation* was $40,000.
Appreciation gains from investment property are generally subject to favorable **capital gains** tax rates.

APPROPRIATION setting aside land for a public use.
Example: Abel plans to develop a subdivision in Pleasantville. In order to obtain permission from the city council, Abel is required to *appropriate* 2 acres to the city for construction of an elementary school.

APPURTENANCE something that is outside the property itself but is considered a part of the property and adds to its greater enjoyment, such as the right to cross another's land (i.e., **easement** or **right-of-way**).
Example: Figure 16.

FIG. 16. APPURTENANCES

APR annual percentage rate.

ARBITRAGE 1. buying in one market, selling simultaneously in another to make a profit.
Example: Graham bought gold in London for $500 per ounce; simultaneously she sold it in New York for $502. The *arbitrage* allowed $2 profit per ounce, less transaction costs.

2. buying one type of security and selling an equivalent to make a profit.

Example: Baker bought bonds for $5,000 that could be converted into 500 shares of stock. Simultaneously, he sold 500 shares of stock at $11 per share. He earned $500 for this *arbitrage*, minus transaction costs.

ARCHITECTURE the manner in which a building is constructed, including the layout, **floor plan,** style and appearance, materials used, and the building technology used.

Example: The *architecture* of the houses in the neighborhood is characteristic of the design common to the 1930s: small rooms, much attention to detail, an elaborate **facade,** high ceilings, and thick walls.

AREA a 2-dimensional space defined by boundaries; such as floor area, area of a lot, and market area.

Example: A rectangular lot is 50 × 100 feet in dimension. Its *area* is 5,000 square feet or 0.11 acre.

AREUEA American Real Estate and Urban Economics Association.

ARM adjustable rate mortgage.

ARM'S LENGTH TRANSACTION a transaction among parties, each of whom acts in his or her own best interest.

Examples: Transactions between the following parties would, in most cases, NOT be considered *arm's length*:
• a husband and wife
• a father and son
• a corporation and one of its subsidiaries

ARREARS 1. at the end of a term.

Example: Interest on mortgage loans is normally paid in *arrears*. This means that interest is paid at the end of a month or other period. Generally, rent and insurance are paid in advance.

2. sometimes used to signify default; overdue in payment.

Example: Jones has not made his scheduled mortgage payments for three months; he is in *arrears*.

ARTESIAN WELL a deep-drilled shaft that reaches water that rises because of natural underground pressure.

Example: Schematic drawing of an *artesian well* (Figure 17).

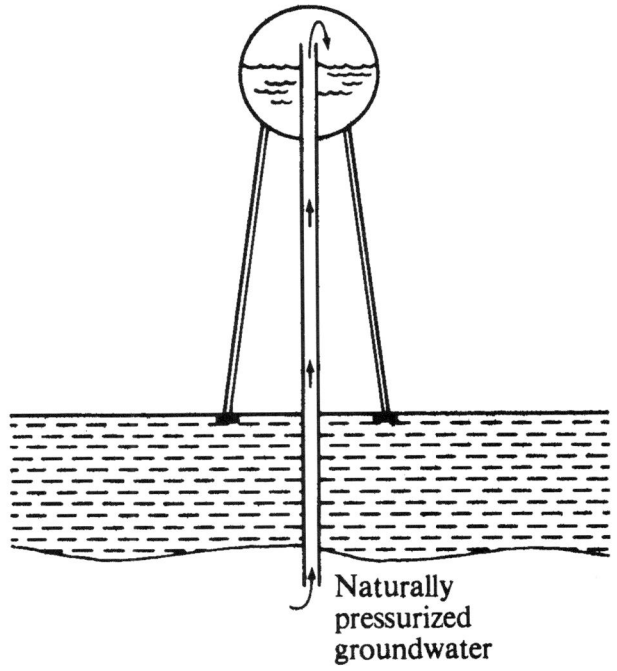

Naturally
pressurized
groundwater

FIG. 17. ARTESIAN WELL

ASA American Society of Appraisers. Also, a senior professional designation offered by the **American Society of Appraisers.** The ASA designation is awarded upon meeting rigorous requirements that include extensive experience, education, and approved demonstration reports. Designations offered include urban and rural real estate, and non-real estate disciplines such as business valuation, machinery and equipment, fine arts, appraisal education, and administration.
Address:
American Society of Appraisers
P.O. Box 17265
Washington, DC 20041

AS IS without guarantees as to condition, as in a sale.
Example: Baker purchases a building from Abel with the understanding that the building is to be conveyed *as is*. When Baker discovers that the roof leaks, Abel is not legally responsible for repairs.

ASKED the amount a property owner sets as a selling price for his property.
Example: Abel has *asked* $75,000 for 20 acres of land, even though its **appraised** value is only $60,000.

ASKING PRICE the list price that an owner would like to receive.

Example: Abel advertises a property for sale at a price of $100,000. The advertised price is Abel's *asking price.*

ASREC American Society of Real Estate Counselors.

ASSEMBLAGE combining of 2 or more parcels of land. See **plottage value.**

Example: Abel buys 2 **adjoining** properties of land for $10,000 each. The large unified tract is worth $25,000. The process is *assemblage.*

ASSESSED VALUATION the value established for property tax purposes.

Example: Abel receives a statement indicating that, in the judgment of the local tax **assessor,** Abel's property is worth $40,000. By law, properties in this jurisdiction are assessed at 75% of **market value.** Thus Abel's *assessed valuation* is $30,000 (75% of $40,000) and property taxes will be based on this assessed amount.

ASSESSMENT 1. the amount of tax or special payment due to a municipality or association.

Example: Abel owns a parcel of land assessed on the tax roll for $40,000. The tax rate is $1.00 per $100 of value. The tax *assessment* for Abel's land is $400.

2. an owner's or lessee's proportionate share of a common expense.

Example: Abel rents office space under a **net lease.** Abel pays an *assessment* each month for maintenance of the building lobby and elevators.

ASSESSMENT RATIO the ratio of assessed value to **market value.**

Example: A county requires a 40% *assessment ratio* on all property to be taxed. Property with a $10,000 market value is therefore assessed at $4,000 (40% of $10,000), and the tax rate is applied to $4,000.

ASSESSMENT ROLL a public record of the assessed value of property in a taxing jurisdiction.

Example: The *assessment roll* of Anytown, USA, lists each individual tract of land within its taxing jurisdiction and shows the assessed value of each. The total assessed value of property is $10 million.

ASSESSOR an official who determines property tax assessments.

Example: Jones inspects Abel's property and estimates its value at $50,000 for property tax purposes. Jones is an *assessor.*

ASSET something of value.
Example: Land, houses, cars, furniture, cash, bank deposits, and securities owned are *assets*.

ASSET DEPRECIATION RANGE generally applies to property purchased before 1981. Limitations on the period over which assets may be depreciated. Generally allows depreciable lives 20% longer or shorter than the guidelines provided by the Internal Revenue Service. Also provides maximum amounts that can be spent annually on assets and still be a deductible repair.
Example: Farm buildings purchased before 1981 may be depreciated over 25 years or within a range of 20 to 30 years, according to the *asset depreciation range.* Up to 5% of the cost can be spent annually and be treated as repair, not as a capital improvement.

ASSIGN to transfer one's property rights or contract rights to another.
Example: Jones has the right, under a **contract of sale,** to conclude the purchase of a house. Jones may *assign* this right to someone else.

ASSIGNEE the person to whom an agreement or contract is sold or transferred.
Example: See **assignor.**

ASSIGNMENT the method by which a right or contract is transferred from one person to another.
Example: A tenant signs an *assignment* giving another the rights to use the leased space.

ASSIGNMENT OF LEASE the transfer of rights to use leased property. The **assignee** acquires the same rights and privileges as the **assignor.** The assignor remains liable unless released by the landlord.
Example: Abel signs a 20-year lease for a warehouse. After 5 years, Abel no longer needs the warehouse and *assigns the lease* to Baker.

ASSIGNOR a party who assigns or transfers an agreement or contract to another.
Example: Davis has an option to buy certain land. She assigns her rights to Baker, so that Baker now has the same rights. Davis is the *assignor.* Baker is the **assignee.**

ASSOCIATE BROKER 1. in some states, a licensed **broker** whose license is held by another broker. 2. in Alabama, a real estate licensee whose status is the same as that of a **salesperson** in other states.

ASSUMABLE LOAN a mortgage loan which allows a new home purchaser to undertake the obligation of the loan with no change in loan terms. This is generally true of loans without **due-on-sale clauses.** Most FHA and VA mortgages are assumable.
Example: Abel sells a home with an *assumable loan* to Baker. Baker takes over the payments of the loan and accepts liability under the mortgage note.

ASSUMPTION FEE a charge levied by a lender on a buyer who assumes the existing loan on the subject property.
Example: When Acton purchased the home, he was able to assume the existing loan, which had very attractive terms, by paying an *assumption fee* of $500 to the lender, Standard Savings Association.

ASSUMPTION OF MORTGAGE the purchase of mortgaged property whereby the buyer accepts liability for the debt that continues to exist. The seller remains liable to the lender unless the lender agrees to release him.
Example: Abel owes a 30-year mortgage loan of $50,000 against his house. Baker wants to buy the house and keep the same mortgage. Baker pays $20,000 cash for the **equity** and *assumes* the mortgage. Baker becomes liable for the debt, but Abel remains liable also.

AT-RISK RULES tax laws that limit the amount of tax losses an investor (particularly a **limited partner**) can claim. *At-risk rules* were extended to real estate by the 1986 tax act, and apply to property placed in service after 1986. This means that losses on real estate investments will be deductible only to the extent of money the equity investor stands to lose.
Example: If an investor has $10,000 at risk in a real estate investment that generates $3,333 per year in tax losses, the losses may be used for only three years. Thereafter, the losses may be used only if the investor contributes more money or property (net of withdrawals) or becomes liable to repay borrowed money. Amount at-risk include:
• cash contributed to the activity
• borrowed money for which the investor is personally liable
• property pledged as security for the real estate activity, provided the property is not used in the activity
An exception is made for qualified third-party non-recourse financing. These loans may be treated as amounts at-risk provided:
• a third-party, unrelated to the investor, provides the loan
• the third-party lender is neither the seller of the property nor related to the seller
• the lender is not paid a fee with respect to the equity investor's investment in the property

Related parties. Non-recourse loans from related parties qualify as amounts at-risk only if the terms are "commercially reasonable" and on substantially the same terms as loans involving unrelated persons.

Partnerships. A partnership's non-recourse financing may increase a general or limited partner's amount at risk provided the financing is qualified non-recourse for both the partner and the partnership. However, the amount treated at risk cannot be more than the total qualified non-recourse financing at the partnership level.

ATTACHMENT legal seizure of property to force payment of a debt.

Example: The landlord obtained an *attachment* that created a **lien** on the tenant's property to enforce payment of back rent.

ATTEST to witness by observation and signature.

Example: Many contracts require a third party to *attest* to the signing by the principals.

ATTORNEY-IN-FACT one who is authorized to act for another under a power of attorney, which may be general or limited in scope.

Example: Collins wishes to sell her home but is planning a 6-month vacation in the Middle East. She gives authorization to her friend Baker to sign the **deed** over to a buyer. Baker becomes her *attorney-in-fact* for this situation.

ATTORNEY'S OPINION OF TITLE a written statement by an attorney, after examination of **public records** and/or **abstracts of title,** that in his or her judgment the title to a particular property is good.

Example: The Chicago Lawyers Land Title Company issued a title insurance policy after they read the *attorney's opinion of title* and accepted whatever risk it described.

ATTORNMENT a tenant's formal agreement to be a tenant of a new landlord.

Example: Abel defaulted on the mortgage against his shopping center, so the Happy Life Insurance Company **foreclosed** and became the landlord. Happy Life asked all tenants to sign an *attornment* recognizing the new landlord.

ATTRACTIVE NUISANCE an appealing but potentially hazardous feature or characteristic of a piece of real estate that may lure trespassers who could suffer harm; in law, the owner of an attractive nuisance must take extraordinary precautions to avoid liability for harm to trespassers.

Example: Glen installs a swimming pool in his backyard. It can lure children to trespass and use it, potentially causing an injury or drowning. To avoid liability, Glen must install unusually high, secure, and/or screening fences to keep them out.

AUCTION a way of marketing property to the highest bidder. **Bids** are taken verbally or simultaneously through mail or telegrams, and the property is sold to the highest bidder. Auctioning real estate may require both an auctioneer's license and a real estate license.

Example: Land in Iowa, since it is relatively homogeneous, lends itself to *auction* sales where it is sold to the highest verbal bidder.

Example: Fannie Mae agrees to buy mortgages once a week via an *auction*. Mortgage sellers state the price or yield they want, and Fannie Mae accepts the highest yields offered.

AUCTIONEER one who conducts an auction.

Example: Prior to the auction, the *auctioneer* placed ads in local papers and made the properties available for inspection. In addition, the *auctioneer* ran the auction by taking bids and providing sales contracts to the winners.

AVULSION the sudden removal of land from one parcel to another, when a body of water, such as a river, abruptly changes its channel. Contrast with **accretion**.

Example: Because of the change in the river's channel, in Figure 18 parcel A gains use of a portion of the land in the original river bed through *avulsion*. Similarly, parcel B loses land which is now covered by the river.

FIG. 18. AVULSION

B

BACKFILL the replacement of excavated earth into a hole or against a structure.
Example: Figure 19.

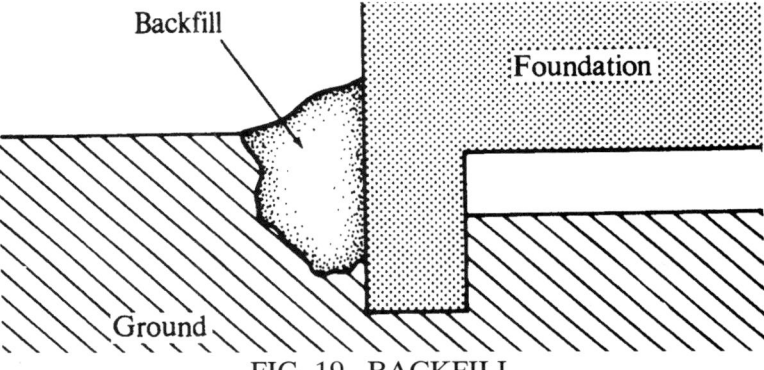

FIG. 19. BACKFILL

BACKUP CONTRACT a contract to buy real estate that becomes effective if a prior contract fails to be consummated.
Example: Abel contracts with Baker to sell a property contingent on Baker's ability to obtain financing within 30 days. In the meantime, Abel arranges a *backup contract* to sell to Collins, should Baker fail to obtain financing.

BALANCE, PRINCIPLE OF in **real estate appraisal,** there is an optimal mix of inputs that, when combined with land, will result in the greatest land value. Inputs, or factors of production, include labor, capital, and entrepreneurship.
Example: Suppose a **subdivider** was trying to determine how large building lots should be, by determining how much could be realized for the land at different **densities** of housing. She finds that 4 lots per acre is the proper balance because it yields the highest land value (see Table 4).

TABLE 4
BALANCING OF LAND VALUES

Lots per Acre	Price of Lot	Total per Acre
1	$25,000	$25,000
2	18,000	36,000
3	14,000	42,000
4	12,000	48,000
5	9,000	45,000
6	7,000	42,000

BALANCE SHEET

BALANCE SHEET a financial statement in table form showing **assets,** liabilities, and **equity,** in which assets equal the sum of **liabilities** plus **equity.**
Example: Table 5.

TABLE 5
BALANCE SHEET

Assets		Liabilities & Equity	
Cash	$ 1,000	Charge account debts	$ 500
Cars	5,000	Auto loan balance	2,000
Furniture	5,000	Home mortgage	28,500
House	50,000	Equity	40,000
Stocks	10,000		
Total assets	$71,000	Total liabilities & equity	$71,000

BALLOON MORTGAGE a mortgage with a **balloon payment.**
Example: The *balloon mortgage* called for payments of $500 per month for 5 years, followed by a **balloon payment** of $50,000.

BALLOON PAYMENT the final payment on a loan, when that payment is greater than the preceding installment payments and pays the loan in full.
Example: A debt requires interest-only payments annually for 5 years, at the end of which time the principal balance (a *balloon payment*) is due, as seen in Figure 20.

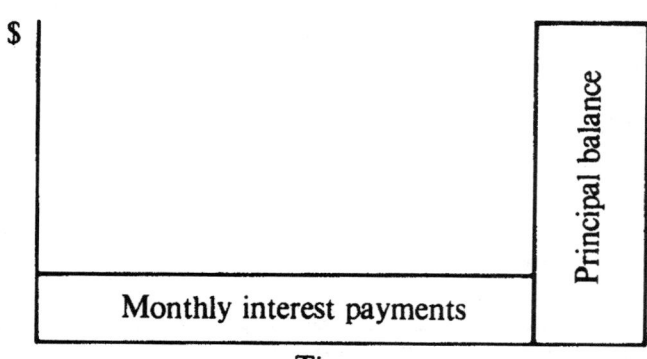

FIG. 20. BALLOON PAYMENT

BAND OF INVESTMENT an income property **appraisal** technique where the overall interest rate is derived from weighting **mortgage and equity** rates.

134

Example: Table 6.

TABLE 6
BAND OF INVESTMENT

Source of purchase capital	Percentage contributed	×	Rate of interest	=	Weighted rate
Mortgage	60%		15%		9%
Equity	40%		20%		8%
Band of investment rate					17%

BANKRUPTCY the financial inability to pay one's debts when due. The debtor seeks relief through court action that may work out or erase debts.
Example: Carter lost his job but continued to live extravagantly on **credit.** When accounts were overdue, Carter filed a *bankruptcy* petition. The court allowed him to pay creditors 10 cents per dollar of debt, payable over 3 years.

BARGAIN AND SALE DEED one in which the **grantor** implies to have or have had an interest in the property but offers no warranties of title to the grantee. This type of deed is typically used in many states to transfer title. Contrast **general warranty deed, quitclaim deed, special warranty deed.**
Example: Abel gives Baker a *bargain and sale deed* which includes no warranty of title but states, "for $10 and other valuable consideration, the grantor does hereby grant and release to the grantee, the following property."

BASE AND MERIDIAN imaginary lines used by **surveyors** to find and describe the location of land. The baseline is east-west; the meridian line is north-south.
Example: Principal *base and meridian* lines for Oklahoma (Figure 21).

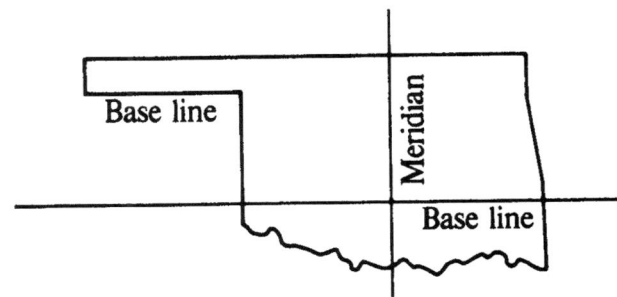

FIG. 21. BASELINE AND MERIDIAN LINE

BASELINE part of the **Rectangular Survey** or **Government Rectangular Survey** method of land description. The *baseline* is the major east-west line to which all north-south measurements refer.
Example: See **base and meridian.**

BASE PERIOD a point of time that serves as a benchmark for reflecting the change in an **index.** The *base period* is usually set equal to 1, 100%, or 100.
Example: The **Consumer Price Index** set the period 1982–1984 as the *base period*, equal to 100. If the index is 150 in 1994, it will have risen 50% from the base period.

BASE RENT the minimum rent due under a lease that has a percentage or participation requirement.
Example: Spinning Records leases retail space in Majestic Mall. Under the lease Spinning Records must pay a *base rent* of $2,000 per month plus 5% of all sales revenue over $50,000 per month.

BASIC INDUSTRY MULTIPLIER in economic base analysis, the ratio of total population in a local area to employment in basic industry. Basic industry is considered to be any concern which attracts income from outside the local area. The jobs added in basic industry may also contribute to the need for local service jobs (telephone operator, nurse, waitress, etc.); and, if the workers have families, additional new people may be brought to the area.
Example: The Maintown economic base has a *basic industry multiplier* of 6. It is estimated that each new job added at Maintown's basic industries will increase the town's population by 6.

BASIS (TAX) the point from which gains, losses, and **depreciation** deductions are computed. Generally the cost or purchase price of an asset.
Example: Collins purchases land for $10,000 and erects a store for $80,000. Her *tax basis* is $90,000. If she then sells the property for $95,000, she has a $5,000 gain. If she instead depreciates the property, the $80,000 cost basis of improvements is depreciable; the $10,000 *basis* of the land remains because land is not depreciable.

BASIS POINT one 100th of 1%.
Example: Mortgage loan interest rates are 12.75% this week. They were 12.25% last week. The increase was 50 *basis points* (1275 minus 1225 equals 50).

BEARER INSTRUMENT a **security** that does not indicate the owner; payable to whoever presents it.
Example: A *bearer instrument* is open to theft because it can be redeemed without proof of legitimate ownership.

BEDROOM COMMUNITY a residential community in the **suburbs,** often near an employment center, but itself providing few employment opportunities.
Example: *Bedroom communities* frequently offer uncrowded schools, uncongested streets, and less noise and air pollution than the nearby industrial city. However, property tax rates are generally higher than in the city.

BEFORE-AND-AFTER-RULE in an **eminent domain** award, many jurisdictions **appraise** the property value before the taking, then the property value after the taking, considering enhancement or injury to the **property** that was the result of **condemnation.**
Example: Farmer Brown's 1,000-acre farm is in the path of a proposed superhighway. The state has condemned a **tract** that is 200 feet wide and 1,000 feet long from the middle of Brown's farm. The state will pay at the rate of $1,500 per acre for the land taken. In addition, Brown seeks damages because the farm, now cut in two, has lost value from reduced accessibility. The remaining land is appraised *before and after* the taking to determine damages to be awarded.

BEFORE-TAX CASH FLOW **cash flow** prior to deducting income tax payments or adding income tax benefits. See **cash throw-off.**
Example: After deducting **debt service** of $500 from a **net operating income** of $1,000, Abel has a *before-tax cash flow* of $500.

BEFORE-TAX EQUITY REVERSION same as **after-tax proceeds from resale,** except it does not consider income taxes.

BELOW-MARKET INTEREST RATE (BMIR) in some government-subsidized housing, the owner is charged a low **interest rate** with the requirement that savings be passed on to **tenants** in the form of reduced **rent.**
Example: The market interest rate is 9% but a certain apartment complex pays only 1% interest because it is a *below-market interest rate* program. The savings must be pased on to tenants.

BENCHMARK a permanently affixed mark that establishes the exact elevation of a place; used by **surveyors** in measuring site elevations, or as a starting point for **surveys.**
Example: The U.S. Coast and Geodetic Survey implants brass markers in the sidewalks of downtown areas to serve as *benchmarks.* The benchmark indicates the official elevation above sea level for the spot at which the marker is placed.

137

BENEFICIARY the person who receives or is to receive the benefits resulting from certain acts.
Example: Whitman takes out a $10,000 life insurance policy with her husband as the *beneficiary*. Should Whitman die, her husband will receive the benefits from the policy.

BEQUEATH to specify by **will** the recipient of personal property. Compare **devise**.
Example: In Abel's will he *bequeaths* his automobile and wrist watch to his son.

BEQUEST that personal property given by the terms of a **will**.
Example: Collins received a set of sterling silverware as a *bequest* from her deceased aunt.

BETTERMENT an improvement to real estate.
Example: Abel purchases a **site** and constructs a building. The building is considered a *betterment* to the site.

BIANNUAL occurring twice a year. Same as **semiannual**. Contrast with **biennial**.
Example: Under a lease, Abel is required to make *biannual* rent payments, one in January and one in July (Figure 22).

FIG. 22. BIANNUAL PAYMENTS

BID the amount someone offers to pay.
Example: Abel places a property for sale at an **asking price** of $90,000. Baker makes a *bid* of $65,000 for the property, indicating he is willing to pay that amount for the property.

BIENNIAL occurring every 2 years.
Example: Abel arranges to pay premiums on a property insurance policy on a *biennial* basis. If the current premium is paid in 1993, the next premium is due in 1995 (Figure 23).

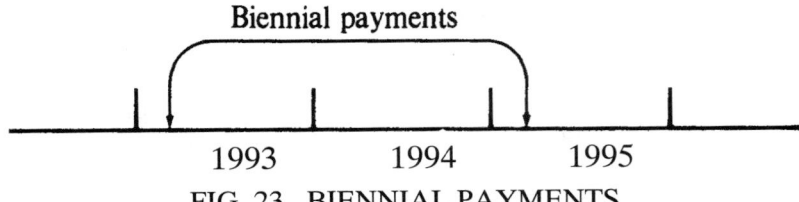

FIG. 23. BIENNIAL PAYMENTS

BILATERAL CONTRACT a contract under which each party promises performance. See **unilateral contract.**
Example: A sales contract is a *bilateral contract,* since the seller promises to **convey** a property and the buyer agrees to pay a specified sum, given certain conditions.

BI-LEVEL a house built on 2 levels in which the main entrance is situated above the lower level but below the upper level.
Example: Drawing of a *bi-level* house (Figure 24):

FIG. 24. BI-LEVEL HOUSE

BILL OF ASSURANCE the name given, in some states, to the total collection of **restrictive covenants** that apply to a group of contiguous lots.
Example: A subdivider gave a *Bill of Assurance* to purchasers of lots to provide comfort that the development had standards for high quality housing, such as minimum home sizes, architectural consistency, and the quality of exterior materials including garages, fences, and auxiliary buildings.

BILL OF SALE a written **instrument** given to pass **title** of personal property from a seller to a buyer. Used when furniture and portable appliances are sold.
Example: Figure 25.

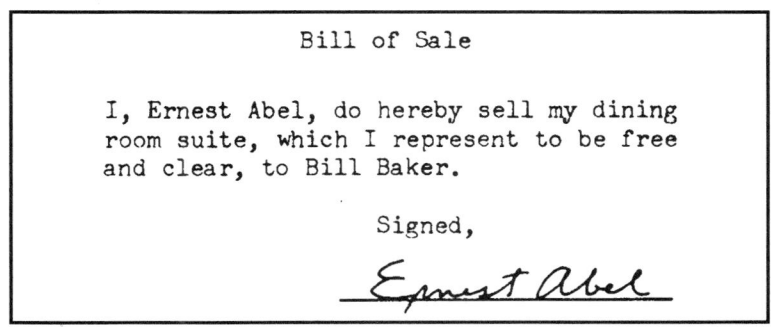

FIG. 25. BILL OF SALE

BINDER an agreement, accompanied by a **deposit,** for the purchase of real estate, to evidence **good faith** on the part of the purchaser.
Example: Abel gave Baker a *binder* on the house; Abel then contacted his attorney to prepare the papers for a contract.

BIWEEKLY LOAN a mortgage which requires principal and interest payments at two-week intervals. The payment is exactly half of what a monthly payment would be. Over a year's time, the 26 payments are equivalent to 13 monthly payments on a comparable mortgage loan. As a result, the loan will amortize much faster than loans with monthly payments.
Example: A 30-year mortgage for $70,000 at 12 percent interest requires monthly payments of $720. A *biweekly loan* for the same amount and interest rate requires a payment of $360 every two weeks. The biweekly mortgage will be fully amortized (paid off) after 19 years.

BLANKET MORTGAGE a single **mortgage** that covers more than one parcel of real estate.
Example: A developer subdivides a tract of land into lots and obtains a *blanket mortgage* on the whole tract. A **release** provision in the mortgage allows the developer to sell individual lots over time without **retiring** the entire mortgage.

BLEEDING A PROJECT 1. in new construction, overstating expenses and fees so as to divert a larger than normal amount of the project costs to the developer's profit.
Example 1: Bugsy's girl, Virginia, was *bleeding* the Flamingo project and put millions aside in a Swiss bank account.
2. managing an existing piece of real estate so as to obtain the higest possible current income from it, to the extent that many normal operating expenses are forgone. Usually this results in rapid deterioration and loss of property value.
Example 2: Maurice owns an apartment building. Instead of keeping it up, he *bleeds the project* by pocketing the money that would normally be used to pay for maintenance, etc.

BLENDED RATE an **interest rate,** applied to a **refinanced** loan, that is higher than the rate on the old loan but lower than the rate offered on new loans. Generally offered by the lender to induce home buyers to refinance existing, low-interest rate loans as an alternative to assuming the existing loan. Compare **assumption of mortgage.**
Example: Jones wishes to sell a home to Brown. Brown can assume the existing loan of $20,000 at an interest rate of 8%. Jones's lender offers the alternative of refinancing the loan for $40,000 at a *blended rate* of 10%. Brown could get a new loan at a rate of 12%.

BLIGHTED AREA a section of a city in which a majority of the structures are dilapidated.
Example: Urban renewal is planned for several *blighted areas* of the city. Within these areas, houses that do not meet **housing codes** are to be rehabilitated or demolished and new buildings constructed.

BLIND POOL an investment program in which monies are invested into an association without investors knowing which properties will be purchased.
Example: Each of 100 investors contributes $5,000 into a joint venture. The **syndicator** has not located the property to be purchased, so the investment money is said to be a *blind pool*.

BLOCKBUSTING a racially discriminatory and illegal practice of coercing a party to sell a home to someone of a minority race or ethnic background, then using scare tactics to cause others in the neighborhood to sell at depressed prices.
Example: A sales agent arranges a sale in which a minority family enters a previously all-white neighborhood. The agent then engages in *blockbusting* by contacting other owners in the neighborhood and informing them that their property's value will fall if they don't sell right away at a depressed offered price.

BLUEPRINT a detailed set of plans used as the guide for construction of a building.
Example: The architects' plans for the building were converted into a *blueprint* and provided to the general contractor prior to construction.

BLUE-SKY LAWS state laws requiring the offeror of securities to give full disclosure, and register the offering as required by federal and state law.
Example: A **syndicator** wishes to sell 10,000 units of a partnership to investors throughout the U.S. He registers the offering with the **Securities and Exchange Commission** and complies with *blue-sky laws* in 50 states. The term comes from fraudulent practices of exaggerated offerings to investors, including part of the blue sky.

BOARD OF EQUALIZATION a government entity whose purpose is to assure uniform property tax assessments.
Example: A *board of equalization* at the local level may review **assessments** to be certain that the assessment for each parcel is fair; at the state level, the board will assure that each county is assessing property at the mandated proportion of market value.

BOARD OF REALTORS® a local group of real estate licensees who are members of the State and **National Association of Realtors®.**
Example: The Springfield *Board of Realtors®* has 200 members. They meet monthly to discuss business matters, and form the **multiple listing** service in Springfield.

BOARD OF ZONING APPEALS see **appeals board.**

BOECKH BUILDING VALUATION MANUAL a book, frequently updated, that offers estimates of the **replacement cost** or **reproduction cost** for different types of buildings.
Address:
Boeckh
525 East Michigan
P.O. Box 664
Milwaukee, WI 53201-0664

BOILER PLATE standard language found in contracts. Preprinted material.
Example: Collins decided to lease her property. At a stationery store she finds a preprinted *boiler plate* form. She fills in rental rates and dates in the blank places, then asks her tenant, Baker, to sign the lease.

BOMA Building Owners and Managers Association.

BONA FIDE in **good faith,** without fraud.
Example: To be certain that the signatures to the deed were *bona fide,* the county clerk insisted they be **notarized.**

BOND a certificate that serves as evidence of a debt and of the terms under which it is undertaken. See **promissory note.**
Example: Abel loans $10,000 to Baker, who gives a **note** or *bond* to evidence the debt (Figure 26).

Bill Baker owes Ernest Abel $10,000, payable at maturity in 10 years with interest payable semiannually at 10%.

Signed

Bill Baker

Bill Baker
August 15, 1993

FIG. 26. BOND

BOOK DEPRECIATION same as **depreciation (accounting).**

BOOK VALUE the carrying amount of an **asset,** as shown on the books of a company. Generally the amount paid for an asset, less depreciation.
Example: X Corporation purchases a building for $100,000, then **depreciates** it by $10,000 on its financial statements. The *book value* was $100,000 and is now $90,000.

BOOT unlike property included to balance the value of like properties exchanged.
Example: In an exchange of property under **Section 1031** of the **Internal Revenue Code,** Collins exchanges her warehouse worth $100,000 and receives Baker's land worth $125,000. Collins pays $15,000 cash and a car worth $10,000 to *boot* in order to equalize the values of properties exchanged. The car and cash are *boot* (Figure 27).

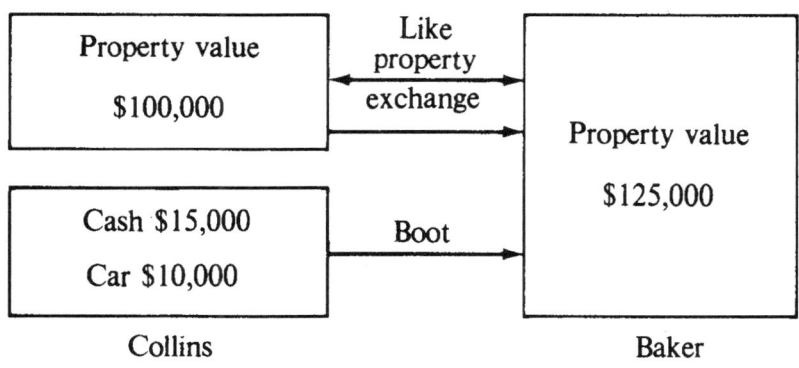

FIG. 27. BOOT

BOTTOMLAND 1. low land near a river, lake, stream, which is often flooded. See **flood plain.**
Example: Figure 28.

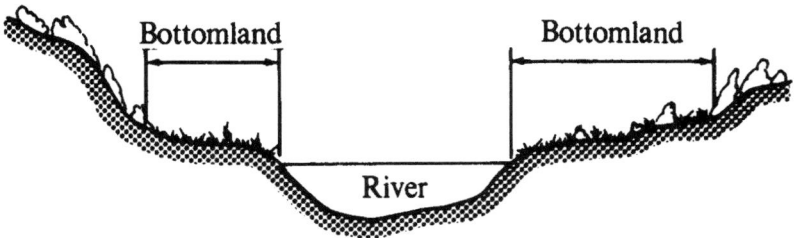

FIG. 28. BOTTOMLAND

2. land in a valley or dale.
Example: Figure 29.

FIG. 29. BOTTOMLAND

BOUNDARY same as **property line.**

BOY beginning of year.
Example: In most leases, rent is due at the beginning of each period. If a commercial lease requires annual payments, rent is due at the *beginning of the year* (*BOY*).

BREACH OF CONTRACT a violation of the terms of a legal agreement; **default.** Breach of contract allows the nonbreaching party to rescind the contract, sue for damages, or sue for performance of the contract.
Example: Baker contracts with owner Brown to purchase a property. When the closing date arrives, Brown refuses to **convey** title to the property. Brown's action is not supported by any special conditions in the sales contract and therefore constitutes a *breach of contract.* Baker may rescind the contract and recover his **deposit,** may sue Brown for any expenses and damages incurred, or may sue to force Brown to sell.

BREAK-EVEN POINT the amount of **rent** or the **occupancy level** needed to pay **operating expenses** and **debt service.** Also called **default** point.

$$\text{Break-even point} = \frac{\text{operating expenses and debt service}}{\text{potential gross income}}$$

Example: Annual operating expenses for a 100-unit apartment complex are estimated at $200,000 per year. Debt service requirements are $250,000 per year. Therefore, total cash requirements are $450,000. If all apartments are rented all year, the **gross income** would be $600,000. The *break-even point is* at 75% occupancy. At that level, gross income would exactly equal cash requirements.

BRIDGE LOAN mortgage financing between the termination of one loan and the beginning of another loan.
Example: Collins, who is a developer, has a construction loan outstanding. She is in the process of negotiating better terms for permanent financing than the commitment previously arranged. She has arranged a *bridge loan* to pay off the construction loan when it is due. When new permanent financing is arranged, that loan will pay off the bridge loan.

BROKER a state-licensed **agent** who, for a fee, acts for property owners in real estate transactions, within the scope of state law. **Example:** A person wishing to sell or lease property often engages a *broker* to arrange the sale or locate tenants. A broker may also be engaged by a prospective buyer or tenant to locate acceptable property.

BROKERAGE 1. the business of being a **broker.**
Example: One may open a *brokerage* office, upon receiving a broker's license, for the purpose of engaging in brokerage.
2. the **commission** received by a broker for his services.
Example: The *brokerage* was $6,000 on the sale of a $100,000 house.

BROWNSTONE, BRICK ROW HOUSE, OR EASTERN TOWNHOUSE a nineteenth-century-style house, usually having 4 or 5 stories with a stoop leading up to the first floor. There are common side walls with a house on either side.
Example: Figure 30.

FIG. 30. BROWNSTONE HOUSE

BUDGET MORTGAGE a **mortgage** that requires monthly payments for taxes and insurance in addition to interest and principal.
Example: Abel borrows $50,000 on a *budget mortgage* at 12% interest. His monthly mortgage payment is $700, which consists of $514 principal and interest, $150 taxes, and $36 insurance.

BUFFER ZONE a transitional area between 2 areas of different predominant land uses.
Example: In Figure 31 a *buffer zone* of **apartments** separates an area of **single-family** houses from a **commercial property** area:

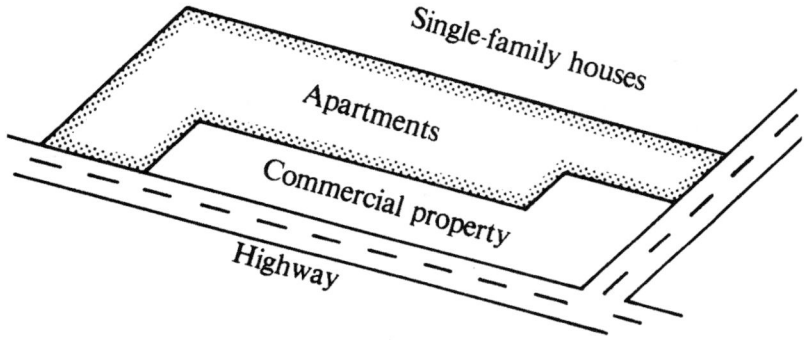

FIG. 31. BUFFER ZONE

BUILDERS AND SPONSORS PROFIT AND RISK ALLOWANCE (BSPRA) an amount above the cost of apartments that is allowed to be included in the project cost for purposes of determining the loan amount in certain government-sponsored programs.
Example: Since the actual cash cost to the developer is $1,827,272 (project cost + land cost), the *BSPRA* reduces the required cash for **equity** to a minimum amount, $27,272 in the example in Table 7.

TABLE 7
EFFECT OF BSPRA UPON LOAN AMOUNT

Project cost	$1,727,272
BSPRA allowance of 10%	172,728
Land cost	100,000
Total cost	$2,000,000
Loan at 90% of cost	$1,800,000

BUILDER WARRANTY a guarantee on the quality of construction offered by the developer or building contractor. See **homeowner warranty program.**
Example: Abel buys a newly built home. The home carries a

146

builder warranty which guarantees that the home is free of structural defects for a period of time.

BUILDING AND LOAN ASSOCIATIONS see **savings and loan associations.**

BUILDING CAPITALIZATION RATE in appraisal, the **capitalization rate** is used to convert an **income stream** into one lump sum value. The rate for the building may differ from that for the land because the building is a wasting asset.
Example: A **discount rate** of 10% is used as the land capitalization rate. The building, with a 50-year useful life, requires a 2% straight-line annual **capital recovery** rate. So the *building capitalization rate* is 12% (10% discount plus 2% capital recovery). If the building generates $15,000 annual income, its estimated value is $125,000 ($15,000 ÷ 0.12 = $125,000). (However, straight-line capital recovery is applicable only when a declining income stream is expected.)

BUILDING CODES regulations established by local governments describing the minimum structural requirements for buildings; includes foundation, roofing, plumbing, electrical, and other specifications for safety and sanitation.
Example: Abel is a developer who wishes to construct houses. He must comply with the standards of the local *building codes* and submit to inspections by a building inspector.

BUILDING EFFICIENCY RATIO see **efficiency ratio.**

BUILDING LINE a line fixed at a certain distance from the front and/or sides of a lot, beyond which the building may not project.
Example: Figure 32.

FIG. 32. BUILDING LINE

147

BUILDING LOAN AGREEMENT an agreement whereby the lender advances money to an owner at specified stages of construction, i.e., upon completion of the foundation, framing, etc. Same as **construction loan** agreement.

BUILDING OWNERS AND MANAGERS ASSOCIATION (BOMA) an organization of practitioners who own and manage buildings, notably office space.
Address:
Building Owners and Managers Association
1221 Massachusetts Avenue NW
Washington, DC 20005

BUILDING PERMIT permission granted by a local government to build a specific structure at a particular site.
Example: Abel desires to construct a small office building at the corner of First and Main. A *building permit* must be obtained from the city to allow the construction to proceed legally.

BUILDING RESIDUAL TECHNIQUE an **appraisal** technique whereby income to land is subtracted from **net operating income** to result in the building income. Building income is capitalized into building value.
Example: Table 8.

TABLE 8
BUILDING RESIDUAL TECHNIQUE

Net operating income	$13,000
Less: Land income	– 5,000
(Land value $50,000 × 10% rate of return)	
Building income	$ 8,000
Divided by building rate of return	÷ .12
(10% + 2% **depreciation**)	
Building value	$66,666

BUILDING RESTRICTIONS provisions in **building codes** that affect the orientation, size, and appearance of a building.
Example: Because of local *building restrictions*, Bond could not put the building as close to the highway as he wished, nor could he construct as large a building as he had envisioned.

BUILD TO SUIT an arrangement whereby a landowner offers to pay to construct on his or her land a building specified by a potential tenant, and then to lease land and building to the tenant.
Example: Beverly wants to open a restaurant. Rather than buy land and then pay to construct the needed facility, Beverly seeks a suitable site whose owner will *build to suit* and then lease to Beverly the land and building.

BUILT-INS appliances, machinery, and other equipment that are constructed as part of a building rather than left freestanding and moveable.
Example: Upon the sale of real estate, there is often a dispute concerning whether or not a **fixture** is **real property** or **personal property.** *Built-ins* normally are considered real property.

BULLET LOAN typically a loan with a 5- to 10-year **term** and no **amortization.** At the end of the term the full amount is due.
Example: Barry borrows $1 million for 5 years at 10% interest to buy commercial **real estate.** If he can't repay the loan or **refinance** it when due, he will lose the **property.**

BUNDLE OF RIGHTS THEORY the theory that ownership of realty implies a group of rights such as occupancy, use and enjoyment, and the right to sell, **bequeath,** give, or **lease** all or part of these rights.
Example: Under the *bundle of rights* concept, Abel may sell mineral rights, hunting rights, **easements,** and other partial interest, then give a **life estate** to his wife with the **remainder** to their daughter.

BUNGALOW a small, early-twentieth-century-style, 1-story house that usually has an open or enclosed front porch.
Example: Figure 33.

Open or enclosed front porch
1 story
Shingle roof

FIG. 33. BUNGALOW

BUREAU OF LAND MANAGEMENT an agency of the U.S. Department of the Interior that oversees the management of much of the land owned by the U.S. government, particularly national forests and other relatively undeveloped land.

Address:
Bureau of Land Management
C Street, between 18th and 19th Streets NW
Washington, DC 20240

BUSINESS DAY a standard day for conducting business. Excludes weekends and holidays.
Example: On Monday, July 1, Abel agrees to buy real estate. Closing will be 5 *business days* later, which is July 9 (Table 9).

TABLE 9
BUSINESS DAYS

		Business days
Tuesday	July 2	1
Wednesday	July 3	2
Thursday	July 4	holiday
Friday	July 5	3
Saturday	July 6	weekend
Sunday	July 7	weekend
Monday	July 8	4
Tuesday	July 9	5

BUY-BACK AGREEMENT a provision in a contract under which the seller agrees to repurchase the property at a stated price upon the occurrence of a specified event within a certain period of time.
Example: The *buy-back agreement* in the sales contract requires the builder-seller to buy the property back if Collins, the buyer-occupant, is transferred by her company within 6 months.

BUY DOWN 1. the action to pay additional **discount points** to a lender in exchange for a reduced rate of interest on a loan. The reduced rate may apply for all or a portion of the loan term. 2. a loan that has been bought down by the seller of the property for the benefit of the buyer.
Example: In order to achieve a sale of a property, Jones arranged for a *buy-down* loan. If a seller agreed to Jones's price, Jones would *buy down* the interest rate for the first 3 years by paying the lender 5% of the loan amount at closing.

BUYER'S BROKER an agent hired by a prospective purchaser to find an acceptable property for purchase. The broker then represents the buyer and negotiates with the seller in the purchaser's best interest.
Example: Abel wishes to purchase a small apartment complex. Abel hires Baker, a licensed real estate broker, to find such a property. Baker is acting as a *buyer's broker* and earns a com-

150

mission from Abel when an acceptable property is found and the owner is willing to sell.

BUYER'S MARKET　a situation where buyers have a wide choice of properties and may negotiate lower prices. Often caused by overbuilding, local population decreases, or economic slump.

Example: Abel can purchase properties below their appraised values because of the existence of a *buyer's market.*

BUY-SELL AGREEMENT　a pact among partners or stockholders under which some agree to buy the interests of others upon some event.

Example: Collins and Baker are partners. In the event Baker dies, Collins has agreed to buy Baker's interest for $25,000. If Collins dies first, Baker will buy her interest for $25,000.

BYLAWS　a set of regulations by which an organization conducts its activities.

Example: An association of **condominium** owners prepares *bylaws* that state the minimum number of owners to conduct a meeting, to decide on policies, to elect officers, and other matters.

C

CAI Community Associations Institute.

CALIFORNIA BUNGALOW a l-story, small, compact, early-twentieth-century house.
Example: Figure 34.

Small, compact shape l story

FIG. 34. CALIFORNIA BUNGALOW

CALIFORNIA RANCH a post–World War II style, 1-story, ground-hugging house with a low, pitched roof.
Example: Figure 35.

Low-pitched roof Picture windows Ground-hugging Sliding windows

l story

FIG. 35. CALIFORNIA RANCH

CALL PROVISIONS clauses in a loan that give the lender the right to accelerate the debt upon the occurrence of a specific event or date. See **acceleration clause.**
Example: Abel, the **mortgage** lender, notices that Baker, the homeowner, has begun to demolish the property. *Call provisions* in the loan allow Abel to claim that the full debt is now due.

CANCELLATION CLAUSE a contract provision that gives the right to terminate obligations upon the occurrence of specified conditions or events.
Example: A *cancellation clause* in a **lease** may allow the landlord to break the lease upon the sale of the building.

CAP in adjustable rate mortgages, a limit placed on adjustments to protect the borrower from large increases in the interest rate or the payment level. See **annual cap, life-of-loan cap, payment cap.**

CAPACITY OF PARTIES one of the requirements for a valid contract. Parties with less than full capacity include **minors,** the mentally insane, and those who are intoxicated.
Example: Collins, at age 17, entered into a contract to buy a tract of land. Collins can void that contract because it was entered into without full legal capacity.

CAPE COD COLONIAL an early-American-style 1½-story compact house that is small and symmetrical with a central entrance. The roof is the steep gable type covered with shingles. The authentic types have low central chimneys, but end chimneys are very common in the new versions. Bedrooms are on the first floor. The attic may be finished into additional bedrooms and a bath. A vine-covered picket fence is traditional.
Example: Figure 36.

FIG. 36. CAPE COD COLONIAL

153

CAPITAL ASSET an asset defined in **Section 1221** of the **Internal Revenue Code** that once received favorable tax treatment upon sale. Excludes **inventory,** property held for resale, property used in a trade or business, copyrights in certain instances, and certain U.S. government obligations.
Example: The dwelling that one owns and lives in, investment land, a limited partnership interest, or securities held for investment are *capital assets.*

CAPITAL CALLS additional money to be invested by equity owners to fund deficits in construction costs or operating costs.
Example: Bugsy's investors were asked for an additional $2 million as *capital calls* due to poor budgeting, cost estimation, cost controls, and project bleeding.

CAPITAL EXPENDITURE an improvement (as distinguished from a **repair**) that will have a life of more than one year. Capital expenditures are generally depreciated over their useful life, as distinguished from repairs, which are subtracted from income of the current year.
Example: Collins adds a new 25-room wing to her motel, at a cost of $250,000. The new wing is a *capital expenditure.*
Example: Baker, a rancher, has a fence that is in such poor condition it cannot be repaired. He makes a $50,000 *capital expenditure* to replace the fence.

CAPITAL GAIN gain on the sale of a **capital asset.** In 1991 and thereafter, the maximum individual tax rate on capital gains is 28%. There are limits on the deduction of **capital losses** against ordinary income.
Example: Collins purchases land, for investment purposes, for $10,000. Thirteen months later she sells it for $14,000. She reports the $4,000 profit as a long-term *capital gain* on her income tax return.

CAPITAL IMPROVEMENT same as **capital expenditure.**

CAPITAL LOSS loss from the sale of a **capital asset.**
Example: Collins, an investor, purchases land for $10,000. Two years later she sells it for $8,000. The $2,000 difference is a *capital loss,* since the land is a capital asset. Note: There are limitations on the amount of loss that can be used to offset **ordinary income.**

CAPITAL RECOVERY see **recapture rate.**

CAPITALIZATION 1. in finance, a process whereby anticipated future income is converted to one lump sum capital value. A **capitalization rate** is divided into the expected periodic income to derive a capital value for the expected income. Sum of **interest rate** and **recapture rate.** See **capitalization rate.**

Example: A property is expected to produce an annual income of $10,000. It is judged to have a value of $80,000, which represents *capitalization* of the $10,000 per year income stream. Also, when taxes on the property increased by $500 per year, the property's value was reduced by $6,000 due to the *capitalization* process.
2. in accounting, setting up an **asset** on the financial records, rather than deducting it currently.
Example: *Capitalization* is required for an asset that has a 15-year **depreciable life;** the cost will be deducted over that time period, not deducted currently.

CAPITALIZATION RATE a rate of return used to derive the capital value of an **income stream.** The formula is

$$\text{Value} = \frac{\text{annual income}}{\text{capitalization rate}}$$

Example: The estimated net operating income of an office building is $12,000 per year. An appraiser decides the appropriate *capitalization rate* is 12%, comprised of a 10% return on investment and 2% for **depreciation.** The estimated value of the building is $100,000.

CAPITALIZE 1. to estimate the present lump sum value of an **income stream.** See **capitalization rate.**
Example: An **income stream** of $1,000 per year expected for 20 years is *capitalized* to result in a value of $8,513, based on a 10% interest rate.
2. to set up the cost of an asset on financial records.
Example: Abel acquires a building at a cost of $100,000. Since the cost cannot be deducted in the year paid, the $100,000 is *capitalized* as an asset and **depreciates** over its estimated useful life.

CAPITALIZED VALUE the value estimated by converting an **income stream** into a lump sum amount.
Example: A small parking lot generates $10,000 of income each year. If the appropriate capitalization rate is 8% for this type of property, considering the quality and duration of the expected income, the *capitalized value* is $125,000. This is computed by dividing the $10,000 income stream by 8% (.08).

CAP RATE same as **capitalization rate.**

CAPTURE RATE the sales or leasing rate of a real estate development compared to the sales or leasing rate of all developments in the market area.
Example: Two thousand condominium units are built in a rapidly growing metropolitan area, including one project of 500 units built by the Gibraltar Development Company. Sales in the area during July are 200 units, of which half are sold by Gibraltar. Gibraltar's *capture rate is 50%.*

CARRYING CHARGES expenses necessary for holding property, such as taxes and interest on idle property or property under construction.
Example: The annual *carrying charges* on a $100,000 tract of land are: $2,000 for taxes and $12,000 for interest.

CARRYOVER BASIS in a tax-deferred exchange, the **adjusted tax basis** of the property surrendered that is used to determine the tax basis of the property acquired. See **basis (tax).**
Example: Abel exchanges land with Baker in a tax-deferred exchange. Abel's **adjusted tax basis** in the **land** given up was $10,000. The *carryover basis* will therefore be $10,000 and (in the absence of **boot**) that will be Abel's tax basis in the land acquired from Baker.

CASH EQUIVALENT the **conversion** of the price of **property** that sold with either favorable or unfavorable financing into the price the property would have sold for had the seller accepted all cash in the transaction.
Example: A **tract** of land sold for $100,000, with $25,000 cash and a $75,000 note to the seller at 6% **interest** with 20-year **amortization.** The market interest rate was 12% for such a mortgage. Although the mortgage carries a $75,000 **face value,** it is worth only $49,000. Therefore, the seller received a *cash equivalent* price of $74,000 ($25,000 cash plus a mortgage worth $49,000) in the transaction. This is much less than the $100,000 face amount.

CASH FLOW periodic amounts available to an **equity** investor after deducting all periodic cash payments from rental income. See **before-tax cash flow, cash throw-off, after-tax cash flow.**
Example: Table 10.

TABLE 10
STATEMENT OF CASH FLOW

Potential gross income	$10,000
Less: Vacancy and collection allowance	– 1,000
Add: Miscellaneous income	+ 500
Effective gross income	$ 9,500
Less: Operating expenses	– 3,000
Less: Replacement reserve	– 500
Net operating income	$ 6,000
Less: Interest	– 4,000
Less: Principal payment	– 500
Cash Flow	$ 1,500

CASH METHOD a method of accounting based on cash receipts and disbursements. Contrast **accrual method.**
Example: Abel, a *cash method* taxpayer, has the carpets in his office building shampooed on December 20 and immediately gets a bill for the service. He pays the bill on January 1 so the tax deduction is taken in the next year.

CASH-ON-CASH same as **equity dividend** rate.

CASH THROW-OFF same as **cash flow.**

CAVEAT EMPTOR "let the buyer beware." The buyer must examine the goods or property and buy at his own risk, except for **latent defects.**
Example: Often a property is offered "as is," with no expressed or implied guarantee of quality or condition. When entering such transactions, *caveat emptor* is a worthy admonishment.

CBD central business district.

CCIM **Certified Commercial Investment Member,** a professional designation of the **Realtors® National Market Institute (RNMI).**

CD certificate of deposit.

CENTRAL BUSINESS DISTRICT (CBD) the downtown section of a city, generally consisting of retail, office, hotel, entertainment, and governmental land uses with some high **density** housing.
Example: Office markets of the CBD are distinguished from those in the suburbs by market analysts.

CERTIFICATE OF DEPOSIT (CD) a type of savings account that carries a specified minimum deposit and **term** and generally provides a higher **yield** than passbook-type savings accounts.
Example: Carny purchased a 3-year *certificate of deposit* from Local Savings and Loan. Carny had to deposit at least $1,000 and could not withdraw the money for 3 years without forfeiting a portion of the interest earned. Carny received a yield of 8% annually.

CERTIFICATE OF ELIGIBILITY issued by the Veterans Administration to those who qualify for a **VA loan.**
Example: A person honorably discharged after serving a certain number of days on active duty in the armed forces is entitled to a *certificate of eligibility.* It indicates eligibility for a VA mortgage loan.

CERTIFICATE OF ESTOPPEL see **estoppel certificate.**

CERTIFICATE OF INSURANCE a document issued by an insurance company to verify the coverage.
Example: Under the **net lease,** the tenant had to keep adequate insurance and provide the landlord with a *certificate of insurance* as evidence.

CERTIFICATE OF NO DEFENSE same as **estoppel certificate.**

CERTIFICATE OF OCCUPANCY a document issued by a local government to a **developer** permitting the structure to be occupied by members of the public. Issuance of the certificate generally indicates that the building is in compliance with public health and **building codes.**
Example: Upon obtaining **zoning** and **subdivision** approvals and passing inspection by code enforcement officials, the developer is issued a *certificate of occupancy.*

CERTIFICATE OF REASONABLE VALUE a document issued by the Veteran's Administration, based on an approved **appraisal.** Establishes a ceiling on the maximum **VA mortgage loan** principal.
Example: A *certificate of reasonable value* (CRV) was received for a home that was under a **contract of sale.** Since the CRV was $1,000 more than the contracted price, the VA lent the full purchase price.

CERTIFICATE OF TITLE an opinion rendered by an attorney as to the status of **title** to a property, according to the public records. See **title search.**
Example: Abel's attorney issues a *certificate of title* that indicates no public record of claims against Abel's ownership of the property.

CERTIFIED COMMERCIAL INVESTMENT MEMBER (CCIM) a designation awarded by the **Realtors National Marketing Institute,** which is affiliated with the **National Association of Realtors®.**
Address:
Realtors National Marketing Institute
430 North Michigan Avenue
Chicago, IL 60611

CERTIFIED GENERAL APPRAISER one qualified to appraise any property, under the **appraiser** certification law recently adopted by most states. Usually requires at least two years of general appraisal experience, 150 hours of education, and passing a state examination.

Example: Jim Weaver met the requirements to be a state *certified general appraiser* and can appraise any property, including those with the involvement of federal government agencies such as the FDIC.

CERTIFIED HISTORIC STRUCTURE see **historic structure.**

CERTIFIED PROPERTY MANAGER (CPM) a professional designation awarded to real estate managers by the **Institute of Real Estate Management,** an affiliate of the **National Association of Realtors®.**
Address:
Institute of Real Estate Management
430 North Michigan Avenue
Chicago, IL 60611

CERTIFIED RESIDENTAL APPRAISER one qualified to **appraise** residences and up to 4 units of housing, under appraiser certification law. Standards call for less education, less experience, and less comprehensive exam than for General Certification.
Example: E.T. Jones is a *certified residential appraiser* and does much of the appraisal work for houses that are VA and FHA financed.

CERTIFIED RESIDENTIAL BROKER (CRB) a designation awarded by the **Realtors National Marketing Institute,** which is affiliated with the **National Association of Realtors®.**
Example: Upon completing the necessary requirements, Abel was awarded the title of *Certified Residential Broker.*

CERTIFIED RESIDENTIAL SPECIALIST (CRS) a professional designation awarded by the **Realtors National Marketing Institute,** based on education and experience in residential sales. Candidates must hold the **GRI** designation.

CHAIN a linear unit of land measurement used in surveying: 66 feet in length. Each chain consists of 100 links.
Example: A plot 66 ft. square measures 1 chain by 1 chain.

CHAIN OF TITLE a history of **conveyances** and **encumbrances** affecting a **title** from the time that the original **patent** was granted, or as far back as records are available. See **abstract of title, certificate of title.**
Example: An abstractor can research title to property going back to the date that the property was granted to the United States. This *chain of title is* helpful in preparing an attorney's **opinion of title,** as to whether the owner has a marketable or **insurable interest.** See **marketable title.**

CHATTEL personal property. Anything owned and tangible, other than real estate. See **personalty.**
Examples: Furniture, automobiles, and jewelry are all *chattels.*

CHATTEL MORTGAGE a pledge of personal property as **security** for a **debt.**
Example: Abel borrows money against his automobile; the lender grants a *chattel mortgage.*

CLEAR TITLE a **marketable title;** one free of **clouds** and disputed interests.
Example: It is necessary to obtain *clear title* in order to convey a **general warranty deed** in a transaction.

CLIENT the one who engages a **broker,** lawyer, accountant, **appraiser,** etc.
Example: Unless otherwise specified in the sales contract, the *client* of the broker, most often the seller, pays the brokerage commission.

CLOSED-END MORTGAGE a mortgage loan whose principal amount cannot be increased during the payout period; contrast with **open-end mortgage.**
Example: Most first mortgages on homes provide the full balance at origination of the loan. No additional debts are allowed under the mortgage because it is a *closed-end mortgage.*

CLOSING 1. the act of transferring ownership of a property from seller to buyer in accordance with a sales contract.
2. the time when a closing takes place.
Example: Abel agrees to purchase a property from Baker. A *closing* is set up for June 15, at which time Abel and Baker will sign all documents and pay all expenses necessary to transfer ownership and secure financing.

CLOSING COSTS various fees and expenses payable by the seller and buyer at the time of a real estate **closing** (also termed transaction costs).
Examples: The following are some closing costs:
• **brokerage** commissions
• lender **discount points**/other fees
• **title insurance** premium
• deed **recording** fees
• loan **prepayment penalty**
• **inspection** and **appraisal** fees
• attorney's fees

CLOSING DATE the date on which the seller delivers the **deed** and the buyer pays for the property.

Example: The sales contract generally establishes a *closing date,* at which time the parties will meet and settle all accounts necessary to transfer **title** to the property.

CLOSING STATEMENT an accounting of funds from a real estate sale, made to both the seller and the buyer separately. Most states require the **broker** to furnish accurate closing statements to all parties to the transaction.
Example: Table 11.

CLOUD ON THE TITLE an outstanding claim or **encumbrance** that, if valid, would affect or impair the owner's **title.** Compare **clear title.**
Example: Abel dies and in his will leaves land to Baker. Abel's widow is contesting the validity of Abel's will. During this period there is a *cloud* on Baker's *title* to the land.

TABLE 11
CLOSING STATEMENT

	Seller		Buyer	
	Debit	Credit	Debit	Credit
Real property		$40,000	$40,000	
Prepaid taxes		670	670	
Sales commission	$2,400			
Survey fee			75	
Cash paid by buyer to close				$40,745
Cash received by seller	38,270			
Totals	$40,670	$40,670	$40,745	$40,745

CLUSTER HOUSING a **subdivision** technique in which detached dwelling units are grouped relatively close together, leaving open spaces as **common areas.**
Example: A *cluster housing* development (Figure 37).

CMO collateralized mortgage obligation.

CODE see **building code, code of ethics, housing code.**

CODE OF ETHICS a statement of principles concerning the behavior of those who subscribe to the code.
Example: All Realtors® are required to subscribe to a *code of ethics* that defines proper professional behavior and practices that are considered unbecoming a professional real estate **agent.**

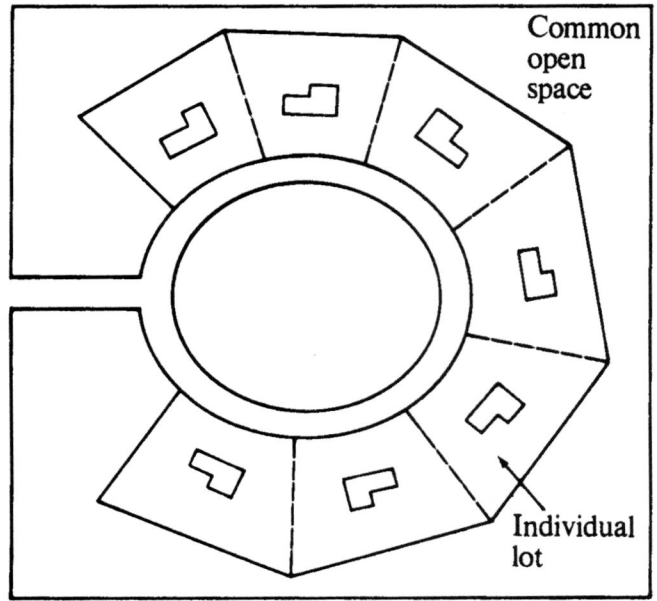

Common open space

Individual lot

FIG. 37. CLUSTER HOUSING

COINSURANCE a clause in an insurance policy stating the minimum percentage of value to be insured in order to collect the full amount of loss.

Example: Abel has a building worth $100,000. He figures that the maximum loss in the event of a disastrous fire will be $60,000, and insures it to $60,000. The policy has an 80% *coinsurance* clause. Since he did not insure it to 80% of its value, he will not receive the full amount of loss. The ratio he will receive is:

$$\frac{\text{amount carried}}{\substack{\text{amount should carry} \\ \text{(property value} \times \text{coinsurance rate)}}} = \frac{\$60,000}{\$80,000} \times \text{loss}$$

= maximum recovery, subject to maximum carried

COLD CANVASS the process of contacting homeowners in an area in order to solicit **listings.**

Example: Abel discovers a growing demand for older homes that are close to the central business district. To increase the number of listings of such homes, Abel *cold canvasses* several older neighborhoods to determine owners' interest in selling.

COLLAPSIBLE CORPORATION a term that applies to some corporations that are dissolved within 3 years. The IRS treats gain on the sale or **liquidation** of the corporation as **ordinary income** to the stockholder.

Example: Abel forms a corporation and is the sole stockholder. The corporation builds 50 houses and estimates that each is worth $10,000 more than it costs. Abel liquidates the corporation and claims a $500,000 **capital gain** on the corporate stock. The **Internal Revenue Service claims** the gain is ordinary income because of the existence of a *collapsible corporation.*

COLLATERAL property pledged as **security** for a **debt.**
Example: A borrower who arranges a **mortgage** loan pledges the property as *collateral.*

COLLATERALIZED MORTGAGE OBLIGATION (CMO) a security backed by a pool of mortgage loans that may be separated into various classes with varying maturities. Note that **REMICs,** introduced by the Tax Reform Act of 1986, are the standard vehicle for investing in mortgage instruments.
Example: Fidelity Savings and Loan pools $2 million worth of home mortgages to create a *collateralized mortgage obligation.* Investors in the *CMO* receive periodic interest and principal payments as well as return of principal as the loans are repaid.

COLOR OF TITLE that which appears to be good title but is not.
Example: Abel gives Baker a **deed** to land that he has never actually owned; Baker farms the land under a *color of title.*

COMMERCIAL BANK a financial institution authorized to provide a variety of financial services, including consumer and business loans (generally short-term), checking services, credit cards and savings accounts. Certain deposits at most commercial banks are insured by the **Federal Deposit Insurance Corporation.** Commercial banks may be members of the **Federal Reserve System.**
Example: Although *commercial banks* do make long-term mortgage loans, they have traditionally concentrated on short-term loans and are good sources for home-improvement loans and second loans secured by home equity.

COMMERCIAL BROKER one who **lists** and sells **commercial property,** which may include shopping, office, industrial, and apartment projects. Contrast **residential broker.**
Example: Collins sells apartment complexes to earn a brokerage fee. She is considered a *commercial broker* despite the fact that apartments are residences.

COMMERCIAL PROPERTY property designed for use by retail, wholesale, office, hotel, or service users.
Example: An investor is interested in purchasing *commercial property* for investment. A **broker** might show the investor

shopping centers, office buildings, hotels and motels, resorts or restaurants.

COMMINGLE to mingle or mix, such as the deposit of another's money in a broker's personal account.
Example: State law prohibits the *commingling* of **earnest money** deposits with a broker's own money. Most states require a separate account for earnest money held by a **broker.**

COMMISSION 1. an amount earned by a real estate broker for his services.
Example: Broker Roberts sells a $100,000 home for a client. At a 6% commission rate the client owes the broker a $6,000 *commission.*
2. the official body that enforces real estate license laws. See Figure 38.
Example: The State Real Estate *Commission* administers the real estate licensing examination, collects license fees, hears testimony from those who claim misconduct on the part of a licensee, and may punish offenders.

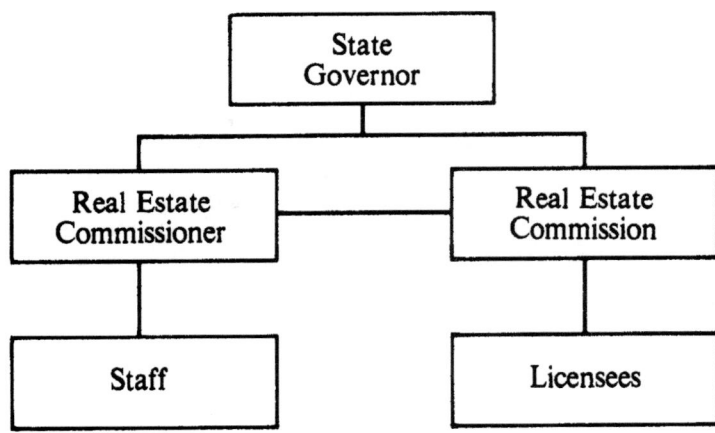

FIG. 38. STATE REAL ESTATE COMMISSION

COMMISSIONER the head administrator of the State **Real Estate Commission.**
Example: As *commissioner,* Jones is responsible for maintaining records of licensees and administering examinations (Figure 38).

COMMISSION SPLIT the arrangement of sharing commissions earned between a sales agent and sponsoring broker, or between the selling broker and listing broker. See **cooperating broker.**
Example: The seller of a $100,000 house paid a $6,000 commission at closing. The *commission split* was 50-50 between

the listing and selling brokers. Each broker then split the fee received with the sales agent responsible for the sale, in accordance with each firm's *commission split* schedule.

COMMITMENT a pledge or promise; a firm agreement.
Example: Collins obtains a *commitment* from a **savings and loan association** for a $100,000 loan on a house she wants to buy. She is then assured of the loan so business will proceed to **closing.**

COMMITMENT FEE a charge required by a lender to lock in specific terms on a loan at the time of application.
Example: When Collins applied for a loan to finance the apartment building she wanted to buy, the mortgage banker agreed to make the loan, at an interest reate of 9% with 2 discount points and covering 90% of value, in exchange for a *commitment fee* of 1% of the loan amount.

COMMITMENT LETTER an official notification to a borrower from a lender indicating that the borrower's loan application has been approved and stating the terms of the prospective loan.
Example: When Standard Mortgage Company completed the loan approval process, they sent Collins a *commitment letter* to inform her of the results. The letter than became a binding promise of Standard's intention to grant Collins the loan at the terms stated.

COMMON AREAS areas of a property that are used by all owners or tenants.
Examples: The following are examples of *common areas:*
• the clubhouse and pool of a condominium development
• the hallways and stairs of an apartment building
• the elevators in an office building
• the mall area of a shopping center

COMMON ELEMENTS in a **condominium,** those portions of the property not owned individually by unit owners but in which an indivisible interest is held by all unit owners. Generally includes the grounds, parking areas, recreational facilities, and external structure of the building. See **community association.**
Example: In a condominium building, each resident unit owner owns the interior space within that unit. The remainder of the building and **site** are *common elements* enjoyed by each resident according to the condominium bylaws. The common elements are maintained by the owners' association, to which each owner pays a fee.

COMMON LAW the body of law that has grown out of legal customs and practices that developed in England. Common law prevails unless superseded by other law.

Example: In many disputes between neighboring landowners over damages from the activities of one or the other, the courts apply *common law* to reach a settlement.

COMMUNITY ASSOCIATION general name for any organization of property owners to oversee some common interest. In a **condominium** or planned unit development, the association has the responsibility of managing the **common elements** in the project. A **homeowners' association** may be established in a **subdivision** to enforce deed **covenants.**

Example: The **Community Associations Institute (CAI)** is a not-for-profit organization to assist in the establishment and operation of *community associations.* Their materials are helpful in setting up the association, maintenance of common elements, enforcing bylaws, and collecting monthly fees.

COMMUNITY ASSOCIATIONS INSTITUTE (CAI) a non-profit educational and research organization concerned with the problems of managing homeowners' associations and other community associations (such as **condominium** owners associations). CAI sponsors educational seminars and publishes various handbooks and brochures.

Address:
Community Associations Institute
3000 South Eads Street
Arlington, VA 22202

COMMUNITY PROPERTY property accumulated through joint efforts of husband and wife and owned by them in equal shares. This doctrine of ownership now exists in Arizona, California, Idaho, Louisiana, Nevada, New Mexico, Texas, and Washington State.

Example: Mary and Jim are getting divorced. During their marriage she inherited $100,000, which is kept in a separate bank account. All other property was acquired during their marriage. Although she never worked outside the home, half of all property acquired by joint effort during the marriage is hers under the *community property* laws of the state. Her $100,000 is entirely her separate property.

COMMUNITY REINVESTMENT ACT a federal law that requires federal regulators of lending institutions to encourage lending within the local area of the institution, particularly to low- and moderate-income residents and those residing in inner-city neighborhoods. See **redlining.**

Example: An auditor from the **Office of Thrift Supervision** made a determination that the Federal Insured Savings Association of Small Town was raising money locally and investing in New York City, not following the *Community Reinvestment Act.*

CO-MORTGAGOR one who signs a **mortgage** contract with another party or parties and is thereby jointly obligated to repay the loan. Generally a co-mortgagor provides some assistance in meeting the requirements of the loan and receives a share of ownership in the encumbered property.
Example: Brown and Jones agree to purchase and share residence in a home. They jointly apply for and receive a mortgage loan to make the purchase and, thereby, become *co-mortgagors.*
Example: Sims wishes to assist her son to purchase a home. Sims provides a portion of the **down payment** money and signs the loan contract as a *co-mortgagor.*

COMPARABLES properties that are similar to the one being sold or appraised. See **market approach.**
Example: A subject property is a detached, 3-bedroom house that is 30 years old and will be bought with an **FHA loan.** *Comparables* would be recently sold houses with similar styling, age, location, and financing. Slight variations in characteristics may be taken into account when making the analysis.

COMPARATIVE SALES APPROACH same as **market comparison approach.**

COMPARATIVE UNIT METHOD an appraisal technique to establish relevant units as a guide to **appraising** the subject property.
Examples:
• Parking garages are compared per parking space.
• Bowling centers are compared per lane.
• Land may be sold per square foot or per **front foot.**

COMPARISON METHOD same as **market comparison approach.**

COMPETENT PARTIES persons legally capable of entering a **contract.** Must be of legal age, not be insane or a drunkard.
Example: If Abel is a **minor** he may generally **void** contracts he entered to buy or sell real estate because the law does not consider him to be a *competent party.*

COMPLETION BOND a legal instrument used to guarantee the completion of a development according to specifications. More encompassing than a **performance bond,** which assures that

one party will perform under a contract on condition that the other party performs. The completion bond assures production of the development without reference to any contract and without the requirement of payment to the **contractor.**

Example: A developer proposes to build a **subdivision** that necessitates a rezoning. The **zoning** commission requires the developer to post a *completion bond* prior to granting a permit for the development.

COMPONENT DEPRECIATION dividing real estate improvements into various parts such as the roof, plumbing, electrical system, and shell, then depreciating each component separately for tax purposes. Eliminated by the 1981 Tax Act, for acquisitions after 1980.

Example: Abel builds a shopping center. The $1 million total cost was spent on the components with useful lives indicated in Table 12. Abel claims *component depreciation* on each part based on its estimated useful life.

TABLE 12
COMPONENT DEPRECIATION

Roof	$100,000	15-year life
Plumbing	100,000	20-year life
Electrical	100,000	15-year life
Heating & A/C	100,000	10-year life
Paving	100,000	15-year life
Building foundation and structure	500,000	50-year life

COMPOUND AMOUNT OF ONE PER PERIOD the amount that a series of deposits of $1.00 per period would grow to if left on deposit with **interest** allowed to compound.

Example: See Table 13 below.

TABLE 13
GROWTH OF ONE AND ONE PER PERIOD
COMPOUNDED AT 8% INTEREST

Year	Compound Amount of 1	Compound Amount of 1 per Period
1	1.0800	1.0800
2	1.1664	2.2464
3	1.2597	3.5061
4	1.3605	4.8666
5	1.4693	6.3359

COMPOUND INTEREST interest paid on the original principal and also on the unpaid interest that has accumulated. Contrast with **simple interest.**
Example: $100 deposited in a 5% savings account earns $5 interest the first year. Its second-year earnings are 5% of $105, or $5.25. Each year, interest is received on previously earned but undistributed interest, so interest compounds.

COMPRESSED BUY-DOWN a **buy-down** loan for which the extent of rate reduction is changed in 6-month intervals. Many buy-downs feature a deep discount in the first year that is reduced gradually each year. The compressed buy-down is a variation of this type with accelerated gradations.
Example: Table 14 compares the interest rate on a regular 3-2-1 buy-down with a *compressed buy-down* of the same form.

TABLE 14
3-2-1 BUY-DOWN AND COMPRESSED BUY-DOWN

Months	Regular	Compressed
1–6	6%	6%
7–12	6	7
13–18	7	8
19–24	7	9
25–36	8	9
37–48	9	9

COMPS appraisal term, short for **comparables.**

CONCESSIONS benefits granted by a seller/**lessor** to induce a sale/**lease.**
Example: Abel is leasing out space in an office building. In order to get the Granite Insurance Co. to sign a lease, Abel offers a *concession* in the form of a $2,000 remodeling allowance.
Example: Baker is converting apartments to **condominium** units. In order to induce tenants to purchase their units, Baker offers a *concession* of a 20% discount on the sales price, available only to tenants.

CONDEMNATION 1. taking private property for public use with compensation to the owner under **eminent domain.** Used by governments to acquire land for streets, parks, schools, etc., and by utilities to acquire necessary property. Compare **appropriation.**
Example: Abel's home is in the **right-of-way** of the new highway. When Abel refused to sell, the highway department acquired the property through *condemnation,* paying Abel an amount based on a **fair market value** appraisal.

2. declaring a structure unfit for use.

Example: The state health department, acting through its *condemnation* powers, prevented use of an old, dilapidated shack because of violations of the **housing code.**

CONDITION(S) provision(s) in a contract that some or all terms of the contract will be altered or cease to exist upon a certain event. See **cancellation clause.**

Example: If a house is destroyed by fire before closing, the buyer is not obligated to complete the purchase.

Example: If a loan that is described as a *condition* cannot be arranged, the buyer is not required to complete the transaction and may receive a refund of any **earnest money.**

CONDITIONAL COMMITMENT an agreement by a lender to provide a loan to a qualified borrower, within a specified time period, but without stating who the borrower will be.

Example: The Solid Rock Development Company is completing a project with 200 condominiums. They arrange financing with the Trusty Mortgage Company to provide 90% loan-to-value financing at a 10% interest rate to qualified buyers. Trusty Mortgage issues a *conditional commitment* and will make such loans to qualified buyers.

CONDITIONAL OFFER purchase contract tendered to the seller that stipulates one or more requirements to be satisfied before the purchaser is obligated to buy.

Example: Baker offers to buy Collins's farm, conditioned on its rezoning for use as a shopping center prior to purchase. If it is not rezoned, Baker can get the earnest money, tendered with the *conditional offer,* refunded.

CONDITIONAL SALES CONTRACT a contract for the sale of property stating that the seller retains **title** until the conditions of the contract have been fulfilled.

Example: A **contract for deed** or a **land contract** is a *conditional sales contract.* Until the buyer makes full payment, the seller retains title to the property.

CONDOMINIUM a system of ownership of individual units in a multiunit structure, combined with joint ownership of commonly used property (sidewalks, hallways, stairs, etc.). See **common elements.**

Example: A midrise *condominium* (Figure 39).

CONDOMINIUM CONVERSION see **conversion.**

CONDOMINIUM DECLARATION see **declaration.**

Individual units

Common elements

Parking

FIG. 39. MIDRISE CONDOMINIUM

CONDOMINIUM OWNERS ASSOCIATION an organization of all unit owners in a **condominium** to oversee the **common elements** and enforce the bylaws. See **community association.**
Example: When Vivian and Paul Carter purchase a unit in the condominium, they are automatically members of the *owners association.* As such, they are entitled to vote on decisions before the association regarding changes in bylaws, development and repair of common elements, and other matters. They are also required to pay a monthly fee to cover expenses of the association.

CONFORMING LOAN a mortgage loan that is eligible for purchase by **FNMA** or **FHLMC.**
Example: In 1992, the maximum size of a loan that could be purchased by FNMA or FHLMC, or *conforming loan,* was $202,300 when secured by a single-family home ($303,450 in Alaska, Hawaii, and Guam.) The limit is revised each year according to the change in average sales price of conventionally financed single-family homes.

CONFORMITY PRINCIPLE an **appraisal** principle that holds that property tends to reach maximum value when the neighborhood is reasonably homogeneous in social and economic activity.
Example: Under the *conformity principle,* a house that cost $300,000 in a neighborhood of $100,000 homes is not worth as much as if it were in a neighborhood of $300,000 homes.

CONSIDERATION anything of value given to induce entering into a **contract;** it may be money, personal services, a product, etc.

171

Example: Abel ran out of gasoline while driving down the highway. Baker, a passing motorist, gave him a ride to the nearest filling station. Abel promised Baker a $50,000 tract of land for his help, but Baker cannot enforce the promise because of the absence of *consideration.*

CONSIGNMENT in real estate finance, the process in which the **FSLIC** replaces the management of an insolvent savings and loan association, but allows the association to continue operating. **Example:** Under the **Southwest Plan,** many savings and loan associations in Texas were placed under a *consignment* program, in which experienced managers from other S&Ls were recruited to run the associations under federal supervision.

CONSOLIDATED METROPOLITAN STATISTICAL AREA (CMSA) see **primary metropolitan statistical area.**

CONSTANT same as **mortgage constant.**

CONSTANT ANNUAL PERCENT same as **mortgage constant.**

CONSTANT PAYMENT LOAN a loan on which equal payments are made periodically so as to pay off the debt when the last payment is made. See **level payment mortgage, variable payment plan.**
Example: Baker obtains a *constant payment loan* to purchase a home. The loan requires a payment of $450 per month (principal and interest) for 30 years. At the end of 30 years, the principal balance will be zero.

CONSTRUCTION LOAN one that finances **subdivision** costs and/or improvements to real estate. See **building loan agreements.**
Example: Collins plans to develop an office building. She receives a **commitment** for permanent financing and approaches a **commercial bank** for a *construction loan.* The bank agrees to advance money as construction progresses (Figure 40).

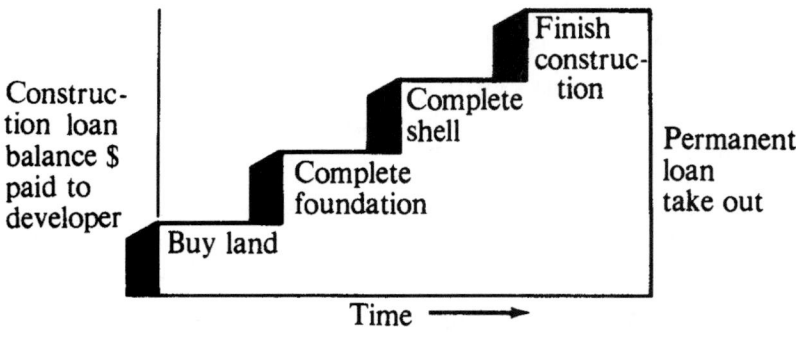

FIG. 40. •CONSTRUCTION LOAN

CONSTRUCTIVE EVICTION the legal term describing a situation in which a lessor's breach of a lease contract causes the lessee (tenant) to cancel the contract and vacate.
Example: Evelyn's landlord keeps coming into her apartment unannounced, in violation of the lease, which requires 24-hour notice. Eventually Evelyn vacates and refuses to pay rent any further, claiming *constructive eviction*, in that the landlord's instrusions violated the lease and her right of **quiet enjoyment.**

CONSTRUCTIVE NOTICE the law presumes that everyone has knowledge of a fact when the fact is a matter of public record.
Example: Abel buys land from Baker, believing that Baker is the owner. Since Carter's **deed** had been properly recorded, Abel had *constructive notice* of Carter's ownership and cannot claim ownership against Carter.

CONSTRUCTIVE RECEIPT 1. for tax purposes, the right to receive money that would be taxable and is taxable, even if receipt is postponed.
Example: Charles received a dividend check on December 20, 1992, but didn't deposit it until January 1993. The money was *constructively received* in 1992 and becomes part of Charles's taxable income for that year.
2. in real estate **exchanges,** the receipt of cash or other non-like-kind property or the acquisition of the right to use or benefit from such cash or property during an exchange transaction.
Example: Cohn entered into a delayed-exchange transaction in which his property was relinquished for property to be delivered later. As part of the transaction, a sum of money was deposited in Cohn's bank account to be used for acquiring the replacement property. Though Cohn never received this cash, the Internal Revenue Service denied nonrecognition of gain because of his *constructive receipt* of the money.

CONSUMER PRICE INDEX the most widely known of many such measures of price levels and inflation that are reported to the U.S. government. It measures and compares, from month to month, the total cost of a statistically determined "typical market basket" of goods and services consumed by U.S. households.
Example: The *Consumer Price Index* for May 1992 stood at 139.7. Compared to the base period of 1982–1984, prices were almost 40% higher.

CONTIGUOUS actually touching; contiguous properties have a common boundary.
Example: Lots A and B in Figure 41 are *contiguous*. Lot C is **adjacent** to A and B but not *contiguous*.

173

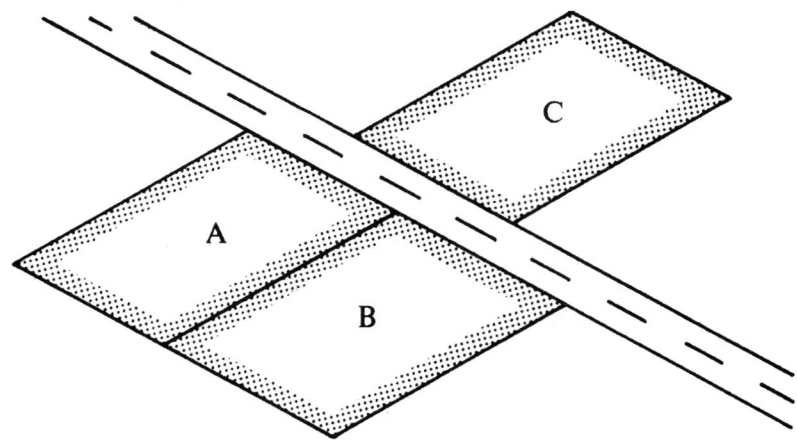

FIG. 41. CONTIGUOUS PROPERTY

CONTINGENCY CLAUSE see **condition.**

CONTOUR MAP a map that displays the **topography** of the **site.** A map with contour lines that indicate various elevations. **Example:** A *contour map* of a building site (Figure 42).

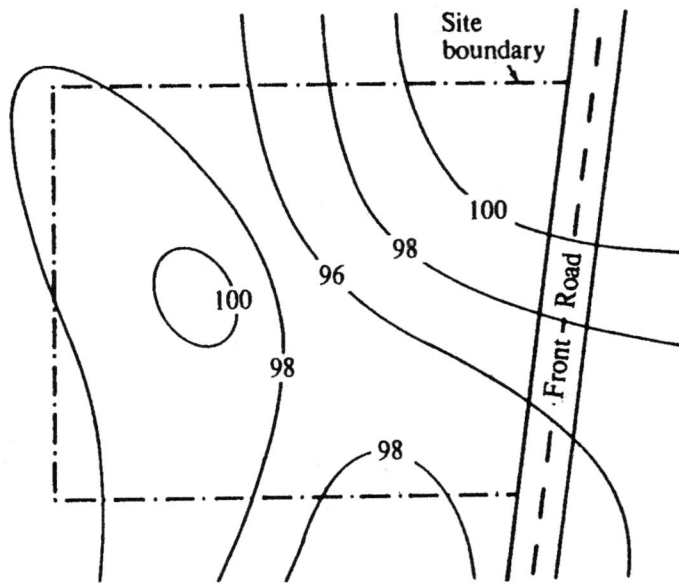

FIG. 42. CONTOUR MAP

CONTRACT an agreement between competent parties to do or not to do certain things for a **consideration.**

174

Example: To have a valid *contract* for the sale of real estate there must be:
1. an **offer**
2. an **acceptance**
3. **competent parties**
4. **consideration**
5. **legal purpose**
6. **written documentation**
7. **description of the property**
8. **signatures by principals** or their **attorney-in-fact**

CONTRACT FOR DEED same as **land contract.**

CONTRACT OF SALE same as **agreement of sale.**

CONTRACTOR one who contracts to supply specific goods or services, generally in connection with development of a property.
Example: Abel is developing a residential **subdivision.** In the course of the project, Abel secures the services of various *contractors,* such as landscapers, carpenters, plumbers, and architects.

CONTRACT PRICE (TAX) in an **installment sale,** for tax purposes, generally the selling price less existing mortgages assumed by the buyer. See also **installment sale.**
Example: Abel sells land for $100,000 subject to an existing $60,000 first mortgage. Abel receives $5,000 cash in the year of sale and a $35,000 second mortgage from the buyer. The *contract price* is $40,000. Note, if Abel's **adjusted tax basis** in the land exceeds the first mortgage, such excess is a payment in the year and reduces the contract price.

CONTRACT RATE same as **face interest rate.**

CONTRACT RENT the amount of rent that has been set forth in a contract. Contrast with **economic rent.**
Example: Abel signs a lease requiring rent payments of $400 per month. The *contract rent is* $400 per month.

CONTRIBUTION a principle of valuation that states that the value of any portion of a property is determined by how it affects the performance of the total property. Therefore, a property is considered a combination of features, each of which adds something to the total value based on its *contribution* to the property's usefulness.
Example: The value of an improvement can be appraised based on the principle of *contribution.* If a swimming pool adds $25,000 to the value of a house in a prestigious San Diego neighborhood, then its *contribution is* $25,000 regardless of what it costs to build.

CONVENTIONAL LOAN 1. a mortgage loan other than one guaranteed by the Veterans Administration or insured by the **Federal Housing Administration.** See **VA loan, FHA loan.**
Example: Abel applies for a *conventional loan* from his **savings and loan association.** If Abel wants to borrow more than 80% of the value of the mortgaged property, he must buy private **mortgage insurance.**
2. a fixed-rate, fixed-term mortgage loan.
Example: Alternative mortgage instruments, by commonly used definition, are not *conventional loans.*
Example: A *conventional mortage loan* requires a fixed principal and interest payment over its term.

CONVERSION 1. changing property to a different use or form of ownership, such as when **apartments** are transformed to **condominiums.**
Example: A **condominium** *conversion* allows existing tenants to remain until the expiration of their **lease** and often allows them to purchase the unit at terms more favorable than those offered to general public.
2. the taking away of property that belongs to another person. See also **involuntary conversion.**
Example: An illegal *conversion* of the landlord's property occurred when the tenant removed the landlord's light fixture from the apartment.
3. a change in the ownership form of a **savings and loan association.**
Example: Friendly Savings applies to the **Federal Home Loan Bank** Board for *conversion* from a **mutual savings bank** to a stockholder-owned company.

CONVERTIBLE ARM an **adustable rate mortgage** that offers the borrower the option to convert payments to a fixed-rate schedule at a specified period within the term of the loan. Conversion is made for a nominal fee, and the interest rate on the fixed-rate loan is determined by a rule specified in the ARM loan agreement.
Example: Conroy obtained a *convertible ARM* that allows him to convert the loan to a fixed-rate loan anytime between the second and tenth year of the loan term. Conversion will cost Conroy $100, and the interest rate on the new loan will be 1 percentage point above the average contract rate on fixed-rate mortgage loans closed in the nation during the previous month. The amortization term of the new loan will be 25 years from the time of conversion.

CONVEY to **deed** or transfer **title** to another.
Example: At the **closing,** Abel will *convey* the property to Baker.

CONVEYANCE the transfer of the **title** of real estate from one to another; the means or medium by which title of real estate is transferred.
Example: A **warranty deed** is most often used as a *conveyance* at the **closing.**

CO-OP 1. an arrangement between 2 real estate **agents** that generally results in splitting the **commission** between them.
Example: Abel obtains a **listing** contract on a piece of property. Baker agrees to find a buyer in exchange for a portion of the commission. Abel and Baker have arranged a *co-op* agreement.
2. a type of housing in which each tenant is a shareholder in a **corporation** that owns the building. Also termed **cooperative.**
Example: Upon moving to New York, Abel obtains an apartment in a *co-op*. This requires purchase of shares in the apartment corporation.

COOPERATING BROKER one who agrees to share the **commission** with another broker. See **commission split.**
Example: The broker who secured the listing is a *cooperating broker* with the one who brought the purchaser. The brokers agree to a **commission split.**

COOPERATIVE a type of corporate ownership of real property whereby stockholders of the corporation are entitled to use a certain dwelling unit or other units of space. Special income tax laws allow the tenant stockholders to deduct interest and property taxes paid by the corporation. See **co-op.**
Example: Apartment buildings in New York City are occasionally converted to *cooperatives*. In simple terms, this requires forming a **corporation** to own the building and selling shares to those who wish to live in the building.

CORPORATION a legal entity properly registered with the secretary of state. Can have **limited liability,** perpetual life, freely transferable shares, and centralized management.
Example: Abel wants to start a real estate **brokerage** business with $10,000 of his own money. He asks his attorney to form a *corporation* with Abel as the sole stockholder. The corporation may **bankrupt** but Abel's other assets are not affected.

CORPOREAL visible or tangible real or personal property.
Example: Buildings, pavement, fences, and the like are *corporeal*. **Easements** are incorporeal.

COSIGNER same as **accommodation party.**

COST APPROACH a method of **appraising** property based on the **depreciated** reproduction or replacement cost (new) of improvements, plus the market value of the **site.**

177

Example: Table 15.

TABLE 15
COST APPROACH

Reproduction cost (new)		$100,000
Minus: Physical deterioration	$25,000	
Functional obsolescence	10,000	
Economic obsolescence	5,000	
Total accrued depreciation	$40,000	– 40,000
Depreciated value of improvements		$ 60,000
Add: Site value		20,000
Value indicated by *cost approach*		$ 80,000

COST ESTIMATNG in construction, the act of predicting the total costs of labor, materials, capital, and professional fees required to construct a proposed project.
Example: When *cost estimating* the new hospital, Superior Engineering Company took into account the current costs of building materials, the labor supply situation, and the short-term interest rates available from local construction lenders.

COST OF LIVING INDEX an indicator of the current price level for goods and services related to some base year.
Example: The Consumer Price Index (CPI), published by the Bureau of Labor Statistics, indicates that the price level for goods and services in April 1992 was 139.5. This means that, on average, prices were 39.5% higher in April 1992 than in 1982–84.

COST-PLUS-PERCENTAGE CONTRACT an agreement on a construction project in which the contractor is provided a specified percentage profit over and above the actual costs of construction. These contracts are considered poor business practice because the contractor has little incentive to hold down costs. A cost-plus-fixed-fee contract is a better approach.
Example: Smith Construction Company entered into a *cost-plus-percentage contract* to build the new high school. Smith will get 10% above the costs of construction. If the project costs $10 million, Smith will receive $11 million to complete the project.

COTENANCY any of a number of forms of multiple ownership such as **tenancy in common** and **joint tenancy.**
Example: Abel and Baker decide to invest in a parcel of land. Both names are to be on the **deed.** Abel and Baker join together as *cotenants;* each owns one half of the property.

COUNSELING the act of advising clients on a variety of real estate investment or development matters.

Example: Abel wishes to invest in an office building. Baker offers *counseling* by advising Abel on how to select a property, how to legally structure the investment and how to maximize after-tax returns from the investment.

COUNSELOR OF REAL ESTATE (CRE) a member of the **American Society of Real Estate Counselors (ASREC).** Membership is based on experience and professional conduct as a real estate counselor.

COUNTEROFFER rejection of an **offer** to buy or sell, with a simultaneous substitute offer.
Example: A property is put on the market. An investor offers $75,000 in cash. The owner rejects the offer but submits a *counteroffer* to sell for $80,000. Offers and counteroffers may be negotiated on factors other than price, e.g., **financing** arrangements, **apportionment** of **closing costs,** inclusion of personal property.

COVENANT NOT TO COMPETE a clause in an agreement where one party promises not to offer to sell or produce the same goods and services in proximity to the other party.
Example: Abel sells his realty firm to Baker. In the sales contract, Abel gives Baker a *covenant not to compete.* This bars Abel from opening a competing realty firm in the same immediate area as Baker.

COVENANT RUNNING WITH THE LAND a covenant restricting or limiting property rights to land, or a deed restriction, in which it is specified that ownership of the land cannot be transferred unless the new owner agrees to continue to abide by the covenant.
Example: A group of owners of building lots agree in a contract (a) that each will use his or her lot only for a single-family dwelling and (b) that each will require that any purchaser of their land agree to the same contract. This contract (covenant) then *runs with the land*, because all owners, present and future, must abide by it.

COVENANTS promises written into **deeds** and other instruments agreeing to performance or nonperformance of certain acts, or requiring or preventing certain uses of the property.
Examples: Deed *covenants* are often used to:
• maintain a land parcel in a specified use, such as residential
• enforce architectural and design standards
• control the **density** of future development
• prohibit certain practices, such as the sale of liquor

CPI consumer price index.

CPM Certified Property Manager, a professional designation of the **Institute of Real Estate Management (IREM).**

CRAM DOWN in **bankruptcy,** the reduction of various classes of **debt** to a lower amount, with acceptance by the bankruptcy court.
Example: The bankruptcy judge considered the $100,000 property value that was encumbered by a $90,000 first mortgage and $25,000 unsecured debt. He allowed $90,000 to the first mortgage holders, and *crammed down* the $25,000 unsecured debt to $10,000.

CRB Certified Real Estate Brokerage Manager, a professional designation of the **Realtors® National Marketing Institute (RNMI).**

CRE Counselor of Real Estate, or member of the **American Society of Real Estate Counselors (ASREC).**

CREATIVE FINANCING any **financing** arrangement other than a traditional **mortgage** from a third-party lending institution.
Examples: *Creative financing* devices include:
• loans from the seller
• **balloon payment** loans
• **wraparound mortgages**
• **assumption of mortgage**
• **sale-leasebacks**
• **land contracts**
• alternative mortgage instruments

CREDIT 1. in finance, the availability of money.
Example: When money and *credit* are readily available, it is easier to buy real estate. Credit policy is determined to a large extent by the **Federal Reserve System.**
2. in accounting, a **liability** or **equity** entered on the right side of the ledger.
Example: In **closing statements,** the *credit* column shows what is due and payable. The buyer is *credited* with amounts paid; the seller is *credited* with the price of the real property and prepaid items.

CREDITOR one who is owed money.
Examples: *Creditors* include:
• bond holders
• loan companies
• mortgage lenders

CREDIT RATING (REPORT) an evaluation of a person's capacity (or history) of debt repayment. Generally available for

individuals from a local retail credit association; for businesses by companies such as Dunn & Bradstreet; and for publicly held bonds by Moody's, Standard & Poors, and Fitch's. Individuals have access to their own files.

Example: Goodmoney Savings Association received and studied the *credit report* on Collins before they issued her a mortgage loan. The report stated credit limits at various stores, current balances, and repayment terms in days. It would have noted **defaults** and slow repayments.

CRS Certified Residential Specialist, a professional designation of the **Realtors® National Marketing Institute (RNMI)**.

CUL-DE-SAC a street with an intersection on one end and a closed turning area on the other. Often valued in the design of residential **subdivisions** for the privacy provided to homes on the street.

Example: A **subdivision** plan showing a *cul-de-sac* (Figure 43).

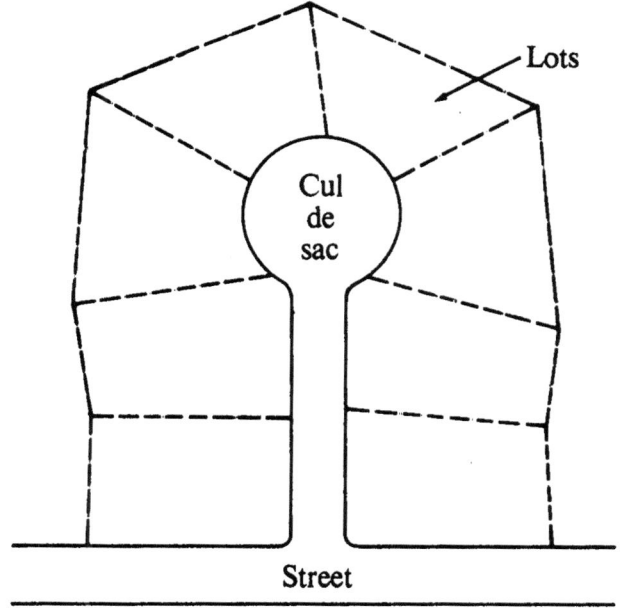

FIG. 43. CUL-DE-SAC

CURABLE DEPRECIATION depreciation or deterioration that can be corrected at a cost less than the value that will be added.

Example: An apartment owner estimates that remodeling the dwelling units would allow an increase in rent of $20 per month. The cost of remodeling is $1,500 per unit. The prevailing **gross rent multiplier** in the neighborhood is 100. Thus the

value added by remodeling is $100 \times \$20 = \$2,000$ per unit. Thus, the outmoded appearance of the units is a form of *curable depreciation.*

CURRENT YIELD a measurement of investment returns based on the percentage relationship of annual cash income to the investment cost. The formula is

$$\text{Current yield} = \frac{\text{current income}}{\text{investment cost}}$$

Example: Abel purchases a parking lot for $10,000. It provides $5,000 of parking revenues each year. Property taxes and insurance total $3,500, leaving $1,500 of annual before-income-tax **cash flow.** The *current yield* is 15%:

$$\frac{\$1,500}{\$10,000} = 15\%$$

CURTESY the right of a husband to all or part of his deceased wife's realty regardless of the provisions of her will. Exists in only a few states.
Example: Under the *curtesy* law of some states, a widower may claim a **life estate** to part of the property left by his deceased wife, provided they had a child in their marriage.

CUSTOM BUILDER one who builds unique houses; contrast with **tract house.**
Example: Abel, a *custom builder*, erects unique homes from plans provided by architects and buyers. Each home is unique, whether built for a specific customer or speculatively.

D

DAMAGES the amount recoverable by a person who has been injured in any manner, including physical harm, property damage, or violated rights, through the act or default of another.
Example: Abel forfeited his **earnest money** to the owner of property as *damages* for failing to purchase as agreed.

DATE OF APPRAISAL same as **appraisal date.**

DATE OF CLOSING see **closing date.**

DCR debt coverage ratio.

DEALER (TAX) one who buys and sells for his or her own account. The merchandise is **inventory,** consequently any gain on the sale is **ordinary income.**
Example: Davis purchases mobile homes from several manufacturers, and sells them to her customers. Davis is a *dealer* and all gains from sales are ordinary income.

DEBENTURE an unsecured **note** or **bond.**
Example: Abel invests in *debentures* of the XYZ Corporation; Baker invests in a **first mortgage** on a building owned by XYZ Corporation. The XYZ Corporation **bankrupts.** Ultimately Baker receives full payment for the mortgage upon the **foreclosure sale.** Abel is a general creditor and receives only 18 cents per dollar owed to him.

DEBIT 1. in a **closing statement** (settlement), an item that is charged to a party. Contrast with **credit.**
Examples: The buyer is charged with these typical *debits:*
• purchase price
• taxes prepaid by seller
• deed recording fees
The seller is charged with these typical debits:
• cost to **retire** existing mortgage principal
• **accrued interest** on mortgage being relieved
• **termite inspection** fee
2. in accounting, entries on the left side of the general ledger. Contrast with **credit.**
Examples: Debits include:
• acquisition cost of **assets**
• amounts of deductible expenses

DEBT an obligation to pay.
Example: Abel borrows $1,000 from Baker and thereby incurs a *debt.*

DEBT COVERAGE RATIO the relationship between **net operating income** (NOI) and **annual debt service** (ADS). Often used as an **underwriting** criterion for **income property** mortgage loans.

Example: Annual debt service for a mortgage loan on a certain office building is $10,000. The property generates $25,000 in annual gross rent, and requires $7,000 for expenses of operation, leaving $18,000 net operating income. The *debt coverage ratio is* 1.80, calculated by the following formula:

$$\frac{NOI}{ADS} = \frac{\$18,000}{\$10,000} = 1.8$$

DEBT/EQUITY RATIO the relationship of these components of **purchase capital.**

Example: Mortgage = $75,000
Equity = $25,000
The *debt/equity ratio* is 3:1. This is equivalent to a 75% **loan-to-value ratio** loan.

DEBT SERVICE see **annual debt service.**

DECLARATION 1. formal pleadings by a plaintiff as to the facts and circumstances that gave rise to his cause of action. Also, a statement made out of court.

Example: The unhappy land buyer offered a *declaration* explaining the claim that the property was misrepresented.

2. a legal document used to create a **condominium.** Includes a description of the property and the uses to which it is restricted, a description of individual ownership units, **common elements,** and procedures for amending the declaration.

Example: A developer constructs apartments and wishes to market them as a condominium. He prepares and records a *declaration*, which describes the division of individual and common ownership, a set of bylaws and a master **deed** for the project.

DECLARATION OF TRUST a written statement by a **trustee** to acknowledge that the property is held for the benefit of another.

Example: A *declaration of trust* was signed by a **trustee** to state that certain valuable land was being held in **trust** for certain orphaned children.

DECLINING BALANCE DEPRECIATION a method of **depreciation,** often used for income tax purposes, whereby a rate is applied to the remaining balance to derive the depreciation deduction. Compare **accelerated depreciation.**

Example: Table 16 shows the depreciation schedule for a property with a **tax basis** of $10,000 and **depreciable** life of 5 years, using the 125% *declining balance* method:

184

TABLE 16
DECLINING BALANCE DEPRECIATION

Year	Remaining balance	Rate*	Annual deduction
1	$10,000	0.25	$2,500
2	7,500	0.25	1,875
3	5,625	0.25	1,406
4	4,219	0.25	1,055
5	3,164	0.25	791

*A 5-year life results in 20% per year depreciation using the straight-line method. The 125% declining balance method results in an annual percentage of 25 for an asset with this life (125% of 20% = 25%).

DECREE an order issued by one in authority; a court order or decision. **Example:** The court issued a *decree* stating that Abel owed $10,000 to Baker for failing to perform under a **contract.**

DEDICATION the gift of land by its owner for a public use and the acceptance of it by a unit of government. See also **appropriation.**
Example: A **developer** of a large **subdivision** makes to the local government a *dedication* of the streets, the flood-prone areas and one **acre** of land for a public school. This obligates the government to **maintenance** of these areas and relieves the developer of a property tax liability on the dedicated lands.

DEED a written document, properly signed and delivered, that conveys **title** to real property. See **general warranty deed, quitclaim deed, special warranty deed.**
Example: In exchange for the agreed upon terms of a **contract,** including the purchase price, at **closing** the seller delivers a *deed* to the buyer.

DEED BOOKS the books, files, or record storage of the **public records** in which county governments keep the deeds and other real estate-related documents that have been filed.
Example: The county courthouse provides rooms full of *deed books* where interested parties, particularly attorneys and title companies, may research ownership records.

DEED IN LIEU OF FORECLOSURE the act of giving property back to a lender without **foreclosure.**
Example: Abel, a builder, has a **construction loan** with a $100,000 balance against the house he is building. He offers the house for sale at $100,000 but no one buys it. He does not have the cash to continue to pay interest on the construction loan, and is in **default.** The lender asks for a *deed in lieu of foreclosure.*

185

DEED OF RELEASE a document, in the form of a **deed,** in which one who has limited rights to a piece of real estate (usually a **mortgagee** or **lienholder**) abandons those rights back to the owner of the real estate; often takes the form of a **quitclaim deed.**
Example: Morgan holds the mortgage on Fillmore's land. Fillmore wishes to sell part of the land. In return for Fillmore paying down the mortgage loan by an agreed amount, Morgan gives Fillmore a *deed of release* to the part to be sold, so that Fillmore can transfer **clear title** to the buyer.

DEED OF TRUST an instrument used in many states in lieu of a **mortgage.** Legal title to the property is **vested** in one or more **trustees** to secure the repayment of the loan.
Example: Abel borrows $50,000 on his property in Texas from the Good Money Savings Association. He gives a *deed of trust* that is held in the name of I.M. Honest, a trustee. If Abel **defaults** it will not be difficult for Good Money to gain possession.

DEED RESTRICTION a clause in a deed that limits the use of land. See **covenants.**
Example: A deed might stipulate that alcoholic beverages are not to be sold on the land for 20 years. This is a *deed restriction.*

DEFAULT failure to fulfill an obligation or promise, or to perform specified acts.
Example: The **contract** required the buyer to close within 3 business days. His failure to appear at **closing** constituted a *default* under the contract.

DEFAULT POINT same as **break-even point.**

DEFEASANCE a clause in a **mortgage** that gives the borrower the right to redeem the property after **default,** usually by paying the full indebtedness and fees incurred.
Example: Graham defaults on the **balloon payment** of the mortgage. Three days later she pays the balance in cash. The *defeasance* clause allows her to redeem the property. It overrides the provision that grants the property to the lender upon default.

DEFECT IN TITLE any recorded **instrument** that would prevent a **grantor** from giving a **clear title.**
Example: A **mechanic's lien** that was recorded against the property when it was remodeled was a *defect in title.* The grantor had to clear the **lien** by paying the amount due the electrician who filed the lien.

DEFENDANT the party sued in an action at law.
Example: Abel brings suit against a former landlord, Baker, for refusing to return a **security deposit.** In the suit, Baker is the *defendant.*

DEFERRED CHARGES nontangible costs that are expected to provide value over a number of years. For accounting or tax purposes, these are to be **amortized** over the life to which they are expected to provide value.
Examples:
• Commissions paid upon **lease** negotiation of a lengthy lease.
• **Mortgage** placement fee for a **permanent mortgage**.

DEFERRED MAINTENANCE in appraisal, a type of physical **depreciation** owing to lack of normal upkeep.
Examples: The appraiser found the following examples of *deferred maintenance* on the subject property:
• broken window glass
• missing roof shingles
• peeling paint
• broken guttering

DEFERRED PAYMENTS payments to be made at some future date.
Example: On a **graduated payment mortgage** the **principal** payments and some interest payments are *deferred* for the first 3 to 5 years.

DEFICIENCY in mortgage finance, the shortfall of funds recovered through the sale of property securing a foreclosed loan compared to the amount of debt, accrued interest, foreclosure expenses, and damages incurred by the lender. See **deficiency judgment.**
Example: A lender foreclosed a mortgage loan with outstanding principal balance of $100,000 and accrued interest of $2,000. At the foreclosure sale, the property brought $80,000. The lender claimed a *deficiency* of $22,000 plus expenses when filing for a judgment in the courts.

DEFICIENCY JUDGMENT a court order stating that the borrower still owes money when the **security** for a loan does not entirely satisfy a defaulted debt.
Example: Upon **default** by the **mortgagor,** a lender **forecloses** on the mortgage. The unpaid balance of the loan is $60,000. The property is sold at public **auction** and brings $50,000. The lender then seeks a *deficiency judgment* against the mortgagor to recover the $10,000 shortage.

DELAYED (TAX-FREE) EXCHANGE a transaction in which a property is traded for the promise to provide a replacement **like-kind property** in the near future. The Tax Reform Act of 1984 allows investment real estate or real property used in a trade or business to be sold with the tax on the gain deferred, provided replacement property is identified within 45 days and

187

closed within 180 days. Other strict requirements must be observed. See also **tax-free exchange.**

DELINQUENCY RATE statistically, the number of loans with delinquent payments divided by the number of loans held in a portfolio. Sometimes, the rate is based on the total dollar volume of the loans instead of number. Generally, delinquency is qualified to include only loans where payments are 3 or more months past due.
Example: In January, ABC Savings reported 15 loans with delinquent payments of 3 or more months. Its loan portfolio at the beginning of the month included 300 loans. Its *delinquency rate* at the end of January was 5%.

DELIVERY transfer of the **possession** of a thing from one person to another.
Example: A man dies leaving no will. A search of his possessions uncovers a **deed** giving valuable land to his nephew. Since the deed has not been *delivered,* the court ruled that the land does not belong to the nephew.

DEMAND LOAN a loan that may be called by the lender at any time.
Example: Abel borrows $10,000 from a bank on a *demand loan* and uses the cash for the downpayment on a parcel of land. The bank may call in the loan and Abel may be forced to sell the property at a distressed price to meet the *demand loan.*

DEMISED PREMISES property subject to lease.
Example: An apartment is rented under a written lease. In the lease, the apartment is referred to as the *demised premises.*

DEMOGRAPHIC pertaining to characteristics of the population, such as race, sex, age, household size, and to population growth and **density.**
Example: As a first step in estimating the demand for new housing units, a **developer** commissions a *demographic* study. The study describes the current population density and rate of growth, the age distribution of the population, and average size of households in the local **market area.**

DEMOLITION destruction and removal of an existing structure from a **site;** necessary to prepare a site for new construction.
Example: A block of old houses in the city is to be converted into a new shopping mall. This conversion will require *demolition* of the houses, site preparation and construction of the mall.

DENSITY the intensity of a land use. See **also land use intensity.**
Example: A 10-acre **subdivision** contains 30 single-family houses. The *density is* 3 dwelling units per **acre.**

DENSITY ZONING laws that restrict **land use intensity.**
Example: A zoning ordinance states that all zones designated "R-2" may contain no more than 4 **detached housing** units per **acre.** This is an example of *density zoning.*

DEP depreciation (appraisal).

DEPLETION a **tax deduction** to account for reduced **land** value due to removing minerals.
Example: The $10,000 tax deduction for *depletion* was allowed because coal was being removed and the land would become virtually worthless when all of the coal was gone.

DEPOSIT money paid in **good faith** to assure performance of a contract. Deposits are commonly used with **sales contracts** and **leases.** If the person who put up the deposit fails to perform, the deposit is forfeited, unless conditions in the contract allow a refund. **Brokers** are to put deposits in a separate checking account pending completion of the contract. See **earnest money.**
Example: Whitman presented a $1,000 check as an earnest money *deposit* on a home she would buy provided she could get a 10% rate, 30-year loan for 80% of the price. The broker deposited the check in an **escrow account,** and refunded it when Whitman could not arrange said loan.

DEPOSIT ACCOUNT an arrangement whereby an individual or organization may place cash under the safekeeping of a financial institution. It is understood that the institution may invest the cash and pay the depositor a specified amount of interest and that the depositor can reclaim the full value of the account according to the agreed upon procedures governing the account.
Example: Town Savings maintains several types of *deposit accounts* for the benefit of its depositors. The accounts provide funds which are used to make mortgage loans.

DEPOSITORY INSTITUTIONS DEREGULATION AND MONETARY CONTROL ACT federal law that represents significant decontrol of federally regulated banks and savings institutions, including gradual phase out of limits on interest rates paid on passbook accounts. **(Regulation Q).**
Example: The *Depository Institutions Deregulation and Monetary Control Act* is a major effort to reform the nation's banking regulations. Among its effects are:
• standardized reserve requirements for banks and **savings and loan associations**
• phase out of deposit interest rate limitations
• authorization for interest-bearing checking accounts
• increased ability for savings and loan associations to make consumer loans
• reduced applicability of state **usury** laws

DEPRECIABLE BASIS see **basis (tax), adjusted tax basis.**

DEPRECIABLE LIFE 1. for tax purposes, the number of years over which the cost of an **asset** may be spread. See **accelerated cost recovery.**
Example: Abel buys an apartment complex. For tax purposes the building has a 27½-year *depreciable life.*
2. for **appraisal** purposes, the estimated useful life of an asset.
Example: Baker buys an apartment complex. An appraiser estimates that the roof will last for 15 years, so it has a 15-year *depreciable life.*

DEPRECIABLE REAL ESTATE (TAX) **realty** that is subject to deductions for **depreciation.** It generally includes property used in a trade or business, or an investment, subject to an allowance for depreciation under **Section 167** of the **Internal Revenue Code.**
Example: Abel buys an apartment complex for $1 million. Of the purchase price, $100,000 is the value of the land, the remaining $900,000 is the value of *depreciable real estate.* Abel uses the **straight-line depreciation** method and a 27½-year remaining depreciable life.

DEPRECIATED COST same as **book value** or **adjusted tax basis.**

DEPRECIATION (ACCOUNTING) allocating the cost of an **asset** over its estimated **useful life.**
Example: Collins buys a warehouse for $550,000. Of the price, $50,000 is for land, which is not subject to depreciation. Of the remaining $500,000, she claims accounting *depreciation* of $10,000 per year over a 50-year **depreciable life,** despite the fact that the property is expected to increase in value because of the location of the land.

DEPRECIATION (APPRAISAL) a charge against the **reproduction cost** (new) of an **asset** for the estimated wear and **obsolescence.** Depreciation may be physical, functional, or economic.
Example: The estimated reproduction cost (new) of a theater being appraised is $500,000. **Wear and tear** sustained during its life is estimated at $100,000. Functional obsolescence caused by lack of air-conditioning and high ceilings causes an estimated loss of $100,000. It is in a decaying area of the city estimated at causing $100,000 of economic obsolescence. Total *depreciation is* estimated at $300,000.

DEPRECIATION METHODS accounting technique of allocating the cost of an asset over its **useful life.**
Example: Table 17 is a depreciation schedule for a $1,000 asset with a depreciable life of 4 years, using 3 methods.

TABLE 17
DEPRECIATION METHODS

		Annual Depreciation	
Year	Straight Line	Double Declining Balance	Sum-of-Years-Digits
1	$250	$500	$400
2	250	250	300
3	250	125	200
4	250	62	100

DEPRECIATION RECAPTURE when real property is sold at a gain and **accelerated depreciation** had been claimed, the owner may be required to pay a tax at ordinary rates to the extent of the excess accelerated depreciation. Excess depreciation on residential real estate after 1980 is recaptured; all depreciation on commercial property after 1980 is recaptured when an accelerated method had been used, under **Section 1250** of the **Internal Revenue Code.** See Figure 44.
Note: The importance of *depreciation recapture* for real estate was minimized by the Tax Reform Act of 1986, which mandated straight-line depreciation for buildings bought after 1986 and eliminated favorable tax rates on long-term capital gains after 1987.

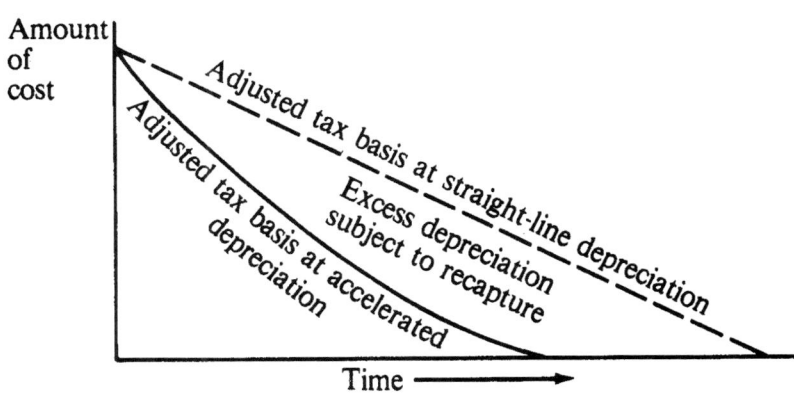

FIG. 44. DEPRECIATION RECAPTURE

DEPTH TABLES a set of percentages indicating the proportion of **site** value attributable to each additional amount of depth in the lot. **Example:** A commonly used *depth table* (Figure 45). (Compare with **four-three-two-one rule.**)

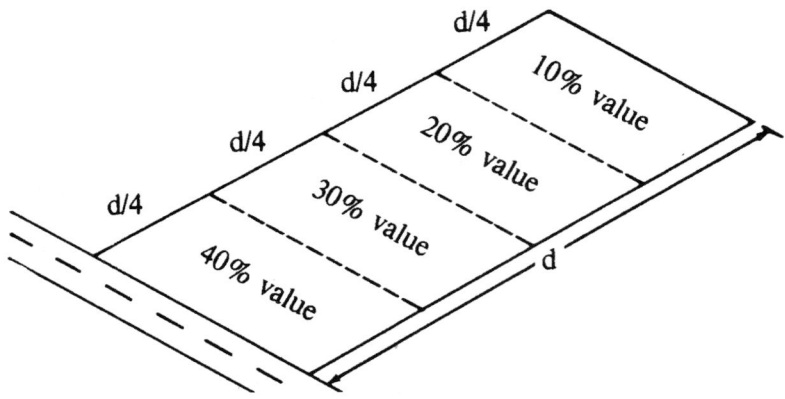

FIG. 45. DEPTH TABLE

DESCRIPTION formal depiction of the dimensions and location of a property; generally included in **deeds, leases, sales contracts,** and **mortgage** contracts for **real property.** See **government rectangular survey, lot and block, metes and bounds,** for specific methods of legal description. See also **plat.**
Example: A **sales contract** is executed. A portion of the contract contains a *description* of the property that simply states the street address of the house. In the deed conveyed at **closing** a more precise metes and bounds *description* is included based upon a **survey** of the property.

DESCRIPTIVE MEMORANDUM a term used to describe an offering circular of property or securities when a **prospectus** is not required.
Example: A **syndicator** prepared a *descriptive memorandum* about the property after receiving an exemption from registering the offering by the **Securities and Exchange Commission (SEC).**

DESCENT the acquisition of property by an heir when the deceased leaves no will.
Example: Abel dies without having prepared a will. His wife and son are awarded **title** to Abel's estate by the courts. They are said to acquire title by *descent.*

DESIGNATED REAL ESTATE INSTRUCTOR (DREI) a **real estate** teacher, typically of licensing preparation courses, who has been designated by the **Real Estate Educators Association.**
Example: In order to qualify as a *DREI*, Don had to demonstrate classroom teaching techniques to a panel of teachers who judged his effectiveness. Don also offered experience and expertise in real estate law.

DETACHED HOUSING **residential** buildings in which each **dwelling** unit is surrounded by freestanding walls and is generally sited on a separate lot. Contrast with **duplex, row house, town house.**
Example: Figure 46.

Detached housing Town houses

FIG. 46. DETACHED HOUSING

DEVELOPER one who transforms **raw land** to **improved** property by use of labor, capital, and **entrepreneur** efforts.
Example: Abel buys 25 acres of land for $10,000 per **acre.** After putting in streets and utilities, dividing it into l00 lots, and building homes on each lot, Abel sells the homes. Abel is a *developer.*

DEVELOPMENT the process of adding improvements on or to a parcel of land. Such improvements may include drainage, utilities, subdividing, access, buildings, and any combination of these elements. Also the project where such improvements are being made.
Example: Baker, a developer, acquired a large parcel of land and began the preparation of detailed plans and securing of government permits. Later, the site will be prepared and construction will commence. The *development* will be the first phase of a large multi-use subdivision.

DEVELOPMENT LOAN same as **construction loan.**

DEVISE a gift of real estate by **will** or last testament. Compare **bequeath.**
Example: In his will, Abel *devises* his home to his daughter. He **bequeaths** his automobile to his son.

DEVISEE one who inherits real estate through a will.
Example: Abel dies. The *devisee* in his will receives his land.

DIRECT CAPITALIZATION dividing the **net operating income** by an overall **capitalization rate** to estimate value. See **capitalized value.**
Example: Table 18.

TABLE 18
DIRECT CAPITALIZATION

Gross income	$100,000
Operating expenses	– 40,000
Net operating income	$ 60,000
Capitalization rate	÷ 0.12
Value estimate	$500,000

DIRECT COSTS costs that are readily identified in the construction of real estate, such as labor, materials, and contractor's overhead and profit. Contrast with **indirect costs.**
Example: *Direct costs* for an apartment building were $2 million; indirect costs, such as architect's fees, interest during construction, and builder's overhead and profit allowance, totaled $500,000.

DIRECTIONAL GROWTH the location or direction toward which a city is growing.
Example: The *directional growth* of Boomtown is toward the northeast (Figure 47).

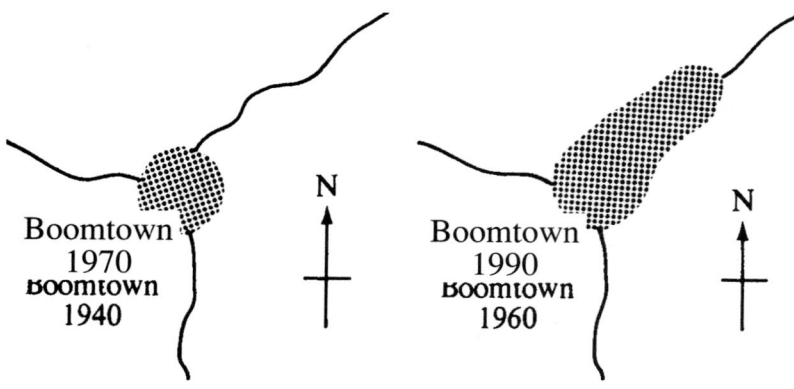

FIG. 47. DIRECTIONAL GROWTH

DIRECT REDUCTION MORTGAGE a loan that requires both **interest** and **principal** with each payment such that the level payment will be adequate for **amortization** over the loan's term. See **level payment mortgage.**
Example: Collins borrows $50,000 at 10% interest over a 30-year term, using a *direct reduction mortgage.* Her monthly principal and interest payment of $438.79 will fully amortize (pay off) the loan over 30 years.

DIRECT SALES COMPARISON APPROACH same as **market comparison approach.**

DISCHARGE IN BANKRUPTCY the release of a bankrupt party from the obligation to repay **debts** that were, or might have been, proved in a **bankruptcy** proceeding.
Example: A real estate resort **developer** filed for bankruptcy. He owned 2,000 unsold vacation lots, and owed $2 million on land acquisition loans. The court granted a *discharge in bankruptcy* for these loans and allowed the creditor to dispose of the lots.

DISCLAIMER 1. a statement whereby responsibility is rejected.
Example: Abel, a certified public accountant, is asked to write up the **financial statements** of Baker without testing (auditing) the validity of the statements. Abel's report provides a *disclaimer* in which he states that he did not examine the financial statements and does not accept responsibility for their accuracy. 2. renunciation of ownership of **property.**
Example: Because they were no longer profitable, Baker *disclaimed* apartments that had become dilapidated.

DISCLOSURE STATEMENT a statement required by law, in which sellers of particular kinds of property, or under certain circumstances, must reveal specified information to potential buyers.
Examples:
• Most states require sellers of real estate to disclose any "dangerous condition" to potential buyers.
• Many sellers of investment interests in real estate are required to disclose their own interest and even profit potential.
• Sellers of **time-share** interests must disclose which portions of the project will be retained by the developer, and the costs and conditions of use by time-share buyers.

DISCOUNT the difference between the **face amount** of an obligation and the amount advanced or received.
Example: Abel sells land for $100,000 and receives a $60,000 mortgage at 7% interest as part of the payment. Abel then sells the mortgage (the right to collect payments on the mortgage) at a $15,000 *discount,* thereby receiving $45,000.

DISCOUNT BROKER a licensed broker who provides brokerage services for a lower commission than that typical in the market. Generally, the services provided are less extensive than those of a full service broker. Many discount brokers charge a flat fee rather than a percentage of the selling price. See **flat fee broker.**
Example: Henson, a *discount broker,* offers to list a property for a 3% commission. Henson will refer prospective buyers to the seller and prepare a sales contract. The seller is expected to show the property and negotiate directly with the buyer.

DISCOUNTED CASH FLOW a method of investment analysis in which anticipated future cash income from the investment is estimated and converted into a rate of return on initial investment based on the time value of money. In addition, when a required rate of return is specified, a net present value of the investment can be estimated.
Example: An asset may be purchased for $1,000. It is expected to generate $100 in income per year for 10 years, after which time it is expected to sell for $1,200. *Discounted cash flow* analysis shows that the internal rate of return on the investment is expected to be 11.2% per year.

DISCOUNTED LOAN one that is offered or traded for less than its face value. See **discount, discount points.**
Example: When the Deavers sold their house, they accepted a second mortgage as part of the purchase price. The Deavers then sold the loan to an investor for 75% of its face value. The purchaser of this *discounted loan* is entitled to all interest and principal payments stipulated in the mortgage contract.

DISCOUNTED PRESENT VALUE see **discounted cash flow, net present value.**

DISCOUNTING the process of estimating the present value of an **income stream** by reducing expected **cash flow** to reflect the **time value of money.** *Discounting* is the opposite of compounding. Mathematically they are reciprocals. See **discounted cash flow, net present value.**
Example: If the sale of land expected to be $1 million in the year 2000 was discounted to a present value in 1994 at a 15% risk rate, it would provide a value today of approximately $432,000.

DISCOUNT POINTS amounts paid to the lender (usually by the seller) at the time of origination of a loan, to account for the difference between the market interest rate and the lower face rate of the note (often required when **VA loans** are used).
Example: At the time of loan application, conventional mortgages are being made at 15%. The maximum rate on an FHA loan is 14½ % with 4 *discount points* added to compensate for the lower face rate of interest. If the loan is for $50,000, the points will require an additional payment of $2,000 at closing. (The 4 points equals 4% of $50,000, which is $2,000.)

DISCOUNT RATE 1. a **compound interest** rate used to convert expected future income into a present value. See **capitalization rate, present value of annuity, present value of one.**
Example: A *discount rate* of 10% applied to a $100 sum expected to be received in one year results in a present value of $90.90. (The **present value of one** for one year is 0.909.)

2. the rate charged member banks who borrow from the **Federal Reserve System.** Same as **rediscount rate.**
Example: See **rediscount rate.**

DISCRIMINATION applying special treatment (generally unfavorable) to an individual solely on the basis of the person's race, religion, or sex.
Example: Abel is accused of *discrimination* under the Fair Housing Laws because he refused to rent apartments to nonwhite families.

DISINTERMEDIATION situation when deposits are removed from a financial intermediary, such as a **savings and loan association,** and invested in other **assets,** generally for the purpose of obtaining higher yields.
Example: Figure 48.

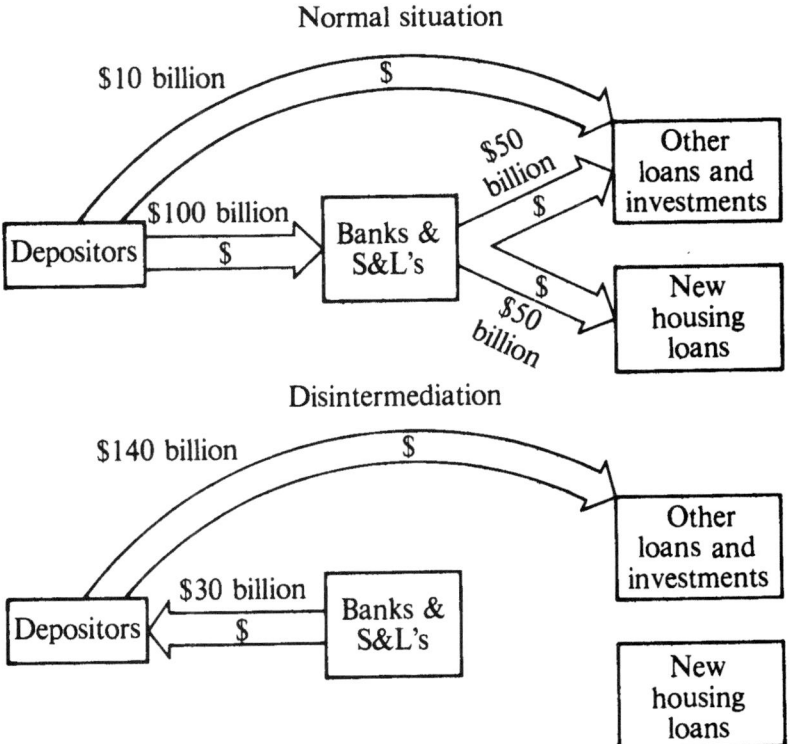

FIG. 48. DISINTERMEDIATION

DISPOSSESS PROCEEDINGS the legal process by a **landlord** to remove a **tenant** and regain possession of property. See **eviction.**
Example: After not having received rent for 3 months, the landlord began *dispossess proceedings* to eject the tenant.

DISTRAINT the legal right of a **landlord** to seize a tenant's personal property to satisfy payment of back rent.
Example: Abel is 6 months in **arrears** on rent. Landlord Baker obtains a court order to seize Abel's furniture to satisfy the rent due. Baker is exercising his right of *distraint.*

DISTRESSED PROPERTY real estate that is under **foreclosure** or impending foreclosure because of insufficient income production.
See **workout.**
Example: An **apartment building** is financed with **mortgages** that require $25,000 in **annual debt service.** Because of high vacancies and rising expenses, **net operating income** drops to $20,000. The owners have ceased making loan payments because their resources are insufficient to pay the **negative cash flow.** The property is considered *distressed property.*

DOCUMENTARY EVIDENCE evidence in the form of written or printed papers.
Example: During court proceedings, a **sales contract** was entered in the record as *documentary evidence* of the agreement made between the **plaintiff** and the **defendant.**

DOMICILE the state in which one makes his or her principal residence.
Example: Mason's job requires her to travel throughout the United States. Although she owns property in several states, Mason's *domicile* is New York, where she has her principal residence. Mason is subject to the laws of New York concerning automobile registration, voting rights, payment of taxes, and other matters.

DOMINANT TENEMENT land that benefits from an **easement** on another property. The other property, which usually is **adjacent,** is the **servient tenement.**
Example: In Figure 49 the owner of Parcel A has a right-of-way easement to the road by going across Parcel B.

DONEE a recipient, as of a gift.
Example: Collins was the *donee* of an **estate;** she takes the **property** as a gift.

DONOR one who gives.
Example: Whitman was the *donor* of land that she gave to charity; she had owned the land in **fee simple.**

DORMER 1. a window projecting through a sloping roof (single dormer).
2. the roofed structure containing such a window (shed dormer).
Example: Figure 50.

FIG. 49. DOMINANT TENEMENT

FIG. 50. DORMER WINDOWS

DOUBLE DECLINING BALANCE a method of **depreciation** for tax purposes whereby twice the **straight-line** rate is applied to the remamlng depreciable balance of an asset. See **declining balance depreciation.**

Example: Table 19 is a depreciation schedule for a property with depreciable basis of $10,000 and **depreciable life** of 5 years, using the **double declining balance** method.

TABLE 19
DOUBLE DECLINING BALANCE

Year	Remaining balance	Rate*	Annual deduction
1	$10,000	.40	$4,000
2	6,000	.40	2,400
3	3,600	.40	1,440
4	2,160	.40	864
5	1,296	.40	518

*.40 = twice the straight-line rate of 20% per year for a 5-year life asset.

DOUBLE TAXATION taxation of the same income at 2 levels. **Example:** A corporation earns $25,000 of **net income.** The corporation pays a $5,000 corporate income tax, then distributes $20,000 in dividends to its shareholders, who pay an $8,000 tax on this dividend income. The corporation's earnings are subject to *double taxation.*

DOWER under **common law,** the legal right of a wife or child to part of a deceased husband's or father's property. See **curtesy.** **Example:** In some states a widow can enforce *dower* rights to claim part of her deceased husband's **estate,** regardless of provisions in his will.

DOWN PAYMENT the amount one pays for property in addition to the **debt** incurred. **Example:** Abel buys a house for $50,000. He arranges a $30,000 **first mortgage** and a $5,000 **second mortgage.** The *down payment* he needs is $15,000, which he pays in cash at **closing.**

DOWNZONING the act of **rezoning** a tract of land for a less intensive use than the existing use or permitted use. **Example:** Arlington had a booming single-family residential market, but was not attracting industry. The owner of a large tract of land zoned for industrial use asked for a *downzoning* to **single-family housing** use to develop the land immediately.

DRAGNET CLAUSE a provision in a **mortgage** that pledges several properties as **collateral.** A **default** on one mortgage constitutes a default on the one with the *dragnet.* **Example:** A real estate investor was in financial straits. She failed to pay a certain **mortgage.** The holder of the mortgage on a different property, which was not in **default,** enforced the *dragnet* clause in its mortgage by **foreclosing.**

DRAW a periodic advance of funds from a construction lender to a **developer. Construction loans** generally provide for a schedule of draws, either at regular intervals during construction or pending construction of specific segments of the structures. **Example:** A developer arranges a construction loan of $500,000. The funds are to be advanced in a series of *draws* as follows:
- $50,000 upon completion of final plans and **specifications**
- $200,000 upon completion of the foundation
- $150,000 upon completion of the frame, external surfaces, and roof
- $100,000 upon internal finishing

DRY MORTGAGE same as **nonrecourse** mortgage.

DUAL AGENCY the situation in which an agent represents more than one party to a transaction.
Example: In certain real estate transactions involving exchange of real estate, it is not uncommon for one broker to arrange the swap, representing both parties and thereby creating a *dual agency*.

DUAL CONTRACT the illegal or unethical practice of providing 2 different **contracts** for the same transaction.
Example: Abel wants to purchase a home from a builder for $144,000 but has no cash for the **down payment.** The builder suggests that they prepare a fictitious contract for $160,000 and try to borrow 90% of $160,000. The bank's attorney discusses the *dual contract* and explains that they could be guilty of attempted **fraud.**

DUE-ON-SALE CLAUSE a provision in a **mortgage** that states the loan is due upon the sale of the property.
Example: Collins owes on a $30,000 mortgage loan against her house at an 8% interest rate. She wants to sell the house to a buyer who will assume the mortgage. The lender says that the $30,000 loan is *due upon the sale* of the house so it cannot be assumed by the buyer. The lender adds that he will waive the due-on-sale provision if the interest rate is escalated to 16%.

DUMMY an individual or **entity** that stands in the place of the **principal** to a transaction.
Example: Abel wants to borrow from a bank $100,000 to build houses to sell. Abel requests his attorney to establish a *dummy* **corporation** with $500 of **equity.** The dummy borrows the $100,000 from the bank and, in turn, lends it to Abel as a **non-recourse** loan.

DUPLEX 1. two dwelling units under one roof.
Example: General floor plan for a *duplex* (Figure 51).
2. an apartment having rooms on two floors.
Example: An artist in a Manhattan *duplex* apartment enjoyed the sunlight that came in from the upper floor to his studio below.

DURESS compulsion to do something because of a threat.
Example: Abel tells Baker that unless Baker will sell his property to Abel for $1,000, Abel will physically harm Baker. Baker signs the **contract** under *duress,* but can later **void** it by showing he acted under duress.

DUTCH AUCTION a bidding process in which the asking price is lowered gradually until someone places a qualifying bid.
Example: The home was offered in a *dutch auction* beginning at $150,000. The auctioneer lowered the price gradually in $5,000 increments until a bidder was found willing to pay $120,000. Therefore, the home was sold for $120,000.

FIG. 51. DUPLEX FLOOR PLAN

DUTCH COLONIAL an early-American-style, moderate-sized, 2-to 2½-story house with a gambrel roof and eaves that flare outward. **Example:** Figure 52.

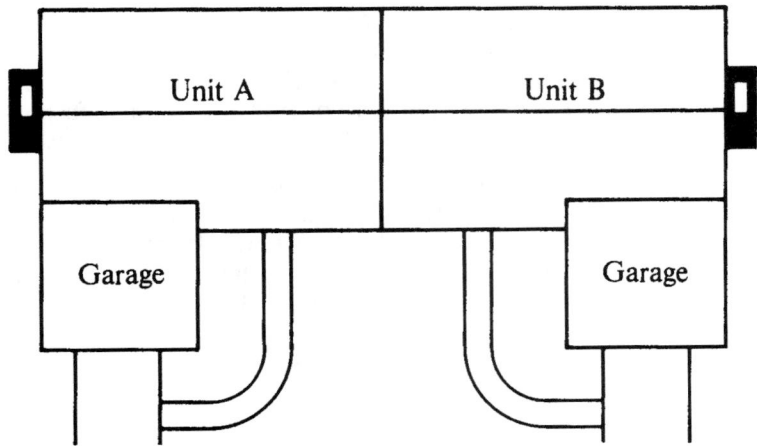

FIG. 52. DUTCH COLONIAL HOUSE

DWELLING a place of residence.
 Examples: The following are *dwellings:*
 • apartment
 • hotel
 • mobile home
 • nursing home
 • single-family house

E

EARNEST MONEY a **deposit** made by a purchaser of real estate to evidence **good faith.**
Example: It is customary for the buyer to give the seller *earnest money* at the time a **sales contract** is signed. The earnest money generally is credited to the **down payment** at **closing.** Until closing a **broker** must hold earnest money in a separate account. See also **commingle.**

EASEMENT the right, privilege, or interest that one party has in the land of another.
Example: The right of public utility companies to lay their lines across others' property is a utility *easement.*

EASEMENT BY NECESSITY the right of an owner to cross over another's property for a special necessary purpose.
Example: Figure 53.

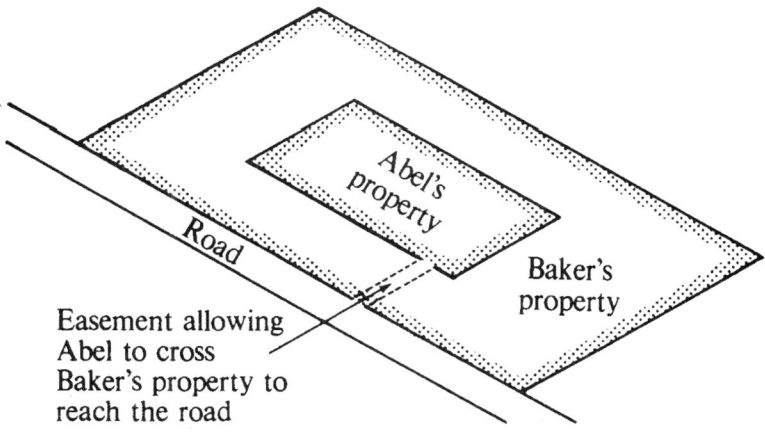

FIG. 53. EASEMENT BY NECESSITY

EASEMENT BY PRESCRIPTION continued use of another's property for a special purpose can ripen into a permanent use if conditions are met.
Example: Although Abel can reach the highway by another path, for the last 10 years, Abel has been traveling across Baker's property to reach the highway. Since Abel has been doing this for the length of time required by state law, Abel can continue to do so despite Baker's protests, because Abel has achieved an *easement by prescription* (Figure 54).

203

FIG. 54. EASEMENT BY PRESCRIPTION

EASTLAKE HOUSE a nineteenth-century-style house with three-dimensional ornamentation made with a chisel, gouge, and lathe rather than the scroll saw. Many of the parts of the ornamentation resemble furniture legs and knobs. This distinctive type of ornamentation is the major characteristic of this style and separates the Eastlake-style house from the Queen Anne or Carpenter Gothic style.
Example: Figure 55.

FIG. 55. EASTLAKE HOUSE

ECONOMIC BASE industry within a geographic **market area** that provides employment opportunities that are essential to support the community.
Example: Steel is the *economic base* for Pittsburgh. For each steelworker added to the economic base there is another job added in service employment (physician, lawyer, switchboard operator, barber). Each new job brings 2 people to the community (spouse, children, nonworking parents, etc.).

ECONOMIC DEPRECIATION loss of value from all causes outside the property itself. See **depreciation (appraisal).**
Example: An expensive private home may drop in value when an industrial plant is built nearby. This is a form of *economic depreciation* that must be considered in the appraisal of the property.

ECONOMIC LIFE that remaining period for which real estate **improvements** are expected to generate more income than **operating expenses** cost. See **useful life.**
Example: Figure 56.

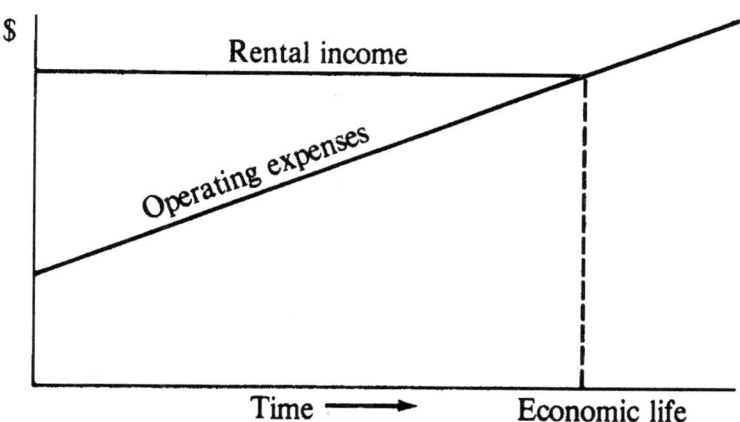

FIG. 56. ECONOMIC LIFE

ECONOMIC OBSOLESCENCE same as **economic depreciation.**

ECONOMIC RENT 1. in economics, the cost commanded by a factor that is unique or inelastic in supply.
Example: The portion of rental income attributable to the land is often considered *economic rent,* since the land will exist no matter what the rental rate. In this context, *economic rent* carries a connotation of being "unearned" by its owner.
2. in appraisal, the **market rent.** Contrast with **contract rent.**
Example: Big Buy Foods is using a store for $1,000 per month

205

rent. If the landlord could rent the store on a new lease now, it would command $4,000 per month. The $1,000 is the **contract rent** and the $4,000 is the *economic rent.*

EFFECTIVE AGE the age of a property based on the amount of **wear and tear** it has sustained. Contrast with **actual age.**
Example: Collins's house was built 12 years ago. Because she keeps it in excellent condition it shows only as much wear as a typical 5-year-old house. Collins's house therefore has an *effective age* of 5 years.

EFFECTIVE GROSS INCOME for income-producing **property,** potential **gross income,** less a vacancy and collection allowance, plus miscellaneous income.
Example: An office building rents for $12 per square foot and contains 100,000 leasable square feet. A 5% vacancy and collection allowance is expected. A small concession stand provides $1,000 of annual revenue. *Effective gross income* is shown in Table 20.

TABLE 20
EFFECTIVE GROSS INCOME

Potential gross income:		
$12 × 100,000	=	$1,200,000
Less: Vacancy and		
collection allowance, 5%	−	60,000
Add: Miscellaneous income	+	1,000
Effective gross income		$1,141,000

EFFECTIVE RATE the true rate of return considering all relevant **financing** expenses. See **annual percentage rate.**
Example: Abel borrows $10,000 on a one-year bank loan. He pays 2 **discount points** and a 10% **face interest rate.** He repays the loan at the end of the year, with interest. Since he really received only $9,800 at the start of the loan and repaid $11,000, the *effective rate* was greater than 10%. It was approximately 12.25%.

EFFICIENCY RATIO the proportion of a building's area that is leasable space.
Example: An office building contains 200,000 square feet of space. Of this amount, 10,000 square feet are taken up by elevators and other physical plant equipment. Another 5,000 square feet are taken up by the sales and management office. Restrooms and hallways occupy 30,000 square feet. The lobby is 5,000 square feet. Total space available for lease is 150,000 square feet. The *efficiency ratio* is 150,000:200,000, or 75%.

EFFICIENCY UNIT OR APARTMENT a small dwelling unit, often consisting of a single room, within a multifamily structure. In most cases, kitchen and bath facilities are not complete.
Example: Figure 57 shows the floor plan of a typical efficiency apartment.

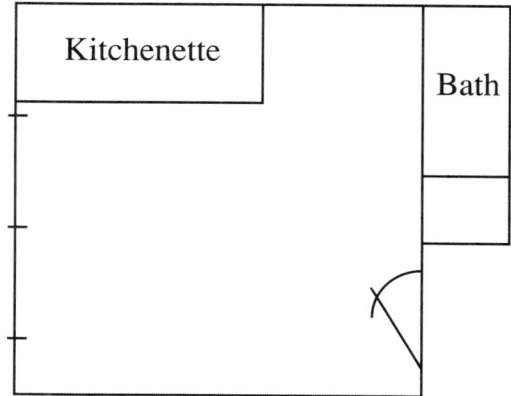

FIG. 57. EFFICIENCY APARTMENT

EGRESS access from a land parcel to a public road or other means of exit.
Example: Figure 58.

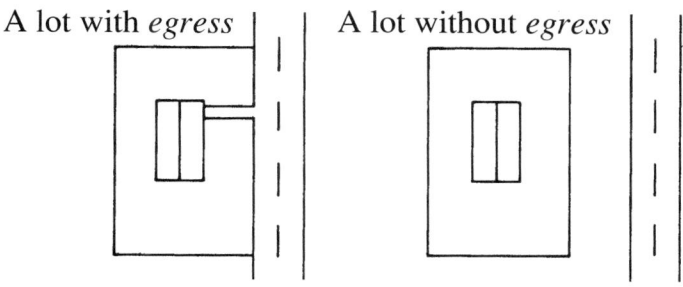

FIG. 58. EGRESS

EJECTMENT action to regain possession of **real property,** when there is no lease.
Example: The holder of a **conditional sales contract,** through an action in *ejectment,* regains possession when the buyer **defaults.**

ELIZABETHAN OR HALF TIMBER STYLE an English-style, 2- or 2½-story house, often with part of the second story overhanging the first. It has less stone work and is less fortlike than the Tudor. Stone and stucco walls with half timbers are most common.
Example: Figure 59.

FIG. 59. ELIZABETHAN-STYLE HOUSE

ELLWOOD TECHNIQUE in the **appraisal** of mortgaged **income property,** a technique used to estimate the present value of the **property.** The **appraiser** determines and **discounts** to a present value the annual cash flow to the equity owner and the expected **resale proceeds.** Those amounts are added together to derive the equity value, then added to the mortgage balance to offer a property value estimate. The late L. W. Ellwood provided **capitalization rate** tables that accelerate the process.

Example: An equity owner expects to receive $10,000 of annual cash flow for 10 years, then $100,000 upon resale. A $500,000 mortgage is currently on the property. Using 12% as the appropriate **equity yield rate,** Table 21 illustrates the Ellwood technique.

TABLE 21
ELLWOOD TECHNIQUE

Present value of cash flow:		
$10,000		
× 5.65 Annuity factor at 12%	=	$ 56,500
Present value of **reversion:**		
$100,000		
× .322 Present value factor at 12%	=	32,200
Value of equity		$ 88,700
Add: Mortgage balance		500,000
Property value		$588,700

EMBLEMENT a growing crop. Annual crops are generally considered **personal property.**
Example: Abel, a **tenant,** planted corn on Baker's land. Three days prior to harvesting, Baker informs Abel that the **land lease** has expired. Abel has the right to *emblements* and so can harvest the corn.

EMINENT DOMAIN the right of the government or a public utility to acquire property for necessary public use by **condemnation;** the owner must be fairly compensated.
Example: Ready Watts Electric Company is granted the power of *eminent domain* by the state government. This allows the company to acquire private property for specified purposes through the process of condemnation.

EMPTY NESTERS a couple whose children have established separate households; important segment of the housing market, since empty nesters often seek to reduce the amount of housing space they occupy. Thus empty nesters are one source of demand for smaller housing units.
Example: The Etons have raised 2 children, who are now grown and have families of their own. As *empty nesters,* the Etons no longer have need for the big 4-bedroom home they occupy. They purchase a 2-bedroom **town house,** which provides all the space they require.

ENCROACHMENT a building, a part of a building, or an obstruction that physically intrudes upon, overlaps, or **trespasses** upon the property of another.
Example: A part of the building on lot A is an *encroachment* on lot B. This situation probably occurred because of a faulty **survey** of lot A (Figure 60).

FIG. 60. ENCROACHMENT

ENCUMBRANCE any right to or interest in land that affects its value. Includes outstanding **mortgage** loans, unpaid taxes, **easements, deed restrictions.**
Example: *Encumbrances* on Blackacres include 3 mortgages, 4 **leases,** a **mechanic's lien,** and a deed restriction preventing the sale of alcoholic beverages on the land.

END LOAN same as **permanent mortgage.**

ENDORSEMENT 1. the act of signing one's name, as the payee, on the back of a check or **note,** with or without further qualification; the signature itself.
Example: Figure 61.
2. offering support or credibility to a statement.
Example: The American Association of Homebuilders *endorses* the use of brick as a construction material.

Pay $1000 to Mary Johns on August 20, 1994. *John Jones*	*Mary John* Endorsement
Front	Back

FIG. 61. ENDORSEMENTS

ENERGY EFFICIENT as applied to buildings, generally indicating the existence of extra insulation, weatherproofing, and/or special features and equipment designed to reduce the cost of energy for heating, cooling and hot water.
Example: An *energy efficient* home might have an extra layer of insulation in the attic and walls, a relatively airtight exterior, a heat pump, and a solar hot water heater. An *energy efficient* furnace might be designed to burn fuel more completely and capture more of the heat generated.

ENERGY TAX CREDITS a reduction in income tax, generally based on the cost of installing insulation and other energy-saving devices.
Note: At the federal level, *energy tax credits* generally expired before 1987 and were not renewed by the 1986 Tax Act.

ENTITY the legal form under which property is owned. See also **corporation, limited partnership, partnership.**
Examples: The benefits and risks of owning real property may vary depending on the *entity* that is formed. Among the options are:
• corporation
• individual ownership (see **tenancy** entries)

210

- **joint venture**
- **limited partnership**
- **partnership**
- **real estate investment trust**

ENTREPRENEUR an individual who generates business activity. A businessman or businesswoman. Often associated with one who takes business risks.
Example: Businesses owned by *entrepreneurs* include:
- auto dealerships
- restaurants
- retail stores
- wholesale distributing companies

ENVIRONMENTAL IMPACT STATEMENT (EIS) an analysis of the expected effects of a development or action on the surrounding natural and fabricated environment. Such statements are required for many federally supported developments under the National Environmental Policy Act of 1969.
Example: Abel seeks to develop a large **subdivision** and obtain **FHA-**insured financing for lot purchasers. Abel must prepare an *environmental impact statement* detailing the effects the development will have on the natural and fabricated environment.

ENVIRONMENTAL PROTECTION AGENCY (EPA) an agency of the U.S. government established to enforce federal pollution abatement laws and to implement various pollution prevention programs.
Example: The *Environmental Protection Agency* requires **permits** for the siting of manufacturing facilities that may introduce pollution into the air or public waters. The *EPA* also provides grants to local governments to assist in construction of sewage treatment plants.

EOY end of year.
Example: Most mortgage loans call for payments at the end of each period. If a loan requires annual payments, a payment would be due at the *end of the year (EOY)*.

EPA Environmental Protection Agency.

EQUAL CREDIT OPPORTUNITY ACT a federal law, enacted in 1974, to discourage discrimination by lenders on the basis of sex or marital status. Amended in 1976 to prohibit discrimination on the basis of age, race, color, religion, national origin, or receipt of public assistance.
Example: Collins, a divorced woman, is denied a **mortgage** loan by a local **savings and loan association.** She feels she would have obtained the loan if she were a man. She sues the

savings and loan under the *Equal Credit Opportunity Act.* Her steady, permanent part-time earnings are to be considered in granting the loan.

EQUALIZATION BOARD a government agency that determines the fairness of taxes levied against properties.
Example: Abel feels the **market value** estimate of his property made by the tax **assessor** is too high. Appeals to the assessor do not result in satisfying Abel's complaint. Abel may take his case to the *Equalization Board* in the hope of reducing the amount of his **assessment.**

EQUITABLE CONVERSION a legal doctrine in some states in which, under a **contract of sale,** buyers and sellers are treated as though the **closing** had taken place in that the seller in possession has an obligation to take care of the property. See **equitable title.**
Note: A contract of sale may specify which party incurs risk of loss until closing.
Example: Though the legal **title** has not passed, the law holds that there has been an *equitable conversion* that effectively **vests** the property in the buyer.

EQUITABLE TITLE the interest held by one who has agreed to purchase but has not yet closed the transaction.
Example: Collins has agreed in writing to buy Baker's house, with closing to be arranged in 2 weeks. In the interim, valuable minerals are found on the property. Since Collins has *equitable title*, the minerals belong to her. Similarly, if the property were **condemned** for public use, the value gain or loss would be hers.

EQUITY the interest or value that the owner has in real estate over and above the **liens** against it.
Example: A property has a **market value** of $100,000. The owner currently owes $60,000 in **mortgage** loans that are against the property. The owner's *equity* is $40,000. See Table 22.

TABLE 22
EQUITY

Market value	$100,000
Liens	− 60,000
Equity	$ 40,000

EQUITY BUILDUP the gradual increase in a **mortgagor's equity** in a property caused by **amortization** of loan principal.
Example: Echols bought a home for $20,000 cash plus a mortgage loan of $80,000, the total cost being $100,000. After 5 years, Echols had worked the outstanding principal of the loan

down to $76,000. Assuming the home was still worth at least $100,000, Echols now has an additional $4,000 in equity because of *equity buildup.*

EQUITY DIVIDEND the annual **cash flow** that an equity investor receives. See **before-tax cash flow, cash-on-cash** return.

EQUITY KICKER see **kicker.**

EQUITY OF REDEMPTION the right of an owner to redeem property securing a loan that has been accelerated prior to **foreclosure.** See **statutory right of redemption.**
Example: Abel's property is about to be foreclosed because he has not met his **mortgage** obligation. If he raises enough money before the loan is foreclosed, he may reclaim the property by paying the **principal, interest,** and legal expenses, under *equity of redemption* laws. Depending on state law, he may be able to reclaim the property after foreclosure.

EQUITY PARTICIPATION same as **participation mortgage.**

EQUITY YIELD RATE the **rate of return** on the **equity** portion of an investment, taking into account periodic **cash flow** and the proceeds from resale. Considers the timing and amounts of cash flow after **annual debt service,** but not income taxes. See **after-tax equity yield.**

EROSION the gradual wearing away of land through processes of nature, as by streams and winds.
Examples:
• Deep gullies cut into unvegetated earth, caused by rainwater *erosion*
• The Grand Canyon formed by *erosion* from the Colorado River
• The Sphinx in Egypt, disfigured by wind *erosion*

ERRORS AND OMISSIONS INSURANCE liability protection against professional malpractice, mistakes in business dealings by insured, etc.
Example: Read estate **brokers** usually have *errors and omission insurance* to protect against claims arising from mistakes they and their agents make in their representation of clients.

ESCALATOR CLAUSE a provision in a **lease** that requires the **tenant** to pay more rent based on an increase in costs. Same as **stop clause.**
Example: A lease requires the tenant to pay increases in real estate taxes over the amount in the base year. Taxes were $1,000 for the base year and $1,250 for the following year. The tenant's rent is *escalated* by $250.

ESCAPE CLAUSE a provision in a contract that allows one or more of the parties to cancel all or part of the contract if certain events or situations do or do not happen.
Example: Mary agrees to buy Joe's house for $100,000; the **contract of sale** includes an *escape clause* that allows Mary to cancel the contract if she cannot obtain approval for a mortgage loan of $80,000 within 60 days.

ESCHEAT the **reversion** of property to the state in the event that the owner dies without leaving a will and has no legal heirs.
Example: Abel dies without a will. No heirs are found. His property *escheats* to the state.

ESCROW an agreement between 2 or more parties providing that certain instruments or property be placed with a third party for safekeeping, pending the fulfillment or performance of a specified act or condition.
Example: The **deed** to the property and the **earnest money** were both placed in *escrow* pending fulfillment of other conditions to the **contract.**

ESCROW ACCOUNT same as **trust account.**

ESCROW AGENT any person engaged in the business of receiving **escrows** for deposit or delivery.
Example: The **title** company is serving as the *escrow agent*. It holds the **earnest money** and **deed,** pending fulfillment of other conditions to the **contract** (Figure 62).

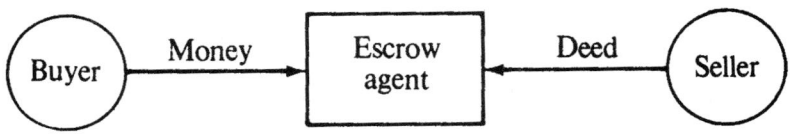

FIG. 62. ESCROW AGENT

ESCROW CLOSING term meaning the same as **closing,** especially in states where **deeds of trust** are used instead of **mortgages.**
Example: Elaine sold her land in California to Connie. The title company acted as escrow agent. Elaine surrendered her deed to them and Connie gave her purchase money to them, thus effecting an *escrow closing.*

ESTATE the degree, nature, and extent of interest that a person has in **real property.**
Example: The highest form of an *estate* is **fee simple,** under which the owner can use the property at will and dispose of it without restriction.

ESTATE AT SUFFERANCE the wrongful occupancy of property by a tenant after the **lease** has expired. See **dispossess proceedings.**
Example: Abel's lease expired and he remained on the property. He has an *estate at sufferance* and may be ejected at the landlord's whim.

ESTATE AT WILL the occupation of real estate by a tenant for an indefinite period, terminable by one or both parties at will.
Example: Under an *estate at will,* the landlord may evict the tenant at any time, and the tenant may vacate at any time. The tenant may have certain rights, however, such as ownership of **emblements** (crops as a result of annual cultivation).

ESTATE FOR LIFE an interest in property that terminates upon the death of a specified person. See **life estate.**
Example: Abel deeded his wife an *estate for her life.* When she dies the property will go to Abel's son. She may use the property and may not commit **waste,** but normal **wear and tear** is acceptable.

ESTATE FOR YEARS an interest in land allowing possession for a specified and limited time.
Example: The **tenant** under a 5-year **lease** holds an *estate for years.*

ESTATE IN REVERSION an **estate** left by the **grantor** for himself or herself, to begin after the termination of some particular estate granted by him or her.
Example: All landlords have an *estate in reversion* which becomes theirs to possess when the **lease** expires.

ESTATE IN SEVERALTY see **tenancy in severalty.**

ESTATE TAX a tax based on the value of property left by the deceased. Since 1987, the estate and gift tax laws exempt approximately $600,000 of property.
Example: Abel dies, leaving $800,000 worth of **assets.** The estate of Abel will pay an *estate tax.* Abel's heirs may also be liable for an **inheritance tax** under their state law.

ESTOPPEL a doctrine of law that stops one from later denying facts which that person once acknowledged were true and others accepted on **good faith.**
Example: Abel signs a certificate acknowledging that he owes $10,000 on a **mortgage** as of a certain date. Later he contends that he owed only $5,000. Abel is prevented from asserting this new contention under *estoppel.*

ESTOPPEL CERTIFICATE a document by which the **mortgagor** (borrower) certifies that the mortgage debt is a **lien** for the amount stated. The debtor is thereafter prevented from claiming that the balance due differs from the amount stated.
Example: The Good Money Savings Association asks Abel to sign an *estoppel certificate,* which he does. Good Money Savings then sells the mortgage to Baker, who buys with confidence. Abel is later estopped (prevented) from denying that he owed the money.

ESTOVERS the legally supported right to take necessities from property. Contrast with **waste.**
Example: Mason has a **life estate** on property. She needs to cut timber for firewood to heat the residence. The **remainderman,** Baker, complains that Mason is damaging the property. The law supports Mason's use of the *estovers* as she has been doing.

ET AL. abbreviation of the Latin *et alii* "and others."
Example: Property owned by John Jones and several others may be referenced as "John Jones, *et al.*"

ET CON abbreviation of the Latin *et conjunx.* Legal term signifying "and husband." See **et ux.**
Example: Hereby signed and delivered by Ellen Smith *et con.*

ET UX abbreviation of the Latin *et uxor,* which means "and wife."
Example: A house is sold by Bill Baker *et ux.* Baker and his wife both must sign the **deed.**

EVALUATION a study of potential **property** uses, but not to determine its present value.
Examples: Evaluations include studies as to the market and **marketability** of a property, **feasibility, highest and best use,** land use, and supply and demand.

EVICTION a legal proceeding by a **lessor** (landlord) to recover possession of property.
Example: When the **tenant** fails to comply with the **lease** agreement (skipping rent payments, unauthorized use of the property, etc.), the landlord may seek *eviction* of the tenant. If successful, this action will terminate the rights of the tenant to use the property.

EVICTION, ACTUAL exists where one is removed from the property, either by force or by process of law.
Example: An apartment tenant may be subject to *actual eviction,* in which case, a notice will be served requiring the tenant to vacate the apartment within a specified time interval.

EVICTION, CONSTRUCTIVE exists when, through the fault of the landlord, physical conditions of the property render it unfit for the purpose for which it was leased.
Example: A landlord may allow the physical condition of an apartment building to deteriorate to the point that the premises are no longer safe for occupancy. A tenant may be able to terminate the **lease,** order *constructive eviction,* and end **liability** for future rent payments.

EVICTION, PARTIAL exists where the possessor of the property, such as a tenant, is deprived of a portion thereof.
Example: A law firm leases a floor of an office building. The **landlord** wishes to make substantial modifications to one side of the building. Because of the disruption caused by the work, the tenant and landlord agree to a *partial eviction* from the property affected by construction. The tenant's rent is reduced accordingly.

EVIDENCE OF TITLE documents, such as **deeds,** that demonstrate ownership.
Example: The property owner kept the **deed** in a bank vault because it is important *evidence of title.*

EXAMINATION OF TITLE research of the **title** to a piece of real estate; less thorough than a **title search,** usually concentrates on recent records.
Example: Al Legal, attorney-at-law, prepared a *title examination* for a building that was sold. The same building had sold two years earlier, and Legal had prepared a title search then; he found no reason to duplicate efforts for the more recent sale.

EXCESS ACCELERATED DEPRECIATION the accumulated difference between **accelerated depreciation** claimed for tax purposes and what **straight-line depreciation** would have been. Generally, *excess accelerated depreciation* is recaptured (taxed) as **ordinary income** upon a sale, instead of receiving more favorable **capital gains** treatment. See **depreciation recapture.**
Note: Since the 1986 Tax Act, the significance of accelerated depreciation has been diminished becaused only straight-line may be claimed for **real estate** acquired since then, and the tax rate differential between ordinary income and capital gains has been minimized.

EXCESS RENT when the **rent** of an existing **lease** exceeds the rental rate on comparable existing space. Should the lease expire or the **tenant** break the lease, the new rate will probably be at market rates.

217

Example: Two years ago the Data Intensive Corporation signed a 5-year lease on office space in downtown Metropolis at $25 per square foot. Overbuilding of office space caused the market rental rate of that space to decline to $20. The $5 paid above **market rent** is considered *excess rent*. This is part of the leased fee value, but a prospective buyer of that building should recognize that the excess rent will diminish upon lease expiration, or perhaps sooner.

EXCHANGE under **Section 1031** of the **Internal Revenue Code, likekind property** used in a trade or business or held as an investment can be exchanged tax-free. See also **boot, realized gain, recognized gain, delayed (tax-free) exchange.**
Example: Collins *exchanges* her farm worth $100,000, but subject to a $20,000 **mortgage,** for Baker's apartments worth $80,000.

EXCLUSIVE AGENCY LISTING employment **contract** giving only one **broker,** for a specified time, the right to sell the property and also allowing the owner alone to sell the property without paying a **commission.**
Example: Graham gives Quick Sale Realty an *exclusive agency listing* on her house. If an agent of Quick Sale or any other **brokerage** firm sells the house during the time of the listing, Quick Sale is entitled to the commission. If Graham sells the house herself, no commission is earned.

EXCLUSIVE RIGHT TO SELL LISTING employment **contract** giving the **broker** the right to collect **commission** if the property is sold by anyone, including the owner, during the term of the agreement. See also **multiple listing service.**
Example: Abel gives Quick Sale Realty an *exclusive right to sell listing* on his house. If the house is sold during the time of the listing, Quick Sale is entitled to a commission.

EXCULPATORY CLAUSE a provision in a **mortgage** allowing the borrower to surrender the property to the lender without personal **liability** for the loan.
Example: Abel buys land for $100,000, paying $40,000 cash and gives a $60,000 mortgage to the seller with an *exculpatory clause*. The **market value** of the land drops suddenly to $55,000. Abel abandons the mortgaged property, losing the $40,000 investment but keeping everything else he owns.

EXECUTE to sign a **contract;** sometimes, to perform a contract fully.
Example: Generally when a buyer and seller sign a **sales contract,** they *execute* the contract.

EXECUTED CONTRACT a **contract** whose terms have been completely fulfilled.
Example: At the **closing,** all parties signed the contract, which made it an *executed contract.*

EXECUTOR a person named in a **will** to carry out its provisions for the disposition of the estate.
Example: Abel specifies in his will that his attorney shall serve as its *executor.* The attorney, at the appropriate time, assures that Abel's property is distributed according to the will.

EXECUTORY CONTRACT a **contract** under which one or more parties has not yet performed.
Example: Abel orally has agreed to buy Baker's land, and Baker's attorney has drafted a contract. At this stage it is *executory* because neither Abel nor Baker has signed it.

EXECUTRIX a woman who performs the duties of an **executor.**
Example: Abel appoints his wife as *executrix* for his estate. She will not need a real estate **license** to sell the property he leaves.

EXEMPTION an amount provided by law that reduces taxable income or taxable value.
Example: Personal exemptions, generally based on the number of people in a household, reduce taxable income.
Example: Homestead exemptions, offered in many jurisdictions, reduce the value of real estate that would otherwise be subject to **ad valorem tax.**

EXPENSE RATIO a comparison of the **operating expenses** to **potential gross income.** This ratio can be compared over time and with that of other properties to determine the relative operating efficiency of the **property** considered.
Example: An apartment complex generates potential gross income of $1 million annually and incurs operating expenses of $400,000 over the same time period. The *expense ratio* of 40% can be compared to its historical rate and to that of other competitive properties. The comparison may disclose reasons for differences that may be used to bolster the property's efficiency.

EXPOSURE (MARKET) the advertising, whether free or paid, of property that is for sale.
Examples: Real estate agents provide market *exposure* through such devices as:
• classified ads in local papers
• for sale signs on the premises
• inclusion in **multiple listing service**
• displays in their office

219

EXTENDED COVERAGE insurance that covers specific incidences normally excluded from standard insurance policies.
Example: A homeowner who lives **adjacent** to a golf course discovers that the standard homeowners' insurance policy does not cover damage due to errant golf balls. An *extended coverage* policy may be obtained, however, to cover such damage.

EXTENSION an agreement between 2 parties to extend the time period specified in a **contract.**
Example: When a tenant is unable to **vacate** the property at the termination of the **lease,** an *extension* may be granted by the **landlord.**
Example: When a seller fails to clear the title in time for a **closing,** an *extension* of the closing date may be granted.

F

FACADE the outside front wall of a building.
Examples: *Facade* materials for a building include:
• aluminum
• brick
• glass
• masonry
• wood

FACE AMOUNT same as **face value.**

FACE INTEREST RATE the percentage interest that is shown on the loan document. Compare with **annual percentage rate, effective rate.**
Example: A mortgage has an 8% *face interest rate,* $10,000 **face value,** and 30-year **amortization** term. If market interest rates are 12%, the **market value** of the loan is $7,200.

FACE VALUE the dollar amount, shown by words and/or numbers, on a document. Compare with **market value; see amortization.**
Example: A **mortgage** has a *face value* of $10,000, **amortization** term of 30 years, and 8% **face interest rate.** It will be amortized in 13 years to $8,000 by annual payments.

FAIR CREDIT REPORTING ACT a federal law that allows individuals to examine and correct information used by **credit** reporting services.
Example: Abel wishes to purchase property from Baker under an **installment land contract.** Baker refuses to make the contract because of Abel's poor **credit rating.** Under the *Fair Credit Reporting Act,* Abel may demand disclosure of Baker's source of information and then take steps to correct any misinformation in the report.

FAIR MARKET RENT the amount that a property would command if it were now available for **lease.** Contrast with **contract rent.** See **economic rent, rent control, Section 8 housing.**
Example: The *fair market rent* for an apartment is estimated at $400 per month. Under **Section 8,** the **tenant** is required to pay 20% of income toward rent; the **landlord** would receive a payment from the government to make up the difference.

221

FAIR MARKET VALUE a term, generally used in **property tax** and **condemnation** legislation, meaning the **market value** of a property.
Example: Property taxes generally are assessed at some ratio of *fair market value.*
Example: When property is condemned for public use, the owner is entitled to be compensated at *fair market value.*

FALSE ADVERTISING describing property in a misleading fashion.
Examples: Examples of false advertising might include:
• representing a property as not being in a **floodplain** when, in fact, it is
• stating, without **caveat**, that a property will appreciate in value
• denying structural flaws that are known to exist

FANNIE MAE nickname for **Federal National Mortgage Association.**

FAR floor-area ratio.

FARMER'S HOME ADMINISTRATION (FmHA) an agency, within the U.S. Department of Agriculture, that administers assistance programs for purchasers of homes and farms in small towns and rural areas.
Example: Abel wishes to develop housing for the elderly in a rural area. He may apply to the *Farmer's Home Administration* for a special 40-year **mortgage** loan.

FDIC Federal Deposit Insurance Corporation.

FEASIBILITY STUDY a determination of the likelihood that a proposed development will fulfill the objectives of a particular investor.
Example: A *feasibility study* of a proposed **subdivision** should:
• estimate the demand for housing units in the area
• estimate the **absorption rate** for the project
• discuss legal and other considerations
• forecast **cash flows**
• approximate investment returns likely to be produced

FEDERAL an early-American-style house that is box-shaped and has a flat roof.
Example: Figure 63.

Ornamentation

Box-like shape

Flat roof

Belvedere

Chimneys protrude through roof

Balustrade

FIG. 63. FEDERAL-STYLE HOUSE

FEDERAL DEPOSIT INSURANCE CORPORATION (FDIC)
a public corporation, established in 1933; insures up to $100,000 for each depositor in most **commercial banks** and **savings and loan associations.** Has own reserves and can borrow from the U.S. Treasury.
Example: The First National Bank becomes insolvent and cannot pay depositors who want to withdraw their money. The *FDIC* pays each depositor the full **prinicpal** amount, up to $100,000, if a merger with a healthy bank cannot be arranged.

FEDERAL FAIR HOUSING LAW a federal law that forbids **discrimination** on the basis of race, color, sex, religion, handicap, familial status, or national origin in the selling or renting of homes and apartments. See **steering.**
Example: Broker Abel is contacted by a black couple wishing to purchase a home. Although homes are currently for sale in several all-white neighborhoods, Abel maintains there are no houses available in these areas. Abel may be prosecuted under the *Federal Fair Housing Law.*

223

FEDERAL HOME LOAN BANK SYSTEM a federally created banking system primarily intended to assure **liquidity** to qualified thrift lenders. The Office of Thrift Supervision was established to replace the Federal Home Loan Bank Board, as part of the **Financial Institutions Reform, Recovery and Enforcement Act** of 1988 **(FIRREA)**.

FEDERAL HOME LOAN MORTGAGE CORPORATION (FHLMC) an organization that purchases **mortgage** loans, mostly from **savings and loan associations.**
Example: ABC Savings and Loan Association sells mortgage loans to the *Federal Home Loan Mortgage Corporation* to gain funds for originating new mortgage loans.

FEDERAL HOUSING ADMINISTRATION (FHA) an agency, within the U.S. Department of Housing and Urban Development, that administers many loan programs, loan **guarantee** programs, and **loan insurance** programs designed to make more housing available.
Example: Abel wishes to purchase a home but lacks funds for a large **down payment.** Through a program provided by the *Federal Housing Administration,* Abel may obtain a loan for up to 97% of the purchase price.

FEDERAL HOUSING FINANCE BOARD a federal agency created under the **Financial Institutions Reform, Recovery and Enforcement Act (FIRREA)** to regulate and supervise the 12 district Federal Home Loan Banks. The functions of the Board were the responsibility of the Federal Home Loan Bank Board prior to passage of the Act.
Example: Figure 64.

FIG. 64. FEDERAL HOUSING FINANCE BOARD

FEDERAL LAND BANK an agency of the federal government that makes mortgage loans on rural property to farmers and to

individuals who provide services to farmers and ranchers. Loans are made at below-market interest rates. Borrowers are required to purchase stock in their local land bank association, which serves as additional security for the loan.
Address: The *Federal Land Bank* operates through regional and district offices located throughout the nation.

FEDERALLY RELATED MORTGAGE a **mortgage loan** that is, in some way, subject to federal law because it is guaranteed, insured, or otherwise regulated by a government agency such as the **Federal Housing Administration (FHA), Veterans Administration (VA), Federal National Mortgage Association (FNMA),** or **Federal Home Loan Mortgage Corporation (FHLMC).**
Example: To borrow on a *federally related mortgage*, certain things must be done in an appropriate way, including use of a **state-certified appraiser.**

FEDERAL NATIONAL MORTGAGE ASSOCIATION (FNMA) a corporation that specializes in buying mortgage loans, mostly from **mortgage bankers.** It adds **liquidity** to the mortgage market. Nicknamed **Fannie Mae,** FNMA is owned by its stockholders, who elect 10 to its Board of Directors. The U.S. president appoints the other 5 directors.
Example: A mortgage banker originates conventional and **FHA loans** and periodically sells them to the *Federal National Mortgage Association.*

FEDERAL RESERVE SYSTEM the central federal banking system that regulates and provides services to member **commercial banks.** Also has the responsibility for conducting federal monetary policy.
Example: The system consists of the Federal Reserve Board and a series of regional Federal Reserve Banks.

FEDERAL REVENUE STAMPS stamps that, when affixed to a transaction document, indicate payment of a federal tax imposed upon the transaction. These have not been required since 1968.

FEDERAL SAVINGS AND LOAN INSURANCE CORPORATION (FSLIC) prior to passage of **FIRREA,** the agency that provided deposit insurance to most **savings and loan associations.** The 1990 law abolished the agency and placed its functions under the **Federal Deposit Insurance Corporation.**

FEDERAL TAX LIEN a **debt** attached against **property** for unpaid federal taxes; most often used by the **Internal Revenue Service** to attach property for payment of owner's unpaid income taxes.

Example: Cecil sold his home but could not receive the equity because of the *federal tax lien* arising out of his failure to pay federal income taxes.

FEDERAL TRADE COMMISSION (FTC) a federal agency, headquartered in Washington, DC, that regulates advertising and other promotion and sales practices of firms engaged in interstate commerce. The FTC does *not* regulate interstate land sales (HUD), anticompetitive activities (JUSTICE), or sale of securities (SEC).
Example: Abel, a builder, was found guilty of false television advertising by the *FTC.*

FEE SIMPLE or FEE ABSOLUTE or FEE SIMPLE ABSOLUTE absolute ownership of **real property;** owner is entitled to the entire property with unconditional power of disposition during the owner's life, and upon his death the property descends to the owner's designated heirs.
Example: The only power that can require Abel to sell his land is **eminent domain;** he owns the property in *fee simple,* so there is no other interest.

FEE SIMPLE DEFEASIBLE a type of property ownership in which the grant of **title** or duration of ownership is dependent on a specified condition.
Example: A *fee simple defeasible* may be granted on the condition that the property be used for an orphanage home (termed "fee simple subject to a condition subsequent").
Example: A *fee simple defeasible* may be granted as long as the property is held as a wildlife refuge (termed "fee simple determinable").

FHA **Federal Housing Administration.**

FHA MORTGAGE LOAN a **mortgage** loan insured by the FHA. See **Federal Housing Administration.**
Example: Abel wishes to purchase a home but has insufficient cash to make a large down payment. By obtaining an *FHA mortgage loan,* Abel may borrow more than the customary 80% of value, with the FHA insuring the loan amount.

FHLB **Federal Home Loan Bank.**

FHLMC **Federal Home Loan Mortgage Corporation;** nicknamed Freddie Mac.

FIABCI see **International Real Estate Federation.**

FIDELITY BOND an assurance, generally purchased by an employer, to cover employees who are entrusted with valuable property or funds.

Example: A landlord employs a resident manager who, among other duties, collects the **rent.** To safeguard these funds during the collection process, the landlord purchases a *fidelity bond* on the resident manager.

FIDUCIARY one who acts, in a financial role, in the best interests of others.
Examples:
• A **broker** is a *fiduciary* for the seller.
• A banker is a *fiduciary* for the bank's depositors.
• An attorney may be a *fiduciary* for the client.
• A **trustee** is a *fiduciary* for the **beneficiaries.**

FIFTEEN-YEAR MORTGAGE a fixed-rate, level-payment mortgage loan with a maturity of 15 years.
Example: In the 1980s, *15-year mortgages* became popular as a way to reduce the amount of interest paid over the life of the mortgage loan. Although the monthly payment is somewhat higher than that of a comparable 30-year loan, the interest savings are substantial.

FILTERING DOWN the process whereby, over time, a housing unit or neighborhood is occupied by progressively lower-income residents.
Example: Many older residences near the downtown of big cities were once occupied by the upper classes, but have *filtered down* to the relatively poor. At some point in the filtering process, many large houses may be converted into rented **multifamily housing.**

FINAL VALUE ESTIMATE in an **appraisal** of **real estate,** the appraiser's value conclusion.
Example: An appraiser has determined these 3 amounts of value based on each appraisal approach:

Cost approach	$600,000
Market comparison approach	575,000
Income approach	560,000

She then reconciles these amounts, decides which is most relevant, and offers a *final value estimate*. If the income approach is considered most indicative of purchaser behavior, the amount may be $560,000 to $570,000, depending on the relative weight assigned to each approach.

FINANCE CHARGE interest or certain other fees charged to a **credit** customer.
Example: A customer makes purchases of $400 on credit. Payment is made one month later. Based on an annual percentage rate of interest of 18%, a *finance charge* of $6.00 ($\frac{.18}{12} \times \400) is added to the bill.

227

FINANCIAL FEASIBILITY the ability of a proposed land use or change of land use to justify itself from an economic point of view. *Financial feasibility* is one test of the **highest and best use** of land, but not the only test. Nor does the financial feasibility of a project make it the most rewarding use of the land.
Example: A proposed small office building will cost $1 million to build, including **direct costs** and **indirect costs.** It is expected to generate $150,000 in annual **net operating income.** Building investors require a 12% **rate of return** on the $1 million investment, or $120,000, so this project is *financially feasible.*

FINANCIAL INSTITUTIONS REFORM, RECOVERY AND ENFORCEMENT ACT (FIRREA) a federal law passed in 1990 that restructured the regulatory and deposit insurance apparatus dealing with savings and loan associations and changed the rules under which federally regulated S&Ls operate. See **Federal Housing Finance Board, Office of Thrift Supervision, Resolution Trust Corporation.**
Example: The *FIRREA* was intended to address the major problem of failing S&Ls due to mounting nonperforming loans held in portfolio, as well as to make reforms that would prevent the problem from recurring. Often referred to as the "S&L bailout," the law represents a large expenditure of federal funds to pay off depositors at failed associations. The law also created the Resolution Trust Corporation, which is charged with managing and liquidating the assets of associations seized by the government. The **Federal Savings and Loan Insurance Corporation** was abolished by the law, and its insurance and regulatory responsibilites were brought under the **Federal Deposit Insurance Corporation,** which also insures commercial banks.

FINANCIAL INTERMEDIARY a firm, such as a bank or savings and loan association, which performs the function of collecting deposits from individuals and investing them in loans and other securities. Also includes credit unions and mutual savings banks. See **disintermediation.**
Example: First National Bank serves as a *financial intermediary* by taking in deposits and placing them in mortgage loans and various securities. In doing so, the bank links individual investors with demanders of credit and the financial markets.

FINANCIAL LEVERAGE the use of borrowed money to complete an investment purchase.
Example: The effects of *financial leverage* on return on **equity** are shown in Table 23.
Note: If **debt service** required is high compared to income, effect of leverage may be to *reduce* return to equity.

TABLE 23
FINANCIAL LEVERAGE TABLE

No leverage		Leverage with 50% debt	
Cost	$100,000	Cost	$100,000
Debt	0	Debt	$50,000
Equity	$100,000	Equity	$50,000
Income	$20,000	Income	$20,000
Debt service	0	Debt service	− 7,500
Cash to equity	$20,000	Cash to equity	$12,500
Return on equity	$\dfrac{20{,}000}{100{,}000} = 0.20$	Return on equity	$\dfrac{12{,}500}{50{,}000} = 0.25$

FINANCIAL MANAGEMENT RATE OF RETURN (FMRR)
a method of measuring investment performance that is a varia-
tion on the **internal rate of return** method. The user specifies
2 after-tax reinvestment rates:
i_L: a safe, liquid rate, obtainable for liquid deposits.
i_R: a run-of-the-mill rate, which can be earned from typical
investments over a long term.
Negative cash flows are generally **discounted** to a present value
at the i_L rate, inflows are compounded to the investment resale
date at i_R. The FMRR is the rate that equates the present value of
negative cash flows to the future value of inflows.
Example: An investment requires a $10,000 negative cash flow
for the first 3 years, then offers $8,500 of cash inflows for years
4-10. If i_L is 5%, the negative cash flows have a present value of
$27,232. If i_R is 10%, the cash inflows will become $80,641.
The *FMRR* is 11.47% because that is the rate at which $27,232
would grow to $80,641 in 10 years with **compound interest.**

FINANCIAL STATEMENT one that shows income and
expenses for an accounting period, or **assets, liabilities,** and
equity as of a point in time.
Example: Table 24.

TABLE 24
FINANCIAL STATEMENT

Income statement		Balance sheet			
		Assets		Liabilities & equity	
Rental income	$5,000				
Interest expense	−2,000				
Depreciation	−1,000	Buildings	$40,000	Mortgage	$30,000
Real estate taxes	− 500	Land	10,000	Equity	20,000
Net income	$1,500	Total	$50,000	Total	$50,000

FINANCING borrowing money to buy property. See **creative financing.**
Examples: The following are examples of *financing:*
• obtaining a **mortgage** loan on a purchase
• **assumptions of a mortgage** from a seller
• arranging for the seller to take a loan as part of the purchase price
• arranging an **installment sale**

FINDER'S FEE money paid to someone other than a **broker** who locates suitable property or a purchaser. Prohibited or limited in most states.
Example: Broker Abel has a **listing** on a particular property. Baker knows several people interested in such property. Abel arranges with Baker to provide a *finder's fee* should one of the **prospects** identified by Baker purchase the property.

FINISH OUT ALLOWANCE a provision in a lease for an office or retail space that provides a certain sum or amount per square foot to the **tenant** to customize the space provided.
Example: A retail tenant leases space for 5 years at a $10 per square foot annual rental rate. The **lessor** provides four concrete walls and a concrete floor, and will pay the tenant *a finish out allowance* of up to $4 per square foot for costs to customize the space.

FIREPROOF having all exposed surfaces constructed of noncombustible materials or protected by such materials.
Example: The exterior surface of the building was composed of brick, aluminum siding, and asbestos shingles, thereby making the exterior *fireproof.*

FIRE-RESISTIVE able to withstand exposure to flame of a specified intensity or for a specified time. Compare **fireproof.**
Example: The interior walls in the house were made of *fire-resistive* material. The walls were designed to resist igniting at temperatures below 1,000 degrees if not exposed for more than one hour.

FIRM COMMITMENT an irrevocable agreement that commits one of the parties to perform a certain act; most common in reference to commitments by lenders to provide financing.
Example: Good Money Bankers made a *firm commitment* to finance a shopping center that had been **preleased.**

FIRREA see **Financial Institutions Reform, Recovery and Enforcement Act.**

FIRST MORTGAGE a **mortgage** that has priority as a **lien** over all other mortgages. In cases of **foreclosure** the first mort-

gage will be satisfied before other mortgages. Also called **senior mortgage.** See **junior mortgage, second mortgage.**

Example: A property costing $100,000 is financed with a *first mortgage* of $75,000, a second mortgage of $15,000, and $10,000 in cash. If the borrower **defaults** and the property is sold upon foreclosure for $80,000, the holder of the *first mortgage* will receive the full amount of the unpaid **principal** plus legal expenses. The second mortgage holder will receive any excess after the first mortgage has been satisfied.

FIRST REFUSAL RIGHT same as **right of first refusal.**

FIRST-YEAR DEPRECIATION same as **additional first-year depreciation.**

FISCAL YEAR a continuous 12-month time interval used for financial reporting; the period starts on any date after January 1 and ends one year later.

Example: For agencies of the federal government, *fiscal year* 1994 refers to the time between October 1, 1993 and September 30, 1994.

FIXED EXPENSES in the operation of **real estate,** those expenses that remain the same regardless of occupancy. Contrast with **variable expenses.**

Examples: Insurance and interest expenses are expected to be the same cost, regardless of the occupancy of a building, so they are *fixed.* By contrast, the cost of utilities and office cleaning will vary with occupancy.

FIXED PAYMENT MORTGAGE a loan secured by real property which features a periodic payment of interest and principal which is constant over the term of the loan. All *fixed payment mortgages* are **fixed rate mortgages,** but some fixed rate mortgages may have variable payments, such as a **graduated payment mortgage.**

Example: A *fixed payment mortgage* calls for 360 monthly payments of interest and principal of $1,000. Added to that amount is a payment to an escrow account for taxes and insurance which may change from year to year.

FIXED-RATE MORTGAGE a loan secured by real property featuring an interest rate that is constant for the term of the loan. Contrast with **adjustable rate mortgage.**

Example: A *fixed-rate mortgage* is originated with an interest rate of 10% for a term of 30 years. The rate will remain at 10% until the loan is retired or the **due-on-sale clause** is exercised at resale of the property.

FIXING-UP EXPENSES (TAX) expenses incurred for the purpose of physically preparing a personal residence for sale. Qualified fixing-up expenses may be deducted from the sale price to determine the price that must be spent in the purchase of another residence to defer **capital gains** taxes on the sale of the old one.

Example: Abel spends $500 for painting and repairs on a home prior to sale. The house sells for $75,500 and costs $7,000 in transaction costs. The adjusted sales price is calculated in Table 25.

TABLE 25
FIXING-UP EXPENSES

Sale price	$75,500
Fixing-up expenses	– 500
Selling expenses	– 7,000
Adjusted sales price	$68,000

Abel must spend at least $68,000 on a new residence to avoid **capital gains** on the sale.

FIXTURES **improvements** or **personal property** attached to the land so as to become part of the real estate. Tests to determine whether an item is a fixture include:
• intent of the parties (was it intended to remain?)
• method of annexation (how is it affixed?)
• relation of the parties (was it expected to be part of a tenant's business?)
• adaptation of the article (is it essential to the building?)
Example: Abel sells his house. The contract of sale includes all of the real estate. Baker, the buyer, believes that the ceiling fan in the dining room is a *fixture*, but Abel claims it as **personal property.**

FLAT 1. an apartment, generally on one level.
Example: A 2-room *flat* is an apartment having 2 rooms.
2. a **level payment mortgage or lease** requirement.
Example: A **flat lease** is one that requires level payments each month or other specified period.

FLAT FEE BROKER a licensed broker who charges a fixed fee for the provision of brokerage services instead of a commission based on a percentage of the sales price of the property. See **discount broker.**
Example: Kramden, a *flat fee broker,* charges $5,000 to arrange the sale of a home, no matter what price is agreed upon by the buyer and seller. If a sale is not consummated within the term of the listing contract, no fee is paid.

FLAT LEASE a rental agreement that requires periodic level rent payments.

Example: Pattern of payments for a one-year *flat lease* with monthly payments (Figure 65).

Flat lease payments

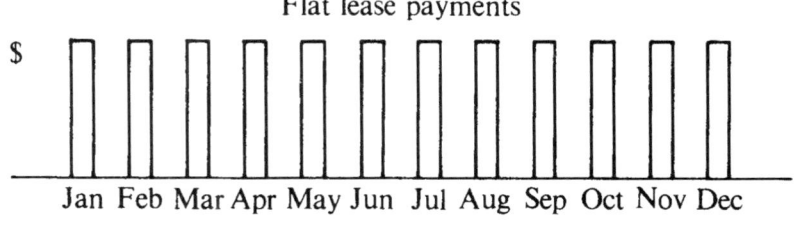

FIG. 65. FLAT LEASE

FLOAT 1. the interval of time after a deposit or withdrawal is made and before the transaction is credited or deducted.

Example: Abel writes a check to pay a **debt** to Baker. Baker deposits the check in a bank other than the one used by Abel. Abel's bank may have a *float* of 2 or 3 days before Baker's bank collects the money.

2. the difference between a **variable interest rate** and the **index** to which it is pegged.

Example: A bank makes construction loans at 3% over the **prime rate.** The 3% is the *float.*

3. to incur a debt.

Example: To fund a project, Atlas Company may *float* a loan or *float* a **bond** issue.

FLOATING RATE an interest rate that is not fixed over the term of a loan, bond, or other fixed-income security, but is allowed to vary according to the change in a specified **index.** See **adjustable-rate mortgage.**

Example: Financial Securities Company created a *floating-rate* mutual fund based on a portfolio of adjustable-rate mortgages. The yield on the fund varies from year to year, depending on the interest rates charged on the ARMs in portfolio.

FLOOD INSURANCE an insurance policy that covers property damage due to natural flooding. Flood insurance is offered by private insurers but is subsidized by the federal government.

Example: Abel owns a home within an area defined as a 100-year **floodplain.** If the local community is participating in a special federal program, Abel may purchase *flood insurance* to cover damage from periodic flooding.

FLOODPLAIN a level land area subject to periodic flooding from a **contiguous** body of water. Floodplains are delineated by

the expected frequency of flooding. For example, an annual floodplain is expected to flood once each year.
Example: Figure 66.

FIG. 66. FLOODPLAIN

FLOOR-AREA RATIO (FAR) the arithmetic relationship of the total square feet of a building to the square footage of the land area.

$$\text{Formula: floor-area ratio} = \frac{\text{building area}}{\text{land area}}$$

Example: In Figure 67, the floor-area ratio is $0.25 \left(\dfrac{50' \times 50'}{100' \times 100'} \right)$.

100 ft | 50 ft

50 ft

100 ft

FIG. 67. FLOOR AREA

FLOOR LOAN the minimum that a lender is willing to advance. See also **gap loan**.
Example: Abel, a lender, agrees to a $700,000 floor on a $1,000,000 permanent loan. When construction is complete, the borrower will receive a $700,000 *floor loan*; when the property is 80% occupied the full $1,000,000 will be loaned.

FLOOR PLAN the arrangement of rooms in a building, or a one-plane diagram of that arrangement.
Example: The home is difficult to sell because of its awkward *floor plan.* One must pass through a bedroom to enter the master bedroom. There is no direct access from the garage to the kitchen and the living room is too small.

FmHA Farmer's Home Administration.

FMRR financial management rate of return.

FMV fair market value.

FNMA Federal National Mortgage Association, which buys and sells existing residential mortgages; nicknamed **Fannie Mae.**

FORBEARANCE a policy of restraint in taking legal action to remedy a **default** or other breach of contract, generally in the hope that the default will be cured, given additional time.
Example: Because of a slowdown in the local economy, loan delinquencies increased dramatically at First Savings. Considering that most of the borrowers were long-term customers of the bank and had always honored their commitments, First Savings adopted a policy of *forbearance* in dealing with overdue payments. Every effort would be made to avoid foreclosure and give the borrowers time to bring the loans up to date.

FORCE MAJEURE an unavoidable cause of delay or of failure to perform a **contract** obligation in time.
Example: A *force majeure* clause is often inserted in a construction contract to protect the **contractor** from delays due to weather, labor disputes, and other unavoidable incidents.

FORECLOSURE a termination of the **equity of redemption** of a **mortgagor** or the **grantee** in the property covered by the **mortgage. Statutory foreclosure** is effected without recourse to courts, but must conform to laws (statutes). **Judicial foreclosure** submits the process to court supervision. See **default, foreclosure sale, statutory right of redemption.**
Example: The lender *forecloses* to gain possession of mortgaged land after the borrower missed 3 payments.

FORECLOSURE SALE the public sale of a mortgaged property following foreclosure of the loan secured by that property. Depending on the type of foreclosure proceeding, the sale may be administered by the courts (**judicial foreclosure**) or by an appointed trustee (**statutory foreclosure**). Proceeds of the sale are used to satisfy the claims of the mortgagee primarily, with any excess going to the mortgagor.

Example: Anyone may bid on properties sold at a *foreclosure sale*. As a practical matter, however, most properties are acquired by the lender, often for the amount owed on the foreclosed loan.

FORFEITURE loss of money or anything else of value because of failure to perform under **contract.**
Example: Because Baker, the prospective purchaser, failed to keep up payments under the **land contract,** he *forfeited* all his rights to the property.

FOUR-THREE-TWO-ONE RULE for an area with commercial lots of uniform depth, the idea that 40% of the value lies in the front quarter, 30% in the next quarter, then 20%, and 10%. If part of the property is **condemned** by **eminent domain,** this provides some guidance as to the value of the part taken. (Compare with **depth tables.**)
Example: A commercial lot would sell for $100,000. Its value is divided into percentages as shown in Figure 68.

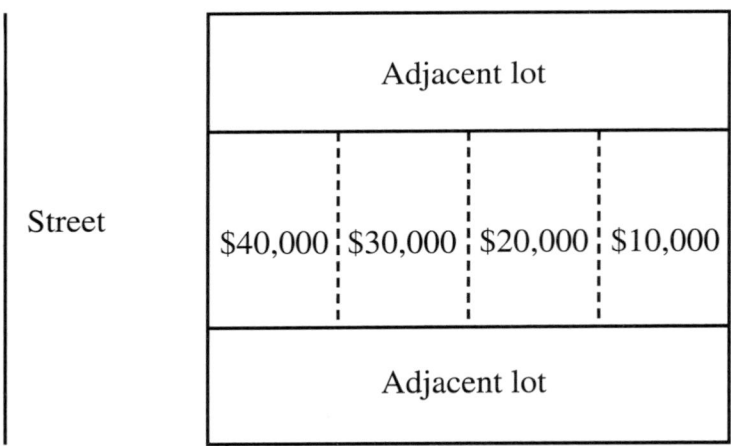

FIG. 68. 4-3-2-1 RULE

FPM flexible payment mortgage.

FRACTIONAL INTEREST ownership of some but not all of the rights in **real estate.**
Examples:
• **Leasehold**
• **Easement**
• Hunting rights

FRAME HOUSE a house constructed with a wooden frame over which is placed some form of siding or **veneer.**
Example: Figure 69.

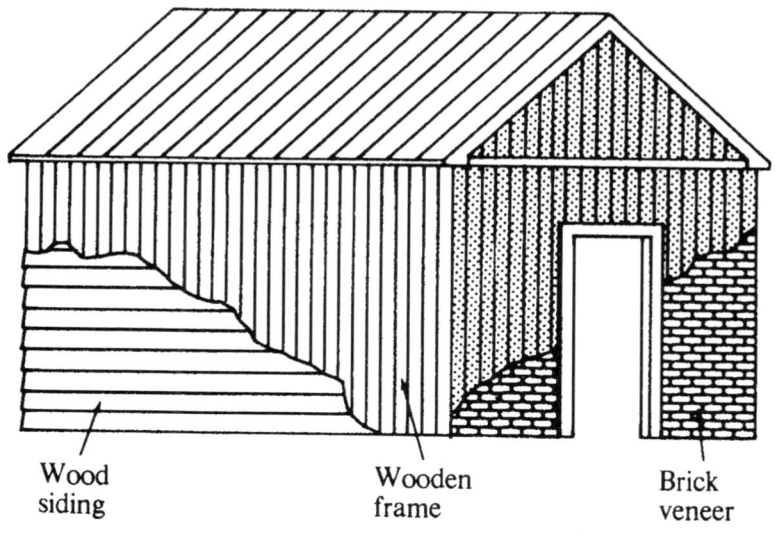

Wood siding Wooden frame Brick veneer

FIG. 69. FRAME HOUSE

FRANCHISE an arrangement between a franchisor and franchisee through which the franchisee uses the company name of the franchisor and is provided specified business services in exchange for a franchise fee. The fee is usually an initial purchase requirement plus an ongoing percentage of gross sales of the business.
Example: In real estate brokerage, locally owned firms may operate as *franchises* of such national companies as Century 21, Gallery of Homes, and Red Carpet. The franchisor advertises the name and logo of the company, offers training for salespersons, and offers or provides other services to the franchisee.

FRAUD the intentional use of deception to cause another person to suffer loss.
Example: Abel purchases property from Baker. Abel later discovers that Baker did not hold **title** to the property and had no right to sell. Baker was guilty of *fraud* and is liable for damages suffered by Abel in the purchase of the property.

FREDDIE MAC nickname for **Federal Home Loan Mortgage Corporation.**

237

FREE AND CLEAR TITLE **title** to a property without **encumbrances.** Generally used to refer to a property free of **mortgage** debt. See **clear title, marketable title.**
Example: *Free and clear title* is generally desired by the purchaser of a property. This requires clearing any **clouds on the title** and satisfying any **liens** that may exist.

FREEHOLD an interest in **real estate** without a predetermined time span.
Example: A **fee simple** or a **life estate** is considered *a freehold* estate because there is not a specified time limit. A **lease** is less than freehold because it has a specified termination date.

FRENCH PROVINCIAL a French-style formal, 1½- to 2½-story house that is perfectly balanced with a high, steep hip roof and curve-headed upper windows that break through the cornice.
Example: Figure 70.

FIG. 70. FRENCH PROVINCIAL HOUSE

FRONTAGE the linear distance of a piece of land along a lake, river, street, or highway.

Example: Road *frontage* (Figure 71).

FIG. 71. ROAD FRONTAGE PROPERTY

Example: Lake *frontage* (Figure 72).

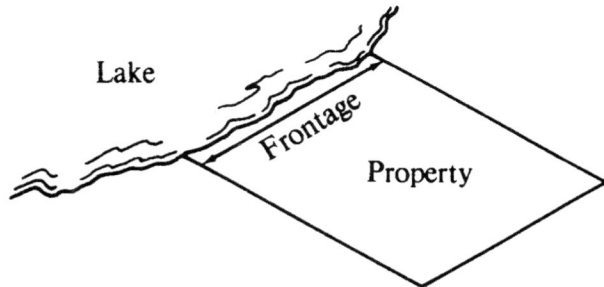

FIG. 72. LAKE FRONTAGE PROPERTY

FRONT FOOT a standard measurement of land, applied at the **frontage** of its street line. Used for lots of generally uniform depth in downtown areas.

Example: The lot in Figure 73 sold for $30,000, or $300 per *front foot*.

FIG. 73. FRONT FOOTAGE

239

FRONT MONEY cash necessary to start a development project.
Example: *Front money* is generally required for purchasing a **site,** preparing plans and studies, obtaining **permits,** and obtaining loan **commitments.**

FSBO for sale by owner. A term referring to properties on the market that are not listed with a real estate broker. Pronounced "fizzbo."
Example: The Mathers are attempting to find a buyer for their home by placing an ad in the paper and putting up a sign in the yard. Such activities indicate the existence of a *FSBO.*

FSLIC Federal Savings and Loan Insurance Corporation.

FTC Federal Trade Commission.

FULL DISCLOSURE a requirement to reveal all information pertinent to a transaction.
Example: Under *full disclosure,* a **broker** is required to give the buyer all known facts about the physical, financial, and economic condition of the subject property.

FULLY AMORTIZED LOAN one having payments of **interest** and **principal** that are sufficient to **liquidate** the loan over its term. Self-liquidating.
Examples:
• $10,000 at 10% interest with 10 annual payments of $1,627.45.
• $100,000 at 9% interest with 360 monthly payments of $804.62.

FULLY INDEXED RATE in conjunction with **adjustable rate mortgages,** the interest rate indicated by the sum of the current value of the **index** and **margin** applied to the loan. This rate is the interest rate which is used to calculate monthly payments in the absence of constraints imposed by the **initial rate** or **caps.** See **teaser rate, adjustable rate mortgage.**
Example: An adjustable rate mortgage is indexed to the one-year treasury bill rate. The current value of the index is 6%. A margin of 2.5 percentage points is applied to the loan. The *fully indexed rate* is 8.5%. However, the loan has an initial rate of 7.5% which determines the interest rate for the first year. When the rate is adjusted, the *fully indexed rate* rises to 10%. A cap of 2 percentage points limits the adjustment in the rate to only 9.5%. If there had been no cap, the interest rate would have risen to 10%.

FUNCTIONAL DEPRECIATION loss of value from all causes within the property, except those due to physical deterioration. See **obsolescence.**

Example: A poor **floor plan** or outdated plumbing fixtures are types of *functional depreciation.*

FUNCTIONAL MODERN OR CONTEMPORARY HOUSE
a post-World War II style house with an exterior style that is an integral part of the overall design. Its function is to enclose some living areas with modern materials while integrating the indoor and outdoor space into one unit.
Example: Figure 74.

FIG. 74. FUNCTIONAL MODERN HOUSE

FUNCTIONAL OBSOLESCENCE same as **functional depreciation.**

FUTURE INTEREST a property right or estate that may not be enjoyed until some time in the future.
Example: When a **life estate** is created, the **remainder** is a *future interest.*
Example: The lender's right to a portion of net **appreciation,** under a **shared appreciation mortgage,** is a *future interest.*

FUTURE WORTH OF ONE same as **compound amount of one.**

FUTURE WORTH OF ONE PER PERIOD same as **compound amount of one per period.**

FY fiscal year.

G

GABLE ROOF one with a triangle, with the ridge forming an angle at the top and each eave forming an angle at the bottom.
Example: Figure 75.

FIG. 75. GABLE ROOF

GAIN an increase in money or **property** value. See **capital gain, realized gain, recognized gain.**
Example: Abel sells for $10,000 land that he bought for $4,000. He recognizes a $6,000 gain excluding property and income taxes.

GAMBREL ROOF one having two slopes on two sides with a steeper lower slope than the upper, flatter sections.
Example: Figure 76.

FIG. 76. GAMBREL ROOF

GAP LOAN one that fills the difference between the **floor loan** and the full amount of the **permanent loan.**
Example: A **developer** arranges a permanent **mortgage** that will fund $1,000,000 when the apartments she is building are 80% occupied. From completion of construction until 80% occupancy is reached, the mortgage is only $700,000. The developer arranges a *gap loan* of $300,000 for the **rent-up period.**

GARDEN APARTMENTS a housing complex whereby some or all **tenants** have access to a lawn area.

242

Example: Abel is now enjoying a steak that he grilled outside his *garden apartment* (Figure 77).

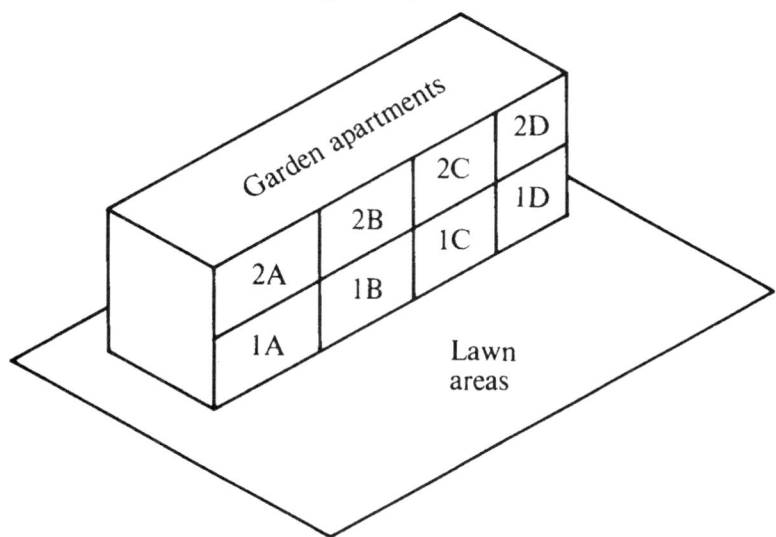

FIG. 77. GARDEN APARTMENTS

GEM growing equity mortgage.

GENERAL CONTRACTOR one who constructs a building or other **improvement** for the owner or **developer.** May retain a construction labor force or use **subcontractors.** See **contractor.**
Example: Collins, a landowner, has architectural plans and **specifications** for an office building. She enters into a **contract** with Baker, a *general contractor,* to build the structure. Baker hires subcontractors who put up the foundation, walls, roof, electrical and plumbing systems, etc.

GENERAL LIEN a **lien** that includes all of the property owned by the debtor, rather than a specific property.
Example: Abel failed to pay 3 months of rent and moved out. Baker, the **landlord,** obtained a *general lien* against Abel by going to secure a **judgment** against Abel. If Abel doesn't pay the back rent, Baker will apply for a specific lien against Abel's furniture and then have it sold.

GENERAL PARTNER in a **partnership,** a partner whose **liability** is not limited. All partners in an ordinary partnership are general partners. A **limited partnership** must have at least one general partner.
Example: The *general partner* in a limited partnership is the **syndicator** who arranges the purchase, seeks investors, and assumes all liabilities of the partnership.

243

GENERAL WARRANTY DEED a **deed** in which the **grantor** agrees to protect the **grantee** against any other claim to **title** of the property and provides other promises. See **warranty deed.**
Example: Abel received a *general warranty deed* for land he bought from Baker. Five years later a defect is found. Mrs. Cabel, whose deceased husband sold the land to Baker, actually owns one half of the property. Abel can claim restitution from Baker for the half because the deed warranties against all defects.

GENTRIFICATION the displacement of lower-income residents by higher-income residents in a neighborhood. Generally occurs when an older neighborhood is rehabilitated or revitalized.
Example: In the past, many large older homes in Inman Park, Atlanta, had been converted to boarding houses. Recently, middle-income families have been buying these houses and converting them back into **single-family homes.** The lower-income residents are often forced to move to surrounding areas and are replaced by the middle-income renovators. As this process is repeated, *gentrification* of the neighborhood occurs.

GEORGIAN a large, English-style, formal 2- or 3-story rectangular house that is characterized by its classic lines and ornamentation.
Example: Figure 78.

FIG. 78. GEORGIAN-STYLE HOUSE

GIFT DEED a **deed** for which **consideration** is love and affection and no material consideration is involved.
Example: Abel, who is on the brink of **bankruptcy, executes** a *gift deed* to his wife. Since there is no consideration and the apparent reason for the transfer was to remove the property from the reach of Abel's creditors, the deed might not be valid. In other situations the gift deed would be upheld.

GIFT TAX federal tax upon a monetary gift to a relative or friend. Generally, each person may give up to $10,000 per year to each **donee** without imposition of a federal gift tax. On higher gifts, there may be a gift tax, or the gift may affect the **donor's estate tax.**
Example: Mr. and Mrs. Abel together give $20,000 this year to each of 3 sons ($60,000 total). There will be no *gift tax* imposed.

GI LOAN same as **VA loan.**

GIM **gross income multiplier.**

GINNIE MAE nickname for **Government National Mortgage Association.**

GINNIE MAE PASS THROUGH a **pass-through certificate** secured by a pool of mortgage loans insured by the Government National Mortgage Association, an arm of the federal government.
Ginnie Mae pass throughs often provide high yields with security to investors, although the returns may be affected by the pattern of loan repayments on the mortgages in the pool.

GLA **gross leasable area.**

GNMA **Government National Mortgage Association (Ginnie Mae).**

GOOD AND MARKETABLE TITLE **title** to a piece of real estate that can be shown, usually by **title search** or **abstract of title** to be vested in the **owner of record,** and free of claims or **liens** that would impair its marketability.

GOOD AND MERCHANTABLE TITLE same as **good and marketable title.**

GOOD FAITH an act done honestly.
Example: Abel pays $1,000 to Baker as a *good faith* **deposit** on land Baker offers for sale. Baker doesn't own the land and doesn't plan to buy it, so his acceptance of the deposit was not in *good faith.*

GOOD FAITH MONEY see **earnest money.**

GOOD TITLE see **good and marketable title.**

GOODWILL a business **asset** of **intangible value** created by customer and supplier relations.
Example: Diversified Enterprises, Inc. bought Acme Hardware Co. They paid a total of $200,000, which included $100,000 for the **property,** $50,000 for **inventory,** and $50,000 for *goodwill.*

GOVERNMENT NATIONAL MORTGAGE ASSOCIATION (GNMA) a government organization to assist in housing finance. There are 2 main programs:
1. to **guarantee** payments to investors in mortgage-backed securities
2. to absorb the **write-down** of low-interest rate loans that are used to finance **low-income housing**
See **secondary mortgage market.**
Example: Good Money Mortgage Bankers, who have originated $3 million of **FHA** and **VA mortgages,** have issued **participation mortgage** certificates, backed by the mortgages, to investors. *GNMA* guarantees the participation certificates (Figure 79). See **pass-through certificates.**

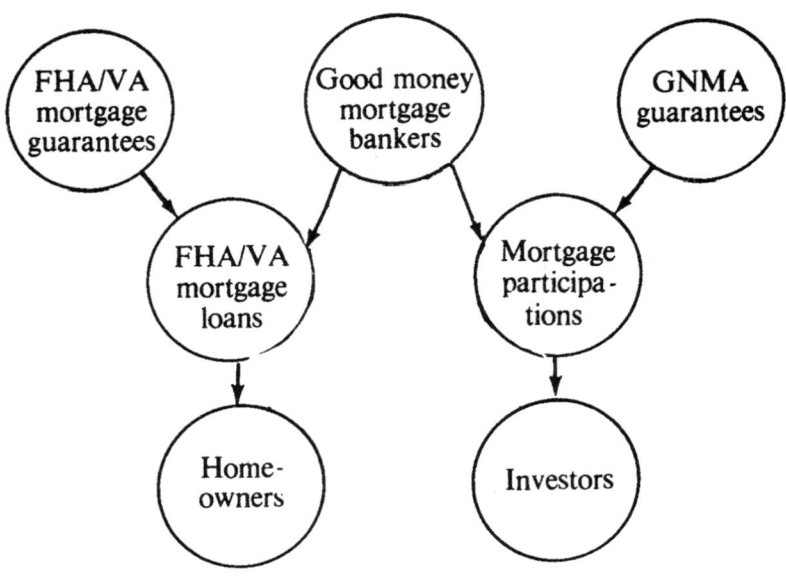

FIG. 79.
GNMA GUARANTEED PARTICIPATION CERTIFICATES

GOVERNMENT RECTANGULAR SURVEY a rectangular system of land **survey** that divides a district into 24-square mile **quadrangles** from the **meridian** (north-south line) and the

baseline (east-west line); the tracts are divided into 6-mile-square parts called *townships,* which are in turn divided into 36 tracts, each 1 mile square, called **sections.**

Example: *Government Rectangular Survey* System (Figure 80).

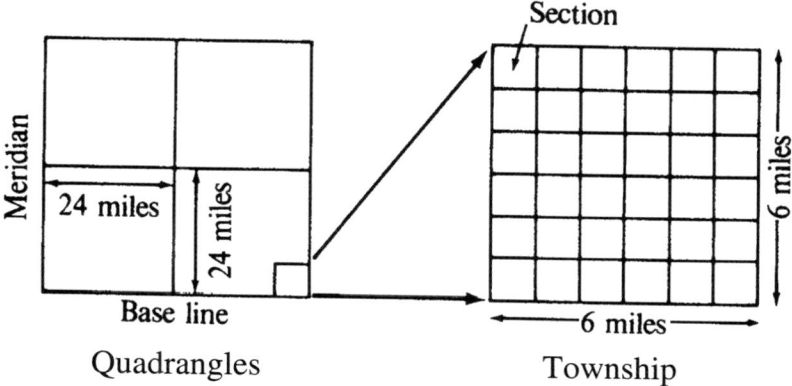

FIG. 80. GOVERNMENT RECTANGULAR SURVEY

GOVERNMENT-SPONSORED ENTERPRISE (GSE) a quasi-governmental organization that is privately owned but was created by the government and retains certain privileges not afforded totally private entities.

Example: Both the **Federal National Mortgage Association** and the **Federal Home Loan Mortgage Corporation** are *government-sponsored enterprises* that were created by the federal government but transferred to private owners. Both organizations have the implicit backing of the U.S. Treasury, which allows them to raise funds at lower interest rates than other private concerns.

GPM graduated-payment mortgage.

GRACE PERIOD the period during which one party may fail to perform without being considered in **default.**

Example: Rent is due on the first of each month, but the tenant requested and received a 10-day *grace period* from the landlord. If rent is paid on or before the 10th, the tenant is not in default.

GRADE 1. ground level at the foundation.

Example: Part A of the building in Figure 81 is above *grade*; Part B is below *grade*.

2. to prepare a smooth surface on a site.

Example: Machinery was brought to the **site** to *grade* the **land** in preparation for the foundation.

247

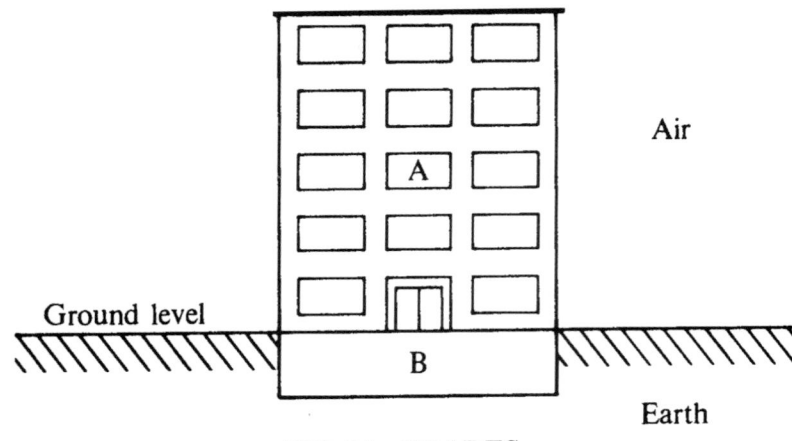

FIG. 81. GRADES

GRADED LEASE same as **graduated lease.**

GRADIENT the slope or rate of increase or decrease in the elevation of a surface; usually expressed as a percentage:

$$\text{Gradient} = \frac{\text{vertical rise or fall}}{\text{horizontal distance}}$$

Example: The lot in Figure 82 has a 10% *gradient:*

FIG. 82. GRADIENT

GRADUATED LEASE a lease that provides for graduated changes, at stated intervals, in the amount of rent.
Example: A 5-year *graduated lease* calls for annual rent increases of 5%. The yearly payments are shown in Figure 83.

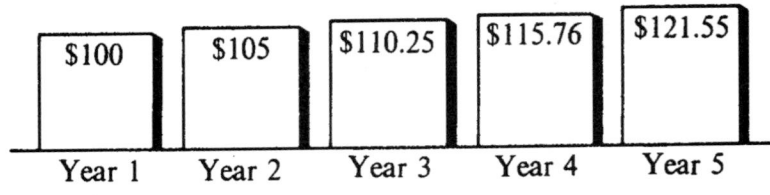

FIG. 83. GRADUATED LEASE

GRADUATED-PAYMENT MORTGAGE (GPM) a mortgage requiring lower payments in early years than in later years. Payments increase in steps each year until the installments are sufficient to amortize the loan.

Example: A *GPM* may be made in which monthly payments rise by a set percentage after each year for the first 4 years. The payments would look like Figure 84.

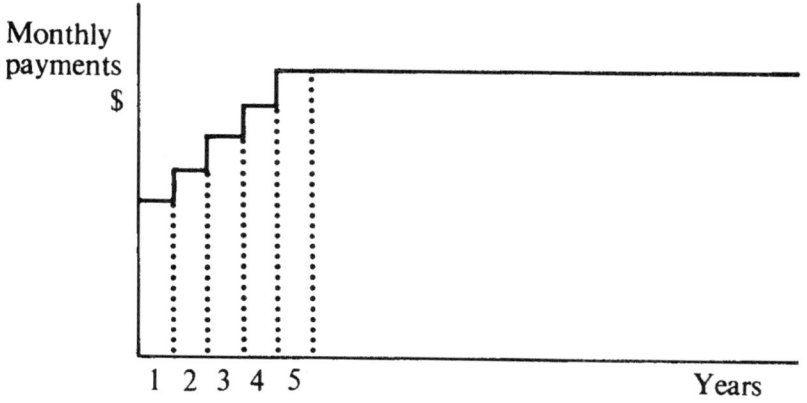

FIG. 84. GRADUATED-PAYMENT MORTGAGE

GRADUATE REALTORS® INSTITUTE (GRI) an educational program sponsored by the **National Association of Realtors®** or State Boards.

Example: Broker Abel attends 3 approved courses offered by the California Association of Realtors®, and he passes the examinations. His new business cards read: Broker Albert Abel, *GRI*.

GRANDFATHER CLAUSE when a law is changed or a new law is passed, those whose specific activity was legal under the previous law are often allowed to continue, by virtue of this provision.

Example: All real estate **brokers** are allowed to continue to practice as brokers after licensure requirements increase. The new law affects only new **licensees;** old licensees are *grandfathered.*

GRANT a technical term used in deeds of **conveyance** of property to indicate a transfer.

Example: In a **deed,** Abel *grants* his land to his daughter in **fee simple.**

GRANTEE the party to whom the **title** to **real property** is conveyed; the buyer.

Example: Edith Andrew Abel is the *grantee* under a **deed** from her father, Albert Abel.

GRANTOR anyone who gives a **deed.**

249

Examples: *Grantors* include:
- an individual (former) owner
- a bankruptcy **trustee**
- a **guardian** for an **incompetent**

GRANTOR/GRANTEE INDEX a reference kept with **public records** that cross-indexes **grantors** and **grantees** with one another and the properties they relate to.
Example: By visiting the county courthouse records room, you can trace property ownership history. If you know who the current owner is, cross-reference the name(s) to the *grantor/grantee index* to discover prior owners.

GRI graduate of the Realtors® Institute, which is affiliated with the **National Association of Realtors®**. See **Graduate Realtors® Institute.**

GRM gross rent multiplier.

GROSS AREA the total floor area of a building, usually measured from its outside walls.
Example: The *gross area* of a 2-story office building (Figure 85) that completely covers a 100' x 100' tract of land is 20,000 square feet (10,000 square feet for each story). Exterior walls, interior hallways, stairwells, and utility rooms absorb 4,000 square feet, so the **net leasable area** is 16,000 square feet.

FIG. 85. GROSS AREA

GROSS INCOME total income from property before any expenses are deducted.

Example: A building with 10,000 net rentable square feet of floor space rents for an average of $10 per square foot. **Concessions** in the lobby produce an additional $20,000 in annual income. An average 5% **vacancy rate** is maintained. Two measures of *gross income* are shown in Table 26.

TABLE 26
GROSS INCOME

Total **rent** income	$100,000	(10,000 × $10)
Concession income	+ 20,000	
Potential gross income	$120,000	
Vacancy loss	− 5,000	(.05 × $100,000)
Effective gross income	$115,000	

GROSS INCOME MULTIPLIER (GIM) same as **gross rent multiplier.**

GROSS LEASABLE AREA the floor area that can be used by **tenants.** Generally measured from the center of joint partitions to outside wall surfaces. Contrast **net leasable area.**
Example: Figure 86.

FIG. 86. GROSS LEASABLE AREA

Of the 20,000 gross leasable square feet on each floor, approximately 25% is used for purposes of common use.

GROSS LEASE a lease of property whereby the landlord **(lessor)** is responsible for paying all property expenses, such as taxes, insurance, utilities, and repairs.

Example: In a certain apartment complex the **landlord** pays for all utilities and taxes. The lease is a *gross lease,* since the landlord receives rent as a gross figure and must pay **operating expenses.**

GROSS POSSIBLE RENT same as **potential gross income.**

GROSS PROFIT RATIO in an **installment sale,** the relationship between the gross profit (gain) and the **contract price.** The resulting fraction is applied to periodic receipts from the buyer to determine the taxable gain from each receipt.

Example: Land, held as a **capital asset** by Collins, is sold for $10,000. Collins' tax basis was $4,000, so the resulting gain was $6,000. The *gross profit ratio* is 60% ($6,000 divided by $10,000 equals 60%). Collins accepted a $1,000 cash **down payment** with the $9,000 balance of the price to be paid over 3 years. Of each amount paid toward the principal, 60% is gain to be taxed and the balance is a nontaxable return of capital. See **contract price.**

GROSS RENT MULTIPLIER (GRM) the sales price divided by the **contract** rental rate.

Example: The sales price is $40,000; the gross monthly **contract rent** is $400; the *GRM* = $40,000 ÷ $400 = 100. GRM may also be expressed as the number of years of rent equaling the purchase price ($40,000 ÷ $4,800 annual rent = a *GRM* of 8.333).

GROUND LEASE one that rents the land only.

Example: The landowner, Abel, gives a 50-year *ground lease* to Baker. Baker must pay $5,000 per year rent. At the end of the 50-year period, Abel owns the land **free and clear** and whatever **improvements** that Baker left on the property.

GROUND RENT the rent earned by leased land.

Example: The Good Title Company owns an office building situated on a **site** owned by the Widget Makers Retirement Fund. The site is leased to Good Title on a long-term basis and requires the payment of *ground rent* to the Widget Makers Retirement Fund on a semiannual basis.

GROWING-EQUITY MORTGAGE (GEM) a **mortgage** loan in which the payment is increased by a specific amount each year, with the additional payment amount applied to **principal** retirement. As a result of the added principal retirement, the **maturity** of the loan is significantly shorter than a comparable **level-payment mortgage.**

Example: Long purchased her home with a *growing-equity mortgage.* Long's monthly payments will increase by 5% each year, with the increased amount applied to principal. Long will

retire the loan in about half the time required to retire a comparable loan with fixed payments.

(TO) GUARANTEE (A LOAN) to agree to **indemnify** the holder of a loan all or a portion of the unpaid **principal** balance in case of **default** by the borrower. See also **VA mortgage loan.**
Example: Abel takes out a **VA mortgage loan** to purchase a home. The Veterans Administration *guarantees* the loan. In case foreclosure is threatened because Abel fails to make the payments, the VA will reimburse the lender for losses up to the amount guaranteed.

GUARANTY an assurance provided by one party that another party will perform under a contract.
Example: Fred Garrison is an experienced developer. His daughter, Ruth, decides to branch out and start her own company. The construction lender requires a *guaranty* from Fred Garrison before granting Ruth Garrison a loan for her first project.

GUARDIAN one appointed by a court to administer the personal affairs or property of an individual who is not capable of such duties.
Example: The *guardian* of an orphan **minor** signs a **deed** to sell property inherited by the minor, to pay the minor's educational expenses.

GUIDELINE LIVES **depreciable lives,** for buildings and equipment, that are used in trade or business. Generally applied to **assets** bought before 1981; the **accelerated cost recovery system** applies to depreciable assets bought in 1981–1986; the modified accelerated cost recovery system applies to purchases after 1986.
Example: *Guideline lives* for certain assets:
• apartments—40 years
• dwellings—45 years
• hotels—40 years
• warehouses—60 years

H

HABENDUM CLAUSE the "to have and to hold" clause that defines or limits the quantity of the **estate** granted in the **deed.**
Example: The *habendum clause* "to have and to hold for one's lifetime" creates a **life estate.**

HALF BATH a room in a residence which contains a toilet and wash basin but no bathing facilities, such as a bathtub or shower stall. A three-quarter bath contains a shower but no bathtub.
Example: The two-story home has two full baths upstairs and a *half bath* downstairs.

HANDYMAN'S SPECIAL in real estate classified advertising, generally refers to a house that requires extensive repair and remodeling, selling at a relatively low price.
Example: The Williamses looked at a *handyman's special* that needed new carpeting and repainting. They bought it for $50,000, spent $12,000 (not counting the value of their own labor) to repair it, then resold it for $75,000, providing them with a $13,000 profit.

HANGOUT the remaining balance of a loan when the **term** of the loan is beyond the term of a **lease.**
Example: A lender offers a 30-year loan on property that is leased to Big Buy Foods for the next 25 years. In 25 years the loan balance will be $100,000, which is the *hangout*. The lender estimates that the land value in 25 years will greatly exceed $100,000, so concern for the hangout is minimized.

HAZARD INSURANCE a form of insurance that protects against certain risks, such as from fires or storms.
Example: Mortgage lenders frequently require that owners maintain *hazard insurance,* at least to the extent of the mortgage debt.

HEARING a formal procedure, with issues of fact or law to be tried, in which parties have a right to be heard. Similar to a trial and may result in a final order.
Example: State **real estate commissions** hold *hearings* to investigate complaints filed against licensed salespersons.

HECTARE a metric land measurement equal to about 2.471 **acres** or about 107,637 square feet.
Example: Abel sold 6 *hectares* of land in Puerto Rico for $20,000.

HEIR one who inherits **property.**
Example: A person can decide on *heirs* by leaving a **valid** will. If one dies **intestate,** state laws determine who the heirs are.

HEIRS AND ASSIGNS a term often found in **deeds** and **wills** to grant a **fee simple** estate.

Example: Abel wills property to "Baker, *heirs and assigns.*" Upon inheriting the property, Baker can sell it or will it to **heirs.**

HEREDITAMENTS any property, whether real or personal, tangible or intangible, that may be inherited.
Example: Buildings, lands, and **leaseholds** are examples of *hereditaments.*

HIGHEST AND BEST USE an **appraisal** term meaning the legally and physically possible use that, at the time of appraisal, is most likely to produce the greatest net return to the land and/or buildings over a given period.
Example: A vacant lot in the city is valued at $10,000 if developed for a **single-family house,** $20,000 as an **apartment building,** $25,000 as a retail store, and $30,000 as a small chemical processing plant. Because of **restrictions** on water supply and disposal, the chemical plant is not physically or legally possible. **Zoning** laws prohibit commercial development. Therefore, the *highest and best use* of the lot is for an apartment building.

HIGH-RISE generally a building that exceeds 6 stories in height and is equipped with elevators.
Example: A *high-rise* building is constructed to include retail space on the first floor, 8 floors of office space, 10 floors of **condominium** units, and a club/restaurant on the 20th floor.

FIG. 87. HIGH VICTORIAN ITALIANATE HOUSE

255

HIGH VICTORIAN ITALIANATE a nineteenth-century-style house with three different kinds of window arches, the primary distinguishing characteristic of this style. The arches are straight-sided, flat-topped and rectangular.
Example: Figure 87.

HIP ROOF one formed by four walls sloped in different directions with the two longer sides forming a ridge at the top.
Example: Figure 88.

FIG. 88. HIP ROOF

HISTORIC DISTRICT a designated area where the buildings are considered to have some significant historic character. Such designation makes the area eligible for certain federal assistance programs and protects the area from clearance in conjunction with federally sponsored programs.
Example: Older areas, such as the French Quarter in New Orleans, enjoy protection by being designated as *historic districts.*

HISTORIC STRUCTURE a building that is officially recognized for its historic significance has special status under the 1976 Tax Reform Act, which encourages **rehabilitation** and discourages **demolition** or substantial alteration of the structure. In 1981 a special tax law allowed a 25% **tax credit** for rehabilitation of **certified historic structures,** reduced to 20% in 1986.
Example: Because the old office building was designated a certified *historic structure*, its owner decided to restore the building to take advantage of allowable tax deductions.

HOLDBACK money not paid until certain events have occurred, such as a **floor loan** of a **loan commitment** or **retainage** on a construction contract.
Example: On a $1,000,000 loan the lender has a $300,000 *holdback* until the property is 80% rented.
Example: The developer has a 10% *holdback* from subcontractors until the building **inspection** is complete.

HOLDER IN DUE COURSE one who acquires a **bearer instrument** in **good faith** and is eligible to keep it even though it may have been stolen.

Example: Abel receives from Baker a $100 bill in payment of rent on his apartment. Police inform Abel that the bill was stolen by Baker from Cobb. Since the bill is bearer paper and Abel accepted it without knowing about the theft, he became a *holder in due course* and is allowed to keep it.

HOLD HARMLESS CLAUSE in a **contract,** a clause whereby one party agrees to protect another party from claims.
Example: Big Buy Foods is leasing property from its landlord, Lucky Lessors. A customer is injured by a falling light fixture, and she sues both Big Buy Foods and Lucky Lessors. In the **lease,** Big Buy Foods agreed to a *hold harmless clause* whereby they **indemnified** Lucky Lessors against such events.

HOLDING COMPANY one that owns or controls another company(ies).
Example: Banks and public utilities are often owned or controlled by a *holding company.* Sometimes this arrangement allows more latitude for business practices than the operating company can achieve alone.

HOLDING COSTS same as **carrying costs.**

HOLDING PERIOD the time span of ownership, often for investment real estate.
Example: Some investors prefer short *holding periods* (under 5 years) in an attempt to retain high levels of financial **leverage.** Others hold property longer to reduce frequent **transaction costs** and avoid **depreciation recapture.**

HOLDOUT a landowner in the path of an **assemblage** who attempts to realize the highest possible price by refusing to sell in the early stages of assemblage.
Example: While downtown lots were being assembled for future use as a bus depot, Harold *held out* for a price of $200 per square foot for his land.

HOLDOVER TENANT a **tenant** who remains in possession of leased property after the expiration of the lease **term.** See **tenancy at sufferance.**
Example: Abel leases an apartment for one year. At the end of the year, Abel is still in the process of finding a new home. As a *holdover tenant,* Abel may be evicted or allowed to remain on a month-to-month basis by continuing to pay rent, at the landlord's discretion.

HOME EQUITY CONVERSION the process of liquidating all or a portion of the **equity** in one's home. See **home equity loan, reverse annuity mortgage.**

Example: The Hudsons own a home valued at $100,000, on which they have a mortgage loan in the amount of $60,000. By refinancing the loan for $80,000, they can obtain cash in the amount of $20,000 through *home equity conversion.*

HOME EQUITY LOAN a loan secured by a second mortgage on one's principal residence, generally to be used for some non-housing expenditure.
Example: *Home equity loans* became popular in the late 1980s as a way to finance purchases or consolidate existing debts while retaining tax-deductible status for the interest paid on the loan.

HOME IMPROVEMENT LOAN a loan, usually secured by a mortgage on the home, used to pay for major remodeling, reconstruction, or additions to the home.
Example: In order to add an extra bedroom, remodel the kitchen, and construct a swimming pool in the backyard, the Holmeses took out a *home improvement loan* from their local savings and loan association.

HOME INSPECTOR a professional who evaluates the structural and mechanical condition of a home prior to its being sold. Some states require home inspectors to be bonded or licensed.
Example: Before closing on their new home, the Felixes hired a *home inspector* to check the condition of the structure. The inspector discovered an unsafe furnace burner and a leaking faucet. The seller agreed to have the problems repaired before the closing.

HOME LOAN see **mortgage.**

HOMEOWNERS' ASSOCIATION an organization of the homeowners in a particular **subdivision,** planned unit development, or **condominium;** generally for the purpose of enforcing **deed** restrictions or managing the **common elements** of the development. See **community association.**
Example: All unit owners of the Lakefront Condominiums are members of the Lakefront *Homeowners' Association.* The Association maintains the pool, grounds, and building structure, and regulates use of common elements. They assess each owner a $75 monthly fee.

HOMEOWNERSHIP the state of living in a structure that one owns. Contrasted with being a renter or **tenant** in one's home.
Example: *Homeownership* is a goal of many families. It provides security from the decisions of landlords, pride of ownership, and investment advantages in exchange for undertaking the responsibilities of a property owner.

HOMEOWNERSHIP RATE the percentage ratio of owner-occupied dwelling units to total occupied dwelling units in an area.
Example: In 1989, the *homeownership rate* for the United States was 63.9%, indicating the proportion of all households owning the home in which they lived. Within the population, the rate varies greatly by age and type of household. Again for 1989, the rate for householders under age 35 was 39.1%, while for those over 65 it was 75.8%. Married couple families had a rate of 78.3%, but single households had only a 48.2% rate.

HOMEOWNER'S ONCE-IN-A-LIFETIME EXCLUSION see **over age 55 home sale exemption.**

HOMEOWNER'S POLICY an insurance policy designed especially for homeowners. Usually protects the owner from losses caused by most common disasters, theft, and **liability.** Coverage and costs vary widely.
Example: Whitman acquired a *homeowner's policy* for an annual premium of $500. It insures her home from fire losses (up to $100,000), theft (of household goods, excluding jewelry, paintings, stamp collections, silverware), and gives up to $300,000 of **liability** protection.

HOMEOWNERS' WARRANTY PROGRAM (HOW) a private insurance program that protects purchasers of newly constructed homes, when the builder participates in the program, against structural and mechanical faults.
Example: Abel purchases a new home. The builder participates in the HOW program and provides Abel with a *homeowner's warranty* to cover any faults or oversights in the construction.

HOMEOWNER WARRANTY INSURANCE same as **homeowner warranty program.**

HOMESTEAD status provided to a homeowner's principal residence by some state statutes; protects home against **judgments** up to specified amounts.
Example: *Homestead* laws in Texas prevent a lender, other than the **mortgage** lender, from forcing the sale of one's principal residence to satisfy a **debt**.

HOMESTEAD EXEMPTION in some jurisdictions, a reduction in the **assessed value** allowed for one's principal residence.
Example: The *homestead exemption* in Georgia enables a homeowner, upon application, to get $5,000 subtracted from the assesor's **appraisal** of the home. This reduces the property tax burden.

HOMOGENEOUS uniform, of like characteristics or quality. Opposite of heterogeneous. The values of an area tend to be maximized when properties are *homogeneous,* because low-valued or unusual properties are likely to reduce the value of other nearby properties of higher cost.
Example: The houses in the neighborhood were *homogeneous,* all single-family, one-story buildings with brick exteriors. They were readily marketable with asking and selling prices in a tight range.

HORIZONTAL PROPERTY LAWS state statutes that enable **condominium** ownership of property. Whereas property laws generally recognize **ownership rights** to all space from the center of the earth to some distance in the air, condominium laws allow individual ownership to be split on a horizontal plane that generally limits the unit owner's interest to the inside dimensions of the unit. See **common elements.**
Example: Before passage of *horizontal property laws,* all owners in a condominium were obligated under each individual mortgage loan in the complex. If one owner **defaulted,** the lender could **foreclose** on the entire condominium. Now, to secure a loan, each owner pledges only his or her limited interest in the condominium.

HOUSING AFFORDABILITY INDEX an indicator of the proportion of the population that can afford to buy the average home sold during the current period.
Example: There are many types of *housing affordability indexes* in use. One of the most well-known is the index compiled by the **National Association of Realtors®.** The index is formed by the ratio of a percentage of the average income of all families in the area to the monthly loan payment needed to purchase the average-priced home sold in that area. An index value of 1.00 indicates that half of the families in the area could afford to buy the average home. The higher the index, the more affordable housing should be in the area.

HOUSING AND URBAN DEVELOPMENT (HUD) DEPARTMENT a U.S. government agency established to implement certain federal housing and community development programs.
Example: Mason desires to develop a housing project for low-income families. She applies to the *Department of Housing and Urban Development* for a special low-interest loan for the development.

HOUSING CODE a local government **ordinance** that sets minimum standards of safety and sanitation for existing residential buildings. Contrast to **building codes,** which pertain to new construction.

Example: Because of violations of the *housing code,* including a badly leaking roof and rat infestation, the old apartment building was condemned.

HOUSING STARTS an estimate of the number of dwelling units on which construction has begun during a stated period.
Example: During the last month, *housing starts* were 20% lower than the same month a year ago, reflecting a lower demand for new houses caused by high **mortgage** rates.

HOW homeowners' warranty program.

HUD Department of Housing and Urban Development.
Example: This federal agency attempts to assure decent, safe, and sanitary housing for all Americans, and investigates complaints of discrimination in housing.

HUD-1 FORM same as **Uniform Settlement Statement.**

HUNDRED PERCENT LOCATION see **one-hundred percent location.**

HVAC an acronym that refers to the climate control system in buildings (**H**eat, **V**entilation, and **A**ir-**C**onditioning).

HYPOTHECATE to pledge a thing as security without having to give up possession of it.
Example: Through use of a **mortgage** or **deed of trust,** the buyer *hypothecates* a newly acquired home to the lender or **trustee.** The buyer uses and controls the property.

I

IAAO International Association of Assessing Officers.

IMPLIED CONTRACT created by actions but not necessarily written or spoken. See also **statute of frauds.**
Example: Abel posts a for-sale sign on his property that says, "See Your Broker." Davis submits an offer through her **broker** and buys the property. Abel refuses to pay the broker, who then goes to court contending that the sign created an *implied contract.*

IMPLIED EASEMENT See **easement by prescription.**

IMPLIED WARRANTY one that is not written but exists under the law. Contrasted with "expressed."
Example: Under the law in several states there is an *implied warranty* **of habitability** for apartments leased to tenants. This means that the tenant has the right to a dwelling that is fit for living, i.e., there are no **building code** violations.

IMPROVED LAND land that has some improvements. Land that has been partially or fully developed for use.
Examples: Any of the following activities on a piece of **raw land** will result in *improved land:*
• landscaping and grading
• installation of utilities
• construction of roads, curbs, and/or gutters
• construction of buildings

IMPROVEMENT RATIO the relative value of **improvements** to the value of **unimproved property.**
Example: Land worth $250,000 was improved with a $1 million building. The improvement ratio is $1 million to $250,000, or 4:1.

IMPROVEMENTS those additions to **raw land,** such as buildings, streets, sewers, etc., tending to increase value.
Example: A hypothetical example of how *improvement* costs may affect property and land values is shown in Table 27.

TABLE 27
IMPROVEMENT COSTS

Improvement	Cost of improvement	Total property value	Value of land
None	$ 0	$ 500	$ 500
Curbs, drainage, & utilities	3,000	5,000	2,000
House	70,000	85,000	15,000
Apartment building	250,000	290,000	40,000

IMPOUND ACCOUNT a fund set aside for future needs. See **reserve fund, escrow account.**
Example: Each month a homeowner deposits ¹⁄₁₂ of the estimated annual property tax and insurance premium requirements into an impound account, so that the balance will be sufficient to pay amounts when they come due.

IMPUTED INTEREST implied interest. In a **mortgage** that states an insufficient interest rate, the law will impute that the rate is higher, and the **principal** is less.
Example: Abel sells property to Baker. Baker gives Abel a portion of the price in cash and Abel takes a **note** for the remainder. Since the gain on the sale is taxable at **capital gains** rates and the interest paid on the note is taxed as **ordinary income,** it is in Abel's favor to set a higher price in exchange for charging a low rate of interest on the note. If this is done, the **Internal Revenue Service** will consider a portion of the principal paid on the note as *imputed interest* and tax that portion as ordinary income.

INCHOATE unfinished, begun but not completed. In real estate, this can apply to **dower** or **curtesy** rights prior to the death of a spouse.
Example: Collins dies, leaving dower rights *inchoate.* Her children by a former marriage sue her widower to recover her share of property he sold.

INCOME the money or other benefit coming from the use of property, skill, or business.
Examples: In real estate, *income* may be produced by:
• rents
• fees
• royalties
• sales of crops, timber, or livestock
• revenues derived from business activities on the property

INCOME APPROACH a method appraising real estate based on the property's anticipated future income. The formula for appraisal by the income approach is

$$\frac{\text{Expected annual income}}{\text{Capitalization rate}} = \text{Market value}$$

See **capitalization** and **gross rent multiplier.**
Example: A property is expected to produce a **net operating income** of $100,000 yearly. Recent sales data indicate that the **capitalization rate** for **comparable** properties is 10%. By the *income approach,* the property has a market value of

$$\frac{\$100,000}{.10} = \$1,000,000$$

INCOME/EXPENSE RATIO see **expense ratio.**

INCOME MULTIPLIER the relationship of price to income. See **gross rent multiplier.**

INCOME PARTICIPATION see **participation mortgage.**

INCOME PROPERTY real estate that generates rental income.
Examples: The following are types of *income property:*
• apartment buildings
• shopping centers
• office buildings
• industrial properties and warehouses
• resort and recreational properties
• hotels, motels, and restaurants
The following are generally not considered income property:
• personal residences
• undeveloped land (rental income is minimal)
• schools, churches, parks

INCOME STREAM a regular flow of money generated by a business or investment.
Example: A **net lease** that pays $1,000 per month **rent** for 10 years provides an *income stream.*

INCOMPETENT one not legally capable of completing a **contract.** Includes the mentally ill, minors, and others considered incapable.
Example: Abel, a mentally retarded individual, inherited $100,000, and wants to buy a tract of land. He enters into a contract, but his legal guardian **voids** it because the land is worth under $5,000. It is voidable because Abel is *incompetent.*

INCORPORATE 1. to form a **corporation** under regulations provided by the Secretary of State.
Example: Abel intends to enter the real estate **brokerage** business and wishes to protect his personal **assets.** He retains a lawyer to whom he pays a $1,000 fee to *incorporate* the business. Abel is the sole stockholder and chairman of the board of directors. Abel's personal assets are protected because **liability** is limited to the assets owned by the corporation.
2. to provide a geographic area the legal status of a political subdivision of the state.
Example: A large **subdivision** outside a large city petitions the state legislature to *incorporate* as an independent city. The residents of the incorporated area may elect representatives and tax themselves to provide services.

INCORPOREAL PROPERTY legal interests in real property that do not entail the right of possession. See **easement, license.**

INCURABLE DEPRECIATION a defect that cannot be cured or that is not financially practical to cure; a defect in the "bone structure" of a building. Compare **curable depreciation.**
Example: It is estimated that if a specific house had a more convenient **floor plan,** it would sell for an additional $5,000. The cost of rearranging the partitions to improve the plan is $10,000. The poor floor plan is *incurable depreciation.*

INDEMNIFY 1. to protect another person against loss or damage.
Example: FHA mortgage loans *indemnify* the lender against the risk of a buyer's **default.**
2. to compensate a party for loss or damage.
Example: Upon **foreclosure,** the FHA *indemnified* the lender for losses on the defaulted loan.

INDENTURE a written agreement made between 2 or more persons having different interests.
Example: The *indenture* **trustee** enforces the agreement made between the **bond** issuer (borrower) and the lender.

INDEPENDENT APPRAISAL a value estimate provided by someone who does not participate in the income or value of the property.
Example: An **appraiser's** certification should show independence from the transaction. Those who cannot provide *independent appraisals* include owners, lenders, and property managers.

INDEPENDENT CONTRACTOR a **contractor** who is self-employed.
Example: Collins, a real estate salesperson, is an *independent contractor* engaged by **broker** Baker. She has not received any income in the last 3 months but is unable to collect unemployment insurance because she is an *independent contractor.* Last year she paid a self-employment tax instead of social security.

INDEPENDENT FEE APPRAISER one who estimates the value of property, has no interest in the property, and is not associated with a lending association or other investor.
Example: Some lenders have appraisers on their salaried staff; others hire *independent fee appraisers.*

INDEX 1. a statistic that indicates some current economic or financial condition. Indexes are often used to make adjustments in wage rates, rental rates, loan interest rates, and pension benefits set by long-term contracts.
Example: Office building rental rates are sometimes adjusted in relation to the consumer price *index.*

2. to adjust contract terms according to an index. See **indexed loan.**
Example: Mortgage interest rates on **adjustable rate mortgages** are often *indexed* to the average mortgage rate for all lenders or the average cost of funds for all lenders.

INDEXED LOAN a long-term loan in which the **term,** payment, **interest rate,** or **principal** amount may be adjusted periodically according to a specific **index.** The index and the manner of adjustment are generally stated in the loan contract.
Example: An **adjustable rate mortgage** is an *indexed loan.* At specific intervals the **face interest rate** on the loan may be changed according to variations in the specified **index.**

INDEX LEASE a rental agreement that requires changes in rent based on a published record of cost changes. See **cost of living index.**
Example: A landlord makes an *index lease* with initial rent at $10,000 per year, adjusted annually by the Consumer Price Index (CPI). If the CPI is 100 at the time of the lease and increases to 110 in the second year, the rent for the second year will be $10,000 \times 1.10 = \$11,000$.

INDIRECT COSTS costs not directly associated with the **structure,** but incurred during the construction period. Also called soft costs. Contrast with **direct costs.**
Examples:
• Real estate taxes
• Administrative costs
• Professional fees
• Insurance
• Lease up

INDUSTRIAL PARK an area designed and **zoned** for manufacturing and associated activities.
Example: Figure 89.

INDUSTRIAL PROPERTY property used for industrial purposes, such as factories.
Examples: Types of *industrial property*:
• factory-office multiuse property
• factory-warehouse multiuse property
• heavy manufacturing buildings
• industrial parks
• light manufacturing buildings
• research and development parks

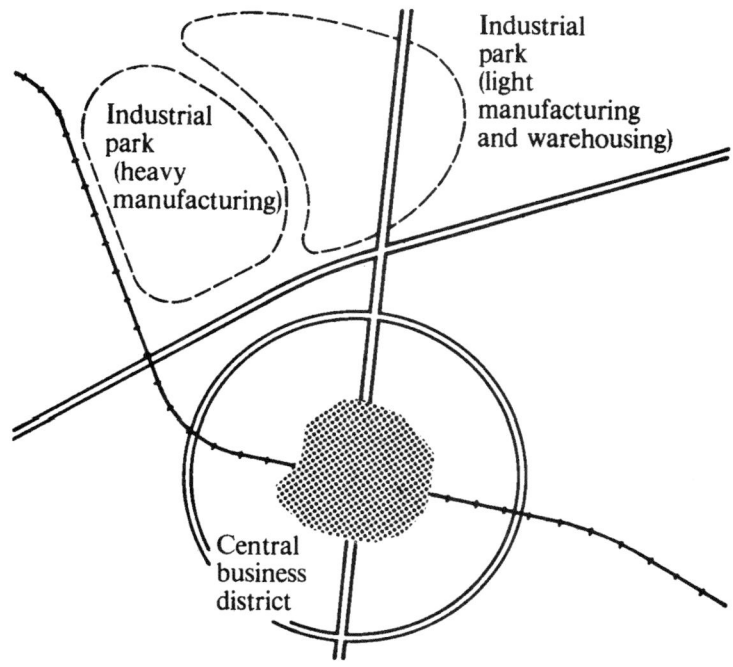

FIG. 89. INDUSTRIAL PARK

INFLATION a loss in the purchasing power of money; an increase in the general price level. Generally measured by the Consumer Price Index, published by the Bureau of Labor Statistics.
Example: Real estate is considered a hedge against *inflation* because it tends to be long-lasting and holds its value in real terms. As the value of the dollar drops, real estate tends to command more dollars. A home that was purchased in 1967 for $50,000, resold in 1976 for $100,000 and in 1993 for $200,000. The home did nothing to cause its price to change; inflation caused the house to command more dollars.

INFORMATION REPORTING reports provided to the Internal Revenue Service (IRS), such as commissions earned by real estate sales agents and real estate transactions of home sellers, reported by the broker.
Example: In January, Baker files a form 1099 with the IRS for real estate transactions she brokered during the past year. Such *information reporting* is required by the Tax Reform Act of 1986.

INFRASTRUCTURE the basic public works of a city or subdivision, including roads, bridges, sewer and water systems, drainage systems, and essential public utilities.

267

Example: After many years of neglect, the city council realized that there was a need to invest in the *infrastructure* of the city. Accordingly, they embarked on a major program of road improvements and reconstruction of water and sewerage lines throughout the city.

INHERITANCE TAX a tax, based on property **value,** imposed in some states on those who acquire property from a decedent. Compare **estate tax.**
Example: An estate tax is based on the value of all property left by the decedent, whereas an *inheritance tax* is based on the amount that an **heir** receives.

INJUNCTION an order issued under the seal of a court to restrain one or more parties to a legal proceeding, from performing an act deemed inequitable to another party or parties in the proceeding.
Example: Abel begins serving alcoholic drinks on property he bought from Baker. Baker claims that a **deed restriction** prevents consumption of such beverages on the property, and sues Abel. Since the trial is set several months ahead, Baker requests an *injunction* to prevent the sale of drinks until the trial.

INNER CITY generally the older and more urbanized area of a large city surrounding the **central business district.** The term often refers to densely populated blighted **areas** characterized by low-income residents and a high proportion of minority racial and ethnic groups.
Examples:
• Many inner city neighborhoods have been **rehabilitated** by **urban renewal** projects.
• Violence is a problem in some inner city schools.
• The mayor promises a construction program to rehabilitate the inner city.

IN REM Latin: "against the thing." A proceeding against the property directly, as distinguished from a proceeding against a person (used in taking land for nonpayment of taxes, etc.)
Example: Baker cannot collect on his past due loan from Abel. Baker, through court action, secures a **judgment** *in rem* against a building lot owned by Abel, which causes a lien against the lot.

INSIDE LOT in a **subdivision,** a lot surrounded on each side by other lots, as opposed to a corner lot, which has road **frontage** on at least 2 sides.
Example: An *inside lot* **adjoining** a corner lot (Figure 90).

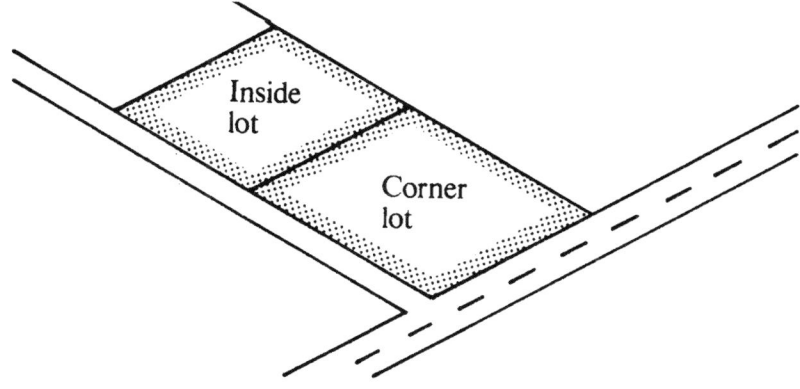

FIG. 90. INSIDE LOT

INSPECTION a physical scrutinizing review of property or of documents.
Example: *Inspections* may be required for the following purposes:
• compliance with **building codes**
• sale requirements as to property conditions, such as wood-destroying insects or structural soundness
• legal review of documents such as **leases** and **mortgages** to determine whether they are as purported

INSTALLMENTS parts of the same **debt,** payable at successive periods as agreed; payments made to reduce a **mortgage.**
Example: Abel purchases a property with a **land contract.** The contract calls for a payment of $30,000 at **closing,** with 10 annual *installments* of $15,000 each.

INSTALLMENT CONTRACT same as **land contract.**

INSTALLMENT SALE when a seller accepts a **mortgage** for part of the sale, the tax on the gain is paid as the mortgage **principal** is collected. See also **contract price, gross profit ratio, imputed interest.**
Example: Collins sells for $10,000 her land that she bought 3 years ago for $4,000. Her gain is $6,000. She received 10% ($1,000) as a cash **down payment** and a 90% ($9,000) **purchase money mortgage.** She will report 10% of the gain in the year of sale and the balance as she collects the principal of the purchase money mortgage. To do so, on her tax return she reports the sale as an installment sale. See Table 28.

TABLE 28
INSTALLMENT SALE

	Year of sale	Year 1	Year 2	Year 3
Principal paid	$1,000	$3,000	$3,000	$3,000
Taxable gain	600	1,800	1,800	1,800
Interest income	0	900	600	300

INSTALLMENT TO AMORTIZE ONE DOLLAR a mathematically computed factor derived from **compound interest** functions that offers the level periodic payment required to retire a $1.00 loan within a certain time frame. The periodic installment must exceed the periodic interest rate. See **amortization, amortization schedule.**
Examples:
• $.2638 is required to amortize $1.00 at 10% interest, with 5 yearly payments.
• $.1627 is required to amortize $1.00 at 10% interest with 10 yearly payments.
• $.1175 is required to amortize $1.00 at 10% interest, with 20 yearly payments.

INSTITUTE OF REAL ESTATE MANAGEMENT (IREM) a professional organization of property managers. Affiliated with the **National Association of Realtors®.** Publishes the *Journal* of *Property Management.*
Address:
Institute of Real Estate Management
430 North Michigan Avenue
Chicago, IL 60611

INSTITUTIONAL LENDER financial intermediaries who invest in loans and other securities on behalf of their depositors or customers; lending and investment activities are regulated by laws to limit risk.
Example: *Institutional lenders* are a prime source of real estate loans. Many organizations, such as **savings and loan associations** and **commercial banks,** originate loans directly; others, such as insurance companies, lend through **mortgage brokers.**

INSTRUMENT a written legal document, created to establish the rights and liabilities of the parties to it.
Examples: The following are examples of instruments:
• **deed**
• mortgage

- land contract
- lease
- assignment

INSURABLE INTEREST an **interest** in a person or property that would cause one a loss if that person or property were injured. Must be present to collect from an insurance policy.
Example: The Good Money Savings Association lent $50,000 on Abel's house. Yesterday the house was destroyed by fire. Good Money can collect on its insurance policy, because they were insured and had an *insurable interest.* Five Star Savings also had an insurance policy on the home but had no **lien,** so they couldn't collect.

INSURABLE TITLE a **title** that can be insured by a **title insurance** company.
Example: In some **contracts** for the sale of **real estate** the buyer must receive *insurable title* or he is not obligated to purchase the property.

INSURABLE VALUE the cost of total replacement of destructible improvements to a property.
Example: Although the market value of the home was $100,000, its *insurable value* was $75,000, based on an allocation of $25,000 to the land and replacement costs of $75,000 for the structure and other man-made improvements.

INSURANCE COVERAGE total amount and type of insurance carried.
Example: The owner maintained $100,000 of hazard *insurance coverage* on the property, and $300,000 of **liability** *insurance coverage.* The **hazard insurance** coverage was adequate to meet the 80% **coinsurance** requirement in the policy.

INSURANCE (MORTGAGE) a service, generally purchased by a borrower, that will **indemnify** the lender in case of **foreclosure** of the loan. Indemnification is generally limited to losses suffered by the lender in the foreclosure process. See **FHA mortgage loan, private mortgage insurance.**
Example: Abel took out a **home loan** covered by *mortgage insurance.* After one year, Abel **defaulted** on the loan and the lender foreclosed. Abel owed $50,000, but the foreclosure sale produced only $40,000 in proceeds. The insurance company paid the lender the difference of $10,000.

INTANGIBLE VALUE value that cannot be seen or touched.
Example: The **goodwill** of an established business is an *intangible value.*

271

INTEREST 1. cost of the use of money.
Example: Lenders require payment of *interest* at a specified rate, to compensate for risk, deferment of benefits, inflation, and administrative burdens.
2. the type and extent of ownership.
Example: One may hold either a partial or **fee simple** *interest* in a property. That *interest* entitles one to specific ownership rights.

INTEREST DEDUCTIONS (UNDER THE 1986 TAX ACT)

Investment Interest. Investment interest deductions are limited to net investment income, which includes interest, dividends, long-term capital gains and income or loss from working interests in oil and gas interests. However, net investment income includes neither rental nor other passive activity income or loss, nor interest paid to buy an ownership in a passive activity.
Construction Interest. Interest incurred during the construction and development of most real estate (but not a personal residence) must be capitalized, and deducted over its depreciable life beginning when the property is ready to be placed in service or sold.
Business Interest. Interest incurred in an active trade or business in which the investor materially participates is fully deductible.
Housing Interest. Interest on up to $1 million of acquisition debt (used to purchase or improve a home) plus $100,000 of home equity debt is tax deductible. This may be claimed for a principal residence plus one vacation home (provided the owner used it personally for the greater of 14 days or 10% of the time it is rented). Debt incurred before October 13, 1987, is not subject to the $1 million limit though limits exist, based on home costs, medical and educational expenses.

Points paid on a mortgage to acquire a principal residence may be deductible if they are customary in the geographic area; points paid for other purposes such as refinancing are amortized (deducted evenly each year over the life of the loan) rather than deducted currently.
Consumer Interest. Interest on credit cards and auto loans has not been deductible since 1990.

INTEREST-ONLY LOAN a loan in which interest is payable at regular intervals until loan **maturity,** when the full loan balance is due. Does not require **amortization.** Contrast with **self-amortizing mortgage.**
Example: Land was bought with a 5-year *interest-only loan of* $100,000 at 12%. The **interest** of $12,000 was paid annually for 4 years. The $100,000 **principal,** together with the last $12,000 interest payment, was due at the end of the fifth year.

INTEREST RATE 1. the percentage of a sum of money charged for its use.

2. the **rate of return** on an investment.

Example: A $50,000 mortgage loan is made at 12% interest and 4 **discount points.** The contract *interest rate is* 12% and determines the monthly payment amount. The **effective rate** of interest, which incorporates the effects of the discount points, is 12.55% and is the rate of return to the lender if the loan runs to maturity.

INTERIM FINANCING a loan, including a **construction loan,** used when the property owner is unable or unwilling to arrange permanent financing. Generally arranged for less than 3 years, used to gain time for financial or market conditions to improve.

Example: Monroe developed an office building but, in the expectation of falling **interest rates,** does not wish to use permanent financing at this time. He arranges a 2-year *interim* loan, during which time he seeks favorable permanent financing.

INTERNAL RATE OF RETURN (IRR) the true annual rate of earnings on an investment. Equates the value of cash returns with cash invested. Considers the application of **compound interest** factors. Requires a trial-and-error method for solution. The formula is

$$\sum_{t-1}^{n} \frac{\text{periodic } \textit{cash flow}}{(1 + i)^t} = \text{investment amount}$$

where i = internal rate of return
t = each time interval
n = total time intervals
Σ = summation

Example: Abel sells for $20,000 land that he bought 4 years earlier for $10,000. There were no **carrying charges** or **transaction costs.** The *internal rate of return* was about 19%. That is the annual rate at which compound interest must be paid for $10,000 to become $20,000 in 4 years.

Example: Baker received $3,000 per year for 5 years on a $10,000 investment. The *internal rate of return* was about 15%.

INTERNAL REVENUE CODE the law, passed by Congress, that specifies how and what income is to be taxed, and what may be deducted from taxable income.

Example: Court cases, regulations, revenue rules, and revenue procedures attempt to properly interpret the *Internal Renenue Code.*

INTERNAL REVENUE SERVICE (IRS) an agency of the federal government that is responsible for the administration and collection of federal income taxes. The IRS prints and distributes tax forms and audits tax returns.

273

Addresses:
Regional Offices
- Andover, MA 05501
- Atlanta, GA 31101
- Austin, TX 73301
- Cincinnati, OH 45999
- Fresno, CA 93888
- Holtsville, NY 00501
- Kansas City, MO 64999
- Memphis, TN 37501
- Ogden, UT 84201
- Philadelphia, PA 19255

INTERNATIONAL ARCHITECTURE an early-twentieth-century-style house whose design is very simple with no ornamentation. The windows appear to be continuous rather than appearing to be holes in the walls.
Example: Figure 91.

FIG. 91. INTERNATIONAL ARCHITECTURE

INTERNATIONAL ASSOCIATION OF ASSESSING OFFICERS (IAAO) a professional organization of property tax **assessors.** Awards the designation of Certified Assessment Evaluator (CAE). Publishes the quarterly *Assessors Journal.*
Address:
International Association of Assessing Officers
1313 East 60th Street
Chicago, IL 60637

INTERNATIONAL REAL ESTATE FEDERATION an organization with worldwide membership that is devoted to encouraging private rights to **real estate.** The international abbreviation is FIABCI; its American chapter is an affiliate of the **National Association of Realtors®.**

274

Address:
FIABCI
777 14th Street NW
Washington, DC 20005

INTERNATIONAL RIGHT OF WAY ASSOCIATION
(IR/WA) an individual membership association (no corporate membership) that offers courses covering various phases of **right-of-way** work. Educational curriculum includes law, engineering, **appraisal.** Offers a designation, SR/WA, and a bimonthly magazine.
Address:
International Right of Way Association
13650 S. Grammercy Place, Ste. 100
Gardena, CA 90249
(310) 538-0233

INTERSTATE LAND SALES ACT a federal law, administered by the Department of **Housing and Urban Development** (HUD), which requires certain disclosures and advertising procedures when selling land to purchasers in other states.
Example: Rollins, a developer, has a 200-acre **subdivision** in Florida and wishes to market lots nationally. Under the *Interstate Land Sales Act,* she must register with the Office of Interstate Land Sales Registration (OILSR, a division of HUD), and make certain disclosures in the **prospectus** sent to prospective purchasers.

INTERVAL OWNERSHIP same as **time-sharing.**

INTER VIVOS during one's life.
Example: Abel makes an *inter vivos* gift of $10,000 to each of 3 children. The children spend the $10,000 and may inherit more money if Abel names them in the **will** he is preparing.

INTESTATE 1. (adj.) having made no valid will.
2. (noun) a person who dies leaving no will or leaving one that is defective. Property goes to the legal **heirs** of the intestate.
Example: If Doris dies *intestate,* her heirs under state law will inherit her property. If she leaves no heirs her property will **escheat.**

INVENTORY property held for sale or to be used in the manufacture of goods held for sale. Does not qualify for **capital gains** tax treatment.
Examples: Examples of *inventory* are:
• raw materials
• work-in-progress
• finished goods

To a builder, property under construction and property completed are *inventory.* To a **subdivider,** vacant lots are *inventory.*

INVERSE CONDEMNATION a legal procedure to obtain compensation when a property **interest** has been taken or diminished in value by a government activity.
Example: Abel owns a home near a public airport. The city constructs a new runway that sends air traffic directly over Abel's house, seriously diminishing Abel's enjoyment of his property. Abel may sue for *inverse condemnation* and, if successful, may force the airport authority to take Abel's house in exchange for just compensation.

INVESTMENT ANALYSIS a study of the likely return from a proposed real estate investment with the objective of evaluating the amount an investor may pay for it, the investment's suitability to that investor, or the feasibility of a proposed real estate development. Appraised value is based on a synthesis of people in the market whereas *investment analysis is* based on the value to a specific investor.
There are various methods of *investment analysis,* including:
• Cash on cash return
• Payback period
• Internal rate of return
• Net present value
Each provides some measure of the estimated return on an investment, based on various assumptions and investment horizons.

INVESTMENT LIFE CYCLE the time span from acquisition of an investment to final disposition.
Example: The best way to measure the **rate of return** from an *investment* is over its *life cycle.* All relevant investment contributions, **cash flows,** and resale proceeds are known (Figure 92).

FIG. 92. INVESTMENT LIFE CYCLE

INVESTMENT TAX CREDIT a reduction in income tax generally based on the cost and life of certain assets purchased.
Note: This was abolished by the Tax Reform Act of 1986; but see **rehabilitation tax credit** and **low-income housing (qualified).**

INVESTMENT VALUE the estimated value of a certain real estate investment to a particular individual or institutional investor. May be greater or less than **market value,** depending on the investor's particular situation.
Example: The *investment value* of vacant land in the path of growth would be greater for a young aggressive investor who has time to wait for fruition than for an elderly widow who needs cash flow for living costs. Similarly, the *investment value* of a **tax shelter** investment is greater for a high-tax-bracket investor than for a tax-exempt pension plan.

INVOLUNTARY CONVERSION **condemnation** or sudden destruction by nature.
Example: A property is taken by **eminent domain** for the purpose of constructing a public highway. This *involuntary conversion* of the property is contrasted with a sale that the owner enters into voluntarily.

INVOLUNTARY LIEN a **lien** imposed against property without consent of the owner (unpaid taxes, special assessments, etc.). Compare **mortgage lien.**
Example: The **absentee** land **owner** was not notified of the past-due tax bill. The tax **assessor** placed a lien on the property that was an *involuntary lien,* since the owner did not take action to cause the lien.

INWOOD ANNUITY FACTOR a number that, when multiplied by the periodic payment from a **level payment income stream,** indicates the present value of the income stream, based on a specific interest rate. Same formula as that for **annuity factor.**
Example: An investment is expected to provide income of $100 per month for 10 years. At the end of 10 years the investment has no value. At an interest rate of 10%, the present value (PV) of the investment is

$$PV = \$100 \times 75.67 = \$7,567$$

where 75.67 is the *Inwood annuity factor.*

INWOOD TABLES a set of **annuity factors** for various **interest rates** and **maturities.** See **Inwood annuity factor.**
Example: The *Inwood tables* show that the right to receive $1.00 at the end of each year for 10 years at 15% interest is worth $5.02 as of the beginning of the first year.

277

IREM Institute of Real Estate Management.

IRR internal rate of return.

IRREVOCABLE incapable of being recalled or revoked; unchangeable.
Example: The bank issued an *irrevocable* **letter of credit** stating that if the terms of the **contract** were met the bank would lend the money requested.

IRS Internal Revenue Service.

IR/WA International Right of Way Association.

ITALIAN VILLA a Latin-style, massive 2- or 3-story house of masonry with large overhanging eaves.
Example: Figure 93.

FIGURE 93. ITALIAN VILLA

J

JEOPARDY danger, **risk.**
Example: Property pledged as **security** for a delinquent loan is in *jeopardy* of **foreclosure.**

JOINT AND SEVERAL LIABILITY a **creditor** can demand full repayment from any and all of those who have borrowed. Each borrower is **liable** for the full debt, not just the **prorated** share.
Example: Abel and Baker are **general partners.** Together they borrow (or the **partnership** borrows) $10,000 from a bank, agreeing to *joint and several liability.* Upon **default,** the bank can collect the remaining balance of the $10,000 from either party.

JOINT TENANCY ownership of **realty** by 2 or more persons, each of whom has an **undivided interest** with the **right of survivorship.** Typically used by related persons.
Example: Abel and Baker own land in *joint tenancy.* Each owns half of the entire (undivided) property. Upon Abel's death, Baker will own the entire property, and vice versa.

JOINT VENTURE an agreement between 2 or more parties who invest in a single business or property. See also **limited partnership, tenancy in common.**
Example: Abel and Baker form a *joint venture* to explore for minerals on Cobb's land. Abel and Baker use a **tenancy in common** arrangement for ownership of the mineral rights.

JUDGMENT a decree of a court stating that one individual is indebted to another and fixing the amount of the indebtedness.
Example: As a result of Abel's failure to pay disputed rent, the landlord obtained a court decision, or *judgment,* against Abel.

JUDGMENT CREDITOR one who has received a court decree or **judgment** for money due from the **judgment debtor.**
Example: To enforce the judgment awarded by court, the *judgment creditor* filed a **lien** against the **judgment debtor** Abel.

JUDGMENT DEBTOR one against whom a **judgment** has been issued by a court for money owed, and that remains unsatisfied.
Example: A judgment was entered into against Abel for nonpayment of rent. Abel is the *judgment debtor.*

JUDGMENT LIEN the claim upon the property of a debtor resulting from a **judgment.**
Example: Abel won't pay his debt to Baker. After establishing the debt in court, Baker may be allowed by the court to put *a judgment lien* on Abel's **real estate.**

JUDICIAL FORECLOSURE having a defaulted debtor's property sold where the court ratifies the price paid.
Example: Happy Mortgage Company is owed $50,000 on a first mortgage by Mr. Baker. At *judicial foreclosure,* Happy Mortgage Company **bids** $30,000 for the property, which is more than anyone else bids. They then claim the property and are awarded a $20,000 **deficiency judgment** against Mr. Baker.

JUNIOR LIEN same as **junior mortgage.**

JUNIOR MORTGAGE a **mortgage** whose claim against the property will be satisfied only after prior mortgages have been repaid. See **first mortgage, second mortgage.**
Example: Property is purchased for $100,000. A first mortgage is obtained covering $75,000 of the price. To reduce the cash requirements, a *junior mortgage* is arranged to cover $15,000 of the price. The remaining $10,000 is cash **equity.**

JURISDICTION geographic or topical area of authority for a specific government entity.
Example: The *jurisdiction* of the Lower Valley Consolidated Appraisal District is a 3-county area surrounding the city of Valleyview. The federal district court has *jurisdiction* in all cases involving violation of federal law.

JUST COMPENSATION the amount paid to the owner of a property when it is acquired under **eminent domain.** See **condemnation.**
Example: Property is condemned to construct a sewage treatment plant. The owner is entitled to *just compensation* equal to the **fair market value** of the property taken.

K

KICKER a payment required by a **mortgage** in addition to normal **principal** and **interest.** See **participation loan.**
Example: Abel obtains a loan to purchase a retail store building. The lender requires a *kicker* equal to 10% of gross sales in excess of $100,000 per month, in addition to principal and interest.

KIOSK an independent stand from which merchandise is sold, often placed in the common area of a regional **shopping center.**
Example: Figure 94.

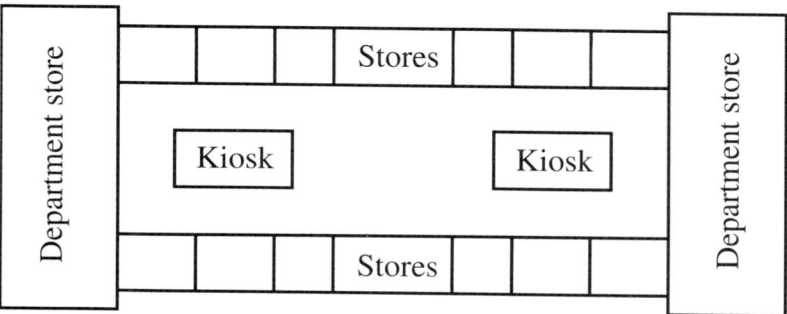

FIG. 94. KIOSK

L

LACHES undue delay or negligence in asserting one's legal rights, possibly leading to **estoppel** of the negligent party's suit.
Example: Abel was estopped by *laches* after he knowingly delayed telling an **adjacent** property owner of an **encroachment.**

LAND the surface of the earth; any part of the surface of the earth. (Note: Legal definitions often distinguish land from water.)
Example: Extent of *land* as **real property** (Figure 95). **Air rights** may be limited to some defined altitude. Added **improvements** are distinguished from *land.*

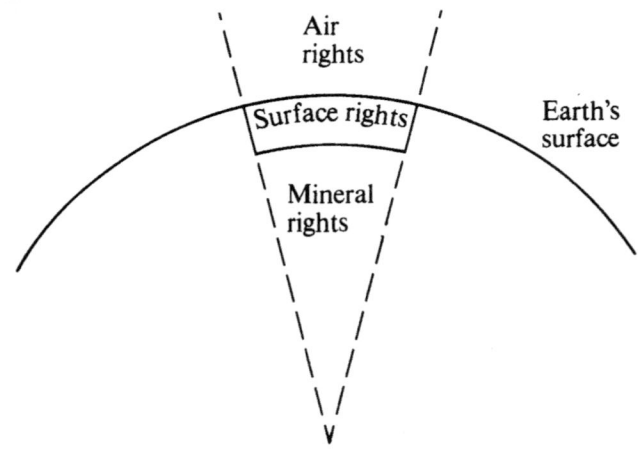

FIG. 95. EXTENT OF LAND OWNERSHIP

LAND BANKING the activity of purchasing land that is not presently needed for use.
Example: The Burger Company buys 8 **sites** that they plan to use 10 years from now. Wendy Ronald is in charge of *land banking* for The Burger Company.

LAND/BUILDING RATIO a ratio of relative values of the land to **improvements.** Contrast with **improvement ratio.**
Examples:
• A **shopping center** has a *land-to-building ratio* of 40% ($4 million land to $10 million building).
• An office building has a *land-to-building ratio* of 10% ($1 million land to $10 million building).

LAND CONTRACT a real estate **installment** selling arrangement whereby the buyer may use, occupy, and enjoy land, but no **deed** is given by the seller (so no **title** passes) until all or a

specified part of the sale price has been paid. Same as **contract for deed** and **installment land contract.**

Example: Collins buys a recreational lot. Under the *land contract* she signed, she must pay $500 down and $100 per month for 7 years; then she is to receive a **general warranty deed.**

LAND ECONOMICS the branch of economics that concentrates upon the economic attributes of land and the economics of agriculture.

Example: A study of *land economics* is helpful to estimate the value of farm land prices.

LAND LEASE only the ground is covered by the lease. See **ground lease.**

Example: Abel arranges a *land lease* from Baker for 50 years at a net annual rent of $5,000. Abel builds a shopping center on the land. At the end of 50 years the entire property will revert to Baker (Figure 96).

Building owner pays $5,000 per year rent on land

FIG. 96. LAND LEASE

LANDLOCKED the condition of a lot that has no access to a public thoroughfare except through an **adjacent** lot. See **egress.** Compare with **easement, right-of-way.**

Example: Figure 97.

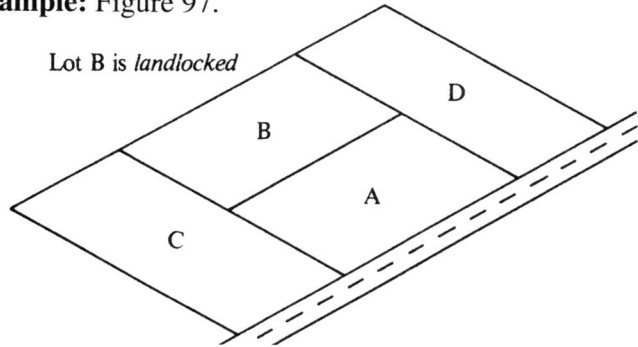

Lot B is *landlocked*

FIG. 97. LANDLOCKED PROPERTY

LANDLORD one who rents property to another; a **lessor.** A property owner who surrenders the right to use property for a specific time in exchange for the receipt of rent.
Example: *Landlord*-tenant relationship (Figure 98).

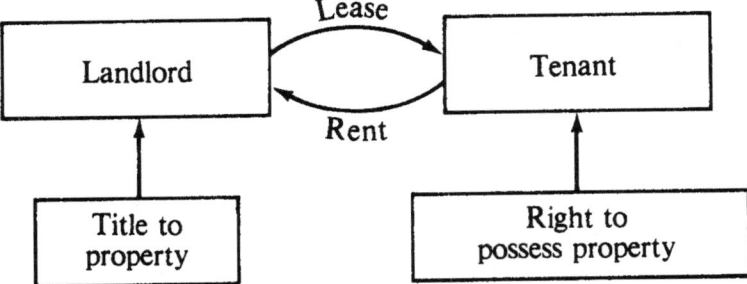

FIG. 98. LANDLORD-TENANT RELATIONSHIP

LANDMARK a fixed object serving as a **boundary** mark for a tract of land. Same as **monument.**
Example: The tree and rail line may serve as *landmarks* in a land **description** (Figure 99).

FIG. 99. LANDMARKS

LAND RESIDUAL TECHNIQUE in **appraisal,** a method of estimating the value of land when given **the net operating income (NOI)** and value of **improvements.** Used for **feasibility** analysis and **highest and best use.** See **income approach.**
Example: A property generates $10,000 net operating income ($15,000 rent less $5,000 operating expenses). The improvements cost $70,000 to construct and claim a 12% rate of return (10% interest plus 2% depreciation), which is $8,400. The

remaining $1,600 income is capitalized at a 10% rate (divided by .10) to result in a $16,000 land value using the *land residual technique*. See Table 29.

TABLE 29
LAND RESIDUAL TECHNIQUE

Property NOI	$10,000
Income to improvement	– 8,400
Income to land	$1,600
Divided by required rate (10%)	$16,000 Land value

LAND SALE-LEASEBACK the sale of land and simultaneous leasing of it by the seller, who becomes the **tenant.**
Example: Collins owns land and wants to raise cash to build a shopping center on it. She sells the land for $100,000 to Baker and leases it back for 50 years at a $5,000 annual rent. Collins can use the land for the lease **term** provided she pays the annual rent, so she builds the shopping center after the *land sale-leaseback* (Figure 100).

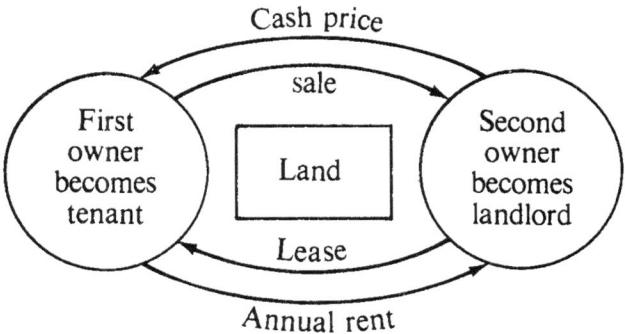

FIG. 100. LAND SALE-LEASEBACK

LANDSCAPE ARCHITECT a professional who designs building sites, subdivisions, and other projects which require work on drainage, grading, vegetation, installation of utilities and site improvements.
Example: On the office park project, a *landscape architect* advised the developer on the placement of drainage sewers, parking lots, plantings and other landscaping requirements.

LAND, TENEMENTS, AND HEREDITAMENTS a phrase used in early English law to express all sorts of **real estate.**
Example: The **bundle of rights** in real estate is expressed by the phrase *land, tenements and hereditaments*. It includes all **interests** in real estate.

LAND USE INTENSITY a measure of the extent to which a land parcel is developed in conformity with **zoning** ordinances.
Example: Under a local zoning ordinance, **developers** might be allowed a maximum *land use intensity* of 4,000 square feet of **improvements** per **acre** of land.

LAND USE PLANNING an activity, generally conducted by a local government, that provides public and private land use recommendations consistent with community policies. Generally used to guide decisions on **zoning.**
Example: As part of its *land use planning* efforts, the city planning department prepared maps of existing land uses, forecasts of future development, a list of planned new roads, **utility** extensions, and waste disposal facilities, a map of environmentally sensitive areas, and a map showing recommended future land uses.

LAND USE REGULATION government **ordinances,** codes, and permit requirements intended to make the private use of land and natural resources conform to policy standards. See also **zoning.**
Examples: Local governments have several types of *land use regulation*. Commonly used types are:
• building codes
• curb-cut permit systems
• historic preservation laws
• housing codes
• subdivision regulations
• tree-cutting laws
• zoning

LAND USE SUCCESSION a change in the predominant use of a **neighborhood** or area over time. See also **neighborhood life cycle.**
Example: As the neighborhood aged, it began to make a transition from large **single-family housing** to **apartment buildings** through the process of *land use succession.*

LATENT DEFECTS flaws that are hidden but are apt to surface later.
Example: A building was found to have *latent defects* in the form of poor construction of subfloors and improper foundation support.

LATE PAYMENTS a fee added to a bill after the expiration of a specific grace period. Such payments are intended to encourage timely payment of the bill.
Example: Largetown Federal Savings requires an additional 5% in *late payments* when a mortgage payment is made after the fifteenth of the month.

LEASE a **contract** in which, for a payment called **rent,** the one entitled to the **possession** of real property (**lessor**) transfers those rights to another (**lessee**) for a specified period of time.
Example: Abel leases office space from Baker. Under the *lease* signed by the parties, Abel is allowed to conduct business activities within the office space, subject to specified **restrictions,** for a specified period of time. Baker is entitled to receive a specified amount of rent payments according to a specified schedule of payments.

LEASED FEE the landlord's ownership interest of a **property** that is under **lease.**
Example: Land in Hawaii is under a lease to an individual who built a home on it. The landowner's interest is the *leased fee.* Its value is based on the anticipated income from **rent.**

LEASEHOLD the **interest** or **estate** on which a **lessee** (**tenant**) of **real estate** has a **lease.**
Example: Mason possesses a long-term lease on a property. She may obtain a loan with the *leasehold* pledged as **collateral.** If the **contract rent** required by the lease is lower than **market rents,** Mason's *leasehold* will have a positive value.

LEASEHOLD IMPROVEMENTS fixtures attached to real estate that are generally acquired or installed by the **tenant.** Upon expiration of the **lease,** the tenant can generally remove them, provided such action does not damage the property nor conflict with the lease.
Examples: Cabinets, light fixtures, and window treatments of a retail store in a leased building are *leasehold improvements.*

LEASEHOLD MORTGAGE a **lien** on the tenant's **interest** in **real estate.**
Example: Abel is leasing land from Baker under a 50-year lease. Abel builds a shopping center and borrows money from the Big Money Assurance Company to do so. Big Money Assurance Company secures the loan with a *leasehold mortgage.* The mortgage will be lower in priority (subordinate) to land lease because the lease was contracted first. Had the mortgage been arranged before the lease, the mortgage would have priority. The holder of a prior **lien** has first claim to the income and assets if in default.

LEASEHOLD VALUE the value of a tenant's interest in a **lease,** especially when the **rent** is below market and the lease has a long remaining **term.**
Example: When land rent for an acre of Manhattan was $10,000 per year, a knowledgeable investor bought the rights of a 99-year

lease. A comparable **tract** today commands $150,000 annual rent. The *leasehold value* of the subject property is the present value of the bargain rent ($140,000) over the remaining lease term.

LEASE WITH OPTION TO PURCHASE a lease that gives the **lessee** (**tenant**) the right to purchase the property at an agreed-upon price under certain conditions.
Example: Abel *leases* property with an *option to purchase.* He must pay $500 per month rent for 5 years; after that he may buy the property (but is not forced to buy) for $100,000.

LEGAL AGE the official standard of maturity upon which one is held legally responsible for one's acts. Contracts for the sale or lease of real estate by a minor are voidable by the minor. See **minor.**
Example: Young, aged 17, signed a contract to purchase a home. Because Young was not of *legal age,* the seller could not enforce the contract when Young later decided not to go through with the purchase.

LEGAL DESCRIPTION legally acceptable identification of **real estate** by one of the following:
• the **government rectangular survey**
• metes and bounds
• recorded **plat** (**lot and block** number)
Example: The seller was required to include a *legal description* in the **deed**.

LEGAL NAME the name one has for official purposes.
Example: Though friends call him Fast Buck Jones, his *legal name is* Ferdinand Buchanan Jones. He may sign **contracts** with the name Ferdinand B. Jones.
Example: The *legal name* of GM is General Motors, Incorporated.

LEGAL NOTICE notification of others using the method required by law. See **constructive notice, notice.**
Example: Abel wishes to **rescind** an **offer** to buy real estate that has not been accepted by Baker. Abel sends a telegram and registered letter to Baker as *legal notice.*
Example: Collins bought land. She recorded the **deed** in the county courthouse as *legal notice* of ownership.

LEGAL RESIDENCE generally one's permanant home.
Example: Although President Gardner lives in Washington, DC, and has a vacation home in New England, he claims Houston as his *legal residence* because he maintains a permanent home there.

LEGAL TITLE a collection of rights of ownership that are defined or recognized by law or that could be successfully defended in a court of law.

Example: *Legal title* is vested in the mortgage lender in **title theory states**, although the real owner has constructive ownership.

LEGATEE one who receives property by **will.** See **devisee.**

Example: Garrison wills all her property to Baker. Upon Garrison's death, Baker is the *legatee.*

LENDER PARTICIPATION see **participation mortgage.**

LESSEE a person to whom property is rented under a **lease.** A **tenant.** Compare with **lessor.**

Example: In the arrangement shown in Figure 101, Baker is the *lessee.*

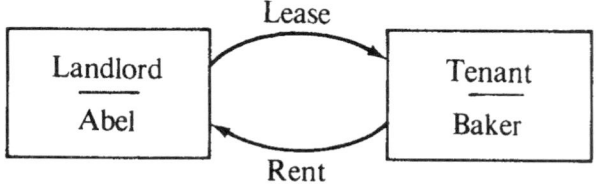

FIG. 101. LESSEE

LESSOR one who rents property to another under a **lease.** A **landlord.** Compare with **lessee.**

Example: In the arrangement shown in Figure 102, Abel is the *lessor.*

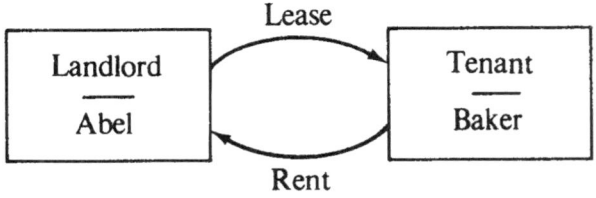

FIG. 102. LESSOR

LESS THAN FREEHOLD ESTATE an **estate** in land that has a predetermined time span; most commonly a **leasehold.**

Example: A five-year lease on land is considered a *less than freehold estate.*

LET to rent a property to a tenant.

Example: Larry *lets* an apartment to Simon for $300 per month.

LETTER OF COMMITMENT official notification to a borrower of the lender's intent to grant a loan. Generally specifies the terms of the loan and sets a date for the **closing.**
Example: Four weeks after applying for a mortgage loan, the Longs received a *letter of commitment* stating that the loan was approved and that the interest rate would be 9.5% and the term 30 years.

LETTER OF CREDIT an arrangement, with specified conditions, whereby a bank agrees to substitute its credit for a customer's.
Example: Abel, from Atlanta, wishes to buy property from Baker in Boston. Abel arranges a *letter of credit* with the Atlanta Trust Company Bank to pay Baker upon **closing** in Boston.

LETTER OF INTENT the expression of a desire to enter into a **contract** without actually doing so.
Example: After a preliminary meeting, the Five Stars Development Company writes to a landowner, "We wish to enter into a contract to buy your land and will further pursue this matter in coming days. This *letter of intent* does not commit either party to purchase, sell, or lease."

LEVEL ANNUITY see **annuity.**

LEVEL-PAYMENT INCOME STREAM see **annuity.**

LEVEL-PAYMENT MORTGAGE requires the same payment each month (or other period) for full **amortization.** See **mortgage constant, flat.**
Example: Abel borrows $50,000 to buy a house. The *level-payment mortgage* at 15% interest, payable over 30 years, requires a $632.50 monthly payment for **principal** and **interest.** That payment will be constant over the life of the loan.

LEVERAGE use of borrowed funds to increase purchasing power and, ideally, to increase the profitability of an investment. See **positive leverage, reverse leverage.**
Example: Collins wishes to invest in real estate. The property costs $100,000 and produces **net operating income** of $10,000 per year. If purchased with all cash, Collins' annual **rate of return** is 10% ($10,000 ÷ $100,000). If she *leverages* the investment by borrowing $75,000, her return may be higher. If the debt cost is 8% ($6,000) annually, the *leverage* results in a return of 16% ($4,000 ÷ $25,000). However, if the debt cost is 12% ($9,000), the *leverage* produces a return of 4% ($1,000 ÷ $25,000).

LEVY to legally impose or collect that which is due.
Example: A tax assessor *levies* a tax.
Example: A judge *levies* a fine.

LIABILITY 1. a **debt** or financial obligation. Contrast with **asset.**
Example: One who borrows $75,000 for a **mortgage** loan incurs a *liability* to repay that loan.
Example: A **general partner** in a **partnership** has a personal *liability* for debts of the partnership in the event the partnership cannot repay its debt.
2. a potential loss.
Example: One should purchase sufficient *liability* insurance to protect against possible legal claims of someone who gets injured on one's property.

LIABILITY INSURANCE protection for a property owner from claims arising from injuries or damage to other people or property.
Example: Abel slipped on a broken step on the walkway in an apartment complex owned by Baker. Baker's *liability insurance* pays Abel for the doctor and hospital fees.

LIABLE responsible or obligated. Contrast with **exculpatory clause** and **nonrecourse.**
Example: One who borrows a **mortgage** loan generally becomes personally *liable* for its repayment. The lender can look to the **property** or the borrower personally for repayment.

LIBOR London Interbank Offered Rate. The rate that international banks dealing in Eurodollars charge each other for large loans. Some domestic banks use this rate as an **index** for **adjustable rate mortgages.**
Example: European lenders offered to finance a hotel in California at the *LIBOR* rate plus three percentage points, adjusted monthly.

LICENSE 1. permission.
Example: If Abel did not secure *license* to cross Baker's property, it would be a **trespass.**
2. a right granted by a state to an individual to operate as a real estate **broker** or salesperson.
Example: The **real estate commission** issued a salesperson *license* to Rollins (Figure 103). Working under the supervision of her broker, Rollins can sell and lease real estate owned by others.

State Real Estate Commission
—— 1993 ——

The Real Estate Commission hereby certifies that this License is issued in accordance with all legal requirements and shall remain in force and effect during the year shown above as long as the broker conforms with all obligations of the law.

	FILE	LICENSE
Charlie Baker	025	360245
101 Maple Road		
Springfield, MA 90001	October 15, 1995	

Application for annual certification of this license must be made between Sept 1st and Nov. 30th.

ADMINISTRATOR, THE REAL ESTATE COMMISSION
P.O. BOX 12188 CAPITOL STATION

THIS LICENSE MUST BE PROMINENTLY DISPLAYED IN THE OFFICE OF THE BROKER NAMED HEREON.

FIG. 103. LICENSE

LICENSED APPRAISER generally an **appraiser** who meets certain state requirements, but lacks the experience or expertise of a certified appraiser. See **Certified General Appraiser, Certified Residential Appraiser.**

LICENSEE one who holds a real estate **license;** a licensed salesperson or **broker.** See **licensing examination.**
Example: A pocket card is held by *licensees.* The employing broker displays licenses in the office.

LICENSE LAWS laws that govern the activities of real estate salespersons.
Example: Abel, an unlicensed individual, sold a farm for Baker and a house owned by Collins. Under state *license laws* each violation subjects Abel to a $10,000 fine and a year imprisonment, or both.

LICENSING EXAMINATION a written test given to a prospective real estate **broker** or salesperson to determine ability to represent the public in a real estate transaction. Most states offer examinations on at least 5 dates each year.
Example: Educational Testing Services (ETS) in Princeton, New Jersey, and American College Testing (ACT) in Iowa City, Iowa, prepare *licensing examinations* for most states. Some states prepare their own *licensing examination.*

LIEN a charge against property making it **security** for the payment of a **debt, judgment, mortgage,** or taxes; it is a type of **encumbrance.** A specific lien is against certain property only. A **general lien** is against all of the property owned by the debtor.
Example: Abel failed to pay the **contractor** for work performed on his home. The contractor files a **mechanic's lien** against the property for the amount due.

LIENHOLDER one who holds, or benefits from, a **lien.**
Example: Albert held a **mortgage** on the property, which made him a *lienholder.*

LIEN, JUNIOR a **lien** that will be paid after earlier liens have been paid. See **junior mortgage, subordination.**
Example: Abel obtains a **mortgage** loan from Solid Savings to finance the acquisition of a property. To reduce the **down payment,** he takes out a **second mortgage** with Baker, an investor. Solid Savings has a first lien and has first **priority** to **foreclosure** sale proceeds in case of a **default.** Baker has a *junior lien* and is entitled to whatever remains, up to the debt and costs, after Solid Savings is **indemnified.**

LIEN-THEORY STATES states whose laws give a **lien** on property to secure debt. Contrasted with **title theory states** in which the lender becomes the **title** owner. In either case the borrower has the right to use and enjoy the property in the absence of **default;** in the event of default, lenders may **foreclose.**
Example: After **closing** the sale of a home in a *lien-theory state,* the lender acquires a **first mortgage** and may foreclose upon certain default.

LIFE ESTATE a **freehold** interest (in **real property**) that expires upon the death of the owner or some other specified person (**pur autre vie**).
Example: A retired couple purchase a *life estate* in a retirement village apartment unit. Upon death of both husband and wife, ownership of the unit will revert to the owner's association, who may then resell to another couple.

LIFE OF LOAN CAP a contractual limitation on the maximum interest rate that can be applied to an adjustable rate mortgage during the term of the loan. See **adjustable rate mortgage;** contrast with **annual cap.**
Example: An adjustable rate mortgage is offered at the initial interest rate of 7.5% and has a *life of loan cap* of 5 percentage points. At no time during the term of the loan can the interest rate rise above 12.5%, regardless of how much the index rises.

LIFE TENANT one who is allowed to use property for life or the lifetime of another designated person. See **life estate.**
Example: Graham owns a life estate in a home. As a *life tenant,* Graham may enjoy full ownership rights to the home during her lifetime.

LIKE-KIND PROPERTY property having the same nature. See also **Section 1031** and **tax-free exchange.**
Example: Under the **Internal Revenue Code,** apartments and land are considered *like-kind property,* but animals of different sexes are not.

LIMITED LIABILITY the restriction of one's potential losses to the amount invested. The absence of personal liability. See **at-risk rules.**
Example: *Limited liability is* provided to stockholders in a **corporation** and limited partners of a **limited partnership.** Those parties cannot lose more than they contribute to the corporation, unless they agree to become personally liable. For example, if Collins buys stock in a corporation for $1,000, she cannot lose more than that amount. However, many lenders require personal guarantees of major stockholders before lending to corporations.

LIMITED PARTNERSHIP one in which there is at least one partner who is passive and limits **liability** to the amount invested, and at least one partner whose liability extends beyond monetary investment. See **general partner, partnership.**
Example: Abel, a syndicator, forms a *limited partnership* with Price, Stone, and Wise. Abel invests his time and talent, is the general partner, and owns 10% of the partnership. Price, Stone, and Wise each invested $30,000 cash and were limited partners. They buy property with a $90,000 **down payment** and a $500,000 mortgage. The property drops in value by $250,000. Price, Stone, and Wise lose their equity, and Abel, the general partner, is responsible for additional losses (Figure 104).

Abel	Price	Stone	Wise
General partner	Limited partner	Limited partner	Limited partner
Entrepreneur and manager	Passive investor	Passive investor	Passive investor

FIG. 104. LIMITED PARTNERSHIP

LINCOLN GRADUATE CENTER an organization that offers real estate education, especially appraisal courses.
Address:
Lincoln Graduate Center
P.O. Box 12528
San Antonio, TX 78212

LINEAL FOOT a measure of one foot, in a straight line, along the ground.
Example: Land along Campbell Road typically is sold at $100 per *lineal foot*. This assumes a standard depth for all lots along the road.

LINE OF CREDIT an agreement whereby a financial institution promises to lend up to a certain amount without the need to file another application.
Example: Happy Homes Brokers, Inc., has a *line of credit* under which they can borrow up to $50,000 at 3% above the **prime rate** through The Goodmoney National Bank.

LIQUIDATE 1. to dissolve a business.
Example: A **corporation's** only asset is **real estate** which is encumbered by a **mortgage.** The stockholders decide to *liquidate* the corporation. They may have the corporation sell the real estate, **retire** the mortgage, and distribute the **resale proceeds** to stockholders. The corporation is said to be *liquidated.*
2. to **retire debts.**
Example: Abel *liquidates* a $1,000 **debt** by paying it off in full with cash.

LIQUIDATED DAMAGES an amount agreed upon in a contract that one party will pay the other in the event of a **breach of the contract.**
Example: Abel engages a builder to erect a house. The **contract** says that if the builder fails to complete it by March 1, 1995, the builder will pay $50 per day thereafter until completion, as *liquidated damages.*

LIQUIDITY ease of converting **assets** to cash.
Example: Common stocks and U.S. savings bonds have good *liquidity.* **Real estate** and many types of collectibles generally have poor *liquidity.*

LIS PENDENS Latin: "suit pending." Recorded **notice** of the filing of a suit, the outcome of which may affect **title** to a certain land.
Example: The unpaid **mortgage** holder filed a **foreclosure** suit. She gave notice of *lis pendens* to make others aware of the suit pending.

LIST to obtain a **listing.**
>**Example:** Baker wanted to *list* as many properties as possible under an **exclusive right to sell** so he would earn a commission no matter who sold the property.

LISTING 1. a written engagement **contract** between a principal and an **agent,** authorizing the agent to perform services for the principal involving the latter's property.
2. a record of property for sale by a **broker** who has been authorized by the owner to sell.
3. the property so listed.
>**Example:** Abel employs Baker to find a buyer for his home by giving Baker a *listing* contract. When prospective buyers visit Baker, they will examine the *listings* in Baker's office. If interested, a prospective buyer may wish to visit the *listing.*

LISTING BROKER (AGENT) the licensed real estate **broker** (agent) who secures a **listing** of the property. Contrast with **selling broker (agent).**
>**Example:** For most sales, the *listing broker* and the **selling broker** share commissions equally. In some locales, notably for new homes, the *listing broker* earns only 1%, whereas the **selling broker** earns 3% of the selling price.

LITIGATION the act of carrying on a lawsuit.
>**Example:** *Litigation* is a contest in court to enforce a right.

LITTORAL part of the shore zone of a large body of water. Compare with **riparian rights.**
>**Example:** Lot A has *littoral* land, and Lot B has **riparian** land (Figure 105).

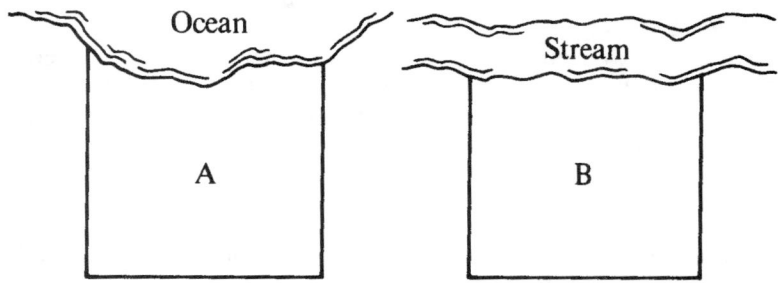

FIG. 105. LITTORAL VS. RIPARIAN LAND

LOAN APPLICATION document required by a lender prior to issuing a **loan commitment.** The application generally includes the following information:
1. name of the borrower
2. amount and terms of the loan

3. description of the subject property to be mortgaged

4. borrower's financial and employment data

Example: Lowry wishes to borrow money to purchase a home. At Friendly Savings, she completes a *loan application* and pays an application fee. Friendly Savings will **appraise** the house, examine Lowry's **credit rating,** and verify certain information on the application prior to approving or disapproving the application.

LOAN APPLICATION FEE a charge required by a loan originator to be paid by the borrower to cover the credit report, property appraisal and other incidental expenses associated with underwriting the loan. The fee is generally not refundable.
Example: Home Mortgage Company charges a *loan application fee* of $250 to process a mortgage application. The prospective property buyer/mortgage borrower brings the purchase contract to a loan officer at Home Mortgage Company.

LOAN CLOSING see **closing.**

LOAN COMMITMENT an agreement to lend money, generally of a specified amount, at specified terms at some time in the future.
Example: Before commencing development, Abel obtained a *loan commitment* from a construction lender. Also, he was required to get a **takeout financing** commitment for a **permanent mortgage.**

LOAN CONSTANT same as **mortgage constant.**

LOAN CORRESPONDENT see **mortgage correspondent.**

LOAN COVERAGE RATIO same as **debt coverage ratio.**

LOAN ORIGINATION FEE see **origination fees.**

LOAN PACKAGE the collection of documents associated with a specific loan application.
Example: A *loan package* for a home loan may contain the application form, various verifications of borrower's income and financial resources, a credit evaluation, and an appraisal of the mortgaged property.

LOAN POINTS see **discount points.**

LOAN SERVICING see **servicing.**

LOAN-TO-VALUE RATIO (LTV) the portion of the amount borrowed compared to the cost or value of the property purchased.
Example: Abel bought a $100,000 house and arranged a $90,000 **mortgage** loan, resulting in a 90% *loan-to-value ratio.*

Home mortgages at more than an 80% *LTV* ratio generally require **mortgage insurance.**

"LOCATION, LOCATION, LOCATION" the "three most important things about real estate"; a popular statement that emphasizes the importance of location with respect to the value of urban real estate.
Example: Value of real estate depends largely on where it is. However, many other elements besides *location* also affect value.

LOCKED-IN INTEREST RATE the rate promised by a lender at the time of loan application. The promise is a legal commitment of the lender, though there may be qualifications or contingencies that allow the lender to charge a higher rate. On home loans, the lock-in is customarily provided for 1% of the amount borrowed, though often it is free of charge. On income property loans, a lock-in generally requires a **commitment fee** from the loan applicant.
Example: When Lewis applied for a mortgage loan, the lender assured her that the loan would carry a rate of 9% interest. This *locked-in interest rate* represented a guarantee from the lender in the event that the loan is approved and Lewis follows through by accepting the loan. The lock-in will expire 45 days from the application date.

LOG CABIN an early-American-style house of unfinished logs.
Example: Figure 106.

Chimneys at ends

Shingle covered gable roof

Unfinished logs

FIG. 106. LOG CABIN

298

LONG-TERM CAPITAL GAIN for income tax purposes, the gain on a **capital asset** held long enough to qualify for special tax considerations.
Note: The highest rate for individuals in 1991 and thereafter for *long-term capital gains* is 28%.

LONG-TERM FINANCING same as **permanent mortgage.**

LONG-TERM LEASE generally, a commercial lease of 5 years or longer, or a residential lease longer than 1 year.

LOT AND BLOCK a method of locating a parcel of land. See **legal description.**
Example: The shaded property in Figure 107 is *lot* 4, *block* B of Rolling Acres **subdivision,** in Lincoln County, New Mexico.

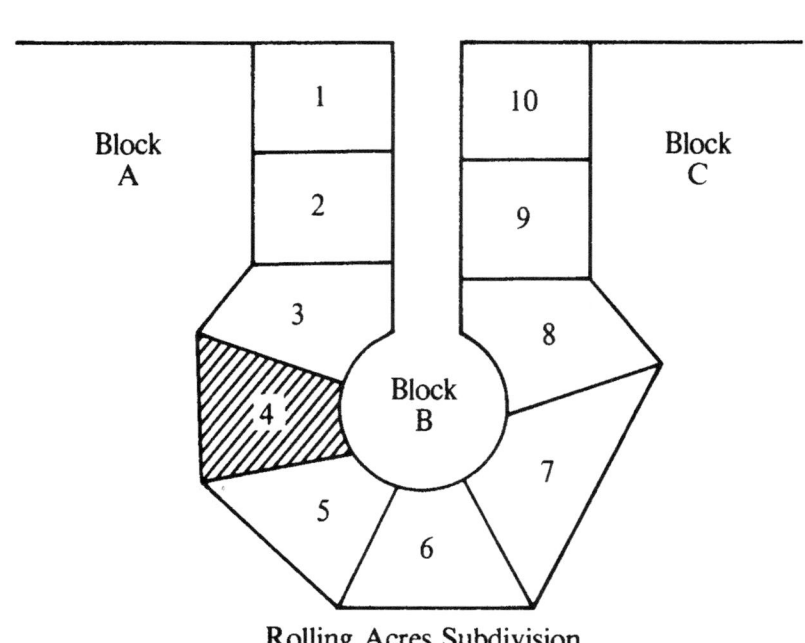

Rolling Acres Subdivision

FIG. 107. LOT AND BLOCK

LOT LINE a line bounding a lot as described in a property **survey.**
Example: Figure 108.

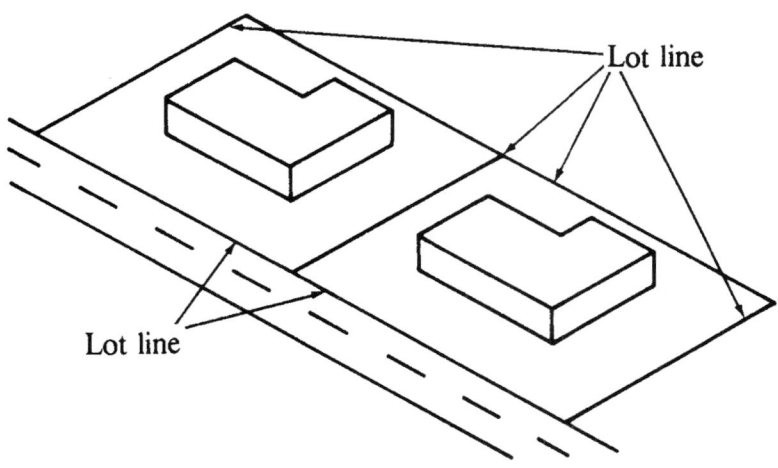

FIG. 108. LOT LINES

LOW-BALL OFFER an offer from a prospective property buyer that is much lower than the listing price. Such an offer may indicate the buyer's belief that the property will not attract many good offers and that the asking price is unrealistic. Also, it probably means the buyer is interested in the property only if it can be purchased at a bargain price.
Example: Although the house was listed at $80,000, Lowry made a *low-ball offer* of $40,000. The seller was at first insulted by the low offer, yet eventually agreed to sell the home to Lowry for $55,000.

LOW-INCOME HOUSING (QUALIFIED) housing that is eligible for special tax credits of up to 9% of their cost (4% in certain situations) under the 1986 tax act. Strict rules must be followed concerning tenant qualification, certification, and project financing.

LTV loan-to-value ratio.

L/V loan-to-value ratio.

M

MACRS modified accelerated cost recovery system. See **accelerated cost recovery system.**

MAI Member, Appraisal Institute.
Example: To acquire the designation *MAI*, an **appraiser** must pass several written proficiency examinations, perform acceptable appraisal work for a specific period of time, and prepare a demonstration narrative appraisal report. The *MAI* signifies the appraiser is qualified to appraise a broad range of **real estate** types.
Address:
Appraisal Institute
875 North Michigan Avenue
Chicago, IL 60611

MAINTENANCE activities required to compensate for **wear and tear** on a property. See **deferred maintenance.**
Example: Among the duties of **property management** is *maintenance* of the property. This includes routine upkeep of the building, repair and periodic painting as needed, keeping all mechanical parts in working order, and lawn maintenance.

MAINTENANCE FEE an assessment by a **homeowners' association** or a **condominium owners' association,** to pay costs of operating the **common elements.**
Example: A condominium association assesses each owner a *maintenance fee* of $100 per month for lawn maintenance and insurance costs.

MAJORITY 1. the age at which one is no longer a **minor** and is fully able to conduct one's own affairs; *majority* (full legal age) is 18 to 21 years, depending on the state.
Example: Abel, under 18 years of age, enters into a **contract** to buy land. Because he has not attained *majority,* he may void the contract if he chooses. Baker, the seller, is bound to the contract unless Abel voids it.
2. more than half.
Example: The bylaws of the **condominium owners' association** require a *majority* of the owners who vote to change to another management firm.

MALL a public area connecting individual stores in a **shopping center;** generally enclosed. Also, an enclosed shopping center.
Example: A large shopping *mall* was being developed south of town. It was designed to include over 40 stores connected by an enclosed and air-conditioned *mall.*

MANAGEMENT AGREEMENT a **contract** between the owner of property and someone who agrees to manage it. Fees are generally 4–10% of the rental income. See **property management.**
Example: Abel has a *management agreement* with Baker for a 200-unit apartment complex. The contract provides that Baker will receive 5% of the rental income, and he will perform all duties concerning leasing, operating, and managing the property. He will maintain a separate bank checking account for receipts and disbursements, provide monthly accounting statements, and manage the property with competence.

MANAGEMENT FEE the cost of professional **property managment.** The fee is typically set at a fixed percentage of total rental income generated by the property managed.
Example: Acme Managment Company is employed by several property owners to oversee and collect rent for their properties. Acme's standard *management fee* is 5% of gross rental income.

MANSARD ROOF one having two slopes on all four sides, with the lower slope steeper than the upper, flatter sections.
Example: Figure 109.

FIG. 109. MANSARD ROOF

MANUFACTURED HOME see **mobile home, mobile home park.**

MARGIN a constant amount added to the value of the **index** for the purpose of adjusting the interest rate on an **adjustable rate mortgage.**
Example: An adjustable rate mortgage is indexed to the 1 year Treasury yield and has a *margin* of 3 percentage points. If the index is currently 6%, the fully indexed rate on the loan is 9% (6% index plus 3% *margin*).

MARGINAL PROPERTY property that is barely profitable to use.
Example: The sale of cotton that has been efficiently raised **yields** $100; yet the cotton cost $99.99 to raise. The land on

which the cotton was raised is therefore considered *marginal property.*
Example: A tract of undeveloped land is deemed *marginal property* because of lack of access to a roadway.

MARGINAL TAX BRACKET the amount of income tax that an investor would pay on the next dollar of income. Generally, the marginal rate is higher than the average rate because of the progressive tax rate structure.
Example: Morris, a married taxpayer who files a joint return, earns $90,000, on which an $18,000 federal income tax payment is required. This tax represents an average rate of 20% ($18,000 ÷ $90,000 = 20%). If he were to earn $1,000 more, the tax would increase by $330, because he is in the 33% *marginal tax bracket.*

MARITAL DEDUCTION the tax-free amount one transfers by **will** to one's spouse. The 1981 tax act allows an unlimited amount to be transferred without federal estate tax.
Example: The concept of a *marital deduction* is to treat husband and wife as one economic unit. Since 1981, a federal **estate tax** will be due only on taxable property that passes to another generation.

MARKETABILITY STUDY an analysis, for a specific client, of the likely sales of a specific type of real estate product.
Note: A **market analysis** or study is an effort to glean information from the market on prices, **rents,** and type of product that is selling. A *marketability study* presumes a particular product and seeks to determine its **market price** and rate of sales.

MARKETABLE TITLE a **title** so free from defect that a court will enforce the title's acceptance by a purchaser. Compare **cloud on the title.**
Example: Through a divorce settlement, Collins obtained certain ownership rights to a property. She now wishes to sell the property. To obtain a *marketable title,* she must obtain a **quitclaim deed** from her former husband, thereby curing a defect in her title.

MARKET ANALYSIS a study of the supply and demand conditions in a specific area for a specific type of property or service. A *market analysis* report is generally prepared by someone with experience in real estate, economics, or marketing. It serves to help decide what type of project to develop and is also helpful in arranging permanent and construction financing for a proposed development.
Example: The developer commissioned a *market analysis* to evaluate the need for luxury apartments in the St. Louis subur-

ban market. Copies of the report were supplied to prospective lenders for this type of development.

MARKET APPROACH same as **market comparison approach.**

MARKET AREA a geographic region from which one can expect the primary demand for a specific product or service provided at a fixed location.
Example: A regional shopping center has a larger *market area* than a neighborhood shopping center.
Example: A developer estimates that the *market area* for a **subdivision** covers the northeast section of the metropolitan area.

MARKET COMPARISON APPROACH one of 3 **appraisal approaches.** Value is estimated by analyzing sales prices of similar properties (**comparables**) recently sold.
Example: The subject property is a 3-bedroom, 2-bath house. Two recently sold comparables are found. The appraiser, using the *market comparison approach*, sets up Table 30.

TABLE 30
MARKET COMPARISON APPROACH

Subject	Comparable # 1	Comparable #2
Sale price	$170,500	$167,000
Date of sale	last week	3 months ago (+$1,000)
3 bedrooms	3 bedrooms	3 bedrooms
2 baths	2½ baths (– $2,500)	2 baths
Adjusted price	$168,000	$168,000

The subject property is appraised for $168,000.

MARKET DATA APPROACH same as **market comparison approach.**

MARKET DELINEATION the process of defining the geographic extent of the demand for a specific property.
Example: The *market delineation* for a new regional shopping center showed that shoppers are likely to be drawn from a 2-county area.

MARKET PRICE the actual price paid in a market transaction. Contrast with **market value.**
Example: A home was offered for sale at $100,000. It was appraised for $93,000, and actually sold for $95,000 in an **arm's length transaction.** The *market price* is $95,000.

MARKET RENT the **rent** that a comparable unit would command if offered in the competitive market. Contrast with **contract rent.**

Example: Long rents an apartment to Towns for $900 per month. Similar units are renting for $950 per month. The apartment's *market rent* is $950 per month.

MARKET SEGMENTATION the process of defining the socio-economic characteristics of the demand for a specific property or properties.
Example: *Market segmentation* shows that the tenants for a new garden apartment complex are likely to be young married couples with incomes between $40,000 and $60,000.

MARKET STUDY see **market analysis.**

MARKET VALUE the theoretical highest price a buyer, willing but not compelled to buy, would pay, and the lowest price a seller, willing but not compelled to sell, would accept.
Example: An **appraisal** of a home indicates its *market value* is $150,000. In a normally active market, the home should sell for this amount if allowed to stay on the market for a reasonable time. The owner may, however, **deed** the home to a relative for $250. The owner may also grow impatient and sell for $140,000. Conversely, an anxious buyer may be found who pays $160,000. Finally, the owner may provide favorable financing and sell for $170,000.

MASONRY construction made from brick, cement block, or stone.
Example: The ground floor of the house shown in Figure 110 is made of *masonry*. The upper floor is wooden frame with wooden siding.

FIG. 110. MASONRY CONSTRUCTION, FIRST FLOOR

MASS APPRAISING typically used by tax assessors, an effort to determine salient characteristics of properties in a given submarket, to allow an approximation of value for each. Sophisticated statistical techniques are used frequently in *mass appraising*.

Example: Through use of multiple **regression** statistics, the tax assessor developed the formula in Table 31 to estimate the value of homes in a certain neighborhood.

TABLE 31
MASS APPRAISAL

Add:	Intercept	=	$20,000
	Baths above 1	=	10,000
	Size/per square-foot	=	45
	Garage	=	12,000
	Age/per year	=	− 1,000
	Fireplace	=	5,000

A 2,000-square-foot home, 10 years old, with one fireplace, a garage, and two baths would be assessed at $127,000 as follows:

Intercept	Baths	Size	Garage	Age
$20,000 +	$10,000 +	$45(2,000) +	$12,000 +	10(−$1,000) +

Fireplace	Assessment
$5,000 =	$127,000

MASTER DEED used by a condominium developer or converter for recording a **condominium** development. It divides a single property into individually owned units, includes restrictions on their use and provides for ownership of common areas.

Example: When a New York apartment building was converted into a condominium, the converter filed a *master deed* with the city to reflect separate ownership of individual units.

MASTER LEASE a controlling **lease.** Contrast with **sublease.** Note that one cannot grant a greater interest in real estate than one has; so if a *master lease* is for a 5-year term, a sublease cannot legally exceed 5 years.

Example: Abel leases 10,000 square feet of retail space to Baker. Baker then subleases the space to 5 different **tenants.** The lease between Abel and Baker is the *master lease.*

MASTER LIMITED PARTNERSHIP an ownership vehicle, especially used for real estate or oil and gas ventures. It is generally formed by a "roll up" of existing **limited partnerships** that own property, and typically has the advantage of ownership interests that are more marketable than individual limited partnerships.

Example: A real estate entrepreneur has syndicated 30 properties over the past 5 years, with each as a separate limited partnership. All were brought together as one large entity, a *master limited partnership*, with interests that were readily marketable.

MASTER MORTGAGE LOAN the mortgage debt existing on a building used for cooperative housing. While each co-op tenant-shareholder is obligated for a portion of the loan, this debt is separate from the loans that may have been used to purchase the individual co-op shares.
Example: When the Morgans bought a co-op apartment, they became co-mortgagors in the *master mortgage loan* that was used to buy the building by the co-op organization. They are allowed to deduct a prorated share of mortgage interest on their federal income tax return.

MASTER PLAN a document that describes, in narrative and with maps, an overall development concept. The *master plan* is used to coordinate the preparation of more detailed plans or may be a collection of detailed plans. The plan may be prepared by a local government to guide private and public development or by a **developer** on a specific project.
Example: The city planners checked to see if the **zoning** request complied with the city's *master plan.*
Example: The *master plan* for further development of the resort **condominium** is displayed in the sales office.

MATERIAL FACT a fact that is germane to a particular situation; one that participants in the situation such as a trial, may reasonably be expected to consider.
Example: If *material facts* about the investment property lying in a **floodplain** had been communicated to the buyer, he would not have bought. He is now charging **misrepresentation** against the seller and the **broker.**

MATERIALMAN a person who supplies materials used in the construction or repair of a building or other property.
Example: Since the *materialman* was not paid for lumber, he filed a **mechanic's lien** against the property.

MATERIAL PARTICIPATION a tax term introduced by the 1986 tax act, defined as year-round active involvement in the operations of a business activity on a regular, continuous and substantial basis. Three main factors to consider in determining the presence of *material participation* are:
• Is the activity the taxpayer's principal trade or business?
• How close is the taxpayer to the business?
• Does the taxpayer have knowledge and experience in the enterprise?

Retired Farmers A special exception is provided for retired farmers who are considered to continue to participate materially in that activity after retirement, as does the spouse of deceased farmers.

Limited Partners Limited partnership interests are considered inherently passive. However, the IRS may draft regulations to prevent persons from using the limited partnership vehicle for any business enterprise simply to generate passive income to offset passive losses.

MATURITY the due date of a loan.

Example: A **mortgage** loan may have a *maturity* of 30 years. Periodic payments are established so that the loan **principal** will **amortize** by the *maturity* date.

Example: A bond may have a *maturity* of 20 years. Generally, **interest** only will be paid, with the full principal repaid at *maturity*.

MBA 1. **Mortgage Bankers Association** of America.
2. Masters of Business Administration.

MECHANIC'S LIEN a **lien** given by law upon a building or other **improvement** upon land, and upon the land itself, as **security** for the payment for labor done and materials furnished for improvement.

Example: The unpaid plumber filed a *mechanic's lien* against the property while it was under construction. The builder had to satisfy the lien in order to give **clear title** to the buyer.

MEETING OF THE MINDS agreement, by all parties to a **contract,** to the exact terms thereof.

Example: To have a *meeting of the minds* there must be:
1. an **offer** and **acceptance**
2. considering the subject property
3. **consideration**
4. **terms**

MERCHANTABLE TITLE see **marketable title.**

MERGER the fusion of 2 or more interests, such as businesses or investments.

Examples: Examples of *mergers* are:
• conglomerates—corporations that are not customers or suppliers to each other or competitors
• corporations—union of 2 or more by transferring property to one that survives, and issuing its shares to stockholders of the corporation that ceases to exist

MERIDIAN a longitudinal reference line that traverses the earth in a north-south direction; all meridians circle the earth through

the equator and converge at the north and south poles; used by **surveyors** in describing property under the **government rectangular survey method.**
Example: Figure 111.

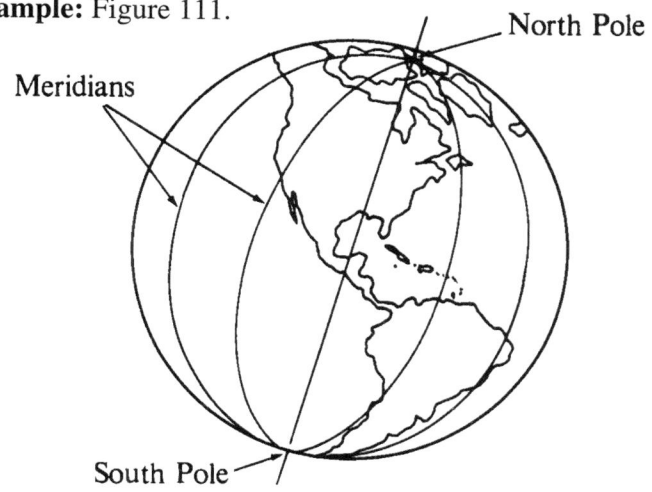

FIG. 111. MERIDIANS

METES AND BOUNDS a land **description** method that details all the **boundary** lines of land, together with their terminal points and angles.
Example: *Metes and bounds* description: Beginning at a point on the northeasterly corner of the intersection of South St. and West Rd.; running thence northerly along West Rd. 200 feet, thence easterly parallel to South St. 150 feet; thence southerly parallel to West Rd. 200 feet; thence westerly along South St. 150 feet to the point of beginning (Figure 112).

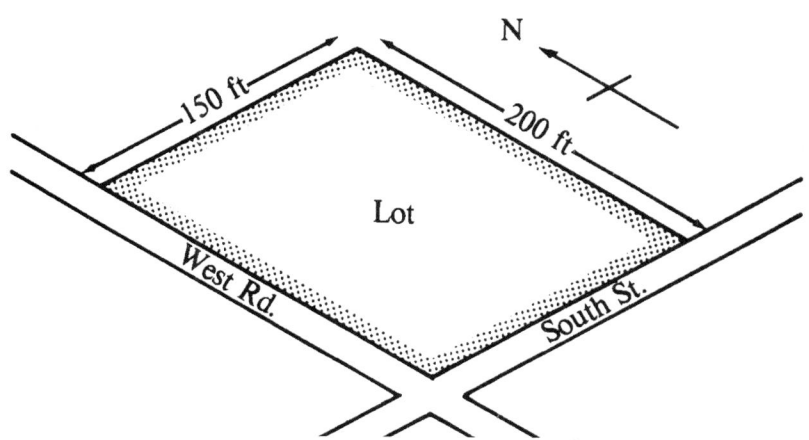

FIG. 112. METES AND BOUNDS

309

METROPOLITAN STATISTICAL AREA (MSA) one or more counties having a population of at least 50,000 (see Table 32). A **Consolidated Metropolitan Statistical Area (CMSA)** is an area with two or more **Primary Metropolitan Statistical Areas (PMSA)**. A CMSA must also include at least 1 million people.

TABLE 32
STATISTICAL AREA REQUIREMENTS

MSA or PMSA	Minimum Population
Level A	1,000,000
Level B	250,000
Level C	100,000
Level D	50,000

Example: The *metropolitan statistical area* of Atlanta, Georgia, covers 15 counties and contains over 2 million people.

MGIC Mortgage Guaranty Insurance Corporation.

MILKING A PROJECT see **bleeding a project.**

MILL one tenth of a cent. Used in expressing tax rates on a per-dollar basis.
Example: A tax rate of 60 *mills* means that taxes are 6 cents per dollar of **assessed valuation.**

MILLAGE RATE a tax rate applied to property. Each **mill** represents $1 of tax **assessment** per $1,000 of assessed property value.
Example: The *millage rate* for property taxes in the Bumpton school district is 20 mills. A home with assessed value of $100,000 pays $2,000 a year in property taxes to the district.

MINERAL LEASE an agreement that provides the lessee the right to excavate and sell minerals on the property of the lessor or to remove and sell petroleum and natural gas from the pool underlying the property of the lessor. In return, the lessor receives a royalty payment based on the value of the minerals removed.
Example: The Minavers own a piece of land in Texas that is part of an area covering a large oil reserve. Big Strike Oil Company offers them a *mineral lease* that pays the Minavers a pro-rated share of oil revenues in exchange for the right to place a well at locations within the reserve area.

MINERAL RIGHTS the privilege of gaining **income** from the sale of oil, gas, and other valuable resources found on land.
Example: Abel purchases a property that contains underground oil deposits. Abel may:
• develop these *mineral rights* by drilling a well
• sell the rights for a price to an oil company
• **lease** the rights to an oil company in exchange for a royalty

MINIMUM LOT AREA the smallest building lot area allowed in a **subdivision,** generally specified by a **zoning ordinance.**
Example: Baker owns land that is zoned "R-4." If Baker develops the land, it must be used for residential purposes and lots must have a *minimum lot area* of ¼ acre.

MINI-WAREHOUSE a building separated into relatively small lockable individual units, typically with a garage-door-styled opening, that provide storage. Units are typically rented month to month and are sized from 5' × 5' to 25' × 25'.
Example: A typical 10' × 20' *mini-warehouse* can be rented for $75 per month to be used for storage of excess household goods.

MINOR a person under the age of **majority** specified by law (18 to 21 years, depending on the state).
Example: Contracts for the sale or use of real estate, entered into by a *minor,* are voidable by the minor. Note that the other party is bound; only the minor may void them.

MISREPRESENTATION an untrue statement, whether unintentional or deliberate. It may be a form of nondisclosure where there is a duty to disclose or the planned creation of a false appearance. Where there is misrepresentation of **material fact,** the person injured may sue for **damages** or **rescind** the **contract.** See **false advertising.**
Example: The **broker** represented the home as being structurally sound. The broker did not know that **termites** were destroying the wood. The buyer sued the broker for *misrepresentation.*

MISSION HOUSE a nineteenth-century-style house that looks like the old mission churches and houses of Southern California. The doors and windows are arch-shaped.
Example: Figure 113.

FIG. 113. MISSION HOUSE

311

MISTAKE an unintentional error made in preparing a **contract;** may be corrected by mutual consent of all parties without voiding contract.

Example: Abel and Baker agree to a sales contract for a property located at 100 Main Street. In preparing the contract the address is listed as 100 Main Blvd. The *mistake* is discovered at the **closing,** and correction is made with the consent of both parties.

MLS multiple listing service.

MOBILE HOME a dwelling unit (Figure 114) manufactured in a factory and designed to be transported to a **site** and semipermanently attached.

Example: One option for low-cost housing is purchase of a *mobile home,* which generally costs much less than site-built housing. *Mobile homes* may be placed on the purchaser's lot or in a **mobile home park** for a monthly rental.

FIG. 114. MOBILE HOME

MOBILE HOME PARK a **subdivision** of plots designed for siting of mobile homes. Plots are generally leased to mobile home owners and include **utilities,** parking space, and access to utility roads. Many parks also include such **amenities** as swimming pools and clubhouses.

Example: A typical *mobile home park* design (Figure 115).

MODEL UNIT a representative home, apartment, or office space used as part of a sales campaign to demonstrate the design, structure, and appearance of units in a development.

Example: A **developer** constructs a *model unit* in an effort to **prelease** units in a development. Prospective tenants are invited to tour the *model unit* to gain an appreciation for the design and appearance of the development.

FIG. 115. MOBILE HOME PARK

MODERNIZE to alter a property by installing up-to-date equipment, making contemporary cosmetic improvements, and deleting obsolete facilities.
Example: The redeveloper *modernized* the apartment building by installing dishwashers, wall-to-wall carpeting, a new gas furnace and by removing the coal storage bin.

MODULAR HOUSING dwelling units constructed from components **prefabricated** in a factory and erected on the **site.**
Example: In a *modular housing* project, site preparation may be performed while structural panels are being fabricated by mass production techniques in a factory. The panels are then shipped to the site and erected in place.

MOISTURE BARRIER a layer of foil, plastic, or paper used in the construction of exterior walls, ceilings, and foundations to prevent moisture penetration into wooden members or insulation.
Example: The *moisture barrier* in an exterior wall (Figure 116).

MONETARY INSTITUTION DEREGULATION ACT same as **Depository Institutions Deregulation and Monetary Control Act.**

MONTEREY ARCHITECTURE a nineteenth-century-style, 2-story house with a balcony across the front at the second-floor level.
Example: Figure 117.

313

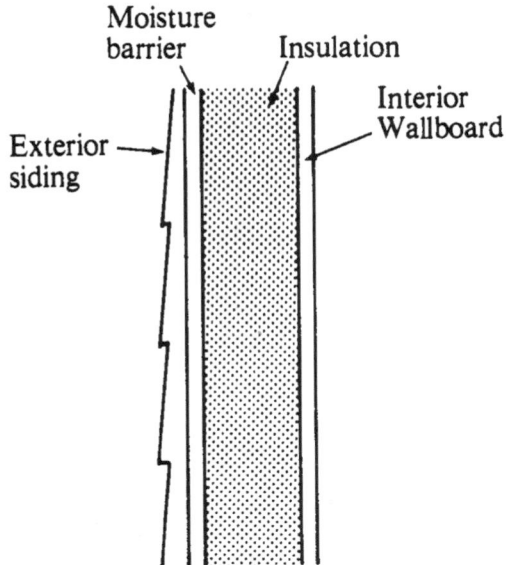

Moisture
barrier

Insulation

Interior
Wallboard

Exterior
siding

FIG. 116. MOISTURE BARRIER

Balcony across front at second floor

Shingle
roof

2 stories

Rail simple
iron or wood

FIG. 117. MONTEREY ARCHITECTURE

MONTH-TO-MONTH TENANCY lease agreement extendable or cancelable each month.

Example: Abel rents an apartment from Baker on a *month-to-month tenancy* basis. Abel may remain as long as he pays rent and Baker does not give notice to cancel the lease. Abel may also cancel the lease upon giving notice.

314

MONUMENT a fixed object and point established by **surveyors** to determine land locations.
Example: See **landmark.**

MORATORIUM a time period during which a certain activity is not allowed.
Example: Fair City passes an **ordinance** that establishes a 6-month *moratorium* on condominium **conversions.** During the period, no one may legally convert an apartment complex into **condominium** units.

MORTGAGE a written **instrument** that creates a **lien** upon **real estate** as **security** for the payment of a specified debt.
Example: Lowry wants to buy a home. She needs a loan to complete the purchase. As **collateral,** Lowry offers a *mortgage* on the property to the lender.
Note that the borrower gives the *mortgage*, which pledges the property as collateral. The lender gives the loan.

MORTGAGE ASSUMPTION same as **assumption of mortgage.**

MORTGAGE-BACKED SECURITY a bond or other financial obligation secured by a pool of mortgage loans. See **collateralized mortgage obligations, REMICs.**
Example: The Sachs Mortgage Broker Company purchased $100 million worth of mortgage loans on private homes. To fund the purchase, Sachs created a *mortgage-backed security* secured by the pool of mortgages and sold the security to investors.

MORTGAGE BANKER one who originates, sells, and services **mortgage** loans. Most loans are insured or guaranteed by a government agency or private mortgage insurer. See **mortgage insurance.**
Example: The Mortgage Store, a *mortgage banker,* originates 100 loans totaling $5,000,000. They sell this package of loans to an out-of-state investor for $5,010,000. They continue to collect monthly payments from homeowners and assure that property taxes are paid and insurance is maintained. They charge the investor an annual fee of ⅜ of 1% of the loan **principal,** each month remitting to the investor the rest of the monthly payments from homeowners.

MORTGAGE BANKERS ASSOCIATION OF AMERICA (MBA) an organization that provides educational programs and other services for **mortgage bankers.** Offers the Certified Mortgage Banker (CMB) designation. Publishes *Mortgage Banker* magazine.

Address:
Mortgage Bankers Association of America
1125 Fifteenth Street NW
Washington, DC 20005

MORTGAGE BONDS tax-exempt securities sold by municipal and state authorities for the purpose of providing low-interest rate **mortgage** loans to qualified individuals. For most programs, mortgage borrowers must be first-time home buyers with moderate income.
Example: Local Housing Finance Agency, a creation of the city of Local, sold $50 million of *mortgage bonds.* The proceeds from the sale were used to originate loans through local mortgage lenders for first-time home buyers within the city. Interest on the bonds was tax-exempt to the bondholders, thereby allowing the agency to borrow money at an **interest rate** below 8%. The mortgage loans could be originated at rates below 9% at a time when market mortgage interest rates were above 10%.

MORTGAGE BROKER one who, for a fee, places loans with investors, but does not service such loans.
Example: The Ace Development Company wants to build a shopping center. A *mortgage broker* charges a 1% fee for each construction loan (placed with a commercial bank) and the permanent loan (placed with an insurance company).

MORTGAGE COMMITMENT an agreement between a lender and a borrower to lend money at a future date, subject to the conditions described in the agreement.
Example: Baker wishes to build a home. Construction will require 6 months. Baker obtains a *mortgage commitment* from Home Town Savings and Loan for permanent financing of the home at the time of its completion.

MORTGAGE CONSTANT the percentage ratio between the annual **debt service** and the loan **principal.** The formula is

$$\frac{\text{Ann. debt serv.}}{\text{Loan prin.}} = \text{mort. const.}$$

Example: A loan of $10,000 at 12% interest for 5 years requires annual payments of $2,774. The *mortgage constant* is

$$\frac{2,744}{10,000} = .2774 \text{ or } 27.74\%$$

Annual debt service for the loan is

$$0.2774 \times \$10,000 = \$2,774$$

316

MORTGAGE CORRESPONDENT one who services loans for a fee. Compare **mortgage broker.**
Example: The Good Money Savings Association bought a package of 1,000 loans in another state. They arrange with a *mortgage correspondent* to collect monthly payments, pay real estate taxes, and assure that the property is insured. The *mortgage correspondent* keeps as a fee 3/8 of 1% of the mortgage balance each year.

MORTGAGE DISCOUNT amount of **principal** that lenders deduct at the beginning of the loan. See **discount points.**
Example: Abel obtains a mortgage loan in the amount of $50,000. The loan is discounted by 2 **points,** each point equaling 1% of the **principal.** At **closing** Abel will receive $49,000, yet will owe $50,000. The $1,000 difference is the *mortgage discount.*

MORTGAGEE one who holds a **lien** on property or **title** to property, as **security** for a debt.
Example: Abel obtains a **mortgage** loan from Homebuyers Savings. Homebuyers Savings serves as the *mortgagee.*

MORTGAGEE IN POSSESSION situation in which a lender takes possession and control of a mortgaged property upon foreclosure of the loan secured by the mortgage. The lender possesses the property, collecting any income produced, until it is sold at the foreclosure sale.
Example: Following nonpayment of debt service for a period of 6 months, Savings Bank filed for foreclosure of the loan. Fearing damages to the property, Savings immediately took possession under an action of *mortgagee in possession.*

MORTGAGE-EQUITY TECHNIQUE same as **Ellwood technique.**

MORTGAGE GUARANTEE INSURANCE CO. (MGIC) a private company that insures, to lenders, loan repayment in the event of **default** and/or **foreclosure.** See **mortgage insurance.**
Example: Collins wants to arrange a loan for 90% of the cost of the home she is buying. The lender applies to *MGIC* for **private mortgage insurance.** MGIC accepts and, for a **premium,** stands willing to accept any losses on the mortgages up to 25% of the **principal.**

MORTGAGE INSURANCE 1. a policy that guarantees repayment of a mortgage loan in the event of death or, possibly, disability of the **mortgagor.**
2. protection for the lender in the event of **default,** usually covering the top 25% of the amount borrowed.

317

See **private mortgage insurance.**
Example: Manning obtains a mortgage loan and, for an additional monthly **premium,** purchases *mortgage insurance.* Should Manning die before loan **maturity,** the policy will pay the remaining balance of the loan. This protects Manning's survivors from losing the property because of inability to continue the loan payments, and also protects the **mortgagee.**

MORTGAGE INSURANCE PREMIUM (MIP) the fee paid by a mortgagor to obtain **mortgage insurance** on a mortgage loan. The fee may be collected as a lump sum at loan closing or as a periodic amount included in the monthly payment, or both.
Example: To obtain a mortgage loan insured by the FHA, the borrower must pay a *mortgage insurance premium* equal to 3.8% of the loan amount. Depending on the loan-to-value ratio, there may be a monthly premium as well.

MORTGAGE LIEN an **encumbrance** on property used to secure a loan. The holder of the **lien** has a claim to the property in case of loan **default.** The **priority** of the claim depends on the order of **recording** and any **subordination** agreements. Thus a **first mortgage** generally has prior claim to all other mortgage lien holders. See also **second mortgage.**
Example: Minton obtains a mortgage loan to purchase a house. Minton signs a **note** and mortgage contract. The lender obtains a *mortgage lien* on the house. Should Minton default on the loan, the lender may **foreclose** and exercise the lien to force a sale, the proceeds of which are used to satisfy Minton's debt.

MORTGAGE OUT to obtain financing in excess of the cost to construct a project. In the mid 1980s **developers** could mortgage out by obtaining a permanent **loan commitment** based on a high percentage of the completed project's value. This enabled the developer to borrow more than the cost of developing the project. Since then, opportunities to mortgage out have been virtually eliminated by lower **loan-to-value ratios,** higher **capitalization rates** and higher construction costs.
Example: A proposed office building is projected to produce annual **net operating income** of $100,000. At a capitalization rate of 10%, the building is worth $1,000,000. A **takeout** loan commitment is obtained for 80% of value, or $800,000. The developer requires only $750,000 to purchase the land and construct the building. The $50,000 excess represents the results of the developer *mortgaging out.*

MORTGAGE POOL a collection of loans of similar nature which are sold as a unit in the secondary market or used to back a security which is then sold in the capital markets.

Example: Lenders Mortgage Company packaged a *mortgage pool* consisting of $50 million worth of VA guaranteed loans. The package was sold to a group of investors who each put up a minimum of $25,000.

MORTGAGE RELIEF acquired freedom from mortgage debt, generally through **assumption of mortgage** by another party or **debt** retirement. In a tax-free exchange, mortgage relief is considered **boot** received. In many foreclosures, where the sole property is the sole collateral for the loan, or the borrower fails to pay anything in addition to the real estate, the transaction is treated for tax purposes as a sale for the mortgage debt. If the taxpayer's basis is less than the mortgage relief, the difference is a taxable gain.
Example: Collins exchanged her mortgaged office building, receiving land worth $25,000 and *mortgage relief* of $75,000. The total value received was $100,000.
Example: Eric owed $650,000 on a home upon foreclosure. Because his tax basis of the home was $400,000, a $250,000 gain is realized, but may be postponed if a new residence is purchased for $650,000 within 2 years.

MORTGAGOR one who pledges property as **security** for a loan.
Example: Abel obtains a mortgage loan from Homebuyers Savings. Abel serves as a *mortgagor*.

MOST PROBABLE SELLING PRICE the property's most likely selling price when not all the conditions required for a **market value** estimate are relevant.
Example: An **appraiser** estimated a property's most likely sales price at $100,000, assuming a sale within 20 days, whereas its market value of $120,000 might require up to 6 months to realize.

MULTIFAMILY HOUSING a type of residential structure with more than one **dwelling** unit in the same building.
Example: *Multifamily housing* is divided into 2 categories:
2–4 dwelling units: **duplexes,** triplexes, and quadraplexes
5 or more units: apartment buildings
Multifamily housing may be tenant-occupied, owner-occupied (as in a **condominium** or cooperative project), or mixed (as many duplexes with the owner occupying one side).

MULTIPLE LISTING an arrangement among a group of real estate **brokers;** they agree in advance to provide information about some or all of their **listings** to the others and also agree that **commissions** on sales of such listings will be split between listing and selling brokers.
Example: A broker lists a home under an **exclusive right to sell.** The broker belongs to a *multiple listing* association. After 5 days

the broker turns in a description of the home to the association. Any cooperating broker can sell the home and will receive half of the commission. The broker who obtained the **exclusive right to sell** is assured of earning half the commission upon the sale.

MULTIPLE LISTING SERVICE (MLS) an association of real estate **brokers** that agrees to share **listings** with one another. The listing broker and the selling broker share the **commission.** The MLS usually distributes a book with all listings to its members, updating the book frequently. Prospective buyers benefit from the ability to select from among many homes from any member broker.
Example: Abel and Baker, both brokers, are members of the *multiple listing service.* A home that was listed by Abel under an **exclusive right to sell** is sold by Baker. The two brokers share the commission.

MULTIPLIER a factor, used as a guide, applied by multiplication to derive or estimate an important value.
Example: A **gross rent multiplier** of 6 means that property renting for $12,000 per year can be sold for 6 times that amount, or $72,000.
Example: A population *multiplier* of 2 means that, for each job added, 2 people will be added to a city's population.

MUNIMENTS OF TITLE documents, such as **deeds** or **contracts,** one uses to indicate ownership.
Example: In order to register **title** under the **Torrens system,** the owner offered *muniments of title*.

MUTUAL SAVINGS BANKS mostly in the northeastern U.S., these state-chartered banks are owned by the depositors and operated for their benefit. Most of these banks hold a large portion of their **assets** in home mortgage loans.
Example: Abel deposits his savings in a *mutual savings bank* in New York. As a depositor-shareholder, Abel receives a proportionate distribution of the bank's earnings.

N

NAA National Apartment Association.

NACORE National Association of Corporate Real Estate Executives.

NAHB National Association of Home Builders.

NAR National Association of Realtors®.

NAREB National Association of Real Estate Brokers.

NARELLO National Association of Real Estate License Law Officials.

NATIONAL APARTMENT ASSOCIATION (NAA) an organization of apartment owners, with local chapters in metropolitan areas, that provides information and services for members concerning apartment rentals, **lease** forms, occupancy rates, and other matters.
Address:
National Apartment Association
1101 14th Street NW
Washington, DC 20005

NATIONAL ASSOCIATION OF CORPORATE REAL ESTATE EXECUTIVES (NACORE) membership includes those active with purchasing, selling, and managing **real estate** held by **corporations.**
Address:
National Association of Corporate Real Estate Executives
471 Spencer Drive, S, Suite 8
West Palm Beach, FL 33409

NATIONAL ASSOCIATION OF HOME BUILDERS (NAHB) an organization of home builders, providing educational, political information and research services. Publishes a monthly magazine, *Builder.*
Address:
National Association of Home Builders
15th and M Street, NW
Washington, DC 20005

NATIONAL ASSOCIATION OF INDEPENDENT FEE APPRAISERS (NAIFA) an organization of **real estate appraisers** that offers these professional designations:
• **IFA**—Member

321

- **IFAS**—Senior member
- **IFAC**—Appraiser-counselor

Address:
National Association of Independent Fee Apprasiers
7501 Murdoch Avenue
St. Louis, MO 63119

NATIONAL ASSOCIATION OF MASTER APPRAISERS
an association that offers the Master Senior Appraiser (MSA) designation. Requires education but little or no experience.
Address:
National Association of Master Appraisers
P.O. Box 12528
San Antonio, TX 78212

NATIONAL ASSOCIATION OF REAL ESTATE BROKERS
(NAREB) an organization mostly of minority real estate sales-persons and **brokers** who are called **Realtists.**
Address:
National Association of Real Estate Brokers
9th floor, Suite 900
1101 14th Street, NW
Washington, DC 20005

NATIONAL ASSOCIATION OF REAL ESTATE LICENSE LAW OFFICIALS (NARELLO)
membership is composed of commissioners from state real estate licensing agencies.
Address:
National Association of Real Estate License Law Officials
2580 South 90th Street
Omaha, NE 68124

NATIONAL ASSOCIATION OF REALTORS® (NAR)
an organization of **Realtors®,** devoted to encouraging profession-alism in **real estate** activities. There are over 600,000 members of NAR, 50 state associations, and several affiliates. Members are required to abide by the **Code of Ethics** of the NAR.
Address:
National Association of Realtors®
430 North Michigan Avenue
Chicago, IL 60611

NATIONAL ASSOCIATION OF REVIEW APPRAISERS AND MORTGAGE UNDERWRITERS
an organization that awards the Certified Review Appraiser (CRA) designation.
Address:
National Association of Review Appraisers and Mortgage Underwriters
8715 Via de Commercio
Scottsdale, AZ 85285

NATIONAL FLOOD INSURANCE PROGRAM see **flood insurance.**

NATIONAL REALTY COMMITTEE a group whose membership is primarily composed of large, high-profile owners and **developers.** Their paramount concern is the legislative arena, especially the government's policy toward real estate finance, taxation, and investment.
Address:
National Realty Committee
1250 Connecticut Avenue, Suite 630
Washington, DC 20036

NATIONAL SOCIETY OF REAL ESTATE APPRAISERS an affiliate of the National Association of Real Estate Brokers that offers the professional designations RA, CRA, MREA.
Address:
National Society of Real Estate Appraisers
1265 East 105th Street
Cleveland, OH 44108

NATURAL VACANCY RATE the average **vacancy rate** for a rental property market that would result if supply and demand were in balance. The level to which vacancy rates adjust over the long term. A benchmark by which current vacancy rates in the market are considered high or low.
Example: During a period of rapid popoulation growth, apartment vacancy rates fell to less than 1%. The *natural vacancy rate* for the local market was 5%. Because of the unusually low vacancy rate, rent soared and plans were started on new apartment developments in the area.

NEGATIVE AMORTIZATION an increase in the **outstanding balance** of a loan resulting from the failure of periodic **debt service** payments to cover required interest charged on the loan. Generally occurs under **indexed loans** for which the applicable **interest rate** may be changed without affecting the monthly payments. *Negative amortization* will occur if the indexed interest rate is increased.
Example: A loan is originated at 15% interest with a **maturity** of 30 years. The interest rate may be adjusted each 6 months, but monthly payments remain a constant $632. After 6 months, the interest rate is raised to 16.5%, which would require a monthly payment of $692 to fully amortize the loan. At the new interest rate, $687 is required to pay interest. The $55 difference between the payment and interest due is added to the principal in month 7 as *negative amortization* (Figure 118).

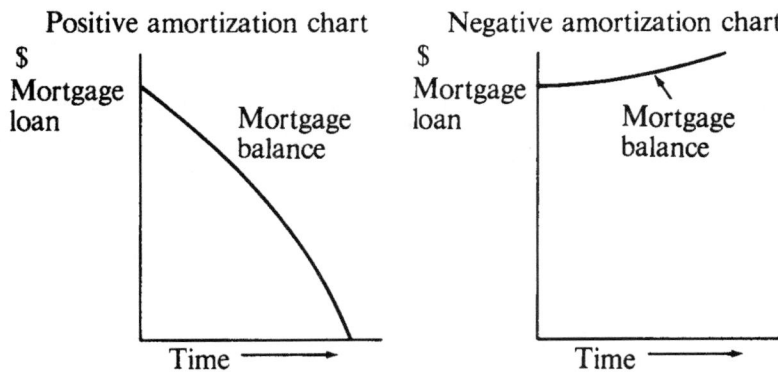

Positive amortization chart

Negative amortization chart

FIG. 118. NEGATIVE AMORTIZATION

NEGATIVE CASH FLOW situation in which a property owner must make an outlay of funds to operate a property.

Example: Baker acquires an apartment building with the first year income statement shown in Table 33. Baker must spend $5,000 to operate the building for the first year, because of a *negative cash flow*.

TABLE 33
NEGATIVE CASH FLOW

Potential **gross income:**	$50,000
Vacancy loss	− 5,000
Effective gross income	$45,000
Operating expenses	−30,000
Net operating income	$15,000
Debt service	−20,000
Negative cash flow before tax	$5,000

NEGATIVE LEVERAGE same as **reverse leverage.**

NEGOTIABLE INSTRUMENT a promise to pay money, transferable from one person to another.

Example: Abel gave Baker a *negotiable instrument* that contained a promise to pay $1,000 on July 22 of this year. Baker sold the note for $900 cash to Collins by endorsing and delivering it. Collins became a **holder in due course.**

NEGOTIATION the process of bargaining that precedes an agreement. Successful negotiation generally results in a **contract** between the parties.

Example: Nelson wishes to purchase a property from Newman. Nelson is willing to pay up to a certain price and desires certain **conditions** placed on the sale. Newman will accept any-

thing over a certain price and may be willing to help finance the purchase for a higher price. In *negotiation* Nelson and Newman attempt to come to an agreement over the price and conditions. When they agree, a sales contract is **executed.**

NEIGHBORHOOD a district or locality characterized by similar or compatible land uses. *Neighborhoods* are often identified by a place name and have boundaries composed of major streets, barriers, or abrupt changes in land use.
Example: Residential *neighborhoods* are often identified with a **subdivision,** an elementary school attendance zone, a major public facility, such as a college, or a small town within a larger urban area. Homes in the neighborhood are of similar style, age, and value.
Example: Commercial *neighborhoods* are generally associated with a major road, shopping center, or **central business district.**
Example: Industrial *neighborhoods* are generally identified by common use of a transportation linkage.

NEIGHBORHOOD LIFE CYCLE a generalized pattern that describes the physical and social changes that residential areas experience over time. See also **abandonment, filtering down, urban renewal, land use succession.**
Example: Richard Andrews' *neighborhood life cycle* (Figure 119).

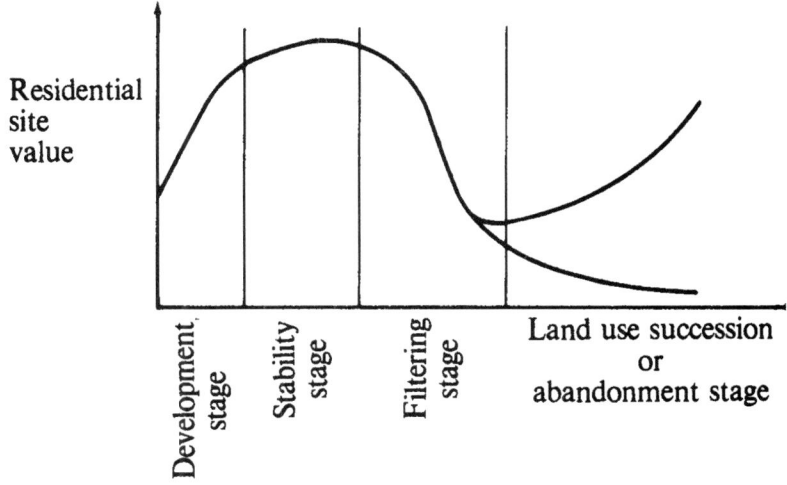

FIG. 119. NEIGHBORHOOD LIFE CYCLE

NET INCOME 1. in accounting, the amount remaining after all expenses have been met.
Example: Table 34.
2. in **appraisal,** same as **net operating income.**

325

TABLE 34
NET INCOME STATEMENT

Rental income		$10,000
Less:		
Utilities	$ 1,500	
Property taxes	1,000	
Management fee	500	
Maintenance expenses	2,000	
Interest	2,000	
Depreciation	1,000	
Income taxes	1,000	
Subtotal		− 9,000
Net income		$1,000

NET INCOME MULTIPLIER a factor that, when applied by multiplication to a property's **net operating income,** results in a property value estimate.
Example: A duplex generates $20,000 of gross rental income and requires $8,000 of **operating expenses,** providing $12,000 of net operating income. If similar properties in the area typically sell for 10 times net operating income, this duplex would be worth $120,000 (10 × $12,000) using the *net income multiplier.*

NET LEASABLE AREA in a building or project, floor space that may be rented to tenants. The area upon which rental payments are based. Generally excludes common areas and space devoted to the heating, cooling, and other equipment of a building.
Example: A building with 10 floors, each containing 3,000 square feet of space, may have a *net leasable area* of 25,000 square feet. Elevators, hallways, etc., absorb the remaining 5,000 square feet.

NET LEASE a **lease** whereby, in addition to the rent stipulated, the lessee (tenant) pays such expenses as taxes, insurance, and **maintenance.** The landlord's rent receipt is thereby "net" of those expenses.
Example: Baker leases retail space from Abel on a *net lease.* Abel can expect to receive the full rent without deducting for **operating expenses,** which are paid by Baker. In practice, various levels of net leases are often used to designate arrangements where the tenant pays only some types of expenses and the landlord pays other types.

NET LISTING a listing in which the broker's **commission** is the excess of the sale price over an agreed-upon (net) price to the seller; illegal in some states.

Example: Abel agrees to sell Baker's house on a *net listing.* They set the net price at $70,000. Abel finds a buyer willing to pay $75,000. Abel's commission is $5,000. Note that should Abel find a buyer offering $70,000, Abel would earn no commission.

NET OPERATING INCOME (NOI) income from property or business after **operating expenses** have been deducted, but before deducting income taxes and financing expenses **(interest** and **principal payments).** The formula is:

NOI = gross income − operating expenses

Example: A property produces rental income of $100,000 during the year. The expenses incurred are shown in Table 35.

TABLE 35
NET OPERATING INCOME

Operating expenses:	
Maintenance	$20,000
Insurance	5,000
Property taxes	10,000
Management	10,000
Utilities	15,000
Total operating expenses	$60,000

NOI = $100,000 − $60,000 = $40,000 (*net operating income*)

Debt service:*	
Interest	$18,000
Principal	2,000
	$20,000
Income taxes*	($5,000)

*Excluded from the computation.

NET PRESENT VALUE a method of determining whether expected performance of a proposed investment promises to be adequate. See also **internal rate of return, present value of one.** **Example:** A proposed land investment requires $10,000 of cash now, and is expected to be resold for $25,000 in 4 years. For the **risks** involved, the investor seeks a 20% **discount rate** (same as **compounded rate of return).** The $25,000 amount to be received in 4 years, when discounted by 20% annually, is worth $12,056 now. Since the investment costs $10,000, the *net present value* is $2,056.

$$\frac{\$25,000}{(1 + 0.20)^4} - \$10,000 = \$2,056$$

NET SPENDABLE INCOME same as **after-tax cash flow.**

NET WORTH the excess of **assets** over **liabilities.** The amount
of **equity.**
Example: Table 36:

**TABLE 36
NET WORTH**

Balance Sheet			
Assets		Liabilities	
Land	$10,000	Mortgage	$75,000
Buildings	90,000	Net worth	25,000
Total	$100,000	Total	$100,000

NET YIELD the return on an investment after subtracting all
expenses. See also **current yield, yield to maturity.**
Example: Equity paid for an investment is $10,000. **Net
income** is $1,000. Therefore, the investment generates a $1,000
net yield.

NEW ENGLAND COLONIAL an early-American-style, 2½-
story boxlike house that is generally symmetrical, square, or
rectangular with side or rear wings. The traditional material is
narrow clapboard siding. The roof is usually the gable type
covered with shingles.
Example: Figure 120.

FIG. 120. NEW ENGLAND COLONIAL

NEW ENGLAND FARMHOUSE an early-American-style house that is simple and box-shaped. The traditional material for the exterior siding is white clapboard. A steep pitched roof is used to shed heavy snow.
Example: Figure 121.

White clapboard

Steep, pitched roof
simple box shape

FIG. 121. NEW ENGLAND FARMHOUSE

NEW TOWN a large mixed-use development designed to provide residences, general shopping, services, and employment. The basic concept of a new town is to construct a community in a previously undeveloped area under a central plan, to avoid unplanned development. Some European and South American countries use new towns to attract population into less developed regions.
Example: The popularity of *new towns* reached a peak in the early 1970s under financial assistance from the federal government. Possibly the most famous modern *new towns* in the U.S. are Columbia, Maryland and Reston, Virginia. *New towns* have been developed to serve as national capitals, such as Washington DC; Brasilia, Brazil; and Canberra, Australia.

NLA net leasable area.

NO BID decision by the **Veterans Administration,** when a loan it has guaranteed goes into default, to pay the guarantee amount to the lender instead of acquiring the property in foreclosure. The result is that often the lender obtains the property at the sale. The VA guarantees 60% of the loan amount or a fixed amount (currently $27,500), whichever is lower.

Example: A VA *no bid* is usually a losing proposition for a lender holding the loan. The VA resorts to the practice when it determines the property has declined enough in value to make paying the guarantee the less expensive alternative. This leaves the lender to look to the property to cover its loses on the loan in excess of the VA contribution.

NOI net operating income.

NOMINAL LOAN RATE same as **face interest rate.**

NOMINEE one who, in a limited sense, acts for or represents another.
Example: Davis, with consent, used her secretary's name as the **grantee** to property she bought. Her secretary was considered her *nominee.* Simultaneously, her secretary **deeded** the property to Davis. There was a **mortgage** on the property. Davis acquired the property from the *nominee* **subject to** the mortgage. By doing so, Davis is not personally liable for the mortgage loan.

NO MONEY DOWN general term referring to real estate acquisition strategies based on seller-provided financing and/or existing loan assumption and minimal use of cash down payments. It is a method of achieving maximum profits from real estate investments.
Example: Allen purchased three houses using a *no money down* strategy. In one transaction, Allen assumed the existing mortgage of $55,000, gave the seller a note for an additional $30,000 and transferred ownership of an automobile worth $5,000 to finance the $90,000 house with no cash down payment.

NONCONFORMING USE a use that violates **zoning** regulations or codes but is allowed to continue because it began before the zoning **restriction** was enacted.
Example: Carter owns a commercial building constructed in 1920. In 1935, the city enacted a **zoning ordinance** that prescribes residential use for the area in which the building is located. Under *nonconforming use,* the building may remain, but Carter is restricted in the extent to which he may improve or restore the building.

NONDISTURBANCE CLAUSE 1. an agreement in mortgage contracts on income-producing property that provides for the continuation of **leases** in the event of loan **foreclosure.**
Example: The tenant was concerned that he would be **evicted** if the landlord went **bankrupt.** He insisted on a *nondisturbance clause* so the lease would continue in the event of foreclosure.
2. an agreement in a sales contract, when the seller retains **mineral rights,** that provides that exploration of minerals will not interfere with surface development.

Example: When the seller negotiated the **oil and gas lease,** she was assured by the oil company that the property could be conveyed with a *nondisturbance clause.*

NONEXCLUSIVE LISTING same as **open listing.**

NONRECOURSE no personal **liability.** Lenders may take the property pledged as **collateral** to satisfy a **debt,** but have no **recourse** to other **assets** of the borrower.
Example: Downing purchases a property with a *nonrecourse* loan. Should Downing **default,** the lender may **foreclose** and acquire the property but is barred from seeking a **judgment** against other properties held by Downing.

NORMAL WEAR AND TEAR physical **depreciation** arising from age and ordinary use of the property.
Example: An **appraiser** estimates that a certain type of carpeting, subject to *normal wear and tear,* should have a physical life of 5 years.

NOTARIZE to attest in one's capacity as a **notary public,** to the genuineness of a signature.
Example: Before a county clerk will record certain types of documents, they must be *notarized* to assure the signature is not forged.

NOTARY PUBLIC an officer who is authorized to take **acknowledgments** to certain types of documents, such as **deeds, contracts,** and **mortgages,** and before whom **affidavits** may be sworn.
Example: Eakins and Finwick agree to transfer a piece of property. At the **closing,** a *notary public* serves to witness the signing of all documents.

NOTE a written **instrument** that acknowledges a **debt** and promises to pay.
Example: Greer borrows money from Thrifty Savings to purchase a home. Greer signs a *note* to acknowledge the debt, to promise to pay under specified terms, and to prescribe a procedure for curing **default.** A **mortgage** will also be signed that pledges the home to the lender as **security** for the note.

NOTICE official communication of a legal action or one's intent to take an action. See also **public offering, public sale.**
Example: A landlord may be required to give a tenant 30 days' *notice* before terminating the **lease.**
Example: A lender may be required to give a debtor *notice* that a **default** has occurred before initiating **foreclosure** proceedings. See **notice of default.**

Example: Recording a deed serves to give **constructive notice** to the public of one's ownership of a property.

NOTICE OF DEFAULT a letter sent to a defaulting party as a reminder of the **default.** May state a **grace period** and the **penalties** for failing to cure the default.
Example: Vacation Lot Sales Corp. sent a *notice of default* to Abel. It offered a 7-day grace period, after which they would consider his **interest** as forfeited unless he paid the delinquent **installment.**

NOTICE TO QUIT 1. a notice to a tenant to **vacate** rented property.
Example: After the lease expired the tenant remained in **possession.** The landlord sent a *notice to quit* by January 31.
2. sometimes used by a tenant who intends to vacate on a certain date.

NOTORIOUS POSSESSION generally acknowledged **possession of real estate.** One of the requirements to gain ownership of real estate through **adverse possession.**
Example: A squatter, who was in *notorious possession* of land, was thought by neighbors to be the owner of record.

NOVATION a 3-party agreement whereby one party is released from a **contract** and another party is substituted.
Example: Baker wants to buy Abel's home and assume the mortgage. Abel wants to be released from all mortgage **liability.** Good Money Savings Association cooperates. The three sign a *novation* whereby Baker is substituted for Abel on the mortgage.

NPV net present value.

NUISANCE a land use whose associated activities are incompatible with surrounding land uses.
Examples: Zoning laws and private **deed restrictions** are used to prevent the development of *nuisances,* such as:
• activities that produce noxious fumes or air pollution in residential areas
• commercial uses that generate large volumes of automobile traffic in residential areas
• junkyards in highly visible areas
• activities considered socially offensive, such as sale of pornographic materials, in residential areas

NULL AND VOID that which cannot be legally enforced, as with a **contract** provision that is not in conformance with the law.
Example: Ivenson sells a property and places in the **deed** a **covenant** that the property may never be sold to someone of a minority race. Since this provision is in defiance of the U.S. Constitution, it could never be enforced and is thereby *null and void.*

O

OAR overall rate of capitalization. Same as **overall rate of return**.

OBLIGEE the person in whose favor an obligation is entered into.
Example: Jackson promises to manage the property of Kindall, an out-of-town investor. In this arrangement, Kindall is the *obligee;* Jackson is the **obligor.**

OBLIGOR the person who binds himself or herself to another; one who has engaged to perform some obligation; one who makes a **bond.**
Example: See obligee.

OBSOLESCENCE a loss in value due to reduced desirability and usefulness of a structure because its design and construction has become obsolete; loss due to a structure's becoming old-fashioned, not in keeping with modern needs, with consequent loss of income. See **economic depreciation, functional depreciation, functional obsolescence.**
Examples: An old house may suffer from the following examples of *obsolescence:*
• rooms of improper size
• features no longer useful, such as a coal chute with a gas-fired furnace
• out-of-date plumbing, heating, and electrical fixtures and systems
• inadequate insulation
• unsuitable architectural style
• construction materials that require excessive **maintenance**
• undesirable location

OCCUPANCY AGREEMENT, LIMITED one that allows a prospective buyer to obtain **possession** under a temporary arrangement, usually prior to **closing.**
Example: Abel, the seller, signs a *limited occupancy agreement* with Baker that allows Baker possession of the property at rent of $25 per day for up to 30 days or the day of closing, whichever occurs first.

OCCUPANCY LEVEL percentage of currently rented units in a building, city, neighborhood, or complex. Contrast with **vacancy rate.**
Example: Today the Holiday Hotel has 90 of its 100 rooms booked and filled. Its *occupancy level* is 90%. Conversely, its vacancy rate is 10%.

333

OFFER an expression of willingness to purchase a property at a specified price.
Example: Lincoln places a property on the market. Murray makes an *offer* to buy the property for $150,000. Lincoln may accept the offer, reject the offer, or propose a **counteroffer.**

OFFER AND ACCEPTANCE see **agreement of sale.**

OFFEREE one who receives an offer. Generally a buyer offers a purchase contract to an owner, which makes the owner the *offeree.* When the seller offers a contract to a buyer, the buyer is the *offeree.*
Example: Brewster offers Smithton a contract in which Brewster offers to pay $120,000 for a property. Smithton is the *offeree.*

OFFEROR one who extends an offer to another.
Example: Brewster offers Smithton $120,000 for a property. Brewster is the *offeror.*

OFFICE BUILDING a structure primarily used for the conduct of business, such as administration, clerical services, and consultation with clients and associates. Such buildings can be large or small and may house one or more business concerns.
Example: From a large *office building* in downtown, the XYZ Corporation controlled its nationwide system of factories and outlets.

OFFICE OF INTERSTATE LAND SALES REGISTRATION (OILSR) a division of the U.S. Department of **Housing and Urban Development** that regulates offerings of land for sale across state lines. See **Interstate Land Sales Act.**
Example: Norwood **subdivides** a large land parcel in Arizona and wishes to market the lots to investors across the nation. Norwood is required to register the offering with *OILSR* and follow certain procedures intended to inform buyers of the characteristics of their investment.

OFFICE OF THRIFT SUPERVISION (OTS) a federal agency created by **FIRREA** to regulate and supervise federally chartered **savings and loan associations**. The *OTS* takes over the thrift regulatory duties exercised by the Federal Home Loan Bank Board prior to passage of the Act. The new agency is part of the Treasury Department.

OFFICE PARK a planned development specially designed for **office buildings** and supportive facilities, such as restaurants. Some office parks, such as a research park or a medical services park, are designed to attract specific tenants.

Example: After several large corporations located in the new *office park*, the park became a major employment center for the city.

OFF-SITE COSTS expenditures related to construction that are spent away from the place of construction.
Example: Owens is developing a **subdivision.** Certain *off-site costs* are incurred, such as the costs of extending roads, sewers, and water lines to the **site.** Site costs include landscaping and other site **improvements.**

OFF-SITE IMPROVEMENTS the portions of a **subdivision** or development that are not directly on the lots to be sold.
Example: Access streets, curbs, sewers, and utility connections are common examples of *off-site improvements.*

OIL AND GAS LEASE an agreement that gives the right to explore for oil, gas, and sometimes other minerals and to extract them from the ground. Provisions include the granting of subsurface and surface rights, **lease** duration, **extension** terms, royalties, surface damages, **assignments,** and **warranties.** See **mineral rights.**
Example: In an *oil and gas lease,* the owner is to receive $100 per acre as a bonus payment, and one eighth of the value of minerals found on the property.

OILSR Office of Interstate Land Sales Registration.

ONE-HUNDRED-PERCENT LOCATION the particular spot in an urban area where land value and rents are the highest; the "best" location.
Example: Broadway and 42nd Street was thought of as the highest-priced property, the *100% location,* in New York City. Other locations could be judged as percentages of that property's value.

OPEN-END MORTGAGE a **mortgage** under which the **mortgagor** (borrower) may secure additional funds from the **mortgagee** (lender), usually stipulating a ceiling amount that can be borrowed.
Example: Poole obtains an *open-end mortgage* to purchase a home. Under the mortgage agreement, Poole may borrow additional funds over the **maturity** of the loan as long as the unpaid **principal** does not exceed 80% of the home's **appraised** value.

OPEN HOUSE a method of showing a home for sale whereby the home is left open for inspection by interested parties.
Example: A **broker** advertises an *open house* to promote the sale of a **listing.** On the specified date, prospective buyers may inspect the house during the hours of the *open house.*

OPEN HOUSING a condition under which housing units may be purchased or **leased** without regard for racial, ethnic, color, or religious characteristics of the buyers or tenants.
Example: The intent of government antidiscrimination laws applied to housing is to provide *open housing* under which anyone with sufficient funds may purchase or rent available housing units.

OPEN LISTING a **listing** given to any number of **brokers** without **liability** to compensate any except the one who first secures a buyer who is ready, willing, and able to meet the terms of the listing or secures the seller's **acceptance** of another **offer.** The sale of the property automatically terminates all open listings.
Example: Quarry offers an *open listing* to 2 brokers, Ridley and Sims. Ridley presents a buyer who eventually purchases the property. Ridley is entitled to a **commission;** Sims is not.

OPEN MORTGAGE a **mortgage** that has **matured** or is overdue and is therefore open to **foreclosure** at any time.
Example: Towns sells a property to Udall. Towns provides financing for the sale in the form of a 5-year, **interest-only** loan. At the end of 5 years, Udall does not pay the **principal** and Towns allows the loan to become an *open mortgage.* This arrangement allows Udall to pay off the loan at any time or Towns to call the loan at any time.

OPEN SPACE land, within a developed area, that is left undeveloped and serves as an **amenity** to surrounding occupants.
Example: A 20-acre **planned unit development** contains 12 acres that are covered by structures and pavement. The remaining 8 acres are left in *open space.*

OPERATING EXPENSE RATIO the mathematical relationship derived by dividing **operating expenses** by **potential gross income**.
Examples: Apartments generally have *operating expense ratios* between 30% and 50%; this figure may be exceeded where the lessor pays utilities or in low rent areas. Office buildings often have higher *operating expense ratios* (40% to 60%), because more intensive management and maintenance, such as cleaning services, are provided.

OPERATING EXPENSES amounts paid to maintain property, such as **property taxes, utilities, hazard insurance.** Excludes **financing** expenses and **depreciation.**

Examples: The following are expenses incurred in operating a property: Operating expenses
• maintenance
• management
• real estate taxes
• hazard and liability insurance
• utilities
• supplies
The following are not categorized as operating expenses:
• debt service
 principal payments
 interest
 loan fees
 participation payments
• depreciation
• income taxes

OPERATING INCOME same as **net operating income**.

OPERATING LEASE a **lease** between the **lessee** and the sublessee who actually occupies and uses the property. See **sublease.**
Example: Figure 122.

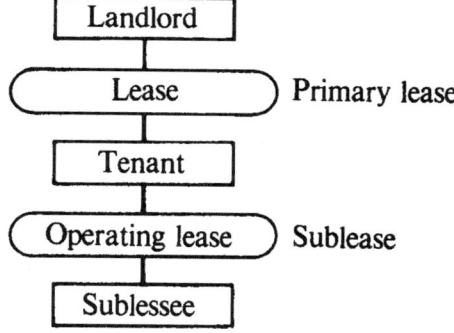

FIG. 122. OPERATING LEASE

OPERATING LEVERAGE automatic increases in the **net operating income** or **cash flow** of income-producing real estate when income and expenses increase at the same rate; further enhanced when expenses are fixed.
Example: In the example shown in Table 37, **gross income** and **operating expense** both increase by 5% in a year, while **debt service** is fixed. The cash flow increases by 30% because of *operating leverage.*

TABLE 37
EFFECT OF OPERATING LEVERAGE

	Year 1	Year 2
Gross income	$10,000	$10,500
Less: Operating expense	– 4,000	– 4,200
Net operating income	$ 6,000	$ 6,300
Less: Debt service	– 5,000	– 5,000
Cash flow	$ 1,000	$ 1,300

OPINION OF TITLE a certificate, generally from an attorney, as to the validity of **title** to property being sold. See **title abstract.**
Example: Based upon the attorney's *opinion of title,* the **title insurance** company insured title to the property.

OPPORTUNITY COST a term used in economics; when taking a particular action, the loss of the value of the next-best action.
Example: Jim had to choose between two investment properties because he did not have the resources to buy both. Each cost the same; the better one offered a 10% return on investment, the other only 9%. Jim's *opportunity cost* of the better one (which he bought) was measured as the 9% return of the one he did not buy and, therefore, had to do without.

OPTION the right to purchase or **lease** a property upon specified terms within a specified period.
Example: Moore purchases an *option* on a piece of land. The option runs 90 days and costs $500 per acre. If Moore wishes to purchase the land, she has 90 days to exercise her right and may buy the land for $5,000 per acre. If she decides not to purchase, she **forfeits** the $500 per acre.

OPTIONEE one who receives or purchases an option.
Example: Brewster pays Smithton $5,000 for the right to purchase a property for $120,000 within the next year. Brewster is the *optionee.*

OPTIONOR one who gives or sells an option.
Example: Brewster pays Smithton $5,000 for the right to purchase a property for $120,000 within the next year. Smithton is the *optionor.*

OPTION TO PURCHASE a contract that gives one the right (but *not* the obligation) to buy a property, within a certain time, for a specified amount, and subject to specified conditions.
Example: Marco needs two adjacent parcels of land for a project he wishes to build. He can obtain an *option to purchase*

338

one of them; if he is able to buy the other, he can use his option to buy the first one. If he cannot buy the other, he can let the option expire.

ORAL CONTRACT a verbal agreement. With few exceptions, verbal agreements for the sale or use of **real estate** are unenforceable. In most states, contracts for the sale or rental of real estate are, unless they are in writing, unenforceable under the **Statute of Frauds.** Verbal leases for a year or less are often acceptable.
Example: Abel agrees to sell property to Baker. Their contract is oral. Abel changes his mind. He faces no **penalty** because *oral contracts* for the sale of real estate are unenforceable.

ORDINANCES municipal rules governing the use of land.
Examples: Local governments may pass *ordinances* to:
• specify certain land uses in certain areas
• regulate **nuisances**
• specify the manner in which structures are constructed or maintained
• specify the manner in which **subdivisions** are designed
• regulate rental practices
• regulate condominium **conversion** practices

ORDINARY AND NECESSARY BUSINESS EXPENSES a tax term that allows a current deduction for business expenses. Contrasted with **capital expenditures** and unreasonable expenses.
Example: Each day the apartment manager enjoyed a 3-martini lunch with his friend. He claimed a tax deduction for the lunch expense. The **Internal Revenue Service** contests the deductions because they were not *ordinary and necessary business expenses.*

ORDINARY ANNUITY a series of equal payments, each payment occurring at the end of each equally spaced period.
Example: For a lender the **income stream** from a standard, fixed rate mortgage loan provides an *ordinary annuity* (Figure 123).

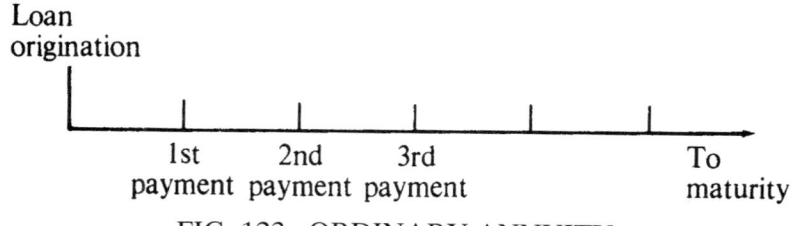

FIG. 123. ORDINARY ANNUITY

ORDINARY INCOME defined by the **Internal Revenue Code** to include salaries, fees, **commissions,** interests, dividends, and

many other items. Taxed at regular tax rates. Contrasted with long-term **capital gains,** which receive more favorable tax treatment.

Example: Abel would prefer to convert *ordinary income* into long-term capital gains. He wants to change the nature of property he has from **inventory** to investment.

ORDINARY LOSS for income tax purposes a loss that is deductible against **ordinary income.** Usually more beneficial to a taxpayer than a **capital loss,** which has limitations on deductibility.

Example: The sale of **inventory** at a loss results in an *ordinary loss,* whereas the sale of an investment at a loss results in a capital loss.

ORE, OREO other real estate, other real estate owned. Generally, foreclosed property held by lending institutions. An account at banks or savings and loan associations that includes property other than real estate used for bank operations.

Example: The **Office of Thrift Supervision (OTS)** monitors real estate loans at lending institutions and places foreclosed real estate on the *ORE* list. When *ORE* exceeds 2% of an institution's assets, the OTS takes steps to reduce losses and safeguard the institution.

ORIENTATION the position of a structure on a **site** relative to sunlight angles and prevailing winds.

Example: A house in Figure 124 has a north-south *orientation* designed to maximize the natural heating effect of the sun in the winter:

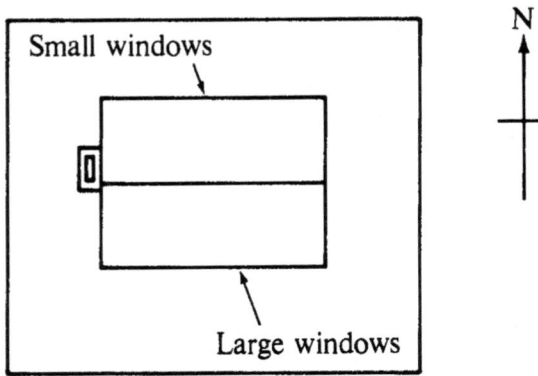

FIG. 124. ORIENTATION

ORIGINAL EQUITY the amount of cash initially invested by the underlying **real estate** owner. Distinguished from **sweat equity, capital calls.**

Example: Oliver paid $25,000 cash as *original equity* and borrowed $75,000 to purchase a $100,000 vacation home. His laborious efforts to remodel added $20,000 through sweat equity, and inflation raised the value by another $10,000.

ORIGINATION FEES charges to a borrower to cover the costs of issuing the loan, such as **credit** checks, **appraisal,** and **title** expenses.
Example: The lender issued a $50,000 **mortgage** loan and charged a 1% *origination fee* ($500).

OTHER PEOPLE'S MONEY borrowed funds invested in a money-making venture. This term implies that debt can be used to maximize investment profits or minimize risk of personal loss.
Example: Through the use of *other people's money*, Otis was able to amass a sizable portfolio of investment properties. His principle was to borrow as much as possible and invest the proceeds in new properties.

OUTSTANDING BALANCE the amount currently owed on a **debt.**
Example: Whitman borrowed $10,000. She then paid $1,200 of interest and $500 toward **principal.** Her *outstanding balance* is $9,500 ($10,000 minus $500).

OVERAGE in leases for retail stores, amounts to be paid, based on gross sales, over the **base rent.** See **percentage lease.**
Example: Winfield leases retail space in a shopping center. The lease calls for a base rent of $2,500 per month plus 5% of gross sales over $10,000. The first month, Winfield has sales of $20,000. In addition to the $2,500 base rent, Winfield pays an *overage* of $500 [.05 × ($20,000 - $10,000)].

OVER AGE 55 HOME SALE EXEMPTION in taxation, an individual over age 55 can sell a principal residence at a gain and exclude up to $125,000 of the gain from taxation. Allowed regardless of the purchase of another home. Must have used the property as a **principal residence** for 3 of the last 5 years.
Example: Abel, *over age 55*, sells his principal residence, which he has lived in for the last 3 years, at a $150,000 gain. He may exclude $125,000 of the gain from taxation. The rest of the gain is taxable as a **capital gain.**

OVERALL CAPITALIZATION RATE same as **overall rate of return**.

OVERALL RATE OF RETURN (OAR) the percentage relationship of **net operating income** divided by the purchase price of property. See **capitalization rate.**

Example: Property that sells for $1,000,000 is anticipated to produce a net operating income of $100,000 per year. The indicated *overall rate of return* is 0.10 or 10% $\left(\dfrac{\$100,000}{\$1,000,000} \right)$.

OVERBUILDING a situation in a given area where there has been more real estate construction than the market can economically support.
Example: In many cities in the 1980s, office space was *overbuilt*: there was more space than potential tenants wanted to rent; as a result, much space either went unrented or rented at unusually low rates.

OVERIMPROVEMENT a land use considered too intense for the land.
Example: A proposed house costs $100,000 to construct on a **site** valued at $20,000. It is estimated that the completed house would have a market value of only $110,000. The proposed house is an *overimprovement* of the site.

OVERRIDE 1. a fee paid to someone higher in the organization, or above a certain amount.
Example: In the agreement the salesman was required to pay an *override* of 10% of his gross **commissions** to the managing **broker.**
2. an **estate** carved out of a working interest in an **oil or gas lease.**
Example: The *overriding* **royalty** required 2% of the production of the well be paid to the attorney who negotiated the oil lease.

OWNER FINANCING same as **seller financing**.

OWNER OCCUPANT a tenant of a residence who also owns the property.
Example: Homer lives in a home that he also owns. Landon owns a home but rents it to Renton. Homer is an *owner occupant,* Landon is an **absentee owner,** and Renton is a rental tenant.

OWNER OF RECORD the person(s) who, according to the **public records**, is/are the owner(s) of a particular property.
Example: An attorney searching the title found Helen to be the *owner of record*, even though she had assigned her interest to anonymous foreign investors who were the beneficial owners.

OWNERSHIP FORM methods of owning **real estate,** which affect **income** tax, **estate tax,** continuity, **liability, survivorship,** transferability, disposition at death and at **bankruptcy.**

Examples: *Ownership* forms include:
- **corporation**
- joint tenancy
- **limited partnership**
- **partnership**
- **Subchapter S corporation**
- **tenancy by the entireties**
- **tenancy in common**
- **tenancy in severalty**

OWNERSHIP IN SEVERALTY see **tenancy in severalty**.

OWNERSHIP RIGHTS TO REALTY **possession,** enjoyment, control, and disposition. See also **fee tail, interest, tenancy.**
Example: By virtue of **title** to the property, Overton enjoys full *ownership rights to realty*. This enables Overton to use the property, **lease** out the property, pledge it as **security** on loans, and sell the property within the restrictions of the law.

P

PACKAGE MORTGAGE a **mortgage** arrangement whereby the **principal** amount loaned is increased because **personalty** (e.g., appliances) as well as **realty** serve as **collateral.**
Example: Simmons applied for a *package mortgage* in order to spread the cost of appliances over 25 years and to pay for them with her home mortgage payment.

PAD SITE an individual freestanding site for a retailer, often adjacent to a larger **shopping center**.
Example: Figure 125.

FIG. 125. PAD SITE

P&I principal and interest (payment).

PAPER **credit** given, evidenced by a written obligation that is backed by **property.**
Example: Dunn sells his property for $100,000. He receives $20,000 cash and $80,000 of *paper* that is payable over 20 years at 10% interest.

PAPER PROFIT an increase in value above original cost or **basis** that would be realized if the property were sold; however, the property is not offered for sale.

Example: Phyllis purchased a **tract** of land for $100,000 that was recently appraised at $150,000. Her *paper profit* is $50,000.

PARCEL a piece of property under one ownership; a lot in a **subdivision.**
Example: In order to construct the highway, the state must acquire parts of *parcels* A and C in Figure 126. *Parcels* B and D are unaffected.

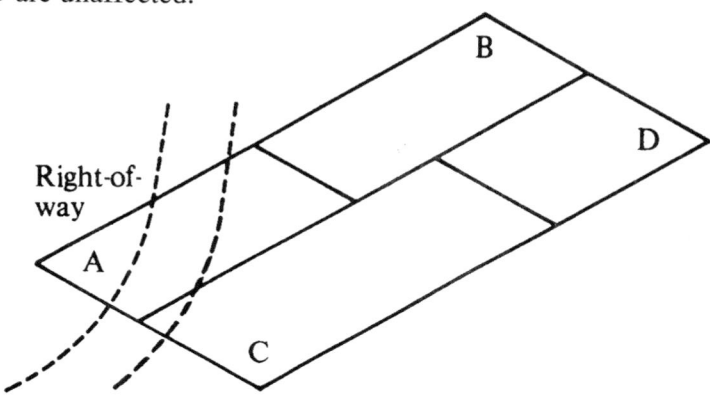

FIG. 126. PARCELS OF LAND

PAROL EVIDENCE oral evidence, rather than that contained in documents. The parol evidence rule states that when parties put their agreement in writing, all previous oral agreements merge into the written agreement. The written agreement cannot be contradicted by oral testimony, unless there was a **mistake** or **fraud.**
Example: Carter agrees to buy a house from Dooley, and both sign a written agreement. Carter later argues that Dooley said he'd pay all the loan **discount points.** Under the *parol evidence* rule, courts will interpret the **contract** as it is written.

PARTIAL INTEREST 1. ownership of a part of the **ownership rights** to a parcel of real estate.
Examples: Mineral rights, easements on another's property, etc.
2. infrequently used to describe an **undivided interest** in property shared with several other owners.

PARTIALLY AMORTIZED LOAN one that requires some payments toward **principal** but does not fully retire the **debt,** thereby requiring a **balloon payment.**
Example: A 30-year **amortization schedule** is provided for a loan that balloons in 10 years. Originally $100,000 of principal at 10% interest, this *partially amortized loan* balance will be reduced to $90,311 when it matures.

PARTIAL RELEASE a provision in a **mortgage** that allows some of the property pledged to be freed from serving as **collateral.**

Example: Baker sold 3 acres of land (Figure 127), and accepted a $30,000 purchase money mortgage. *Partial releases* in the mortgage require that, upon each $10,000 **principal** payment, one acre be freed from serving as collateral. The sequence of release was **platted,** and described in the mortgage.

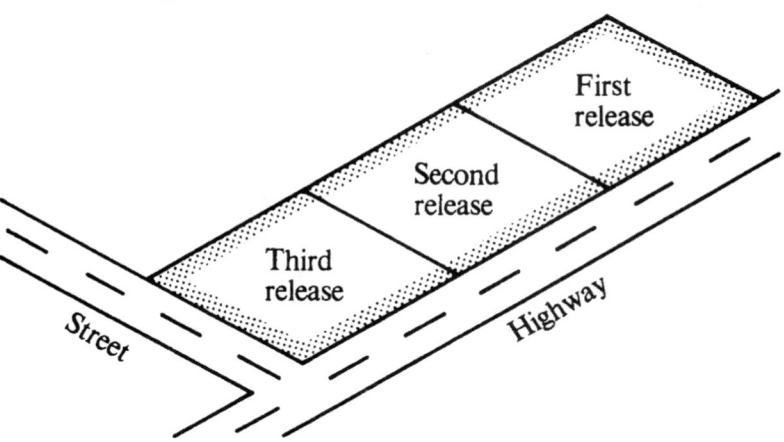

FIG. 127. PARTIAL RELEASE

PARTIAL TAKING acquisition by **condemnation** of only part of the property or some property rights.

Examples: Situations calling for *partial takings* (Figure 128).

FIG. 128. PARTIAL TAKINGS

PARTICIPATION (or PARTICIPATING) MORTGAGE one that allows the lender to share in part of the income or resale proceeds.

Example: A loan is given on an office building. In addition to a fixed payment of **principal** and **interest,** the lender is entitled to 2% of gross rental income. This is a *participation loan* in which the lender participates in the **income stream** provided by the property.

PARTITION the division of **real property** between those who own it with **undivided interest.**

Example: Abel and Baker own land by **tenancy in common** until they *partition* it. Thereafter, each owns a particular tract of land (Figure 129).

Before partition	After partition	
Abel and Baker, as tenants in common, are owners of one parcel.	Abel owns this half.	Baker owns this half.

FIG. 129. PARTITION

PARTNERSHIP an agreement between 2 or more entities to go into business or invest. Either partner may bind the other, within the scope of the partnership. Each partner is liable for all the partnelship's debts. A partnership normally pays no taxes, but merely files an information return. The individual partners pay personal income tax on their share of **income.** See also **general partner, limited partnership.** Compare with **corporation.**

Example: Abel and Baker form a *partnership* to buy land. The partnership owns the property, rather than Abel and Baker.

PARTY WALL a wall built along the line separating 2 properties, partly on each **parcel.** Either owner has the right to use the wall and has an **easement** over that part of the **adjoining** owner's land covered by the wall.

Example: The structures built on lots A and B in Figure 130 are separated by a *party wall.*

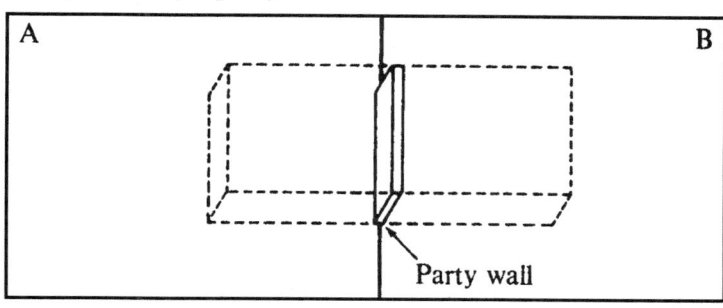

FIG. 130. PARTY WALL

PASSIVE ACTIVITY INCOME under the 1986 tax act, is generated by: 1. any trade or business conducted for profit in which the taxpayer does not materially participate. 2. any rental activity, whether or not the taxpayer materially participates.

Rental activities are presumed to be passive. These include all activities that generate income from payments for the use of property rather than for the performance of services. Rental activities include long-term rentals of apartments, net leased property, office equipment, and automobiles. In contrast, the rental of hotel rooms or transient apartments and short-term car rentals are not passive because of the extent of services provided.

Because rental real estate is a passive activity, owners may not use losses to shelter other types of income. These are exceptions: 1. Phase-out for property acquired before October 22, 1986, the enactment date of the 1986 tax act. Losses on property acquired before then were allowed as follows:

1987	65%
1988	40%
1989	20%
1990	10%

Property acquired after the October 22, 1986, date is not eligible for the phase-out.
2. Real estate dealers.
3. **"Active" participants** in rental real estate are allowed to shelter up to $25,000 per year of losses against nonpassive income. A less stringent definition of active participation is provided as compared to **material participation.**
4. Mortgage interest on a principal or second residence is not subject to these rules even when the residence is rented out.
5. A closely held *C* corporation (other than a personal services corporation) may use passive losses and credits to offset its net active income, but not portfolio income. An *S* corporation may not apply passive losses and credits against other income.
Example: Paul bought an apartment complex in 1988, which generated a $30,000 tax loss. If Paul meets the test of an active investor, up to $25,000 of the loss may be used to offset active or portfolio income. If not, the entire loss remains suspended until Paul earns passive income.

PASSIVE INCOME 1. generally, income from **rents, royalties,** dividends, interest, and gains from the sale of securities.
2. a new meaning created by the Tax Reform Act of 1986, distinguishes *passive income* or loss from **active income** and **portfolio income.** See **passive activity income.**

PASSIVE INCOME GENERATOR a business or investment that produces **passive income** which can be used to offset passive losses.

Example: Perry owns rental real estate which provides a tax loss. Under the 1986 tax act, the loss may be offset by passive income, but not by **portfolio income** or **active income.** Without a *passive income generator* to offset the loss, the loss will be carried forward in a suspense account.

PASSIVE INVESTOR 1. one who invests money but does not manage the business or property.
2. See **passive income, portfolio income.**
Example: Dooley has neither time nor skills to manage the property that he wants to invest in. He forms a **partnership** with a real estate syndicator who will devote time and expertise to manage the property for profit. Dooley contributes money but not effort, so he is a *passive investor.*

PASSIVE SOLAR HEATING a system of features incorporated into a building's design to use and maximize the effects of the sun's natural heating capability. See **active solar heating**.
Example: *Passive solar heating* systems use some type of collection and storage element, such as a water-filled partition, which is exposed to the sun during the day and radiates heat to the structure at night. Other features, such as south-facing windows, site **orientation,** roof overhangs, are included to enhance the effects of the sun's heat.

PASS-THROUGH CERTIFICATES (OR SECURITIES) interests in a pool of mortgages sold by **mortgage bankers** to investors. Money collected as monthly mortgage payments is distributed to those who own certificates. Often **guaranteed** by **Ginnie Mae.**
Example: A mortgage banker sells $5,000,000 of *pass-through certificates* in $10,000 denominations, supported by an equal amount of **VA** and **FHA mortgages.** Monthly collections of **interest** and **principal** are remitted to certificate holders, except for $^{44}\!/_{100}$ of 1% of the annual principal, kept by the mortgage banker as a **servicing** fee (Figure 131).

PATENT **conveyance** of **title** to government land.
Example: The federal government grants a *patent* on land they sell to a mining company.

PAYBACK PERIOD the amount of time required for cumulative estimated future income from an investment to equal the amount initially invested. It is used to compare alternative investment opportunities.
Example: Purchase of an apartment building requires an equity investment of $20,000. Annual cash flow is expected to be $2,000. The *payback period* for the investment is 10 years.

349

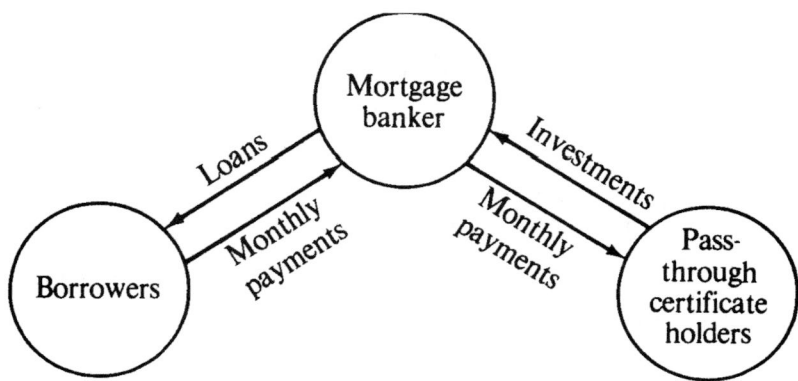

FIG. 131. PASS-THROUGH CERTIFICATES

PAYMENT CAP a contractual limit on the percentage amount of adjustment allowed in the monthly payment for an adjustable rate mortgage at any one adjustment period. Generally it does not affect the interest rate charged. If the allowable payment does not cover interest due on the principal at the adjusted rate of interest, **negative amortization** will occur.
Example: An adjustable rate mortgage has a *payment cap* of 7% a year. The monthly payment in year 1 is $500. When the interest rate is adjusted in year 2, the new payment would be $550 to pay interest and amortize the principal. However, due to the *payment cap,* the maximum payment for year 2 is $535.

PENALTY money one will pay for breaking a law or violating part or all of the **terms** of a **contract.**
Example: *Penalties* are often imposed for:
• prepaying a loan
• failing to complete a contract of sale
• breaking a lease

PENTHOUSE a luxury housing unit located on the top floor of a high-rise building.
Example: A *penthouse* (Figure 132).

PERCENTAGE LEASE a lease of property in which the rental is based on a percentage of the volume of sales made upon the leased premises. It usually stipulates a minimum rental and is regularly used for retailers who are **tenants.** See **overage.**
Example: The *percentage lease* required the jewelry store to pay as additional rent 6% of annual sales in excess of $100,000. The **base rent** is $6,000 per year.

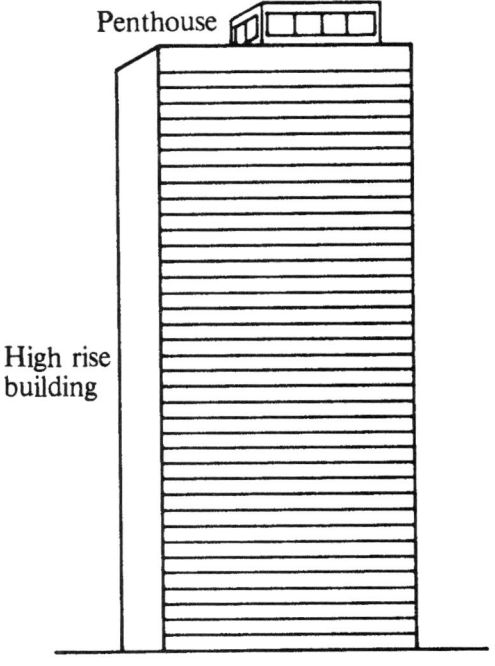

Penthouse

High rise
building

FIG. 132. PENTHOUSE

PERCENTAGE RENT rent payable under a **percentage lease**. Typically the percentage applies to sales in excess of a pre-established base amount of the dollar sales volume.
Examples: Typical *percentage rents* in a neighborhood **shopping center** are shown in Table 38.

TABLE 38
TYPICAL PERCENTAGE RENTS

Card & gift shop	5.0 to 8.0%
Drugstore	2.5 to 4.0%
Liquor and wine shop	1.5 to 5.0%
Pet shop	5.0 to 8.0%
Restaurant	4.0 to 7.0%
Supermarket	1.0 to 2.0%

Adapted from *Dollars & Cents of Shopping Centers*, Urban Land Institute, Washington, D.C., 1990.

PERCOLATION TEST a procedure to measure the drainage characteristics of the soil on a lot. Required in the proper design of septic tank drainfields.
Example: Carter is developing a **subdivision** in the county. As part of site preparation, Carter runs *percolation tests* on the soil.

From this information, the engineer can determine the proper size of the lots and placement of septic tanks.

PERFORMANCE in contract law, the completion of duties and obligations specified in a **contract**.
Example: Patty, the tenant, and Bruce, the landlord, agreed upon the terms of the lease. The lease expired after the *performance* of the parties.

PERFORMANCE BOND one issued by an insurance company; posted by a party who is to perform certain work. If the work is not performed, the insurer promises to complete the work or pay damages up to the amount of the bond. Contrast with **completion bond.**
Example: The contract requires the **contractor** to put up a $10,000 *performance bond.* If the contractor fails to do the job, the property owner has assurances of compensatory payment from the insurance company.

PERMANENT MORTGAGE a mortgage for a long period of time (over 10 years).
Example: The **savings and loan association** promises to originate a 25-year **self-amortizing** *permanent mortgage* when construction is completed. A permanent **mortgage commitment** is often needed before a **construction** loan can be arranged.

PERMIT a document, issued by a government regulatory authority, that allows the bearer to take some specific action.
Example: An occupancy *permit* allows the owner of a building to occupy or rent the building.
Example: A building *permit* allows a builder to construct or modify a structure.

PERPETUITY the condition of being never ending. Most states attempt to outlaw perpetuities because of potential problems. A perpetual income stream may cause bankruptcy. A **deed** that keeps property in a family in *perpetuity* can cause financial hardship.
Example: A bank offers to pay a 10% interest rate in *perpetuity*. A $10,000 deposit should receive $1,000 annual income for as long as the deposit remains in the account.

PERSON in law, an **entity** having legal responsibility. Legally, a natural person is a human being who has reached **majority.** (Compare with **minor.**) An artificial person may be a **corporation**; in some instances **partnerships,** governments, and certain other bodies are considered persons.
Example: When negotiating a contract it is important to deal with a **person**; otherwise the contract may be unenforceable.

352

PERSONAL PROPERTY same as **personalty.**

PERSONAL RESIDENCE the dwelling unit that one claims as one's primary home. This dwelling establishes one's legal residence for voting, tax, and legal purposes.
Example: Mr. Pierce owned houses in several different cities, with the one in San Francisco serving as his *personal residence.*

PERSONALTY personal property, i.e., all **property** that is not **realty.** Property that is movable, not fixed to land. See **chattel.**
Examples: The following are *personalty*:
• appliances not permanently attached to **real property**
• cash and securities
• furniture and household items
• **mobile homes** not permanently affixed to a **site**
• vehicles

PER STIRPES a legal method of distributing an **estate** to include the descendants of a deceased legatee, whose share is apportioned among linear descendants.
Example: A person dies intestate. State Law requires a *per stirpes* distribution of assets. The decedent had 4 children. Three are surviving; the fourth child died as an adult and left 5 children. The estate is divided into 4 equal parts. Each surviving child of the decedent gets one fourth, and the 5 orphaned grandchildren, as a group, share one fourth.

PHOTOVOLTAIC the process of converting light directly into electricity using specially designed silicon cells.
Example: The house has a *photovoltaic* system which supplies power to the filter pumps of the swimming pool.

PHYSICAL DEPRECIATION OR DETERIORATION the loss of value from all causes of age and action of the elements.
Example: Sources of *physical depreciation:*
• breakage
• deferred maintenance
• effects of age on construction material
• normal wear and tear

PIGGYBACK LOAN 1. a combination of the **construction loan** with the permanent **loan commitment.**
Example: The permanent lender would issue a commitment at a 15% rate, effective upon completion of construction. As assurance that the loan will be borrowed even if rates are lower later, the commitment is *piggybacked* to the construction loan, and must be drawn down upon **retiring** the construction loan.
2. one mortgage held by more than one lender, with one lender holding the rights of the others in **subordination.**

PITI

Example: A loan is made for 90% of the home price; 80% of the price is supplied by a **savings and loan association,** 10% by an individual, who then has a *piggyback loan.* The piggyback agreement allows the S&L to have priority in **foreclosure.**

PITI see **Principal, Interest, Taxes and Insurance Payment.**

PLAINTIFF the person who brings a lawsuit. Contrast with **defendant.**
Example: A *plantiff* sued for **specific performance** to force the owner of land to sell at the agreed upon terms.

PLANNED UNIT DEVELOPMENT (PUD) a **zoning** classification that allows flexibility in the design of a **subdivision.** Planned Unit Development zones generally set an overall **density** limit for the entire subdivision, allowing the dwelling units to be clustered to provide for common open space. See also **cluster housing, common areas.**
Example: A typical *planned unit development* (Figure 133).

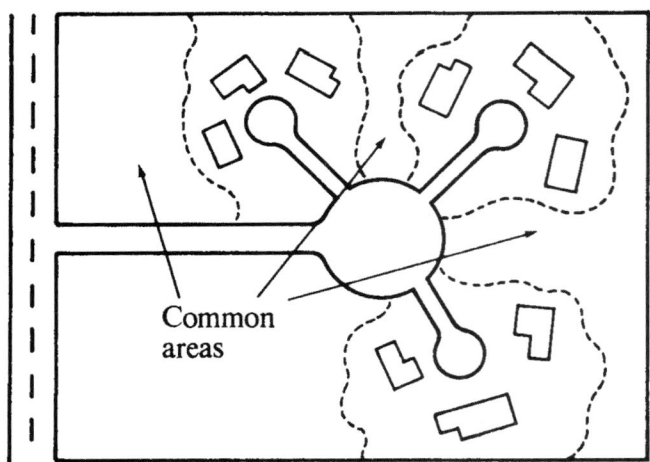

Common areas

FIG. 133. PLANNED UNIT DEVELOPMENT

PLANNING COMMISSION a group of citizens appointed by local government officials to conduct hearings and recommend amendments to the **zoning ordinance.** The planning commission generally oversees the work of a professional planning department, which prepares a comprehensive plan. May also be called a planning board, zoning commission, or zoning board, depending on locality.
Example: Moore wishes to have her land **rezoned** from low **density** to high density **residential.** She submits her request to the *planning commission.* The commission holds a public hear-

ing and asks the planning department to evaluate the change. Following the review, the commission makes a recommendation to the city council on whether or not to grant the request.

PLAT a plan or map of a specific land area. See also **description, government rectangular survey.**
Example: *Plat* of a **subdivision** (Figure 134).

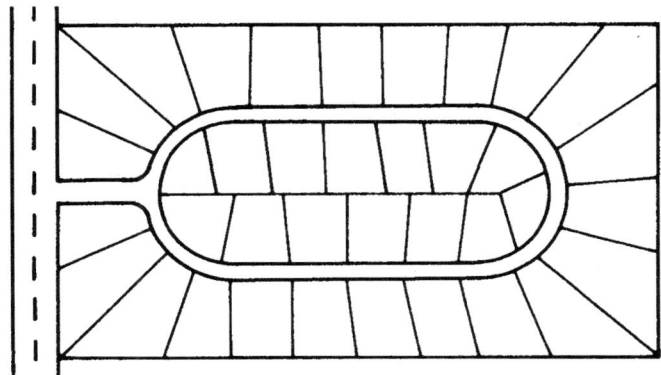

FIG. 134. PLAT OF A SUBDIVISION

PLAT BOOK a public record containing maps of land, showing the division of the land into streets, blocks, and lots and indicating the measurements of the individual **parcels.**
Example: Sample entry in a *plat book* for property number 001 in district 07-510-AZ (Figure 135).

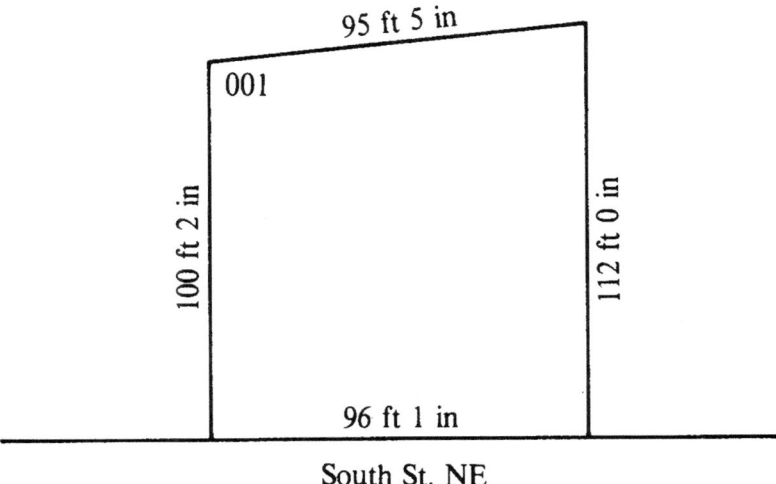

FIG. 135. SAMPLE PLAT BOOK ENTRY

PLEDGED ACCOUNT MORTGAGE (PAM) a type of home purchase loan under which a sum of cash contributed by the owner is set aside in an account pledged to the lender. The account is drawn down during the initial years of the loan to supplement periodic mortgage payments. The effect is to reduce the payment amounts in early years. See **graduated payment mortgage.** Compare with **collateral.**
Example: Abel obtains a *pledged account mortgage.* The loan **principal** is $40,000 and Abel makes a down payment of $10,000. $5,000 of this amount is put in a pledged account. Abel makes payments based on a mortgage principal of $45,000 but the payments are reduced in the first 3 years by drawing upon the $5,000 pledged account.

PLOT PLAN a diagram showing the proposed or existing use of a specific **parcel** of land.
Example: A *plot plan* submitted to a **zoning** review board (Figure 136).

FIG. 136. PLOT PLAN

PLOTTAGE creating **plottage value** of land by assembling small, adjacent parcels of land into a larger, more useful parcel.
Example: Three small, old adjacent buildings were acquired for $250,000 each, then demolished for $50,000. The resulting large, clear tract of land was estimated to be worth $1 million; the **plottage** value was $200,000.

PLOTTAGE VALUE increment in the value of land comprised by **assemblage** of smaller plots into one ownership.
Example: A and B are adjacent lots, each worth $10,000 (Figure 137). By combining them under one owner the entire **tract** becomes large enough for use as a restaurant site, worth $50,000. The *plottage value* is $30,000.

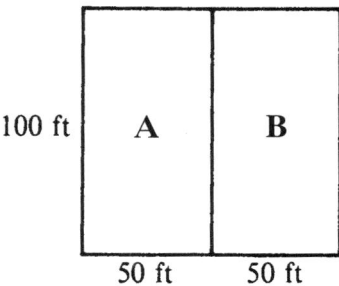

Two lots valued at $10,000 each

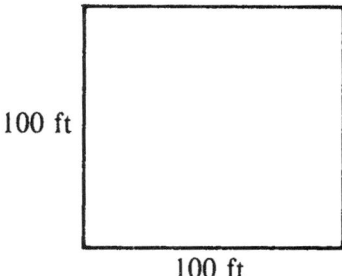

Lots combined with value of $50,000

FIG. 137. PLOTTAGE VALUE

PMI private mortgage insurance.

POCKET CARD required for salespersons and **brokers** in most states. Issued by the state licensing agency, it identifies its holder as a **licensee** and must be carried at all times.
Example: Figure 138.

POINTS fees paid to induce lenders to make a **mortgage** loan. Each point equals 1% of the loan **principal**. Points have the effect of reducing the amount of money advanced by the lender. Same as *discount points.*
Example: Mortgage lenders commonly charge one *point* as a loan **origination fee.** Additional points may be charged to raise the loan **yield** to current **market interest rates.** If only one point is required, a borrower requesting a loan of $50,000 would actually receive only $49,500. The $500 cost of the point is a **closing** cost.

```
,-------------------------------------------.
|        Real Estate Broker Identification Card      |
|                                                    |
|        Expires  3-1-92                             |
|                                                    |
|                                                    |
|            Charlie Baker                           |
|            101 Maple Road                           |
|            Springfield, MA 90001                    |
|                                                    |
|  FILE   025        LICENSE  360245                  |
|     (NOT A LICENSE — FOR IDENTIFICATION ONLY)       |
`-------------------------------------------'
```

FIG. 138. POCKET CARD

POLICE POWER the right of any governmental body to enact and enforce regulations for the order, safety, health, morals, and general welfare of the public.
Example: Types of *police power* mechanisms applied to **real property:**
• **condemnation** proceedings
• **housing codes**
• public **nuisance** ordinances
• **rent controls**
• special operating **licenses**
• **subdivision** regulations
• **zoning**

PORTFOLIO INCOME interest, dividends, royalties (unless earned in the ordinary course of business) and gains from the sale of property that generates this type of income. Under the Tax Reform Act of 1986 this type of income cannot be used to offset passive activity losses. See **passive income.**

POSITIVE CASH FLOW same as **cash flow**.

POSITIVE LEVERAGE the use of borrowed funds that increases the return on an investment.
Example: See **leverage**.

POSSESSION the holding, control, or custody of property for one's use, either as owner or person with another right. See also **ownership rights to realty, title.**
Examples: Actual *possession:* within immediate occupancy
Adverse *possession:* see definition
Constructive *possession:* as stated in the public record

POTENTIAL GROSS INCOME the amount of income that could be produced by a real property assuming no vacancies or

collection losses. Does not include miscellaneous income. Contrast with **cash flow, net operating income.**

Example: An office building has 10,000 square feet of rentable space and rents for an average of $12 per square foot. *Potential gross income* for the building is $120,000 per year. Concessions on the ground floor that contribute $1,000 of annual revenue, and a 5% vacancy and collection allowance are not included in *potential gross income*

POWER OF ATTORNEY an **instrument** authorizing a person to act as the **agent** of the person granting it. See **attorney-in-fact.**

Example: Abel is going on a 6-month vacation to China. He wants to sell his house in Colorado for $75,000 but will not be present to sign the **deed.** He gives his trusted friend Baker the *power of attorney* so Baker may deed the property to a **grantee** while Abel is in China.

POWER OF SALE a clause sometimes inserted in **mortgages** or **deeds of trust**; grants the lender (or **trustee**) the right to sell the property upon certain **default.** The property is to be sold at **auction** but court authority is unnecessary.

Example: The **savings and loan association** exercises the *power of sale* clause in the mortgage by selling the defaulted property at public auction for $100,000. Since the debt was $60,000 and expenses of sale $5,000, the $35,000 surplus belongs to the borrower.

PRAIRIE HOUSE an early-twentieth-century-style house with a long, low roof line, continuous row of windows and an unornamented exterior. Designed to satisfy the physical and psychological needs of the inhabitants, it is unlike the traditional concept of a house that is a box subdivided into smaller boxes (rooms), each with some doors and windows. Architectural development is credited to Frank Lloyd Wright.

Example: Figure 139.

FIG. 139. PRAIRIE HOUSE

PRECLOSING a rehearsal of the **closing** whereby **instruments** are prepared and signed by some or all parties to the **contract.** Used when closings are expected to be complicated.
Example: *Preclosings* are used when there are many parties to an agreement. This sometimes occurs when there are multiple loans to be arranged and/or multiple buyers or sellers, as when **syndicating** property or converting an apartment complex to a **condominium.**

PREEXISTING USE see **nonconforming use.**

PREFABRICATED 1. constructed, as building components, in a factory prior to being erected or installed on the construction site. 2. constructed, as a house, of prefabricated components. See **modular housing.**
Example: The **subdivision** is developed with *prefabricated* housing. The roof, exterior walls, and interior partitions are *prefabricated* in a factory in Dallas.

PRELEASE to obtain **lease** commitments in a building or complex prior to its being available for occupancy.
Example: As a requirement for obtaining a **permanent mortgage,** a developer must *prelease* 50% of the space in the office building.

PREMISES land and **tenements;** an **estate**; the subject matter of a **conveyance.**
Example: In selling the property, Carter **deeds** the *premises* to Dawson. Dawson later **leases** the *premises* to Enwright.

PREMIUM 1. the cost of an insurance policy.
Example: Annual or monthly *premiums* are generally required for **hazard insurance, liability insurance,** and life insurance. **Title insurance** *premiums* are paid only once.
2. the value of a **mortgage** or **bond** in excess of its **face amount.**
Example: When the face rate of a mortgage exceeds the prevailing **market interest rate**, the mortgage may be worth a *premium* over its **face value.**

PREPAID EXPENSES amounts that are paid prior to the period they cover.
Example: Simmons pays the full **premium** on a 3-year insurance policy. When her accountant prepares Abel's financial statement, the proportionate value of the unused premium is presented as a *prepaid expense.*

PREPAID INTEREST interest paid in advance of the time it is earned.

Example: Prior to 1968, up to 5 years of prepaid interest could be deducted from taxable income; until 1976 up to one year could be deducted. Since then *prepaid interest* has not been deductible. An exception is for **points** paid to purchase one's residence, provided that the practice and amount is customary in the local area.

PREPAYMENT CLAUSE a clause in a **mortgage** that gives a **mortgagor** (borrower) the privilege of paying the mortgage indebtedness before it becomes due. Sometimes there is a **penalty** for prepayment, with **waiver** of the interest that is not yet due. **Example:** The *prepayment clause* in the mortgage allows the unpaid **principal** to be **retired** by the owner with a 1% penalty.

PREPAYMENT PENALTY fees paid by borrowers for the privilege of **retiring** a loan early. **Example:** Abel borrowed $50,000 last year at 15% interest on a 30-year mortgage. If he pays the remaining **principal** now, in one lump sum, there will be a 5% *prepayment penalty* that amounts to $2,500.

PREPAYMENT PRIVILEGE the right of a borrower to **retire** a loan before **maturity.** **Example:** A loan on **commercial property** is closed (no *prepayment privilege*) for the first 5 years. Afterwards it can be prepaid without **penalty.**

PREPAYMENTS advance payments of expenses such as insurance and taxes, often into an escrow account. **Example:** At the closing of a residence they bought, the Pollards made *prepayments* equal to 14 months of hazard insurance and 6 months of property taxes.

PRESALE sale of proposed properties, such as **condominiums**, before construction begins. **Example:** The developer *presold* 40% of the condominium units at a $5,000 **discount** for each unit before construction began. Based on the *presales*, the developer was able to get a favorable **construction loan.**

PRESCRIPTION acquiring rights through **adverse possession.** **Example:** For years, Fulson, owner of a **landlocked** parcel, has continually and openly crossed the property of Grissom to reach the highway. Fulson eventually acquires an **easement** by *prescription* to the access route, thus preventing Grissom from blocking his way.

PRESENT VALUE OF ANNUITY the value now of a level stream of income to be received each period for a finite number of periods. See **ordinary annuity.**

$$\text{Present value of annuity} = \frac{1 - \dfrac{1}{(1+i)^n}}{i}$$

where i = interest rate
n = number of periods

Example: The *present value of an annuity* of $1.00 per year for 10 years, discounted at 12%, is $5.65. Selected present values of annuity factors for annual income of 1 are shown in Table 39.

TABLE 39
PRESENT VALUE TABLE

Life of the annuity (years)	Discount rates			
	5%	10%	15%	20%
1	.952	.909	.870	.833
2	1.859	1.736	1.626	1.528
3	2.723	2.487	2.283	2.016
4	3.546	3.170	2.855	2.589
5	4.329	3.791	3.352	2.991
10	7.722	6.144	5.019	4.192
15	10.380	7.606	5.847	4.675
20	12.462	8.514	6.259	4.870
25	14.094	9.077	6.464	4.948
30	15.372	9.427	6.566	4.979

PRESENT VALUE OF ONE the value today of an amount to be received in the future, based on a **compound interest** rate.
Example: At a 12% interest rate, the receipt of one dollar one year from now has a *present value* of $.89286 (slightly more than 89 cents). One dollar to be received in 2 years has a *present value* of $.79719 (under 80 cents). Factors are based on the following formula:

$$\text{Present worth (1 factor)} = \frac{1}{(1+i)^n}$$

where i= interest rate
n = number of periods

See Table 40.

TABLE 40
PRESENT VALUE OF ONE

Number of years until $1 is received			
Rates			
5%	10%	15%	20%
.952381	.909291	.869565	.833333
.907029	.826446	.756144	.694444
.863838	.751315	.657516	.578704
.822702	.683014	.571753	.482253
.783526	.620921	.497177	.401878
.613913	.385543	.247185	.161506
.481017	.239392	.122894	.064905
.376889	.148644	.061100	.026084
.295302	.092296	.030377	.010482
.231377	.057308	.015103	.004212

with row labels: 1, 2, 3, 4, 5, 10, 15, 20, 25, 30

PRETAX INCOME the amount earned from a business or investment before deducting income taxes.
Example: *Pretax income* of $50,000 was earned from a **mini-warehouse** operation, according to its accountant. Income taxes of $15,000 reduced the **after-tax income** to $35,000.

PRICE-LEVEL-ADJUSTED MORTGAGE a loan whose payment is adjusted according to the rate of inflation. The payments are generally quite low, typically 3 to 5% annually of the debt. This type of mortgage is not commonly used in the U.S.
Example: A *price-level-adjusted mortgage* is made for $100,000. Monthly payments in the first year are $400. After the first year, the principal balance is reduced to $98,000. The inflation rate for the year was 10%. The principal balance is adjusted to $107,800 and the payments for the second year are increased to $440 per month.

PRIMARY LEASE a **lease** between the owner and a tenant whose **interest,** all or in part, has been sublet.
Example: Figure 140.

PRIMARY METROPOLITAN STATISTICAL AREA (PMSA) a classification of the U.S. Census Bureau applied to cities with the following classifications. Within a metropolitan area with a population of one million or more, there may be areas that would qualify as metropolitan areas on their own, yet are linked to other cities in close proximity. These individual areas are called Primary Metropolitan Statistical Areas, while the metropolitan area containing these PMSAs is called a Consolidated Metropolitan Statistical Area (CMSA).

Example: Dallas and Fort Worth, Texas, are each classified as *Primary Metropolitan Statistical Areas*, while the Dallas-Fort Worth area is a *Consolidated Metropolitan Statistical Area*.

PRIMARY MORTGAGE MARKET that portion of the credit market that originates mortgage loans, including institutional lenders, such as savings and loan associations and banks, and mortgage bankers and brokers. Contrast with **secondary mortgage market.**

The *primary mortgage market* originates and services mortgage loans. Many of these loans are packaged and sold in the secondary mortgage market.

PRIME CONTRACTOR see **general contractor.**

PRIME RATE the lowest commercial **interest rate** charged by banks on short-term loans to their most credit-worthy customers. The prime rate is not the same as the long-term mortgage rate, though it may influence long-term rates. Also, it is not the same as the consumer loan rate that is charged on personal property loans and credit cards. Mortgage rates and consumer loan rates are generally higher than the prime rate, but exceptions occur at times.
Example: The Chemical Bank and the Chase Manhattan Bank offer a *prime rate* of 7%. Texaco is a prime customer and at that rate may borrow loans up to 270 days. Chemical Bank offers construction loans at 4 **points** over the *prime rate*.

FIG. 140. PRIMARY LEASE

PRIME TENANT in a shopping center or office building, the tenant who occupies the most space. Prime tenants are considered creditworthy and attract customers or traffic to the center. See also **anchor tenant.**

Example: Huntley is developing an office building with 40,000 square feet of leasable space. Of this, 20,000 square feet are **preleased** to a *prime tenant*, Diesoil. The **credit rating** and prestige of the prime tenant allow Huntley to obtain **financing** and prelease the remaining space to other tenants.

PRINCIPAL 1. the one who owns or will use property.
Example: The *principals* to the **lease** are the **landlord** and **tenant**; *principals* to a sale are the buyer and seller.
2. one who contracts for the services of an **agent** or **broker,** the broker's or agent's **client.**
Example: Grey wishes to purchase a shopping center. Grey engages Jamison, a mortgage broker, to arrange **financing**. Jamison arranges a loan in the name of the *principal,* Grey. The loan is payable as **interest** only for 5 years, with the *principal* payable as a **balloon payment** at the end of year 5.
3. the amount of money raised by a mortgage or other loan, as distinct from the **interest** paid on it.
Example: Abel arranged a loan with $100,000 principal on his home. The first monthly payment is $1,200 including $1,000 interest and $200 that **amortized** the *principal.*

PRINCIPAL AND INTEREST PAYMENT (P&I) a periodic payment, usually paid monthly, that includes the **interest** charges for the period plus an amount applied to **amortization** of the **principal** balance. Commonly used with amortizing loans. See **mortgage constant, amortization.**
Example: A $1,200 annual *principal and interest payment* is required by a $10,000 **face value** amortizing mortgage at a 10% **interest rate.** $1,000 of the first year payment is required for interest; $200 reduces the outstanding balance to $9,800.

PRINCIPAL BROKER the licensed broker responsible for the operations conducted by the brokerage firm.
Example: As *principal broker,* Collins receives a 10% **override** on all sales **commissions** earned by the other **agents.**

PRINCIPAL, INTEREST, TAXES and INSURANCE PAYMENT (PITI) the periodic (typically monthly) payment required by an amortizing loan that includes **escrow** deposits. Each periodic payment includes a **principal and interest payment** plus a contribution to the escrow account set up by the lender to pay insurance premiums and property taxes on the mortgaged property.

Example: Abel's monthly *PITI payment* is $950. This includes $750 for **principal and interest,** $150 for **ad valorem taxes,** and $50 for insurance.

PRINCIPAL MERIDIAN one of the prime **meridians** used in the **government rectangular survey** method of land **description** to locate **range lines.**
Example: *Principal meridians* within the state of California are shown in Figure 141.

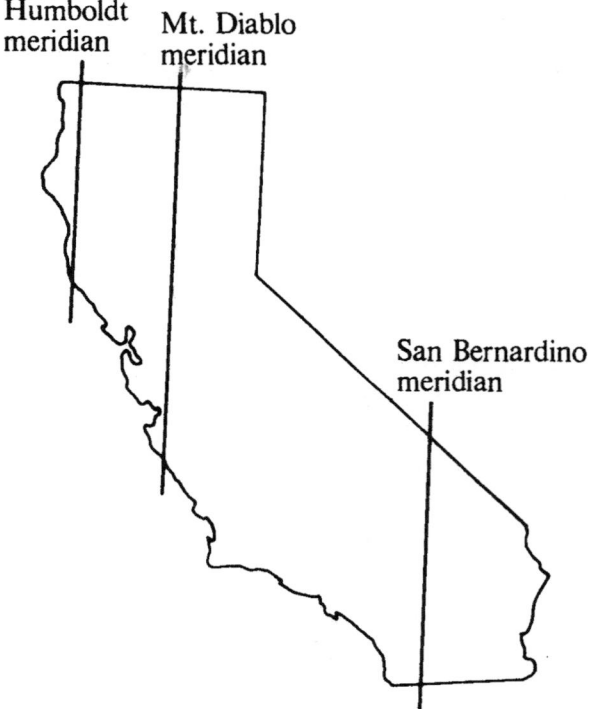

FIG. 141. PRINCIPAL MERIDIANS

PRINCIPAL RESIDENCE the place one lives in most of the time. May be a single-family house, **condominium,** trailer, or houseboat. To defer **capital gain** taxes on the profit from a home, the home must be used as the taxpayer's *principal residence.*
Example: Collins spends 10 months each year living in a rented apartment in downtown Seattle. She spends 2 months in a home she owns in San Diego. The rented apartment is her *principal residence.*

PRIORITY legal precedence; having preferred status. Generally, upon **foreclosure,** lenders are repaid according to priority.

Example: Abel's home was foreclosed and sold for $25,000. Unpaid taxes and attorney's fees were accorded *priority,* and paid in full. The rest of the sales proceeds was applied against the **first mortgage.** There was nothing for the **second mortgage,** because it was lower in *priority.*

PRIVATE MORTGAGE INSURANCE **default** insurance on conventional loans, provided by private insurance companies. See **mortgage insurance.**
Example: Lawton wishes to obtain a home purchase loan covering 90% of value. The lender requires Lawton to acquire *private mortgage insurance* as a condition for granting any loan for more than 80% of value.

PRIVATE OFFERING an investment or business offered for sale to a small group of investors, generally under exemptions to registration allowed by the **Securities and Exchange Commission** and state securities registration laws.
Example: The **syndicator** prepared a *private offering* of the **equity** in the apartments. Up to 35 persons are allowed to participate in the purchase. If more persons are allowed, the **syndicator** must register a **public offering** with the state securities commissioner or the U.S. Securities and Exchange Commission (SEC).

PROBATE OR PROVE to establish the validity of the will of a deceased person.
Example: Hughes died. The **executor** appealed to the *probate* court that a certain document was the **valid** will that Hughes left.

PROCEEDS FROM RESALE same as **resale proceeds.**

PROCURING CAUSE a legal term that means the cause resulting in accomplishing a goal. Used in **real estate** to determine whether a **broker** is entitled to a **commission.**
Example: A real estate broker introduced parties and they agreed to enter into a transaction to sell a home. The broker claimed she was entitled to a commission but had to show in court that she was the *procuring cause.*

PRO-FORMA STATEMENT (from Latin *pro forma,* "according to form"). Financial statements showing what is expected to occur.
Example: The **broker** prepared a *pro-forma* statement for the prospective purchaser (Table 41). It showed expected cash flows for the property:

367

TABLE 41
PRO-FORMA STATEMENT

Pro-forma Cash Flow Statement
Next Year, Projected

Rental income		$10,000
Taxes	−$2,000	
Utilities	−$1,000	
Miscellaneous	− 500	
Subtotal expenses		−3,500
Cash flow		$6,500

PROGRESS PAYMENTS in construction, loan payments issued to the builder as building is completed. See **draw**.
Example: For the $100,000 **construction loan,** the *progress payments* were $20,000 upon buying the lot and a like amount upon pouring the foundation, roofing, wiring, and completion of all work.

PROJECTION PERIOD the time duration for estimating future **cash flows** and the **resale proceeds** from a proposed real estate investment.
Example: A 10-year *projection period* is typically used in a **discounted cash flow** analysis of income-producing real estate.

PROMISSORY NOTE a promise to pay a specified sum to a specified **person** under specified **terms.** See also **note.**
Example: Figure 142.

```
                Promissory Note

    I, June Monroe, do promise to pay City
Finance Co. the sum of $50,000. Repayment is
to be made in the form of 300 equal payments
at 12% interest, or $526.61 payable on the
1st of each month, beginning 8/1/88 until the
total debt is satisfied.

              Signed,

                June Monroe
                7/15/88
```

FIG. 142. PROMISSORY NOTE

PROPERTY 1. the rights that one individual has in lands or goods to the exclusion of all others; rights gained from the ownership of wealth. See **real property, personalty, possession, title.**
Example: An individual may own *property* with the associated rights to enjoyment, control over others' use of the property, and disposition, subject to government-imposed **restrictions.** Groups of individuals may own *property,* with ownership rights shared collectively. Governments may also own *property,* held for public use.
2. real estate
Example: The appraiser needed to inspect the *property* prior to establishing its value.

PROPERTY LINE the recorded **boundary** of a plot of land.
Example: Figure 143.

FIG. 143. PROPERTY LINE

PROPERTY MANAGEMENT the operation of property as a business, including rental, rent collection, **maintenance,** etc.
Example: The following tasks are often required in the ownership of property:
Property management
• accounting and reporting
• leasing
• maintenance and repair
• paying taxes
• provision of utilities and insurance
• remodeling
• rent rate setting and collection
Investment management
• acquisition and disposition
• development and rehabilitation feasibility

- financing
- income tax accounting

PROPERTY REPORT required by the **Interstate Land Sale Act** for the sale of **subdivisions** of 50 lots or more, if the subdivisions are not otherwise exempt. Filed with HUD's **Office of Interstate Land Sales Registration (OILSR).**
Example: A subdivider wishes to sell lots in a 55-lot development, through an interstate commerce promotional plan. She is required to file a property report with OILSR.

PROPERTY RESIDUAL TECHNIQUE in **appraisal,** a method for estimating the value of property based on estimated future income and the **reversionary value** of the building and land. See **income approach. Example:** Table 42.

TABLE 42
PROPERTY RESIDUAL TECHNIQUE

Level annual **net operating income**		$10,000
Multiplied by: **annuity factor** of appropriate rate for number of years (say 12%, 30 years)		× 8.0552
Value of income		$80,552
Estimated *property residual* in 30 years	$50,000	
Multiply by: Present worth of one factor at 12%	× .03338	
Present worth of reversion		$1,669
Estimated property value		$82,221

PROPERTY TAX a government **levy** based on the **market value** of privately owned property. Sometimes referred to as **ad valorem tax** or real estate tax.
Example: Homeville assesses a property tax at the rate of $.50 per $100 of market value. Kilmer pays a tax of $500 on a property valued at $100,000.

PROPRIETARY LEASE in a cooperative apartment building, the lease a corporation provides to the stockholders which allows them to use a certain apartment unit under the conditions specified.
Example: The Coopers purchase a unit in a cooperative on Fifth Avenue. Their ownership provides 450 shares of stock in the cooperative and a *proprietary lease* to a unit in the apartment building.

PRO RATA an equal amount, according to the fraction held by each.
Example: A owns 40%, B owns 30%, C owns 20%, and D owns 10%. A $100 *pro rata* distribution is paid to the owners: A received $40, B received $30, C received $20, D received $10.

PRORATE to allocate between seller and buyer their proportionate share of an obligation paid or due; for example, to prorate real **property taxes** or insurance.
Example: Property taxes were $730, assessed for the calendar year and paid by the seller on April 30. The property was sold on September 15 (Figure 144). It is necessary to *prorate* property taxes so that the buyer and seller each pay a proportionate share for his or her ownership period. There are 107 days from September 15 to December 31. Therefore the buyer must pay $214 at **closing,** based on a daily rate of $2.

FIG. 144. PRORATE

PROSPECT a **person** considered likely to buy. A prospective purchaser.
Example: All of the persons who request further information about the advertised property are considered *prospects.*

PROSPECTUS a printed descriptive statement about a business or investment that is for sale, to invite the interest of prospective investors.
Example: A **syndicator** prepared a *prospectus* that disclosed all **material facts** about the property being offered. Before it is approved by the SEC or state securities commissioner, it is called a **red herring.** If it need not be approved, it is called a **descriptive memorandum.**

PROXY a person who represents another, particularly in some meeting. Also, the document giving to another the authority to represent.
Example: Abel could not be at the **cooperative** apartment association's annual meeting, so he cast his vote by *proxy.*

PUBLIC HOUSING government-owned housing units made available to low-income individuals and families at no cost or for nominal rental rates. Contrast with **low-income housing.**

371

Example: The Metropolitan Housing Authority operates several *public housing* projects for those who cannot afford decent housing on the rental market.

PUBLIC LANDS acreage held by the government for conservation purposes. Public lands are generally undeveloped, with limited activities such as grazing, wildlife management, recreation, timbering, mineral development, water development, and hunting.
Example: Many western states, such as Alaska and Nevada, have large amounts of *public lands.* A part of this area is held by the federal government and is dedicated to national parks, wilderness, and wildlife refuges. Some oil and mineral exploration is allowed under **lease** to private firms.

PUBLIC OFFERING soliciting the general public for the sale of investment units. Generally requires approval by the SEC and/or state securities agencies. Contrast with **private offering.**
Example: The **syndicator** who wishes to sell **limited partnership** interests to over 35 investors should register this *public offering* with the SEC or state securities commissioner.

PUBLIC RECORD usually refers to land transaction records kept at the county courthouse.
Example: Documents that are evidence of real estate transactions should be taken to the county courthouse to be officially entered in the *public record.* Recording gives **constructive notice** of a document's existence.

PUBLIC SALE an **auction** sale of property with **notice** to the general public.
Example: After **foreclosure**, a *public sale* was effected. It was advertised in the local newspaper in advance. The property was auctioned off on the courthouse steps to the highest bidder.

PUD planned unit development.

PUEBLO OR ADOBE HOUSE an early-twentieth-century house that is made of adobe brick or some other material made to look like adobe brick. The characteristic projecting roof beams are called vigas.
Example: Figure 145.

PUFFING overstating the qualities of a property.
Example: "This house has the most efficient floor plan of any home in the world" is an example of a salesperson's *puffing.*

Projecting roof beams (viga)

Real or simulated adobe brick

Flat roof

Massive looking

FIG. 145. PUEBLO OR ADOBE HOUSE

PUNCH LIST an enumeration of items that need to be corrected prior to a sale.
Example: The buyer refuses to close the purchase until the builder fixes the leaky roof and replaces the defective carpeting—the 2 items on the buyer's *punch list.*

PUR AUTRE VIE for the life of another. An **estate** one person grants to another, only for the duration of the life of a third person.
Example: Abel grants a **life estate** to Baker to use Abel's ranch until Baker's wife dies. Baker has a life estate *pur autre vie.*

PURCHASE AGREEMENT same as **contract of sale.**

PURCHASE CAPITAL the amount of money used to purchase real estate, regardless of the source.
Example: The **equity** owner supplied $25,000 and the mortgage lender provided $75,000, totaling the $100,000 of *purchase capital* that was required to complete the transaction.

PURCHASE MONEY MORTGAGE a **mortgage** given by a **grantee** (buyer) to a **grantor** (seller) in part payment of the purchase price of **real estate.**
Example: Lamar wishes to purchase a house from Murphy. The sale price is $75,000. Lamar will assume Murphy's existing mortgage in the amount of $50,000. In addition, Lamar gives Murphy a *purchase money mortgage* of $15,000, plus $10,000 in cash to close the sale.
Note: a purchase money mortgage can be a **first mortgage** or junior lien, depending on its **priority.**

373

Q

QUADRANGLE a square-shaped land area, 24 miles on each side used in the **government rectangular survey** method of land **description.** Each quadrangle contains 16 **townships.**
Example: See example for **government rectangular survey.**

QUALIFIED THRIFT LENDER a lender who specializes in home mortgage finance under the rules established by **FIRREA.** One requirement is that the lender hold at least 70% of its portfolio in residential mortgage loans and mortgage-backed securities. Qualifying lenders are eligible for advances from the district Federal Home Loan Bank.
Example: Under the new rules, commercial banks and credit unions, in addition to savings and loan associations, can enjoy the privileges of affiliation with the Federal Home Loan Banks by becoming *qualified thrift lenders.*

QUANTITY SURVEY a method used by **appraisers** to estimate **reproduction cost** (new) of an **improvement**; detailed cost estimate of all materials, labor, and overhead required to reproduce a structure. See **cost approach.**
Example: A simplified *quantity survey* estimate of reproduction cost (new) is shown in Table 43.

TABLE 43
QUANTITY SURVEY

Item	Cost
site preparation	$ 5,000
cement	10,000
masonry	15,000
lumber	25,000
fasteners	5,000
siding	15,000
roof cover	10,000
labor	30,000
fees	5,000
financing	10,000
Total cost	$130,000

QUEEN ANNE HOUSE a nineteenth-century-style house that is unique-looking, multistory, and irregular in shape with a vari-

ety of surface textures, materials, and colors. The term Queen Anne has come to be applied to any Victorian house that cannot be otherwise classified.
Example: Figure 146.

FIG. 146. QUEEN ANNE HOUSE

QUIET ENJOYMENT the right of an owner or any other **person** legally entitled to **possession** to the use of property without interference.
Example: The landlord, unhappy with a low rental rate, continually blocks the driveway of the tenant. The tenant sues for *quiet enjoyment.*

QUIET TITLE (ACTION) court action to settle a **title** dispute.
Example: People may use *quiet title action* to:
• substantiate the **title** of a squatter
• extinguish **easements**
• release a **dower** interest
• remove any **cloud on title**

QUIET TITLE SUIT (OR ACTION) a suit in court to remove a defect, **cloud on the title,** or suspicion regarding legal rights of an owner to a certain **parcel** of **real property.**
Example: In an *action to quiet title*, the landowner of record brought the **adverse possessor** to court, which required him to establish his claim or be forever barred from claiming the property.

QUITCLAIM DEED a **deed** that conveys only the **grantor's** rights or interest in real estate, without stating the nature of the rights and with no **warranties** of ownership. Often used to remove a possible **cloud on the title.** Contrast with **general warranty deed.**
Example: It is discovered during a **title** search that a certain property was at one time held by a **partnership** that later **abandoned** the property. To obtain a **marketable title,** the current owner obtains *quitclaim deeds* from all partners in the old partnership.

R

RAM reverse annuity mortgage.

RANCH HOUSE originally a low, rambling, one-story house typical of the western United States; now used to describe almost any one-story house.

RANGE LINES lines parallel to a **principal meridian,** marking off the land into 6-mile strips known as ranges; they are numbered east or west of a principal meridian in the **Government Rectangular** Survey. See **baseline.**
Example: Figure 147.

FIG. 147. RANGE LINES

RATE OF INTEREST same as **interest rate.**

RATE OF RETURN the percentage relationship between the earnings and the cost of an investment. See **internal rate of return, overall rate of return.**
Example: Nickson deposits $100 in a savings account. At the end of the year Nickson receives a payment of $10. Nickson's *rate of return* is 10%.

RATE OF RETURN OF INVESTMENT same as **recapture rate.**

RAW LAND acreage with no added **improvements,** such as landscaping, drainage, streets, **utilities,** and structures.
Example: The developer bought 50 acres of *raw land* upon which to develop a **subdivision.**

377

READY, WILLING, AND ABLE capable of an action and disposed to act.
Example: A home is listed with a **broker** who finds a *ready, willing and able* person who agrees to buy under the terms of the **listing.** The seller refuses to sell. The broker has earned a **commission** because she fulfilled the requirements of the listing.

REAL ESTATE 1. in law, land and everything more or less attached to it. Ownership below to the center of the earth and above to the heavens. Distinguished from **personal property.** Same as **realty.**
Example: Figure 148.
2. in business, the activities concerned with ownership and use transfers of the physical property.
Example: The following are engaged in *real estate* business activities:
• **accountants**
• **appraisers**
• attorneys
• **brokers**
• counselors
• government regulators
• **mortgage brokers**
• mortgage lenders
• salespersons
• **surveyors**
• **title** companies

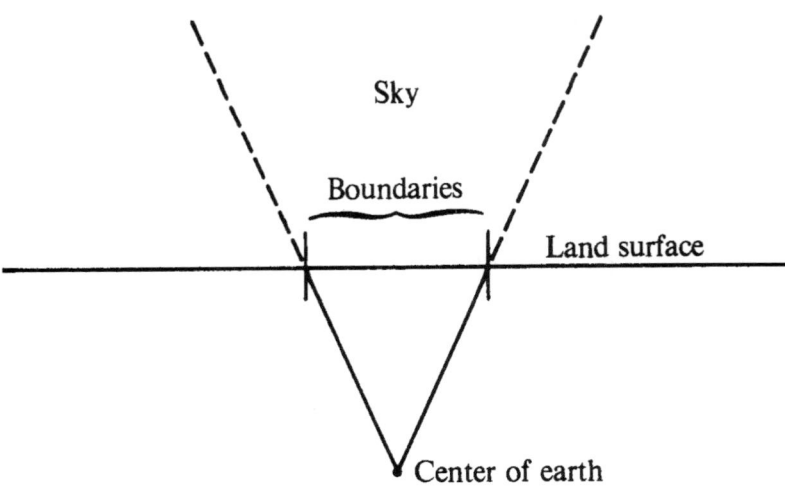

FIG. 148. REAL ESTATE

REAL ESTATE AGENT see **agent.**

REAL ESTATE BOARD see **Board of REALTORS®.**

REAL ESTATE BROKER see **broker.**

REAL ESTATE COMMISSION state agency that enforces real estate **license** laws.
Example: The *Real Estate Commission* is usually comprised of between 5 and 15 members who are appointed for a term (2 to 6 years) by the governor, generally confirmed by the state senate. They enforce the real estate laws and regulations, subject to judicial authority. The real estate **commissioner,** a full time employee of the Real Estate Commission, conducts the routine activities of licensing, collecting fees, and other matters.

REAL ESTATE EDUCATORS ASSOCIATION a professional organization primarily composed of persons who teach **real estate** in junior colleges and proprietary license preparation schools.
Address:
Real Estate Educators Association
One Illinois Center, #200
111 East Wacker Drive
Chicago, IL 60601-4298

REAL ESTATE INVESTMENT TRUST (REIT) a real estate mutual fund, allowed by income tax laws to avoid the corporate income tax. It sells shares of ownership and must invest in real estate or **mortgages.** It must meet certain other requirements, including minimum number of shareholders, widely dispersed ownership, **asset** and income tests. If it distributes 95% of its income to shareholders, it is not taxed on that income, but shareholders must include their share of the *REIT's* income in their personal tax returns.
Example: During the early 1970s, many *real estate investment trusts* were created. They raised money from investors for investment in mortgages and real estate **equities.** An individual could buy shares on the stock market in such a **trust.** Its unique feature is to allow small investors to participate, without **double taxation,** in large real estate ventures. The trust is not subject to corporate income tax as long as it complies with the tax requirements for a *REIT*.

REAL ESTATE MARKET the potential buyers and sellers of real property at the current time, and the current transaction activity for real property. It includes markets for various property types, such as housing market, office market, condominium market, land market.
Example: The local *real estate market* is very active. There have been a record number of sales and there still are many properties on the market.

REAL ESTATE MORTGAGE INVESTMENT CONDUIT (REMIC) The Tax Reform Act of 1986 created a new entity, the *REMIC*. The purpose of a *REMIC is* to hold a fixed pool of mortgages and issue interests in itself to mortgage investors. A *REMIC* may be a partnership, corporation, trust, or separate pool of assets. *REMICs* are intended to become the exclusive means for issuing multiple-class mortgage backed securities in a form that avoids the corporate double tax.

Substantially all of a *REMIC's* assets must be qualified mortgages (mortgages secured by real estate) but it may also hold some short-term liquid assets that produce interest income, and assets held in a special reserve fund, and foreclosed properties.

All interests in a *REMIC* must be classified as regular or residual. Regular interests entitle the holder to interest and principal income, through debt, stock or some other ownership form. Residual interests provide income that is more contingent in nature.

A *REMIC* will not, in general, be a taxable entity, although it must comply with tax requirements and is subject to a 100% tax on prohibited transactions. Regular interest holders will be taxed as if their interests were debt obligations subject to their share of the *REMIC's* income on an accrual basis. Gain or loss on the sale of a regular interest will be ordinary to the extent of their share of original issue discount. Residual interest holders generally receive their share of *REMIC* income as ordinary. (Although the Tax Reform Act of 1986 makes no distinction in rates for capital gains after 1987, the character of capital gains remains in the tax code, perhaps paving the way for a rate distinction in the future.)

REAL ESTATE OWNED (REO) property acquired by a lender through foreclosure and held in inventory. Commonly referred to as REO.
Example: Because of a large number of recent mortgage foreclosures, the bank's *real estate owned* has grown to 5% of all assets, or $25 million.

REAL ESTATE SALESPERSON see **salesperson.**

REAL ESTATE SETTLEMENT PROCEDURES ACT (RESPA) a law that states how **mortgage** lenders must treat those who apply for federally related real estate loans on property with 1–4 dwelling units. Intended to provide borrowers with more knowledge when they comparison shop for mortgage money.
Example: Within 3 days after Abel applies for a loan on a house he wants to buy, the lender is to provide a **good faith** estimate of settlement (**closing**) costs, and a booklet about *RESPA*. In addition, one day before closing, the borrower is

entitled to review the closing papers, including all amounts that are known at that time.

REALIZED GAIN in a tax-free exchange, a gain that has occurred financially, but is not necessarily taxed. See **boot, recognized gain, Section 1031.**
Example: Abel's land has a tax **basis** of $10,000. Its **market value** is $75,000. He exchanges the land, tax-free under Section 1031, for Baker's warehouse, which was appraised at $75,000. Abel's *realized gain* is $65,000. None of Abel's *realized gain* is recognized, because he did not receive boot.

REAL PROPERTY the rights to use real estate. Sometimes also defined as **real estate.**
Examples: *Real property* includes, but is not limited to:
• personal residence owned in **fee simple**
• a **life estate** to a farm
• rights to use land under a **lease**
• **easements** and other partial interests

REALTIST a member of the **National Association of Real Estate Brokers,** a group comprised of mainly minority brokers.
Example: Abel, a black real estate broker, paid dues to the National Association of Real Estate Brokers and subscribed to its code of ethics. Abel is a *Realtist.*

REALTOR® a professional in real estate who subscribes to a strict **Code of Ethics** as a member of the local and state boards and of the **National Association of Realtors®.**
Example: Many of the general public are surprised to discover that only about 40% of licensed real estate brokers are eligible to use the designation *Realtor®.*

REALTOR®-ASSOCIATE a licensed salesperson (not **broker**) who is a member of the **National Association of Realtors®.**
Example: Downing passed the salesperson's **licensing exam** and is sponsored by a Realtor®-Broker. Upon being sworn in to the national and state association, Downing is appropriately described as a *Realtor®-Associate.*

REALTORS® NATIONAL MARKETING INSTITUTE (RNMI) an affiliate of the **National Association of Realtors®;** mainly concerned with educational programs and literature for members.
Address:
Realtors® National Marketing Institute
430 North Michigan Avenue
Chicago, IL 60611

REALTY same as **real estate.**

REAPPRAISAL LEASE a **lease** where the rental level is periodically reviewed by independent **appraisers.** Often, the **lessor** and **lessee** will each select an appraiser; if they do not agree on a value, they will choose a third appraiser.
Example: In the 20-year *reappraisal lease*, Big Buy Foods agrees to pay the landlord an annual rent of 12% of the property value. Every 5 years the property will be reappraised to determine the rent.

REASSESSMENT the process of revising or updating the value estimate of property for **ad valorem tax** purposes.
Example: Local **property tax** assessors are required to periodically conduct a *reassessment* of all property. Value estimates are revised based on recent sales and other data, and tax **assessments** are based on the new estimates.

REBATE 1. a refund resulting from a purchase or tax.
Example: To encourage sales of the **condominium** project, the developer offered a $2,500 *rebate to* each purchaser.
2. a kickback of a charge, often illegal if done without knowledge of all parties.
Example: The broker accepted a $50 *rebate* from the insurer each time he sold a home carrying a homeowner's **warranty.**

RECAPTURE CLAUSE in a contract, a clause permitting the party who grants an **interest** or right to take it back under certain conditions.
Example: Carter grants a **lease** to Frank's Furniture, with rent set at 6% of retail sales. The lease contains a *recapture clause* whereby Carter can regain the property unless sales are over $1 million per year.

RECAPTURE OF DEPRECIATION same as **depreciation recapture.**

RECAPTURE RATE in **appraisal,** a term used to describe the rate of recovery of an investment in a **wasting asset.** This rate is added to the **discount rate** to derive a **capitalization rate** in appraisal terminology. May be based on the straight-line, **sinking fund,** or annuity method.
Example: A building with a 50-year estimated **useful life** has a 2% straight-line *recapture rate.* At a discount rate of 10%, the capitalization rate is 12%.

RECASTING the process of adjusting a loan arrangement, especially under the threat of **default.** See **workout.**

Example: Pope owns an apartment building with a **mortgage** loan requiring **debt service** of $25,000 per year. Because of a period of high vacancies, Pope's **net operating income** falls to $20,000 per year. To eliminate the **negative cash flow,** Pope appeals to the lender to *recast* the loan by extending the **maturity** and reducing the **interest rate** for the next 2 years.

RECIPROCITY mutual agreement to accept, such as a state's **acceptance,** as **valid** the real estate **license** one has earned in another state.
Example: In the absence of *reciprocity,* Moore must take a new examination to obtain a real estate license in the state to which she moves. With *reciprocity* she needs only to present her previously earned license.

RECOGNIZED GAIN in a **tax-free exchange,** the portion of gain that is taxable. A **realized gain** will generally be recognized to the extent of **boot** received. See **Section 1031.**
Example: Abel's land has a **tax basis** of $10,000. It is worth $75,000. He exchanges the land under Section 1031 for Baker's warehouse worth $70,000 and $5,000 of cash. Of Abel's $65,000 realized gain, $5,000 will be *recognized.*

RECONCILIATION in **appraisal,** the process of adjusting **comparables** to estimate the value of the subject being appraised.
Example: An **appraiser** arrives at the market value estimates shown in Table 44 following application of the 3 traditional approaches.

TABLE 44
RECONCILIATION

Market comparison:	$85,000
Cost approach:	$89,000
Income approach:	$84,000

In *reconciliation,* the appraiser considers the appropriateness of each approach to the subject, the quality of available data, and the amount of judgmental **adjustment** required to reach each estimate. Following this review, the appraiser settles on an estimate of $85,000 as her opinion of **market value.**

RECONVEYANCE occurs when a **mortgage** debt is **retired.** The lender **conveys** the property back to the **equity** owner, free of the debt.
Example: The *reconveyance* took place after Abel paid off the loan; Abel promptly **recorded** the *reconveyance* **instrument.**

RECORDING the act of entering in a book of public records **instruments** affecting the **title** to **real property.** Recording in this manner gives **notice** to the world of facts recorded. See **constructive notice, ownership rights to realty.**
Example: By *recording* the **deed** from a sale of property, the purchaser assumes that all subsequent interested parties are given notice of the purchaser's ownership **interests** in the property. **Leases and liens** may also be recorded.

RECOURSE the ability of a lender to claim money from a borrower in **default,** in addition to the property pledged as **collateral.**
Example: Ross obtains a **mortgage** loan from Local Savings. Should Ross default on the loan, Local Savings may **foreclose** and force the sale of the mortgaged property. Should the sale fail to satisfy the unpaid loan **principal,** Local Savings has *recourse* to other assets of Ross.

RECOVERY FUND generally administered by the **Real Estate Commission.** Requires **licensees** to contribute, then reimburses aggrieved persons who are unable to collect from **brokers** for wrongdoings.
Example: A typical state's *recovery fund* law requires all new licensees to contribute $10 to the fund. Anytime the fund account balance drops below $500,000, all licensees will be assessed. Payments from the fund to an aggrieved person may not exceed $10,000; total payments on behalf of any licensee may not exceed $25,000. The recovery fund pays only when the broker does not.

RECTANGULAR SURVEY same as **government rectangular survey method.**

REDEMPTION, EQUITY OF same as **equity of redemption.**

REDEMPTION PERIOD the period during which a former owner can reclaim **foreclosed** property. See **equity of redemption.**
Example: Collins's property was foreclosed. If she acts within her state's *redemption period,* she can reclaim her property by paying the **debt** and legal fees.

REDEVELOP the process of demolition of the existing improvements and construction of new improvements on a site. The new improvements are often of a different type from the old.
Example: Since the old building has outgrown its usefulness, the owner plans to *redevelop* the site as the location of a new office tower.

RED HERRING a proposed **prospectus** that has not been approved by the **Securities and Exchange Commission** (SEC) or state securities commission. See **public offering.**

Example: A *red herring* is shown in Table 45.

TABLE 45
RED HERRING PROSPECTUS

Proposed Prospectus

A registration statement has been filed with the Securities and Exchange Commission but is subject to change. The securities described herein may not be sold until approval becomes effective.

REDISCOUNT RATE the rate of interest charged to member banks when they borrow from the **Federal Reserve System.** Also called **discount rate.**
Example: The First and Citizens Banks borrows funds from the Federal Reserve for one day and is charged interest at the *rediscount rate.*

REDLINING the illegal practice of refusing to originate **mortgage** loans in certain neighborhoods on the basis of race or ethnic composition.
Example: A **savings and loan association** may be accused of practicing *redlining* if it is found that no loans have been originated in predominantly nonwhite neighborhoods. The term derives from the alleged practice of drawing a red line on a map around certain neighborhoods to designate them as off limits for loan approvals.

REDUCTION CERTIFICATE a document in which the **mortgagee** (lender) acknowledges the sum due on the **mortgage** loan. Used when mortgaged property is sold and the buyer assumes the debt.
Example: Abel buys Baker's home and agrees to assume the existing mortgage. They obtain a *reduction certificate* from the mortgage lender stating that the remaining balance is $34,567.89.

REEVALUTION LEASE same as **reappraisal lease.**

REFERRAL the act of suggesting the use of a certain **broker.**
Example: Smith receives several **listings** based on *referrals* from former customers.
Example: A broker agrees to pay a 1% *referral* fee to out-of-state brokers who suggest families that are moving into the area.

385

REFINANCE to replace an old loan(s) with a new loan(s).
Example: Garner has a $30,000 loan against her house, which is worth $200,000. She desires cash to pay for a college education. By *refinancing* the home with a new $150,000 loan, she will realize $115,000 in cash after paying $5,000 in **transaction costs.** See Table 46.

TABLE 46
REFINANCING STATEMENT

New loan	$150,000
Old debt	− 30,000
Cost of loan	− 5,000
Refinancing: cash proceeds	$115,000

Example: Arthur owes $100,000 at 12% interest on a loan with 15 years left, borrowed 10 years ago at 12% interest. Current interest rates for 15-year loans are 9%. Arthur can refinance and reduce his payment from $1,200 per month to $1,014 per month.

REGENCY HOUSE an English-style 2- or 3-story symmetrical house with a hip roof. A small octagonal window over the front door is traditional.
Example: Figure 149.

Simple informal style

Small octagonal window

Brick

Double-hung windows

Hip roof

1 chimney at side

FIG. 149. REGENCY HOUSE

386

REGIONAL SHOPPING CENTER a type of **shopping center** containing 300,000 to 900,000 square feet of shopping space and at least one major department store.

REGISTRAR the person who is to maintain accurate official records, such as for **deeds, mortgages,** and other recorded **documents.**
Example: After **closing,** the buyer brought the deed to the *registrar* of deeds for **recording** in the county records.

REGRESSION a statistical technique used to estimate mathematical models of economic and other processes. It is used to find a mathematical expression which best fits the relationship between a group of random variables as indicated by a sample of data.
Example: An appraiser wants to find the relationship between sales prices for homes and their physical characteristics. Data are collected on the prices of a group of homes and their size, number of rooms, location and age. Linear *regression* is used to analyze the relationship expressed by the data. The *regression* model can then be used to estimate prices for other similar houses on the market.

REGULATION D a regulation of the **Securities and Exchange Commission** that sets forth conditions necessary for a **private offering** exemption.
Example: Syndicator Stuart wants to sell **35 limited partnership** interests in an office building. He applies for an exemption under Rule 146 of *Regulation D* to avoid the need of registering a **public offering;** he thereby saves over $100,000 and avoids a 4-month delay.

REGULATION Q a federal law that specified the maximum interest rates that banks and **savings and loan associations** could pay on various types of deposits. It was phased out by the **Depository Institutions Deregulations and Monetary Control Act of 1980.**
Example: Under *Regulation Q,* Hometown Savings could offer no more than a 5% yield on its passbook accounts. Today, it can offer any rate required to attract deposits.

REGULATION Z a federal regulation requiring **creditors** to provide full disclosure of the terms of a loan. Compliance is compulsory for anyone who arranges **credit** for more than 5 sales of **residential** real estate in a year. **Terms** of the loan must be disclosed. The **interest rate** must be stated as an **annual percentage rate** (APR).
See also **rescind, rescission.**
Example: Figure 150.

```
Convenient Savings and Loan                          Account number: 4862-98

  Michael Jones
  500 Walnut Court, Little Creek, U.S.A.
```

Annual Percentage Rate The cost of your credit as a yearly rate	Finance Charge The dollar amount the credit will cost you	Amount Financed The amount of credit provided to you or on your behalf	Total of Payments The amount you will have paid after you have made all payments as scheduled
15.37%	$177,970.44	$43,777	$221,548.44

Your payment schedule will be:

Number of Payments	Amount of Payments	When Payments Are Due
12	$446.62	Monthly beginning 6/1/88
12	$479.67	" " 6/1/89
12	$515.11	" " 6/1/'90
12	$553.13	" " 6/1/91
12	$593.91	" " 6/1/92
300	varying from $637.68 to $627.37	" " 6/1/93

Security: You are giving a security interest in the property being purchased.

Late Charge: If a payment is late, you will be charged 5% of the payment.

Prepayment: If you pay off early, you
☒ may ☐ will not ☐ have to pay a penalty.
☒ may ☐ will not ☐ be entitled to a refund of part of the finance charge.

Assumption: Someone buying your home cannot assume the remainder of the mortgage on the original terms.

See your contract documents for any additional information about nonpayment, default, any required repayment in full before the scheduled date, and prepayment refunds and penalties.

e means an estimate

FIG. 150. REGULATION Z

REHABILITATE to restore a structure to a condition of good repair.

Example: An old building has deteriorated to the point of prohibiting profitable operation. The owner faces the choice of **demolition** of the structure and rebuilding or *rehabilitation* to restore the building to a competitive position.

REHABILITATION TAX CREDIT the Tax Reform Act of 1986 provides a 20% tax credit for rehabilitating certified historic structures, and a 10% credit for other buildings that were

placed in service after 1936. However, there are certain conditions or requirements that are imposed.
- The credit may be used to offset a maximum of $25,000 of nonpassive income, but is phased out on a 50% basis between $200,000 and $250,000 of adjusted gross income. Thus, the credit is not of use to high income investors.
- The tax basis of the property is reduced by the full amount of the credit.
- Transition rules are provided for those with binding contracts for rehabilitations between March 1, 1986, and October 22, 1986; these rules require such property be placed in service before 1994.

REINVESTMENT RATE the **interest rate** an investor is assumed to be able to earn on intermediate **cash flow** in the projection of a terminal value. See **financial management rate of return.**

REIT real estate investment trust.

RELEASE CLAUSE in a **mortgage,** a clause that gives the owner the privilege of paying off a portion of the mortgage indebtedness, thus freeing a portion of the property from the mortgage.
See **partial release.**
Example: Smith, a **developer,** is **subdividing** land that is **financed** under a mortgage. A *release clause* in the mortgage allows Smith to sell individual lots from the **tract** by retiring portions of the loan. Without the clause, Smith would have to **retire** the entire loan before selling any lots.

RELEASE OF LIEN to free real estate from a **mortgage.** See **partial release.**
Example: Reynolds owns 100 **acres** of land that is mortgaged for $10,000. If she pays the $10,000, the land will be *released* from the lender's **lien** on the property.

RELICTION gradual subsidence of waters, leaving dry land.
Example: As the Great Salt Lake in Utah becomes smaller by evaporation, *reliction* occurs. Generally the new land belongs to the party who owned the rights to the water area (Figure 151).

RELOCATION CLAUSE a **lease** stipulation that allows the landlord to move the tenant within the building.
Example: The landlord of an office building requires *relocation clauses* in all leases for space that does not include an entire floor. When a new client wishes to lease an entire floor, the landlord may relocate tenants in such a way as to provide the desired space.

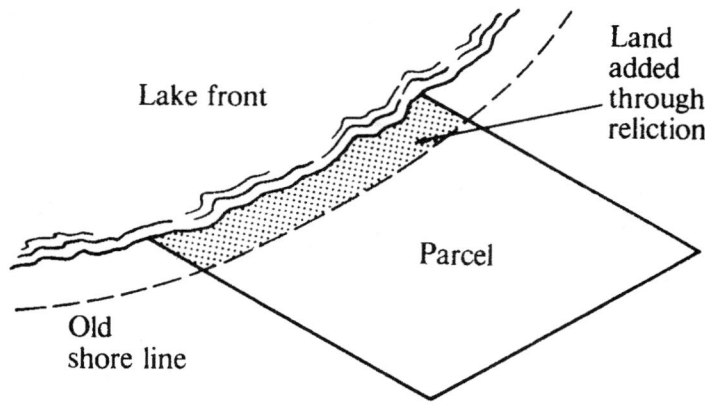

Lake front

Land added through reliction

Old shore line

Parcel

FIG. 151. RELICTION

RELOCATION NETWORK a geographically diversified group of independent real estate brokerage companies, generally not members of a franchise, that share information with one another concerning potential customers.
Example: A broker in Atlanta, Georgia, lists a home for sale which is owned by a family who is moving to Dallas, Texas. The broker, who is a member of a certain *relocation network,* finds a counterpart member/broker in Dallas and refers the family to the Dallas broker. If they buy a home through the Dallas broker, the Atlanta broker will receive a referral fee.

RELOCATION SERVICE a company which contracts with other firms to arrange the relocation of employees from one city to another. The service generally handles the sale of the employee's home and purchase of a new home. Furniture-moving services may be included also.
Example: The Beeker Company wishes to open a new office in Denver. Most of the staff for the new office will be relocated from Miami. Beeker hires a *relocation service* to sell the employees' homes and to help them find new homes in the Denver area.

REMAINDER an **estate** that takes effect after the termination of a prior estate, such as a **life estate.**
Example: At the death of her husband, Polly Rowen inherits a **life estate** in their home. The *remainder* is **devised** to their son, Paul Rowen. When Polly dies, Paul will gain **title** to the house. Paul is the **remainderman.**

REMAINDERMAN the person who is to receive **possession** of the property after the death of a **life tenant.**
Example: See example under **remainder.**

REMIC Real Estate Mortgage Investment Conduit.

REMODEL to change the appearance and functional utility of a building. This may include painting, repairing, and replacing of fixtures and equipment.
Example: The Moodys wish to *remodel* the kitchen in their home. They plan to refinish the cabinets, repaint the walls, install a new floor covering, and replace the range and sink.

RENEGOTIATE to legally revise the **terms** of a **contract.**
Example: Abel owes $10,000 to Baker at 7% interest. Abel and Baker *renegotiate* so that Baker agrees to lend $15,000 at 13 interest instead of the original loan.

RENEWAL OPTION the right, but not the obligation, of a **tenant** to continue a **lease** at specified **term** and **rent.**
Example: Abel leases property from Baker for 20 years at $500 monthly rent. A *renewal option* in the lease gives Abel the right to continue leasing for 5 years beyond the original term (Figure 152).

FIG. 152. RENEWAL OPTION

RENOVATE general term applied to the process of upgrading an existing improvement. Usually there is an attempt to keep the same general appearance of the building with new materials or to return the building to its original appearance.
Example: The city bought several dilapidated homes in the neighborhood. They plan to *renovate* the homes by bringing them up to the current housing code standards. The renovated homes will be sold to city residents.

RENT a charge for the use of space. See **contract rent, economic rent.**
Example: Abel allows Baker to use property, provided that Baker pays $500 per month (Figure 153). The charge is *rent.*

RENTABLE AREA same as **net leasable area.**

RENTAL RATE the periodic charge per unit for the use of a property. The period may be a month, quarter, or year. The unit may be a dwelling unit, square foot, or other unit of measurement.
Example: The *rental rate* for the 2-bedroom apartments is $750 per month. The *rental rate* for office space is $18 per square foot per year.

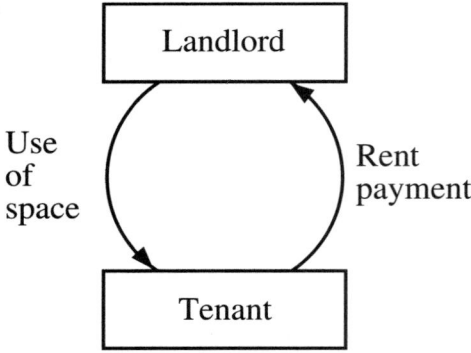

FIG. 153. RENT

RENT BID MODELS a conceptual tool used to explain how land is allocated in competitive markets. The model is based on the assumption that space is controlled by the activity which offers the highest bid for the site.
Example: A simple *rent bid model* of urban land is formulated. The model predicts that commercial uses will occupy land near the city center, while residential land will spread around the core.

RENT CONCESSION see **concession.**

RENT CONTROL laws that govern the rate that may be charged for space.
Example: Since the 1940s, apartment owners in New York City have been restricted by law in the rent that they may charge. *Rent control* laws have been adopted by Boston, Washington, D.C., Los Angeles, and many cities in New Jersey, among others.

RENT-FREE PERIOD a portion of the term of a lease when no rent is required. It is offered by a landlord as a rental concession to attract tenants.
Example: In order to attract tenants to the new office building, the landlord is offering a 3-month *rent-free period* to all tenants who sign a 2-year lease.

RENT MULTIPLIER see **gross rent multiplier.**

RENT-UP PERIOD the time it takes for newly constructed properties to be fully occupied.
Example: Figure 154.

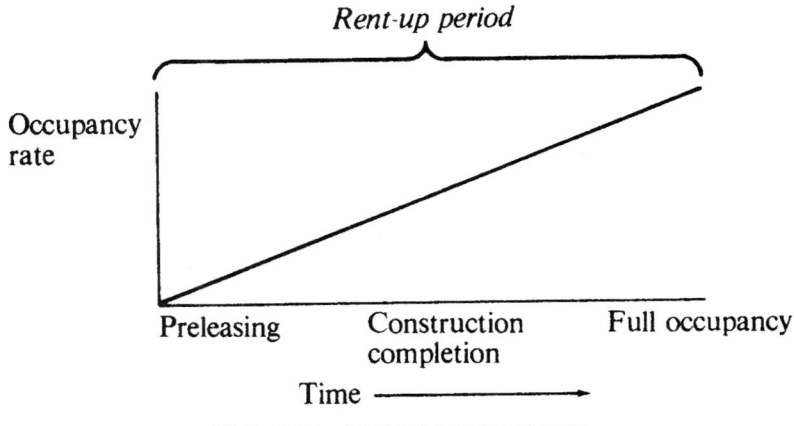

FIG. 154. RENT-UP PERIOD

REO see **real estate owned.**

REPAIRS work performed to return property to a former condition without extending its **useful life,** as distinguished from **capital improvements.** In **income property,** repairs are an **operating expense** for accounting and tax purposes.
Examples: Patching a hole in the roof (but not replacing the roof) and mending (but not rebuilding) a fence are *repairs.*

REPLACEMENT COST the cost of erecting a building to replace or serve the functions of a previous structure. See **reproduction cost.**
Example: Abel wishes to insure a building against accidental destruction. The policy should be written so that in the event of destruction of the building, Abel may replace it with a structure that serves an identical function. Therefore, Abel should insure the building in an amount equal to its *replacement cost,* which is likely to be greater than its **market value.**

REPLACEMENT RESERVE an amount set aside from **net operating income** to pay for the eventual wearing out of short-lived **assets.** See **reserve fund.**
Example: Singer buys new apartments, each containing $1,000 worth of carpeting and appliances that have a 10-year **useful life.** Each year she deposits $100 in a *replacement reserve* account to pay for recarpeting in 10 years.

REPRODUCTION COST the cost of exact duplication of a property as of a certain date. Reproduction differs from replacement in that replacement requires the same functional utility for a property, whereas reproduction is an exact duplication. See **replacement cost.**

393

Example: In the **cost approach** to property valuation, the **appraiser** estimates the *reproduction cost* of the subject structure. Various deductions are then made to account for **depreciation** in value from the time the building was constructed. These deductions reflect the fact that the building is not new, may not be of modern design, and may have suffered adverse effects due to its location.

RESALE PRICE in a projection of real estate investment performance, the assumed selling price a **property** could fetch at the end of the **projection period.** See **resale proceeds.**

RESALE PROCEEDS the amount a former owner receives upon a sale after paying **transaction costs,** remaining debt, and, sometimes, income taxes. Same as **proceeds from resale.** **Example:** Table 47.

TABLE 47
RESALE PROCEEDS

Selling price		$100,000
Less: Commissions	$5,000	
Closing costs	1,000	
Unpaid mortgage	60,000	
Capital gains tax	14,000	– 80,000
Resale proceeds		$20,000

RESCIND to withdraw an **offer** or contract. **Regulation** Z allows a 3-day period in which to *rescind* certain credit transactions.
Example: Abel offers to buy a certain house from Baker. Before Baker accepts, Abel *rescinds* the offer and, therefore, is not obligated to follow through on the purchase.

RESCISSION the act of cancelling or terminating a **contract.** Rescission is allowed when the contract was induced by **fraud, duress, misrepresentation,** or **mistake. Regulation** Z allows one to **rescind** certain credit transactions within 3 business days (not applicable to **first mortgages** on a home); purchasers of certain land that must be registered by **Department of Housing and Urban Development** (HUD) may rescind within 3 business days. See **rescind.**
Example: *Rescission* was allowed by the court for a contract that Abel was induced to enter on the threat of death.

RESERVE FUND an account maintained to provide funds for anticipated expenditures required to maintain a building. A reserve may be required by a lender in the form of an **escrow** to pay upcoming taxes and insurance costs. A **replacement reserve** may

be maintained to provide for **replacement cost** of short-lived components, such as carpets, heating equipment, or roofing. Deposit of money into such a fund does not achieve a tax deduction.

Example: A **property management** firm anticipates that property taxes will be due in 6 months, insurance must be renewed in 2½ years, and carpeting must be replaced in 6 years. Accordingly, they establish a *reserve fund* by depositing a portion of monthly revenues in an account. Monies from the fund will be used at the appropriate time to meet the future expenditures.

RESERVE PRICE in an **auction** or other bidding procedure, an established amount below which the seller is not obligated to accept a winning bid.

Example: Before the auction, a *reserve price* of $45,000 was set for the home. Since the highest bid was only $39,000, the seller could withdraw the property from the sale.

RESIDENCE the place where one lives, particularly the **dwelling** in which one lives. See **domicile.**

Example: Baker owns several houses, one of which is Baker's *residence,* another is a vacation home, and the others are **income properties** rented to tenants.

RESIDENTIAL pertaining to housing. See **residential property.**

RESIDENTIAL BROKER one who **lists** and sells houses or **condominiums.** Contrast with **commercial broker.**

Example: Baker earned a livelihood as a *residential broker* selling **single-family housing.**

RESIDENTIAL MEMBER (RM) a professional designation once offered by the **American Institute of Real Estate Appraisers.** It is being exchanged or phased out in favor of the **SRA** designation offered by the Appraisal Institute.

Example: Collins passed several examinations, prepared demonstration **appraisal** reports, and acquired several years of experience in the appraisal of **residential property.** She has been awarded the *RM* designation, which acknowledges her skills as a residential appraiser. She may exchange that for the SRA designation.

RESIDENTIAL PROPERTY 1. in real estate **brokerage** terminology, owner-occupied housing.

Example: Rollins is in *residential* real estate. She secures **listings** for **single-family housing** and sells homes.

2. in income taxation terminology, rental units used for **dwelling** purposes, not of a transient (hotel, motel) nature. To qualify as residential, at least 80% of a building's income should be derived from dwelling units.

Example: *Residential* rental *property* owners may be subject to different methods of **depreciation (accelerated cost recovery)** and/or **depreciation recapture** than **commercial property** owners.

RESIDENTIAL SALES COUNCIL affiliate of the **Realtors®** **National Marketing Institute** of the **National Association of Realtors®** that provides educational and promotional materials for members, most of whom are involved in residential real estate sales or brokerage.
Address:
Residential Sales Council
430 North Michigan Avenue
Chicago, IL 60611

RESIDENTIAL SERVICE CONTRACT an insurance **contract** or home **warranty,** generally for one year, covering the plumbing, mechanical, and electrical systems of a home. It is available in most areas upon the purchase of an existing home. Either the buyer or seller can pay for the contract.
Example: Ricky and Rebecca Miller purchase a home. The sellers paid $300 for a *residential service contract.* Three months later, the air-conditioner compressor breaks and costs $800 to repair. The Millers must pay the $100 deductible, and the contract covers the balance of the cost of repair.

RESIDENT MANAGER one who supervises the care of an apartment complex while living in one of the units in the complex.
Example: Carter employs Downs as a *resident manager.* Downs's duties include showing vacant units to prospective tenants, making sure the building is kept clean, and providing entry to repair persons. In return, Downs receives an apartment rent-free.

RESIDUAL value or income remaining after deducting an amount necessary to meet fixed obligations.
Example: After deducting **operating expenses, debt service,** and income taxes from **gross income,** the **equity** investor is entitled to the *residual.*
Note: There is no assurance that a *residual* will exist.
In **appraisal,** a portion of stabilized **net operating income** is deducted to support the value of the **improvements.** The *residual* net operating income is then left to support the value of the **site.**

RESIDUAL TECHNIQUES a method of estimating the value of a building or land, given values of one and **rate of return.** See **building residual technique, land residual technique.**

RESOLUTION TRUST CORPORATION (RTC) a federal agency created by **FIRREA** to manage and resolve insolvent savings and loan associations placed into its conservatorship or receivership. The agency is supervised by the **Federal Deposit Insurance Corporation.**
Example: The *RTC* is charged with liquidating the assets left over from the "S&L crisis," the problem that prompted passage of FIRREA. The agency is funded through special appropriations and proceeds from the sale of seized assets. Presumably, the agency will be dissolved once all assets are sold.

RESPA Real Estate Settlement Procedures Act.

RESPONDEAT SUPERIOR in **agency** law, the doctrine that a **principal** is liable for the acts of an **agent.**
Example: A real estate **agent** misrepresented the facts about property that was offered for sale. The injured party sued the **agent** and the **broker.** The **broker** was held liable under the doctrine of *respondeat superior.*

RESTORE to return a building to its original quality and appearance. While modern materials are used, the emphasis is on faithful reproduction of the original style.
Example: The Hollys bought an old Victorian-style home which had been converted into a duplex. They plan to *restore* the home by removing partitions, refinishing the hardwood floors, repairing the fireplaces, and making other improvements to return the building to its original style.

RESTRAINT ON ALIENATION a limiting condition on the right to transfer property. If the condition is against public policy or is unreasonable, courts will **void** the condition.
Example: The **deed** that Lowell received when she bought property specifies that she may not resell the property to certain ethnic minorities. Since the clause is illegal, she went to court to remove this *restraint on alienation.*

RESTRICTION a limitation placed upon the use of property, contained in the **deed** or other written **instrument** in the **chain of title** or in local **ordinances** pertaining to land use. See **encumbrance.**
Examples: The ownership of property is subject to several *restrictions.* A deed **covenant** may restrict development alternatives, as may a local **zoning ordinance. Easements** may restrict use of parts of the property. **Liens** may restrict sales. **Building** codes may restrict construction practices.

RESTRICTIVE COVENANT a **covenant** or **deed restriction** that limits the property rights of the owner.

Example: A *restrictive covenant* was placed on property to prevent the sale of alcoholic beverages on the land for the next 50 years.

RETAIL GRAVITATION the drawing power of a shopping center; generally, the larger the center, the greater its ability to draw from distant areas.

RETAINAGE in a construction **contract,** money earned by a **contractor** but not paid to the contractor until the completion of construction or some other agreed-upon date.
Example: The **general contractor** earns $5,000 upon pouring the foundation, plus $15,000 upon completion of the frame, plus $10,000 upon completion of the roof. Of each payment, 10% is held back as *retainage.* It is paid after a **certificate of occupancy** is issued.

RETALIATORY EVICTION the requirement that a tenant vacate a unit in response to a complaint from the tenant concerning the condition of the building. Landlord-tenant laws in many states forbid such **evictions** if proper channels are taken to lodge the complaint.
Example: Six months after Romney moved into an apartment, the heating system stopped operating. The landlord failed to repair the system, and Romney filed a formal complaint with the city **housing code** enforcement office. When the landlord received notice from the city to repair the system, he evicted Romney in a *retaliatory eviction.* The eviction was stopped in court.

RETIRE (A DEBT) to pay off the **principal** on a loan, thereby fulfilling the obligation under the loan contract. See also **amortization.**
Example: When Smith made the last monthly payment on his mortgage loan, he *retired* the debt.
Example: Jones arranged to *retire* her home improvement loan by paying an amount equal to the remaining principal balance.

RETURN ON EQUITY see **equity dividend, equity yield rate.**

REVALUATION CLAUSE see **reappraisal lease.**

REVENUE STAMPS stamps that are affixed to deeds (and, in some states, other documents affecting real estate) and that indicate the payment of the state's deed transfer (or other transfer) tax. **Federal revenue stamps** have not been used since 1968, but many states have substituted their own.
Example: A state requires $1 of *revenue stamps* to be attached to deeds for each $1,000 of purchase price. There were $50 of stamps on Dan's deed, so appraisers assumed he paid $50,000 for the land, though he could have paid less.

REVERSE ANNUITY MORTGAGE a type of **mortgage,** designed for elderly homeowners with substantial **equity,** by which a lender periodically (monthly, for example) pays an amount to the borrower. The loan balance increases with interest and periodic payments, causing **negative amortization.**
Example: Roper, age 70, who retired from his job, owns his home **free and clear** of any **liens.** His pension is inadequate to pay expenses. He seeks a *reverse annuity mortgage* that will pay him $200 per month. At a 15% interest rate, he will owe $55,043 in 10 years.

REVERSE LEVERAGE a situation in which financial benefits from ownership accrue at a lower rate than the mortgage interest rate. See **leverage.**
Example: Net-leased property is purchased for $100,000 with a $75,000 mortgage at 12% interest and $25,000 of **equity.** The net rent is $10,000 per year; interest expense is $9,000 per year. The $1,000 difference (**cash flow**) provides a 4% return to the equity owner. In the absence of debt, the owner would receive a 10% return. *Reverse leverage* works against the property owner.

REVERSION the right of a **lessor** to **possess** leased property upon the termination of a **lease.**
Example: Evans purchases the home of Felker, a senior citizen, and leases the home back to Felker for life. Evans has the right to receive rental payments from Felker plus a *reversion* in the property at Felker's death.

REVERSIONARY FACTOR the mathematical factor that indicates the present worth of one dollar to be received in the future. Same as **present value of one.** The formula is

$$\text{Reversionary factor} = \frac{1}{(1+i)^n}$$

where i = interest rate
n = number of years (or periods)
Example: The *reversionary factor* for 30 years at 12% is .03338. The present value of the receipt of land that will be worth $50,000 in 30 years is $1,690 (.03338 × $50,000).

REVERSIONARY INTEREST the **interest** a person has in property upon the termination of the preceding **estate.**
Example: Abel is the **remainderman** in property that was granted to Baker for life. Abel has a *reversionary interest* in the property.

REVERSIONARY VALUE the value of property at the expiration of a certain time period.

Example: A **lease** will expire in 30 years. The landlord estimates that the *reversionary value* of the property will be $50,000; that is, the property can be sold in 30 years for $50,000.

REVOCATION an act of recalling a power of authority conferred, as a revocation of a **power of attorney,** a **license,** an **agency,** etc.
Example: The *revocation* of Abel's broker's license, caused by his fraudulent acts, prevented him from earning a living in **real estate.**

REZONING an action to change the designation of a subject **parcel** or group of parcels on the **zoning** map. The effect of a rezoning is to change the permitted uses for the affected parcels. See **downzoning.**
Example: Brown, whose property was zoned for low-**density** residential, petitioned the city for a *rezoning* to allow construction of an **apartment building.**

RIDER an amendment or **attachment** to a **contract.**
Example: A *rider* to Owen's **homeowner's policy** insured the valuable paintings against fire and theft losses.

RIGHT OF FIRST REFUSAL the opportunity of a party to match the **terms** of a proposed contract before the contract is **executed**.
Example: In some states, tenants whose apartments are converted to **condominiums** are given a *right of first refusal* for the unit when it is sold. This means the tenant may purchase the unit at the same price and terms of any outside purchaser.

RIGHT OF REDEMPTION same as **equity of redemption.**

RIGHT OF SURVIVORSHIP the right of a surviving joint tenant to acquire the **interest** of a deceased joint owner; the distinguishing feature of both **joint tenancy** and **tenancy by the entirety.**
Example: Frank Adams and Anna Adams own property as joint tenants with the *right of survivorship*. When either dies, the entire property will pass to the other without **probate.**

RIGHT-OF-WAY 1. the right to use a particular path for **access** or passage; a type of **easement.**
Example: Lot A has acquired a *right-of-way* across lot B (Figure 155).
2. the areas of subdivisions **dedicated** to government for use for streets, roads, and other public access to lots.
Example: A section of a subdivision with a *right-of-way* for a public road (Figure 156).

400

FIG. 155. RIGHT-OF-WAY

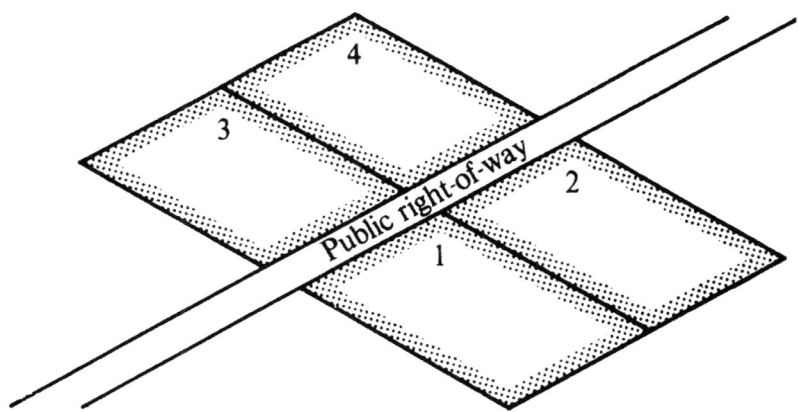

FIG. 156. RIGHT-OF-WAY

RIPARIAN OWNER one who owns land bounding upon a lake, river, or other body of water. See also **littoral.**
Example: The owner of lot A in Figure 157 is a *riparian owner,* whose ownership rights include access to the river and use of its waters, or **riparian rights.** The owner of lot B has no riparian rights.

RIPARIAN RIGHTS rights pertaining to the use of water on, under, or **adjacent** to one's land. May be qualified to avoid **nuisance** and pollution. Riparian rights are recognized in most eastern states but rarely in western states, where they recognize **usufructory rights.**
Example: See **riparian owner.**

401

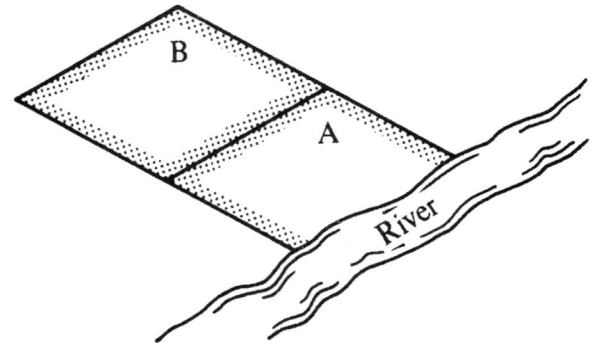

FIG. 157. RIPARIAN OWNER

RISK 1. uncertainty or variability. The possibility that returns from an investment will be greater or less than forecast. Diversification of investments provides some protection against risk.
Examples: Types of *risk* in real estate:
• business risk—rents, vacancies, or **operating expenses** vary from projected amounts
• interest risk—property may be subject to a higher rate **mortgage** than the **market rate**
• market rental rate—a long-term lease may lock the owner into low rents
• principal risk—resale proceeds may be less than anticipated
2. the possibility of a loss. Insurance can offer protection against certain risks.
Example: Owners insure buildings against *risk* of loss caused by fires, storms, and other hazards by taking out a **hazard insurance** policy.

RISK-FREE RATE the **interest rate** on the safest investments, such as federal government obligations.

ROD a linear unit of measurement equal to 16½ feet.
Example: A certain lot has 165 feet, or 10 *rods,* of road **frontage.**

ROLLOVER LOAN a type of **mortgage** loan, commonly used in Canada, in which the **amortization** of **principal** is based on a long **term** but the **interest rat**e is established for a much shorter term. The loan may be extended, or rolled over, at the end of the shorter term at the current market interest rate.
Example: Abel obtains a *rollover loan.* The amortization term is 30 years. The interest rate is 14% for 2 years. After 2 years, Abel must renew the loan at the going interest rate or **refinance** with a new loan.

ROW HOUSE single-family dwelling units attached to one another by common walls, generally with a common **facade.** See **townhouse.**

Example: A group of *row houses* (Figure 158).

FIG. 158. A GROUP OF ROW HOUSES

ROYALTY money paid to a property owner for extraction of some valuable resource from the land.

Example: Richman owns a 500-**acre** ranch in west Texas. An oil company negotiates a **lease** with Richman to explore for oil on the ranch. Under the agreement, Richman will receive a *royalty* in proportion to the number of barrels of oil pumped from the ranch.

RRM **renegotiated rate mortgage.**

RULE OF 72's an approximation of the time it takes for money to double when earning **compound interest.** Divide the percentage rate into 72 to derive the number of years to double the **principal.**

Example: A $1,000 **certificate of deposit** pays a 9% interest rate with annual compounding. In about 8 years the balance will be $2,000 ($72 \div 9\% = 8$ years).

RULE OF 78's a method for computing unearned interest used on installment loans with **add-on interest.** The number 78 is based on the sum of the digits from 1 to 12.

Example: A 12-month loan is made for $1,000 with 8% add-on interest. The loan payments are based on a total of $1,080, payable at the rate of $90 per month for 12 months. If the borrower prepays the loan at the end of 1 month, $\frac{12}{78}$ of the $80 interest is charged; the balance of interest is refunded. If the borrower prepays at the end of the second month, $\frac{12+11}{78} = \frac{23}{78}$ is charged. Prepayment at the end of the eleventh month results in a $\frac{1}{78}$ refund.

403

RUN WITH THE LAND an expression indicating a right or **restriction** that affects all current and future owners of a property. Contrasted to an agreement, between a current owner and other parties, that is not passed on to future owners in a **deed.**
Example: A **covenant,** written into the **deed,** prohibits the property from being used as a liquor store. The restriction *runs with the land,* and all future owners are restrained from violating the covenant.

RURBAN AREAS on the fringe of urban development, that are in the process of being developed for urban uses.
Example: Figure 159.

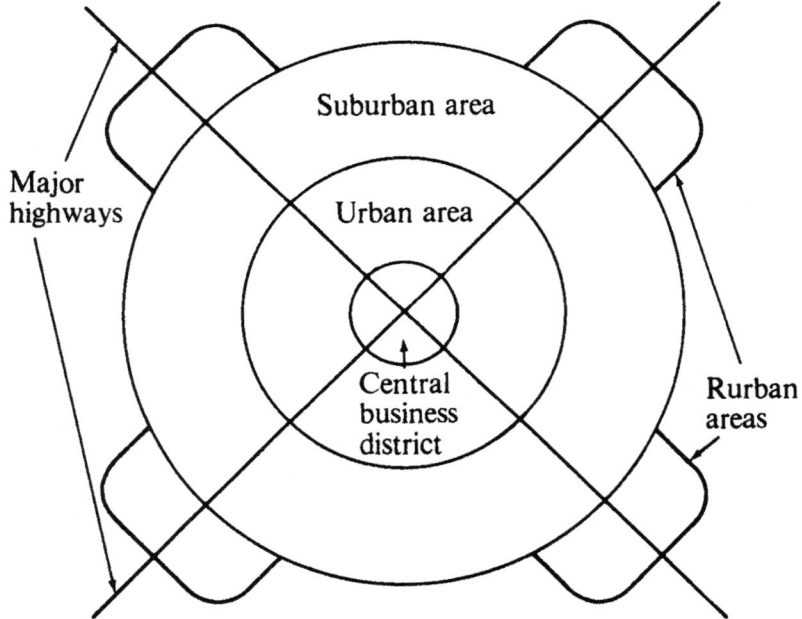

FIG. 159. RURBAN AREAS

RURAL pertaining to the area outside the larger and moderate-sized cities and surrounding population concentrations. Generally characterized by farms, ranches, small towns, and unpopulated regions. Compare with **suburb.**
Example: Garrison grew up on a farm in a *rural* area of Indiana. She later moved to Chicago and lived in a suburban town nearby. Garrison invested in *rural* land, hoping to be able to return at retirement.

R VALUE a measure of the heat conductivity of material. The higher the *R value,* the better the material serves as insulation

from heat transfer. *R value* generally applies to insulating materials, roofs, exterior walls, and windows and doors.

Example: The walls in a building have an estimated *R value* of 20. Fiberglass insulation with an *R value* of 34 was installed in the walls to make the building more energy efficient.

R/W right-of-way.

S

SAFE RATE an **interest rate** provided by relatively low-**risk** investments such as high-grade **bonds** or well-secured **first mortgages.** See **financial management rate of return.**

SALES CONTRACT a **contract** by which the buyer and seller agree to the **terms** of sale. Same as **agreement of sale, earnest money** contract.
Example: Carter and Dooley sign a *sales contract,* which specifies the property to be sold, type of **deed, closing date,** price, **financing** conditions, and other details.

SALE-LEASEBACK the simultaneous purchase of property and **lease** back to the seller. The lease portion of the transaction is generally long-term. The seller-lessee in the transaction is converted from an owner to a tenant.
Example: ABC Corporation owns an office building. It arranges a *sale-leaseback* for the building **site** with the Carpenters Pension Fund. ABC receives cash and a 25-year lease to the site. In addition, ABC might **depreciate** the value of the building for income taxes. The Fund receives an **income stream** for 25 years and a **reversion** to the property at the end of the lease.

SALES COMPARISON APPROACH same as **market comparison approach.**

SALESPERSON one who is licensed to deal in real estate or perform any other act enumerated by state real estate **license** laws, while under the supervision of a **broker** licensed by the state.
Example: A *salesperson* arranges a 90-day **listing** on a house, which is accepted by the broker. Another *salesperson* shows the home to a prospective buyer. The sale is closed, and **commissions** are collected by the broker and shared with the *salespersons.*

SALES PRICE the amount of money required to be paid for real estate according to a **contract,** or previously paid.
Example: The *sales price* consisted of $30,000 cash plus the buyer's **assumption of** a $70,000 **mortgage,** for a $100,000 total.

SALTBOX COLONIAL OR (IN SOUTH) CATSLIDE an early-American-style, 2- or 2½-story house that is square or rectangular with a steep gable roof that extends down to the first floor in the rear.
Example: Figure 160.

406

Steep gable roof
extended to first
floor in rear

Large central chimney

2 or 2½ stories

Square or
rectangular
shape

No windows
in rear

Small glass
panes in
double-hung
windows

FIG. 160. SALTBOX COLONIAL HOUSE

SALVAGE VALUE the estimated **value** that an **asset** will have
at the end of its **useful life.**
Example: An appraiser estimates the useful life of a building at
40 years; she also estimates that the building's *salvage value*
would be $10,000 in 40 years. Consequently, all but $10,000 of
the building cost is to be **depreciated** over 40 years.

SAM shared appreciation mortgage.

SAMDA CONTRACTOR a middleman who is responsible for
the management and disposition of a specific group of assets
controlled by the **Resolution Trust Corporation.** The respon-
sibility is created by the Standard Asset Management and Dis-
position Agreement (SAMDA) entered into by the contractor
and the RTC.
Example: All assets held by the RTC are managed through
SAMDA contractors. Each contractor has responsibility for a
specific portfolio of real properties, loans, and/or securities.
Actual property management, loan servicing, and marketing
operations are performed by subcontractors employed by the
SAMDA contractor.

S&L savings and loan association.

SANDWICH LEASE lease held by a **lessee** who becomes a
lessor by subletting. Typically, the sandwich leaseholder is nei-
ther the owner nor the user of the property. See **sublease.**
Example: Figure 161.

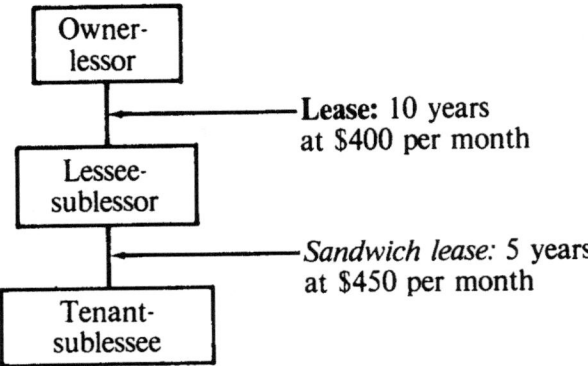

FIG. 161. SANDWICH LEASE

SATISFACTION PIECE an **instrument** for recording and acknowledging final payment of a **mortgage** loan.
Example: After the mortgage loan was paid off, the borrower received a *satisfaction piece,* which she promptly **recorded,** officially.

SAVINGS AND LOAN ASSOCIATIONS (S&Ls) depository institutions that specialize in originating, servicing, and holding **mortgage** loans, primarily on owner-occupied, **residential property.**
Example: Traditionally, *savings and loan associations* were distinguished from **commercial banks** by their emphasis on long-term home mortgage loans, separate regulations and deposit insurance mechanisms, and their affiliation with the **Federal Home Loan Bank System.** Passage of **FIRREA** in 1990 destroyed most of these divisions. Today all depository institutions are eligible for affiliation with the Home Loan Bank System if they are willing to specialize in home mortgages.

SBA Small Business Administration.

SCALE the proportional relationship between the dimensions of a drawing, plan, or model to the dimensions of the physical object it represents.
Example: A **subdivision** plan is prepared at a *scale* in which 1 inch equals 1,000 feet. A distance of 1 inch on the drawing is intended to signify 1,000 feet on the **site.**
Example: A *scale* model of a building has a *scale* of 1 to 25. Each inch on the model represents 25 inches on the actual building.

SCENIC EASEMENT an **encumbrance** on the **title** to a property to preserve it in a more-or-less natural or undeveloped state. See **easement.**

Example: Smith owns a house with a view of the ocean (Figure 162). Snyder owns the property between the Smith house and the beach. To preserve the view of the ocean, Smith purchases a *scenic easement* to Snyder's property. Snyder is then prevented from developing the property in such a manner as to obstruct Smith's view.

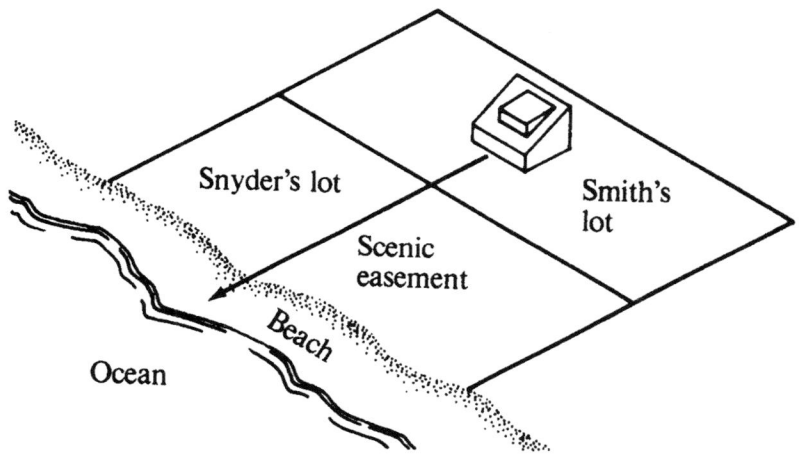

FIG. 162. SCENIC EASEMENT

SEASONED LOAN a loan on which several payments have been collected.
Example: The seller accepts a **second mortgage** on the property sold. After he collects 12 months of payments, the loan is considered *seasoned* and can more easily be sold to a second mortgage investor.

SEC Securities and Exchange Commission.

SECONDARY FINANCING see **junior mortgage, second mortgage.**

SECONDARY MORTGAGE MARKET the mechanisms available to buy and sell mortgages, mainly residential **first mortgages.** There is no set meeting place for the secondary mortgage market. **FNMA** and **Freddie Mac** hold **auctions** weekly to buy those mortgages offered at the highest **effective rate. Bids** are collected from all over the country.
Example: The Good Money Mortgage Bankers originated 100 residential first mortgages with a total **face value** of $5 million. They sell the mortgages in the *secondary mortgage market* for a $1,000 profit on each.

SECOND HOME a residence that is not one's **principal residence.** Under the Tax Reform Act of 1986, a taxpayer may deduct interest on 2 personal residences.
Example: Senator Goodwill maintains his principal residence in Hometown, Iowa, and a *second home* in Washington, D.C. He is allowed to deduct interest paid on both as an itemized deduction.

SECOND MORTGAGE a **subordinated lien,** created by a mortgage loan, over the amount of a **first mortgage.** Second mortgages are used at purchase to reduce the amount of a cash **down payment** or in **refinancing** to raise cash for any purpose. See **subordination.**
Example: A house costs $100,000. Available **financing** is a mortgage loan covering 80% of value, or $80,000. The required cash **down payment** is $20,000. A *second mortgage* is available for an additional $10,000 of value, reducing the down payment to $10,000. The *second mortgage* will generally carry a higher **interest rate** than the first mortgage to reflect the inferior position and greater **risk** of the second mortgage.

SECTION (OF LAND) one square mile in the **government rectangular survey.** There are 36 sections in a 6-mile square **township.**
Example: A township, containing 36 *sections* (Figure 163).

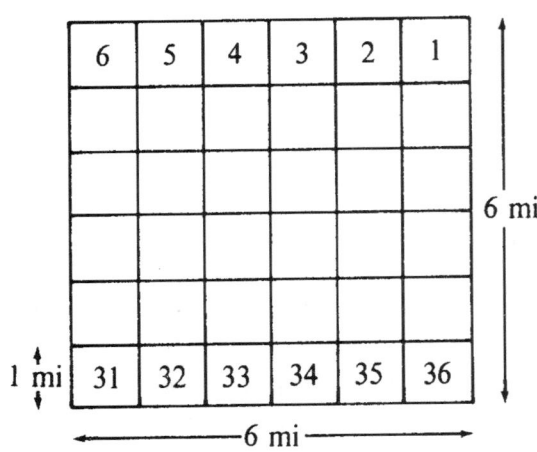

FIG. 163. SECTIONS OF LAND

SECTION 8 HOUSING privately owned rental **dwelling** units participating in the low-income rental assistance program created by 1974 amendments to Section 8 of the 1937 Housing Act. Under the program, landlords receive rent subsidies on behalf

410

of qualified low-income tenants, allowing the tenants to pay a limited proportion of their incomes toward the rent.
Example: A **landlord** elects to participate in the *Section 8 housing* program. A prospective tenant's income is $800 per month—low enough to qualify for the program. A **fair market rent** for the unit is established by the **Department of Housing and Urban Development** as $200 per month. The tenant pays 20% of income, or $160 per month, and HUD supplements $40 per month to the landlord.

SECTION 167 the part of the **Internal Revenue Code** that deals with **depreciation.**
Example: Improvements to **real estate** are depreciable in accordance with *Section 167* of the Internal Revenue Code.

SECTION 1031 the section of the **Internal Revenue Code** that deals with tax-deferred **exchanges** of certain property. General rules for a tax-deferred **exchange** of real estate are:
The properties must be:
1. exchanged or qualify as a **delayed exchange**
2. **like-kind property** (real estate for real estate)
3. held for use in a trade or business or held as an investment
See also **boot.**
Example: Under *Section 1031,* Lowell trades her **appreciated** land for Baker's shopping center. **Equities** are the same. Lowell's adjusted tax basis in the land becomes her adjusted tax basis in the shopping center.

SECTION 1034 the section of the **Internal Revenue Code** dealing with sales of personal residences. Generally, there is no **recognized gain** or loss on the sale of a personal residence, provided another one is purchased within 2 years of the sale date of the old one. The new one must cost at least as much as the adjusted sales price of the old one (sales price, less expenses of sale, less fixing-up expenses).
Example: Under *Section 1034,* Abel can defer tax on the $10,000 gain on the home he sold for $65,000 by buying a new one that costs more.

SECTION 1221 the part of the **Internal Revenue Code** that defines a **capital asset.** It actually states what is not a capital asset.
Examples: Under *Section 1221* the following are not **capital assets:**
• inventory (such as lots of a subdivider)

411

- receivables collected in the course of business (such as **notes** received from the sale of lots by a **subdivider**)
- copyrights and the like held by the creator or certain other parties
- certain U.S. securities
 The following are capital assets:
- the personal **residence** thal one owns
- **raw land** held as an investment
- **mortgages** held as investments

Note: The importance of capital gains has been diminished by the Tax Reform Act of 1986 which applies the same tax rate to capital gains after 1987 as it does to ordinary income. However, there remain important distinctions as to capital loss limitations, so *Section 1221* remains relevant.

SECTION 1231 the section of the **Internal Revenue Code** that deals with **assets** used in a trade or business. Generally, gains on *Section 1231* assets are taxed at **capital gains** rates (except for **depreciation recapture**) and losses are **tax deductible** as **ordinary income.** See also **Section 1245, Section 1250.**
Examples: *Section 1231* assets include:
- vehicles used in business
- machinery used in business
- hotels, office buildings, warehouses, apartments

SECTION 1245 the section of the **Internal Revenue Code** dealing with **gains** from **personal property** on which **depreciation** had been claimed. Generally, gains are taxed at **capital gains** rate except to the extent of depreciation claimed.
Note: The Tax Reform Act of 1986 provides the same tax rate for ordinary income as for capital gains after 1987. Therefore the nature of the gain has diminished in importance, though *Section 1245* remains in the Internal Revenue Code.

SECTION 1250 the section of the **Internal Revenue Code** dealing with **gains** from **real estate** on which **accelerated depreciation** had been claimed. Under the Tax Reform Act of 1986, the tax rate for ordinary income is the same as for capital gains after 1987, and straight-line depreciation is mandated for most buildings. Consequently, the importance of *Section 1250* has been minimized. Under prior law, gains on **residential property** were generally treated as **capital gains** except to the extent of accelerated depreciation claimed (Figure 164 and Table 48). Gains on nonresidential property on which accelerated depreciation was claimed were all **recaptured** to the extent of gain or depreciation, whichever is less.

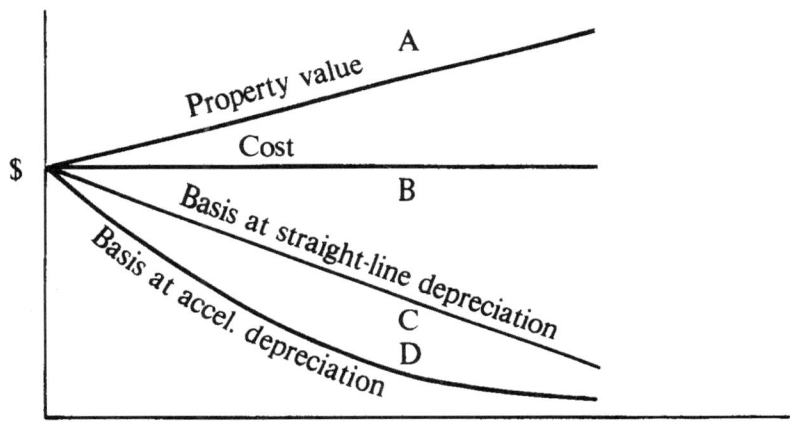

FIG. 164.
ACCELERATED DEPRECIATION SUBJECT TO
SECTION 1231, 1245, OR 1250

TABLE 48
TREATMENT OF GAIN
AFTER USE OF DEPRECIATION METHOD

1. Accelerated Method

	Nonresidential	Residential
Capital gain	A — B	A — C
Ordinary income	B — D	C — D

2. Straight-line

	Nonresidential	Residential
Capital gain	A — B	A — C
Ordinary income	none	none

SECURITIES AND EXCHANGE COMMISSION (SEC) the federal agency created in 1934 to carry out the provisions of the Securities Exchange Act. Generally, the agency seeks to protect the investing public by preventing **misrepresentation, fraud,** manipulation, and other abuses in the securities markets.
Example: The *Securities and Exchange Commission* requires their review of proposed **public offerings** of securities, registration of listed securities, and other matters. They do not, however, guarantee the investor against loss.

SECURITIZATION the process of creating a security marketable in the capital markets and backed by a package of assets such as mortgage loans. See **real estate mortgage investment conduit, mortgage pools, collateralized mortgage obligation.**

Example: Mortgage loans insured by the Federal Housing Administration are good assets for *securitization.* A lender can organize a pool of such loans and create a collateralized mortgage obligation for sale to investors.

SECURITY 1. property that serves as **collateral** for a **debt.**
Example: Real estate serves as *security* for a **mortgage** loan. In the event of **default** on the loan, the lender may sell the property to satisfy the debt.
2. a document that serves as evidence of ownership.
Examples: The following are securities:
• common and preferred stocks
• **bonds**
• **mortgages**
 The **Securities and Exchange Commission** defines **limited partnership** interests and **condominiums** and **cooperatives** in certain situations as *securities.*

SECURITY DEPOSIT a cash payment required by a landlord, to be held during the **term** of a **lease** to offset damages incurred due to actions of the tenant. Such damages may include physical damage to the property, theft of property, failure to pay back rent and breaking the lease. **Forfeiture** of the deposit does not absolve the tenant of further financial **liability.** Laws in most states require landlords to hold the deposit in a separate account and refund the amount within a specified time after termination of the lease.
Example: A landlord requires a *security deposit* equal to one month's rent, payable at the signing of the lease. An additional deposit is required for tenants with pets. At termination of the lease, the landlord inspects the rented unit. If there is no reason for forfeiture, the landlord refunds the deposit within 30 days.

SECURITY INTEREST an interest in **real estate** in which the real estate serves as **collateral.**
Example: A **mortgage** lender holds a *security interest* in real estate. He doesn't own the real estate, but does have a **lien** against it.

SEED MONEY amounts needed to begin a real estate development, prior to being able to borrow under a **mortgage** loan. Required costs include those for a **feasibility study, loan application** and **loan commitment** fees, attorney and accountant fees, land **option** costs, and others. See **front money.**
Example: To begin a $2,000,000 **condominium** development, about 2% of the total cost is needed as *seed money.*

SEE-THROUGH BUILDING a vacant building.
Example: The term originated with overbuilt glass office buildings in Houston during the late 1980s. Without **tenants** or furniture, looking from the outside you could see right through the glass facades of these buildings.

SEISIN the **possession of realty** by one who claims to own a **fee simple** estate or a **life estate** or other salable **interest.** See also **ownership rights to realty, title.**
Example: *Seisin* is used to describe the **possession** of real estate by one who claims a **freehold** interest.

SELF-AMORTIZING MORTGAGE one that will **retire** itself through regular **principal and interest payments.** Contrast with **balloon mortgage, interest-only loan.**
Example: Collins borrowed $100,000 with a *self-amortizing mortgage* at 12% **interest** with a 30-year **term. Principal and interest payments** are $1,029 each month for the 30 years, at the end of which her loan will be amortized fully.

SELF-HELP the efforts of a landlord to cure a **default** on the **lease** without aid of legal proceedings. In most states, self-help remedies are not considered a legitimate substitute for a legal **eviction.**
Example: When Simmons's tenant fell 3 months behind in rent, Simmons changed the locks on the apartment and cut off the heat. The tenant took Simmons to court and forced him to follow eviction procedures in lieu of these *self-help* activities.

SELLER FINANCING a debt instrument taken back by the seller as part of the purchase price for a property. Such financing is used as an inducement to a sale when normal third-party financing is expensive or unavailable and in situations where the existing, first-lien loan may be assumed by the buyer but the difference between the existing debt and sales price exceeds the cash resources of the buyer. Seller financing may be in the form of a **senior mortgage** or a **junior mortgage.**
Example: The Sextons offer their home for sale with an asking price of $100,000. The existing mortgage may be assumed by the buyer and has a principal of $40,000. One buyer offers to meet the Sextons's price on the condition that they provide *seller financing* in the form of a second mortgage of $40,000 subordinated to the existing loan. Another buyer will pay the asking price if the Sextons take back a note for $75,000 in addition to $25,000 in cash.

SELLER'S MARKET economic conditions that favor sellers, reflecting rising prices and market activity. Contrast with **buyer's market.**

Example: *Seller's markets* in real estate are often caused by:
• population influx
• lower interest rates
• lack of building activity

SELLING BROKER (AGENT) the licensed real estate **broker (agent)** that brings forth the buyer. Contrast with **listing broker (agent).**
Example: Abel was the *selling broker* under a multiple listing agreement. He showed the property to Collins, the buyer. Abel will share the **commission** with the listing broker.

SEMIANNUAL twice a year; same as **biannual.**

SENIOR MORTGAGE same as **first mortgage.**

SENIOR RESIDENTIAL APPRAISER see **SRA.**

SENSITIVITY ANALYSIS a technique of investment analysis whereby different values of certain key variables are tested to see how sensitive investment results are to possible change in assumptions. It is a method of evaluating the riskiness of an investment.
Example: *Sensitivity analysis* was applied to a certain income property investment. It was found that forecasting a 15% vacancy rate produced a rate of return on investment of 16% versus an 18% rate of return for a 5% vacancy factor. On the other hand, varying the property's appreciation rate from 10% per year to 5% reduced the return from 20% to 4%.

SEPARATE PROPERTY property acquired by either spouse prior to marriage or by gift or **devise** after marriage, as distinct from **community property.**
Example: At a divorce trial, each party tries to show that property owned prior to marriage or acquired in his or her own right is *separate property.*

SERVICING the act of billing, collecting payment, and filing reports for a **mortgage** loan; may also include loan analysis, **default** followup, and management of tax and insurance **escrow** accounts. Often performed for a fee by **mortgage bankers** after loans are sold to investors.
Example: Gray, a mortgage banker, originates loans and markets them in groups to large investors. On each loan originated, Gray receives a monthly fee for *servicing,* thereby freeing the investors of loan management burdens. The fee is ⅜ of 1% of the loan balance.

SERVIENT TENEMENT contrast with **dominant tenement.**

SETBACK the distance from the curb or other established line within which no buildings may be erected. See also **building line.**
Example: A 50-ft setback is shown in Figure 165.

FIG. 165. SETBACK

SETTLEMENT same as **closing.**

SETTLEMENT STATEMENT same as **closing statement.**

SEVERALTY the ownership of **real property** by an individual as an individual. See **tenancy in severalty.**
Example: The owner in *severalty* enjoys working the land without partners in its ownership.

SEVERANCE DAMAGES an element of **value** arising out of a **condemnation** to which a **tract** was a part.
Example: The state highway department needed a strip of land 100 feet wide from the middle of Dooley's farm. They awarded $1,000 per **acre** for the land taken, plus $15,000 *severance damages* for Dooley's inconvenience in getting from one side of the highway to the other.

SEWER a system of pipes, containments, and treatment facilities for the disposal of plumbing wastes.
Example: A sanitary *sewer* collects waste water from individual buildings and homes, for treatment and disposal at a public facility.
Example: To prevent flooding, a storm *sewer* collects water drainage from streets and other surfaces.

SHARED APPRECIATION MORTGAGE a residential loan with a fixed **interest rate** set below **market rates,** with the lender entitled to a specified share of **appreciation** in property **value** over a specified time interval. Loan payments are set to **amortize** the loan over a long-term **maturity,** but repayment is generally required after a much shorter term. The amount of appreciation is established by sale of the home or by **appraisal** if no sale is made.
Example: Hogan obtains a *shared appreciation mortgage.* The interest rate on the loan is 10%, with the lender receiving ⅓ of any appreciation after 10 years. At the end of 10 years, Hogan does not wish to sell the home. An appraisal is made to establish the appreciation amount. Hogan must **retire** the loan by **refinancing** with a new loan the amount of the unpaid balance plus the appreciation share.

SHARED EQUITY MORTGAGE a home **loan** in which the lender is granted a share of the **equity,** thereby allowing the lender to participate in the proceeds from resale. After satisfying the unpaid balance of the loan, the borrower splits the residue of the proceeds with the lender. Shared equity plans often require the lender to buy a portion of the equity by providing a portion of the **down payment.**
Example: Ingram obtains a *shared equity mortgage* from a **mortgage banker.** The lender provides one half of the necessary down payment. Ingram makes loan payments on a fixed-rate, level payment basis. At resale, Ingram and the lender split the proceeds after repayment of the balance of the loan.

SHED ROOF one having a single, sloped side.
Example: Figure 166.

FIG. 166. SHED ROOF

SHOPPING CENTER a collection of retail stores with a common parking area and generally one or more large department, discount, or food stores; sometimes including an enclosed **mall** or walkway. See also **anchor tenant.**

Example: *Shopping centers* developed after World War II as population shifted to the suburbs. Providing a variety of stores with easy access and ample parking, the centers became a strong alternative to downtown retail centers. Types of shopping centers are shown in Table 49.

TABLE 49
SHOPPING CENTER CHARACTERISTICS

Center type	Leading tenant (Basis for classification)	Typical GLA* (sq. ft.)	General range in GLA (sq. ft.)	Usual minimum site area (acres)	Minimum population support required
Neighbor-hood	Supermarket	50,000	30,000–100,000	3–10	3,000–40,000
Community	Junior department store, large variety, discount or department store	150,000	100,000–300,000	10–30	40,000–150,000
Regional	One or more full-line department store(s)	400,000	300,000–900,000	10–60	150,000 or more
Super-regional	Three or more full-line department store(s)	800,000	500,000–1.5 million or more	15–100 or more	300,000 or more

*Gross leasable area
Source: International Council of Shopping Centers

SHORT FORM an **instrument,** seldom more than 2 pages, that refers to another document. The short form is often recorded in lieu of a cumbersome longer document.
> **Example:** The Giant Development Company leased part of a shopping center to Malee's Department Store. The **lease** required 150 printed pages. A *short-form* lease was recorded.

SHORT-TERM CAPITAL GAIN gain on the sale of a **capital asset** that was held, generally, for less than 6 months. A taxpayer's *short-term capital gains* and losses are merged, the net is then merged with net long-term capital gains.
> **Example:** An investor sold land that was owned for 4 months at a $10,000 profit. The sale was the investor's only capital transaction that year, so the $10,000 *short-term capital gain* is added to ordinary income.

SIMPLE INTEREST a method of calculating the future value of a sum assuming that interest paid is not compounded, i.e., that interest is paid only on the **principal.** See also **compound interest.**
Example: An account is established paying *simple interest* of 10% on a principal of $1,000. Table 50 shows the current value of the account for the next 5 years.

TABLE 50
SIMPLE INTEREST

Year	Value
1	$1,100
2	1,200
3	1,300
4	1,400
5	1,500

SINGLE-FAMILY HOUSING a type of residential structure designed to include one **dwelling.** Adjacent units may share walls and other structural components but generally have separate access to the outside and do not share plumbing and heating equipment.
Examples: *Single-family housing* includes:
• **detached housing** units
• **town houses**
• **zero lot line** homes

SINKING FUND an account that, when compounded, will equal a specified sum after a specified time period. See **compound interest.**
Example: The Johnsons wish to buy a home 3 years from now. They estimate the **down payment** will equal $5,000. To accumulate the necessary money, they set up a *sinking fund* at the local bank. At 5% interest, the fund requires monthly deposits of $129. After 36 payments, the account will contain $5,000.

SIOR Society of Industrial and Office Realtors®.

SITE a plot of land prepared for or underlying a structure or development. The location of a property.
Example: The Smith Building is located on a half-**acre** *site* in downtown Smithville. Several new buildings are being constructed on *sites* nearby.

SITE ASSESSMENT (ENVIRONMENTAL) an evaluation of a site, prior to acquisition of title to the property, for the existence of hazardous waste. Under the Comprehensive Environmental

Response, Compensation, and Liability Act of 1980 (CERCLA), as amended by the Superfund Amendments and Reauthorization Act of 1986 (SARA), anyone acquiring title to a site is responsible for environmental damages resulting from hazardous wastes on the site. However, there are legal defenses for landowners who conduct proper site assessments prior to acquisition.

Example: A CERCLA *site assessment* may be conducted in two phases. A phase I assessment involves research into previous uses of the site and whether a hazardous waste condition is likely to exist. If evidence from this phase suggests a problem, a phase II assessment is conducted to discover the extent of the problem. Either assessment requires the use of an environmental consultant and special legal counsel.

SITE PLAN a document which describes how a parcel of land is to be improved. It includes the outlines of all structures and site improvements, such as driveways, parking lots, landscaping and utility connections.

Example: The *site plan* indicates that the office tower will be set back 100 feet from the street and be surrounded by surface parking for 2,000 cars.

SITUS the economic attributes of location, including the relationship between the property and surrounding properties, as well as distant points of interest and the linkages to those points. *Situs* is considered to be the aspect of location that contributes to the market value of a real property.

Example: The *situs* of a commercial property includes surrounding commercial establishments, the location of suppliers' warehouses, competing establishments, and the homes of employees and customers.

SMALL BUSINESS ADMINISTRATION (SBA) a federal government agency in Washington, D.C., that encourages small business.

Example: The *SBA* offers low-interest rate loans to qualified businessmen and businesswomen.

Address:
Small Business Administration
1441 L Street NW
Washington, DC 20416

SMSA standard metropolitan statistical area.

**SOCIETY OF INDUSTRIAL AND OFFICE REALTORS®
(SIOR)** an organization, affiliated with the **National Association of Realtors®,** whose members are mainly concerned with the sale of warehouses, factories, and other **industrial property.** Confers *SIOR* designation.

SOCIETY OF REAL ESTATE APPRAISERS

Address:
Society of Industrial and Office Realtors
777 14th Street NW, #400
Washington, DC 20005-3279

SOCIETY OF REAL ESTATE APPRAISERS (SREA) an organization that merged with the **American Institute of Real Estate Appraisers** in 1991 to form the **Appraisal Institute.**

SOFT MARKET a market in which demand has shrunk or supply has grown faster than demand and in which sales at reasonable prices have become more difficult; a **buyer's market.**
Example: In a *soft market*, a buyer or lessee is able to negotiate a better deal.

SOFT MONEY 1. in a development or an investment, money contributed that is **tax-deductible.**
Example: Equity required for a development is $100,000, of which 50% is promised to be tax-deductible and therefore is *soft money.*
2. sometimes used to describe costs that do not physically go into construction, such as interest during construction, architect's fees, legal fees, etc.

SOIL BANK land held out of agricultural production in an effort to stabilize commodity prices and promote soil conservation. Subsidies to farmers participating in the soil bank program are provided by the U.S. Department of Agriculture.
Example: A farmer normally plants her land in corn. To avoid a surplus of corn production, the federal government pays the farmer to hold the land out of production for a year. The farmer is participating in the *soil bank* program.

SOLAR HEATING, HOT WATER see **active solar heating, passive solar heating.**

SOLE PROPRIETORSHIP ownership of a business, with no formal entity as a vehicle or structure. Contrast with **corporation, limited partnership, partnership.**
Example: Jessica goes into the real estate appraising business with all business activities in her own name and no partners. She is a *sole proprietor.*

SOUTHERN COLONIAL a large, early-American-style, 2- or 3-story frame house with a characteristic colonnade extending across the front. The roof extends over the colonnade.
Example: Figure 167.

FIG. 167. SOUTHERN COLONIAL HOUSE

SOUTHWEST PLAN an effort by the Federal Home Loan Bank to reconcile the problem of insolvent **savings and loan associations** in Texas in the late 1980s. Under the plan, insolvent S&Ls were placed under a **consignment** program through which they continued to operate with management assigned by the **FSLIC.** The plan was terminated by the passage of **FIRREA.**

SPANISH VILLA a Latin-style, asymmetrical, 1- to 3-story house with painted stucco exterior walls and red tile roof. **Example:** Figure 168.

FIG. 168. SPANISH VILLA

423

SPEC HOUSE a **single-family** dwelling constructed in anticipation of finding a buyer.
Example: Keene, a **developer,** is convinced there is local demand for 3-bedroom houses priced in the $80,000 range. Keene therefore constructs a number of *spec houses* and mounts a marketing campaign.

SPECIAL AGENT one who is engaged to act for another, with limited authority.
Example: A real estate **broker,** engaged by an owner to find a buyer, is considered a *special agent* of the owner.

SPECIAL ASSESSMENT an **assessment** made against a property to pay for a public **improvement** by which the assessed property is supposed to be especially benefited.
Example: The Lawsons own a house in a developing section of the city. When the city constructs curbs and gutters along their street, the Lawsons are levied a *special assessment,* in the form of a one-time tax, to pay for the construction.

SPECIALIST IN REAL ESTATE SECURITIES (SRS) a professional designation awarded by the **Real Estate Securities and Syndication Institute (RESSI).** Qualification is based on experience, education, examination, and demonstration of expertise in preparing a **syndication** report.

SPECIAL USE PERMIT a right granted by a local **zoning** authority to conduct certain activities within a zoning district. Such activities are considered conditional uses, which are permitted within the zone only upon special approval of the zoning authority. Also termed a "conditional use permit."
Example: A local government allows, as a conditional use, the operation of parking lots within its high-**density** residential zoning districts. A landowner wishing to operate a parking lot must obtain a *special use permit* following review of the plans of the development.

SPECIAL WARRANTY DEED a **deed** in which the **grantor** limits the title **warranty** given to the **grantee** to anyone claiming by, from, through, or under him, the grantor. The grantor does not warrant against **title** defects arising from conditions that existed before he owned the property. See **warranty deed.**
Example: Because of **bankruptcy** of its owner, a property goes under trusteeship. When the property is sold to satisfy creditor claims, the **trustee** conveys a *special warranty deed to* the buyer. This provides the buyer with warranty against claims incurred only during the time the property was held by the trustee.

SPECIFICATIONS detailed instructions provided in conjunction with plans and blueprints for construction. Specifications may stipulate the type of materials to be used, special construction techniques, dimensions, and colors.
Examples: The building *specifications* state that:
• number 3 lumber shall be used for all framing
• studs are to be on 16-inch centers
• all exterior surfaces shall be painted white

SPECIFIC PERFORMANCE a legal action in which the court requires a party to a **contract** to perform the **terms** of the contract when he has refused to fulfill his obligations. Used in real estate, since each **parcel** of land is unique.
Example: Baker agrees in writing to sell his house to Abel. Baker changes his mind when his adult daughter decides to buy the house. Baker offers to refund Abel's **earnest money** and pay living expenses for one month, but Abel insists on buying the house as agreed and sues for *specific performance*.

SPECULATIVE BUILDING land development or construction with no formal commitment from the end users of the finished product. Contrast with **custom building,** where the builder is under contract to produce a specific structure. The speculative builder anticipates that a demand exists or will form for the product when it is put on the market.
Examples:
• A developer subdivides a tract and markets the lots.
• A builder produces houses and puts them up for sale.
• A developer converts a building into condominiums and looks for buyers.
• A builder constructs a shopping center and leases space.

SPECULATOR one who invests with the anticipation that an event or series of events will occur to increase the value of the investment.
Example: The value of **single-family houses** has been appreciating rapidly for several months. Munson, a *speculator,* purchases several houses in anticipation that this rapid rate of appreciation will continue.

SPENDABLE INCOME same as **after-tax cash flow.**

SPLIT-LEVEL also called tri-level; a popular style of home, best suited for side-to-side slopes, in which a 1-story wing is attached between the levels of a 2-story wing.

SPOT ZONING the act of rezoning a **parcel** of land where all surrounding parcels are zoned for a different use, in particular where

the rezoning creates a use which is incompatible with surrounding land uses. Spot **zoning** is generally disallowed in the courts. **Example:** Figure 169 may be construed as *spot zoning*.

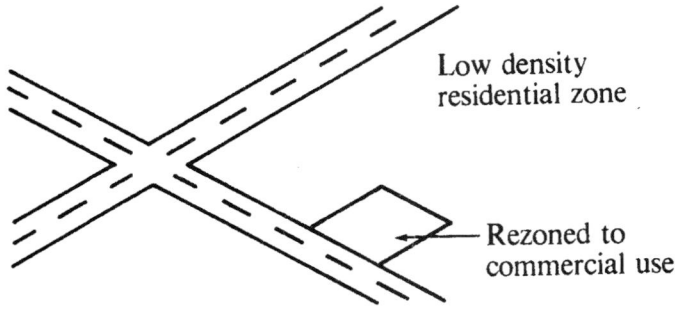

Low density
residential zone

Rezoned to
commercial use

FIG. 169. SPOT ZONING

SPREAD 1. the difference between the **bid** price and **asking price.**
Example: The buyer offers to pay $1,000 per **acre,** but the seller asks $1,300. The *spread* is $300.
2. the difference between the cost of money and the earnings rate.
Example: Good Money Savings and Loan pays an average interest rate of 10% to its depositors. It earns an average of 12% on its investments. The 2-point *spread* is adequate to pay **operating expenses** and leave some profit.

SPREADING AGREEMENT an agreement that extends the **collateral** of a loan to include several properties.
Example: Abel owns 7 shopping centers; all have **first mortgages.** He wants to borrow $5 million from a lender. The lender insists he sign a *spreading agreement* that gives a second **lien** on all 7 shopping centers.

SQUARE FOOTAGE the area, measured in square feet, of a piece of **real estate.** Generally measured from outside the exterior walls in the case of structures.
Example: The outside dimension of a rectangular home is 40 × 50 feet. Its *square footage* is 2,000.

SQUATTER'S RIGHTS the legal allowance to use the property of another in absence of an attempt by the owner to force **eviction;** this right may eventually be converted to **title** to the property over time by **adverse possession,** if recognized by state law.
Example: Various poor families take up residence in a vacant building, acquiring *squatter's rights.* Since ownership of the property is uncertain, no one attempts to evict the families.

SRA a person who is a Senior Residential Appraiser, a designation originally granted by the **Society of Real Estate Appraisers** for

residential **appraisers,** now offered by the Appraisal Institute.
Example: To assure that the appraiser was ethical and qualified, Good Money Savings Association engaged one with the *SRA* designation.

SREA Senior Real Estate Analyst, the highest designation once awarded by the **Society of Real Estate Appraisers.** *SREA*s could exchange this designation for the MAI.
Example: A complicated **condemnation** of multiuse properties required the services of an *SREA*.

SRPA Senior Real Property Appraiser. Once awarded by the **Society of Real Estate Appraisers** to those qualified to appraise **residential** and income-producing **property.** *SRPA*s are offered an opportunity to become MAIs upon meeting further experience and examination requirements.
Example: The *SRPA* is careful in estimating the **market value** of the subject office building. She considers all **appraisal** approaches before arriving at a value estimate.

STABLE MORTGAGE a mortgage loan instrument that combines fixed and adjustable rates in the same loan. The rate applied to the loan is a blend of a fixed rate and a rate that varies according to an **index.** The loan is a creation of General Electric Capital Mortgage Service, Inc. and **FNMA.**
Example: There are two versions of the *stable mortgage*: one with a 50/50 mix and one with a 75/25 mix of fixed and adjustable rates. If the loan is originated at an interest rate of 9% and the index justifies changing to the adjustable portion of the ratio to 10%, the 50/50 option would carry a rate of 9½%, while the 75/25 option would adjust to 9¼%.

STANDARD METROPOLITAN STATISTICAL AREA (SMSA) see **Metropolitan Statistical Area.**

STANDBY COMMITMENT a **commitment** by a lender to make available a sum of money at specified terms for a specified period. A **standby fee** is charged for this commitment. The borrower retains the **option** of closing the loan or allowing the commitment to lapse.
Example: See **standby fee.**

STANDBY FEE the sum required by a lender to provide a standby **commitment.** See **standby loan.** The fee is **forfeited** should the loan not be closed within a specified time.
Example: A **developer** obtains a **standby loan** on a project to be developed. The developer hopes **interest rates** will decline during the construction period so that permanent **financing** may

427

be arranged with **terms** better than those on the standby loan. However, a permanent loan commitment is required to obtain a **construction loan.** The developer pays a *standby fee* to compensate the lender for making the standby loan commitment. At the completion of construction, the developer has the **option** of exercising the **standby commitment** or forfeiting the fee.

STATE-CERTIFIED APPRAISER see **certified general appraiser, certified residental appraiser.**

STATUTE a law established by an act of legislature.
Example: When a bill is passed by the legislature and signed by the governor, it becomes a state *statute.* Similarly, when a bill is passed by Congress and signed by the president, it becomes a federal *statute.*

STATUTE OF FRAUDS a state law that provides that certain **contracts** must be in writing in order to be enforceable. Applied to **deeds, mortgages,** and other **real estate** contracts, with the exception of **leases** for periods shorter than one year.
Example: An oral contract for the sale of land is considered unenforceable under the *statute of frauds.*

STATUTE OF LIMITATIONS a specified statutory period after which a claimant is barred from enforcing his claim by suit.
Example: Abel bought a **limited partnership** interest in a real estate transaction. The **syndicator** failed to mention in the **prospectus** that the land is in a flood-prone area. Abel discovers the fact and sues 4 years later but is barred from collecting under the *statute of limitations.*

STATUTORY FORECLOSURE an foreclosure proceeding not conducted under court supervision. Contrast with **judicial foreclosure.**
Example: In many states, deeds of trust are used as mortgage instruments. In these cases, foreclosure sales are handled through a trustee acting according to the law and the stipulations of the mortgage contract. This process is a type of *statutory foreclosure.*

STATUTORY RIGHT OF REDEMPTION the legal right of a **mortgagor** to redeem the property after it has been sold at a **foreclosure sale.** This right is granted by state law for a limited period of time, depending on the state.
Example: In Alabama, a debtor has up to one year after foreclosure to regain possession of the property by paying up all indebtedness. In Texas, no such *statutory right of redemption* exists, so that all foreclosure sales are final unless overturned by the courts on procedure.

STEERING an illegal practice of limiting the housing shown to a certain ethnic group.

Example: Though the minority couple wanted to be shown all available rental housing that they could afford, the unlicensed person *steered* them from certain neighborhoods.

STEP LOAN a type of **adjustable-rate mortgage** for which the interest rate is adjusted only once during the term of the loan. Therefore, the loan shares some of the features of both fixed-rate and adjustable-rate loans.

Example: A typical *step loan* features a fixed interest rate for the first 7 years of the term. The interest rate is then adjusted according to an index to better match current market interest rates. Some loans also have caps that limit how much the interest rate may be raised.

STEPPED-UP BASIS an income tax term used to describe a change in the **adjusted tax basis** of property, allowed for certain transactions. The old basis is increased to **market value** upon inheritance, as opposed to a **carry-over basis** in the event of a **tax-free exchange.**

Example: Dooley dies, leaving land worth $100,000. The land was purchased for $20,000, but the heirs receive a *stepped-up basis* to the **fair market value** at death. The $80,000 **unrealized gain** to Dooley escapes **capital gains** tax.

STEP-UP LEASE see **graduated lease.**

STICK-STYLE OR CARPENTER GOTHIC HOUSE a nineteenth-century-style house with exposed framing members, high steep roofs, complex silhouettes, diagonal braces, and a large amount of gingerbread trim.

Example: Figure 170.

STIPULATIONS the **terms** within a written **contract.**

Example: A sales contract contains *stipulations* concerning the type of **financing** the buyer must be able to obtain, the price, proration of **closing** cost between buyer and seller, and the date and location of the closing.

STOP CLAUSE in a **lease, stipulates** an amount of **operating expense** above which the tenant must bear. Often the base amount is the amount of expense for the first full year of operation under the lease.

Example: The *stop clause* requires the tenant to pay all **utilities** in excess of $2,500 per year. If utilities are less than that amount, the landlord pays them.

STRAIGHT LEASE see **flat lease.**

Exposed framing members

High steep roof

Lots of "Gingerbread"

Ornate windows and doors

Complex silhouette

FIG. 170. STICK-STYLE HOUSE

STRAIGHT-LINE DEPRECIATION equal annual reductions in the **book value** of property. It is used in accounting for replacement and tax purposes. See **depreciation (accounting).**
Example: A property has a **depreciable basis** of $275,000. For tax purposes, a **useful life** of 27½ years is used with no **salvage value.** Using *straight-line depreciation,* the book value of the property is decreased by $10,000 ($275,000/27.5) per year. The tax deduction for depreciation is $10,000 per year.

STRAIGHT-LINE RECAPTURE RATE the part of a **capitalization rate** that accounts for the annual erosion of a **wasting asset** by assuming an equal amount of loss in value each year of the **useful life** of the asset.
Example: A retail building's **useful life** is estimated at 50 years. The *straight-line recapture rate* is 2% per year, which will recover the asset cost over its estimated useful life. The 2% should be added to the **discount rate** to derive the **capitalization rate.**

STRAW MAN one who purchases property that is, in turn, **conveyed** to another for the purpose of concealing the identity of the eventual purchaser.

Example: A **developer** is assembling land, for a **subdivision,** from a large number of individually owned plots. To avoid the possibility that a few landowners will hold out for high prices, the developer uses *straw men* to purchase the **parcels. Agents** of the developer purchase plots in their own names and later convey the land to the developer.

STRICT FORECLOSURE a foreclosure proceeding in which the **mortgagee** has the right to possess the mortgaged property directly upon default on the mortgage agreement. This type of foreclosure is rarely used in contemporary markets.
Example: Under a *strict foreclosure* proceeding, the lender requested the court to order the delinquent borrower to pay the debt within the next 2 months. When the borrower failed to do so, the lender took possession of the property and canceled the indebtedness.

STRIP DEVELOPMENT OR STRIP SHOPPING CENTER a form of commercial land use in which each establishment is afforded direct access to a major thoroughfare; generally associated with intensive use of signs to attract passers-by. Generally without an **anchor tenant**.
Example: Map of *strip development* (Figure 171).

Auto parts store	Fast food	Tire store	Car wash	Service station

Fast food	Shoe store	Hardware store	Fast food

FIG. 171. STRIP DEVELOPMENT

STRUCTURE any constructed improvement to a **site.**
 Examples: *Structures* include:
 • buildings
 • fencing and enclosures
 • garages
 • gazebos, greenhouses, and kiosks
 • sheds and utility buildings

SUBAGENCY the relationship under which a sales agent tries to sell a property listed with another agent. This situation is common under a **multiple listing service (MLS).** A listing contract is taken by a listing broker and entered into the MLS, from which any member broker may sell the property. The listing broker and the selling broker split the commission.
Example: Any broker attempting to sell properties in the multiple listing service inventory does so under a *subagency* agreement stipulating the right of each agent to a portion of the commission.

SUBCHAPTER S CORPORATION a **corporation** with a limited number of stockholders (35 or fewer) that elects not to be taxed as a regular corporation, and meets certain other requirements. Shareholders include, in their personal tax return, their pro-rata share of **capital gains, ordinary income, tax preference** items, and so on. See **passive income.**
Example: To avoid **double taxation,** the ABC Real Estate Corporation elects *Subchapter S* status. Its shareholders will include corporate income in their own tax return, whether or not they receive a dividend. The corporation itself will not pay an income tax, but will file a tax return.

SUBCONTRACTOR one who performs services under **contract** to a **general contractor.**
Example: A general contractor agrees to construct a building for a **developer.** The contractor arranges with individual *subcontractors* who are specifically responsible to the contractor for performance of carpentry, plumbing, electrical, and masonry work.

SUBDIVIDER one who partitions a **tract** of land for the purpose of selling the individual plots. If the land is improved in any way, the subdivider becomes a **developer.**
Example: Olsen, a *subdivider,* purchases a 100-acre tract of land. The tract is subdivided into 5-acre plots that are marketed to investors and developers.

SUBDIVIDING dividing a **tract** of land into smaller tracts.
Example: See **subdivider.**

SUBDIVISION a **tract** of land divided into lots suitable for homebuilding purposes. Some states and localities require that a subdivision **plat** be recorded.
Example: A residential *subdivision* (Figure 172).

SUBJECT PROPERTY in appraisal, the property being appraised.
Example: The *subject property* compares favorably with other homes in the neighborhood.

FIG. 172. RESIDENTIAL SUBDIVISION

SUBJECT TO acquiring property with an existing mortgage, but not becoming **personally liable** for the debt. Contrast with **assumption of mortgage.**
Example: Abel bought **land** for $1,000 cash, *subject to* a $99,000 mortgage. If Abel defaults on the **mortgage** he will lose the cash **down payment** but is not responsible for the $99,000 **debt.**

SUBJECT TO MORTGAGE circumstance in which a buyer takes **title** to mortgaged **real property** but is not personally liable for the payment of the amount due. The buyer must make payments in order to keep the property; however, with default, only the buyer's **equity** in that property is lost. Contrast **assumption of mortgage.**
Example: Queen purchases a house from Parsons *subject to* the existing *mortgage.* Parson's mortgage has an outstanding balance of $40,000 and the sales price is $60,000. Queen pays Parsons $20,000 in cash and takes over the payments on the mortgage. Should Queen **default,** Parsons is liable under the **promissory note** given to the lender.

SUBLEASE a **lease** from a **lessee** to another lessee. The new lessee is a sublessee or subtenant. See **sandwich lease.**
Example: Acme, Inc., leases office space under a 10-year lease. Acme wishes to relocate but cannot break the lease. With the landlord's permission, Acme finds a subtenant, Medcorp, to sign a *sublease* for the space. Medcorp pays rent to Acme, which, in turn, continues to pay rent to the landlord.

SUBLET see **sublease.**

SUBORDINATED GROUND LEASE a **lease** where the **mortgage** has priority over the **ground lease.**
Example: Pruable holds a $3-million **mortgage lien** on a **shopping center.** The **property** owner, Dealmaker, sells the land to Subru for $1 million and agrees to **lease** it back for $100,000 annual **rent** over 30 years. When Dealmaker fails to pay Pruable the interest due, Pruable **forecloses** on the entire property. Because of the *subordinated ground lease*, Pruable gains **title** to the land and building.

SUBORDINATION moving to a lower **priority,** as a **lien** would if it changes from a **first mortgage** to a **second mortgage.**
Example: The land seller who held a first mortgage allowed *subordination* so the **development loan** could be arranged. In return the seller is promised mortgage **retirement** in 2 years.

SUBORDINATION CLAUSE a clause or document that permits a **mortgage** recorded at a later date to take **priority** over an existing mortgage.
Example: Even though the **first mortgage** was recently **retired,** the **second mortgage** remained a second mortgage. The *subordination clause* in the second mortgage provided that a mortgage that replaces the existing first mortgage will become a first mortgage; the second mortgage will not move up in priority.

SUBSTITUTION in appraisal, the principle that market value is indicated by the value of another property with similar utility. A typical buyer is assumed to be indifferent to substituting one property for the other.
Example: By the principle of *substitution,* the market value of a property can be estimated by analyzing sales prices of comparable properties.

SUBSURFACE RIGHTS same as **mineral rights.**

SUBURB a town or unincorporated developed area in close proximity to a city. Suburbs, largely residential, are often dependent on the city for employment and support services; generally characterized by low-**density** development relative to the city.
Example: Figure 173.

SUMMARY POSSESSION same as **eviction, actual.**

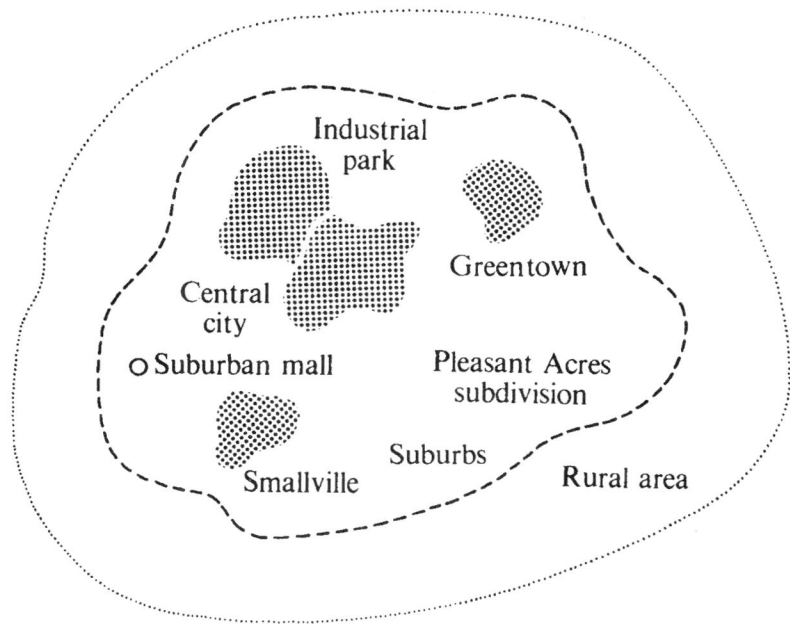

FIG. 173. SUBURB

SUM-OF-YEARS-DIGITS DEPRECIATION in tax and accounting, a method of allocating the cost of an **asset** over its **useful life.** It requires a fraction to be computed each year, which is applied against the depreciable amount. The numerator is the number of years left to be depreciated. The denominator is the sum of the years digits of the depreciable life. The formula for the denominator is:

$$\frac{N(N+1)}{2}$$

where N = the depreciable life. See **accelerated depreciation.**
Example: An automobile used in business cost $10,000 and has a 4-year depreciable life. *Sum-of-the-years-digits depreciation* results in the deductions shown in Table 51.

TABLE 51
SUM-OF-YEARS-DIGITS DEPRECIATION

Year	Fraction	Asset	Depreciation deduction
1	$\frac{4}{10}$	$10,000	$4,000
2	$\frac{3}{10}$	10,000	3,000
3	$\frac{2}{10}$	10,000	2,000
4	$\frac{1}{10}$	10,000	1,000

435

SUMP as part of a drainage system, a pit in the basement to collect excess moisture and liquids. To avoid flooding, a *sump pump* may be installed to remove accumulated water in the sump pit.

Example: Figure 174.

FIG. 174. SUMP DRAINAGE SYSTEM

SUNSPACE a room, generally with glass walls and roof, designed to collect solar heat.

Example: By adding a *sunspace* to the south side of their home, the Sols were able to save money on their winter heating bills.

SUPERADEQUACY a component of **real estate** that is beyond what is needed in the structure.

Example: Air conditioning in an Alaskan home would be a *superadequacy.*

SURETY one who guarantees the performance of another.

Example: Ridley employs a **contractor** to construct a house. Under the **contract,** the contractor is required to obtain a **performance bond** against failure to perform the work. Ace Bonding Co. provides the bond, thereby acting as a *surety.* Should the contractor fail to perform, Ace compensates Ridley for damages.

SURFACE RIGHTS the right to use and modify the surface area of real property. In Texas, *surface rights* are subservient to **mineral rights.** In the absence of an agreement to the contrary, an oil driller who owns the mineral rights may operate anywhere on the surface of the property. See **air rights.**

Example: Though the landowner retained the *surface rights* to the land, his ability to build was limited because he had sold off the air rights.

SURRENDER the cancellation of a **lease** by mutual consent of the **lessor** and the **lessee.**

Example: Simmons rents a house under a 2-year lease. Simmons is forced to move due to a job transfer. The landlord agrees to allow Simmons to *surrender* the **premises** if Simmons finds an acceptable new tenant.

SURVEY 1. the process by which a **parcel** of land is measured and its area ascertained.
2. the plan showing the measurements, boundaries, area, and contours.
Example: A simplified *survey* (Figure 175).

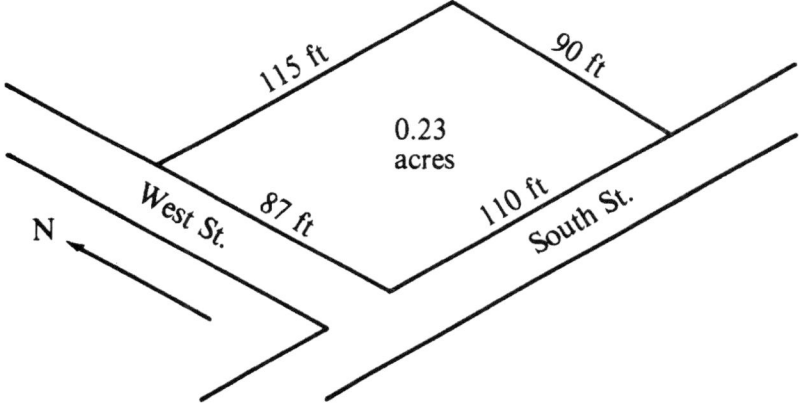

FIG. 175. SURVEY

SURVEYOR one who prepares **surveys.**
Example: Prior to selling her property, Collins had to hire a *surveyor* to prepare a survey of the land.

SURVIVORSHIP the right of a joint tenant or tenants to maintain ownership rights following the death of another joint tenant. Survivorship prevents heirs of the deceased from making claims against the property. See **joint tenancy.**
Example: Travers and Vance Mead are brothers who own an apartment building, with the right of survivorship. When Travers Mead dies, Vance Mead, through *survivorship,* becomes sole owner of the building.

SWEAT EQUITY value added to a property due to **improvements** as a result of work performed personally by the owner.
Example: The Watsons purchase an old house for $20,000. Working in their spare time, the Watsons repair and repaint the structure to the point that the property is valued at $30,000. The $10,000 increment is *sweat equity*.

SWEETENER something included in a transaction to make it more acceptable.

Example: The seller agreed to pay insurance for up to one year as a *sweetener* for the buyer.

SWISS CHALET a Swiss-style 1½- to 2½-story, gable roof house with extensive natural decorative woodwork on the exterior.
Example: Figure 176.

Gable roof · 1½ to 2½ stories · Large glass windows · Natural wood look · Decorative wood work · Open porches · Curved cornice

FIG. 176 SWISS CHALET

SYD sum-of-years-digits (method of depreciation).

SYNDICATION a method of selling property whereby a sponsor (or **syndicator**) sells interests to investors. May take the form of a **partnership, limited partnership, tenancy in common, corporation, or Subchapter S Corporation.**
Example: A *syndication* was formed whereby limited partnership interests were sold to investors. The partnership bought land with the **equity** raised.

SYNDICATOR a person in business who sells an investment in shares or units.
Example: Collins, licensed as both a real estate **broker** and a **securities** salesperson, is a *syndicator*. She contracts with investors to buy shopping centers, then sells **partnership** interests conveying ownership in the centers to 30 different investors.

T

TACKING adding on to a time period.

Example: A squatter was on property for 10 years, moved away for one year, then returned for 10 years. If he were allowed to *tack* both 10-year periods, his claim to **squatter's rights** to the land would be a strong one.

TAKEOUT FINANCING a **commitment** to provide permanent **financing** following construction of a planned project. The takeout commitment is generally predicated upon specific conditions, such as a certain percentage of unit sales or leases, for the permanent loan to "takeout" the **construction loan.** Most construction lenders require takeout financing.

Example: Young, a developer, applied for a construction loan on a small office building. The construction lender requires Young to obtain *takeout financing* in the form of a commitment from a permanent lender. The takeout loan will be granted following construction and leasing of at least 65% of **net rentable area** to creditworthy tenants.

TAKING 1. acquisition of a **parcel** of land through **condemnation.**

Example: The Highway Department acquires much of its **right-of-way** for new roads through *takings*. These are usually parcels whose owners are unwilling to settle on a price through negotiation.

2. in land use law, application of **police power** restrictions to a parcel of land that are so restrictive as to preclude any reasonable use.

Example: A local community zone is a parcel of land for agricultural use. The owner argues the land is unsuitable for growing crops but could be used for building homes. The owner's argument is the **zoning** is a *taking* of the property without just compensation, which is contrary to the Fourteenth Amendment to the U.S. Constitution.

TANDEM PLAN a program of the **Government National Mortgage Association (GNMA)** working together with the **Federal National Mortgage Association (FNMA)** to provide low-interest rate home loans.

Example: Under the *tandem* plan, FNMA purchases qualified low-interest rate mortgages at a discount from GNMA. GNMA absorbs the loss as a subsidy to the qualified low-income home buyer.

TANGIBLE PROPERTY real estate and other valuables which can be seen and touched.
Example: A home, farm, furniture and fixtures are types of *tangible properties.* In contrast, a deed, mortgage, or stock certificate are intangibles in that they represent ownership in something but are not the thing itself.

TAX a charge levied upon persons or things by a government.
Examples:
• ad valorem *tax*
• county *tax*
• excise *tax*
• income *tax*
• property *tax*
• sales *tax*
• school *tax*
• use *tax*

TAXABLE VALUE see **assessed value.**

TAX AND INSURANCE ESCROW an account required by a mortgage lender to fund annual property tax assessments and hazard insurance premiums for the mortgaged property. Funded through monthly contributions by the mortgagor. See **PITI.**
Example: When the mortgage loan was originated, a *tax and insurance escrow* was set up by the lender to pay tax and insurance expenses. The borrower's monthly mortgage payment was increased by an amount necessary to accumulate a balance in the account sufficient to cover these expenses.

TAX ASSESSOR see **assessor.**

TAX BASE the collective value of property, income or other taxable activity or assets subject to a tax. Tax revenues are computed as the tax base times the tax rate. For property taxation, the tax base is the total assessed value of all taxable property less exemptions.
Example: American Widgetworks plans to build a new plant in Centerville. The plant will add $15 million to the property *tax base* of the city.

TAX BASIS same as **basis (tax);** see **adjusted tax basis.**

TAX BRACKET marginal rate for income taxes; the percentage of each additional dollar in income required to be paid as income taxes.
Example: Abel is considering an investment that will produce $1,000 in taxable income for the next year. Abel's taxable income is currently $20,000, which places Abel in the 28% *tax*

440

bracket. Thus, should Abel make the investment, $280 of the $1,000 will be paid in taxes.

TAX CREDIT a reduction against income tax payments that would otherwise be due. Contrast with **tax deductions** that reduce taxable income .
Examples: *Tax credits* that are available to real estate owners include:
• rehabilitation tax credits for older properties and **historic structures**
• low-income housing

TAX DEDUCTIBLE a type of expense that can be used to reduce taxable income. See **tax deduction.**
Example: Interest and **ad valorem** taxes are generally *tax deductible* for all types of property. **Depreciation,** repairs, **maintenance, utilities,** and other ordinary and necessary expenses are *tax deductible* for **income property.**

TAX DEDUCTION one that can be used to reduce taxable income. See **tax deductible.** Contrast with **tax credit.**
Example: Abel has a $75,000 annual salary and $25,000 worth of *tax deductions.* Taxes for the year are figured on taxable income of $50,000.

TAX DEED the type of instrument given to a **grantee** by a government that had claimed the **property** for unpaid taxes.
Example: The city acquired a **parcel** of land because the former owner failed to pay **ad valorem** taxes. The city then auctioned it. Baker, the highest bidder, received a *tax deed* as evidence of ownership.

TAX-EXEMPT PROPERTY **real property** that is not subject, in whole or in part, to **ad valorem** property taxes.
Examples: In many local communities, the following types of property are *tax-exempt property:*
• churches
• government land and buildings
• **homesteads** (in part)
• solar-powered heating systems

TAX FORECLOSURE the process of enforcing a lien against property for nonpayment of delinquent property taxes. Taxing authorities hold a superior lien against all taxable property to enforce the payment of their taxes. See **foreclosure.**
Example: The owner of the old apartment house had failed to pay property taxes on the building for the past 2 years. The county was forced to pursue a *tax foreclosure* against the property and have it sold at auction.

TAX-FREE EXCHANGE same as tax-deferred exchange. See **Section 1031.**

TAX LIEN a **debt** attached against **property** for failing to pay taxes.
Example: A *tax lien* may be imposed for failing to pay the following taxes:
- city
- county
- estate
- income
- payroll
- sales
- school

TAX MAP a document showing the location, dimensions, and other information pertaining to a **parcel** of land subject to **property taxes.** Maps are generally bound into books and kept as public records at the local tax office.
Example: A *tax map* showing parcel 65 in district A5-300 (Figure 177).

FIG. 177. TAX MAP

TAX PREFERENCE ITEMS certain types of **income** or deductions that are added to adjusted **gross income** to calculate the **alternative minimum tax.**
Examples: *Tax preference items* in 1987 and thereafter include:
- **depreciation** on **real estate** to the extent it exceeds 40-year **straight-line depreciation**

442

- **accelerated depreciation** on leased **personal property** to the extent it exceeds **straight-line depreciation**
- bargain element of an incentive stock option
- certain rapid write-offs
- losses from passive activity investment
- certain itemized deductions (state and local income taxes, real estate taxes, medical expenses not greater than 10% of adjusted gross income)
- miscellaneous deductions in excess of 2% of adjusted gross income
- all interest expense, except home mortgage interest and investment interest, to the extent of net investment income
- interest on certain tax exempt bonds issued after August 7, 1986
- the excess of value deducted over the cost of property given to charitable organizations.

TAX RATE the ratio of a tax **assessment** to the amount being taxed.
Example: In a certain community, the *tax rate* for **property taxes** is $0.35 per $100 of **assessed value.** A home is valued at $20,000. A **homestead exemption** of $2,000 is allowed for this type of property. The tax collected is

$$\$0.35 \times \frac{(\$20,000 - \$2,000)}{\$100} = \$63.00$$

TAX ROLL the list of all properties subject to a tax in a county or other property taxing jurisdiction. It identifies all properties and indicates their assessed values.
Example: A *tax roll* was prepared by the county tax assessor's office, showing $100 million worth of assessed value in the jurisdiction. The county commissioners needed to collect $1 million of taxes to run the government this year, so they applied a 10 mill tax rate to the tax roll.

TAX SALE the sale of property after a period of nonpayment of taxes. The **grantee** receives a **tax deed.** In most states the **defaulting** party has a **redemption period** during which he may pay the unpaid taxes, interest, court costs, and the purchase price to redeem the property.
Example: The failure to pay property **ad valorem** taxes resulted in a *tax sale* of Abel's land. Since the property was worth more than the back taxes, Abel erred by failing to pay.

TAX SHELTER an investment that produces after-tax income that is greater than before-tax income. The investment may produce **before-tax cash flow** while generating losses to shield, from taxation, income from sources outside the investment.

Example: Dunn purchases an income-producing property which provides *tax shelter*. In the first year, the property produces a **net operating income** of $100,000. **Debt service** is $80,000, of which $75,000 is **interest**. Dunn's **before-tax cash flow** is $20,000. First-year **depreciation** is $50,000, so that a tax loss is generated as shown in Table 52.

TABLE 52
TAX SHELTER

$100,000	Net operating income
− 75,000	Interest deduction
− 50,000	Depreciation deduction
($25,000)	Taxable income (loss)

Dunn not only pays no tax on the $20,000 cash flow but might be allowed to shelter $25,000 of income from other sources. The Tax Reform Act of 1986 places limits and restrictions on the deductibility of passive losses. See **passive income, active participation, material participation.**

TAX STOP a clause in a **lease** that stops a **lessor** from paying **property taxes** above a certain amount. See **escalator clause, stop clause.**
Example: The *tax stop* in the lease required the tenant to pay all property taxes in excess of $1,200.

TDR transferable development rights.

TEASER RATE a contract interest rate charged on an adjustable-rate mortgage for the initial adjustment interval that is significantly lower than the fully indexed rate at the time. It is an incentive to encourage borrowers to accept adjustable-rate mortgage loans. In general, the interest rate reverts to the fully indexed rate at the first adjustment date. See **fully indexed rate.**
Example: An adjustable rate mortgage is indexed to the average contract rate for mortgage loans made by all lenders. Although the current average rate is 10%, the loan is offered at a *teaser rate* of 8%.

TENANCY the right of possession of real property. May refer to ownership or occupancy. See **tenancy in common, joint tenancy.**

TENANCY AT SUFFERANCE tenancy established when a person who had been a lawful tenant wrongfully remains in **possession** of property after expiration of a **lease.**
Example: A *tenant at sufferance* may be ejected from the property anytime the landlord decides to do so.

TENANCY AT WILL a **license** to use or occupy lands and buildings at the will of the owner. The tenant may decide to leave the property at any time or must leave at the landlord's will. Agreement may be oral or written. See also **emblements.**
Example: Under an oral agreement, Abel is using Baker's property. Baker may ask Abel to leave at any time; Abel may leave at any time.

TENANCY BY THE ENTIRETY an **estate** that exists only between husband and wife with equal right of **possession** and enjoyment during their joint lives and with the **right of survivorship**—i.e., when one dies, the property goes to the surviving tenant. Recognized in some states.
Example: A married couple owns property as *tenants by the entirety.* Neither can convey his or her part of the property during their lives unless the other consents. A creditor of only one spouse is generally prevented from claiming property held by the other spouse in *tenancy by the entirety.* Divorced spouses become tenants in common. See **tenancy in common.**

TENANCY FOR LIFE same as **life estate.**

TENANCY FOR YEARS created by a **lease** for a fixed term, such as 2 months, 3 years, 10 years, and so on.
Example: Big Buy Groceries leased a building for 10 years, beginning April 1, 1984, and ending March 31, 1994, 10 years later. The company has a *tenancy for years.*

TENANCY FROM YEAR TO YEAR same as **leasehold.**

TENANCY IN COMMON an ownership of **realty** by 2 or more persons, each of whom has an **undivided interest,** without the right of **survivorship.** Upon the death of one of the owners, the ownership share of the decedent is inherited by the party or parties designated in the decedent's **will.** Compare with **partition. See syndication.**
Example: A syndicate is formed using a *tenancy in common.* Under this arrangement all of the investors have to sign the deed for the entire property to be conveyed. Each tenant may convey his or her share independently.

TENANCY IN SEVERALTY ownership of property by one person or one legal entity (corporate ownership).
Example: Abel owns land as a *tenancy in severalty.* He enjoys the absence of partners or cotenants.

TENANT one who is given **possession** of real estate for a fixed period or at will. See **lessee, tenancy at will.**
Example: Enwright signs a **lease** to rent office space. Enwright is a *tenant* of the office building.

TENANT FIXTURES **fixtures** added to leased real estate by a **lessee** that, by contract or by law, may be removed by the lessee upon expiration of the lease.
Example: Joseph leased a building to use for a dry-cleaning business. Much of Joseph's equipment had to be attached firmly to the building; however, since the fixtures were used in his business, they were *tenant fixtures*, and he could remove them when the lease expired.

TENDER 1. an **offer** to perform an obligation, together with actual performance or evidence of present ability to perform.
2. to perform under a contract.
3. to pay or deliver.
Example: Abel thought Baker would **default** under the **sales contract** but did not know for certain until Baker *tendered* the deed.

TENEMENTS 1. possessions that are permanent and fixed; structures attached to land.
Example: Real property consists of *tenements* and *hereditaments*: tenements are the physical and legal property that may be enjoyed by the owner; hereditaments are property one can pass on to one's heirs.
2. older apartment units.
Example. In the inner city, many people live in *tenements*.

TENURE the nature of an occupant's ownership rights; an indication of whether one is an owner or a tenant.
Example: For economic analysis, one may differentiate the occupied housing stock by *tenure*: one portion may be owner-occupied; the other portion may be renter-occupied.

TENURE IN LAND the mode in which a person holds an **estate** in lands.
Example: If one purchases all rights to real estate, *tenure in land* is **fee simple** ownership. A tenant's *tenure in land* is a **leasehold**.

TERM the period of time during which something is in effect.
Example: Fowler leases an apartment for a *term* of one year. At the end of the year, Fowler moves from the apartment and buys a house. To finance the purchase, Fowler gets a mortgage loan with a *term* of 30 years. At the end of 30 years, the loan will be paid off.

TERM, AMORTIZATION for a loan, the period of time during which **principal and interest** payments must be made; generally the time needed to amortize the loan fully.
Example: *Amortization terms* of 25 and 30 years are commonly used on real estate mortgage loans. Monthly principal and interest payments are set to fully liquidate loans over the term.

TERMITE CLAUSE a provision in a sales contract that allows the buyer to have the property inspected for termite infestation. In general, if termites are discovered, the buyer may require the seller to treat the property or the buyer may cancel the contract. Most clauses now use the term **wood-destroying insects** to protect against other types of insects that harm structures, such as the powder post beetle and old house borer.
Example: Under the *termite clause* in the sales contract, the buyer may get the home inspected before the closing. The seller will pay to exterminate any termites found. The buyer pays for the inspection.

TERMITE INSPECTION an examination of a structure by qualified personnel to determine the existence of infestation by **termites.** Often required by the **terms** of a **sales contract.** See **wood-destroying insect.**
Example: Gross sells a house to Handy. As protection for Handy, the sales contract stipulates that a *termite inspection* will be performed at Gross' expense and the sale is contingent on a finding of no termite infestation.

TERMITES insects that bore into wood and destroy it.
Example: *Termites* are a threat to any wooden structure or members of a structure. *Termites* generally act to weaken support members in proximity to the ground or in contact with it. *Termites* are often confused with winged adult ants. The differences are shown in Figure 178.

TERM LOAN one with a set maturity date, typically without **amortization.**
Example: Terry purchased a tract of land for $15,000, and borrowed $10,000 from a lender with a 5-year *term loan*. The interest rate is 10% annually; the entire principal is due at the end of the 5-year term.

TERMS conditions and arrangements specified in a **contract.**
Example: A **sales contract** will generally include *terms* relating to the price, **financing** available to the buyer, contingencies based on the condition of the property, **how to prorate closing costs,** and items of personal property included in the sale. See also **as is, cancellation clause, contingency clause.**

TESTAMENT a **will.** Generally to dispose of personal property. Common usage employs the words **will,** *testament,* and *last will and testament* as synonyms.
Example: Ewen wrote her *testament* that directed the disposition of her property upon her death.

WINGED ANT

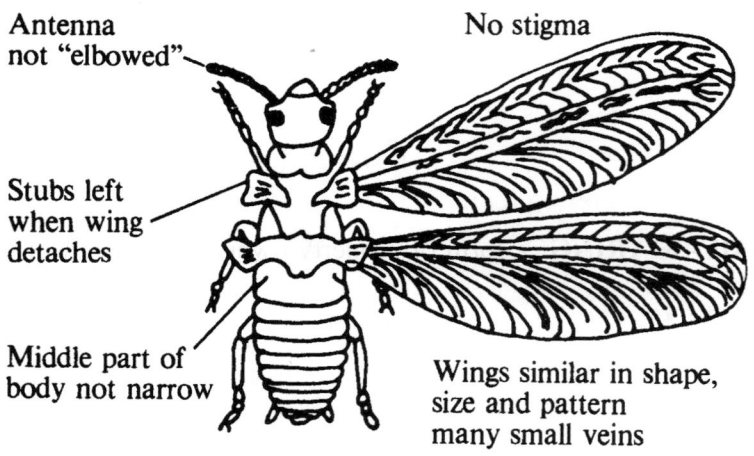

TERMITE

FIG. 178. DISTINGUISHING TERMITES FROM ANTS

TESTATE having made a valid **will.** Contrast with **intestate.**
Example: A person who dies *testate* has left a will disposing of property.

TESTATOR a person who makes a **will.**
Example: By will the *testator* left his property to his wife.

TESTATRIX a woman who makes a **will.**
Example: By will the *testatrix* left her property to her husband.

448

TESTIMONIUM a clause that cites the act and date in a **deed** or other **conveyance.** Before signing a deed, the grantor should make sure that everything is in order, e.g., the spelling of names and legal descriptions. This is the *testimonium* clause.
Example: *Testimonium* clause: "In witness whereof, the parties to these presents have hereunto set their hands and seals this day and year written above."

THIRD PARTY one who is not directly involved in a transaction or **contract** but may be involved or affected by it.
Example: An apartment owner sells the property to a **condominium** converter. The **tenants,** as *third parties,* may be forced to move or buy their units at the expiration of their **lease.**
Example: A trusted *third party* was designated as **escrow** agent by the **principals.**

TIL truth-in-lending law. See **Regulation Z.**

TIME IS OF THE ESSENCE a phrase that, when inserted in a **contract,** requires that all references to specific dates and times of day noted in the contract be interpreted exactly. In its absence extreme delays might be acceptable.
Example: A **sales contract** contains the clause: *time is of the essence.* This statement reinforces the content of other clauses, such as the time provided to the buyer to arrange **financing** and the date of **closing.**

TIME-SHARING a form of property ownership under which a **property** is held by a number of people, each with the right of **possession** for a specified time interval. Time-sharing is most commonly applied to resort and vacation properties.
Example: Ingram is an owner in a *time-sharing* arrangement for a lakefront cottage. Ingram is entitled to use the cottage each year from July 1 to July 15. Use of the property during the remainder of the year is divided among other owners. All property expenses are paid by an owner's association to which Ingram pays an annual fee.

TIME VALUE OF MONEY a concept that money available now is worth more than the same amount in the future because of its potential earning capacity.
Example: See **present value of one, present value of annuity.**

TITLE evidence that the owner of land is in lawful **possession** thereof; evidence of ownership. See also **adverse possession,** certificate of title, **clear title, color of title, cloud on the title, marketable title.**
Example: *Title* to land does not merely imply that a person has the right of **possession,** because one may have the right to pos-

session and have no title. Title does ordinarily signify rights to possession in addition to evidence of ownership.

Example: Abel sold land to Baker. *Title* to the **property** was transferred at closing by the deed Baker received.

TITLE ABSTRACT see **abstract of title.**

TITLE COMPANY one in the business of examining **title** to real estate and/or issuing **title insurance.**

Example: The Chicago Lawyer Title Company searched courthouse records to be sure that Whitman would get **marketable title** on a house she planned to buy. They charged a $500 one-time **premium.** The bank wouldn't issue a loan without the policy.

TITLE DEFECT an unresolved claim against the ownership of property which prevents presentation of a marketable title. Such claims may arise from failure of the owner's spouse, or former part owner, to sign a deed, current liens against the property, or an interruption in the title records to a property. See **cloud on the title.**

Example: Prior to the closing, the attorney for the title insurance company discovered a *title defect* which delayed the transaction. It seems the property had once been owned by the seller's parents and a deed had never been signed over to the seller.

TITLE INSURANCE an insurance policy that protects the holder from loss sustained by **defects in the title.**

Example: When property is purchased, most **mortgage** lenders require the buyer to obtain *title insurance.* After a satisfactory **title search** and in exchange for a one-time **premium,** the title company insures the buyer against most claims to the title of the property.

TITLE REPORT a document indicating the current state of the **title,** such as **easements, covenants, liens** and any **defects.** The title report does not describe the **chain of title.** See **abstract of title.**

Example: A buyer wishes to assure receipt of **clear title** to a property. The buyer authorizes a *title search* by an experienced attorney. The attorney examines the public records for all recorded encumbrances and past claims. The attorney renders to the buyer an **abstract of the title.**

TITLE SEARCH an examination of the public records to determine the ownership and **encumbrances** affecting **real property.**

Example: A buyer wishes to assure receiving **clear title** to a property. The buyer authorizes a *title search* by an experienced attorney. The attorney examines the public records for all recorded encumbrances and past claims. The attorney renders to the buyer an **abstract of the title.**

TITLE THEORY STATES states in which the law splits the **title** of mortgaged property into legal title, held by the lender, and **equitable title,** held by the borrower. The borrower gains full title to the property upon **retiring** the mortgage debt. The lender is granted more immediate cure to a **default** than in **lien theory states.** Contrast with **lien theory states.**
Example: In *title theory states,* mortgage lenders may possess the property upon default of the borrower. In **lien theory states,** lenders must go through the process of **foreclosure.**

TO HAVE AND TO HOLD CLAUSE see **habendum clause.**

TOPOGRAPHY the state of the surface of the land; may be rolling, rough, flat, etc.
Example: The *topography* in Oklahoma is mostly flat; in West Virginia, mountainous; in Ohio, rolling.

TORRENS SYSTEM a **title** registration system used in some states; the condition of the **title** can easily be discovered without resorting to a **title search.**
Example: A property owner in Chicago wishes to register the property under the *Torrens System.* An application is made with the appropriate court. Following a title examination and **notice** to all who wish to make a claim, the court issues a **certificate of title** setting forth the nature of the applicant's title. When the owner sells the property, a new certificate is issued to the buyer. Anyone establishing a claim to the property following registration is compensated from a special fund for any losses suffered.

TORT a wrongful act that is neither a crime nor a **breach of contract,** but that renders the perpetrator **liable** to the victim for damages.
Examples:
• **nuisance**
• **trespass**
• negligence
An example of negligence is a landlord's failure to fix reported defective wiring. The law provides remedy for damages from resulting fire.

TOWN HOUSE a **dwelling** unit, generally having 2 or more floors and attached to other similar units via **party walls.** Town houses are often used in **planned unit developments** and **condominium** developments, which provide for clustered or attached housing and common open space. See **cluster housing, row house, brownstone.**
Example: Figure 179.

FIG. 179. TOWN HOUSES

TOWNSHIP a 6-mile square **tract** delineated by **government rectangular survey.**
Example: 16 *townships* (Figure 180).

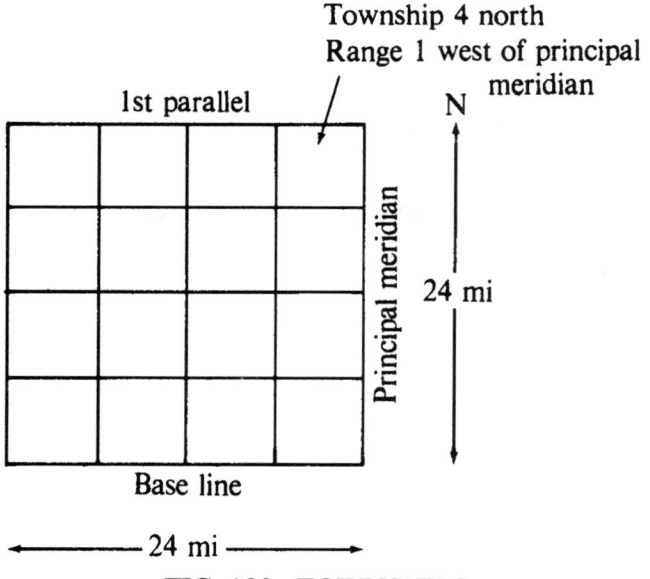

FIG. 180. TOWNSHIPS

TRACK RECORD a developer's or builder's reputation for producing on a timely and economical basis. A good track record can be helpful in arranging financing or attracting investors for a new project.
Example: The developer had a reputation for completing projects within schedule and budget, as well as for being able to lease up the buildings within 2 years of completion. This good

track record allowed the developer to get good terms on construction loans.

TRACT a **parcel** of land, generally held for **subdividing; a subdivision.**
Example: Reynolds, a **subdivider** purchases a *tract* of land. For marketing purposes, she subdivides the *tract* into lots (Figure 181).

75 ft	75 ft	75 ft	70 ft	70 ft
1	2	3	4	5

200 ft

South St.

FIG. 181. TRACT

TRACT HOUSE a dwelling that has a similar style and **floor plan** to those of all other houses in a development. Contrast with **custom builder.**
Example: Pleasant Acres is a **subdivision** of *tract houses.* Each home is a 3-bedroom ranch-style house with the same basic floor plan.

TRADE AREA same as **market area.**

TRADE FIXTURE articles placed in rented buildings by the tenant to help carry out trade or business. The tenant can remove the **fixtures** before the expiration of the **lease,** but if the tenant fails to do so shortly after the lease expires, the fixtures become the landlord's property.
Examples: *Trade fixtures* include:
• bar stools
• neon signs
• decorative or functional light fixtures
• stoves and refrigerators

TRANSACTION COSTS the costs associated with buying and selling **real estate.**

453

Examples: The following are *transaction costs:*
- **appraisal** fees
- **brokerage** commission
- legal fees
- mortgage **discount points**
- mortgage **origination fees**
- recording fees
- **survey** fees
- **title search**

TRANSFERABLE DEVELOPMENT RIGHTS the permission to increase the intensity of development for 1 parcel in exchange for decreasing the density of an adjacent parcel.

Example: In downtown Big City, there were 2 adjacent vacant parcels of land, upon which zoning permitted a 10-story building on each. Using the *transferable development rights*, the owner of tract A sold to the owner of tract B, the right to build a 20-story building on tract B; but A's land must be used as a park for the next 50 years.

TRANSFER DEVELOPMENT RIGHTS a type of **zoning ordinance** that allows owners of property zoned for low-density development or conservation use to sell development rights to other property owners. The development rights purchased permit the landowners to develop their **parcels** at higher **densities** than otherwise. The system is designed to provide for low-density uses, such as historic preservation, without unduly penalizing some landowners.

Example: Under a *transfer development rights* system, a landowner whose property is restricted to open space is assigned development rights in proportion to some overall desirable density for the jurisdiction. The landowner cannot utilize the rights but may sell them on the open market to landowners in other locations who are allowed to develop their properties. The rights may be used to develop additional structures on the unrestricted properties. In this way, restricted areas may be maintained as open space without completely destroying the development value of the properties.

TRANSFER TAX one paid upon the passing of **title** to property or to a valuable **interest.**

Example: In a state that imposes a high *transfer tax* on the sale of **real estate,** the seller formed a **corporation** as the owner of a valuable building and sold stock that was subject to a lower transfer tax. The state is claiming that it was a sale of real estate.

TRESPASS unlawful entry or **possession** of property.

Example: Thompson rents an apartment from Turner. When Thompson is away, Turner enters with a passkey and checks on

the apartment's condition. Even though Turner owns the property, he is guilty of *trespass,* since the right to possession has been granted to Thompson exclusively. It is possible for Turner to reserve the right to enter the property periodically.
Example: Smith fenced in his farm and posted signs to prevent *trespass* by hunters.

TRI-LEVEL see **split-level.**

TRIPLE-A TENANT one with an excellent credit record.
Example: The U.S. Postal Service and the American Telephone and Telegraph Company are examples of *triple-A tenants*, because they are unlikely to default on the lease.

TRIPLE-NET LEASE one in which the tenant is to pay all **operating expenses** of the property; the landlord receives a net rent.
Example: Big Buy Supermarkets enters into a *triple-net lease.* They are to pay for all the taxes, **utilities,** insurance, repairs, janitorial services, and license fees; any **debt service** and the landlord's income taxes are the responsibility of the landlord.

TRUST an arrangement whereby property is transferred to a trusted **third party** (trustee) by a **grantor** (trustor). The **trustee** holds the property for the benefit of another (**beneficiary**).
Example: An **inter vivos** *trust* was established by a living person who gave her warehouse to a trustee for the benefit of her children.
Example: A testamentary *trust* was established upon the death of a trustor, according to his **will.**

TRUST ACCOUNT a separate bank account segregated from a broker's own funds, in which the **broker** is required by state law to deposit all monies collected for clients. In some states called an **escrow account.**
Example: A broker who fails to deposit **earnest money** into a separate *trust account* may be held **liable** for penalties under the state's real estate **license** laws.

TRUST DEED a **conveyance** of real estate to a **third party** to be held for the benefit of another. Commonly used in some states in place of **mortgages** that conditionally convey **title** to the lender.
Example: Same as **deed of trust.**

TRUSTEE one who holds property in **trust** for another to secure performance of an obligation; the neutral party in a **trust deed** transaction.
Example: Johnson purchases property and finances it with a **deed of trust** from a lender. The **title company** is the *trustee,* holding legal title to the property pending Johnson's satisfaction of the debt. Should Johnson **default** on the loan, the trustee may sell the property to satisfy the debt.

TRUSTEE'S DEED same as **deed of trust.**

TRUSTEE'S SALE a **foreclosure sale** conducted by a trustee under the stipulations of a **deed of trust.**
Example: When a deed of trust is exercised, a specific trustee is designated. Upon default, the trustee is authorized to foreclose the mortgage and put the property up for a *trustee's sale.* The proceeds of the sale are distributed by the trustee according to the priorities listed in the deed of trust.

TRUTH IN LENDING see **Regulation Z.**

TUDOR an English-style imposing-looking house with fortress lines. Siding is chiefly stone and brick with some stucco and half timbers. Windows and doors have moulded cement or stone trim around them.
Example: Figure 182.

FIG. 182. TUDOR

TURNKEY PROJECT a development in which a **developer** completes the entire project on behalf of a buyer; the developer turns over the keys to the buyer at completion.
Example: Many government-owned public housing projects are *turnkey projects.* A private developer undertakes all activities necessary to producing the project, including land purchases, **permits,** plans, and construction, and sells the project to the housing authority.

U

UCC **Uniform Commercial Code.**

ULI **Urban Land Institute.**

UNDERIMPROVEMENT a structure or development of lower cost than the **highest and best use** of the site. Compare with **overimprovement.**
Example: Construction of a $40,000 bungalow on a vacant lot in a **neighborhood** of $100,000 homes would represent an *underimprovement* of the **site.**

UNDERLYING MORTGAGE refers to the first mortgage when there is a **wraparound mortgage.**
Example: A wraparound for $100,000 includes a $60,000 *underlying mortgage* in its balance, so the additional funds provided by the wrap are $40,000.

UNDERWRITER one who insures another or takes certain **risks.** In **mortgage** lending, the one who approves or denies a loan based on the property and the applicant. In securities, it is the **broker** that sells the issue and, unless sold on a "best efforts" basis, agrees to purchase the shares not bought by the public.
Example: The *underwriter* analyzed the loan submission package carefully, because she didn't want her firm to accept excessive risk.

UNDIVIDED INTEREST an ownership right to use and possession of a property that is shared among co-owners, with no one co-owner having exclusive rights to any portion of the property. Compare with **partition.**
Example: Ten investors form a **tenancy in common** and purchase a 100-**acre** tract of land. Each cotenant obtains an *undivided interest* in the property. All decisions as to the use and disposition of the land are made collectively by all cotenants. No one cotenant may unilaterally mortgage, develop, or sell a portion of the **tract.**

UNEARNED INCREMENT an increase in the **value** of real estate unrelated to effort on the part of the owner; often due to an increase in population.
Example: Murphy buys a **tract** of land in the county for $2,000 per **acre.** As the city grows, the surrounding county begins to develop, with paved highways eventually extended to Murphy's land. Murphy sells the land for $5,000 per acre, realizing an *unearned increment* in value of $3,000 per acre.

UNENCUMBERED PROPERTY real estate with **free and clear title.**
Example: Nash owns an *unencumbered property.* Nash's **interest** is **fee simple,** there are no **mortgage, vendor, mechanic's** or **tax liens** on the property, no restrictive covenants exist, and no easements have been granted.

UNIFORM COMMERCIAL CODE (UCC) a group of laws to standardize the state laws that are applicable to commercial transactions. Few of the laws have relevance to **real estate.**
Example: The *Uniform Commercial Code* applies to **chattel mortgages, promises, commercial paper, securities, etc.**

UNIFORM RESIDENTIAL APPRAISAL REPORT a standard form for reporting the appraisal of a dwelling. This form is required for use by the major secondary mortgage purchasers. It provides numerous checklists and appropriate definitions and certifications that are printed on the form.
Example: A real estate appraiser estimated the value of a house and wrote, on the *Uniform Residential Appraisal Report*, all of the relevant information for the property.

UNIFORM SETTLEMENT STATEMENT the form prescribed by the **Real Estate Settlement Procedures Act** for **federally related mortgages,** which must be prepared by whoever handles a **closing,** must contain certain relevant closing information, and must be given to buyer and seller.

UNIFORM STANDARDS OF PROFESSIONAL APPRAISAL PRACTICES (USPAP) a set of requirements covering research and reportings promulgated by the **Appraisal Foundation,** and adhered to by its members.
Example: Table 53.

TABLE 53
UNIFORM STANDARDS OF
PROFESSIONAL APPRAISAL PRACTICES

Standard Number	Applies to
1	Real Property Appraisal
2	Real Property Appraisal, Reporting
3	Review Appraisal and Reporting
4	Real Estate/Real Property Counseling
5	Real Estate/Real Property Reporting
6	Mass Appraisal and Reporting
7	Personal Property Appraisal
8	Personal Property Appraisal, Reporting
9	Business Appraisal
10	Business Appraisal, Reporting

UNILATERAL CONTRACT an obligation given by one party contingent on the performance of another party, but without obligating the second party to perform. Compare with **bilateral contract.**

Example: A **broker** makes a *unilateral contract* with her associates. She offers a trip to Hawaii to any salesman who sells one million dollars of property during the month. None of the salesmen is obligated to meet the goal, but the broker is obligated to provide the trip should any salesman perform the feat.

UNIMPROVED PROPERTY land that has received no development, construction, or **site** preparation. See **raw land.**

Example: O'Brien is **subdividing** a **tract** of land and selling lots to investors. In all marketing materials, O'Brien must disclose the fact that the land is *unimproved property* that must receive extensive development before being suitable for urban uses.

UNINCORPORATED ASSOCIATION an organization formed by a group of people. If the organization has too many characteristics of a **corporation** it may be treated like one for income tax purposes.

Example: Many **condominium** associations, **limited partnerships,** and real estate investment **trusts** are examples of *unincorporated associations.*

UNIT in multifamily residential property, a suite of rooms making up a residence for 1 tenant. It is generally characterized by a private entrance and some method of individuality from other units in the building or complex.

Example: The apartment building has 45 dwelling *units.* Each *unit* has a private bath and kitchen. Some are 2-bedroom *units* and others have 3 bedrooms.

UNIT-IN-PLACE METHOD a technique used by **appraisers** to estimate the **reproduction cost** (new) of a structure. The method involves estimating the cost of producing and installing individual components, such as the foundation, exterior walls, and plumbing. Similar methods include the trade-breakdown method and segregated-costs method. See **cost approach.**

Example: A simplified cost estimate using the *unit-in-place method* is shown in Table 54.

TABLE 54
UNIT-IN-PLACE METHOD

Item	Cost per unit ($/ft^2)	Cost
Foundation 1500 ft^2	2	$3,000
Walls 1600 ft^2	4	6,400
Roof 1500 ft^2	3	4,500
Flooring 1500 ft^2	2	3,000
Plumbing		2,500
Heating		1,500
Electrical		2,000
Total		$22,900
Fees, interest and overhead (10%)		2,290
Reproduction cost (new)		$25,190

UNREALIZED GAIN the excess of current **market value** over cost for an asset that is unsold.
Example: Collins bought land for $10,000; she had an offer to sell it for $15,000, but decided to keep the land. Her *unrealized gain* is $5,000.

UNRECORDED DEED an **instrument** that transfers **title** from one party (**grantor**) to another party (**grantee**) without providing public **notice** of change in ownership. **Recording** is essential to protect one's **interest** in **real estate.**
Example: Uncas purchases a lakefront lot from Upson. At closing, Uncas receives a **deed** but fails to record it at the county courthouse. In the meantime, Upson fraudulently sells the lot to Ustinov. Ustinov's attorney does a **title search** but, because of the *unrecorded deed,* does not turn up the sale to Uncas. When Uncas discovers what has occurred, he is forced to pursue legal proceedings against Upson for recovery. Ustinov, who purchased in **good faith,** owns the land.

UPSET PRICE same as **reserve price.**

URAR **Uniform Residential Appraisal Report.**

URBAN LAND INSTITUTE (ULI) a nonprofit organization providing research and information on land use and development. Among the many publications of the ULI are the periodicals, *Urban Land* and *Environmental Comment,* and several development guides for specific types of land use.
Address:
Urban Land Institute
625 Indiana Avenue NW
Washington, DC 20004
(202) 624-7000

URBAN PROPERTY **real estate** located in an urban area, generally characterized by relatively high-**density** development and extensive availability of city water and sewer services.
Example: Typical development of 3 types of property is shown in Table 55.

TABLE 55
URBAN PROPERTY

Urban	Suburban	Rural
High-rise office	Office parks	Farms
High-rise apartment	Industrial parks	Low-density housing
Department stores	Shopping centers	Recreational lands
Public buildings	Garden apartments	Summer camps
Moderate density single-family housing	Low-density housing	

URBAN RENEWAL the process of redeveloping deteriorated sections of the city, often through **demolition** and new construction. Although urban renewal may be privately funded, it is most often associated with government renewal programs.
Example: Most large cities have experienced some *urban renewal* in the last 20 years. The typical program attempts to demolish concentrations of dilapidated housing and attract **developers** of middle-income or mixed housing. Often, however, urban renewal areas become **sites** for new public buildings, such as civic auditoriums, sports arenas, and universities.

USEFUL LIFE the period of time over which a building is expected to provide a competitive return. *Useful life* provides the basis for allowable **depreciation** deductions on properties acquired prior to 1981. For tax purposes, this was replaced in 1981 by the **accelerated cost recovery system.**
Example: A property acquired in 1980 has a **depreciable basis** of $100,000 and a *useful life* of 25 years. Using **straight-line depreciation,** the owner may deduct $4,000 per year for tax reporting.

USPAP **Uniform Standards of Professional Appraisal Practices,** promulgated by the **Appraisal Foundation.** These are requirements for research and reporting with which a professional appraiser is to comply.

USUFRUCTUARY RIGHTS **interests** that provide for the use of property that belongs to another. Compare with **emblement.**

Example: The owner of land that bounds or contains a natural water channel has a *usufructuary right* to use of the water. The water itself is considered to be held by the public with all **adjacent** property owners holding rights to its use. **Restrictions** on that use vary under state law.

USURY charging a rate of interest greater than that permitted by state law. In most states, usury limits vary according to the type of lender and type of loan. Federal laws have passed to preempt certain usury limits under certain conditions.
Example: The **interest rate** that must comply with *usury* limitation is defined differently in the various states. The stated maximum rate may apply to the **face interest rate, effective rate** to the borrower, or the actual **yield** to the lender. If a loan is found to be usurious, severe penalties may be imposed, including loss of the **principal,** interest, a multiple of the interest, and/or damages.

UTILITIES 1. services, such as water, sewer, gas, electricity, and telephones, that are generally required to operate a building.
2. the periodic charges for such services.
Example: The building will be ready for occupancy as soon as the *utilities* are connected. When available, the *utility* bill is expected to average $100 per month. All *utilities* are paid for by the **landlord.**

UTILITY EASEMENT use of another's property for the purpose of laying gas, electric, water, and sewer lines.
Example: A property owner grants a utility *easement* to the electric power company to extend power lines to the owner's home.

V

VA Veterans Administration.

VACANCY RATE the percentage of all units or space that is unoccupied or not rented. On a **pro-forma** income **statement** a projected vacancy rate is used to estimate the vacancy allowance, which is deducted from potential **gross income** to derive effective gross income.
Example: The *vacancy rate* for apartment units in Boom City is currently 4.5%. For the Hightower Building, the *vacancy rate* is 9.5% (of 100,000 square feet of **net leasable area,** 9,500 square feet are not rented). If this 9.5% *vacancy rate* is expected to be the average through next year, a vacancy allowance of $95,000 (at $10 per square foot) should be deducted from potential rent when projecting income.

VACANT LAND land not currently being used. May have **utilities** and **off-site improvements.** Contrast with **raw land.**
Example: *Vacant land* was cleared and graded for future use as a **shopping center.**

VACATE to move out.
Example: A tenant *vacates* an apartment by terminating occupancy and removing all possessions. The tenant is responsible for **rent** to the end of the **lease** term.

VACATION HOME a dwelling used by the owner occasionally for recreational or resort purposes. It may be rented to others for a portion of the year. Income tax deductions pertaining to *vacation homes* depend on the frequency of use by the owner. Generally, a business loss cannot be claimed on a vacation home. See **second home.**
Example: The Travers have a *vacation home* in the mountains that they use on weekends during the summer. At other times it is rented to strangers on a weekly basis. If business deductions including depreciation exceed income, the loss cannot be deducted.

VALID having legally binding force; legally sufficient and authorized by law.
Examples: A *valid* **deed, will, lease, mortgage,** or other **contract.**

VA LOAN home loan **guaranteed** by the U.S. **Veterans Administration (VA)** under the Servicemen's Readjustment Act of 1944 and later. The VA **guarantees** restitution to the lender in

the event of **default.** The **guaranty** is 60% of the loan, but not more than $27,500. Home must be a principal residence.
Example: Abel, a veteran of the U.S. Army, wishes to purchase a home. Abel may apply for a *VA loan* with the Veterans Administration and, if qualified, may obtain a mortgage loan from a lending institution with no **down payment.**

VALUABLE CONSIDERATION a type of promised payment upon which a promisee can enforce a claim against an unwilling promisor. Includes money, extension of time, and other equivalents for the grant. Distinguished from good **consideration,** which may be love and affection toward a relative, generosity, and the like.
Example: A man promised to give certain land to a suitor of his daughter, provided they marry. This was not considered *valuable consideration*, so the suitor could not enforce it and he did not marry the daughter.

VALUATION 1. estimated worth or price.
Example: The *valuation* of the land is $100,000.
2. the act of estimating the worth of a thing. See **appraisal.**
Example: The *valuation* was prepared in accordance with instructions provided by the tax **assessor.**

VALUE the worth of all the rights arising from ownership; the quantity of one thing that will be given in exchange for another.
Example: A property may have a certain *value* to its owner (value in use) equal to the amount of other property (typically cash) that the owner would be willing to accept in exchange for the property without loss in wealth or well-being. The same property may have a different **market value** (value in exchange) equal to the amount of other property exchanged for the property when many typically motivated buyers and sellers are allowed to interact.

VARA a measurement or unit of length.
Example: The *vara* in Texas is 33⅓ inches. The land size was a 100 *vara* by 100 *vara* square, or 3333 inches by 3333 inches.

VARIABLE EXPENSES property operating costs that increase with occupancy.
Example: The **management fee,** at 5% of actual **rent** collections, and trash removal, at $10 per month per occupied apartment unit, are *variable expenses*.

VARIABLE INTEREST RATE an amount of compensation to a lender that is allowed to vary over the **maturity** of a loan. The

amount of variation is generally governed by an appropriate index. See **variable rate mortgage, renegotiated rate mortgage.** **Example:** A 20-year loan is made with a *variable interest rate.* The initial rate is 14% but may be changed each year in relation to changes in a published index of average loan rates. If, at the end of the first year, the index has risen one percentage **point,** the rate on the loan may be raised to 15%. Similarly, a fall in the index at one point would allow a decrease in the loan rate to 13%.

VARIABLE-MATURITY MORTGAGE a long-term **mortgage** loan, under which the **interest rate** may be adjusted periodically. Payment levels remain the same but the loan **maturity** is lengthened or shortened to achieve the adjustment.
Example: Abel obtains a *variable-maturity mortgage* originated at 12% with a **term** of 25 years. At the end of one year, the interest rate is increased to 12¼%. Abel's monthly payment of $527 remains the same after the adjustment; however, the remaining term is no longer 24 years, but is increased to 27 years.

VARIABLE-PAYMENT PLAN any **mortgage** repayment schedule that provides for periodic change in the amount of monthly payments. Changes may occur as a result of: the expiration of an interest-only period (**flexible payment mortgage**), a planned step-up in payments (**graduated payment mortgage**), or a change in the **interest rate** due to fluctuation in an index (**variable-rate mortgage**).
Example: A loan is made with a *variable-payment plan.* The interest rate on the loan may be adjusted once a year according to a published index. As the interest rate is changed, the monthly payment is adjusted to provide for full **amortization** of the outstanding **principal** over the remaining life of the loan.

VARIABLE-RATE MORTGAGE (VRM) a long-term **mortgage** loan applied to residences, under which the **interest rate** may be adjusted on a 6-month basis over the term of the loan. Rate increases are restricted to no more than ½ **point** per year and 2½ points over the term.
Example: Abel obtains a *variable-rate mortgage* originated at a 12% interest rate. In 6 months, the index upon which the rate is based increases by one percentage point. Abel's rate is adjusted to 12½% and cannot be further increased during the year because of the ½% annual cap.

VARIANCE permission granted by a **zoning** authority to a property owner to allow for a specified violation of the zoning requirements. Variances are generally granted when compliance is impossible without rendering the property virtually unusable.

465

Example: Sherman owns a lot that is zoned for low-**density** housing. Because of the peculiar shape and **topography** of the lot, Sherman cannot build a home with the required minimum floor area without violating the **setback** requirements for the area. Sherman may be granted a *variance* to either construct a smaller dwelling or encroach on the setback line.

VENDEE a buyer. Generally used for **real estate;** one who purchases **personal property** is usually called the buyer.
Example: The *vendee* is the party that pays for the real estate bought.

VENDEE'S LIEN a **lien** against property under a **contract of sale,** to secure the **deposit** paid by a purchaser.
Example: Moore, the vendee (buyer), gave a substantial deposit. Since Moore did not trust the seller, she secured a *vendee's lien* against the property. The lien provides the vendee with a claim against the property should the seller attempt to sell to another party prior to closing.

VENDOR a seller, usually of **real estate.** The term *seller* is commonly used for **personal property.**
Example: The *vendor* receives cash, **notes,** and **mortgage relief** from the **vendor.**

VENDOR'S LIEN see **purchase money mortgage.**

VENEER wood or brick exterior that covers a less attractive and less expensive surface.
Example: Beneath the sturdy-looking oak *veneer* was low-grade hollow board (Figure 183).

VENTURE CAPITAL money raised for high-risk investments.
Example: Money raised for oil exploration, theatrical productions, and the like is considered *venture capital.*

VERIFICATION sworn statements before a duly qualified officer that the contents of an **instrument** are correct.
Example: A tenant takes a landlord to court to recover a **security** deposit. The tenant files a claim describing the **conditions** under which the **deposit** is to be refunded and the manner in which the tenant complied with the conditions. The tenant then supplies *verification* of this description by a sworn statement.

VEST to create an entitlement to a privilege or right.
Example: By crossing Baker's property regularly for 20 years, Abel's right to an easement became *vested*. Baker can no longer prevent Abel from crossing.
Example: If she stays employed by the same **brokerage** firm for 10 years, Collins' right to a pension will *vest.*

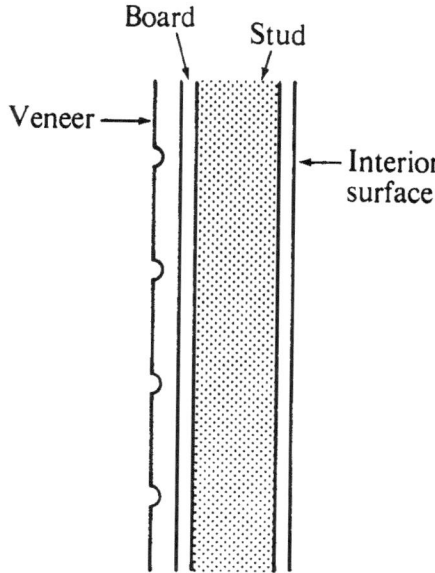

FIG. 183. OAK VENEER

VETERANS ADMINISTRATION (VA) an agency of the federal government that provides services for eligible veterans. Generally, a veteran who has served (beyond basic training) more than 120 days active duty in the armed forces is eligible for a **home loan** with no **down payment.**
Address:
Veterans Administration
810 Vermont Avenue
Washington, DC 20420

VIOLATION an act or a condition contrary to law or to permissible use of **real property.**
Examples: According to most **zoning ordinances,** operating a business from one's home is a *violation* of the restriction for a residential zone. In many cities, owning an occupied **apartment building** with nonfunctioning plumbing is a *violation* of the **housing code.**

VOID having no legal force or effect; unenforceable. See **null and void.**
Example: In a **listing** contract with a **broker,** Smith stipulates that the property be sold only to a person of a certain race. Since the stipulation is contrary to antidiscrimination laws, it is *void* and thereby unenforceable.

VOIDABLE capable of being voided, but not void unless action is taken to void it. A **contract** to **real estate** entered into by a **minor** is voidable only by the minor.

Example: A **landlord** leases an apartment to a minor. The minor may honor the lease and rent the apartment. However, should the minor decide not to rent the apartment, he may void the lease without **liability** for performance. The lease is a *voidable* contract.

VOLUNTARY ALIENATION legal term that describes a sale or gift made by the free will of the seller or donor.

Example: Boyd owned a tract of land with 100 feet of frontage along highway 4, with 200 feet of depth. The highway department condemned a strip that was 20 feet deep along the frontage and paid Boyd $1 per square foot. Boyd sold the remaining land to Collins for $1.25 per square foot by *voluntary alienation.*

VOLUNTARY LIEN a **debt** that the property owner agrees to have recorded. Typically a **mortgage.** Contrast with **involuntary lien.**

Example: The **mortgage** was a *voluntary lien,* since the real estate owner agreed to pledge the property as **security.**

VRM variable-rate mortgage.

W

WAIVER the voluntary renunciation, **abandonment,** or surrender of some claim, right, or privilege.
Example: A **violation** of a contract causes the need for a *waiver* from the other party who does not feel injured.

WALK-THROUGH INSPECTION inspection of premises by a buyer or tenant prior to closing or taking possession.
Example: Before closing the purchase of his new home, Wally was concerned that all repairs agreed to by the seller in the **agreement of sale** had been made. He arranged for a *walk-through inspection* prior to **closing**.

WAREHOUSING (LOAN) the packaging of a number of **mortgage** loans for sale in the **secondary mortgage market** by a financial institution or **mortgage banker** who has originated the loans.
Example: Willard, a mortgage banker, is regularly engaged in loan *warehousing*. He would originate a number of FHA-insured mortgages and sell the package to **FNMA** at **auction.** After origination but before the sale to FNMA, the loans are considered to be in Willard's *warehouse*.

WARRANTY a promise contained in a **contract.**
Example: The **vendee** received a one-year *warranty* from the builder as to the structural soundness of the property.

WARRANTY DEED one that contains a **covenant** that the **grantor** will protect the grantee against any and all claims. Usually contains covenants assuring good **title,** freedom from **encumbrances,** and **quiet enjoyment.** See also **general warranty deed** and **special warranty deed.**
Example: The grantor was willing to give a *warranty deed* because she was confident that she had good title to the property.

WARRANTY OF HABITABILITY an implied assurance given by a **landlord** that an apartment offered for rent is free from safety and health hazards.
Example: Todd signed a one-year **lease** to rent an apartment from Landon. Todd later discovered that the apartment's heating system was not functioning. Todd sought to break the lease, claiming the apartment was deficient under Landon's implied *warranty of habitability*.

469

WASTE unauthorized use or neglect of property by a party with the right to **possession** when another party owns an **interest** in the property. The party may be a **tenant, a mortgagor,** or a **life tenant.**
Example: A tenant neglecting to heat an apartment in the winter with the result of damage to the plumbing.
Example: A mortgagor failing to pay property taxes, thereby risking a tax **foreclosure.**
Example: A life tenant converting a residential property into a production center for some specialized product.

WASTING ASSET something of value that deteriorates over time.
Example: Improvements to land will not last forever, so they are *wasting assets;* in contrast, **land** is not wasting because it will last forever.

WATER RIGHTS see **riparian rights, usufructuary** rights.

WATER TABLE the upper level at which underground water is normally encountered in a particular area.
Example: Cross section showing the *water table* (Figure 184).

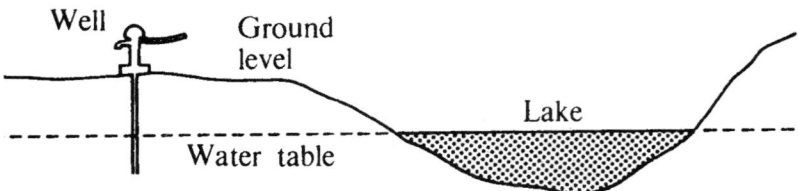

FIG. 184. WATER TABLE

WCR Women's Council of Realtors®.

WEAR AND TEAR physical deterioration of property as the result of use, weathering, and age.
Example: A carpet is expected to last only 8 years because of *wear and tear,* or deterioration resulting from foot traffic and cleaning.

WESTERN ROW HOUSE OR WESTERN TOWN HOUSE a nineteenth-century-style-house usually built to cover an entire street or block. It has common side walls with the house on either side.
Example: Figure 185.

FIG. 185. WESTERN ROW HOUSE

WETLANDS land, such as a marsh or swamp, normally saturated with water.
Example: A typical coastal *wetlands* (Figure 186).

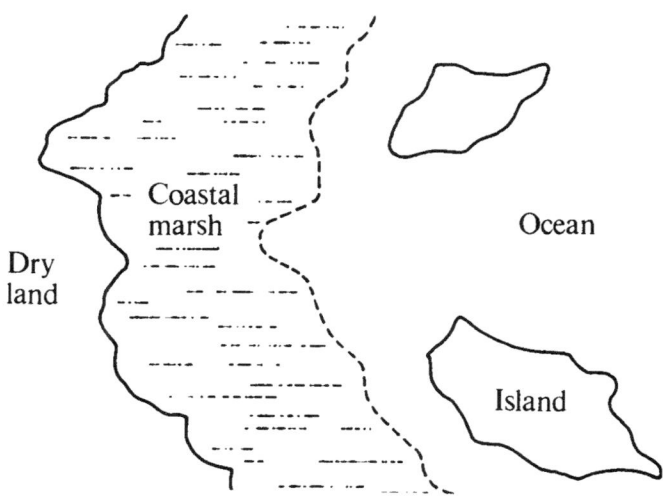

FIG. 186. WETLANDS

WILL the disposition of one's property, to take effect after one's death. Same as **testament.**
Example: If one does not prepare a *will*, state law will govern the disposition of one's property after death.

471

WILLIAMSBURG GEORGIAN OR EARLY GEORGIAN

an English-style house built in Williamsburg and representative of the early Georgian houses built in America throughout the early 1700s. They had simple exterior lines and generally fewer of the decorative devices characteristic of the later Georgian houses. Most were 2- or 3-story rectangular houses with two large chimneys rising high above the roof at each end. **Example:** Figure 187.

2 to 3 stories
Simple exterior lines
Large, high chimneys
Double-hung windows; small panes
Rectangular shape
Simple front

FIG. 187. WILLIAMSBURG GEORGIAN HOUSE

WINDOW an opening in the wall of a building to let in light and air. Most are made of transparent material and have the ability to be opened and closed.
Example: Figure 188.

WITHOUT RECOURSE words used in endorsing a **note** or bill to denote that the holder is not to look to the debtor personally in the event of nonpayment: the creditor has **recourse** only to the property. A form of exculpation. Same as **nonrecourse.** See **endorsement, exculpatory clause.**
Example: Abel insisted that the **mortgage** to the seller be *without recourse.* In the event that the value of the property declines, Abel may lose the property but he loses nothing else.

Fixed

Sliding

Double or single-hung

Casement

Awning

Hopper

Center pivot

Jalousie

FIG. 188. WINDOWS

WOMEN'S COUNCIL OF REALTORS® (WCR) an organization, affiliated with the **National Association of Realtors®**, devoted to preparing women in **real estate** for their emerging

roles in society, to encouraging members to a productive career in real estate, and to developing leadership potential. Publishes *The Real Estate Scene* (monthly) and the *WCR Communiqué* (quarterly).

Address:
Women's Council of Realtors®
430 North Michigan Avenue
Chicago, IL 60611

WOOD-DESTROYING INSECT a term used in certain home **inspection** forms; as a condition for purchase, the property must be free of these insects.

Examples:
• subterranean termites
• dry wood termites
• powder post beetles
• carpenter ants (in some locations)

WORKING CAPITAL the difference between current **assets** and current **liabilities.**
Example: The *working capital* is $2,500 ($4,000 minus $1,500) according to the balance sheet in Table 56.

TABLE 56
WORKING CAPITAL STATEMENT

Assets		Liabilities & equity	
Current		Current	
Cash	$1,000		
Acc'ts receivable	1,000	Accounts payable	$ 500
Inventory	2,000	3-month note	1,000
Current assets	$4,000	Current liabilities	$1,500
Fixed		Long-term	
Land	6,000	Mortgage	10,000
Buildings	10,000	Equity	8,500
Total assets	$20,000	Total liabilities and equity	$20,000

WORKOUT a mutual effort by a property owner and lender to avoid **foreclosure** or **bankruptcy** following a **default;** generally involves substantial reduction in the **debt service** burden during an economic depression. See **distressed property.**
Example: Because of an economic slowdown, the hotel suffered high **vacancy rates** and failed to generate enough income to meet **mortgage** payments. The owner approached the lender about a *workout.* It was agreed to reduce the outstanding loan

principal and extend the **maturity** date to reduce the debt service. In turn the lender would participate in the income when the economy recovered and hotel income exceeded a specified amount. See **participation mortgage.**

WORK TRIANGLE the total distance of the sides of the "triangle" connecting the refrigerator, range, and sink in a home kitchen; experts say that this distance should be between 15 and 21 feet for maximum efficiency.
Example: Figure 189.

FIG. 189. WORK TRIANGLE

WRITE-DOWN to diminish in amount on the records, generally to reflect a **market value** loss.
Example: Bank auditors, upon discovering that a certain **mortgage** was worthless, insisted on a *write-down.* The bank recorded the value decline as a bad debt expense.

WRAPAROUND MORTGAGE a loan arrangement in which an existing loan is retained and an additional loan, larger than the existing loan, is made. The new lender accepts the obligation to make payments on the old loan. The existing loan generally carries an **interest rate** below the rate available on new loans. Consequently, the **yield** to the wraparound lender is higher than the rate charged on the new loan. Sellers are the most common wraparound lenders.
Examples: Figure 190 and Table 57.

Home sale price: $70,000

Wraparound loan:
$60,000 12%
25 years $632 payments

Existing loan:
$40,000 principal
25 years left
9%
$336 payments

FIG. 190. WRAPAROUND MORTGAGE

TABLE 57
WRAPAROUND MORTGAGE

Seller gets $10,000 from buyer
and $20,000 from wraparound
lender.

Wraparound lender makes
payments on existing
mortgage.

Buyer makes payments on
wraparound mortgage.

Lender gets payment of
$632
−336
$296 per month on $20,000
outlay for a yield over 25
years of 17.5%.

WRIT OF EJECTMENT see **ejectment.**

Y

YIELD 1. a measurement of the rate of earnings from an invest-ment. See **current yield, yield to maturity.**
Example: A loan is arranged to *yield* 15% a year to the lender.
2. the productivity of agricultural land.
Example: A farm produces a *yield* of 5,000 bushels of corn per acre.

YIELD TO MATURITY (YTM) the **internal rate of return** on an investment. Considers all inflows and outflows of invest-ment returns and their timing.
Example: An income-producing property requires a $10,000 investment. It promises a $1,000 annual return for 5 years, then resale proceeds of $15,000. The *yield to maturity* is 17.1%. See **internal rate of return** for formulas.

Z

ZERO LOT LINE a form of **cluster housing** development in which individual dwelling units are placed on separately platted lots. They may be attached to one another, but not necessarily. See **planned unit development, plat, row house, town house.** **Example:** A representative *zero lot line* development (Figure 191).

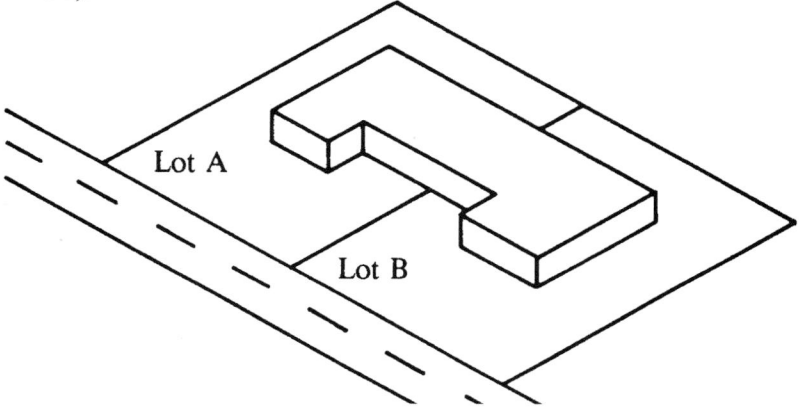

FIG. 191. ZERO LOT LINE

ZONE an area set off by local **ordinance** for specific use, subject to certain **restrictions** or conditions. See **zoning.** **Example:** A zoning map designates various *zones* with associated land use restrictions (Figure 192). C-l: commercial (service station, convenience store, etc.) R-2: low-**density** residential (**single-family** housing) R-4: high-density residential (apartments)

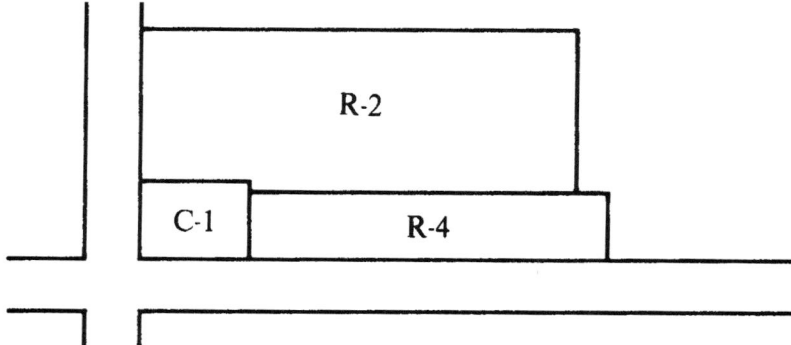

FIG. 192. ZONES

478

ZONING a legal mechanism for local governments to regulate the use of privately owned **real property** by specific application of **police power** to prevent conflicting land uses and promote orderly development. All privately owned land within the jurisdiction is placed within designated zones that limit the type and intensity of development permitted. See **zone.**

Example: Before a **tract** of land may be developed, the intended use must be permitted under the existing *zoning* classification. If the proposed use is not permitted, the developer must apply for an amendment to the **zoning ordinance,** or for rezoning. Such amendments are granted by the local governing body, generally following a public hearing and recommendation from the **planning commission.**

ZONING MAP a map of the local jurisdiction that indicates current **zoning** designations.

Example: A typical *zoning* map (Figure 193).

ZONING ORDINANCE act of city or county or other authorities specifying the type of use to which property may be put in specific areas. See **zone, zoning.**

Example: A typical *zoning ordinance* defines:
- the purpose for which the ordinance is adopted
- the various zoning classifications and permitted uses within each
- **restrictions,** such as height limitations
- the procedure for handling nonconforming uses
- the procedure for granting amendments, **variances,** and hearing appeals
- penalties for **violation** of the ordinance

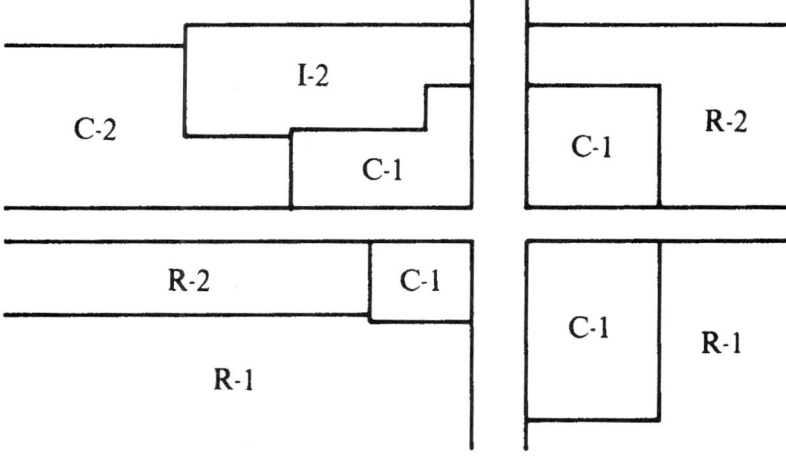

FIG. 193. ZONING MAP

479

USEFUL REAL ESTATE REFERENCES

This section offers selected publications on a wide variety of real estate topics. It is intended as a reference for use by those who want information about a special aspect of real estate, its financing and development. It contains references to recent and relevant articles, books, and monographs on selected topics; it is not an exhaustive list of publications.

The authors are grateful to those helpful in preparing an earlier version of this list. They include (alphabetically): Don Albrecht, Waldo Born, Wayne Etter, Judon Fambrough, Rick Floyd, Charles Gilliland, Terry Grissom, Ted Jones, Robert Lyon, Gary Maler, Ivan Schmedemann, and Arthur Wright.

TOPICS

Agriculture
Apartments
Appraisal (General)
Appraisal (Rural)
Appraisal Terminology and Definitions
Assessment
Associations (Directories)
Bankruptcy
Bibliographies
Brokerage
Capitalization
Careers
Commercial Real Estate
Computers and Calculators
Condemnation
Condominiums and Cooperatives
Construction
Corporate Real Estate
Cost Indexes
Counseling
Demographics
Depreciation
Development
Distressed Properties
Easements
Economics, Land
Eminent Domain
Employee Transfer

Energy
Environment
Feasibility
Finance
Financial Tables
Flood Plain
Foreclosure
Foreign Ownership
Forms
Glossaries
Highest and Best Use
Historic Properties
Home Buying
Home Selling
Hotel/Motel
Housing, Multi-Family
Housing, Single-Family
Housing, Urban
Income Property
Industrial Parks
Industrial Property
Insurance
Investment
Land and Land Use
Land Planning
Law
Leases and Leasehold Interests
Licensing

481

Limited Partnerships	Right of Way
Management (Brokerage)	Rural Properties
Management (Property)	Savings and Loan Associations
Market Analysis	Securitization
Marketing	Shopping Centers
Mathematics	Site Selection
Mineral Leasing	Subdivisions
Mortgage, Alternative Instruments	Syndication
Mortgage Market	Tax (Income)
Multiple Regression	Tax (Property)
Office Buildings	Timber and Timber Land
Parking Facilities	Timesharing
Principles (of Real Estate)	Transfer of Development Rights
Regulations	Waterfront Property
Rent and Rent Control	Water Rights
Retirement Housing	Zoning

AGRICULTURE (SEE RURAL PROPERTIES)

Articles

Gillentine, Thomas G. "Valuation of an Agricultural Operation," *The Appraisal Journal*, October 1986.

Pariser, David B. "Nine Credit Underwriting Standards for Farmer Mac," *Real Estate Finance*, Fall 1989.

Periodicals

Agricultural Economics Research. Superintendent of Documents, Government Printing Office, Washington, DC 20402. Quarterly.

Agricultural Outlook. Superintendent of Documents, Government Printing Office, Washington, DC 20402. Monthly.

Farmline. Superintendent of Documents, Government Printing Office, Washington, DC 20402. 11 issues a year.

Journal of the American Society of Farm Managers and Rural Appraisers. Box 6857, Denver, CO 80206. Semiannual.

APARTMENTS

Articles

Peck, Janet. "Appraising Rental Property in a Soft Market." *The Real Estate Appraiser and Analyst*, Spring 1985.

Books

Kelley, Edward N. *Practical Apartment Management*. Chicago: Institute of Real Estate Management, National Association of Realtors, 1981.

APPRAISAL (GENERAL)

Articles

O'Toole, Janet. "Appraisal Procedures and Real Estate Lending," *The Appraisal Journal*, January 1989.

Pilmer, Charles. "Trouble on the Farm: An Income Analysis is a Must," *The Appraisal Journal*, April 1985.

Periodicals

Appraisal Journal, The. Appraisal Institute, 875 North Michigan Avenue, Chicago, IL 60611. Quarterly.

Appraisal Review Journal. National Association of Review Appraisers, 875 Via de Commercio, Scottsdale, AZ 85258.

Journal of the American Society of Farm Managers and Rural Appraisers. 950 South Cherry Street, Suite 106, Denver, CO 80222.

Real Estate Appraiser. Appraisal Institute, 875 North Michigan Avenue, Chicago, IL 60611. Bimonthly.

Valuation. American Society of Appraisers, P.O. Box 17265, Washington, DC 20041.

Books

The Appraisal of Real Estate. 10th ed. Chicago: Appraisal Institute, 1992.

Friedman, Edith. *Encyclopedia of Real Estate Appraising*, 3rd edition. Englewood Cliffs, NJ: Prentice-Hall, 1978.

Friedman, Jack P., and Ordway, Nicholas. *Income Property Appraisal and Analysis*. 2nd ed. Englewood Cliffs, NJ: Prentice-Hall, 1987.

Harrison, Henry S. *Appraising Residences and Income Property*. New Haven: The H2 Company.

Ring, Alfred, and Boykin, Jack. *The Valuation of Real Estate*. 3rd ed. Englewood Cliffs, NJ: Prentice-Hall, 1986.

Shenkel, William M. *Real Estate Appraisal*. Dallas: South-Western Publishing Co., 1992.

Smith, Halbert, and Beloit, Jerry. *Real Estate Appraisal*. 2nd ed. Dayton, OH: Century VII Publishing Co., 1987.

APPRAISAL (RURAL)

Books

The Appraisal of Rural Property. Chicago: Appraisal Institute, 1983.

APPRAISAL TERMINOLOGY AND DEFINITIONS

Books

Boyce, Byrl N. *Real Estate Appraisal Terminology.* Cambridge, MA: Ballinger Publishing Co., 1984.

The Dictionary of Real Estate Appraisal. Chicago: Appraisal Institute, 2nd edition, 1989.

ASSESSMENT

Articles

Fruitman, Cecilia, and Gloudsman, Robert J. "A Feasibility Study of CAMA for Apartment and Commercial Property." *Property Tax Journal*, March 1989.

Periodicals

Assessment and Valuation Legal Reporter. International Association of Assessing Officers, 1313 East 60th Street, Chicago, IL 60637-9990. Monthly.

Articles

Fisher, Glenn. "Property Taxation and Local Government: Four Hypotheses." *Property Tax Journal*, June 1989.

Mark, Jonathan and Goldberg, Michael. "Multiple Regression Analysis and Mass Assessment: A Review of the Issues." *The Appraisal Journal*, January 1988.

Books

Property Appraisal and Assessment. Chicago: International Association of Assessing Officers, 1990.

ASSOCIATIONS (DIRECTORIES)

Periodicals

CAI News. Community Associations Institute, 1630 Duke Street, Alexandria, VA 22314. Monthly.

Community Association Law Reporter. Community Associations Institute, 1630 Duke Street, Alexandria, VA 22314. Monthly.

Housing and Development Reporter. Warren, Gorham, and Lamont, 210 South Street, Boston, MA 02111.

National Real Estate Investor. Communication Channels, Inc., 6255 Barfield Road, Atlanta, GA 30328. Monthly.

BANKRUPTCY

Articles

De Gannon, Victoria Eve. "Commercial Real Estate Lending from Appraisal to Bankruptcy." *Real Estate Law Journal*, Spring 1992.

Kahn, Beatrice. "What Happens to the OREA if an Anchor Goes Under?" *Real Estate Finance*, Fall 1989.

Melchiorre, Cam. "Battling the Bankruptcy Boom." *Mortgage Banking*, February 1992.

Moskowitz, Stuart S. "Cooperative Apartments: The Enforceability of Transfer Restrictions and the Impact of Bankruptcy." *Real Estate Law Journal*, Fall 1989.

Roswick, Bruce H., and McEvily, Stephanie. "Use Clauses in Shopping Center Leases: What if a Tenant Bankrupts?" *Real Estate Law Journal*, Summer 1985.

Savage, Denise. "Reciprocal Easement Agreements: Assumption and Rejection in Bankruptcy." *Real Estate Law Journal*, Fall 1990.

BIBLIOGRAPHIES

Books

Johnsich, John Robert. *Real Estate Books and Periodicals in Print.* Sacramento, CA: Real Estate Publishing Company, 1988–89 edition.

BROKERAGE

Articles

Colwell, Peter and Marshall, David. "Market Share in the Real Estate Brokerage Industry." *Journal of The American Real Estate and Urban Economics Association*, Winter 1986.

Follain, James. "Why Do Some Salespeople Earn More Than Others," *The Journal of Real Estate Research*, Fall 1987.

Frew, James R., and Jud, G. Donald. "The Value of a Real Estate Franchise," *Journal of The American Real Estate and Urban Economics Association*, Summer 1986.

Johnson, Linda L., Dotson, Michael, and Dunlap, B.J., "Service Quality Determinants and Effectiveness in the Real Estate Brokerage Industry." *The Journal of Real Estate Research*, Summer 1988.

Ridhins, Marsha L., Black, William C., and Sirmans, C.F. "Strategic Orientation and Market Surgery: An Analysis of Residential Real Estate Brokerage Firms." *The Journal of Real Estate Research*, Winter 1987.

Periodicals

Real Estate Today. National Association of Realtors, 430 North Michigan Avenue, Chicago, IL 60611. Monthly.

Books

Lindeman, Bruce. *Real Estate Brokerage Management.* Englewood Cliffs, NJ: Prentice-Hall, 1987.

National Association of Realtors. *Inside the Real Estate Business.* Washington, DC: Acropolis Books, 1982.

CAPITALIZATION

Articles

Bradley, David M. "The Capitalization Rate, the Discount Rate, and Inflation," *The Appraisal Journal*, April 1989.

McCoy, Bowen. "Capitalization Rate in a Dynamic Environment." *Real Estate Issues*, Fall/Winter 1990.

Reynolds, Anthony. "Current Valuation Techniques: A Review," *The Appraisal Journal*, April 1984.

Simonds, Richard R. "Corporate Valuations Using Yield and Direct Capitalization: A Further Clarification." *Property Tax Journal*, June 1990.

Books

Akerson, Charles B. *Capitalization Theory and Technique.* Chicago: Appraisal Institute, 1984.

486

CAREERS

Articles

Collins, Webster A. "One Thousand One-Dollar Decisions—A Primer for a Career in Real Estate Valuation." *The Appraisal Journal*, January 1991.

Wofford, Larry and Preddy, R. Keith. "Assessing Student Perceptions of Real Estate Careers." *Journal of the American Real Estate and Urban Economics Association*, Winter 1980.

Books

Edwards, Kenneth. *Your Successful Real Estate Career.* New York: American Management Association, 1982.

COMMERCIAL REAL ESTATE

Articles

Gelbtuch, Howard C. "The World of Commercial Real Estate: A Look at the Past 15 Years." *The Appraisal Journal*, October 1989.

Kelley, Hugh F. "Forecasting Office Space Demand in Urban Areas," *Real Estate Review*, Fall 1983.

Martin, William B., and English, Wilke D. "Forecasting Demand for Multi-Tenant Office Space." *Commercial Investment Journal*, Winter 1985.

Miles, Mike and McCue, Tom. "Commercial Real Estate Returns." *The Journal of the American Real Estate & Urban Economics Association*, Fall 1984.

Rosen, Kenneth T. "Toward a Model of the Office Building Sector." *AREUEA Journal*, Fall 1984.

Periodicals

Commercial Investment Journal. Realtors National Marketing Institute, 430 N. Michigan Avenue, Chicago, IL 60611.

Real Estate Finance. Federal Research Press, 155 Federal Street, 13th Floor, Boston, MA 02110.

Real Estate Review. Warren, Gorham & Lamont, Inc., 210 South Street, Boston, MA 02111. Quarterly.

COMPUTERS & CALCULATORS

Articles

Kell, Lawrence. "Using Computers in the Counseling Office." *The Appraisal Journal*, October 1986.

Schneider, Howard. "Competing with Computers." *Mortgage Banking*, October 1989.

Books

Dilmore, Gene. *Quantitative Techniques in Real Estate Counseling.* Lexington, MA: Lexington Books, 1981.

CONDEMNATION

Articles

Bailey, Donald. "Appraisal of Real Estate for Purposes of Condemnation." *The Real Estate Appraiser and Analyst*, Summer 1989.

Shedd, Peter J. "Inverse Condemnation: Will the Supreme Court Allow It?" *Real Estate Law Journal*, Spring 1981.

Books

Bonbright, James C. *The Valuation of Property*. Vols I and II. Charlottesville, VA: The Michie Co., 1965.

Condemnation Appraisal Practice. Vol. II. Chicago: Appraisal Institute, 1973.

Real Estate Valuation in Litigation. Chicago: Appraisal Institute, 1983.

CONDOMINIUMS and COOPERATIVES

Articles

Danner, John C. "Cooperative Apartments." *The Real Estate Appraiser and Analyst*, Spring 1985.

Moskowitz, Stuart S. "Cooperative Apartments: The Enforceability of Transfer Restrictions and the Impact of Bankruptcy." *Real Estate Law Journal*, Fall 1989.

Tudzarov, Louise. "Platting the Condominium: Is it Required?" *Real Estate Law Journal*, Summer 1986.

Books

Dombal, Robert W. *Appraising Condominiums: Suggested Data Analysis Techniques.* Chicago: Appraisal Institute, 1981.

Friedman, Jack P. and Harris, Jack. *Keys to Purchasing a Condo or a Co-op*. Hauppauge, New York: Barron's Educational Series, 1990.

CONSTRUCTION

Articles

Ahluwalia, Gopal. "Who are the People Who Build Homes?" *Housing Economics*, January 1988.

Rago, George, and Kimball, William. "Appraising Proposed Income-Producing Property for Construction Lending." *The Appraisal Journal*, October 1989.

West, Robert J. "Construction Loan Cost Model." *The Appraisal Journal*, July 1989.

Periodicals

Builder. National Association of Home Builders, 15th & M Streets NW, Washington, DC 20005. Monthly.

Construction Review. U.S. Department of Commerce, Washington, DC. Bimonthly.

Multi-Housing News. Gralla Publications, 1515 Broadway, New York, NY 10036. Monthly.

Professional Builder/Apartment Business. Cahners Publishing Co. Inc., 270 St. Paul Street, Denver, CO 80206. Monthly.

Books

Boeckh Building Cost Manual. 525 E. Michigan Avenue, Milwaukee, Wisconsin, 53202.

Construction Cost Control Manual. Washington, DC: National Association of Homebuilders, 1982.

Construction Dictionary. Washington, DC: National Association of Homebuilders, 1985.

Dodge Building Cost Calculator. New York: McGraw-Hill Information Systems. Updated regularly.

Marshall Valuation Service. Los Angeles, CA: Marshall & Swift Publication Co. Updated regularly.

CORPORATE REAL ESTATE

Articles

Friedman, Jack P., and Moores, John H. "A Mixed Bag of Blessings: Corporate Real Estate." *Financial Executive*, October 1978.

Glascock, John L., Wallace N. Davidson III, and C.F. Sirmans. "The Gains from Corporate Selloffs: The Case of Real Estate Assets." *AREUEA Journal*, Winter 1991.

Manning, Chris. "Leasing Versus Purchase of Corporate Real Property: Leases with Residual Equity Interests." *The Journal of Real Estate Research*, Spring 1991.

McIntosh, Willard, Davidson, Wallace, and Albert, Joseph. "Capital Budgeting Practices of Corporate Real Estate Executives," *The Appraisal Journal*, January 1987.

Nourse, Hugh O., and Kingery, Dorothy. "Survey Approaches to Disposing of Corporate Real Estate." *The Journal of Real Estate Research*, Fall 1987.

Periodicals

Corporate Real Estate Executive. National Association of Corporate Real Estate Executives, 471 Spencer Drive, West Palm Beach, FL 33409.

Books

Collins, Webster A.; Spaulding, Charles H.; et al. *Real Estate: A Hidden Corporate Asset*. Chicago: American Society of Real Estate Counselors, 1986.

Silverman, Robert A. *Corporate Real Estate Handbook*. New York: McGraw-Hill, 1987.

COST INDEXES

Boeckh Building Cost Manual. 525 E. Michigan Avenue, Milwaukee, WI.

Building Construction Cost Data. Duxbury, MA: Robert Snow Means Company. Annual.

Dodge Services, F. W. Dodge, 1221 Avenue of the Americas, New York, NY 10020.

Marshall Valuation Service, 1617 Beverly Blvd., Los Angeles, CA 90026.

COUNSELING

Articles

Boykin, James H. "Criteria Used in Selecting Appraisers and Consultants." *The Appraisal Journal*, January 1985.

Kell, Lawrence. "Using Computers in the Counseling Office." *The Appraisal Journal*, October 1986.

Mills, Arlen. "Counseling Opportunities for the Appraiser." *The Appraisal Journal*, October 1983.

Periodicals

Real Estate Issues. American Society of Real Estate Counselors, 430 N. Michigan Avenue, Chicago, IL 60611. Quarterly.

Books

Boykin, James H., ed. *Real Estate Counseling.* Chicago: American Society of Real Estate Counselors, 1984.

DEMOGRAPHICS

Articles

McFaul, Francis. "Regional Outlook: State Population and Household Estimates." *Housing Economics*, July 1989.

Schussheim, Morton J. "The Impact of Demographic Change on Housing and Community Development." *The Appraisal Journal*, July 1984.

Periodicals

Annual Survey of Buying Power. Sales and Marketing Management Magazine, Bill Publication Co., New York, NY. Annual.

Current Population Reports. Bureau of the Census, Government Printing Office, Washington, DC.

New One-Family Houses Sold and for Sale. Bureau of the Census, U.S. Department of Commence, Washington, DC.

DEPRECIATION

Articles

Cannaday, Roger E. and Sunderman, Mark A. "Estimation of Depreciation for Single-Family Appraisals." *Journal of the American Society of Real Estate & Urban Economics Association*, Summer 1986.

Derbes, Max J. "Economic Life Concepts." *The Appraisal Journal*, April 1987.

Books

Young, James C., and Dilley, Steven C., eds. *The Tax Reform Act of 1986: The New ACRS Rules.* Paramus, NJ: Prentice-Hall Information Services, 1987.

DEVELOPMENT

Articles

Frew, James and Jud, G. Donald. "A Simulation Model of Commercial Real Estate Development." *The Real Estate Appraiser and Analyst*, Fall 1988.

Peiser, Richard B. "Risk Analysis in Land Development." *AREUEA Journal*, Spring 1984.

Periodicals

National Real Estate Investor. Communication Channels, Inc., 6285 Barfield Road, Atlanta, GA 30328. Monthly.

Books

McMahan, John. *Property Development*. New York: McGraw-Hill, 2nd ed., 1989.

Miles, Mike E, Emil E. Malizia, Marc A. Weiss, Gayle L. Berens, and Ginger Travis. *Real Estate Development Principles and Process*. Chicago: Urban Land Institute, 1991.

DISTRESSED PROPERTIES

Articles

Fransen, Robert A. "Marketing Distressed Properties." *Journal of Property Management*, November/December 1990.

Lesser, David M., and Klug, Loren. "A Borrower's Guide to Real Estate Loan Workouts." *Real Estate Finance*, Summer 1990.

EASEMENTS

Articles

Derbes, Max J. Jr., "Facade Easement Valuation Methodology." *The Appraisal Journal*, April 1988.

Graham, Lannie M. "Prescriptive Easements and a Highest and Best Use Decision." *The Appraisal Journal*, October 1991.

Periodicals

Right Of Way. International Right of Way Association, 13650 South Gramercy Place, Suite 100, Gardena, CA 90249. Bimonthly.

ECONOMICS, LAND

Periodicals

Land Economics. University of Wisconsin Press, Journals Dept., 114 North Murray Street, Madison, WI 53715. Quarterly.

Books

Barlowe, Raleigh. *Land Resource Economics.* 4th ed. Englewood Cliffs, NJ: Prentice-Hall, 1986.

EMINENT DOMAIN

Books

The Federal Law of Eminent Domain. Charlottesville, VA: Federal Law Library, Michie Co., 1982.

EMPLOYEE TRANSFER

Periodicals

Mobility. Ed. Jerry Holloman. Employee Relocation Council, 1720 N Street, NW, Washington, DC 20036.

ENERGY

Articles

Webb, James. "The Influence of Solar Energy Systems on the Value of Dwellings," *Real Estate Appraiser and Analyst*, January–February 1980.

Books

Energy Conservation Opportunities and Strategies. Chicago: Institute of Real Estate Management, 1981.

ENVIRONMENT

Articles

Alvayay, Jaime, and Baen, John. "The Implications of Federal Wetland Protection Programs for the Real Estate Appraisal Industry." *The Journal of Real Estate Research*, Spring 1990.

Bookspan, Shelley. "From the Environment: Asbestos—A Major Real Estate Concern." *Real Estate Law Journal*, Fall 1990.

_____. "From the Environment: Radon—The Risks of a Natural Gas." *Real Estate Law Journal*, Spring 1991.

Entreken, Henry. "Appraisal of a Class III Landfill." *The Appraisal Journal*, October 1987.

Kellman, Mark A., and Triana, Ray F. "CERCLA and Nonjudicial Foreclosure: The Effect of California's Anti-Deficiency Statutes on Unsecured Indemnities." *Real Estate Finance*, Summer 1989.

McGregor, Greg. "Establishing the Level of Care for Site Assessments." *Real Estate Finance*, Winter 1991.

Neal, Larry A. "Taking on Environmental Hazards." *The Real Estate Appraiser and Analyst*, Summer 1987.

Patchin, Peter. "Contaminated Properties—Stigma Revisited." *Appraisal Journal*, April 1991.

Sage, Cindy, and Johns, Joseph G. "From the Environment: Electromagnetic Radiation—A Case for Relevance in Real Estate Transactions and Eminent Domain." *Real Estate Law Journal*, Fall 1991.

Slutsky, David. "Lenders Strategies for Environmental Liabilities." *Mortgage Banking*, October 1987.

Periodicals

Environmental Watch. Chicago: Appraisal Institute.

FEASIBILITY

Articles

Bottum, MacKenzie S. "Retail Gravity Model." *The Appraisal Journal*, April 1989.

Derbes, Max J., Jr. "Feasibility Income Deficiency." *The Appraisal Journal*, January 1989.

Grissom, Terry V. "Appraisal Models and the Feasibility Process." *The Appraisal Journal*, April 1986.

Rowan, Tomothy. "The Use of Computerized Demographic Data Bases in Feasibility Studies." *The Real Estate Appraiser and Analyst*, Winter 1988.

Periodicals

Site Selection Handbook. Conway Data Inc., 40 Technology Park, Norcross, GA. 30092.

Books

Barrett, G. V., and Blair, John P. *How to Conduct and Analyze Real Estate Market and Feasibility Studies*. New York: Van Nostrand Reinhold Company, 1982.

Cannestaso, James C. *Real Estate Financial Feasibility Analysis Handbook & Workbook*. Chicago: Appraisal Institute, 1982.

FINANCE

Articles

Dickens, Thomas L., Samson, William D., and Sirmans, C.F. "The Refinancing Decision for Income-Producing Real Estate." *The Appraisal Journal*, January 1985.

Downs, Anthony. "An Encompassing View of the World of Real Estate Finance." *Mortgage Banking*, July 1987.

Friedman, Jack P. "New Tax Law Gridlocks Avenues for Creative Finance." *The Appraisal Journal*, April 1985.

Ledford, David. "Housing Finance: The Impact of New Capital Regulations." *Housing Economics*, March 1989.

Lesser, David M., and Klug, Loren. "A Borrower's Guide to Real Estate Loan Workouts." *Real Estate Finance*, Summer 1990.

Megbolugbe, Isaac. "Who Uses FHA Insurance and Why." *Housing Economics*, May 1990.

Waller, Neil. "The Residential Refinancing Decision: An After-tax Analysis." *The Real Estate Appraiser and Analyst*, Fall/Winter 1987.

Periodicals

Crittenden Report. Crittenden Publishing Inc., Box 1150, Novato, CA 94948. Weekly.

Federal Home Loan Bank Board Journal. Superintendent of Documents, Government Printing Office, Washington, DC 20402. Monthly.

Mortgage Banking. Mortgage Bankers Association of America, 1125 15th Street NW, Washington, DC 20005. Monthly.

Real Estate Finance. Federal Research Press, 155 Federal Street, 13th Fl., Boston, MA 02110. Quarterly.

Real Estate Finance Journal. Warren, Gorham & Lamont, 210 South Street, Boston, MA 02111-9902.

Books

Brueggeman, William B., Fisher, Jeffrey, and Stone, Leo D. *Real Estate Finance*. 8th ed. Homewood, IL: Richard D. Irwin, 1988.

Friedman, Jack P. and Harris, Jack. *Keys to Real Estate Financing and Refinancing*. Hauppauge, NY: Barron's Educational Series, 1993.

Mason, James J. *AIREA Financial Tables*. Chicago: Appraisal Institute, 1981.

Sirmans, C.F. *Real Estate Finance*. New York: McGraw-Hill, 2nd ed. 1989.

Weidemer, John. *Real Estate Finance*. Englewood Cliffs, NJ: Prentice-Hall, 1986.

FINANCIAL TABLES

Ellwood, L. W. *Ellwood Tables*. Cambridge, MA: Ballinger Publishing Co., 1977.

Friedman, Jack P., and Harris, Jack C. *Adjustable Rate Tables*. Hauppauge, NY: Barron's Educational Series, 2nd ed. 1993.

Friedman, Jack P., and Pearson, Peggy. *Real Estate Finance and Investment Tables*. Englewood Cliffs, NJ: Prentice-Hall, 1983.

FLOOD PLAIN

Flood hazard maps available from: National Flood Insurance Program, Box 34294, Bethesda, MD 20034. Phone: 1-800-638-6620.

Articles

Owens, Robert W., and Roberts, Joe R. "Appraising Floodplain Properties." *The Appraisal Journal*, April 1991.

Sirmans, C.F. "Adjusting Comparable Sales for Floodplain Location." *The Appraisal Journal*, July 1985.

Skantz, Terrance R., and Strickland, Thomas. "House Prices and a Flood Event: An Empirical Investigation of Market Efficiency." *The Journal of Real Estate Research*, Winter 1987.

FORECLOSURE

Articles

Boneparth, Harvey. "Taking a Deed in Lieu of Foreclosure: Pitfalls for the Lender." *Real Estate Law Journal*, Spring 1991.

Kellman, Mark A., and Triana, Ray F. "CERCLA and Nonjudicial Foreclosure: The Effect of California's Anti-Deficiency Statutes on Unsecured Indemnities." *Real Estate Finance*, Summer 1989.

Massa, Michael R. "REO: A Pre-Foreclosure Counseling Solution." *Mortgage Banking*, August 1987.

McGuire, John A. "Foreclosure and Debt Cancellation." *The Journal of Real Estate Taxation*, Winter 1989.

Silverman, Robert A., and Geldzahler, Seth D. "Navigating Through Foreclosure Law." *Mortgage Banking*, February 1992.

Tolzmann, David C. "Troubled Loans." *Mortgage Banking*, July 1988.

Books

Friedman, Jack P. and Harris, Jack. *Keys to Buying a Foreclosed Home.* Hauppauge, NY: Barron's Educational Series, 1992.

FOREIGN OWNERSHIP

Articles

Del Casino, Joseph J. "European Investment in U.S. Office Markets." *The Appraisal Journal*, January 1986.

Her, Mangshar. "Attracting Asian Real Estate: East Meets Southwest." *Real Estate Finance*, Winter 1990.

Hines, Mary Alice. "International Dimensions of Real Estate." *The Appraisal Journal*, October 1988.

Mitchell, Arthur M. "Preparing for the 'Fourth Wave' of Japanese Investment." *Real Estate Finance*, Spring 1988.

Musa, Essayyad, and Green, G. Hayden. "International Real Estate Adjusted Present Value Model." *Real Estate Issues*, Spring/Summer 1990.

Orth, Victor E.J. "Japanese Investment in U.S. Real Estate," *The Appraisal Journal*, January 1990.

Books

Hinds, Dudley S., and Ordway, Nicholas. *International Real Estate Investment*. Chicago: Real Estate Education Co., 1982.

Meyers, Myron. *Foreign Investment in United States Real Estate*. New York: Dow Jones-Irwin, 1982.

U.S. Department of Agriculture. *Monitoring Foreign Ownership of U.S. Real Estate*. (A Report to Congress). Vol. 1, Chapter 2.

Periodicals

International Real Estate Federation, FIABCI, American Chapter, 430 N. Michigan Avenue, Chicago, IL 60611.

FORMS

Books

Arnold, Alvin L. *Modern Real Estate & Mortgage Forms*. New York: Warren, Gorham & Lamont, 1979.

_____, and Smith, Owen T. *Modern Ownership & Investment Forms*. New York: Warren, Gorham & Lamont, 1976.

Kushet, Jack, and Lopatin, Robert. *Modern Real Estate Forms*. New York: Warren, Gorham & Lamont, 1981.

Kushet, Robert, and Lopatin, Robert. *Modern Real Estate Leasing Forms*. New York: Warren, Gorham & Lamont, 1980.

GLOSSARIES

Books

Arnold, Alvin. *Encyclopedia of Real Estate*. Boston: Warren Gorham & Lamont. Boston. Updated annually.

The Dictionary of Real Estate Appraisal. Chicago: Appraisal Institute, 2nd ed., 1989.

Friedman, Jack P., Harris, Jack C., and Lindeman, Bruce. *Dictionary of Real Estate Terms*. 3rd ed. Hauppage, NY: Barron's Educational Series, 1993.

Reilly, John W. *The Language of Real Estate*. 3rd ed. Chicago: Dearborn Financial Publishing Company, 1988.

HIGHEST AND BEST USE

Articles

Dotzour, Mark G., Grissom, Terry V., Liu, Crocker, and Pearson, Thomas. "Highest and Best Use: The Evolving Paradigm." *The Journal of Real Estate Research*, Spring 1990.

Steele, Kent D. "A 'Backdoor' Approach to Highest and Best Use Analysis." *The Appraisal Journal*, January 1991.

Books

Readings in Highest & Best Use. Chicago: Appraisal Institute, 1981.

HISTORIC PROPERTIES

Articles

Asabere, Paul K., Hachey, George, and Grubaugh, Steven. "Architecture, Historic Zoning, and the Value of Homes." *The Journal of Real Estate Finance and Economics*, September 1989 and "Historic Districts and Land Values." *The Journal of Real Estate Research*, Spring 1991.

Derbes, Max J. Jr., "Facade Easement Valuation Methodology." *The Appraisal Journal*, April 1988.

Ford, Deborah Ann. "The Effect of Historic District Designation on Single-Family Home Prices." *AREUEA Journal*, Fall 1989.

Howe, Rex and Hatton, Nikkii C. "New Challenges for the Appraiser: Tax Credit Incentives on Historic Property." *The Real Estate Appraiser and Analyst*, Winter 1983.

Oldham, Sally G. "Historic Properties: Variable Valuations." *Appraisal Journal*, July 1982.

Periodicals

The Old House Journal. Old House Journal Corp., 69A Seventh Ave, Brooklyn, NY 11217. 10 issues per year.

Books

Reynolds, Judith. *Historic Properties: Preservation and the Valuation Process.* Chicago: Appraisal Institute, 1982.

HOMEBUYING

Books

Friedman, Jack P. *Keys to Buying a Home.* Hauppauge, NY: Barron's Educational Series, 1990.

HOME SELLING

Books

Real Estate Advertising Handbook. Chicago: Realtors National Marketing Institute, 1984.

Rosenauer, Johnnie L. *Effective Real Estate Sales & Marketing.* Chicago: Dearborn Financial Publishing Company, 1982.

HOTEL/MOTEL

Articles

Corgel, John. "Hotel/Motel Properties vs. Other Real Estate: A Comparison of Mortgage Terms." *Real Estate Finance*, Spring 1986.

Dempsey, Donald H. "Financing Trends in the Hotel Industry." *Real Estate Finance*, Winter 1991.

Hennessey, Sean. "Economic Studies for Hotels: A Guide for Gathering Basis Data." *The Appraisal Journal*, July 1986.

Nelson, Roland; Messer, Jay L.; and Lawrence J. Allen. "Hotel Enterprise Evaluation." *The Appraisal Journal*, April 1988.

Rushmore, Stephen, and Rubin, Karen. "The Valuation of Hotels and Motels for Assessment Purposes." *The Appraisal Journal*, April 1984.

Periodicals

Cornell Hotel and Restaurant Administration Quarterly. School of Hotel Administration, Cornell University, Statler Hall, Ithaca, NY 14853. Quarterly.

Lodging Hospitality. Penton/IPC, Inc., 1111 Chester Avenue, Cleveland, OH 44114. Monthly.

Books

Rushmore, Stephen. *Hotels and Motels*: *A Guide to Market Analysis and Valuation*. Chicago: Appraisal Institute, 1992.

HOUSING, MULTI-FAMILY

Articles

Crist, Dean. "Multifamily Housing." *Housing Economics*, May 1990.

Dale, Larry. "Fannie Mae's Multifamily Multiproducts." *Mortgage Banking*, July 1988.

Periodicals

Apartment Management Newsletter. Mattco Equities, Inc., 48 West 21st Street, New York, NY 10010-6976. Monthly.

Income/Expense Analysis: *Apartments*. Institute of Real Estate Management. Annual.

Multi-Housing News. Gralla Publications, 1515 Broadway, New York, NY 10036. Monthly.

Books

Downs, James C., Jr. *Principles of Real Estate Management.* Chicago: Institute of Real Estate Management, National Association of Realtors, 1980.

Kelley, Edward N. *Practical Apartment Management.* Chicago: Institute of Real Estate Management, National Association of Realtors, 1981.

HOUSING, SINGLE-FAMILY

Articles

Ahluwalia, Gopal. "Upper Bracket Homes and Home Buyers." *Housing Economics*, July–August 1988.

Holloway, Thomas and Peach, Richard. "Plan Your Long-Range Business Strategy By Anticipating Future Housing Demand." *Mortgage Banking*, June 1988.

Rabianski, Joseph. "The Residential Resale Market." *The Real Estate Appraiser and Analyst*, Fall 1985.

Schussheim, Morton J. "The Impact of Demographic Change on Housing and Community Development." *The Appraisal Journal*, July 1984.

Villanueva, Bob. "Revising the Single Family Home Price Index." *Housing Economics*, September 1990.

Webb, James R., and Rubens, Jack H. "Tax Rates and Implicit Rates of Return on Owner-Occupied Single-Family Housing." *The Journal of Real Estate Research*, Winter 1987.

Periodicals

Existing Home Sales. National Association of Realtors, Economics & Research Division, 777 14th Street NW, Washington, DC 20005. Monthly and annual reports.

Books

Harrison, Henry S. *Houses.* Chicago: Dearborn Financial Publishing, 2nd. ed. 1992.

HOUSING, URBAN

Articles

Goannias, Dimitrios A. "Housing Quality Differentials in Urban Areas." *Journal of Urban Economics*, March 1991.

Books

Sumichrast, Michael, et al. *Housing Fact Book.* Washington, DC: National Association of Home Builders, 1979.

INCOME PROPERTY

Articles

Clapp, John, and Miller, Stephen. "The Theory and Practice of Underwriting Income Property Mortgages." *Appraisal Review Journal*, Fall 1986.

Plattner, Robert H. "Income Property: Factors Affecting Value." *The Real Estate Appraiser and Analyst*, Fall 1986.

Books

Epley, Donald R., and Boykin, James H. *Basic Income Property Appraisal.* Reading, MA: Addison-Wesley, 1983.

Friedman, Jack P., and Ordway, Nicholas. *Income Property Appraisal and Analysis.* Englewood Cliffs, NJ: Prentice-Hall, 1987.

Readings in the Income Capitalization Approach to Real Property Valuation. Vol. II. Chicago: Appraisal Institute, 1985.

INDUSTRIAL PARKS

Articles

Nikols, Carrie. "Tailoring an Acquisition Loan for an Individual Ownership Industrial Park." *Real Estate Finance*, Winter 1990.

Periodicals

The SIOR Professionals. Department of Finance, University of Akron, Akron, OH 44325. Semiannual.

Books

Kinnard, William N., Jr., and Messner, Stephen D. *Industrial Real Estate.* 4th ed. Washington, DC: Society of Industrial and Office Realtors, 1984.

INDUSTRIAL PROPERTY

Articles

Ambrose, Brent W. "An Analysis of the Factors Affecting Light Industrial Property Valuation." *The Journal of Real Estate Research*, Fall 1990.

Gandhi, Devinder, and Rahman, Abdul. "An Econometric Model of Industrial Land Valuation." *Property Tax Journal*, June 1989.

Wheaton, William C. and Torto, Raymond. "An Investment Model of the Demand and Supply for Industrial Real Estate." *AREUEA Journal*, Winter 1990.

Wofford, Larry E. "Significant Trends Affecting Office and Industrial Real Estate: A Twenty-First Century Perspective." *The Appraisal Journal*, January 1987.

Periodicals

Industrial Development. Conway Research, Inc., 40 Technology Park, Norcross, GA 30092. Bimonthly.

Industrial Market Survey. Society of Industrial and Office Realtors, 777 14th Street NW, Washington, DC 20005. Semiannual.

SIOR Reports. Society of Industrial and Office Realtors, 777 14th Street NW, Washington, DC 20005. 10 issues a year.

Articles

Atkins, Robert J., and Shrives, Richard, H. "New Approach to Facilities Location." *Harvard Business Review*, May–June 1968.

Schmeiner, Roger W. "Look Beyond the Obvious in Plant Location." *Harvard Business Review*, January–February 1979.

Books

Kinnard, William N., Jr., and Messner, Stephen D. *Industrial Real Estate.* 2nd ed. Washington, DC: Society of Industrial and Office Realtors, 1984.

Lochmoeller, Donald C., Muncy, Dorothy, Thorne, Oakleigh, and Viets, Mark. *Industrial Development Handbook.* Washington, DC: Urban Land Institute, 1975.

INSURANCE

Articles

Barth, James R., Bradley, Michael G., and Feid, John J. "How Deposit Insurance Went Awry." *Federal Home Loan Bank Board Journal*, February 1989.

Charron, Mark. "Trends in Insurance—1990." *The Journal of Property Management*, January/February 1990.

Christman, Bruce L. "Primer on Fire/Hazard Insurance for the Commercial Real Estate Lender." *Real Estate Finance Journal*, Fall 1991.

Clauretie, Terrance, and Corgel, John B. "Weighing the Risk of Self-Insurance." *Mortgage Banking*, March 1988.

Levine, Mark Lee. "Errors and Omission Insurance: The Appraiser's Friend or Foe." *The Real Estate Appraiser and Analyst*, Summer 1988.

Ordway, Nicholas. "The Banking Insurance Crisis." *Real Estate Finance*, Summer 1987.

Book

Rubin, Harvey W. *Dictionary of Insurance Terms*. New York: Barron's Educational Series, 1987.

INVESTMENT

Articles

Davis, Joseph M. "Cash Flow Model Analysis: Buy the Assumptions, Not the Investments." *The Appraisal Journal*, April 1985.

Del Casino, Joseph J. "An Overview of the Real Estate Investment Marketplace." *The Appraisal Journal*, October 1987.

Hartzell, David, Shulman, David, and Wurtzebach, Charles. "Refining the Analysis of Regional Diversification for Income-Producing Real Estate." *The Journal of Real Estate Research*, Winter 1987.

Locke, Stuart M. "Property Investment Analysis Using Adjusted Present Values." *The Appraisal Journal*, July 1990.

Weinzimmer, Larry and Horvath, Philip. "Incorporating Risk Into Real Estate Investment Analysis: A New Valuation Approach." *The Real Estate Appraiser and Analyst*, Winter 1990.

Periodicals

Commercial Investment Journal. Realtors National Marketing Institute, 430 North Michigan Avenue, Chicago, IL 60611. Quarterly.

Books

Friedman, Jack P. and Harris, Jack. *Keys to Investing in Real Estate*. Hauppauge, NY: Barron's Educational Series, 1993.

Messner, Stephen D., et al. *Marketing Investment Real Estate*. Chicago: Realtors National Marketing Institute, National Association of Realtors, 1982.

Pyhrr, Stephen A., Cooper, James R., Wofford, Larry E., Kapplin, Steven D., and Lapides, Paul D. *Real Estate Investment: Strategy, Analysis & Decision*. New York: John Wiley & Sons, 1989.

Unger, Maurice A. *How to Invest in Real Estate*. New York: McGraw-Hill, 1990.

Wiedemer, John P. *Real Estate Investment Strategy*. Englewood Cliffs, N.J.: Prentice-Hall, 4th ed., 1989.

LAND AND LAND USE

Articles

Alvayay, Jaime, and Baen, John. "The Implications of Federal Wetland Protection Programs for the Real Estate Appraisal Industry." *The Journal of Real Estate Research*, Spring 1990.

Goldman, Ellis G. and Field, Charles G. "Summary of an Article on Reforming Land Use Regulations." *AREUEA Journal*, Summer 1983.

Grissom, Terry V. "Most Probable Land Use Determinations Under Uncertainty." *Appraisal Review Journal*, Spring–Summer 1983.

Books

Netter, Edith. *Land Use Law: Issues for the Eighties*. Chicago: American Planning Association, 1984.

Robinson, Shepard D. *Land Use Guide for Builders, Developers and Planners*. New York: McGraw-Hill, 1981.

Turnbull, Geoffrey K. "Property Taxes and the Transition of Land to Urban Use." *The Journal of Real Estate Finance and Economics*, December 1988.

LAND PLANNING

Periodicals

Journal of the American Planning Association. 1313 East 60th Street, Chicago, IL 60637. Quarterly.

Planning. American Planning Association, 1313 East 60th Street, Chicago, IL 60637. Monthly.

Books

Mandelker, Daniel R., and Cunningham, Roger A. *Land Use Law*. Charlottesville, VA: Michie Co., 1982.

LAW

Articles

Abney, David L. "Disclaiming the Implied Real Estate Common-Law Warranties." *Real Estate Law Journal*, Fall 1988.

Nessen, Robert and Ragalevsky, Stanley. "The Changing Role of Lawyers in Real Estate Transactions." *Real Estate Finance*, Spring 1988.

Periodicals

Real Estate Law Journal. Warren, Gorham & Lamont, Inc. Quarterly.

Real Estate Law Report. Warren, Gorham & Lamont, Inc. Monthly.

Books

Eaton, James D. *Real Estate Valuation in Litigation*. Chicago: Appraisal Institute, 1982.

Jacobus, Charles J., and Levi, Donald R. *Real Estate Law*. Englewood Cliffs, NJ: Prentice-Hall, 1980.

Kratovil, Robert, and Werner, Raymond J. R*eal Estate Law*. 8th ed. Englewood Cliffs, NJ: Prentice-Hall, 1983.

Madison, Michael T., and Dwyer, Jeffrey R. *The Law of Real Estate Financing*. Boston: Warren, Gorham & Lamont, 1981.

McLoughlin, Daniel P. *Principles of Real Estate Law*, New York: McGraw Hill, 1992.

LEASES & LEASEHOLD INTERESTS

Articles

Albert, Joseph and McIntosh, Willard. "Identifying Risk-Adjusted Indifference Rents for Alternative Operating Leases." *The Journal of Real Estate Research*, Fall 1989.

Jones, Robert N., and Roach, Stephen. "Valuation of Long-Term Leases." *The Appraisal Journal*, October 1989.

Manning, Chris. "Leasing Versus Purchase of Corporate Real Property: Leases with Residual Equity Interests." *The Journal of Real Estate Research*, Spring 1991.

Wunder, Gene. "Restrictive Clauses in Shopping Center Leases: A Review." *Real Estate Issues*, Spring/Summer 1988.

Periodicals

Real Estate Leasing Report. Federal Research Press, 210 Lincoln St., Suite 700, Boston, MA 02111.

Books

Friedman, Jack P., and Ordway, Nicholas. *Income Property Appraisal and Analysis.* Englewood Cliffs, NJ: Prentice-Hall, 1987. Chapter 19.

Kusnet, Jack. *Modern Real Estate Leasing Forms.* New York: Warren, Gorham & Lamont, 1980.

Seldin, Maury, ed. *The Real Estate Handbook*, New York: Dow Jones-Irwin, 1980.

Stevenson, Eric., ed. *Financing Income-Producing Real Estate.* New York: McGraw Hill, 1988.

LICENSING

Articles

Guntermann, Karl, and Smith, Richard L., "Licensing Requirements, Enforcement Effort and Complaints Against Real Estate Agents." *The Journal of Real Estate Research*, Summer 1988.

Johnson, Linda L., and Loucks, Christine. "The Effect of Certification and Licensure on Appraisers and Users of Appraisals." *The Appraisal Journal*, October 1988 and "The Effect of State Licensing Regulations on the Real Estate Brokerage Industry." *AREUEA Journal*, Winter 1986.

Shilling, James D., and Sirmans, C.F. "The Effects of Occupational Licensing on Complaints Against Real Estate Agents." *The Journal of Real Estate Research*, Summer 1988.

Books

Friedman, Jack P., and Lindeman, Bruce. *Barron's How to Prepare for Real Estate Licensing Examinations*, 4th Edition, Hauppauge, NY: Barron's Educational Series, 1991.

LIMITED PARTNERSHIPS

Articles

Kapplin, Steven, and Schwartz, Arthur. "Public Real Estate Limited Partnership Returns: A Preliminary Comparison with Other Investments." *AREUEA Journal*, Spring 1988.

Milich, Marvin F. "Master Limited Partnerships." *Real Estate Law Journal*, Summer 1991.

Taylor, Rick J., and Kozub, Robert M. "Real Estate Limited Partnerships: Is a Graceful Exit Possible?" *The Journal of Real Estate Taxation*, Winter 1987.

Books

Lynn, Theodore S., and Goldberg, Harry F. *Real Estate Limited Partnerships*. Somerset, NY: Ronald Press, 1983.

MANAGEMENT (BROKERAGE)

Articles

Johnson, Linda L., Dotson, Michael, and Dunlap, B.J., "Service Quality Determinants and Effectiveness in the Real Estate Brokerage Industry." *The Journal of Real Estate Research*, Summer 1988.

Books

Lindeman, Bruce. *Real Estate Brokerage Management*. Englewood Cliffs, NJ: Prentice-Hall, 1987.

Marcus, Bruce. *Marketing Professional Services in Real Estate*: *Advertising*, *Promotion*, *Public Relations*. Chicago: Realtors National Marketing Institute, 1981.

MANAGEMENT (PROPERTY)

Periodicals

Journal of Property Management. Institute of Real Estate Management, 430 North Michigan Avenue, Chicago, IL 60611. Bimonthly.

Books

Downs, James C., Jr. *Principles of Real Estate Management*. 12th ed. Chicago: Institute of Real Estate Management, 1980.

MARKET ANALYSIS

Articles

Dasso, Jerome. "Techniques of Area Analysis." *The Appraisal Journal*, October 1987.

Fanning, Stephen, and Winslow, Jody. "Guidelines for Defining the Scope of Market Analysis in Appraisal Assignments." *The Appraisal Journal*, October 1988.

Hennessey, Sean. "Economic Studies for Hotels: A Guide for Gathering Basis Data." *The Appraisal Journal*, July 1986.

Kimball, J.R, and Bloomberg, Barbara. "The Demographics of Subdivision Analysis." *The Appraisal Journal*, October 1986.

Morsch, William, and Shaw, William. "Use of Zip Codes in Location Analysis." *The Appraisal Journal*, January 1987.

Seldin, Maury. "A Reclassification of Real Estate and Market Analyses: Toward Improving the Line of Reasoning." *Real Estate Issues*, Spring/Summer 1984.

Vandell, Kerry. "Market Analysis: Can We Do Better?" *The Appraisal Journal*, July 1988.

Weber, Bruce R. "Application of Geographic Information Systems to Real Estate Market Analysis and Appraisal." *The Appraisal Journal*, January 1990.

Books

Barrett, Vincent G., and Blair, John O. *How to Conduct and Analyze Real Estate Market and Feasibility Studies*. New York: Van Nostrand and Reinhold Company, 1982.

Boykin, James H. *Real Estate Counseling*. Englewood Cliffs, NJ: Prentice-Hall, 1984.

Carn, Neil, Joseph Rabianski, Maury Seldin, Ron Racster. *Real Estate Market Analysis: Applications and Technique*. Englewood Cliffs, NJ: Prentice-Hall, 1988.

Clapp, John M. *Handbook for Real Estate Market Analysis*. Englewood Cliffs, NJ: Prentice-Hall, 1987.

Jarchow, Stephen P., editor. *Graaskamp on Real Estate*. Chicago: Urban Land Institute, 1992.

ULI Market Profiles. 7th ed. Chicago: Urban Land Institute, 1992.

Vernor, James D., ed. *Readings in Market Research for Real Estate*. Chicago: Appraisal Institute, 1985.

MARKETING

Articles

Kang, Han Bing, and Gardner, Mona. "Selling Price and Marketing Time in the Residential Real Estate Market." *The Journal of Real Estate Research*, Spring 1989.

Schloemer, Ellen and Jenkins, Russ. "Market Segmentation: The Quantum Leap to Success." *Mortgage Banking*, January 1987

Books

Real Estate Sales Handbook. Chicago: Realtors National Marketing Institute, 1984.

Shenkel, William. *Marketing Real Estate.* Englewood Cliffs, NJ: Prentice-Hall, 1980.

MATHEMATICS

Books

Ordway, Nicholas, Ordway, Kathy, and Tosh, Dennis S. *Real Estate Math Made Easy.* Englewood Cliffs, NJ: Prentice-Hall, 1985.

Ventolo, William L., Jr., Marks, Lynette K., and Allaway, Wellington J. *Mastering Real Estate Mathematics.* 2nd ed. Chicago: Real Estate Education Company, 1984.

MINERAL LEASING

Books

Oil and Gas Law. 8 vols. New York: Matthew Bender & Co.

MORTGAGE, ALTERNATIVE INSTRUMENTS

Periodicals

The Mortgage & Real Estate Executives Report. Warren, Gorham & Lamont, Inc. Twice monthly.

Books

Friedman, Jack P., and Harris, Jack C. *Adjustable Mortgage Loans.* Hauppauge, NY: Barron's Educational Series, 2nd ed. 1993.

MORTGAGE MARKET

Articles

American Real Estate & Urban Economics Association Journal, Spring 1980, Entire issue.

Vartanian, Thomas. "The Garn-St. Germain Depository Institutions Act of 1982," *Housing Finance Review,* April 1983.

MULTIPLE REGRESSION

Articles

Cronan, Timothy; Epley, Donald; and Perry, Larry. "The Use of Rank Transformation and Multiple Regression Analysis in Estimating Residential Property." *The Journal of Real Estate Research*, Fall 1986.

Jensen, David L. "The Use of Multiple Linear Regression in Residual Land Valuation." *Property Tax Journal*, September 1988.

Mark, Jonathan and Goldberg, Michael. "Multiple Regression Analysis and Mass Assessment: A Review of the Issues." *The Appraisal Journal*, January 1988.

Murphy, Lloyd T., III. "Determining the Appropriate Equation in Multiple Regression." *The Appraisal Journal*, October 1989.

OFFICE BUILDINGS

Articles

Bottum, MacKenzie S. "Estimating Economic Obsolescence in Supply-saturated Office Markets." *The Appraisal Journal*, October 1988.

Derbes, Max J., Jr. "Feasibility Income Deficiency." *The Appraisal Journal*, January 1989.

Frew, James and Jud, G. Donald. "The Vacancy Rates and Rent Levels in the Commercial Office Market." *The Journal of Real Estate Research*, Spring 1988.

Glascock, John; Jahanian, Sirin, and Sirmans, C.F. "An Analysis of Office Market Rents: Some Empirical Evidence." *AREUEA Journal*, Spring 1990.

Kelley, Hugh F. "Forecasting Office Space Demand in Urban Areas," *Real Estate Review*, Fall 1983.

Kimball, J.R., and Bloomberg, Barbara. "Office Space Demand Analysis." *The Appraisal Journal*, October 1987.

Kimball, William J. "Measuring an Office Building—1+1 = 2.2." *The Appraisal Journal*, January 1988.

Martin, William B., and English, Wilke D. "Forecasting Demand for Multi-Tenant Office Space." *Commercial Investment Journal*, Winter 1985.

Rosen, Kenneth T. "Toward a Model of the Office Building Sector." *Journal of the American Real Estate and Urban Economics Association*, Fall 1984.

Sullivan, John H. "Renewal Marketing in Office Buildings." *Journal of Property Management*, May/June 1991.

Vernor, James D. "Comparative Lease Analysis Using a Discounted Cash Flow Approach." *The Appraisal Journal*, July 1988.

Voith, Richard and Crone, Theodore. "National Vacancy Rates and the Persistence of Shocks in U.S. Office Markets." *AREUEA Journal*, Winter 1988.

Wheaton, William C. "The Cyclical Behavior of the National Office Market." *AREUEA Journal*, Winter 1987.

Wofford, Larry E. "Significant Trends Affecting Office and Industrial Real Estate: A Twenty-First Century Perspective." *The Appraisal Journal*, January 1987.

Periodicals

Income/Expense Analysis: Office Buildings. Institute of Real Estate Management, Chicago. Annually.

Office Building Experience Exchange Report. Building Owners and Managers Association International (BOMA), Washington, DC.

Books

Bearden, Thomas H., Farber, Joseph, and Trione, Gerard W. *Office Buildings: Development, Marketing and Leasing*. Chicago: American Society of Real Estate Counselors, 1981.

Managing the Office Building. Chicago: Institute of Real Estate Management. 1981.

Roberts, Duane F. *Marketing & Leasing of Office Space*. Chicago: Institute of Real Estate Management, 1979.

Stevenson, Eric, ed. *Financing Income-Producing Real Estate*. New York: McGraw-Hill, 1988.

PARKING FACILITIES

Articles

Cherry, Robert L., Jr. "Liability of Business Property Owners for Injury to Customers in Parking Lots by Criminal Attack from Third Parties." *Real Estate Law Journal*, Fall 1984.

Gottesman, Jerome. "Parking Feasibility Checklist." *Appraisal Digest*, October–November–December 1976.

Kenig, Neil S. "Economic Impact of Current Parking Standards of Office Developments." *Real Estate Issues*, Fall/Winter 1983.

Lindgrin, Gerald E. "Trends Affecting the Planning and Design of Parking Facilities." *Real Estate Issues*, Fall/Winter 1983.

Books

The Dimensions of Parking. 2nd ed. Washington, DC: The Urban Land Institute, 1983.

PRINCIPLES (OF REAL ESTATE)

Books

Dasso, Jerome, and Ring, Alfred. *Real Estate Principles.* 10th ed. Englewood Cliffs, NJ: Prentice-Hall, 1990.

Karvel, George and Unger, Maurice. *Real Estate Principles and Practices.* 9th ed. Dallas: South-Western Publishing Co., 1991.

Seldin, Maury, and Boykin, James H. *The Real Estate Handbook.* 2nd ed. Chicago: Dow Jones Irwin, 1990

Wofford, Larry E., and Clauretie, Terrence M. *Real Estate.* 3rd ed. New York: John Wiley & Sons, 1992.

Wurtzebach, Charles, and Miles, Mike E. *Modern Real Estate.* 4th ed. New York: John Wiley & Sons, 1991.

REGULATIONS

Articles

Goldman, Ellis G. and Field, Charles G. "Summary of an Article on Reforming Land Use Regulations." *AREUEA Journal*, Summer 1983.

Kettlewell, Ursula. "Land Use Regulations as a Barrier to Business and Economic Growth." *The Appraisal Journal*, July 1984.

Sussna, Stephen. "Another Look at Height Restrictions and Air Rights." *The Appraisal Journal*, January 1989.

Periodicals

Housing & Development Reporter. Bureau of National Affairs, 1231 25th Street NW, Washington, DC 20037. Weekly.

Books

Barron, Paul E. *Federal Regulation of Real Estate.* Boston: Warren, Gorham & Lamont, 1985.

RENT AND RENT CONTROL

Articles

Ault, Richard, and Saba, Richard. "The Economic Effects of Long-Term Rent Control: The Case of New York City." *The Journal of Real Estate Finance and Economics*, March 1990.

Fallis, George. "Rent Control: The Citizen, The Market, and The State." *Journal of Real Estate Finance and Economics*, June 1988.

Olson, Edgar O. "What Do Economists Know about the Effect of Rent Control on Housing?" *Journal of Real Estate Finance and Economics*, November 1988.

Rydell, C. Peter, and Michael P. Murray. "How Rent Control Affects Property Taxes." *Property Tax Journal*, March 1987.

RETIREMENT HOUSING

Articles

Bogorad, Leonard. "Rental Retirement Housing: Running Out with Renewed Vigor." *Mortgage Banking*, December 1986.

Festervand, Troy and Lumpkin, James R. "Positioning Retirement Housing Developments via Perceptual Mapping." *Real Estate Finance*, Summer 1990.

Haynes, Joel B. and Elliott, Clifford. "Congregate Living Facilities: The Florida Experience." *The Real Estate Appraiser and Analyst*, Spring 1989.

Rasmussen, John A. "Retirement Community Development: New Trends in Marketing and Financing Concepts." *Real Estate Issues*, Fall/Winter 1986.

Books

Friedman, Jack P. and Harris, Jack. *Keys to Buying a Retirement Home.* Hauppauge, NY: Barron's Educational Series, 1991.

RIGHT OF WAY (SEE EASEMENTS)

Articles

Reiger, Arthur J. "Appraising the Sun: Experience to Date." *Appraisal Journal*, April 1980.

Smith, Walstein, Jr. "Some Enchanting Easements." *Appraisal Journal*, October 1980.

Periodicals

Right of Way. International Right of Way Assn., 13650 South Gramercy Place, Suite 100, Gardena, CA 90249. Bimonthly.

RURAL PROPERTIES

Articles

Everhart, Marion E. "Who is Qualified to Appraise and Review Rural Properties?" *The Real Estate Appraiser and Analyst*, Summer 1989.

Periodicals

Agricultural Economics Research. U.S. Department of Agriculture. Superintendent of Documents, Government Printing Office, Washington, DC 20402. Quarterly.

American Journal of Agricultural Economics. Dept. of Economics, Iowa State University, Ames, IA 50011.

SAVINGS & LOAN ASSOCIATIONS

Articles

Harris, Jack. "The Real Cost of the Savings and Loan Crisis." *Real Estate Finance*, Summer 1990.

Sussman, Allen Z. "Increasing Thrift Industry Capital in Light of Post-FIRREA Asset Constraints." *Real Estate Finance*, Winter 1990.

Periodicals

National Savings & Loan League Journal. National Savings & Loan League, Suite 400, 1101 15th Street, NW, Washington, DC 20005. Monthly.

Savings & Loan News. U.S. League of Savings Associations, 111 East Wacker Drive, Chicago IL 60601. Monthly.

SECURITIZATION

Articles

Avery, Jonathan H. "Securitization and the Appraiser." *Real Estate Finance*, Spring 1987.

Books, Roberta Paula. "Securitization: A Comparison of Hedging Techniques." *Real Estate Finance*, Summer 1989.

Franzetti, Joseph C. "Movements in Commercial Mortgage Securitization." *Mortgage Banking*, July 1991.

Hess, Alan C. and Smith, Clifford W., Jr. "Elements of Mortgage Securitization." *The Journal of Real Estate Finance and Economics*, December 1988.

Jaffee, Dwight M. and Rosen, Kenneth T. "Mortgage Securitization Trends." *Journal of Real Estate Housing*, 1990.

Miller, John H., III, and Betts, Richard M. "The Impact of Securitization on Real Estate Appraisal." *The Appraisal Journal*, October 1986.

Roulac, Stephen E. "Real Estate Securitization: Prologue and Prospects." *Real Estate Finance*, Spring 1988.

SHOPPING CENTERS

Articles

Bottum, MacKenzie S. "Retail Gravity Model." *The Appraisal Journal*, April 1989.

Fisher, Jeffrey, and Lentz, George. "Enterprise Value in Shopping Center Malls: An Empirical Test." *The Journal of Real Estate Research*, Spring 1990.

Gelbtuch, Howard C. "Shopping Centers Are a Business, Too." *The Appraisal Journal*, April 1990 and "The Warehouse Club Industry." *The Appraisal Journal*, April 1990.

Kahn, Beatrice. "What Happens to the OREA if an Anchor Goes Under?" *Real Estate Finance*, Fall 1989.

Kenney, Mark. "Does Shopping Mall Development Create Business Value?" *The Appraisal Journal*, July 1991.

Kimball, William J. "Recent Trends in the Shopping Center Market." *The Appraisal Journal*, July 1991.

Lamm, Robert R. "Selling or Buying Shopping Centers in Today's Market." *Urban Land*, May 1983.

Ordway, Nicholas and Bul, Alexander. "Developing an Index to Classify Shopping Centers." *The Appraisal Journal*, April 1988.

Roswick, Bruce H., and McEvily, Stephanie. "Use Clauses in Shopping Center Leases: What if a Tenant Bankrupts?" *Real Estate Law Journal*, Summer 1985.

Wunder, Gene. "Restrictive Clauses in Shopping Center Leases: A Review." *Real Estate Issues*, Spring/Summer 1988.

Periodicals

Dollars & Cents of Shopping Centers 1993. Chicago: Urban Land Institute. Triennial.

Survey of Buying Power. New York: Sales and Marketing Management.

Books

Davies, R. L., and Rogers, D. S. *Store Location and Store Assessment Research.* New York: Wiley & Sons, 1984.

Managing the Shopping Center. Chicago: Institute of Real Estate Management, 1983.

Shopping Center Development Handbook. Urban Land Institute, Washington, DC: 1985.

Vernor, James D., and Joseph Rabianski, *Shopping Center Appraisal and Analysis.* Chicago: Appraisal Institute, 1992.

SITE SELECTION

Articles

Born, Waldo L., and Williams, B. Earl. "Electronic Data Transmission Pathways: Implications for Site Selection." *The Journal of Real Estate Research*, Fall 1989.

Erickson, Rodney A., and Wasylenko. "Firm Relocation and Site Selection in Surburban Municipalities." *Journal of Urban Economics*, July 1980.

Meyer, Terry G. "Site Selection Vs. Site Evaluation: Techniques for Locating Retail." *Real Estate Issues*, Spring/Summer 1988.

Rabianski, Joseph. "Non-economic Factors in the Site Selection Process." *Real Estate Issues*, Fall/Winter 1982.

Periodicals

Industrial Development Site Selection Handbook. Conway Data, Inc., 40 Technology Park, Norcross, GA 30092-9990.

SUBDIVISIONS

Articles

Kimball, J.R, Bloomberg, Barbara, and Steven A. Jones. "Subdivision Analysis and Valuation." *The Appraisal Journal*, October 1986.

West, Robert J. "Subdivision Analysis: Retail Values." *The Appraisal Journal*, April 1989.

SYNDICATION

Articles

Roulac, Stephen E. "Syndication Emerges to Transform the Real Estate Capital Market." *Real Estate Finance*, Winter 1985.

Seymour, Charles F. "Market Value vs. Syndication Price." *The Appraisal Journal*, July 1986.

Wetterer, Charles. "Syndication Watch: New Life in Private Syndications." *Real Estate Finance*, Fall 1987.

Periodicals

RESSI Review. Real Estate Securities & Syndication Institute, 430 North Michigan Avenue, Chicago, IL 60611. Monthly.

Securities Regulation Law Journal. Warren, Gorham & Lamont, Inc., Boston, MA 02111. Quarterly.

TAXATION (INCOME)

Articles

Bible, Douglas. "Rehabilitation Tax Credits and Rate of Return on Real Estate Under Recent Tax Reform Measures." *The Journal of Real Estate Research*, Winter 1987.

Eichen, Glenn N. "Federal Income Tax Consequences of Debt Restructuring." *Journal of Real Estate Taxation*, Winter, 1988 and Spring 1988.

Friedman, Jack P. "Washington Letter: New Regulations Proposed for Deferred Tax-Free Exchanges." *Real Estate Finance*, Summer 1990.

Friedman, Jack and Harris, Jack. "Tax Reform Encourages 1031 Exchanges." *The Appraisal Journal*, January 1987.

Haight, G. Timothy. "The Effect of the Tax Reform Act of 1986 on Low Income Housing Investments." *The Appraisal Journal*, January 1988.

Stoller, Linda A. "Tax Topics: Passive Income Generators." *Real Estate Finance*, Fall 1987.

Periodicals

Journal of Real Estate Taxation. Warren, Gorham & Lamont, Inc., Boston. MA 02111. Quarterly.

Real Estate Newsletter. Coopers & Lybrand, 222 South Riverside Plaza, Chicago, IL 60606. Quarterly.

Real Estate Tax Ideas. Warren, Gorham & Lamont, Inc., Boston, MA 02111. Monthly.

Books

Kau, James B., and Sirmans, C. F. *Tax Planning for Real Estate Investors*. Englewood Cliffs, NJ: Prentice-Hall, 1980.

Robinson, Gerald J. *Federal Income Taxation of Real Estate*. 3rd ed. New York: Warren, Gorham & Lamont, 1979.

Smith, David A. *Subsidized Housing as a Tax Shelter*. Fair Haven, NJ: Robert A. Stanger Co., 1982.

Young, James C., and Dilley, Steven C., eds. *The Tax Reform Act of 1986*: *Taxation of Real Estate Transactions*. Paramus, NJ: Prentice-Hall Information Services, 1987.

TAX (PROPERTY)

Articles

Blake, D. R. "Property Tax Incidence An Alternative View." *Land Economics*, 1979.

Gilreath, Morgan, Jr. "Appraisal with General Purpose Software: Applying the Income Approach." *Property Tax Journal*, March 1990.

Grissom, Terry V., and Kimball, J. "Using a Loaded Capitalization Rate to Estimate Property Taxes in Various Income Models." *The Appraisal Journal*, July 1989.

Haurin, Donald R. "An Empirical Analysis of Property Tax Equity." *Property Tax Journal*, March 1988.

Jensen, David L. "The Use of Multiple Linear Regression in Residual Land Valuation." *Property Tax Journal*, September 1988.

Turnbull, Geoffrey K. "Property Taxes and the Transition of Land to Urban Use." *The Journal of Real Estate Finance and Economics*, December 1988.

Periodical

Property Tax Journal. Chicago: International Association of Assessing Officers.

TIMBER AND TIMBER LAND

Articles

Anglyn, William. "Timber Assessment Procedures—A Critical Analysis." *The Appraisal Journal*, April 1991.

Gilmore, Terry and Healy, Martin, Jr. "What is Dirt Worth?" *The Appraisal Journal*, July 1991.

Klemperer, David W. "Effects of Inflation and Debt on Old Growth Timber Appraisal." *Appraisal Journal*, January 1985 and "Valuing Young Timber Scheduled for Future Harvest." *Appraisal Journal*, October 1987.

Schuster, Ervin G., and Niccolucci, Michael J. "Comparative Accuracy of Six Timber Appraisal Methods." *The Appraisal Journal*, January 1990.

Periodicals

Forest Farmers. Forest Farmers Association, Box 95385, 4 Executive Park East NE, Atlanta, GA 30347.

TIMESHARING

Articles

Bouillon, Jennifer Wang. "Time-Share Performance: A Survey of Financial Performance from Developers." *Real Estate Issues*, Spring/Summer 1990.

Tuschka, Karl O. "California Real Property Taxation of Time-Share Interests." *Real Estate Issues*, Spring/Summer 1985.

Periodicals

Conroe, Kathleen. *"Valuing the Timeshare Property."The Appraisal Journal*, 1981.

Resort Timesharing Today. CHB Co. Inc., Drawer 730, Los Altos, CA 94022. Monthly.

Timesharing Law Reporter. Land Development Institute, Ltd., 1401 16th Street NW, Washington, DC 20036. Monthly.

TRANSFER OF DEVELOPMENT RIGHTS

Books

Heffley, Dennis S. *Transferable Development Rights: A Spatial Equilibrium Analysis*. Storrs, CT: Center for Real Estate and Urban Economic Studies, 1980.

WATERFRONT PROPERTY

Books

Kline, John E. "An Alternative Method of Valuing Nondevelopable Waterfront Land and Beaches." *The Appraisal Journal*, January 1984.

Rick, William B. *Planning & Developing Water Front Property.* Washington, DC: Urban Land Institute, 1984.

WATER RIGHTS

Articles

Claus, R. James, Large, Donald W. and Claus, Karen E. "Irrigated Agriculture: Economic, Environmental, Disposal, and Legal Problems." *The Appraisal Journal*, July 1987.

Colby, Bonnie G. "Alternative Approaches to Valuing Water Rights." *The Appraisal Journal*, April 1989.

Books

Waters and Water Rights. 7 vols. Indianapolis: The Allen Smith Company, 1967.

ZONING

Articles

Geller, Leslie. "Zoning and the Appraiser." *The Appraisal Journal*, April 1987.

Books

Hinds, Dudley; Carn, Neil; and Ordway, Nicholas. *Winning at Zoning.* New York: McGraw-Hill, 1980.

Mandelker, Daniel R. *Managing our Urban Environment.* Indianapolis: Bobbs-Merrill, 1982.

PUBLISHERS' ADDRESSES

Addison-Wesley Publishing Co.
 Jacob Way
 Reading, MA 01867

American Society of Farm Managers
 & Rural Appraisers
 950 S. Cherry St., #106
 Denver, CO 80222

American Society of Appraisers
 Dulles International Airport
 Box 17265
 Washington, DC 20041

The Appraisal Institute
 875 N. Michigan Avenue
 Chicago, IL 60611

Ballinger Publishing Co.
 54 Church St.
 Cambridge, MA 02139

Barron's Educational Series, Inc.
 250 Wireless Blvd.
 Hauppauge, NY 11788

Bobbs-Merrill Co.
 4300 W. 62nd Street
 Indianapolis, IN 46268

Business One-Irwin
 1818 Ridge Road
 Homewood, IL 60430

Cahners Publishing Company
44 Cook Street
Denver, CO 80206

Communication Channels, Inc.
6255 Barfield Road
Atlanta, GA 30328

Community Associations Institute
1630 Duke Street
Alexandria, VA 22202

Conway Data Inc.
40 Technology Park
Norcross, GA 30092

Crittenden Publishing Inc.
Box 1150
Novato, CA 94948

Environmental Protection Agency
U.S. Government Printing Office
Washington, DC 20402

Employee Relocation Council
1720 N Street NW
Washington, DC 20036

Farm & Land Institute
430 North Michigan Avenue
Chicago, IL 60611

FIABCI
American Chapter
430 N. Michigan Avenue
Chicago, IL 60611

Gralla Publications
1515 Broadway
New York, NY 10036

Institute of Real Estate Management
430 North Michigan Avenue
Chicago, IL 60611

International Association of Assessing Officers
1313 East 60th Street
Chicago, IL 60637-9990

International Right of Way Association
13650 South Gramercy Place, Suite 100
Gardena, CA 90249

McGraw-Hill Book Company
1221 Avenue of the Americas
New York, NY 10020

Mortgage Bankers Association of America
1125 15th Street NW
Washington, DC 20005

National Apartment Association
1111 14th Street NW, Suite 900
Washington, DC 20005

National Association of Review Appraisers
8715 Via de Commercio
Scottsdale, AZ 85258

National Association of Homebuilders
The National Housing Center
15th and M Streets NW
Washington, DC 20005

National Association of Realtors
Economics & Research Division
777 14th Street NW
Washington, DC 20005

Penton/IPC Inc.
1111 Chester Avenue
Cleveland, OH 44114

Prentice-Hall, Inc.
Englewood Cliffs, NJ 07632

Random House, Inc.
201 E. 50th Street
New York, NY 10022

Real Estate Education Company
520 N. Dearborn Street
Chicago, IL 60610

Real Estate Law Institute
Box 12528
San Antonio, TX 78212

Real Estate Publishing Company
Box 41177
Sacramento, CA 95841

Realtors National Marketing Institute
430 N. Michigan
Chicago, IL 60611

School of Hotel Administration
Cornell University
Statler Hall
Ithaca, NY 14853

Scott, Foresman & Co.
1900 E. Lake Ave.
Glenview, IL 60025

South-Western Publishing Co.
13800 Senlac Dr., Suite 100
Dallas, TX 75234

Superintendent of Documents
U.S. Government Printing Office
Washington, DC 20402

University of Wisconsin Press
Journals Dept.
114 North Murray Street
Madison, WI 53715

Urban Land Institute
625 Indiana Avenue, Suite 400
Washington, DC 20004-2930

U.S. Department of Agriculture
Washington, DC 20250

Van Nostrand Reinhold Company
450 W. 33rd Street
New York, NY 10001

Warren, Gorham & Lamont
One Penn Plaza
New York, NY 10119

West Publishing Company
Box 64833
St. Paul, MN 55164-1803

522

MONTHLY MORTGAGE PAYMENTS

The monthly payments table allows you to find out how much you would pay in interest and principal per month on an amortizing mortgage loan. To use the table you must know the following:

1. *The loan interest rate.* Each page is for a different interest rate as shown in the table's heading. Rates range from 5% to 21.75% by .25% intervals.

2. *The amount borrowed.* Amounts are shown in the column on the far left side of each table. To find the payment for an amount in between those shown, add up the payments as shown in the example below.

3. *The maturity or term of the loan.* This is the length of time over which the payments are set to run. Maturities of 10, 15, 20, 25, and 30 years are shown in the top row of each table.

The body of the table shows the monthly payment amount in dollars. This payment does not include escrow payments which may be required by the lender for insurance and property taxes. Such payments would be in addition to the amount shown in the table.

Example: Suppose you wish to borrow $47,850 to buy a home. The maturity of the loan is 25 years and the annual interest rate is 7%. To find the monthly payment, look at the first table where the annual interest rate is 7%. First look at where the row for "40,000" intersects the column for "25" years. The amount is 282.72. Next locate the row for "7,000" and column for "25" and see the amount of 49.48 at their intersection. Likewise, find the "800" row and "25" column (amount is 5.66) and the "50" row and "25" column (amount is .36). The total payment is the sum of these amounts:

40,000	282.72
7,000	49.48
800	5.66
50	.36
47,850	338.22

The total loan amount is $47,850 and the total monthly payment is $338.22.

Example: Suppose your monthly income is $2,000 and you can afford to pay up to 25% of that amount ($500) on mortgage payments. How big a loan can you get?

Assume the loan interest rate is 7% and 30 year loans are available. Look once again at the first table. Find the amount in the table under the "30" column which is closest but lower than 500. You should see the amount of 465.72 in the "70,000" row. The difference between 500 and 465.72 is 34.28. Find the closest lower amount in the "30" column. The answer is 33. 27 in the "5,000" row. You still have 34.28 minus 33.27, or 1.01 to

523

spend. In the "100" row you will find an amount of .67. You still have 1.01 −.67, or .34 to spend. In the "50" row you will find an amount of .34. Now add up all the amounts:

465.72	70,000
33.27	5,000
.67	100
.34	50
500.00	75,150

The highest payment you could afford is $500.00 which, at 7% over 30 years, will provide for a loan of $75,150.

MONTHLY PAYMENTS
ANNUAL INTEREST RATE: 5%

LOAN AMOUNT	LOAN MATURITY (YEARS)				
	10	15	20	25	30
50	0.54	0.40	0.33	0.30	0.27
100	1.07	0.80	0.66	0.59	0.54
200	2.13	1.59	1.32	1.17	1.08
300	3.19	2.38	1.98	1.76	1.62
400	4.25	3.17	2.64	2.34	2.15
500	5.31	3.96	3.30	2.93	2.69
600	6.37	4.75	3.96	3.51	3.23
700	7.43	5.54	4.62	4.10	3.76
800	8.49	6.33	5.28	4.68	4.30
900	9.55	7.12	5.94	5.27	4.84
1,000	10.61	7.91	6.60	5.85	5.37
2,000	21.22	15.82	13.20	11.70	10.74
3,000	31.82	23.73	19.80	17.54	16.11
4,000	42.43	31.64	26.40	23.39	21.48
5,000	53.04	39.54	33.00	29.23	26.85
6,000	63.64	47.45	39.60	35.08	32.21
7,000	74.25	55.36	46.20	40.93	37.58
8,000	84.86	63.27	52.80	46.77	42.95
9,000	95.46	71.18	59.40	52.62	48.32
10,000	106.07	79.08	66.00	58.46	53.69
20,000	212.13	158.16	131.99	116.92	107.37
30,000	318.20	237.24	197.99	175.38	161.05
40,000	424.26	316.32	263.98	233.84	214.73
50,000	530.32	395.40	329.98	292.30	268.41
60,000	636.39	474.48	395.97	350.76	322.10
70,000	742.45	553.55	461.97	409.21	375.78
80,000	848.52	632.63	527.96	467.67	429.46
90,000	954.58	711.71	593.96	526.13	483.14
100,000	1060.64	790.79	659.95	584.59	536.82
110,000	1166.71	869.87	725.95	643.05	590.50
120,000	1272.77	948.95	791.94	701.51	644.19
130,000	1378.84	1028.02	857.94	759.96	697.87
140,000	1484.90	1107.10	923.93	818.42	751.55
150,000	1590.96	1186.18	989.93	876.88	805.23
160,000	1697.03	1265.26	1055.92	935.34	858.91
170,000	1803.09	1344.34	1121.92	993.80	912.59
180,000	1909.16	1423.42	1187.91	1052.26	966.28
190,000	2015.22	1502.49	1253.91	1110.72	1019.96
200,000	2121.28	1581.57	1319.90	1169.17	1073.64
250,000	2651.60	1976.96	1649.88	1461.47	1342.05
300,000	3181.92	2372.35	1979.85	1753.76	1610.46

MONTHLY PAYMENTS
ANNUAL INTEREST RATE: 5.25%

LOAN AMOUNT	LOAN MATURITY (YEARS)				
	10	15	20	25	30
50	0.54	0.41	0.34	0.30	0.28
100	1.08	0.81	0.68	0.60	0.56
200	2.15	1.61	1.35	1.20	1.11
300	3.22	2.42	2.03	1.80	1.66
400	4.30	3.22	2.70	2.40	2.21
500	5.37	4.02	3.37	3.00	2.77
600	6.44	4.83	4.05	3.60	3.32
700	7.52	5.63	4.72	4.20	3.87
800	8.59	6.44	5.40	4.80	4.42
900	9.66	7.24	6.07	5.40	4.97
1,000	10.73	8.04	6.74	6.00	5.53
2,000	21.46	16.08	13.48	11.99	11.05
3,000	32.19	24.12	20.22	17.98	16.57
4,000	42.92	32.16	26.96	23.98	22.09
5,000	53.65	40.20	33.70	29.97	27.62
6,000	64.38	48.24	40.44	35.96	33.14
7,000	75.11	56.28	47.17	41.95	38.66
8,000	85.84	64.32	53.91	47.95	44.18
9,000	96.57	72.35	60.65	53.94	49.70
10,000	107.30	80.39	67.39	59.93	55.23
20,000	214.59	160.78	134.77	119.86	110.45
30,000	321.88	241.17	202.16	179.78	165.67
40,000	429.18	321.56	269.54	239.71	220.89
50,000	536.47	401.95	336.93	299.63	276.11
60,000	643.76	482.34	404.31	359.56	331.33
70,000	751.05	562.72	471.70	419.48	386.55
80,000	858.35	643.11	539.08	479.41	441.77
90,000	965.64	723.50	606.47	539.33	496.99
100,000	1072.93	803.89	673.85	599.26	552.21
110,000	1180.22	884.28	741.24	659.18	607.43
120,000	1287.52	964.67	808.62	719.11	662.65
130,000	1394.81	1045.05	876.01	779.03	717.87
140,000	1502.10	1125.44	943.39	838.96	773.09
150,000	1609.40	1205.83	1010.78	898.88	828.31
160,000	1716.69	1286.22	1078.16	958.81	883.54
170,000	1823.98	1366.61	1145.55	1018.73	938.76
180,000	1931.27	1447.00	1212.93	1078.66	993.98
190,000	2038.57	1527.38	1280.32	1138.58	1049.20
200,000	2145.86	1607.77	1347.70	1198.51	1104.42
250,000	2682.32	2009.71	1684.63	1498.13	1380.52
300,000	3218.79	2411.66	2021.55	1797.76	1656.62

MONTHLY PAYMENTS
ANNUAL INTEREST RATE: 5.5%

LOAN AMOUNT	LOAN MATURITY (YEARS)				
	10	15	20	25	30
50	0.55	0.41	0.35	0.31	0.29
100	1.09	0.82	0.69	0.62	0.57
200	2.18	1.64	1.38	1.23	1.14
300	3.26	2.46	2.07	1.85	1.71
400	4.35	3.27	2.76	2.46	2.28
500	5.43	4.09	3.44	3.08	2.84
600	6.52	4.91	4.13	3.69	3.41
700	7.60	5.72	4.82	4.30	3.98
800	8.69	6.54	5.51	4.92	4.55
900	9.77	7.36	6.20	5.53	5.12
1,000	10.86	8.18	6.88	6.15	5.68
2,000	21.71	16.35	13.76	12.29	11.36
3,000	32.56	24.52	20.64	18.43	17.04
4,000	43.42	32.69	27.52	24.57	22.72
5,000	54.27	40.86	34.40	30.71	28.39
6,000	65.12	49.03	41.28	36.85	34.07
7,000	75.97	57.20	48.16	42.99	39.75
8,000	86.83	65.37	55.04	49.13	45.43
9,000	97.68	73.54	61.91	55.27	51.11
10,000	108.53	81.71	68.79	61.41	56.78
20,000	217.06	163.42	137.58	122.82	113.56
30,000	325.58	245.13	206.37	184.23	170.34
40,000	434.11	326.84	275.16	245.64	227.12
50,000	542.64	408.55	343.95	307.05	283.90
60,000	651.16	490.26	412.74	368.46	340.68
70,000	759.69	571.96	481.53	429.87	397.46
80,000	868.22	653.67	550.31	491.28	454.24
90,000	976.74	735.38	619.10	552.68	511.02
100,000	1085.27	817.09	687.89	614.09	567.79
110,000	1193.79	898.80	756.68	675.50	624.57
120,000	1302.32	980.51	825.47	736.91	681.35
130,000	1410.85	1062.21	894.26	798.32	738.13
140,000	1519.37	1143.92	963.05	859.73	794.91
150,000	1627.90	1225.63	1031.84	921.14	851.69
160,000	1736.43	1307.34	1100.62	982.55	908.47
170,000	1844.95	1389.05	1169.41	1043.95	965.25
180,000	1953.48	1470.76	1238.20	1105.36	1022.03
190,000	2062.00	1552.46	1306.99	1166.77	1078.80
200,000	2170.53	1634.17	1375.78	1228.18	1135.58
250,000	2713.16	2042.71	1719.72	1535.22	1419.48
300,000	3255.79	2451.26	2063.67	1842.27	1703.37

MONTHLY PAYMENTS
ANNUAL INTEREST RATE: 5.75%

LOAN AMOUNT	LOAN MATURITY (YEARS)				
	10	15	20	25	30
50	0.55	0.42	0.36	0.32	0.30
100	1.10	0.84	0.71	0.63	0.59
200	2.20	1.67	1.41	1.26	1.17
300	3.30	2.50	2.11	1.89	1.76
400	4.40	3.33	2.81	2.52	2.34
500	5.49	4.16	3.52	3.15	2.92
600	6.59	4.99	4.22	3.78	3.51
700	7.69	5.82	4.92	4.41	4.09
800	8.79	6.65	5.62	5.04	4.67
900	9.88	7.48	6.32	5.67	5.26
1,000	10.98	8.31	7.03	6.30	5.84
2,000	21.96	16.61	14.05	12.59	11.68
3,000	32.94	24.92	21.07	18.88	17.51
4,000	43.91	33.22	28.09	25.17	23.35
5,000	54.89	41.53	35.11	31.46	29.18
6,000	65.87	49.83	42.13	37.75	35.02
7,000	76.84	58.13	49.15	44.04	40.86
8,000	87.82	66.44	56.17	50.33	46.69
9,000	98.80	74.74	63.19	56.63	52.53
10,000	109.78	83.05	70.21	62.92	58.36
20,000	219.55	166.09	140.42	125.83	116.72
30,000	329.32	249.13	210.63	188.74	175.08
40,000	439.09	332.17	280.84	251.65	233.44
50,000	548.86	415.22	351.05	314.56	291.79
60,000	658.63	498.26	421.26	377.47	350.15
70,000	768.40	581.30	491.47	440.38	408.51
80,000	878.17	664.34	561.68	503.29	466.87
90,000	987.94	747.38	631.89	566.21	525.22
100,000	1097.71	830.43	702.10	629.12	583.58
110,000	1207.48	913.47	772.30	692.03	641.94
120,000	1317.25	996.51	842.51	754.94	700.30
130,000	1427.02	1079.55	912.72	817.85	758.66
140,000	1536.80	1162.59	982.93	880.76	817.01
150,000	1646.57	1245.63	1053.14	943.67	875.37
160,000	1756.34	1328.68	1123.35	1006.58	933.73
170,000	1866.11	1411.72	1193.56	1069.50	992.09
180,000	1975.88	1494.76	1263.77	1132.41	1050.44
190,000	2085.65	1577.80	1333.98	1195.32	1108.80
200,000	2195.42	1660.85	1404.19	1258.23	1167.16
250,000	2744.27	2076.05	1755.23	1572.78	1458.95
300,000	3293.13	2491.26	2106.28	1887.34	1750.74

MONTHLY PAYMENTS
ANNUAL INTEREST RATE: 6%

LOAN AMOUNT	LOAN MATURITY (YEARS)				
	10	15	20	25	30
50	0.56	0.43	0.36	0.33	0.30
100	1.12	0.85	0.72	0.65	0.60
200	2.23	1.69	1.44	1.29	1.20
300	3.34	2.54	2.15	1.94	1.80
400	4.45	3.38	2.87	2.58	2.40
500	5.56	4.22	3.59	3.23	3.00
600	6.67	5.07	4.30	3.87	3.60
700	7.78	5.91	5.02	4.52	4.20
800	8.89	6.76	5.74	5.16	4.80
900	10.00	7.60	6.45	5.80	5.40
1,000	11.11	8.44	7.17	6.45	6.00
2,000	22.21	16.88	14.33	12.89	12.00
3,000	33.31	25.32	21.50	19.33	17.99
4,000	44.41	33.76	28.66	25.78	23.99
5,000	55.52	42.20	35.83	32.22	29.98
6,000	66.62	50.64	42.99	38.66	35.98
7,000	77.72	59.07	50.16	45.11	41.97
8,000	88.82	67.51	57.32	51.55	47.97
9,000	99.92	75.95	64.48	57.99	53.96
10,000	111.03	84.39	71.65	64.44	59.96
20,000	222.05	168.78	143.29	128.87	119.92
30,000	333.07	253.16	214.93	193.30	179.87
40,000	444.09	337.55	286.58	257.73	239.83
50,000	555.11	421.93	358.22	322.16	299.78
60,000	666.13	506.32	429.86	386.59	359.74
70,000	777.15	590.70	501.51	451.02	419.69
80,000	888.17	675.09	573.15	515.45	479.65
90,000	999.19	759.48	644.79	579.88	539.60
100,000	1110.21	843.86	716.44	644.31	599.56
110,000	1221.23	928.25	788.08	708.74	659.51
120,000	1332.25	1012.63	859.72	773.17	719.47
130,000	1443.27	1097.02	931.37	837.60	779.42
140,000	1554.29	1181.40	1003.01	902.03	839.38
150,000	1665.31	1265.79	1074.65	966.46	899.33
160,000	1776.33	1350.18	1146.29	1030.89	959.29
170,000	1887.35	1434.56	1217.94	1095.32	1019.24
180,000	1998.37	1518.95	1289.58	1159.75	1079.20
190,000	2109.39	1603.33	1361.22	1224.18	1139.15
200,000	2220.41	1687.72	1432.87	1288.61	1199.11
250,000	2775.52	2109.65	1791.08	1610.76	1498.88
300,000	3330.62	2531.57	2149.30	1932.91	1798.66

MONTHLY PAYMENTS
ANNUAL INTEREST RATE: 6.25%

LOAN AMOUNT	LOAN MATURITY (YEARS)				
	10	15	20	25	30
50	0.57	0.43	0.37	0.33	0.31
100	1.13	0.86	0.74	0.66	0.62
200	2.25	1.72	1.47	1.32	1.24
300	3.37	2.58	2.20	1.98	1.85
400	4.50	3.43	2.93	2.64	2.47
500	5.62	4.29	3.66	3.30	3.08
600	6.74	5.15	4.39	3.96	3.70
700	7.86	6.01	5.12	4.62	4.32
800	8.99	6.86	5.85	5.28	4.93
900	10.11	7.72	6.58	5.94	5.55
1,000	11.23	8.58	7.31	6.60	6.16
2,000	22.46	17.15	14.62	13.20	12.32
3,000	33.69	25.73	21.93	19.79	18.48
4,000	44.92	34.30	29.24	26.39	24.63
5,000	56.14	42.88	36.55	32.99	30.79
6,000	67.37	51.45	43.86	39.58	36.95
7,000	78.60	60.02	51.17	46.18	43.11
8,000	89.83	68.60	58.48	52.78	49.26
9,000	101.06	77.17	65.79	59.37	55.42
10,000	112.28	85.75	73.10	65.97	61.58
20,000	224.56	171.49	146.19	131.94	123.15
30,000	336.84	257.23	219.28	197.90	184.72
40,000	449.12	342.97	292.37	263.87	246.29
50,000	561.40	428.71	365.47	329.84	307.86
60,000	673.68	514.46	438.56	395.80	369.43
70,000	785.96	600.20	511.65	461.77	431.01
80,000	898.24	685.94	584.74	527.74	492.58
90,000	1010.52	771.68	657.84	593.70	554.15
100,000	1122.80	857.42	730.93	659.67	615.72
110,000	1235.08	943.16	804.02	725.64	677.29
120,000	1347.35	1028.91	877.11	791.60	738.86
130,000	1459.63	1114.65	950.21	857.57	800.43
140,000	1571.91	1200.39	1023.30	923.54	862.01
150,000	1684.19	1286.13	1096.39	989.50	923.58
160,000	1796.47	1371.87	1169.48	1055.47	985.15
170,000	1908.75	1457.61	1242.58	1121.44	1046.72
180,000	2021.03	1543.36	1315.67	1187.40	1108.29
190,000	2133.31	1629.10	1388.76	1253.37	1169.86
200,000	2245.59	1714.84	1461.85	1319.34	1231.43
250,000	2806.98	2143.55	1827.32	1649.17	1539.29
300,000	3368.38	2572.26	2192.78	1979.00	1847.15

530

MONTHLY PAYMENTS
ANNUAL INTEREST RATE: 6.5%

LOAN AMOUNT	LOAN MATURITY (YEARS)				
	10	15	20	25	30
50	0.57	0.44	0.38	0.34	0.32
100	1.14	0.88	0.75	0.68	0.64
200	2.28	1.75	1.50	1.36	1.27
300	3.41	2.62	2.24	2.03	1.90
400	4.55	3.49	2.99	2.71	2.53
500	5.68	4.36	3.73	3.38	3.17
600	6.82	5.23	4.48	4.06	3.80
700	7.95	6.10	5.22	4.73	4.43
800	9.09	6.97	5.97	5.41	5.06
900	10.22	7.85	6.72	6.08	5.69
1,000	11.36	8.72	7.46	6.76	6.33
2,000	22.71	17.43	14.92	13.51	12.65
3,000	34.07	26.14	22.37	20.26	18.97
4,000	45.42	34.85	29.83	27.01	25.29
5,000	56.78	43.56	37.28	33.77	31.61
6,000	68.13	52.27	44.74	40.52	37.93
7,000	79.49	60.98	52.20	47.27	44.25
8,000	90.84	69.69	59.65	54.02	50.57
9,000	102.20	78.41	67.11	60.77	56.89
10,000	113.55	87.12	74.56	67.53	63.21
20,000	227.10	174.23	149.12	135.05	126.42
30,000	340.65	261.34	223.68	202.57	189.63
40,000	454.20	348.45	298.24	270.09	252.83
50,000	567.75	435.56	372.79	337.61	316.04
60,000	681.30	522.67	447.35	405.13	379.25
70,000	794.85	609.78	521.91	472.65	442.45
80,000	908.39	696.89	596.47	540.17	505.66
90,000	1021.94	784.01	671.02	607.69	568.87
100,000	1135.49	871.12	745.58	675.21	632.07
110,000	1249.04	958.23	820.14	742.74	695.28
120,000	1362.59	1045.34	894.70	810.26	758.49
130,000	1476.14	1132.45	969.25	877.78	821.70
140,000	1589.69	1219.56	1043.81	945.30	884.90
150,000	1703.23	1306.67	1118.37	1012.82	948.11
160,000	1816.78	1393.78	1192.93	1080.34	1011.32
170,000	1930.33	1480.89	1267.48	1147.86	1074.52
180,000	2043.88	1568.01	1342.04	1215.38	1137.73
190,000	2157.43	1655.12	1416.60	1282.90	1200.94
200,000	2270.98	1742.23	1491.16	1350.42	1264.14
250,000	2838.72	2177.78	1863.95	1688.03	1580.18
300,000	3406.46	2613.34	2236.73	2025.63	1896.21

MONTHLY PAYMENTS
ANNUAL INTEREST RATE: 6.75%

LOAN AMOUNT	LOAN MATURITY (YEARS)				
	10	15	20	25	30
50	0.58	0.45	0.39	0.35	0.33
100	1.15	0.89	0.77	0.70	0.65
200	2.30	1.77	1.53	1.39	1.30
300	3.45	2.66	2.29	2.08	1.95
400	4.60	3.54	3.05	2.77	2.60
500	5.75	4.43	3.81	3.46	3.25
600	6.89	5.31	4.57	4.15	3.90
700	8.04	6.20	5.33	4.84	4.55
800	9.19	7.08	6.09	5.53	5.19
900	10.34	7.97	6.85	6.22	5.84
1,000	11.49	8.85	7.61	6.91	6.49
2,000	22.97	17.70	15.21	13.82	12.98
3,000	34.45	26.55	22.82	20.73	19.46
4,000	45.93	35.40	30.42	27.64	25.95
5,000	57.42	44.25	38.02	34.55	32.43
6,000	68.90	53.10	45.63	41.46	38.92
7,000	80.38	61.95	53.23	48.37	45.41
8,000	91.86	70.80	60.83	55.28	51.89
9,000	103.35	79.65	68.44	62.19	58.38
10,000	114.83	88.50	76.04	69.10	64.86
20,000	229.65	176.99	152.08	138.19	129.72
30,000	344.48	265.48	228.11	207.28	194.58
40,000	459.30	353.97	304.15	276.37	259.44
50,000	574.13	442.46	380.19	345.46	324.30
60,000	688.95	530.95	456.22	414.55	389.16
70,000	803.77	619.44	532.26	483.64	454.02
80,000	918.60	707.93	608.30	552.73	518.88
90,000	1033.42	796.42	684.33	621.83	583.74
100,000	1148.25	884.92	760.37	690.92	648.60
110,000	1263.07	973.41	836.41	760.01	713.46
120,000	1377.90	1061.90	912.44	829.10	778.32
130,000	1492.72	1150.39	988.48	898.19	843.18
140,000	1607.54	1238.88	1064.52	967.28	908.04
150,000	1722.37	1327.37	1140.55	1036.37	972.90
160,000	1837.19	1415.86	1216.59	1105.46	1037.76
170,000	1952.02	1504.35	1292.62	1174.56	1102.62
180,000	2066.84	1592.84	1368.66	1243.65	1167.48
190,000	2181.67	1681.33	1444.70	1312.74	1232.34
200,000	2296.49	1769.83	1520.73	1381.83	1297.20
250,000	2870.61	2212.28	1900.92	1727.28	1621.50
300,000	3444.73	2654.74	2281.10	2072.74	1945.80

MONTHLY PAYMENTS
ANNUAL INTEREST RATE: 7%

LOAN	LOAN MATURITY (YEARS)				
AMOUNT	10	15	20	25	30
50	0.59	0.45	0.39	0.36	0.34
100	1.17	0.90	0.78	0.71	0.67
200	2.33	1.80	1.56	1.42	1.34
300	3.49	2.70	2.33	2.13	2.00
400	4.65	3.60	3.11	2.83	2.67
500	5.81	4.50	3.88	3.54	3.33
600	6.97	5.40	4.66	4.25	4.00
700	8.13	6.30	5.43	4.95	4.66
800	9.29	7.20	6.21	5.66	5.33
900	10.45	8.09	6.98	6.37	5.99
1,000	11.62	8.99	7.76	7.07	6.66
2,000	23.23	17.98	15.51	14.14	13.31
3,000	34.84	26.97	23.26	21.21	19.96
4,000	46.45	35.96	31.02	28.28	26.62
5,000	58.06	44.95	38.77	35.34	33.27
6,000	69.67	53.93	46.52	42.41	39.92
7,000	81.28	62.92	54.28	49.48	46.58
8,000	92.89	71.91	62.03	56.55	53.23
9,000	104.50	80.90	69.78	63.62	59.88
10,000	116.11	89.89	77.53	70.68	66.54
20,000	232.22	179.77	155.06	141.36	133.07
30,000	348.33	269.65	232.59	212.04	199.60
40,000	464.44	359.54	310.12	282.72	266.13
50,000	580.55	449.42	387.65	353.39	332.66
60,000	696.65	539.30	465.18	424.07	399.19
70,000	812.76	629.18	542.71	494.75	465.72
80,000	928.87	719.07	620.24	565.43	532.25
90,000	1044.98	808.95	697.77	636.11	598.78
100,000	1161.09	898.83	775.30	706.78	665.31
110,000	1277.20	988.71	852.83	777.46	731.84
120,000	1393.30	1078.60	930.36	848.14	798.37
130,000	1509.41	1168.48	1007.89	918.82	864.90
140,000	1625.52	1258.36	1085.42	989.49	931.43
150,000	1741.63	1348.25	1162.95	1060.17	997.96
160,000	1857.74	1438.13	1240.48	1130.85	1064.49
170,000	1973.85	1528.01	1318.01	1201.53	1131.02
180,000	2089.95	1617.89	1395.54	1272.21	1197.55
190,000	2206.06	1707.78	1473.07	1342.88	1264.08
200,000	2322.17	1797.66	1550.60	1413.56	1330.61
250,000	2902.71	2247.07	1938.25	1766.95	1663.26
300,000	3483.25	2696.49	2325.90	2120.34	1995.91

533

MONTHLY PAYMENTS
ANNUAL INTEREST RATE: 7.25%

LOAN AMOUNT	LOAN MATURITY (YEARS)				
	10	15	20	25	30
50	0.59	0.46	0.40	0.37	0.35
100	1.18	0.92	0.80	0.73	0.69
200	2.35	1.83	1.59	1.45	1.37
300	3.53	2.74	2.38	2.17	2.05
400	4.70	3.66	3.17	2.90	2.73
500	5.88	4.57	3.96	3.62	3.42
600	7.05	5.48	4.75	4.34	4.10
700	8.22	6.40	5.54	5.06	4.78
800	9.40	7.31	6.33	5.79	5.46
900	10.57	8.22	7.12	6.51	6.14
1,000	11.75	9.13	7.91	7.23	6.83
2,000	23.49	18.26	15.81	14.46	13.65
3,000	35.23	27.39	23.72	21.69	20.47
4,000	46.97	36.52	31.62	28.92	27.29
5,000	58.71	45.65	39.52	36.15	34.11
6,000	70.45	54.78	47.43	43.37	40.94
7,000	82.19	63.91	55.33	50.60	47.76
8,000	93.93	73.03	63.24	57.83	54.58
9,000	105.67	82.16	71.14	65.06	61.40
10,000	117.41	91.29	79.04	72.29	68.22
20,000	234.81	182.58	158.08	144.57	136.44
30,000	352.21	273.86	237.12	216.85	204.66
40,000	469.61	365.15	316.16	289.13	272.88
50,000	587.01	456.44	395.19	361.41	341.09
60,000	704.41	547.72	474.23	433.69	409.31
70,000	821.82	639.01	553.27	505.97	477.53
80,000	939.22	730.30	632.31	578.25	545.75
90,000	1056.62	821.58	711.35	650.53	613.96
100,000	1174.02	912.87	790.38	722.81	682.18
110,000	1291.42	1004.16	869.42	795.09	750.40
120,000	1408.82	1095.44	948.46	867.38	818.62
130,000	1526.22	1186.73	1027.50	939.66	886.84
140,000	1643.63	1278.02	1106.53	1011.94	955.05
150,000	1761.03	1369.30	1185.57	1084.22	1023.27
160,000	1878.43	1460.59	1264.61	1156.50	1091.49
170,000	1995.83	1551.88	1343.65	1228.78	1159.71
180,000	2113.23	1643.16	1422.69	1301.06	1227.92
190,000	2230.63	1734.45	1501.72	1373.34	1296.14
200,000	2348.04	1825.74	1580.76	1445.62	1364.36
250,000	2935.04	2282.17	1975.95	1807.03	1705.45
300,000	3522.05	2738.60	2371.14	2168.43	2046.54

MONTHLY PAYMENTS
ANNUAL INTEREST RATE: 7.5%

LOAN AMOUNT	LOAN MATURITY (YEARS)				
	10	15	20	25	30
50	0.60	0.47	0.41	0.37	0.35
100	1.19	0.93	0.81	0.74	0.70
200	2.38	1.86	1.62	1.48	1.40
300	3.57	2.79	2.42	2.22	2.10
400	4.75	3.71	3.23	2.96	2.80
500	5.94	4.64	4.03	3.70	3.50
600	7.13	5.57	4.84	4.44	4.20
700	8.31	6.49	5.64	5.18	4.90
800	9.50	7.42	6.45	5.92	5.60
900	10.69	8.35	7.26	6.66	6.30
1,000	11.88	9.28	8.06	7.39	7.00
2,000	23.75	18.55	16.12	14.78	13.99
3,000	35.62	27.82	24.17	22.17	20.98
4,000	47.49	37.09	32.23	29.56	27.97
5,000	59.36	46.36	40.28	36.95	34.97
6,000	71.23	55.63	48.34	44.34	41.96
7,000	83.10	64.90	56.40	51.73	48.95
8,000	94.97	74.17	64.45	59.12	55.94
9,000	106.84	83.44	72.51	66.51	
10,000	118.71	92.71	80.56	73.90	69.93
20,000	237.41	185.41	161.12	147.80	139.85
30,000	356.11	278.11	241.68	221.70	209.77
40,000	474.81	370.81	322.24	295.60	279.69
50,000	593.51	463.51	402.80	369.50	349.61
60,000	712.21	556.21	483.36	443.40	419.53
70,000	830.91	648.91	563.92	517.30	489.45
80,000	949.62	741.61	644.48	591.20	559.38
90,000	1068.32	834.31	725.04	665.10	629.30
100,000	1187.02	927.01	805.60	738.99	699.22
110,000	1305.72	1019.72	886.16	812.89	769.14
120,000	1424.42	1112.42	966.71	886.79	839.06
130,000	1543.12	1205.12	1047.27	960.69	908.98
140,000	1661.82	1297.82	1127.83	1034.59	978.90
150,000	1780.52	1390.52	1208.39	1108.49	1048.83
160,000	1899.23	1483.22	1288.95	1182.39	1118.75
170,000	2017.93	1575.92	1369.51	1256.29	1188.67
180,000	2136.63	1668.62	1450.07	1330.19	1258.59
190,000	2255.33	1761.32	1530.63	1404.09	1328.51
200,000	2374.03	1854.02	1611.19	1477.98	1398.43
250,000	2967.54	2317.53	2013.98	1847.48	1748.04
300,000	3561.04	2781.03	2416.78	2216.97	2097.64

MONTHLY PAYMENTS
ANNUAL INTEREST RATE: 7.75%

LOAN AMOUNT	LOAN MATURITY (YEARS)				
	10	15	20	25	30
50	0.61	0.48	0.42	0.38	0.36
100	1.21	0.95	0.83	0.76	0.72
200	2.41	1.89	1.65	1.52	1.44
300	3.61	2.83	2.47	2.27	2.15
400	4.81	3.77	3.29	3.03	2.87
500	6.01	4.71	4.11	3.78	3.59
600	7.21	5.65	4.93	4.54	4.30
700	8.41	6.59	5.75	5.29	5.02
800	9.61	7.54	6.57	6.05	5.74
900	10.81	8.48	7.39	6.80	6.45
1,000	12.01	9.42	8.21	7.56	7.17
2,000	24.01	18.83	16.42	15.11	14.33
3,000	36.01	28.24	24.63	22.66	21.50
4,000	48.01	37.66	32.84	30.22	28.66
5,000	60.01	47.07	41.05	37.77	35.83
6,000	72.01	56.48	49.26	45.32	42.99
7,000	84.01	65.89	57.47	52.88	50.15
8,000	96.01	75.31	65.68	60.43	57.32
9,000	108.02	84.72	73.89	67.98	64.48
10,000	120.02	94.13	82.10	75.54	71.65
20,000	240.03	188.26	164.20	151.07	143.29
30,000	360.04	282.39	246.29	226.60	214.93
40,000	480.05	376.52	328.39	302.14	286.57
50,000	600.06	470.64	410.48	377.67	358.21
60,000	720.07	564.77	492.58	453.20	429.85
70,000	840.08	658.90	574.67	528.74	501.49
80,000	960.10	753.03	656.77	604.27	573.14
90,000	1080.11	847.16	738.86	679.80	644.78
100,000	1200.12	941.28	820.96	755.34	716.42
110,000	1320.13	1035.41	903.05	830.87	788.06
120,000	1440.14	1129.54	985.15	906.40	859.70
130,000	1560.15	1223.67	1067.24	981.93	931.34
140,000	1680.16	1317.80	1149.34	1057.47	1002.98
150,000	1800.17	1411.92	1231.43	1133.00	1074.63
160,000	1920.19	1506.05	1313.53	1208.53	1146.27
170,000	2040.20	1600.18	1395.62	1284.07	1217.91
180,000	2160.21	1694.31	1477.72	1359.60	1289.55
190,000	2280.22	1788.44	1559.81	1435.13	1361.19
200,000	2400.23	1882.56	1641.91	1510.67	1432.83
250,000	3000.29	2353.20	2052.38	1888.33	1791.04
300,000	3600.34	2823.84	2462.86	2266.00	2149.25

536

MONTHLY PAYMENTS
ANNUAL INTEREST RATE: 8%

LOAN AMOUNT	\multicolumn{5}{c}{LOAN MATURITY (YEARS)}				
	10	15	20	25	30
50	0.61	0.48	0.42	0.39	0.37
100	1.22	0.96	0.84	0.78	0.74
200	2.43	1.92	1.68	1.55	1.47
300	3.64	2.87	2.51	2.32	2.21
400	4.86	3.83	3.35	3.09	2.94
500	6.07	4.78	4.19	3.86	3.67
600	7.28	5.74	5.02	4.64	4.41
700	8.50	6.69	5.86	5.41	5.14
800	9.71	7.65	6.70	6.18	5.88
900	10.92	8.61	7.53	6.95	6.61
1,000	12.14	9.56	8.37	7.72	7.34
2,000	24.27	19.12	16.73	15.44	14.68
3,000	36.40	28.67	25.10	23.16	22.02
4,000	48.54	38.23	33.46	30.88	29.36
5,000	60.67	47.79	41.83	38.60	36.69
6,000	72.80	57.34	50.19	46.31	44.03
7,000	84.93	66.90	58.56	54.03	51.37
8,000	97.07	76.46	66.92	61.75	58.71
9,000	109.20	86.01	75.28	69.47	66.04
10,000	121.33	95.57	83.65	77.19	73.38
20,000	242.66	191.14	167.29	154.37	146.76
30,000	363.99	286.70	250.94	231.55	220.13
40,000	485.32	382.27	334.58	308.73	293.51
50,000	606.64	477.83	418.22	385.91	366.89
60,000	727.97	573.40	501.87	463.09	440.26
70,000	849.30	668.96	585.51	540.28	513.64
80,000	970.63	764.53	669.16	617.46	587.02
90,000	1091.95	860.09	752.80	694.64	660.39
100,000	1213.28	955.66	836.44	771.82	733.77
110,000	1334.61	1051.22	920.09	849.00	807.15
120,000	1455.94	1146.79	1003.73	926.18	880.52
130,000	1577.26	1242.35	1087.38	1003.37	953.90
140,000	1698.59	1337.92	1171.02	1080.55	1027.28
150,000	1819.92	1433.48	1254.66	1157.73	1100.65
160,000	1941.25	1529.05	1338.31	1234.91	1174.03
170,000	2062.57	1624.61	1421.95	1312.09	1247.40
180,000	2183.90	1720.18	1505.60	1389.27	1320.78
190,000	2305.23	1815.74	1589.24	1466.46	1394.16
200,000	2426.56	1911.31	1672.88	1543.64	1467.53
250,000	3033.19	2389.13	2091.10	1929.55	1834.42
300,000	3639.83	2866.96	2509.32	2315.45	2201.30

MONTHLY PAYMENTS
ANNUAL INTEREST RATE: 8.25 %

LOAN AMOUNT	LOAN MATURITY (YEARS)				
	10	15	20	25	30
50	0.62	0.49	0.43	0.40	0.38
100	1.23	0.98	0.86	0.79	0.76
200	2.46	1.95	1.71	1.58	1.51
300	3.68	2.92	2.56	2.37	2.26
400	4.91	3.89	3.41	3.16	3.01
500	6.14	4.86	4.27	3.95	3.76
600	7.36	5.83	5.12	4.74	4.51
700	8.59	6.80	5.97	5.52	5.26
800	9.82	7.77	6.82	6.31	6.02
900	11.04	8.74	7.67	7.10	6.77
1,000	12.27	9.71	8.53	7.89	7.52
2,000	24.54	19.41	17.05	15.77	15.03
3,000	36.80	29.11	25.57	23.66	22.54
4,000	49.07	38.81	34.09	31.54	30.06
5,000	61.33	48.51	42.61	39.43	37.57
6,000	73.60	58.21	51.13	47.31	45.08
7,000	85.86	67.91	59.65	55.20	52.59
8,000	98.13	77.62	68.17	63.08	60.11
9,000	110.39	87.32	76.69	70.97	67.62
10,000	122.66	97.02	85.21	78.85	75.13
20,000	245.31	194.03	170.42	157.69	150.26
30,000	367.96	291.05	255.62	236.54	225.38
40,000	490.61	388.06	340.83	315.38	300.51
50,000	613.27	485.07	426.04	394.23	375.64
60,000	735.92	582.09	511.24	473.07	450.76
70,000	858.57	679.10	596.45	551.92	525.89
80,000	981.22	776.12	681.66	630.76	601.02
90,000	1103.88	873.13	766.86	709.61	676.14
100,000	1226.53	970.14	852.07	788.45	751.27
110,000	1349.18	1067.16	937.28	867.30	826.40
120,000	1471.83	1164.17	1022.48	946.14	901.52
130,000	1594.49	1261.19	1107.69	1024.99	976.65
140,000	1717.14	1358.20	1192.90	1103.83	1051.78
150,000	1839.79	1455.21	1278.10	1182.68	1126.90
160,000	1962.44	1552.23	1363.31	1261.52	1202.03
170,000	2085.10	1649.24	1448.52	1340.37	1277.16
180,000	2207.75	1746.26	1533.72	1419.21	1352.28
190,000	2330.40	1843.27	1618.93	1498.06	1427.41
200,000	2453.05	1940.28	1704.14	1576.90	1502.54
250,000	3066.32	2425.35	2130.17	1971.13	1878.17
300,000	3679.58	2910.42	2556.20	2365.35	2253.80

MONTHLY PAYMENTS
ANNUAL INTEREST RATE: 8.5 %

LOAN MATURITY (YEARS)

	10	15	20	25	30
50	0.62	0.50	0.44	0.41	0.39
100	1.24	0.99	0.87	0.81	0.77
200	2.48	1.97	1.74	1.62	1.54
300	3.72	2.96	2.61	2.42	2.31
400	4.96	3.94	3.48	3.23	3.08
500	6.20	4.93	4.34	4.03	3.85
600	7.44	5.91	5.21	4.84	4.62
700	8.68	6.90	6.08	5.64	5.39
800	9.92	7.88	6.95	6.45	6.16
900	11.16	8.87	7.82	7.25	6.93
1,000	12.40	9.85	8.68	8.06	7.69
2,000	24.80	19.70	17.36	16.11	15.38
3,000	37.20	29.55	26.04	24.16	23.07
4,000	49.60	39.39	34.72	32.21	30.76
5,000	62.00	49.24	43.40	40.27	38.45
6,000	74.40	59.09	52.07	48.32	46.14
7,000	86.80	68.94	60.75	56.37	53.83
8,000	99.19	78.78	69.43	64.42	61.52
9,000	111.59	88.63	78.11	72.48	69.21
10,000	123.99	98.48	86.79	80.53	76.90
20,000	247.98	196.95	173.57	161.05	153.79
30,000	371.96	295.43	260.35	241.57	230.68
40,000	495.95	393.90	347.14	322.10	307.57
50,000	619.94	492.38	433.92	402.62	384.46
60,000	743.92	590.85	520.70	483.14	461.35
70,000	867.91	689.32	607.48	563.66	538.25
80,000	991.89	787.80	694.27	644.19	615.14
90,000	1115.88	886.27	781.05	724.71	692.03
100,000	1239.87	984.75	867.83	805.23	768.92
110,000	1363.85	1083.22	954.61	885.76	845.81
120,000	1487.84	1181.70	1041.40	966.28	922.70
130,000	1611.82	1280.17	1128.18	1046.80	999.59
140,000	1735.81	1378.64	1214.96	1127.32	1076.49
150,000	1859.80	1477.12	1301.74	1207.85	1153.38
160,000	1983.78	1575.59	1388.53	1288.37	1230.27
170,000	2107.77	1674.07	1475.31	1368.89	1307.16
180,000	2231.76	1772.54	1562.09	1449.42	1384.05
190,000	2355.74	1871.02	1648.87	1529.94	1460.94
200,000	2479.73	1969.49	1735.66	1610.46	1537.83
250,000	3099.66	2461.86	2169.57	2013.08	1922.29
300,000	3719.59	2954.23	2603.48	2415.69	2306.75

MONTHLY PAYMENTS
ANNUAL INTEREST RATE: 8.75 %

LOAN AMOUNT	LOAN MATURITY (YEARS)				
	10	15	20	25	30
50	0.63	0.50	0.45	0.42	0.40
100	1.26	1.00	0.89	0.83	0.79
200	2.51	2.00	1.77	1.65	1.58
300	3.76	3.00	2.66	2.47	2.37
400	5.02	4.00	3.54	3.29	3.15
500	6.27	5.00	4.42	4.12	3.94
600	7.52	6.00	5.31	4.94	4.73
700	8.78	7.00	6.19	5.76	5.51
800	10.03	8.00	7.07	6.58	6.30
900	11.28	9.00	7.96	7.40	7.09
1,000	12.54	10.00	8.84	8.23	7.87
2,000	25.07	19.99	17.68	16.45	15.74
3,000	37.60	29.99	26.52	24.67	23.61
4,000	50.14	39.98	35.35	32.89	31.47
5,000	62.67	49.98	44.19	41.11	39.34
6,000	75.20	59.97	53.03	49.33	47.21
7,000	87.73	69.97	61.86	57.56	55.07
8,000	100.27	79.96	70.70	65.78	62.94
9,000	112.80	89.96	79.54	74.00	70.81
10,000	125.33	99.95	88.38	82.22	78.68
20,000	250.66	199.89	176.75	164.43	157.35
30,000	375.99	299.84	265.12	246.65	236.02
40,000	501.31	399.78	353.49	328.86	314.69
50,000	626.64	499.73	441.86	411.08	393.36
60,000	751.97	599.67	530.23	493.29	472.03
70,000	877.29	699.62	618.60	575.51	550.70
80,000	1002.62	799.56	706.97	657.72	629.37
90,000	1127.95	899.51	795.34	739.93	708.04
100,000	1253.27	999.45	883.72	822.15	786.71
110,000	1378.60	1099.40	972.09	904.36	865.38
120,000	1503.93	1199.34	1060.46	986.58	944.05
130,000	1629.25	1299.29	1148.83	1068.79	1022.72
140,000	1754.58	1399.23	1237.20	1151.01	1101.39
150,000	1879.91	1499.18	1325.57	1233.22	1180.06
160,000	2005.23	1599.12	1413.94	1315.43	1258.73
170,000	2130.56	1699.07	1502.31	1397.65	1337.40
180,000	2255.89	1799.01	1590.68	1479.86	1416.07
190,000	2381.21	1898.96	1679.05	1562.08	1494.74
200,000	2506.54	1998.90	1767.43	1644.29	1573.41
250,000	3133.17	2498.63	2209.28	2055.36	1966.76
300,000	3759.81	2998.35	2651.14	2466.44	2360.11

MONTHLY PAYMENTS
ANNUAL INTEREST RATE: 9 %

LOAN AMOUNT	LOAN MATURITY (YEARS)				
	10	15	20	25	30
50	0.64	0.51	0.45	0.42	0.41
100	1.27	1.02	0.90	0.84	0.81
200	2.54	2.03	1.80	1.68	1.61
300	3.81	3.05	2.70	2.52	2.42
400	5.07	4.06	3.60	3.36	3.22
500	6.34	5.08	4.50	4.20	4.03
600	7.61	6.09	5.40	5.04	4.83
700	8.87	7.10	6.30	5.88	5.64
800	10.14	8.12	7.20	6.72	6.44
900	11.41	9.13	8.10	7.56	7.25
1,000	12.67	10.15	9.00	8.40	8.05
2,000	25.34	20.29	18.00	16.79	16.10
3,000	38.01	30.43	27.00	25.18	24.14
4,000	50.68	40.58	35.99	33.57	32.19
5,000	63.34	50.72	44.99	41.96	40.24
6,000	76.01	60.86	53.99	50.36	48.28
7,000	88.68	71.00	62.99	58.75	56.33
8,000	101.35	81.15	71.98	67.14	64.37
9,000	114.01	91.29	80.98	75.53	72.42
10,000	126.68	101.43	89.98	83.92	80.47
20,000	253.36	202.86	179.95	167.84	160.93
30,000	380.03	304.28	269.92	251.76	241.39
40,000	506.71	405.71	359.89	335.68	321.85
50,000	633.38	507.14	449.87	419.60	402.32
60,000	760.06	608.56	539.84	503.52	482.78
70,000	886.73	709.99	629.81	587.44	563.24
80,000	1013.41	811.41	719.78	671.36	643.70
90,000	1140.08	912.84	809.76	755.28	724.16
100,000	1266.76	1014.27	899.73	839.20	804.63
110,000	1393.43	1115.69	989.70	923.12	885.09
120,000	1520.11	1217.12	1079.67	1007.04	965.55
130,000	1646.78	1318.55	1169.64	1090.96	1046.01
140,000	1773.46	1419.97	1259.62	1174.88	1126.47
150,000	1900.13	1521.40	1349.59	1258.80	1206.94
160,000	2026.81	1622.82	1439.56	1342.72	1287.40
170,000	2153.48	1724.25	1529.53	1426.64	1367.86
180,000	2280.16	1825.68	1619.51	1510.55	1448.32
190,000	2406.83	1927.10	1709.48	1594.47	1528.79
200,000	2533.51	2028.53	1799.45	1678.39	1609.25
250,000	3166.88	2535.66	2249.31	2097.99	2011.56
300,000	3800.26	3042.79	2699.17	2517.59	2413.87

MONTHLY PAYMENTS
ANNUAL INTEREST RATE: 9.25%

LOAN AMOUNT	LOAN MATURITY (YEARS)				
	10	15	20	25	30
50	0.65	0.52	0.46	0.43	0.42
100	1.29	1.03	0.92	0.86	0.83
200	2.57	2.06	1.84	1.72	1.65
300	3.85	3.09	2.75	2.57	2.47
400	5.13	4.12	3.67	3.43	3.30
500	6.41	5.15	4.58	4.29	4.12
600	7.69	6.18	5.50	5.14	4.94
700	8.97	7.21	6.42	6.00	5.76
800	10.25	8.24	7.33	6.86	6.59
900	11.53	9.27	8.25	7.71	7.41
1,000	12.81	10.30	9.16	8.57	8.23
2,000	25.61	20.59	18.32	17.13	16.46
3,000	38.41	30.88	27.48	25.70	24.69
4,000	51.22	41.17	36.64	34.26	32.91
5,000	64.02	51.46	45.80	42.82	41.14
6,000	76.82	61.76	54.96	51.39	49.37
7,000	89.63	72.05	64.12	59.95	57.59
8,000	102.43	82.34	73.27	68.52	65.82
9,000	115.23	92.63	82.43	77.08	74.05
10,000	128.04	102.92	91.59	85.64	82.27
20,000	256.07	205.84	183.18	171.28	164.54
30,000	384.10	308.76	274.77	256.92	246.81
40,000	512.14	411.68	366.35	342.56	329.08
50,000	640.17	514.60	457.94	428.20	411.34
60,000	768.20	617.52	549.53	513.84	493.61
70,000	896.24	720.44	641.11	599.47	575.88
80,000	1024.27	823.36	732.70	685.11	658.15
90,000	1152.30	926.28	824.29	770.75	740.41
100,000	1280.34	1029.20	915.87	856.39	822.68
110,000	1408.37	1132.12	1007.46	942.03	904.95
120,000	1536.40	1235.04	1099.05	1027.67	987.22
130,000	1664.44	1337.96	1190.63	1113.30	1069.48
140,000	1792.47	1440.88	1282.22	1198.94	1151.75
150,000	1920.50	1543.80	1373.81	1284.58	1234.02
160,000	2048.54	1646.72	1465.40	1370.22	1316.29
170,000	2176.57	1749.64	1556.98	1455.86	1398.55
180,000	2304.60	1852.56	1648.57	1541.50	1480.82
190,000	2432.64	1955.48	1740.16	1627.13	1563.09
200,000	2560.67	2058.40	1831.74	1712.77	1645.36
250,000	3200.84	2572.99	2289.68	2140.96	2056.70
300,000	3841.00	3087.59	2747.61	2569.16	2468.03

MONTHLY PAYMENTS
ANNUAL INTEREST RATE: 9.5%

LOAN AMOUNT	LOAN MATURITY (YEARS)				
	10	15	20	25	30
50	0.65	0.53	0.47	0.44	0.43
100	1.30	1.05	0.94	0.88	0.85
200	2.59	2.09	1.87	1.75	1.69
300	3.89	3.14	2.80	2.63	2.53
400	5.18	4.18	3.73	3.50	3.37
500	6.47	5.23	4.67	4.37	4.21
600	7.77	6.27	5.60	5.25	5.05
700	9.06	7.31	6.53	6.12	5.89
800	10.36	8.36	7.46	6.99	6.73
900	11.65	9.40	8.39	7.87	7.57
1,000	12.94	10.45	9.33	8.74	8.41
2,000	25.88	20.89	18.65	17.48	16.82
3,000	38.82	31.33	27.97	26.22	25.23
4,000	51.76	41.77	37.29	34.95	33.64
5,000	64.70	52.22	46.61	43.69	42.05
6,000	77.64	62.66	55.93	52.43	50.46
7,000	90.58	73.10	65.25	61.16	58.86
8,000	103.52	83.54	74.58	69.90	67.27
9,000	116.46	93.98	83.90	78.64	75.68
10,000	129.40	104.43	93.22	87.37	84.09
20,000	258.80	208.85	186.43	174.74	168.18
30,000	388.20	313.27	279.64	262.11	252.26
40,000	517.59	417.69	372.86	349.48	336.35
50,000	646.99	522.12	466.07	436.85	420.43
60,000	776.39	626.54	559.28	524.22	504.52
70,000	905.78	730.96	652.50	611.59	588.60
80,000	1035.18	835.38	745.71	698.96	672.69
90,000	1164.58	939.80	838.92	786.33	756.77
100,000	1293.98	1044.23	932.13	873.70	840.86
110,000	1423.37	1148.65	1025.35	961.07	924.94
120,000	1552.77	1253.07	1118.56	1048.44	1009.03
130,000	1682.17	1357.49	1211.77	1135.81	1093.11
140,000	1811.56	1461.92	1304.99	1223.18	1177.20
150,000	1940.96	1566.34	1398.20	1310.55	1261.29
160,000	2070.36	1670.76	1491.41	1397.92	1345.37
170,000	2199.76	1775.18	1584.62	1485.29	1429.46
180,000	2329.15	1879.60	1677.84	1572.66	1513.54
190,000	2458.55	1984.03	1771.05	1660.03	1597.63
200,000	2587.95	2088.45	1864.26	1747.40	1681.71
250,000	3234.93	2610.56	2330.33	2184.24	2102.14
300,000	3881.92	3132.67	2796.39	2621.09	2522.57

MONTHLY PAYMENTS
ANNUAL INTEREST RATE: 9.75%

LOAN AMOUNT	LOAN MATURITY (YEARS)				
	10	15	20	25	30
50	0.66	0.53	0.48	0.45	0.43
100	1.31	1.06	0.95	0.90	0.86
200	2.62	2.12	1.90	1.79	1.72
300	3.93	3.18	2.85	2.68	2.58
400	5.24	4.24	3.80	3.57	3.44
500	6.54	5.30	4.75	4.46	4.30
600	7.85	6.36	5.70	5.35	5.16
700	9.16	7.42	6.64	6.24	6.02
800	10.47	8.48	7.59	7.13	6.88
900	11.77	9.54	8.54	8.03	7.74
1,000	13.08	10.60	9.49	8.92	8.60
2,000	26.16	21.19	18.98	17.83	17.19
3,000	39.24	31.79	28.46	26.74	25.78
4,000	52.31	42.38	37.95	35.65	34.37
5,000	65.39	52.97	47.43	44.56	42.96
6,000	78.47	63.57	56.92	53.47	51.55
7,000	91.54	74.16	66.40	62.38	60.15
8,000	104.62	84.75	75.89	71.30	68.74
9,000	117.70	95.35	85.37	80.21	77.33
10,000	130.78	105.94	94.86	89.12	85.92
20,000	261.55	211.88	189.71	178.23	171.84
30,000	392.32	317.81	284.56	267.35	257.75
40,000	523.09	423.75	379.41	356.46	343.67
50,000	653.86	529.69	474.26	445.57	429.58
60,000	784.63	635.62	569.12	534.69	515.50
70,000	915.40	741.56	663.97	623.80	601.41
80,000	1046.17	847.50	758.82	712.92	687.33
90,000	1176.94	953.43	853.67	802.03	773.24
100,000	1307.71	1059.37	948.52	891.14	859.16
110,000	1438.48	1165.31	1043.38	980.26	945.08
120,000	1569.25	1271.24	1138.23	1069.37	1030.99
130,000	1700.02	1377.18	1233.08	1158.49	1116.91
140,000	1830.79	1483.12	1327.93	1247.60	1202.82
150,000	1961.56	1589.05	1422.78	1336.71	1288.74
160,000	2092.34	1694.99	1517.63	1425.83	1374.65
170,000	2223.11	1800.93	1612.49	1514.94	1460.57
180,000	2353.88	1906.86	1707.34	1604.05	1546.48
190,000	2484.65	2012.80	1802.19	1693.17	1632.40
200,000	2615.42	2118.73	1897.04	1782.28	1718.32
250,000	3269.27	2648.42	2371.30	2227.85	2147.89
300,000	3923.12	3178.10	2845.56	2673.42	2577.47

MONTHLY PAYMENTS
ANNUAL INTEREST RATE: 10%

LOAN	LOAN MATURITY (YEARS)				
AMOUNT	10	15	20	25	30
50	0.67	0.54	0.49	0.46	0.44
100	1.33	1.08	0.97	0.91	0.88
200	2.65	2.15	1.94	1.82	1.76
300	3.97	3.23	2.90	2.73	2.64
400	5.29	4.30	3.87	3.64	3.52
500	6.61	5.38	4.83	4.55	4.39
600	7.93	6.45	5.80	5.46	5.27
700	9.26	7.53	6.76	6.37	6.15
800	10.58	8.60	7.73	7.27	7.03
900	11.90	9.68	8.69	8.18	7.90
1,000	13.22	10.75	9.66	9.09	8.78
2,000	26.44	21.50	19.31	18.18	17.56
3,000	39.65	32.24	28.96	27.27	26.33
4,000	52.87	42.99	38.61	36.35	35.11
5,000	66.08	53.74	48.26	45.44	43.88
6,000	79.30	64.48	57.91	54.53	52.66
7,000	92.51	75.23	67.56	63.61	61.44
8,000	105.73	85.97	77.21	72.70	70.21
9,000	118.94	96.72	86.86	81.79	78.99
10,000	132.16	107.47	96.51	90.88	87.76
20,000	264.31	214.93	193.01	181.75	175.52
30,000	396.46	322.39	289.51	272.62	263.28
40,000	528.61	429.85	386.01	363.49	351.03
50,000	660.76	537.31	482.52	454.36	438.79
60,000	792.91	644.77	579.02	545.23	526.55
70,000	925.06	752.23	675.52	636.10	614.31
80,000	1057.21	859.69	772.02	726.97	702.06
90,000	1189.36	967.15	868.53	817.84	789.82
100,000	1321.52	1074.61	965.03	908.71	877.58
110,000	1453.67	1182.07	1061.53	999.58	965.33
120,000	1585.82	1289.53	1158.03	1090.45	1053.09
130,000	1717.97	1396.99	1254.53	1181.32	1140.85
140,000	1850.12	1504.46	1351.04	1272.19	1228.61
150,000	1982.27	1611.92	1447.54	1363.06	1316.36
160,000	2114.42	1719.38	1544.04	1453.93	1404.12
170,000	2246.57	1826.84	1640.54	1544.80	1491.88
180,000	2378.72	1934.30	1737.05	1635.67	1579.63
190,000	2510.88	2041.76	1833.55	1726.54	1667.39
200,000	2643.03	2149.22	1930.05	1817.41	1755.15
250,000	3303.78	2686.52	2412.56	2271.76	2193.94
300,000	3964.54	3223.83	2895.07	2726.11	2632.72

MONTHLY PAYMENTS
ANNUAL INTEREST RATE: 10.25%

LOAN AMOUNT	LOAN MATURITY (YEARS)				
	10	15	20	25	30
50	0.67	0.55	0.50	0.47	0.45
100	1.34	1.09	0.99	0.93	0.90
200	2.68	2.18	1.97	1.86	1.80
300	4.01	3.27	2.95	2.78	2.69
400	5.35	4.36	3.93	3.71	3.59
500	6.68	5.45	4.91	4.64	4.49
600	8.02	6.54	5.89	5.56	5.38
700	9.35	7.63	6.88	6.49	6.28
800	10.69	8.72	7.86	7.42	7.17
900	12.02	9.81	8.84	8.34	8.07
1,000	13.36	10.90	9.82	9.27	8.97
2,000	26.71	21.80	19.64	18.53	17.93
3,000	40.07	32.70	29.45	27.80	26.89
4,000	53.42	43.60	39.27	37.06	35.85
5,000	66.77	54.50	49.09	46.32	44.81
6,000	80.13	65.40	58.90	55.59	53.77
7,000	93.48	76.30	68.72	64.85	62.73
8,000	106.84	87.20	78.54	74.12	71.69
9,000	120.19	98.10	88.35	83.38	80.65
10,000	133.54	109.00	98.17	92.64	89.62
20,000	267.08	217.99	196.33	185.28	179.23
30,000	400.62	326.99	294.50	277.92	268.84
40,000	534.16	435.98	392.66	370.56	358.45
50,000	667.70	544.98	490.83	463.20	448.06
60,000	801.24	653.97	588.99	555.83	537.67
70,000	934.78	762.97	687.15	648.47	627.28
80,000	1068.32	871.96	785.32	741.11	716.89
90,000	1201.85	980.96	883.48	833.75	806.50
100,000	1335.39	1089.95	981.65	926.39	896.11
110,000	1468.93	1198.95	1079.81	1019.03	985.72
120,000	1602.47	1307.94	1177.98	1111.66	1075.33
130,000	1736.01	1416.94	1276.14	1204.30	1164.94
140,000	1869.55	1525.93	1374.30	1296.94	1254.55
150,000	2003.09	1634.93	1472.47	1389.58	1344.16
160,000	2136.63	1743.92	1570.63	1482.22	1433.77
170,000	2270.16	1852.92	1668.80	1574.86	1523.38
180,000	2403.70	1961.91	1766.96	1667.49	1612.99
190,000	2537.24	2070.91	1865.13	1760.13	1702.60
200,000	2670.78	2179.90	1963.29	1852.77	1792.21
250,000	3338.48	2724.88	2454.11	2315.96	2240.26
300,000	4006.17	3269.85	2944.93	2779.15	2688.31

MONTHLY PAYMENTS
ANNUAL INTEREST RATE: 10.5%

LOAN AMOUNT	LOAN MATURITY (YEARS)				
	10	15	20	25	30
50	0.68	0.56	0.50	0.48	0.46
100	1.35	1.11	1.00	0.95	0.92
200	2.70	2.22	2.00	1.89	1.83
300	4.05	3.32	3.00	2.84	2.75
400	5.40	4.43	4.00	3.78	3.66
500	6.75	5.53	5.00	4.73	4.58
600	8.10	6.64	6.00	5.67	5.49
700	9.45	7.74	6.99	6.61	6.41
800	10.80	8.85	7.99	7.56	7.32
900	12.15	9.95	8.99	8.50	8.24
1,000	13.50	11.06	9.99	9.45	9.15
2,000	26.99	22.11	19.97	18.89	18.30
3,000	40.49	33.17	29.96	28.33	27.45
4,000	53.98	44.22	39.94	37.77	36.59
5,000	67.47	55.28	49.92	47.21	45.74
6,000	80.97	66.33	59.91	56.66	54.89
7,000	94.46	77.38	69.89	66.10	64.04
8,000	107.95	88.44	79.88	75.54	73.18
9,000	121.45	99.49	89.86	84.98	82.33
10,000	134.94	110.55	99.84	94.42	91.48
20,000	269.88	221.09	199.68	188.84	182.95
30,000	404.81	331.63	299.52	283.26	274.43
40,000	539.75	442.17	399.36	377.68	365.90
50,000	674.68	552.71	499.20	472.10	457.37
60,000	809.62	663.25	599.03	566.51	548.85
70,000	944.55	773.79	698.87	660.93	640.32
80,000	1079.49	884.33	798.71	755.35	731.80
90,000	1214.42	994.87	898.55	849.77	823.27
100,000	1349.36	1105.41	998.39	944.19	914.74
110,000	1484.29	1215.95	1098.22	1038.61	1006.22
120,000	1619.23	1326.49	1198.06	1133.02	1097.69
130,000	1754.16	1437.03	1297.90	1227.44	1189.17
140,000	1889.10	1547.57	1397.74	1321.86	1280.64
150,000	2024.04	1658.11	1497.58	1416.28	1372.11
160,000	2158.97	1768.65	1597.41	1510.70	1463.59
170,000	2293.91	1879.19	1697.25	1605.12	1555.06
180,000	2428.84	1989.73	1797.09	1699.53	1646.54
190,000	2563.78	2100.27	1896.93	1793.95	1738.01
200,000	2698.71	2210.81	1996.77	1888.37	1829.48
250,000	3373.39	2763.51	2495.96	2360.46	2286.85
300,000	4048.07	3316.21	2995.15	2832.55	2744.22

MONTHLY PAYMENTS
ANNUAL INTEREST RATE: 10.75%

LOAN AMOUNT	LOAN MATURITY (YEARS)				
	10	15	20	25	30
50	0.69	0.57	0.51	0.49	0.47
100	1.37	1.13	1.02	0.97	0.94
200	2.73	2.25	2.04	1.93	1.87
300	4.10	3.37	3.05	2.89	2.81
400	5.46	4.49	4.07	3.85	3.74
500	6.82	5.61	5.08	4.82	4.67
600	8.19	6.73	6.10	5.78	5.61
700	9.55	7.85	7.11	6.74	6.54
800	10.91	8.97	8.13	7.70	7.47
900	12.28	10.09	9.14	8.66	8.41
1,000	13.64	11.21	10.16	9.63	9.34
2,000	27.27	22.42	20.31	19.25	18.67
3,000	40.91	33.63	30.46	28.87	28.01
4,000	54.54	44.84	40.61	38.49	37.34
5,000	68.17	56.05	50.77	48.11	46.68
6,000	81.81	67.26	60.92	57.73	56.01
7,000	95.44	78.47	71.07	67.35	65.35
8,000	109.08	89.68	81.22	76.97	74.68
9,000	122.71	100.89	91.38	86.59	84.02
10,000	136.34	112.10	101.53	96.21	93.35
20,000	272.68	224.19	203.05	192.42	186.70
30,000	409.02	336.29	304.57	288.63	280.05
40,000	545.36	448.38	406.10	384.84	373.40
50,000	681.70	560.48	507.62	481.05	466.75
60,000	818.04	672.57	609.14	577.26	560.09
70,000	954.38	784.67	710.67	673.47	653.44
80,000	1090.72	896.76	812.19	769.68	746.79
90,000	1227.05	1008.86	913.71	865.89	840.14
100,000	1363.39	1120.95	1015.23	962.10	933.49
110,000	1499.73	1233.05	1116.76	1058.31	1026.83
120,000	1636.07	1345.14	1218.28	1154.52	1120.18
130,000	1772.41	1457.24	1319.80	1250.73	1213.53
140,000	1908.75	1569.33	1421.33	1346.94	1306.88
150,000	2045.09	1681.43	1522.85	1443.14	1400.23
160,000	2181.43	1793.52	1624.37	1539.35	1493.58
170,000	2317.76	1905.62	1725.89	1635.56	1586.92
180,000	2454.10	2017.71	1827.42	1731.77	1680.27
190,000	2590.44	2129.81	1928.94	1827.98	1773.62
200,000	2726.78	2241.90	2030.46	1924.19	1866.97
250,000	3408.47	2802.38	2538.08	2405.24	2333.71
300,000	4090.17	3362.85	3045.69	2886.28	2800.45

MONTHLY PAYMENTS
ANNUAL INTEREST RATE: 11%

LOAN AMOUNT	LOAN MATURITY (YEARS)				
	10	15	20	25	30
50	0.69	0.57	0.52	0.50	0.48
100	1.38	1.14	1.04	0.99	0.96
200	2.76	2.28	2.07	1.97	1.91
300	4.14	3.41	3.10	2.95	2.86
400	5.51	4.55	4.13	3.93	3.81
500	6.89	5.69	5.17	4.91	4.77
600	8.27	6.82	6.20	5.89	5.72
700	9.65	7.96	7.23	6.87	6.67
800	11.02	9.10	8.26	7.85	7.62
900	12.40	10.23	9.29	8.83	8.58
1,000	13.78	11.37	10.33	9.81	9.53
2,000	27.55	22.74	20.65	19.61	19.05
3,000	41.33	34.10	30.97	29.41	28.57
4,000	55.10	45.47	41.29	39.21	38.10
5,000	68.88	56.83	51.61	49.01	47.62
6,000	82.65	68.20	61.94	58.81	57.14
7,000	96.43	79.57	72.26	68.61	66.67
8,000	110.20	90.93	82.58	78.41	76.19
9,000	123.98	102.30	92.90	88.22	85.71
10,000	137.75	113.66	103.22	98.02	95.24
20,000	275.50	227.32	206.44	196.03	190.47
30,000	413.25	340.98	309.66	294.04	285.70
40,000	551.00	454.64	412.88	392.05	380.93
50,000	688.75	568.30	516.10	490.06	476.17
60,000	826.50	681.96	619.32	588.07	571.40
70,000	964.25	795.62	722.54	686.08	666.63
80,000	1102.00	909.28	825.75	784.09	761.86
90,000	1239.75	1022.94	928.97	882.11	857.10
100,000	1377.50	1136.60	1032.19	980.12	952.33
110,000	1515.25	1250.26	1135.41	1078.13	1047.56
120,000	1653.00	1363.92	1238.63	1176.14	1142.79
130,000	1790.75	1477.58	1341.85	1274.15	1238.02
140,000	1928.50	1591.24	1445.07	1372.16	1333.26
150,000	2066.25	1704.90	1548.29	1470.17	1428.49
160,000	2204.00	1818.56	1651.50	1568.18	1523.72
170,000	2341.75	1932.22	1754.72	1666.20	1618.95
180,000	2479.50	2045.88	1857.94	1764.21	1714.19
190,000	2617.25	2159.54	1961.16	1862.22	1809.42
200,000	2755.00	2273.19	2064.38	1960.23	1904.65
250,000	3443.75	2841.49	2580.47	2450.29	2380.81
300,000	4132.50	3409.79	3096.57	2940.34	2856.97

MONTHLY PAYMENTS
ANNUAL INTEREST RATE: 11.25%

LOAN AMOUNT	LOAN MATURITY (YEARS)				
	10	15	20	25	30
50	0.70	0.58	0.53	0.50	0.49
100	1.40	1.16	1.05	1.00	0.98
200	2.79	2.31	2.10	2.00	1.95
300	4.18	3.46	3.15	3.00	2.92
400	5.57	4.61	4.20	4.00	3.89
500	6.96	5.77	5.25	5.00	4.86
600	8.36	6.92	6.30	5.99	5.83
700	9.75	8.07	7.35	6.99	6.80
800	11.14	9.22	8.40	7.99	7.78
900	12.53	10.38	9.45	8.99	8.75
1,000	13.92	11.53	10.50	9.99	9.72
2,000	27.84	23.05	20.99	19.97	19.43
3,000	41.76	34.58	31.48	29.95	29.14
4,000	55.67	46.10	41.98	39.93	38.86
5,000	69.59	57.62	52.47	49.92	48.57
6,000	83.51	69.15	62.96	59.90	58.28
7,000	97.42	80.67	73.45	69.88	67.99
8,000	111.34	92.19	83.95	79.86	77.71
9,000	125.26	103.72	94.44	89.85	87.42
10,000	139.17	115.24	104.93	99.83	97.13
20,000	278.34	230.47	209.86	199.65	194.26
30,000	417.51	345.71	314.78	299.48	291.38
40,000	556.68	460.94	419.71	399.30	388.51
50,000	695.85	576.18	524.63	499.13	485.64
60,000	835.02	691.41	629.56	598.95	582.76
70,000	974.19	806.65	734.49	698.77	679.89
80,000	1113.36	921.88	839.41	798.60	777.01
90,000	1252.53	1037.12	944.34	898.42	874.14
100,000	1391.70	1152.35	1049.26	998.25	971.27
110,000	1530.87	1267.59	1154.19	1098.07	1068.39
120,000	1670.04	1382.82	1259.11	1197.89	1165.52
130,000	1809.21	1498.06	1364.04	1297.72	1262.65
140,000	1948.37	1613.29	1468.97	1397.54	1359.77
150,000	2087.54	1728.52	1573.89	1497.37	1456.90
160,000	2226.71	1843.76	1678.82	1597.19	1554.02
170,000	2365.88	1958.99	1783.74	1697.01	1651.15
180,000	2505.05	2074.23	1888.67	1796.84	1748.28
190,000	2644.22	2189.46	1993.59	1896.66	1845.40
200,000	2783.39	2304.70	2098.52	1996.49	1942.53
250,000	3479.24	2880.87	2623.15	2495.61	2428.16
300,000	4175.08	3457.04	3147.78	2994.73	2913.79

MONTHLY PAYMENTS
ANNUAL INTEREST RATE: 11.5%

LOAN AMOUNT	LOAN MATURITY (YEARS)				
	10	15	20	25	30
50	0.71	0.59	0.54	0.51	0.50
100	1.41	1.17	1.07	1.02	1.00
200	2.82	2.34	2.14	2.04	1.99
300	4.22	3.51	3.20	3.05	2.98
400	5.63	4.68	4.27	4.07	3.97
500	7.03	5.85	5.34	5.09	4.96
600	8.44	7.01	6.40	6.10	5.95
700	9.85	8.18	7.47	7.12	6.94
800	11.25	9.35	8.54	8.14	7.93
900	12.66	10.52	9.60	9.15	8.92
1,000	14.06	11.69	10.67	10.17	9.91
2,000	28.12	23.37	21.33	20.33	19.81
3,000	42.18	35.05	32.00	30.50	29.71
4,000	56.24	46.73	42.66	40.66	39.62
5,000	70.30	58.41	53.33	50.83	49.52
6,000	84.36	70.10	63.99	60.99	59.42
7,000	98.42	81.78	74.66	71.16	69.33
8,000	112.48	93.46	85.32	81.32	79.23
9,000	126.54	105.14	95.98	91.49	89.13
10,000	140.60	116.82	106.65	101.65	99.03
20,000	281.20	233.64	213.29	203.30	198.06
30,000	421.79	350.46	319.93	304.95	297.09
40,000	562.39	467.28	426.58	406.59	396.12
50,000	702.98	584.10	533.22	508.24	495.15
60,000	843.58	700.92	639.86	609.89	594.18
70,000	984.17	817.74	746.51	711.53	693.21
80,000	1124.77	934.56	853.15	813.18	792.24
90,000	1265.36	1051.38	959.79	914.83	891.27
100,000	1405.96	1168.20	1066.43	1016.47	990.30
110,000	1546.56	1285.01	1173.08	1118.12	1089.33
120,000	1687.15	1401.83	1279.72	1219.77	1188.35
130,000	1827.75	1518.65	1386.36	1321.41	1287.38
140,000	1968.34	1635.47	1493.01	1423.06	1386.41
150,000	2108.94	1752.29	1599.65	1524.71	1485.44
160,000	2249.53	1869.11	1706.29	1626.36	1584.47
170,000	2390.13	1985.93	1812.94	1728.00	1683.50
180,000	2530.72	2102.75	1919.58	1829.65	1782.53
190,000	2671.32	2219.57	2026.22	1931.30	1881.56
200,000	2811.91	2336.39	2132.86	2032.94	1980.59
250,000	3514.89	2920.48	2666.08	2541.18	2475.73
300,000	4217.87	3504.58	3199.29	3049.41	2970.88

MONTHLY PAYMENTS
ANNUAL INTEREST RATE: 11.75%

LOAN AMOUNT	LOAN MATURITY (YEARS)				
	10	15	20	25	30
50	0.72	0.60	0.55	0.52	0.51
100	1.43	1.19	1.09	1.04	1.01
200	2.85	2.37	2.17	2.07	2.02
300	4.27	3.56	3.26	3.11	3.03
400	5.69	4.74	4.34	4.14	4.04
500	7.11	5.93	5.42	5.18	5.05
600	8.53	7.11	6.51	6.21	6.06
700	9.95	8.29	7.59	7.25	7.07
800	11.37	9.48	8.67	8.28	8.08
900	12.79	10.66	9.76	9.32	9.09
1,000	14.21	11.85	10.84	10.35	10.10
2,000	28.41	23.69	21.68	20.70	20.19
3,000	42.61	35.53	32.52	31.05	30.29
4,000	56.82	47.37	43.35	41.40	40.38
5,000	71.02	59.21	54.19	51.74	50.48
6,000	85.22	71.05	65.03	62.09	60.57
7,000	99.43	82.89	75.86	72.44	70.66
8,000	113.63	94.74	86.70	82.79	80.76
9,000	127.83	106.58	97.54	93.14	90.85
10,000	142.04	118.42	108.38	103.48	100.95
20,000	284.07	236.83	216.75	206.96	201.89
30,000	426.10	355.25	325.12	310.44	302.83
40,000	568.13	473.66	433.49	413.92	403.77
50,000	710.16	592.07	541.86	517.40	504.71
60,000	852.19	710.49	650.23	620.88	605.65
70,000	994.22	828.90	758.60	724.36	706.59
80,000	1136.25	947.31	866.97	827.84	807.53
90,000	1278.28	1065.73	975.34	931.32	908.47
100,000	1420.31	1184.14	1083.71	1034.80	1009.42
110,000	1562.34	1302.55	1192.09	1138.28	1110.36
120,000	1704.37	1420.97	1300.46	1241.76	1211.30
130,000	1846.40	1539.38	1408.83	1345.24	1312.24
140,000	1988.43	1657.79	1517.20	1448.72	1413.18
150,000	2130.46	1776.21	1625.57	1552.20	1514.12
160,000	2272.49	1894.62	1733.94	1655.68	1615.06
170,000	2414.52	2013.04	1842.31	1759.16	1716.00
180,000	2556.55	2131.45	1950.68	1862.64	1816.94
190,000	2698.58	2249.86	2059.05	1966.12	1917.89
200,000	2840.61	2368.28	2167.42	2069.60	2018.83
250,000	3550.76	2960.34	2709.28	2587.00	2523.53
300,000	4260.91	3552.41	3251.13	3104.40	3028.24

MONTHLY PAYMENTS
ANNUAL INTEREST RATE: 12%

LOAN AMOUNT	LOAN MATURITY (YEARS)				
	10	15	20	25	30
50	0.72	0.61	0.56	0.53	0.52
100	1.44	1.21	1.11	1.06	1.03
200	2.87	2.41	2.21	2.11	2.06
300	4.31	3.61	3.31	3.16	3.09
400	5.74	4.81	4.41	4.22	4.12
500	7.18	6.01	5.51	5.27	5.15
600	8.61	7.21	6.61	6.32	6.18
700	10.05	8.41	7.71	7.38	7.21
800	11.48	9.61	8.81	8.43	8.23
900	12.92	10.81	9.91	9.48	9.26
1,000	14.35	12.01	11.02	10.54	10.29
2,000	28.70	24.01	22.03	21.07	20.58
3,000	43.05	36.01	33.04	31.60	30.86
4,000	57.39	48.01	44.05	42.13	41.15
5,000	71.74	60.01	55.06	52.67	51.44
6,000	86.09	72.02	66.07	63.20	61.72
7,000	100.43	84.02	77.08	73.73	72.01
8,000	114.78	96.02	88.09	84.26	82.29
9,000	129.13	108.02	99.10	94.80	92.58
10,000	143.48	120.02	110.11	105.33	102.87
20,000	286.95	240.04	220.22	210.65	205.73
30,000	430.42	360.06	330.33	315.97	308.59
40,000	573.89	480.07	440.44	421.29	411.45
50,000	717.36	600.09	550.55	526.62	514.31
60,000	860.83	720.11	660.66	631.94	617.17
70,000	1004.30	840.12	770.77	737.26	720.03
80,000	1147.77	960.14	880.87	842.58	822.90
90,000	1291.24	1080.16	990.98	947.91	925.76
100,000	1434.71	1200.17	1101.09	1053.23	1028.62
110,000	1578.19	1320.19	1211.20	1158.55	1131.48
120,000	1721.66	1440.21	1321.31	1263.87	1234.34
130,000	1865.13	1560.22	1431.42	1369.20	1337.20
140,000	2008.60	1680.24	1541.53	1474.52	1440.06
150,000	2152.07	1800.26	1651.63	1579.84	1542.92
160,000	2295.54	1920.27	1761.74	1685.16	1645.79
170,000	2439.01	2040.29	1871.85	1790.49	1748.65
180,000	2582.48	2160.31	1981.96	1895.81	1851.51
190,000	2725.95	2280.32	2092.07	2001.13	1954.37
200,000	2869.42	2400.34	2202.18	2106.45	2057.23
250,000	3586.78	3000.43	2752.72	2633.07	2571.54
300,000	4304.13	3600.51	3303.26	3159.68	3085.84

MONTHLY PAYMENTS
ANNUAL INTEREST RATE: 12.25%

LOAN AMOUNT	LOAN MATURITY (YEARS)				
	10	15	20	25	30
50	0.73	0.61	0.56	0.54	0.53
100	1.45	1.22	1.12	1.08	1.05
200	2.90	2.44	2.24	2.15	2.10
300	4.35	3.65	3.36	3.22	3.15
400	5.80	4.87	4.48	4.29	4.20
500	7.25	6.09	5.60	5.36	5.24
600	8.70	7.30	6.72	6.44	6.29
700	10.15	8.52	7.83	7.51	7.34
800	11.60	9.74	8.95	8.58	8.39
900	13.05	10.95	10.07	9.65	9.44
1,000	14.50	12.17	11.19	10.72	10.48
2,000	28.99	24.33	22.38	21.44	20.96
3,000	43.48	36.49	33.56	32.16	31.44
4,000	57.97	48.66	44.75	42.87	41.92
5,000	72.46	60.82	55.93	53.59	52.40
6,000	86.96	72.98	67.12	64.31	62.88
7,000	101.45	85.15	78.30	75.03	73.36
8,000	115.94	97.31	89.49	85.74	83.84
9,000	130.43	109.47	100.68	96.46	94.32
10,000	144.92	121.63	111.86	107.18	104.79
20,000	289.84	243.26	223.72	214.35	209.58
30,000	434.76	364.89	335.57	321.53	314.37
40,000	579.68	486.52	447.43	428.70	419.16
50,000	724.60	608.15	559.29	535.88	523.95
60,000	869.52	729.78	671.14	643.05	628.74
70,000	1014.44	851.41	783.00	750.23	733.53
80,000	1159.36	973.04	894.86	857.40	838.32
90,000	1304.28	1094.67	1006.71	964.57	943.11
100,000	1449.20	1216.30	1118.57	1071.75	1047.90
110,000	1594.12	1337.93	1230.43	1178.92	1152.69
120,000	1739.04	1459.56	1342.28	1286.10	1257.48
130,000	1883.96	1581.19	1454.14	1393.27	1362.27
140,000	2028.88	1702.82	1566.00	1500.45	1467.06
150,000	2173.80	1824.45	1677.85	1607.62	1571.85
160,000	2318.72	1946.08	1789.71	1714.80	1676.64
170,000	2463.64	2067.71	1901.57	1821.97	1781.43
180,000	2608.56	2189.34	2013.42	1929.14	1886.22
190,000	2753.48	2310.97	2125.28	2036.32	1991.01
200,000	2898.40	2432.60	2237.13	2143.49	2095.80
250,000	3623.00	3040.75	2796.42	2679.36	2619.75
300,000	4347.60	3648.90	3355.70	3215.24	3143.69

MONTHLY PAYMENTS
ANNUAL INTEREST RATE: 12.5%

LOAN AMOUNT	LOAN MATURITY (YEARS)				
	10	15	20	25	30
50	0.74	0.62	0.57	0.55	0.54
100	1.47	1.24	1.14	1.10	1.07
200	2.93	2.47	2.28	2.19	2.14
300	4.40	3.70	3.41	3.28	3.21
400	5.86	4.94	4.55	4.37	4.27
500	7.32	6.17	5.69	5.46	5.34
600	8.79	7.40	6.82	6.55	6.41
700	10.25	8.63	7.96	7.64	7.48
800	11.72	9.87	9.09	8.73	8.54
900	13.18	11.10	10.23	9.82	9.61
1,000	14.64	12.33	11.37	10.91	10.68
2,000	29.28	24.66	22.73	21.81	21.35
3,000	43.92	36.98	34.09	32.72	32.02
4,000	58.56	49.31	45.45	43.62	42.70
5,000	73.19	61.63	56.81	54.52	53.37
6,000	87.83	73.96	68.17	65.43	64.04
7,000	102.47	86.28	79.53	76.33	74.71
8,000	117.11	98.61	90.90	87.23	85.39
9,000	131.74	110.93	102.26	98.14	96.06
10,000	146.38	123.26	113.62	109.04	106.73
20,000	292.76	246.51	227.23	218.08	213.46
30,000	439.13	369.76	340.85	327.11	320.18
40,000	585.51	493.01	454.46	436.15	426.91
50,000	731.89	616.27	568.08	545.18	533.63
60,000	878.26	739.52	681.69	654.22	640.36
70,000	1024.64	862.77	795.30	763.25	747.09
80,000	1171.02	986.02	908.92	872.29	853.81
90,000	1317.39	1109.28	1022.53	981.32	960.54
100,000	1463.77	1232.53	1136.15	1090.36	1067.26
110,000	1610.15	1355.78	1249.76	1199.40	1173.99
120,000	1756.52	1479.03	1363.38	1308.43	1280.72
130,000	1902.90	1602.29	1476.99	1417.47	1387.44
140,000	2049.28	1725.54	1590.60	1526.50	1494.17
150,000	2195.65	1848.79	1704.22	1635.54	1600.89
160,000	2342.03	1972.04	1817.83	1744.57	1707.62
170,000	2488.41	2095.30	1931.45	1853.61	1814.34
180,000	2634.78	2218.55	2045.06	1962.64	1921.07
190,000	2781.16	2341.80	2158.67	2071.68	2027.80
200,000	2927.54	2465.05	2272.29	2180.71	2134.52
250,000	3659.42	3081.32	2840.36	2725.89	2668.15
300,000	4391.30	3697.58	3408.43	3271.07	3201.78

MONTHLY PAYMENTS
ANNUAL INTEREST RATE: 12.75%

LOAN AMOUNT	LOAN MATURITY (YEARS)				
	10	15	20	25	30
50	0.74	0.63	0.58	0.56	0.55
100	1.48	1.25	1.16	1.11	1.09
200	2.96	2.50	2.31	2.22	2.18
300	4.44	3.75	3.47	3.33	3.27
400	5.92	5.00	4.62	4.44	4.35
500	7.40	6.25	5.77	5.55	5.44
600	8.88	7.50	6.93	6.66	6.53
700	10.35	8.75	8.08	7.77	7.61
800	11.83	10.00	9.24	8.88	8.70
900	13.31	11.24	10.39	9.99	9.79
1,000	14.79	12.49	11.54	11.10	10.87
2,000	29.57	24.98	23.08	22.19	21.74
3,000	44.36	37.47	34.62	33.28	32.61
4,000	59.14	49.96	46.16	44.37	43.47
5,000	73.92	62.45	57.70	55.46	54.34
6,000	88.71	74.94	69.23	66.55	65.21
7,000	103.49	87.42	80.77	77.64	76.07
8,000	118.28	99.91	92.31	88.73	86.94
9,000	133.06	112.40	103.85	99.82	97.81
10,000	147.84	124.89	115.39	110.91	108.67
20,000	295.68	249.77	230.77	221.82	217.34
30,000	443.52	374.66	346.15	332.72	326.01
40,000	591.36	499.54	461.53	443.63	434.68
50,000	739.20	624.42	576.91	554.53	543.35
60,000	887.04	749.31	692.29	665.44	652.02
70,000	1034.88	874.19	807.67	776.34	760.69
80,000	1182.72	999.07	923.05	887.25	869.36
90,000	1330.56	1123.96	1038.44	998.15	978.03
100,000	1478.40	1248.84	1153.82	1109.06	1086.70
110,000	1626.24	1373.73	1269.20	1219.96	1195.37
120,000	1774.08	1498.61	1384.58	1330.87	1304.04
130,000	1921.92	1623.49	1499.96	1441.77	1412.71
140,000	2069.76	1748.38	1615.34	1552.68	1521.38
150,000	2217.60	1873.26	1730.72	1663.58	1630.04
160,000	2365.44	1998.14	1846.10	1774.49	1738.71
170,000	2513.28	2123.03	1961.49	1885.39	1847.38
180,000	2661.12	2247.91	2076.87	1996.30	1956.05
190,000	2808.96	2372.80	2192.25	2107.20	2064.72
200,000	2956.80	2497.68	2307.63	2218.11	2173.39
250,000	3696.00	3122.10	2884.53	2772.64	2716.74
300,000	4435.20	3746.52	3461.44	3327.16	3260.08

MONTHLY PAYMENTS
ANNUAL INTEREST RATE: 13%

LOAN AMOUNT	\multicolumn{5}{c}{LOAN MATURITY (YEARS)}				
	10	15	20	25	30
50	0.75	0.64	0.59	0.57	0.56
100	1.50	1.27	1.18	1.13	1.11
200	2.99	2.54	2.35	2.26	2.22
300	4.48	3.80	3.52	3.39	3.32
400	5.98	5.07	4.69	4.52	4.43
500	7.47	6.33	5.86	5.64	5.54
600	8.96	7.60	7.03	6.77	6.64
700	10.46	8.86	8.21	7.90	7.75
800	11.95	10.13	9.38	9.03	8.85
900	13.44	11.39	10.55	10.16	9.96
1,000	14.94	12.66	11.72	11.28	11.07
2,000	29.87	25.31	23.44	22.56	22.13
3,000	44.80	37.96	35.15	33.84	33.19
4,000	59.73	50.61	46.87	45.12	44.25
5,000	74.66	63.27	58.58	56.40	55.31
6,000	89.59	75.92	70.30	67.68	66.38
7,000	104.52	88.57	82.02	78.95	77.44
8,000	119.45	101.22	93.73	90.23	88.50
9,000	134.38	113.88	105.45	101.51	99.56
10,000	149.32	126.53	117.16	112.79	110.62
20,000	298.63	253.05	234.32	225.57	221.24
30,000	447.94	379.58	351.48	338.36	331.86
40,000	597.25	506.10	468.64	451.14	442.48
50,000	746.56	632.63	585.79	563.92	553.10
60,000	895.87	759.15	702.95	676.71	663.72
70,000	1045.18	885.67	820.11	789.49	774.34
80,000	1194.49	1012.20	937.27	902.27	884.96
90,000	1343.80	1138.72	1054.42	1015.06	995.58
100,000	1493.11	1265.25	1171.58	1127.84	1106.20
110,000	1642.42	1391.77	1288.74	1240.62	1216.82
120,000	1791.73	1518.29	1405.90	1353.41	1327.44
130,000	1941.04	1644.82	1523.05	1466.19	1438.06
140,000	2090.35	1771.34	1640.21	1578.97	1548.68
150,000	2239.66	1897.87	1757.37	1691.76	1659.30
160,000	2388.97	2024.39	1874.53	1804.54	1769.92
170,000	2538.28	2150.91	1991.68	1917.32	1880.54
180,000	2687.59	2277.44	2108.84	2030.11	1991.16
190,000	2836.91	2403.96	2226.00	2142.89	2101.78
200,000	2986.22	2530.49	2343.15	2255.67	2212.40
250,000	3732.77	3163.11	2928.94	2819.59	2765.50
300,000	4479.32	3795.73	3514.73	3383.51	3318.60

MONTHLY PAYMENTS
ANNUAL INTEREST RATE: 13.25%

LOAN AMOUNT	LOAN MATURITY (YEARS)				
	10	15	20	25	30
50	0.76	0.65	0.60	0.58	0.57
100	1.51	1.29	1.19	1.15	1.13
200	3.02	2.57	2.38	2.30	2.26
300	4.53	3.85	3.57	3.45	3.38
400	6.04	5.13	4.76	4.59	4.51
500	7.54	6.41	5.95	5.74	5.63
600	9.05	7.70	7.14	6.89	6.76
700	10.56	8.98	8.33	8.03	7.89
800	12.07	10.26	9.52	9.18	9.01
900	13.58	11.54	10.71	10.33	10.14
1,000	15.08	12.82	11.90	11.47	11.26
2,000	30.16	25.64	23.79	22.94	22.52
3,000	45.24	38.46	35.69	34.41	33.78
4,000	60.32	51.27	47.58	45.87	45.04
5,000	75.40	64.09	59.48	57.34	56.29
6,000	90.48	76.91	71.37	68.81	67.55
7,000	105.56	89.73	83.27	80.27	78.81
8,000	120.64	102.54	95.16	91.74	90.07
9,000	135.72	115.36	107.05	103.21	101.32
10,000	150.79	128.18	118.95	114.68	112.58
20,000	301.58	256.35	237.89	229.35	225.16
30,000	452.37	384.53	356.83	344.02	337.74
40,000	603.16	512.70	475.78	458.69	450.31
50,000	753.95	640.87	594.72	573.36	562.89
60,000	904.74	769.05	713.66	688.03	675.47
70,000	1055.53	897.22	832.61	802.70	788.05
80,000	1206.32	1025.39	951.55	917.37	900.62
90,000	1357.11	1153.57	1070.49	1032.04	1013.20
100,000	1507.90	1281.74	1189.44	1146.71	1125.78
110,000	1658.68	1409.92	1308.38	1261.38	1238.36
120,000	1809.47	1538.09	1427.32	1376.05	1350.93
130,000	1960.26	1666.26	1546.27	1490.72	1463.51
140,000	2111.05	1794.44	1665.21	1605.39	1576.09
150,000	2261.84	1922.61	1784.15	1720.06	1688.67
160,000	2412.63	2050.78	1903.09	1834.73	1801.24
170,000	2563.42	2178.96	2022.04	1949.40	1913.82
180,000	2714.21	2307.13	2140.98	2064.07	2026.40
190,000	2865.00	2435.31	2259.92	2178.74	2138.97
200,000	3015.79	2563.48	2378.87	2293.41	2251.55
250,000	3769.73	3204.35	2973.58	2866.76	2814.44
300,000	4523.68	3845.22	3568.30	3440.11	3377.33

MONTHLY PAYMENTS
ANNUAL INTEREST RATE: 13.5%

LOAN AMOUNT	LOAN MATURITY (YEARS)				
	10	15	20	25	30
50	0.77	0.65	0.61	0.59	0.58
100	1.53	1.30	1.21	1.17	1.15
200	3.05	2.60	2.42	2.34	2.30
300	4.57	3.90	3.63	3.50	3.44
400	6.10	5.20	4.83	4.67	4.59
500	7.62	6.50	6.04	5.83	5.73
600	9.14	7.79	7.25	7.00	6.88
700	10.66	9.09	8.46	8.16	8.02
800	12.19	10.39	9.66	9.33	9.17
900	13.71	11.69	10.87	10.50	10.31
1,000	15.23	12.99	12.08	11.66	11.46
2,000	30.46	25.97	24.15	23.32	22.91
3,000	45.69	38.95	36.23	34.97	34.37
4,000	60.91	51.94	48.30	46.63	45.82
5,000	76.14	64.92	60.37	58.29	57.28
6,000	91.37	77.90	72.45	69.94	68.73
7,000	106.60	90.89	84.52	81.60	80.18
8,000	121.82	103.87	96.59	93.26	91.64
9,000	137.05	116.85	108.67	104.91	103.09
10,000	152.28	129.84	120.74	116.57	114.55
20,000	304.55	259.67	241.48	233.13	229.09
30,000	456.83	389.50	362.22	349.70	343.63
40,000	609.10	519.33	482.95	466.26	458.17
50,000	761.37	649.16	603.69	582.83	572.71
60,000	913.65	778.99	724.43	699.39	687.25
70,000	1065.92	908.83	845.17	815.96	801.79
80,000	1218.20	1038.66	965.90	932.52	916.33
90,000	1370.47	1168.49	1086.64	1049.08	1030.88
100,000	1522.74	1298.32	1207.38	1165.65	1145.42
110,000	1675.02	1428.15	1328.12	1282.21	1259.96
120,000	1827.29	1557.98	1448.85	1398.78	1374.50
130,000	1979.57	1687.82	1569.59	1515.34	1489.04
140,000	2131.84	1817.65	1690.33	1631.91	1603.58
150,000	2284.11	1947.48	1811.07	1748.47	1718.12
160,000	2436.39	2077.31	1931.80	1865.04	1832.66
170,000	2588.66	2207.14	2052.54	1981.60	1947.21
180,000	2740.94	2336.97	2173.28	2098.16	2061.75
190,000	2893.21	2466.81	2294.01	2214.73	2176.29
200,000	3045.48	2596.64	2414.75	2331.29	2290.83
250,000	3806.85	3245.80	3018.44	2914.12	2863.53
300,000	4568.22	3894.95	3622.13	3496.94	3436.24

MONTHLY PAYMENTS
ANNUAL INTEREST RATE: 13.75%

LOAN	LOAN MATURITY (YEARS)				
AMOUNT	10	15	20	25	30
50	0.77	0.66	0.62	0.60	0.59
100	1.54	1.32	1.23	1.19	1.17
200	3.08	2.63	2.46	2.37	2.34
300	4.62	3.95	3.68	3.56	3.50
400	6.16	5.26	4.91	4.74	4.67
500	7.69	6.58	6.13	5.93	5.83
600	9.23	7.89	7.36	7.11	7.00
700	10.77	9.21	8.58	8.30	8.16
800	12.31	10.52	9.81	9.48	9.33
900	13.84	11.84	11.03	10.67	10.49
1,000	15.38	13.15	12.26	11.85	11.66
2,000	30.76	26.30	24.51	23.70	23.31
3,000	46.14	39.45	36.77	35.55	34.96
4,000	61.51	52.60	49.02	47.39	46.61
5,000	76.89	65.75	61.28	59.24	58.26
6,000	92.27	78.90	73.53	71.09	69.91
7,000	107.64	92.05	85.78	82.93	81.56
8,000	123.02	105.20	98.04	94.78	93.21
9,000	138.40	118.35	110.29	106.63	104.87
10,000	153.77	131.50	122.55	118.47	116.52
20,000	307.54	263.00	245.09	236.94	233.03
30,000	461.31	394.50	367.63	355.41	349.54
40,000	615.07	526.00	490.17	473.87	466.05
50,000	768.84	657.50	612.71	592.34	582.56
60,000	922.61	789.00	735.25	710.81	699.07
70,000	1076.38	920.50	857.79	829.27	815.58
80,000	1230.14	1052.00	980.33	947.74	932.10
90,000	1383.91	1183.50	1102.87	1066.21	1048.61
100,000	1537.68	1315.00	1225.41	1184.67	1165.12
110,000	1691.45	1446.49	1347.95	1303.14	1281.63
120,000	1845.21	1577.99	1470.49	1421.61	1398.14
130,000	1998.98	1709.49	1593.03	1540.07	1514.65
140,000	2152.75	1840.99	1715.58	1658.54	1631.16
150,000	2306.52	1972.49	1838.12	1777.01	1747.67
160,000	2460.28	2103.99	1960.66	1895.47	1864.19
170,000	2614.05	2235.49	2083.20	2013.94	1980.70
180,000	2767.82	2366.99	2205.74	2132.41	2097.21
190,000	2921.58	2498.49	2328.28	2250.87	2213.72
200,000	3075.35	2629.99	2450.82	2369.34	2330.23
250,000	3844.19	3287.48	3063.52	2961.67	2912.79
300,000	4613.03	3944.98	3676.23	3554.01	3495.34

MONTHLY PAYMENTS
ANNUAL INTEREST RATE: 14%

LOAN AMOUNT	LOAN MATURITY (YEARS)				
	10	15	20	25	30
50	0.78	0.67	0.63	0.61	0.60
100	1.56	1.34	1.25	1.21	1.19
200	3.11	2.67	2.49	2.41	2.37
300	4.66	4.00	3.74	3.62	3.56
400	6.22	5.33	4.98	4.82	4.74
500	7.77	6.66	6.22	6.02	5.93
600	9.32	8.00	7.47	7.23	7.11
700	10.87	9.33	8.71	8.43	8.30
800	12.43	10.66	9.95	9.64	9.48
900	13.98	11.99	11.20	10.84	10.67
1,000	15.53	13.32	12.44	12.04	11.85
2,000	31.06	26.64	24.88	24.08	23.70
3,000	46.58	39.96	37.31	36.12	35.55
4,000	62.11	53.27	49.75	48.16	47.40
5,000	77.64	66.59	62.18	60.19	59.25
6,000	93.16	79.91	74.62	72.23	71.10
7,000	108.69	93.23	87.05	84.27	82.95
8,000	124.22	106.54	99.49	96.31	94.79
9,000	139.74	119.86	111.92	108.34	106.64
10,000	155.27	133.18	124.36	120.38	118.49
20,000	310.54	266.35	248.71	240.76	236.98
30,000	465.80	399.53	373.06	361.13	355.47
40,000	621.07	532.70	497.41	481.51	473.95
50,000	776.34	665.88	621.77	601.89	592.44
60,000	931.60	799.05	746.12	722.26	710.93
70,000	1086.87	932.22	870.47	842.64	829.42
80,000	1242.14	1065.40	994.82	963.01	947.90
90,000	1397.40	1198.57	1119.17	1083.39	1066.39
100,000	1552.67	1331.75	1243.53	1203.77	1184.88
110,000	1707.94	1464.92	1367.88	1324.14	1303.36
120,000	1863.20	1598.10	1492.23	1444.52	1421.85
130,000	2018.47	1731.27	1616.58	1564.89	1540.34
140,000	2173.74	1864.44	1740.93	1685.27	1658.83
150,000	2329.00	1997.62	1865.29	1805.65	1777.31
160,000	2484.27	2130.79	1989.64	1926.02	1895.80
170,000	2639.54	2263.97	2113.99	2046.40	2014.29
180,000	2794.80	2397.14	2238.34	2166.78	2132.77
190,000	2950.07	2530.32	2362.70	2287.15	2251.26
200,000	3105.34	2663.49	2487.05	2407.53	2369.75
250,000	3881.67	3329.36	3108.81	3009.41	2962.18
300,000	4658.00	3995.23	3730.57	3611.29	3554.62

561

MONTHLY PAYMENTS
ANNUAL INTEREST RATE: 14.25%

LOAN AMOUNT	LOAN MATURITY (YEARS)				
	10	15	20	25	30
50	0.79	0.68	0.64	0.62	0.61
100	1.57	1.35	1.27	1.23	1.21
200	3.14	2.70	2.53	2.45	2.41
300	4.71	4.05	3.79	3.67	3.62
400	6.28	5.40	5.05	4.90	4.82
500	7.84	6.75	6.31	6.12	6.03
600	9.41	8.10	7.58	7.34	7.23
700	10.98	9.45	8.84	8.57	8.44
800	12.55	10.79	10.10	9.79	9.64
900	14.11	12.14	11.36	11.01	10.85
1,000	15.68	13.49	12.62	12.23	12.05
2,000	31.36	26.98	25.24	24.46	24.10
3,000	47.04	40.46	37.86	36.69	36.15
4,000	62.71	53.95	50.47	48.92	48.19
5,000	78.39	67.43	63.09	61.15	60.24
6,000	94.07	80.92	75.71	73.38	72.29
7,000	109.75	94.41	88.33	85.61	84.33
8,000	125.42	107.89	100.94	97.84	96.38
9,000	141.10	121.38	113.56	110.07	108.43
10,000	156.78	134.86	126.18	122.30	120.47
20,000	313.55	269.72	252.35	244.59	240.94
30,000	470.32	404.58	378.52	366.88	361.41
40,000	627.10	539.44	504.69	489.18	481.88
50,000	783.87	674.29	630.86	611.47	602.35
60,000	940.64	809.15	757.04	733.76	722.82
70,000	1097.42	944.01	883.21	856.05	843.29
80,000	1254.19	1078.87	1009.38	978.35	963.75
90,000	1410.96	1213.73	1135.55	1100.64	1084.22
100,000	1567.73	1348.58	1261.72	1222.93	1204.69
110,000	1724.51	1483.44	1387.90	1345.22	1325.16
120,000	1881.28	1618.30	1514.07	1467.52	1445.63
130,000	2038.05	1753.16	1640.24	1589.81	1566.10
140,000	2194.83	1888.01	1766.41	1712.10	1686.57
150,000	2351.60	2022.87	1892.58	1834.40	1807.04
160,000	2508.37	2157.73	2018.75	1956.69	1927.50
170,000	2665.14	2292.59	2144.93	2078.98	2047.97
180,000	2821.92	2427.45	2271.10	2201.27	2168.44
190,000	2978.69	2562.30	2397.27	2323.57	2288.91
200,000	3135.46	2697.16	2523.44	2445.86	2409.38
250,000	3919.33	3371.45	3154.30	3057.32	3011.72
300,000	4703.19	4045.74	3785.16	3668.79	3614.07

MONTHLY PAYMENTS
ANNUAL INTEREST RATE: 14.5%

LOAN AMOUNT	LOAN MATURITY (YEARS)				
	10	15	20	25	30
50	0.80	0.69	0.64	0.63	0.62
100	1.59	1.37	1.28	1.25	1.23
200	3.17	2.74	2.56	2.49	2.45
300	4.75	4.10	3.84	3.73	3.68
400	6.34	5.47	5.12	4.97	4.90
500	7.92	6.83	6.40	6.22	6.13
600	9.50	8.20	7.68	7.46	7.35
700	11.09	9.56	8.96	8.70	8.58
800	12.67	10.93	10.24	9.94	9.80
900	14.25	12.29	11.52	11.18	11.03
1,000	15.83	13.66	12.80	12.43	12.25
2,000	31.66	27.32	25.60	24.85	24.50
3,000	47.49	40.97	38.40	37.27	36.74
4,000	63.32	54.63	51.20	49.69	48.99
5,000	79.15	68.28	64.00	62.11	61.23
6,000	94.98	81.94	76.80	74.53	73.48
7,000	110.81	95.59	89.60	86.96	85.72
8,000	126.63	109.25	102.40	99.38	97.97
9,000	142.46	122.90	115.20	111.80	110.22
10,000	158.29	136.56	128.00	124.22	122.46
20,000	316.58	273.11	256.00	248.44	244.92
30,000	474.87	409.66	384.00	372.65	367.37
40,000	633.15	546.21	512.00	496.87	489.83
50,000	791.44	682.76	640.00	621.09	612.28
60,000	949.73	819.31	768.00	745.30	734.74
70,000	1108.01	955.86	896.00	869.52	857.19
80,000	1266.30	1092.41	1024.00	993.74	979.65
90,000	1424.59	1228.96	1152.00	1117.95	1102.11
100,000	1582.88	1365.51	1280.00	1242.17	1224.56
110,000	1741.16	1502.06	1408.00	1366.38	1347.02
120,000	1899.45	1638.61	1536.00	1490.60	1469.47
130,000	2057.74	1775.16	1664.00	1614.82	1591.93
140,000	2216.02	1911.71	1792.00	1739.03	1714.38
150,000	2374.31	2048.26	1920.00	1863.25	1836.84
160,000	2532.60	2184.81	2048.00	1987.47	1959.29
170,000	2690.88	2321.36	2176.00	2111.68	2081.75
180,000	2849.17	2457.91	2304.00	2235.90	2204.21
190,000	3007.46	2594.46	2432.00	2360.12	2326.66
200,000	3165.75	2731.01	2560.00	2484.33	2449.12
250,000	3957.18	3413.76	3200.00	3105.41	3061.40
300,000	4748.62	4096.51	3840.00	3726.50	3673.67

MONTHLY PAYMENTS
ANNUAL INTEREST RATE: 14.75%

LOAN AMOUNT	LOAN MATURITY (YEARS)				
	10	15	20	25	30
50	0.80	0.70	0.65	0.64	0.63
100	1.60	1.39	1.30	1.27	1.25
200	3.20	2.77	2.60	2.53	2.49
300	4.80	4.15	3.90	3.79	3.74
400	6.40	5.54	5.20	5.05	4.98
500	8.00	6.92	6.50	6.31	6.23
600	9.59	8.30	7.80	7.57	7.47
700	11.19	9.68	9.09	8.84	8.72
800	12.79	11.07	10.39	10.10	9.96
900	14.39	12.45	11.69	11.36	11.21
1,000	15.99	13.83	12.99	12.62	12.45
2,000	31.97	27.66	25.97	25.23	24.89
3,000	47.95	41.48	38.96	37.85	37.34
4,000	63.93	55.31	51.94	50.46	49.78
5,000	79.91	69.13	64.92	63.08	62.23
6,000	95.89	82.96	77.91	75.69	74.67
7,000	111.87	96.78	90.89	88.31	87.12
8,000	127.85	110.61	103.87	100.92	99.56
9,000	143.83	124.43	116.86	113.54	112.01
10,000	159.81	138.26	129.84	126.15	124.45
20,000	319.62	276.51	259.68	252.30	248.90
30,000	479.43	414.76	389.51	378.44	373.35
40,000	639.24	553.01	519.35	504.59	497.80
50,000	799.04	691.26	649.18	630.74	622.24
60,000	958.85	829.51	779.02	756.88	746.69
70,000	1118.66	967.76	908.85	883.03	871.14
80,000	1278.47	1106.01	1038.69	1009.18	995.59
90,000	1438.27	1244.26	1168.53	1135.32	1120.03
100,000	1598.08	1382.51	1298.36	1261.47	1244.48
110,000	1757.89	1520.76	1428.20	1387.62	1368.93
120,000	1917.70	1659.01	1558.03	1513.76	1493.38
130,000	2077.50	1797.26	1687.87	1639.91	1617.82
140,000	2237.31	1935.51	1817.70	1766.06	1742.27
150,000	2397.12	2073.76	1947.54	1892.20	1866.72
160,000	2556.93	2212.01	2077.37	2018.35	1991.17
170,000	2716.73	2350.26	2207.21	2144.50	2115.61
180,000	2876.54	2488.51	2337.05	2270.64	2240.06
190,000	3036.35	2626.76	2466.88	2396.79	2364.51
200,000	3196.16	2765.01	2596.72	2522.93	2488.96
250,000	3995.19	3456.27	3245.89	3153.67	3111.19
300,000	4794.23	4147.52	3895.07	3784.40	3733.43

564

MONTHLY PAYMENTS
ANNUAL INTEREST RATE: 15%

LOAN AMOUNT	LOAN MATURITY (YEARS)				
	10	15	20	25	30
50	0.81	0.70	0.66	0.65	0.64
100	1.62	1.40	1.32	1.29	1.27
200	3.23	2.80	2.64	2.57	2.53
300	4.85	4.20	3.96	3.85	3.80
400	6.46	5.60	5.27	5.13	5.06
500	8.07	7.00	6.59	6.41	6.33
600	9.69	8.40	7.91	7.69	7.59
700	11.30	9.80	9.22	8.97	8.86
800	12.91	11.20	10.54	10.25	10.12
900	14.53	12.60	11.86	11.53	11.38
1,000	16.14	14.00	13.17	12.81	12.65
2,000	32.27	28.00	26.34	25.62	25.29
3,000	48.41	41.99	39.51	38.43	37.94
4,000	64.54	55.99	52.68	51.24	50.58
5,000	80.67	69.98	65.84	64.05	63.23
6,000	96.81	83.98	79.01	76.85	75.87
7,000	112.94	97.98	92.18	89.66	88.52
8,000	129.07	111.97	105.35	102.47	101.16
9,000	145.21	125.97	118.52	115.28	113.80
10,000	161.34	139.96	131.68	128.09	126.45
20,000	322.67	279.92	263.36	256.17	252.89
30,000	484.01	419.88	395.04	384.25	379.34
40,000	645.34	559.84	526.72	512.34	505.78
50,000	806.68	699.80	658.40	640.42	632.23
60,000	968.01	839.76	790.08	768.50	758.67
70,000	1129.35	979.71	921.76	896.59	885.12
80,000	1290.68	1119.67	1053.44	1024.67	1011.56
90,000	1452.02	1259.63	1185.11	1152.75	1138.00
100,000	1613.35	1399.59	1316.79	1280.84	1264.45
110,000	1774.69	1539.55	1448.47	1408.92	1390.89
120,000	1936.02	1679.51	1580.15	1537.00	1517.34
130,000	2097.35	1819.47	1711.83	1665.08	1643.78
140,000	2258.69	1959.42	1843.51	1793.17	1770.23
150,000	2420.02	2099.38	1975.19	1921.25	1896.67
160,000	2581.36	2239.34	2106.87	2049.33	2023.12
170,000	2742.69	2379.30	2238.55	2177.42	2149.56
180,000	2904.03	2519.26	2370.22	2305.50	2276.00
190,000	3065.36	2659.22	2501.90	2433.58	2402.45
200,000	3226.70	2799.18	2633.58	2561.66	2528.89
250,000	4033.37	3498.97	3291.98	3202.08	3161.11
300,000	4840.04	4198.76	3950.37	3842.49	3793.34

MONTHLY PAYMENTS
ANNUAL INTEREST RATE: 15.25%

LOAN AMOUNT	LOAN MATURITY (YEARS)				
	10	15	20	25	30
50	0.82	0.71	0.67	0.66	0.65
100	1.63	1.42	1.34	1.31	1.29
200	3.26	2.84	2.68	2.61	2.57
300	4.89	4.26	4.01	3.91	3.86
400	6.52	5.67	5.35	5.21	5.14
500	8.15	7.09	6.68	6.51	6.43
600	9.78	8.51	8.02	7.81	7.71
700	11.41	9.92	9.35	9.11	9.00
800	13.03	11.34	10.69	10.41	10.28
900	14.66	12.76	12.02	11.71	11.57
1,000	16.29	14.17	13.36	13.01	12.85
2,000	32.58	28.34	26.71	26.01	25.69
3,000	48.87	42.51	40.06	39.01	38.54
4,000	65.15	56.68	53.42	52.02	51.38
5,000	81.44	70.84	66.77	65.02	64.23
6,000	97.73	85.01	80.12	78.02	77.07
7,000	114.01	99.18	93.48	91.02	89.92
8,000	130.30	113.35	106.83	104.03	102.76
9,000	146.59	127.51	120.18	117.03	115.61
10,000	162.87	141.68	133.53	130.03	128.45
20,000	325.74	283.36	267.06	260.06	256.90
30,000	488.61	425.03	400.59	390.08	385.34
40,000	651.48	566.71	534.12	520.11	513.79
50,000	814.35	708.38	667.65	650.13	642.23
60,000	977.22	850.06	801.18	780.16	770.68
70,000	1140.09	991.73	934.71	910.19	899.13
80,000	1302.96	1133.41	1068.24	1040.21	1027.57
90,000	1465.83	1275.08	1201.77	1170.24	1156.02
100,000	1628.70	1416.76	1335.30	1300.26	1284.46
110,000	1791.57	1558.43	1468.83	1430.29	1412.91
120,000	1954.44	1700.11	1602.36	1560.32	1541.36
130,000	2117.31	1841.78	1735.89	1690.34	1669.80
140,000	2280.18	1983.46	1869.42	1820.37	1798.25
150,000	2443.05	2125.13	2002.95	1950.39	1926.69
160,000	2605.92	2266.81	2136.48	2080.42	2055.14
170,000	2768.79	2408.48	2270.01	2210.44	2183.58
180,000	2931.65	2550.16	2403.54	2340.47	2312.03
190,000	3094.52	2691.83	2537.07	2470.50	2440.48
200,000	3257.39	2833.51	2670.60	2600.52	2568.92
250,000	4071.74	3541.88	3338.25	3250.65	3211.15
300,000	4886.09	4250.26	4005.90	3900.78	3853.38

MONTHLY PAYMENTS
ANNUAL INTEREST RATE: 15.5%

LOAN AMOUNT	LOAN MATURITY (YEARS)				
	10	15	20	25	30
50	0.83	0.72	0.68	0.66	0.66
100	1.65	1.44	1.36	1.32	1.31
200	3.29	2.87	2.71	2.64	2.61
300	4.94	4.31	4.07	3.96	3.92
400	6.58	5.74	5.42	5.28	5.22
500	8.23	7.17	6.77	6.60	6.53
600	9.87	8.61	8.13	7.92	7.83
700	11.51	10.04	9.48	9.24	9.14
800	13.16	11.48	10.84	10.56	10.44
900	14.80	12.91	12.19	11.88	11.75
1,000	16.45	14.34	13.54	13.20	13.05
2,000	32.89	28.68	27.08	26.40	26.10
3,000	49.33	43.02	40.62	39.60	39.14
4,000	65.77	57.36	54.16	52.79	52.19
5,000	82.21	71.70	67.70	65.99	65.23
6,000	98.65	86.04	81.24	79.19	78.28
7,000	115.09	100.38	94.78	92.39	91.32
8,000	131.53	114.72	108.32	105.58	104.37
9,000	147.97	129.06	121.85	118.78	117.41
10,000	164.42	143.40	135.39	131.98	130.46
20,000	328.83	286.80	270.78	263.95	260.91
30,000	493.24	430.20	406.17	395.93	391.36
40,000	657.65	573.60	541.56	527.90	521.81
50,000	822.06	717.00	676.94	659.88	652.26
60,000	986.47	860.40	812.33	791.85	782.71
70,000	1150.88	1003.80	947.72	923.83	913.17
80,000	1315.29	1147.20	1083.11	1055.80	1043.62
90,000	1479.70	1290.60	1218.50	1187.78	1174.07
100,000	1644.11	1433.99	1353.88	1319.75	1304.52
110,000	1808.52	1577.39	1489.27	1451.72	1434.97
120,000	1972.93	1720.79	1624.66	1583.70	1565.42
130,000	2137.34	1864.19	1760.05	1715.67	1695.88
140,000	2301.75	2007.59	1895.44	1847.65	1826.33
150,000	2466.16	2150.99	2030.82	1979.62	1956.78
160,000	2630.57	2294.39	2166.21	2111.60	2087.23
170,000	2794.98	2437.79	2301.60	2243.57	2217.68
180,000	2959.39	2581.18	2436.99	2375.55	2348.13
190,000	3123.80	2724.58	2572.38	2507.52	2478.59
200,000	3288.21	2867.98	2707.76	2639.49	2609.04
250,000	4110.26	3584.98	3384.70	3299.37	3261.30
300,000	4932.31	4301.97	4061.64	3959.24	3913.56

MONTHLY PAYMENTS
ANNUAL INTEREST RATE: 15.75%

LOAN AMOUNT	LOAN MATURITY (YEARS)				
	10	15	20	25	30
50	0.83	0.73	0.69	0.67	0.67
100	1.66	1.46	1.38	1.34	1.33
200	3.32	2.91	2.75	2.68	2.65
300	4.98	4.36	4.12	4.02	3.98
400	6.64	5.81	5.50	5.36	5.30
500	8.30	7.26	6.87	6.70	6.63
600	9.96	8.71	8.24	8.04	7.95
700	11.62	10.16	9.61	9.38	9.28
800	13.28	11.62	10.99	10.72	10.60
900	14.94	13.07	12.36	12.06	11.93
1,000	16.60	14.52	13.73	13.40	13.25
2,000	33.20	29.03	27.46	26.79	26.50
3,000	49.79	43.54	41.18	40.18	39.74
4,000	66.39	58.06	54.91	53.58	52.99
5,000	82.98	72.57	68.63	66.97	66.24
6,000	99.58	87.08	82.36	80.36	79.48
7,000	116.18	101.60	96.08	93.76	92.73
8,000	132.77	116.11	109.81	107.15	105.97
9,000	149.37	130.62	123.53	120.54	119.22
10,000	165.96	145.14	137.26	133.93	132.47
20,000	331.92	290.27	274.51	267.86	264.93
30,000	497.88	435.40	411.77	401.79	397.39
40,000	663.84	580.53	549.02	535.72	529.85
50,000	829.80	725.66	686.27	669.65	662.31
60,000	995.76	870.79	823.53	803.58	794.78
70,000	1161.72	1015.92	960.78	937.51	927.24
80,000	1327.68	1161.05	1098.03	1071.44	1059.70
90,000	1493.63	1306.18	1235.29	1205.37	1192.16
100,000	1659.59	1451.31	1372.54	1339.30	1324.62
110,000	1825.55	1596.45	1509.79	1473.22	1457.08
120,000	1991.51	1741.58	1647.05	1607.15	1589.55
130,000	2157.47	1886.71	1784.30	1741.08	1722.01
140,000	2323.43	2031.84	1921.55	1875.01	1854.47
150,000	2489.39	2176.97	2058.81	2008.94	1986.93
160,000	2655.35	2322.10	2196.06	2142.87	2119.39
170,000	2821.31	2467.23	2333.31	2276.80	2251.85
180,000	2987.26	2612.36	2470.57	2410.73	2384.32
190,000	3153.22	2757.49	2607.82	2544.66	2516.78
200,000	3319.18	2902.62	2745.07	2678.59	2649.24
250,000	4148.98	3628.28	3431.34	3348.23	3311.55
300,000	4978.77	4353.93	4117.61	4017.88	3973.86

MONTHLY PAYMENTS
ANNUAL INTEREST RATE: 16%

LOAN AMOUNT	LOAN MATURITY (YEARS)				
	10	15	20	25	30
50	0.84	0.74	0.70	0.68	0.68
100	1.68	1.47	1.40	1.36	1.35
200	3.36	2.94	2.79	2.72	2.69
300	5.03	4.41	4.18	4.08	4.04
400	6.71	5.88	5.57	5.44	5.38
500	8.38	7.35	6.96	6.80	6.73
600	10.06	8.82	8.35	8.16	8.07
700	11.73	10.29	9.74	9.52	9.42
800	13.41	11.75	11.14	10.88	10.76
900	15.08	13.22	12.53	12.24	12.11
1,000	16.76	14.69	13.92	13.59	13.45
2,000	33.51	29.38	27.83	27.18	26.90
3,000	50.26	44.07	41.74	40.77	40.35
4,000	67.01	58.75	55.66	54.36	53.80
5,000	83.76	73.44	69.57	67.95	67.24
6,000	100.51	88.13	83.48	81.54	80.69
7,000	117.26	102.81	97.39	95.13	94.14
8,000	134.02	117.50	111.31	108.72	107.59
9,000	150.77	132.19	125.22	122.31	121.03
10,000	167.52	146.88	139.13	135.89	134.48
20,000	335.03	293.75	278.26	271.78	268.96
30,000	502.54	440.62	417.38	407.67	403.43
40,000	670.06	587.49	556.51	543.56	537.91
50,000	837.57	734.36	695.63	679.45	672.38
60,000	1005.08	881.23	834.76	815.34	806.86
70,000	1172.60	1028.10	973.88	951.23	941.34
80,000	1340.11	1174.97	1113.01	1087.12	1075.81
90,000	1507.62	1321.84	1252.14	1223.01	1210.29
100,000	1675.14	1468.71	1391.26	1358.89	1344.76
110,000	1842.65	1615.58	1530.39	1494.78	1479.24
120,000	2010.16	1762.45	1669.51	1630.67	1613.71
130,000	2177.68	1909.32	1808.64	1766.56	1748.19
140,000	2345.19	2056.19	1947.76	1902.45	1882.67
150,000	2512.70	2203.06	2086.89	2038.34	2017.14
160,000	2680.22	2349.93	2226.02	2174.23	2151.62
170,000	2847.73	2496.80	2365.14	2310.12	2286.09
180,000	3015.24	2643.67	2504.27	2446.01	2420.57
190,000	3182.76	2790.54	2643.39	2581.89	2555.04
200,000	3350.27	2937.41	2782.52	2717.78	2689.52
250,000	4187.84	3671.76	3478.15	3397.23	3361.90
300,000	5025.40	4406.11	4173.77	4076.67	4034.28

569

MONTHLY PAYMENTS
ANNUAL INTEREST RATE: 16.25%

LOAN AMOUNT	LOAN MATURITY (YEARS)				
	10	15	20	25	30
50	0.85	0.75	0.71	0.69	0.69
100	1.70	1.49	1.42	1.38	1.37
200	3.39	2.98	2.83	2.76	2.73
300	5.08	4.46	4.24	4.14	4.10
400	6.77	5.95	5.65	5.52	5.46
500	8.46	7.44	7.06	6.90	6.83
600	10.15	8.92	8.47	8.28	8.19
700	11.84	10.41	9.88	9.65	9.56
800	13.53	11.89	11.29	11.03	10.92
900	15.22	13.38	12.70	12.41	12.29
1,000	16.91	14.87	14.11	13.79	13.65
2,000	33.82	29.73	28.21	27.58	27.30
3,000	50.73	44.59	42.31	41.36	40.95
4,000	67.63	59.45	56.41	55.15	54.60
5,000	84.54	74.31	70.51	68.93	68.25
6,000	101.45	89.18	84.61	82.72	81.90
7,000	118.36	104.04	98.71	96.50	95.55
8,000	135.26	118.90	112.81	110.29	109.20
9,000	152.17	133.76	126.91	124.07	122.85
10,000	169.08	148.62	141.01	137.86	136.50
20,000	338.15	297.24	282.01	275.71	272.99
30,000	507.23	445.86	423.02	413.57	409.49
40,000	676.30	594.47	564.02	551.42	545.98
50,000	845.38	743.09	705.03	689.28	682.47
60,000	1014.45	891.71	846.03	827.13	818.97
70,000	1183.53	1040.32	987.04	964.98	955.46
80,000	1352.60	1188.94	1128.04	1102.84	1091.95
90,000	1521.67	1337.56	1269.05	1240.69	1228.45
100,000	1690.75	1486.17	1410.05	1378.55	1364.94
110,000	1859.82	1634.79	1551.05	1516.40	1501.43
120,000	2028.90	1783.41	1692.06	1654.25	1637.93
130,000	2197.97	1932.02	1833.06	1792.11	1774.42
140,000	2367.05	2080.64	1974.07	1929.96	1910.91
150,000	2536.12	2229.26	2115.07	2067.82	2047.41
160,000	2705.19	2377.87	2256.08	2205.67	2183.90
170,000	2874.27	2526.49	2397.08	2343.52	2320.39
180,000	3043.34	2675.11	2538.09	2481.38	2456.89
190,000	3212.42	2823.72	2679.09	2619.23	2593.38
200,000	3381.49	2972.34	2820.10	2757.09	2729.87
250,000	4226.86	3715.42	3525.12	3446.36	3412.34
300,000	5072.23	4458.51	4230.14	4135.63	4094.81

MONTHLY PAYMENTS
ANNUAL INTEREST RATE: 16.5%

LOAN AMOUNT	LOAN MATURITY (YEARS)				
	10	15	20	25	30
50	0.86	0.76	0.72	0.70	0.70
100	1.71	1.51	1.43	1.40	1.39
200	3.42	3.01	2.86	2.80	2.78
300	5.12	4.52	4.29	4.20	4.16
400	6.83	6.02	5.72	5.60	5.55
500	8.54	7.52	7.15	7.00	6.93
600	10.24	9.03	8.58	8.39	8.32
700	11.95	10.53	10.01	9.79	9.70
800	13.66	12.03	11.44	11.19	11.09
900	15.36	13.54	12.87	12.59	12.47
1,000	17.07	15.04	14.29	13.99	13.86
2,000	34.13	30.08	28.58	27.97	27.71
3,000	51.20	45.12	42.87	41.95	41.56
4,000	68.26	60.15	57.16	55.93	55.41
5,000	85.33	75.19	71.45	69.92	69.26
6,000	102.39	90.23	85.74	83.90	83.11
7,000	119.45	105.26	100.03	97.88	96.97
8,000	136.52	120.30	114.32	111.86	110.82
9,000	153.58	135.34	128.61	125.85	124.67
10,000	170.65	150.38	142.90	139.83	138.52
20,000	341.29	300.75	285.79	279.65	277.03
30,000	511.93	451.12	428.68	419.48	415.55
40,000	682.58	601.49	571.57	559.30	554.06
50,000	853.22	751.86	714.46	699.13	692.58
60,000	1023.86	902.23	857.35	838.95	831.09
70,000	1194.50	1052.60	1000.24	978.78	969.61
80,000	1365.15	1202.97	1143.13	1118.60	1108.12
90,000	1535.79	1353.34	1286.02	1258.43	1246.64
100,000	1706.43	1503.71	1428.91	1398.25	1385.15
110,000	1877.07	1654.09	1571.80	1538.07	1523.67
120,000	2047.72	1804.46	1714.69	1677.90	1662.18
130,000	2218.36	1954.83	1857.58	1817.72	1800.70
140,000	2389.00	2105.20	2000.47	1957.55	1939.21
150,000	2559.64	2255.57	2143.36	2097.37	2077.73
160,000	2730.29	2405.94	2286.25	2237.20	2216.24
170,000	2900.93	2556.31	2429.14	2377.02	2354.76
180,000	3071.57	2706.68	2572.03	2516.85	2493.27
190,000	3242.21	2857.05	2714.92	2656.67	2631.79
200,000	3412.86	3007.42	2857.81	2796.49	2770.30
250,000	4266.07	3759.28	3572.26	3495.62	3462.88
300,000	5119.28	4511.13	4286.71	4194.74	4155.45

MONTHLY PAYMENTS
ANNUAL INTEREST RATE: 16.75%

LOAN AMOUNT	LOAN MATURITY (YEARS)				
	10	15	20	25	30
50	0.87	0.77	0.73	0.71	0.71
100	1.73	1.53	1.45	1.42	1.41
200	3.45	3.05	2.90	2.84	2.82
300	5.17	4.57	4.35	4.26	4.22
400	6.89	6.09	5.80	5.68	5.63
500	8.62	7.61	7.24	7.09	7.03
600	10.34	9.13	8.69	8.51	8.44
700	12.06	10.65	10.14	9.93	9.84
800	13.78	12.18	11.59	11.35	11.25
900	15.50	13.70	13.04	12.77	12.65
1,000	17.23	15.22	14.48	14.18	14.06
2,000	34.45	30.43	28.96	28.36	28.11
3,000	51.67	45.64	43.44	42.54	42.17
4,000	68.89	60.86	57.92	56.72	56.22
5,000	86.11	76.07	72.40	70.90	70.27
6,000	103.34	91.28	86.87	85.08	84.33
7,000	120.56	106.50	101.35	99.26	98.38
8,000	137.78	121.71	115.83	113.44	112.44
9,000	155.00	136.92	130.31	127.62	126.49
10,000	172.22	152.14	144.79	141.80	140.54
20,000	344.44	304.27	289.57	283.60	281.08
30,000	516.66	456.40	434.35	425.40	421.62
40,000	688.87	608.53	579.13	567.20	562.16
50,000	861.09	760.67	723.91	709.00	702.70
60,000	1033.31	912.80	868.70	850.80	843.24
70,000	1205.52	1064.93	1013.48	992.60	983.78
80,000	1377.74	1217.06	1158.26	1134.40	1124.32
90,000	1549.96	1369.19	1303.04	1276.20	1264.86
100,000	1722.17	1521.33	1447.82	1418.00	1405.40
110,000	1894.39	1673.46	1592.61	1559.80	1545.94
120,000	2066.61	1825.59	1737.39	1701.60	1686.48
130,000	2238.82	1977.72	1882.17	1843.40	1827.02
140,000	2411.04	2129.86	2026.95	1985.20	1967.56
150,000	2583.26	2281.99	2171.73	2127.00	2108.10
160,000	2755.47	2434.12	2316.52	2268.80	2248.64
170,000	2927.69	2586.25	2461.30	2410.60	2389.18
180,000	3099.91	2738.38	2606.08	2552.40	2529.72
190,000	3272.13	2890.52	2750.86	2694.20	2670.26
200,000	3444.34	3042.65	2895.64	2836.00	2810.80
250,000	4305.43	3803.31	3619.55	3545.00	3513.49
300,000	5166.51	4563.97	4343.46	4254.00	4216.19

MONTHLY PAYMENTS
ANNUAL INTEREST RATE: 17%

LOAN AMOUNT	LOAN MATURITY (YEARS)				
	10	15	20	25	30
50	0.87	0.77	0.74	0.72	0.72
100	1.74	1.54	1.47	1.44	1.43
200	3.48	3.08	2.94	2.88	2.86
300	5.22	4.62	4.41	4.32	4.28
400	6.96	6.16	5.87	5.76	5.71
500	8.69	7.70	7.34	7.19	7.13
600	10.43	9.24	8.81	8.63	8.56
700	12.17	10.78	10.27	10.07	9.98
800	13.91	12.32	11.74	11.51	11.41
900	15.65	13.86	13.21	12.95	12.84
1,000	17.38	15.40	14.67	14.38	14.26
2,000	34.76	30.79	29.34	28.76	28.52
3,000	52.14	46.18	44.01	43.14	42.78
4,000	69.52	61.57	58.68	57.52	57.03
5,000	86.90	76.96	73.34	71.89	71.29
6,000	104.28	92.35	88.01	86.27	85.55
7,000	121.66	107.74	102.68	100.65	99.80
8,000	139.04	123.13	117.35	115.03	114.06
9,000	156.42	138.52	132.02	129.41	128.32
10,000	173.80	153.91	146.68	143.78	142.57
20,000	347.60	307.81	293.36	287.56	285.14
30,000	521.40	461.71	440.04	431.34	427.71
40,000	695.19	615.61	586.72	575.12	570.28
50,000	868.99	769.51	733.40	718.90	712.84
60,000	1042.79	923.41	880.08	862.68	855.41
70,000	1216.59	1077.31	1026.76	1006.46	997.98
80,000	1390.38	1231.21	1173.44	1150.24	1140.55
90,000	1564.18	1385.11	1320.12	1294.02	1283.11
100,000	1737.98	1539.01	1466.80	1437.80	1425.68
110,000	1911.78	1692.91	1613.48	1581.58	1568.25
120,000	2085.57	1846.81	1760.16	1725.36	1710.82
130,000	2259.37	2000.71	1906.84	1869.14	1853.38
140,000	2433.17	2154.61	2053.52	2012.92	1995.95
150,000	2606.96	2308.51	2200.20	2156.70	2138.52
160,000	2780.76	2462.41	2346.88	2300.48	2281.09
170,000	2954.56	2616.31	2493.56	2444.26	2423.65
180,000	3128.36	2770.21	2640.24	2588.04	2566.22
190,000	3302.15	2924.11	2786.92	2731.82	2708.79
200,000	3475.95	3078.01	2933.60	2875.60	2851.36
250,000	4344.94	3847.51	3667.00	3594.50	3564.19
300,000	5213.92	4617.01	4400.40	4313.39	4277.03

MONTHLY PAYMENTS
ANNUAL INTEREST RATE: 17.25%

LOAN AMOUNT	LOAN MATURITY (YEARS)				
	10	15	20	25	30
50	0.88	0.78	0.75	0.73	0.73
100	1.76	1.56	1.49	1.46	1.45
200	3.51	3.12	2.98	2.92	2.90
300	5.27	4.68	4.46	4.38	4.34
400	7.02	6.23	5.95	5.84	5.79
500	8.77	7.79	7.43	7.29	7.23
600	10.53	9.35	8.92	8.75	8.68
700	12.28	10.90	10.41	10.21	10.13
800	14.04	12.46	11.89	11.67	11.57
900	15.79	14.02	13.38	13.12	13.02
1,000	17.54	15.57	14.86	14.58	14.46
2,000	35.08	31.14	29.72	29.16	28.92
3,000	52.62	46.71	44.58	43.73	43.38
4,000	70.16	62.28	59.44	58.31	57.84
5,000	87.70	77.84	74.30	72.89	72.30
6,000	105.24	93.41	89.16	87.46	86.76
7,000	122.77	108.98	104.01	102.04	101.22
8,000	140.31	124.55	118.87	116.62	115.68
9,000	157.85	140.11	133.73	131.19	130.14
10,000	175.39	155.68	148.59	145.77	144.60
20,000	350.78	311.36	297.17	291.53	289.20
30,000	526.16	467.03	445.76	437.30	433.80
40,000	701.55	622.71	594.34	583.06	578.40
50,000	876.93	778.38	742.93	728.83	723.00
60,000	1052.32	934.06	891.51	874.59	867.60
70,000	1227.70	1089.74	1040.09	1020.35	1012.20
80,000	1403.09	1245.41	1188.68	1166.12	1156.79
90,000	1578.47	1401.09	1337.26	1311.88	1301.39
100,000	1753.86	1556.76	1485.85	1457.65	1445.99
110,000	1929.24	1712.44	1634.43	1603.41	1590.59
120,000	2104.63	1868.11	1783.02	1749.18	1735.19
130,000	2280.01	2023.79	1931.60	1894.94	1879.79
140,000	2455.40	2179.47	2080.18	2040.70	2024.39
150,000	2630.78	2335.14	2228.77	2186.47	2168.98
160,000	2806.17	2490.82	2377.35	2332.23	2313.58
170,000	2981.55	2646.49	2525.94	2478.00	2458.18
180,000	3156.94	2802.17	2674.52	2623.76	2602.78
190,000	3332.32	2957.85	2823.11	2769.52	2747.38
200,000	3507.71	3113.52	2971.69	2915.29	2891.98
250,000	4384.64	3891.90	3714.61	3644.11	3614.97
300,000	5261.56	4670.28	4457.53	4372.93	4337.96

MONTHLY PAYMENTS
ANNUAL INTEREST RATE: 17.5%

LOAN AMOUNT	LOAN MATURITY (YEARS)				
	10	15	20	25	30
50	0.89	0.79	0.76	0.74	0.74
100	1.77	1.58	1.51	1.48	1.47
200	3.54	3.15	3.01	2.96	2.94
300	5.31	4.73	4.52	4.44	4.40
400	7.08	6.30	6.02	5.92	5.87
500	8.85	7.88	7.53	7.39	7.34
600	10.62	9.45	9.03	8.87	8.80
700	12.39	11.03	10.54	10.35	10.27
800	14.16	12.60	12.04	11.83	11.74
900	15.93	14.18	13.55	13.30	13.20
1,000	17.70	15.75	15.05	14.78	14.67
2,000	35.40	31.50	30.10	29.56	29.33
3,000	53.10	47.24	45.15	44.33	43.99
4,000	70.80	62.99	60.20	59.11	58.66
5,000	88.49	78.73	75.25	73.88	73.32
6,000	106.19	94.48	90.30	88.66	87.98
7,000	123.89	110.23	105.35	103.43	102.65
8,000	141.59	125.97	120.40	118.21	117.31
9,000	159.29	141.72	135.45	132.98	131.97
10,000	176.98	157.46	150.50	147.76	146.64
20,000	353.96	314.92	300.99	295.51	293.27
30,000	530.94	472.38	451.49	443.26	439.90
40,000	707.92	629.84	601.98	591.02	586.54
50,000	884.90	787.29	752.48	738.77	733.17
60,000	1061.88	944.75	902.97	886.52	879.80
70,000	1238.86	1102.21	1053.46	1034.28	1026.43
80,000	1415.84	1259.67	1203.96	1182.03	1173.07
90,000	1592.81	1417.13	1354.45	1329.78	1319.70
100,000	1769.79	1574.58	1504.95	1477.53	1466.33
110,000	1946.77	1732.04	1655.44	1625.29	1612.96
120,000	2123.75	1889.50	1805.94	1773.04	1759.60
130,000	2300.73	2046.96	1956.43	1920.79	1906.23
140,000	2477.71	2204.41	2106.92	2068.55	2052.86
150,000	2654.69	2361.87	2257.42	2216.30	2199.49
160,000	2831.67	2519.33	2407.91	2364.05	2346.13
170,000	3008.65	2676.79	2558.41	2511.81	2492.76
180,000	3185.62	2834.25	2708.90	2659.56	2639.39
190,000	3362.60	2991.70	2859.39	2807.31	2786.02
200,000	3539.58	3149.16	3009.89	2955.06	2932.66
250,000	4424.48	3936.45	3762.36	3693.83	3665.82
300,000	5309.37	4723.74	4514.83	4432.59	4398.98

MONTHLY PAYMENTS
ANNUAL INTEREST RATE: 17.75%

LOAN AMOUNT	LOAN MATURITY (YEARS)				
	10	15	20	25	30
50	0.90	0.80	0.77	0.75	0.75
100	1.79	1.60	1.53	1.50	1.49
200	3.58	3.19	3.05	3.00	2.98
300	5.36	4.78	4.58	4.50	4.47
400	7.15	6.37	6.10	5.99	5.95
500	8.93	7.97	7.63	7.49	
600	10.72	9.56	9.15	8.99	8.93
700	12.51	11.15	10.67	10.49	10.41
800	14.29	12.74	12.20	11.98	11.90
900	16.08	14.34	13.72	13.48	13.39
1,000	17.86	15.93	15.25	14.98	14.87
2,000	35.72	31.85	30.49	29.95	29.74
3,000	53.58	47.78	45.73	44.93	44.61
4,000	71.44	63.70	60.97	59.90	59.47
5,000	89.29	79.63	76.21	74.88	74.34
6,000	107.15	95.55	91.45	89.85	89.21
7,000	125.01	111.48	106.69	104.83	104.07
8,000	142.87	127.40	121.93	119.80	118.94
9,000	160.73	143.33	137.17	134.78	133.81
10,000	178.58	159.25	152.41	149.75	148.67
20,000	357.16	318.50	304.82	299.50	297.34
30,000	535.74	477.75	457.24	449.24	446.01
40,000	714.32	636.99	609.64	598.99	594.68
50,000	892.90	796.24	762.06	748.74	743.35
60,000	1071.48	955.49	914.47	898.48	892.02
70,000	1250.06	1114.73	1066.88	1048.23	1040.69
80,000	1428.64	1273.98	1219.28	1197.97	1189.36
90,000	1607.22	1433.23	1371.70	1347.72	1338.03
100,000	1785.80	1592.47	1524.11	1497.47	1486.70
110,000	1964.38	1751.72	1676.51	1647.21	1635.37
120,000	2142.96	1910.97	1828.93	1796.96	1784.04
130,000	2321.54	2070.21	1981.34	1946.70	1932.71
140,000	2500.11	2229.46	2133.74	2096.45	2081.37
150,000	2678.69	2388.71	2286.15	2246.20	2230.04
160,000	2857.27	2547.95	2438.56	2395.94	2378.71
170,000	3035.85	2707.20	2590.97	2545.69	2527.38
180,000	3214.43	2866.45	2743.38	2695.43	2676.05
190,000	3393.01	3025.70	2895.79	2845.18	2824.72
200,000	3571.59	3184.94	3048.20	2994.93	2973.39
250,000	4464.49	3981.18	3810.25	3743.66	3716.74
300,000	5357.38	4777.41	4572.30	4492.39	4460.08

MONTHLY PAYMENTS
ANNUAL INTEREST RATE: 18%

LOAN AMOUNT	LOAN MATURITY (YEARS)				
	10	15	20	25	30
50	0.91	0.81	0.78	0.76	0.76
100	1.81	1.62	1.55	1.52	1.51
200	3.61	3.23	3.09	3.04	3.02
300	5.41	4.84	4.63	4.56	4.53
400	7.21	6.45	6.18	6.07	6.03
500	9.01	8.06	7.72	7.59	7.54
600	10.82	9.67	9.26	9.11	9.05
700	12.62	11.28	10.81	10.63	10.55
800	14.42	12.89	12.35	12.14	12.06
900	16.22	14.50	13.89	13.66	13.57
1,000	18.02	16.11	15.44	15.18	15.08
2,000	36.04	32.21	30.87	30.35	30.15
3,000	54.06	48.32	46.30	45.53	45.22
4,000	72.08	64.42	61.74	60.70	60.29
5,000	90.10	80.53	77.17	75.88	75.36
6,000	108.12	96.63	92.60	91.05	90.43
7,000	126.13	112.73	108.04	106.23	105.50
8,000	144.15	128.84	123.47	121.40	120.57
9,000	162.17	144.94	138.90	136.57	135.64
10,000	180.19	161.05	154.34	151.75	150.71
20,000	360.38	322.09	308.67	303.49	301.42
30,000	540.56	483.13	463.00	455.23	452.13
40,000	720.75	644.17	617.33	606.98	602.84
50,000	900.93	805.22	771.66	758.72	753.55
60,000	1081.12	966.26	925.99	910.46	904.26
70,000	1261.30	1127.30	1080.32	1062.21	1054.96
80,000	1441.49	1288.34	1234.65	1213.95	1205.67
90,000	1621.67	1449.38	1388.99	1365.69	1356.38
100,000	1801.86	1610.43	1543.32	1517.44	1507.09
110,000	1982.04	1771.47	1697.65	1669.18	1657.80
120,000	2162.23	1932.51	1851.98	1820.92	1808.51
130,000	2342.42	2093.55	2006.31	1972.66	1959.22
140,000	2522.60	2254.60	2160.64	2124.41	2109.92
150,000	2702.79	2415.64	2314.97	2276.15	2260.63
160,000	2882.97	2576.68	2469.30	2427.89	2411.34
170,000	3063.16	2737.72	2623.64	2579.64	2562.05
180,000	3243.34	2898.76	2777.97	2731.38	2712.76
190,000	3423.53	3059.81	2932.30	2883.12	2863.47
200,000	3603.71	3220.85	3086.63	3034.87	3014.18
250,000	4504.64	4026.06	3858.29	3793.58	3767.72
300,000	5405.57	4831.27	4629.94	4552.30	4521.26

MONTHLY PAYMENTS
ANNUAL INTEREST RATE: 18.25%

LOAN AMOUNT	10	15	20	25	30
		LOAN MATURITY (YEARS)			
50	0.91	0.82	0.79	0.77	0.77
100	1.82	1.63	1.57	1.54	1.53
200	3.64	3.26	3.13	3.08	3.06
300	5.46	4.89	4.69	4.62	4.59
400	7.28	6.52	6.26	6.15	6.12
500	9.09	8.15	7.82	7.69	7.64
600	10.91	9.78	9.38	9.23	9.17
700	12.73	11.40	10.94	10.77	10.70
800	14.55	13.03	12.51	12.30	12.23
900	16.37	14.66	14.07	13.84	13.75
1,000	18.18	16.29	15.63	15.38	15.28
2,000	36.36	32.57	31.26	30.75	30.56
3,000	54.54	48.86	46.88	46.13	45.83
4,000	72.72	65.14	62.51	61.50	61.11
5,000	90.90	81.43	78.13	76.88	76.38
6,000	109.08	97.71	93.76	92.25	91.66
7,000	127.26	114.00	109.39	107.63	106.93
8,000	145.44	130.28	125.01	123.00	122.21
9,000	163.62	146.56	140.64	138.37	137.48
10,000	181.80	162.85	156.26	153.75	152.76
20,000	363.60	325.69	312.52	307.49	305.51
30,000	545.40	488.54	468.78	461.24	458.26
40,000	727.20	651.38	625.04	614.98	611.01
50,000	908.99	814.23	781.29	768.72	763.76
60,000	1090.79	977.07	937.55	922.47	916.51
70,000	1272.59	1139.91	1093.81	1076.21	1069.26
80,000	1454.39	1302.76	1250.07	1229.96	1222.01
90,000	1636.18	1465.60	1406.33	1383.70	1374.76
100,000	1817.98	1628.45	1562.58	1537.44	1527.51
110,000	1999.78	1791.29	1718.84	1691.19	1680.26
120,000	2181.58	1954.13	1875.10	1844.93	1833.01
130,000	2363.38	2116.98	2031.36	1998.68	1985.76
140,000	2545.17	2279.82	2187.61	2152.42	2138.51
150,000	2726.97	2442.67	2343.87	2306.16	2291.26
160,000	2908.77	2605.51	2500.13	2459.91	2444.01
170,000	3090.57	2768.35	2656.39	2613.65	2596.76
180,000	3272.36	2931.20	2812.65	2767.39	2749.51
190,000	3454.16	3094.04	2968.90	2921.14	2902.26
200,000	3635.96	3256.89	3125.16	3074.88	3055.01
250,000	4544.95	4071.11	3906.45	3843.60	3818.76
300,000	5453.94	4885.33	4687.74	4612.32	4582.51

MONTHLY PAYMENTS
ANNUAL INTEREST RATE: 18.5%

LOAN AMOUNT	LOAN MATURITY (YEARS)				
	10	15	20	25	30
50	0.92	0.83	0.80	0.78	0.78
100	1.84	1.65	1.59	1.56	1.55
200	3.67	3.30	3.17	3.12	3.10
300	5.51	4.94	4.75	4.68	4.65
400	7.34	6.59	6.33	6.23	6.20
500	9.18	8.24	7.91	7.79	7.74
600	11.01	9.88	9.50	9.35	9.29
700	12.84	11.53	11.08	10.91	10.84
800	14.68	13.18	12.66	12.46	12.39
900	16.51	14.82	14.24	14.02	13.94
1,000	18.35	16.47	15.82	15.58	15.48
2,000	36.69	32.94	31.64	31.15	30.96
3,000	55.03	49.40	47.46	46.73	46.44
4,000	73.37	65.87	63.28	62.30	61.92
5,000	91.71	82.33	79.10	77.88	77.40
6,000	110.06	98.80	94.92	93.45	92.88
7,000	128.40	115.26	110.74	109.03	108.36
8,000	146.74	131.73	126.56	124.60	123.84
9,000	165.08	148.19	142.38	140.18	139.32
10,000	183.42	164.66	158.19	155.75	154.80
20,000	366.84	329.31	316.38	311.50	309.59
30,000	550.26	493.96	474.57	467.25	464.39
40,000	733.67	658.61	632.76	623.00	619.18
50,000	917.09	823.27	790.95	778.75	773.98
60,000	1100.51	987.92	949.14	934.50	928.77
70,000	1283.92	1152.57	1107.33	1090.24	1083.57
80,000	1467.34	1317.22	1265.52	1245.99	1238.36
90,000	1650.76	1481.88	1423.71	1401.74	1393.16
100,000	1834.17	1646.53	1581.90	1557.49	1547.95
110,000	2017.59	1811.18	1740.09	1713.24	1702.74
120,000	2201.01	1975.83	1898.28	1868.99	1857.54
130,000	2384.42	2140.49	2056.47	2024.73	2012.33
140,000	2567.84	2305.14	2214.66	2180.48	2167.13
150,000	2751.26	2469.79	2372.85	2336.23	2321.92
160,000	2934.67	2634.44	2531.04	2491.98	2476.72
170,000	3118.09	2799.10	2689.23	2647.73	2631.51
180,000	3301.51	2963.75	2847.42	2803.48	2786.31
190,000	3484.92	3128.40	3005.61	2959.23	2941.10
200,000	3668.34	3293.05	3163.80	3114.97	3095.89
250,000	4585.42	4116.32	3954.75	3893.72	3869.87
300,000	5502.51	4939.58	4745.70	4672.46	4643.84

MONTHLY PAYMENTS
ANNUAL INTEREST RATE: 18.75%

LOAN AMOUNT	LOAN MATURITY (YEARS)				
	10	15	20	25	30
50	0.93	0.84	0.81	0.79	0.79
100	1.86	1.67	1.61	1.58	1.57
200	3.71	3.33	3.21	3.16	3.14
300	5.56	5.00	4.81	4.74	4.71
400	7.41	6.66	6.41	6.32	6.28
500	9.26	8.33	8.01	7.89	7.85
600	11.11	9.99	9.61	9.47	9.42
700	12.96	11.66	11.21	11.05	10.98
800	14.81	13.32	12.82	12.63	12.55
900	16.66	14.99	14.42	14.20	14.12
1,000	18.51	16.65	16.02	15.78	15.69
2,000	37.01	33.30	32.03	31.56	31.37
3,000	55.52	49.95	48.04	47.33	47.06
4,000	74.02	66.59	64.06	63.11	62.74
5,000	92.53	83.24	80.07	78.88	78.43
6,000	111.03	99.89	96.08	94.66	94.11
7,000	129.53	116.53	112.09	110.43	109.79
8,000	148.04	133.18	128.11	126.21	125.48
9,000	166.54	149.83	144.12	141.99	141.16
10,000	185.05	166.47	160.13	157.76	156.85
20,000	370.09	332.94	320.26	315.52	313.69
30,000	555.13	499.41	480.38	473.27	470.53
40,000	740.17	665.87	640.51	631.03	627.37
50,000	925.21	832.34	800.64	788.79	784.21
60,000	1110.25	998.81	960.76	946.54	941.05
70,000	1295.30	1165.27	1120.89	1104.30	1097.89
80,000	1480.34	1331.74	1281.02	1262.06	1254.73
90,000	1665.38	1498.21	1441.14	1419.81	1411.57
100,000	1850.42	1664.67	1601.27	1577.57	1568.41
110,000	2035.46	1831.14	1761.40	1735.33	1725.25
120,000	2220.50	1997.61	1921.52	1893.08	1882.09
130,000	2405.54	2164.08	2081.65	2050.84	2038.94
140,000	2590.59	2330.54	2241.78	2208.60	2195.78
150,000	2775.63	2497.01	2401.90	2366.35	2352.62
160,000	2960.67	2663.48	2562.03	2524.11	2509.46
170,000	3145.71	2829.94	2722.16	2681.87	2666.30
180,000	3330.75	2996.41	2882.28	2839.62	2823.14
190,000	3515.79	3162.88	3042.41	2997.38	2979.98
200,000	3700.84	3329.34	3202.54	3155.14	3136.82
250,000	4626.04	4161.68	4003.17	3943.92	3921.03
300,000	5551.25	4994.01	4803.80	4732.70	4705.23

MONTHLY PAYMENTS
ANNUAL INTEREST RATE: 19%

LOAN AMOUNT	LOAN MATURITY (YEARS)				
	10	15	20	25	30
50	0.94	0.85	0.82	0.80	0.80
100	1.87	1.69	1.63	1.60	1.59
200	3.74	3.37	3.25	3.20	3.18
300	5.61	5.05	4.87	4.80	4.77
400	7.47	6.74	6.49	6.40	6.36
500	9.34	8.42	8.11	7.99	7.95
600	11.21	10.10	9.73	9.59	9.54
700	13.07	11.79	11.35	11.19	11.13
800	14.94	13.47	12.97	12.79	12.72
900	16.81	15.15	14.59	14.38	14.31
1,000	18.67	16.83	16.21	15.98	15.89
2,000	37.34	33.66	32.42	31.96	31.78
3,000	56.01	50.49	48.63	47.94	47.67
4,000	74.67	67.32	64.83	63.91	63.56
5,000	93.34	84.15	81.04	79.89	79.45
6,000	112.01	100.98	97.25	95.87	95.34
7,000	130.68	117.81	113.45	111.84	111.23
8,000	149.34	134.64	129.66	127.82	127.12
9,000	168.01	151.46	145.87	143.80	143.01
10,000	186.68	168.29	162.07	159.77	158.89
20,000	373.35	336.58	324.14	319.54	317.78
30,000	560.02	504.87	486.21	479.31	476.67
40,000	746.69	673.16	648.28	639.08	635.56
50,000	933.37	841.44	810.35	798.84	794.45
60,000	1120.04	1009.73	972.42	958.61	953.34
70,000	1306.71	1178.02	1134.48	1118.38	1112.23
80,000	1493.38	1346.31	1296.55	1278.15	1271.12
90,000	1680.05	1514.59	1458.62	1437.92	1430.01
100,000	1866.73	1682.88	1620.69	1597.68	1588.90
110,000	2053.40	1851.17	1782.76	1757.45	1747.79
120,000	2240.07	2019.46	1944.83	1917.22	1906.68
130,000	2426.74	2187.74	2106.89	2076.99	2065.57
140,000	2613.42	2356.03	2268.96	2236.76	2224.45
150,000	2800.09	2524.32	2431.03	2396.52	2383.34
160,000	2986.76	2692.61	2593.10	2556.29	2542.23
170,000	3173.43	2860.89	2755.17	2716.06	2701.12
180,000	3360.10	3029.18	2917.24	2875.83	2860.01
190,000	3546.78	3197.47	3079.31	3035.60	3018.90
200,000	3733.45	3365.76	3241.37	3195.36	3177.79
250,000	4666.81	4207.19	4051.72	3994.20	3972.24
300,000	5600.17	5048.63	4862.06	4793.04	4766.68

MONTHLY PAYMENTS
ANNUAL INTEREST RATE: 19.25%

LOAN AMOUNT	LOAN MATURITY (YEARS)				
	10	15	20	25	30
50	0.95	0.86	0.83	0.81	0.81
100	1.89	1.71	1.65	1.62	1.61
200	3.77	3.41	3.29	3.24	3.22
300	5.65	5.11	4.93	4.86	4.83
400	7.54	6.81	6.57	6.48	6.44
500	9.42	8.51	8.21	8.09	8.05
600	11.30	10.21	9.85	9.71	9.66
700	13.19	11.91	11.49	11.33	11.27
800	15.07	13.61	13.13	12.95	12.88
900	16.95	15.32	14.77	14.57	14.49
1,000	18.84	17.02	16.41	16.18	16.10
2,000	37.67	34.03	32.81	32.36	32.19
3,000	56.50	51.04	49.21	48.54	48.29
4,000	75.33	68.05	65.61	64.72	64.38
5,000	94.16	85.06	82.01	80.90	80.47
6,000	112.99	102.07	98.41	97.07	96.57
7,000	131.82	119.09	114.82	113.25	112.66
8,000	150.65	136.10	131.22	129.43	128.76
9,000	169.48	153.11	147.62	145.61	144.85
10,000	188.31	170.12	164.02	161.79	160.94
20,000	376.62	340.23	328.04	323.57	321.88
30,000	564.93	510.35	492.05	485.35	482.82
40,000	753.24	680.46	656.07	647.14	643.76
50,000	941.55	850.58	820.08	808.92	804.70
60,000	1129.86	1020.69	984.10	970.70	965.64
70,000	1318.17	1190.81	1148.11	1132.48	1126.58
80,000	1506.48	1360.92	1312.13	1294.27	1287.52
90,000	1694.79	1531.03	1476.14	1456.05	1448.46
100,000	1883.10	1701.15	1640.16	1617.83	1609.40
110,000	2071.41	1871.26	1804.17	1779.62	1770.34
120,000	2259.72	2041.38	1968.19	1941.40	1931.28
130,000	2448.03	2211.49	2132.20	2103.18	2092.22
140,000	2636.34	2381.61	2296.22	2264.96	2253.16
150,000	2824.65	2551.72	2460.23	2426.75	2414.10
160,000	3012.95	2721.83	2624.25	2588.53	2575.04
170,000	3201.26	2891.95	2788.26	2750.31	2735.98
180,000	3389.57	3062.06	2952.28	2912.09	2896.92
190,000	3577.88	3232.18	3116.29	3073.88	3057.86
200,000	3766.19	3402.29	3280.31	3235.66	3218.80
250,000	4707.74	4252.86	4100.38	4044.57	4023.50
300,000	5649.29	5103.44	4920.46	4853.49	4828.20

MONTHLY PAYMENTS
ANNUAL INTEREST RATE: 19.5%

LOAN AMOUNT	LOAN MATURITY (YEARS)				
	10	15	20	25	30
50	0.95	0.86	0.83	0.82	0.82
100	1.90	1.72	1.66	1.64	1.63
200	3.80	3.44	3.32	3.28	3.26
300	5.70	5.16	4.98	4.92	4.89
400	7.60	6.88	6.64	6.56	6.52
500	9.50	8.60	8.30	8.20	8.15
600	11.40	10.32	9.96	9.83	9.78
700	13.30	12.04	11.62	11.47	11.41
800	15.20	13.76	13.28	13.11	13.04
900	17.10	15.48	14.94	14.75	14.67
1,000	19.00	17.20	16.60	16.39	16.30
2,000	38.00	34.39	33.20	32.77	32.60
3,000	56.99	51.59	49.79	49.15	48.90
4,000	75.99	68.78	66.39	65.53	65.20
5,000	94.98	85.98	82.99	81.91	81.50
6,000	113.98	103.17	99.58	98.29	97.80
7,000	132.97	120.37	116.18	114.67	114.10
8,000	151.97	137.56	132.78	131.05	130.40
9,000	170.96	154.76	149.37	147.43	146.70
10,000	189.96	171.95	165.97	163.81	163.00
20,000	379.91	343.90	331.94	327.61	325.99
30,000	569.86	515.85	497.90	491.41	488.98
40,000	759.81	687.79	663.87	655.21	651.97
50,000	949.77	859.74	829.84	819.01	814.97
60,000	1139.72	1031.69	995.80	982.81	977.96
70,000	1329.67	1203.63	1161.77	1146.61	1140.95
80,000	1519.62	1375.58	1327.74	1310.41	1303.94
90,000	1709.57	1547.53	1493.70	1474.21	1466.93
100,000	1899.53	1719.47	1659.67	1638.01	1629.93
110,000	2089.48	1891.42	1825.64	1801.81	1792.92
120,000	2279.43	2063.37	1991.60	1965.61	1955.91
130,000	2469.38	2235.32	2157.57	2129.41	2118.90
140,000	2659.34	2407.26	2323.54	2293.21	2281.89
150,000	2849.29	2579.21	2489.50	2457.01	2444.88
160,000	3039.24	2751.16	2655.47	2620.81	2607.88
170,000	3229.19	2923.10	2821.43	2784.62	2770.87
180,000	3419.14	3095.05	2987.40	2948.42	2933.86
190,000	3609.10	3267.00	3153.37	3112.22	3096.85
200,000	3799.05	3438.94	3319.33	3276.02	3259.85
250,000	4748.81	4298.68	4149.17	4095.02	4074.80
300,000	5698.57	5158.41	4979.00	4914.02	4889.76

583

MONTHLY PAYMENTS
ANNUAL INTEREST RATE: 19.75%

LOAN AMOUNT	LOAN MATURITY (YEARS)				
	10	15	20	25	30
50	0.96	0.87	0.84	0.83	0.83
100	1.92	1.74	1.68	1.66	1.66
200	3.84	3.48	3.36	3.32	3.31
300	5.75	5.22	5.04	4.98	4.96
400	7.67	6.96	6.72	6.64	6.61
500	9.59	8.69	8.40	8.30	8.26
600	11.50	10.43	10.08	9.95	9.91
700	13.42	12.17	11.76	11.61	11.56
800	15.33	13.91	13.44	13.27	13.21
900	17.25	15.65	15.12	14.93	14.86
1,000	19.17	17.38	16.80	16.59	16.51
2,000	38.33	34.76	33.59	33.17	33.01
3,000	57.49	52.14	50.38	49.75	49.52
4,000	76.65	69.52	67.17	66.33	66.02
5,000	95.81	86.90	83.97	82.92	82.53
6,000	114.97	104.28	100.76	99.50	99.03
7,000	134.13	121.65	117.55	116.08	115.54
8,000	153.29	139.03	134.34	132.66	132.04
9,000	172.45	156.41	151.14	149.24	148.55
10,000	191.61	173.79	167.93	165.83	165.05
20,000	383.21	347.58	335.85	331.65	330.10
30,000	574.81	521.36	503.77	497.47	495.14
40,000	766.41	695.15	671.69	663.29	660.19
50,000	958.01	868.93	839.62	829.11	825.24
60,000	1149.61	1042.72	1007.54	994.93	990.28
70,000	1341.21	1216.50	1175.46	1160.76	1155.33
80,000	1532.82	1390.29	1343.38	1326.58	1320.37
90,000	1724.42	1564.08	1511.31	1492.40	1485.42
100,000	1916.02	1737.86	1679.23	1658.22	1650.47
110,000	2107.62	1911.65	1847.15	1824.04	1815.51
120,000	2299.22	2085.43	2015.07	1989.86	1980.56
130,000	2490.82	2259.22	2183.00	2155.68	2145.60
140,000	2682.42	2433.00	2350.92	2321.51	2310.65
150,000	2874.02	2606.79	2518.84	2487.33	2475.70
160,000	3065.63	2780.57	2686.76	2653.15	2640.74
170,000	3257.23	2954.36	2854.68	2818.97	2805.79
180,000	3448.83	3128.15	3022.61	2984.79	2970.83
190,000	3640.43	3301.93	3190.53	3150.61	3135.88
200,000	3832.03	3475.72	3358.45	3316.43	3300.93
250,000	4790.04	4344.65	4198.06	4145.54	4126.16
300,000	5748.04	5213.57	5037.68	4974.65	4951.39

MONTHLY PAYMENTS
ANNUAL INTEREST RATE: 20%

LOAN AMOUNT	LOAN MATURITY (YEARS)				
	10	15	20	25	30
50	0.97	0.88	0.85	0.84	0.84
100	1.94	1.76	1.70	1.68	1.68
200	3.87	3.52	3.40	3.36	3.35
300	5.80	5.27	5.10	5.04	5.02
400	7.74	7.03	6.80	6.72	6.69
500	9.67	8.79	8.50	8.40	8.36
600	11.60	10.54	10.20	10.08	10.03
700	13.53	12.30	11.90	11.75	11.70
800	15.47	14.06	13.60	13.43	13.37
900	17.40	15.81	15.29	15.11	15.04
1,000	19.33	17.57	16.99	16.79	16.72
2,000	38.66	35.13	33.98	33.57	33.43
3,000	57.98	52.69	50.97	50.36	50.14
4,000	77.31	70.26	67.96	67.14	66.85
5,000	96.63	87.82	84.95	83.93	83.56
6,000	115.96	105.38	101.93	100.71	100.27
7,000	135.28	122.95	118.92	117.50	116.98
8,000	154.61	140.51	135.91	134.28	133.69
9,000	173.94	158.07	152.90	151.07	150.40
10,000	193.26	175.63	169.89	167.85	167.11
20,000	386.52	351.26	339.77	335.70	334.21
30,000	579.77	526.89	509.65	503.54	501.31
40,000	773.03	702.52	679.53	671.39	668.41
50,000	966.28	878.15	849.42	839.23	835.51
60,000	1159.54	1053.78	1019.30	1007.08	1002.62
70,000	1352.80	1229.41	1189.18	1174.92	1169.72
80,000	1546.05	1405.04	1359.06	1342.77	1336.82
90,000	1739.31	1580.67	1528.95	1510.61	1503.92
100,000	1932.56	1756.30	1698.83	1678.46	1671.02
110,000	2125.82	1931.93	1868.71	1846.30	1838.13
120,000	2319.07	2107.56	2038.59	2014.15	2005.23
130,000	2512.33	2283.19	2208.48	2181.99	2172.33
140,000	2705.59	2458.82	2378.36	2349.84	2339.43
150,000	2898.84	2634.45	2548.24	2517.68	2506.53
160,000	3092.10	2810.08	2718.12	2685.53	2673.63
170,000	3285.35	2985.71	2888.01	2853.37	2840.74
180,000	3478.61	3161.34	3057.89	3021.22	3007.84
190,000	3671.86	3336.97	3227.77	3189.06	3174.94
200,000	3865.12	3512.60	3397.65	3356.91	3342.04
250,000	4831.40	4390.75	4247.07	4196.13	4177.55
300,000	5797.68	5268.90	5096.48	5035.36	5013.06

MONTHLY PAYMENTS
ANNUAL INTEREST RATE: 20.25%

LOAN AMOUNT	LOAN MATURITY (YEARS)				
	10	15	20	25	30
50	0.98	0.89	0.86	0.85	0.85
100	1.95	1.78	1.72	1.70	1.70
200	3.90	3.55	3.44	3.40	3.39
300	5.85	5.33	5.16	5.10	5.08
400	7.80	7.10	6.88	6.80	6.77
500	9.75	8.88	8.60	8.50	8.46
600	11.70	10.65	10.32	10.20	10.15
700	13.65	12.43	12.03	11.90	11.85
800	15.60	14.20	13.75	13.59	13.54
900	17.55	15.98	15.47	15.29	15.23
1,000	19.50	17.75	17.19	16.99	16.92
2,000	38.99	35.50	34.37	33.98	33.84
3,000	58.48	53.25	51.56	50.97	50.75
4,000	77.97	71.00	68.74	67.95	67.67
5,000	97.46	88.74	85.93	84.94	84.58
6,000	116.95	106.49	103.11	101.93	101.50
7,000	136.45	124.24	120.30	118.92	118.42
8,000	155.94	141.99	137.48	135.90	135.33
9,000	175.43	159.74	154.67	152.89	152.25
10,000	194.92	177.48	171.85	169.88	169.16
20,000	389.84	354.96	343.70	339.75	338.32
30,000	584.75	532.44	515.55	509.62	507.48
40,000	779.67	709.92	687.39	679.49	676.64
50,000	974.59	887.40	859.24	849.36	845.80
60,000	1169.50	1064.88	1031.09	1019.23	1014.96
70,000	1364.42	1242.36	1202.93	1189.11	1184.12
80,000	1559.33	1419.84	1374.78	1358.98	1353.28
90,000	1754.25	1597.32	1546.63	1528.85	1522.44
100,000	1949.17	1774.80	1718.47	1698.72	1691.60
110,000	2144.08	1952.28	1890.32	1868.59	1860.76
120,000	2339.00	2129.76	2062.17	2038.46	2029.92
130,000	2533.91	2307.24	2234.01	2208.34	2199.08
140,000	2728.83	2484.72	2405.86	2378.21	2368.23
150,000	2923.75	2662.20	2577.71	2548.08	2537.39
160,000	3118.66	2839.67	2749.55	2717.95	2706.55
170,000	3313.58	3017.15	2921.40	2887.82	2875.71
180,000	3508.49	3194.63	3093.25	3057.69	3044.87
190,000	3703.41	3372.11	3265.10	3227.57	3214.03
200,000	3898.33	3549.59	3436.94	3397.44	3383.19
250,000	4872.91	4436.99	4296.18	4246.80	4228.99
300,000	5847.49	5324.39	5155.41	5096.15	5074.78

MONTHLY PAYMENTS
ANNUAL INTEREST RATE: 20.5%

LOAN AMOUNT	LOAN MATURITY (YEARS)				
	10	15	20	25	30
50	0.99	0.90	0.87	0.86	0.86
100	1.97	1.80	1.74	1.72	1.72
200	3.94	3.59	3.48	3.44	3.43
300	5.90	5.39	5.22	5.16	5.14
400	7.87	7.18	6.96	6.88	6.85
500	9.83	8.97	8.70	8.60	8.57
600	11.80	10.77	10.43	10.32	10.28
700	13.77	12.56	12.17	12.04	11.99
800	15.73	14.35	13.91	13.76	13.70
900	17.70	16.15	15.65	15.48	15.41
1,000	19.66	17.94	17.39	17.20	17.13
2,000	39.32	35.87	34.77	34.39	34.25
3,000	58.98	53.81	52.15	51.58	51.37
4,000	78.64	71.74	69.53	68.77	68.49
5,000	98.30	89.67	86.91	85.96	85.61
6,000	117.95	107.61	104.29	103.15	102.74
7,000	137.61	125.54	121.68	120.34	119.86
8,000	157.27	143.47	139.06	137.53	136.98
9,000	176.93	161.41	156.44	154.72	154.10
10,000	196.59	179.34	173.82	171.91	171.22
20,000	393.17	358.67	347.64	343.81	342.44
30,000	589.75	538.01	521.45	515.71	513.66
40,000	786.34	717.34	695.27	687.61	684.88
50,000	982.92	896.68	869.08	859.51	856.10
60,000	1179.50	1076.01	1042.90	1031.41	1027.31
70,000	1376.08	1255.35	1216.71	1203.31	1198.53
80,000	1572.67	1434.68	1390.53	1375.21	1369.75
90,000	1769.25	1614.02	1564.34	1547.11	1540.97
100,000	1965.83	1793.35	1738.16	1719.01	1712.19
110,000	2162.41	1972.69	1911.98	1890.91	1883.40
120,000	2359.00	2152.02	2085.79	2062.81	2054.62
130,000	2555.58	2331.36	2259.61	2234.71	2225.84
140,000	2752.16	2510.69	2433.42	2406.62	2397.06
150,000	2948.74	2690.03	2607.24	2578.52	2568.28
160,000	3145.33	2869.36	2781.05	2750.42	2739.49
170,000	3341.91	3048.70	2954.87	2922.32	2910.71
180,000	3538.49	3228.03	3128.68	3094.22	3081.93
190,000	3735.07	3407.37	3302.50	3266.12	3253.15
200,000	3931.66	3586.70	3476.31	3438.02	3424.37
250,000	4914.57	4483.38	4345.39	4297.52	4280.46
300,000	5897.48	5380.05	5214.47	5157.03	5136.55

MONTHLY PAYMENTS
ANNUAL INTEREST RATE: 20.75%

LOAN AMOUNT	LOAN MATURITY (YEARS)				
	10	15	20	25	30
50	1.00	0.91	0.88	0.87	0.87
100	1.99	1.82	1.76	1.74	1.74
200	3.97	3.63	3.52	3.48	3.47
300	5.95	5.44	5.28	5.22	5.20
400	7.94	7.25	7.04	6.96	6.94
500	9.92	9.06	8.79	8.70	8.67
600	11.90	10.88	10.55	10.44	10.40
700	13.88	12.69	12.31	12.18	12.13
800	15.87	14.50	14.07	13.92	13.87
900	17.85	16.31	15.83	15.66	15.60
1,000	19.83	18.12	17.58	17.40	17.33
2,000	39.66	36.24	35.16	34.79	34.66
3,000	59.48	54.36	52.74	52.18	51.99
4,000	79.31	72.48	70.32	69.58	69.32
5,000	99.13	90.60	87.90	86.97	86.64
6,000	118.96	108.72	105.48	104.36	103.97
7,000	138.78	126.84	123.06	121.76	121.30
8,000	158.61	144.96	140.64	139.15	138.63
9,000	178.43	163.08	158.21	156.54	155.96
10,000	198.26	181.20	175.79	173.94	173.28
20,000	396.51	362.40	351.58	347.87	346.56
30,000	594.77	543.59	527.37	521.80	519.84
40,000	793.02	724.79	703.16	695.73	693.12
50,000	991.28	905.98	878.94	869.67	866.40
60,000	1189.53	1087.18	1054.73	1043.60	1039.68
70,000	1387.78	1268.37	1230.52	1217.53	1212.95
80,000	1586.04	1449.57	1406.31	1391.46	1386.23
90,000	1784.29	1630.76	1582.10	1565.40	1559.51
100,000	1982.55	1811.96	1757.88	1739.33	1732.79
110,000	2180.80	1993.15	1933.67	1913.26	1906.07
120,000	2379.06	2174.35	2109.46	2087.19	2079.35
130,000	2577.31	2355.54	2285.25	2261.12	2252.62
140,000	2775.56	2536.74	2461.04	2435.06	2425.90
150,000	2973.82	2717.93	2636.82	2608.99	2599.18
160,000	3172.07	2899.13	2812.61	2782.92	2772.46
170,000	3370.33	3080.33	2988.40	2956.85	2945.74
180,000	3568.58	3261.52	3164.19	3130.79	3119.02
190,000	3766.84	3442.72	3339.98	3304.72	3292.29
200,000	3965.09	3623.91	3515.76	3478.65	3465.57
250,000	4956.36	4529.89	4394.70	4348.31	4331.96
300,000	5947.63	5435.86	5273.64	5217.97	5198.36

588

MONTHLY PAYMENTS
ANNUAL INTEREST RATE: 21%

LOAN AMOUNT	LOAN MATURITY (YEARS)				
	10	15	20	25	30
50	1.00	0.92	0.89	0.88	0.88
100	2.00	1.84	1.78	1.76	1.76
200	4.00	3.67	3.56	3.52	3.51
300	6.00	5.50	5.34	5.28	5.27
400	8.00	7.33	7.12	7.04	7.02
500	10.00	9.16	8.89	8.80	8.77
600	12.00	10.99	10.67	10.56	10.53
700	14.00	12.82	12.45	12.32	12.28
800	16.00	14.65	14.23	14.08	14.03
900	18.00	16.48	16.00	15.84	15.79
1,000	20.00	18.31	17.78	17.60	17.54
2,000	39.99	36.62	35.56	35.20	35.07
3,000	59.98	54.92	53.33	52.79	52.61
4,000	79.98	73.23	71.11	70.39	70.14
5,000	99.97	91.54	88.89	87.99	87.67
6,000	119.96	109.84	106.66	105.58	105.21
7,000	139.96	128.15	124.44	123.18	122.74
8,000	159.95	146.45	142.22	140.78	140.28
9,000	179.94	164.76	159.99	158.37	157.81
10,000	199.94	183.07	177.77	175.97	175.35
20,000	399.87	366.13	355.53	351.94	350.69
30,000	599.80	549.19	533.30	527.90	526.03
40,000	799.73	732.25	711.06	703.87	701.37
50,000	999.66	915.31	888.83	879.84	876.71
60,000	1199.59	1098.37	1066.59	1055.80	1052.05
70,000	1399.53	1281.43	1244.35	1231.77	1227.39
80,000	1599.46	1464.49	1422.12	1407.74	1402.73
90,000	1799.39	1647.56	1599.88	1583.70	1578.07
100,000	1999.32	1830.62	1777.65	1759.67	1753.41
110,000	2199.25	2013.68	1955.41	1935.63	1928.75
120,000	2399.18	2196.74	2133.18	2111.60	2104.09
130,000	2599.11	2379.80	2310.94	2287.57	2279.42
140,000	2799.05	2562.86	2488.70	2463.53	2454.77
150,000	2998.98	2745.92	2666.47	2639.50	2630.11
160,000	3198.91	2928.98	2844.23	2815.47	2805.44
170,000	3398.84	3112.04	3022.00	2991.43	2980.79
180,000	3598.77	3295.11	3199.76	3167.40	3156.13
190,000	3798.70	3478.17	3377.53	3343.36	3331.46
200,000	3998.63	3661.23	3555.29	3519.33	3506.81
250,000	4998.29	4576.53	4444.11	4399.16	4383.51
300,000	5997.95	5491.84	5332.93	5278.99	5260.21

MONTHLY PAYMENTS
ANNUAL INTEREST RATE: 21.25%

LOAN AMOUNT	LOAN MATURITY (YEARS)				
	10	15	20	25	30
50	1.01	0.93	0.90	0.90	0.89
100	2.02	1.85	1.80	1.79	1.78
200	4.04	3.70	3.60	3.57	3.55
300	6.05	5.55	5.40	5.35	5.33
400	8.07	7.40	7.19	7.13	7.10
500	10.09	9.25	8.99	8.91	8.88
600	12.10	11.10	10.79	10.69	10.65
700	14.12	12.95	12.59	12.47	12.42
800	16.13	14.80	14.38	14.25	14.20
900	18.15	16.65	16.18	16.03	15.97
1,000	20.17	18.50	17.98	17.81	17.75
2,000	40.33	36.99	35.95	35.61	35.49
3,000	60.49	55.48	53.93	53.41	53.23
4,000	80.65	73.98	71.90	71.21	70.97
5,000	100.81	92.47	89.88	89.01	88.71
6,000	120.97	110.96	107.85	106.81	106.45
7,000	141.14	129.46	125.83	124.61	124.19
8,000	161.30	147.95	143.80	142.41	141.93
9,000	181.46	166.44	161.78	160.21	159.67
10,000	201.62	184.94	179.75	178.01	177.41
20,000	403.23	369.87	359.49	356.01	354.81
30,000	604.85	554.80	539.24	534.01	532.21
40,000	806.46	739.73	718.98	712.02	709.62
50,000	1008.08	924.67	898.73	890.02	887.02
60,000	1209.70	1109.60	1078.47	1068.02	1064.42
70,000	1411.31	1294.53	1258.22	1246.02	1241.83
80,000	1612.92	1479.46	1437.96	1424.03	1419.23
90,000	1814.54	1664.40	1617.71	1602.03	1596.63
100,000	2016.15	1849.33	1797.45	1780.03	1774.03
110,000	2217.77	2034.26	1977.19	1958.03	1951.44
120,000	2419.38	2219.19	2156.94	2136.04	2128.84
130,000	2621.00	2404.13	2336.68	2314.04	2306.24
140,000	2822.61	2589.06	2516.43	2492.04	2483.65
150,000	3024.23	2773.99	2696.17	2670.04	2661.05
160,000	3225.84	2958.92	2875.92	2848.05	2838.45
170,000	3427.46	3143.86	3055.66	3026.05	3015.85
180,000	3629.07	3328.79	3235.41	3204.05	3193.26
190,000	3830.69	3513.72	3415.15	3382.05	3370.66
200,000	4032.30	3698.65	3594.89	3560.06	3548.06
250,000	5040.38	4623.32	4493.62	4450.07	4435.08
300,000	6048.45	5547.98	5392.34	5340.08	5322.09

MONTHLY PAYMENTS
ANNUAL INTEREST RATE: 21.5%

LOAN AMOUNT	LOAN MATURITY (YEARS)				
	10	15	20	25	30
50	1.02	0.94	0.91	0.91	0.90
100	2.04	1.87	1.82	1.81	1.80
200	4.07	3.74	3.64	3.61	3.59
300	6.10	5.61	5.46	5.41	5.39
400	8.14	7.48	7.27	7.21	7.18
500	10.17	9.35	9.09	9.01	8.98
600	12.20	11.21	10.91	10.81	0.77
700	14.24	13.08	12.73	12.61	12.57
800	16.27	14.95	14.54	14.41	14.36
900	18.30	16.82	16.36	16.21	16.16
1,000	20.34	18.69	18.18	18.01	17.95
2,000	40.67	37.37	36.35	36.01	35.90
3,000	61.00	56.05	54.52	54.02	53.85
4,000	81.33	74.73	72.70	72.02	71.79
5,000	101.66	93.41	90.87	90.03	89.74
6,000	121.99	112.09	109.04	108.03	107.69
7,000	142.32	130.77	127.21	126.03	125.63
8,000	162.65	149.45	145.39	144.04	143.58
9,000	182.98	168.13	163.56	162.04	161.53
10,000	203.31	186.81	181.73	180.05	179.47
20,000	406.61	373.62	363.46	360.09	358.94
30,000	609.91	560.43	545.19	540.13	538.41
40,000	813.22	747.24	726.92	720.17	717.87
50,000	1016.52	934.05	908.65	900.21	897.34
60,000	1219.82	1120.86	1090.37	1080.25	1076.81
70,000	1423.13	1307.66	1272.10	1260.29	1256.27
80,000	1626.43	1494.47	1453.83	1440.33	1435.74
90,000	1829.73	1681.28	1635.56	1620.37	1615.21
100,000	2033.04	1868.09	1817.29	1800.42	1794.67
110,000	2236.34	2054.90	1999.01	1980.46	1974.14
120,000	2439.64	2241.71	2180.74	2160.50	2153.61
130,000	2642.95	2428.51	2362.47	2340.54	2333.08
140,000	2846.25	2615.32	2544.20	2520.58	2512.54
150,000	3049.55	2802.13	2725.93	2700.62	2692.01
160,000	3252.86	2988.94	2907.65	2880.66	2871.48
170,000	3456.16	3175.75	3089.38	3060.70	3050.94
180,000	3659.46	3362.56	3271.11	3240.74	3230.41
190,000	3862.77	3549.37	3452.84	3420.78	3409.88
200,000	4066.07	3736.17	3634.57	3600.83	3589.34
250,000	5082.59	4670.22	4543.21	4501.03	4486.68
300,000	6099.10	5604.26	5451.85	5401.24	5384.01

MONTHLY PAYMENTS
ANNUAL INTEREST RATE: 21.75%

LOAN	LOAN MATURITY (YEARS)				
AMOUNT	10	15	20	25	30
50	1.03	0.95	0.92	0.92	0.91
100	2.05	1.89	1.84	1.83	1.82
200	4.10	3.78	3.68	3.65	3.64
300	6.15	5.67	5.52	5.47	5.45
400	8.20	7.55	7.35	7.29	7.27
500	10.25	9.44	9.19	9.11	9.08
600	12.30	11.33	11.03	10.93	10.90
700	14.35	13.21	12.87	12.75	12.71
800	16.40	15.10	14.70	14.57	14.53
900	18.45	16.99	16.54	16.39	16.34
1,000	20.50	18.87	18.38	18.21	18.16
2,000	41.00	37.74	36.75	36.42	36.31
3,000	61.50	56.61	55.12	54.63	54.46
4,000	82.00	75.48	73.49	72.84	72.62
5,000	102.50	94.35	91.86	91.05	90.77
6,000	123.00	113.22	110.23	109.25	108.92
7,000	143.50	132.09	128.61	127.46	127.08
8,000	164.00	150.96	146.98	145.67	145.23
9,000	184.50	169.83	165.35	163.88	163.38
10,000	205.00	188.69	183.72	182.09	181.54
20,000	410.00	377.38	367.44	364.17	363.07
30,000	615.00	566.07	551.15	546.25	544.60
40,000	819.99	754.76	734.87	728.33	726.13
50,000	1024.99	943.45	918.58	910.41	907.67
60,000	1229.99	1132.14	1102.30	1092.49	1089.20
70,000	1434.99	1320.83	1286.01	1274.58	1270.73
80,000	1639.98	1509.52	1469.73	1456.66	1452.26
90,000	1844.98	1698.21	1653.44	1638.74	1633.79
100,000	2049.98	1886.90	1837.16	1820.82	1815.33
110,000	2254.97	2075.59	2020.87	2002.90	1996.86
120,000	2459.97	2264.28	2204.59	2184.98	2178.39
130,000	2664.97	2452.97	2388.30	2367.07	2359.92
140,000	2869.97	2641.66	2572.02	2549.15	2541.46
150,000	3074.96	2830.35	2755.73	2731.23	2722.99
160,000	3279.96	3019.04	2939.45	2913.31	2904.52
170,000	3484.96	3207.73	3123.17	3095.39	3086.05
180,000	3689.95	3396.42	3306.88	3277.47	3267.58
190,000	3894.95	3585.11	3490.60	3459.56	3449.12
200,000	4099.95	3773.80	3674.31	3641.64	3630.65
250,000	5124.93	4717.24	4592.89	4552.05	4538.31
300,000	6149.92	5660.69	5511.47	5462.45	5445.97

LOAN PROGRESS TABLES
(Remaining Balance per $1,000 Original Loan)

Loan progress tables allow you to determine how much is still owed on a mortgage loan during the loan term. To use the tables you must know the following:

1. *The annual interest rate on the loan.* The rate is shown at the top of each table, and each table is for a different rate. Rates range from 5% to 21.75% by .25% intervals.

2. *The original amount borrowed.* The amounts in the table are per $1,000 of original loan. If the original principal was $30,000 then multiply the amount in the table by 30.

3. *The maturity of the loan.* The table shows amounts for 10, 15, 20, 25 and 30 year maturities.

4. *The age of the loan.* This is the number of years since the loan was originated and is shown in the left-most column.

The amounts shown in the table are the remaining balance of the loan at the end of the period shown.

Example: Suppose you obtained a mortgage loan 3½ years ago for $48,500. The interest rate is 7% and the maturity is 20 years. How much do you still owe on the loan?

Find the 7% table. Look at the row for "3.5" age of loan. At the intersection of this row with the "20" column is the amount of 908.94. Multiply this amount by the number of thousands originally borrowed (48.5) to get $44,083.59, the existing balance of the loan.

Example: Suppose you want to know how much interest you paid last year on your mortgage loan so you can deduct the amount from your taxable income. The amount of interest is the difference between your total payments over the year and the amount the loan amortized principal. You can find this latter amount with aid of the table.

Suppose the loan had been originated 5 years ago for $50,000. The interest rate is 7% and maturity is 30 years. At the beginning of last year the loan was 4 years old. At that time the amount owed was $954.75 ("4.0" row, "30" column) per thousand, or $47,737.50 total (50 times 954.75). At the end of the year, the 5-year old loan had a balance of $941.32 per thousand, or $47,066.00. The balance amortized by $47,737.50 minus $47,066.00, or $671.50, during the year. The total monthly payments were $332.66 times 12, or $3,991.92. Total interest paid was $3,991.92 minus $671.50, or $3,320.42.

Example: Suppose you take out a loan today at 7% for 25 years. How long will it take to pay off half of the principal?

Look down the column for 25 year loans. At the 17 year row the amount is 518.41. This is slightly more than half the original $1,000 of principal. The 18 year row shows 468.29, which is less than half. Therefore, you will pay off half the principal some time during the 17th year of the loan.

REMAINING BALANCE PER $1000 OF ORIGINAL LOAN
ANNUAL INTEREST RATE: 5%

AGE OF LOAN	LOAN MATURITY (YEARS)				
	10	15	20	25	30
0.5	960.96	977.32	985.25	989.82	992.72
1.0	920.93	954.06	970.13	979.38	985.25
1.5	879.88	930.22	954.62	968.68	977.59
2.0	837.81	905.77	938.73	957.71	969.74
2.5	794.66	880.71	922.43	946.46	961.69
3.0	750.43	855.01	905.72	934.93	953.44
3.5	705.09	828.67	888.59	923.10	944.98
4.0	658.59	801.66	871.02	910.98	936.30
4.5	610.92	773.97	853.01	898.55	927.41
5.0	562.05	745.57	834.55	885.80	918.29
5.5	511.94	716.46	815.62	872.74	908.94
6.0	460.57	686.62	796.21	859.34	899.35
6.5	407.90	656.02	776.31	845.61	889.53
7.0	353.90	624.65	755.91	831.53	879.45
7.5	298.53	592.48	735.00	817.09	869.12
8.0	241.77	559.50	713.55	802.29	858.53
8.5	183.57	525.69	691.57	787.11	847.67
9.0	123.90	491.03	669.02	771.55	836.54
9.5	62.72	455.49	645.91	755.60	825.13
10.0	0.00	419.05	622.22	739.25	813.42
11.0		343.39	573.02	705.29	789.12
12.0		263.86	521.30	669.59	763.58
13.0		180.25	466.93	632.07	736.73
14.0		92.38	409.79	592.62	708.51
15.0		0.00	349.72	551.16	678.84
16.0			286.57	507.58	647.66
17.0			220.20	461.77	614.88
18.0			150.43	413.61	580.42
19.0			77.09	362.99	544.20
20.0			0.00	309.78	506.13
21.0				253.85	466.10
22.0				195.05	424.04
23.0				133.25	379.81
24.0				68.29	333.33
25.0				0.00	284.47
26.0					233.11
27.0					179.12
28.0					122.36
29.0					62.71
30.0					0.00

REMAINING BALANCE PER $1000 OF ORIGINAL LOAN
ANNUAL INTEREST RATE: 5.25%

AGE OF LOAN	LOAN MATURITY (YEARS)				
	10	15	20	25	30
0.5	961.46	977.78	985.66	990.19	993.04
1.0	921.89	954.96	970.95	980.12	985.90
1.5	881.27	931.54	955.84	969.78	978.57
2.0	839.57	907.50	940.33	959.16	971.04
2.5	796.77	882.82	924.41	948.27	963.31
3.0	752.84	857.49	908.07	937.08	955.38
3.5	707.73	831.48	891.29	925.60	947.24
4.0	661.43	804.78	874.07	913.82	938.88
4.5	613.90	777.38	856.39	901.72	930.30
5.0	565.11	749.24	838.24	889.30	921.49
5.5	515.02	720.36	819.61	876.55	912.45
6.0	463.61	690.72	800.49	863.46	903.17
6.5	410.83	660.29	780.86	850.02	893.64
7.0	356.65	629.05	760.70	836.23	883.86
7.5	301.03	596.98	740.02	822.07	873.82
8.0	243.94	564.06	718.78	807.54	863.52
8.5	185.33	530.26	696.98	792.62	852.94
9.0	125.16	495.57	674.60	777.31	842.08
9.5	63.40	459.96	651.63	761.58	830.93
10.0	0.00	423.40	628.05	745.44	819.48
11.0		347.36	578.99	711.87	795.67
12.0		267.22	527.29	676.49	770.58
13.0		182.77	472.82	639.21	744.14
14.0		93.78	415.41	599.92	716.28
15.0		0.00	354.92	558.52	686.92
16.0			291.17	514.89	655.98
17.0			223.99	468.92	623.38
18.0			153.20	420.47	589.03
19.0			78.61	369.42	552.82
20.0			0.00	315.63	514.67
21.0				258.93	474.47
22.0				199.20	432.11
23.0				136.24	387.46
24.0				69.91	340.42
25.0				0.00	290.85
26.0					238.61
27.0					183.56
28.0					125.55
29.0					64.42
30.0					0.00

REMAINING BALANCE PER $1000 OF ORIGINAL LOAN
ANNUAL INTEREST RATE: 5.5%

AGE OF LOAN	LOAN MATURITY (YEARS)				
	10	15	20	25	30
0.5	961.95	978.23	986.07	990.55	993.36
1.0	922.84	955.85	971.75	980.83	986.53
1.5	882.65	932.85	957.03	970.84	979.51
2.0	841.33	909.21	941.90	960.58	972.30
2.5	798.87	884.91	926.35	950.03	964.88
3.0	755.23	859.93	910.37	939.19	957.26
3.5	710.37	834.26	893.95	928.04	949.43
4.0	664.26	807.88	877.07	916.59	941.38
4.5	616.87	780.76	859.72	904.82	933.11
5.0	568.17	752.89	841.88	892.72	924.61
5.5	518.10	724.24	823.55	880.28	915.87
6.0	466.65	694.80	804.71	867.49	906.88
6.5	413.76	664.54	785.35	854.36	897.65
7.0	359.41	633.43	765.44	840.85	888.16
7.5	303.54	601.46	744.99	826.97	878.40
8.0	246.12	568.60	723.96	812.71	868.38
8.5	187.10	534.83	702.35	798.04	858.07
9.0	126.43	500.12	680.14	782.97	847.48
9.5	64.08	464.44	657.31	767.48	836.60
10.0	0.00	427.77	633.84	751.56	825.41
11.0		351.34	584.94	718.38	802.09
12.0		270.59	533.27	683.32	777.46
13.0		185.30	478.70	646.29	751.43
14.0		95.19	421.04	607.17	723.94
15.0		0.00	360.13	565.84	694.90
16.0			295.78	522.18	664.22
17.0			227.81	476.06	631.80
18.0			156.00	427.34	597.56
19.0			80.14	375.87	561.39
20.0			0.00	321.49	523.18
21.0				264.05	482.81
22.0				203.37	440.17
23.0				139.26	395.12
24.0				71.54	347.53
25.0				0.00	297.25
26.0					244.14
27.0					188.04
28.0					128.76
29.0					66.15
30.0					0.00

REMAINING BALANCE PER $1000 OF ORIGINAL LOAN
ANNUAL INTEREST RATE: 5.75%

AGE OF LOAN	LOAN MATURITY (YEARS)				
	10	15	20	25	30
0.5	962.44	978.67	986.46	990.90	993.66
1.0	923.79	956.72	972.53	981.53	987.14
1.5	884.01	934.13	958.20	971.88	980.42
2.0	843.08	910.89	943.44	961.96	973.51
2.5	800.95	886.97	928.26	951.75	966.40
3.0	757.60	862.35	912.64	941.24	959.08
3.5	712.99	837.01	896.56	930.42	951.55
4.0	667.08	810.94	880.02	919.29	943.80
4.5	619.84	784.11	862.99	907.84	935.83
5.0	571.21	756.50	845.46	896.06	927.62
5.5	521.18	728.09	827.43	883.93	919.17
6.0	469.69	698.85	808.87	871.44	910.48
6.5	416.70	668.76	789.78	858.60	901.54
7.0	362.17	637.79	770.12	845.38	892.33
7.5	306.05	605.92	749.90	831.77	882.86
8.0	248.30	573.13	729.09	817.77	873.11
8.5	188.87	539.38	707.67	803.37	863.08
9.0	127.71	504.65	685.62	788.54	852.76
9.5	64.77	468.91	662.94	773.28	842.13
10.0	0.00	432.13	639.60	757.58	831.20
11.0		355.32	590.85	724.80	808.37
12.0		273.98	539.23	690.07	784.19
13.0		187.84	484.56	653.30	758.58
14.0		96.61	426.66	614.36	731.47
15.0		0.00	365.35	573.11	702.75
16.0			300.41	529.44	672.34
17.0			231.64	483.18	640.13
18.0			158.81	434.19	606.02
19.0			81.68	382.31	569.89
20.0			0.00	327.37	531.63
21.0				269.19	491.12
22.0				207.56	448.21
23.0				142.30	402.77
24.0				73.19	354.64
25.0				0.00	303.68
26.0					249.70
27.0					192.54
28.0					132.00
29.0					67.89
30.0					0.00

REMAINING BALANCE PER $1000 OF ORIGINAL LOAN
ANNUAL INTEREST RATE: 6%

AGE OF LOAN	LOAN MATURITY (YEARS)				
	10	15	20	25	30
0.5	962.93	979.11	986.85	991.23	993.95
1.0	924.73	957.58	973.30	982.20	987.72
1.5	885.37	935.40	959.34	972.89	981.30
2.0	844.81	912.55	944.96	963.30	974.68
2.5	803.03	889.00	930.14	953.42	967.87
3.0	759.97	864.74	914.86	943.24	960.84
3.5	715.60	839.74	899.13	932.75	953.60
4.0	669.89	813.98	882.92	921.94	946.15
4.5	622.79	787.44	866.21	910.80	938.46
5.0	574.26	760.09	849.00	899.32	930.54
5.5	524.25	731.91	831.26	887.50	922.39
6.0	472.73	702.88	812.98	875.31	913.98
6.5	419.64	672.96	794.15	862.76	905.32
7.0	364.94	642.13	774.75	849.82	896.39
7.5	308.57	610.37	754.76	836.49	887.20
8.0	250.49	577.65	734.16	822.76	877.72
8.5	190.65	543.92	712.94	808.61	867.96
9.0	128.99	509.18	691.07	794.02	857.90
9.5	65.46	473.38	668.53	779.00	847.54
10.0	0.00	436.49	645.31	763.52	836.86
11.0		359.32	596.74	731.13	814.51
12.0		277.38	545.17	696.75	790.79
13.0		190.40	490.42	660.25	765.61
14.0		98.05	432.29	621.49	738.87
15.0		0.00	370.58	580.34	710.49
16.0			305.06	536.66	680.35
17.0			235.50	490.28	648.36
18.0			161.65	441.04	614.39
19.0			83.24	388.77	578.32
20.0			0.00	333.27	540.04
21.0				274.35	499.39
22.0				211.79	456.23
23.0				145.37	410.41
24.0				74.86	361.77
25.0				0.00	310.12
26.0					255.29
27.0					197.08
28.0					135.28
29.0					69.66
30.0					0.00

REMAINING BALANCE PER $1000 OF ORIGINAL LOAN
ANNUAL INTEREST RATE: 6.25%

AGE OF LOAN	LOAN MATURITY (YEARS)				
	10	15	20	25	30
0.5	963.41	979.54	987.23	991.56	994.23
1.0	925.66	958.43	974.05	982.85	988.28
1.5	886.71	936.66	960.46	973.87	982.14
2.0	846.54	914.19	946.44	964.61	975.81
2.5	805.08	891.01	931.97	955.05	969.28
3.0	762.32	867.10	917.05	945.18	962.54
3.5	718.21	842.44	901.65	935.01	955.58
4.0	672.69	816.99	885.77	924.51	948.41
4.5	625.74	790.73	869.38	913.68	941.01
5.0	577.30	763.65	852.47	902.51	933.37
5.5	527.32	735.70	835.03	890.98	925.50
6.0	475.77	706.88	817.04	879.09	917.37
6.5	422.58	677.14	798.47	866.83	908.99
7.0	367.71	646.45	779.32	854.17	900.34
7.5	311.10	614.80	759.56	841.11	891.41
8.0	252.69	582.15	739.18	827.64	882.21
8.5	192.44	548.46	718.15	813.75	872.71
9.0	130.28	513.70	696.46	799.41	862.91
9.5	66.16	477.84	674.08	784.62	852.81
10.0	0.00	440.85	650.99	769.36	842.38
11.0		363.32	602.59	737.38	820.52
12.0		280.80	551.08	703.35	797.26
13.0		192.97	496.26	667.12	772.50
14.0		99.49	437.92	628.56	746.15
15.0		0.00	375.81	587.52	718.10
16.0			309.72	543.85	688.25
17.0			239.37	497.36	656.48
18.0			164.50	447.88	622.67
19.0			84.81	395.22	586.68
20.0			0.00	339.18	548.38
21.0				279.52	507.61
22.0				216.04	464.22
23.0				148.46	418.04
24.0				76.54	368.89
25.0				0.00	316.58
26.0					260.90
27.0					201.64
28.0					138.57
29.0					71.44
30.0					0.00

599

REMAINING BALANCE PER $1000 OF ORIGINAL LOAN
ANNUAL INTEREST RATE: 6.5%

AGE OF LOAN	LOAN MATURITY (YEARS)				
	10	15	20	25	30
0.5	963.89	979.96	987.60	991.88	994.50
1.0	926.58	959.27	974.79	983.49	988.82
1.5	888.05	937.89	961.56	974.82	982.96
2.0	848.24	915.81	947.89	965.87	976.90
2.5	807.13	893.00	933.77	956.63	970.64
3.0	764.66	869.44	919.19	947.08	964.17
3.5	720.79	845.10	904.12	937.21	957.49
4.0	675.48	819.96	888.56	927.02	950.60
4.5	628.68	793.99	872.49	916.49	943.47
5.0	580.33	767.17	855.89	905.62	936.11
5.5	530.39	739.46	838.74	894.39	928.51
6.0	478.80	710.85	821.03	882.79	920.65
6.5	425.52	681.28	802.73	870.81	912.54
7.0	370.48	650.75	783.83	858.43	904.16
7.5	313.62	619.21	764.31	845.64	895.51
8.0	254.90	586.63	744.14	832.44	886.57
8.5	194.24	552.97	723.31	818.79	877.33
9.0	131.58	518.21	701.80	804.70	867.79
9.5	66.86	482.30	679.57	790.15	857.94
10.0	0.00	445.21	656.61	775.11	847.76
11.0		367.32	608.41	743.54	826.39
12.0		284.22	556.97	709.85	803.58
13.0		195.55	502.09	673.91	779.25
14.0		100.94	443.53	635.56	753.29
15.0		0.00	381.05	594.64	725.59
16.0			314.39	550.98	696.03
17.0			243.26	504.40	664.50
18.0			167.37	454.70	630.85
19.0			86.40	401.67	594.95
20.0			0.00	345.09	556.65
21.0				284.72	515.78
22.0				220.30	472.18
23.0				151.57	425.65
24.0				78.24	376.01
25.0				0.00	323.04
26.0					266.53
27.0					206.23
28.0					141.89
29.0					73.24
30.0					0.00

REMAINING BALANCE PER $1000 OF ORIGINAL LOAN
ANNUAL INTEREST RATE: 6.75%

AGE OF LOAN	LOAN MATURITY (YEARS)				
	10	15	20	25	30
0.5	964.36	980.38	987.96	992.19	994.76
1.0	927.50	960.09	975.51	984.10	989.34
1.5	889.37	939.11	962.63	975.75	983.74
2.0	849.94	917.40	949.31	967.10	977.94
2.5	809.16	894.96	935.54	958.16	971.95
3.0	766.99	871.74	921.29	948.92	965.75
3.5	723.37	847.74	906.55	939.35	959.34
4.0	678.26	822.90	891.32	929.47	952.71
4.5	631.61	797.22	875.56	919.24	945.85
5.0	583.35	770.67	859.26	908.66	938.76
5.5	533.45	743.20	842.40	897.72	931.42
6.0	481.84	714.79	824.96	886.40	923.84
6.5	428.46	685.41	806.93	874.70	915.99
7.0	373.25	655.02	788.28	862.60	907.87
7.5	316.16	623.59	769.00	850.08	899.48
8.0	257.11	591.09	749.05	837.14	890.80
8.5	196.04	557.48	728.42	823.75	881.83
9.0	132.88	522.71	707.09	809.90	872.54
9.5	67.56	486.76	685.02	795.58	862.94
10.0	0.00	449.57	662.20	780.77	853.01
11.0		371.34	614.19	749.61	832.12
12.0		287.65	562.83	716.28	809.77
13.0		198.15	507.90	680.63	785.87
14.0		102.41	449.14	642.50	760.30
15.0		0.00	386.30	601.71	732.95
16.0			319.07	558.09	703.70
17.0			247.17	511.42	672.41
18.0			170.26	461.51	638.95
19.0			87.99	408.12	603.15
20.0			0.00	351.01	564.86
21.0				289.93	523.91
22.0				224.59	480.10
23.0				154.71	433.24
24.0				79.96	383.12
25.0				0.00	329.51
26.0					272.17
27.0					210.84
28.0					145.23
29.0					75.06
30.0					0.00

REMAINING BALANCE PER $1000 OF ORIGINAL LOAN
ANNUAL INTEREST RATE: 7%

AGE OF LOAN	LOAN MATURITY (YEARS)				
	10	15	20	25	30
0.5	964.83	980.79	988.31	992.48	995.01
1.0	928.40	960.90	976.21	984.70	989.84
1.5	890.68	940.31	963.68	976.64	984.49
2.0	851.63	918.98	950.70	968.30	978.95
2.5	811.18	896.89	937.26	959.66	973.21
3.0	769.30	874.02	923.35	950.71	967.27
3.5	725.94	850.34	908.94	941.44	961.12
4.0	681.03	825.82	894.02	931.85	954.75
4.5	634.53	800.42	878.57	921.91	948.15
5.0	586.37	774.13	862.57	911.62	941.32
5.5	536.51	746.90	846.00	900.97	934.24
6.0	484.87	718.70	828.84	889.93	926.92
6.5	431.40	689.50	811.08	878.51	919.33
7.0	376.03	659.27	792.68	866.68	911.47
7.5	318.70	627.96	773.63	854.43	903.34
8.0	259.33	595.54	753.90	841.74	894.92
8.5	197.85	561.97	733.48	828.61	886.19
9.0	134.19	527.20	712.32	815.01	877.16
9.5	68.26	491.20	690.42	800.92	867.81
10.0	0.00	453.93	667.74	786.33	858.12
11.0		375.35	619.93	755.59	837.71
12.0		291.10	568.66	722.62	815.82
13.0		200.75	513.69	687.27	792.35
14.0		103.88	454.75	649.37	767.18
15.0		0.00	391.54	608.72	740.19
16.0			323.77	565.14	711.25
17.0			251.09	518.41	680.22
18.0			173.16	468.29	646.94
19.0			89.60	414.56	611.26
20.0			0.00	356.94	573.00
21.0				295.15	531.98
22.0				228.90	487.98
23.0				157.86	440.81
24.0				81.68	390.23
25.0				0.00	335.99
26.0					277.83
27.0					215.47
28.0					148.60
29.0					76.89
30.0					0.00

REMAINING BALANCE PER $1000 OF ORIGINAL LOAN
ANNUAL INTEREST RATE: 7.25%

AGE OF LOAN	LOAN MATURITY (YEARS)				
	10	15	20	25	30
0.5	965.29	981.20	988.66	992.77	995.25
1.0	929.30	961.70	976.90	985.28	990.32
1.5	891.99	941.49	964.70	977.51	985.21
2.0	853.30	920.53	952.06	969.46	979.92
2.5	813.19	898.80	938.96	961.11	974.43
3.0	771.60	876.27	925.37	952.45	968.73
3.5	728.49	852.92	911.28	943.47	962.83
4.0	683.78	828.70	896.67	934.16	956.71
4.5	637.44	803.59	881.52	924.51	950.37
5.0	589.38	777.56	865.82	914.51	943.79
5.5	539.56	750.57	849.54	904.14	936.97
6.0	487.90	722.59	832.66	893.38	929.90
6.5	434.34	693.57	815.16	882.23	922.56
7.0	378.82	663.49	797.01	870.67	914.96
7.5	321.24	632.30	778.20	858.68	907.08
8.0	261.55	599.97	758.70	846.26	898.91
8.5	199.67	566.44	738.47	833.37	890.44
9.0	135.50	531.68	717.50	820.01	881.65
9.5	68.97	495.64	695.77	806.16	872.55
10.0	0.00	458.28	673.23	791.80	863.10
11.0		379.37	625.63	761.48	843.16
12.0		294.55	574.46	728.88	821.73
13.0		203.37	519.46	693.83	798.69
14.0		105.36	460.34	656.16	773.92
15.0		0.00	396.79	615.67	747.29
16.0			328.47	572.14	718.67
17.0			255.03	525.35	687.90
18.0			176.08	475.06	654.83
19.0			91.22	420.99	619.28
20.0			0.00	362.87	581.06
21.0				300.39	539.98
22.0				233.23	495.82
23.0				161.03	448.35
24.0				83.42	397.32
25.0				0.00	342.47
26.0					283.50
27.0					220.12
28.0					151.98
29.0					78.73
30.0					0.00

REMAINING BALANCE PER $1000 OF ORIGINAL LOAN
ANNUAL INTEREST RATE: 7.5 %

AGE OF LOAN	LOAN MATURITY (YEARS)				
	10	15	20	25	30
0.5	965.75	981.59	988.99	993.05	995.48
1.0	930.19	962.49	977.57	985.84	990.78
1.5	893.28	942.65	965.71	978.35	985.91
2.0	854.96	922.06	953.40	970.58	980.85
2.5	815.19	900.69	940.61	962.52	975.60
3.0	773.89	878.50	927.35	954.14	970.14
3.5	731.03	855.46	913.57	945.45	964.48
4.0	686.53	831.55	899.27	936.42	958.61
4.5	640.34	806.73	884.43	927.05	952.51
5.0	592.39	780.96	869.02	917.33	946.17
5.5	542.61	754.21	853.03	907.23	939.60
6.0	490.93	726.44	836.42	896.75	932.78
6.5	437.29	697.62	819.18	885.87	925.69
7.0	381.60	667.69	801.29	874.57	918.34
7.5	323.79	636.63	782.72	862.85	910.71
8.0	263.78	604.38	763.43	850.68	902.78
8.5	201.49	570.90	743.42	838.04	894.56
9.0	136.82	536.15	722.64	824.93	886.02
9.5	69.69	500.08	701.06	811.31	877.15
10.0	0.00	462.63	678.67	797.18	867.95
11.0		383.40	631.29	767.27	848.48
12.0		298.02	580.24	735.04	827.50
13.0		206.01	525.22	700.32	804.89
14.0		106.85	465.93	662.89	780.52
15.0		0.00	402.03	622.56	754.27
16.0			333.18	579.10	725.97
17.0			258.98	532.27	695.48
18.0			179.02	481.80	662.62
19.0			92.86	427.41	627.21
20.0			0.00	368.80	589.05
21.0				305.64	547.93
22.0				237.57	503.62
23.0				164.22	455.86
24.0				85.18	404.40
25.0				0.00	348.95
26.0					289.18
27.0					224.78
28.0					155.38
29.0					80.59
30.0					0.00

REMAINING BALANCE PER $1000 OF ORIGINAL LOAN
ANNUAL INTEREST RATE: 7.75%

AGE OF LOAN	LOAN MATURITY (YEARS)				
	10	15	20	25	30
0.5	966.20	981.98	989.32	993.32	995.70
1.0	931.07	963.26	978.22	986.38	991.22
1.5	894.56	943.80	966.69	979.17	986.57
2.0	856.61	923.57	954.70	971.67	981.74
2.5	817.17	902.54	942.24	963.88	976.72
3.0	776.17	880.69	929.28	955.78	971.50
3.5	733.55	857.98	915.82	947.36	966.07
4.0	689.26	834.37	901.83	938.61	960.43
4.5	643.23	809.83	887.28	929.52	954.57
5.0	595.38	784.33	872.17	920.07	948.48
5.5	545.65	757.82	856.45	910.24	942.14
6.0	493.96	730.26	840.12	900.03	935.56
6.5	440.23	701.63	823.15	889.42	928.72
7.0	384.39	671.86	805.50	878.39	921.61
7.5	326.35	640.92	787.17	866.92	914.22
8.0	266.02	608.77	768.11	855.00	906.54
8.5	203.32	575.35	748.30	842.62	898.55
9.0	138.14	540.61	727.71	829.74	890.25
9.5	70.41	504.50	706.31	816.36	881.63
10.0	0.00	466.97	684.06	802.45	872.66
11.0		387.42	636.91	772.97	853.66
12.0		301.49	585.97	741.12	833.13
13.0		208.65	530.95	706.71	810.95
14.0		108.35	471.50	669.54	786.99
15.0		0.00	407.28	629.38	761.11
16.0			337.90	586.00	733.14
17.0			262.95	539.14	702.93
18.0			181.97	488.51	670.30
19.0			94.50	433.81	635.04
20.0			0.00	374.72	596.96
21.0				310.89	555.81
22.0				241.93	511.36
23.0				167.43	463.34
24.0				86.95	411.46
25.0				0.00	355.42
26.0					294.87
27.0					229.46
28.0					158.80
29.0					82.47
30.0					0.00

REMAINING BALANCE PER $1000 OF ORIGINAL LOAN
ANNUAL INTEREST RATE: 8%

AGE OF LOAN	LOAN MATURITY (YEARS)				
	10	15	20	25	30
0.5	966.65	982.37	989.64	993.58	995.91
1.0	931.95	964.02	978.86	986.91	991.65
1.5	895.83	944.93	967.65	979.96	987.21
2.0	858.25	925.06	955.97	972.73	982.60
2.5	819.13	904.38	943.82	965.21	977.80
3.0	778.43	882.86	931.18	957.38	972.80
3.5	736.07	860.46	918.02	949.23	967.60
4.0	691.99	837.16	904.33	940.75	962.19
4.5	646.11	812.90	890.08	931.92	956.56
5.0	598.37	787.66	875.26	922.74	950.70
5.5	548.69	761.40	859.82	913.18	944.60
6.0	496.98	734.06	843.77	903.24	938.25
6.5	443.17	705.61	827.05	892.89	931.65
7.0	387.18	676.01	809.66	882.11	924.77
7.5	328.91	645.20	791.56	870.90	917.62
8.0	268.26	613.14	772.73	859.24	910.18
8.5	205.15	579.77	753.13	847.10	902.43
9.0	139.48	545.05	732.73	834.46	894.37
9.5	71.13	508.92	711.50	821.32	885.98
10.0	0.00	471.31	689.41	807.63	877.25
11.0		391.45	642.49	778.58	858.71
12.0		304.97	591.68	747.11	838.62
13.0		211.30	536.65	713.03	816.88
14.0		109.86	477.06	676.12	793.32
15.0		0.00	412.52	636.14	767.82
16.0			342.62	592.85	740.19
17.0			266.92	545.97	710.27
18.0			184.94	495.19	677.87
19.0			96.16	440.20	642.78
20.0			0.00	380.65	604.78
21.0				316.15	563.62
22.0				246.30	519.05
23.0				170.65	470.78
24.0				88.73	418.50
25.0				0.00	361.88
26.0					300.56
27.0					234.16
28.0					162.24
29.0					84.35
30.0					0.00

REMAINING BALANCE PER $1000 OF ORIGINAL LOAN
ANNUAL INTEREST RATE: 8.25%

AGE OF LOAN	LOAN MATURITY (YEARS)				
	10	15	20	25	30
0.5	967.10	982.75	989.95	993.84	996.11
1.0	932.81	964.77	979.49	987.42	992.05
1.5	897.09	946.04	968.58	980.73	987.83
2.0	859.87	926.52	957.22	973.76	983.42
2.5	821.09	906.19	945.38	966.49	978.83
3.0	780.68	885.00	933.04	958.92	974.05
3.5	738.57	862.92	920.19	951.04	969.07
4.0	694.70	839.91	906.79	942.82	963.88
4.5	648.98	815.94	892.83	934.26	958.47
5.0	601.35	790.97	878.29	925.34	952.84
5.5	551.72	764.94	863.14	916.04	946.97
6.0	500.00	737.82	847.35	906.36	940.85
6.5	446.12	709.57	830.90	896.27	934.48
7.0	389.97	680.13	813.76	885.75	927.83
7.5	331.47	649.45	795.90	874.80	920.91
8.0	270.51	617.49	777.29	863.38	913.70
8.5	206.99	584.18	757.89	851.48	906.19
9.0	140.81	549.48	737.69	839.09	898.36
9.5	71.85	513.32	716.64	826.17	890.20
10.0	0.00	475.65	694.70	812.72	881.70
11.0		395.48	648.02	784.09	863.62
12.0		308.45	597.35	753.00	843.98
13.0		213.96	542.34	719.25	822.66
14.0		111.38	482.60	682.61	799.52
15.0		0.00	417.76	642.83	774.39
16.0			347.35	599.64	747.11
17.0			270.91	552.75	717.49
18.0			187.92	501.84	685.33
19.0			97.82	446.57	650.42
20.0			0.00	386.57	612.52
21.0				321.42	571.36
22.0				250.69	526.68
23.0				173.89	478.18
24.0				90.52	425.51
25.0				0.00	368.34
26.0					306.26
27.0					238.86
28.0					165.69
29.0					86.25
30.0					0.00

607

REMAINING BALANCE PER $1000 OF ORIGINAL LOAN
ANNUAL INTEREST RATE: 8.5%

AGE OF LOAN	LOAN MATURITY (YEARS)				
	10	15	20	25	30
0.5	967.54	983.12	990.26	994.08	996.30
1.0	933.67	965.51	980.10	987.91	992.44
1.5	898.34	947.13	969.50	981.47	988.41
2.0	861.48	927.97	958.44	974.75	984.21
2.5	823.03	907.97	946.90	967.74	979.83
3.0	782.91	887.11	934.86	960.43	975.26
3.5	741.06	865.34	922.30	952.80	970.49
4.0	697.40	842.64	909.20	944.84	965.51
4.5	651.84	818.95	895.53	936.53	960.32
5.0	604.32	794.24	881.27	927.87	954.90
5.5	554.74	768.45	866.39	918.83	949.25
6.0	503.02	741.56	850.87	909.40	943.36
6.5	449.06	713.50	834.68	899.57	937.21
7.0	392.76	684.22	817.79	889.30	930.79
7.5	334.03	653.68	800.17	878.60	924.10
8.0	272.76	621.82	781.78	867.43	917.11
8.5	208.84	588.58	762.60	855.78	909.83
9.0	142.15	553.90	742.59	843.62	902.23
9.5	72.58	517.72	721.72	830.94	894.30
10.0	0.00	479.97	699.94	817.70	886.02
11.0		399.52	653.51	789.50	868.39
12.0		311.95	602.98	758.80	849.20
13.0		216.64	547.99	725.39	828.31
14.0		112.90	488.13	689.03	805.57
15.0		0.00	422.99	649.45	780.83
16.0			352.08	606.37	753.90
17.0			274.91	559.49	724.58
18.0			190.92	508.46	692.68
19.0			99.50	452.92	657.95
20.0			0.00	392.48	620.16
21.0				326.69	579.03
22.0				255.08	534.26
23.0				177.15	485.53
24.0				92.32	432.50
25.0				0.00	374.78
26.0					311.95
27.0					243.58
28.0					169.16
29.0					88.16
30.0					0.00

REMAINING BALANCE PER $1000 OF ORIGINAL LOAN
ANNUAL INTEREST RATE: 8.75%

AGE OF LOAN	LOAN MATURITY (YEARS)				
	10	15	20	25	30
0.5	967.98	983.48	990.56	994.32	996.48
1.0	934.52	966.23	980.69	988.38	992.81
1.5	899.58	948.21	970.39	982.19	988.98
2.0	863.08	929.39	959.63	975.71	984.97
2.5	824.96	909.73	948.38	968.95	980.78
3.0	785.13	889.19	936.64	961.88	976.41
3.5	743.53	867.74	924.37	954.50	971.85
4.0	700.08	845.33	911.56	946.79	967.08
4.5	654.69	821.92	898.18	938.74	962.09
5.0	607.28	797.47	884.20	930.33	956.89
5.5	557.76	771.94	869.60	921.55	951.45
6.0	506.03	745.26	854.34	912.37	945.77
6.5	452.00	717.39	838.41	902.78	939.84
7.0	395.56	688.29	821.77	892.77	933.65
7.5	336.60	657.88	804.38	882.31	927.17
8.0	275.02	626.12	786.22	871.39	920.41
8.5	210.69	592.95	767.25	859.97	913.35
9.0	143.50	558.30	747.44	848.05	905.98
9.5	73.31	522.10	726.74	835.60	898.27
10.0	0.00	484.29	705.13	822.60	890.22
11.0		403.55	658.96	794.82	873.04
12.0		315.45	608.58	764.51	854.28
13.0		219.32	553.62	731.45	833.82
14.0		114.44	493.65	695.37	811.49
15.0		0.00	428.21	656.00	787.13
16.0			356.82	613.05	760.56
17.0			278.92	566.18	731.56
18.0			193.92	515.05	699.91
19.0			101.19	459.25	665.39
20.0			0.00	398.38	627.72
21.0				331.96	586.62
22.0				259.49	541.77
23.0				180.41	492.84
24.0				94.14	439.46
25.0				0.00	381.20
26.0					317.65
27.0					248.30
28.0					172.64
29.0					90.08
30.0					0.00

REMAINING BALANCE PER $1000 OF ORIGINAL LOAN
ANNUAL INTEREST RATE: 9%

AGE OF LOAN	LOAN MATURITY (YEARS)				
	10	15	20	25	30
0.5	968.41	983.84	990.85	994.55	996.66
1.0	935.37	966.95	981.27	988.84	993.17
1.5	900.81	949.28	971.26	982.88	989.52
2.0	864.67	930.79	960.79	976.64	985.70
2.5	826.87	911.46	949.84	970.12	981.70
3.0	787.34	891.25	938.38	963.29	977.52
3.5	746.00	870.11	926.41	956.16	973.15
4.0	702.76	847.99	913.88	948.69	968.58
4.5	657.54	824.87	900.77	940.89	963.80
5.0	610.24	800.68	887.07	932.73	958.80
5.5	560.78	775.38	872.74	924.19	953.57
6.0	509.04	748.93	857.75	915.26	948.11
6.5	454.94	721.26	842.07	905.92	942.39
7.0	398.36	692.32	825.68	896.15	936.41
7.5	339.18	662.06	808.53	885.94	930.15
8.0	277.28	630.41	790.60	875.25	923.61
8.5	212.55	597.31	771.85	864.08	916.77
9.0	144.85	562.68	752.23	852.40	909.61
9.5	74.05	526.48	731.72	840.18	902.13
10.0	0.00	488.61	710.26	827.39	894.30
11.0		407.58	664.35	800.05	877.55
12.0		318.96	614.14	770.13	859.23
13.0		222.02	559.22	737.41	839.20
14.0		115.98	499.14	701.62	817.28
15.0		0.00	433.43	662.48	793.31
16.0			361.55	619.66	767.09
17.0			282.94	572.82	738.40
18.0			196.94	521.60	707.03
19.0			102.88	465.56	672.72
20.0			0.00	404.27	635.19
21.0				337.23	594.13
22.0				263.90	549.23
23.0				183.69	500.11
24.0				95.96	446.38
25.0				0.00	387.62
26.0					323.34
27.0					253.03
28.0					176.13
29.0					92.01
30.0					0.00

REMAINING BALANCE PER $1000 OF ORIGINAL LOAN
ANNUAL INTEREST RATE: 9.25%

AGE OF LOAN	LOAN MATURITY (YEARS)				
	10	15	20	25	30
0.5	968.84	984.20	991.13	994.77	996.83
1.0	936.20	967.65	981.84	989.29	993.51
1.5	902.03	950.32	972.11	983.55	990.03
2.0	866.24	932.17	961.92	977.54	986.39
2.5	828.77	913.17	951.26	971.25	982.58
3.0	789.53	893.27	940.09	964.66	978.58
3.5	748.44	872.44	928.39	957.76	974.40
4.0	705.42	850.62	916.14	950.54	970.03
4.5	660.36	827.77	903.32	942.97	965.44
5.0	613.19	803.85	889.89	935.05	960.64
5.5	563.78	778.80	875.82	926.75	955.61
6.0	512.05	752.57	861.10	918.07	950.35
6.5	457.88	725.10	845.68	908.97	944.84
7.0	401.15	696.33	829.53	899.45	939.07
7.5	341.75	666.21	812.62	889.47	933.02
8.0	279.55	634.67	794.91	879.03	926.69
8.5	214.42	601.64	776.37	868.09	920.06
9.0	146.21	567.05	756.96	856.64	913.12
9.5	74.79	530.83	736.63	844.65	905.86
10.0	0.00	492.91	715.34	832.09	898.25
11.0		411.61	669.70	805.17	881.93
12.0		322.47	619.66	775.65	864.05
13.0		224.72	564.78	743.28	844.43
14.0		117.53	504.61	707.79	822.92
15.0		0.00	438.63	668.88	799.34
16.0			366.29	626.20	773.48
17.0			286.96	579.41	745.12
18.0			199.97	528.10	714.03
19.0			104.59	471.84	679.93
20.0			0.00	410.15	642.55
21.0				342.50	601.55
22.0				268.32	556.60
23.0				186.98	507.31
24.0				97.80	453.27
25.0				0.00	394.00
26.0					329.02
27.0					257.76
28.0					179.62
29.0					93.95
30.0					0.00

611

REMAINING BALANCE PER $1000 OF ORIGINAL LOAN
ANNUAL INTEREST RATE: 9.5%

AGE OF LOAN	LOAN MATURITY (YEARS)				
	10	15	20	25	30
0.5	969.26	984.54	991.40	994.98	996.99
1.0	937.03	968.34	982.39	989.72	993.83
1.5	903.24	951.35	972.94	984.20	990.52
2.0	867.81	933.53	963.03	978.41	987.06
2.5	830.66	914.86	952.65	972.35	983.42
3.0	791.71	895.28	941.76	965.99	979.60
3.5	750.88	874.74	930.34	959.32	975.61
4.0	708.07	853.22	918.37	952.33	971.41
4.5	663.18	830.65	905.81	945.00	967.02
5.0	616.12	806.99	892.65	937.31	962.41
5.5	566.78	782.18	878.86	929.25	957.58
6.0	515.05	756.17	864.39	920.81	952.51
6.5	460.82	728.90	849.22	911.95	947.20
7.0	403.95	700.31	833.32	902.66	941.63
7.5	344.33	670.33	816.65	892.93	935.80
8.0	281.82	638.91	799.17	882.72	929.67
8.5	216.29	605.95	780.84	872.02	923.26
9.0	147.57	571.41	761.63	860.79	916.53
9.5	75.53	535.18	741.48	849.03	909.47
10.0	0.00	497.21	720.36	836.70	902.08
11.0		415.64	675.00	810.20	886.19
12.0		325.99	625.14	781.08	868.73
13.0		227.43	570.32	749.07	849.54
14.0		119.09	510.07	713.88	828.44
15.0		0.00	443.83	675.20	805.24
16.0			371.03	632.69	779.75
17.0			290.99	585.95	751.72
18.0			203.02	534.57	720.91
19.0			106.31	478.09	687.05
20.0			0.00	416.01	649.82
21.0				347.77	608.90
22.0				272.75	563.92
23.0				190.29	514.47
24.0				99.64	460.12
25.0				0.00	400.37
26.0					334.69
27.0					262.50
28.0					183.14
29.0					95.90
30.0					0.00

REMAINING BALANCE PER $1000 OF ORIGINAL LOAN
ANNUAL INTEREST RATE: 9.75%

AGE OF LOAN	LOAN MATURITY (YEARS)				
	10	15	20	25	30
0.5	969.68	984.88	991.67	995.18	997.14
1.0	937.85	969.02	982.93	990.13	994.14
1.5	904.43	952.36	973.75	984.82	991.00
2.0	869.36	934.87	964.12	979.25	987.69
2.5	832.53	916.52	954.00	973.41	984.22
3.0	793.88	897.25	943.38	967.27	980.58
3.5	753.30	877.02	932.24	960.82	976.76
4.0	710.71	855.78	920.54	954.06	972.74
4.5	665.99	833.49	908.26	946.96	968.53
5.0	619.05	810.09	895.37	939.51	964.11
5.5	569.78	785.53	881.83	931.68	959.47
6.0	518.05	759.74	867.62	923.47	954.59
6.5	463.75	732.68	852.71	914.84	949.48
7.0	406.75	704.26	837.05	905.79	944.11
7.5	346.91	674.43	820.62	896.29	938.47
8.0	284.10	643.12	803.36	886.32	932.55
8.5	218.16	610.25	785.25	875.84	926.34
9.0	148.94	575.74	766.24	864.85	919.82
9.5	76.28	539.52	746.28	853.31	912.97
10.0	0.00	501.49	725.33	841.20	905.79
11.0		419.67	680.25	815.14	890.32
12.0		329.51	630.57	786.42	873.28
13.0		230.15	575.82	754.76	854.51
14.0		120.66	515.50	719.89	833.81
15.0		0.00	449.02	681.45	811.01
16.0			375.76	639.10	785.88
17.0			295.03	592.42	758.19
18.0			206.07	540.99	727.68
19.0			108.03	484.31	694.05
20.0			0.00	421.85	656.99
21.0				353.03	616.16
22.0				277.18	571.16
23.0				193.60	521.57
24.0				101.50	466.93
25.0				0.00	406.71
26.0					340.36
27.0					267.23
28.0					186.65
29.0					97.85
30.0					0.00

613

REMAINING BALANCE PER $1000 OF ORIGINAL LOAN
ANNUAL INTEREST RATE: 10%

AGE OF LOAN	LOAN MATURITY (YEARS)				
	10	15	20	25	30
0.5	970.09	985.22	991.93	995.38	997.29
1.0	938.66	969.68	983.45	990.53	994.44
1.5	905.62	953.35	974.54	985.43	991.45
2.0	870.89	936.19	965.17	980.07	988.30
2.5	834.39	918.15	955.33	974.43	984.99
3.0	796.03	899.19	944.98	968.51	981.52
3.5	755.71	879.26	934.10	962.28	977.86
4.0	713.33	858.32	922.67	955.74	974.02
4.5	668.79	836.30	910.65	948.87	969.99
5.0	621.97	813.17	898.02	941.64	965.74
5.5	572.76	788.85	884.75	934.04	961.28
6.0	521.05	763.28	870.80	926.06	956.60
6.5	466.69	736.42	856.13	917.66	951.67
7.0	409.55	708.18	840.72	908.84	946.49
7.5	349.50	678.50	824.52	899.57	941.05
8.0	286.38	647.31	807.50	889.83	935.33
8.5	220.04	614.52	789.60	879.58	929.32
9.0	150.31	580.06	770.79	868.82	923.00
9.5	77.03	543.84	751.02	857.51	916.36
10.0	0.00	505.77	730.24	845.61	909.38
11.0		423.70	685.45	819.98	894.33
12.0		333.03	635.96	791.65	877.71
13.0		232.88	581.30	760.37	859.34
14.0		122.23	520.90	725.81	839.06
15.0		0.00	454.19	687.62	816.64
16.0			380.49	645.44	791.89
17.0			299.07	598.85	764.54
18.0			209.13	547.37	734.32
19.0			109.77	490.50	700.94
20.0			0.00	427.68	664.07
21.0				358.28	623.33
22.0				281.62	578.33
23.0				196.92	528.62
24.0				103.36	473.70
25.0				0.00	413.03
26.0					346.01
27.0					271.97
28.0					190.18
29.0					99.82
30.0					0.00

REMAINING BALANCE PER $1000 OF ORIGINAL LOAN
ANNUAL INTEREST RATE: 10.25%

AGE OF LOAN	LOAN MATURITY (YEARS)				
	10	15	20	25	30
0.5	970.50	985.55	992.19	995.57	997.43
1.0	939.46	970.34	983.96	990.92	994.72
1.5	906.80	954.33	975.31	986.01	991.88
2.0	872.42	937.49	966.20	980.85	988.88
2.5	836.24	919.76	956.62	975.42	985.73
3.0	798.17	901.11	946.54	969.71	982.41
3.5	758.11	881.48	935.92	963.70	978.92
4.0	715.94	860.82	924.75	957.37	975.25
4.5	671.58	839.08	913.00	950.71	971.38
5.0	624.88	816.20	900.63	943.71	967.31
5.5	575.75	792.13	887.61	936.33	963.03
6.0	524.04	766.79	873.92	928.57	958.52
6.5	469.62	740.13	859.50	920.41	953.78
7.0	412.35	712.07	844.33	911.81	948.79
7.5	352.09	682.54	828.37	902.77	943.54
8.0	288.67	651.47	811.57	893.25	938.01
8.5	221.93	618.77	793.89	883.24	932.20
9.0	151.69	584.36	775.28	872.70	926.08
9.5	77.78	548.14	755.70	861.60	919.64
10.0	0.00	510.03	735.10	849.93	912.86
11.0		427.72	690.60	824.72	898.22
12.0		336.56	641.31	796.80	882.01
13.0		235.61	586.73	765.88	864.05
14.0		123.81	526.29	731.64	844.17
15.0		0.00	459.35	693.72	822.15
16.0			385.22	651.72	797.76
17.0			303.12	605.21	770.76
18.0			212.20	553.71	740.85
19.0			111.51	496.66	707.72
20.0			0.00	433.49	671.04
21.0				363.53	630.42
22.0				286.06	585.43
23.0				200.25	535.61
24.0				105.23	480.43
25.0				0.00	419.32
26.0					351.65
27.0					276.71
28.0					193.71
29.0					101.79
30.0					0.00

615

REMAINING BALANCE PER $1000 OF ORIGINAL LOAN
ANNUAL INTEREST RATE: 10.5%

AGE OF LOAN	LOAN MATURITY (YEARS)				
	10	15	20	25	30
0.5	970.91	985.87	992.43	995.76	997.56
1.0	940.26	970.98	984.46	991.29	994.99
1.5	907.96	955.29	976.06	986.58	992.29
2.0	873.93	938.77	967.21	981.61	989.44
2.5	838.07	921.35	957.88	976.38	986.43
3.0	800.29	903.00	948.06	970.87	983.27
3.5	760.49	883.66	937.70	965.07	979.93
4.0	718.54	863.29	926.79	958.95	976.42
4.5	674.35	841.83	915.30	952.50	972.72
5.0	627.78	819.21	903.18	945.71	968.82
5.5	578.72	795.38	890.42	938.56	964.71
6.0	527.02	770.27	876.98	931.02	960.38
6.5	472.55	743.81	862.81	923.07	955.81
7.0	415.15	715.93	847.88	914.70	951.00
7.5	354.68	686.56	832.15	905.88	945.94
8.0	290.96	655.61	815.58	896.59	940.60
8.5	223.82	623.00	798.11	886.80	934.97
9.0	153.08	588.64	779.71	876.48	929.05
9.5	78.54	552.43	760.32	865.61	922.80
10.0	0.00	514.28	739.90	854.15	916.22
11.0		431.74	695.69	829.37	901.99
12.0		340.10	646.62	801.85	886.18
13.0		238.36	592.13	771.30	868.63
14.0		125.40	531.65	737.38	849.15
15.0		0.00	464.49	699.73	827.52
16.0			389.94	657.93	803.51
17.0			307.17	611.51	776.85
18.0			215.28	559.99	747.25
19.0			113.26	502.79	714.39
20.0			0.00	439.28	677.91
21.0				368.77	637.41
22.0				290.49	592.45
23.0				203.59	542.53
24.0				107.11	487.11
25.0				0.00	425.58
26.0					357.27
27.0					281.44
28.0					197.24
29.0					103.77
30.0					0.00

REMAINING BALANCE PER $1000 OF ORIGINAL LOAN
ANNUAL INTEREST RATE: 10.75%

AGE OF LOAN	LOAN MATURITY (YEARS)				
	10	15	20	25	30
0.5	971.31	986.19	992.67	995.93	997.69
1.0	941.04	971.61	984.95	991.65	995.25
1.5	909.12	956.24	976.79	987.12	992.68
2.0	875.43	940.02	968.19	982.35	989.97
2.5	839.89	922.91	959.11	977.31	987.11
3.0	802.40	904.86	949.54	972.00	984.09
3.5	762.85	885.82	939.44	966.39	980.90
4.0	721.13	865.73	928.79	960.48	977.54
4.5	677.11	844.54	917.55	954.24	974.00
5.0	630.67	822.18	905.69	947.66	970.26
5.5	581.68	798.59	893.18	940.72	966.32
6.0	530.00	773.71	879.98	933.39	962.15
6.5	475.48	747.46	866.06	925.67	957.76
7.0	417.95	719.76	851.37	917.52	953.13
7.5	357.27	690.54	835.87	908.92	948.25
8.0	293.25	659.72	819.52	899.84	943.09
8.5	225.71	627.20	802.28	890.27	937.65
9.0	154.47	592.90	784.08	880.17	931.92
9.5	79.30	556.71	764.89	869.52	925.86
10.0	0.00	518.53	744.64	858.28	919.48
11.0		435.75	700.74	833.92	905.64
12.0		343.63	651.88	806.81	890.23
13.0		241.11	597.50	776.63	873.08
14.0		127.00	536.98	743.04	854.00
15.0		0.00	469.62	705.66	832.76
16.0			394.66	664.06	809.12
17.0			311.22	617.76	782.81
18.0			218.37	566.23	753.53
19.0			115.02	508.87	720.95
20.0			0.00	445.04	684.68
21.0				374.00	644.31
22.0				294.94	599.39
23.0				206.94	549.39
24.0				109.00	493.74
25.0				0.00	431.81
26.0					362.88
27.0					286.16
28.0					200.78
29.0					105.76
30.0					0.00

REMAINING BALANCE PER $1000 OF ORIGINAL LOAN
ANNUAL INTEREST RATE: 11%

AGE OF LOAN	LOAN MATURITY (YEARS)				
	10	15	20	25	30
0.5	971.71	986.50	992.91	996.10	997.81
1.0	941.83	972.24	985.42	991.99	995.50
1.5	910.26	957.17	977.50	987.64	993.06
2.0	876.92	941.26	969.15	983.05	990.48
2.5	841.70	924.45	960.32	978.21	987.75
3.0	804.50	906.70	950.99	973.08	984.87
3.5	765.21	887.95	941.14	967.67	981.83
4.0	723.70	868.14	930.74	961.96	978.62
4.5	679.86	847.22	919.75	955.92	975.23
5.0	633.55	825.12	908.14	949.55	971.65
5.5	584.64	801.77	895.88	942.81	967.86
6.0	532.97	777.12	882.93	935.70	963.86
6.5	478.40	751.07	869.25	928.19	959.64
7.0	420.76	723.56	854.80	920.25	955.18
7.5	359.87	694.50	839.53	911.87	950.47
8.0	295.55	663.81	823.41	903.01	945.49
8.5	227.62	631.38	806.38	893.66	940.24
9.0	155.86	597.14	788.39	883.78	934.69
9.5	80.06	560.97	769.39	873.35	928.82
10.0	0.00	522.76	749.32	862.32	922.63
11.0		439.77	705.73	838.38	909.17
12.0		347.17	657.09	811.67	894.16
13.0		243.86	602.83	781.87	877.41
14.0		128.60	542.29	748.62	858.72
15.0		0.00	474.74	711.52	837.87
16.0			399.37	670.12	814.61
17.0			315.28	623.94	788.66
18.0			221.46	572.42	759.70
19.0			116.79	514.93	727.39
20.0			0.00	450.78	691.34
21.0				379.22	651.12
22.0				299.38	606.25
23.0				210.29	556.19
24.0				110.90	500.33
25.0				0.00	438.00
26.0					368.47
27.0					290.89
28.0					204.33
29.0					107.75
30.0					0.00

REMAINING BALANCE PER $1000 OF ORIGINAL LOAN
ANNUAL INTEREST RATE: 11.25%

AGE OF LOAN	LOAN MATURITY (YEARS)				
	10	15	20	25	30
0.5	972.10	986.80	993.14	996.27	997.93
1.0	942.60	972.85	985.88	992.32	995.73
1.5	911.39	958.09	978.20	988.15	993.41
2.0	878.39	942.48	970.08	983.74	990.96
2.5	843.49	925.97	961.49	979.07	988.37
3.0	806.58	908.51	952.41	974.13	985.62
3.5	767.55	890.04	942.80	968.91	982.72
4.0	726.26	870.51	932.64	963.39	979.65
4.5	682.60	849.86	921.90	957.55	976.41
5.0	636.42	828.02	910.54	951.38	972.97
5.5	587.59	804.92	898.52	944.85	969.34
6.0	535.94	780.49	885.82	937.94	965.50
6.5	481.32	754.65	872.38	930.64	961.44
7.0	423.56	727.32	858.16	922.91	957.15
7.5	362.46	698.43	843.13	914.74	952.61
8.0	297.85	667.86	827.23	906.10	947.81
8.5	229.52	635.54	810.42	896.96	942.73
9.0	157.26	601.36	792.64	887.30	937.36
9.5	80.83	565.20	773.83	877.08	931.67
10.0	0.00	526.97	753.94	866.27	925.67
11.0		443.77	710.66	842.75	912.59
12.0		350.71	662.26	816.44	897.97
13.0		246.63	608.12	787.01	881.61
14.0		130.21	547.56	754.10	863.32
15.0		0.00	479.83	717.28	842.86
16.0			404.07	676.11	819.97
17.0			319.34	630.06	794.37
18.0			224.56	578.55	765.74
19.0			118.56	520.94	733.72
20.0			0.00	456.50	697.90
21.0				384.42	657.84
22.0				303.81	613.03
23.0				213.65	562.91
24.0				112.80	506.86
25.0				0.00	444.16
26.0					374.03
27.0					295.60
28.0					207.87
29.0					109.75
30.0					0.00

REMAINING BALANCE PER $1000 OF ORIGINAL LOAN
ANNUAL INTEREST RATE: 11.5%

AGE OF LOAN	LOAN MATURITY (YEARS)				
	10	15	20	25	30
0.5	972.49	987.10	993.36	996.43	998.04
1.0	943.36	973.45	986.32	992.64	995.96
1.5	912.52	958.99	978.87	988.64	993.75
2.0	879.86	943.67	970.99	984.40	991.42
2.5	845.27	927.46	962.63	979.90	988.95
3.0	808.65	910.29	953.79	975.15	986.34
3.5	769.87	892.11	944.43	970.11	983.57
4.0	728.81	872.86	934.51	964.78	980.64
4.5	685.33	852.47	924.01	959.13	977.53
5.0	639.28	830.89	912.89	953.15	974.25
5.5	590.53	808.03	901.12	946.82	970.77
6.0	538.91	783.83	888.65	940.11	967.08
6.5	484.24	758.20	875.45	933.01	963.18
7.0	426.36	731.06	861.47	925.50	959.04
7.5	365.06	702.32	846.67	917.54	954.67
8.0	300.16	671.90	830.99	909.11	950.03
8.5	231.43	639.68	814.40	900.18	945.13
9.0	158.66	605.56	796.82	890.73	939.93
9.5	81.60	569.43	778.21	880.72	934.43
10.0	0.00	531.17	758.51	870.12	928.60
11.0		447.77	715.55	847.02	915.90
12.0		354.25	667.38	821.11	901.66
13.0		249.40	613.37	792.06	885.69
14.0		131.83	552.81	759.49	867.79
15.0		0.00	484.90	722.97	847.71
16.0			408.77	682.03	825.20
17.0			323.40	636.11	799.97
18.0			227.67	584.63	771.67
19.0			120.34	526.91	739.93
20.0			0.00	462.19	704.36
21.0				389.62	664.46
22.0				308.24	619.73
23.0				217.01	569.58
24.0				114.71	513.34
25.0				0.00	450.28
26.0					379.58
27.0					300.31
28.0					211.42
29.0					111.75
30.0					0.00

620

REMAINING BALANCE PER $1000 OF ORIGINAL LOAN
ANNUAL INTEREST RATE: 11.75%

AGE OF LOAN	LOAN MATURITY (YEARS)				
	10	15	20	25	30
0.5	972.88	987.40	993.57	996.58	998.14
1.0	944.12	974.04	986.76	992.95	996.17
1.5	913.63	959.87	979.53	989.11	994.08
2.0	881.31	944.85	971.87	985.03	991.86
2.5	847.03	928.93	963.75	980.71	989.51
3.0	810.70	912.04	955.14	976.13	987.02
3.5	772.18	894.15	946.01	971.27	984.38
4.0	731.34	875.17	936.33	966.12	981.58
4.5	688.04	855.05	926.07	960.66	978.61
5.0	642.13	833.72	915.19	954.87	975.46
5.5	593.46	811.11	903.66	948.73	972.13
6.0	541.86	787.13	891.43	942.22	968.59
6.5	487.16	761.71	878.46	935.32	964.84
7.0	429.16	734.76	864.72	928.01	960.86
7.5	367.66	706.19	850.14	920.25	956.65
8.0	302.47	675.90	834.69	912.03	952.18
8.5	233.35	643.78	818.31	903.31	947.44
9.0	160.07	609.73	800.95	894.07	942.41
9.5	82.37	573.63	782.53	884.27	937.09
10.0	0.00	535.36	763.01	873.89	931.44
11.0		451.76	720.38	851.20	919.11
12.0		357.80	672.45	825.69	905.24
13.0		252.17	618.58	797.02	889.65
14.0		133.45	558.02	764.80	872.14
15.0		0.00	489.96	728.58	852.45
16.0			413.45	687.86	830.31
17.0			327.45	642.10	805.43
18.0			230.79	590.66	777.47
19.0			122.13	532.84	746.03
20.0			0.00	467.84	710.70
21.0				394.79	670.99
22.0				312.67	626.35
23.0				220.37	576.17
24.0				116.62	519.76
25.0				0.00	456.37
26.0					385.10
27.0					305.00
28.0					214.96
29.0					113.76
30.0					0.00

REMAINING BALANCE PER $1000 OF ORIGINAL LOAN
ANNUAL INTEREST RATE: 12%

AGE OF LOAN	LOAN MATURITY (YEARS)				
	10	15	20	25	30
0.5	973.26	987.69	993.78	996.73	998.24
1.0	944.87	974.61	987.18	993.25	996.37
1.5	914.73	960.74	980.17	989.56	994.39
2.0	882.74	946.01	972.73	985.64	992.28
2.5	848.79	930.37	964.84	981.49	990.05
3.0	812.74	913.77	956.46	977.07	987.67
3.5	774.48	896.15	947.56	972.39	985.16
4.0	733.86	877.45	938.11	967.41	982.48
4.5	690.74	857.60	928.09	962.14	979.64
5.0	644.97	836.52	917.44	956.53	976.63
5.5	596.39	814.15	906.15	950.58	973.43
6.0	544.82	790.40	894.15	944.27	970.04
6.5	490.07	765.20	881.42	937.57	966.44
7.0	431.96	738.44	867.91	930.45	962.61
7.5	370.27	710.03	853.56	922.90	958.55
8.0	304.78	679.88	838.34	914.88	954.24
8.5	235.27	647.87	822.17	906.37	949.67
9.0	161.48	613.89	805.01	897.33	944.81
9.5	83.15	577.82	786.80	887.74	939.65
10.0	0.00	539.54	767.46	877.56	934.18
11.0		455.75	725.15	855.29	922.20
12.0		361.34	677.47	830.18	908.71
13.0		254.96	623.75	801.89	893.50
14.0		135.08	563.21	770.02	876.37
15.0		0.00	494.99	734.10	857.06
16.0			418.13	693.63	835.30
17.0			331.51	648.02	810.78
18.0			233.91	596.64	783.16
19.0			123.93	538.73	752.03
20.0			0.00	473.48	716.95
21.0				399.95	677.42
22.0				317.10	632.88
23.0				223.74	582.69
24.0				118.54	526.14
25.0				0.00	462.41
26.0					390.60
27.0					309.69
28.0					218.51
29.0					115.77
30.0					0.00

REMAINING BALANCE PER $1000 OF ORIGINAL LOAN
ANNUAL INTEREST RATE: 12.25%

AGE OF LOAN	LOAN MATURITY (YEARS)				
	10	15	20	25	30
0.5	973.63	987.97	993.98	996.87	998.33
1.0	945.61	975.18	987.59	993.54	996.56
1.5	915.83	961.59	980.80	990.00	994.68
2.0	884.17	947.15	973.57	986.23	992.68
2.5	850.52	931.79	965.90	982.24	990.56
3.0	814.77	915.48	957.74	977.99	988.30
3.5	776.76	898.13	949.07	973.47	985.90
4.0	736.36	879.70	939.85	968.67	983.34
4.5	693.43	860.11	930.06	963.57	980.63
5.0	647.80	839.29	919.65	958.14	977.75
5.5	599.31	817.16	908.58	952.38	974.69
6.0	547.76	793.64	896.82	946.25	971.43
6.5	492.98	768.64	884.32	939.74	967.97
7.0	434.75	742.07	871.04	932.82	964.29
7.5	372.87	713.84	856.92	925.47	960.38
8.0	307.10	683.82	841.91	917.65	956.22
8.5	237.19	651.93	825.97	909.34	951.81
9.0	162.89	618.02	809.01	900.51	947.11
9.5	83.93	581.99	791.00	891.13	942.12
10.0	0.00	543.69	771.85	881.15	936.82
11.0		459.73	729.87	859.28	925.20
12.0		364.88	682.45	834.58	912.07
13.0		257.74	628.88	806.67	897.23
14.0		136.72	568.36	775.15	880.47
15.0		0.00	500.01	739.54	861.55
16.0			422.79	699.32	840.16
17.0			335.56	653.88	816.01
18.0			237.03	602.55	788.72
19.0			125.73	544.57	757.90
20.0			0.00	479.08	723.09
21.0				405.09	683.76
22.0				321.52	639.33
23.0				227.11	589.15
24.0				120.47	532.46
25.0				0.00	468.42
26.0					396.08
27.0					314.36
28.0					222.06
29.0					117.79
30.0					0.00

REMAINING BALANCE PER $1000 OF ORIGINAL LOAN
ANNUAL INTEREST RATE: 12.5%

AGE OF LOAN	LOAN MATURITY (YEARS)				
	10	15	20	25	30
0.5	974.01	988.25	994.18	997.00	998.42
1.0	946.34	975.74	987.99	993.81	996.75
1.5	916.91	962.43	981.40	990.42	994.96
2.0	885.58	948.26	974.39	986.80	993.06
2.5	852.25	933.19	966.93	982.96	991.04
3.0	816.77	917.15	958.99	978.87	988.89
3.5	779.03	900.08	950.54	974.51	986.60
4.0	738.86	881.92	941.55	969.88	984.17
4.5	696.11	862.59	931.98	964.95	981.58
5.0	650.62	842.02	921.80	959.70	978.82
5.5	602.21	820.14	910.97	954.12	975.88
6.0	550.70	796.84	899.44	948.17	972.76
6.5	495.88	772.06	887.17	941.85	969.44
7.0	437.55	745.68	874.11	935.12	965.90
7.5	375.47	717.61	860.22	927.96	962.14
8.0	309.41	687.74	845.43	920.34	958.13
8.5	239.12	655.96	829.70	912.23	953.87
9.0	164.31	622.13	812.95	903.61	949.33
9.5	84.71	586.14	795.14	894.42	944.51
10.0	0.00	547.84	776.18	884.65	939.37
11.0		463.70	734.53	863.19	928.09
12.0		368.43	687.37	838.88	915.31
13.0		260.53	633.96	811.36	900.85
14.0		138.36	573.48	780.19	884.46
15.0		0.00	505.00	744.90	865.91
16.0			427.44	704.93	844.90
17.0			339.62	659.67	821.11
18.0			240.16	608.41	794.17
19.0			127.54	550.37	763.67
20.0			0.00	484.64	729.12
21.0				410.21	690.00
22.0				325.93	645.69
23.0				230.48	595.53
24.0				122.40	538.71
25.0				0.00	474.38
26.0					401.53
27.0					319.02
28.0					225.60
29.0					119.80
30.0					0.00

REMAINING BALANCE PER $1000 OF ORIGINAL LOAN
ANNUAL INTEREST RATE: 12.75%

AGE OF LOAN	LOAN MATURITY (YEARS)				
	10	15	20	25	30
0.5	974.37	988.52	994.37	997.13	998.51
1.0	947.07	976.29	988.38	994.08	996.92
1.5	917.98	963.25	981.99	990.82	995.23
2.0	886.98	949.36	975.19	987.35	993.43
2.5	853.96	934.57	967.94	983.65	991.50
3.0	818.77	918.80	960.21	979.71	989.46
3.5	781.28	902.01	951.98	975.52	987.28
4.0	741.33	884.11	943.21	971.05	984.95
4.5	698.77	865.04	933.86	966.28	982.48
5.0	653.43	844.72	923.91	961.21	979.84
5.5	605.11	823.08	913.30	955.80	977.03
6.0	553.63	800.01	902.00	950.04	974.03
6.5	498.78	775.44	889.96	943.90	970.84
7.0	440.34	749.25	877.13	937.36	967.44
7.5	378.08	721.36	863.46	930.39	963.82
8.0	311.74	691.63	848.89	922.96	959.96
8.5	241.05	659.96	833.37	915.05	955.85
9.0	165.74	626.22	816.84	906.62	951.47
9.5	85.50	590.27	799.22	897.64	946.80
10.0	0.00	551.96	780.45	888.07	941.83
11.0		467.67	739.14	867.01	930.88
12.0		371.97	692.24	843.10	918.46
13.0		263.33	639.01	815.96	904.35
14.0		140.00	578.57	785.15	888.34
15.0		0.00	509.97	750.17	870.16
16.0			432.08	710.46	849.53
17.0			343.67	665.39	826.10
18.0			243.29	614.22	799.51
19.0			129.35	556.13	769.32
20.0			0.00	490.18	735.05
21.0				415.32	696.14
22.0				330.33	651.97
23.0				233.86	601.83
24.0				124.33	544.92
25.0				0.00	480.30
26.0					406.95
27.0					323.67
28.0					229.14
29.0					121.83
30.0					0.00

REMAINING BALANCE PER $1000 OF ORIGINAL LOAN
ANNUAL INTEREST RATE: 13%

AGE OF LOAN	LOAN MATURITY (YEARS)				
	10	15	20	25	30
0.5	974.74	988.79	994.56	997.26	998.59
1.0	947.79	976.82	988.76	994.33	997.09
1.5	919.04	964.06	982.57	991.21	995.48
2.0	888.37	950.45	975.96	987.88	993.77
2.5	855.65	935.92	968.92	984.32	991.95
3.0	820.75	920.43	961.40	980.53	990.00
3.5	783.52	903.90	953.38	976.49	987.92
4.0	743.80	886.27	944.83	972.18	985.70
4.5	701.43	867.46	935.70	967.57	983.34
5.0	656.22	847.39	925.97	962.67	980.82
5.5	608.00	825.98	915.59	957.43	978.13
6.0	556.56	803.15	904.51	951.84	975.26
6.5	501.68	778.78	892.69	945.88	972.19
7.0	443.14	752.80	880.08	939.52	968.93
7.5	380.69	725.07	866.63	932.74	965.44
8.0	314.06	695.50	852.29	925.51	961.72
8.5	242.99	663.94	836.98	917.79	957.76
9.0	167.17	630.29	820.66	909.55	953.53
9.5	86.29	594.38	803.24	900.77	949.01
10.0	0.00	556.08	784.66	891.40	944.20
11.0		471.62	743.69	870.74	933.58
12.0		375.51	697.07	847.23	921.50
13.0		266.13	644.01	820.47	907.75
14.0		141.66	583.63	790.02	892.11
15.0		0.00	514.91	755.36	874.30
16.0			436.71	715.92	854.04
17.0			347.71	671.04	830.97
18.0			246.43	619.96	804.73
19.0			131.17	561.84	774.86
20.0			0.00	495.69	740.87
21.0				420.40	702.19
22.0				334.73	658.17
23.0				237.23	608.07
24.0				126.27	551.06
25.0				0.00	486.18
26.0					412.34
27.0					328.31
28.0					232.68
29.0					123.85
30.0					0.00

REMAINING BALANCE PER $1000 OF ORIGINAL LOAN
ANNUAL INTEREST RATE: 13.25%

AGE OF LOAN	LOAN MATURITY (YEARS)				
	10	15	20	25	30
0.5	975.10	989.05	994.74	997.38	998.67
1.0	948.50	977.35	989.12	994.57	997.24
1.5	920.09	964.85	983.12	991.58	995.72
2.0	889.75	951.51	976.71	988.38	994.10
2.5	857.34	937.25	969.87	984.97	992.36
3.0	822.72	922.03	962.56	981.32	990.51
3.5	785.74	905.76	954.75	977.43	988.53
4.0	746.25	888.39	946.41	973.27	986.42
4.5	704.06	869.84	937.50	968.82	984.16
5.0	659.01	850.02	927.98	964.07	981.75
5.5	610.88	828.85	917.82	959.00	979.17
6.0	559.48	806.24	906.96	953.59	976.42
6.5	504.57	782.10	895.37	947.80	973.49
7.0	445.93	756.30	882.98	941.63	970.35
7.5	383.29	728.75	869.75	935.03	966.99
8.0	316.39	699.33	855.62	927.98	963.41
8.5	244.93	667.90	840.53	920.45	959.59
9.0	168.60	634.33	824.41	912.41	955.50
9.5	87.08	598.47	807.20	903.82	951.14
10.0	0.00	560.17	788.80	894.65	946.48
11.0		475.57	748.18	874.38	936.19
12.0		379.05	701.84	851.26	924.44
13.0		268.94	648.96	824.89	911.04
14.0		143.32	588.64	794.80	895.76
15.0		0.00	519.83	760.47	878.32
16.0			441.32	721.30	858.42
17.0			351.75	676.62	835.73
18.0			249.57	625.65	809.83
19.0			132.99	567.50	780.29
20.0			0.00	501.15	746.59
21.0				425.46	708.14
22.0				339.11	664.27
23.0				240.60	614.23
24.0				128.22	557.14
25.0				0.00	492.01
26.0					417.70
27.0					332.93
28.0					236.21
29.0					125.88
30.0					0.00

REMAINING BALANCE PER $1000 OF ORIGINAL LOAN
ANNUAL INTEREST RATE: 13.5%

AGE OF LOAN	LOAN MATURITY (YEARS)				
	10	15	20	25	30
0.5	975.45	989.30	994.92	997.49	998.74
1.0	949.20	977.87	989.48	994.81	997.39
1.5	921.13	965.63	983.67	991.94	995.95
2.0	891.11	952.55	977.45	988.87	994.41
2.5	859.00	938.56	970.80	985.59	992.76
3.0	824.67	923.60	963.69	982.08	991.00
3.5	787.95	907.60	956.08	978.33	989.12
4.0	748.68	890.49	947.95	974.32	987.10
4.5	706.69	872.19	939.25	970.03	984.95
5.0	661.78	852.62	929.95	965.44	982.64
5.5	613.75	831.69	920.01	960.53	980.18
6.0	562.39	809.31	909.37	955.28	977.54
6.5	507.46	785.37	897.99	949.67	974.72
7.0	448.72	759.78	885.83	943.67	971.71
7.5	385.90	732.40	872.82	937.25	968.48
8.0	318.72	703.13	858.90	930.38	965.04
8.5	246.87	671.82	844.02	923.04	961.35
9.0	170.04	638.34	828.11	915.19	957.41
9.5	87.87	602.54	811.09	906.79	953.19
10.0	0.00	564.25	792.90	897.81	948.68
11.0		479.50	752.62	877.94	938.70
12.0		382.59	706.56	855.21	927.29
13.0		271.75	653.88	829.22	914.23
14.0		144.98	593.63	799.49	899.30
15.0		0.00	524.72	765.49	882.23
16.0			445.92	726.61	862.70
17.0			355.79	682.14	840.37
18.0			252.71	631.28	814.83
19.0			134.82	573.11	785.61
20.0			0.00	506.59	752.20
21.0				430.50	714.00
22.0				343.49	670.30
23.0				243.98	620.32
24.0				130.16	563.16
25.0				0.00	497.79
26.0					423.03
27.0					337.53
28.0					239.74
29.0					127.91
30.0					0.00

REMAINING BALANCE PER $1000 OF ORIGINAL LOAN
ANNUAL INTEREST RATE: 13.75%

AGE OF LOAN	LOAN MATURITY (YEARS)				
	10	15	20	25	30
0.5	975.81	989.56	995.09	997.60	998.81
1.0	949.90	978.37	989.83	995.03	997.53
1.5	922.16	966.40	984.19	992.29	996.17
2.0	892.46	953.58	978.16	989.34	994.71
2.5	860.66	939.85	971.70	986.19	993.14
3.0	826.61	925.15	964.79	982.82	991.47
3.5	790.14	909.41	957.38	979.20	989.67
4.0	751.10	892.55	949.45	975.33	987.75
4.5	709.30	874.51	940.97	971.19	985.70
5.0	664.54	855.18	931.88	966.75	983.49
5.5	616.61	834.49	922.14	962.00	981.14
6.0	565.29	812.34	911.72	956.92	978.61
6.5	510.34	788.62	900.56	951.47	975.91
7.0	451.51	763.22	888.61	945.64	973.01
7.5	388.51	736.02	875.82	939.40	969.91
8.0	321.05	706.90	862.12	932.71	966.59
8.5	248.82	675.72	847.45	925.55	963.04
9.0	171.48	642.33	831.75	917.89	959.23
9.5	88.67	606.58	814.93	909.68	955.16
10.0	0.00	568.30	796.92	900.89	950.80
11.0		483.43	757.00	881.41	941.12
12.0		386.12	711.22	859.07	930.03
13.0		274.56	658.74	833.46	917.32
14.0		146.65	598.57	804.09	902.74
15.0		0.00	529.59	770.43	886.02
16.0			450.49	731.83	866.86
17.0			359.82	687.58	844.89
18.0			255.85	636.84	819.70
19.0			136.66	578.67	790.82
20.0			0.00	511.98	757.71
21.0				435.52	719.75
22.0				347.85	676.23
23.0				247.35	626.33
24.0				132.11	569.12
25.0				0.00	503.53
26.0					428.33
27.0					342.11
28.0					243.26
29.0					129.93
30.0					0.00

629

REMAINING BALANCE PER $1000 OF ORIGINAL LOAN
ANNUAL INTEREST RATE: 14%

AGE OF LOAN	LOAN MATURITY (YEARS)				
	10	15	20	25	30
0.5	976.15	989.80	995.25	997.71	998.88
1.0	950.59	978.87	990.16	995.25	997.67
1.5	923.18	967.15	984.71	992.62	996.38
2.0	893.80	954.58	978.85	989.79	994.99
2.5	862.30	941.11	972.58	986.77	993.51
3.0	828.53	926.67	965.86	983.52	991.91
3.5	792.32	911.19	958.65	980.04	990.21
4.0	753.51	894.59	950.92	976.31	988.37
4.5	711.90	876.79	942.64	972.31	986.41
5.0	667.29	857.71	933.76	968.03	984.31
5.5	619.46	837.26	924.23	963.43	982.05
6.0	568.19	815.33	914.02	958.50	979.63
6.5	513.22	791.83	903.08	953.22	977.04
7.0	454.29	766.62	891.35	947.56	974.26
7.5	391.12	739.61	878.77	941.49	971.28
8.0	323.38	710.64	865.28	934.98	968.09
8.5	250.77	679.59	850.82	928.00	964.66
9.0	172.93	646.30	835.33	920.52	960.99
9.5	89.47	610.61	818.71	912.50	957.06
10.0	0.00	572.34	800.89	903.90	952.84
11.0		487.34	761.32	884.80	943.46
12.0		389.65	715.84	862.85	932.69
13.0		277.37	663.56	837.62	920.31
14.0		148.32	603.48	808.62	906.07
15.0		0.00	534.43	775.29	889.72
16.0			455.06	736.98	870.92
17.0			363.84	692.95	849.31
18.0			259.00	642.35	824.47
19.0			138.50	584.19	795.93
20.0			0.00	517.34	763.12
21.0				440.51	725.41
22.0				352.21	682.08
23.0				250.72	632.27
24.0				134.07	575.02
25.0				0.00	509.22
26.0					433.60
27.0					346.68
28.0					246.78
29.0					131.96
30.0					0.00

REMAINING BALANCE PER $1000 OF ORIGINAL LOAN
ANNUAL INTEREST RATE: 14.25%

AGE OF LOAN	LOAN MATURITY (YEARS)				
	10	15	20	25	30
0.5	976.50	990.04	995.41	997.81	998.94
1.0	951.27	979.36	990.49	995.46	997.80
1.5	924.19	967.89	985.20	992.94	996.57
2.0	895.13	955.57	979.53	990.23	995.26
2.5	863.93	942.35	973.44	987.32	993.85
3.0	830.44	928.17	966.90	984.20	992.34
3.5	794.49	912.94	959.89	980.85	990.71
4.0	755.90	896.59	952.35	977.26	988.97
4.5	714.49	879.05	944.27	973.40	987.09
5.0	670.03	860.21	935.59	969.26	985.08
5.5	622.30	839.99	926.28	964.81	982.93
6.0	571.08	818.29	916.28	960.04	980.61
6.5	516.10	795.00	905.55	954.91	978.13
7.0	457.08	770.00	894.02	949.41	975.46
7.5	393.72	743.16	881.66	943.51	972.60
8.0	325.72	714.35	868.39	937.18	969.52
8.5	252.73	683.43	854.14	930.37	966.22
9.0	174.38	650.24	838.84	923.07	962.68
9.5	90.28	614.61	822.43	915.24	958.88
10.0	0.00	576.36	804.81	906.83	954.80
11.0		491.25	765.59	888.11	945.72
12.0		393.18	720.40	866.54	935.25
13.0		280.19	668.34	841.69	923.20
14.0		150.00	608.36	813.05	909.31
15.0		0.00	539.24	780.06	893.30
16.0			459.61	742.05	874.86
17.0			367.86	698.26	853.61
18.0			262.14	647.79	829.13
19.0			140.34	589.65	800.93
20.0			0.00	522.66	768.43
21.0				445.48	730.98
22.0				356.55	687.84
23.0				254.08	638.13
24.0				136.03	580.86
25.0				0.00	514.87
26.0					438.83
27.0					351.23
28.0					250.29
29.0					134.00
30.0					0.00

REMAINING BALANCE PER $1000 OF ORIGINAL LOAN
ANNUAL INTEREST RATE: 14.5%

AGE OF LOAN	LOAN MATURITY (YEARS)				
	10	15	20	25	30
0.5	976.84	990.28	995.57	997.91	999.00
1.0	951.95	979.83	990.80	995.66	997.92
1.5	925.19	968.61	985.69	993.24	996.76
2.0	896.44	956.54	980.18	990.65	995.51
2.5	865.54	943.58	974.27	987.85	994.18
3.0	832.33	929.64	967.92	984.86	992.74
3.5	796.64	914.66	961.09	981.63	991.19
4.0	758.28	898.57	953.75	978.17	989.53
4.5	717.06	881.27	945.86	974.44	987.74
5.0	672.75	862.67	937.38	970.44	985.83
5.5	625.13	842.69	928.27	966.14	983.76
6.0	573.96	821.22	918.48	961.52	981.55
6.5	518.96	798.14	907.96	956.55	979.16
7.0	459.85	773.34	896.65	951.21	976.60
7.5	396.33	746.68	884.49	945.47	973.85
8.0	328.06	718.03	871.43	939.31	970.90
8.5	254.69	687.24	857.39	932.68	967.72
9.0	175.83	654.15	842.30	925.56	964.30
9.5	91.08	618.59	826.08	917.90	960.63
10.0	0.00	580.36	808.66	909.67	956.69
11.0		495.14	769.80	891.33	947.89
12.0		396.71	724.91	870.14	937.73
13.0		283.01	673.07	845.67	925.99
14.0		151.68	613.19	817.40	912.44
15.0		0.00	544.02	784.75	896.78
16.0			464.14	747.04	878.70
17.0			371.86	703.48	857.81
18.0			265.29	653.17	833.68
19.0			142.19	595.06	805.82
20.0			0.00	527.94	773.63
21.0				450.42	736.45
22.0				360.87	693.51
23.0				257.45	643.92
24.0				137.98	586.63
25.0				0.00	520.46
26.0					444.03
27.0					355.76
28.0					253.80
29.0					136.03
30.0					0.00

REMAINING BALANCE PER $1000 OF ORIGINAL LOAN
ANNUAL INTEREST RATE: 14.75%

AGE OF LOAN	LOAN MATURITY (YEARS)				
	10	15	20	25	30
0.5	977.17	990.51	995.72	998.00	999.05
1.0	952.61	980.30	991.11	995.85	998.03
1.5	926.18	969.32	986.16	993.54	996.94
2.0	897.74	957.50	980.82	991.05	995.76
2.5	867.14	944.78	975.08	988.37	994.49
3.0	834.21	931.09	968.91	985.48	993.12
3.5	798.77	916.36	962.26	982.38	991.65
4.0	760.64	900.51	955.11	979.04	990.07
4.5	719.61	883.46	947.41	975.45	988.36
5.0	675.46	865.11	939.13	971.59	986.53
5.5	627.96	845.36	930.22	967.43	984.56
6.0	576.83	824.11	920.64	962.95	982.44
6.5	521.83	801.25	910.32	958.14	980.16
7.0	462.63	776.64	899.22	952.95	977.70
7.5	398.94	750.17	887.27	947.38	975.06
8.0	330.40	721.68	874.42	941.38	972.21
8.5	256.65	691.02	860.58	934.92	969.15
9.0	177.29	658.04	845.70	927.97	965.86
9.5	91.89	622.54	829.68	920.49	962.31
10.0	0.00	584.35	812.45	912.45	958.50
11.0		499.02	773.95	894.48	949.98
12.0		400.23	729.37	873.67	940.12
13.0		285.83	677.75	849.57	928.70
14.0		153.37	617.98	821.67	915.47
15.0		0.00	548.78	789.37	900.16
16.0			468.65	751.96	882.43
17.0			375.87	708.65	861.90
18.0			268.43	658.50	838.13
19.0			144.04	600.43	810.60
20.0			0.00	533.19	778.73
21.0				455.33	741.83
22.0				365.19	699.10
23.0				260.81	649.63
24.0				139.94	592.34
25.0				0.00	526.01
26.0					449.20
27.0					360.27
28.0					257.29
29.0					138.06
30.0					0.00

REMAINING BALANCE PER $1000 OF ORIGINAL LOAN
ANNUAL INTEREST RATE: 15%

AGE OF LOAN	LOAN MATURITY (YEARS)				
	10	15	20	25	30
0.5	977.51	990.74	995.87	998.09	999.11
1.0	953.27	980.76	991.41	996.04	998.14
1.5	927.16	970.01	986.61	993.82	997.10
2.0	899.03	958.43	981.44	991.43	995.99
2.5	868.73	945.96	975.87	988.86	994.78
3.0	836.07	932.51	969.87	986.09	993.48
3.5	800.89	918.03	963.40	983.11	992.09
4.0	762.99	902.43	956.43	979.89	990.58
4.5	722.16	885.62	948.93	976.43	988.96
5.0	678.17	867.50	940.84	972.69	987.21
5.5	630.77	847.99	932.13	968.67	985.32
6.0	579.70	826.97	922.74	964.34	983.29
6.5	524.68	804.32	912.63	959.67	981.11
7.0	465.41	779.91	901.73	954.64	978.75
7.5	401.55	753.62	890.00	949.22	976.21
8.0	332.74	725.30	877.35	943.38	973.48
8.5	258.61	694.78	863.72	937.09	970.53
9.0	178.75	661.90	849.04	930.32	967.35
9.5	92.70	626.48	833.23	923.02	963.93
10.0	0.00	588.31	816.18	915.15	960.25
11.0		502.89	778.05	897.54	952.00
12.0		403.74	733.78	877.11	942.43
13.0		288.66	682.39	853.39	931.31
14.0		155.07	622.74	825.86	918.41
15.0		0.00	553.51	793.90	903.44
16.0			473.14	756.80	886.06
17.0			379.86	713.74	865.89
18.0			271.58	663.76	842.47
19.0			145.89	605.74	815.29
20.0			0.00	538.39	783.74
21.0				460.22	747.12
22.0				369.49	704.61
23.0				264.16	655.26
24.0				141.91	597.99
25.0				0.00	531.51
26.0					454.34
27.0					364.76
28.0					260.78
29.0					140.09
30.0					0.00

REMAINING BALANCE PER $1000 OF ORIGINAL LOAN
ANNUAL INTEREST RATE: 15.25%

AGE OF LOAN	LOAN MATURITY (YEARS)				
	10	15	20	25	30
0.5	977.83	990.96	996.01	998.18	999.16
1.0	953.92	981.21	991.70	996.21	998.25
1.5	928.13	970.70	987.05	994.09	997.26
2.0	900.31	959.35	982.04	991.80	996.20
2.5	870.30	947.11	976.64	989.34	995.06
3.0	837.92	933.91	970.80	986.67	993.83
3.5	803.00	919.67	964.51	983.80	992.50
4.0	765.33	904.31	957.73	980.70	991.06
4.5	724.69	887.74	950.41	977.36	989.52
5.0	680.85	869.87	942.51	973.76	987.85
5.5	633.57	850.59	933.99	969.87	986.05
6.0	582.56	829.79	924.80	965.68	984.11
6.5	527.53	807.35	914.89	961.15	982.01
7.0	468.18	783.15	904.20	956.27	979.75
7.5	404.15	757.04	892.66	951.01	977.31
8.0	335.08	728.88	880.22	945.33	974.68
8.5	260.58	698.50	866.80	939.20	971.85
9.0	180.21	665.73	852.32	932.59	968.79
9.5	93.52	630.38	836.71	925.46	965.49
10.0	0.00	592.25	819.86	917.78	961.93
11.0		506.75	782.08	900.53	953.94
12.0		407.25	738.13	880.47	944.65
13.0		291.48	686.98	857.12	933.84
14.0		156.76	627.46	829.96	921.26
15.0		0.00	558.20	798.34	906.62
16.0			477.61	761.56	889.59
17.0			383.84	718.76	869.77
18.0			274.72	668.95	846.71
19.0			147.75	610.99	819.87
20.0			0.00	543.55	788.64
21.0				465.08	752.31
22.0				373.77	710.02
23.0				267.51	660.82
24.0				143.87	603.57
25.0				0.00	536.95
26.0					459.43
27.0					369.23
28.0					264.26
29.0					142.12
30.0					0.00

REMAINING BALANCE PER $1000 OF ORIGINAL LOAN
ANNUAL INTEREST RATE: 15.5%

AGE OF LOAN	LOAN MATURITY (YEARS)				
	10	15	20	25	30
0.5	978.16	991.18	996.14	998.26	999.20
1.0	954.57	981.65	991.98	996.38	998.34
1.5	929.09	971.37	987.48	994.35	997.41
2.0	901.58	960.25	982.63	992.16	996.41
2.5	871.86	948.25	977.38	989.79	995.33
3.0	839.76	935.29	971.71	987.23	994.16
3.5	805.09	921.29	965.59	984.47	992.89
4.0	767.65	906.17	958.98	981.49	991.53
4.5	727.21	889.84	951.85	978.27	990.05
5.0	683.53	872.20	944.14	974.79	988.46
5.5	636.36	853.15	935.81	971.03	986.74
6.0	585.41	832.58	926.81	966.97	984.88
6.5	530.38	810.36	917.10	962.59	982.88
7.0	470.95	786.36	906.61	957.85	980.71
7.5	406.76	760.43	895.28	952.74	978.37
8.0	337.43	732.44	883.04	947.21	975.84
8.5	262.55	702.20	869.82	941.25	973.11
9.0	181.68	669.54	855.55	934.81	970.16
9.5	94.34	634.27	840.13	927.85	966.98
10.0	0.00	596.18	823.48	920.33	963.54
11.0		510.59	786.07	903.45	955.81
12.0		410.76	742.43	883.75	946.80
13.0		294.31	691.52	860.78	936.28
14.0		158.46	632.14	833.98	924.02
15.0		0.00	562.87	802.71	909.71
16.0			482.07	766.25	893.02
17.0			387.81	723.71	873.55
18.0			277.86	674.09	850.84
19.0			149.61	616.20	824.35
20.0			0.00	548.68	793.45
21.0				469.91	757.41
22.0				378.04	715.36
23.0				270.86	666.31
24.0				145.84	609.09
25.0				0.00	542.35
26.0					464.49
27.0					373.67
28.0					267.73
29.0					144.15
30.0					0.00

REMAINING BALANCE PER $1000 OF ORIGINAL LOAN
ANNUAL INTEREST RATE: 15.75%

AGE OF LOAN	LOAN MATURITY (YEARS)				
	10	15	20	25	30
0.5	978.48	991.39	996.28	998.34	999.25
1.0	955.21	982.09	992.25	996.54	998.44
1.5	930.04	972.02	987.90	994.60	997.56
2.0	902.83	961.14	983.19	992.50	996.61
2.5	873.40	949.37	978.10	990.23	995.58
3.0	841.58	936.64	972.60	987.77	994.47
3.5	807.16	922.88	966.65	985.12	993.27
4.0	769.95	908.00	960.21	982.24	991.97
4.5	729.71	891.90	953.25	979.14	990.56
5.0	686.19	874.50	945.72	975.78	989.04
5.5	639.13	855.68	937.58	972.15	987.40
6.0	588.25	835.33	928.78	968.22	985.63
6.5	533.22	813.32	919.26	963.97	983.70
7.0	473.71	789.52	908.97	959.38	981.63
7.5	409.36	763.79	897.84	954.41	979.38
8.0	339.77	735.96	885.80	949.04	976.95
8.5	264.52	705.86	872.79	943.23	974.32
9.0	183.15	673.32	858.71	936.95	971.48
9.5	95.16	638.13	843.49	930.16	968.41
10.0	0.00	600.07	827.03	922.81	965.09
11.0		514.42	789.99	906.28	957.61
12.0		414.26	746.67	886.95	948.87
13.0		297.13	696.01	864.35	938.64
14.0		160.17	636.77	837.91	926.69
15.0		0.00	567.50	807.00	912.70
16.0			486.50	770.85	896.35
17.0			391.77	728.58	877.24
18.0			281.00	679.15	854.88
19.0			151.47	621.35	828.73
20.0			0.00	553.76	798.16
21.0				474.71	762.41
22.0				382.28	720.60
23.0				274.20	671.71
24.0				147.80	614.54
25.0				0.00	547.69
26.0					469.51
27.0					378.10
28.0					271.19
29.0					146.18
30.0					0.00

REMAINING BALANCE PER $1000 OF ORIGINAL LOAN
ANNUAL INTEREST RATE: 16%

AGE OF LOAN	LOAN MATURITY (YEARS)				
	10	15	20	25	30
0.5	978.80	991.60	996.41	998.41	999.29
1.0	955.84	982.51	992.52	996.70	998.52
1.5	930.98	972.67	988.30	994.84	997.69
2.0	904.07	962.01	983.74	992.83	996.79
2.5	874.93	950.47	978.81	990.65	995.82
3.0	843.38	937.97	973.46	988.29	994.77
3.5	809.22	924.44	967.67	985.74	993.62
4.0	772.24	909.80	961.40	982.97	992.39
4.5	732.20	893.94	954.62	979.98	991.05
5.0	688.84	876.77	947.27	976.74	989.60
5.5	641.90	858.18	939.31	973.23	988.03
6.0	591.08	838.05	930.70	969.43	986.33
6.5	536.05	816.25	921.38	965.31	984.49
7.0	476.47	792.66	911.28	960.86	982.50
7.5	411.96	767.11	900.35	956.03	980.35
8.0	342.12	739.45	888.51	950.81	978.01
8.5	266.50	709.50	875.70	945.16	975.48
9.0	184.63	677.07	861.82	939.04	972.75
9.5	95.98	641.97	846.80	932.41	969.79
10.0	0.00	603.95	830.54	925.23	966.58
11.0		518.24	793.86	909.05	959.34
12.0		417.75	750.86	890.08	950.86
13.0		299.96	700.46	867.84	940.92
14.0		161.87	641.37	841.77	929.27
15.0		0.00	572.11	811.21	915.61
16.0			490.91	775.39	899.60
17.0			395.73	733.39	880.82
18.0			284.14	684.16	858.82
19.0			153.34	626.45	833.02
20.0			0.00	558.80	802.78
21.0				479.49	767.32
22.0				386.52	725.77
23.0				277.53	677.05
24.0				149.77	619.94
25.0				0.00	552.99
26.0					474.50
27.0					382.50
28.0					274.65
29.0					148.21
30.0					0.00

REMAINING BALANCE PER $1000 OF ORIGINAL LOAN
ANNUAL INTEREST RATE: 16.25%

AGE OF LOAN	LOAN MATURITY (YEARS)				
	10	15	20	25	30
0.5	979.11	991.81	996.53	998.49	999.33
1.0	956.46	982.93	992.77	996.85	998.61
1.5	931.91	973.30	988.70	995.07	997.82
2.0	905.30	962.86	984.28	993.14	996.97
2.5	876.45	951.54	979.49	991.05	996.05
3.0	845.17	939.28	974.30	988.79	995.05
3.5	811.27	925.98	968.67	986.33	993.96
4.0	774.52	911.57	962.56	983.67	992.79
4.5	734.67	895.94	955.95	980.79	991.51
5.0	691.48	879.00	948.78	977.66	990.13
5.5	644.66	860.64	941.01	974.27	988.63
6.0	593.90	840.73	932.58	970.59	987.01
6.5	538.88	819.15	923.44	966.61	985.25
7.0	479.23	795.76	913.54	962.29	983.34
7.5	414.57	770.40	902.81	957.60	981.27
8.0	344.47	742.91	891.17	952.53	979.03
8.5	268.48	713.11	878.55	947.02	976.60
9.0	186.10	680.80	864.88	941.06	973.96
9.5	96.81	645.78	850.05	934.59	971.10
10.0	0.00	607.81	833.98	927.58	968.01
11.0		522.04	797.67	911.74	961.01
12.0		421.24	755.00	893.13	952.79
13.0		302.79	704.86	871.26	943.13
14.0		163.59	645.93	845.55	931.77
15.0		0.00	576.68	815.35	918.43
16.0			495.30	779.85	902.74
17.0			399.67	738.13	884.31
18.0			287.28	689.11	862.66
19.0			155.21	631.50	837.21
20.0			0.00	563.80	807.30
21.0				484.23	772.15
22.0				390.74	730.85
23.0				280.86	682.31
24.0				151.74	625.27
25.0				0.00	558.23
26.0					479.46
27.0					386.88
28.0					278.09
29.0					150.24
30.0					0.00

REMAINING BALANCE PER $1000 OF ORIGINAL LOAN
ANNUAL INTEREST RATE: REMAINING BALANCE PER $1000 OF ORIGINAL LOAN ANNUAL INTEREST RATE:16.5%

AGE OF LOAN	LOAN MATURITY (YEARS)				
	10	15	20	25	30
0.5	979.42	992.01	996.65	998.56	999.37
1.0	957.08	983.33	993.02	996.99	998.69
1.5	932.83	973.92	989.08	995.29	997.94
2.0	906.52	963.70	984.80	993.44	997.14
2.5	877.95	952.60	980.15	991.44	996.26
3.0	846.95	940.56	975.11	989.27	995.31
3.5	813.30	927.49	969.64	986.91	994.28
4.0	776.77	913.31	963.70	984.34	993.16
4.5	737.13	897.91	957.25	981.56	991.95
5.0	694.10	881.20	950.25	978.55	990.63
5.5	647.40	863.07	942.66	975.27	989.20
6.0	596.71	843.38	934.41	971.71	987.65
6.5	541.70	822.02	925.46	967.86	985.97
7.0	481.98	798.83	915.75	963.67	984.14
7.5	417.17	773.65	905.21	959.12	982.15
8.0	346.82	746.33	893.77	954.19	980.00
8.5	270.46	716.68	881.35	948.83	977.66
9.0	187.59	684.50	867.87	943.02	975.12
9.5	97.63	649.56	853.24	936.71	972.37
10.0	0.00	611.65	837.37	929.86	969.38
11.0		525.83	801.43	914.36	962.61
12.0		424.72	759.08	896.11	954.64
13.0		305.62	709.21	874.59	945.25
14.0		165.30	650.44	849.25	934.19
15.0		0.00	581.22	819.40	921.15
16.0			499.67	784.23	905.80
17.0			403.59	742.80	887.71
18.0			290.41	693.99	866.40
19.0			157.08	636.49	841.30
20.0			0.00	568.75	811.73
21.0				488.95	776.89
22.0				394.93	735.84
23.0				284.18	687.49
24.0				153.71	630.53
25.0				0.00	563.42
26.0					484.37
27.0					391.24
28.0					281.52
29.0					152.27
30.0					0.00

REMAINING BALANCE PER $1000 OF ORIGINAL LOAN
ANNUAL INTEREST RATE: 16.75%

AGE OF LOAN	LOAN MATURITY (YEARS)				
	10	15	20	25	30
0.5	979.72	992.20	996.77	998.62	999.41
1.0	957.69	983.73	993.26	997.13	998.76
1.5	933.74	974.52	989.45	995.50	998.06
2.0	907.72	964.52	985.30	993.73	997.30
2.5	879.44	953.64	980.79	991.81	996.47
3.0	848.71	941.82	975.90	989.72	995.57
3.5	815.31	928.98	970.58	987.46	994.59
4.0	779.02	915.02	964.80	984.99	993.52
4.5	739.58	899.86	958.51	982.31	992.37
5.0	696.72	883.38	951.69	979.40	991.11
5.5	650.14	865.46	944.27	976.24	989.75
6.0	599.52	846.00	936.20	972.80	988.26
6.5	544.51	824.85	927.44	969.06	986.65
7.0	484.73	801.86	917.92	965.00	984.90
7.5	419.76	776.88	907.57	960.59	983.00
8.0	349.17	749.73	896.32	955.80	980.93
8.5	272.45	720.23	884.10	950.59	978.68
9.0	189.07	688.17	870.82	944.92	976.24
9.5	98.46	653.32	856.38	938.77	973.58
10.0	0.00	615.46	840.70	932.08	970.70
11.0		529.60	805.13	916.92	964.16
12.0		428.20	763.12	899.01	956.43
13.0		308.45	713.51	877.86	947.30
14.0		167.02	654.92	852.88	936.53
15.0		0.00	585.73	823.38	923.80
16.0			504.01	788.54	908.77
17.0			407.51	747.40	891.02
18.0			293.54	698.81	870.06
19.0			158.95	641.43	845.30
20.0			0.00	573.66	816.06
21.0				493.63	781.53
22.0				399.12	740.76
23.0				287.50	692.60
24.0				155.68	635.73
25.0				0.00	568.56
26.0					489.24
27.0					395.57
28.0					284.94
29.0					154.29
30.0					0.00

REMAINING BALANCE PER $1000 OF ORIGINAL LOAN
ANNUAL INTEREST RATE: 17%

AGE OF LOAN	LOAN MATURITY (YEARS)				
	10	15	20	25	30
0.5	980.03	992.39	996.88	998.69	999.44
1.0	958.29	984.12	993.49	997.26	998.83
1.5	934.64	975.12	989.80	995.70	998.17
2.0	908.91	965.32	985.79	994.01	997.45
2.5	880.92	954.66	981.42	992.17	996.66
3.0	850.46	943.06	976.67	990.17	995.81
3.5	817.31	930.44	971.50	987.99	994.88
4.0	781.25	916.71	965.87	985.61	993.87
4.5	742.01	901.77	959.75	983.03	992.77
5.0	699.32	885.52	953.08	980.23	991.57
5.5	652.86	867.83	945.84	977.17	990.27
6.0	602.31	848.58	937.95	973.85	988.85
6.5	547.32	827.64	929.37	970.23	987.31
7.0	487.47	804.86	920.03	966.30	985.63
7.5	422.36	780.07	909.87	962.01	983.80
8.0	351.52	753.09	898.82	957.36	981.82
8.5	274.43	723.74	886.79	952.29	979.66
9.0	190.56	691.81	873.70	946.77	977.31
9.5	99.30	657.06	859.46	940.77	974.75
10.0	0.00	619.25	843.97	934.24	971.96
11.0		533.36	808.77	919.40	965.64
12.0		431.67	767.10	901.84	958.15
13.0		311.27	717.76	881.05	949.28
14.0		168.74	659.35	856.43	938.79
15.0		0.00	590.20	827.28	926.36
16.0			508.34	792.78	911.65
17.0			411.41	751.93	894.24
18.0			296.67	703.57	873.62
19.0			160.83	646.31	849.21
20.0			0.00	578.53	820.31
21.0				498.28	786.10
22.0				403.28	745.59
23.0				290.80	697.64
24.0				157.65	640.87
25.0				0.00	573.65
26.0					494.08
27.0					399.88
28.0					288.35
29.0					156.32
30.0					0.00

REMAINING BALANCE PER $1000 OF ORIGINAL LOAN
ANNUAL INTEREST RATE: 17.25%

AGE OF LOAN	LOAN MATURITY (YEARS)				
	10	15	20	25	30
0.5	980.32	992.58	996.99	998.75	999.47
1.0	958.89	984.50	993.72	997.38	998.90
1.5	935.54	975.70	990.15	995.90	998.27
2.0	910.10	966.11	986.26	994.28	997.59
2.5	882.38	955.66	982.03	992.51	996.84
3.0	852.19	944.28	977.41	990.59	996.04
3.5	819.30	931.88	972.39	988.49	995.15
4.0	783.46	918.37	966.91	986.21	994.19
4.5	744.43	903.65	960.95	983.73	993.14
5.0	701.90	887.62	954.45	981.02	992.00
5.5	655.57	870.16	947.37	978.07	990.76
6.0	605.10	851.13	939.65	974.86	989.41
6.5	550.11	830.40	931.25	971.36	987.93
7.0	490.21	807.82	922.10	967.54	986.33
7.5	424.96	783.22	912.13	963.39	984.57
8.0	353.87	756.42	901.26	958.86	982.67
8.5	276.42	727.23	889.43	953.93	980.59
9.0	192.05	695.42	876.54	948.56	978.33
9.5	100.13	660.77	862.49	942.71	975.86
10.0	0.00	623.02	847.19	936.33	973.18
11.0		537.10	812.36	921.82	967.06
12.0		435.12	771.02	904.60	959.81
13.0		314.10	721.96	884.16	951.19
14.0		170.47	663.74	859.90	940.97
15.0		0.00	594.64	831.11	928.84
16.0			512.63	796.94	914.45
17.0			415.30	756.39	897.36
18.0			299.79	708.26	877.09
19.0			162.70	651.14	853.02
20.0			0.00	583.35	824.46
21.0				502.90	790.57
22.0				407.42	750.34
23.0				294.10	702.60
24.0				159.61	645.94
25.0				0.00	578.69
26.0					498.88
27.0					404.16
28.0					291.75
29.0					158.34
30.0					0.00

REMAINING BALANCE PER $1000 OF ORIGINAL LOAN
ANNUAL INTEREST RATE: 17.5%

AGE OF LOAN	LOAN MATURITY (YEARS)				
	10	15	20	25	30
0.5	980.62	992.77	997.10	998.81	999.50
1.0	959.48	984.88	993.94	997.50	998.96
1.5	936.42	976.27	990.48	996.08	998.37
2.0	911.27	966.88	986.72	994.53	997.72
2.5	883.83	956.64	982.62	992.84	997.02
3.0	853.91	945.47	978.14	991.00	996.25
3.5	821.27	933.29	973.25	988.98	995.41
4.0	785.66	920.00	967.92	986.79	994.50
4.5	746.83	905.51	962.11	984.40	993.50
5.0	704.47	889.70	955.77	981.79	992.42
5.5	658.27	872.45	948.86	978.94	991.23
6.0	607.87	853.65	941.32	975.83	989.94
6.5	552.91	833.13	933.09	972.44	988.53
7.0	492.95	810.75	924.12	968.75	986.99
7.5	427.55	786.34	914.33	964.72	985.31
8.0	356.22	759.72	903.66	960.32	983.48
8.5	278.41	730.68	892.02	955.52	981.48
9.0	193.54	699.00	879.31	950.29	979.31
9.5	100.97	664.45	865.46	944.59	976.93
10.0	0.00	626.77	850.35	938.37	974.34
11.0		540.82	815.89	924.17	968.43
12.0		438.58	774.90	907.29	961.40
13.0		316.93	726.12	887.20	953.04
14.0		172.19	668.09	863.30	943.09
15.0		0.00	599.05	834.86	931.25
16.0			516.91	801.03	917.16
17.0			419.18	760.78	900.41
18.0			302.91	712.89	880.47
19.0			164.58	655.92	856.75
20.0			0.00	588.14	828.53
21.0				507.49	794.96
22.0				411.54	755.01
23.0				297.39	707.49
24.0				161.58	650.95
25.0				0.00	583.68
26.0					503.64
27.0					408.42
28.0					295.14
29.0					160.36
30.0					0.00

REMAINING BALANCE PER $1000 OF ORIGINAL LOAN
ANNUAL INTEREST RATE: REMAINING BALANCE PER $1000 OF
ORIGINAL LOAN ANNUAL INTEREST RATE: 17.75%

AGE OF LOAN	LOAN MATURITY (YEARS)				
	10	15	20	25	30
0.5	980.91	992.95	997.20	998.86	999.53
1.0	960.06	985.24	994.15	997.62	999.02
1.5	937.29	976.83	990.81	996.26	998.46
2.0	912.42	967.64	987.17	994.78	997.85
2.5	885.27	957.60	983.19	993.15	997.18
3.0	855.61	946.65	978.84	991.39	996.46
3.5	823.22	934.68	974.09	989.45	995.66
4.0	787.85	921.61	968.91	987.34	994.79
4.5	749.22	907.33	963.25	985.04	993.84
5.0	707.03	891.74	957.07	982.52	992.81
5.5	660.96	874.72	950.32	979.77	991.68
6.0	610.64	856.13	942.94	976.77	990.44
6.5	555.69	835.82	934.89	973.49	989.09
7.0	495.68	813.65	926.10	969.91	987.62
7.5	430.14	789.43	916.49	966.00	986.01
8.0	358.57	762.98	906.00	961.73	984.26
8.5	280.40	734.10	894.55	957.07	982.34
9.0	195.04	702.56	882.04	951.98	980.24
9.5	101.81	668.11	868.38	946.41	977.95
10.0	0.00	630.49	853.46	940.34	975.46
11.0		544.53	819.37	926.46	969.75
12.0		442.02	778.71	909.91	962.94
13.0		319.75	730.23	890.17	954.82
14.0		173.92	672.39	866.62	945.13
15.0		0.00	603.42	838.54	933.58
16.0			521.16	805.05	919.80
17.0			423.04	765.10	903.37
18.0			306.02	717.46	883.77
19.0			166.46	660.64	860.39
20.0			0.00	592.87	832.51
21.0				512.05	799.26
22.0				415.65	759.60
23.0				300.67	712.30
24.0				163.55	655.89
25.0				0.00	588.61
26.0					508.36
27.0					412.66
28.0					298.51
29.0					162.37
30.0					0.00

REMAINING BALANCE PER $1000 OF ORIGINAL LOAN
ANNUAL INTEREST RATE: 18%

AGE OF LOAN	LOAN MATURITY (YEARS)				
	10	15	20	25	30
0.5	981.20	993.12	997.30	998.91	999.56
1.0	960.63	985.60	994.35	997.73	999.08
1.5	938.15	977.38	991.13	996.43	998.55
2.0	913.57	968.38	987.60	995.01	997.97
2.5	886.69	958.55	983.74	993.46	997.34
3.0	857.30	947.80	979.52	991.76	996.65
3.5	825.16	936.04	974.91	989.90	995.90
4.0	790.02	923.19	969.87	987.87	995.07
4.5	751.59	909.13	964.36	985.66	994.17
5.0	709.57	893.76	958.33	983.23	993.18
5.5	663.63	876.95	951.74	980.58	992.10
6.0	613.40	858.58	944.53	977.68	990.93
6.5	558.47	838.48	936.65	974.50	989.64
7.0	498.40	816.51	928.03	971.04	988.23
7.5	432.73	792.49	918.60	967.24	986.68
8.0	360.92	766.22	908.30	963.10	985.00
8.5	282.40	737.49	897.03	958.56	983.16
9.0	196.54	706.08	884.71	953.61	981.14
9.5	102.65	671.74	871.24	948.18	978.94
10.0	0.00	634.19	856.51	942.26	976.53
11.0		548.23	822.80	928.69	971.01
12.0		445.45	782.48	912.46	964.42
13.0		322.57	734.29	893.07	956.53
14.0		175.66	676.66	869.88	947.10
15.0		0.00	607.76	842.15	935.83
16.0			525.38	809.00	922.36
17.0			426.89	769.36	906.24
18.0			309.13	721.97	886.98
19.0			168.34	665.31	863.95
20.0			0.00	597.57	836.41
21.0				516.57	803.48
22.0				419.73	764.12
23.0				303.95	717.05
24.0				165.51	660.78
25.0				0.00	593.49
26.0					513.05
27.0					416.87
28.0					301.87
29.0					164.38
30.0					0.00

REMAINING BALANCE PER $1000 OF ORIGINAL LOAN
ANNUAL INTEREST RATE: 18.25%

AGE OF LOAN	LOAN MATURITY (YEARS)				
	10	15	20	25	30
0.5	981.48	993.29	997.40	998.97	999.58
1.0	961.20	985.95	994.55	997.83	999.13
1.5	939.01	977.91	991.43	996.59	998.63
2.0	914.70	969.11	988.02	995.23	998.09
2.5	888.10	959.48	984.28	993.75	997.49
3.0	858.97	948.93	980.19	992.12	996.83
3.5	827.08	937.38	975.71	990.34	996.12
4.0	792.17	924.74	970.80	988.39	995.33
4.5	753.95	910.90	965.43	986.25	994.48
5.0	712.11	895.74	959.55	983.91	993.54
5.5	666.30	879.15	953.12	981.35	992.51
6.0	616.14	860.99	946.07	978.55	991.38
6.5	561.24	841.11	938.36	975.48	990.15
7.0	501.13	819.34	929.92	972.12	988.80
7.5	435.32	795.51	920.67	968.44	987.32
8.0	363.27	769.42	910.55	964.42	985.71
8.5	284.39	740.85	899.47	960.01	983.94
9.0	198.04	709.58	887.34	955.18	982.00
9.5	103.50	675.34	874.05	949.90	979.88
10.0	0.00	637.86	859.51	944.12	977.55
11.0		551.91	826.17	930.85	972.23
12.0		448.88	786.20	914.95	965.84
13.0		325.40	738.30	895.90	958.19
14.0		177.39	680.88	873.06	949.01
15.0		0.00	612.06	845.69	938.02
16.0			529.58	812.88	924.84
17.0			430.72	773.55	909.04
18.0			312.23	726.42	890.11
19.0			170.22	669.93	867.42
20.0			0.00	602.22	840.22
21.0				521.06	807.62
22.0				423.79	768.55
23.0				307.21	721.72
24.0				167.48	665.60
25.0				0.00	598.33
26.0					517.70
27.0					421.06
28.0					305.23
29.0					166.40
30.0					0.00

REMAINING BALANCE PER $1000 OF ORIGINAL LOAN
ANNUAL INTEREST RATE: 18.5%

AGE OF LOAN	LOAN MATURITY (YEARS)				
	10	15	20	25	30
0.5	981.76	993.46	997.49	999.01	999.61
1.0	961.77	986.29	994.74	997.93	999.18
1.5	939.85	978.44	991.73	996.75	998.71
2.0	915.83	969.82	988.42	995.45	998.19
2.5	889.49	960.38	984.80	994.02	997.63
3.0	860.63	950.04	980.83	992.46	997.01
3.5	828.99	938.69	976.48	990.75	996.33
4.0	794.31	926.26	971.71	988.88	995.59
4.5	756.29	912.63	966.48	986.82	994.77
5.0	714.62	897.70	960.75	984.57	993.87
5.5	668.95	881.32	954.47	982.10	992.89
6.0	618.88	863.37	947.58	979.39	991.82
6.5	564.00	843.70	940.03	976.42	990.64
7.0	503.84	822.13	931.76	973.17	989.35
7.5	437.90	798.49	922.69	969.60	987.94
8.0	365.62	772.58	912.75	965.69	986.38
8.5	286.39	744.18	901.85	961.41	984.68
9.0	199.54	713.05	889.91	956.71	982.82
9.5	104.35	678.92	876.81	951.57	980.78
10.0	0.00	641.51	862.46	945.92	978.54
11.0		555.56	829.48	932.96	973.39
12.0		452.29	789.86	917.38	967.21
13.0		328.21	742.26	898.66	959.78
14.0		179.13	685.06	876.17	950.85
15.0		0.00	616.33	849.15	940.13
16.0			533.76	816.68	927.24
17.0			434.54	777.67	911.76
18.0			315.33	730.80	893.16
19.0			172.10	674.49	870.81
20.0			0.00	606.82	843.95
21.0				525.52	811.68
22.0				427.84	772.91
23.0				310.47	726.33
24.0				169.44	670.36
25.0				0.00	603.11
26.0					522.30
27.0					425.22
28.0					308.56
29.0					168.40
30.0					0.00

REMAINING BALANCE PER $1000 OF ORIGINAL LOAN
ANNUAL INTEREST RATE: 18.75%

AGE OF LOAN	LOAN MATURITY (YEARS)				
	10	15	20	25	30
0.5	982.04	993.63	997.58	999.06	999.63
1.0	962.32	986.63	994.93	998.03	999.23
1.5	940.68	978.95	992.01	996.90	998.78
2.0	916.94	970.52	988.82	995.65	998.30
2.5	890.88	961.28	985.31	994.29	997.76
3.0	862.27	951.13	981.46	992.79	997.17
3.5	830.88	939.99	977.23	991.15	996.53
4.0	796.43	927.76	972.59	989.35	995.82
4.5	758.62	914.34	967.50	987.37	995.05
5.0	717.13	899.62	961.91	985.20	994.20
5.5	671.58	883.46	955.78	982.82	993.26
6.0	621.60	865.72	949.05	980.20	992.24
6.5	566.75	846.26	941.67	977.33	991.11
7.0	506.55	824.89	933.56	974.18	989.87
7.5	440.48	801.45	924.66	970.72	988.52
8.0	367.97	775.72	914.90	966.93	987.03
8.5	288.39	747.48	904.19	962.76	985.40
9.0	201.05	716.49	892.43	958.19	983.61
9.5	105.20	682.47	879.52	953.18	981.64
10.0	0.00	645.14	865.36	947.67	979.48
11.0		559.21	832.75	935.00	974.51
12.0		455.70	793.48	919.74	968.53
13.0		331.03	746.17	901.36	961.32
14.0		180.87	689.20	879.22	952.63
15.0		0.00	620.57	852.55	942.17
16.0			537.91	820.42	929.58
17.0			438.35	781.73	914.40
18.0			318.42	735.13	896.13
19.0			173.98	678.99	874.11
20.0			0.00	611.38	847.60
21.0				529.95	815.66
22.0				431.86	777.19
23.0				313.71	730.86
24.0				171.40	675.05
25.0				0.00	607.83
26.0					526.87
27.0					429.35
28.0					311.89
29.0					170.41
30.0					0.00

REMAINING BALANCE PER $1000 OF ORIGINAL LOAN
ANNUAL INTEREST RATE: 19%

AGE OF LOAN	LOAN MATURITY (YEARS)				
	10	15	20	25	30
0.5	982.31	993.79	997.67	999.10	999.65
1.0	962.87	986.96	995.11	998.12	999.27
1.5	941.51	979.45	992.29	997.04	998.85
2.0	918.04	971.21	989.20	995.85	998.39
2.5	892.24	962.15	985.80	994.54	997.89
3.0	863.90	952.20	982.06	993.11	997.33
3.5	832.76	941.26	977.96	991.53	996.72
4.0	798.54	929.24	973.45	989.80	996.05
4.5	760.94	916.03	968.49	987.90	995.31
5.0	719.62	901.51	963.05	985.81	994.50
5.5	674.21	885.57	957.06	983.51	993.61
6.0	624.32	868.04	950.48	980.98	992.63
6.5	569.50	848.78	943.26	978.21	991.56
7.0	509.25	827.62	935.32	975.16	990.37
7.5	443.06	804.37	926.59	971.80	989.07
8.0	370.32	778.82	917.01	968.12	987.65
8.5	290.39	750.75	906.47	964.08	986.08
9.0	202.56	719.89	894.90	959.63	984.36
9.5	106.05	685.99	882.18	954.74	982.46
10.0	0.00	648.74	868.20	949.38	980.38
11.0		562.83	835.96	936.99	975.59
12.0		459.10	797.04	922.04	969.79
13.0		333.85	750.04	903.99	962.80
14.0		182.61	693.29	882.19	954.35
15.0		0.00	624.77	855.87	944.15
16.0			542.03	824.10	931.84
17.0			442.13	785.72	916.97
18.0			321.51	739.39	899.02
19.0			175.86	683.45	877.34
20.0			0.00	615.90	851.17
21.0				534.34	819.56
22.0				435.86	781.40
23.0				316.95	735.33
24.0				173.37	679.69
25.0				0.00	612.51
26.0					531.40
27.0					433.46
28.0					315.20
29.0					172.41
30.0					0.00

REMAINING BALANCE PER $1000 OF ORIGINAL LOAN
ANNUAL INTEREST RATE: 19.25%

AGE OF LOAN	LOAN MATURITY (YEARS)				
	10	15	20	25	30
0.5	982.58	993.94	997.75	999.15	999.67
1.0	963.41	987.28	995.28	998.21	999.31
1.5	942.32	979.95	992.56	997.18	998.92
2.0	919.12	971.88	989.57	996.04	998.48
2.5	893.60	963.01	986.27	994.79	998.00
3.0	865.52	953.24	982.65	993.41	997.48
3.5	834.62	942.50	978.66	991.90	996.90
4.0	800.63	930.68	974.28	990.24	996.26
4.5	763.24	917.68	969.45	988.40	995.56
5.0	722.09	903.38	964.15	986.39	994.79
5.5	676.83	887.64	958.31	984.17	993.94
6.0	627.02	870.32	951.88	981.73	993.01
6.5	572.23	851.27	944.81	979.05	991.98
7.0	511.95	830.32	937.04	976.10	990.85
7.5	445.63	807.26	928.48	972.85	989.60
8.0	372.67	781.89	919.07	969.28	988.24
8.5	292.39	753.98	908.71	965.34	986.73
9.0	204.07	723.27	897.32	961.02	985.08
9.5	106.90	689.49	884.78	956.26	983.25
10.0	0.00	652.32	870.99	951.02	981.25
11.0		566.44	839.12	938.93	976.62
12.0		462.49	800.55	924.28	971.01
13.0		336.66	753.86	906.56	964.22
14.0		184.35	697.34	885.10	956.01
15.0		0.00	628.93	859.13	946.07
16.0			546.13	827.70	934.03
17.0			445.90	789.65	919.47
18.0			324.59	743.60	901.83
19.0			177.74	687.85	880.49
20.0			0.00	620.37	854.66
21.0				538.70	823.39
22.0				439.84	785.54
23.0				320.17	739.72
24.0				175.32	684.26
25.0				0.00	617.14
26.0					535.89
27.0					437.54
28.0					318.50
29.0					174.41
30.0					0.00

REMAINING BALANCE PER $1000 OF ORIGINAL LOAN
ANNUAL INTEREST RATE: 19.5%

AGE OF LOAN	LOAN MATURITY (YEARS)				
	10	15	20	25	30
0.5	982.84	994.10	997.83	999.19	999.69
1.0	963.95	987.59	995.45	998.29	999.35
1.5	943.13	980.43	992.82	997.31	998.98
2.0	920.20	972.54	989.92	996.22	998.57
2.5	894.94	963.85	986.73	995.02	998.12
3.0	867.12	954.27	983.22	993.70	997.62
3.5	836.47	943.73	979.35	992.25	997.07
4.0	802.71	932.11	975.09	990.65	996.46
4.5	765.52	919.31	970.39	988.89	995.80
5.0	724.55	905.21	965.22	986.95	995.06
5.5	679.43	889.68	959.52	984.81	994.25
6.0	629.72	872.58	953.24	982.46	993.36
6.5	574.96	853.73	946.33	979.86	992.38
7.0	514.65	832.98	938.71	977.01	991.30
7.5	448.20	810.11	930.32	973.86	990.11
8.0	375.02	784.93	921.08	970.39	988.80
8.5	294.39	757.18	910.90	966.57	987.35
9.0	205.59	726.62	899.69	962.36	985.76
9.5	107.76	692.96	887.33	957.73	984.01
10.0	0.00	655.87	873.73	952.62	982.08
11.0		570.03	842.23	940.80	977.61
12.0		465.86	804.01	926.46	972.18
13.0		339.47	757.63	909.06	965.60
14.0		186.10	701.35	887.95	957.61
15.0		0.00	633.06	862.33	947.92
16.0			550.20	831.24	936.16
17.0			449.66	793.51	921.89
18.0			327.66	747.74	904.57
19.0			179.63	692.20	883.56
20.0			0.00	624.80	858.07
21.0				543.02	827.13
22.0				443.79	789.60
23.0				323.39	744.05
24.0				177.28	688.78
25.0				0.00	621.72
26.0					540.34
27.0					441.60
28.0					321.79
29.0					176.41
30.0					0.00

REMAINING BALANCE PER $1000 OF ORIGINAL LOAN
ANNUAL INTEREST RATE: 19.75%

AGE OF LOAN	LOAN MATURITY (YEARS)				
	10	15	20	25	30
0.5	983.11	994.25	997.91	999.23	999.71
1.0	964.48	987.90	995.61	998.37	999.39
1.5	943.93	980.90	993.07	997.43	999.04
2.0	921.27	973.18	990.27	996.39	998.65
2.5	896.27	964.67	987.18	995.25	998.22
3.0	868.71	955.28	983.77	993.98	997.75
3.5	838.30	944.93	980.02	992.59	997.23
4.0	804.77	933.51	975.87	991.05	996.66
4.5	767.79	920.91	971.30	989.36	996.02
5.0	727.00	907.02	966.26	987.49	995.32
5.5	682.02	891.70	960.70	985.43	994.55
6.0	632.40	874.80	954.57	983.15	993.70
6.5	577.68	856.16	947.81	980.65	992.77
7.0	517.33	835.60	940.35	977.88	991.73
7.5	450.77	812.93	932.12	974.83	990.59
8.0	377.36	787.93	923.05	971.47	989.34
8.5	296.40	760.35	913.05	967.76	987.95
9.0	207.10	729.94	902.01	963.66	986.42
9.5	108.62	696.40	889.84	959.15	984.73
10.0	0.00	659.40	876.42	954.17	982.87
11.0		573.60	845.28	942.63	978.56
12.0		469.23	807.41	928.59	973.31
13.0		342.27	761.35	911.50	966.92
14.0		187.85	705.31	890.73	959.16
15.0		0.00	637.15	865.45	949.71
16.0			554.25	834.71	938.22
17.0			453.40	797.31	924.24
18.0			330.73	751.82	907.24
19.0			181.51	696.49	886.56
20.0			0.00	629.18	861.40
21.0				547.31	830.80
22.0				447.73	793.58
23.0				326.59	748.31
24.0				179.24	693.23
25.0				0.00	626.24
26.0					544.75
27.0					445.63
28.0					325.06
29.0					178.40
30.0					0.00

REMAINING BALANCE PER $1000 OF ORIGINAL LOAN
ANNUAL INTEREST RATE: 20%

AGE OF LOAN	LOAN MATURITY (YEARS)				
	10	15	20	25	30
0.5	983.37	994.39	997.99	999.26	999.73
1.0	965.00	988.20	995.77	998.45	999.43
1.5	944.72	981.36	993.31	997.55	999.10
2.0	922.32	973.81	990.61	996.56	998.73
2.5	897.59	965.48	987.61	995.46	998.32
3.0	870.28	956.27	984.31	994.25	997.88
3.5	840.12	946.11	980.66	992.91	997.38
4.0	806.82	934.88	976.64	991.44	996.84
4.5	770.04	922.48	972.19	989.81	996.24
5.0	729.43	908.79	967.28	988.01	995.57
5.5	684.59	893.68	961.85	986.02	994.84
6.0	635.07	876.99	955.86	983.83	994.03
6.5	580.39	858.55	949.25	981.40	993.13
7.0	520.01	838.20	941.95	978.73	992.14
7.5	453.34	815.72	933.88	975.77	991.05
8.0	379.71	790.90	924.98	972.51	989.85
8.5	298.40	763.50	915.15	968.90	988.52
9.0	208.62	733.23	904.29	964.92	987.05
9.5	109.48	699.81	892.30	960.53	985.42
10.0	0.00	662.91	879.06	955.68	983.63
11.0		577.15	848.29	944.40	979.47
12.0		472.59	810.77	930.65	974.39
13.0		345.08	765.02	913.89	968.20
14.0		189.59	709.24	893.44	960.65
15.0		0.00	641.21	868.51	951.44
16.0			558.27	838.12	940.22
17.0			457.12	801.05	926.53
18.0			333.78	755.85	909.84
19.0			183.39	700.73	889.49
20.0			0.00	633.52	864.67
21.0				551.57	834.40
22.0				451.64	797.50
23.0				329.78	752.50
24.0				181.19	697.63
25.0				0.00	630.72
26.0					549.13
27.0					449.64
28.0					328.32
29.0					180.39
30.0					0.00

REMAINING BALANCE PER $1000 OF ORIGINAL LOAN
ANNUAL INTEREST RATE: 20.25%

AGE OF LOAN	LOAN MATURITY (YEARS)				
	10	15	20	25	30
0.5	983.62	994.54	998.06	999.30	999.74
1.0	965.52	988.50	995.92	998.52	999.46
1.5	945.50	981.82	993.55	997.66	999.15
2.0	923.36	974.43	990.93	996.71	998.80
2.5	898.89	966.27	988.03	995.67	998.42
3.0	871.84	957.24	984.83	994.51	998.00
3.5	841.92	947.26	981.29	993.22	997.53
4.0	808.85	936.23	977.38	991.81	997.01
4.5	772.28	924.03	973.05	990.24	996.44
5.0	731.85	910.54	968.26	988.51	995.81
5.5	687.16	895.63	962.97	986.59	995.11
6.0	637.74	879.14	957.12	984.47	994.33
6.5	583.10	860.92	950.66	982.13	993.48
7.0	522.69	840.76	943.51	979.54	992.54
7.5	455.90	818.48	935.60	976.68	991.49
8.0	382.05	793.84	926.86	973.51	990.34
8.5	300.41	766.61	917.20	970.01	989.06
9.0	210.14	736.49	906.52	966.14	987.65
9.5	110.34	703.20	894.71	961.86	986.09
10.0	0.00	666.38	881.65	957.13	984.36
11.0		580.69	851.24	946.12	980.34
12.0		475.93	814.08	932.66	975.43
13.0		347.88	768.65	916.21	969.43
14.0		191.34	713.12	896.10	962.09
15.0		0.00	645.24	871.51	953.12
16.0			562.26	841.46	942.16
17.0			460.83	804.72	928.75
18.0			336.84	759.82	912.37
19.0			185.27	704.92	892.34
20.0			0.00	637.82	867.86
21.0				555.80	837.93
22.0				455.53	801.35
23.0				332.96	756.63
24.0				183.14	701.97
25.0				0.00	635.15
26.0					553.46
27.0					453.62
28.0					331.57
29.0					182.37
30.0					0.00

REMAINING BALANCE PER $1000 OF ORIGINAL LOAN
ANNUAL INTEREST RATE: 20.5%

AGE OF LOAN	LOAN MATURITY (YEARS)				
	10	15	20	25	30
0.5	983.88	994.68	998.13	999.33	999.76
1.0	966.03	988.78	996.07	998.59	999.49
1.5	946.27	982.26	993.78	997.77	999.20
2.0	924.39	975.04	991.24	996.87	998.87
2.5	900.18	967.04	988.44	995.86	998.51
3.0	873.38	958.19	985.34	994.75	998.11
3.5	843.71	948.40	981.90	993.52	997.66
4.0	810.86	937.55	978.10	992.16	997.17
4.5	774.51	925.55	973.88	990.65	996.63
5.0	734.26	912.26	969.22	988.98	996.03
5.5	689.71	897.55	964.06	987.14	995.36
6.0	640.39	881.27	958.35	985.09	994.63
6.5	585.79	863.24	952.03	982.83	993.81
7.0	525.36	843.29	945.03	980.32	992.91
7.5	458.45	821.20	937.28	977.55	991.91
8.0	384.40	796.75	928.70	974.48	990.80
8.5	302.42	769.68	919.21	971.08	989.58
9.0	211.67	739.72	908.70	967.32	988.22
9.5	111.21	706.55	897.06	963.16	986.72
10.0	0.00	669.84	884.19	958.55	985.06
11.0		584.20	854.15	947.79	981.18
12.0		479.26	817.34	934.62	976.43
13.0		350.67	772.23	918.47	970.61
14.0		193.09	716.95	898.69	963.48
15.0		0.00	649.22	874.45	954.74
16.0			566.22	844.74	944.03
17.0			464.51	808.33	930.91
18.0			339.88	763.72	914.83
19.0			187.15	709.06	895.12
20.0			0.00	642.07	870.97
21.0				559.98	841.38
22.0				459.39	805.12
23.0				336.13	760.69
24.0				185.09	706.24
25.0				0.00	639.52
26.0					557.76
27.0					457.57
28.0					334.80
29.0					184.35
30.0					0.00

REMAINING BALANCE PER $1000 OF ORIGINAL LOAN
ANNUAL INTEREST RATE: 20.75%

AGE OF LOAN	LOAN MATURITY (YEARS)				
	10	15	20	25	30
0.5	984.12	994.81	998.20	999.36	999.77
1.0	966.53	989.06	996.21	998.66	999.52
1.5	947.03	982.69	994.00	997.88	999.24
2.0	925.41	975.63	991.55	997.01	998.94
2.5	901.46	967.80	988.83	996.05	998.59
3.0	874.91	959.13	985.82	994.99	998.21
3.5	845.48	949.51	982.49	993.81	997.79
4.0	812.87	938.86	978.79	992.50	997.33
4.5	776.72	927.05	974.70	991.05	996.81
5.0	736.65	913.95	970.16	989.44	996.24
5.5	692.24	899.45	965.12	987.66	995.61
6.0	643.03	883.36	959.55	985.69	994.90
6.5	588.48	865.54	953.37	983.50	994.12
7.0	528.02	845.79	946.51	981.08	993.26
7.5	461.01	823.89	938.92	978.39	992.31
8.0	386.74	799.63	930.50	975.42	991.25
8.5	304.42	772.73	921.18	972.12	990.07
9.0	213.19	742.92	910.84	968.46	988.77
9.5	112.07	709.88	899.38	964.41	987.32
10.0	0.00	673.26	886.68	959.92	985.72
11.0		587.70	857.00	949.42	981.99
12.0		482.58	820.55	936.52	977.39
13.0		353.46	775.76	920.68	971.75
14.0		194.85	720.75	901.22	964.82
15.0		0.00	653.17	877.32	956.31
16.0			570.16	847.96	945.85
17.0			468.18	811.88	933.00
18.0			342.91	767.57	917.22
19.0			189.03	713.14	897.84
20.0			0.00	646.28	874.02
21.0				564.14	844.77
22.0				463.24	808.83
23.0				339.29	764.69
24.0				187.04	710.46
25.0				0.00	643.85
26.0					562.02
27.0					461.50
28.0					338.02
29.0					186.33
30.0					0.00

657

REMAINING BALANCE PER $1000 OF ORIGINAL LOAN
ANNUAL INTEREST RATE: 21%

AGE OF LOAN	LOAN MATURITY (YEARS)				
	10	15	20	25	30
0.5	984.37	994.95	998.27	999.39	999.79
1.0	967.03	989.34	996.34	998.72	999.55
1.5	947.78	983.12	994.21	997.98	999.29
2.0	926.42	976.21	991.84	997.15	999.00
2.5	902.72	968.55	989.21	996.23	998.67
3.0	876.42	960.04	986.30	995.21	998.31
3.5	847.24	950.61	983.06	994.08	997.92
4.0	814.85	940.14	979.47	992.82	997.48
4.5	778.91	928.51	975.49	991.43	996.98
5.0	739.03	915.62	971.06	989.89	996.44
5.5	694.77	901.31	966.16	988.17	995.84
6.0	645.66	885.43	960.71	986.27	995.17
6.5	591.15	867.81	954.67	984.15	994.42
7.0	530.67	848.25	947.96	981.81	993.60
7.5	463.56	826.55	940.52	979.21	992.68
8.0	389.08	802.47	932.26	976.32	991.67
8.5	306.43	775.75	923.10	973.12	990.54
9.0	214.72	746.09	912.93	969.57	989.29
9.5	112.94	713.19	901.65	965.62	987.90
10.0	0.00	676.67	889.13	961.24	986.36
11.0		591.18	859.81	951.00	982.76
12.0		485.90	823.71	938.38	978.32
13.0		356.25	779.25	922.84	972.85
14.0		196.60	724.51	903.70	966.11
15.0		0.00	657.09	880.13	957.82
16.0			574.07	851.11	947.61
17.0			471.84	815.38	935.04
18.0			345.94	771.37	919.55
19.0			190.91	717.18	900.48
20.0			0.00	650.44	877.00
21.0				568.26	848.08
22.0				467.06	812.47
23.0				342.44	768.62
24.0				188.98	714.62
25.0				0.00	648.13
26.0					566.24
27.0					465.40
28.0					341.22
29.0					188.31
30.0					0.00

REMAINING BALANCE PER $1000 OF ORIGINAL LOAN
ANNUAL INTEREST RATE: 21.25%

AGE OF LOAN	LOAN MATURITY (YEARS)				
	10	15	20	25	30
0.5	984.61	995.08	998.33	999.42	999.80
1.0	967.52	989.61	996.48	998.78	999.58
1.5	948.53	983.53	994.42	998.07	999.33
2.0	927.42	976.78	992.13	997.28	999.05
2.5	903.97	969.28	989.58	996.40	998.75
3.0	877.92	960.94	986.76	995.43	998.41
3.5	848.98	951.68	983.62	994.34	998.03
4.0	816.82	941.39	980.13	993.14	997.61
4.5	781.09	929.96	976.25	991.80	997.15
5.0	741.39	917.26	971.95	990.31	996.63
5.5	697.28	903.14	967.16	988.66	996.06
6.0	648.27	887.46	961.85	986.82	995.42
6.5	593.82	870.04	955.94	984.78	994.71
7.0	533.32	850.68	949.38	982.51	993.92
7.5	466.10	829.18	942.08	979.99	993.04
8.0	391.42	805.28	933.98	977.20	992.07
8.5	308.44	778.73	924.98	974.09	990.99
9.0	216.25	749.23	914.98	970.63	989.79
9.5	113.81	716.46	903.87	966.79	988.46
10.0	0.00	680.04	891.52	962.53	986.97
11.0		594.63	862.57	952.52	983.50
12.0		489.19	826.82	940.18	979.20
13.0		359.03	782.69	924.93	973.90
14.0		198.35	728.21	906.11	967.36
15.0		0.00	660.96	882.88	959.28
16.0			577.95	854.21	949.32
17.0			475.47	818.81	937.01
18.0			348.96	775.10	921.82
19.0			192.79	721.16	903.06
20.0			0.00	654.56	879.91
21.0				572.35	851.33
22.0				470.86	816.05
23.0				345.58	772.49
24.0				190.92	718.73
25.0				0.00	652.35
26.0					570.42
27.0					469.27
28.0					344.41
29.0					190.28
30.0					0.00

REMAINING BALANCE PER $1000 OF ORIGINAL LOAN
ANNUAL INTEREST RATE: 21.5%

AGE OF LOAN	LOAN MATURITY (YEARS)				
	10	15	20	25	30
0.5	984.85	995.20	998.39	999.45	999.81
1.0	968.00	989.87	996.60	998.84	999.60
1.5	949.26	983.94	994.62	998.16	999.37
2.0	928.41	977.33	992.40	997.41	999.11
2.5	905.21	969.99	989.94	996.57	998.82
3.0	879.41	961.82	987.20	995.63	998.50
3.5	850.71	952.73	984.16	994.59	998.14
4.0	818.77	942.62	980.77	993.43	997.75
4.5	783.25	931.38	977.00	992.15	997.30
5.0	743.74	918.87	972.80	990.72	996.81
5.5	699.78	904.95	968.14	989.12	996.26
6.0	650.88	889.47	962.95	987.35	995.66
6.5	596.48	872.24	957.18	985.38	994.98
7.0	535.96	853.08	950.76	983.19	994.23
7.5	468.65	831.77	943.61	980.75	993.39
8.0	393.76	808.06	935.66	978.04	992.46
8.5	310.45	781.69	926.82	975.02	991.42
9.0	217.78	752.34	916.99	971.66	990.27
9.5	114.68	719.70	906.05	967.93	988.98
10.0	0.00	683.39	893.88	963.77	987.56
11.0		598.07	865.28	954.01	984.20
12.0		492.48	829.88	941.93	980.05
13.0		361.81	786.08	926.98	974.92
14.0		200.11	731.88	908.48	968.56
15.0		0.00	664.81	885.58	960.70
16.0			581.80	857.24	950.97
17.0			479.09	822.18	938.93
18.0			351.97	778.79	924.02
19.0			194.67	725.09	905.58
20.0			0.00	658.64	882.75
21.0				576.40	854.51
22.0				474.64	819.56
23.0				348.70	776.30
24.0				192.86	722.78
25.0				0.00	656.54
26.0					574.57
27.0					473.13
28.0					347.59
29.0					192.24
30.0					0.00

REMAINING BALANCE PER $1000 OF ORIGINAL LOAN
ANNUAL INTEREST RATE: 21.75%

AGE OF LOAN	LOAN MATURITY (YEARS)				
	10	15	20	25	30
0.5	985.09	995.33	998.45	999.48	999.82
1.0	968.48	990.13	996.73	998.90	999.63
1.5	949.99	984.33	994.81	998.25	999.41
2.0	929.39	977.88	992.67	997.53	999.16
2.5	906.44	970.69	990.29	996.72	998.89
3.0	880.88	962.68	987.63	995.83	998.58
3.5	852.42	953.77	984.68	994.83	998.25
4.0	820.71	943.83	981.39	993.72	997.87
4.5	785.40	932.77	977.72	992.48	997.45
5.0	746.07	920.45	973.64	991.11	996.98
5.5	702.26	906.73	969.09	989.57	996.46
6.0	653.47	891.44	964.03	987.86	995.88
6.5	599.13	874.42	958.38	985.96	995.24
7.0	538.60	855.45	952.10	983.84	994.52
7.5	471.18	834.33	945.10	981.48	993.72
8.0	396.09	810.81	937.31	978.85	992.82
8.5	312.46	784.61	928.62	975.92	991.83
9.0	219.31	755.43	918.95	972.66	990.72
9.5	115.56	722.92	908.18	969.03	989.49
10.0	0.00	686.72	896.18	964.98	988.12
11.0		601.49	867.94	955.45	984.88
12.0		495.75	832.90	943.63	980.87
13.0		364.58	789.43	928.97	975.90
14.0		201.86	735.51	910.78	969.73
15.0		0.00	668.62	888.22	962.07
16.0			585.63	860.22	952.57
17.0			482.68	825.49	940.79
18.0			354.97	782.41	926.17
19.0			196.54	728.97	908.03
20.0			0.00	662.67	885.54
21.0				580.42	857.63
22.0				478.39	823.00
23.0				351.82	780.05
24.0				194.79	726.77
25.0				0.00	660.67
26.0					578.67
27.0					476.95
28.0					350.76
29.0					194.21
30.0					0.00

661

MORTGAGE VALUE TABLES
(Value of Amortizing Mortgage Loans as Percentage of Face Value)

Mortgage loans can be an investment medium as well as a method for financing a home purchase. When viewed as an investment, a loan has a market value just as a share of stock or a bond. The value of the loan depends in part on the face interest rate of the loan compared with current interest rates. The following tables provide the relative value of mortgage loans for various combinations of face rates and market rates.

To use the tables, you need the following information:

1. *The interest rate on the loan* (face interest rate). Each page covers a different rate ranging from 6% to 17.75% in intervals of .25%.

2. *The yield demanded by secondary investors* (yield to maturity). Even though the loan is contracted at a certain interest rate, the yield may be raised or lowered by adjusting the price paid for the loan. The yield to maturity is the rate desired by the investor. Each page covers yields from 10 to 19.00% in .25% intervals.

3. *The remaining term of the loan.* How many years will the loan run after being purchased by the investor? The tables cover terms of 10, 15, 20, 25, and 30 years. Use the column which is closest to the actual remaining term.

4. *The remaining balance of the loan* (face value). What is the balance of the loan when the investor makes the purchase?

Example. A home seller provides a loan as part of the sales arrangement. After holding the loan for two years, the seller decides to sell the loan to secondary investors. The loan still has 23 years until maturity and a remaining principal balance of $45,000. The interest rate on the loan is 6%. If investors require a yield to maturity of 15% on 25-year amortizing home mortgage loans, what is the loan worth in the market?

Look at the first table. At the top is listed the "FACE INTEREST RATE" of 6%. Under the column for "YIELD TO MATURITY" find the yield of 15.0%. Follow this row over to the column under "TERM OF LOAN 25" (this is the closest to the actual term of 23 years). The value factor is 50.303. That is, the loan is worth 50.303 cents per dollar of face value. Multiply this percentage by the balance of the loan, or $45,000. The result is $22,636, which is the market value of the loan.

Example. A home seller is willing to provide financing to assist in making a sale. The seller makes an offer to provide a loan at 6% interest over a term of 20 years. The seller intends to sell the loan to investors who desire a yield to maturity of 12%. What should be the amount of the loan if the seller wants to get $50,000 cash from its sale?

Look at the table for "FACE INTEREST RATE" of 6%. Under the column "YIELD TO MATURITY" find the rate 12.0%. Follow the row to the column under "TERM OF LOAN 20." The value factor is 65.066. Divide the value desired, $50,000, by the percentage value factor, .65066, to obtain the result of $76,845. This is the face value of the loan which serves the seller's purpose.

663

VALUE OF AMORTIZING MORTGAGE LOANS
AS PERCENTAGE OF FACE VALUE
FACE INTEREST RATE: 6%

YIELD TO MATURITY	TERM OF LOAN (YEARS)				
	10	15	20	25	30
10.00	84.010	78.527	74.240	70.903	68.319
10.25	83.137	77.422	72.983	69.550	66.907
10.50	82.277	76.339	71.759	68.239	65.543
10.75	81.430	75.281	70.568	66.969	64.227
11.00	80.596	74.244	69.409	65.737	62.957
11.25	79.774	73.229	68.280	64.544	61.729
11.50	78.964	72.236	67.180	63.386	60.543
11.75	78.167	71.263	66.109	62.263	59.396
12.00	77.382	70.312	65.066	61.174	58.287
12.25	76.608	69.379	64.049	60.117	57.215
12.50	75.846	68.466	63.058	59.091	56.177
12.75	75.095	67.571	62.093	58.095	55.172
13.00	74.355	66.695	61.151	57.127	54.199
13.25	73.626	65.837	60.233	56.187	53.257
13.50	72.908	64.996	59.338	55.274	52.344
13.75	72.200	64.172	58.465	54.387	51.459
14.00	71.503	63.365	57.613	53.524	50.600
14.25	70.816	62.574	56.782	52.685	49.768
14.50	70.139	61.798	55.971	51.869	48.961
14.75	69.471	61.038	55.180	51.076	48.177
15.00	68.814	60.293	54.407	50.303	47.416
15.25	68.165	59.563	53.653	49.552	46.677
15.50	67.526	58.847	52.917	48.820	45.960
15.75	66.896	58.144	52.198	48.108	45.262
16.00	66.276	57.456	51.495	47.414	44.584
16.25	65.664	56.781	50.809	46.738	43.925
16.50	65.060	56.118	50.139	46.079	43.284
16.75	64.466	55.469	49.483	45.437	42.661
17.00	63.879	54.831	48.843	44.812	42.054
17.25	63.301	54.206	48.217	44.202	41.463
17.50	62.731	53.593	47.605	43.607	40.888
17.75	62.169	52.990	47.007	43.026	40.328
18.00	61.615	52.400	46.422	42.460	39.782
18.25	61.068	51.820	45.849	41.907	39.250
18.50	60.529	51.251	45.289	41.368	38.732
18.75	59.998	50.692	44.742	40.841	38.227
19.00	59.473	50.144	44.205	40.327	37.734

VALUE OF AMORTIZING MORTGAGE LOANS
AS PERCENTAGE OF FACE VALUE
FACE INTEREST RATE: 6.25%

YIELD TO MATURITY	TERM OF LOAN (YEARS)				
	10	15	20	25	30
10.00	84.963	79.789	75.742	72.594	70.161
10.25	84.080	78.666	74.459	71.209	68.710
10.50	83.210	77.566	73.211	69.866	67.310
10.75	82.353	76.490	71.996	68.566	65.959
11.00	81.510	75.437	70.813	67.305	64.654
11.25	80.678	74.406	69.661	66.083	63.393
11.50	79.860	73.397	68.539	64.898	62.175
11.75	79.053	72.409	67.446	63.748	60.997
12.00	78.259	71.441	66.382	62.633	59.859
12.25	77.477	70.494	65.345	61.551	58.757
12.50	76.706	69.566	64.334	60.500	57.691
12.75	75.946	68.657	63.349	59.480	56.659
13.00	75.198	67.767	62.388	58.490	55.660
13.25	74.461	66.895	61.452	57.527	54.693
13.50	73.735	66.041	60.538	56.592	53.755
13.75	73.019	65.203	59.647	55.684	52.846
14.00	72.314	64.383	58.779	54.800	51.965
14.25	71.619	63.579	57.931	53.942	51.110
14.50	70.934	62.791	57.104	53.106	50.281
14.75	70.259	62.019	56.296	52.294	49.476
15.00	69.594	61.262	55.508	51.503	48.695
15.25	68.938	60.520	54.739	50.733	47.936
15.50	68.292	59.792	53.987	49.984	47.199
15.75	67.655	59.079	53.254	49.255	46.482
16.00	67.027	58.379	52.537	48.545	45.786
16.25	66.408	57.693	51.837	47.852	45.109
16.50	65.798	57.020	51.153	47.178	44.451
16.75	65.196	56.360	50.484	46.521	43.811
17.00	64.604	55.713	49.831	45.880	43.188
17.25	64.019	55.077	49.193	45.256	42.581
17.50	63.442	54.454	48.568	44.647	41.990
17.75	62.874	53.842	47.958	44.052	41.415
18.00	62.313	53.242	47.361	43.473	40.855
18.25	61.760	52.653	46.777	42.907	40.309
18.50	61.215	52.074	46.206	42.355	39.776
18.75	60.678	51.507	45.647	41.815	39.257
19.00	60.148	50.950	45.100	41.289	38.751

VALUE OF AMORTIZING MORTGAGE LOANS
AS PERCENTAGE OF FACE VALUE
FACE INTEREST RATE: 6.5%

YIELD TO MATURITY	TERM OF LOAN (YEARS)				
	10	15	20	25	30
10.00	85.923	81.063	77.260	74.305	72.025
10.25	85.030	79.922	75.952	72.887	70.536
10.50	84.150	78.805	74.679	71.513	69.098
10.75	83.284	77.712	73.439	70.181	67.711
11.00	82.431	76.642	72.233	68.891	66.371
11.25	81.590	75.595	71.058	67.640	65.077
11.50	80.763	74.569	69.913	66.427	63.827
11.75	79.947	73.565	68.799	65.250	62.618
12.00	79.144	72.582	67.713	64.109	61.449
12.25	78.353	71.620	66.655	63.001	60.318
12.50	77.573	70.677	65.624	61.926	59.224
12.75	76.805	69.754	64.619	60.882	58.164
13.00	76.049	68.849	63.639	59.868	57.139
13.25	75.303	67.963	62.683	58.883	56.145
13.50	74.569	67.095	61.752	57.926	55.183
13.75	73.844	66.245	60.843	56.996	54.250
14.00	73.131	65.411	59.957	56.092	53.345
14.25	72.429	64.595	59.092	55.213	52.468
14.50	71.736	63.794	58.248	54.358	51.616
14.75	71.053	63.010	57.425	53.526	50.790
15.00	70.381	62.241	56.621	52.717	49.988
15.25	69.718	61.487	55.836	51.929	49.209
15.50	69.064	60.747	55.070	51.162	48.452
15.75	68.420	60.022	54.321	50.415	47.717
16.00	67.785	59.312	53.590	49.688	47.003
16.25	67.159	58.615	52.876	48.980	46.308
16.50	66.542	57.931	52.178	48.290	45.632
16.75	65.934	57.260	51.496	47.617	44.975
17.00	65.334	56.602	50.830	46.961	44.335
17.25	64.742	55.957	50.179	46.322	43.712
17.50	64.159	55.323	49.542	45.699	43.106
17.75	63.584	54.702	48.919	45.090	42.515
18.00	63.018	54.092	48.310	44.497	41.940
18.25	62.459	53.494	47.714	43.918	41.379
18.50	61.907	52.906	47.132	43.353	40.833
18.75	61.364	52.329	46.562	42.801	40.300
19.00	60.828	51.763	46.004	42.262	39.781

VALUE OF AMORTIZING MORTGAGE LOANS
AS PERCENTAGE OF FACE VALUE
FACE INTEREST RATE: 6.75%

YIELD TO MATURITY	TERM OF LOAN (YEARS)				
	10	15	20	25	30
10.00	86.889	82.347	78.792	76.033	73.908
10.25	85.986	81.188	77.458	74.582	72.380
10.50	85.096	80.053	76.160	73.176	70.905
10.75	84.220	78.943	74.896	71.813	69.482
11.00	83.357	77.856	73.665	70.493	68.107
11.25	82.507	76.792	72.467	69.213	66.779
11.50	81.670	75.751	71.300	67.972	65.496
11.75	80.845	74.730	70.163	66.768	64.255
12.00	80.033	73.732	69.056	65.600	63.056
12.25	79.233	72.754	67.977	64.466	61.895
12.50	78.444	71.797	66.925	63.366	60.772
12.75	77.668	70.859	65.900	62.298	59.686
13.00	76.903	69.940	64.901	61.260	58.633
13.25	76.149	69.040	63.927	60.252	57.614
13.50	75.406	68.158	62.977	59.273	56.626
13.75	74.674	67.294	62.050	58.321	55.668
14.00	73.953	66.448	61.146	57.396	54.740
14.25	73.242	65.618	60.264	56.497	53.840
14.50	72.542	64.805	59.404	55.622	52.966
14.75	71.852	64.008	58.564	54.771	52.118
15.00	71.171	63.227	57.744	53.943	51.295
15.25	70.501	62.461	56.943	53.137	50.496
15.50	69.840	61.710	56.162	52.352	49.719
15.75	69.188	60.973	55.399	51.588	48.965
16.00	68.546	60.251	54.653	50.844	48.232
16.25	67.913	59.543	53.925	50.119	47.519
16.50	67.289	58.848	53.213	49.413	46.825
16.75	66.674	58.167	52.518	48.724	46.151
17.00	66.068	57.499	51.838	48.054	45.494
17.25	65.470	56.843	51.174	47.399	44.855
17.50	64.880	56.200	50.525	46.761	44.233
17.75	64.299	55.568	49.889	46.139	43.627
18.00	63.726	54.949	49.268	45.532	43.037
18.25	63.160	54.341	48.661	44.939	42.461
18.50	62.603	53.744	48.067	44.361	41.901
18.75	62.053	53.158	47.485	43.796	41.354
19.00	61.511	52.583	46.916	43.245	40.821

VALUE OF AMORTIZING MORTGAGE LOANS
AS PERCENTAGE OF FACE VALUE
FACE INTEREST RATE: 7%

YIELD TO MATURITY	TERM OF LOAN (YEARS)				
	10	15	20	25	30
10.00	87.860	83.642	80.340	77.779	75.812
10.25	86.947	82.465	78.980	76.294	74.244
10.50	86.047	81.312	77.656	74.856	72.731
10.75	85.162	80.184	76.367	73.463	71.271
11.00	84.289	79.081	75.112	72.112	69.861
11.25	83.430	78.000	73.890	70.802	68.499
11.50	82.583	76.942	72.700	69.533	67.182
11.75	81.749	75.906	71.541	68.301	65.910
12.00	80.928	74.892	70.412	67.106	64.680
12.25	80.119	73.899	69.312	65.947	63.489
12.50	79.322	72.926	68.240	64.821	62.337
12.75	78.536	71.973	67.194	63.728	61.223
13.00	77.763	71.040	66.176	62.667	60.143
13.25	77.000	70.126	65.182	61.636	59.097
13.50	76.250	69.230	64.214	60.634	58.084
13.75	75.509	68.352	63.269	59.661	57.102
14.00	74.780	67.493	62.347	58.714	56.150
14.25	74.061	66.650	61.448	57.794	55.226
14.50	73.353	65.824	60.570	56.899	54.330
14.75	72.655	65.014	59.714	56.028	53.460
15.00	71.967	64.221	58.878	55.181	52.616
15.25	71.289	63.443	58.062	54.357	51.796
15.50	70.621	62.680	57.265	53.554	51.000
15.75	69.962	61.932	56.487	52.773	50.226
16.00	69.313	61.199	55.726	52.011	49.474
16.25	68.673	60.480	54.984	51.270	48.742
16.50	68.042	59.774	54.258	50.548	48.031
16.75	67.420	59.082	53.549	49.843	47.339
17.00	66.807	58.403	52.856	49.157	46.666
17.25	66.202	57.737	52.179	48.488	46.010
17.50	65.606	57.084	51.517	47.835	45.372
17.75	65.018	56.442	50.869	47.198	44.750
18.00	64.438	55.813	50.236	46.577	44.145
18.25	63.867	55.196	49.617	45.971	43.555
18.50	63.303	54.589	49.011	45.379	42.980
18.75	62.747	53.994	48.418	44.802	42.419
19.00	62.199	53.410	47.838	44.238	41.872

VALUE OF AMORTIZING MORTGAGE LOANS
AS PERCENTAGE OF FACE VALUE
FACE INTEREST RATE: 7.25%

YIELD TO MATURITY	TERM OF LOAN (YEARS)				
	10	15	20	25	30
10.00	88.839	84.949	81.903	79.543	77.735
10.25	87.916	83.753	80.516	78.025	76.127
10.50	87.006	82.582	79.166	76.554	74.576
10.75	86.110	81.437	77.852	75.129	73.079
11.00	85.228	80.316	76.573	73.748	71.633
11.25	84.359	79.218	75.327	72.408	70.236
11.50	83.503	78.144	74.114	71.110	68.887
11.75	82.660	77.091	72.933	69.850	67.582
12.00	81.829	76.062	71.782	68.628	66.320
12.25	81.011	75.053	70.660	67.442	65.100
12.50	80.205	74.065	69.567	66.291	63.919
12.75	79.411	73.097	68.501	65.174	62.776
13.00	78.629	72.150	67.463	64.088	61.669
13.25	77.858	71.221	66.450	63.034	60.596
13.50	77.099	70.312	65.463	62.009	59.557
13.75	76.350	69.420	64.499	61.014	58.550
14.00	75.613	68.547	63.560	60.046	57.574
14.25	74.886	67.691	62.643	59.105	56.627
14.50	74.170	66.852	61.748	58.189	55.708
14.75	73.464	66.030	60.875	57.299	54.816
15.00	72.769	65.224	60.023	56.433	53.951
15.25	72.083	64.434	59.191	55.590	53.110
15.50	71.408	63.659	58.379	54.769	52.294
15.75	70.741	62.899	57.585	53.970	51.500
16.00	70.085	62.155	56.810	53.191	50.729
16.25	69.438	61.424	56.053	52.433	49.979
16.50	68.800	60.708	55.314	51.694	49.249
16.75	68.171	60.005	54.591	50.974	48.540
17.00	67.551	59.315	53.885	50.272	47.849
17.25	66.939	58.639	53.194	49.588	47.177
17.50	66.336	57.975	52.519	48.920	46.523
17.75	65.742	57.324	51.859	48.269	45.886
18.00	65.156	56.685	51.213	47.634	45.265
18.25	64.578	56.058	50.582	47.014	44.660
18.50	64.008	55.442	49.964	46.409	44.070
18.75	63.446	54.838	49.360	45.818	43.495
19.00	62.892	54.244	48.768	45.241	42.934

669

VALUE OF AMORTIZING MORTGAGE LOANS
AS PERCENTAGE OF FACE VALUE
FACE INTEREST RATE: 7.5%

YIELD TO MATURITY	TERM OF LOAN (YEARS)				
	10	15	20	25	30
10.00	89.822	86.265	83.479	81.324	79.676
10.25	88.889	85.051	82.066	79.772	78.028
10.50	87.969	83.862	80.690	78.268	76.438
10.75	87.063	82.699	79.351	76.811	74.904
11.00	86.172	81.560	78.047	75.398	73.422
11.25	85.293	80.445	76.777	74.029	71.990
11.50	84.428	79.354	75.541	72.702	70.607
11.75	83.575	78.286	74.336	71.414	69.269
12.00	82.735	77.240	73.163	70.165	67.976
12.25	81.908	76.216	72.020	68.952	66.725
12.50	81.093	75.212	70.906	67.775	65.515
12.75	80.290	74.230	69.820	66.633	64.343
13.00	79.500	73.267	68.761	65.523	63.209
13.25	78.720	72.324	67.729	64.445	62.110
13.50	77.952	71.401	66.723	63.398	61.045
13.75	77.195	70.496	65.741	62.380	60.012
14.00	76.450	69.609	64.783	61.390	59.012
14.25	75.715	68.740	63.849	60.428	58.041
14.50	74.991	67.888	62.937	59.492	57.099
14.75	74.278	67.053	62.047	58.582	56.185
15.00	73.575	66.235	61.178	57.696	55.298
15.25	72.881	65.432	60.330	56.834	54.436
15.50	72.198	64.645	59.502	55.995	53.599
15.75	71.525	63.874	58.694	55.178	52.786
16.00	70.861	63.118	57.904	54.382	51.996
16.25	70.207	62.376	57.132	53.607	51.227
16.50	69.561	61.648	56.378	52.851	50.479
16.75	68.925	60.934	55.642	52.115	49.752
17.00	68.299	60.234	54.922	51.397	49.044
17.25	67.680	59.547	54.218	50.698	48.355
17.50	67.071	58.873	53.530	50.015	47.685
17.75	66.470	58.212	52.857	49.350	47.031
18.00	65.877	57.563	52.199	48.700	46.395
18.25	65.293	56.926	51.555	48.066	45.775
18.50	64.717	56.301	50.926	47.448	45.170
18.75	64.148	55.687	50.310	46.844	44.581
19.00	63.588	55.085	49.707	46.254	44.006

VALUE OF AMORTIZING MORTGAGE LOANS
AS PERCENTAGE OF FACE VALUE
FACE INTEREST RATE: 7.75%

YIELD TO MATURITY	TERM OF LOAN (YEARS)				
	10	15	20	25	30
10.00	90.814	87.593	85.071	83.122	81.636
10.25	89.870	86.360	83.630	81.535	79.948
10.50	88.940	85.153	82.228	79.998	78.319
10.75	88.024	83.972	80.864	78.509	76.746
11.00	87.123	82.816	79.535	77.066	75.228
11.25	86.234	81.684	78.241	75.666	73.761
11.50	85.359	80.576	76.981	74.309	72.344
11.75	84.497	79.491	75.754	72.993	70.973
12.00	83.648	78.429	74.558	71.716	69.649
12.25	82.812	77.389	73.393	70.477	68.367
12.50	81.988	76.370	72.258	69.274	67.127
12.75	81.177	75.372	71.151	68.106	65.926
13.00	80.377	74.395	70.072	66.972	64.764
13.25	79.589	73.438	69.021	65.870	63.637
13.50	78.813	72.500	67.995	64.799	62.546
13.75	78.047	71.581	66.994	63.759	61.489
14.00	77.294	70.680	66.018	62.748	60.463
14.25	76.551	69.798	65.066	61.764	59.469
14.50	75.819	68.933	64.137	60.808	58.504
14.75	75.097	68.085	63.230	59.877	57.568
15.00	74.387	67.254	62.345	58.972	56.658
15.25	73.686	66.439	61.481	58.091	55.776
15.50	72.995	65.641	60.637	57.233	54.918
15.75	72.314	64.857	59.813	56.398	54.085
16.00	71.643	64.089	59.008	55.584	53.275
16.25	70.981	63.336	58.222	54.792	52.487
16.50	70.329	62.597	57.453	54.020	51.721
16.75	69.686	61.873	56.703	53.267	50.976
17.00	69.052	61.162	55.969	52.534	50.251
17.25	68.427	60.464	55.252	51.819	49.545
17.50	67.811	59.780	54.550	51.121	48.858
17.75	67.203	59.108	53.865	50.441	48.188
18.00	66.604	58.449	53.194	49.777	47.536
18.25	66.014	57.803	52.538	49.129	46.901
18.50	65.431	57.168	51.897	48.497	46.282
18.75	64.856	56.545	51.269	47.880	45.678
19.00	64.290	55.933	50.655	47.277	45.089

671

VALUE OF AMORTIZING MORTGAGE LOANS
AS PERCENTAGE OF FACE VALUE
FACE INTEREST RATE: 8%

YIELD TO MATURITY	TERM OF LOAN (YEARS)				
	10	15	20	25	30
10.00	91.810	88.930	86.676	84.936	83.613
10.25	90.856	87.679	85.208	83.315	81.884
10.50	89.915	86.453	83.780	81.744	80.216
10.75	88.990	85.254	82.389	80.223	78.605
11.00	88.078	84.080	81.036	78.748	77.050
11.25	87.180	82.931	79.717	77.318	75.548
11.50	86.295	81.806	78.434	75.931	74.096
11.75	85.424	80.705	77.183	74.586	72.692
12.00	84.566	79.626	75.965	73.281	71.335
12.25	83.720	78.570	74.778	72.015	70.023
12.50	82.887	77.536	73.621	70.786	68.752
12.75	82.067	76.523	72.494	69.592	67.523
13.00	81.259	75.531	71.394	68.433	66.332
13.25	80.462	74.559	70.323	67.308	65.179
13.50	79.677	73.607	69.278	66.214	64.061
13.75	78.903	72.674	68.258	65.150	62.978
14.00	78.141	71.760	67.264	64.117	61.928
14.25	77.391	70.864	66.294	63.112	60.909
14.50	76.650	69.985	65.347	62.135	59.921
14.75	75.921	69.125	64.423	61.184	58.962
15.00	75.202	68.281	63.521	60.259	58.031
15.25	74.494	67.454	62.641	59.359	57.126
15.50	73.796	66.643	61.781	58.482	56.248
15.75	73.107	65.848	60.941	57.629	55.394
16.00	72.429	65.068	60.121	56.798	54.565
16.25	71.760	64.303	59.320	55.988	53.758
16.50	71.100	63.553	58.537	55.199	52.974
16.75	70.450	62.817	57.772	54.430	52.211
17.00	69.810	62.096	57.025	53.681	51.468
17.25	69.178	61.387	56.294	52.950	50.745
17.50	68.555	60.693	55.580	52.237	50.041
17.75	67.940	60.011	54.881	51.542	49.356
18.00	67.335	59.342	54.198	50.863	48.688
18.25	66.738	58.685	53.529	50.201	48.037
18.50	66.149	58.041	52.876	49.555	47.402
18.75	65.568	57.408	52.236	48.925	46.784
19.00	64.995	56.787	51.610	48.309	46.181

VALUE OF AMORTIZING MORTGAGE LOANS
AS PERCENTAGE OF FACE VALUE
FACE INTEREST RATE: 8.25%

YIELD TO MATURITY	TERM OF LOAN (YEARS)				
	10	15	20	25	30
10.00	92.812	90.279	88.295	86.767	85.607
10.25	91.848	89.008	86.800	85.111	83.837
10.50	90.897	87.764	85.345	83.506	82.129
10.75	89.962	86.546	83.928	81.952	80.480
11.00	89.040	85.355	82.549	80.445	78.888
11.25	88.132	84.188	81.207	78.984	77.350
11.50	87.238	83.046	79.899	77.568	75.863
11.75	86.357	81.928	78.625	76.193	74.426
12.00	85.489	80.834	77.384	74.861	73.037
12.25	84.635	79.762	76.175	73.567	71.693
12.50	83.792	78.712	74.996	72.311	70.392
12.75	82.963	77.683	73.848	71.092	69.133
13.00	82.146	76.676	72.728	69.908	67.914
13.25	81.340	75.689	71.636	68.758	66.733
13.50	80.547	74.723	70.572	67.641	65.589
13.75	79.765	73.775	69.533	66.555	64.480
14.00	78.995	72.847	68.520	65.499	63.405
14.25	78.236	71.938	67.532	64.472	62.362
14.50	77.487	71.046	66.568	63.474	61.350
14.75	76.750	70.173	65.626	62.503	60.368
15.00	76.024	69.316	64.708	61.558	59.415
15.25	75.307	68.476	63.811	60.638	58.489
15.50	74.601	67.653	62.935	59.743	57.590
15.75	73.905	66.846	62.080	58.871	56.716
16.00	73.220	66.054	61.244	58.022	55.866
16.25	72.544	65.278	60.428	57.194	55.040
16.50	71.877	64.516	59.631	56.389	54.237
16.75	71.220	63.770	58.852	55.603	53.456
17.00	70.572	63.037	58.090	54.837	52.695
17.25	69.933	62.318	57.346	54.091	51.955
17.50	69.303	61.613	56.618	53.363	51.235
17.75	68.682	60.920	55.906	52.652	50.533
18.00	68.070	60.241	55.210	51.960	49.849
18.25	67.466	59.575	54.529	51.283	49.183
18.50	66.871	58.920	53.864	50.623	48.533
18.75	66.284	58.278	53.212	49.979	47.900
19.00	65.705	57.648	52.574	49.350	47.282

VALUE OF AMORTIZING MORTGAGE LOANS
AS PERCENTAGE OF FACE VALUE
FACE INTEREST RATE: 8.5%

YIELD TO MATURITY	TERM OF LOAN (YEARS)				
	10	15	20	25	30
10.00	93.822	91.637	89.928	88.613	87.618
10.25	92.847	90.348	88.405	86.922	85.807
10.50	91.886	89.085	86.923	85.283	84.058
10.75	90.940	87.849	85.481	83.695	82.371
11.00	90.008	86.640	84.076	82.157	80.741
11.25	89.090	85.455	82.709	80.665	79.167
11.50	88.186	84.296	81.377	79.218	77.645
11.75	87.296	83.161	80.079	77.815	76.175
12.00	86.419	82.050	78.815	76.454	74.753
12.25	85.555	80.962	77.584	75.133	73.377
12.50	84.704	79.896	76.384	73.850	72.046
12.75	83.865	78.853	75.214	72.605	70.757
13.00	83.039	77.830	74.073	71.396	69.510
13.25	82.225	76.829	72.961	70.221	68.301
13.50	81.423	75.848	71.877	69.080	67.130
13.75	80.632	74.886	70.819	67.971	65.995
14.00	79.854	73.944	69.788	66.893	64.894
14.25	79.086	73.021	68.781	65.844	63.827
14.50	78.330	72.116	67.799	64.825	62.791
14.75	77.585	71.229	66.840	63.833	61.786
15.00	76.850	70.360	65.905	62.868	60.810
15.25	76.126	69.507	64.991	61.928	59.863
15.50	75.413	68.672	64.099	61.014	58.942
15.75	74.709	67.852	63.228	60.124	58.048
16.00	74.016	67.048	62.377	59.256	57.179
16.25	73.332	66.261	61.546	58.412	56.333
16.50	72.658	65.488	60.734	57.589	55.511
16.75	71.994	64.729	59.940	56.786	54.712
17.00	71.340	63.986	59.165	56.004	53.933
17.25	70.694	63.256	58.406	55.242	53.176
17.50	70.057	62.540	57.665	54.498	52.438
17.75	69.429	61.837	56.940	53.773	51.720
18.00	68.810	61.148	56.231	53.065	51.020
18.25	68.200	60.472	55.538	52.375	50.338
18.50	67.598	59.807	54.860	51.701	49.673
18.75	67.004	59.155	54.196	51.042	49.025
19.00	66.419	58.515	53.547	50.400	48.393

674

VALUE OF AMORTIZING MORTGAGE LOANS
AS PERCENTAGE OF FACE VALUE
FACE INTEREST RATE: 8.75%

YIELD TO MATURITY	TERM OF LOAN (YEARS)				
	10	15	20	25	30
10.00	94.836	93.006	91.574	90.475	89.645
10.25	93.850	91.697	90.024	88.748	87.791
10.50	92.879	90.415	88.514	87.075	86.003
10.75	91.923	89.161	87.045	85.454	84.276
11.00	90.981	87.934	85.615	83.883	82.609
11.25	90.053	86.732	84.222	82.359	80.998
11.50	89.140	85.555	82.866	80.882	79.441
11.75	88.239	84.403	81.545	79.450	77.937
12.00	87.353	83.276	80.258	78.060	76.482
12.25	86.480	82.171	79.004	76.711	75.074
12.50	85.619	81.090	77.782	75.401	73.712
12.75	84.772	80.030	76.591	74.130	72.394
13.00	83.937	78.993	75.429	72.896	71.117
13.25	83.114	77.976	74.297	71.696	69.881
13.50	82.303	76.980	73.193	70.531	68.683
13.75	81.504	76.004	72.116	69.399	67.521
14.00	80.717	75.048	71.065	68.298	66.395
14.25	79.942	74.111	70.040	67.228	65.303
14.50	79.177	73.193	69.040	66.186	64.244
14.75	78.424	72.293	68.064	65.174	63.215
15.00	77.681	71.410	67.111	64.188	62.217
15.25	76.949	70.545	66.181	63.229	61.248
15.50	76.228	69.697	65.272	62.296	60.306
15.75	75.517	68.865	64.385	61.387	59.391
16.00	74.816	68.050	63.519	60.501	58.501
16.25	74.125	67.250	62.672	59.639	57.636
16.50	73.444	66.466	61.845	58.798	56.795
16.75	72.773	65.696	61.037	57.979	55.977
17.00	72.111	64.941	60.248	57.181	55.181
17.25	71.458	64.201	59.475	56.402	54.406
17.50	70.815	63.474	58.721	55.643	53.651
17.75	70.180	62.761	57.982	54.903	52.916
18.00	69.554	62.061	57.261	54.180	52.200
18.25	68.937	61.375	56.555	53.475	51.502
18.50	68.329	60.700	55.864	52.787	50.822
18.75	67.729	60.039	55.188	52.115	50.159
19.00	67.137	59.389	54.527	51.459	49.512

675

VALUE OF AMORTIZING MORTGAGE LOANS
AS PERCENTAGE OF FACE VALUE
FACE INTEREST RATE: 9%

YIELD TO MATURITY	TERM OF LOAN (YEARS)				
	10	15	20	25	30
10.00	95.856	94.384	93.233	92.351	91.687
10.25	94.860	93.056	91.655	90.588	89.791
10.50	93.878	91.755	90.118	88.880	87.962
10.75	92.912	90.482	88.623	87.226	86.196
11.00	91.960	89.237	87.167	85.622	84.490
11.25	91.022	88.017	85.749	84.067	82.843
11.50	90.099	86.823	84.368	82.560	81.251
11.75	89.189	85.654	83.023	81.097	79.712
12.00	88.293	84.510	81.712	79.679	78.224
12.25	87.410	83.389	80.435	78.302	76.784
12.50	86.541	82.291	79.191	76.965	75.391
12.75	85.684	81.217	77.978	75.668	74.043
13.00	84.840	80.164	76.796	74.408	72.737
13.25	84.008	79.132	75.643	73.183	71.473
13.50	83.189	78.121	74.519	71.994	70.247
13.75	82.381	77.131	73.422	70.838	69.059
14.00	81.585	76.161	72.353	69.714	67.908
14.25	80.802	75.210	71.309	68.622	66.791
14.50	80.029	74.278	70.291	67.559	65.707
14.75	79.267	73.364	69.297	66.525	64.655
15.00	78.517	72.469	68.327	65.520	63.634
15.25	77.777	71.591	67.380	64.541	62.643
15.50	77.048	70.730	66.455	63.588	61.680
15.75	76.329	69.886	65.552	62.660	60.744
16.00	75.621	69.058	64.670	61.756	59.834
16.25	74.923	68.247	63.808	60.876	58.949
16.50	74.234	67.451	62.966	60.018	58.089
16.75	73.556	66.670	62.143	59.182	57.252
17.00	72.887	65.904	61.339	58.367	56.438
17.25	72.227	65.152	60.553	57.572	55.645
17.50	71.576	64.415	59.785	56.797	54.873
17.75	70.935	63.691	59.033	56.041	54.122
18.00	70.303	62.981	58.298	55.304	53.389
18.25	69.679	62.284	57.579	54.584	52.676
18.50	69.064	61.600	56.876	53.881	51.980
18.75	68.458	60.929	56.188	53.196	51.302
19.00	67.860	60.270	55.515	52.526	50.640

VALUE OF AMORTIZING MORTGAGE LOANS
AS PERCENTAGE OF FACE VALUE
FACE INTEREST RATE: 9.25%

YIELD TO MATURITY	TERM OF LOAN (YEARS)				
	10	15	20	25	30
10.00	96.884	95.774	94.906	94.243	93.745
10.25	95.877	94.426	93.300	92.444	91.806
10.50	94.885	93.106	91.735	90.701	89.936
10.75	93.908	91.815	90.213	89.013	88.130
11.00	92.946	90.551	88.731	87.376	86.386
11.25	91.998	89.313	87.287	85.789	84.702
11.50	91.065	88.102	85.882	84.251	83.074
11.75	90.145	86.915	84.512	82.758	81.501
12.00	89.240	85.754	83.179	81.311	79.979
12.25	88.348	84.617	81.879	79.906	78.507
12.50	87.468	83.503	80.612	78.542	77.083
12.75	86.603	82.412	79.378	77.218	75.705
13.00	85.750	81.344	78.174	75.932	74.370
13.25	84.909	80.297	77.001	74.682	73.077
13.50	84.081	79.272	75.856	73.469	71.824
13.75	83.264	78.266	74.740	72.289	70.609
14.00	82.460	77.282	73.651	71.142	69.432
14.25	81.668	76.317	72.589	70.027	68.290
14.50	80.887	75.371	71.552	68.943	67.182
14.75	80.117	74.444	70.541	67.888	66.106
15.00	79.359	73.536	69.553	66.862	65.062
15.25	78.611	72.645	68.589	65.863	64.049
15.50	77.874	71.772	67.648	64.890	63.064
15.75	77.148	70.915	66.728	63.943	62.107
16.00	76.432	70.075	65.830	63.021	61.177
16.25	75.726	69.252	64.953	62.122	60.272
16.50	75.030	68.444	64.096	61.247	59.393
16.75	74.344	67.651	63.259	60.394	58.537
17.00	73.668	66.874	62.440	59.562	57.704
17.25	73.001	66.111	61.640	58.751	56.894
17.50	72.344	65.363	60.857	57.960	56.105
17.75	71.695	64.629	60.092	57.189	55.336
18.00	71.056	63.908	59.344	56.436	54.587
18.25	70.426	63.201	58.613	55.702	53.858
18.50	69.805	62.507	57.897	54.985	53.146
18.75	69.192	61.826	57.197	54.285	52.453
19.00	68.587	61.157	56.511	53.602	51.777

VALUE OF AMORTIZING MORTGAGE LOANS
AS PERCENTAGE OF FACE VALUE
FACE INTEREST RATE: 9.5%

YIELD TO MATURITY	TERM OF LOAN (YEARS)				
	10	15	20	25	30
10.00	97.916	97.172	96.591	96.148	95.816
10.25	96.899	95.805	94.956	94.313	93.835
10.50	95.896	94.465	93.364	92.535	91.923
10.75	94.909	93.155	91.815	90.812	90.077
11.00	93.936	91.873	90.306	89.142	88.295
11.25	92.978	90.617	88.837	87.524	86.573
11.50	92.035	89.388	87.407	85.954	84.910
11.75	91.105	88.184	86.013	84.431	83.301
12.00	90.190	87.006	84.655	82.954	81.746
12.25	89.289	85.852	83.333	81.521	80.242
12.50	88.400	84.722	82.043	80.129	78.786
12.75	87.525	83.616	80.787	78.779	77.377
13.00	86.663	82.531	79.562	77.467	76.013
13.25	85.813	81.469	78.368	76.192	74.691
13.50	84.977	80.429	77.203	74.954	73.411
13.75	84.151	79.409	76.067	73.750	72.169
14.00	83.339	78.410	74.959	72.580	70.966
14.25	82.538	77.431	73.878	71.443	69.799
14.50	81.748	76.472	72.823	70.337	68.666
14.75	80.971	75.531	71.793	69.260	67.567
15.00	80.204	74.609	70.788	68.213	66.500
15.25	79.448	73.705	69.807	67.194	65.464
15.50	78.704	72.819	68.849	66.202	64.457
15.75	77.969	71.950	67.913	65.236	63.479
16.00	77.246	71.098	66.999	64.295	62.528
16.25	76.533	70.263	66.106	63.378	61.604
16.50	75.829	69.443	65.234	62.485	60.705
16.75	75.136	68.639	64.382	61.615	59.830
17.00	74.453	67.851	63.549	60.766	58.979
17.25	73.779	67.077	62.734	59.939	58.151
17.50	73.114	66.318	61.938	59.132	57.344
17.75	72.459	65.573	61.159	58.345	56.559
18.00	71.813	64.842	60.398	57.577	55.793
18.25	71.176	64.124	59.653	56.828	55.048
18.50	70.548	63.420	58.925	56.097	54.321
18.75	69.929	62.728	58.212	55.383	53.612
19.00	69.318	62.050	57.515	54.685	52.921

VALUE OF AMORTIZING MORTGAGE LOANS
AS PERCENTAGE OF FACE VALUE
FACE INTEREST RATE: 9.75%

YIELD TO MATURITY	TERM OF LOAN (YEARS)				
	10	15	20	25	30
10.00	98.955	98.582	98.290	98.067	97.901
10.25	97.927	97.194	96.626	96.195	95.877
10.50	96.914	95.835	95.006	94.382	93.923
10.75	95.916	94.506	93.429	92.625	92.038
11.00	94.934	93.205	91.894	90.922	90.217
11.25	93.965	91.931	90.399	89.271	88.458
11.50	93.012	90.684	88.943	87.670	86.758
11.75	92.072	89.463	87.525	86.117	85.115
12.00	91.148	88.268	86.144	84.611	83.526
12.25	90.237	87.097	84.798	83.148	81.989
12.50	89.339	85.951	83.486	81.729	80.501
12.75	88.454	84.828	82.207	80.351	79.061
13.00	87.583	83.728	80.961	79.013	77.667
13.25	86.724	82.651	79.746	77.713	76.317
13.50	85.879	81.595	78.560	76.450	75.008
13.75	85.044	80.561	77.404	75.223	73.740
14.00	84.223	79.547	76.277	74.029	72.510
14.25	83.414	78.554	75.177	72.869	71.318
14.50	82.616	77.581	74.103	71.741	70.161
14.75	81.830	76.627	73.055	70.643	69.038
15.00	81.056	75.691	72.033	69.575	67.947
15.25	80.292	74.774	71.034	68.535	66.889
15.50	79.539	73.875	70.059	67.524	65.860
15.75	78.797	72.994	69.107	66.538	64.861
16.00	78.066	72.129	68.177	65.578	63.889
16.25	77.345	71.282	67.269	64.644	62.945
16.50	76.634	70.450	66.381	63.733	62.026
16.75	75.934	69.635	65.514	62.845	61.133
17.00	75.243	68.835	64.666	61.979	60.263
17.25	74.562	68.049	63.837	61.136	59.417
17.50	73.891	67.279	63.027	60.313	58.592
17.75	73.228	66.523	62.235	59.510	57.790
18.00	72.576	65.782	61.460	58.727	57.008
18.25	71.932	65.054	60.702	57.963	56.246
18.50	71.297	64.339	59.961	57.217	55.503
18.75	70.671	63.638	59.236	56.488	54.779
19.00	70.054	62.950	58.526	55.777	54.073

679

VALUE OF AMORTIZING MORTGAGE LOANS
AS PERCENTAGE OF FACE VALUE
FACE INTEREST RATE: 10%

YIELD TO MATURITY	TERM OF LOAN (YEARS)				
	10	15	20	25	30
10.00	100.000	100.000	100.000	100.000	100.000
10.25	98.961	98.592	98.307	98.091	97.932
10.50	97.937	97.214	96.659	96.242	95.937
10.75	96.928	95.866	95.055	94.451	94.011
11.00	95.936	94.546	93.493	92.714	92.151
11.25	94.957	93.254	91.972	91.030	90.354
11.50	93.994	91.989	90.491	89.398	88.618
11.75	93.044	90.750	89.048	87.814	86.939
12.00	92.110	89.538	87.643	86.278	85.316
12.25	91.189	88.351	86.273	84.787	83.746
12.50	90.282	87.188	84.939	83.340	82.227
12.75	89.388	86.049	83.638	81.935	80.756
13.00	88.508	84.933	82.370	80.570	79.332
13.25	87.640	83.840	81.133	79.245	77.953
13.50	86.785	82.769	79.927	77.957	76.616
13.75	85.942	81.720	78.751	76.705	75.321
14.00	85.112	80.692	77.604	75.489	74.065
14.25	84.295	79.684	76.485	74.305	72.846
14.50	83.488	78.697	75.392	73.155	71.665
14.75	82.694	77.729	74.327	72.035	70.517
15.00	81.911	76.780	73.286	70.946	69.404
15.25	81.139	75.850	72.270	69.886	68.322
15.50	80.379	74.938	71.278	68.854	67.272
15.75	79.629	74.044	70.310	67.849	66.251
16.00	78.890	73.167	69.363	66.871	65.259
16.25	78.162	72.307	68.439	65.918	64.294
16.50	77.443	71.464	67.536	64.989	63.356
16.75	76.735	70.636	66.654	64.083	62.443
17.00	76.037	69.825	65.791	63.201	61.555
17.25	75.349	69.029	64.948	62.341	60.690
17.50	74.671	68.247	64.124	61.501	59.848
17.75	74.001	67.481	63.318	60.683	59.028
18.00	73.342	66.728	62.529	59.884	58.230
18.25	72.691	65.990	61.758	59.105	57.451
18.50	72.050	65.265	61.004	58.344	56.693
18.75	71.417	64.554	60.266	57.602	55.953
19.00	70.793	63.855	59.544	56.876	55.232

VALUE OF AMORTIZING MORTGAGE LOANS
AS PERCENTAGE OF FACE VALUE
FACE INTEREST RATE: 10.25%

YIELD TO MATURITY	TERM OF LOAN (YEARS)				
	10	15	20	25	30
10.00	101.050	101.428	101.722	101.946	102.111
10.25	100.000	100.000	100.000	100.000	100.000
10.50	98.965	98.602	98.323	98.115	97.962
10.75	97.946	97.235	96.692	96.288	95.996
11.00	96.943	95.896	95.103	94.518	94.096
11.25	95.954	94.585	93.556	92.802	92.262
11.50	94.981	93.302	92.049	91.137	90.489
11.75	94.021	92.046	90.582	89.523	88.775
12.00	93.077	90.816	89.152	87.957	87.117
12.25	92.147	89.612	87.759	86.437	85.514
12.50	91.230	88.432	86.401	84.962	83.963
12.75	90.327	87.277	85.078	83.529	82.461
13.00	89.437	86.146	83.788	82.138	81.007
13.25	88.560	85.037	82.530	80.787	79.599
13.50	87.696	83.951	81.304	79.474	78.234
13.75	86.845	82.887	80.107	78.198	76.911
14.00	86.006	81.844	78.941	76.957	75.629
14.25	85.180	80.822	77.802	75.751	74.385
14.50	84.365	79.820	76.691	74.578	73.178
14.75	83.562	78.839	75.607	73.437	72.006
15.00	82.771	77.877	74.548	72.327	70.869
15.25	81.991	76.933	73.515	71.246	69.765
15.50	81.223	76.008	72.506	70.194	68.692
15.75	80.465	75.101	71.520	69.170	67.650
16.00	79.718	74.212	70.558	68.172	66.637
16.25	78.982	73.340	69.618	67.200	65.652
16.50	78.256	72.484	68.699	66.253	64.694
16.75	77.541	71.645	67.801	65.330	63.761
17.00	76.836	70.822	66.924	64.431	62.855
17.25	76.140	70.014	66.066	63.554	61.972
17.50	75.455	69.222	65.228	62.698	61.112
17.75	74.778	68.444	64.408	61.864	60.275
18.00	74.112	67.681	63.606	61.049	59.459
18.25	73.455	66.932	62.822	60.255	58.664
18.50	72.806	66.197	62.055	59.479	57.890
18.75	72.167	65.475	61.304	58.722	57.134
19.00	71.537	64.767	60.570	57.983	56.398

681

VALUE OF AMORTIZING MORTGAGE LOANS
AS PERCENTAGE OF FACE VALUE
FACE INTEREST RATE: 10.5%

YIELD TO MATURITY	TERM OF LOAN (YEARS)				
	10	15	20	25	30
10.00	102.107	102.866	103.457	103.905	104.235
10.25	101.046	101.418	101.705	101.921	102.080
10.50	100.000	100.000	100.000	100.000	100.000
10.75	98.971	98.613	98.340	98.138	97.992
11.00	97.957	97.255	96.725	96.334	96.054
11.25	96.958	95.926	95.151	94.585	94.181
11.50	95.974	94.625	93.619	92.888	92.371
11.75	95.005	93.351	92.126	91.243	90.621
12.00	94.051	92.104	90.672	89.647	88.929
12.25	93.110	90.882	89.256	88.098	87.293
12.50	92.184	89.686	87.875	86.594	85.709
12.75	91.271	88.514	86.529	85.134	84.176
13.00	90.372	87.367	85.217	83.716	82.692
13.25	89.486	86.242	83.938	82.339	81.254
13.50	88.614	85.141	82.690	81.001	79.861
13.75	87.753	84.062	81.473	79.700	78.511
14.00	86.906	83.004	80.287	78.436	77.202
14.25	86.071	81.968	79.129	77.207	75.932
14.50	85.247	80.952	77.999	76.011	74.700
14.75	84.436	79.956	76.896	74.848	73.504
15.00	83.637	78.981	75.819	73.716	72.343
15.25	82.849	78.024	74.768	72.615	71.216
15.50	82.072	77.086	73.742	71.543	70.121
15.75	81.307	76.166	72.740	70.499	69.057
16.00	80.552	75.264	71.761	69.482	68.023
16.25	79.808	74.379	70.805	68.491	67.017
16.50	79.075	73.512	69.871	67.526	66.039
16.75	78.352	72.661	68.958	66.586	65.088
17.00	77.639	71.826	68.065	65.669	64.162
17.25	76.937	71.007	67.193	64.775	63.261
17.50	76.244	70.203	66.340	63.903	62.383
17.75	75.560	69.414	65.506	63.052	61.529
18.00	74.887	68.640	64.691	62.222	60.696
18.25	74.223	67.881	63.893	61.413	59.885
18.50	73.568	67.135	63.113	60.622	59.094
18.75	72.922	66.404	62.349	59.851	58.323
19.00	72.285	65.685	61.602	59.097	57.571

682

VALUE OF AMORTIZING MORTGAGE LOANS
AS PERCENTAGE OF FACE VALUE
FACE INTEREST RATE: 10.75%

YIELD TO MATURITY	TERM OF LOAN (YEARS)				
	10	15	20	25	30
10.00	103.169	104.312	105.203	105.876	106.371
10.25	102.097	102.844	103.421	103.855	104.171
10.50	101.040	101.407	101.688	101.897	102.049
10.75	100.000	100.000	100.000	100.000	100.000
11.00	98.976	98.623	98.357	98.162	98.022
11.25	97.966	97.275	96.757	96.379	96.110
11.50	96.972	95.956	95.199	94.650	94.263
11.75	95.993	94.664	93.681	92.974	92.478
12.00	95.029	93.399	92.203	91.347	90.752
12.25	94.079	92.161	90.762	89.769	89.081
12.50	93.143	90.947	89.358	88.237	87.465
12.75	92.221	89.759	87.989	86.749	85.901
13.00	91.312	88.596	86.655	85.304	84.386
13.25	90.417	87.455	85.354	83.901	82.919
13.50	89.535	86.339	84.086	82.537	81.497
13.75	88.666	85.244	82.848	81.212	80.119
14.00	87.809	84.172	81.641	79.924	78.783
14.25	86.966	83.121	80.464	78.671	77.487
14.50	86.134	82.091	79.315	77.453	76.230
14.75	85.314	81.081	78.193	76.268	75.010
15.00	84.507	80.091	77.099	75.115	73.825
15.25	83.710	79.121	76.030	73.992	72.675
15.50	82.926	78.170	74.987	72.900	71.558
15.75	82.152	77.237	73.967	71.836	70.472
16.00	81.390	76.322	72.972	70.800	69.416
16.25	80.638	75.425	72.000	69.791	68.390
16.50	79.897	74.546	71.050	68.807	67.392
16.75	79.167	73.683	70.121	67.849	66.421
17.00	78.447	72.836	69.214	66.914	65.476
17.25	77.737	72.005	68.327	66.003	64.557
17.50	77.037	71.190	67.460	65.115	63.661
17.75	76.346	70.391	66.612	64.248	62.789
18.00	75.666	69.606	65.783	63.403	61.940
18.25	74.995	68.836	64.971	62.578	61.112
18.50	74.333	68.080	64.178	61.772	60.305
18.75	73.680	67.338	63.402	60.986	59.518
19.00	73.036	66.609	62.642	60.218	58.750

683

VALUE OF AMORTIZING MORTGAGE LOANS
AS PERCENTAGE OF FACE VALUE
FACE INTEREST RATE: 11%

YIELD TO MATURITY	TERM OF LOAN (YEARS)				
	10	15	20	25	30
10.00	104.237	105.768	106.960	107.859	108.518
10.25	103.153	104.280	105.149	105.800	106.274
10.50	102.086	102.822	103.386	103.805	104.109
10.75	101.035	101.396	101.670	101.873	102.018
11.00	100.000	100.000	100.000	100.000	100.000
11.25	98.980	98.633	98.373	98.184	98.050
11.50	97.976	97.295	96.789	96.423	96.166
11.75	96.986	95.985	95.246	94.715	94.344
12.00	96.012	94.703	93.743	93.058	92.583
12.25	95.052	93.447	92.278	91.450	90.879
12.50	94.106	92.217	90.850	89.889	89.231
12.75	93.175	91.012	89.459	88.374	87.635
13.00	92.257	89.832	88.103	86.902	86.090
13.25	91.353	88.676	86.780	85.472	84.593
13.50	90.462	87.544	85.490	84.083	83.142
13.75	89.583	86.434	84.232	82.733	81.737
14.00	88.718	85.346	83.005	81.421	80.373
14.25	87.866	84.281	81.808	80.145	79.051
14.50	87.025	83.236	80.640	78.904	77.769
14.75	86.197	82.213	79.500	77.696	76.524
15.00	85.381	81.209	78.387	76.522	75.316
15.25	84.577	80.226	77.300	75.378	74.142
15.50	83.784	79.261	76.239	74.265	73.002
15.75	83.002	78.315	75.203	73.181	71.894
16.00	82.232	77.388	74.191	72.126	70.817
16.25	81.473	76.478	73.202	71.098	69.771
16.50	80.724	75.586	72.236	70.096	68.752
16.75	79.986	74.711	71.293	69.119	67.762
17.00	79.259	73.853	70.370	68.168	66.798
17.25	78.541	73.010	69.468	67.240	65.860
17.50	77.834	72.184	68.587	66.335	64.946
17.75	77.136	71.373	67.724	65.452	64.056
18.00	76.449	70.577	66.881	64.590	63.190
18.25	75.771	69.797	66.057	63.750	62.345
18.50	75.102	69.030	65.250	62.929	61.522
18.75	74.443	68.278	64.461	62.128	60.719
19.00	73.792	67.539	63.688	61.346	59.936

VALUE OF AMORTIZING MORTGAGE LOANS
AS PERCENTAGE OF FACE VALUE
FACE INTEREST RATE: 11.25%

YIELD TO MATURITY	TERM OF LOAN (YEARS)				
	10	15	20	25	30
10.00	105.311	107.234	108.729	109.853	110.676
10.25	104.216	105.725	106.888	107.757	108.388
10.50	103.138	104.247	105.096	105.725	106.179
10.75	102.076	102.801	103.352	103.757	104.047
11.00	101.031	101.386	101.654	101.850	101.989
11.25	100.000	100.000	100.000	100.000	100.000
11.50	98.986	98.644	98.390	98.207	98.078
11.75	97.986	97.315	96.821	96.467	96.221
12.00	97.002	96.015	95.293	94.779	94.424
12.25	96.032	94.742	93.804	93.142	92.687
12.50	95.076	93.495	92.353	91.552	91.005
12.75	94.135	92.274	90.938	90.008	89.378
13.00	93.208	91.077	89.560	88.509	87.802
13.25	92.294	89.905	88.215	87.053	86.275
13.50	91.394	88.757	86.904	85.639	84.796
13.75	90.506	87.632	85.625	84.263	83.362
14.00	89.632	86.529	84.378	82.927	81.972
14.25	88.771	85.449	83.161	81.627	80.624
14.50	87.922	84.390	81.973	80.363	79.315
14.75	87.086	83.352	80.814	79.133	78.046
15.00	86.261	82.335	79.683	77.937	76.813
15.25	85.448	81.337	78.578	76.772	75.616
15.50	84.648	80.360	77.500	75.639	74.454
15.75	83.858	79.400	76.447	74.535	73.324
16.00	83.080	78.460	75.418	73.460	72.226
16.25	82.313	77.538	74.413	72.413	71.158
16.50	81.556	76.634	73.431	71.392	70.120
16.75	80.810	75.746	72.472	70.398	69.110
17.00	80.076	74.876	71.534	69.429	68.126
17.25	79.351	74.022	70.617	68.483	67.170
17.50	78.636	73.184	69.721	67.561	66.238
17.75	77.931	72.362	68.844	66.662	65.330
18.00	77.237	71.556	67.987	65.785	64.446
18.25	76.552	70.764	67.149	64.929	63.585
18.50	75.876	69.987	66.329	64.093	62.745
18.75	75.210	69.224	65.527	63.277	61.927
19.00	74.553	68.475	64.742	62.481	61.128

VALUE OF AMORTIZING MORTGAGE LOANS
AS PERCENTAGE OF FACE VALUE
FACE INTEREST RATE: 11.5%

YIELD TO MATURITY	TERM OF LOAN (YEARS)				
	10	15	20	25	30
10.00	106.390	108.709	110.508	111.860	112.844
10.25	105.284	107.178	108.637	109.725	110.511
10.50	104.195	105.680	106.816	107.656	108.259
10.75	103.122	104.214	105.043	105.652	106.086
11.00	102.066	102.780	103.317	103.709	103.987
11.25	101.025	101.375	101.637	101.826	101.959
11.50	100.000	100.000	100.000	100.000	100.000
11.75	98.990	98.653	98.405	98.229	98.106
12.00	97.996	97.336	96.853	96.510	96.275
12.25	97.016	96.045	95.339	94.843	94.503
12.50	96.051	94.780	93.864	93.224	92.788
12.75	95.100	93.542	92.427	91.652	91.129
13.00	94.163	92.329	91.025	90.126	89.522
13.25	93.240	91.141	89.659	88.643	87.965
13.50	92.331	89.977	88.326	87.202	86.457
13.75	91.434	88.836	87.027	85.802	84.995
14.00	90.551	87.719	85.759	84.441	83.578
14.25	89.681	86.624	84.522	83.118	82.203
14.50	88.823	85.550	83.315	81.831	80.869
14.75	87.978	84.498	82.137	80.578	79.575
15.00	87.145	83.467	80.987	79.360	78.318
15.25	86.324	82.456	79.865	78.174	77.098
15.50	85.515	81.464	78.768	77.020	75.913
15.75	84.717	80.492	77.698	75.896	74.761
16.00	83.931	79.539	76.652	74.801	73.641
16.25	83.156	78.604	75.631	73.735	72.552
16.50	82.392	77.687	74.633	72.696	71.494
16.75	81.639	76.788	73.658	71.683	70.464
17.00	80.896	75.906	72.705	70.696	69.461
17.25	80.164	75.040	71.773	69.734	68.486
17.50	79.442	74.191	70.862	68.795	67.536
17.75	78.730	73.357	69.971	67.880	66.610
18.00	78.028	72.539	69.100	66.986	65.709
18.25	77.336	71.737	68.248	66.114	64.831
18.50	76.654	70.949	67.415	65.264	63.975
18.75	75.981	70.176	66.599	64.433	63.140
19.00	75.317	69.416	65.801	63.622	62.326

VALUE OF AMORTIZING MORTGAGE LOANS
AS PERCENTAGE OF FACE VALUE
FACE INTEREST RATE: 11.75%

YIELD TO MATURITY	TERM OF LOAN (YEARS)				
	10	15	20	25	30
10.00	107.476	110.192	112.299	113.877	115.023
10.25	106.359	108.641	110.398	111.703	112.645
10.50	105.258	107.123	108.547	109.597	110.350
10.75	104.174	105.637	106.745	107.557	108.134
11.00	103.107	104.183	104.992	105.580	105.995
11.25	102.056	102.759	103.284	103.662	103.928
11.50	101.020	101.365	101.620	101.803	101.931
11.75	100.000	100.000	100.000	100.000	100.000
12.00	98.996	98.664	98.422	98.251	98.133
12.25	98.006	97.356	96.884	96.553	96.327
12.50	97.031	96.074	95.385	94.905	94.580
12.75	96.070	94.819	93.924	93.305	92.888
13.00	95.124	93.590	92.500	91.751	91.250
13.25	94.191	92.385	91.112	90.242	89.664
13.50	93.273	91.205	89.758	88.775	88.126
13.75	92.367	90.049	88.437	87.349	86.636
14.00	91.475	88.916	87.148	85.964	85.192
14.25	90.596	87.806	85.892	84.617	83.790
14.50	89.729	86.718	84.665	83.306	82.431
14.75	88.876	85.651	83.468	82.032	81.111
15.00	88.035	84.606	82.299	80.791	79.830
15.25	87.205	83.581	81.159	79.584	78.586
15.50	86.388	82.576	80.045	78.409	77.378
15.75	85.582	81.591	78.957	77.265	76.204
16.00	84.787	80.625	77.894	76.150	75.063
16.25	84.005	79.677	76.856	75.065	73.953
16.50	83.233	78.748	75.842	74.007	72.874
16.75	82.472	77.836	74.851	72.976	71.824
17.00	81.722	76.942	73.883	71.971	70.802
17.25	80.982	76.064	72.936	70.991	69.808
17.50	80.253	75.203	72.010	70.036	68.839
17.75	79.533	74.358	71.105	69.104	67.896
18.00	78.824	73.530	70.220	68.194	66.978
18.25	78.125	72.716	69.354	67.307	66.082
18.50	77.436	71.917	68.507	66.440	65.210
18.75	76.756	71.133	67.678	65.595	64.359
19.00	76.085	70.364	66.867	64.769	63.529

VALUE OF AMORTIZING MORTGAGE LOANS
AS PERCENTAGE OF FACE VALUE
FACE INTEREST RATE: 12%

YIELD TO MATURITY	TERM OF LOAN (YEARS)				
	10	15	20	25	30
10.00	108.566	111.684	114.100	115.904	117.211
10.25	107.438	110.112	112.168	113.692	114.788
10.50	106.326	108.573	110.287	111.549	112.449
10.75	105.231	107.067	108.457	109.472	110.191
11.00	104.153	105.593	106.675	107.460	108.011
11.25	103.091	104.150	104.940	105.508	105.905
11.50	102.045	102.737	103.250	103.616	103.870
11.75	101.014	101.354	101.603	101.780	101.902
12.00	100.000	100.000	100.000	100.000	100.000
12.25	99.000	98.674	98.437	98.272	98.160
12.50	98.015	97.375	96.915	96.595	96.379
12.75	97.045	96.103	95.430	94.966	94.655
13.00	96.089	94.857	93.983	93.385	92.986
13.25	95.147	93.636	92.573	91.848	91.369
13.50	94.219	92.440	91.197	90.356	89.803
13.75	93.304	91.268	89.855	88.905	88.284
14.00	92.403	90.120	88.546	87.494	86.812
14.25	91.515	88.995	87.269	86.123	85.384
14.50	90.640	87.892	86.022	84.790	83.999
14.75	89.777	86.811	84.806	83.492	82.654
15.00	88.928	85.752	83.619	82.230	81.349
15.25	88.090	84.713	82.460	81.001	80.081
15.50	87.264	83.694	81.328	79.805	78.850
15.75	86.450	82.696	80.223	78.640	77.654
16.00	85.648	81.716	79.143	77.506	76.491
16.25	84.857	80.756	78.089	76.401	75.360
16.50	84.077	79.814	77.058	75.325	74.260
16.75	83.308	78.890	76.051	74.275	73.190
17.00	82.551	77.984	75.067	73.253	72.149
17.25	81.803	77.094	74.105	72.255	71.136
17.50	81.067	76.222	73.165	71.283	70.149
17.75	80.340	75.365	72.245	70.334	69.188
18.00	79.624	74.525	71.346	69.408	68.252
18.25	78.918	73.700	70.466	68.505	67.339
18.50	78.221	72.891	69.605	67.623	66.450
18.75	77.534	72.096	68.763	66.763	65.583
19.00	76.857	71.317	67.940	65.922	64.738

VALUE OF AMORTIZING MORTGAGE LOANS
AS PERCENTAGE OF FACE VALUE
FACE INTEREST RATE: 12.25%

YIELD TO MATURITY	TERM OF LOAN (YEARS)				
	10	15	20	25	30
10.00	109.662	113.185	115.911	117.942	119.409
10.25	108.523	111.592	113.948	115.691	116.940
10.50	107.399	110.032	112.038	113.510	114.557
10.75	106.294	108.506	110.179	111.397	112.257
11.00	105.205	107.012	108.368	109.349	110.036
11.25	104.132	105.550	106.605	107.363	107.890
11.50	103.076	104.118	104.889	105.438	105.817
11.75	102.035	102.716	103.216	103.570	103.813
12.00	101.010	101.344	101.587	101.758	101.875
12.25	100.000	100.000	100.000	100.000	100.000
12.50	99.005	98.684	98.453	98.293	98.186
12.75	98.025	97.394	96.945	96.636	96.430
13.00	97.059	96.132	95.475	95.027	94.729
13.25	96.108	94.895	94.042	93.463	93.082
13.50	95.171	93.683	92.644	91.944	91.486
13.75	94.246	92.495	91.281	90.468	89.939
14.00	93.336	91.331	89.951	89.033	88.440
14.25	92.439	90.191	88.654	87.638	86.985
14.50	91.555	89.073	87.388	86.280	85.574
14.75	90.684	87.978	86.152	84.960	84.204
15.00	89.826	86.904	84.946	83.676	82.874
15.25	88.979	85.851	83.769	82.425	81.583
15.50	88.145	84.819	82.619	81.208	80.328
15.75	87.323	83.807	81.496	80.023	79.109
16.00	86.512	82.815	80.400	78.869	77.925
16.25	85.714	81.841	79.328	77.745	76.773
16.50	84.926	80.887	78.281	76.649	75.652
16.75	84.150	79.950	77.259	75.582	74.562
17.00	83.384	79.032	76.259	74.541	73.502
17.25	82.629	78.130	75.282	73.526	72.469
17.50	81.885	77.246	74.326	72.536	71.464
17.75	81.152	76.378	73.392	71.571	70.485
18.00	80.428	75.527	72.478	70.629	69.531
18.25	79.715	74.691	71.585	69.710	68.602
18.50	79.011	73.871	70.710	68.812	67.696
18.75	78.318	73.065	69.855	67.937	66.813
19.00	77.633	72.275	69.018	67.081	65.951

VALUE OF AMORTIZING MORTGAGE LOANS
AS PERCENTAGE OF FACE VALUE
FACE INTEREST RATE: 12.5%

YIELD TO MATURITY	TERM OF LOAN (YEARS)				
	10	15	20	25	30
10.00	110.765	114.695	117.732	119.990	121.615
10.25	109.614	113.081	115.739	117.700	119.100
10.50	108.479	111.500	113.798	115.481	116.673
10.75	107.362	109.954	111.910	113.332	114.331
11.00	106.263	108.440	110.071	111.248	112.069
11.25	105.179	106.958	108.281	109.228	109.884
11.50	104.112	105.507	106.537	107.269	107.772
11.75	103.060	104.086	104.838	105.369	105.731
12.00	102.025	102.696	103.184	103.525	103.757
12.25	101.005	101.334	101.571	101.737	101.848
12.50	100.000	100.000	100.000	100.000	100.000
12.75	99.010	98.694	98.469	98.314	98.212
13.00	98.035	97.414	96.976	96.677	96.480
13.25	97.074	96.160	95.520	95.086	94.802
13.50	96.127	94.932	94.100	93.541	93.177
13.75	95.194	93.729	92.715	92.039	91.601
14.00	94.274	92.550	91.365	90.579	90.074
14.25	93.369	91.394	90.047	89.159	88.592
14.50	92.475	90.262	88.761	87.779	87.155
14.75	91.596	89.152	87.506	86.436	85.760
15.00	90.729	88.064	86.281	85.129	84.405
15.25	89.874	86.997	85.085	83.857	83.090
15.50	89.031	85.951	83.917	82.619	81.813
15.75	88.201	84.925	82.777	81.413	80.571
16.00	87.382	83.919	81.663	80.239	79.364
16.25	86.575	82.933	80.575	79.095	78.191
16.50	85.780	81.966	79.512	77.980	77.050
16.75	84.995	81.017	78.473	76.894	75.940
17.00	84.223	80.086	77.457	75.835	74.860
17.25	83.460	79.172	76.464	74.803	73.808
17.50	82.709	78.276	75.494	73.796	72.785
17.75	81.967	77.397	74.545	72.814	71.787
18.00	81.237	76.534	73.617	71.855	70.816
18.25	80.516	75.687	72.709	70.920	69.869
18.50	79.805	74.856	71.821	70.007	68.947
18.75	79.105	74.040	70.953	69.116	68.047
19.00	78.414	73.239	70.103	68.246	67.170

VALUE OF AMORTIZING MORTGAGE LOANS
AS PERCENTAGE OF FACE VALUE
FACE INTEREST RATE: 12.75%

YIELD TO MATURITY	TERM OF LOAN (YEARS)				
	10	15	20	25	30
10.00	111.872	116.213	119.563	122.048	123.830
10.25	110.709	114.578	117.539	119.719	121.269
10.50	109.563	112.976	115.568	117.462	118.798
10.75	108.436	111.409	113.650	115.275	116.413
11.00	107.325	109.875	111.783	113.156	114.110
11.25	106.230	108.373	109.965	111.101	111.885
11.50	105.153	106.904	108.194	109.108	109.735
11.75	104.090	105.464	106.469	107.176	107.656
12.00	103.045	104.055	104.789	105.301	105.647
12.25	102.015	102.675	103.151	103.481	103.702
12.50	101.000	101.324	101.555	101.715	101.821
12.75	100.000	100.000	100.000	100.000	100.000
13.00	99.015	98.704	98.484	98.335	98.237
13.25	98.044	97.433	97.005	96.717	96.529
13.50	97.088	96.189	95.564	95.145	94.874
13.75	96.145	94.969	94.157	93.617	93.269
14.00	95.217	93.775	92.786	92.132	91.714
14.25	94.302	92.604	91.448	90.688	90.205
14.50	93.400	91.456	90.142	89.284	88.742
14.75	92.511	90.332	88.867	87.918	87.321
15.00	91.636	89.229	87.623	86.589	85.942
15.25	90.772	88.148	86.408	85.295	84.603
15.50	89.921	87.088	85.223	84.035	83.302
15.75	89.082	86.049	84.064	82.809	82.038
16.00	88.256	85.030	82.933	81.615	80.810
16.25	87.441	84.031	81.828	80.451	79.615
16.50	86.637	83.050	80.748	79.317	78.453
16.75	85.845	82.089	79.693	78.213	77.323
17.00	85.065	81.146	78.662	77.136	76.223
17.25	84.294	80.220	77.654	76.085	75.152
17.50	83.535	79.312	76.668	75.061	74.110
17.75	82.787	78.421	75.704	74.062	73.095
18.00	82.049	77.547	74.762	73.088	72.106
18.25	81.321	76.689	73.840	72.136	71.142
18.50	80.603	75.847	72.938	71.208	70.202
18.75	79.896	75.020	72.056	70.302	69.286
19.00	79.198	74.209	71.193	69.416	68.393

VALUE OF AMORTIZING MORTGAGE LOANS
AS PERCENTAGE OF FACE VALUE
FACE INTEREST RATE: 13%

YIELD TO MATURITY	TERM OF LOAN (YEARS)				
	10	15	20	25	30
10.00	112.985	117.740	121.404	124.115	126.052
10.25	111.811	116.083	119.348	121.746	123.446
10.50	110.653	114.460	117.347	119.451	120.930
10.75	109.514	112.872	115.400	117.227	118.503
11.00	108.393	111.319	113.504	115.072	116.158
11.25	107.287	109.797	111.658	112.982	113.893
11.50	106.199	108.308	109.860	110.956	111.704
11.75	105.126	106.849	108.108	108.991	109.589
12.00	104.070	105.422	106.402	107.084	107.543
12.25	103.030	104.024	104.739	105.234	105.564
12.50	102.004	102.654	103.119	103.437	103.649
12.75	100.995	101.314	101.540	101.694	101.795
13.00	100.000	100.000	100.000	100.000	100.000
13.25	99.020	98.713	98.499	98.355	98.261
13.50	98.054	97.452	97.035	96.756	96.577
13.75	97.102	96.217	95.607	95.203	94.943
14.00	96.164	95.006	94.214	93.693	93.360
14.25	95.240	93.820	92.856	92.224	91.825
14.50	94.329	92.658	91.529	90.796	90.335
14.75	93.431	91.518	90.235	89.407	88.889
15.00	92.547	90.401	88.972	88.055	87.485
15.25	91.675	89.306	87.739	86.739	86.122
15.50	90.816	88.232	86.535	85.459	84.798
15.75	89.968	87.179	85.358	84.211	83.511
16.00	89.134	86.147	84.210	82.997	82.260
16.25	88.311	85.134	83.088	81.814	81.044
16.50	87.499	84.141	81.991	80.661	79.861
16.75	86.699	83.167	80.920	79.537	78.711
17.00	85.911	82.212	79.873	78.442	77.591
17.25	85.133	81.274	78.849	77.374	76.501
17.50	84.366	80.354	77.849	76.332	75.440
17.75	83.610	79.452	76.870	75.317	74.407
18.00	82.865	78.566	75.913	74.325	73.400
18.25	82.130	77.696	74.977	73.358	72.419
18.50	81.405	76.843	74.061	72.414	71.462
18.75	80.690	76.006	73.166	71.492	70.530
19.00	79.985	75.183	72.289	70.592	69.621

VALUE OF AMORTIZING MORTGAGE LOANS
AS PERCENTAGE OF FACE VALUE
FACE INTEREST RATE: 13.25%

YIELD TO MATURITY	TERM OF LOAN (YEARS)				
	10	15	20	25	30
10.00	114.104	119.275	123.254	126.191	128.283
10.25	112.918	117.596	121.167	123.783	125.630
10.50	111.749	115.952	119.136	121.449	123.070
10.75	110.599	114.344	117.159	119.188	120.599
11.00	109.466	112.770	115.234	116.997	118.213
11.25	108.349	111.228	113.359	114.872	115.908
11.50	107.250	109.720	111.534	112.812	113.681
11.75	106.167	108.242	109.756	110.814	111.528
12.00	105.101	106.796	108.023	108.875	109.446
12.25	104.050	105.380	106.335	106.994	107.432
12.50	103.014	103.993	104.690	105.168	105.483
12.75	101.995	102.634	103.087	103.395	103.596
13.00	100.990	101.304	101.524	101.673	101.770
13.25	100.000	100.000	100.000	100.000	100.000
13.50	99.025	98.723	98.514	98.375	98.285
13.75	98.063	97.471	97.064	96.795	96.624
14.00	97.116	96.245	95.650	95.260	95.012
14.25	96.183	95.044	94.271	93.767	93.449
14.50	95.263	93.866	92.924	92.315	91.933
14.75	94.357	92.711	91.611	90.902	90.462
15.00	93.464	91.580	90.328	89.528	89.033
15.25	92.583	90.470	89.076	88.190	87.646
15.50	91.715	89.383	87.854	86.888	86.298
15.75	90.859	88.316	86.659	85.620	84.989
16.00	90.016	87.270	85.493	84.385	83.716
16.25	89.185	86.244	84.354	83.182	82.478
16.50	88.365	85.238	83.241	82.010	81.275
16.75	87.558	84.252	82.153	80.868	80.104
17.00	86.761	83.284	81.090	79.754	78.964
17.25	85.976	82.334	80.051	78.668	77.855
17.50	85.202	81.402	79.035	77.609	76.775
17.75	84.438	80.487	78.042	76.576	75.723
18.00	83.685	79.590	77.070	75.569	74.699
18.25	82.943	78.709	76.120	74.585	73.700
18.50	82.211	77.845	75.190	73.625	72.727
18.75	81.489	76.996	74.281	72.688	71.778
19.00	80.777	76.164	73.391	71.773	70.853

VALUE OF AMORTIZING MORTGAGE LOANS
AS PERCENTAGE OF FACE VALUE
FACE INTEREST RATE: 13.5%

YIELD TO MATURITY	TERM OF LOAN (YEARS)				
	10	15	20	25	30
10.00	115.227	120.818	125.113	128.276	130.521
10.25	114.030	119.117	122.995	125.827	127.822
10.50	112.850	117.452	120.933	123.455	125.217
10.75	111.688	115.823	118.926	121.157	122.703
11.00	110.544	114.229	116.972	118.930	120.276
11.25	109.416	112.667	115.069	116.770	117.930
11.50	108.306	111.139	113.216	114.676	115.664
11.75	107.212	109.643	111.411	112.644	113.473
12.00	106.136	108.178	109.653	110.674	111.355
12.25	105.075	106.743	107.940	108.761	109.306
12.50	104.029	105.338	106.270	106.905	107.323
12.75	102.999	103.962	104.642	105.103	105.403
13.00	101.985	102.614	103.056	103.352	103.545
13.25	100.985	101.294	101.508	101.652	101.744
13.50	100.000	100.000	100.000	100.000	100.000
13.75	99.029	98.732	98.528	98.394	98.309
14.00	98.073	97.490	97.093	96.833	96.670
14.25	97.130	96.273	95.693	95.316	95.080
14.50	96.201	95.080	94.326	93.840	93.537
14.75	95.286	93.910	92.993	92.404	92.040
15.00	94.384	92.764	91.691	91.007	90.586
15.25	93.494	91.640	90.420	89.647	89.175
15.50	92.618	90.539	89.179	88.323	87.804
15.75	91.754	89.458	87.967	87.034	86.471
16.00	90.903	88.399	86.783	85.779	85.176
16.25	90.063	87.360	85.627	84.556	83.917
16.50	89.236	86.341	84.497	83.365	82.692
16.75	88.420	85.341	83.393	82.204	81.501
17.00	87.616	84.361	82.313	81.072	80.342
17.25	86.823	83.399	81.259	79.968	79.213
17.50	86.041	82.455	80.227	78.891	78.114
17.75	85.270	81.529	79.219	77.841	77.044
18.00	84.510	80.620	78.233	76.817	76.002
18.25	83.760	79.728	77.268	75.817	74.986
18.50	83.021	78.852	76.324	74.841	73.996
18.75	82.292	77.992	75.401	73.889	73.030
19.00	81.573	77.149	74.498	72.959	72.089

VALUE OF AMORTIZING MORTGAGE LOANS
AS PERCENTAGE OF FACE VALUE
FACE INTEREST RATE: 13.75%

YIELD TO MATURITY	TERM OF LOAN (YEARS)				
	10	15	20	25	30
10.00	116.357	122.369	126.982	130.369	132.766
10.25	115.148	120.647	124.832	127.881	130.020
10.50	113.956	118.960	122.739	125.470	127.371
10.75	112.783	117.310	120.702	123.134	124.814
11.00	111.628	115.696	118.719	120.871	122.344
11.25	110.489	114.114	116.788	118.676	119.959
11.50	109.369	112.566	114.907	116.547	117.654
11.75	108.264	111.051	113.075	114.483	115.425
12.00	107.177	109.567	111.291	112.480	113.270
12.25	106.105	108.114	109.552	110.536	111.186
12.50	105.049	106.691	107.857	108.650	109.169
12.75	104.009	105.297	106.205	106.818	107.216
13.00	102.985	103.932	104.595	105.039	105.326
13.25	101.975	102.594	103.025	103.311	103.494
13.50	100.981	101.284	101.494	101.632	101.720
13.75	100.000	100.000	100.000	100.000	100.000
14.00	99.034	98.742	98.543	98.414	98.332
14.25	98.083	97.509	97.122	96.871	96.715
14.50	97.145	96.301	95.735	95.371	95.146
14.75	96.220	95.117	94.381	93.912	93.623
15.00	95.310	93.956	93.060	92.492	92.144
15.25	94.411	92.817	91.770	91.110	90.709
15.50	93.527	91.702	90.511	89.765	89.314
15.75	92.654	90.607	89.281	88.455	87.958
16.00	91.794	89.534	88.079	87.179	86.641
16.25	90.947	88.482	86.906	85.936	85.360
16.50	90.111	87.450	85.759	84.725	84.115
16.75	89.287	86.437	84.638	83.545	82.903
17.00	88.475	85.444	83.543	82.395	81.724
17.25	87.674	84.470	82.472	81.273	80.576
17.50	86.885	83.514	81.426	80.179	79.458
17.75	86.106	82.576	80.402	79.112	78.369
18.00	85.338	81.655	79.401	78.071	77.309
18.25	84.582	80.752	78.422	77.055	76.276
18.50	83.835	79.865	77.464	76.063	75.268
18.75	83.099	78.994	76.527	75.095	74.286
19.00	82.373	78.139	75.610	74.149	73.329

695

VALUE OF AMORTIZING MORTGAGE LOANS
AS PERCENTAGE OF FACE VALUE
FACE INTEREST RATE: 14%

YIELD TO MATURITY	TERM OF LOAN (YEARS)				
	10	15	20	25	30
10.00	117.492	123.928	128.859	132.470	135.017
10.25	116.271	122.184	126.678	129.942	132.225
10.50	115.067	120.476	124.554	127.492	129.531
10.75	113.883	118.805	122.487	125.119	126.930
11.00	112.716	117.169	120.474	122.819	124.419
11.25	111.567	115.568	118.514	120.588	121.993
11.50	110.435	114.000	116.606	118.426	119.649
11.75	109.319	112.465	114.747	116.328	117.383
12.00	108.222	110.963	112.936	114.293	115.191
12.25	107.140	109.491	111.171	112.318	113.071
12.50	106.073	108.050	109.451	110.401	111.020
12.75	105.024	106.639	107.775	108.540	109.035
13.00	103.989	105.256	106.141	106.732	107.112
13.25	102.969	103.901	104.548	104.976	105.250
13.50	101.965	102.575	102.994	103.270	103.445
13.75	100.975	101.274	101.478	101.612	101.696
14.00	100.000	100.000	100.000	100.000	100.000
14.25	99.039	98.752	98.558	98.433	98.355
14.50	98.092	97.528	97.150	96.908	96.759
14.75	97.158	96.328	95.777	95.426	95.211
15.00	96.239	95.153	94.436	93.983	93.707
15.25	95.332	94.000	93.127	92.579	92.247
15.50	94.439	92.870	91.849	91.212	90.828
15.75	93.557	91.761	90.600	89.881	89.450
16.00	92.689	90.675	89.381	88.584	88.110
16.25	91.833	89.609	88.190	87.321	86.808
16.50	90.989	88.564	87.026	86.091	85.541
16.75	90.158	87.539	85.889	84.892	84.309
17.00	89.338	86.533	84.778	83.723	83.110
17.25	88.529	85.546	83.691	82.583	81.942
17.50	87.732	84.578	82.629	81.471	80.806
17.75	86.945	83.628	81.591	80.387	79.699
18.00	86.170	82.695	80.575	79.329	78.620
18.25	85.406	81.780	79.581	78.297	77.569
18.50	84.652	80.882	78.610	77.289	76.545
18.75	83.909	80.000	77.659	76.305	75.546
19.00	83.176	79.135	76.728	75.344	74.572

VALUE OF AMORTIZING MORTGAGE LOANS
AS PERCENTAGE OF FACE VALUE
FACE INTEREST RATE: 14.25%

YIELD TO MATURITY	TERM OF LOAN (YEARS)				
	10	15	20	25	30
10.00	118.632	125.495	130.745	134.580	137.275
10.25	117.399	123.728	128.531	132.011	134.436
10.50	116.184	121.999	126.376	129.522	131.697
10.75	114.988	120.307	124.279	127.111	129.053
11.00	113.810	118.651	122.237	124.774	126.500
11.25	112.649	117.029	120.249	122.508	124.033
11.50	111.506	115.442	118.312	120.311	121.650
11.75	110.380	113.887	116.426	118.180	119.346
12.00	109.271	112.366	114.589	116.113	117.118
12.25	108.179	110.876	112.798	114.106	114.962
12.50	107.102	109.416	111.053	112.159	112.877
12.75	106.042	107.987	109.352	110.268	110.858
13.00	104.998	106.587	107.694	108.431	108.903
13.25	103.968	105.215	106.077	106.647	107.010
13.50	102.954	103.871	104.501	104.914	105.175
13.75	101.955	102.554	102.963	103.230	103.397
14.00	100.970	101.264	101.463	101.592	101.672
14.25	100.000	100.000	100.000	100.000	100.000
14.50	99.043	98.761	98.572	98.451	98.377
14.75	98.101	97.546	97.178	96.945	96.803
15.00	97.173	96.356	95.818	95.479	95.274
15.25	96.257	95.188	94.490	94.053	93.789
15.50	95.355	94.044	93.193	92.664	92.347
15.75	94.465	92.921	91.926	91.312	90.946
16.00	93.588	91.821	90.689	89.995	89.584
16.25	92.724	90.742	89.481	88.712	88.260
16.50	91.872	89.683	88.300	87.462	86.972
16.75	91.032	88.645	87.146	86.243	85.719
17.00	90.204	87.627	86.018	85.056	84.499
17.25	89.388	86.627	84.916	83.898	83.312
17.50	88.583	85.647	83.838	82.768	82.157
17.75	87.789	84.685	82.784	81.667	81.031
18.00	87.006	83.741	81.754	80.592	79.935
18.25	86.235	82.814	80.746	79.543	78.866
18.50	85.474	81.905	79.760	78.519	77.825
18.75	84.723	81.012	78.795	77.520	76.810
19.00	83.983	80.135	77.851	76.544	75.819

VALUE OF AMORTIZING MORTGAGE LOANS
AS PERCENTAGE OF FACE VALUE
FACE INTEREST RATE: 14.5%

YIELD TO MATURITY	TERM OF LOAN (YEARS)				
	10	15	20	25	30
10.00	119.777	127.070	132.639	136.696	139.539
10.25	118.533	125.281	130.394	134.087	136.654
10.50	117.306	123.530	128.207	131.560	133.869
10.75	116.098	121.817	126.080	129.111	131.182
11.00	114.909	120.140	124.008	126.737	128.586
11.25	113.737	118.498	121.991	124.435	126.079
11.50	112.583	116.890	120.027	122.204	123.656
11.75	111.446	115.316	118.113	120.039	121.314
12.00	110.327	113.776	116.249	117.939	119.049
12.25	109.224	112.267	114.432	115.901	116.859
12.50	108.137	110.789	112.662	113.923	114.739
12.75	107.067	109.342	110.937	112.002	112.686
13.00	106.012	107.924	109.255	110.137	110.699
13.25	104.973	106.535	107.614	108.325	108.775
13.50	103.949	105.175	106.015	106.565	106.910
13.75	102.939	103.841	104.455	104.853	105.102
14.00	101.945	102.535	102.933	103.190	103.349
14.25	100.966	101.255	101.449	101.573	101.649
14.50	100.000	100.000	100.000	100.000	100.000
14.75	99.049	98.770	98.586	98.470	98.399
15.00	98.111	97.565	97.206	96.981	96.845
15.25	97.186	96.383	95.859	95.532	95.336
15.50	96.276	95.224	94.543	94.121	93.870
15.75	95.377	94.088	93.258	92.748	92.446
16.00	94.492	92.973	92.003	91.410	91.062
16.25	93.620	91.881	90.777	90.107	89.715
16.50	92.759	90.809	89.579	88.837	88.406
16.75	91.911	89.758	88.409	87.600	87.132
17.00	91.076	88.726	87.265	86.394	85.893
17.25	90.251	87.714	86.146	85.217	84.687
17.50	89.438	86.722	85.053	84.070	83.512
17.75	88.637	85.748	83.984	82.951	82.368
18.00	87.847	84.792	82.938	81.860	81.253
18.25	87.068	83.853	81.916	80.794	80.167
18.50	86.299	82.932	80.915	79.754	79.109
18.75	85.541	82.028	79.937	78.739	78.076
19.00	84.794	81.141	78.979	77.748	77.070

VALUE OF AMORTIZING MORTGAGE LOANS
AS PERCENTAGE OF FACE VALUE
FACE INTEREST RATE: 14.75%

YIELD TO MATURITY	TERM OF LOAN (YEARS)				
	10	15	20	25	30
10.00	120.928	128.652	134.541	138.821	141.809
10.25	119.671	126.841	132.264	136.171	138.877
10.50	118.433	125.068	130.046	133.604	136.047
10.75	117.214	123.333	127.888	131.117	133.316
11.00	116.013	121.636	125.787	128.706	130.678
11.25	114.830	119.973	123.740	126.369	128.130
11.50	113.665	118.346	121.748	124.103	125.668
11.75	112.517	116.752	119.807	121.904	123.287
12.00	111.387	115.193	117.916	119.772	120.986
12.25	110.273	113.665	116.073	117.702	118.759
12.50	109.176	112.169	114.278	115.693	116.605
12.75	108.095	110.703	112.528	113.743	114.520
13.00	107.030	109.268	110.821	111.848	112.500
13.25	105.981	107.862	109.158	110.008	110.544
13.50	104.947	106.484	107.536	108.220	108.649
13.75	103.928	105.134	105.953	106.483	106.812
14.00	102.925	103.812	104.410	104.794	105.030
14.25	101.936	102.516	102.904	103.151	103.303
14.50	100.961	101.245	101.434	101.554	101.627
14.75	100.000	100.000	100.000	100.000	100.000
15.00	99.054	98.780	98.600	98.488	98.421
15.25	98.120	97.583	97.233	97.016	96.887
15.50	97.200	96.410	95.899	95.584	95.397
15.75	96.293	95.259	94.595	94.189	93.950
16.00	95.400	94.131	93.323	92.831	92.543
16.25	94.519	93.025	92.079	91.507	91.175
16.50	93.651	91.940	90.864	90.218	89.844
16.75	92.794	90.875	89.677	88.961	88.550
17.00	91.951	89.831	88.516	87.736	87.290
17.25	91.118	88.807	87.382	86.541	86.064
17.50	90.298	87.802	86.273	85.377	84.870
17.75	89.488	86.815	85.188	84.240	83.708
18.00	88.691	85.847	84.128	83.132	82.575
18.25	87.904	84.897	83.091	82.050	81.471
18.50	87.128	83.965	82.076	80.994	80.395
18.75	86.363	83.050	81.083	79.963	79.346
19.00	85.609	82.151	80.112	78.956	78.323

VALUE OF AMORTIZING MORTGAGE LOANS
AS PERCENTAGE OF FACE VALUE
FACE INTEREST RATE: 15%

YIELD TO MATURITY	TERM OF LOAN (YEARS)				
	10	15	20	25	30
10.00	122.083	130.242	136.452	140.952	144.084
10.25	120.815	128.408	134.141	138.261	141.105
10.50	119.564	126.613	131.892	135.655	138.230
10.75	118.334	124.857	129.704	133.130	135.455
11.00	117.122	123.138	127.573	130.682	132.775
11.25	115.927	121.455	125.497	128.309	130.186
11.50	114.751	119.808	123.476	126.008	127.684
11.75	113.592	118.195	121.507	123.776	125.266
12.00	112.451	116.616	119.590	121.610	122.927
12.25	111.327	115.069	117.721	119.509	120.665
12.50	110.219	113.554	115.900	117.469	118.476
12.75	109.128	112.071	114.125	115.489	116.357
13.00	108.053	110.618	112.395	113.565	114.305
13.25	106.994	109.194	110.707	111.697	112.318
13.50	105.950	107.800	109.062	109.882	110.392
13.75	104.921	106.433	107.457	108.117	108.525
14.00	103.908	105.094	105.892	106.402	106.716
14.25	102.910	103.782	104.365	104.735	104.960
14.50	101.925	102.496	102.874	103.113	103.257
14.75	100.956	101.235	101.420	101.535	101.605
15.00	100.000	100.000	100.000	100.000	100.000
15.25	99.058	98.788	98.614	98.506	98.442
15.50	98.129	97.601	97.260	97.051	96.928
15.75	97.214	96.436	95.938	95.635	95.457
16.00	96.312	95.294	94.647	94.256	94.028
16.25	95.422	94.174	93.386	92.912	92.638
16.50	94.545	93.075	92.154	91.603	91.286
16.75	93.681	91.998	90.950	90.327	89.971
17.00	92.829	90.941	89.773	89.083	88.691
17.25	91.989	89.904	88.622	87.870	87.445
17.50	91.160	88.886	87.498	86.687	86.232
17.75	90.343	87.888	86.398	85.533	85.051
18.00	89.538	86.908	85.322	84.408	83.900
18.25	88.744	85.946	84.270	83.309	82.778
18.50	87.961	85.002	83.241	82.237	81.685
18.75	87.188	84.076	82.234	81.190	80.620
19.00	86.427	83.166	81.249	80.168	79.580

VALUE OF AMORTIZING MORTGAGE LOANS
AS PERCENTAGE OF FACE VALUE
FACE INTEREST RATE: 15.25%

YIELD TO MATURITY	TERM OF LOAN (YEARS)				
	10	15	20	25	30
10.00	123.245	131.839	138.370	143.090	146.365
10.25	121.964	129.983	136.027	140.359	143.339
10.50	120.702	128.166	133.746	137.713	140.418
10.75	119.459	126.389	131.527	135.149	137.599
11.00	118.236	124.649	129.366	132.664	134.876
11.25	117.030	122.945	127.261	130.255	132.246
11.50	115.843	121.277	125.212	127.919	129.705
11.75	114.672	119.644	123.216	125.653	127.248
12.00	113.521	118.046	121.271	123.455	124.873
12.25	112.386	116.480	119.376	121.322	122.575
12.50	111.267	114.947	117.529	119.251	120.351
12.75	110.166	113.446	115.729	117.240	118.199
13.00	109.081	111.975	113.975	115.288	116.115
13.25	108.011	110.534	112.264	113.391	114.096
13.50	106.958	109.122	110.595	111.548	112.139
13.75	105.919	107.738	108.968	109.757	110.243
14.00	104.897	106.383	107.380	108.016	108.405
14.25	103.889	105.055	105.832	106.323	106.622
14.50	102.895	103.753	104.320	104.677	104.892
14.75	101.916	102.477	102.845	103.075	103.213
15.00	100.951	101.226	101.406	101.517	101.583
15.25	100.000	100.000	100.000	100.000	100.000
15.50	99.063	98.798	98.628	98.523	98.462
15.75	98.138	97.619	97.287	97.086	96.968
16.00	97.228	96.463	95.978	95.685	95.516
16.25	96.330	95.329	94.699	94.321	94.104
16.50	95.445	94.217	93.449	92.992	92.731
16.75	94.572	93.126	92.228	91.697	91.395
17.00	93.712	92.056	91.035	90.434	90.095
17.25	92.864	91.006	89.868	89.203	88.829
17.50	92.028	89.976	88.728	88.002	87.597
17.75	91.203	88.966	87.612	86.831	86.397
18.00	90.390	87.974	86.522	85.688	85.228
18.25	89.588	87.000	85.455	84.573	84.089
18.50	88.798	86.045	84.411	83.485	82.978
18.75	88.018	85.107	83.390	82.422	81.896
19.00	87.249	84.186	82.391	81.384	80.840

VALUE OF AMORTIZING MORTGAGE LOANS
AS PERCENTAGE OF FACE VALUE
FACE INTEREST RATE: 15.5%

YIELD TO MATURITY	TERM OF LOAN (YEARS)				
	10	15	20	25	30
10.00	124.411	133.443	140.295	145.234	148.651
10.25	123.118	131.565	137.920	142.462	145.577
10.50	121.844	129.726	135.608	139.776	142.611
10.75	120.590	127.926	133.357	137.174	139.747
11.00	119.354	126.165	131.166	134.652	136.983
11.25	118.137	124.441	129.032	132.207	134.312
11.50	116.939	122.753	126.954	129.836	131.731
11.75	115.757	121.100	124.930	127.536	129.235
12.00	114.595	119.482	122.959	125.305	126.823
12.25	113.449	117.898	121.037	123.140	124.489
12.50	112.320	116.346	119.165	121.038	122.231
12.75	111.208	114.826	117.340	118.998	120.045
13.00	110.113	113.337	115.561	117.016	117.928
13.25	109.033	111.879	113.826	115.091	115.877
13.50	107.970	110.450	112.134	113.220	113.891
13.75	106.921	109.049	110.484	111.402	111.965
14.00	105.889	107.678	108.875	109.635	110.098
14.25	104.872	106.333	107.304	107.917	108.287
14.50	103.868	105.015	105.772	106.246	106.530
14.75	102.880	103.724	104.276	104.620	104.825
15.00	101.906	102.458	102.817	103.038	103.169
15.25	100.946	101.217	101.392	101.499	101.562
15.50	100.000	100.000	100.000	100.000	100.000
15.75	99.067	98.807	98.641	98.541	98.483
16.00	98.148	97.636	97.313	97.119	97.008
16.25	97.241	96.489	96.017	95.735	95.574
16.50	96.348	95.363	94.750	94.386	94.179
16.75	95.467	94.259	93.512	93.071	92.822
17.00	94.599	93.177	92.302	91.789	91.502
17.25	93.742	92.114	91.119	90.540	90.216
17.50	92.898	91.071	89.962	89.321	88.965
17.75	92.066	90.048	88.831	88.132	87.746
18.00	91.245	89.044	87.726	86.972	86.559
18.25	90.436	88.059	86.644	85.840	85.402
18.50	89.638	87.092	85.586	84.736	84.274
18.75	88.850	86.143	84.551	83.657	83.175
19.00	88.074	85.211	83.538	82.604	82.102

VALUE OF AMORTIZING MORTGAGE LOANS
AS PERCENTAGE OF FACE VALUE
FACE INTEREST RATE: 15.75%

YIELD TO MATURITY	TERM OF LOAN (YEARS)				
	10	15	20	25	30
10.00	125.583	135.055	142.228	147.385	150.941
10.25	124.278	133.154	139.820	144.572	147.820
10.50	122.991	131.293	137.476	141.847	144.808
10.75	121.725	129.472	135.195	139.206	141.901
11.00	120.479	127.689	132.973	136.647	139.093
11.25	119.250	125.944	130.810	134.165	136.381
11.50	118.040	124.236	128.704	131.759	133.760
11.75	116.848	122.563	126.652	129.425	131.227
12.00	115.674	120.926	124.653	127.161	128.777
12.25	114.518	119.322	122.705	124.964	126.407
12.50	113.378	117.751	120.807	122.831	124.114
12.75	112.256	116.213	118.957	120.760	121.894
13.00	111.150	114.706	117.153	118.749	119.745
13.25	110.060	113.230	115.394	116.795	117.663
13.50	108.987	111.784	113.679	114.897	115.646
13.75	107.929	110.367	112.006	113.052	113.690
14.00	106.886	108.978	110.375	111.259	111.794
14.25	105.859	107.618	108.783	109.515	109.955
14.50	104.847	106.284	107.229	107.819	108.171
14.75	103.849	104.977	105.713	106.169	106.440
15.00	102.866	103.696	104.234	104.564	104.759
15.25	101.897	102.439	102.789	103.002	103.127
15.50	100.942	101.208	101.378	101.481	101.541
15.75	100.000	100.000	100.000	100.000	100.000
16.00	99.072	98.816	98.654	98.558	98.502
16.25	98.157	97.655	97.340	97.153	97.046
16.50	97.255	96.515	96.055	95.784	95.630
16.75	96.366	95.398	94.800	94.449	94.252
17.00	95.490	94.302	93.573	93.149	92.912
17.25	94.625	93.226	92.374	91.881	91.607
17.50	93.773	92.171	91.202	90.644	90.336
17.75	92.933	91.136	90.055	89.437	89.098
18.00	92.104	90.120	88.934	88.260	87.893
18.25	91.288	89.123	87.838	87.112	86.718
18.50	90.482	88.144	86.765	85.991	85.573
18.75	89.687	87.183	85.716	84.896	84.456
19.00	88.904	86.240	84.689	83.827	83.367

VALUE OF AMORTIZING MORTGAGE LOANS
AS PERCENTAGE OF FACE VALUE
FACE INTEREST RATE: 16%

YIELD TO MATURITY	TERM OF LOAN (YEARS)				
	10	15	20	25	30
10.00	126.759	136.673	144.168	149.542	153.236
10.25	125.442	134.749	141.727	146.688	150.068
10.50	124.143	132.866	139.351	143.922	147.010
10.75	122.865	131.023	137.039	141.243	144.058
11.00	121.607	129.219	134.787	138.646	141.208
11.25	120.367	127.453	132.594	136.128	138.455
11.50	119.146	125.725	130.459	133.687	135.794
11.75	117.942	124.032	128.379	131.319	133.222
12.00	116.758	122.375	126.353	129.022	130.735
12.25	115.590	120.752	124.379	126.792	128.329
12.50	114.440	119.162	122.454	124.628	126.001
12.75	113.307	117.606	120.579	122.527	123.748
13.00	112.191	116.081	118.751	120.487	121.566
13.25	111.091	114.587	116.968	118.504	119.452
13.50	110.008	113.124	115.230	116.578	117.404
13.75	108.939	111.689	113.534	114.706	115.419
14.00	107.888	110.284	111.880	112.887	113.494
14.25	106.851	108.907	110.267	111.118	111.627
14.50	105.829	107.558	108.692	109.397	109.816
14.75	104.822	106.235	107.155	107.723	108.058
15.00	103.830	104.938	105.655	106.094	106.352
15.25	102.851	103.667	104.191	104.509	104.694
15.50	101.887	102.421	102.761	102.966	103.085
15.75	100.937	101.198	101.364	101.463	101.520
16.00	100.000	100.000	100.000	100.000	100.000
16.25	99.077	98.825	98.668	98.574	98.522
16.50	98.166	97.672	97.365	97.185	97.084
16.75	97.269	96.541	96.093	95.832	95.685
17.00	96.384	95.432	94.850	94.512	94.324
17.25	95.512	94.344	93.634	93.225	92.999
17.50	94.652	93.276	92.446	91.970	91.709
17.75	93.803	92.228	91.284	90.746	90.453
18.00	92.967	91.200	90.147	89.552	89.229
18.25	92.143	90.191	89.036	88.387	88.036
18.50	91.329	89.200	87.949	87.249	86.874
18.75	90.527	88.228	86.885	86.138	85.740
19.00	89.737	87.273	85.844	85.054	84.635

VALUE OF AMORTIZING MORTGAGE LOANS
AS PERCENTAGE OF FACE VALUE
FACE INTEREST RATE: 16.25%

YIELD TO MATURITY	TERM OF LOAN (YEARS)				
	10	15	20	25	30
10.00	127.940	138.299	146.115	151.704	155.535
10.25	126.611	136.352	143.641	148.809	152.319
10.50	125.300	134.446	141.233	146.004	149.216
10.75	124.010	132.581	138.889	143.286	146.220
11.00	122.740	130.756	136.608	140.651	143.327
11.25	121.488	128.969	134.385	138.097	140.532
11.50	120.256	127.220	132.221	135.621	137.832
11.75	119.041	125.507	130.113	133.218	135.221
12.00	117.846	123.830	128.059	130.888	132.697
12.25	116.667	122.188	126.058	128.626	130.255
12.50	115.506	120.579	124.108	126.430	127.892
12.75	114.363	119.004	122.208	124.299	125.604
13.00	113.237	117.461	120.355	122.229	123.390
13.25	112.126	115.949	118.548	120.218	121.244
13.50	111.033	114.469	116.786	118.264	119.165
13.75	109.955	113.017	115.067	116.365	117.150
14.00	108.893	111.596	113.391	114.519	115.197
14.25	107.847	110.203	111.756	112.725	113.302
14.50	106.815	108.837	110.160	110.979	111.464
14.75	105.799	107.498	108.602	109.281	109.679
15.00	104.797	106.186	107.082	107.629	107.947
15.25	103.810	104.900	105.598	106.021	106.265
15.50	102.837	103.639	104.148	104.455	104.631
15.75	101.877	102.402	102.733	102.931	103.044
16.00	100.932	101.189	101.350	101.446	101.500
16.25	100.000	100.000	100.000	100.000	100.000
16.50	99.081	98.833	98.680	98.591	98.541
16.75	98.175	97.689	97.391	97.217	97.121
17.00	97.282	96.567	96.131	95.879	95.740
17.25	96.402	95.466	94.899	94.573	94.395
17.50	95.534	94.385	93.694	93.300	93.085
17.75	94.677	93.325	92.517	92.059	91.810
18.00	93.833	92.284	91.365	90.847	90.568
18.25	93.001	91.263	90.238	89.665	89.357
18.50	92.180	90.261	89.136	88.511	88.177
18.75	91.371	89.277	88.058	87.384	87.027
19.00	90.573	88.311	87.003	86.284	85.905

VALUE OF AMORTIZING MORTGAGE LOANS
AS PERCENTAGE OF FACE VALUE
FACE INTEREST RATE: 16.5%

YIELD TO MATURITY	TERM OF LOAN (YEARS)				
	10	15	20	25	30
10.00	129.127	139.931	148.069	153.873	157.839
10.25	127.785	137.961	145.562	150.936	154.575
10.50	126.462	136.033	143.122	148.091	151.425
10.75	125.161	134.146	140.747	145.334	148.385
11.00	123.879	132.300	138.434	142.662	145.449
11.25	122.615	130.491	136.182	140.071	142.613
11.50	121.371	128.721	133.989	137.559	139.873
11.75	120.145	126.988	131.853	135.122	137.223
12.00	118.939	125.292	129.772	132.759	134.662
12.25	117.750	123.630	127.744	130.464	132.184
12.50	116.578	122.002	125.768	128.238	129.786
12.75	115.424	120.409	123.842	126.076	127.465
13.00	114.287	118.848	121.964	123.976	125.217
13.25	113.166	117.318	120.133	121.936	123.040
13.50	112.063	115.820	118.348	119.955	120.930
13.75	110.974	114.351	116.606	118.029	118.885
14.00	109.903	112.913	114.908	116.156	116.903
14.25	108.847	111.503	113.250	114.336	114.980
14.50	107.806	110.121	111.633	112.565	113.114
14.75	106.780	108.767	110.055	110.843	111.304
15.00	105.769	107.440	108.514	109.167	109.546
15.25	104.773	106.138	107.010	107.536	107.839
15.50	103.791	104.862	105.541	105.948	106.181
15.75	102.822	103.611	104.107	104.402	104.570
16.00	101.868	102.384	102.706	102.896	103.004
16.25	100.928	101.180	101.337	101.429	101.481
16.50	100.000	100.000	100.000	100.000	100.000
16.75	99.086	98.842	98.693	98.607	98.559
17.00	98.185	97.707	97.416	97.249	97.157
17.25	97.296	96.592	96.168	95.925	95.793
17.50	96.420	95.499	94.947	94.634	94.464
17.75	95.556	94.426	93.754	93.374	93.170
18.00	94.704	93.374	92.587	92.146	91.909
18.25	93.864	92.340	91.445	90.946	90.681
18.50	93.035	91.326	90.328	89.776	89.483
18.75	92.219	90.331	89.236	88.633	88.316
19.00	91.413	89.354	88.167	87.517	87.177

VALUE OF AMORTIZING MORTGAGE LOANS
AS PERCENTAGE OF FACE VALUE
FACE INTEREST RATE: 16.75%

YIELD TO MATURITY	TERM OF LOAN (YEARS)				
	10	15	20	25	30
10.00	130.318	141.570	150.030	156.046	160.146
10.25	128.964	139.577	147.490	153.068	156.835
10.50	127.629	137.626	145.017	150.183	153.639
10.75	126.315	135.717	142.610	147.387	150.554
11.00	125.022	133.849	140.267	144.677	147.576
11.25	123.746	132.019	137.985	142.050	144.698
11.50	122.491	130.229	135.763	139.502	141.917
11.75	121.254	128.475	133.599	137.031	139.229
12.00	120.036	126.759	131.490	134.634	136.630
12.25	118.836	125.078	129.436	132.307	134.116
12.50	117.653	123.431	127.433	130.049	131.683
12.75	116.489	121.819	125.481	127.857	129.328
13.00	115.341	120.240	123.579	125.727	127.047
13.25	114.210	118.692	121.724	123.659	124.838
13.50	113.097	117.176	119.915	121.649	122.698
13.75	111.998	115.691	118.150	119.696	120.623
14.00	110.917	114.235	116.429	117.797	118.612
14.25	109.851	112.809	114.750	115.951	116.661
14.50	108.800	111.411	113.111	114.155	114.768
14.75	107.765	110.041	111.512	112.409	112.931
15.00	106.745	108.698	109.951	110.709	111.147
15.25	105.739	107.381	108.427	109.055	109.415
15.50	104.748	106.090	106.939	107.445	107.733
15.75	103.771	104.824	105.485	105.877	106.098
16.00	102.808	103.583	104.066	104.350	104.509
16.25	101.859	102.365	102.679	102.862	102.964
16.50	100.923	101.171	101.324	101.413	101.462
16.75	100.000	100.000	100.000	100.000	100.000
17.00	99.091	98.851	98.706	98.623	98.578
17.25	98.193	97.724	97.441	97.280	97.193
17.50	97.309	96.618	96.204	95.971	95.845
17.75	96.437	95.532	94.995	94.693	94.532
18.00	95.578	94.467	93.813	93.447	93.253
18.25	94.730	93.422	92.656	92.231	92.006
18.50	93.894	92.396	91.524	91.044	90.791
18.75	93.069	91.389	90.417	89.885	89.607
19.00	92.256	90.400	89.334	88.754	88.451

VALUE OF AMORTIZING MORTGAGE LOANS
AS PERCENTAGE OF FACE VALUE
FACE INTEREST RATE: 17%

YIELD TO MATURITY	TERM OF LOAN (YEARS)				
	10	15	20	25	30
10.00	131.514	143.215	151.996	158.225	162.457
10.25	130.147	141.199	149.423	155.205	159.098
10.50	128.800	139.226	146.918	152.279	155.856
10.75	127.475	137.295	144.480	149.445	152.727
11.00	126.169	135.405	142.106	146.697	149.705
11.25	124.882	133.554	139.794	144.033	146.786
11.50	123.615	131.742	137.543	141.450	143.965
11.75	122.366	129.968	135.350	138.944	141.238
12.00	121.138	128.232	133.214	136.514	138.602
12.25	119.926	126.532	131.132	134.155	136.051
12.50	118.733	124.866	129.104	131.865	133.583
12.75	117.558	123.235	127.126	129.642	131.194
13.00	116.400	121.637	125.199	127.483	128.880
13.25	115.259	120.072	123.319	125.385	126.640
13.50	114.135	118.538	121.487	123.348	124.468
13.75	113.026	117.035	119.699	121.367	122.364
14.00	111.935	115.563	117.955	119.442	120.323
14.25	110.859	114.120	116.254	117.570	118.344
14.50	109.799	112.706	114.594	115.749	116.424
14.75	108.754	111.320	112.974	113.978	114.560
15.00	107.725	109.961	111.392	112.255	112.751
15.25	106.710	108.629	109.848	110.578	110.994
15.50	105.710	107.323	108.340	108.945	109.288
15.75	104.723	106.042	106.868	107.355	107.629
16.00	103.751	104.787	105.430	105.807	106.017
16.25	102.793	103.555	104.025	104.298	104.450
16.50	101.849	102.347	102.652	102.829	102.926
16.75	100.918	101.162	101.311	101.396	101.443
17.00	100.000	100.000	100.000	100.000	100.000
17.25	99.095	98.859	98.718	98.639	98.595
17.50	98.202	97.741	97.466	97.311	97.228
17.75	97.322	96.643	96.240	96.016	95.896
18.00	96.455	95.565	95.042	94.752	94.598
18.25	95.599	94.508	93.871	93.519	93.334
18.50	94.755	93.470	92.724	92.315	92.101
18.75	93.923	92.451	91.602	91.140	90.900
19.00	93.103	91.451	90.505	89.993	89.728

VALUE OF AMORTIZING MORTGAGE LOANS
AS PERCENTAGE OF FACE VALUE
FACE INTEREST RATE: 17.25%

YIELD TO MATURITY	TERM OF LOAN (YEARS)				
	10	15	20	25	30
10.00	132.716	144.868	153.970	160.409	164.771
10.25	131.337	142.828	151.363	157.348	161.364
10.50	129.977	140.832	148.825	154.381	158.076
10.75	128.639	138.879	146.355	151.507	154.902
11.00	127.322	136.967	143.951	148.722	151.838
11.25	126.023	135.095	141.609	146.021	148.877
11.50	124.745	133.262	139.329	143.402	146.016
11.75	123.484	131.468	137.107	140.862	143.250
12.00	122.244	129.712	134.943	138.398	140.576
12.25	121.022	127.991	132.835	136.007	137.989
12.50	119.818	126.307	130.780	133.685	135.486
12.75	118.632	124.657	128.777	131.431	133.063
13.00	117.463	123.040	126.824	129.242	130.717
13.25	116.312	121.457	124.920	127.116	128.444
13.50	115.177	119.906	123.064	125.050	126.242
13.75	114.059	118.386	121.253	123.042	124.107
14.00	112.957	116.896	119.487	121.091	122.037
14.25	111.872	115.437	117.763	119.193	120.030
14.50	110.802	114.006	116.082	117.347	118.082
14.75	109.748	112.604	114.440	115.552	116.192
15.00	108.709	111.230	112.838	113.804	114.357
15.25	107.685	109.882	111.274	112.104	112.576
15.50	106.675	108.561	109.747	110.449	110.845
15.75	105.680	107.266	108.255	108.837	109.163
16.00	104.699	105.996	106.799	107.267	107.528
16.25	103.733	104.750	105.376	105.738	105.938
16.50	102.779	103.528	103.985	104.248	104.392
16.75	101.840	102.329	102.626	102.796	102.888
17.00	100.914	101.154	101.298	101.380	101.425
17.25	100.000	100.000	100.000	100.000	100.000
17.50	99.100	98.868	98.731	98.654	98.613
17.75	98.211	97.758	97.490	97.341	97.262
18.00	97.336	96.668	96.276	96.060	95.946
18.25	96.473	95.598	95.089	94.810	94.663
18.50	95.621	94.548	93.928	93.589	93.413
18.75	94.782	93.518	92.792	92.398	92.194
19.00	93.954	92.506	91.680	91.235	91.006

VALUE OF AMORTIZING MORTGAGE LOANS
AS PERCENTAGE OF FACE VALUE
FACE INTEREST RATE: 17.5%

YIELD TO MATURITY	TERM OF LOAN (YEARS)				
	10	15	20	25	30
10.00	133.922	146.526	155.949	162.598	167.089
10.25	132.530	144.463	153.309	159.495	163.634
10.50	131.158	142.444	150.738	156.488	160.300
10.75	129.808	140.468	148.237	153.575	157.081
11.00	128.479	138.535	145.801	150.751	153.974
11.25	127.168	136.641	143.429	148.013	150.971
11.50	125.878	134.788	141.120	145.359	148.070
11.75	124.607	132.973	138.869	142.784	145.265
12.00	123.355	131.197	136.678	140.286	142.554
12.25	122.122	129.457	134.542	137.862	139.930
12.50	120.907	127.752	132.461	135.509	137.392
12.75	119.710	126.084	130.432	133.225	134.935
13.00	118.531	124.449	128.455	131.006	132.555
13.25	117.369	122.847	126.526	128.851	130.250
13.50	116.224	121.278	124.646	126.756	128.017
13.75	115.095	119.741	122.812	124.721	125.853
14.00	113.984	118.234	121.023	122.743	123.754
14.25	112.889	116.758	119.277	120.819	121.718
14.50	111.809	115.311	117.574	118.948	119.743
14.75	110.745	113.893	115.911	117.128	117.827
15.00	109.697	112.503	114.289	115.357	115.966
15.25	108.663	111.140	112.704	113.634	114.159
15.50	107.645	109.804	111.158	111.956	112.404
15.75	106.640	108.494	109.647	110.322	110.698
16.00	105.651	107.209	108.171	108.731	109.040
16.25	104.675	105.949	106.730	107.181	107.428
16.50	103.713	104.713	105.322	105.670	105.861
16.75	102.765	103.501	103.945	104.198	104.335
17.00	101.831	102.312	102.600	102.764	102.851
17.25	100.909	101.145	101.285	101.364	101.407
17.50	100.000	100.000	100.000	100.000	100.000
17.75	99.104	98.877	98.743	98.669	98.630
18.00	98.220	97.774	97.514	97.371	97.295
18.25	97.349	96.692	96.311	96.103	95.995
18.50	96.490	95.630	95.135	94.866	94.727
18.75	95.643	94.588	93.985	93.659	93.491
19.00	94.807	93.565	92.858	92.480	92.286

VALUE OF AMORTIZING MORTGAGE LOANS
AS PERCENTAGE OF FACE VALUE
FACE INTEREST RATE: 17.75%

YIELD TO MATURITY	TERM OF LOAN (YEARS)				
	10	15	20	25	30
10.00	135.133	148.191	157.934	164.791	169.410
10.25	133.728	146.105	155.260	161.646	165.907
10.50	132.344	144.063	152.657	158.599	162.526
10.75	130.982	142.064	150.124	155.646	159.263
11.00	129.640	140.109	147.657	152.785	156.112
11.25	128.318	138.194	145.255	150.010	153.068
11.50	127.016	136.319	142.916	147.320	150.127
11.75	125.733	134.484	140.637	144.710	147.283
12.00	124.471	132.687	138.418	142.179	144.534
12.25	123.226	130.927	136.255	139.722	141.874
12.50	122.000	129.204	134.147	137.337	139.300
12.75	120.792	127.516	132.093	135.022	136.809
13.00	119.603	125.863	130.090	132.773	134.396
13.25	118.430	124.243	128.137	130.589	132.060
13.50	117.275	122.656	126.233	128.466	129.795
13.75	116.136	121.101	124.375	126.403	127.601
14.00	115.015	119.578	122.563	124.398	125.473
14.25	113.910	118.085	120.796	122.449	123.409
14.50	112.820	116.621	119.070	120.553	121.407
14.75	111.746	115.187	117.387	118.708	119.463
15.00	110.689	113.781	115.744	116.913	117.577
15.25	109.646	112.403	114.139	115.166	115.745
15.50	108.618	111.052	112.573	113.466	113.965
15.75	107.605	109.726	111.043	111.810	112.236
16.00	106.606	108.427	109.548	110.197	110.555
16.25	105.622	107.153	108.089	108.626	108.920
16.50	104.651	105.903	106.662	107.096	107.331
16.75	103.694	104.677	105.269	105.604	105.785
17.00	102.751	103.474	103.906	104.150	104.280
17.25	101.821	102.294	102.575	102.732	102.815
17.50	100.904	101.136	101.273	101.349	101.389
17.75	100.000	100.000	100.000	100.000	100.000
18.00	99.109	98.885	98.755	98.684	98.647
18.25	98.230	97.791	97.538	97.400	97.328
18.50	97.363	96.717	96.346	96.146	96.043
18.75	96.508	95.663	95.181	94.922	94.790
19.00	95.665	94.628	94.041	93.727	93.568

711

PREMIUMS FOR ASSUMABLE LOANS
(Maximum Premiums for Assumable Loans as Percentage of Loan Balance)

Homes are often sold with a provision for the buyer to assume the existing mortgage, rather than arrange new financing. Some older loans carry interest rates below the rates charged on new loans. When the buyer assumes such a loan (and the lender does not have the authority to escalate the rate), monthly loan payments will be lower than for a comparable loan at the higher market rate of interest. Consequently, buyers are often willing to pay a higher price for the home because of the assumable mortgage.

The tables which follow provide indications of the highest additional price sellers should expect to receive for specific assumable loans. At the premium shown in the table, a buyer would be indifferent between assuming the loan and arranging new financing, assuming the buyer has enough additional cash to pay the premium. In the actual market, the price will be set through negotiation between buyer and seller, so the actual premium paid for the favorable assumption tends to be lower than the maximum indicated in the table.

To use the tables, you need the following information:

1. *The market value of the home with new financing.* How much would the home be worth if the assumable loan did not exist? A knowledgeable real estate appraiser should be able to provide an indication.

2. *The interest rate on new financing* (current rate). What is the current interest rate on new mortgage loans with a maturity similar to the remaining term on the assumable loan? The tables cover current rates ranging from 9% to 18% in .25% intervals.

3. *The interest rate on the assumable loan* (face interest rate). This is the rate you are paying on the existing loan and that the buyer will be paying on the assumed loan. In some cases, lenders may raise the rate above what the seller has paid but keep it below that of new financing. The rate charged to the buyer is the rate to use. The tables cover face rates from 6% to 17.75% in intervals of .25%.

4. *The remaining term of the existing loan.* How many more years are left on the loan that will be assumed? The tables cover terms of 15, 20, 25, 27, and 30 years. Select the term which is closest to the actual remaining term on the loan.

5. *The remaining balance of the assumable loan.* How much is still owed on the existing loan? This represents the amount of the purchase price that will be covered by the assumed loan.

Example. A home is valued at $60,000. The owner has an assumable loan with a remaining principal balance of $30,000 and a 21-year remaining term. The loan may be assumed at the existing interest rate of 6%. What is the maximum price the seller can expect to receive if the current market interest rate for 20-year loans is 14%?

Look at the first table covering face interest rates of 6%. Look down the "CURRENT RATE" column to find 14.00%. Follow this row over to the column under 20-year remaining term. (The table has no 21-year re-

maining term column, so use the column which most closely matches the actual remaining term in the problem.) The premium listed in the table is 42.387%. Multiply this percentage by the remaining balance of the assumed loan, or $30,000. The result is $12,716 which is added to the home's market value of $60,000. The home could sell for as much as $72,716 owing to the assumable loan.

Example. A home is for sale. The seller wants $70,000 cash which is in line with prices of similar homes on the market. Alternatively, the seller is willing to provide financing for $50,000 of the price with an amortizing loan at 10% interest over 25 years. If the financing is included, the seller will demand a higher price. If current mortgage interest rates for 25-year loans is 15%, what is the highest price a buyer should pay under the favorable financing arrangement?

Look for the table with a "FACE INTEREST RATE" of 10%. Follow down the "CURRENT RATE" column to find 15.00%. Follow this row to the "25" column and read the premium of 29.054%. Multiply this percentage by the balance of $50,000 to obtain the amount of $14,527. The buyer could pay up to $70,000 plus $14,527, or $84,527, for the home with the seller financing.

MAXIMUM PREMIUM FOR ASSUMABLE LOANS
AS PERCENTAGE OF LOAN BALANCE
FACE INTEREST RATE: 6%

CURRENT RATE	REMAINING TERM OF LOAN (YEARS)				
	15	20	25	27	30
9.00	16.801	20.372	23.224	24.193	25.487
9.25	18.008	21.776	24.765	25.776	27.122
9.50	19.188	23.140	26.256	27.305	28.697
9.75	20.343	24.468	27.699	28.783	30.216
10.00	21.473	25.760	29.097	30.211	31.681
10.25	22.578	27.017	30.450	31.591	33.093
10.50	23.661	28.241	31.761	32.927	34.457
10.75	24.719	29.432	33.031	34.219	35.773
11.00	25.756	30.591	34.263	35.469	37.043
11.25	26.771	31.720	35.456	36.679	38.271
11.50	27.764	32.820	36.614	37.851	39.457
11.75	28.737	33.891	37.737	38.986	40.604
12.00	29.688	34.934	38.826	40.085	41.713
12.25	30.621	35.951	39.883	41.150	42.785
12.50	31.534	36.942	40.909	42.183	43.823
12.75	32.429	37.907	41.905	43.185	44.828
13.00	33.305	38.849	42.873	44.156	45.801
13.25	34.163	39.767	43.813	45.099	46.743
13.50	35.004	40.662	44.726	46.013	47.656
13.75	35.828	41.535	45.613	46.901	48.541
14.00	36.635	42.387	46.476	47.763	49.400
14.25	37.426	43.218	47.315	48.601	50.232
14.50	38.202	44.029	48.131	49.414	51.039
14.75	38.962	44.820	48.924	50.205	51.823
15.00	39.707	45.593	49.697	50.973	52.584
15.25	40.437	46.347	50.448	51.720	53.323
15.50	41.153	47.083	51.180	52.447	54.040
15.75	41.856	47.802	51.892	53.154	54.738
16.00	42.544	48.505	52.586	53.842	55.416
16.25	43.219	49.191	53.262	54.511	56.075
16.50	43.882	49.861	53.921	55.163	56.716
16.75	44.531	50.517	54.563	55.798	57.339
17.00	45.169	51.157	55.188	56.416	57.946
17.25	45.794	51.783	55.798	57.018	58.537
17.50	46.407	52.395	56.393	57.605	59.112
17.75	47.010	52.993	56.974	58.177	59.672
18.00	47.600	53.578	57.540	58.735	60.218

MAXIMUM PREMIUM FOR ASSUMABLE LOANS
AS PERCENTAGE OF LOAN BALANCE
FACE INTEREST RATE: 6.25%

CURRENT RATE	REMAINING TERM OF LOAN (YEARS)				
	15	20	25	27	30
9.00	15.464	18.761	21.393	22.286	23.478
9.25	16.691	20.193	22.971	23.909	25.157
9.50	17.889	21.586	24.497	25.477	26.775
9.75	19.063	22.940	25.975	26.991	28.335
10.00	20.211	24.258	27.406	28.455	29.839
10.25	21.334	25.541	28.791	29.871	31.290
10.50	22.434	26.789	30.134	31.240	32.690
10.75	23.510	28.004	31.434	32.564	34.041
11.00	24.563	29.187	32.695	33.846	35.346
11.25	25.594	30.339	33.917	35.086	36.607
11.50	26.603	31.461	35.102	36.287	37.825
11.75	27.591	32.554	36.252	37.451	39.003
12.00	28.559	33.618	37.367	38.578	40.141
12.25	29.506	34.655	38.449	39.670	41.243
12.50	30.434	35.666	39.500	40.729	42.309
12.75	31.343	36.651	40.520	41.756	43.341
13.00	32.233	37.612	41.510	42.752	44.340
13.25	33.105	38.548	42.473	43.718	45.307
13.50	33.959	39.462	43.408	44.655	46.245
13.75	34.797	40.353	44.316	45.566	47.154
14.00	35.617	41.221	45.200	46.449	48.035
14.25	36.421	42.069	46.058	47.308	48.890
14.50	37.209	42.896	46.894	48.142	49.719
14.75	37.981	43.704	47.706	48.952	50.524
15.00	38.738	44.492	48.497	49.740	51.305
15.25	39.480	45.261	49.267	50.506	52.064
15.50	40.208	46.013	50.016	51.251	52.801
15.75	40.921	46.746	50.745	51.975	53.518
16.00	41.621	47.463	51.455	52.681	54.214
16.25	42.307	48.163	52.148	53.367	54.891
16.50	42.980	48.847	52.822	54.035	55.549
16.75	43.640	49.516	53.479	54.686	56.189
17.00	44.287	50.169	54.120	55.320	56.812
17.25	44.923	50.807	54.744	55.937	57.419
17.50	45.546	51.432	55.353	56.539	58.010
17.75	46.158	52.042	55.948	57.125	58.585
18.00	46.758	52.639	56.527	57.697	59.145

MAXIMUM PREMIUM FOR ASSUMABLE LOANS
AS PERCENTAGE OF LOAN BALANCE
FACE INTEREST RATE: 6.5%

CURRENT RATE	REMAINING TERM OF LOAN (YEARS)				
	15	20	25	27	30
9.00	14.114	17.133	19.541	20.357	21.445
9.25	15.360	18.594	21.156	22.021	23.169
9.50	16.578	20.014	22.718	23.627	24.830
9.75	17.770	21.396	24.231	25.179	26.431
10.00	18.937	22.740	25.695	26.680	27.975
10.25	20.078	24.048	27.113	28.130	29.464
10.50	21.195	25.321	28.487	29.533	30.902
10.75	22.288	26.561	29.819	30.890	32.289
11.00	23.358	27.767	31.109	32.204	33.629
11.25	24.405	28.942	32.360	33.475	34.923
11.50	25.431	30.087	33.573	34.706	36.173
11.75	26.435	31.201	34.750	35.898	37.382
12.00	27.418	32.287	35.891	37.053	38.551
12.25	28.380	33.345	36.999	38.173	39.682
12.50	29.323	34.376	38.074	39.258	40.776
12.75	30.246	35.381	39.118	40.310	41.836
13.00	31.151	36.361	40.132	41.331	42.861
13.25	32.037	37.317	41.117	42.321	43.855
13.50	32.905	38.248	42.074	43.282	44.817
13.75	33.755	39.157	43.004	44.215	45.750
14.00	34.589	40.043	43.908	45.120	46.655
14.25	35.405	40.908	44.787	46.000	47.532
14.50	36.206	41.752	45.642	46.855	48.384
14.75	36.990	42.575	46.474	47.685	49.210
15.00	37.759	43.379	47.283	48.492	50.012
15.25	38.513	44.164	48.071	49.277	50.791
15.50	39.253	44.930	48.838	50.041	51.548
15.75	39.978	45.679	49.585	50.783	52.283
16.00	40.688	46.410	50.312	51.506	52.997
16.25	41.385	47.124	51.020	52.209	53.692
16.50	42.069	47.822	51.710	52.894	54.368
16.75	42.740	48.504	52.383	53.561	55.025
17.00	43.398	49.170	53.039	54.211	55.665
17.25	44.043	49.821	53.678	54.843	56.288
17.50	44.677	50.458	54.301	55.460	56.894
17.75	45.298	51.081	54.910	56.061	57.485
18.00	45.908	51.690	55.503	56.647	58.060

717

MAXIMUM PREMIUM FOR ASSUMABLE LOANS
AS PERCENTAGE OF LOAN BALANCE
FACE INTEREST RATE: 6.75%

CURRENT RATE	REMAINING TERM OF LOAN (YEARS)				
	15	20	25	27	30
9.00	12.753	15.489	17.670	18.408	19.391
9.25	14.019	16.979	19.322	20.112	21.160
9.50	15.257	18.427	20.921	21.758	22.864
9.75	16.468	19.837	22.469	23.348	24.507
10.00	17.653	21.208	23.967	24.885	26.092
10.25	18.812	22.542	25.418	26.371	27.620
10.50	19.947	23.840	26.824	27.808	29.095
10.75	21.057	25.104	28.187	29.199	30.518
11.00	22.144	26.335	29.507	30.544	31.893
11.25	23.208	27.533	30.787	31.847	33.221
11.50	24.249	28.700	32.028	33.108	34.504
11.75	25.270	29.837	33.232	34.330	35.745
12.00	26.268	30.944	34.400	35.513	36.944
12.25	27.246	32.023	35.534	36.660	38.105
12.50	28.203	33.075	36.634	37.771	39.228
12.75	29.141	34.100	37.703	38.849	40.314
13.00	30.060	35.099	38.740	39.895	41.367
13.25	30.960	36.073	39.748	40.909	42.386
13.50	31.842	37.023	40.727	41.894	43.374
13.75	32.706	37.950	41.679	42.849	44.332
14.00	33.552	38.854	42.604	43.777	45.260
14.25	34.382	39.736	43.503	44.678	46.160
14.50	35.195	40.596	44.378	45.554	47.034
14.75	35.992	41.436	45.229	46.405	47.882
15.00	36.773	42.256	46.057	47.232	48.705
15.25	37.539	43.057	46.863	48.036	49.504
15.50	38.290	43.838	47.648	48.818	50.281
15.75	39.027	44.601	48.412	49.579	51.035
16.00	39.749	45.347	49.156	50.319	51.768
16.25	40.457	46.075	49.881	51.040	52.481
16.50	41.152	46.787	50.587	51.741	53.175
16.75	41.833	47.482	51.276	52.425	53.849
17.00	42.501	48.162	51.946	53.090	54.506
17.25	43.157	48.826	52.601	53.738	55.145
17.50	43.800	49.476	53.239	54.370	55.767
17.75	44.432	50.111	53.861	54.986	56.373
18.00	45.051	50.732	54.468	55.586	56.963

718

MAXIMUM PREMIUM FOR ASSUMABLE LOANS
AS PERCENTAGE OF LOAN BALANCE
FACE INTEREST RATE: 7%

CURRENT RATE	REMAINING TERM OF LOAN (YEARS)				
	15	20	25	27	30
9.00	11.381	13.829	15.779	16.439	17.315
9.25	12.667	15.348	17.469	18.184	19.130
9.50	13.924	16.825	19.105	19.869	20.878
9.75	15.154	18.262	20.688	21.498	22.563
10.00	16.358	19.660	22.221	23.072	24.188
10.25	17.535	21.020	23.706	24.594	25.756
10.50	18.688	22.344	25.144	26.066	27.269
10.75	19.816	23.633	26.537	27.490	28.729
11.00	20.919	24.888	27.888	28.868	30.139
11.25	22.000	26.110	29.198	30.202	31.501
11.50	23.058	27.300	30.467	31.493	32.818
11.75	24.094	28.459	31.699	32.744	34.090
12.00	25.108	29.588	32.894	33.956	35.320
12.25	26.101	30.688	34.053	35.131	36.511
12.50	27.074	31.760	35.179	36.269	37.663
12.75	28.027	32.806	36.272	37.373	38.777
13.00	28.960	33.824	37.333	38.444	39.857
13.25	29.874	34.818	38.364	39.483	40.903
13.50	30.770	35.786	39.366	40.491	41.916
13.75	31.648	36.731	40.339	41.470	42.898
14.00	32.507	37.653	41.286	42.420	43.850
14.25	33.350	38.552	42.206	43.343	44.774
14.50	34.176	39.430	43.101	44.239	45.670
14.75	34.986	40.286	43.972	45.111	46.540
15.00	35.779	41.122	44.819	45.958	47.384
15.25	36.557	41.938	45.643	46.781	48.204
15.50	37.320	42.735	46.446	47.582	49.000
15.75	38.068	43.513	47.227	48.362	49.774
16.00	38.801	44.274	47.989	49.120	50.526
16.25	39.520	45.016	48.730	49.858	51.258
16.50	40.226	45.742	49.452	50.576	51.969
16.75	40.918	46.451	50.157	51.276	52.661
17.00	41.597	47.144	50.843	51.957	53.334
17.25	42.263	47.821	51.512	52.621	53.990
17.50	42.916	48.483	52.165	53.268	54.628
17.75	43.558	49.131	52.802	53.899	55.250
18.00	44.187	49.764	53.423	54.514	55.855

MAXIMUM PREMIUM FOR ASSUMABLE LOANS
AS PERCENTAGE OF LOAN BALANCE
FACE INTEREST RATE: 7.25%

CURRENT RATE	REMAINING TERM OF LOAN (YEARS)				
	15	20	25	27	30
9.00	9.997	12.153	13.869	14.448	15.218
9.25	11.303	13.702	15.598	16.235	17.078
9.50	12.579	15.207	17.270	17.960	18.871
9.75	13.829	16.672	18.889	19.628	20.599
10.00	15.051	18.097	20.457	21.240	22.265
10.25	16.247	19.484	21.975	22.798	23.873
10.50	17.418	20.834	23.446	24.305	25.424
10.75	18.563	22.148	24.871	25.763	26.921
11.00	19.684	23.427	26.252	27.173	28.367
11.25	20.782	24.673	27.592	28.539	29.764
11.50	21.856	25.886	28.890	29.862	31.113
11.75	22.909	27.067	30.150	31.142	32.418
12.00	23.939	28.218	31.372	32.383	33.680
12.25	24.947	29.340	32.558	33.586	34.900
12.50	25.935	30.433	33.709	34.751	36.081
12.75	26.903	31.499	34.826	35.881	37.224
13.00	27.850	32.537	35.912	36.978	38.331
13.25	28.779	33.550	36.966	38.041	39.404
13.50	29.688	34.537	37.991	39.074	40.443
13.75	30.580	35.501	38.986	40.076	41.450
14.00	31.453	36.440	39.954	41.048	42.426
14.25	32.309	37.357	40.895	41.993	43.373
14.50	33.148	38.252	41.811	42.911	44.292
14.75	33.970	39.125	42.701	43.804	45.184
15.00	34.776	39.977	43.567	44.671	46.049
15.25	35.566	40.809	44.410	45.514	46.890
15.50	36.341	41.621	45.231	46.334	47.706
15.75	37.101	42.415	46.030	47.132	48.500
16.00	37.845	43.190	46.809	47.908	49.271
16.25	38.576	43.947	47.567	48.664	50.021
16.50	39.292	44.686	48.306	49.399	50.751
16.75	39.995	45.409	49.026	50.116	51.460
17.00	40.685	46.115	49.728	50.813	52.151
17.25	41.361	46.806	50.412	51.493	52.823
17.50	42.025	47.481	51.080	52.156	53.477
17.75	42.676	48.141	51.731	52.801	54.114
18.00	43.315	48.787	52.366	53.431	54.735

MAXIMUM PREMIUM FOR ASSUMABLE LOANS
AS PERCENTAGE OF LOAN BALANCE
FACE INTEREST RATE: 7.5%

CURRENT RATE	REMAINING TERM OF LOAN (YEARS)				
	15	20	25	27	30
9.00	8.603	10.462	11.941	12.439	13.100
9.25	9.929	12.041	13.708	14.268	15.007
9.50	11.225	13.575	15.418	16.034	16.845
9.75	12.494	15.068	17.074	17.741	18.616
10.00	13.735	16.521	18.676	19.390	20.324
10.25	14.949	17.934	20.228	20.985	21.972
10.50	16.138	19.310	21.732	22.527	23.562
10.75	17.301	20.649	23.189	24.019	25.096
11.00	18.440	21.953	24.602	25.463	26.578
11.25	19.555	23.223	25.971	26.861	28.010
11.50	20.646	24.459	27.298	28.214	29.393
11.75	21.714	25.664	28.586	29.525	30.731
12.00	22.760	26.837	29.835	30.795	32.024
12.25	23.784	27.980	31.048	32.026	33.275
12.50	24.788	29.094	32.225	33.219	34.485
12.75	25.770	30.180	33.367	34.376	35.657
13.00	26.733	31.239	34.477	35.498	36.791
13.25	27.676	32.271	35.555	36.586	37.890
13.50	28.599	33.277	36.602	37.643	38.955
13.75	29.504	34.259	37.620	38.668	39.988
14.00	30.391	35.217	38.610	39.664	40.988
14.25	31.260	36.151	39.572	40.631	41.959
14.50	32.112	37.063	40.508	41.571	42.901
14.75	32.947	37.953	41.418	42.484	43.815
15.00	33.765	38.822	42.304	43.371	44.702
15.25	34.568	39.670	43.166	44.234	45.564
15.50	35.355	40.498	44.005	45.074	46.401
15.75	36.126	41.306	44.822	45.890	47.214
16.00	36.882	42.096	45.618	46.685	48.005
16.25	37.624	42.868	46.393	47.458	48.773
16.50	38.352	43.622	47.149	48.211	49.521
16.75	39.066	44.358	47.885	48.944	50.248
17.00	39.766	45.078	48.603	49.658	50.956
17.25	40.453	45.782	49.302	50.354	51.645
17.50	41.127	46.470	49.985	51.032	52.315
17.75	41.788	47.143	50.650	51.693	52.969
18.00	42.437	47.801	51.300	52.337	53.605

MAXIMUM PREMIUM FOR ASSUMABLE LOANS
AS PERCENTAGE OF LOAN BALANCE
FACE INTEREST RATE: 7.75%

CURRENT RATE	REMAINING TERM OF LOAN (YEARS)				
	15	20	25	27	30
9.00	7.196	8.755	9.993	10.411	10.963
9.25	8.542	10.364	11.800	12.281	12.917
9.50	9.858	11.927	13.548	14.088	14.799
9.75	11.147	13.449	15.240	15.835	16.614
10.00	12.407	14.929	16.878	17.522	18.364
10.25	13.640	16.370	18.465	19.154	20.052
10.50	14.847	17.772	20.002	20.732	21.681
10.75	16.028	19.136	21.491	22.259	23.254
11.00	17.184	20.465	22.934	23.736	24.772
11.25	18.316	21.759	24.334	25.166	26.239
11.50	19.424	23.019	25.691	26.551	27.656
11.75	20.509	24.246	27.007	27.892	29.027
12.00	21.571	25.442	28.284	29.192	30.351
12.25	22.611	26.607	29.523	30.451	31.633
12.50	23.630	27.742	30.726	31.672	32.873
12.75	24.628	28.849	31.894	32.855	34.074
13.00	25.605	29.928	33.028	34.003	35.236
13.25	26.562	30.979	34.130	35.117	36.363
13.50	27.500	32.005	35.201	36.198	37.454
13.75	28.419	33.006	36.241	37.247	38.511
14.00	29.320	33.982	37.252	38.266	39.537
14.25	30.202	34.934	38.236	39.256	40.531
14.50	31.067	35.863	39.192	40.217	41.496
14.75	31.915	36.770	40.123	41.151	42.432
15.00	32.746	37.655	41.028	42.059	43.342
15.25	33.561	38.519	41.909	42.942	44.224
15.50	34.359	39.363	42.767	43.801	45.082
15.75	35.143	40.187	43.602	44.637	45.915
16.00	35.911	40.992	44.416	45.449	46.725
16.25	36.664	41.778	45.208	46.241	47.513
16.50	37.403	42.547	45.980	47.011	48.279
16.75	38.128	43.297	46.733	47.761	49.024
17.00	38.838	44.031	47.466	48.492	49.749
17.25	39.536	44.748	48.181	49.204	50.455
17.50	40.220	45.450	48.879	49.897	51.142
17.75	40.892	46.135	49.559	50.574	51.812
18.00	41.551	46.806	50.223	51.233	52.464

MAXIMUM PREMIUM FOR ASSUMABLE LOANS
AS PERCENTAGE OF LOAN BALANCE
FACE INTEREST RATE: 8%

CURRENT RATE	REMAINING TERM OF LOAN (YEARS)				
	15	20	25	27	30
9.00	5.779	7.034	8.029	8.364	8.806
9.25	7.146	8.673	9.875	10.277	10.808
9.50	8.482	10.266	11.661	12.126	12.736
9.75	9.790	11.816	13.390	13.912	14.595
10.00	11.070	13.324	15.064	15.638	16.387
10.25	12.321	14.792	16.685	17.307	18.116
10.50	13.547	16.220	18.256	18.921	19.784
10.75	14.746	17.611	19.777	20.483	21.395
11.00	15.920	18.964	21.252	21.994	22.950
11.25	17.069	20.283	22.682	23.457	24.452
11.50	18.194	21.566	24.069	24.873	25.904
11.75	19.295	22.817	25.414	26.245	27.308
12.00	20.374	24.035	26.719	27.574	28.665
12.25	21.430	25.222	27.985	28.862	29.977
12.50	22.464	26.379	29.214	30.111	31.248
12.75	23.477	27.506	30.408	31.321	32.477
13.00	24.469	28.606	31.567	32.495	33.668
13.25	25.441	29.677	32.692	33.635	34.821
13.50	26.393	30.722	33.786	34.740	35.939
13.75	27.326	31.742	34.850	35.814	37.022
14.00	28.240	32.736	35.883	36.856	38.072
14.25	29.136	33.706	36.888	37.868	39.091
14.50	30.015	34.653	37.865	38.851	40.079
14.75	30.875	35.577	38.816	39.807	41.038
15.00	31.719	36.479	39.741	40.736	41.969
15.25	32.546	37.359	40.641	41.639	42.874
15.50	33.357	38.219	41.518	42.517	43.752
15.75	34.152	39.059	42.371	43.372	44.606
16.00	34.932	39.879	43.202	44.203	45.435
16.25	35.697	40.680	44.012	45.012	46.242
16.50	36.447	41.463	44.801	45.800	47.026
16.75	37.183	42.228	45.570	46.568	47.789
17.00	37.904	42.975	46.320	47.315	48.532
17.25	38.613	43.706	47.050	48.043	49.255
17.50	39.307	44.420	47.763	48.753	49.959
17.75	39.989	45.119	48.458	49.444	50.644
18.00	40.658	45.802	49.137	50.119	51.312

MAXIMUM PREMIUM FOR ASSUMABLE LOANS
AS PERCENTAGE OF LOAN BALANCE
FACE INTEREST RATE: 8.25%

CURRENT RATE	REMAINING TERM OF LOAN (YEARS)				
	15	20	25	27	30
9.00	4.350	5.297	6.047	6.299	6.631
9.25	5.738	6.966	7.933	8.256	8.680
9.50	7.095	8.589	9.757	10.145	10.654
9.75	8.423	10.169	11.523	11.972	12.558
10.00	9.721	11.705	13.233	13.737	14.393
10.25	10.992	13.200	14.889	15.443	16.163
10.50	12.236	14.655	16.494	17.094	17.871
10.75	13.454	16.072	18.048	18.691	19.520
11.00	14.645	17.451	19.555	20.236	21.112
11.25	15.812	18.794	21.016	21.732	22.650
11.50	16.954	20.101	22.433	23.180	24.137
11.75	18.072	21.375	23.807	24.583	25.574
12.00	19.166	22.616	25.139	25.942	26.963
12.25	20.238	23.825	26.433	27.259	28.307
12.50	21.288	25.004	27.689	28.536	29.608
12.75	22.317	26.152	28.908	29.774	30.867
13.00	23.324	27.272	30.092	30.974	32.086
13.25	24.311	28.364	31.242	32.139	33.267
13.50	25.277	29.428	32.359	33.270	34.411
13.75	26.225	30.467	33.445	34.367	35.520
14.00	27.153	31.480	34.501	35.433	36.595
14.25	28.062	32.468	35.528	36.468	37.638
14.50	28.954	33.432	36.526	37.473	38.650
14.75	29.827	34.374	37.497	38.450	39.632
15.00	30.684	35.292	38.442	39.400	40.585
15.25	31.524	36.189	39.362	40.324	41.511
15.50	32.347	37.065	40.257	41.222	42.410
15.75	33.154	37.920	41.129	42.096	43.284
16.00	33.946	38.756	41.978	42.946	44.134
16.25	34.722	39.572	42.806	43.773	44.960
16.50	35.484	40.369	43.611	44.579	45.763
16.75	36.230	41.148	44.397	45.364	46.544
17.00	36.963	41.910	45.163	46.128	47.305
17.25	37.682	42.654	45.909	46.872	48.045
17.50	38.387	43.382	46.637	47.598	48.765
17.75	39.080	44.094	47.348	48.305	49.467
18.00	39.759	44.790	48.040	48.995	50.151

MAXIMUM PREMIUM FOR ASSUMABLE LOANS
AS PERCENTAGE OF LOAN BALANCE
FACE INTEREST RATE: 8.5%

CURRENT RATE	REMAINING TERM OF LOAN (YEARS)				
	15	20	25	27	30
9.00	2.910	3.545	4.047	4.216	4.438
9.25	4.319	5.246	5.973	6.216	6.535
9.50	5.696	6.899	7.836	8.148	8.555
9.75	7.044	8.507	9.640	10.015	10.503
10.00	8.363	10.072	11.387	11.819	12.382
10.25	9.652	11.595	13.078	13.564	14.193
10.50	10.915	13.077	14.717	15.251	15.942
10.75	12.151	14.519	16.305	16.883	17.629
11.00	13.360	15.924	17.843	18.463	19.259
11.25	14.545	17.291	19.335	19.992	20.833
11.50	15.704	18.623	20.782	21.473	22.355
11.75	16.839	19.921	22.185	22.907	23.825
12.00	17.950	21.185	23.546	24.296	25.247
12.25	19.038	22.416	24.867	25.642	26.623
12.50	20.104	23.616	26.150	26.947	27.954
12.75	21.147	24.786	27.395	28.212	29.243
13.00	22.170	25.927	28.604	29.440	30.490
13.25	23.171	27.039	29.779	30.631	31.699
13.50	24.152	28.123	30.920	31.786	32.870
13.75	25.114	29.181	32.029	32.908	34.005
14.00	26.056	30.212	33.107	33.997	35.106
14.25	26.979	31.219	34.156	35.055	36.173
14.50	27.884	32.201	35.175	36.083	37.209
14.75	28.771	33.160	36.167	37.082	38.214
15.00	29.640	34.095	37.132	38.053	39.190
15.25	30.493	35.009	38.072	38.997	40.137
15.50	31.328	35.901	38.986	39.915	41.058
15.75	32.148	36.772	39.876	40.808	41.952
16.00	32.952	37.623	40.744	41.678	42.821
16.25	33.739	38.454	41.588	42.523	43.667
16.50	34.512	39.266	42.411	43.347	44.489
16.75	35.271	40.060	43.214	44.149	45.288
17.00	36.014	40.835	43.996	44.930	46.067
17.25	36.744	41.594	44.758	45.691	46.824
17.50	37.460	42.335	45.502	46.433	47.562
17.75	38.163	43.060	46.227	47.156	48.280
18.00	38.852	43.769	46.935	47.861	48.980

MAXIMUM PREMIUM FOR ASSUMABLE LOANS
AS PERCENTAGE OF LOAN BALANCE
FACE INTEREST RATE: 8.75%

CURRENT RATE	REMAINING TERM OF LOAN (YEARS)				
	15	20	25	27	30
9.00	1.461	1.780	2.032	2.116	2.227
9.25	2.890	3.511	3.998	4.160	4.373
9.50	4.288	5.194	5.900	6.134	6.440
9.75	5.656	6.833	7.742	8.042	8.433
10.00	6.994	8.426	9.525	9.886	10.355
10.25	8.303	9.976	11.252	11.669	12.209
10.50	9.585	11.486	12.925	13.393	13.997
10.75	10.839	12.955	14.546	15.061	15.724
11.00	12.066	14.385	16.117	16.676	17.391
11.25	13.268	15.778	17.641	18.238	19.002
11.50	14.445	17.134	19.118	19.751	20.559
11.75	15.597	18.455	20.550	21.217	22.063
12.00	16.724	19.742	21.940	22.636	23.518
12.25	17.829	20.996	23.289	24.012	24.926
12.50	18.910	22.218	24.599	25.346	26.288
12.75	19.970	23.409	25.870	26.639	27.606
13.00	21.007	24.571	27.104	27.893	28.883
13.25	22.024	25.703	28.304	29.110	30.119
13.50	23.020	26.807	29.469	30.291	31.317
13.75	23.996	27.884	30.601	31.438	32.479
14.00	24.952	28.935	31.702	32.551	33.605
14.25	25.889	29.960	32.773	33.632	34.697
14.50	26.807	30.960	33.814	34.682	35.756
14.75	27.707	31.936	34.826	35.703	36.785
15.00	28.590	32.889	35.812	36.695	37.783
15.25	29.455	33.819	36.771	37.660	38.752
15.50	30.303	34.728	37.704	38.598	39.694
15.75	31.135	35.615	38.613	39.511	40.609
16.00	31.950	36.481	39.499	40.399	41.499
16.25	32.750	37.328	40.361	41.264	42.364
16.50	33.534	38.155	41.202	42.105	43.205
16.75	34.304	38.963	42.021	42.925	44.023
17.00	35.059	39.752	42.819	43.723	44.819
17.25	35.799	40.525	43.598	44.501	45.594
17.50	36.526	41.279	44.357	45.259	46.349
17.75	37.239	42.018	45.097	45.998	47.084
18.00	37.939	42.739	45.820	46.718	47.800

726

MAXIMUM PREMIUM FOR ASSUMABLE LOANS
AS PERCENTAGE OF LOAN BALANCE
FACE INTEREST RATE: 9%

CURRENT RATE	REMAINING TERM OF LOAN (YEARS)				
	15	20	25	27	30
9.00	0.000	0.000	0.000	0.000	0.000
9.25	1.451	1.763	2.007	2.088	2.195
9.50	2.869	3.477	3.949	4.105	4.309
9.75	4.258	5.144	5.829	6.054	6.347
10.00	5.616	6.767	7.649	7.938	8.313
10.25	6.944	8.345	9.412	9.759	10.209
10.50	8.245	9.882	11.120	11.521	12.038
10.75	9.518	11.377	12.774	13.225	13.804
11.00	10.763	12.833	14.378	14.874	15.510
11.25	11.983	14.251	15.933	16.471	17.157
11.50	13.177	15.632	17.440	18.016	18.749
11.75	14.346	16.978	18.903	19.513	20.288
12.00	15.490	18.288	20.321	20.964	21.776
12.25	16.611	19.565	21.698	22.369	23.216
12.50	17.709	20.809	23.035	23.732	24.609
12.75	18.783	22.022	24.332	25.053	25.957
13.00	19.836	23.204	25.592	26.334	27.263
13.25	20.868	24.357	26.817	27.577	28.527
13.50	21.879	25.481	28.006	28.784	29.753
13.75	22.869	26.578	29.162	29.955	30.941
14.00	23.839	27.647	30.286	31.092	32.092
14.25	24.790	28.691	31.378	32.197	33.209
14.50	25.722	29.709	32.441	33.270	34.293
14.75	26.636	30.703	33.475	34.313	35.345
15.00	27.531	31.673	34.480	35.327	36.366
15.25	28.409	32.620	35.459	36.312	37.357
15.50	29.270	33.545	36.412	37.271	38.320
15.75	30.114	34.448	37.340	38.203	39.256
16.00	30.942	35.330	38.244	39.111	40.166
16.25	31.753	36.192	39.124	39.994	41.051
16.50	32.549	37.034	39.982	40.854	41.911
16.75	33.330	37.857	40.818	41.691	42.748
17.00	34.096	38.661	41.633	42.506	43.562
17.25	34.848	39.447	42.428	43.301	44.355
17.50	35.585	40.215	43.203	44.075	45.127
17.75	36.309	40.967	43.959	44.830	45.878
18.00	37.019	41.702	44.696	45.566	46.611

MAXIMUM PREMIUM FOR ASSUMABLE LOANS
AS PERCENTAGE OF LOAN BALANCE
FACE INTEREST RATE: 9.25%

CURRENT RATE	REMAINING TERM OF LOAN (YEARS)				
	15	20	25	27	30
9.00	− 1.472	− 1.795	− 2.048	− 2.133	− 2.244
9.25	0.000	0.000	0.000	0.000	0.000
9.50	1.439	1.744	1.981	2.060	2.162
9.75	2.848	3.442	3.900	4.051	4.246
10.00	4.226	5.094	5.757	5.975	6.255
10.25	5.574	6.700	7.556	7.835	8.194
10.50	6.894	8.265	9.299	9.634	10.064
10.75	8.185	9.787	10.987	11.374	11.870
11.00	9.449	11.269	12.624	13.059	13.614
11.25	10.687	12.713	14.211	14.689	15.298
11.50	11.898	14.118	15.749	16.268	16.926
11.75	13.085	15.488	17.242	17.797	18.499
12.00	14.246	16.821	18.689	19.278	20.021
12.25	15.383	18.121	20.094	20.713	21.493
12.50	16.497	19.388	21.458	22.105	22.917
12.75	17.588	20.622	22.782	23.454	24.295
13.00	18.656	21.826	24.068	24.763	25.630
13.25	19.703	22.999	25.318	26.033	26.923
13.50	20.728	24.144	26.531	27.265	28.176
13.75	21.734	25.260	27.711	28.461	29.391
14.00	22.718	26.349	28.858	29.623	30.568
14.25	23.683	27.411	29.973	30.751	31.710
14.50	24.629	28.448	31.057	31.847	32.818
14.75	25.556	29.459	32.112	32.912	33.894
15.00	26.464	30.447	33.138	33.947	34.938
15.25	27.355	31.411	34.137	34.954	35.951
15.50	28.228	32.352	35.110	35.933	36.936
15.75	29.085	33.272	36.057	36.885	37.893
16.00	29.925	34.170	36.979	37.812	38.823
16.25	30.748	35.047	37.878	38.714	39.728
16.50	31.556	35.904	38.753	39.592	40.607
16.75	32.349	36.742	39.606	40.447	41.463
17.00	33.126	37.560	40.438	41.280	42.296
17.25	33.889	38.360	41.249	42.092	43.106
17.50	34.637	39.143	42.040	42.882	43.895
17.75	35.371	39.908	42.811	43.653	44.664
18.00	36.092	40.656	43.564	44.405	45.413

MAXIMUM PREMIUM FOR ASSUMABLE LOANS
AS PERCENTAGE OF LOAN BALANCE
FACE INTEREST RATE: 9.5%

CURRENT RATE	REMAINING TERM OF LOAN (YEARS)				
	15	20	25	27	30
9.00	−2.954	−3.602	−4.111	−4.281	−4.503
9.25	−1.460	−1.775	−2.022	−2.103	−2.209
9.50	0.000	0.000	0.000	0.000	0.000
9.75	1.429	1.728	1.957	2.033	2.130
10.00	2.828	3.409	3.852	3.997	4.184
10.25	4.195	5.044	5.687	5.896	6.165
10.50	5.535	6.636	7.465	7.733	8.077
10.75	6.845	8.185	9.188	9.510	9.923
11.00	8.127	9.694	10.858	11.230	11.705
11.25	9.383	11.163	12.476	12.895	13.427
11.50	10.612	12.593	14.046	14.507	15.090
11.75	11.816	13.987	15.569	16.068	16.699
12.00	12.994	15.345	17.046	17.580	18.254
12.25	14.148	16.667	18.479	19.046	19.758
12.50	15.278	17.957	19.871	20.467	21.214
12.75	16.384	19.213	21.221	21.844	22.623
13.00	17.469	20.438	22.533	23.181	23.987
13.25	18.531	21.632	23.808	24.477	25.309
13.50	19.571	22.797	25.046	25.735	26.589
13.75	20.591	23.933	26.250	26.957	27.831
14.00	21.590	25.041	27.420	28.143	29.034
14.25	22.569	26.122	28.557	29.294	30.202
14.50	23.528	27.177	29.663	30.413	31.334
14.75	24.469	28.207	30.740	31.501	32.433
15.00	25.391	29.212	31.787	32.558	33.500
15.25	26.295	30.193	32.806	33.586	34.536
15.50	27.181	31.151	33.798	34.585	35.543
15.75	28.050	32.087	34.764	35.558	36.521
16.00	28.902	33.001	35.705	36.504	37.472
16.25	29.737	33.894	36.622	37.425	38.396
16.50	30.557	34.766	37.515	38.322	39.295
16.75	31.361	35.618	38.385	39.195	40.170
17.00	32.149	36.451	39.234	40.045	41.021
17.25	32.923	37.266	40.061	40.874	41.849
17.50	33.682	38.062	40.868	41.681	42.656
17.75	34.427	38.841	41.655	42.468	43.441
18.00	35.158	39.602	42.423	43.236	44.207

729

MAXIMUM PREMIUM FOR ASSUMABLE LOANS
AS PERCENTAGE OF LOAN BALANCE
FACE INTEREST RATE: 9.75%

CURRENT RATE	REMAINING TERM OF LOAN (YEARS)				
	15	20	25	27	30
9.00	− 4.447	− 5.423	− 6.190	− 6.445	− 6.778
9.25	− 2.931	− 3.565	− 4.058	− 4.222	− 4.434
9.50	− 1.450	− 1.758	− 1.996	− 2.075	− 2.177
9.75	0.000	0.000	0.000	0.000	0.000
10.00	1.418	1.710	1.933	2.005	2.099
10.25	2.806	3.374	3.805	3.944	4.123
10.50	4.165	4.994	5.618	5.819	6.077
10.75	5.494	6.571	7.375	7.633	7.962
11.00	6.795	8.106	9.078	9.388	9.783
11.25	8.069	9.601	10.729	11.088	11.542
11.50	9.316	11.057	12.330	12.733	13.242
11.75	10.537	12.475	13.883	14.326	14.885
12.00	11.732	13.856	15.389	15.870	16.474
12.25	12.903	15.202	16.852	17.366	18.011
12.50	14.049	16.514	18.271	18.817	19.499
12.75	15.172	17.793	19.649	20.223	20.939
13.00	16.272	19.039	20.987	21.587	22.333
13.25	17.349	20.254	22.287	22.910	23.683
13.50	18.405	21.440	23.550	24.194	24.992
13.75	19.439	22.596	24.777	25.441	26.260
14.00	20.453	23.723	25.971	26.652	27.490
14.25	21.446	24.823	27.131	27.827	28.682
14.50	22.419	25.897	28.259	28.970	29.839
14.75	23.373	26.945	29.357	30.080	30.962
15.00	24.309	27.967	30.425	31.159	32.053
15.25	25.226	28.966	31.465	32.208	33.111
15.50	26.125	29.941	32.476	33.228	34.140
15.75	27.006	30.893	33.462	34.221	35.139
16.00	27.871	31.823	34.422	35.187	36.111
16.25	28.718	32.731	35.356	36.127	37.055
16.50	29.550	33.619	36.267	37.042	37.974
16.75	30.365	34.486	37.155	37.933	38.867
17.00	31.165	35.334	38.021	38.801	39.737
17.25	31.951	36.163	38.864	39.647	40.583
17.50	32.721	36.973	39.687	40.471	41.408
17.75	33.477	37.765	40.490	41.275	42.210
18.00	34.218	38.540	41.273	42.058	42.992

MAXIMUM PREMIUM FOR ASSUMABLE LOANS
AS PERCENTAGE OF LOAN BALANCE
FACE INTEREST RATE: 10%

CURRENT RATE	REMAINING TERM OF LOAN (YEARS)				
	15	20	25	27	30
9.00	− 5.950	− 7.258	− 8.283	− 8.623	− 9.067
9.25	− 4.412	− 5.367	− 6.109	− 6.354	− 6.673
9.50	− 2.910	− 3.529	− 4.007	− 4.164	− 4.367
9.75	− 1.439	− 1.740	− 1.971	− 2.046	− 2.144
10.00	0.000	0.000	0.000	0.000	0.000
10.25	1.408	1.693	1.909	1.978	2.068
10.50	2.786	3.341	3.758	3.892	4.063
10.75	4.134	4.945	5.550	5.743	5.989
11.00	5.454	6.507	7.286	7.534	7.849
11.25	6.746	8.028	8.970	9.268	9.646
11.50	8.011	9.509	10.602	10.947	11.382
11.75	9.250	10.952	12.186	12.573	13.061
12.00	10.462	12.357	13.722	14.149	14.684
12.25	11.649	13.727	15.213	15.675	16.254
12.50	12.812	15.061	16.660	17.155	17.773
12.75	13.951	16.362	18.065	18.590	19.244
13.00	15.067	17.630	19.430	19.982	20.668
13.25	16.160	18.867	20.755	21.333	22.047
13.50	17.231	20.073	22.043	22.643	23.384
13.75	18.280	21.249	23.295	23.916	24.679
14.00	19.308	22.396	24.511	25.151	25.935
14.25	20.316	23.515	25.695	26.351	27.154
14.50	21.303	24.607	26.845	27.516	28.335
14.75	22.271	25.673	27.965	28.649	29.483
15.00	23.220	26.714	29.054	29.750	30.596
15.25	24.150	27.730	30.114	30.821	31.678
15.50	25.062	28.722	31.146	31.862	32.728
15.75	25.956	29.690	32.150	32.875	33.749
16.00	26.833	30.637	33.129	33.860	34.741
16.25	27.693	31.561	34.082	34.820	35.706
16.50	28.536	32.464	35.011	35.754	36.644
16.75	29.364	33.346	35.917	36.663	37.557
17.00	30.175	34.209	36.799	37.549	38.445
17.25	30.971	35.052	37.659	38.412	39.310
17.50	31.753	35.876	38.499	39.253	40.152
17.75	32.519	36.682	39.317	40.073	40.972
18.00	33.272	37.471	40.116	40.872	41.770

MAXIMUM PREMIUM FOR ASSUMABLE LOANS
AS PERCENTAGE OF LOAN BALANCE
FACE INTEREST RATE: 10.25%

CURRENT RATE	REMAINING TERM OF LOAN (YEARS)				
	15	20	25	27	30
9.00	− 7.462	− 9.105	− 10.390	− 10.815	− 11.369
9.25	− 5.903	− 7.182	− 8.174	− 8.501	− 8.925
9.50	− 4.379	− 5.312	− 6.030	− 6.266	− 6.570
9.75	− 2.887	− 3.492	− 3.955	− 4.106	− 4.300
10.00	− 1.428	− 1.722	− 1.946	− 2.018	− 2.111
10.25	0.000	0.000	0.000	0.000	0.000
10.50	1.398	1.677	1.885	1.952	2.038
10.75	2.765	3.308	3.712	3.841	4.004
11.00	4.104	4.897	5.482	5.668	5.904
11.25	5.415	6.444	7.198	7.437	7.738
11.50	6.698	7.951	8.863	9.150	9.511
11.75	7.954	9.418	10.477	10.809	11.225
12.00	9.184	10.848	12.043	12.416	12.883
12.25	10.388	12.241	13.563	13.973	14.486
12.50	11.568	13.599	15.038	15.483	16.037
12.75	12.723	14.922	16.471	16.947	17.539
13.00	13.854	16.212	17.862	18.367	18.993
13.25	14.963	17.470	19.213	19.745	20.401
13.50	16.049	18.696	20.526	21.082	21.766
13.75	17.113	19.893	21.802	22.380	23.089
14.00	18.156	21.059	23.043	23.640	24.371
14.25	19.178	22.198	24.249	24.864	25.615
14.50	20.180	23.309	25.422	26.053	26.822
14.75	21.161	24.393	26.563	27.209	27.994
15.00	22.123	25.452	27.673	28.332	29.131
15.25	23.067	26.485	28.754	29.424	30.235
15.50	23.992	27.494	29.806	30.487	31.308
15.75	24.899	28.480	30.830	31.520	32.350
16.00	25.788	29.442	31.828	32.525	33.363
16.25	26.660	30.382	32.800	33.504	34.348
16.50	27.516	31.301	33.747	34.457	35.306
16.75	28.355	32.199	34.670	35.385	36.239
17.00	29.178	33.076	35.569	36.288	37.145
17.25	29.986	33.934	36.446	37.169	38.028
17.50	30.778	34.772	37.302	38.027	38.888
17.75	31.556	35.592	38.136	38.864	39.725
18.00	32.319	36.394	38.951	39.679	40.541

MAXIMUM PREMIUM FOR ASSUMABLE LOANS
AS PERCENTAGE OF LOAN BALANCE
FACE INTEREST RATE: 10.5%

CURRENT RATE	REMAINING TERM OF LOAN (YEARS)				
	15	20	25	27	30
9.00	−8.986	−10.965	−12.511	−13.021	−13.686
9.25	−7.404	−9.009	−10.252	−10.661	−11.191
9.50	−5.859	−7.108	−8.068	−8.382	−8.787
9.75	−4.346	−5.257	−5.952	−6.179	−6.470
10.00	−2.866	−3.457	−3.905	−4.049	−4.235
10.25	−1.418	−1.705	−1.921	−1.991	−2.080
10.50	0.000	0.000	0.000	0.000	0.000
10.75	1.387	1.660	1.862	1.926	2.008
11.00	2.745	3.275	3.666	3.790	3.946
11.25	4.074	4.849	5.415	5.594	5.819
11.50	5.375	6.381	7.112	7.341	7.629
11.75	6.649	7.874	8.757	9.033	9.379
12.00	7.896	9.328	10.353	10.672	11.071
12.25	9.118	10.744	11.902	12.261	12.707
12.50	10.314	12.125	13.406	13.801	14.291
12.75	11.486	13.471	14.866	15.294	15.824
13.00	12.633	14.783	16.284	16.742	17.308
13.25	13.758	16.062	17.661	18.147	18.746
13.50	14.859	17.310	18.999	19.511	20.139
13.75	15.938	18.527	20.300	20.835	21.489
14.00	16.996	19.713	21.564	22.120	22.798
14.25	18.032	20.871	22.793	23.368	24.068
14.50	19.048	22.001	23.989	24.581	25.300
14.75	20.044	23.104	25.152	25.760	26.496
15.00	21.019	24.181	26.284	26.905	27.657
15.25	21.976	25.232	27.385	28.019	28.784
15.50	22.914	26.258	28.457	29.103	29.879
15.75	23.834	27.260	29.501	30.156	30.943
16.00	24.736	28.239	30.518	31.182	31.977
16.25	25.621	29.195	31.509	32.180	32.983
16.50	26.488	30.129	32.474	33.152	33.961
16.75	27.339	31.042	33.414	34.098	34.912
17.00	28.174	31.935	34.331	35.020	35.838
17.25	28.993	32.807	35.225	35.918	36.739
17.50	29.797	33.660	36.097	36.793	37.617
17.75	30.586	34.494	36.948	37.646	38.471
18.00	31.360	35.309	37.778	38.478	39.304

MAXIMUM PREMIUM FOR ASSUMABLE LOANS
AS PERCENTAGE OF LOAN BALANCE
FACE INTEREST RATE: 10.75%

CURRENT RATE	REMAINING TERM OF LOAN (YEARS)				
	15	20	25	27	30
9.00	− 10.519	− 12.838	− 14.645	− 15.241	− 16.015
9.25	− 8.915	− 10.849	− 12.344	− 12.834	− 13.469
9.50	− 7.348	− 8.915	− 10.118	− 10.510	− 11.016
9.75	− 5.813	− 7.033	− 7.962	− 8.264	− 8.651
10.00	− 4.312	− 5.203	− 5.876	− 6.093	− 6.371
10.25	− 2.844	− 3.421	− 3.855	− 3.994	− 4.171
10.50	− 1.407	− 1.688	− 1.897	− 1.964	− 2.049
10.75	0.000	0.000	0.000	0.000	0.000
11.00	1.377	1.643	1.838	1.900	1.978
11.25	2.725	3.243	3.621	3.740	3.890
11.50	4.044	4.801	5.350	5.521	5.737
11.75	5.336	6.319	7.026	7.247	7.522
12.00	6.601	7.797	8.653	8.918	9.248
12.25	7.839	9.238	10.231	10.538	10.919
12.50	9.053	10.642	11.763	12.108	12.535
12.75	10.241	12.011	13.251	13.630	14.099
13.00	11.404	13.345	14.696	15.107	15.614
13.25	12.545	14.646	16.099	16.540	17.081
13.50	13.661	15.914	17.463	17.930	18.503
13.75	14.756	17.152	18.788	19.280	19.881
14.00	15.828	18.359	20.076	20.590	21.217
14.25	16.879	19.536	21.329	21.863	22.513
14.50	17.909	20.685	22.547	23.100	23.770
14.75	18.919	21.807	23.732	24.302	24.990
15.00	19.909	22.901	24.885	25.470	26.175
15.25	20.879	23.970	26.008	26.606	27.325
15.50	21.830	25.013	27.100	27.710	28.442
15.75	22.763	26.033	28.164	28.785	29.528
16.00	23.678	27.028	29.200	29.831	30.584
16.25	24.575	28.000	30.209	30.848	31.610
16.50	25.454	28.950	31.193	31.839	32.608
16.75	26.317	29.879	32.151	32.804	33.579
17.00	27.164	30.786	33.086	33.744	34.524
17.25	27.995	31.673	33.997	34.660	35.443
17.50	28.810	32.540	34.885	35.552	36.339
17.75	29.609	33.388	35.752	36.422	37.211
18.00	30.394	34.218	36.597	37.270	38.060

MAXIMUM PREMIUM FOR ASSUMABLE LOANS
AS PERCENTAGE OF LOAN BALANCE
FACE INTEREST RATE: 11%

CURRENT RATE	REMAINING TERM OF LOAN (YEARS)				
	15	20	25	27	30
9.00	− 12.061	− 14.723	− 16.792	− 17.473	− 18.357
9.25	− 10.435	− 12.700	− 14.448	− 15.020	− 15.759
9.50	− 8.846	− 10.734	− 12.180	− 12.651	− 13.257
9.75	− 7.290	− 8.821	− 9.984	− 10.361	− 10.844
10.00	− 5.768	− 6.960	− 7.859	− 8.148	− 8.518
10.25	− 4.280	− 5.149	− 5.800	− 6.008	− 6.274
10.50	− 2.822	− 3.386	− 3.805	− 3.939	− 4.109
10.75	− 1.396	− 1.670	− 1.873	− 1.937	− 2.018
11.00	0.000	0.000	0.000	0.000	0.000
11.25	1.367	1.627	1.816	1.875	1.950
11.50	2.705	3.211	3.577	3.691	3.834
11.75	4.015	4.754	5.285	5.450	5.656
12.00	5.297	6.257	6.942	7.153	7.417
12.25	6.553	7.722	8.550	8.805	9.121
12.50	7.783	9.150	10.111	10.405	10.769
12.75	8.988	10.541	11.626	11.957	12.365
13.00	10.168	11.897	13.098	13.462	13.910
13.25	11.324	13.220	14.528	14.923	15.407
13.50	12.456	14.510	15.917	16.340	16.858
13.75	13.566	15.768	17.267	17.716	18.263
14.00	14.654	16.995	18.579	19.052	19.627
14.25	15.719	18.192	19.855	20.350	20.949
14.50	16.764	19.360	21.096	21.610	22.231
14.75	17.787	20.500	22.304	22.835	23.476
15.00	18.791	21.613	23.478	24.026	24.684
15.25	19.774	22.700	24.622	25.184	25.858
15.50	20.739	23.761	25.735	26.310	26.998
15.75	21.685	24.797	26.819	27.405	28.106
16.00	22.612	25.809	27.874	28.471	29.183
16.25	23.522	26.798	28.902	29.509	30.229
16.50	24.414	27.764	29.904	30.519	31.248
16.75	25.289	28.707	30.881	31.502	32.238
17.00	26.147	29.630	31.832	32.460	33.202
17.25	26.990	30.532	32.760	33.394	34.140
17.50	27.816	31.413	33.665	34.303	35.054
17.75	28.627	32.276	34.548	35.190	35.944
18.00	29.423	33.119	35.410	36.055	36.810

MAXIMUM PREMIUM FOR ASSUMABLE LOANS
AS PERCENTAGE OF LOAN BALANCE
FACE INTEREST RATE: 11.25%

CURRENT RATE	REMAINING TERM OF LOAN (YEARS)				
	15	20	25	27	30
9.00	− 13.614	− 16.620	− 18.952	− 19.718	− 20.710
9.25	− 11.966	− 14.564	− 16.565	− 17.218	− 18.061
9.50	− 10.355	− 12.566	− 14.255	− 14.804	− 15.509
9.75	− 8.777	− 10.621	− 12.019	− 12.470	− 13.048
10.00	− 7.234	− 8.729	− 9.853	− 10.215	− 10.676
10.25	− 5.725	− 6.888	− 7.757	− 8.035	− 8.388
10.50	− 4.247	− 5.096	− 5.725	− 5.926	− 6.179
10.75	− 2.801	− 3.352	− 3.757	− 3.885	− 4.047
11.00	− 1.386	− 1.654	− 1.850	− 1.911	− 1.989
11.25	0.000	0.000	0.000	0.000	0.000
11.50	1.356	1.610	1.793	1.850	1.922
11.75	2.685	3.179	3.533	3.643	3.779
12.00	3.985	4.707	5.221	5.379	5.576
12.25	5.258	6.196	6.858	7.062	7.313
12.50	6.505	7.647	8.448	8.693	8.995
12.75	7.726	9.062	9.992	10.274	10.622
13.00	8.923	10.440	11.491	11.809	12.198
13.25	10.095	11.785	12.947	13.297	13.725
13.50	11.243	13.096	14.361	14.741	15.204
13.75	12.368	14.375	15.737	16.144	16.638
14.00	13.471	15.622	17.073	17.505	18.028
14.25	14.551	16.839	18.373	18.827	19.376
14.50	15.610	18.027	19.637	20.112	20.685
14.75	16.648	19.186	20.867	21.360	21.954
15.00	17.665	20.317	22.063	22.574	23.187
15.25	18.663	21.422	23.228	23.754	24.384
15.50	19.640	22.500	24.361	24.901	25.546
15.75	20.600	23.553	25.465	26.018	26.676
16.00	21.540	24.582	26.540	27.104	27.774
16.25	22.462	25.587	27.587	28.161	28.842
16.50	23.366	26.569	28.608	29.191	29.880
16.75	24.254	27.528	29.602	30.193	30.890
17.00	25.124	28.466	30.572	31.170	31.874
17.25	25.978	29.383	31.517	32.121	32.830
17.50	26.816	30.279	32.439	33.048	33.762
17.75	27.638	31.156	33.338	33.952	34.670
18.00	28.444	32.013	34.215	34.833	35.554

MAXIMUM PREMIUM FOR ASSUMABLE LOANS
AS PERCENTAGE OF LOAN BALANCE
FACE INTEREST RATE: 11.5%

CURRENT RATE	REMAINING TERM OF LOAN (YEARS)				
	15	20	25	27	30
9.00	− 15.176	− 18.529	− 21.124	− 21.975	− 23.076
9.25	− 13.505	− 16.439	− 18.693	− 19.428	− 20.374
9.50	− 11.872	− 14.408	− 16.341	− 16.968	− 17.772
9.75	− 10.273	− 12.431	− 14.064	− 14.591	− 15.263
10.00	− 8.709	− 10.508	− 11.860	− 12.293	− 12.844
10.25	− 7.178	− 8.637	− 9.725	− 10.071	− 10.511
10.50	− 5.680	− 6.816	− 7.656	− 7.922	− 8.259
10.75	− 4.214	− 5.043	− 5.652	− 5.844	− 6.086
11.00	− 2.780	− 3.317	− 3.709	− 3.833	− 3.987
11.25	− 1.375	− 1.637	− 1.826	− 1.885	− 1.959
11.50	0.000	0.000	0.000	0.000	0.000
11.75	1.347	1.595	1.771	1.826	1.894
12.00	2.664	3.147	3.490	3.595	3.726
12.25	3.955	4.661	5.157	5.310	5.497
12.50	5.220	6.136	6.776	6.971	7.212
12.75	6.458	7.573	8.348	8.583	8.871
13.00	7.671	8.975	9.874	10.146	10.478
13.25	8.859	10.341	11.357	11.662	12.035
13.50	10.023	11.674	12.798	13.134	13.543
13.75	11.164	12.973	14.198	14.563	15.005
14.00	12.281	14.241	15.559	15.950	16.422
14.25	13.376	15.478	16.882	17.297	17.797
14.50	14.450	16.685	18.169	18.606	19.131
14.75	15.502	17.863	19.422	19.878	20.425
15.00	16.533	19.013	20.640	21.114	21.682
15.25	17.544	20.135	21.826	22.317	22.902
15.50	18.536	21.232	22.980	23.486	24.087
15.75	19.508	22.302	24.104	24.623	25.239
16.00	20.461	23.348	25.199	25.730	26.359
16.25	21.396	24.369	26.265	26.807	27.448
16.50	22.313	25.367	27.304	27.856	28.506
16.75	23.212	26.342	28.317	28.877	29.536
17.00	24.094	27.295	29.304	29.872	30.539
17.25	24.960	28.227	30.266	30.841	31.514
17.50	25.809	29.138	31.205	31.786	32.464
17.75	26.643	30.029	32.120	32.706	33.390
18.00	27.461	30.900	33.014	33.604	34.291

737

MAXIMUM PREMIUM FOR ASSUMABLE LOANS
AS PERCENTAGE OF LOAN BALANCE
FACE INTEREST RATE: 11.75%

CURRENT RATE	REMAINING TERM OF LOAN (YEARS)				
	15	20	25	27	30
9.00	− 16.749	− 20.449	− 23.309	− 24.244	− 25.452
9.25	− 15.054	− 18.326	− 20.834	− 21.650	− 22.698
9.50	− 13.399	− 16.262	− 18.439	− 19.144	− 20.046
9.75	− 11.778	− 14.253	− 16.121	− 16.722	− 17.489
10.00	− 10.192	− 12.299	− 13.877	− 14.382	− 15.023
10.25	− 8.641	− 10.398	− 11.703	− 12.119	− 12.645
10.50	− 7.123	− 8.547	− 9.597	− 9.930	− 10.349
10.75	− 5.637	− 6.745	− 7.557	− 7.813	− 8.134
11.00	− 4.183	− 4.992	− 5.580	− 5.764	− 5.995
11.25	− 2.759	− 3.284	− 3.662	− 3.780	− 3.928
11.50	− 1.365	− 1.620	− 1.803	− 1.860	− 1.931
11.75	0.000	0.000	0.000	0.000	0.000
12.00	1.336	1.578	1.749	1.802	1.867
12.25	2.644	3.116	3.447	3.548	3.673
12.50	3.926	4.615	5.095	5.241	5.420
12.75	5.181	6.076	6.695	6.882	7.112
13.00	6.410	7.500	8.249	8.475	8.750
13.25	7.615	8.888	9.758	10.019	10.336
13.50	8.795	10.242	11.225	11.518	11.874
13.75	9.951	11.563	12.651	12.973	13.364
14.00	11.084	12.852	14.036	14.386	14.808
14.25	12.194	14.108	15.383	15.759	16.210
14.50	13.282	15.335	16.694	17.092	17.569
14.75	14.349	16.532	17.968	18.388	18.889
15.00	15.394	17.701	19.209	19.647	20.170
15.25	16.419	18.841	20.416	20.872	21.414
15.50	17.424	19.955	21.591	22.062	22.622
15.75	18.409	21.043	22.735	23.221	23.796
16.00	19.375	22.106	23.850	24.348	24.937
16.25	20.323	23.144	24.935	25.446	26.047
16.50	21.252	24.158	25.993	26.514	27.126
16.75	22.164	25.149	27.024	27.554	28.176
17.00	23.058	26.117	28.029	28.567	29.198
17.25	23.936	27.064	29.009	29.555	30.192
17.50	24.797	27.990	29.964	30.517	31.161
17.75	25.642	28.895	30.896	31.455	32.104
18.00	26.470	29.780	31.806	32.369	33.022

MAXIMUM PREMIUM FOR ASSUMABLE LOANS
AS PERCENTAGE OF LOAN BALANCE
FACE INTEREST RATE: 12%

CURRENT RATE	REMAINING TERM OF LOAN (YEARS)				
	15	20	25	27	30
9.00	− 18.329	− 22.381	− 25.504	− 26.524	− 27.838
9.25	− 16.612	− 20.223	− 22.985	− 23.882	− 25.032
9.50	− 14.934	− 18.126	− 20.548	− 21.330	− 22.330
9.75	− 13.291	− 16.085	− 18.189	− 18.864	− 19.724
10.00	− 11.684	− 14.099	− 15.904	− 16.480	− 17.211
10.25	− 10.112	− 12.168	− 13.692	− 14.176	− 14.788
10.50	− 8.573	− 10.287	− 11.549	− 11.947	− 12.449
10.75	− 7.067	− 8.457	− 9.472	− 9.791	− 10.191
11.00	− 5.593	− 6.675	− 7.460	− 7.705	− 8.011
11.25	− 4.150	− 4.940	− 5.508	− 5.685	− 5.905
11.50	− 2.737	− 3.250	− 3.616	− 3.729	− 3.870
11.75	− 1.354	− 1.603	− 1.780	− 1.835	− 1.902
12.00	0.000	0.000	0.000	0.000	0.000
12.25	1.326	1.563	1.728	1.778	1.840
12.50	2.625	3.085	3.405	3.502	3.621
12.75	3.897	4.570	5.034	5.174	5.345
13.00	5.143	6.017	6.615	6.795	7.014
13.25	6.364	7.427	8.152	8.368	8.631
13.50	7.560	8.803	9.644	9.895	10.197
13.75	8.732	10.145	11.095	11.377	11.716
14.00	9.880	11.454	12.506	12.815	13.188
14.25	11.005	12.731	13.877	14.213	14.616
14.50	12.108	13.978	15.210	15.571	16.001
14.75	13.189	15.194	16.508	16.890	17.346
15.00	14.248	16.381	17.770	18.173	18.651
15.25	15.287	17.540	18.999	19.420	19.919
15.50	16.306	18.672	20.195	20.632	21.150
15.75	17.304	19.777	21.360	21.812	22.346
16.00	18.284	20.857	22.494	22.960	23.509
16.25	19.244	21.911	23.599	24.078	24.640
16.50	20.186	22.942	24.675	25.166	25.740
16.75	21.110	23.949	25.725	26.225	26.810
17.00	22.016	24.933	26.747	27.257	27.851
17.25	22.906	25.895	27.745	28.262	28.864
17.50	23.778	26.835	28.717	29.242	29.851
17.75	24.635	27.755	29.666	30.197	30.812
18.00	25.475	28.654	30.592	31.128	31.748

MAXIMUM PREMIUM FOR ASSUMABLE LOANS
AS PERCENTAGE OF LOAN BALANCE
FACE INTEREST RATE: 12.25%

CURRENT RATE	REMAINING TERM OF LOAN (YEARS)				
	15	20	25	27	30
9.00	− 19.920	− 24.323	− 27.711	− 28.815	− 30.235
9.25	− 18.180	− 22.132	− 25.148	− 26.125	− 27.376
9.50	− 16.479	− 20.001	− 22.668	− 23.527	− 24.623
9.75	− 14.814	− 17.928	− 20.267	− 21.016	− 21.968
10.00	− 13.185	− 15.911	− 17.942	− 18.589	− 19.409
10.25	− 11.592	− 13.948	− 15.691	− 16.243	− 16.940
10.50	− 10.032	− 12.038	− 13.510	− 13.974	− 14.557
10.75	− 8.506	− 10.179	− 11.397	− 11.779	− 12.257
11.00	− 7.012	− 8.368	− 9.349	− 9.655	− 10.036
11.25	− 5.550	− 6.605	− 7.363	− 7.598	− 7.890
11.50	− 4.118	− 4.889	− 5.438	− 5.607	− 5.817
11.75	− 2.716	− 3.216	− 3.570	− 3.679	− 3.813
12.00	− 1.344	− 1.587	− 1.758	− 1.811	− 1.875
12.25	0.000	0.000	0.000	0.000	0.000
12.50	1.316	1.547	1.707	1.755	1.814
12.75	2.606	3.055	3.364	3.457	3.570
13.00	3.868	4.525	4.973	5.108	5.271
13.25	5.105	5.958	6.537	6.709	6.918
13.50	6.317	7.356	8.056	8.263	8.514
13.75	7.505	8.719	9.532	9.772	10.061
14.00	8.669	10.049	10.967	11.237	11.560
14.25	9.809	11.346	12.362	12.660	13.015
14.50	10.927	12.612	13.720	14.042	14.426
14.75	12.022	13.848	15.040	15.385	15.796
15.00	13.096	15.054	16.324	16.691	17.126
15.25	14.149	16.231	17.575	17.961	18.417
15.50	15.181	17.381	18.792	19.195	19.672
15.75	16.193	18.504	19.977	20.397	20.891
16.00	17.185	19.600	21.131	21.565	22.075
16.25	18.159	20.672	22.255	22.703	23.227
16.50	19.113	21.719	23.351	23.811	24.348
16.75	20.050	22.741	24.418	24.889	25.438
17.00	20.968	23.741	25.459	25.940	26.498
17.25	21.870	24.718	26.474	26.963	27.531
17.50	22.754	25.674	27.464	27.961	28.536
17.75	23.622	26.608	28.429	28.933	29.515
18.00	24.473	27.522	29.371	29.881	30.469

MAXIMUM PREMIUM FOR ASSUMABLE LOANS
AS PERCENTAGE OF LOAN BALANCE
FACE INTEREST RATE: 12.5%

CURRENT RATE	REMAINING TERM OF LOAN (YEARS)				
	15	20	25	27	30
9.00	− 21.519	− 26.277	− 29.929	− 31.116	− 32.641
9.25	− 19.756	− 24.051	− 27.321	− 28.378	− 29.730
9.50	− 18.033	− 21.887	− 24.798	− 25.734	− 26.926
9.75	− 16.346	− 19.781	− 22.355	− 23.178	− 24.222
10.00	− 14.695	− 17.732	− 19.990	− 20.708	− 21.615
10.25	− 13.081	− 15.739	− 17.700	− 18.320	− 19.100
10.50	− 11.500	− 13.798	− 15.481	− 16.010	− 16.673
10.75	− 9.954	− 11.910	− 13.332	− 13.776	− 14.331
11.00	− 8.440	− 10.071	− 11.248	− 11.614	− 12.069
11.25	− 6.958	− 8.281	− 9.228	− 9.520	− 9.884
11.50	− 5.507	− 6.537	− 7.269	− 7.494	− 7.772
11.75	− 4.086	− 4.838	− 5.369	− 5.531	− 5.731
12.00	− 2.696	− 3.184	− 3.525	− 3.629	− 3.757
12.25	− 1.334	− 1.571	− 1.737	− 1.787	− 1.848
12.50	0.000	0.000	0.000	0.000	0.000
12.75	1.306	1.531	1.686	1.732	1.788
13.00	2.586	3.024	3.323	3.412	3.520
13.25	3.840	4.480	4.914	5.042	5.198
13.50	5.068	5.900	6.459	6.624	6.823
13.75	6.271	7.285	7.961	8.160	8.399
14.00	7.450	8.635	9.421	9.651	9.926
14.25	8.606	9.953	10.841	11.099	11.408
14.50	9.738	11.239	12.221	12.506	12.845
14.75	10.848	12.494	13.564	13.874	14.240
15.00	11.936	13.719	14.871	15.203	15.595
15.25	13.003	14.915	16.143	16.495	16.910
15.50	14.049	16.083	17.381	17.752	18.187
15.75	15.075	17.223	18.587	18.974	19.429
16.00	16.081	18.337	19.761	20.164	20.636
16.25	17.067	19.425	20.905	21.322	21.809
16.50	18.034	20.488	22.020	22.449	22.950
16.75	18.983	21.527	23.106	23.547	24.060
17.00	19.914	22.543	24.165	24.617	25.140
17.25	20.828	23.536	25.197	25.658	26.192
17.50	21.724	24.506	26.204	26.674	27.215
17.75	22.603	25.455	27.186	27.663	28.213
18.00	23.466	26.383	28.145	28.628	29.184

741

MAXIMUM PREMIUM FOR ASSUMABLE LOANS
AS PERCENTAGE OF LOAN BALANCE
FACE INTEREST RATE: 12.75%

CURRENT RATE	REMAINING TERM OF LOAN (YEARS)				
	15	20	25	27	30
9.00	− 23.128	− 28.241	− 32.157	− 33.427	− 35.057
9.25	− 21.341	− 25.980	− 29.504	− 30.641	− 32.092
9.50	− 19.595	− 23.782	− 26.938	− 27.950	− 29.237
9.75	− 17.885	− 21.644	− 24.453	− 25.349	− 26.484
10.00	− 16.213	− 19.563	− 22.048	− 22.836	− 23.830
10.25	− 14.578	− 17.539	− 19.719	− 20.406	− 21.269
10.50	− 12.976	− 15.568	− 17.462	− 18.055	− 18.798
10.75	− 11.409	− 13.650	− 15.275	− 15.781	− 16.413
11.00	− 9.875	− 11.783	− 13.156	− 13.581	− 14.110
11.25	− 8.373	− 9.965	− 11.101	− 11.451	− 11.885
11.50	− 6.904	− 8.194	− 9.108	− 9.389	− 9.735
11.75	− 5.464	− 6.469	− 7.176	− 7.391	− 7.656
12.00	− 4.055	− 4.788	− 5.301	− 5.456	− 5.647
12.25	− 2.675	− 3.151	− 3.481	− 3.581	− 3.702
12.50	− 1.324	− 1.555	− 1.715	− 1.763	− 1.821
12.75	0.000	0.000	0.000	0.000	0.000
13.00	1.297	1.516	1.665	1.710	1.763
13.25	2.567	2.995	3.283	3.369	3.471
13.50	3.811	4.436	4.855	4.978	5.126
13.75	5.031	5.843	6.383	6.541	6.731
14.00	6.225	7.214	7.868	8.058	8.286
14.25	7.396	8.552	9.312	9.532	9.795
14.50	8.544	9.858	10.716	10.964	11.258
14.75	9.668	11.133	12.082	12.355	12.679
15.00	10.771	12.377	13.411	13.708	14.058
15.25	11.852	13.592	14.705	15.023	15.397
15.50	12.912	14.777	15.965	16.302	16.698
15.75	13.951	15.936	17.191	17.546	17.962
16.00	14.970	17.067	18.385	18.757	19.190
16.25	15.969	18.172	19.549	19.935	20.385
16.50	16.950	19.252	20.683	21.082	21.547
16.75	17.911	20.307	21.787	22.200	22.677
17.00	18.854	21.338	22.864	23.288	23.777
17.25	19.780	22.346	23.915	24.348	24.848
17.50	20.688	23.332	24.939	25.381	25.890
17.75	21.579	24.296	25.938	26.388	26.905
18.00	22.453	25.238	26.912	27.370	27.894

MAXIMUM PREMIUM FOR ASSUMABLE LOANS
AS PERCENTAGE OF LOAN BALANCE
FACE INTEREST RATE: 13%

CURRENT RATE	REMAINING TERM OF LOAN (YEARS)				
	15	20	25	27	30
9.00	− 24.745	− 30.215	− 34.395	− 35.748	− 37.481
9.25	− 22.935	− 27.919	− 31.697	− 32.913	− 34.463
9.50	− 21.166	− 25.688	− 29.088	− 30.176	− 31.557
9.75	− 19.434	− 23.516	− 26.561	− 27.530	− 28.754
10.00	− 17.740	− 21.404	− 24.115	− 24.972	− 26.052
10.25	− 16.083	− 19.348	− 21.746	− 22.500	− 23.446
10.50	− 14.460	− 17.347	− 19.451	− 20.109	− 20.930
10.75	− 12.872	− 15.400	− 17.227	− 17.795	− 18.503
11.00	− 11.319	− 13.504	− 15.072	− 15.557	− 16.158
11.25	− 9.797	− 11.658	− 12.982	− 13.390	− 13.893
11.50	− 8.308	− 9.860	− 10.956	− 11.292	− 11.704
11.75	− 6.849	− 8.108	− 8.991	− 9.259	− 9.589
12.00	− 5.422	− 6.402	− 7.084	− 7.290	− 7.543
12.25	− 4.024	− 4.739	− 5.234	− 5.382	− 5.564
12.50	− 2.654	− 3.119	− 3.437	− 3.533	− 3.649
12.75	− 1.314	− 1.540	− 1.694	− 1.739	− 1.795
13.00	0.000	0.000	0.000	0.000	0.000
13.25	1.287	1.501	1.645	1.688	1.739
13.50	2.548	2.965	3.244	3.325	3.423
13.75	3.783	4.393	4.797	4.915	5.056
14.00	4.994	5.786	6.307	6.459	6.640
14.25	6.180	7.144	7.776	7.959	8.175
14.50	7.342	8.471	9.204	9.415	9.665
14.75	8.482	9.765	10.593	10.831	11.111
15.00	9.599	11.028	11.945	12.207	12.515
15.25	10.694	12.261	13.261	13.545	13.878
15.50	11.768	13.465	14.541	14.846	15.202
15.75	12.821	14.642	15.789	16.112	16.489
16.00	13.853	15.790	17.003	17.344	17.740
16.25	14.866	16.912	18.186	18.543	18.956
16.50	15.859	18.009	19.339	19.710	20.139
16.75	16.833	19.080	20.463	20.846	21.289
17.00	17.788	20.127	21.558	21.953	22.409
17.25	18.726	21.151	22.626	23.032	23.499
17.50	19.646	22.151	23.668	24.083	24.560
17.75	20.548	23.130	24.683	25.108	25.593
18.00	21.434	24.087	25.675	26.107	26.600

MAXIMUM PREMIUM FOR ASSUMABLE LOANS
AS PERCENTAGE OF LOAN BALANCE
FACE INTEREST RATE: 13.25%

CURRENT RATE	REMAINING TERM OF LOAN (YEARS)				
	15	20	25	27	30
9.00	− 26.371	− 32.200	− 36.643	− 38.079	− 39.914
9.25	− 24.538	− 29.869	− 33.900	− 35.195	− 36.843
9.50	− 22.746	− 27.604	− 31.247	− 32.410	− 33.885
9.75	− 20.991	− 25.399	− 28.678	− 29.719	− 31.033
10.00	− 19.275	− 23.254	− 26.191	− 27.118	− 28.283
10.25	− 17.596	− 21.167	− 23.783	− 24.603	− 25.630
10.50	− 15.952	− 19.136	− 21.449	− 22.170	− 23.070
10.75	− 14.344	− 17.159	− 19.188	− 19.817	− 20.599
11.00	− 12.770	− 15.234	− 16.997	− 17.541	− 18.213
11.25	− 11.228	− 13.359	− 14.872	− 15.336	− 15.908
11.50	− 9.720	− 11.534	− 12.812	− 13.202	− 13.681
11.75	− 8.242	− 9.755	− 10.814	− 11.135	− 11.528
12.00	− 6.796	− 8.023	− 8.875	− 9.132	− 9.446
12.25	− 5.380	− 6.335	− 6.994	− 7.192	− 7.432
12.50	− 3.993	− 4.690	− 5.168	− 5.310	− 5.483
12.75	− 2.634	− 3.087	− 3.395	− 3.486	− 3.596
13.00	− 1.304	− 1.524	− 1.673	− 1.717	− 1.770
13.25	0.000	0.000	0.000	0.000	0.000
13.50	1.277	1.486	1.625	1.666	1.715
13.75	2.529	2.936	3.205	3.283	3.376
14.00	3.755	4.350	4.740	4.853	4.988
14.25	4.956	5.729	6.233	6.378	6.551
14.50	6.134	7.076	7.685	7.860	8.067
14.75	7.289	8.389	9.098	9.300	9.538
15.00	8.420	9.672	10.472	10.700	10.967
15.25	9.530	10.924	11.810	12.061	12.354
15.50	10.617	12.146	13.112	13.384	13.702
15.75	11.684	13.341	14.380	14.672	15.011
16.00	12.730	14.507	15.615	15.925	16.284
16.25	13.756	15.646	16.818	17.144	17.522
16.50	14.762	16.759	17.990	18.331	18.725
16.75	15.748	17.847	19.132	19.488	19.896
17.00	16.716	18.910	20.246	20.614	21.036
17.25	17.666	19.949	21.332	21.711	22.145
17.50	18.598	20.965	22.391	22.780	23.225
17.75	19.513	21.958	23.424	23.822	24.277
18.00	20.410	22.930	24.431	24.838	25.301

MAXIMUM PREMIUM FOR ASSUMABLE LOANS
AS PERCENTAGE OF LOAN BALANCE
FACE INTEREST RATE: 13.5%

CURRENT RATE	REMAINING TERM OF LOAN (YEARS)				
	15	20	25	27	30
9.00	− 28.006	− 34.194	− 38.900	− 40.418	− 42.354
9.25	− 26.149	− 31.828	− 36.112	− 37.485	− 39.230
9.50	− 24.333	− 29.529	− 33.415	− 34.653	− 36.220
9.75	− 22.556	− 27.290	− 30.804	− 31.916	− 33.318
10.00	− 20.818	− 25.113	− 28.276	− 29.271	− 30.521
10.25	− 19.117	− 22.995	− 25.827	− 26.714	− 27.822
10.50	− 17.452	− 20.933	− 23.455	− 24.240	− 25.217
10.75	− 15.823	− 18.926	− 21.157	− 21.847	− 22.703
11.00	− 14.229	− 16.972	− 18.930	− 19.532	− 20.276
11.25	− 12.667	− 15.069	− 16.770	− 17.290	− 17.930
11.50	− 11.139	− 13.216	− 14.676	− 15.120	− 15.664
11.75	− 9.643	− 11.411	− 12.644	− 13.018	− 13.473
12.00	− 8.178	− 9.653	− 10.674	− 10.981	− 11.355
12.25	− 6.743	− 7.940	− 8.761	− 9.007	− 9.306
12.50	− 5.338	− 6.270	− 6.905	− 7.094	− 7.323
12.75	− 3.962	− 4.642	− 5.103	− 5.239	− 5.403
13.00	− 2.614	− 3.056	− 3.352	− 3.440	− 3.545
13.25	− 1.294	− 1.508	− 1.652	− 1.694	− 1.744
13.50	0.000	0.000	0.000	0.000	0.000
13.75	1.268	1.472	1.606	1.645	1.691
14.00	2.510	2.907	3.167	3.242	3.330
14.25	3.727	4.307	4.684	4.792	4.920
14.50	4.920	5.674	6.160	6.299	6.463
14.75	6.090	7.007	7.596	7.764	7.960
15.00	7.236	8.309	8.993	9.187	9.414
15.25	8.360	9.580	10.353	10.571	10.825
15.50	9.461	10.821	11.677	11.917	12.196
15.75	10.542	12.033	12.966	13.226	13.529
16.00	11.601	13.217	14.221	14.500	14.824
16.25	12.640	14.373	15.444	15.741	16.083
16.50	13.659	15.503	16.635	16.948	17.308
16.75	14.659	16.607	17.796	18.124	18.499
17.00	15.639	17.687	18.928	19.269	19.658
17.25	16.601	18.741	20.032	20.385	20.787
17.50	17.545	19.773	21.109	21.472	21.886
17.75	18.471	20.781	22.159	22.532	22.956
18.00	19.380	21.767	23.183	23.565	23.998

MAXIMUM PREMIUM FOR ASSUMABLE LOANS
AS PERCENTAGE OF LOAN BALANCE
FACE INTEREST RATE: 13.75%

CURRENT RATE	REMAINING TERM OF LOAN (YEARS)				
	15	20	25	27	30
9.00	− 29.650	− 36.198	− 41.167	− 42.766	− 44.803
9.25	− 27.769	− 33.797	− 38.334	− 39.784	− 41.625
9.50	− 25.930	− 31.463	− 35.593	− 36.905	− 38.563
9.75	− 24.130	− 29.192	− 32.939	− 34.122	− 35.612
10.00	− 22.369	− 26.982	− 30.369	− 31.433	− 32.766
10.25	− 20.647	− 24.832	− 27.881	− 28.833	− 30.020
10.50	− 18.960	− 22.739	− 25.470	− 26.318	− 27.371
10.75	− 17.310	− 20.702	− 23.134	− 23.885	− 24.814
11.00	− 15.696	− 18.719	− 20.871	− 21.531	− 22.344
11.25	− 14.114	− 16.788	− 18.676	− 19.251	− 19.959
11.50	− 12.566	− 14.907	− 16.547	− 17.045	− 17.654
11.75	− 11.051	− 13.075	− 14.483	− 14.907	− 15.425
12.00	− 9.567	− 11.291	− 12.480	− 12.837	− 13.270
12.25	− 8.114	− 9.552	− 10.536	− 10.830	− 11.186
12.50	− 6.691	− 7.857	− 8.650	− 8.885	− 9.169
12.75	− 5.297	− 6.205	− 6.818	− 6.999	− 7.216
13.00	− 3.932	− 4.595	− 5.039	− 5.170	− 5.326
13.25	− 2.594	− 3.025	− 3.311	− 3.395	− 3.494
13.50	− 1.284	− 1.494	− 1.632	− 1.672	− 1.720
13.75	0.000	0.000	0.000	0.000	0.000
14.00	1.258	1.457	1.586	1.624	1.668
14.25	2.491	2.878	3.129	3.200	3.285
14.50	3.699	4.265	4.629	4.732	4.854
14.75	4.883	5.619	6.088	6.221	6.377
15.00	6.044	6.940	7.508	7.668	7.856
15.25	7.183	8.230	8.890	9.076	9.291
15.50	8.298	9.489	10.235	10.444	10.686
15.75	9.393	10.719	11.545	11.775	12.042
16.00	10.466	11.921	12.821	13.071	13.359
16.25	11.518	13.094	14.064	14.332	14.640
16.50	12.550	14.241	15.275	15.559	15.885
16.75	13.563	15.362	16.455	16.754	17.097
17.00	14.556	16.457	17.605	17.919	18.276
17.25	15.530	17.528	18.727	19.053	19.424
17.50	16.486	18.574	19.821	20.159	20.542
17.75	17.424	19.598	20.888	21.236	21.631
18.00	18.345	20.599	21.929	22.287	22.691

MAXIMUM PREMIUM FOR ASSUMABLE LOANS
AS PERCENTAGE OF LOAN BALANCE
FACE INTEREST RATE: 14%

CURRENT RATE	REMAINING TERM OF LOAN (YEARS)				
	15	20	25	27	30
9.00	− 31.302	− 38.212	− 43.443	− 45.122	− 47.258
9.25	− 29.396	− 35.775	− 40.563	− 42.091	− 44.026
9.50	− 27.534	− 33.407	− 37.778	− 39.164	− 40.913
9.75	− 25.711	− 31.101	− 35.081	− 36.336	− 37.911
10.00	− 23.928	− 28.859	− 32.470	− 33.602	− 35.017
10.25	− 22.184	− 26.678	− 29.942	− 30.959	− 32.225
10.50	− 20.476	− 24.554	− 27.492	− 28.402	− 29.531
10.75	− 18.805	− 22.487	− 25.119	− 25.929	− 26.930
11.00	− 17.169	− 20.474	− 22.819	− 23.536	− 24.419
11.25	− 15.568	− 18.514	− 20.588	− 21.219	− 21.993
11.50	− 14.000	− 16.606	− 18.426	− 18.976	− 19.649
11.75	− 12.465	− 14.747	− 16.328	− 16.804	− 17.383
12.00	− 10.963	− 12.936	− 14.293	− 14.699	− 15.191
12.25	− 9.491	− 11.171	− 12.318	− 12.659	− 13.071
12.50	− 8.050	− 9.451	− 10.401	− 10.682	− 11.020
12.75	− 6.639	− 7.775	− 8.540	− 8.765	− 9.035
13.00	− 5.256	− 6.141	− 6.732	− 6.905	− 7.112
13.25	− 3.901	− 4.548	− 4.976	− 5.101	− 5.250
13.50	− 2.575	− 2.994	− 3.270	− 3.350	− 3.445
13.75	− 1.274	− 1.478	− 1.612	− 1.650	− 1.696
14.00	0.000	0.000	0.000	0.000	0.000
14.25	1.248	1.442	1.567	1.603	1.645
14.50	2.472	2.850	3.092	3.160	3.241
14.75	3.672	4.223	4.574	4.674	4.789
15.00	4.847	5.564	6.017	6.145	6.293
15.25	6.000	6.873	7.421	7.575	7.753
15.50	7.130	8.151	8.788	8.966	9.172
15.75	8.239	9.400	10.119	10.319	10.550
16.00	9.325	10.619	11.416	11.636	11.890
16.25	10.391	11.810	12.679	12.918	13.192
16.50	11.436	12.974	13.909	14.166	14.459
16.75	12.461	14.111	15.108	15.381	15.691
17.00	13.467	15.222	16.277	16.564	16.890
17.25	14.454	16.309	17.417	17.717	18.058
17.50	15.422	17.371	18.529	18.841	19.194
17.75	16.372	18.409	19.613	19.936	20.301
18.00	17.305	19.425	20.671	21.004	21.380

MAXIMUM PREMIUM FOR ASSUMABLE LOANS
AS PERCENTAGE OF LOAN BALANCE
FACE INTEREST RATE: 14.25%

CURRENT RATE	REMAINING TERM OF LOAN (YEARS)				
	15	20	25	27	30
9.00	− 32.962	− 40.234	− 45.726	− 47.486	− 49.721
9.25	− 31.032	− 37.762	− 42.801	− 44.406	− 46.435
9.50	− 29.147	− 35.359	− 39.972	− 41.431	− 43.270
9.75	− 27.301	− 33.020	− 37.232	− 38.557	− 40.218
10.00	− 25.495	− 30.745	− 34.580	− 35.778	− 37.275
10.25	− 23.728	− 28.531	− 32.011	− 33.092	− 34.437
10.50	− 21.999	− 26.376	− 29.522	− 30.494	− 31.697
10.75	− 20.307	− 24.279	− 27.111	− 27.981	− 29.053
11.00	− 18.651	− 22.237	− 24.774	− 25.549	− 26.500
11.25	− 17.029	− 20.249	− 22.508	− 23.194	− 24.033
11.50	− 15.442	− 18.312	− 20.311	− 20.915	− 21.650
11.75	− 13.887	− 16.426	− 18.180	− 18.706	− 19.346
12.00	− 12.366	− 14.588	− 16.113	− 16.568	− 17.118
12.25	− 10.876	− 12.798	− 14.106	− 14.495	− 14.962
12.50	− 9.416	− 11.053	− 12.159	− 12.485	− 12.877
12.75	− 7.987	− 9.352	− 10.268	− 10.537	− 10.858
13.00	− 6.587	− 7.694	− 8.431	− 8.647	− 8.903
13.25	− 5.215	− 6.077	− 6.647	− 6.813	− 7.010
13.50	− 3.871	− 4.501	− 4.914	− 5.034	− 5.175
13.75	− 2.554	− 2.963	− 3.230	− 3.306	− 3.397
14.00	− 1.264	− 1.463	− 1.592	− 1.629	− 1.672
14.25	0.000	0.000	0.000	0.000	0.000
14.50	1.239	1.428	1.549	1.583	1.623
14.75	2.454	2.822	3.055	3.121	3.197
15.00	3.644	4.182	4.521	4.616	4.726
15.25	4.812	5.510	5.947	6.069	6.211
15.50	5.956	6.807	7.336	7.483	7.653
15.75	7.079	8.074	8.688	8.858	9.054
16.00	8.179	9.311	10.005	10.197	10.416
16.25	9.258	10.519	11.288	11.499	11.740
16.50	10.317	11.700	12.538	12.767	13.028
16.75	11.355	12.854	13.757	14.002	14.281
17.00	12.373	13.982	14.944	15.205	15.501
17.25	13.373	15.084	16.102	16.377	16.688
17.50	14.353	16.162	17.232	17.519	17.843
17.75	15.315	17.216	18.333	18.632	18.969
18.00	16.259	18.246	19.408	19.718	20.065

MAXIMUM PREMIUM FOR ASSUMABLE LOANS
AS PERCENTAGE OF LOAN BALANCE
FACE INTEREST RATE: 14.5%

CURRENT RATE	REMAINING TERM OF LOAN (YEARS)				
	15	20	25	27	30
9.00	− 34.630	− 42.266	− 48.019	− 49.858	− 52.190
9.25	− 32.677	− 39.758	− 45.048	− 46.728	− 48.850
9.50	− 30.767	− 37.320	− 42.174	− 43.706	− 45.633
9.75	− 28.898	− 34.947	− 39.391	− 40.785	− 42.530
10.00	− 27.070	− 32.639	− 36.697	− 37.962	− 39.539
10.25	− 25.281	− 30.394	− 34.087	− 35.233	− 36.654
10.50	− 23.530	− 28.207	− 31.560	− 32.593	− 33.869
10.75	− 21.817	− 26.080	− 29.111	− 30.039	− 31.182
11.00	− 20.140	− 24.008	− 26.737	− 27.568	− 28.586
11.25	− 18.498	− 21.991	− 24.435	− 25.175	− 26.079
11.50	− 16.890	− 20.027	− 22.204	− 22.859	− 23.656
11.75	− 15.316	− 18.113	− 20.039	− 20.615	− 21.314
12.00	− 13.776	− 16.249	− 17.939	− 18.442	− 19.049
12.25	− 12.267	− 14.432	− 15.901	− 16.336	− 16.859
12.50	− 10.789	− 12.662	− 13.923	− 14.294	− 14.739
12.75	− 9.342	− 10.937	− 12.002	− 12.314	− 12.686
13.00	− 7.924	− 9.255	− 10.137	− 10.394	− 10.699
13.25	− 6.535	− 7.614	− 8.325	− 8.531	− 8.775
13.50	− 5.175	− 6.015	− 6.565	− 6.723	− 6.910
13.75	− 3.841	− 4.455	− 4.853	− 4.968	− 5.102
14.00	− 2.535	− 2.933	− 3.190	− 3.263	− 3.349
14.25	− 1.255	− 1.449	− 1.573	− 1.608	− 1.649
14.50	0.000	0.000	0.000	0.000	0.000
14.75	1.230	1.414	1.530	1.563	1.601
15.00	2.435	2.794	3.019	3.082	3.155
15.25	3.617	4.141	4.468	4.559	4.664
15.50	4.776	5.457	5.879	5.995	6.130
15.75	5.912	6.742	7.252	7.393	7.554
16.00	7.027	7.997	8.590	8.752	8.938
16.25	8.119	9.223	9.893	10.076	10.285
16.50	9.191	10.421	11.163	11.364	11.594
16.75	10.242	11.591	12.400	12.619	12.868
17.00	11.274	12.735	13.606	13.841	14.107
17.25	12.286	13.854	14.783	15.032	15.313
17.50	13.278	14.947	15.930	16.193	16.488
17.75	14.252	16.016	17.049	17.324	17.632
18.00	15.208	17.062	18.140	18.426	18.747

MAXIMUM PREMIUM FOR ASSUMABLE LOANS
AS PERCENTAGE OF LOAN BALANCE
FACE INTEREST RATE: 14.75%

CURRENT RATE	REMAINING TERM OF LOAN (YEARS)				
	15	20	25	27	30
9.00	− 36.306	− 44.306	− 50.319	− 52.237	− 54.666
9.25	− 34.329	− 41.762	− 47.301	− 49.058	− 51.272
9.50	− 32.396	− 39.289	− 44.383	− 45.987	− 48.002
9.75	− 30.503	− 36.883	− 41.557	− 43.020	− 44.849
10.00	− 28.652	− 34.541	− 38.821	− 40.152	− 41.809
10.25	− 26.841	− 32.264	− 36.171	− 37.379	− 38.877
10.50	− 25.068	− 30.046	− 33.604	− 34.698	− 36.047
10.75	− 23.333	− 27.888	− 31.117	− 32.103	− 33.316
11.00	− 21.636	− 25.787	− 28.706	− 29.593	− 30.678
11.25	− 19.973	− 23.740	− 26.369	− 27.162	− 28.130
11.50	− 18.346	− 21.748	− 24.103	− 24.810	− 25.668
11.75	− 16.752	− 19.807	− 21.904	− 22.530	− 23.287
12.00	− 15.193	− 17.916	− 19.772	− 20.322	− 20.986
12.25	− 13.665	− 16.073	− 17.702	− 18.183	− 18.759
12.50	− 12.169	− 14.278	− 15.693	− 16.108	− 16.605
12.75	− 10.703	− 12.528	− 13.743	− 14.097	− 14.520
13.00	− 9.268	− 10.821	− 11.848	− 12.146	− 12.500
13.25	− 7.862	− 9.158	− 10.008	− 10.254	− 10.544
13.50	− 6.484	− 7.536	− 8.220	− 8.417	− 8.649
13.75	− 5.134	− 5.953	− 6.483	− 6.634	− 6.812
14.00	− 3.812	− 4.410	− 4.794	− 4.903	− 5.030
14.25	− 2.516	− 2.904	− 3.151	− 3.221	− 3.303
14.50	− 1.245	− 1.434	− 1.554	− 1.588	− 1.627
14.75	0.000	0.000	0.000	0.000	0.000
15.00	1.220	1.400	1.512	1.543	1.579
15.25	2.417	2.767	2.984	3.044	3.113
15.50	3.590	4.101	4.416	4.503	4.603
15.75	4.741	5.405	5.811	5.923	6.050
16.00	5.869	6.677	7.169	7.304	7.457
16.25	6.975	7.921	8.493	8.648	8.825
16.50	8.060	9.136	9.782	9.957	10.156
16.75	9.125	10.323	11.039	11.232	11.450
17.00	10.169	11.484	12.264	12.474	12.710
17.25	11.193	12.618	13.459	13.683	13.936
17.50	12.198	13.727	14.623	14.862	15.130
17.75	13.185	14.812	15.760	16.011	16.292
18.00	14.153	15.872	16.868	17.131	17.425

MAXIMUM PREMIUM FOR ASSUMABLE LOANS
AS PERCENTAGE OF LOAN BALANCE
FACE INTEREST RATE: 15%

CURRENT RATE	REMAINING TERM OF LOAN (YEARS)				
	15	20	25	27	30
9.00	− 37.990	− 46.355	− 52.626	− 54.623	− 57.148
9.25	− 35.988	− 43.775	− 49.563	− 51.394	− 53.699
9.50	− 34.031	− 41.267	− 46.599	− 48.275	− 50.376
9.75	− 32.115	− 38.826	− 43.730	− 45.262	− 47.173
10.00	− 30.242	− 36.452	− 40.952	− 42.349	− 44.084
10.25	− 28.408	− 34.141	− 38.261	− 39.533	− 41.105
10.50	− 26.613	− 31.892	− 35.655	− 36.809	− 38.230
10.75	− 24.857	− 29.704	− 33.130	− 34.174	− 35.455
11.00	− 23.138	− 27.573	− 30.682	− 31.624	− 32.775
11.25	− 21.455	− 25.497	− 28.309	− 29.156	− 30.186
11.50	− 19.808	− 23.476	− 26.008	− 26.766	− 27.684
11.75	− 18.195	− 21.507	− 23.776	− 24.451	− 25.266
12.00	− 16.616	− 19.590	− 21.610	− 22.208	− 22.927
12.25	− 15.069	− 17.721	− 19.509	− 20.035	− 20.665
12.50	− 13.554	− 15.900	− 17.469	− 17.928	− 18.476
12.75	− 12.071	− 14.125	− 15.489	− 15.885	− 16.357
13.00	− 10.618	− 12.395	− 13.565	− 13.904	− 14.305
13.25	− 9.194	− 10.707	− 11.697	− 11.982	− 12.318
13.50	− 7.800	− 9.062	− 9.882	− 10.116	− 10.392
13.75	− 6.433	− 7.457	− 8.117	− 8.305	− 8.525
14.00	− 5.094	− 5.892	− 6.402	− 6.547	− 6.716
14.25	− 3.782	− 4.365	− 4.735	− 4.839	− 4.960
14.50	− 2.496	− 2.874	− 3.113	− 3.180	− 3.257
14.75	− 1.235	− 1.420	− 1.535	− 1.567	− 1.605
15.00	0.000	0.000	0.000	0.000	0.000
15.25	1.212	1.386	1.494	1.524	1.558
15.50	2.399	2.740	2.949	3.006	3.072
15.75	3.564	4.062	4.365	4.448	4.543
16.00	4.706	5.353	5.744	5.851	5.972
16.25	5.826	6.614	7.088	7.217	7.362
16.50	6.925	7.846	8.397	8.546	8.714
16.75	8.002	9.050	9.673	9.841	10.029
17.00	9.059	10.227	10.917	11.102	11.309
17.25	10.096	11.378	12.130	12.330	12.555
17.50	11.114	12.502	13.313	13.528	13.768
17.75	12.112	13.602	14.467	14.695	14.949
18.00	13.092	14.678	15.592	15.833	16.100

MAXIMUM PREMIUM FOR ASSUMABLE LOANS
AS PERCENTAGE OF LOAN BALANCE
FACE INTEREST RATE: 15.25%

CURRENT RATE	REMAINING TERM OF LOAN (YEARS)				
	15	20	25	27	30
9.00	− 39.683	− 48.412	− 54.941	− 57.016	− 59.635
9.25	− 37.656	− 45.796	− 51.831	− 53.737	− 56.132
9.50	− 35.675	− 43.253	− 48.823	− 50.570	− 52.757
9.75	− 33.736	− 40.777	− 45.910	− 47.510	− 49.503
10.00	− 31.839	− 38.370	− 43.090	− 44.552	− 46.365
10.25	− 29.983	− 36.027	− 40.359	− 41.692	− 43.339
10.50	− 28.166	− 33.746	− 37.713	− 38.926	− 40.418
10.75	− 26.389	− 31.527	− 35.149	− 36.250	− 37.599
11.00	− 24.649	− 29.366	− 32.664	− 33.661	− 34.876
11.25	− 22.945	− 27.261	− 30.255	− 31.154	− 32.246
11.50	− 21.277	− 25.212	− 27.919	− 28.727	− 29.705
11.75	− 19.644	− 23.216	− 25.653	− 26.377	− 27.248
12.00	− 18.046	− 21.271	− 23.455	− 24.100	− 24.873
12.25	− 16.480	− 19.376	− 21.322	− 21.893	− 22.575
12.50	− 14.947	− 17.529	− 19.251	− 19.753	− 20.351
12.75	− 13.446	− 15.729	− 17.240	− 17.679	− 18.199
13.00	− 11.975	− 13.975	− 15.288	− 15.667	− 16.115
13.25	− 10.534	− 12.264	− 13.391	− 13.715	− 14.096
13.50	− 9.122	− 10.595	− 11.548	− 11.820	− 12.139
13.75	− 7.738	− 8.968	− 9.757	− 9.981	− 10.243
14.00	− 6.383	− 7.380	− 8.016	− 8.196	− 8.405
14.25	− 5.055	− 5.832	− 6.323	− 6.462	− 6.622
14.50	− 3.753	− 4.320	− 4.677	− 4.777	− 4.892
14.75	− 2.477	− 2.845	− 3.075	− 3.139	− 3.213
15.00	− 1.226	− 1.406	− 1.517	− 1.548	− 1.583
15.25	0.000	0.000	0.000	0.000	0.000
15.50	1.202	1.372	1.477	1.505	1.538
15.75	2.381	2.713	2.914	2.969	3.032
16.00	3.537	4.022	4.315	4.394	4.484
16.25	4.671	5.301	5.679	5.781	5.896
16.50	5.783	6.551	7.008	7.131	7.269
16.75	6.874	7.772	8.303	8.445	8.605
17.00	7.944	8.965	9.566	9.726	9.905
17.25	8.994	10.132	10.797	10.974	11.171
17.50	10.024	11.272	11.998	12.189	12.403
17.75	11.034	12.388	13.169	13.375	13.603
18.00	12.026	13.478	14.312	14.530	14.772

MAXIMUM PREMIUM FOR ASSUMABLE LOANS
AS PERCENTAGE OF LOAN BALANCE
FACE INTEREST RATE: 15.5%

CURRENT RATE	REMAINING TERM OF LOAN (YEARS)				
	15	20	25	27	30
9.00	− 41.383	− 50.477	− 57.263	− 59.415	− 62.128
9.25	− 39.331	− 47.825	− 54.107	− 56.086	− 58.570
9.50	− 37.326	− 45.246	− 51.053	− 52.871	− 55.142
9.75	− 35.363	− 42.736	− 48.096	− 49.764	− 51.837
10.00	− 33.443	− 40.295	− 45.234	− 46.760	− 48.651
10.25	− 31.565	− 37.920	− 42.462	− 43.857	− 45.577
10.50	− 29.726	− 35.608	− 39.776	− 41.049	− 42.611
10.75	− 27.926	− 33.357	− 37.174	− 38.332	− 39.747
11.00	− 26.165	− 31.166	− 34.652	− 35.703	− 36.983
11.25	− 24.441	− 29.032	− 32.207	− 33.158	− 34.312
11.50	− 22.753	− 26.954	− 29.836	− 30.694	− 31.731
11.75	− 21.100	− 24.930	− 27.536	− 28.308	− 29.235
12.00	− 19.482	− 22.959	− 25.305	− 25.996	− 26.823
12.25	− 17.898	− 21.037	− 23.140	− 23.755	− 24.489
12.50	− 16.346	− 19.165	− 21.038	− 21.583	− 22.231
12.75	− 14.826	− 17.340	− 18.998	− 19.477	− 20.045
13.00	− 13.337	− 15.561	− 17.016	− 17.434	− 17.928
13.25	− 11.879	− 13.826	− 15.091	− 15.452	− 15.877
13.50	− 10.450	− 12.134	− 13.220	− 13.529	− 13.891
13.75	− 9.049	− 10.484	− 11.402	− 11.662	− 11.965
14.00	− 7.678	− 8.875	− 9.635	− 9.849	− 10.098
14.25	− 6.333	− 7.304	− 7.917	− 8.088	− 8.287
14.50	− 5.015	− 5.772	− 6.246	− 6.378	− 6.530
14.75	− 3.724	− 4.276	− 4.620	− 4.715	− 4.825
15.00	− 2.458	− 2.817	− 3.038	− 3.099	− 3.169
15.25	− 1.217	− 1.392	− 1.499	− 1.528	− 1.562
15.50	0.000	0.000	0.000	0.000	0.000
15.75	1.193	1.359	1.459	1.487	1.517
16.00	2.364	2.687	2.881	2.933	2.992
16.25	3.511	3.983	4.265	4.341	4.426
16.50	4.637	5.250	5.614	5.712	5.821
16.75	5.741	6.488	6.929	7.046	7.178
17.00	6.823	7.698	8.211	8.346	8.498
17.25	7.886	8.881	9.460	9.613	9.784
17.50	8.929	10.038	10.679	10.848	11.035
17.75	9.952	11.169	11.868	12.051	12.254
18.00	10.956	12.274	13.028	13.224	13.441

MAXIMUM PREMIUM FOR ASSUMABLE LOANS
AS PERCENTAGE OF LOAN BALANCE
FACE INTEREST RATE: 15.75%

CURRENT RATE	REMAINING TERM OF LOAN (YEARS)				
	15	20	25	27	30
9.00	− 43.090	− 52.551	− 59.592	− 61.821	− 64.626
9.25	− 41.014	− 49.861	− 56.389	− 58.441	− 61.013
9.50	− 38.985	− 47.247	− 53.290	− 55.178	− 57.533
9.75	− 36.998	− 44.703	− 50.290	− 52.024	− 54.177
10.00	− 35.055	− 42.228	− 47.385	− 48.975	− 50.941
10.25	− 33.154	− 39.820	− 44.572	− 46.028	− 47.820
10.50	− 31.293	− 37.476	− 41.847	− 43.177	− 44.808
10.75	− 29.472	− 35.195	− 39.206	− 40.420	− 41.901
11.00	− 27.689	− 32.973	− 36.647	− 37.751	− 39.093
11.25	− 25.944	− 30.810	− 34.165	− 35.168	− 36.381
11.50	− 24.236	− 28.704	− 31.759	− 32.667	− 33.760
11.75	− 22.563	− 26.652	− 29.425	− 30.244	− 31.227
12.00	− 20.926	− 24.653	− 27.161	− 27.897	− 28.777
12.25	− 19.322	− 22.705	− 24.964	− 25.623	− 26.407
12.50	− 17.751	− 20.807	− 22.831	− 23.418	− 24.114
12.75	− 16.213	− 18.957	− 20.760	− 21.280	− 21.894
13.00	− 14.706	− 17.153	− 18.749	− 19.207	− 19.745
13.25	− 13.230	− 15.394	− 16.795	− 17.195	− 17.663
13.50	− 11.784	− 13.679	− 14.897	− 15.242	− 15.646
13.75	− 10.367	− 12.006	− 13.052	− 13.347	− 13.690
14.00	− 8.978	− 10.375	− 11.259	− 11.507	− 11.794
14.25	− 7.618	− 8.783	− 9.515	− 9.719	− 9.955
14.50	− 6.284	− 7.229	− 7.819	− 7.983	− 8.171
14.75	− 4.977	− 5.713	− 6.169	− 6.295	− 6.440
15.00	− 3.696	− 4.234	− 4.564	− 4.655	− 4.759
15.25	− 2.439	− 2.789	− 3.002	− 3.060	− 3.127
15.50	− 1.208	− 1.378	− 1.481	− 1.509	− 1.541
15.75	0.000	0.000	0.000	0.000	0.000
16.00	1.184	1.346	1.442	1.468	1.498
16.25	2.345	2.660	2.847	2.897	2.954
16.50	3.485	3.945	4.216	4.289	4.370
16.75	4.602	5.200	5.551	5.644	5.748
17.00	5.698	6.427	6.851	6.963	7.088
17.25	6.774	7.626	8.119	8.249	8.393
17.50	7.829	8.798	9.356	9.502	9.664
17.75	8.864	9.945	10.563	10.724	10.902
18.00	9.880	11.066	11.740	11.915	12.107

MAXIMUM PREMIUM FOR ASSUMABLE LOANS
AS PERCENTAGE OF LOAN BALANCE
FACE INTEREST RATE: 16%

CURRENT RATE	REMAINING TERM OF LOAN (YEARS)				
	15	20	25	27	30
9.00	− 44.805	− 54.632	− 61.928	− 64.232	− 67.129
9.25	− 42.704	− 51.906	− 58.678	− 60.802	− 63.461
9.50	− 40.650	− 49.256	− 55.534	− 57.490	− 59.928
9.75	− 38.640	− 46.677	− 52.489	− 54.289	− 56.521
10.00	− 36.673	− 44.168	− 49.542	− 51.195	− 53.236
10.25	− 34.750	− 41.727	− 46.688	− 48.204	− 50.068
10.50	− 32.866	− 39.351	− 43.922	− 45.311	− 47.010
10.75	− 31.023	− 37.039	− 41.243	− 42.512	− 44.058
11.00	− 29.219	− 34.787	− 38.646	− 39.804	− 41.208
11.25	− 27.453	− 32.594	− 36.128	− 37.182	− 38.455
11.50	− 25.725	− 30.459	− 33.687	− 34.644	− 35.794
11.75	− 24.032	− 28.379	− 31.319	− 32.185	− 33.222
12.00	− 22.375	− 26.353	− 29.022	− 29.803	− 30.735
12.25	− 20.752	− 24.379	− 26.792	− 27.495	− 28.329
12.50	− 19.162	− 22.454	− 24.628	− 25.257	− 26.001
12.75	− 17.606	− 20.579	− 22.527	− 23.087	− 23.748
13.00	− 16.081	− 18.751	− 20.487	− 20.983	− 21.566
13.25	− 14.587	− 16.968	− 18.504	− 18.941	− 19.452
13.50	− 13.124	− 15.230	− 16.578	− 16.960	− 17.404
13.75	− 11.689	− 13.534	− 14.706	− 15.036	− 15.419
14.00	− 10.284	− 11.880	− 12.887	− 13.168	− 13.494
14.25	− 8.907	− 10.267	− 11.118	− 11.354	− 11.627
14.50	− 7.558	− 8.692	− 9.397	− 9.592	− 9.816
14.75	− 6.235	− 7.155	− 7.723	− 7.879	− 8.058
15.00	− 4.938	− 5.655	− 6.094	− 6.215	− 6.352
15.25	− 3.667	− 4.191	− 4.509	− 4.596	− 4.694
15.50	− 2.421	− 2.761	− 2.966	− 3.022	− 3.085
15.75	− 1.198	− 1.364	− 1.463	− 1.490	− 1.520
16.00	0.000	0.000	0.000	0.000	0.000
16.25	1.175	1.332	1.426	1.450	1.478
16.50	2.328	2.635	2.815	2.863	2.916
16.75	3.459	3.907	4.168	4.238	4.315
17.00	4.568	5.150	5.488	5.577	5.676
17.25	5.656	6.366	6.775	6.882	7.001
17.50	6.724	7.554	8.030	8.154	8.291
17.75	7.772	8.716	9.254	9.393	9.547
18.00	8.800	9.853	10.448	10.602	10.771

MAXIMUM PREMIUM FOR ASSUMABLE LOANS
AS PERCENTAGE OF LOAN BALANCE
FACE INTEREST RATE: 16.25%

CURRENT RATE	REMAINING TERM OF LOAN (YEARS) 15	20	25	27	30
9.00	− 46.527	− 56.720	− 64.270	− 66.649	− 69.637
9.25	− 44.401	− 53.957	− 60.972	− 63.169	− 65.914
9.50	− 42.323	− 51.271	− 57.783	− 59.808	− 62.327
9.75	− 40.289	− 48.658	− 54.694	− 56.560	− 58.869
10.00	− 38.299	− 46.115	− 51.704	− 53.420	− 55.535
10.25	− 36.352	− 43.641	− 48.809	− 50.385	− 52.319
10.50	− 34.446	− 41.233	− 46.004	− 47.449	− 49.216
10.75	− 32.581	− 38.889	− 43.286	− 44.610	− 46.220
11.00	− 30.756	− 36.608	− 40.651	− 41.862	− 43.327
11.25	− 28.969	− 34.385	− 38.097	− 39.201	− 40.532
11.50	− 27.220	− 32.221	− 35.621	− 36.625	− 37.832
11.75	− 25.507	− 30.113	− 33.218	− 34.130	− 35.221
12.00	− 23.830	− 28.059	− 30.888	− 31.714	− 32.697
12.25	− 22.188	− 26.058	− 28.626	− 29.371	− 30.255
12.50	− 20.579	− 24.108	− 26.431	− 27.101	− 27.892
12.75	− 19.004	− 22.208	− 24.299	− 24.899	− 25.604
13.00	− 17.461	− 20.355	− 22.229	− 22.763	− 23.390
13.25	− 15.949	− 18.548	− 20.218	− 20.692	− 21.244
13.50	− 14.469	− 16.786	− 18.264	− 18.681	− 19.165
13.75	− 13.017	− 15.067	− 16.365	− 16.729	− 17.150
14.00	− 11.596	− 13.391	− 14.519	− 14.834	− 15.197
14.25	− 10.203	− 11.756	− 12.725	− 12.993	− 13.302
14.50	− 8.837	− 10.160	− 10.979	− 11.205	− 11.464
14.75	− 7.498	− 8.602	− 9.281	− 9.467	− 9.679
15.00	− 6.186	− 7.082	− 7.629	− 7.778	− 7.947
15.25	− 4.900	− 5.598	− 6.021	− 6.135	− 6.265
15.50	− 3.639	− 4.148	− 4.455	− 4.538	− 4.631
15.75	− 2.402	− 2.733	− 2.931	− 2.984	− 3.044
16.00	− 1.189	− 1.350	− 1.446	− 1.472	− 1.500
16.25	0.000	0.000	0.000	0.000	0.000
16.50	1.167	1.320	1.409	1.433	1.459
16.75	2.311	2.609	2.783	2.828	2.879
17.00	3.433	3.869	4.121	4.187	4.260
17.25	4.534	5.101	5.427	5.512	5.605
17.50	5.615	6.306	6.700	6.802	6.915
17.75	6.675	7.483	7.941	8.060	8.190
18.00	7.716	8.635	9.153	9.286	9.432

MAXIMUM PREMIUM FOR ASSUMABLE LOANS
AS PERCENTAGE OF LOAN BALANCE
FACE INTEREST RATE: 16.5%

CURRENT RATE	REMAINING TERM OF LOAN (YEARS)				
	15	20	25	27	30
9.00	− 48.257	− 58.816	− 66.618	− 69.072	− 72.149
9.25	− 46.105	− 56.016	− 63.273	− 65.541	− 68.371
9.50	− 44.003	− 53.294	− 60.038	− 62.131	− 64.731
9.75	− 41.944	− 50.646	− 56.905	− 58.836	− 61.222
10.00	− 39.931	− 48.069	− 53.873	− 55.651	− 57.839
10.25	− 37.961	− 45.562	− 50.936	− 52.571	− 54.575
10.50	− 36.033	− 43.122	− 48.091	− 49.593	− 51.425
10.75	− 34.146	− 40.747	− 45.334	− 46.712	− 48.385
11.00	− 32.300	− 38.434	− 42.662	− 43.924	− 45.449
11.25	− 30.491	− 36.182	− 40.071	− 41.225	− 42.613
11.50	− 28.721	− 33.989	− 37.559	− 38.611	− 39.873
11.75	− 26.988	− 31.853	− 35.122	− 36.080	− 37.223
12.00	− 25.292	− 29.772	− 32.759	− 33.628	− 34.662
12.25	− 23.630	− 27.744	− 30.464	− 31.252	− 32.184
12.50	− 22.002	− 25.768	− 28.238	− 28.948	− 29.786
12.75	− 20.409	− 23.842	− 26.076	− 26.715	− 27.465
13.00	− 18.848	− 21.964	− 23.976	− 24.548	− 25.217
13.25	− 17.318	− 20.133	− 21.936	− 22.446	− 23.040
13.50	− 15.820	− 18.348	− 19.955	− 20.406	− 20.930
13.75	− 14.351	− 16.606	− 18.029	− 18.426	− 18.885
14.00	− 12.913	− 14.908	− 16.156	− 16.503	− 16.903
14.25	− 11.503	− 13.250	− 14.336	− 14.636	− 14.980
14.50	− 10.121	− 11.633	− 12.565	− 12.822	− 13.114
14.75	− 8.767	− 10.055	− 10.843	− 11.058	− 11.304
15.00	− 7.440	− 8.514	− 9.167	− 9.345	− 9.546
15.25	− 6.138	− 7.010	− 7.536	− 7.678	− 7.839
15.50	− 4.862	− 5.541	− 5.948	− 6.058	− 6.181
15.75	− 3.611	− 4.107	− 4.402	− 4.481	− 4.570
16.00	− 2.384	− 2.706	− 2.896	− 2.947	− 3.004
16.25	− 1.180	− 1.337	− 1.429	− 1.454	− 1.481
16.50	0.000	0.000	0.000	0.000	0.000
16.75	1.158	1.307	1.393	1.416	1.441
17.00	2.293	2.584	2.751	2.794	2.843
17.25	3.408	3.832	4.075	4.138	4.207
17.50	4.501	5.053	5.366	5.447	5.536
17.75	5.574	6.246	6.626	6.723	6.830
18.00	6.626	7.413	7.854	7.967	8.091

MAXIMUM PREMIUM FOR ASSUMABLE LOANS
AS PERCENTAGE OF LOAN BALANCE
FACE INTEREST RATE: 16.75%

CURRENT RATE	REMAINING TERM OF LOAN (YEARS)				
	15	20	25	27	30
9.00	− 49.993	− 60.918	− 68.971	− 71.500	− 74.666
9.25	− 47.817	− 58.082	− 65.580	− 67.918	− 70.832
9.50	− 45.689	− 55.324	− 62.299	− 64.459	− 67.139
9.75	− 43.607	− 52.640	− 59.122	− 61.116	− 63.579
10.00	− 41.570	− 50.030	− 56.047	− 57.886	− 60.146
10.25	− 39.577	− 47.490	− 53.068	− 54.762	− 56.835
10.50	− 37.626	− 45.017	− 50.183	− 51.741	− 53.639
10.75	− 35.717	− 42.610	− 47.387	− 48.819	− 50.554
11.00	− 33.849	− 40.267	− 44.677	− 45.990	− 47.576
11.25	− 32.019	− 37.985	− 42.050	− 43.253	− 44.698
11.50	− 30.229	− 35.763	− 39.502	− 40.602	− 41.917
11.75	− 28.475	− 33.599	− 37.031	− 38.034	− 39.229
12.00	− 26.759	− 31.490	− 34.634	− 35.547	− 36.630
12.25	− 25.078	− 29.436	− 32.307	− 33.137	− 34.116
12.50	− 23.431	− 27.433	− 30.049	− 30.800	− 31.683
12.75	− 21.819	− 25.481	− 27.857	− 28.534	− 29.328
13.00	− 20.240	− 23.579	− 25.727	− 26.337	− 27.047
13.25	− 18.692	− 21.724	− 23.659	− 24.204	− 24.838
13.50	− 17.176	− 19.915	− 21.649	− 22.135	− 22.698
13.75	− 15.691	− 18.150	− 19.696	− 20.127	− 20.623
14.00	− 14.235	− 16.429	− 17.797	− 18.176	− 18.612
14.25	− 12.809	− 14.750	− 15.951	− 16.282	− 16.661
14.50	− 11.411	− 13.111	− 14.155	− 14.442	− 14.768
14.75	− 10.041	− 11.512	− 12.409	− 12.653	− 12.931
15.00	− 8.698	− 9.951	− 10.709	− 10.915	− 11.147
15.25	− 7.381	− 8.427	− 9.055	− 9.224	− 9.415
15.50	− 6.090	− 6.939	− 7.445	− 7.581	− 7.733
15.75	− 4.824	− 5.485	− 5.877	− 5.981	− 6.098
16.00	− 3.583	− 4.066	− 4.350	− 4.425	− 4.509
16.25	− 2.365	− 2.679	− 2.862	− 2.911	− 2.964
16.50	− 1.171	− 1.324	− 1.413	− 1.436	− 1.462
16.75	0.000	0.000	0.000	0.000	0.000
17.00	1.149	1.294	1.377	1.399	1.422
17.25	2.276	2.559	2.720	2.761	2.807
17.50	3.382	3.796	4.029	4.089	4.155
17.75	4.468	5.005	5.307	5.384	5.468
18.00	5.533	6.187	6.553	6.646	6.747

MAXIMUM PREMIUM FOR ASSUMABLE LOANS
AS PERCENTAGE OF LOAN BALANCE
FACE INTEREST RATE: 17%

CURRENT RATE	REMAINING TERM OF LOAN (YEARS)				
	15	20	25	27	30
9.00	− 51.736	− 63.028	− 71.331	− 73.932	− 77.186
9.25	− 49.534	− 60.154	− 67.892	− 70.300	− 73.297
9.50	− 47.383	− 57.360	− 64.565	− 66.792	− 69.551
9.75	− 45.276	− 54.641	− 61.344	− 63.402	− 65.939
10.00	− 43.215	− 51.996	− 58.225	− 60.125	− 62.457
10.25	− 41.199	− 49.423	− 55.205	− 56.958	− 59.098
10.50	− 39.226	− 46.918	− 52.279	− 53.893	− 55.856
10.75	− 37.295	− 44.480	− 49.445	− 50.929	− 52.727
11.00	− 35.405	− 42.106	− 46.697	− 48.061	− 49.705
11.25	− 33.554	− 39.794	− 44.033	− 45.285	− 46.786
11.50	− 31.742	− 37.543	− 41.450	− 42.596	− 43.965
11.75	− 29.968	− 35.350	− 38.944	− 39.992	− 41.238
12.00	− 28.232	− 33.214	− 36.514	− 37.470	− 38.602
12.25	− 26.532	− 31.132	− 34.155	− 35.025	− 36.051
12.50	− 24.866	− 29.104	− 31.865	− 32.655	− 33.583
12.75	− 23.235	− 27.126	− 29.642	− 30.357	− 31.194
13.00	− 21.637	− 25.199	− 27.483	− 28.129	− 28.880
13.25	− 20.072	− 23.319	− 25.385	− 25.966	− 26.640
13.50	− 18.538	− 21.487	− 23.348	− 23.868	− 24.468
13.75	− 17.035	− 19.699	− 21.367	− 21.830	− 22.364
14.00	− 15.563	− 17.955	− 19.442	− 19.853	− 20.323
14.25	− 14.120	− 16.254	− 17.570	− 17.931	− 18.344
14.50	− 12.706	− 14.594	− 15.749	− 16.065	− 16.424
14.75	− 11.320	− 12.974	− 13.978	− 14.251	− 14.560
15.00	− 9.961	− 11.392	− 12.255	− 12.488	− 12.751
15.25	− 8.629	− 9.848	− 10.578	− 10.774	− 10.994
15.50	− 7.323	− 8.340	− 8.945	− 9.107	− 9.288
15.75	− 6.042	− 6.868	− 7.355	− 7.485	− 7.629
16.00	− 4.787	− 5.430	− 5.807	− 5.906	− 6.017
16.25	− 3.555	− 4.025	− 4.298	− 4.370	− 4.450
16.50	− 2.347	− 2.652	− 2.829	− 2.875	− 2.926
16.75	− 1.162	− 1.311	− 1.396	− 1.418	− 1.443
17.00	0.000	0.000	0.000	0.000	0.000
17.25	1.141	1.282	1.361	1.382	1.405
17.50	2.259	2.534	2.689	2.729	2.772
17.75	3.357	3.760	3.984	4.042	4.104
18.00	4.435	4.958	5.248	5.322	5.402

MAXIMUM PREMIUM FOR ASSUMABLE LOANS
AS PERCENTAGE OF LOAN BALANCE
FACE INTEREST RATE: 17.25%

CURRENT RATE	REMAINING TERM OF LOAN (YEARS)				
	15	20	25	27	30
9.00	− 53.487	− 65.144	− 73.695	− 76.370	− 79.710
9.25	− 51.260	− 62.233	− 70.209	− 72.687	− 75.766
9.50	− 49.083	− 59.403	− 66.836	− 69.130	− 71.966
9.75	− 46.952	− 56.649	− 63.571	− 65.692	− 68.303
10.00	− 44.868	− 53.970	− 60.409	− 62.369	− 64.771
10.25	− 42.828	− 51.363	− 57.348	− 59.157	− 61.364
10.50	− 40.832	− 48.825	− 54.381	− 56.050	− 58.076
10.75	− 38.879	− 46.355	− 51.507	− 53.045	− 54.902
11.00	− 36.967	− 43.951	− 48.722	− 50.136	− 51.838
11.25	− 35.095	− 41.609	− 46.021	− 47.321	− 48.877
11.50	− 33.262	− 39.329	− 43.402	− 44.595	− 46.016
11.75	− 31.468	− 37.107	− 40.862	− 41.954	− 43.250
12.00	− 29.712	− 34.943	− 38.398	− 39.396	− 40.576
12.25	− 27.991	− 32.835	− 36.007	− 36.917	− 37.989
12.50	− 26.307	− 30.780	− 33.685	− 34.514	− 35.486
12.75	− 24.657	− 28.777	− 31.431	− 32.184	− 33.063
13.00	− 23.040	− 26.824	− 29.242	− 29.924	− 30.717
13.25	− 21.457	− 24.920	− 27.116	− 27.732	− 28.444
13.50	− 19.906	− 23.064	− 25.050	− 25.604	− 26.242
13.75	− 18.386	− 21.253	− 23.042	− 23.538	− 24.107
14.00	− 16.896	− 19.487	− 21.091	− 21.532	− 22.037
14.25	− 15.437	− 17.763	− 19.193	− 19.584	− 20.030
14.50	− 14.006	− 16.082	− 17.347	− 17.692	− 18.082
14.75	− 12.604	− 14.440	− 15.552	− 15.852	− 16.192
15.00	− 11.230	− 12.838	− 13.804	− 14.065	− 14.357
15.25	− 9.882	− 11.274	− 12.104	− 12.326	− 12.576
15.50	− 8.561	− 9.747	− 10.449	− 10.636	− 10.845
15.75	− 7.266	− 8.255	− 8.837	− 8.991	− 9.163
16.00	− 5.996	− 6.799	− 7.267	− 7.391	− 7.528
16.25	− 4.750	− 5.376	− 5.738	− 5.833	− 5.938
16.50	− 3.528	− 3.985	− 4.248	− 4.317	− 4.392
16.75	− 2.329	− 2.626	− 2.796	− 2.840	− 2.888
17.00	− 1.154	− 1.298	− 1.380	− 1.401	− 1.425
17.25	0.000	0.000	0.000	0.000	0.000
17.50	1.132	1.269	1.346	1.366	1.387
17.75	2.242	2.510	2.659	2.697	2.738
18.00	3.332	3.724	3.940	3.995	4.054

MAXIMUM PREMIUM FOR ASSUMABLE LOANS
AS PERCENTAGE OF LOAN BALANCE
FACE INTEREST RATE: 17.5%

CURRENT RATE	REMAINING TERM OF LOAN (YEARS)				
	15	20	25	27	30
9.00	− 55.244	− 67.267	− 76.065	− 78.812	− 82.238
9.25	− 52.991	− 64.318	− 72.531	− 75.078	− 78.238
9.50	− 50.790	− 61.452	− 69.113	− 71.471	− 74.385
9.75	− 48.634	− 58.662	− 65.802	− 67.986	− 70.671
10.00	− 46.526	− 55.949	− 62.598	− 64.618	− 67.089
10.25	− 44.463	− 53.309	− 59.495	− 61.361	− 63.634
10.50	− 42.444	− 50.738	− 56.488	− 58.211	− 60.300
10.75	− 40.468	− 48.237	− 53.575	− 55.164	− 57.081
11.00	− 38.535	− 45.801	− 50.751	− 52.215	− 53.974
11.25	− 36.641	− 43.429	− 48.013	− 49.360	− 50.971
11.50	− 34.788	− 41.120	− 45.359	− 46.597	− 48.070
11.75	− 32.973	− 38.869	− 42.784	− 43.920	− 45.265
12.00	− 31.196	− 36.678	− 40.286	− 41.326	− 42.554
12.25	− 29.457	− 34.542	− 37.862	− 38.813	− 39.930
12.50	− 27.752	− 32.461	− 35.509	− 36.377	− 37.392
12.75	− 26.084	− 30.432	− 33.225	− 34.014	− 34.935
13.00	− 24.449	− 28.455	− 31.006	− 31.723	− 32.555
13.25	− 22.847	− 26.526	− 28.851	− 29.500	− 30.250
13.50	− 21.278	− 24.646	− 26.756	− 27.343	− 28.017
13.75	− 19.741	− 22.812	− 24.721	− 25.248	− 25.853
14.00	− 18.234	− 21.023	− 22.743	− 23.215	− 23.754
14.25	− 16.758	− 19.277	− 20.819	− 21.240	− 21.718
14.50	− 15.311	− 17.574	− 18.948	− 19.321	− 19.743
14.75	− 13.893	− 15.911	− 17.128	− 17.456	− 17.827
15.00	− 12.503	− 14.289	− 15.357	− 15.644	− 15.966
15.25	− 11.140	− 12.704	− 13.634	− 13.881	− 14.159
15.50	− 9.804	− 11.158	− 11.956	− 12.167	− 12.404
15.75	− 8.494	− 9.647	− 10.322	− 10.500	− 10.698
16.00	− 7.209	− 8.171	− 8.731	− 8.878	− 9.040
16.25	− 5.949	− 6.730	− 7.181	− 7.298	− 7.428
16.50	− 4.713	− 5.322	− 5.670	− 5.761	− 5.861
16.75	− 3.501	− 3.945	− 4.198	− 4.264	− 4.335
17.00	− 2.312	− 2.600	− 2.764	− 2.805	− 2.851
17.25	− 1.145	− 1.285	− 1.364	− 1.385	− 1.407
17.50	0.000	0.000	0.000	0.000	0.000
17.75	1.123	1.257	1.331	1.350	1.370
18.00	2.226	2.486	2.629	2.666	2.705

MAXIMUM PREMIUM FOR ASSUMABLE LOANS
AS PERCENTAGE OF LOAN BALANCE
FACE INTEREST RATE: 17.75%

CURRENT RATE	REMAINING TERM OF LOAN (YEARS)				
	15	20	25	27	30
9.00	-57.008	-69.397	-78.440	-81.258	-84.769
9.25	-54.729	-66.410	-74.859	-77.473	-80.714
9.50	-52.503	-63.507	-71.394	-73.817	-76.808
9.75	-50.323	-60.682	-68.039	-70.284	-73.041
10.00	-48.191	-57.934	-64.791	-66.870	-69.410
10.25	-46.105	-55.260	-61.646	-63.569	-65.907
10.50	-44.063	-52.657	-58.599	-60.375	-62.526
10.75	-42.064	-50.124	-55.646	-57.287	-59.263
11.00	-40.109	-47.657	-52.785	-54.298	-56.112
11.25	-38.194	-45.255	-50.010	-51.404	-53.068
11.50	-36.319	-42.916	-47.320	-48.602	-50.127
11.75	-34.484	-40.637	-44.710	-45.889	-47.283
12.00	-32.687	-38.418	-42.179	-43.260	-44.534
12.25	-30.927	-36.255	-39.722	-40.712	-41.874
12.50	-29.204	-34.147	-37.337	-38.243	-39.300
12.75	-27.516	-32.093	-35.022	-35.848	-36.809
13.00	-25.863	-30.090	-32.773	-33.525	-34.396
13.25	-24.243	-28.137	-30.589	-31.272	-32.060
13.50	-22.656	-26.233	-28.466	-29.085	-29.795
13.75	-21.101	-24.375	-26.403	-26.962	-27.601
14.00	-19.578	-22.563	-24.398	-24.901	-25.473
14.25	-18.085	-20.796	-22.449	-22.899	-23.409
14.50	-16.621	-19.070	-20.553	-20.954	-21.407
14.75	-15.187	-17.387	-18.708	-19.063	-19.463
15.00	-13.781	-15.744	-16.913	-17.226	-17.577
15.25	-12.403	-14.139	-15.166	-15.440	-15.745
15.50	-11.052	-12.573	-13.466	-13.702	-13.965
15.75	-9.726	-11.043	-11.810	-12.012	-12.236
16.00	-8.427	-9.548	-10.197	-10.367	-10.555
16.25	-7.153	-8.089	-8.626	-8.766	-8.920
16.50	-5.903	-6.662	-7.096	-7.208	-7.331
16.75	-4.677	-5.269	-5.604	-5.690	-5.785
17.00	-3.474	-3.906	-4.150	-4.212	-4.280
17.25	-2.294	-2.575	-2.732	-2.772	-2.815
17.50	-1.136	-1.273	-1.349	-1.368	-1.389
17.75	0.000	0.000	0.000	0.000	0.000
18.00	1.115	1.245	1.316	1.334	1.353

DISCOUNT POINT TABLE
(Effective Annual Interest Rates on Loan Held to Maturity)

The following tables indicate the effective interest rate paid over the term of a mortgage loan when discount points are charged at origination. Discount points are commonly charged to either or both the seller and buyer when a home mortgage loan is made. Each point is equal to 1% of the amount borrowed on the loan. Points are generally considered interest. Their effect is to raise the interest rate above the rate stated in the mortgage contract. The tables assume that loans run to their full amortization term. If the loan is paid off before maturity, the effective rate is higher than that shown in the table. The difference is not substantial, however, unless the loan is paid off in the early part of the term.

To use the table, you must know the following items:

1. *The loan maturity.* There are two tables each for loans with maturities of 15, 20, 25, and 30 years.

2. *The contract or face rate of interest.* This is the rate of interest stated in the mortgage contract. Contract rates are shown in the left-most column of each table. One table covers rates from 7% to 13.75% and the other from 14% to 20.75% in .25% increments.

3. *The number of discount points charged.* These are listed in the heading of each table and vary from 1 to 5 points.

Example: A loan with a maturity of 15 years is originated at a contract rate of 10%. If three points are charged and the loan is held to maturity, what is the effective annual rate of interest?

Look at the first table for 15-year loans. Find "10.00" in the column under "CONTRACT RATE." Follow this row across to the column under "3 DISCOUNT POINTS." This is the effective interest rate of 10.54%

Example. A loan is originated for 15 years at a contract interest rate of 14. 5%. If the lender wants to earn an effective rate of 15.5% on the loan, how many discount points should be charged?

Look at the second table for 15-year loans. Find the row under "CONTRACT RATE" for 14.50%. Follow this row across until a rate of at least 15.5% is found. The column under "5 DISCOUNT POINTS" shows an effective rate of 15.55%, so the lender should charge 5 points.

EFFECTIVE INTEREST RATE
ON LOAN HELD TO MATURITY
LOAN TERM: 15 YEARS

CONTRACT RATE	DISCOUNT POINTS				
	1	2	3	4	5
7.00	7.16	7.33	7.49	7.66	7.83
7.25	7.41	7.58	7.75	7.92	8.09
7.50	7.66	7.83	8.00	8.17	8.35
7.75	7.92	8.08	8.25	8.43	8.60
8.00	8.17	8.34	8.51	8.68	8.86
8.25	8.42	8.59	8.76	8.94	9.12
8.50	8.67	8.84	9.02	9.19	9.37
8.75	8.92	9.09	9.27	9.45	9.63
9.00	9.17	9.35	9.52	9.70	9.89
9.25	9.42	9.60	9.78	9.96	10.14
9.50	9.67	9.85	10.03	10.21	10.40
9.75	9.93	10.10	10.29	10.47	10.66
10.00	10.18	10.36	10.54	10.72	10.91
10.25	10.43	10.61	10.79	10.98	11.17
10.50	10.68	10.86	11.05	11.24	11.43
10.75	10.93	11.11	11.30	11.49	11.68
11.00	11.18	11.37	11.56	11.75	11.94
11.25	11.43	11.62	11.81	12.00	12.20
11.50	11.69	11.87	12.06	12.26	12.46
11.75	11.94	12.13	12.32	12.51	12.71
12.00	12.19	12.38	12.57	12.77	12.97
12.25	12.44	12.63	12.83	13.03	13.23
12.50	12.69	12.88	13.08	13.28	13.49
12.75	12.94	13.14	13.34	13.54	13.74
13.00	13.19	13.39	13.59	13.79	14.00
13.25	13.45	13.64	13.85	14.05	14.26
13.50	13.70	13.90	14.10	14.31	14.52
13.75	13.95	14.15	14.35	14.56	14.77

EFFECTIVE INTEREST RATE
ON LOAN HELD TO MATURITY
LOAN TERM: 15 YEARS

CONTRACT RATE	DISCOUNT POINTS				
	1	2	3	4	5
14.00	14.20	14.40	14.61	14.82	15.03
14.25	14.45	14.66	14.86	15.08	15.29
14.50	14.70	14.91	15.12	15.33	15.55
14.75	14.95	15.16	15.37	15.59	15.81
15.00	15.21	15.42	15.63	15.84	16.07
15.25	15.46	15.67	15.88	16.10	16.32
15.50	15.71	15.92	16.14	16.36	16.58
15.75	15.96	16.18	16.39	16.61	16.84
16.00	16.21	16.43	16.65	16.87	17.10
16.25	16.46	16.68	16.90	17.13	17.36
16.50	16.72	16.94	17.16	17.38	17.62
16.75	16.97	17.19	17.41	17.64	17.87
17.00	17.22	17.44	17.67	17.90	18.13
17.25	17.47	17.69	17.92	18.16	18.39
17.50	17.72	17.95	18.18	18.41	18.65
17.75	17.97	18.20	18.43	18.67	18.91
18.00	18.23	18.46	18.69	18.93	19.17
18.25	18.48	18.71	18.94	19.18	19.43
18.50	18.73	18.96	19.20	19.44	19.69
18.75	18.98	19.22	19.45	19.70	19.95
19.00	19.23	19.47	19.71	19.96	20.20
19.25	19.48	19.72	19.97	20.21	20.46
19.50	19.74	19.98	20.22	20.47	20.72
19.75	19.99	20.23	20.48	20.73	20.98
20.00	20.24	20.48	20.73	20.98	21.24
20.25	20.49	20.74	20.99	21.24	21.50
20.50	20.74	20.99	21.24	21.50	21.76
20.75	21.00	21.24	21.50	21.76	22.02

EFFECTIVE INTEREST RATE
ON LOAN HELD TO MATURITY
LOAN TERM: 20 YEARS

CONTRACT RATE	DISCOUNT POINTS				
	1	2	3	4	5
7.00	7.13	7.26	7.40	7.53	7.67
7.25	7.38	7.51	7.65	7.79	7.93
7.50	7.63	7.77	7.90	8.04	8.18
7.75	7.88	8.02	8.16	8.30	8.44
8.00	8.14	8.27	8.41	8.55	8.70
8.25	8.39	8.53	8.67	8.81	8.96
8.50	8.64	8.78	8.92	9.07	9.21
8.75	8.89	9.03	9.18	9.32	9.47
9.00	9.14	9.28	9.43	9.58	9.73
9.25	9.39	9.54	9.68	9.83	9.99
9.50	9.64	9.79	9.94	10.09	10.24
9.75	9.90	10.04	10.19	10.35	10.50
10.00	10.15	10.30	10.45	10.60	10.76
10.25	10.40	10.55	10.70	10.86	11.02
10.50	10.65	10.80	10.96	11.11	11.27
10.75	10.90	11.06	11.21	11.37	11.53
11.00	11.15	11.31	11.47	11.63	11.79
11.25	11.40	11.56	11.72	11.88	12.05
11.50	11.66	11.81	11.98	12.14	12.31
11.75	11.91	12.07	12.23	12.40	12.57
12.00	12.16	12.32	12.49	12.65	12.82
12.25	12.41	12.57	12.74	12.91	13.08
12.50	12.66	12.83	13.00	13.17	13.34
12.75	12.91	13.08	13.25	13.42	13.60
13.00	13.17	13.33	13.51	13.68	13.86
13.25	13.42	13.59	13.76	13.94	14.12
13.50	13.67	13.84	14.02	14.19	14.38
13.75	13.92	14.09	14.27	14.45	14.63

EFFECTIVE INTEREST RATE
ON LOAN HELD TO MATURITY
LOAN TERM: 20 YEARS

CONTRACT RATE	DISCOUNT POINTS				
	1	2	3	4	5
14.00	14.17	14.35	14.53	14.71	14.89
14.25	14.42	14.60	14.78	14.97	15.15
14.50	14.68	14.86	15.04	15.22	15.41
14.75	14.93	15.11	15.29	15.48	15.67
15.00	15.18	15.36	15.55	15.74	15.93
15.25	15.43	15.62	15.80	16.00	16.19
15.50	15.68	15.87	16.06	16.25	16.45
15.75	15.94	16.12	16.32	16.51	16.71
16.00	16.19	16.38	16.57	16.77	16.97
16.25	16.44	16.63	16.83	17.03	17.23
16.50	16.69	16.89	17.08	17.28	17.49
16.75	16.94	17.14	17.34	17.54	17.75
17.00	17.19	17.39	17.59	17.80	18.01
17.25	17.45	17.65	17.85	18.06	18.27
17.50	17.70	17.90	18.11	18.32	18.53
17.75	17.95	18.15	18.36	18.57	18.79
18.00	18.20	18.41	18.62	18.83	19.05
18.25	18.45	18.66	18.87	19.09	19.31
18.50	18.71	18.92	19.13	19.35	19.57
18.75	18.96	19.17	19.39	19.61	19.83
19.00	19.21	19.42	19.64	19.86	20.09
19.25	19.46	19.68	19.90	20.12	20.35
19.50	19.71	19.93	20.15	20.38	20.61
19.75	19.97	20.19	20.41	20.64	20.87
20.00	20.22	20.44	20.67	20.90	21.13
20.25	20.47	20.70	20.92	21.16	21.39
20.50	20.72	20.95	21.18	21.42	21.66
20.75	20.97	21.20	21.44	21.67	21.92

EFFECTIVE INTEREST RATE
ON LOAN HELD TO MATURITY
LOAN TERM: 25 YEARS

CONTRACT RATE	DISCOUNT POINTS				
	1	2	3	4	5
7.00	7.11	7.23	7.34	7.46	7.58
7.25	7.36	7.48	7.59	7.71	7.83
7.50	7.61	7.73	7.85	7.97	8.09
7.75	7.87	7.98	8.10	8.23	8.35
8.00	8.12	8.24	8.36	8.48	8.61
8.25	8.37	8.49	8.61	8.74	8.86
8.50	8.62	8.74	8.87	8.99	9.12
8.75	8.87	9.00	9.12	9.25	9.38
9.00	9.12	9.25	9.38	9.51	9.64
9.25	9.38	9.50	9.63	9.76	9.90
9.50	9.63	9.76	9.89	10.02	10.16
9.75	9.88	10.01	10.14	10.28	10.41
10.00	10.13	10.26	10.40	10.53	10.67
10.25	10.38	10.52	10.65	10.79	10.93
10.50	10.63	10.77	10.91	11.05	11.19
10.75	10.88	11.02	11.16	11.30	11.45
11.00	11.14	11.28	11.42	11.56	11.71
11.25	11.39	11.53	11.67	11.82	11.97
11.50	11.64	11.78	11.93	12.08	12.23
11.75	11.89	12.04	12.18	12.33	12.49
12.00	12.14	12.29	12.44	12.59	12.74
12.25	12.40	12.54	12.69	12.85	13.00
12.50	12.65	12.80	12.95	13.11	13.26
12.75	12.90	13.05	13.21	13.36	13.52
13.00	13.15	13.30	13.46	13.62	13.78
13.25	13.40	13.56	13.72	13.88	14.04
13.50	13.65	13.81	13.97	14.14	14.30
13.75	13.91	14.07	14.23	14.39	14.56

EFFECTIVE INTEREST RATE
ON LOAN HELD TO MATURITY
LOAN TERM: 25 YEARS

CONTACT RATE	DISCOUNT POINTS				
	1	2	3	4	5
14.00	14.16	14.32	14.48	14.65	14.82
14.25	14.41	14.57	14.74	14.91	15.08
14.50	14.66	14.83	15.00	15.17	15.34
14.75	14.91	15.08	15.25	15.43	15.60
15.00	15.17	15.34	15.51	15.68	15.86
15.25	15.42	15.59	15.77	15.94	16.12
15.50	15.67	15.84	16.02	16.20	16.39
15.75	15.92	16.10	16.28	16.46	16.65
16.00	16.17	16.35	16.53	16.72	16.91
16.25	16.43	16.61	16.79	16.98	17.17
16.50	16.68	16.86	17.05	17.24	17.43
16.75	16.93	17.12	17.30	17.49	17.69
17.00	17.18	17.37	17.56	17.75	17.95
17.25	17.44	17.62	17.82	18.01	18.21
17.50	17.69	17.88	18.07	18.27	18.47
17.75	17.94	18.13	18.33	18.53	18.73
18.00	18.19	18.39	18.59	18.79	19.00
18.25	18.44	18.64	18.84	19.05	19.26
18.50	18.70	18.90	19.10	19.31	19.52
18.75	18.95	19.15	19.36	19.57	19.78
19.00	19.20	19.40	19.61	19.82	20.04
19.25	19.45	19.66	19.87	20.08	20.30
19.50	19.70	19.91	20.13	20.34	20.56
19.75	19.96	20.17	20.38	20.60	20.83
20.00	20.21	20.42	20.64	20.86	21.09
20.25	20.46	20.68	20.90	21.12	21.35
20.50	20.71	20.93	21.15	21.38	21.61
20.75	20.97	21.19	21.41	21.64	21.87

EFFECTIVE INTEREST RATE
ON LOAN HELD TO MATURITY
LOAN TERM: 30 YEARS

CONTRACT RATE	DISCOUNT POINTS				
	1	2	3	4	5
7.00	7.10	7.20	7.30	7.41	7.52
7.25	7.35	7.45	7.56	7.67	7.77
7.50	7.60	7.71	7.81	7.92	8.03
7.75	7.85	7.96	8.07	8.18	8.29
8.00	8.11	8.21	8.32	8.44	8.55
8.25	8.36	8.47	8.58	8.69	8.81
8.50	8.61	8.72	8.83	8.95	9.07
8.75	8.86	8.97	9.09	9.21	9.32
9.00	9.11	9.23	9.34	9.46	9.58
9.25	9.36	9.48	9.60	9.72	9.84
9.50	9.62	9.73	9.85	9.98	10.10
9.75	9.87	9.99	10.11	10.23	10.36
10.00	10.12	10.24	10.37	10.49	10.62
10.25	10.37	10.50	10.62	10.75	10.88
10.50	10.62	10.75	10.88	11.01	11.14
10.75	10.88	11.00	11.13	11.26	11.40
11.00	11.13	11.26	11.39	11.52	11.66
11.25	11.38	11.51	11.64	11.78	11.92
11.50	11.63	11.76	11.90	12.04	12.18
11.75	11.88	12.02	12.16	12.30	12.44
12.00	12.13	12.27	12.41	12.55	12.70
12.25	12.39	12.53	12.67	12.81	12.96
12.50	12.64	12.78	12.92	13.07	13.22
12.75	12.89	13.03	13.18	13.33	13.48
13.00	13.14	13.29	13.44	13.59	13.74
13.25	13.39	13.54	13.69	13.85	14.00
13.50	13.65	13.80	13.95	14.10	14.26
13.75	13.90	14.05	14.21	14.36	14.52

EFFECTIVE INTEREST RATE
ON LOAN HELD TO MATURITY
LOAN TERM: 30 YEARS

CONTRACT RATE	DISCOUNT POINTS 1	2	3	4	5
14.00	14.15	14.31	14.46	14.62	14.78
14.25	14.40	14.56	14.72	14.88	15.05
14.50	14.66	14.81	14.97	15.14	15.31
14.75	14.91	15.07	15.23	15.40	15.57
15.00	15.16	15.32	15.49	15.66	15.83
15.25	15.41	15.58	15.74	15.92	16.09
15.50	15.66	15.83	16.00	16.17	16.35
15.75	15.92	16.09	16.26	16.43	16.61
16.00	16.17	16.34	16.51	16.69	16.87
16.25	16.42	16.59	16.77	16.95	17.14
16.50	16.67	16.85	17.03	17.21	17.40
16.75	16.92	17.10	17.29	17.47	17.66
17.00	17.18	17.36	17.54	17.73	17.92
17.25	17.43	17.61	17.80	17.99	18.18
17.50	17.68	17.87	18.06	18.25	18.45
17.75	17.93	18.12	18.31	18.51	18.71
18.00	18.19	18.38	18.57	18.77	18.97
18.25	18.44	18.63	18.83	19.03	19.23
18.50	18.69	18.89	19.08	19.29	19.49
18.75	18.94	19.14	19.34	19.55	19.76
19.00	19.20	19.40	19.60	19.81	20.02
19.25	19.45	19.65	19.86	20.07	20.28
19.50	19.70	19.90	20.11	20.33	20.54
19.75	19.95	20.16	20.37	20.59	20.81
20.00	20.21	20.41	20.63	20.85	21.07
20.25	20.46	20.67	20.88	21.11	21.33
20.50	20.71	20.92	21.14	21.37	21.59
20.75	20.96	21.18	21.40	21.62	21.85

GRADUATED PAYMENT MORTGAGES
(Monthly Payment per $1,000 of Principal)

The following tables allow you to compute a payment schedule for a common form of graduated payment mortgage loan. This type of loan features a 5-year period in the beginning of the loan term in which monthly payments are lower than with a conventional fixed-payment loan. For each year of this period, monthly payments are increased by 7.5% compared with the previous year. The payment reaches its highest level in the sixth year and is constant over the remaining term of the loan.

The table allows you to calculate what the payments will be for each year of the initial term and the constant payment for the remaining term. You will need the following information:

1. *The interest rate on the loan.* Interest rates ranging from 8% to 21.75% in .25% intervals are listed in the left-most column of the tables.

2. *The amount of the loan.* The factors in the tables represent the monthly payment in dollars for each thousand dollars of original loan principal. To calculate the payments for your loan, you must multiply the factor by the number of thousands in the loan amount.

Example. A graduated payment mortgage, following the form of FHA 245 plan III, is originated at 12% interest. The amount of the loan is $55,500. What is the monthly payment in the first year? In the sixth year?

Find the column under "INTEREST RATE" and look for the rate of 12.00%. Follow this row to the column under "YEAR 1st." The factor is 7.91. Multiply this factor by 55.5 to obtain the first-year payment of $439.01.

Now follow the row for the 12% interest rate to the column under "YEAR 6-30." The factor shown is 11.36. Multiplying this factor by 55.5 gives $630.48, the payment in the sixth year and every year thereafter.

Example. You can afford to pay up to $400 in monthly payments in the first year. If the interest rate on graduated payment mortgages is 15%, how much can you afford to borrow?

Look under "INTEREST RATE" to find 15.00 (second page of tables). The factor under the 1st year is 9.90. Divide $400 by the factor to obtain 40.4. Multiply this figure by $1,000 to obtain the maximum loan you can afford, $40,400.

GRADUATED PAYMENT MORTGAGE
MONTHLY PAYMENT PER $1000 OF PRINCIPAL
FHA 245 PLAN III
LOAN TERM = 30 YEARS

INTEREST RATE	YEAR					
	1	2	3	4	5	6–30
7.00	4.97	5.34	5.74	6.17	6.63	7.13
7.25	5.10	5.48	5.89	6.34	6.81	7.32
7.50	5.23	5.63	6.05	6.50	6.99	7.52
7.75	5.37	5.77	6.21	6.67	7.17	7.71
8.00	5.51	5.92	6.37	6.85	7.36	7.91
8.25	5.65	6.07	6.53	7.02	7.55	8.11
8.50	5.79	6.23	6.69	7.19	7.73	8.31
8.75	5.93	6.38	6.86	7.37	7.93	8.52
9.00	6.08	6.53	7.02	7.55	8.12	8.73
9.25	6.22	6.69	7.19	7.73	8.31	8.94
9.50	6.37	6.85	7.36	7.92	8.51	9.15
9.75	6.52	7.01	7.54	8.10	8.71	9.36
10.00	6.67	7.17	7.71	8.29	8.91	9.58
10.25	6.82	7.33	7.88	8.47	9.11	9.79
10.50	6.97	7.50	8.06	8.66	9.31	10.01
10.75	7.13	7.66	8.24	8.85	9.52	10.23
11.00	7.28	7.83	8.42	9.05	9.73	10.46
11.25	7.44	8.00	8.60	9.24	9.93	10.68
11.50	7.60	8.17	8.78	9.44	10.14	10.90
11.75	7.75	8.34	8.96	9.63	10.36	11.13
12.00	7.91	8.51	9.15	9.83	10.57	11.36
12.25	8.07	8.68	9.33	10.03	10.78	11.59
12.50	8.24	8.85	9.52	10.23	11.00	11.82
12.75	8.40	9.03	9.71	10.43	11.22	12.06
13.00	8.56	9.20	9.89	10.64	11.43	12.29
13.25	8.73	9.38	10.08	10.84	11.65	12.53
13.50	8.89	9.56	10.28	11.05	11.87	12.77
13.75	9.06	9.74	10.47	11.25	12.10	13.00
14.00	9.23	9.92	10.66	11.46	12.32	13.24
14.25	9.39	10.10	10.86	11.67	12.54	13.49
14.50	9.56	10.28	11.05	11.88	12.77	13.73
14.75	9.73	10.46	11.25	12.09	13.00	13.97

GRADUATED PAYMENT MORTGAGE
MONTHLY PAYMENT PER $1000 OF PRINCIPAL
FHA 245 PLAN III
LOAN TERM = 30 YEARS

INTEREST RATE	\ 1	YEAR \ 2	\ 3	\ 4	\ 5	\ 6–30
15.00	9.90	10.65	11.44	12.30	13.22	14.22
15.25	10.07	10.83	11.64	12.51	13.45	14.46
15.50	10.25	11.01	11.84	12.73	13.68	14.71
15.75	10.42	11.20	12.04	12.94	13.91	14.96
16.00	10.59	11.39	12.24	13.16	14.15	15.21
16.25	10.77	11.57	12.44	13.37	14.38	15.46
16.50	10.94	11.76	12.64	13.59	14.61	15.71
16.75	11.12	11.95	12.85	13.81	14.85	15.96
17.00	11.29	12.14	13.05	14.03	15.08	16.21
17.25	11.47	12.33	13.25	14.25	15.32	16.47
17.50	11.65	12.52	13.46	14.47	15.55	16.72
17.75	11.82	12.71	13.66	14.69	15.79	16.98
18.00	12.00	12.90	13.87	14.91	16.03	17.23
18.25	12.18	13.10	14.08	15.13	16.27	17.49
18.50	12.36	13.29	14.29	15.36	16.51	17.75
18.75	12.54	13.48	14.49	15.58	16.75	18.01
19.00	12.72	13.68	14.70	15.81	16.99	18.27
19.25	12.90	13.87	14.91	16.03	17.23	18.53
19.50	13.09	14.07	15.12	16.26	17.48	18.79
19.75	13.27	14.26	15.33	16.48	17.72	19.05
20.00	13.45	14.46	15.54	16.71	17.96	19.31
20.25	13.63	14.66	15.76	16.94	18.21	19.57
20.50	13.82	14.85	15.97	17.17	18.45	19.84
20.75	14.00	15.05	16.18	17.39	18.70	20.10
21.00	14.19	15.25	16.39	17.62	18.95	20.37
21.25	14.37	15.45	16.61	17.85	19.19	20.63
21.50	14.56	15.65	16.82	18.08	19.44	20.90
21.75	14.74	15.85	17.04	18.31	19.69	21.16
22.00	14.93	16.05	17.25	18.55	19.94	21.43
22.25	15.12	16.25	17.47	18.78	20.19	21.70
22.50	15.30	16.45	17.68	19.01	20.44	21.97
22.75	15.49	16.65	17.90	19.24	20.69	22.24

Depreciation Rates

The Tax Reform Act of 1986

The body of these tables shows the rate of depreciation that may be claimed each year for assets eligible for depreciation. The tables shown here include those offered by the Tax Reform Act of 1986 and those used for standard accounting purposes.

Depreciation deductions may be claimed for tax purposes on most structural assets or equipment used in a trade or business. These deductions may be thought of as providing a tax incentive for the use of productive assets, allowing for the cost of assets to be recovered over time, or as an allowance for exhaustion, wear and tear, and normal obsolescence.

To be eligible for depreciation deductions, an asset must be used in a trade or business or held for the production of income. This excludes personal cars or residences since they are not used in a trade or business. It also excludes land since land does not wear out. For example, a single family home that is rented to a tenant can be depreciated, but not the land under it.

Depreciation under the Tax Reform Act of 1986. The Tax Reform Act of 1986 (TRA) prescribed the rate at which asset cost may be depreciated each year. This is based on the class of property. Classes include 3-, 5-, 7-, 10-, 15-, 20-, 27½-, 31½-year life property. Apartment buildings and other residential rental properties are generally in the 27½-year category; most other buildings such as offices and retail stores are depreciable over a 31½-year life. The depreciation to be claimed is shown in the following tables as a fraction of original cost.

For personal property, such as refrigerators and furniture, the annual depreciation allowance under TRA will vary depending on the year it is placed in service. For real estate, the allowance for the first and last year depends upon the month placed in service.

To use the tables you need to know the year the property was placed in service (for buildings the month is needed), the recovery class, and the asset cost. Select the appropriate table considering the year and class of property. For most personal property (short-lived) find the intersection of the class life (year) with the year of use. Apply the rate in the table to the asset cost. For a building, find the column for the month it was placed in service. Multiply the rate by the building cost to derive the annual depreciation allowance.

Example. A warehouse was acquired in July 1988 for $1,000,000, exclusive of land. How much depreciation may be deducted under TRA in 1988 and 1989? Turn to the table which offers recovery amounts for nonresidential real property other than low-income housing. The intersection of July with year 1 provides the number .015. Thus, 1.5% of the asset cost, or $15,000 for the warehouse, is deductible in 1988. The intersection of July with recovery year 2 provides .032. Therefore 3.2% of the asset cost, or $32,000 may be deducted in the second year (1989).

Example. What are the first and second year deductions for furniture that cost $500 and is placed in service in 1990? Most furniture is in the 7-year property class, so you may find the column for 7-year property. The appropriate first year rate is .143. Then 14.3 percent of its cost may be deducted in 1990 regardless of the month of acquisition. This is a $71.50 deduction. The second year rate is .245. The second year deduction is 24.5% of $500 or $122.50.

Example. A duplex was purchased for rental use in January 1990 at a cost of $125,000. Of the purchase price $25,000 was for land, leaving $100,000 to be depreciated. How much depreciation may be claimed in 1990 and each year thereafter?

Locate the table with the heading: Annual Straight-Line Depreciation Rates For Real Estate, $27^1/_2$ Year Residential Real Property. At the intersection of Jan with Recovery Year 1 you will find .035. In the first year of ownership 3.5% of the cost is allowed for tax purposes as depreciation, which is $3,500 for a $100,000 asset. From years 2 through 27 3.6% may be claimed, providing a $3,600 annual tax deduction.

ANNUAL STRAIGHT-LINE DEPRECIATION RATES FOR REAL ESTATE

27½-YEAR RESIDENTIAL REAL PROPERTY

Recovery Year(s)	Jan	Feb	Mar	Apr	May	Jun	Jul	Aug	Sep	Oct	Nov	Dec
1	.035	.032	.029	.026	.023	.020	.017	.014	.011	.008	.005	.002
2-27	.036	.036	.036	.036	.036	.036	.036	.036	.036	.036	.036	.036
28	.029	.032	.035	.036	.036	.036	.036	.036	.036	.036	.036	.036
29	0	0	0	.002	.005	.008	.011	.014	.017	.020	.023	.026
Total	1.000	1.000	1.000	1.000	1.000	1.000	1.000	1.000	1.000	1.000	1.000	1.000

31½-YEAR NONRESIDENTIAL REAL PROPERTY

Recovery Years(s)	Jan	Feb	Mar	Apr	May	Jun	Jul	Aug	Sep	Oct	Nov	Dec
1	.030	.028	.025	.022	.020	.017	.015	.012	.009	.007	.004	.001
2-27	.032	.032	.032	.032	.032	.032	.032	.032	.032	.032	.032	.032
28	.010	.012	.015	.018	.020	.023	.025	.028	.031	.032	.032	.032
29	0	0	0	0	0	0	0	0	0	.001	.004	.007
Total	1.000	1.000	1.000	1.000	1.000	1.000	1.000	1.000	1.000	1.000	1.000	1.000

UNOFFICIAL ALTERNATIVE DEPRECIATION SYSTEM FOR REAL ESTATE
DEPRECIATION RATES FOR 27 OR 31 YEAR REAL PROPERTY (40 YEARS)*

Recovery Year(s)	Jan	Feb	Mar	Apr	May	Jun	Jul	Aug	Sep	Oct	Nov	Dec
1	.024	.022	.020	.018	.016	.014	.011	.009	.007	.005	.003	.001
2-40	.025	.025	.025	.025	.025	.025	.025	.025	.025	.025	.025	.025
41	.001	.003	.005	.007	.009	.011	.014	.016	.018	.020	.022	.024
Total	1.000	1.000	1.000	1.000	1.000	1.000	1.000	1.000	1.000	1.000	1.000	1.000

STRAIGHT-LINE DEPRECIATION FOR PROPERTY OTHER THAN REAL ESTATE

ACRS Class	First Recovery Year	Other Recovery Years		Last Recovery Year		Depreciation Total
		Years	%	Year	%	
3-Year	.167	2-3	.333	4	.167	1.000
5-Year	.100	2-5	.200	6	.100	1.000
7-Year	.071	2-7	.143	8	.071	1.000
10-Year	.050	2-10	.100	11	.050	1.000
15-Year	.033	2-15	.067	16	.029	1.000
20-Year	.025	2-20	.050	21	.025	1.000

APPENDIX

House Cross Section

Description of Number Parts in House

1—Collar beam	18—Girder
2—Ceiling joist	19—Footing for foundation wall
3—Chimney cap	20—Foundation drain tile
4—Chimney pots	21—Diagonal subflooring
5—Chimney flashing	22—Foundation wall
6—Rafters	23—Termite shield
7—Roof boards	24—Wall studs
8—Stud	25—Pilaster
9—Eave trough or gutter	26—Window casing
10—Downspout or leader gooseneck	27—Wainscoting
11—Frieze	28—Baseboard
12—Door jamb	29—Floor joists
13—Basement stair riser	30—Fire brick
14—Stair stringer	31—Newel cap
15—Girder post	32—Window sash
16—Chair rail	33—Mantel
17—Furring strips	34—Newel

FIGURE 188

ABBREVIATIONS

A/C air conditioning

ACRS accelerated cost recovery system

ADR asset depreciation range

AIREA American Institute of Real Estate Appraisers

ALTA American Land Title Association

AMI alternative mortgage instrument

AML adjustable mortgage loan

APA American Planning Association

app appreciation (in appraisal terminology)

APR annual percentage rate

AREUEA American Real Estate and Urban Economics Association

ARM adjustable rate mortgage

ASA American Society of Appraisers

ASREC American Society of Real Estate Counselors

BOMA Building Owners and Managers Association

CAI Community Associations Institute

CBD central business district

CCIM Certified Commercial-Investment Member (RNMI)

CD certificate of deposit

CPI consumer price index (see cost of living index)

CPM Certified Property Manager (IREM)

CRB Certified Real Estate Brokerage Manager (RNMI)

CRE Counselor in Real Estate (ASREC)

CRS Certified Residential Specialist (RNMI)

DCR debt coverage ratio

dep depreciation (in appraisal terminology)

EIS environmental impact statement

EPA Environmental Protection Agency

FAR floor-area ratio

FDIC Federal Deposit Insurance Corporation

FHA Federal Housing Administration

FHLB Federal Home Loan Bank

FHLMC Federal Home Loan Mortgage Corporation (Freddie Mac)

FmHA Farmers Home Administration

FMRR financial management rate of return

FMV fair market value

FNMA Federal National Mortgage Association (Fannie Mae)

FPM flexible payment mortgage

FSLIC Federal Savings and Loan Insurance Corporation

FTC Federal Trade Commission

FY fiscal year

GEM growing equity mortgage

GIM gross income multiplier

GNMA Government National Mortgage Association (Ginnie Mae)

GPM graduated payment mortgage

GRI Graduate, Realtors® Institute

GRM gross rent multiplier

784

HOW homeowners warranty

HUD Department of Housing and Urban Development

HVAC heating, ventilation, and air conditioning

IAAO International Association of Assessing Officers

IRA individual retirement account

IREM Institute of Real Estate Management

IRR internal rate of return

IRS Internal Revenue Service

IRWA International Right-of-Way Association

L/V loan-to-value ratio

MAI Member, Appraisal Institute (AIREA)

MBA Mortgage Bankers Association of America

MGIC Mortgage Guaranty Insurance Corporation

MLS multiple listing service

MMC money market certificate of deposit

NAA National Apartment Association

NACORE National Association of Corporate Real Estate Executives

NAHB National Association of Home Builders

NAR National Association of Realtors®

NAREB National Association of Real Estate Brokers

NARELLO National Association of Real Estate Licensing Law Officials

NOI net operating income

NOW negotiable order of withdrawal (account)

NPV net present value

OAR overall rate of capitalization

OILSR Office of Interstate Land Sales Registration

PAM pledged account mortgage

P & I principal and interest (payment)

PITI principal, interest, taxes and insurance (payment)

PMI private mortgage insurance

PUD planned unit development

RAM reverse annuity mortgage

REIT real estate investment trust

RESPA Real Estate Settlement Procedures Act

RESSI Real Estate Securities and Syndication Institute

RM Residential Member (AIREA)

RNMI Realtors® National Marketing Institute

RRM renegotiated rate mortgage

R/W right-of-way

SAM shared appreciation mortgage

SBA Small Business Administration

SEC Securities and Exchange Commission

SIR Society of Industrial Realtors®

S&L savings and loan association

SMSA standard metropolitan statistical area

SRA Senior Residential Appraiser (SREA)

APPENDIX

SREA Senior Real Estate Analyst (SREA)

SREA Society of Real Estate Appraisers

SRPA Senior Real Property Appraiser (SREA)

SYD sum-of-the-years-digits (method of depreciation)

TDR transferable development rights

TIL truth-in-lending law

UCC Uniform Commercial Code

ULI Urban Land Institute

VA Veterans Administration

VRM variable rate mortgage

WCR Women's Council of Realtors

YTM yield to maturity

MEASUREMENT TABLES

ENGLISH SYSTEM

Linear Measure

12 inches (in or ")	= 1 foot (ft or ')
3 feet	= 1 yard (yd)
5½ yards	= 1 rod (rd), pole, or perch (16½ feet)
40 rods	= 1 furlong (fur)
	= 220 yards
	= 660 feet
6076.11549 feet	= 1 international nautical mile

Gunter's or Surveyor's Chain Measure

7.92 inches (in)	= 1 link
100 links	= 1 chain (ch)
	= 4 rods
	= 66 feet
80 chains	= 1 statute mile (mi)
	= 320 rods
	= 5,280 feet

Area Measure

Squares and cubes of units are sometimes abbreviated by using "superior" figures. For example, ft^2 means square foot, and ft^3 means cubic foot.

144 square inches	= 1 square foot (ft^2)
9 square feet	= 1 square yard (yd^2)
	= 1,296 square inches
30¼ square yards	= 1 square rod (rd^2)
	= 272¼ square feet
160 square rods	= 1 acre
	= 4,840 square yards
	= 43,560 square feet
640 acres	= 1 square mile (mi^2)
1 mile square	= 1 section (of land)
6 miles square	= 1 township
	= 36 sections
	= 36 square miles

APPENDIX

METRIC SYSTEM

Linear Measure

10 millimeters (mm)	= 1 centimeter (cm)
10 centimeters	= 1 decimeter (dm)
	= 100 millimeters
10 decimeters	= 1 meter (m)
	= 1,000 millimeters
10 meters	= 1 dekameter (dam)
10 dekameters	= 1 hectometer (hm)
	= 100 meters
10 hectometers	= 1 kilometer (km)
	= 1,000 meters

Area Measure

100 square millimeters (mm^2)	= 1 square centimeter (cm^2)
10,000 square centimeters	= 1 square meter (m^2)
	= 1,000,000 square millimeters
100 square meters	= 1 are (a)
100 ares	= 1 hectare (ha)
	= 10,000 square meters
100 hectares	= 1 square kilometer (km^2)
	= 1,000,000 square meters

EQUIVALENTS BETWEEN ENGLISH AND METRIC SYSTEMS

Lengths

angstrom	= 0.1 nanometer (exactly)
	= 0.000 1 micron (exactly)
	= 0.000 000 1 millimeter (exactly)
	= 0.000 000 004 inch
1 cable's length	= 120 fathoms
	= 720 feet
	= 219.456 meters (exactly)
1 centimeter (cm)	= 0.3937 inch
1 chain (ch), (Gunter's or surveyor's)	= 66 feet
	= 20.1168 meters (exactly)
1 chain (engineer's)	= 100 feet
	= 30.48 meters (exactly)
1 decimeter (dm)	= 3.937 inches
1 dekameter (dam)	= 32.808 feet
1 fathom	= 6 feet
	= 1.8288 meters (exactly)

1 foot (ft)	=	0.3048 meters (exactly)
1 inch (in)	=	2.54 centimeters (exactly)
1 kilometer (km)	=	0.621 mile
	=	3,280.8 feet
1 league (land)	=	3 statute miles
	=	4.828 kilometers
1 link (Gunter's or surveyor's)	=	7.92 inches
	=	0.201 meter
1 link (engineer's)	=	1 foot
	=	0.305 meter
1 meter (m)	=	39.37 inches
	=	1.094 yards
1 mile (mi) (statute or land)	=	5,280 feet
	=	1.609 kilometers
1 international nautical mile (INM)	=	1,852 kilometers (exactly)
	=	1.150779 statute miles
	=	6,076.11549 feet
1 rod (rd), pole, or perch	=	16½ feet
	=	5½ yards
	=	5.029 meters
1 yard (yd)	=	0.9144 meter (exactly)

Areas or Surfaces

1 acre	=	43,560 square feet
	=	4,840 square yards
	=	0.405 hectare
1 are (a) (100 square meters)	=	119.599 square yards
	=	0.025 acre
1 hectare (ha) (10,000 square meters)	=	2.471 acres
[1 square (building)]	=	100 square feet
1 square centimeter (cm²)	=	0.155 square inch
1 square decimeter (dm²)	=	15.500 square inches
1 square foot (ft²)	=	929.030 square centimeters
1 square inch (in²)	=	6.452 square centimeters
1 square kilometer (km²)	=	247.105 acres
	=	0.386 square mile
	=	1,196 square yards
1 square meter (m²)	=	10.764 square feet
1 square mile (mi²)	=	640 acres 258.999 hectares
1 square millimeter (mm²)	=	0.002 square inch
1 square rod (rd²), sq. pole, or sq. perch	=	25.293 square meters
1 square yard (yd²)	=	0.836 square meter

MATHEMATICAL FORMULAS

To find the **CIRCUMFERENCE** of a:

Circle—Multiply the diameter by 3.14159265 (usually 3.1416).

To find the **AREA** of a:

Circle—Multiply the square of the diameter by .785398 (usually .7854).

Rectangle—Multiply the length of the base by the height.

Sphere (surface)—Multiply the square of the radius by 3.1416 and multiply by 4.

Square—Square the length of one side.

Trapezoid—Add the length of the 2 parallel sides, multiply by the height and divide by 2.

Triangle—Multiply the length of the base by the height and divide by 2.

REAL ESTATE FORMS AND WORKSHEETS

Standard real estate forms that are mentioned in the text are reproduced in this section for the convenience of the reader. Although they have been reduced to fit on the page, these forms are more than adequate for anyone who wishes to become familiar with their contents.

In addition several worksheets are provided to facilitate analyses that must be prepared by the prospective home buyer or home seller.

The following forms and worksheets are included:
Qualifying Income Worksheet
Debt Obligation Worksheet
Residential Purchase Agreement and Deposit Receipt
Residential Loan Application
Request for Verification of Employment
Request for Verification of Deposit
Seller's Estimated Receipts Worksheet
Settlement Statement
Form 2119 Sale or Exchange of Principal Residence
Form 3903 Moving Expenses

APPENDIX

Debt Obligations Worksheet

For all entries, use average monthly payment.

Loans from lending institutions and credit companies (if term of loan is at least ten months):

Creditor	Payment
_____	_____
_____	_____
_____	_____

Credit cards and lines of credit (if balance maintained):

Source	Payment
_____	_____
_____	_____
_____	_____

Mortgage debt on rental property or second home:

Property	Payment
_____	_____

Child support: _____
Alimony: _____

Total obligations: _____

Qualifying Income Worksheet

Source of Income	Borrower	Spouse
Annual Salary:	_____	_____

Variable income (list annual average for last two years):

	Borrower	Spouse
Overtime pay:	_____	_____
Bonus pay:	_____	_____
Commissions:	_____	_____
Second job:	_____	_____
Self-employment:	_____	_____

Investment income (list average if at least $1,200 per year):

	Borrower	Spouse
Interest:	_____	_____
Dividends:	_____	_____
Royalties:	_____	_____
Rental property net operating income:	_____	_____
Business profits:	_____	_____

Other income (optional):

	Borrower	Spouse
Alimony:	_____	_____
Child support:	_____	_____
Welfare:	_____	_____
Social security:	_____	_____
Pension:	_____	_____

	Borrower	Spouse
Total income:	_____	_____

Add two totals: _____
Monthly income (divide by 12): _____

Note: All income listed must be consistent and expected to continue in the future. The lender may ask you to verify past income.

RESIDENTIAL PURCHASE AGREEMENT AND DEPOSIT RECEIPT

RECEIVED from _____

_____, hereinafter designated as PURCHASER, the amount set forth below as **DEPOSIT** on account of the

PURCHASE PRICE of $_____ (_____

_____**DOLLARS),**

for the real property in the City of_____, County of_____, State of_____,

described as_____, upon the following **TERMS AND CONDITIONS:**

1. FINANCING TERMS. *(Also refer to Items 8,9, and 10 on the reverse side)*

A. $_____ **DEPOSIT** evidenced by ☐ Cash, ☐ Cashiers Check, ☐ Note, ☐ Personal Check, ☐ Other:_____,

held uncashed until acceptance and one day thereafter deposited with:_____

B. $_____ **ADDITIONAL CASH DEPOSIT in escrow** ☐ within_____days from acceptance, ☐ upon removal of all contingencies.

C. $_____ **BALANCE OF CASH PAYMENT at close of escrow.**

FIRST LOAN

D. $_____ **PROCEEDS FROM NEW FIRST LOAN:** ☐ FHA, ☐ VA, ☐ CONVENTIONAL ☐ FIXED RATE,

☐ OTHER:_____

for _____ years, with Interest not to exceed _____%, payable at approximately $_____ p/mo,

☐ including Taxes and Insurance, with the balance due not less than _____ years. ☐ Other terms:_____

_____. Loan fee not to exceed _____% plus $_____

Seller agrees to pay discount points not to exceed_____%. Purchaser agrees to pay discount points not to exceed

_____%. FHA – MIP to be ☐ Financed, ☐ Paid in Cash.

E. $_____ **EXISTING FIRST LOAN:** ☐ ASSUMPTION OF, ☐ SUBJECT TO existing first loan of record:

☐ FHA, ☐ VA, ☐ CONVENTIONAL, ☐ PRIVATE _____ ☐ FIXED RATE, ☐ OTHER: _____

payable at $_____ per month, with interest currently at _____%, ☐ including Taxes and Insurance,

with Interest Rate to be adjusted not to exceed _____%. Other terms: _____

Held by: _____ Assumption Fee, if any, not to exceed_____%.

All charges related to assumption shall be paid by Purchaser.

☐ **ASSUMPTION OF VA LOAN WITH RELEASE OF LIABILITY:** Purchaser shall assume Seller's Potential Indemnity

Liability to the U.S. Government for the repayment of the loan.

F. $_____ **SELLER FINANCING:** First Loan secured by the property, payable at $_____ per month, or more, including

_____% interest, with the balance due _____ years from date of conveyance, ☐ due on sale.

A late charge of $_____ shall be due on monthly payments tendered more than _____ days late.

JUNIOR LOANS

G. $_____ **PROCEEDS FROM NEW SECOND LOAN:** ☐ FIXED RATE ☐ OTHER:_____

amortization _____ years, with Interest not to exceed _____%, payable at approximately $_____ p/mo,

with the balance due not less than _____ years. ☐ Other terms:_____

_____. Loan fee not to exceed _____%.

H. $_____ **EXISTING SECOND LOAN** ☐ ASSUMPTION OF, ☐ SUBJECT TO existing second loan of record:

☐ FIXED RATE, ☐ Other:_____

payable at $_____ per month, with interest currently at _____%. Interest Rate to be adjusted

to: _____%. Other terms: _____

Held by: _____ Assumption Fee, if any, not to exceed_____%.

All charges related to assumption shall be paid by purchaser.

I. $_____ **SELLER FINANCING:** ☐ SECOND, ☐ THIRD LOAN secured by the property, payable at $_____ per

month, or more, including _____% interest, with the balance due _____ years from date of conveyance, ☐ due on sale.

A late charge of $_____ shall be due on monthly payments tendered more than _____ days late.

J. $_____ **OTHER FINANCIAL TERMS:** ☐ BELOW, ☐ IN ATTACHED ADDENDUM

K. $_____ **BONDS AND ASSESSMENTS** of record assumed by Purchaser. (See Item 22 on page 101-R.2)

L. $_____ **TOTAL PURCHASE PRICE** (not including closing costs). Any net differences between the approximate balances

of encumbrances shown above, which are to be assumed or taken subject to, and the actual balances of said encumbrances

at close of escrow shall be adjusted in ☐ Cash, ☐ Other:_____

M. LOAN APPROVAL: Conditioned upon Lender's ☐ written, ☐ verbal LOAN APPROVAL within _____ days of acceptance, per Item 8

on reverse side.

2. ADDITIONAL TERMS AND CONDITIONS:

3. ADDENDUM. Addendum(s), identified as _____, signed by the parties, is attached.

4. SELLER'S PROPERTY DISCLOSURE STATEMENT [Professional Publishing Form 109.1 & 109.2 or 109.5 CAL] ☐ is, ☐ is not to be provided to Purchaser.

(continued on reverse side)

PROVISIONS ON REVERSE SIDE ARE PART OF THIS AGREEMENT Purchaser's Initials: [_____] [_____] Seller's Initials: [_____] [_____]

FORM 101-R.1 (12-87) COPYRIGHT © 1985, BY PROFESSIONAL PUBLISHING CORP. 122 PAUL DR. SAN RAFAEL, CA 94903. (415)472-1964 **PROFESSIONAL PUBLISHING**

793

APPENDIX

. . . PROPERTY DISCLOSURE STATEMENT *(continued)*. On or before delivery of the accepted offer or counter offer, **Purchaser shall receive, in addition to any Transfer Statements required by law, a Property Disclosure Statement prepared and signed by Seller. If Purchaser is not satisfied with any condition of the property disclosed in the statement, and which was not previously known to Purchaser, he may terminate the transaction by written notice delivered to Seller's broker or agent** *within 72 hours of receipt* **of Seller's Property Disclosure Statement, or notify Seller's broker or agent in writing** *within said 72 hours* **of Purchaser's election to order additional inspections of the property by appropriate professionals.**

If Purchaser is not satisfied with the result of any such inspections, he may terminate the transaction by written notice delivered to Seller's broker or agent, together with copies of all inspection reports, *within fifteen (15) days of receipt* **of Seller's Property Disclosure Statement.**

Purchaser understands that Seller's Property Disclosure Statement is not a substitute for property inspections by professionals, including but not limited to engineers, architects, general contractors, and structural pest control operators, and Purchaser has the opportunity to retain and pay for such professionals as he believes are appropriate. Purchaser understands and acknowledges that the brokers and agents in the transaction cannot warrant the condition of the property or guarantee that all defects have been disclosed by Seller.

Seller agrees to hold all brokers and agents in the transaction harmless and to defend and indemnify them from any claim, demand, action or proceedings resulting from any omission or alleged omission by Seller in his Property Disclosure Statement. Unless otherwise required by this agreement, (*i.e., Clause #26, MAINTENANCE*) Seller shall not be obligated to make any repair or remedy any defect set forth in his Property Disclosure Statement.

5. TIME. Time is of the essence of this agreement. All modifications and extensions shall be in writing and signed by all parties.

6. DEFINITIONS. The term "Broker" includes cooperating brokers and all sales persons, and the term "days" means calendar days unless otherwise specified.

7. CONDITIONS SATISFIED IN WRITING. Each condition contained herein shall be satisfied according to its terms or waived in writing by the party responsible within the time specified (or any extension thereof agreed to by the parties in writing), or this agreement shall be null and void and all deposits returned to Purchaser less expenses incurred by Purchaser to the date of cancellation of this transaction. This paragraph contemplates that each party shall diligently pursue the completion of this transaction.

8. LOAN APPROVAL. Within the number of days and in the manner specified under **Item 1-M,** Purchaser shall provide Seller with evidence of loan commitment for the New Financing, from a lender of Purchaser's choice, and/or consent to assumption of Existing Financing provided for in this agreement. Purchaser shall use his best efforts to qualify for and obtain said financing and shall complete and submit a loan application **within five (5) days of acceptance.**

8A. LOAN CLOSING. In the event a loan commitment and/or consent is obtained but not honored without fault of Purchaser, this agreement shall be null and void and all deposits returned to Purchaser less expenses incurred by Purchaser to the date of cancellation of this transaction.

9. EXISTING LOANS.
LOAN DOCUMENTS. Seller shall **within three (3) days of acceptance,** provide Purchaser with copies of all Notes and Deeds of Trust or Mortgages to be assumed or taken subject to, and **within five (5) days of receipt** thereof Purchaser shall in writing notify Seller of his approval or disapproval of such terms, which shall not be unreasonably withheld. **Within three (3) days of acceptance,** Seller shall submit written request for a current Beneficiary Statement on the above loan or loans.

10. SELLER FINANCING. In the event of Seller Financing, Purchaser shall furnish Seller **within three (3) days of acceptance,** a customary financial statement for the sole purpose of credit approval, which approval shall not be unreasonably withheld. Purchaser authorizes Seller to engage the services of a reputable credit reporting agency for this purpose at Purchaser's expense and Seller shall notify Purchaser **within ten (10) days of receipt** of financial statement, of approval or disapproval of Purchaser's credit.

11. EXAMINATION OF TITLE. Fifteen (15) days from date of acceptance hereof are allowed the Purchaser to examine the title to the property and to report in writing any valid objections thereto. Any exceptions to the title, which would be disclosed by examination of the records, shall be deemed to have been accepted unless reported in writing **within said fifteen (15) days.** If Purchaser objects to any exceptions to the title, Seller shall use due diligence to remove such exceptions at his own expense **before close of escrow.** But if such exceptions cannot be removed **before close of escrow,** all rights and obligations hereunder may, at the election of the Purchaser, terminate and the deposit shall be returned to Purchaser, unless he elects to purchase the property subject to such exceptions.

12. ENCUMBRANCES. In addition to any encumbrances referred to herein, Purchaser shall take title to the property subject to: [1] Real Estate Taxes not yet due, and [2] Covenants, Conditions, Restrictions, Rights of Way, and Easements of record, if any, which do not materially affect the value or intended use of the property. Such encumbrances shall be deemed approved unless written notice to the contrary is delivered to Seller or his agent **within fifteen (15) days of acceptance.**

13. PRORATIONS. Rents, taxes, interest, and other expenses of the property to be prorated as of the date of recordation of the deed. Security deposits, advance rentals, or considerations involving future lease credits shall be credited to Purchaser.

13A. REASSESSMENT. Purchaser is advised that the property may be reassessed as of the date of conveyance which may result in a tax increase.

14. INSURANCE. Purchaser to obtain hazard insurance prepaid for one year in an amount satisfactory to the loan holders and covering one hundred percent replacement cost of improvements, and to name holders of the secured loans as additional loss payees. Purchaser agrees further to annually increase said insurance if necessary, to equal the current replacement cost of the property during the term of the loan holders' mortgages. In the event of Seller Financing, Purchaser shall instruct the insurance carrier to deliver to Seller before close of escrow a certificate providing for 30 days written notice in the event of cancellation.

14A. DESTRUCTION OF IMPROVEMENTS. If the improvements of the property are destroyed, materially damaged, or found to be materially defective prior to close of escrow, Purchaser may terminate the transaction by written notice delivered to Seller's broker or agent, and all deposits shall be returned to Purchaser. In the event Purchaser does not elect to terminate the agreement, Purchaser shall be entitled to receive in addition to the property any insurance proceeds payable on account of the damage or destruction.

15. NOTICES. By acceptance hereof Seller warrants that he has no notice of violations relating to the property from City, County, or State agencies.

15A. ACCESS TO PROPERTY. Seller agrees to provide reasonable access to the property to Purchaser and inspectors representing Purchaser as provided in this agreement and to representatives of lending institutions for appraisal purposes.

16. DUE ON SALE CLAUSE. IF the note and deed of trust or mortgage for any existing loan contains an acceleration or DUE ON SALE clause, the lender may demand full payment of the entire loan balance as a result of this transaction. Both parties acknowledge that they are not relying on any representation by the other party or the broker with respect to the enforceability of such a provision in existing notes and deeds of trust or mortgages, or deeds of trust or mortgages to be executed in accordance with this agreement. Both parties have been advised by the broker to seek independent legal advice with respect to these matters.

17. BALLOON PAYMENT. Both parties acknowledge they have not received or relied upon any statements or representations made to them by Broker regarding availability of funds, or rate of interest at which funds might be available, when Purchaser becomes obligated to refinance or pay off the remaining balance of any loan pursuant to the terms of this agreement.

18. DEFAULT. In the event that Purchaser shall default in the performance of this agreement, unless the parties have agreed to a provision for liquidated damages, Seller may, subject to any rights of the Broker herein, retain Purchaser's deposit on account of damages sustained and may take such actions as he deems appropriate to collect such additional damages as may have been actually sustained, and Purchaser shall have the right to take such action as he deems appropriate to recover such portion of the deposit as may be allowed by law. **In the event that Purchaser shall so default, unless Purchaser and Seller have agreed to liquidated damages, Purchaser agrees to pay the Broker(s) entitled thereto such commissions as would be payable by Seller in the absence of such default.** Purchaser's obligation to said Broker(s) shall be in addition to any rights which said Broker(s) may have against Seller in the event of default. In the event legal action is instituted by the Broker(s), or any party to this agreement, or arising out of the execution of this agreement or the sale, or to collect commissions, the prevailing party shall be entitled to receive from the other party a reasonable attorney fee to be determined by the court in which such action is brought.

19. FOREIGN INVESTMENT AND REAL PROPERTY TAX ACT. The Foreign Investment and Real Property Tax Act requires a buyer purchasing real property from a foreign person to withhold tax from the sale proceeds unless an exemption applies. Seller agrees to provide Purchaser with a certification establishing that no federal income tax is required to be withheld under the act, or to consent to withholding of tax from the proceeds of sale as required, unless it is established that the transaction is exempt because the purchase price is $300,000 or less and the Purchaser intends to use the property as his residence.

FORM 101-R.1(a) (12-87) COPYRIGHT © 1985, BY PROFESSIONAL PUBLISHING CORP., 122 PAUL DR., SAN RAFAEL, CA 94903, (415) 472-1964 **PROFESSIONAL PUBLISHING**

NCR (No Carbon Required) Property Address _____ **PAGE 3 of 4 PAGES**

20. CLOSING on or before _____, or within _____ **days of acceptance**, whichever is later, both parties shall deposit with an authorized Escrow Holder, to be selected by ☐ **Purchaser,** ☐ **Seller,** all funds and instruments necessary to complete the sale in accordance with the terms hereof. ☐ Signed Escrow Instructions to be delivered to Escrow Holder **within _____ days of acceptance**. The representations and warranties shall not be terminated by conveyance of the property. Escrow Fee to be paid by_____. Transfer Tax(es), if any, to be paid by _____.

21. EVIDENCE OF TITLE in the form of ☐ a policy of _____ Title Insurance, ☐ Other: _____ paid by _____, who shall order a Preliminary Title Report **within _____ days of acceptance.**

22. BONDS. The amount of any bond or assessment which is a lien shall be ☐ paid by Seller, ☐ assumed by Purchaser.

23. PHYSICAL POSSESSION. Physical possession, with all keys and garage door openers, shall be delivered to Purchaser (check either item [1] or item [2]) : ☐ 1. UPON recordation of the deed. ☐ 2. AFTER recordation, **but not later than midnight of**_____. Unless Seller has vacated the premises prior to recordation of the deed, Seller agrees to pay Purchaser $_____ per day from recordation to date possession is delivered and to leave in escrow a sum equal to the above per diem amount multiplied by the number of days from date of closing to date allowed above for delivery of possession. Said sum to be disbursed to the persons entitled thereto on the date possession is delivered.

24. FIXTURES. All items permanently attached to the property, including attached floor coverings, draperies with hardware, shades, blinds, window and door screens, storm sash, combination doors, awnings, light fixtures, television antennas, electric garage door openers with controls, outdoor plants and trees, are included in the purchase price free of liens, EXCLUDING:_____

25. PERSONAL PROPERTY. The following personal property, on the premises when inspected by Purchaser, is included in the purchase price and shall be transferred to Purchaser by a Bill of Sale at close of escrow. No warranty is implied as to the condition of said property:_____

26. MAINTENANCE. Seller covenants that the heating, air-conditioning (if any), electrical, sewer, septic system, drainage, sprinkler (if any), and plumbing systems including the water heater, as well as built-in appliances and other mechanical apparatus shall be in **normal working order** on the date occupancy is delivered. Seller shall replace any cracked or broken glass including windows, mirrors, shower and tub enclosures. Until occupancy is delivered Seller shall maintain landscaping, grounds and pool (if any). Seller agrees to deliver the property in a neat and clean condition with all debris removed. The following items are specifically excluded from the above: _____

Purchaser and Seller understand and acknowledge that Broker shall not in any circumstances be liable for any breach in this clause.

27. PROVISIONS ON THE REVERSE SIDE. The provisions marked ☒ below, printed in full on the reverse side, are included in this agreement.

☐ A. **Pest Control Inspection,** paid by ☐ **Purchaser,** ☐ **Seller**
☐ B. **Existing Pest Control Report** Dated:_____,
 By _____.
☐ C. **"As Is,"** but Subject to Purchaser's Approval
☐ D. Waiver of Pest Control Inspection
☐ E. Roof Inspection Report within _____ days of acceptance
☐ F. City and County inspections within _____ days of acceptance
☐ G. Condominium Disclosure
☐ H. Home Protect. Ctr. ☐ paid by _____
 ☐ waived by _____
☐ I. Arbitration Clause

☐ J. Contingent upon the sale of_____
☐ K. Inspection of Property Condition, Pool, and Septic Tank, approved within _____ days of receipt of report(s)
☐ L. VA Appraisal Clause
☐ M. FHA Appraisal Clause
☐ N. Smoke Detectors provided by _____
☐ O. Flood Hazard Zone

28. EXPIRATION. This offer shall expire unless a copy with Seller's written acceptance is delivered to Purchaser or the Purchaser's agent on or before _____ o'clock ☐ AM ☐ PM, on _____, 19____.

29. OWNER OCCUPANCY. Purchaser ☐ does, ☐ does not intend to occupy the property as Purchaser's residence.

30. TITLE shall vest as _____, unless otherwise designated in Escrow Instructions.
(The manner of taking title may have significant legal and tax consequences. If in doubt, Purchasers should obtain advice from legal or tax counsel.)

31. AGENCY DECLARATION. The following agency relationship(s) are hereby confirmed.

_____is the agent of (check one): _____is the agent of (check one):
(Name of Listing Agent) (Name of Selling Agent if not the same as the Listing Agent)

☐ the seller exclusively; or ☐ the buyer exclusively; or ☐ the seller exclusively; or
☐ both the buyer and seller. ☐ both the buyer and seller.

The undersigned Purchaser **has read all 4 pages of this agreement** and hereby acknowledges receipt of a copy of pages 1, 2, 3 and 4. Purchaser acknowledges further that he has not received or relied upon statements or representations by the undersigned Broker which are not herein expressed.

_____ Purchaser's Broker DATED: _____ TIME: _____
By _____ _____ Purchaser
Broker's Initials: _____ Dated: _____ _____ Purchaser

ACCEPTANCE

Seller accepts the foregoing offer and agrees to sell the herein described property for the price and on the terms and conditions herein specified. Subject to: _____

COMMISSION. Seller hereby irrevocably assigns and agrees to pay to _____, the Broker in this transaction, in Cash from proceeds at close of escrow, for services rendered:_____

In the event that Purchaser defaults and fails to complete the sale, the Broker shall be entitled to receive one-half of Purchaser's deposit, but not more than the commission earned, without prejudice to Broker's rights to recover the balance of the commission from Purchaser. The mutual rescission of this agreement by Purchaser and Seller shall not relieve said parties of their obligations to Broker hereunder. This agreement shall not limit the rights of Broker provided for in any listing or other agreement which may be in effect between Seller and Broker, except that the amount of the commission shall be as specified herein.

The undersigned Seller **has read all 4 pages of this agreement** and hereby acknowledges receipt of a copy of pages 1, 2, 3 and 4. Broker is hereby authorized to deliver a signed copy to Purchaser and to disclose the terms of sale to Multiple Listing Service or Real Estate Board members.

_____ Seller's Broker DATED: _____ TIME: _____
By _____ _____ Seller
Broker's Initials: _____ Dated: _____ _____ Seller
Purchaser acknowledges receipt of a copy of the accepted agreement. DATE: _____ TIME: _____ _____ Purchaser

FORM **101-R.2** (12-87) COPYRIGHT © 1985, BY PROFESSIONAL PUBLISHING CORP., 122 PAUL DR., SAN RAFAEL, CA 94903, (415) 472-1964 **PROFESSIONAL PUBLISHING**

APPENDIX

_____ **27-A. PEST CONTROL INSPECTION.** The main building and all attached structures to be inspected by a licensed structural pest control operator. Seller to pay for: (1) Elimination of infestation and/or infection of wood-destroying pests or organisms, (2) For repair of damage caused by such infestation and/or infection, (3) For correction of conditions which caused said damage and (4) For repair of plumbing and other leaks affecting wood members, including repair of leaking stall showers, in accordance with said pest control operator's report. Seller shall not be responsible for preventive work where no damage is found, except where required for FHA or VA financing.

If the inspecting structural pest control operator shall recommend further inspection of inaccessible areas, Purchaser may require that said areas be inspected. If any infestation or infection is discovered by such inspection, the additional cost of such inspection and additional required work shall be paid by Seller. If no such infestation or infection is discovered, the additional cost of inspecting such inaccessible areas and the work required to return the property to its original condition shall be paid by Purchaser.

Funds for work specified in said report to be done at Seller's expense shall be held in escrow and disbursed by escrow holder upon receipt of Notice of Work Completed by a licensed structural pest control operator selected by Seller certifying that the property is free of evidence of active infestation or infection.

As soon as the same are available, copies of the report, and any certification or other proof of completion of the work shall be delivered to the agents of Purchaser and Seller who are authorized to receive the same on behalf of their principals.

_____ **27-B. EXISTING PEST CONTROL REPORT ACCEPTED BY PURCHASER.** Purchaser accepts existing pest control report on the property by the licensed structural pest control operator listed under Item 27-B. Seller's obligations shall be as set forth in Item 27-A above.

_____ **27-C. AS IS, BUT SUBJECT TO PURCHASER'S APPROVAL OF INSPECTION REPORT.** Property to be purchased in its present condition with no charge to Seller for any pest control work. However, Purchaser shall have the right to have the property inspected and to obtain a report from a licensed structural pest control operator. Purchaser shall be deemed to have approved said report unless written notice to the contrary is delivered to Seller or his agent **within fifteen (15) days of acceptance.** In the event Purchaser does not approve the report, he may have his deposit returned and both parties shall be relieved of all obligations hereunder. Purchaser acknowledges that he has not received or relied upon any representations by either the Broker or the Seller, with respect to the condition of the property.

_____ **27-D. WAIVER OF PEST CONTROL INSPECTION.** Purchaser has satisfied himself about the condition of the property and agrees to purchase the property in its present condition without the benefit of a structural pest control inspection.

Purchaser acknowledges that he has not received or relied upon any representations by either the Broker or the Seller, with respect to the condition of the property.

_____ **27-E. ROOF INSPECTION.** Purchaser, at his expense, may order a roof inspection report from a licensed general or roofing contractor. **Within the number of days specified under Item 27-E,** copies of the report shall be delivered to the agents of Purchaser and Seller who are authorized to receive the same on behalf of their principals.

Within three (3) days following receipt of the report, Seller may [a]: elect to pay the cost of all work recommended by such report; or [b]: elect to pay none or only a portion of the cost of such work. Written notice of such election shall be delivered to Purchaser or his agent.

In the event Seller does not agree to pay for all such work, Purchaser may elect to pay the balance of the cost of such work or terminate all rights and obligations to the parties under this agreement. Written notice of such election shall be delivered to Seller or his agent **within seven (7) days following receipt** of Seller's notice. In the event of such termination, Purchaser shall be entitled to a full refund of all deposits excluding the cost of the above roof inspection report. If no written election is made **within seven (7) days,** Purchaser shall have no right to terminate this agreement, and Seller shall be responsible for the cost of that portion of the work which he elected to pay.

In the event Seller shall have elected to pay the cost of all such work, he shall have the right to have such work performed by a licensed general or roofing contractor of his choice.

_____ **27-F. CITY AND COUNTY INSPECTION REPORT.** Local ordinance requires that the property be inspected **or a report issued** for compliance with local building and permit regulations, standards and ordinances as a condition to sale or transfer. **Within the number of days specified under Item 27-F** Seller shall notify the appropriate local agency to cause the property to be inspected, **or to issue the required report** at the earliest practicable date. If Seller is unable or unwilling to pay for correction of any violations shown in the report, this agreement shall terminate and all deposits be returned to Purchaser, unless Purchaser agrees to pay the cost of corrections required.

_____ **27-G. CONDOMINIUM DISCLOSURE.** Purchaser shall take title subject to Condominium Declaration, Covenants, Conditions and Restrictions, Articles of Incorporation, By-Laws, Rules and Regulations currently in force, and Financial Statements of the condominium owners association, to be delivered to Purchaser for his approval **within five (5) days of acceptance.** Purchaser shall be deemed to have approved said documents unless written notice to the contrary is delivered to Seller or his agent **within five (5) days of receipt** by Purchaser, in which case Purchaser may have his deposit returned and both parties shall be relieved of all obligations hereunder.

In addition, Seller shall deliver to Purchaser before close of escrow a written statement from the condominium owners association documenting the amount of any delinquent assessments including penalties, attorney's fees, and other charges provided for in the management documents. Such charges shall be credited to Purchaser at close of escrow.

_____ **27-H. HOME PROTECTION CONTRACT,** paid for by the party specified under **Item 27-H,** shall become effective upon close of escrow for not less than one year, unless both parties have waived such Home Protection Contract, as specified under **Item 27-H.** The brokers herein have informed both parties that such protection programs are available, but do not approve or endorse any particular program.

_____ **27-I. ARBITRATION.** Purchaser, Seller and Broker(s) agree that in the event any party defaults in the performance of the obligations of such party under the agreement, or in the event there is a dispute between any of them with respect to their obligations under the agreement, or their obligations arising out of the purchase and sale, exchange or lease of the property, that the matter shall be submitted to arbitration in accordance with the Commercial Rules of Arbitration of the American Arbitration Association.

The parties do further agree that the party or parties prevailing in such arbitration shall be entitled to receive from the other party or parties a reasonable attorney's fee and all costs incurred in connection with the arbitration in an amount to be determined by the arbitrator or arbitrators, and in the event that any party shall fail to pay the amount due under the award of the arbitrator or arbitrators, and legal action is commenced for the enforcement of the award, the prevailing party or parties shall be entitled to receive a reasonable attorney's fee incurred in such action to be determined by the court in which such action is brought.

The parties further agree that they shall each have the rights of discovery set forth in provisions of local law, which is by this reference incorporated herein.

_____ **27-J. CONTINGENCY RELEASE CLAUSE.** Subject to the sale and conveyance of "Purchaser's Property," described in **Item 27-J,** within the time specified for closing of Seller's property, Seller shall have the right to continue to offer the herein property for sale and to accept offers subject to the rights of Purchaser. Should Seller accept such an offer, then Purchaser shall be given written notice of such acceptance. In the event Purchaser will not waive this condition in writing **within three (3) days** of receipt of such notice, then this agreement shall be terminated and all deposits be returned to Purchaser and escrow cancelled. Said notice may be personally delivered or mailed by certified mail and addressed to Purchaser, in care of his agent identified herein. In the event of mailing, such notice shall be deemed to have been given on the day following the date of mailing evidenced by the postmark on the envelope containing such notice.

_____ **27-K. INSPECTION OF PHYSICAL CONDITION OF PROPERTY, POOL, SEPTIC TANK.** Inspection report(s) of physical condition of the property including swimming pool, wells, if any, by a representative of Purchaser's choice and at Purchaser's expense to be ordered **within two (2) days of acceptance.** Seller to provide a septic tank inspection report at his expense. Approval of the report(s), at the discretion of the Purchaser, to be given in writing **within the number of days of receipt of said report(s) specified under Item 27-K,** which approval shall not be unreasonably withheld. In the event Purchaser does not approve of the report, he may have his deposit returned and both parties shall be relieved of all obligations hereunder. Seller, or seller's agent, to be provided with copies of the report(s).

_____ **27-L. VA APPRAISED VALUE CLAUSE.** It is expressly agreed that, notwithstanding any other provisions of this contract, the Purchaser shall not incur any penalty by forfeiture of earnest money or otherwise be obligated to complete the purchase of the property described herein, if the contract purchase price or cost exceeds the Reasonable Value of the property established by the Veterans Administration. The Purchaser shall, however, have the privilege and option of proceeding with the consummation of this contract without regard to the amount of the Reasonable Value established by the Veterans Administration. Escrow Fee to be paid by Seller.

_____ **27-M. FHA APPRAISED VALUE CLAUSE.** It is expressly agreed that, notwithstanding any other provisions of this contract, the Purchaser shall not be obligated to complete the purchase of the property described herein or to incur any penalty by forfeiture of earnest money deposits or otherwise unless the Seller has delivered to the Purchaser a written statement, issued by the Federal Housing Commissioner, setting forth the appraised value of the property for mortgage insurance purposes of not less than $_____, which statement the Seller hereby agrees to deliver to the Purchaser promptly after such appraised value statement is made available to the Seller. The Purchaser shall, however, have the privilege and option of proceeding with the consummation of this contract without regard to the amount of the appraised valuation made by the Federal Housing Commissioner.

The appraised valuation is arrived at to determine the maximum mortgage the Department of Housing and Urban Development will insure. HUD does not warrant the value or the condition of the property. The Purchaser should satisfy himself/herself that the price and condition of the property are acceptable.

_____ **27-N. SMOKE DETECTORS.** In accordance with local ordinance smoke detectors shall be installed at the expense of the party indicated under **Item 27-N.** If required, said smoke detectors shall be inspected by the appropriate City or County agency prior to close of escrow and a compliance report obtained.

_____ **27-O. FLOOD HAZARD ZONE.** Purchaser has been advised that the property is located in an area which the Secretary of HUD has found to have special flood hazards and that it will be necessary to purchase flood insurance in order to obtain any loan secured by the property from any federally regulated financial institution or a loan insured or guaranteed by an agency of the U.S. Government.

FORM 101-R.2(a) (12-87) COPYRIGHT © 1965, BY PROFESSIONAL PUBLISHING CORP., 122 PAUL DR., SAN RAFAEL, CA 94903. (415) 472-1964 **PROFESSIONAL PUBLISHING**

Residential Loan Application

MORTGAGE APPLIED FOR	☐ Conventional ☐ VA	☐ FHA ☐	Amount $	Interest Rate %	No. of Months	Monthly Payment Principal & Interest $	Escrow/Impounds (to be collected monthly) ☐ Taxes ☐ Hazard Ins. ☐ Mtg. Ins. ☐
Prepayment Option							

Subject Property

Property Street Address	City	County	State	Zip	No. Units
Legal Description (Attach description if necessary)				Year Built	

Purpose of Loan: ☐ Purchase ☐ Construction-Permanent ☐ Construction ☐ Refinance ☐ Other (Explain)

Complete this line if Construction-Permanent or Construction Loan ☞	Lot Value Data	Original Cost	Present Value (a)	Cost of Imps. (b)	Total (a + b)	ENTER TOTAL AS PURCHASE PRICE IN DETAILS OF PURCHASE.
	Year Acquired $	$	$	$	$	

Complete this line if a Refinance Loan			Purpose of Refinance	Describe Improvements [] made [] to be made	
Year Acquired	Original Cost	Amt. Existing Liens			
$	$			Cost: $	

Title Will Be Held In What Name(s)	Manner In Which Title Will Be Held
Source of Down Payment and Settlement Charges	

This application is designed to be completed by the borrower(s) with the lender's assistance. The Co-Borrower Section and all other Co-Borrower questions must be completed and the appropriate box(es) checked if ☐ another person will be jointly obligated with the Borrower on the loan, or ☐ the Borrower is relying on income from alimony, child support or separate maintenance or on the income or assets of another person as a basis for repayment of the loan, or ☐ the Borrower is married and resides, or the property is located, in a community property state.

Borrower				Co-Borrower			
Name		Age	School Yrs	Name		Age	School Yrs
Present Address	No. Years ☐ Own ☐ Rent			Present Address	No. Years ☐ Own ☐ Rent		
Street				Street			
City/State/Zip				City/State/Zip			
Former address if less than 2 years at present address				Former address if less than 2 years at present address			
Street				Street			
City/State/Zip				City/State/Zip			
Years at former address ☐ Own ☐ Rent				Years at former address ☐ Own ☐ Rent			
Marital Status ☐ Married ☐ Separated ☐ Unmarried (incl. single, divorced, widowed)	DEPENDENTS OTHER THAN LISTED BY CO-BORROWER NO AGES			Marital Status ☐ Married ☐ Separated ☐ Unmarried (incl. single, divorced, widowed)	DEPENDENTS OTHER THAN LISTED BY BORROWER NO AGES		
Name and Address of Employer	Years employed in this line of work or profession? ____ years Years on this job ____ ☐ Self Employed*			Name and Address of Employer	Years employed in this line of work or profession? ____ years Years on this job ____ ☐ Self Employed*		
Position/Title	Type of Business			Position/Title	Type of Business		
Social Security Number ***	Home Phone	Business Phone		Social Security Number ***	Home Phone	Business Phone	

Gross Monthly Income				Monthly Housing Expense**			Details of Purchase	
Item	Borrower	Co-Borrower	Total	Rent	PRESENT	PROPOSED	Do Not Complete If Refinance	
Base Empl. Income	$	$	$	First Mortgage (P&I)	$	$	a. Purchase Price	$
Overtime				Other Financing (P&I)			b. Total Closing Costs (Est.)	
Bonuses				Hazard Insurance			c. Prepaid Escrows (Est.)	
Commissions				Real Estate Taxes			d. Total (a + b + c)	$
Dividends/Interest				Mortgage Insurance			e. Amount This Mortgage	()
Net Rental Income				Homeowner Assn. Dues			f. Other Financing	()
Other† (Before completing, see notice under Describe Other Income below.)				Other:			g. Other Equity	()
				Total Monthly Pmt.	$	$	h. Amount of Cash Deposit	()
				Utilities			i. Closing Costs Paid by Seller	()
Total	$	$	$	Total	$	$	j. Cash Reqd. For Closing (Est.)	$

Describe Other Income

⇨ B—Borrower C—Co-Borrower	NOTICE: † Alimony, child support, or separate maintenance income need not be revealed if the Borrower or Co-Borrower does not choose to have it considered as a basis for repaying this loan.	Monthly Amount
		$

If Employed In Current Position For Less Than Two Years, Complete the Following

B/C	Previous Employer/School	City/State	Type of Business	Position/Title	Dates From/To	Monthly Income
						$

These Questions Apply To Both Borrower and Co-Borrower

If a "yes" answer is given to a question in this column, please explain on an attached sheet.

	Borrower Yes or No	Co-Borrower Yes or No
Are there any outstanding judgments against you?	____	____
Have you been declared bankrupt within the past 7 years?	____	____
Have you had property foreclosed upon or given title or deed in lieu thereof in the last 7 years?	____	____
Are you a party to a law suit?	____	____
Are you obligated to pay alimony, child support, or separate maintenance?	____	____
Is any part of the down payment borrowed?	____	____
Are you a co-maker or endorser on a note?	____	____

	Borrower Yes or No	Co-Borrower Yes or No
Are you a U.S. citizen?	____	____
If "no," are you a resident alien?	____	____
If "no," are you a non-resident alien?	____	____
Explain Other Financing or Other Equity (if any):		

*FHLMC/FNMA require business credit report, signed Federal Income Tax returns for last two years; and, if available, audited Profit and Loss Statement plus balance sheet for same period.
**All Present Monthly Housing Expenses of Borrower and Co-Borrower should be listed on a combined basis.
***Optional for FHLMC
FHLMC 65 Rev. 10/86

797

Fannie Mae Form 1003 Rev. 10/86

APPENDIX

Federal National Mortgage Association

REQUEST FOR VERIFICATION OF EMPLOYMENT

INSTRUCTIONS: LENDER- Complete items 1 thru 7. Have applicant complete item 8. Forward directly to employer named in item 1.
EMPLOYER-Please complete either Part II or Part III as applicable. Sign and return directly to lender named in item 2.

PART I · REQUEST

1. TO *(Name and address of employer)*	2. FROM*(Name and address of lender)*

3. SIGNATURE OF LENDER	4. TITLE	5. DATE	6. LENDER'S NUMBER *(optional)*

I have applied for a mortgage loan and stated that I am now or was formerly employed by you. My signature below authorizes verification of this information.

7. NAME AND ADDRESS OF APPLICANT *(Include employee or badge number)*	8. SIGNATURE OF APPLICANT

PART II · VERIFICATION OF PRESENT EMPLOYMENT

EMPLOYMENT DATA

EMPLOYMENT DATA	PAY DATA		
9. APPLICANT'S DATE OF EMPLOYMENT	12A. CURRENT BASE PAY (Enter Amount and Check Period) ☐ ANNUAL ☐ HOURLY ☐ MONTHLY ☐ OTHER ☐ WEEKLY *(Specify)* $ _____	12C. FOR MILITARY PERSONNEL ONLY PAY GRADE	

12B. EARNINGS				12C.	TYPE	MONTHLY AMOUNT
10. PRESENT POSITION					BASE PAY	$
	TYPE	YEAR TO DATE	PAST YEAR			
11. PROBABILITY OF CONTINUED EMPLOYMENT					RATIONS	$
13. IF OVERTIME OR BONUS IS APPLICABLE, IS ITS CONTINUANCE LIKELY?	BASE PAY	$	$		FLIGHT OR HAZARD	$
	OVERTIME	$	$		CLOTHING	$
					QUARTERS	$
	COMMISSIONS	$	$		PRO PAY	$
OVERTIME ☐ YES ☐ NO						
BONUS ☐ YES ☐ NO	BONUS	$	$		OVER SEAS OR COMBAT	$

14. REMARKS *(if paid hourly, please indicate average hours worked each week during current and past year)*

PART III · VERIFICATION OF PREVIOUS EMPLOYMENT

15. DATES OF EMPLOYMENT	16. SALARY/WAGE AT TERMINATION PER (Year) (Month) (Week) BASE _____ OVERTIME _____ COMMISSIONS _____ BONUS _____
17. REASON FOR LEAVING	18. POSITION HELD

19. SIGNATURE OF EMPLOYER	20. TITLE	21. DATE

The confidentiality of the information you have furnished will be preserved except where disclosure of this information is required by applicable law. The form is to be transmitted directly to the lender and is not to be transmitted through the applicant or any other party.

PREVIOUS EDITION WILL BE USED UNTIL STOCK IS EXHAUSTED

FNMA Form 1005
Rev. June 78

This Statement and any applicable supporting schedules may be completed jointly by both married and unmarried co-borrowers if their assets and liabilities are sufficiently joined so that the Statement can be meaningfully and fairly presented on a combined basis; otherwise separate Statements and Schedules are required (FHLMC 65A/FNMA 1003A). If the co-borrower section was completed about a spouse, this statement and supporting schedules must be completed about that spouse also. ☐ Completed Jointly ☐ Not Completed Jointly

Assets		Liabilities and Pledged Assets				

Indicate by (*) those liabilities or pledged assets which will be satisfied upon sale of real estate owned or upon refinancing of subject property

Description	Cash or Market Value	Creditors' Name, Address and Account Number		Acct. Name if Not Borrower's	Mo. Pmt. and Mos. Left to Pay	Unpaid Balance
Cash Deposit Toward Purchase Held By	$	Installment Debts (Include "revolving" charge accounts)			$ Pmt./Mos.	$
		Co.	Acct. No.			
Checking and Savings Accounts (Show Names of Institutions (Account Numbers) Bank, S & L or Credit Union		Addr.				
		City				
Addr.		Co.	Acct. No.			
City		Addr.				
Acct. No.		City				
Bank, S & L or Credit Union		Co.	Acct. No.			
Addr.		Addr.				
City		City				
Acct. No.		Co.	Acct. No.			
Bank, S & L or Credit Union		Addr.				
		City				
Addr.		Co.	Acct. No.			
City		Addr.				
Acct. No.		City				
Stocks and Bonds (No./Description)		Other Debts including Stock Pledges				
		Real Estate Loans Co.	Acct. No.			
		Addr.				
		City				
Life Insurance Net Cash Value Face Amount $		Co.	Acct. No.			
		Addr.				
Subtotal Liquid Assets		City				
Real Estate Owned (Enter Market Value from Schedule of Real Estate Owned)		Automobile Loans Co.	Acct. No.			
Vested Interest in Retirement Fund		Addr.				
Net worth of Business Owned (ATTACH FINANCIAL STATEMENT)		City				
Automobiles Owned (Make and Year)		Co.	Acct. No.			
		City				
Furniture and Personal Property		Alimony/Child Support/Separate Maintenance Payments Owed to				
Other Assets (Itemize)						
		Total Monthly Payments			$	
Total Assets	A $	Net Worth (A minus B) $			Total Liabilities	B $

Statement of Assets and Liabilities

SCHEDULE OF REAL ESTATE OWNED (If Additional Properties Owned Attach Separate Schedule)

Address of Property (Indicate S if Sold, PS if Pending Sale or R if Rental being held for income)	Type of Property	Present Market Value	Amount of Mortgages & Liens	Gross Rental Income	Mortgage Payments	Taxes, Ins. Maintenance and Misc.	Net Rental Income
		$	$	$	$	$	$
TOTALS →		$	$	$	$	$	$

List Previous Credit References

B-Borrower C-Co-Borrower	Creditor's Name and Address	Account Number	Purpose	Highest Balance	Date Paid
				$	

List any additional names under which credit has previously been received _____

AGREEMENT. The undersigned applies for the loan indicated in this application to be secured by a first mortgage or deed of trust on the property described herein, and represents that the property will not be used for any illegal or restricted purpose, and that all statements made in this application are true and are made for the purpose of obtaining the loan. Verification may be obtained from any source named in this application. The original or a copy of this application will be retained by the lender, even if the loan is not granted. The undersigned ☐ intend or ☐ do not intend to occupy the property as their primary residence.

I/we fully understand that it is a federal crime punishable by fine or imprisonment, or both, to knowingly make any false statements concerning any of the above facts as applicable under the provisions of Title 18, United States Code, Section 1014.

_____ Date _____ _____ Date _____
Borrower's Signature Co-Borrower's Signature

Information for Government Monitoring Purposes

The following information is requested by the Federal Government for certain types of loans related to a dwelling, in order to monitor the lender's compliance with equal credit opportunity and fair housing laws. You are not required to furnish this information, but are encouraged to do so. The law provides that a lender may neither discriminate on the basis of this information, nor on whether you choose to furnish it. However, if you choose not to furnish it, under Federal regulations this lender is required to note race and sex on the basis of visual observation or surname. If you do not wish to furnish the above information, please check the box below. (Lender must review the above material to assure that the disclosures satisfy all requirements to which the Lender is subject under applicable state law for the particular type of loan applied for.)

Borrower: ☐ I do not wish to furnish this information
Race/National Origin:
☐ American Indian, Alaskan Native ☐ Asian, Pacific Islander
☐ Black ☐ Hispanic ☐ White
☐ Other (specify): _____
Sex: ☐ Female ☐ Male

Co-Borrower: ☐ I do not wish to furnish this information
Race/National Origin:
☐ American Indian, Alaskan Native ☐ Asian, Pacific Islander
☐ Black ☐ Hispanic ☐ White
☐ Other (specify): _____
Sex: ☐ Female ☐ Male

To Be Completed by Interviewer

This application was taken by:
☐ face to face interview
☐ by mail
☐ by telephone

_____ Interviewer _____ Name of Interviewer's Employer

_____ Interviewer's Phone Number _____ Address of Interviewer's Employer

FHLMC Form 65 Rev. 10/86

REVERSE

799

Fannie Mae Form 1003 Rev. 10/86

Federal National Mortgage Association
REQUEST FOR VERIFICATION OF DEPOSIT

INSTRUCTIONS: LENDER - Complete Items 1 thru 8. Have applicant(s) complete Item 9. Forward directly to depository named in Item 1.
DEPOSITORY - Please complete Items 10 thru 15 and return DIRECTLY to lender named in Item 2.

PART I - REQUEST

1. TO (Name and address of depository)	2. FROM (Name and address of lender)

3. SIGNATURE OF LENDER	4. TITLE	5. DATE	6. LENDER'S NUMBER (Optional)

7. INFORMATION TO BE VERIFIED

TYPE OF ACCOUNT	ACCOUNT IN NAME OF	ACCOUNT NUMBER	BALANCE
			$
			$
			$
			$

TO DEPOSITORY: I have applied for a mortgage loan and stated in my financial statement that the balance on deposit with you is as shown above. You are authorized to verify this information and to supply the lender identified above with the information requested in Items 10 thru 12. Your response is solely a matter of courtesy for which no responsibility is attached to your institution or any of your officers.

8. NAME AND ADDRESS OF APPLICANT(s)	9. SIGNATURE OF APPLICANT(s)

TO BE COMPLETED BY DEPOSITORY

PART II - VERIFICATION OF DEPOSITORY

10. DEPOSIT ACCOUNTS OF APPLICANT(s)

TYPE OF ACCOUNT	ACCOUNT NUMBER	CURRENT BALANCE	AVERAGE BALANCE FOR PREVIOUS TWO MONTHS	DATE OPENED
		$	$	
		$	$	
		$	$	
		$	$	

11. LOANS OUTSTANDING TO APPLICANT(s)

LOAN NUMBER	DATE OF LOAN	ORIGINAL AMOUNT	CURRENT BALANCE	INSTALLMENTS (Monthly/Quarterly)	SECURED BY	NUMBER OF LATE PAYMENTS
		$	$	$ per		
		$	$	$ per		
		$	$	$ per		

12. ADDITIONAL INFORMATION WHICH MAY BE OF ASSISTANCE IN DETERMINATION OF CREDIT WORTHINESS:
(Please include information on loans paid-in-full as in Item 11 above)

13. SIGNATURE OF DEPOSITORY	14. TITLE	15. DATE

The confidentiality of the information you have furnished will be preserved except where disclosure of this information is required by applicable law. The form is to be transmitted directly to the lender and is not to be transmitted through the applicant or any other party.

PREVIOUS EDITION WILL BE USED UNTIL STOCK IS EXHAUSTED

FNMA Form 1006
Rev. June 78

SELLER'S ESTIMATED RECEIPTS
ALL FIGURES ARE APPROXIMATE

Date_____

PROPERTY DESCRIPTION	SELLER'S NAME

		Seller Receives
SELLING PRICE		$
OUTSTANDING MORTGAGES		
1st Mortgage	$	
2nd Mortgage		
Other Encumbrances		
Subtract Total Mortgages →		$
Gross Equity →		$

LESS SELLER'S ESTIMATED EXPENSES

	Seller Pays	
Title Insurance Policy	$	
Attorneys Fees		
Release of Lien		
Survey of Property		
Escrow Fees		
Termite Inspection		
Recording Fees		
Brokers Professional Service Fee		
Prepayment Penalty On Loan		
Photographs		
Loan Discount Fee		
Home Warranty		
...........		
...........		
...........		
Total Estimated Expenses →	$	
ESTIMATED RECEIPTS →	$	

Note: 1. These figures are only estimated and are subject to verification by the Seller.
2. Prorations of taxes, interest and insurance are not included on this statement.
3. Our insurance estimates are based on minimum coverage since types and amounts of coverage varies so much from individual to individual.

Notes: _____

APPENDIX

A

B. TYPE OF LOAN

1. ☐ FHA	2. ☐ FMHA	3. ☐ CONV. UNINS.
4. ☐ VA	5. ☐ CONV. INS.	
6. File Number:		7. Loan Number:
8. Mortgage Insurance Case Number:		

SETTLEMENT STATEMENT
U.S. DEPARTMENT OF HOUSING AND URBAN DEVELOPMENT

C. NOTE: *This form is furnished to give you a statement of actual settlement costs. Amounts paid to and by the settlement agent are shown. Items marked "(p.o.c.)" were paid outside the closing, they are shown here for informational purposes and are not included in the totals. WARNING: It is a crime to knowingly make false statements to the United States on this or any other similar form. Penalties upon conviction can include a fine and imprisonment. For details see: Title 18U, S. Code Section 1001 and Section 1010.* PREVIOUS EDITION IS OBSOLETE

D. NAME OF BORROWER:
 ADDRESS:

E. NAME OF SELLER:
 ADDRESS:

F. NAME OF LENDER:
 ADDRESS:

SELLER'S IDENTIFICATION NUMBER:

G. PROPERTY LOCATION: STREET:
 LEGAL:

☐ PRINCIPAL RESIDENCE ☐ OTHER REAL ESTATE

H. SETTLEMENT AGENT: UNIVERSITY TITLE COMPANY
 ADDRESS: 1021 UNIVERSITY DRIVE EAST, COLLEGE STATION, TX 77841

SETTLEMENT AGENT'S IDENTIFICATION NUMBER: 74-1753734

I. SETTLEMENT DATE:

PLACE OF SETTLEMENT:
 ADDRESS:

J. SUMMARY OF BORROWER'S TRANSACTION		K. SUMMARY OF SELLER'S TRANSACTION	
100. GROSS AMOUNT DUE FROM BORROWER		**400. GROSS AMOUNT DUE TO SELLER:**	
101. Contract sales price		401. Contract sales price	
102. Personal property		402. Personal property	
103. Settlement charges to borrower (line 1400)		403.	
104.		404.	
105.		405.	
Adjustments for items paid by seller in advance		*Adjustments for items paid by seller in advance*	
106. City/town taxes to		406. City/town taxes to	
107. County taxes to		407. County taxes to	
108. Assessments to		408. Assessments to	
109.		409.	
110.		410.	
111.		411.	
112.		412.	
120. GROSS AMOUNT DUE FROM BORROWER		**420. GROSS AMOUNT DUE TO SELLER**	
200. AMOUNTS PAID BY OR IN BEHALF OF BORROWER:		**500. REDUCTIONS IN AMOUNT DUE TO SELLER:**	
201. Deposit or earnest money		501. Excess deposit (see instructions)	
202. Principal amount of new loan(s)		502. Settlement charges to seller (line 1400)	
203. Existing loan(s) taken subject to		503. Existing loan(s) taken subject to	
204.		504. Payoff of first mortgage loan	
205.		505. Payoff of second mortgage loan	
206.		506.	
207.		507.	
208.		508.	
209.		509.	
Adjustments for items unpaid by seller		*Adjustments for items unpaid by seller*	
210. City/town taxes to		510. City/town taxes to	
211. County taxes to		511. County taxes to	
212. Assessments to		512. Assessments to	
213.		513.	
214.		514.	
215.		515.	
216.		516.	
217.		517.	
218.		518.	
219.		519.	
220. TOTAL PAID BY/FOR BORROWER		**520. TOTAL REDUCTIONS AMOUNT DUE SELLER**	
300. CASH AT SETTLEMENT FROM/TO BORROWER		**600. CASH AT SETTLEMENT TO/FROM SELLER**	
301. Gross amount due from borrower (line 120)		601. Gross amount due to seller (line 420)	
302. Less amounts paid by/for borrower (line 220)	()	602. Less reductions in amount due seller (line 520)	()
303. CASH (☐ FROM) (☐ TO) BORROWER		**603. CASH (☐ FROM) (☐ TO) SELLER**	

SOLICITATION: You are required by law to provide **UNIVERSITY TITLE COMPANY** with your correct taxpayer identification number. If you do not provide **UNIVERSITY TITLE COMPANY** with your correct taxpayer identification number, you may be subject to civil or criminal penalties imposed by law.

Under penalties of perjury, I certify that the number shown on this statement is my correct taxpayer identification number.

_____ _____ _____
Seller's Signature Seller's Signature Seller's Signature

The information contained in Blocks E, G, H, I, and on line 401 (or if line 401 has an asterick, line 403 and 404) is important tax information and is being furnished to the Internal Revenue Service. If you are required to file a return, a negligence penalty or other sanction will be imposed on you if this item is required to be reported and the IRS determines that it has not been reported.

L. SETTLEMENT CHARGES

		PAID FROM BORROWER'S FUNDS AT SETTLEMENT	PAID FROM SELLER'S FUNDS AT SETTLEMENT
700.	**TOTAL SALES/BROKER'S COMMISSION based on price $** @ % =		
	Division of commission (line 700) as follows:		
701.	$ to		
702.	$ to		
703.	Commission paid at Settlement (Money retained by broker applied to commission $ _____)		
704.			
800.	**ITEMS PAYABLE IN CONNECTION WITH LOAN**		
801.	Loan Origination Fee %		
802.	Loan Discount %		
803.	Appraisal Fee to		
804.	Credit Report to		
805.	Lender's Inspection Fee		
806.	Mortgage Insurance Application Fee to		
807.	Assumption Fee		
808.			
809.			
900.	**ITEMS REQUIRED BY LENDER TO BE PAID IN ADVANCE**		
901.	Interest from to @ $ /day		
902.	Mortgage Insurance Premium for months to		
903.	Hazard Insurance Premium for years to		
904.	years to		
905.			
1000.	**RESERVES DEPOSITED WITH LENDER**		
1001.	Hazard insurance month @ $ per month		
1002.	Mortgage insurance month @ $ per month		
1003.	City property taxes month @ $ per month		
1004.	County property taxes month @ $ per month		
1005.	Annual assessments month @ $ per month		
1006.	month @ $ per month		
1007.	month @ $ per month		
1008.	month @ $ per month		
1100.	**TITLE CHARGES**		
1101.	Settlement or closing fee to		
1102.	Abstract or title search to		
1103.	Title examination to		
1104.	Title insurance binder to		
1105.	Document preparation to		
1106.	Notary fees to		
1107.	Attorney's fees to		
	(includes above items numbers:		
1108.	Title insurance to		
	(includes above items numbers:		
1109.	Lender's coverage $		
1110.	Owner's coverage $		
1111.			
1112.			
1113.			
1200.	**GOVERNMENT RECORDING AND TRANSFER CHARGES**		
1201.	Recording fees: Deed $; Mortgage $; Release $		
1202.	City/county tax/stamps: Deed $; Mortgage $		
1203.	State tax/stamps: Deed $; Mortgage $		
1204.			
1205.			
1300.	**ADDITIONAL SETTLEMENT CHARGES**		
1301.	Survey to		
1302.	Pest inspection to		
1303.			
1304.			
1305.			
1306.			
1307.			
1400.	**TOTAL SETTLEMENT CHARGES (enter on lines 103, Section J and 502, Section K)**		

I have carefully reviewed the HUD-1 Settlement Statement and to the best of my knowledge and belief, it is a true and accurate statement of all receipts and disbursements made on my account in this transaction. I further certify that I have received a copy of the HUD-1 Settlement Statement.

Borrower _____ Seller _____

The HUD-1 Settlement Statement which I have prepared is a true and accurate account of this transmission. I have caused or will cause funds to be disbursed in accordance with this statement.

Settlement Agent _____ Date _____

WARNING: It is a crime to knowingly make false statements to the United States on this or any other similar form. Penalties upon conviction can include a fine and imprisonment. For details see: Title 18 U. S. Code Section 1001 and Section 1010.

HUD-1
RESPA HB 4305 2

367 11-92

Form **3903**	**Moving Expenses**	OMB No. 1545-0062

Department of the Treasury
Internal Revenue Service

▶ Attach to Form 1040.

▶ See separate instructions.

19**92**

Attachment
Sequence No. **62**

Name(s) shown on Form 1040

Your social security number

1	Enter the number of miles from your **old home** to your **new workplace**	**1**
2	Enter the number of miles from your **old home** to your **old workplace**	**2**
3	Subtract line 2 from line 1. Enter the result but not less than zero. ▶	**3**

If line 3 is 35 or more miles, complete the rest of this form. If line 3 is less than 35 miles, you may not deduct your moving expenses. This rule does not apply to members of the armed forces.

Caution: *If you are a member of the armed forces, see the instructions before continuing.*

Part I Moving Expenses

Note: *Any payments your employer made for any part of your move (including the value of any services furnished in kind) should be included on your W-2 form. Report that amount on* **Form 1040, line 7.** *See* **Reimbursements** *in the instructions.*

Section A—Transportation of Household Goods

4	Transportation and storage for household goods and personal effects	**4**

Section B—Expenses of Moving From Old To New Home

5	Travel and lodging **not** including meals	**5**
6	Total meals **6**	
7	Multiply line 6 by 80% (.80)	**7**
8	Add lines 5 and 7 .	**8**

Section C—Pre-move Househunting Expenses and Temporary Quarters
(for any 30 days in a row after getting your job)

9	Pre-move travel and lodging **not** including meals	**9**
10	Temporary quarters expenses **not** including meals	**10**
11	Total meal expenses for both pre-move househunting and temporary quarters **11**	
12	Multiply line 11 by 80% (.80)	**12**
13	Add lines 9, 10, and 12	**13**

Section D—Qualified Real Estate Expenses

14	Expenses of (check one): a ☐ selling or exchanging your old home, or ⎫ b ☐ if renting, settling an unexpired lease. ⎭ .	**14**
15	Expenses of (check one): a ☐ buying your new home, or ⎫ b ☐ if renting, getting a new lease. ⎭	**15**

Part II Dollar Limits and Moving Expense Deduction

16	Enter the **smaller** of: • The amount on line 13, or • $1,500 ($750 if married filing a separate return and at the end of 1992 you lived with your spouse who also started work in 1992). ⎱ . .	**16**
17	Add lines 14, 15, and 16	**17**
18	Enter the **smaller** of: • The amount on line 17, or • $3,000 ($1,500 if married filing a separate return and at the end of 1992 you lived with your spouse who also started work in 1992). ⎱ · ·	**18**
19	Add lines 4, 8, and 18. Enter the total here and on Schedule A, line 18. This is your **moving expense** deduction . ▶	**19**

For Paperwork Reduction Act Notice, see separate instructions. Cat. No. 12490K Form **3903** (1992)

367 11-92

Form **2119**	**Sale of Your Home**	OMB No. 1545-0072

▶ **Attach to Form 1040 for year of sale.**

Department of the Treasury
Internal Revenue Service

▶ **See separate Instructions.** ▶ **Please print or type.**

19~~92~~

Attachment
Sequence No. **20**

Your first name and initial. If a joint return, also give spouse's name and initial. Last name

Your social security number

Fill In Your Address Only If You Are Filing This Form by Itself and Not With Your Tax Return

Present address (no., street, and apt. no., rural route, or P.O. box no. if mail is not delivered to street address)

Spouse's social security number

City, town or post office, state, and ZIP code

Part I General Information

1 Date your former main home was sold (month, day, year) ▶ | **1** | / | / |

2 Face amount of any mortgage, note (e.g., second trust), or other financial instrument on which you will get periodic payments of principal or interest from this sale (see instructions) . . . | **2** | |

3 Have you bought or built a new main home? ☐ Yes ☐ No

4 Is or was any part of either main home rented out or used for business? If "Yes," see instructions . . . ☐ Yes ☐ No

Part II Gain on Sale (Do not include amounts you deduct as moving expenses.)

5 Selling price of home. Do not include personal property items that you sold with your home . | **5** | |

6 Expense of sale. Include sales commissions, advertising, legal, etc. | **6** | |

7 Amount realized. Subtract line 6 from line 5 | **7** | |

8 Basis of home sold (see instructions) | **8** | |

9 **Gain on sale.** Subtract line 8 from line 7 | **9** | |

- If line 9 is zero or less, **stop here** and attach this form to your return.
- If line 3 is "Yes," you **must** go to Part III or Part IV, whichever applies. Otherwise, go to line 10.

10 If you haven't replaced your home, do you plan to do so within the replacement period (see instructions)? ☐ Yes ☐ No

- If line 10 is "Yes," stop here, attach this form to your return, and see **Additional Filing Requirements** in the instructions.
- If line 10 is "No," you **must** go to Part III or Part IV, whichever applies.

Part III One-Time Exclusion of Gain for People Age 55 or Older (If you are not taking the exclusion, go to Part IV now.)

11 Who was age 55 or older on date of sale? ☐ You ☐ Your spouse ☐ Both of you

12 Did the person who was age 55 or older own and use the property as his or her main home for a total of at least 3 years (except for short absences) of the 5-year period before the sale? If "No," go to Part IV now . . ☐ Yes ☐ No

13 **If line 12 is "Yes,"** do you elect to take the one-time exclusion? If "No," go to Part IV now ☐ Yes ☐ No

14 At time of sale, who owned the home? ☐ You ☐ Your spouse ☐ Both of you

15 Social security number of spouse at time of sale if you had a different spouse from the one above at time of sale. If you were not married at time of sale, enter "None" ▶ | **15** | |

16 **Exclusion.** Enter the **smaller** of line 9 or $125,000 ($62,500, if married filing separate return). Then, go to line 17 | **16** | |

Part IV Adjusted Sales Price, Taxable Gain, and Adjusted Basis of New Home

17 Subtract line 16 from line 9 | **17** | |

- If line 17 is zero, stop here and attach this form to your return.
- If line 3 is "Yes," go to line 18 now.
- If you are reporting this sale on the installment method, stop here and see the line 2 instructions.
- All others, stop here and **enter the amount from line 17 on Schedule D, line 2 or line 10.**

18 Fixing-up expenses (see instructions for time limits) | **18** | |

19 Add lines 16 and 18 | **19** | |

20 **Adjusted sales price.** Subtract line 19 from line 7 | **20** | |

21a Date you moved into new home (month, day, year) ▶ | / | / | b Cost of new home | **21b** | |

22 Subtract line 21b from line 20. If the result is zero or less, enter -0- | **22** | |

23 **Taxable gain.** Enter the **smaller** of line 17 or line 22 | **23** | |

- If line 23 is zero, go to line 24 and attach this form to your return.
- If you are reporting this sale on the installment method, see the line 2 instructions and go to line 24.
- All others, **enter the amount from line 23 on Schedule D, line 2 or line 10,** and go to line 24.

24 Postponed gain. Subtract line 23 from line 17 | **24** | |

25 **Adjusted basis of new home.** Subtract line 24 from line 21b | **25** | |

Sign Here Only If You Are Filing This Form by Itself and Not With Your Tax Return

Under penalties of perjury, I declare that I have examined this form, including attachments, and to the best of my knowledge and belief, it is true, correct, and complete.

Your signature Date Spouse's signature Date

▶ _____ ▶ _____

If a joint return, both must sign.

For Paperwork Reduction Act Notice, see separate instructions. Cat. No. 11710J Form **2119** (1992)

INDEX

Asterisks indicate entries that appear in the Glossary.

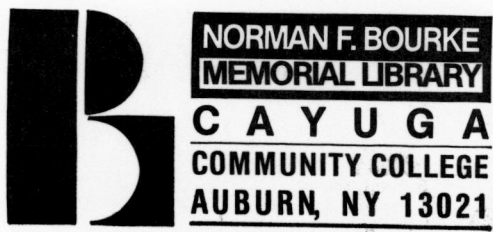